Territorial Growth of the United States

THE ORIGINAL UNITED STATES
(By Treaty with Britain, 1783)

THE ORIGINAL THIRTEEN COLONIES

MASON-DIXON LINE

(Seized from Spain, 1810, 1813)

FLORIDA
(By Treaty with Spain, 1819)

MAINE
VT.
N.H.
MASS.
CONN.
R.I.
NEW YORK
PENNSYLVANIA
NEW JERSEY
DELAWARE
MARYLAND
WEST VIRGINIA
VIRGINIA
KENTUCKY
NORTH CAROLINA
TENNESSEE
SOUTH CAROLINA
GEORGIA
OHIO
INDIANA
ILLINOIS
MICHIGAN
WISCONSIN
MINNESOTA
IOWA
MISSOURI
ARKANSAS
MISSISSIPPI
ALABAMA
LOUISIANA
FLORIDA

Lake Superior
Lake Michigan
Lake Huron
Lake Ontario
Lake Erie
St. Lawrence R.
Ohio R.
Mississippi R.

36°30'N

GULF OF MEXICO
ATLANTIC OCEAN
BAHAMAS
CUBA
DOMINICAN REPUBLIC
HAITI

PUERTO RICO
(Acquired from Spain, 1898)

VIRGIN IS.
(Acquired from Denmark, 1916-1917)

PUERTO RICO
VIRGIN ISLANDS

| 0 | 50 | 100 Miles |
| 0 | 50 | 100 Kilometers |

| 0 | 200 | 400 Miles |
| 0 | 200 | 400 Kilometers |

Albers Equal-Area Projection

THE ENDURING VISION

A HISTORY OF THE AMERICAN PEOPLE

Third Edition

Paul S. Boyer
University of Wisconsin, Madison

Clifford E. Clark, Jr.
Carleton College

Joseph F. Kett
University of Virginia

Neal Salisbury
Smith College

Harvard Sitkoff
University of New Hampshire

Nancy Woloch
Barnard College

D. C. Heath and Company
Lexington, Massachusetts   Toronto

Address editorial correspondence to:
D. C. Heath and Company
125 Spring Street
Lexington, MA 02173

Acquisitions: James Miller
Development: Sylvia Mallory
Editorial Production: Kathleen Deselle
Design: Henry Rachlin
Photo Research: Sharon Donahue, Bruce Carson, and Mary Lang
Art Editing: Gary Crespo
Production Coordination: Lisa Merrill and Dick Tonachel
Permissions: Margaret Roll

International Standard Book Number: 0-669-39771-7

Library of Congress Catalog Number: 94-74553

10 9 8 7 6 5

ABOUT THE AUTHORS

Paul S. Boyer, Merle Curti Professor of History at the University of Wisconsin, Madison, earned his Ph.D. from Harvard University. An editor of *Notable American Women, 1607–1950* (1971), he also coauthored *Salem Possessed: The Social Origins of Witchcraft* (1974), for which, with Stephen Nissenbaum, he received the John H. Dunning Prize of the American Historical Association. His other published works include *Urban Masses and Moral Order in America, 1820–1920* (1978), *By the Bomb's Early Light: American Thought and Culture at the Dawn of the Atomic Age* (1985), *When Time Shall Be No More: Prophecy Belief in Modern American Culture* (1992), and *Promises to Keep: The United States Since World War II* (1995). His articles and essays have appeared in *American Quarterly, The New Republic,* and other journals. He is an elected member of the American Antiquarian Society and the Society of American Historians.

Clifford E. Clark, Jr., M. A. & A. D. Hulings Professor of American Studies and professor of history at Carleton College, earned his Ph.D. from Harvard University. He has served as both the chair of the History Department and director of the American Studies program at Carleton. Clark is the author of *Henry Ward Beecher: Spokesman for a Middle-Class America* (1978), *The American Family Home, 1800–1960* (1986), and *The Intellectual and Cultural History of Anglo-America Since 1789* in the General History of the Americas. He also has edited and contributed to *Minnesota in a Century of Change: The State and Its People Since 1900* (1989). A past member of the Council of the American Studies Association, Clark is active in the fields of material culture studies and historic preservation, and he serves on the Northfield, Minnesota, Historical Preservation Commission.

Joseph F. Kett, professor of history at the University of Virginia, received his Ph.D. from Harvard University. His works include *The Formation of the American Medical Profession: The Role of Institutions, 1780–1860* (1968), *Rites of Passage: Adolescence in America, 1790–Present* (1977), *The Pursuit of Knowledge Under Difficulties: From Self-Improvement to Adult Education in America, 1750–1990* (1994), and *The Dictionary of Cultural Literacy* (1988), of which he is coauthor. A former History Department chair at Virginia, he also has participated on the Panel on Youth of the President's Science Advisory Committee, has served on the Board of Editors of the *History of Education Quarterly*, and is a past member of the Council of the American Studies Association.

Neal Salisbury, professor of history at Smith College, received his Ph.D. from the University of California, Los Angeles. The author of *Manitou and Providence: Indians, Europeans, and the Making of New England, 1500–1643* (1982) and *The Indians of New England: A Critical Bibliography* (1982), he also has contributed numerous articles to journals and edited collections, most recently to the forthcoming *Cambridge History of the Native Peoples of the Americas.* He has been awarded fellowships by the Smithsonian Institution, the National Endowment for the Humanities, the Charles Warren Center for Studies in American History at Harvard University, and the National Humanities Center. Formerly chair of the History Department at Smith, he is active in the fields of colonial and Native American history, has served on the editorial board of the journal *Ethnohistory,* and coedits a book series, Cambridge Studies in North American Indian History.

Harvard Sitkoff, professor of history at the University of New Hampshire, earned his Ph.D. from Columbia University. He is the author of *A New Deal for Blacks* (1978) and *The Struggle for Black Equality, 1954–1992* (1981, 1992), coeditor of *A History of Our Time* (1982, 1987, 1991), and editor of *Fifty Years*

Later: The New Deal Evaluated (1985). A contributor to numerous edited collections, he also has published articles in many journals, among them *The American Quarterly, The Journal of American History, The Journal of Southern History,* and *The Wilson Quarterly.*

Nancy Woloch received her Ph.D. from Indiana University. She is the author of *Women and the American Experience* (1984, 1994, 1996), editor of *Early American Women: A Documentary History, 1600–1900* (1992), and coauthor, with Walter LaFeber and Richard Polenberg, of *The American Century: A History of the United States Since the 1890s* (1986, 1992). Her most recent book is *Muller v. Oregon: A Brief History with Documents* (1996). She teaches American history and American Studies at Barnard College, Columbia University.

PREFACE

Writing a textbook sometimes seems a labor of Sisyphus. It is not enough to push the rock uphill once; the job must be done over and over, revising the book to keep it current with the best recent scholarship, responding to users' criticisms, rethinking our own conclusions, and all the while squirming under our editors' pleas that all the changes be made without lengthening the text.

Yet the rigors of this task are mitigated by the enthusiastic reception that our colleagues and students have given *The Enduring Vision* ever since its first edition in 1990. It is indeed a pleasure to realize that our efforts are producing a textbook from which hundreds of thousands of undergraduates are learning to think about the subtleties of American history, not merely memorizing facts, and with which historians with many different expectations find they can teach creatively. It was in the spirit of keeping such a diverse and warmly responsive audience satisfied that we prepared this Third Edition. We have tried to improve the readability, to give more attention to the peoples and cultures of the borderland communities in the South and West, and to continue weaving in the story of Americans' encounters with the natural environment. We hope that the results continue to please you.

One major change that will be of interest to instructors who may be rethinking the chronological divisions of the traditional two-semester survey course is D. C. Heath's decision to publish the twentieth-century chapters separately. Of course, the complete *Enduring Vision* is still available in two volumes. Volume One extends from the origins through Reconstruction (Chapters 1–16), and Volume Two, from Reconstruction to the present day (Chapters 16–33). The new twentieth-century version (Chapters 22–33, plus some material from Chapter 21) will serve the needs of those who teach a semester- or quarter-length course that begins with imperialism and the Spanish-American War and then takes up domestic developments with the Progressive Era.

Adopters' comments, as well as our own sense of the "rightness" of things, guided us in introducing these substantive changes in the Third Edition:

- Along with the origins of English colonization, Chapter 2 now discusses the beginnings of the Spanish, French, and Dutch colonies in North America; some of this material formerly appeared in Chapter 4.

- We have substantially overhauled Chapter 3: a new section, "The Spread of Slavery," combines coverage of the Caribbean colonies and the origin of Carolina; another new section, "The Middle Colonies," gives greater attention to this region's ethnic and religious pluralism; and the section "Rivals for North America" encompasses developments in the French and Spanish colonies. In keeping with our decision to give more attention to the borderlands, a new "Place in Time" essay focuses on Taos and the Pueblo revolt.

- Some condensation in Chapter 4 has made it possible to add a new subsection, "Colonial Farmers and the Environment," and to expand discussion of colonial women and of the French and Spanish colonies (particularly Louisiana).

- Chapter 5 now offers more British perspectives on the coming of the Revolution.

- Chapter 6 revises and extends the discussion of women in the new republic.

- In the chapters on antebellum America and the Civil War and Reconstruction, changes mainly involved compressing and streamlining some complex material. There is a new "Place in Time" essay in Chapter 11 on Frances Trollope's efforts to market popular culture in Cincinnati, new material on George Catlin's paintings of the American Indian, and—in line with recent scholarship—a new synthesis of the rise of the Republican party. The Civil War in the trans-Mississippi West also receives more attention.

- Users of the split version will find a new Prologue for Volume Two, tracing changes in attitudes toward the natural environment from the first years of settlement to the present.

- Chapter 17 offers more coverage of Mexican-American women.

- Chapter 18 now emphasizes the importance of coal as the cheap energy source that literally fueled American industrial expansion; it also expands the coverage of working women in the late nineteenth century and of the Homestead strike.

- Chapter 19's assessment of urban political bosses emphasizes how they exploited as well as helped immigrants.

- Chapter 20 offers new material on the "stem family" and on sports—racism in the boxing ring and the commercialization of sports at the turn of the century.

- Chapter 21 gives more analysis of populist ideology and of women's participation in the populist movement.

- Chapter 22 expands its discussion of Progressive Era social problems, such as drug and alcohol abuse, and of the origins and function of the Federal Reserve System.

- Chapter 23 now includes more material on the World War I combat experience and on the war's impact on the American economy and on progressivism.

- Chapter 24 more fully discusses revivalism and women's presence in both higher education and the workplace; and a new "Place in Time" essay explores the vibrancy and rich diversity of the Harlem Renaissance, as well as the bleaker realities of Harlem life in the 1920s.

- Chapter 25 also offers a new "Place in Time" profile, on Cimarron County, Oklahoma, bringing alive the human and ecological meaning of the Dust Bowl. The chapter features more discussion of depression-era economic thought, including Keynesianism.

- Chapter 26's analysis of the coming of World War II now includes a fuller treatment of isolationism's ideological roots.

- Chapter 27 provides updated coverage of the experience of blacks, Native Americans, and Chicanos during World War II, as well as of the Holocaust. A new "Place in Time" essay looks at life in wartime Honolulu.

- Chapter 29 gives more attention to nuclear-power plants and to the origins of the troubling nuclear-waste problem.

- Chapter 30 critically reexamines the Kennedy presidency in the light of recent scholarship.

- Chapter 31 offers an expanded discussion of the rise of the gay-power movement.

- Chapter 32's reorganized treatment of the Ford, Carter, and Reagan administrations smoothly synthesizes political, economic, social, and international developments. The inevitable compression of political coverage as these administrations recede has opened up opportunities for more synthesis of such trends as the revolution in mass marketing, mass entertainment, and the growing political clout of evangelical Christians.

- Chapter 33 analyzes the Clinton administration's first two years and offers a considered assessment of the major political shift represented by the Republican victory in the 1994 elections. A new "Place in Time" essay on contemporary Miami explores issues of cultural diversity and social conflict in a fascinating multiethnic American city.

- Throughout, we have updated bibliographies and suggestions for further reading.

Reflecting the best efforts of its authors and editors, this textbook also rests on the scholarly work of literally hundreds of historians over the years. We hope that you will find it helpful in making sense of America's unique historical experience, and in conveying your own research to your students.

Special Features

A range of useful study aids has been built into *The Enduring Vision*. Each chapter begins with a vignette of a person or an event that both swiftly draws the reader into the atmosphere and issues of the times and establishes the chapter's main themes. In every chapter a two-page, illustrated essay called "A Place in Time" delves into a single community's experiences. Tables and chronological charts on special topics occur regularly throughout the text, and each chapter closes with a Conclusion, a Chronology of pivotal events and developments, annotated For Further Reading recommendations for the student, and a lengthy Additional Bibliography. The Appendix provides statistical tables; handy reference lists; and the text of the Declaration of Independence, the Articles of Confederation, and the Constitution (with its amendments). The full-color design of *The Enduring Vision* features hundreds of photographs, paintings, and cartoons and almost 200 maps and graphs. Informative captions enrich the art program.

Supplementary Resources

An outstanding program of supplementary resources is available with this textbook. Included are:

- *Critical Reading: U.S. History and The Enduring Vision,* by Connie Cantrell

  This **all-new**, concise guide, developed for students by a reading specialist, offers a wealth of critical-reading exercises keyed to *The Enduring* Vision, Third Edition. Students will develop skills in such areas as previewing the text, discerning main arguments, identifying supporting material, and mastering other aspects of reading and studying history.

- *Student Guide with Map Exercises*, Third Edition, by Barbara Blumberg

  Keyed chapter-by-chapter to the textbook, the *Student Guide with Map Exercises,* available in one- and two-volume editions, provides an outline-summary of major topics and themes and includes several features guiding the student in chapter review and self-testing. Map exercises sharpen students' knowledge of and skills in understanding U.S. historical geography.

- *Reading and Writing American History: An Introduction to the Historian's Craft*, by Peter Charles Hoffer and William W. Stueck

  This skills-based sourcebook, featuring discussions of the nature of historical inquiry, readings, and hands-on exercises, is available in two brief volumes to complement students' reading of their American history textbook.

- *Surveying the Land: Skills and Exercises in U.S. Historical Geography*, by Robert Grant

  This two-volume supplement strengthens students' understanding of U.S. geography and illuminates its shaping role in historical events. Comprising thirty-two units, *Surveying the Land* builds basic geographic literacy and develops map-reading proficiency through a blend of descriptive narrative and mapping exercises.

- *Getting the Most out of Your U.S. History Course: The History Student's Vade Mecum*, Third Edition, by Neil R. Stout

  With suggestions on reading the textbook, inter-

preting maps and graphs, taking lecture notes, preparing for exams, and more, the *Vade Mecum* is a convenient pocket-size handbook for beginning college students.

- *Enduring Voices Document Sets*, Third Edition, by James J. Lorence

  This one-of-a-kind, two-volume reader, organized to follow the chapter sequence of *The Enduring Vision,* presents discrete sets of primary sources, with each set built around a "problem" closely related to a major theme in the corresponding textbook chapter.

- *Regional Document Sets:*

  Document Sets for the South in U.S. History, by Richard Purday

  Document Sets for Texas and the Southwest in U.S. History, by J'Nell Pate

  Document Sets for California and the West in U.S. History, by Iris Engstrand

  These three unique collections of documents are designed to enhance students' understanding of regional history. They provide rich opportunities for students to work with primary sources and to explore matters of keen regional interest that are linked to larger questions in U.S. history.

- *Instructor's Guide*, Third Edition, by Robert Grant and James J. Lorence

  This indispensable instructor's resource provides introductory how-to essays and student handouts, followed by teaching suggestions and strategies tied to each chapter of *The Enduring Vision*, Third Edition. Also included are detailed guidelines for using the *Enduring Voices Document Sets* in the classroom.

- *Test Item File*, Third Edition, by Kenneth Blume

  This rich bank of identification, multiple-choice, essay, and map questions covers all the main topics and themes of *The Enduring Vision*. Questions suitable for midterm and final exams are included.

- *Computerized Testing* for IBM and Macintosh computers

  Available for Macintosh and IBM-compatible computers, this electronic test generator provides the same questions as the printed test bank, but in convenient electronic format.

- *The D. C. Heath U.S. History Transparency Set*, 1996 Edition

Approximately 150 full-color maps and graphs are offered in this valuable two-volume collection of overhead-transparency acetates.

- *An American Portfolio* Videodisc

    This CAV-format disc for instructors provides thousands of still images of historic events, personages, and artifacts; twenty-seven minutes of full-motion historical video footage; and numerous historical maps showing change over time.

- *What Makes America Different?* Videodisc and Videotape

    This video features lively conversations among the authors of *The Enduring Vision* on the topic of what makes the American historical experience unique.

- Audiocassette for U.S. History

    This audio anthology of songs, speeches, and radio broadcasts affords students another link to important events from the nation's past.

An All-New CD-ROM Designed for Students

With this new edition comes the debut of a revolutionary concept in CD-ROMs—*EnVision: A Student Guide to U.S. History to Accompany The Enduring Vision. EnVision*, an all-new interactive study aid for students, offers extensive banks of documentary, map, and other resources; a large bank of self-tests with which students can review course material and prepare confidently for exams; and "big-picture" overviews of the main periods and themes of American history, presented by authors of *The Enduring Vision*. The full text of *The Enduring Vision*, Third Edition, is included as a handy reference. Students will learn history in a whole new, exciting way with this innovative resource, the ideal complement to *The Enduring Vision*.

In Conclusion—and with Thanks

In the supplements program as well as in the textbook, our goal has been to make teaching and learning American history enjoyable and stimulating. We would value any comments you and your students have as you navigate through your course using *The Enduring Vision* and its supplements; don't hesitate to write to us.

We wish to extend our sincere gratitude to the many people at D. C. Heath and Company who worked hand in hand with us as we planned and executed this revision. Senior editor James Miller and editorial director Sylvia Mallory—our editors now on all three editions of the textbook—ably coordinated all stages of the revision. Supplements developmental editor Pat Wakeley, production editor Kathleen Deselle, designer Henry Rachlin, photo editors Sharon Donahue, Bruce Carson, and Mary Lang, permissions editor Margaret Roll, and production coordinators Lisa Merrill and Dick Tonachel played crucial roles in the production and design of the textbook and its ancillary program. Marketing manager Kenneth Rust and marketing associate Alyssa Chung got the word out about the new edition in their usual thorough and timely fashion. We warmly thank them all.

We also owe a debt of gratitude to the many colleagues who provided reviews for this edition of *The Enduring Vision*: **Tyler Anbinder,** George Washington University; **Kevin Boyle,** University of Massachusetts, Amherst; **Diane Britton,** University of Toledo; **Gregory Bush,** University of Miami; **Brian Cannon,** Brigham Young University; **Kathleen Carter**, High Point University; **Paul Cunningham,** Catonsville Community College; **Christine Daniels,** Michigan State University; **Sam Elworthy**, Rutgers University; **Scott Garrett,** Paducah Community College; **Gregory Gordon,** College of Lake County; **John Jameson,** Kent State University; **Timothy Keirn,** California State University, Long Beach; **Gary Kornblith,** Oberlin College; **Virginia Laas,** Missouri Southern University; **Ralph Levering,** Davidson College; **Larry Menna,** State University of New York, Farmingdale; **Larry Peterson,** North Dakota State University; **William Robbins,** Oregon State University; **Yolanda Romero,** North Lake College; **Ronald Schlundt,** University of Maryland, European Division; **Sally Schwartz,** Marquette University; **Stanley Underdal,** San Jose State University; **Edward Weller,** San Jacinto College South; and **Gerald Wilson**, Duke University. Finally, we thank the countless others—instructors and students alike—who have taken the time to send in their thoughtful and constructive suggestions over the years. The book is much better for our having listened to them.

P. B.   N. S.
C. C.   H. S.
J. K.   N. W.

CONTENTS

5

THE ROAD TO REVOLUTION, 1744–1776

126

6

THE FORGE OF NATIONHOOD, 1776–1788

162

9

THE TRANSFORMATION OF
AMERICAN SOCIETY,
1815–1840

266

10

POLITICS, RELIGION, AND REFORM
IN THE AGE OF JACKSON

298

11

LIFE, LEISURE, AND CULTURE,
1840–1860

332

TECHNOLOGY AND ECONOMIC GROWTH 334

12

THE OLD SOUTH AND SLAVERY,
1800–1860

364

KING COTTON 366

16

THE CRISES OF RECONSTRUCTION, 1865–1877

498

17

THE TRANS-MISSISSIPPI WEST

534

22

THE PROGRESSIVE ERA

698

27

WAGING GLOBAL WAR, 1939–1945

866

28

COLD WAR AMERICA, 1945–1952

900

29

AMERICA AT MIDCENTURY

928

MAPS

CHARTS, GRAPHS, and TABLES

The Enduring Vision

Harvest Time (detail)
by Carl William Hahn, 1875

ENDURING VISION, ENDUR

This is the story of America and of the visions that Americans have shared. The first vision was of the land itself. For the Siberian adventurers who crossed the land bridge from Asia, for the Europeans who began to arrive in the sixteenth century, and for the later immigrants who poured in by the tens of millions, North America offered a haven for new beginnings. If life was hard elsewhere, it would be better here. And once here, the lure of the land continued. If times were tough in the East, they would be better in the West. New Englanders migrated to Ohio; Ohioans migrated to Kansas; Kansans migrated to California. For Africans the migration to America was forced and brutal. But after the Civil War, newly freed southern blacks embraced the vision and dreamed of new opportunities elsewhere:

> I got my ticket,
> Leaving the thicket,
> And I'm a-heading for the Golden Shore!

For most of American history, the vision of the land celebrated its beauty, its diversity, and its ability to provide sustenance and even wealth to those who exploited its fertility and its resources. But within this shared vision were deep-seated tensions. Whereas Native Americans regarded the land and other natural phenomena as spiritual forces to be feared and respected, many Europeans and their descendants considered nature a force to be conquered. The very abundance of America's natural resources led many to think of these resources as infinitely abundant and exploitable. In moving from one locale to another, some sought only to escape starvation or oppression, while others pursued wealth and power no matter the environmental consequences. Regardless of their motives and conditions, migrants often left behind a land bereft of wild animals, its fertility depleted by ing, its waters dammed and polluted or together. If the land today remains part of the visi it is only because we realize its vulnerability, rather than its immunity, to pollution and exploitation.

But the vision involves more than simply a love of the land. It also entails a commitment to an ongoing process: the process of creating a just social order. In pursuing this goal, Americans have sought to blend the best from their intellectual and cultural traditions with new, experimental social forms, a pattern often leading to bitter debates. Over thousands of years, Native Americans worked in this way to construct ideal social orders as they refined their relationships with one another and with the land around them. For the past five hundred years, immigrants from all over the world have pursued comparable ideals, both within their communities and in the nation at large.

Central to the American vision of the good society is the notion of individual freedom. To be sure, our commitment to freedom has frequently faltered in practice. The Puritans who sought freedom of worship for themselves often denied it to others. Southern whites who cheered the Declaration of Independence lived by the labor of black slaves. Many a wealthy employer conveniently forgot that economic exploitation can extinguish freedom as effectively as political tyranny or military force. And through much of our history, women—half the population—were relegated to second-class status. Yet the battered vision endured, prodding a sometimes reluctant nation to confront and explore its full meaning.

But freedom can be an empty and cheerless thing unless one is also part of a social group. The novelist O. E. Rölvaag, describing the emotions of a

...grant farm
...ured this feeling of

...tury ...
...solation so profound settled upon
...t she seemed unable to think at all. . . .
*She threw herself back in the grass and looked
up into the heavens. But darkness and infinitude
lay there, also—the sense of utter desolation still
remained. . . . Suddenly, for the first time, she realized the full extent of her loneliness. . . .*

Thus the vision must also be one of community. Puritan leader John Winthrop, addressing a group of fellow immigrants aboard the *Arbella* on their way to
America in 1630, eloquently summed up this dimension of the vision: "We must delight in each other,
make others' conditions our own, rejoice together,
mourn together, labor and suffer together: always having before our eyes our commission and community
. . . as members of the same body."

The family, the town, the neighborhood, the
church, the ethnic group, and the nation itself have
been ways by which Americans have woven into
their lives a web of social meaning. And *community*
is not just a high-sounding abstraction; it has political implications. If we are not just a fragmented collection of self-absorbed individuals but also a *people,* what obligations do we owe each other? What
limitations on our freedom are we willing to accept
in order to be part of a social group? In struggling
with tough questions like these, we have further defined our vision of America.

Finally, this vision is one of renewal and new beginnings. The story of America is part of the human
story, and thus it has its dark and shameful passages
as well as its bright moments of achievement. Arrogance, injustice, callous blindness to suffering, and
national self-delusion have all figured in our history.
But balancing the times when we lost our way are
the moments when we found our bearings and returned to the hard task of defining what America at
its best might truly be.

This, then, is the essence of the vision: a vision
not of a foreordained national destiny unfolding ef-
fortlessly but of a laborious, often frustrating struggle to define what our common life as a people shall

be. For all the failures and the wrong turns, it remains a vision rooted in hope, not despair. In 1980
Jesse de la Cruz, a Mexican-American woman who
had fought for years to improve conditions for California's migrant workers, summed up the philosophy that kept her going: "Is America progressing toward the better? . . . We're the ones that are gonna
do it. We have to keep on struggling. . . . With us,
there's a saying: *La esperanza muere al último.*
Hope dies last. You can't lose hope. If you lose hope,
that's losing everything."

No sentiment could better sum up the enduring
vision of American history.

AN ANCIENT HERITAGE

"The land was ours before we were the land's." So begins the poem "The Gift Outright," which the aged
Robert Frost read at President John F. Kennedy's inauguration in 1961. Frost's poem meditates on the inter-
relatedness of history, geography, and human consciousness. At first, wrote Frost, North American
settlers merely possessed the land; but then, in a subtle spiritual process, they became possessed by it.
Only by entering into this deep relationship with the
land itself—"such as she was, such as she would become"—did their identity as a people fully take shape.

Frost's poem speaks of the encounter of English
colonists with a strange new continent of mystery and
promise; but of course, what the Europeans called the
"New World" was in fact the homeland of the Native
American peoples whose ancestors had been "possessed by" the land for at least fifteen thousand years.
Native Americans had undergone an immensely long
process of settling the continent, developing divergent
cultures, discovering agriculture, and creating a rich
spiritual life tightly interwoven with the physical environment that sustained them. We cannot fully comprehend the past five hundred years of American history
without first understanding how, for thousands of
years before then, Indians created the human habitats
that non-natives and their descendants would occupy
and transform.

To comprehend the American past, we first must
know the American land itself. The patterns of
weather; the undulations of valley, plain, and moun-

tain; the shifting mosaic of sand, soil, and rock; the intricate network of rivers, streams, and lakes—these have profoundly influenced U.S. history. North America's fundamental physical characteristics have shaped human events from the earliest migrations from Asia to the later cycles of agricultural and industrial development, the rise of cities, the course of politics, and even the basic themes of American literature, art, and music. Geology, geography, and environment are among the fundamental building blocks of human history.

This prologue tells the story of the land itself: its geological origins; its reshaping by eons of lifting, sinking, erosion, and glaciation; the opportunities and limitations that it presents to human endeavor. It reminds us of the ultimate dependence of human beings on their environment.

It is sobering to begin the study of American history by contrasting the recent rise of a rich, complex human society on this continent with the awesomely slow pace by which the North American environment took form. Geologists trace the oldest known rocks on the continent back some 3 billion years when a single landmass, called Pangaea by geologists, encompassed

Volcanic Eruption, Hawaii

Formation of the Continents
After the break-up of the supercontinent of Pangaea, drifting land masses gradually formed today's continents.

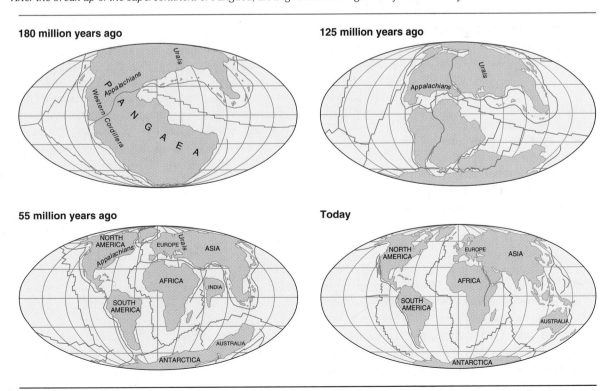

all the earth's dry surfaces. The rocky "floor" known as the Canadian Shield first became visible on the surface of what is now Canada during the earliest geologic era, the Precambrian, which ended 500 million years ago. Halfway between that remote age and the present, during the Paleozoic ("ancient life") era, forests covered much of what would eventually be the United States. From this organic matter, America's enormous coal reserves would be created, the largest yet discovered in the entire world. About 180 million years ago, during the Mesozoic ("middle life") era—the age of the dinosaurs—Pangaea began to break apart. By a process known as continental drift—which continues today at the rate of a few centimeters a year—today's continents were eventually formed. As a result, most plant and animal life in each of the earth's major landmasses—the Americas, Eurasia-Africa, Australia, and Antarctica—evolved in isolation from life in the others for 180 million years. As environmental historian Alfred W. Crosby puts it, "The ancestors of American buffalos, Eurasian cattle, and Australian kangaroos shambled and hopped down diverging paths of evolution." The overseas expansion of Europeans in the past five centuries has brought an abrupt end to that isolation, with some far-reaching consequences in North America that are noted in the chapters that follow.

So enormous a gulf of time separates the origins of North America from the beginning of human history that, if those 180 million years were compressed into the space of a single twenty-four-hour day, everything that has happened since the Indians' ancestors first migrated here would flash by in the last half-second before midnight, and the New World's history since Columbus would occupy about five-thousandths of a second. In considering the sweep of geologic time, one inevitably wonders how ephemeral human history itself may yet prove to be.

Many millions of years after North America's initial separation, violent movements of the earth's crust thrust up the Pacific Coastal, Sierra Nevada, and Cascade ranges on the continent's western edge. As the dinosaurs were dying out, toward the end of the Mesozoic some 65–70 million years ago, the vast, shallow sea that washed over much of west-central North America disappeared, having been replaced by the Rocky Mountains. By then, the decay and fossilization of plant and animal life were creating North America's once great petroleum deposits, which until a generation ago seemed almost limitless. Within the last 50 million years, volcanic eruptions raised the cones that now form the Hawaiian Islands, twenty-five hundred

miles southwest of California. Active Pacific-rim volcanoes and powerful earthquakes all over the continent dramatically demonstrate that the molding of the American landscape still continues.

Between 2 million and ten thousand years ago, four great glaciations left a tremendous imprint on the land. The Ice Age staggers the imagination. During periods of maximum glacial expansion, a carpet of ice as thick as thirteen thousand feet extended over most of Canada and crept southward into what is now New England, New York State, and much of the Midwest. As we shall see in Chapter 1, the first humans to inhabit North America—ancestors of American Indians—arrived as temperatures rose and the glaciers began their most recent, slow retreat northward. While the earth has been relatively stable during the last few thousand years, earthquakes in California and elsewhere remind us that the continents continue to drift and that the world as we know it is not static but in a state of steady change.

THE CONTINENT AND ITS REGIONS

As the glacial ice melted at last, raising the world's oceans to their present level, North America slowly warmed. The ensuing differences in climate, physical features, and organic life were the basis of America's extraordinary geographic diversity. Geographic diversity contributed, in turn, to the remarkable diversity of regional cultures that later emerged, first among American Indians and then among the non-native peoples who settled in America after Columbus's voyages. Geographic variety also made possible the United States' rise to political and economic preeminence in the modern world.

The West

With its severe climate and profuse wildlife, Alaska still evokes the land that ancient North America's earliest migrants discovered. Indeed, Alaska's far north resembles a world from which ice caps have just retreated—a treeless tundra of grasses, lichens, and stunted shrubs. This region, the Arctic, is a stark wilderness in winter, reborn in fleeting summers of colorful flowers and returning birds. In contrast, the subarctic of central Alaska and Canada is a heavily forested country known as taiga. Here rises North America's highest peak,

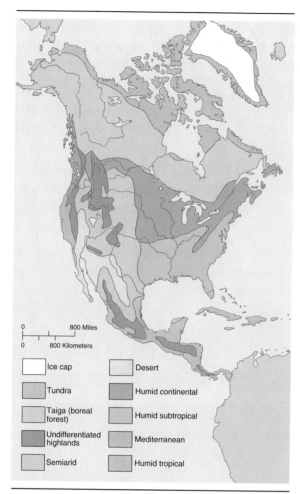

North American Climatic Regions

Legend:
- Ice cap
- Tundra
- Taiga (boreal forest)
- Undifferentiated highlands
- Semiarid
- Desert
- Humid continental
- Humid subtropical
- Mediterranean
- Humid tropical

0 — 800 Miles
0 — 800 Kilometers

more uniformly temperate than anywhere else in North America. From Anchorage and the Alaska panhandle to a little south of San Francisco Bay, winters are cool, humid, and foggy, and the coast's dense forest cover includes the largest living organisms on earth, the giant sequoia (redwood) trees. Along the southern California coast, winds and currents generate a warmer, "Mediterranean" climate, and vegetation includes a heavy growth of shrubs and short trees, scattered stands of oak, and grasses able to endure prolonged seasonal drought.

The rugged Sierra Nevada, Cascade, and coastal ranges stretch the length of British Columbia, Washington, Oregon, and California. Their majestic peaks trap abundant Pacific Ocean moisture that gigantic clockwise air currents carry eastward. Between the ranges nestle flat, fertile valleys—California's Central Valley (formed by the San Joaquin and Sacramento rivers), Oregon's Willamette Valley, and the Puget

Mendenhall Glacier, Alaska

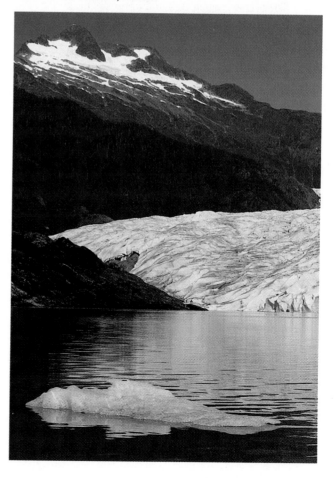

20,320-foot Mt. McKinley, or Denali. Average temperatures in the subarctic range from the fifties above zero in summer to well below zero in the long, dark winters, and the soil is permanently frozen except during summer surface thaws.

The expanse from Alaska's glacier-gouged and ruggedly mountainous Pacific shore southward to northern California forms the Pacific Northwest. Only a few natural harbors break the shoreline, but they include the magnificent anchorages of Puget Sound and San Francisco Bay. Offshore, cool currents and warm winds make possible rich coastal fisheries.

The Pacific coastal region is in some ways a world apart. Vegetation and animal life, isolated from the rest of the continent by mountains and deserts, include many species unfamiliar farther east. Warm, wet westerly winds blowing off the Pacific create a climate

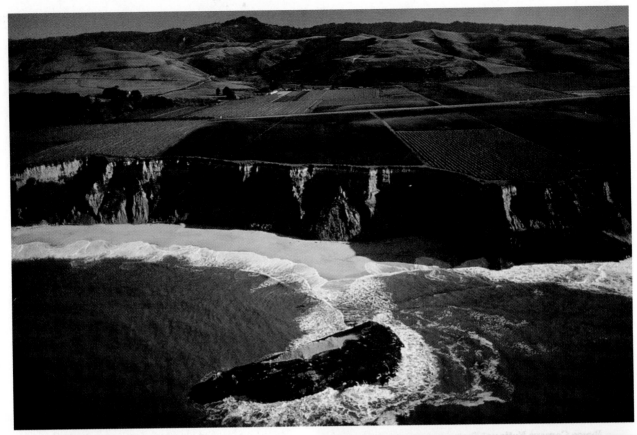

Coastal Farming, Northern California

Sound region in Washington—that have become major agricultural centers in recent times.

Well east of the Pacific coastal band lies the Great Basin, encompassing Nevada, western Utah, southern Idaho, and eastern Oregon. The few streams here have no outlet to the sea. Much of the Great Basin was once covered by an inland sea holding glacial meltwater, a remnant of which survives in Utah's Great Salt Lake. Today, however, the Great Basin is dry and severely eroded, a cold desert rich in minerals, imposing in its austere grandeur and lonely emptiness. North of the basin, the Columbia and Snake rivers, which drain the plateau country of Idaho and eastern Washington and Oregon, provide plentiful water for farming.

Western North America's "backbone" is the Rocky Mountains. In turn, the Rockies form part of the immense mountain system that reaches from Alaska to the Andes of South America. Elevations in the Rockies rise from a mile above sea level at Denver at the foot of the mountains to permanently snowcapped

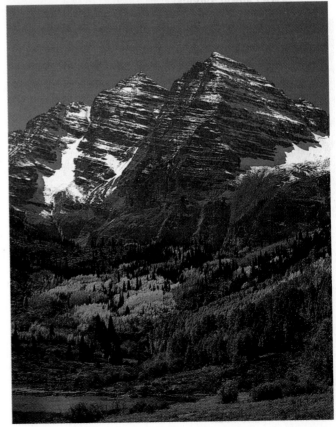

Maroon Bells of the Rocky Mountains, near Aspen, Colorado

peaks more than fourteen thousand feet above sea level. Beyond the front range of the Rockies lies the Continental Divide, the watershed separating the rivers flowing eastward into the Atlantic from those draining westward into the Pacific. The climate and vegetation of the Rocky Mountain high country resemble Arctic and subarctic types.

Arizona, southern Utah, western New Mexico, and southeastern California form America's southwestern desert. The climate is arid, searingly hot on summer days and cold on winter nights. Adapted to stringent environmental conditions, many plants and animals here could not survive elsewhere. Dust storms, cloudbursts, and flash floods have everywhere carved, abraded, and twisted the rocky landscape. Nature's fantastic sculpture appears on the most monumental scale in the Grand Canyon, where for 20 million years the Colorado River has been cutting down to Precambrian bedrock.

In the face of such tremendous natural forces, human activity might well seem paltry and transitory. Yet here the first crop cultivation began in what is now the

Lakes and Marshes in the Great Basin During the Last Ice Age

The Great Basin's extensive lakes and marshes during the last Ice Age contrast starkly with the diminished amount of surface water in the region today.

SOURCE: W. F. Ruddiman and H. E. Wright, Jr., eds. "North America and Adjacent Oceans During the Last Deglaciation." *The Geology of North America* K–3 (1987): 241.

Bryce Canyon National Park, Utah, at sunset

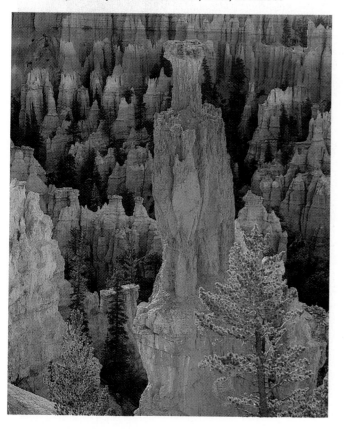

continental United States. Indian peoples later modified their societies and cultures in order to establish elaborate irrigation systems. Such systems are maintained today by Pueblo Indian and Hispanic communities in the region.

The Heartland

North America's heartland comprises the area extending eastward from the Rockies to the Appalachians. This vast region forms one of the world's largest drainage systems. From it the Great Lakes empty into the North Atlantic through the St. Lawrence River, and the Mississippi-Missouri-Ohio river network flows southward into the Gulf of Mexico. Where the drainage system originates, at the northern and western reaches of the Great Lakes region, lie some of the world's richest deposits of iron and copper ore.

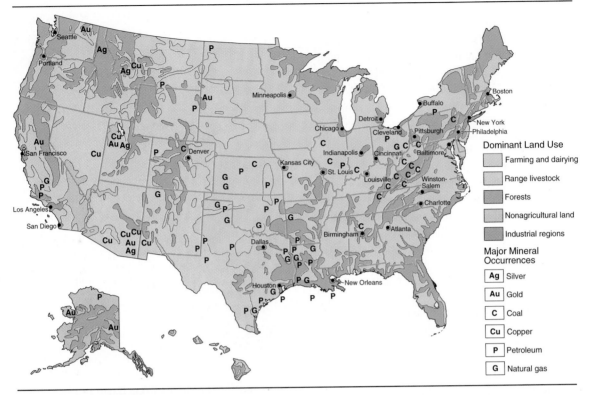

Present-Day U.S. Agriculture, Industry, and Resources

Confluence of the Mississippi and Ohio Rivers near Cairo, Illinois

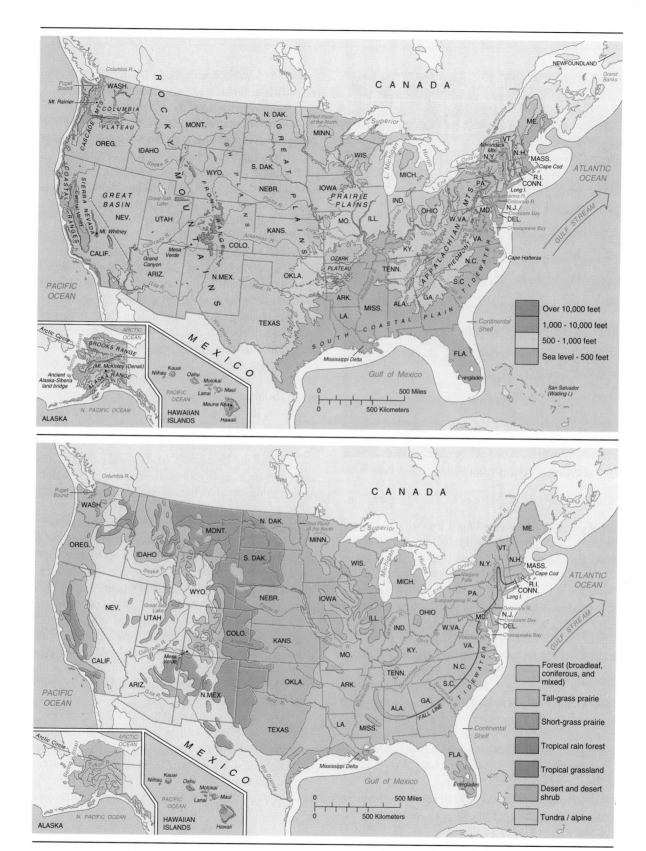

Above, **Physiographic Map of the United States** *Below,* **Natural Vegetation of the United States**

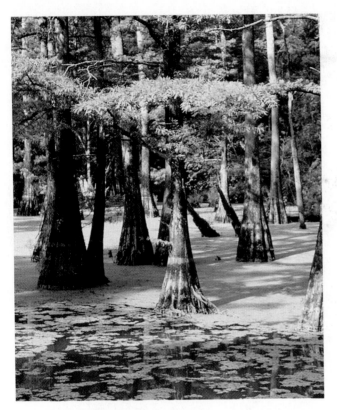

Cypress Pond in Bayou Country

In our own time, the heartland's waterways have offered a splendid means of carrying this mineral wealth to nearby coal-producing areas for processing but in so doing have spawned widespread environmental pollution.

The Mississippi—the "Father of Waters" to nearby Algonquian-speaking Indians, and one of the world's longest rivers—carries a prodigious volume of water and silt. It has changed course many times in geological history. The lower Mississippi (below the junction with the Ohio River) meanders constantly. In the process, the river deposits rich sediments throughout its broad, ancient floodplain. Indeed, the Missisippi has carried so much silt over the millennia that in its lower stretches, the river flows *above* the surrounding valley, which it catastrophically floods when its high banks (levees) are breached. Over millions of years, such riverborne sediment covered what was once the westward extension of the Appalachians in northern Mississippi and eastern Arkansas. Only the Ozark Plateau and Ouachita Mountains remain exposed, forming the hill country of southern Missouri, north-central Arkansas, and eastern Oklahoma. These uplands have evolved into an economically and culturally distinctive region—beautiful but isolated and impoverished.

Below New Orleans the Mississippi empties into the Gulf of Mexico through an enormous delta with an intricate network of grassy swamps known as bayous. The Mississippi Delta offers good farm soil, capable of supporting a large population. Swarming with waterfowl, insects, alligators, and marine plants and animals, this environment has nurtured a distinctive way of life for the Indian, white, and black peoples who have inhabited it.

North of the Ohio and Missouri rivers, themselves products of glacial runoff, Ice Age glaciation molded the American heartland. Because the local terrain was generally flat prior to glaciation, the ice sheets distributed glacial debris quite evenly. Spread even farther by wind and rivers, this fine-ground glacial dust slowly created the fertile farm soil of the Midwest. Glaciers also dug out the five Great Lakes (Superior, Huron, Michigan, Ontario, and Erie), collectively the world's largest body of fresh water. Water flowing from Lake Erie to the lower elevation of Lake Ontario created Niagara Falls, comparable only to the Grand Canyon as testimony to nature's power.

Most of the heartland's eastern and northern sectors were once heavily forested. To the west thick, tall-grass prairie covered Illinois and parts of adjoining states, as well as much of the Missouri River basin and the middle Arkansas River basin (Oklahoma and central Texas). Beyond the Missouri the prairie gave way to short-grass steppe—the Great Plains, cold in winter, blazing hot in summer, and always dry. The great distances that separate the heartland's prairies and Great Plains from the moderating effects of the oceans have made this region's annual temperature range the most extreme in North America. As the traveler moves westward, elevations rise gradually, winds howl ceaselessly, trees grow only along streambeds, long droughts alternate with violent thunderstorms and tornadoes, and water and wood are ever scarcer.

Now much of this forested, grassy world is forever altered. The heartland has become open farming country. Gone are the flocks of migratory birds that once darkened the daytime skies of the plains; gone are the free-roaming bison. Forests now only fringe the heartland: in the lake country of northern Minnesota and Wisconsin, on Michigan's upper peninsula, and across the hilly uplands of the Appalachians, southern Indiana, and the Ozarks. The settlers who displaced the region's Indian inhabitants have done most of the plowing up of prairie grass and felling of trees since the

Bison on South Dakota Prairie

Grain Harvesting in America's Heartland

early nineteenth century. Destruction of the forest and grassy cover has made the Midwest both a "breadbasket" for the world market and, during intervals of drought, a "dust bowl."

The Atlantic Seaboard

The eastern edge of the heartland is marked by the ancient Appalachian Mountain chain, which over the course of 200 million years has been ground down to gentle ridges paralleling one another southwest to northeast. Between the ridges lie fertile valleys such as Virginia's Shenandoah. The Appalachian hill country's wealth is in thick timber and mineral beds—particularly the Paleozoic coal deposits—whose heavy exploitation since the nineteenth century has accelerated destructive soil erosion in this softly beautiful, mountainous land.

Cades Cove, Great Smoky Mountains; Tennessee Strip Mining
The impact of human hands is dramatically apparent in these two starkly contrasting Appalachian hill-country scenes.

Descending gently from the Appalachians' eastern slope is the piedmont ("foot of the mountain"). In this broad, rolling upland extending from Alabama to Maryland, the rich red soil has been ravaged in modern times by excessive cotton and tobacco cultivation. The piedmont's modern piney-woods cover constitutes "secondary growth" replacing the sturdy hardwood trees that Native Americans and pioneering whites and blacks once knew. The northward extension of the piedmont from Pennsylvania to New England has

Pemigewasset Wilderness, White Mountains, New Hampshire

more broadleaf vegetation, a harsher winter climate, and (through the Hudson and Connecticut river valleys) somewhat better access to the piedmont itself. But unlike the piedmont, upstate New York and New England were shaped by glaciation: the terrain here comprises hills contoured by advancing and retreating ice, and numerous lakes scoured out by glaciers. Belts of debris remain, and in many places granite boulders shoulder their way up through the soil. Though picturesque, the land is the despair of anyone who has tried to plow it.

From southeastern Massachusetts and Rhode Island to south-central Alabama runs the fall line, the boundary between the relatively hard rock of the interior and the softer sediment of the coastal plain. Rivers crossing the fall line drop quickly to near sea level, thus making a series of rapids that block navigation upstream from the coast.

The character of the Atlantic coastal plain varies strikingly from south to north. In the extreme south, at the tip of the Florida peninsula, the climate and vegetation are subtropical. The southern coastal lands running north from Florida to Chesapeake Bay and the mouth of the Delaware River compose the tidewater region. This is a wide, rather flat lowland, heavily wooded with a mixture of broadleaf and coniferous

Tidewater Wetlands, North Carolina

Oyster Men, Chesapeake Bay, Maryland

dian and Maine coasts, where at the end of the Ice Age the rising ocean half covered glaciated mountains and valleys, oceangoing craft may find numerous small anchorages. South of Massachusetts Bay, the Atlantic shore and the Gulf of Mexico coastline form a shoreline of sandy beaches and long barrier islands paralleling the mainland. Tropical storms boiling up from the open seas regularly lash North America's Atlantic shores, and at all times brisk winds make coastal navigation treacherous.

Crossing the Atlantic east to west can daunt even skilled mariners, particularly those battling against powerful winds by sail. Here, on one of the world's stormiest seas, the mighty Gulf Stream current sweeps from southwest to northeast. Winds off the North American mainland also trend steadily eastward, and dangerous icebergs floating south from Greenland's waters threaten every ship. Little wonder that in 1620 the *Mayflower* Pilgrims' first impulse on landing was to sink to their knees in thanks to God for having transported them safely across "the vast and furious ocean." Many a vessel went to the bottom.

But for millennia, the Atlantic coastal region of North America offered a welcoming haven to settlers. For example, ten thousand years ago, ancient Indian hunters followed a warming climate eastward across the Appalachians to the coast. During the first millennium A.D., eastern peoples began adopting the Woodland culture and agriculture from the heartland. Offshore, well within their reach, lay such productive fishing grounds as the Grand Banks and Cape Cod's

forests, ribboned with numerous small rivers, occasionally swampy, and often miserably hot and humid in summer. North of Delaware Bay, the coastal lowlands narrow and flatten to form the New Jersey Pine Barrens, Long Island, and Cape Cod—all of these created by the deposit of glacial debris. Here the climate is noticeably milder than in the interior. North of Massachusetts Bay, the land back of the immediate shoreline becomes increasingly mountainous.

Many large rivers drain into the Atlantic: the St. Lawrence, flowing out of the Great Lakes northeastward through eastern Canada; the Connecticut in New England; the Hudson, Delaware, Susquehanna, and Potomac in what are now the Middle Atlantic states; the Savannah in the South. Most of these originally carried glacial meltwater. The Susquehanna and the Potomac filled in the broad, shallow Chesapeake Bay, teeming with marine life and offering numerous anchorages for oceangoing ships.

North America's true eastern edge is not the coastline but the offshore continental shelf, whose relatively shallow waters extend as far as 250 miles into the Atlantic before plunging deeply. Along the rocky Cana-

The Tip of Cape Cod, Massachusetts

coastal bays, where cool-water upwellings on the continental shelf had lured swarms of fish and crustaceans. "The abundance of sea-fish are almost beyond believing," wrote a breathless English settler in 1630, "and sure I should scarce have believed it, except I had seen it with my own eyes."

A Legacy and a Challenge

At least three thousand miles of open sea separates North America from Europe and Africa; and Asia, except for the subarctic region where Alaska and Siberia once joined, lies even more distant.

A lingering sense of isolation stimulated European-descended Americans' hopes of keeping "Old World" problems away from the pristine "New World," just as North America's fertile soil, extensive forests, and rich mineral resources long conjured up visions of limitless wealth. But population growth, intensive agriculture, industrialization, urbanization, and a hunger for consumer goods have stretched to the limits the American land's ability to maintain a modern society without irreversible ecological damage. And only in the twentieth century have Americans learned that global transportation networks and instantaneous communication make isolation impossible. At last, as ecologist Aldo Leopold put it, they have begun discovering that the earth's people "are only fellow voyagers in the odyssey of evolution." And that lesson has been hard learned. "It required 19 centuries to define decent man-to-man conduct and the process is only half-done," Leopold admonished; "it may take as long to evolve a code of decency for man-to-land conduct."

It is in evolving such a code, however, that the Native American legacy may yet prove most enduring. Interacting constantly with their physical environments, Indians considered themselves spiritually related to the land and all living beings that shared it. In recapturing a sense that the land—its life-sustaining bounty and its soul-sustaining beauty—is itself of inestimable value and not merely a means to the end of material growth, future American generations may reestablish a sense of historical and cultural continuity with their Native American precursors. Thereby they can truly be possessed by their land instead of simply being its possessors.

Chronology

c. 3,000,000,000 B.C.	Formation of oldest known rocks in present-day North America.
c. 500,000,000 B.C.	Precambrian era ends; Paleozoic era begins. Earliest forms of animal life appear.
c. 250,000,000 B.C.	Supercontinent of Pangaea forms.
c. 225,000,000 B.C.	Paleozoic era ends; Mesozoic era begins. First dinosaurs appear.
c. 210,000,000 B.C.	Appalachian Mountains emerge.
c. 180,000,000 B.C.	Pangaea begins to break up.
c. 65,000,000 B.C.	Mesozoic era ends; Cenozoic era begins. Dinosaurs become extinct. Rocky Mountains form.

Trilobite from Mesozoic era

c. 50,000,000 B.C.	Hawaiian Islands emerge.
c. 20,000,000 B.C.	Grand Canyon begins to form.
c. 5,000,000 B.C.	Earliest human ancestors appear in Africa.
c. 2,000,000 B.C.	Ice Age begins.
c. 300,000– 100,000 B.C.	Humans spread throughout Eastern Hemisphere.
c. 120,000 B.C.	Wisconsin glaciation begins.
c. 40,000– 15,000 B.C.	Ancestors of Native Americans cross Alaska-Siberian land bridge.
c. 10,000 B.C.	Ice Age ends. Wisconsin glaciation retreats from North America. Native Americans begin to spread throughout Western Hemisphere.
A.D. 1492	Christopher Columbus's first voyage to the Western Hemisphere.

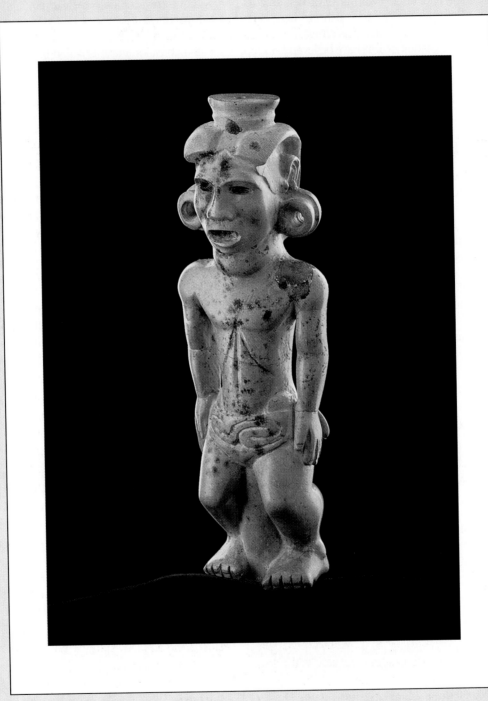

Adena Stone Effigy Pipe
c. 400–100 B.C.

1

AMERICA BEGINS

Hiawatha had known the depths of despair. For years his people, the group of Indian nations known as the Iroquois, had been beset by a destructive, seemingly endless cycle of violence and revenge. Families, villages, and nations fought one another, and neighboring Indians attacked relentlessly. When Hiawatha tried to restore peace among his own Onondaga people, an evil sorcerer who opposed peace caused the deaths of his seven beloved daughters. Grief-stricken and angry, Hiawatha wandered alone into the forest. After several days he reached the shore of a lake, where he experienced a series of visions. First he saw a flock of wild ducks suddenly fly up from the lake, taking the water with them. Hiawatha walked onto the dry lake bed, gathering and stringing the beautiful purple and white shells that lay there. He saw the shells, called wampum, as symbolic "words" of condolence that, when properly presented, would soothe grief, no matter how intense. Then he met a holy man named Deganawidah ("the Peacemaker"), who presented him the beads and spoke the appropriate words, one to dry his weeping eyes, another to open his ears to the words of peace and reason, a third to clear his throat so that he himself could once again speak peacefully and reasonably. Deganawidah and Hiawatha then took the wampum to the five Iroquois nations. To each they introduced the ritual of condolence as a new message of peace. The Iroquois subsequently submerged their differences

and created a council of chiefs and a confederacy, based on the condolence ritual. Thus was born the powerful League of the Iroquois.

Although it is an oral tradition couched in the language of supernatural religion, the story of Hiawatha and Deganawidah depicts a concrete event in American history. Archaeological evidence at Iroquois sites corroborates the sequence of bloody warfare followed by peace and dates the league's origins at some time between the late fourteenth and the mid-fifteenth century. As with all of American history before the arrival of Europeans and their system of writing, archaeological evidence and oral traditions, examined critically, are our principal sources of knowledge about the past. In this case the story refers to an event of importance not only for pre-Columbian history but for the period of European contact with Native Americans as well. For the Iroquois Confederacy was a significant diplomatic and military force throughout the colonial period and has inspired and intrigued many non-Indians down to the present, despite the fact that it was established prior to, and entirely independently of, the Europeans' arrival.

The founding of the League of the Iroquois marked just one moment in a long history that began more than ten thousand years before Christopher Columbus's first voyage. Over that time an indigenous American history unfolded, utterly separate from that of the Eastern Hemisphere.

Some native peoples eked out their existences in precarious environments, whereas others enjoyed affluence and prosperity; some lived in small bands, whereas others lived in large cities; some believed that the first humans came from the sky, whereas others maintained that they originated underground. Wherever and however they lived and whatever they believed, native peoples together made North America a human habitat and gave it a history.

THE FIRST AMERICANS

Like the slow but relentless shaping of the planet itself, the origins of the human species extend back to the mists of prehistoric time. More than 5 million years ago, direct human ancestors evolved in the temperate grasslands of Africa. Between three hundred thousand and one hundred thousand years ago, humans began migrating through much of the Old World. During the last glaciation, which geologists term Wisconsin, hunting bands pursuing large game animals moved from Central Asia into Siberia. Between forty thousand and fifteen thousand years ago, some of these bands began crossing the broad land bridge then connecting Siberia to Alaska. In so doing, they became the first Americans.

Most Native Americans are descended from these earliest migrants. A few, however, trace their lineage to later arrivals. About nine thousand years ago, Athapaskan-speaking peoples crossed the land bridge and spread over much of northern and western Canada and southern and central Alaska. Some of them later migrated southward to form the Apaches and Navajos in the Southwest, as well as smaller groups elsewhere. Eskimos and Aleuts began crossing the Bering Sea—which had submerged the land bridge—from Siberia between five thousand and four thousand years ago, and the Hawaiian Islands remained uninhabited until after A.D. 300.

The Peopling of North America

About 10,000 B.C. the Ice Age was nearing its end. Melting glaciers had opened up an ice-free corridor leading from Alaska to the northern Plains. Bands of hunters moved through this corridor, and others probably trav-

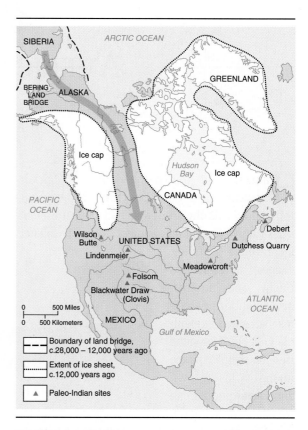

The First Americans
The arrow shows the "ice corridor" through which most ancestors of Native Americans passed before dispersing throughout the Western Hemisphere.
SOURCE: Dean R. Snow, *The Archaeology of North America* (New York: Chelsea House Publishers, 1989).

eled south along the Pacific coast by boat. As they emerged from the glacier-covered north, they discovered a hunter's paradise. Giant mammoths, mastodons, horses, camels, bison, caribou, and moose, as well as smaller species, roamed the continent innocent of the ways of human predators. So bountiful and accommodating was this new environment that the Paleo-Indians, as archaeologists call these hunters, fanned out and proliferated with astonishing speed. By 9000 B.C. descendants of the first Americans had dispersed throughout the Western Hemisphere.

Most Paleo-Indians dwelled in bands of about fifteen to fifty people. The men hunted; the women prepared the food and cared for the children. Members of a band lived together during the spring and summer and split into smaller groups of one or two families for the fall and winter. Although they moved constantly, they generally remained within informally defined

A Folsom Point
The Folsom point is the most common of the Paleo-Indian fluted spear points. This point is shown just as it was found, imbedded between two ribs of the extinct Bison taylori.

boundaries. An exception occurred when they traveled to favored quarries to obtain jasper or flint for making tools and spear points. At such sites they encountered other bands, with whom they traded, intermarried, and participated in religious ceremonies.

Even before leaving Alaska the Paleo-Indians had developed distinctly American ways. Their most characteristic innovation was their "fluted" points, so-called for their shape, which permitted fitting them on spears. Although fluted points have been found throughout the Western Hemisphere, none has been uncovered in Siberia. Around 9000 B.C. many of the big-game species such as the mammoths and mastodons became extinct. The effectiveness of the Paleo-Indian hunters may have contributed to this demise, but the animals were also doomed by the warming climate, which brought ecological changes that undermined the food chain on which they depended. In other words, the replacement of the big-game mammals by humans marked part of a larger process of ecological change associated with the end of the Ice Age.

Archaic Societies

The warming of the earth's atmosphere continued until about 4000 B.C., with far-reaching effects on the North American continent. Sea levels rose, flooding shallow offshore areas, and glacial runoff in the interior filled the Great Lakes, the Mississippi River basin, and other waterways. As the glaciers receded northward, so did the arctic and subarctic environments that had previously extended far into what are now the "lower 48" states of the United States. Treeless plains and evergreen forests gave way to deciduous forests in the East, grassland prairies on the Plains, and desert in much of the West. An immense range of flora and fauna, both on land and in the waters, came to characterize the American landscape. We are familiar with many of these same plants and animals today.

Just as the Paleo-Indians had flourished in settings south of the glaciers, so their descendants now prospered in the abundance and diversity of their new environments. Instead of focusing most of their food gathering energy on big game, these Archaic peoples, as archaeologists term native North Americans from c. 8000 B.C. to 1500 B.C., lived off wide varieties of smaller mammals, fish, and wild plants. As they used the resources of their environments more efficiently, their communities required less land area and could

Archaic Hunting Aid
This duck decoy was made 2,000 to 3,000 years ago by a hunter living at Lovelock Cave in the Humboldt Basin of west-central Nevada.

support larger populations. Although the size of populations and territories of hunting-gathering bands in the Great Basin and Southwest changed little from Paleo-Indian times, people in parts of the East and Midwest now resided in villages with larger populations for all or most of the year. For example, a year-round village that flourished near Kampsville, Illinois, from 3900 to 2800 B.C., supported 100 to 150 people. It could do so because the residents knew how and when to procure fish and mussels from local lakes, in addition to the deer and other mammals, birds, nuts, and seeds available in the surrounding area.

Archaic peoples diversified other aspects of their lives as well. Besides using many more varieties of stone, they utilized bone, shell, copper, horn, ivory, asphalt, clay, and leather to make such objects as tools, weapons, utensils, and ornaments. Although many of these materials were available locally, the Native Americans obtained others through exchanges, both with neighbors and through long-distance trade networks. Archaeological evidence gives some indication of the extent and importance of this long-distance trade. Obsidian (a glassy black volcanic rock) from the Yellowstone region, copper from the Great Lakes, and marine shells from the coasts appear at sites hundreds and even thousands of miles from their points of origin. Archaic peoples, as well as Indians who encountered Europeans several millenia later, thought that such minerals contained supernatural power. A few large sites, among them Indian Knoll in western Kentucky, which dates to 2500–2000 B.C., served as major centers of interregional trade.

Trade networks were routes not only for materials but also for ideas about their uses. By means of these pathways, the techniques developed in one locale for making material objects, procuring food, or utilizing the medicinal properties of plants were carried to other areas, transcending the narrow boundaries of community, language, and ethnicity. Out of such diffusions of ideas arose regional cultural patterns (see below). Trade also served to spread religious beliefs, as exemplified in ideas and practices relating to death. Human burials became more elaborate during the Archaic era as Native Americans in many regions buried the dead with their personal possessions as well as with objects fashioned from obsidian, copper, shell, and other highly valued substances. They often sprinkled the flexed corpses with bright red hematite, a source of iron, so that they resembled a baby at birth. Ideas of death as a kind of rebirth remained widespread in North America at the time Europeans began arriving many centuries later.

Archaic Americans did not distinguish among themselves on the basis of class or rank, or centralize political power in the hands of one person or a few individuals. However, the growing complexity of their diets and of their technologies led them to sharpen many of the distinctions between women's and men's roles. Men took responsibility for fishing as well as hunting, whereas women harvested and prepared the products of wild plants, including the grinding and milling of seeds. Men and women each made the tools needed for their tasks. In general, men's activities entailed travel, and women's activities kept them close to the village, where they bore and raised children. These role distinctions are apparent in the burials at Indian Knoll, where tools relating to hunting, fishing, woodworking, and leatherworking were usually buried with men and those relating to nut cracking and seed grinding with women. Yet gender-specific distinctions by no means applied to all activities, for objects used by shamans, or religious healers, were distributed equally between male and female graves.

THE INDIANS' CONTINENT

By 1500 B.C. Indians in parts of North America were shaping new ways of life and new institutions, transcending the Archaic cultures developed over the preceding millennia. Most post-Archaic Americans remained in small bands consisting of a few families and continued to rely on combinations of hunting, fishing, and gathering. But others developed more specialized methods of food production and more actively shaped their environments to their own needs. In the Southwest, the Southeast, and the Northeast the advent of agriculture and of large centers of trade and population marked a radical departure from Archaic patterns and from the foraging way of life still followed by Indians in other regions.

Despite the discrepancies emerging among native societies, the ties between them grew strong. Trade networks carrying goods and ideas over geographic distances and across linguistic, ethnic, and cultural divides continued to proliferate. In this way the bow and arrow and ceramic pottery spread throughout the Americas, from the smallest bands to the largest cities.

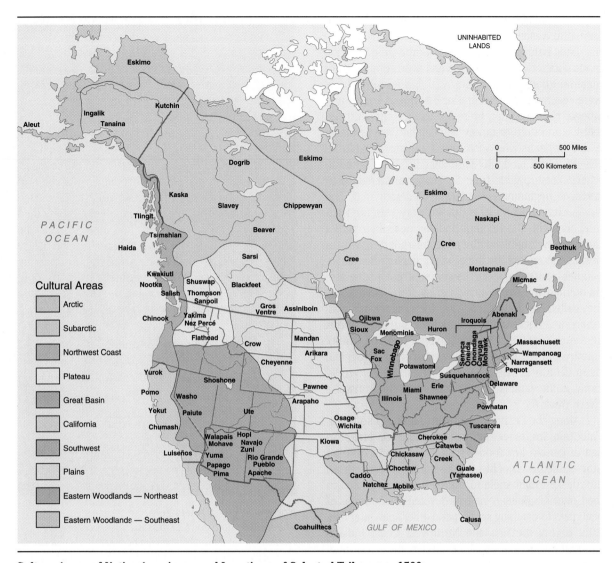

Culture Areas of Native Americans and Locations of Selected Tribes, A.D. 1500
"Culture area" is a convention enabling archaeologists and anthropologists to generalize about regional patterns among pre-Columbian Native American cultures.

And Indians virtually everywhere retained their preferences for seasonal food procurement and for living in communities based on kinship, often abandoning or resisting more centralized systems that proved unworkable or oppressive.

The Northern and Western Perimeters

In western Alaska, where the first Americans had arrived thousands of years earlier, the post-Archaic period marked the beginning of a new, arctic way of life.

The Eskimos and Aleuts had brought highly sophisticated tools and weapons from their Siberian homeland. Combining ivory, bone, and other materials, they fashioned harpoons and spears for the pursuit of sea mammals and—in the case of the Eskimos—caribou. Through their continued contacts with Siberia, the Eskimos were making and using the first bows and arrows, the first ceramic pottery, and the first pit houses (structures set partially below ground level) in the Americas by 1500 B.C. As they perfected their ways of living in the cold tundra regions of the far north, many

Eskimos spread across upper Canada to the shores of Labrador, western Newfoundland, and Greenland.

Long before the arrival of Columbus, the Eskimos made contact with Europeans and used some of their material goods. From about A.D. 1, a few iron tools were reaching western Alaska by way of Russia and Siberia. However, they were too few in number to affect Eskimo culture in any substantial way. Contacts with Europeans were more direct and sustained in areas of Greenland, Newfoundland, and Labrador, where Norse people from Scandinavia attempted to colonize, beginning in the late tenth century A.D. The Norse exchanged metal goods for ivory with the Eskimos and with the Beothuk Indians near their settlement in Newfoundland. But peaceful trade gave way to hostile encounters. By the eleventh century the native peoples' resistance to the newcomers' colonizing ambitions led the Norse to withdraw from Vinland, as they called Newfoundland. As a Norse leader, dying after losing a battle with some natives, put it, "There is fat around my belly! We have won a fine and fruitful country, but will hardly be allowed to enjoy it." Several more centuries would pass before Europeans would enjoy, at the expense of native peoples, the fruits of a "New World."

Along the Pacific coast, from Alaska to southern California, improvements in the production and storage of certain key foods enabled Indians to develop more settled ways of life. On the Northwest coast, from the Alaskan panhandle to northern California, and in the Columbia Plateau, natives devoted brief periods of each year to catching salmon and other spawning fish. After drying the fish, the Northwest Coast Indians stored it in quantities sufficient to last the year round. As a result, their seasonal movements gave way to a settled lifestyle in permanent villages consisting of cedar-plank houses. Plateau Indians constructed villages with pit houses where they ate salmon through the summer. They left the villages in spring and fall for hunting and gathering.

By A.D. 1 many villages on the Northwest coast numbered several hundred people. Trade and warfare with interior groups strengthened the power of chiefs and other leading figures, whose families were distinguished from those of commoners by their wealth and prestige. These leading families proclaimed their status most conspicuously in elaborate totem poles depicting supernatural beings supposedly linked to their ancestors and in potlatches, ceremonies in which they gave away or destroyed much of their material wealth. From

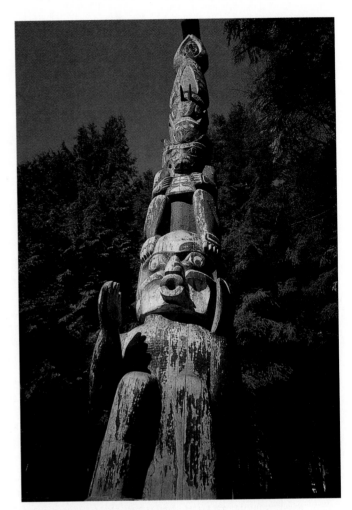

Northwest Coast Totem Pole
The most famous form of artistic expression among Northwest Coast Indians, totem poles served various purposes. Some advertised the genealogy and accomplishments of a clan, family, or individual. Others celebrated a successful potlatch. A few seem to have been intended to ridicule an enemy or simply to express the maker's whimsy and skill.

the time of the earliest contacts, Europeans were awestruck by the artistic and architectural achievements of the Northwest Coast Indians. "What must astonish most," wrote a French explorer in 1791, "is to see painting everywhere, everywhere sculpture, among a nation of hunters."

At about the same time as native peoples in the Northwest, Indians on the coast and in the interior valleys of what is now California became more settled. Residing in villages of about one hundred people, each established near large oak groves, they devoted extensive time and effort to processing acorns. After the fall harvest, the Indians ground the acorns into meal, leached them of their bitter tannic acid, and then roasted, boiled, or baked the nuts prior to eating or storing them. In the face of intense competition for acorns, native Californians defined territorial boundaries more rigidly than elsewhere in pre-Columbian North America and combined several villages under the leadership of a single chief. The chiefs conducted trade, diplomacy, and religious ceremonies with neighboring groups and, when necessary, led their people in battle. Along with the resources of game, fish, and plants available to them, acorns enabled the Indians of California to prosper. As a Spanish friar arriving in California from Mexico in 1770 wrote, "This land exceeds all the preceding territory in fertility and abundance of things necessary for sustenance."

The end of the Archaic period is less noticeable in the Great Basin than almost anywhere else in North America. This region's warm, dry climate was almost as forbidding to humans as that of the frigid Arctic. Foraging bands continued to move over the area, depending primarily on hunting small mammals and harvesting seeds and piñon (pine) nuts. Little change occurred until about the fourteenth or fifteenth century A.D., when Paiute, Ute, and Shoshone Indians fanned over the Great Basin from their homeland in southeastern California, absorbing or displacing the earlier inhabitants. Although the newcomers' way of life was essentially the same as that of the older groups, their more efficient seed processing enabled them to support larger populations, which in turn occupied ever-larger territories.

The Hawaiian Islands were not part of indigenous North America but rather of Oceania. By 3000 B.C. the Austronesian peoples of Australia, New Guinea, and nearby smaller islands had developed agriculture and crafted pottery, tools and other objects of stone and shell, and giant outrigger canoes for voyaging on the high seas. About 1600 B.C. some Austronesians began settling the formerly uninhabited islands of the south Pacific, but only in the fourth century A.D. did voyagers from the Marquesas Islands reach Hawaii, the northern extremity of Polynesia.

For the next four hundred years, these first Hawaiians lived in self-sufficient communities, cultivating sweet potatoes, yams, and taro (whose starchy root they made into a fermented paste) and exploiting a rich variety of fish and shellfish. Each community dis-

A Hawaiian Chief
This portrait was drawn by a member of Captain James Cook's expedition in 1778.

tinguished sharply between commoners and chiefs. The latter included a paramount chief as well as various lesser rulers who could prove kinship with him. As in parts of North America, Hawaiian chiefs collected food and craft goods from subordinate communities and allies. Unlike their counterparts in North America, these chiefs occasionally waged war for territorial conquest and the subjugation of other peoples.

When Europeans began arriving in Hawaii in the late eighteenth century, the islands numbered about four hundred thousand people, with communities averaging about two hundred individuals each. Thereafter European diseases had effects similar to those on the mainland: within half a century the native population plummeted to 130,000 and by 1890 to 40,000.

The Southwest

Although the peoples of the Northwest coast and California cultivated tobacco, they never farmed food-bearing plants. With their abundant food sources, they had little incentive to hazard the additional risks that agriculture would have entailed, especially in California, with its dry summers. However, elsewhere in North America agriculture became central to Indian life. In the arid Southwest, natives concentrated much of their communities' energy on irrigation in order to feed themselves by farming. In the humid Eastern Woodlands, on the other hand, plant cultivation came more easily. But in both regions, the advent of agriculture was a long, slow process that never entirely displaced other food-procuring activities.

Farming began in the Western Hemisphere about 5000 B.C.—just as agriculture was being introduced to Europe from southwestern Asia—when Indians living in the Tehuacán Valley of central Mexico experimentally planted the seeds of certain wild plants they customarily harvested. Among these were squash, maize (corn), and eventually beans. Slowly, the techniques of plant domestication spread in all directions. The earliest North American evidence is at Bat Cave in western New Mexico, where archaeologists have found maize and squash remains dating to about 3500 B.C. Yet for thousands of years more, farming remained only a minor activity for hunter-gatherers in both Mexico and the Southwest. Substantial changes in southwestern life began only after 400 B.C., when the introduction (probably from Mexico) of a more drought-resistant strain of maize enabled the inhabitants to move from the highlands to the drier lowlands. In the centuries that followed, populations rose throughout the region, and native culture was transformed. The two most influential new cultural traditions were the Hohokam and the Anasazi.

The Hohokam emerged during the third century B.C. when ancestors of the Pima and Papago Indians began farming in the Gila River and Salt River valleys of southern Arizona. Hohokam peoples built elaborate canal systems for irrigation that enabled them to harvest two crops per year, an astonishing achievement in such an arid environment. To construct and maintain their canals, the Hohokam people needed large, coordinated work forces. They built permanent villages, usually consisting of several hundred people. Although many such villages remained independent, others joined confederations in which several towns were linked by canals. The central village in each confederation coordinated labor, trade, and religious and political life for all the communities connected to it.

Essentially a local creation, Hohokam culture nevertheless drew extensively on materials and ideas from outside the Southwest. From about the sixth century A.D., the large villages had ball courts and platform mounds like those found throughout Mexico at the time. As in Mexico, ball games were major public events in Hohokam villages. Although no evidence of their rules survives, they probably resembled the Mexican game, in which play was rough, players could not use their hands, and the losers sacrificed some of their material possessions. Mexican influence was also apparent in the creations of Hohokam artists, who worked in clay, stone, turquoise, and shell. Archaeologists have unearthed such artifacts as rubber balls, macaw feathers, and copper bells among the Mexican items found at Hohokam sites. Artists used seashells from California in pottery, as backing for turquoise mosaics, and as material for intricate etchings.

Among the last southwesterners to make farming the focus of their subsistence were a people known as the Anasazi, a Navajo term meaning "ancient ones." Their culture originated in the Four Corners area where Arizona, New Mexico, Colorado, and Utah meet. By the sixth century A.D., the Anasazi people were only beginning to harvest beans, live in permanent villages with pit houses, make pottery (although they had crafted elaborately coiled baskets for centuries), use the bow and arrow, and domesticate turkeys—practices already adopted by most of their southwestern neighbors. Yet over the next six centuries, these ancestors of the modern Pueblo Indians expanded over a wide region and became the most powerful people in the region. And while they traded with Indians in Mexico, California, and elsewhere, the Anasazis borrowed little in the way of artistic or cultural ideas. Instead their neighbors borrowed from them.

One of the distinguishing characteristics of Anasazi culture was its architecture. Early Anasazi houses were round, with walls of stone slabs or clay plaster and domed roofs of logs and mud, supported by four central posts. They also featured underground storage cists, ventilator shafts, and small holes in the floor known as *sipapus*. The Anasazis and modern Pueblos maintain that the first humans reached the earth from underground, following a long and tortuous journey through several underworlds. Symbolizing this journey, the sipapu was a sacred place in each family's house. As village populations increased after the sixth century, often reaching one hundred or more houses, the Anasazis shifted to above-ground, rectangular apartments. However, they retained the form of the pit house in their *kivas*, round, partly underground structures in which the men held religious ceremonies. To this day Anasazi-style apartments and kivas are central features of Pueblo Indian architecture in the Southwest.

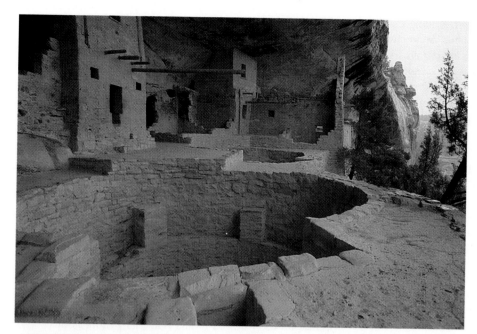

(top left) **Anasazi Cliffside Balcony House with Kiva, Mesa Verde, Colorado**
Some Anasazi peoples, most notably those at Mesa Verde in southwestern Colorado, built their villages in cliffside caves.

(bottom left) **Pueblo Bonito, Chaco Canyon**
Pueblo Bonito illustrates the richness and grand scale of Anasazi architecture.

These roads were perfectly straight; their builders even carved out stairs or footholds in the sides of steep cliffs rather than go around them. The largest of the villages, Pueblo Bonito, had about 1,200 inhabitants and was the home of two Great Kivas, each about fifty feet in diameter. People traveled from the outlying towns to Chaco Canyon for religious rituals. In addition, the canyon was the center of a turquoise industry that manufactured beads for trade with Mexico, and its pueblos supplied the outliers with food in times of drought. The ability of canyon residents to grow enough vegetables and other crops to feed themselves and others lay in their system of controlling rainwater runoff through small dams, terraces, and other devices.

From the beginning of the tenth century to the middle of the twelfth, during an unusually wet period in the Southwest, the Anasazis expanded over much of what is today northern New Mexico and Arizona. The population of some villages grew to more than a thousand. In Chaco Canyon in present-day northwestern New Mexico, a cluster of twelve villages forged a powerful confederation numbering about fifteen thousand people. A system of roads radiated out of the canyon to satellite pueblos located as far as sixty-five miles away.

The classic Anasazi culture, as manifested at Chaco Canyon, Mesa Verde in southwestern Colorado, Canyon de Chelly in northeastern Arizona, and other sites, came to an end in the twelfth and thirteenth centuries. Although Chaco Canyon's somewhat earlier collapse may have been triggered by a cutoff of its turquoise trade with Mexico, the overriding cause of the Anasazi demise was drought. Suddenly, the amount of available farmland was drastically reduced for a population that had grown rapidly during the preceding centuries. The great Anasazi centers were abandoned as the inhabitants dispersed. Most formed new pueblos on or near the upper Rio Grande, whereas others moved south to establish the Zuni and Hopi pueblos. Descendants of the Anasazis still inhabit many of these pueblos. Other large agricultural communities, such as those of the Hohokam, also dispersed when drought came. With farming peoples now clustered in the few areas with enough water, the drier lands of the Southwest attracted the foraging Apaches and Navajos, whose arrival at the end of the fourteenth century ended their long migration from northwestern Canada.

The Eastern Woodlands

Whereas the Hohokam and Anasazi peoples built large villages and created centralized or confederated political systems as a consequence of deciding to farm for most of their food, natives on the Northwest coast and in California enlarged and consolidated their societies in the absence of agriculture. Nonfarming Indians in much of the Eastern Woodlands—that vast stretch of land from the Mississippi Valley to the Atlantic Ocean—likewise experimented with village life and political centralization without farming. But after doing so, they developed an extraordinarily productive agriculture.

In 1200 B.C. about five thousand people had concentrated in a single village at Poverty Point on the Mississippi River in Louisiana. The village was flanked by two large mounds and surrounded by six concentric embankments, the outermost of which spanned more than half a mile in diameter. During the spring and autumn equinoxes, a person standing on the larger mound could watch the sun rise directly over the village center. As with similar communities of the period in Mexico, solar observations were the basis for religious beliefs as well as for a calendar. Poverty Point also lay at the center of a much larger political and economic unit. The settlement imported large quantities of quartz, copper, obsidian, crystal, and other sacred materials from throughout eastern North America and then redistributed them to nearby communities. These communities almost certainly supplied some of the labor for the earthworks. Although

Poverty Point was built by local inhabitants, its general design and organization suggest the influence of the Olmec peoples of Mexico. For reasons that are unclear, Poverty Point flourished for only about three centuries and then declined. Nevertheless, it foreshadowed later developments in the Mississippi Valley.

A different kind of mound-building culture, called Adena, emerged in the Ohio Valley in the fifth century B.C. Adena villages were smaller than Poverty Point, rarely exceeding four hundred inhabitants. But Adena people spread over a wide area and built hundreds of mounds, most of them containing graves. The largest, Grave Creek Mound in West Virginia, was 240 feet in diameter, 70 feet high, and contained 72,000 tons of soil. The treatment of Adena dead varied widely, indicating differences in social or political status. Some corpses were cremated, others were placed in round clay basins, and still others were given elaborate tombs. Some burials contained just a few utilitarian grave goods, whereas others had many more goods and a greater variety, including pipes and other finely crafted objects.

The Adena mounds constituted the heart of a religious movement whose adherents were diffused over much of the Northeast. Although many Adena burial practices, such as the inclusion of grave goods and the spreading of red hematite on some corpses, were familiar in the Northeast, the burial rituals themselves and many of the manufactured objects were new. Many of these objects were distributed throughout the Northeast via trade networks during the period in which Adena culture flourished.

During the first century B.C., Adena culture evolved into a more complex and widespread culture known as Hopewell. Hopewell ceremonial centers were even larger and more elaborate than their Adena predecessors. They proliferated not only in the Ohio Valley but also in the Illinois River valley. Some centers contained two or three dozen mounds within enclosures of several square miles. The variety and quantity of goods buried with members of the elite were also greater. The people surrounded some corpses with thousands of freshwater pearls or copper ornaments or with sheets of mica, quartz, or other sacred substances. Hopewell artisans fashioned a wide variety of effigies, ornaments, and jewelry, which their owners wore to their graves. The raw materials for these objects originated in locales throughout America east of the Rockies. Through trade networks Hopewell influence spread over much of the Eastern Woodlands—to

Great Serpent Mound, Ohio
This well-known mound, built for religious ceremonies rather than for burials, depicts a 1,254-foot-long snake devouring an egg or a frog.

Poverty Point, Louisiana
This perspective sketch shows the large mound located just outside the concentric rings, as well as a smaller mound in the upper right. The earthworks symbolized Poverty Point's importance as a regional center for trade and religious ceremonies.

communities as far away as Wisconsin, Missouri, Florida, and New York. Some of these, such as Marksville in Louisiana, emulated the Ohio centers in almost every detail, but others were more selective, imitating Hopewell mounds, copper work, or pottery. Although the great Hopewell centers of the Ohio and Illinois valleys were abandoned in the fifth century A.D. for reasons that are unclear, they had an enormous influence on subsequent developments in eastern North America.

Remarkably, the people who created the sophisticated Hopewell culture were hunter-gatherers rather than farmers. Archaic Indians in Kentucky and Missouri had cultivated small amounts of squash as early as 2500 B.C., and maize first appeared in eastern North America by 300 B.C. But agriculture became a dietary mainstay for Woodlands people only between the seventh and twelfth centuries A.D., as women moved beyond gathering and minor cultivating activities to become the major producers of food.

Mississippian Engraved Shell
Engraved conch shells, often with highly abstract designs, were among the goods traded by Mississippian peoples in the Southeast.

Major Mississippian Centers
SOURCE: Jay A. Levenson, ed., *Art in the Age of Exploration: Circa 1492* (New Haven, Conn.: Yale University Press, 1991).

The first full-time farmers in the East were Indians living on the floodplains of the Mississippi River and its major tributaries. They developed a new culture, called Mississippian, that incorporated elements of Hopewell culture and ideas from Mexico into their indigenous traditions. The volume of Mississippian craft production and long-distance trade dwarfed those of Adena and Hopewell cultures. At the same time, Mississippian towns, numbering hundreds or even thousands of people, were built around open plazas like those of central Mexico. Large platform mounds stood next to the plazas, topped by sumptuous religious temples and the residences of chiefs and other elites. Religious ceremonies focused on the worship of the sun as the source of agricultural fertility. The people considered chiefs to be related to the sun. When a chief died, his wives and servants were killed so that they could accompany him to the afterlife. Largely in connection with their religious and funeral rituals, Mississippian artists produced highly sophisticated work in clay, stone, shell, copper, wood, and other materials.

Many Mississippian centers were built not by local natives but by outsiders seeking to combine farming and riverborne trade. Local natives often were coerced into bringing corn and goods to a new center and pay-

ing homage to its chief. By the tenth century most Mississippian centers were part of even larger systems, based on trade and on shared religious beliefs and dominated by a single "super-center." The most powerful such system centered around Cahokia (see "A Place in Time"), located near modern St. Louis.

For two and a half centuries, Cahokia reigned supreme in the American heartland. Beginning in the thirteenth century, however, Cahokia and its allied centers began to experience shortages of food and other resources. Soon they were challenged militarily by neighboring peoples and, as a result, the inhabitants fled to the countryside. By the fifteenth century, Indians in the central Mississippi Valley were living (like their Archaic forebears) in small villages linked by reciprocity rather than coercion. Similar developments led to the decline of some temple-mound centers in the Southeast, but in this region new centers arose to take their place. Thus the decline of Etowah in northwestern Georgia near the end of the fourteenth century was followed by the rise of Coosa nearby. But Coosa and the other remaining centers were abandoned after 1500 as a result of European diseases.

The demise of Mississippian culture, like that of the Hopewell, ended a trend toward political centralization among Indians in eastern North America. In spite of their decline, however, the Mississippians profoundly affected native culture in the East. They spread new strains of maize and beans, along with many of the techniques and tools to cultivate these crops, enabling women to weave agriculture into the fabric of village life among the Iroquois and other Indians throughout the region. Only in portions of northern New England and the upper Great Lakes was the growing season for maize (one hundred frost-free days) generally too short for it to be a reliable crop. Some eastern Indians, searching for new farmlands, took the new ways to the river valleys of the plains, where they interacted peacefully with the region's hunting peoples.

Indian hands tended eastern North America's lands with skill and care. Over much of the region, great expanses of hardwood trees formed open, park-like tracts, free of underbrush (which the Indians had systematically burned) but rich with grass and berry bushes that attracted a profusion of game. The Woodland peoples' "slash-and-burn" method of land management was environmentally sound and economically productive. Men cleared the land by burning underbrush and destroying the larger trees' bark. Then, amid the leafless deadwood, women planted corn, beans, and pumpkins in soil enriched by ash. After several years of abundant harvests, yields declined, and the Indians moved on to a new site to repeat the process. Soon groundcover reclaimed the abandoned clearing, restoring fertility naturally, and the Indians could return.

The Indians rotated their crops to prevent soil depletion and diversified their food-producing activities (fishing, hunting, and gathering wild plants, as well as farming) to avoid dependence on a single food source. Later Europeans, importing a system in which land was divided into individual plots and valued according to the wealth it yielded, ignored and even belittled strategies that would have allowed natural resources to renew themselves.

By A.D. 1500 the North American continent presented a remarkable variety of human cultures, societies, and historical experiences. As they had for thousands of years, small, mobile hunting bands peopled the Arctic, Subarctic, Great Basin, and much of the Plains. More stable societies, based on fishing or gath-ering, predominated along the Pacific coast, whereas village-based agriculture was typical in the Eastern Woodlands and the river valleys of the Southwest and Plains. Finally, Mississippian urban centers still prevailed in portions of the Southeast.

Despite the vast differences among Native Americans, much bound them together. Trade facilitated the exchange not only of goods but of new ideas, techniques, and beliefs. Thus the bow and arrow, ceramic pottery, and certain beliefs and rituals surrounding the burial of the dead came to characterize Indians everywhere. Indians also shared a preference for the independent, kin-based communities that generally had characterized indigenous North America, a preference that probably was reinforced by the failure of such highly centralized systems as Cahokia and the Anasazi centers during the thirteenth century.

NEW WORLD PEOPLES ON THE EVE OF EUROPEAN CONTACT

In 1492 the entire Western Hemisphere had a population of about 75 million. Native Americans clustered most thickly in Mexico and Central America, the Caribbean islands, and Peru. But North America was not an empty wasteland. In 1492 between 7 million and 10 million Indians lived north of present-day Mexico, unevenly distributed. Sparse populations of nomads inhabited the Great Basin, the high plains, and the northern forests. Fairly dense concentrations, however, thrived along the Pacific coast, in the Southwest and Southeast, in the Mississippi Valley, and along the Atlantic coast. All these peoples grouped themselves in several hundred nations and tribes, speaking many diverse languages and dialects. But the most important Indian social groups were the family, the village, and—in many societies—the clan. Within these spheres Native Americans fed themselves, reared their children, and interacted with one another and with the spiritual forces surrounding them.

Family and Community

Kinship cemented all Indian societies together. Ties to cousins, aunts, and uncles created complex patterns of social obligation. So did membership in clans—the large networks of kin groups who reckoned their

Cahokia in 1200

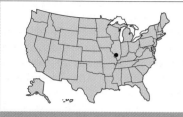

Artist's Rendering of Cahokia

This contemporary painting conveys Cahokia's grand scale. Not until the late eighteenth century did another North American city (Philadelphia) surpass the population of Cahokia, ca. 1200.

Between the tenth and thirteenth centuries, a city of about 20,000 people flourished near the confluence of the Mississippi and Missouri rivers. Called Cahokia, it filled more than 6 square miles and contained more than 120 earthworks. At its center a four-terraced structure called Monk's Mound covered 15 acres (more than the Great Pyramids of Egypt) and rose 100 feet at its highest point. Surrounding the city, a 125-square-mile metropolitan area encompassed 10 large towns and more than 50 farming villages. In addition, Cahokia dominated a vast network of commercial and political alliances extending over much of the American heartland.

Cahokia's beginnings lay in the seventh century A.D., as Native Americans in the East were shifting to farming as their primary means of procuring food. In search of better soil, several small villages moved to the low floodplain extending eastward from the Mississippi around what is now the Illinois side of greater St. Louis. Around A.D. 900 these villages began their transformation into a city with the construction of several mounds. Within another two centuries, a stockade enclosed Monk's Mound and numerous other public structures, and most of the city's residents lived on the outside.

Cahokia was ideally situated for a position of preeminence in mid-America. Its fertile land yielded surplus agricultural crops, which the women harvested, and the river provided rich supplies of fish and mussels. Game and wild plants abounded in nearby uplands. The city had ready access not only to the Mississippi and Missouri rivers but to the Ohio and Illinois, where Adena and Hopewell peoples had previously developed extensive trade networks based on shared religious beliefs. Cahokia and other Mississippian societies drew on Hopewell beliefs and new ideas from Mexico as they erected even more complex political, economic, and religious institutions. By the twelfth century, some scholars believe, Cahokia was the capital of a potential nation-state.

Archaeology provides evidence of what Cahokians made and left in the ground as well as clues to their social structure, trade networks, and beliefs. Work gangs dug the soil for the mounds with shovels made of wood and stone and then carried the dirt in baskets to construction sites, often more than half a mile away. Much of this backbreaking labor undoubtedly was drawn from neighboring towns, which also contributed agricultural surpluses to feed specialized artisans and elites in the city. The artisans produced pottery, shell beads, copper ornaments, clothing, stone tools, and a range of other goods. The raw materials for these objects were brought to Cahokia from locations all over eastern and central North America as tribute—payment by Indian societies dependent on Cahokia—or in return for the finished products. The coordination of labor, trade, and other activities also required a sizable class of managers or overseers. Atop all these were the political and religious leaders, whose overpowering roles are confirmed by French accounts, recorded in the eighteenth century, of a similar society among the Natchez Indians of the lower Mississippi River.

Archaeologists also find evidence of social ranking at Cahokia in the treatment of the dead. Most people were buried in mass graves outside the city, but more prestigious commoners were placed in ridgetop mounds, and those of highest status in conical mounds. In the single most remarkable mound, an adult male was laid out on a platform of twenty thousand beads, made from shells originating in the Gulf of Mexico. He was surrounded by bushels of mica from the Appalachians, a sheet of rolled copper from Lake Superior, and quivers of arrows from communities throughout the Mississippi Valley. This extraordinary man did not go to his grave alone. An adjacent pit contained the bodies of fifty young females in

Sandstone Tablet Depicting Birdman

Stone Spud
A spud was used in ceremonies as a symbol of authority.

their late teens and early twenties; another held the remains of four men whose heads and hands were cut off; and a third included three men and three women. French authors describe how, when a Natchez ruler died, his wife, servants, guards, and others personally attached to him were killed so that they could accompany him in the afterlife. The people called this ruler the Great Sun to denote his position as earthly representative of the sun, the central focus of Mississippian religion. This and burials like it at Cahokia appear to be based on similar beliefs.

By 1200 Cahokia had reached its peak. During the century that followed, it declined in size and power, while other centers in the Southeast and Midwest surpassed it. Although the causes of this decline are not certain, the archaeological evidence provides clues. First, neighboring communities were having increasing difficulty producing enough crops to feed themselves and the many Cahokians who did not grow their own food. Second, the city's demands for fuel and construction materials was seriously reducing the supply of wood in and around Cahokia. This depletion of the forests also deprived residents of the animals and wild plants on which they depended for food. Third, the strengthening of the stockade surrounding central Cahokia suggests that the elites were facing a military challenge from inside or outside the city, or both. Finally, the trade networks that formerly brought tribute to Cahokia and carried away the city's finished products had collapsed. Taken together, these trends indicate that a combination of environmental factors and resistance to centralized authority probably led to Cahokia's downfall. By the time the French explorer La Salle passed through in 1682, Cahokia was a small village of Illinois Indians who, like other native peoples of the region, had abandoned Mississippian religious and political systems for the autonomous villages of their ancestors.

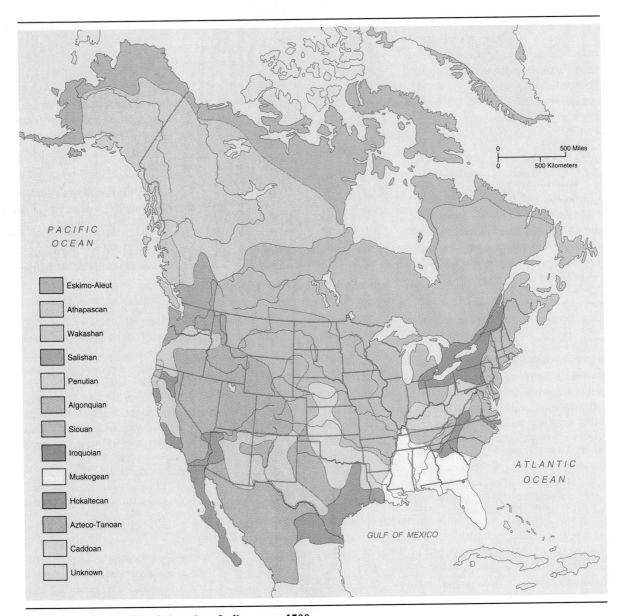

Language Groups of North American Indians, A.D. 1500
The several hundred languages spoken by North American native peoples in A.D. 1500 were derived from just a dozen basic language groups.
SOURCE: **Dean Snow,** *The Archaeology of North America: American Indians and Their Origins* (London: Thames and Hudson, Ltd., 1976).

descent from a common ancestor who embodied the admired qualities of some animal. Depending on the culture, clan membership could descend from either the mother or the father. Clans linked widely scattered groups within a tribe. Several different clans usually dwelled together in a single Indian village.

Kinship bonds counted for much more in Indian society than did the nuclear families that married couples and their children formed. Indians did not necessarily expect spouses to be bound together forever, but kinship lasted for life. Thus Native Americans could accept the divorce of a married couple without feeling a threat to the social order. Customs regulating marriages varied considerably, but strict rules always prevailed. In most cultures young people married in their teens, after winning social acceptance as adults and (generally) after a period of sexual experimentation. Sometimes male leaders took more than one wife, but nuclear families never stood alone. Instead, strong ties of residence and deference bound each couple to one or both sets of parents, producing what social scientists call extended families.

Kinship was also the basis for armed conflict. Indian societies typically considered homicide a matter to be resolved by the extended families of the victim and the perpetrator. If the perpetrator's family offered a gift that the victim's family considered appropriate, the question was settled. If not, the victim's kin might seek to avenge the killing by armed retaliation. If necessary, chiefs and other leaders intervened to resolve disputes between families within the same band, village, or tribe. But disputes between members of different groups could escalate into war. Densely populated societies that competed for scarce resources, as on the Northwest and California coasts, and centralized societies that attempted to dominate trade networks through coercion, such as Hopewell and Mississippian, experienced frequent and intense intergroup warfare. Some scholars believe that the warfare among the Iroquois in Hiawatha's time was a symptom of the political instability accompanying the collapse of a Mississippian center in the upper Ohio valley. Still, warfare remained a low-level affair in most of North America. An exasperated New England officer, writing of his effort to obtain Indian allies in the early seventeenth century, described a battle between two Indian groups as "more for pastime than to conquer and subdue enemies." He concluded that "they might fight seven years and not kill seven men."

Women did the cultivating among most agricultural Indians outside the Southwest. For Indian women, field work easily meshed with child care, as did such other tasks as preparing animal hides and gathering wild vegetation. Men did jobs that took them away from the women and children: hunting, fishing, trading, negotiating, and fighting. With women producing the greater share of the food supply, these communities accorded women more power than did European societies. Among the Iroquois of upstate New York, for example, the women collectively owned the fields, distributed food, and played a weighty role in

Chumash Baskets
California Indians, including the Chumash, gathered, prepared, and stored acorns and other foods in baskets crafted by specialized weavers.

tribal councils. In New England, women sometimes served as *sachems,* or chiefs.

In the Southwest, wresting a living from the severe environment demanded concentrated effort, but the native peoples succeeded remarkably well. The population was comparatively dense: a hundred thousand people may have lived in the pueblos in the early sixteenth century, and intensive cultivation also supported large river-valley settlements. As in the rest of North America, extended families formed the foundation of southwestern village life in both the pueblos and the river valleys.

Southwestern patterns of property ownership and gender roles differed, not only from those of Native Americans elsewhere but also among local cultures. Unlike Indians in other regions, here men and women shared agricultural labor. River-valley peoples of the Southwest owned land privately and passed it through the male line, and men dominated decision making. In pueblo society (which in this respect resembled societies in the Northeast and Southeast), land was communally owned, and women played an influential role in community affairs. A pueblo woman could end a marriage simply by tossing her husband's belongings out the door and sending him back to his kinfolk. Moreover, clan membership passed in the mother's line. Yet pueblo communities depended on secret male societies to perform the rituals that would secure the gods' blessing and ensure life-giving rain. More than with other Indians, pueblo society strictly subordinated the individual to the group and demanded rigorous cooperation.

Indian Religion and Social Values

Most Indians explained the origin and destiny of the human race in myths told by storytellers during religious ceremonies. In the beginning, said the Iroquois, was the sky world of unchanging perfection. From it fell a beautiful pregnant woman, whom the birds saved from plunging into the limitless ocean. On the back of a tortoise who rose from the sea, birds created the earth's soil, in which the woman planted seeds carried during her fall. From these seeds sprang all nature; from her womb, the human race.

Native American religions revolved around the conviction that all nature was alive, pulsating with a spiritual power—*manitou,* in the Algonquian languages, *orenda* in the Iroquoian, *wakan* in the Siouan. A mysterious, awe-inspiring force that could affect human life for both good and evil, such power united all nature in an unbroken web. Manitou encompassed "every thing which they cannot comprehend," wrote the Puritan leader Roger Williams, one of the few Europeans who genuinely tried to understand the northeastern Indians' spiritual world. Their belief in supernatural power led most Native Americans to seek constantly to conciliate all the spiritual forces in nature: living things, rocks and water, sun and moon, even ghosts and witches. For example, Indians were careful to pray to the spirits of the animals they hunted, justifying the killing of just enough game to sustain themselves. To Native Americans, humanity was only one link in the great chain of living nature. The Judeo-Christian view that God had given humanity domination over nature was very strange to them.

Indians had many ways of gaining access to spiritual power. One was through dreaming: most Native Americans took very seriously the visions that came to them in sleep. Some also sought access to the supernatural by artificially altering their consciousness through difficult physical ordeals. Young men in many societies commonly endured a traumatic rite of passage before gaining recognition as adults. Such a rite often involved a "vision quest"—going alone into a forest or up a mountain, fasting, and awaiting the mystical experience in which an animal spirit would reveal

itself as a protective guide and offer a glimpse of the future. Girls went through comparable rituals at the onset of menstruation to initiate them into the spiritual world from which female reproductive power flowed. Moreover, entire communities often practiced collective power-seeking rituals such as the Sun Dance, performed by Indians of the Plains and Great Basin (see Chapter 17).

Although on occasion all Indians tried to communicate directly with the spiritual world, they normally relied on shamans for help in understanding the unseen. The shamans were healers who used both medicinal plants and magical chants, but their role in Indian society went further. They interpreted dreams, guided vision quests, invoked war or peace spirits, and figured prominently in community councils. Chiefs had to maintain respectful relations with their people's shamans, who by the sixteenth century were organized into priesthoods in some societies in the Southeast and Southwest.

Even as they grew larger and more complex, Indian societies maintained the strong sense of interdependence forged over thousands of years by Paleo-Indians and their successors. As a result, they demanded a strong degree of conformity and close cooperation. From early childhood Indians learned to be accommodating and reserved—slow to reveal their own feelings before they could sense others'. Although few Native American peoples favored physical punishment in child rearing, Indian parents punished psychologically, by shaming. Throughout life the fear of becoming an isolated social outcast (a status that could mean death) forced individual Indians to maintain strict self-control. Communities took decisions by consensus, and leaders articulated slowly emerging agreements in memorable, persuasive, often passionate oratory. Shamans and chiefs therefore had to be dramatic orators. Noted John Smith, they spoke in public "with vehemency and so great passions that they sweat till they drop and are so out of breath they scarce can speak."

Because Indians highly valued consensus building in everyday life, their leaders' authority depended primarily on the respect that they invoked rather than what they could demand by compulsion. Distributing gifts was central to establishing and maintaining leadership within a Native American community, as a French observer in early seventeenth-century Canada clearly understood: "For the savages have that noble quality, that they give liberally, casting at the feet of him whom they will honor the present that they give him. But it is with hope to receive some reciprocal kindness, which is a kind of contract, which we call . . . 'I give thee, to the end thou shouldst give me.' "

Thus for Indians, trade was not merely an economic activity by which they acquired useful goods. It was also a means of ensuring goodwill with other peoples and of building their own prestige. European visitors almost always found Native Americans eager to barter. For many centuries, trade among the Indians had spanned the continent. The Hurons of southern Ontario and the Pueblo Indians of the Southwest produced large agricultural surpluses for trade, and southwestern turquoise found its way to Mexico and the Great Plains. Flint and other tool-making materials, salt, dyes, furs, exotic minerals and shells, and (in hard times) food and seeds were major objects of trade. So was tobacco, which Indians regarded primarily as a ceremonial drug, its fragrant smoke symbolizing the union of heaven and earth. Native Americans eagerly assimilated into their own way of life the new goods that European traders offered. Metal tools they valued for their practical, labor-saving benefits, and dyed cloth and glass objects quickly took on symbolic, prestige-enhancing qualities.

"They love not to be encumbered with too many utensils," remarked an early-seventeenth-century English visitor. Rather, prestige counted for everything in Native American societies. If Indians did accumulate possessions, it was primarily with the aim of giving them away, to win prestige. The most spectacular example of such gift-exchanging rituals was the Pacific Northwest potlatch ceremony. When a northwestern community's social hierarchy was shaken, an aspiring new leader would invite his neighbors to a potlatch, at which he would give away or destroy most of what he owned, all the while chanting about his own greatness and taunting his rivals. Those who received were expected later to give away even more. He who could give away the most gained the highest prestige and accumulated the greatest number of people obligated to him.

Scholars have used the word *reciprocity* to characterize Native American religious and social values. Reciprocity involved mutual give-and-take, but its aim was not to confer equality. Instead, societies based on reciprocity tried to maintain equilibrium and interdependence between individuals of unequal power and prestige. In their religious thinking, too, Indians applied the concept of reciprocity, in viewing nature as a web of interdependent spiritual powers into which humans had to fit. And in social organization, the Indians' principle of reciprocity required that communities be places of face-to-face, lifelong interaction. Trade and gift giving solidified such reciprocal bonds. The Indians' faith in social reciprocity also underlay their idea of property rights. They believed that the people of one area might agree to share with others the right to use the land for different but complementary purposes: hunting, gathering, farming, trapping, or traveling. The notion (then emerging in Europe) that property ownership conferred perpetual and exclusive control of land was alien to Indians.

But Native American society was hardly a simple, noncompetitive world. All Indian cultures possessed a strong sense of order. Custom, the demands of social conformity, and the rigors of nature strictly regulated life, and the people's everyday affairs mingled with the spiritual world at every turn. Nature and the supernatural world could sometimes be frightening. For example, Indians feared ghosts and believed that nonconformists could invoke evil spirits by witchcraft—the most dreaded crime in Indian cultures. Much in Indian religions involved placating the evil spirits that caused sickness and death. The pueblo peoples, whose existence depended on rainfall, expressed their gratitude by performing frequent rituals. And even in the Southwest, where stress on cooperation minimized competition, Indian life had an intensely competitive side. Individuals and communities eagerly strove to show physical prowess in ritualized games like lacrosse, and some bet enthusiastically on the outcome. "They are so bewitched with these . . . games, that they will lose sometimes all they have," said an Englishman of the Massachusett Indians about 1630. Such games served not only as recreation but also as a means of acquiring prestige.

The breakdown of order in Indian communities could bring fearful consequences: accusations of witchcraft, demands for revenge against wrongdoers, war against enemies. Going to war or exacting personal revenge was a ritualized way of restoring order that had broken down. A captured male could expect death after prolonged torture. Indian men learned from early childhood to inflict (and to bear) physical pain out of loyalty to kin and neighbors; they knew that they must withstand torture without flinching and death without fear. Endurance was central to Indian life.

CONCLUSION

Well before the first Siberian hunters crossed the Bering land bridge, geographic isolation and ecological variety had been the Americas' most striking characteristics. Isolation made possible Native Americans' social and cultural development untouched by alien influences and lethal epidemics. (The effects of Norse colonization were minimized because they were brief, involved few people, and above all because the Norse did not carry the epidemic diseases brought by later colonizers.) Meanwhile, great climatic and geographic variations among North American regions helped ensure that native cultures—all shaped significantly by their natural environments—would be extremely diverse.

When Europeans "discovered" America in 1492, they did not, as they thought, enter an unchanging world of simple savages. Instead, for thousands of years, native cultures and societies had transformed the North American continent into a human habitat. Indians had tapped the secrets of the land and the environment so as to be able to sustain themselves and flourish in almost every ecological zone. Over the millennia they learned the properties, uses, and values of plants, animals, soils, rocks, and other minerals, as well as the cycles of months, seasons, and years. And the Indians transformed the landscape, as evidenced by their hunting camps, villages, and cornfields and by the web of roads and trails connecting them to one another. But for Indians, these discoveries and accomplishments were not the basis for pride in their ability to conquer nature. Rather, they saw themselves as participants in a natural and supernatural order that pervaded the universe, and their attitudes, as expressed in their religious practices, were ones of gratitude and constant concern lest they violate that order.

These beliefs did not necessarily make all Indians careful conservationists. Plains hunters, stampeding herds of bison (an essential food source) over cliffs, often killed more animals than they could eat. There is evidence, moreover, that eastern Indians may sometimes have lost control of their fires and burned more land than intended. But the depletion of species in such cases was only temporary; Indians did not act consistently enough to prevent their renewal. However, other Indian actions were more consistent and hence more consequential. One reason for the decline of the great Anasazi centers in the Southwest and of the Mississippian center of Cahokia was the excessive demands placed on their environments by large concentrations of people. In these instances, Indians seemed to have learned the obvious lessons and abandoned destructive ways of life.

After 1500 a new attitude toward the land made itself felt in North America. "A people come from under the world, to take their world from them"—thus an early-seventeenth-century Virginia Indian characterized the English invaders of his homeland. Indeed, the modern society that since the seventeenth century has arisen on the Indians' ancient continent bears little resemblance to the world that the Native Americans once knew.

CHRONOLOGY

c. 5,000,000 B.C	Earliest human ancestors appear in Africa.
c. 2,000,000 B.C.	Ice Age begins.
c. 300,000–100,000 B.C.	Humans spread throughout Eastern Hemisphere.
c. 120,000 B.C.	Wisconsin glaciation begins.
c. 40,000–15,000 B.C.	Ancestors of Native Americans cross Alaska-Siberian land bridge.
c. 10,000 B.C.	Ice Age ends. Wisconsin glaciation retreats from North America.
c. 10,000–9000 B.C.	Paleo-Indians spread throughout Western Hemisphere.
c. 9000 B.C.	Extinction of big-game mammals.
c. 8000 B.C.	Archaic era begins.
c. 7000 B.C.	Athapaskan-speaking peoples arrive in North America.
c. 5000 B.C.	First domesticated plants grown in Western Hemisphere.
c. 3500 B.C.	First domesticated plants grown in North America.
c. 3000–2000 B.C.	Inuit and Aleut peoples arrive in North America.

c. 1500 B.C.	Archaic era ends.
	Bow and arrow and ceramic pottery introduced in North America.
c. 1200 B.C.	Poverty Point flourishes in Louisiana.
c. 400–100 B.C.	Adena culture flourishes in Ohio Valley.
c. 250 B.C.	Hohokam culture begins in Southwest.
c. 100 B.C.	Anasazi culture begins in Southwest.
c. 100 B.C.–A.D. 600	Hopewell culture thrives in Midwest.

Hopewell Claw Artifact

c. A.D. 300	First people arrive at Hawaiian Islands.
c. A.D. 700	Mississippian culture begins.
c. A.D. 900	Stockade and first mounds built at Cahokia.
	Anasazi expansion begins.
c. A.D. 1000–1100	Norse settlement of Vinland flourishes on Newfoundland.
c. A.D. 1150	Anasazi peoples disperse to form pueblos.
c. A.D. 1200–1300	Cahokia declines.
c. A.D. 1400	League of the Iroquois formed.
A.D. 1492	Christopher Columbus begins permanent European colonization of Western Hemisphere.

FOR FURTHER READING

John Bierhorst, *The Mythology of North America* (1985). An excellent introduction to Native American mythology, organized regionally.

Brian Fagan, *Ancient North America: The Archaeology of a Continent* (1991). An informative, comprehensive introduction to the continent's history before Europeans' arrival.

Åke Hultkrantz, *The Religions of the American Indians* (1979). A stimulating discussion by the leading scholar on the subject.

Gwyn Jones, *The Norse Atlantic Saga,* rev. ed. (1986). A single volume combining recent scholarship on Norse, Eskimos, and Indians with translations of the most important sagas.

Alvin M. Josephy, Jr., *America in 1492: The World of the Indian Peoples Before the Arrival of Columbus* (1992). Outstanding essays on life in the Western Hemisphere on the eve of European contact.

William C. Sturtevant, gen. ed., *Handbook of North American Indians* (20 vols. projected, 1978–   ). A partially completed reference work providing basic information on the history and culture of virtually every known native society, as well as surveys of regional archaeology and essays on topics of special interest.

ADDITIONAL BIBLIOGRAPHY

History and Anthropology

Harold E. Driver, *Indians of North America,* 2d ed. (1969); Charles Hudson, *The Southeastern Indians* (1976); Alvin Josephy, Jr., *The Indian Heritage of America,* 2d ed. (1991); Alice B. Kehoe, *North American Indians: A Comprehensive Account,* 2d ed. (1992); Eleanor Burke Leacock and Nancy Oestrich Lurie, eds., *North American Indians in Historical Perspective* (1971); Richard J. Perry, *Western Apache Heritage: People of the Mountain Corridor* (1991); Helen C. Rountree, *The Powhatan Indians: Their Traditional Culture* (1989); Wilcomb E. Washburn, *The Indian in America* (1975).

Archaeology

Brian M. Fagan, *The Great Journey: The Peopling of Ancient America* (1987); Stuart J. Fiedel, *Prehistory of the Americas,* 2d ed. (1992); Melvin Fowler, *The Cahokia Atlas: A Historical Atlas of Cahokia Archaeology* (1989); Kendrick Frazier, *People of Chaco: A Canyon and Its Culture* (1986); Patricia Galloway, ed., *The Southeastern Ceremonial Complex: Artifacts and Analysis* (1989); Jesse Jennings, ed., *Ancient North Americans* (1983); Patrick Vinton Kirch, *Feathered Gods and Fishhooks: An Introduction to Hawaiian Archaeology and Prehistory* (1985); Lynda Norene Shaffer, *Native Americans Before 1492: The Moundbuilding Centers of the Eastern Woodlands* (1992); Stuart Struever and Felicia Antonelli Holton, *Koster: Americans in Search of Their Prehistoric Past* (1980).

Religion and World View

Paul Radin, *The Trickster: A Study in American Indian Mythology* (1972); Elisabeth Tooker, ed., *Native North American Spirituality of the Eastern Woodlands* (1979); Velerio Valeri, *Kingship and Sacrifice: Ritual and Society in Ancient Hawaii* (1985); Christopher Vecsey, *Imagine Ourselves Richly: Mythic Narratives of North American Indians* (1988); Ray A. Williamson, *Living the Sky: The Cosmos of the American Indian* (1987); Paul Zolbrod, *Diné bahane': The Navajo Creation Story* (1984).

Demography

David E. Stannard, *American Holocaust: The Conquest of the New World* (1992) and *Before the Horror: The Population of Hawai'i on the Eve of Western Contact* (1989); Russell Thornton, *American Indian Holocaust and Survival: A Population History Since 1492* (1987).

**Bartholomew Gosnold Trading with the Indians
at Martha's Vineyard, Massachusetts** *(detail)*
by Theodore De Bry, 1634

TRANSATLANTIC ENCOUNTERS AND COLONIAL BEGINNINGS
1492–1630

At ten o'clock on a moonlit night, the tense crew spotted a glimmering light. Then at two the next morning came the shout "Land! Land!" At daybreak they entered a shallow lagoon. The captain, Christopher Columbus (inset), rowed ashore, the royal flag fluttering in the breeze. "And, all having rendered thanks to the Lord, kneeling on the ground, embracing it with tears of joy for the immeasurable mercy of having reached it, [he] rose and gave this island the name San Salvador." The date was October 12, 1492. The place was a tiny tropical island less than four hundred miles southeast of present-day Florida.

Besides his crew, the only witnesses to Columbus's landing were a band of Taíno Indians peeking from the jungle as he claimed for his queen the island that they called Guanahaní. Soon curiosity overcame their fears. Gesturing and smiling, the Taínos walked down to the beach, where the newcomers quickly noticed the cigars they offered and the gold pendants in their noses.

The voyagers learned to savor the islanders' tobacco and to trade for golden ornaments as they sailed on among the West Indies, searching for the emperor of China's capital city. Although Columbus had found no potentates, he sensed that fabulous wealth lay within his grasp. He was sure that he had reached Asia—the Indies. Two months later, bringing with him some "Indians" and various souvenirs, he

sailed home to tell of "a land to be desired and, once seen, never to be left."

Perhaps some Taínos would have agreed with the astonished Canadian Indian who saw his first shaggily bearded white man in 1632: "O, what an ugly man! Is it possible that any woman would look with favor on such a man?" Later Indians' accounts of their first sightings of Europeans also speak of wonder at seeing white-sailed "canoes" descending as from the sky and of fascination with the strangers' "magic"—their guns, gunpowder, durable metal pots and tools, and glass beads. Because the strangers were seldom prepared to survive unaided, the hospitable native people had ample opportunity to make themselves useful.

But the potential for deep misunderstanding was already present. From his first day in the New World, Columbus thought like a benevolent colonial master. "They should be good servants and of quick intelligence, . . . and I believe that they would easily be made Christians, for it appeared to me that they had no creed." The Europeans would soon realize that Native Americans were neither gullible fools nor humble servants. Disillusioned, the newcomers would begin to see the Indians as lazy and deceitful "savages." Meanwhile, the Native Americans found much of the Europeans' "magic"—which included their diseases as well as their material goods— very destructive. In much of what is now Latin

America, the coming of the Europeans quickly turned into conquest. In the future United States and Canada, European mastery would come more slowly. More than one hundred years would pass before truly self-sustaining colonies were established. Nevertheless, from the moment of Columbus's landing on October 12, 1492, the American continents became the stage for the encounter of Native American, European, and African peoples.

AFRICAN AND EUROPEAN PEOPLES

The Eastern Hemisphere gave birth to the human race. For several million years, early humans went forth in waves from Africa's warm grasslands to people the globe. Then, as in the Americas, a great range of societies arose over a span of at least five thousand years before 1492. Stretching from West Africa and Europe to Siberia and Polynesia, complex networks of peaceful or aggressive interactions, cultural influences, and long-range trade linked many of these societies. Many Asian, African, and European peoples lived in hunter-gatherer or agricultural communities. But throughout the Eastern Hemisphere—as also in Mexico and Peru—there existed powerful states with armed forces, bureaucracies, religious institutions, proud aristocracies, and toiling common people.

West Africa and Its Peoples

For almost five thousand years, the vast, barren Sahara Desert has lain between much of Africa and the rest of the world. In addition, West Africa was effectively isolated from the land to its north by the prevailing Atlantic winds, which could bring old-fashioned sailing ships south but hampered them from returning north. Moreover, the yellow fever rampant in the West African rain-forest coastline helped ward off outside intruders. If contracted in youth, yellow fever could be survived with lifelong immunity, but it generally killed adult newcomers lacking such defenses.

Nevertheless, between the formidable Sahara and the forbidding coast, a broad swath of grassland (savanna) offered a hospitable shelter. By about 3000 B.C., people here were growing grain and herding livestock. Late in the first millennium B.C., when knowledge of iron metallurgy reached the grasslands, the region's people began carrying their culture outward, eventually leaving their imprint on almost all of sub-Saharan Africa. By the sixteenth century, sub-Saharan Africa, twice the size of the United States, had a population of perhaps 20 million.

Despite its seeming isolation, West Africa looked northward. Camel caravans crossed the Sahara, and an important trade in gold and salt developed with North Africa's Mediterranean coast. From A.D. 600 to 1600, there arose in the grassland a series of West African empires—Ghana, Mali, and Songhai—that imposed tribute on their subject populations and taxed the merchant communities at the southern end of the caravan routes. Islam spread into West Africa from its Middle Eastern birthplace, and by the late eleventh century, the grassland empires became at least nominally Muslim. Their rulers kept records in Arabic and irregularly enforced Islamic law, but it was their wealth that made them famous throughout the Islamic world. By 1492 the last of the great West African empires, Songhai, stood at the height of its glory, with a bureaucracy and a vigorous army dominating much of the interior. Songhai's major city, Timbuktu, boasted flourishing markets and a famous Islamic university.

Compared with the grassland empires, coastal West Africa was relatively insignificant. In Senegambia at Africa's westernmost bulge, several small Islamic states took root. Infestation by the tsetse fly, the carrier of sleeping sickness, kept livestock-herding peoples out of Guinea's coastal forests, but many small states arose here, too, during the first millennium A.D. Among these was Benin, where artisans had been fashioning magnificent ironwork for centuries.

Then in the fifteenth century, Guinea's population rose. Foreign demands for gold that Africans panned from streams or dug from the earth touched off the spurt. Grassland warriors and merchants poured into Guinea and Senegambia, seeking new opportunities and on occasion founding or expanding the region's tiny states. Similarly thirsting for fresh opportunities were the Portuguese, who in the mid-fifteenth century used new maritime techniques to sail up and down West Africa's coast in search of gold and slaves.

West African political leaders differed sharply in the amounts and kinds of political power they wielded. Grassland emperors claimed semigodlike status, which they only thinly disguised when they adopted Islam. Rulers of smaller kingdoms depended largely on their ability to persuade, to conform to custom, and

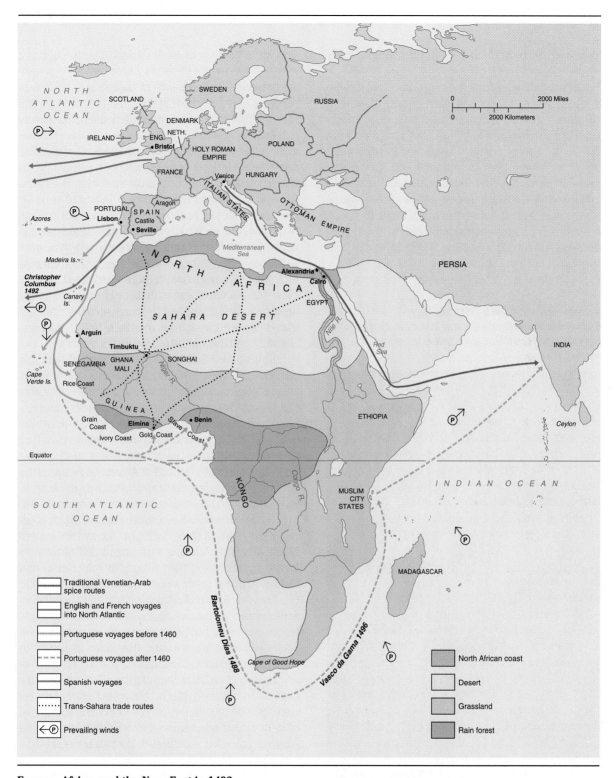

Europe, Africa, and the Near East in 1492

In 1492 Europeans had little knowledge of the outside world apart from the Mediterranean basin and Africa's west coast. Since the Azores, the Canary Islands, and the Cape Verde Islands had been explored recently in the eastern Atlantic, many Europeans were not surprised when Columbus encountered new islands farther west in 1492.

sometimes to redistribute wealth justly among their people.

In sub-Saharan Africa, the cohesiveness of kinship groups knitted society together. From childhood, Africans found themselves in a network of interlocking, mutual obligations to kinfolk. Not just parents but also aunts, uncles, distant cousins, and persons sharing clan ties formed an African's kin group and claimed his or her first loyalty. Africans held their grandparents in highest esteem and accorded village or clan elders great deference. In centuries to come, the tradition of strong extended families would help enslaved Africans in the New World to endure the breakup of nuclear families by sale.

Mali Horseman, c. 13th–14th century
This terra-cotta figure originated in Mali, one of several powerful empires in West Africa before the arrival of Europeans.

Some aspects of West African family structure were interpreted by Christian Europeans as demeaning to women and evidence of "barbarism." One was polygyny, the custom whereby a man married several wives and maintained numerous households. A second was bridewealth, a prospective husband's payment to his bride's kin before marriage. Christian Europeans interpreted both practices as demeaning to women and evidence of "barbarism." But an African man did not "buy" a wife; in effect, he posted bond for good behavior and acknowledged the relative prestige of his own and his bride's kin groups. Marrying several wives could cost a man heavily, so polygyny was largely confined to higher-status men who needed to establish marriage ties with more than one kin group. West African wives generally kept lifelong links with their own kin group, and in many societies children traced descent through the mother's, not the father's, bloodline. All this buttressed women's standing.

Kinship also informed attitudes toward land and property. To West Africans, kin groups not only enjoyed inalienable rights to the soil that their ancestors had always cultivated but also had a duty to honor ancestors and earth spirits by properly cultivating the land. Like Native Americans, Africans did not treat land as a commodity to be bought and sold.

Cultivation was difficult in Africa and required the labor of both genders. As in all tropical regions, scorching sunlight and frequent downpours prevented humus (slowly decaying vegetative matter) from accumulating in the African soil. Like Indians in eastern North America, Africans maintained soil fertility by practicing slash-and-burn tillage. In the coastal rain forests, Africans grew root crops, primarily yams. On the grasslands the staff of life was grain, which in Senegambia meant rice. In the seventeenth and eighteenth centuries, both rice and its Senegambian cultivators would be transplanted (the latter as slaves) to the North American mainland.

Religion permeated African life. West African, like Native American, religions recognized spiritual presences pervading nature. The power of earth spirits and of agricultural ancestors reinforced the esteem that Africans accorded to cultivators. In the eighteenth century, Europeans got an authentic glimpse of African religion from Olaudah Equiano, a West African who eventually managed to buy his freedom from slavery:

The natives believe that there is one Creator of all things, and that he lives in the sun, [and] . . . that he governs events. . . . Some . . . believe in the transmigration of souls [reincarnation] to some degree. Those spirits, who are not transmigrated, such as their dear friends or relations, they believe always attend them, and guard them from the bad spirits of their foes. For this reason, they always, before eating . . . put some small portion of the meat and pour some of their drink, on the ground for them; and they often make oblations [offerings] of the blood of beasts or fowls at their graves.

Magic and the placating of spiritual powers were important in West African life, and, as with Native Americans, the responsibility for maintaining contact with the spirit world fell to shamans. Africans explained misfortunes in terms of witchcraft, much as did Indians and Europeans. But African religion differed from other traditions in its focus on ancestor worship, in which departed forebears were venerated as spiritual guardians.

Africa's magnificent artistic traditions were also steeped in religion. The ivory, cast-iron, and wood sculpture of West Africa, whose bold design would help mold the twentieth-century Western world's modern art, was used in ceremonies reenacting creation myths and honoring spirits. A strong moralistic streak ran through African folk tales. Oral reciters transmitted these stories in dramatic public presentations with ritual masks, dance, and music of a highly complex rhythmic structure now appreciated as one of the foundations of jazz.

Much in traditional African culture seemed to clash with the great monotheistic religions, Islam and Christianity. Among Africans, Islam appealed primarily to merchants trading with Muslim North Africa and the Middle East and to the grassland rulers eager to consolidate their power. Even these ambitious emperors were incompletely Islamicized—some learned with dismay that Islam limited them to four wives. By the sixteenth century, Islam had only begun to affect the daily lives of grassland cultivators and artisans. Christianity, arriving in West Africa with the Portuguese in the fifteenth and sixteenth centuries, demanded that Africans break even more radically with their traditional culture, but until the nineteenth century had little impact.

European Culture and Society

When Columbus landed on San Salvador in 1492, Europe was approaching the height of a mighty cultural revival, the Renaissance. Contemporary intellectuals and poets believed that their age was witnessing a return to the standards of ancient Greek and Roman civilization. After a century-long economic recession, money had accumulated to pay for magnificent architecture, and wealthy patrons commissioned master painters and sculptors to create works glowing with idealized human beauty. Renaissance scholars strove to reconcile ancient philosophy with Christian faith, to explore the mysteries of nature, to map the world, and to explain the motions of the heavens.

But European society was quivering with tension. The era's artistic and intellectual creativity was partly inspired by intense social and spiritual stress, as Renaissance Europeans groped for stability by glorifying order, hierarchy, and beauty. A concern for power and rank ("degree") dominated European life between the fifteenth and seventeenth centuries. William Shakespeare (1564–1616), who expressed Renaissance values with incomparable eloquence, wrote:

The heavens themselves, the planets and this center [earth]
Observe degree, priority, and place . . .
Take but degree away, untune that string,
And hark, what discord follows!

Gender, wealth, inherited position, and political power affected every European's status, and few lived outside the reach of some political authority's claim to tax and impose laws upon them. But this order was shaky. Conflicts between states, between religions, and between rich and poor constantly threatened the balance. A few late-medieval and sixteenth-century revolts had democratic overtones, but the authorities mercilessly suppressed these uprisings. To most Europeans, especially elites, democracy in practice meant mob rule and the destruction of social distinctions. All the more eagerly, then, did they cling to visions of order and hierarchy.

At the top of the European hierarchy were kings, in the process of consolidating their power as heads of nation-states. (A handful of republics existed, the most important of which were the aristocratic city-states of Venice and Florence.) Lacking broad support, kings often waged wars with mercenary armies that cost mountains of money. The kings' forces spread disease and misery everywhere; they were "an unchristian, cursed tribe whose trade consists of gouging, pillaging, burning, murdering, gambling, drinking, whoring, blaspheming, willfully killing husbands and fathers, persecuting peasants . . . , stripping fields, and demanding tribute," a German chronicler wrote in 1531.

Rule by a woman frightened sixteenth-century people, especially in England, where Mary I and then Elizabeth I reigned for half a century (1553–1558 and 1558–1603, respectively). Not only did Europeans consider governance a male responsibility, but they also knew that a queen's marriage would ultimately transfer the crown to either a foreign dynasty or some domestic noble family. In this dangerous situation, Mary blundered repeatedly and saved the day only by dying soon. Elizabeth I, however, took her nation's interests to heart. Remaining the unmarried "virgin queen," she artfully managed Parliament, which represented the nation's landowning upper class and merchants. Parliament flooded her with advice, usually trying to push her further than she thought it prudent to go in dealing with political and religious issues. But by cleverly managing patronage—the distribution of royal favors and political offices—and by choosing shrewd advisers, Elizabeth remained in control of the nation's intricate political system and guided England through a perilous half-century.

As Elizabeth demonstrated, monarchs' power depended on gaining the cooperation of the upper classes, usually by consulting such representative institutions as Parliament. The men who dominated these institutions generally saw officeholding as a form of property owning and a legitimate way to improve their fortunes. No monarch could ride roughshod over such men, and by defending their own liberties, they were also preserving the principle of limited government against encroaching despotism.

All was not well with the upper classes, however, especially in England. To maintain status, they were expected to spend freely even if they could not afford to. Among the titled nobility, or aristocracy, only the eldest son inherited estates; younger sons normally had to fend for themselves in a world of shrinking opportunities. A stagnant economy also pinched many among the gentry—the "respectable" landowners without titles who traditionally lived without doing manual labor and played a prominent role in local government and Parliament.

At the bottom of the social heap toiled the ordinary people. In the overwhelmingly rural Europe of the times, peasants composed between 70 percent and 80 percent of the population. Peasants ranged from a few prosperous families with large holdings, such as the English yeomen, to landless laborers who barely scraped by on odd jobs. Taxes, rents, and other dues to landlords and Catholic church officials were heavy, and poor harvests or war drove even well-to-do peasants to starvation.

Conditions among the peasants were made even worse by a sharp rise in population. After the plague epidemic known as the Black Death killed approximately one-third of Europe's people in the late fourteenth century, the population remained low for another half-century. But as the fear of mass death subsided and Europeans resumed having large families, the number of people increased dramatically, from about 55 million in 1450 to almost 100 million by 1600. But without corresponding improvements in technology and agriculture, output did not rise to meet growing demand. Northern European and English peasant families cultivated wheat or rye, barley, and oats on long strips scattered through their village's three or more fields; one field lay fallow every third year to restore fertility. Yields were pitifully low. Families had to cooperate in plowing, sowing, and harvesting, as well as in grazing their livestock on the fallow field and the jointly owned "commons," or pastureland and forest. With new land at a premium, the commons were a tempting prize for landlords, especially the English gentry, to "enclose"—that is, to convert to private property. Peasants who had no *written* title to their land were especially vulnerable, but yeomen with strong titles often kept their land, and a few even profited by enclosing.

European towns were numerous but small, typically with several thousand inhabitants each. A great metropolis like London, whose population ballooned from fifty-five thousand in 1550 to two hundred thousand in 1600, was quite exceptional. But all towns were dirty and disease-ridden, and townspeople lived close-packed with their neighbors.

Unappealing as sixteenth-century towns might seem today, ambitious (or desperate) men and women of the time viewed them as growing, dynamic centers of opportunity. Immigration from the countryside—rather than an excess of urban births over deaths—accounted for towns' expansion. Most of the displaced country people who flocked into towns remained at the bottom of the social order, however, as servants or laborers who often failed to accumulate enough money to marry and live independently. Manufacturing took place in household workshops, where subordinate workers were dependent on an artisan master. Successful artisans and merchants formed guilds to control employment, prices, and the sale of goods. Dominated by the richest citizens, urban governments enforced social conformity by "sumptuary laws" that forbade dressing inappropriately to one's social rank.

The consequences of rapid population growth were particularly acute in England, where the number of people doubled from about 2.5 million in 1500 to 5 million in 1620. In parts of the countryside, landowners united to divide the commons among themselves, raise sheep, and grow rich selling wool. But with textile-manufacturing technology largely unchanged, per capita output and real household income among textile workers fell. In effect, more workers competed for fewer jobs in the face of diminishing European markets for English cloth and rapidly rising prices for food. Enclosures aggravated unemployment, forcing large numbers of people to wander the countryside in search of work and so making England's population highly mobile. To the upper and middle classes, these poor "vagabonds" seemed to threaten law and order. To control them, Parliament passed "Poor Laws" that ordered vagrants whipped and sent home, where hardpressed taxpayers maintained them on relief.

Thus the hopes and ambitions that drew thousands into towns usually gave way to frustration. Some in England blamed the well-to-do, whom they charged with raising prices, goading the poor to revolt, and giving too little to charity. But others, such as the writer Thomas Nashe, spread the blame more widely:

> From the rich to the poor ... there is ambition, or swelling above their states [proper place in society]; the rich citizen swells against the pride of the prodigal courtier; the prodigal courtier swells against the wealth of the citizen. One company swells against another. ... The ancients [elderly], they oppose themselves against the younger, and suppress them and keep them down all that they may. The young men, they call [the elderly] dotards, and swell and rage. ...

Conservative moralists like Nashe condemned "overreaching" (individuals' attempts to rise in society) and stoutly upheld the values of old-fashioned social reciprocity. As in America and Africa, traditional society in Europe rested on maintaining long-term, reciprocal relationships. But because its aim was the smooth functioning of social relationships between individuals of unequal status, European reciprocity required the upper classes to act with self-restraint and

Decline in Real Wages in England, 1500–1700

This index of real wages, which measures the drop in purchasing power due to inflation and declining wages, indicates that as the Great Migration began around 1630, living standards for English workers had suffered a steady reduction of about 60 percent since the base year, 1500.

SOURCE: E. H. Phelps Brown and S. V. Hopkins, "Builders' Wage-Rates, Prices and Population: Some Further Evidence," *Economica,* XXVI (1959): 18–38; adapted from D. C. North and R. P. Thomas, *The Rise of the Western World: A New Economic History* (Cambridge: Cambridge University Press, 1973), 111.

dignity, and the lower classes to show deference to their "betters." It also demanded strict economic regulation to ensure that sellers charged a "just price"—one that covered costs and allowed the seller a "reasonable" living standard but that barred him from taking advantage of buyers' and borrowers' misfortunes or of shortages to make "excessive" profits.

Yet for several centuries Europeans had been compromising the ideals of traditional economic behavior. "In the Name of God and of Profit," thirteenth-century Italian merchants had written on their ledgers. By the sixteenth century, nothing could stop the charging of interest on borrowed money or sellers' price increases in response to demand. New forms of business organization slowly spread in the commercial world—especially the impersonal joint-stock company with many investors (see below), the ancestor of the modern corporation. Demand rose for capital investment,

The Banker and His Wife, *by Quentin Metsys, 1514 Despite religious admonitions against excessive material gain, some sixteenth-century Europeans sought to reconcile profit with piety. In this portrait, a banker weighs gold coins to ensure their accurate value as his wife, watching him, holds a prayer book.*

and so did the supply of accumulated wealth. Slowly a new economic outlook took form that justified both the unimpeded acquisition of wealth and unregulated economic competition, and insisted that individuals owed one another nothing but the money necessary to settle each market transaction. This new outlook, the central value system of capitalism or the "market economy," was the opposite of traditional demands for the strict regulation of economic activity to ensure social reciprocity and maintain "just prices."

Sixteenth- and seventeenth-century Europeans therefore held conflicting attitudes toward economic enterprise and social change, and their ambivalence remained unresolved. In Europe itself and in transplanted Europeans' colonial communities, a restless desire for fresh opportunity kept life simmering with competitive tension. But those who prospered still sought the security and prestige provided by traditional social distinctions, whereas the poor longed for the age-old values that they hoped would restrain irresponsible greed. Almost all intellectuals and clergymen defended traditional standards. When Europeans violated these standards, they did so with a

bad conscience. Thus ideal and reality remained far apart.

Fundamental change in European society could also be seen in the growing importance of the nuclear family. The tradition of broad kinship networks did survive in the sense that nuclear families prudently tried to retain the goodwill of distant relatives, but these networks seldom overruled the male head of each nuclear family. In a common cliché of the age, the nuclear family was a "little commonwealth." The father's government within the family was supposed to mirror God's rule over Creation and kings' lordship over their subjects. Even grown sons and daughters regularly knelt for their father's blessing. The ideal, according to a German writer, was that "wives should obey their husbands and not seek to dominate them; they must manage the home efficiently. Husbands . . . should treat their wives with consideration and occasionally close an eye to their faults." In practice, the father's domination often had to make room for the wife's responsibility in managing family affairs and helping to run the farm or the workshop. And repeated male complaints (such as that of an English author in 1622) about wives "who think themselves every way as good as their husbands, and no way inferior to them," suggested that male domination had its limits.

Europeans and Their God

"In the beginning God created the heaven and the earth. . . . And God said, Let us make man in our image . . . and let them have dominion . . . over all the earth. . . . So God created man in his own image, . . . male and female he created them." Sixteenth-century Europeans firmly believed in this biblical explanation of the origins of the world and its peoples. Christianity, to which the vast majority of Europeans adhered, taught that Jesus Christ, God's Son, had redeemed sinners by suffering crucifixion and rising from the dead. Equally vivid was their belief in the devil, Satan, whom God had hurled from heaven soon after the Creation and who ceaselessly lured people to damnation by tempting them to do evil. The non-Christian European minority encompassed small Jewish communities and Muslims in the Balkans and in Spain. But all Europe's population—Christians, Jews, and Muslims—worshiped a single supreme being, based on the God of the Old Testament.

Although Christianity had sunk deep roots into Europeans' consciousness by the sixteenth century, many also retained beliefs that originated outside the Christian tradition. Virtually all Europeans feared witches, and many thought that individuals could manipulate nature by invoking unseen spiritual powers—that is, by magic. Many also looked to astrology, which insisted that a person's fate depended on the conjunction of various planets and stars. Everyone envisioned nature as a "chain of being" infused by God with life and tingling with spiritual forces. Deeply embedded in European folklore, such supernaturalism also marked the "high culture" of educated Europeans. Indeed, the sixteenth-century European "mentality" had more in common with Indian and African mind sets than any of these traditional belief systems have with more modern world views.

The Catholic church, based in Rome, taught that Christ's sacrifice was repeated every time a priest said Mass, and that divine grace flowed to sinners through the sacraments that consecrated priests alone could administer—above all, baptism, confession, and the Eucharist (communion). The Church was a huge network of clergymen, set apart from laypeople by the fact that they did not marry. At the top was the pope, the "vicar (representative) of Christ," whose authority reached everywhere in Europe but Russia, Greece, and the Balkan Peninsula.

The papacy wielded awesome spiritual power. Fifteenth- and early-sixteenth-century popes claimed the authority to dispense extra blessings, or "indulgences," to repentant sinners in return for such "good works" as donating money to the Church. Indulgences promised time off from future punishment in purgatory, where souls atoned for sins they had already confessed and been forgiven. (Hell, from which there was no escape, awaited those who died unforgiven.) Given people's anxieties over "sinful" behavior, indulgences were enormously popular. The jingle of one successful indulgence seller in early-sixteenth-century Germany promised that

> As soon as the coin in the cash box rings,
> The soul from purgatory's fire springs.

But the sale of indulgences provoked charges that the materialism and corruption infecting economic life had spread to the Church. In 1517 the German friar Martin Luther (1483–1546) attacked the practice. When the papacy tried to silence him, Luther broadened his criticism to encompass the Mass, purgatory, priests, and the pope. Luther's revolt initiated the Protestant Reformation, which changed Christianity forever.

To Luther, indulgence selling and similar examples of clerical corruption were evil not just because they bilked people. The Church, he charged, also wronged people by giving them false confidence that they could "earn" salvation by doing good works. His own agonizing search for salvation had convinced Luther that God alone chose whom to save from damnation and that believers could trust only God's love. "I did not love a just and angry God, but rather hated and murmured against him," recalled Luther. "Night and day I pondered until I saw the connection between the justice of God and the [New Testament] statement that 'the just shall live [be saved] by faith.' ... Thereupon I felt myself to be reborn and to have gone through open doors into paradise." Luther's spiritual struggle and experience of being "reborn" constituted a classic conversion experience—the heart of Protestant religion as it soon would be preached and practiced in northern Europe and North America.

A religious prophet of genius, Luther was socially conservative and politically naive. His assault on the Church's abuses won a fervent following among the German public, but Luther and his followers could carry out their program only with the aid of the German princes and city-states. Protestantism* thus had to allow civil governments' broad control over reformed religion. Luther's dream of rallying all Christendom around God's Word soon crumbled.

Protestant reformers could not even agree on what God's Word really meant. Thus Luther and the great French reformer John Calvin (1509–1564) interpreted salvation quite differently. Calvin insisted on the stark doctrine of predestination, in which an omnipotent God "predestined" most sinful humans to hell, saving only a few to exemplify his grace. And Calvinists and Lutherans, as the followers of the two Reformation leaders came to be called, were equally horrified by more radical Protestants such as the Anabaptists, who appealed strongly to women and common people with their criticisms of the rich and powerful and sought to restrict baptism to "converted" adults. Most Anabaptists were pacifists, and some renounced private property and lived communally. Judging the Anabaptists a threat to the social order, governments and mainstream churches persecuted them.

Still another disappointment for Protestants was the Catholic church's remarkable resilience. Catholic

*The word *Protestant* comes from the *protest* of Luther's princely supporters against Holy Roman Emperor Charles V's anti-Lutheran policies.

John Calvin, *by Hans Holbein the Younger,*
Sixteenth Century
Calvin was trained as a classical scholar before his religious conversion. He brought to Protestant theology a scholar's erudition, a lawyer's appreciation of the importance of God's sovereignty over Creation, and a religious zealot's intense faith.

fection. Second, Protestantism placed a high value on reading. Luther's own conversion had sprung from his long study of the Bible, and Protestants demanded that God's Word be translated from Latin into spoken languages and read carefully by believers. The new faith was spread best by the newly invented printing press; wherever Protestantism became established, basic education and religious indoctrination followed. Third, Protestantism denied that God had endowed priests with special powers. Instead, Luther claimed, the church was a "priesthood of all believers." Protestant reformers insisted that laypeople take responsibility for their own spiritual and moral conditions. Finally, the Reformation and Counter-Reformation reinforced a new crusading spirit in Europe, recently bolstered by Spain's fifteenth-century expulsions of Muslims and of Jews who refused to become Christians. Coinciding with the emergence of nation-states and overseas expansion, this spirit frequently gave Europeans a justification for assuming themselves superior to the non-Christian peoples of the Americas and Africa and for seizing their land, resources, and labor.

Along with its innovations, the Reformation had a conservative side. It created a yearning in many people for the simplicity and purity of the ancient Christian church. Protestantism condemned the replacement of traditional reciprocity by marketplace values and, more than Catholicism, questioned the pursuit of excessive wealth. In a world of troubling change, it could forge individuals of strong moral determination and equip them with the fortitude to survive and prosper. Protestantism's greatest appeal was to all those— ordinary individuals, merchants, and aristocrats alike—who brooded over their chances for salvation and valued the steady performance of duty.

Those in all camps who hoped that Christian concord would overcome religious quarrels were sadly disillusioned. Religious warfare consumed much of western and central Europe from the mid-sixteenth to the mid-seventeenth century, and international rivalries in western Europe, particularly between Catholic Spain and Protestant England, assumed a religious dimension. In England the crown itself was heavily entangled in domestic religious strife. King Henry VIII (ruled 1509–1547) wanted a legitimate male heir to ensure political stability. But his queen, Catherine of Aragon, failed to bear a son, and so Henry asked the pope to annul his marriage. After the pope denied Henry's request, the king had Parliament, in a series of acts in 1533–1534, dissolve his marriage and proclaim

reform had begun in Spain even before Luther's revolt, and soon the papacy vigorously attacked corruption and combated Protestant viewpoints on major religious issues. The popes also sponsored a new religious order fervently committed to the papacy: the Jesuits, whose members would distinguish themselves for centuries as missionaries and royal advisers. This Catholic revival, the Counter-Reformation, brought into existence the modern Roman Catholic church.

The Reformation era left four major legacies. First, it created almost all the major Christian traditions that would eventually take root in American soil: Protestantism, Catholicism, and many radical Protestant impulses that would flower into dozens of denominations and visionary groups striving for human per-

Major Religions in Europe, c. 1560
Sixteenth-century Europe teemed with religious change and conflict.

him "supreme head" of the Church of England (or Anglican church). He then used his new position to seize vast tracts of land owned by Catholic monastic orders and to sell them to members of the gentry as a means of raising revenue.

The Rise of Puritanism in England

Religion remained a source of trouble in England for well over a century after Henry's break with Rome. His sale of monastic lands created a vested interest against returning to the old order. But Henry never quite decided whether he was a Protestant. Under Edward VI (ruled 1547–1553), the church veered sharply toward Protestantism; then Mary I tried to restore Catholicism, in part by burning several hundred Protestants at the stake.

The reign of Elizabeth I marked a crucial watershed. After "Bloody Mary," most English people were ready to become Protestant; *how* Protestant was the divisive question. A militant but minority Calvinist movement called Puritanism had arisen. Puritans demanded a wholesale "purification" of the Church of England from "popish [Catholic] abuses." As Calvinists, they affirmed salvation by predestination, denied Christ's presence in the Eucharist, and believed that a learned sermon was the heart of true worship. They wished to free each congregation and its minister from outside interference by bishops and encouraged lay members (nonclergy) to participate in parish affairs. Puritans also objected to certain ceremonies and practices inherited from Catholicism, such as the Mass, elaborate church decoration, kneeling, and the use of priestly vestments or communion rails—the latter two implying that the clergy were separate from, and superior to, their congregations.

Insisting that it was not sufficient for a person to lead an outwardly moral life, Puritans argued that Christians must forge a commitment to serve God through a special act of spiritual rebirth termed the *conversion experience.* At this moment of being "reborn," a soul confronted the horrifying truth of its own unworthiness and felt the transcending power of God's saving grace. Through a process known as sanctification, the new convert was cemented to God as a "saint," or member of the "elect." Whereas membership in the Church of England was automatic for anyone born in England, only saints could join Puritan congregations.

For many Puritans, the conversion process was understandably a tortuous one. Poverty, loneliness, and fear so pervaded England that no one could avoid feeling anxious over the future. Chronic unemployment and low wages constantly tempted the hard-pressed to become petty cheats. Even honest individuals had difficulty showing charity, because they found life so insecure. Unable to make a decent living, many had to fight the impulse to desert their families and the urge to drown their sorrows in drink. Because the faltering economy forced half of all men and women to delay marriage until after age twenty-five, young adults had to battle temptation through much of their lives. In such desperate times, it was natural for many to doubt that they could set the example expected of saints.

In preparing for spiritual rebirth, Puritans struggled to master their own wills, to internalize a highly idealistic code of ethics, and to forge the inner strength to survive in a world of economic and moral chaos. By the time of his or her redemption, a Puritan had undergone a radical personality transformation that replaced doubt with certainty. This reorientation of character produced the Puritans' strong sense of purpose, willingness to sacrifice, and ironclad discipline. The conversion experience molded individuals like the Puritan military and political leader Oliver Cromwell, who felt that, because he had conquered himself, he could conquer any enemy.

The severe self-discipline and righteousness demanded of Puritans appealed to certain elements of English society more than others. The new religion attracted only a few from the titled nobility, with their inherited wealth and privileges, and from the desperate poor, whose lives were consumed by the quest for physical survival. Puritanism's primary appeal lay instead among the small but growing number of people between the extremes of English society—landowning gentry, university-educated clergymen and intellectuals, merchants, shopkeepers, artisans, and yeoman farmers. Self-discipline had become central to both the secular and spiritual dimensions of these people's lives. From their ranks, and particularly from the farmers, artisans, and clergymen, would later come the settlers of New England (see Chapter 3).

Elizabeth distrusted Puritan militancy but also, after 1570, when the pope declared her a heretic and urged Catholics to overthrow her, she regarded English Catholics as potential traitors. She and her advisers gradually forged a strong Church of England that satisfied most Protestants in matters of belief and practice.

By courting influential Puritans and embracing militant anti-Catholicism, Elizabeth maintained most Puritans' loyalty. But religious tensions resurfaced in England after her death.

James I (ruled 1603–1625), the founder of England's Stuart dynasty, bitterly opposed Puritan efforts to eliminate the office of bishop. The monarchy's right to name bishops greatly strengthened its power because bishops composed about a quarter of the House of Lords, the upper chamber of Parliament, which at the time had a strong voice in enacting laws. Bishops also controlled the clergy and thus could silence ministers whose sermons or writings criticized government policies. James made it clear that he saw Puritan attacks on bishops as a direct threat to himself when he snapped, "No bishop, no king."

Under Elizabeth, most Puritans had come to expect that they would eventually tansform the Church of England into independent congregations of "saints." But James's position undermined that hope, leading many Puritans to become *Separatists* who insisted

that saints had to separate themselves from the corrupt state church. During James's reign, some Separatists moved to Calvinist Holland, and a few of these led the founding of Plymouth Plantation in New England (see below). *Non-Separatists,* in contrast, believed that the Church of England could be reformed from within. Some of them would lead the later colonization of Massachusetts Bay and Connecticut (see Chapter 3).

After Charles I became king in 1625, Anglican authorities undertook a systematic campaign to eliminate Puritan influence within the church. With the king's backing, bishops insisted that services be conducted according to the Book of Common Prayer, which prescribed rituals similar to Catholic practices, and they dismissed Puritan ministers who refused to perform these "High Church" rites. Church courts, which judged cases involving religious law, harassed the Puritan laity with fines or excommunication.

The Puritan's spiritual discontent was reinforced by England's poor economic situation. Between 1550 and 1650, wages fell by half. Bad harvests and depressions plagued England. A 30 percent rise in population from 1590 to 1640 spawned massive unemployment. When economic crisis and the outbreak of the Thirty Years' War on the European continent prevented Germany from importing large amounts of English cloth after 1618, a deep recession gripped England's weaving industry, taking a severe toll on the heavily Puritan southeastern counties. For Puritans, these problems contributed to England's spiritual and moral malaise. Dwindling economic opportunities made leading a godly life difficult for many. One Puritan minister wrote that everyone in England was tempted "to pluck his means, as it were, out of his neighbor's throat." Such conditions led many Puritans to consider migrating to New England after 1629 (see Chapter 3).

EUROPEAN EXPANSION

Europeans' outward thrust began centuries before Columbus's first voyage in 1492. In the tenth century, Norse voyagers from Scandinavia had reached North America (see Chapter 1). They established a settlement in Newfoundland and may have explored the New England coast. But the Norse soon abandoned and eventually almost forgot America, and the direction of European expansion changed. A series of crusading armies after 1096 struggled (ultimately in vain) to wrest Palestine from Muslim control. A brisk trade with the Middle East began in these years as Europeans sold cloth and bought silks and the spices they needed to preserve food and spark up a monotonous diet. Some thirteenth-century merchants such as Marco Polo even traveled overland to East Asia to buy directly from the Chinese. By the fourteenth and fifteenth centuries, the highly profitable spice and silk trade had enriched well-placed Italian merchants despite the era's generally depressed economic conditions. With their personal fortunes, the merchants financed the cultural flowering of the early Renaissance as well as the consolidation of domestic power and overseas expansion by the European monarchs.

Seaborne Expansion

Around 1460 a century of depression and population stagnation ended in Europe. An era of renewed economic and population growth opened. As Europeans competed for commercial advantage, they projected their power overseas.

Important changes in maritime technology occurred at this dawn of European expansion. In the early fifteenth century, shipbuilders and mariners along Europe's stormy Atlantic coast added the triangular Arab sail to the heavy cargo ships they used for voyaging between England and the Mediterranean. They created a more maneuverable vessel, the caravel, that could sail against the wind. Sailors also mastered the compass and astrolabe, by which they got their bearings on the open sea. Without this "maritime revolution," European exploration would have been impossible.

Renaissance scholars' search for more accurate readings of ancient texts forced fifteenth-century Europeans to look at their world with new eyes. The great ancient Greek authority on geography was Ptolemy, but Renaissance scholars had to correct his data when they tried to draw accurate maps. Thus Renaissance "new learning" combined with older Arabic and European advances in mathematics to sharpen Europeans' geographic sense.

The impetus to explore new worlds first arose in impoverished Portugal. Here zeal for continuing the struggle against the Muslims who were slowly being driven out of Spain and Portugal combined with an anxious search for new markets. Prince Henry "the Navigator" of Portugal (1394–1460) embodied both urges. Henry encouraged Portuguese seamen to pilot the new caravels farther down the African coast, searching for weak spots in Muslim defenses and for

An Astrolabe
A device for calculating the position and altitude of the sun, stars, and planets, the astrolabe was one of the world's oldest scientific instruments. It was known to the ancient Greeks and perfected by the medieval Arabs. Ocean navigators found it indispensable. This brass English astrolabe, dating to 1326, may be the oldest such European instrument extant.

opportunities to trade profitably. At the time of his death, the Portuguese had established a profitable slaving station at Arguin, and by the late fifteenth century, they had penetrated south of the equator. In 1488 Bartolomeu Días reached the Cape of Good Hope at Africa's southern tip. The Portuguese king John II seized the opportunity to open up direct contact with India, circumventing the Arabs and Venetians. In 1498 Vasco da Gama led a Portuguese fleet around the Cape of Good Hope and on to India.

Ultimately the Portuguese failed to destroy traditional Venetian-Arab commercial links, although for a century they remained an imperial presence in the Indian Ocean and present-day Indonesia. Already, however, they had brought Europeans face-to-face with black Africans.

The "New Slavery" and Racism

Slavery was well established in fifteenth-century West Africa, as elsewhere. The grassland emperors, as well as individual families, depended on slaves. But most slaves or their children were absorbed into African families over time. The eighteenth-century West African Olaudah Equiano, who had suffered enslavement by the British, explained the fate of war captives in his native society:

> How different was their condition from that of the slaves in the West Indies! With us they do no more work than other members of the community, even their master. Their food, clothing, and lodging, were nearly the same as [free people's], except that they were not permitted to eat with those who were born free. . . . Some of these slaves even have slaves under them, as their own property, and for their own use.

Outsiders—first Muslims then Europeans—turned African slavery into an intercontinental business and tore slaves from their native societies. One fifteenth-century Italian who witnessed Portuguese and Muslim slave trading noted that the Arabs "also have many Berber horses, which they trade, and take to the Land of the Blacks, exchanging them with the rulers for slaves. Ten or fifteen slaves are given for one of these horses, according to their quality. . . . These slaves are brought to the market town of Hoden; there they are divided. . . . [Some] are taken . . . and sold to the Portuguese leaseholders [of Arguin]. As a result every year the Portuguese carry away from [Arguin] a thousand slaves."

Equiano's eighteenth-century testimony starkly captures slaves' experience in earlier centuries too. Brought on a European slave ship, he wrote:

> I was now persuaded that I had got into a world of bad spirits, and that they were going to kill me. Their complections differing so much from ours, their long hair, and the languages they spoke . . . united to confirm me in this belief. . . . Quite overpowered with shock and horror, I . . . fainted. When I recovered a little, I found some black people around me, who I believed were some of those who brought me on board, and had been receiving their pay. . . . I asked them if we were not to be eaten by those white men. . . . They told me I was not. [But] soon after this the blacks who had brought me on board went off, and left me abandoned to despair. . . . I found some of my own nation [and] inquired . . . what was to be done with us? They gave me to understand that we were to be carried to these white people's country to work for them. I then was a

> little revived . . . but still I feared I should be put to death, the white people looked, as I thought, so savage. . . .

The Portuguese found slave trading lucrative and kept out competitors until about 1600. Although in 1482 they built an outpost, Elmina, on West Africa's Gold Coast, they exploited existing African commercial and social patterns. Often Portuguese merchants traded slaves and local products to other Africans for gold. The local African kingdoms were too strong for the Portuguese to attack, and black rulers traded—or chose not to trade—according to their own self-interest.

West African societies changed with the coming of Portuguese slavers. In Guinea and Senegambia, which supplied the bulk of sixteenth-century slaves, small kingdoms expanded to "service" the trade. Some of their rulers became comparatively rich. Farther south, in present-day Angola, the kings of Kongo used the slave trade to consolidate their power and voluntarily adopted Christianity. Kongo flourished until the late sixteenth century, when attackers from the interior destroyed it.

The slave-trading African kings and their communities used the trade as a way of disposing of "undesirables," including slaves whom they already owned, lawbreakers, and persons accused of witchcraft. But most slaves were simply victims of raids or wars. Muslim and European slave trading greatly stimulated conflicts among African communities.

Although European societies had used slaves since the time of ancient Greece and Rome, there were ominous differences in the European slavery that arose once the Portuguese began voyaging to West Africa. First, the new slave trade was a high-volume business that expanded steadily. Between 1500 and 1600, perhaps 250,000 African slaves would land in the Western Hemisphere, and 50,000 would die en route. Another 200,000 would arrive between 1601 and 1621. Before the Atlantic slave trade finally ended in the nineteenth century, nearly 12 million Africans would be shipped in terrible conditions across the sea. Slavery on this scale had been unknown to Europeans since the collapse of the Roman Empire. Second, African slaves were treated exceptionally harshly. In medieval Europe slaves had primarily performed domestic service, but by 1450 the Portuguese and Spanish created large slave-labor plantations on their Atlantic and Mediterranean islands. These plantations produced sugar for European markets, using capital supplied by Italian investors to buy African slaves who toiled until death. In short, the African slaves owned by Europeans were destined for exhausting, mindless labor. By 1600 the "new slavery" had become a brutal link in a commerce that ultimately would encompass all major Western nations.

Finally, race became the explicit basis of the "new slavery." Africans' blackness and their alien religion dehumanized them in European eyes. As their racial prejudice hardened, Europeans justified enslaving blacks with increasing ease. From the fifteenth century onward, European Christianity made few attempts to soften slavery's rigors, and race defined a slave. Because the victims of the "new slavery" were physically distinctive as well as culturally alien, slavery became a lifelong, hereditary, and despised status.

Europeans Reach America

Europeans' varying motivations for expanding their horizons converged in the fascinating, contradictory figure of Christopher Columbus (1451–1506), the son of a weaver from the Italian port of Genoa. Columbus's maritime experience, self-taught geographical learning, and keen imagination led him to conclude that Asia could be reached by sailing westward across the Atlantic. By the early 1480s this idea obsessed him. Religious fervor led Columbus to dream of carrying Christianity around the globe and liberating Jerusalem from Muslim rule, but he also burned with ambition to win wealth and glory.

Columbus would not be the first European to venture far out into the Atlantic. Besides the early Norse, fifteenth-century English fishermen may already have sailed as far west as the Grand Banks and even the North American coast. But Columbus was unique in the persistence with which he hawked his "enterprise of the Indies" around the royal courts of western Europe. John II of Portugal showed interest until Días's discovery of the Cape of Good Hope promised a surer way to India. Finally, in 1492, hoping to break a threatened Portuguese monopoly on direct trade with Asia, the rulers of newly united Spain—Queen Isabella of Castile and King Ferdinand of Aragon—accepted Columbus's offer. Picking up the westward-blowing trade winds at the Canary Islands, Columbus's three small ships reached San Salvador within a month.

Columbus's success derived in part from a gigantic miscalculation. The West Indies lay about where he expected to find Japan, for he had combined Marco Polo's overestimate of Asia's eastward thrust with Ptolemy's underestimate of the earth's circumference. Another ancient Greek mathematician's calculation was close to the true circumference, and this figure was generally accepted by knowledgeable fifteenth-century Europeans; hence the skepticism that Columbus had aroused.

Word of Columbus's discovery caught Europeans' imaginations. It also induced Isabella and John II in 1494 to sign the Treaty of Tordesillas, which divided all future discoveries between Castile and Portugal. Meanwhile, Isabella had sent Columbus back to explore further, and he established a colony on Hispaniola, the Caribbean island today occupied by Haiti and the Dominican Republic. Columbus proved a poor administrator, and after his last voyages (1498–1502), he was shunted aside. He died an embittered man, convinced that he had reached the threshold of Asia, only to be cheated of his rightful rewards.

England's Henry VII (ruled 1485–1509) ignored Castile's and Portugal's claims of exclusive rights to new discoveries. In 1497 he sent an Italian navigator known in England as John Cabot westward into the Atlantic, tacking against the eastward winds of these latitudes. Cabot claimed for England Nova Scotia, Newfoundland, and the rich Grand Banks fisheries. Like Columbus, Cabot thought that he had reached Asia.

The more Columbus and others explored, the more apparent it became (to everyone except himself) that a vast landmass blocked the route to Asia. In 1500 the Portuguese claimed Brazil, and other voyages soon revealed a continuous coastline from the Caribbean to Brazil. In 1507 this landmass got its name when a publisher brought out a collection of voyagers' tales. One of the chroniclers was an Italian named Amerigo Vespucci. With a shrewd marketing touch, the publisher devised a catchy name for the new continent: America.

Getting past America and reaching Asia remained the early explorers' primary aim. In 1513 the Spaniard Vasco Núñez de Balboa chanced upon the Pacific Ocean when he crossed the narrow isthmus of Panama. Then in 1519 the Portuguese Ferdinand Magellan, sailing under the Castilian flag, began a voyage around the world by way of the stormy Magellan Straits at South America's southern tip. In an incredible feat of endurance, he crossed the Pacific to the Philippines, only to die fighting with local natives. One of his five ships and fifteen emaciated sailors finally returned to Spain in 1522, the first people to have sailed around the world. But Europeans hoped for easier access to East

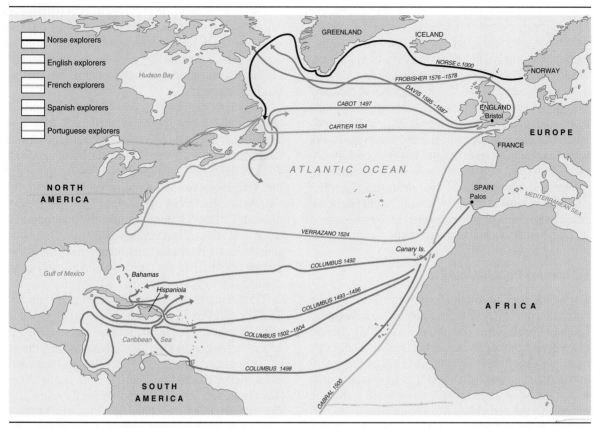

Major Transatlantic Explorations, 1000–1587
Following Columbus's 1492 voyage, Spain's rivals soon began laying claim to parts of the New World based on the voyages of Cabot for England, Cabral for Portugal, and Verrazano for France. Later English and French exploration focused on finding a passage to Asia around or through Canada.

Asia's fabled wealth. The French king Francis I accepted the challenge of finding a "northwest passage" to Asia. In 1524 he dispatched the Italian navigator Giovanni da Verrazano, who explored the North American coast from the Carolinas to Newfoundland. In three subsequent voyages between 1534 and 1542 the French explorer Jacques Cartier carefully probed the coasts of Newfoundland, Quebec, and Nova Scotia and ascended the St. Lawrence as far as present-day Montreal. Although encountering large numbers of Native Americans, Verrazano and Cartier found no gold and no northwest passage.

The Conquerors

Columbus was America's first slave trader and the first of the Spanish conquerors, or *conquistadores.* At his

struggling colony on Hispaniola, he began exporting Indian slaves and created *encomiendas*—grants for the right to extract labor and other tribute from the Indians of a designated district. Other *conquistadores* would soon transplant this practice to the American mainland.

From the beginning *encomiendas* harshly exploited the native people, who died in droves from overwork, malnutrition, and disease. Then Portuguese slavers stepped in, supplying shiploads of Africans to replace the perishing Indians. Spanish friars who came to Hispaniola to convert the Indians quickly sent back grim reports of Indian exploitation; and King Ferdinand (who had made money by selling *encomiendas*) felt sufficiently shocked to attempt to forbid the practice. No one, however, worried about the African slaves' fate.

Spanish Map of the Antilles, 1519

This map offers a rare glimpse of Spain's initial stronghold in the Caribbean islands, centering on what is now Haiti. The decorative figures are Africans, imported to replace Indian labor lost to disease and harsh treatment.

Soon Spanish settlers were fanning out through the Caribbean in search of Indian slaves and gold. In 1519 the restless nobleman Hernán Cortés (1485–1547) led a small band of followers to the Mexican coast. Destroying his boats and gathering Indian allies, he marched inland over towering mountain passes to conquer Mexico.

Spaniards had dreamed of a prize such as Mexico ever since they reached America. Mexico was rich: an impressive civilization had been evolving there for three thousand years, culminating in the mighty Aztec Empire. It was exotic: the priests and soldiers who dominated the empire raided neighboring peoples to seize victims for grisly human sacrifices. And Mexico was highly organized. The three hundred thousand inhabitants of the capital, Tenochtitlán, enjoyed fresh water supplied by means of elaborate engineering works; their urban society was highly stratified; and artisans produced a profusion of finely crafted pottery as well as stone, copper, silver, and gold implements. "We were amazed and said that it was like the enchantments they tell of [in stories], and some of our soldiers even asked whether the things that we saw were not a dream?" recalled one of Cortés's soldiers of his first glimpse of Tenochtitlán's pyramids, lakes, and causeways. Certainly the golden gifts that the Aztecs offered in the vain hope of buying off the invaders were no dream. "They picked up the gold and fingered it like monkeys," recalled an Indian. "Their bodies swelled with greed, and their hunger was ravenous. They hungered like pigs for that gold."

Cortés attacked and swiftly prevailed. He owed his astonishing victories partly to firearms and horses, which terrified the Aztecs, and partly to initial Aztec

Cortés's Entrance into Veracruz, *c. 1550*
The ancient Mexicans called Veracruz the "Place of Precious Stones." Mexican Lienzo de Tlaxcala's pictorial description shows Cortés transporting cannons on his march through Mexico.

suppositions that the Spanish were the white, bearded gods whose return ancient legends had foretold. His success also resulted from his boldness and cunning, the Aztec emperor Moctezuma's fears, epidemics among the Indians, and the revolt of the Aztecs' subject peoples. By 1521 Cortés had overthrown the Aztecs and begun to build Mexico City on the ruins of Tenochtitlán. Soon the last Aztec emperor suffered defeat and execution, and within twenty years Central America lay at the Spaniards' feet. New Spain was born.

During the rest of the sixteenth century, other *conquistadores* and officials consolidated a great Hispanic empire stretching from New Spain (Mexico) to Chile. Subduing Native Americans and enriching themselves never troubled the *conquistadores'* consciences. Before a battle a herald would read the *requerimiento,* a proclamation in Spanish demanding the Indians' conversion to Christianity and blaming them for bloodshed if they resisted. From the beginning, however, the Spanish church and government worried that the *conquistadores* were becoming too powerful and abusive. The monarchs sent over hundreds of bureaucrats to govern in the hierarchical European manner and to defend Indian rights. Armies of Spanish friars established missions among the Indians, sometimes lessening the native people's suffering, other times increasing it, and often clashing with civilian authorities. The whole system was too cumbersome. "I obey, but I do not fulfill" became a standard bureaucratic dodge.

The human cost of the conquest was enormous. Mourned a vanquished Aztec:

Broken spears lie in the roads;
We have torn our hair in our grief.
The houses are roofless now . . .
And the walls are splattered with gore . . .
We have pounded our hands in despair
Against the adobe walls.

When Cortés landed in 1519, central Mexico's population had been about 25 million. By 1600 it had shrunk to between 1 million and 2 million. Peru and other regions experienced similar devastation. America had witnessed the greatest demographic disaster in world history.

Warfare, forced labor, starvation, and mass slaughter accounted for some of the catastrophe, but the greatest killers were <u>microbes</u>. Native Americans lacked antibodies to European and African infections—above all, the deadly, highly communicable smallpox. From the first years of contact, frightful epidemics decimated Indian communities. In the West Indian islands, the entire native population perished within fifty years, and devastation from disease facilitated the colonization of mainland North America. "The people began to die very fast, and many in a short space," an Englishman later remarked, adding that the deaths invariably occurred after Europeans had visited an Indian village. From early in the sixteenth century, raging epidemics of smallpox and other alien maladies scourged the defenseless Indians. Whole villages perished at once, with no one left to bury the dead. Up to 90 percent of the native population in some areas was lost.

Yet the "Columbian exchange"—the biological encounter of the Old and New Worlds—was not limited to deadly germs. In addition to diseases, sixteenth-century Europeans brought horses, cattle, sheep, swine, chickens, wheat and other grains, coffee, sugar cane, numerous fruits and garden vegetables, and an astonishing variety of weeds to America. In the next century, African slaves carried rice and yams with them across the Atlantic. The list of American gifts to the Eastern Hemisphere was equally impressive: corn, many varieties of beans, white and sweet potatoes, the tropical root crop manioc, tomatoes, squash, pumpkins, peanuts, vanilla, cacao, avocados, pineapples, chilis, tobacco, and turkeys. Often several centuries passed before new plants became widely accepted across the ocean; for example, many Europeans suspected that potatoes and tomatoes were either poisons or aphrodisiacs until the nineteenth century, and Indians at first had to be forced to grow wheat. European weeds and domestic animals drastically altered many environments in the Western Hemisphere, especially in North America, overwhelming indigenous plantlife and thereby driving away wild animals who fed on those plants. In this way, colonists' ways of life impinged directly on the lives of native peoples. Settlers' crops, intensively cultivated on lands never replenished by lying fallow, often exhausted American soil. But the worldwide exchange of food products also enriched human diets and later made possible enormous population growth.

Another dimension of the transatlantic encounters was the mixing of peoples. Throughout the sixteenth century, between one hundred thousand and three hundred thousand Spaniards immigrated, 90 percent of them male. Particularly in towns, a racially blended people emerged as these men married Indian women, giving rise to the large *mestizo* (mixed Spanish-Indian) population of Mexico and other Latin American countries. *Métis,* as the French termed people of both Indian and European descent, would appear in lesser proportions in the French and English colonies of North America. Throughout the Americas, particularly in plantation colonies, European men fathered *mulatto* children with African women, most of them slaves, and African-Indian unions occurred in nearly all regions. But the context for these population transfers and mixtures was the massive migrations of Europeans and enslaved Africans and the wholesale extermination of Native Americans through disease and violence.

The Americas supplied seemingly limitless wealth for Spain. Not only did some Spaniards grow rich from West Indian sugar plantations and Mexican sheep and cattle ranches, but immense quantities of silver crossed the Atlantic after rich mines in Mexico and Peru began producing in the 1540s. A robust trade between America and Spain grew up, which Castilian officials tried to regulate. Spain took in far more American silver than its economy could absorb, setting off inflation that eventually engulfed all Europe. Bent on dominating Europe, the Spanish kings needed ever more American silver to pay their armies. Several times they went bankrupt, and their efforts to squeeze more taxes from their subjects provoked in the 1560s the revolt of Spain's rich Netherlands provinces—modern Belgium, Holland, and Luxembourg. In the end, gaining access to American wealth cost Spain dearly.

The bloody history of Spain's American conquests and efforts to dominate Europe helped spin the "Black Legend"—Protestant Europeans' vision of a tyrannical, fanatically Catholic Spain intent on conquering everything in sight. Ironically, much of the Black Legend's lurid picture of American horrors derived from the writings of a devout Spanish friar, Bartolomé de Las Casas (1474–1566), who had repented his own participation (as a layman) in the subjugation of Hispaniola. By the end of the sixteenth century, Las Casas's noble hopes of justice for the Indians lay in ruins. The Spanish church became increasingly bureaucratic, intolerant, and restrictive. All this fueled the Black Legend. As Spain's struggle to reconquer the Netherlands and to dominate France spilled ominously near their homeland, Protestant Britons shuddered. But they also looked for opportunities across the Atlantic with which to strike back at Spain—and to enrich themselves.

Footholds in North America

As early as 1510, the flow of wealth from the New World to Spain attracted swarms of Europeans. For the rest of the century, Europeans grew familiar with the North American coast through exploratory voyages, fishing expeditions, a small-scale fur trade, and piracy and smuggling. But except for a Spanish base at St.

Augustine, Florida, their attempts to plant colonies failed. These failures did not stem from lack of effort. Would-be conquerors and colonizers tried many times to establish the presence of Spain, France, or England on North American soil. But they predicated their efforts on unrealistic expectations of fabulous wealth and pliant natives.

As the seventeenth century dawned, the ravaging of Indian populations owing to disease, and the rise of English, French, and Dutch power finally made colonization possible. By 1614 Spain, England, France, and the Netherlands had established secure North American bases. Within another decade, each colony developed a distinct economic orientation, and patterns of Indian relations and geographic expansion. The first quarter of the seventeenth century marked the formative period of North America's modern history.

New Spain's Northern Frontier

The Spanish had built their American empire by subduing the Aztec and other Indian states, whose riches had attracted the invaders like a magnet. The dream of more such finds drew would-be *conquistadores* to the borderlands north of Mexico. "As it was his object to find another treasure like that . . . of Peru," a witness wrote of one such man, Hernando de Soto, he "would not be content with good lands nor pearls."

The earliest of these invaders was Juan Ponce de León, the conqueror of Puerto Rico, who in 1512–1513 and again in 1521 trudged through Florida in search of gold and slaves. His quest ended in death in an Indian skirmish. The most astonishing early expedition began in Florida in 1527. After provoking several attacks by Apalachee Indians, the three hundred explorers were separated into several parties. All were thought to have perished until eight years later, when four survivors, led by Alvar Nuñez Cabeza de Vaca and including the African slave Estevanico, arrived in northern Mexico. They had sailed to the Texas coast, where they were shipwrecked. They then walked west to New Mexico and turned south, living among many different Indian groups. They arrived in Mexico in 1536. Cabeza de Vaca's account of their journey is the most compelling European literary work on North America before permanent colonization.

Cabeza de Vaca provided direct inspiration for the two most formidable attempts at Spanish conquest. De Soto and his party in 1539–1543 blundered

The Spanish and Portuguese Empires, 1610
By 1610 Spain dominated Latin America, including Portugal's possessions. Having devoted its energies to exploiting Mexico and the Caribbean, Spain had not yet expanded into what is now the United States, aside from establishing outposts in Florida and New Mexico.

from Tampa Bay to the Appalachians to southern Texas. Scouring the land for gold, de Soto harried the Indians mercilessly. "Think, then," an Indian chief appealed to him vainly,

> what must be the effect on me and mine, of the sight of you and your people, whom we have at no time seen, astride the fierce brutes, your horses, entering with such speed and fury into my country, that we had no tidings of your coming—things so absolutely new, as to strike awe and terror into our hearts.

Although de Soto died without finding gold or conquering any Indians, his and other expeditions caused epidemics that destroyed most of the remaining Mississippian societies. By the time Europeans returned to the southeastern interior late in the seventeenth century, only the Natchez on the lower Mississippi River still inhabited their sumptuous temple-mound center and remained under the rule of a Great Sun. Depopulated groups like the Cherokees and Creeks had adopted the less centralized village life of other eastern Indians.

As de Soto roamed the Southeast, some Spanish officials in Mexico were drawn by rumors that the fabled Seven Golden Cities of Cíbola lay to the north. In 1538 they launched an expedition, guided by Estevanico, to find them. Estevanico was killed by Zuni Indians, but the Spanish were certain that the Zunis' pueblo was one of the golden cities. In 1540–1542, Francisco Vásquez de Coronado led a massive expedition bent on conquest. Coronado plundered several pueblos and roamed from the Grand Canyon to Kansas before returning to Mexico, finding no gold but embittering many Native Americans. Other expeditions, along the California coast and up the Colorado River, likewise proved fruitless.

For several decades after these failed ventures, Spain's principal interest north of Mexico and the Caribbean lay in establishing strategic bases to keep out French and English intruders. In 1565 Spain established the first successful European settlement in North America, a powerful fortress at St. Augustine, Florida. Despite efforts to strengthen Florida and to build forts linking it to Mexico, St. Augustine remained only a military stronghold and a base for a chain of re-

ligious missions extending north to Chesapeake Bay. Rejecting missionary efforts to reorder their lives, the Indians rebelled and forced the closing of all the missions before 1600.

Franciscan missionaries renewed their efforts in Florida in the early seventeenth century and secured the nominal allegiance of about 16,000 Guale and Timucuan Indians. But epidemics in the 1610s killed about half the converts.

Meanwhile, in the 1580s, Spanish friars had returned to the southwestern pueblo country, preaching Christianity and scouting the area's potential wealth. Encouraged by their reports, in 1598 Juan de Oñate led five hundred Spaniards, mestizos, Mexican Indians, and African slaves into the upper Rio Grande Valley, where he proclaimed the royal colony of New Mexico, distributed *encomiendas,* and demanded tribute from the pueblo-dwelling Indians.

The new colony barely survived. The Spanish government replaced Oñate in 1606 because of mismanagement and excessive brutality toward the Indians. His successor founded Santa Fe in 1610, but many colonists established ranches nearer the pueblos in order to exploit Indian labor. New Mexico survived primarily through the efforts of Franciscan missionaries. By 1630 they had converted about 20,000 Indians (contrary to their claim of 500,000) and established more than 50 missions in the Rio Grande Valley and westward 250 miles to the Hopi villages in Arizona.

**Indian View of
Spanish Colonizers**
*This pictograph—a painting
or drawing on rock—was
sketched in the early colonial
period in Cañón del Muerto,
Arizona.*

France: Initial Failures and Canadian Success

In 1534 Jacques Cartier of France, searching for the northwest passage, identified the St. Lawrence River as one of North America's two primary avenues of entry. After 1600 this river would become the center of French colonization. (The other such avenue, used by the French in later years, was the Mississippi River.) Before finally planting permanent American colonies, however, France experienced more than a half-century of failure.

France made the first attempt at European colonization in North America in 1541, when Cartier led ten ships carrying four hundred soldiers, three hundred sailors, and a few women to the St. Lawrence Valley. Cartier had already alienated many Indians along the St. Lawrence during two previous expeditions, and his construction of a fortified settlement on Indian land cut off all possibility of native support. Over the next two years, the French suffered heavy casualties from Indian attacks and from scurvy (for which the Indians could have shown them a cure) before abandoning the colony.

The failed French expedition seemed to verify the Spanish opinion, voiced by the cardinal of Seville, that "this whole coast as far [south] as Florida is utterly unproductive." The next French effort at colonization came in 1562, when French Huguenots (Calvinists) briefly established a base in what is now South Carolina. In 1564 the Huguenots founded a settlement near modern-day Jacksonville, Florida, which the Spanish destroyed a year later, massacring all 132 male defenders. These failures, along with a civil war between French Catholics and Huguenots, temporarily discouraged the French from further attempts at colonization.

Meanwhile, French and other European fishers were working the plenteous Grand Banks fisheries of the North Atlantic. Going ashore to dry their fish, some

European Settlements in Eastern North America, 1565–1625

Except for St. Augustine, Florida, and Santa Fe, New Mexico, all European settlements founded before 1607 were abandoned by 1625. Despite the migration of ten thousand Europeans to North America's Atlantic coast by 1625, the total number of Spanish, English, French, and Dutch on the continent was then about eighteen hundred, of whom two-thirds lived in Virginia. For French and Spanish settlement in the late colonial period, see the map on p. 118.

Battle of Lake Champlain, 1609

French soldiers and their Indian allies attack a band of Mohawk Iroquois. In this decisive battle, the French escalated the intensity of warfare in the Northeast with their introduction of firearms.

French sailors bartered with coastal Indians for skins of the beaver, a species almost extinct in Europe. By the late sixteenth century, as European demand for beaver hats skyrocketed, a French-dominated fur trade blossomed. Before the end of the century, French traders were returning annually to sites from Newfoundland to Maine and along the lower St. Lawrence.

Unlike explorers such as de Soto and colonizers such as those at Roanoke, the traders recognized the importance of reciprocity in dealing with the Indians. Consequently, they were generally more successful. In exchange for pelts, they traded metal tools such as axes and knives, cloth, and glass beads. Seen by the Europeans as "trinkets," glass beads to the Indians had the same supernatural power as quartz, mica, and other sacred substances obtained via trade networks for thousands of years. By the next century specialized factories in Europe would be producing both cloth and glass for the "Indian trade."

Between 1598 and 1604, a series of government-sponsored French fur-trading outposts appeared in Acadia (modern-day Nova Scotia). But only in 1608 did the first enduring French settlement on Canadian soil begin, founded by Samuel de Champlain at Quebec, far up the St. Lawrence River. Champlain wintered there with twenty-eight men, of whom twenty died.

Shrewdly understanding how to keep his settlement going, Champlain the next year joined nearby Indians in a battle with some Mohawk Iroquois at Lake Champlain. Using guns to defeat the dreaded Mohawks, the French secured the allegiance of several Indian nations, including the powerful Hurons. Through the latter, the French gained access to the thick beaver pelts of the Canadian interior and pledged to protect their Indian allies from the Iroquois. These economic and diplomatic arrangements defined the course of New France's history for the rest of the seventeenth century.

The Enterprising Dutch

By 1588 the independence of the northern, Dutch-speaking part of Spain's rebellious Netherlands provinces was secure, although the southern Netherlands—modern Belgium and Luxembourg—would remain under Spanish rule until 1713. The Dutch Republic was one of the seventeenth century's great powers. Mighty at sea, the Hollanders built an empire stretching from Brazil to West Africa to what is now Indonesia. North America was for them a relatively minor sphere of activity. Even so, the Dutch played a key role in colonizing the continent.

As early as 1609, the Dutch East India Company had become interested in North America when Henry Hudson sailed up the broad, deep river that today bears his name. The next year Dutch ships were sailing up the Hudson to trade with Indians. Among the most eager customers of the Dutch were Mohawk Iroquois,

New Amsterdam

After the Dutch "purchase" of Manhattan Island, the fortified settlement of New Amsterdam grew only slowly, as this view from 1651 (the earliest known depiction) clearly shows. Except for the tip, the island remained farmland or forest. Corn brought by canoe-paddling Indians also helped feed the settlement. Note the windmill, where grain was ground.

smarting from their defeat by the French the year before. In 1614 a Dutch trading company built Fort Nassau near what would become Albany, and established the colony of New Netherland. In 1625 the Dutch erected another fort on an island at the mouth of the Hudson. The colony's director-general, Peter Minuit, bought the island from local Indians in 1626 and began a second settlement there. The Dutch named the island Manhattan and the settlement New Amsterdam.

New Netherlanders lived by the fur trade. Through the Mohawks, they relied on the Iroquois Confederacy, much as the French depended on the Hurons. To stimulate a flow of furs to New Netherland, in the 1620s Dutch traders obtained from the Indians of Long Island Sound large quantities of wampun (tiny seashells traditionally denoting spiritual power, which Native Americans had long traded throughout the continent's interior) and used it to buy beaver pelts inland. Backed respectively by the French and the Dutch, Hurons and Iroquois became embroiled in an ever-deepening contest to control the movement of goods between Europeans and Indians.

Elizabethan England and the Wider World

In 1558, when Elizabeth I became queen, England was a minor power and stood on the sidelines as Spain and France grappled for supremacy in Europe. England's initial claims to North America had by now receded, although hundreds of English fishing vessels voyaged annually to North American shores and to the Grand Banks. The English remained preoccupied with charting the direction of their religious Reformation and coping with domestic instability.

This instability, however, helped propel Elizabethan expansion. Shipping its unemployed poor overseas seemed a good solution to England's economic woes. "Surplus" English people transplanted to the colonies across the ocean might not only provide raw markets for English cloth but also produce valuable export commodities. And the gentry of England's West Country (the southwestern peninsula jutting out into the Atlantic) itched for action. They were restless men, used to the sea, linked by family ties and Puritan sympathies, and frustrated by customs that limited the amount of family property inherited by younger sons. Francis Drake, John Hawkins, Humphrey Gilbert, and Walter Raleigh all fit this description and stood ready to lead England's overseas adventure.

But Spain blocked the way. When Elizabeth came to the throne, England and Spain were enjoying friendly relations. With the queen's support, Hawkins in the early 1560s made a tidy fortune raiding the Guinea coast for slaves and selling them legally to the Spanish; and Elizabeth stood by as the Spanish wiped out France's Florida colony in 1564. But the English worried about Spain's intervention in France's civil wars and its determined effort to crush the Netherlands revolt, as well as about the pope's call for Elizabeth's overthrow. Furthermore, by now the English had no incentive to trade legally with Spanish America: in 1568 the Spanish authorities in Mexico had chased Hawkins and Drake from the Caribbean. Secretly, Elizabeth stepped up her aid to Calvinist rebels in France and the Netherlands, and to "sea dogs" like Hawkins and Drake—from whose voyages she took a share of the plunder. In the 1570s she encouraged merchants to invest in Atlantic-oriented ventures.

Meanwhile, England's position in Ireland was deteriorating. As early as 1565, English troops fought to impose Tudor rule throughout the island. The conflict intensified when the pope and the Spanish began directly aiding Irish Catholics' resistance to the English. In the ensuing war that ground on through the 1580s, the English drove the Irish clans out of their strongholds, especially in northern Ireland, or Ulster, and established their own settlements ("plantations") of English and Scottish Protestant settlers. Since Irish resistance did not depend on fortified cities or large armies, English commanders had to develop new tactics to subdue the mobile, armed Irish people, who could easily disappear into bogs and forests. The English practiced total war to break the rebellious population's spirit, inflicting starvation and mass slaughter by destroying villages in the winter.

Elizabeth's generals justified these atrocities by claiming that the Irish were "savages." Ireland thus furnished precedents for strategies that the English later employed against North American Indians, whose customs, religion, and method of fighting likewise seemed to absolve the English from guilt in waging exceptionally cruel warfare. Fighting in Ireland and settling fellow citizens there, English colonizers such as Gilbert and Raleigh gained practical experience that they later applied in America.

England had two objectives in the Western Hemisphere in the 1570s. The first was to find the northwest passage to Asia and if possible to discover gold on the way; the second, in Drake's words, was to "singe the king of Spain's beard" by raiding Spanish fleets and ports from Spain to the West Indies. The search for the northwest passage only led to such embarrassments as explorer Martin Frobisher's return from the Canadian Arctic with a shipload of "fool's gold." However, privateering raids on the Spanish were both spectacularly successful and profitable for Drake's and Hawkins's financial backers, including merchants, gentry, government leaders, and Elizabeth herself. The most breathtaking enterprise was Drake's voyage around the world (1577–1580) in quest of sites for colonies. During this voyage he sailed up the California coast and entered Drake's Bay, north of San Francisco.

Now deadly rivals, Spain and England sought to plant strategic bases against each other. In 1572 the

Spanish tried to fortify a Jesuit mission on the Chesapeake Bay. They failed, largely because Powhatan Indians resisted. Securing a royal patent (charter) to start an English colony in Newfoundland, Gilbert took five ships there in 1583 but drowned on his return voyage. In 1584 Gilbert's half-brother Raleigh acquired the patent. Raleigh dispatched Arthur Barlowe to explore the coast farther south, closer to the Spanish—the region that the English had already named Virginia in honor of their virgin queen. Barlowe returned singing the praises of Roanoke Island, but the colony Raleigh established there proved to be the costliest failure yet in England's brief imperial history (see "A Place in Time").

In 1588 England won a spectacular naval victory over the Armada, a huge invasion fleet sent into the English Channel by Spain's Philip II. This famous victory preserved England's independence and demonstrated that the kingdom could repel attacks although it had little offensive military might. The war churned on as before. In 1595 Drake and Hawkins died fighting in the Caribbean. Raleigh wasted his political influence and physical health in fruitless quests for the legendary gilded king ("El Dorado") in South America. England, France, and the Netherlands formed an alliance to dismember the Spanish Empire, but the French backed out. Only the Netherlanders' naval assaults on Spanish and Portuguese* outposts around the world had devastating effects. England made no further moves to carve out American colonies until after 1600.

Yet overseas expansion still lured individual Englishmen. To sustain public interest in the New World, in 1589 and again in 1601 Richard Hakluyt published monumental collections of explorers' accounts, *The Principal Navigations, Voyages, and Discoveries of the English Nation.* But neither the English crown nor Parliament would agree to spend money on colonies, and Roanoke's failure had proved that private fortunes were inadequate to finance successful settlements. Only joint-stock companies—business corporations that would amass capital through sales of stock to the public—could raise funds for American settlement. Such stock offerings produced large sums, but with limited risk for each investor. England's government henceforth would leave colonization to the private initiative of individuals or business groups and would

---

*Between 1580 and 1640, Portugal and its colonies were united with Spain.

spend no substantial sums on any colonies until the eighteenth century.

The Beginnings of English Colonization: Virginia

The hopes of would-be colonial investors rose after 1600 as Anglo-Spanish relations took a new turn. Elizabeth died in 1603, and her cousin, the king of Scotland, ascended the English throne as James I. The cautious and peace-loving king signed a truce with Spain in 1604. Seriously alarmed by Dutch naval victories, the Spanish considered England the lesser danger. The new Spanish king, Philip III, therefore conceded what his predecessors had always refused: a free hand to another power in part of the Americas. Spain renounced its claims to Virginia; England could now colonize unmolested.

On April 10, 1606, James I granted a charter authorizing overlapping grants of land in Virginia to two separate joint-stock companies, one based in London and the other in Plymouth. The Virginia Company of Plymouth received a grant extending south from modern Maine to the Potomac River, and the Virginia Company of London's lands ran north from Cape Fear to the Hudson River. The colonists would be business employees, not citizens of a separate political jurisdiction, and the stockholders of each company would regulate

their behavior. Both companies dispatched colonists in 1607.

The Virginia Company of Plymouth sent 120 men to Sagadahoc, at the mouth of the Kennebec River. Half left in 1608 after alienating the Abenaki Indians and enduring a hard Maine winter, and the rest went back to England a year later with Raleigh Gilbert (Humphrey's son) when he returned home to collect an inheritance. Soon thereafter the company disbanded.

The Virginia Company of London barely avoided a similar failure. Its first expedition included many members of the gentry, most of whom expected riches to fall into their laps. They chose a site on the James River in May 1607 and named it Jamestown. Discipline quickly fell apart after the discovery of iron pyrite sparked a fool's gold rush, and, as at Roanoke, the colonists neglected to plant crops. When relief ships arrived in January 1608 with reinforcements, only 38 survivors remained out of 105 immigrants.

Short of workers who could farm, fish, hunt, and do carpentry, Virginia also needed effective leadership on the council directing its affairs. The council's first president hoarded supplies, and its second was lazy and indecisive. In September 1608 the councilors turned to a brash soldier of fortune whose eagerness to settle arguments with his fists had landed him in irons for most of the 1607 voyage: the magnificent braggart Captain John Smith.

Artifacts from Early Virginia

This double-edged sword (shown with fragments of its guard and pommel) and elaborate pipe tamper (featuring a man wearing armor and smoking a pipe) were unearthed at Flowerdew Hundred, an early English settlement near present-day Hopewell, Virginia, and date from the first half of the seventeenth century.

Only twenty-eight years old and of yeoman origin, Smith had experience fighting Spaniards and Turks that prepared him well to assume control in Virginia. Organizing all but the sick in work gangs, he ensured sufficient food and housing for winter. Applying lessons learned in his soldiering days, he laid down rules for maintaining sanitation and hygiene to limit disease. Above all, he brought order through military discipline. During the winter of 1608–1609, Virginia lost just a dozen men out of two hundred.

Smith also became the colony's best diplomat. After local Native Americans captured him in late 1607, Smith displayed such courage that Powhatan, the leader of the nearby Powhatan Confederacy, arranged an elaborate reconciliation ceremony in which his daughter, Pocahontas, "saved" Smith's life during a mock execution. Smith maintained satisfactory relations with the Powhatan Confederacy in part through his personality, but he also employed calculated demonstrations of English military strength to mask the settlers' actual weakness.

John Smith prevented Virginia from disintegrating as Sagadahoc had. But when he returned to England in 1609 after being wounded in a gunpowder explosion, discipline again crumbled. Expecting the Indians to provide them with corn, the colonists had not laid away sufficient food for the winter. Consequently, relations with the Powhatans deteriorated. A survivor of the winter wrote:

> So lamentable was our scarcity, that we were constrained to eat dogs, cats, rats, snakes, toadstools, horsehides, and what not; one man out of the misery endured, killing his wife powdered her up [with flour] to eat her, for which he was burned. Many besides fed on the corpses of dead men, . . . and indeed so miserable was our estate that the happiest day that some of them hoped to see was when the Indians had killed a mare, they wishing whilst she was boiling that Sir Thomas Smythe [Treasurer of the Virginia Company] was upon her back in the kettle.

Of the five hundred residents at Jamestown in September 1609, about four hundred died by May 1610. But an influx of new recruits, coupled with the imposition of military rule, enabled Virginia to win the first Anglo-Powhatan War (1610–1614). By 1611 the colony had already expanded forty miles beyond Jamestown, to modern-day Richmond. The English population remained small, however, just 380 in 1616, and it had yet to produce anything of value for the stockholders.

Tobacco emerged as Virginia's economic salvation. John Rolfe, an Englishman who married Pocahontas after the war, spent several years perfecting a salable variety of tobacco and began planting it in Virginia. By 1619 the product commanded high prices, and that year Virginia exported large amounts of the crop. Thereafter the Virginia Company poured supplies and settlers into the colony.

To attract labor and capital, the company awarded fifty-acre grants ("headrights") to anyone paying his or her own passage or the transit of a laborer. By paying the passage of their indentured servants, some enterprising planters accumulated sizable tracts of land. Despite the uncertainty of life in Virginia, thousands of single young men and a few hundred women calculated that uncertainty was preferable to continued unemployment and poverty in England. In return for their passage, the servants worked for a fixed term, usually four to seven years. The Virginia Company also abandoned military rule and provided for an assembly to be elected by the "inhabitants" (apparently meaning only the planters). Although the assembly's actions were subject to the company's veto, its establishment in 1619 did mark the beginnings of representative government in North America.

By 1622 Virginia still faced three serious problems. First, local officials systematically defrauded the shareholders by embezzling treasury funds, overcharging for supplies, and using company laborers to work their own tobacco fields. They profited, but the company sank deep into debt. Second, the colony's population suffered from an exceptionally high death rate. The majority of fatalities stemmed from malnutrition owing to the poor diets of the servants, or from salt poisoning, typhus, or dysentery, contracted when the settlers drank the salty, polluted water from the lower James River. Most of the 3,500 immigrants entering Virginia from 1618 to 1622 died within three years. Finally, relations with the Powhatans steadily worsened after Pocahontas died in England in 1617, and Powhatan a year later. Leadership passed to Opechancanough, who at first sought to accommodate the English. But relentless expansion led to Indian discontent and to the rise of a powerful shaman, Nemattenew, who urged the Powhatans to resist the English to the death. After some settlers killed Nemattenew, the Indians launched a surprise attack in 1622 that killed 347 of the 1,240 colonists. With much of their livestock destroyed, spring planting prevented, and disease spreading through cramped fortresses, hundreds more colonists died in the ensuing months.

"We found the people most gentle, loving, and faithful, void of all guile and treason, and such as live after the manner of the golden age. . . . The earth bringeth forth all things in abundance, as at the first creation, without toil or labor." Arthur Barlowe, who wrote these glowing words in 1584 after returning to England from Roanoke Island, on the coast of North Carolina, thought that he had found a paradise. To be sure, the Algonquian-speaking Roanoke Indians seemed (to Barlowe) to fight cruel and bloody wars that had left them "marvelously wasted" and the country "desolate." (He was unaware of the prior impact of Spanish-induced epidemics and wars.) But this was all the more reason that they should welcome English protection. To establish friendly reciprocity, the Roanokes' chief, Winginia, immediately offered to trade.

He beckoned us to come and sit by him, and being set he made all signs of joy and welcome, striking on his head and breast and afterwards on ours to show that we were all one, smiling and making show the best he could of all love and familiarity. After he had made a long speech unto us, we presented him with divers [various] things, which he received very joyfully and thankfully.

Sir Walter Raleigh (1552?–1618),
by an unknown artist
Raleigh was the foremost advocate of colonization at the English court.

Shortly thereafter Barlowe returned home, taking two kidnapped Roanokes to impress them with the wealth and size of England, teach them the English language, and publicize their venture.

The voyagers had been sent by Sir Walter Raleigh, who dreamed of founding an American colony where English, Indians, and even Africans liberated from Spanish slavery could live together productively. Barlowe reported just what Raleigh wanted to hear. Raleigh persuaded Queen Elizabeth to dispatch ships and a company of soldiers to launch a colony at Roanoke, accompanied by painter John White and scientist Thomas Harriot.

At first all went well. Harriot carefully studied native culture, and White captured the Indians' life in paintings of extraordinary delicacy. Native Americans eagerly traded and shared their corn—which they grew with amazing ease: "Their country corn," Barlowe had already reported, "groweth three times in five months. . . . They cast the corn into the ground, breaking a little of the soft turf with a wooden matlock, or pickax. . . . They have also beans very fair of divers colors and wonderful plenty. Some growing naturally and some in their gardens. . . . " Given such abundance and native hospitality, the English wondered why they should work at all.

So the English refused to try growing their own food, expecting the Indians to feed them. By the first winter, they had outlived their welcome. Fearing that the Roanokes were about to attack them, the English killed Winginia in June 1586. When Raleigh's friend Drake arrived soon after with a shipload of Africans whom he had rescued from the Spanish and planned to settle at Roanoke, most of the English were ready to quit. Casually abandoning the blacks, the English sailed back across the Atlantic.

Raleigh did not give up yet. He sent another expedition in the summer of 1586 commanded by Richard Grenville, who left 15 men at Roanoke before hurrying off to fight the Spanish. In 1587 Raleigh dispatched White back to Roanoke with 110 settlers and their last Indian friend, Manteo, whom the English baptized and proclaimed "lord" of the local Indians. White found no trace of the little English garrison. Leaving the settlers (including his newborn granddaughter), he went home to bring more supplies.

But Spain's attack in the English Channel intervened. Drake and every other English seaman were needed to help repel the Armada of 1588. Not until 1590 could White return to Roanoke—and found only rusty armor, moldy books, and the word *CROATOAN* cut into a post. What had happened to the "lost colony"? Were the settlers killed by Indians? Did they starve or die in a hurricane or drown attempting to join the friendly Indians at Cape Hatteras? One theory is that they were absorbed into the Lumbee Indians of North Carolina; another, that they moved closer to Chesapeake Bay, only to be wiped out by the Powhatan Confederacy when the next English settlement was planted at Jamestown, in 1607. Historians will probably never know with certainty.

Roanoke's brief history illustrated several stubborn realities about early European experiences in North America. First, even a large-scale, well-financed colonizing effort could fail, given the settlers' unpreparedness for the American environment. Second, colonists did not bring enough provisions for the first winter and consistently disdained growing their own food. Although some early English settlers were curious and open-minded about the Indians' way of life, all assumed that the natives would submit to their authority and feed them while they looked for gold—a sure recipe for trouble. Third, colonizing attempts would have to be self-financing: financially strapped monarchs like Elizabeth I would not throw good money after bad into America. Fourth, conflict with the Spanish hung menacingly over every European attempt to gain a foothold in North America.

(Below) **A Carolina Indian Mother and Child;** *(Bottom)* **A Carolina Indian Warrior in Body Paint**

(Below) **Carolina Indians Fishing,** *by John White, 1585*
Using canoes, weirs, nets, and spears, coastal Indians depended on fishing as an important source of their food.

After the Virginia Company sent more men, Governor Francis Wyatt reorganized the settlers and took the offensive during the second Anglo-Powhatan War (1622–1632). Using tactics developed during the Irish war, Wyatt inflicted widespread starvation by destroying food supplies, conducted winter campaigns to drive Indians from their homes when they would suffer most, and fought (according to John Smith) as if he had "just cause to destroy them by all means possible." By 1625 the English had effectively won the war, and the Indians had lost their best chance of driving out the intruders.

The clash left the Virginia Company bankrupt and James I concerned over complaints against its officers. After receiving a report critical of the company's management, James revoked its charter in 1624 and Virginia became a royal colony. Only about five hundred colonists now lived in Virginia, including a handful of Africans who had been brought in since 1619.* So the roots from which Virginia's Anglo-American and African-American peoples later grew were fragile indeed.

The Origins of New England: Plymouth Plantation

Still another colonial venture was begun in the early seventeenth century by the English who settled New England. In 1614 the ever-enterprising John Smith, exploring its coast, gave New England its name. "Who," he asked, "can but approve this most excellent place, both for health and fertility?" An admirer of Cortés, Smith planned to conquer its "goodly, strong, and well-proportioned [Indian] people" and establish an English colony there. But his hopes came to naught. As for the region's native peoples, a terrible epidemic devastated the coastal tribes by about 90 percent in 1616–1618. Later visitors found the ground littered with the "bones and skulls" of the unburied dead, and acres of overgrown cornfields.

Against this tragic backdrop, in 1620 the Virginia Company of London gave a patent to some London merchants headed by Thomas Weston for a settlement. Weston sent over 24 families (a total of 102 people) in a small, leaky ship called the *Mayflower*. The colonists promised to send lumber, furs, and fish back to Weston in England for seven years, after which they would own the tract.

The expedition's leaders—but only half its members—belonged to a small religious community from the town of Scrooby in northern England. The group was made up of Separatist Puritans who had withdrawn from the Church of England and fled to the Netherlands to practice their religion freely. But fearing that their children were assimilating into Dutch culture, they decided to immigrate to America under Weston's sponsorship.

In November 1620 the *Mayflower* landed at Plymouth Bay, outside the bounds of Virginia. Knowing that they had no legal right to be there, the expedition's leaders insisted that all the adult males in the group (including Non-Separatists) sign the Mayflower Compact before they landed. By this document they constituted themselves a "civil body politic"—that is, a civil government—under James I's sovereignty and established the colony of Plymouth Plantation.

Weakened by their journey and unprepared for winter, half the Pilgrims, as they came to be known, died within four months of landing. Those still alive in the spring of 1621 owed much to the aid of two English-speaking Indians. One was Squanto, a local Patuxet Indian who had been taken to Spain as a slave some years earlier, escaped to England, and made himself useful to potential colonizers. Returning, he learned that most of the two thousand Patuxets had perished in the recent epidemic. The other friendly Indian, an Abenaki from Maine named Samoset, had experience trading with the English. To prevent the Pilgrims from stealing their food, the Indians taught the newcomers how to grow corn. The alliance that Squanto and Samoset arranged between Plymouth and local Wampanoag Indians headed by chief Massasoit united two weak parties. But with their firearms the colonists became the dominant partner, forcing the Indians to acknowledge English sovereignty. The Pilgrims' first harvest of 1621 was marked by a ceremony cementing the relationship, "at which time . . . we exercised our arms, many of the Indians coming amongst us, . . . some 90 men, whom for three days we entertained and feasted." This ceremony was the basis for Thanksgiving, a holiday established in the nineteenth century.

Plymouth's relations with the Native Americans worsened, however. News of the Virginia massacre of 1622 hastened the colony's militarization under the leadership of a professional soldier, Miles Standish, who threatened Plymouth's Indian "allies" with its monopoly of firepower. For although Massasoit remained

---

*Whether or not these first Africans were—or remained—slaves is unknown. The emergence of Virginia's African-American population will be traced in Chapter 3.

Early Plymouth Colony
After barely surviving their first winter, the settlers ensured their future by building simple houses and using Indian techniques to grow corn.

loyal, many other Indians were offended by the colonists' conduct.

Relations with Native Americans also enabled Plymouth to become economically self-sufficient. Systematically cheated by their English sponsors, after seven years the colonists had sunk so deeply into debt that they faced fifteen years' additional labor to free themselves. Fishing failed to be profitable, but some farmers, having turned from communal farming to individually owned plots, produced corn surpluses, which they traded to Abenakis in Maine for furs. In 1627 Plymouth agreed with the Dutch to divide the fur and wampum trade in New England. By the time Plymouth finally freed itself of obligations, the settlement had grown to several hundred people on Cape Cod and in the southeastern corner of present-day Massachusetts.

At first an almost insignificant group, the Pilgrims were only one of several small English bands that immigrated to New England in the 1620s. Their importance was twofold. First, they would help inspire the later American vision of sturdy, self-reliant, God-fearing folk crossing the Atlantic to govern themselves freely. Second, they foreshadowed the methods that later generations of European-Americans would use to gain mastery over Indians. In both respects, the Pilgrims were the vanguard of a massive, voluntary migration of Puritans to New England in the 1630s.

CONCLUSION

The founding of colonies in North America occurred as part of the process by which Europe haltingly entered a new, "modern" era. Commercial capitalism, nation-states, and post-medieval Christianity all emerged during the sixteenth century. But they did not entirely displace economies based on subsistence and reciprocity, local communities rooted in centuries-old customs, and widespread beliefs in supernatural forces independent of the Christian God. Expansion and colonization strengthened the "modern" forces by providing new fields for investment and profit, and new foundations for national power. The overseas ventures also enabled European leaders and ideologues to portray Native Americans and Africans as "savages" whose cultures and customs "civilized" Europeans should avoid at all cost.

The displacement of Indians and the enslavement of Africans underlined the early history of European settlement in America. Despite devastation by disease, however, Native Americans yielded only slowly to foreign incursions. As for Africans, even the horrors of the Atlantic slave trade did not strip them entirely of their heritage, which they later nurtured into a distinctive African-American culture.

During the first third of the seventeenth century, the general outlines of European land claims in North America emerged, as did the basic elements of the various colonies' economic life. In New Mexico and Florida, Spain advanced as far north as seemed worthwhile to protect their Mexican and Caribbean conquests. Virginia's victory over the Indians there strengthened the English position in the Chesapeake, where tobacco had become the principal commercial crop. Here and in the fragile Plymouth colony, English settlers depended primarily on farming. New France and New Netherland existed mainly to trade in furs. To one degree or another, all these enterprises depended for their success or security on maintaining stable relations with at least some Native Americans.

Given the thousands of lives lost and the fortunes wasted, the first tiny European outposts in North America may seem a minor achievement. By the 1630s they were just beginning to take on an air of permanence, leading discontented Europeans to imagine that new societies could be created across the Atlantic free from Europe's inherited problems or without painful labor. These dreamers seldom dared to cross the ocean, and those who did generally lost their illusions—or their lives—when faced with the rigors of a strange environment. The transplantation of Europeans into North America was hardly a story of inevitable triumph.

CHRONOLOGY

c. 600–1600	Rise of the great West African empires.
c. 1000	Norse establish a small settlement at Vinland (Newfoundland).
1096	European Crusades begin in Middle East.
1271–1295	Marco Polo travels to East Asia.
c. 1400–1600	Renaissance era—first in Italy, then elsewhere in Europe.
1440	Portuguese slave trade in West Africa begins.
1488	Bartolomeu Días reaches the Cape of Good Hope.
1492	Christopher Columbus lands at San Salvador.
1497	John Cabot reaches Nova Scotia and Newfoundland.
1512–1521	Juan Ponce de León explores Florida.
1513	Vasco Núñez de Balboa views the Pacific Ocean.
1517	Protestant Reformation begins in Germany.
1519	Ferdinand Magellan embarks on round-the-world voyage.
	Hernán Cortés begins conquest of Aztec empire.
1524	Giovanni da Verrazano explores the Atlantic coast of North America.
1534	Church of England breaks from Roman Catholic church.
1534–1542	Jacques Cartier explores eastern Canada for France.
1539–1543	de Soto explores the southeastern United States.
1540–1542	Francisco Vásquez de Coronado explores the southwestern United States.

1558	Elizabeth I becomes queen of England.
1565	St. Augustine founded by Spanish.
1565–1580s	English attempt to subdue Ireland.
1577	Francis Drake circumnavigates the globe.
1578	Humphrey Gilbert secures a patent to establish an English colony in Newfoundland.
1584–1587	Roanoke colony explored and founded.
1588	English defeat the Spanish Armada.
1598	New Mexico colony founded.
1603	James I becomes king of England.
1607	English found colonies at Jamestown and Sagadahoc.
1608	Samuel de Champlain founds Quebec.
1609	Henry Hudson explores the Hudson River for the Dutch Republic.
1610–1614	First Anglo-Powhatan War.
1614	New Netherland colony founded.
1619	Large exports of tobacco from Virginia begin.
	First Africans arrive in Virginia.
1620	Mayflower Compact signed; Plymouth Plantation founded.
1622–1632	Second Anglo-Powhatan War.
1624	James I revokes Virginia Company's charter.

Elizabeth I

FOR FURTHER READING

J. F. A. Ajayi and Michael Crowder, eds., *History of West Africa,* vol. I (1972). A comprehensive collection of essays covering the period prior to 1800.

Robert J. Berkhofer, Jr., *The White Man's Indian: Images of the American Indian from Columbus to the Present* (1978). A penetrating analysis of the shaping of European and American attitudes, ideologies, and policies toward Native Americans.

Carl Bridenbaugh, *Vexed and Troubled Englishmen, 1590–1642* (1968). A highly readable account of England at the outset of the colonial era.

Alfred W. Crosby, Jr., *Ecological Imperialism: The Biological Expansion of Europe, 900–1900* (1986). An outstanding discussion of the environmental and medical history of European overseas colonization.

D. W. Meinig, *The Shaping of America, vol. I: Atlantic America, 1492–1800* (1986). A geographer's engrossing study of Euro-peans' encounter with North America and the rise of colonial society.

J. H. Parry, *The Age of Reconnaissance* (1963). A comprehensive analysis of European exploration and the rise of European overseas empires from the fifteenth to the seventeenth century.

David B. Quinn, *North America from Earliest Discoveries to First Settlements: The Norse Voyages to 1612* (1977). A thorough, learned account of European exploration, based on a wide range of scholarship.

Kirkpatrick Sale, *The Conquest of Paradise: Christopher Columbus and the Columbian Legacy* (1990). A polemical but informed critique of Columbus and his role in opening the Americas to European exploitation.

Eric Wolf, *Europe and the People Without History* (1982). An anthropologist's sweeping view of the causes and consequences of Europe's worldwide expansion.

ADDITIONAL BIBLIOGRAPHY

Africa and Slavery

Philip Curtin, *The Atlantic Slave Trade: A Census* (1969) and *Economic Change in Precolonial Africa: Senegambia in the Era of the Slave Trade* (1975); David Brion Davis, *The Problem of Slavery in Western Culture* (1966); Winthrop D. Jordan, *White over Black: American Attitudes Toward the Negro, 1550–1812* (1968); Paul E. Lovejoy, *Transformations in Slavery: A History of Slavery in Africa* (1983); Patrick Manning, *Slavery and African Life: Occidental, Oriental, and African Slave Trades* (1990); Roland Oliver and Anthony Atmore, *The African Middle Ages, 1400–1800* (1981); Walter Rodney, *A History of the Upper Guinea Coast, 1545–1800* (1970); John Thornton, *Africa and Africans in the Making of the Atlantic World, 1400–1680* (1992); Jon Vogt, *Portuguese Rule on the Gold Coast, 1469–1682* (1979).

Europe

Fernand Braudel, *The Mediterranean and the Mediterranean World in the Age of Philip II,* 2d ed. (1966; English trans., 1972) and *Civilization and Capitalism, 15th–18th Centuries* (3 vols., 1979; English trans., 1981); Peter Burke, *Popular Culture in Early Modern Europe* (1978); Patrick Collinson, *The Elizabethan Puritan Movement* (1967); Natalie Z. Davis, *Society and Culture in Early Modern France* (1975); Ralph Davis, *Rise of the Atlantic Economies* (1973); J. H. Elliott, *Imperial Spain, 1479–1716* (1963); Christopher Hill, *Society and Puritanism in Pre-Revolutionary England,* 2d ed. (1967); Peter Laslett, *The World We Have Lost: England Before the Industrial Age,* 3d ed. (1984); Stephen Ozment, *The Age of Reform, 1250–1550* (1980); Simon Schama, *An Embarrassment of Riches: Dutch Culture in the Golden Age* (1987); Lawrence Stone, *The Crisis of the English Aristocracy, 1558–1641,* abridged ed. (1965); Penry Williams, *The Tudor Regime* (1979); Keith Wrightson, *English Society, 1580–1680* (1982).

European Expansion and Colonization

Kenneth R. Andrews, *Trade, Plunder, and Settlement: Maritime Enterprise and the Genesis of the British Empire, 1480–1630* (1984); Nicholas P. Canny, *The Elizabethan Conquest of Ireland: A Pattern Established, 1565–1576* (1976); Alfred W. Crosby, Jr., *The Columbian Exchange: Biological and Cultural Consequences of 1492* (1972); W. J. Eccles, *France in America,* rev. ed. (1990); J. H. Elliott, *The Old World and the New, 1492–1650* (1970); Lewis Hanke, *The Spanish Struggle for Justice in the Conquest of America* (1965); Karen Ordahl Kupperman, *Roanoke: The Abandoned Colony* (1984); James Lockhart and Stuart B. Schwartz, *Early Latin America: A History of Colonial Spanish America and Brazil* (1983); William H. McNeill, *Plagues and Peoples* (1976); J. H. Parry, *The Establishment of the European Hegemony: Trade and Expansion in the Age of Renaissance* (1966); William D. Phillips, Jr., and Carla Rahn Phillips, *The Worlds of Christopher Columbus* (1992); Oliver Rink, *Holland on the Hudson: An Economic and Social History of Dutch New York* (1986); Carol O. Sauer, *Sixteenth Century North America* (1971); Marcel Trudel, *The Beginnings of New France, 1524–1663* (1973); David J. Weber, *The Spanish Frontier in North America* (1992).

Native Americans

James Axtell, *After Columbus: Essays in the Ethnohistory of Colonial North America* (1988); Charles Hudson and Carmen C. Tesser, eds., *The Forgotten Centuries: Indians and Europeans in the American South, 1521–1704* (1994); Francis Jennings, *The Invasion of America: Indians, Colonialism, and the Cant of Conquest* (1975); Calvin Martin, *Keepers of the Game: Indian-Animal Relationships and the Fur Trade* (1978); Daniel K. Richter, *The Ordeal of the Longhouse: The Peoples of the Iroquois League in the Era of European Colonization* (1992); Helen C. Rountree, *Pocahontas's People: The Powhatan Indians of Virginia Through Four Centuries* (1990); Neal Salisbury, *Manitou and Providence: Indians, Europeans, and the Making of New En-gland, 1500–1643* (1982); Russell Thornton, *American Indian Holocaust and Survival: A Population History Since 1492* (1987); Bruce G. Trigger, *Natives and Newcomers: Canada's "Heroic Age" Reconsidered* (1985); J. Leitch Wright, Jr., *The Only Land They Knew: The Tragic Story of the American Indians in the Old South* (1981).

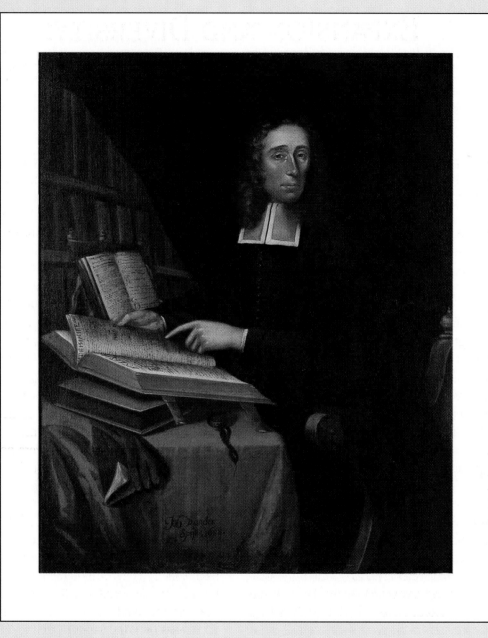

Increase Mather
by John Vander Spriett, 1688

3

EXPANSION AND DIVERSITY: THE RISE OF COLONIAL AMERICA

On the West Indian island of Barbados in 1692, a widowed Englishwoman named Sarah Horbin counted up her relatives to see who might deserve bequests of property in case her only son—a sailor being held for ransom in a North African prison—died. Through her kinsman John Seabury of Barbados, she had kept in contact with a dozen Seabury cousins in Massachusetts. She had also remained in touch with several Virginia relatives in the Empereur family and with a kinsman of her husband's, Andrew Rouse, who lived in the frontier zone between Virginia and Florida then simply called Carolina.

Sarah Horbin and her far-flung clan were part of a great migration of English, Dutch, French, Spanish, Irish, Scottish, and German women and men who built new communities in North America and the Caribbean during the seventeenth century. By 1700 there were more than 250,000 people of European birth or parentage, most of them English, within the modern-day United States. The vast exodus provided North America with its first large wave of immigrant settlers.

The Europeans were joined by a second movement of peoples during the seventeenth century—that of some three hundred thousand West Africans, mostly to the West Indies. But whereas Europeans might at least hope to realize economic opportunity or religious freedom, Africans and their progeny would be the property of others for as long as they lived. Although statistically improbable, it is possible to imagine that in the locales inhabited by Sarah Horbin and her kin in Massachusetts, Virginia, and Carolina was a parallel set of relatives, this one originating along the west coast of Africa between Senegambia and Angola. The vast majority of Africans taken to the Caribbean and North America during the seventeenth century went to the sugar plantations of Sarah Horbin's neighbors in Barbados and elsewhere in the West Indies; a small but distinct minority, to the mainland plantation colonies of the Southeast; and a scattered few to other regions.

These two vast migrations were possible only because of a third demographic upheaval, the depopulation and uprooting of Native Americans. Having begun in the sixteenth century, the process continued in the seventeenth, primarily as a result of epidemic diseases but also because of warfare and other factors arising from the European invasion of Indian lands. Although many native populations partly recovered, it is likely that about 1 million Indians died as a result of contact with Europeans by 1700. Sarah Horbin and her various kin settled not in wildernesses but in lands long inhabited and worked by Native Americans.

Although dominated by English immigrants, the wealth and vitality of the English colonies at the end of the seventeenth century resulted from the unequal encounter of peoples from three continents.

THE NEW ENGLAND WAY

In the late 1620s, as England's religious and political environment grew threatening and the economy worsened, many Puritans became interested in colonizing New England. Separatist Puritans (the "Pilgrims") had established Plymouth in 1620, and a few hundred others had drifted into the region over the next decade. But not until 1630 did large-scale migration begin. Building communities based on religious ideals, this larger, more formidable group of Puritans founded America's first utopian, or ideal, society.

A City upon a Hill

In 1628 several Puritan merchants obtained a charter to settle north of Plymouth colony between the Charles and Merrimack rivers. Organizing as the Massachusetts Bay Company, they took advantage of a gap in their charter and agreed in 1629 to move the seat of their colony's government to New England. Like Plymouth, Massachusetts Bay would be self-governed rather than controlled from England by stockholders, proprietors, or the crown.

After four hundred Puritans arrived at Salem, Massachusetts, in 1629, the company in 1630 sent out its "great fleet" of eleven ships and seven hundred passengers under Governor John Winthrop. In midvoyage Winthrop delivered a lay sermon titled "A Model of Christian Charity," describing the colony as a utopian alternative to old England.

Winthrop boldly announced that "we shall be as a city upon a hill, the eyes of all people are upon us." The settlers would build a godly community whose compelling example would shame England into repenting. The English government would then truly reform the church, and a revival of piety would create a nation of saints.

Winthrop denounced the self-destructive economic jealousy that bred class hatred. God intended that "in all times some must be rich and some poor," the governor explained, in order that the saints could display virtue appropriate to their station in life. The rich had an obligation to show charity and mercy; those less wealthy should live out their faith in God's will by demonstrating patience and fortitude. God expected the state's rulers to keep the greedy among the rich from exploiting the needy and to prevent the lazy among the poor from burdening their fellow citizens.

In outlining a divine plan in which all people, rich and poor, depended on one another, Winthrop's sermon expressed a conservative European's understanding of social reciprocity (see Chapter 2) and voiced the Puritans' deep dismay with the economic forces battering—and changing—English society. Winthrop wanted charity to moderate the drive for profit, so that goods would be exchanged, wages set, and interest calculated in a manner that would allow a decent life for all. He expected the rich to serve God with their money, giving generously in time of need, and the less

John Winthrop
During the passage to America, Winthrop urged his shipmates to build a society about which "men shall say of succeeding plantations: 'The Lord make it like that of New England.'"

The Great English Migration, 1630–1660
During the great transatlantic English migration, the present-day United States received just one-third of English immigrants. The West Indies attracted twice as many colonists as went to the Chesapeake, and over four times as many as settled in New England.

fortunate to sacrifice their time to serve in church, government, or the military.

Winthrop's shipboard sermon exemplified the main difference between New England's settlement and English colonization elsewhere. Other colonists would display the acquisitive impulses transforming England, but in New England, as one minister put it, "Religion and profit [would] jump together." While hoping for prosperity, Puritans believed there were limits to legitimate commercial behavior. They thought that moral self-restraint—or if need be, the government—should prevent merchants from taking advantage of shortages to squeeze out "excessive" profits. Above all, they hoped to turn religious idealism into a renewed sense of community. "It is a great thing," wrote an early New Englander, "to be a foundation stone in such a spiritual building." Massachusetts Bay would not be an extension of England but an alternative to it.

Winthrop and the great fleet arrived in June 1630 at Boston harbor, and by fall six towns had sprung up in the city's modern limits. During the unusually severe first winter, 30 percent of Winthrop's party died, and an additional 10 percent went home in the spring. By mid-1631, however, thirteen hundred new settlers had landed, and more were on the way. The worst was over. The colony would never suffer another starving time. In contrast to early Virginia, Massachusetts Bay attracted disciplined, motivated men and women of modest means who established the colony on a firm basis within a year.

Settlers and Natives

Also in contrast to the settlement of Virginia, the colonization of New England began with little sustained resistance from Native Americans, whose numbers were drastically reduced by the ravages of disease. After one epidemic killed about 90 percent of New England's coastal Indians between 1616 and 1618 (see Chapter 2), a second inflicted comparable casualties on Indians throughout the Northeast in 1633–1634. Having dwindled from twenty thousand in 1600 to a few dozen survivors by the mid-1630s, the Massachusett Indians sold most of their land to the English. During the 1640s Massachusetts Bay passed laws prohibiting them from practicing their own religion and encouraging missionaries to convert them to Christianity. Beginning in 1651 they surrendered much of their independence and moved into "praying towns" like Natick, a reserva-

tion established by the colony. In the praying towns Puritan missionary John Eliot hoped to teach the Native Americans Christianity and English ways.

The expansion of English settlement farther inland, however, aroused Indian resistance. As settlers moved into the Connecticut River Valley, beginning in 1633, friction developed with the Pequots, who controlled the trade in furs and wampum with New Netherland. After tensions escalated into violence, the English in 1637 took decisive action. Having gained the support of the Mohegan and Narragansett Indians, they waged a ruthless campaign, using tactics similar to those devised by the English to break Irish resistance during the 1570s (see Chapter 2). In a predawn attack English troops surrounded and set fire to a Pequot village at Mystic, Connecticut, and then cut down all who tried to escape. Several hundred Pequots, mostly women and children, were killed. Although their Narragansett allies protested that "it is too furious, and slays too many men," the Puritans found in the grisly massacre a cause for celebration. Wrote Plymouth's Governor William Bradford,

> It was a fearful sight to see them [the Pequots] thus frying in the fire and the streams of blood quenching the same, and horrible was the stink and scent thereof; but the victory seemed a sweet sacrifice, and they [the English] gave the praise to God, who had wrought so wonderfully for them, thus to enclose their enemies in their hands and give them so speedy a victory over so proud and insulting an enemy.

By late 1637 Pequot resistance was crushed, with surviving Pequots being taken by pro-English Indians as captives or by the English as slaves. English settlement of the new colonies of Connecticut and New Haven could now proceed unimpeded.

The Development of a Puritan Orthodoxy

As Non-Separatists, Massachusetts Puritans considered themselves spiritual members of the Church of England, but they created a system of self-governing congregations (congregationalism) that completely ignored the authority of Anglican bishops. (Except for the Separatists of Plymouth and Rhode Island, most New England Puritans were Non-Separatists.) More than any other person, the Reverend John Cotton shaped American congregationalism. This clergyman's prestige was so great that, according to a fellow

Two Sketches of an Early Plymouth Meetinghouse *(above);* **Interior of the "Old Ship Church," Hingham, Massachusetts** *(left)*
One early New Englander boasted that his community's meetinghouse had been erected "by our own vote, framed by our own hammers and saws, and by our own hands set in the convenientest place for us all." Hingham's First Parish Meeting House (1681, left) was built by ship carpenters. They simply constructed a ship's keel in reverse for the interior roof.

minister, Massachusetts settlers "could hardly believe that God would suffer Mr. Cotton to err."

Cotton's plan for governing the New England church placed control of each congregation squarely in the hands of the male saints (church members). By majority vote these men chose their minister, elected a board of "elders" to handle finances, decided who else deserved recognition as saints, and otherwise ran the church. In contrast, in a typical English parish, a powerful gentry family would select a new pastor (subject to a bishop's formal approval), and all other important decisions would be made by the parish council, or vestry, which was virtually always composed of wealthy landlords. New England congregationalism thus allowed for far more broad-based control of the church than did Anglicanism.

New England congregationalism fused elements of separating and nonseparating Puritanism. Congregational churches followed the Separatist tradition by allowing only saints to take communion and baptize their children, but as in Non-Separatist practice, they obliged all adults to attend services and pay set rates (or tithes) for their support. New England thus had a state-sponsored, or "established," church, whose relationship to civil government was symbolized by the fact that a single building—called a meetinghouse rather than a church—was used for both religious services and town business.

This "New England Way" also diverged from English practices by setting higher standards for identifying the elect. English Puritans usually accepted as saints those who could correctly profess the faith, had repented their sins, and lived free of scandal. Massachusetts Puritans, however, insisted that candidates for membership provide a soul-baring "relation," or account, of their conversion before the congregation.

English Puritans strongly criticized the conversion relation as an unnecessary barrier to membership that would intimidate humble saints who were hesitant to reveal their spiritual travails in public. Many early Puritans shared the reluctance of Jonathan Fairbanks, who refused to give a public profession of grace before the church in Dedham, Massachusetts, for several years, until the faithful persuaded him with many "loving conferences." The conversion relation would emerge as the New England Way's most vulnerable point and a major cause of its eventual demise.

New Englanders, like most European Protestants, could scarcely imagine conversion without literacy. Young people read the Bible to feel the quickening of God's grace, and saints often recorded their lapses and spiritual insights in diaries. In 1647 Massachusetts Bay enacted the Old Deluder Act, ordering every town of fifty or more households to appoint one teacher to whom all children could come for instruction, and every town of at least one hundred households to maintain a grammar school. The law's name derived from its declaration that "one chief project of that old deluder, Satan, [is] to keep men from knowledge of the Scriptures" by encouraging ignorance. By 1671 most other Puritan colonies enacted similar laws, which represented New England's first step toward public education. But none of these laws required school attendance, and boys were more likely to be taught reading and especially writing than were girls.

However diligent laypeople might be in reading the Bible and indoctrinating their children, clergymen had responsibility for leading saints to repentance and stimulating piety. The minister's role was to stir his parishioners' faith with direct, logical, and moving sermons understandable by average listeners, not just by a well-educated elite. The Puritans' preference for this "plain style" of preaching did not contradict their desire for a highly educated clergy, for ministers also had to uphold orthodoxy and be alert for signs of heresy. To produce learned ministers, Massachusetts founded Harvard College in 1636.

Harvard not only trained ministers but also offered instruction in the arts and sciences. Freshmen entered Harvard as young teenagers after demonstrating an ability to write and speak Latin and a knowledge of Greek grammar. Harvard offered a single curriculum emphasizing classical languages, logic, philosophy, and divinity. From 1642 to 1671, the college produced 201 graduates, including 111 ministers. Harvard's alumni made New England the only part of England's overseas empire to possess a college-educated elite during the seventeenth century, and they ensured that the New England Way would not falter for lack of properly trained clergy.

Dissenting Puritans

The values articulated by Winthrop, Cotton, and other New England leaders reinforced social order and religious conformity. Without order and conformity, the leaders feared, divisiveness among Puritans over questions such as church-state relations, church membership, economic individualism, and the role of women would lead to a splintering of the colonists and their failure in the eyes of God. Despite the leaders' efforts, some Puritans entertained quite radical ideas and insisted on expressing them.

Among the first to challenge the New England Way was Roger Williams, who arrived in 1631. Williams was one of those rare individuals who stir controversy without making personal enemies. Radiating the joy of serving God, he quickly became one of the most respected and popular figures in Massachusetts. But Williams questioned the legal basis of congregationalism. Once he began to insist that church and state be entirely separate, the Massachusetts Bay government moved to silence him.

Puritans agreed that the church must be free of state control, and they opposed theocracy (government run by clergy). However, they believed that a holy commonwealth required cooperation between church and state. Williams took a different stance, arguing that civil government should remain absolutely uninvolved with religious matters, whether blasphemy (cursing God), failure to pay tithes, refusal to attend worship, or swearing oaths on the Bible in court. He derived this position from the sixteenth-century Anabaptist tradition (see Chapter 2), which held that the elect must limit their association with society's sinners to protect God's church from contamination. Williams opposed any kind of compulsory church service or interference with private religious beliefs, not because he felt that all religions deserved equal respect (for he did not) but because he feared that the state would corrupt the church and its saints.

Believing that the very purpose of founding Massachusetts Bay was to protect true religion and prevent heresy, the political authorities declared Williams's opinions subversive and banished him in 1635. At his friend Winthrop's suggestion, he went south with four companions to a place that he called Providence, which he purchased from the Narragansett Indians. At Williams's invitation, a steady stream of dissenters drifted to the group of settlements near Providence on Narragansett Bay, which in 1647 joined to form Rhode Island colony. (Orthodox Puritans scorned the place as "Rogues Island.") True to Williams's ideals, Rhode Island was the only New England colony to practice religious toleration. Growing slowly, the colony's four towns had eight hundred settlers by 1650.

A second major challenge to the New England Way came from Anne Hutchinson, whom Winthrop described as "a woman of haughty and fierce carriage, of a nimble wit and active spirit." The controversy surrounding Hutchinson was especially ironic since her ideas derived from the much-respected John Cotton's theology. Cotton insisted that true congregationalism required the saints to be entirely free of religious or political control by anyone who had not undergone a conversion experience. His refusal to give any authority or power over religion to the nonelect applied even to those who led upright, blameless lives—until they had been reborn spiritually.

Anne Hutchinson extended Cotton's main point—that the saints must be free from interference by the nonelect—into a broad attack on clerical authority. Dissatisfied with her own minister, she charged that he was not among the elect, and asserted that the saints in his congregation could ignore his views. She eventually alleged that all the colony's ministers except John Cotton and her brother-in-law John Wheelwright had not been saved and so lacked authority over saints like herself.

By casting doubt on the clergy's spiritual state, Hutchinson undermined its authority over laypersons. Critics charged that her beliefs would delude individuals into imagining that they were accountable to no one but themselves. They branded her followers Antinomians, meaning those opposed to the rule of law. Hutchinson bore the additional liability of being a woman who stepped outside her prescribed role by voicing her criticisms at public meetings attended by men. The authorities would have prosecuted Hutchinson had she been a man, but her gender made her an even more dangerous foe.

By 1636 Massachusetts Bay split into two camps. Hutchinson's supporters included Boston merchants (like her husband) who disliked the government's economic restrictions on their business; young men chafing against the rigid control of church elders; and most women, protesting their second-class status in church affairs. In 1636 the Antinomians were strong enough to have their candidate elected governor, but they suffered defeat with Winthrop's return to office in 1637.

The victorious Winthrop brought Hutchinson to trial for heresy before the Massachusetts Bay legislature (the General Court). While John Cotton watched nervously, the legislators peppered her with questions. Hutchinson's knowledge of Scripture was so superior to that of her interrogators, however, that she would have been acquitted had she not claimed to have communicated directly with the Holy Spirit. Like virtually all Christians, orthodox Puritans believed that God had ceased to make known matters of faith by personal revelation since New Testament times. Thus Hutchinson's own words were sufficient to condemn her.

The General Court banished the leading Antinomians from the colony, and some of the others voluntarily followed them to Rhode Island, New Hampshire, or back to England. The largest group, led by Hutchinson, settled in Rhode Island. After her husband died, Hutchinson moved to New Netherland, where in 1643 she was killed in that colony's war with local Indians (see below).

Antinomianism's defeat was followed by new restrictions on women's independence and on equality within those Puritan congregations that had previously acted more evenhandedly on matters of gender. Increasingly, women were prohibited from assuming the kind of public religious roles claimed by Hutchinson, and even required to relate their conversion experiences in private to their ministers rather than publicly before their congregations.

The most fundamental threat to Winthrop's city upon a hill was that the people would abandon the ideal of a close-knit community to pursue self-interest. Although most Puritans welcomed the chance to found villages dedicated to stability, self-discipline, and a sense of mutual obligation, a large minority had come to America to find prosperity and social mobility. The most visibly ambitious colonists were merchants, whose activities fueled New England's economy but whose way of life challenged its ideals.

Merchants fit uneasily into a religious utopia that idealized social reciprocity and equated financial shrewdness with greed. They also clashed repeatedly with government leaders, who were trying to regulate prices so that consumers would not suffer from the chronic shortage of manufactured goods that afflicted New England.

In 1635, when the Massachusetts General Court forbade the sale of any item above 5 percent of its cost, Robert Keayne of Boston and other merchants objected. These men argued that they had to sell some goods at higher rates in order to offset their losses from other sales, shipwrecked cargoes, and inflation. In 1639, after selling nails at 25 percent to 33 percent above cost, Keayne was fined heavily in court and was forced to make a humiliating apology before his congregation.

Though a pious Puritan whose annual profits averaged just 5 percent, Keayne symbolized the dangerous possibility that a headlong rush for profits would lead New Englanders to forget that they were their brothers' keepers. "Worldly gain was not the end design of the people of *New-England*," warned the Reverend John Higginson, "but *Religion*." Controversies like the one involving Keayne were part of a struggle for New England's soul. At stake was the Puritans' ability and desire insulate their city upon a hill from a market economy that, they feared, would strangle the spirit of community within a harsh new world of frantic competition.

Power to the Saints

To preserve the New England Way, the Puritans evolved political and religious institutions with far more popular participation than those in England. Unlike the Virginia Company of London, the Massachusetts Bay Company established its headquarters in America (see above). Massachusetts did not require voters or officeholders to own property but bestowed full citizenship on every adult male accepted as a saint. By 1641 about 55 percent of the colony's twenty-three hundred men could vote. By contrast, English property requirements allowed fewer than 30 percent of adult males to vote.

In 1634, after public protest that the governor and council held too much power, each town gained the option of sending two delegates to the General Court.

In 1644 the General Court became a bicameral (two-chamber) lawmaking body when the towns' deputies separated from the Governor's Council to form the House of Representatives.

In 1639 the new towns of Hartford, Windsor, and Wethersfield adopted a government, designed by Thomas Hooker, called the Fundamental Orders of Connecticut. Hooker modeled his government after that of Massachusetts Bay, except that voting and officeholding were opened to all adult male landowners.

The southwestern portion of modern-day Connecticut remained outside this agreement. Under John Davenport, a minister who felt that both Massachusetts Bay and Connecticut allowed too much moral laxness, this region set the strictest standards for verifying sainthood and based its laws most closely upon Old Testament examples. In 1643 the eight towns of this area united as the colony of New Haven.

England's basic unit of local government was the county court. Its members, the justices of the peace, not only decided legal cases as judges but also performed administrative tasks and assessed taxes. Gaining office by royal appointment rather than election, English justices were always members of the gentry selected because of their wealth and political connections. By contrast, New England's county courts functioned primarily as courts of law, and the vital unit of local administration was the town meeting. Town meetings decentralized authority over political and economic decisions to a degree unknown in either England or its other overseas colonies.

New England legislatures established a town by awarding a grant of land to several dozen heads of families. These men then laid out the settlement, organized its church, distributed land among themselves, set local tax rates, and made local laws. Each town determined its own qualifications for voting and holding office in the town meeting, although custom dictated that all male taxpayers (including non-saints) be allowed to participate. The meeting could exclude anyone from settling in town, and it could grant the right of sharing in any future land distributions to newcomers, whose children would inherit this privilege.

Community Life

The local economy and environment left their stamp on New England towns. Of these communities the seaports often seemed least tight-knit because of their transient population, whereas towns in Plymouth

Land Divisions in Sudbury, Massachusetts, 1639–1656

Like other first-generation settlers, John Goodnow lived on a small house lot near the meetinghouse. He pastured his livestock on "common" fields owned by the town and grew crops on thirty-four acres in five separate locations at a distance from his house.

SOURCE: Sumner Chilton Powell, *Puritan Village: The Formation of a New England Town* (Middletown, Conn.: Wesleyan University Press, 1963). Reprinted by permission.

colony tended to be little more than a few stores, a mill, and a meetinghouse serving farmers dwelling over a wide distance. Nevertheless, towns in Massachusetts, Connecticut, and what would become New Hampshire (part of Massachusetts until 1679) were broadly uniform, since most were farm communities resembling traditional English villages.

The founders usually granted each family a one-acre house lot (just enough for a vegetable garden) within a half-mile of the meetinghouse. The town meeting also gave each household strips of land or small fields farther out for its crops and livestock. Often an individual owned several parcels of land in different locations and had the right to graze a few extra animals on the town "commons."

Few aspects of early New England life are more revealing than the first generation's attempt in many, but not all, towns to keep settlement tightly clustered by granting families no more land than they needed to support themselves. Dedham's forty-six founders, for example, received 128,000 acres from Massachusetts Bay in 1636 yet gave themselves just 3,000 acres by 1656, or about 65 acres per family. The rest remained in trust for future generations.

With families clustered within a mile of one another, New England towns' physical settings were conducive to traditional reciprocity. In some parts of England, meanwhile, this mode of land division was coming to seem inefficient as farmers tried to produce a greater surplus for sale by consolidating their landholdings. Reinforcing New England's sense of local community were the town meetings, in which all property-owning males participated, and the congregations, whose Sunday services everyone attended whether or not they were members. The region's generally compact system of settlement forced people to interact with each other and also established an atmosphere of mutual watchfulness that promoted godly order.

Puritan Families

To the Puritans, society's foundation rested not upon the individual but upon the "little commonwealth"—the nuclear family. *Well ordered families,*" declared minister Cotton Mather in 1699, "naturally produce a *Good Order* in other *Societies.*" In a proper Puritan family, the wife, children, and servants dutifully obeyed

Seventeenth-Century Fashions
Made of heavy oxhide in the mid-1640s, this English coat was owned by Mass-
achusetts Bay governor George Leverett. The woman's shoe was fashioned in
England or New England around 1650. Stylish English men and women
alike wore high beaver hats beginning in the early 1600s. In 1634 the
Massachusetts General Court restricted the right to wear them to
people holding property valued at two hundred pounds or more.

the husband. According to John Winthrop, a "true wife" thought of herself "in subjection to her husband's authority."

New Englanders defined matrimony as a contract subject to state regulation rather than a religious sacrament and so were married by justices of the peace instead of ministers. As a civil institution, a marriage could be dissolved by the courts in cases of desertion, bigamy, adultery, or physical cruelty. By permitting divorce, Puritans diverged radically from practices in England, where Anglican authorities rarely annulled marriages and civil divorces required a special act of Parliament. Still, New Englanders saw divorce as a remedy fit only for extremely wronged spouses, such as the Plymouth woman who discovered that her husband was simultaneously married to women in Boston, Barbados, and England. Massachusetts courts allowed just twenty-seven divorces from 1639 to 1692.

Because Puritans believed that healthy families were crucial to the community's welfare, they intervened whenever they discovered truly serious problems in a household. The courts disciplined unruly youngsters, disobedient servants, disrespectful wives, and violent or irresponsible husbands whose behavior

seemed dangerous or unusually disruptive to a family. Churches also censured, and sometimes expelled, spouses who did not maintain domestic tranquillity. Negligent parents, one minister declared, "not only wrong each other, but they provoke God by breaking his law."

Although New England wives enjoyed significant legal protections against spousal violence and nonsupport and also had more freedom than their English counterparts to escape a failed marriage, they suffered the same legal disabilities as all Englishwomen. English common law allowed a wife no property rights independently of her husband unless he consented to a special prenuptial agreement giving her control over any property that she already owned. Only if a husband had no other heirs or wrote a will awarding his widow full control over their possessions could she claim rights over household property, although the law reserved lifetime use of a third of the estate for her support.

In contrast to England, New England benefited from a remarkably benign disease environment. Although settlements were compact, minimal travel occurred between towns, especially in the winter, when people were most susceptible to infection. Furthermore, easy access to land allowed families an adequate diet, which improved resistance to disease and lowered death rates associated with childbirth.

Consequently, New Englanders lived long and raised large families. Life expectancy for men reached 65, and women lived nearly that long. More than 80 percent of all infants survived long enough to get married. The 58 men and women who founded Andover, Massachusetts, for example, had 247 children; by the fourth generation, the families of their descendants numbered 2,000 (including spouses who married in from other families). Despite the relatively small size and short duration of the Puritan exodus to New England (just 20,000 immigrants landed from 1630 to 1642, after which few newcomers arrived), the fact that about 70 percent of all settlers came as members of family groups soon resulted in a population evenly divided between males and females. This balance permitted rapid population growth without heavy immigration.

Most immigrants had little or no capital; instead they relied on the labor of their large, healthy families to sustain them and secure their futures. Male heads of households managed the family's scattered crops and livestock, conducted most of its business transactions, and represented it in town government. Besides bearing, nursing, and rearing children, wives had charge of most labor in the house, barn, and garden. In addition, they contributed to their communities by assisting at childbirths and aiding the poor and vulnerable, especially women living alone.

Lacking any legal right to share in town land divisions until they became their fathers' heirs, the founding generation's sons depended on their parents to provide them with acreage for a farm. Parents encouraged sons to delay marriage and work for them in return for a bequest of land at a later date. Young males often stayed at home to till their fathers' fields until their late twenties, when they finally received their own land. Because the average family raised three or four boys to adulthood, parents could depend on thirty to forty years of work if their sons delayed marriage until about age twenty-six.

Keeping sons dependent also ensured that the family line would continue in the hands of capable, experienced men. While daughters performed equally vital labor, their future lay with another family—the one into which they would marry. Being young, with many childbearing years ahead of them, enhanced their value to that family. Thus first-generation women, on average, were only 21 when they married.

Families with more sons and daughters enjoyed a labor surplus that allowed them to send their children to work as apprentices or hired hands for others. However, this system of family labor was inefficient for two reasons. First, the available supply of labor could not expand in times of great demand. Second, parents were reluctant to force their own children to work as hard as strangers. Nevertheless, family labor was the only system that most New Englanders could afford.

Saddled with the burdens of a short growing season, rocky soil salted with gravel, and a system of land distribution in which farmers cultivated widely scattered strips, the colonists managed to feed large families and keep ahead of their debts, but few became wealthy from farming. Seeking greater fortunes than agriculture offered, some seventeenth-century New Englanders turned lumbering, fishing, fur trading, shipbuilding, and rum distilling into major industries employing perhaps a fifth of all adults full-time and offering seasonal work to many natives and settlers alike. As its economy became more diversified, New England prospered. But in the process, its inhabitants grew more worldly, only to discover that fewer and fewer of their children were emerging as saints.

The Demise of the Puritan Errand

As New Englanders struggled to make a living and curb dissent, England fell into chaos. Charles I's efforts to impose taxes without Parliament's consent sparked a civil war in 1642. Alienated by years of religious harassment, Puritans gained control of the revolt, beheaded Charles in 1649, and eventually replaced the king with "Lord High Protector" Oliver Cromwell. After Cromwell's death, a provisional English government recalled the Stuarts and in 1660 crowned Charles II king.

The Stuart restoration doomed Puritanism in England. High Church Anglicans ruthlessly expelled Puritan ministers from their parishes and passed harsh laws forbidding Separatists from establishing churches and schools. One English saint summed up Puritan disillusionment: "God has spit in our face." The Restoration also left American Puritans without a mission. A generation of New England ministers had inspired their congregations to hope that their example would shame England into establishing a truly reformed church. However, having conquered a wilderness and built their city upon a hill, New Englanders discovered after 1660 that the eyes of the world were no longer fixed on them.

Simultaneously with the demise of English Puritanism, an internal crisis gripped the New England Way. The turmoil stemmed from the failure of the founding generation's children to declare themselves saints. The first generation believed that they had accepted a holy contract, or covenant, with God, which obliged them to establish a scripturally ordained church and charge their descendants with its preservation. In return for upholding this New England Way, God would make the city upon a hill prosper and shield it from corruption.

Relatively few second-generation Puritans, on the other hand, were willing to join the elect by making the required conversion relation before their congregation. By 1650, for example, fewer than half the adults in John Winthrop's congregation were saints. The principal reason was the second generation's reluctance to subject themselves to a grilling before relatives and friends. All children who matured in Puritan towns must have witnessed at least one person suffer an ordeal like that of Sarah Fiske. For more than a year, Fiske answered petty charges of speaking uncharitably about her relatives—especially her husband, Phineas—and then was admitted to the Wenham, Massachusetts, church only after publicly denouncing herself as worse "than any toad."

Because Puritan churches baptized only babies born to saints, the unwillingness of the second generation to submit to the conversion relation confronted their parents with the prospect that their own grandchildren would remain unbaptized unless standards for church membership were loosened. In 1662 a convention of clergy and laity devised a compromise known as the Half-Way Covenant, which permitted the children of all baptized members, including nonsaints, to receive baptism. This covenant allowed the founders' descendants to transmit church membership to their children, but it left these offspring "halfway" members who could not take communion or vote in church affairs. When forced to choose between a church system founded on a pure membership of the elect and one that embraced the entire community, New Englanders, after bitter struggles in many congregations, sacrificed purity for community.

The Half-Way Covenant signaled the end of the New England Way. The elect had been unable to bring up a new generation of saints whose religious fervor equaled their own. Most adults chose to remain in "halfway" status for life, and the saints became a shrinking minority as the third and fourth generations matured. Sainthood tended to flow in certain families, and by the 1700s there were more women among the elect than men in most congregations. But since women could not vote in church affairs, religious authority stayed in male hands. Nevertheless, ministers publicly recognized women's role in upholding piety and the church itself.

Expansion and Native Americans

As the settlers grew and prospered, the Native Americans declined. Although Indians began to recover from the initial epidemics by midcentury, the settlers brought new diseases such as diphtheria, measles, and tuberculosis, as well as new outbreaks of smallpox, that took heavy tolls. New England's Indian population had been reduced from 125,000 in 1600 to 10,000 in 1675.

Native Americans felt the English presence in other ways. The fur trade, which initially benefited interior natives, became a burden after midcentury. Once Indians began hunting for trade instead of just for their own subsistence needs, they quickly depleted the beavers and other fur-bearing animals of the region. And because English traders customarily advanced trade goods on credit to Indian hunters before the hunting season, the lack of pelts pushed many natives into debt. In this situation traders such as John Pynchon of Springfield, Massachusetts, began taking Indian land as collateral and selling it to settlers.

Elsewhere, English townsmen, eager to expand their agricultural output and provide land for their sons, voted themselves much larger amounts of land after 1660 and insisted that their scattered parcels be consolidated. For example, Dedham, Massachusetts, which distributed only three thousand acres from 1636 to 1656, allocated five times as much in the next dozen years. Rather than continue living closely together, many farmers built homes on their outlying tracts, thereby coming into closer proximity to native settlements and the Indians' hunting, gathering, and fishing areas.

Colonizing New England, 1620–1674

Puritan expansion reached its maximum extent in the seventeenth century just before King Philip's War, which erupted as a result of the pressure of white expansion on Indian communities. Frontier expansion did not resume in New England until after 1715.

SOURCE: Frederick Merk, *History of the Westward Movement.* Copyright © 1979 by Lois Bannister Merk. Reprinted by permission of Alfred A. Knopf, Inc.

As the settlements expanded, they put new pressures on the natives and the land alike. As early as 1642, Miantonomi, a Narragansett sachem (chief), warned other New England Indians:

These English having gotton our land, they with scythes cut down the grass, and with axes fell the trees; their cows and horses eat the grass, and their hogs spoil our clam banks, and we shall all be starved.

Within a generation, Miantonomi's fears were being borne out. By clearing away extensive stands of trees for fields and for use as fuel and building material, colonial farmers inadvertently altered an entire ecosystem. Deer were no longer attracted, and the wild plants upon which the Indians depended for food and medicine could not grow. The soil became drier and flooding more frequent in the face of this deforestation. The settlers also introduced domestic livestock, which, according to English custom, ran wild. Pigs damaged Indian cornfields (until the natives adopted the alien practice of fences) and shellfish gathering sites. English cattle and horses quickly devoured native grasses, which the settlers then replaced with English varieties.

With the native religious leaders, and their practices, powerless to halt the alarming decline of Indian population, land, and food sources, many Indians became demoralized. In their despair some turned to alcohol, increasingly available during the 1660s despite colonial efforts to suppress its sale to Native Americans. Interpreting the crisis as one of belief, others joined those Indians who had already converted to Christianity. By 1675 Puritan missionaries had established about thirty praying towns in eastern Massachusetts and Plymouth and on the islands of Martha's Vineyard and Nantucket. Supervised by missionaries, each praying town nevertheless had its own Native American magistrate, usually a sachem, and many praying congregations had Indian preachers. Although the missionaries struggled to convert the Indians to "civilization," by which they meant English culture and life-styles as well as to Christianity, most praying Indians integrated the new faith with their native cultural identities. This practice reinforced the hostility of most settlers, who believed that all Indians were irrevocably "savage" and heathen.

Anglo-Indian conflict became acute during the 1670s because of pressure imposed on unwilling Indians to sell their land and to accept missionaries and the legal authority of colonial courts. Tension ran especially high in the Plymouth colony, where the English had engulfed the Wampanoags and forced a number of humiliating concessions on their leader Metacom, or "King Philip," the son of Massasoit, the Pilgrims' onetime ally.

In 1675 Plymouth hanged three Wampanoags for killing a Christian Indian and threatened to arrest Metacom. A minor incident in which several Wampanoags were shot while burglarizing a farmhouse led to a steady escalation of violence; and Metacom soon organized about two-thirds of the Native Americans, including perhaps a third of all Christian Indians, into a military alliance. "But little remains of my ancestor's domain, I am resolved not to see the day when I have no country," Metacom declared as he and his followers ignited the conflict known as King Philip's War.

Metacom's forces—unlike the Indian combatants in the Pequot War, few of whom had fought with guns—were as well armed as the colonists. The Indians attacked 52 of New England's 90 towns (of which 12 were entirely destroyed), burned 1,200 houses, slaughtered 8,000 head of cattle, and killed 600 colonists.

The tide turned against Metacom in 1676 after the Mohawk Indians of New York and many Christian Indians joined the English against him. English militiamen destroyed their enemies' food supplies and sold hundreds of captives into slavery, including Metacom's wife and child. "It must have been as bitter as death to him," wrote Puritan clergyman Cotton Mather, "to lose his wife and only son, for the Indians are marvellously fond and affectionate toward their children." Perhaps three thousand Indians starved or fell in battle, including Metacom himself, and many more fled to New York and Canada.

King Philip's War reduced southern New England's Indian population by almost 40 percent and eliminated overt resistance to white expansion. It also deepened English hostility toward Native Americans, even the Christian Indians who fought Philip. In Massachusetts ten praying towns were disbanded and all Indians restricted to the remaining four; all Indian courts were dismantled; and "guardians" were appointed to supervise the reservations. "There is a cloud, a dark cloud upon the work of the Gospel among the poor Indians," mourned John Eliot. In the face of poverty and discrimination, remaining Indians managed to maintain their communities and cultural identities. To make

up for the loss of traditional sources of sustenance, many worked as seamen or indentured servants, served in England's wars against the French in Canada, or made and sold baskets and other wares.

Economics, Gender, and Satan in Salem

In the three decades after the Half-Way Covenant's adoption in 1662, New Englanders endured an endless stream of sermons called jeremiads (after ancient Israel's prophet Jeremiah), in which the clergy berated them for failing to preserve the idealism of the region's founding generation. The ministers most bitterly complained about their parishioners' increasing tendency to forget, as one minister emphasized in 1663, "that New-England is originally a plantation of Religion, not a plantation of trade." The jeremiads indicted New Englanders for becoming more worldly and more individualistic, even blaming them for calamities like King Philip's War and the Dominion of New England (see Chapter 4), saying that God caused these as punishments or tests of his wayward saints.

In attacking the colonists' behavior, the clergy recognized that social and economic changes were undermining the New England Way. The dispersal of settlers away from town centers, besides putting pressure on Native Americans, generated friction between the townspeople settled near the meetinghouse, who usually dominated politics, and the "outlivers," whose distance from the town center generally limited their influence over town affairs. By the late seventeenth century, moreover, the region's occupational structure had become more complex, especially in its several port cities, and the distribution of wealth was growing more uneven. These developments undermined the spirit of community by sowing jealousy and creating the anxiety that a small minority might be profiting at the majority's expense. At the same time, New England's rising involvement in international trade led many individuals—in both cities and the countryside—to act more competitively, aggressively, and impersonally toward one another. John Winthrop's vision of a religiously oriented community sustained by a sense of reciprocity and charity was giving way to a world increasingly like the materialistic, acquisitive society that the original immigrants had fled in England.

Nowhere in New England did these trends have more disturbing effects than in Salem, Massachusetts, which grew rapidly after 1660 to become the region's second largest port. Trade made Salem prosperous but also destroyed the relatively equal society of humble fishermen and farmers that had once existed. A sharp distinction emerged between the port's residents—especially its rich merchants—and outlying farmers. Prior to 1661 the richest 10 percent of Salem residents owned 21 percent of the town's property, but by 1681 the richest tenth possessed 62 percent of all wealth.

Salem's farmers lost not only social standing to the merchants but also political power. Before 1665 twice as many farmers as merchants had held the town meeting's highest offices, but thereafter, merchant officeholders outnumbered those who were farmers by six to one. Salem became highly vulnerable to internal conflict between its prosperous merchants and its agricultural folk.

About six miles west of Salem's meetinghouse lay the precinct of Salem Village (now Danvers), an economically stagnant district whose residents resented Salem Town's political domination. The village was divided between supporters of the Porter and Putnam families. Well connected with the merchant elite, the Porters enjoyed political prestige in Salem Town and lived in the village's eastern section, whose residents farmed richer soils and benefited somewhat from Salem Town's prosperity. In contrast, most Putnams lived in Salem Village's less fertile western half, had little chance to share in Salem Town's commercial expansion, and had lost the political influence that they once held in town. The Porter-Putnam rivalry mirrored the tensions between Salem's urban and rural dwellers.

In late 1691 several Salem Village girls encouraged an African slave woman, Tituba, to tell fortunes and talk about sorcery. When the girls later began behaving strangely, villagers assumed that they were victims of witchcraft. Pressed to identify their tormenters, the girls named two local white women and Tituba.

So far the incident was not unusual. Until the late seventeenth century, belief in witchcraft was very strong at all levels of European and American society. Witches were people (nearly always women) whose pride, envy, discontent, or greed supposedly led them to sign a pact with the devil. Thereafter they allegedly used *maleficium* (the devil's supernatural power of evil) to torment neighbors and others by causing illness, destroying property, or—as with the girls in Salem Village—inhabiting or "possessing" their victims' bodies and minds. Apart from *maleficium*, wit-

nesses usually claimed that witches displayed aggressive, unfeminine behavior. And a disproportionate number of the 342 accused witches in New England were women who had either no living sons or no living brothers. As a result, they had inherited, or stood to inherit in the future, property beyond the one-third of a husband's estate normally bequeathed to widows. In other words, most witches were assertive women who had, once had, or soon might have more economic power and independence than many men. For New Englanders, who felt the need to limit both female independence and economic individualism, witches symbolized the dangers awaiting those who disregarded such limits. In most witchcraft accusations in New England, there was only one defendent and the case never went to trial. The few exceptions to this rule were tried with little fanfare. Events in Salem Village, on the other hand, led to a colonywide panic.

By April 1692 the girls had denounced two prosperous farm wives long considered saints in the local church, and they had identified the village's former minister as a wizard (male witch). Fears of witchcraft soon overrode doubts about the girls' credibility and led local judges to sweep aside normal procedural safeguards. Specifically the judges ignored the law's ban on "spectral evidence"—testimony that a spirit resembling the accused had been seen tormenting a victim. Thereafter accusations multiplied until the jails overflowed with accused witches.

The pattern of hysteria in Salem Village reflected that community's internal divisions. Most charges came from the village's troubled western division, especially from Putnam family members, who lodged 46 of the 141 formal indictments. With two exceptions, those named as witches lived outside the village's western half; they primarily included people connected economically or by marriage to the Porters—though no Porters were themselves named as witches—and several members of wealthy Salem Town families.

Anxieties concerning gender and age also influenced who became victims. Two-thirds of all accusers were "possessed" girls or young women aged eleven to twenty, and more than half had lost one or more parents in conflicts between Indians and settlers in Maine. They and other survivors had fled to Massachusetts, where most were now servants in other families' households. They most frequently named as witches middle-aged wives and widows—women

The Geography of Witchcraft: Salem Village, 1692

Geographic patterns of witchcraft testimony mirrored tensions within Salem Village. Accused witches and their defenders lived mostly in the village's eastern division or in Salem Town, whereas their accusers overwhelmingly resided in the village's western sector.

SOURCE: Adapted from Paul Boyer and Stephen Nissenbaum, *Salem Possessed: The Social Origins of Witchcraft* (Cambridge, Mass.: Harvard University Press, 1974).

who had avoided the poverty and uncertainty they themselves faced. At the same time, the "possessed" accusers gained momentary power and prominence by voicing the anxieties and hostilities of many others in their community and by virtually dictating the course of events in and around Salem for several months.

The number of persons facing trial multiplied quickly. Those found guilty desperately tried to stave off death by implicating others. As the pandemonium spread beyond Salem, fear dissolved ties of friendship and family. A minister heard himself condemned by his own granddaughter. A seven-year-old girl helped send her mother to the gallows. A wife and daughter facing death testified against their own husband and father. Fifty persons saved themselves by confessing. Twenty others who would neither disgrace their own name nor betray the guiltless went to their graves.

Shortly before she was hanged, a victim of the

Petition of Mary Easty, 1690 *(Detail)*

In her petition Easty swore that "I know not the least thing of witchcraft."

witch hunters named Mary Easty begged the court to come to its senses: "I petition your honors not for my own life, for I know I must die ... [but] if it be possible, that no more innocent blood be shed."

By late 1692 most Massachusetts ministers had come to doubt that justice was being done. They objected that spectral evidence, which was crucial in most convictions, lacked legal credibility because the devil could manipulate it. New Englanders, concluded Increase Mather, a leading clergyman, had fallen victim to a deadly game of "blind man's buffet" set up by Satan and were "hotly and madly, mauling one another in the dark." Backed by the clergy (and alarmed by an accusation against his wife), Governor William Phips forbade any further imprisonments for witchcraft in October—by which time over a hundred individuals were in jail and twice that many stood accused—and shortly thereafter he suspended all trials. Phips ended the terror in early 1693 by pardoning all those convicted or suspected of witchcraft.

The witchcraft hysteria reflected profound anxieties over social change in New England. The underlying causes for this tension were evident in the antagonism of Salem Village's communally oriented farmers toward the competitive, individualistic, and impersonal way of life represented by Salem Town. In this clash of values, the rural villagers assumed the symbolic role of purging their city upon a hill of its commercial witches, only to leave the landscape desecrated by their gallows.

By the last years of the seventeenth century, the New England Way had lost its relevance for the generation reaching maturity. Eighteenth-century New Englanders would be far less willing to accept society's right to restrict their personal behavior and economic freedom. True to their Puritan roots, the people would retain strong religious convictions and an extraordinary capacity for perseverance. Out of these roots now grew the traits of ingenuity, shrewdness, and a sharp eye for opportunity, on which New Englanders would build a thriving international commerce—and later an industrial revolution.

Throughout the seventeenth century, as New England moved away from its roots, the Chesapeake colony to the south also underwent a radical transformation that gave it a new prominence. But the differences between the two regions remained as great as ever.

CHESAPEAKE SOCIETY

Virginia's survival was no longer at stake when James I took control of the colony in 1624 from the bankrupt Virginia Company. The company had built a colony but destroyed itself in the process. Charles I and his successors refused to spend any significant amount of money on Virginia, even for the governors whom they appointed—whose salaries instead came from local taxes.

Royal indifference worked to the colonial elite's advantage by minimizing outside interference. Virginia's leading planters experimented with various systems of local administration and succeeded in forcing reluctant governors to cooperate with their legislature. The environment and the dominant regional crop—tobacco—determined the colonists' destiny. Similar forces shaped life in Maryland and northeastern North Carolina, which, with Virginia, evolved a common Chesapeake culture.

State and Church in Virginia

King James I disliked representative government and planned to rule Virginia through a governor of his own choosing, who would appoint and dismiss advisers to a newly created council. But Virginians petitioned repeatedly that their elected assembly be revived. In 1628 the new king, Charles I, grudgingly relented, but only to induce the assembly to lay a tax on tobacco exports that would transfer the cost of the colony's government from the crown to Virginia's taxpayers.

After 1630 the need for additional taxes led royal governors to call regular assemblies. The small number of elected representatives, or burgesses, initially met as a single body with the council to pass laws. During the 1650s the legislature split into two chambers—the House of Burgesses and the Governor's Council, whose members held lifetime appointments. Later other royal colonies all established bicameral legislatures like Virginia's.

Local government varied widely during Virginia's first quarter-century. All individuals who commanded the militia, enforced the law, or held courts were appointed to office rather than elected. After experimenting with various institutions of local administration, in 1634 Virginia's settlers adopted England's county-court system. The courts' members, or justices of the peace, acted as judges; they also set local tax rates, paid county officials, and saw to the construction and maintenance of roads, bridges, and public buildings. As in England, this system was undemocratic, for the justices and the sheriffs, who administered the counties during the courts' recesses, gained office by the royal governor's appointment instead of by citizens' votes. Everywhere south of New England, unelected county courts would become the basic unit of local government by 1710.

In contrast to Puritan New England, Virginia had as its established church the Church of England. First instituted in 1618, Anglican vestries governed each parish. The six vestrymen handled all church finances, determined who was deserving of poor relief, and investigated complaints against the minister. The taxpayers, who were legally obliged to pay fixed rates to the Anglican church, elected vestries until 1662, when the assembly made them self-perpetuating and independent of the voters.

Because few counties supported more than one parish, many residents could not conveniently attend services. A chronic shortage of clergymen left many communities without functioning congregations. In 1662 just ten ministers served Virginia's forty-five parishes. Compared to New Englanders, Chesapeake dwellers felt religion's influence lightly.

Virginia's First Families

Virginia encountered great difficulty in developing a social elite able and willing to provide disinterested public service. The gentry sent by the Virginia Company to supervise its affairs were rarely suited for a frontier society. By 1630 all but a few of these gentlemen had either died or returned to England.

The next cycle of leaders were primarily middle class in origins, but over time they acquired great wealth. Some had built large estates by defrauding Virginia Company stockholders. Others were rough-hewn gamblers who risked all on tobacco and won big. From 1630 to 1660, these individuals dominated Virginia's council and became even richer through land grants, tax exemptions, and public salaries. Because they had few or no children to assume their place in society, however, their influence died with them.

From 1660 to 1675, a third cycle of immigrants, who generally arrived after 1645, assumed political

Colonizing the Chesapeake, 1607–1660
The native-settler frontier moved slowly westward until after Indian defeat in the Third Anglo-Powhatan War (1644–1646). By 1700, when the European and African population had reached 110,000, newcomers had spread virtually throughout the tidewater.

power. Principally members of English merchant families engaged in trade with Virginia, they had become planters. They usually emigrated with wealth, education, and burning ambition. By 1670 they controlled the council. Most of them profited from "public" service by obtaining huge land grants.

Unlike their predecessors, this group bequeathed their wealth and power to future generations, later known as the First Families of Virginia. Among them were the Burwell, Byrd, Carter, Harrison, Lee, Ludwell, Randolph, and Taylor families. The First Families would dominate Virginia politics for two centuries, and four of the first five American presidents would be descended from them.

Maryland

Until 1632 successful English colonization had resulted from the ventures of joint-stock companies, but afterward the crown repeatedly made presents of the Virginia Company's forfeited territory to reward English politicians. Overseas settlement thereafter resulted from grants of crown land to proprietors, who assumed the responsibility for peopling, governing, and defending their colonies.

In 1632 the first such grant went to Lord Baltimore (Cecilius Calvert) for a large tract of land north of the Potomac River and east of Chesapeake Bay, which he named Maryland in honor of England's Queen Henrietta Maria. Lord Baltimore also secured freedom from royal taxation, the power to appoint all sheriffs and judges, and the privilege of creating a local nobility. The only checks on the proprietor's power were the crown's control of war and trade and the requirement that an elected assembly approve all laws.

With Charles I's agreement, Lord Baltimore intended to create an overseas refuge for English Catholics, who constituted about 2 percent of England's population. Although English Catholics were rarely molested and many (like the Calverts) were very wealthy, they could not worship in public, had to pay tithes to the Anglican church, and could not hold political office.

In making Maryland a Catholic haven, Baltimore had to avoid antagonizing English Protestants. He sought to accomplish this by transplanting to the Chesapeake the old English institution of the manor— an estate on which a lord could maintain private law courts and employ as his chaplain a Catholic priest. Local Catholics could then come to the manor to hear Mass and receive the sacraments privately. Baltimore adapted Virginia's headright system (see Chapter 2) by offering wealthy English Catholic aristocrats large land grants on condition that they bring settlers at their own cost. Anyone transporting five adults (a requirement raised to twenty by 1640) received a two-thousand-acre manor. Baltimore hoped that this arrangement would allow Catholics to survive and prosper in Maryland while making it unnecessary to pass any special laws alarming to Protestants.

Maryland's initial colonization proceeded quite smoothly. In 1634 the first two hundred settlers landed.

Maryland was the first colony spared a starving time, thanks to the Calvert family's careful study of Virginia's early history. The new colony's success showed that English overseas expansion had come of age. Baltimore, however, stayed in England, governing as an absentee proprietor, and few Catholic settlers went to Maryland. From the outset, Protestants formed the majority of the population. Maryland became a society of independent landowners because land prices were low and few settlers consequently were willing to become tenants on the manors. These conditions doomed the Calvert family's dream of creating on the Chesapeake a manorial system of mostly Catholic lords collecting rents. By 1675 all of Maryland's sixty nonproprietary manors had evolved into plantations.

There was little religious tension in Maryland in the colony's first years, but the situation worsened over time. The Protestant majority dominated the colonial assembly's elective lower house, but many Catholics (including several Calvert relatives) became large landowners, held high public office in the colony, and dominated the appointive upper house. Serious religious problems first emerged in 1642, when Catholics and Protestants in the capital at St. Mary's argued over use of the city's chapel, which the two groups had shared until then. As antagonisms intensified, Baltimore drafted the Act for Religious Toleration, which the assembly passed in 1649. Baltimore hoped that the statute would reinforce the Catholic minority's legal rights, but the law also reflected his consistent support for freedom of conscience. The toleration act was America's first law affirming liberty of worship. However, it did not protect non-Christians, nor did it separate church and state, since it empowered the government to punish religious offenses such as blasphemy.

The toleration act did not secure religious peace. In 1654 the Protestant majority barred Catholics from voting, ousted Governor William Stone (himself a Protestant), and repealed the toleration act. In 1655 Stone raised an army of both faiths to regain the government but was defeated at the Battle of the Severn River. The victors imprisoned Stone and hanged three Catholic leaders. Catholics in Maryland actually experienced more trouble than did their counterparts during the English Civil War, in which Catholics were seldom molested by the victorious Puritans.

Maryland remained in Protestant hands until 1658. Ironically, Lord Baltimore resumed control by order of the Puritan authorities then ruling England. Even so, the Calverts encountered enormous obstacles in governing Maryland during the next four decades because of Protestant resistance to any political influence by Catholics.

Tobacco Shapes a Way of Life

Compared to colonists in New England's compact towns (where five hundred people often lived within a mile of the meetinghouse), Chesapeake residents had few neighbors. A typical community comprised about two dozen families in an area of twenty-five square miles, or about six persons per square mile. Friendship networks seldom extended beyond a three-mile walk from one's farm and rarely included more than twenty adults. Many, if not most, Chesapeake inhabitants lived in a constricted world much like that of Robert Boone, a Maryland farmer described by an Annapolis paper as having died at age seventy-nine "on the same Plantation where he was born in 1680, from which he never went 30 Miles in his Life."

The isolated folk in Virginia and Maryland and in the unorganized settlements of what would become North Carolina shared a way of life shaped by one overriding fact: their future depended on the price of tobacco. Tobacco had dominated Chesapeake agriculture since 1618, when demand for the crop exploded and prices spiraled to dizzying levels. The boom ended in 1629 after prices sank a stunning 97 percent, from a high of 36 pence per pound to a penny. After stabilizing near 2.4 pence, tobacco rarely again fetched more than 10 percent of its former high.

Despite its plunge, tobacco stayed profitable as long as it sold for over two pence per pound *and* was cultivated on fertile soil near navigable water. The plant grew best on level ground with good internal drainage, so-called light soil, which was usually found beside rivers. Locating a farm along Chesapeake Bay or the region's web of rivers also minimized transportation costs by permitting tobacco to be loaded on ships at wharves near one's home. Perhaps 80 percent of all Chesapeake homes lay within a half-mile of a riverbank, and most within just six hundred feet of the shoreline.

From such waterfront bases, wealthy planters built wharves that served not only as depots for tobacco exports but also as distribution centers for imported goods. The planters' control of both export and import commerce stunted the growth of towns and the

Pattern of Settlement in Surry County, Virginia, 1620–1660

Unlike the New England colonists, whose settlements were usually nucleated around a town center (see the map of Sudbury, Massachusetts, on page 60), the Chesapeake population distributed itself thinly along the banks of rivers and creeks.

SOURCE: Thad W. Tate and David Ammerman, eds., *The Chesapeake in the Seventeenth Century* (Chapel Hill: University of North Carolina Press, 1979). Published for the Institute of Early American History and Culture. Reprinted by permission.

emergence of a powerful merchant class. Urbanization therefore proceeded slowly in the Chesapeake, even in a capital like Maryland's St. Mary's, which as late as 1678 was still a mere hamlet of thirty scattered houses.

Although the tobacco crash left small producers struggling to support themselves, cultivating the "weed" could generate a large income for anyone with a sizable work force. Tobacco thus sustained a sharp demand for labor that lured about 110,000 English to the Chesapeake from 1630 to 1700. Ninety percent of these immigrants were indentured servants. Men were more valued as field hands than women, so 80 percent of servants were males, usually in their twenties.

Mortality, Gender, and Kinship

So few women immigrated to the Chesapeake in the early years of colonization that barely a third of all male servants could find brides before 1650. Furthermore, marriage occurred relatively late, because most inhabitants immigrated as servants whose indentures forbade them to wed before completing their term of labor. Their own scarcity gave women a great advantage in negotiating favorable marriages. Female indentured servants often found prosperous planters to be their suitors and to buy their remaining time of service.

Death ravaged seventeenth-century Chesapeake society mercilessly and left domestic life exceptionally fragile. Before 1650 the greatest killers were diseases contracted from contaminated water: typhoid, dysentery, and salt poisoning. After 1650 malaria became endemic as sailors, arriving from Africa, along with a few Africans, carried it into the marshy lowlands, where the disease was spread rapidly by mosquito bites. Life expectancy in the 1600s was about forty-eight for men and forty-four for women—slightly less than in England but nearly twenty years less than in New England. Servants died at horrifying rates, with perhaps 40 percent going to their graves within six years of arrival, and 70 percent by age forty-nine. Such high death rates severely crippled family life. Half of all people married in Charles County, Maryland, during the late 1600s became widows or widowers within seven years. The typical Maryland family saw half of its four children die in childhood.

Chesapeake women who lost their husbands tended to enjoy greater property rights than widows elsewhere. To ensure that their own children would inherit the family estate in the event that their widows remarried, Chesapeake men often wrote wills giving their wives perpetual and complete control of their estates. A widow in such circumstances gained economic independence yet still faced enormous pressure to marry a man who could produce income by farming her fields.

The prevalence of early death produced complex households in which stepparents might raise children with two or three different surnames. Mary Keeble of Middlesex County, Virginia, bore seven children before being widowed at age 29, whereupon she immediately married Robert Beverley, a prominent planter. Mary died in 1678 at age 41 after having five children by Beverley, who then married Katherine Hone, a widow with one child. Upon Beverley's death in 1687, Katherine quickly wed Christopher Robinson, who had just lost his wife and needed a mother for his four children. Christopher and Katherine's household included children named Keeble, Beverley, Hone, and Robinson. This tangled chain of six marriages among seven people eventually produced twenty-five children who lived at least part of their lives with one or more stepparents.

The combination of predominantly male immigration and devastating death rates notably retarded population growth. Although the Chesapeake had received perhaps 110,000 English immigrants between 1630 and 1700, its white population stood at just 69,000 in 1700. By contrast, a benign disease environment and a more balanced gender ratio among the 25,000 immigrants to New England during the 1600s allowed that region's white population to climb to 91,000 by 1700.

The Chesapeake's dismal demographic history began improving in the late seventeenth century. By then resistance acquired from childhood immunities allowed native-born residents to survive into their fifties, or ten years longer than immigrants. As the number of families slowly rose, the ratio of men to women became more equal, since half of all children were girls. By 1690 an almost even division existed between the genders. Thereafter, the white population grew primarily through an excess of births over deaths rather than through immigration, so that by 1720 the Chesapeake was primarily a native-born society.

Tobacco's Troubles

The massive importation of servants into the seventeenth-century Chesapeake widened the gap between rich and poor. Taking advantage of the headright system, a few planters built up large landholdings and then earned substantial incomes from their servants' labor. The servants' lot was harsh. Most were poorly fed, clothed, and housed. The exploitation of Chesapeake labor was unequaled anywhere in the English-speaking world outside the West Indies.

Servants faced a bleak future when their indentures ended. Having received no pay, they entered into freedom without savings. Virginia obliged masters to provide a new suit of clothes and a year's supply of corn to a freed servant. Maryland required these items plus a hoe and an ax and gave the right to claim fifty

Tobacco Prices, 1618–1710

Even after its great plunge in the 1620s, tobacco remained profitable until about 1660, when its price fell below the break-even point—the income needed to support a family or pay off a farm mortgage.

SOURCE: Russell R. Menard, "The Chesapeake Economy, 1618–1720: An Interpretation" (unpublished paper presented at the Johns Hopkins University Seminar on the Atlantic Community, November 20, 1973) and "Farm Prices of Maryland Tobacco, 1659–1710," *Maryland Historical Magazine*, LVIII (Spring 1973): 85.

acres whenever an individual could pay to have the land surveyed and deeded.

Maryland's policy of reserving fifty acres for former servants permitted many of its so-called freedmen to become landowners. Two-thirds of all Chesapeake servants went to Virginia, however, where no such entitlement existed. After 1650 Virginia speculators monopolized most of the light soil along riverbanks so essential for a profitable farm, and freedmen found land ever more unaffordable. Upward mobility was possible, but few achieved it.

After 1660 upward mobility almost vanished from the Chesapeake as the price of tobacco fell far below profitable levels, to a penny a pound. So began a depression lasting over fifty years. Despite their own tobacco losses, large planters earned other income from rents, interest on loans, some shopkeeping, and government fees.

Most landowners held on by offsetting tobacco losses with small sales of corn and cattle to the West Indies. A typical family nevertheless inhabited a shack barely twenty feet by sixteen feet and owned no more property than Adam Head of Maryland possessed when he died in 1698: three mattresses without bedsteads, a chest and barrel that served as table and chair, two pots, a kettle, "a parcell of old pewter," a gun, and some books. Most tobacco farmers lacked furniture, lived on mush or stew because they had just one pot, and slept on the ground—often on a pile of rags. Having fled poverty in England or the Caribbean for the promise of a better life, they found utter destitution in the Chesapeake.

Servants who completed their indentures after 1660 fared even worse, for the depression slashed wages well below the level needed to build savings and in this way placed landownership beyond their means. Lacking capital, those living as tenants could not afford to breed cattle for the West Indies, and they had little corn to sell after meeting their own needs. Ex-servants formed a frustrated and embittered underclass that seemed destined to remain landless and poor.

Bacon's Rebellion

By the 1670s these bleak conditions trapped most Virginia landowners in a losing battle against poverty and left the colony's freedmen verging on despair. Both groups were capable of striking out in blind rage if an opportunity presented itself to stave off economic disaster. In 1676 this human powder keg exploded in violence that left hundreds of Indians dead, dozens of plantations looted, and Virginia's capital, Jamestown, burned. The person who lit the match was Nathaniel Bacon, a wealthy, well-educated young Englishman who had immigrated to Virginia in 1674 and established a plantation. He was a bold man and an inspiring speaker, and Governor William Berkeley, a distant relative, had immediately appointed him to the council.

Virginia had been free of serious conflict with Native Americans since the Third Anglo-Powhatan War (1644–1646). During that struggle, forces under Opechancanough, then nearly a century old but able to direct battles from a litter, killed five hundred of the colony's eight thousand whites before meeting defeat. By 1653 tribes encircled by English settlement began agreeing to remain within boundaries set by the government—in effect, on reservations. White settlement then expanded north to the Potomac River, and by 1675 Virginia's four thousand Indians were greatly outnumbered by forty thousand whites.

As in New England, tensions flared between natives struggling against depopulation and nearby settlers bent on altering the landscape. In Virginia tensions ran particularly high because Governor Berkeley and a few friends held a fur-trade monopoly that profited from friendly relations with some of the frontier Indians. As a result, settler resentments against the governor became fused with those against Indians. In June 1675 a dispute between some Doeg Indians and a Virginia farmer escalated until a force of Virginia and Maryland militia pursuing the Doegs murdered fourteen friendly Susquehannocks and then executed five of their chiefs during a peace conference. The violence was now unstoppable.

Governor Berkeley proposed defending the panic-stricken frontier with an expensive chain of forts linked by patrols. Stung by low tobacco prices and taxes that took almost a quarter of their yearly incomes, small farmers preferred the less costly solution of waging a war of extermination. Despite orders from Berkeley not to retaliate, three hundred settlers elected Bacon to lead them against nearby Indians in April 1676. Bacon's expedition found only peaceful Indians but massacred them anyway.

When he returned in June 1676, Bacon sought authority to wage war "against all Indians in generall." Bacon's newfound popularity forced the governor to grant his demand. The legislature voted a program designed to appeal to both hard-pressed taxpayers and ex-servants desperate for land. The assembly defined as enemies any Indians who left their villages without English permission (even if they did so out of fear of attack by Bacon), and declared their lands forfeited. Bacon's troops were free to plunder all "enemies" of their furs, guns, wampum, and corn harvests and also to keep Indian prisoners as slaves. The assembly's incentives for enlisting were directed at land-bound buccaneers eager to get rich quickly by seizing land and enslaving any Indians who fell into their clutches.

But Berkeley soon had second thoughts about letting Bacon's thirteen hundred men continue their frontier slaughter and called them back. The governor's order spared more Indians from attack, leading Bacon's

Virginia Indian, c. 1645
At the time that this contemporary sketch was made, Virginia's white settlers and Indians were embroiled in the Third Anglo-Powhatan War.

men to rebel and march on Jamestown. Forcing Berkeley to flee across Chesapeake Bay, the rebels burned Jamestown, offered freedom to any Berkeley supporters' servants or slaves who joined the rebels, and then looted their enemies' plantations. At the very moment of triumph, however, Bacon died of dysentery in late 1676, and his followers dispersed.

The tortured course of Bacon's Rebellion revealed a society under deep internal stress. The revolt began as an effort to displace escalating tensions within white society onto local Indians. Because social success in Virginia depended on accumulating land and labor, farmers and landless ex-servants alike responded enthusiastically to the prospect of taking Indian lands, stealing their furs, wampum, and harvests, and enslaving prisoners. So easily did the insurrection disintegrate into an excuse for settlers of all classes to plunder other whites, however, that it appears that the rebels were driven by economic opportunism as well as by racism. Bacon's Rebellion was an outburst of long pent-up frustrations by marginal taxpayers and ex-servants, driven to desperation by the tobacco depression, as well as by wealthier planters excluded from Berkeley's circle of favorites.

Slavery

Bacon's Rebellion exposed the crackling tensions underlying class relations among Chesapeake whites. This social instability derived in large part from the massive importation of indentured servants, who later became free agents in an economy that offered them little but poverty while their former masters seemingly prospered. But even before Bacon's Rebellion, the acute potential for class conflict was diminishing as Chesapeake planters gradually substituted black slaves for white servants.

Racial slavery developed in three stages in the Chesapeake. Africans first began appearing from 1619 to 1640. Although Anglo-Virginians carefully distinguished blacks from whites in official documents—in a manner that seems to show a tendency to discriminate according to race—they did not assume that every African sold was a slave rather than a servant destined for eventual freedom. The same was true for Indians captured in the colony's wars. Some Africans gained their freedom, and a few, mostly on Virginia's eastern shore, had their own tobacco farms. During the second phase, spanning the years 1640–1660, unmistakable evidence survives that growing numbers of blacks and some Indians were treated as slaves and that their children inherited that status, in contrast to white indentured servants, who had fixed terms of service. In the final phase, after 1660, whites officially recognized slavery and regulated it by law. Maryland first defined slavery as a lifelong, inheritable, racial status in 1661. Virginia followed suit in 1670. By 1705 strict legal codes defined the place of slaves in society and set standards of racial etiquette. By then free blacks had all but disappeared from the Chesapeake. Although this period saw slavery mature into a legal system, many of the specific practices enacted into law were evolving into custom before 1660.

Slavery was never considered a status appropriate for any European or any Christian. Although the English could have enslaved enemies such as the Irish and Spanish, they always reserved this complete denial of human rights for nonwhites. The English embarked on

slavery as an "unthinking decision," one in which they unconsciously acted on the basis of a profoundly negative, emotional response to nonwhites, assuming that they were inferior to themselves—and so uniquely suited for slavery.

As late as 1660, fewer than a thousand slaves lived in Virginia and Maryland. The number in bondage first became truly significant in the 1680s, when the Chesapeake's slave population (by now almost entirely black, owing to Indian decline) almost tripled, rising from forty-five hundred to about twelve thousand. By 1700 nearly twenty thousand slaves resided in the region, and they made up 22 percent of the inhabitants. Even so, indentured servants still composed half of all unfree laborers in 1700.

Having been made possible by racism, slavery replaced indentured servitude for economic reasons. First, it became more difficult to import indentured servants as the seventeenth century advanced, because a gradual decline in England's population

Tobacco Label
The slave's central role in growing tobacco and serving his white master (here enjoying a smoke) is depicted.

Kasitzky's Best Virginia *LONDON.*

between 1650 and 1700 reduced the number of people willing to emigrate overseas. As England's population decreased, labor became more valuable at home, and wages rose by about 50 percent. Second, before 1690 the Royal African Company, which held a monopoly on selling slaves to the English colonies, shipped nearly all its cargoes to the West Indies, a situation that left few blacks available for sale to the Chesapeake. During the 1690s this monopoly was broken, and rival companies soon expanded the supply of slaves. Large shipments of Africans then began reaching the Chesapeake.

The emergence of slavery relaxed the economic strains within white society that had helped precipitate Bacon's Rebellion. Gradually after 1690, nonslaveowning whites came to see themselves as sharing a common interest with upper-class planters in maintaining social control over a black race regarded as alien and threatening. Slavery's establishment as the principal form of labor in the Chesapeake was part of a larger trend among England's plantation colonies, one that began in the Caribbean and spread to the new mainland colony of Carolina.

THE SPREAD OF SLAVERY: THE CARIBBEAN AND CAROLINA

Simultaneously with the expansion of European colonization in mainland North America, a second wave of settlement swept the West Indies. Between 1630 and 1642 almost 60 percent of the seventy thousand English who emigrated went to the Caribbean or to the Western Atlantic provisioning base at Bermuda.

The English West Indies strongly influenced English North America. The Caribbean islands became the major market for New England's surplus foodstuffs, dried fish, and lumber. In the 1640s the English West Indians began adapting their economy to large-scale slave labor and devising a code of social conduct for nonwhites. In this way, the West Indies pioneered techniques of racial control that would later appear in the mainland colonies' plantation societies.

After 1660 a large outmigration of English islanders added significantly to English North America's population. Most of the migrants went to the Chesapeake and to Carolina, thereby introducing the habits

and prejudices of plantation slaveholding, as well as some slaves, to the mainland colonies. By 1710, the population of Carolina, like that of the Caribbean colonies, was predominantly black and enslaved.

The Chaotic Caribbean

In the sixteenth century, Spain claimed all the Caribbean, but the Spanish eventually concentrated on holding the four largest islands: Hispaniola, Puerto Rico, Cuba, and Jamaica. Successful English and French colonies appeared in the Caribbean only after Spain and the Dutch Republic went to war in 1621. Gambling that the Dutch would distract Spain from launching attacks against isolated outposts, English freebooters began seizing islands vacated by the Spanish. St. Kitts (St. Christopher) was first in 1624, and by 1640 the English had established nearly twenty communities from the Bahamas to the waters off Nicaragua. Spanish troops soon destroyed most of these fledgling settlements but left the English entrenched on St. Kitts, Barbados, Montserrat, Nevis, and Antigua. Later, in 1655, Jamaica also fell to an English force. Similarly, the French seized several islands in the Antilles and the western half of Hispaniola, which they called St. Domingue.

Born of war, England's West Indian colonies matured in turmoil. Between 1640 and 1713 every major island but Barbados suffered at least one invasion by Carib Indians, Spaniards, French, or Dutch. After 1680 pirates from the Bahamas menaced English shipping until the Royal Navy exterminated them during the 1720s. Seven slave revolts rocked the English islands prior to 1713, and they left a bitter legacy of racial hatred on the crowded West Indies.

Life in the Caribbean went on amid the constant violence inflicted on Catholic by Protestant, slave by master, and humans by nature. Of the seventy-four settlers who founded Barbados in 1627, only six remained alive just eleven years later. A bubonic-plague epidemic killed an estimated one-third of the islanders from 1647 to 1649. Up to five thousand militiamen (every sixth Englishman in the Caribbean) perished while fighting to capture Jamaica from Spain in the 1650s. Hundreds regularly lost their lives in hurricanes. In 1692 an earthquake killed almost seven thousand Jamaicans out of a population of forty thousand. Malaria and yellow fever never ceased their slaughter. Immigrants usually died less than twenty years after arriving, at about thirty-eight years of age.

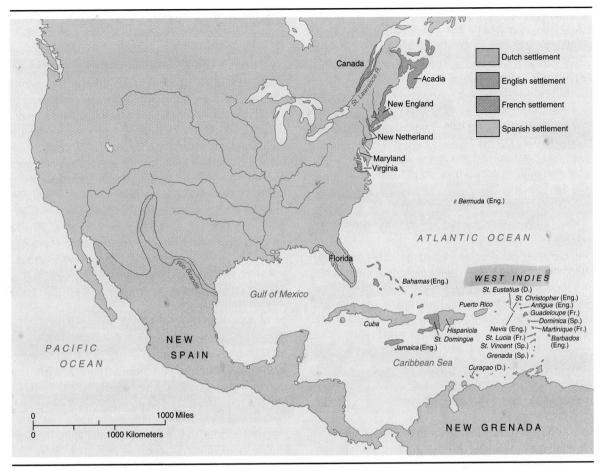

The Caribbean Colonies, 1660

Aside from Jamaica, England's sugar colonies were clustered in the eastern Caribbean's Leeward Islands. Lying within easy reach of seaborne attack, every English island but Barbados was the scene of major fighting.

Sugar and Slaves

As in the Chesapeake, a strong demand for tobacco led the first English settlers in the Caribbean to cultivate that plant almost exclusively. Although low prices inhibited upward mobility, through the 1630s the English West Indies remained a society with a large percentage of independent landowners, an overwhelmingly white population, and no extreme inequality of wealth.

During the early 1640s an alternative to tobacco appeared that rapidly revolutionized the islands' economy and society. Dutch merchants familiar with Portuguese methods of sugar production in Brazil began encouraging English planters to raise and process sugar cane, which the Dutch would then market.

Sugar could make a settler fabulously wealthy because European demand for the new sweetener was virtually unquenchable. But sugar manufacture was also a complex process that required grinding, boiling, refining, and (for rum) distilling the cane immediately after cutting—before it lost its sweetness—and therefore was a very costly venture. Besides a large labor force, a sugar producer needed a mill, several caldrons, a still, and a number of outbuildings. Growing sugar required more capital than ordinary tobacco farmers possessed or could borrow as long as tobacco prices stayed low. Aggressively buying land, a few sugar planters on Barbados closed off opportunity to small farmers by bidding up real-estate prices about 1,000 percent from 1643 to 1650. By 1680 a mere 7 percent of property owners held over half the agricultural acreage on Barbados, which grew 60 percent of the sugar exported to England. A typical sugar planter owned an estate of two hundred acres, whereas most white Barbadians scratched a pitiful living from farms of ten acres or less.

Because the profit from sugar vastly exceeded that from any other crop, West Indian planters soon turned all available acreage into cane fields. They deforested every English island except mountainous Jamaica and greatly reduced the amount of land available for grain and livestock. The West Indies then quickly became dependent on outside sources for lumber and foodstuffs, and a flourishing market thus opened up for New England farmers, fishermen, and loggers.

Because planters needed three times as many workers per acre to raise cane as tobacco, rising sugar production greatly multiplied the demand for labor. Before 1640 West Indians had imported white servants who signed an indenture, or contract, to work without pay for four to six years in return for free passage to America. After 1640, however, sugar planters increasingly purchased enslaved Africans from the Dutch to do common field work and instead employed the indentured servants who came from Britain as overseers or skilled artisans.

Although slavery had died out in England after the eleventh century, English immigrants to the Caribbean quickly copied the example set there by Spanish slaveowners. On Barbados, for example, English newcomers imposed slavery on both blacks and Indians immediately after settling on that island in 1627. The Barbadian government in 1636 condemned every black brought there to life-

long bondage. All other English islanders likewise plunged into slaveowning with gusto.

Sugar planters preferred black slaves to white servants because slaves could be driven harder and maintained less expensively. Unlike European servants, who wilted in the tropics, Africans could endure Caribbean conditions, because they had grown up in a hot, humid climate. Indentured servants could use their contracts to demand decent food, clothes, and housing; but slaves, as mere property, had no rights, and masters could spend the bare minimum necessary to keep them alive. Most servants ended their indentures after four years, just as they were becoming efficient workers, but slaves toiled on until death. Although slaves initially cost two to four times more than servants, they proved a more economical long-term investment. In this way the profit motive and the racism that emerged with the "new slavery" (see Chapter 2) reinforced one another.

By 1670 the sugar revolution had transformed the British West Indies into a predominantly slave society. In 1713 blacks outnumbered whites by a margin of four to one. Although the number of blacks shot up from approximately 40,000 in 1670 to 130,000 in 1713, the white population remained stable at about 33,000 because the planters' preference for slave labor greatly reduced the importation of indentured servants after 1670.

African Slaves Making Sugar

This drawing, published in 1665, shows slaves feeding sugar cane into a cattle-driven mill, which turns it into juice. Other slaves then boil the liquid.

Declining demand for white labor in the West Indies diverted the flow of English immigration from the islands to mainland North America and so contributed to population growth there. Furthermore, because the expansion of West Indian sugar plantations priced land beyond the reach of most whites, perhaps thirty thousand people left the islands from 1655 to 1700. Most whites who quit the West Indies also migrated to the mainland colonies—especially Carolina.

West Indian Society

At the bottom of Caribbean society were the slaves, who lived under a ruthless system of racial control imposed by the islands' European minority through laws known as slave codes. In 1661 Barbados passed the first comprehensive slave code, which served as a model for all colonies in the Caribbean and several on the North American mainland. The Barbados code professed to guarantee decent treatment for slaves (as did certain laws protecting indentured servants), but it failed to define an adequate diet or shelter, aside from requiring masters to furnish each woman with a dress and every man with a pair of pants and a hat. In effect, the code allowed owners to let their slaves run almost naked, house them in rickety shacks, and work them to exhaustion. Moreover, the Barbados code stripped slaves of all legal rights protected under English law. Unlike white servants, slaves could not be tried by juries. The law gave slaves no guarantee of a fair legal hearing and did not even forbid testimony obtained by torture.

In this way, West Indian governments allowed masters almost complete control over their human property. Their laws purposefully placed no limits on how or why a master could punish a slave. As a result, slaves suffered vicious beatings and whippings. If a master killed a slave, he could not be punished unless a jury determined that he acted intentionally, and even then he could only be fined, not jailed or executed. The slave codes effectively legalized assault, battery, manslaughter, and murder.

Slave codes, moreover, left those in bondage defenseless against *all* whites, not just their masters. Slaves could not testify in court against free people. Barbados allowed any ordinary white who caught a slave at large without a pass to give him a "moderate whipping," which could include beatings of up to fifty lashes.

Finally, slave codes attempted to terrorize those in bondage into obedience through cruel and extreme punishments. Judges could order ears sliced off for theft of food, have slaves torn limb from limb for allegedly poisoning masters, and sentence rebels to be burned alive. Heads or other body parts of executed slaves often dangled gruesomely in public places to generate an atmosphere of dread.

Mortality among blacks was especially frightful, even by Caribbean standards. Sugar production required arduous labor, but it was so profitable that planters had little incentive to keep their slaves healthy; they could well afford to replace those killed by overwork. Slaves usually arrived on the islands as men and women in their early twenties, and within ten years most were dead of exhaustion and abuse. So rapidly did the planters wear out field hands that, although they imported 264,000 Africans to the English West Indies before 1700, the slave population stood at just 100,000 in that year.

Despite these appalling conditions, enslaved Africans did what they could to maintain a semblance of normal existence. They were more likely than island whites to start families, since the ratio of male to female slaves neared equality by 1670. (Still, a staggering mortality rate among slave spouses cut most marriages short, and half or more of all slave children died before age five.) In their daily lives, slaves retained much of their native heritage. African music survived in work songs and ceremonial dances and chants, including the mournful laments in which newly arrived Africans grieved over their fate. Very few converted to Christianity; most clung to faith in ancestral spirits, and some committed suicide in the belief that their ghosts would return home. They also re-created African family structures, as well as marriage and funeral customs. In the end the islands' black culture displayed a stronger African imprint than did the African-American way of life that emerged on the North American mainland.

Among white islanders, family cohesion was weak. Because about 80 percent of servants were male, most English settlers led wild lives as bachelors. Not until after 1700 did a sufficient number of white women inhabit the islands to give all white men the option of marriage. Even then high death rates robbed most children of at least one parent well before they reached maturity.

Organized religion withered in the English Caribbean. The majority of churches had no minister, and aside from the small Jewish minority, most whites rarely attended services. English islanders spent far more time in taverns drinking rum (popularly known as Old Kill-Devil) than in church. According to an old Caribbean joke, upon founding a new settlement, the Spanish first constructed a church, the Dutch first built a fort, and the English immediately set up a barroom. If drinking habits on Bermuda in the 1620s were typical, the average English islander consumed well over a gallon of distilled liquor each month.

English residents demonstrated little sense of community. The rich generally hired overseers to manage their estates and retired in luxury to England. The poor left in droves for other colonies. In sum, the English Caribbean was a society of materialistic fortune seekers trying to get rich quickly before death overtook them, and of slaves being worked to death.

The West Indian colonies were the first of England's overseas possessions to evolve into plantation societies. The most extreme examples of labor exploitation, racial subordination, and social stratification could indeed be found in these Caribbean colonies, but a similar pattern of development also characterized English settlements in Chesapeake Bay and in the coastal region known as Carolina.

Carolina: The First Restoration Colony

During the 1650s settlers from New England and the English West Indies established several struggling, unauthorized little outposts along the swampy coast between Virginia and Spanish Florida. In 1663 King Charles II (who had assumed the throne when the Stuart monarchy was restored in 1660) bestowed this unpromising coast on several English supporters, making it the first of several Restoration colonies. The grateful proprietors named their colony Carolina in honor of Charles (*Carolus* in Latin).

Carolina grew haltingly at first. The proprietors organized the existing settlements in the northern part of their domain as a separate district and established a bicameral legislative body for it. Then in 1669 one of the proprietors, Anthony Ashley Cooper, speeded up settlement by offering immigrants fifty-acre land grants for every family member, indentured servant, or slave they brought in. Cooper's action marked a turning point. In 1670 settlement of southern Carolina began when two hundred Barbadian and English settlers landed near modern-day Charleston, "in the very chops of the Spanish." Here, in the settlement they called Charles Town, they formed the colony's nu-

cleus, with their own bicameral legislature distinct from that of the northern district.

Cooper and his secretary—John Locke, later acclaimed as one of the great philosophers of the age—devised an intricate plan for Carolina's settlement and government. Their Fundamental Constitutions of Carolina attempted to ensure the colony's stability by decreeing that political power and social rank should accurately reflect settlers' landed wealth. Thus they invented three orders of nobility, with "proprietors" on top, "landgraves" in the middle, and "caciques" at the bottom. Together this elite would hold two-fifths of all land, make laws through a Council of Nobles, and dispense justice through manorial law courts. Ordinary Carolinians with smaller landholdings were expected to defer to nobility, although they would enjoy religious toleration and the benefits of English common law.

The reality of Carolina's early settlement bore small resemblance to Locke's scheme. New arrivals who could get all the land they needed saw little reason to obey pseudofeudal lords and all but ignored most of the plans drawn up for them across the Atlantic.

Until the 1680s most settlers were small landowners from Barbados or the mainland colonies, along with some French Huguenots. Southern Carolinians raised livestock and exported deerskins and Indian slaves (see below), and colonists in northern Carolina exported tobacco, lumber, and pitch, giving local people the name tarheels. These activities did not at first produce enough profit to warrant maintaining many slaves, and so self-sufficient white families predominated in the area.

But Carolina had not been created so that settlers could merely eke out a marginal existence. Like the first Virginians, southern Carolinians sought a staple crop that could make them rich. By the early 1690s, they found it—rice. The grain was introduced by slaves from Senegambia, where it constituted the basic foodstuff. Because rice, like sugar, enormously enriched a few men with capital to invest in costly dams, dikes, and slaves, it remade southern Carolina into a society resembling that of the West Indies. By earning annual profits of 25 percent, rice planters within a generation became the only colonial elite whose wealth rivaled that of the Caribbean sugar planters.

The Carolina rice planters' huge profits had to be reaped at someone's expense, however. No matter how inhumanly they might be driven, indentured English servants simply could not survive in humid rice paddies swarming with malaria-bearing mosquitoes.

Tuscarora Resistance, 1711
Defending their homeland against an influx of settlers, the Tuscaroras captured Baron Christoph von Graffenried, leader of the Swiss community at New Bern. Graffenried drew this sketch, which depicts him being held along with an English trader, John Lawson, and an African slave. Lawson was later executed.

The planters' solution was to import an ever-growing force of African slaves, who possessed two major advantages for masters. First, perhaps 15 percent of the Africans taken to Carolina had cultivated rice in their homeland, and their expertise was vital in teaching whites how to raise the unfamiliar crop. Second, many Africans had developed partial immunity to malaria, the infectious and deadly disease transmitted by mosquito bites, which was endemic to coastal regions of West Africa and which African-born slaves (and infected slave ships' crews) carried to the New World. (Tragically, the antibody that helps ward off malaria also tends to produce the sickle-cell trait, a hereditary genetic condition often fatal to those children who inherit it.) These two advantages made possible commercial rice production in Carolina. A great demand for black slave labor resulted, for a typical rice planter farming 130 acres needed sixty-five slaves. The proportion of slaves in southern Carolina's population spurted from 17 percent in 1680 to 67 percent in 1720. Carolina was Britain's sole mainland colony with a black majority.

Rice thrived only within a forty-mile-wide coastal strip extending from Cape Fear to present-day Georgia. The hot, humid, marshy lowlands quickly became infested with malaria. Carolinians grimly joked that the rice belt was a paradise in spring, an inferno in summer, and a hospital in the wet, chilly fall. In the worst months, planters' families usually escaped to the relatively cool and more healthful climate of Charles Town and let overseers supervise their harvests.

As long as Europeans outnumbered Africans, race relations could be somewhat relaxed. But as a black majority emerged and swelled, whites increasingly relied on force and fear to control their slaves, adopting many of the galling restrictions and gruesome punishments imposed on slaves in Barbados. Bondage in the mainland colony was becoming as cruel and harsh as in the West Indies.

White Carolinians' attitudes toward Native Americans likewise hardened into exploitation and violence. In the 1670s traders in southern Carolina armed nearby Indians and encouraged them to raid Spanish missions in Florida. These allies captured unarmed Guale, Apalachee, and Timucua Indians at the missions and traded them, along with deerskins, to the Carolinians for guns and other European goods. The English then sold the enslaved Indians, mostly to planters in the West Indies. By the mid-1680s the Carolinians had extended the trade inland through alliances with the Yamasees (Guale Indians who had fled the inadequate protection of the Spanish in Florida) and the Creeks, a powerful confederacy centered in what is now western Georgia and northern Alabama. For three decades these Indians terrorized the Spanish and other Indians in the region with their slave raids. No statistical records of Carolina's Indian slave trade survive, but a recent study estimates that the number of Native Americans enslaved was in the tens of thousands. Once shipped to the West Indies, most died quickly because they lacked immunities to both European and tropical diseases.

Conflict came to northern Carolina in 1711 when the Tuscarora Indians, provoked by white encroachments on their land and by several instances of whites kidnapping Indians as slaves, destroyed New Bern, a frontier settlement of seven hundred Swiss immigrants. Northern Carolina enlisted the aid of southern Carolina and its well-armed Indian allies. By 1713, with a thousand of their people killed or enslaved (about one-fifth of the total population), the Tuscaroras surrendered. Nearly half the survivors eventually migrated to New York, where they became the Sixth Nation of the Iroquois Confederacy.

Having helped defeat the Tuscaroras, Carolina's Indian allies resented a growing number of incidents of cheating, violence, and enslavement perpetrated by English traders, and encroachments on their land by settlers. In 1715 the Yamasees, who were most seriously affected by these incidents, led a coordinated series of attacks on English trading houses and settlements. Only by enlisting the aid of the Cherokee Indians, and allowing four hundred slaves to bear arms, could the colony crush the uprising. Yamasees not killed or captured were driven back to Florida or to the Creek nation.

The first two generations of white settlers and black slaves had cleared the unhealthy coastal regions and developed Carolina's profitable exports. With help from Indian allies, they had extinguished resistance from hostile Native Americans. In realizing these formidable accomplishments, they had received little aid from the faraway proprietors, whose main activities had been grabbing land for themselves, vetoing laws passed by the assemblies, and appointing unpopular governors. Carolinians came to regard the proprietors as indifferent even to their defense. After southern Carolinians overthrew proprietary rule in 1719 (Carolina's fourth major rebellion), the British monarchy intervened and by 1729 created two royal colonies, North Carolina and South Carolina.

THE MIDDLE COLONIES

Between the Chesapeake and New England, a third mainland colonial region, the middle colonies, emerged slowly at first. New Netherland and New Sweden were small commercial outposts, although the Dutch colony began to grow and flourish at midcentury. But in 1664, England seized New Netherland from the Dutch, and in 1681 King Charles II authorized a new colony where New Sweden had stood. These actions resulted in three additional Restoration colonies—New York, New Jersey, and Pennsylvania. By the end of the seventeenth century, the middle colonies composed North America's fastest-growing region.

Precursors: New Netherland and New Sweden

New Netherland became North America's first multi-ethnic society. Barely half the settlers were Dutch; most of the rest were Germans, French, Scandinavians, and Africans, free as well as enslaved. In 1643 the population included Protestants, Catholics, Jews, and Muslims, and eighteen European and African languages were spoken. But religion counted for little (in 1642 the colony had seventeen taverns but not one place of worship), and the settlers' get-rich-quick attitude had long sapped company profits as private individuals persisted in trading illegally in furs. In 1639 the company bowed to the inevitable and legalized private fur trading.

Privatization led to a rapid influx of guns into the hands of New Netherland's Iroquois allies, giving them a distinct advantage over other natives. As overhunting depleted local supplies of beaver skins and as smallpox epidemics took their toll, the Iroquois encroached on pro-French rival Indians in a quest for pelts and for captives, who could be adopted into Iroquois families to replace the dead. After 1648 the Iroquois, in a series of bloody "beaver wars," dispersed the Hurons and other French allies, incorporating many members of these nations into their own ranks. Then they attacked the French settlements along the St. Lawrence. "They come like foxes, they attack like lions, they disappear like birds," wrote a French Jesuit of the Iroquois.

Although the Dutch allied successfully with the Iroquois, their relations with their nearer Indian neighbors were the worst of any Europeans. With its greedy settlers and military weakness, New Netherland had largely itself to blame. In 1643 all-out war erupted when Dutch forces massacred previously friendly Algonquian-speaking Indians and by 1645 the Dutch could temporarily prevail only with English help and by inflicting terrible atrocities. But the fighting had cut New Netherland's Indian population from sixteen hundred to seven hundred.

Another European challenger dangerously distracted the Dutch in their war with the Algonquians. In 1638 Sweden had planted a small fur-trading colony in the lower Delaware Valley. Trading with the

Delaware (or Lenni Lenape) Indians, New Sweden diverted many furs from New Netherland. Annoyed, in 1655 the Dutch colony's governor, Peter Stuyvesant, marched his militia against New Sweden. The four hundred residents of the rival colony peacefully accepted Dutch annexation. But New Netherland paid dearly for the victory. The Algonquians attacked during the militia's absence, this time destroying many scattered settlements and forcing Stuyvesant to ransom Dutch captives.

Tiny though they were, the Dutch and Swedish colonies were historically significant. New Netherland had attained a population of 9,000 and featured a wealthy, thriving port city by the time it came under English rule in 1664. Even short-lived New Sweden left a mark—the log cabin, that durable symbol of the American frontier, which Finnish settlers in the Swedish colony first introduced to the continent. Above all, the two colonies bequeathed an environment characterized by ethnic and religious diversity that would continue in England's "middle colonies."

English Conquests: New York and the Jerseys

Like Carolina, the English colonies of New York and New Jersey had their origins in the speculative enterprise of Restoration courtiers close to King Charles II. Here too upper-class proprietors hoped to create a hierarchical society in which they could profit from settlers' rents. These plans for the most part failed in New Jersey, as in Carolina. Only in New York did they come close to success.

In 1664, waging war against the Dutch Republic, Charles II dispatched a naval force to conquer New Netherland. Weakened by clashes with local Indians, Dutch governor Peter Stuyvesant and four hundred poorly armed civilians surrendered peacefully. Nearly all the Dutch (including Stuyvesant himself) remained in the colony on generous terms.

Charles II made his brother James, Duke of York, proprietor of the new province and renamed it New York. When the duke became King James II in 1685, he proclaimed New York a royal colony. Immigration from New England, Britain, and France boosted the population from nine thousand in 1664 to twenty thousand in 1700, of whom just 44 percent were descended from the original New Netherlanders.

New York's governors rewarded their most influential political supporters, both Dutch and English, with large land grants. By 1703 five families held approximately 1.75 million acres (about half the area

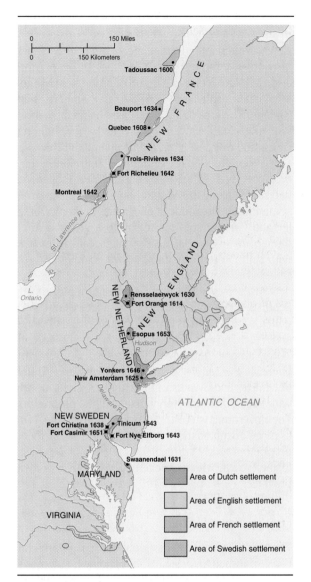

The Riverine Colonies of New France, New Netherland, and New Sweden, c. 1650
So that they could easily buy furs trapped by Indians farther inland, England's imperial rivals located their colonies along major river routes to the interior. The French settled along the St. Lawrence, the Dutch along the Hudson, and the Swedes along the Delaware.

east of the Hudson River and south of Albany), which they withheld from sale in hope of creating manors with numerous rent-paying tenants. Earning an enormous income from their rents over the next half-century, the New York *patroons* (the Dutch name for manor lords) by 1750 formed a landed elite second only in wealth to the Carolina rice planters.

Ambitious plans likewise collided with American realities in New Jersey, which also was carved out of New Netherland. Immediately after the Dutch province's conquest in 1664, the Duke of York awarded New Jersey to a group of proprietors headed by William Penn, John Lord Berkeley, and Sir Philip Carteret. The area at the time was inhabited by about four thousand Delaware Indians and a few hundred Dutch and Swedes. From the beginning the New Jersey proprietors had difficulty controlling their province. By 1672 several thousand New Englanders had settled along the Atlantic shore. After the quarrelsome Puritans renounced allegiance to them, Berkeley and Carteret sold the region to a group of even more contentious religious dissenters, called Quakers, who split the territory into the two colonies of West Jersey (1676) and East Jersey (1682).

East Jersey's new proprietors, a group of mostly Scottish Quakers, could no more successfully work with the local Puritans than had Berkeley and Carteret, and West Jersey's English Quakers squabbled constantly among themselves. The Jerseys' Quakers, Anglicans, Puritans, Scottish Presbyterians, Dutch Calvinists, and Swedish Lutherans got along poorly with each other and even worse with the proprietors. The governments collapsed between 1698 and 1701 as mobs disrupted the courts. In 1702 the disillusioned proprietors finally surrendered their political powers to the crown, which proclaimed New Jersey a royal province.

Quaker Pennsylvania

The noblest attempt to carry out European-born concepts of justice and stability in founding a colony began in 1681. That year Charles II paid off a huge debt by making a supporter's son, William Penn, the proprietor of the last unallocated tract of American territory at the king's disposal. Penn (1644–1718) had two aims in developing his colony. First, he was a Quaker and wanted to launch a "holy experiment" based on the teachings of the radical English preacher George Fox. Second, "though I desire to extend religious freedom," he explained, "yet I want some recompense for my trouble."

Quakers in late-seventeenth-century England stood well beyond the fringe of respectability. They appealed strongly to men and women at the bottom of the economic ladder, and they challenged the conventional foundation of the social order. George Fox, the

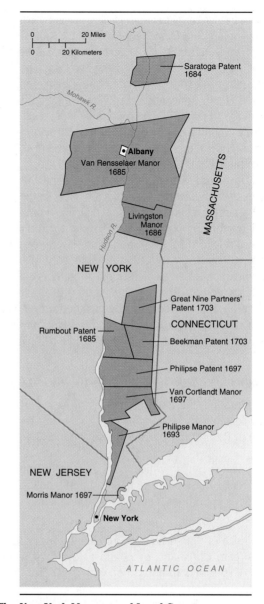

The New York Manors and Land Grants
Between 1684 and 1703, English governors awarded most of the best land east of the Hudson River as manors to prominent politicians—the majority of them Dutch—whose heirs became the wealthiest elite in the rural northern colonies.

movement's originator, had received his inspiration while wandering civil war–torn England's byways and searching for spiritual meaning among distressed common people. Tried on one occasion for blasphemy, he warned the judge to "tremble at the word

Abraham Wendell, *by an unknown artist, c. 1737*
The well-to-do Albany patroon *Abraham Wendell is shown standing before his land, stream, and mill.*

of the Lord" and was ridiculed as a "quaker." Fox's followers called themselves the Society of Friends, but the name Quaker stuck. They were among the most radical of the many religious sects born in England during the 1640s and 1650s.

The core of Fox's theology was his belief that the Holy Spirit or "Inner Light" could inspire every soul. Mainstream Christians, by contrast, found any such claim of special communication with God highly suspicious, as Anne Hutchinson's banishment from Massachusetts Bay colony in 1637 had revealed. Although trusting direct inspiration, Quakers also took great pains to ensure that individual opinions would not be mistaken for God's will. They felt confident that they understood Inner Light only after having reached near-unanimous agreement through intensive and searching discussion led by "Public Friends"—ordinary laypeople. In their simple religious services ("meetings"), Quakers sat silently until the Inner Light prompted one of them to speak.

Some of their beliefs led English Quakers to behave in ways that seemed disrespectful to government and the social elite and so aroused fierce hostil-

ity. For example, insisting that individuals deserved recognition for their spiritual state rather than their wealth or family status, Quakers refused to tip their hats to their social betters. For the same reason, they would not use the pronoun *you* (customarily employed when commoners spoke to members of the gentry), instead addressing everyone *thee* and *thou* as a token of equality. By wearing their hats in court, moreover, Quakers appeared to mock the state's authority; and by taking literally Scripture's ban on swearing oaths, they seemed to place themselves above the law. The Friends' refusal to bear arms appeared unpatriotic and cowardly to many. Finally, Quakers accorded women unprecedented equality. The Inner Light, Fox insisted, could "speak in the female as well as the male." A number of fiery Quaker proselytizers were women, including Mary Dyer, a former Antinomian who was exiled to Rhode Island. She helped organize Quaker groups there, and eventually was condemned for sedition and hanged in Massachusetts in 1660.

Not all Quakers came from the bottom of society. The movement's emphasis on quiet introspection and its refusal to adopt a formal creed also attracted well-educated and well-to-do individuals disillusioned by the quarreling of rival faiths. The possessor of a great fortune, William Penn was hardly a typical Friend, but there were significant numbers of merchants among the estimated sixty thousand Quakers in the British Isles in the early 1680s. Moreover, the industriousness that the Society of Friends encouraged in its members ensured that many humble Quakers were already accumulating money and property.

Quakers in England faced intense pressure to conform to the established church, but they throve on persecution. The courts severely fined those absent from Anglican services. Constables commonly collected fines by seizing Quakers' farm tools, equipment, or livestock and by destroying their looms or workbenches. Between 1660 and 1685, fifteen thousand Quakers were jailed, and many others suffered public whippings or facial disfigurements. Through all this adversity, they won a reputation for industriousness, even in prison. Jailed in 1669, William Penn found his fellow Quaker inmates busily engaged at crafts like weaving and spinning and absorbed in prayer during their work breaks. "The jail by that means became a meeting-house and a workhouse," Penn proudly wrote, "for *they would not be idle anywhere.*"

Much care lay behind the Quaker migration to Pennsylvania that began in 1681, and it resulted in the most successful initial transplantation of Europeans in any North American colony. Penn sent an advance party to the Delaware Valley, where about five thousand Delaware Indians and one thousand Swedes and Dutch already lived. After an agonizing voyage in which one-third of the passengers died, Penn arrived in 1682. Choosing a site for the capital, he named it Philadelphia—the "City of Brotherly Love." By 1687 some eight thousand settlers had joined Penn across the Atlantic. Most were Quakers from the British Isles, but they also included Presbyterians, Baptists, Anglicans, and Catholics, as well as Lutherans and radical sectarians from Germany—all attracted by Pennsylvania's religious toleration. Because most Quakers immigrated in family groups rather than as single males, a high birthrate resulted, and the population grew rapidly. In 1698 a Quaker reported that in Pennsylvania one seldom met "any young Married Woman but hath a Child in her belly, or one upon her lap."

As planned by its founder, Pennsylvania offered Friends the freedom not only to live diligently but also to make laws according to their ideals. Having experienced persecution, Penn hated intolerance and arbitrary government. Thus in drafting the colony's Frame of Government (constitution), he proposed "to leave myself and my successors [as proprietor] no power of doing mischief, that the will of One man may not hinder the good of the whole company." After wavering between authoritarian and more democratic plans, Penn finally opted for a system with a strong executive branch (a governor and governor's council) and granted the lower legislative chamber (the assembly) only limited powers. Friends, forming the majority of the colony's population, dominated this elected assembly. Penn named Quakers and their supporters as governor, judges, and sheriffs. Hardly a democrat, he feared "the ambitions of the populace which shakes the Constitution," and he intended to check "the rabble" as much as possible. Because he also insisted on the orderly disposition of property and hoped to avoid unseemly wrangling, he carefully oversaw land sales in the colony. To prevent haphazard growth and social turmoil in Philadelphia, Penn designed the city with a grid plan, laying out the streets at right angles and reserving small areas for parks.

Good planning ensured that Pennsylvania suffered no initial "starving time." The colony was also fortunate in experiencing no large-scale wars for seventy years. Partly this resulted from the reduced Native American population in the Delaware Valley. To the Indians, Penn expressed a wish "to live together as Neighbours and Friends," and he tried to buy land fairly from them.

Pennsylvania seemed an ideal colony—intelligently organized, well financed, tolerant, open to all industrious settlers, and largely at peace with the Indians. Rich, level lands and a lengthy growing season produced bumper crops. Sharp West Indian demand for its grain quickly generated widespread prosperity and by 1700 made Philadelphia a major port.

But like other attempts to base new American societies on preconceived plans or lofty ideals, Penn's "peaceable kingdom" soon bogged down in human bickering. In 1684 the founder returned to England to resolve boundary disputes with adjacent Maryland, and in his absence (until 1699) the settlers quarreled incessantly. Although Penn spent much money on his colony, an opposition party attacked his efforts to monopolize foreign trade and to make each landowner pay him a small annual fee. Bitter struggles between Penn's supporters in the governor's council and opponents in the assembly deadlocked the government. From 1686 to 1688, the legislature passed no laws and the council once ordered the lower house's speaker arrested. Penn's brief return to Pennsylvania from 1699 to 1701 helped little, but just before he sailed home, he made the legislature a unicameral (one-chamber) assembly and allowed it to initiate measures.

In addition, religious conflict shook Pennsylvania during the 1690s, when George Keith, a college-educated Public Friend, urged Quakers to adopt a formal creed. This would have changed the democratically functioning Quaker sect—in which the humblest member had equal authority in interpreting the Inner Light—into a more traditional church dominated by an educated clergy. The majority of Quakers rejected Keith's views in 1692, whereupon he joined the Church of England, taking some Quakers with him. Keith's departure began a major decline in the Quaker share of Pennsylvania's population. The proportion fell further once Quakers ceased immigrating in large numbers after 1710.

William Penn met his strongest opposition in the counties on the lower Delaware River, where the best lands had been taken up by Swedes and Dutch. In 1704 these counties gained the right to elect their own legislature, but Penn continued to name their governor. Although the new colony of Delaware's separation temporarily strengthened the proprietor's party in what remained of Pennsylvania, by then the founder's dream of a harmonious society was dashed.

William Penn's Map of Philadelphia, *c. 1681;*
Portrait of Penn, *by Francis Place*
Central to William Penn's master plan for Philadelphia was the idea that each residence should stand in the middle of its plot, encircled by gardens and orchards. This pastel portrait is thought to be the most accurate likeness of Penn extant.

Sadness darkened Penn's last years. Having sunk a fortune into Pennsylvania, he later spent some months in a debtor's prison and died in debt. Long before, he had despaired at having to battle with the legislature's politicians, bent on economic and political advantage. As early as 1685, he begged them, "For the love of God, me, and the poor country, be not so governmentish; so noisy and open in your disaffection."

Despite Penn's anguish, his colony was a solid success. It and the other middle colonies soon demonstrated that British America could benefit by encouraging pluralism. New York and New Jersey successfully integrated New Netherland's Swedish and Dutch population; and Pennsylvania, New Jersey, and Delaware refused to require residents to pay support for any official church. Meanwhile, England's European rivals, France and Spain, were also extending their claims in North America.

RIVALS FOR NORTH AMERICA

In marked contrast to England's compact settlements, France and Spain had established far-flung inland networks of fortified trading posts and missions. To offset the English colonists' superiority in numbers, France and Spain enlisted Native Americans as trading partners and military allies, and the two Catholic nations

had far more success than English Protestants in converting Indians to Christianity. By 1720 missionaries, fur traders, soldiers, and merchants—and relatively few farmers—had spread French and Spanish influence through two-thirds of the present-day United States.

England's rivals exercised varying degrees of control in developing their American colonies. Louis XIV's France, the supreme power in late-seventeenth-century Europe, poured in state resources, whereas Spain, then in deep decay, made little attempt to influence North American affairs from afar. In both cases, local officials and settlers assumed the primary burden for extending imperial control.

France Claims a Continent

France's King Louis XIV (reigned 1661–1715) sought to subordinate his American colony to French interests. His principal adviser, Jean-Baptiste Colbert, was a forceful proponent of the doctrine of *mercantilism* (see Chapter 4), according to which colonies should provide their home country with raw materials it lacked and with markets for its manufactured output of Louis In this way, the nation would no... ...nce's new val countries for trade. A... ...st Indies, and export hoped that New ... ...furs, ship... ...pr...

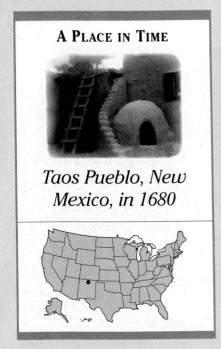

Taos Pueblo, New Mexico, in 1680

Since 1675 Native American leaders from many New Mexico pueblos had gathered regularly at Taos to plan the overthrow of Spanish rule. Hostile to the Spanish from the time of their arrival, Taos had become the center of a wider movement after Popé, a religious leader of San Juan Pueblo, fled there to avoid persecution by the Spanish.

In August 1680 Popé and his cohorts were ready to act. On the morning of August 10, some Taos Indians and their Apache allies attacked the homes of the seventy Spanish colonists residing near Taos and killed all but two. Then, with Indians from neighboring pueblos, they proceeded south and joined a massive siege of New Mexico's capital, Santa Fe. Thus began the Pueblo Revolt of 1680, the most significant event in the history of the colonial Southwest.

Taos's leading role in the revolt is not surprising, for it had long been a meeting-place for Native Americans from near and far and a center of anti-Spanish resistance. Before the Spanish arrived, Taos was a major center of trade between the farming Pueblo Indians and buffalo-hunting Apaches to the north and east. An early Spanish expedition reported some Apaches returning from Taos, "where they sell meat, hides, tallow, suet, and salt in exchange for cotton, blankets, pottery, maize, and some small green stones [turquoise]."

After establishing New Mexico in 1598, the Spanish collected corn as tribute from the pueblos. As a result, Pueblo Indians could no longer send their surplus crops to Taos and other trade centers for exchange with the Apaches. Having come to depend on corn, Apaches now raided pueblos for the grain. When Taos resisted colonial rule in 1602, Spanish troops waged a punitive raid on the pueblo. Four years later, Taos, two other trade centers, and several Apache bands urged the other pueblos to join them in overthrowing the Spanish. But most of the pueblos, fearing the Apaches, responded by strengthening their ties to the Spanish.

For the next seven decades, the Taos Indians struggled to retain their independence from the Spanish. On two occasions they destroyed Franciscan missions in their pueblo, only to watch as the churches were rebuilt under the protection of Span-

Diego de Vargas
Leader of the Spanish reconquest of New Mexico.

ish soldiers. The Taos also maintained their ties with the Apaches. In 1640 some Taos fled to live near friendly Apaches in Kansas, where they remained until Spanish troops forcibly returned them home in 1662. Meanwhile, the Spanish raided Taos and another pueblo where some Apaches lived, slaying all Apache men and enslaving Apache women and children.

For more than half a century, most of the other pueblos tried to accommodate Spanish rule and Catholicism. But during the 1660s they grew disillusioned. For several consecutive years their crops withered under the effects of sustained drought. Drought-induced starvation plus deadly epidemic diseases sent their population plummeting from about 80,000 in 1598 to just 17,000 in the 1670s. Riding horses stolen from the Spanish, Apaches inflicted more damage than ever in their raids. Reeling under the effects of these catastrophes, Christian Indians returned to traditional Pueblo beliefs and ceremonies in hopes of restoring the spiritual balance that had brought ample rainfall, good health, and

Taos Pueblo, North House Block, 1880

peace before the Spanish arrived. Seeking to suppress Pueblo religion as "witchcraft" and "idolatry," missionaries entered sacred, underground kivas, destroyed religious objects, and publicly whipped native religious leaders and their followers.

Matters came to a head in 1675 when Governor Juan Francisco Treviño ordered soldiers to sack the kivas and to arrest the religious leaders. Three leaders were sent to the gallows, a fourth hanged himself, and forty-three others—including Popé—were whipped, jailed, and sentenced to be sold as slaves. In response, armed warriors from several pueblos converged on Santa Fe and demanded the prisoners' release. With most of his soldiers off fighting the Apaches, Governor Treviño complied.

Despite this concession, there was now no cooling of Pueblo resentment against the Spanish. Besides Popé and his Taos host, El Saca, the leaders gathered at Taos included Luis Tupatú, Antonio Mala-

cate, and others whose Christian names signified that earlier they had been baptized. Some were of mixed Pueblo-Spanish ancestry, and one leader, Domingo Naranjo, combined Pueblo, Mexican Indian, and African ancestors. They and many of their followers had attempted to reconcile conversion to Christianity and subjection to Spanish rule with their identities as Indians. But the natives' deteriorating conditions and the cruel intolerance of the Spanish turned them against Catholicism. At each pueblo, rebels destroyed the churches and religious paraphernalia and killed those missionaries who did not escape. Then they "plunge[d] into the rivers and wash[ed] themselves with amole," a native root, in order to undo their baptisms. As a follower later testified, Popé also called on the Indians "to break and enlarge their cultivated fields, saying now they were as they had been in ancient times, free from the labor they had per-

formed for the religious and the Spaniards." In rejecting Christianity and the Spanish, Pueblo Indians from throughout New Mexico did what many Taos had urged them to do for decades.

The siege of Santa Fe led to the expulsion of the Spanish from New Mexico for twelve years. By the time Diego de Vargas, leading the Spanish reconquest, reached Taos in September 1692, most pueblos had already resubmitted to Spanish rule. Suspicious as always of Spanish intentions, the Taos retreated to the mountains until Vargas consented to pardon them. Once returned to their community, ninety-six of them agreed to be baptized, and two leaders told Vargas of a new plot against him. Nevertheless, many Taos people continued to resent the Spanish, and in 1696 they joined Indians from several other villages in an abortive uprising. Thereafter suspicions of the Spanish lingered, but Taos did not again attempt to overthrow them.

timber for those colonies and for the French navy. To begin realizing these goals, they revoked the charter of the private New France Company in 1663 and placed the colony under royal direction. They then sought to stifle the Iroquois threat to New France's economy and to encourage French immigration to Canada.

For more than half a century, and especially since the "beaver wars," the Iroquois had limited New France's productivity by intercepting convoys of beaver pelts from the interior. After assuming control of the colony, the royal government sent fifteen hundred soldiers (most of whom eventually became settlers) to stop Iroquois interference with the French fur trade. In 1666 these troops marched into present-day New York, panicking the local Mohawks into fleeing without a fight. Sobered by the burning of four villages well stocked with winter food, the Iroquois Confederacy made a peace that lasted until 1680. Subsequently, New France enormously expanded its North American fur exports.

Meanwhile, the French crown energetically built up New France's population by dispatching about six hundred settlers each year. About half were indentured servants who received land after three years' work and could marry among the "king's girls," female orphans shipped over with dowries.

But many French male immigrants quickly spurned farming in the St. Lawrence Valley, instead swarming westward in search of furs. By 1670 one-fifth of them were *coureurs de bois*—independent traders unconstrained by government authority or dubious pasts. Living and intermarrying with the Indians, the *coureurs* built for France an empire based on alliances with Canadian and Great Lakes Indians from whom the French exchanged furs for European goods, including guns to use against the Iroquois and other rivals.

Alarmed by the rapid expansion of England's colonies, France then boldly sought to contain the English, as well as to prevent Spain from linking Florida with New Mexico, by dominating the North American heartland. As early as 1672, fur trader Louis Jolliet and Jesuit missionary Jacques Marquette became the first Europeans known to have reached the upper Mississippi River (near modern Prairie du Chien, Wisconsin); they later paddled twelve hundred miles downstream, to the Mississippi's junction with the Arkansas River. Ten years later, the Sieur de La Salle, an ambitious upper-class adventurer, descended the entire Mis-

sissippi to the Gulf of Mexico. When he reached the delta, La Salle formally claimed all the Mississippi basin—half the territory of the present-day continental United States—for Louis XIV, in whose honor he named the territory Louisiana.

Having asserted title to this vast empire, the French began settling the southern gateway into it. In 1698 the first colonizers arrived near the mouth of the Mississippi. A year later, the French erected a fort near present-day Biloxi, Mississippi. In 1702 they occupied what is now Mobile, Alabama, as a fur-trading station.

The Spanish Borderlands

English and French expansion did not go unnoticed by the Spanish. They grew alarmed when La Salle temporarily occupied an outpost near modern-day Houston from 1685 to 1687. To defend their borderland holdings, Spanish authorities in Mexico proclaimed the province of Texas (or Tejas) in 1691. But no permanent Spanish settlements appeared there until 1716 (see Chapter 4).

Spanish preoccupation with New Mexico was a primary reason for this neglect of Texas. By 1680 about 2,300 Europeans—many of them scattered on isolated *ranchos* (ranches)—and 17,000 Pueblo Indians lived in New Mexico's Rio Grande Valley, compared with 80,000 natives in 1598 when the Spanish arrived. That year a Pueblo religious leader named Popé led a revolt, culminating nearly a century of grievances and sparked by Spanish efforts to outlaw the rituals central to the Pueblo peoples' way of life (see "A Place in Time"). The Indians killed 400 colonists (including most priests), captured Santa Fe, and drove the survivors south to El Paso. The Pueblo peoples held New Mexico until 1692, and their resistance continued to threaten Spanish rule until the end of the century.

In Florida, an even older colony than New Mexico, the Spanish fared no better. Before 1680 the colony faced periodic rebellions from Guale, Timucua, and Apalachee Indians protesting forced labor and the religious discipline imposed by Franciscan missionaries. Beginning in the 1680s, Creek and other slave raiders allied to Carolina added to the effects of recurrent diseases in reducing the number of Indians in Florida. When a new round of warfare erupted in Europe at the end of the decade, Spain was ill prepared to defend its beleaguered North American colonies.

CONCLUSION

In less than a century, from 1630 to 1715, European colonization transformed the map of North America. From a series of scattered settlements, Europeans now laid claim to most of the area composing the present-day United States east of the Rocky Mountains. A casual look at a map based on European claims as of 1715 would suggest that France and Spain were the dominant powers, for together they surrounded the seaboard-clinging English by land, from Florida to the Mississippi Valley to Canada. But the demographic and economic reality was quite different. By 1700 the European population of England's North American colonies was about 250,000, compared with 15,000 for the French holdings and 4,500 for the Spanish.

Within the English colonies, several distinct regions had emerged. The southern colonies, emulating the English West Indies, concentrated primarily on the specialized production of plantation crops using slave labor. New England's Puritanism had grown less utopian and more wordly as the inhabitants gradually reconciled their religious views with the realities of a commercial economy. In between New England and the South, the middle colonies, with their ethnic and religious pluralism, embraced the market economy with less hesitation. During the first half of the eighteenth century, these diverse, rapidly expanding colonial regions would be effectively integrated into the first empire in history rooted in commercial capitalism.

CHRONOLOGY

1627	English establish Barbados.
1630	John Winthrop, "A Model of Christian Charity." Massachusetts Bay colony founded.
1630–1660	The great English migration to North America.
1633	First English settlements in Connecticut.
1634	Cecilius Calvert (Lord Baltimore) founds proprietary colony of Maryland.
1635	Roger Williams banished from Massachusetts Bay; founds Providence, Rhode Island, in 1636.
1636	Harvard College established.
1637	Anne Hutchinson tried by Massachusetts Bay colony and banished to Rhode Island. Pequot War.
1638	New Sweden established.
1639	Fundamental Orders of Connecticut.
1640s	Large-scale slave-labor system takes hold in the West Indies.
1642	English Civil War begins.
1643	New Haven colony founded.
1644	Williams obtains permission to establish a legal government in Rhode Island.
1644–1646	Third Anglo-Powhatan War in Virginia.
1649	Maryland's Act for Religious Toleration. King Charles I beheaded. Five Nations Iroquois disperse Hurons.
1651	First New England "praying town" established at Natick, Massachusetts.
1653	First Indian reservation established in Virginia.
1655	New Netherland annexes New Sweden.
1660	Charles II becomes king of England.
1661	Barbados government creates first comprehensive slave code. Maryland defines slavery as a lifelong, inheritable racial status.
1662	Half-Way Covenant drafted.
1663	Carolina founded as English colony. New France made a royal colony.
1664	English conquer the Dutch colony of New Netherland, which becomes the English colony of New York. New Jersey established.
1670	Settlement of southern Carolina begins. Virginia defines slavery as a lifelong, inheritable racial status.
1672	Louis Jolliet and Jacques Marquette explore the Mississippi River.
1675–1676	King Philip's War in New England.
1676	Bacon's Rebellion in Virginia. Quakers organize the colony of West Jersey.
1680–1692	Pueblo revolt in New Mexico.
1681	William Penn founds the Pennsylvania colony.

1682   Quakers organize the colony of East Jersey.

The Sieur de La Salle descends the Mississippi River to the Gulf of Mexico and claims the Mississippi basin for France.

Sieur de La Salle

1690s   Collapse of the Royal African Company's monopoly on selling slaves to the English colonies; large shipments of Africans begin reaching the Chesapeake.

1691   Spain establishes province of Texas.

1692–1693   Salem witchcraft trials.

1698   French begin settlements near the mouth of the Mississippi River.

1711–1713   Tuscarora War in Carolina.

1715–1716   Yamasee War in Carolina.

FOR FURTHER READING

Paul Boyer and Stephen Nissenbaum, *Salem Possessed: The Social Origins of Witchcraft* (1974). A study of the witchcraft episode as the expression of social conflict in one New England community.

William Cronon, *Changes in the Land: Indians, Colonists, and the Ecology of New England* (1983). A pioneering study of the interactions of Native Americans and European settlers with the New England environment.

W. J. Eccles, *France in America*, rev. ed. (1991). An interpretive overview of French colonization in North America and the Caribbean by a distinguished scholar.

Jack P. Greene, *Pursuits of Happiness: The Social Development of Early Modern British Colonies and the Formation of American Culture* (1988). A brilliant synthesis of the colonial history of British America.

Winthrop D. Jordan, *The White Man's Burden: Historical Origins of Racism in the United States* (1974). A brief yet definitive analysis of racism's origins.

Carol F. Karlsen, *The Devil in the Shape of a Woman: Witchcraft in Colonial New England* (1987). An examination of the relationship between witchcraft episodes and gender in New England society.

Edmund S. Morgan, *American Slavery, American Freedom: The Ordeal of Colonial Virginia* (1975). The most penetrating analysis yet written on the origins of southern slavery.

Alan Simpson, *Puritanism in Old and New England* (1955). A good brief introduction to Puritanism.

David J. Weber, *The Spanish Frontier in North America* (1992). A masterful synthesis of Spanish colonial history north of the Caribbean and Mexico.

ADDITIONAL BIBLIOGRAPHY

Early New England

David Grayson Allen, *In English Ways: The Movement of Societies and the Transferral of English Local Law and Custom* (1981); Virginia DeJohn Anderson, *New England's Generation: The Great Migration and the Formation of Society and Culture in the Seventeenth Century* (1991); James Axtell, *The School upon a Hill: Education and Society in Colonial New England* (1974); Bernard Bailyn, *The New England Merchants in the Seventeenth Century* (1955); Emery Battis, *Saints and Sectaries: Anne Hutchinson and the Antinomian Controversy in the Massachusetts Bay Colony* (1962); Sacvan Bercovitch, *The Puritan Origins of the American Self* (1975); Charles L. Cohen, *God's Caress: The Psychology of Puritan Religious Experience* (1986); David Cressy, *Coming Over: Migration and Communication Between England and New England in the Seventeenth Century* (1987); Andrew Delbanco, *The Puritan Ordeal* (1989); John Demos, *A Little Commonwealth: Family Life in Plymouth Colony* (1970), *Entertaining Satan: Witchcraft and the Culture of Early New England* (1982), and *The Unredeemed Captive: A Family Story from Early America* (1994); Stephen Foster, *Their Solitary Way: The Puritan Social Ethic in the First Century of Settlement in New* *England* (1971); Richard Godbeer, *The Devil's Dominion: Magic and Religion in Early New England* (1992); Philip Greven, *Four Generations: Population, Land, and Family in Colonial Andover, Massachusetts* (1970); Philip F. Gura, *A Glimpse of Sion's Glory: Puritan Radicalism in New England, 1620–1660* (1984); David D. Hall, *Worlds of Wonder, Days of Judgment: Popular Religious Belief in Early New England* (1990); Stephen Innes, *Labor in a New Land: Economy and Society in Seventeenth-Century Springfield* (1983); David Thomas Konig, *Law and Society in Puritan Massachusetts, 1629–1692* (1979); Kenneth A. Lockridge, *A New England Town: The First Hundred Years: Dedham, Massachusetts, 1636–1736* (1970); John F. Martin, *Profits in the Wilderness: Entrepreneurship and the Founding of New England Towns in the Seventeenth Century* (1991); Edmund S. Morgan, *The Puritan Dilemma: The Story of John Winthrop* (1958); Carla Gardina Pestana, *Quakers and the Baptists in Colonial Massachusetts* (1991); Darrett B. Rutman, *Winthrop's Boston: A Portrait of a Puritan Town, 1630–1649* (1965); Laurel Thatcher Ulrich, *Good Wives: Image and Reality in the Lives of Women in the Northern New England, 1650–1750* (1982).

The Southern Colonies

Timothy H. Breen and Stephen Innes, *"Myne Own Ground": Race and Freedom on Virginia's Eastern Shore, 1640–1676* (1980); Lois Green Carr et al., *Colonial Chesapeake Society* (1988) and *Robert Cole's World: Agriculture and Society in Early Maryland* (1990); Carville Earle, *The Evolution of a Tidewater Settlement Pattern: All Hallow's Parish, Maryland, 1650–1783* (1975); Ivor Noël Hume, *Martin's Hundred*, rev. ed. (1991); David W. Jordan, *Foundations of Representative Government in Maryland* (1988); Daniel C. Littlefield, *Rice and Slavery: Ethnicity and the Slave Trade in Colonial South Carolina* (1981); Gloria L. Main, *Tobacco Colony: Life in Early Maryland, 1650–1720* (1982); James R. Perry, *Formation of a Society on Virginia's Eastern Shore, 1615–1655* (1990); Darret B. Rutman and Anita S. Rutman, *A Place in Time: Middlesex County, Virginia, 1650–1750* (1984); Thad Tate and David Ammerman, eds., *The Chesapeake in the Seventeenth Century: Essays on Anglo-American Society* (1979); Wilcomb E. Washburn, *The Governor and the Rebel: A History of Bacon's Rebellion in Virginia* (1957); Robert Weir, *Colonial South Carolina: A History* (1983); Peter H. Wood, *Black Majority: Negroes in Colonial South Carolina from 1670 Through the Stono Rebellion* (1974).

The West Indies

Hilary M. Beckles, *White Servitude and Black Slavery in Barbados, 1627–1715* (1989); Philip P. Boucher, *Cannibal Encounters: Europeans and Island Caribs, 1492–1763* (1992); Carl Bridenbaugh and Roberta Bridenbaugh, *No Peace Beyond the Line: The English in the Caribbean, 1624–1690* (1972); Richard S. Dunn, *Sugar and Slaves: The Rise of the Planter Class in the English West Indies, 1624–1713* (1972); Richard B. Sheridan, *Sugar and Slavery: An Economic History of the British West Indies, 1623–1775* (1973).

The Middle Colonies

Thomas J. Archdeacon, *New York City, 1664–1710: Conquest and Change* (1976); Richard S. Dunn and Mary Maples Dunn, eds., *The World of William Penn* (1986); Joyce D. Goodfriend, *Before the Melting Pot: Society and Culture in Colonial New York City, 1664–1730* (1991); Barry Levy, *Quakers and the American Family: British Settlement in the Delaware Valley* (1988); Donna Merwick, *Possessing Albany, 1630–1710: The Dutch and English Experiences* (1990); Gary B. Nash, *Quakers and Politics: Pennsylvania, 1681–1726* (1968); Robert C. Ritchie, *The Duke's Province: A Study of New York Politics and Society, 1664–1691* (1977); Oliver A. Rink, *Holland on the Hudson: An Economic and Social History of Dutch New York* (1986).

French and Spanish Colonies

Donald E. Chipman, *Spanish Texas, 1519–1821* (1992); Louise Dechêne, *Habitants and Merchants in Seventeenth-Century Montreal* (1992); W. J. Eccles, *Canada Under Louis XIV, 1663–1701* (1964); Ramón A. Gutiérrez, *When Jesus Came, the Corn Mothers Went Away: Marriage, Sexuality, and Power in New Mexico, 1500–1846* (1991); Richard Colebrook Harris, *The Seigneurial System in Early Canada* (1966).

Indian-European Relations

James Axtell, *The Invasion Within: The Contest of Cultures in Colonial North America* (1985); Jack D. Forbes, *Apache, Navaho, and Spaniard* (1960); Francis Jennings, *The Invasion of America: Indians, Colonialism, and the Cant of Conquest* (1975); Elizabeth A. H. John, *Storms Brewed in Other Men's Worlds: The Confrontation of Indians, Spanish, and French in the Southwest, 1540–1795* (1975); Douglas Edward Leach, *Flintlock and Tomahawk: New England in King Philip's War* (1958); James H. Merrell, *The Indians' New World: Catawbas and Their Neighbors from European Contact Through the Era of Removal* (1989); Daniel K. Richter, *The Ordeal of the Longhouse: The Peoples of the Iroquois League in the Era of European Colonization* (1992); Helen C. Rountree, *Pocahontas's People: The Powhatan Indians of Virginia Through Four Centuries* (1990); Neal Salisbury, *Manitou and Providence: Indians, Europeans, and the Making of New England, 1500–1643* (1982); Richard White, *The Middle Ground: Indians, Empires, and Republics in the Great Lakes Region, 1650–1815* (1991).

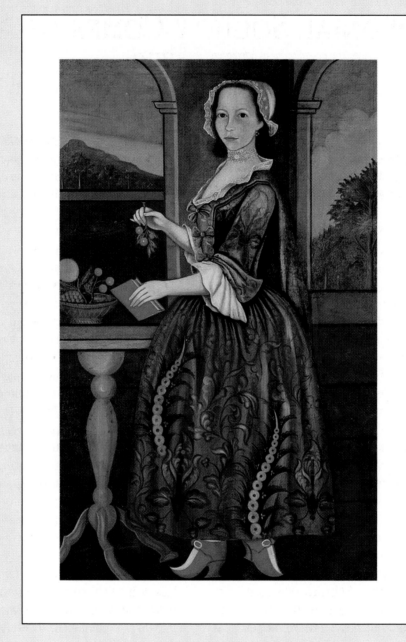

Mrs. Harme Gansevoort (Magdalena Bouw)

by Pieter Vanderlyn, c. 1740

COLONIAL SOCIETY COMES OF AGE
1660–1750

Alexander Garden was furious with the young Anglican minister George Whitefield (inset). Just over from England, Whitefield was stating publicly that Garden's ministers were unsaved and endangering their parishioners' souls. Garden, as the bishop of London's commissary (representative) in Charles Town, South Carolina, was responsible for the Church of England's well-being in the southern British colonies. He thought that he had plenty to contend with already—most pressingly, the numbing indifference of most of his flock—and did not appreciate this impudent outsider's accusations. With Whitefield's descent on the colonies like a hurricane, Garden sensed that 1740 would not be a good year for established religion.

Calling Whitefield in for an interview and demanding that he explain his repeated attacks, Garden got more than he bargained for. Whitefield claimed that Garden "was as ignorant as the rest" of the local clergy because he failed to teach the central Calvinist doctrine of salvation by predestination (see Chapter 2). And Whitefield threatened to speak out against the commissary if Garden refused to condemn dancing and other public entertainments. Garden shot back that Whitefield would be suspended if he preached in any church in the province—to which Whitefield retorted that he would treat such an action as he would an order from the pope. The meeting ended with Garden shouting, "Get out of my house!"

Garden got Whitefield out of his house but not out of his hair. The two men carried their dispute to the public. Garden accused Whitefield of jeopardizing the stability of colonial society. Whitefield accused the Anglican clergy of abandoning Calvinist doctrine in favor of the cold heresy of reason. An extraordinary orator, Whitefield stirred his listeners' passions, calling forth an "enthusiasm" for religion that undermined traditional order and deference. He inspired members of congregations to think themselves as good as, if not superior to, their ministers; wives, to question their husbands' piety; children, to claim divine grace that their parents did not feel; and common people, including slaves and subjugated Indians, to insist that they were the equal of anyone else.

That was Whitefield's greatest crime—to be heard throughout America. He became the first national figure in North America, traveling thousands of miles to spread his critique of the established religious order. Everywhere he went, the people poured out by the thousands to listen and feel, to sense individually the overwhelming power of a direct connection with God.

Sweeping through British North America in the 1740s, Whitefield encountered a vibrant society, a rapidly growing economy, and the beginnings of a richly diverse culture. By 1750 the colonies could claim the world's largest concentration of overseas Europeans; besides those of English stock, significant numbers descended from German, Irish, Scottish, Dutch, and French settlers. North America was also the enforced home of a burgeoning African population, by now slowly becoming both English-speaking and Christian. Geographically, however, the people remained isolated from one another.

Whitefield found it quicker to make the hazardous, disease-ravaged transatlantic voyage than to go overland from New England to Georgia.

A generation of imperial crisis and war with the French from 1685 to 1713 had forged among Anglo-America's whites a strong sense of shared allegiance to the English crown and of deeply felt Protestant heritage. Then, during an era of peace between 1713 and 1744, British Americans' provincialism faced the dual challenge of two vital yet conflicting European cultural currents. The first of these was the Enlightenment—the dissemination among the educated public of faith in reason rooted in an appreciation of natural science—which found its foremost American exponent in Benjamin Franklin. The second current was the religious revival pulsing across Protestant Europe in the 1730s and 1740s, one of whose greatest prophets was George Whitefield. That Franklin and Whitefield became the first two Anglo-American public figures to win fame not only throughout the colonies but also in the entire Western world testifies to America's active participation in the culture of the age.

The peace and prosperity that characterized mid-eighteenth-century British North America would have astonished seventeenth-century colonists, clinging to their uncertain footholds on the edge of the transatlantic wilderness. But even though by 1740 life was becoming reasonably stable and secure, especially for upper-class Anglo-Americans, the Great Awakening let loose spiritual and social tremors that jolted colonial self-confidence. Alexander Garden's nervousness was hardly unreasonable.

RESTORATION AND REBELLION

Although the English had established colonies as early as 1607, with the founding of Virginia, England made no serious effort to weld its colonies into a coherent empire until King Charles II (ruled 1660–1685) assumed the throne. Charles's ascension, marking the "restoration" of the Stuart monarchy in England, ended two decades of civil war and experimentation with republican rule. Almost immediately, English authorities undertook a concerted policy that sought to expand the nation's overseas trade at the expense of its rivals and to subordinate its colonies to English commercial interests and political authority. Efforts to tighten royal control over the colonies ended in 1689 after the "Glorious Revolution" in England forced King James II into exile.

Stuart Policies

After the Restoration, Parliament passed laws collectively known as the Navigation Acts designed to benefit England's commercial interests. Expanding upon a 1651 law, the Navigation Acts of 1660 and 1663 barred colonial merchants from exporting such commodities

The Restoration Colonies

England's Restoration colonies were carved out of the claims or earlier colonial territory of rival European powers. Spain claimed the territory chartered as Carolina in 1663. Out of England's takeover of Dutch New Netherland in 1664 came the colonies of New York, East Jersey, West Jersey, Pennsylvania, and Delaware.

as sugar and tobacco anywhere except to England, and from importing goods in non-English ships. The act of 1672 provided administrative machinery to enforce these rules. The Restoration also set in motion a new wave of colony building that gave England control of the North American coast from Maine to South Carolina (see Chapter 3).

English domestic politics figured prominently in the Restoration government's plans for America. Charles II had clamoring supporters to reward. The Navigation Acts favored powerful commercial interests in England. The king entrusted the creation of the new colonies to important English politicians—the proprietors who organized settlement, oversaw governance (subject to loose control from London), and expected to profit handsomely. But, as earlier in Maryland, their plans collided with the colonists' determination to better themselves.

One of the Restoration's least effective initiatives was an effort to strengthen the Church of England in North America. Lamenting the sorry state of religious affairs in the Chesapeake, an Anglican minister in Maryland in 1660 described that colony as a "Sodom of uncleaness [sic] & a Pest house of iniquity." But because educated English clergy resisted taking American parishes, the reform of American Anglicanism never got very far. Neither did royal attempts to reorganize New England and to impose Anglicanism on its recalcitrant Puritans.

Royal Centralization

As the sons of a king executed by Parliament, the last two Stuart monarchs disliked representative government. Charles II called Parliament into session rarely after 1674, and not at all from 1681 until his death in 1685. James II (ruled 1685–1688) hoped to reign as an "absolute" monarch like France's Louis XIV, who never had to face a national parliament. Not surprisingly, neither English king had much sympathy for the American colonial assemblies.

Royal intentions of extending direct political control to North America first became evident in New York. The proprietor, Charles II's brother James, the Duke of York, considered elected assemblies "of dangerous consequence" and forbade legislatures to meet from 1664 to 1682. He relented from 1682 to 1686 but thereafter called none. Meanwhile, Charles showed a clear preference for naming high-ranking army men as colonial governors. Despite their new civilian status,

these governors were the militia's commanders in chief, and their background made them well suited to crushing civilian dissent with armed force. From 1660 to 1685, Charles appointed former army officers to about 90 percent of all gubernatorial positions, thereby compromising the time-honored English tradition of holding the military strictly accountable to civilian authority. By 1680 such "governors general" ruled 60 percent of all American colonists. James II later continued this policy.

Ever resentful of outside meddling, New Englanders proved most stubborn in defending self-government and resisting Stuart policies. As early as 1661, the Massachusetts assembly politely but firmly declared its citizens exempt from all laws and royal decrees from England except for a declaration of war. The colony ignored the Navigation Acts and continued welcoming Dutch traders. "The New England men break through and . . . trade to any place that their interest lead them," claimed Virginia's governor William Berkeley.

Soon Charles II targeted Massachusetts for special punishment. In 1679 he carved out of its territory a new royal colony, New Hampshire. Then in 1684 he declared Massachusetts itself a royal colony and revoked its charter, the very foundation of the Puritan city upon a hill. Puritan minister Increase Mather responded by openly calling on colonists to resist even to the point of martyrdom.

Royal centralization in America culminated after James II ascended to the throne. In 1686 the new king consolidated Massachusetts, New Hampshire, Connecticut, Rhode Island, and Plymouth into a single administrative unit, the Dominion of New England. He added New York and the Jerseys in 1688. With this bold stroke, all legislatures in these colonies ceased to exist, and still another former army officer, Sir Edmund Andros, became the governor of the Dominion of New England, at Boston.

Massachusetts burned with hatred for the new governor. By "Exercise of an arbitrary Government," preached Salem's minister, "ye wicked walked on Every Side & ye Vilest of men ware [sic] exalted." Andros was indeed arbitrary. He suppressed the legislature, limited towns to a single annual meeting, and jailed prominent citizens to crush protests. Furthermore, Andros hit a raw nerve by forcing a Boston Puritan congregation to share its meetinghouse with an Anglican minister, and he strictly enforced the Navigation Acts. "You have no more privileges left you,"

Andros reportedly told a group of outraged colonists, "than not to be sold for slaves." Other than his soldiers and a handful of recently arrived Anglican immigrants, however, Andros had no base of support in Massachusetts.

Tensions also ran high in New York, where Catholics held high political and military posts under the Duke of York's rule. By 1688 citizens feared that these Catholic officials would betray the colony to France. When Andros's local deputy, Captain Francis Nicholson, allowed the harbor's forts to deteriorate and reacted skeptically to rumors of Indian hostility, New Yorkers suspected the worst.

The Glorious Revolution in England and America

New England Puritans' fury at Andros's forcing them to tolerate Anglicanism was matched by English Protestants' growing worries about the Stuarts' predilection for Catholicism. The Duke of York became a Catholic in 1676, and Charles II converted on his deathbed. Both rulers violated Parliament's laws by issuing decrees that allowed Catholics to hold high office and worship openly. When seven Anglican bishops denounced one such edict in 1688, James II tried them as state enemies. English Protestants' fears that they would have to accept Catholicism intensified after both kings expressed their preference for allying with France just as Louis XIV was launching new persecutions of that country's Protestants in 1685.

The English tolerated James II's Catholicism only because his heirs, his daughters Mary and Anne, had remained Anglican. Then in 1688 James's wife bore a son, who would be raised—and might someday reign—as a Catholic. Aghast at the thought of a Catholic monarchy, some English politicians asked Mary and her husband, William of Orange (the Dutch Republic's leader) to intervene. When William and Mary led a small army to England in November 1688, most royal troops defected to them, and James II fled to France.

This bloodless revolution of 1688, also called the Glorious Revolution, created a "limited monarchy" as defined by England's Bill of Rights of 1689. The crown promised to summon Parliament annually, sign all its bills, and respect traditional civil liberties. The Glorious Revolution's vindication of limited representative government burned deeply into the English political consciousness, and Anglo-Americans never forgot it. Anglo-Americans not only came to share English

King William and Queen Mary
This plate, made in England in about 1700, depicts the monarchs who assumed the throne after the Glorious Revolution.

Protestants' pride in the Glorious Revolution but also struck their own blows for liberty. Soon Massachusetts, New York, and Maryland all rose up against local representatives of the Stuart regime.

News that England's Protestant leaders had risen up against James II electrified New Englanders. On April 18, well before confirmation of the English revolt's success, Boston's militia arrested Andros and his councilors. (The governor tried to flee in women's clothing but was caught after an alert guard spotted a "lady" in army boots.) The "sensible Gentlemen" of Massachusetts—the old political leaders—acted in the name of William and Mary, risking their necks should James return to power in England. Massachusetts and every other New England colony swiftly resumed self-government.

William and Mary would have preferred continuing the Dominion, but in the face of single-minded colonial determination to break it up, they wisely desisted. They gave official consent to dismantling the Dominion and restored to the citizens of Connecticut and Rhode Island the right of electing their own governors. However, they kept Massachusetts a royal colony, and, though allowing the province to absorb Plymouth and Maine, refused to let it regain New Hampshire.

In other respects, too, Massachusetts won only a partial victory. Despite Increase Mather's lobbying in London, the new royal charter of 1691 reserved to the crown the right of appointing the governor. Moreover, property ownership, not church membership, became the criterion for voting. Worst of all, the Puritan colony had to tolerate Anglicans, who were proliferating in the port towns. In a society trembling at divine displeasure over its ungodliness (see Chapter 3), this was indeed bitter medicine to swallow.

New York's counterpart of the anti-Stuart uprising was Leisler's Rebellion. Emboldened by news of Boston's April 18 coup and startled by rumors that Andros's deputy Nicholson had threatened to burn New York, the city's militia—consisting mainly of Dutch and other non-English artisans and shopkeepers—seized the harbor's main fort on May 31, 1689. With his authority strangled, Nicholson sailed for England. Captain Jacob Leisler of the militia took over command of the colony, repaired its run-down defenses, and called elections for an assembly. When English troops arrived at New York in 1691 and Leisler denied them entry to key forts for fear that their commander was loyal to James II, a skirmish resulted, and Leisler was arrested.

"Hott brain'd" Leisler unwittingly had set his own downfall in motion. He had jailed many elite New Yorkers for questioning his authority, only to find that his former enemies had gained the new governor's ear and persuaded him to charge Leisler with treason for firing on royal troops. In the face of popular outrage, a packed jury found Leisler and his son-in-law, Jacob Milborne, guilty. Both men went to the gallows insisting that they were dying "for the king and queen and the Protestant religion."

Quickly wresting control of the council and legal system, Leisler's enemies used the courts to plunder their opponents' estates. Their rampage ceased in 1695, when Parliament reversed Leisler's and Milborne's convictions and ordered them reburied with full honors. Leislerians and their opponents fought ruthlessly to defeat each other; but not until most of their leaders had died, in about 1720, did Jacob Leisler's vengeful ghost cease stalking New York.

News of England's Glorious Revolution heartened Maryland's Protestant majority, which had long chafed under Catholic rule. Hoping to prevent a repetition of religion-tinged uprisings that had flared in 1676 and 1681, Lord Baltimore sent a messenger from England in early 1689 to command Maryland's obedience to William and Mary. But the courier died en route. The colony's Protestants widely began to fear that their proprietor was a traitor who supported James II.

Soon John Coode, a leader of the 1681 revolt, and three others organized the Protestant Association to secure Maryland for William and Mary. These conspirators seem to have been motivated far more by their exclusion from high public office than by religion, for three of the four had Catholic wives. Coode's group seized the capital in July 1689, removed all Catholics from office, and requested that the crown take over the colony. They got their wish. Maryland became a royal province in 1691, and in 1692 it made the Church of England the established religion. Catholics, who composed less than one-fourth of the population, lost the right to vote and thereafter could worship only in private. Maryland stayed in royal hands until 1715, when the fourth Lord Baltimore joined the Church of England and regained his proprietorship.

The revolutionary events of 1688–1689 decisively changed the colonies' political climate by reestablishing legislative government and ensuring religious freedom for Protestants. Dismantling the Dominion of New England and directing governors to call annual assemblies, William and Mary allowed colonial elites to reassert control over local affairs and encouraged American political leaders to identify their interests with England. A foundation was thus laid for an empire based on voluntary allegiance rather than submission to raw power imposed from faraway London. The crowning of William and Mary opened a new era in which Americans drew rising confidence from their relationship to the English throne. "As long as they reign," wrote a Bostonian who helped topple Andros, "New England is secure."

A Generation of War

The Revolution of 1688 ushered in a quarter-century of warfare that convulsed both Europe and the colonies. In 1689 England joined a general European coalition against France's Louis XIV, who supported James II's claim to the English crown. The resulting War of the League of Augsburg (which Anglo-Americans called King William's War) was the first struggle to embroil the colonies in European rivalries.

With the outbreak of King William's War, New Yorkers and Yankees launched a two-pronged invasion of Canada (New France) in 1690, with one prong aimed at Montreal and the second at Quebec. Lack of supplies caused the Anglo-American expedition marching on Montreal to disintegrate in the New York wilderness. Meanwhile, their strength sapped by smallpox, half-rations, and insufficient ammunition, two thousand Massachusetts militiamen eventually abandoned a lengthy siege of Quebec. The war then took the form of cruel but inconclusive border raids against civilians on both sides, carried out by English and French troops and their Indian allies.

Already weary from a new wave of wars with pro-French Indians in the Ohio Valley, the Five Nations of the Iroquois bore the bloodiest fighting in King William's War. Standing almost alone against their foes, the Five Nations faced overwhelming odds. Not only did their English allies meet with little success intercepting enemy war parties, but the French had enlisted virtually all other Indians from Maine to the Great Lakes as combatants. In 1691 every Mohawk and Oneida war chief died in battle; by 1696 French armies had destroyed the villages of every Iroquois nation but the Cayugas and Oneidas.

Although the Anglo-French war ended in 1697, the Iroquois staggered under Algonquian invasions until 1700. By then one-quarter of the Five Nations' 2,000 warriors had been killed or taken prisoner, or had fled to Canada. The total Iroquois population declined 20 percent over twelve years, from 8,600 to 7,000. (By comparison, fewer than 900 English and Dutch, and perhaps no more than 400 French, died during the same period.)

By 1700 Iroquois society was divided into three factions—pro-English, pro-French, and neutralists. Under the impact of war, the neutralists succeeded in defining a new direction for Iroquois diplomacy. In the "Grand Settlement" of 1701, the Five Nations of the Iroquois made peace with France and its Indian allies in exchange for access to western furs while redefining their British alliance to exclude military cooperation. Skillful negotiations brought the exhausted Iroquois far more success than had war by allowing them to keep control of their lands, rebuild their decimated population, and gain recognition as holding the balance of power in the Northeast.

In 1702 European war again erupted when England fought France and Spain in the War of the Spanish Succession, called Queen Anne's War by England's American colonists. This conflict taught Anglo-Americans painful lessons about their military weakness. French and Indian raiders from Canada destroyed several towns in Massachusetts and Maine. The Spanish invaded southern Carolina and nearly took Charles

Town in 1706. Enemy warships captured many colonial vessels and landed looting parties along the Atlantic coast. Colonial sieges of Quebec and St. Augustine ended as expensive failures.

English forces had more success than those of the colonies, seizing the Hudson Bay region, as well as Newfoundland and Acadia (henceforth called Nova Scotia). Although Britain kept these gains in the peace of 1713, the French and Indian hold on the continent's interior remained unbroken.

The most important consequence of the colonial wars for Anglo-Americans was political, not military. The wars instilled in them a profound sense of dependence on Great Britain. The clashes with France vividly reminded Americans of the loyalty they owed William and Mary for ousting James II, who the colonists believed would have persecuted Protestants and ruled despotically. Anglo-Americans also came to recognize their own military weakness and the extent to which their shipping needed the Royal Navy's protection. Even as a new generation of English colonists matured, war was thus reinforcing their sense of British identity by buttressing their loyalty to the crown.

A MATURING COLONIAL ECONOMY AND SOCIETY

Britons who visited mid-eighteenth-century America were generally impressed at the sight of a sophisticated society and widespread economic prosperity. "The nobleness of the town," wrote an English naval officer after first viewing New York in 1756, "surprized me more than the fertile appearance of the country. I had no idea of finding a place in America, consisting of near 2,000 houses, elegantly built of brick, raised on an eminence and the streets paved and spacious, . . . but such is this city that very few in England can rival it in its show." Seven years later, when issuing orders for demobilizing royal troops stationed in the colonies, General Jeffrey Amherst advised his regimental commanders to discourage their men from returning to the British Isles to be mustered out because "I would much rather they would take their Discharges in this country, where they can get their Livelyhood by working Easier than at Home."

The prosperity and social development that European visitors recorded, as well as the underlying rapid population growth and wide expansion of frontier settlement, were relatively new. By 1750 the colonies' brisk economic growth had been underway for fifty to seventy-five years, depending on the region. Throughout the first half of the eighteenth century, colonial exports climbed steadily and allowed Anglo-Americans to enjoy a relatively high standard of living because of protections established by Parliament.

British Economic Policy Toward America

Between 1651 and 1733, Parliament enacted a series of laws governing commerce between the British Isles and the overseas colonies. Historians label the rules of trade set forth in these laws the "navigation system," and they use the word *mercantilism* to describe the assumptions on which these laws rested. Both the navigation system and mercantilist thinking remained vigorously alive from the late seventeenth to the late eighteenth century, and they deeply affected North America's relationship with Great Britain.

Mercantilism was not a carefully elaborated economic theory. Rather, the word refers to European policy makers' aim of guaranteeing prosperity by making their own country as self-sufficient as possible—by eliminating dependence on foreign suppliers, damaging foreign competitors' commercial interests, and increasing their nation's net stock of gold and silver by selling more abroad than they bought. Mercantilist policies generally had the additional effect of favoring special interests such as chartered companies and merchants' guilds. Mercantilism was the antithesis of a competitive free-market system, which received its first great theoretical defense in Scottish economist Adam Smith's *The Wealth of Nations,* published in 1776. Until that revolutionary year, mercantilist thinking would dominate British economic policy almost unchallenged.

Parliament enacted England's first Navigation Act in 1651 to undercut the Dutch Republic's economic preponderance. Dutch shippers and merchants then controlled oceanic trade and probably owned three-quarters of northern Europe's commercial vessels; few English could compete with the well-financed and experienced Dutch traders. By the Navigation Acts, Parliament sought to exclude the Dutch from English trade and thereby to force England to build up its own merchant marine. Immediately after the Stuart restoration in 1660, Parliament reiterated these rules and also began protecting English manufactures from foreign competition. By 1750 a long series of Navigation Acts were in force, affecting the colonial economy in four major ways.

First, the laws limited all imperial trade to *British* ships, defined as those with British ownership and whose crews were three-quarters British. For purposes of this legislation, Parliament classified all colonists, including slaves, as British. When Parliament began strictly to enforce this requirement in the late seventeenth century, American colonists and some elements of the English business community alike objected, because the Dutch offered better prices, credit, and merchandise. After 1700, however, when Britain's merchant marine became equal to its Dutch competitors, this cause for complaint evaporated.

This new shipping restriction not only contributed to Great Britain's rise as Europe's foremost shipping nation but also laid the foundations for an American merchant marine. By the 1750s one-third of all imperial vessels were American-owned, mostly by merchants in New England and the middle colonies. The swift growth of this merchant marine diversified the northern colonial economy and made it more self-sufficient. The expansion of colonial shipping in turn hastened urbanization by creating a need for centralized docks, warehouses, and repair shops in America. By 1770 Philadelphia was the British Empire's second-largest port, after London, and New York City was not far behind. Shipbuilding emerged as a major colonial industry in these years, and by 1770 one-third of the "British" merchant marine was actually American-built.

The second major way in which the Navigation Acts affected the colonies lay in their barring the export of certain "enumerated goods" to foreign nations unless these items first passed through England or Scotland. The mainland's chief "controlled" items were tobacco, rice, furs, indigo (a Carolina plant that produced a blue dye), and naval stores (masts, hemp, tar, and turpentine). Parliament never restricted grain, livestock, fish, lumber, or rum, which altogether made up 60 percent of colonial exports. Furthermore, American exporters of tobacco and rice—the chief commodities affected by enumeration—had their burdens reduced by two significant concessions. First, Parliament gave Americans a monopoly over the British market by excluding foreign tobacco, even though this hurt the British consumers. (Rice planters enjoyed a natural monopoly because they had no competitors.) Second, Parliament tried to minimize the added cost of landing tobacco and rice in Britain (where customs officials collected duties on both) by refunding these duties on all tobacco and rice that the colonists later shipped to other countries. About 85 percent of all American tobacco and rice was eventually reexported and sold outside the British Empire.

The navigation system's third impact on the colonies was to encourage economic diversification in America. Parliament used British tax money to pay modest bounties to Americans producing such items as silk, iron, dyes, hemp, and lumber, which Britain would otherwise have had to import from other countries, and it raised the price of commercial rivals' imports by imposing protective tariffs on them.

On the surface, the trade laws' fourth consequence for the colonies was negative: they forbade Americans from competing with British manufacturers. In practice, however, this prohibition had little effect, for it banned only *large-scale* manufacturing of certain products, most notably clothing; colonial tailors, hatters, and housewives could continue to make any item of dress in their households or small shops. Manufactured by low-paid labor, British clothing imports to America generally undersold whatever the colonists could have produced at their higher labor costs. For this reason, Americans failed to establish a profitable clothing industry until after 1820. The colonists were free to produce iron, however, and by 1770 they had built 250 ironworks employing thirty thousand men, a work force larger than the entire population of Georgia or of any provincial city. At the American Iron Company's complex of eleven forges and furnaces near Ringwood, New Jersey, five hundred workers manned eleven furnaces that annually consumed eight square miles of timber as fuel. By 1770 British North America produced more iron than England and Wales, and only Sweden and Russia exceeded the colonies' output.

Colonial complaints against the navigation system raged in the late seventeenth century but rarely were heard after 1700. The trade regulation primarily burdened tobacco and rice exporters, whose income nevertheless was reduced by less than 3 percent. The commercial laws did increase the cost of non-British merchandise imported into the colonies, but seldom by enough to encourage smuggling (except in the case of tea from India and molasses from the French Caribbean). Anglo-American commerce provided mu-

tual advantages for Britain and its colonies, and when Americans lost their trading rights in 1783, their commerce declined greatly. Although Parliament intended the laws to benefit only Britain, the navigation system had far from crippled the provincial economy. Rather, British North America's economy grew at a per capita rate of 0.6 percent annually from 1650 to 1770, a pace twice that of Britain.

A Burgeoning, Diversifying Population

In 1751 Pennsylvania businessman, publicist, and scientist Benjamin Franklin (1706–1790) wrote in an essay, *Observations Concerning the Increase of Mankind and the Peopling of the Colonies*, that "people increase in proportion to the number of marriages, and that is greater in proportion to the ease and convenience of supporting a family. When families can be easily supported, more persons marry, and earlier in life." Cities, he noted, retarded such growth: they were unhealthy and contained many people too poor to marry and rear families. But British America, with its small cities and great expanses of rural space, clearly seemed destined to grow and flourish. Estimating the colonies' population at 1 million, Franklin calculated that this number would double every twenty-five years. He exulted, "What an accession of power to the British empire!" Franklin knew whereof he spoke: he was the tenth child among seventeen siblings. He estimated colonial growth trends with amazing precision, and modern research has confirmed his reasoning about the factors driving population change in his era.

After 1700, when life expectancy and family size in the South rose to levels typical of the North, British North America's growth rate far outpaced Great Britain's. Colonial women had an average of eight children and forty-two grandchildren; British women at the time typically bore five infants and had fifteen grandchildren. The ratio of England's population to that of the mainland colonies plummeted from 20 to 1 (1700) to 3 to 1 (1775).

Fully half of all colonial women bore more than eight children. This exceptionally high birthrate produced families like that of New Jersey resident Daniel Robbins, described in the *New England Weekly Journal* in 1733. By the time Robbins was 66, his wife had 13 children, of whom 11 had married and borne 62 offspring of their own. None of the Robbins's descendants had yet died, and more grandchildren were on the way. "Thus it appears," the *Weekly Journal* declared, "that said Daniel Robbins has successfully kept and fulfilled that great and necessary Commandment of *Multiply, be Fruitful,* and *Replenish the Earth.*" Such remarkable fertility was responsible for two-thirds of colonial population growth after 1700.

In the eighteenth century, immigration continued to contribute significantly to colonial population growth, although it became less important than natural increase. In the forty years after Queen Anne's War, the colonies absorbed 350,000 newcomers, 40 percent of them (140,000) African-born slaves who had survived a sea crossing of sickening brutality. All but a few enslaved immigrants originated along the west coast of Africa between Senegambia and Angola. Whereas most planters made few distinctions as to Africans' backgrounds, many in South Carolina expressly sought slaves from Gambia and nearby regions for their rice-growing experience.

Conditions aboard slave ships were appalling by any standard. Olaudah Equiano was an enslaved Ibo from the area that today is Nigeria. Equiano, who eventually became free, Christian, and an abolitionist, recalled being put aboard a Barbados-bound ship in 1756:

> *I was soon put down under the decks, and there I received such salutation in my nostrils as I had never experienced in my life; so that, with the loathsomeness of the stench, and crying together, I became so sick and low that I was not able to eat, nor had I the least desire to taste any thing. . . . On my refusing to eat, one of them [white men] held me fast by the hands, and laid me across I think the windlass while the other flogged me severely. . . . Could I have got over the nettings, I would have jumped over the side, but I could not.*

The approximately 210,000 whites who immigrated during these years included a sharply reduced share from England compared to the seventeenth century. Whereas between 1630 and 1700 an average

Architect's Plan of a Slave Ship
This plan graphically depicts the crowded, unsanitary conditions under which slaves were transported across the Atlantic.

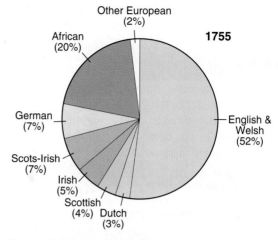

Distribution of Non-Indian Nationalities Within the British Mainland Colonies, 1700–1755

The impact of heavy immigration from 1720 to 1755 can be seen in the reduction of the English and Welsh stock from four-fifths of all colonists to a slight majority; in the doubling of the African-American population; and in the sudden influx of Germans and Irish, who together composed a fifth of all Anglo-Americans by 1755. For a more detailed breakdown of African origins, see the map on page 109.

SOURCE: Thomas L. Purvis, "The European Ancestry of the United States Population," *William & Mary Quarterly,* LXI (1984): 85–101.

of 2,000 English settlers landed annually (constituting 90 percent of all European immigrants), after 1713 the English contribution dropped to about 500 a year. Rising employment and higher wages in eighteenth-century England simply made voluntary immigration to America far less attractive than before. But economic hardship elsewhere in the British Isles and northern Europe supplied a steady stream of immigrants, and their coming ensured that white North Americans were growing more ethnically diverse.

The largest European contingent comprised 100,000 newcomers from Ireland, two-thirds of them "Scots-Irish" descendants of sixteenth-century Scottish Presbyterians who had settled in northern Ireland. After 1718 Scots-Irish fled to America to escape rack renting (frequent increases in farm rents), and they commonly came as complete families. In contrast, 90 percent of all Catholic Irish immigrants arrived as unmarried male indentured servants. Rarely able to find Catholic wives, they generally abandoned their faith to marry Protestant women.

Meanwhile, from Germany came a wave of 65,000 settlers, most of them refugees from terrible economic conditions in the Rhine Valley. Wartime devastation had compounded the misery of Rhenish peasants, many of whom were squeezed onto plots of land too small to feed a family. One-third of these people financed their voyage as "redemptioners"—that is, they had sold themselves or their children as indentured servants.

Most Germans were either Lutherans or Calvinists. But a significant minority belonged to small, pacifist religious sects that desired above all to be left alone.

Overwhelmingly, the eighteenth-century immigrants were poor. Those who became indentured servants had to give one to four years of work to an urban or rural master, who might well exploit them cruelly. Servants could be sold or rented out, beaten, granted minimal legal protection, kept from marrying, and sexually harassed; and attempted escape usually meant an extension of their service. But at the end of their term, most managed to collect "freedom dues," which could help them to marry and acquire land.

Few immigrants settled permanently in those parts of North America where land was relatively scarce and expensive—New England, New Jersey, lower New York, and the southern tidewater. New Englanders in particular did not welcome people who might become public charges: "these confounded Irish will eat us all up," snorted one Bostonian. Philadelphia became the immigrants' primary port of entry. So many foreigners went to Pennsylvania that by 1755 the English accounted for only one-third of that colony's population; the rest were mostly Germans, and Scots-Irish.

Rising numbers of immigrants also traveled to the piedmont region, stretching along the eastern slope of the Appalachians. A significant German community developed in upper New York, and thousands of other

Immigration and Frontier Expansion, to 1755
A sharp rise in the importance of African slaves made much of the southern tidewater a predominantly black region. Immigrants from Germany, Ireland, and Scotland tended to settle in the piedmont. A significant Jewish population emerged in the seaports.

Germans as well as Scots-Irish fanned southward from Pennsylvania into western Maryland. Many more from Germany and Ireland arrived in the second-most-popular gateway to eighteenth-century America, Charles Town, whence they moved on to settle the Carolina piedmont. There they raised grain, livestock, and to-

bacco, generally without slaves. After 1750 both streams of immigration merged with an outpouring of Anglo-Americans from the Chesapeake in the rolling, fertile hills of western North Carolina. In 1713 few Anglo-Americans had lived more than fifty miles from the sea, but by 1750 one-third of all colonists resided in the piedmont.

English-descended colonists did not relish the influx of so many foreigners. Franklin spoke for many when he asked in his 1751 essay on population,

> *why should the Palatine boors [Germans] be suffered to swarm into our settlements, and, by herding together, establish their language and manners, to the exclusion of ours? Why should Pennsylvania, founded by the English, become a colony of aliens, who will shortly be so numerous as to Germanize us instead of us Anglicizing them, and will never adopt our language or customs any more than they can acquire our complexion?*

In the same ungenerous spirit, Franklin objected to the slave trade largely because it would increase America's black population at the expense of industrious whites.

On another occasion, Franklin suggested that the colonists send rattlesnakes to Britain in return for the convict laborers dumped on American shores. Deportation of lawbreakers to America had been common enough in the seventeenth century, and between 1718 and 1783, some thirty thousand convicts arrived. A few were murderers; most were thieves; some were guilty of the most trivial offenses, like a young Londoner who "got intoxicated with liquor, and in that condition attempted to snatch a handkerchief from the body of a person in the street to him unknown. . . ." Convicts were sold as servants on arrival. Relatively few continued to commit crimes in America, and some managed eventually to establish themselves as backcountry farmers. But like many contemporary Americans, colonists seldom wished to absorb the victims of other nations' social problems.

Eighteenth-Century Living Standards

Propelled by a tenfold increase in the volume of exports, colonial living standards in general rose dramatically in the years from 1700 to 1770. Nowhere was Americans' newfound prosperity more evident than in the Chesapeake, which in the late seventeenth century had been a region of impoverished tenants battered by depressed tobacco prices. Not only did tobacco exports triple from 1713 to 1774, but prices slowly crept upward, in large part owing to a 75 percent reduction in marketing costs. The Chesapeake economy further benefited from sharply higher exports of wheat and corn, which by 1770 equaled 25 percent of tobacco sales. Thus within three generations of Bacon's Rebellion, the Chesapeake had ceased to be a region locked in pervasive poverty.

Poverty was the lot mainly of slaves and of a small underclass of whites attempting to farm marginal-quality soil. At the same time, a landholding small-planter element arose, so large that perhaps 30 percent of all white families owned slaves. Atop Chesapeake society, moreover, an elite of wealthy large landowners and slavemasters flourished after about 1700.

Living standards were highest in the mid-Atlantic, spanning the area from New York south to Delaware. In 1770 per capita wealth here exceeded the colonial average by 40 percent. These colonies' striking prosperity owed much to rich soils, a long-term climatic warming that lengthened the growing season after 1700, and brisk demand for livestock, wheat, and corn in the West Indies and (to a lesser extent) southern Europe.

Of all colonial regions, New England prospered least. Though hardly poor, Yankees were on average only half as wealthy as colonists elsewhere. Plagued by mediocre soil and a short growing season, New Englanders had to import grain to feed themselves. Yankees sent two-thirds of their livestock, lumber, and fish exports to the West Indies, and although their cattle raising remained profitable, a long-term decline in lumber prices stung the local economy. By the 1750s most New England towns had become overpopulated, bursting with more young men than could acquire enough land to support a family. In subsequent decades only migration to the frontier—to Vermont, Maine, Nova Scotia, Pennsylvania, and upper New York—would ease the pressure.

Many New Englanders survived economically by turning to the sea. By 1700 the Yankee merchant marine and fishing industry were the largest in the colonies, providing employment for every seventh man. This prosperity came at a heavy cost, however, for the sea was cruel and took perhaps every fifth sailor to a watery grave. For this reason, the balcony on a ship captain's home from which his wife could watch for her husband's return to harbor became known as the widow's walk.

Taken as a whole, the American colonies by the mid-eighteenth century enjoyed a standard of living that greatly exceeded that of Scotland or Ireland and approximated that of England and Wales. Steady overseas demand for colonial products spawned a prosperity that enabled Americans to consume a huge volume of British products. Consequently, the share of British exports sold to the colonies spurted from just 5 percent in 1700 to almost 40 percent by 1760. "You may depend upon it," remarked Pennsylvania judge William Allen in commenting on prospects for self-improvement, "this is one of the best poor man's countries in the world."

Rural Men and Women

Although the benefits of rising living standards were widespread, the colonial population enjoyed these advantages unevenly. With few exceptions—Benjamin Franklin is the best known—true affluence was reserved for those born wealthy. For the rest, personal success was limited and came only through hard work, if at all.

Because the vast majority of landowners had just enough acreage for a working farm, they could not provide their children with land of their own when they married. Moreover, since couples typically started having children in their mid-20s, had their last babies sometime after 40, and lived past 60, all but their youngest children would be approaching middle age before receiving any inheritance. Even children who obtained inheritances before turning 30 rarely got more than a sixth or seventh of their parents' estate, because most families wrote wills that divided property evenly—or almost so—among all daughters and sons. A young male had to build savings to buy farm equipment by working (from about age 16 to 23) as a field hand for his father or neighbors. Because mortgages usually required down payments of 33 percent, a young husband normally supported his growing family by renting a farm from the local gentry until his early or mid-30s.

Landownership came quickest to those farmers who could find seasonal or part-time work. Some learned a craft like carpentry that earned money year-round. Many more trapped furs, gathered honey and beeswax, or made cider, shingles, turpentine, or wampum. Whenever possible, farmers found wintertime jobs draining meadows, clearing fields, or fencing

Women's Work

Rural women were responsible for most household and garden tasks. This print, dating to 1780, shows young women tending onions in Wethersfield, Connecticut.

land for wealthier landowners who did not own slaves or indentured servants. Such nonagricultural work might gain an industrious farmer half again of his total income from selling crops and livestock.

Families worked off mortgages slowly because the long-term cash income from a farm (6 percent) about equaled the interest on borrowed money (5–8 percent). After making a down payment of one-third, a husband and wife generally satisfied the next third upon inheriting shares of their deceased parents' estates. They paid off the final third when their children reached their teens and the family could thus expand farm output with two or three full-time workers. Only by their late 50s, just as their youngest offspring got ready to leave home, could most colonial parents hope to free themselves of debt.

In general, the more isolated a community or the less productive its farmland, the more self-sufficiency

and bartering its people practiced, although only the remotest settlements were completely self-sufficient. Almost all rural families depended heavily on wives' and daughters' production. Women contributed to their household's financial success by manufacturing items that the family would otherwise have had to purchase. Besides cooking, cleaning, and washing, wives preserved food, boiled soap, made clothing, and tended the garden, dairy, orchard, poultry house, and pigsty. Women often sold dairy products to neighbors or export merchants, spun yarn into cloth for tailors, knitted various garments for sale, and even vended their own hair for wigs. A farm family's ability to feed itself and its animals was worth about half of its cash income (a luxury that few European tenants had), and women did no less than men in meeting this end.

Legally, however, colonial American women found themselves constrained (see Chapter 3). A woman's single most autonomous decision was her choice of a husband. Once married, she lost control of her dowry (unless she was a New Yorker subject to old Dutch custom, which allowed her somewhat more authority). Still, widows controlled between 8 and 10 percent of all property in eighteenth-century Anglo-America, and some—among them Eliza Pinckney of South Carolina, a prominent political leader and the mother of two Revolutionary-era leaders—owned and managed several large estates.

Colonial Farmers and the Environment

The rapid expansion of English settlement hastened the transformation of the environment east of the Appalachians. Whereas the earliest colonists farmed land already cleared and cultivated by Native Americans, eighteenth-century settlers usually first had to remove trees from their plots. Despite the labor involved, farmers and planters, especially those using slave labor, preferred the most heavily forested areas, where the soil was most fertile. In New England farmers also had to clear innumerable heavy rocks—debris from the last Ice Age—with which they then built walls around their fields. And colonists everywhere used timber to construct their houses, barns, and fences and to provide fuel for heating and cooking. Farmers and planters also sold firewood to the inhabitants of colonial cities and towns. Only six years after Georgia's founding, a colonist noted that there was "no more firewood in Savannah; . . . it must be bought from the plantations for which reason firewood is already right expensive."

In removing the trees (deforestation), farmers drove away bears, panthers, wild turkeys, and other forest animals while attracting grass- and seed-eating rabbits, mice, and possums. By removing protection from winds and, in summer, from the sun, deforestation also produced warmer summers and colder winters, so that it actually reinforced the demand for wood as fuel. By hastening the runoff of spring waters, it led both to heavier flooding and drier streambeds in most areas and, where water could not escape, to more extensive swamps. In turn, less stable temperatures and water levels, along with impediments created by mills and by the floating of timbers downstream, rapidly reduced the number of fish in colonial waters. Writing in 1766, naturalist John Bartram noted that fish "abounded formerly when the Indians lived much on them & was very numerous," but that "now there is not the 100th or perhaps the 1000th [portion of] fish to be found."

Deforestation dried and hardened the soil, but colonists' crops had even more drastic effects. Native Americans, recognizing the soil-depleting effects of intensive cultivation, rotated their crops regularly so that fields could lie fallow (unplanted) and thereby be replenished with vital nutrients. But many colonial farmers either did not have enough land to leave some unplanted or were unwilling to sacrifice short-term profits for possible long-term benefits. As early as 1637, one New England farmer discovered that his soil "after five or six years [of planting corn] grows barren beyond belief and puts on the face of winter in the time of summer." Chesapeake planters' tobacco yields declined after only three or four years in the same plot. Like farmers elsewhere, they used animal manure to fertilize their food crops but not their tobacco, fearing that manure would spoil the taste for consumers. As Chesapeake tobacco growers moved inland to hillier areas, away from rivers and streams, they also contributed to increased soil erosion. By 1750, to remain productive, many Chesapeake farmers were shifting their crop from tobacco to wheat.

Because they confronted a more serious shortage of land and resources, well-to-do Europeans were already turning their attention to conservation and "scientific" farming. But most colonists ignored such techniques, either because they could not afford to implement them or because they believed that American land, including that still held by Indians, would sustain them and future generations indefinitely.

The Urban Paradox

The cities were colonial America's economic paradox. They shipped the livestock, grain, and lumber that enriched the countryside but were caught in a downward spiral of declining opportunity.

After 1740 economic success proved ever more elusive for the 4 percent of colonists who lived in cities. Poverty escalated rapidly in the three major seaports of Philadelphia, New York, and Boston. Debilitating ocean voyages left many immigrants too weak to work, and every incoming ship from Europe carried numerous widows and orphans. Moreover, the cities' poor rolls always bulged with the survivors of mariners lost at sea, as well as with unskilled, landless men, women (often widowed), and children from the countryside. High population density and poor sanitation in urban locales allowed contagious diseases to run rampant, so that half of all city children died before age twenty-one and urban adults lived ten years less on average than country folk.

Even the able-bodied found cities economically treacherous. Early-eighteenth-century urban artisans typically trained apprentices and employed them as journeymen for many years until the latter opened their own shops. After 1750, however, more and more employers kept their labor force only as long as business was brisk, and released workers when sales slowed; in 1751 a shrewd Benjamin Franklin recommended this practice as an intelligent way to use expensive labor. Recessions hit more frequently after 1720 and created longer spells of unemployment. As urban populations ballooned, wages correspondingly tended to shrink, and the cost of rents, food, and firewood shot up.

Urban poverty grew from insignificance before 1700 into a major problem in the mid-eighteenth century. By 1730 Boston could no longer shelter its destitute in the almshouse built in 1685, and by 1741 the town had declared every sixth citizen too poor to pay taxes. Not until 1736 did New York need a poorhouse (for just forty people), but by 1772, 4 percent of its residents (over eight hundred people) required public assistance to survive. The number of Philadelphia families listed as poor on tax rolls jumped from 3 percent in 1720 to 11 percent by 1760.

Wealth, on the other hand, remained highly concentrated in eighteenth-century colonial cities. For example, New York's wealthiest 10 percent owned about 45 percent of the property throughout the eighteenth century. Similar patterns existed in Boston and Philadelphia. Set alongside the growth of a poor underclass in these cities, such statistics underscored the polarization of status and wealth in urban America on the eve of the Revolution.

Economic frustration disposed townspeople to turn to violence to defend their interests. Before 1710 few serious disorders disrupted Boston, but between that year and 1750, the city experienced five major riots, aimed at closing a public market operated by wealthy merchants, stopping the navy from drafting sailors, or halting wartime profiteering. However, colonists used force only as a last resort to curb public nuisances. They usually achieved their goals through intimidation or property damage, after which they disbanded and let the law resume its course.

Most southern cities were little more than large towns. Charles Town, however, became North America's fourth-largest city. South Carolina's capital offered gracious living to the wealthy planters who flocked to their townhouses during the months of worst heat and insect infestation on their plantations. But shanties on the city's outskirts sheltered a growing crowd of destitute whites. The colony encouraged whites to immigrate in hopes of reducing blacks' numerical preponderance, but some European newcomers could not reach frontier farms or find any work except as ill-paid roustabouts. Like their counterparts in northern port cities, Charles Town's poor whites competed for work with urban slaves whose masters rented out their labor, and racial tensions simmered.

Although middle-class women in cities and large towns performed somewhat less manual drudgery than their country cousins, they nonetheless managed complex households that often included servants, slaves, apprentices, and other nonfamily members. While raising poultry and vegetables as well as sewing and knitting, urban wives purchased their cloth and most of their food in daily trips to public markets. Many had one or more household servants, usually young single women or widows, to help with cooking, cleaning, and laundering—tasks that required more attention than in the country because of higher urban standards of cleanliness and appearance. Wives also worked in family businesses located (unlike in modern times) in owners' homes.

Less affluent wives and widows housed boarders rather than servants, and many spun and wove cloth in their homes for local merchants. But especially in Boston, where conditions were the grimmest, many widows with children had to look to the community for relief. Whereas their Puritan forebears had deemed it one's Christian duty to care for poor dependents, affluent Bostonians turned an increasingly wary eye toward the needy. Preaching in 1752, the city's leading minister, Charles Chauncy, lamented "the Swarms of Children, of both Sexes, that are continually strolling and playing about the Streets of our Metropolis, cloathed in Rags, and brought up in Idleness and Ignorance," and another clergyman warned that charity for widows and their children was money "worse than Lost."

Slavery's Wages

From 1713 to 1754, five times as many slaves poured onto mainland North America as in all the preceding years. The proportion of blacks in the colonies doubled, rising from 11 percent at the beginning of the century to 20 percent by midcentury. Slavery was primarily a southern institution, but 15 percent of its victims lived north of Maryland, mostly in New York and New Jersey. By 1750 every seventh New Yorker was a slave.

Because West Indian and Brazilian slave buyers outbid the mainland colonists, a mere 5 percent of transported Africans were ever sold within the present-day United States. Unable to buy as many male field hands as they needed, mainland masters had no choice but to accept numerous female workers, and they protected their investments by maintaining the slaves' health. These factors promoted family formation and increased life expectancy far beyond the levels in the Caribbean, where family life was unstable and high death rates resulted from overwork and disease (see Chapter 3). On the mainland by 1750, the rate of natural increase for blacks almost equaled that for whites, and in some areas American-born slaves outnumbered those born in Africa.

For slaves, the economic progress achieved in colonial America by about 1750 meant primarily that masters could usually afford to keep them healthy. Rarely, however, did masters choose to make their human chattels comfortable. A visitor to a Virginia plantation from Poland (where most peasants lived in dire poverty) gave this impression of slaves' quality of life:

We entered some Negroes huts—for their habitations cannot be called houses. They are far more miserable than the poorest of the cottages of our peasants. The husband and wife sleep on a miserable bed, the children on the floor . . . a little kitchen furniture amid this misery . . . a teakettle and cups . . . five or six hens, each with ten or fifteen chickens, walked there. That is the only pleasure allowed to the negroes.

To maintain slaves, masters normally spent just 40 percent of the amount paid for the upkeep of indentured servants. Whereas white servants ate two hundred pounds of beef or pork yearly, most slaves consumed only fifty pounds of meat. The value of the beer and hard cider given to a typical servant alone equaled the expense of feeding and clothing the average slave. Masters usually provided adult slaves with eight quarts of corn and a pound of pork each week but expected them to grow their own vegetables, forage for wild fruits, and perhaps raise poultry.

Blacks as a Percentage of the Total Population in the British Colonies, 1650–1770

Wide differences developed in the racial composition of Britain's American colonies. By the mid-eighteenth century, the Caribbean sugar islands were almost 90 percent black, whereas the mainland colonies north of Maryland had become about 95 percent white. By 1750 slaves composed almost 40 percent of all mainland colonists south of Pennsylvania.

SOURCE: Robert W. Fogel and Stanley L. Engerman, *Time on the Cross* (Boston: Little, Brown, 1974), 21.

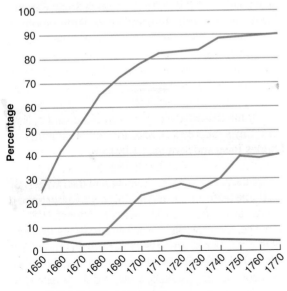

——— British Caribbean colonies
——— Southern British mainland colonies
——— Northern British mainland colonies

Slaves worked for a far longer portion of their lives than whites. Slave children went to the fields as part-time helpers soon after reaching seven years and began working full-time between eleven and fourteen. Whereas most white women worked in their homes, barns, and gardens, female slaves routinely tended tobacco or rice crops, even when pregnant, and often worked outdoors in winter. Most slaves toiled until they died, although those who survived to their sixties rarely performed hard labor.

The rigors of bondage did not, however, crush its victims' spirits. Slaves proved resourceful at maximizing opportunities within a harsh, confining system. For example, some slaves accumulated small amounts of property by establishing exclusive rights over their gardens and poultry, and a few sold food to their masters. In 1769, for example, Thomas Jefferson made several purchases like the following:

gave negro for watermelon	7 pence
paid Fanny for 6 chickens	2 shillings
paid Cato for 1 doz eggs	3 pence

House slaves widely insisted on being tipped by guests for shining shoes and stabling horses. They sometimes sought presents aggressively on holidays, as a startled New Jersey tutor on a Virginia plantation discovered in 1774 when slaves demanding gifts of cash roused him from bed early Christmas morning.

In the South Carolina and Georgia rice country, slaves working under the highly favorable task system had control of about half their waking hours. Under tasking, each slave spent some hours caring for a quarter-acre—usually a half-day—after which his or her duties ended. By 1750 this system permitted certain slaves to keep hogs and sell surplus vegetables in Charles Town. A remarkable but atypical slave named Sampson earned enough money in his off-hours to hire another to work his own task, and became free in 1728.

But the independence of South Carolina's slaves and the fact that they constituted a majority of the colony's population aroused planters' fears that they were losing control of "their" blacks. For example, a 1735 law, noting that many Africans wore "clothes much above the condition of slaves," imposed a dress code limiting slaves' apparel to fabrics worth less than ten shillings per yard and even prohibited their wearing the cast-off clothes of their owners. Of even greater concern were gatherings of large numbers of blacks uncontrolled by whites. In 1721 Charles Town enacted a 9:00 P.M. curfew for blacks, while South Carolina's

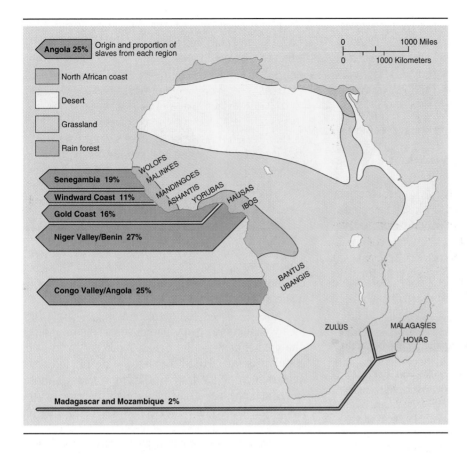

African Origins of North American Slaves, 1690–1807

Virtually all slaves brought to English North America came from West Africa, between Senegambia and Angola. Most were captured or bought inland and marched to the coast, where they were sold to African merchants who in turn sold them to European slave traders.

assembly placed all local slave patrols under the colonial militia. Slaves responded to the colony's vigilance and harsher punishments with increased instances of arson, theft, flight, and violence.

Tensions erupted in 1739 when South Carolina was rocked by a powerful slave uprising, the Stono Rebellion. It began when twenty slaves robbed guns and ammunition from a store twenty miles from Charles Town, at the Stono River Bridge. Marching under a makeshift flag and crying "Liberty!" they collected eighty men and headed for Spanish Florida, a well-known refuge for runaways (see "A Place in Time"). Along the way they burned seven plantations and killed twenty whites, but they spared a Scottish innkeeper who "was a good Man and kind to his slaves." Within a day mounted militia surrounded the slaves by a riverbank, cut them down mercilessly, and spiked a rebel head on every milepost between that spot and Charles Town. Disturbances elsewhere in the colony required more than a month to suppress, with insurgents generally "put to the most cruel Death." Thereafter white apprehension ran high, expressed in

a new slave code that would remain essentially in force until the Civil War. The code kept South Carolina slaves under constant surveillance. Furthermore, it threatened masters with fines for not disciplining slaves and required legislative approval for manumission (freeing of individual slaves). The Stono Rebellion thus speeded South Carolina's emergence as a rigid, racist, and fear-ridden society.

By midcentury slaves made up 20 percent of New York City's population and formed a majority in Charles Town and Savannah. City life offered slaves advantages, most notably the chance for those with skills to hire themselves out and keep part of their wages. By 1770 one-tenth of Savannah's slaves lived in rented rooms away from their owners. Though still in bondage, these blacks forced urban whites to allow them a substantial measure of personal freedom. But although city life afforded slaves greater freedom of association than the plantation did, it did not extend to them the opportunities being realized by their owners. In 1712 rebellious slaves in New York City killed nine whites in a calculated attack. As a result thirteen slaves

John Potter and His Family
*The Potters of Matunuck,
Rhode Island, relax at tea. In
commissioning a portrait depicting themselves at leisure
and attended by a black slave,
the Potters proclaimed their
elite status.*

were hanged, one was starved to death, three were burned at the stake, and one was broken on the wheel. Six others committed suicide to avoid similar tortures. In 1741 a wave of thefts and fires attributed to New York slaves led to the torture and hanging of thirteen slaves and four whites (alleged accomplices), the burning of an additional thirteen slaves, and the sale of seventy more to the West Indies.

The Rise of the Colonial Elites

"A man who has money here, no matter how he came by it, he is everything, and wanting [lacking] that he's a mere nothing, let his conduct be ever so irreproachable." Thus a Rhode Islander in 1748 described how colonial Americans defined high status. But once having achieved wealth, a man was expected by his contemporaries to behave with an appropriate degree of responsibility, to display dignity and generosity, and to be a community leader. His wife must be a skillful household manager and, in the presence of men, a refined yet deferring hostess. In short, they were to act like a "gentleman" and a "lady."*

Before 1700 the colonies' class structure was less readily apparent, because the rural elite's more limited resources were spent buying land, servants, or slaves instead of luxuries. In 1715 a traveler visiting one of Virginia's richest planters, Robert Beverley, noticed that his host owned "nothing in or about his house but just what is necessary, . . . [such as] good beds but no

---

*In the eighteenth century, the words *gentleman* and *lady* referred to individuals who not only conformed to socially accepted standards of behavior but also belonged to the upper class, or *gentry*.

curtains and instead of cane chairs he hath stools made of wood."

After 1720 well-to-do colonists began displaying their wealth more openly, particularly in their housing. The greater gentry—the richest 2 percent, who held about 15 percent of all property—constructed residences such as the Low House, New Jersey's most splendid home in 1741, and the Shirley mansion in Virginia. The lesser gentry, or second-wealthiest 2 to 10 percent, who held about 25 percent of all property, typically lived in a more modest fieldstone dwelling such as Pennsylvania's Lincoln homestead or a wood-frame house such as Whitehall in Rhode Island. In contrast, middle-class farmers commonly inhabited one-story wooden buildings with four small rooms and a loft.

Colonial gentlemen and ladies also exhibited their wealth after 1720 by living in imitation of the European "grand style." They wore costly English fashions, drove carriages instead of wagons, and bought expensive chinaware, books, furniture, and musical instruments. They pursued a gracious life by studying foreign languages, learning formal dances, and cultivating polite manners. In sports men's preference shifted to horse racing (on which they bet avidly) and away from cockfighting, a less elegant diversion. A few young colonial males even got an English education. By midcentury the elite's taste for consumer goods was spreading to the middle class and helping to fuel a "consumer revolution" in the British Empire.

For Chesapeake gentlemen, debt was a problem even if they lived virtuously. Tobacco planters were perpetually short of cash and in debt to British merchants who bought their crops and sold them imported goods on credit at high prices. Noted the Maryland assembly in 1697, "The trade of this province ebbs and flows according to the rise or fall of tobacco in the market of England." Planters could respond only in two ways. First, they could strive for as much self-sufficiency as possible on their estates—for example, by training their slaves to manufacture glass, bricks, tools, nails, and carriages. Second, they could diversify away from the region's tobacco monoculture (dependence on a single staple crop) by growing wheat or cutting timber. Self-sufficiency and diversification became more widely accepted objectives as the eighteenth century wore on, and after 1750 respected landowners like George Washington and Thomas Jefferson strongly advocated them.

Elites and Colonial Politics

Colonial gentlemen not only monopolized wealth but also dominated politics. Governors invariably appointed members of the greater gentry to sit on their councils and as judges on the highest courts. Most representatives elected to the legislatures' lower houses (assemblies) also ranked among the wealthiest 2 percent, as did majors and colonels in the militia. In contrast, members of the lesser gentry sat less often in the legislature, but they commonly served as justices of the peace on the county courts and as militia officers up to captain.

Colonial America's only high-ranking elected officeholders were the members of the legislature's lower house. But outside New England (where any voter could hold office), legal requirements barred 80 percent of white men from running for the assembly, most often by specifying that a candidate must own a minimum of a thousand acres. (Farms then averaged 180 acres in the South and 120 acres in the mid-Atlantic colonies.) Even had there been no such property qualifications, however, few ordinary citizens could have afforded the high costs of elective office. Assemblymen received only living expenses, which might not fully cover the cost of staying at their province's capital, much less compensate a farmer or an artisan for his absence from farm or shop for six to ten weeks a year. Even members of the gentry grumbled about legislative duty, many of them viewing high office as "a sort of tax on them to serve the public at their own Expense besides the neglect of their business," according to Governor Lewis Morris of New Jersey.

For these reasons, political leadership fell to certain wealthy families with a tradition of public service.

Nine families, for example, provided one-third of Virginia's royal councilors during the century after 1680. John Adams, a rising young Massachusetts politician, estimated that most towns in his colony chose their legislators from among just three or four families.

The colonies set liberal qualifications for male voters, but all provinces excluded women, blacks (free as well as slaves), and Indians from elections. In seven colonies voters had to own land (usually forty to fifty acres), and the rest demanded that an elector have enough property to furnish a house and work a farm with his own tools. About 40 percent of free men could not meet these requirements, but nearly all of these were indentured servants, single sons still living with parents, or young men just beginning family life. Most white males in British North America would vote by age forty, whereas two-thirds of all men in England and nine-tenths in Ireland could not and would never vote.

In rural areas voter participation was low unless a vital issue was at stake. The difficulties of voting limited the average rural turnout to about 45 percent. (This rate of participation was, however, better than in typical U.S. elections today, apart from those for president.) Most governors called elections according to no set pattern, so that elections might lapse for years and suddenly be held on very short notice. Voters in isolated areas thus often had no knowledge of an upcoming contest. The fact that all polling took place at the county seat discouraged many electors from traveling long distances over poor roads to vote. In several colonies voters had to state their choice publicly, often face-to-face with the candidates. This procedure naturally inhibited participation on the part of those who might dissent. Finally, the absence of political parties also played a role in the turnout: no institutional means existed to stimulate popular interest in politics and to mobilize voters in support of candidates. Office seekers nominated themselves and usually ran on their reputation rather than issues that might spur public interest.

In view of these factors, indifference toward politics was not uncommon by the mid-eighteenth century. For example, to avoid paying legislators' expenses at the capital, numerous Massachusetts towns refused to choose assemblymen; in 1763, 64 of 168 towns held no elections. Thirty percent of men elected to South Carolina's assembly neglected to take their seats from 1731 to 1760, including a majority of those chosen in 1747 and 1749. Apathy would have been even greater

Charles County, Maryland, Courthouse and Ordinary
In the Chesapeake colonies, community life usually centered on the county courthouse and a few other buildings on a cleared parcel. On election days, voters were treated to drinks in the nearby ordinary (tavern) by candidates before proceeding to the courthouse and voting orally and publicly.

had candidates not freely plied voters with alcohol. This "swilling the planters with bumbo" was most popular among Virginians: George Washington dispensed almost two quarts of liquor for each voter at the courthouse when first elected to the assembly in 1758. Such practices helped the elite in most eighteenth-century colonies build up a tradition of community leadership that would serve them well in the years of revolutionary crisis after 1763.

Only in the major seaports did a truly competitive political life flourish. Voter turnout was relatively high in the cities because of greater population density, better communications, and the use of secret ballots (except in New York). Furthermore, the cities' acute economic difficulties stimulated political participation among urban voters, ever hopeful that the government might ease their problems. In politics as in economics, cities were an exception to the general pattern for Anglo-America.

The most significant political development after 1700 was the rise of the assembly as the preponderant force in American government. Except in Connecticut and Rhode Island (where voters elected their governor), the crown or the proprietors in England chose each colony's governor, who except in Massachusetts in turn named a council, or upper house of the legislature. Thus the assembly became the vehicle through which members of the gentry asserted their own interests. Until 1689 governors and councils took the initiative in drafting laws, and the assemblies rather passively followed their lead; but thereafter, the assemblies assumed a more central role in politics.

Colonial leaders argued that their legislatures should exercise the same rights as those won by Parliament in its seventeenth-century struggle with royal authority. Indeed, Americans saw their assemblies as miniature Houses of Commons, and they assumed that governors possessed only those powers exercised by the British crown. Since Parliament had won supremacy over the monarchy through the Bill of Rights in 1689, colonials felt that their governors had strictly limited powers and should defer to the assemblies in cases of disagreement.

The lower houses steadily asserted their prestige and authority by refusing to permit outside meddling in their proceedings, taking firm control over taxes and budgets, and especially by keeping a tight rein on executive salaries. Although governors had considerable powers (including the right to veto acts, call or dismiss assembly sessions at will, and schedule elections anytime), they were vulnerable to legislatures' financial pressure because they received no salary from British sources and relied on the assemblies for income. Only through this "power of the purse" could assemblies force governors to sign laws opposed by the crown.

Moreover, because the British government had little interest in eighteenth-century colonial politics, the assemblies could seize considerable power at the governors' expense. The Board of Trade, which Parliament established in 1696, was charged with monitoring American developments and advising the crown on colonial affairs. But aside from its first decade and a vigorous period from 1748 to 1753, the board's small, inefficient staff lacked the vision and energy to provide the strong support needed by embattled governors wrestling to maintain royal authority. The board could have easily frustrated the assemblies' rise to power by persuading the crown to disallow objectionable colonial laws signed by the governors; but of 8,563 acts sent from the mainland between 1696 and 1776, the board had just 469 disapproved. The Board of Trade's ineffectiveness left a vacuum in royal policy that allowed the colonies to become self-governing in most respects except for trade regulation, restrictions on printing money, and declaring war. This autonomy, reinforced by self-assertive assemblies, would haunt British authorities when they attempted to exercise more direct rule after 1763 (see Chapter 5).

Thus during the first half of the eighteenth century, many colonists flourished and some grew wealthy. At the same time, however, class distinctions became more sharply etched. But British North America had no centuries-old institutions to bolster aristocratic privilege: no hereditary nobility, powerful bureaucracy, standing army, or royal court. Even the Anglican church was weak, lacking American bishops. Despite the absence of such institutions, its hold on colonial wealth, along with social expectations, largely sufficed to ensure that the American upper class would dominate public life in the colonies.

COMPETING FOR A CONTINENT

The first half of the eighteenth century witnessed the rapid transformation of North America as Europeans competed among themselves in expanding their territorial claims, engaging in more intensive trade and warfare alike with Native Americans, and opening up new areas for settlement by colonists. Native Americans welcomed some of these new developments and resisted others, depending on how they thought their livelihoods would be affected.

France and Native Americans

With the conclusion of the War of Spanish Succession in 1713, France aggressively resumed expanding and strengthening its North American empire, particularly the colony of Louisiana. Founded in 1718, New Orleans soon became the colony's capital and port. Louisiana's staunchest Indian allies were the Choctaws, through whom the French hoped to counter both the rapidly expanding influence of Carolina's traders and the weakening presence of the Spanish in the Southeast. But inroads by the persistent Carolinians led the Choctaws by the 1730s to become bitterly divided into pro-English and pro-French factions.

In no time Louisiana acquired a foul reputation, and few French immigrated there willingly. To boost its population, the government sent paupers and criminals there, recruited German refugees, and encouraged large-scale slave imports. By 1732 two-thirds of

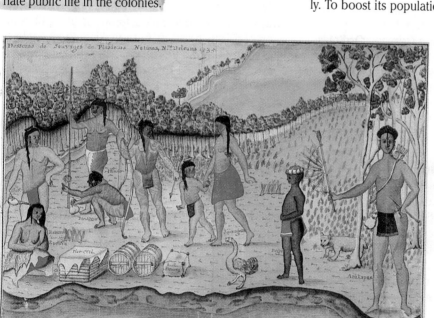

Intercultural Trade in Colonial Louisiana
Alexandre de Batz, a French visitor in 1735, depicted an important dimension of Louisiana's economy in this drawing of Indians from several nations gathering to trade near New Orleans. Trade goods, including cured skins, kegs of fat, and bear oil, are lined up in the foreground.

lower Louisiana's fifty-eight hundred people were slaves. Life was dismal, even for whites. A thoroughly corrupt government ran the colony. With Louisiana's sluggish export economy failing to sustain them, settlers and slaves found other means of survival. Like the Indians, they hunted, fished, gathered wild plants, and cultivated gardens. In 1727 a priest described how some free settlers eventually prospered: "A man with his wife or partner clears a little ground, builds himself a house on four piles, covers it with sheets of bark, and plants corn and rice for his provisions; the next year he raises a little more for food, and has also a field of tobacco; if at last he succeeds in having three or four Negroes, then he is out of difficulties."

But many red, white, and black Louisianans depended on exchanges with one another in order to be "out of difficulties." Indians provided corn, bear oil, tallow (for candles), and above all deerskins to European merchants in return for blankets, kettles, axes, chickens, hogs, guns, and alcohol. Indians from west of the Mississippi brought horses and cattle, usually stolen from Spanish ranches in Texas. Familiar with cattle from their homelands, West African slaves managed many of Louisiana's herds, and some became rustlers and illicit traders of beef.

With Canada and Louisiana secure, the French sought to counter growing British influence in and around the Ohio Valley. After the valley was largely emptied of natives during wars with the Iroquois in the seventeenth century, the Iroquois' adoption of neutrality in 1701 (see Chapter 3) encouraged Indian refugees to settle there. Nations such as the Kickapoos and Mascoutens returned from the upper Great Lakes, while others, among them Shawnees and Delawares, arrived from the east to escape English encroachments. Hoping to secure commercial and diplomatic ties with these natives, the French expanded their trade activities. Detroit and several other French posts ballooned into sizable villages housing Indians, French, and mixed-ancestry *métis*. But with English traders increasingly active in the region, most Indians preferred a more independent course.

Although the French generally were more successful among Indians than the English, by no means did they enjoy universal success. The Carolina-supported Chickasaws frequently attacked the French and their native allies on the Mississippi River. Although ultimately unsuccessful, the Fox Indians led a long effort

Huron (Wyandotte) Woman
Her cloth dress, glass beads, and iron hoe reflect the influence of French trade on this woman and other Indians of the Great Lakes–Ohio region in the eighteenth century.

to prevent French traders from making direct contact with Sioux Indians to the west. And the French in 1729–1730 brutally suppressed the Natchez Indians, the last of the Mississippian peoples, in order to open up land in Louisiana for tobacco and sugar production.

By 1744 French fur traders had explored as far west as North Dakota and Colorado and were buying beaver pelts and Indian slaves on the Great Plains. At the instigation of these traders and their British competitors, trade goods, including guns, spread to Native Americans throughout central Canada and then to the Plains. Meanwhile, Indians in the Great Basin and southern Plains were acquiring horses, thousands of which had been left behind by the Spanish when they fled New Mexico during the Pueblo Revolt of 1680. Adopting the horse and gun, Indians such as the Lakota Sioux and Comanches moved to the Plains and built a new, highly mobile way of life based on the pursuit of buffalo.

Only at widely scattered places between Louisiana and Canada did the French attempt to settle, most notably in modern-day Missouri and Illinois. By 1750 France had an immense domain, but one that depended on often precarious relations with nearby Native Americans.

Native Americans and British Expansion

As in the seventeenth century, the rapid expansion of colonial settlement was made possible by the depopulation and dislocation of Native Americans. Epidemic diseases, environmental changes, war, and political pressures on Indians to cede land and to emigrate all combined to open up new lands for the immigrants. Pennsylvania, where William Penn's idealism was rapidly waning, coerced the Delaware Indians into selling more than fifty thousand acres between 1729 and 1734. In 1735 the colony's leaders (William Penn's sons and his former secretary) produced a patently fraudulent treaty in which the Delawares allegedly had agreed in 1686 to sell their land as far west as a man could walk in a day and a half. The colony then blazed a trail and hired three men to walk west as fast as they could. The men covered nearly sixty miles, meaning that the Delawares, in what became known as the Walking Purchase, had to cede an additional twelve hundred square miles of land. Despite the protests of Delaware elders who had been alive in 1686 and remembered no such treaty, the Delawares were forced to move under Iroquois supervision. The proprietors then sold these lands to settlers and speculators at a large profit. Within a generation the Delawares' former lands were among the most productive in the British Empire.

In helping to remove the Delawares from Pennsylvania, the Iroquois sought to accommodate the English while consolidating their own power. Late in the seventeenth century, the Iroquois had agreed with several colonies, from Maryland to Massachusetts, to relocate Indians whose lands were sought by colonists. Under these agreements, known collectively as the Covenant Chain, Indians were moved to areas of what are now New York and Pennsylvania on the periphery of the Iroquois' own homeland, where they could serve as buffers against English expansion. The removal of the Delawares marked Pennsylvania's entry into the Covenant Chain. In so grouping other Native Americans around them and in incorporating the Tuscaroras as the sixth nation of their confederacy (see Chapter 3), the Iroquois established a center of Native American power distinct from, but cooperative with, the British.

Indians elsewhere along the frontier of settlement likewise confronted pressures from settlers on one side and from the Iroquois on the other. Typical of these were the Catawbas of the Carolina piedmont. After the defeat of the Yamasees (whose cause the Catawbas supported) in 1716, Carolina settlers moved uncomfortably close to some Catawba villages, provoking the kind of environmental upheavals experienced earlier by Indians in New England and other settled regions (see Chapter 3). Most Catawbas abandoned these villages to join more remote Catawbas who engaged in the deerskin trade. Having escaped the settlers, the Catawbas, however, faced rising conflict with the Iroquois, who, after making peace with the Indian allies of New France in 1701, looked south when launching raids for captives to adopt into their ranks. To counter the Iroquois, whose alliances with most of the northern colonies left them well armed, the Catawbas turned to South Carolina. By ceding land and helping defend that colony against outside Indians, the Catawbas received guns, food, and clothing. Their relationship with the English allowed the Catawbas the security they needed to strengthen their traditional institutions. However, the growing gap in numbers between them and the settlers, and their competition with the settlers for resources, made the Indians vulnerable and dependent.

British Settlement in the South: Georgia

Parliament's chartering of the colony of Georgia in 1732 represented a new expansionist thrust. Parliament intended Georgia as a refuge where bankrupt debtors (who typically rotted in English jails until they repaid their debts) could settle, their presence protecting South Carolina against attacks from Spanish Florida to the south. Meanwhile, the new colony's sponsors hoped that Georgia would flourish by exporting expensive commodities like wine and silk. Parliament even spent money to ensure the success of the colony, which became the only North American province besides Nova Scotia in which the British government actually invested funds.

Under tough-minded James Oglethorpe (1696–1785), who dominated the provincial board of trustees, Georgia took shape slowly during its first decade. Oglethorpe founded the port of entry, Savannah, in 1733, and by 1740 a small contingent of 2,800 colonists had settled in the colony. Almost half the immigrants came from Germany, Switzerland, and Scotland, and most had their overseas passage paid by the government. A small number of Jews were among the early settlers. Georgia thus began as the least English of all the colonies. In 1740 Oglethorpe led a massive assault on Florida (see "A Place in Time"). Although failing to seize St. Augustine, he led 650 men in repelling 3,000 Spanish troops and refugee South Carolina slaves who counterattacked Georgia in 1742. When peace returned in 1744, Georgia's survival was assured.

Oglethorpe hated slavery and tried to ban it from Georgia. "They live like cattle," he wrote to the trustees after viewing Charles Town's slave market. "If we allow slaves, we act against the very principles by which we associated together, which was to relieve the distressed." Slavery, he thought, degraded blacks, made whites lazy, and presented a terrible risk. South Carolina's Stono Rebellion of 1739 particularly alarmed him. Oglethorpe worried that wherever whites relied on a slave labor force, they courted slave revolts, which the Spanish could then exploit. But most of all, he recognized that slavery undermined the economic position of poor whites like those he sought to settle in Georgia.

At Oglethorpe's insistence, Parliament made Georgia the only colony where slavery was forbidden. He also pushed through a requirement that landholdings be no larger than 500 acres. These mea-sures were aimed at keeping rural Georgia populated by white, independent farmer-soldiers, ready to leap to the colony's defense and uncorrupted by the urge to speculate in real estate or build up slave-labor plantations.

But Oglethorpe's well-intentioned plans failed completely. Few debtors arrived because Parliament set impossibly stringent conditions for their release from prison. Limitations on settlers' rights to sell or enlarge their holdings, as well as the ban on slavery, also kept settlement low. Raising exotic export crops proved impractical; as in South Carolina, only rice yielded a profit. Oglethorpe struggled against economic reality for a decade and then gave up. In 1750 the trustees finally legalized slavery, and other restrictions on the market for land also fell by the wayside. As a result, Georgia boomed. The population rose from four thousand residents in 1750 (including up to a thousand hitherto illegal slaves) to twenty-three thousand inhabitants in 1770, 45 percent of them blacks.

Georgia's settlement completed British colonization of the Atlantic seaboard. Having held Georgia against Spain and pushed the frontier west 150 miles, British expansion virtually halted after 1750. Anglo-Americans would not settle beyond the Appalachians until the 1760s. Nevertheless, the colonial population continued to grow rapidly, doubling every twenty-six years—almost exactly what Franklin had predicted in 1751. Had this rate continued, the U.S. population to-

James Oglethorpe and the Indians

In 1734 Oglethorpe visited London with Creek Indians who had sold him land. Here the Creeks meet with Englishmen who have invested in the Georgia colony.

Yuchi Ceremony, 1736
A German visitor to Georgia drew this watercolor, which he titled A Festival. *The guns hanging inside the shelter were probably acquired from English traders in South Carolina.*

day would number around 850 million, second only to China's.

Spain's Struggles

While endeavoring to maintain its empire in the face of Native American, French, and British adversaries, Spain spread its language and culture over much of North America, especially in the Southwest.

Seeking to repopulate New Mexico with settlers after the Pueblo Revolt (see Chapter 3), Spain gave land grants of approximately twenty-six square miles wherever ten or more families founded a town. Strong fortifications arose to protect against Indian attacks, now coming primarily from the Apaches. As in the early New England towns, the settlers built homes on small lots around the church plaza, farmed separate fields nearby, grazed livestock at a distance, and shared a community woodlot and pasture.

The livestock-raising *ranchos,* radiating out for many miles from little clusters of houses, monopolized vast tracts along the Rio Grande and blocked further town settlement. On the *ranchos* mounted cattle and sheep herders *(vaqueros)* created the way of life later associated with the American cowboy—featuring lariat and roping skills, cattle drives, roundups, and livestock brandings.

By 1750 the population of New Mexico numbered just 3,800 Spanish, half of them in four towns, and

8,400 Pueblos (an astonishing 50 percent reduction since 1680). Most Pueblos were integrated into New Mexico society and, although many had converted to Catholicism, they also practiced their traditional religion. On the colony's borders, the Navajos and Apaches, whose raids once menaced Spanish and Pueblos alike, had made peace with New Mexico in order to gain its support against even more fearsome raids by armed and mounted Utes from the north and Comanches from the east.

Spain established Texas in order to counter growing French influence among the Comanches and other Native Americans on the southern Plains. Colonization began in 1716, when Spaniards established four missions and a small garrison. The most flourishing of these was San Antonio de Valero, where friars constructed a fortified mission building later famous as the Alamo. But the Indians of Texas preferred trading with the French to farming, Christianity, and the ineffective protection of the Spanish. Lack of security also deterred Hispanic settlement, so that by 1760 only 1,200 Spaniards faced periodic raids by French, Comanches, and other Indians.

Spain's position in Florida was equally precarious. After 1715 the neutrality of the Creeks enabled the Spanish to compete with the English and French in the southeastern deerskin trade, though with limited effectiveness, and to sponsor Indian counterraids into Carolina. In addition, the Spanish offered freedom to any

Mose, Florida, in 1740

The Spanish presence in Florida was always tenuous and, after English colonists established Charles Town in Carolina in 1670, vulnerable to outside attack. During the eighteenth century Spain retained its hold in Florida by enlisting the support of Native Americans and Africans alienated by the English. In particular, by promising freedom to slaves who fled from Carolina to Florida and converted to Catholicism, the Spanish bolstered their population and defenses. The black community of Mose, established near St. Augustine in 1738, vividly demonstrated the importance of these immigrants.

Blacks had lived in Florida since the founding of St. Augustine in 1565. In 1683, after Indians armed by Carolina began attacking and capturing Florida mission Indians for sale into slavery, the Spanish colony formed a black militia unit. In 1686 fifty-three blacks and Indians conducted a counterraid into Carolina and returned with, among other prizes, thirteen of the governor's slaves. In subsequent diplomatic negotiations between the two colonies, Florida's governor, Diego de Quiroga, refused English demands that he return the blacks, instead giving them wage-paying jobs. Soon other Carolina slaves were making their way to Florida. Spain's King Charles II ruled in 1693 that all arriving slaves should be given their freedom, "so that by their example and my liberality others will do the same."

With Spain deliberately encouraging Carolina slaves to escape to Florida, the numbers rose further, especially during the Yamasee War (1715–1716), when the English were nearly crushed by a massive uprising of Indians. In 1726 a former South Carolina slave, Francisco Menéndez, was appointed to command a militia unit consisting of his fellow Carolinians to defend against an expected English invasion. The Spanish built a fortified village for Menéndez's men and their families in 1738 and called it Gracia Real de Santa Teresa de Mose, usually shortened to Mose, an Indian name for the location.

Mose was strategically placed just two miles north of St. Augustine, so that its residents served as both sentries and a buffer for the capital. Spanish and English documents, along with recent archaeological excavations, reveal that it had sturdy earthen walls "lined round with prickly royal" (a thorny plant) and was surrounded by a moat. A stone fort was the most prominent structure inside the walls. Outside the fort the one hundred residents planted fields and gathered shellfish from the banks of a nearby saltwater stream. In a letter to the Spanish king, Florida's governor, Manuel de Montiano, praised Menéndez for having "distinguished himself in the establishment and cultivation of Mose, . . . [and] doing all he could so that the rest of his subjects, following his example, would apply themselves and learn good customs."

For its residents Mose symbolized their new status as freed men and women. Most had been born in West Africa and then enslaved and carried to Carolina. After escaping they had lived among friendly Indians who helped them make their way to the Spanish colony. Mose was their own community, their first since being taken from Africa. In agreeing to live there, they understood the price they might have to pay. Writing to the king in 1738, they declared themselves "the most cruel enemies of the English," who were ready to shed

English Map of St. Augustine and Mose, 1762
Mose is indicated as "Negroe Fort"; "Indian Town" is a settlement of pro-Spanish Indians.

Ft. Mose Watercolor

Artist's reconstruction of Mose, based on archaeological and documentary evidence.

now, after twelve years of assimilation in the capital city, seemed a mark of second-class citizenship.

In 1763 Spain ceded Florida to Britain in the Treaty of Paris (see Chapter 5). Spanish authorities evacuated the people of Mose and allotted them homesteads in Matanzas, Cuba. But the meager provisions given the blacks proved inadequate, and many, including Francisco Menéndez, soon moved to Havana. In 1783 another Treaty of Paris returned Florida to Spain (see Chapter 6), and the following year, a new Florida governor resumed the policy of granting freedom to escaped slaves. Hearing the news and recalling Florida's earlier reputation, hundreds of slaves responded. But now Spain proceeded more cautiously with the slaveholders' government to Florida's north; in 1790 U.S. Secretary of State Thomas Jefferson persuaded the Spanish to rescind the policy of granting freedom to escaped slaves. In 1819 the United States annexed Florida, and in 1845 it joined the Union as a slave state.

Puerto Rican Sergeant,

Seventeenth Century
This free black sergeant belonged to a Spanish militia unit in Puerto Rico, similar to the one based at Mose.

their "last drop of blood in defense of the Great Crown of Spain and the Holy Faith."

The importance of Florida's free blacks and their town was demonstrated in 1740 when Georgia's governor, James Oglethorpe, led a massive force of Georgia and South Carolina troops, Indian allies, and seven warships in an invasion of Florida. The English captured Mose in May after all its residents were evacuated, but Menéndez's militia and other troops recaptured the town a month later in a fierce battle that helped Oglethorpe decide to withdraw. (The British called the battle Bloody Mose.) But English destruction of the town and the Spanish crown's refusal to fund its rebuilding led Mose's residents to move into St. Augustine. For twelve years they lived among the Spanish as laborers, seamen, and hunters and in other capacities. In 1752 a new governor had Mose rebuilt and ordered the blacks to return to their former town despite their express "desire to live in complete liberty." To reside in the town, which they once had cherished as a symbol of their freedom,

English-owned slaves who escaped and made their way to Florida (see "A Place in Time").

The Spanish saw Georgia's founding in 1733 as a bold new threat to Florida, and planned, but then cancelled, an all-out invasion in 1737. When war broke out between England and Spain in 1739, the two sides attempted invasions of one another without success. Even though Spain had resisted the English, its reputa-

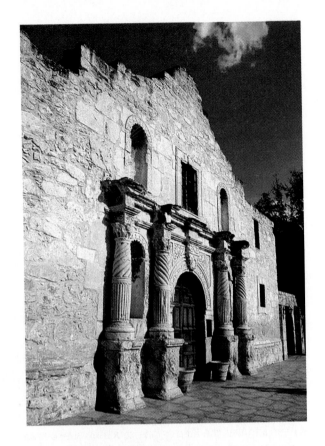

The Alamo

As the center of Franciscan missionary efforts in Texas, this church was a critical bulwark for Spain on its fragile northern frontier. It later became the symbol of Texan independence from Mexico (see Chapter 13).

French and Spanish Occupation of North America, to 1750

French fur traders became entrenched along the Great Lakes and upper Mississippi River between 1666 and 1700, after which they built many settlements in territory claimed by Spain along the Gulf of Mexico. Spanish colonization was concentrated in Florida, central Texas, and the Rio Grande Valley.

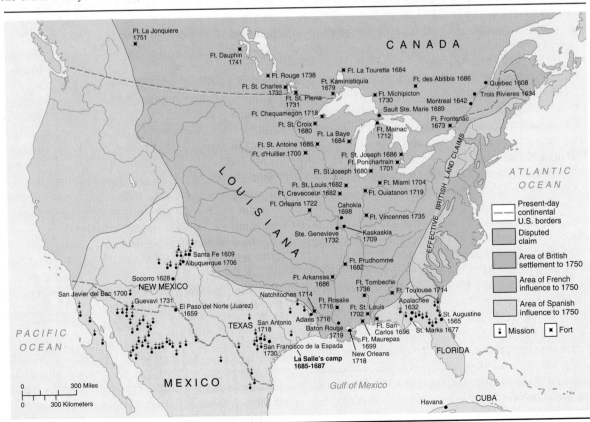

tion as "the sick man of Europe" clearly applied equally in North America.

By the mid-eighteenth century, Spain controlled much of the Southeast and Southwest, while France exercised influence in the Mississippi, Ohio, and Missouri River valleys, as well as around the Great Lakes and in Canada. Both empires, spread thin, depended heavily on Indian goodwill or acquiescence. In contrast, British North America was compact, densely populated by non-Indians, and aggressively expansionist.

ENLIGHTENMENT AND AWAKENING

Anglo-America was probably the world's most literate society in the eighteenth century. Perhaps 90 percent of New England's adult white male population and 40 percent of the women could write well enough to sign documents, thanks to the region's traditional support for primary education. Among white males elsewhere in the colonies, the literacy rate varied from about 35 percent to more than 50 percent. (In England, by contrast, no more than one-third of all males could read and write.) But how readily most of these people could (or would) read a book or write a letter was another matter. Ordinary Americans' reading fare at best encompassed only a few well-thumbed books: an almanac, a psalter, and the Bible. They inhabited a world of oral culture, in which ideas and information passed through the spoken word—a conversation with neighbors, an exchange of pleasantries with the local gentleman, a hot debate at the town meeting, a sermon by the minister. When uttered with feeling and sincerity, spoken words could move them with tremendous force.

However, members of the gentry, well-to-do merchants, educated ministers, and some self-improving artisans and farmers also lived in the world of print culture. Though costly, books, newspapers, and writing paper could open up eighteenth-century European civilization to reading men and women. And a rich, exciting world it was. Great advances in natural science seemed to explain the laws of nature; human intelligence appeared poised to triumph over ignorance and prejudice; life itself looked as if it would at last become pleasant. For those who had the time to read and think, an age of optimism and progress had dawned: the Enlightenment. Upper-class Americans could not resist its charms and could be powerfully moved by the promise of its written words.

The Enlightenment in America

Anglo-American intellectuals like the self-taught scientist Benjamin Franklin drew their inspiration from Enlightenment ideals, which combined confidence in human reason with skepticism toward beliefs not founded on science or strict logic. One source of Enlightenment thought lay in the writings of English physicist Sir Isaac Newton (1642–1727), who in 1687 explained how universal gravitation ruled the universe. Newton's work captured Europe's imagination by demonstrating the harmony of natural laws and stimulated others to search for rational principles in medicine, law, psychology, and government.

In the second quarter of the eighteenth century, no American more fully embodied the Enlightenment spirit than Franklin. Born in Boston in 1706, Franklin migrated to Philadelphia at age seventeen. He brought along skill as a printer, considerable ambition, and insatiable intellectual curiosity. In 1727 he gathered a small group of young men, mostly aspiring artisans like himself, into a club called the Junto, whose members pledged themselves to debate highbrow questions and to collect useful information for their "mutual improvement."

In moving to Philadelphia, Franklin put himself in the right place at the right time, for the city was growing much more rapidly than Boston and was attracting English and Scottish merchants who shared Franklin's zest for learning. These men nudged Franklin's career along by lending him books and securing him printing contracts. In 1732 Franklin began to publish *Poor Richard's Almanack,* a collection of maxims and proverbs that made him famous. By age forty-two Franklin had earned enough money to retire and devote himself to science and community service.

These dual goals—science and community benefit—were intimately related in Franklin's mind, for he believed that all true science would be useful in the sense of making everyone's life more comfortable. For example, experimenting with a kite, Franklin demonstrated in 1752 that lightning was electricity, a discovery that led to the useful lightning rod. Building on his Junto activities, Franklin organized the American Philosophical Society in 1743 to encourage "all philosophical experiments that let light into the nature of things, tend to increase the power of man over matter, and multiply the conveniences and pleasures of life." By 1769 this society had blossomed into an inter-colonial network of amateur scientists.

Franklin left his mark on Philadelphia in other ways. He established its first volunteer fire company—complete with engine—in 1736, inspired the creation of a circulating library that held America's finest collection of scientific books, and in 1740 helped to found an academy that became the College of Philadelphia (now the University of Pennsylvania). From this institution sprang the colonies' first medical school in 1765.

Although several southern plantation owners, including Thomas Jefferson, ardently championed progress through science, the Enlightenment's primary centers in America were the seaboard cities, where the latest books and ideas from Europe circulated and gentlemen and self-improving artisans met in small societies to investigate nature. In the eyes of many of these individuals, the ideal was the Royal Society in London, the foremost learned society in the English-speaking world. Franklin and Cotton Mather became members of the Royal Society. In this respect, the Enlightenment, at least initially, strengthened the ties between colonial and British elites. Although confident that science would benefit everyone, the Enlightenment's followers envisioned progress as gradual and proceeding from the top down. They trusted reason far more than they trusted the common people, whose judgment, especially on religious matters, seemed too easily deranged.

Just as Newton inspired the scientific bent of Enlightenment intellectuals, English philosopher John Locke's *Essay Concerning Human Understanding* (1690) led many to embrace "reasonable" or "rational" religion. Locke contended that ideas, including religion, are not inborn but are acquired by toilsome investigation of and reflection upon experience. To most Enlightenment intellectuals, the best argument for the existence of God seemingly could be derived through study of the harmony and order of nature, which pointed to a rational Creator. Some individuals carried this argument a step further by insisting that where the Bible conflicted with reason, one should follow the dictates of reason rather than the Bible. Those, such as Franklin and Jefferson, who took the argument furthest were called Deists. Deists concluded that God, having created a perfect universe, did not miraculously intervene in its workings but rather left it alone to operate according to natural laws.

Americans influenced by the Enlightenment usually described themselves as Christians and attended church. But they feared Christianity's excesses, particularly as indulged in by fanatics who persecuted others in religion's name, and by "enthusiasts" who claimed miraculous visions and direct mandates from God. Mindful of Locke's caution that a human can never be *absolutely* certain of anything but his or her own existence, they distrusted zealots. Typically, Franklin contributed money to most of the churches in Philadelphia but thought that religion's value lay in its encouragement of virtue and morality rather than in theological hair splitting.

Prior to 1740 colonial intellectuals usually associated fanaticism and bigotry with the bygone days of the early Puritans, and they looked on their own time as an era of progressive reasonableness. But a series of religious revivals known as the Great Awakening would soon shatter their complacency.

The Great Awakening

Viewing the world as orderly and predictable, rationalists were inclined to a sense of smug self-satisfaction. Franklin took the occasion of writing his will in 1750 to thank God for giving him "such a mind, with moderate passions" and "such a competency of this world's goods as might make a reasonable mind easy." But many Americans lacked a comfortable competency of worldly goods and lived neither orderly nor predictable lives. For example, in 1737 and 1738 an epidemic of diphtheria, a contagious throat disease, killed every tenth child under sixteen from New Hampshire to Pennsylvania. Such an event starkly reminded the colonists of the fragility of earthly life and turned their thoughts to religion.

A quickening of religious fervor began at scattered places in the colonies in the mid-1730s. Then in the 1740s, an outpouring of passionate Christian revivalism swept all of British North America. This "Great Awakening" cut across lines of class, status, and education. Even many elites found themselves caught up in it, realizing the inadequacy of reason alone to move their hearts. Above all, the Great Awakening represented an unleashing of anxiety and longing among ordinary people living in a world of oral culture—anxiety about sin, and longing for salvation. And the answers that they received were conveyed through the spoken word. Some preachers of the Great Awakening were themselves ntellectuals, comfortable amid the books and ideas of the print culture. But for all, religion was primarily a matter of emotional commitment.

In contrast to rationalists, who stressed the human potential for betterment, the ministers who roused their congregations into outbursts of religious fervor during the Great Awakening's revivals depicted the emptiness of material comfort, the utter corruption of human nature, the fury of divine wrath, and the need for immediate repentance. Although he was a brilliant thinker, well aware of contemporary philosophy and science, the Congregationalist Jonathan Edwards, who led a revival at Northampton, Massachusetts, in 1735, drove home this message with breathtaking clarity. "The God that holds you over the pit of Hell, much as one holds a spider or other loathsome insect over the fire, abhors you," Edwards intoned in one of his famous sermons, "Sinners in the Hands of an Angry God." "His wrath toward you burns like fire; He looks upon you as worthy of nothing else but to be cast into the fire."

Even before Edwards's Northampton revival, two men in central New Jersey—the Presbyterian minister William Tennent and the Dutch Reformed minister Theodore Frelinghuysen—had stimulated conversions in prayer meetings called the Refreshings. But the event that brought these isolated threads of revival together was the arrival in 1739 of the charismatic George Whitefield, an English clergyman who had been stoking the fires of revival in the Anglican church. So overpowering was Whitefield's presence that some joked that he could make crowds swoon simply by uttering "Mesopotamia." Crowds exceeding twenty thousand could hear his booming voice clearly, and many wept at his eloquence.

Whitefield's American tour inspired thousands to seek salvation. Most converts were young adults in their late twenties. In Connecticut alone, the number joining churches jumped from 630 in 1740 to 3,217 in 1741, and within four years of Whitefield's arrival, every fifth man and woman under forty-five had been "born again."

Whitefield's allure was so mighty that he even awed potential critics. Hearing him preach in Philadelphia, Benjamin Franklin first vowed to contribute nothing to the collection but gradually melted. So admirably did Whitefield conclude his sermon, Franklin recalled, "that I empty'd my Pocket wholly into the Collector's Dish, Gold and all." But divisions over the revivals quickly developed in Whitefield's wake and were widened by the tactics of some of his more extreme followers. For example, after leaving Boston in October 1740, Whitefield invited Gilbert Tennent (William's son) to follow "in order to blow up the divine flame lately kindled there." Denouncing Boston's established clergymen as "dead Drones" and lashing out at aristocratic fashion, Tennent built a following among the city's poor and downtrodden. So did another firebrand,

the Congregationalist James Davenport, who once preached to his Southold, New York, congregation for twenty-four hours.

Exposing colonial society's social divisions, Tennent and Davenport corroded support for the revivals among established ministers and officials. Increasingly, the lines hardened between the revivalists, known as New Lights, and the rationalist clergy, or Old Lights, who dominated the Anglican, Presbyterian, and Congregational churches. In 1740 Gilbert Tennent published *The Danger of an Unconverted Ministry,* which hinted that most Presbyterian ministers lacked saving grace and hence were bound for hell, and urged their parishioners to abandon them for the New Lights. By thus sowing the seeds of doubt about individual ministers, Tennent was undermining one of the foundations of social order, for if the people could not trust their own ministers, whom could they trust?

Old Light rationalists fired back. In 1742 Charles Chauncy, a well-known Boston Congregationalist, condemned the revival as an epidemic of the "enthusiasm" that Enlightened intellectuals so loathed. Chauncy particularly blasted those enthusiasts who mistook the ravings of their overheated imaginations for direct communications from God. He even provided a kind of checklist for spotting enthusiasts: look for "a certain wildness" in their eyes, the "quakings and tremblings" of their limbs, and foaming at the mouth, Chauncy suggested. Put simply, the revival had unleashed "a sort of madness."

The Great Awakening opened unprecedented splits in American Protestantism. In 1741 New and Old Light Presbyterians formed rival branches that did not reunite until 1758, when the revivalists emerged victorious. The Anglicans lost many members to New Light preachers, especially to Presbyterians and Baptists. Congregationalists splintered so badly that within twenty years of 1740, New Lights had seceded from one-third of all churches and formed separate parishes.

In Massachusetts and Connecticut, where the Congregational church was established by law, the secession of New Light parishes provoked bitter conflict. To force New Lights into paying tithes to their former church, Old Lights repeatedly denied new parishes legal status. Connecticut passed repressive laws forbidding revivalists to preach or perform marriages, and the colony expelled many New Lights from the legislature. In Connecticut's Windham County, an extra story had to be added to the jail to hold all the New Lights arrested for not paying tithes. Elisha Paine, a revivalist imprisoned at Windham for illegal preaching, continued giving sermons from his cell and drew such crowds that

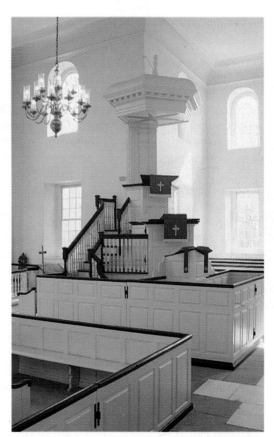

Baptist Meetinghouse and Anglican Church Interiors, Eighteenth-Century Virginia

The New Light Baptist structure (above) reflects the members' poverty as well as their preference for equality, simplicity, and intimacy in their services. The Old Light Anglican church (right) expresses an emphasis on hierarchy, formality, and distance among members. In particular, compare the relationship of minister to congregation in each church.

his followers built bleachers nearby to hear him. Paine and his fellow victims generated widespread sympathy for the New Lights, who finally won control of Connecticut's assembly in 1759.

Although New Lights made steady gains until the 1770s, the Great Awakening peaked in 1742. The revival then crested everywhere but in Virginia, where its high point came after 1755 with an upsurge of conversions by Baptists, who also suffered legal harassment.

For all the commotion it raised at the time, the Great Awakening's long-term effects exceeded its immediate impact. First, the revival started the decline in the influence of Quakers (who were not significantly affected by the Great Awakening), Anglicans, and Congregationalists. As these churches' importance waned, the number of Presbyterians and Baptists increased after 1740, and that of Methodists (pro-revival offshoots of Anglicanism) rose after 1770. Ever since the late 1700s, these three churches have dominated American Protestantism. Second, the Great Awakening stimulated the founding of new colleges, for existing colleges were scarred in their opponents' eyes by their affiliations with either Old or New Lights. In 1746 New Light Presbyterians established the College of New Jersey (Princeton). Then followed King's College

(Columbia) for Anglicans in 1754, the College of Rhode Island (Brown) for Baptists in 1764, Queen's College (Rutgers) for Dutch Reformed in 1766, and Dartmouth College for Congregationalists in 1769. Third, the revival went beyond the ranks of white society to draw many African-Americans and Native Americans to Protestantism for the first time. The revivals' oral and communal dimensions, along with their emphasis on piety over intellectual learning as the key to God's grace, enabled some members of both these groups to combine aspects of their traditional cultures with Protestant Christianity. The Great Awakening marked the real emergence of black Protestantism, which was almost nonexistent before 1740. New Lights reached out to slaves, some of whom joined white churches and even preached at revival meetings. Conversions came slowly, but by 1790 many blacks were Christians. Meanwhile, a few New Light preachers became missionaries to Indians still residing in the colonies. Among their converts were some Indians who had previously rejected Protestant missionaries. A few Christian Indians, such as Samson Occom, a Mohegan born in Connecticut, became widely known as preachers themselves. Despite these breakthroughs, blacks and

Reverend Samson Occom, Mohegan Indian Preacher

Born in a wigwam in Connecticut, Occom converted to Christianity under the influence of the Great Awakening and preached to other Native Americans. But he grew disillusioned with the treatment of his people by whites and, after the American Revolution, joined an exodus of Indians from New England to upstate New York.

Indians still faced considerable discrimination in colonial churches, even among New Lights.

The Great Awakening also gave added prominence to women in colonial religion. For several decades ministers had singled out women—who constituted the majority of church members—as embodying the Christian ideal of piety. Now some New Light churches, mostly Baptist and Congregationalist, began to grant women the right to speak and vote in church meetings. And like Anne Hutchinson a century earlier, some women moved from leading women's prayer and discussion groups to presiding over meetings that included men. One such woman, Sarah Osborn of Newport, Rhode Island, conducted "private praying Societies Male and female" that included black slaves in her home. In 1770 Osborn and her followers won a bitter fight over their congregation's choice of a new minister. While most assertive women were prevented by detractors from exercising as much power as Osborn, none was persecuted as Hutchinson had been in Puritan New England.

Finally the revivals had the unintended effect of fostering religious toleration by blurring theological differences among New Lights. Although an Anglican who helped found Methodism, George Whitefield preached with Presbyterians such as Gilbert Tennent and Congregationalists like Jonathan Edwards. By emphasizing inner experience over doctrinal and institutional fine points, revivalism helped to prepare Americans to accept denominational pluralism, which emerged after the Revolution as the best means of accommodating religious diversity.

Historians have disagreed over whether the Great Awakening had political as well as religious effects. Although Tennent and Davenport called the poor "God's people" and flayed the wealthy, they never advocated a social revolution, and the Awakening did not produce any distinct political ideology. Yet by empowering ordinary people to criticize those in authority, the revivals laid some of the groundwork for political revolutionaries a generation later, who would contend that royal government in America had grown corrupt and unworthy of obedience.

CONCLUSION

The aura of sanctified purpose around George Whitefield and his religious revival lingered even after his death in Boston in 1770. In September 1775 a ragtag army of American rebels, marching through Massachusetts, paused on their way to attack the British stronghold at Quebec. Hoping to win a blessing for their risky venture, they broke open a tomb and prayed over a holy man's remains. The corpse was George Whitefield's.

By the 1750s the British mainland colonies had taken on the look of mature societies. For fifty years their population and wealth had been rising impressively. The mainland provinces were more populous than Scotland and almost one-third the size of England. White colonists' standard of living far exceeded those of Scotland and Ireland and equaled that of England. Literacy had spread widely in the northern colonies, and by 1766 Anglo-America had more institutions of higher learning than England, Scotland, and Ireland together. A self-confident Anglo-American upper class had garnered expertise in law, trade, finance, and politics.

Together Britain and its colonies had become a far more formidable presence in North America than their French and Spanish rivals. But after France was vanquished and Spain further weakened in the Seven Years' War (1756–1763), latent tensions in the colonies' relations with Britain developed into irreconcilable differences.

CHRONOLOGY

1651–1733	Parliament creates the navigation system to regulate British imperial commerce.
1660	Restoration of the Stuart dynasty to English throne.
1685	Duke of York becomes King James II of England.
1686–1689	Dominion of New England.
1688	Glorious Revolution in England; James II deposed.
1689	William and Mary ascend to English throne. Protestant Association seizes power in Maryland. Leisler's Rebellion in New York.
1689–1697	King William's War (in Europe, War of the League of Augsburg).
1690	John Locke, *Essay Concerning Human Understanding.*
1698	French begin settlements near the mouth of the Mississippi River.
1701	Iroquois adopt neutrality policy toward European powers.
1702–1713	Queen Anne's War (in Europe, War of the Spanish Succession).

1716	San Antonio founded.
1718	New Orleans founded.
1729–1730	French war on Natchez Indians in Louisiana.
1732	Georgia colony chartered. Benjamin Franklin begins publishing *Poor Richard's Almanack.*
1734	"Walking Purchase" of Delaware Indians in Pennsylvania.
1735	Jonathan Edwards leads revival in Northampton, Massachusetts.
1736	Benjamin Franklin establishes first American fire company, at Philadelphia.
1739	Great Awakening begins. Stono Rebellion in South Carolina.
1739–1744	Anglo-Spanish War.
1743	Benjamin Franklin founds American Philosophical Society.
1750	Slavery legalized in Georgia.

Jonathan Edwards

FOR FURTHER READING

Bernard Bailyn, *The Peopling of British North America: An Introduction* (1986). A brief interpretive overview of the causes and effects of European immigration to British North America.

Bernard Bailyn and Philip D. Morgan, eds., *Strangers Within the Realm: Cultural Margins of the First British Empire* (1991). Essays by leading historians examine the interplay of ethnicity and empire occurring in North America, the Caribbean, Scotland, and Ireland.

Richard L. Bushman, *From Puritan to Yankee: Character and the Social Order in Connecticut, 1690–1765* (1967). The best examination of social and cultural transformation in any eighteenth-century colony.

Rhys Isaac, *The Transformation of Virginia, 1740–1790* (1982). Pulitzer Prize–winning study of class relationships, race relations, and folkways during the Great Awakening and American Revolution.

John J. McCusker and Russell R. Menard, *The Economy of British America, 1607–1789,* rev. ed. (1991). A comprehensive discussion of the colonial economy in light of current scholarship.

James H. Merrell, *The Indians' New World: Catawbas and Their Neighbors from European Contact Through the Era of Removal* (1989). A pathbreaking examination, with broad implications for understanding the Native American past, of the interaction between South Carolina colonists and Catawba Indians.

Gary B. Nash, *The Urban Crucible: The Northern Seaports and the Origins of the American Revolution,* abridged ed. (1986). A study of social, economic, and political change in Boston, New York, and Philadelphia during the eighteenth century.

Timothy Silver, *A New Face on the Countryside: Indians, Colonists, and Slaves in South Atlantic Forests, 1500–1800* (1990). A highly readable discussion of the interactions of humans and their environment in one region.

Peter H. Wood, *Black Majority: Negroes in Colonial South Carolina from 1670 Through the Stono Rebellion* (1974). An engrossing study of slavery, racism, and African-American life in the Lower South.

ADDITIONAL BIBLIOGRAPHY

Rebellion and Imperial Warfare

Lois Green Carr and David W. Jordan, *Maryland's Revolution of Government, 1689–1692* (1974); Richard R. Johnson, *Adjustment to Empire: The New England Colonies, 1675–1715* (1981); David S. Lovejoy, *The Glorious Revolution in America, 1660–1692* (1972); Stephen Saunders Webb, *The Governors General: The English Army and the Definition of the Empire, 1569–1681* (1979).

British Colonial Society and Economy

Ida Altman and James Horn, eds., *"To Make America": European Emigration in the Early Modern Period* (1991); Richard L. Bushman, *The Refinement of America: People, Houses, Cities* (1992); Karen Calvert, *Children in the House: The Material Culture of Early Childhood, 1600–1800* (1992); James Deetz, *In Small Things Forgotten: The Archaeology of Early American Life* (1977); A. Roger Ekirch, *Bound for America: The Transportation of British Convicts to the Colonies, 1718–1775* (1987); Joyce D. Goodfriend, *Before the Melting Pot: Society and Culture in Colonial New York City, 1664–1730* (1991); Christine Leigh Heyrman, *Commerce and Culture: The Maritime Communities of Colonial Massachusetts, 1690–1750* (1984); Stephen Innes, ed., *Work and Labor in Early America* (1988); Sung Bok Kim, *Landlord and Tenant in Colonial New York: Manorial Society, 1664–1775* (1978); Michael Kammen, *Empire and Interest: The American Colonies and the Politics of Mercantilism* (1970); Allan Kulikoff, *Tobacco and Slaves: The Development of Southern Cultures in the Chesapeake, 1680–1800* (1986); James T. Lemon, *The Best Poor Man's Country: A Geographical Study of Early Southeastern Pennsylvania* (1972); Barry Levy, *Quakers and the American Family: British Settlement in the Delaware Valley* (1988); James Leyburn, *The Scotch-Irish: A Social History* (1989); Peter C. Mancall, *Valley of Opportunity: Economic Culture Along the Upper Susquehanna, 1700–1800* (1991); Marcus Rediker, *Between the Devil and Deep Blue Sea: Merchant Seamen, Pirates, and the Anglo-American Maritime World, 1700–1750* (1989); Sharon V. Salinger, *"To Serve Well and Faithfully": Labor and Indentured Servants in Pennsylvania, 1682–1800* (1987); Marylynn Salmon, *Women and the Law of Property in Early America* (1986); Beverly Smaby, *The Transformation of Moravian Bethelem: From Communal Mission to Family Economy* (1988); Daniel Blake Smith, *Inside the Great House: Family Life in Eighteenth-Century Chesapeake Society* (1980); Phinizy Spalding, *Oglethorpe in America* (1977); Laurel Thatcher Ulrich, *Good Wives: Image and Reality in the Lives of Women in Northern New England, 1650–1763* (1982).

Blacks and Slavery

Ira Berlin, "Time, Space, and the Evolution of Afro-American Society in British Mainland North America," *American Historical Review* 85 (1980): 44–78; Philip D. Curtin, *The Atlantic Slave Trade: A Census* (1969); Winthrop D. Jordan, *White over Black: American Attitudes Toward the Negro, 1550–1812* (1968); Jane Landers, "Gracia Real de Santa Teresa de Mose: A Free Black Town in Spanish Colonial Florida," *American Historical Review* 95 (1990): 9–30; Edgar J. McManus, *Black Bondage in the North* (1973); Edmund S. Morgan, *American Slavery, American Freedom: The Ordeal of Colonial Virginia* (1975); Gerald W. Mullin, *Flight and Rebellion: Slave Resistance in Eighteenth-Century Virginia* (1972); William D. Piersen, *Black Yankees: The Development of an Afro-American Subculture in Eighteenth-Century New England* (1988); Mechal Sobel, *The World They Made Together: Black and White Values in Eighteenth-Century Virginia* (1987).

Native Americans

Richard Aquila, *The Iroquois Restoration: Iroquois Diplomacy on the Colonial Frontier, 1701–1754* (1983); James Axtell, *The Invasion Within: The Contest of Cultures in Colonial North America* (1985); Gregory Evans Dowd, *A Spirited Resistance: The North American Indian Struggle for Unity, 1745–1815* (1992); Tom Hatley, *The Dividing Paths: Cherokees and South Carolinians Through the Era of Revolution* (1993); Preston Holder, *The Hoe and the Horse on the Plains: A Study of Cultural Development Among North American Indians* (1970); Elizabeth A. H. John, *Storms Brewed in Other Men's Worlds: The Confrontations of Indians, Spanish, and French in the Southwest, 1540–1795* (1975); Michael N. McConnell, *A Country Between: The Upper Ohio Valley and Its Peoples, 1724–1774* (1992); Daniel K. Richter, *The Ordeal of the Longhouse: The Peoples of the Iroquois League in the Era of European Colonization* (1992); Daniel H. Usner, Jr., *Indians, Settlers, and Slaves in a Frontier Exchange Economy: The Lower Mississippi Valley Before 1783* (1992); Richard White, *The Middle Ground: Indians, Empires and Republics in the Great Lakes Region, 1650–1815* (1991); Peter H. Wood et al., eds., *Powhatan's Mantle: Indians in the Colonial Southeast* (1989); J. Leitch Wright, Jr., *The Only Land They Knew: The Tragic Story of the American Indians in the Old South* (1981).

French and Spanish Colonies

J. M. Bumsted, *The Peoples of Canada: A Pre-Confederation History* (1992); Donald E. Chipman, *Spanish Texas, 1519–1821* (1992); W. J. Eccles, *France in America*, rev. ed. (1991); Ramon A. Gutiérrez, *When Jesus Came, the Corn Mothers Went Away: Marriage, Sexuality, and Power in New Mexico, 1500–1846* (1991); Richard Colebrook Harris, *The Seigneurial System in Early Canada* (1966); Gerald E. Poyo and Gilberto M. Hinojosa, eds., *Tejano Origins in Eighteenth-Century San Antonio* (1991); David J. Weber, *The Spanish Frontier in North America* (1992).

The Enlightenment, Religion, and Politics

Bernard Bailyn, *The Origins of American Politics* (1968); Patricia Bonomi, *A Factious People: Politics and Society in Colonial New York* (1971) and *Under the Cope of Heaven: Religion, Society, and Politics in Colonial America* (1986); Richard D. Brown, *Knowledge Is Power: The Diffusion of Information in Early America, 1700–1865* (1991); Jon Butler, *Awash in a Sea of Faith: Christianizing the American People* (1990); Edwin S. Garstad, *The Great Awakening in New England* (1957); Jack P. Greene, *The Quest for Power: The Lower Houses of Assembly in the Southern Royal Colonies, 1689–1776* (1963); Frank Lambert, *"Pedlar in Divinity": George Whitefield and the Transatlantic Revivals* (1994); Kenneth A. Lockridge, *The Diary and Life of William Byrd II of Virginia* (1988) and *On the Sources of Patriarchal Rage: The Commonplace Books of William Byrd and Thomas Jefferson and the Gendering of Power in the Eighteenth Century* (1992); Sally Schwartz, *A Mixed Multitude: The Struggle for Toleration in Colonial Pennsylvania* (1987); Harry S. Stout, *The New England Soul: Preaching and Religious Culture in Colonial New England* (1988); Charles S. Sydnor, *American Revolutionaries in the Making: Political Practices in Washington's Virginia* (1965); Michael Warner, *The Letters of the Republic: Publication and the Public Sphere in Eighteenth-Century America* (1990); Marilyn J. Westerkamp, *Triumph of the Laity: Scots-Irish Piety and the Great Awakening, 1625–1760* (1988); Esmond Wright, *Franklin of Philadelphia* (1986).

Captain and Mrs. John Purves *(detail)*
by Henry Benbridge, 1775

5

THE ROAD TO REVOLUTION
1744–1776

In 1769 Benjamin Franklin (inset) was an agent for several American colonial assemblies and living in London, where he obtained an anonymous English pamphlet entitled *Good Humour*. Franklin bristled at the unknown author's charges that the colonists' recent opposition to parliamentary taxes represented *"a posture of hostility* against Great Britain." "There was no Posture of Hostility in America," Franklin angrily scribbled in the margin, "but Britain put herself in a Posture of Hostility against America."

As Franklin wrote those words, a constitutional crisis gripped the British Empire and was markedly affecting Britain's relationship with its overseas colonies. The conflict between Britain and the American colonies arose suddenly after 1763, when Parliament attempted to reorganize its suddenly enlarged empire by tightening control over economic and political affairs in the colonies. Long accustomed to benefiting economically from the empire while legislating for themselves, colonists resisted this unexpected effort to centralize decision making in London. Leaders like Franklin interpreted Britain's clampdown as calculated antagonism, intended to deprive the colonists of their prosperity and their relative independence.

As telling as they were, Franklin's words represented only one of many perspectives on unfolding events. For other colonists, the conflict was more than a constitutional crisis. In the port cities, crowds of poor and working people engaged in direct, often violent demonstrations against British authority. Sometimes they acted in concert with elite radicals; at other times, in defiance. Settlers in the remote "backcountry" of several colonies invoked the language and ideas of urban radicals when resisting the monopolies of large landowners and the policies of colonial governments dominated by seaboard elites. These movements reflected social-economic tensions within the colonies and the emergence of distinctly nonelite views on the crisis. By the same token, the growing participation of women in colonial resistance brought to the fore yet another perspective on the crisis. Moreover, colonial protests did not arise in a vacuum but rather drew from ideas and opposition movements in Britain and elsewhere in Europe.

Taken as a whole, colonial resistance involved many kinds of people with many outlooks. It arose most immediately from a constitutional crisis within the British Empire, but it also reflected deep democratic stirrings in America and in the north Atlantic world generally. These stirrings would erupt in the American Revolution, beginning in 1776, and then in the French Revolution, which began in 1789.

Despite their apprehension over parliamentary taxes, colonial politicians usually expressed their opposition peacefully from 1763 to 1775, through such tactics as legislative resolutions and commercial boycotts. Few lost their lives during the twelve years prior to the battles at Lexington and Concord, the first military clashes of the Revolution, and all of those killed were American civilians rather than royal officials or soldiers. Even after fighting broke out, some colonists agonized for more than a year over whether to sever their political relationship with England—which even native-born Americans sometimes referred to affectionately as "home." Of all the world's colonial peoples, none became rebels more reluctantly than did Anglo-Americans in 1776.

IMPERIAL WARFARE

Between 1713, when Queen Anne's War ended, and the early 1740s, the American colonies enjoyed a generation of peace, punctuated only by a brief war with Spain fought in Georgia from 1739 to 1742. But the war with Spain was symptomatic of renewed tensions between England on one hand and France and Spain on the other for overseas empire. That conflict merged with a second one in central Europe between Austria and Prussia, leading to an international war known as the War of the Austrian Succession (1740–1748). After a "diplomatic revolution" in which Austria dropped its alliance with Britain for one with France, leading Britain to align with Prussia, the conflict resumed as the Seven Years' War (1756–1763). In both wars the Anglo-French conflict was fought not in Europe but on the high seas; in India (where the two powers competed for influence among local rulers); and in North America. Although these conflicts originated in rivalries among the great powers of Europe, few colonists doubted that King George's War was also *their war*, or that their prosperity depended on a British victory in the Seven Years' War.

Yet these wars produced an ironically mixed effect. On one hand, they fused the bonds between the British and the Anglo-Americans. Fighting side by side, shedding their blood in the same cause, the British and the American colonists came to rely on each other as rarely before. At the same time, the conclusion of each war planted the seeds first of misunderstanding, then of suspicion, and finally of hostility between the two former compatriots.

King George's War

King George's War largely followed the pattern of earlier conflicts under William and Mary and Queen Anne (see Chapter 3). Few battles involved more than six hundred men, and most of the skirmishes consisted of raids and counterattacks in the Northeast, in which many civilians were killed and others captured, especially by French and Indians attacking New England frontier towns. Although prisoners were exchanged at the end of each conflict, some captives, particularly women and children, elected to remain with the French or Indians.

King George's War produced just one major engagement. In 1745 almost four thousand New Englanders under William Pepperell of Maine assaulted the French bastion of Louisbourg on the northern tip of Nova Scotia, which guarded the entrance to the St. Lawrence River. Unable to bring artillery with them, the New Englanders obtained siege guns by storming the enemy's outer batteries and then captured ammunition from several unsuspecting French supply ships that sailed into their clutches. For almost seven weeks they shelled Louisbourg, lobbing in nine thousand cannonballs and six hundred bombs until every building was either crumbling or on fire. On June 17, 1745, Pepperell took the fortress and almost 1,500 prisoners, at a loss of only 167 of his troops.

The colonists did not enjoy the fruits of victory for long. After three more years of inconclusive warfare, Britain and France signed the Treaty of Aix-la-Chapelle in 1748, exchanging Louisbourg for a British outpost in India that the French had taken during the war. The memory of how their stunning achievement at Louisbourg went for naught would rankle the colonists for a decade.

A Fragile Peace

King George's War had failed to establish either Britain or France as the dominant power in North America, and each side soon began preparations for another war. Although there were many points of contention between the two powers, it was the Ohio Valley that became the tinderbox for conflict.

For more than half a century, the region had attracted refugee Indians—Delawares from Pennsylvania, Shawnees returning to their homeland from Pennsylvania and South Carolina, and others driven there by colonial expansion and fur-trade rivalries (see Chapter 4). Even some Iroquois, eager for new trading opportunities, had moved to the area, where they became known as Mingos. Initially welcomed as trade partners and bulwarks against English expansion, these Indians increasingly irritated the French by their independence, in particular the willingness of some to deal with Pennsylvania traders and even to fight against the

"Join or Die," 1754

Benjamin Franklin published this well-known cartoon just before the Albany Congress convened. The snake symbolized the colonies' considerable divisions—a disunity that political leaders would have to struggle against in years to come.

French in King George's War. The French derided these Indians as "republicans" for their defiance of all outside authority—French, English, and Iroquois.

For the next decade and a half, the "republican" Indians sought to balance the English and French against each other while the two powers grew ever less patient with the Indians' neutrality. After the war Virginia pressured some Iroquois leaders into ceding land occupied by Delawares so that the colony's agents could build a fortified trading post at the junction of the Allegheny and Monongahela rivers—the site of modern Pittsburgh. As a result the Delawares and other "republican" Indians began to fear that the English were the greater threat to their independence.

By 1752 the Ohio Valley was the subject of competing claims by Virginia, Pennsylvania, France, and the Iroquois, as well as by the Indians who actually lived there. The next year the French began building a chain of forts in order to recapture control of trade with the Indians from Virginians and Pennsylvanians. Virginia retaliated by sending a twenty-one-year-old surveyor and speculator, George Washington, to demand that the French abandon their forts on the Alleghany River, but the French refused. Returning in 1754 with three hundred colonial militiamen and one hundred British regulars, Washington found the French already constructing Fort Duquesne at the juncture of the rivers. After killing and seizing members of a small French force, Washington's men built a crude defensive position about sixty miles southeast called Fort

Necessity. The French retaliated swiftly and effectively. On July 4, 1754, after losing one-fourth of his men in a daylong battle, Washington surrendered Fort Necessity to an enemy force four times larger than his own and led the survivors home.

Sensing the need to resolve differences among themselves and to restore the confidence of the Indians in the face of an almost certain response by France, delegates from seven colonies north of Virginia gathered in mid-1754 at Albany, New York, to lay plans for their mutual defense. By showering the wavering Iroquois with thirty wagonloads of presents, the colonists kept them neutral for the moment. (But virtually all Indians in Ohio itself now supported the French.) The delegates then endorsed a proposal for a colonial confederation, the so-called Albany Plan of Union, largely based on the ideas of Pennsylvania's Franklin and Massachusetts's Thomas Hutchinson. The plan called for a "Grand Council" representing all the colonial assemblies, with a crown-appointed "president general" as its executive officer. The Grand Council would devise policies regarding military defense and Indian affairs, and if necessary, it could demand funds from the colonies according to an agreed-upon formula. Although it provided a precedent for later American unity, the Albany Plan came to nothing, primarily because no colonial legislature would surrender the least control over its powers of taxation, even to fellow Americans and in the face of grave mutual danger.

The Seven Years' War in America

Although France and Britain remained at peace in Europe until 1756, Washington's action at Fort Necessity created a virtual state of war in North America. In response, nearly eight thousand colonists enlisted during 1755 to attack French strongholds menacing New York and Nova Scotia. That same year, British general Edward Braddock and a thousand regular troops arrived in North America to take Fort Duquesne.

Stiff-necked and scornful of colonial soldiers, Braddock expected his disciplined British regulars to make short work of the enemy and only dimly perceived the strength and resourcefulness of the forces gathering against him. Washington's failure in the Ohio Valley and Braddock's arrogance had lost them all Indian support. On July 9, 1755, about 850 French, Canadians, and Indians ambushed Braddock's force of 2,200 Britons and Virginians nine miles east of Fort Duquesne. Riddled by three hours of steady fire from

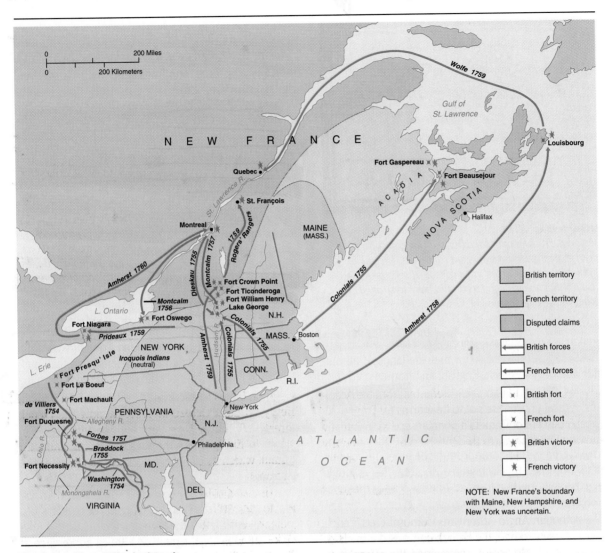

The Seven Years' War in America

After experiencing major defeats early in the war, Anglo-American forces turned the tide against the French by taking Fort Duquesne in late 1757 and Louisbourg in 1758. After Canada fell in 1760, the fighting shifted to Spain's Caribbean colonies.

an unseen foe, Braddock's troops retreated. Nine hdred regular and provincial soldiers died in Braddock's defeat, including the general himself, compared to just twenty-three on the French side.

Following this engagement, Indian raids convulsed Pennsylvania, Maryland, Virginia, and even parts of New Jersey—all colonies that had escaped attack in previous wars. Meanwhile, neither of two Anglo-American armies that marched against the French fortresses at Niagara and Crown Point in New York

reached its objective in 1755. The only successful British expedition that year was undertaken by two thousand New Englanders who seized two French forts near Nova Scotia. This campaign was memorable less for its military significance than for its tragic aftermath. Following the takeover of the French forts, the governor of Nova Scotia ordered the troops to drive thousands of local French-Canadian civilians, the Acadians, from their homes—often with nothing more than they could carry in their arms—and to burn their

New British Fort, 1759
After the French abandoned Crown Point on Lake Champlain, British troops occupied it and built a greatly expanded fortress. This watercolor was painted by a British officer.

villages. This cruel expulsion stemmed from the Acadians' refusal to promise not to bear arms for France. Almost 5 percent of Canada's population was eventually deported in this way to the British colonies, especially Maryland and Pennsylvania. But facing poverty and intense anti-French, anti-Catholic prejudice, most Acadians moved on to Louisiana. There they became known as Cajuns.

Although Anglo-Americans outnumbered French forces twenty to one, the French commander in chief, Louis Joseph Montcalm, maintained the offensive in 1756 and 1757. A daring and resourceful general, Montcalm benefited from large numbers of French regulars in Canada, overwhelming Indian support (including even that of the Iroquois), and the mobilization of nearly every able-bodied Canadian into a militia that fought with the courage of desperate men. In contrast, the American colonies balked at providing many troops and frequently sent poorly trained men who had been enlisted for only a few months. "I would rather have no Troops," wrote a despairing British colonel in 1757, "than to be at the Trouble & expence to form them, & when they could begin to be able to perform their Duty, be oblig'd to disband them."

Confronted by the numerically superior but disorganized Anglo-Americans, the French seized Fort Oswego on Lake Ontario in 1756 and took Fort William Henry on Lake George in 1757. By now the French threatened central New York and western New England. In Europe, too, the war was going badly for Britain, which by 1757 seemed to be facing defeat on all fronts.

In this dark hour, two developments turned the tide for the British. First, the Iroquois and most Ohio Indians, sensing that the French were gaining too decisive an advantage, agreed at a treaty conference at Easton, Pennsylvania, in 1758 to abandon their support of the French. Their subsequent withdrawal from Fort Duquesne enabled the British to capture it and other French forts. Although some Indians stayed out of the fighting, others actively joined the British cause.

The second decisive development occurred when one of the British ministers, William Pitt, took control of military affairs in the royal cabinet and reversed the downward course. Imaginative and single-minded in his conception of Britain's imperial destiny, Pitt saw himself as the man of the hour. "I know," he declared, "that I can save this country and that no one else can." True to his word, Pitt reinvigorated British patriotism throughout the empire. By the war's end, he was the colonists' most popular hero, the symbol of what Americans and the English could accomplish when united.

Hard pressed in Europe by France and its allies (which included Spain after 1761), Pitt preferred not to send large numbers of British regulars to America. Fewer than four thousand British troops arrived on the mainland from mid-1757 until New France's defeat. Rather, Pitt believed that the key to crushing New France lay in the mobilization of colonial soldiers. To encourage the colonies to assume the military burden, he promised that if they raised the necessary men, Parliament would bear most of the cost of fighting the war.

Pitt's offer to free Americans from the war's financial burdens generated unprecedented support. The colonies organized twenty-one thousand troops in 1758, more soldiers than the crown sent to the mainland during the entire war, and raised an equal number in 1759. The resulting offensive under General Jeffrey Amherst captured Fort Duquesne and Louisbourg by late 1758 and drove the French from northern New York the next year. In September 1759 Quebec fell after General James Wolfe defeated Montcalm on the Plains of Abraham outside that city, where both commanders died in battle. French resistance ended in 1760, when Montreal surrendered.

France ceded all its territories on the North American mainland by the Treaty of Paris of 1763, which officially ended the Seven Years' War in both America and Europe. France gave Britain all of its lands east of the Mississippi and transferred title to its claims west of that river to Spain, which also gained New Orleans. In return for Cuba, which a British expedition had taken over in 1762, Spain ceded Florida to Britain. Spain's vast American empire thus remained intact, but France's formerly extensive holdings were reduced to a few tiny fishing islands off Newfoundland and several thriving sugar isl in the West Indies. Britain reigned supreme in eastern North America.

IMPERIAL REORGANIZATION

Following the Seven Years' War, Britain sought to finance its greatly expanded empire through a series of revenue measures imposed on Britons and colonists alike, and to exercise more direct control over its colonies. Opposition movements arose in both Britain and its colonies in mainland North America, from Massachusetts to Georgia, to protest not only the new measures' economic costs but what many people regarded

George III, *Studio of A. Ramsay, c. 1767*
Although unsure of himself and emotionally little more than a boy upon his accession to the English throne, George III possessed a deep moral sense and a fierce determination to rule as well as to reign.

as a dangerous extension of tyrannical power. In America this confrontation quickly escalated into a principled conflict over the colonies' relationship with Parliament in Britain.

These measures coincided with the beginning of the reign of George III (ruled 1760–1820), who ascended to the throne at age twenty-two. In contrast to his immediate predecessors, George I and George II, who had been largely content to let veteran politicians in Parliament run the country, the new king distrusted the British political establishment. He was determined to have a strong influence on government policy, but he wished to reign as a constitutional monarch who cooperated with Parliament and worked through prime ministers. However, neither his experience, his temperament, nor his philosophy suited George III to the formidable task of selecting satisfactory prime ministers to oversee the passage of imperial laws. Frequent clashes of personality and policy prompted the king to make abrupt changes in leadership at the very time when British government was trying to implement a massive reorganization of the empire. George's first prime minister, his friend and former tutor Lord Bute, lasted only from 1760 to 1763. Then in quick succession came the ministry of George Grenville from 1763 to 1765, that of the Marquis of Rockingham in 1766, the ministry of the ailing William Pitt in 1766, and a period of uncertain leadership that ended only in 1770, with the appointment of the ministry led by Frederick, Lord North.

Friction Among Allies

An extraordinary coalition of Britons, colonists, and Native Americans had achieved the victory over France in North America. But the return of peace brought deep-seated tensions among these allies back to the surface.

In England, public opinion assumed that credit for the victory belonged to the professional soldiers

European Powers in the New World Before 1754 and in 1763

The Treaty of Paris (1763) divided France's North American empire between Britain and Spain. Hoping to prevent unnecessary violence between whites and Indians, Britain forbade any new white settlements west of the Appalachians' crest in the Proclamation of 1763.

sent over from Britain. In fact, however, two of every five regulars who served had enlisted in America. Benjamin Franklin once complained that, although the force that captured two French forts on Nova Scotia's border in 1755 comprised two thousand Massachusetts troops and fewer than three hundred British regulars, "yet it could not be discovered by the Account . . . published in the London Gazette, that there was a single New England man concern'd in the Affair."

Although realizing that the newly formed colonial units would not perform as well as veteran regiments, Pitt had nevertheless placed the American enlistees in charge of vital support roles: forming the reserve force in battle, performing essential supply functions, and holding frontier forts. This plan had the advantage of freeing the greatest number of British regulars for combat against the highly trained French. But British officers in America regularly complained about the quality of colonial troops, not only their inability to fight but also their tendency to return home—even in the midst of campaigns—when their terms were up or when they were not paid on time. For their part, colonial soldiers complained of British officers who, as one put it, contemptuously treated their troops "but little better than slaves."

Tensions between British officers and colonial civilians also flared, with officers complaining about colonists' unwillingness to provide food and shelter and colonists resenting the officers' arrogant manners. One general groused that South Carolina planters were "extremely pleased to have Soldiers to protect their Plantations but will feel no inconveniences for them." Quakers in the Pennsylvania assembly, acting from their pacifist convictions, refused to vote funds to support the war effort, while assemblies in New York and Massachusetts opposed the quartering of British troops on their soil as an encroachment on their English liberties. English authorities regarded such actions as affronts to the king's prerogative and as stifling Britain's efforts to defend its territories.

Pitt's promise to reimburse the colonial assemblies for their military expenses also angered many Britons, who concluded that the colonists were escaping scot-free from the war's financial burden. The colonies had already profited enormously from the war, as military contracts and spending by British troops brought an influx of British currency into the hands of farmers, artisans, and merchants. Some colonial merchants, moreover, had continued their illicit trade with the French West Indies during the conflict,

so that they were not only violating the Navigation Acts but trading with the enemy. Meanwhile, Britain's national debt had nearly doubled during the war, from £72 million to over £132 million. At a time when the total debt of all the colonies collectively amounted to £2 million, the interest charges alone on the British debt came to more than £4 million a year. This debt was assumed by landowners through a land tax and, increasingly, by ordinary consumers through excise duties on a wide variety of items, including beer, tea, salt, and bread.

But many colonists felt equally burdened. Those who profited during the war spent their additional incomes on goods imported from Britain, the annual value of which doubled during the war's brief duration. Along with a parallel movement in Britain, the consumption of tea, wine, mass-produced textiles, ceramics, and metalware by members of the middle class was fueling Britain's economy, particularly its manufacturing sector. And it was transforming the habits and tastes of thousands of people who previously had made or purchased locally nearly everything they consumed. But the wartime boom in the colonies ended as abruptly as it had begun when peace returned in 1760. To maintain their new middle-class lifestyles, colonists went into debt. British creditors obliged their American merchant customers by extending the usual period for remitting payments from six months to a year. Nevertheless, many recently prosperous colonists suddenly found themselves overloaded with debts and in many cases bankrupt. As colonial indebtedness to Britain grew, some Americans began to suspect the British of deliberately plotting to "enslave" the colonies.

Victory over the French did not end the British need for revenue, for the settlement of the war spurred new Anglo-Indian conflicts that drove the British debt even higher. With the French vanquished, Ohio and Great Lakes Indians recognized that they could no longer play the two imperial rivals off against one another. Their fears that the British would treat them as subjects rather than allies were confirmed when General Amherst decided to cut expenses by refusing to distribute food, ammunition, and other gifts. Moreover, squatters from the colonies were moving onto Indian lands in some areas and harassing the occupants, and many Indians feared that the British occupation was intended to support these incursions.

As tensions mounted, a Delaware religious prophet named Neolin attracted a large following by calling for a complete repudiation by Indians of European culture, material goods, and alliances. Meanwhile, other Native Americans hoped that the French would return so they could once again balance the two powers against each other. Political leaders such as Pontiac, an Ottawa Indian, drew on these sentiments to forge an explicitly anti-British movement. During the spring and summer of 1763, they sacked eight British forts near the Great Lakes and besieged two others at Pittsburgh and Detroit. But over the next three years, shortages of food and ammunition, a smallpox epidemic (triggered when British officers at Fort Pitt distributed deliberately infected blankets at a peace parley), and a recognition that the French would not return led the Indians to make peace with Britain. Although word of the uprising spread to Indians in the Southeast and Mississippi Valley, the effective diplomacy of British agent John Stuart prevented violence from erupting in these areas.

Despite the uprising's failure, the Native Americans had not been decisively defeated. Hoping to conciliate the Indians and end the frontier fighting, the British government issued the Proclamation of 1763, by which it asserted direct control of land transactions, settlement, trade, and other activities of non-Indians west of the Appalachian crest. The government's goal was to restore order to the process of colonial expansion by replacing the authority of the various (and often competing) colonies with that of the crown. The proclamation recognized existing Indian land titles everywhere west of the "proclamation line" until such time as tribal governments agreed to cede their land through treaties. Although calming Indian fears, the proclamation angered the colonies by subordinating their western claims to imperial authority and by slowing expansion.

The uprising was also a factor in the British government's decision that ten thousand British soldiers should remain in North America to occupy the new western territories and to intimidate the Indian, French, and Spanish inhabitants. The British expected to spend £220,000 annually to maintain these troops, but the actual expense soared to nearly twice that figure. With the £20,000 needed to establish civil governments in Canada and Florida factored in, the burden of maintaining control over Britain's newly acquired territories would reach almost half a million pounds a year, fully 6 percent of Britain's peacetime budget. Britons considered it perfectly reasonable for the colonists to help offset this expense, which the

colonists, however, saw as none of their responsibility. Although the troops would help to offset the colonies' unfavorable balance of payments with Britain, they appeared to many Americans as a "standing army" that in peacetime could only threaten their liberty. With the French menace to their security removed, increasing numbers of colonists saw westward expansion onto Indian lands as a way to prosperity, and they viewed British troops, enforcing the Proclamation of 1763, as hindering rather than enhancing that expansion.

The Writs of Assistance

Even before the Seven Years' War was over, British attempts to halt American merchants from trading with the enemy in the French West Indies produced a crackdown on smuggling. In 1760 the royal governor of Massachusetts authorized revenue officers to employ a document called a writ of assistance to seize illegally imported goods. The writ was a general search warrant that permitted customs officials to enter any ships or buildings where smuggled goods might be hidden. Because the document required no evidence of probable cause for suspicion, most English legal authorities considered it unconstitutional. The writ of assistance also threatened the traditional respect accorded the privacy of a family's place of residence, since most merchants conducted business from their homes. The writ allowed a customs agent to ransack a merchant's house in search of illegal goods, even if there was no evidence of lawbreaking.

Writs of assistance proved a powerful weapon against smuggling. In quick reaction to the writs, merchants in Boston, virtually the smuggling capital of the colonies, hired lawyer James Otis to challenge the constitutionality of these warrants. Arguing his case before the Massachusetts supreme court in 1761, Otis proclaimed that "an act against the Constitution is void"—even one passed by Parliament. But the court, heavily influenced by the opinion of Chief Justice Thomas Hutchinson, who noted the continuing use of identical writs in England, ruled against the Boston merchants.

Despite having lost the case, Otis had expressed with absolute clarity the fundamental conception of many, both in Britain and in the colonies, of Parliament's role under the British constitution. The British constitution was not a written document but a collection of customs and accepted principles that guaranteed certain rights to all citizens. Most British politicians assumed that Parliament's laws were themselves part of the constitution and hence that Parliament could alter the constitution at will. Like other colonists, Otis contended that Parliament possessed no authority to violate any of the traditional "rights of Englishmen," and he asserted that there were limits "beyond which if Parliaments go, their Acts bind not."

The Sugar Act

In 1764, just three years after Otis's court challenge, Parliament passed the Sugar Act with the goal of raising £100,000, a sum that would offset one-fifth of the military expenses in North America. Its enactment triggered a new round of tension between Britain and the colonies, for the Sugar Act ended Britain's long-standing policy of exempting colonial trade from revenue-raising measures. The Navigation Acts had not been designed to bring money into the British treasury but rather to benefit the imperial economy indirectly, by stimulating trade and protecting English manufacturers from foreign competition. The taxes that Parliament levied on colonial products entering Britain were paid by English importers who passed them on to consumers; they were not taxes paid by American producers. So little revenue did the Navigation Acts bring in (just £1,800 in 1763) that they did not even pay for the cost of their own enforcement, which came to about £8,000.

The Sugar Act amended the old Molasses Act of 1733, which had taxed all foreign molasses entering British America at 6 pence per gallon. Parliament had never intended this law to raise revenue but rather to serve as a protective tariff excluding French West Indian molasses from entering British North America, where colonists distilled it into rum. But colonists simply continued to import the cheaper French molasses, bribing customs officials into taking 1½ pence per gallon to look the other way when it was unloaded. Aware of the widespread bribery, Parliament assumed, erroneously, that rum drinkers could stomach a 3 pence duty per gallon.

New taxes were not the only feature of the Sugar Act objectionable to American merchants. The act also stipulated that colonists could export lumber, iron, skins, hides, whalebone, logwood, and many other commodities to foreign countries only if the shipments landed first in Britain. Previously, American ships had taken these products directly to the

Netherlands or the German states, where captains purchased local goods and then sailed straight back to the colonies. By channeling this trade through Britain, Parliament hoped that colonial shippers would purchase more *imperial* wares for the American market and buy fewer goods from foreign competitors. Moreover, by slapping a heavy tax on the formerly thriving American business of carrying duty-free Portuguese wine from Madeira and the Azores to the colonists, the law also aimed to increase English merchants' sales of European wine. By interfering with a profitable trade developed through American enterprise, the Sugar Act had the perverse effect of creating a new category of smuggling where none had existed before, because many colonial merchants ultimately ignored the law, which in their view senselessly sacrificed their interests.

The Sugar Act also vastly complicated the requirements for shipping colonial goods. A captain now had to fill out a confusing series of documents to certify his trade as legal, and the absence of any of them left his entire cargo liable to seizure. Moreover, the Sugar Act defined oceanic commerce so broadly that much of the trade between colonies, never before regulated, became subject to complex rules for compliance. The law's petty regulations made it virtually impossible for many colonial shippers to avoid committing technical violations of the Sugar Act, even if they traded in the only manner possible under local circumstances.

Finally, the Sugar Act disregarded many traditional English protections for a fair trial. First, the law allowed customs officials to transfer smuggling cases from the colonial courts, in which juries decided the outcome, to vice-admiralty courts, where a judge alone gave the verdict. Because the Sugar Act (until 1768) awarded vice-admiralty judges 5 percent of any confiscated cargo, judges had a financial incentive to find defendants guilty. Second, until 1767 the law did not permit defendants to be tried where their offense allegedly had taken place (usually their home province) but required all cases to be heard in the vice-admiralty court at Halifax, Nova Scotia. Third, the law reversed normal courtroom procedures, which presumed innocence until guilt was proved, by requiring the defendant to disprove the prosecution's charge.

The Sugar Act was no idle threat. British prime minister George Grenville ordered the navy to enforce the measure, and it did so vigorously. A Boston resident complained in 1764 that "no vessel hardly comes in or goes out but they find some pretense to seize and detain her." That same year, Pennsylvania's chief justice reported that customs officers were extorting fees from small boats carrying lumber across the Delaware River to Philadelphia from New Jersey and seemed likely "to destroy this little River-trade."

Rather than pay the 3 pence tax, Americans continued smuggling molasses until 1766. Then, to discourage smuggling, Britain lowered the duty to 1 penny—less than the customary bribe American shippers paid to get their cargoes past inspectors. The law thereafter raised about £30,000 annually in revenue until 1775.

Colonial opponents hesitated to denounce the Sugar Act as unconstitutional, for it seemingly only amended the Molasses Act. Although nine provincial legislatures protested that in passing the Sugar Act, Parliament had abused its authority to regulate trade, seven of these objected on narrow grounds—either to its economic consequences for distillers or to its denial of traditional guarantees of a fair trial. Thus opposition to the Sugar Act remained fragmented and ineffective. The law's burden fell overwhelmingly on Massachusetts, New York, and Pennsylvania; other provinces had little interest in resisting a measure that did not affect them directly. In the end, the Sugar Act's immediate impact was minor. Soon a far more controversial issue would overshadow it—the Stamp Act.

The Stamp Act

The revenue raised by the Sugar Act did little to ease Britain's financial crisis. The national debt continued to rise, and the British public groaned under the weight of the second-highest tax rates in Europe. Particularly irritating to Britons was the fact that by 1765 their rates averaged 26 shillings per person, whereas the colonial tax burden varied from ½ to 1½ shillings per inhabitant, or barely 2 percent to 6 percent of the British rate. Well aware of how lightly the colonists were taxed, Grenville thought that fairness demanded a larger contribution to the empire's expenses in North America.

To force the colonists to pay their share of imperial expenses, Parliament passed the Stamp Act in March 1765. The law obliged Americans to purchase and use special stamped (watermarked) paper for newspapers, customs documents, various licenses, college diplomas, and numerous legal forms necessary for recovering debts, buying land, and making wills. As with the Sugar Act, any violators would face prosecution in vice-admiralty courts, without juries.

The prime minister projected yearly revenues of £60,000 to £100,000, which would offset 12 percent to 20 percent of North American military expenses. Unlike the Sugar Act, which was an *external* tax—one levied on imports as they entered the colonies—the Stamp Act was an *internal* tax, or a duty levied directly on property, goods, and government services in the colonies. Whereas external taxes were intended to regulate trade and fell mainly on merchants and ship captains, internal taxes were designed to raise revenue

Tax Stamps
Under the Stamp Act, all legal and commercial documents had to bear tax stamps such as the one shown here in close-up.

for the crown and had far wider effects. In the case of the Stamp Act, anyone who made a will, transferred property, borrowed money, or bought playing cards or newspapers would pay the tax.

To Grenville and most of his supporters in Britain, the new tax seemed a small price for the benefits of the empire, especially since Britons had been paying a similar tax since 1695. Nevertheless, some in England, most notably William Pitt, objected in principle to Britain's levying an internal tax on the colonies. They emphasized that the colonists had never been subject to British revenue bills and noted that they taxed themselves through their own elected assemblies.

Grenville and his followers agreed with Pitt that Parliament could not tax any British subjects unless they enjoyed representation in that body. But, they contended, Americans *were* represented in Parliament, even if no one in the colonies actually elected any members. Americans, the prime minister claimed, shared the same status as the majority of British adult males, who either lacked sufficient property to vote or lived in large cities like Sheffield, Manchester, and Birmingham—some more populous than the entire colony of Georgia in the mid-1760s—which had no seats in Parliament. Such people were considered to be "virtually" represented in Parliament. The theory of virtual representation held that every member of Parliament stood above the narrow interests of his constituents and considered the welfare of *all* subjects when deciding issues. By definition, then, no Briton was represented by any particular individual in the House of Commons, but rather all imperial subjects, including Americans, could depend on each member of Parliament to protect their well-being.

Grenville and his supporters also denied that the colonists were entitled to any exemption from British taxation because they elected their own assemblies. These legislative bodies were allegedly no different from English or Scottish town councils, whose local powers to pass laws and taxes did not nullify Parliament's authority over them. Accordingly, colonial assemblies were an adaptation to unique American circumstances and possessed no more power than Parliament allowed them to exercise. But Grenville's position clashed directly with the stance of many colonists who had been arguing for several decades that their assemblies exercised legislative powers equivalent to those of the House of Commons in Britain (see Chapter 4).

The Colonial Perspective

To many colonists the Stamp Act seemed to force them either to confront the issue of parliamentary taxation head-on or surrender any claim to meaningful rights of self-government. However much they might admire and respect Parliament, few colonists imagined that it represented them. American spokesmen accepted the theory of virtual representation as valid for England and Scotland, but they denied that it could be extended to inhabitants of the colonies. In their view, unless a lawmaker shared the interests of his constituents, he would have no personal stake in opposing bills contrary to their welfare.

To many colonists Parliament's passage of the Stamp Act demonstrated both its indifference to their interests and the shallowness of the theory of virtual representation. Colonial agents in London had lobbied against passage of the law, and provincial legislatures had sent petitions—carefully worded statements of principle—warning against passage, but all to no avail. Parliament had dismissed the petitions without a hearing. Parliament "must have thought us Americans all a parcel of Apes and very tame Apes too," concluded Christopher Gadsden of South Carolina, "or they would have never ventured on such a hateful, baneful experiment."

Although the colonists rejected Parliament's claim to tax them, they did concede that it possessed *limited* powers of legislation. For example, they be-

lieved that Parliament could standardize legal procedures throughout the realm to permit every British subject equal access to royal justice. The colonists also accepted the practical necessity for Parliament to regulate the empire's trade, even if their commerce was inconvenienced in the process.

Anglo-Americans considered the essential obligation of British allegiance to be loyalty to the crown, and their one unequivocal duty to be helping to defend the empire in wartime. The colonists insisted that they enjoyed a substantial measure of self-governance similar to that of Ireland, whose Parliament alone could tax its people but could not interfere with laws, like the Navigation Acts, passed by the British Parliament. In a speech before the Boston town meeting opposing the Sugar Act, James Otis expressed Americans' basic argument: "that by [the British] Constitution, every man in the dominions is a free man: that no parts of His Majesty's dominions can be taxed without consent: that every part has a right to be represented in the supreme or some subordinate legislature." In essence, the colonists assumed that the empire was a loose federation in which their legislatures possessed considerable autonomy, rather than an extended nation governed directly from London.

Resisting the Stamp Act

Unlike the Sugar Act, the Stamp Act generated a political storm that rumbled through all the colonies in 1765. Nearly every rank in society was caught up in the tempest—unskilled workers, artisans, small farmers, planters, and merchants; blacks as well as whites; women as well as men. Before the protest was over, upper-class community leaders had assumed direction of the colonial resistance movement.

In late May, Patrick Henry, a twenty-nine-year-old Virginia lawyer with a talent for fiery oratory, dramatically conveyed the rising spirit of resistance. Henry persuaded the Virginia House of Burgesses to adopt several strongly worded resolutions denying Parliament's power to tax the colonies, and in the debate over the resolutions, the Speaker of the House cut him off just short of his uttering a treasonous wish that "some good American would stand up for his country"—presumably by assassinating the British tyrant responsible. Rather garbled accounts of Henry's resolutions electrified other Americans, and by the year's end, eight other colonial legislatures took a firm stand against British taxation.

Stamp Act Protest
A Boston crowd burns bundles of the special watermarked paper intended for use as stamps.

Meanwhile, grass-roots resistance to the law was taking shape. In Boston by late summer, a group of mostly middle-class artisans, shopkeepers, and businessmen joined together as the Loyal Nine to fight the Stamp Act. They recognized that the stamp distributors, who alone could accept money for watermarked paper, were the law's weak link. If the public could pressure them into resigning before taxes became due on November 1, the Stamp Act would become inoperable. The Loyal Nine would propel Boston to the forefront of resistance.

It was no accident that Boston set the pace in opposing Parliament. Bostonians lived primarily by trade and distilling, and in 1765 they were not living well. No other port suffered so much from the Sugar Act's trade restrictions. The law burdened rum producers with a heavy tax on molasses, dried up a flourishing business of importing Portuguese wines, and prohibited the direct export of many New England products to prof-

itable overseas markets. The city, moreover, was still struggling to recover from a great fire in 1760 that had burned 176 warehouses and left every tenth family homeless.

Widespread economic distress produced an explosive situation in Boston. A large segment of its population blamed British policies for the town's hard times. The situation was unusually dangerous because Bostonians were accustomed to forming large crowds to engage in pointed but symbolic political expression. The high point of each year was November 5, Guy Fawkes Day, when thousands gathered to commemorate the failure of a Catholic plot in England in 1605 to blow up Parliament and kill King James I. On that day each year, crowds from the North End and the South End customarily burned gigantic effigies of the pope as well as of local political leaders and other elite figures, and generally satirized the behavior of the "better sort." High spirits sometimes overflowed into violent confrontations in which the two crowds battled each other with fists, stones, and barrel staves. In August 1765 the Loyal Nine oversaw a truce between the two groups that united them under a South End shoemaker named Ebenezer MacIntosh.

The morning of August 14 found a likeness of Boston's stamp distributor, Andrew Oliver, swinging from a tree guarded by a menacing crowd. Oliver apparently did not realize that the Loyal Nine were warning him to resign immediately, so at dusk MacIntosh and several hundred shouting followers demolished a new building of Oliver's at the dock. Thereafter, the Loyal Nine withdrew and the crowd continued on its own. The men surged toward Oliver's house, where they ceremoniously beheaded his effigy and "stamped" it to pieces, an exercise designed in part to give him time to flee to safety. The crowd then shattered the windows of his home, smashed his furniture, and even tore out the paneling. When Lieutenant Governor Thomas Hutchinson and the sheriff tried to disperse the crowd, they were driven off under a barrage of rocks. Surveying his devastated home the next morning, Oliver announced his resignation.

Bitterness against the Stamp Act unleashed spontaneous, contagious violence. Twelve days after the first Boston riot, Bostonians demolished the elegant home of Thomas Hutchinson. This attack occurred in part because smugglers held grudges against Hutchinson for certain decisions he had given as chief justice and also because many financially pinched citizens saw him as a symbol of the royal policies crippling Boston's already troubled economy and their own livelihoods. In their view, wealthy officials "rioted in luxury," with homes and fancy furnishings that cost hundreds of times the annual incomes of most Boston working men. Others lashed out in reaction to Hutchinson's efforts to stop the destruction of his brother-in-law Andrew Oliver's house. Ironically, Hutchinson privately opposed the Stamp Act.

Violence nearly got completely out of hand in Newport, Rhode Island. As in Boston, a working-class crowd organized by merchants quickly assumed a life of its own, but in this case the mob turned on the merchants themselves. After the rowdies burned the effigies and sacked the homes of three stamp distributors, an English seaman named John Webber assumed leadership. Webber threatened to destroy the merchants' homes and warehouses unless they paid a large sum, and publicly humiliated the sheriff. One of the deposed stamp masters—who was also the colony's attorney general—ended Webber's threats by clapping him in jail.

Meanwhile, groups similar to the Loyal Nine but calling themselves Sons of Liberty began forming throughout the colonies. The Sons of Liberty directed their violence against property and invariably left avenues of escape for their victims. No one was killed or tarred and feathered, although some stamp distributors had their pride deeply wounded.

After Webber's rampage and the frenzied assault on Hutchinson's mansion, the leaders of the Sons of Liberty sought to prevent more such incidents, lest they alienate elite opponents of the tax. They directed public demonstrations with firm discipline and sometimes used military formations to maneuver hundreds of protesters like a small army. Especially fearful that a royal soldier or revenue officer might be shot or killed, the Sons of Liberty forbade their followers to carry weapons, even when facing armed adversaries. Realizing the value of martyrs, they resolved that the only lives lost over the issue of British taxation would come from their own ranks.

In October 1765 representatives of nine colonial assemblies met in New York City in the so-called Stamp Act Congress. The session was remarkable for the colonies' agreement on and bold articulation of the general principle that Parliament lacked authority to levy taxes outside Great Britain and to deny any person a jury trial. Only once before had a truly intercolonial meeting taken place—the Albany Congress, in 1754—

and, as we have seen, its plea for unity had fallen on deaf ears. In 1765 the colonial response was entirely different. "The Ministry never imagined we could or would so generally unite in opposition to their measures," wrote a Connecticut delegate to the congress, "nor I confess till I saw the Experiment made did I."

By late 1765 most stamp distributors had resigned or fled, and, without the watermarked paper required by law, most royal customs officials and court officers were refusing to perform their duties. In response, legislators compelled the reluctant officials to resume operation by threatening to withhold their pay. At the same time, merchants obtained sailing clearances by insisting that they would sue if cargoes spoiled while delayed in port. By late December the courts and harbors of almost every colony were again functioning.

Thus the colonial upper class assumed control of the public outcry against the Stamp Act. Respectable gentlemen moved to keep an explosive situation from getting out of hand by taking over leadership of local Sons of Liberty groups, by coordinating protest through the Stamp Act Congress, and by having colonial legislatures restore normal business. Colonial leaders feared that chaos was about to break out, particularly if British troops landed to enforce the Stamp Act. An influential Pennsylvanian, John Dickinson, summed up how colonial elites envisioned the dire consequences of revolutionary turmoil: "a multitude of Commonwealths, Crimes, and Calamities, Centuries of mutual jealousies, Hatreds, Wars of Devastation, till at last the exhausted provinces shall sink into savagery under the yoke of some fortunate Conqueror."

Such extreme consequences did not come to pass, though the Stamp Act remained in effect. To force its repeal, New York's merchants agreed on October 31, 1765, to boycott all British goods, and businessmen in other cities soon followed their example. Because American colonists purchased about 40 percent of England's manufactures, this nonimportation strategy put the English economy in danger of recession. The colonial boycotts consequently triggered panic within England's business community, whose members descended on Parliament to warn that the Stamp Act's continuation would stimulate a wave of bankruptcies, massive unemployment, and political unrest.

For reasons unconnected with the Stamp Act, George Grenville had fallen from George III's favor in mid-1765 and had been succeeded by the Marquis of Rockingham. The new prime minister hesitated to advocate repeal because the overwhelming majority within the House of Commons was outraged at colonial defiance of the law. Then in January 1766 William Pitt, a steadfast opponent of the Stamp Act, boldly denounced all efforts to tax the colonies, declaring, "I rejoice that America has resisted." Parliamentary support for repeal thereafter grew, though only as a matter of practicality, not as a surrender of principle. In March 1766 Parliament revoked the Stamp Act, but only in conjunction with passage of the Declaratory Act, which affirmed parliamentary power to legislate for the colonies "in all cases whatsoever."

Because the Declaratory Act was written in general language, Americans interpreted its meaning to their advantage. Most colonial political leaders recognized that the law was modeled after an earlier statute of 1719 regarding Ireland, which was considered exempt from British taxation. The measure therefore seemed no more than a parliamentary exercise in saving face to compensate for the Stamp Act's repeal, and Americans ignored it. The House of Commons, however, intended that the colonists take the Declaratory Act literally to mean that they could not claim exemption from *any* parliamentary statute, including a tax law. The Stamp Act crisis thus ended in a fundamental disagreement between Britain and America over the colonists' political rights.

Although the Stamp Act crisis had not resolved the underlying philosophical differences between Britain and America, most colonists eagerly put the events of 1765 behind them, and they showered both king and Parliament with loyal statements of gratitude for the Stamp Act's repeal. The Sons of Liberty disbanded. Anglo-Americans manifestly still possessed a deep emotional loyalty to "Old England" and concluded with relief that their active resistance to the law had slapped Britain's leaders back to their senses. Nevertheless, the crisis led many to ponder British policies and actions more deeply than ever before.

Ideology, Religion, and Resistance

The Stamp Act and the conflicts that arose around it revealed a chasm between England and its colonies that startled Anglo-Americans. For the first time, some sensed a sinister quality to the imperial relationship that they previously had taken for granted and valued. In their efforts to grasp the significance of their new perceptions, a number of educated colonists turned to the works of philosophers, historians, and political writers. Many more, both educated and uneducated, looked to religion.

By the 1760s the colonists already were widely familiar with the political writings of European Enlightenment thinkers, particularly John Locke (see Chapter 4). Locke argued that humanity originated in a state of nature in which people enjoyed the "natural rights" of life, liberty, and property. Thereafter, people entered into a "social contract" in order to form governments that would protect those rights. A government that encroached on natural rights, then, broke its contract with the people. In such cases, people could resist their government, although Locke cautioned against outright rebellion except in the most extreme cases. To many colonial readers, Locke's concept of natural rights appeared to justify opposition to arbitrary legislation by Parliament.

Among the most widely read authors in the colonies were a group of English political writers known as oppositionists. According to John Trenchard, Thomas Gordon, and others belonging to this group, Parliament—consisting of the freely elected representatives of the people—formed the foundation of England's unique political liberties and protected those liberties against the inherent corruption and tyranny of executive power. But since 1720, the oppositionists argued, prime ministers had exploited the treasury's vast resources to provide pensions, contracts, and profitable offices to politicians or had bought elections by bribing voters in small boroughs. Most members of Parliament, in their view, no longer represented the true interests of their constituents; rather, they had sold their souls for financial gain and joined in a "conspiracy against liberty." Often referring to themselves as the "country party," these oppositionists feared that a power-hungry "court party" of nonelected officials close to the king was using a corrupted Parliament to gain absolute power for themselves.

During the 1760s and 1770s, a group of English radicals, most notably Joseph Priestley and James Burgh, drew on both Enlightenment and oppositionist authors to fashion a wide-ranging critique of English government and a new way of thinking about politics. At the heart of all political relationships, they argued, a struggle raged between the aggressive extension of artificial *power,* as represented by corrupt governments, and the natural *liberty* of the people. To protect their liberty, a free people had to avoid moral corruption in their own lives and resist the encroachments of power, or tyranny. Above all, they had to remain alert for "designs" or "conspiracies" against liberty wherever they might appear.

Influenced by such ideas, a number of colonists detected a diabolical conspiracy behind British policy during the Stamp Act crisis. John Adams referred to the actions of Massachusetts lieutenant governor Thomas Hutchinson as "serpentine wiles," and James Otis characterized a group of pro-British Rhode Islanders as a "little, dirty, drinking, drabbing, contaminated knot of thieves, beggars, and transports . . . made up of Turks, Jews, and other infidels, with a few renegade Christians and Catholics." Joseph Warren of Massachusetts noted that the act not unreasonably "induced some to imagine that the minister designed by this to force the colonies into a rebellion, and from thence to take occasion to treat them with severity, and, by military power, to reduce them to servitude." Over the next decade, a proliferation of pamphlets denounced British efforts to "enslave" the colonies through excessive taxation and the imposition of officials, judges, and a standing army directed from London. In such assaults on liberty and natural rights, some Americans found principled reasons for opposing British policies and actions.

Many colonists also followed the lead of Massachusetts assemblyman Samuel Adams, who expressed hope that America would become a "Christian Sparta." By linking religion and ancient history, Adams was combining two of colonial leaders' most potent rhetorical appeals in rallying public protest. Almost every eighteenth-century American had been steeped in Protestantism since childhood; and all whose education had gone beyond the basics had imbibed Greek and Latin learning, as well as seventeenth-century English literature. All these hallowed traditions, Americans believed, confirmed the legitimacy of their cause. "Having been initiated in youth, in the doctrines of civil liberty, as they were taught by such men as Plato . . . [and] Cicero . . . among the ancients; and such as . . . Milton [and] Locke . . . among the moderns," wrote the minister Jonathan Mayhew, "[and] having earlier still learnt from the holy scriptures, that wise, brave, and virtuous men were always friends of liberty . . . I would not, I cannot now, relinquish the fair object of my youthful affections, LIBERTY. . . ."

Recalling in later years the inspiring debate over the Stamp Act that he had witnessed in Virginia's House of Burgesses in 1765, Thomas Jefferson said of Patrick Henry that "he appeared to me to speak as Homer wrote." Jefferson was a typical educated man of his day in revering the ancient republics of Greece and Rome for their supposedly stern, virtuous devotion to liberty. The pamphlets, speeches, and public declarations that gentlemen like Jefferson and Dickinson wrote resounded with quotations from the ancient classics. These allusions served as constant reminders to upper-class Americans of the righteous dignity of their cause. But appeals to ordinary Americans had to draw upon deeper wellsprings of belief. Significantly, the power of Henry's oratory also reflected his ability (unique among Virginia political leaders) to evoke the colonists' religious fervor, which the Great Awakening had stirred.

Beginning with the Stamp Act protest, New England's clergymen mounted their pulpits and summoned their flocks to stand up for God and liberty. "A just regard to our liberties . . . is so far from being

A Patriot View of British Officials, 1766
This Boston editorial cartoon depicts Lord Bute (left) and another British official as enslaved to the devil.

displeasing to God that it would be ingratitude to him who has given them to us to . . . tamely give them up," exhorted one minister. "We are bound in conscience to stand fast in the liberty with which Christ has made us free." Not quite so quickly, but in the end with equally heartfelt intensity, Baptist and other dissenting preachers took up the cause. Only Anglican ministers, whose church was headed by the king, tried to stay neutral or opposed the protest; and many pacifist Quakers kept out of the fray. But to most American Protestant clergymen, memories of battling for the Lord in the old Calvinist tradition proved too powerful to resist.

Voicing such a message, "the black regiment" of clergymen in their dignified gowns exerted an enormous influence on public opinion. Far more Americans heard sermons than had access to newspapers or pamphlets, and ministers always got a respectful hearing at town meetings. Community leaders' proclamations of days of "fasting and public humiliation"—in colonial America, a familiar means of focusing public attention on an issue and invoking divine aid—inspired sermons on the theme of God's sending the people woes only to strengthen and sustain them until victory. Even Virginia gentlemen not notable for their piety felt moved by such proclamations and ordered their families to comply. Moreover, protest leaders' calls for boycotting British luxuries meshed neatly with traditional pulpit warnings against frivolity and wastefulness. Few ordinary Americans escaped the unceasing public reminders that community solidarity against British tyranny and "corruption" meant rejecting sin and obeying God.

The ebbing of the Stamp Act crisis momentarily took the urgency out of such extreme views. But the alarm that Britain's actions raised in the minds of many colonists was not easily put to rest. After a hiatus of two years, it was clear that British and American views of the colonies' place in the empire remained as far apart as ever.

ERA OF ANGLO-AMERICAN CRISIS

From 1767 to 1773, Parliament pursued a confrontational policy that gradually corroded Americans' trust of Britain. The British government's actions in these years created a climate of fear and alienation that left most colonists convinced that the Stamp Act had not been an isolated mistake but part of a deliberate design to undermine colonial self-governance. In this they were joined by growing numbers in Britain who questioned policies that were economically costly and actions that seemed to threaten Britons and colonists alike.

The Quartering Act

In August 1766, in a move arising out of British politics, George III dismissed the Rockingham government and summoned William Pitt to form a cabinet. An opponent of taxing the colonies, Pitt had the potential to repair the Stamp Act's damage, for no man was more respected in America. Pitt's health collapsed in March 1767 however, and effective leadership passed to his chancellor of the exchequer (or treasurer) Charles Townshend.

Just as Townshend took office, a conflict arose with the New York legislature over the Quartering Act of 1765. This law ordered colonial legislatures to pay for certain goods needed by soldiers stationed within their respective borders. The necessary items were relatively inexpensive barracks supplies such as candles, windowpanes, mattress straw, polish, and a small liquor ration. The Quartering Act applied only to troops in settled areas, not on the frontier. It did not force citizens to accept soldiers in private homes or require legislatures to build new barracks. Just five colonies fell under its provisions, and four of these generally complied.

Despite its seemingly petty stipulations, the law aroused resentment, for it constituted an *indirect* tax; that is, although it did not (like the Stamp Act) empower royal officials to collect money directly from the colonists, it obligated particular assemblies to raise a stated amount of revenue by whatever means they considered appropriate. The act fell lightly or not at all on most colonies; but New York, where more soldiers were stationed than in any other province, found compliance very burdensome and refused to grant any supplies.

New York's resistance to indirect taxation produced a torrent of anti-American feeling in the House of Commons, whose members remained bitter at having had to withdraw the Stamp Act. Townshend responded by drafting the New York Suspending Act, which threatened to nullify all laws passed by the colony after October 1, 1767, if the assembly still refused to vote the supplies. By the time that George III signed the measure in June, however, New York had already appropriated the necessary funds.

Although New York's retreat averted further confrontation, the conflict over the Quartering Act revealed the full extent of anticolonial sentiment in the House of Commons. The incident demonstrated that British leaders would not hesitate to defend Parliament's sovereignty through the most drastic of all steps: by interfering with American claims to self-governance. What Townshend and others did not realize was that such a course of action would soon undermine a loyal people's political allegiance.

The Townshend Duties

The new wave of British resentment toward the colonies coincided with an outpouring of British frustration over the government's failure to cut taxes from wartime levels. Discontent raged among the landed gentry, whose members took advantage of their domination of the House of Commons to slash their own taxes by 25 percent in 1767. This move cost the government £500,000 and prompted Townshend to propose laws that would tax imports entering America and increase colonial customs revenue.

Townshend sought to tax the colonists by exploiting an oversight in their arguments against the Stamp Act. In confronting the Stamp Act, Americans had emphasized their opposition to *internal* taxes, but had said little about Parliament's right to tax imports as they entered the colonies. Townshend and other British leaders chose to interpret this silence as evidence that the colonists accepted Britain's right to tax their trade—to impose *external* taxes. Yet not all British politicians were so mistaken. "They will laugh at you," predicted a now wiser George Grenville, "for your distinctions about regulations of trade." Brushing aside Grenville's warnings, Parliament passed Townshend's Revenue Act of 1767 (popularly called the Townshend duties) in June and July 1767. The new law taxed glass, paint, lead, paper, and tea imported into the colonies.

On the surface, Townshend's contention that the Americans would submit to this external tax on imports was convincing, for the colonists had long accepted Parliament's right to regulate their overseas trade and had in principle acknowledged taxation as a legitimate form of regulation. Even the Sugar Act had not primarily aroused opposition in the colonies because it imposed taxes; rather, Americans had protested the law because it instituted impractical regulations for conducting trade and violated traditional guarantees of a fair trial.

Townshend's Revenue Act differed significantly from what Americans had long seen as a legitimate way of regulating trade through taxation. To the colonists, charging a duty was a lawful way for British authorities to control trade only if that duty excluded foreign goods by making them prohibitively expensive to consumers. The Revenue Act of 1767, however, set moderate rates that did not price goods out of the colonial market; clearly, its purpose was to collect money for the treasury. Thus from the colonial standpoint, Townshend's duties were taxes just like the Stamp Act duties.

Although Townshend had introduced the Revenue Act in response to the government's budgetary problems, he had an ulterior motive for establishing an American source of revenue. Traditionally, royal governors had depended on colonial legislatures to vote their salaries; for their part, the legislatures had often refused to allocate these salaries until governors had signed certain bills to which they were opposed. Through the Revenue Act, Townshend hoped to establish a fund that would pay the salaries of governors and other royal officials in America, thus freeing them from the assemblies' control. In effect, by stripping the assemblies of their most potent weapon, the power of the purse, the Revenue Act threatened to tip the balance of constitutional power away from elected colonial representatives and toward unelected royal officials.

In reality the Revenue Act would never yield anything like the income that Townshend anticipated. Of the various items taxed, only tea produced any significant revenue—£20,000 of the £37,000 that the law was expected to yield. And because the measure would serve its purpose only if British tea were affordable to colonial consumers (who could easily smuggle Dutch tea), Townshend eliminated £60,000 worth of import fees paid on East Indian tea entering Britain before transhipment to America. On balance, the Revenue Act *worsened* the British treasury's deficit by £23,000. By 1767 Britain's financial difficulties were more an excuse for, than the driving force behind, political demands to tax the colonies. From Parliament's standpoint, the conflict with America was becoming a test of national will over the *principle* of taxation.

The Colonists' Reaction

Parliament gave the colonists little time to plan resistance against the Townshend duties. Americans only learned of the Revenue Act shortly before it went into operation, and they hesitated over the appropriate response. The strong-arm tactics that sent stamp tax collectors into panicky flight would not work against the Townshend duties, which the navy could easily collect offshore, safe from any Sons of Liberty.

Resistance to the Revenue Act remained weak until December 1767, when John Dickinson published twelve essays entitled *Letters from a Farmer in Pennsylvania*. The son of a Maryland planter and himself the owner of a large country estate in Delaware, Dickinson was actually a highly successful Philadelphia lawyer. But with most colonists living on farms, his title suggested that his sentiments lay with those of ordinary people. The essays, which appeared in nearly every colonial newspaper, emphasized that, although Parliament could regulate trade by voting duties capable of providing small amounts of "incidental revenue," it had no right to tax commerce for the single purpose of raising revenue. In other words, the legality of any external tax depended on its intent. No tax designed to produce revenue could be considered constitutional unless a people's elected representatives voted for it. Dickinson said nothing that the colonists had not stated or implied during the Stamp Act crisis. Rather, his contribution lay in persuading Americans that the many arguments that they had marshaled against the Stamp Act also applied to the Revenue Act.

Soon after publication of Dickinson's *Letters,* James Otis, the Boston lawyer famed for his arguments in the writs-of-assistance case, chaired a Boston town meeting that asked the Massachusetts legislature to oppose the Townshend duties. In response, the assembly in early 1768 called on Samuel Adams to draft a "circular letter" to every other legislature. Harvard-educated yet possessing a flair for the push-and-shove of local politics, Adams had helped organize the Sons of Liberty in Boston in 1765. Adams's circular letter forthrightly condemned both taxation without representation and the threat to self-governance posed by Parliament's making governors and other royal officials financially independent of the legislatures. Nonetheless, the document acknowledged Parliament as the "supreme legislative Power over the whole Empire," and it advocated no illegal activities.

Samuel Adams

A central player in the drive for American liberty, Adams wrote in 1774 that "I wish for a permanent union with the mother country, but only in terms of liberty and truth. No advantage that can accrue to America from such a union, can compensate for the loss of liberty."

Virginia's assembly warmly approved Adams's eloquent message and sent out a more strongly worded circular letter of its own, urging all colonies to oppose imperial policies that would "have an immediate tendency to enslave them." But most colonial legislatures reacted indifferently to these letters. In fact, resistance to the Revenue Act might have disintegrated in time had the British government not overreacted to the circular letters.

Indeed, parliamentary leaders regarded even the mild Massachusetts letter as "little better than an incentive to Rebellion." Disorganized by Townshend's sudden death in 1767, the king's Privy Council directed Lord Hillsborough, first appointee to the new post of secretary of state for the colonies, to express the government's displeasure. Hillsborough flatly told the Massachusetts assembly to disown its letter, forbade all overseas assemblies to endorse it, and commanded royal governors to dissolve any colonial legislature that violated his instructions. George III later commented that he never met "a man of less judgment than Lord

The Alternative of Williamsburg, *by Philip Dawe, 1775*
In this cartoon, armed patriots in Williamsburg, Virginia,
obtain a merchant's written agreement not to import British
goods. The "alternative" is the containers of tar and feath-
ers hanging in the background.

Hillsborough." A wiser man might have tried to divide
the colonists by appealing to their sense of British patriotism, but Hillsborough had chosen a course guaranteed to unite them in anger.

To protest Hillsborough's crude bullying, many
legislatures previously indifferent to the Massachusetts circular letter now adopted it enthusiastically.
The Massachusetts House of Representatives voted
92–17 not to recall its letter. The number 92 immediately acquired symbolic significance for Americans;
colonial politicians on more than one occasion drank
92 toasts in tipsy salutes to Massachusetts's action. In
obedience to Hillsborough, royal governors responded by dismissing legislatures in Massachusetts
and elsewhere. These moves played directly into the
hands of Samuel Adams, James Otis, and John Dickinson, who wished to ignite widespread opposition to
the Townshend duties.

Although increasingly outraged over the Revenue
Act, the colonists still needed some effective means of
pressuring Parliament for its repeal. One approach,
nonimportation, seemed especially promising because it offered an alternative to violence and would
distress Britain's economy. In August 1768 Boston's
merchants therefore adopted a nonimportation agreement, and the tactic slowly spread southward. "Save
your money, and you save your country!" became the
watchword of the Sons of Liberty, who began reorganizing after two years of inactivity. Not all colonists
supported nonimportation, however. Its effectiveness
ultimately depended on the compliance of merchants,
whose livelihood relied, in turn, on buying and selling
imports. In several major communities, including
Philadelphia and Baltimore, merchants continued buying British goods until early 1769, and Charles Town
(Charleston), South Carolina, did not cut off its purchases until July 1769. Far from complete, the boycott
probably kept out no more than 40 percent of all imports from Britain.

"Wilkes and Liberty"

The exclusion of 40 percent of imports seriously affected many people in Britain and thus heightened
pressure there, too, for repeal of the Townshend duties.
Hardest hit were merchants and artisans dealing in
consumer goods. Their protests formed part of a larger
movement that arose during the 1760s in opposition to
the domestic and foreign policies of George III and a
Parliament dominated by wealthy landowners. The
leader of this movement was John Wilkes, a fiery London editor and member of Parliament who had first
gained notoriety in 1763, when his newspaper regularly
and irreverently denounced George III's policies. The
government had finally arrested Wilkes for seditious libel, but to great popular acclaim, he had won his case
in court. The government, however, had succeeded in
shutting down his newspaper and in persuading members of the House of Commons to deny Wilkes his seat.
After again offending the government with a publication, Wilkes had fled to Paris.

Wilkes returned to England in 1768, defying a
warrant for his arrest, and ran again for Parliament. By
this time the Townshend acts and other government
policies were stirring up widespread protests. Merchants and artisans in London, Bristol, and other cities
demanded the dismissal of the "obnoxious" ministers
who were "ruining our manufactories by invidiously
imposing and establishing the most impolitic and unconstitutional taxations and regulations on your
Majesty's colonies." They were joined by (nonvoting)

weavers, coal heavers, seamen, and other workers who protested low wages and high prices that stemmed in part from government policies. All these people rallied around the cry, "Wilkes and liberty!"

After he again was elected to Parliament, Wilkes was arrested. The next day, twenty to forty thousand angry "Wilkesites" massed on St. George's Fields, outside the prison where he was being held. When members of the crowd began throwing stones, soldiers and police responded with gunfire, killing eleven protesters. The "massacre of St. George's Fields" had given the movement some martyrs. Wilkes and an associate were elected to the seat twice more and were both times denied their seats by other legislators. Meanwhile, the imprisoned Wilkes was besieged by outpourings of popular support, from the colonies as well as from Britain. Some Virginians sent him tobacco, and the South Carolina assembly voted to contribute £1,500 to help defray his debts. He maintained a regular correspondence with the Boston Sons of Liberty and, upon his release in April 1770, was hailed in a massive Boston celebration as "the illustrious martyr to Liberty."

Wilkes's cause sharpened the political thinking of government opponents in Britain and the colonies alike. Thousands of voters in English cities and towns signed petitions to Parliament protesting its refusal to seat Wilkes as an affront to the electorate's will. Like the colonists, they regarded the theory of "virtual representation" in Parliament as a sham. Fearing arbitrary government actions, some of them formed a Society of the Supporters of the Bill of Rights "to defend and maintain the legal, constitutional liberty of the subject." And while more "respectable" opponents of the government such as William Pitt and Edmund Burke disdained Wilkes for courting the "mob," his movement emboldened them to speak more forcefully against the government, especially on its policies toward the colonies. For the colonists themselves, Wilkes and his following made clear that Parliament and the government represented a small if powerful minority whose authority could be legitimately questioned.

Women and Colonial Resistance

The tactical value of nonimportation was not restricted to damaging Britain's economy. It also hinged on colonists convincing the British—and one another—that all Americans were determined to sustain resistance, and on demonstrating that the American cause

rested on the foundations of impeccable morality and sensible moderation. In this respect, the nonimportation movement provided a unique opportunity for women to join the protest against unconstitutional laws.

The enlistment of women in the colonial protest movement unfolded slowly. Calling themselves the Daughters of Liberty, upper-class female patriots had played a minor part in defeating the Stamp Act. Some had attended political rallies during the Stamp Act crisis, and others had reinforced colonial resolve by turning a cold shoulder to men unwilling to resist Grenville's tax.

In contrast, women assumed a highly visible role during the Townshend crisis. To protest the Revenue Act's tax on tea, more than three hundred "mistresses of families" in Boston denounced the consumption of the beverage in early 1770. In some ways, such nonconsumption was a more effective tactic than nonimportation, for although a minority of merchants might ignore nonimportation on the basis of principle or financial interest, a refusal by colonists to consume imports would chill merchants' economic incentive to continue bringing in English products.

Nonconsumption agreements therefore soon became popular and were extended to include English manufactures (mostly clothing) as well as tea. Again women played a vital role, because the boycott would fail unless the colonists replaced British imports with apparel of their own making. Responding to leaders' pleas that they expand domestic cloth production, women of all social ranks, even those who customarily did not weave their own fabric or sew their own clothing, organized spinning bees. These events attracted intense publicity as evidence of American determination to fight parliamentary taxation. The colonial cause, noted a New York woman, had enlisted "a fighting army of amazons . . . armed with spinning wheels."

Spinning bees not only helped undermine the masculine prejudice that women had no place in public life but also endowed spinning and weaving, previously considered routine household tasks, with special political virtue. "Women might recover to this country the full and free enjoyment of all our rights, properties and privileges," exclaimed the Reverend John Cleaveland of Ipswich, Massachusetts, in 1769; he then added with more than usual honesty that this "is more than the men have been able to do."

Spinning bees, combined with female support for boycotting tea, dramatically demonstrated American determination. Colonial leaders were waging a battle

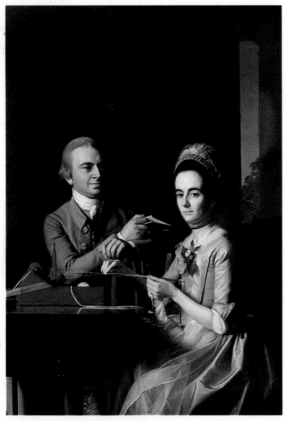

Mr. and Mrs. Thomas Mifflin,
by John Singleton Copley, 1773
The Mifflins were prominent Philadelphians. Thomas, a merchant in his early years, sat in the Pennsylvania assembly and the First Continental Congress and was later an officer in the Continental Army. An ardent supporter of the American cause, Sarah Morris Mifflin here demonstrates her patriotism by spinning her own thread.

to convince public opinion in Britain that their society would stand firm in opposing unconstitutional taxes. Only if the British people believed that Americans—male and female alike—were truly united would they accept repeal of the Townshend duties. Female participation in symbolic protests forced the British public to appreciate the depth of colonial commitment to maintaining the nonimportation agreements.

Customs Racketeering

Besides taxing colonial imports, Townshend sought to increase revenues through closer British surveillance of colonial trade. At the same time as he submitted his

Revenue Act of 1767, he introduced legislation creating the American Board of Customs Commissioners, whose members would strictly enforce the Navigation Acts. This law raised the number of port officials, funded the construction of a colonial coast guard, and provided money for secret informers. In the face of lax enforcement, including widespread bribery of customs officials by colonial shippers and merchants, Towshend wanted the board to bring honesty, efficiency, and more revenue to overseas customs operations. But the law quickly drew protests because of the ways it was enforced and because it assumed those accused to be guilty until they could prove otherwise.

The new legal provisions awarded an informer one-third of the value of all goods and ships appropriated through a conviction of smuggling. The fact that fines could be tripled under certain circumstances provided an even greater incentive to seize illegal cargoes. Smuggling cases were heard in vice-admiralty courts, moreover, where the probability of conviction was extremely high.

Revenue agents commonly filed charges for technical violations of the Sugar Act, even when no evidence existed of intent to conduct illegal trade. They most often exploited the provision that declared any cargo illegal unless it had been loaded or unloaded with a customs officer's written authorization. Many vessels transporting lumber or tobacco found it impossible to comply, because they typically picked up these items piecemeal at a succession of small wharves far from a customhouse. Even a captain who threw rotting provisions overboard while at sea could be found guilty of illegally unloading. One common device by which customs officials created opportunities for seizures was to accommodate local circumstances by bending the rules for a time and then suddenly to enforce the letter of the law.

Customs commissioners also fanned angry passions by invading the traditional rights of sailors. Long-standing maritime custom allowed a ship's crew to supplement their incomes by making small sales between ports. Anything stored in a sailor's chest was considered private property that did not have to be listed as cargo on the captain's manifest and so was exempt from the regulations of the Navigation Acts. After 1767, however, revenue agents began treating such belongings as cargo, thus establishing an excuse to seize the entire ship. Under this new policy, crewmen saw their trunks ruthlessly broken open by arrogant inspectors and then lost trading stock worth several months' wages because it was not listed on the captain's loading papers.

The commissioners thus embarked on a program of "customs racketeering" that constituted little more than a system of legalized piracy. The board's program fed an upsurge in popular violence. Above all, customs commissioners' use of informers provoked retaliation. The *Pennsylvania Journal* in 1769 scorned these agents as "dogs of prey, thirsting after the fortunes of worthy and wealthy men." By betraying the trust of employers, and sometimes of friends, informers aroused wild hatred in their victims and were roughly handled whenever found. Nearly all instances of tarring and feathering in these years were acts of private revenge against informers rather than acts of political reprisal.

Sailors developed deep hatred for customs officers who had seized their property, and eagerly awaited chances to get even. Not surprisingly, after 1767 inspectors fell increasingly victim to riots dominated by vengeful seamen. By enforcing the letter of the law, commissioners created a superheated climate that made such riots and assaults inevitable.

Nowhere were customs agents and informers more detested than in Boston, where in June 1768 citizens finally retaliated against their tormentors. The occasion was the seizure, on a technicality, of the colonial merchant John Hancock's sloop *Liberty*. A crowd tried to prevent the towing of Hancock's ship and then began assaulting customs agents. Growing to several hundred as it surged through the streets, the mob drove all revenue inspectors from Boston.

Hancock, reportedly North America's richest merchant and a leading opponent of British taxation, had become a chief target of the customs commissioners. In 1768 the commissioners used a perjured statement from a customs inspector to seize the *Liberty* for allegedly avoiding £700 in duties on Madeira wine worth £3,000. By then requesting the payment of triple charges on the wine, they made Hancock liable for a total fine of £9,000, an amount almost thirteen times greater than the taxes supposedly evaded.

Hancock's case forced Americans to reevaluate their former acceptance of the principle that Parliament had limited authority to pass laws for them. Prior to 1768 colonial leaders had single-mindedly denied Britain's power to tax them, without considering that freedoms of equal importance might also be jeopardized by other kinds of legislation. But by 1770 many argued that measures like the Sugar Act and the act creating the American Board of Customs Commissioners seriously endangered property rights and civil liberties. They expanded their opposition from a rejection of taxation without representation to a more broadly based rejection of legislation without representation. By 1774 there would emerge a new consensus that Parliament possessed no lawmaking authority over the colonies except the right to regulate imperial commerce through statutes like the old Navigation Acts.

By 1770 the British government, aware of its customs officers' excesses, began reforming the service. The smuggling charges against Hancock were finally dropped because the prosecution feared that Hancock would appeal a conviction to England, where honest officials would take action against the persons responsible for violating his rights. But although the abuses largely ended by the early 1770s, the damage had been done. Townshend's American Board of Customs Commissioners contributed enormously to the colonists' growing suspicion of British motives and their progressive alienation from England.

Repeal of the Townshend Duties

In January 1770 Lord North became prime minister. Although described as a "great, heavy, booby-looking man" and noted for occasionally sleeping through debates in the House of Commons, North had ability and would retain his office until 1782. North favored eliminating most of the Townshend duties to prevent the American commercial boycott from widening, but to underscore British authority, he insisted on retaining the tax on tea. Parliament agreed, and in April 1770, giving in for the second time in three years to colonial pressure, it repealed most of the Townshend duties.

Parliament's partial repeal produced a dilemma for American politicians. They considered it intolerable that taxes remained on tea, the most profitable item for the royal treasury. Colonial leaders were unsure whether they should press on with the nonimportation agreement until they achieved total victory, or whether it would suffice to maintain a selective boycott of tea. When the nonimportation movement collapsed in July 1770, colonists resisted external taxation by voluntary agreements not to drink British tea. Through nonconsumption they succeeded in limiting revenue from tea to about one-sixth the level originally expected. This amount was far too little to pay the salaries of royal governors as Townshend had intended.

Yet American leaders took little satisfaction in having forced Parliament to compromise. The tea duty remained as a galling reminder that Parliament refused to retreat from the broadest possible interpretation of the Declaratory Act. Thus although the crisis passed in 1770, its legacy lingered long afterward. The tax on tea acted like a festering sore that slowly poisoned relations between Britain and its colonies. The Townshend crisis had begun the gradual process by which a loyal people lost all sense of allegiance to their king and country.

The Boston Massacre

As another consequence of the violence stirred up by the customs commissioners, a force of seventeen hundred British troops landed in Boston during the six weeks after October 1, 1768. Regarding the troops as a "standing army" that threatened their liberty, as well as a financial burden, Bostonians resented the soldiers' presence.

Boston rapidly took on the atmosphere of an occupied city and crackled with tension as armed sentries and resentful civilians traded insults. The mainly Protestant townspeople found it especially galling that many soldiers were Irish Catholics and a few, mostly drummers, were blacks. The majority of enlisted men, moreover, were free to seek employment following the morning muster.

Often agreeing to work for less than local laborers, they generated fierce hostility in a community plagued by persistently high unemployment.

Still, Bostonians endured their first winter as a garrison town without undue trouble and saw half the British troops sail home in mid-1769. Relations between the remaining soldiers and the city's poorer civilians then abruptly worsened. The deep-seated resentment against all who upheld British authority suddenly boiled over on February 22, 1770, when an unpopular customs informer fired bird shot at several children bombarding his house with rocks and killed an eleven-year-old German boy. While elite Bostonians had disdained the unruly exchanges between soldiers and crowds, the horror at a child's death momentarily united the community. "My Eyes never beheld such a funeral," wrote John Adams. "A vast Number of Boys walked before the Coffin, a vast Number of Women and Men after it. . . . This Shews there are many more Lives to spend if wanted in the Service of their country."

Although the army had played no part in the shooting, it became a natural target for popular frustration and rage. A week after the boy's funeral, ten-

The Boston Massacre, 1770,
Engraving by Paul Revere Shortly after this incident, one Bostonian observed that "unless there is some great alteration in the state of things, the era of the independence of the colonies is much nearer than I once thought it, or now wish it."

sions between troops and Boston civilians erupted at the guardpost protecting the customs office. When an officer tried to disperse a crowd led by Crispus Attucks, a seaman of African and Native American descent, his men endured a steady barrage of flying objects and dares to shoot. One soldier finally did fire, after having been knocked down by a block of ice, and the others pulled their triggers without orders. Their uneven volley hit eleven persons, five of whom, including Attucks, died.

The shock that followed the March 5 bloodshed marked the emotional high point of the Townshend crisis. Royal authorities in Massachusetts tried to defuse the situation in Boston by isolating all British soldiers on a fortified island in the harbor, and Governor Thomas Hutchinson promised that the soldiers who had fired would be tried. Patriot leader John Adams, an opponent of crowd actions, served as their attorney. Adams intended not only to demonstrate Americans' commitment to impartial justice but also "to lay before [the people of Boston], the Law as it stood, that they might be apprized of the Dangers . . . which must arise from intemperate heats and irregular commotions." All but two of the soldiers were acquitted, and the ones found guilty suffered only a branding on their thumbs.

Burning hatreds produced by an intolerable situation underlay the "Boston Massacre," as it came to be called in conscious recollection of the "St. George's Fields Massacre" of Wilkesites in London two years earlier. The shooting of unarmed American civilians by British soldiers, and the light punishment given the soldiers, forced the colonists to confront the stark possibility that the British government was bent on coercing and suppressing them through naked force.

The Committees of Correspondence

Although Lord North's government virtually ignored the colonies from mid-1770 to 1772, the brief truce ended on June 9, 1772, when the customs schooner *Gaspee* ran aground near Providence, Rhode Island. One of the last revenue cutters to engage in customs racketeering by plundering cargoes for technical violations of the Sugar Act, the *Gaspee* had acquired an odious reputation among Rhode Islanders. Its crew had frequently landed to steal fruit, unfenced livestock, and firewood, and the captain was said to be "more imperious and haughty than the Grand Turk himself." Now helplessly stuck in the mud, the *Gaspee* presented a tempting target for local inhabitants. That night, more than one hundred disguised men burned it to the waterline.

The British government dispatched a commission to look into the attack, with instructions to send all suspects to England for trial. The investigators failed to identify any raiders and came back empty-handed. Nevertheless, colonists were alarmed that the ministry intended to dispense with another essential civil liberty, an accused citizen's right to be tried by a local jury.

In the fall of 1772, meanwhile, Lord North's ministry was preparing to implement Townshend's goal of paying the royal governors' salaries out of customs revenue. The colonists had always viewed this intention to free the governors from legislative domination as a fundamental threat to representative government. In response, Samuel Adams persuaded Boston's town meeting to request that every Massachusetts community appoint persons responsible for exchanging information and coordinating measures to defend colonial rights. Of approximately 260 towns, about half immediately established "committees of correspondence," and most others did so within a year. From Massachusetts the idea spread throughout New England.

The committees of correspondence were the colonists' first attempt to maintain close and continuing political cooperation over a wide area. By linking almost every interior community to Boston through a network of dedicated activists, the system allowed Adams to conduct a campaign of political education for all of Massachusetts, and increasingly for all New England. Adams sent out messages for each town's local committee to read at its own town meeting, which would then debate the issues and adopt a formal resolution. Forcing tens of thousands of citizens to consider evidence that their rights were in danger, the system committed them to take a personal stand by voting.

Adams's most successful venture in whipping up public alarm came in June 1773, when he publicized certain letters of Massachusetts governor Thomas Hutchinson that Benjamin Franklin had obtained. Massachusetts town meetings discovered through the letters that their own chief executive had advocated "an abridgement of what are called English liberties" and "a great restraint of natural liberty." The publication of the Hutchinson correspondence confirmed American suspicions that a plot was afoot to destroy basic freedoms.

Meanwhile, in reaction to the *Gaspee* commission's instructions, Patrick Henry, Thomas Jefferson, and Richard Henry Lee proposed in March 1773 that

Virginia establish colony-level committees of correspondence. Within a year every province but Pennsylvania had followed its example. By early 1774 colonial leaders were linked by a communications web for the first time since 1766.

In contrast to the brief, intense Stamp Act crisis, the dissatisfaction spawned by the Townshend duties and the American Board of Customs Commissioners persisted and gradually poisoned relations between Britain and America. In 1765 feelings of loyalty and affection toward Britain had remained strong in America and thus had helped disguise the depth of the division over the constitutional issue of taxation. By 1773, however, colonial allegiance was becoming conditional and could no longer be assumed.

Frontier Tensions

Although most of the conflicts between colonists and British officials took place in the eastern seaports, tensions along the frontier contributed to a continuing sense of crisis among natives, settlers, and colonial authorities. These stresses were rooted in the rapid growth of both the colonial population and the economy. This growth had spurred the migration of people and capital to the Appalachian frontier, where colonists and their governments sought access to Indian land. Land pressures and the lack of adequate revenue from the colonies left the British government utterly helpless in enforcing the Proclamation of 1763. Speculators such as George Washington sought western land because "any person who . . . neglects the present opportunity of hunting out good Lands will never regain it." Settlers, traders, hunters, and thieves also trespassed on Indian land, and a growing number of instances of violence by colonists toward Indians were going unpunished. In the meantime, the British government was unable to maintain garrisons at many of its forts, to enforce violations of laws and treaties, and to provide gifts to its native allies. Under such pressure, Britain and the Iroquois agreed in the Treaty of Fort Stanwix (1768) to grant land along the Ohio River that was occupied by the Shawnees, Delawares, and Cherokees to the government of Pennsylvania and Virginia. The Shawnees now assumed leadership of the "republican" Indians who, along with the Cherokees, sensed that no policy of appeasement could stop colonial expansion.

The Treaty of Fort Stanwix resolved the conflicting claims of Pennsylvania and Virginia in Ohio at the Indians' expense. But other frontier disputes led directly to

conflict among the colonists themselves. Settlers moving west in Massachusetts in the early 1760s found their titles challenged by some of New York's powerful landlords. When two of the landlords threatened tenants with eviction in 1766, the New Englanders made common cause with the tenants in an armed uprising, calling themselves Sons of Liberty after the Stamp Act protestors. In 1769, in what is now Vermont, settlers from New Hamsphire also came into conflict with New York. After four years of guerrilla warfare, the New Hampshire settlers, calling themselves the Green Mountain Boys, established an independent government. Unrecognized at the time, it eventually became the government of Vermont. A third group of New England settlers, from Connecticut, settled in the Wyoming Valley of Pennsylvania, where they clashed in 1774 with Pennsylvanians claiming title to the same land.

Expansion also provoked conflicts between frontier settlers and their colonial governments. In North Carolina a group known as the Regulators aimed to redress the grievances of settlers living in the colony's western regions. The westerners, underrepresented in the colonial assembly, had found themselves exploited by dishonest, self-serving officeholders appointed by eastern politicians. The Regulator movement climaxed on May 16, 1771, at the battle of Alamance Creek. Leading an army of perhaps thirteen hundred easternmilitiamen, North Carolina's royal governor defeated about twenty-five hundred Regulators in a clash that produced almost three hundred casualties. Although the Regulator uprising then disintegrated, it crippled the colony's subsequent ability to resist British authority.

An armed Regulator movement also arose in South Carolina, in this case to counter the government's unwillingness to prosecute bandits who were terrorizing the settlers. But the South Carolina government did not dispatch its militia to the frontier for fear that the colony's restive slave population might use the occasion to revolt. Instead it conceded to the principal demands of the Regulators by establishing four new judicial circuits and allowing jury trials in the newly settled areas.

Although not directly related to one another, these frontier episodes all reflect the tensions generated by a rising land-hungry population and its willingness to defy established authorities and resort to violence. As tensions mounted between colonists and British authorities in older settled areas, the frontier dweller's anxious mood spread.

TOWARD INDEPENDENCE

Although the British Empire remained superficially tranquil in early 1773, it had resolved none of its underlying constitutional problems. To a large degree, Americans ignored the continued taxation of tea because of a widespread expectation that Lord North would eventually have the duty repealed. Parliament suddenly blasted this unrealistic hope when it passed the Tea Act in 1773. This measure set off a chain reaction that started with the Boston Tea Party in late 1773 and was followed by Parliament's attempt to retaliate through the Coercive Acts in 1774, the First Continental Congress in September 1774, the outbreak of fighting in April 1775, and the colonists' declaration of their independence in July 1776.

The Tea Act

Colonial smuggling and nonconsumption had taken a heavy toll on Britain's East India Company, which enjoyed a legal monopoly on importing tea into the British Empire. By 1773, with tons of tea rotting in its warehouses, the East India Company was teetering on the brink of bankruptcy. But Lord North could not let the company fail. Not only did it pay substantial duties on the tea it imported into Britain, but it also provided huge indirect savings for the government by maintaining British authority in India at its own expense.

If the company could only control the colonial market, North reasoned, its chances for returning to profitability would greatly increase. Americans supposedly consumed more than a million pounds of tea each year, but by 1773 they were purchasing just one-quarter of it from the company. In May 1773, to save the beleaguered East India Company from financial ruin, Parliament passed the Tea Act, which eliminated all remaining import duties on tea entering England and thus lowered the selling price to consumers. (Ironically, the same saving could have been accomplished by repealing the Townshend tax, which would have ended colonial objections to the company's tea and produced enormous goodwill toward the British government.) To lower the price further, the Tea Act also permitted the company to sell its tea directly to consumers rather than through wholesalers.

These two concessions reduced the cost of East India Company tea in the colonies well below the price of all smuggled competition. Parliament expected simple economic self-interest to overcome American scruples about buying taxed tea. With the resulting revenue, the British government would finally be able to achieve Townshend's goal of making the royal governors independent of colonial assemblies by paying their salaries.

But the Tea Act alarmed many Americans, above all because they saw in it a menace to colonial representative government. By making taxed tea competitive in price with smuggled tea, the law in all likelihood would raise revenue, which the British government would use to pay royal governors. The law thus threatened to corrupt Americans into accepting the principle of parliamentary taxation by taking advantage of their weakness for a frivolous luxury. Quickly, therefore, the committees of correspondence decided to resist the importation of tea, though without violence and without the destruction of private property. Either by pressuring the company's agents to refuse acceptance or by intercepting the ships at sea and ordering them home, the committees would keep East India Company cargoes from being landed. In Philadelphia an anonymous "Committee for Tarring and Feathering" warned harbor pilots not to guide any ships carrying tea into port.

In Boston, however, this strategy failed. On November 28, 1773, the first ship came under the jurisdiction of the customhouse, to which duties would have to be paid on its cargo within twenty days. Otherwise, the cargo would be seized from the captain and the tea claimed by the company's agents (who included two of Governor Hutchinson's sons) and placed on sale. When Samuel Adams, John Hancock, and other leading citizens repeatedly asked the customs officers to issue a special clearance for the ship's departure, they found themselves blocked by the governor's refusal to compromise.

On the evening of December 16, Samuel Adams convened a meeting in Old South Church. He informed the five thousand citizens of Hutchinson's insistence upon landing the tea, told them that the grace period would expire in a few hours, and announced that "this meeting can do no more to save the country." About fifty young men disguised as Indians then yelled a few war whoops and headed for the wharf, followed by most of the crowd.

The disciplined band assaulted no one and damaged nothing but the hated cargo. Thousands lined the waterfront to see them heave forty-five tons of tea overboard. For almost an hour, the onlookers stood silently transfixed, as if at a religious service, while they peered through the crisp, cold air of a moonlit night. The only sounds were the steady chop of hatchets breaking open wooden chests and the soft splash of tea on the water. When their work was finished, the participants left quietly, and the town lapsed into a profound hush—"never more still and calm," according to one observer.

The Coercive Acts

Boston's "Tea Party" inflamed the British. Lord North fumed that only "New England fanatics" could imagine themselves oppressed by inexpensive tea. A Welsh member of Parliament drew wild applause by declaring that "the town of Boston ought to be knocked about by the ears, and destroy'd." In vain did the great parliamentary orator Edmund Burke plead for the one action that could end the crisis. "Leave America . . . to tax herself. . . . Leave the Americans as they anciently stood. . . ." The British government, however, swiftly asserted its authority by enacting four Coercive Acts that, together with the unrelated Quebec Act, became known to many colonists as the "Intolerable Acts."

The first of the Coercive Acts, the Boston Port Bill, became law on April 1, 1774. It ordered the navy to close Boston harbor unless the Privy Council certified

by June 1 that the town had arranged to pay for the ruined tea. Lord North's cabinet deliberately imposed this impossibly short deadline in order to ensure the harbor's closing, which would lead to serious economic distress. The government therefore refused to let a group of London merchants post bond for the necessary £9,000.

The second Coercive Act, the Massachusetts Government Act, had actually been under consideration before the Boston Tea Party. This law revoked the Massachusetts charter and restructured the government to make it less democratic. The colony's upper house would no longer be elected annually by the assembly but appointed for life by the crown. The governor gained absolute control over the naming of all judges and sheriffs. Jurymen, previously elected, were now appointed by sheriffs. Finally, the new charter forbade communities to hold more than one town meeting a year without the governor's permission. These changes brought Massachusetts into line with other royal colonies, but the colonists interpreted them as evidence of hostility toward representative government.

The final two Coercive Acts—the Administration of Justice Act and a new Quartering Act—rubbed salt into the wounds. The first of these permitted any person charged with murder while enforcing royal authority in Massachusetts (such as the British soldiers

"Boston Cannonaded"
In this pro-resistance cartoon, Britain's ministers harass and force tea down the throat of America, depicted as an innocent woman. Note that one minister carries a copy of the (Boston) Port Bill (1774) that forced the closing of the city's harbor.

indicted for the Boston Massacre) to be tried in England or in other colonies. The second went beyond the Quartering Act of 1766 by allowing the governor to requisition *empty* private buildings for housing troops. These measures, along with the appointment of General Thomas Gage, Britain's military commander in North America, as the new governor of Massachusetts, struck New Englanders as proof of a plan to place them under a military despotism.

Americans learned of the Quebec Act along with the previous four statutes and associated it with them. Intended to cement loyalty to Britain among conquered French-Canadian Catholics, the law established Roman Catholicism as Quebec's official religion. This provision alarmed Protestant Anglo-Americans, who widely associated Catholicism with arbitrary government. Furthermore, the Quebec Act gave Canada's governors sweeping powers but established no legislature. It also permitted property disputes (but not criminal cases) to be decided by French law, which did not use juries. Additionally, the law extended Quebec's territorial claims south to the Ohio River and west to the Mississippi, a vast area populated by Native Americans and some French. Although covered by the Proclamation of 1763, the region was claimed by several colonies.

The "Intolerable Acts" convinced New Englanders that the crown was plotting to corrode traditional English liberties throughout North America. Many believed that after starving Boston into submission, the governor of Massachusetts would appoint corrupt sheriffs and judges to crush political dissent through rigged trials. The Quartering Act would repress any resistance by forcing troops on an unwilling population. The Administration of Justice Act, which the colonists cynically called the Murder Act, would encourage massacres by preventing local juries from convicting soldiers who killed civilians. Once resistance in Massachusetts had been smashed, the Quebec Act would serve as a blueprint for extinguishing representative government throughout the colonies. Parliament would revoke every colony's charter and introduce a government like Quebec's. Elected assemblies, freedom of religion for Protestants, and jury trials would all disappear.

Intended by Parliament simply to punish Massachusetts—and particularly that rotten apple in the barrel, Boston—the acts instead pushed most colonies to the brink of revolution. Repeal of these laws became, in effect, the colonists' nonnegotiable demand. Of the twenty-seven reasons justifying the break with Britain that the Americans cited in their 1776 Declaration of Independence, six concerned these statutes.

Virginia's response was particularly important because that colony could provide more military manpower than any other. Sentiment for active resistance first solidified in the Virginia assembly, whose members returned to their counties and enlisted the local gentry in the cause of firmly opposing the offensive laws. As the upper class quickly pulled together, the leading planters undertook a program of political education for the colony's ordinary citizens, who up to that point had been apathetic about the Anglo-American confrontation. On public occasions such as court days and militia musters, the gentry spoke repeatedly of the need to support Massachusetts, persuading voters to commit themselves to resistance by signing petitions against the Coercive Acts. Within two years the gentry had mobilized Virginia's free population overwhelmingly against Parliament, and it was clear that if war broke out, the British Army would face united resistance not only in New England but also in Virginia.

The First Continental Congress

In response to the "Intolerable Acts," the extralegal committees of correspondence of every colony but Georgia sent delegates to a Continental Congress in Philadelphia. Among those in attendance when the Congress assembled on September 5, 1774, were the colonies' most prominent politicians: Samuel and John Adams of Massachusetts; John Jay of New York; Joseph Galloway and John Dickinson of Pennsylvania; and Patrick Henry, Richard Henry Lee, and George Washington of Virginia. The fifty-six delegates had come together to find a way of defending American rights short of war, and in interminable dinner parties and cloakroom chatter, they took one another's measure.

The First Continental Congress opened by endorsing a set of extreme statements of principle called the Suffolk Resolves that recently had placed Massachusetts in a state of passive rebellion. Adopted by delegates at a convention of Massachusetts towns just as the Continental Congress was getting under way, the resolves declared that the colonies owed no obedience to any of the Coercive Acts, that a provisional government should collect all taxes until the former Massachusetts charter was restored, and that defensive measures should be taken in the event of an attack by royal troops. The Continental Congress also voted to boycott all British goods after December 1 and to cease exporting almost all goods to Britain and its West Indian possessions after September 1775 unless a reconciliation had been accomplished. This agreement, the Continental Association, would be enforced by locally elected committees of "observation" or "safety," whose members in effect were usurping control of American trade from the royal customs service.

Such bold defiances were not to the liking of all delegates. Jay, Dickinson, Galloway, and other moderates who dominated the middle-colony contingent most feared the internal turmoil that would surely accompany a head-on confrontation with Britain. These "trimmers" (John Adams's scornful phrase) vainly opposed nonimportation and tried unsuccessfully to win endorsement of Galloway's plan for a "Grand Council," an American legislature that would share with Parliament the authority to tax and govern the colonies.

Finally, however, the delegates summarized their principles and demands in a petition to the king. This document conceded to Parliament the power to regulate colonial commerce, but it argued that all previous parliamentary efforts to impose taxes, enforce laws through admiralty courts, suspend assemblies, and unilaterally revoke charters were unconstitutional. By addressing the king rather than Parliament, Congress was imploring George III to end the crisis by dismissing those ministers responsible for passing the Coercive Acts.

The Fighting Begins

Most Americans hoped that their resistance would jolt Parliament into renouncing all authority over the colonies except trade regulation. But a minority of the colonial elite took alarm, and bonds between men formerly united in outlook sometimes snapped. John Adams's onetime friend Jonathan Sewall, for example, charged that the Congress had made the "breach with the parent state a thousand times more irreparable than it was before." Fearing that Congress was enthroning "their *High Mightinesses,* the MOB," he and like-minded Americans fell back on their loyalty to the

Battle of Lexington
James Pike, a Massachusetts militiaman, recorded the clash at Lexington on his powder horn: The other side shows British "regulars, the aggressors," assaulting "provincials defending" a Liberty Tree.

king. In England meanwhile, George III sniffed rebellion in the Congress's actions. His instincts, and those of American loyalists, were correct. A revolution was indeed brewing.

To solidify their defiance, the American resistance leaders coerced waverers and loyalists (or "Tories," as they were often called). Thus the elected committees that Congress had created to enforce the Continental Association often turned themselves into vigilantes, compelling merchants who still traded with Britain to burn their imports and make public apologies, browbeating clergymen who preached pro-British sermons, and pressuring Americans to adopt simpler diets and dress in order to relieve their dependence on British imports. Additionally, in colony after colony, the committees took on government functions by organizing volunteer military companies and extralegal legislatures. By the spring of 1775, colonial patriots had established provincial "congresses" that paralleled and rivaled the existing colonial assemblies headed by royal governors.

The uneasy calm was first broken in April 1775, in Massachusetts. There as elsewhere, citizens had prepared for the worst by collecting arms and organizing extralegal militia units (locally known as minutemen) whose members could respond instantly to an emergency. The British government ordered Massachusetts governor Gage to quell the "rude rabble" by arresting the principal patriot leaders. Aware that most of these had already fled Boston, Gage instead sent 700 British soldiers on April 19, 1775, to seize military supplies that the colonists had stored at Concord. Two couriers, William Dawes and Paul Revere, quickly alerted nearby towns of the British troops' movements and target. At Lexington about seventy minutemen hastily drawn up on the town green attempted to oppose the soldiers. After a confused skirmish in which eight minutemen died and a single redcoat was wounded, the British pushed on to Concord. There they found few munitions but encountered a growing swarm of armed Yankees (see "A Place in Time"). When some minutemen mistakenly became convinced that the town was being burned, they exchanged fire with the British regulars and touched off a running battle that continued most of the sixteen miles back to Boston. By day's end the redcoats had lost 273 men, and they had gained some respect for Yankee courage.

These engagements awakened the countryside, and by the evening of April 20, some twenty thousand New Englanders were besieging the British garrison in Boston. On May 10 the Green Mountain Boys, led by Ethan Allen, overran Fort Ticonderoga on Lake Champlain, partly with the intent of using its captured cannon in the siege of Boston. That same day, the Second Continental Congress convened in Philadelphia. Most delegates still opposed independence and at Dickinson's urging agreed to send a "loyal message" to George III. Dickinson composed what became known as the Olive Branch Petition; excessively polite, it nonetheless presented three demands: a cease-fire at Boston, repeal of the Coercive Acts, and negotiations to establish guarantees of American rights. Events quickly overtook this effort at reconciliation. The Olive Branch Petition reached London at the same time as news of a battle fought just outside Boston on June 17. In this engagement British troops attacked colonists entrenched on Breed's Hill and Bunker Hill. Although successfully dislodging the Americans, the British suffered 1,154 casualties out of 2,200 men, compared to a loss of 311 Yankees. After Bunker Hill the British public wanted retaliation, not reconciliation, and on August 23 the king proclaimed New England in a state of rebellion. In December Parliament declared all the colonists rebellious and made their ships subject to seizure.

The Failure of Reconciliation

Despite the turn of events, most Americans clung to hopes of reconciliation. Even John Adams, who believed in the inevitability of separation, described himself as "fond of reconciliation, if we could reasonably entertain Hopes of it on a constitutional basis." Yet the same Americans who pleaded for peace passed measures that Britain could only construe as rebellious. Before the delegates to the Continental Congress even heard about the Battle of Bunker Hill, they voted to establish an "American continental army" and appointed George Washington its commander.

Still, most Americans resisted independence, partly because they clung to the notion that evil ministers rather than the king were forcing unconstitutional measures on them and partly because they expected that saner heads would rise to power in Britain. On both counts they were wrong. The Americans exaggerated the influence of Pitt, Burke, Wilkes (who finally took his seat in Parliament in 1774), and their other friends in Britain. For example, when Burke proposed in March 1775 that Parliament acknowledge the colonists' right to raise and dispose of taxes, he was voted down by a thumping majority in Parliament. Lord North's sole counterproposal was to allow the colonists to tax themselves, but on condition that they collect whatever sum Parliament ordered. This concession amounted to no more than involuntary self-taxation.

The Americans' sentimental attachment to the king, the last emotional barrier to their accepting independence, finally crumbled in January 1776 with the publication of Thomas Paine's *Common Sense.* A failed corsetmaker and schoolmaster, Paine immigrated to the colonies from England late in 1774 with a letter of introduction from Benjamin Franklin, a penchant for radical politics, and a gift for writing plain and pungent prose that anyone could understand.

Paine told Americans what they had been unable to bring themselves to say: kingship was an institution rooted in superstition, dangerous to liberty, and inappropriate to Americans. The king was "the royal brute" and a "hardened, sullen-tempered Pharaoh." Whereas previous writers had maintained that an English conspiracy against American liberty was being directed by certain corrupt politicians, Paine argued that such a conspiracy was rooted in the very institutions of monarchy and empire. Moreover, he argued, America had no economic need for the British connection. As he put it, "The commerce by which she [America] hath enriched herself are the necessaries of life, and will always have a market while eating is the custom in Europe." In addition, he pointed out, the events of the preceding six months

Concord, Massachusetts, in 1775

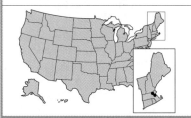

About 2 A.M. on April 19, 1775, the alarm bell in Concord, Massachusetts, started to ring furiously. Normally, it summoned men to turn out with fire buckets, but on this night drowsy citizens (including the town's minister, Reverend William Emerson) ambled toward the town square clutching muskets. Concord's minutemen were gathering to oppose 750 British troops marching to seize arms and ammunition stored in their town. Concord's mobilization on that chilly spring night was sure evidence that the colonies were teetering on the brink of revolution.

Until recently, the citizens had been loyal British subjects. Like other rural New Englanders, they had been indifferent to the British Empire's political crisis until they had debated Boston's circular letter of November 20, 1772. Thereafter, Concord's town meeting endorsed a steady flow of correspondence from Boston denouncing unconstitutional parliamentary laws. In June 1774, 80 percent of Concord's men signed a strongly worded pledge to boycott British goods until the Coercive Acts were repealed. By March 6, 1775, all but three men in town had sworn to uphold the Continental Congress against Massachusetts's royal governor, General Thomas Gage. Within the brief span of thirty months, Concord had shed its apathy and become united in resisting the Coercive Acts.

As dawn approached, the townspeople hid bullets and gunflints throughout their houses, concealed gunpowder in the woods, and buried cannon and muskets. Fifteen-year-old Milicent Barrett, the granddaughter of the minutemen's colonel, supervised teenage girls in the manufacture of cartridges. Reinforcements for Concord's 150 minutemen arrived from nearby towns. Word came that the British had opened fire on Lexington's minutemen, but no one knew if blood had been shed.

At daybreak Captain David Brown marched his company toward Lexington and promptly ran into the British. Sizing up the situation, Brown swung back to Concord with drums beating and fifes squealing. "We had grand music," Corporal Amos Barrett later recalled. Badly outnumbered, Colonel James Barrett evacuated the town center and took up position on high ground overlooking the Concord River bridge to await reinforcements.

After posting a guard at the bridge, just out of the minutemen's range, the British scoured the town for military equipment. Much of what little remained behind was saved by the town's women, who outwitted redcoats sent to search their homes. Mrs. Amos Wood tricked an officer who correctly suspected the presence of hidden ammunition into believing that a locked room sheltered panic-stricken women. "I forbid anyone entering this room," commanded the chivalrous Englishman. Hannah Barnes bluffed a search party out of entering a room that contained a chest filled with money needed to buy additional military supplies.

The British regulars dumped five hundred pounds of bullets into a pond, destroyed sixty barrels of flour, and found two cannon. They also accidentally set fire to the courthouse and a blacksmith shop, which they saved before serious damage

"The White Cockade"
Fifer Luther Blanchard and drummer Francis Barker played this martial tune shortly before the skirmish near the bridge.

A View of the Town of Concord, 1775, *by Ralph Earl*

resulted. But the minutemen on the ridge became enraged by the rising smoke.

"Will you let them burn the town down?" screamed hotheaded Lieutenant Joseph Hosmer at Colonel Barrett. Now commanding four hundred men, Barrett decided to reenter the town and led his men toward the hundred redcoats guarding the bridge. The British withdrew across the river and fired several warning shots. One round wounded Luther Blanchard, a fifer who had been merrily playing a marching tune. Suddenly, smoke billowed from the British ranks and musketballs whistled across the water. Captain Isaac Davis and Private Abner Hosmer, volunteers from nearby Acton, fell dead. "For God's sake, fire," shouted Captain Jonathan Buttrick to his Concord company, which shot a volley at the British that killed three soldiers and wounded nine others.

The skirmish lasted only two or three minutes. The British withdrew to the town center. The minutemen crossed the river but then broke ranks and milled about in confusion. Both sides kept their distance until noon, when the British started to march back to Boston.

The British delay in leaving Concord allowed hundreds of minutemen to arrive from neighboring towns. At Meriam's Corner, these reinforcements began harassing the redcoats in a running battle that continued for sixteen miles. "Every man," recalled Private Thaddeus Blood, "was his own commander." By day's end almost three hundred royal troops were killed, wounded, or missing, and eighty colonists lay dead or injured.

Concord citizens escaped the day with slight losses: four men wounded, none dead. The war, however, had barely begun, and during the coming months, Concord sent off every able-bodied man between the ages of eighteen and forty to serve in the army. After the war the fight at the bridge assumed mythic dimensions for Americans, who celebrated the patriots who dared death at "the rude bridge that arched the flood" and "fired the shot heard 'round the world." But Concord citizens were too familiar with the events to romanticize

British Looters
A colonial cartoonist caught the redcoats in a looting spree during their retreat from Concord.

them. In 1792 they unemotionally tore up the historic bridge and built a more convenient crossing several hundred yards downriver.

had made independence a reality. Finally, Paine linked America's awakening nationalism with the sense of religious mission felt by many in New England and elsewhere when he proclaimed, "We have it in our power to begin the world over again. A situation, similar to the present, hath not happened since the days of Noah until now." America, in Paine's view, would be not only a new nation but a new *kind* of nation, a model society founded on new principles and unburdened by the oppressive beliefs and institutions of the European past.

Printed in both English and German, *Common Sense* sold more than one hundred thousand copies within three months, equal to one for every fourth or fifth adult male. The Connecticut Gazette described it as "a landflood that sweeps all before it." By the spring of 1776, Paine's pamphlet had dissolved lingering allegiance to George III and removed the last psychological barrier to independence.

Independence at Last

John Adams described the movement toward independence as a coach drawn by thirteen horses, which could not reach its destination any faster than the slowest ones were willing to run. New England was already in rebellion, and Rhode Island declared itself independent in May 1776. The middle colonies hesitated to support revolution because they feared, correctly, that the war would largely be fought over control of Philadelphia and New York. Following the news in April that North Carolina's congressional delegates were authorized to vote for independence, the South began pressing for separation. Virginia's extralegal legislature soon instructed its delegates at the Second Continental Congress to propose independence, which Richard Henry Lee did on June 7. Formally adopting Lee's resolution on July 2, Congress created the United States of America.

The task of drafting a statement to justify the colonies' separation from England fell to Virginia delegate Thomas Jefferson. Congress reviewed his manuscript on July 3 and approved it the next day. The Declaration of Independence never mentioned Parliament by name—even though the central point of dispute since 1765 had been Parliament's legislative powers—because Congress was unwilling to imply, even indirectly, that it held any authority over America. Jefferson instead followed Paine and focused on the king, citing George III's "repeated injuries and usurpations" against the colonies. And he drew on a familiar line of thinking when he added that the king's actions had as their "direct object the establishment of an absolute tyranny over these states."

Also like Paine, Jefferson elevated the colonists' grievances from a dispute over English freedoms to a struggle of universal dimensions. In the tradition of Locke and other Enlightenment figures, Jefferson argued that the English government had violated its contract with the colonists, thereby giving them the right to replace it with a government of their own design. His eloquent emphasis on the equality of all individuals and their natural entitlement to justice, liberty, and self-fulfillment expressed the Enlightenment's deepest longing for a government that would rest on neither legal privilege nor the exploitation of the majority by the few.

Jefferson addressed the Declaration of Independence as much to Americans uncertain about the wisdom of independence as to world opinion, for he wanted to convince his fellow citizens that social and political progress could no longer be accomplished within the British Empire. The declaration never claimed that perfect justice and equal opportunity existed in the United States; rather, it challenged the Revolutionary generation and all who later inherited the nation to bring this ideal closer to reality.

CONCLUSION

The most moving section of the Declaration of Independence's original draft was directed to the people of England, whom Jefferson regretfully reminded that "we might have been a free and great people together." Congress eliminated these words, which expressed the feelings of most Americans all too well, for in a civil war it is never wise to dwell on the matter of shedding common blood. Throughout the long imperial crisis, Americans had repeatedly pursued the goal of reestablishing the empire as it had functioned before 1763, when colonial trade was protected and encouraged—not taxed and plundered—by the Navigation Acts, and when colonial assemblies had exercised exclusive power over taxation and internal legislation. These reluctant revolutionaries now had to face the might of Europe's greatest imperial power and win their independence on the battlefield. They also had to decide to what degree they would implement the idealistic vision evoked in Jefferson's declaration. Neither task would prove simple or easy.

CHRONOLOGY

1744–1748 King George's War (in Europe, the War of Austrian Succession, 1740–1748).

1754–1760 Seven Years' War (in Europe, 1756–1763).

1760 George III becomes king of Great Britain.
Massachusetts controversy over writs of assistance.

1763–1766 Indian uprising in Ohio Valley and Great Lakes.

1763 Proclamation of 1763.

1764 Sugar Act.

1765 Stamp Act.
First Quartering Act.
Loyal Nine formed in Boston to oppose the Stamp Act.
Sons of Liberty band together throughout the colonies.
Stamp Act Congress.
Colonists begin boycott of British goods.

1766 Stamp Act repealed.
Declaratory Act.

1767 New York Suspending Act.
Revenue Act (Townshend duties).
John Dickinson, *Letters from a Farmer in Pennsylvania.*
American Board of Customs Commissioners created.

Commemorative Teapot, 1766

1768 Massachusetts "circular letter."
Boston merchants adopt the colonies' first nonimportation agreement.
John Hancock's ship *Liberty* seized by Boston customs commissioner.
British troops arrive in Boston.
First Treaty of Fort Stanwix.
John Wilkes elected to Parliament; arrested.
St. George's Fields Massacre in London.

1770 Townshend duties, except tea tax, repealed.
Boston Massacre.

1771 Battle of Alamance Creek in North Carolina.

1772 *Gaspee* incident in Rhode Island.
Committees of correspondence begin in Masschusetts and rapidly spread.

1773 Tea Act.
Boston Tea Party.

1774 Coercive Acts.
Quebec Act.
First Continental Congress meets in Philadelphia and adopts Suffolk Resolves.
Continental Association.

1775 Battles of Lexington and Concord.
Second Continental Congress meets.
Olive Branch Petition.
Battles at Breed's Hill and Bunker Hill.

1776 Thomas Paine, *Common Sense.*
Declaration of Independence.

FOR FURTHER READING

Bernard Bailyn, *The Ideological Origins of the American Revolution* (1967). Pulitzer Prize–winning examination of the political heritage that shaped colonial resistance to British authority.

Edward Countryman, *The American Revolution* (1985). An outstanding introduction to the Revolution and its background.

Robert A. Gross, *The Minutemen and Their World* (1976). An eloquent and evocative examination of Concord, Massachusetts, in the Revolutionary era.

Pauline Maier, *From Resistance to Revolution: Colonial Radicals and the Development of American Opposition to Britain, 1765–1776* (1972). An insightful, definitive examination of how colonial leaders strove to force the repeal of unconstitutional laws with a minimum use of violence.

Robert Middlekauff, *The Glorious Cause: The American Revolution, 1763–1789* (1982). A judicious, learned, and highly readable narrative of the events leading to Independence.

Edmund S. Morgan and Helen M. Morgan, *The Stamp Act Crisis: Prologue to Revolution*, rev. ed. (1963). The most penetrating, and now classic, analysis of colonial constitutional principles regarding the limits on Parliament's taxing power.

Robert R. Palmer, *The Age of the Democratic Revolution: Vol. I, The Challenge* (1959). Bancroft Prize–winning examination of the American Revolution in comparison to events in England, Ireland, and France.

Gordon S. Wood, *The Radicalism of the American Revolution* (1991). A sweeping account of the Revolution's long-range impact on American society.

ADDITIONAL BIBLIOGRAPHY

The Military Background

Fred Anderson, *A People's Army: Massachusetts Soldiers and Society in the Seven Years' War* (1984); Sylvia R. Frey, *The British Soldier in America: A Social History of Military Life in the Colonial Period* (1981); John Shy, *Toward Lexington: The Role of the British Army in the Coming of the America Revolution* (1965); Ian K. Steele, *Betrayals: Fort William Henry and the "Massacre"* (1990).

Native Americans and the Frontier

David H. Corkran, *The Creek Frontier, 1540–1783* (1967); Gregory Evans Dowd, *A Spirited Resistance: The North American Indian Struggle for Unity, 1745–1815* (1992); Tom Hatley, *The Dividing Paths: Cherokees and South Carolinians Through the Era of Revolution* (1993); Dorothy V. Jones, *License for Empire: Colonialism by Treaty in Early America* (1982); Francis Jennings, *Empire of Fortune: Crowns, Colonies and Tribes in the Seven Years' War in America* (1988); Michael N. McConnell, *A Country Between: The Upper Ohio Valley and Its Peoples, 1724–1774* (1992); Richard White, *The Middle Ground: Indians, Empires, and Republics in the Great Lakes Region, 1650–1815* (1991).

Taxing and Regulating Trade

Thomas C. Barrow, *Trade and Empire: The British Customs Service in Colonial America* (1967); Oliver M. Dickerson, *The Navigation Acts and the American Revolution* (1951); Michael Kammen, *Empire and Interest: The American Colonies and the Politics of Mercantilism* (1970); John W. Tyler, *Smugglers and Patriots: Boston Merchants and the Advent of the American Revolution* (1986); Carol Ubbelohde, *The Vice-Admiralty Courts and the American Revolution* (1960).

Constitutional Issues

Richard L. Bushman, *King and People in Provincial Massachusetts* (1985); Jack P. Greene, *Peripheries and Center: Constitutional Development in the Extended Politics of the British Empire and the United States, 1607–1788* (1987); Jerrilyn G. Marston, *King and Congress* (1987); Edmund S. Morgan, *Inventing the People: The Rise of Popular Sovereignty in England and America* (1988); John G. A. Pocock, *Three British Revolutions: 1641, 1688, 1776* (1980); Jack R. Pole, *Political Representation in England and the Origins of the American Republic* (1966); John P. Reid, *Constitutional History of the American Revolution: The Authority of Rights* (1986), *Constitutional History of the American Revolution: The Power to Tax* (1987).

Religious Influences

Ruth H. Bloch, *Visionary Republic: Millennial Themes in American Thought, 1756–1800* (1985); Patricia U. Bonomi, *Under the Cope of Heaven: Religion, Society, and Politics in Colonial America* (1986); Jack P. Greene and William G. McLoughlin, *Preachers and Politicians: Two Essays on the Origin of the American Revolution* (1977); Nathan O. Hatch, *The Sacred Cause of Liberty: Republican Thought and the Millennium in Revolutionary New England* (1977).

Resistance

David Ammerman, *In the Common Cause: American Response to the Coercive Acts of 1774* (1974); Michael Bellesiles, *Revolutionary Outlaws: Ethan Allen and the Struggle for Independence* (1993); John L. Brooke, *The Heart of the Commonwealth: Society and Political Culture in Worcester County, Massachusetts, 1713–1861* (1989); Richard D. Brown, *Revolutionary Politics in Massachusetts: The Boston Committees of Correspondence and the Towns, 1772–1774* (1970); Marc Egnal, *A Mighty Empire: The Origins of the American Revolution* (1988); Jay Fleigelman, *Prodigals and Pilgrims: The American Revolution Against Patriarchal Authority, 1750–1800* (1982); Michael G. Kammen, *A Rope of Sand: The Colonial Agents, British Politics, and the American Revolution* (1968); Benjamin W. Labaree, *The Boston Tea Party* (1964); Edmund S. Morgan and Helen M. Morgan, *The Stamp Act Crisis: Prologue to Revolution*, rev. ed. (1963); Gary B.

Nash, *The Urban Crucible: The Northern Seaports and the Origins of the American Revolution,* abridged ed. (1986); Mary Beth Norton, *Liberty's Daughters: The Revolutionary Experience of American Women, 1750–1800* (1980); John Sainsbury, *Disaffected Patriots: London Supporters of Revolutionary America, 1769–1782* (1987); Peter Shaw, *American Patriots and the Rituals of Revolution* (1981); Neil R. Stout, *The Perfect Crisis: The Beginnings of the Revolutionary War* (1976); Peter D. G. Thomas, *The Townshend Duties Crisis: The Second Phase of the American Revolution, 1767–1773* (1987); Robert W. Tucker and David C. Hendrickson, *The Fall of the First British Empire: Origins of the War of American Independence* (1982); Hiller B. Zobel, *The Boston Massacre* (1970).

Biographies

Bernard Bailyn, *The Ordeal of Thomas Hutchinson* (1974); Richard R. Beeman, *Patrick Henry: A Biography* (1974); Milton E. Flower, *John Dickinson: Conservative Revolutionary* (1983); Eric Foner, *Tom Paine and Revolutionary America* (1976); Pauline Maier, *The Old Revolutionaries: Political Lives in the Age of Samuel Adams* (1980); Dumas Malone, *Jefferson the Virginian* (1948).

George Washington [1777]
by Charles Peale Polk, c. 1792–1793

6

THE FORGE OF NATIONHOOD
1776–1788

In November 1775 General George Washington ordered Colonel Henry Knox (inset) to bring the British artillery recently captured at Fort Ticonderoga to the siege of Boston. Washington knew firsthand of the difficulties of wilderness travel, especially in the winter, and he must have wondered if this city-bred officer was up to the task. Only twenty-five years old and a Boston bookseller with little experience in the woods, Knox was nevertheless the army's senior artillerist, largely because he had read several books on the subject while business in his store was dull.

Knox and his men built crude sleds to haul their fifty-nine cannons through dense forest covered by two feet of snow. On good days they moved these sixty tons of artillery about seven miles. On two very bad ones, they shivered for hours in freezing water while retrieving guns that had fallen through the ice at river crossings. As their oxen grew weak from overexertion and poor feed, the men had to throw their own backs into pulling the cannons across New York's frozen landscape. On reaching the Berkshire Mountains in western Massachusetts, their pace slowed to a crawl as they trudged uphill through snow-clogged passes. Forty days and three hundred miles after leaving Ticonderoga, Knox and his exhausted New Yorkers reported to Washington in late January 1776. The Boston bookseller had more than proved himself: he had accomplished one of the Revolution's great feats of endurance.

The guns from Ticonderoga placed the outnumbered British in a hopeless position and forced them to evacuate Boston on March 17, 1776. A lifelong friendship formed between Washington and Knox. Knox served on the Virginian's staff throughout the war and accepted his request to be the nation's first secretary of war in 1789.

Friendships like the one between Washington and Knox were almost as revolutionary as the war that produced them. Because inhabitants of different colonies had little opportunity to become acquainted before 1775, their outlooks had remained narrowly confined within the borders of their provinces. This localism was well entrenched at the start of the war. George Washington at first described New Englanders as "an exceeding dirty and nasty people." Yankee soldiers irritated troops from distant colonies such as Virginia with smug assumptions of superiority expressed in their popular marching song "Chester," whose rousing lyrics rang out:

Let tyrants shake their iron rod,
and slavery clank her galling chains.
We fear them not, we trust in God.
New England's *God forever reigns.*

The Revolution gave northerners and southerners their first real chance to learn what they had in common, and they soon developed mutual admiration. George Washington, who in the war's early days dismissed New England officers as "the most indifferent kind of people I ever saw," changed his mind after meeting men like Henry Knox.

In July 1776 the thirteen colonies had out of desperation declared independence and established a new nation. But only as a result of the collective hardships experienced during eight years of terrible fighting did the inhabitants of the thirteen states cease to see themselves simply as military allies and begin to accept each other as fellow citizens.

The return of peace in 1783 left Americans with a false sense of security. Major problems remained unsolved and ignored, particularly the power and authority of the national government relative to that of the states. With the ratification of the Constitution, the United States arrived at a resolution of this fundamental question, thereby completing the process whereby thirteen colonies became a single nation.

America's First Civil War

The Revolution was both a collective struggle that marched a sizable portion of the American people against Britain and a civil war between inhabitants of North America. Eventually, it would degenerate into a brothers' war of the worst kind, conducted without restraint, mutual respect, or compassion. From a military standpoint, the Revolution's outcome depended not only on the ability of the supporters of independence, called the patriots, or Whigs, to wear down the British army but also on the rebels' success in suppressing fellow North Americans' opposition to independence.

Loyalists and Other British Sympathizers

As late as January 1776, most colonists still hoped that declaring independence from Britain would not be necessary. Not surprisingly, when separation came six months later, many Americans remained unconvinced that it was justified. About 20 percent of all whites either opposed the rebellion actively or refused to support the Continental Congress unless threatened with fines or imprisonment. Although these internal enemies of the Revolution called themselves loyalists, they were "Tories" to their Whig foes. Whigs remarked, but only half in jest, that "a tory was a thing with a head in England, a body in America, and a neck that needed stretching."

Loyalists avowed many of the same political values as did the patriots. Like the rebels, they usually opposed Parliament's claim to tax the colonies. Many loyalists thus found themselves fighting for a cause with which they did not entirely agree, and as a result many of them would change sides during the war. Most doubtless shared the apprehension expressed in 1775 by the Reverend Jonathan Boucher, a well-known Maryland loyalist, who preached with two loaded pistols lying on his pulpit cushion: "For my part I equally dread a Victory by either side."

Loyalists disagreed, however, with the patriots' insistence that only independence could preserve the colonists' constitutional rights. The loyalists denounced separation as an illegal act certain to ignite an unnecessary war. Above all, they retained a profound

A British View of the Loyalists

This British cartoon depicts Americans as "savage" Indian warriors massacring helpless loyalists. It is also critical of Prime Minister Lord Shelburne for failing to protect the loyalists.

reverence for the crown and deeply believed that if they failed to defend their king, they would sacrifice their personal honor.

The most important factor in determining loyalist strength in any area was the degree to which prominent local Whigs had successfully convinced the mass of voters that representative government was endangered by the king and Parliament. Town leaders in New England, the Virginia gentry, and the rice planters of South Carolina's seacoast all vigorously pursued a program of political education and popular mobilization from 1772 to 1776. Repeatedly explaining the issues at public meetings, these elites shook the mass of citizens from their apathy and persuaded the overwhelming majority in favor of resistance. As a result, probably no more than 5 percent of whites in these areas were committed loyalists in 1776. Where the leading families acted indecisively, however, their communities remained divided when the fighting began. Because the gentry of New York and New Jersey were especially reluctant to declare their allegiance to either side, the proportion of loyalists was highest there. Those two states eventually furnished about half of the twenty-one thousand Americans who fought in loyalist military units.

The next most significant factor influencing loyalist military strength was the geographic distribution of recent British immigrants, who closely identified with their homeland, not America, and overwhelmingly opposed independence. Among these newcomers were thousands of British soldiers who had served in the Seven Years' War and then remained in the colonies, usually in New York, where they could obtain land grants of two hundred acres. Furthermore, more than 125,000 English, Scots, and Irish landed from 1763 to 1775—the greatest number of Britons to arrive during any dozen years of the colonial era. Major centers of loyalist sympathy existed wherever large concentrations of such British-born people lived. In New York, Georgia, and the backcountry of North and South Carolina, where the native-born Britons were heavily concentrated, the proportion of loyalists among whites probably ranged from 25 percent to 40 percent in 1776. In wartime the British army organized many Tory units comprising immigrants from the British Isles, including the Loyal Highland Emigrants, the North Carolina Highlanders, and the Volunteers of Ireland. After the war foreign-born loyalists composed a majority of those compensated by the British for property losses during the Revolution—including

three-quarters of all such claimants from the Carolinas and Georgia.

Other minorities supported the British cause, not out of loyalty to the crown but from a perception that an independent American republic would pose the greater threat to their own liberty and independence. A small number of German, Dutch, and French religious congregations that resisted use of the English language felt indebted to the British government for their religious freedom and doubted that their rights would be as safe in an independent nation dominated by Anglo-Americans. Yet on balance, these ethnic and religious minorities provided few loyalists. The great majority of German colonists in Pennsylvania, Maryland, and Virginia, for example, had embraced emergent American republicanism by 1776 and would overwhelmingly support the Revolutionary cause.

Canada's French Catholics composed the most significant white minority to hold pro-British sympathies. Although the British had conquered them in the Seven Years' War, the Quebec Act of 1774 guaranteed their religious freedom and their continued use of French civil law. Remembering that the American colonists had denounced this measure and demanded its repeal, French Catholics worried that their privileges would disappear if they were absorbed into an independent Protestant America.

Canadian anxieties intensified in mid-1775, when the Continental Congress ordered Continental forces to "free" Canada from British tyranny unless this action was "disagreeable" to the French population. In reality, Congress cared little what the French-Canadians thought, for Congress believed that a conquest of Canada was essential to block a British invasion from the north. In 1775 Continental armies (one of them led by Benedict Arnold, a fervent patriot who later turned traitor) marched into Canada and attacked Quebec but suffered defeat on December 31, 1775. French Catholics emerged from the shock of invasion more loyal to the crown than ever before. The rebels never even attempted to win over three other mainland colonies—Nova Scotia and East and West Florida—whose small populations of mainly recent immigrants were firmly dominated by British military authorities.

The British cause would also draw significant wartime support from nonwhites. As a deeply alienated group within society, slaves quickly realized that the Revolution was not intended to benefit them. In 1766, when a group of African-American slaves, inspired by the protests against the Stamp Act, had marched through Charles Town, South Carolina, shouting "Liberty!" they had faced arrest for inciting a rebellion. By 1775 it was the British who most often offered liberty to enslaved African-Americans. For example, in 1775 Lord Dunmore, governor of Virginia, promised freedom to any slave who enlisted in the cause of restoring royal authority. About eight hundred blacks joined him before he fled the colony. Meanwhile, hundreds of South Carolina slaves had escaped and taken refuge on British ships in Charles Town's harbor. During the war at least twenty thousand American slaves ran away to sign on as laborers or soldiers in the Royal Army. Among the Whig slaveholders who saw many of his slaves escape to British protection was Thomas Jefferson.

Although the Native American population was divided, most supported the British. Indians along the frontier recognized the danger to their homelands posed by expansion-minded Anglo-Americans. As had been the case since midcentury, tensions ran especially high in the Ohio Country. There, Shawnees, Delawares, Mingos, and other Indians continued to bristle at white incursions, as did the Cherokees to the south. Native Americans in the upper Great Lakes, after the uprising of 1763 (see Chapter 5), had developed good rapport with British agents in the former French forts and were solidly in the British camp. The Iroquois and Creek confederacies, whose neutrality had been a source of strength until the French defeat in 1760, were now divided. The Creeks' allegiance reflected each village's earlier trade ties with either Britain or Spain (the latter leaned toward the colonists' cause). Most Iroquois followed the lead of the English-educated Mohawk chief Joseph Brant in supporting Britain. Only the Oneidas and Tuscaroras, influenced by Congregationalist missionary Samuel Kirkland, sided with the rebels. Native Americans in upper New England and the Canadian maritime provinces and in the Illinois and Wabash valleys initially took an anti-British stand because of earlier ties with the French, though many of them became alienated from the colonists during the war. Most of the dwindling number of Indians living in the established colonies favored the rebellion.

Toward loyalists collectively, Whigs reserved an intense hatred, far greater than their antipathy toward the British army, and loyalists responded with equal venom. Each side saw its cause as so sacred that opposition by a fellow American was an unforgivable act of betrayal. The worst atrocities committed during the war were inflicted by Americans upon each other.

The Opposing Sides

Britain entered the war with two major advantages. First, in 1776 the 11 million inhabitants of the British Isles greatly outnumbered the 2.5 million colonists, one-third of whom were either slaves or loyalists. Second, Britain possessed the world's largest navy and one of its best professional armies. Nevertheless, the royal military establishment grew during the war years to a degree that strained Britain's resources. The army more than doubled from 48,000 to 111,000 men, not only in North America but also in the British Isles and the West Indies. To meet its manpower needs, the British government had to raise the recruiting bonuses paid to get men to enlist, lower physical requirements, widen age limits, and sometimes enroll soldiers forcibly. But even these measures failed to provide the required numbers. Without hiring 30,000 German mercenaries known as Hessians and later enlisting 21,000 loyalists, Britain could not have met its manpower needs.

Despite its smaller population, the new nation mobilized its people more effectively than did Britain. By the end of the war, the rebels had enlisted or drafted into the Continental Army or the state militias perhaps half of all free males from age sixteen to forty-five—about 220,000 troops—compared to the 162,000 Britons, loyalists, and Hessians who served in the British army.

Britain's ability to crush the rebellion was further weakened by the decline in its seapower that had resulted from peacetime budget cuts after 1763. Midway through the war, half of the Royal Navy's ships sat in dry dock awaiting major repairs. Although the navy expanded rapidly from 18,000 to 111,000 sailors, it lost 42,000 men to desertion and 20,000 to disease or wounds. In addition, Britain's merchant marine suffered mightily from raids by the numerous American privateers newly outfitted from the colonies' thriving merchant marine. During the war rebel privateers and the fledgling U.S. Navy would capture over 2,000 British merchant vessels and 16,000 crewmen.

Britain could ill afford these losses, for it faced a colossal task in trying to supply its troops in America. Although at one time or another the British army controlled all the major American cities, British soldiers ventured into the agricultural hinterland only at their peril and hence could not easily round up supplies. In fact, almost all the food consumed by the army, a third

Woodcut from "A New Touch on the Times. . . . By a Daughter of Liberty, Living in Marblehead," 1779
Americans on the home front as well as in the front lines experienced stunning wartime hardships. This illustration of a female partisan holding a musket accompanied a poem by Molly Gutridge, whose theme was women's sacrifice and suffering in a seaport economy upset by war.

guerrilla skirmishes and were also effective in intimidating loyalists and in requisitioning war supplies, they lacked the training to fight pitched battles. Congress recognized that independence would never be secured if the United States relied on guerrilla tactics, avoided major battles, and allowed the British to occupy all major population centers. Moreover, because European powers would interpret U.S dependence on guerrilla warfare as evidence that Americans could not drive out the British army, that strategy would doom efforts by the Continental Congress to gain foreign loans and diplomatic recognition.

The Continental Army thus had to fight in the standard European fashion of the times. Professional eighteenth-century armies relied on expert movements of mass formations. Victory often depended on rapid maneuvers to crush an enemy's undefended flank or rear. Attackers needed exceptional skill in close-order drill in order to fall on an enemy before the enemy could re-form and return fire. Because muskets had a range of under one hundred yards, armies in battle were never far apart. Battles usually occurred in open country with space for maneuver. The troops advanced within musket range of each other, stood upright without cover, and fired volleys at one another until one line weakened from its casualties. Discipline, training, and nerve were essential if soldiers were to stay in ranks while comrades fell beside them. The stronger side then attacked at a quick walk with bayonets drawn and drove off its opponents.

In 1775 Britain possessed a well-trained army with a strong tradition of discipline and bravery under fire. In contrast, the Continental Army had neither an inspirational heritage nor many experienced officers or sergeants who might turn raw recruits into crack units. Consequently, the Americans experienced a succession of heartbreaking defeats in the war's early years. Yet to win the war, the Continentals did not have to destroy the British army but only prolong the rebellion until Britain's taxpayers lost patience with the struggle. Until then, American victory would hinge heavily on the ability of one man to keep his army fighting despite defeat. He was George Washington.

of a ton per soldier per year, had to be imported from Britain. Seriously overextended, the navy barely kept the army supplied and never effectively blockaded American ports.

Mindful of the enormous strain that the war imposed, British leaders faced serious problems maintaining their people's support for the conflict. The war more than doubled the national debt, thereby adding further to the burdens of a people already paying record taxes. The politically influential landed gentry could not be expected to vote against their pocketbooks forever.

The United States faced different but no less severe wartime problems. First, one-fifth of its free population openly favored the British. Second, although the state militias sometimes performed well in hit-and-run

George Washington

Few generals ever looked and acted the role as much as Washington. He spoke with authority and comported himself with dignity. At six feet two inches, he stood a half-foot taller than the average man of his day.

Powerfully built, athletic, and hardened by a rugged outdoor life, he was one of the war's few generals whose presence on the battlefield could inspire troops to heroism.

Washington's military experience began at age twenty-two, when he had taken command of a Virginia regiment raised to resist French claims in the Ohio Valley (see Chapter 5). He had lost his first battle to a force vastly outnumbering his own. A year later, at Braddock's defeat, he had placed himself at the point of greatest danger and had two horses killed under him, besides having his hat shot off and his coat ripped by five bullets. Washington's early military experience—his mistakes and lost battles—taught him lessons that he might not have learned from easy, glorious victories. He discovered the dangers of overconfidence and the need for determination in the face of defeat. He also learned much about American soldiers, especially that they performed best when led by example and treated with respect.

With Virginia's borders safe from attack in 1758, Washington had resigned his commission and become a tobacco planter. He had sat in the Virginia House of Burgesses, where his influence had grown, not because he thrust himself into every issue but because others respected him and sought his opinion. Having emerged as an early, though not outspoken, opponent of parliamentary taxation, he had also sat in the Continental Congress. In the eyes of the many who valued his advice and remembered his military experience, Washington was the logical choice to head the Continental Army.

The Battle of Princeton (1777), *by James Peale, c. 1790*
In the battle's first phase, fought south of the town, the American advance guard clashed with redcoats who were en route to Trenton, where they planned to link up with Lord Cornwallis. The British had the upper hand until George Washington and the main Continental force arrived, attacked, and drove them off.

War in Earnest

Henry Knox's successful transport of artillery from Ticonderoga to Boston prompted the British to evacuate Boston in March 1776 and to move on to New York, which they wished to seize and use as a base for conquering New England. Under two brothers—General William Howe and Admiral Richard, Lord Howe—130 warships carrying 32,000 royal troops landed near New York harbor in the summer of 1776. Defending New York, America's second-largest city, were 18,000 poorly trained soldiers under George Washington.

On August 27, 15,000 of William Howe's men nearly overwhelmed the 10,500 troops whom Washington had stationed on Long Island, just across a river from New York City. Inflicting over 1,000 casualties while losing fewer than 400 men, the British were on the verge of annihilating the Americans. But Washington executed a masterful night evacuation to New York City, saving 9,500 soldiers and most of his artillery from certain capture. He himself was the last American to board a boat.

By the third week of September 1776, the Continental Army around New York included more than 16,000 men fit to bear arms. Over the next three months, the British killed or took prisoner one-quarter of these troops and drove the survivors into headlong retreat across New Jersey. By early December, when Washington crossed the Delaware River from New Jersey into Pennsylvania, he had fewer than 7,000 troops fit for duty. Thomas Paine accurately described these demoralizing days as "the times that try men's souls."

With the British in striking distance of Philadelphia, Washington decided to seize the offensive before the morale of his army and country collapsed completely. On Christmas night, 1776, he led his troops back into New Jersey and attacked a Hessian garrison at Trenton, where he captured 918 Germans and lost only 4 Continentals. Washington then attacked 1,200 British at Princeton on January 3, 1777, and killed or took captive one-third of them while sustaining only 40 casualties.

These American victories at Trenton and Princeton had several important consequences. At a moment when defeat seemed inevitable, they boosted civilian and military morale. In addition, by checking the British offensive, they frustrated Howe's plans to pacify New Jersey by persuading inhabitants opposed to or skeptical of independence to rally to the British cause. Although nearly 5,000 New Jerseyans with loyalist sympathies swore allegiance to the crown late in 1776, Washington's victories forced the British early in 1777 to remove virtually all their New Jersey garrisons to New York, while Washington established winter quarters at Morristown, New Jersey, only twenty-five miles from New York City.

As long as they had enjoyed the support of the redcoats, New Jersey's loyalists had plundered local Whigs. Now stripped of British protection, the loyalists fell prey to the rebel militia, who drove thousands of loyalists into British-held New York, where many joined the Royal Army. Although some loyalists formed guerrilla bands and raided their former neighbors, New Jersey loyalism never recovered from the blow it received when the British evacuated the state early in 1777. The state militia became a relentless police force dedicated to rooting out political dissent. The militia disarmed known loyalists, jailed their leaders, and kept a constant watch on suspected Tories. Ironically, the British themselves contributed to the undermining of New Jersey loyalism, for prior to the Battle of Trenton, British commanders had failed to prevent an orgy of looting by their troops that damaged loyalists and Whigs equally. Surrounded by armed enemies and facing constant danger of arrest, most loyalists who remained in the state bowed to the inevitable and swore allegiance to the Continental Congress; more than a few ex-loyalists themselves joined the rebel militia.

The same process was eventually repeated following British invasions of New York in 1777, Georgia in 1778, and the Carolinas in 1779. Upon regaining the upper hand, Whig militias ruthlessly pursued loyalists aiding the redcoats, forced many to flee, and coerced most into renouncing the crown.

Not all loyalists shifted sides, however. The war drove perhaps one of every six loyalists into exile in Canada, Britain, or the West Indies. Twenty percent of all New Yorkers may have left the United States by 1784. When the British evacuated Savannah in 1782, 15 percent of all whites in Georgia accompanied them. Most of those who departed were evidently British immigrants. Whether loyalists changed sides or became political refugees, loyalism declined as a force during the war. By 1782 few active loyalists remained outside British lines.

The War in the North, 1776–1779

Following the British evacuation of Boston, the war shifted to New York City, which the British held from 1776 to 1783. In 1777 Britain's success in taking Philadelphia was offset by defeat in upstate New York. The hard-fought battle of Monmouth Court House, New Jersey, ended the northern campaigns in 1778.

The Turning Point

Shortly after the battles of Trenton and Princeton, the Marquis de Lafayette, a young French aristocrat, joined Washington's staff. Lafayette was twenty years old, highly idealistic, very brave, and infectiously optimistic. Given Lafayette's close connections with the French court, his presence in America indicated that the French king, Louis XVI, might recognize U.S. independence and perhaps declare war on Britain. Before recognizing the United States, however, Louis wanted proof that the Americans could win a major battle, a feat they had not yet accomplished.

Louis did not have to wait long. In the summer of 1777, the British planned a two-pronged assault intended to crush American resistance in New York State and thereby isolate New England. Pushing off from Montreal, a force of regulars and their Iroquois allies, marching under Lieutenant Colonel Barry St. Leger, would proceed south along Lake Ontario and invade central New York from Fort Oswego in the west, while General John Burgoyne would lead the main British force south from Quebec through eastern New York and link up with St. Leger near Albany.

The British would have faced a formidable task under any circumstances; but to complicate matters, General William Howe, the British commander in chief in North America, chose to launch a *second* major campaign in the summer of 1777, which was aimed at the American capital, Philadelphia. Howe intended to draw the Continentals south to the defense of their capital, defeat them in battle, and then use Philadelphia as a base for building loyalist support in the mid-Atlantic region. Howe's fateful decision to move against Philadelphia meant that neither he nor the modest force that he had left behind in New York City under General Henry Clinton could decisively aid St. Leger or Burgoyne if their invasion of New York misfired.

Unfortunately for Howe, nothing went according to plan in New York. St. Leger's force of 1,900 British and Iroquois advanced a hundred miles and halted to besiege 750 New York Continentals at Fort Stanwix. Unable to take the post after three weeks, St. Leger retreated in late August 1777.

Meanwhile, on July 6 Burgoyne's 8,300 British and Hessians had taken Fort Ticonderoga, about a hundred miles north of Albany. But by now Burgoyne's supply lines were overstretched, and a force that he dispatched to seize supplies at Bennington, Vermont, was repulsed with heavy losses. Along with the 900 troops that Burgoyne had detached to garrison Fort Ticonderoga, his losses in Vermont depleted his army and gave General Horatio Gates time to collect nearly 17,000 American troops for an attack. Gates fought two indecisive battles near Saratoga in the fall, inflicting another 1,200 casualties on Burgoyne. Surrounded and hopelessly outnumbered, Burgoyne's 5,800 troops honorably laid down their arms on October 17, 1777.

The diplomatic impact of the Battle of Saratoga rivaled its military significance and made it the war's turning point. Early in December 1777, news of the battle reached France, where Benjamin Franklin had recently arrived as the U.S. ambassador. Although one of America's wealthiest, wisest, and most sophisticated men, Franklin shrewdly captured the French imagination by appearing in a fur cap and playing the part of an innocent backwoods philosopher. Turning himself into the French court's latest fad, Franklin won widespread French sympathy for the United States. Then with the victory at Saratoga, France became convinced that the Americans could win the war and thus deserved diplomatic recognition.

In February 1778 France therefore formally recognized the United States. Four months later, it went to war with Britain. Spain declared war on Britain in 1779, but as an ally of France, not the United States, and the Dutch Republic joined them in the last days of 1780. Now facing a coalition of enemies, Britain had no allies.

The American allies soon made their presence felt. Between 1779 and 1781, Spanish troops based in Louisiana drove the British from West Florida, effectively preventing Britain from taking the Mississippi Valley. Beginning in 1781, French troops also contributed to rebel victories. Moreover, Britain sent thousands of soldiers to Ireland and the West Indies to guard against French invasion, thus reducing the manpower available to fight in the United States. The French and Spanish navies, which together approximately equaled the British fleet, won several large battles, denied Britain control of the sea, and punctured the Royal Navy's blockade.

The Continentals Mature

While Gates and Burgoyne maneuvered in upstate New York, Howe landed 18,000 troops near Philadelphia in late August. With Washington at their head and Lafayette at his side, 16,000 Continentals paraded through the imperiled city on August 24, 1777. "They marched twelve deep," John Adams wrote to his wife Abigail, "and yet took up above two hours in passing by." Adams noted that the troops were well armed and uniformed but that they did not keep their heads straight or wear their hats cocked properly—in short, they still had not acquired "quite the air of soldiers." They would pay a fearful price for their lack of training when they met Howe's professionals.

The two armies collided on September 11, 1777, at Brandywine Creek, Pennsylvania. In the face of superior British discipline, not only did most Continental units crumble but Congress soon fled Philadelphia in panic, enabling Howe to occupy the city. Howe again defeated Washington at Germantown on October 4. In one month's bloody fighting, 20 percent of the Continentals were killed, wounded, or captured.

In early December 1777, 11,000 tentless American survivors huddled around campfires at Whitemarsh, Pennsylvania. Short on rations and chilled to the bone from marching into a wall of sleet, they took a full week to walk to their winter quarters fourteen miles away. A fourth of them had worn out at least one shoe, and on days when the roads froze, they suffered horribly on the ice-covered ridges. Washington later remembered that "you might have tracked the army from White Marsh to Valley Forge by the blood of their feet."

While the British army rested comfortably eighteen miles away in Philadelphia, the Continentals stumbled around the bleak hills of Valley Forge, building crude huts. Despite some lapses in morale and discipline, the troops somehow preserved a sense of humor, which they occasionally demonstrated by joining together in a thousand voices to squawk like crows watching a cornfield. Underlying these squawks was real hunger: James Varnum reported on December 20 that his Connecticut and Rhode Island troops had gone the two previous days without meat and three days without bread.

The army slowly regained its strength but still lacked training. The Continentals had forced Burgoyne to surrender more by their overwhelming numbers than by their skill. Indeed, when Washington's men had met Howe's forces on equal terms, they lost badly. The Americans mainly lacked the ability to march as compact units and maneuver quickly. Regiments often straggled single-file into battle and then wasted precious time forming to attack, and few troops were expert in bayonet drill.

The Continental Army's ill-trained recruits received a desperately needed boost in February 1778, when the German soldier of fortune Friedrich von Steuben arrived at Valley Forge. The short, squat Steuben did not look like a soldier, but this earthy German instinctively liked Americans and became immensely popular. He had a talent for motivating men (sometimes by staging humorous tantrums featuring a barrage of German, English, and French swearing);

but more important, he possessed administrative genius. In a mere four months, General Steuben almost single-handedly turned the army into a formidable fighting force.

General Henry Clinton, now British commander in chief, evacuated Philadelphia in mid-1778 and marched to New York. The Continental Army got its first opportunity to demonstrate Steuben's training when it caught up with Clinton's rear guard at Monmouth Court House, New Jersey, on June 28, 1778. Although the Americans initially faltered, General Washington re-formed them along a strong defensive position. Clinton ordered his best units against Washington's line, only to see them thrown back at bayonet point. The battle raged for six hours in one-hundred-degree heat until Clinton broke off contact. Expecting to renew the fight at daybreak, the Americans slept on their arms, but Clinton's army slipped away before then. The British would never again win easily, except when they faced more militiamen than Continentals.

The Battle of Monmouth ended the contest for the North. Clinton occupied New York, which the Royal Navy made safe from attack. Washington kept his army nearby to watch Clinton. Meanwhile, the Whig militia hunted down the last few Tory guerrillas and extinguished loyalism.

Friedrich von Steuben
The Prussian-born Steuben arrived in the United States in December 1777. Although the government and the army alike felt deep disillusionment over the value of foreign officers at that time, the talented Steuben overcame this disability and was appointed the Continental Army's major-general in 1778.

Frontier Campaigns

A different kind of war developed west of the Appalachians and along the western borders of New York and Pennsylvania. The numbers engaged in these frontier skirmishes were relatively small, but the fighting was fierce and the stakes—for the new nation, for the British, and for Indians in the region—were high. In 1776 few Anglo-Americans had a clear notion of the western boundaries of the new nation; by 1783, when the Peace of Paris concluded the war, the new nation was able to assert its claim to the Mississippi River as

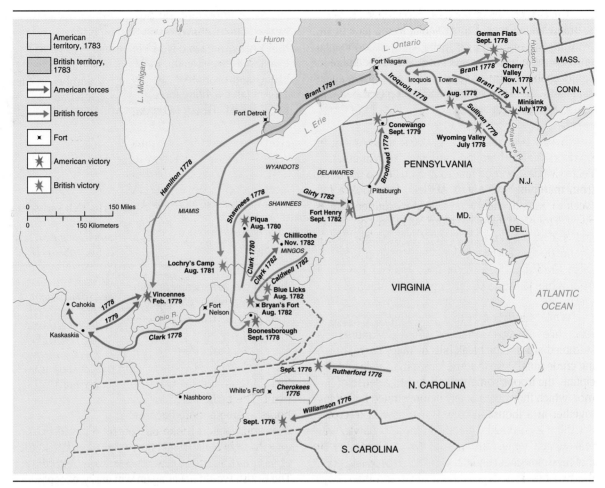

The War in the West, 1776–1779

George Rogers Clark's victory at Vincennes in 1779 gave the United States effective control of the Ohio Valley. Carolina militiamen drove attacking Cherokees far back into the Appalachians in 1776. In retaliation for their raids on New York and Pennsylvania, John Sullivan inflicted widespread starvation on the Iroquois by burning their villages and winter food supplies in 1779.

its western border. So although the frontier campaigns did not determine the outcome of the war, they had a significant impact on the future shape of the United States.

Frontier fighting erupted first in the South, where Cherokees began attacking settlers from Virginia to Georgia in 1776. After suffering heavy losses, the southern colonies recovered and organized retaliatory expeditions. Within a year these expeditions had burned most Cherokee towns, forcing the Cherokees to sign treaties that ceded most of their land in South Carolina and substantial tracts in North Carolina and Tennessee.

Elsewhere the intense fighting lasted longer. Natives and settlers fought for two years in Kentucky with neither side gaining a clear advantage. Then in June 1778 British troops moved into the areas settled by French farmers in what are now Illinois and Indiana. To counter these movements, Colonel George Rogers Clark led 175 Kentucky militiamen north of the Ohio River. After capturing and losing the French community of Vincennes on the Wabash River, Clark retook the settlement for good in February 1779. With the British unable to offer assistance, the Indians were vulnerable. In May, John Bowman led a second

Kentucky unit in a campaign that destroyed most Shawnee villages, and in August a move northward from Pittsburgh by Daniel Brodhead inflicted similar damage on the Delawares and the Seneca Iroquois. Although these raids depleted their populations and food supplies, most Ohio Indians resisted the Americans until the war's end.

In the East meanwhile, pro-British Iroquois, led by the gifted Mohawk leader Joseph Brant, devastated the Pennsylvania and New York frontiers in 1778. They killed 340 Pennsylvania militia at Wyoming, Pennsylvania, and probably slew an equal number in their other raids. In 1779 the U.S. general John Sullivan retaliated by invading the Iroquois country with 3,700

The War in the South, 1778–1781

By 1780 Britain held the South's major cities, Charles Town and Savannah, but could not establish control over the backcountry because of resistance from Nathanael Greene's Continentals. By invading Virginia, Lord Cornwallis placed himself within striking distance of Washington's U.S. and French forces, a decision that rapidly led to the British surrender at Yorktown in October 1781.

Continentals and several hundred Tuscaroras and Oneidas. Sullivan fought just one battle, near present-day Elmira, New York, in which his artillery routed Brant's warriors. After he burned two dozen Indian villages and destroyed a million bushels of corn, most Iroquois fled without food into Canada. Untold hundreds starved during the next winter, when more than sixty inches of snow fell.

In 1780 Brant's thousand warriors fell upon the Tuscaroras and Oneidas and then laid waste to Pennsylvania and New York for two years. But this final whirlwind of Iroquois fury masked reality: Sullivan's campaign had destroyed the Iroquois peoples' heartland; their population had declined by about one-third during the eight-year war.

Victory in the South

After 1778, as Britain formulated a new strategy that reflected changed circumstances, the war's focus shifted to the South. With the entry of France and Spain into the war, the conflict had acquired international dimensions; Britain was suddenly locked in a struggle that raged from India to Gibraltar to the West Indies and the American mainland. By securing ports in the South, the British would acquire the flexibility to move their forces back and forth between the West Indies and the United States as necessity dictated. In addition, the South looked like a relatively easy target. General Henry Clinton recalled that in 1778 a British force of 3,500 troops had taken Savannah, Georgia, without great difficulty, and he expected that a renewed invasion of the South would tap a huge reservoir of loyalist support. In sum, the British plan was to seize key southern ports and, with the aid of loyalist militiamen, move back toward the North, pacifying one region after another.

The plan unfolded smoothly at first. Sailing from New York with 9,000 troops, Clinton forced the surrender of Charles Town, South Carolina, and its 3,400-man garrison on May 12, 1780. Clinton then returned to New York with a third of his army, leaving mopping-up operations in the South to Lord Charles Cornwallis, now in command of British forces in that region. However, the British quickly found that there were fewer loyalists than they had expected. The Carolinas and Georgia did contain a sizable loyalist population, whose members enlisted by the thousands in royal militia units. Most were British immigrants, and Scots were especially prominent. But southern loyalism had

American Foot Soldiers, Yorktown Campaign, *by Jean-Baptiste-Antoine DeVerger, 1781*

suffered a serious blow in 1776, when the Cherokees had attacked the Carolina frontier and killed residents indiscriminately. Numerous Tories had switched sides, joining the rebel militia to defend their homes. After the British capture of Charles Town, the loyalist militia, embittered by countless instances of harsh treatment under patriot rule, lost little time in taking revenge. Patriots struck back whenever possible. So began an escalating cycle of revenge, retribution, and retaliation that engulfed the Lower South through 1782.

This southern war became intensely personal. Individuals often chose sides not for political reasons but to avenge an outrage perpetrated by the other. For example, Thomas Sumter and Andrew Pickens, South Carolina's two foremost rebel guerrillas, both took up arms after Tories plundered their plantations in 1780. And when another South Carolinian, the Tory William Cunningham, learned that his brother had been whipped to death by patriot militiamen, he grimly walked sixty miles to find and to kill the officer responsible. Afterward, while leading loyalist guerrillas, Cunningham earned the nickname Bloody Bill.

But the southern conflict was not all personal feuds and guerrilla warfare. After the capture of Charles Town, Congress sent General Horatio Gates to take command in the South. With only a small force of Continentals at his disposal, however, Gates had to rely on poorly trained militiamen. In August 1780 Cornwallis inflicted a crushing defeat on Gates at Camden, South Carolina. Fleeing after firing a single volley, Gates's militia left his badly outnumbered Continentals to be overrun. Camden was the worst rebel defeat of the war.

Washington and Congress responded by relieving Gates of command and sending General Nathanael Greene to confront Cornwallis. Greene subsequently fought three major battles between March and September 1781, and he lost all of them. "We fight, get beat, rise, and fight again," he wrote back to Washington. Still, Greene won the campaign, for he gave the Whig militia the protection they needed to hunt down loyalists, stretched British supply lines until they began to snap, and sapped Cornwallis's strength by inflicting much heavier casualties than the British general could afford. Greene's dogged resistance forced Cornwallis to leave the Carolina backcountry in American hands and to lead his battered troops into Virginia.

Secure in New York City, Clinton wanted Cornwallis to return to Charles Town and renew his Carolina campaign; but Cornwallis had a mind of his own and established a new base at Yorktown, Virginia, near the coast. From Yorktown Cornwallis hoped to fan out into Virginia and Pennsylvania, but he never got the chance. Cornwallis's undoing began on August 30, 1781, when a French fleet from the West Indies, commanded by Admiral De Grasse, dropped anchor off the Virginia coast and landed troops near Yorktown. Soon Lafayette joined them, leading a small force of Continentals. Meanwhile, Washington made enough feints at New York City to prevent Clinton from coming to Cornwallis's aid and then moved his army south to tighten the noose around the British. Trapped in Yorktown, Cornwallis's 6,000 British stood off 8,800 Americans and 7,800 French for three weeks. They finally surrendered with military honors on October 19, 1781.

The Peace of Paris

"Oh God!" Lord North exclaimed upon hearing of Yorktown, "It's all over." Indeed, Cornwallis's surrender drained the will of England's overtaxed people to fight and forced the government to commence peace negotiations. John Adams, Benjamin Franklin, and John Jay were America's principal diplomats at the peace talks in Paris, which began in June 1782.

Military realities largely influenced the terms of the peace. Britain recognized American independence and stipulated the evacuation of all royal troops from U.S. soil. Although the vast majority of Americans lived in the thirteen states clustered near the eastern seaboard, the British had little choice but to award the United States all lands east of the Mississippi, for by 1783

twenty thousand Anglo-Americans lived west of the Appalachians, and Clark's victories had given Americans control of the Northwest. The treaty also gave the United States important fishing rights off the Grand Banks of Canada.

On the whole, the settlement was highly favorable to the United States, but it did not resolve all disputes. In a separate treaty, Britain transferred East and West Florida back to Spain, but the boundaries designated by this treaty were ambiguous. Spain interpreted the treaty to mean that it regained the same Florida territory that it had ceded to Britain in 1763. But Britain's treaty with the United States named the thirty-first parallel as the Floridas' northern border, well south of the area claimed by Spain. Spain and the United States would dispute the northern boundary of Florida until 1795.

The Peace of Paris also planted the seeds of several future disputes between Britain and the United States. Although the United States promised to urge the state legislatures to compensate loyalists for their property losses and agreed that no legal bars would prevent British creditors from collecting prewar debts, several state governments later refused to pay back loyalists and erected barriers against British creditors. In response, the British failed to honor their treaty pledge to return slaves confiscated by their troops.

Notably missing in the Peace of Paris was any reference to the Native Americans, most of whom had supported the British in order to avert the alternative— an independent American republic that would be no friend to Indian interests. In effect the treaty left the native peoples to deal with this new republic on their own, without any provision for their status or treatment. Not surprisingly, many Native Americans did not acknowledge the new nation's claims to sovereignty over their territory.

The Peace of Paris ratified American independence, but winning independence had exacted a heavy price. At least 5 percent of all free white males aged sixteen to forty-five died in the war. If the present-day U.S. population fought a war with comparable casualties, 2.5 million people would be killed. Only the Civil War produced a higher ratio of casualties to the nation's population. Furthermore, although the war secured American independence, it did not settle two important issues: what kind of society America was to become and what sort of government the new nation would possess. Yet the war had a profound impact on both questions.

recognized American Independence
— rec– American Territory

REVOLUTIONARY SOCIETY

Two forces shaped the social effects of the Revolution: first, the principles articulated in the Declaration of Independence; and second, the dislocations caused by the war itself. These factors combined to change relationships between members of different classes, races, and genders momentously.

Egalitarianism

Between 1700 and 1760, social relations between elites and the common people had grown more formal, distant, and restrained. Members of the colonial gentry had emphasized their social position by living far beyond the means of ordinary families. By the late 1760s, however, many in the upper classes began wearing homespun rather than imported English clothes in support of the boycott of British goods and subsequently watched their popularity soar. When the First Families of Virginia organized minutemen companies in 1775, they threw away their expensive militia uniforms and dressed in homespun hunting shirts; then even the poorest farmer would not be too embarrassed to enlist because of his humble appearance. By 1776 some of the more visible distinctions of wealth had been noticeably reduced.

Then came war, which accelerated the erosion of class differences by forcing the gentry, who held officers' rank, to show respect to the ordinary folk serving as privates. Indeed, the soldiers demanded to be treated with consideration, especially in light of the ringing words of the Declaration of Independence, "All men are created equal." The soldiers would follow commands, but not if they were addressed as inferiors. General Steuben reported to a European army officer, "You say to your soldier, 'Do this,' and he doeth it, but I am obliged to say 'This is the reason why you ought to do that,' and he does it."

The best officers realized this fact immediately. Some, among them General Israel Putnam of Connecticut, went out of their way to show that they felt no superiority to their troops. While inspecting a regiment digging fortifications around Boston in 1776, Putnam saw a large stone nearby and told a noncommissioned officer to throw it onto the outer wall. The individual protested, "Sir, I am a corporal." "Oh," replied Putnam,

"I ask your pardon, sir." The general then dismounted his horse and hurled the rock himself, to the immense delight of the troops working there.

A majority of men of military age were exposed to treatment of this sort in the course of the war. Soldiers came to expect that their worth as individuals would be recognized by their officers, at least within the limits of the army. After these common soldiers returned to civilian life, they retained a sense of self-esteem and insisted on respectful treatment. As these feelings of personal pride gradually translated into political behavior and beliefs, candidates took care not to scorn the common people. The war thus subtly but fundamentally democratized Americans' political assumptions.

The gentry's sense of social rank also diminished as they met men who rose through ability rather than through advantages of wealth or family. The war produced numerous examples like James Purvis, the illiterate son of a nonslaveowning Virginia farmer, who joined the First Virginia Regiment as a private in 1775, soon rose to sergeant, and then taught himself to read and write so that he could perform an officer's duties. Captain Purvis fought through the entire war and impressed his well-born officers as "an uneducated man, but of sterling worth." As elites saw more and more middle-class farmers and even artisans performing responsibilities previously thought to be above their station in life, they developed a new appreciation that a person's merit was not always related to his wealth.

This new emphasis on equality did not extend to propertyless males, women, and nonwhites, but it undermined the tendency to believe that wealth or distinguished family background conferred a special claim to public office. "One should consider himself as good a man as another," declared the *New Jersey Gazette* in 1780, "and not be brow beaten or intimidated by riches or supposed superiority." After the war a fraternal organization of veteran Continental Army officers, the Society of the Cincinnati, evoked widespread alarm because its charter gave membership to sons and their descendants who, it was feared, might evolve into a hereditary aristocracy.

In short, Revolutionary-generation Americans came to insist that virtue and sacrifice defined a citizen's worth independently of his wealth. Voters widely began to view members of the "natural aristocracy"—those who had demonstrated fitness for government service by personal accomplishments—as the ideal candidates for political office. This natural aristocracy criminal. Free blacks could expect no more than grudging toleration, and few slaves ever gained their freedom.

Although the United States was a "white man's country" in 1776, the war opened some opportunities to African-Americans. Amid the confusion of war, some slaves, among them Jehu Grant of Rhode Island, ran off and posed as freemen. Grant later recalled his excitement "when I saw liberty poles and the people all engaged for the support of freedom, and I could not but like and be pleased with such a thing." Black men also made their way into the Continental Army. Even though the army late in 1775 forbade the enlistment of any African-Americans, black soldiers were already fighting in units during the siege of Boston, and the ban on black enlistments started to collapse in 1777. All states but Georgia and South Carolina eventually recruited black soldiers.

In contrast to the twenty thousand who joined British forces, approximately five thousand African-Americans served in the Continental forces, most from the North. The majority were slaves serving with their masters' consent, usually in integrated units. In 1781 a German mercenary described Rhode Island's black regiment as "the most neatly dressed, the best under arms, and the most precise in its maneuvers."

For the most part, these wartime opportunities for African-Americans grew out of the army's need for manpower rather than a white commitment to equal justice. In fact, until the mid-eighteenth century, few in the Western world had criticized slavery at all. Like disease and sin, slavery was considered part of the natural order. But in the decade before the Revolution, American opposition to slavery had swelled. The first American prohibition against slaveowning came from the annual leadership conference (known as the yearly meeting) of the New England Quakers in 1770. The yearly meetings of New York and Philadelphia Quakers followed suit in 1776, and by 1779 Quaker slaveowners had freed 80 percent of their slaves.

Although the Quakers aimed mainly to abolish slaveholding within their own ranks, the Declaration of Independence's broad assertion of natural rights and human equality spurred a more general attack on the institution of slavery. Between 1777 and 1784, Vermont, Pennsylvania, Massachusetts, Rhode Island, and Connecticut ended slavery. New York did so in 1799, and New Jersey in 1804. New Hampshire, unmoved by petitions like that written in 1779 by Portsmouth slaves demanding liberty "to dispose of our lives, freedom,

Revolutionary War Sailor,
by an unknown artist, c. 1780

had room for a few self-made men such as Benjamin Franklin, as well as for those, like Jefferson and John Hancock, born into wealth. Voters still elected the wealthy to office, but not if they flaunted their money. And members of the gentry increasingly acted like the "harmless aristocrats" of Virginia described by Judge St. George Tucker, who "never failed to pull off their hats to a poor man whom they met, and generally appeared to me to shake hands with every man in a Court-yard or a Church-yard."

A Revolution for Black Americans

The wartime situation of African-Americans contradicted the ideals of equality and justice for which Americans were fighting. About five hundred thousand black persons—20 percent of the total population—inhabited the United States in 1776, of whom all but about twenty-five thousand lived in bondage. Even those who were free could not vote, lived under curfews and other galling restrictions, and lacked the guarantees of equal justice held by the poorest white and property," never freed its slaves; but by 1810 there were none in the state.

The movement against slavery reflected the Enlightenment's emphasis on gradual change, initiated by leaders who carefully primed public opinion. The Revolutionary generation, rather than advocating slavery's immediate abolition, favored steps that would weaken the institution and in this way bring about its eventual demise. Most state abolition laws provided for gradual emancipation, typically declaring all children born of a slave woman after a certain date—often July 4—free. (Such individuals still had to work, without pay, for their mother's master for up to twenty-eight years.) Furthermore, the Revolution's leaders did not press for decisive action against slavery in the South, out of fear that widespread southern emancipation would either bankrupt or end the Union. They argued that the United States, already deeply in debt as a result of the war, could not finance immediate abolition in the South, and any attempt to do so without compensation would drive that region into secession. "Great as the evil is," observed Virginia's James Madison in 1787, "a dismemberment of the union would be worse."

Yet even in the South, slavery worried the consciences of some Whigs. When one of his slaves ran off to join the British and later was recaptured, Madison concluded that it would be hypocritical to punish the runaway "merely for coveting that liberty for which we have paid the price of so much blood." Still, Madison did not free the slave, and no state south of Pennsylvania abolished slavery. Nevertheless, every state but North Carolina passed laws making it possible for masters to manumit (set free) slaves without posting large sums of money as bond for their good behavior. By 1790 the number of free blacks in Virginia and Maryland had risen from about four thousand in 1775 to nearly twenty-one thousand, or about 5 percent of all African-Americans there.

These "free persons of color" faced the future as destitute, second-class citizens. Most had purchased their freedom by spending their small cash savings earned in off-hours and were past their physical prime. Once free, they found whites reluctant to hire them or to pay equal wages. Black ship carpenters in Charleston (formerly Charles Town), South Carolina, for example, earned one-third less than their white coworkers in 1783. Under such circumstances, most free blacks remained poor laborers or tenant farmers. However, even under such extreme disadvantages,

Phillis Wheatley, African-American Poet
Though a slave, Wheatley was the best-known poet in America at the time of the Revolution. Some of her poems linked the liberty sought by the colonists with a plea for the liberty of slaves. Despite her fame, Wheatley died in poverty in 1784.

some free blacks became landowners or skilled artisans. One who achieved considerable fame was Benjamin Banneker of Maryland, a self-taught mathematician and astronomer. Later, in 1789, he served on the commission that designed Washington, D.C., and after 1791 he published a series of almanacs.

Free blacks relied on one another for help. Self-help among African-Americans largely flowed through religious channels. Because many white congregations spurned them and because racially separate churches provided mutual support, self-pride, and a sense of accomplishment, free blacks began founding their own Baptist and Methodist congregations after the Revolution. In 1787 black Methodists in Philadelphia started the congregation that by 1816 would become the African Methodist Episcopal church. Black churches, a great source of inner strength and community cohesion for African-Americans ever since, had their origins in the Revolutionary period.

Most states granted important civil rights to free blacks during and after the Revolution. Free blacks

Sarah Livingston Jay and Her Children,
by James Sharpless, 1798
Jay was not only the devoted mother pictured here but a shrewd political observer who was married to the politician, diplomat, and chief justice John Jay.

had not participated in colonial elections, but those who were male and met the property qualification gained this privilege everywhere by the 1780s. Most northern states repealed or stopped enforcing curfews or other colonial laws restricting their freedom of movement. These same states generally changed their laws to guarantee free blacks equal treatment in court hearings.

The Revolution neither ended slavery nor brought equality to free blacks, but it did begin a process by which slavery eventually could be extinguished. In half the nation, human bondage had been outlawed and white southerners increasingly viewed slavery as a necessary evil—an attitude that implicitly recognized its immorality. Slavery had begun to crack, and free blacks had made some gains. But this shift proved short-lived, as events in the 1790s squelched the move toward egalitarianism.

Women in the New Republic

"To be adept in the art of Government is a prerogative to which your sex lay almost exclusive claim," wrote Abigail Adams to her husband John in 1776. She was one of the era's shrewdest political commentators and her husband's political confidante and best friend, but she had no public role. Indeed, for most women and almost all men in the 1780s, a woman's duty was to maintain her household and raise her children.

Apart from the fact that some states eased women's difficulties in obtaining divorces, the Revolution did not significantly affect the legal position of women. Women did not gain any new political rights, although New Jersey's 1776 constitution did not exclude white female property holders from voting, which they did in significant numbers until barred (along with free blacks) in 1807. The assumption that women were naturally dependent—either as children subordinate to their parents or as wives to their husbands—continued to dominate discussions of the female role. Nevertheless, the Revolutionary War and contemporary ideological currents emphasizing liberty and equality were significant for white American women.

Women's support of colonial resistance before Independence (see Chapter 5) broadened into an even wider range of support activities during the war. Female "camp followers," many of them soldiers' wives, served military units on both sides by cooking and laundering and by nursing the wounded. A few women, by disguising themselves as men, even joined in the fighting. Many more women remained at home, where they managed families, households, farms, and businesses on their own. After her civilian husband was seized by loyalists and turned over to the British on Long Island, Mary Silliman of Fairfield, Connecticut, tended to her four children (and bore a fifth), oversaw several servants and slaves, ran a commercial farm that had to be evacuated when the British attacked Fairfield, and launched appeals for her husband's release. Despite often enormous struggles, such experiences boosted women's confidence in their abilities to think and act on matters traditionally reserved for men.

As with African-Americans, the Revolutionary era witnessed the beginnings of a challenge to traditional attitudes toward women. American republicans increasingly recognized the right of a woman to choose her husband—a striking departure from the tradition whereby marriages were approved or even arranged by fathers. Thus in 1790, on the occasion of his daughter's marriage, Jefferson wrote to a friend that, following "the usage of my country, I scrupulously suppressed my wishes, [so] that my daughter might indulge her sentiments freely." Outside elite circles, such independence was apparent even before the Revolution. Especially in the Northeast, daughters increasingly got pregnant by prospective husbands, thus forcing their fathers to consent to their marrying in order to avoid a public scandal. For example, Mary Brown's father objected to her wedding John Chamberlain in Hallowell, Maine, in May 1792. In December he finally consented and the couple wed, just two days before their daughter's birth. By becoming pregnant, northeastern woman also secured for themselves economic support in a region where an exodus of young, unmarried men left a growing number of women single.

White women also had fewer children overall than their mothers and grandmothers. In Sturbridge, Massachusetts, women in the mid-eighteenth century averaged nearly nine children per marriage, compared with just six in the first decade of the nineteenth century. Whereas 40 percent of Quaker women had nine or more children before 1770, only 14 percent bore that many thereafter. Such statistics testify to declining farm sizes and urbanization, both of which were incentives for having fewer children. But they also indicate that women were finding some relief from the near-constant state of pregnancy and nursing that consumed their forebears.

As women's roles expanded, so too did republican notions of male-female relations. "I object to the word 'obey' in the marriage-service," wrote a female author calling herself Matrimonial Republican, "because it is a general word, without limitations or definition." "The obedience between man and wife," she continued, "is, or ought to be mutual." Lack of mutuality was one reason for a rising number of divorce petitions from women, from fewer than 14 per year in Connecticut before the Revolution, to 45 in 1795. A few women also challenged the sexual double standard that allowed men to indulge in extramarital affairs while their female partners, single or married, were condemned. Writing in 1784, an author calling herself Daphne pointed out how a woman whose illicit affair was exposed was "forever deprive[d] . . . of all that renders life valuable," while "the base [male] betrayer is suffered to triumph in the success of his unmanly

arts, and to pass unpunished even by a frown." Daphne called on her "sister Americans" to "stand by and support the dignity of our own sex" by publicly condemning seducers rather than their victims.

Gradually, the subordination of women, which once was taken for granted, became the subject of debate. In the essay "On the Equality of the Sexes," written in 1779 and published in 1790, Massachusetts essayist and poet Judith Sargent Murray contended that the genders had equal intellectual ability and deserved equal education. "We can only reason from what we know," she wrote, "and if an opportunity of acquiring knowledge hath been denied us, the inferiority of our sex cannot fairly be deduced from there." Murray hoped that "sensible and informed" women would improve their minds rather than rush into marriage (as she had at eighteen), and would instill republican ideals in their children.

Like many of her contemporaries, Murray supported "republican motherhood." Republicans emphasized the importance of educating women in the values of liberty and independence in order to strengthen virtue in the new nation. It was the duty of women to inculcate these values in their sons as well as their daughters. Even so conservative a man as John Adams reminded his daughter that she was part of "a young generation, coming up in America . . . [and] will be responsible for a great share of the duty and opportunity of educating a rising family, from whom much will be expected." After 1780 the urban upper class founded numerous private schools, or academies, for girls, and these provided to American women their first widespread opportunity for advanced education. Massachusetts also established an important precedent in 1789, when it forbade any town to exclude girls from its elementary schools.

Although the great struggle for female political equality would not begin until the nineteenth century, the frequent Revolutionary-era assertions that women were intellectually and morally men's peers provoked scattered calls late in the eighteenth century for political equality. In 1793 Priscilla Mason, a young woman graduating from one of the female academies, blamed "*Man, despotic man*" for shutting women out of the church, the courts, and government. In her salutatory oration, she urged that a women's senate be established by Congress to evoke "all that is human—all that is *divine* in the soul of woman."

Priscilla Mason had pointed out a fundamental limitation to republican egalitarianism: besides being a virtuous wife and mother, there was little a woman could *do* with her education.

Native Americans and the Revolution

For Native Americans, the consequences of the United States' triumph over Britain were less certain. Whereas Revolutionary ideology held out at least an abstract hope for blacks, women, and others seeking equal rights and status in American society, it made no provision for the many Indians who sought to maintain some degree of political and cultural independence. Moreover, in an overwhelmingly agrarian society like the United States, the Revolution's implicit promise of equal economic opportunity for all citizens set the stage for territorial expansion beyond the areas already settled, thereby threatening Indian landholdings. Even where Indians retained land, the influx of settlers posed dangers to them in the form of deadly diseases, farming practices inimical to Indian subsistence (see Chapter 3), and alcohol. Indians were all the more vulnerable because, during the three decades encompassed by the Seven Years' War and the Revolution (1754–1783), the native population east of the Mississippi had declined by about half, and many Indian communities had been uprooted.

In the face of these uncertainties, Native Americans continued their efforts to incorporate the most useful aspects of European culture into their own. From the beginning of the colonial period, Indians had selectively adopted European-made goods of cloth, metal, glass, and other materials into their lives. But Native Americans did not give up their older ways altogether; rather, their clothing, tools, weapons, utensils, and other material goods combined elements of the old and the new. Indians, especially those no longer resisting American expansion, also selectively participated in the American economy by working occasionally for wages or by selling food, crafts, or other products. This interweaving of the new with the traditional characterized Indian communities up and down the newly independent states, such as the Seneca Iroquois town of Jenuchshadago (see "A Place in Time"). Even Indians west of the settled areas, who hoped to avert the takeover of their lands by the new republic, looked to the British in Canada or the Spanish in Florida for trade as well as for diplomatic and military support.

Native Americans, then, did not remain stubbornly rooted in traditional ways, nor did most of them resist participation in a larger world dominated by Europeans or Euro-Americans. But they did insist on retaining control of their communities and their ways of life. As a group of Iroquois bluntly told an Anglo-American missionary in 1745, "We are Indians and do not wish to be transformed into white men. The English are our Brethren, but we never promised to become what they are." In the Revolution's aftermath, it remained unclear whether the new nation would accommodate Native Americans on such terms.

The Revolution and Social Change

The American Revolution left the overall distribution of wealth in the nation unchanged. Because the 3 percent of Americans who fled abroad as loyalists represented a cross section of society, their departure left the new nation's class structure unaltered. Loyalists' confiscated estates tended to be bought up by equally well-to-do Whig gentlemen. Overall, the American upper class seems to have owned about as much of the national wealth in 1783 as it did in 1776.

In short, the Revolution did not obliterate social distinctions nor even challenge most of them. Class distinctions, racial injustice, and the subordination of women persisted into the nineteenth century. In particular, the institution of slavery survived intact in the South, where the vast majority of slaves lived. Yet the Revolutionary era set in motion significant social changes. Increasingly, the members of the gentry had to earn respect by demonstrating their competence and by treating the common people with dignity. The Revolution dealt slavery a decisive blow in the North, greatly enlarged the free-black population, and awarded free people of color important political rights. Although the momentous era did not bring women political equality, it placed new issues pertaining to the relations between the genders on the agenda of national debate. And inevitably, the social changes wrought by the Revolution shaped the new nation's momentous political debates.

FORGING NEW GOVERNMENTS

Americans had drawn many political conclusions from the imperial crisis of the 1760s, including the conviction that without vigilance by the people, governments would become despotic. But before the Declaration of

Independence was written, few Americans had given much thought to forming governments of their own. Although guiding and inspiring the rebels, the Continental Congress lacked the sovereign powers usually associated with governments, including the authority to impose taxes.

During the war years, rebels quickly recognized the need to establish government institutions to sustain the war effort and to buttress the United States' claim to independent nationhood. But the task of forging a government would prove arduous, in part because of the inevitable upheavals of war. In addition, the state governments that Americans formed after the Declaration of Independence reflected two different and often conflicting impulses: on one hand, the traditional ideas and practices that had guided Anglo-Americans for much of the eighteenth century; on the other, the republican ideals that found a receptive audience in America in the 1760s and early 1770s.

"Can America be happy under a government of her own?" asked Thomas Paine in 1776. He answered his own question: "as happy as she pleases: she hath a blank sheet to write upon."

Tradition and Change

In establishing the Revolutionary state governments, patriots relied heavily on ideas about government inherited from the colonial experience. For example, most Whigs took for granted the value of bicameral legislatures. As we have seen, the colonial legislatures in the royal provinces had consisted of two houses: an elected lower chamber (or assembly) and an upper chamber (or council) appointed by the governor or chosen by the assembly. These two-part legislatures resembled Parliament's division into the House of Commons and House of Lords and symbolized the assumption that a government should give separate representation to aristocrats and common people.

Despite the Revolution's democratic tendencies, few questioned the long-standing practice of setting property requirements for voters and elected officials. In the prevailing view, only the ownership of property, especially land, made it possible for voters to think and act independently. Whereas tenant farmers and hired laborers might sell their votes or vote against their best judgment to avoid displeasing their landlords or employers, property holders could express their opinions freely. The association be-

tween property and citizenship was so deeply ingrained that even radicals such as Samuel Adams opposed allowing all males—much less women—to vote and hold office.

The notion that elected representatives should exercise independent judgment in leading the people rather than simply carry out the popular will also survived from the colonial period and restricted the democratization of politics. Although Americans today take political parties for granted, the idea of parties as necessary instruments for identifying and mobilizing public opinion was alien to the eighteenth-century political temper, which equated parties with "factions"— selfish groups that advanced their own interests at the expense of the public good. In general, candidates for office did not present voters with a clear choice between policies calculated to benefit rival interest groups; instead, they campaigned on the basis of their personal reputations and fitness for office. As a result, voters did not know where office seekers stood on specific issues and hence found it hard to influence government actions.

Another colonial practice that persisted into the 1770s and 1780s was the equal (or nearly equal) division of legislative seats among all counties or towns, regardless of differences in population. Inasmuch as representation had never before been apportioned according to population, a minority of voters normally elected a majority of assemblymen. Additionally, many offices that later would become elective—such as sheriffs and justices of county courts—were appointive in the eighteenth century.

In sum, the colonial experience provided no precedent for a democratization of the United States during the Revolutionary era. Yet without intending to extend political participation, political elites found themselves pulled in a democratic direction by the logic of the imperial crisis of the 1760s and 1770s. The colonial assemblies, the most democratic parts of colonial government, had led the fight against British policy during Americans' ideological clash with England, whereas the executive branch of colonial governments, filled by royal governors and their appointees, had repeatedly locked horns with the assemblies. Colonists entered the Revolution dreading executive officeholders and convinced that even elected governors could no more be trusted with power than could monarchs. Recent history seemed to confirm the message hammered home by British "country party" ideology (see Chapter 5) that those in

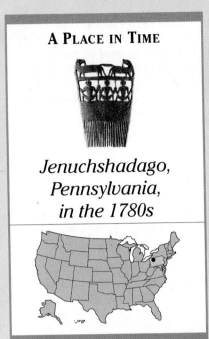

In the Revolution's aftermath, hundreds of new settlements sprang up west of the old colonial frontier. The best known of these settlements were inhabited by white pioneers who had streamed across the Appalachians in search of new lands and new opportunities. Many Native Americans in the West also took up new settlements—not to realize hopes and dreams but to regroup in the wake of a disastrous war in which they had lost family members and friends, homes, and land. Such was the case for the two hundred or three hundred Senecas who gathered during the early 1780s at the old town of Jenuchshadago, also known as Cornplanter's Town (after the name of their *sachem,* or chief), on the west bank of the Allegheny River just south of the New York–Pennsylvania boundary.

The Senecas and the other four original members of the Iroquois Confederacy had developed a rich culture and a sophisticated political and military organization that served them well as Dutch, French, and English moved in around them to trade, settle, and extend their empires. Seneca life had changed drastically after the mid-eighteenth century, when the movement of English colonists into the Ohio Valley upset the balance of power that had maintained peace between Indians and Europeans and between Britain and France. During the Revolution the Senecas, like most Iroquois, had sided with the British in hopes of restraining the settlers' westward push. In 1779 U.S. forces had raided Iroquois country and systematically burned every Seneca village, field, and fruit grove. After the war most Iroquois had moved to British Canada, prepared to continue the fight against the United States. But the Senecas, as the westernmost of the Iroquois, were less familiar than other Iroquois with the British, and most had declined to move.

The Senecas of Jenuchshadago were a demoralized people in the 1780s. During the recent war the symbol of Iroquois unity—the confederacy's central council fire at Onondaga—had been allowed to die out for the first time since the Confederacy's formation about four centuries earlier, owing to differences among the Iroquois people over which side to support. Thereafter Iroquois had fought one another. At the war's end the Senecas who remained in their homeland had been re-

Ki-In-Twog-Ky (Cornplanter), *1796*

Seneca reservations

LAKE ONTARIO

TUSCARORA RESERVATION

Genesee R.

Canandaigua L.

Black Rock
Buffalo

Cayuga L.

LAKE ERIE

Seneca L.

Salamanca
Cold Spring
Genesingunta
Olean
Warren
Jenuchshadago
Ceres
Genesee R.

Susquehanna R.

Meadville
Oil City
Ft. Franklin
Allegheny R.

0   40 Miles
0   40 Kilometers

Seneca Reservations, 1790

Pressured after the American Revolution to give up most of their land, the Senecas now lived in a few widely separated villages.

SOURCE: *The Death and Rebirth of the Seneca* by Anthony F. C. Wallace. Copyright © 1969 by Anthony F. C. Wallace. Reprinted by permission of Alfred A. Knopf, Inc.

Seneca Cradleboard

viled for abandoning the Confederacy by fellow Iroquois who moved to Canada. These and other Indians had called for continuing the war against the United States. The authority and prestige of Cornplanter and other sachems had been undermined when they accepted bribes for agreeing to additional cessions of land. On several occasions white interlopers had killed innocent Indians, including two of Cornplanter's relatives.

Repudiated by all those around them, the Senecas also had been diminished as a people. Only eighteen hundred of a prewar population of four thousand survived, scattered in small villages on widely separated tracts of land. Beyond those who had died in combat, many had perished from starvation in the winter following the U.S. raids and from smallpox epidemics in the winters of 1776–1777 and 1781–1782. The effects of liquor aggravated their health problems. Indians who hunted, logged, or worked in other capacities for whites were paid in the unfamiliar medium of cash but found little to spend it on except liquor. Many Senecas drank to excess, and some died from alcohol-induced illness or violence linked to alcoholism.

Despite their sufferings and the tenuousness of their situation, the people of Jenuchshadago survived, and so did many of their cultural traditions. The isolation of the town, located as it was on a narrow

strip of land between steep cliffs and the river, helped shield residents from many of the more destructive outside influences that undermined native cultures elsewhere after the Revolution. The fertile floodplain enabled the women to reap bountiful harvests of corn, beans, and squash, the Senecas' dietary mainstays for about a thousand years. The men and boys hunted bears, deer, elk, and turkeys. At sites downriver the people returned annually for maple sugaring and spearfishing. And along the riverbank and clifftops grew medicinal herbs whose efficacy brought fame to the healers of Jenuchshadago among the Senecas.

The community itself also nurtured aspects of traditional culture. Between the river and the village lay Jenuchshadago's burial ground, now used with greater frequency than ever. In the middle of town was the ceremonial center where the Indians each year burned a white dog as part of the traditional midwinter ceremony. Nearby stood Cornplanter's house and the two or three dozen other dwellings in the village. Although they no longer lived in multifamily longhouses as many had before the war, the people of Jenuchshadago had reconstituted some of the most important components of a traditional Iroquois community.

The continuity in their ways of life, institutions, and ceremonies was the basis

for Seneca survival during the difficult period after the Revolution. Yet many remained uncertain at the end of the 1780s on the question of religion, for the cumulative destruction of the war and its aftermath implied that traditional religion had failed. In their spiritual torment some found the message of American missionaries attractive, but others sought to escape through alcohol. Among the residents of Jenuchshadago was Cornplanter's young half-brother, Handsome Lake. After a bout with alcoholism and severe illness, Handsome Lake would emerge in 1799 to lead a revival among the Senecas that would accommodate traditional religion to the Indians' new circumstances.

183b

power tended to become either corrupt or dictatorial. Consequently, Revolutionary statesmen proclaimed the need to strengthen legislatures at the governors' expense.

Despite their preference for vesting power in popularly elected legislatures, Revolutionary leaders described themselves as republicans rather than democrats. Although used interchangeably today, these words had different connotations in the eighteenth century. At worst, democracy suggested mob rule; at best, it implied the concentration of power in the hands of an uneducated multitude. In contrast, republicanism presumed that government would be entrusted to capable leaders, elected for their superior talents and wisdom. For most republicans, the ideal government would delicately balance the interests of different classes to prevent any one group from gaining absolute power. Some, including John Adams, thought that a republic could include a hereditary aristocracy or even a monarchy as part of this balance, but most thought otherwise. Having blasted one king in the Declaration of Independence, most political leaders had no desire to enthrone another. Still, their rejection of hereditary aristocracy and monarchy posed a problem for republicans as they set about drafting state constitutions: how to maintain balance in government amid pervasive distrust of executive power.

Reconstituting the States

The state governments that Americans constructed during the Revolution reflected a struggle between more radical, democratic elements and elites who would minimize popular participation. In keeping with colonial practice, eleven of the thirteen states maintained bicameral legislatures. In all but a few states, the great majority of officeholders, at both the state and the county level, were still appointed rather than elected. The most radical constitution, Pennsylvania's, attempted to ensure that election districts would be roughly equal in population, so that a minority of voters could not elect a majority of legislators. Nine of the thirteen states reduced property requirements for voting, but none abolished such qualifications entirely, and most of the reductions were modest.

Yet the persistence of these conservative features should not obscure the pathbreaking components of the state constitutions. Above all, they were *written* documents whose adoption usually required popular ratification and which could be changed only if the people voted to amend them. In short, Americans jettisoned the British conception of a constitution as a body of customary arrangements and practices, insisting instead that constitutions were written compacts that defined and limited the powers of rulers. Moreover, as a final check on government power, the revolutionary constitutions spelled out citizens' fundamental rights. By 1784 all state constitutions included explicit bills of rights that outlined certain freedoms beyond government control. In sum, governments were no longer to serve as the final judge of the constitutionality of their activities.

The earliest of those new state constitutions severely limited executive power in particular. In most states the governor became an elected official, and elections themselves occurred far more frequently. Prior to 1776 colonial elections, typically called at the governor's pleasure, most often took place every three or four years. In contrast, after 1776 each state scheduled annual elections except South Carolina, which held them every two years. In most states the power of appointments was transferred from the governor to the legislature. Legislatures usually appointed judges and could reduce their salaries or impeach them (try them for wrongdoing). By relieving governors of most appointive powers, denying them the right to veto laws, and making them subject to impeachment, the constitutions turned governors into figureheads who simply chaired an executive council that made militia appointments and supervised financial business. (Pennsylvania actually eliminated the office of governor altogether.)

As the new state constitutions weakened the executive branch and vested more power in the legislatures, they also made the legislatures, especially the upper chambers, more responsive to the will of the people. Nowhere could the governor appoint the upper chamber. Eight constitutions written before 1780 allowed voters to select both houses of the legislature, one (Maryland) used a popularly chosen "electoral college" for its upper house, and the remaining "senates" were filled by vote of their assemblies. Pennsylvania and Georgia abolished the upper house and substituted a single-chamber (unicameral) legislature. Americans' assault on the executive branch and their enhancement of legislative authority reflected their bitter memories of royal governors who had acted arbitrarily to prorogue (dismiss) assemblies and control government through their power of appointment, and it underscored the influence of "country-party" ideologues, who had warned that republics' undoing began with executive usurpation of authority.

In the first flush of revolutionary enthusiasm, elites had to content themselves with state governments dominated by popularly elected legislatures. Gradually, however, wealthier landowners, bankers, merchants, and lawyers reasserted their desires for centralized authority and the political prerogatives of wealth. In Massachusetts an elite-dominated convention in 1780 pushed through a constitution stipulating stiff property qualifications for voting and holding office, state senate districts that were apportioned according to property values, and a governor with considerable powers in making appointments and vetoing legislative measures. The Massachusetts constitution signaled a general trend. Georgia and Pennsylvania substituted bicameral for unicameral legislatures by 1790. Other states raised property qualifications for members of the upper chamber in a bid to encourage the "senatorial element" and to make room for men of "Wisdom, remarkable integrity, or that Weight which arises from property."

The elites' deference to the principle of balanced government revealed a central feature of their thought. Gradations among social classes and restrictions on the expression of popular will troubled them far less than the prospect of tyranny by those in power. But elites also believed that social divisions, if deep-seated and permanent, could jeopardize republican liberty. Although more committed to liberty than to equality, some republican leaders attempted to implement major social changes through legislation by the new state governments. In Virginia, for example, between 1776 and 1780, Thomas Jefferson drafted a series of bills to promote greater equality. In October 1776 he persuaded the Virginia legislature to abolish entails, legal requirements that prevented an heir and all his descendants from selling or dividing an estate. Although entails were easy to break through special laws—Jefferson himself had escaped from the restrictions of one—he hoped that their elimination would strip wealthy families of the opportunity to amass land continuously and become an overbearing aristocracy. Through Jefferson's efforts, Virginia also ended primogeniture, the legal requirement that the eldest son inherit all a family's property in the absence of a will. Thereby, Jefferson hoped to ensure a continuous division of wealth. By 1791 no state provided for primogeniture, and just two allowed entails.

These years also witnessed the end of state-established churches in most of the country. New England, whose religious climate was the nation's most conservative, resisted this reform, and the Congregational church continued to collect tithes (church taxes) until 1817 in New Hampshire, 1818 in Connecticut, and 1833 in Massachusetts. But in every state where colonial taxpayers had supported the Anglican church, such support was abolished by 1786. Thomas Jefferson best expressed the ideal behind disestablishment in his Statute for Religious Freedom (1786), whose preamble resounded with a defense of religious freedom at all times and places. "Truth is great," proclaimed Jefferson, "and will prevail if left to itself."

The American Revolution, wrote Thomas Paine in 1782, was intended to ring in "a new era and give a new turn to human affairs." This was an ambitious declaration and seemed to conflict with elites' tendency to borrow from the past institutions such as state senates and property requirements for voting. Paine's point was not that the unique features of some constitutions, such as the termination of primogeniture and the disestablishment of the Anglican church, outweighed the traditional elements of the constitutions. Instead, he was expressing the republican ideal that *all* political institutions now were being judged by the standard of whether they served the public good rather than the interests of the powerful few. More than any single innovation of the era, it was this new way of thinking that made American politics revolutionary.

The Articles of Confederation

As with their revolt against Britain and their early state constitutions, Americans' first national government reflected widespread fears of centralized authority and its potential for corruption. In 1776 John Dickinson, who had stayed in Congress despite having refused to sign the Declaration of Independence, drafted a proposal for a national government, which he called the Articles of Confederation. Congress adopted a weakened version of the Articles and sent it to the states for ratification in 1777.

The Articles explicitly reserved to each state "its sovereignty, freedom and independence" and established a form of government in which Americans were citizens of their own states first and of the United States second. As John Adams later explained, the Whigs of 1776 never thought of "consolidating this vast Continent under one national Government" but instead

State Claims to Western Lands, and State Cessions to the Federal Government, 1782–1802

Eastern states' surrender of land claims paved the way for new state governments in the West. Georgia was the last state to cede its western lands, in 1802.

erected "a Confederacy of States, each of which must have a separate government."

Under the Articles, the national government consisted of a single-chamber national Congress, elected by the state legislatures, in which each state had only one vote. Congress could request funds from the states but could enact no tax of its own without every state's approval, nor could it regulate interstate or overseas commerce. The Articles did not provide for an executive branch. Rather, congressional committees oversaw financial, diplomatic, and military affairs. Nor was there a judicial system by which the national government could compel allegiance to its laws.

The Articles would not become operational until approved by all thirteen state legislatures. Twelve states

agreed to the new government by 1779, but Maryland delayed, refusing to sign until all states claiming lands north of the Ohio River turned these territories over to the United States. Maryland lawmakers wanted to keep Virginia and New York from expanding to such a degree that they would dominate the new nation. Beginning in 1781, northwestern claims by individual states were abandoned, and the Articles finally became law in March 1781.

With the Confederation in place, the United States had taken a critical step in defining the role of national sovereignty in relation to the sovereignty of the individual states. Whereas the Continental Congress had directed most of the war effort without defined powers, the nation now had a formal govern-

imposing imported duties on each other

ment. Nevertheless, the Whigs' misgivings left the Confederation government severely limited in important respects.

Finance and Trade
Under the Confederation

Perhaps the greatest challenge facing the Confederation was putting the nation on a sound financial footing. Winning the war cost the nation's six hundred thousand taxpayers a staggering $160 million, a sum that exceeded by 2,400 percent the taxes raised to pay for the Seven Years' War. To finance the War for Independence, which cost far more than could be immediately collected through taxation, the government borrowed funds from abroad and printed its own paper money, called Continentals. Lack of public faith in the government destroyed 98 percent of the value of the Continentals from 1776 to 1781, an inflationary disaster that gave rise to the expression "not worth a Continental."

Faced with a desperate financial situation, Congress turned to a wealthy, self-made Philadelphia merchant, Robert Morris, who in 1781 became the nation's superintendent of finance. Morris proposed that the states authorize the collection of a national import duty of 5 percent to finance the congressional budget and to guarantee interest payments on the war debt. Because the Articles stipulated that every state had to approve the levying of national taxes, the import duty failed to pass in 1782 when Rhode Island alone rejected it.

Hoping to panic the country into creating a regular source of national revenue, Morris and New York congressman Alexander Hamilton then engineered a dangerous gamble known later as the Newburgh Conspiracy. In 1783 the two men secretly persuaded some army officers, then encamped at Newburgh, New York, to threaten a coup d'etat unless the treasury obtained the taxation authority needed to raise their pay, which was months in arrears. But George Washington, learning of the conspiracy before it was carried out, ended the plot by delivering a speech that appealed to his officers' honor and left them unwilling to proceed. Although Morris may never have intended that a coup actually occur, his willingness to take such a risk demonstrated the new nation's perilous financial straits and the vulnerability of its political institutions.

When peace came in 1783, Morris found it impossible to secure adequate funding for the United States. That year, Congress sent another tax measure to the

got together in Phil & tried to amend articles → start all over

states, but once again a single legislature, this time New York's, blocked it. From then on, the states steadily decreased their contributions to Congress. By the late 1780s, the states had fallen behind nearly 80 percent in providing the funds that Congress requested to operate the government and honor the national debt.

Nor did the Confederation succeed in prying trade concessions from Britain. Before Independence, almost 60 percent of northern exports had gone to the West Indies, and New England's maritime community had employed approximately 15 percent of all adult males. After Independence, however, Britain quickly slapped strict limitations on U.S. commerce. The new republic's ships lost all rights to carry cargoes to the West Indies and faced high customs fees for landing products in Great Britain. For the most part, American foodstuffs, lumber, and tobacco were welcome in Britain only if they arrived in British ships. Because half of all U.S. exports went to Great Britain or its West Indian colonies, these restrictions allowed British shippers to increase their share of the Atlantic trade at American expense. The loss of this trade contributed mightily to an economic depression that gripped the nation beginning in 1784.

The Confederation and the West

Another formidable challenge confronting the Confederation was the postwar settlement and administration of western lands. Settlers and speculators were determined to possess these lands, and Native Americans were just as determined to keep them out. At the same time, Britain and Spain sought to contain the new nation's territorial expansion.

After the states surrendered claims to more than 160 million acres north of the Ohio River, Congress established uniform procedures for surveying this land in the Ordinance of 1785. The law established as the basic unit of settlement a township six miles square. Every township would be subdivided into thirty-six sections of 640 acres each, one of which would be reserved as a source of income for schools. Subsequently, in the Northwest Ordinance of 1787, Congress defined the steps for the creation and admission of new states. This law designated the area north of the Ohio River as the Northwest Territory and provided for its later division into states. It forbade slavery while the region remained a territory, although the citizens could legalize the institution after statehood (as Illinois almost did in 1824).

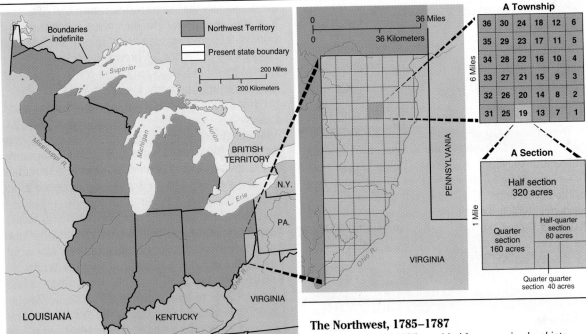

The Northwest, 1785–1787

The Ordinance of 1785 provided for surveying land into townships, each supporting four families on a 160-acre plot (approximately 25 people per square mile). In 1787 the Northwest Ordinance stipulated that states would ultimately be created in the region

The Northwest Ordinance outlined three stages for admitting states into the Union. First, during the initial years of settlement, Congress would appoint a territorial governor and judges. Second, as soon as five thousand adult males lived in a territory, the people would write a temporary constitution and elect a legislature that would pass the territory's laws. Third, when the total population reached sixty thousand, the settlers would write a state constitution, which Congress would have to approve before granting statehood.

The Ordinance of 1785 and the Northwest Ordinance became the Confederation's major contributions to American life. These laws set the basic principles for surveying the frontier, allowed territorial government at an early stage of settlement, and provided reasonable standards for obtaining statehood. Both measures served as models for organizing territories later acquired west of the Mississippi River. The Northwest Ordinance also established a significant precedent for banning slavery from certain territories. But because Indians, determined to keep out white settlers, controlled virtually the entire region north of the Ohio River, the Confederation's ordinances respecting the Northwest had no immediate effect.

The Northwest Territory seemed to offer enough rich land to guarantee future citizens landownership for centuries. This fact satisfied American republican sentiment, which placed great importance upon opening the West for settlement out of fears that the rapidly growing U.S. population would quickly exhaust the land east of the Appalachians and so create a large class of tenants and poor laborers who would lack the property needed to vote. By poisoning politics through class conflict, such a development would undermine the equality that republicans thought essential for a healthy nation. In the anticipated westward push by whites, Thomas Jefferson and other republican thinkers hoped to avoid conflict with the northwestern Indians by assimilating them into white society. However, since Native Americans had no desire to abandon their own cultures, republican anxieties over preserving economic opportunity by giving white settlers access to western lands made war inevitable.

Joseph Brant, *by Wilhelm von Moll Berczy, c. 1800*
In the 1780s several Indian leaders—among them Brant (a Mohawk), Blue Jacket (a Shawnee), and Little Turtle (a Miami)—worked to create a northwestern Indian confederation that would strengthen Native American resolve not to bargain with land-hungry whites.

At postwar treaty negotiations, Native Americans repeatedly heard U.S. commissioners scornfully declare, "You are a subdued people . . . we claim the country by conquest." Under threats of continued warfare, some Indian leaders initially gave in. The Iroquois, who had suffered heavily during the war, lost about half their land in New York and Pennsylvania in the second Treaty of Fort Stanwix (1784). In the treaties of Fort McIntosh (1785) and Fort Finney (1786), the Delawares and Shawnees, respectively, were obliged to recognize American sovereignty over their lands. But most Indians reacted with outrage and repudiated these treaties on the grounds that their negotiators lacked the authority to give up their nations' lands.

The Indians' resistance also stemmed from their confidence that the British—still a presence in the West—would provide the arms and ammunition they needed to defy the United States. Britain had refused to abandon seven forts on the nation's northwestern frontier, officially because several state legislatures had blocked the collection of prewar debts owed British merchants and had also refused to compensate loyalists for wartime property losses. In April 1784, however, well before Britain knew about the violation of these provisions of the peace treaty, its colonial office had secretly ordered the governor of Canada to hold those forts. With Indian support, Britain hoped eventually to reestablish its claim to the Northwest Territory.

The Mohawk Joseph Brant emerged as the initial inspiration behind Indian resistance to white encroachments. Courageous in battle, skillful in diplomacy, and highly educated (he had translated the Bible into Iroquois), Brant became a minor celebrity when he visited King George at London in 1785. At British-held Fort Detroit in 1786, he helped organize the northwestern Indians into a military alliance to exclude white settlers north of the Ohio River. But Brant and his Mohawks, who had relocated beyond American reach in Canada, could not win support from Iroquois such as the Senecas of Jenuchshadago, who had chosen to remain in New York. John Sullivan's campaign of 1779 had left the Six Nations unwilling to risk another such invasion.

The Confederation confronted similar problems in the Southeast, where Spain and its Indian allies took steps to prevent American settlers from encroaching on their lands. The Spanish found a brilliant ally in the Creek leader Alexander McGillivray. In a series of fraudulent treaties, two Creeks had surrendered extensive territory to Georgia that McGillivray intended to regain. Patiently holding back his followers for three years, McGillivray negotiated a secret treaty with Spain that promised the Creeks weapons so that they could protect themselves "from the Bears and other fierce Animals." When McGillivray finally unleashed his forces in 1786, he assaulted only occupants on the disputed lands and wisely offered a cease-fire after winning his objective. Eager to avoid voting taxes for a costly war, Georgia politicians let him keep the land.

Spain also sought to prevent American infiltration by denying western settlers permission to ship their crops down the Mississippi River to New Orleans. Having negotiated a separate treaty with Britain (see above), Spain had not signed the Peace of Paris, by which Britain promised the United States export rights down the Mississippi, and in 1784 the Spanish closed New Orleans to Anglo-American commerce.

To negotiate trading privileges at New Orleans, the United States sent John Jay to Spain. Jay failed to win concessions, but he returned with a treaty that opened up valuable Spanish markets to eastern merchants and renounced Spanish claims to disputed southwestern lands—at the cost, however, of relinquishing American export rights through New Orleans for twenty years. Although Congress rejected this Jay-Gardoqui Treaty in 1786, the treaty infuriated westerners and southerners, whose interests seemed to have been sacrificed to benefit northern commerce.

Shays's Rebellion

Without an outbreak of violence in Massachusetts late in 1786, the Confederation might have tottered on indefinitely. The depression that had begun in 1784 struck especially hard in Massachusetts after the state lost its best market, the British West Indies. To worsen matters, the state legislature voted early in 1786 to pay off its Revolutionary debt in three years. This ill-considered policy necessitated a huge tax hike. Meanwhile, the state's unfavorable balance of payments with Britain had produced a shortage of specie (gold and silver coin) because British creditors refused any other currency. Fearing a flood of worthless paper notes, Massachusetts bankers and merchants insisted that they, too, be paid in specie, while the state mandated the same for payment of taxes. At the bottom of this cycle of debt were thousands of small family farmers who rarely handled hard currency. As with small farmers throughout America, those in Massachusetts were accustomed to paying each other and local creditors in goods such as grain and wool and sometimes with a service such as shoeing a horse or helping to build a barn. Creditors allowed debts from local customers to run for months and years at a time. The notion of immediately paying all debts and taxes owed in hard currency was not only alien to but impossible for many.

The plight of Massachusetts farmers was especially severe in the western counties, where agriculture was least profitable. Farmers held public meetings, as they had more than a decade earlier, to discuss "the Suppressing of tyrannical government." This time, however, they meant the Massachusetts government rather than the British. Late in 1786 farmer and former Revolutionary War officer Daniel Shays led some two thousand angry men in an attempt to shut down the courts in three of these western counties, and thereby stop sheriffs' auctions for unpaid taxes and prevent foreclosures on farm mortgages. Although routed by state troops after several skirmishes, sympathizers of Shays won control of the Massachusetts legislature in 1787, cut taxes, and secured a pardon for their leader.

Shays's supporters had limited objectives, were dispersed with relatively little bloodshed, and never seriously posed the danger of anarchy. But his uprising, and similar but less militant movements in other states, symbolized for critics of the weak national government the Republic's fragility under the Confederation. By threatening to seize weapons from a federal arsenal at Springfield, Massachusetts, the Shaysites unintentionally enabled nationalists to argue that the United States had become vulnerable to "mobocracy." At the same time, rumors were flying that the Spanish had offered export rights at New Orleans to westerners if they would secede from the Union. Nationalists sowed fears that the United States was on the verge of coming apart.

Not everyone shared these apprehensions. In contrast to New England, the mid-Atlantic and southern states were emerging from the depression, thanks to rising tobacco and food exports to Europe. Taxpayers in these sections, moreover, were paying off war debts easily. Furthermore, the regions' numerous small farming families, living in relatively isolated communities and trading largely with neighbors, were in quiet times widely indifferent to national politics. But the minority of people intensely dissatisfied with the Confederation was growing. Urban artisans, for example, hoped for a stronger national government that would impose a uniformly high tariff and thereby protect them from foreign competition. Merchants and shippers wanted a government powerful enough to secure trading privileges for them, and land speculators and western settlers preferred a government capable of pursuing a more activist policy against the Indians. To these groups were now added economic and political elites who saw in Shays's Rebellion a sign of worse things to come.

Shortly before the outbreak of the rebellion, delegates from five states had assembled at Annapolis, Maryland. They had intended to discuss means of promoting interstate commerce but instead called for a general convention to propose amendments to the Articles of Confederation. Accepting their suggestion, Congress asked the states to appoint delegations to meet in Philadelphia.

The Philadelphia Convention

In May 1787 fifty-five delegates from every state but Rhode Island began gathering at the Pennsylvania State House in Philadelphia, later known as Independence Hall. Among them were figures with an established reputation like George Washington, Benjamin Franklin, John Dickinson, and Robert Morris, as well as talented newcomers such as Alexander Hamilton and James Madison. Most were wealthy and in their thirties or forties, and nineteen owned slaves. More than half had legal training.

The convention immediately closed its sessions to the press and the public, kept no *official* journal, and even appointed chaperones to accompany the aged and talkative Franklin to dinner parties lest he disclose details of what was happening. Although these measures opened the members of the convention to the charge of acting undemocratically and conspiratorially, the delegates thought secrecy essential to ensure themselves freedom of debate without fear of criticism from home.

The delegates shared a "continental" or "nationalist" perspective, instilled through their extended involvement with the national government. Thirty-nine had sat in Congress, where they had seen the Articles' defects firsthand. In the postwar years, they had become convinced that unless the national government were freed from the state legislatures' control, the country would fall victim to foreign aggression or simply disintegrate.

The convention faced two basic issues. The first was whether to tinker with the Articles, as the state legislatures had formally instructed the delegates to do, or to scrap the Articles and draw up an entirely new frame of government. The second fundamental question was how to balance the conflicting interests of large and small states. James Madison of Virginia, who had entered Congress in 1780 at twenty-nine, proposed an answer to each issue. Despite his youth and almost frail build, Madison commanded enormous respect for his profound knowledge of history and the passionate intensity that he brought to debates.

Madison's Virginia Plan, introduced by his fellow Virginian Edmund Randolph in late May, boldly called for the establishment of a national government rather than a federation of states. Madison's blueprint gave Congress virtually unrestricted rights of legislation and taxation, the power to veto any state law, and authority to use military force against the states. As delegate Charles Pinckney of South Carolina immediately saw, the Virginia Plan was designed "to abolish the State Govern[men]ts altogether." The Virginia Plan specified a bicameral legislature and fixed representation in both houses of Congress proportionally to each state's population. The voters would elect the lower house, which would then choose delegates to the upper chamber from nominations submitted by the legislatures. Both houses would jointly name the country's president and judges.

Madison's scheme aroused immediate opposition, however, especially his call for state representation

The Assembly Room in Independence Hall
Much history was made in this room. The Declaration of Independence was signed here in 1776, and the constitutional-convention delegates met in this chamber in 1787.

James Madison
Although one of the Philadelphia Convention's youngest delegates, Madison of Virginia was among its most politically astute. He played a central role in the Constitution's adoption.

according to population—a provision highly favorable to his own Virginia. On June 15 William Paterson of New Jersey offered a counterproposal, the so-called New Jersey Plan, which recommended a single-chamber congress in which each state had an equal vote, just as under the Articles.

Despite their differences over representation, Paterson's and Madison's proposals alike would have strengthened the national government at the states' expense. No less than Madison, Paterson wished to empower Congress to raise taxes, regulate interstate commerce, and use military force against the states. The New Jersey Plan, in fact, was the first to define congressional laws and treaties as the "supreme law of the land"; it would also have established courts to force reluctant states to accept these measures.

The New Jersey Plan was highly significant because it exposed the convention's great stumbling block: the question of representation. The Virginia Plan would have given the four largest states a majority in both houses. The New Jersey Plan would have al-

lowed the seven smallest states, which included just 25 percent of all Americans, to control Congress. By July 2 the convention had arrived "at a full stop," as Roger Sherman of Connecticut noted. To end the impasse, the delegates assigned a member from each state to a "grand committee" dedicated to compromise. The panel adopted a proposal offered earlier by the Connecticut delegation: an equal vote for each state in the upper house and proportional voting in the lower house. Madison and the Virginians doggedly fought this so-called Connecticut Compromise, but they were voted down on July 17. The convention overcame the remaining hurdles rather easily in the next two months.

As finally approved on September 17, 1787, the Constitution of the United States was an extraordinary document, and not merely because it successfully reconciled the conflicting interests of the large and small states. Out of hard bargaining among different states' representatives emerged the Constitution's delicate balance between the desire of nearly all delegates for a stronger national government and their fear that governments tended to grow despotic. The Constitution augmented national authority in several ways. Although it did not incorporate Madison's proposal to give Congress a veto over state laws, it vested in Congress the authority to lay and collect taxes, to regulate interstate commerce, and to conduct diplomacy. States could no longer coin money, interfere with contracts and debts, or tax interstate commerce. All acts and treaties of the United States became "the supreme law of the land." All state officials had to swear to uphold the Constitution, even against acts of their own states. The national government could use military force against any state.

These provisions added up to a complete abandonment of the principle on which the Articles of Confederation had rested: that the United States was a federation of independent republics known as states, with all authority concentrated in their legislatures. Yet still concerned about too centralized a federal system, the Constitution's framers devised two ways to restrain the power of the new national government. First, they established three distinct branches—executive, legislative, and judicial—within the national government; and second, they designed a system of checks and balances to prevent any one branch from dominating the other two. The framers systematically applied to the national government the principle of a *functional* separation of powers, an idea that had been evolving in the states since about 1780. In the bicameral Congress, states' equal representation in the Senate was offset by the proportional representation, by population, in the House; and each chamber could block hasty measures demanded by the other. Furthermore, where the state constitutions had deliberately weakened the executive, the Constitution gave the president the power to veto acts of Congress; but to prevent capricious use of the veto, Congress could override the president by a two-thirds majority in each house. The president could conduct diplomacy, but only the Senate could ratify treaties. The president named his cabinet, but only with Senate approval. The president and all his appointees could be removed from office by a joint vote of Congress, but only for "high crimes," not for political disagreements.

To further ensure the independence of each branch, the Constitution provided that the members of one branch would not choose those of another, except for judges, whose independence was protected by lifetime appointment. For example, the president was to be selected by an electoral college, whose members the states would select as their legislatures saw fit. The state legislatures also elected the members of the Senate, whereas the election of delegates to the House of Representatives was achieved by popular vote.

In addition to checks and balances, the founders improvised a novel form of federalism—that being a system of shared power and dual lawmaking by the national and state governments—in order to place limits on central authority. Not only did the state legislatures have a key role in electing the president and senators, but the Constitution could be amended by the votes of three-fourths of the state legislatures. Thus, the convention devised a form of government that differed significantly from Madison's plan to establish a "consolidated" national government entirely independent of, and superior to, the states.

A key assumption behind federalism was that the national government would limit its activities to foreign affairs, national defense, regulating interstate commerce, and coining money. Most other political matters were left to the states. Regarding slavery in particular, each state retained full authority.

The dilemma confronting the Philadelphia convention revolved around whether slaves should be considered persons or property. For most purposes, the southern states regarded slaves as the property of their owners. But given that slaves constituted substantial proportions of southern populations, these states' delegates wished to count them as persons when it came to determining representation in the House of Representatives. Northern delegates hailed from states that were abolishing slavery, and hesitated to give southern states a political advantage by allowing them to count people who had no civil or political rights. But as property owners themselves, northern delegates were even more hesitant to question southern planters' notions of property rights, no matter what form the property took. Accordingly, they agreed to allow three-fifths of all slaves to be counted for congressional representation. The Constitution also forbade any state's people to prevent the return of runaway slaves to another state. The Constitution did limit slavery to the extent of permitting Congress to ban the importation of slaves after 1808, and by not repudiating Congress's earlier ban on slavery in the Northwest Territory.

Although leaving much authority to the states, the Constitution established a national government clearly superior to the states in several spheres, and it utterly abandoned the notion of a federation of virtually independent states. Having thus strengthened national authority, the convention had to face the issue of ratification. For two reasons, it seemed unwise to submit the Constitution to state legislatures for ratification. First, the framers realized that the state legislatures would reject the Constitution, which shrank their power relative to the national government. Second, most of the framers repudiated the idea—implicit in ratification by existing state legislatures—that the states composed the foundation of the new government. The opening words of the Constitution—"We the People of the United States"—underlined the delegates' growing conviction that the government had to be based on the consent of the American people themselves, "the fountain of all power" in Madison's words.

In the end, the Philadelphia Convention provided for the Constitution's ratification by special state conventions composed of delegates elected by the people. Approval by only nine such conventions would put the new government in operation. Because any state refusing to ratify the Constitution would remain under the Articles, the possibility existed that the country might divide into two nations.

Under the Constitution the framers expected the nation's "natural aristocracy" to continue exercising political leadership; but did they also intend to rein in the democratic currents set in motion by the Revolution? In one respect they did, by curtailing what most nationalists considered the excessive power of popularly elected legislatures. But the Constitution made no attempt to control faction and disorder by suppressing liberty—a "remedy," wrote Madison, that would be "worse than the disease." The framers did provide for one crucial democratic element in the new government, the House of Representatives. Equally important, the Constitution recognized the American people as the ultimate source of political legitimacy. Moreover, by making the Constitution flexible and amendable (though not easily amendable) and by dividing political power among competing branches of government, the framers made it possible for the national government to be slowly democratized in ways unforeseen in 1787, without turning into a tyranny of ideologues or temporary majorities. Madison eloquently expressed the founders' intention of controlling the dangers inherent in any society:

If men were angels, no government would be necessary. If angels were to govern men, neither external nor internal controls on government would be necessary. In framing a government which is to be administered by men over men, the great difficulty lies in this: You must first enable the government to control the governed; and in the next place, oblige it to control itself. A dependence on the people is no doubt the primary control on the government; but experience has taught mankind the necessity of external precautions.

Ratification

The Constitution's supporters began the campaign for ratification without significant national support. Most Americans had expected that the Philadelphia Convention would offer only limited amendments to the Articles. A majority therefore hesitated to adopt the radical restructuring of government that had been proposed. Undaunted, the Constitution's friends moved decisively to marshal political support. In a clever stroke, they called themselves Federalists, a term that implied that the Constitution balanced the relationship between the national and state governments and thereby

lessened the opposition of those hostile to a centralization of national authority.

The Constitution's opponents commonly became known as Antifederalists. This negative-sounding title probably hurt them, for it did not convey the crux of their argument against the Constitution—that it was not "federalist" at all since it failed to balance the power of the national and state governments. Indeed, many Antifederalists doubted whether any such balance was possible. In their view, either the national or the state governments would dominate the Republic; no even division of power could be achieved. By augmenting national authority, Antifederalists maintained, the Constitution would ultimately doom the states.

The Antifederalist arguments reflected a deep-seated Anglo-American suspicion of concentrated power, expressed from the time of the Stamp Act crisis (see Chapter 5) through the War of Independence and during the framing of the first state constitutions and the Articles of Confederation. Unquestionably, the Constitution gave the national government unprecedented authority in an age when almost all writers on politics taught that the sole means of preventing despotism was to restrain the power of government officials. Compared to a national government, which inevitably would be distant from the people in an era when news traveled slowly, the state governments struck Antifederalists as far more responsive to the popular will. "The vast Continent of America cannot be long subjected to a Democracy if consolidated into one Government. You might as well attempt to rule Hell by Prayer," wrote a New England Antifederalist. True, the framers had devised a system of checks and balances to guard against tyranny, but no one could be certain that the untried scheme would work. For all its checks and balances, in addition, the Constitution nowhere contained ironclad guarantees that the new government would protect the liberties of individuals or the states. The absence of a bill of rights made an Antifederalist of Madison's nationalist ally and fellow Virginian, George Mason, the author of the first such state bill in 1776.

Although the Antifederalists advanced some formidable arguments, they confronted a number of disadvantages in publicizing their cause. While Antifederalist ranks included prominent political figures, among them Patrick Henry and Richard Henry Lee, the Federalists claimed most of the country's

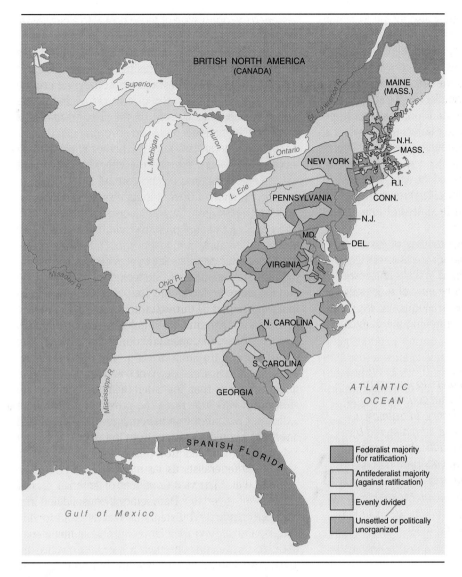

Federalist and Anti-federalist Strongholds, 1787–1790
Federalists drew their primary backing from densely populated areas along major transportation routes, where trade, mobility, and frequent contact with people in other states encouraged a nationalistic identity. Antifederalist support came from interior regions where geographic isolation bred a localistic perspective. However, some frontier regions, among them Georgia and western Virginia, voted for a strong central government that would push back the Indians or the Spanish.

wealthiest and most honored men. And no Antifederalist had the stature of George Washington or Benjamin Franklin. Moreover, most American newspapers were pro-Constitution and did not hesitate to bias their reporting in favor of the Federalist cause. Finally, as state and local leaders, the Antifederalists lacked their opponents' contacts and experience at the national level, acquired through service in the officer corps of the Continental Army or in Congress.

The Federalists' advantages in funds and political organizing proved decisive. The Antifederalists failed to create a sense of urgency among their supporters, as-

suming incorrectly that a large majority would rally to them. Only one-quarter of the voters turned out to elect delegates to the state ratifying conventions, however, and most had been mobilized by Federalists.

Federalist delegates prevailed in eight conventions between December 1787 and May 1788, in all cases except one by margins of at least two-thirds. Such lopsided votes reflected the Federalists' organizational skills and aggressiveness rather than the degree of popular support for the Constitution. Advocates of the new plan of government did indeed ram through approval in some states "before it can be digested or deliberately considered," in the words of a Pennsylvania Antifederalist. Only Rhode Island and North Carolina rejected the Constitution and thus refused to join the new United States.

But unless Virginia and New York ratified, the new government would not be workable. In both states (and elsewhere) antifederalist sentiment ran high among small farmers, who saw the Constitution as a scheme favoring city dwellers and monied interests. Prominent political leaders in these two states called for refusing ratification, including New York governor George Clinton and Virginia's Richard Henry Lee, George Mason, Patrick Henry, and future president James Monroe.

The Constitution became the law of the land on June 21, 1788, when the ninth state, New Hampshire, ratified by the close vote of 57–47. At that moment debate was still under way in the Virginia convention. The Federalists won crucial support from the representatives of the Alleghany counties—modern West Virginia—who wanted a strong national government capable of ending Indian raids across the Ohio River. Western Virginians' votes, combined with James Madison's logic and the growing support for the Constitution among tidewater planters, proved too much for Henry's spellbinding oratory. On June 25 the Virginia delegates ratified by a narrow 53 percent majority.

The struggle was even closer and more hotly contested in New York. Antifederalists had solid control of the state convention and would probably have voted down the Constitution, but then news arrived of New Hampshire's and Virginia's ratification. The Federalist forces, led by Alexander Hamilton and John Jay, began hinting strongly that if the convention voted to reject, pro-Federalist New York City would secede from the state and join the Union alone, leaving upstate New York a landlocked enclave. When a number of Antifederalist delegates took alarm at this threat and switched sides, New York ratified on July 26, by a 30–27 vote.

So the Antifederalists went down in defeat, and they did not survive as a political movement. Yet they left an important legacy. At their insistence, the Virginia, New York, and Massachusetts conventions ratified the Constitution with the accompanying request that the new charter be amended to include a bill of rights protecting Americans' basic freedoms. So widespread was the public demand for a bill of rights that it became an inevitable item on the new government's agenda, even as the states were choosing members of Congress and as presidential electors were unanimously designating George Washington president of the United States.

Antifederalists' objections in New York also stimulated a response in the form of one of the greatest works of political analysis ever written: *The Federalist,* a series of eighty-five newspaper essays penned by Alexander Hamilton, James Madison, and John Jay. *The Federalist* papers probably had little or no influence on the voting in the New York State convention. Rather, their importance lay in providing a glimpse of the framers' intentions in designing the Constitution, and thus powerfully shaping the American philosophy of government. The Constitution, insisted *The Federalist*'s authors, had a twofold purpose: first, to defend the minority's rights against majority tyranny; and second, to prevent a stubborn minority from blocking well-considered measures that the majority believed necessary for the national interest. Critics, argued *The Federalist,* had no reason to fear that the Constitution would allow a single economic or regional interest to dominate. In the most profound essay in the series, *Federalist* No. 10, Madison rejected the Antifederalist argument that establishing a republic for a nation as large as the United States would unleash a chaotic contest for power and ultimately leave the majority exploited by a minority. "Extend the sphere," Madison insisted, "and . . . you make it less probable that a majority of the whole will have a common motive to invade the rights of other citizens, . . . [or will be able to] act in unison with each other." The country's very size and diversity would theoretically neutralize the attempts of factions to manipulate unwise laws through Congress.

Madison's analysis was far too optimistic, however. As the Antifederalists predicted, the Constitution afforded enormous scope for special interests to influence the government. The great challenge for Madison's generation would be how to maintain a government that would provide equal benefits to all but at the same time accord special privileges to none.

CONCLUSION

The entry of North Carolina into the Union in late 1789 and of Rhode Island in May 1790 marked the final triumph of the nationalism born of the War for Independence. The devastating eight-year conflict swept up half of all men of military age and made casualties of one-fifth of these. Never before had such a large part of the population been called on to make sacrifices in a common cause of this magnitude.

The collective experience of fighting together as countrymen made many veterans self-consciously American. After several years in the army, General Nathanael Greene of Rhode Island condemned the "prejudices" of those with "local attachments." "I feel the cause and not the place," Greene said; "I would as soon go to Virginia [to fight] as stay here [New England]." The distractions of peace almost allowed this sentiment to evaporate, but the Constitution offered the firmest proof that a growing number of Americans now felt comfortable viewing themselves as a common people rather than citizens of allied states.

CHRONOLOGY

1770 Yearly meeting of New England Quakers prohibits slaveowning—first American ban on slaveholding.

1775 Virginia governor Lord Dunmore promises freedom to any slave assisting in the restoration of royal authority.

1776 British troops evacuate Boston.
British defeat American forces under George Washington in fighting around New York City.
American victory in Battle of Trenton.
Cherokees attack North Carolina frontier.

1777 American victory in Battle of Princeton.
British general John Burgoyne surrenders at Saratoga.
Battle of Brandywine Creek; British occupy Philadelphia.
British general William Howe defeats Washington at Battle of Germantown.
Congress approves Articles of Confederation.

1778 France formally recognizes the United States.
France declares war on Britain.
Philadelphia evacuated by British general Henry Clinton; Battle of Monmouth Court House (New Jersey).
British occupy Savannah.
Joseph Brant leads Iroquois attacks in western Pennsylvania and New York.

1779 Spain declares war on Britain.
George Rogers Clark's recapture of Vincennes.
John Sullivan leads U.S. raids in Iroquois country.
Judith Murray writes "On the Equality of the Sexes" (published 1790).

George Rogers Clark

1780 British seize Charles Town.
Dutch Republic declares war on Britain.

1781 Articles of Confederation become law.
Battle of Yorktown; British general Charles Cornwallis surrenders.

1782 British evacuate Savannah.
Paris peace negotiations begin.
Rhode Island rejects national import duty.

1783 Peace of Paris.
Newburgh Conspiracy.
Treaty of Augusta.

1784 Spain closes New Orleans to American trade.
Economic depression begins.
Second Treaty of Fort Stanwix.

1785   Ordinance of 1785.
        Treaty of Fort McIntosh.

1786   Congress rejects Jay-Gardoqui Treaty.
        Treaty of Fort Finney.
        Joseph Brant organizes Indian resistance to
        U.S. expansion.
        Virginia adopts Thomas Jefferson's Statute for
        Religious Freedom.

1786–1787 Shays's Rebellion in Massachusetts.

1787   Northwest Ordinance.
        Philadelphia Convention; federal Constitution
        signed.

1788   Alexander Hamilton, James Madison, and
        John Jay, *The Federalist.*
        Federal Constitution becomes law.

FOR FURTHER READING

Edward Countryman, *The American Revolution* (1985). An excellent introduction to developments from the Revolution through ratification of the Constitution.

Jack P. Greene, ed., *The American Revolution: Its Character and Limits* (1987). Leading scholars' analysis of how Americans dealt with the problem of applying their political ideals to an imperfect society without endangering the nation's survival.

Robert Middlekauff, *The Glorious Cause: The American Revolution, 1763–1789* (1982). A comprehensive account of military and political developments through the Philadelphia Convention.

Mary Beth Norton, *Liberty's Daughters: The Revolutionary Experience of American Women, 1750–1800* (1980). A wide-ranging study of changes in the lives and roles of women during the Revolutionary era.

Benjamin Quarles, *The Negro in the American Revolution* (1961). An authoritative study of blacks' role in the Revolution and its consequences for them.

Charles Royster, *A Revolutionary People at War: The Continental Army and American Character* (1980). An illuminating analysis of how Revolutionary Americans created and fought in an army.

Gordon Wood, *The Creation of the American Republic, 1776–1787* (1969). Comprehensive treatment of the evolution of American political thought from the first state governments to the Philadelphia Convention.

ADDITIONAL BIBLIOGRAPHY

The Military Struggle

Richard Buel, Jr., *Dear Liberty: Connecticut's Mobilization for the Revolutionary War* (1980); Robert M. Calhoon, *The Loyalists in Revolutionary America, 1760–1781* (1973); E. Wayne Carp, *To Starve the Army at Pleasure: Continental Army Administration and American Political Culture, 1775–1783* (1984); Jonathan R. Dull, *A Diplomatic History of the American Revolution* (1985); Barbara Graymont, *The Iroquois in the American Revolution* (1972); Don Higginbotham, *The War of American Independence: Military Attitudes, Policies, and Practice, 1763–1789* (1983); Ronald Hoffman and Peter J. Albert, eds., *Arms and Independence: The Military Character of the American Revolution* (1984); Ronald Hoffman and Thad W. Tate, eds., *An Uncivil War: The Southern Backcountry During the American Revolution* (1985); James O'Donnell, *Southern Indians in the American Revolution* (1973); Steven Rosswurm, *Arms, Country, and Class: The Philadelphia Militia and the "Lower Sort" in the Era of the American Revolution* (1987); John Shy, *A People Numerous and Armed: Reflections on the Military Struggle for American Independence* (1976); Paul H. Smith, *Loyalists and Redcoats: A Study in British Revolutionary Policy* (1964); Jack M. Sosin, *The Revolutionary Frontier, 1763–1783* (1967).

Revolutionary Society

Ira Berlin and Ronald Hoffman, eds., *Slavery and Freedom in the Age of the American Revolution* (1983); Joy Day Buel and Richard Buel, Jr., *The Way of Duty: A Woman and Her Family in Revolutionary America* (1984); Jeffrey J. Crow and Larry E. Tise, *The Southern Experience in the American Revolution* (1978); Sylvia R. Frey, *Water from the Rock: Black Resistance in a Revolutionary Age* (1991); Ronald Hoffman and Peter J. Albert, eds., *Women in the Age of the American Revolution* (1989); Rhys Isaac, *The Transformation of Virginia, 1740–1790* (1982); Michael Kammen, *A Season of Youth: The American Revolution and the Historical Imagination* (1978); Linda K. Kerber, *Women of the Republic: Intellect and Ideology in Revolutionary America* (1980); Duncan J. MacLeod, *Slavery, Race, and the American Revolution* (1974); Jackson Turner Main, *The Social Structure of Revolutionary America* (1965); Gary B. Nash, *Race and Revolution* (1990); Gary B. Nash and Jean R. Soderlund, *Freedom by Degrees: Emancipation in Pennsylvania and Its Aftermath* (1991); Anthony F. C. Wallace, *The Death and Rebirth of the Seneca* (1969); Gordon S. Wood, *The Radicalism of the American Revolution* (1992).

Politics and Constitutionalism

Willi Paul Adams, *The First American Constitutions: Republican Ideology and the Making of the State Constitutions in the Revolutionary Era* (1980); Richard Beeman et al., eds., *Beyond Confederation: Origins of the Constitution and American National Identity* (1987); Herman Belz et al., eds., *To Form a More Perfect Union: The Critical Ideas of the Constitution* (1992); John L. Brooke, *The Heart of the Commonwealth: Society and Political Culture in Worcester County, Massachusetts, 1713–1861* (1989); Robert A. Gross, ed., *In Debt to Shays: The Bicentennial of an Agrarian Rebellion* (1993); Van Beck Hall, *Politics Without*

Parties: Massachusetts, 1780–1791 (1972); Donald S. Lutz, *Origins of American Constitutionalism* (1988); Forrest McDonald, *E Pluribus Unum: The Formation of the American Republic, 1776–1790* (1965) and *Novus Ordo Seclorum: The Intellectual Origins of the Constitution* (1985); Jackson T. Main, *The Antifederalists: Critics of the Constitution, 1781–1788* (1961) and *Political Parties Before the Constitution* (1973); Cathy D. Matson and Peter S. Onuf, *Union of Interests: Political and Economic Thought in Revolutionary America* (1990); Anne M. Ousterhout, *A State Divided: Opposition in Pennsylvania to the American Revolution* (1987); J. G. A. Pocock, *The Machiavellian Moment: Florentine Political Thought and the Atlantic Republican Tradition* (1975); Jack N. Rakove, *The Beginnings of National Politics: An Interpretive History of the Continental Congress* (1979); Norman K. Risjord, *Chesapeake Politics, 1781–1800* (1978); David P. Szatmary, *Shays' Rebellion: The Making of an Agrarian Insurrection* (1980).

Biographies

James T. Flexner, *Washington: The Indispensable Man* (1974); Isabel Thompson Kelsay, *Joseph Brant, 1743–1807: Man of Two Worlds* (1984); Ralph Ketcham, *Benjamin Franklin* (1966) and *James Madison: A Biography* (1971); Dumas Malone, *Jefferson and the Rights of Man* (1951); Sheila L. Skemp, *William Franklin: Son of a Patriot, Servant of a King* (1990).

Silk Embroidery
Rachel Breck Hooker, Early Nineteenth Century

7

LAUNCHING THE NEW REPUBLIC
1789–1800

Early in 1789 a mysterious stranger from New Orleans named André Fagot appeared in Nashville, Tennessee. Fagot was officially there to talk business with local merchants, but in reality he was a Spanish agent sent to stir up discontent. For years, westerners had agonized over the American government's failure to win Spanish permission for them to export crops through New Orleans (inset), without which their settlements would never flourish. Fagot made westerners a tempting offer—unrestricted

export privileges at New Orleans, which promised to ensure them prosperity. But in return, they would have to request that Spain annex Tennessee to its Louisiana colony.

Fagot found many local residents willing to discuss becoming Spanish subjects. One of his more enthusiastic contacts was a young lawyer recently arrived from the Carolinas. Aware that poor communities could support only poor lawyers, the Carolinian was drawn irresistibly to the plot. Learning that Spain would give valuable land grants in the lower Mississippi Valley to anyone who renounced U.S. citizenship, the lawyer began visiting Spanish Louisiana regularly to investigate settling there. Fagot probably placed little reliance on this brash conspirator, who had a wild temper and a reputation for gambling and drinking. In 1789 he seemed just another frontier opportunist. But in little more than a quarter-century, the Nashville lawyer would become the country's most popular hero and the symbol of American nationalism. He was Andrew Jackson.

The fact that even Jackson could talk secession to Spanish agents underscores the fragility of the United States in 1789, one year after the Constitution's ratification. North Carolina (which controlled Tennessee territory) and Rhode Island had not yet joined the Union. Westerners appeared to be abandoning the new government. The United States faced the prospect that foreign powers would slice off western territory. The nation could conceivably have disintegrated into several smaller republics, much as Latin America would splinter into numerous nations after rebelling against Spain in the early nineteenth century.

Few incoming American presidents have confronted as many grave problems as did George Washington in 1789. The West might well have separated from the Union. Indians and frontier whites fought endlessly. Foreign restrictions on U.S. exports threatened the nation's economy. The treasury was bankrupt, and the government's credit in shambles.

Some of the most serious obstacles facing the United States in 1789 were overcome by the time Washington's second administration ended in 1797, but only at the price of unleashing fiercely emotional party divisions among citizens. By 1798 a sense of crisis gripped the nation. The party in power resorted to political repression. Fearing that a fair election might be impossible and that the national government was slipping into despotism, the opposing party desperately tried to justify the right of state legislatures to veto federal laws. In the election of 1800, each side damned the other in increasingly irresponsible rhetoric. Only when the election had been settled—by the narrowest of margins—could it be said that the United States had managed to avoid dissolution and preserve civil liberties for its citizens.

THE FRAGILE NEW NATION

By 1789 six years had elapsed since Britain had recognized U.S. independence, but for many Americans peace had brought problems rather than prosperity. Restrictions on export markets endangered the livelihoods of innumerable farmers, sailors, and merchants. Foreign efforts to prevent Americans from settling the frontier frustrated influential land speculators and toiling pioneers. The Confederation's default on the national debt had injured tens of thousands of Revolutionary creditors from all levels of society by delaying their compensation, and even after 1788 there was no guarantee that the new government would honor their claims fully. All these conditions had helped convince prominent Americans that a new constitution and a new government were desperately needed. But Antifederalists had not disappeared from public life, and supporters of the new government faced enormous pressure to succeed.

In the first two decades under the Constitution, it proved impossible for the government to devise policies that would provide equal benefits throughout the land. The different regions' interests varied greatly and often conflicted. Other fissures also became apparent in American society: among blacks, Indians, and whites; between emerging capitalists and wage-earning workers; above all, among citizens who interpreted the republican ideology of the Revolutionary years in different ways.

Regional and ideological conflicts would split the new nation's Congress, first into factions and then into hostile parties—just what the Constitution's framers had hoped to avoid. And political polarization would also bring into focus something else that few members of the Philadelphia Convention had favored: a rising demand for a *democratic* republic.

The West and the South

Most U.S. territory from the Appalachians to the Mississippi River belonged to those peoples whom the Declaration of Independence had condemned as "merciless Indian savages." Divided into more than eighty tribes and numbering perhaps 150,000 people in 1789, these Native Americans were struggling to preserve their way of life. During the Revolutionary War, patriot forces had dealt the Iroquois and Cherokees a punishing series of blows. But most Indians, although bloodied, continued to resist threats to their land. Tribes in the Ohio Valley formed a defensive confederacy in 1786 (see Chapter 6). The powerful southeastern nations refused to acknowledge American rule. Great Britain openly backed Indian resistance in the Northwest, and Spain armed the southeastern Native Americans. As the Constitution took effect, the federal government faced the prospect of having to force Britain and Spain to abandon the Indians and then of negotiating land purchases from them.

Confronting the inland Indians were approximately two hundred thousand settlers who had established homesteads on the frontier. Although their ranks included some well-to-do planters and merchants, most families found life exceedingly harsh. Above all, frontier settlers were isolated and vulnerable. By 1786 a succession of Indian war parties spread death, destruction, and anxiety from Pennsylvania to Georgia. In Kentucky alone, where just 74,000 settlers lived in 1790, more than 1,500 pioneers were killed or captured in Indian raids from 1784 to 1790—a casualty rate twice as high as that of the Revolutionary War. Frontier people retaliated ruthlessly. "The people of Kentucky," wrote an army officer trying to end the fighting, "will carry on private expeditions against the Indians and kill them whenever they meet them, and I do not believe there is a jury in all Kentucky [that] will punish a man for it."

Whites could conquer the Indians only by mustering overwhelming military force and threatening entire tribes with starvation by ravaging their villages and stocks of winter food. Such large-scale operations lay beyond the capability of poorly equipped, ill-trained frontier militia. This fact became obvious in 1786, when a lack of supplies forced 1,200 Kentuckians marching under George Rogers Clark against the Indians of the Great Lakes region to abandon their campaign. If Clark, who had prevailed against enormous odds during the Revolution, found himself thus overwhelmed, clearly only federal forces could defeat the Indians. But in 1789 the U.S. Army's total strength was 672 soldiers, less than half the number of warriors that the northwestern Indian confederation could raise. Little wonder that the weakness of the U.S. government caused many frontier folk to despair—and to decide that the United States had forfeited their loyalty. Clark spoke for untold Kentuckians in 1788 when he declared that "no property or person is safe under a government so weak as that of the United States."

Nevertheless, militia raids across the Ohio River did force the Miamis, Shawnees, and Delawares gradually to evacuate southern Indiana and Ohio. These Indians' withdrawal northward, toward the Great Lakes, tempted whites to make their first settlements in what is now Ohio. In the spring of 1788, about fifty New Englanders sailed down the Ohio River in a bullet-proof barge named the *Mayflower* and founded the town of Marietta. That same year, some Pennsylvanians and New Jerseyites established a second community north of the Ohio, on the site of modern-day Cincinnati. By then the contest for the Ohio Valley was nearing a decisive stage.

Westerners felt a special bitterness toward the British. The recent enemy's continued occupation of seven forts on American soil seemed the mainspring of the unceasing border fighting. Royal diplomats justified this violation of the Peace of Paris by citing certain states' failure to compensate loyalists for confiscated property and to honor prewar debts owed by U.S. citizens. But these complaints served only as pretexts for retarding American expansion westward until Britain could sponsor an Indian buffer state south of the Great Lakes and possibly annex the region to Canada. Meanwhile, the lingering British presence in the Northwest allowed Canadian fur traders to maintain a brisk business there.

Having failed to prevent American settlers from occupying territory it claimed in the Southeast, Spain sought to win the newcomers' allegiance by offering them citizenship. Noting that Congress under the Articles of Confederation seemed ready to accept the permanent closing of New Orleans in return for Spanish concessions elsewhere (see Chapter 6), many westerners began talking openly of secession. "I am decidedly of the opinion," wrote Kentucky's attorney general in 1787, "that this western country will in a few years Revolt from the Union and endeavor to erect an Independent Government." In 1788 Tennessee conspirators boldly advertised their flirtation with Spain by

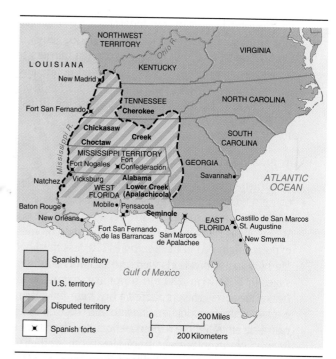

Disputed Territorial Claims, Spain and the United States, 1783–1796
The two nations' claims to lands east of the Mississippi and north of the thirty-first parallel were a principal point of contention until the Treaty of San Lorenzo was ratified in 1796.

naming a large district along the Cumberland River after Spain's governor in New Orleans. Most westerners who accepted Spanish favors and gold meant only to pocket badly needed cash in return for vague promises of goodwill. The episode showed, however, that leading citizens were susceptible to foreign manipulation and subversion. As young Andrew Jackson concluded in 1789, making some arrangements with the Spanish seemed "the only immediate way to obtain peace with the Savage [Indians]."

Meanwhile, southerners watched the deterioration of Anglo-American fortunes in the West with concern. Many southern citizens had acquired a personal stake in trans-Appalachian affairs because Virginia and North Carolina had rewarded Revolutionary soldiers with western land. Whether these veterans intended to move west themselves or to profit by selling their rights to others, all wanted to see the western territories prosper. Hoping to make a quick fortune in land speculation, southern planters (including George Washington) had borrowed heavily to buy frontier real estate; but uncertainty about the West's future made them worry that land prices would crash. By 1789 a potent combination of small farmers and landed gentry in the South had become enraged at foreign barriers to frontier expansion and eagerly supported politicians, among them Thomas Jefferson and James Madison, who advocated strong measures against the British and Spanish.

Regional Economies

The frustrations of southern planter-speculators were compounded by the failure of their principal crops, tobacco and rice, to return to prewar export levels. Whereas nearly two-thirds of the mainland colonies' exports originated in the South in 1770, less than half the new nation's exports were produced by southern states in 1790. In an effort to stay afloat, many Chesapeake tobacco growers shifted to wheat, and others expanded their production of hemp. But these changes had little effect on the region as a whole. The South's failure to recover its export base, along with barriers to westward expansion, contributed to nagging uncertainties about its future.

In the mid-Atlantic region, particularly Pennsylvania and New York, agricultural production benefited from a steady demand for foodstuffs and by 1788 had largely recovered from the Revolution's ravages. As famine stalked Europe, American farmers in the Delaware and Hudson River valleys prospered from climbing export prices.

New Englanders were not so fortunate. A short growing season and poor soil kept yields so low, even in the best of times, that farmers barely produced enough grain for local consumption. New Englanders also faced both high taxes to repay the money borrowed to finance the Revolution and a tightening of credit that spawned countless lawsuits against debtors. These problems had sparked Shays's Rebellion in 1786 and still defied solution. Whereas most southern states had largely eliminated their war debts and the Middle Atlantic states had made great progress in managing theirs, New England taxpayers remained under a crushing obligation. Economic depression only aggravated the region's chronic overpopulation. Young New England men continued migrating to the frontier or to the cities, and their discontent and restless mobility loosened the bonds of parental authority and left many women without marriage prospects.

British restrictions against trading with the West Indies (see Chapter 6) fell especially hard on New England. Resourceful captains took cargoes to the French West Indies, Scandinavia, and even China. Some even smuggled foodstuffs to the British West Indies under the very nose of the Royal Navy. Nevertheless, by 1791 discriminatory British treatment had reduced the number of seamen in the Massachusetts cod and whale fisheries by 42 percent compared to the 1770s. Recognizing that Great Britain could not be forced to grant trade concessions, New England's leaders preferred to solve the problem through peaceful accommodation, an approach entirely opposite to western and southern preferences for direct confrontation with Britain—even at the risk of war.

Entrepreneurs, Artisans, and Wage Earners

After 1783, through the enterprise of an ambitious, aggressive class of businessmen, the northern economy became less dependent on farming. Most of these individuals had begun as merchants, and they now used their profits to invest in factories, ships, government bonds, and banks (see "A Place in Time"). These men believed that the United States would gain strength if Americans balanced agriculture with banking, manufacturing, and commerce, and they wanted to limit American dependence on imported British manufactures. They also insisted that the nation needed a healthy merchant marine standing ready to augment U.S. naval forces in wartime.

Such entrepreneurs stimulated a flurry of innovative business ventures that pointed toward the future. The country's first private banks were founded in the 1780s in Philadelphia, Boston, and New York. Philadelphia merchants created the Pennsylvania Society for the Encouragement of Manufactures and the Useful Arts in 1787. This organization promoted the immigration of English artisans familiar with the latest industrial technology, including Samuel Slater (see Chapter 9), a pioneer of American industrialization who helped establish a cotton-spinning mill at Pawtucket, Rhode Island, in 1793. In 1791 investors from New York and Philadelphia started the Society for the Encouragement of Useful Manufactures, which attempted to demonstrate the potential of large-scale industrial enterprises by building a factory town at Paterson, New Jersey. That same year, New York merchants and insurance underwriters organized America's first formal association for trading government bonds, out of which the New York Stock Exchange evolved.

Certificate of the "New York Mechanick Society"
In the face of changing times and narrowing opportunity, many urban artisans organized societies to set wages and working hours.

Many of these early enterprises ended in financial ruin, however, because they proved premature or unrealistic. Not a few of their promoters shared the fate of Philadelphia businessman Robert Morris, who had signed both the Declaration of Independence and Constitution yet would spend three years in a debtors' prison after 1798. But the vision of these men was ultimately vindicated, for as often happens, failure preceded success: in the nineteenth century, the United States gradually became an industrial society.

Yet in 1789 the northeastern cities remained overwhelmingly preindustrial, without large factories. Half the urban work force consisted of "mechanics," whose ranks included both master artisans and journeymen. Mechanics manufactured goods by hand, typically in workshops where the master and his family employed a few journeymen or apprentices. Journeymen changed jobs frequently; those hired in Samuel Ashton's Philadelphia cabinet shop, for example, stayed an average of just six months between 1795 and 1803. Moreover, well-to-do artisan households, as well as professional and upper-class families, employed numerous servants. And masters and other employers could draw upon the growing ranks of low-paid day workers, who included most free blacks and many orphans, widows, and drifters.

Mechanics tended to follow in their fathers' occupational footsteps. They lived in close-knit neighborhoods with others who practiced their trade and with whom they enjoyed such traditional pastimes as drinking, marching, and "mobbing." Their wives and daughters often helped in the shop but rarely sought outside employment unless widowed or orphaned. Despite their industriousness and thrift, mechanics faced stiff competition from British manufacturers, who increasingly used labor-saving machinery and unskilled, low-paid labor. Consequently, American mechanics were disposed to support political leaders willing to raise the price of imported British goods through a national tariff. Most mechanics had supported the Constitution, hoping that it would create a strong and assertive national government.

A few artisans succeeded in adapting techniques of large-scale production to their crafts. The textile-finishing, printing, furniture-making, and construction trades most successfully exploited new technology or unskilled wage labor; they offered many opportunities for master artisans to establish flourishing family businesses. But most mechanics were either reluctant to abandon traditional household-oriented shops for an impersonal factory system or else could not modernize for lack of credit, which was scarce and expensive. Many artisans thus found opportunity shrinking, and they responded by organizing societies to set wages and working hours. Over the long run, the artisan community would contract as the mechanics themselves became wage earners working for entrepreneurial industrialists; but in the 1790s these trends were only beginning to emerge.

In 1789 virtually all politically conscious Americans—entrepreneurs and merchants, urban mechanics and frontier settlers, nationalists and Antifederalists, northerners and southerners—expressed their hopes for the nation's future in terms of republican ideals. These lofty goals of selfless service to the general good had helped community leaders rally the public behind them in resisting British encroachments since the 1760s. Republican ideology had guided the men who hammered out state constitutions and the new federal Constitution, and it had also helped Antifederalists state their case against the Constitution. Now in the 1790s, how to interpret republican ideals, with their abiding distrust of government power, became a nagging question in the cut-and-thrust of everyday politics. Most Americans thought that they knew what republican virtue meant, and most tended to condemn rivals' views as the road to corruption. Noting in *The Federalist* the numerous divergent meanings of the word

From 1790 to 1800, Philadelphia was the United States' capital, largest city, main financial market, and intellectual and scientific center. Home to forty-four thousand people in 1790, by 1800 Philadelphia almost doubled its population. This growth occurred despite a series of frightful yellow-fever epidemics, which cost thousands of lives and sent wealthier residents (including President Washington and the entire federal government) fleeing each summer while the disease raged. A constant stream of country people and foreign immigrants poured in, and large numbers of Germans, French, Irish, and Scots kept Philadelphia's population diverse.

The dynamism and diversity of Philadelphia's economy made for a society consisting of several distinct layers.

The City or Port of Philadelphia on the River Delaware from Kensington,
by William Birch, 1800
This engraving illustrates Philadelphia's remarkable growth in little more than a century. From the large elm under which William Penn was said to have first negotiated with the Delaware Indians (see Chapter 4), it looks across the Delaware River to the busiest port in North America.

The richest 10 percent of Philadelphians owned about half the city's wealth. This upper crust included old Quaker merchant families, recent wartime profiteers, and hustling new entrepreneurs. Philadelphia was still a preindustrial city entirely dependent on foreign trade for its existence, and most of its wealthiest men made their fortunes in commerce.

Philadelphia's economic environment was treacherous, however. Given rapidly changing market conditions, merchants had to be ever ready to act decisively. They repeatedly gambled everything in hopes of developing new overseas markets for Delaware Valley foodstuffs or of expanding the sphere within which they could retail European-made imports. But overseas trade was the most nerve-wracking of all Philadelphia businesses. From 1785 to 1791, bankruptcies reduced the number of trading firms from 514 to 440. Of the sixty-five wealthiest traders operating in 1779, only nine were still in business seventeen years later. The survivors were calculating, daring, and grasping.

In 1776, into this competitive commercial world came the half-blind French immigrant Stephen Girard. Relying on a quick mind and a scrappy, abrasive personality, Girard struggled for years just to avoid bankruptcy. But he exemplified the traits necessary for commercial success in Philadelphia—a determination to conduct his business personally (even when laid up with a painful head wound) and a willingness to take chances. "Since I have not as much as I desire, it seems necessary for me to take some risks or remain always poor." By 1795 he ranked high among the city's wealthiest individuals.

Girard's phenomenal success stemmed from his refusal to imitate conservative businessmen, who demonstrated a "prudence that will risk nothing." He and his fellow entrepreneurs helped propel Philadelphia into the industrial age. They provided two essential elements that would transform the city's economy—capital amassed from foreign trade, and a

Absalom Jones,
by Raphael Peale, 1810
Born a slave, Jones was allowed to study and work for pay; eventually he bought his freedom. He became a businessman, co-founder of the African Methodist Episcopal Church, and a stalwart in Philadelphia's free-black community.

readiness to take chances by investing in manufacturing.

Amid the shifting sands of precarious commerce and embryonic industrial capitalism, the wealthier families in the 1790s helped a flourishing, cultured city continue to prosper. The well-to-do could even afford to send their daughters to the Young Ladies' Academy, founded in 1787 by Dr. Benjamin Rush. "The patriot—the hero—the legislator," Dr. Rush grandly proclaimed, "would find the sweetest reward for their toils, in the approbation of their wives"—and how better could young women bestow this approval than by being educated themselves? Among the subjects that they studied was bookkeeping.

Most Philadelphians belonged to artisan families practicing such trades as carpentry, bricklaying, tailoring, and leatherworking. These crafts supplied the city's elite with elegant imitations of the latest European styles in dress, furniture, and housing. The better endowed artisans, along with small merchants and

professional men, lived fairly comfortably, if not opulently.

Such was not the case for the thousands of Philadelphians known to those in the upper and middle ranks as the lower sort. Employed as porters, woodcutters, washer-women, dock workers, seamen, and in dozens of other occupations, the "lower sort" provided vital services but led lives of uncertainty. When they had work at all, it was temporary and low paying. They had higher rates of illness and death than other Philadelphians because of their poor diets and living conditions and their inability to afford smallpox immunizations. Many received relief and charity or spent time in the almshouse, workhouse, or jail. Among the "lower sort" in 1790 were 1,840 African-Americans, all but 301 of whom were free. (Pennsylvania had enacted gradual emancipation in 1780.) Whereas some slaves had been trained in a skilled trade such as blacksmithing, young free men of color found themselves excluded from crafts and relegated to menial work. Still, free blacks strove to improve their lot: this largest free black community in North America maintained seven schools and three churches, all of which were segregated.

Philadelphia's bustling commerce and unequal distribution of wealth produced social strain. Journeymen printers and leatherworkers, for example, organized and struck in a vain attempt to avoid becoming permanent wage earners. Yet the "lower sort" largely avoided politics, and the city's most notable political pressure group of the 1790s did not promote class conflict. In this organization, Philadelphia's Democratic Society, artisan masters rubbed shoulders with members of the professional elite like Dr. Rush and famed scientist David Rittenhouse—and with entrepreneur Stephen Girard. What united these republican enthusiasts were a conviction that individuals of talent and ambition ought not be held back by special interests, an admiration for revolutionary France, and a determination to preserve the liberty so hard won in the American Revolution.

republican, James Madison had concluded that "no satisfactory one would ever be found."

CONSTITUTIONAL GOVERNMENT TAKES SHAPE

Traveling slowly over the nation's miserable roads, the men entrusted with launching the federal experiment began assembling in New York, the new national capital, in March 1789. Because so few members were on hand, Congress opened its session a month late. George Washington did not arrive until April 23 and only took his oath of office a week later.

The slowness of these first halting steps, however, disguised the seriousness of the tasks at hand. The country's elected leaders had to make far-reaching decisions on several critical questions left unresolved by the Constitution's framers. For example, the Constitution gave the president no formal responsibility for preparing a legislative agenda, although it allowed him wide discretion by directing him to make periodic reports on the state of the Union and by permitting him to recommend matters for Congress's consideration. The Philadelphia Convention likewise had not specified whether cabinet officers would be accountable to Congress or to the president. Nor did the Constitution say how the federal court system should be structured. Finally, widespread distrust of any government unrestrained by a bill of rights required that Congress prepare amendments for the states' consideration, but the exact scope and character of these amendments remained to be determined. "We are in a wilderness," wrote James Madison, "without a footstep to guide us."

Consequently, even though the Constitution had been ratified as the supreme law of the land, its framers' intentions might still have been reversed. The First Congress could easily have weakened presidential authority, limited access to federal courts, or passed amendments resurrecting features of the Articles of Confederation. Antifederalists conceivably could have convoked another constitutional convention, ostensibly to prepare a bill of rights but actually to rewrite the entire Constitution. In 1789 the nation's future remained unsettled in these, as in many other, regards.

Defining the Presidency

No office in the new government aroused more suspicion than the presidency. Many feared that the president's powers could make him a virtual king. Public apprehension remained in check only because of George Washington's reputation for honesty. Washington tried to calm fears of unlimited executive power.

The Constitution mentioned the executive departments only in passing, required the president to obtain the Senate's approval for his nominees to head these bureaus, and made all executive personnel liable to impeachment. Otherwise, Congress was free to determine the organization and accountability of what became known as the cabinet. The first cabinet, established by Congress, consisted of four departments, headed by the secretaries of state, treasury, and war and by the attorney general. Vice President John Adams's tie-breaking vote defeated a proposal that would have forbidden the president from dismissing cabinet officers without Senate approval. This outcome reinforced the president's authority to make and carry out policy; it also separated the powers of the executive and legislative branches beyond what the Constitution required, and so made the president a more equal partner with Congress.

President Washington suggested few laws to Congress. Rarely did he speak out against opponents of government policy, and generally he limited his public statements to matters of foreign relations and military affairs. He deferred to congressional decisions concerning domestic policy whenever possible and cast only two vetoes during his eight-year tenure (1789–1797).

Washington tried to reassure the public that he was above favoritism and conflicts of interest. Believing himself duty-bound to seek advice from a wide range of opinions, he balanced his cabinet with southerners and northeasterners. When Secretary of State Thomas Jefferson opposed certain policies of Secretary of the Treasury Alexander Hamilton, Washington implored Jefferson not to leave his post, even though the president supported Hamilton.

"He is polite with dignity, affable without familiarity, distant without haughtiness, grave without austerity, modest, wise, and good." So Abigail Adams, the wife of the vice president, described Washington. Once the government had settled into Philadelphia (the nation's capital from 1790 to 1800), the president enjoyed the private company of wealthy citizens, but he felt truly comfortable only at his Virginia estate, Mount Vernon, or on the Pennsylvania farm he rented. More than any other national leader, Washington sincerely strove to understand the aspirations of the two groups that dominated American society—northeastern merchants and entrepreneurs, and southern planters. Like most republican leaders, he believed that the proper role for ordinary citizens was not to set policy through elections but rather to choose well-educated, politically sophisticated men who would make laws in the people's best interest, though independently of direct popular influence.

The president endured rather than enjoyed the pomp of office. Suffering from a variety of ailments that grew as the years passed, Washington longed to escape the presidency. Only with difficulty was he persuaded to accept reelection in 1792. He dreaded dying while in office and thus setting the precedent for a lifetime presidency. With great anxiety he realized that "the preservation of the sacred fire of liberty and the destiny of the republican model of government are . . . *deeply,* perhaps *finally,* staked on the experiment entrusted to the hands of the American people." Should he contribute to that experiment's failure, he feared, his name would live only as an "awful monument."

National Justice and the Bill of Rights

The Constitution merely authorized Congress to establish federal courts below the level of the Supreme Court; it had offered no guidance as to how the judicial system should be structured. And although the Constitution specifically barred the federal government from committing such abuses as passing ex post facto laws* and bills of attainder,† the absence of a comprehensive bill of rights had led several delegates at Philadelphia to refuse to sign the Constitution and had been a major point of attack by Antifederalists. The task of filling in these gaps fell to the First Congress.

In 1789 many citizens feared that the new federal courts would ride roughshod over local customs. Every state had gradually devised a unique, time-honored blend of judicial procedures appropriate to local cir-

---

*Ex post facto law: a law criminalizing previously legal actions and punishing those who have been engaging in such actions.

†Bill of attainder: a legislative act proclaiming a person's guilt and stipulating punishment without a judicial trial.

cumstances. Any attempt to force states to abandon their legal heritage would have produced strong counterdemands that federal justice be narrowly restricted. Bowing to such sentiments, Congress might have drastically curtailed the scope and power of the federal judiciary or limited the federal judicial system to the Supreme Court. Congress might also have forbidden federal judges to accept cases from the states on a range of subjects (as permitted by Article III, Section 2). Such actions by Congress would have tipped the balance of power in the new nation to the states.

But when it passed the Judiciary Act of 1789, which created the federal-court system, Congress did not seek to hobble the national judiciary. Yet the act managed to quiet popular apprehensions by establishing in each state a federal district court that operated according to local procedures. As the Constitution stipulated, the Supreme Court exercised final jurisdiction. Congress had struck a reasonable compromise that respected state traditions while offering wide access to federal justice.

Behind the movement for a bill of rights lay Americans' long-standing fear that a strong central government would lead to tyranny. Many Antifederalists believed that the best defense against tyranny would be to strengthen the powers of state governments at the expense of the federal government, but many more Americans wanted simply to guarantee basic personal liberties. James Madison, who had been elected to the House of Representatives, battled fiercely to keep the Constitution's opponents from undermining the powers essential for a firm national government. It was Madison who played the leading role in drafting the ten amendments that became known as the Bill of Rights when ratified by the states in December 1791.

Madison insisted that the first eight amendments guarantee personal liberties, not strip the national government of any necessary authority. The First Amendment guaranteed the most fundamental freedoms of expression—religion, speech, press, and political activity—against federal interference. The Second Amendment ensured that each state could form its own citizen militia. Like the Third Amendment, it sought to protect citizens from what eighteenth-century Britons and Americans alike considered the most sinister embodiment of tyrannical power: standing armies. The Fourth through Eighth amendments limited the police powers of the state by guaranteeing individuals' fair treatment in legal and judicial proceedings. The Ninth and Tenth amendments reserved to the people or to the states powers not allocated to the federal government under the Constitution, but Madison headed off proposals to limit federal power more explicitly. In general, the Bill of Rights imposed no serious check on the framers' nationalist objectives.

Once the Bill of Rights was in place, the federal judiciary moved decisively to establish its authority. In 1793, in *Chisholm* v. *Georgia*, the Supreme Court ruled that a state could be sued in federal courts by nonresidents. In 1796 the Court declared its right to determine the constitutionality of congressional statutes in *Hylton* v. *United States* and to strike down state laws in *Ware* v. *Hylton*. But Congress decided that the Court had encroached too far on states' authority in *Chisholm*, and in 1794 it voted to overturn this decision through a constitutional amendment. Ratified in 1798, the Eleventh Amendment revised Article III, Section 2, so that private citizens could no longer undermine states' financial autonomy by using federal courts to sue another state's government in civil cases and claim money from that state's treasury. The defeat of *Chisholm* stands as one of the handful of instances in American history whereby the Supreme Court was subsequently overruled by a constitutional amendment.

By endorsing the Eleventh Amendment, Congress expressed its recognition that federal power could threaten vital local interests. Such awareness had been growing since the early 1790s, rupturing the nationalist coalition that had written the Constitution, secured its ratification, and dominated the First Congress. A dramatic sign of this split was James Madison's shift from nationalist to critic of excessive federal power in 1790–1791. Up to this time, Madison and most of his fellow nationalists had not thought very deeply about how federal power should be used. The chief exception was Alexander Hamilton, whose bold program alienated many like-minded nationalists by demonstrating that federal policies could be shaped to reward special interests.

NATIONAL ECONOMIC POLICY AND ITS CONSEQUENCES

Realizing that war would jeopardize national survival, Washington concentrated his attention on diplomacy and military affairs. His reluctance to become involved with pending legislation enabled his energetic secretary of the treasury, Alexander Hamilton, to set the administration's domestic priorities. Hamilton quickly emerged as the country's most imaginative and dynamic statesman by formulating a sweeping program for national economic development. But Hamilton's agenda proved deeply divisive.

Hamilton and His Objectives

Born in the West Indies in 1755, Hamilton had sailed to New York in 1772 to enroll at King's College (now Columbia University), where he had emerged as a passionate defender of American rights. He had entered the Continental Army in 1775, distinguished himself in battle several times, and won the nickname the Little Lion.

During his four years on Washington's staff, Hamilton developed an exceptionally close relationship with his commander in chief. Hamilton's mother had been the mistress of a Scottish merchant who had abandoned her and their children when Alexander was about ten. For Hamilton, Washington helped fill the emotional void created by his own father's desertion. At the same time, for the childless Washington, Hamilton became almost a son. Hamilton thus gained extraordinary influence over Washington, who despite misgivings frequently supported the younger man's policies.

Hamilton formulated his financial proposals to strengthen the nation against foreign enemies and also to lessen the threat of disunion. In his mind, the most immediate danger concerned national security: the possibility of war with Great Britain, Spain, or both. The Republic could finance a full-scale war only by borrowing heavily, but because Congress under the Articles of Confederation had failed to redeem or pay interest on the Revolutionary debt, the nation's credit had been seriously weakened abroad and at home. The country's economy also seemed unequal to fighting a major European power. War with Britain would mean a blockade, which would strangle commerce and stop the importation of necessary manufactured goods. French assistance had overcome this danger during the Revolution; but France's navy had declined greatly since 1783 (while the British navy had vastly improved). Moreover, growing political instability in France was transforming America's wartime ally into an uncertain friend. Unless the United States achieved self-sufficiency in the manufacture of vital industrial products and maintained a strong merchant marine ready for combat, Hamilton reasoned, its chances of surviving a second war with Britain appeared slim.

Hamilton also feared that the Union might disintegrate because of Americans' tendency to think first of their local loyalties and interests. Born outside the thirteen colonies, he felt little personal identification with his adopted state, New York, or any other American locale. Instead, his six years in the Continental Army produced a burning nationalistic faith. For him, the Constitution's adoption had been a close victory of national over state authority. Now he worried that the states might reassert power over the new government. If this happened, he doubted whether the nation could prevent ruinous trade discrimination between states, deter foreign aggression, and avoid civil war.

Both his wartime experiences and his view of human nature forged Hamilton's political beliefs. An enthusiastic young patriot who had fought bravely during the Revolution's darkest hours, Hamilton had grown profoundly disillusioned by civilian profiteering. Like many disappointed idealists, he became a cynic who believed that few could live up to his own standards. Thus, he came to share the conviction of many other nationalists that the Republic's population (like the rest of humanity) would never show limitless self-sacrifice and virtue. Hamilton concluded that the federal government's survival depended on building support among politically influential citizens through a straightforward appeal to their financial interests. Private ambitions would then serve the national welfare.

Charming and brilliant, vain and handsome, a notorious womanizer, and thirsting for fame and power, Hamilton himself exemplified the worldly citizen whose fortunes he hoped to link to the Republic's future. But to the growing ranks of his opponents, Hamilton would embody the dark forces luring the Republic to its doom—a man who, Jefferson wrote, believed in "the necessity of either force or corruption to govern men."

Report on the Public Credit

Seeking guidance on how to restore the nation's credit worthiness, in 1789 Congress directed the Treasury Department to evaluate the status of the Revolutionary debt. Hamilton seized the opportunity to devise policies that would at once strengthen the country's credit, enable it to defer paying its debt, and entice a key sector of the upper class to place their prestige and capital at its service. Congress received his Report on the Pub-

Continental Currency

lic Credit in January 1790. The report listed $54 million in U.S. debt: $42 million owed to Americans, and the rest to foreigners. Hamilton estimated that on top of the national debt, the states had debts of $25 million, an amount that included several million dollars that the United States had promised to reimburse, such as Virginia's expenses in defending settlements in the Ohio Valley.

Hamilton's first major recommendation was that the federal government support the national debt by "funding" it—that is, raising the $54 million needed to honor the debt by selling an equal sum in new securities. Purchasers of these securities would choose from several combinations of federal "stock" and western lands. Those who wished could retain their original bonds and earn 4 percent interest. All of the options would reduce interest payments on the debt from the full 6 percent set by the Confederation Congress. Hamilton knew that creditors would not object to this reduction because their investments would now be more valuable and more secure.

Second, the report proposed that the federal government pay off the state debts remaining from the Revolution. Such obligations would be funded along with the national debt in the manner described above.

Hamilton argued that the continued failure of certain states to honor their obligations would undermine U.S. credit in overseas markets. Although this reasoning contained a kernel of truth, it masked his most important motive. He saw the federal assumption of state debts as a chance for the national government to win the gratitude and loyalty of state creditors by honoring their claims before the remaining states could pay

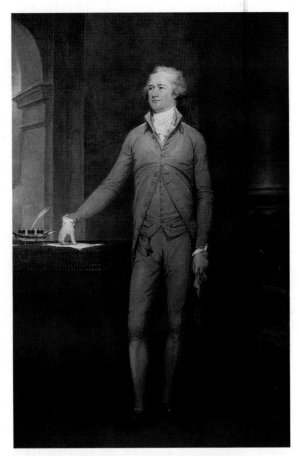

Alexander Hamilton, *by John Trumbull, 1792*
*Hamilton's self-confident pride clearly shines through in
this portrait, painted at the height of his influence in the
Washington administration.*

them. Since legislatures awash in debt wanted to avoid piling more taxes on the voters, they would accept any relief, regardless of Hamilton's actual intentions.

Hamilton exhorted the government to use the money earned by selling federal lands in the West to pay off the $12 million owed to Europeans as quickly as possible. The Treasury could easily accumulate the interest owed on the remaining $42 million by collecting customs duties on imports and excise taxes on whiskey distillers. In addition, Hamilton proposed that money owed to American citizens should be made a permanent debt. That is, he urged that the government *not* attempt to repay the $42 million principal but instead keep paying interest to people wishing to hold bonds as an investment. If Hamilton's recommendation were adopted, the only burden on the taxpayers

would be the small annual cost of interest. It would then be possible to uphold the national credit at minimal expense, without ever having to pay off the debt itself.

Hamilton advocated a perpetual debt above all as a lasting means of uniting the economic fortunes of the nation's creditors to the United States. In an age when financial investments were notoriously risky, the federal government would protect the savings of wealthy bond holders through conservative policies but still offer an interest rate competitive with the Bank of England's. The guarantee of future interest payments would act as the explicit link uniting the interests of the moneyed class with those of the government. Few other investments would entail so little risk.

Hamilton's Report on the Public Credit provoked immediate controversy. Although no one in Congress doubted that its provisions would fully restore the country's fiscal reputation, many objected that those least deserving of reward would gain the most. The original owners of more than three-fifths of the debt certificates issued by the Continental Congress (ranging from George Washington to Revolutionary patriots of modest means) had long before sold theirs at a loss, many out of dire financial necessity. Foreseeing Hamilton's intentions, wealthy speculators, on the other hand, had by then accumulated large holdings at the expense of unsuspecting original owners. Now these astute speculators stood to reap huge gains, even collecting interest that had fallen due before they had purchased the certificates. "That the case of those who parted with their securities from necessity is a hard one, cannot be denied," Hamilton admitted. But making exceptions would be even worse.

To Hamilton's surprise, Madison—his longtime colleague and initially a supporter of the plan—emerged as one of the chief opponents of reimbursing current holders at face value. Sensing opposition to the plan in his home state of Virginia, Madison now tried but failed to obtain compensation for original owners who had sold their certificates. Congress rejected his suggestions primarily because some members feared that they would weaken the nation's credit. Hamilton's policy was defensible, but it generated widespread resentment because it rewarded rich profiteers while ignoring the wartime sacrifices of ordinary citizens.

Opposition to assuming the state debts also ran high. Only Massachusetts, Connecticut, and South Carolina had failed to make effective provisions for paying their creditors. Understandably, the issue stirred the fiercest indignation in the South, which except for South Carolina had extinguished 83 percent of its debt. To allow residents of the laggard states to escape heavy taxes while others had liquidated theirs at great expense seemed to reward irresponsibility. Many Virginians, among them Madison, opposed Hamilton not only for reasons of high principle but also because of their state's self-interest. South Carolina became the sole southern state that supported Hamilton's policies.

Southern hostility almost defeated assumption. In the end, however, Hamilton managed to save his proposal by exploiting the strong desire among Virginians to relocate the national capital in their region. Virginians expected that moving the capital would make their state the crossroads of the country and thus help preserve its position as the nation's largest, most influential state. In return for the northern votes necessary to transfer the capital to the Potomac River, Hamilton secured enough Virginians' support to win the battle for assumption. Yet the debate over state debts alienated most southerners by confirming their suspicions that other regions monopolized the benefits of a stronger union.

Congressional enactment of the Report on the Public Credit dramatically reversed the nation's fiscal standing. Thereafter, Europeans grew so enthusiastic for U.S. bonds that by 1792 some securities were selling at 10 percent above face value.

Reports on the Bank and Manufactures

In December 1790 the secretary of the treasury presented Congress with a second message, the Report on a National Bank. Having managed to restore full faith in greatly undervalued certificates, Hamilton in effect had significantly expanded the stock of capital available for investment. He intended to direct that money toward projects that would diversify the national economy through a federally chartered bank.

The proposed bank would raise $10 million through a public stock offering. The Treasury would hold one-fifth of the stock and name one-fifth of the directors, but four-fifths of the control would fall to private hands. Private investors could purchase shares by paying for three-quarters of their value in government bonds. In this way, the bank would capture a significant portion of the recently funded debt and make it available for loans; it would also receive a substantial and steady flow of interest payments from the Trea-

sury. Anyone buying shares under these circumstances had little chance of losing money and was positioned to profit handsomely.

Hamilton argued that the Bank of the United States would cost the taxpayers nothing and greatly benefit the nation. It would provide a safe place for the federal government to deposit tax revenues, make inexpensive loans to the government when taxes fell short, and help relieve the scarcity of hard cash by issuing paper notes that would circulate as money. Furthermore, it would possess authority to regulate the business practices of state banks. Above all, the bank would provide much needed credit to expand the economy.

Finally, Hamilton called for American economic self-sufficiency. He admired the "prodigious effect" on Great Britain's national wealth that the recent expansion of factories had stimulated in that nation, and he wanted to encourage similar industrialization in the United States. His Report on Manufactures of December 1791 advocated protective tariffs on foreign imports to foster domestic manufacturing, which in turn would both attract immigrants and create national wealth. Elsewhere the secretary called for assisting the merchant marine against British trade restrictions by reducing duties on goods imported into the United States on American ships and by offering subsidies (called bounties) for fishermen and whalers. These measures would also indirectly protect the national bank's loans to industrialists and shippers.

Hamilton's Challenge to Limited Government

In the eyes of many of the new government's supporters, Hamilton's plan to establish a permanent national debt violated the principle of equality among citizens; it seemed to favor the interests of public creditors over those of other Americans. Hamilton's critics also denounced his proposal for a national bank, interpreting it as a dangerous scheme that would give a small, elite group special power to influence the government.

The bank issue drew Thomas Jefferson into the ranks of Hamilton's opponents. It was almost an article of faith among Revolutionary-generation Americans like Madison and Jefferson that the Bank of England had undermined the integrity of government in Britain. Shareholders of the new Bank of the United States could just as easily become the tools of unscrupulous politicians. If significant numbers in

Congress also owned bank stock, they would likely vote in support of the bank even at the cost of the national good. To Jefferson, the bank was "a machine for the corruption of the legislature [Congress]." Representative John Taylor of Virginia predicted that its vast wealth would enable the bank to take over the country, which would thereafter, he quipped, be known as the United States of the Bank.

Opponents' strongest argument against the bank was their claim of its unconstitutionality. The Constitution gave Congress no specific authorization to issue charters of incorporation; indeed the constitutional convention had rejected a proposal giving Congress just such power. Unless Congress adhered to a "strict interpretation" of the Constitution, critics argued, the central government might oppress the states and trample individual liberties, just as Parliament had done to the colonies. Strictly limiting the powers of the government seemed the surest way of preventing the United States from degenerating into a corrupt despotism, as Britain had.

Congress approved the bank by only a thin margin. Doubtful of the bank's constitutionality, Washington turned for advice to both Jefferson and Hamilton. Jefferson distrusted banking and did not want to extend government power beyond the letter of the Constitution. "To take a single step beyond the boundaries thus specifically drawn around the powers of Congress is to take possession of a boundless field of power no longer susceptible of any definition," warned Jefferson. Hamilton fought back, urging Washington to sign the bill. Because Congress could enact all measures "necessary and proper" (Article I, Section 8), Hamilton contended that the only unconstitutional activities were those actually *forbidden* to the national government. In the end, the president accepted Hamilton's cogent argument for a "loose interpretation" of the Constitution. In February 1791 the Bank of the United States obtained a charter guaranteeing its existence for twenty years. Washington's acceptance of the principle of loose interpretation was the first victory for those advocating an active, assertive national government.

Madison and Jefferson also strongly opposed Hamilton's proposal to encourage industry through protective tariffs on foreign manufactures. They viewed such protectionism as an unfair subsidy promoting uncompetitive industries that would founder without government support. Moreover, tariffs doubly injured the majority of citizens, first by imposing heavy import taxes that were passed on to consumers and then by reducing the incentive for American manufacturers to produce goods at a lower cost than imports. Together these results unjustifiably raised prices. The only beneficiaries would be those shielded from overseas competition and institutions, like the bank, that lent them money. Fearing that American cities might develop a dangerous class of dependent and politically volatile poor people, Jefferson and Madison saw industrialization as a potential menace to the Republic's stability.

Congress ultimately refused to approve a high protective tariff. Nevertheless, Hamilton succeeded in setting higher duties on goods imported into the United States by British vessels than on items carried by American ships. As a result, the tonnage of such goods carried by the American merchant marine more than tripled from 1789 to 1793. Congress also approved subsidies for New England's beleaguered whale and cod fisheries in 1792.

Hamilton's Legacy

Hamilton's attempt to erect a base of political support by appealing to economic self-interest proved highly successful. His arrangements for rescuing the nation's credit provided enormous gains for the speculators, merchants, and other "monied men" of the port cities who by 1790 held most of the Revolutionary debt. As holders of bank stock, these same groups had yet another reason to use their prestige on behalf of national authority. Assumption of the state debts liberated taxpayers from a crushing burden in New England, New Jersey, and South Carolina. Hamilton's efforts to promote industry, commerce, and shipping struck a responsive chord among the Northeast's budding entrepreneurs and hard-pressed artisans.

Those attracted to Hamilton's policies called themselves Federalists, in large part to imply (incorrectly) that their opponents had formerly been Antifederalists. Despite the Federalists' effort to associate themselves with the Constitution, they actually favored a "consolidated" (centralized) national government instead of a truly federal system with substantial powers left to the states. Federalists dominated public opinion in New England, New Jersey, and South Carolina besides enjoying considerable support in Pennsylvania and New York.

However, Hamilton's program sowed dissension in sections of the country where Federalist economic policies provided few benefits. Resentment ran high among those who felt that the government appeared to be rewarding special interests. This situation appeared a perversion of the common understanding that the Constitution had been ratified to bring equal advantages to all Americans. Southern reaction to Hamilton's program, for example, was overwhelmingly negative. Few southerners (aside from some wealthy Charleston merchants) had retained Revolutionary certificates until 1789. By that date only South Carolina of all the southern states had any significant remaining Revolutionary debt. The Bank of the United States had few southern stockholders, and it allocated very little capital for loans there.

Hamilton's plans for commercial expansion and industrial development likewise seemed irrelevant to the interests of the West, where agriculture promised to be exceptionally profitable if only the right to export through New Orleans would be guaranteed. In Pennsylvania and New York, too, the uneven impact of Hamiltonian policies generated dissatisfaction. Resentment against a national economic program whose main beneficiaries seemed to be eastern "monied men" and Yankees who refused to pay their debts gradually united westerners, southerners, and many individuals in the mid-Atlantic region into a political coalition that challenged the Federalists for control of the government and called for a return to the "true principles" of republicanism.

The Whiskey Rebellion

Hamilton's financial program not only sparked an angry political debate in Congress but also helped ignite a civil insurrection called the Whiskey Rebellion. Severely testing the federal government's authority, this insurrection was the young republic's first serious crisis.

To augment the national government's revenue from import duties, Hamilton had recommended an excise tax on domestically produced whiskey. He insisted that his proposal would distribute the expense of financing the national debt evenly across the United States. He even alleged that the country's morals would improve if higher prices induced Americans to drink less liquor, a contention enthusiastically endorsed by Philadelphia's College of Physicians.

Though Congress complied with Hamilton's request in March 1791, many members doubted that Americans (who on average annually imbibed six gallons of hard liquor per adult) would submit tamely to sobriety. James Jackson of Georgia, for example, warned the administration that his constituents "have long been in the habit of getting drunk and that they will get drunk in defiance of a dozen colleges or all the excise duties which Congress might be weak or wicked enough to pass."

The accuracy of Jackson's prophecy became apparent in September 1791, when a crowd tarred and feathered an excise agent near Pittsburgh. Western Pennsylvanians found the new tax especially burdensome. Unable to ship their crops to world markets through Spanish New Orleans, most farmers had grown accustomed to distilling their rye or corn into alcohol, which could be carried across the Appalachians at a fraction of the price charged for bulky grain. Hamilton's excise equaled 25 percent of whiskey's retail value, enough to wipe out a frontier farmer's profit.

The law furthermore specified that all trials concerning tax evasion be conducted in federal courts. Any western Pennsylvanian indicted for noncompliance thus had to travel three hundred miles to Philadelphia. Not only would the accused then face a jury of unsympathetic easterners, but he would have to bear the cost of a long journey and lost earnings while at court, in addition to fines and other court penalties if found guilty. Consequently, western Pennsylvanians had justifiable reasons for complaining that local circumstances made the whiskey tax excessively burdensome.

Moreover, Treasury officials rarely enforced the law rigorously outside western Pennsylvania. An especially diligent excise inspector lived near Pittsburgh. His efforts to collect the tax increasingly enraged local residents and in time touched off massive resistance.

Initially, most residents preferred to protest the tax peacefully, through mass meetings and petitions to Congress. Only a frustrated minority resorted to violence, not only attacking federal revenue officers but even turning on their own neighbors, destroying property and occasionally pinning down farmers with rifle fire for hours. Despite such tactics, popular opposition to the whiskey tax became increasingly militant.

In a scene reminiscent of colonial protests against Britain, large-scale resistance erupted in July 1794.

One hundred men attacked a U.S. marshal serving sixty delinquent taxpayers with summonses to appear in court at Philadelphia. A crowd of five hundred burned the chief revenue officer's house after a shootout with federal soldiers assigned to protect him. Roving bands torched buildings, assaulted tax collectors, chased government supporters from the region, and flew a flag symbolizing an independent country that they hoped to create from six western counties.

The frontier turmoil played directly into the Washington administration's hands. Echoing British denunciation of colonial protests, Hamilton blasted the rebellion as simple lawlessness, in particular because Congress had reduced the tax rate per gallon in 1792 and just recently had voted to allow state judges in western Pennsylvania to hear trials. Washington concluded that failure to respond strongly to the uprising would encourage similar outbreaks in other frontier areas where lax enforcement had allowed distillers to escape paying taxes.

Washington accordingly summoned 12,900 militiamen from Pennsylvania, Maryland, Virginia, and New Jersey to march west under his command. Opposition evaporated once the troops reached the Appalachians, and the president left Hamilton in charge of making arrests. Of about 150 suspects seized, Hamilton sent twenty in irons to Philadelphia. Two men received death sentences, but Washington eventually pardoned them both, noting that one was a "simpleton" and the other "insane."

The Whiskey Rebellion was a milestone in determining limits on public opposition to federal policies. In the early 1790s, many Americans still assumed that it was legitimate to protest unpopular laws using the same tactics with which they had blocked parliamentary measures like the Stamp Act. Indeed, western Pennsylvanians had justified their resistance with exactly such reasoning. Before 1794 the question of how far the people might go in resisting federal laws remained unresolved because, as Washington declared, "We had given no testimony to the world of being able or willing to support our government and laws." But by firmly suppressing the first major challenge to national authority, Washington served notice that if citizens wished to change the law, they could do so only through constitutional procedures—by making their dissatisfaction known to their elected representatives and if necessary by electing new representatives.

THE UNITED STATES IN A HOSTILE WORLD

By 1793 disagreements over foreign affairs had emerged as the primary source of friction in American public life. The political divisions created by Hamilton's financial program hardened into ideologically oriented factions that argued vehemently over whether the country's foreign policy should be pro-French or pro-British.

The United States faced a particularly hostile international environment in the 1790s. European powers restricted American trade, supported Indian raids on the frontier, strengthened and expanded their North American empires, and maintained military garrisons on U.S. soil. Because the new nation's economic well-being depended heavily on exports, foreign-policy issues loomed large in national politics. Disputes over foreign relations would poison public life from 1793 to 1815.

Foreign Powers and Native Americans in the West

The most serious perils to the nation's future rose from British, Spanish, and Native American efforts to resist U.S. expansion farther westward.

Spain's efforts were a facet of its larger attempt to counter potential rivals for North American territory—Russia and Britain on the Pacific; Britain and the United States in the Mississippi Valley. In the 1740s, Russian traders in Siberia had crossed the Bering Sea and had begun trading with Alaskan natives for sea-otter pelts, frequently using brutal force and spreading deadly diseases in the process. Meanwhile, Britain was searching for the "Northwest Passage," a route that would link the Canadian interior with the Pacific. Sensing twin threats to its previously unchallenged monopoly in the north Pacific, Spain boldly expanded its empire northward from Mexico by establishing "New California," a long stretch of coast from San Diego to Sonoma (north of San Francisco), beginning in 1769. Efforts to encourage large-scale Hispanic immigration to New California failed, so that the colony was sustained primarily by its religious missions. Spanish colonists' spreading of epidemic and venereal diseases among coastal Californian natives precipitated a decline in the Indians' numbers

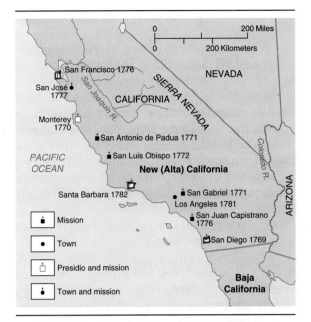

Spanish Settlements in New California, 1784
While the United States was struggling to establish its independence, Spain was extending its empire northward along the Pacific coast.

from about 72,000 in 1770 to about 18,000 by 1830. Survivors who did not escape were placed in missions, where priests sought to Christianize and "civilize" them by imposing rigid disciplinary measures and putting them to work in vineyards and in other enterprises. Meanwhile, Spain strengthened its position in the Southwest by making peace with the Comanches, Navajos, and most of the Apache nations that had previously threatened its settlements.

Revitalized by its far western successes, Spain, along with Britain and the Native Americans, constituted a formidable barrier to U.S. aims in the Mississippi Valley.

In the early years of Washington's administration, Spanish officials commonly bribed numerous well-known political figures in Tennessee and Kentucky, among them a former general on Washington's staff, James Wilkinson, whose unscrupulous intrigues would continue well past 1800. Thomas Scott, a congressman from western Pennsylvania, meanwhile schemed with the British. Between 1791 and 1796, the federal government anxiously admitted Vermont, Kentucky, and Tennessee to the Union, partly in the hope of strengthening their sometimes flickering loyalty to the United States.

Consulting with the Senate as the Constitution required, President Washington nevertheless tried to keep tight control of foreign policy. Realizing that he could not quickly resolve the complex western problem, he pursued a course of patient diplomacy that was intended "to preserve the country in peace if I can, and to be prepared for war if I cannot." The prospect of peace improved in 1789 when Spain unexpectedly opened New Orleans to American commerce, although exports remained subject to a 15 percent duty that westerners bitterly resented. Still, secessionist sentiment gradually subsided.

Washington now moved to weaken Spanish influence in the West by neutralizing Spain's most important ally, the Creek Indians. The Creeks numbered more than twenty thousand, including perhaps five thousand warriors, and they bore a fierce hostility toward Georgian settlers, whom they called *Ecunnaunuxulgee*, or "the greedy people who want our lands." In 1790 the Creek leader Alexander McGillivray

Stimafachki of the Koasati Creeks,
by John Trumbull, 1790
This portrait was sketched during the U.S.–Creek conference that resulted in the Treaty of New York.

signed the Treaty of New York with the United States. The treaty permitted American settlers to occupy lands in the Georgia piedmont fought over since 1786, but in other respects preserved Creek territory against U.S. expansion. Washington insisted that Georgia restore to the Creeks' allies, the Chickasaws and Choctaws, the vast area along the Mississippi River known as the Yazoo Tract, which Georgia claimed and had begun selling off to white land speculators.

Hoping to conclude a similar agreement with Great Britain's Indian allies, the United States sent an envoy to the Great Lakes tribes in 1790. The Miamis responded by burning a captured American to death. Late that same year, the president's first effort to force peace through military action failed when General Josiah Harmar abandoned his march against the Miamis after the loss of nearly two hundred of his soldiers. A second campaign ended in disaster on November 4, 1791, when Indians killed nine hundred men out of a force of fourteen hundred led by General Arthur St. Clair.

While employing military force, the Washington administration, led by Secretary of War Henry Knox, also sought to pacify the Indians through a benevolent policy similar to that proclaimed by the British in 1763 (see Chapter 5). Alarmed by the chaos on the frontier, where trespassers invaded Indian lands and the native peoples rejected U.S. claims to sovereignty, the government formally recognized Indian title as secure and inalienable except by the "free consent" of the Indians themselves. To reinforce this policy, Congress passed laws prohibiting trespassing on Indian lands, punishing crimes committed there by non-Indians, outlawing alcohol, and regulating trade. In addition, the administration sought to encourage Indians to leave off their "savage" ways and become "civilized," by which it meant above all abandoning communal landownership and seasonal migrations for hunting, gathering, and fishing. By adopting private property and a strictly agricultural way of life, Knox and others thought, Indians would find a niche for themselves in American society while making much additional land available for non-Indians.

Knox recognized that his "civilization" policy would have limited appeal. Although most Indians were receptive to European material goods, they were unwilling to give up their traditional ways entirely and assimilate into an alien culture. And most whites were averse to integrating Native Americans into their society. Accordingly, the United States continued to pres-

sure most Native Americans to sell their lands and move farther west.

With many Indians opposed to abandoning both their lands and their cultures, and with St. Clair's defeat in 1791, Washington's frontier policy lay in a shambles. Not only had two military expeditions suffered defeat in the Northwest Territory, but in 1792 the Spanish had persuaded the Creeks to renounce their treaty with the federal government and to resume hostilities. Ultimately, the damage done to U.S. prestige by these setbacks convinced many Americans that the combined strength of Britain, Spain, and the Native Americans could be counterbalanced only by an alliance with France.

France and Factional Politics

One of the most momentous events in history, the French Revolution began in 1789 with the meeting (for the first time in almost two centuries) of France's legislative assembly, the Estates General. Americans remained fundamentally sympathetic to the revolutionary cause as the French abolished nobles' privileges, wrote a constitution, and bravely repelled invading armies from Austria and Prussia. France became a republic early in 1793; it then proclaimed a war of all peoples against all kings, in which it assumed that the United States would eagerly enlist.

Enthusiasm for a pro-French foreign policy raged in the South and on the frontier, in particular after France went to war against Spain and Great Britain in 1793. Increasingly, western settlers and southern speculators in frontier lands hoped for a decisive French victory in Europe that, they reasoned, would leave Britain and Spain militarily too exhausted to continue meddling in the West. The United States could then insist on free navigation of the Mississippi, force the evacuation of British garrisons, and end both nations' support of Indian resistance.

Moreover, a slave uprising in France's Caribbean colony of Saint Domingue (later renamed Haiti), in which the British became involved, soon generated passionate anti-British sentiment in the South. White southerners grew alarmed for the future of slavery and their own lives as thousands of terrified French planters fled to the United States from Saint Domingue with accounts of how British invaders in 1793 had supported the rebellious slaves. The blacks had fought with determination and inflicted heavy casualties on the French. Southern whites concluded that the British had intentionally sparked a bloodbath on the island and worried that a British-inspired race war would engulf the South as well. Anti-British hysteria even began to undermine South Carolina's loyalty to Federalist policies.

After 1790 American reactions to the French Revolution diverged sharply in the North and the South, in large measure for economic reasons. In the North merchants' growing antagonism toward France reflected not only their conservatism but also their strong awareness that good relations with Britain were essential for their region's prosperity. Virtually all the nation's merchant marine operated from northern ports, and by far the largest share of U.S. foreign trade was with Great Britain. Merchants, shippers, and ordinary sailors in New England, Philadelphia, and New York feared that an alliance with France would provoke British retaliation against this valuable commerce, and they argued that the United States could win valuable concessions by demonstrating friendly intentions toward Great Britain. Indeed, important members of Parliament, including Prime Minister William Pitt the Younger, seemed to favor liberalizing trade with the United States.

Southerners had no such reasons to favor Britain. Southern spokesmen like Jefferson and Madison viewed Americans' reliance on British commerce as a menace to national self-determination and wished to divert most U.S. trade to France. Jefferson and Madison repeatedly demanded that British imports be reduced through the imposition of discriminatory duties on cargoes shipped from England and Scotland in British vessels. Their recommendations gravely threatened ties with Britain, which sold more manufactured goods to the United States than to any other country. In the heat of the debate, Federalist opponents of a discriminatory tariff warned that the English would not stand by while a weak French ally pushed them into depression. If Congress adopted this program of trade retaliation, Hamilton predicted in 1792, "there would be, in less than six months, an open war between the United States and Great Britain."

After declaring war on Britain and Spain in 1793, France actively tried to embroil the United States in the conflict. The French dispatched Edmond Genet as minister to the United States with orders to mobilize republican sentiment in support of France, enlist American mercenaries to conquer Spanish territories and attack British shipping, and strengthen the treaty of alliance between the two nations. Much to the French government's disgust, however, President Washington issued a proclamation of American neutrality on April 22.

Meanwhile, Citizen Genet (as he was known in French Revolutionary style) had arrived on April 8. He found no shortage of southern volunteers for his American Foreign Legion despite America's official neutrality. Making generals of George Rogers Clark of Kentucky and Elisha Clarke of Georgia, Genet directed them to seize the Spanish garrisons at New Orleans and St. Augustine. Clark openly defied Washington's Neutrality Proclamation by advertising for recruits for his mission in Kentucky newspapers; Clarke began drilling three hundred troops on the Florida border. But the French failed to provide adequate funds for either campaign. And as for the American recruits, although all were willing to fight for France, few were willing to fight for free, and so both expeditions eventually disintegrated in 1794 for lack of French money to supply them.

However, Genet did not need funds to outfit privateers, whose crews were paid from captured plunder. By the summer of 1793, almost a thousand Americans were at sea in a dozen ships flying the French flag. These privateers seized more than eighty British vessels and towed them to U.S. ports, where French consuls sold the ships and cargoes at auction.

The British Crisis

Even though the Washington administration swiftly closed the nation's harbors to Genet's buccaneers and requested the French ambassador's recall, his exploits provoked an Anglo-American crisis. George III's ministers decided that only a massive show of force would deter further American aggression. Accordingly, on November 6, 1793, the Privy Council issued secret orders confiscating any foreign ships trading with French islands in the Caribbean. The council purposely delayed publishing these instructions until after most American ships carrying winter provisions to the Caribbean left port, so that their captains would not know that they were sailing into a war zone. The Royal Navy then seized more than 250 American vessels, a high price for Genet's troublemaking.

Meanwhile, the U.S. merchant marine was suffering a second galling indignity—the drafting of its crewmen into the Royal Navy. Thousands of British sailors, including numerous naval deserters, had previously fled to U.S. ships, where they hoped to find an easier life than under the tough, poorly paying British system. In late 1793 British naval officers began routinely inspecting American crews for British subjects, whom they then impressed (forcibly enlisted) as the king's sailors. Overzealous commanders sometimes broke royal orders by taking U.S. citizens, and in any case the British did not recognize former subjects' right to adopt American citizenship. Impressment scratched a raw nerve in most Americans, who recognized that their government's willingness to defend its citizens from such contemptuous abuse was a critical test of national character.

Next the British boldly challenged the United States for control of the West. In February 1794 Canada's royal governor delivered an inflammatory speech at an Indian council, denying U.S. claims north of the Ohio River and urging his listeners to destroy every white settlement in the Northwest. Soon British troops were building an eighth garrison on U.S. soil, Fort Miami, near present-day Toledo, Ohio. Meanwhile, the Spanish encroached further upon territory owned by the United States by building Fort San Fernando in 1794 at what is now Memphis, Tennessee.

Hoping to halt the drift toward war, Washington launched a desperate diplomatic initiative in 1794. He sent Chief Justice John Jay to Great Britain, dispatched Thomas Pinckney to Spain, and authorized General Anthony Wayne to negotiate a treaty with the Indians of the Ohio Valley.

Having twice defeated federal armies, the Indians scoffed at Washington's peace offer. But the tide turned as "Mad Anthony" Wayne led three thousand regulars and Kentucky militiamen deep into the Indian homeland and ruthlessly razed every village within his reach. On August 20, 1794, his troops routed a thousand Indians at the Battle of Fallen Timbers just two miles from British Fort Miami. Wayne's army marched past the post in a provocative victory parade and then built an imposing stronghold to challenge British authority in the Northwest, appropriately named Fort Defiance. Indian morale plummeted. In August 1795 Wayne compelled twelve northeastern tribes to sign the Treaty of Greenville, which opened most of modern-day Ohio to white settlement and ended Indian hostilities for sixteen years.

Wayne's success allowed John Jay to win a major diplomatic victory in London: a British promise to withdraw troops from American soil. He also managed to gain access to West Indian markets for small American ships, but only by bargaining away U.S. rights to load cargoes of sugar, molasses, and coffee from the Caribbean. On other points, Jay found the British unyielding. Aside from fellow Federalists, few Americans could interpret Jay's Treaty as preserving peace with honor.

Jay's Treaty left Britain free not only to violate American neutrality but also to ruin a profitable commerce by restricting U.S. trade with French ports during wartime. Many opponents, moreover, passionately decried Jay's failure to end impressment and predicted that Great Britain would thereafter force even more Americans into the Royal Navy. And southerners re-

Negotiating the Treaty of Greenville

In this detail of a contemporary painting believed to have been done by a member of General Wayne's staff, Chief Little Turtle of the Miamis speaks to Wayne, who stands with one hand behind his back.

sented that Jay had not achieved their long-sought goal of compensation for slaves taken away by the British army during the Revolution. As the Federalist-dominated Senate ratified the treaty by a one-vote margin in 1795, Jay nervously joked that he could find his way across the country by the fires of rallies burning him in effigy.

Despite its unpopularity, Jay's Treaty probably represented the most that a weak, politically divided United States could have extracted from mighty Britain. Although enormously unpopular, the treaty was one of the Washington administration's major accomplishments. First, it defused an explosive crisis with Great Britain before war became inevitable. Second, it ended a twelve-year British occupation of U.S. territory. Third, the treaty provided for the settlement, by arbitration, of the claims of British merchants who were owed American debts from before 1776, and it also arranged for U.S. citizens' compensation for property seized by the Royal Navy in 1793 and 1794 (though these accounts were not finally settled until 1804).

Although the Senate rejected the provision granting limited trading rights with the West Indies in return for a British monopoly over certain commodities, Jay's Treaty played a critical role in stimulating an enormous expansion of American trade. British governors in the West Indies used the treaty's ratification as an excuse to proclaim their harbors open to U.S. ships. Other British officials permitted Americans to develop a thriving commerce with India, even though this trade infringed on the East India Company's monopoly. Within a few years after 1795, American exports to the British Empire shot up 300 percent.

On the heels of Jay's Treaty came an unqualified diplomatic triumph engineered by Thomas Pinckney. Ratified in 1796, the Treaty of San Lorenzo with Spain (also called Pinckney's Treaty) won westerners the right of unrestricted, duty-free access to world markets via the Mississippi River. Spain also promised to recognize the thirty-first parallel as the United States' southern boundary, to dismantle all fortifications on American soil, and to discourage Indian attacks against western settlers.

By 1796 the Washington administration thus had successfully defended the country's territorial integrity, restored peace to the frontier, opened the Mississippi for western exports, made it possible for northeastern shippers to regain British markets, and kept the nation out of a dangerous European war. As the popular outcry over Jay's Treaty demonstrated, however, the nation's foreign policy had left Americans much more deeply divided in 1796 than they had been in 1789.

Battling for the Nation's Soul

Besides distrusting centralized executive authority, colonial and Revolutionary Americans feared organized political parties. Labeling parties "factions," Americans (and many Britons) assumed that such groups were formed by corrupt conspirators operating against the liberties of the people. Neither the Constitution nor *The Federalist* had envisioned political parties, and none existed in 1789 when Washington became president. By the end of his second term, however, politically conscious Americans had split into two hostile parties, Federalists and Republicans.

The unfolding struggle transcended the economic and sectional differences so evident in earlier disputes about Hamiltonian finance and the possibility of war with Britain. After 1796 a battle raged over the very future of representative government, culminating in the election of 1800, whose outcome would determine whether the nation's political elite could accommodate demands from ordinary citizens for a more active and influential role in determining government policy. No issue was more important or hotly argued than the matter of officeholders' accountability to their constituents.

Ideological Confrontation

By the mid-1790s the French Revolution had led many Americans to reassess their political values. American attitudes toward events in France divided sharply after that nation's revolutionary regime turned radical in 1793–1794, sending thousands of "counterrevolutionaries" to the guillotine. The polarization of American opinion assumed a strongly, though not completely, regional dimension.

For northern Federalists, revolutionary France became an abomination—"an open hell," thundered Massachusetts Federalist Fisher Ames, "still ringing with agonies and blasphemies, still smoking with sufferings and crimes." New England was the United States' most conservative, religiously oriented region, and most of its people came to detest the French

The Republican Court, *by Daniel Huntington Federalists emphasized the dignity of the national government by staging sumptuous balls and formal receptions. Administration critics saw these affairs as an effort to emulate European court life. Washington, although mindful of upholding presidential dignity, found public functions tedious, and his stiff formality often masked his personal discomfort.*

government's disregard for civil rights and its attempt to substitute the adoration of Reason for the worship of God. Middle Atlantic businessmen, who were perhaps less religious than New Englanders but hardly less conservative, condemned French leaders as evil radicals who incited the poor against the rich. A minority of well-off northern merchants and professional men, however, continued to look favorably upon the French Revolution, primarily out of loyalty to deeply felt republican principles.

Federalists trembled at the thought of guillotines and "mob rule" looming in the United States' future. Memories of Shays's Rebellion and the Whiskey Rebellion reinforced their fears. So did the tendency of artisans in Philadelphia and New York to bandy the French revolutionary slogan "Liberty, Equality, Fraternity" and to admire pro-French political leaders such as Jefferson. Moreover, Citizen Genet had openly encouraged vocal opposition to the Washington administration until the faction in the French government that he represented fell from power—and even more troubling, he had found hundreds of Americans willing to fight for France. Federalists worried that all of this was just the tip of an iceberg.

By the mid-1790s Federalist leaders had concluded that it was unwise and perhaps dangerous to involve the public too deeply in politics. The people, they believed, were not evil-minded but simply undependable and could easily fall prey to a rabble rouser such as Genet. As Senator George Cabot of Massachusetts put it, "The many do not think at all." For Federalists, democracy meant "government by the passions of the multitude," though they also felt that the people, if properly led, could stand as a powerful (but passive) bulwark against anarchy. Indeed, they *did* trust ordinary property owners to judge a candidate's personal fitness for high office. Federalists consequently argued that citizens need not be presented with choices over policy during elections; instead, voters ought to choose candidates according to their personal merits. Thus they favored a representative government, in which elected officials would rule in the people's name but would be independent of direct popular influence.

Preserving order, the Federalists maintained, required demonstrating the dignity of the government and forging a close, visible relationship between the government and the upper class. Such a spectacle would not only reassure citizens that their future was in competent hands but also set high standards that few radicals could meet. As early as 1789, Vice President John Adams had tried to give the president and

George Washington, *by James Sharples, 1795*

other high officials such royal-sounding titles as "His High Mightiness." (Adams had failed amid much ridicule, including being lampooned as "His Rotundity.") During the 1790s government officials continued to dramatize their social distance from average citizens. Members of Congress and the cabinet dressed in high fashion, traveled in expensive coaches, appeared with retinues of servants, and attended endless formal dinners and balls, which served as grand opportunities for the upper class to flaunt its wealth. Federalists insisted that they ruled of and for the people, but they took pains to symbolize that their government was not by the people.

The Federalists aimed to limit public office to wise and virtuous men who would vigilantly protect liberty. This objective was consistent with eighteenth-century fears that corruption and unchecked passion would undermine society, for in republican theory a "virtuous" government need not be directly responsible to public opinion. If (as many assumed) democracy meant "mob rule," then political virtue and direct democracy were incompatible. The Federalists' profound suspicion of the common people therefore was deeply rooted not only in old-fashioned social reciprocity (see Chapter 2) and in conservative colonial

political traditions but also in republican ideology itself.

A very different understanding of republican ideology influenced Jefferson, Madison, and others alienated by Federalist measures. Although some critics of the administration surfaced in New England and the Middle Atlantic states, opposition ran particularly high in the South. Indeed, the southern interpretation of republicanism stressed the corruption inherent in a powerful government dominated by a highly visible few, and white southerners widely insisted that liberty would be safe only if power were diffused among virtuous, independent citizens. With their own labor force consisting of enslaved blacks rather than of free white wage workers, southern elites feared popular participation in politics far less than their northern counterparts. Furthermore, few southern planters were strongly religious, and many had absorbed the Enlightenment's faith that the free flow of ideas would inevitably ensure progress. They also felt confident of their ability to lead (and be elected by) the smaller farmers. Consequently, many white southerners felt exhilarated by the events unfolding in France; they saw the French as fellow republicans, carrying on a work of universal revolution that would replace hereditary privilege with liberty, equality, and brotherhood. Unlike northern Federalists, nervous about urban mobs, southern planters faced the future with optimism and viewed attempts to inhibit widespread political participation as unworthy of educated gentlemen.

Self-interest, too, drove men like Jefferson and Madison to rouse ordinary citizens' concerns about civic affairs. Political apathy was widespread in the early 1790s, a situation that favored the Federalists by making it unlikely that they would be criticized for passing unwise laws. If, however, the Federalists could be held accountable to the public, they would think twice before enacting measures opposed by the majority; or if they persisted in advocating misguided policies, they would ultimately be removed from office. Such reasoning led Jefferson, a wealthy landowner and large slaveholder, to say, "I am not among those who fear the people; they and not the rich, are our dependence for continued freedom."

Organized efforts to turn public opinion against the Federalists had begun in October 1791 with the publication of the nation's first opposition newspaper, the *National Gazette.* Then in 1793–1794, popular dissatisfaction with the government's policies led to the formation of dozens of Democratic (or Republican) societies, primarily in seaboard cities but also in the rural South and in frontier towns. Their memberships ranged from planters and merchants to artisans and sailors. Conspicuously absent were clergymen, the poor, and nonwhites.

Sharply critical of the Federalists, the societies spread dissatisfaction with the Washington administration's policies. Because many of the clubs arose during Genet's ministry, and because all of them also acclaimed revolutionary France, Federalists assumed (wrongly) that their members were acting as foreign agents. Federalists interpreted their emotional appeals to ordinary people as demagoguery and denounced the societies' followers as "democrats, mobocrats, & all other kinds of rats."

The Federalists feared that the societies would grow into revolutionary organizations. Washington privately warned that "if [the clubs] were not counteracted (not by prosecutions, the ready way to make them grow stronger) or did not fall into disesteem . . . they would shake the government to its foundation." During the Whiskey Rebellion, the president publicly denounced "certain self-created societies." So great was his prestige that the societies temporarily broke up. But by attacking them, Washington had at last ended his nonpartisan stance and identified himself unmistakably with the Federalists. The censure would cost him dearly.

The Republican Party

Neither Jefferson nor Madison belonged to a Democratic society. However, these private clubs helped publicize administration critics' views, and they initiated into political activity numerous voters who would later support Jefferson's and Madison's Republican party. Ironically, Madison had earlier been one of the most outspoken opponents of political parties.

In the early 1790s, politically active Americans believed that deliberately organizing a political faction or party was a corrupt, subversive action. The Constitution's framers had neither wanted nor planned for political parties, and in *The Federalist* No. 10, Madison had claimed that the Constitution would prevent the rise of national political factions. Republican ideology commonly assumed that factions or parties would fill Congress with politicians of little ability and less integrity, pursuing selfish goals at the expense of national welfare. Good citizens, it was assumed, would

shun partisan scheming. These ideals, however, began to waver as controversy mounted over Hamilton's program and foreign policy. President Washington still tried to set an example of impartial leadership by seeking advice from both camps. (He did not know that in their partisan zeal both Hamilton and Jefferson maintained indiscreet contacts with British and French diplomats, respectively.) But Jefferson finally resigned from the cabinet in 1793, and thereafter even the president could not halt the widening political split. Each side saw itself as the guardian of republican virtue and attacked the other as an illegitimate "cabal" (faction).

In 1794 party development reached a decisive stage. Shortly after Washington had openly identified himself with Federalist policies, followers of Jefferson who called themselves Republicans* successfully attacked the Federalists' "pro-British" leanings in many local elections and won a slight majority in the House of Representatives. The election signaled the Republicans' transformation from a faction of officeholders to a broad-based party capable of coordinating local political campaigns throughout the nation.

Federalists and Republicans alike used the press to mold public opinion in the 1790s. In this decade American journalism came of age as the number of newspapers multiplied from 92 to 242, mostly in New England and the Middle Atlantic states. By 1800 newspapers had perhaps 140,000 paid subscribers (about one-fifth of the eligible voters), and their secondhand readership probably exceeded 300,000. Newspapers of both camps were libelous and irresponsible. They cheapened the quality of public discussion through incessant fear mongering and character assassination. Republicans stood accused of plotting a reign of terror and of wishing to turn the nation over to France. Federalists faced charges of favoring a hereditary aristocracy and even of planning to establish an American dynasty by marrying off John Adams's daughter to George III. Such tactics whipped up mutual distrust and made political debate emotional and subjective. Nevertheless, the newspaper warfare stimulated many citizens to become politically active, even if for the wrong reasons.

Behind the inflammatory rhetoric, the Republicans' central charge was that the Federalists had evolved into a faction bent on enriching wealthy citi-

---

*Jefferson and Madison preferred the party name *Republican* rather than the radical-sounding *Democratic*.

zens at the taxpayers' expense. In 1794 a Republican writer claimed that Federalist policies would create "a privileged order of men . . . who shall enjoy the honors, the emoluments, and the patronage of government, without contributing a farthing to its support." Although almost every Republican leader, too, was well born, Republicans asserted that the Federalists planned to recreate the atmosphere of a European court through highly publicized state dinners, formal balls, and other dazzling entertainments. The Republicans erred in claiming that their opponents were scheming to introduce legal privilege, aristocracy, and monarchy. But they correctly identified the Federalists' fundamental assumption: that citizens' worth could be measured in terms of their money.

Republican charges that the president secretly supported alleged Federalist plots to establish a monarchy enraged Washington. "By God," Jefferson reported him swearing, "he [the president] would rather be in his grave than in his present situation . . . he had rather be on his farm than to be made *emperor of the world.*" Furthermore, the president took alarm at the stormy debate over Jay's Treaty, and he dreaded the nation's polarization into hostile factions. Republicans' abuse sharply stung him. "As for you, sir," sneered Thomas Paine in a pamphlet, "treacherous in private friendship . . . and a hypocrite in public life, the world will be puzzled to decide whether you are an apostate or an impostor, whether you have abandoned good principles or ever had any." Lonely and surrounded by mediocre advisers after Hamilton's return to private life, Washington decided in the spring of 1796 to retire after two terms. Four years earlier, Madison had drafted the president's parting message to the nation; but now Washington called on Hamilton to give a sharp political twist to his Farewell Address.

The heart of Washington's message was a vigorous condemnation of political parties. Partisan alignments, he insisted, endangered the republic's survival, especially if they became entangled in disputes over foreign policy. Washington warned that the country's safety depended on citizens' avoiding "excessive partiality for one nation and excessive dislike of another." Otherwise, independent-minded "real patriots" would be overwhelmed by demagogues championing foreign causes and paid by foreign governments. Aside from scrupulously fulfilling its existing treaty obligations and maintaining its foreign commerce, the United States must avoid "political connection" with Europe and its wars. If the United States gathered its strength under "an efficient government," it could defy any foreign challenge; but if it became sucked into Europe's quarrels, violence, and corruption, then the republican experiment was doomed. Washington and Hamilton had skillfully turned the central argument of republicanism against their Republican critics. They had also evoked a vision of America virtuously isolated from foreign intrigue and power politics, which would remain a potent inspiration until the twentieth century.

Washington left the presidency in 1797 and died in 1799. Like many later presidents, he went out amid a barrage of criticism. During his brief retirement, the nation's political division into Republicans and Federalists hardened. Each party consolidated its hold over particular states and groups of voters, leaving the electorate almost equally divided.

The Election of 1796

As the election of 1796 approached, the Republicans cultivated a large, loyal body of voters. Their efforts to marshal support marked the first time since the Revolution that the political elite had effectively mobilized ordinary Americans to take an interest in public affairs. The Republicans' constituency included the Democratic societies, workingmen's clubs, and immigrant-aid associations.

Immigrants became a prime target for Republican recruiters. During the 1790s the United States absorbed perhaps twenty thousand French refugees from Saint Domingue and more than sixty thousand Irish, including some conspirators exiled for plotting against British rule. Although potential immigrant voters were few—composing less than 2 percent of the electorate—the Irish in particular could exert crucial influence in Pennsylvania and New York, where public opinion was closely divided and a few hundred immigrant voters could tip the balance away from the Federalists. In short, Irish immigrants could provide the Republicans with a winning margin in the two states, and the Republicans' pro-French and anti-British rhetoric ensured enthusiastic Irish support.

In 1796 the presidential candidates were Vice President John Adams, supported by the Federalists, and the Republicans' Jefferson. Republicans expected to win as many southern electoral votes and congressional seats as the Federalists counted on in New England, New Jersey, and South Carolina. The crucial

Adams Family Farm; John Adams, *by Gilbert Stuart, 1826 (Detail) The Adamses hailed from Quincy, Massachusetts. John Adams was born in the house at the right; his son, John Quincy Adams, in the saltbox at the left. Soon after the elder Adams's death, John Quincy Adams, himself now president, commissioned a final portrait; this gentle and distinguished canvas was the result.*

"swing" states were Pennsylvania and New York, where the Republicans tried mightily to tip the balance by wooing the large immigrant (particularly Irish) vote. In the end, however, the Republicans took Pennsylvania but not New York, and so Jefferson lost the presidency by just three electoral votes. The Federalists narrowly regained control of the House and maintained their firm grip on the Senate. But by a political fluke possible under the Constitution at the time, Jefferson became vice president.*

The new president exemplified both the strengths and the weaknesses of an intellectual. His brilliance, insight, and idealism have rarely been equaled among American presidents. Like most intellectuals, however, Adams was more comfortable with ideas than with people, more theoretical than practical, and rather inflexible. He inspired trust and often admiration but could not command personal loyalty. His wisdom and historical vision were drowned out in highly emotional political debate. Adams's rational, reserved personality was likewise ill suited to inspiring the

*The Constitution then stipulated that the presidential candidate with the second-highest electoral vote would become vice president. This was one example of the Constitution's failure to provide for political partisanship.

electorate, and he ultimately proved unable to unify the country.

The French Crisis

Adams was initially fortunate, however, that French provocations produced a sharp backlash against the Republicans. The French interpreted Jay's Treaty as an American attempt to assist the British in their war against France. On learning of Jefferson's defeat, the French ordered the seizure of American ships carrying goods to British ports; and within a year the French had plundered more than three hundred vessels. The French government rubbed in its contempt for the United States by directing that every American captured on a British naval ship (even those involuntarily impressed) should be hanged.

Hoping to avoid war, Adams sent a peace commission to Paris. But the French foreign minister, Charles de Talleyrand, refused to meet the delegation, instead promising through three unnamed agents ("X, Y, and Z") that talks could begin after he received $250,000 and France obtained a loan of $12 million. This barefaced demand for a bribe became known as the XYZ Affair. Americans reacted to it with outrage.

"Millions for defense, not one cent for tribute" became the nation's battle cry as the 1798 congressional elections began.

The XYZ Affair discredited the Republicans' foreign policy views, but the party's leaders compounded the damage by refusing to condemn French aggression and opposing Adams's call for defensive measures. The Republicans tried to excuse French behavior, whereas the Federalists rode a wave of militant patriotism. In the 1798 elections, Jefferson's supporters were routed almost everywhere, even in the South.

Congress responded to the XYZ Affair by arming fifty-four ships to protect American commerce. The new warships were at once put to use in what has become known as the Quasi-War—an undeclared Franco-American naval conflict in the Caribbean from 1798 to 1800, during which U.S. forces seized ninety-three French privateers at the loss of just one vessel. The British navy meanwhile extended the protection of its convoys to America's merchant marine. By early 1799 the French were a nuisance but no longer a serious threat at sea.

Despite the president's misgivings, the Federalists in Congress tripled the regular army to ten thousand men in 1798, with an automatic expansion of land forces to fifty thousand in case of war. But the risk of a land war with the French was minimal. In reality, the Federalists primarily wanted a military force ready in the event of a civil war, for the crisis had produced near-hysteria about conspiracies that were being hatched by French and Irish malcontents flooding into the United States.

Federalists were well aware that the French legation was not only engaged in espionage but also making treasonous suggestions to prominent persons. The government knew, for example, that in 1796 General Victor Collot had traveled from Pittsburgh to New Orleans under orders to investigate the prospects for establishing a pro-French, independent nation west of the mountains, and also that he had examined strategic locations to which rebellious frontier dwellers might rally. The State Department heard in 1798 that France had created in the West "a party of mad Americans ready to join with them at a given Signal."

The Alien and Sedition Acts

The Federalists, moreover, insisted that the likelihood of open war with France required stringent legislation to protect national security. In 1798 the Federalist-dominated Congress accordingly passed four measures known collectively as the Alien and Sedition Acts. Adams neither requested nor particularly wanted these laws, but he deferred to Federalist congressional leaders and signed them.

The least controversial of the four laws, the Alien Enemies Act, was designed to prevent wartime spying or sabotage. This measure outlined procedures for determining whether the citizens of a hostile country posed a threat to the United States; if so, they were to be deported or jailed. The law established fundamental principles for protecting national security and respecting the rights of enemy citizens. It was to operate only if Congress declared war and so was not used until the War of 1812 (see Chapter 8).

Second, the Alien Friends Act was a peacetime statute enforceable until June 25, 1800. It authorized the president to expel any foreign residents whose activities he considered dangerous. The law did not require proof of guilt, on the assumption that spies would hide or destroy evidence of their crime. Republicans maintained that the law's real purpose was to deport prominent immigrants critical of Federalist policies.

Republicans also denounced the third law, the Naturalization Act. This measure increased the residency requirement for U.S. citizenship from five to fourteen years (the last five continuously in one state), with the purpose of reducing Irish voting.

Finally came the Sedition Act, the only one of these measures enforceable against U.S. citizens. Although its alleged purpose was to distinguish between free speech and attempts at encouraging others to violate federal laws or to overthrow the government, the act nevertheless defined criminal activity so broadly that it blurred any real distinction between sedition and legitimate political discussion. Thus it forbade an individual or group "to oppose any measure or measures of the United States"—wording that could be interpreted to ban any criticism of the party in power. Another clause made it illegal to speak, write, or print any statement about the president that would bring him "into contempt or disrepute." Under such restrictions, for example, a newspaper editor might face imprisonment for disapproving of an action by Adams or his cabinet members. The Federalist *Gazette of the United States* expressed the twisted logic of the Sedition Act perfectly: "It is patriotism to write in favor of our government—it is sedition to write against it."

Sedition cases were heard by juries, which could decide if the defendant had really intended to stir up rebellion or was merely expressing political dissent. But whatever way one looked at it, the Sedition Act interfered with free speech. Ingeniously, the Federalists wrote the law to expire in 1801 (so that it could not be turned against them if they lost the next election) and to leave them free meanwhile to heap abuse on the *vice* president, Jefferson.

Federalist enforcement of the first of the repressive new laws, the Alien Friends Act, produced mixed results. The president signed a deportation order for French agent Collot, who escaped capture. No expulsions were actually carried out under the law, although two of Collot's assistants and several dozen other French sailed home before they could be forcibly removed from the country.

The real target of Federalist repression was the U.S. opposition press. Four of the five largest Republican newspapers were charged with sedition just as the election of 1800 was getting under way. The attorney general used the Alien Friends Act to threaten an Irish journalist, John Daly Burk, with expulsion (Burk went underground instead). Scottish editor Thomas Callender was on the verge of being deported when he suddenly qualified for citizenship. Now unable to expel Callender, the government tried him for sedition before an all-Federalist jury, which sent him to prison for criticizing the president.

Federalist leaders never intended to fill the jails with Republican martyrs. Rather, they wanted to use a small number of highly visible prosecutions to intimidate most journalists and candidates into keeping quiet during the election of 1800. The attorney general charged seventeen persons with sedition and won ten convictions. Among the victims was the Republican congressman Matthew Lyon of Vermont ("Ragged Matt, the democrat," to the Federalists), who spent four months in prison for publishing a blast against Adams.

Vocal criticism of Federalist repression erupted only in Virginia and Kentucky. During the summer of 1798, militia commanders in these states mustered their regiments, not to drill but to hear speeches demanding that the federal government respect the Bill of Rights. Entire units then signed petitions denouncing the Alien and Sedition Acts. The symbolic implications of these protests were sobering. Young men stepped forward to sign petitions on drumheads with a pen in one hand and a gun in the other, as older officers who had fought in the Continental Army looked on approvingly. It was not hard to imagine Kentucky rifles being

substituted for quill pens as the men who had led one revolution took up arms again.

Ten years earlier, opponents of the Constitution had warned that giving the national government extensive powers would eventually endanger freedom. By 1798 their prediction had come true. Shocked Republicans realized that because the Federalists controlled all three branches of the government, neither the Bill of Rights nor the system of checks and balances protected individual liberties. In this context, the doctrine of states' rights was advanced as a means of preventing the national government from violating basic freedoms.

Madison and Jefferson anonymously wrote two manifestos on states' rights that the assemblies of Virginia and Kentucky officially endorsed in 1798. Madison's Virginia Resolutions and Jefferson's Kentucky Resolutions declared that the state legislatures had never surrendered their right to judge the constitutionality of federal actions and that they retained an authority called interposition, which enabled them to protect the liberties of their citizens. A set of Kentucky Resolutions adopted in November 1799 added that objectionable federal laws might be "nullified" by the states. The terms *interposition* and *nullification* were not defined, but the intention was obviously to prevent residents from being tried for breaking an unconstitutional law. The Virginia and Kentucky legislatures must have understood that interposition would ultimately challenge the jurisdiction of federal courts and perhaps require that state militia march into a federal courtroom to halt proceedings at bayonet point.

Although no other states endorsed these resolutions (most in fact expressed disapproval), their passage demonstrated the great potential for violence in the late 1790s. So did a minor insurrection called the Fries Rebellion, which broke out in 1799 when crowds of Pennsylvania German farmers released prisoners jailed for refusing to pay taxes needed to fund the national army's expansion. Fortunately, the disturbance collapsed just as federal cavalry arrived, and the only casualties were several head of rebellious cattle shot by trigger-happy soldiers.

The nation's leaders increasingly acted as if a crisis were imminent. Vice President Jefferson hinted that events might push the southern states into secession from the Union. The normally sensible President Adams hid guns in his home. After passing through Richmond and learning that state officials were purchasing thousands of muskets for the militia, an alarmed Supreme Court justice wrote in January 1799 that "the General Assembly of Virginia are pursuing steps which will lead directly to civil war." A tense atmosphere hung over the Republic as the election of 1800 neared.

The Election of 1800

In the election the Republicans rallied around Jefferson for president and the wily New York politician Aaron Burr for vice president. The Federalists meanwhile became mired in wrangling between Adams and the extreme "High Federalists" who looked to Alexander Hamilton for guidance. That the nation survived the election of 1800 without a civil war or the disregard of voters' wishes owed much to the good sense of the more moderate leaders of both parties. Thus Jefferson and Madison discouraged radicalism that might provoke intervention by the national army, while Adams rejected High Federalist demands that he ensure victory by deliberately sparking an insurrection or asking Congress to declare war on France.

"Nothing but an open war can save us" argued Adams's High Federalist secretary of the treasury. But when the president suddenly discovered the French willing to seek peace in 1799, he proposed a special diplomatic mission. "Surprise, indignation, grief & disgust followed each other in quick succession," said a Federalist senator on hearing the news. Adams obtained Senate approval for his envoys only by threatening to resign and so make Jefferson president, an action that he later described with justifiable pride as "the most disinterested . . . in my whole life." The High Federalists were so outraged that they tried unsuccessfully to dump Adams. Hamilton denounced him as a fool, but this ill-considered maneuver rallied most New Englanders around their stubborn, upright president.

Adams's negotiations with France did not achieve a settlement until 1801, but the expectation that normal—and perhaps friendly—relations with the French would resume prevented the Federalists from exploiting charges of Republican sympathy for the enemy. Without the immediate threat of war, moreover, voters grew resentful that in merely two years, taxes had soared 33 percent to support an army that had done nothing except chase terrified Pennsylvania farmers. As the danger of war receded, voters gave the Federalists less credit for standing up to France and

more blame for ballooning the national debt by $10 million.

Two years after their triumph in the 1798 elections, support for the Federalists had eroded sharply. High Federalists who had hoped for war spitefully withheld the backing that Adams needed to win. The Republicans meanwhile redoubled their efforts to elect Jefferson. They were especially successful in mobilizing voters in Philadelphia and New York, where artisans, farmers, and some entrepreneurs were ready to forsake the Federalists, whom they saw as defenders of entrenched privilege and upstart wealth. As a result, popular interest in politics rose sharply. Voter turnouts in 1800 leaped to more than double those of 1788, rising from about 15 percent to almost 40 percent, and in hotly contested Pennsylvania and New York more than half the eligible voters participated.

Playing on their opponent's reputation as a religious free thinker, the Federalists forged a case against Jefferson that came down to urging citizens to vote for "GOD—AND A RELIGIOUS PRESIDENT; or impiously declare for JEFFERSON—AND NO GOD!!!" But this ploy did not prevent thousands of deeply religious Baptists, Methodists, and other dissenters from voting Republican. Nor did voters know that Adams was scarcely more conventional in his religious views than Jefferson.

Adams lost the presidency by just 8 electoral votes out of 138. He would have won if his party had not lost control of New York's state senate, which chose the electors, after a narrow defeat in New York City. Unexpectedly, Jefferson and his running mate Burr also carried South Carolina because their backers made lavish promises of political favors to that state's legislators.

Although Adams lost, Jefferson's election was not assured. Because all 73 Republican electors voted for both their party's nominees, the electoral college deadlocked in a Jefferson-Burr tie.* The choice of president devolved upon the House of Representatives, where thirty-five ballots over six days produced no result. Finally, Delaware's only representative, a Federalist, abandoned Burr and gave Jefferson the presidency by history's narrowest margin.

---

*The Twelfth Amendment (ratified in 1804) eliminated the possibility of such problems. It stipulated that electors vote for presidential and vice-presidential candidates as a pair; no longer would the runner-up in the presidential contest become vice president.

DEFERRING EQUALITY

The election of 1800 did not make the United States more democratic. Rather, it prevented rigidly antidemocratic prejudices from blocking future political liberalization. The Republican victory also repudiated the Federalist willingness, so evident in Hamilton's plans, to create a base of support for the government through special-interest legislation. Such self-serving goals led critics like Madison to condemn the Federalists for "substituting the motive of private interest for public duty." After 1800 government policies would be judged by Jefferson's standard of "equal rights for all, special privileges for none."

But not all Americans won equal rights. Women and African-Americans took almost no part in politics, and few people felt that they should. As for the Native Americans, the nation's diplomatic gains came largely at their expense. Moreover, in the Republic's early years, white Americans lost much of the idealism that Revolutionary ideology had inspired, and they began to assume that racial minorities could never be more than second-class citizens at best.

Indians in the New Republic

By 1795 eastern Indians had suffered severe reductions in population and territory. Innumerable deaths had resulted from battle, famine, exposure to the elements during flight from enemies, and disease. From 1775 to 1795, the Cherokees declined from 16,000 to 10,000 and the Iroquois fell from about 9,000 to 4,000. Meanwhile, in the quarter-century before 1800, Indians forfeited more land than the area inhabited by whites in 1775. Settlers crowded Indians onto reservations (often illegally), liquor dealers and criminals trespassed on Indian lands, and government agents and missionaries pressured Native Americans to give up their communal lands and traditional cultures.

In the face of such losses and pressures, many Indians became demoralized. Unable to strike back at whites, Indians often consumed enormous quantities of whiskey and inflicted violence on one another. The situation among the Iroquois was all too typical. "The Indians of the Six Nations," wrote a federal offi-

Sauk Chief, *c. 1805*
This portrait probably depicts Wa Pawni Ha, a seventeen-year-old leader of the Sauk nation.

cial in 1796, "have become given to indolence, drunkenness, and thefts, and have taken to killing each other."

The Indians' predicament spawned a profound social and moral crisis within tribes threatened by the settlers' expansion. Among those most afflicted were the Seneca Iroquois. But beginning in 1799, a Seneca prophet, Handsome Lake, led his people in one of the most resourceful efforts to resolve this crisis. Overcoming his own problems with liquor, he sought to end alcoholism among Indians by appealing to their religious traditions. Even more radically, he welcomed Quaker missionaries and federal aid earmarked for teaching Euro-American agricultural methods to Iroquois men, who had to look for new livelihoods after the loss of most of their lands and the demise of the fur trade. More traditional Indians rejected the notion that Indian men should work like white farmers; said one, only "squaws and hedgehogs are made to scratch the ground." But many Iroquois men welcomed the change. It was the women who resisted most, because they stood to lose their collective ownership of farmland, their control of the food supply, and their place in tribal councils. Women who did not accept Handsome Lake's and the Quakers' urging to exchange farming for housewifery found themselves ac-

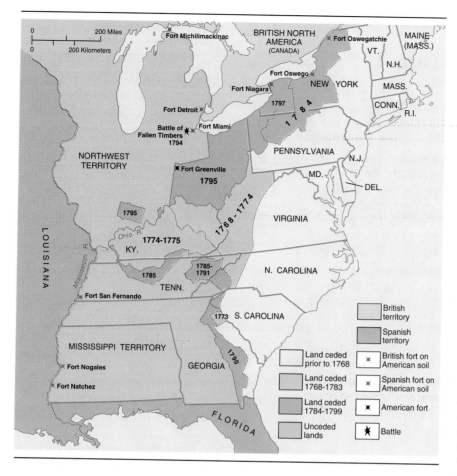

Indian Land Cessions, 1768–1799

Between 1768 and 1775, western Indians sold off vast territories, mostly hunting grounds in mountainous regions. The upheavals of the Revolutionary War, followed by conflicts with U.S. military forces from 1784 to 1799, led to large cessions of inhabited Indian lands.

cused of witchcraft, and some were killed. As a result of such conflicts between traditional and new ways, cultural change among the Senecas and other tribes proceeded slowly.

Redefining the Color Line

The Republic's first years marked the high tide of African-Americans' Revolutionary era success in bettering their lot. Although racism had not disappeared, Jefferson's eloquent words "all men are created equal" had awakened many whites' consciences. By 1790, 8 percent of all African-Americans enjoyed freedom—many having purchased liberty or earned it through wartime service. Ten years later, 11 percent controlled their own fate. Various state reforms meanwhile attempted to improve slaves' conditions. In 1791, for example, the North Carolina legislature declared that the former "distinction of criminality between the murder

of a white person and one who is equally an human creature, but merely of a different complexion, is disgraceful to humanity" and authorized the execution of whites who murdered slaves. By 1794 most states had outlawed the Atlantic slave trade.

Hesitant measures to ensure free blacks' legal equality also appeared in the 1780s and early 1790s. Most states dropped restrictions on their freedom of movement and protected their property. Of the sixteen states in the Union by 1796, all but three either permitted free blacks to vote or made no specific attempt to exclude them. But by then a countertrend was reversing many of the Revolutionary era advances for free blacks. Before the 1790s ended, abolitionist sentiment ebbed, slavery became more entrenched, and whites demonstrated unmistakable reluctance to accept even free blacks as fellow citizens.

Federal law led the way in restricting blacks' rights. When Congress established procedures for

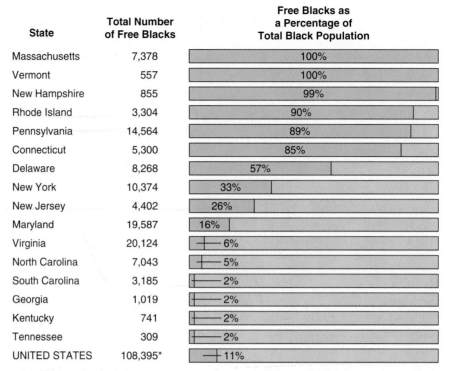

State	Total Number of Free Blacks	Free Blacks as a Percentage of Total Black Population
Massachusetts	7,378	100%
Vermont	557	100%
New Hampshire	855	99%
Rhode Island	3,304	90%
Pennsylvania	14,564	89%
Connecticut	5,300	85%
Delaware	8,268	57%
New York	10,374	33%
New Jersey	4,402	26%
Maryland	19,587	16%
Virginia	20,124	6%
North Carolina	7,043	5%
South Carolina	3,185	2%
Georgia	1,019	2%
Kentucky	741	2%
Tennessee	309	2%
UNITED STATES	108,395*	11%

Number and Percentage of Free Blacks, by State, 1800

Within a generation of the Declaration of Independence, a large free black population emerged that included every ninth African-American. In the North, only in New Jersey and New York did most blacks remain slaves. Almost half of all free blacks lived in the South. Every sixth black in Maryland was free by 1800.

SOURCE: U.S. Bureau of the Census.

* Total includes figures from the District of Columbia, Mississippi Territory, and Northwest Territory. These areas are not shown on the chart.

naturalizing aliens in 1790, it limited eligibility to foreign whites. The federal militia law of 1792 required whites to enroll in local units but allowed states to exclude free blacks, an option that state governments increasingly chose. The navy and the marine corps forbade nonwhite enlistments in 1798. Delaware stripped free blacks of the vote in 1792, and by 1807 Maryland, Kentucky, and New Jersey had followed suit. Free blacks continued to vote and serve in integrated militia organizations in many localities after 1800 (including the slave states of North Carolina and Tennessee), but the number of places that treated them as the political equals of whites dropped sharply in the early 1800s.

An especially revealing indication of changing racial attitudes occurred in 1793, when Congress enacted the Fugitive Slave Law. This law required judges to award possession of a runaway slave upon any formal request by a master or his representative. Accused runaways not only were denied a jury trial but also were sometimes refused permission to present evidence of their freedom. Slaves' legal status as property

disqualified them from claiming these constitutional privileges, of course, but the Fugitive Slave Law denied *free* blacks the legal protections that the Bill of Rights guaranteed them as citizens. Congress nevertheless passed this measure without serious opposition. The law marked a striking departure from the atmosphere of the 1780s, when state governments had invariably given whites and free blacks the same legal privileges. By 1793 white Americans clearly found it easy to forget that the Constitution had not limited citizenship to their race, and fewer of them felt honor-bound to protect black rights.

The bloody slave revolt on Saint Domingue notably undermined the trend toward abolition and reinforced the kind of fears that spawned racism. Reports of the slaughter of French slaveowners made white Americans more reluctant to criticize slavery in the United States and helped transform the image of blacks from that of victims of injustice to one of a potential menace. In August 1800 smoldering southern white fears were kindled when a slave insurrection broke out near Virginia's capital, Richmond. Having

Slave Artifacts

These objects, uncovered at the site of slave quarters on a large plantation, were used by African-Americans after the day's work was finished. They include part of a fiddle bow, a fragment of a writing slate, pencils, a penknife, dominoes, marbles, and a jew's harp.

secretly assembled weapons, more than a thousand slaves planned to march on Richmond. State militiamen, called out by Governor James Monroe, swiftly put down the conspiracy and executed some thirty-five slaves, including the leader, Gabriel Prosser. "I have nothing more to offer than what General Washington would have had to offer, had he been taken by the British officers and put to trial by them," said one rebel before his execution. "I have ventured my life in endeavoring to obtain the liberty of my countrymen, and I am a willing sacrifice to their cause."

Gabriel's Rebellion confirmed whites' anxieties that Saint Domingue's terrifying experience could be replayed on American soil. For years thereafter, isolated uprisings occurred, and rumors persisted that a massive revolt was brewing. Antislavery sentiment diminished quickly. By 1810 abolitionists ceased to exert political influence, and not until the 1830s would the antislavery movement recover from the damage inflicted by the Saint Domingue revolt.

A different kind of development would also strengthen slavery. During the 1790s demand in the British textile industry stimulated the cultivation of cotton in coastal South Carolina and Georgia. The soil and climate were ideal for growing long-staple cotton, a variety whose fibers could be separated easily from its seed by squeezing it through rollers. In the South's upland and interior regions, however, the only cotton that would thrive was the short-staple variety, whose seed stuck so tenaciously to the fibers that rollers crushed the seeds and ruined the fibers. It was as if southerners had discovered gold only to find that they could not mine it. But in 1793 a Connecticut Yankee, Eli Whitney, rescued the South by inventing a cotton gin that successfully separated the fibers of short-staple cotton from the seed. Quickly copied and improved upon by others, Whitney's invention removed a major obstacle to the spread of cotton cultivation. It gave a new lease on life to plantation slavery and undermined the doubts of those who considered slavery economically outmoded.

By the time Thomas Jefferson assumed the presidency in 1801, free blacks had suffered a subtle erosion of their substantial political gains since 1776, and slaves were no closer to freedom. Two vignettes poignantly communicate the plight of African-Americans. By arrangement with her late husband, Martha Washington freed the family's slaves in 1800, a year after George died. But many of the freed blacks remained impoverished and dependent on the Washington estate because Virginia law prohibited the education of blacks and otherwise denied them the opportunities to realize their freedom. Meanwhile, across the Potomac, work was proceeding on the new national capital that would bear the first president's name. Enslaved blacks performed most of thelabor. African-Americans were manifestly losing ground.

CONCLUSION

The United States had survived the perils of birth. First George Washington had steered the country through the initial uncertain years under the new Constitution. But even before his retirement, an outbreak of bitter political strife led to the formation of distinct political parties and threatened the unity of the still fragile new nation. Then a peaceful transfer of power, unprecedented in history, occurred when the Federalists allowed Thomas Jefferson to become president. By 1801 the dangers of civil war and national disintegration had abated, though they had not vanished. Ideological hatreds remained strong, and the West's allegiance to the Union was by no means assured. Racial tensions were growing, not diminishing. It remained to be seen whether Jefferson's liberal version of republicanism could serve as a better philosophy of government than the Federalists' conservative republicanism.

CHRONOLOGY

1787   Pennsylvania Society for the Encouragement of Manufactures and the Useful Arts established.

1789   First Congress convenes in New York.

Washington sworn in as first president.

Judiciary Act of 1789.

French Revolution begins.

Inaugural Commemorative Mug

1790   Alexander Hamilton submits his Report on the Public Credit and Report on a National Bank to Congress.

Treaty of New York.

1791   Bank of the United States is granted a twenty-year charter.

Vermont admitted to the Union.

Bill of Rights ratified.

Slave uprising begins in French colony of Saint Domingue.

Society for the Encouragement of Useful Manufactures founded.

Hamilton submits his Report on Manufactures to Congress.

1792   Washington reelected president.

Kentucky admitted to the Union.

1793   Fugitive Slave Law.

Chisholm v. *Georgia.*

Large-scale exodus of French planters from Saint Domingue to the United States.

France declares war on Britain and Spain.

Washington's Neutrality Proclamation.

Citizen Genet arrives in United States.

Democratic societies established.

1794   Whiskey Rebellion in western Pennsylvania.

A Contemporary Cartoon, "The Exciseman"

1794   General Anthony Wayne's forces rout Indians in the Battle of Fallen Timbers.

1795   Treaty of Greenville.

Jay's Treaty with Britain ratified.

1796   *Hylton* v. *United States.*

Ware v. *Hylton.*

Tennessee admitted to the Union.

Treaty of San Lorenzo (Pinckney's Treaty) ratified.

Washington's Farewell Address.

John Adams elected president.

1798   XYZ Affair.

Alien and Sedition Acts.

Eleventh Amendment to the Constitution ratified.

1798–1799   Virginia and Kentucky Resolutions.

1798–1800   United States fights Quasi-War with France.

1799   Fries Rebellion in Pennsylvania.

1800   Gabriel's Rebellion in Virginia.

Thomas Jefferson elected president.

FOR FURTHER READING

Joyce Appleby, *Capitalism and a New Social Order: The Republican Vision of the 1790s* (1984). A brief, penetrating analysis of Jeffersonian ideology.

Stanley Elkins and Eric McKitrick, *The Age of Federalism: The Early American Republic, 1788–1800* (1993). A magisterial account of politics and diplomacy through the election of 1800.

Richard Hofstadter, *The Idea of a Party System: The Rise of Legitimate Opposition in the United States, 1780–1840* (1969). A classic account of how and why America's founders, originally fearing political parties, came to embrace them.

Drew R. McCoy, *The Elusive Republic: Political Economy in Jeffersonian America* (1980). An insightful portrayal of the influ-

ence of economic considerations on early national political thought.

James M. Smith, *Freedom's Fetters: The Alien and Sedition Laws and American Civil Liberties,* rev. ed. (1966). The most comprehensive study of the country's first great crisis in civil rights.

Laurel Thatcher Ulrich, *A Midwife's Tale: The Life of Martha Ballard, Based on Her Diary, 1785–1812* (1990). A Pulitzer Prize–winning study of a woman's life in rural America.

Anthony F. C. Wallace, *The Death and Rebirth of the Seneca* (1969). An anthropologist's masterful account of the Senecas' devastation during the Revolution and their remarkable cultural recovery afterward.

ADDITIONAL BIBLIOGRAPHY

Early National Society

Ira Berlin, *Slaves Without Masters: The Free Negro in the Antebellum South* (1974); James Essig, *Bonds of Wickedness: American Evangelicals Against Slavery, 1770–1808* (1982); Alfred N. Hunt, *Haiti's Influence on Antebellum America* (1989); Robert McColley, *Slavery and Jeffersonian Virginia* (1964); Gary B. Nash, *Forging Freedom: The Formation of Philadelphia's Black Community, 1720–1840* (1990) and *Race and Revolution* (1991); Curtis P. Nettles, *The Emergence of a National Economy, 1775–1815* (1962); Howard B. Rock, *Artisans of the New Republic: The Tradesmen of New York City in the Age of Jefferson* (1979); George C. Rogers, Jr., *Charleston in the Age of the Pinckneys* (1969); Bernard W. Sheehan, *Seeds of Extinction: Jeffersonian Philanthropy and the American Indian* (1973); Billy G. Smith, *The "Lower Sort": Philadelphia's Laboring People, 1750–1800* (1990); Charles G. Steffen, *The Mechanics of Baltimore: Workers and Politics in the Age of Revolution, 1763–1812* (1984); Alan Taylor, *Liberty Men and Great Proprietors: The Revolutionary Settlement on the Maine Frontier, 1760–1820* (1990); Shane White, *Somewhat More Independent: The End of Slavery in New York City, 1770–1810* (1991).

Diplomatic, Military, and Western Affairs

Harry Ammon, *The Genet Mission* (1973); Colin G. Calloway, *Crown and Calumet: British-Indian Relations, 1783–1815* (1987); Alexander DeConde, *Entangling Alliance: Politics and Diplomacy Under George Washington* (1958), Gregory Evans Dowd, *A Spirited Resistance: The North American Indian Struggle for Unity, 1745–1815* (1992); Felix Gilbert, *To the Farewell Address: Ideas of Early American Foreign Policy* (1961); Reginald Horsman, *The Frontier in the Formative Years, 1783–1815* (1970); Richard H. Kohn, *Eagle and Sword: The Federalists and the Creation of the Military Establishment in America, 1783–1802* (1975); Daniel G. Lang, *Foreign Policy in the Early Republic: The Law of Nations and the Balance of Power* (1985); Bradford Perkins, *The First Rapprochement: England and the United States, 1795–1805* (1955); Charles R. Ritcheson, *Aftermath of Revolution: British Policy Toward the United States, 1783–1795* (1969); Thomas P. Slaughter, *The Whiskey Rebellion: Frontier Epilogue to the American Revolution* (1986); Wiley Sword, *President Washington's Indian War: The Struggle for the Old Northwest, 1790–1795* (1985); Mary K. B. Tachau, *Federal Courts in the Early Republic: Kentucky, 1789–1816* (1978); Richard White, *The Middle Ground: Indians, Empires, and Republics in the Great Lakes Region, 1650–1815* (1991); J. Leitch Wright, *Britain and the American Frontier, 1783–1815* (1975).

Politics

Lance Banning, *The Jeffersonian Persuasion: Evolution of a Party Ideology* (1978); Richard Beeman, *The Old Dominion and the New Nation, 1788–1801* (1972); Rudolph M. Bell, *Party and Faction in American Politics: The House of Representatives, 1789–1801* (1974); Richard Buel, Jr., *Securing the Revolution: Ideology in American Politics, 1789–1815* (1972); E. James Ferguson, *The Power of the Purse: A History of American Public Finance, 1776–1790* (1961); Paul Goodman, *The Democratic Republicans of Massachusetts* (1964); John F. Hoadley, *Origins of American Political Parties, 1789–1803* (1986); Ralph Ketcham, *Presidents Above Party: The First American Presidency, 1789–1829* (1984); John C. Miller, *The Federalist Era, 1789–1801* (1960); Peter S. Onuf, ed., *Jeffersonian Legacies* (1993); Thomas L. Pangle, *The Spirit of Modern Republicanism: The Moral Vision of the American Founders and the Followers of Locke* (1988); Lisle A. Rose, *Prologue to Democracy: The Federalists in the South, 1789–1800* (1968); Robert A. Rutland, *The Birth of the Bill of Rights, 1776–1791* (1955); Bernard Schwartz, *The Great Rights of Mankind* (1977); Donald H. Stewart, *The Opposition Press of the Federalist Period* (1969); Gerald Strouzh, *Alexander Hamilton and the Idea of Republican Government* (1970); Alfred F. Young, *The Democratic Republicans of New York: The Origins, 1763–1797* (1967); John Zvesper, *Political Philosophy and Rhetoric: A Study of the Origins of American Party Politics* (1977).

Biographies

Jacob E. Cooke, *Alexander Hamilton* (1982); Marcus Cunliffe, *George Washington: Man and Monument* (1958); John Mack Faragher, *Daniel Boone: The Life and Legend of an American Pioneer* (1992); John Ferling, *John Adams: A Life* (1992); Ralph Ketcham, *James Madison: A Biography* (1971); Forrest McDonald, *Alexander Hamilton: A Biography* (1979); Dumas Malone, *Jefferson and the Ordeal of Liberty* (1962); Richard B. Morris, *John Jay: The Nation and the Court* (1967); Merrill Peterson, *Thomas Jefferson and the New Nation: A Biography* (1970); Peter Shaw, *The Character of John Adams* (1976).

Portrait of Samuel Chester Reid
by John Wesley Jarvis, 1815

JEFFERSONIANISM AND THE ERA OF GOOD FEELINGS

Arriving at a diplomatic reception in 1803, the British minister to the United States, Anthony Merry, was aghast to find the American president, Thomas Jefferson, "ACTUALLY STANDING IN SLIPPERS DOWN AT THE HEELS." Such "utter slovenliness and indifference to appearances," Merry concluded, could only be "intended as an insult, not to me personally, but to the sovereign I represented." In fact, Jefferson intended no insult. He never paid much attention to his dress and believed that pomp and fanfare had gotten out of hand in the administrations of George Washington and John Adams. Jefferson's casual dress, including his penchant for wearing slippers on public occasions, reflected both his personal preference and his desire to restore "republican simplicity" to the American government. That same desire led Jefferson to walk to his inaugural and then back to his boardinghouse, and later to substitute written messages for personal appearances before Congress.

The appearance of the new capital, Washington (inset), reinforced Merry's impression of Americans' shabbiness. Designed for the traffic of London and the elegance of Versailles, Washington possessed neither in 1800. It could boast of two public buildings of note, the president's mansion and the Capitol, both unfinished and separated by a mile and a half of swampy terrain. The best that could be said for the place, a British visitor observed, was that the partridges nesting around the Capitol's wall provided excellent shooting.

Washington's spare arrangements mirrored conditions in the young nation. In 1800 the two most populous states, Virginia and Pennsylvania, contained fewer than fourteen inhabitants per square mile. At a time when London reported more than a million inhabitants and Paris more than half a million, no American city held even seventy thousand people. The poor quality or utter lack of roads forced Americans to live very isolated from each other. Stagecoaches running between Baltimore and Washington, for example, had to pass through a virtually trackless forest. To get to Washington from Monticello, his home in Virginia, President Jefferson had to cross five rivers that lacked bridges.

This isolation ensured that the political horizons of most Americans were limited by the physical boundaries of their own towns or villages. Republicans and Federalists clashed venomously in Washington, but in many rural areas, neither party aroused intense support. The outgoing president, John Adams, had not seen himself as the leader of a political party. The incoming president, Thomas Jefferson, did play the role of party leader and in this respect was a more modern figure than Adams. But neither Jefferson's Republicans nor the rival Federalists had any effective grass roots organization. However sharp the clashes between Republicans and Federalists in Washington, national issues only occasionally concerned ordinary Americans. Women, slaves, and the propertyless were legally barred from voting, and even those citizens who were eligible to vote often found national issues remote and uninteresting. Few voters ever laid eyes on a president. Jefferson, for example, had not been in New England since 1784, and he never did venture west of the Appalachian Mountains or south of Virginia.

Despite its deeply ingrained localism, America was to experience the most extraordinary national events between 1800 and 1820. In swift succession, the United States would double its land area; survive a bizarre scheme by a former vice president to divide the Union; stop all its trade with Europe in an effort to avoid war, and then go to war anyway and nearly lose; conclude a peace more favorable than it had a right to expect; and almost disintegrate in a battle over statehood for Missouri while simultaneously profiting from European power concessions that would extend its territorial claims from the Atlantic to the Pacific.

The intrusion of so dizzying a sequence of events upon a society known for its sleepy provinciality was not altogether accidental. Because communications were poor, the age proved congenial to adventurers like Jefferson's vice president, Aaron Burr, who hatched wild conspiracies with the hope of succeeding before his plans became common knowledge. Furthermore, the strength of local attachments among the common people somewhat insulated leaders like Jefferson and his successor, James Madison, from their constituents. This insulation, in turn, enabled Jefferson and Madison to view politics on a grand scale. In their eyes, politics was more a process for transforming philosophical ideas into realities than for accommodating the special needs of diverse groups.

America's newness also contributed to the philosophical or ideological cast of its politics. Because there had never before been a transfer of political power from a defeated party to a victorious party, no one was sure how the Republicans would behave in office or what would become of the Federalists. The absence of precedents that might have quietly settled certain issues meant that seemingly minor questions such as replacement of Federalist officeholders became occasions for major philosophical clashes between the Republicans and the Federalists. In sum, one of the tasks that faced Jefferson and Madison was to devise and gain popular acceptance of ground rules to guide the operations of republican government.

THE AGE OF JEFFERSON

Although basically a dispassionate man, Thomas Jefferson aroused deep emotions in others. His admirers saw him as a vigilant defender of popular liberty, an aristocrat who trusted the people. His detractors, pointing to his doubts about some Christian doctrines and to his early defense of the French Revolution, portrayed him as an infidel and a frenzied radical. Jefferson had so many facets that it was hard not to misunderstand him. Trained in law, he spent much of his prepresidential life in public office—as governor of Virginia, secretary of state under Washington, and vice president under John Adams. His interests included the violin, architecture, languages, and science. He designed his own mansion, Monticello, in Virginia; studied Latin, Greek, French, Italian, Anglo-Saxon, and several Native American languages; and served for nearly twenty years as president of the American Philosophical Society, the nation's first and foremost scientific organization. He viewed himself as a stronger friend of equality than either Washington or Adams; yet he owned more than two hundred slaves.

History convinced Jefferson that republics collapsed from within, not from without. Hostile neighbors notwithstanding, the real threat to freedom was posed by governments that progressively undermined popular liberty. Taxes, standing armies, and corrupt officials had made governments the masters, rather than the servants, of the people. Anyone who doubted this lesson of history needed only to look at the French Revolution; Jefferson had greeted it with hope and then watched in dismay as Napoleon Bonaparte assumed despotic power in 1799.

To prevent the United States from sinking into tyranny, Jefferson advocated that state governments retain considerable authority. He reasoned that in a vast republic marked by strong local attachments, state

The World of Thomas Jefferson at Monticello
Jefferson spent much of his adult life building and remodeling Monticello, his "simple and elegant" Virginia mansion, and he died there on July 4, 1826, fifty years to the day after the signing of the Declaration of Independence. Preferring the useful to the showy, he omitted the grand staircase evident in other mansions, designed the house to appear smaller than it actually was, and filled it with labor-saving gadgets.

governments were more immediately responsive to the popular will than was the government in Washington. He also believed that popular liberty required popular virtue. For republican theorists like Jefferson, virtue consisted of a disposition to place the public good ahead of one's private interests and to exercise vigilance to keep governments from growing out of control. To Jefferson, the most vigilant and virtuous people were educated farmers, who were accustomed to act and think with sturdy independence. The least vigilant were the inhabitants of cities. Jefferson regarded cities as breeding grounds for mobs and as menaces to liberty. When the people "get piled upon one another in large cities, as in Europe," he wrote, "they will become corrupt as in Europe."

Despite his deep philosophical beliefs, Jefferson was not impractical. Of all the charges leveled at him by contemporaries, the most inaccurate was that he was a dreamy philosopher incapable of governing. "What is practicable," he wrote, "must often control pure theory." He studied science not because he liked to ponder abstract puzzles but because he believed that every scientific advance would increase human happiness. All true knowledge was useful knowledge. This practical cast of mind revealed itself both in his inventions—he designed an improved plow and a gadget for duplicating letters—and in his presidential agenda.

Jefferson's "Revolution"

Jefferson described his election as a revolution, but the revolution he sought was to restore the country to the liberty and tranquillity it had known before Alexander Hamilton's economic program and John Adams's Alien and Sedition Acts: to reverse the drift into despotism that he had detected during the 1790s. One alarming sign of this drift was the growth of the national debt by $10 million under the Federalists. Jefferson and his secretary of the treasury, the Swiss-born Albert Gallatin, objected to the debt on both political and economic grounds. Hamilton had argued that by giving creditors a financial stake in the health of the federal government, a national debt would strengthen that government. Jefferson and Gallatin disagreed. Merely to pay the interest on the debt, there would have to be taxes, which Jefferson and Gallatin opposed for many of the same reasons that they opposed the debt. Taxes would suck money from industrious farmers, the backbone of the Republic, and put it in the hands of wealthy creditors, parasites who lived off interest

Explosion of the *Intrepid*
In September 1804 the American fireship Intrepid, *loaded with powder and intending to penetrate Tripoli harbor and explode enemy ships, blew up before reaching its target, killing Captain Richard Somers and his crew. Seven months earlier, commanded by Lieutenant Stephen Decatur, the* Intrepid *had destroyed the American frigate* Philadelphia, *which had fallen into Tripolitan hands. Britain's Lord Nelson reportedly described Decatur's exploit as "the most bold and daring act of the age."*

payments. Increased tax revenues might also tempt the government to create a standing army, always a threat to liberty.

Jefferson and Gallatin induced Congress to repeal most internal taxes, and they slashed expenditures by closing some embassies overseas and reducing the army. The navy was a different matter. In 1801 Jefferson ordered a naval squadron into action in the Mediterranean against the so-called Tripolitan (or Barbary) pirates of North Africa. For centuries, the Muslim rulers of Tripoli, Morocco, Tunis, and Algiers had solved their own budgetary problems by engaging in piracy and extorting tribute in exchange for protection; seamen whom they captured were held for ransom or sold into slavery. Most European powers handed over the fees demanded, but Jefferson calculated that going to war would be cheaper than paying high tribute to maintain peace. Although suffering its share of reverses during the ensuing fighting, the United States did not come away empty-handed. In 1805 it was able to conclude a peace treaty with Tripoli for roughly half the price that it had been paying annually for protection.

Jefferson was not a pacifist and would continue to use the navy to gain respect for the American flag, but he and Gallatin placed economy ahead of military preparedness. Gallatin calculated that the nation could be freed of debt in sixteen years if administrations held the line on expenditures. In Europe, the Peace of Amiens (1802) brought a temporary halt to the hostilities between Britain and France that had threatened American shipping in the 1790s, and buoyed Jefferson's confidence that minimal military preparedness was a sound policy. The Peace of Amiens, he wrote, "removes the only danger we have to fear. We can now proceed without risks in demolishing useless structures of expense, lightening the burdens of our constituents, and fortifying the principles of free government." This may have been wishful thinking, but it rested on a sound economic calculation, for the vast territory of the United States could never be secured from attack without astronomical expense.

Jefferson and the Judiciary

In his inaugural address, Jefferson reminded Americans that their agreements were more basic than their disagreements. "We have called by different name brothers of the same principle," he proclaimed. "We are all republicans; we are all federalists." He was enough of a realist to know that the political conflict would not evaporate, but he sincerely hoped to allay fear of the Republican party and to draw moderate Federalists over to his side. There was a chance of success. He and John Adams had once been friends. The two shared many views, and each was suspicious of Hamilton. But the eventual reconciliation between Adams and Jefferson (they renewed their friendship after Jefferson's presidency), and more generally between Federalists and Republicans, would not occur during Jefferson's administration, largely because of bitter feelings over the composition and control of the judiciary.

In theory, Jefferson believed that talent and virtue rather than political affiliation were the primary qualifications for judgeships. In theory, Federalists believed the same, but they rarely had detected either talent or virtue among Republicans, and in 1800 not a single Republican sat on the federal judiciary. For Republicans, the crowning blow was the Federalist-sponsored Judiciary Act, passed on February 27, 1801. On the surface, this law had a nonpartisan purpose. By creating sixteen new federal judgeships, the act promised to relieve Supreme Court justices of the burden of riding far from Washington to hear cases. But the act contained several features that struck Jefferson as objectionable, including a provision to reduce the number of justices on the Supreme Court from six to five. This provision threatened both to strip Jefferson of his first opportunity to appoint a justice and to perpetuate Federalist domination of the judiciary.

Recalling the federal courts' zealousness in enforcing the Alien and Sedition Acts, and dismayed by the absence of Republicans on the federal judiciary, Jefferson saw in the Judiciary Act of 1801 a confirmation of his fears that the Federalists were retreating into the judiciary as a stronghold, "and from that battery all the works of Republicanism are to be beaten down and erased." Any lingering doubts Jefferson might have had about Federalist intentions were swept away by the actions of outgoing president John Adams during his last days in office. Between December 12, 1800, the day on which Adams's defeat in the election became clear, and March 4, 1801, the date of Jefferson's inauguration, Adams appointed several last-minute, or "midnight," judges. All federal judges appointed by Adams under provisions of the Judiciary Act were prominent Federalists. Some had been defeated for office during the election of 1800. One had captained a loyalist regiment during the Revolution, and three were brothers or brothers-in-law of John Marshall, the Federalist chief justice who was also the reputed author of the Judiciary Act of 1801.

Some radical Jeffersonians believed that judges should be elected, but Jefferson himself had no quarrel with the practice of appointing judges to serve during "good behavior" (normally for life); indeed, he thought that an independent judiciary was vital to the success of republican government. But the Federalists seemed to be turning the judiciary into an arm of their party, and in defiance of the popular will. Ironically, it was not the midnight appointments that Adams actually made but one that he left unfinished that stiffened Jefferson's resolve to seek repeal of the Judiciary Act. On his last day in office, Adams appointed an obscure Federalist, William Marbury, as justice of the peace in the District of Columbia but then failed to deliver Marbury's commission before midnight. With Jefferson in office, the new secretary of state, James Madison, refused to release the commission. Marbury petitioned the Supreme Court for a writ of mandamus,* ordering Madison to make the delivery. Chief Justice Marshall then called on Madison to show cause why he should not be compelled to hand over the commission. Although the Supreme Court did not decide the case of *Marbury* v. *Madison* until 1803, Jefferson detected in Marshall's maneuvers the early signs of still another Federalist scheme to use the judiciary to advance partisan interests, and in 1802 he won congressional repeal of the Judiciary Act. The Federalists were in despair. The Constitution, moaned Federalist senator Gouverneur Morris, "is dead. It is dead."

As John Marshall would soon demonstrate, however, the Federalist judiciary was alive and brimming with energy. Like Jefferson, Marshall was a Virginian, but he was the son of an ordinary farmer, not an aristocrat. Marshall's service in the Continental Army during the Revolution had instilled in him (as in Alexander Hamilton) a burning attachment to the Union rather than to any state, and in the 1790s he had embraced the Federalist party. In 1803 Marshall's long-awaited decision in *Marbury* v. *Madison* came down. From the perspective of constitutional history, Marshall's decision would have immense significance, for in it he declared an act of Congress unconstitutional. Specifically, he denied Marbury's petition for a writ of mandamus (to force Madison to deliver his commission) on grounds that Congress had exceeded its constitutional authority when, in the Judiciary Act of 1789, it had granted the Court the authority to issue such a writ. This was the first time the Court declared an act of Congress unconstitutional. It would not do so again until 1857, but the justices had set an important precedent.

---

*Mandamus: an order from a higher court commanding that a specified action be taken.

John Marshall, *by Chester Harding*
*In his three decades as chief justice of the Supreme
Court, Marshall greatly strengthened the power of both
the Court and the national government, each of which
he thought vital to preserving the intrinsic rights of life,
liberty, and property.*

Marshall's decision, however, had a different significance for Jefferson. Along with most mainstream Republicans, Jefferson thought that the courts did have a right to engage in judicial review (that is, to declare legislative acts unconstitutional). As far as judicial review went, Jefferson merely held that courts had no *exclusive* right of review; other branches of the government should also have the right to review the constitutionality of measures before them. Since Marshall's decision in *Marbury* did not assert that courts alone could declare laws unconstitutional, Jefferson

had no quarrel with the principle of judicial review as Marshall advanced it. What infuriated Jefferson was that Marshall used part of his decision to lecture Madison on his moral duty (as opposed to his legal obligation) to have delivered the commission to Marbury. This gratuitous lecture—really a lecture to Jefferson as Madison's superior—struck Jefferson as another example of Federalist partisanship with respect to the judiciary.

While the *Marbury* decision was brewing, the Republicans had already taken the offensive against the judiciary by moving to impeach (charge with wrongdoing) two Federalist judges, John Pickering of the New Hampshire District Court and Samuel Chase of the U.S. Supreme Court. The particulars of the two cases differed. Pickering was an insane alcoholic who behaved in a bizarre manner in court. In one case, he decided against the prosecution before hearing any of its witnesses and then taunted the district attorney that even if he could present forty thousand witnesses, "they will not alter the decree." Chase, a notoriously partisan Federalist, had rigorously enforced the Sedition Act of 1798 and had jailed several Republican editors, including one whom Jefferson had befriended. To Republicans, Chase was the devil incarnate; all of them knew that Chase's name formed the correct ending of a popular ditty:

> *Cursed of thy father, scum of all that's base,*
> *Thy sight is odious, and thy name is . . .*

Despite these differing details, the two cases raised the same issue. The Constitution provided that federal judges could be removed solely by impeachment, which could be considered only in cases of "Treason, Bribery and other high Crimes and Misdemeanors." Was impeachment an appropriate way to get rid of judges who were insane or excessively partisan? Despite misgivings among Federalists and some Republicans about charging an obviously insane man with crimes and misdemeanors, the Senate voted to convict Pickering on March 12, 1804. That same day, the House of Representatives voted to indict Chase. John Randolph, one of Jefferson's supporters in Congress, so completely botched the prosecution of Chase that he failed to obtain the necessary two-thirds majority for conviction on any of the charges. But even if Randolph had done a competent job, Chase might still have gained acquittal, because moderate Republicans were coming to doubt whether impeachment was a solution to the issue of judicial partisanship.

Chase's acquittal ended Jefferson's skirmishes with the judiciary. Although his radical followers continued to attack the principles of judicial review and an appointed judiciary as undemocratic, Jefferson objected to neither. He merely challenged Federalist use of judicial power for political goals. Yet there was always a gray area between law and politics. Federalists did not necessarily see a conflict between protecting the Constitution and advancing their party's cause. Nor did they use their control of the federal judiciary to undo Jefferson's "revolution" of 1800. The Marshall court, for example, upheld the constitutionality of the repeal of the Judiciary Act of 1801. For his part, Jefferson never proposed to impeach Marshall. In supporting the impeachments of Pickering and Chase, Jefferson was trying to make the judiciary more responsive to the popular will by challenging a pair of judges whose behavior had been outrageous. No other federal judge would be impeached for more than fifty years.

The Louisiana Purchase

Jefferson's goal of avoiding foreign entanglements would remain beyond reach as long as European powers had large landholdings in North America. In 1800 Spain, a weak and declining power, controlled East and West Florida as well as the vast Louisiana Territory. The latter alone was equal in size to the United States at that time. In the Treaty of San Ildefonso (October 1, 1800), Spain ceded the Louisiana Territory to France, which was fast emerging under Napoleon Bonaparte as the world's foremost military power. It took six months for news of the treaty to reach Jefferson and Madison but only a few minutes for them to grasp its significance.

Jefferson had long dreamed of an "empire of liberty" extending across North America and even into South America, an empire to be gained not by military conquest but by the inevitable expansion of the free and virtuous American people. An enfeebled Spain constituted no real obstacle to this expansion. As long as Louisiana had belonged to Spain, time was on the side of the United States. But Bonaparte's capacity for mischief was boundless. What if Bonaparte and the British reached an agreement that gave England a free hand in the Mediterranean and France a license to ex-

pand into North America? Then the United States would be sandwiched between the British in Canada and the French in Louisiana. What if Britain refused to cooperate with France? In that case, Britain might use its naval power to seize Louisiana before the French took control, thereby trapping the United States between British forces in the South and West as well as in the North and West.

Although Americans feared these two possibilities, Bonaparte actually had a different goal. During the 1790s he had dreamed of a French empire in the Middle East, but his defeat by the British fleet at the Battle of the Nile in 1798 had blasted this dream. Now Bonaparte devised a plan for a new French empire, this one bordering the Caribbean and the Gulf of Mexico. The fulcrum of the empire was to be the Caribbean island of Santo Domingo (today comprising Haiti and the Dominican Republic). He wanted to use Louisiana not as a base from which to threaten the United States but as a breadbasket for an essentially Caribbean empire. His immediate task was to subdue Santo Domingo, where a bloody slave revolution in the 1790s had resulted by 1800 in the takeover of the government by the black statesman Toussaint L'Ouverture (see Chapter 7). Bonaparte dispatched an army to reassert French control and to reestablish slavery, but yellow fever and fierce resistance on the part of former slaves combined to destroy the army.

As a slaveholder himself, Jefferson tacitly approved Bonaparte's attempted reconquest of Santo Domingo; as a nationalist, he continued to fear a French presence in Louisiana. This fear intensified in October 1802, when the Spanish colonial administrator in New Orleans issued an order prohibiting the deposit of American produce in New Orleans for transshipment to foreign lands. Because American farmers west of the Appalachians depended on New Orleans as a port for the cash crops that they shipped down the Mississippi River, the order was a major provocation to Americans. The order had in fact originated in Spain, but most Americans assumed that it had come from Bonaparte, who, although he now owned Louisiana, had not yet taken possession of it. An alarmed Jefferson wrote to a friend that "the day that France takes possession of N. Orleans . . . we must marry ourselves to the British fleet and nation."

The combination of France's failure to subdue Santo Domingo and the termination of American rights

The Louisiana Purchase and the Exploration of the West
The explorations of Lewis and Clark demonstrated the vast extent of the area purchased from France.

to deposit produce in New Orleans stimulated two crucial decisions, one by Jefferson and the other by Bonaparte, that ultimately resulted in the United States' purchase of Louisiana. First, Jefferson nominated James Monroe and Robert R. Livingston to negotiate with France for the purchase of New Orleans and as much of the Floridas as possible. (Because West Florida had repeatedly changed hands between France, Britain, and Spain, no one was sure who owned it.) Meanwhile, Bonaparte, mindful of his military failure in Santo Domingo and of American opposition to French control of Louisiana, had concluded that his projected Caribbean empire was not worth the cost. In addition,

he planned to recommence the war in Europe and needed cash. Accordingly, he decided to sell *all* of Louisiana. After some haggling between the American commissioners and Bonaparte's minister, Talleyrand, a price of $15 million was settled upon. (One-fourth of the total represented an agreement by the United States to pay French debts owed to American citizens.) For this sum the United States gained an immense, uncharted territory west of the Mississippi River. No one knew its exact size; Talleyrand merely observed that the bargain was noble. But the purchase virtually doubled the area of the United States at a cost, omitting interest, of 13½¢ an acre.

Because Jefferson's commissioners had exceeded their instructions, however, the president had doubts about the constitutionality of the purchase. No provision of the Constitution explicitly gave the government authority to acquire new territory or to incorporate it into the Union. Jefferson therefore drafted a constitutional amendment that authorized the acquisition of territory and prohibited the American settlement of Louisiana for an indefinite period. Fearing that an immediate and headlong rush to settle the area would lead to the destruction of the Native Americans and to an orgy of land speculation, Jefferson wanted to control development so that Americans could advance "compactly as we multiply." Few Republicans, however, shared Jefferson's constitutional reservations, and the president himself soon began to worry that ratification of an amendment would take too long and that Bonaparte might in the meantime change his mind about selling Louisiana. Consequently, he quietly dropped the amendment and submitted the treaty to the Senate, where it was quickly ratified.

It is easy to make too much of Jefferson's dilemma over Louisiana. He was wedded to strict construction of the Constitution, believing that the Constitution should be interpreted according to its letter. But he was also committed to the principle of establishing an "empire of liberty." Doubling the size of the Republic would guarantee land for American farmers, the backbone of the Republic and the true guardians of liberty. Like the principle of states' rights to which Jefferson also subscribed, strict construction was not an end in itself but a means to promote republican liberty. If that end could be achieved by some way other than strict construction, so be it. In addition, Jefferson was alert to practical considerations. Most Federalists opposed the Louisiana Purchase on the grounds that it would decrease the relative importance of their strongholds on the eastern seaboard. As the leader of the Republican party, Jefferson saw no reason to hand the Federalists an issue by dallying over ratification of the treaty.

The Lewis and Clark Expedition

Louisiana dazzled Jefferson's imagination. Here was an immense territory about which Americans knew virtually nothing. No one was sure of its western boundary. A case could be made for the Pacific Ocean, but Jefferson was content to claim that Louisiana extended at least to the mountains west of the Missis-

sippi. No one, however, was certain of the exact location of these mountains, because few Americans had ever seen them. Jefferson himself had never been more than fifty miles west of his home in Virginia. Thus the Louisiana Purchase was both a bargain and a surprise package.

Even before the acquisition of Louisiana, Jefferson had planned an exploratory expedition; picked its leader, his personal secretary and fellow Virginian Lieutenant Meriwether Lewis; and sent him to Philadelphia for a crash course in sciences such as zoology, astronomy, and botany that were relevant to exploration. Jefferson instructed Lewis to trace the Missouri River to its source, cross the western highlands, and follow the best water route to the Pacific. In requesting congressional funding for the expedition, Jefferson stressed the commercial possibilities that it might uncover; along the line of the Missouri and beyond, the Indians' trade in pelts might be diverted from Canada to the south. But the advance of scientific knowledge probably had a higher priority for Jefferson. His specific instructions to Lewis focused on the need to obtain accurate measurements of latitude and longitude; to gather information about Native American languages and customs; and to learn about climate, plants, birds, reptiles, insects, and volcanoes.

Setting forth from St. Louis in May 1804, Lewis, his second-in-command William Clark, and about fifty others followed the Missouri River and then the Snake and Columbia rivers. In the Dakota country, Lewis and Clark hired a French-Canadian fur trader, Toussaint Charbonneau, as a guide and interpreter. Slow-witted and inclined to panic in crises, Charbonneau proved a mixed blessing, but his wife, Sacajawea, who accompanied him on the trip, made up for his failings. A Shoshone and probably no more than sixteen years old in 1804, Sacajawea had been stolen by a rival tribe and then claimed by Charbonneau, perhaps in settlement for a gambling debt. When first encountered by Lewis and Clark, she had just given birth to a son; indeed, her infant's presence helped to reassure Native American tribes of the expedition's peaceful intent. Additionally, Sacajawea showed Lewis and Clark how to forage for wild artichokes and other plants, often their only food, by digging into the dens where rodents stored them. Clutching her baby, she rescued most of the expedition's scientific instruments after a storm capsized one of its boats on the Missouri River.

William Clark and Meriwether Lewis,
by Charles Willson Peale Clark, the brother of the famed Indian fighter George Rogers Clark, fought at the Battle of Fallen Timbers. He later became the governor of Missouri and an outspoken advocate of the interests of the Native Americans, whom he had opposed in his youth. Lewis grew up near Jefferson's Virginia home and later served as his personal secretary.

Plains Pipe Bowl
Instructed by Jefferson to acquaint themselves with the Indians' "ordinary occupations in the arts," Lewis and Clark collected this Lakota sacred pipe, whose red stone symbolized the flesh and blood of all people and whose smoke represented the breath that carries prayers to the Creator. Considering pipes sacred objects, Indians used them to seal contracts and treaties and to perform ceremonial healing.

The group finally reached the Pacific Ocean in November 1805 and then returned to St. Louis, but not before collecting a mass of scientific information, including the disturbing fact that more than three hundred miles of mountains separated the Missouri from the Columbia. It also produced a sprinkling of tall tales, many of which Jefferson believed, about gigantic Indians, soil too rich to grow trees, and a mountain composed of salt. Jefferson's political opponents railed that he would soon be reporting the discovery of a molasses-filled lake. For all the ridicule, the expedition stimulated rather than dampened interest in the West.

The Election of 1804

Jefferson's acquisition of Louisiana left the Federalists dispirited and without a popular national issue. As the election of 1804 approached, the main threat to Jefferson was not the Federalist party but his own vice president, Aaron Burr. In 1800 Burr had tried to take advantage of a tie in the electoral college to gain the

off

The Election of 1804

Candidates	Parties	Electoral Vote
THOMAS JEFFERSON	Democratic-Republican	162
Charles C. Pinckney	Federalist	14

presidency, a betrayal in the eyes of most Republicans, who assumed that he had been nominated for the vice presidency. Although the adoption in 1804 of the Twelfth Amendment, which required separate and distinct ballots in the electoral college for the presidency and vice presidency, put an end to the possibility of an electoral tie for the presidency, it did not put an end to Burr. Between 1801 and 1804, Burr entered into enough intrigues with the Federalists to convince the Republicans that it would be unsafe to renominate him for the vice presidency. The Republicans in Congress rudely dumped Burr in favor of George Clinton. Without a hope of success, the Federalists nominated Charles C. Pinckney and Rufus King and then watched their candidates go down in complete and crushing defeat in the election. The Federalists carried only two states, failing to hold even Massachusetts. Jefferson's overwhelming victory brought his first term to a fitting close; between 1801 and 1804, the United States had doubled its territory, taken steps to pay off its debt, and remained at peace. In short, Jefferson basked in the sun of success.

THE GATHERING STORM

The sky was not cloudless for long. In gaining control of Louisiana, the United States had benefited from the preoccupation of European powers with their own struggles. The nation would again benefit from this preoccupation between 1814 and 1823. But between 1803 and 1814, the renewal of the Napoleonic wars in Europe turned the United States into a pawn in a chess game played by others and helped to make Jefferson's second term far less successful than his first. In fact, the very success of his first administration contained the germs of problems that would plague his second term. As long as the two parties could compete on a more or less even basis, as in the election of 1800,

leaders within each party could demand unity as requisite for victory. But as the Federalist opposition weakened, unity among Republicans became less important, and they increasingly fell victim to internal squabbles.

Jefferson's Coalition Fragments

For the moment, the election of 1804 eliminated the Federalists as a force in national politics. More troubling to Republicans than Federalist opposition was factionalism within their own party, much of it the product of the inventive and perverse mind of Aaron Burr. Burr suffered a string of reverses in 1804. After being denied renomination as vice president, he entered into a series of intrigues with a faction of despairing and extreme (or "High") Federalists in New England. Led by Senator Timothy Pickering of Massachusetts, these High Federalists plotted to sever the Union by forming a pro-British "Northern Confederacy," composed of Nova Scotia (part of British-owned Canada), New England, New York, and even Pennsylvania. Although most Federalists disdained the plot, Pickering and others settled on Burr as their leader and helped him gain the Federalist nomination for the governorship of New York. Alexander Hamilton, who had thwarted Burr's plans for the presidency in 1800 by throwing his weight behind Jefferson, now foiled Burr a second time by allowing the publication of his "despicable opinion" of Burr. Defeated by a Republican in the election for New York's governor, Burr challenged Hamilton to a duel and mortally wounded him at Weehawken, New Jersey, on July 11, 1804.

Under indictment in two states for his murder of Hamilton, Burr, still vice president, now hatched a scheme so bold that it gained momentum initially because his political opponents seriously doubted that even Burr was capable of such machinations. He allied himself with the unsavory general James Wilkinson, the military governor of the Louisiana Territory. Wilkinson had been on Spain's payroll intermittently as a secret agent since the 1780s. Together, Burr and Wilkinson conspired to separate the western states into an independent confederacy south of the Ohio River. In addition, Wilkinson had long entertained the idea of an American conquest of Mexico, and Burr now added West Florida as a possible target. They presented these ideas to westerners as having the covert support of the administration, to the British as a way to attack Spanish-owned Mexico and West Florida, and to the Spanish (removing Mexico and West Florida as targets) as a way to divide up the United States.

Jefferson, who described Burr as a crooked gun that never shot straight, let the plot germinate for more than a year before taking action. By the fall of 1806, Burr and about sixty followers had left their staging ground, an island in the upper Ohio River, and were making their way down the Ohio and Mississippi rivers to join Wilkinson at Natchez. But Wilkinson was not there to greet Burr and his several boatloads of conspirators. Recognizing that Jefferson was now moving against Burr and that the British were uninterested in supporting the plot, Wilkinson wrote to Jefferson to report the conspiracy and then took refuge in New Orleans, where he proclaimed himself the most loyal of the president's followers.

A few weeks later, in October 1806, Jefferson officially denounced the conspiracy. Now Burr panicked. He tried to escape to West Florida but was intercepted; brought back to Richmond, he was put on trial for treason. Chief Justice Marshall presided at the trial and charged the jury that the prosecution had to prove not merely that Burr had treasonable intentions but also that he had committed treasonable acts, a virtually impossible task inasmuch as the conspiracy had fallen apart before Burr accomplished what he had planned. Jefferson was furious, but Marshall was merely following the clear wording of the Constitution, which deliberately made treason difficult to prove. The jury returned a verdict of "not proved," which Marshall entered as "not guilty." Still under indictment for his murder of Hamilton, Burr fled to Europe, where he tried to interest Napoleon in making peace with Britain as a prelude to a proposed Anglo-French invasion of the United States and Mexico. He returned to the United States in 1812 and, in keeping with his reputation as a womanizer, fathered two illegitimate children in his seventies and was divorced for adultery at eighty. Perhaps the most puzzling man in American history, he died in 1836.

Jefferson and the Quids

Besides the Burr conspiracy, Jefferson faced a challenge from a group of Republicans known as the Quids,* who were led by the president's fellow Vir-

ginian John Randolph. A man of abounding eccentricities and acidic wit, Randolph stood squarely in the tradition of the "country" ideology of the 1770s, the set of beliefs that celebrated the honest wisdom of the farmer against the corruption of rulers and "court" hangers-on and that warned against the tendency of all governments to encroach on liberty. Jefferson had started out with the same beliefs but had gradually recognized their limitations. Country ideology was a stance for those out of power, an ideology of opposition rather than governance. In gaining political power, Jefferson had learned to compromise. Randolph, in contrast, remained frozen in an earlier time period. He denounced every change as a decline from the purity of 1776 and once said that he would throw all politicians to the dogs if he had less respect for dogs.

After serving in the House of Representatives between 1801 and 1805, Randolph turned on Jefferson. First, he blasted Jefferson for backing a compromise in the Yazoo land scandal. In 1795 the Georgia legislature had sold the huge "Yazoo" tract (35 million acres comprising most of present-day Alabama and Mississippi) for a fraction of its value to four land companies that had bribed virtually the entire legislature. Responding to public outrage, the next legislature canceled the sale, but not before many investors had purchased land. The scandal posed a moral challenge for Jefferson because some of the purchasers, knowing nothing of the bribery, had bought the land in good faith. It presented a political challenge, too, because some of the buyers were northerners whom Jefferson hoped to woo to the Republican party. In 1803 a federal commission awarded 5 million acres to Yazoo investors as a compromise. For Randolph, the compromise was itself a scandal—further evidence of the decay of republican virtue.

Randolph next collided with Jefferson over the president's request for a congressional appropriation to purchase East and West Florida from Spain. Characteristically, Randolph raged less at the idea of obtaining the Floridas than at Jefferson's apparent act of deception in requesting money for extraordinary diplomatic expenses without officially informing Congress of the real object of the expenditures. In fact, Jefferson had privately informed members of Congress, including Randolph, of his plans for the purchase; but to Randolph, it all seemed like another betrayal of virtue.

---

*Quid: a name taken from the Latin *tertium quid,* or "third thing"; roughly, a dissenter.

The Suppression of American Trade

Burr's acquittal and Randolph's taunts shattered the aura of invincibility that had surrounded Jefferson after the Louisiana Purchase and the election of 1804. Now foreign affairs began to pose an even sharper challenge to his administration. In 1803 the Peace of Amiens collapsed. Britain and France resumed their war. As a neutral, the United States prospered at Britain's expense. American vessels carried sugar and coffee from French and Spanish colonies in the Caribbean to Europe. This trade not only provided Napoleon with supplies but also drove down the price of sugar and coffee from the British West Indies by adding to the glut of these commodities on the world markets. Understandably, the British concluded that American prosperity was the cause of Britain's economic difficulties.

The basis of the American prosperity was the re-export trade—an American adaptation to the British Rule of 1756, which stated that trade closed in time of peace could not be opened in time of war. For example, in peacetime, France usually restricted to French ships the transportation of products such as sugar from the French West Indies. According to the Rule of 1756, the ships of a neutral country such as the United States could not replace French ships as carriers now that the war between France and Britain made French vessels fair game for the British navy. The American response to the Rule of 1756 was the "broken voyage." American vessels would carry produce from the Spanish and French West Indies to an American port, unload it and pass it through customs, then reload it and reexport it to Europe as *American* produce. Between 1795 and 1805, the British tolerated broken voyages but thereafter charted a new course. Seeking now to strangle French commerce as well as to defeat Napoleon's armies, Britain pursued total war against France. A sign of the new policy was a British court's decision in the 1805 *Essex* case declaring broken voyages illegal.

The British followed the *Essex* decision in May 1806 with the first of several trade regulations known as Orders in Council, which established a blockade of French-controlled ports on the continent of Europe. Napoleon responded with his so-called Continental System, a series of counterproclamations that ships obeying British regulations would be subject to seizure by France. In effect, this Anglo-French war of decrees outlawed virtually all U.S. trade: if an American ship complied with British regulations, it became a French target, and vice versa.

Both Britain and France seized American ships, but British seizures were far more humiliating to Americans. France was a weaker naval power than Britain; much of the French fleet had been destroyed by the British at the Battle of Trafalgar in October 1805. Accordingly, most of France's seizures of American ships occurred in European ports where American ships had been lured by Napoleon's often inconsistent enforcement of his Continental System. In contrast, British warships hovered just beyond the American coast. Off New York, for example, the Royal Navy stopped and searched virtually every American vessel. At times, U.S. ships had to line up a few miles from the American coast to be searched by the Royal Navy.

Impressment

On top of these provocations, the British added that of impressment. At issue was the seizure from American merchant ships, and the subsequent pressing into service, of purported British sailors who had deserted from the Royal Navy.

British sailors had good reason to be discontented with the navy. Aside from the fact that discipline on the Royal Navy's "floating hells" was often brutal, wages were much lower than on American ships. The pay of an able-bodied seaman on a British ship was only around seven dollars a month, compared to twenty-five to thirty-five dollars a month on American ships. As a result, at a time when war intensified Britain's need for sailors, the Royal Navy suffered a high rate of desertion to U.S. ships; for example, in 1807 the American frigate *Constitution* carried a crew of 419 men, of whom 149 were British subjects.

Impressed sailors led harrowing lives that included frequent escapes and recaptures. One seaman suffered impressment on eleven separate occasions; another, on the verge of his third recapture, drowned himself rather than spend another day in the Royal Navy. The British practice of impressment was not only cruel to individuals but galling to American pride, because many deserters from the Royal Navy had acquired American naturalization papers and become American citizens. The British impressed these men anyway on the principle that once a Briton, always a Briton. At times, the British also impressed American-born citizens, despite documentation proving their

American birth. Between 1803 and 1812, the British impressed over six thousand American citizens. Although impressment did less damage to the American economy than the seizure of ships, it was more humiliating.

Any doubts Americans had about British arrogance evaporated in June 1807 when a British warship, HMS *Leopard,* patrolling off Hampton Roads, Virginia, attacked an unsuspecting American frigate, USS *Chesapeake,* and forced it to surrender. The British then boarded the vessel and seized four supposed deserters. One, a genuine deserter, was later hanged; the other three were former Britons, now American citizens, who had "deserted" only from impressment. Even the British had never before asserted their right to seize deserters off government ships. The so-called *Chesapeake* Affair enraged the country. Jefferson remarked that he had not seen so belligerent a spirit in America since 1775. Yet while making some preparations for war, the president sought peace—first by conducting fruitless negotiations with Britain to gain redress for the *Chesapeake* outrage, and second by steering the Embargo Act through Congress in December 1807.

The Embargo Act

By far the most controversial legislation of either of Jefferson's administrations, the Embargo Act prohibited vessels from leaving American ports for foreign ports. Technically, it prohibited only exports, but its practical effect was to stop imports as well, for few foreign ships would venture into American ports if they had to leave without cargo. Amazed by the boldness of the act, a British newspaper described the embargo as "little short of an absolute secession from the rest of the civilized world."

Jefferson advocated the embargo as a means of "peaceable coercion." By restricting French and British (especially British) trade with the United States, he hoped to pressure both nations into respecting American neutrality. But the embargo did not have the effect that Jefferson intended. Although British sales to the United States dropped 50 percent between 1807 and 1808, the British quickly found new markets in South America, where rebellions against Spanish rule had flared up, and in Spain itself, where a revolt against Napoleon had opened trade to British shipping. Furthermore, the Embargo Act itself contained some loopholes. For example, it allowed American ships blown off course to put in at European ports if necessary; suddenly, many captains were reporting that adverse winds had forced them across the Atlantic. Treating the embargo as a joke, Napoleon seized whatever American ships he could lay hands on and then informed the United States that he was only helping to enforce the embargo. The British were less amused, but the embargo confirmed their view that Jefferson was an ineffectual philosopher, an impotent challenger compared with Napoleon.

The harshest effects of the embargo were felt not in Europe but in the United States. Some thirty thousand American seamen found themselves out of work. Merchants stumbled into bankruptcy by the hundreds, and jails swelled with debtors. A New York City newspaper ruefully noted that the only activity still flourishing in the city was prosecution for debt. Farmers, too, were devastated. Unable to export their produce or sell

The Embargo Act
This nasty lampoon of the Embargo Act portrays the tiny Madison, left, parroting Jefferson's policy. Here Madison is made to say: "France wants an embargo & must have it," an expression of the widespread view that the embargo favored the French at America's expense.

it at a decent price to hard-pressed urban dwellers, many farmers could not earn enough cash to pay their debts. In desperation, one farmer in Schoharie County, New York, sold his cattle, horses, and farm implements, worth eight hundred dollars before the embargo, for fifty-five dollars. Speculators who had purchased land expecting to sell it later at a higher price also took a beating, because cash-starved farmers stopped buying land. "I live and that is all," wrote one New York speculator. "I am doing no business, cannot sell anybody property, nor collect any money."

The embargo fell hardest on New England and particularly on Massachusetts, which in 1807 had twice the ship tonnage per capita of any other state and more than a third of the entire nation's ship tonnage in foreign trade. For a state so dependent on foreign trade, the embargo was a calamity. Wits reversed the letters of *embargo* to form the phrase "O grab me."

The picture was not entirely bleak. The embargo forced a diversion of merchants' capital into manufacturing. In short, unable to export produce, Americans began to make products. Before 1808 the United States had only fifteen mills for fashioning cotton into textiles; by the end of 1809, an additional eighty-seven mills had been constructed. But none of this comforted merchants already ruined or mariners driven to soup kitchens. Nor could New Englanders forget that the source of their misery was a policy initiated by one of the "Virginia lordlings," "Mad Tom" Jefferson, who knew little about New England and who had a dogmatic loathing of cities, the very foundations of New England's prosperity. A Massachusetts poet wrote:

> *Our ships all in motion once whitened the ocean,*
> *They sailed and returned with a cargo;*
> *Now doomed to decay they have fallen a prey*
> *To Jefferson, worms, and embargo.*

The Election of 1808

Even before the Embargo Act, Jefferson had announced that he would not be a candidate for reelection. With his blessing, the Republican congressional caucus nominated James Madison and George Clinton for the presidency and vice presidency, whereas the Federalists countered with Charles C. Pinckney and Rufus King, the same ticket that had made a negligible showing in 1804. In 1808 the Federalists staged a modest comeback, gaining twenty-four congressional seats. Still, Madison won 122 of 175 electoral votes for

The Election of 1808

Candidates	Parties	Electoral Vote
JAMES MADISON	Democratic-Republican	122
Charles C. Pinckney	Federalist	47
George Clinton	Democratic-Republican	6

president, and the Republicans retained comfortable majorities in both houses of Congress.

Several factors contributed to the Federalists' revival in 1808. First, the embargo gave them the national issue that they had long lacked. Also, younger Federalists, represented by men like Harrison Gray Otis of Massachusetts and Robert G. Harper of South Carolina, were making their influence felt. Old-time Federalists, expecting the voters to defer naturally to gentlemen, had refused to campaign actively for votes, and they judged it disgraceful that their Republican opponents treated voters to barbecues and staged mass meetings. The younger Federalists, on the other hand, deliberately imitated the vote-winning techniques that had proved successful for the Republicans.

The Failure of Peaceable Coercion

To some contemporaries, the diminutive "Little Jemmy" Madison (he was only five feet, four inches tall) seemed a weak and shadowy figure alongside the commanding presence of Jefferson. But in fact, Madison brought to the presidency an intelligence and a capacity for systematic thought that matched Jefferson's. Like Jefferson, Madison believed that American liberty had to rest on the virtue of the people and that that virtue was critically tied to the growth and prosperity of agriculture. More clearly than Jefferson, Madison also recognized that agricultural prosperity depended on the vitality of American trade, for Americans would continue to enter farming only if they could get their crops to market. In particular, the British West Indies, dependent on the United States for much of their lumber and grain, struck Madison as a natural trading partner for the United States. Britain alone could not fully supply the West Indies. Therefore, if the United States embargoed its own trade with the West Indies, Madison reasoned, the British would be forced to their knees before Americans could suffer severe losses from the embargo. Britain, he wrote, was "more vulnerable in her commerce than in her armies."

The problem was that the American embargo was coercing no one. Increased trade between Canada and the West Indies after 1808 made a shambles of Madison's plan to pressure Britain by blocking American trade to the West Indies. On March 1, 1809, Congress repealed the Embargo Act and substituted the weaker, although face-saving, Non-Intercourse Act. This act opened American trade to all nations except Britain and France and authorized the president to restore trade with either nation if it ceased to violate neutral rights. But the act failed to persuade the British or the French to respect American shipping. Grasping at straws, Madison then negotiated an agreement with David Erskine, the British minister in Washington, to reopen American trade in return for a British promise to revoke its Orders in Council. That same day, June 10, 1809, some six hundred American ships sailed for Britain. But Erskine had acted without orders. British Foreign Secretary George Canning disavowed the Erskine agreement as soon as he got wind of it, and Madison was forced to reembargo trade with Britain.

Madison called Canning's policy a "mixture of fraud and folly," but Canning thought that he was pursuing a level-headed course of action and had trouble understanding American belligerence. Canning and most British statesmen saw the world as containing a few great powers like Britain and France and innumerable small and weak powers. When great powers waged war against each other, there were no neutrals. Weak nations such as the United States should logically seek the protection of a great power. Since Britain was a natural trading partner for the United States, Americans should recognize, the reasoning went, that their best interests would be served by peacefully submitting to dependency on Britain. The problem was that Jefferson and Madison refused to accept this British conception of power relationships. In their view, the United States, however weak its military, was a nation founded on majestic principles that made it morally superior to Europe. The outgrowth of vanity and ambition, Europe's wars were of no concern to Americans. Jefferson wrote of France and England: "The one is a den of robbers and the other of pirates."

As an economic boom swept across Britain in 1809, the failure of the American policy of peaceable coercion was becoming obvious. Nor was that policy having a noticeable impact on France. Holding the same view of international power relations as the British, Napoleon tried to manipulate the United States into a collision course with Britain. Confronted by implacable hostility from Britain and France, Congress continued to drift. In May 1810 it substituted Macon's Bill No. 2 for the Non-Intercourse Act. The Macon legislation reopened trade with Britain and France and then offered a clumsy bribe to each: if either Britain or France repealed its restrictions on neutral shipping, the United States would halt all commerce with the other. Jumping at the opportunity presented by Macon's Bill No. 2, Napoleon promised to repeal his edicts against American trade. Madison snapped at the bait and proclaimed non-intercourse against Britain. But Napoleon had no intention of respecting American neutrality. His plan all along had been to trick the Americans into a posture of hostility toward Britain, and he continued to seize American ships spotted in French-controlled ports. Peaceable coercion had become a fiasco.

The Push into War

Madison soon found himself faced not only by a hostile Britain and France but by militants within his own party who demanded more aggressive policies. Most of these men were southerners and westerners. Coming from regions where honor was a sacred word, they were infuriated by insults to the American flag. In addition, when an economic recession struck the South and West between 1808 and 1810, South Carolina's John C. Calhoun and others realized that British policies were wrecking the economies of their regions. Consequently, a war spirit began to pulsate in the veins of several young congressmen elected in 1810. Drawn mainly from the South and West, these hotbloods formed a cohesive group, dubbed the "war hawks," in the House of Representatives. Their leader was a thirty-four-year-old Kentuckian, Henry Clay, who preferred war to the "putrescent pool of ignominious peace." With the support of the other war hawks, such as Calhoun, Richard M. Johnson of Kentucky, and William R. King of North Carolina—all of them future vice presidents—Clay was elected to the speakership of the House over the aging Nathaniel Macon, the author of Macon's Bill No. 2.

Tecumseh and the Prophet

Voicing a more emotional and pugnacious nationalism than Jefferson and Madison, the war hawks called for the expulsion of the British from Canada and the Spanish from the Floridas. Their demands merged with western settlers' fears that the British in Canada were actively recruiting the Indians to halt the march of American settlement. These fears, groundless but plausible, became intense when the Shawnee chief Tecumseh and his half-brother the Prophet sought to unite several tribes in Ohio and the Indiana territory against American settlers. Demoralized by the continu-

Tenskwatawa, the Prophet

In periods of crisis, the Native American cultures often gave rise to prophets—religious revivalists of sorts—such as Tecumseh's brother Tenskwatawa. Known to non-Indians as the Prophet, Tenskwatawa tried to revive traditional Indian values and customs such as the common ownership of land and the wearing of animal skins and furs. His religious program blended with Tecumseh's political program to unite the western tribes.

ing loss of Native American lands to the whites and by the ravages of Native American society by alcoholism, Tecumseh and the Prophet (himself a reformed alcoholic) tried to unify their people and revive traditional Native American virtues. Both men believed that the Indians had to purge themselves of liquor and other corrupting messengers of white civilization as part of this revival. For example, to express his rejection of the whites' ways, Tecumseh long refused to learn English.

The aspirations of these Shawnee leaders set them on a collision course with Governor William Henry Harrison of the Indiana Territory. A wily bargainer, Harrison had purchased much of central and western Indiana from the Miami and the Delaware Indians in the Treaty of Fort Wayne (1809) for the paltry sum of ten thousand dollars. When Tecumseh's Shawnee people had refused to sign the treaty, however, Harrison began to regard the brilliant and charismatic Native American leader as an enemy.

With white settlers in Indiana convinced that Tecumseh's effort to unite the Indians was a scheme inspired by the British, Harrison gathered an army in September 1811 and marched against a Shawnee encampment, the Prophet's Town, at the junction of the Wabash and Tippecanoe rivers. Then in November the Shawnees, led by the Prophet (Tecumseh was off recruiting Creek Indians), attacked Harrison. In the ensuing Battle of Tippecanoe, the Shawnees were beaten, the Prophet's Town was destroyed, and the Prophet was discredited in Tecumseh's eyes for his premature attack. Ironically, the Battle of Tippecanoe, which made Harrison a national hero, accomplished precisely what it had been designed to prevent. Never before a British agent, Tecumseh now joined with the British.

Congress Votes for War

By the spring of 1812, President Madison had reached the decision that war with Britain was inevitable. On June 1 he sent his war message to Congress. Meanwhile, an economic depression struck Britain, partly because the American policy of restricting trade with that country had finally started to work. Under pressure from its merchants, Britain repealed the Orders in Council on June 23, but by then Congress, unaware that the British were contemplating repeal of the orders, had passed the declaration of war. It was still possible, of course, for Madison to revoke the declaration now that the maritime issue had been partly settled.

The British cabinet believed that he would do so. What the British failed to comprehend, however, was how much more belligerent American political leaders, particularly Republicans, had become between 1810 and 1812.

Although both war hawks and westerners had contributed to this hostile mood, neither held the key to the vote in favor of war. The war hawks composed a minority within the Republican party; the West was still too sparsely settled to have many representatives in Congress. Rather, the votes of Republicans in populous states like Pennsylvania, Maryland, and Virginia were the main force propelling the war declaration through Congress. Most opposition to war came from Federalist strongholds in Massachusetts, Connecticut, and New York. Because Federalists were so much stronger in the Northeast than elsewhere, congressional opposition to war revealed a sectional as well as a party split. In general, however, southern Federalists opposed the war declaration, whereas northern Republicans supported it. In other words, the vote for war followed party lines more closely than sectional lines. Much like James Madison himself, the typical Republican advocate of war had not wanted war in 1810 nor even in 1811 but had been led by the accumulation of grievances to demand it in 1812.

The Causes of the War

In his war message, Madison listed impressment, the continued presence of British ships in American waters, and British violations of neutral rights as grievances that justified war. But none of these complaints was new. Taken together, they do not fully explain why Americans went to war in 1812 rather than earlier—for example, in 1807 after the *Chesapeake* affair. Madison also listed British incitement of the Indians as a stimulus for war. This grievance of recent origin contributed to war feeling in the West. "The War on the Wabash," a Kentucky newspaper proclaimed, "is purely British. The British scalping knife has filled many habitations both in this state as well as in the Indiana Territory with widows and orphans." But the West had too few American inhabitants to account for the nation's being propelled into war. A more important underlying cause was the economic recession that affected the South and West after 1808—and the conviction, held by John C. Calhoun and others, that British policy was damaging America's economy. Finally, the fact that Madison rather than Jefferson was president in 1812 was of ma-

jor importance. Jefferson had believed that the only motive behind British seizures of American ships was Britain's desire to block American trade with Napoleon. Hence Jefferson had concluded that time was on America's side; the seizures would stop as soon as the war in Europe ceased. In contrast, Madison had become persuaded that Britain's real motive was to strangle American trade once and for all and thereby eliminate the United States as a trading rival. War or no war in Europe, Madison saw Britain as a menace to America. In his war message, he stated flatly that Britain was meddling with American trade not because that trade interfered with Britain's "belligerent rights" but because it "frustrated the monopoly which she covets for her own commerce and navigation."

THE WAR OF 1812

The popular American war slogan in June 1812 was "Free Trade and Sailors' Rights," and maritime issues had indeed been the centerpiece of Madison's war message. Yet Americans marched rather than sailed to war; they aimed at Canada, not at the British fleet. There were several reasons for this strategy. First, the growth of Canadian exports to the West Indies after 1808 had convinced Madison that Canada was not a snowbound wasteland but a key prop of the British Empire, an indispensable component of Britain's designs to strangle American trade. Moreover, an attack on Canada seemed a practical tactic. Between 1800 and 1812, the Republicans had consistently preferred economy to preparedness. They had shrunk the national debt from $83 million to $27.5 million, and as a result the American navy contained only six frigates, three sloops of war, and a number of smaller vessels, including gunboats. A brainchild of Jefferson, the gunboats were little more than floating gun docks designed for harbor defense. They often sank when they ventured out to sea and at times could not even hold anchor in harbors. When a hurricane blew one gunboat eight miles inland onto a cornfield, the Federalists mordantly toasted it as the finest ship "upon earth."

Unable to challenge Britain at sea, Americans looked north to Canada as a practical objective. Few Americans expected a prolonged or difficult struggle. The United States outstripped Canada in everything: 25 to 1 in population, 9 to 1 in militia, 7 to 5 in regular army soldiers. Furthermore, not only were the best British troops in Europe fighting Napoleon but three out of every five settlers in Canada were Americans from New York, Pennsylvania, and Connecticut. These settlers, now technically Canadians, had been lured north by cheap land but feared the British more than they feared their kin on the American side. To Jefferson, the conquest of Canada seemed "a mere matter of marching."

Expectations of an easy victory, however, rested on a much shakier foundation than many Americans realized. First, the British had an invaluable ally in the Native Americans, who proved to be terrifying as well as tough warriors. Although not the only ones to commit atrocities, the Indians struck fear in beholders by dangling scalps from their belts. The British quickly learned to play on this fear, in some cases forcing Americans to surrender by hinting that the Indians might be uncontrollable in battle. Second, most American generals were aged and incompetent, and one of the only good ones, Andrew Jackson, was long denied a federal commission, on political grounds. And the American state militias were filled with Sunday soldiers who "hollered for water half the time, and whiskey the other. . . ." Their lack of training aside, few militiamen really understood the goals of the war. In fact, outside Congress, there simply was not much blood lust in 1812. In New England, where opposition to the war was widespread, the people had little stomach for an invasion of Canada. (The loyal minority in New England, however, did provide the army with more regiments than either the middle states or the South.) President Madison was able to raise only 10,000 one-year volunteers out of the 50,000 authorized by Congress. In Kentucky, the home of the prominent war hawk Henry Clay, only 400 answered the first call for volunteers. This lukewarm response in all sections indicates not only that most people viewed Canada as remote but also that national political issues did not necessarily penetrate deeply into American society in 1812. Local attachments remained stronger than national ones.

The military campaigns of the war developed in two broad phases. From the summer of 1812 to the spring of 1814, the Americans assumed the offensive position, launching a succession of poorly coordinated and generally unsuccessful attacks on Canada. From the spring of 1814 into early 1815, the British took the offensive and achieved some spectacular victories while losing key battles.

On to Canada

[handwritten: briefly mention to help support a point]

Whereas some Americans wanted to commence the war with an attack on Montreal, the ardor of western politicians dictated that the opening offensive occur in the West. In July 1812 sixty-year-old General William Hull led an American army from Detroit into Canada, but the ingenious Tecumseh cut his supply line. Hull then retreated to Detroit. Unnerved by the sight of Tecumseh and by the hint of the British commander, General Isaac Brock, that "the numerous body of Indians who have attached themselves to my troops will be beyond my control the moment the contest commences," Hull surrendered two thousand men to thirteen hundred British and Native American troops.

Now the British concentrated their strength against a mixed force of regulars and New York militia menacing Canada north of Niagara Falls. While the American regulars marched into Canada, the New York militiamen, contending that they had volunteered only to protect their homes, not to invade Canada, refused to cross their state line. As the militia looked on from the American side, a detachment of American regulars was crushed by the British at the Battle of Queenston (October 13, 1812). Again the daunting Indian presence proved decisive. Winfield Scott, later to become a candidate for the presidency of the United States, negotiated the American surrender as Mohawk Indians were attacking his men. The third American offensive of 1812 never got off the ground. The sixty-two-year-old general Henry Dearborn was to have moved on Montreal via Lake Champlain. He had advanced twenty miles north of Plattsburgh by November 19, when the militia refused to go any farther. Thus Dearborn returned to Plattsburgh.

Under General William Henry Harrison, the Americans renewed their offensive in 1813 and tried to retake Detroit. A succession of reverses convinced Harrison that offensive operations were futile as long as the British controlled Lake Erie. During the winter of 1812–1813, Captain Oliver H. Perry constructed a little fleet of vessels out of green wood, cannon captured in a raid on York (Toronto), and supplies dragged across the snow from Pittsburgh to his headquarters at Presqu'ile (Erie). Perry encountered and destroyed a British squadron at Put-in-Bay on the western end of Lake Erie on September 10, 1813, reporting, "We have met the enemy, and they are ours." Losing control of Lake Erie, the British pulled back from Detroit, but Harrison overtook and defeated a combined British and Indian force at the Battle of the Thames on October 5. Tecumseh, now a legend among the whites, died in the battle; Colonel Richard Johnson's claim, never proved, to have killed Tecumseh later contributed to Johnson's election as vice president of the United States.

The Naval War

Even before their victory at Put-in-Bay, Americans had achieved sensational successes on the high seas. Republican tightfistedness had not altogether succeeded in starving the United States Navy. However small, the navy had entered the war with three of the largest and fastest frigates afloat—the *Constitution,* the *United States,* and the *President.* On August 19, 1812, the *Constitution* destroyed HMS *Guerrière* in the mid-Atlantic and on December 29 wrecked HMS *Java* off Brazil. But U.S. victories had more psychological than strategic value. Although they gave Americans something to cheer, the British clamped a blockade on the American coast, starting with Delaware Bay and Chesapeake Bay in the fall of 1812 and extending to New York in the spring of 1813 and to New England in the spring of 1814. The *United States* was now corked in the bottle of New York harbor, the *President* in New Haven, and the *Constitution* in Boston. Nor did Perry's victory on Lake Erie and Harrison's at the Battle of the Thames

hasten the conquest of Canada. Efforts to invade Canada in the Niagara area and to gain control of Lake Ontario failed.

The British Offensive

Britain's military fortunes crested in the spring of 1814. After his disastrous invasion of Russia in 1812 and a series of defeats in 1813, France's Napoleon abdicated as emperor in April 1814, and Britain began to move regulars from Europe to North America. The British quickly found, however, that earlier defeats had toughened the Americans, who were now fighting to defend their homes rather than to invade Canada. The first sign of trouble for the British came on the Niagara front in July 1814, when attacking redcoats were stopped by fierce American resistance at the battles of Chippewa (July 5) and Lundy's Lane (July 25).

The main British thrust came not on the Niagara front but down Lake Champlain. At the head of ten thousand British veterans, the largest and best-equipped British army ever sent to North America, General Sir George Prevost advanced south via the lake at the end of August and reached Plattsburgh on September 6. Prevost's plan was to split the New England states from the rest of the country. At Plattsburgh, however, he encountered a well-entrenched American army. Resolving that he had to control the

The *Constitution* Ranging Alongside the *Guerrière*,
*by Michael Felice Corne,
1812 (Detail)*
The Constitution *won more battles than any other early American frigate. Its most famous victory was over H.M.S.* Guerrière *in August 1812. Known affectionately as Old Ironsides, it was saved from demolition in 1830 by the poet Oliver Wendell Holmes, became a schoolship for the U.S. Naval Academy, was nearly confiscated by the fledgling Confederate navy in 1861, and today survives as a naval relic in Boston harbor.*

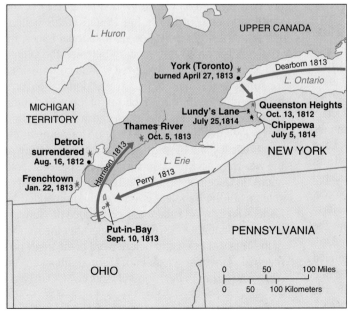

Major Battles of the War of 1812

Most of the war's major engagements occurred on or near the United States' northern frontier; but the Royal Navy blockaded the entire Atlantic coast, and the British army penetrated as far south as Washington and New Orleans.

Dolley Madison, *by Gilbert Stuart, 1804*
As the attractive young wife of Secretary of State James Madison, Dolley Madison acted virtually as the nation's First Lady during the administration of Jefferson, a widower. Friendly, tactful, and blessed with an unfailing memory for names and events, she added to her reputation as an elegant hostess after her husband became president.

lake before attacking Plattsburgh, Prevost called up his fleet, but an American naval squadron under Captain Thomas Macdonough defeated the British squadron on September 11. Dispirited, Prevost abandoned the campaign.

Ironically, the British achieved a far more spectacular success in an operation originally designed merely as a diversion from their main thrust down Lake Champlain. In 1814 a British army sailed from Bermuda for Chesapeake Bay, landed near Washington, and on August 24 met a larger American force, composed mainly of militia, at Bladensburg, Maryland. The Battle of Bladensburg quickly became the "Bladensburg races" as the American militia fled, almost without firing a shot. The British then descended on Washington. Madison, who had witnessed the Bladensburg fiasco, escaped into the Virginia hills. His wife, Dolley, pausing only long enough to load her sil-

ver, a bed, and a portrait of George Washington onto her carriage, hastened to join her husband, while British troops ate the supper prepared for the Madisons at the presidential mansion. Then they burned the mansion along with other public buildings in Washington. A few weeks later, the British attacked Baltimore, but after failing to crack its defenses, they broke off the operation.

The Treaty of Ghent   *discusses what we got out of it.*

In August 1814 negotiations to end the war commenced between British and American commissioners at Ghent, Belgium. The British appeared to command a strong position. Having frustrated American designs on Canada, they stood poised for their Lake Champlain initiative. In reality, however, their position was not as strong as it appeared and would grow weaker as negotiations progressed.

With Napoleon's abdication as emperor, Britain's primary goal had become a favorable and lasting peace in Europe; the British had little to gain from prolonging a minor war in America. Mindful of their superior military position, they demanded territorial concessions from the United States. The American naval victory at Plattsburgh, however, brought home to Britain the fact that after two years of fighting, the British controlled neither the Great Lakes nor Lake Champlain. Similarly, the spectacular raid on Washington had no strategic significance, and so the British gave way on the issue of territorial concessions. The final treaty, signed on Christmas Eve 1814, restored the status quo ante bellum*: the United States neither gained nor lost territory. Several additional issues, including the fixing of a boundary between the United States and Canada, were referred to joint commissions for future settlement. Nothing was done about impressment, but with Napoleon out of the way, neutral rights became a dead issue. Because there was no longer a war in Europe, there were no longer neutrals.

Ironically, the most dramatic American victory of the war came after the conclusion of the peace negotiations. In December 1814 a British army, composed of veterans of the Napoleonic wars and commanded by General Sir Edward Pakenham, descended on New Orleans. On January 8, 1815, two weeks after the signing of the Treaty of Ghent but before word of the treaty had reached America, Pakenham's force attacked an American army under General Andrew ("Old Hick-

---

*Status quo ante bellum: Latin for the state of affairs before the war.

Peace Medal
Bearing the president's portrait, peace medals such as this were given as gifts to Native Americans in the Old Northwest during the War of 1812. At the same time, the British were wooing the Indians with silver medals bearing the image of George III.

The Election of 1812

Candidates	Parties	Electoral Vote
JAMES MADISON	Democratic-Republican	128
DeWitt Clinton	Federalist	89

ory") Jackson. Already a legend for his ferocity as an Indian fighter, Jackson inspired little fear among the British, who advanced into battle far too confidently, but he did strike enough terror in his own men to prevent another American rout. In an hour of gruesome carnage, Jackson's troops shredded the line of advancing redcoats, killing Pakenham and inflicting more than two thousand casualties while losing only thirteen Americans.

The Hartford Convention

Because the Treaty of Ghent had already concluded the war, the Battle of New Orleans had little significance for diplomats. Indirectly, however, it had an impact on domestic politics by eroding Federalist strength.

The comeback that the Federalists had made in the election of 1808 had continued into the 1812 campaign. Buoyed by hostility to the war in the Northeast, the Federalists had thrown their support behind DeWitt Clinton, an antiwar Republican. Although Madison won the electoral vote 128 to 89, Clinton carried all of New England except Vermont, as well as New York and New Jersey. American military setbacks in the war intensified Federalist disdain for the new Madison administration. Indeed, from their bastions in New England (see "A Place in Time"), Federalists saw a nation misruled for over a decade by Republican bunglers.

Jefferson's attack on the judiciary had seemed to threaten the rule of law. His purchase of Louisiana, a measure of doubtful constitutionality, had enhanced Republican strength and reduced the relative importance of Federalist New England in the Union. The Embargo Act had severely damaged New England's commerce. Now "Mr. Madison's War" was bringing fresh misery to New England in the form of the British blockade. A few Federalists began to talk of New England's secession from the Union. Most, however, rejected the idea, believing that they would soon benefit from popular disfavor with the war and spring back into power.

In late 1814 a Federalist convention met in Hartford, Connecticut. Although some advocates of secession were present, moderates took control and passed a series of resolutions summarizing New England's grievances. At the root of these grievances lay the belief that New England was becoming a permanent minority in a nation dominated by southern Republicans who failed to understand New England's commercial interests. Accordingly, the convention proposed to amend the Constitution to abolish the three-fifths clause (which gave the South a disproportionate share of votes in Congress by allowing it to count slaves as a basis of representation), to require a two-thirds vote of Congress to declare war and to admit new states into the Union, to limit the president to a single term, to prohibit the election of two successive presidents from the same state, and to bar embargoes lasting more than sixty days. As bold as these proposals were, their timing was disastrous for the Federalists. News of the Treaty of Ghent and of Jackson's victory at New Orleans dashed the Federalists' hopes of gaining broad popular support. The goal of the Hartford Convention had been to assert states' rights rather than disunion, but to many the proceedings smelled of a traitorous plot. The restoration of peace, moreover, stripped the Federalists of the primary grievance that had fueled the convention. In the election of 1816, Republican James Monroe, Madison's hand-picked successor, swept the nation over negligible Federalist opposition. He would

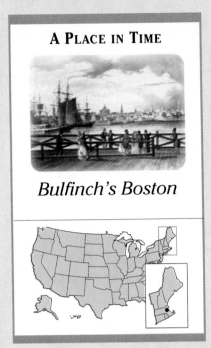

Bulfinch's Boston

During the first quarter of the nineteenth century, Boston shed its quaint colonial-era character and was transformed into a bustling commercial and cultural hub and one of the most important towns in the independent nation. Formerly a community dotted with frame houses and boxy brick residences—most with gardens and orchards—Boston became a prosperous seaport in the Republic's early years. Stately brick homes with heavy oak doors and multipaned windows sprang up in many quarters, giving whole neighborhoods a newly formal air. These were the residences of the town's elite, many of whom, after the Revolution, had risen to new heights of prosperity.

Success in maritime industry underlay Boston's metamorphosis. Shipping, cod fishing, whaling, and trade in sea-otter pelts (obtained in the Pacific Northwest, and especially prized in China) thrived in the port town. Graceful sailing ships bobbed gently in the harbor, blending into a riot of masts. Bostonians going about their daily business on the waterfront passed wharf after wharf lined with brick warehouses and countinghouses that had sprouted to manage Bostonians' widening sea trade. In the mid-1790s eighty humming quays gave the harborfront streets a distinctively commercial flavor.

A highly profitable commerce with the East Indies, China, and Europe, along with shipping to ports in the Indies and elsewhere in the United States, fueled the furious seaside activity. Boston merchants and sea captains built substantial fortunes from their shipping and fishing ventures; some voyages realized profits of more than $100,000, a huge take for the times. The spices, teas, silks, and fine porcelain they brought home were eagerly sought by their fellow elites.

New England cotton manufacturers benefited handsomely too after the Revolution. Savvy Yankees began to turn a former home industry into a large-scale business operation that supplied the duck and canvas for the harbor's panorama of sails. The fledgling American navy also needed sails; those for the *Constitution* had to be made in an old grain storehouse because no other town structure was long enough.

Even before the imposition of the embargo that stifled these lucrative enterprises, Boston, the home of many of President Thomas Jefferson's most bitter Federalist critics, among them George Cabot and Harrison Gray Otis, was a thorn in Jefferson's side. A Federalist elite ran the city, dominating its politics and culture as well as its maritime economy. Composing the elite were not only the merchants upon whom the town's commercial prosperity rested but also the lawyers who controlled its judicial offices, as well as men who had made a fortune in real estate. These uppercrust Bostonians supported the town's cultural institutions, such as the Boston Athenaeum, the nation's largest private library; the American Academy of Arts and Sciences; and Harvard College in nearby Cambridge. Austere and even frigid in their manners, Boston's Federalist leaders were a study in contrast to friendly, backslapping Virginia squires.

Following a grand tour of Europe, the architect Charles Bulfinch, in love with the classical style that he had seen in ancient Roman ruins, designed the majestic Massachusetts State House (completed in 1798) and the gracious mansions on Beacon Hill from which Boston's Federalists

Charles Bulfinch,
by Mather Brown, 1786
Bulfinch learned about architecture as a boy by browsing in the well-stocked architectural library of his maternal grandfather, the wealthy Charles Apthorp. In the 1780s Bulfinch's interest was further stimulated by his visits to Rome, Florence, and London and by the encouragement of Thomas Jefferson.

looked down upon "their" prosperous city. Bulfinch did more than cater to the elite; the scion of colonial aristocrats, he was part of the elite and served as Boston's police chief. The vast majority of Bostonians, of course, shared none of the privileges and splendor enjoyed by Bulfinch and others of the elite; artisans, mariners, and laborers looked up to Beacon Hill, not down from it. Yet even when Jefferson's Republicans began to score victories in Massachusetts, Boston stayed solidly Federalist.

How could the Federalists retain their political control for so long? Part of the answer is that Boston artisans and laborers remembered how the elite families had supported the Revolution and the Constitution. In addition, the Federalist elite profited from the attitude still prevailing among the common people that social superiors deserved respect and even obedience. Historians call this attitude deference, and there was a lot of it in Boston. To secure deference, the elite paid careful attention to dress. Powdered wigs, lace ruffles, silk stockings, and gold canes were all part of a carefully fashioned image that members of the elite projected when they walked the streets. This attention to image was important, especially among elite

Massachusetts State House
Like Jefferson, Bulfinch admired the classical style of ancient Greece and Rome. But Bulfinch was less inclined than Jefferson to copy ancient buildings literally. Bulfinch's design for the Massachusetts State House reflects the symmetry of neoclassicism; unlike Jefferson's plan for the Virginia Capitol, it is not based on any particular Roman structure.

families like the Cabots and the Lowells, recent arrivals to Boston who had made their fortunes during and after the Revolution. If deference showed any sign of weakening, the Boston elite could and did fall back on its control of elections. Until 1822, for example, Boston Brahmins beat back efforts to establish decentralized polling places. All Bostonians voted in Faneuil Hall under the eyes of the elite, and only after presenting evidence of property owning.

Bulfinch advised young men against becoming architects, for he believed that few new buildings would be constructed in Boston. His attitude reflected the fact that Boston's population had grown by only 10 percent between 1743 and 1790. Immigrants avoided stuffy Federalist Boston. Adventurers and radicals found New York and Philadelphia more congenial. Yet even as Bulfinch designed his stately mansions, the city was changing. Its population rose from 18,000 in 1790 to nearly 34,000 in 1810, and to 58,000 in 1826. By the 1820s the city had become too large and diverse to follow the leadership of a single elite. By the late 1820s, new political alignments had shattered Federalist domination of Boston's politics.

The Tea Party, *by Henry Sargent, c. 1821*
Bulfinch's Federalist patrons craved elegant interiors and could afford wall-to-wall carpeting. Tea parties like this unified as well as entertained Boston's elite.

The Election of 1816

Candidates	Parties	Electoral Vote
JAMES MONROE	Democratic-Republican	183
Rufus King	Federalist	34

The Election of 1820

Candidates	Parties	Electoral Vote
JAMES MONROE	Democratic-Republican	231
John Quincy Adams	Independent Republican	1

win reelection in 1820 with only a single dissenting electoral vote. As a force in national politics, the Federalists were finished.

THE AWAKENING OF AMERICAN NATIONALISM

The United States emerged from the War of 1812 bruised but intact. In its first major war since the Revolution, the American republic had demonstrated not only that it could fight on even terms against a major power but also that republics could fight wars without turning themselves into despotisms. The war produced more than its share of symbols of American nationalism. Whitewash cleared the smoke damage to the

presidential mansion; thereafter, it became known as the White House. The British attack on Fort McHenry, guarding Baltimore, prompted a young observer, Francis Scott Key, to compose "The Star-Spangled Banner." The Battle of New Orleans boosted Andrew Jackson onto the stage of national politics and became a source of legends about why the Americans had won the battle. It appears to most scholars today that the British lost because Pakenham's men, advancing within range of Jackson's riflemen and cannon, unaccountably paused and became sitting ducks. But in the wake of the battle, Americans spun a different tale. The legend arose that Jackson owed his victory not to Pakenham's blundering tactics but to hawk-eyed Kentucky frontiersmen whose rifles picked off the British with unerring accuracy. In fact, many frontiersmen in Jackson's army had not carried rifles; even if they had, gunpowder smoke would have obscured the enemy. But none of this mattered at the time. Just as Americans preferred militia to professional soldiers, they chose to believe that their greatest victory of the war was the handiwork of mere amateurs.

Madison's Nationalism and the Era of Good Feelings

The War of 1812 had three major political consequences. First, it eliminated the Federalists as a national political force. Second, it went a long way toward convincing the Republicans that the nation was strong and resilient, capable of fighting a war while maintaining the liberty of its people. The third consequence was an outgrowth of the first two. With the Federalists tainted by disloyalty and with fears about the fragility of republics fading, Republicans increas-

Manuscript for "The Star-Spangled Banner" *(Detail)*

> O say can you see, ~~through~~ by the dawn's early light,
> what so proudly we hail'd at the twilight's last gleaming,
> whose broad stripes & bright stars through the perilous fight
> O'er the ramparts we watch'd, were so gallantly streaming?
> And the rocket's red glare, the bomb bursting in air,
> Gave proof through the night that our flag was still there,
> O say does that star spangled banner yet wave
> O'er the land of the free & the home of the brave?

ingly embraced some doctrines long associated with the Federalists. In a message to Congress in December 1815, Madison called for federal support for internal improvements, tariff protection for the new industries that had sprung up during the embargo, and the creation of a new national bank. (The charter of the first Bank of the United States had expired in 1811.) In Congress another Republican, Henry Clay of Kentucky, proposed similar measures, which he called the American System, with the aim of making the young nation economically self-sufficient and free from dependency on Europe. In 1816 Congress chartered the Second Bank of the United States and enacted a moderate tariff. Federal support for internal improvements proved to be a thornier problem. Madison favored federal aid in principle but believed that a constitutional amendment was necessary to authorize it. Accordingly, he vetoed an internal-improvements bill passed in 1817.

As Republicans adopted positions that they had once disdained, an "Era of Good Feelings" dawned on American politics. A Boston newspaper, impressed by the warm reception accorded President Monroe while touring New England, coined the phrase in 1817. It has stuck as a description of Monroe's two administrations, from 1816 to 1824. Compared with Jefferson and Madison, Monroe was neither brilliant, polished, nor wealthy, but he keenly desired to heal the political divisions that a stronger intellect and personality might have inflamed. The phrase "Era of Good Feelings" reflects not only the war's elimination of some divisive issues but also Monroe's conscious effort to avoid political controversies. But the good feelings were paperthin. Madison's 1817 veto of the internal-improvements bill revealed the persistence of disagreements about the role of the federal government under the Constitution. Furthermore, the embargo, the War of 1812, and the continuation of slavery had aroused sectional animosities that a journalist's phrase about good feelings could not dispel. Not surprisingly, the postwar consensus began to unravel almost as soon as Americans recognized its existence.

John Marshall and the Supreme Court

Jefferson's old antagonist John Marshall continued to preside over the Supreme Court during the Monroe administrations and in 1819 issued two opinions that stunned Republicans. The first case, *Dartmouth College* v. *Woodward,* centered on the question of whether New Hampshire could transform a private corporation, Dartmouth College, into a state university.

Marshall concluded that the college's original charter, granted to its trustees by George III in 1769, was a contract. Since the Constitution specifically forbade states to interfere with contracts, New Hampshire's effort to turn Dartmouth into a state university was unconstitutional. The implications of Marshall's ruling were far-reaching. Charters or acts of incorporation provided their beneficiaries with various legal privileges and were sought by businesses as well as by colleges. In effect, Marshall said that once a state had chartered a college or business, it surrendered both its power to alter the charter and, in large measure, its authority to regulate the beneficiary.

A few weeks later, the chief justice handed down an even more momentous decision in the case of *McCulloch* v. *Maryland.* The issue here was whether the state of Maryland had the power to tax a national corporation, specifically the Baltimore branch of the Second Bank of the United States. The bank was a national corporation, chartered by Congress, but most of the stockholders were private citizens who reaped whatever profits the bank made. Speaking for a unanimous Court, Marshall ignored these private features of the bank and concentrated instead on two issues. First, did Congress have the power to charter a national bank? Nothing in the Constitution, Marshall conceded, explicitly granted this power. But the Constitution did authorize Congress to lay and collect taxes, to regulate interstate commerce, and to declare war. Surely these enumerated powers, he reasoned, implied a power to charter a bank. Marshall was clearly engaging in a broad, or "loose," rather than strict, construction (interpretation) of the Constitution. The second issue was whether a state could tax an agency of the federal government that lay within its borders. Marshall argued that any power of the national government, express or implied, was supreme within its sphere. States could not interfere with the exercise of federal powers. A tax by Maryland on the Baltimore branch was such an interference and hence was plainly unconstitutional.

Marshall's decision in the *McCulloch* case dismayed many Republicans. Although Madison and Monroe had supported the establishment of the Second Bank of the United States, the bank had made itself unpopular by tightening its loan policies during the summer of 1818. This contraction of credit triggered a severe depression, the Panic of 1819, that gave rise to considerable distress throughout the country, especially among western farmers. At a time when the bank was widely blamed for the panic, Marshall's ruling stirred controversy by placing the bank beyond the regulatory power of any state government. His decision, indeed, was as much an attack on state sovereignty as it was a defense of the bank. The Constitution, Marshall argued, was the creation not of state governments but of the people of *all* the states and thus was more fundamental than state laws. His reasoning assailed the Republican theory, best expressed in the Virginia and Kentucky resolutions of 1798–1799, that the Union was essentially a compact among states. Republicans had continued to view state governments as more immediately responsive to the people's will than was the federal government and to regard the compact theory of the Union as a guarantor of popular liberty. As Republicans saw it, Marshall's *McCulloch* decision, along with his decision in the *Dartmouth College* case, stripped state governments of the power to impose the will of their people upon corporations.

The Missouri Compromise

The fragility of the Era of Good Feelings again became apparent in the prolonged controversy between 1819 and 1821 over the territory of Missouri. In February 1819 the House of Representatives was considering a bill to admit Missouri as a slave state. James Tallmadge, Jr., a New York Republican, offered an amendment that prohibited the further introduction of slaves into Missouri and provided for the emancipation, at age twenty-five, of all slave offspring born after Missouri's admission as a state. Following bitter debate, the House approved the bill with Tallmadge's amendment. The Senate, after an equally rancorous debate, struck the amendment from the Missouri bill. In each chamber the vote on the Tallmadge amendment followed sectional lines, with the South virtually unanimously opposed to the provisions regarding slavery and the North predominantly in support. "This momentous question," Jefferson worried, "like a fire bell in the night, awakened and filled me with terror."

American politics had long been torn by sectional conflict, and slavery had at times figured in this discord, notably in the debate at the Constitutional Convention over the three-fifths clause. Yet prior to 1819, slavery had not been the primary factor in sectional division. Issues like Alexander Hamilton's economic program and the Jay Treaty had done more than slavery to polarize the country along sectional lines. During the 1790s Jefferson's main fear had been that Federalist economic policies were favoring northern

commercial development at the expense of southern agriculture. After 1800 Federalist opposition to the Louisiana Purchase and to the War of 1812 grew mainly out of concern that the now dominant Republicans were sacrificing New England's political and commercial interests to those of the South and West. The Hartford Convention of 1814 had been a reaction not so much to the spread of slavery as to the decline of New England's political influence.

For various reasons, the Missouri question thrust slavery into the center of this long-standing sectional conflict. In 1819 the Union had eleven free and eleven slave states. The admission of Missouri as a slave state would upset this balance to the advantage of the South. Noting that every president since John Adams had been a Virginian, Federalists portrayed the admission of Missouri as part of a conspiracy to perpetuate the rule of Virginia slaveholders. Republicans countered by pointing to the relatively sudden emergence in the House of Representatives of a vocal antislavery block, which included many northern Federalists, and to the growing number of Federalist-dominated societies in the North that promoted the manumission (freeing) of slaves. In response to these developments, some Republicans began to view all efforts to restrict slavery as part of a plot by the Federalists to divide northern and southern Republicans and thus regain political power. In sum, by 1819 the slavery issue had become intertwined with the prevailing distrust between the parties and between the sections.

Virtually every issue that was to wrack the Union during the next forty years was present in the controversy over Missouri: southern charges that the North was conspiring to destroy the Union and to end slavery; accusations by northerners that southerners were conspiring to extend the institution. For a while, leaders doubted that the Union would survive the crisis. House Speaker Henry Clay wrote that the words *civil war* and *disunion* were commonly uttered, almost without emotion. But a series of congressional agreements in 1820 and 1821, known collectively as the Missouri Compromise, resolved the crisis.

The first of these agreements involved the balance between slave states and free states. At the same time that Congress was considering statehood for Missouri, Maine was seeking admission as a free state. In 1820 Congress agreed to admit Maine as a free state, to pave the way for Missouri's admission as a slave state, and to prohibit slavery in the remainder of the Louisiana Purchase territory north of 36° 30′ (the

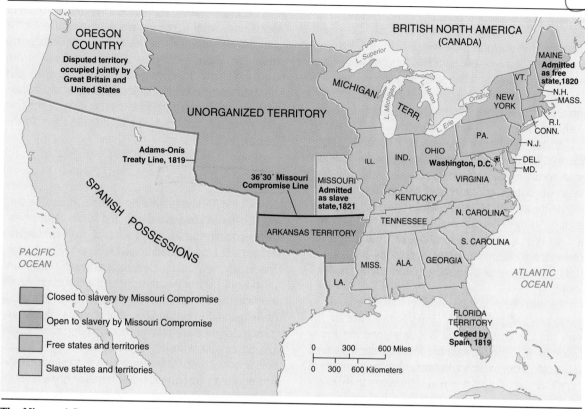

OREGON COUNTRY
Disputed territory occupied jointly by Great Britain and United States

BRITISH NORTH AMERICA (CANADA)

MAINE
Admitted as free state, 1820

UNORGANIZED TERRITORY

MICHIGAN TERR.

VT.
N.H.
MASS.
NEW YORK
R.I.
CONN.
PA.
N.J.

Adams-Onís Treaty Line, 1819

36°30′ Missouri Compromise Line

MISSOURI
Admitted as slave state, 1821

ILL.
IND.
OHIO
Washington, D.C.
DEL.
MD.

SPANISH POSSESSIONS

VIRGINIA
KENTUCKY
N. CAROLINA
TENNESSEE

ARKANSAS TERRITORY

S. CAROLINA

PACIFIC OCEAN

LA.
MISS.
ALA.
GEORGIA

ATLANTIC OCEAN

FLORIDA TERRITORY
Ceded by Spain, 1819

Closed to slavery by Missouri Compromise

Open to slavery by Missouri Compromise

Free states and territories

Slave states and territories

0   300   600 Miles
0   300   600 Kilometers

The Missouri Compromise, 1820–1821

The Missouri Compromise temporarily quelled controversy over slavery by admitting Maine as a free state and Missouri as a slave state, and by prohibiting slavery in the remainder of the Louisiana Purchase north of 36° 30′.

southern boundary of Missouri). But compromise did not come easily. The components of the eventual compromise passed by close and ominously sectional votes. Additionally, no sooner had the compromise been forged than it nearly fell apart. As a prelude to statehood, Missourians drafted a constitution that prohibited free blacks from entering their territory. This provision raised a thorny question, for some eastern states recognized free people of color as citizens, who, as such, were protected from discrimination by the federal Constitution, which clearly stated that "Citizens of each State shall be entitled to all Privileges and Immunities of Citizens in the several States." Balking at Missourians' exclusion of free blacks, antislavery northerners barred Missouri's admission into the Union until 1821, when Henry Clay engineered a new agreement. This second Missouri Compromise prohibited Missouri from discriminating against citizens of other states but left open the issue of whether free blacks were citizens.

The Missouri Compromise was widely viewed as a southern victory. The South had gained admission of Missouri, whose acceptance of slavery was controversial, while conceding to the North the admission of Maine, whose rejection of slavery inspired no controversy at all. Yet the South had conceded to freedom a vast block of territory north of 36° 30′. Although much of this territory was unorganized Indian country that some viewed as unfit for white habitation, it would not remain a wilderness for long. Also, the Missouri Compromise reinforced the principle, originally set down by the Northwest Ordinance of 1787, that Congress had the right to prohibit slavery in some territories. Southerners had implicitly accepted the argument that slaves were not like other forms of property that could be moved from place to place at will.

Foreign Policy Under Monroe

American foreign policy between 1816 and 1824 reflected more consensus than conflict. The end of the Napoleonic Wars and the signing of the Treaty of Ghent had removed most of the foreign-policy disagreements between Federalists and Republicans. Moreover, Monroe was fortunate to have as his secretary of state an extraordinary diplomat, John Quincy Adams. An austere and scholarly man whose library equaled his house in monetary value, Adams was a tough negotiator and a fervent nationalist. Although he was the son of the last Federalist president, he had been the only Federalist in the Senate to support the Louisiana Purchase. He later backed the embargo, joined the Republican party, served as minister to Russia, and was one of the negotiators of the Treaty of Ghent.

As secretary of state, Adams moved quickly to strengthen the peace with Great Britain. During his term the United States and Britain signed the Rush-Bagot Treaty of 1817, which effectively demilitarized the Great Lakes by severely restricting the number of ships that the two powers could maintain there. Next the British-American Convention of 1818 fixed the boundary between the United States and Canada from the Lake of the Woods west to the Rockies and restored to Americans the same fishing rights off Newfoundland that they had enjoyed before the War of 1812. As a result of these two agreements, for the first time since independence, the United States had a secure border with British-controlled Canada and could turn its attention southward and westward.

Adams's dealings with the Spanish, who still owned East Florida and claimed West Florida, were also successful. It had never been clear whether the Louisiana Purchase included West Florida. Acting as if it did, the United States in 1812 had simply added a slice of West Florida to the state of Louisiana and another slice to the Mississippi Territory. In 1818 Andrew Jackson, the American military commander in the South, seizing upon the pretext that Florida was both a base for Seminole Indian raids into American soil and a refuge for fugitive slaves, invaded East Florida, hanged two British subjects, and captured Spanish forts. Jackson had acted without explicit orders, but Adams supported the raid, guessing correctly that it would panic the Spanish into further concessions. In 1819 Spain agreed to the Adams-Onís (or Transcontinental) Treaty. By its terms, Spain ceded East Florida

to the United States, renounced its claims to all of West Florida, and agreed to a southern border of the United States west of the Mississippi that ran north along the Sabine River (separating Texas from Louisiana) and then westward along the Red and Arkansas rivers to the Rocky Mountains, finally following the forty-second parallel to the Pacific. For the first time, the United States had a legitimate claim to the Pacific coast.

The Monroe Doctrine

John Quincy Adams had long believed that God and nature had ordained that the United States would eventually span the entire continent of North America. Throughout his negotiations leading up to the Adams-Onís Treaty, he made it clear to Spain that if the Spanish did not concede some of their territory in North America, the United States might seize all of it, including Texas and even Mexico. Americans were fast acquiring a reputation as an aggressive people. Yet Spain was concerned with larger issues than American encroachment. Its primary objective was to suppress the revolutions against Spanish rule that had broken out in South America. To accomplish this goal, Spain sought support from the European monarchs who had organized the Holy Alliance in 1815. The brainchild of the tsar of Russia, the Holy Alliance aimed to quash revolutions everywhere in the name of Christian principles, and by 1822 its members talked of helping Spain suppress the South American revolutions. But Britain refused to join the Holy Alliance; British foreign minister George Canning proposed that the United States and Britain issue a joint statement opposing any European interference in South America while pledging that neither would annex any part of Spain's old empire in the New World.

While sharing Canning's opposition to European intervention in the New World, Adams preferred that the United States make a declaration of policy on its own rather than "come in as a cock-boat in the wake of the British man-of-war." Specifically, Adams rejected Canning's insistence on a joint Anglo-American pledge never to annex any part of Spain's former territories, for Adams wanted to keep the United States' freedom to annex Texas or Cuba, should their inhabitants one day "solicit a union with us."

This was the background of the Monroe Doctrine, as President Monroe's message to Congress on December 2, 1823, later came to be called. The message, largely written by Adams, announced three key principles: that unless American interests were involved, the United States' policy was to abstain from European wars; that the "American continents" were not "subjects for future colonization by any European power"; and that the United States would construe any attempt at European colonization in the New World as an "unfriendly act."

Europeans widely derided the Monroe Doctrine as a mere unilateral pronouncement by the United States. Fear of the British navy, not the Monroe Doctrine, prevented the Holy Alliance from intervening in South America. With hindsight, however, the Europeans would have taken the doctrine more seriously, for it had important implications. First, by pledging itself not to interfere in European wars, the United States was excluding the possibility that it would support revolutionary movements in Europe. For example, Adams opposed the United States' recognition of Greek patriots, who were then fighting against Turkish domination. Second, by keeping open its options to annex territory in the Americas, the United States was using the Monroe Doctrine to claim a preeminent position in the New World.

CONCLUSION

Although the diplomatic achievements of John Quincy Adams and James Monroe were formidable, the greatest accomplishment of the early Republic's leaders was to fashion a workable body of political institutions and customs to govern the young nation. The framers of the Constitution had not anticipated the rise of political parties, and when Jefferson took office in 1801, it was unclear how a victorious party would behave. The range of possibilities was great. Some feared that the Republicans would amend the Constitution to ensure their political ascendancy. One reason why Jefferson's early actions against the judiciary had terrified Federalists was that they viewed his maneuverings as part of a larger plan to destroy them.

As it turned out, Jefferson did not destroy the Federalists; they destroyed themselves. Until the embargo, they failed to come up with a popular national issue, and then they rode opposition to the embargo and to the War of 1812 for too long. When the war ended, a surge of national pride swept the Federalists aside. The election of 1800 had generated anxiety bordering on hysteria; that of 1820 produced yawns. Indeed, the nation was almost too peaceful. Federalist collapse and the embrace by the Republicans of former Federalist policies like the tariff and national banking blurred divisions once sharp.

James Monroe's reelection in 1820 marked the high point of the Republican surge. Even as Republicans congratulated themselves on the emergence of an era of apparent good feelings, the signs of future divisions were growing. The furor over the Missouri Compromise shattered sectional harmony. Subtle changes were starting to occur in American society—changes that would create new political issues and divisions by 1830.

CHRONOLOGY

1800–1801	John Adams's midnight appointments.
1801	Thomas Jefferson's inauguration.
1802	Repeal of the Judiciary Act of 1801.
	Yazoo land compromise.
	American right of deposit at New Orleans revoked.
1803	*Marbury* v. *Madison*.
	Conclusion of the Louisiana Purchase.
1804	Judge John Pickering convicted by the Senate.
	Impeachment of Justice Samuel Chase.
	Aaron Burr kills Alexander Hamilton in a duel.
	Jefferson elected to a second term.
1804–1806	Lewis and Clark expedition.
1805	Start of the Burr conspiracy.
	Chase acquitted by the Senate.
	Essex case.

1806	British government issues the first Order in Council.
1807	Burr acquitted of treason. *Chesapeake* Affair. Embargo Act passed.
1808	James Madison elected president.
1809	Non-Intercourse Act passed; Embargo Act repealed.
1810	Macon's Bill No. 2.
1811	Battle of Tippecanoe.
1812	Orders in Council revoked. United States declares war on Britain. Madison reelected to a second term. General William Hull surrenders at Detroit. USS *Constitution* defeats HMS *Guerrière*. Battle of Queenston.
1813	Battle of Lake Erie (Put-in-Bay). Battle of the Thames.
1814	Battles of Chippewa and Lundy's Lane. Battle of Bladensburg.

James Madison

1814   British burn Washington, D.C.

	Captain Thomas Macdonough's naval victory at the Battle of Plattsburgh. Hartford Convention. Treaty of Ghent signed.
1815	Battle of New Orleans.
1816	James Monroe elected president. Second Bank of the United States chartered.
1817	Rush-Bagot Treaty.
1818	British-American Convention of 1818. Andrew Jackson invades East Florida.
1819	Adams-Onís (Transcontinental) Treaty. *Dartmouth College* v. *Woodward*. *McCulloch* v. *Maryland*.
1820	Monroe reelected to a second term.
1820–1821	Missouri Compromise.
1823	Monroe Doctrine.

FOR FURTHER READING

Henry Adams, *History of the United States During the Administrations of Jefferson and Madison,* 9 vols. (1889–1891). A classic study by the great-grandson of John Adams.

Drew R. McCoy, *The Last of the Fathers: James Madison and the Republican Legacy* (1989). The best recent book on Madison.

Forrest McDonald, *The Presidency of Thomas Jefferson* (1976). A lively overview.

Dumas Malone, *Jefferson and His Time,* vols. 4 and 5 (1970, 1974). An extremely comprehensive biography.

Merrill Peterson, *Thomas Jefferson and the New Nation: A Biography* (1970). The best one-volume biography of Jefferson.

Marshall Smelser, *The Democratic Republic, 1801–1815* (1968). A thorough general work.

J. C. A. Stagg, *Mr. Madison's War: Politics, Diplomacy and Warfare in the Early Republic* (1983). An important reinterpretation of the causes of the War of 1812.

G. Edward White, *The Marshall Court and Cultural Change, 1815–1835* (1991). A seminal reinterpretation of the Supreme Court under John Marshall.

ADDITIONAL BIBLIOGRAPHY

Political Ideologies

Joyce Appleby, *Capitalism and a New Social Order: The Republican Vision of the 1790s* (1984); Lance Banning, *The Jeffersonian Persuasion: Evolution of a Party Ideology* (1978); Drew McCoy, *The Elusive Republic: Political Economy in Jeffersonian America* (1980); Steven Watts, *The Republic Reborn* (1987).

Political Parties

James Banner, *To the Hartford Convention: The Federalists and the Origins of Party Politics in the Early Republic, 1789–1815* (1967); Noble E. Cunningham, *The Jeffersonian Republicans and Power: Party Operations, 1801–1809* (1963); David Hackett Fischer, *The Revolution of American Conservatism: The Federalist Party in the Era of Jeffersonian Democracy* (1965); Ronald P. Formisano, *The Transformation of Political Culture: Massachusetts Parties, 1790s–1840s* (1983); Robert M. Johnstone, Jr., *Jefferson and the Presidency: Leadership in the Young Republic* (1978); Linda K. Kerber, *Federalists in Dissent: Imagery and Ideology in Jeffersonian America* (1970); Shaw Livermore, *The Twilight of Federalism: The Disintegration of the Federalist*

Party, 1815–1830 (1962); Alan Taylor, *Liberty Men and Great Proprietors: The Revolutionary Settlement on the Maine Frontier* (1990); James S. Young, *The Washington Community: 1800–1828* (1966).

Political Leaders

Thomas P. Abernethy, *The Burr Conspiracy* (1954); Robert Dawidoff, *The Education of John Randolph* (1979); Milton Lomask, *Aaron Burr*, 2 vols. (1979, 1982); Samuel Eliot Morison, *Harrison Gray Otis, 1765–1848: The Urbane Federalist* (1962); Robert Shalhope, *John Taylor of Caroline: Pastoral Republican* (1978).

Law and the Judiciary

Leonard Baker, *John Marshall: A Life in Law* (1974); Albert J. Beveridge, *John Marshall*, 4 vols. (1916–1919); Richard E. Ellis, *The Jeffersonian Crisis: Courts and Politics in the Young Republic* (1971); Charles G. Haines, *The Role of the Supreme Court in American Government and Politics, 1789–1835* (1944); Peter C. Hoffer and N. E. H. Hull, *Impeachment in America, 1635–1805* (1984); Morton J. Horwitz, *The Transformation of American Law, 1780–1860* (1977).

The War of 1812 and Its Prologue

Pierre Berton, *The Invasion of Canada* (1980); Roger H. Brown, *The Republic in Peril* (1964); A. L. Burtt, *The United States, Great Britain, and British North America* (1940); Harry L. Coles, *The War of 1812* (1965); Donald R. Hickey, *The War of 1812: A Forgotten Conflict* (1989); Reginald Horsman, *The Causes of the War of 1812* (1962); Bradford Perkins, *Prologue to War: England and the United States, 1805–1812* (1961); Julius W. Pratt, *Expansionists of 1812* (1925); Burton Spivak, *Jefferson's English Crisis: Commerce, Embargo, and the Republican Revolution* (1979).

Nationalism and Sectionalism

Harry Ammon, Jr., *James Monroe: The Quest for National Identity* (1971); George Dangerfield, *The Awakening of American Nationalism, 1815–1828* (1965) and *The Era of Good Feelings* (1952); Don E. Fehrenbacher, *The South and Three Sectional Crises* (1980); Glover Moore, *The Missouri Compromise, 1819–1821* (1953); Donald L. Robinson, *Slavery in the Structure of American Politics, 1765–1820* (1971).

John Quincy Adams and the Monroe Doctrine

Samuel F. Bemis, *John Quincy Adams and the Foundations of American Foreign Policy* (1949); Walter LaFeber, ed., *John Quincy Adams and the American Continental Empire* (1965); Ernest R. May, *The Making of the Monroe Doctrine* (1975); Dexter Perkins, *Hands Off: A History of the Monroe Doctrine* (1951) and *The Monroe Doctrine, 1823–1826* (1927).

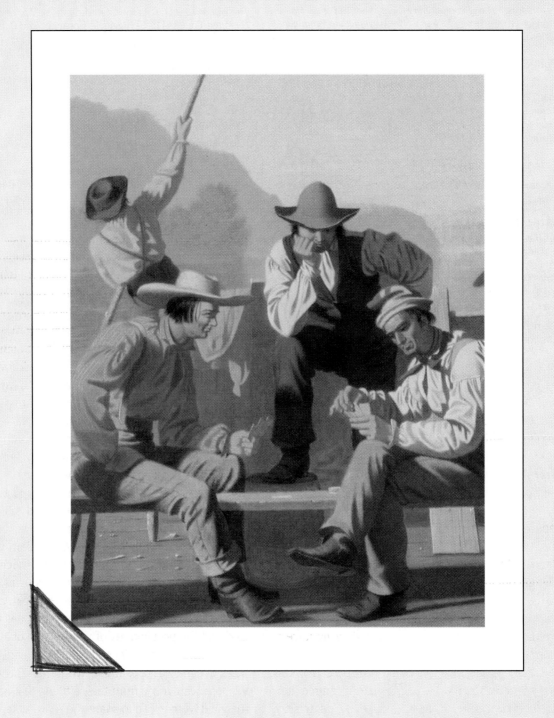

Raftsmen Playing Cards *(detail)*
by George Caleb Bingham, 1847

THE TRANSFORMATION OF AMERICAN SOCIETY 1815–1840

In 1835 William Kirkland and his wife, Caroline, left the private school that they had run in Geneva, New York, and moved to Detroit, in the Michigan Territory. William's plan was simple. He and Caroline would teach in Detroit long enough to earn money to invest in land. Detroit was being flooded by immigrants from the East who, as Caroline wrote, "came to buy land,—not to clear and plough, but as men buy a lottery ticket or dig for gold—in the hope of unreasonable and unearned profits." Although William intended to found a settle-

ment in the wilderness rather than merely to buy and sell land, he, too, hoped to get rich in the West.

Reared in cultivated refinement in New York City and educated at excellent Quaker schools, Caroline had her own notions about the West. The novels and travelers' accounts that she had read projected conflicting but invariably rosy images of the frontier: the West was a land of boundless treasure, a vast garden eager to yield the fruits of its soil, and a romantic wilderness through which one could easily drive a carriage on a moonlit night.

After serving for a year as the principal of a school for young women in Detroit, William acquired thirteen hundred acres of land in Livingston County, sixty miles northwest of Detroit, and laid out his settlement around the village of Pinckney. But life in Pinckney failed to live up to the Kirklands' expectations. Instead of a quaintly romantic cottage, Caroline found herself forced to live in a tiny log cabin, far too small for her fancy eastern furniture. Equally disconcerting to the Kirklands was westerners' attitude toward others' possessions. Frontier people thought that they had a right to borrow anything that Caroline owned, with no more than a blunt declaration that "you've got plenty." "For my own part," Caroline related, "I have lent my broom, my thread, my tape, my spoons, my cat, my thimble, my scissors, my shawl, my shoes; and have been asked for my combs and brushes: and my husband, for his shaving apparatus and his pantaloons."

Other surprises were in store for the Kirklands. Accustomed to servants, Caroline found that even poor western girls refused to hire themselves out permanently as household help. As William noted, occasionally a poor girl would enter service long enough to earn money for a new dress, "but never as a regular calling, or with an acknowledgement of inferior station." Yet the Kirklands gradually realized that the peculiarities of westerners sprang not from selfishness or laziness but from an underlying belief in equality. For example, westerners' penchant for borrowing arose from their attitude that frontier men and women had to share and share alike, or go under.

Caroline turned her experiences in Michigan to good advantage by writing a fictionalized account of them, *A New Home—Who'll Follow?* (1839). Justly hailed as the first realistic account of western life, *A New Home* established Caroline's literary reputation, which she continued to build after she and William returned to New York in 1843.

Between 1815 and 1840, many Americans like the Kirklands ventured into the West and had their visions of easy living punctured by the harsh realities of the frontier. Even those who remained in the East had to adjust—to the successive waves of economic and social change that swept the nation after the conclusion of the War of 1812. For westerners and easterners alike, improvements in transportation (the so-called transportation revolution) were spearheaded by the completion in 1825 of the Erie Canal. This "revolution" both stimulated interregional trade and migration and encouraged an unprecedented development of towns and cities. The new urban dwellers, in turn, formed a market not only for agricultural produce but also for the products of the industries springing up in New England and the major northeastern cities.

Viewed superficially, these changes did not greatly affect the way most Americans lived. Whether in 1815 or 1840, the majority of Americans dwelled outside of cities, practiced agriculture for a living, and traveled on foot or by horse. Yet this surface impression of continuity is misleading, because by 1840 many farmers had moved to the West. The nature of farming had also changed, as farmers increasingly raised crops for sale in distant markets rather than merely for their families' consumption. Although most Americans still depended on agriculture, by 1840 alternatives to farming abounded. The rise of such alternatives, in turn, affected some of the most basic social relationships: between parents and children, and between wives and husbands.

WESTWARD EXPANSION AND THE GROWTH OF THE MARKET ECONOMY

The spark that ignited these changes was the spread of Americans across the Appalachian Mountains. In 1790 the vast majority of the people resided east of the

mountains and within a few hundred miles of the Atlantic Ocean. But by 1840 one-third lived between the Appalachians and the Mississippi River. In this area, known at the time as the West, settlers were buffeted by a succession of unexpected social and economic forces.

The Sweep West

This outward thrust of the population occurred in a series of bursts. The first began even before the 1790s and was reflected in the admission of four new states into the Union between 1791 and 1803: Vermont, Kentucky, Tennessee, and Ohio. Then, after an interlude of over ten years that saw the admission of only one new state, Louisiana, six states entered the Union between 1816 and 1821: Indiana, Mississippi, Illinois, Alabama, Maine, and Missouri. Even as Indiana and Illinois were gaining statehood, settlers were pouring farther west into Michigan. Ohio's population jumped from 45,000 in 1800 to 581,000 by 1820 and 1,519,000 by 1840; Michigan's, from 5,000 in 1810 to 212,000 by 1840.

An adventuring spirit carried Americans far beyond the Mississippi. On an exploring expedition in the Southwest in 1806, Zebulon Pike sighted the Colorado peak that was later named after him. The Lewis and Clark expedition whetted interest in the Far West. In 1811 a New York merchant, John Jacob Astor, founded the fur-trading post of Astoria at the mouth of the Columbia River in the Oregon Country. In the 1820s and 1830s, fur traders also operated along the Missouri River from St. Louis to the Rocky Mountains and beyond. At first, whites relied on the Native Americans to bring them furs, but during the 1820s white trappers or "mountain men"—among them, Kit Carson, Jedediah Smith, and the mulatto Jim Beckwourth—gathered furs on their own while performing astounding feats of survival in harsh surroundings.

Jedediah Smith was representative of these men. Born in the Susquehanna Valley of New York in 1799, Smith moved west with his family to Pennsylvania and Illinois and in 1822 signed on with an expedition bound for the upper Missouri River. In the course of this and subsequent explorations, he was almost killed by a grizzly bear in the Black Hills of South Dakota, learned from the Native Americans to trap beaver and shoot buffalo, crossed the Mojave Desert into California, explored California's San Joaquin Valley, and hiked back across the Sierras and the primeval Great Basin to the Great Salt Lake, a trip so forbidding that even the Native Americans avoided it.

The Mountain Men

Rocky Mountain trappers or "mountain men" were among the most colorful and individualistic of nineteenth-century Americans. Entrepreneurs who trapped beavers for their pelts (which were used until the 1830s to make hats), the mountain men were also hunters, explorers, and adventurers who lived "a wild Robin Hood kind of life" with "little fear of God and none at all of the Devil."

Their exploits popularized in biographies, the mountain men became legends in their own day. They were, however, atypical migrants. For most pioneer settlers, the West meant the area between the Appalachians and the Mississippi River, the region today known as the Midwest, and before 1840 very few ventured into the Far West. In contrast to Jedediah Smith, whose unquenchable thirst for adventure led to his death at the hands of Comanches in 1831, most pioneers sought stability and security. The newspaper reports, pamphlets, and letters home that told easterners what to expect in the West usually stressed that western living was bountiful rather than harsh or even risky. A legislator in the Missouri Territory wrote in 1816 that in the states west of the Appalachians, "there neither is, nor, in the nature of things, can there ever be, any thing like poverty there. All is ease, tranquility and comfort."

Western Society and Customs

In their desire for stability, pioneers usually migrated as families rather than as individuals. Because they needed to get their crops to market, most settlers between 1790 and 1820 clustered near the navigable rivers of the West, especially the magnificent water system created by the Ohio and Mississippi rivers. Only with the spread of canals in the 1820s and 1830s, and later of railroads, did westerners feel free to venture far from rivers. In addition, westerners often clustered with people who hailed from the same region back east. For instance, in 1836 a group of farmers from nearby towns met at Castleton, Vermont, listened to a minister intone from the Bible, "And Moses sent them to spy out the land of Canaan," and soon established the town of Vermontville in Michigan. Other migrants to the West were less organized than these latter-day descendants of the Puritans, but most hoped to settle among familiar faces in the West. Finding southerners already well entrenched in Indiana, for example, New Englanders tended to prefer Michigan.

Far from seeking isolation, most westerners craved sociability. Even before there were towns and cities in the West, farm families joined with their neighbors in group sports and festivities. Men met for games that, with a few exceptions like marbles (popular among all ages), were tests of strength or agility. These included wrestling, lifting weights, pole jumping

Merrymaking at a Wayside Inn,
by Pavel Svinin
Country inns served as social centers for rural neighborhoods as well as stopping places for travelers. Although this painting evokes rustic charm, guests at inns complained of the stale odor of rum, pie crusts that tasted like leather, cheese that defied digestion, and a lack of privacy that made them look forward to the crack of the coachman's whip and another day on the road.

(for distance rather than height), and a variant of the modern hammer toss. Some of these games were brutal. In gander pulling, horseback riders competed to pull the head off a gander whose neck had been stripped of feathers and greased. Women usually combined work and play in quilting and sewing parties, carpet tackings, and even chicken and goose pluckings. Social activities brought the genders together. Group corn huskings usually ended with dances; and in a variety of "hoedowns" and "frolics," even westerners who in theory might disapprove of dancing promenaded to singing and a fiddler's tune.

Within western families, there was usually a clear division of labor between men and women. Men performed most of the heaviest labor such as cutting down trees and plowing fields, but women had many chores. Women usually rose first in the morning, because their work included milking the cows as well as preparing breakfast. Women also fashioned the coverlets that warmed beds in unheated rooms, and prior to the spread of factory-made clothing in the 1830s, they made shirts, coats, pants, and dresses on home spinning wheels for family use. They often helped butcher hogs. They knew that the best way to bleed a hog was to slit its throat while it was still alive, and after the bleeding, they were adept at scooping out the innards,

washing the heart and liver, and hanging them to dry. There was nothing dainty about the work of pioneer women.

Most western sports and customs had been transplanted from the East. Gander pulling, for example, had been a popular pastime in Virginia before it made its way to the frontier. Yet the West had a character of its own. Before 1830 few westerners could afford elegant living. Cowpaths did double duty as sidewalks in country towns. The West contained no more than a sprinkling of elegant mansions. Even in the wealthy cotton-growing regions of Alabama and Mississippi, most planters lived in rough conditions prior to 1830. Their relative lack of refinement made westerners easy targets for easterners' contemptuous jibes. Criticisms of the West as a land of half-savage yokels tended, in turn, to give rise to counterassertions by westerners that they lived in a land of honest democracy and that the East was soft and decadent. The exchange of insults fostered a regional identity among westerners that further shaped their behavior. Priding themselves on their simple manners, westerners were often not only hostile to the East but also intolerant of those westerners who had pretensions to gentility. On one occasion, a traveler who hung up a blanket in a tavern to cover his bed from public gaze had it promptly ripped down. On another, a woman who improvised a screen behind which to retire in a crowded room was dismissed as "stuck up." And a politician who rode to a public meeting in a buggy instead of on horseback lost votes.

The Federal Government and the West

Of the various causes of expansion to the Mississippi from 1790 to 1840, the one that operated most generally and uniformly throughout the period was the growing strength of the federal government. Even before the Constitution's ratification, several states had ceded their western land claims to the national government, thereby creating the bountiful public domain. The Land Ordinance of 1785 had set forth plans for surveying and selling parcels of this public treasure to settlers. The Northwest Ordinance of 1787 provided for the orderly transformation of western territories into states. The Louisiana Purchase of 1803 brought the entire Mississippi River under American control, and the Transcontinental Treaty of 1819 wiped out the last vestiges of Spanish power east of the Mississippi. The federal government directly stimulated settlement of its expanding landholdings by inducing soldiers to enlist during the War of 1812 in return for promises of land after the war. With 6 million acres allotted to these so-called military bounties, many former soldiers pulled up roots and tried farming in the West. To facilitate westward migration, Congress authorized funds in 1816 for continued construction of the National Road, a highway begun in 1811 that reached Wheeling, Virginia, on the Ohio River, in 1818 and Vandalia, Illinois, by 1838. Soon the road was thronged with settlers. "Old America seems to be breaking up," a traveler on the National Road wrote in 1817. "We are seldom out of sight, as we travel on this grand track towards the Ohio, of family groups before and behind us."

Although whites gained innumerable advantages from having a more powerful national government behind them, the rising strength of that government brought misery to the Indians. Virtually all the foreign-policy successes during the Jefferson, Madison, and Monroe administrations worked to the Native Americans' disadvantage. Both the Louisiana Purchase and the Transcontinental Treaty stripped them of Spanish protection. In the wake of the Louisiana Purchase, Lewis and Clark bluntly told the Indians that they must "shut their ears to the counsels of bad birds" and listen henceforth only to the Great Father in Washington. The outcome of the War of 1812 also worked against the Native Americans; indeed, the Indians were the only real losers of the war. Early in the negotiations leading to the Treaty of Ghent, the British had insisted on the creation of an Indian buffer state in the Old Northwest, between the United States and Canada. But after the American victory at the Battle of Plattsburgh, the British dropped the demand and essentially abandoned the Indians to the Americans.

The Removal of the Indians

As white settlers poured into the West, they found in their path sizable pockets of Indians, particularly in the South. The Cherokees, Creeks, Choctaws, Chickasaws, and Seminoles—whom non–Native Americans collectively called the Five Civilized Tribes—occupied large parts of Tennessee, Georgia, Alabama, Mississippi, and Florida. Years of commercial dealings and intermarriage with non-Indians had created in all these tribes an influential minority of mixed-bloods, who had heeded the call of white missionaries to embrace Christianity and agriculture. Among the Cherokees, for example, not only was agriculture practiced, but some Native Americans built looms and gristmills and even owned slaves. One of their chiefs, Sequoyah, devised a written form of the Cherokee language, whereas other Cherokees published their own newspaper, the *Cherokee Phoenix.*

In whites' eyes, these were extraordinary accomplishments, and the federal government welcomed them as signs of advancing "civilization" among the Indians. But "civilizing" the Native Americans did not always work to the federal government's advantage. Although some assimilated mixed-bloods willingly sold tribal lands to the government and moved west, others, recognizing that their prosperity depended on commercial dealings with whites, resisted removal. In addition, within the "civilized" tribes, the majority of Indians were full-bloods. Although some full-bloods willingly moved west, most were keen to retain their ancestral lands in the East and were contemptuous both of whites and of mixed-bloods who bartered away tribal land to whites. When the Creek mixed-blood chief William McIntosh sold to the government all Creek lands in Georgia and two-thirds of Creek lands in Alabama in the Treaty of Indian Springs (1825), other Creeks executed him.

As whites' demands for Native American lands reached the boiling point during the 1820s, the traditional policy of negotiating treaties piecemeal with the Indians came under fire. Andrew Jackson embodied the whites' new militancy. Jackson was one of the first prominent government officials to recognize that the balance of power between Native Americans and whites had shifted drastically since the American Revolution. His victory over the Creeks at the Battle of Horseshoe Bend in 1814 had convinced him that the Indians were much weaker than whites often realized. And because they were weakening, Jackson could see no justification for continuing "the farce of treating with the Indian tribes." The Indians were not independent nations, Jackson argued, but were subject to the laws of whatever state they resided in.

When Jackson became president in 1829, he promptly instituted a more coercive removal policy. His policy reflected not only his disdain for the Indians but also his conviction that, as long as the Indians stayed in the East, the "real" Indians who still retained their "savage" ways would be exploited by mercenary whites and self-serving mixed-bloods. In 1830 he secured from a divided Congress passage of the Indian Removal Act, which granted the president funds and authority to remove Native Americans by force if necessary. By then, Georgia and other states were putting overwhelming pressure on the Indians. Resolutions pushed through the Georgia legislature provided that after 1830 Native Americans could not be parties to or witnesses in legal cases involving whites. By the late 1820s, the Creeks in Georgia and Alabama started to move west. In 1836 the Georgia militia attacked Creeks still in the state, and when starving Creeks raided white settlements for food, federal troops finished the job begun by the militia. In 1836 fifteen thousand Creek Indians, most of the Creek nation, were removed—many in chains and handcuffs—and resettled west of the Mississippi.

A similar fate befell the other "civilized" tribes of the South. Treaties signed in 1830 and 1832 achieved the removal of the Choctaws from Mississippi and the Chickasaws from northern Alabama and northern Mississippi. The visiting Frenchman Alexis de Tocqueville witnessed the arrival of the Choctaws, including "the wounded, the sick, newborn babies, and the old men on the point of death," at Memphis on the Mississippi. "I saw them embark to cross the great river, and the sight will never fade from my memory. Neither sob nor complaint rose from that silent assembly. Their afflictions were of long standing, and they felt them to be irremediable." Most Seminoles were removed from

Political Cartoon of Jackson and Native Americans
This cartoon, which depicts Native Americans as children or dolls subject to father Andrew Jackson, was intended as a satire on Jackson's policy of forcibly removing the Indians to reservations. The painting in the upper right corner pointedly depicts the goddess Liberty trampling a tyrant.

Florida, but only after a bitter war between 1835 and 1842 that cost the federal government $20 million.

The Cherokees, the most assimilated of the southern tribes, tried legal resistance to removal, but to no avail. In 1827 the Cherokees proclaimed themselves an independent republic within Georgia. When the Georgia legislature subsequently passed laws extending the state's jurisdiction over this "nation," the Cherokees petitioned the U.S. Supreme Court for an injunction to halt the execution of Georgia's legislation. In the case of *Cherokee Nation v. Georgia* (1831), Chief Justice John Marshall ruled that the Cherokees were neither a state nor a foreign nation and hence lacked standing to bring suit. But Marshall acknowledged that prolonged occupancy gave the Cherokees a right to their land, and a year later, he clarified the Cherokees' legal

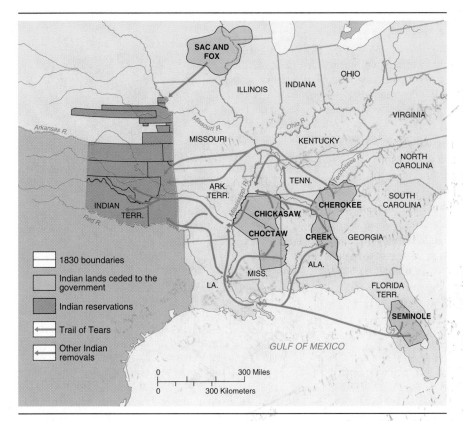

The Removal of the Native Americans to the West, 1820–1840

The so-called Trail of Tears, followed by the Cherokees, was one of several routes along which various tribes migrated on their forced removal to reservations west of the Mississippi.

position in *Worcester* v. *Georgia,* by holding that they were a "domestic dependent nation" entitled to federal protection from molestation by Georgia.

But Marshall's decision had little impact. Jackson ignored it, reportedly sneering, "John Marshall has made his decision; now let him enforce it." The Cherokees themselves were divided into a majority antiremoval faction and a minority proremoval faction. Federal agents persuaded a proremoval chief to sign the Treaty of New Echota (1835), which ceded all Cherokee land to the United States for $5.6 million and free transportation west. Most Cherokees denounced the treaty, and on June 22, 1839, a party of Cherokees took revenge by murdering its three principal signers, including a former *Cherokee Phoenix* editor. But the Cherokees' fate had already been sealed. Between 1835 and 1838, bands of Cherokees straggled west to the Mississippi along the so-called Trail of Tears. Unlike the Creeks, the Cherokees policed their own removal, but this fact did not lessen their physical and spiritual sufferings. Between 2,000 and 4,000 of the 16,000 migrating Cherokees died (see "A Place in Time").

Indians living in the Northwest Territory fared no better. A series of treaties extinguished their land titles, and most moved west of the Mississippi. The removal of the northwestern Indians was notable for two uprisings. The first, led by Red Bird, a Winnebago chief, began in 1827 but was quickly crushed. The second was led by a Sac and Fox chief, Black Hawk, who resisted removal until 1831 and then moved his people west of the Mississippi, only to return the following year. In June 1832 federal troops and Illinois militia furiously attacked his band and virtually annihilated Black Hawk's followers as they tried to recross the Mississippi into Iowa. Black Hawk's downfall induced the other Old Northwest tribes to cede their lands. Between 1832 and 1837, the United States acquired nearly 190 million acres of Indian land in the Northwest for $70 million in gifts and annuities.

The Agricultural Boom

In pushing Indians from the path of white settlers, the federal government was responding to whites' demands for land and more land. Depleted soil and overcrowding had long driven eastern farmers west, but after the War of 1812, a new incentive—the bounding prices of agricultural commodities such as wheat, corn, and cotton—pulled settlers westward in search

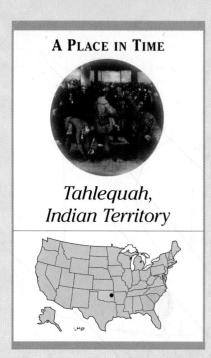

Tahlequah, Indian Territory

The sufferings of the southeastern Indian tribes along the Trail of Tears did not end when the Cherokees, Choctaws, Creeks, Chickasaws, and other nations arrived in the Indian Territory that is now Oklahoma. Most of the tribes found that the federal government failed to deliver fully on promises of supplies and that white merchants, who had contracted to feed the Native Americans until they could raise their own crops, often cheated them. At times, white contractors bought up Indian claims for corn rations for cash, which the Indians then spent on whiskey. One white agent reported seeing two thousand drunken Creeks, more than 10 percent of the entire tribe, on a single day in 1837.

Yet left to their own devices, the southeastern Indians were thriving in their new western home by the 1840s. In addition to establishing farms and small

Chief John Ross,
by John Rubens Smith, 1841
After becoming the principal chief of the eastern Cherokees in 1828, Ross, who was only one-eighth Cherokee himself, emerged as a leading opponent of Jackson's Indian-removal policy.

Cherokee Hunter,
by Baroness Hyde de Neuville, 1820
On the eve of their removal to the West, the Cherokees and the other southeastern tribes had increasingly abandoned their traditional hunting, fishing, and gathering for agriculture and trade.

factories, the Native Americans developed a passion for education. With the aid of white missionaries, they built elementary schools and academies. They operated printing presses that turned out schoolbooks, hymnals, and catechisms in the Creek, Choctaw, and Cherokee languages as well as in English. Some historians have concluded that the Native Americans' school system was the best west of the Mississippi in the 1840s. As white Americans trekked to Texas and California during that decade, moreover, they came to depend on the food and other supplies that they purchased from the transplanted southeastern Indians.

With prosperity, the tribes gradually overcame their internal political divisions. Rival Cherokee factions, for example, united in 1839 and established a government seat at Tahlequah, a village in present-day eastern Oklahoma, near the Illinois River. But the "civilized" tribes continued to suffer from raids by the nomadic prairie Indians such as the Osages and Comanches. In June 1843 Tahlequah became the scene of a most extraordinary

273a

Tahlequah Council, 1843,
by John Mix Stanley
The seventeen-tribe council of the summer of 1843 was intended to establish friendly ties between the Cherokee exiles and the Indian Territory's Plains peoples.

council of tribes. Some four thousand delegates from seventeen Indian nations, including the seven-foot-tall Osage leader Black Dog and the son of Tecumseh, crowded into Tahlequah to hear the presiding Cherokee chief, John Ross, proclaim: "By peace our condition has been improved in the pursuits of civilized life. We should, therefore, extend the hand of peace from tribe to tribe, till peace is established between every nation of red men within the reach of our voice." In addition to destroying a thousand gallons of whiskey, the council agreed on a compact that provided for punishment of offenders from one tribe who raided another tribe.

No Indian council, however, could remove the source of intertribal raiding: the steady shrinkage of the nomadic Indians' hunting grounds caused by the relentless advance of white settlement and by the very prosperity of the "civilized" Indians. Reduced to near starvation, the Osages and Comanches continued to raid the settled tribes' livestock until these nomads themselves were forced onto reservations.

Choctaw Girls
These young Choctaws, members of one of the Five Civilized Tribes, were photographed in the Oklahoma Indian Territory.

273b

of better farmland. Several factors accounted for the skyrocketing farm prices. First, Britain and France, exhausted by the Napoleonic Wars, were importing wheat and corn from America, and the United States had swiftly captured former British markets in the West Indies and former Spanish markets in South America. In addition, the beginnings of industrialization in New England even before the war combined with the westward migration of New England farmers to create a demand in the eastern United States for western foodstuffs. So as domestic and foreign demand intensified, commodity prices rose between 1815 and 1819. The West's splendid river systems made it possible for farmers in Ohio to ship wheat and corn down the Ohio River to the Mississippi and then down the Mississippi to New Orleans. There wheat and corn were either sold or transshipped to the East, the West Indies, South America, or Europe. Just as government policies made farming in the West possible, high prices for foodstuffs made it attractive.

As the prospect of raising wheat and corn pulled farmers toward the Old Northwest, Eli Whitney's invention of the cotton gin in 1793 (see Chapter 7) cleared the path for settlement of the Old Southwest, particularly the states of Alabama and Mississippi on the Gulf of Mexico. After the War of 1812, the explosive thrust of small farmers and planters from the seaboard South into the Old Southwest resembled a gold rush. By 1817 "Alabama fever" gripped the South; settlers bid the price of good land up to thirty dollars to fifty dollars an acre. By 1820 Alabama and Mississippi produced half of the nation's cotton. Stimulated by the seemingly bottomless demand of the British textile industry for raw cotton, cotton production tripled between 1816 and 1826, and the story was only beginning. Between 1831 and 1836, the value of cotton exports rose 300 percent. Accounting for less than a quarter of all American exports between 1802 and 1807, cotton composed just over half by 1830, and nearly two-thirds by 1836.

The Rise of the Market Economy

To farmers, the high prices of agricultural commodities between 1815 and 1819 appeared an unmixed blessing. Most planned to grow enough food to feed their families (called subsistence agriculture) *and* a cash crop like wheat or cotton to sell in local or distant markets (called commercial agriculture, or the "market economy"). Farming for markets was not new;

many farmers had done so during the colonial era. What was new after the War of 1812 was the extent to which farmers entered the market economy. High crop prices tempted many former subsistence farmers into the commercial economy. Often these individuals had little experience with commercial dealings and little idea of what they were getting into. Commercial agriculture exposed farmers to innumerable new risks. First, cash crops like wheat and cotton were sold to people whom the farmers themselves frequently never met, in places that they never saw. Second, farmers had no control over the fluctuations of distant markets. Furthermore, there was inevitably an interval, often a long one, between harvesting a cash crop and selling it. To sustain themselves during the interval, farmers had to borrow money. Thus commercial agriculture forced farmers into short-term debt in the hope of long-term profit.

The debt was frequently worse than most had expected. In the first place, many western farmers had to borrow money to buy their land. The roots of this indebtedness for land lay, in turn, in the federal government's inability to devise an effective policy for transferring the public domain directly into the hands of small farmers.

Federal Land Policy

Partisan and sectional pressures buffeted federal land policy like a kite in a March wind. The result was a succession of land laws passed between 1796 and 1820, each of which sought to undo the damage caused by its predecessors.

At the root of early federal land policy lay a preference for the orderly settlement of the public domain. To this end, the Ordinance of 1785 divided public lands into townships of six miles square each and then subdivided each township into one-mile-square lots (usually called sections) of 640 acres. The architects of the ordinance did not expect that ordinary farmers could afford to purchase 640-acre sections; rather, they assumed that farmers who shared ties based on religion or region of origin would band together to purchase sections. This outcome would ensure that compatible settlers would live on adjoining lots in what amounted to rural neighborhoods, and it would make the task of government much easier than if settlers were to live in isolation on widely scattered homesteads.

Political developments in the 1790s undermined the expectations of the ordinance's framers. Because their political bases lay in the East, the Federalists were reluctant to encourage headlong settlement of the West, but at the same time they were eager to raise revenue for the federal government from land sales. They reconciled these goals—retarding actual settlement while gaining revenue—by encouraging the sale of huge tracts of land to wealthy speculators who did not intend to farm the land but instead planned to hold it until its value rose, and then sell off parcels to farmers. In the 1790s land speculators swarmed through the area east of the Appalachians. The Holland Land Company, for example, composed mainly of Dutch investors, bought up much of western New York and western Pennsylvania. A federal land law passed in 1796 reflected Federalist aims by maintaining the minimum purchase at 640 acres at a minimum price of two dollars an acre, and by allowing only a year for complete payment.

Believing that the small farmer was the backbone of the Republic, and fully aware of Republican political strength in the West, Thomas Jefferson and the Republicans took a different tack. Starting in 1800, federal land laws increasingly reflected the Republicans' desire to ease the transfer of the public domain to farmers. Accordingly, the land law of 1800 dropped the minimum purchase to 320 acres and allowed up to four years for full payment but kept the minimum purchase price at $2.00 an acre. In 1804 the minimum purchase came down to 160 acres, in 1820 to 80 acres, and in 1832 to 40 acres. The minimum price also declined from $2.00 an acre in 1800 to $1.64 in 1804 and to $1.25 in 1820.

Although the government steadily liberalized its land policy, speculators always remained one step ahead of Congress. Long before 1832, speculators were selling 40-acre lots to farmers. Farmers actually preferred these small lots (and rarely bought more than 160 acres), because the "farm" they purchased typically was a forest. A new landowner could clear no more than ten to twelve acres of trees a year. But small lots carried a price. All land in the public domain was sold at auction, usually for much more than the two-dollar minimum. With agricultural prices soaring, speculators assumed that land would continue to rise in value and accordingly were willing to bid high on new land, which they resold to farmers at hefty prices.

The growing availability of credit after the War of 1812 fed speculation. The chartering of the Second Bank of the United States in 1816 had the dual effect of increasing the amount of money in circulation and stimulating the chartering of private banks within states (state banks). The circulation of all banks grew from $45 million in bank notes in 1812 to $100 million in 1817. The stockholders and directors of these banks viewed them less as a sound investment for their capital (many directors actually had very little capital when they started state banks) than as agencies that could lend them money for land speculation. Secretary of the Treasury William H. Crawford observed in 1820 that banks had been incorporated "not because there was capital seeking investment, not because the places where they were established had commerce and manufacturers which required their fostering aid; but because men without active capital wanted the means of obtaining loans, which their standing in the community would not command from banks or individuals having real capital and established credit." In short, banks were founded so that they could lend their directors money for personal investment in land speculation. The result was an orgy of land speculation between 1815 and 1819. In 1819 sales of public land were over 1,000 percent greater than the average in 1800–1814.

The Speculator and the Squatter

Nevertheless, most of the public domain eventually found its way into the hands of small farmers. Because speculators gained nothing by holding land for prolonged periods, they were only too happy to sell it when the price was right. In addition, a familiar frontier type, the squatter, exerted a restraining influence on the speculator.

Even before the creation of the public domain, squatters had helped themselves to western land; George Washington himself had been unable to drive squatters off lands that he owned in the West. Squatters were an independent and proud lot, scornful of their fellow citizens, who were "softened by Ease, enervated by Affluence and Luxurious Plenty, & unaccustomed to Fatigues, Hardships, Difficulties or dangers." Disdaining land speculators above all, squatters formed claims associations to police land auctions and prevented speculators from bidding up the price of land. Squatters also pressured Congress to allow them "preemption" rights—that is, the right to purchase at the minimum price land that they had already settled on and improved. Seeking to undo the pernicious effects of its own laws, Congress responded by passing special preemption laws for squatters in specific areas and finally, in 1841, acknowledged a general right of preemption.

But preemption laws were of no use to farmers who arrived after speculators had already bought up land. Having spent their small savings on livestock, seed, and tools, these settlers then had to buy land from speculators on credit at vicious interest rates that ranged as high as 40 percent. Saddled by steep indebtedness, many western farmers had no choice but to skimp on subsistence crops while expanding cash crops in the hope of paying off their creditors. Farmers in these years were not merely entering the market economy; they were lunging into it.

Countless farmers who had carried basically conservative expectations to the West and who had hoped to establish self-sufficient farms in a land of abundance quickly became economic adventurers. Wanting land that they could call their own, but forced to raise cash crops in a hurry, many farmers worked their acreage to exhaustion and thus had to keep moving in search of new land. The phrase "the moving frontier" refers not only to the obvious fact that with each passing decade the line of settlement shifted farther west but also to the fact that the same people kept moving. The experience of Abraham Lincoln's parents, who migrated from the East through several farms in Kentucky and then to Indiana, was representative of the westward trek.

The Panic of 1819

In 1819 the land boom collapsed like a house of cards, the victim of a financial panic. The state banks' loose practices contributed mightily to the panic. Like the Bank of the United States, these banks issued their own bank notes. In the absence of any national system of paper money, these notes served as a circulating medium. A bank note was just a piece of paper with a printed promise from the bank's directors to pay the bearer ("redeem") on demand a certain amount of specie (gold or silver coinage). State banks had long emitted far more bank notes than they could redeem, and these notes had fueled the economic boom after 1815. With credit so readily available, farmers borrowed money to buy more land and to plant more crops, confident that they could repay their loans when they sold their crops. After 1817, however, the combination of bumper crops in Europe and a business recession in Britain trimmed the foreign demand for U.S. wheat, flour, and cotton—at the

very time when American farmers were becoming more dependent on agricultural exports to pay their debts.

In reaction to the overemission of state bank notes, the Bank of the United States, in the summer of 1818, began to insist that state banks redeem in specie their notes that were held by the Bank of the United States. Because the Bank of the United States had more branches than any state bank, notes of state banks were often presented by their holders to branches of the Bank of the United States for redemption. Whenever the Bank of the United States redeemed a state bank note in specie, it became a creditor of the state bank. In turn, to pay their debts to the Bank of the United States, the state banks had no choice but to force farmers and land speculators to repay loans. The result was a general curtailment of credit throughout the nation, but particularly in the West.

The biggest losers were the land speculators, who had bought huge tracts with the expectation that prices would rise but now found prices tumbling. Land that had once sold for as much as $69 an acre dropped to $2 an acre. Land prices fell, in turn, because the credit squeeze drove down the market prices of staples like wheat, corn, cotton, and tobacco. Cotton, which sold for 32¢ a pound in 1818, sank as low as 17¢ a pound in 1820. Since farmers could not get much cash for their crops, they could not pay the debts that they had incurred to buy land. Since speculators could not collect money owed them by farmers, the value of land that they still held for sale collapsed.

The significance of the panic lay not only in the economic damage it did but also in the conclusions that many Americans drew from it. First, the panic left a bitter taste about banks, particularly the Bank of the United States, which was widely blamed for the hard times. In addition, the panic dramatized the vulnerability of American factories to cheap foreign competition (a vulnerability evident even before the economic downturn) and thereby stimulated demands for the protection of domestic industries. These demands would lead to the passage of higher tariffs in 1824 and 1828. Finally, plummeting prices for cash crops demonstrated how much farmers were coming to depend on distant markets. In effect, it took a severe business reverse to show farmers the extent to which they had become entrepreneurs. The fall in the prices of cash crops intensified the search for better forms of transportation to reach those faraway markets. If the cost of transporting crops could be cut, farmers could keep a larger share of the value of their crops and thereby adjust to falling prices.

The Transportation Revolution: Steamboats, Canals, and Railroads

Most forms of transportation available to Americans in 1820 had severe drawbacks. The great rivers west of the Appalachians ran primarily from north to south and hence could not by themselves connect western farmers with eastern markets. The National Road, with its crushed-stone surface, was a well-built highway that advanced farther west each year. In addition, between 1815 and 1825, several northern states chartered private companies to build toll roads (turnpikes). But roads could not solve the nation's transportation problems. Aside from the fact that horse-drawn wagons could carry only limited produce, roads were expensive to maintain. After 1825 investment in turnpikes slackened, and the interest of both public and private investors shifted toward the development of waterways.

In 1807 Robert R. Livingston and Robert Fulton successfully introduced a steamboat popularly known as the *Clermont* on the Hudson River. Livingston and Fulton soon gained a monopoly from the New York legislature to run a ferry service on the Hudson between New York and New Jersey. So spectacular were their profits that rival entrepreneurs secured a license from Congress to operate a competing ferry service and thereby challenged the Livingston-Fulton monopoly. A long court battle followed. Finally, in 1824 the U.S. Supreme Court decided against the monopoly in the famous case of *Gibbons* v. *Ogden*. Speaking for a unanimous Court, Chief Justice John Marshall ruled that commerce included not merely the exchange of products but navigation as well. This was an important finding, because the Constitution clearly empowered Congress to regulate commerce "among the several States." In the event of a conflict between state and congressional regulation of commerce, Marshall continued, the congressional power must prevail. Thus Marshall upheld the competitors (who had a license from Congress) and effectively broke the Livingston-Fulton monopoly. In the wake of Marshall's decision, state efforts to establish monopolies over river trade quickly collapsed. The number of steamboats operating on western rivers jumped from 17 in 1817 to 69 in 1820 and to 727 by 1855.

Interior of a Flatboat,
by Charles-Alexandre Lesueur, 1826
Not all flatboats that carried produce and pioneers on American rivers were floating rafts. Many had roomy interiors that accommodated whole families, provisions, and even barn animals.

Prior to the introduction of steamboats on the Mississippi, flatboats (often just rafts) carried produce downriver. Since they were unable to navigate upstream, the flatboats were broken up and sold for firewood in New Orleans. The return voyage was made either by foot or horse through Indian country, or by sailing vessels from New Orleans to Philadelphia or New York and then by foot or horse across the Appalachians to the West. Keelboats—similar to flatboats but moved by a rudder—could make the upstream voyage, though at a snail's pace. It took a keelboat three or four months to complete the 1,350-mile journey from New Orleans to Louisville. In contrast, steamboats could travel upstream at a relatively fast speed. As early as 1817, a steamboat made the trip in twenty-five days. Moreover, although the English had developed steam-propulsion technology in the eighteenth century, between 1820 and 1840 Americans discovered many practical techniques for increasing the effectiveness of steamboats. The gradual introduction of long, shallow hulls made steamboats suitable for use in shallow water (particularly the stretch of the Mississippi-Ohio river system from Louisville to Pittsburgh). The result was an extension of the navigation season; hot, dry summer weather that lowered water levels no longer forced steamboats out of service.

Erie Canal, *by John William Hill, 1831 Construction of the Erie Canal was a remarkable feat—all the more so because the United States did not possess a single school of engineering at the time. The project's heroes were lawyers and merchants who taught themselves engineering, and brawny workmen, often Irish immigrants, who hacked a waterway through the forests and valleys of New York.*

Steamboats became more ornate as well as more practical. To compete for passengers, they began to offer luxurious cabins and lounges (called saloons). The saloon of the *Eclipse,* a Mississippi steamboat, was the length of a football field and featured skylights, chandeliers, a ceiling crisscrossed by Gothic arches, and mahogany furniture covered with velvet. Such "elegance bordering on magnificence" helped to reassure westerners that whatever easterners might say, they were not savage backwoods people but polished and urbane citizens. Yet most steamboat passengers only glimpsed this elegance. Saloons were reserved for the small minority who booked "cabin" passage. The majority of travelers purchased "deck" passage, which entitled them to sleep on a cotton bale if they were lucky enough to find one, on the floor if they were not.

Whether cabin or deck passengers, all steamboat travelers confronted the hazards of this mode of navigation. Fires were common—not surprisingly, in view of the fact that steamboats needed huge furnaces and often carried combustible cargoes like oil and hay. Collisions claimed many lives. The worst, occurring in 1837 on the Mississippi, killed several hundred Creek Indians who were being transported by steamer to reservations in the West. Submerged snags often cracked the fragile hulls of fast-moving steamers: British novelist Charles Dickens described the Mississippi above Cairo, Illinois, as "an enormous ditch . . . choked and obstructed everywhere by huge logs and whole forest trees." Moreover, because little was

known about the reaction of metals under stress, boiler explosions destroyed many steamboats, not to mention their passengers. So common were such explosions that one company introduced a line of steamboats on the Hudson River that, for safety's sake, carried the passengers in tow on a barge.

Once steamboats had demonstrated the feasibility of upriver navigation, popular enthusiasm for internal improvements shifted away from turnpikes and toward canals. As late as 1816, the United States had only a hundred miles of canals. Not only did Americans know little about building canals in these early years, but the capital required to construct them was mindboggling. Even Thomas Jefferson dismissed the idea of canals as "little short of madness." However, the invention of the steamboat, the abundance of western settlers desperate for access to markets, and the natural endowment of the Great Lakes combined to make the lure of canals irresistible. Canals offered the prospect of connecting the superb Mississippi-Ohio river system with the Great Lakes, and the Great Lakes with eastern markets.

The construction of the Erie Canal was the first major canal project. Started by New York State in 1817, the canal at its completion stretched for 363 miles between Albany and Buffalo. The Erie Canal was ten times longer than any previous American canal and by far the longest in the Western world. More than a waterway, it was a capstone of the sometimes fragile Era of Good Feelings, a symbol of American ingenuity and peaceful progress. As part of the celebration of its completion in 1825, a procession of American steamboats formed a perfect circle of salute around two British warships anchored in New York Harbor. The British responded by striking up "Yankee Doodle," to which the Americans replied with "God Save the King." Through the Erie Canal, New York City was linked by inland waterways (the Hudson River, the canal itself, and Lake Erie) all the way to Ohio.

Major Rivers, Roads, and Canals, 1825–1860

Railroads and canals increasingly tied the economy of the Midwest to that of the Northeast.

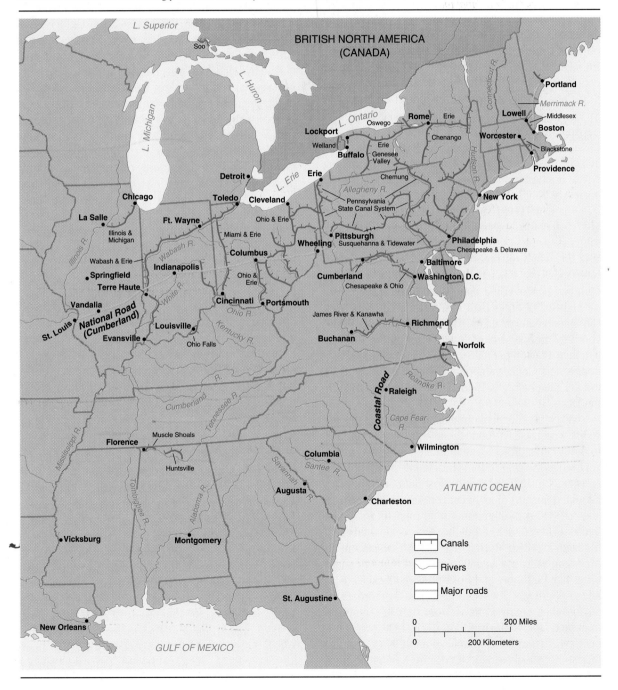

In New England the Blackstone Canal (1824–1828) created a water highway between Worcester, Massachusetts, and the Narragansett Bay in Rhode Island. By 1834 the Main Line (or Pennsylvania) Canal connected eastern Pennsylvania with Pittsburgh. The Main Line Canal was an even more remarkable feat of engineering than the Erie because it crossed the Allegheny Mountains with the aid of a railroad. Canal boats on this system had to be built in collapsible sections; they were disassembled upon reaching the mountains and then carried up one side and down the other on cable cars. As these canals spread like fingers from east to west, a similar system of canals was under construction from west to east. By 1836 the Ohio and Erie Canal stretched from Portsmouth on the Ohio River to Cleveland on Lake Erie. From Lake Erie, packets and steamboats could carry produce to the Erie Canal and on to Albany and New York City. In 1836, 365,000 bushels of western wheat entered the milling city of Rochester on the Erie Canal and left as 369,000 barrels of flour bound for eastern New York.

The canal boom drastically cut shipping costs. In 1817, just before construction began on the Erie Canal, the cost of transporting wheat from Buffalo to New York City was three times the market value of wheat in New York City, whereas the transportation costs for corn and oats over the same route were, respectively, six and twelve times their market value in New York City. Average freight charges between Buffalo and New York City dropped from 19¢ a ton per mile in 1817 to less than 2¢ a ton per mile in 1830. Throughout the nation, canals reduced shipping costs from 20¢ to 30¢ a ton per mile before 1815 to 2¢ to 3¢ a ton per mile by the 1830s.

When another economic depression hit in the late 1830s, various states found themselves overcommitted to costly canal projects and ultimately scrapped many. Yet even as the canal boom was ending, railroads were spreading. In 1825 the world's first railroad devoted to general transportation began operation in England, and by 1840 some three thousand miles of track had been laid in America, about the same as the total canal mileage in 1840. During the 1830s, investment in American railroads actually exceeded that in canals. Cities like Baltimore and Boston, which lacked major inland waterway connections, turned to railroads to enlarge their share of the western market. The Baltimore and Ohio Railroad, chartered in 1828, took business away from the Chesapeake and Ohio Canal farther south. Blocked by its Berkshire Mountains from

building a canal to the Erie, Massachusetts chartered the Boston and Worcester Railroad in 1831 and the Western Railroad (from Worcester to Albany) in 1833.

Faster, cheaper to build, and able to reach more places, railroads had obvious advantages over canals and also contributed to the growth of communities that were remote from waterways. But railroads' potential was only slowly realized. Most early railroads ran between cities in the East rather than from east to west and carried more passengers than freight. Not until 1849 did freight revenues exceed passenger revenues, and not until 1850 was the East Coast connected by rail to the Great Lakes.

Several factors explain the relatively slow spread of interregional railroads. Unlike canals, which were built directly by state governments, most railroads were constructed by private corporations seeking quick profits. To minimize their original investment, railroad companies commonly resorted to cost-cutting measures such as covering wooden rails with iron bars. As a result, although relatively cheap to build, American railroads needed constant repairs and were even more vulnerable than canals to economic fluctuations. In contrast, although expensive to construct, canals needed relatively little maintenance and were kept in operation for decades after railroads appeared. Moreover, it remained cheaper to ship bulky commodities such as iron ore, coal, and nonperishable agricultural produce by canal.

The Growth of the Cities

The transportation revolution contributed to the rapid growth of towns and cities. In 1820 only 6.1 percent of the population lived in places of 2,500 or more inhabitants, and only two cities, New York and Philadelphia, had more than 100,000 people. Four of the ten largest cities in the United States in 1820 had fewer than 15,000 inhabitants. The next forty years witnessed, in relative terms, the most rapid urbanization in American history. By 1860 nearly 20 percent of the population lived in places of 2,500 or more. New York City's population rose from 124,000 in 1820 to 800,000 in 1860. By 1860 there were eight American cities larger than the largest city in 1820. An even more revealing change was the transformation of sleepy villages of a few hundred into thriving towns of several thousand. In 1820 only 56 incorporated towns could boast between 2,500 and 10,000 inhabitants; by 1850 there were over 350 such towns. The Erie Canal transformed

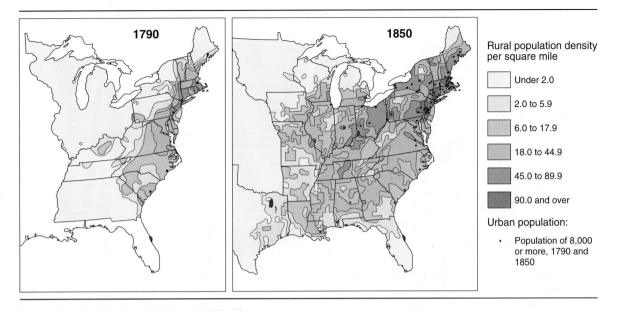

Population Distribution, 1790 and 1850

By 1850 high population density characterized parts of the Midwest as well as the Northeast.

SOURCE: *1900 Census of Population, Statistical Atlas,* plates 2 and 8.

Rochester, New York, for example, from a village of a few hundred people in 1817 to a thriving town of 9,000 by 1830.

City and town growth occurred with dramatic suddenness, especially in the West. Pittsburgh, Cincinnati, and St. Louis were little more than villages in 1800. The War of 1812 stimulated the growth of Pittsburgh, whose iron forges provided shot and weapons for American soldiers, and Cincinnati, which became a staging ground for attacks on the British in the Old Northwest. Meanwhile, St. Louis acquired some importance as a fur-trading center. Then between 1815 and 1819, the agricultural boom and the introduction of the steamboat transformed all three places from outposts with transient populations of hunters, traders, and soldiers into bustling cities. Cincinnati's population, for example, nearly quadrupled between 1810 and 1820 and doubled in the 1820s.

With the exception of Lexington, Kentucky, whose lack of access to water forced it into relative stagnation after 1820, all the prominent western cities were river ports: Pittsburgh, Cincinnati, and Louisville on the Ohio; St. Louis and New Orleans on the Mississippi. Except for Pittsburgh, all were essentially commercial hubs rather than manufacturing centers and were flooded by individuals extremely eager to make

money. In 1819 land speculators in St. Louis were bidding as much as a thousand dollars an acre for lots that had sold for thirty dollars an acre in 1815. Waterfronts endowed with natural beauty were swiftly overrun by stores and docks. "Louis Ville, by nature is beautiful," a visitor wrote, "but the handy Work of *Man* has instead of improving destroy'd the works of Nature and made it a detestable place."

The transportation revolution acted like a fickle god, selecting some cities for growth while sentencing others to relative decline. Just as the steamboat had elevated the river cities over land-locked Lexington, the completion of the Erie Canal shifted the center of western economic activity toward the Great Lakes. The result was a gradual decline in the importance of river cities and a rise between 1830 and 1860 in the importance of lake cities such as Buffalo, Cleveland, Detroit, Chicago, and Milwaukee. In 1830 nearly 75 percent of all western city dwellers lived in the river ports of New Orleans, Louisville, Cincinnati, and Pittsburgh, but by 1840 the proportion had dropped to 20 percent.

The growth of cities and towns was spurred initially by the transportation revolution and the development of interregional trade. Urban expansion received an added boost from the rise of manufacturing between 1815 and 1840.

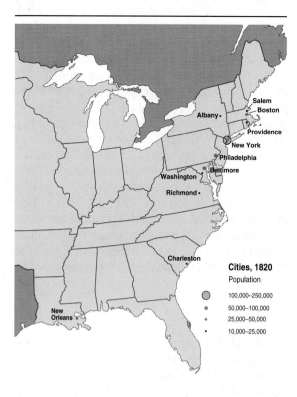

Cities, 1820

Population

●	100,000–250,000
●	50,000–100,000
●	25,000–50,000
●	10,000–25,000

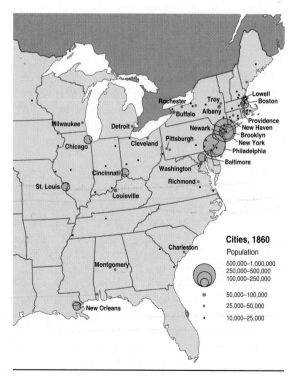

Cities, 1860

Population

	500,000–1,000,000
	250,000–500,000
	100,000–250,000
●	50,000–100,000
●	25,000–50,000
●	10,000–25,000

American Cities, 1820 and 1860

In 1820 most cities were seaports. By 1860, however, cities dotted the nation's interior and included San Francisco on the West Coast. This change occurred in large measure because of the transportation revolution.

SOURCE: *Statistical Abstract of the United States.*

THE RISE OF MANUFACTURING

Today we customarily equate the word *manufacturing* with industrialization—that is, with large factories, machinery, and mass production. But the literal meaning of *manufacturing* is "making by hand." During the colonial era, most products were made by hand, either in households or in the workshops of skilled artisans. The period between 1815 and 1860 marked a transition from colonial to modern manufacturing. Household, or "cottage," industries declined, whereas large factories and power-driven machinery came to dominate the production of cotton textiles. But small shops were still responsible for a great deal of manufacturing. As late as 1860, the average manufacturing establishment contained only eight workers.

Few Americans believed in 1860 that they lived in an industrial society; most continued to think of the United States as a nation of farmers and small producers. This self-image, however, was misleading. By 1850 the 20 percent of the labor force engaged in manufacturing produced about 30 percent of the national output. Furthermore, industrialization was starting to affect many crafts besides textile making.

Industrialization was not a single occurrence, a kind of tidal wave that washed away traditional forms of manufacturing. Rather, it was a gradual process with several distinct stages. First, the tasks involved in making a product were subdivided, so that instead of making a whole product, each worker made only a part. Next, workers were gathered into factories with rooms devoted to specialized operations performed by hand or by simple machines. Finally, power-driven machinery replaced fabrication by hand. These three stages arrived quickly and almost simultaneously in New England's cotton textile industry, but many crafts—including the making of shoes, hats, guns, trunks, and saddles—experienced at least the first two stages before 1860. Many variations of this pattern appeared between 1815 and 1860. In some crafts, task subdivision and simple machinery were introduced without the creation of large factories. In others, like shoe manufacturing, the subdivision of tasks and the emergence of large factories occurred before the introduction of power-driven machinery. Because industrialization occurred gradually and unevenly, people did not always realize that hand fabrication by skilled artisans was becoming obsolete and that machines would soon tumble artisans from their pedestals.

Causes of Industrialization

A host of factors stimulated industrialization. The Embargo Act of 1807 persuaded merchants barred from foreign trade to redirect their capital into factories. The War of 1812 sparked support for protective tariffs to end American economic dependence on Europe; particularly in the 1820s, tariffs reduced imports of English cloth and contributed to the 15.4 percent average annual rise in American cloth products between 1815 and 1833. Improvements in transportation made it possible for manufacturers to sell finished products in distant markets and provided an incentive to increase production. In addition, a popular preference for factory-made rather than homemade products developed wherever the transportation revolution reached. Household production declined not only in cities but in rural areas along canals and railroads and never gained a secure footing in the West. The more farmers went into the business of selling as well as raising crops, the more they were inclined to buy articles like shoes and clothes rather than make them.

Immigration was also vital. Five million people migrated from Europe to the United States between 1790 and 1860, most of them to pursue economic opportunity. The majority were German or Irish, but the smaller number of British immigrants played the key role in launching industrialization. In Britain industrialization was a generation ahead of the United States, and by 1790 Britain had a class of artisans who understood the workings of machines. For example, Samuel Slater, who immigrated to the United States in 1789, had learned the "mystery" of textile production in England. Although British laws forbade emigration by skilled "mechanics," Slater disguised himself and brought his knowledge of machines to eager Americans.

Although Britain had a head start in developing the technology relevant to industrialization, Americans made contributions of their own. Unlike Britain, America had no craft organizations (called guilds) that tied artisans to a single trade. As a result, American artisans freely experimented with machines outside their craft. In the 1790s wagon maker Oliver Evans of Delaware, for example, built an automated flour mill that required only a single supervisor to look on as the grain poured in from one side and was discharged from the other as flour. In addition, the relatively high wages paid to American workers gave manufacturers an incentive to find substitutes for expensive hand labor in order to make products as quickly and cheaply as possible. After inventing the cotton gin, Eli Whitney in 1798 filled a government contract for ten thousand muskets by using unskilled workers to make identical parts that could be interchanged from musket to musket. The idea of interchangeable parts actually originated in Europe, but the United States led all nations in applying the idea in factories—so much so that it came to be called the American system of manufacturing.

New England Industrializes

New England became America's first industrial region. The gradual strangulation of American trade by Britain's Orders in Council, Napoleon's Continental System, and Jefferson's embargo hit New England more severely than regions less dependent on European trade. Incentives were thus provided for New England's merchants to invest in manufacturing. In addition, New England's rivers were numerous, swift-flowing, and ideally suited to provide water power for mills. At the same time, the region's soil, thin and rocky in many places, forced young men off the land and into the westward flow of migration, leaving villages and towns with a surplus of young women. The textile mills that multiplied in New England after 1815 depended on the labor of the sisters who had stayed at home while their brothers headed west or moved to the cities.

Within New England the main innovation came in the manufacture of cotton textiles. In 1790 Samuel Slater arrived in Pawtucket, Rhode Island, and established there the first permanent American mill for spinning cotton into yarn through the use of the spinning frame invented by the Englishman Richard Arkwright. Starting with nine workers, Slater had a hundred by 1800 and constructed other mills around Rhode Island and Massachusetts. Slater's mills performed only two of the many operations needed to turn raw cotton into clothing: carding, or fashioning broad laps of cotton into fine strands or slivers, and spinning these strands into yarn. The actual weaving of yarn Slater contracted out to women working in their homes. This "putting-out" system reinforced rather than challenged the traditional position of household, or "cottage," industry.

The incorporation in 1813 of the Boston Manufacturing Company by a group of merchant capitalists called the Boston Associates began a new chapter in the relationship between factories and cottage industries. Starting with a capital stock of $400,000 (more than ten times the stock of a typical Rhode Island mill), the Boston Manufacturing Company in quick succession established cotton textile factories in the Massachusetts towns of Waltham on the Charles River and Lowell on the Merrimack. By 1836 the Boston Associates had a total investment of $6.2 million in eight companies employing more than six thousand workers.

Size was not the only factor that distinguished these new mills from Slater's. In contrast to Slater's mills, the Waltham and Lowell factories produced finished products and thus challenged the cottage industries that Slater's system had sustained. Additionally, the Waltham and Lowell mills upset the traditional ordering of New England society to a degree that Slater never contemplated. Slater had sought to preserve tradition by hiring entire families to work in his mill complexes, just as entire families had traditionally worked on farms. He hired men to raise crops on nearby land owned by the factory and their wives and children to tend the machines inside. Under this arrangement, children were never out of parental sight for long. In contrast, 80 percent of the workers in the mills operated by the Boston Manufacturing Company were unmarried women between the ages of fifteen and thirty, who had been lured from New England's farms by the promise of factory work. Mary Paul, a Vermont teenager, settled her doubts about leaving home for work in Lowell by concluding that "I . . . must work where I can get more pay." Although these young women often wrote home, they rarely saw their parents. In place of traditional family discipline, the Waltham and Lowell operatives, as the mill workers were called, experienced new kinds of restraints. The Boston capitalists who financed the mills did not personally oversee them; rather, they delegated oversight to managers, who imposed their own forms of discipline on the work force. Operatives had to live either in boardinghouses built by the factory owners or in licensed private dwellings. Company regulations required operatives to attend church on the Sabbath, to observe a 10:00 P.M. curfew, and to accept what one minister called the "moral police of the corporations." At least initially, most young female operatives submitted without complaint to the "moral police."

Mill Girls
New England's humming textile mills were a magnet for untold numbers of independence-seeking young women in antebellum America.

A major reason why the corporations enforced high moral standards was to give the mills a good reputation so that New England farm girls would continue to be attracted into factory work. Yet mill conditions were far from attractive. To prevent the threads from snapping, the factories had to be kept humid. To create this condition, overseers nailed the windows shut and sprayed the air with water. Operatives also had to contend with flying dust and the deafening roar of the machines. Then keener competition and a worsening economy in the late 1830s led the mill owners to reduce wages and speed up work schedules. Such conditions were common in nineteenth-century factories, but in Lowell and Waltham they were intensified by the basic impersonality of the system. Each of the major groups that contributed to the system lived in a self-contained world. The Boston Associates raised capital but rarely visited the factories. Their agents, all men, gave orders to the operatives, mainly women. Some 800 Lowell mill women quit work in 1834 to protest a reduction in wages. Two years later, there was another "turnout," this time involving 1,500 to 2,000 women. These were the largest strikes in American history to that date, noteworthy as strikes not only of employees against employers but also of women against men.

Manufacturing in New York City and Philadelphia

With their large size, reliance on female labor, and dependence on machinery, the Lowell and Waltham textile mills were the most conspicuous examples of industrialization before 1840. In contrast to such planned factory towns, cities like New York and Philadelphia during the 1820s and 1830s witnessed an industrialization that lacked even the appearance of orderliness, depended far less on machinery and on female workers, occurred in small firms as well as in large ones, and encompassed a greater range of products, including shoes, saddles, tools, rope, hats, and gloves.

Although diverging from the Lowell-Waltham model, the factories of New York and Philadelphia exposed workers to some of the same forces encountered by New England mill girls. By expanding the market for manufactures, the transportation revolution had turned some urban artisans, auctioneers, and merchants into aggressive merchandisers who scoured the country for orders. As a result, by 1835 New York City's ready-made clothing industry, for example, was supplying cheap dungarees and shirts to western farmers and even southern slaves; in the 1840s it was providing expensive suits for well-to-do customers. In turn, the possibility of reaching distant markets intensified competition and spurred entrepreneurs to slash the cost of their products by increasing output, cutting wages, or both. In New England the Boston Associates had responded by introducing machines, but New York City lacked an easily harnessable source of water power, and before 1840 few machines existed that could speed up the fabrication of products like shoes. Thus factory owners in cities like New York and Philadelphia had to use different tactics to increase their share of the marketplace: they hired large numbers of unskilled or semiskilled workers, many of them women, and paid them low wages to perform simple, specialized hand operations like

stitching cloth and soling shoes. In place of the colonial artisan who had fabricated the whole shoe on demand for a customer, such unskilled or semiskilled laborers no longer made whole shoes and rarely even saw a customer.

This subdivision of tasks (without the use of machines) characterized a great deal of industrialization before 1840 and occurred in a variety of work settings. In the boot and shoe industry that developed after 1820 in eastern Massachusetts, especially at Lynn, workers were gradually gathered into large factories to perform specialized operations in different rooms. In metropolises like New York and Philadelphia, the pattern was a little different. Here, although some large factories appeared in nearly all crafts, much of the subdivision of tasks took place in small shops, garrets, or homes. Because of the population density in these cities, it was unnecessary to gather workers into large factories. Middlemen could simply subcontract tasks out to widows, immigrants, and others who would fashion parts of shoes or saddles or dresses anywhere that light would enter. "We have been in some fifty cellars in different parts of the city," a New York *Tribune* reporter wrote in 1845, "each inhabited by a shoe-maker and his family. The floor is made of rough plank laid loosely down, and the ceiling is not quite so high as a tall man. The walls are dark and damp and . . . the miserable room is lighted only by a shallow sash partly projecting above the surface of the grounds and by the little light that struggles from the steep and rotting stairs. In this apartment often lives the man and his work bench, the wife, and five or six children of all ages; and perhaps a palsied grandfather and grandmother and often both. . . . Here they work, here they cook, they eat, they sleep, they pray. . . ."

In further contrast to places like Lowell and Waltham, which had not even existed in the eighteenth century, New York and Philadelphia were home to artisans with proud craft traditions and independence. Those with a highly marketable skill like cutting leather or clothing continued to earn good wages. Others grew rich by turning themselves into entrepreneurs who spent less time making products than taking trips to obtain orders and who then hired workers to fill the orders. Thus industrialization did not reduce all artisans to misery. But many artisans, even though skilled, found themselves on the downslope. Increasingly faced with factory competition, they could either eke out a living as independent artisans by working longer hours and skimping on food or other necessaries, or enter factories at low wages as semiskilled or unskilled workers.

In the late 1820s, skilled artisans in New York, Philadelphia, and other cities began to form trade unions and "workingmen's" political parties to protect their interests. Disdaining association with unskilled workers, most of these groups initially sought to restore privileges and working conditions that artisans had once enjoyed rather than to act as leaders of unskilled workers. But the steady deterioration of working conditions in the early 1830s tended to throw skilled and unskilled workers into the same boat. When coal heavers in Philadelphia struck for a ten-hour day in 1835, they were quickly joined by carpenters, cigar makers, shoemakers, leather workers, and other artisans in the United States' first general strike.

The emergence of organized worker protest underscored the mixed blessings of economic development. Although some benefited from the new commercial and industrial economy, others found their economic position deteriorating. By the 1830s many Americans wondered whether their nation was truly a land of equality.

EQUALITY AND INEQUALITY

Observers of antebellum (pre–Civil War) America sensed changes sweeping the country but had trouble describing them or agreeing on their direction. Some insisted that wealth was "universally diffused." Others, like the New York merchant Philip Hone, portrayed an unhappy society marked by extremes of "costly luxury" and "squalid misery."

One of the most astute of these observers was the French nobleman Alexis de Tocqueville, who spent nine months in America in 1831–1832. Although Tocqueville filled his private journals with references to inequality, in his two-volume *Democracy in America* (1835, 1840) he cited the "general equality of condition among the people" as the fundamental shaping force of American society. Inclined to view everything in comparative terms, Tocqueville, while certainly recognizing inequality, thought that wealth was more evenly distributed in the United States than in France and that, regardless of an individual's wealth, Americans believed that one person was as good as another. American servants insisted on being called the "help" and viewed as neighbors invited to assist in running a

household rather than as permanent menials. Similarly, whereas in France merchants were disdained by the titled nobility, in America merchants thought themselves equal to anyone.

Historians continue to argue about the meaning and extent of equality in antebellum America, but by using refined techniques of measurement they have drawn a more detailed portrait of antebellum society than the profile sketched by contemporaries. The following discussion applies mainly to northern society. We examine the South, whose "peculiar institution" of slavery created a distinctive social structure and set of social relationships, in Chapter 12.

Growing Inequality: The Rich and the Poor

The gap between the rich and the poor, which had increased during the late eighteenth century, widened further during the first half of the nineteenth century. Although Americans portrayed them as oases of equality, farm areas contained a good deal of inequality. In 1850 the poorest 40 percent of native-born farmers owned less than one hundred dollars worth of property, whereas the richest 30 percent to 40 percent of farmers owned three-fourths or more of the total farm property. But the truly striking inequalities developed in the cities, where a small fraction of the people owned a huge share of urban wealth. In Boston, for example, the richest 10 percent of the population owned a little over half of the city's real estate and personal property in 1771. By 1833 the richest 4 percent owned 59 percent of the wealth, and by 1848 nearly two-thirds of the wealth. By 1848, 81 percent of Boston's population owned only 4 percent of its wealth. In New York City, the richest 4 percent owned nearly half the wealth in 1828 and more than two-thirds by 1845. These statistics are representative of trends that affected all major cities.

Although commentators celebrated the self-made American who rose "from rags to riches," few individuals actually accumulated their wealth in this way. The vast majority of those who became extremely rich started out with considerable wealth. Fewer than five of every hundred wealthy individuals started poor, and close to ninety of every hundred started rich. The old-fashioned way to make money was to inherit it, marry into more, and then invest wisely. There were just enough instances of fabulously successful poor boys like John Jacob Astor, who built a fur-trading empire,

View of St. Louis, *by Leon Pomarede, 1832*
When the trans-Mississippi fur trade declined in the 1830s, the steamboats plying the Mississippi and Missouri rivers became the key to St. Louis's expansion. With under 5,000 inhabitants in 1820, the city contained 100,000 by the 1850s. Population growth drove up the value of choice lots and contributed to the widening distance between social classes.

to sustain popular belief in the rags-to-riches myth, but not enough to turn that myth into a reality.

Their splendid residences as well as their wealth set the rich apart. The urban rich built imposing mansions clustered in neighborhoods. In 1828 over half of the 500 wealthiest families in New York City lived on only 8 of the city's more than 250 streets. During the early 1830s, half of Boston's wealthy families lived on but 8 of its 325 streets. Social clubs also separated the rich from others. The Philadelphia Club, founded in 1834, was a stronghold for proper Philadelphians. By the late 1820s, New York City had a club so exclusive that it was called just The Club. Tocqueville noted that in America "the wealthiest and most enlightened live

among themselves." Yet Tocqueville was also struck by how the rich feigned respect for equality when they moved about in public. They rode in ordinary rather than sumptuous carriages, brushed elbows easily with the less privileged, and avoided the conspicuous display of wealth that marked their private lives.

At the opposite end of the social ladder were the poor. By today's standards, most antebellum Americans were poor: they lived "close to the margin" of poverty, depended heavily on their children's labor to meet expenses, had little money to spend on medical care or recreation, and were subject to unemployment, not just during general economic downturns but from month to month, even in times of prosperity.

Freezing weather, for instance, could temporarily throw day laborers, factory workers, and boatmen out of work. In 1850 an estimated three out of eight males over the age of twenty owned little more than their clothing and the cash in their pockets.

In evaluating economic status, it is important to recognize that statistics on the distribution of wealth to some extent mask the fact that the accumulation of property takes place over an entire lifetime and increases with age. With its extraordinarily high birthrate, antebellum America was overwhelmingly a nation of young people with little property; not all of them would remain propertyless as they grew older.

Also keep in mind that when antebellum Americans themselves spoke of poverty, they were not thinking of the condition of hardship that affected most people. Instead, they were referring to a state of dependency, a total inability to fend for oneself, that affected *some* people. They often called this dependency *pauperism*. The absence of health insurance and old-age pensions condemned many infirm and aged people to pauperism. Widows whose children had left home might also have a hard time avoiding pauperism. Contemporaries usually classified all such people as the "deserving" poor and contrasted them with the "undeserving" poor—such as indolent loafers and drunkards whose poverty was self-willed. Most moralists claimed that America was happily free of a permanent class of paupers. They assumed that since pauperism resulted either from circumstances beyond anyone's control, such as old age and disease, or from voluntary decisions to squander money on liquor, it could not afflict entire groups generation after generation.

This assumption was comforting but also misleading, because a class of people who could not escape poverty was emerging in the major cities during the first half of the nineteenth century. One source of this class was immigration. As early as 1801, a New York newspaper called attention to boatloads of immigrants with large families, without money or health, and *"expiring from the want of sustenance."* The arrival of huge numbers of Irish immigrants during the 1840s and 1850s made a bad situation worse. The Irish were among the poorest immigrants ever to arrive in America. Fleeing famine in Ireland, they found even worse conditions in noxious slums like New York's infamous Five Points district. Starting with the conversion of a brewery into housing for hundreds of people

in 1837, the Five Points became probably the worst slum in America.

The Irish were not only poor but, as Catholics, also belonged to a church despised by the Protestant majority. In short, they were different and had little claim on the kindly impulses of most Protestants. But even the Protestant poor came in for rough treatment in the years between 1815 and 1840. The more Americans convinced themselves that success was within everyone's grasp, the less they accepted the traditional doctrine that poverty was ordained by God, and the more they were inclined to hold the poor responsible for their own poverty. Ironically, even as many Americans blamed the poor for being poor, they practiced discrimination that kept some groups mired in enduring poverty. Nowhere was this more true than in the case of northern free blacks.

Free Blacks in the North

Prejudice against blacks was deeply ingrained in white society throughout the nation. Although slavery had largely disappeared in the North by 1820, laws penalized blacks in many ways. One form of discrimination was to restrict the blacks' right to vote. In New York State, for example, a constitutional revision of 1821 eliminated property requirements for white voters but kept them for blacks. Rhode Island banned blacks from voting in 1822; Pennsylvania did so in 1837. Throughout the half-century after 1800, blacks could vote on equal terms with whites in only one of the nation's major cities, Boston. Efforts were made to bar free blacks from migrating to other states and cities. Missouri's original constitution authorized the state legislature to prevent blacks from entering the state "under any pretext whatsoever." Free blacks were often barred from public conveyances and facilities and were either excluded from public schools in major cities or forced into segregated schools. Segregation was the rule in northern jails, almshouses, and hospitals. But of all restrictions on free blacks, the most damaging was the social pressure that forced them into the least skilled and lowest-paying occupations throughout the northern cities. Recollecting his youthful days in Providence, Rhode Island, in the early 1830s, the free black William J. Brown wrote: "To drive carriages, carry a market basket after the boss, and brush his boots, or saw wood and run errands was as high as a colored man could rise." Although a few free blacks became successful entrepreneurs and grew moder-

DANCING FOR EELS, 1820 CATHARINE MARKET.

Dancing for Eels, Catharine Market, 1820

Expressive dancing was part of African-American street festivals in the eighteenth-century cities. Fearing that such street dancing perpetuated white stereotypes of blacks, antislavery whites and black leaders tried to suppress it after 1800, but black dancing survived in dance cellars in New York City's Five Points slum. As this sketch indicates, blacks sometimes danced in public for applause, "a bunch of eels" or other fish, and perhaps money. The black at the left is "patting juba," which meant keeping time by hand clapping or by beating hands against legs. "Juba" also became the nickname of William Henry Lane. After seeing Lane perform in 1842 in a Five Points cellar, the novelist Charles Dickens labeled him "the greatest dancer known."

ately wealthy, urban free blacks were only half as likely as city dwellers in general to own real estate.

The "Middling Classes"

The majority of antebellum Americans lived neither in splendid wealth nor in grinding poverty. Most belonged to what men and women of the time called the middling classes. Even though the wealthy owned an increasing proportion of all wealth, most people's standard of living rose between 1800 and 1860, particularly between 1840 and 1860, when per capita income grew at an annual rate of around 1.5 percent.

Americans applied the term *middling classes* to farmers and artisans, whose ideal was self-employ-

ment. Commentators viewed them as steady and dependable, the nation's sturdy "producers." Yet life in the middle was unpredictable, filled with jagged ups and downs. Words like *farmer* and *artisan* were often misleading, for they gave a greater impression of steadiness and stability than was really the case. For example, Asa G. Sheldon, born in Massachusetts in 1788, described himself in his autobiography as a farmer, offered advice on growing corn and cranberries, and gave speeches about the glories of farming. Although Sheldon undoubtedly knew a great deal about farming, he actually spent very little time tilling the soil. In 1812 he began to transport hops from New England to brewers in New York City, and he soon extended this business to Philadelphia and Baltimore. He invested his profits in land, but rather than farm the land, he made money selling its timber. When a business setback forced him to sell his property, he was soon back in operation "through the disinterested kindness of friends," who lent him money with which he purchased carts and oxen. These he used to get contracts for filling in swamps in Boston and for clearing and grading land for railroads. From all this and from the backbreaking labor of the Irish immigrants he hired to do the shoveling, Sheldon the "farmer" grew prosperous. But his prosperity in fact owed little to farming.

The increasingly commercial and industrial economy of antebellum America created opportunities for success and forced individuals like Sheldon to adapt. Not everyone, though, had an opportunity for success. Had it not been for the intervention of wealthy friends, Sheldon would have ended up in a poorhouse. Many lacked kindly friends with money to lend. Some, like Sheldon, rose. Others, like Allan Melville, father of novelist Herman Melville, slipped down the slope. An enterprising import merchant, Allan Melville had an abounding faith in his nation, in "our national Eagle, 'with an eye that never winks and a wing that never tires,' " and in the inevitable triumph of honesty and prudence. The Melvilles lived comfortably in Albany and New York City, but in the late 1820s, Melville's business, never robust, sagged. By 1830 he was begging his father for a loan of $500, proclaiming that "I am destitute of resources and without a shilling—without immediate assistance I know not what will become of me." He got the $500 plus an additional $3,000, but the downward spiral continued. In 1832 he died, broken in spirit and nearly insane.

The case of artisans also illustrates the perils of life in the middling classes. During the colonial period, artisans had formed a proud and cohesive group whose members often attained the goal of self-employment. They owned their own tools, made their own products on order from customers, boarded their apprentices and journeymen in their homes, and passed their skills on to their children. By 1850, in contrast, artisans had entered a new world of economic relationships. This was true even of a craft like carpentry that did not experience any industrial or technological change. Town and city growth in the wake of the transportation revolution created a demand for housing. Some carpenters, usually those with access to capital, became contractors who took orders for more houses than they could build themselves and who then hired large numbers of journeymen to do the construction work. Likewise, as we have seen, in the early industrialization of shoe manufacturing during the 1820s, some shoemakers spent less time crafting shoes than making trips to obtain orders for their products, then hired workers to fashion parts of shoes. In effect, the old class of artisans was splitting into two new groupings. On one side were artisans who had become entrepreneurs; on the other, journeymen with little prospect of self-employment.

An additional characteristic of the middling classes (one that they shared with the poor) was a high degree of transiency, or "spatial mobility." Farmers who cultivated land intensively in order to raise a cash crop and so get out of debt exhausted their land quickly and had to move on. Artisans displaced from skilled jobs by machines found that much unskilled work was seasonal and that they had to move from job to job to survive. Canal workers and boatmen had to secure new work when waterways froze. Even for city dwellers, to shift jobs often meant changing residences, for the cities were spreading out at a much faster rate than was public transportation. Some idea of the degree of transiency can be gained from a survey made by the Boston police on Saturday, September 6, 1851. At a time when Boston's population was 145,000, the survey showed that from 6:30 A.M. to 7:30 P.M., 41,729 people entered the city and 42,313 left.

The multiplying risks and opportunities that confronted Americans both widened the gap between social classes and increased the psychological burdens on individuals. Commercial and industrial growth also placed pressure on such basic social relationships as those between lawyers and their clients, ministers and their parishioners, and children and their parents.

THE REVOLUTION IN SOCIAL RELATIONSHIPS

Following the War of 1812, the growth of interregional trade, commercial agriculture, and manufacturing disrupted many traditional social relationships and forged new ones. Two broad generalizations encompass these changes. First, Americans questioned authority to an unprecedented degree. In 1775 they had rebelled against their king. Now, it seemed, they were rebelling as well against their lawyers, physicians, ministers, and even their parents. An attitude of individualism sprouted and took firm root in antebellum America. Once *individualism* had meant nothing more than selfishness, but now Americans used the word to signify positive qualities: self-reliance and the conviction that each person was the best judge of his or her own true interests. Ordinary Americans might still agree with the opinions of their leaders, but only after they had thought matters through on their own. Those with superior wealth, education, or social position could no longer expect the automatic deference of the common people.

Second, even as Americans widely proclaimed themselves a nation of self-reliant individualists and questioned the traditional basis of authority, they sought to construct new foundations for authority. For example, among middle-class women, the idea developed that they possessed a "separate sphere" of authority in the home. In addition, individuals increasingly joined with others in these years to form voluntary associations through which they might influence the direction that their society would take.

The Attack on the Professions

The first phase in this alteration of social relationships was the erosion of traditional forms of authority. In the swiftly changing antebellum society, claims to social superiority were questioned as never before. The statesman Harrison Gray Otis put it in a nutshell in 1836: "Everywhere the disposition is found among those who live in the valleys to ask those who live on the hills, 'How came we here and you there?' "

Intense criticism of lawyers, physicians, and ministers exemplified this assault on authority. As far back as the 1780s, Benjamin Austin, a radical Boston artisan, had complained that lawyers needlessly prolonged and confused court cases so that they could charge high fees. Between 1800 and 1840, a wave of religious revivals known as the Second Great Awakening (see Chapter 10) sparked new attacks on the professions. Some revivalists blasted the clergy for creating complicated theologies that ordinary men and women could not comprehend, for drinking expensive wines, and for fleecing the people. One religious revivalist, Elias Smith, extended the criticism to physicians, whom he accused of inventing Latin and Greek names for diseases in order to disguise their own ignorance of how to cure them.

Attacks on the learned professions peaked between 1820 and 1850. In medicine a movement arose under the leadership of Samuel Thomson, a farmer's son with little formal education, to eliminate all barriers to entry into the medical profession. Thomson believed that anyone could understand the principles of medicine and become a physician. His crusade was remarkably successful. By 1845 every state had repealed laws that required licenses and education to practice medicine. Meanwhile, attacks on lawyers sharpened, and relations between ministers and their parishioners grew tense and acrimonious. In colonial New England, ministers had usually served a single parish for life, but by the 1830s a rapid turnover of ministers was becoming the norm as finicky parishioners commonly dismissed clergymen whose theology displeased them. Ministers themselves were becoming more ambitious—more inclined to leave small, poor congregations for large, wealthy ones.

The increasing commercialization of the economy contributed both to the growing number of professionals and to the attacks on them. The rise of the market economy intensified the demand for lawyers and physicians; the number of medical schools, for example, grew from one in 1765 to twenty in 1830 and sixty-five in 1860. Like so many other antebellum Americans, these freshly minted lawyers and doctors often were transients without deep roots in the towns that they served and without convincing claims to social superiority. Describing lawyers and physicians, a contemporary observer wrote: "Men dropped down into their places as from clouds. Nobody knew who or what they were, except as they claimed, or as a surface view of their character indicated." A horse doctor one day would the next day hang up his sign as "Physician and Surgeon" and "fire at random a box of his pills into your bowels, with a vague chance of hitting some disease unknown to him, but with a better prospect of killing the patient, whom or whose administrator he charged some ten dollars a trial for his marksmanship."

The questioning of authority was particularly sharp on the frontier. Here, to eastern and foreign visitors, it seemed that every man they met was a "judge," "general," "colonel," or "squire." In a society in which everyone was new, such titles were easily adopted but just as easily challenged. Where neither law nor custom sanctioned claims of superiority, would-be gentlemen substituted an exaggerated sense of personal honor. Obsessed with their fragile status, many of these "gentlemen" reacted testily to the slightest insult. Dueling became a widespread frontier practice. At a Kentucky militia parade in 1819, a colonel's dog jogged onto the field and sat at his master's knee. Enraged by this breach of military decorum, the regiment's general ran the dog through with his dress sword. A week later, general and colonel met with pistols at ten paces. The colonel was killed; the general, crippled for life.

The Challenge to Family Authority

In contrast to the public, philosophical attacks on the learned professions, children engaged in a quiet questioning of parental authority. Economic change created new opportunities that forced young people to choose between staying at home to help their parents and venturing out on their own. Writing to her parents in Vermont shortly before taking a job in a Lowell textile mill, eighteen-year-old Sally Rice quickly got to the point: "I must of course have something of my own before many more years have passed over my head and where is that something coming from if I go home and earn nothing. You may think me unkind but how can you blame me if I want to stay here. I have but one life to live and I want to enjoy myself as I can while I live."

A similar desire for independence propelled young men to leave home at earlier ages than in the past and to strike out on their own. Although the great migration to the West was primarily a movement of entire families, movement from farms to towns and cities within regions was frequently spearheaded by restless and single young people. Two young men in Virginia put it succinctly: "All the promise of life seemed to us to be at the other end of the rainbow— somewhere else—anywhere else but on the farm. . . . And so all our youthful plans had as their chief object the getting away from the farm."

Antebellum Americans also widely wished to be free of close parental supervision, and their changing attitudes influenced courtship and marriage. Many young people who no longer depended on their parents for land insisted on privacy in courting and wanted to decide for themselves when to marry. Increasingly, too, romantic love between the partners rather than parental preferences determined decisions to marry. Whereas seventeenth-century Puritans had advised young people to choose marriage partners whom they *could* love, by the early 1800s, young men and women viewed romantic love as the indispensable basis for a successful marriage. "In affairs of love," a young lawyer in Maine wrote, "young peoples hearts are generally much wiser than old peoples heads."

One sign of young people's growing control over courtship and marriage was the declining likelihood that the young women of a family would marry in their exact birth order. Traditionally, fathers had wanted their daughters to marry in the order of their birth, to avoid planting the suspicion that there was something wrong with one or more of them. Toward the end of the eighteenth century, however, the practice ceased to be customary, as daughters were making their own marital decisions. Another mark of the times was the growing number of long engagements. Having made the decision to marry, some young women were reluctant to tie the knot, fearing that marriage would snuff out their independence. For example, Caroline and William Kirkland were engaged for seven years before their marriage in 1828. Equally striking was the increasing number of young women who chose not to marry. Catharine Beecher, the daughter of the prominent minister Lyman Beecher, broke off her engagement to a young man during the 1820s, despite her father's pressure to marry him. She later renewed the engagement, but after her fiancé's death in a shipwreck, she remained single for the rest of her life.

Thus young people lived more and more in a world of their own. Not surprisingly, moralists reacted with alarm and flooded the country with books of advice to youth such as William Alcott's *The Young Man's Guide*, which went through thirty-one editions between 1833 and 1858. The number of such advice books sold in antebellum America was truly vast, but to an amazing extent, they all said the same thing. They did not advise young men and women to return to farms, and they assumed that parents had little control over them. Rather, their authors exhorted youths to develop habitual rectitude, self-control, and "character." It was an age not just of the self-made adult but also of the self-made youth.

Wives, Husbands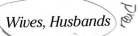

Another class of advice books pouring from the antebellum presses counseled wives and husbands on their rights and duties. These were a sign that relations between spouses, too, were changing. Young men and women who, as teenagers, had grown accustomed to making decisions on their own were more likely than their ancestors to approach wedlock as a compact between equals. Of course, wives remained unequal to their husbands in many tangible ways, the most obvious being the continuation into the 1830s of the traditional legal rule that married women could not own property. But relations between wives and husbands were changing during the 1820s and 1830s toward a form of equality.

One source of the change was the rise of a potent ideology known as the doctrine of separate spheres. Traditionally, women had been viewed as subordinate to men in all spheres of life. Now middle-class men and women developed a kind of separate-but-equal doctrine that portrayed men as superior in making money and governing the world and women as superior for their moral influence on family members. One of the most important duties assigned to the sphere of women was the raising of children. During the eighteenth century, ministers had addressed sermons to fathers to remind them of their duty to govern the family, but by the 1830s child-rearing manuals increasingly appealed to mothers rather than fathers. "How entire and perfect is this dominion over the unformed character of your infant," the popular writer Lydia Sigourney proclaimed in her *Letters to Mothers* (1838). Advice books instructed mothers to discipline their children by loving them and withdrawing affection when they misbehaved rather than by using corporal punishment. A whipped child might become more obedient but would remain sullen and bitter. In contrast, the gentler methods advised in manuals promised to penetrate to the child's heart, to make the child want to do the right thing.

The idea of a separate women's sphere blended with a related image of the family and the home as secluded refuges from a society marked by commotion and disorder. The popular culture of the 1830s and 1840s painted an alluring portrait of the pleasures of

Ingersell Family in 1818
This watercolor of a Maine family captures the large size of antebellum families and the importance they attached to children. The parents point toward the infant Peggy. But childhood was short. Five-year-old Solomon on the bottom left is dressed as a child, but his older brothers to his left, respectively twelve and nine, are clothed as adults, and Eli grips a paper scroll rather than Solomon's butterfly.

home life through songs like "Home, Sweet Home" and poems such as Henry Wadsworth Longfellow's "The Children's Hour" and Clement Moore's "A Visit from St. Nicholas." The publication of Moore's poem coincided with the growing popularity of Christmas as a holiday season in which family members gathered to exchange warm affection. Even the physical appearance of houses changed as architects offered new designs for the ideal home. The prominent architect Andrew Jackson Downing published plans for peaceful single-family homes that he hoped would offset the

"spirit of unrest" and the feverish pace of American life. He wrote of the ideal home: "There should be something to love. There must be nooks about it, where one would love to linger; windows, where one can enjoy the quiet landscape at his leisure; cozy rooms, where all fireside joys are invited to dwell."

As a prophet, Downing deserves high marks, because one of the motives that has impelled many Americans to flee cities for suburbs in the twentieth century has been the desire to achieve ownership of a single-family residence. However, in the 1820s and 1830s, this ideal was beyond the reach of most people—not just blacks, immigrants, and sweatshop workers, but much of the middle class as well. In the countryside, although middle-class farmers still managed productive households, these were anything but tranquil: wives milked cows and bled hogs, and children fetched wood, drove cows to pasture, and chased blackbirds from cornfields. In the cities, middle-class families often had to sacrifice their privacy by taking in boarders to supplement family income.

Still, the doctrine of separate spheres for men and women, and the image of the home as a calming refuge from a harsh world, were powerful ideals, and virtually the only ones projected in antebellum magazines. Although they were ideals rather than descriptions of reality, they did intersect with the real world at *some* points. For example, the decline of cottage industries and the rising number of urban families headed by merchants, lawyers, or brokers (all of whom worked away from their homes) gave married women more time to spend on child rearing. Above all, even if they could not afford to live in a Downing-designed house, married women found that they could use the doctrine of separate spheres and the image of the home as a refuge to gain new power within their families. A subtle implication of the doctrine of separate spheres was that women should have control not only over the discipline of children but also over the more fundamental issue of the number of children that they would bear.

In 1800 the United States had one of the highest birthrates ever recorded. The average American woman bore 7.04 children. It is safe to say that married women had become pregnant as often as possible. In the prevailing farm economy, children were valuable for carrying out essential tasks and, as time passed, for relieving aging parents of the burden of heavy farm labor. Most parents had assumed that the more children, the better. However, the spread of a commercial economy raised troublesome questions about

idea of separate spheres

children's economic value. Unlike a farmer, a merchant or lawyer could not send his children to work at the age of seven or eight. The average woman, who had borne 7.04 children in 1800, was bearing only 5.02 by 1850, and 3.98 by 1900. The birthrate remained high among blacks and among many immigrant groups, but it slumped drastically among native-born whites, particularly in towns and cities. The birthrate also declined in rural areas, but more sharply in rural villages than on farms, and more sharply in the East, where land was scarce, than in the West, where abundant land created continued incentives for parents to have many children.

For the most part, the decline in the birthrate was accomplished by abstinence from sexual intercourse, by *coitus interruptus* (withdrawal of the penis before ejaculation), or by abortion. By the 1840s such abortionists as New York City's notorious Madame Restell advertised remedies for "female irregularities," a common euphemism for unwanted pregnancies. There were no foolproof birth-control devices, and as much misinformation as information circulated about the techniques of birth control. Nonetheless, interest in birth-control devices was intensifying. In 1832 Charles Knowlton, a Massachusetts physician, described the procedure for vaginal douching in his book *Fruits of Philosophy*. Although Knowlton was frequently prosecuted and once jailed for obscenity, efforts to suppress his ideas only resulted in their being publicized even more. By 1865 popular tracts had familiarized Americans with a wide range of birth-control methods, including the rubber condom and the vaginal diaphragm. Whatever the method, the decision to limit family size was usually reached jointly by wives and husbands. Economic and ideological considerations blended together. Husbands could note that the economic value of children was declining; wives, that having fewer children would give them more time to nurture each one and thereby carry out the duties of the woman's sphere.

Supporters of the ideal of separate spheres did not advocate full legal equality for women. Indeed, the idea of separate spheres was an explicit *alternative* to legal equality. But the concept did enhance women's power within marriage by justifying their demands for influence over such vital issues as child rearing and the frequency of pregnancies. In addition, it allowed some women a measure of independence from the home. For example, it sanctioned Catharine Beecher's travels to lecture women on better ways to raise children and manage their households.

Horizontal Allegiances and the Rise of Voluntary Associations

 read

As some forms of authority, such as that of parents over their children and of husbands over their wives, were weakening, Americans devised new ways through which individuals could extend their influence over others. The pre–Civil War period witnessed the widespread substitution of *horizontal* allegiances for *vertical* allegiances. An example of vertical allegiance is found in the traditional patriarchal family, wherein a wife and children looked up to the father for leadership. Another example occurs in the small eighteenth-century workshop, where apprentices and journeymen took direction from the master craftsman and even lived in the craftsman's house, subject to his authority. Common to these examples is the idea of authority flowing from the top down. In a vertical allegiance, people in a subordinate position identify their best interests with the interests of their superiors rather than with those of other individuals in the same subordinate position.

When social relationships began to assume a horizontal form, several new patterns emerged. Although the older kind of vertical relationships did not disappear, they became less important in people's lives. Relationships now arose that linked those in a similar position. For example, in large textile mills during the 1830s, many operatives discovered that they had more in common with each other than with their managers and overseers. Similarly, wives were increasingly inclined to form associations that bound them with other married women. Young men formed associations with other young men. None of these associations was intended to overthrow traditional authority. Many of them in fact professed to strengthen the family or community. But all represented the substitution of new allegiances for old ones.

A sign of the change can be seen in the large number of voluntary associations formed in the 1820s and 1830s. These were associations that arose apart from government and sought to accomplish some goal of value to their members. Tocqueville observed that in France the government stood at the head of every enterprise but that in America "you will be sure to find an association."

At the most basic level, the voluntary associations encouraged sociability. As transients and newcomers flocked into towns and cities, they tended to join with others who shared similar characteristics, experiences, or interests. Gender was the basis of many voluntary societies. Of twenty-six religious and charitable associations in Utica, New York, in 1832, for instance, one-third were exclusively for women. Race was still another basis for voluntary associations. Although their names did not indicate it, Boston's Thompson Literary and Debating Society, its Philomathean Adelphic Union for the Promotion of Literature and Science, and New York City's Phoenix Society were all organizations for free blacks.

Promoting sociability was not the only benefit of voluntary associations. These associations also allowed their members to assert their influence at a time when traditional forms of authority were weakening. For example, voluntary associations proved compatible with the idea that women had a separate sphere. As long as a woman could argue that her activities were in the best interests of the home, she could escape the kitchen long enough to join maternal associations (where mothers exchanged ideas about child rearing), temperance associations (where they promoted absti-

nence from alcoholic beverages), and moral-reform societies. These latter societies, which multiplied in the 1830s and 1840s, combated prostitution.

Temperance and moral-reform societies had a dual purpose. They sought to suppress well-known vices *and* to enhance women's power over men. Temperance advocates assumed that intemperance was a male vice. Moral reformers attributed the prevalence of prostitution to the lustfulness of men who, unable to control their passions, exploited poor and vulnerable girls. While exhorting prostitutes to give up their line of work, moral reformers also tried to shame brothel patrons into chastity by publishing their names in newspapers. Just as strikes in Lowell in the 1830s were a form of collective action by working women, temperance and moral-reform societies represented collective action by middle-class women to increase their influence in society. Here, as elsewhere, the tendency of the times was to forge new forms of horizontal allegiance between like-minded Americans.

CONCLUSION

Alexis de Tocqueville described the United States of the 1830s as remarkable not for "the marvellous grandeur of some undertakings" but for the "innumerable multitude of small ones." In fact, a number of grand enterprises *were* undertaken between 1815 and 1840, among them the construction of the Erie Canal and the establishment of the Lowell mills. But Tocqueville was basically correct. The distinguishing feature of the period was the amount of small to medium-size enterprises that Americans embarked upon: commercial farms of modest proportions, railroads that ran for a few hundred miles, manufacturing companies that employed five to ten workers.

The changes of the period were modest in comparison to those that would come in the late nineteenth century, when industrial firms routinely employed hundreds of workers and railroads spanned the continent. Nevertheless, to antebellum Americans, it seemed as if the world of their ancestors was breaking apart. In 1800 no human or machine had been able to sustain motion at more than ten miles an hour. The railroads changed that. In 1800 it had been natural to assume that the limits of trade were set by the limits of rivers.

Canals changed that. Everywhere traditional assumptions about what was "natural" were being challenged.

As traditional assumptions eroded, new ones took their place. Ties to village leaders and even to parents weakened, but new bonds with the like-minded and with age peers emerged. Individualism became a major force in the sense that a widening circle of Americans insisted on the right to shape their own economic destinies. "No man in America is contented to be poor," a magazine proclaimed, "or expects to continue so." Yet Americans did not desire isolation from each other. Voluntary associations based on the personal preferences of their members, rather than on custom, proliferated. A host of advice books aimed at young people, wives, and husbands tried to teach Americans how to play the new roles thrust upon them by economic and social change. The marriage manual was as much a part of antebellum America as the Erie Canal or the Boston Manufacturing Company.

The social transformations of 1815 to 1840 not only changed the private lives of Americans but also brought a host of new political issues to the fore, as we shall see in Chapter 10.

CHRONOLOGY

1790   Samuel Slater opens his first Rhode Island mill for the production of cotton yarn.

1793   Eli Whitney invents the cotton gin.

Eli Whitney

1807   Robert R. Livingston and Robert Fulton introduce the steamboat *Clermont* on the Hudson River.

1811   Construction of the National Road begins at Cumberland, Maryland.

1813   Incorporation of the Boston Manufacturing Company.

1816   Second Bank of the United States chartered.

1817   Erie Canal started.

1819   Economic panic, ushering in four-year depression.

1820–1850   Growth of female moral-reform societies.

1820s   Expansion of New England textile mills.

1824   *Gibbons* v. *Ogden*.

1825   Completion of the Erie Canal.

1828   Baltimore and Ohio Railroad chartered.

1830   Indian Removal Act passed by Congress.

1831   *Cherokee Nation* v. *Georgia*.

       Alexis de Tocqueville begins visit to the United States to study American penitentiaries.

1832   *Worcester* v. *Georgia*.

1834   First strike at the Lowell mills.

1837   Economic panic begins a depression that lasts until 1843.

1840   System of production by interchangeable parts perfected.

FOR FURTHER READING

Rowland Berthoff, *An Unsettled People: Social Order and Disorder in American History* (1971). A stimulating interpretation of American social history.

Ray A. Billington, *Westward Expansion: A History of the American Frontier* (1949). The standard study of westward movement and settlement.

Carl Degler, *At Odds: Women and the Family in America from the Revolution to the Present* (1980). A fine overview of the economic and social experiences of American women.

Harry N. Scheiber, *The Ohio Canal Era: A Case Study of Government and the Economy, 1820–1861* (1969). An analysis that speaks volumes about economic growth in the early republic.

Sean Wilentz, *Chants Democratic: New York City and the Rise of the American Working Class, 1788–1850* (1983). A stimulating synthesis of economic, social, and political history.

ADDITIONAL BIBLIOGRAPHY

Agriculture and the Westward Movement

Charles Danhof, *Change in Agriculture: The Northern United States, 1820–1870* (1969); Robert Feller, *The Public Lands in Jacksonian Politics* (1984); Paul W. Gates, *The Farmer's Age: Agriculture, 1815–1860* (1960); William H. Goetzmann, *Explorations and Empire: The Explorer and the Scientist in the Winning of the American West* (1966); Hildegard B. Johnson, *Order Upon the Land* (1976); Malcolm Rohrbough, *The Land Office Business: The Settlement and Administration of American Public Lands, 1789–1837* (1968); Michael Williams, *Americans and Their Forests* (1989).

Indians

Robert F. Berkhofer, Jr., *The White Man's Indian: Images of the American Indian from Columbus to the Present* (1979); John R. Finger, *The Eastern Band of Cherokees, 1819–1900* (1984); Michael D. Green, *The Politics of Indian Removal: Creek Government and Society in Crisis* (1982); Joseph Herring, *The Enduring Indians of Kansas* (1990); William G. McLoughlin, *Cherokee Renascence in the New Republic* (1987); Roy H. Pearce, *The Savages of America* (1965); Richard Slotkin, *Regeneration Through Violence: The Mythology of the American Frontier, 1600–1860* (1973); Wilcomb E. Washburn, *The Indian in*

America (1975); J. Leitch Wright, Jr., *Creeks and Seminoles* (1986).

The Transportation Revolution

Albert Fishlow, *American Railroads and the Transformation of the Ante-Bellum Economy* (1965); Robert W. Fogel, *Railroads and American Economic Growth: Essays in Econometric History* (1964); Carter Goodrich, *Government Promotion of American Canals and Railroads, 1800–1890* (1960); Erik F. Haites, James Mak, and Gary M. Walton, *Western River Transportation: The Era of Early Internal Development, 1800–1860* (1975); Harry N. Scheiber, *The Ohio Canal Era: A Case Study of Government and the Economy, 1820–1861* (1969); R. E. Shaw, *Erie Water West* (1966); George R. Taylor, *The Transportation Revolution, 1815–1860* (1951).

Communities

Jeffrey S. Adler, *Yankee Merchants and the Making of the Urban West* (1991); Stuart Blumin, *The Urban Threshold: Growth and Change in a Nineteenth-Century American Community* (1976); Don H. Doyle, *The Social Order of a Frontier Community: Jacksonville, Illinois, 1825–1870* (1978); Clyde Griffen and Sally Griffen, *Natives and Newcomers: The Ordering of Opportunity in Mid-Nineteenth-Century Poughkeepsie* (1978); David Hamer, *New Towns in the New World* (1990); Paul Johnson, *A Shopkeeper's Millennium: Society and Revivals in Rochester, New York, 1815–1837* (1978); Steven J. Ross, *Workers on the Edge: Work, Leisure, and Politics in Industrializing Cincinnati, 1788–1890* (1985); Richard C. Wade, *The Urban Frontier* (1964); Anthony F. C. Wallace, *Rockdale: The Growth of an American Village in the Early Industrial Revolution* (1977).

Immigrants

Rowland Berthoff, *British Immigrants in Industrial America* (1953); Kathleen N. Conzen, *Immigrant Milwaukee, 1836–1860* (1976); Jay P. Dolan, *The Immigrant Church: New York's Irish and German Catholics, 1815–1860* (1975); Oscar Handlin, *Boston's Immigrants: A Study in Acculturation*, rev. ed. (1959); Marcus L. Hansen, *The Atlantic Migration, 1607–1860* (1940); Philip Taylor, *The Distant Magnet: European Emigration to the United States of America* (1971); Carl Wittke, *The Irish in America* (1956).

Technology

Siegfried Giedion, *Mechanization Takes Command* (1948); H. J. Habakkuk, *American and British Technology in the Nineteenth Century* (1962); Otto Mayr and Robert C. Post, eds., *Yankee Enterprise: The Rise of the American System of Manufactures* (1981); Merritt R. Smith, *Harpers Ferry Armory and the New Technology* (1977).

Manufacturing and Economic Growth

W. Elliot Brownlee, *Dynamics of Ascent* (1974); Stuart Bruchey, *The Roots of American Economic Growth, 1607–1861* (1965); Christopher Clark, *The Roots of Rural Capitalism: Western Massachusetts, 1780–1860* (1990); Thomas C. Cochran, *Frontiers of Change: Early Industrialism in America* (1981); Alan Dawley, *Class and Community: The Industrial Revolution in Lynn* (1976); Thomas Dublin, *Women at Work: The Transformation of Work and Community in Lowell, Massachusetts, 1826–1860* (1979); Bruce Laurie, *Working People of Philadelphia, 1800–1850* (1980); Judith A. McGaw, *Most Wonderful Machine: Mechanization and Social Change in Berkshire Paper Making, 1815–1885* (1987); Douglass North, *The Economic Growth of the United States, 1790–1860* (1961); Ronald Schultz, *The Republic of Labor: Philadelphia Artisans and the Politics of Class, 1720–1830* (1993); Peter Temin, *The Jacksonian Economy* (1969); Barbara Tucker, *Samuel Slater and the Origins of the American Textile Industry, 1790–1860* (1984).

Rich and Poor

Elizabeth Blackmar, *Manhattan for Rent, 1785–1850* (1989); Leonard P. Curry, *The Free Black in Urban America, 1800–1850* (1981); Paul A. Gilje, *The Road to Mobocracy: Popular Disorder in New York City, 1763–1834* (1987); Peter Knights, *The Plain People of Boston, 1830–1860* (1971); Edward Pessen, *Riches, Class, and Power Before the Civil War* (1973); Stephan Thernstrom, *Poverty and Progress* (1964).

Professions

Daniel H. Calhoun, *Professional Lives in America: Structure and Aspiration, 1750–1850* (1965); Donald M. Scott, *From Office to Profession: The New England Ministry, 1750–1850* (1978); Richard Shryock, *Medical Licensing in America, 1650–1965* (1967); William B. Skelton, *An American Profession of Arms: The Army Officer Corps, 1784–1861* (1993).

Women and the Family

Jeanne Boydston, *Home and Work* (1990); Nancy F. Cott, *The Bonds of Womanhood: 'Woman's Sphere' in New England, 1780–1835* (1977); Suzanne Lebsock, *The Free Women of Petersburg: Status and Culture in a Southern Town, 1784–1860* (1984); James C. Mohr, *Abortion in America: The Origins and Evolution of National Policy, 1800–1900* (1978); Glenda Riley, *Women and Indians on the Frontier, 1825–1915* (1984); Ellen K. Rothman, *Hands and Hearts: A History of Courtship in America* (1987); Mary Ryan, *Cradle of the Middle Class: The Family in Oneida County, New York, 1790–1865* (1981); Kathryn K. Sklar, *Catharine Beecher: A Study in American Domesticity* (1973); Christine Stansell, *City of Women: Sex and Class in New York, 1789–1860* (1986); Gwendolyn Wright, *Building the Dream: A Social History of Housing in America* (1981).

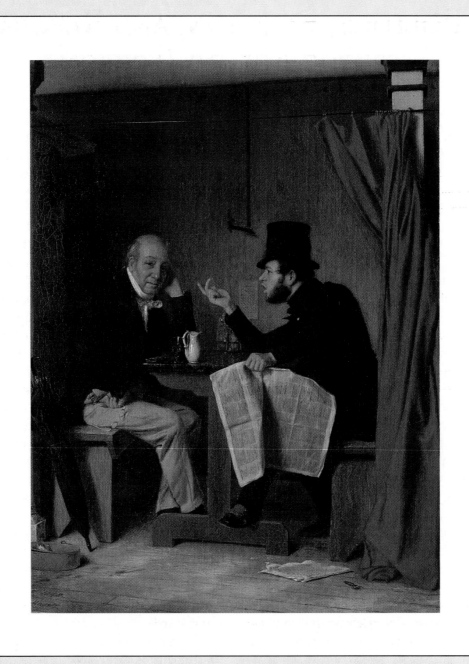

Politics in an Oyster House
by Richard Caton Woodville, 1848

POLITICS, RELIGION, AND REFORM IN THE AGE OF JACKSON

In 1824 the Marquis de Lafayette (inset), former major general in the Continental Army and a Revolutionary War hero, accepted the invitation of President James Monroe and Congress and revisited the United States. For thirteen months as "the Nation's Guest," Lafayette traveled to every state and received a welcome that fluctuated between warm and tumultuous. There seemed no limits to what Americans would do to show their admiration for this "greatest man in the world." "There were," one contemporary wrote, "*La Fayette* boots—*La Fayette* hats—*La Fayette* wine—and *La Fayette* everything." In New York City, some fervid patriots tried to unhitch the horses from Lafayette's carriage and pull it up Broadway themselves.

Lafayette had contributed mightily to the Revolution's success. Americans venerated him as a living embodiment of the entire Revolutionary generation fast passing from the scene. The majority of Americans alive in 1824 had been born since George Washington's death in 1799. John Adams and Thomas Jefferson survived, but they were along in years. Both would die on July 4, 1826, fifty years to the day after the signing of the Declaration of Independence. Seizing on Washington's remark that he loved Lafayette "as my own son," Americans toasted the Frenchman as a cherished member of the family of Revolutionary heroes. In Charleston the toast ran: "WASHINGTON, our Common Father—*you* his favorite *son*"; in New Jersey, "LA FAYETTE, a living monument of greatness, virtue, and faithfulness still exists—a second Washington is now among us."

The festive rituals surrounding Lafayette's visit symbolized Americans' conviction that they had remained true to their heritage of republican liberty. The embers of conflict between Federalists and Republicans that once had seemed to threaten the Republic's stability had cooled; the Era of Good Feelings still reigned over American politics in 1824. Yet even as Americans were turning Lafayette's visit into an affirmation of their ties to the Founders, those ties were fraying in the face of new challenges. Westward migration, growing economic individualism, and increasing sectional conflict over slavery shaped politics mightily between 1824 and 1840. The impact of economic and social change shattered old assumptions and contributed to a vigorous new brand of politics.

This transformation led to the birth of a second American party system, in which two new parties, the Democrats and the Whigs, replaced the Republicans and the Federalists. More was at work here than a change of names. The new parties took advantage of the transportation revolution to spread their messages to the farthest corners of the nation and to arouse voters in all sections. The new parties' leaders were more effective than their predecessors at organizing grass roots support, more eager to make government responsive to the popular will, and more likely to enjoy politics and welcome conflict as a way to sustain interest in political issues.

Not all Americans looked to politics as the pathway to their goals. Some, in fact, viewed politics as suited only to scoundrels and could identify with the sentiments of the Detroit workingman who wrote in 1832 that he "did not vote. I'll [have] none of sin." Despairing of politics, many men and women became active in reform movements pursuing various goals, among them the abolition of slavery, the suppression of the liquor trade, improved public education, and equality for women. Strongly held religious beliefs impelled reformers into these causes, while simultaneously increasing their distrust of politics. Yet even reformers hostile to politics gradually found that the success of their reforms depended on their ability to influence the political process.

During the 1820s and 1830s, the political and reform agendas of Americans diverged increasingly from those of the Founders. The Founders had feared popular participation in politics, enjoyed their wine and rum, left an ambiguous legacy on slavery, and displayed only occasional interest in women's rights. Yet even as Americans shifted their political and social priorities, they continued to venerate the Founders, who in death meant even more than in life. Histories of the United States, biographies of Revolutionary patriots, and torchlight parades that bore portraits of Washington and Jefferson alongside those of Andrew Jackson all helped to reassure the men and women of the young nation that they were remaining loyal to their republican heritage.

THE TRANSFORMATION OF AMERICAN POLITICS, 1824–1832

In 1824 Andrew Jackson and Martin Van Buren, who would lead the Democratic party in the 1830s, and John Quincy Adams and Henry Clay, who would help to guide the rival National Republican (or Whig) party in the 1830s, all belonged to the same political party— the Republican party of Thomas Jefferson. Yet by 1824 the Republican party was coming apart at the seams under pressures generated by industrialization in New England, the spread of cotton cultivation in the South,

and westward expansion. These forces sparked issues that would become the basis for the new political division between Democrats and Whigs. In general, those Republicans (augmented by a few former Federalists) who retained Jefferson's suspicion of a strong federal government and preference for states' rights became Democrats; those Republicans (along with many former Federalists) who believed that the national government should actively encourage economic development became Whigs.

Regardless of which path a politician chose, all leaders in the 1820s and 1830s had to adapt to the rising democratic idea of politics as a forum for the expression of the will of the common people rather than as an activity that gentlemen conducted for the people. Gentlemen could still be elected to office, but their success now depended less on their education or wealth than on their ability to identify and follow the will of the majority. Americans still looked up to their political leaders, but the leaders could no longer look down on the people.

Democratic Ferment

The process by which politics gradually became more democratic took several forms. In one state after another, the requirement, common in the eighteenth century, that voters own property was scaled down to a stipulation that voters merely pay poll taxes. Maryland, South Carolina, Massachusetts, Connecticut, and New York all liberalized their suffrage laws for white voters between the 1790s and 1821, and none of the eight new states admitted between 1796 and 1821 required voters to own property. Moreover, written ballots replaced the old custom of voting aloud (called *viva voce* or "stand up" voting), which had enabled social superiors to influence their inferiors at the polls. Many appointive offices became elective. Although the electoral college remained in place, the practice of allowing state legislatures to choose presidential electors gave way to the selection of electors by popular vote. In 1800, rather than voting for Thomas Jefferson or John Adams, most Americans could do no more than vote for the men who would vote for the men who would vote for Jefferson or Adams. By 1824, however, legislatures chose electors in only six states, and by 1832 in only one (South Carolina).

Nothing did more to undermine the old barriers to the people's expression of their will than a fierce tug-of-war between the Republicans and the Federalists in the 1790s and early 1800s. Because party survival depended on the ability to win elections, political parties had to court voters. First the Republicans and then the Federalists learned to woo voters by staging grand barbecues at which men from Massachusetts to Maryland washed down free clams and oysters with free beer and whiskey. Wherever one party was in the minority, it sought to increase the number of eligible voters in order to turn itself into the majority party. In the South, where the Republicans were strong, they showed little interest in increasing the size of the electorate; but in the North, they built a following by advocating expanded suffrage. Federalists played the same game when it suited them; the initiator of suffrage reform in Maryland, for example, was an aristocratic Federalist.

The democratization of politics developed at an uneven pace, however. As late as 1820, the Republican and Federalist parties continued to be organized from the top down. To nominate candidates, for example, both parties relied on the caucus, a meeting of party members in the legislature, rather than on popularly elected nominating conventions. Moreover, few party leaders rushed to embrace the *principle* of universal white manhood suffrage. Even the newly admitted western states tried at first to imitate the suffrage restrictions of the East and abandoned them only when it became clear that in a region where nearly everyone's land title was in dispute, to require property ownership for voting merely invited fraud. Nor did the democratization of politics necessarily draw more voters to the polls. Waning competition between the Republicans and the Federalists between 1816 and 1824 deprived voters of clear choices and turned national politics into a boring spectacle.

Yet no one could mistake the tendency of the times: to oppose the people or democracy had become a formula for political suicide. The people, a Federalist moaned, "have become too saucy and are really beginning to fancy themselves equal to their betters." Whatever their convictions, politicians learned to adjust.

The Election of 1824

Partially submerged political tensions surfaced in the election of 1824 and inflicted sudden death on the Era of Good Feelings. Even before the election, President Monroe's Republican coalition was cracking under pressure from its rival sectional components. In 1824 five candidates, all Republicans, ended up vying for the presidency. John Quincy Adams emerged as New En-gland's favorite. South Carolina's brilliant John C. Calhoun contended with Georgia's William Crawford, an old-school Jeffersonian, for southern support. Out of the West marched Henry Clay of Kentucky, ambitious, crafty, and confident that his American System of protective tariffs and federally supported internal improvements would endear him to the manufacturing regions of the East as well as to the New West.

Clay's belief that he was holding a solid block of western states was punctured by the rise of a fifth candidate, Andrew Jackson of Tennessee. At first, none of the other candidates took Jackson seriously. But he was popular on the frontier and in the South and stunned his rivals by gaining the support of opponents of the American System from Pennsylvania and other northern states.

Although the Republican congressional caucus chose Crawford as the party's official candidate early in 1824, the caucus could no longer unify the party. Three-fourths of the Republicans in Congress had refused to attend the caucus. Crawford's already diminished prospects evaporated when he suffered a paralyzing stroke. Impressed by Jackson's support, Calhoun withdrew from the race and ran unopposed

The Election of 1824

Candidates	Parties	Electoral Vote	Popular Vote	Percentage of Popular Vote
JOHN QUINCY ADAMS	Democratic-Republican	84	108,740	30.5
Andrew Jackson	Democratic-Republican	99	153,544	43.1
William H. Crawford	Democratic-Republican	41	46,618	13.1
Henry Clay	Democratic-Republican	37	47,136	13.2

for the vice presidency. In the election, Jackson won more popular and electoral votes than any other candidate (Adams, Crawford, and Clay) but failed to gain a majority, as required by the Constitution. Thus the election was thrown into the House of Representatives, whose members had to choose from the three top candidates—Jackson, Adams, and Crawford. Hoping to forge an alliance between the West and Northeast in a future bid for the presidency, Clay gave his support to Adams. Clay's action secured the presidency for Adams, but when Adams promptly appointed Clay his secretary of state, Jackson's supporters raged that a "corrupt bargain" had cheated Jackson of the presidency. Although there is no evidence that Adams had traded Clay's support for an explicit agreement to appoint Clay his secretary of state (an office from which Jefferson, Madison, Monroe, and Adams himself had risen to the presidency), the allegation of a corrupt bargain was widely believed. It formed a cloud that hung over Adams's presidency.

John Quincy Adams as President

Adams's appointment of Clay as his secretary of state was the first of several clumsy miscalculations that cloaked his presidency in controversy. Basically, Adams failed to understand the changing political climate. In his first annual message to Congress in December 1825, the president made a series of proposals that might have won acclaim in 1815 but that only antagonized interests that had grown more powerful and alert in the ensuing decade. He proposed, for example, a program of federal support for internal improvements, an idea that had gained support from Republicans like Henry Clay, the architect of the American System, after the War of 1812. Between 1819 and 1825, however, opponents of the American System had multiplied. Strict Jeffersonians (often called Old Republicans), among them the Virginian John Randolph, had consistently attacked federal aid for internal improvements as unconstitutional, but they were no longer the mainstays of the opposition. Adams's call for federal support for improvements came within a few months of New York's completion of the Erie Canal. Because New York had built the canal with its own money, its senator, Martin Van Buren, opposed federal aid for internal improvements; such support would only enable other states to construct rival canals.

John Quincy Adams
This photo captures John Quincy Adams's austerity, determination, integrity, and respect for knowledge.

In addition, Adams infuriated southerners by proposing to send American delegates to a conference of newly independent Latin American nations in Panama. Southerners feared that U.S. attendance would imply recognition of Haiti, a black republic that had gained its independence from France through a slave revolution. Both the sharp debate over the Missouri Compromise in 1819–1820 and the discovery of a planned slave revolt in South Carolina in 1822 (organized by a free black, Denmark Vesey) had shaken southern slaveholders and generated hostility to Adams's proposal. If Adams had simply recognized that he was antagonizing important groups and responded by seeking new bases of support, he might have saved himself. But he clung to an increasingly obsolete notion of the president as a custodian of the public good who stayed aloof from factions and parties. Far from purging his political opponents, he appointed several to high office and thereby alienated even his friends. As late as 1829, he wrote blithely, "I have no wish to fortify myself by the support of any party whatever."

The Rise of Andrew Jackson

As Adams's popularity declined, Andrew Jackson's rose. Jackson's victory over the British in the Battle of New Orleans in 1815 had given him a national reputation. The fact that he was a Tennessee slaveholder, a renowned Indian fighter, and a militant advocate of Indian removal endeared Jackson to the South. Where Adams tried to uphold treaties between the federal government and the Indians that gave the Native Americans the option of staying in the East, Jackson urged that southerners be allowed a free hand in pushing the Indians further westward. Southerners praised Jackson's stance as a noble application of the Jeffersonian principle of states' rights and recognized that it would satisfy their hunger for land. Furthermore, as the only presidential candidate in the election of 1824 with no connection to the Monroe administration, Jackson was in an ideal position to capitalize on what John C. Calhoun called "a vague but widespread discontent" in the wake of the Panic of 1819 that left people with "a general mass of disaffection to the Government" and "looking out anywhere for a leader."

Jackson's supporters swiftly established committees throughout the country. Two years before the election of 1828, towns and villages across the United States buzzed with furious but unfocused political activity. With the exception of the few remaining Federalists, almost everyone called himself a Republican. Some Republicans were "Adams men," others were "Jackson men," and still others styled themselves "friends of Clay." Amid all the confusion, few realized that a new political system was being born. The man most alert to the signs of the times was Martin Van Buren, who was to become vice president during Jackson's second term and president upon Jackson's retirement.

Van Buren exemplified a new breed of politician. A tavernkeeper's son, he had started his political career in county politics and worked his way up to New York's governorship. In Albany he built a powerful political machine, the Albany Regency, composed mainly of men like himself from the lower and middling ranks. His arch rival in New York politics, DeWitt Clinton, was all that Van Buren was not—tall, handsome, aristocratic, and brilliant. But Van Buren

had a geniality that made ordinary people feel comfortable and an uncanny ability to sense in which direction the political winds were about to blow. Van Buren loved politics, which he viewed as a wonderful game; he was one of the first prominent American politicians to make personal friends from among his political enemies.

The election of 1824 convinced Van Buren of the need for renewed two-party competition. Without the discipline imposed by a strong opposition party, the Republicans in 1824 had splintered into sectional pieces. No candidate had secured an electoral majority, and the House of Representatives had decided the outcome amid charges of intrigue and corruption. It would be better, Van Buren concluded, to let all the shades of opinion in the nation be reduced to two. Then the parties would clash, and a clear popular winner would emerge. Jackson's strong showing in the election persuaded Van Buren that "Old Hickory" could lead a new political party. In the election of 1828, this party, which gradually became known as the Democratic party, put up Jackson for president and Calhoun for vice president. Its opponents, increasingly calling themselves the National Republicans, rallied behind Adams and his running mate, treasury secretary Richard Rush. Slowly but surely, the second American party system was taking shape.

The Election of 1828

The 1828 campaign was a vicious, mudslinging affair. The National Republicans attacked Jackson as a murderer (between duels and military executions, he was directly responsible for several men's deaths), a drunken gambler, and an adulterer. The adultery charge stemmed from the fact that in 1791 Jackson had married Rachel Robards, and each erroneously believing that her divorce from her first husband had become final. "Ought a convicted adulteress and her paramour husband," the Adams men taunted, "be placed in the highest office of this free and Christian land?" Jackson's supporters replied in kind. They accused Adams of wearing silk underwear, being rich, being in debt, and having gained favor with the tsar of Russia by trying to provide him with a beautiful American prostitute.

Although both sides engaged in mudslinging, Jackson's men had better aim. Charges by Adams's supporters that Jackson was an illiterate backwoodsman only added to Jackson's popular appeal by making him seem just like an ordinary citizen. Jackson's supporters portrayed the clash as one between "the *democracy* of the *country,* on the one hand, and a *lordly purse-proud aristocracy* on the other." Jackson, they said, was the common man incarnate—his mind unclouded by learning, his morals simple and true, his will fierce and resolute. In contrast, Jackson's men represented Adams as an aristocrat, a dry scholar whose learning obscured the truth, a man who could write but not fight. Much of this, of course, was wild exaggeration. Jackson was a wealthy planter, not a simple backwoodsman. But it was what people wanted to hear. Uncorrupt, natural, plain, Jackson was presented as the common man's image of his better self.

The election swept Jackson into office with more than twice the electoral vote of Adams. Yet the popular vote, much closer, made it clear that the people were not simply responding to the personalities or images of the candidates (though these factors dominated the campaign). The vote also reflected the strongly sectional bases of the new parties. The popular vote was close only in the middle states and the Northwest. Adams gained double Jackson's vote in New England; Jackson received double Adams's vote in the South, and nearly triple Adams's vote in the Southwest.

The Election of 1828

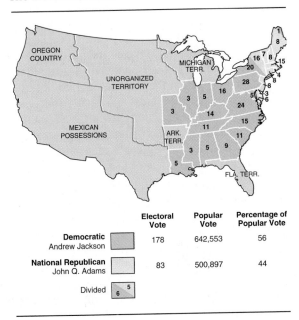

		Electoral Vote	Popular Vote	Percentage of Popular Vote
Democratic Andrew Jackson		178	642,553	56
National Republican John Q. Adams		83	500,897	44
Divided	5	6		

Jackson in Office

For all its fanfare, the campaign had revealed little about Jackson's stands on major issues. On such key questions as federal aid for internal improvements and the tariff, Jackson had sent out conflicting signals. In Tennessee he had aggressively pursued wealth and opposed legislation for the relief of debtors. Yet he understood the popular feelings that had carried him to the presidency and he would use the office to express the will of the majority.

His first policy on coming to office was to openly support the principle of "rotation in office"—the removal of officeholders of the rival party—which critics called the spoils system. Jackson did not invent this policy: many of his predecessors had employed it. Nor did he pursue it with unusual thoroughness, for he removed only about one-fifth of the federal officeholders whom he inherited from Adams. But Jackson defended removal on new and democratic grounds. The duties of officeholders were so plain and simple, he argued, that any intelligent man could perform them. By moving civil servants into and out of office at will, Jackson hoped not only to give as many individuals as possible a chance to work for the government but also to prevent the emergence of an elite bureaucracy that operated beyond the will of the people.

Although Jackson's policy toward the civil service ruffled feathers, it did not produce deep sectional or ideological division. But the issues of federal support for internal improvements and protective tariffs ignited sectional controversy. The South had fewer canals and roads than other sections and, in 1830, fewer plans to build them. Its main cash crop, cotton, was nonperishable and could be transported by rivers and the ocean. Accordingly, southerners were cool toward spending federal money for internal improvements. Jackson, whose firmest political base was in the South, became convinced that federal support for internal improvements was a lavish giveaway program prone to corruption. He also believed that such funding violated the principle that Congress could appropriate money only for objectives shared by *all* Americans, such as national defense, not for the objectives of particular sections or interests. Accordingly, in 1830 Jackson vetoed a bill to provide federal support for a road in Kentucky between Maysville and Lexington.

Coupled with the almost simultaneous passage of the Indian Removal Act (see Chapter 9), the Maysville

Road veto enhanced Jackson's popularity in the South. The tariff issue, however, sternly tested the South's allegiance to Jackson. In 1828, while John Quincy Adams was still in office, Jackson's supporters in Congress had contributed to the final passage of a bill that favored western agricultural interests by raising tariffs (import taxes) on imported hemp, wool, fur, flax, and liquor as well as New England manufacturing interests by raising the tariff on imported textiles. The South, which had few industries to protect from foreign competition, was left high and dry, for tariffs effectively raised the cost of manufactured goods for southerners. Jackson's followers had assumed that the support of the South could be taken for granted in the upcoming election and that embittered southerners would blame the Adams administration for this "Tariff of Abominations." In reality, Jackson rather than Adams would bear the brunt of the South's ire over the tariff.

Nullification

The tariff of 1828 laid the basis for a rift between Jackson and his vice president, John C. Calhoun, that was to shake the foundations of the Republic. Early in his career, Calhoun had been an ardent nationalist. He had entered Congress in 1811 as a "war hawk," supported the protectionist tariff of 1816, and dismissed strict construction of the Constitution as refined philosophical nonsense. During the late 1820s, however, Calhoun the nationalist gradually became Calhoun the states' rights sectionalist. The reasons for his shift were complex. He had supported the tariff of 1816 essentially as a measure conducive to national defense in the wake of the War of 1812. By encouraging fledgling industries, he had reasoned, the tariff would free the United States from dependence upon Britain and provide revenue for military preparedness. By 1826, however, few Americans perceived national defense as a priority. Furthermore, the infant industries of 1816 had grown into troublesome adolescents that demanded higher and higher tariffs.

There was also the matter of Calhoun's fierce ambition. He longed to be president. Jackson had stated that he would serve only one term, and as vice president, Calhoun assumed that he would succeed Jackson. To do so, however, he had to maintain the support of his native South Carolina and of the South in general. As the center of cotton production shifted to the Southwest—Alabama and Mississippi—South Carolina's economy declined during the 1820s, and South Carolinians largely blamed protective tariffs. Tariffs not only drove up the price of manufactured goods but also threatened to reduce the sale of British textile products in the United States. Such a reduction might eventually lower the British demand for southern cotton and cut cotton prices. The more New England industrialized, the clearer it became that tariff laws were pieces of sectional legislation. New Englanders like Massachusetts's eloquent Daniel Webster swung toward protectionism; southerners responded with militant hostility.

Calhoun followed the Virginia and Kentucky resolutions of 1798–1799 in viewing the Union as a compact by which the states had conferred limited and specified powers on the federal government. Although the Constitution did empower Congress to levy tariffs, Calhoun insisted that only tariffs that raised revenue for such common purposes as defense were constitutional. Set so high that it deterred foreign exporters from shipping their products to the United States, the tariff of 1828 could raise little revenue, and hence it failed to meet Calhoun's criterion of constitutionality: that federal laws benefit everyone *equally*. In 1828 Calhoun anonymously wrote the widely circulated *South Carolina Exposition and Protest,* in which he spelled out his argument that the tariff of 1828 was unconstitutional and that aggrieved states therefore had the right to nullify, or override, the law within their borders.

Vehement opposition to tariffs in the South, and especially in South Carolina, rested on more than economic considerations, however. Southerners feared that a federal government that passed tariff laws favoring one section over another might also pass laws meddling with slavery. Because Jackson himself was a slaveholder, the fear of federal interference with slavery was perhaps farfetched. But South Carolinians, long apprehensive of assaults on their crucial institution of slavery, had many reasons for concern. South Carolina was one of only two states in which blacks composed a majority of the population in 1830. Moreover, in 1831 a bloody slave revolt led by Nat Turner boiled up in Virginia. That same year, William Lloyd Garrison established *The Liberator,* an abolitionist newspaper. These developments were enough to convince many troubled South Carolinians that a line had to be drawn against tariffs and possible future interference with slavery.

Jackson Versus Calhoun

Like Calhoun, Jackson was strong-willed and proud. Unlike Calhoun, he was already president and the leader of a national party that included supporters in pro-tariff states like Pennsylvania (which had gone for Jackson in the election of 1828). Thus to retain key northern support while soothing the South, Jackson devised two policies.

The first was to distribute surplus federal revenue to the states. Tariff schedules kept some goods out of the United States but let many others in for a price. The price, in the form of duties on imports, became federal revenue. In these years before federal income taxes, tariffs were a major source of federal revenue. Jackson hoped that this revenue, fairly distributed among the states, would remove the taint of sectional injustice from the tariff and force the federal government to restrict its own expenditures. All of this was good Jeffersonianism. Second, Jackson hoped to ease tariffs down from the sky-high tariff of 1828.

Calhoun disliked the idea of distributing federal revenue to the states because he believed that such a policy could become an excuse to maintain tariffs forever. But he was loath to break openly with Jackson. Between 1828 and 1831, Calhoun muffled his protest, hoping that Jackson would lower the tariff and that he, Calhoun, would retain both Jackson's favor and his chances for the presidency. Congress did pass new, slightly reduced tariff rates in 1832, but these did not come close to satisfying South Carolinians.

Before passage of the tariff of 1832, however, two personal issues had ruptured relations between Calhoun and Jackson. In 1829 Jackson's secretary of war, John H. Eaton, married the widowed daughter of a Washington tavernkeeper. By her own account, Peggy O'Neale Timberlake was "frivolous, wayward, [and] passionate." While still married to a naval officer away on duty, Peggy had acquired the reputation of flirting with Eaton, who boarded at her father's tavern. After her husband's death and her marriage to Eaton, she and Eaton were snubbed socially by Calhoun's wife and by his friends in the cabinet. Jackson, who never forgot how his own wife had been wounded by slander during the campaign of 1828, not only befriended the Eatons but concluded that Calhoun had initiated the snubbing to discredit him and to advance Calhoun's own presidential aspirations.

To make matters worse, in 1830 Jackson received convincing documentation of his suspicion that in 1818, Calhoun, as secretary of war under President Monroe, had urged that Jackson be punished for his unauthorized raid into Spanish Florida. The revelation that Calhoun had tried to stab him in the back in 1818, combined with the snubbing of the Eatons, convinced Jackson that he had to "destroy [Calhoun] regardless of what injury it might do me or my administration." A symbolic confrontation occurred between Jackson and Calhoun at a Jefferson Day dinner in April 1830. Jackson proposed the toast, "Our Union: It must be preserved." Calhoun responded: "The Union next to Liberty the most dear. May we always remember that it can only be preserved by distributing equally the benefits and burdens of the Union."

The stage was now set for a direct clash between the president and his vice president over nullification. In 1831 Calhoun acknowledged his authorship of the *South Carolina Exposition and Protest.* In November 1832 a South Carolina convention nullified the tariffs of 1828 and 1832 and forbade the collection of customs duties within the state. Jackson reacted quickly. He despised nullification, calling it an "abominable doctrine" that would reduce the government to anarchy, and he berated the South Carolina nullifiers as "unprincipled men who would rather rule in hell, than be subordinate in heaven." Jackson even began to send arms to loyal Unionists in South Carolina, and in December 1832 he issued a proclamation that while promising South Carolinians further tariff reductions, lambasted nullification as itself unconstitutional. The Constitution, he emphasized, had established "a single nation," not a league of states.

The crisis eased in March 1833, when Jackson signed into law two measures—"the olive branch and the sword," in one historian's words. The olive branch was the tariff of 1833 (also called the Compromise Tariff), which provided for a gradual but significant lowering of duties between 1833 and 1842. The sword was the Force Bill, authorizing the president to use arms to collect customs duties in South Carolina. Although South Carolina did not abandon nullification in principle—in fact, it nullified the Force Bill—it construed the Compromise Tariff as a concession and rescinded its nullification of the tariffs of 1828 and 1832.

Like most of the accommodations by which the Union lurched from one sectional crisis to the next before the Civil War, the Compromise of 1833 grew out of a mixture of partisanship and statesmanship. The moving spirit behind the Compromise Tariff was Kentucky's senator Henry Clay, who had long favored high

Andrew Jackson, *by Thomas Sully, 1845*

John C. Calhoun, *by Charles Bird King, c. 1825*
Jackson, defeated in the presidential election of 1824,
won handily four years later. The magnetic Calhoun,
Jackson's vice president, broke with Jackson over nullifi-
cation and the Peggy Eaton affair and resigned the vice
presidency in 1832.

tariffs. A combination of motives brought Clay and the nullifiers together in favor of tariff reduction. Clay feared that without concessions to South Carolina on tariffs, the Force Bill would produce civil war. Furthermore, he was apprehensive that without compromise, the principle of protective tariffs would disappear under the wave of Jackson's immense popularity. In short, Clay would rather take responsibility for lowering tariffs than allow the initiative on tariff questions to pass to the Jacksonians. For their part, the nullifiers hated Jackson and defiantly toasted "Andrew Jackson: On the soil of South Carolina he received an humble birthplace. May he not find in it a traitor's grave!" Although recognizing that South Carolina had failed to gain support for nullification from other southern states and that they would have to bow to pressure, the nullifiers preferred that Clay, not Jackson, be the hero of the hour. So they supported Clay's Compromise Tariff. Everywhere Americans now hailed Clay as the Great Compromiser. Even Martin Van Buren frankly stated that Clay had "saved the country."

The Bank Veto

One reason Jackson signed Clay's compromise tariff into law was that he did not have strong convictions about an alternative. Inclined to react passionately to most issues, Jackson was relatively open-minded on the subject of tariffs. In sharp contrast, as a result of some disastrous financial speculations early in his career, Jackson was deeply suspicious of all banks, all paper money, and all exclusive monopolies. On each count, the Bank of the United States was a likely target.

In 1816 the Second Bank of the United States had received a twenty-year charter from Congress. As a creditor of state banks, the Bank of the United States could contract the lending capacity of the state banks whenever it chose by demanding that they redeem in specie (gold or silver coinage) their bank notes that were held by the Bank of the United States. Because most banks emitted more notes than they could redeem in specie, the Bank of the United States exerted an often healthy restraint on excessive lending by state banks.

Many aspects of the Bank of the United States, however, made it controversial. As we have seen, its decision to contract credit precipitated the Panic of 1819, for which it was widely blamed. Furthermore, at a time when privilege was coming under fire, the bank was undeniably a privileged institution. First, it was the official depository for federal revenue, a fact that greatly increased its capacity to lend money and that gave it a commanding position over all state banks. Second, although the federal government accorded it privileges not available to any other bank, the Bank of the United States was only remotely under the federal government's control. The bank's stockholders were private citizens—a "few monied capitalists," in Jackson's words. In addition, although chartered by Congress, the bank was located not in Washington but in Philadelphia; and the federal government allowed the bank's directors (a majority of whom were government appointees) considerable independence. Finally, the bank's president, the aristocratic Nicholas Biddle, viewed himself as a public servant whose duty was to keep the bank above politics.

In his first annual message to Congress in 1829, Jackson questioned "both the constitutionality and expediency" of the Bank of the United States. Strongly influenced by Henry Clay, Biddle resolved to seek recharter of the bank in 1832, four years before its existing charter expired. With his eyes on the presidential election of 1832, Clay sensed that a pro-bank stand would boost his own chances in the election. Although Biddle and Clay secured congressional approval to recharter, Jackson promptly vetoed the recharter bill. He denounced the bank as a private and privileged monopoly that drained the West of specie, was immune to taxation by states (as Chief Justice Marshall had established in his 1819 *McCulloch* v. *Maryland* decision), gathered inordinate power into the hands of a few men, and made "the rich richer and the potent more powerful." Failing to persuade Congress to override Jackson's veto, Clay now pinned his hopes on gaining the presidency himself.

The Election of 1832

By 1832 Jackson's views on major issues were considerably clearer than in 1828. The Indian Removal Act, his vetoes of the Maysville Road Bill and the recharter of the Bank of the United States, his policy of distributing federal revenues, and his lowering of tariffs all marked him as a strong defender of states' rights. But at the same time, his vigorous response to nullification had established him as a staunch Unionist. States' rights and Unionism were compatible doctrines. Although he cherished the Union, Jackson believed that the states were far too diverse to accept strong, purposeful direction from the federal government. The safest course was to allow the states considerable freedom, so that they would remain contentedly within the Union and reject dangerous doctrines like nullification.

Despite earlier statements to the contrary, Jackson ran again, selecting Martin Van Buren, now clearly the heir apparent, as his running mate to replace Calhoun, who had resigned. Against Jackson the National Republicans put up Henry Clay. Clay's platform was his American System of protective tariffs, national banking, and federal support for internal improvements. The election of 1832, the first in which national nominating conventions chose the candidates, was more issue-oriented than the vicious campaign of 1828. But Jackson continued to benefit from his great personal popularity. He carried 219 electoral votes to Clay's 49 and even took pro-bank and pro-tariff Pennsylvania. Clay's economic nationalism made him popular in pro-tariff New England. But Clay could not topple

The Election of 1832

Candidates	Parties	Electoral Vote	Popular Vote	Percentage of Popular Vote
ANDREW JACKSON	Democratic	219	687,502	55.0
Henry Clay	National Republican	49	530,189	42.4
William Wirt	Anti-Masonic	7	33,108	2.6
John Floyd	National Republican	11		

Jackson's stronghold in the South, whereas Jackson chalked up support in the North and West as well as the South. Secure in office for another four years, Jackson was ready to finish the job of dismantling the Bank of the United States.

THE BANK CONTROVERSY AND THE SECOND PARTY SYSTEM

Coming late in Andrew Jackson's first term, the veto of the bank's recharter had relatively little impact on the election of 1832. However, between 1833 and 1840, banking became an issue that ignited extraordinary popular passion. In no period of American history have issues relating to banking generated keener public interest than during these seven years. Jackson's veto of recharter unleashed a tiger that threatened to devour all banks.

Why did banking so raise people's temperature? Part of the answer lay in the fact that the U.S. government did not issue paper currency of its own; there were no "official" dollar bills as we know them today. Paper money took the form of notes (promises to redeem in specie) emitted by private banks. As a consequence, private bankers had enormous influence over economic transactions and could easily be viewed by ordinary people as sinister. In addition, a basic issue lurked behind most of the banking debates of the 1830s. What sort of society would the United States become? If paper money circulated in abundance, businessmen and farmers could readily obtain loans to open factories or buy more land. Such an economy would be speculative in the sense that it would raise expectations for profit while posing risks. A sudden slump in the prices of industrial or agricultural products would leave businessmen and farmers mired in debt. Furthermore, a speculative economy would not benefit everyone equally. Factory owners would reap profits, but their employees would have to perform poorly paid and often unhealthy work. Would the United States be a nation that embraced swift economic development, even at the price of allowing some to get rich quickly off investments while others languished? Or would it be a nation characterized by more modest growth in traditional molds, but one anchored by "honest" manual work and frugality?

Before the answer to any of these [...] clear, the banking issue dramaticall[...] American politics. It contributed might[...] gence of opposition to the Democrats a[...] expansion of popular interest in politics.

The War on the Bank

Once reelected, Jackson could have allowed the bank to die a natural death when its charter ran out in 1836. But Jackson and several of his rabid followers viewed the bank as a kind of dragon that would grow new limbs as soon as old ones were cut off. As one radical Jacksonian put it, were the bank allowed to escape with a breath of life, "it will soon recover its wonted strength, its whole power to injure us, and all hope of its destruction must forever be renounced." When Biddle, anticipating further moves against the bank by Jackson, began to call in the bank's loans and contract credit during the winter of 1832–1833, Jacksonians saw their darkest fears confirmed. The bank, Jackson assured Van Buren, "is trying to kill me, but I will kill it." Accordingly, Jackson embarked on a controversial policy of removing federal deposits from the Bank of the United States and placing them in state banks.

Once in place, the policy of removing deposits only raised a new and even thornier issue. Those state banks that became the depositories for federal revenue could use that revenue as the basis for issuing more paper money and for extending more loans. In short, the removal policy enabled state banks to increase their lending capacity. But Jackson hated both paper money and a speculative economy in which capitalists routinely took out large loans. The policy of removal seemed a formula for producing exactly the kind of economy that Jackson wanted to abolish. Jackson recognized the danger and hoped to sharply limit the number of state banks that would become depositories for federal revenue. But as state banks increasingly clamored for the revenue, the number of state-bank depositories soon multiplied beyond Jackson's expectations. There were twenty-three by the end of 1833. Critics dubbed them "pet banks" because they were usually selected for their loyalty to the Democratic party. During the next few years, fueled by paper money from the pet banks and by an influx of foreign specie to purchase cotton and for investment in canal projects, the economy entered a heady expansion. Jackson could not stem the tide. In 1836, pressured by Congress, he reluctantly signed into law the Deposit

Jackson Versus the Bank
Andrew Jackson, aided by Martin Van Buren (center), attacks the Bank of the United States, which, like the many-headed serpent Hydra of Greek mythology, keeps sprouting new heads. The largest head belongs to Nicholas Biddle, the bank's president.

Act, which both increased the number of deposit banks and loosened federal control over them.

Jackson's policy of removing deposits deepened a split within his own Democratic party between advocates of soft money (paper) and those of hard money (gold or silver coinage, or specie). Both sides agreed that the Bank of the United States was evil, but for different reasons. Soft-money Democrats resented the bank's role in periodically contracting credit and restricting the lending activities of state banks; their hard-money counterparts disliked the bank because it sanctioned an economy based on paper money. Prior to the Panic of 1837, the soft-money position was more popular among Democrats outside Jackson's inner circle of advisers than within that circle. For example, western Democrats had long viewed the Bank of the United States' branch in Cincinnati as inadequate to supply their need for credit and favored an expansion of banking activity.

Aside from Jackson and a few other figures within the administration, the most articulate support for hard money came from a faction of the Democratic party in New York called the Locofocos. The Locofocos grew out of various "workingmen's" parties that had sprouted during the late 1820s in northern cities and that called for free public education, the abolition of imprisonment for debt, and a ten-hour workday. Most of these parties had collapsed within a few years, but in New York the "workies" had gradually been absorbed by the Democratic party. Once in the party, the workingmen were hard to keep in line. Composed of a mixture of intellectuals and small artisans and journey-

men threatened by economic change, they worried about inflation, preferred to be paid in specie, and distrusted banks and paper money. In 1835 a faction of workingmen had broken away from Tammany Hall, the main Democratic party organization in New York City, and held a dissident meeting in a hall whose candles were illuminated by a newfangled invention, the "loco foco," or match. Thereafter, these radical workingmen were known as Locofocos.

The Rise of Whig Opposition

During Jackson's second term, the opposition National Republican party changed its name to the Whig party. More important, the opposition began to broaden its base in both the South and the North. Jackson's magnetic personality had swept him to victory in 1828 and 1832. But as the profile of Jackson's administration became more sharply delineated—as Jackson's vague Jeffersonianism of 1829 gave way to hard-and-fast positions against the Bank of the United States, federal aid for internal improvements, protective tariffs, and nullification—the opposition drew into its fold increasing numbers alienated by Jackson's policies.

Jackson's crushing of nullification, for example, led some of its southern supporters into the Whig party, not because the Whigs favored nullification but because they opposed Jackson. Jackson's war on the Bank of the United States produced the same result. His policy of removing deposits from the bank pleased some southerners but dismayed others who had been satisfied with the bank and who did not share westerners' mania for even cheaper and easier credit. Jackson's opposition to federal aid for internal improvements also alienated some southerners who feared that the South would languish behind the North unless it began to push ahead with improvements. Because so much southern capital was tied up in slavery, pro-improvement southerners looked to the federal government for aid, and when they were met with a cold shoulder, they drifted into the Whig party. None of this added up to an overturning of the Democratic party in the South; the South was still the Democrats' firmest base. But the Whigs were making significant inroads, particularly in southern market towns and among planters who had close ties to southern bankers and merchants.

Meanwhile, in the North, social reformers were infusing new vitality into the opposition to Jackson. These reformers wanted to improve American society by attacking the sale of liquor, opposing slavery, bettering public education, and elevating public morality. Most opponents of liquor (temperance reformers) and most public-school reformers gravitated to the Whigs. Whig philosophy was more compatible with the reformers' goals than with Democratic ideals. Where Democrats maintained that the government should not impose a uniform standard of conduct on a diverse society, the Whigs' commitment to Clay's American System implied an acceptance of active intervention by the government to change society. Reformers wanted the government to play a positive role specifically by suppressing the liquor trade and by establishing centralized systems of public education. Thus a shared sympathy for active government programs tended to unite Whigs and reformers.

Reformers also indirectly stimulated new support for the Whigs from native-born Protestant workers. The reformers, themselves almost all Protestants, widely distrusted immigrants, especially the Irish, who viewed drinking as a normal recreation and who, as Catholics, suspected (correctly) that the public schools favored by reformers would teach Protestant doctrines. The rise of reform agitation and its frequent association with the Whigs drove the Irish into the arms of the Democrats but, by the same token, gained support for the Whigs from many native-born Protestant workers who were contemptuous of the Irish.

No source of Whig strength, however, was more remarkable than Anti-Masonry, a protest movement against the secrecy and exclusiveness of the Masonic lodges, which had long provided prominent men with fraternal fellowship and exotic rituals. The spark that set off the Anti-Masonic crusade was the abduction and disappearance in 1826 of William Morgan, a stonemason in Genesee County, New York, who had threatened to expose Masonic secrets. Every effort to solve the mystery of Morgan's disappearance ran into a stone wall because local officials were themselves Masons seemingly bent on obstructing the investigation. Throughout the Northeast the public became increasingly aroused against the Masonic order, and rumors spread that Masonry was a powerful conspiracy of the rich to suppress popular liberty, a secret order of men who loathed Christianity, and an exclusive retreat for drunkards.

By 1836 the Whigs had become a national party with widespread appeal. In both the North and South, they attracted those with close ties to the market economy—commercial farmers, planters, merchants, and bankers. In the North they also gained support from reformers, evangelical clergymen (especially Presbyterians and Congregationalists), Anti-Masons, and manufacturers. In the South they appealed to some former nullificationists; Calhoun himself briefly became a Whig. Everywhere the Whigs assailed Jackson as an imperious dictator, "King Andrew I"; indeed, they had taken the name "Whigs" to associate their cause with that of the American patriots who had opposed King George III in 1776.

The Election of 1836

As the election of 1836 approached, the Whigs lacked only a national leader. Henry Clay came close, but he was scarred by many political battles and additionally could not shake his reputation as a man who spent his days at the gaming table and his nights in brothels. Unable to agree on a single candidate, the Whigs ran four sectional candidates: William Henry Harrison of Ohio in the Old Northwest, Hugh Lawson White of Tennessee and W. P. Mangum of North Carolina in the South, and Daniel Webster of Massachusetts in the East. The Whig strategy was to prevent Vice President Martin Van Buren, the Democratic candidate, from gaining the required majority of electoral votes. That

The Election of 1836

Candidates	Parties	Electoral Vote	Popular Vote	Percentage of Popular Vote
MARTIN VAN BUREN	Democratic	170	765,483	50.9
William H. Harrison	Whig	73		
Hugh L. White	Whig	26	739,79	49.1
Daniel Webster	Whig	14		
W. P. Mangum	Whig	11		

would force the election into the House of Representatives, where the Whigs thought that they had a chance to win.

Van Buren, whose star in the Democratic party had risen as Calhoun's had fallen, captured 170 electoral votes to 124 for the four Whigs combined. The Whig strategy obviously had backfired, but there were signs of trouble ahead for the Democrats. In the South the Whigs ran virtually even in the popular vote and captured Georgia and Tennessee. Even in the southern states held by Van Buren, the Democratic proportion of the popular vote was much smaller than in 1832; in North Carolina, for example, it dropped from 70 percent to 53 percent.

The Panic of 1837

Jackson left office in March 1837 in a sunburst of glory. Hailed as "the greatest man of his age," he returned to his Nashville home in a triumphant procession. But the public's mood quickly became less festive, for no sooner was Van Buren in office than a severe depression began.

The years 1835 and 1836 had witnessed a speculative boom fed by Jackson's policy of removing federal deposits from the Bank of the United States and placing them in state banks. In 1830 there were 329 banks in the nation with a total capital of $110 million. By 1835 the number of banks had increased to 704, with a total capital of $231 million. The value of bank notes in circulation grew from $61 million in 1830 to $149 million in 1837. Commodity prices rose an average of 13 percent a year in 1835 and 1836. Land sales skyrocketed. States made new commitments to build canals. Then in May 1837, prices began to tumble, and bank after bank suspended specie payments. After a short rally, the economy crashed again in 1839. The Bank of the United States, which had continued to operate as a

state bank with a Pennsylvania charter, failed. Nicholas Biddle himself was charged with fraud and theft. Banks throughout the nation once again suspended specie payments.

The ensuing depression was far more severe and prolonged than the economic downturn of 1819. Those lucky enough to find work saw their wage rates drop by roughly one-third between 1836 and 1842. In despair, many workers turned to the teachings of William Miller, a New England religious enthusiast whose reading of the Bible convinced him that the end of the world was imminent. Dressed in black coats and stovepipe hats, Miller's followers roamed urban sidewalks and rural villages in search of converts. Many Millerites sold their possessions and purchased white robes to ascend into heaven on October 22, 1843, the date on which Millerite leaders calculated the world would end. Ironically, by then the worst of the depression was over; but at its depths in the late 1830s and early 1840s, the economic slump fed the gloom that made poor people receptive to Miller's predictions.

The origins of the depression were both national and international. In July 1836 Jackson had issued a proclamation called the Specie Circular, which provided that after August 15 only specie was to be accepted in payment for public lands. The Specie Circular was one of Jackson's final affirmations of his belief that paper money encouraged people to embark on speculative, get-rich-quick schemes, sapped "public virtue," and robbed "honest labour of its earnings to make knaves rich, powerful and dangerous." He hoped that the Specie Circular would reverse the damaging effects of the Deposit Act of 1836, which he had signed reluctantly. The Specie Circular took the wind out of the speculative boom by making banks hesitant to issue more of the paper money that was fueling the boom, because western farmers eager to buy public lands would now demand that banks immediately redeem their paper in specie. Although the Specie Circular chilled bankers' confidence, it was not the sole or even the major reason for the depression. There were international causes as well, most notably the fact that in 1836, Britain, in an effort to restrain the outflow of British investment, checked the flow of specie from its shores to the United States.

The Search for Solutions

Van Buren came to office with a well-deserved reputation as a crafty politician; contemporaries called him the "sly fox" and the "little magician." Now he had to act decisively, for the depression was causing misery not only for ordinary citizens but for the Democratic party as well. Railing against "Martin Van Ruin," the Whigs in 1838 swept the governorship and most of the legislative seats in Van Buren's own New York.

To regain the political initiative, the president called for the creation of an Independent Treasury. Instead of depositing its revenue in state banks, the federal government would keep the revenue itself and thereby withhold public money from the grasp of business corporations. Introduced in Congress in 1837, the Independent Treasury Bill finally passed in 1840. With a flourish, Van Buren signed it into law on July 4, 1840; his supporters hailed it as America's second Declaration of Independence.

The establishment of the Independent Treasury reflected the basic Jacksonian suspicion of an alliance between the federal government and banking. From the moment that it was introduced, the Independent Treasury Bill promised not only to give the Democrats a clear national issue around which to rally but to get the federal government out of the banking business. But the Independent Treasury proposal failed to address the banking issue on the state level. Jackson's dismemberment of the Bank of the United States had not slowed the establishment of state banks, whose number by 1840 had grown to over nine hundred. Although holding charters from state governments, these banks were privately controlled institutions whose loans to businessmen and farmers fueled the kind of speculative economy that Jacksonians feared.

Whigs and Democrats differed sharply in their approach to the multiplication of state banks. Eager to encourage economic development, Whigs in New York and elsewhere introduced the idea of "free banking." Free banking allowed any group to start a bank as long as its members met general state requirements.

In the eyes of Whigs, Jackson's Specie Circular, not banks themselves, had caused the depression. In contrast, Democrats took a different view of both the causes of the depression and the value of state banks. Disillusioned by the collapse of the speculative boom of 1835–1836, a growing number of Democrats blamed the depression on banks and paper money and adopted the hard-money stance long favored by Jackson and his advisers. In Louisiana and Arkansas, Democrats successfully prohibited banks altogether. Elsewhere, Democrats imposed severe legislative restrictions on banks—for example, by banning the emission of paper money in small denominations. In sum, after 1837 the Democrats became an antibank, hard-money party.

The Election of 1840

Despite the depression, Van Buren gained his party's renomination. Avoiding their mistake of 1836, the Whigs settled on a single candidate, Ohio's William Henry Harrison, and ran former Virginia senator John Tyler as vice president. Harrison, sixty-seven years old and barely eking out a living on a farm, was picked because he had few enemies. Early in the campaign, the Democrats made a fatal mistake by ridiculing Harrison as "Old Granny," a man who desired only to spend his declining years in a log cabin sipping cider. Without knowing it, the Democrats had handed the Whigs the

The Election of 1840

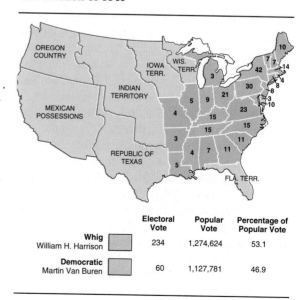

		Electoral Vote	Popular Vote	Percentage of Popular Vote
Whig William H. Harrison		234	1,274,624	53.1
Democratic Martin Van Buren		60	1,127,781	46.9

The Federal-Abolition–Whig Trap

This Democratic cartoon from the 1840 campaign linked the Whigs to the discredited Federalists and to the unpopular abolitionists. An unwary voter, seeking a harmless sip of hard cider, is about to be entrapped by the log cabin, the campaign symbol of the Whig William Henry Harrison.

most famous campaign symbol in American history. The Whigs immediately reminded the public that Harrison had been a rugged frontiersman, the hero of the Battle of Tippecanoe, and a defender of all frontier people who lived in log cabins.

Refusing to publish a platform, the Whigs ran a "hurrah" campaign. They used log cabins for headquarters, sang log-cabin songs, gave out log-cabin cider, and called their newspaper the *Log Cabin.* For a slogan, they trumpeted "Tippecanoe and Tyler too." When not celebrating log cabins, they attacked Van Buren as a soft aristocrat who lived in "regal splendor." Whereas Harrison was content to drink hard cider from a plain mug, the Whigs observed, Van Buren had turned the White House into a palace fit for an oriental despot and drank fine wines from silver goblets while he watched people go hungry in the streets.

The election results gave Harrison a clear victory. Van Buren carried only seven states and failed even to hold his own New York. The depression would have made it difficult, if not impossible, for any Democrat to have triumphed in 1840, but Van Buren had other disabilities besides the economic collapse. Unlike Harrison and Jackson, he had no halo of military glory.

Moreover, Van Buren ran a surprisingly sluggish campaign. Prior to 1840 the Whigs had been slower than the Democrats to mobilize voters by new techniques. But in 1840 it was Van Buren who directed his campaign the old-fashioned way by writing encouraging letters to key supporters, whereas Harrison broke with tradition and went about the country (often on railroads) campaigning. Ironically, Van Buren, the master politician, was beaten at his own game.

The Second Party System Matures

In losing the presidency in 1840, Van Buren actually received 400,000 more popular votes than any previous presidential candidate. The total number of votes cast in presidential elections had risen from 1.2 million in 1828 to 1.5 million in 1836 to 2.4 million in 1840. The leap in the size of the popular vote between 1836 and 1840, 60 percent, is the greatest proportional jump between consecutive elections in American history. Neither lower suffrage requirements nor population growth was the main cause of this change. Rather, the spurt in the popular vote resulted from a jump in the percentage of eligible voters who *chose* to vote. In the three elections before 1840, the proportion of white males who voted had fluctuated between 55 percent and 58 percent; in 1840 it rose to 80 percent.

Both the depression and the frenzy of the log-cabin campaign had jolted previously indifferent voters into going to the polls. Yet voter turnouts stayed up even after prosperity returned in the 1840s. The second party system, which had been developing slowly since 1828, reached a high plateau in 1840 and remained there for more than a decade. What gave politicians their appeal in the eyes of ordinary people were not only their rousing campaign techniques but also the strong contrasts and simple choices that they could present. The gradual hardening of the line between the two parties stimulated enduring popular interest in politics.

No less than the tariff and banking issues, reform also aroused partisan passions by 1840. Yet many of the seeds of the reform movements that burst upon the national scene in the 1830s were initially sown in the field of religion rather than politics.

THE RISE OF POPULAR RELIGION

In *Democracy in America,* Alexis de Tocqueville pointed out an important difference between France and the United States. "In France I had almost always seen the spirit of religion and the spirit of freedom pursuing courses diametrically opposed to each other; but in America I found that they were intimately united, and that they reigned in common over the same country." From this assertion Tocqueville drew a startling conclusion: religion was "the foremost of the political institutions" of the United States.

In calling religion a political institution, Tocqueville did not mean that Americans gave special political privileges to any particular denomination. Rather, he was referring to the way in which religious impulses reinforced American democracy and liberty. Just as Americans demanded that politics be made accessible to the average person, they insisted that ministers preach doctrines that appealed to ordinary people. The most successful ministers were those who used plain words to move the heart, not those who tried to dazzle their listeners with theological complexities. Increasingly, too, Americans demanded theological doctrines that put individuals in charge of their own religious destiny. They thrust aside the Calvinist doctrine that God had arbitrarily selected some people for salvation and others for damnation and substituted the belief that anyone could attain heaven.

Thus heaven as well as politics became democratized in these years. This harmony between religious and democratic impulses owed much to a series of religious revivals known as the Second Great Awakening.

The Second Great Awakening

The Second Great Awakening had begun in Connecticut during the 1790s and set ablaze one section of the nation after another during the following half-century. At first, educated Congregationalists and Presbyterians such as Yale University's president Timothy Dwight had dominated the revivals. But as they moved from Connecticut to frontier states like Tennessee and Kentucky, the revivals had undergone striking changes that were typified by the rise of camp meetings. Camp meetings were gigantic revivals in which members of several denominations gathered together in sprawling open-air camps for up to a week to hear revivalists proclaim that the Second Coming of Jesus was near and that the time for repentance was now. The most famous camp meeting had occurred at Cane Ridge, Kentucky, in August 1801, when a huge crowd had come together on a hillside to listen to thunderous sermons and to sing hymns and experience the influx of divine grace. One eyewitness vividly described the meeting:

> *At night, the whole scene was awfully sublime. The ranges of tents, the fires, reflecting light amidst the branches of the towering trees; the candles and lamps illuminating the encampment; hundreds moving to and fro, with lights or torches, like Gideon's army; the preaching, praying, singing, and shouting, all heard at once, rushing from different parts of the ground, like the sound of many waters, was enough to swallow up all the powers of contemplation.*

The Cane Ridge revival had been an episode of the larger Great Kentucky Revival of 1800–1801. Among the distinguishing features of these frontier revivals was the appearance of "exercises" in which men and women rolled around like logs, jerked their heads furiously (a phenomenon known simply as "the jerks"),

Methodist Camp Meeting
Frontier revivals occurred outdoors, lasted for days, and attracted an abundance of women and children as well as men.

and grunted like animals (the "barking exercise"). Observing the apparent pandemonium that had broken loose, critics had blasted the frontier frenzy for encouraging fleshly lust more than spirituality and complained that in revivals, "more souls were begot than saved." In fact, the early frontier revivals had challenged traditional religious customs. The most successful frontier revivalist preachers were not college graduates but ordinary farmers and artisans who had experienced powerful religious conversions and who had contempt for learned ministers with their dry expositions of doctrine.

No religious denomination had been more successful on the frontier than Methodists. With fewer than seventy thousand members in 1800, the Methodists had by 1844 become America's largest Protestant denomination, claiming a little over a million members. in contrast to New England Congregationalists and Presbyterians, Methodists emphasized that religion was primarily a matter of the heart rather than the head. Too, the frontier Methodists disdained a "settled" ministry—that is, ministers tied to fixed parishes. Instead, they preferred itinerant circuit riders—young, unmarried men—who moved on horseback from place to place and preached in houses, open fields, or wherever else listeners gathered.

Although the frontier revivals disrupted religious custom, they also worked to promote law, order, and a sense of morality on the frontier. Drunken rowdies who tried to invade camp meetings met their match in brawny itinerants like the Methodist Peter Cartwright. It was not only in camp meetings that Cartwright and his peers sought to raise the moral standard of the frontier. The basic unit of Methodist discipline on the frontier was the "class." When revivals broke up, the converted formed these tiny groups of twelve or so members who met weekly to provide mutual encouragement of both religion and morality. During these class meetings, Methodists chastised each other for drunkenness, fighting, fornication, gossiping, and even sharp business practices.

Eastern Revivals

By the 1820s the Second Great Awakening had begun to shift back to the East. The hottest revival fires blazed in an area of western New York known as the Burned-Over District. No longer a frontier, western New York teemed with descendants of Puritans who hungered for religious experience and with people drawn by the hope of wealth after the completion of the Erie Canal. At this time it was a fertile field of high expectations and bitter discontent.

The man who harnessed these anxieties to religion was Charles G. Finney. Finney began his career as a lawyer, but after a religious conversion in 1821, which he described as a "retainer from the Lord Jesus Christ to plead his cause," he became a Presbyterian minister and conducted revivals in towns along the canal like Rome and Utica. Although he also found time for trips to New York and Boston, his greatest "harvest" came in the thriving canal city of Rochester in 1830–1831.

The Rochester revival had several features that justify Finney's reputation as the "father of modern revivalism." First, it was a citywide revival in which all denominations participated. Finney was a pioneer of cooperation among Protestant denominations. In addition, in Rochester and elsewhere, Finney introduced devices for speeding conversions. Among these were the "anxious seat," a bench to which those ready for conversion were led so that they could be made objects of special prayer, and the "protracted meeting," which went on nightly for up to a week. Finney's emphasis on special revival techniques sharply distinguished him from eighteenth-century revivalists, including Jonathan Edwards. Whereas Edwards had portrayed revivals as the miraculous work of God, Finney made them out to be human creations. The divine spirit flowed in revivals, but humans made them happen. Finally, although a Presbyterian, Finney flatly rejected the Calvinist belief that humans had a natural and nearly irresistible inclination to sin (the doctrine of "human depravity"). Rather, he affirmed, sin was purely a voluntary act; no one *had* to sin. Men and women could will themselves out of sin just as readily as they had willed themselves into it. Indeed, he declared, it was theoretically possible for men and women to will themselves free of all sin—to live perfectly. Those who heard Finney and similar revivalists came away convinced that they had experienced the washing away of all past guilt and the beginning of a new life. "I have been born again," a young convert wrote. "I am three days old when I write this letter."

The assertions that people could live without sin ("perfectionism") and that revivals were human contrivances made Finney a controversial figure. Yet his ideas came to dominate "evangelical" Protestantism, forms of Protestantism that focused on the need for an emotional religious conversion. He was successful because he told people what they wanted to hear: that their destinies were in their own hands. A society that celebrated the "self-made" individual found plausible Finney's assertion that even in religion, people could make of themselves what they chose. Moreover, compared to most frontier revivalists, Finney had an unusually dignified style. Taken together, these factors gave him a potent appeal to merchants, lawyers, and small manufacturers in the towns and cities of the North. Finally, more than most revivalists, Finney recognized that without the mass participation of women, few revivals would have gotten off the ground. During the Second Great Awakening, female converts outnumbered male converts by about two to one. Finney encouraged women to give public testimonials of their religious experiences in church, and he often converted husbands by first converting their wives and daughters. After a visit by Finney, Melania Smith, the wife of a Rochester physician who had little time for religion, greeted her husband with a reminder of "the woe which is denounced against the families which call not on the Name of the Lord." Soon Dr. Smith heeded his wife's pleading and joined one of Rochester's Presbyterian churches.

Critics of Revivals: The Unitarians

Whereas some praised revivals for saving souls, others doubted that they produced permanent changes in behavior and condemned them for encouraging "such extravagant and incoherent expressions, and such enthusiastic fervor, as puts common sense and modesty to the blush."

One small but influential group of revival critics was the Unitarians. The basic doctrine of Unitarianism—that Jesus Christ was less than fully divine—had gained quiet acceptance among religious liberals during the eighteenth century. However, it was not until the early nineteenth century that Unitarianism emerged as a formal denomination with its own churches, ministry, and national organization. In New England in these years, hundreds of Congregational churches were torn apart by the withdrawal of socially prominent families who had embraced Unitarianism and by legal battles over which group—Congregationalists or Unitarians—could occupy church property. Although Unitarians won relatively few converts outside New England, their tendency to attract the wealthy and educated gave them influence beyond their numbers.

Unitarians criticized revivals as uncouth emotional exhibitions and argued that moral goodness should be cultivated by a gradual process of "character building," in which the individual learned to model his or her behavior on that of Jesus rather than by a sudden emotional conversion as in a revival. Yet Unitarians and revivalists shared the belief that human behavior could be changed for the better. Both rejected the Calvinist emphasis on innate human wickedness. William Ellery Channing, a Unitarian leader, claimed that Christianity had but one purpose: "the perfection of human nature, the elevation of men into nobler beings."

The Rise of Mormonism

The Unitarians' assertion that Jesus Christ was human rather than divine challenged a basic doctrine of orthodox Christianity. Yet Unitarianism proved far less controversial than another of the new denominations of the 1820s and 1830s, the Church of Jesus Christ of Latter-day Saints, or Mormons. Its founder, Joseph Smith, grew to manhood in one of those families that seemed in constant motion to and fro but never up. After moving his family nearly twenty times in ten years, Smith's

Mormon Migrants
*Persecution of the Mormons raged in Missouri in the 1830s, and in 1838 the state's governor
ordered the militia to kill the Mormons or drive them from the state. By 1839 most Mormons
had left. Many resettled in Nauvoo, Illinois, only to migrate again to Deseret in the late 1840s.*

ne'er-do-well father settled in Palmyra, New York, in the
heart of the Burned-Over District. As a boy, Smith's
imagination teemed with plans to find buried treasure,
while his religious views were convulsed by the conflicting claims of the denominations that thrived in the
region. "Some were contending for the Methodist faith,
some for the Presbyterian, and some for the Baptists,"
Smith later wrote. He wondered who was right and
who wrong, or whether they were "all wrong together."

The sort of perplexity that Smith experienced was
widespread in the Burned-Over District, but his resolution of the confusion was unique. Smith claimed that
an angel led him to a buried book of revelation and to
special stones for use in translating it. He completed
his translation of this Book of Mormon in 1827. The
Book of Mormon tells the story of an ancient Hebrew

prophet, Lehi, whose descendants came to America
and created a prosperous civilization that looked forward to the appearance of Jesus as its savior. Jesus had
actually appeared and performed miracles in the New
World, the book claimed, but the American descendants of Lehi had departed from the Lord's ways and
quarreled among themselves. God had cursed some
with dark skin; these were the American Indians, who,
when later discovered by Columbus, had forgotten
their history.

Despite his astonishing claims, Smith quickly
gathered followers. The appeal of Mormonism lay
partly in its positioning of America at the center of
Christian history and partly in Smith's assertion that he
had discovered a new revelation. The idea of an additional revelation beyond the Bible appeared to some to

resolve the turmoil created by the Protestant denominations' inability to agree on what the Bible said or meant.

Smith and his followers steadily moved west from New York to Ohio and Missouri. Then they migrated to Illinois, where they built a model city, Nauvoo, and a magnificent temple supported by thirty huge pillars. By moving to these areas, the Mormons hoped to draw closer to the Indians, whose conversion was one of their goals, and to escape persecution. Smith's claim to have received a new revelation virtually guaranteed a hostile reception for the Mormons wherever they went, because Smith had seemingly undermined the authority of the Bible, one of the two documents (the other being the Constitution) upon which the ideals of the American republic rested.

Smith added fuel to the fire when he reported in 1843 that he had received still another revelation, this one sanctioning the Mormon practice of having multiple wives, or polygyny. Although Smith did not publicly proclaim polygyny as a doctrine, its practice among Mormons was a poorly kept secret. Smith's self-image also intensified the controversy that boiled around Mormonism. He refused to view himself merely as the founder of another denomination; instead, he saw himself as a prophet of the kingdom of God and was called a "Second Mohammed." Mormonism would be to Christianity what Christianity had been to Judaism: an all-encompassing, higher form of religion. In 1844 he announced his candidacy for the presidency of the United States. But the state of Illinois was already moving against him. Charged with treason, he was jailed in Carthage, Illinois, and along with his brother, murdered there by a mob in June 1844.

Despite persecution, the Mormons won converts, not only in the United States but in the teeming slums of English factory cities from which Mormon agents brought thousands to America. In the thirty years after 1840, the number of Mormons grew from six thousand to two hundred thousand. After Smith's death a new leader, Brigham Young, led the main body of Mormons from Nauvoo to the Great Salt Lake Valley in Utah, which then was still under the control of Mexico. There Mormons established an independent republic, the state of Deseret. A thousand miles from Illinois, they prospered. Their isolation, combined with the firm control of Young, the "Old Boss," kept the rank and file in line. Polygyny, which Young officially proclaimed as a church doctrine, did not produce the hoped-for increase in Mormon numbers, but it did guarantee that

Mormons would remain a people apart from the mainstream of American society. Above all, the Mormons were industrious and deeply committed to the welfare of other Mormons. Cooperation among Mormons took several forms, not the least of which was the practice of devoting each Mormon's "surplus" production to public projects like irrigation. Mormons transformed the valley into a rich oasis. When Utah came under American control after the Mexican War, they dominated its government.

Although Mormonism is one of the few religions to have originated in the United States, the antebellum Mormons pushed against the currents of standard American religion and society. They rejected the Bible as the sole source of revelation, substituted polygyny for monogamy, and elevated economic cooperation above competitiveness. Mormonism appealed to the downtrodden and insecure rather than to the prosperous and secure. It offered the downcast an explicit alternative to dominant religious and social practices. In this respect, Mormonism mirrored the efforts of several religious communal societies whose members resolutely set themselves apart from society. In general, these religious communitarians were less numerous, controversial, and long-lasting than the Mormons, but one group among them, the Shakers, has continued to fascinate Americans.

The Shakers

The leader of the Shakers (who derived their name from a convulsive religious dance that was part of their ceremony) was Mother Ann Lee, the illiterate daughter of an English blacksmith. Lee had set sail for America in 1774, and her followers soon organized a tightly knit community in New Lebanon, New York. In this and in other communities, the Shakers proved themselves able artisans. Shaker furniture became renowned for its beauty and strength. But for all their achievements as artisans, the Shakers were fundamentally otherworldly and hostile to materialism. Lee insisted that her followers abstain from sexual intercourse, believed that the end of the world was imminent, and derived many of her doctrines from trances and heavenly visions that she claimed to have. Among these doctrines was her conviction that at the Second Coming, Jesus would take the form of a woman, herself.

Her teachings about the evils of sexual relations would quickly have doomed the Shakers to extinction had it not been for the spread of religious revivalism in

1790. Turning up at Cane Ridge and other revival sites, Shaker missionaries made off with converts whom the revivals had loosened from their traditional religious moorings. At their peak during the second quarter of the nineteenth century, the Shakers numbered about six thousand in eight states.

Shakers and Mormons chose to live apart from society. But the message of most evangelical Protestants, including Charles G. Finney, was that religion and economic individualism—a person's pursuit of wealth— were compatible. Most revivalists told people that getting ahead in the world was acceptable as long as they were honest, temperate, and bound by the dictates of their consciences. By encouraging assimilation into rather than retreat from society, evangelicalism provided a powerful stimulus to the manifold reform movements of the 1820s and 1830s.

THE AGE OF REFORM

Despite rising popular interest in politics between 1824 and 1840, large numbers of people were excluded from politics. Women were not allowed to vote, and blacks generally suffered rather than benefited from the gradual liberalization of voting requirements. By 1860 most northern states denied free people of color the right to vote. Too, the political parties did not welcome the intrusion of controversial issues like slavery, nor did they show much interest in women's rights.

During the 1820s and 1830s, unprecedented numbers of men and women overcame these limits of political parties by joining organizations that aimed to improve society. Slavery's abolition, women's rights, temperance, better treatment of criminals and the insane, public education, and even the establishment of perfect, utopian communities were high on various reformers' agenda. Although they occasionally cooperated with political parties, especially the Whigs, reformers gave their loyalty to their causes, not to parties. Indeed, politics struck most reformers as a sorry spectacle that allowed a man like Andrew Jackson, a duelist who married a divorcee, to become president and that routinely rewarded persons who would sacrifice any principle for victory at the polls.

Reformers believed that they were on God's side on any issue. Religious revivalism contributed to their intense moralism. Virtually all prominent temperance reformers of the 1820s and 1830s, for example, had been inspired initially by revivals. But revivalism and reform were not always so intimately linked. Influential school reformers and women's rights advocates were frequently religious liberals either hostile or indifferent to revivals. And although some abolitionists owed their first flush of idealism to revivals, others did not, and almost all came to criticize the churches for condoning slavery. Yet even those reformers opposed to revivalism borrowed the evangelical preachers' language and psychology by portraying drunkenness, ignorance, and inequality as sins that called for immediate repentance and change.

Reform had a dark side. Reformers did not hesitate to coerce people into change by calling for the legal prohibition of liquor and for compulsory education. For criminals, they designed penitentiaries on highly repressive principles. While assailing intemperance with fury, they frequently ignored the slums and working conditions that stimulated drinking.

Although the reform movements appealed to those excluded from or repelled by politics, most lacked the political parties' national organizations. New England and those parts of the Midwest settled by New Englanders were hotbeds of reform. In contrast, southerners actively suppressed abolition, displayed only mild interest in temperance and education reform, ignored women's rights, and saw utopian communities as proof of the mental instability of northern reformers.

The War on Liquor

Agitation for temperance (either total abstinence from alcoholic beverages, or moderation in their use) intensified during the second quarter of the nineteenth century. Temperance reformers addressed a growing problem. The spread of the population across the Appalachians stimulated the production and consumption of alcohol. Before the transportation revolution, western farmers, unable to get their grain to markets, commonly distilled it into spirits. Annual per capita consumption of rum, whiskey, gin, and brandy rose until it exceeded seven gallons by 1830, nearly triple today's rate. By the late 1820s, the average adult male drank a half-pint of liquor a day. With some justification, reformers saw alcoholic excess as a male indulgence whose bitter consequences (spending wages on liquor instead of food) fell on women and children.

Politicians in a Country Bar,
by James Clooney, 1844
The temperance movement did not deter politicians from soliciting voters in taverns.

Not surprisingly, millions of women would march behind the temperance banner during the nineteenth century.

There had been agitation against intemperance before 1825, but that year the Connecticut revivalist Lyman Beecher ushered in a new phase when, in six widely acclaimed lectures, he thundered against all use of alcohol. A year later, evangelical Protestants created the American Temperance Society, the first national temperance organization. By 1834 some five thousand state and local temperance societies were loosely affiliated with the American Temperance Society. Where as previous temperance supporters had advised moderation in the use of spirits, the American Temperance Society followed Beecher in demanding total abstinence. The society flooded the country with tracts denouncing the "amazing evil" of strong drink and urged churches to expel any members who condoned alcohol.

Among the main targets of the evangelical temperance reformers were moderate drinkers among the laboring classes. In the small shops where a handful of journeymen and apprentices worked informally, passing the jug every few hours was a time-honored way to relieve fatigue and monotony. But with the rise of large factories, new demands arose for a disciplined work force. Factory owners with precise production schedules to meet needed orderly and steady workers. Thus evangelical temperance reformers quickly gained manufacturers' support. In East Dudley, Massachusetts, for example, three factory owners refused to sell liquor in factory stores, calculating that any profits from the sale would be more than offset by lost working time and "the scenes of riot and wickedness thus produced."

Workers showed little interest in temperance before the late 1830s. But after the Panic of 1837, a new stage of temperance agitation sprang up in the form of the Washington Temperance Societies. Starting in Baltimore in 1840, the Washingtonians were more likely to be mechanics (workingmen) and laborers than ministers and manufacturers. Many were reformed drunkards, and most had concluded that their survival in the harsh climate of depression depended on their commitment to sobriety and frugality. For example, Charles T. Woodman, a baker, had been forced by the collapse of his business to flee Boston for Philadelphia to escape his creditors. Like most Washingtonians, Woodman blamed his ruin on the revival of his "old habit" of drink. The forces dislocating workers in the late 1830s were often far beyond their control. Part of the appeal of temperance was that it lay *within* their control. Take care of temperance, a Washingtonian assured a Baltimore audience, and the Lord would take care of the economy.

For all their differences from earlier temperance associations, the Washingtonians reflected the impact of revivals even more than did the American Temperance Society. Viewing drinking as sinful, they held "experience meetings," in which members described their "salvation" from liquor and their "regeneration" through abstinence (or "teetotalism"*). Their wives joined "Martha Washington" societies, in which they pledged to smell their husbands' breath each night and paraded with banners that read "Teetotal or No Husband." The Washingtonians spread farther and faster than any other antebellum temperance organization.

As temperance won new supporters, anti-alcohol crusaders gradually shifted their tactics from calls that individuals abstain to demands that cities and towns, and even states, ban all traffic in liquor. This shift from moral suasion to legal prohibition was controversial even within the movement. But by the late 1830s, prohibition was scoring victories. In 1838 Massachusetts prohibited the sale of distilled spirits in amounts less than fifteen gallons, thereby restricting small purchases by individual drinkers; in 1851 Maine banned the manufacture and sale of all intoxicating beverages. Controversial though these laws were, the temperance movement earned a measure of success. After rising steadily between 1800 and 1830, per capita consumption of distilled spirits began to fall during the 1830s. The rate of consumption during the 1840s was less than half that in the 1820s.

Public-School Reform

No less than temperance reformers, school reformers worked to encourage orderliness and thrift in the common people. Rural America's so-called district schools provided reformers with one of their main targets. One-room log or clapboard cabins containing pupils aged anywhere from three to twenty or more, the district schools taught farmers' children to read and count but little more. Those who attended the district schools never forgot their primitive conditions or harsh discipline: "the wood-pile in the yard, the open fireplace, the backless benches," and the floggings until "the youngster vomited or wet his breeches."

For all their drawbacks, the district schools enjoyed popular and financial support from rural parents. But reformers saw these schools in a different light, insisting that schools had to equip children for the emerging competitive and industrial economy. The most articulate and influential of the reformers, Horace Mann of Massachusetts, in 1837 became the first secretary of his state's newly created board of education,

and for the next decade, he promoted a sweeping transformation of public education. Mann's goals included shifting the burden of financial support for schools from parents to the state, grading the schools (that is, classifying pupils by age and attainment), extending the school term from two or three months to as many as ten months, introducing standardized textbooks, and compelling attendance. In place of loosely structured schools that were mere appendages of the family, Mann and other reformers advocated highly structured institutions that would occupy most of the child's time and energy.

School reformers hoped not only to combat ignorance but to spread uniform cultural values by exposing all children to identical experiences. Children would arrive at school at the same time and thereby learn punctuality. Graded schools that matched children against their age peers would stimulate the competitiveness needed in a rapidly industrializing society. Children would all read the same books and absorb such common sayings as "Idleness is the nest in which mischief lays its eggs." The McGuffey readers, which sold 50 million copies between 1836 and 1870, created a common curriculum and preached industry, honesty, sobriety, and patriotism.

Although school reform made few gains in the South (see Chapter 12), much of the North remodeled its schools along the lines advocated by Mann, and in 1852 Massachusetts passed the nation's first compulsory school law. Success did not come easily, however. Educational reformers faced challenges from farmers, who were satisfied with the informality of the district schools, and from urban Catholics led by New York City's Bishop John Hughes, who pointed out that the textbooks used in public schools contained anti-Catholic and anti-Irish barbs. And in both rural and urban areas, the laboring poor opposed compulsory education as a menace to parents dependent on their children's wages.

Yet school reformers prevailed, in part because their opponents, rural Protestants and urban Catholics, were incapable of cooperating with each other. In part, too, reformers succeeded by gaining influential allies. For example, their stress on free, tax-supported schools won the backing of the urban workingmen's parties that arose in the late 1820s; and their emphasis on punctuality appealed to manufacturers, who needed a disciplined work force. The new ideas also attracted reform-minded women, who recognized that the grading of schools would ease women's entry into

---

*Teetotal: coined by an English laborer at a temperance meeting in 1834, *teetotal* was merely an emphatic form of *total*.

teaching. People of the times widely believed that a woman could never control the assortment of three- to twenty-year-olds found in a one-room schoolhouse, but managing a class of eight- or nine-year-olds was a different matter. Catharine Beecher accurately predicted that school reform would render teaching a suitable profession for women. Women gradually did take the place of men in the classroom wherever school reform left its mark. By 1900 about 70 percent of the nation's schoolteachers were women.

School reform also appealed to native-born Americans alarmed by the swelling tide of immigration. The public school emerged as the favorite device by which reformers forged a common American culture out of an increasingly diverse society. "We must decompose and cleanse the impurities which rush into our midst" through the "one infallible filter—the SCHOOL."

School reformers were assimilationists in the sense that they hoped to use public education to give children common values through shared experiences. In one respect, however, these reformers wore blinders on the issue of assimilation, for few stressed the integration of black and white children. When black children were fortunate enough to get any schooling, it was usually in segregated schools. Black children who entered integrated public schools met with such virulent prejudice that black leaders in northern cities frequently preferred segregated schools.

Abolition

Antislavery sentiment among whites flourished in the Revolutionary era but declined in the early nineteenth century. The main antislavery organization founded between 1800 and 1830 was the American Colonization Society (1817), which displayed little moral outrage against slavery. The society proposed a plan for gradual emancipation, with compensation to the slaveowner, and the shipment of freed blacks to Africa. This proposal attracted support from some slaveholders in the Upper South who would never have dreamed of a general emancipation.

At its core, colonization was hard-hearted and softheaded. Colonizationists assumed that blacks were a degraded race that did not belong in American society, and they underestimated the growing dependence of the South's economy on slavery. Confronted by a soaring demand for cotton and other commodities, few southerners were willing to free their slaves, even if compensated. In any event, the American Coloniza-

tion Society never had enough funds to buy freedom for more than a fraction of slaves. Between 1820 and 1830, only 1,400 blacks migrated to Liberia, and most were already free. In striking contrast, the American slave population, fed by natural increase (the excess of births over deaths), rose from 1,191,000 in 1810 to more than 2,000,000 in 1830.

During the 1820s the main source of radical opposition to slavery was blacks themselves. Blacks had little enthusiasm for colonization. Most American blacks were native- rather than African-born. How, they asked, could they be sent back to a continent that they had never left? "We are *natives* of this country," a black pastor in New York proclaimed. "We only ask that we be treated as well as *foreigners.*" In opposition to colonization, blacks formed scores of abolition societies. In 1829 the Boston free black David Walker published an *Appeal* for a black rebellion to crush slavery.

Not all whites acquiesced to the continuance of slavery. In 1821 the Quaker Benjamin Lundy began a newspaper, the *Genius of Universal Emancipation*, and put forth proposals that no new slave states be admitted, that the internal slave trade be outlawed, that the three-fifths clause of the Constitution be repealed, and that Congress abolish slavery wherever it had the authority to do so. In 1828 Lundy hired a young New Englander, William Lloyd Garrison, as an assistant editor. Prematurely bald and with steel-rimmed glasses, and typically donning a black suit and black cravat, Garrison looked more like a schoolmaster than a rebel. But in 1831, when he launched his own newspaper, *The Liberator*, he quickly established himself as the most famous and controversial white abolitionist. "I am in earnest," Garrison wrote. "I will not equivocate—I will not excuse—I will not retreat a single inch—AND I WILL BE HEARD."

Garrison's battle cry was "immediate emancipation." In place of exiling blacks to Africa, he substituted the truly radical notion that blacks should enjoy civil (or legal) equality with whites. He greeted slaves as "a Man and a Brother," "a Woman and a Sister." Even Garrison, however, did not think that all slaves could be freed overnight. "Immediate emancipation" meant that all people had to realize that slavery was sinful and its continued existence intolerable.

Garrison quickly gained support from the growing number of black abolitionists. A black barber in Pittsburgh sent Garrison sixty dollars to help with *The Liberator*. Black agents sold subscriptions and three-fourths of *The Liberator*'s subscribers in the early

The Antislavery Alphabet
Viewing children as morally pure and hence as natural opponents of slavery, abolitionists produced antislavery toys, games, and, as we see here, alphabet books.

years were black. The escaped slave Frederick Douglass and a remarkable freed slave who named herself Sojourner Truth proved eloquent lecturers against slavery. Douglass could rivet an audience with an opening line. "I appear before the immense assembly this evening as a thief and a robber," he gibed. "I stole this head, these limbs, this body from my master, and ran off with them."

Relations between black and white abolitionists were not always harmonious. White abolitionists called for legal equality for blacks but not necessarily for social equality. Not without racial prejudice, they preferred light- to dark-skinned Negroes and, Garrison excepted, were hesitant to admit blacks to antislavery societies. Yet the prejudices of white abolitionists were mild compared to those of most whites. A white man or woman could do few things less popular in the 1830s than become an abolitionist. Mobs, often including colonizationists, repeatedly attacked abolitionists. For example, a Boston mob, searching for a British abolitionist in 1835, found Garrison instead and dragged him through town on the end of a rope. An abolitionist editor, Elijah Lovejoy, was murdered by a mob in Alton, Illinois, in 1837.

Abolitionists drew on the language of revivals and described slavery as sin, but the Protestant churches did not rally behind abolition as strongly as behind temperance. Lyman Beecher roared against the evils of strong drink but whimpered about those of slavery and in 1834 tried to suppress abolitionists at Cincinnati's Lane Theological Seminary. In response, Theodore Dwight Weld, an idealistic follower of Charles G. Finney, led a mass withdrawal of students. These "Lane rebels" formed the nucleus of abolitionist activity at the antislavery Oberlin College.

As if external hostility were not enough, abolitionists argued continually with each other. The American Anti-Slavery Society, founded in 1833, was the scene of several battles between Garrison and prominent New York and midwestern abolitionists such as the brothers Lewis and Arthur Tappan, Theodore Dwight Weld, and James G. Birney. One of the issues between the two sides was whether abolitionists should enter politics as a distinct party. In 1840 Garrison's opponents ran Birney for president on the ticket of the newly formed Liberty party. As for Garrison himself, he was increasingly rejecting *all* laws and governments, as well as political parties, as part of his doctrine of "nonresistance." In 1838 he and his followers had founded the New England Non-Resistance Society. The starting point of the doctrine was the fact that slavery depended on force. Garrison then added that all governments ultimately rested on force; even laws passed by elected legislatures needed police enforcement. Because Garrison viewed force as the opposite of Christian love, he concluded that Christians should refuse to vote, hold office, or have anything to do with government. It is a small wonder that many abolitionists thought of Garrison as extreme, or "ultra."

The second issue that divided the American Anti-Slavery Society concerned the role of women in the abolitionist movement. In 1837 Angelina and Sarah Grimké, daughters of a South Carolina slaveholder, embarked on an antislavery lecture tour of New England. Women had become deeply involved in antislavery societies during the 1830s, but always in female auxiliaries affiliated with those run by men. What made the Grimké sisters so controversial was that they drew mixed audiences of men and women to their lectures at a time when it was thought indelicate for women to speak before male audiences. Clergymen chastised the Grimké sisters for lecturing men rather than obeying them.

Such criticism backfired, however, because the Grimkés increasingly took up the cause of women's rights. In 1838 each wrote a classic of American feminism. Sarah produced her *Letters on the Condition of Women and the Equality of the Sexes,* and Angelina contributed her *Letters to Catharine E. Beecher* (Lyman Beecher's daughter and a militant opponent of female equality). Some abolitionists tried to dampen the feminist flames. The abolitionist poet John Greenleaf Whittier dismissed women's grievances as "paltry" compared to the "great and dreadful wrongs of the slave." Even Theodore Dwight Weld, who had married Angelina Grimké, wanted to subordinate women's rights to antislavery. But the fiery passions would not be extinguished. Garrison, welcoming the controversy, promptly espoused women's rights and urged that women be given positions equal to men in the American Anti-Slavery Society. In 1840 the election of a woman, Abby Kelley, to a previously all-male committee split the American Anti-Slavery Society wide open. A substantial minority of pro-feminist delegates left—some to join the Liberty party, others to follow Lewis Tappan into the new American and Foreign Anti-Slavery Society.

The disruption of the American Anti-Slavery Society did not greatly damage abolitionism. The national society had never had much control over the local societies that had grown swiftly during the mid-1830s. By 1840 there were more than fifteen hundred local societies, principally in Massachusetts, New York, and Ohio. By circulating abolitionist tracts, newspapers, and even chocolates with antislavery messages on their wrappers, these local societies kept the country ablaze with agitation.

One of the most disruptive abolitionist techniques was to flood Congress with petitions calling for an end to slavery in the District of Columbia. Congress had no time to consider all the petitions, but to refuse to address them meant depriving citizens of their right to have petitions heard. In 1836 southerners secured congressional adoption of the "gag rule," which automatically tabled abolitionist petitions and thus prevented discussion of them in Congress. Ex-president John Quincy Adams, then a representative from Massachusetts, led the struggle against the gag rule and finally secured its repeal in 1845. The debate over the gag rule subtly shifted the issue from the abolition of slavery to the constitutional rights of free expression and petitioning Congress. Members of Congress with little sympathy for abolitionists found themselves attacking the South for suppressing the right of petition. In a way, the gag-rule episode vindicated Garrison's tactic of stirring up emotions on the slavery issue. By holding passions over slavery at the boiling point, Garrison kept the South on the defensive. The less secure southerners felt, the more they were tempted into clumsy overreactions like the gag rule.

Women's Rights

The position of American women in the 1830s contained many contradictions. Women could not vote. If married, they had no right to own property (even inherited property) or to retain their own earnings. Yet the spread of reform movements provided women with unprecedented opportunities for public activity without challenging the prevailing belief that their proper sphere was the home. By suppressing liquor, for example, women could claim that they were transforming wretched homes into nurseries of happiness.

The argument that women were natural guardians of the family was double-edged. It justified reform activities on behalf of the family, but it undercut women's demands for legal equality. Let women attend to their sphere, the counterargument ran, and leave politics and finance to men. So deeply ingrained was sexual inequality, indeed, that most feminists did not start out intending to attack it. Instead, their experiences in other reform movements, notably abolition, led them to the issue of women's rights.

Among the early women's rights advocates who started their reform careers as abolitionists were the Grimké sisters, the Philadelphia Quaker Lucretia Mott, Lucy Stone, and Abby Kelley. Like abolition, the cause of women's rights revolved around the conviction that differences of race and gender were unimportant and incidental. "Men and women," Sarah Grimké wrote, "are CREATED EQUAL! They are both moral and accountable beings, and whatever is *right* for man to do,

Most newspapers ridiculed the Seneca Falls convention that Stanton and Mott organized to advance women's rights. More than three hundred people attended.

Lucretia Mott   **Elizabeth Cady Stanton**

is *right* for woman." The most articulate and aggressive advocates of women's rights, moreover, tended to gravitate to William Lloyd Garrison rather than to more moderate abolitionists. Garrison, himself a vigorous feminist, repeatedly stressed the peculiar degradation of women under slavery. The early issues of *The Liberator* contained a "Ladies' Department" headed by a picture of a kneeling slave woman imploring, "Am I Not a Woman and a Sister?" It was common knowledge that slave women were vulnerable to the sexual demands of white masters. Garrison denounced the South as a vast brothel and described slave women as "treated with more indelicacy and cruelty than cattle."

Although their involvement in abolition aroused advocates of women's rights, the discrimination they encountered within the abolition movement infuriated them and impelled them to make women's rights a separate cause. In the 1840s Lucy Stone became the first abolitionist to lecture solely on women's rights. When Lucretia Mott and other American women tried to be seated at the World's Anti-Slavery Convention in London in 1840, they were relegated to a screened-off section. The incident made a sharp impression not only on Mott but on Elizabeth Cady Stanton, who had elected to accompany her abolitionist husband to the meeting as a honeymoon trip. In 1848 Mott and Stanton organized a women's rights convention at Seneca Falls, New York, that proclaimed a Declaration of Sentiments. Modeled on the Declaration of Independence, the Seneca Falls Declaration began with the assertion that "all men and women are created equal." The convention passed twelve resolutions,

and only one, a call for the right of women to vote, failed to pass unanimously; but it did pass. Ironically, after the Civil War, the call for woman suffrage became the main demand of women's rights advocates for the rest of the century.

Although its crusaders were resourceful and energetic, women's rights had less impact than most other reforms. Temperance and school reform were far more popular, and abolitionism created more commotion. Women would not secure the right to vote throughout the nation until 1920, fifty-five years after the Thirteenth Amendment would abolish slavery. One reason for the relatively slow advance of women's rights was that piecemeal gains—such as married women securing the right to own property in several states by the Civil War—satisfied many women. The cause of women's rights also suffered from a close association with abolitionism, which was unpopular. In addition, the advance of feminism was slowed by the competition that it faced from the alternative ideal of domesticity. By sanctioning activities in reforms such as temperance and education, the cult of domesticity provided many women with worthwhile pursuits beyond the family. In this way, it blunted the edge of female demands for full equality.

Penitentiaries and Asylums

Reform efforts took shape during the 1820s to combat poverty, crime, and insanity by establishing highly regimented institutions, themselves products of striking new assumptions about the causes of deviancy.

Charlestown Jail
The military precision of prisoners' movements in the courtyard of the Charlestown (Massachusetts) jail reflected the belief of reformers that the character of wrongdoers would be reshaped by order and discipline.

In the colonial era, Americans had viewed poverty as neither the fault of its victims nor a sign of a defective social order. Rather, poverty was seen as a permanent condition of society, ordained by God to test Christians' humility and charity. Men and women thought of crime, too, as an enduring feature of society. Faced with punishment, individual criminals might mend their ways, but new lawbreakers would take their place. So ingrained were the defects of human nature that some would always choose the way of crime.

Several developments undermined these assumptions during the first half of the nineteenth century. Not only were poverty and crime rising, but in the swiftly growing cities, each was more visible than in the past. Alarmed legislators launched investigations into the causes of both indigence and crime, from which they concluded that deviant behavior often resulted from exposure to drunken fathers and broken homes. The failure of parental discipline, not the will of God or the wickedness of human nature, lay at the root of evil.

Few Americans would have reached these conclusions (or even undertaken the investigations that led to them) had it not been for their growing belief that the moral qualities of the individual were changeable rather than fixed. Both religious revivalists and reformers increasingly came to think that human nature could be altered by the right combination of moral influences. Most grasped the optimistic implications. "The study of the *causes* of crime," William Ellery Channing concluded, "may lead us to its *cure.*"

To cure crime, reformers created substitutes for parental discipline, most notably the penitentiary. Penitentiaries were prisons marked by an unprecedented degree of order and discipline. Of course, colonial Americans had incarcerated criminal offenders, but jails had been used mainly to hold prisoners awaiting trial or to lock up debtors. For much of the eighteenth century, the threat of the gallows rather than of imprisonment had deterred wrongdoers. In contrast, nineteenth-century reformers believed that rightly managed, penitentiaries would bring about the sincere reformation of offenders.

To purge offenders' violent habits, reformers usually insisted on solitary confinement. Between 1819 and 1825, New York built penitentiaries at Auburn and Ossining (Sing Sing), in which prisoners were confined by night in small, windowless cells. By day they could work together but never speak and rarely even look at each other. Some reformers criticized this "Auburn system" for allowing too much contact and preferred the rival "Pennsylvania system," in which each prisoner spent all of his or her time in a single cell (each with a walled courtyard for exercise) and received no news or visits from the outside.

Antebellum America also witnessed a remarkable transformation in the treatment of poor people. The prevailing colonial practice of offering relief to the poor by supporting them in a household ("outdoor relief") gradually gave way to the construction of almshouses for the infirm poor and workhouses for the able-bodied poor ("indoor relief"). The argument for indoor relief was much the same as the argument for penitentiaries: plucking the poor from their demoralizing surroundings and exposing them to a highly regimented institution could change them

The Oneida Community

The most controversial of the antebellum experiments in communitarian utopianism, the Oneida community in New York State challenged conventional notions of religion, property, gender roles, marriage, sex, dress, and motherhood. Contemporaries dismissed its founder, John Humphrey Noyes, as a licentious crackpot, and Oneida as the "utopia of obscenity." Yet by the standards of utopian experiments, Oneida passed the test of time, achieved considerable economic prosperity, and continued to attract new members long after the collapse of less radical utopian experiments.

Little in Noyes's background—he had been born in 1811 into a well-connected Vermont family—marked him as an iconoclast. But Noyes came of age at a time when America was boiling over with radical religious doctrines that contained the seeds of still more unsettling social principles, and he possessed a penchant for carrying ideas to their logical conclusions,

however extreme, and for leading his willing followers into uncharted regions of experience.

Converted in a Vermont revival in 1831, Noyes studied theology at Yale, where he came under the influence of Nathaniel W. Taylor, a theologian who pried Congregationalism from its Calvinist heritage by emphasizing that sin resulted from the individual's choice rather than from any divine plan. This interpretation left open the possibility that some people could achieve freedom from all sin—the doctrine of perfectionism. In 1834 Noyes startled his peers by asserting that he had achieved this perfect state. When, in response, the orthodox clergy revoked his license to preach, he announced that he would go on preaching just as they were free to go on sinning.

In the late 1830s Noyes began to gather disciples at Putney, Vermont, and to attack monogamous marriage. Because monogamy involved an exclusive attach-

Bag Bee
Communal work, shown here in the form of a "bee" (gathering) for making traveling bags, complemented Noyes's belief in the communal ownership of property.

ment to one person, Noyes viewed it as selfish and suited only to sinners. Soon he put his theory into practice by acknowledging his love for Mary Cragin, the wife of one of the Putney perfectionists, while Noyes's wife Harriet disclosed her own affection for Mary's husband. Noyes did not intend to divorce Harriet; rather, he proclaimed that among the perfect, all men would be married to all women and all women to all men—the doctrine of "complex marriage." When the Putney perfectionists recruited two young sisters from the village—one only fifteen years old—to their circle, the villagers exploded in outrage. Indicted for adultery with Mary Cragin, Noyes moved his little colony of the sinless to Oneida County in western New York in 1848.

To ordinary minds, Noyes was an advocate of free love. In reality, Noyes tied complex marriage to "male continence"; that is, men could engage in sexual intercourse with women, but they had to discipline themselves to withhold ejaculation (*coitus reservatus*). In this way, they not only practiced birth control but also demonstrated their perfect self-mastery. Like the Shakers, the Oneida community grew at first by attracting converts rather than by natural increase.

Consistent with Noyes's loathing of any form of proprietorship, whether of people or things, Oneidans renounced private property and practiced communism. But they accepted the profit motive in dealing with outsiders, the "worldlings." When an Oneidan invented an improved animal trap, the community marketed it through a Chicago dealer. In contrast to most other utopian communities, which cherished agriculture as a soothing alternative to the frenzied pace of industry, Oneidans fabricated and sold a wide array of products, including embroidered gentlemen's slippers, silk goods, mop handles, wheel spokes, and silverware. As the community prospered, its membership rose from under one hundred in 1849 to nearly three hundred by 1875.

Yet Noyes's unconventional ideas left their stamp even on work routines in Oneida's homes and factories. Although Noyes believed that women were less perfect than men, he mechanized domestic work wherever possible, insisted that males perform kitchen duties alongside

John Humphrey Noyes
Noyes possessed a magnetic attraction for women and commanded the unswerving loyalty of his female followers.

women, and allowed women to work in the community's stores and factories. Indeed, Noyes bitterly criticized the idea of a separate sphere for women, with its exclusive assignment of females to household duties. Oneida women not only worked outside the home but *looked* as if they did. They preferred pantaloons to unwieldy hoop skirts and cut their hair short in an age when middle-class women enhanced their coiffures by purchasing false hair.

Obsessed by the dream of elevating all humanity to perfection, Noyes in 1867 launched Oneida on its boldest experiment: the breeding of a perfect race by means of "stirpiculture." Stirpiculture* necessitated modifying male continence to allow consummation, but Noyes continued to abhor free love. Although individuals could voice preferences for sexual mates and veto proposed candidates, the final decision was left to a committee of elders, headed by "Father" Noyes. Like most educated people of his day, Noyes believed that moral and spiritual as well as physical qualities would be transmitted to children (the doctrine of "acquired characteristics"), and accordingly, he saw to it that the "more perfect," usually the older members of the community, mated with

---

*Stirpiculture: from the Latin *stirps*—a root or strain.

Harriet Holton
Having heard of Noyes's doctrine of perfection, Harriet Holton had rushed to hear him preach, judged his face to "shine like an angel's," and fallen in love.

"less perfect" younger members—old men with young women, and young men with older women.

Noyes's influence over matings provoked dissent from Oneida's younger women, who faced criticism and even expulsion whenever they fell in love with men their own age and who suspected that stirpiculture too conveniently rationalized the lust of old men (including the ever prolific "Father" Noyes) for young women. Mounting outside criticism in the 1870s found the community weak and divided. In 1879 Noyes exiled himself to Canada to avoid prosecution (although local and state officials could not identify any law that he had broken); that same year, Oneidans renounced the doctrine of complex marriage. In 1881 they formally abandoned communism.

Oneida is more remarkable for its persistence than for its ultimate collapse. Despite the hostility of the clergy, Noyes usually maintained good relations with nearby worldlings, who found jobs in Oneida's factories. At the same time, the radical doctrines on which the experiment rested gave Oneida a degree of cohesion lacking at Brook Farm. By embracing a seemingly outlandish sexual doctrine, Oneidans, like Mormons, effectively burned their bridges to the world, and when they abandoned complex marriage, their unity dissolved.

into virtuous, productive citizens. However lofty the motives behind workhouses and almshouses, the results were often abysmal. In 1833 a legislative committee found that the inmates of the Boston House of Industry were packed seven to a room and included unwed mothers, the sick, and the insane as well as the poor.

As for insane people, those living in a workhouse such as the Boston House of Industry were relatively well off, for many experienced even worse treatment by confinement in prisons. In 1841 an idealistic Unitarian schoolteacher, Dorothea Dix, was teaching a Sunday school class in a jail in East Cambridge, Massachusetts, and discovered there insane people kept in an unheated room. Dix pursued her investigation and visited jails and almshouses throughout the state. In 1843 she presented a memorial to the state legislature, which described the insane confined "in *cages, closets, cellars, stalls, pens! Chained, naked, beaten with rods, and lashed into obedience.*" With the support of Horace Mann and the Boston reformer Samuel G. Howe, she encouraged legislatures to build insane asylums, and by the time of the Civil War, twenty-eight states, four cities, and the federal government had constructed public mental institutions.

Penitentiaries, workhouses, and insane asylums all reflected the same optimistic belief that deviancy could be erased by resettling deviants in the right environment. But what was the "right" environment? In some aspects, the answer was clear-cut. Heated rooms were better than frigid ones, and sober parents preferable to drunkards. But reformers demanded much more than warm rooms and responsible parents. Reformers were convinced that the unfettered freedom and individualism of American society were themselves defects in the environment and that the poor, criminal, and insane needed extraordinary regimentation if they were to change. Prison inmates were to march around in lock step; in workhouses the poor, treated much like prisoners, were often forbidden to leave or receive visitors without permission. The idealism behind such institutions was genuine, but later generations would question reformers' underlying assumptions.

Utopian Communities

The belief that individuals could live perfectly, which tinged most antebellum reform movements, took its most extreme form in the experimental societies or "utopian" communities that flourished in these years. Although varying widely in their philosophies and arrangements, utopian communities had some common features. Their founders were intellectuals who designed their communities as alternatives to the prevailing competitive economy and as models whose success would inspire imitation. Unlike the Shakers and the Mormons, the utopians did not claim to have visions of God or visits from angels. Nor did they burn their bridges to society.

American interest in utopian communities first spurted during the 1820s. In 1825 British industrialist and philanthropist Robert Owen founded the New Harmony community in Indiana. Owen had already acquired a formidable reputation (and a fortune) from his management of cotton mills at New Lanark, Scotland. His innovations at New Lanark had substantially improved his workers' educational opportunities and living conditions and left him convinced that similar changes could transform the lives of working people everywhere. He saw the problem of the early industrial age as social rather than political. If social arrangements could be perfected, all vice and misery would disappear; human character was formed, "without exception," by people's surroundings or environment. The key to perfecting social arrangements lay, in turn, in the creation of small, planned communities—"Villages of Unity and Mutual Cooperation," each to contain a perfect balance of occupational, religious, and political groups.

Lured to the United States by cheap land and by Americans' receptivity to experiments, Owen confidently predicted that by 1827 the northern states would embrace the principles embodied in New Harmony. Unfortunately, by 1827 there was little left to embrace, for the community had quickly fallen apart. New Harmony had attracted more than its share of idlers and fanatics, and Owen had spent too much time on the road publicizing the community and not enough time managing it. He had clashed with clergymen, who still believed that Original Sin, not environment, shaped human character. Yet Owenism survived the wreckage of New Harmony. The ideas that human character was formed by environment and that cooperation was superior to competition had a potent impact on urban workers for the next half-century. Owen's ideas, for example, impelled workingmen's leaders to support educational reform during the late 1820s.

In the early 1830s, the utopian impulse weakened, only to revive amid the economic chaos of the late 1830s and 1840s. Appalled by the misery that came with economic depression, small bands of idealists gathered anew in experimental communities whose names—Hopedale, Fruitlands, Brook Farm—suggested idyllic retreats. Their founders' visions were fired by intense but unconventional forms of Christianity. Adin Ballou, a Universalist minister who founded Hopedale, near Milford, Massachusetts, described it as a "miniature Christian republic." Brook Farm, near Boston, was mainly the creation of a group of religious philosophers called transcendentalists. Most transcendentalists, including Ralph Waldo Emerson and George Ripley, had started as Unitarians but sought to revitalize Unitarianism—and indeed, all denominations—by proclaiming the infinite spiritual capacities of ordinary men and women.

Like other utopias, Brook Farm was both a retreat and a model. Convinced that the competitive commercial life of the cities was unnatural, philosophers welcomed the opportunity to engage in elevated discussions after a day perspiring in the cabbage patch. Although Brook Farm never had more than a hundred residents, it attracted several renowned writers. Emerson visited it, and novelist

Nathaniel Hawthorne lived there for a period; Brook Farm's literary magazine, *The Dial*, became a forum for transcendentalist ideas about philosophy, art, and literature (also see Chapter 11).

Few utopias enjoyed success to match their ambition. Brook Farm disbanded in 1849; Hopedale, in 1853. In general, utopian communities were less durable and attracted fewer people than religious communities such as those of the Shakers and Mormons. In contrast to the religious communitarians, the utopians kept open their avenues to society and moved back and forth between their communities and antislavery or women's rights conventions. With the notable exception of the Oneida community (see "A Place in Time"), utopians neither sought nor attained the kind of grip on the allegiance of their members held by a Mother Ann Lee or a Joseph Smith.

Widely derided as fit only for eccentrics, the antebellum utopias nevertheless exemplified in extreme form the idealism and hopefulness that permeated nearly all reform in the Age of Jackson.

CONCLUSION

During the 1820s and 1830s, American society burst beyond its traditional physical and intellectual boundaries. Everywhere the old leadership provided by the Revolutionary generation gave way to new leaders born after 1775. Surrounded by weak foreign neighbors and at peace with the great powers of Europe, Americans, without much restraint from traditional or external threats, grappled with the implications of a changing society.

Political parties, religious revivals, and reform movements responded to social change in ways that were novel and inventive but never uniform. By reducing the innumerable interests and opinions that composed American society to two alternatives—the Democrats and the Whigs—the second party system gave direction to the conflicts that were created by economic and social change. Those excluded from politics or dismayed by the compromises into which politicians routinely entered turned to the churches and to reform movements as vehicles for change. Yet religion and reform were not simply alternatives to politics, for each intersected politics at scores of points. The closer one drew to 1840, the greater were the number of intersections. Temperance advocates began to demand legal prohibition of liquor; some abolitionists turned to the Liberty party; some feminists demanded the vote; utopians became political targets. Politics became a medium that even those antagonistic to politics had to understand.

CHRONOLOGY

1800–1801	Great Kentucky Revival.
1817	American Colonization Society founded.
1824	John Quincy Adams elected president by the House of Representatives.

1826	American Temperance Society organized.
1828	Andrew Jackson elected president.
	Congress passes the "Tariff of Abominations."
	John Calhoun anonymously writes *South*

1828 *Carolina Exposition and Protest.*

1830 Jackson's Maysville Road Bill veto.

Indian Removal Act.

1830–1831 Charles G. Finney's Rochester revival.

1831 William Lloyd Garrison starts *The Liberator.*

1832 Jackson vetoes recharter of the Bank of the United States.

Jackson reelected president.

South Carolina Nullification Proclamation.

William Lloyd Garrison

1833 Force Bill.

Compromise Tariff.

American Anti-Slavery Society founded.

South Carolina nullifies the Force Bill.

1834 Whig party organized.

1836 Congress imposes the gag rule.

Deposition Act.

Specie Circular.

Martin Van Buren elected president.

1837 Horace Mann becomes secretary of the Massachusetts Board of Education.

1837 Economic depression sets in.

Elijah Lovejoy murdered by proslavery mob.

Grimké sisters set out on lecture tour of New England.

1838 Garrison's New England Non-Resistance Society founded.

Publication of Sarah Grimké's *Letters on the Condition of Women and the Equality of the Sexes* and Angelina Grimké's *Letters to Catharine E. Beecher.*

1839 Depression deepens as the Bank of the United States fails.

1840 Independent Treasury Act passed.

William Henry Harrison elected president.

First Washington Temperance Society started.

1841 Dorothea Dix begins exposé of prison conditions.

Brook Farm Community founded.

1848 Seneca Falls Convention.

John Humphrey Noyes starts the Oneida Community.

Dorothea Dix

FOR FURTHER READING

Lee Benson, *The Concept of Jacksonian Democracy: New York as a Test Case* (1961). A major revisionist interpretation of the period.

William W. Freehling, *Prelude to Civil War* (1966). A major study of the nullification crisis.

Richard P. McCormick, *The Second American Party System: Party Formation in the Jacksonian Era* (1966). An influential work stressing the role of political leaders in shaping the second party system.

Edward Pessen, *Jacksonian America: Society, Personality, and Politics,* rev. ed. (1979). A comprehensive interpretation of the period that emphasizes the lack of real democracy in American society and politics.

Robert V. Remini, *Henry Clay: Statesman for the Union* (1991).

An important new biography of the leading Whig statesman of the period.

Arthur M. Schlesinger, Jr., *The Age of Jackson* (1945). A classic study, now dated in some of its interpretations but still highly readable.

Fred Somkin, *Unquiet Eagle: Memory and Desire in the Idea of American Freedom, 1815–1860* (1967). A penetrating study of American political values.

Ronald G. Walters, *American Reformers, 1815–1860* (1978). A balanced study that addresses the negative as well as positive aspects of nineteenth-century reform.

Chilton Williamson, *American Suffrage: From Property to Democracy, 1760–1860* (1960). The standard study of changing requirements for voting.

ADDITIONAL BIBLIOGRAPHY

Political Leaders

Donald B. Cole, *Martin Van Buren and the American Political System* (1984); James C. Curtis, *The Fox at Bay: Martin Van Buren and the Presidency, 1837–1841* (1970); Richard B. Latner, *The Presidency of Andrew Jackson: White House Politics, 1829–1837* (1979); John Niven, *Martin Van Buren and the Romantic Age* (1983); Merrill D. Peterson, *The Great Triumvirate: Webster, Clay*

and Calhoun (1987); Leonard L. Richards, *The Life and Times of Congressman John Quincy Adams* (1986); Major L. Wilson, *The Presidency of Martin Van Buren* (1984).

Political Parties

Jean H. Baker, *Affairs of Party: The Political Culture of Northern Democrats in the Mid-Nineteenth Century* (1983); Ronald P.

Formisano, *The Birth of Mass Political Parties, 1827–1861* (1971) and *The Transformation of American Political Culture: Massachusetts Parties, 1790s–1840s* (1983); Paul Goodman, *Towards a Christian Republic: Antimasonry and the Great Tradition in New England, 1826–1836* (1988); Daniel W. Howe, *The Political Culture of the American Whigs* (1980); Robert V. Remini, *The Election of Andrew Jackson* (1963); and *Andrew Jackson and the Course of American Empire* (1977); Harry L. Watson, *Jacksonian Politics and Community Conflict: The Emergence of the Second American Party System in Cumberland County, North Carolina* (1981); Sean Wilentz, *Chants Democratic: New York City and the Rise of the American Working Class, 1788–1850* (1983).

Banking and the Economy

Bray Hammond, *Banks and Politics in America from the Revolution to the Civil War* (1957); John M. McFaul, *The Politics of Jacksonian Finance* (1972); William G. Shade, *Banks or No Banks: The Money Question in Western Politics* (1972); James Roger Sharp, *The Jacksonians Versus the Banks: Politics in the United States After the Panic of 1837* (1970); Peter Temin, *The Jacksonian Economy* (1965).

Religious Revivals

Sydney E. Ahlstrom, *A Religious History of the American People*, 2 vols. (1975); Leonard J. Arrington, *The Mormon Experience* (1979) and *Brigham Young: American Moses* (1985); John Boles, *The Great Revival, 1787–1805* (1972); Whitney Cross, *The Burned-Over District* (1950); Nathan O. Hatch, *The Democratization of American Christianity* (1989); Donald G. Mathews, *Religion in the Old South* (1977); Stephen J. Stein, *The Shaker Experience in America* (1992).

Relationships Between Religion and Reform

Gilbert Barnes, *The Anti-Slavery Impulse* (1933); Clifford S. Griffin, *Their Brothers' Keepers: Moral Stewardship in the United States* (1960); Mary Ryan, *Cradle of the Middle Class: The Family in Oneida County, New York, 1790–1865* (1981); Timothy L. Smith, *Revivalism and Social Reform* (1957).

Temperance

Jed Dannenbaum, *Drink and Disorder: Temperance Reform in Cincinnati from the Washingtonian Revival to the WCTU* (1984); Ian Tyrrell, *Sobering Up: From Temperance to Prohibition in Antebellum America* (1979).

Educational Reform

Carl F. Kaestle, *Pillars of the Republic: Common Schools and American Society, 1780–1860* (1983); Carl F. Kaestle and Maris A. Vinovskis, *Education and Social Change in Nineteenth-Century Massachusetts* (1980); Michael B. Katz, *The Irony of Early School Reform* (1968); Stanley K. Schultz, *The Culture Factory: Boston Public Schools 1789–1860* (1973).

Abolitionists

Robert H. Abzug, *Passionate Liberator: Theodore Dwight Weld and the Dilemma of Reform* (1890); William Cheek and Aimee Lee Cheek, *John Mercer Langston and the Fight for Black Freedom, 1829–1865* (1989); David B. Davis, *The Problem of Slavery in the Age of Revolution, 1770–1823* (1975); Hugh Davis, *Joshua Leavitt: Evangelical Abolitionist* (1990); Lawrence J. Freidman, *Gregarious Saints: Self and Community in American Abolitionism, 1830–1870* (1982); Louis Gerteis, *Morality and Utility in American Antislavery Reform* (1987); Blanche Glassman Hersh, *The Slavery of Sex: Feminist Abolitionists in America* (1978); William McFeely, *Frederick Douglass* (1991); Jane A. Pease and William H. Pease, *They Who Would Be Free: Blacks' Search for Freedom, 1830–1861* (1974); Lewis Perry, *Radical Abolitionism: Anarchy and the Government of God in Antislavery Thought* (1973); Benjamin Quarles, *Black Abolitionists* (1969); Leonard L. Richards, *"Gentlemen of Property and Standing": Anti-Abolition Mobs in Jacksonian America* (1970); Ronald G. Walters, *The Antislavery Appeal: American Abolitionists After 1830* (1976); Bertram Wyatt-Brown, *Lewis Tappan and the Evangelical War Against Slavery* (1969).

Women's Rights

Lois Banner, *Elizabeth Cady Stanton* (1980); Barbara J. Berg, *The Remembered Gate—The Woman and the City, 1800–1860* (1978); Carl N. Degler, *At Odds: Women and the Family in America from the Revolution to the Present* (1980); Ellen C. DuBois, *Feminism and Suffrage: The Emergence of an Independent Women's Movement in America, 1848–1869* (1978); Lori D. Ginzberg, *Women and the Work of Benevolence* (1990); Elisabeth Griffith, *In Her Own Right: The Life of Elizabeth Cady Stanton* (1984); Gerda Lerner, *The Grimké Sisters from South Carolina: Rebels Against Slavery* (1967); Jean Fagan Yellin, *Women and Sisters: The Antislavery Feminists in American Culture* (1989).

Institutional Reformers

Gerald W. Grob, *Mental Institutions in America: Social Policy to 1875* (1973); W. David Lewis, *From Newgate to Dannemora: The Rise of the Penitentiary* (1965); Robert Mennel, *Thorns and Thistles* (1973); David Rothman, *The Discovery of the Asylum* (1971).

Utopian Communities

Michael Barkun, *Crucible of the Millennium* (1986); Arthur E. Bestor, *Backwoods Utopias: The Sectarian and Owenite Phases of Communitarian Utopianism in America, 1663–1829* (1950); Michael Fellman, *The Unbounded Frame: Freedom and Community in Nineteenth-Century America Utopianism* (1973); Lawrence Foster, *Women, Family, and Utopia* (1991); Carl J. Guarneri, *Utopian Alternative: Fourierism in Nineteenth-Century America* (1991); Carol Kolmerten, *Women in Utopia* (1990).

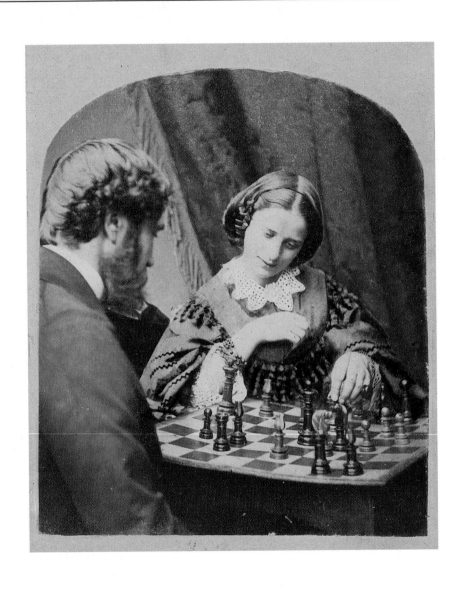

Chess Game
mid-1860s, hand-colored stereograph

11

LIFE, LEISURE, AND CULTURE
1840–1860

Americans, wrote Alexis de Tocqueville, "care but little for what has been, but they are haunted by visions of what will be." British novelist Charles Dickens remarked that while the watchword of the English was "All right," that of Americans was "Go ahead." Indeed, a belief in irreversible progress captivated Americans in the 1840s and 1850s. Each passing year seemed to offer new evidence for Thomas Jefferson's prediction that Europe "will have to lean on our shoulders and hobble along by our side."

Inventiveness and material betterment loomed large in American conceptions of progress. Agricultural innovations such as the McCormick reaper helped farmers produce a surplus of food despite a

swiftly rising population. Americans could confidently brush aside the gloomy forecast of Britain's Thomas Malthus, who at the end of the eighteenth century had argued that a growing population would exhaust its food supply and suffer famine. During the two decades before the Civil War, material progress also affected transportation and industry. Railroads ribboned their way throughout the eastern United States. The widening use of steam power and the perfection of manufacturing on the principle of interchangeable parts contributed to lower commodity prices and a gradual rise in real wages. The evidence of prosperity lay not only in higher wages but in the multiplication of conveniences that transformed such daily activities as cooking, eating, and drinking.

American achievements in agriculture, industry, and transportation led to growing demands in these years that the United States throw off any lingering cultural dependence on Europe. Some contemporaries began to insist that Americans read books written by their compatriots, and others called for the development of a distinctiveAmerican literary and artistic style. No less than economic innovation, literary and artistic inventiveness made a mark on antebellum America. The period between 1820 and 1860 produced Washington Irving, the first American man of letters to gain fame throughout Europe; James Fenimore Cooper, the first American novelist to make a living continuously and exclusively by his writing; Henry Wadsworth Longfellow, the first nationally famous American poet; Edgar Allan Poe, the first and only American to invent a new literary genre, the detective story; and the Hudson River school of painting, the first native school of American painting. In 1820 a British critic had asked rhetorically, "In the four quarters of the Globe, who reads an American book?" By 1860 the answer was clear, for Europeans and Americans alike had learned to cherish Irving, Cooper, Ralph Waldo Emerson, Nathaniel Hawthorne, and other luminaries of what is often called the American Renaissance.

For the most part, antebellum Americans equated material, cultural, and moral progress. Samuel F. B. Morse, for example, expected that his invention of the telegraph in 1844 would not only speed communication but end war as well. Similar high expectations greeted other innovations. Advances in the technology of printing, a clergyman enthused in 1851, "multiply the word of God literally with every minute."

Yet progress had its darker side. Spread unevenly throughout the society, technological advances neither prevented nor ameliorated the depression of the late 1830s and early 1840s and had little positive impact on the poor. Periodic cholera epidemics reminded Americans that technology, in the shape of railroads and steamboats, could transport disease as well as food. Leading writers of the period, among them the philosopher and essayist Henry David Thoreau, questioned the easy assumption that material progress would stimulate moral progress. For the first time, widespread anxieties arose about the despoliation of the American landscape, and conscious efforts were launched to preserve enclaves of nature as parks and retreats safe from progress.

TECHNOLOGY AND ECONOMIC GROWTH

As evidence that they were a progressive people, Americans increasingly pointed to the march of "technology." The word *technology* was popularized after 1829 to describe how an understanding of scientific principles could be used to transform the practical conveniences of life. "We have invented more useful machines within twenty years," a Bostonian wrote in the 1830s, "than have been invented in all Europe." To those familiar with the progress of invention, *DeBow's Review* observed in 1846, "scarcely anything now will appear impossible."

Belief in the progressive effects of technology sprang from widely varying quarters. In 1836 the conservative Whig Daniel Webster contended that machines would advance civilization because they could perform the work of ten people without consuming food or clothing. At the other end of the political spectrum, a Lowell mill girl and labor organizer, Sarah Bagley, wrote in 1847: "It is emphatically the age of improvement. The arts and sciences have been more fully developed and the great mass of society are feeling its improvement." Practical science promised to make everyone's life more comfortable. The benefits of technology seemed to be democratic.

Woman at Singer Sewing Machine
Asked to repair a sewing machine that did not do continuous stitching, Isaac M. Singer invented one that did. Patented in 1851, the Singer machine quickly dominated the market. Although most early sewing machines were used in factories, some had made their way into households by 1860.

The technical innovations that transformed the quality of life in antebellum America included the steam engine, the cotton gin, the reaper, the use of interchangeable parts in manufacturing, the sewing machine, and most dazzling of all, the telegraph. Several of these innovations, including the steam engine and the principle of interchangeable parts, had originated in Europe. But Americans had a flair for investing in others' inventions and for perfecting their own, to the point where the inventions became profitable. Improvements in Eli Whitney's cotton gin between 1793 and 1860, for example, led to an eightfold increase in the amount of cotton that could be ginned in a day. Of course, technology did not benefit everyone. Improvements in the cotton gin served to rivet slavery firmly in place by making the South more dependent on cotton.

Technology also rendered many traditional skills obsolete and thereby undercut the position of artisans. But technology contributed to improvements in transportation and increases in productivity, which in turn lowered commodity prices and raised the living standards of a sizable body of free Americans between 1840 and 1860.

Agricultural Advancement

Before the Civil War, relatively few settlers ventured into the treeless and semiarid Great Plains that stretched west of Missouri, Iowa, and Minnesota. After 1830, however, settlement increasingly edged west of the woodlands of Ohio and Kentucky into parts of Indiana, Michigan, and Illinois, where flat grasslands (prairies) alternated with forests. Farmers had long assumed that the soil beneath forests was fertile, but some worried that the prairie's matted sod, which was difficult to break for planting, would no more sustain crops than trees.

Settlers who ventured into Indiana and Illinois were perplexed to discover treeless areas in otherwise humid regions, and only a few correctly guessed the reason: Native Americans regularly had set fire to undergrowth to hold back forests. But farmers quickly adapted to the new environment, in part because east of the Great Plains there were always some forested areas to afford ample timber for housing and fencing. Inventions also helped; in 1837 John Deere devised a steel-tipped plow that would cut in half the labor required to clear an acre of prairie.

Wheat became to midwestern farmers what cotton was to their southern counterparts. "The wheat crop is the great crop of the North-west, for exchange purposes," an agricultural journal noted in 1850. "It pays debts, buys groceries, clothing and lands, and answers more emphatically the purposes of trade among farmers than any other crop." Technological advances speeded the harvesting as well as the planting of wheat on the midwestern prairies. Using the traditional hand sickle consumed huge amounts of time and labor, all the more so because cut wheat had to be picked up and bound. Inventors in Europe had experimented since the eighteenth century with horse-drawn machines to replace sickles. But until Cyrus McCormick came on the scene, the absence of the right combination of technical skill and business enterprise had relegated mechanical reapers to the realm of tinkerers' dreams. In 1834 McCormick, a Virginian, patented a mechanical reaper that drew on but improved previous designs. Opening a factory in Chicago in 1847, McCormick manufactured reapers by mass production and introduced aggressive marketing techniques such as deferred payments and money-back guarantees. By harvesting grain seven times more rapidly than traditional methods, and with half the labor force, the reaper guaranteed the preeminence of wheat on the midwestern prairies of

He That Tilleth the Land Shall be Satisfied, c. 1850
This painting celebrates the American ideal of the family farm.

Illinois, Indiana, Iowa, and Missouri. McCormick sold 80,000 reapers by 1860, and this was only the beginning. During the Civil War, he made immense profits by selling more than 250,000 reapers.

Ironically, just as a Connecticut Yankee, Eli Whitney, had stimulated the foundation of the Old South's economy by his invention of the cotton gin, Cyrus McCormick, a proslavery southern Democrat, would help the North win the Civil War. Indeed, the North provided the main market for McCormick's reaper and for the models of his many competitors; the South, with its reliance on slave labor, had far less incentive to mechanize agriculture. The reaper would keep northern agricultural production high at a time when labor shortages caused by troop mobilization might otherwise have slashed production.

Although Americans proved resourceful at inventing and marketing machines to speed planting and harvesting, they farmed wastefully. With land abundant, farmers were more inclined to look for virgin soil than to improve "worn out" soil. But a movement for agricultural improvement in the form of more efficient use of the soil did develop before 1860, mainly in the East. Confronted by the superior fertility of western soil, easterners who did not move west or take jobs in factories increasingly experimented with new agricultural techniques. In Orange County, New York, for example, farmers fed their cows the best clover and bluegrass and emphasized cleanliness in the processing of dairy products. Through these practices, they produced a superior butter that commanded more than double the price of ordinary butter. Still other eastern farmers turned to the use of fertilizers to keep their wheat production competitive with that of the bountiful midwestern prairies. By fertilizing their fields with plaster left over from the construction of the James River Canal, Virginia wheat growers raised their average yield per acre to fifteen bushels by the 1850s, up from only six bushels in 1800. Similarly, during the 1840s American cotton planters began to import guano, left by the droppings of sea birds on islands off Peru, for use as a fertilizer. Fertilizers helped eastern cotton farmers close the gap created by the superior fertility of southwestern soil for cotton.

Technology and Industrial Progress

Although Americans had made several important technical innovations before 1820, the early growth of American manufacturing depended mainly on *imported* technology. Gradually, however, American industries gained a reputation abroad for their own innovations. As early as 1835, a British observer reported that a woolen mill in Lowell, Massachusetts, contained a remarkable number of labor-saving contrivances. In 1853 a small-arms factory in England reequipped itself with machine tools (machines that shaped metal products) manufactured by two firms in the backwoods of Vermont. Americans had relatively few reservations about investing in technology. After finishing a tour of American factories in 1854, a noted British engineer concluded that "wherever [machinery] can be introduced as a substitute for manual labor, it is universally and willingly resorted to."

During the 1840s and 1850s, American industries advanced toward perfecting manufacturing by the use of interchangeable parts. Eli Whitney had introduced this idea (often called the American system of manufacturing) to the United States in 1798, but in Whitney's day the manufacture of guns or other items by the use of interchangeable parts required a great deal of time-consuming hand filing before the parts could be fitted together. In the 1840s American factories immeasurably improved the quality of their machine tools and thereby eliminated much of the need for hand filing. As a result, it became possible to substitute parts that were made in one year for those fabricated in another. In 1853 a British commission investigating American technology looked on in amazement as the superintendent of the Springfield, Massachusetts, armory ordered rifles produced in ten consecutive years to be stripped and their parts reassembled at random.

The American system of manufacturing contained several distinctive advantages. Traditionally, damage to any part of a mechanical contrivance had rendered the whole useless, for no new part would fit. With the perfection of manufacturing by interchangeable parts, however, replacements could be ordered for damaged parts. In addition, the improved machine tools upon which the American system depended enabled entrepreneurs to push inventions swiftly into mass production. The likelihood that inventions would quickly enter production in turn attracted investors. By the 1850s Connecticut firms like Smith and Wesson were mass-producing the revolving pistol, which Samuel Colt had invented in 1836. Sophisticated machine tools made it possible, a manufacturer wrote, to increase production "by confining a worker to one particular limb of a pistol until he had made two thousand." The sewing machine, invented in 1846 by Elias Howe, entered mass production only two years later.

Americans also displayed an eagerness to eliminate the constraints of time and space. An impatient people inhabiting a huge area, they seized enthusiastically on Samuel F. B. Morse's invention of the telegraph in 1844. "The advantages to be derived from the adoption of the Electric Telegraph," a British engineer noted in 1854, "have in no country been more promptly appreciated than in the United States. A system of communication that annihilates distance was felt to be of vital importance, both politically and commercially, in a country so vast, and having a population so widely scattered." The speed with which Americans formed telegraph companies and erected lines stunned the British. "No private interests can oppose the passage of a line through any property," the same British engineer wrote. "There are no committees, no counsel, no long array of witnesses and expensive hearings; compensation is made simply for damage done, the amount being assessed by a jury, and generally on a most moderate estimate. With a celerity that is surprising a company is formed, a line is built, and operations are commenced." Although telegraph lines usually transmitted political and commercial messages, some cities adapted them for reporting fires. By the early 1850s, Boston had an elaborate system of telegraph stations from which news of a blaze could be swiftly transmitted to fire companies throughout the city. Whatever their use, telegraph lines spread rapidly. By 1852 more than fifteen thousand miles of lines connected cities as distant as Quebec, New Orleans, and St. Louis.

The Railroad Boom

The same penchant for overcoming the natural limits imposed by time and space drove antebellum Americans to make an extraordinary investment in railroads. To an even greater degree than the telegraph, the railroad embodied progress through technology.

In 1790 even European royalty could travel no faster than fourteen miles an hour, and that only with frequent changes of horses. Yet by 1850 an ordinary American could travel on a train at three times that speed. The swift, comfortable transport that American railroads provided for the common man and woman dramatized the democratic promise of technology more vividly than any other technological innovation of the time.

In Europe railroads usually had several classes of travel. The common people were traditionally herded into crowded cars and seated on wooden benches or chairs. Only those who paid to travel first-class enjoyed a modicum of luxury. In contrast, in America there was only *one* class of railroad travel (except for blacks, who were often forced to sit separately). Furthermore, American inventors introduced a level of comfort that astonished Europeans. They experimented with adjustable upholstered seats that could be turned in whatever direction the train was traveling and that could be converted into couches at night. In effect, everyone could travel first-class. Americans, a Frenchman observed, had "a perfect passion for railroads" and loved them "as a lover loves his mistress."

Yet in the 1830s little about the railroads appeared lovable. The first trains were drawn by horses rather than by locomotives; a few actually used sails for power. Those with locomotives showered their passengers' clothing with sparks, for the riding cars were often open to the air. In the absence of brakes, passengers at times had to get out and pull trains to stops. Without means of illumination, trains rarely ran at night. Scheduling posed problems because the United States did not adopt standard time until 1883 (see Chapter 18); at noon in Boston, it was twelve minutes before noon in New York. Moreover, trains en route faced innumerable delays. Because most railroads owned only a single track, trains had to wait on sidings for other trains to pass. Since a train's whereabouts remained a mystery once it had left a station, such waits on the sidings could seem interminable.

Between 1840 and 1860, a stunning transformation occurred in the size of the rail network and in the power and convenience of trains. Railroad track increased from three thousand to thirty thousand miles. Passengers now traveled in flat-roofed coaches. Illumination by kerosene lamps made night travel possible. Locomotives gained in power to the point where they no longer had to be pulled uphill by horses or by stationary engines. Fifty thousand miles of telegraph wires enabled dispatchers to communicate with trains en route and to reduce delays.

Passengers nevertheless still confronted inconveniences. Sleeping accommodations remained crude and schedules erratic. Since individual railroads continued to use track of different gauges, frequent changes of train (eight between Charleston and Philadelphia in the 1850s) remained a necessity. Yet nothing could slow the advance of railroads or cure Americans' mania for them. By 1860 the United States had more track than the rest of the nations of the world combined.

Just as canals had spearheaded the first phase of the transportation revolution, railroads led the second

Railroad Growth, 1850–1860

Rail ties between the East and the Midwest greatly increased during the railroad "boom" of the 1850s.

phase during the 1840s and 1850s. Canals were not abandoned; the Erie Canal, for example, did not reach its peak volume until 1880. But railroads, providing much faster transport and being less vulnerable to winter frosts, gradually overtook canals, first in passenger and then in freight traffic. By 1860 the value of goods transported by railroad greatly exceeded that carried by canals.

As late as 1860, few rail lines extended west of the Mississippi, but railroads had spread like spiderwebs east of the great river. The 1840s saw vigorous railroad construction in New England; by 1850 Massachusetts had half of the track that it would possess in 1950. Elsewhere to the east of the Mississippi, the railroad boom developed mainly in the 1850s, when twenty-two thousand miles of track were added to the nation's rail network. In the South railroads transformed places like Chattanooga and Atlanta into thriving commercial

hubs. The most important development of the 1850s, however, lay in the forging of rail lines between the East and the Midwest (or "Old Northwest"). The New York Central and the Erie railroads joined eastern New York to Buffalo; the Pennsylvania Railroad connected Philadelphia and Pittsburgh; and the Baltimore and Ohio linked Baltimore to Wheeling, Virginia (now West Virginia). Simultaneously, intense construction in Ohio, Indiana, and Illinois created trunk lines that joined each of these routes. By 1860 rail lines ran from Buffalo to Cleveland, Toledo, and Chicago; from Pittsburgh to Fort Wayne; and from Wheeling to Cincinnati and on to St. Louis.

The completion of rail links between the East and the Midwest rerouted much of the commerce of the nation's interior. Before the 1850s most of the agricultural surplus of the Upper Mississippi Valley had made its way down the river to New Orleans for transshipment to the East. Although a railroad between New Orleans and Cincinnati was finally completed in 1859, the earlier completion of the east-west trunk lines had already deflected the flow of grain, livestock, and dairy products directly to the East, bypassing the Mississippi Valley. Gradually, Chicago supplanted New Orleans as the nation's main interior commercial hub. In 1849 Chicago had virtually no rail service, but by 1860 eleven railroads radiated from it.

Too, the forging of east-west rail trunks dramatically stimulated the settlement and agricultural development of the Midwest. By 1860 Illinois, Indiana, and Wisconsin had replaced Pennsylvania, Ohio, and New York as the leading wheat-growing states. Although settlers usually arrived in advance of the railroads, the trains gave hot pursuit. Furthermore, by enabling midwestern farmers to speed their produce to the East, railroads greatly increased the value of their farms and thereby promoted additional settlement. By encouraging settlement, moreover, railroads indirectly stimulated the industrial development of the Midwest, because new settlers needed lumber for fences and houses, and mills to grind wheat into flour. Cities like Chicago, Davenport, Iowa, and Minneapolis grew not only as railroad hubs but as centers of lumber and flour trade.

Railroads also propelled the growth of small towns along their routes. The Illinois Central Railroad, which had more track than any other railroad in 1855, made money not only from its traffic but also from real-estate speculation. Purchasing land for stations along its route, the Illinois Central then laid out towns

The Express Train
Antebellum depictions of trains usually showed their smoke as harmless, cloudlike puffs, but this picture renders the real color more accurately and menacingly.

around the stations. The selection of Manteno, Illinois, as a stop of the Illinois Central, for example, transformed the site from a crossroads without a single house in 1854 into a bustling town of nearly a thousand in 1860, replete with hotels, lumberyards, grain elevators, and gristmills. (The Illinois Central even dictated the naming of streets. In the towns along its route, streets running east and west were always named after trees, and those running north and south were numbered. Soon one town looked much like the next.) By the Civil War, few thought of the railroad-linked Midwest as a frontier region or viewed its inhabitants as pioneers.

As the nation's first big business, the railroads transformed the conduct of business. During the early 1830s, railroads, like canals, depended on financial aid from state governments. With the onset of depression in the late 1830s, however, state governments scrapped overly ambitious railroad projects. Convinced that railroads burdened them with high taxes and blasted hopes, voters turned against state aid, and in the early 1840s, several states amended their constitutions to bar state funding for railroads and canals. The federal government took up some of the slack, but federal aid did not provide a major stimulus to railroads before 1860. Rather, part of the burden of finance passed to city and county governments in agricultural areas that wanted to attract railroads. Municipal governments, for example, often gave railroads rights-of-way, grants of land for stations, and public funds.

The dramatic expansion of the railroad network in the 1850s, however, strained the financing capacity of local governments and required a turn toward private investment, which had never been absent from the picture. Well aware of the economic benefits of railroads, individuals living near them had long purchased railroad securities issued by governments and had directly bought stock in railroads, often paying by contributing their labor to building the railroads. But the large railroads of the 1850s needed more capital than such small investors could generate. Gradually, the center of railroad financing shifted to New York City, and in fact, it was the railroad boom of the 1850s that helped make Wall Street the nation's greatest capital market. The securities of all the leading railroads were traded on the floor of the New York Stock Exchange during the 1850s. In addition, the growth of railroads turned New York City into the center of modern investment firms. The investment firms evaluated the securities of railroads in Toledo or Davenport or Chattanooga and then found purchasers for these securities in New York, Philadelphia, Paris, London, Amsterdam, and Hamburg. Controlling the flow of funds to railroads, the investment bankers began to exert influence over the railroads' internal affairs by supervising administrative reorganizations in times of trouble. A Wall Street analyst noted in 1851 that railroad men seeking financing "must remember that money is power, and that the [financier] can dictate to a great extent his own terms."

Rising Prosperity

Technological advances also improved the lives of consumers by bringing down the price of many commodities. For example, clocks that cost $50 to fabricate by hand in 1800 could be produced by machine for 50¢ by 1850. In addition, the widening use of steam power contributed to a 25 percent rise in the average worker's real income (actual purchasing power) between 1840 and 1860. Early–nineteenth-century factories, which had depended on water wheels to propel their machines, of necessity had to shut down when the rivers or streams that powered the wheels froze. With the spread of steam engines, however, factories could stay open longer and workers could increase their annual wages by working more hours. Cotton textile workers were among those who benefited: although their hourly wages showed little gain, their average annual wages rose from $163 in 1830 to $176 in 1849 to $201 by 1859.

The growth of towns and cities also contributed to an increase in average annual wages. Farmers experienced the same seasonal fluctuations as laborers in the early factories. In sparsely settled rural areas, the onset of winter traditionally brought hard times; as demand for agricultural labor slumped, few alternatives existed to take up the slack. "A year in some farming states such as Pennsylvania," a traveler commented in 1823, "is only of eight months duration, four months being lost to the laborer, who is turned away as a useless animal." In contrast, densely populated towns and cities offered more opportunities for year-round work. The urban dockworker thrown out of his job as a result of frozen waterways might find work as a hotel porter or an unskilled indoor laborer.

Towns and cities also provided women and children with new opportunities for paid work. (Women and children had long performed many vital tasks on farms, but rarely for pay.) The wages of children between the ages of ten and eighteen came to play an integral role in the nineteenth-century family economy. Family heads who earned more than $600 a year might have been able to afford the luxury of keeping their children in school, but most breadwinners were fortunate if they made $300 a year. Although the cost of many basic commodities fell between 1815 and 1860 (another consequence of the transportation revolution), most families lived close to the margin. Budgets of working-class families in New York City and Philadelphia during the early 1850s reveal annual expenditures of $500–$600, with more than 40 percent spent on food, 25–30 percent on rent, and most of the remainder on clothing and fuel. Such a family obviously could not survive on the annual wages of the average male head of the household. It needed the wages of the children and, at times, those of the wife as well.

Life in urban wage-earning families was not necessarily superior to life in farming communities. A farmer who owned land, livestock, and a house did not have to worry about paying rent or buying fuel for cooking and heating, and rarely ran short of food. Many Americans continued to aspire to farming as the best of all occupations. But to purchase, clear, and stock a farm involved a considerable capital outlay that could easily amount to five hundred dollars, and the effort promised no rewards for a few years. The majority of workers in agricultural areas did not own farms and were exposed to the seasonal fluctuations in demand for agricultural labor. In many respects, they were worse off than urban wage earners.

The economic advantages that attended living in cities help explain why so many Americans moved to urban areas during the first half of the nineteenth century. As a further attraction, during the 1840s and 1850s, cities also provided their residents with an unprecedented range of comforts and conveniences.

THE QUALITY OF LIFE

In addition to large-scale transformations in production, transportation, and income, the two decades before the Civil War witnessed subtle alterations in the quality of everyday life in the United States. Less visible and dramatic than those wrought by the railroad, these changes in everyday experiences occurred for the most part within the privacy of homes and affected such routine activities as eating, drinking, and washing. Technological improvements in these years made the daily home-life experiences of Americans far more comfortable. "Think of the numberless contrivances and inventions for our comfort and luxury which the last half dozen years have brought forth," the poet Walt Whitman exclaimed to his readers, and you will "bless your star that fate has cast your lot in the year of Our Lord 1857." Indeed, the patent office in Washington was flooded with sketches of reclining seats, sliding tables, beds convertible into chairs, lounges convertible into cradles, street-sweeping machines, and fly traps. Machine-made furniture began to transform the interiors of houses. Stoves revolutionized heating and cooking. By bringing fresh vegetables to city dwellers, railroads stimulated important changes in diet.

Despite all the talk of comfort and progress, however, many Americans experienced little improvement in the quality of their lives. Technological advances made it possible for the middle class to enjoy luxuries formerly reserved for the rich but often widened the distance between the middle class and the poor. At a time when the interiors of urban, middle-class homes were becoming increasingly lavish, the urban poor congregated in cramped and unsightly tenements. In addition, some aspects of life remained relatively unaffected by scientific and technical advances. Medical science, for example, made a few advances before 1860, but none that rivaled the astonishing changes wrought by the railroad and the telegraph.

The benefits rather than the limitations of progress, however, gripped the popular imagination. Few Americans accepted the possibility that progress could neglect such an important aspect of everyday life as health. Confronted by the failure of the medical profession to rival the achievements of Cyrus McCormick and Samuel F. B. Morse, Americans embraced popular health movements that sprang up outside the medical profession and promised to conquer disease by the precepts of diet and regimen.

Housing

During the early 1800s, urban dwellings had grown far more standardized. Builders had responded to the swift growth of cities by erecting quickly constructed row houses—uniform attached dwellings increasingly made of brick. Whereas city dwellers in the eighteenth century usually had lived in unattached frame houses of one or two stories, all of which looked different and faced in different directions, their nineteenth-century counterparts were more likely to inhabit row houses. Some praised the uniformity of row houses as democratic, but others condemned the structures as monotonous. "The great defect in the houses," an English visitor observed, "is their extreme uniformity—when you have seen one, you have seen all."

The average row house was narrow and long, fifteen to twenty feet across, thirty to forty feet from front to back. Most had open spaces in the rear for gardens, pigs, privies, and cisterns. Row houses were not all alike. In the nineteenth century, middle-class row houses were larger (3 to 3½ stories) than working-class row houses (2 to 2½ stories). Between 1830 and 1860, moreover, the interiors of middle-class row houses became more elaborate than those of common laborers. Such features as cast-iron balconies (especially popular in the South), elegant doors, curved staircases, carved columns between rooms, and rooms with fanciful, asymmetrical shapes distinguished the row houses of the middle class from those of the less fortunate. The most fashionable urban residences surrounded small parks ringed by iron fences and contained "Place" rather than "Street" in their addresses.

As land values rose in the early nineteenth century (as much as 750 percent in Manhattan between 1785 and 1815), renting rather than owning homes became more common. By 1815 more than half of the homes in the large cities were rented, usually by artisans, jour-neymen, and day laborers. Soaring land values also led to the subdividing of many row houses for occupancy by several families or boarders. The worst of these subdivided houses were called tenements and became the usual habitats of Irish immigrants and free blacks.

In rural areas, the quality of housing depended on the date of settlement as much as on social class. In recently settled areas, the standard dwelling was a rude, one-room log cabin with floors made of split logs that allowed drafts to seep in, roofs that let in snow, crude chimneys made of sticks and clay, and windows covered by oiled paper or cloth. As rural communities matured, however, log cabins gave way to frame houses of two or more rooms with glass windows and better insulation. Most of these houses were built on a principle known as the balloon frame. Originally, *balloon frame* was a term used by traditional artisans to express their contempt for houses that appeared so flimsily constructed as to risk blowing away. In place of foot-thick heavy timbers that were laboriously fitted together, the balloon-frame house had a skeleton of thin sawed timbers nailed together in such a way that every strain ran against the grain of the wood. The strength of balloon-frame houses soon confounded their critics, whereas their simplicity and cheapness endeared them to western builders with neither the time nor the skill to cut heavy beams and fit them into each other.

Home Furniture

Furniture trends between 1840 and 1860 revealed the widening gap between the life-styles of the prosperous and those of the poor. Families in the middle and upper classes increasingly decorated their parlors with a style of furniture known as French antique or rococo. Rococo furniture reflected both the affluence and the formality of middle- and upper-class families. In such households, the ideal parlor required a seven-piece matched set: an armchair for the husband, a smaller and less expensive lady's chair for his wife, a sofa, and four parlor chairs for guests and children. Rococo furniture was by definition ornate. Upholstered chairs, for example, displayed intricate scrolls depicting vines, leaves, or flowers and had curved legs with ornamental feet (called cabriole legs). The heavily upholstered backs of sofas often contained designs of rose blossoms topped by carved medallions. Artisans framed hanging mirrors with intricately fashioned and gilded moldings that depicted birds, flowers, and even young

Family Group
This daguerreotype, taken about 1852, reveals the little things so important to etching a middle-class family's social status: curtains; a wall hanging; a piano with scrolled legs; a small desk with elegantly curved legs; a pet; ladies posed in nonproductive but "improving" activities (music, reading); and a young man seemingly staring into space—and perhaps pondering how to pay for it all.

women. The finished products frequently weighed so much that they threatened to tumble from the wall.

The highly ornamented rococo furniture marked its possessors as people of substantial wealth. At the same time, the rise of mass production in such furniture centers as Grand Rapids, Michigan, and Cincinnati brought the rococo style within the financial reach of the middle class and thereby helped close the gap between the truly wealthy (who often imported their furniture from France) and those who were merely well off. Unable to afford even mass-produced rococo pieces, however, the great majority of Americans had to be content with simpler furniture. Technological advances in the fabrication of furniture tended to level taste between the middle and upper classes while simultaneously marking those classes off from everyone else.

Heating, Cooking, and Diet

In the 1840s the transportation and industrial revolutions affected such basic household features as heating, cooking, and diet. As soon as the transportation revolution had opened distant markets, some iron foundries began to specialize in the production of cast-

iron stoves. In urban areas, stoves were rapidly displacing open hearths for both heating and cooking by the late 1840s.

Even though most of the heat from open hearths was lost up the chimney, country people continued to prefer them to stoves, partly because their labor in clearing the land had left them with an abundance of wood. Wood could be used in stoves, too, but only if laboriously chopped into small pieces. In contrast, city dwellers, who had to pay for wood, increasingly preferred coal-fired stoves. Before 1830 English and Welsh immigrants had taught Americans how to hew coal (that is, mine it with heavy instruments), and the discovery in eastern Pennsylvania of a superior variety of coal called anthracite guaranteed a steady supply.

Coal, however, had its drawbacks. A faulty coal-burning stove could fill a room with poisonous carbon monoxide, and coal left a dirty residue that fouled urban air and blackened the snow. But coal burned longer and hotter than wood and reduced the time and expense that urban families had traditionally devoted to acquiring fuel. Stoves were also superior to hearths for cooking. Householders could leave meals

Popping Corn

Popping kernels of corn by heating them, a skill that the colonists acquired from the Indians, was a popular pastime in antebellum homes.

unattended on stoves, and they no longer ran the danger of scorching their clothing while bending to reach into open flames. In addition, they could cook several dishes at once on a stove. In this way, stoves contributed to the growing variety of the American diet.

As more and more people congregated in towns and cities, and as transportation improved, urban markets for the sale of country produce multiplied. Into America's towns and cities railroads brought fresh vegetables, which in the eighteenth century had been absent even from lavish banquet tables. By 1860 Boston and St. Louis each had ten large public markets. Even small towns in the Midwest were likely to have public markets by the 1840s.

Despite the improvements brought about by the transportation revolution, personal diets were still subject to seasonal fluctuations. Only the rich could afford fruit out of season, for they alone could afford to buy sugar in sufficient quantities to preserve fruit. (The Florida and California citrus fruit industries still lay in the future.) Indeed, preserving almost any kind of food presented problems. Although Americans pioneered technical advances in the harvesting and storing of ice before 1840, home iceboxes were rare before 1860. One contemporary writer recommended that housewives bury meat in the snow to keep it from spoiling, but salt remained the most widely used preservative. One reason antebellum Americans ate more pork than beef was that salt affected the taste of pork less objectionably than it did the flavor of beef.

Water and Sanitation

Rural homes rarely had running water. Water was brought in from wells, springs, or cisterns; used; carried outside again; and dumped. During the early 1800s, the same had been true in cities, but with increasing population density, alarm rose about the threat to well water posed by leakage from outdoor privies. In response, some cities had constructed public waterworks. In 1823 Philadelphia had completed a system that brought water along aqueducts and through pipes from the Schuylkill and Delaware rivers to street hydrants. Visiting Philadelphia in 1842, Charles Dickens marveled that the city "is most bountifully provided with fresh water, which is showered and jerked about, and turned on, and poured off every where." During the 1840s and 1850s, several other major cities constructed similar waterworks. New York City completed the Croton aqueduct (which brought water into the city from reservoirs to the north) in the 1840s, and Cleveland, Detroit, Hartford, Louisville, and Cincinnati built waterworks during the 1850s. By 1860 sixty-eight public water systems operated in the United States.

Although these municipal water systems were among the most impressive engineering triumphs of the age, their impact is easily exaggerated. Many small cities like Rochester and Poughkeepsie, New York, had no waterworks in 1860. As late as 1862, Louisville had only 239 houses connected to its system. The 53,000 customers of New York City's system in 1856 only

The Beauties of Street Sprinkling,
by Thomas Worth, 1856 Street sprinklers controlled flying dust, but they also created slick surfaces that sent unwary pedestrians flying.

composed less than a tenth of the city's population. Even with the establishment of waterworks, few houses had running water; the incoming water usually ended its journey at a street hydrant. As in rural areas, families had to carry water into and out of houses. Moreover, houses blessed with running water rarely possessed hot water. Before one could take a bath, water had to be heated on the stove or over the fireplace. Not surprisingly, people rarely bathed. A New England physician claimed in 1832 that not one in five of his patients took one bath a year. Fewer than fourteen hundred baths served New York City in 1855.

Because Americans bathed infrequently, their bodily odors undoubtedly were pungent, but so were smells of every sort. Even fashionable residential streets often contained stables backed by mounds of manure. Municipal sanitation departments were virtually nonexistent. Street cleaning was mainly the responsibility of private contractors, who gained a reputation for slackness in discharging their duties. To supplement the work of such undependable contractors, Americans relied on hogs, which they let roam freely and scavenge. (Scavenging hogs that turned down the wrong street often made tasty dinners for the poor.) The abundance of outdoor privies added to the stench. Flush toilets were rare outside of cities, and within cities provisions for sewerage lagged behind those for waterworks. With a population of 178,000 in 1860, Boston had only about five thousand flush toilets, a far higher ratio of toilets to people than most cities could report. Americans normally answered calls of nature by trips to outdoor privies, whose unpleasant smells they suppressed mainly by the application of shovelsful of dirt.

Comforts and conveniences later taken for granted were still rare in 1860. Conveniences like stoves and folding beds that made their way into the home, far from liberating women from housework, merely elevated the standards of housekeeping. In her widely popular *Treatise on Domestic Economy* (1841), Catharine Beecher used technological advances to justify her contention that women had a duty to make every house a "glorious temple" by utilizing space and other resources more efficiently. None of this, however, changes the fact that middle-class antebellum Americans increasingly boasted of how comfortable their lives were becoming and pointed to the steady improvement in wages, diet, and water supplies as tangible marks of betterment.

Disease and Health

Despite a slowly rising standard of living, Americans remained vulnerable to disease. Between 1793, when an outbreak of yellow fever had devastated Philadelphia, and 1918–1919, when an influenza epidemic killed more than half a million Americans (and at least 20 million people worldwide), epidemics posed a constant but unpredictable threat. In 1832–1833 the combined effects of cholera and yellow fever had killed perhaps a fifth of New Orleans's population. Cholera returned to the United States in 1849 and carried off 10 percent of St. Louis's population while dealing staggering blows to most other cities.

Although not the only threats to health, epidemic diseases were the most visible and feared dangers. With grim irony, the transportation revolution increased the peril from epidemics. The cholera epidemic of 1832 had the dubious distinction of being America's first national epidemic. Its course followed that of the transportation revolution. One route of the epidemic ran from New York City up the Hudson River, across the Erie Canal to Ohio, and down the Ohio River to the Mississippi and New Orleans; the other route followed shipping up and down the East Coast from New York City.

Each major antebellum epidemic of cholera or yellow fever intensified public calls for the establishment of municipal health boards, and by the 1850s most major cities had formed such agencies. However, so few powers did city governments give them that the boards could not even enforce the reporting of diseases. The inability of physicians to find a satisfactory explanation for epidemic diseases led to a general distrust of the medical profession and contributed to making public health a low-priority issue.

Prior to 1860 no one understood that tiny organisms called bacteria caused both cholera and yellow fever. Rather, rival camps of physicians battled furiously and publicly over the merits of the "contagion" theory versus those of the "miasm" theory. Insisting that cholera and yellow fever were transmitted by touch, contagionists called for vigorous measures to quarantine affected areas. In contrast, supporters of the miasm theory argued that poisonous gases (miasms) emitted by rotting vegetation or dead animals carried disease through the air. The miasm theory led logically to the conclusion that swamps should be drained and streets cleaned. Neither theory, however, was consistent with the evidence. Quarantines failed to check cholera and yellow fever (an argument against the contagionist theory), and many residents of filthy slums and stinking, low-lying areas contracted neither of the two diseases (a refutation of the miasm theory). Confronted by this inconclusive debate between medical experts, municipal leaders refused to delegate more than advisory powers to health boards dominated by physicians. After the worst epidemic in the city's history, a New Orleans editor stated in 1853 that it was "much safer to follow the common sense and unbiased opinion of the intelligent mass of the people than the opinions of medical men . . . based upon hypothetical theories."

Although most epidemic diseases baffled antebellum physicians, a basis for forward strides in surgery was laid during the 1840s by the discovery of anesthetics. Prior to 1840 young people often entertained themselves at parties by inhaling nitrous oxide, or "laughing gas," which produced sensations of giddiness and painlessness; and semicomical demonstrations of laughing gas became a form of popular entertainment. (Samuel Colt, the inventor of the revolver, had begun his career as a traveling exhibitor of laughing gas.) But nitrous oxide had to be carried around in bladders, which were difficult to handle, and in any case, few recognized its surgical possibilities. Then in 1842 Crawford Long, a Georgia physician who had attended laughing-gas frolics in his youth, employed sulfuric ether (an easily transportable liquid with the same properties as nitrous oxide) during a surgical operation. Long failed to follow up on his discovery, but four years later William T. G. Morton, a dentist, successfully employed sulfuric ether during an operation at Massachusetts General Hospital in Boston. Within a few years, ether came into wide use in American surgery.

The discovery of anesthesia improved the public image of surgeons, long viewed as brutes who hacked away at agonized patients. Furthermore, by making longer operations possible, anesthesia encouraged surgeons to take greater care than previously during surgery. Nevertheless, the failure of most surgeons to recognize the importance of clean hands and sterilized instruments partially offset the benefits of anesthesia before 1860. In 1843 Boston physician and poet Oliver Wendell Holmes, Sr., published an influential paper on how the failure of obstetricians to disinfect their hands often spread a disease called puerperal fever among mothers giving birth in hospitals. Still, the medical profession only gradually accepted the importance of disinfection. Operations remained as dangerous as the diseases or wounds that they tried to heal. The mortality rate for amputations hovered around 40 percent, and during the Civil War, 87 percent of soldiers who suffered abdominal wounds died from them.

Popular Health Movements

Doubtful of medicine and skeptical of the benefits of public health, antebellum Americans turned to a variety of therapies and regimens that promised to give them healthier and longer lives. One popular response to disease was hydropathy, or the "water cure," which filtered into the United States from Europe during the 1840s. By the mid-1850s the United States had twenty-seven hydropathic sanatoriums, which claimed to offer by cold baths and wet packs "an abundance of water of dewy softness and crystal transparency, to cleanse, renovate, and rejuvenate the disease-worn and dilapidated system." The water cure held a special attraction for well-off women, partly because hydropathics professed to relieve the pain associated with childbirth and menstruation and partly because hydropathic sanatoriums were congenial gathering places in which middle-class women could relax and exercise in private.

In contrast to the water cure, which necessitated the time and expense of a trip to a sanatorium, a health system that anyone could adopt was propounded by Sylvester Graham, a temperance reformer turned popular health advocate. Alarmed by the 1832 cholera epidemic, Graham counseled changes in diet and regimen as well as total abstinence from alcohol. Contending that Americans ate too much, he urged them to substitute vegetables, fruits, and coarse, whole-grain bread (called Graham bread) for meat and to abstain from spices, coffee, and tea as well as from alcohol. Soon Graham added sexual "excess" (by which he meant most sex) to his list of forbidden indulgences. Vegetables were preferable to meat, according to Graham, because they provoked less hunger. The food cravings of the "flesh-eater" were "greater and more imperious" than those of the vegetarian.

Many of Graham's most enthusiastic disciples were reformers. Grahamites had a special table at the Brook Farm community. Until forced out by outraged parents and hungry students, one of Graham's followers ran the student dining room at reformist Oberlin College. Much like Graham, reformers traced the evils of American society to the unnatural cravings of its people. Abolitionists, for example, contended that slavery intensified white men's lust and contributed to the violent behavior of white southerners. Similarly, Graham believed that eating meat stimulated lust and other aggressive impulses.

Yet Graham's doctrines attracted a broad audience that extended beyond the perimeters of the reform movements. Many towns and cities had boardinghouses whose tables were set according to his principles. His books sold well, and his public lectures were thronged. Like hydropathy, Grahamism addressed the popular desire for better health at a time when orthodox medicine seemed to do more damage than good. Graham used religious phrases that were familiar to churchgoers and then channeled those concepts toward nonreligious goals. Luxury was "sinful," disease resembled hell, and health was a kind of heaven on earth. In this way, he provided simple and familiar assurances to an audience as ignorant as he was of the true causes of disease.

Phrenology

The belief that each person was ultimately the master of his or her own destiny marked the popular antebellum health movements. A similar impulse underlay phrenology, the most popular of the scientific fads that swept antebellum America.

The creation of the Viennese physician Franz J. Gall, phrenology centered on the idea that the human mind was composed of thirty-seven distinct faculties, or "organs," each localized in a different part of the brain. Phrenologists thought that the degree of each organ's development determined the shape of the skull, so that they could accurately analyze an individual's character by examining the bumps and depressions of the skull.

Transported to the United States in the 1830s, phrenology first commanded serious attention from educated dabblers in science. In the 1840s it entered a new phase in the hands of the brothers Orson and Lorenzo Fowler. Orson Fowler originally intended to become a Protestant missionary. Instead, he became a missionary for phrenology and opened a publishing house in New York City (Fowlers and Wells) that marketed books on phrenology everywhere. When some critics argued that phrenology was godless because it eliminated the idea of the human soul, the Fowlers pointed to a huge organ called Veneration to establish that people were naturally religious. When others said that phrenology was pessimistic because a person presumably could not change the shape of his or her skull, the Fowlers retorted that every desirable organ could be improved by exercise. Lorenzo Fowler reported that several of his skull bumps had actually grown. Orson Fowler wrapped it all into a tidy slogan: "Self-Made, or Never-Made."

Drawing phrenological charts of oneself or one's friends became a parlor game of sorts during the 1840s and 1850s, but phrenology appealed to Americans less as a pastime than as a "practical" science. In a mobile and individualistic society where people routinely transacted business with strangers, phrenology promised to provide at a glance a quick assessment of others. Merchants used phrenological charts to pick suitable clerks, and young women induced their fiancés to undergo phrenological analyses before tying the knot. Before phrenology, a supporter declared, "the wisest of men had no means of deciding, with anything like certainty, the talents or character of a stranger."

Phrenology did not cure disease, but phrenologists had close ties to the popular health movement. Fowlers and Wells issued the *Water-Cure Journal* after 1848 and brought out Sylvester Graham's *Lectures on the Science of Human Life.* Orson Fowler filled his popular phrenological books with tips on the evils of coffee, tea, meat, spices, and sex that could have been plucked from Graham's writings. As a "science," phrenology sprang from the same impulse as the health movements—the belief that anyone could understand and obey the "laws" of life.

Unlike hydropathy, phrenology did not require any investment of money. Unlike Grahamism, it did not call for painful abstinence. Easily understood and practiced by the average person, and filled with the promise of universal betterment, phrenology was the ideal science for antebellum America. Just as Americans invented machines to better their lives, they were not above inventing "sciences" that promised human betterment.

DEMOCRATIC PASTIMES

Between 1830 and 1860 technology increasingly transformed leisure by making Americans more dependent on recreation that could be manufactured and sold. People purchased this commodity in the form of cheap newspapers and novels as well as affordable tickets to plays, museums, and lectures.

Just as the Boston Associates had daringly capitalized on new technology to produce textiles at Lowell and Waltham, imaginative entrepreneurs utilized technology to make and sell entertainment. Men like James Gordon Bennett, one of the founders of the penny press in America, and P. T. Barnum, the greatest showman of the nineteenth century, amassed fortunes by sensing what people wanted and then employing available technology to satisfy their desire. To a degree, indeed, these men induced the public to want what they had to sell. Barnum, for example, had a genius for using newspaper publicity to pique popular interest in curiosities that he was about to exhibit.

Bennett and Barnum thought of themselves as purveyors of democratic entertainment. They would sell their wares cheaply to anyone. Barnum's famous American museum in New York City catered to a wide

variety of social classes that paid to view paintings, dwarfs, mammoth bones, and other attractions. By marketing the American Museum as family entertainment, Barnum helped break down barriers that had long divided the pastimes of husbands from those of their wives. Similarly, the racy news stories in Bennett's *New York Herald* provided its vast audience with a common stock of information and topics for conversation. In these ways, the impact of technology on amusement was democratic.

Technology also ignited the process by which individuals became spectators rather than the creators of their own amusements. Americans had long found ways to enjoy themselves. Even the gloomiest Puritans had indulged in games and sports. After 1830, however, the burden of providing entertainment began to shift from individuals to entrepreneurs who supplied ways to entertain the public.

Newspapers

In 1830 the typical American newspaper was a mere four pages long, with the front and back pages devoted almost wholly to advertisements. The second and third pages contained editorials, details of ship arrivals and of their cargoes, reprints of political speeches, and notices of political events. Few papers depended on their circulation for profit; even the most prominent papers had a daily circulation of only one thousand to two thousand. Rather, papers often relied on subsidies from political parties or factions. When a party gained power, it inserted paid political notices only in papers loyal to it. "Journalists," a contemporary wrote, "were usually little more than secretaries dependent upon cliques of politicians, merchants, brokers, and office seekers for their prosperity and bread."

As a result, newspapers could be profitable without being particularly popular. Because of their potential for profit, new papers were constantly being established. But most had limited appeal. The typical paper sold for six cents an issue at a time when the average daily wage was less than a dollar. Papers often seemed little more than published bulletin boards. Merely records of events, they typically lacked the exciting news stories and eye-catching illustrations that later generations would take for granted.

The 1830s witnessed the beginnings of a stunning transformation. Technological changes, most of which originated in Europe, vastly increased both the supply of paper (still made from rags) and the speed

Newspaper Boy, *by Edward Bannister, 1869*
Newsboys such as this one poignantly painted by the black artist Edward Bannister were a familiar sight on nineteenth-century street corners.

of printing presses. The substitution of steam-driven cylindrical presses for flatbed hand presses led to a tenfold increase in the number of printed pages that could be produced in an hour. Enterprising journalists, among them the Scottish-born James Gordon Bennett, grasped the implications of the new technology. Newspapers could now rely on vast circulation rather than on political subsidies to turn a profit. To gain circulation, journalists like Bennett slashed the price of newspapers. In 1833 the *New York Sun* became America's first penny newspaper, and Bennett's *New York Herald* followed in 1835. By June 1835 the combined daily circulation of New York's three penny papers reached 44,000; in contrast, before the dawn of the penny press in 1833, the city's eleven dailies had a combined daily circulation of only 26,500. Spearheaded by the penny papers, the combined daily circulation of newspapers throughout the nation rose from roughly 78,000 in 1830 to 300,000 by 1840. The number of weekly newspapers spurted from 65 in 1830 to 138 in 1840.

Cheapness was not the only feature of the penny papers. Dependent on circulation and advertising rather than on subsidies, the penny press revolutionized the marketing and format of papers. Where single copies of the six-cent papers were usually available only at the printer's office, newsboys hawked the penny papers on busy street corners. Moreover, the penny papers subordinated the recording of political and commercial events to human-interest stories of robberies, murders, rapes, and abandoned children. They dispatched reporters to police courts and printed transcripts of trials. As sociologist Michael Schudson observes, "The penny press invented the modern concept of 'news.' " Rather than merely recording events, the penny papers wove events into gripping stories. They invented not only news but also news reporting. Relying on party stalwarts to dispatch copies of speeches and platforms, and reprinting news items from other papers, the older six-cent papers did little, if any, reporting. In contrast, the penny papers employed their own correspondents and were the first papers to use the telegraph to speed news to readers.

Some penny papers were little more than scandal sheets, but the best, like Bennett's *New York Herald* and Horace Greeley's *New York Tribune* (1841), pioneered modern financial and political reporting. From its inception, the *Herald* contained a daily "money article" that substituted the analysis and interpretation of financial events for the dull recording of commercial facts. "The spirit, pith, and philosophy of commercial affairs is what men of business want," Bennett wrote. The relentless snooping of the *Tribune*'s Washington reporters outraged politicians. In 1848 *Tribune* correspondents were temporarily barred from the House floor for reporting that Representative Sawyer of Ohio ate his lunch (sausage and bread) each day in the House chamber, picked his teeth with a jackknife, and wiped his greasy hands on his pants and coat.

The Popular Novel

Like newspapers, novels became enormously popular between 1830 and 1860. Of course, novels had been read long before 1830, and some authors, among them the Scot Sir Walter Scott, had gained a wide following. But the cost of novels before 1830 had restricted their sales. Each of Scott's novels, for example, was issued in a three-volume set that retailed for as much as thirty dollars. During the 1830s and 1840s, the impact of the transportation revolution and technical advances in printing brought down the price of novels. As canals and railroads opened crossroads stores to the latest fiction, publishers in New York and Philadelphia vied to deliver inexpensive novels to the shelves. By the 1840s cheap paperbacks that sold for as little as seven cents began to flood the market.

Those who did not purchase such fictional books could read serializations in newspapers that were devoted mainly to printing novels. The most successful of these story papers was the *New York Ledger*, which a young Scotch-Irish immigrant, Robert Bonner, started in the mid-1840s. Like James Gordon Bennett, the lord of the penny press, Bonner had a genius for identifying what the public wanted and for launching publicity extravaganzas. To herald the serialization of one novel, Bonner spent twenty thousand dollars and arranged the firing of a one-hundred-gun salute in City Hall Park. By 1860 the *Ledger* had an astonishing weekly circulation of four hundred thousand.

The most popular fiction on the market in the 1840s and 1850s was the sentimental novel, which sought to evoke feelings or emotions. The tribulations of orphans and the deaths of children filled the pages of these tearjerkers. In Susan Warner's *The Wide, Wide World* (first serialized in 1850), the heroine burst into tears on an average of every other page for two volumes. Sentimentalism was not confined to novels. The popular writer Lydia Sigourney wrote a poem on the death of a canary that had accidentally been starved to death.

Women contributed the main audience for sentimental novels. This genre was a kind of women's fiction, written by women about women and mainly for women. The most lucrative occupation open to women before the Civil War, writing often attracted those in desperate need of cash. Hard times had lured many renowned female novelists into the field. Susan Warner, for example, had been brought up in luxury and then tossed into poverty by the financial ruin of her father in the Panic of 1837. Mrs. E. D. E. N. Southworth, who gained fame and fortune from *The Hidden Hand* (first serialized in 1859) and other novels, turned to writing after a broken marriage left her supporting two children on a teacher's salary of $250 a year.

Women's fiction dealt with more than the flow of tears. A major theme in the novels of Susan Warner and Mrs. Southworth was that women could conquer any obstacle. Women's novels challenged the stereotype of the male as the trusty provider and of the female as the delicate dependent by portraying men as liars, drunken lechers, or vicious misers and depicting women as re-sourceful and strong-willed. In the typical plot, a female orphan or a spoiled rich girl thrown on hard times, or a dutiful daughter plagued by a drunken father, learned grittily to master every situation. The moral was clear. Women could overcome trials and make the world a better place. Few of the novelists were active feminists, but their writings provided a glimpse into the private feelings of their female readers.

The Theater

During the 1850s novelists like the Englishman Charles Dickens and the American Harriet Beecher Stowe, the author of *Uncle Tom's Cabin*, were as well known through dramatizations of their work as by sales of their books. Antebellum theaters were large (twenty-five hundred to four thousand seats in some cities) and crowded by all classes. With seats as cheap as twelve cents and rarely more than fifty cents, the typical theater audience included lawyers and merchants and their wives, artisans and clerks, sailors and noisy boys, and a sizable body of prostitutes. Prostitutes usually sat in the top gallery, called the third tier, "that dark, horrible, guilty" place. The presence of prostitutes in theaters was taken for granted; the only annoyance came when they left the third tier to solicit customers in the more expensive seats.

The prostitutes in attendance were not the only factor that made the antebellum theater vaguely disreputable. Theatrical audiences were notoriously rowdy. They showed their feelings by stamping their feet, whistling, hooting at villains, and throwing potatoes or garbage at the stage when they did not like the characters or the acting. Individual actors developed huge followings, and the public displayed at least as much interest in the actors as in the plays. In 1849 a long-running feud between the leading American actor, Edwin Forrest, and the popular British actor William Macready ended with a riot at New York City's Astor Place that left twenty people dead.

The Astor Place riot demonstrated the broad popularity of the theater. Forrest's supporters included a following of Irish workers who loathed the British and appealed to the "working men" to rally against the "aristocrat" Macready. Macready, who projected a more polished and intellectual image than Forrest, attracted the better-educated classes. Had not all classes patronized the theater, the deadly riot probably would never have occurred.

The plays themselves were as diverse as the audiences. Most often performed were melodramas, whose plots resembled those of sentimental novels. Vice was punished, virtue rewarded, and the heroine finally married the hero. Yet the single most popular dramatist was William Shakespeare. In 1835 audiences in Philadelphia witnessed sixty-five performances of Shakespeare's plays. Americans who may never have read a line of Shakespeare grew familiar with Othello, King Lear, Desdemona, and Shylock. Theatrical managers adapted Shakespeare to a popular audience. They highlighted the swordfights and assassinations, cut some speeches, omitted minor characters, and pruned words or references that might have offended the audience's sense of propriety. For example, they substituted *pottels* for *urinals* and quietly advanced Juliet's age at the time that she falls in love with Romeo from fourteen to eighteen. They occasionally changed sad endings to happy ones. The producers even arranged for short performances or demonstrations between acts of Shakespeare—and indeed, of every play. During such an interlude, the audience might have observed a brief impersonation of Tecumseh or Aaron Burr, jugglers and acrobats, a drummer beating twelve drums at once, or a three-year-old who weighed a hundred pounds.

Minstrel Shows

The Yankee or "Brother Jonathan" figure who served as a stock character in many antebellum plays helped audiences to form an image of the ideal American as rustic, clever, patriotic, and more than a match for city slickers and decadent European aristocrats. In a different way, the minstrel shows that Americans thronged to see in the 1840s and 1850s forged enduring stereotypes that buttressed white Americans' sense of superiority by diminishing black people.

Minstrel shows arose in northern cities in the 1840s, as blackfaced white men took to the stage to present an evening of songs, dances, and humorous sketches. Minstrelsy borrowed some authentic elements of African-American culture, especially dances characterized by the sliding, shuffling step of southern blacks, but most of the songs had origins in white culture. Such familiar American songs as Stephen Foster's "Camptown Races" and "Massa's in the Cold Ground," which first aired in minstrel shows, reflected white Americans' notions of how blacks sang more than it represented authentic black music. In addition, the images of blacks projected by minstrelsy both catered to and reinforced the prejudices of the working-class

Dan Bryant, the Minstrel
Bryant was one of many antebellum popularizers of black minstrelsy. One of the earliest known minstrelsy performances occurred in Boston in 1799, when the white man Gottlieb Graupner, reportedly made up as a black, sang and accompanied himself on the banjo.

whites who dominated the audience of minstrel shows. Minstrel troupes usually depicted blacks as stupid, clumsy, and obsessively musical and emphasized the Africanness of blacks by giving their characters names like the Ethiopian Serenaders and their acts titles like the Nubian Jungle Dance and the African Fling. At a time of intensifying political conflict over race, minstrel shows planted images and expectations about blacks' behavior through stock characters. These included Uncle Ned, the tattered, humble, and docile slave, and Zip Coon, the arrogant urban free black who paraded around in a high hat, long-tailed coat, and green vest and who lived off his girlfriends' money. Minstrels lampooned blacks who assumed public roles by portraying them as incompetent stump speakers who called Patrick Henry "Henry Patrick," referred to John Hancock as "Boobcock," and confused the word *statute* with *statue*.

By the 1850s major cities from New York to San Francisco had several minstrel theaters. Touring professional troupes and local amateur talent even brought minstrelsy to small towns and villages. Mark Twain later recalled how minstrelsy had burst upon Hannibal, Missouri, in the early 1840s as "a glad and stunning surprise." So popular was the craze that minstrels even visited the White House and entertained Presidents John Tyler, James K. Polk, Millard Fillmore, and Franklin Pierce.

P. T. Barnum

Like Frances Trollope (see "A Place in Time") but on a grander scale, P. T. Barnum understood how to turn the antebellum public's craving for entertainment into a profitable business. As a young man in his native Bethel, Connecticut, Barnum savored popular journalism by starting a newspaper, the *Herald of Freedom*, that assailed wrongdoing in high places. Throughout his life, he thought of himself as a public benefactor and pointed to his profits as proof that he gave people what they wanted. Yet honesty was never his strong suit. As a small-town grocer in Connecticut, he regularly cheated his customers on the principle that they were trying to cheat him. Barnum, in short, was a hustler raised in the land of the Puritans, a cynic and an idealist rolled into one.

After moving to New York City in 1834, Barnum started a new career as an entrepreneur of popular entertainment. His first venture exhibited a black woman, Joice Heth, whom Barnum billed as the 169-year-old former slave nurse of George Washington. Barnum neither knew nor cared how old Joice was (in fact, she was probably around 80); it was enough that people would pay to see her. Strictly speaking, he cheated the public, but he knew that many of his customers shared his doubts about Joice's age. Determined to expose Barnum's gimmick, some poked her to see whether she was really a machine rather than a person. He was playing a game with the public, and the public with him.

In 1841 Barnum purchased a run-down museum in New York City, rechristened it the American Museum, and opened a new chapter in the history of popular entertainment. The founders of most earlier museums had intended an educational purpose. They exhibited stuffed birds and animals, specimens of rock, and portraits. Most of these museums, however, had languished for want of public interest. Barnum, in contrast, made piquing public curiosity the main goal. To attract people, he added collections of curiosities and faked exhibits. Visitors to the American Museum could see ventriloquists, magicians, albinos, a five-year-old midget whom Barnum named General Tom Thumb and later took on a tour of Europe, and the "Feejee Mermaid," a shrunken oddity that Barnum billed as "positively asserted by its owner to have been taken alive in the Feejee Islands." By 1850 the American Museum had become the best-known museum in the nation and a model for popular museums in other cities.

Blessed with a genius for publicity, Barnum recognized that newspapers could invent as well as report news. One of his favorite tactics was to puff his exhibits by writing letters (under various names) to newspapers, in which he would hint that the scientific world was agog over some astonishing curiosity of nature that the public could soon see for itself at the American Museum. But Barnum's success rested on more than publicity. A staunch temperance advocate, he provided regular lectures at the American Museum on the evils of alcohol and soon gave the place a reputation as a center for safe family amusement. Finally, Barnum tapped the public's insatiable curiosity about natural wonders. In 1835 the editor of the *New York Sun* had boosted his circulation by claiming that a famous astronomer had discovered pelicans and winged men on the moon. At a time when each passing year brought new technological wonders, the public was ready to believe in anything, even the Feejee Mermaid.

THE QUEST FOR NATIONALITY IN LITERATURE AND ART

Sentimental novels, melodramas, minstrel shows, and the American Museum belonged to the world of popular culture. All these genres lacked the dignity and originality that would endear them to those seeking cultural expressions that would reflect the American national spirit and command respect abroad. The limits of the popular genres—with their frequent crudity and their interchangeable plots, characters, and themes—did not escape the notice of reflective observers. During the 1830s Ralph Waldo Emerson emerged as the most influential spokesman for those who sought a national literature and art.

"Our day of dependence, our long apprenticeship to the learning of other lands, draws to a close," Emerson announced in his address "The American Scholar"

Frances Trollope Invents Popular Culture in Cincinnati

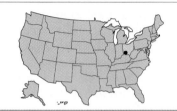

Words like *pioneer* and *frontier* still evoke images of a West of majestic forests and wide, rushing rivers, of buckskin-clad settlers and Indians in loincloths. But in fact, throughout the early–nineteenth-century westward migrations, cities were a colorful and vital part of the western fabric.

Located on the Ohio River in a vast agricultural basin that spread from Ohio to parts of Kentucky and Indiana, Cincinnati was positioned astride the major east-west and north-south trade routes, and its growth was nothing short of remarkable. A mere village of 750 inhabitants in 1788, it had become the West's leading city and the nation's ninth-largest city by 1820. By 1850 its industrial and commercial output was exceeded only by that of New York and Philadelphia.

Early Cincinnatians developed an edginess about criticism, to which they responded by crowning their city with one grand title after another: Queen of the West; Athens of the West; Wonder of the West; the Second Boston; and the Infant Hercules. Cincinnati's very success in attracting settlers aroused envy in the East, especially among journalists, who routinely disparaged it as a pestilence-ridden haven of roughnecks, devoid of culture and refinement.

Already sensitive to these insults, Cincinnati dwellers, especially its fledgling

Republicans at Theatre
Snoring or chatting their way through a performance of Shakespeare's Hamlet, *these Americans display the boorish manners that so annoyed Frances Trollope.*

high society of merchants, professionals, and their spouses, found more cause to complain with the publication in 1832 of Frances Trollope's *The Domestic Manners of the Americans.* This account of the British-born Trollope's four-year residence in America, including two in Cincinnati, made Cincinnati famous as a symbol of American crassness and materialism. Wealthy men there, she related, spent their time spitting, talking about the price of produce and hogs (a leading hog-packing center, Cincinnati acquired "Porkopolis" as another of its many nicknames), and spitting again. Excluded from all conversation about business or politics, the city's society ladies were ignored even by their husbands and passed their hours evaluating each other's dresses down to the last pin.

The Domestic Manners of the Americans would earn a small fortune for

Frances Trollope,
by Auguste Hervieu, c. 1832
With the publication of Domestic Manners of the Americans *at the age of fifty-three, Frances Trollope began a new life as a writer of novels and travel books. She made enough money to overcome the financial catastrophes that overtook her husband and to keep her family together, and she communicated her self-discipline to her son Anthony, who became a famous novelist. Not surprisingly, her fictional heroines were as strong and aggressive as she herself.*

Frances Trollope, and not a moment too soon. When she composed the book, she was in her early fifties, with four children and a husband in England who was on the verge of financial and nervous collapse. Accompanied by her son Henry and Henry's tutor, a French artist and political refugee named Auguste Hervieu, Trollope had arrived in Cincinnati in 1828 after a brief sojourn at Nashoba, an interracial utopian community in Tennessee. Nothing about her seemed quite right to Cincinnatians, who did not relish an intellectual woman, particularly one with utopian and abolitionist leanings and most especially a married woman who traveled without her husband but accompanied by a handsome Frenchman. But like the country boy P. T. Barnum in New York City, she was an outsider who recognized something that the locals missed: that urban resources could be marshaled to create new forms of popular entertainment.

Reasoning that Cincinnatians probably found the place as dull as she did and that they would pay to experience the weird and exotic, she soon grasped the commercial possibilities of one of the city's few cultural institutions, the Western Museum. Founded in 1819 to house western scientific collections, the museum had been sliding into financial ruin: Cincinnatians would not pay to look at stuffed birds and animal bones, even if western. Trollope and the museum's director, the French-born Joseph Dorfeuille, boldly conceived the idea of replacing the scientific exhibits with displays evoking mystery, dread, and romance.

With Hervieu's aid, she helped Dorfeuille to construct two such exhibits. The first, "The Invisible Girl," was housed in a room exotically decorated with wax figures drawn from characters in ancient Greek and Egyptian mythology. A mysterious voice rose from behind a machine-made cloud to answer questions (three to a customer) from the audience in a variety of known and unknown languages. The voice of this "Invisible Girl" was actually that of Trollope's son, Henry, who had studied Latin and Greek in England and who could fake or invent other languages. Most of the time the "girl" spoke gibberish, but customers considered her

a multilingual wonder. So successful was this show that the team of Trollope, Hervieu, and Dorfeuille quickly mounted another, "The Infernal Regions," a fancifully fearsome exhibit of hell with mechanical and wax figures depicting imps, snakes, demons, goblins, and the Evil One, and with the tension heightened by blackouts punctuated by "horrid groans" and "terrible shrieks." The view, one observer recorded, "is calculated to awaken serious but not unprofitable reflections." Such was the crush of visitors to the exhibit that an electrified fence had to be installed to deter them from touching the figures.

Trollope's next scheme was a "bazaar," a kind of nineteenth-century shopping mall rolled into a single building. Designed in the exotic Egyptian or "arabesque" style, the emporium boasted a coffeehouse, a bar, an art gallery, and sundry rooms devoted to selling jewelry, sculpture, and clothing. Unlike her other ventures, the bazaar failed dismally, partly because she ran out of (borrowed) money to construct it and partly because, in contrast to her silent partnership in the museum exhibits, her sponsorship of the bazaar was public knowledge. With additional backing someone else probably would have succeeded, for Trollope had grasped what Barnum would later discover: that there was a hungry market for popular culture as long as exhibits, whether mysterious or outlandish, were lifelike, made at least a pretense at edification, and did not remind Americans too much of America.

Trollope left the city after the collapse of her bazaar, sorry that she had ever entered it. But she had left her mark. Successful purveyors of popular culture not only in Cincinnati but also in the East would follow her formula. Painters, for example, found that, although Cincinnatians lacked interest in western landscapes, they would pay to see "panoramas." Popular artists accordingly painted football-field–long canvases that depicted such subjects as events in the life of Napoleon and that were gradually unrolled before their viewers. These "moving pictures" foreshadowed the newsreels of the twentieth century.

Compared to the paintings of the Hudson River school (see p. 357), popular art was notable for its lack of symbolism or abstraction. Popular cultural exhibits catered to their viewers' pretensions toward refinement by routinely drawing on classical, mythological, or European themes, but they also featured an obsession with the "authentic" and the lifelike that gave customers the feeling that they were part of the scene itself.

The Bazaar
Detractor's called it Trollope's Folly, but with its arabesque windows, Egyptian columns, and Moorish dome, Frances Trollope's Bazaar was splendid relief from Cincinnati's monotony. Its plans called for a basement housing a barroom and coffee house, a main floor for the bazaar itself, and a top floor with a ballroom and arched mosaics in the style of the Alhambra in Spain.

(1837). For too long, Emerson affirmed, Americans had deferred to European precedents in literature and learning. Now the time had come for the American people to trust themselves. Let "the single man plant himself indomitably on his instincts and there abide," and "the huge world will come round to him."

Contemporaries proclaimed "The American Scholar" an intellectual Declaration of Independence and praised Emerson for having "cut the cable" that still moored the United States to European thought. Yet Emerson's plea for cultural autonomy was hardly new; ever since the Revolution, Americans had been calling for cultural as well as political independence from Britain. In the 1780s Noah Webster, the famous compiler of textbooks and dictionaries that substituted phonetic American spellings for British spellings, had warned that basing American literature on European taste and manners was as foolish as constructing "a durable and stately edifice . . . upon the mouldering pillars of antiquity."

"The American Scholar" had an electrifying effect for several reasons. First, as Emerson recognized, the democratic spirit of the age had made Americans more self-reliant. Successful in their political and material lives, they no longer felt the need to defer to European standards. In addition, the dramatic impact of Emerson's address reflected his ability to adapt an international literary movement known as romanticism to American conditions. Originating in Europe in the second half of the eighteenth century, romanticism challenged the rival impulse known as classicism (or neoclassicism). Classicists described standards of beauty and taste as universal and decreed that the most desirable literary productions display elegance and polish. In contrast, romantics argued that each nation had to discover its own unique literary genius. They further insisted that great literature reflect not only national character but also the most profound emotions of the writer. Where classicists expected that all fine literature and art would conform to an identical standard of elegance, romantics sought individuality in literary and artistic expression.

As we have seen, during the 1830s the transcendentalist movement emerged as a challenge to Unitarianism, and in their literary work, Emerson and other transcendentalists evolved a uniquely American form of romanticism. Dismissing the prevailing idea that all knowledge came through the senses, transcendentalists argued instead that such basic conceptions as those of God and freedom were inborn. Knowledge re-

sembled sight—an instantaneous, direct perception of truth. Emerson concluded that learned people enjoyed no special advantages in the pursuit of truth. All persons could see the truth if only they would trust the promptings of their hearts. Applied to the United States, transcendentalist doctrine led to the exhilarating conclusion that a young, democratic society could produce as noble a literature and art as the more traditional societies of Europe. Although such a fledgling, democratic society might lack elegance and polish, it could draw upon the inexhaustible resources of the common people.

Literary Geography

Emerson's "The American Scholar" coincided with a flowering of distinctively American literature and art, often called the American Renaissance, that had been gaining momentum since the 1820s. By 1837 the American public had grown as familiar with native-born authors such as Washington Irving and James Fenimore Cooper as with such lions of the British literary world as Sir Walter Scott and Charles Dickens. Emerson did not initiate this outpouring of native talent, but he expressed its ideals and helped shape its direction.

Of all the regions of the United States, New England had the most fertile soil for literature. Its poets ranged from the urbane Henry Wadsworth Longfellow and polished Boston aristocrats like Oliver Wendell Holmes, Sr., and James Russell Lowell to the farm-born, self-taught Quaker John Greenleaf Whittier. Boston also became the home of George Bancroft, William Hickling Prescott, Francis Parkman, and John Lothrop Motley, the four most distinguished historians of the antebellum period. Twenty miles from Boston lay Concord, the home of Emerson, Nathaniel Hawthorne, the eccentric Henry David Thoreau, and the brilliant philosopher and critic Margaret Fuller. Not far from Concord lay Fruitlands, a utopian community where Louisa May Alcott, the author of *Little Women* (1868), passed part of her childhood under the sometimes dizzying influence of her unworldly father, Bronson Alcott. Farther to the west was Amherst, the residence of Emily Dickinson. Shy and reclusive, she lived out her entire fifty-six years on the same street ("I do not go from home," she stated with characteristic pithiness), where she wrote exquisite poems that examined, in her own words, every splinter in the groove of the brain. Dreading the corruption of her art

Louisa May Alcott, c. 1858
Raised in bleak if genteel poverty, Louisa May Alcott first gained recognition for her sketches of her experiences as a nurse in a military hospital during the Civil War. The publication of Little Women, *her largely autobiographical novel of New England family life, brought her fame and enough money to support herself and her sisters.*

by commercialism, she staunchly refused to publish her verse.

Most New Englanders did not share Emily Dickinson's horror of publicity. Nineteenth-century New England writers and publishers widely exported their region's culture. By the end of the century, schoolchildren throughout the nation were turning pages of Longfellow's *Evangeline* (1847) and *The Song of Hiawatha* (1855), Whittier's *Snow-Bound* (1866), and Lowell's antislavery *The Biglow Papers* (1848). What had begun as a regional culture became enshrined as a national culture, and for this reason alone, New England's literary renaissance deserves special recognition.

New England, however, always faced a challenge from New York, the home of Irving, Cooper, and later of Walt Whitman and Herman Melville. Even before

the flowering of American literature, New York had abounded with literary clubs, composed for the most part of wealthy young lawyers and merchants. It was in New York that the wealthy and gifted Irving had made his reputation with the publication of the comedic *Diedrich Knickerbocker's A History of New York* (1809). After serving in the War of 1812, Irving had left the United States for Europe and had not returned until 1832. Yet his *Sketch Book* (1820), which contained "Rip Van Winkle" and "The Legend of Sleepy Hollow," continued to endear him to Americans, who displayed a boastful pride in the literary accomplishments of their best-known writer.

The literary flowering affected all regions. Southerners such as William Gilmore Simms, the author of *The Yemassee* (1835), acquired reputations that spread beyond their native section. Although he did most of his writing in New York and Philadelphia, Edgar Allan Poe was a Virginian by upbringing and emotional identification. In the lower and westerly regions of the Old South, Augustus B. Longstreet and Johnson J. Hooper crafted humorous sketches that captured a kind of backcountry roguishness and rowdiness so extravagant that it became hilarious. Longstreet's *Georgia Scenes* (1835) described gander pulling, eye gouging, and other frontier pastimes. Hooper's *Some Adventures of Captain Simon Suggs* (1846) related how Suggs cheated his own father at cards to obtain a horse and how he went to a camp meeting to get religion and came away with the contents of the collection box instead.

Not all antebellum writers, however, have passed the test of time. Irving's writings now strike critics as examples of a comfortable second-ratedness. Although polished poets, neither Longfellow nor Whittier was notably innovative. Dickinson was a genius, but although born in 1830, she did most of her writing after 1860. In retrospect, regional humorists like Longstreet and Hooper are significant mainly because they foreshadowed a far greater humorist, Mark Twain.

Yet within the large circle of antebellum writers, the genius of seven individuals continues to shine: Cooper, Emerson, Thoreau, Whitman, Hawthorne, Melville, and Poe. Cooper and Emerson basked in public esteem in their day, but neither Hawthorne nor Poe gained the popular audience that each believed he deserved. The antebellum public largely ignored the remaining three—Thoreau, Whitman, and Melville. Creativity rather than popularity became the unifying characteristic of these seven writers. Each challenged existing literary conventions and created new ones. Cooper demonstrated the possibility of writing a novel using distinctively American literary themes. Emerson gave a new direction to an old literary form, the essay. Thoreau wrote about nature in a way that captured not only its beauty but its constant activity. By breaking with the conventions of rhyme and meter, Whitman breathed new vitality into poetry. As a writer of both short fiction and poetry, Poe went far to free literature from the insistence that it preach a moral and to establish the principle that fiction and poetry be judged by the pleasure that they imparted. Hawthorne and Melville turned the novel into a vehicle for exploring the depths of human psychology.

James Fenimore Cooper and the Stirrings of Literary Independence

Until well after 1800, British literature had dominated American literary taste. With the publication of *Waverley* (1814), a historical novel set in Britain in the 1740s, the star of Sir Walter Scott had begun its spectacular ascent on the American horizon. Americans had named more than a dozen towns Waverley; advertisements for subsequent novels by Scott had borne the simple caption, "By the author of *Waverley*."

Because he wrote historical novels under Scott's influence, James Fenimore Cooper, born in 1789, has often been called the American Scott. But this designation is misleading, for the enormously popular Cooper was remarkably creative in his own right. His most important innovation was to introduce the frontiersman Natty Bumppo ("Leatherstocking") as a fictional character. In *The Pioneers* (1823), Natty appears as an old man settled on the shores of Lake Otsego in upstate New York. Although Natty is a hunter, he blames the farmers for the wanton destruction of game and for turning the silent and majestic forests into deserts of tree stumps. As a spokesman for nature against the march of civilization, Natty immediately became a popular figure, and in subsequent novels such as *The Last of the Mohicans* (1826), *The Pathfinder* (1840), and *The Deerslayer* (1841), Cooper unfolded Natty's life for an appreciative reading public.

Cooper's success marked the first step in a process that saw Americans develop an imaginative literature of their own. They still read British novels, but they increasingly enjoyed American writers. In 1800

American authors accounted for a negligible proportion of the output of American publishers. By 1830, 40 percent of the books published in the United States were written by Americans; and by 1850, 75 percent.

Emerson, Thoreau, and Whitman

Emerson's advocacy of a national literature extended beyond his urgings in "The American Scholar." In writings of his own, he tried (not always successfully) to capture the brisk language of the common people of the United States. Furthermore, he encouraged younger American writers like Thoreau and Whitman. Whitman, extravagantly patriotic, contrasted sharply with Emerson and Thoreau, who often criticized the materialism and aggressiveness of their compatriots. The ideal of nationality in literature clearly did not always mean the uncritical celebration of Americans and American policies. But the uniquely American prose or poetry that flowed from the pens of these three writers did share a strong common feature: it emphasized the spontaneous and vivid expression of personal feelings over learned analysis, which the writers associated with European traditions.

Born in 1803, Emerson served briefly as a Unitarian minister. During the 1830s he carved out a new career for himself as a public lecturer. The topics of his addresses, most of which he published as essays, appeared to be broad and general: "Beauty," "Nature," "Power," "Representative Men," and "New England Reformers." But a unique pungency and vividness characterized his language. For example, in "The American Scholar," in which Emerson emphasized the importance of independent thought on the part of the true scholar, his language was striking: "Let him [the scholar] not quit his belief that a popgun is a popgun, though the ancient and honorable of the earth affirm it to be the crack of doom." Equally remarkable was Emerson's way of developing his subjects. A contemporary compared listening to Emerson to trying to see the sun in a fog; one could see light but never the sun itself. As a transcendentalist who believed that knowledge reflected the voice of God within every person and that truth was inborn and universal, Emerson never amassed evidence or presented systematic arguments to prove his contentions. Rather, he relied on a sequence of vivid and arresting though often unconnected assertions. The argument was hard to follow (one listener thought she might have better understood Emerson if she had stood on her head), but the overall effect dazzled the audience.

Emerson had a magnetic attraction for intellectually inclined young men and women who did not fit easily into American society. Henry David Thoreau, born in 1817 in Concord, Massachusetts, where Emerson took up residence during the 1830s, was representative of the younger Emersonians. Yet a crucial difference separated the two men. Adventurous in thought, Emerson was basically unadventurous in action. As contemplative as Emerson, Thoreau was more of a doer. At one point, Thoreau went to jail rather than pay his poll tax. This revenue, he knew, would support the war against Mexico, which he viewed as part of a southern conspiracy to extend slavery. The experience led Thoreau to write *Civil Disobedience* (1849), in which he defended the right to disobey unjust laws.

In the spring of 1845, Thoreau moved a few miles from Concord into the woods near Walden Pond. There he constructed a simple cabin on land owned by Emerson and spent the next two years providing for his wants away from civilization. Thoreau's stated purpose in retreating to Walden was to write a description (later published) of a canoe trip that he and his brother had taken down the Concord and Merrimack rivers in 1839. During his stay in the woods, however, he conceived and wrote a much more important book, *Walden* (1854). A contemporary described *Walden* as "the logbook of his woodland cruise," and indeed, Thoreau filled its pages with descriptions of hawks and wild pigeons, his invention of raisin bread, his trapping of the woodchucks that despoiled his vegetable garden, and his construction of a cabin for exactly $28.50. Few writers have matched Thoreau's ability to capture both the details and the cycles of nature and to give the reader the sensation of being present at the scene. But true to transcendentalism, Thoreau had a larger message. His woodland retreat taught him that he (and by implication, others) could satisfy material wants with only a few weeks' work each year and thereby leave more time for reexamining life's purpose. The problem with Americans, he said, was that they turned themselves into "mere machines" to acquire wealth without asking why. Thoreau bore the uncomfortable truth that material and moral progress were not as intimately related as Americans liked to think.

One of Ralph Waldo Emerson's qualities was an ability to sympathize with such dissimilar personalities

Walt Whitman
Whitman is today considered one of the major nineteenth-century poets, but in his day many derided his verse as indecent. In 1865 Whitman lost his job with the U.S. government when his superiors found out that he was the author of Leaves of Grass.

as Thoreau and Walt Whitman—the former eccentric, reclusive, and critical; the latter self-taught, outgoing, exuberant, and in love with virtually everything about America except slavery. Born in 1819, Whitman left school at eleven and became a printer's apprentice and later a journalist and editor for various newspapers in Brooklyn, Manhattan, and New Orleans. A familiar figure at Democratic party functions, he marched in the vanguard of party parades and put his pen to the service of the party's free-soil wing.

Journalism gave Whitman an intimate knowledge of ordinary Americans; the more he knew them, the more he liked them. His reading of Emerson nurtured his belief that America was to be the cradle of a new citizen in whom natural virtue would flourish unimpeded by European corruption, a man like Andrew Jackson, that "massive, yet most sweet and plain character." The threads of Whitman's early career came together in his major work, *Leaves of Grass*, a book of poems first published in 1855 and reissued with additions in subsequent years.

Leaves of Grass shattered most existing poetic conventions. Not only did Whitman write in free verse (that is, most of his poems had neither rhyme nor meter), but the poems were also lusty and blunt at a time when delicacy reigned in the literary world. Whitman wrote of "the scent of these armpits finer than prayer" and "winds whose soft-tickling genitals rub against me." No less remarkably, Whitman intruded himself into his poems, one of which he titled "Song of Walt Whitman" (and later retitled "Song of Myself"). Although Whitman thought well of himself, it was not egotism that propelled him to sing of himself. Rather, he viewed himself—crude, plain, self-taught, and passionately democratic—as the personification of the American people. He was

> Comrade of raftsmen and coalmen, comrade
>   of all who shake hands and welcome to
>   drink and meat,
> A learner with the simplest, a teacher of the
>   thoughtfullest.

By 1860 Whitman had acquired a considerable reputation as a poet. Nevertheless, the original edition of *Leaves* (a run of only about eight hundred copies) was ignored or derided as a "heterogeneous mass of bombast, egotism, vulgarity, and nonsense." One reviewer suggested that it was the work of an escaped lunatic. Only Emerson and a few others reacted enthusiastically. Within two weeks of publication, Emerson, never having met Whitman, wrote: "I find it the most extraordinary piece of wit and wisdom that America has yet contributed." Emerson had long called for the appearance of "the poet of America" and knew in a flash that in Whitman, that poet had arrived.

Hawthorne, Melville, and Poe

In "The American Scholar," Emerson called upon American writers to create a democratic literature by comprehending "the near, the low, the common"—the everyday experiences of ordinary Americans. However exhilarating a message, Emerson's plea had a negligible impact on the major writers of fiction during the 1840s and 1850s—Nathaniel Hawthorne, Herman Melville, and Edgar Allan Poe. Hawthorne, for example, set *The Scarlet Letter* (1850) in New England's Puritan past, *The House of the Seven Gables* (1851) in a mansion haunted not by ghosts but by memories of the past, and *The Marble Faun* (1859) in Rome. Poe set several of his short stories such as "The Murders in the Rue Morgue" (1841), "The Masque of the Red Death" (1842), and "The Cask of Amontillado" (1846) in Europe; as one critic has noted, "His art could have been produced as easily had he been born in Europe." Melville did draw materials and themes from his own experiences as a sailor and from the lore of the New England whaling industry, but for his novels *Typee* (1846), *Omoo* (1847), and *Mardi* (1849), he picked the exotic setting of islands in the South Seas; and for his masterpiece *Moby-Dick* (1851), the ill-fated whaler *Pequod*. If the only surviving documents from the 1840s and 1850s were its major novels, historians would face an impossible task in describing the appearance of antebellum American society.

The unusual settings favored by these three writers partly reflected their view that American life lacked the materials for great fiction. Hawthorne, for example, bemoaned the difficulty of writing about a country "where there is no shadow, no antiquity, no mystery, no picturesque and gloomy wrong, nor anything but a commonplace prosperity in broad and simple daylight, as is happily the case with my dear native land." In addition, psychology rather than society riveted the attention of these three writers; each probed the depths of the human mind rather than the intricacies of social relationships. Their preoccupation with analyzing the mental states of their characters grew out of their underlying pessimism about the human condition. Emerson, Whitman, and (to a degree) Thoreau optimistically believed that human conflicts could be resolved if only individuals followed the promptings of their better selves. In contrast, Hawthorne, Melville, and Poe saw individuals as bundles of conflicting forces that, even with the best intentions, might never be reconciled.

Their pessimism led them to create characters obsessed by pride, guilt, a desire for revenge, or a quest for perfection and then to set their stories along the byways of society, where they would be free to explore the complexities of human motivation without the jarring intrusion of everyday life. For example, in *The Scarlet Letter* Hawthorne turned to the Puritan past in order to examine the psychological and moral consequences of the adultery committed by Hester Prynne and the minister Arthur Dimmesdale. So completely did Hawthorne focus on the moral dilemmas of his central characters that he conveyed little sense of the social life of the Puritan village in which the novel is set. Melville, who dedicated *Moby-Dick* to Hawthorne, shared the latter's pessimism. In the novel's Captain Ahab, Melville created a frightening character whose relentless and futile pursuit of the white whale fails to fill the chasm in his soul and brings death to all of his mates save the narrator, Ishmael. Poe also channeled his pessimism into creative achievements of the first rank. In perhaps his finest short story, "The Fall of the House of Usher" (1839), he demonstrated an uncanny ability to weave the symbol of a crumbling mansion with the mental agony of a crumbling family.

Hawthorne, Melville, and Poe did not heed Emerson's call to write about the everyday experiences of their fellow Americans. Nor did they follow Cooper's lead by creating distinctively American heroes. Yet each contributed to an indisputably American literature. Ironically, their conviction that the lives of ordinary Americans provided inadequate materials for fiction led them to create a uniquely American fiction, one marked less by the description of the complex social relationships of ordinary life than by the analysis of moral dilemmas and psychological states. In this way, they unintentionally fulfilled a prediction made by Alexis de Tocqueville that writers in democratic nations, while rejecting many of the traditional sources of fiction, would explore the abstract and universal questions of human nature.

American Landscape Painting

American painters also sought to develop nationality in art between 1820 and 1860. Lacking a mythic past of the sort represented by the gods and goddesses of the ancient world that Europeans called upon, Americans subordinated history and figure painting to landscape painting. Yet just as Hawthorne had complained about the flat, commonplace character of American society, the painters of the Hudson River school recognized that the American landscape lacked the European landscape's "poetry of decay" in the form of ruined castles and crumbling temples. Like everything else in the United States, the landscape was fresh, relatively unencumbered by the human imprint. This fact posed a challenge to the Hudson River school painters.

The Hudson River school flourished from the 1820s to the 1870s. Numbering more than fifty painters, it is best represented by Thomas Cole, Asher Durand, and Frederic Church. All three men painted scenes of the region around the Hudson River, a waterway that Americans compared in majesty to the Rhine. But none was exclusively a landscapist. Some of Cole's most popular paintings were allegories, including *The Course of Empire*, a sequence of five canvases depicting the rise and fall of an ancient city and clearly implying that luxury doomed republican virtue. Nor did these artists paint only the Hudson. Church, a student of Cole and internationally the best known of the three, painted the Andes Mountains during an extended trip to South America in 1853. After the Civil War, the German-born Albert Bierstedt applied many Hudson River school techniques in his monumental canvases of the Rocky Mountains.

The works of Washington Irving and the opening of the Erie Canal had sparked artistic interest in the Hudson during the 1820s. After 1830 the writings of Emerson and Thoreau popularized a new view of nature. Intent on cultivating land, the pioneers of Kentucky and Ohio had deforested a vast area. One traveler complained that Americans would rather view a wheat field or a cabbage patch than a virgin forest. But Emerson, Thoreau, and landscape architects like Frederick Law Olmsted glorified nature; "in wildness is the preservation of the world," Thoreau wrote. Their outlook blended with growing popular fears that, as one contemporary expressed it in 1847, "The axe of civilization is busy with our old forests." As the "wild and picturesque haunts of the Red Man" became "the abodes of commerce and the seats of civilization," he concluded, "it behooves our artists to rescue from its grasp the little that is left before it is too late."

The Hudson River painters wanted to do more than preserve a passing wilderness. Their special contribution to American art was to emphasize emotional effect over accuracy. Cole's use of rich coloring, billowing clouds, massive gnarled trees, towering peaks, and deep chasms so heightened the dramatic impact of his paintings that the poet and editor William Cullen Bryant compared them to "acts of religion." Similar motifs marked Church's paintings of the Andes Mountains, which used erupting volcanoes and thunderstorms to evoke dread and a sense of majesty. Lacking the ruined castles and crumbling temples that dotted European landscapes, the Americans strove to capture the natural grandeur of their own landscape.

Like Cole, the painter George Catlin also tried to preserve a vanishing America. Observing a delegation of Indians passing through Philadelphia in 1824, Catlin

Rainmaking Among the Mandan, 1837–1839

**The Author Painting a Chief at
the Base of the Rocky Mountains, 1850**

Tchow-ee-put-o-kaw, 1834

*George Catlin's paintings preserved the faces, customs, and habitats of the Indian
tribes whose civilization was collapsing in the face of white advance.*

resolved on his life's work: to paint as many Native Americans as possible in their pure and "savage" state. Journeying up the Missouri River in 1832, he sketched at a feverish pace, and in 1837 he first exhibited his "Indian gallery" of 437 oil paintings and thousands of sketches of faces and customs from nearly fifty tribes.

Catlin's Indian paintings made him famous, but his romantic view of Indians as noble savages ("the Indian mind is a beautiful blank") was a double-edged sword. Catlin's admirers delighted in his portrayals of dignified Indians but shared his view that such noble creatures were "doomed" to oblivion by the march of progress.

While painters sought to preserve a passing America on canvas, landscape architects aimed at creating little enclaves of nature that might serve as sources of spiritual refreshment to harried city dwellers. Starting with the opening of Mount Auburn Cemetery near Boston in 1831, "rural" cemeteries with pastoral names such as "Harmony Grove" and "Greenwood" sprang up near major cities and quickly became tourist attractions, so much so that one orator described them as designed for the living rather than the dead. In 1858 New York City chose a plan drawn by Frederick Law Olmsted and Calvert Vaux for its proposed Central Park. Olmsted (who became the park's chief architect) and Vaux wanted the park to look as much like the countryside as possible, showing nothing of the surrounding city. A bordering line of trees screened out buildings, drainage pipes were dug to create lakes, and four sunken thoroughfares were cut across the park to carry traffic. The effect was to make Central Park an idealized version of nature, "picturesque" in that it would remind visitors of the landscapes that they had seen in pictures. Thus nature was made to mirror art.

The "Diffusion" of Knowledge

Just as Emerson contended that the democratizing spirit of his age would encourage Americans to discover their cultural identity, many of his contemporaries argued that in a democratic society, the educated had a duty to "diffuse" or spread enlightenment among the common people. Some hoped that inexpensive books and magazines would automatically bring fine literature to the masses. Reflecting on the declining cost of printed material, a clergyman concluded in 1841 that "genius sends its light into cottages." Many others, however, feared that the public would prefer the sensational penny-press fiction and the predictable sentimental novels to more elevating intellectual fare, and they pointed to the need for organized efforts to instruct and uplift American minds.

Advocates of systematic popular instruction turned not only to the public schools but also to lyceum lectures to popularize knowledge. The brainchild during the 1820s of Josiah Holbrook, an eccentric Connecticut inventor and educator, lyceums were essentially local organizations that sponsored public lectures. The topics and audiences of these lectures were diverse. In the winter of 1851–1852, for example, the lyceum in Belfast, Maine, sponsored lectures on astronomy, biology, physiology, geology, conversation, reading, the cultivation of memory, popular illusions concerning the Middle Ages, Iceland, the equality of the human condition, the true mission of women, and the domestic life of the Turks. Audiences usually included professional men, merchants, farmers, artisans, and a large number of middle-class women.

The lecturers were also a diverse lot. Prior to 1840 most were well-known locals who wished to show off their learning before admiring neighbors. But between 1840 and 1860, the spread of railroads contributed to the creation of a group of nationally known lecturers, a virtual road show of the American Renaissance. Emerson, for example, delivered some sixty lectures in Ohio alone between 1850 and 1867. Known in the 1830s as a radical and eccentric Yankee philosopher, he acquired a reputation throughout the North as a venerable sage by 1860. Another popular lecturer, the poet and world traveler Bayard Taylor, enthralled audiences everywhere with his descriptions of Arabia, Greece, Russia, and Japan. Taylor's frequent appearances in the garb of a cossack or an Arab (complete with scimitar) only heightened the effect. Tickets to lectures sold for as little as twelve cents, but so large were the crowds (up to two thousand) that some literary figures could command the then astounding fee of $125 per lecture. Most lecturers were content with more modest rewards; one stalwart of the lyceum circuit claimed that he did it for "F.A.M.E.—Fifty and My Expenses." Herman Melville, no more popular as a lecturer than as a novelist, pledged, "If they will pay expenses and give a reasonable fee, I am ready to lecture in Labrador or on the Isle of Desolation off Patagonia."

Railroads, the spread of public education, and lower costs for newspapers and books helped bring audiences and lecturers together. Newspapers, for example, announced the comings and goings of lecturers. Bayard Taylor began to receive invitations to lecture only after the public had read his published accounts of his travels. Originating in New England, lyceums expanded quickly across the northern states and made inroads into the South.

The spread of lyceums revealed a broad popular hunger for knowledge and refinement. By 1840 thirty-five hundred towns had lyceums. Yet 1840 was also the year of the log-cabin campaign, which blasted Martin Van Buren for displays of refinement as fully as Andrew Jackson's supporters had earlier gouged John Quincy Adams for being a man of learning. Americans clearly were of two minds on the subject of learning.

This ambivalence toward refined knowledge was nowhere sharper than in the West. Westerners often prided themselves on their rough ways. Western almanacs sprinkled stories of Davy Crockett and other unlettered western heroes among their weather predictions and planting advice, and some western writers fiercely resisted cultural penetration from the East. Yet the West was filled with eastern missionaries who were eager to dispel the notion that westerners were crude backwoods folk and who cultivated learning as well as Protestantism by building scores of colleges, academies, and lyceum halls. In 1800 there was only one college in what is now the Midwest; by 1850 there were nearly seventy, more than in any other region. "They drive schools along with them, as shepherds drive their flocks," clergyman Henry Ward Beecher observed of westerners. "They have herds of churches, academies, lyceums, and their religious and educational institutions go lowing along the western plains, as Jacob's herd lowed along the Syrian hills." Western newspapers sometimes railed at transplanted easterners for "namby-pamby, uptownish" lyceum lectures, but audiences still flocked to listen to emissaries of eastern refinement.

The movement to popularize knowledge bridged the cultural gap between classes but never closed it. Furthermore, the popularization of culture carried a hidden price tag. In bringing learning and art to the masses, creative thinkers had to soften their ideas. Lyceum lecturers, for example, usually avoided controversy. Even Emerson, whose early pronouncements on religion were extremely controversial, learned to pull his punches on the lyceum circuit. Although his epigrammatic style of presenting his ideas made him eminently quotable, his vagueness made it possible to quote him on both sides of most issues.

CONCLUSION

Hailed as progressive and democratic, technological advances transformed the lives of millions of Americans between 1840 and 1860. The introduction of the mechanical reaper increased wheat production and substantiated a federal official's contention in 1860 that "the ratio of increase of the principal agricultural products of the United States had more than kept pace with the increase of population." The gradual introduction of steam power reduced the vulnerability of factories to the vagaries of the weather, stretched out the employment season, and increased both productivity and annual income. The widespread introduction of coal-burning stoves not only warmed houses but, in conjunction with the spread of railroads, brought greater variety to the American diet. Technology also left an enduring mark on leisure pursuits. By bringing down the cost of printing, technical advances stimulated the rise of the penny press and the inexpensive novel, vastly increased the size of the reading public, and encouraged efforts to popularize knowledge.

Even dissenters usually directed their fire at technology's effects rather than at technology itself. Sylvester Graham wanted Americans to return to simpler lives, but he understood that vegetarianism depended on railroads to bring fresh produce into cities. The bright possibilities rather than the dark potential of technology impressed most antebellum Americans. Yet technology scarcely obliterated class and ethnic differences, nor did it quiet sectional strife. Even as the penny press and the telegraph spread throughout the nation, Americans were finding that speedier communication could not bridge their differences over slavery.

CHRONOLOGY

1820 Washington Irving, *The Sketch Book*.

Washington Irving

1823 Philadelphia completes the first urban water-supply system.

James Fenimore Cooper, *The Pioneers*.

1826 Josiah Holbrook introduces the idea for lyceums.

Cooper, *The Last of the Mohicans*.

1831 Mount Auburn Cemetery opens.

1832 A cholera epidemic strikes the United States.

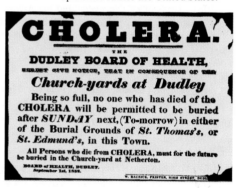

1833 The *New York Sun*, the first penny newspaper, is established.

1834 Cyrus McCormick patents the mechanical reaper.

1835 James Gordon Bennett establishes the *New York Herald*.

1837 Ralph Waldo Emerson, "The American Scholar."

1841 P. T. Barnum opens the American Museum.

1842 Edgar Allan Poe, "The Murders in the Rue Morgue."

1844 Samuel F. B. Morse patents the telegraph.

The American Art Union is established.

Poe, "The Raven."

1846 W. T. G. Morton successfully uses anesthesia.

1849 Second major cholera epidemic.

Astor Place theater riot leaves twenty dead.

1850 Nathaniel Hawthorne, *The Scarlet Letter*.

Nathaniel Hawthorne

1851 Hawthorne, *The House of the Seven Gables*.

Herman Melville, *Moby-Dick*.

Erie Railroad completes its line to the West.

1852 Pennsylvania Railroad completes its line between Philadelphia and Pittsburgh.

1853 Ten small railroads are consolidated into the New York Central Railroad.

1854 Henry David Thoreau, *Walden*.

1855 Walt Whitman, *Leaves of Grass*.

1856 Pennsylvania Railroad completes Chicago link.

Illinois Central completed between Chicago and Cairo, Illinois.

1857 Baltimore–St. Louis rail service completed.

1858 Frederick Law Olmsted is appointed architect in chief for Central Park.

Frederick Law Olmsted

FOR FURTHER READING

Carl Bode, *The Anatomy of American Popular Culture, 1840–1861* (1959). A useful general survey.

Mary Kupiec Cayton, *Emerson's Emergence: Self and Society in the Transformation of New England, 1800–1845* (1989). A sensitive interpretation of the major figure in the American Renaissance.

Ann Douglas, *The Feminization of American Culture* (1977). An analysis of the role of the middle-class women and liberal ministers in the cultural sphere during the nineteenth century.

Siegfried Giedion, *Mechanization Takes Command* (1948). An interpretive overview of the impact of technology on Europe and America.

Barbara Novak, *Nature and Culture: American Landscape Painting, 1825–1875* (1982). An insightful study of the relationships between landscape painting and contemporary religious and philosophical currents.

Gwendolyn Wright, *Building the Dream: A Social History of Housing in America* (1981). An exploration of the ideologies and policies that have shaped American housing since Puritan times.

ADDITIONAL BIBLIOGRAPHY

Technology, Progress, and the Standard of Living

Ruth Schwartz Cowan, *More Work for Mother: The Ironies of Household Technology from the Open Hearth to the Microwave* (1983); Durand Echeverria, *Mirage in the West: A History of the French Image of American Society to 1815* (1957); H. J. Habakkuk, *American and British Technology in the Nineteenth Century* (1962); Dolores Hayden, *The Grand Domestic Revolution: A History of Feminist Designs for American Homes, Neighborhoods, and Cities* (1981); David A. Hounshell, *From the American System to Mass Production, 1800–1932* (1984); John F. Kasson, *Civilizing the Machine: Technology and Republican Values in America, 1776–1900* (1976); Jack Larkin, *Reshaping Everyday Life, 1790–1849* (1988); Susan Strasser, *Never Done: A History of American Housework* (1983).

Railroads

Eugene Alvarez, *Travel on Southern Antebellum Railroads, 1828–1860* (1974); Alfred D. Chandler, *The Visible Hand: The Managerial Revolution in American Business* (1977); Stewart H. Holbrook, *The Story of American Railroads* (1947); Edward C. Kirkland, *Men, Cities and Transportation: A Study in New England History, 1820–1900* (1948); Robert J. Parks, *Democracy's Railroads: Public Enterprise in Michigan* (1972); John F. Stover, *American Railroads* (1961).

Disease and Health

John D. Davies, *Phrenology: Fad and Science* (1955); John S. Haller, Jr., *American Medicine in Transition, 1840–1910* (1981); Stephen Nissenbaum, *Sex, Diet, and Debility in Jacksonian America: Sylvester Graham and Health Reform* (1980); Martin S. Pernick, *A Calculus of Suffering: Pain, Professionalism, and Anesthesia in Nineteenth-Century America* (1985); Charles Rosenberg, *The Cholera Years: The United States in 1832, 1849, and 1866* (1962); Paul Starr, *The Social Transformation of American Medicine* (1982).

Popular Culture

Richard D. Brown, *Knowledge Is Power: The Diffusion of Information in Early America, 1700–1865* (1989); Daniel A. Cohen, *Pillars of Salt, Monuments of Grace: New England Crime Literature and the Origins of American Popular Culture, 1674–1860* (1993); Ann Fabian, *Card Sharps, Dream Books, and Bucket Shops: Gambling in 19th-Century America* (1990); David Grimsted, *Melodrama Unveiled: American Theater and Culture, 1800–1850* (1968); Karen Halttunen, *Confidence Men and Painted Women: A Study in Middle-Class Culture in America, 1830–1870* (1982); Neil Harris, *Humbug: The Art of P. T. Barnum* (1973); Dan Schiller, *Objectivity and the News: The Public and the Rise of Commercial Journalism* (1981); Michael Schudson, *Discovering the News: A Social History of American Newspapers* (1978); Donald Scott, "The Popular Lecture," *Journal of American History* 66 (March 1980): 791–809; Robert C. Toll, *Blacking Up: The Minstrel Show in Nineteenth-Century America* (1974); Ronald J. Zboray, *A Fictive People: Antebellum Economic Development and the American Reading Public* (1993).

Literature

Nina Baym, *Woman's Fiction: A Guide to Novels by and About Women in America, 1820–1870* (1978); Vincent Buranelli, *Edgar Allan Poe* (1977); Mary Kupiec Cayton, *Emerson's Emergence: Self and Society in the Transformation of New England, 1800–1845* (1989); William Charvat, *The Profession of Authorship in America, 1800–1870* (edited by Matthew J. Bruccoli, 1968); David Levin, *History as Romantic Art: Bancroft, Prescott, Motley, and Parkman* (1963); Kenneth S. Lynn, *Mark Twain and Southwestern Humor* (1972); Lucy Maddox, *Removals: Nineteenth-Century American Literature and the Politics of Indian Affairs* (1991); James Mellow, *Nathaniel Hawthorne in His Time* (1980); Benjamin T. Spencer, *The Quest for Nationality: An American Literary Campaign* (1957); Tony Tanner, *The Reign of Wonder: Naiveté and Reality in American Literature* (1965); Larzer Ziff, *Literary Democracy: The Declaration of Cultural Independence in America* (1981).

Visual Arts

Elizabeth Barlow, *Frederick Law Olmsted's New York* (1972); Thomas Bender, *Toward an Urban Vision: Ideas and Institutions in Nineteenth-Century America* (1975); Albert Fein, *Frederick Law Olmsted and the Environmental Tradition* (1972); Neil Harris, *The Artist in American Society: The Formative Years, 1790–1860* (1966); Lee Clark Mitchell, *Witness to a Vanishing America* (1981); Raymond J. O'Brien, *Landscape and Scenery of the Lower Hudson Valley* (1981); Nancy Rash, *The Painting and Politics of George Caleb Bingham* (1991); Laura Wood Roper, *FLO: A Biography of Frederick Law Olmsted* (1973); Bryan J. Wolf, *Romantic Re-Vision: Culture and Consciousness in Nineteenth-Century American Painting and Literature* (1982).

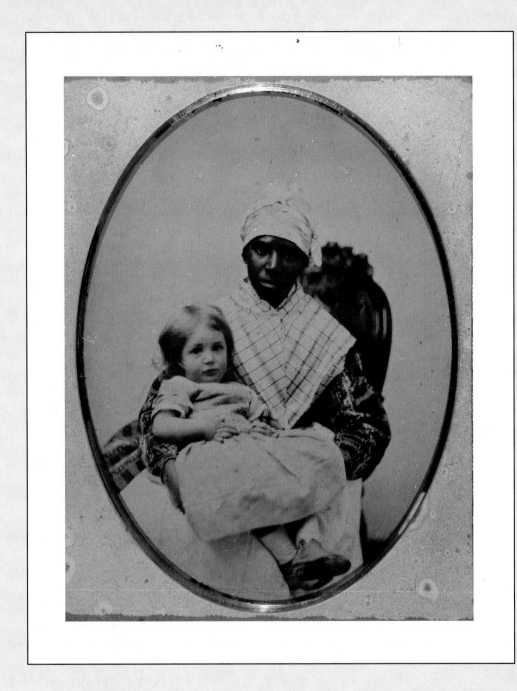

**Charlotte Helen
and Her Faithful Nurse, Lydia**
1857

THE OLD SOUTH AND SLAVERY
1800–1860

During the winter of 1831–1832, an intense debate over the future of slavery galvanized Virginians. A slave insurrection led by Nat Turner in August 1831 aroused new anxieties, particularly among the nonslave-holding whites in the western part of the state. "What is to be done?" an editorial writer in the *Richmond Enquirer* queried. "Oh my God, I don't know, but something must be done." Plans for a gradual emancipation of slaves, one of them advanced by Thomas Jefferson's grandson, leaped onto the state's political agenda. For a period, opponents of slavery held the initiative and protested against the institution with a fury that would have cheered antislavery northerners. Slavery, according to one Virginian, was "a mildew which has blighted in its course every region it has touched from the creation of the world." In the words of another, slavery "is ruinous to whites; retards improvements; roots out our industrious population; banishes the yeomanry from the country; and deprives the spinner, the weaver, the smith, the shoemaker, and the carpenter of employment and support." In the end, the advocates of emancipation were defeated, but only narrowly, and mainly because the state legislature was grossly malapportioned in favor of eastern slaveholders and against western nonslaveholders.

However narrow, the defeat of Virginia's emancipationists at the start of the 1830s marked a point of no return for the region known to history as the

Old South. The Old South gradually took shape between the 1790s and 1860. As late as the American Revolution, *south* referred more to a direction than to a place. But by the 1850s, southerners were publishing books with titles like *Sociology for the South* and *Social Relations in Our Southern States* that took for granted the South's separate regional identity. The distinctive feature of the Old South was that it condoned slavery at a time when the institution had come under attack everywhere else in the civilized world. In 1775 slavery had known no sectional boundaries in America. However, by 1800 nearly every northern state had either abolished slavery or adopted a plan for the gradual emancipation of slaves within its borders, and Congress banned the importation of slaves in 1808. Thereafter, opposition to slavery intensified, not only in the United States, but in Europe and South America. Without too much exaggeration, Senator James Buchanan of Pennsylvania proclaimed in 1842, "All Christendom is leagued against the South upon the question of domestic slavery."

Virginians' debate over slavery in 1831–1832 underscored the internal divisions within Virginia and the South as a whole. In every southern state, nonslaveholding farmers, or yeomen, composed a majority of the white population throughout the antebellum period. Furthermore, among the states that would secede and in 1861 form the Confederate

States of America, there was a basic distinction between the Upper South (Virginia, North Carolina, Tennessee, and Arkansas) and the Lower, or Deep, South (South Carolina, Georgia, Florida, Alabama, Mississippi, Louisiana, and Texas). Socially and economically, the Upper South relied far less than the Lower South on slavery and on cotton. With varied agricultural economies based on the raising of wheat, tobacco, hemp, vegetables, and livestock, the states of the Upper South in many ways resembled the free states of the North. Politically, the Upper South approached secession far more reluctantly than the Lower South.

For all its internal variety, however, the Old South possessed strong bonds of unity that derived from slavery. The defense of slavery gradually united white opinion in the South. After reaching a climax in Virginia in 1831–1832, southern white opposition to slavery steadily weakened, and most whites came to dread the thought of a general emancipation of slaves. In the final analysis, the Upper and Lower Souths were merely parts of a single Old South, because slavery gave southern society such a distinctive cast. Although reminded by daily contact with whites of the contempt in which their race was held, blacks could do little to escape bondage. Slavery scarred all social relationships in the Old South: between blacks and whites, among whites, and even among blacks. Without slavery there never would have been an Old South.

KING COTTON

The traditional cash crops of the South declined in the late eighteenth century. That old standby tobacco, a crop notorious for depleting soil nutrients, depended on foreign markets that were essentially undependable, especially after independence stripped American trade of British protection. Tidewater Virginia, once the center of tobacco production, had dwindled economically to a shadow of its former self. North Carolina, whose soil had been depleted by tobacco, so languished that contemporaries called it the Rip Van Winkle of the Union. Rice provided the coastal region of South Carolina with a major cash crop, but it could not be grown inland. Cotton growing was also confined to seaboard areas. Indeed, in 1790 the South's population was concentrated in states bordering on the Atlantic. Three out of every four southerners lived in Maryland, Virginia, North Carolina, and South Carolina, and one out of every three in Virginia alone.

The contrast between the South of 1790 and that of 1850 was stunning. By 1850 only one out of every seven white southerners lived in Virginia. One out of every three white southerners lived in seven flourishing states (Alabama, Arkansas, Florida, Louisiana, Mississippi, Missouri, and Texas) admitted to the Union after 1800. What transformed the stagnant South of 1800 into the dynamic and bustling South of 1850? The answer, in a word, is cotton. The growth of the British textile industry in the late eighteenth

Value of Cotton Exports as a Percentage of All U.S. Exports, 1800–1860
By 1840 cotton accounted for more than half of all U.S. exports.

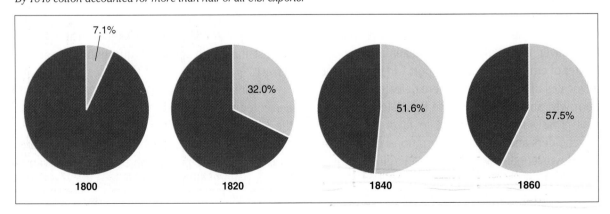

century had created a huge demand for cotton and provided a stimulus to the development of the cotton gin. The removal of the Indians (see Chapter 9) opened the way to the expansion of cotton production in new territories. Armed with cotton gins, settlers swept into Alabama and Mississippi after 1815. By 1860 Mississippi had become the leading cotton producer in the nation, and settlers had already pushed farther west, into east Texas. At its peak the cotton belt (or "Cotton Kingdom") stretched from South Carolina, Georgia, and northern Florida in the east through Alabama, Mississippi, central and western Tennessee, and Louisiana, and from there on to Arkansas and Texas.

The Lure of Cotton

To British traveler Basil Hall, it seemed that all southerners could talk about was cotton. "Every flow of wind from the shore wafted off the smell of that useful plant; at every dock or wharf we encountered it in huge piles or pyramids of bales, and our decks were soon choked with it. All day, and almost all night long, the captain, pilot, crew, and passengers were talking of nothing else." With its warm climate, wet springs and summers, and relatively dry autumns, the Lower South was especially suited to the cultivation of cotton. In contrast to the sugar industry, which thrived in southeastern Louisiana, cotton required neither expensive irrigation canals nor costly machinery. Sugar was a rich man's crop that demanded a considerable capital investment to grow and process. But cotton could be grown profitably on any scale. A cotton farmer did not even need to own a gin; commercial gins were available. Nor did a cotton farmer have to own slaves; in 1860, 35 percent to 50 percent of all farmers in the cotton belt owned no slaves. Cotton was profitable for anyone, even nonslaveholders, to grow; it promised to make poor men prosperous and rich men kings.

Although modest cotton cultivation did not require slaves, large-scale cotton growing and slavery grew together. As the southern slave population nearly doubled between 1810 and 1830, cotton employed three-fourths of all southern slaves. Owning slaves made it possible to harvest vast tracts of cotton speedily, a crucial advantage because a sudden rainstorm at harvest time could pelt cotton to the ground and soil it. Slaveholding also enabled planters to increase their cotton acreage and hence their profits.

Growth of Cotton Production and the Slave Population, 1790–1860

Cotton and slavery rose together in the Old South.

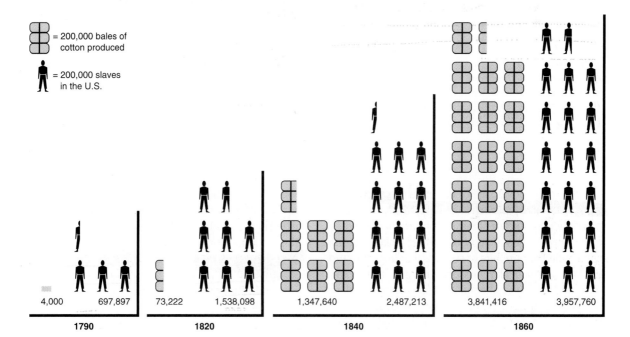

= 200,000 bales of cotton produced

= 200,000 slaves in the U.S.

1790	1820	1840	1860
4,000 — 697,897	73,222 — 1,538,098	1,347,640 — 2,487,213	3,841,416 — 3,957,760

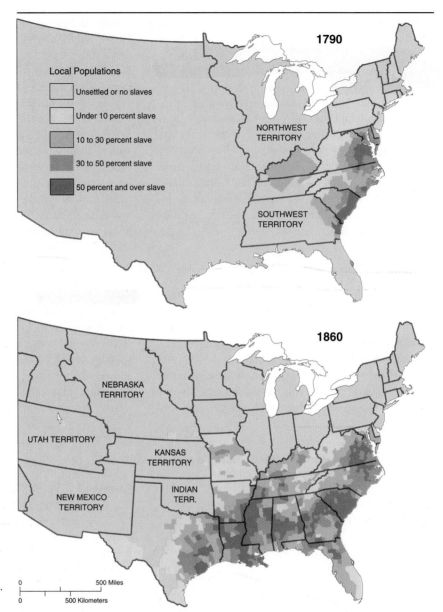

Distribution of Slaves, 1790 and 1860

In 1790 the majority of slaves resided along the southeastern seaboard. By 1860, however, slavery had spread throughout the South, and slaves were most heavily concentrated in the Deep South states.

SOURCE: Reprinted with permission of McGraw-Hill, Inc. from *Ordeal by Fire: The Civil War and Reconstruction* by James M. McPherson. Copyright 1982 by Alfred A. Knopf, Inc.

An added advantage of cotton lay in its compatibility with the production of corn. Corn could be planted earlier or later than cotton and harvested before or after. Since the cost of owning a slave was the same whether or not he or she was working, corn production enabled slaveholders to utilize slave labor when slaves were not employed on cotton. Nonslaveholding cotton growers also found it convenient to raise corn, and by 1860 the acreage devoted to corn in the Old South actually *exceeded* that devoted to cotton. Corn fed both families and the livestock that flourished in the South (in 1860 the region had two-thirds of the nation's hogs). From an economic standpoint, corn and cotton gave the South the best of both worlds. Fed by intense demands in Britain and New England, the price of cotton remained high, with the result that money flowed into the South. Because of southern self-sufficiency in growing corn and in raising

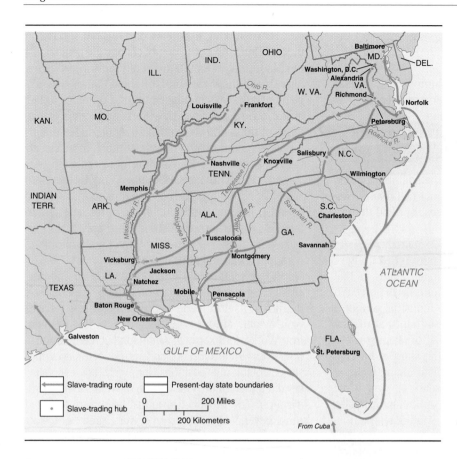

The Internal Slave Trade, 1810–1860

An internal slave trade developed after the slavetrade with Africa ended in 1808. With the growth of cotton production, farmers in the Upper South found it profitable to sell their slaves to planters in the Lower South.

hogs that thrived on the corn, money was not drained out of the region to pay for food produced in the North. In 1860 the twelve wealthiest counties in the United States were all in the South.

Ties Between the Lower and Upper South

Sugar and cotton were the main cash crops in the Lower South. The agriculture of the Upper South, founded on tobacco, hemp, wheat, and vegetables, depended far less than that of the Lower South on a few great cash crops. Yet the Upper South identified with the Lower South rather than with the agricultural regions of the free states. The reasons were social, political, and even psychological. Many settlers in states like Alabama and Mississippi had come from Upper South states like Virginia and North Carolina. All white southerners benefited from the three-fifths clause of the Constitution, which enabled them to count slaves as a basis for congressional representation. All southerners were stung by abolitionists' criti-

cisms of slavery, drawing no distinction between the Upper and Lower South. Importantly, too, economic ties linked the Upper and Lower South. The profitability of cotton and sugar in the Lower South increased the value of slaves throughout the South. Between 1790 and 1860, perhaps a million or more slaves were herded across state lines in the Old South. Roughly three-fourths of these slaves moved with their masters, whereas the remainder were sold as individuals. The sale of slaves from states with declining or stagnant plantation economies (Maryland, Virginia, and South Carolina) to those with booming economies (Alabama, Mississippi, Louisiana, Arkansas, and Texas) became a huge business. Arguing against a proposal for the gradual emancipation of slaves, Professor Thomas R. Dew of Virginia's College of William and Mary stated in 1832, "Virginia is, in fact, a *negro* raising State for other States; she produces enough for her own supply, and six thousand a year for sale." Without the sale of its slaves, Dew concluded, "Virginia will be a desert."

The North and South Diverge: Economic Patterns

The South had emerged from a slump in the last quarter of the eighteenth century to become a region of dynamic change between 1800 and 1860. But it had changed in ways that only widened the distance between it and the North. At a time when the North was rapidly urbanizing, the South remained predominantly rural. In 1820 the proportion of the southern population living in urban areas was about half that of New England and the mid-Atlantic states; by 1860 the proportion had dropped to a third.

One reason for the rural character of the South was that it contained very little industry. Although a third of the population of the United States in 1850 lived there, the South accounted for only 10 percent of the nation's manufacturing. The industrial output of the entire South in 1850 was less than that of New Hampshire and only one-third that of Massachusetts. Between 1840 and 1860, the South's share of the capital invested in American manufacturing actually *declined,* from 20 percent to 16 percent.

Yet the South had advocates of both industrialization and factories. A minority of southerners, among them editor J. D. B. De Bow of New Orleans, applauded industrialization as a way to revive the economies of older states such as Virginia and South Carolina, to retard migration to the Southwest, to reduce the South's dependency on northern manufactured products, and by proving that slavery had not transformed the South into a backwater, to quiet "the slanderous tongue of northern fanatics." Pleas for industrialization met with some success as a few large manufacturing companies took root. In South Carolina William Gregg, a prosperous Charleston jewelry merchant, zealously advocated industrialization after touring New England's textile mills in 1844. A year later, he started the Graniteville Manufacturing Company, which owned nine thousand spindles and three hundred looms by the late 1840s. Graniteville became a company town, with lumber mills, gristmills, and a machine shop as well as textile mills. In Richmond Joseph Reid Anderson guided the Tredegar Iron Works to success. By 1860 the Tredegar Works ranked fourth among the nation's largest producers of iron products, and during the Civil War, it contributed greatly to the Confederate cause. Farther southwest, Daniel Pratt constructed an industrial village near Montgomery, Alabama, in which he produced cotton textiles and ginned raw cotton.

These striking examples of industrial success in the Old South, however, do not change the general picture. Industrial output in the South ran somewhat behind that of the West and far behind that of New England and the Middle Atlantic states. Compared to factories in New England, New York, and Pennsylvania, those of the South were small; they produced mainly for nearby markets; and they were much more closely tied to agriculture. The leading northern industries turned hides into tanned leather and leather into shoes, or cotton into threads and threads into suits. In contrast, although the South had some textile and shoe factories, its leading industries were only a step removed from agriculture. They turned grain into flour, corn into meal, and trees into lumber.

If the South could develop some large and successful industries, why did it not develop more? Slavery did not in itself impede industrial growth, for slaves were widely employed in factories. In the Tredegar Iron Works, for example, Anderson overcame opposition from white workers and introduced slaves into skilled rolling-mill positions. Indirectly, however, slavery did undercut the enthusiasm of whites for industrialization. The prospect of industrial slavery troubled most slaveholders. Slaves who were hired out to factory masters in cities like New Orleans and Richmond could pass themselves off as free, and they often acted as if they were free by negotiating better working conditions and by shifting from factory to factory. The same objection applied to small rural workshops. Even rural factories drew slaves off the plantations, where discipline could be more easily enforced. A Virginia planter who rented his slaves to an iron manufacturer complained that they made money by working overtime and "got the habit of roaming about and *taking care of themselves.*"

White laborers, of course, could be employed in factories. William Gregg proved at Graniteville that supposedly unruly southern whites could be forged into a disciplined labor force. But any effort to introduce extensive industrialization faced a major problem: to raise capital for industrialization, planters would have had to sell their slaves. They had little incentive to do so. Cash crops like cotton and sugar were proven winners, whereas the benefits of industrialization remained remote and doubtful. Moreover, industrialization threatened to disrupt social relations, a southerner contended, by introducing "filthy, overcrowded, licentious factories" and by attracting antislavery white immigrants to the South. As long as southerners believed that an economy founded on

Port and City of New Orleans, *by Marie Adrien Persac, 1858*
The South's largest city, New Orleans was the main port of exit for cotton and Mississippi Valley produce. It was also a major entry port for immigrants, many of whom followed the Mississippi River north in order to avoid working in a slave society.

industrializing in South → risky

why would you change if you're already making a ton of money

cash crops would remain profitable, they had little reason to leap into the uncertainties of industrialization.

The North and South Diverge: Education in a Cotton Economy

Compared to the antebellum North, the Old South made only meager provisions for public elementary schools. Flurries of enthusiasm for public education periodically swept the South, but without much effect. Southerners flatly rejected the idea of compulsory education, which was gaining ground in the North by the 1850s, and they were reluctant to tax property to support education. The idea of educating slaves in any kind of school became increasingly abhorrent to southern legislatures; indeed, lawmakers made it a crime even to teach slaves to read. Some public aid flowed to state universities and to schools for white paupers, but for most whites, the only available schools were private. As a result, white illiteracy, which

had been more extensive in the South than in the North during the eighteenth century, remained high in the South even as it declined in the North during the antebellum period. For example, nearly 60 percent of the North Carolinians who enlisted in the United States Army before the Civil War were illiterate. The comparable proportion for northern enlistees was less than 30 percent.

Various factors help explain why the South lagged behind the North in the field of public education. Because the Lower South's economy relied so heavily on cotton, state revenues rose and fell with the price of cotton, and so did legislative enthusiasm for education. In addition, the South's low population density made it difficult to provide public schools for all children. The idea of having a public school within walking distance of each child was appealing until one realized just how far each child would have to walk. But a low population density did not stop midwestern states from energetically promoting public education. The most probable reason for the South's failure to develop effective public schools was widespread indifference to the idea.

As was true of southern arguments in favor of industrialization, pro-education proclamations were bountiful, but these issued from a small segment of the leadership and often fell on deaf ears. Agricultural, self-sufficient, and independent, the middling and poor whites of the South remained unconvinced of the need for public education. They had little dependency on the printed word, few complex commercial transactions, and infrequent dealings with urban people. Even the large planters, some of whom did support public education, had a less intense commitment to it than did northern manufacturers. Whereas many northern businessmen accepted Horace Mann's argument that public schools would create a more orderly and alert work force, planters had no need for an educated white work force, for they already had a black one that they were determined to keep illiterate lest it acquire through books ideas about freedom.

Cotton and Southern Progress

Because the South diverged so sharply from the North, it is tempting to view the South as backward and lethargic, doomed to be bypassed by the more energetic northern states. Increasingly, northerners associated the spread of cities and factories with progress. Finding few cities and factories in the South, they concluded that the region was a stranger to progress as well. A northern journalist wrote of white southerners in the 1850s: "They work little, and that little, badly; they earn little, they sell little; they buy little, and they have little—very little—of the common comforts and consolations of civilized life."

Yet the white South did not lack progressive features. In 1840 per capita income in the white South was only slightly below the national average, and by 1860 it exceeded the national average. Although it is true that southerners made few contributions to technology to rival those of northerners, many southerners had a progressive zeal for agricultural improvement. The Virginian Edmund Ruffin, who allegedly touched off the Civil War by firing the first cannon on Fort Sumter in 1861 and committed suicide in despair at the South's defeat in 1865, was an enthusiastic supporter of crop rotation and of the use of fertilizer and an important figure in the history of scientific agriculture.

Rather than viewing the Old South as economically backward, it is better to see it merely as different. Cotton was a wonderful crop, and southerners could

hardly be blamed for making it their ruler. "No! You dare not make war upon cotton; no power on earth dares to make war upon it," a senator from South Carolina proclaimed in 1858. "Cotton is king."

SOCIAL RELATIONS IN THE WHITE SOUTH

Antislavery northerners often charged that slavery twisted the entire social structure of the South out of shape. By creating a permanent black underclass of bond servants, they alleged, slavery robbed lower-class whites of the incentive to work, reduced them to shiftless misery, and rendered the South a premodern throwback in an otherwise progressive age. Stung by northern allegations that slavery turned the white South into a region of rich planters and poor common folk, southerners retorted that the real center of white inequality was the North, where merchants and financiers paraded in fine silks and never soiled their hands with manual labor.

In reality, the white South was a curious mix of aristocratic and democratic, premodern and modern features. Although it contained considerable class inequality, property ownership was widespread. Rich planters occupied seats in state legislatures out of proportion to their numbers in the population, but they did not necessarily get their way, nor did their political agenda always differ from that of other whites. Practices like slaveholding and dueling not only survived but intensified in the Old South at a time when they were dying out elsewhere in the civilized world. Visitors to the South sometimes thought that they were traveling backward in time. "It seems as if everything had stopped growing, and was growing backwards," novelist Harriet Beecher Stowe wrote of the South. Yet like northerners, white southerners were restless, acquisitive, eager to make money, skillful at managing complex commercial enterprises, and when they chose, capable of becoming successful industrialists.

The Social Groups of the White South

Although all agricultural regions of the South contained slaveholders and nonslaveholders, there was considerable diversity within each group. Some slaveholders in every southern state owned vast estates, magnificent homes, and hundreds of slaves, but most lived more modestly. In 1860 one-quarter of all white families in the South owned slaves. Of these, nearly half owned fewer than five slaves, and nearly three-quarters had fewer than ten slaves. Only 12 percent owned twenty or more slaves, and only 1 percent had a hundred or more. Large slaveholders clearly were a minority within a minority. Nonslaveholders also formed a diverse group. Most were landowners whose farms drew on the labor of family members, but the South also contained nonslaveholding whites who squatted on land in the so-called pine barrens or piney woods and who scratched out a livelihood by raising livestock, hunting and fishing, and planting a few acres of corn, oats, or sweet potatoes.

Despite all the diversity, one might reasonably divide the South's social structure into four main groups—the planters, the small slaveholders, the yeomen (or family farmers), and the people of the pine barrens—although even this classification is a little arbitrary. Historians usually classify as planters those who owned twenty or more slaves, the minimum number considered necessary for specialized plantation agriculture. Yet in any group of twenty slaves, some were likely to be too old and others too young to work. Arguably, a planter needed more than twenty slaves to run a plantation. Similarly, those with fewer than twenty slaves are usually described as small slaveholders, but an obvious difference separated an individual who owned ten to nineteen slaves and one who owned fewer than five. The former was close to becoming a planter; the latter was only a step removed from a yeomen. A great deal depended on where one lived. In the low country and delta regions of the South, the planters dominated; most small slaveholders in these areas had dealings with the planters and looked to them for leadership. In the hilly upland regions, the yeomen were dominant, and small slaveholders tended to acquire their outlook.

Of course, many lawyers, physicians, merchants, and artisans, who did not fall into any of these four main groups, also made the Old South their home. But because the South was fundamentally rural and agricultural, those outside of agriculture usually identified their interests with one or another of the four agricultural groups. Rural artisans and merchants had innumerable dealings with the yeoman. Urban merchants and lawyers depended on the planters and absorbed their outlook on most issues. Similarly, slave traders relied on the plantation economy for their livelihood.

Nathan Bedford Forrest, the uneducated son of a humble Tennessee blacksmith, made a fortune as a slave trader in Natchez, Mississippi. When the Civil War broke out, Forrest enlisted in the Confederate army as a private and rose swiftly to become the South's greatest cavalry general. "That devil Forrest," the Yankees called him. Plantation slavery directed Forrest's allegiances as surely as it did those of planters like Jefferson Davis, the Confederacy's president.

Planters and Plantation Mistresses

With porticoed mansion and fields teeming with slaves, the plantation still stands at the center of the popular image of the Old South. This romanticized view, reinforced by novels and motion pictures like *Gone with the Wind*, is not entirely misleading, for the South contained plantations that travelers found "superb beyond description." Whether devoted to cotton, tobacco, rice, or sugar, the plantations were characterized by a high degree of division of labor. In the 1850s Bellmead, a tobacco plantation on Virginia's James River, was virtually an agricultural equivalent of a factory village. Its more than one hundred slaves were classified into the domestic staff (butlers, waiters, seamstresses, laundresses, maids, and gardeners), the pasture staff (shepherds, cowherds, and hog drivers), outdoor artisans (stonemasons and carpenters), indoor artisans (blacksmiths, carpenters, shoemakers, spinners, and weavers), and field hands. Such a division of labor was inconceivable without abundant slaves and land. Wade Hampton's cotton plantation near Columbia, South Carolina, encompassed twenty-four hundred acres. With such resources, it is not surprising that large plantations could generate incomes that contemporaries viewed as immense ($20,000–$30,000 a year).

During the first flush of settlement in the piedmont and trans-Appalachian South, in the eighteenth century, most well-off planters had been content to live in simple log cabins. In contrast, between 1810 and 1860, elite planters often vied with each other to build stately mansions. Some, like Lyman Hardy of Mississippi, hired architects. Hardy's "Auburn," built in 1812 near Natchez, featured Ionic columns and a portico thirty-one feet long and twelve feet deep. Others copied designs from books like Andrew Jackson Downing's *The Architecture of Country Houses* (1850), which sold sixteen thousand copies between 1850 and 1865.

However impressive, these were not typical planters. The wealth of most planters, especially in

Colonel and Mrs. James A. Whiteside, Son Charles and Servants,
by James A. Cameron, c. 1858–1859
*This portrait captures the patriarchy as well as the graciousness that whites associated with
the ideal plantation. Not only the slave waiter and nurse but the planter's wife appear overshadowed by the master's presence.*

states like Alabama and Mississippi, consisted primarily
in the value of their slaves rather than in such finery as
expensive furniture or silver plate. In monetary terms,
slaves were worth a great deal, as much as seventeen
hundred dollars for a field hand in the 1850s. Planters
could convert their wealth into cash for purchasing luxuries only by selling slaves. A planter who sold his
slaves ceased to be a planter and relinquished the
South's most prestigious social status. Not surprisingly,
most planters clung to large-scale slaveholding, even if
it meant scrimping on their life-styles. A northern journalist observed that in the Southwest, men worth millions lived as if they were not worth hundreds.

Planters had to worry constantly about profitability, for the fixed costs of operating plantations—including hiring overseers, housing and feeding slaves, and
maintaining cotton gins and other equipment—were
considerable. Their drive for profits led planters to
search constantly for more and better land, to organize
their slaves into specialized work gangs for maximum
efficiency, and to make their plantations self-sufficient
in food. Their quest for profits also impelled planters to
cultivate far-flung commercial connections. Like any
commodity, cotton went up and down in price. Sometimes the fluctuations were long term; more often, the
price fluctuated seasonally. In response to these rises
and falls, planters assigned their cotton to commercial
agents in cities. These agents held the cotton until the
price was right and extended credit to enable the
planters to pay their bills before the cotton was sold.
Thus indebtedness became part of the plantation economy. Persistent debt intensified the planters' quest for

more profits to escape from the burden of debt. Planters enjoyed neither repose nor security.

Plantation agriculture placed psychological strains as well as economic burdens on planters and their wives. Frequent moves disrupted circles of friends and relatives, all the more so because migration to the Southwest carried families into progressively less settled, more desolate areas. In 1850 those regions of the South with thriving plantation economies—notably Alabama, Mississippi, and southeastern Louisiana—had only recently emerged from the frontier stage.

For plantation women, migration to the Southwest often amounted to a fall from grace, for many of them had grown up in seaboard elegance, only to find themselves in isolated regions, surrounded by slaves, and bereft of the companionship of white social peers. "I am sad tonight, sickness preys on my frame," wrote a bride who moved to Mississippi in 1833. "I am alone and more than 150 miles from any near relative in the wild woods of an Indian nation." At times wives lacked even their husbands' companionship. Plantation agriculture kept men on the road, scouting new land for purchase, supervising outlying plantations, and transacting business in New Orleans or Memphis.

Planters and their wives found various ways to cope with their isolation from civilized society. Many spent long periods of time in cities and left the management of plantations to overseers. In 1850 fully one-half the planters in the Mississippi Delta were absentees living in or near Natchez or New Orleans rather than on their plantations. Yet in 1850 only 30 percent of planters with a hundred or more slaves employed white overseers; the majority managed their own estates. In response, many made plantation life more sociable by engaging in lavish hospitality. But hospitality imposed enormous burdens on plantation wives, who might have to entertain as many as fifteen people for breakfast and attend to the needs of visitors who stayed for days. Indeed, in the plantation economy, wives had even less leisure than their husbands. Aside from raising their own children and caring for guests, plantation mistresses supervised house slaves, made carpets and clothes, looked after outlying buildings like smokehouses and dairies, and planted garden fruits and vegetables. Plantation women were anything but the delicate idlers of legend. In the absence of their husbands or fathers, they frequently kept the plantation accounts.

Among the greatest sorrows of some plantation mistresses was the presence of the mulatto children, who stood as daily reminders of their husbands' infidelity. Mary Boykin Chesnut, an astute Charleston woman and famous diarist, commented, "Any lady is ready to tell you who is the father of all the mulatto children in everybody's household but her own. These, she seems to think, drop from clouds." Insisting on sexual purity for white women, southern men followed a looser standard for themselves. After the death of his wife, the brother of the famous abolitionist sisters Sarah and Angelina Grimké fathered three mulatto children. The gentlemanly code usually tolerated such transgressions as long as they were not paraded in public—but at times, even if they were. Richard M. Johnson of Kentucky, the man who allegedly killed Tecumseh during the War of 1812, was elected vice president of the United States in 1836 despite having lived openly for years with his black mistress.

The isolation, drudgery, and humiliation that planters' wives experienced turned very few against the system. When the Civil War came, they supported the Confederacy as enthusiastically as any group. However much they might hate living as white islands in a sea of slaves, they recognized no less than their husbands that their wealth and position depended on slavery.

The Small Slaveholders

In 1860, 88 percent of all slaveholders owned fewer than twenty slaves, and most of these possessed fewer than ten slaves. Some slaveowners were not even farmers: one out of every five was employed outside of agriculture, usually as a lawyer, physician, merchant, or artisan.

As a large and extremely diverse group, small slaveholders experienced conflicting loyalties and ambitions. In the upland regions, they absorbed the outlook of yeomen (nonslaveowning family farmers), the numerically dominant group. Typically, small upland slaveholders owned only a few slaves and rarely aspired to become large planters. In contrast, in the low country and delta regions, where planters formed the dominant group, small slaveholders often aspired to planter status. In these planter-dominated areas, someone with ten slaves could realistically look forward to the day when he would own thirty. The deltas were thus filled with ambitious and acquisitive individuals who linked success to owning more slaves. Whether one owned ten slaves or fifty, the logic of slaveholding was much the same. The investment in slaves could be justified only by setting them to work on profitable crops. Profitable crops demanded, in turn, more and better land. Much like the planters, the small slaveholder of the low country and delta areas were restless and footloose.

The social structure of the deltas was fluid but not infinitely so. Small slaveholders were usually younger than large slaveholders, and many hoped to become planters in their own right. But as the antebellum period wore on, a clear tendency developed toward the geographical segregation of the small slaveholders from the planters in the cotton belt. Small slaveholders led the initial push into the cotton belt in the 1810s and 1820s, whereas the large planters, reluctant to risk transporting their hundreds of slaves into the still turbulent new territory, remained in the seaboard South. Gradually, however, the large planters ventured into Alabama and Mississippi. Colonel Thomas Dabney, a planter originally from tidewater Virginia, made several scouting tours of the Southwest before moving his family and slaves to the region of Vicksburg, Mississippi, where he started a four-thousand-acre plantation. The small slaveholders already on the scene at first resented Dabney's genteel manners and misguided efforts to win friends. He showed up at house raisings to lend a hand, but the hands he lent were not his own, which remained gloved, but those of his slaves. The small slaveholders muttered about transplanted Virginia snobs. Dabney responded to complaints simply by buying up much of the best land in the region. In itself, this was no loss to the small slaveholders. They had been first on the scene, and it was their land that the Dabneys of the South purchased. Dabney and men like him quickly turned the whole region from Vicksburg to Natchez into one of large plantations. The small farmers took the proceeds from the sale of their land, bought

more slaves, and moved elsewhere to grow cotton. Small slaveholders gradually transformed the region from Vicksburg to Tuscaloosa, Alabama, into a belt of medium-size farms with a dozen or so slaves on each.

The Yeomen

Nonslaveholding family farmers, or yeomen, composed the largest single group of southern whites. Most were landowners. Landholding yeomen, because they owned no slaves of their own, frequently hired slaves at harvest time to help in the fields. In an area where the land was poor, like eastern Tennessee, the landowning yeomen were typically subsistence farmers, but most grew some crops for the market. Whether they engaged in subsistence or commercial agriculture, they controlled landholdings far more modest than those of the planters—more likely in the range of fifty to two hundred acres than five hundred or more acres. Yeomen could be found anywhere in the South, but they tended to congregate in the upland regions. In the seaboard South, they populated the piedmont region of Georgia, South Carolina, North Carolina, and Virginia; in the Southwest they usually lived in the hilly upcountry, far from the rich alluvial soil of the deltas. A minority of yeomen did not own land. Typically young, these men resided with and worked for landowners to whom they were related.

The leading characteristic of the yeomen was the value that they attached to self-sufficiency. As non-

Ye Southern Planter, *1838*
Although they aspired to be leisured gentlemen and live in mansions, most planters resided in modest dwellings and actively managed their estates.

slaveholders, they were not carried along by the same logic that impelled slaveholders to acquire more land and plant more cash crops. Although most yeomen raised cash crops, relative to planters, they devoted a higher proportion of their acreage to subsistence crops like corn, sweet potatoes, and oats than to cash crops. The ideal of the planters was profit with modest self-sufficiency; that of the yeomen, self-sufficiency with modest profit.

Yeomen dwelling in the low country and delta regions dominated by planters were often dismissed as "poor white trash." But in the upland areas, where they constituted the dominant group, the yeomen were highly respectable. There they coexisted peacefully with the slaveholders, who typically owned only a few slaves (large planters were rare in the upland areas). Both the small slaveholders and the yeomen were essentially family farmers. With or without the aid of a few slaves, fathers and sons cleared the land and plowed, planted, and hoed the fields. Wives and daughters planted and tended vegetable gardens, helped at harvest, occasionally cared for livestock, cooked, and made clothes for the family.

In contrast to the far-flung commercial transactions of the planters, who depended on distant commercial agents to market their crops, the economic transactions of yeomen usually occurred within the neighborhood of their farms. Yeomen often exchanged their cotton, wheat, or tobacco for goods and services from local artisans and merchants. In some areas they sold their surplus corn to the herdsmen and drovers who made a living in the South's upland regions by specializing in the raising of hogs. Along the French Broad River in eastern Tennessee, some twenty thousand to thirty thousand hogs were fattened for market each year; at peak season, a traveler would see a thousand hogs a mile. When driven to market, the hogs were quartered at night in huge stock stands, veritable hog "hotels," and fed with corn supplied by the local yeomen.

The People of the Pine Barrens

One of the most controversial groups in the Old South comprised independent whites of the wooded "pine barrens." In a region marked by slaveholding, widespread landownership, and agriculture, these people stood out as deviants. Composing about 10 percent of southern whites, they were neither slaveholders nor (as a rule) landowners nor primarily farmers. Rather, they typically put up crude cabins, cleared a few acres of surrounding land (on which they usually squatted), planted some corn between tree stumps, and grazed hogs and cattle in the woods. Their simple diet—cornmeal and pork supplemented by fish and game—did not differ much from that of the yeomen or slaves. But their way of life was different. They did not raise cash crops, nor did they engage in the daily routine of orderly work that marked family farmers. With their ramshackle houses and handful of stump-strewn acres, they appeared to be lazy and shiftless.

Antislavery northerners cited the people of the pine barrens as proof that slavery degraded nonslave-holding whites. A southern defender of slavery, Daniel R. Hundley, summarized the antislavery argument: "Look at the Poor Whites of the South, . . . and behold the fruits of slavery." Then he attacked the argument. The pine barrens folk were poor, he conceded, but unlike the paupers of the northern cities, they could fend for themselves. Hundley's contention was well founded. The people of the pine barrens acquired a degree of self-sufficiency to which the South's climate and customs contributed. Mild winters made it possible to graze livestock in the woods for much of the year. Furthermore, the South retained the legal tradition (rapidly being dismantled in the antebellum North) of treating unfenced and unimproved land as available for public use. Despite complaints, the people of the pine barrens (along with many yeomen) hunted on land belonging to others as long as it was neither enclosed nor improved.

The economic independence of the pine barrens dwellers shaped their attitudes toward work. The men were reluctant to hire themselves out as farm laborers, and even when they did, they refused to perform "slave" tasks like caring for cattle and fetching wood and water. The women had similar attitudes. They might sew or quilt on hire, but they refused to become servants.

It is misleading to think of these people as victimized or oppressed. Many lived in the pine barrens out of choice. The grandson of a farmer who had migrated from Emanuel County, Georgia, to the Mississippi pine barrens explained his grandfather's motives in these words: "The truth is it looks like Emanuel County. The turpentine smell, the moan of the winds through the pine trees, and nobody within fifty miles of him, [were] too captivating . . . to be resisted, and he rested there."

Conflict and Consensus in the White South

Planters tangled with yeomen on several issues in the Old South. With their extensive economic dealings and need for credit, planters and their urban commercial allies inclined toward the Whig party, which was generally more sympathetic to banking and economic development. Cherishing their self-sufficiency, and economically independent, the yeomen tended to be Democrats.

The occasions for conflict between these groups were minimal, however, and an underlying political unity reigned in the South. Especially in the Lower South, each of the four main social groups—planters, small slaveholders, yeomen, and pine barrens people—tended to cluster in different regions. The delta areas that planters dominated contained relatively small numbers of yeomen. In other regions small slaveowners, families with ten to fifteen slaves, predominated. In the upland areas far from the deltas, the yeomen congregated. And the people of the pine barrens lived in a world of their own. There was more geographical intermingling of groups in the Upper South than in the Lower, but throughout the South each group attained a degree of independence from the others. With widespread landownership and relatively few factories, the Old South basically was not a place where whites worked for other whites, and this tended to minimize friction among whites.

In addition, the white South's political structure was sufficiently democratic to prevent any one social group from gaining exclusive control over politics. It is true that in both the Upper and the Lower South, the majority of state legislators were planters. Large planters, those with fifty or more slaves, were represented in legislatures far out of proportion to their numbers in the population. Yet these same planters owed their election to the popular vote. The white South was affected by the same democratic currents that swept northern politics between 1815 and 1860, and the newer states of the South had usually entered the Union with democratic constitutions that included universal white manhood suffrage—the right of all adult white males to vote.

Although yeomen often voted for planters, the nonslaveowners did not issue their elected representatives a blank check to govern as they pleased. During the 1830s and 1840s, Whig planters who favored banks faced intense and often successful opposition from Democratic yeomen. These yeomen blamed banks for the Panic of 1837 and pressured southern legislatures to restrict bank operations. On banking issues, nonslaveholders got their way often enough to nurture their belief that they ultimately controlled politics and that slaveholders could not block their goals.

Conflict over Slavery

Nevertheless, there was considerable potential for conflict between the slaveholders and nonslaveholders. The white carpenter who complained in 1849 that "unjust, oppressive, and degrading" competition from slave labor depressed his wages surely had a point. Between 1830 and 1860, slaveholders gained an increasing proportion of the South's wealth while declining as a proportion of its white population. The size of the slaveholding class shrank from 36 percent of the white population in 1831 to 31 percent in 1850 to 25 percent in 1860. A Louisiana editor warned in 1858 that "the present tendency of supply and demand is to concentrate all the slaves in the hands of the few, and thus excite the envy rather than cultivate the sympathy of the people." That same year, the governor of Florida proposed a law guaranteeing to each white person the ownership of at least one slave. Some southerners began to support the idea of Congress's reopening the African slave trade to increase the supply of slaves, bring down their price, and give more whites a stake in the institution.

As the debate over slavery in Virginia during 1831–1832 (see this chapter's introduction) attests, slaveholders had good reasons for uncertainty over the allegiance of nonslaveholders to the "peculiar institution" of slavery. The publication in 1857 of Hinton R. Helper's *The Impending Crisis of the South,* which called upon nonslaveholders to abolish slavery in their own interest, revealed the persistence of white opposition to slavery. On balance, however, slavery did not create profound and lasting divisions between the South's slaveholders and nonslaveholders. Although antagonism to slavery flourished in parts of Virginia up to 1860, proposals for emancipation dropped from the state's political agenda after 1832. In Kentucky, a state with a history of antislavery activity that dated back to the 1790s, calls for emancipation were revived in 1849 in a popular referendum. But the pro-emancipation forces went down to crushing defeat. Thereafter, the continuation of slavery ceased to be a political issue in Kentucky and elsewhere in the South.

The rise and fall of pro-emancipation sentiment in the South raises a key question. Since the majority of white southerners were nonslaveholders, why did they not attack the institution more consistently? To look ahead, why were so many of them to fight ferociously and die bravely during the Civil War in defense of an institution in which they appeared not to have had any real stake? There are various answers to these questions. First, some nonslaveholders hoped to become slaveholders. Second, most simply accepted the racist assumptions upon which slavery rested. Whether slaveholders or nonslaveholders, white southerners dreaded the likelihood that emancipation might encourage "impudent" blacks to entertain ideas of social equality with whites. Blacks might demand the right to sit next to whites in railroad cars and even make advances to white women. "Now suppose they [the slaves] was free," a white southerner told a northern journalist in the 1850s, "you see they'd all think themselves just as good as we; of course they would if they was free. Now just suppose you had a family of children, how would you like to hev a niggar steppin' up to your darter?" Slavery, in short, appealed to whites as a legal, time-honored, and foolproof way to enforce the social subordination of blacks. Finally, no one knew where the slaves, if freed, would go or what they would do. After 1830 a dwindling minority of northerners and southerners still dallied with the idea of colonizing freed blacks in Africa, but that alternative increasingly seemed unrealistic in a society where slaves numbered in the millions. Without colonization, southerners concluded, emancipation would produce a race war. In 1860 Georgia's governor sent a blunt message to his constituents, many of them nonslaveholders: "So soon as the slaves were at liberty thousands of them would leave the cotton and rice fields . . . and make their way to the healthier climate of the mountain region [where] we should have them plundering and stealing, robbing and killing." There was no mistaking the conclusion. Emancipation would not merely deprive slaveholders of their property, it would jeopardize the lives of nonslaveholders.

The Proslavery Argument

Between 1830 and 1860, as slaveholders and non-slaveholders closed ranks behind slavery, southern intellectuals constructed a defense of the institution as a positive good rather than a necessary evil. Some found defenses of slavery in the Bible, especially in St. Paul's order that servants obey their masters. Others, including the Virginian George F. Holmes, tried to establish slavery as both an ancient and a progressive institution by noting that the slave society of ancient Athens had produced Plato and Aristotle and that Roman slaveholders had laid the basis of Western civilization. Another Virginian, George Fitzhugh, turned the tables on antislavery northerners by contrasting the plight of northern "wage slaves"—white factory workers—with the conditions of black slaves in the South. Whereas northern mill owners discarded wage earners when they were too old or too sick to work, Fitzhugh argued, southern masters gave continuous care to their slave property, attending to their health, clothing, and discipline.

But as they sought to establish slavery's congruence with humanitarian and progressive impulses, southerners increasingly suppressed open discussion of slavery within the South. In the 1830s southerners seized and burned abolitionist literature mailed to the South. In Kentucky the abolitionist editor Cassius Marcellus Clay positioned two cannons and a powder keg to protect his press, but in 1845 a mob dismantled it anyway. By 1860 any southerner found with a copy of Helper's *The Impending Crisis* had every reason to fear for his life.

The rise of the proslavery argument coincided with a shift in the position of the southern churches on slavery. During the 1790s and early 1800s, some Protestant ministers had assailed slavery as immoral. By the 1830s, however, most members of the clergy had convinced themselves that slavery was not only compatible with Christianity but also necessary for the proper exercise of the Christian religion. Like the proslavery intellectuals, clergymen contended that slavery provided the opportunity to display Christian responsibility toward one's inferiors, and it helped blacks develop Christian virtues like humility and self-control. With this conclusion solidified, southerners increasingly attacked antislavery evangelicals in the North for disrupting the allegedly superior social arrangement of the South. In 1844 the Methodist Episcopal church split into northern and southern wings. In 1845 Baptists formed a separate Southern Convention. Even earlier, southerners and conservative northerners had combined in 1837 to drive the antislavery New School Presbyterians out of that denomination's

THE NEGRO IN HIS OWN COUNTRY.

THE NEGRO IN AMERICA.

Proslavery propagandists contrasted what they believed to be the black's African savagery with the blessings of civilization on an American plantation.

main body. All this added up to a profound irony. In 1800 southern evangelicals had been more critical of slavery than southerners as a whole. Yet the evangelicals effectively seceded from national church organizations long before the South seceded from the Union.

HONOR AND VIOLENCE IN THE OLD SOUTH

Almost everything about the Old South struck northern visitors as extreme. Although inequality certainly flourished in the North, no group in northern society was as deprived as the slaves. The Irish immigrants who arrived in the North in great waves in the 1840s often owned no property, but unlike the slaves, they were not in themselves a form of property. Not only did northerners find the gap between the races in the South extreme, but individual southerners seemed to run to extremes. One minute they were hospitable and gracious; the next, savagely violent. Abolitionists were not the only ones to view the Old South as a land of extremes. "The Americans of the South," Alexis de Tocqueville asserted, "are brave, comparatively ignorant, hospitable, generous, easy to irritate, violent in their resentments, without industry or the spirit of enterprise."

Violence in the White South

No one who lived in a southern community, a northern journalist noted in the 1850s, could fail to be impressed with "the frequency of fighting with deadly weapons." Throughout the colonial and antebellum periods, violence deeply colored the daily lives of white southerners. In the 1760s a minister described backcountry Virginians "biting one anothers Lips and Noses off, and gowging one another—that is, thrusting out anothers Eyes, and kicking one another on the Cods [genitals], to the Great damage of many a Poor Woman." In the 1840s a New York newspaper described a fight between two raftsmen on the Mississippi that started when one accidentally bumped the other into shallow water. When it was over, one raftsmen was dead; the other boasted, "I can lick a steamboat. My fingernails is related to a sawmill on my mother's side, . . . and the brass buttons on my coat have all been boiled in poison." Gouging out eyes became a specialty of sorts among poor whites. On one occasion, a South Carolina judge entered his court to find a plaintiff, a juror, and two witnesses all missing one eye. Stories of eye gougings and ear bitings lost nothing in the telling and became part of the folklore of the Old South. Mike Fink, a legendary southern fighter and hunter, boasted that he was so mean that in infancy, he refused his mother's milk and cried out for a bottle of whiskey. Yet beneath the folklore lay the reality of violence that gave the Old South a murder rate as much as ten times higher than that of the North.

The Code of Honor and Dueling

At the root of most violence in the white South lay intensified feelings of personal pride that themselves reflected the inescapable presence of slaves. Every day of their lives, white southerners saw slaves who were degraded, insulted, and powerless to resist. This experience had a searing impact on whites, for it encouraged them to react violently to even trivial insults in order to demonstrate that they had nothing in common with slaves. Among gentlemen this exaggerated pride took the form of a code of honor. In this context, honor can best be defined as an extraordinary sensitivity to one's reputation, a belief that one's self-esteem depends on the judgment of others. In the antebellum North, moralists celebrated a rival ideal, character—the quality that enabled an individual to behave in a steady fashion regardless of how others acted toward him or her. A person possessed of character acted out of the promptings of conscience. In contrast, in the honor culture of the Old South, the slightest insult, as long as it was perceived as intentional, could become the basis for a duel (see "A Place in Time").

Formalized by British and French officers during the Revolutionary War, dueling gained a secure niche in the Old South as a means by which gentlemen dealt with affronts to their honor. To outsiders, the incidents that sparked duels seemed so trivial as to be scarcely credible: a casual remark accidentally overheard, a harmless brushing against the side of someone at a public event, even a hostile glance. Yet dueling did not necessarily terminate in violence. Dueling constituted part of a complex code of etiquette that governed relations among gentlemen in the Old South and, like all forms of etiquette, called for a curious sort of self-restraint. Gentlemen viewed dueling as a refined alternative to the random violence of lower-class life. The code of dueling did not dictate that the insulted party leap at his antagonist's throat or draw his pistol at the perceived moment of insult. Rather, he was to remain cool, bide his time, settle on a choice of weapons, and agree to a meeting place. In the interval, negotiations between friends of the parties sought to clear up the "misunderstanding" that had evoked the challenge. In

this way, most confrontations ended peaceably rather than on the field of honor at dawn.

Although dueling was as much a way of settling disputes peaceably as of ending them violently, the ritual could easily terminate in a death or maiming. Dueling did not allow the resolution of grievances by the courts, a form of redress that would have guaranteed a peaceful outcome. As a way of settling personal disputes that involved honor, recourse to the law struck many southerners as cowardly and shameless. Andrew Jackson's mother told the future president, "The law affords no remedy that can satisfy the feelings of a true man."

In addition, dueling rested on the assumption that a gentleman could recognize another gentleman and hence would know when to respond to a challenge. Nothing in the code of dueling compelled a gentleman to duel someone beneath his status, because such a person's opinion of a gentleman hardly mattered. An insolent porter who insulted a gentleman might get a whipping but did not merit a challenge to a duel. Yet it was often difficult to determine who was a gentleman. The Old South teemed with pretentious, would-be gentlemen. A clerk in a country store in Arkansas in the 1850s found it remarkable that ordinary farmers who hung around the store talked of their honor and that the store's proprietor, a German Jew, kept a dueling pistol.

The Southern Evangelicals and White Values

With its emphasis on the personal redress of grievances and its inclination toward violence, the ideal of honor had a potential for conflict with the values preached by the southern evangelical churches, notably the Baptists, Methodists, and Presbyterians. These evangelical denominations were on the rise even before the Great Kentucky Revival of 1800–1801 and continued to grow in the wake of the revival. With just forty-eight thousand southern members in 1801, for example, the Methodists reported eighty thousand by 1807. All of the evangelical denominations stressed humility and self-restraint, virtues that stood in contrast to the entire culture of show and display that buttressed the extravagance and violence of the Old South.

Prior to 1830 most southern gentlemen looked down on the evangelicals as uncouth fanatics, and even after 1830 evangelical values scarcely dominated the South's white leadership. But evangelicals gradually shed their image as illiterate backwoods people by

Edgefield District, South Carolina, in the Antebellum Era

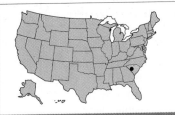

Located on the western edge of South Carolina near the Georgia border, Edgefield District combined features of the aristocratic low country, to which it was linked by the Savannah River, and the yeoman-dominated upland regions of the Old South. Most Edgefield whites were small farmers or agricultural workers. In 1860 a majority did not own any slaves, and a sizable minority had no land. Yet the invention of the cotton gin had attracted wealthy low-country planters to Edgefield, and by 1860 the district had become the state's leading cotton producer. These planters formed the nucleus of the district's elite. By 1860 the wealthiest 10 percent of white heads of household in Edgefield controlled 57 percent of the district's real and personal property. Intermarriage strengthened ties within the elite. By the Civil War, the leading families, among them the Butlers, Bonhams, Brookses, Simkinses, and Pickenses, had intermarried.

Black slaves were the basis of upper-crust Edgefield's wealth. By 1860 slaves outnumbered whites by 50 percent in the district. The vast majority of Edgefield's black bond servants were field slaves. Almost all of those dwelling on the great plantations worked under the "gang" system, by which they were divided into a number of groups, each performing a specified amount of work. (The gang system stood in contrast to the "task" system, in which individual slaves carried out designated chores.) The plantations' "plow gangs" comprised strong young men and occasionally some women, whereas "hoe gangs" generally included elderly slaves and women. A small number of Edgefield's slaves were skilled artisans who did blacksmithing and carpentry on the district's omnipresent farms. Whether field hands or skilled artisans, most slaves lived with their families in simple, rude one-room cabins in close prox-

Pierce Mason Butler
A leading Edgefield politician, Butler was befriended early in his career by John Calhoun, who secured an army commission for him. Joining Calhoun in the early 1830s in support of nullification, Butler was elected governor of South Carolina in 1836. He led the Palmetto regiment in the Mexican War and was killed in action in 1847.

Francis Wilkinson Pickens
Pickens came to Edgefield to study and practice law. A relative of Calhoun, he favored nullification. Elected governor of South Carolina just before its secession from the Union in 1860, Pickens once said that "before a free people can be dragged into a war, it must be in defense of great national right as well as national honor."

Presentation Sword and Ceramic Jar
Decorative arts in Edgefield ranged from this presentation sword owned by P. M. Butler, which symbolized the valor and military honor associated with the role of the southern planter class, to slave-made pottery such as this jar produced in one of the district's ten or so clayworks. Wheel-thrown and painted with alkaline glazes, the jar gets its distinctive appearance from having been taken from the kiln while red-hot and then thrust into a pit of pine needles.

imity to the dwellings of other slaves. An Edgefield black born into slavery in 1852 recalled that the slaves "had houses of weatherboards, big enough for [a] chicken coop—man, wife, and chillun [live] dere."

Only one-quarter of Edgefield's whites owned twenty or more of such slaves in 1860. This elite minority accounted for possession of nearly two-thirds of the district's slaves. Using their slaves not only as agrarian workers but as collateral for loans, the great planters agreed with John C. Calhoun's northern-bred son-in-law Thomas Green Clemson—the owner of the Edgefield plantation called Canebreak—that "slaves are the most valuable property in the South, being the basis of the whole southern fabric." Yet despite the yawning gap between the wealth of the planters and the income of most other whites, class conflict did not convulse antebellum Edgefield's white society, which as a whole was tightly unified. Verbal assaults on "aristocrats" did sweep through the district from time to time, but lawyers (whom the people treated with suspicion because they did not work with their hands) rather than planters bore the brunt of these attacks.

Religion contributed mightily to this harmony reigning within Edgefield's white society. Indeed, religion was at the core of

both family life and community life in the district and significantly molded the world view of the people. Although many churches dotted the countryside, so dispersed was Edgefield's population—the district contained only two incorporated towns—that ministers were limited. Thus devout Episcopalian planters and zealous Baptist yeomen farmers often found themselves sitting side by side listening to whatever traveling preacher had happened through their neighborhood. As a further boon to white solidarity, Edgefield's small farmers depended on the plantation lords to gin and market their cotton, and during the harvest they often rented slaves from the great planters. Nonslaveholding yeomen were likelier than small slaveowners to be dissatisfied with their lot in life, and many moved west into the states of Georgia, Alabama, Mississippi, and Louisiana rather than stay and complain about the rich. Nearly 60 percent of Edgefield's white heads of household in 1850 no longer resided in the district in 1860.

The code of honor further unified the whites. Like southern gentlemen elsewhere, Edgefield's male elite saw affronts to honor behind every bush. Two military officers once fought a duel because one questioned the other's chess moves. Louis Wigfall, an Edgefield planter who later served as a Confederate senator

from Texas and who was rumored to be "half drunk all the time," posted signs denouncing as cowards those who refused to accept his innumerable challenges to duels. Yet however much the code of honor set individual against individual, it could unify a region. For example, in 1856 Preston Brooks, a U.S. congressman from Edgefield, brutally caned Massachusetts senator Charles Sumner on the Senate floor after Sumner had delivered an antislavery oration that dealt roughly with one of Brooks's relatives. As Representative Brooks later wrote to his constituents, it was not just the honor of a relative that he sought to defend. Rather, he had set himself up as a "sentinel" guarding the honor of every white South Carolinian against the slanderous tongues of northerners. By the mid-1850s growing attitudes like this were demonstrating that the battle lines clearly had been drawn between southerners and northerners. The time seemed to be fast approaching when, as Edgefield newspaper editor Arthur Simkins observed, southern planters' "rich blessings . . . inherited from a virtuous ancestry" would lead them to band together to strongly oppose "mobocratic tendencies in American society" flourishing in the Northeast's "larger cities and more populous manufacturing towns."

founding colleges like Randolph Macon (Methodist, 1830) and Wake Forest (Baptist, 1838) and by exhorting pious women, who composed two-thirds of the membership of evangelical churches, to make every home "a sanctuary, a resting place, a shadow from the heats, turmoils, and conflicts of life, and an effectual barrier against ambition, envy, jealousy, and selfishness." During the 1830s evangelical values and practices like revivalism began to penetrate even the Episcopal church, the denomination long preferred by the gentry.

Southern evangelicals rarely attacked honor as such, but they railed against dueling, brawling, intemperance, and gambling and, in the words of a Georgia woman, the *Revenge, Ambition, Pride* that undergirded these practices. By the 1860s the South contained many Christian gentlemen like the bible-quoting Presbyterian general Thomas J. "Stonewall" Jackson, fierce in a righteous war but a sworn opponent of strong drink, the gaming table, and the duel.

LIFE UNDER SLAVERY

Slavery, the institution that lay at the root of the code of honor and other distinctive features of the Old South, has long inspired controversy among historians. Some have portrayed slavery as a benevolent institution in which blacks lived contentedly under kind masters; others, as a cruel and inhuman system that drove slaves into constant rebellion. Neither view is accurate, but both contain a germ of truth. There were kind masters who accepted the view expressed by a Baptist minister in 1854: "Give your servants that which is just and equal, knowing that you also have a Master in heaven." Moreover, some slaves developed genuine affection for their masters. Yet slavery was an inherently oppressive institution that forcefully appropriated the life and labor of one race for the material benefit of another. Despite professions to the contrary by apologists for slavery, the vast majority of slaveholders exploited the labor of blacks to earn a profit. Kind masters might complain about cruel overseers, but the masters hired and paid the overseers to get as much work as possible out of blacks. When the master of one plantation chastised his overseer for "barbarity," the latter replied, "Do you not remember what you told me the time you employed me that [if] I failed to make you good crops I

would have to leave?" Indeed, kindness was a double-edged sword, for the benevolent master came to expect grateful affection from his slaves and then interpreted that affection as loyalty to the institution of slavery. In fact, blacks felt little, if any, loyalty to slavery. When northern troops descended upon plantations during the Civil War, masters were dismayed to find many of their most trusted slaves deserting to Union lines.

Although the kindness or cruelty of masters made some difference to slaves, the most important determinants of their experiences under slavery depended on such impersonal factors as the kind of agriculture in which they were engaged, whether they resided in rural or urban areas, and whether they lived in the eighteenth or nineteenth century. The experiences of slaves working on cotton plantations in the 1830s differed drastically from those of slaves in 1700, for reasons unrelated to the kindness or brutality of masters.

The Maturing of the Plantation System

Slavery changed significantly between 1700 and 1830. In 1700 the typical slave was a young man in his twenties who had recently arrived aboard a slave ship from Africa or the Caribbean and worked in company with other recent arrivals on isolated small farms. Drawn from different African regions and cultures, few such slaves spoke the same language. Because commercial slave ships contained twice as many men as women, and because slaves were widely scattered, blacks had difficulty finding sexual partners and creating a semblance of family life. Furthermore, as a result of severe malnutrition, black women who had been brought to North America on slave ships bore relatively few children. Thus the slave trade had a devastating effect on natural increase among blacks. Without importations, the number of slaves in North America would have declined between 1710 and 1730.

In contrast, by 1830 the typical North American slave was as likely to be female as male, had been born in America, spoke a form of English that made possible communication with other slaves, and worked in the company of numerous other slaves on a plantation. The key to the change lay in the rise of plantation agriculture in the Chesapeake and South Carolina during the eighteenth century. Plantation slaves had an easier time finding mates than those on the remote farms of the early 1700s. As the ratio between slave men and women fell into balance, marriages occurred with increasing frequency between slaves on the same or nearby plantations. The native-born slave population rose after 1730 and soared after 1750. Importations of African slaves gradually declined after 1760, and Congress banned them in 1808.

Work and Discipline of Plantation Slaves

In 1850 the typical slave experience was to work on a large farm or plantation with at least ten fellow bond servants. Almost three-quarters of all slaves that year were owned by masters with ten or more slaves, and just over one-half lived in units of twenty or more slaves. To understand the daily existence of the typical antebellum slave, then, requires an examination of the work and discipline routines common on large-scale farming operations.

The day of antebellum plantation slaves usually began an hour before sunrise with the sounding of a horn or bell. After a sparse breakfast, slaves marched to the fields. A traveler in Mississippi described a procession of slaves on their way to work. "First came, led by an old driver carrying a whip, forty of the largest and strongest women I ever saw together; they were all in a simple uniform dress of bluish check stuff, the skirts reaching little below the knee; their legs and feet were bare; they carried themselves loftily, each having a hoe over the shoulder, and walking with a free, powerful swing." Then came the plow hands, "thirty strong, mostly men, but few of them women. . . . A lean and vigilant white overseer, on a brisk pony, brought up the rear."

As this account indicates, slave men and women worked side by side in the fields. Female slaves who did not labor in the fields scarcely idled their hours away. A former slave, John Curry, described how his mother milked cows, cared for the children whose mothers worked in the fields, cooked for field hands, did the ironing and washing for her master's household, and took care of her own seven children. Plantations never lacked tasks for slaves of either gender. As former slave Solomon Northup noted, "ploughing, planting, picking cotton, gathering the corn, and pulling and burning stalks, occupies the whole of the four seasons of the year. Drawing and cutting wood, pressing cotton, fattening and killing hogs, are but incidental labors." Regardless of the season, the slave's day stretched from dawn to dusk. Touring the South in the 1850s, Frederick Law Olmsted prided himself on rising early and riding late but added, "I always found the negroes in the field when I first looked out, and generally had to wait for the negroes to come from the field to have my horse fed when I stopped for the night." When darkness made field work impossible, slaves toted cotton bales to the ginhouse, gathered up wood for supper fires, and

Black Women and Men on a Trek Home, South Carolina
Much like northern factories, large plantations made it possible to impose discipline and order on their work force. Here black women loaded down with cotton join their men on the march home after a day in the fields.

fed the mules. Weary from their labors, they slept in log cabins on wooden planks. "The softest couches in the world," a former bondsman wryly observed, "are not to be found in the log mansions of a slave."

Although virtually all antebellum Americans worked long hours, no laboring group experienced the same combination of long hours and harsh discipline as did slave field hands. Northern factory workers did not have to put up with drivers who, like one described by Olmsted, walked among the slaves with a whip, "which he often cracked at them, sometimes allowing the lash to fall lightly upon their shoulders." The lash did not always fall lightly. The annals of American slavery contain stories of repulsive brutality. Pregnant slave women were sometimes forced to lie in depressions in the ground and endure whipping on their backs, a practice that supposedly protected the fetus while abusing the mother. The disciplining and punishment of slaves was often left to white overseers and black drivers rather than to masters. "Dat was de meanest devil dat ever lived on the Lord's green earth," a former Mississippi slave said of his driver. The barbaric discipline meted out by others twinged the conscience of many a master. But even masters who professed Christianity viewed the disciplining of slaves as a priority—indeed, as a Christian duty to ensure the slaves' proper "submissiveness." The black abolitionist Frederick Douglass, once a slave, recalled that his worst master had been converted at a Methodist camp meeting. "If religion had any effect on his character at all," Douglass related, "it made him more cruel and hateful in all his ways."

Despite the relentless, often brutal discipline, plantation agriculture gave a minority of slaves opportunities for advancement, not from slavery to freedom but from unskilled and exhausting field work to semi-skilled or skilled indoor work. Some slaves developed skills like blacksmithing and carpentry and learned to operate cotton gins. Others were trained as cooks, butlers, and dining-room attendants. These house slaves became legendary for their arrogant disdain of field hands and poor whites. The legend often distorted the reality, for house slaves were as subject to discipline as field slaves. "I liked the field work better than I did the house work," a female slave recalled. "We could talk and do anything we wanted to, just so we picked the cotton." Such sentiments were typical, but skilled slave artisans and house servants were greatly valued and treated accordingly; they occupied higher rungs than field hands on the social ladder of slavery.

The Slave Family

Masters thought of slaves as naturally promiscuous and flattered themselves into thinking that they alone held slave marriages together. Masters did have an incentive to encourage slave marriages in order to bring new slaves into the world and to discourage slaves from running away. Some masters baked wedding cakes for slaves and later arbitrated marital disputes. James Henry Hammond, the governor of South Carolina and a large slaveholder, noted in his diary how he "flogged Joe Goodwyn and ordered him to go back to his wife. Ditto Gabriel and Molly and ordered them to come together. Separated Moses and Anny finally."

Yet this picture of benevolent masters holding together naturally promiscuous slaves is misleading. The keenest challenge to the slave family came not from the slaves themselves but from slavery. The law provided neither recognition of nor protection for the slave family. Although some slaveholders were reluctant to break slave marriages by sale, such masters could neither bequeath this reluctance to their heirs nor avoid economic hardships that might force them to sell off slaves. The reality, one historian has calculated, was that on average, a slave would witness in a lifetime the sale of eleven family members.

Naturally, the commonplace buying and selling of slaves severely disrupted the slaves' attempts to create a stable family life. Poignant testimony to the effects of sale on slave families, and to the desire of slaves to remain near their families, was provided by an advertisement for a runaway slave in North Carolina in 1851. The advertisement described the fugitive as presumed to be "lurking in the neighborhood of E. D. Walker's, at Moore's Creek, who owns most of his relatives, or Nathan Bonham's who owns his mother; or, perhaps, near Fletcher Bell's, at Long Creek, who owns his father." Small wonder that a slave preacher pronounced a slave couple married "until death or *distance* do you part."

Aside from their disruption by sale, slave families experienced separations and degradations from other sources. The marriage of a slave woman gave her no protection against the sexual demands of a master nor, indeed, of any white. The slave children of white masters at times became targets of the wrath of white mistresses. Sarah Wilson, the daughter of a slave and her white master, remembered that as a child, she was "picked on" by her mistress until the master ordered his wife to let Sarah alone because she "got big, big

The Land of the Free and The Home of the Brave,
by Henry Byam Martin, 1833 White southerners could not escape the fact that much of the Western world loathed their "peculiar institution." In 1833, when a Canadian sketched this Charleston slave auction, Britain abolished slavery in the West Indies.

blood in her." Slave women who worked in the fields usually were separated from their children by day; young sons and daughters often were cared for by the aged or by the mothers of other children. When slave women took husbands from nearby (rather than their own) plantations, the children usually stayed with the mother. Hannah Chapman remembered that her father tried to visit his family under cover of darkness "because he missed us and us longed for him." But if his master found him, "us would track him the nex' day by de blood stains."

Despite enormous obstacles, the relationships within slave families were often intimate and, where possible, long-lasting. In the absence of legal protection, slaves developed their own standards of family morality. A southern white woman observed that slaves "did not consider it wrong for a girl to have a child before she married, but afterwards were extremely severe upon anything like infidelity on her part." When given the opportunity, slaves sought to solemnize their marriages before clergymen. White clergymen who accompanied the Union army into Mississippi and Louisiana in the closing years of the Civil War conducted thousands of marriage rites for slaves who had long viewed themselves as married and who now desired a formal ceremony and registration.

Although slaves tried to solemnize their marriage vows in the same fashion as whites, the slave family did not merely copy the customs of white families. In white families, for example, the parent-child bond overrode all others; slaves, in contrast, emphasized ties between children and their grandparents, uncles, and aunts as well as parents. Such broad kinship ties

marked the West African cultures from which many slaves had originally been brought to America, and they were reinforced by the separations between children and one or both parents that routinely occurred under slavery. Frederick Douglass never knew his father and saw his mother infrequently, but he vividly remembered his grandmother, "a good nurse, and a capital hand at making nets for catching shad and herring." In addition, slaves often created "fictive" kin networks; in the absence of uncles and aunts, they simply named friends their uncles, aunts, brothers, or sisters. In effect, slaves invested non-kin relations with symbolic kin functions. In this way, they helped protect themselves against the involuntary disruption of family ties by forced sale and established a broader community of obligation. When plantation slaves greeted each other as "brudder," they were not making a statement about actual kinship but about obligations they felt for each other. Apologists for slavery liked to argue that a "community of interests" bound masters and slaves together. In truth, the real community of interests was the one that slaves developed among themselves in order to survive.

The Longevity, Diet, and Health of Slaves

In general, slaves in the United States reproduced faster and lived longer than slaves elsewhere in the Western Hemisphere. The evidence comes from a compelling statistic. In 1825, 36 percent of all slaves in the Western Hemisphere lived in the United States, whereas Brazil accounted for 31 percent. Yet of the 10 million to 12 million African slaves who had been imported to the New

World between the fifteenth and nineteenth centuries, only some 550,000 (about 5 percent) had come to North America, whereas 3.5 million (nearly 33 percent) had been taken to Brazil. Mortality had depleted the slave populations of Brazil and the Caribbean to a far greater extent than in North America.

Several factors account for the different rates between the United States on the one hand and Brazil and the Caribbean on the other. First, the gender ratio among slaves equalized more rapidly in North America, encouraging earlier and longer marriages and more children. Second, because growing corn and raising livestock were compatible with cotton cultivation, the Old South produced plenty of food. The normal ration for a slave was a peck of cornmeal and three to four pounds of fatty pork a week. Slaves often supplemented this nutritionally unbalanced diet with vegetables grown in small plots that masters allowed them to farm and with catfish and game. In the barren winter months, slaves ate less than in the summer; in this respect, however, they did not differ much from most whites.

As for disease, slaves had greater immunities to both malaria and yellow fever than did whites, but they suffered more from cholera, dysentery, and diarrhea. In the absence of privies, slaves usually relieved themselves behind bushes; urine and feces washed into the sources of drinking water and caused many diseases. Yet slaves developed some remedies that, though commonly ridiculed by whites, were effective against stomach ailments. For example, the slaves' belief that eating white clay would cure dysentery and diarrhea rested on a firm basis, for we know now that kaolin, an ingredient of white clay, is a remedy for these ailments.

Although slave remedies were often more effective than those of white physicians, slaves experienced higher mortality rates than whites. At any age, a slave faced a shorter life than a white, but most strikingly in infancy. Rates of infant mortality for slaves were at least twice those of whites. Between 1850 and 1860, fewer than two out of three black children survived to the age of ten. Whereas the worst mortality occurred on plantations in disease-ridden, low-lying areas, pregnant, overworked field hands often miscarried or gave birth to weakened infants even in healthier regions. Masters allowed pregnant women to rest, but rarely enough. "Labor is conducive to health," a Mississippi planter told a northern journalist; "a healthy woman will rear most children."

Slaves off Plantations

Although plantation agriculture gave some slaves, especially males, opportunities to acquire specialized skills, it imposed a good deal of supervision on them. The greatest opportunities for slaves were reserved for those who worked off plantations and farms, either as laborers in extractive industries like mining and lumbering or as artisans in towns and cities. Because the lucrative cotton growing attracted so many whites onto small farms, a perennial shortage of white labor plagued almost all the nonagricultural sectors of the southern economy. As a consequence, there was a steady demand for slaves to drive wagons, to work as stevedores (ship-cargo handlers) in port cities, to man river barges, and to perform various tasks in mining and lumbering. In 1860 lumbering employed sixteen thousand workers, most of them slaves who cut trees, hauled them to sawmills, and fashioned them into useful lumber. In sawmills black engineers fired and fixed the steam engines that provided power. In iron-ore ranges and ironworks, slaves not only served as laborers but occasionally supervised less skilled white workers. In addition, just as mill girls composed the labor force of the booming textile industry in New England, slave women and children worked in the South's fledgling textile mills.

Behind all of this were some basic, long-standing features of southern society. Even before the rise of cotton, the profitability of southern cash crops like rice and indigo had pulled white labor out of towns and cities and indirectly provided considerable scope for slaves to work as skilled artisans. In the eighteenth century, cities like Charleston and Savannah had a large class of highly skilled slave blacksmiths and carpenters. This tradition continued into the next century and affected both enslaved and free blacks. Whether slave or free, blacks generally found it easier to work in skilled occupations in southern cities than in northern cities during the antebellum period. Not only did tradition open up skilled crafts to blacks, but the South did not attract the same flow of immigrant labor to compete with blacks as did the North.

As a result, despite slavery's stranglehold on black society, some southern blacks had opportunities in cities that were denied to blacks in northern cities. For the most part, enslaved blacks who worked in factories or in extractive industries like lumbering and mining were not owned by their employers. Rather, they were hired out by their rural masters to urban employers. If conditions in factories or mines deteriorated to the point where slaves grew ill or died, rural masters would refuse to provide urban employers with more slaves. So it was in the interest of white supervisors to keep conditions of work for slaves off the plantations at a tolerable level. Watching the loading of a steamboat with cotton bales, Frederick Law Olmsted was amazed to see slaves sent to the top of the bank to roll the bales down to Irishmen who stowed them on the ship. Asking the reason for this arrangement, Olmsted was told, "The niggers are worth too much to be risked here; if the Paddies [Irish] are knocked overboard, or get their backs broke, nobody loses anything."

Life on the Margin: Free Blacks in the Old South

Free blacks were more likely than southern blacks in general to live in cities. In 1860 one-third of the free blacks in the Upper South and more than half in the Lower South were urban.

The relatively specialized economies of the cities provided free people of color with opportunities to become carpenters, coopers (barrel makers), barbers, and even small traders. A visitor to an antebellum southern market would find that most of the meat, fish, vegetables, and fruit had been prepared for sale by free blacks. Urban free blacks formed their own fraternal orders and churches; a church run by free blacks was often the largest house of worship in a southern city. In New Orleans free blacks had their own literary journals and opera. In Natchez a free black barber, William Tiler Johnson, invested the prof-

its of his shop in real estate, acquired stores that he rented out, purchased slaves and a plantation, and even hired a white overseer.

As Johnson's career suggests, some free blacks were highly successful. But free blacks were always vulnerable in southern society and became more so as the antebellum period wore on. Although free blacks continued to increase in absolute numbers (a little more than a quarter-million free people of color dwelled in the South in 1860), the rate of growth of the free black population slowed after 1810. Between 1790 and 1810, this population had more than tripled, to 108,265. The reason for the slowdown after 1810 was that fewer southern whites were setting slaves free. Until 1820 masters with doubts about the rightness of slavery frequently manumitted (freed) their black mistresses and mulatto children, and some set free their entire work forces. In the wake of the Nat Turner rebellion in 1831 (see below), laws restricting the liberties of free blacks were tightened. During the mid-1830s, for example, most southern states made it a felony to teach blacks to read and write. Every southern state forbade free blacks to enter that state, and in 1859 Arkansas ordered all free blacks to leave.

So although a free black culture flowered in cities like New Orleans and Natchez, that culture did not reflect the conditions under which most free blacks lived. Free blacks were tolerated in New Orleans, in part because there were not too many of them. A much higher percentage of blacks were free in the Upper South than in the Lower South. Furthermore, although a disproportionate number of free blacks lived in cities, the majority lived in rural areas, where whites lumped them together with slaves. Even a successful free black like William Tiler Johnson

Street Scene
Early New Orleans contained a large population of free blacks. Note the contrast here between the woman on the right wearing a slave collar and the well-dressed free black on the left.

could never dine or drink with whites. When Johnson attended the theater, he sat in the colored gallery.

The position of free blacks in the Old South contained many contradictions. So did their minds. As the offspring, or the descendants of offspring, of mixed liaisons, a disproportionate number of free blacks had light brown skin. Some of them were as color-conscious as whites and looked down on "darky" field hands and coal-black laborers. Yet as whites' discrimination against free people of color intensified during the late antebellum period, many free blacks realized that such a future as they had was as blacks, not as whites. Feelings of racial solidarity grew stronger among free blacks in the 1850s, and after the Civil War, the leaders of the freed slaves were usually blacks who had been free before the war.

Slave Resistance

The Old South contained the seeds of organized slave insurrections. In the delta areas of the Lower South, where blacks outnumbered whites, enslaved blacks experienced continuous forced labor on plantations and communicated their bitterness to each other in the slave quarters. Free blacks in the cities could have provided leadership for rebellions. Rumors of slave conspiracies flew around the southern white community, and all whites knew of the massive black insurrection that had destroyed French rule in Santo Domingo.

Yet only three organized rebellions occurred in the Old South, and taken together, they illustrate more the futility than the possibility of a slave insurrection. In 1800 Virginia slave Gabriel Prosser's planned slave uprising was betrayed by other slaves, and Prosser and his followers were executed. That same year, a South Carolina slave, Denmark Vesey, won fifteen hundred dollars in a lottery and bought his freedom. Purchasing a carpentry shop in Charleston and becoming a preacher at that city's African Methodist Episcopal church, Vesey built a cadre of dedicated black followers, including a slave of the governor of South Carolina and a black conjurer named Gullah Jack. In 1822 they devised a plan to attack Charleston and seize all the city's arms and ammunition, but they were betrayed by other slaves and executed.

The Nat Turner rebellion, which occurred in 1831 in Southampton County, Virginia, was the only one of the three slave insurrections to result in the death of whites. Gloomy and introspective by nature, Nat Turner taught himself to read and write in childhood and became a prodigious reader of the Bible. He gained recognition from slaves as a preacher of electrifying sermons delivered in woodland clearings or in the shacks where slaves gathered to hear "real preachin'." Soon he added a reputation for visions and prophecy; he told, for example, of seeing white and black angels warring in the sky. Yet for all his gifts—a white later said that Turner had "a mind capable of attaining anything"—Turner's life was one of onerous field work, punctuated by a sale that separated him from his wife and that reminded him that whites measured his value only in cash.

In 1831 Turner's conviction of the injustice of slavery, intensified by his reading of the Bible and by his own experiences, boiled over. Slaves who had long venerated him as a prophet now took him as their "general." In August he set out with a handful of slaves armed with axes and clubs. Gathering recruits as they moved from plantation to plantation, Turner

Black Society in the Old South, c. 1860

Slaves greatly outnumbered free blacks in the Old South. Most slaves were owned by masters with ten or more slaves.

SOURCES: *Eighth Census of the United States, 1860: Population by Age, Sex, Race;* and Lewis C. Gray, *History of Agriculture in the Southern United States* (New York: Kelley, 1933).

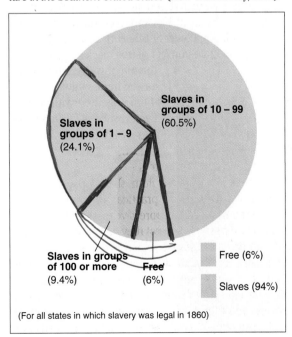

Slaves in groups of 10 – 99 (60.5%)

Slaves in groups of 1 – 9 (24.1%)

Slaves in groups of 100 or more (9.4%)

Free (6%)

Free (6%)

Slaves (94%)

(For all states in which slavery was legal in 1860)

and his followers killed all white men, women, and children they encountered. Before the rebellion was suppressed and Turner hanged, fifty-five whites had been slain, a number roughly equal to Turner's force at its peak strength.

Turner's rebellion stunned the South. In the widely circulated *Confessions of Nat Turner*, which Turner dictated to a white lawyer while awaiting execution, Turner's steadfast belief in the justice of his cause flashed again. When asked, "Do you not find yourself mistaken now?," Turner replied, "Was not Christ crucified?" In company with the earlier slave uprising in Santo Domingo, Turner's rebellion convinced white southerners of the ever-present threat of a slave insurrection. Yet neither the Turner rebellion nor the Prosser and Vesey plots ever had a chance of success. The latter two were conspiracies that never got off the ground. During the Turner rebellion, several slaves alerted their masters to the threat, less out of loyalty to slavery than from a correct assessment of Turner's chances. Despite constant fears of slave rebellion, the Old South experienced far less in the way of organized rebellion than did the Caribbean region and South America.

Why is this so? First, although slaves formed a majority in South Carolina and a few other states, they did not constitute a *large* majority in any state. Second, in contrast to the Caribbean, an area of absentee landlords and sparse white population, the white presence in the Old South was formidable, and the whites had all the guns and soldiers. The rumors of slave conspiracies that periodically swept the white South demonstrated to blacks the promptness with which whites could muster forces and mount slave patrols. Third, the development of family ties among slaves made them reluctant to risk death and leave their children parentless. Finally, blacks who ran away or plotted rebellions had no allies. Southern Indians routinely captured runaway slaves and exchanged them for rewards; some Indians even owned slaves.

Short of rebellion, slaves could try to escape to freedom in the North. Perhaps the most ingenious, Henry Brown, induced a friend to ship him from Richmond to Philadelphia in a box and won immediate fame as "Box" Brown. Some light mulattoes passed as whites. More often, fugitive slaves borrowed, stole, or forged passes from plantations or obtained papers describing them as free. Frederick Douglass borrowed a sailor's papers in making his escape from Baltimore to New York City in 1838. Some former

slaves, among them Harriet Tubman and Josiah Henson, made repeated trips back to the South to help other slaves escape. These sundry methods of escape fed the legend of the "Underground Railroad," supposedly an organized network of safe houses owned by white abolitionists who spirited blacks to freedom. In reality, fugitive slaves owed very little to abolitionists. Some white sympathizers in border states did provide safe houses for blacks, but these houses were better known to watchful slave catchers than to most blacks.

Escape to freedom was a dream rather than an alternative for most blacks; out of millions of slaves, probably fewer than a thousand escaped to the North. Yet slaves often ran away from masters, not to escape to freedom but to visit spouses or avoid punishment. Most runaways remained in the South; indeed, some returned to former, kinder masters. During the eighteenth century, African slaves had often run away in groups to the interior and sought to create self-sufficient colonies or villages of the sort that they had known in Africa. But once the United States had acquired Florida, long a haven for runaways, few uninhabited places remained in the South to which slaves could escape.

Despite poor prospects for permanent escape, slaves could disappear for prolonged periods into the free black communities of southern cities. Because whites in the Old South depended so heavily on black labor, slaves enjoyed a fair degree of practical freedom to drive wagons to market and to come and go when they were off plantations. Slaves hired out or sent to a city might overstay their leave and even pass themselves off as free. The experience of slavery has sometimes been compared to the experience of prisoners in penitentiaries or on chain gangs, but the analogy is misleading. The supervision that slaves experienced was sometimes intense (for example, when working at harvest time under a driver), but often lax; it was irregular rather than consistent.

The fact that antebellum slaves frequently enjoyed some degree of practical freedom did not change the underlying oppressiveness of slavery. But it did give slaves a sense that they had certain rights on a day-to-day basis, and it helped to deflect slave resistance into forms that were essentially furtive rather than open and violent. Theft was so common that planters learned to keep their tools, smokehouses, closets, and trunks under lock and key. Overworked field hands might leave valuable tools out to rust, or

St. Catherine's Island, Georgia, Slave Quarters
Judged by their whitewashed exteriors, these slave cabins attached to a large cotton plantation belonged to the better class of slave housing, which did not differ much from the accommodations available to the white working class. Southern agricultural periodicals advised the regular white-washing of slave cabins as a health measure. But the quality of slave cabins varied and most fell below this standard.

feign illness, or simply refuse to work. As an institution, slavery was vulnerable to such tactics; unlike free laborers, slaves could not be fired for negligence or malingering. Frederick Law Olmsted found slaveholders in the 1850s afraid to inflict punishment on slaves "lest the slave should abscond, or take a sulky fit and not work, or poison some of the family, or set fire to the dwelling, or have recourse to any other mode of avenging himself."

Olmsted's reference to arson and poisoning reminds us that not all furtive resistance was peaceful. Arson and poisoning, both common in African culture as forms of vengeance, were widespread in the Old South, and the fear of each was even more so. Masters afflicted by dysentery and similar ailments never knew for sure that they had not been poisoned.

Arson, poisoning, work stoppages, and negligence were alternatives to violent rebellion. Yet these furtive forms of resistance differed from rebellion. The goal of rebellion was freedom from slavery. The goal of furtive resistance was to make slavery bearable. The kind of resistance that slaves usually practiced sought to establish customs and rules that would govern the conduct of masters as well as that of slaves without challenging the institution of slavery as such. Most slaves would have preferred freedom but settled for less. "White folks do as they please," an ex-slave said, "and the darkies do as they can."

THE EMERGENCE OF AFRICAN-AMERICAN CULTURE

A distinctive culture emerged among blacks in the slave quarters of antebellum plantations. This culture drew on both African and American sources, but it was more than a mixture of the two. Enslaved blacks gave a distinctive twist to the American as well as African components of their culture.

The Language of Slaves

Before slaves could develop a common culture, they had to be able to communicate with each other. During the colonial period, verbal communication among slaves had often been difficult, for most slaves had been born in Africa, which contained an abundance of cultures and languages. The captain of a slave ship noted in 1744,

> As for the languages of Gambia *[in West Africa]*, they are so many and so different that the Natives on either Side of the River cannot understand each other; which, if rightly consider'd, is no small happiness to the Europeans *who go thither to trade for slaves.*

In the pens into which they were herded before shipment and on the slave ships themselves, however, Africans developed a "pidgin"—that is, a language that has no native speakers but in which people with different native languages can communicate. Pidgin is not unique to black people. When Tarzan announced, "Me Tarzan, you Jane," he was speaking English pidgin. Nor is English pidgin the only form of pidgin; slaves that were sent to South America developed Spanish and Portuguese pidgins.

Many of the early African-born slaves learned English pidgin poorly or not at all, but as American-born slaves came to compose an increasingly large proportion of all slaves, English pidgin took root. Indeed, it became the only language most slaves knew. Like all pidgins, this was a simplified language. Slaves usually dropped the verb *to be* (which had no equivalent in African tongues) and either ignored or confused genders. Instead of saying "Mary is in the cabin," they said, "Mary, he in cabin." To negate, they substituted *no* for *not,* saying, "He no wicked." English pidgin

Reed Basket, *1860*
A Florida slave artisan used traditional African skills in making this basket.

contained several African words. Some, like *banjo,* became part of standard English; others, like *goober* (peanut), became part of southern white slang. Although they picked up pidgin terms, whites ridiculed field hands' speech. Some slaves, particularly house servants and skilled artisans, learned to speak standard English but had no trouble understanding the pidgin of field hands. However strange pidgin sounded to some, it was indispensable for communication among slaves.

African-American Religion

The development of a common language marked the first step in the forging of African-American culture. No less important was the religion of the slaves.

Africa contained rich and diverse religious customs and beliefs. Some of the early slaves were Muslims; a few had acquired Christian beliefs either in Africa or in the New World. But the majority of the slaves transported from Africa were neither Muslims nor Christians but rather worshipers in one of many native African religions. Most of these religions, which whites lumped together as heathen, drew little distinction between the spiritual and material worlds. Any event or development, from a storm to an earthquake or an illness, was assumed to stem from supernatural forces. These forces were represented by God, by spirits that inhabited the woods and waters, and by the spirits of ancestors. In addition, the religions of West Africa, the region from which most American slaves originally came, attached special significance to water, which suggested life and hope.

The majority of the slaves brought to America in the seventeenth and eighteenth centuries were young men who may not have absorbed much of this religious heritage before their enslavement. In any case, Africans differed from each other in their specific beliefs and practices. For these reasons, African religions could never have unified blacks in America. Yet some Africans probably clung to their beliefs during the seventeenth and eighteenth centuries, a tendency made easier by the fact that whites undertook few efforts before the 1790s to convert slaves to Christianity. Furthermore, dimly remembered African beliefs such as the reverence for water may have predisposed slaves to accept Christianity when they were finally urged to do so, because water had a symbolic significance for Christians, too, in the sacrament of baptism. The Christianity preached to slaves by Methodist and Baptist revivalists during the late eighteenth and nineteenth centuries, moreover, resembled African religions in that Christianity also drew few distinctions between the sacred and the secular. Just as Africans believed that a crop-destroying drought or a plague resulted from supernatural forces, the early revivalists knew in theirhearts that every drunkard who fell off his horse and every Sabbath-breaker struck by lightning had experienced a deliberate and direct punishment from God.

By the 1790s blacks formed about a quarter of the membership of the Methodist and Baptist denominations. Yet masters continued to fear that a Christianized slave would be a rebellious slave. Converted slaves in fact played a significant role in each of the three major slave rebellions in the Old South. The leaders of Gabriel Prosser's rebellion in 1800 used the Bible to prove that slaves, like the ancient Israelites, could prevail against overwhelming numbers. Denmark Vesey read the Bible, and most of the slaves executed for joining his conspiracy belonged to Charleston's African Methodist church. Nat Turner was both a preacher and a prophet.

Despite the "subversive" impact of Christianity on some slaves, however, these uprisings, particularly the Nat Turner rebellion, actually stimulated Protestant missionaries to intensify their efforts to convert slaves. Missionaries pointed to the self-taught Turner to prove

that slaves would hear about Christianity in any event and that organized efforts to convert blacks were the only way to ensure that slaves learned correct versions of Christianity, which emphasized obedience rather than rebellion. Georgia missionary and slaveholder Charles Colcock Jones reassuringly told white planters of the venerable black preacher who, upon receiving some abolitionist tracts in the mail, promptly turned them over to the white authorities for destruction. A Christian slave, the argument ran, would be a better slave rather than a bitter slave. For whites, the clincher was the split of the Methodists, Baptists, and Presbyterians into northern and southern wings by the mid-1840s. Now, they argued, it had finally become safe to convert slaves, for the churches had rid themselves of their antislavery wings. Between 1845 and 1860, the number of black Baptists doubled.

The experiences of Christianized blacks in the Old South illustrate many of the contradictions of life under slavery. Urban blacks often had their own churches, but in the rural South, where the great majority of blacks lived, slaves worshiped in the same churches as whites. Although the slaves sat in segregated sections, they heard the same sermons and sang the same hymns as whites. Some black preachers actually developed followings among whites, and Christian masters were sometimes disciplined by biracial churches for abusing Christian slaves in the same congregation. The churches were, in fact, the most interracial institutions in the Old South. Yet none of this meant that Christianity was an acceptable route to black liberation. Ministers went out of their way to remind slaves that spiritual equality was not the same as civil equality. The effort to convert slaves gained momentum only to the extent that it was becoming certain that Christianity would not change the basic inequality of southern society.

Although they listened to the same sermons as whites, slaves did not necessarily draw the same conclusions. It was impossible to Christianize the slaves without telling them about the Chosen People, the ancient Jews whom Moses led from captivity in Pharaoh's Egypt into the Promised Land of Israel. Inevitably, slaves drew parallels between their own condition and the Jews' captivity. Like the Jews, blacks concluded, they themselves were "de people of de Lord." If they kept the faith, then, like the Jews, they too would reach the Promised Land. The themes of the Chosen People and the Promised Land ran through the sacred songs, or "spirituals," that blacks sang, to the point where Moses and Jesus almost merged:

> *Gwine to write to Massa Jesus,*
> *To send some Valiant Soldier*
> *To turn back Pharaoh's army, Hallelu!*

A listener could interpret a phrase like "the Promised Land" in several ways; it could refer to Israel, to heaven, or to freedom. From the perspective of whites, the only permissible interpretations were Israel and heaven, but some blacks, like Denmark Vesey, thought of freedom as well. The ease with which slaves constructed alternative interpretations of the Bible also reflected the fact that many plantations contained black preachers, slaves trained by white ministers to spread Christianity among blacks. When in the presence of masters or white ministers, these black preachers usually just repeated the familiar biblical command, "Obey your master." Often, however, slaves met for services apart from whites, usually on Sunday evenings but during the week as well. Then the message changed. A black preacher in Texas related how his master would say "tell them niggers iffen they obeys the master they goes to Heaven." The minister quickly added, "I knowed there's something better for them, but I daren't tell them 'cept on the sly. That I done lots. I tells 'em iffen they keep praying, the Lord will set 'em free."

Some slaves privately interpreted Christianity as a religion of liberation from the oppression of slavery, but most recognized that their prospects for freedom were slight. On the whole, Christianity did not turn them into revolutionaries. Neither did it necessarily turn them into model slaves. It did, however, provide slaves with a view of slavery different from their masters' outlook. Where the masters argued that slavery was a benign and divinely ordained institution in blacks' best interests, Christianity told them that slavery was really an affliction, a terrible and unjust institution that God had allowed in order to test their faith. For having endured slavery, he would reward blacks. For having created it, he would punish masters.

Black Music and Dance

Compared to the prevailing cultural patterns among elite whites, the culture of blacks in the Old South was extremely expressive. In religious services, blacks shouted "Amen" and let their bodily movements reflect their feelings long after white religious observances, some of which had once been similarly expressive, had grown sober and sedate. Frederick Law Olmsted recorded how, during a slave service in New Orleans during the 1850s, parishioners "in indescribable expression of ecstasy" exclaimed every few moments: "Glory! oh yes! yes!—sweet Lord! sweet Lord!"

Slaves also expressed their feelings in music and dance. Drawing on their African musical heritage, which used hand clapping to mark rhythm, American slaves made rhythmical hand clapping—called patting juba—an indispensable accompaniment to dancing, because southern law forbade them to own "drums, horns, or other loud instruments, which may call together or give sign or notice to one another of their wicked designs and intentions." Slaves also played an African instrument, the banjo, and beat tin buckets as a substitute for drums. Whatever instrument they played, their music was tied to bodily movement. Sometimes slaves imitated white dances like the minuet, but in a way that ridiculed the high manners of their masters. More often, they expressed themselves in a dance African in origin, emphasizing shuffling steps and bodily contortions rather than the erect precision of whites' dances.

Whether at work or at prayer, slaves liked to sing. Work songs describing slave experiences usually consisted of a leader's chant and a choral response:

> *I love old Virginny*
> *So ho! boys! so ho!*
> *I love to shuck corn*
> *So ho! boys! so ho!*
> *Now's picking cotton time*
> *So ho! boys! so ho!*

Masters encouraged such songs, believing that singing induced the slaves to work harder and that the innocent content of most work songs proved that the slaves were happy. Recalling his own past, Frederick Douglass came closer to the truth when he observed that "slaves sing most when they are most unhappy. The songs of the slave represent the sorrows of his heart; and he is relieved by them, only as an aching heart is relieved by its tears."

Blacks also sang religious songs, later known as spirituals. The origin of spirituals is shrouded in obscurity, but it is clear that by 1820 blacks at camp meetings had improvised what one white described as "short scraps of disjointed affirmations, pledges, or prayers

The Banjo Lesson,
by Henry O. Tanner, c. 1893
Tanner, a black artist, captured African-Americans' rich musical traditions and close family bonds in this evocative painting. Africans brought the banza, or banjo, to the Americas. Crafted from gourds and animal hides, the instruments shown above were made and played by slaves.

lengthened out with long repetition choruses." As this description suggests, whites usually took a dim view of spirituals and tried to make slaves sing "good psalms and hymns" instead of "the extravagant and nonsensical chants, and catches, and hallelujah songs of their own composing." Indeed, when around whites, blacks often sang hymns like those of Isaac Watts and other great white evangelicals, but nothing could dampen slaves' enthusiasm for songs of their own making.

Spirituals reflected the potent emphasis that the slaves' religion put on deliverance from earthly travails. To a degree, the same was true of white hymns, but spirituals were more direct and concrete. Slaves sang, for example,

In that morning, true believers,
In that morning,
We will sit aside of Jesus
In that morning,
If you should go fore I go,
In that morning,
You will sit aside of Jesus
In that morning,
True believers, where your tickets
In that morning,
Master Jesus got your tickets
In that morning.

Another spiritual proclaimed, "We will soon be free, when the Lord will call us home."

CONCLUSION

The emergence of an African-American culture was one among many features that made the Old South distinctive. With its huge black population, lack of industries, and dispersed white population, the South seemed a world apart. Even while finding individual southerners agreeable, northerners increasingly recognized the differences between their region and the South in the antebellum years. Whether or not they believed that the federal government should tamper with slavery, northerners grew convinced that slavery had cut the South off from progress and had turned it into a region of "sterile land, and bankrupt estates."

Conversely, to most white southerners, the North, and especially the industrial Northeast, appeared to be the region that deviated from the march of progress. Southerners felt most Americans—indeed, most people throughout the world—practiced agriculture and that agriculture made the South a more comfortable place for millions than factories rendered the North. In reaction to northern assaults on slavery, southerners portrayed the institution as a time-honored and benevolent response to the natural inequality of the black and white races. Southerners pointed to the slaves' adequate nutrition, their embrace of evangelical Protestantism, the affection of some slaves for their masters, and even their work songs as evidence of the slaves' contentment.

In reality, few if any slaves accepted slavery. Although slaves rebelled infrequently and had little chance for permanent escape, they often engaged in covert resistance to their bondage. The slaves embraced Christianity, but they understood it differently from whites. Whereas Christianity taught whites the need to make slaves submissive, it taught slaves the gross injustice of human bondage.

CHRONOLOGY

1790s	Methodists and Baptists start to make major strides in converting slaves to Christianity.
1793	Eli Whitney invents the cotton gin.
1800	Gabriel Prosser leads a slave rebellion in Virginia.
1808	Congress prohibits external slave trade.
1812	Louisiana, the first state formed out of the Louisiana Purchase, is admitted to the Union.
1816–1819	Boom in cotton prices stimulates settlement of the Southwest.
1817	Mississippi enters the Union.
1819	Alabama enters the Union.
1819–1820	Missouri Compromise.
1822	Denmark Vesey's conspiracy is uncovered in South Carolina.
1831	William Lloyd Garrison starts *The Liberator*. Nat Turner leads a slave rebellion in Virginia.
1832	Virginia legislature narrowly defeats a proposal for gradual emancipation. Virginia's Thomas R. Dew writes an influential defense of slavery.
1835	Arkansas admitted to the Union.
1837	Economic panic begins, lowering cotton prices.
1844–1845	Methodist Episcopal and Baptist churches split into northern and southern wings over slavery.
1845	Florida and Texas admitted to the Union.
1849	Sugar production in Louisiana reaches its peak.
1849–1860	Period of high cotton prices.
1857	Hinton R. Helper, *The Impending Crisis of the South.*
1859	John Brown's raid on Harpers Ferry.
1860	South Carolina secedes from the Union.

FOR FURTHER READING

John B. Boles, *Black Southerners, 1619–1869* (1983). An excellent synthesis of scholarship on slavery.

Orville Vernon Burton, *In My Father's House Are Many Mansions: Family and Community in Edgefield, South Carolina* (1985). An extremely valuable study of the South Carolina upcountry.

Wilbur J. Cash, *The Mind of the South* (1941). A brilliant interpretation of southern history.

Bruce Collins, *White Society in the Antebellum South* (1985). A very good, brief synthesis of southern white society and culture.

William J. Cooper, *Liberty and Slavery: Southern Politics to 1860* (1983). A valuable synthesis and interpretation of recent scholarship on the antebellum South in national politics.

Clement Eaton, *The Growth of Southern Civilization, 1790–1860* (1961). A fine survey of social, economic, and political change.

Robert W. Fogel, *Without Consent or Contract: The Rise and Fall of American Slavery* (1989). A comprehensive reexamination of the slaves' productivity and welfare.

Robert W. Fogel and Stanley L. Engerman, *Time on the Cross: The Economics of American Negro Slavery* (1974). A controversial book that uses mathematical models to analyze the profitability of slavery.

Eugene D. Genovese, *Roll, Jordan, Roll: The World the Slaves Made* (1974). The most influential work on slavery in the Old South written during the last twenty years; a penetrating analysis of the paternalistic relationship between masters and slaves.

James Oakes, *The Ruling Race: A History of American Slaveholders* (1982). An important attack on the ideas of Eugene D. Genovese.

James Oakes, *Slavery and Freedom: An Interpretation of the Old South* (1990). A study stressing slavery's development in the context of liberal capitalism.

U. B. Phillips, *American Negro Slavery* (1918), and *Life and Labor in the Old South* (1929). Works marred by racial prejudice but containing a wealth of information about slavery and the plantation system.

Kenneth M. Stampp, *The Peculiar Institution: Slavery in the Ante-Bellum South* (1956). A standard account of the black experience under slavery.

Additional Bibliography

The Economic and Social Structure of the White South

William L. Barney, *The Road to Secession* (1972); Fred Bateman and Thomas Weiss, *A Deplorable Scarcity: The Failure of Industrialism in the Slave Economy* (1981); Orville V. Burton and Robert McMath, eds., *Class, Conflict, and Consensus* (1982); Mary B. Chesnut, *A Diary from Dixie* (edited by Ben Ames Williams, 1949); Blanche Henry Clark, *The Tennessee Yeoman, 1840–1860* (1942); Catherine G. Clinton, *The Plantation Mistress: Women's World in the Old South* (1982); Barbara J. Fields, *Slavery and Freedom on the Middle Ground: Maryland During the Nineteenth Century* (1985); Elizabeth Fox-Genovese, *Within the Plantation Household: Black and White Women of the Old South* (1988); Eugene Genovese, *The Political Economy of Slavery* (1965); Steven Hahn, *The Roots of Southern Populism: Yeomen Farmers and the Transformation of the Georgia Upcountry, 1850–1890* (1983); Daniel R. Hundley, *Social Relations in Our Southern States* (1860); Suzanne Lebsock, *The Free Women of Petersburg: Status Culture in a Southern Town, 1784–1860* (1984); Forrest McDonald and Grady McWhiney, "The Antebellum Southern Herdsman: A Reinterpretation," *Journal of Southern History* 41 (May 1975): 147–166; Frank L. Owsley, *Plain Folk of the Old South* (1949); Anne F. Scott, *The Southern Lady: From Pedestal to Politics, 1830–1930* (1970); Herbert Weaver, *Mississippi Farmers, 1850–1860* (1945); Ralph A. Wooster, *Politicians, Planters, and Plain Folk* (1975); Gavin Wright, *The Political Economy of the Cotton South* (1978).

The Values of the White South

David F. Allmendinger, Jr., *Ruffin: Family and Reform in the Old South* (1990); Edward L. Ayers, *Vengeance and Justice: Crime and Punishment in the Nineteenth-Century American South* (1984); David T. Bailey, *Shadow on the Church: Southwestern Evangelical Religion and the Issue of Slavery, 1783–1860* (1985); Dickson D. Bruce, *Violence and Culture in the Antebellum South* (1979); William J. Cooper, *The South and the Politics of Slavery, 1829–1856* (1978); James D. Essig, *The Bonds of Wickedness: American Evangelicals Against Slavery, 1770–1808* (1982); Drew G. Faust, *A Sacred Circle: The Dilemma of the Intellectual in the Old South, 1840–1860* (1977) and *James Henry Hammond and the Old South: A Design for Mastery* (1982); John Hope Franklin, *The Militant South* (1966); George M. Fredrickson, *The Black Image in the White Mind: The Debate on Afro-American Character and Destiny, 1817–1914* (1971) and *White Supremacy: A Comparative Study in American and South African History* (1981); Alison G. Freehling, *Drift Toward Dissolution: The Virginia Slavery Debate of 1831–1832* (1982); Elliott J. Gorn, " 'Gouge and Bite, Pull Hair and Scratch': The Social Significance of Fighting in the Southern Backcountry," *American Historical Review* XC (February 1985): 18–43; Michael Hindus, *Prison and Plantation: Crime, Justice, and Authority in Massachusetts and South Carolina, 1767–1878* (1980); John McCardell, *The Idea of a Southern Nation: Southern Nationalists and Southern Nationalism* (1979); Donald G. Mathews, *Religion in the Old South* (1977); Ronald Takaki, *A Pro-Slavery Crusade: The Agitation to Reopen the African Slave Trade* (1980); J. Mills Thornton, *Politics and Power in a Slave Society: Alabama, 1800–1860* (1978); Larry E. Tise, *Proslavery: A History of the Defense of Slavery in America, 1701–1840* (1987); Bertram Wyatt-Brown, *Southern Honor: Ethics and Behavior in the Old South* (1982).

Black Experience and Culture in the Old South

Ira Berlin, *Slaves Without Masters: The Free Negro in the Antebellum South* (1974); John Blassingame, *The Slave Community* (1972); Leonard P. Curry, *The Free Black in Urban America, 1800–1850: The Shadow of the Dream* (1981); Carl N. Degler, *Neither Black Nor White: Slavery and Race Relations in Brazil and the United States* (1971); Dena J. Epstein, *Sinful Tunes and Spirituals: Black Folk Music to the Civil War* (1977); Claudia D. Goldin, *Urban Slavery in the American South, 1820–1860*

(1976); Herbert G. Gutman, *The Black Family in Slavery and Freedom, 1759–1925* (1976); Vincent Harding, *There Is a River: The Black Struggle for Freedom in America* (1981); Jacqueline Jones, *Labor of Love, Labor of Sorrow: Black Women, Work, and the Family from Slavery to the Present* (1985); Lawrence W. Levine, *Black Culture and Black Consciousness: Afro-American Folk Thought from Slavery to Freedom* (1977); Stephen B. Oates, *The Fires of Jubilee* (1975); Leslie H. Owens, *This Species of Property: Slave Life and Slave Culture in the Old South* (1976); Albert J. Raboteau, *Slave Religion* (1978); George P. Rawick, *From Sundown to Sunup: The Making of a Black Community* (1972); Jon Michael Spencer, *Black Hymnody* (1992); Robert S. Starobin, *Industrial Slavery in the Old South* (1970); Michael Tadman, *Speculators and Slaves: Traders and Slaves in the Old South* (1989).

California Forty-Niner
c. 1850

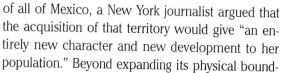

IMMIGRATION, EXPANSION, AND SECTIONAL CONFLICT 1840–1848

Considering themselves uniquely civilized and progressive, many antebellum Americans found the idea that God had ordained the spread of their civilization over all of North America irresistible. "Americans regard this continent as their birthright," proclaimed Sam Houston, the first president of the independent republic of Texas, in 1847. Those whom Americans saw as less civilized, notably the Indians and the Mexicans, could rightfully be dispossessed of their land in order to make way for "our mighty march."

This was not idle talk. In less than a thousand days of feverish activity during the administration of President James K. Polk, the United States increased its land area by 50 percent. The nation not only annexed Texas and successfully negotiated with Britain to acquire that part of Oregon south of the forty-ninth parallel but also fought a war with Mexico that led to the acquisition of California and New Mexico. Americans justified these takeovers on some of the same grounds that they had used earlier to dispossess the Indians of their lands. South Carolina's John C. Calhoun boasted that nothing could prevent Americans, "an industrious and civilized race," from "passing into an uninhabited country where the power of the owners is not sufficient to keep them out." Some commentators even contended that expansion was a blessing in disguise for peoples whom Americans deemed less progressive than themselves. Calling in 1848 for the annexation of all of Mexico, a New York journalist argued that the acquisition of that territory would give "an entirely new character and new development to her population." Beyond expanding its physical boundaries, the United States swelled dramatically in population during the 1840s and 1850s, in part because of a spectacular rise in European immigration. The number of immigrants who entered the United States in these two decades alone exceeded the nation's entire population in 1790. European immigration soared during the mid-1840s, at the same time that the nation plunged into expansion.

Although antebellum immigration and territorial expansion had different sources, the two developments became closely linked. For example, as the penny press whipped up fervor for expansion among the urban immigrant masses, they increasingly championed efforts to push the national boundary to the Pacific Ocean. Most immigrants, moreover, supported the Democratic party, which embraced expansion far more enthusiastically than the rival Whig party. The immigrant vote helped to tip the election of 1844 to the Democrats and brought an ardent expansionist, James K. Polk, to the White House.

Beyond these direct connections between immigration and expansion, immigration indirectly stimulated expansion. New immigrants, particularly the Irish, crowded into cities and factory towns in search of work at a time when the post-1837 depression kept the wages of native-born workers low. Ugly outbursts of anti-immigrant feeling reflected the mounting tensions between the immigrant and native-born populations. A number of influential Democrats concluded that the best solution to the intensifying class and ethnic conflict lay in expanding the national boundaries, bringing more land under cultivation, and attracting immigrants to that land, in the process recapturing the ideal of America as a nation of self-sufficient farmers.

Moreover, Democrats advocated expansion as a means of reducing strife between the sections. Expansion into Oregon would gratify the North; expansion into Texas would please the South. Some influential Democrats even argued that Texas would become a kind of highway along which slaves and free blacks alike would wend their way over the horizon and into Mexico. In this way, the argument ran, expansion would gradually drive the sectionally divisive issue of race out of politics.

In reality, expansion brought sectional antagonism to the boiling point, split the Democratic party in the late 1840s, and set the nation on the path to the Civil War.

NEWCOMERS AND NATIVES

Between 1815 and 1860, 5 million European immigrants landed in the United States. Of these, 4.2 million arrived between 1840 and 1860; 3 million of them came in the single decade from 1845 to 1854. This ten-year period witnessed the largest immigration proportionate to the total population (then around 20 million) in American history. The Irish led the way as a source of immigration between 1840 and 1860, with the Germans running a close second. Smaller contingents continued to immigrate to the United States from England, Scotland, and Wales, and a growing number came from Norway, Sweden, Switzerland, and Holland. But by 1860 three-fourths of the 4.1 million foreign-born Americans were either Irish or German.

Expectations and Realities

A desire for religious freedom drew some immigrants to the United States. For example, when Mormon missionaries actively recruited converts in the slums of English factory towns, a number of English migrated to America. Many emigrants from Norway were Quakers fleeing persecution by the official Lutheran clergy. But a far larger number of Europeans sailed for America to better their economic condition. Their hope was fed by a continuous stream of travelers' accounts and letters from relatives describing America as a utopia for poor people. German peasants learned that they could purchase a large farm in America for the price of renting a small one in Germany. English men and women were told that enough good peaches and apples were left rotting in the orchards of Ohio to sink the British fleet.

Hoping for the best, emigrants often encountered the worst. Their problems began at ports of embarkation, where hucksters frequently sold them worthless tickets and where ships scheduled to leave in June might not sail until August. Countless emigrants spent precious savings in waterfront slums while awaiting departure. The ocean voyage itself proved terrifying; many emigrants had never set foot on a ship. Most sailed on cargo ships as steerage passengers, where, for six weeks or more, they endured quarters almost as crowded as on slave ships.

For many emigrants, the greatest shock came when they landed. "The folks aboard ship formed great plans for their future, all of which vanished quickly after landing," wrote a young German from Frankfurt in 1840. Immigrants quickly discovered that farming in America was a perilous prospect at best. Aside from lacking the capital to start a farm, most immigrants had to confront the fact that farming in the United States bore little resemblance to farming in Europe. European farmers valued the associations of their communities. Their social and cultural lives revolved around villages that were fringed by the fields that they worked. In contrast, as many immigrants quickly learned, American farmers lived in relative isolation. They might belong to rural neighborhoods in which farmers on widely scattered plots of land met occasionally at revivals or militia musters. But they lacked the compact village life of European farmers, and they possessed an individualistic psychology that led them to speculate in land and to move frequently.

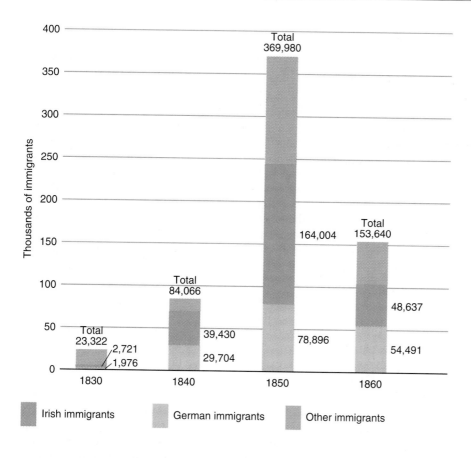

German, Irish, and Total Immigration, 1830–1860
Irish and German immigrants led the more than tenfold growth of immigration between 1830 and 1860.

SOURCE: U.S. Bureau of the Census, *Historical Statistics of the United States, Colonial Times to 1970*, Bicentennial Edition (Washington, D.C., 1975).

Despite the shocks and dislocations caused by migration, certain patterns emerged in the distribution of immigrants within the United States. Initially shaped by trade routes, these patterns were then perpetuated by custom. Most of the Irish settlers before 1840 departed from Liverpool on sailing ships that carried English manufactures to eastern Canada and New England in return for timber. On arrival in America, few of these Irish had the capital to become farmers, and hence they crowded into the urban areas of New England, New York, Pennsylvania, and New Jersey, where they could more easily find jobs. In contrast, German emigrants usually left from continental ports on ships engaged in the cotton trade with New Orleans. However, deterred from settling in the South by the presence of slavery, the oppressive climate, and the lack of economic opportunity, the Germans congregated in the upper Mississippi and Ohio valleys, especially in Illinois, Ohio, Wisconsin, and Missouri. Geographical concentration also characterized most of the smaller groups of immigrants. More than half of the Norwegian immigrants, for example, settled in Wisconsin, where they typically became farmers.

Immigrants were usually less likely to pursue agriculture in the New World than in Europe. Both the Germans and, to an even greater degree, the Irish tended to concentrate in cities. By 1860 these two groups formed more than 60 percent of the population of St. Louis; nearly half the population of New York City, Chicago, Cincinnati, Milwaukee, Detroit, and San Francisco; and well over a third that of New Orleans, Baltimore, and Boston. These fast-growing cities created an intense demand for the labor of people with strong backs and a willingness to work for low wages. Irish construction gangs built the houses, new streets, and aqueducts that were changing the face of urban America and dug the canals and railroads that threaded together the rapidly developing cities. A popular song recounted the fate of the thousands of Irishmen who died of cholera contracted during the building of a canal in New Orleans:

Ten thousand Micks, they swung their picks,
* To build the New Canal*
But the choleray was stronger 'n they.
* An' twice it killed them awl.*

The cities provided the sort of community life that seemed lacking in farming settlements. Immigrant societies like the Friendly Sons of St. Patrick took root in cities and combined with associations like the Hibernian Society for the Relief of Emigrants from Ireland to welcome the newcomers.

The Germans

In the mid-nineteenth century, the Germans were an extremely diverse group. In 1860 Germany was not a nation-state like France or Britain, but a collection of principalities and small kingdoms. German immigrants thought of themselves as Bavarians, Westphalians, or Saxons rather than as Germans. Moreover, the German immigrants included Catholics, Protestants (usually Lutherans), and Jews as well as a sprinkling of freethinkers who denounced the ritual, clergy, and doctrines of all religions. Although few in number, these critics were vehement in their attacks on the established churches. A pious Milwaukee Lutheran complained in 1860 that he could not drink a glass of beer in a saloon "without being angered by anti-Christian remarks or raillery against preachers."

German immigrants came from a wide range of social classes and occupations. The majority had engaged in farming, but a sizable minority were professionals, artisans, and tradespeople. Heinrich Steinweg, an obscure piano maker from Lower Saxony, arrived in New York City in 1851, anglicized his name to Henry Steinway, and in 1853 opened the firm of Steinway and Sons, which quickly achieved international acclaim for the quality of its pianos. Levi Strauss, a Jewish tailor from Bavaria, migrated to the United States in 1847. Upon hearing of the discovery of gold in California in 1848, Strauss gathered rolls of cloth and sailed for San Francisco. When a miner told him of the need for durable work trousers, Strauss fashioned a pair of overalls from canvas. To meet a quickly skyrocketing demand, he opened a factory in San Francisco; his cheap overalls, later known as blue jeans or Levi's, made him rich and famous.

For all their differences, the Germans were bound together by their common language, which strongly induced recent immigrants to the United States to congregate in German neighborhoods. Even prosperous Germans bent on climbing the social ladder usually did so within German neighborhoods. Germans formed their own militia and fire companies, sponsored parochial schools in which German was the language of instruction, started German-language newspapers, and organized their own balls and singing groups. The range of voluntary associations among Germans was almost as broad as among native-born Americans.

Other factors beyond their common language brought unity to the German immigrants. Ironically, the Germans' diversity also promoted their solidarity. For example, because they were able to supply their own doctors, lawyers, teachers, journalists, merchants, artisans, and clergy, the Germans had little need to go outside their own neighborhoods. Moreover, economic self-sufficiency conspired with the strong bonds of their language to encourage a clannish psychology among the German immigrants. Although they admired the Germans' industriousness,

German Winter Gardens
A well-known beer hall on lower Manhattan's Bowery, the German Winter Gardens were famous for music and sociability.

native-born Americans resented their economic success and disdained their clannishness. German refugee Moritz Busch complained that "the great mass of Anglo-Americans" held the Germans in contempt. The Germans responded by becoming even more clannish. In turn, their psychological separateness made it difficult for the Germans to be as politically influential as the Irish immigrants.

The Irish

Between 1815 and 1860, Irish immigration to the United States passed through several stages. Irish soldiers who fought against the United States in the War of 1812 had returned to their homeland with reports that America was a paradise filled with fertile land and abundant game, a place where "all a man wanted was a gun and sufficient ammunition to be able to live like a prince." Among the Irish who subsequently emigrated between 1815 and the mid-1820s, Protestant small landowners and tradespeople in search of better economic opportunity predominated.

From the mid-1820s to the mid-1840s, the character of Irish immigration to the United States gradually changed. Increasingly, the immigrants were Catholics drawn from the poorer classes, many of them tenant farmers whom Protestant landowners had evicted as "superfluous." Protestant or Catholic, rich or poor, 800,000 to a million Irish immigrants entered the United States between 1815 and 1844. Then, between 1845 and the early 1850s, a blight destroyed every harvest of Ireland's potatoes, virtually the only food of the peasantry, and spawned one of the most gruesome famines in history. The Great Famine inflicted indescribable suffering on the Irish peasantry and killed perhaps a million people. One landlord characterized the surviving tenants on his estate as no more than "famished and ghastly skeletons." To escape the ravages of famine, 1.8 million Irish migrated to the United States in the decade after 1845.

Overwhelmingly poor and Catholic, the Irish usually entered the work force at or near the bottom. The popular image of Paddy with his pickax and Bridget the maid contained a good deal of truth. Irish men in the cities dug cellars and often lived in them; outside the cities, they dug canals and railroad beds. Irish women often became domestic servants. Compared to other immigrant women, a high proportion of Irish women entered the work force, if not as maids then often as textile workers. By the 1840s Irish women were displacing native-born women in the textile mills of Lowell and Waltham. Poverty drove Irish women to work at early ages, and the outdoor, all-season work performed by their husbands turned many of them into working widows. Winifred Rooney became a nursemaid at the age of seven and an errand girl at eleven. She then learned needlework, a skill that helped her support her family after her husband's early death. The high proportion of employed Irish women reflected more than their poverty. Compared to the predominantly male German immigrants, more than half of the Irish immigrants were women, most of whom were single adults. In both Ireland and America, the Irish usually married late, and many never married. For Irish women to become self-supporting was only natural.

The lot of most Irish people was harsh. One immigrant described the life of the average Irish laborer in America as "despicable, humiliating, [and] slavish"; there was "no love for him—no protection of life—[he] can be shot down, run through, kicked, cuffed, spat upon—and no redress, but a response of 'served the damn son of an Irish b____ right, damn him.' " Yet some Irish struggled up the social ladder. In Philadelphia, which had a more varied industrial base than Boston, Irish men made their way into iron foundries, where some became foremen and supervisors. Other Irish rose into the middle class by opening grocery and liquor stores.

The varied occupations pursued by Irish immigrants brought them into conflict with two quite different groups. The poorer Irish who dug canals and cellars, hauled cargo on the docks, washed laundry for others, and served white families competed directly with equally poor free blacks. This competition stirred up Irish animosity toward blacks and a hatred of abolitionists. At the same time, enough Irish men eventually secured skilled or semiskilled jobs that clashes with native-born white workers became unavoidable.

Anti-Catholicism, Nativism, and Labor Protest

The hostility of native-born whites toward the Irish often took the form of anti-Catholicism. Anti-Catholicism had been a strong, if latent, impulse among American Protestants since the early Puritan days. The surge of Irish immigration during the second quarter of the nineteenth century revived anti-Catholic fever. For example, in 1834 rumors circulated among Boston Protestants that a Catholic convent in nearby Charlestown contained dungeons and torture chambers. The mother superior turned away a

Defenders of the True Faith
This cartoon portrays the mob that attacked a Roman Catholic convent in Charlestown, Massachusetts, in 1834, as composed of bigoted ruffians who flatter themselves that their deed will live as a heroic act in the national memory.

delegation of officials demanding to inspect the convent. Soon the building lay in ashes, the victim of a Protestant mob. In 1835 Samuel F. B. Morse, the future inventor of the telegraph, warned that the despotic governments of Europe were systematically flooding the United States with Catholic immigrants as part of a conspiracy to destroy republican institutions. "We must first stop this leak in the ship," he wrote, "through which the muddy waters from without threaten to sink us." That same year, the combative evangelical Protestant Lyman Beecher issued *A Plea for the West*, a tract in which he warned faithful Protestants of an alleged Catholic conspiracy to send immigrants to the West in sufficient numbers to dominate the region. A year later, the publication of Maria Monk's best-selling *Awful Disclosures of the Hotel Dieu Nunnery in Montreal* rekindled anti-Catholic hysteria. Although Maria Monk was actually a prostitute who had never lived in a convent, she professed to be a former nun. In her book, she described how the mother superior forced nuns to submit to the lustful advances of priests who entered the convent by a subterranean passage.

As Catholic immigration swelled in the 1840s, Protestants mounted a political counterattack. It took the form of nativist (anti-immigrant) societies with names like the American Republicans and the United Order of Americans. Although usually started as secret or semi-secret fraternal orders, most of these societies developed political offshoots. One, the Order of the Star-Spangled Banner, would evolve by 1854 into the "Know-Nothing," or American, party and would become a major political force in the 1850s. During the 1840s, however, nativist parties enjoyed only brief moments in the sun. These occurred mainly during flare-ups over local issues, such as whether students in predominantly Catholic neighborhoods should be allowed to use the Catholic Douay rather than Protestant King James version of the Bible for the scriptural readings that began each school day. In 1844, for example, after the American Republican party (which opposed any concessions to Catholics) won some offices in Philadelphia elections, fiery Protestant orators mounted soapboxes to denounce "popery," and Protestant mobs descended on Catholic neighborhoods. Before the militia quelled these "Bible Riots," thirty buildings lay in charred ruins and at least sixteen people had been killed.

Nativism fed on an explosive mixture of fears and discontents. Protestants thought that their doctrine that each individual could interpret the Bible was more democratic than Catholicism, which made doctrine the province of the pope and bishops. In addition, at a time when the wages of native-born artisans and journeymen were being depressed by the subdivision of tasks and by the aftermath of the Panic of 1837 (see Chapter 10), many Protestant workers concluded that Catholic immigrants, often desperately poor and willing to work for anything, were threats to their jobs. In reaction, Protestant artisans joined nativist societies.

Nativist outbursts were not labor's only response to the wage cuts that accompanied the depression. Some agitators began to advocate land reform as a solution to workers' economic woes. Americans had long cherished the notion that a nation so blessed by abundant land as the United States need never give rise to a permanent class of factory "wage slaves." In 1844 the English-born radical George Henry Evans organized the National Reform Association and rallied supporters with the slogan "Vote Yourself a Farm." Evans advanced neo-Jeffersonian plans for the establishment of "rural republican townships," composed of 160-acre plots for workers. He quickly gained the backing of artisans who preferred such "agrarian" notions to a further advance of the industrial order that was undermining their position. Evans was also supported by a number of middle-class intellectuals, among them Horace Greeley, the editor of the *New York Tribune*.

Land reformers argued that workers' true interests could never be reconciled with an industrial order in which factory operatives sold their labor for wages. By engaging in wage labor, they said, workers abandoned any hope of achieving economic independence. These reformers most appealed to articulate and self-consciously radical workers, particularly artisans and small masters whose independence was being threatened by factories and who feared that American labor was "fast verging on the servile dependence" common in Europe. But land reform offered little to factory operatives and wage-earning journeymen who completely lacked economic independence. In an age when a horse cost the average worker three months' pay and most factory workers dreaded "the horrors of wilderness life," the idea of solving industrial problems by resettling workers on farms seemed a pipe dream.

The land reformers believed that only a fundamental restructuring of economic relations would improve the condition of workers. They therefore opposed strikes for short-term wage increases. In contrast, labor unions, less idealistic in their goals, were more sympathetic to strikes. Unions had flourished in a number of cities during the mid-1830s and then experienced a resurgence in the mid-1840s as the effects of the depression wore off. They appealed to several groups indifferent to land reform. For example, as refugees from an agricultural society, desperately poor Irish immigrants could more realistically hope to improve their status through unions and strikes rather than through farming. The most celebrated strike in the New York City area in the 1840s was organized by Irish dockworkers in Brooklyn. Women workers also unionized in the 1840s. In 1845 tailoresses and seamstresses organized the Ladies Industrial Association in New York City; their leader, Elizabeth Gray, proclaimed, "Too long have we been bound down by tyrant employers."

Agitation by labor unionists generated considerable commotion in the 1840s and resulted in a few victories for workers. In the landmark case of *Commonwealth* v. *Hunt* (1842), the Massachusetts Supreme Court ruled that labor unions, or "combinations," were not illegal monopolies that restrained trade. But because less than 1 percent of the work force belonged to a labor union during the 1840s, the impact of unions was sharply limited.

Although immigrant and native-born workers at times united to support land reform or unions, profound divisions along ethnic and religious lines split the antebellum working class. Even after labor had gained a modest victory in the *Commonwealth* v. *Hunt* decision, employers freely fired union agitators and replaced them with cheap immigrant labor. "Hundreds of honest laborers," a labor paper reported in 1848, "have been dismissed from employment in the manufactories of New England because they have been suspected of knowing their rights and daring to assert them." This kind of repression effectively blunted agitation for the ten-hour day (at a time when workers typically toiled for twelve to fourteen hours). The drive for a shorter workday had gained support in the 1840s from a number of organizations, among them the Lowell Female Reform Association.

During the 1830s and 1840s, tensions between native-born and immigrant workers inevitably became intertwined with the political divisions of the second party system.

Labor Protest and Immigrant Politics

Very few immigrants had ever cast a vote in an election prior to their arrival in America, and only a small fraction were refugees from political persecution. Political upheavals had erupted in Austria and several of the German states in the turbulent year of 1848 (the so-called Revolutions of 1848), but among the million German immigrants to the United States, only about ten thousand were political refugees, or "Forty-Eighters."

Once they had settled in the United States, however, many immigrants became politically active. They quickly found that urban political organizations, some of them dominated by earlier immigrants, would help them to find lodging and employment—in return for votes. Both the Irish and the Germans identified overwhelmingly with the Democratic party. An obituary of 1837 that described a New Yorker as a "warm-hearted Irishman and an unflinching Democrat" could have been written of millions of other Irish. Similarly, the Germans became stalwart supporters of the Democrats in cities like Milwaukee and St. Louis.

The immigrants' worries about staying financially afloat partly explain their widespread Democratic support. Andrew Jackson had given the Democratic party an antiprivilege and anti-aristocratic coloration, and most immigrants, especially the Irish, saw the Democrats as more sympathetic than the Whigs to the common people. Moreover, many Irish immigrants turned to the Democrats because antislavery was more closely identified in the North with the Whig party than with the Democratic party. The Irish loathed abolitionism out of fear that emancipated slaves would migrate north and compete with them for unskilled jobs.

Beyond these economic considerations, most Irish and German immigrants saw the Whigs as more of a threat than the Democrats to their moral and religious values. The Whigs' identification with temperance reform, for example, pushed the Irish and Germans toward the Democrats, for both immigrant groups had hearty traditions of drinking. The fact that some prominent temperance reformers were also leading anti-Catholics further strengthened the allegiance of Catholic immigrants to the anti-temperance Democrats. Public-school reform, a major Whig goal, also drew fire from immigrants. The Irish looked upon school reform as a menace to the Catholicism of their children; the Germans saw it as a threat to the integrity of their language and culture.

Liquor regulations and school laws were city or state concerns rather than federal responsibilities, but the two major parties proved adept at attracting voters who initially had been aroused by local issues. For example, nativists usually voted for Whigs rather than for the candidates of one of the overtly nativist parties like the American Republicans. The Democratic party that the immigrants so widely supported in their battles over local matters served them as a kind of school of broad, national principles. It taught them to venerate George Washington, to revere Thomas Jefferson and Andrew Jackson, and to view "monied capitalists" as parasites who would tremble when the people spoke. It introduced immigrants to Democratic newspapers, Democratic picnics, and Democratic parades. The Democrats, by identifying their party with all that they thought best about the United States, helped give immigrants a sense of themselves as Americans. By the same token, the Democratic party introduced immigrants to national issues. It redirected political loyalties that often had been forged on local issues into the arena of national politics. During the 1830s the party had persuaded immigrants that national measures like the Bank of the United States and the tariff, seemingly remote from their daily lives, were vital to them. Now during the 1840s, the Democrats would try to convince immigrants that national expansion advanced their interests.

THE WEST AND BEYOND

As late as 1840, Americans who referred to the West still meant the area between the Appalachian Mountains and the Mississippi River or just beyond, a region that included much of the present-day Midwest. Beyond the states bordering the Mississippi lay an inhospitable region unlike any that the earlier settlers had ever known. Those who ventured west of Missouri encountered the Great Plains, a semiarid plateau with few trees. Winds sucked the moisture from the soil. Bands of nomadic Indians—including the Pawnees, Kiowas, and Sioux—roamed this territory and gained sustenance mainly from the buffalo. They ate its meat, wore its fur, and covered their dwellings with its hide. Aside from some well-watered sections of northern Missouri and eastern Kansas and Nebraska, the Great Plains presented would-be farmers with massive obstacles.

The formidable barrier of the Great Plains did not stop settlement of the West in the long run. Temporarily, however, it shifted public interest toward the verdant region lying beyond the Rockies, the Far West.

The Far West

With the Transcontinental (or Adams-Onís) Treaty of 1819, the United States had given up to Spain its claims to Texas west of the Sabine River. This had left Spain in undisputed possession not only of Texas but also of California and the vast territory of New Mexico. Combined, California and New Mexico included all of present-day California and New Mexico as well as modern Nevada, Utah, and Arizona, and parts of Wyoming and Colorado. Two years later, a series of revolts against Spanish rule had culminated in the independence of Mexico and in Mexico's takeover of all North American territory previously claimed by Spain. The Transcontinental Treaty also had provided for Spain's cessation to the United States of its claims to the country of Oregon north of the forty-second parallel (the northern boundary of California). Then in

Trails to the West, 1840
By 1840 several trails carried pioneers from Missouri and Illinois to the West.

1824 and 1825, Russia abandoned its claims to Oregon south of 54°40′ (the southern boundary of Alaska). In 1827 the United States and Britain, each of which had claims to Oregon based on discovery and exploration, revived an agreement (originally signed in 1818) for joint occupation of the territory between 42° and 54°40′, a colossal area that contemporaries could describe no more precisely than the "North West Coast of America, Westward of the Stony [Rocky] Mountains" and that included all of modern Oregon, Washington, and Idaho as well as parts of present-day Wyoming, Montana, and Canada.

Collectively, Texas, New Mexico, California, and Oregon composed an area larger than Britain, France, and Germany combined. Such a vast region should have tempted any nation, but during the 1820s Mexico, Britain, and the United States viewed the Far West as a remote and shadowy frontier. By 1820 the American line of settlement had only reached Missouri, well over 2,000 miles (counting detours for mountains) from the West Coast. El Paso on the Rio Grande and Taos in New Mexico lay, respectively, 1,200 and 1,500 miles north of Mexico City. Britain, of course, was many thousands of miles from Oregon.

Far Western Trade

The earliest American and British outposts on the West Coast were trading centers established by merchants who had reached California and Oregon by sailing around South America and up the Pacific. Between the late 1790s and the 1820s, for example, Boston merchants had built a thriving exchange of coffee, tea, spices, cutlery, clothes, and hardware—indeed, anything that could be bought or manufactured in the eastern United States—for furs (especially those of sea otters), cattle, hides, and tallow (rendered from cattle fat and used for making soap and candles). Between 1826 and 1828 alone, Boston traders took more than 6 million cattle hides out of California; in the otherwise undeveloped California economy, these hides, called "California banknotes," served as the main medium of exchange. During the 1820s the British Hudson's Bay Company developed a similar trade in Oregon and northern California.

The California trade occasioned little friction with Mexico. Producing virtually no manufactured goods, Hispanic people born in California (called *californios*) were as eager to buy as the traders were to sell—so eager that they sometimes rowed out to the vessels laden with goods, thus sparing the traders the trip ashore. Those traders who did settle in California, like the American Thomas O. Larkin and the Swiss-born John Sutter, quickly learned to speak Spanish and became assimilated into Mexican culture.

Farther south, trading links developed during the 1820s between St. Louis and Santa Fe along the famed Santa Fe Trail. The Panic of 1819 left the American Midwest short of cash and its merchants burdened by unsold goods. Pulling themselves up from adversity, however, plucky midwesterners loaded wagon trains with tools, utensils, clothing, windowpanes, and household sundries each spring and rumbled westward to Santa Fe, where they traded their merchandise for mules and New Mexican silver. To a far greater extent than had Spain, Mexico welcomed this trade. Indeed, by the 1830s more than half the goods entering New Mexico by the Santa Fe Trail trickled into the mineral-rich interior provinces of Mexico such as Chihuahua and Sonora, with the result that the Mexican silver peso, which midwestern traders brought back with them, quickly became the principal medium of exchange in Missouri.

Some Americans ventured north from Santa Fe to trap beaver in what is today western Colorado and eastern Utah. The profitability of the beaver trade also encouraged merchants and trappers like the "mountain man" Jedidiah Smith (see Chapter 9) to venture directly from St. Louis into the Rockies in competition with both the Santa Fe traders and agents of the Hudson's Bay Company. On the Green River in Mexican territory, the St. Louis–based trader William Ashley in 1825 inaugurated an annual rendezvous or encampment where traders exchanged beaver pelts for supplies, thereby saving themselves the trip to St. Louis. With the aid of Ashley's encampments, the St. Louis traders gradually wrested the beaver trade from their competitors in Santa Fe.

For the most part, American traders and trappers operating on the northern Mexican frontier in the 1820s and 1830s posed more of a threat to the beaver than to Mexico's provinces. (If silk hats had not become fashionable in Europe in the mid-1830s, the beaver might have been hunted to extinction.) Not only did the Mexican people of California and New Mexico depend on the American trade for manufactured goods, but Mexican officials in both provinces relied on customs duties to support their governments. In New Mexico the government often had to await the arrival of the annual caravan of traders from St. Louis before it could pay its officials and soldiers.

Although the relations between Mexicans and Americans were mutually beneficial during the 1820s, the potential for conflict was never absent. Spanish-speaking, Roman Catholic, and accustomed to a more hierarchical society, the Mexicans formed a striking contrast to the largely Protestant, individualistic Americans. And although few American traders themselves became permanent residents of Mexico, many returned with glowing reports of the climate and fertility of Mexico's northern provinces. By the 1820s American settlers were already moving into eastern Texas. At the same time, the ties that bound the central government of Mexico to its northern frontier provinces were starting to fray.

Mexican Government in the Far West

Spain, and later Mexico, recognized that the key to controlling the frontier provinces lay in promoting their settlement by civilized Hispanic people—that is, by Spaniards, Mexicans, and Indians who had embraced Catholicism and agriculture. The mission had long been the key instrument of Spanish expansion on the frontier. By the early nineteenth century, missions

Mission San Gabriel, *by Ferdinand Deppe, 1832*
The San Gabriel Mission was founded in 1771 in southern California, partly with the intent of converting the local Indians, who are shown here settled in a thatched hut, to Catholicism. In 1781 the Spanish governor set out from this mission to found El Pueblo de Nuestra Señora la Reina de Los Angelos Porciúncula, now usually known simply as Los Angeles.

stretched up the California coast from San Diego to San Francisco and into the interior of New Mexico and Texas.

The Spanish mission combined political, economic, and religious goals—an arrangement alien to the American separation of church and state. The Franciscan priests who staffed the missions were paid government agents who endeavored to convert the Native Americans and to settle them on mission lands. By 1823 more than twenty thousand Indians lived on the lands of the twenty-one California missions. To protect the missions, the Spanish often constructed forts, or presidios, near them. San Francisco was the site of a mission and a presidio founded in 1776 and did not develop as a town until the 1830s.

Dealt a blow by the successful struggle for Mexican independence, Spain's system of missions and presidios declined in the late 1820s and 1830s. The Mexican government gradually "secularized" the missions by distributing their lands to ambitious government officials and private ranchers. Freed from the supervision of Franciscan priests, some former mission-dwelling Native Americans became forced laborers in white communities, but many returned to their nomadic ways and joined with Indians who had always resisted the missions. During the 1820s and 1830s, these "barbaric Indians"—notably, the Comanches, Apaches, Navajos, and Utes—terrorized the Mexican frontier by stealing livestock and carrying off Hispanic women and children. Apaches and Comanches attacked New

Watermelon Race
As Americans advanced into the Southwest, they became familiar with such colorful Mexican customs as the watermelon race shown here.

Mexico and Texas, and the Comanches swept into northern Mexico, striking within 150 miles of Mexico City. The legislature of the Mexican state of Chihuahua complained in 1846 that "we travel the roads at their [the Indians'] whim; we cultivate the land where they wish and in the amount that they wish."

Mexican policy was partly responsible for this upsurge in terrorism. With the secularization of the missions, Hispanic ranchers had turned some Native Americans into virtual slaves on ranches now bloated by the addition of former mission lands. In addition, Mexican frontier dwellers thought little of raiding Native American tribes for domestic servants. "To get Indian girls to work for you," a descendant of Hispanic settlers recalled, "all you had to do was organize a company against the Navahos or Utes or Apaches and kill all the men you could and bring captive the children." In short, the "barbaric Indians" had many scores to settle with the Mexicans.

Because the overofficered and corrupt Mexican army had little taste for frontier fighting, Mexican settlers on the frontier could not rely on the military for protection against the Indians. Consequently, few Mexicans ventured into the undeveloped, lawless territories. Few areas in the Western Hemisphere potentially so rich were so underpopulated. In 1836 New Mexico contained about 30,000 people of Hispanic culture; California, about 3,200; and Texas, 4,000. Far from their government in Mexico City,

which often seemed indifferent to their welfare, and dependent on American traders for the necessities of civilization, the Mexicans of the frontier provinces formed only a frail barrier against the advance of American settlement.

The American Settlement of Texas

Unlike the provinces of New Mexico and California, the Mexican state known as Coahuila-Texas lacked the natural protection of mountains and deserts. During the post-1815 cotton boom, small bands of southern farmers began to push across the Sabine River into eastern Texas in search of more land for cotton cultivation. In addition, after the Panic of 1819, many debt-ridden Americans in the Midwest and South found flight into Texas a convenient escape from creditors. By 1823 some three thousand Americans lived in eastern Texas. In 1824 the Mexican government began actively to encourage American colonization of Texas as a way to bring in manufactured goods (of which the Mexicans produced virtually none) and to gain protection against the Indians. Expecting that American settlers would live peacefully under Mexican rule, the Mexican government bestowed generous land grants on agents (known as *empresarios*) who contracted to bring Americans into Texas. The most successful of these *empresarios*, Stephen F. Austin, had attracted some three hundred American families to

Texas by 1825. Other *empresarios* followed suit, and by 1830 some seven thousand Americans lived in Texas, more than double the Mexican population dwelling there.

Although Mexico gained some advantages from the American immigration into Texas, the Americans proved a mixed blessing to the Mexican people. Some unscrupulous American traders, like the notorious Harlan Coffee, provoked the Indians to raid Mexican settlements and seize livestock to trade for American liquor and guns. Other American immigrants were roust-abouts who moved to Texas to escape debts and sheriffs. But even law-abiding Americans posed a problem. Unlike the relatively assimilated American traders in California, the settlers of Texas were farming families who dwelled in eastern Texas, apart from the Mexicans who had congregated in the western part of the state. Although naturalized as Mexican citizens, the American settlers distrusted the Mexicans and complained constantly about the creaking, erratic Mexican judicial system. Above all, Mexico had not bargained for the size and speed of the American immigration. The Amercans, reported Mexican general Manual Mier y Terán in 1828, had established farming communities before the Mexicans were even aware of their presence. Four years later, Mier y Terán ran a sword through his heart in despair over Mexico's inability to stem and control the American advance.

As early as 1826, an American *empresario*, Haden Edwards, led a revolt against Mexican rule, but Mexican forces, aided by Stephen F. Austin, quickly crushed the uprising. Although, like Austin, most Americans were still willing to live in Texas as naturalized Mexican citizens, during the early 1830s, the allegiance of the Americans to the Mexican government was severely eroded. In 1830 Mexico closed Texas to further immigration from the United States and, having emancipated its own slaves in 1829, forbade the introduction of more slaves to Texas. The latter measure struck directly at the Americans, many of whom were slaveholders. However, Mexico lacked the military might to enforce its decrees. Between 1830 and 1834, the number of Americans in Texas doubled. In 1834 Austin secured repeal of the 1830 prohibition on American immigration, and by 1835 an estimated one thousand Americans a month were crossing into Texas. In 1836 Texas contained some 30,000 white Americans, 5,000 black slaves, and 4,000 Mexicans.

As American immigration swelled, Mexican politics grew increasingly unstable. "The political charac-

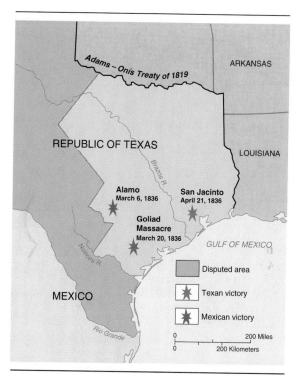

Major Battles in the Texas Revolution, 1835–1836
Sam Houston's victory at San Jacinto was the decisive action of the war and avenged the massacres at the Alamo and Goliad.

ter of this country," Austin wrote, "seems to partake of its geological features—all is volcanic." From its inception, the government of the Mexican republic had rested on a precarious balance between liberals (or federalists), who favored popular liberty and decentralized government, and conservative centralists, who sought to concentrate power in the hands of military and church officials in Mexico City. In 1834 Mexican president Antonio López de Santa Anna ousted leading liberals from his government and began to restrict the powers of the regimes in Coahuila-Texas and other Mexican states. His actions ignited a series of rebellions in the Mexican states, the most important of which became known as the Texas Revolution.

The Texas Revolution

Santa Anna's brutality in crushing most of the rebellions alarmed Austin and others. Austin initially had taken a moderate position. He hoped to cooperate with Mexican liberals to restore the Mexican Constitution of 1824 and to secure greater autonomy for Texas

Sam Houston
This photo shows Houston as a prosperous and successful elder statesman. But in his youth Houston had a reputation for wildness. In 1829 he resigned Tennessee's governorship and lived for three years among the Cherokees.

within Mexico. At the outset, he did not favor Texas's independence from Mexico. When Santa Anna invaded Texas in the fall of 1835, however, Austin cast his lot with the more radical Americans who wanted independence.

At first, Santa Anna's army met with success. In late February 1836, his force of 4,000 men laid siege to San Antonio, whose 200 Texan defenders retreated into an abandoned mission, the Alamo. After repelling repeated attacks and inflicting more than 1,500 casualties on Santa Anna's army, the remaining 187 Texans, including such famed frontiersmen as Davy Crockett and Jim Bowie, were wiped out to the last man on March 6. A few weeks later, Mexican troops massacred some 350 Texas prisoners at Goliad.

Even before these events, Texas delegates had met in a windswept shed in the village of Washington, Texas, and declared Texas independent of Mexico. The rebels by then had settled on a military leader, Sam Houston, for their president. A giant man who wore

leopard-skin vests, Houston retreated east to pick up recruits (mostly Americans who crossed the border to fight Santa Anna). Houston turned and surprised Santa Anna on a prairie near the San Jacinto River in April. Shouting "Remember the Alamo," Houston's army of eight hundred tore through the Mexican lines, killing nearly half of Santa Anna's men in fifteen minutes and taking Santa Anna himself prisoner. Houston then forced Santa Anna to sign a treaty (which the Mexican government never ratified) recognizing the independence of Texas.

American Settlements in California, New Mexico, and Oregon

California and New Mexico, both less accessible than Texas, exerted no more than a mild attraction for American settlers during the 1820s and 1830s. Only a few hundred Americans resided in New Mexico in 1840; that same year, California contained perhaps four hundred Americans. A contemporary observed that the Americans living in California and New Mexico during these years "are scattered throughout the whole Mexican population, and most of them have Spanish wives. . . . They live in every respect like the Spanish."

Yet the beginnings of change were already evident. California's Hispanic population generally welcomed American immigration as a way to encourage economic development. In addition, some Americans who settled in California before 1840 sent back highly favorable reports of the region to induce immigration. One story, tongue-in-cheek, told of a 250-year-old man who had to leave the region when he finally wanted to die. Such reports produced their intended effect. During the 1840s an ever-widening stream of Americans migrated to the interior Sacramento Valley, where they lived geographically and culturally apart from the Mexicans. For these land-hungry settlers, no sacrifice seemed too great if it led to California.

Oregon, with its abundant farmland, beckoned settlers from the Mississippi Valley. During the 1830s missionaries like the Methodist Jason Lee moved into Oregon's Willamette Valley, and by 1840 the area contained some five hundred Americans. Enthusiastic reports sent back by Lee piqued interest in Oregon. An orator in Missouri described Oregon as a "pioneer's paradise" where "the pigs are running around under the great acorn trees, round and fat and already cooked, with knives and forks sticking in them so that you can cut off a slice whenever you are hungry." Indeed, to some, Oregon seemed even more attractive than California. Oregon was already jointly occupied by Britain and the United States, and its prospects for eventual U.S. annexation appeared better than California's.

The Overland Trail

Whether bound for California or Oregon, the pioneers faced a four-month journey across terrain that was all the more terrifying because little was known about it. The eastern press teemed with horror stories, mostly fictitious, of Indian massacres. Assuming that they would have to fight their way across the plains, settlers prepared for the trip by buying enough guns for an army from merchants in the rival jump-off towns of Independence and St. Joseph, Missouri. In reality, the pioneers were more likely to shoot themselves or each other by accident than to be shot by the usually cooperative Indians, and much more likely to be scalped by the inflated prices charged by merchants in Independence or "St. Joe" than by the Native Americans.

Once embarked, the emigrants faced new hardships and hazards: kicks from mules, oxen that collapsed from thirst, overloaded wagons that broke down. Trails were difficult to follow—at least until they became littered by the debris of broken wagons

and by the bleached bones of oxen. After 1845 guidebooks helped emigrants to chart their course, but these often understated the distance across such formidable barriers as the Great Salt Desert. The Donner party, which set out from Illinois in 1846, lost so much time following the advice of one such book that its members became snowbound in the High Sierra and reached California only after its survivors had turned to cannibalism.

Emigrants responded to the challenges of the overland trail by cooperating closely with each other. Most set out in huge wagon trains rather than as individuals. Reflecting firmly entrenched traditions, husbands depended on their wives to pack and unpack the wagon each day, to milk the cows brought along to stock the new farms in the West, and to cook. Women, too, assisted with the childbirths that occurred on the trail at about the same frequency as in the nation as a whole. Men yoked and unyoked the oxen, drove the wagons and stock, and formed hunting parties.

Between 1840 and 1848, an estimated 11,500 emigrants followed an overland trail to Oregon, and some 2,700 reached California. These numbers were modest and concentrated in the years from 1844 to 1848. Yet even small numbers could make a huge difference in the Far West, for the British could not effectively settle Oregon at all, and the Mexican population in California was small and scattered. By 1845 California clung to Mexico by the thinnest of threads. The territory's Hispanic population, the californios, felt little allegiance to Mexico, which they contemptuously referred to as the "other shore." Nor did they feel any allegiance to the United States. Some californios wanted independence from Mexico; others looked to the day when California might

Conestoga Wagon
Originating in southeastern Pennsylvania around 1750, drawn by four or six horses or mules, and distinguished by its slanting gates and its cloth cover supported by bows of bent wood, the conestoga wagon served for a century as the ship of American inland commerce.

become a protectorate of Britain or perhaps even France. But these *californios*, with their shaky allegiances, now faced a growing number of American settlers whose political sympathies were not at all divided.

THE POLITICS OF EXPANSION

The major issue that arose as a by-product of westward expansion was whether the United States should annex the independent Texas republic. In the mid-1840s the Texas-annexation issue generated the kind of political passions that banking questions had ignited in the 1830s, and became entangled with equally unsettling issues relating to California, New Mexico, and Oregon. Between 1846 and 1848, a war with Mexico and a dramatic confrontation with Britain settled all these questions on terms favorable to the United States.

Yet at the start of the 1840s, western issues occupied no more than a tenuous position on the national political agenda. From 1840 to 1842, questions relating to economic recovery—notably, banking, the tariff, and internal improvements—dominated the attention of political leaders. Only after politicians failed to address the economic issues coherently did opportunistic leaders thrust issues relating to expansion to the top of the political agenda.

The Whig Ascendancy

The election of 1840 brought the Whig candidate William Henry Harrison to the presidency and installed Whig majorities in both houses of Congress. The Whigs had raced to power with a program, based on Henry Clay's American System, to stimulate economic recovery, and they had excellent prospects of success. They quickly repealed Van Buren's darling, the Independent Treasury. They then planned to substitute some kind of national "fiscal agent," which, like the defunct Bank of the United States, would be a private corporation chartered by Congress and charged with regulating the currency. The Whigs also favored a tariff, but with a twist. In the past, Whigs had supported a "protective" tariff, one set so high as to discourage the importation of goods that would compete with the products of American industries. Now the Whigs proposed a modification in the form of a "revenue" tariff, one high enough to provide "incidental"

protection for American industries but low enough to allow most foreign products to enter the United States. The duties collected on these imports would accrue to the federal government as revenue. The Whigs then planned to distribute this revenue to the states for internal improvements, a measure as popular among southern and western Whigs as the tariff was among northeastern Whigs.

The Whig agenda might have breezed into law had it not been for the untimely death of Harrison after only one month in office. With Harrison's demise, Vice President John Tyler, an upper-crust Virginian who had been put on the ticket in 1840 to strengthen the Whigs' appeal in the South, assumed the presidency. From virtually every angle, the new president proved a disaster for the Whigs.

A former Democrat, Tyler had broken with Jackson over nullification, but he continued to favor the Democratic philosophy of states' rights. As president, he repeatedly used the veto to shred his new party's program. In August 1841 a Whig bill to create a new national bank became the first casualty of Tyler's veto. Stunned, the Whig majority in Congress quickly passed a modified banking bill, only to see Tyler veto it as well.

Congressional Whigs fared little better on the issues of the tariff and the distribution of tariff revenues to the states. The Compromise Tariff of 1833 had provided for a gradual scaling down of tariff duties, until none was to exceed 20 percent by 1842. Amid the depression of the early 1840s, however, the provision for a 20 percent maximum tariff appeared too low to generate revenue. Without revenue, the Whigs would have no money to distribute among the states for internal improvements and no program with national appeal. In response, the Whig congressional majority passed two bills in the summer of 1842 that simultaneously postponed the final reduction of tariffs to 20 percent and ordered distribution to the states to proceed. Tyler promptly vetoed both bills. Tyler's mounting vetoes infuriated the Whig leadership. "Again has the imbecile, into whose hands accident has placed the power, vetoed a bill passed by a majority of those legally authorized to pass it," screamed the *Daily Richmond Whig*. Some Whigs talked of impeaching Tyler. Finally, in August, Tyler, needing revenue to run the government, signed a new bill that maintained some tariffs above 20 percent but abandoned distribution to the states.

Tyler's erratic course confounded and disrupted his party. By maintaining some tariffs above 20 percent, the tariff of 1842 satisfied northern manufacturers, but by abandoning distribution, it infuriated many southerners and westerners. Northern Whigs succeeded in passing the bill with the aid of many northern Democrats, particularly pro-tariff Pennsylvanians, whereas large numbers of Whigs in the Upper South and West opposed the tariff of 1842.

In the congressional elections of 1842, the Whigs paid a heavy price for failing to enact their program. Although retaining a slim majority in the Senate, they lost control of the House to the Democrats. Now the nation witnessed one party in control of the Senate, its rival in control of the House, and a president who appeared to belong to neither party.

Tyler and the Annexation of Texas

Although a political maverick disowned by his party, Tyler ardently desired a second term as president. Domestic issues offered him little hope of building a popular following, but foreign policy was another matter. In 1842 Tyler's secretary of state, Daniel Webster, concluded a treaty with Great Britain, represented by Lord Ashburton, that settled a long-festering dispute over the boundary between Maine and the Canadian province of New Brunswick. Awarding more than half of the disputed territory to the United States, the Webster-Ashburton Treaty was popular in the North. Tyler reasoned that if he could now arrange for the annexation of Texas, he would build a national following.

The issue of slavery, however, had long clouded every discussion of Texas. By the late 1830s antislavery northerners viewed proposals to annex Texas as part of an elaborate southern conspiracy to extend American territory south into Mexico, Cuba, and Central America, thus allowing for an unlimited number of new slave states while the British presence in Canada would limit the number of free states. In fact, some southerners talked openly of creating as many as four or five slave states out of the vast territory encompassed by Texas.

Nevertheless, in the summer of 1843, Tyler launched a propaganda campaign for Texas annexation. He justified his crusade by reporting that he had learned of certain British designs on Texas, which Americans, he argued, would be prudent to forestall. Tyler's campaign was fed by reports from his unofficial agent in London, Duff Green, a protégé of John C. Calhoun and a man whom John Quincy Adams contemptuously dismissed as an "ambassador of slavery." Green assured Tyler that as a prelude to undermining slavery in the United States, the British would pressure Mexico to recognize the independence of Texas in return for the abolition of slavery there. Calhoun, who became Tyler's secretary of state early in 1844, embroidered these reports with fanciful theories of British plans to use abolition as a way to destroy rice, sugar, and cotton production in the United States and gain for itself a monopoly on all three staples.

In the spring of 1844, Calhoun and Tyler submitted to the Senate for ratification a treaty, secretly drawn up, annexing Texas to the United States. Among the supporting documents accompanying the treaty was a letter from Calhoun to Richard Pakenham, the British foreign minister in Washington, that defended slavery as beneficial to blacks, the only way to protect them from "vice and pauperism." Antislavery northerners no longer had to look under the carpet for evidence that the impulse behind annexation lay in a desire to protect and extend slavery; now they needed only to read Calhoun's words. Both Martin Van Buren, the leading northern Democrat, and Henry Clay, the most powerful Whig, came out against immediate annexation, on grounds that annexation would provoke the kind of sectional conflict that each had sought to bury. By a vote of 35 to 16, the treaty went down to crushing defeat in the Senate. Decisive as it appeared, however, this vote only postponed the final decision on annexation to the upcoming election of 1844.

The Election of 1844

Tyler's ineptitude turned the presidential campaign into a free-for-all. The president hoped to succeed himself in the White House, but he lacked a base in either party. Testing the waters as an independent, he could not garner adequate support and was forced to drop out of the race.

Henry Clay had a secure grip on the Whig nomination. Martin Van Buren appeared to have an equally firm grasp on the Democratic nomination, but the issue of Texas annexation split his party. Trying to appease all shades of opinion within his party, Van Buren stated that he would abide by whatever Congress might decide on the annexation issue. Van Buren's attempt to evade the issue succeeded only in alienating

1844 Campaign Banner
Clay hoped to convince the public that the Whig programs of high tariffs and the distribution of tariff revenues would restore prosperity, here represented by a well-dressed farmer and his well-fed horse.

the modest number of northern annexationists, led by Michigan's former governor Lewis Cass, and the much larger group of southern annexationists. At the Democratic convention, Van Buren and Cass effectively blocked each other's nomination. The resulting deadlock was broken by the nomination of James K. Polk of Tennessee, the first "dark-horse" presidential nominee in American history.

Although little known outside the South, the slaveholding Polk was the favorite of southern Democrats, who accurately described him as the "bosom friend of [Andrew] Jackson, and a pure whole-hogged Democrat, the known enemy of banks and distribution." On the Texas issue, Polk supported immediate "reannexation," a curious turn of phrase that reflected Andrew Jackson's belief that Texas had been part of the Louisiana Purchase until unwisely ceded to Spain by the Transcontinental Treaty of 1819. Indeed, Polk followed Old Hickory's lead so often that he became known as Young Hickory.

Gibing "Who is James K. Polk?" the Whigs derided Polk's nomination. Polk himself marveled at his turn of fortune, for he had lost successive elections for the governorship of Tennessee. Yet he proved a wily campaign strategist. To satisfy pro-tariff Pennsylvania Democrats, Polk adjusted his position on the tariff to hold out some hope for protection. In addition, Polk and supporters like Senator Robert J. Walker of Mississippi managed to convince many northerners that the annexation of Texas would advance their interests. By foiling alleged British plans to abolitionize Texas,

Walker contended, annexation would make Texas a safe haven for slavery and draw both slaves and free blacks away from states bordering the North. Failure to annex, on the other hand, would prevent the westward dispersal of the South's slave population, intensify racial tensions in the existing slave states, and increase the chances of a race war that would spill over into the North. However farfetched, Walker's arguments played effectively on the racial phobias of many northerners and helped Polk detach annexation from Calhoun's narrow, pro-southern defense of it.

In contrast to the Democrats, who established a clear direction in their arguments, Clay kept muddying the waters. In the spring of 1844, he had opposed the annexation treaty. Then he sent conflicting messages to his followers throughout the summer of 1844, saying that he had nothing against annexation as long as it would not disrupt sectional harmony. Finally, in September 1844 he again came out against annexation. Clay's shifts on annexation alienated his southern supporters and prompted a small but influential body of northern antislavery Whigs to desert to the Liberty party, which had been organized in 1840. Devoted to the abolition of slavery by political action, the Liberty party nominated Ohio's James G. Birney for the presidency.

Annexation was not the sole issue of the campaign. The Whigs infuriated Catholic immigrant voters by nominating Theodore Frelinghuysen as Clay's running mate. A leading Presbyterian layman, Frelinghuysen gave "his head, his hand, and his heart" to temperance and an assortment of other Protestant causes. His presence on their ticket fixed the image of the Whigs as the orthodox Protestant party and roused the largely Catholic foreign-born voters to turn out in large numbers for the Democrats.

On the eve of the election in New York City, so many Irish marched to the courthouse to be qualified for voting that the windows had to be left open for people to get in and out. "Ireland has reconquered the country which England lost," an embittered Whig moaned. Polk won the electoral vote 170–105, but his margin in the popular vote was only 38,000 out of 2.6 million votes cast, and he lost his own state of Tennessee by 113 votes. In most states the two main parties contended with each other on close terms, a sign of the maturity of the second party system. A shift of 6,000 votes in New York, where the immigrant vote and Whig defections to the Liberty party hurt Clay, would have given Clay both the state and the presidency.

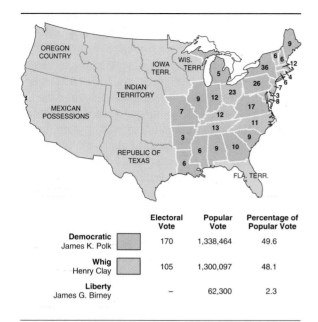

	Electoral Vote	Popular Vote	Percentage of Popular Vote
Democratic James K. Polk	170	1,338,464	49.6
Whig Henry Clay	105	1,300,097	48.1
Liberty James G. Birney	–	62,300	2.3

The Election of 1844

Manifest Destiny

The election of 1844 demonstrated one incontestable fact: the annexation of Texas had more national support than Clay had realized. The surging popular sentiment for expansion that made the underdog Polk rather than Clay the man of the hour reflected a growing conviction among the people that America's natural destiny was to expand into Texas and all the way to the Pacific Ocean.

Expansionists emphasized extending the "area of freedom" and talked of "repelling the contaminating proximity of monarchies upon the soil that we have consecrated to the rights of man." For contemporary young Americans like Walt Whitman, such restless expansionism knew few limits. "The more we reflect upon annexation as involving a part of Mexico, the more do doubts and obstacles resolve themselves away," Whitman wrote. "Then there is California, on the way to which lovely tract lies Santa Fe; how long a time will elapse before they shine as two new stars in our mighty firmament?"

Americans awaited only a phrase to capture this ebullient spirit of continentalism. In 1845 John L. O'Sullivan, a New York Democratic journalist, wrote of "our manifest destiny to overspread and to possess the whole of the continent which Providence has given us

for the development of the great experiment of liberty and federated self-government entrusted to us."

Advocates of Manifest Destiny used lofty language and routinely invoked God and Nature to sanction expansion. Inasmuch as most proponents of Manifest Destiny were Democrats, many of whom supported the annexation of Texas, northern Whigs frequently dismissed Manifest Destiny as a smoke screen aimed at concealing the evil intent of expanding slavery. In reality, many advocates of Manifest Destiny were neither supporters of slavery nor zealous annexationists. Oregon and California loomed more prominently in their minds than Texas. For despite their flowery phrases, these expansionists rested their case on hard material calculations. Most blamed the post-1837 depression on the failure of the United States to acquire markets for its agricultural surplus and saw the acquisition of Oregon and California as solutions. A Missouri Democrat observed that "the ports of Asia are as convenient to Oregon as the ports of Europe are to the eastern slope of our confederacy, with an infinitely better ocean for navigation." An Alabama Democrat praised California's "safe and capacious harbors," which, he assured, "invite to their bosoms the rich commerce of the East."

Expansionists desired more than profitable trade routes, however. At the heart of their thinking lay an impulse to preserve the predominantly agricultural character of the American people and thereby to safeguard democracy. Most expansionists associated the industrialization that was transforming America with social stratification and class strife, and many saw the concentration of impoverished Irish immigrants in cities and factory towns as evidence of the common people's shrinking opportunities for economic advancement. After a tour of New England mill towns in 1842, John L. O'Sullivan warned Americans that should they fail to encourage alternatives to factories, the United States would sink to the level of Britain, a nation that the ardent Democratic expansionist James Gordon Bennett described as a land of "bloated wealth" and "terrible misery."

Most Democratic expansionists came to see the acquisition of new territory as a logical complement to their party's policies of low tariffs and opposition to centralized banking. Where tariffs and banks tended to "favor and foster the factory system," expansion would provide farmers with land and with access to foreign markets for their produce. As a consequence, Americans would continue to become farmers, and the foundations of the Republic would remain secure. The acquisition of California and Oregon would provide enough land and harbors to sustain not only the 20 million Americans of 1845 but the 100 million that some expansionists projected for 1900 and the 250 million that O'Sullivan predicted for 1945.

The expansionists' message, especially as delivered by the penny press in such newspapers as Bennett's *New York Herald*, made sense to the laboring poor of America's antebellum cities. The *Herald*, the nation's largest-selling newspaper in the 1840s, played upon the anxieties of its working-class readers by arguing relentlessly for the expulsion of the British from Oregon and for thwarting alleged British plans to abolitionize the United States. These readers, many of them fiercely antiblack, anti-British Irish immigrants, welcomed any efforts to open up economic opportunities for the common people. Most also favored the perpetuation of slavery, for the freeing of slaves would throw masses of blacks into the already intense competition for jobs.

The expansionists with whom these laboring-class readers sided drew ideas from Thomas Jefferson, John Quincy Adams, and other leaders of the early Republic who had proclaimed the American people's right to displace uncivilized or European people from the path of their westward movement. Early expansionists, however, had feared that overexpansion might create an ungovernable empire. Jefferson, for example, had proposed an indefinite restriction on the settlement of Louisiana. In contrast, the expansionists of the 1840s, citing the virtues of the telegraph and the railroad, believed that the problem of distance had been "literally annihilated." James Gordon Bennett claimed that the telegraph would render the whole nation as compact and homogeneous as New York City. Ironically, although many expansionists pointed with alarm to the negative effects of industrialization on society, their confidence in technology convinced them that the nation could expand with minimal risk to the people.

Polk and Oregon

The most immediate impact of the growing spirit of Manifest Destiny was to escalate the issue of Oregon. To soften northern criticism of the still-pending annexation of Texas, the Democrats had included in their platform for the election of 1844 the assertion that American title "to the whole of the Territory of Oregon is clear and unquestionable." Taken literally, the plat-

form committed the party to acquire the entire area between California and 54°40′, the southern boundary of Alaska. Since Polk had not yet been elected, the British could safely ignore this extraordinary claim for the moment, and in fact, the Oregon issue had aroused far less interest during the campaign than had the annexation of Texas. But in his inaugural address, Polk reasserted the "clear and unquestionable" claim to the "country of Oregon." If by this Polk meant all of Oregon, then the United States, which had never before claimed any part of Oregon north of the forty-ninth parallel, had executed an astounding and belligerent reversal of policy.

Polk's objectives in Oregon, however, were more subtle than his language. He knew that the United States could never obtain all of Oregon without a war with Britain, and he wanted to avoid that. He proposed to use the threat of hostilities to persuade the British to accept what they had repeatedly rejected in the past: a division of Oregon at the forty-ninth parallel. Such a division would give the United States both the excellent deep-water harbors of Puget Sound and the southern tip of British-controlled Vancouver Island. For their part, the British had long held out for a division along the Columbia River, which entered the Pacific Ocean far south of the forty-ninth parallel.

Polk's comments in his inaugural speech roused among westerners a furious interest in acquiring the whole territory. Mass meetings adopted such resolutions as "We are all for Oregon, and *all* Oregon in the West" and "The Whole or None!" Furthermore, each passing year brought new American settlers into Oregon. Even John Quincy Adams, who advocated neither the annexation of Texas nor the 54°40′ boundary for Oregon, believed that the American settlements in Oregon gave the United States a far more reasonable claim to the territory than mere exploration and discovery gave the British. The United States, not Britain, Adams contended, was the nation bound "to make the wilderness blossom as the rose, to establish laws, to increase, multiply, and subdue the earth," all "at the first behest of God Almighty."

In April 1846 Polk secured from Congress the termination of joint British-American occupation of Oregon and promptly gave Britain the required one-year's notice. With joint occupation abrogated, the British could either go to war over American claims to 54°40′ or negotiate. They chose to negotiate. Although the British raged against "that ill-regulated, overbearing, and aggressive spirit of American democ-

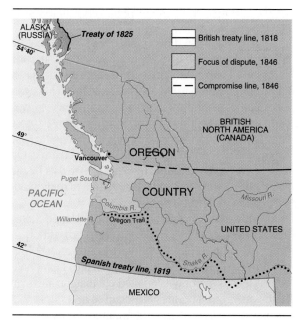

Oregon Boundary Dispute

Although demanding that Britain cede the entire Oregon Territory south of 54°40', the United States settled for a compromise at the forty-ninth parallel.

racy," they had too many domestic and foreign problems to welcome a war over what Lord Aberdeen, the British foreign secretary, dismissed as "a few miles of pine swamp." The ensuing treaty provided for a division at the forty-ninth parallel, with some modifications. Britain retained all of Vancouver Island as well as navigation rights on the Columbia River. The Senate ratified the treaty (with the proviso that Britain's navigation rights on the Columbia were merely temporary) on June 15, 1846.

The Origins of the Mexican War

Even as Polk was challenging Britain over Oregon, the United States and Mexico moved steadily toward war. The impending conflict had both remote and immediate causes. One long-standing grievance lay in the failure of the Mexican government to pay some $2 million in debts owed to American citizens. In addition, bitter memories of the Alamo and of the Goliad massacre continued to arouse in Americans a loathing of Mexicans. Above all, the issue of Texas embroiled relations between the two nations. Mexico still hoped to regain Texas or at least to keep it independent of the United

States. Once in control of Texas, the Mexicans feared, the United States might seize other Mexican provinces, perhaps even Mexico itself, and treat the citizens of Mexico much as it had treated its slaves.

Unfortunately for Mexico, Polk's election boosted the strength of pro-annexation forces in the United States. The arguments that Polk and Senator Robert J. Walker had put forth during the election campaign of 1844 had persuaded many northerners of the national, rather than purely sectional, benefits of annexing Texas. Recognizing the growing popularity of annexation, both houses of Congress passed a resolution in February 1845 to annex Texas. Soon after taking office, Polk dispatched agents to the Texas republic to gain acceptance of annexation. Some Texans feared that annexation would provoke an invasion of Texas by Mexico, which had never formally recognized Texas's independence and which now served notice that it "would consider equivalent to a declaration of war against the Mexican Republic the passage of an act for an incorporation of Texas with the territory of the United States."

Confronted by Texan timidity and Mexican belligerence, Polk moved on two fronts. To sweeten the pot for the Texans, he supported their claim to the Rio Grande as the southern boundary of Texas. This claim ran counter to Mexico's view that the Nueces River, a hundred miles northeast of the Rio Grande, bounded Texas. The area between the Nueces and the Rio Grande was largely uninhabited, but the stakes were high. Although only a hundred miles southwest of the Nueces at its mouth on the Gulf of Mexico, the Rio Grande meandered west and then north for nearly two thousand miles and encircled a huge slice of territory, including part of New Mexico. The Texas that Polk proposed to annex thus encompassed far more land than the Texas that had gained independence from Mexico in 1836. Reassured by Polk's support, a Texas convention voted overwhelmingly on July 4, 1845, to accept annexation. In response to Mexican war preparations, Polk then made a second move, ordering American troops under General Zachary Taylor to the edge of the disputed territory. Taylor took up a position at Corpus Christi, a tiny Texas outpost situated just south of the Nueces and hence in territory still claimed by Mexico.

Never far from Polk's thoughts in his insistence on the Rio Grande boundary lay his desire for California and for its fine harbors of San Diego and San Francisco. In fact, Polk had entered the White House with the firm intention of extending American control over

California. By the summer of 1845, his followers were openly proclaiming that if Mexico went to war with the United States over Texas, "the road to California will be open to us." Then in October 1845, Polk received a dispatch from Thomas O. Larkin, the American consul at Monterey, California, that warned darkly of British designs on California but ended with the optimistic assurance that the Mexicans in California would prefer American to British rule. Larkin's message gave Polk the idea that California might be acquired by the same methods as Texas: revolution followed by annexation.

Visions of new territorial acquisitions were dancing merrily in Polk's mind when Texas accepted annexation in July 1845. With Taylor's troops at Corpus Christi, the next move belonged to Mexico. Unfortunately, Mexico had difficulty making any firm moves, for its politics had again slipped into turmoil with the ouster of Santa Anna by General José Herrera in December 1844. Herrera's own position in Mexican politics was shaky, and prodded by the British, he agreed to receive a delegation from the United States to reach an amicable settlement. Simultaneously, Polk, locked in a war of words with the British over Oregon, decided to give negotiations with Mexico a try. In November 1845 he sent an emissary, the Spanish-speaking John Slidell, to Mexico City. Slidell's final instructions were to gain Mexican recognition of the annexation of Texas, including the Rio Grande boundary, in return for the United States' assumption of all financial claims on the part of American citizens against the Mexican government. Polk also authorized Slidell to offer up to $25 million for New Mexico and California or, failing this, to offer $5 million for New Mexico alone.

By the time Slidell reached Mexico City on December 6, 1845, the threat of a military revolt led by General Mariano Paredes had pushed the Herrera government to the brink of collapse. Too weak to negotiate any concessions to the United States, Herrera refused to receive Slidell. In response to Mexico's refusal to negotiate, Polk now ordered Taylor to march from Corpus Christi southward to the north bank of the Rio Grande. Still viewing the Rio Grande as the key to the Far West, Polk hoped that Taylor's presence on the river would spur the Mexicans to attack. Mexican aggression, the president anticipated, would unify Americans and would quiet northerners who were suspiciously contrasting Polk's willingness to compromise on Oregon with his continuing belligerence toward Mexico. Polk had no intention of compromising

on the Texas boundary, but if it came to war, he wanted a united country behind him.

On May 9, 1846, Polk notified his cabinet that he could no longer await a Mexican attack and that he must send a war message to Congress. A few hours after the cabinet adjourned, news arrived that a Mexican force had crossed the Rio Grande and ambushed two companies of Taylor's troops. Now the prowar press had its martyrs. "American blood has been shed on American soil!" one of Polk's followers proclaimed. On May 11 Polk informed Congress that war "exists by the act of Mexico herself" and called for a $10 million appropriation to fight the war.

Polk's disarming assertion that the United States was already at war provoked furious opposition in Congress, where John C. Calhoun briefly united with antislavery Whigs to protest the president's high-handedness. Polk's opponents pointed out that the Mexican attack on Taylor's troops had occurred in territory that no previous administration had claimed as part of the United States. By announcing that war already existed, moreover, Polk seemed to be undercutting Congress's power to declare war and using a mere border incident as a pretext for plunging the nation into a general war to acquire more slave territory. The pro-Whig *New York Tribune* warned its readers that Polk was "precipitating you into a fathomless abyss of crime and calamity." Antislavery poet James Russell Lowell of Massachusetts wrote of the Polk Democrats:

> *They just want this Californy*
> *So's to lug new slave-states in*
> *To abuse ye, an' to scorn ye,*
> *An' to plunder ye like sin.*

But Polk had maneuvered the Whigs into a corner. Few Whigs could forget that the opposition of the Federalists to the War of 1812 had wrecked the Federalist party, and few wanted to appear unpatriotic by refusing to support Taylor's beleaguered troops. Swallowing their outrage, most Whigs backed appropriations for war against Mexico.

Throughout the negotiations with Britain over Oregon and with Mexico over Texas, Polk had demonstrated his ability to pursue his goals unflinchingly. A humorless, austere man who banned dancing and liquor at White House receptions, Polk inspired little personal warmth, even among his supporters. But he possessed clear objectives and a single-mindedness in their pursuit. At every point, he had encountered opposition on the home front: from Whigs who saw him as a reckless adventurer; from northerners of both parties opposed to any expansion of slavery; and from John C. Calhoun, who loathed Polk for his high-handedness and feared that a war with Britain would strip the South of its market for cotton. Yet Polk triumphed over all opposition, in part because of his opponents' fragmentation, in part because of expansion's popular appeal, and in part because of the weakness of his foreign antagonists. Reluctant to fight over Oregon, Britain chose to negotiate. Too weak to negotiate, Mexico chose to fight over territory that it had already lost (Texas) and for territories over which its hold was feeble (California and New Mexico).

The Mexican War

Most European observers expected Mexico to win the war. With a regular army four times the size of the American forces, Mexico had the added advantage of fighting on home ground. The United States, which had botched its one previous attempt to invade a foreign nation, Canada in 1812, now had to sustain offensive operations in an area remote from American settlements.

In contrast to the Europeans, expansionists in the United States hardly expected the Mexicans to fight at all. A leading Democrat confidently predicted that Mexico would offer only "a slight resistance to the North American race" because its mixed Spanish and Indian population had been degraded by "amalgamation." Newspaper publisher James Gordon Bennett proclaimed that the "imbecile" Mexicans were "as sure to melt away at the approach of [American] energy and enterprise as snow before a southern sun."

In fact, the Mexicans fought bravely and stubbornly, though with little success. In May 1846 Taylor, a sixty-two-year-old veteran of the War of 1812, defeated the Mexicans in two battles north of the Rio Grande and then crossed the river to defeat them again at Matamoros and to capture the major northern Mexican city of Monterrey in September. Taylor's victories touched off a wave of enthusiasm in the United States. Recruiting posters blared, "Here's to Old Zach! Glorious Times! Roast Beef, Ice Cream, and Three Months' Advance!" Already the Whigs were touting Taylor, "Old Rough and Ready," for the presidency in 1848.

After taking the supposedly impregnable Monterrey, however, Taylor, starved for supplies, granted the Mexicans an armistice by which he pledged not to pursue them for eight weeks. Eager to undercut Taylor's popularity, and judging him "wholly unqualified for the command he holds," Polk now stripped Taylor of half his men and assigned them to General Winfield Scott. Polk ordered Scott to prepare an amphibious assault on Vera Cruz, a city on the Gulf of Mexico far to the south, and to proceed overland to Mexico City. Before Scott could attack Vera Cruz, however, Taylor gained even greater fame. Seeking to win an easy victory over Taylor's depleted army, Santa Anna, who had made another of his many comebacks in Mexican politics, led an army of twenty thousand men north to dislodge Taylor. The two armies met at the Battle of Buena Vista, February 22–23, 1847. After a series of futile charges, Santa Anna's men, demoralized by the superior American artillery, retreated.

While Taylor was winning fame in northern Mexico, and before Scott had launched his attack on Vera Cruz, American forces farther north were dealing decisive blows to the remnants of Mexican rule in New Mexico and California. In the spring of 1846, Colonel Stephen Kearny marched an army from Fort Leavenworth, Kansas, toward Santa Fe. Like the pioneers on the Oregon Trail, Kearny's men faced immense natural obstacles as they marched over barren ground. Finally reaching New Mexico, Kearny took the territory by a combination of bluff, bluster, and perhaps bribery, without firing a shot. The Mexican governor, following his own advice that "it is better to be thought brave than to be so," fled at Kearny's approach. After suppressing a brief rebellion by Mexicans and Indians, Kearny sent a detachment of his army south into Mexico. There, having marched fifteen hundred miles from Fort Leavenworth, these troops joined Taylor in time for the Battle of Buena Vista.

Like New Mexico, California fell easily into American hands. In 1845 Polk had ordered Commodore John D. Sloat and his Pacific Squadron to occupy California's ports in the event of war with Mexico. To ensure victory, Polk also dispatched a courier overland with secret orders for one of the most colorful and important actors in the conquest of California, John C. Frémont. A Georgia-born adventurer, Frémont had married Jessie Benton, the daughter of the powerful senator Thomas Hart Benton of Missouri. Benton used his influence to have accounts of Frémont's explorations in the Northwest (mainly written by Jessie Benton Frémont) published as government documents. All of this earned glory for Frémont as "the Great Pathfinder." Finally overtaken by Polk's courier in

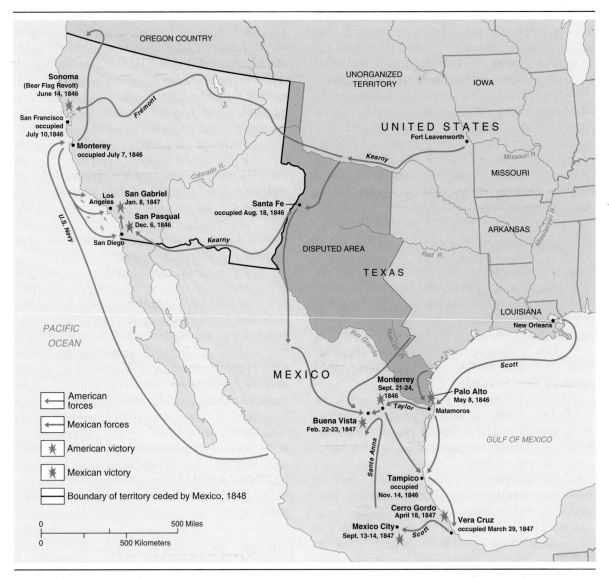

Major Battles of the Mexican War
*The Mexican War's decisive campaign began with General Winfield Scott's capture
of Vera Cruz and ended with his conquest of Mexico City.*

Oregon, Frémont was instructed to proceed to California and to "watch over the interests of the United States." Interpreting his orders liberally, Frémont rounded up some American insurgents, seized the town of Sonoma, and proclaimed the independent "Bear Flag Republic" in June 1846. The combined efforts of Frémont, Sloat, his successor David Stockton, and Stephen Kearny (who arrived in California after capturing New Mexico) quickly established American control over California.

The final and most important campaign of the war saw the conquest of Mexico City itself. In March 1847 Winfield Scott landed near Vera Cruz at the head of twelve thousand men and quickly pounded the city into submission. Moving inland, Scott encountered Santa Anna at the seemingly impregnable pass of Cerro Gordo, but a young captain in Scott's command, Robert E. Lee, helped to find a trail that led around the Mexican flank to a small peak overlooking the pass. There Scott planted howitzers and, on April

18, stormed the pass and routed the Mexicans. Scott now moved directly on Mexico City. Taking the key fortresses of Churubusco and Chapultepec (where another young captain, Ulysses S. Grant, was cited for bravery), Scott took the city on September 13, 1847.

In virtually all these encounters on Mexican soil, the Mexicans were numerically superior. In the final assault on Mexico City, Scott commanded eleven thousand troops against Santa Anna's twenty-five thousand. But doom stalked the Mexican army. Hampered by Santa Anna's nearly unbroken string of military miscalculations, the Mexicans fell victim to the vastly superior American artillery and to the ability of the Americans to organize massive military movements. The "barbarians of the North" (as the Mexicans called the American soldiers) died like flies from yellow fever, and they carried into battle the agonies of venereal disease, which they picked up (and left) in every Mexican town they took. But the Americans benefited from the unprecedented quality of their weapons, supplies, and organization.

By the Treaty of Guadalupe Hidalgo (February 2, 1848), Mexico ceded Texas with the Rio Grande boundary, New Mexico, and California to the United States. In return, the United States assumed the claims of American citizens against the Mexican government and paid Mexico $15 million. Although the United States gained the present states of California, Nevada, New Mexico, Utah, most of Arizona, and parts of Colorado and Wyoming, some rabid expansionists in the Senate denounced the treaty because it failed to include all of Mexico. But the acquisition of California, with its excellent Pacific ports of San Diego and San Francisco, satisfied Polk. Few senators, moreover, wanted to annex the mixed Spanish and Indian population of Mexico. A writer in the *Democratic Review* expressed the prevailing view that "the annexation of the country [Mexico] to the United States would be a calamity," for it would incorporate into the United States "ignorant and indolent half-civilized Indians," not to mention "free negroes and mulattoes" left over from the British slave trade. In this way, the virulent racism of American leaders allowed the Mexicans to retain part of their nation. On March 10, 1848, the Senate ratified the treaty by a vote of 38 to 10.

The Mexican War in the Popular Mind

Occurring amid the rise of the penny press and the popular novel, the Mexican War became the most fully reported war that America had yet fought and the first

conflict in which war correspondents were employed. The extensive coverage given to battlefield victories fueled the soaring nationalism and helped to submerge political divisions. "We are now all Whigs and all Democrats," an Indiana newspaper declared.

Romance as well as patriotism gripped the popular mind. Writers portrayed the war as evidence that the noble, chivalric streak in the American character could prevail over the grasping materialism of American society. To a generation fed on the historical novels of Sir Walter Scott, it seemed that the age of chivalry had returned. Innumerable popular war novels, with titles like *The Texan Ranger; or, The Maid of Matamoros*, mingled patriotism and romance by relating how American soldiers routed Mexican men only to fall in love with Mexican women.

The main beneficiary of the publicity swirling out of the war was Zachary Taylor. Taylor had the right combination of qualities to enchant a people in search of heroes. To those who danced to the hastily composed "Rough and Ready Polka" and the "General Taylor Quick Step," Taylor's military genius seemed equaled only by his democratic bearing and conspicuously ordinary manner. In contrast to the more soldierly Winfield Scott ("Old Fuss and Feathers"), Taylor went into battle wearing a straw hat and plain brown coat. To an idolizing public, even Taylor's short stature and inclination to corpulence became an advantage; some said that he resembled Napoleon.

The war made Taylor a military hero. The conflicts that spun out of the war would now boost his political career.

Intensifying Sectional Divisions

Despite the wartime patriotic enthusiasm, sectional conflict sharpened between 1846 and 1848. To a degree, this conflict intensified over issues unrelated to expansion. Many of the problems stemmed from Polk's uncompromising and literal-minded Jacksonianism.

Once in office, Polk not only had restored the Independent Treasury, a measure that dismayed the Whigs, but also had eroded the unity of his own party by pursuing Jacksonian policies on tariffs and internal improvements. The numerous northern Democrats who supported a modestly protective tariff had taken heart during the 1844 campaign from Polk's promise to combine a revenue tariff with a measure of protection. But Polk's administration, glutted with southerners, quickly abandoned any talk of protection. The tariff of 1846, fashioned by Robert J. Walker, who became

Patriotism and the Mexican War
U.S. soldiers commonly wore tall hats known as shako caps during the Mexican War. The caps were adorned with decorative plates showing the eagle spreading its wings, the symbol of Manifest Destiny. Inexpensive and mass-produced lithographs such as the one above, depicting the Battle of Sacramento, aroused patriotic support for the war.

Polk's secretary of the treasury, slashed all duties to the minimum necessary for revenue. Polk then disappointed western Democrats, thirsting for federal aid for internal improvements, by vetoing a law that they supported, the Rivers and Harbors Bill of 1846. To these western Dem-ocrats, this veto appeared to be another sign of the prosouthern tilt of Polk's presidency and did more to weaken western support for Polk than his abandonment of the fight for the 54°40′ boundary of Oregon.

Ultimately, however, sectional conflict over tariffs and internal improvements proved far less important than the battles generated by territorial expansion. Polk held true to his belief that expansion had provided an "additional guaranty for the preservation of the Union itself." Like most Jacksonian Democrats, he saw the bursting of the nation's boundaries as a way to disperse the population, weaken dangerous tendencies toward centralized government, and retain the agricultural and democratic character of the United States. In Polk's judgment, expansion would accomplish these

objectives whether the new territory acquired were slave or free. Focusing attention on slavery in the territories struck him as "not only unwise but wicked." The Missouri Compromise, prohibiting slavery north of 36°30′, impressed him as a simple and permanent solution to the problem of territorial slavery.

Yet many northerners were coming to see slavery in the territories as a profoundly disruptive issue that could not be resolved merely by extending the 36°30′ line to the Pacific. Some antislavery Whigs, especially those from abolitionist strongholds in New England and Ohio, opposed *any* extension of slavery, on moral grounds. But these Whigs, still a minority in their party, posed no immediate threat to Polk. A more damaging challenge emerged within Polk's own party: from a group of northern Democrats who, though not viewing slavery as morally evil, feared that extension of slavery into California and New Mexico (parts of each lay south of 36°30′) would deter free laborers from settling those territories. These Democrats argued that competition with slave labor clearly degraded free labor, that the westward extension of slavery would create a barrier to the westward migration of free labor, and that such a barrier would intensify the social problems already evident in the East: excessive concentration of population, labor protest, class strife, and social stratification.

The Wilmot Proviso

A young Democratic congressman from Pennsylvania, David Wilmot, became the spokesman for these disaffected northern Democrats. On a sizzling night in August 1846, he introduced an amendment to an appropriations bill for the upcoming negotiations with Mexico over Texas, New Mexico, and California. This amendment, known as the Wilmot Proviso, stipulated that slavery be prohibited in any territory acquired by the negotiations. Neither an abolitionist nor a critic of Polk on tariff policy, Wilmot spoke for those loyal Democrats who had supported the annexation of Texas on the assumption that Texas would be the last slave state. Wilmot's intention was not to split his party along sectional lines but to hold Polk to what Wilmot and other northern Democrats took as an implicit understanding: Texas for the slaveholders, California and New Mexico for free labor. With strong northern support, the proviso passed in the House but stalled in the Senate. Polk refused to endorse it, and most southern Democrats opposed any barrier to the expansion of slavery south of the Missouri Compromise line. Accepting the view that the westward extension of slavery would reduce the concentration of slaves in the older regions of the South and thus lessen the chances of a slave revolt, southern Democrats tried to put as much distance as possible between themselves and Wilmot.

The proviso raised unsettling constitutional issues. Calhoun and fellow southerners contended that since slaves were property, slaveholders enjoyed the Constitution's protection of property and could carry their slaves wherever they chose. This position led to the conclusion (drawn explicitly by Calhoun) that the Missouri Compromise of 1820, prohibiting slavery in the territories north of 36°30′, was unconstitutional. On the other side were many northerners who cited the Northwest Ordinance of 1787, the Missouri Compromise, and the Constitution itself, which gave Congress the power to "make all needful rules and regulations respecting the territory or other property belonging to the United States," as justification for congressional legislation over slavery in the territories. With the election of 1848 approaching, politicians of both sides, eager to hold their parties together and avert civil war, searched frantically for a middle ground.

The Election of 1848

Having asserted that their policies of national banking and high tariffs alone could pull the nation out of the depression, the Whigs had watched in dismay as prosperity returned under the Democrat Polk's program of an independent treasury and low tariffs. Never before had Clay's American System seemed so irrelevant. But the Wilmot Proviso gave the Whigs a political windfall, for, originating in the Democratic party, the proviso enabled the Whigs to portray themselves as the only dependable friends of the South.

These considerations inclined the majority of Whigs toward Zachary Taylor. As a Louisianian and large slaveholder, Taylor had an obvious appeal to the South. As a political newcomer who had never voted in a presidential election, he had no loyalty to Clay's American System. As a war hero, he might have a broad national appeal. Nominating Taylor, the Whigs presented him as an ideal man "without regard to creeds or principles" and ran him without any platform.

The Election of 1848

Candidates	Parties	Electoral Vote	Popular Vote	Percentage of Popular Vote
ZACHARY TAYLOR	Whig	163	1,360,967	47.4
Lewis Cass	Democratic	127	1,222,342	42.5
Martin Van Buren	Free-Soil		291,263	10.1

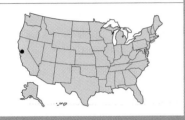

San Francisco in the Gold Rush

San Francisco became a favorite destination for newcomers in the gold rush. Its population spurted from 1,000 in 1849 to 50,000 in 1856. Few American towns had presented less likely prospects for growth. The Spanish had constructed a presidio and a mission on the site in 1776, and a small town, Yerba Buena, had sprung up around the mission. But when the United States took possession of Yerba Buena in July 1846, the town stretched for only a few streets in each direction and contained a mere 150 people who huddled amid its low mountains and fog-enshrouded sand hills. Arriving in the summer of 1846, a boatload of 200 Mormons more than doubled the population of Yerba Buena, which became San Francisco in 1847.

The gold rush transformed the town into "a pandemonium of a city" in the words of John Woodhouse Audubon, who became stranded there by Christmas 1849, on his way to the gold fields. San Francisco quickly emerged as the main supply depot for miners and prospectors in the interior. At first, virtually all commodities that passed through the city originated outside of California. Lumber came from Maine and Oregon, flour from Chile and Virginia, sugar from Hawaii, and manufactured goods from the eastern states and Britain. This reliance on imports shaped the town's occupational structure between 1849 and 1853. San Francisco's economy was so top-heavy with merchants and storekeepers that those willing to drive carts (draymen) or unload ships or build houses could command wages that elsewhere would have seemed unbelievable. A New England–born lawyer seriously considered giving up his practice to

Montgomery Street, San Francisco, 1850, *daguerreotype by Frederick Coombs*
In the view of historian William H. Goetzmann and art historian William N. Goetzmann, San Francisco was "the final living embodiment of Manifest Destiny, a golden dream city of great instant wealth."

become a drayman, for "they pay a man to drive a cart fifteen to twenty dollars a day," a generous wage at the time. By the mid-1850s the establishment of iron foundries and flour mills relieved the growing city's dependence on imports, but the supply of commodities remained uncertain, and commodity prices continued to gyrate crazily. Flour that cost $10 a barrel one month might jump to $19 the next. Real-estate prices also soared during the early rush, particularly near the waterfront. The city's economy was vulnerable to crashes as precipitous as its booms. A commercial panic in 1855 produced nearly two hundred bankruptcies and left close to $7 million in uncollectable debts.

The variety of San Francisco's population rivaled the volatility of its economy. Emigrants came from all around the world. By the 1850s the Irish outnumbered every other group of foreign-born immigrants. Many Irish were convicts who arrived by way of Australia, to which they had been exiled as punishment for their crimes. China, France, and Italy, nations that did not contribute many immigrants to other parts of the United States before 1860, all sent sizable contingents to San Francisco. Part of the city's tiny black population was also foreign-born. Richard Dalton, for example, came from the West Indies as a steward on a steamer and then labored on the ships that plied the Sacramento and San Joaquin rivers to Sacramento and Stockton. Indeed, no other U.S. city contained people from more parts of the world, and only two, St. Louis and Milwaukee, had a higher proportion of foreign-born residents in 1860. In addition, by the early 1850s, San Francisco contained six to ten times as many men as women.

In a city bursting with rival ethnic and racial groups and lacking the constraints imposed by family responsibilities, violence became a principal noncommercial activity. Audubon reported how the place teemed with men "more blasphemous, and with less regard for God and his commands than all I have ever seen on the Mississippi." A young clergyman-wrote in 1851 that "most of our citizens if not all go armed" and confessed that he carried a harmless-looking cane, which "will be found to contain a sword

San Francisco Saloon, *by Frank Marryat*
Mexicans, Chinese, Yankees, and southerners drink together in an ornate San Francisco saloon in the booming gold-rush days.

two-and-a-half feet long." The city's small fledgling police force posed little challenge to criminals. For protection, some entrepreneurs organized disbanded soldiers into an extralegal force called the Hounds. Unfortunately, the Hounds soon terrorized the people whom they were supposed to protect. In response, in 1851 San Francisco's merchants organized the first of several Committees of Vigilance, which patrolled the streets, deported undesirables, and tried and hanged thieves and murderers.

The vigilantes turned out during subsequent outbursts of lawlessness. In 1855 a gambler named Charles Cora insulted the wife of William Richardson, a U.S. marshal. Richardson then insulted Cora's mistress, a prostitute. A crusading editor, William King, joined the fight on Richardson's side, and a political hack and longtime antagonist of King, James Casey, added his barbs to the fray. The outcome revealed much about law and order in early San Francisco. Richardson armed himself and sought out Cora in a saloon, only to be shot to death by Cora; Casey shot and killed King on a street. Vigilantes then seized Cora and Casey, tried them in secret, and hanged them.

These incidents underscore the city's religious and ethnic tensions as well as its atmosphere of easy violence. Richardson was a southerner and a Protestant, and his supporter King crusaded against the Catholic church. Although less than models of virtue, their opponents Cora and

Casey had been raised Catholic and resented attacks on the religion of their parents. Americans thought of the Far West as a land of opportunity where past antagonisms and traditions would be eradicated, but all the divisions of the larger society were reproduced in San Francisco. The major racial, regional, religious, and ethnic groups kept their distance from each other. Blacks were forced to sit in segregated parts of theaters and to attend segregated schools. Southern and New England Protestants worshiped at different churches. Emigrants from Europe also divided on the basis of language and nationality. German, Polish, Russian, and Anglo-American Jews each maintained separate religious congregations.

Regional and ethnic antagonisms even threatened at times to disrupt the harmony within the city's political parties. Transplanted southerners and Irish immigrants, for example, vied with each other for control of the Democratic party. But at election time, these groups laid aside their antagonisms and united against the rival parties. The Germans usually joined the Irish to ally with the Democrats, whereas the Whigs (and later the Republicans) drew support from former New Englanders, from temperance advocates, and from some immigrants who resented the brash and brawling Irish. In this way, party politics gave coherence to the city's divisions and provided a generally peaceful outlet for the populace's overheated tempers.

Because Wilmot was one of their own, the Democrats faced a greater challenge. They could not ignore the issue of slavery in the territories, but if they embraced the positions of either Wilmot or Calhoun, they would suffer an unmendable sectional fracture. With Polk declining to stand for reelection, the Democrats nominated Lewis Cass of Michigan, who solved their problem by evolving a doctrine of "squatter sovereignty," or popular sovereignty as it was later called. Cass argued that the issue of slavery in the territories should be kept out of Congress "and left to the people of the confederacy in their respective local governments." In other words, let the actual settlers in each territory decide the issue for themselves. Cass's position benefited from both its arresting simplicity and its vagueness. Was he saying that Congress had the power to prohibit slavery in the territories but, in the interests of sectional harmony, should leave the issue to each territory? Or did he mean that Congress lacked any power to legislate on slavery in the territories? As a further complication, the doctrine of squatter sovereignty did not establish a clear time frame for territorial action. Did the doctrine mean that the first territorial legislature could abolish slavery, or did it intend that the final decision on slavery had to await the moment of admission to the Union? In actuality, few Democrats wanted definitive answers to these questions. The very vagueness of squatter sovereignty added to its appeal, for Democrats north and south were free to interpret it to their own advantage to their constituents.

Although both parties tried to steer around the issue of slavery in the territories, neither one fully succeeded. A pro–Wilmot Proviso faction of the Democratic party in New York, called the Barnburners, broke away from the party. Proclaiming their dedication to "Free Trade, Free Labor, Free Speech, and Free Men," the Barnburners courted Liberty party abolitionists and antislavery "Conscience" Whigs, who were dismayed by their party's nomination of the slaveholding Taylor. In August 1844 Barnburners, Conscience Whigs, and former Liberty party adherents met in Buffalo, created the Free-Soil party, and nominated Martin Van Buren on a platform opposing any extension of slavery. Van Buren's motives in accepting this third-party nomination reflected both lingering bitterness at his rejection by the Democrats in 1844 (a defeat engineered largely by Lewis Cass) and alarm at the increasingly southern domination of the party under Polk.

The Whig candidate, Taylor, benefited from the opposition's alienation of key northern states over the tariff issue, from Democratic disunity over the Wilmot Proviso, and from his glowing military record. He captured a majority of the electoral votes in both the North and the South. Although failing to carry any state, the Free-Soil party ran well enough in the North to demonstrate the grass roots popularity of opposition to the extension of slavery. Defections to the Free-Soilers, for example, probably cost the Whigs the state of Ohio. Van Buren wrote that the new party had gained "more than we had any right to expect." Indeed, by showing that opposition to the spread of slavery had far greater popular appeal than the abolitionism of the old Liberty party, the Free-Soilers sent the Whig and Democratic parties a message that these parties would be unable to ignore in future elections.

The California Gold Rush

When Wilmot had first made public his proviso, the issue of slavery in the Far West was more abstract than practical, because Mexico had not yet ceded any territory and relatively few Americans resided in either California or New Mexico. Nine days before the signing of the Treaty of Guadalupe Hidalgo, however, an American carpenter discovered gold while constructing a sawmill in the foothills of California's Sierra Nevada range. A frantic gold rush was on within a few months. A San Francisco paper complained that "the whole country from San Francisco to Los Angeles, and from the shore to the base of the Sierra Nevada, resounds with the sordid cry to gold, GOLD, GOLD! while the field is left half-planted, the house half-built, and everything neglected but the manufacture of shovels and pickaxes." (Deprived of its staff, advertisers, and subscribers, the newspaper then suspended publication.) By December 1848 pamphlets with titles like *The Emigrant's Guide to the Gold Mines* had hit the streets of New York City. To speed the gold-rushers to their destination, builders constructed sleek clipper ships like Donald McKay's *Flying Cloud*, which made the eighteen-thousand-mile trip from New York to San Francisco around Cape Horn in a record eighty-nine days on its maiden voyage in 1851. But most gold-rushers traveled overland. Overland immigrants to California rose from 400 in 1848 to 25,000 in 1849 and to 44,000 in 1850 (see "A Place in Time").

With the gold rush, the issue of slavery in the Far West became practical as well as abstract, and immediate rather than remote. In 1849 gold attracted a hundred thousand newcomers to California, including Mexicans, free blacks, and slaves brought by planters from the South. White prospectors loathed the thought of competing with any of these groups and wanted to drive all of them out of the gold fields. Spawned by disputed claims and prejudice, violence mounted, and demands grew for a strong civilian government in California to replace the ineffective military government left over from the war. Polk began to fear that without a satisfactory congressional solution to the slavery issue, Californians might organize a government independent of the United States. The gold rush thus guaranteed that the question of slavery in the Mexican cession would be the first item on the agenda for Polk's successor and, indeed, for the nation.

CONCLUSION

By calling their destiny manifest, Americans of the 1840s implied that they had no other course than to annex Texas, seize California and New Mexico, and secure the lion's share of Oregon. Obstacles might arise, but most believed that barriers to expansion would melt away in the face of a dynamic and resolute people.

This image of expansion as inevitable had deep roots in the experiences and values of the American people. Fed by immigration, the population continued to grow dramatically; by 1850 the United States had nearly five times its population in 1800. The fate of Mexican rule in Texas was sealed as much by the overwhelming numerical superiority of the American settlers as by Sam Houston's brilliant victory at the Battle of San Jacinto. In addition, expansion rested on a sequence of propositions that seemed self-evident to many antebellum Americans: that a nation of farmers would never experience sustained misery; that given the chance, most Americans would rather work on farms than in factories; and that expansion would provide more land for farming, reduce the dangerous concentration of people in cities, and restore opportunity for all.

Beyond all the talk of inevitable expansion, however, Americans saw their society's divisions deepen in the 1840s, not only between native-born and immigrant people but also between northerners and southerners. Expansion proved so controversial that it split the Democratic party over the Wilmot Proviso, widened the gap between northern and southern Whigs, and spurred the emergence of the Free-Soil party. Victorious over Mexico and enriched by the discovery of gold in California, Americans counted the blessings of expansion in these years but began to fear its costs.

CHRONOLOGY

1818   The United States and Britain agree on joint occupation of Oregon for a ten-year period.

1819   Transcontinental (Adams-Onís) Treaty.

1821   Mexico gains independence from Spain.

1822   Stephen F. Austin founds the first American community in Texas.

Stephen F. Austin

1824–1825   Russia abandons its claims to Oregon south of 54°40′.

1826   Haden Edwards leads an abortive rebellion against Mexican rule in Texas.

1827   The United States and Britain renew their agreement on joint occupation of Oregon for an indefinite period.

1830   Mexico closes Texas to further American immigration.

1834   Antonio López de Santa Anna comes to power in Mexico.

1834   Austin secures repeal of the ban on American immigration into Texas.

1835   Santa Anna invades Texas.

1836   Texas declares its independence from Mexico.
Fall of the Alamo.
Goliad massacre.
Battle of San Jacinto.

1840   William Henry Harrison elected president.

1841   Harrison dies; John Tyler becomes president.
Tyler vetoes Whig National Banking Bill.

1842   Whigs abandon distribution.
Webster-Ashburton Treaty.

1843   Tyler launches campaign for Texas annexation.

1844   Philadelphia Bible Riots.
Senate rejects treaty annexing Texas.
James K. Polk elected president.

1845   Congress votes joint resolution to annex Texas.
Texas accepts annexation by the United States.
Mexico rejects Slidell mission.

1846   Congress ends the joint occupation of Oregon.
Zachary Taylor defeats the Mexicans in two battles north of the Rio Grande.
The United States declares war on Mexico.

1846   John C. Frémont proclaims the Bear Flag Republic in California.

Congress votes to accept a settlement of the Oregon boundary issue with Britain.
Walker Tariff (tariff of 1846).
Colonel Stephen Kearny occupies Santa Fe.
Wilmot Proviso introduced.
Taylor takes Monterrey.

1847   Taylor defeats Santa Anna at the Battle of Buena Vista.
Vera Cruz falls to Winfield Scott.
Mexico City falls to Scott.
Lewis Cass's principle of "squatter sovereignty."

1848   Gold discovered in California.
Treaty of Guadalupe Hidalgo signed.
Taylor elected president.

FOR FURTHER READING

Ray A. Billington, *The Far Western Frontier, 1830–1860* (1956). A comprehensive narrative of the settlement of the Far West.

William R. Brock, *Parties and Political Conscience: American Dilemmas, 1840–1850* (1979). An excellent interpretive study of the politics of the 1840s.

William H. Goetzmann, *When the Eagle Screamed: The Romantic Horizon in American Diplomacy, 1800–1860* (1966). A lively overview of antebellum expansionism.

Maldwyn A. Jones, *American Immigration* (1960). An excellent brief introduction to immigration.

Patricia Nelson Limerick, *Legacy of Conquest* (1987). A provocative interpretation of western history.

Charles G. Sellers, *James K. Polk: Continentalist, 1843–1846* (1966). An outstanding political biography.

Henry Nash Smith, *Virgin Land: The American West as Symbol and Myth* (1950). A classic study of westward expansion in the American mind.

ADDITIONAL BIBLIOGRAPHY

Immigration, Nativism, and Labor Protest

Tyler Anbinder, *Nativism and Slavery: The Northern Know Nothings and the Politics of the 1850s* (1992); Lee Benson, *The Concept of Jacksonian Democracy: New York as a Test Case* (1961); Ray A. Billington, *The Protestant Crusade, 1800–1860: A Study of the Origins of Nativism* (1938); R. A. Burchell, *The San Francisco Irish, 1848–1880* (1980); Kathleen Conzen, *Immigrant Milwau-kee, 1836–1860* (1976); Hasia R. Diner, *Erin's Daughter in America* (1983); Oscar Handlin, *Boston's Immigrants*, rev. ed. (1969); Bruce Laurie, *Working People of Philadelphia, 1800–1850* (1980); Bruce Levine, *The Spirit of 1848: German Immigrants, Labor Conflict, and the Coming of the Civil War* (1992); Lawrence J. McCaffrey, *The Irish Diaspora in America* (1984); Kerby A. Miller, *Emigrants and Exiles: Ireland and the Irish*

Exodus to North America (1985); Norman Ware, *The Industrial Worker, 1840–1860* (1964); Sean Wilentz, *Chants Democratic: New York City and the Rise of the American Working Class, 1788–1850* (1984); Carl Wittke, *The Irish in America* (1956).

The Far West

John W. Caughey, *The California Gold Rush* (1975); Malcolm Clark, Jr., *Eden Seekers: The Settlement of Oregon, 1818–1862* (1981); Douglas H. Daniels, *Pioneer Urbanities: A Social and Cultural History of Black San Francisco* (1980); Arnoldo De Leon, *They Called Them Greasers: Anglo Attitudes Toward Mexicans in Texas, 1821–1900* (1983); John Mack Faragher, *Women and Men on the Overland Trail* (1979); William H. Goetzmann, *Exploration and Empire: The Explorer and the Scientist in the Winning of the American West* (1966); Neal Harlow, *California Conquered: War and Peace on the Pacific, 1846–1850* (1982); Theodore J. Karaminski, *Fur Trade and Exploration: Opening of the Far Northwest, 1821–1852* (1983); Frederick Merk, *History of the Westward Movement* (1978); Leonard Pitt, *The Decline of the Californios: A Social History of the Spanish-Speaking Californians, 1846–1890* (1966); Alfred Robinson, *Life in California* (1891); John I. Unruh, Jr., *The Plains Across: Overland Emigrants and the Trans-Mississippi West, 1840–1860* (1979); David J. Weber, *The Mexican Frontier, 1821–1846: The American Southwest Under Mexico* (1982).

The Politics and Diplomacy of Expansion

K. Jack Bauer, *The Mexican War, 1846–1848* (1974); Paul H. Bergeron, *The Presidency of James K. Polk* (1987); William C. Binkley, *The Texas Revolution* (1952); Gene M. Brack, *Mexico Views Manifest Destiny* (1976); Seymour Connor and Odie Faulk, *North America Divided: The Mexican War, 1846–1848* (1971); William J. Cooper, *Liberty and Slavery: Southern Politics to 1860* (1983); Bernard DeVoto, *The Year of Decision, 1846* (1943); Norman A. Graebner, *Empire on the Pacific: A Study in American Continental Expansion* (1955); Thomas R. Hietala, *Manifest Design: Anxious Aggrandizement in Late Jacksonian America* (1985); Reginald Horsman, *Race and Manifest Destiny: The Origins of American Racial Anglo-Saxonism* (1981); Robert W. Johannsen, *To the Halls of the Montezumas: The Mexican War in the American Imagination* (1985); Ernest McPherson Lander, Jr., *Reluctant Imperialist: Calhoun, the South Carolinian, and the Mexican War* (1980); Frederick Merk, *Slavery and the Annexation of Texas* (1972); David M. Pletcher, *The Diplomacy of Annexation: Texas, Oregon, and the Mexican War* (1973); Joseph G. Raybeck, *Free Soil: The Election of 1848* (1970); John H. Schroeder, *Mr. Polk's War: American Opposition and Dissent, 1846–1848* (1971); Charles G. Sellers, *James K. Polk: Jacksonian, 1795–1843* (1957); Joel H. Silbey, *The Shrine of Party: Congressional Voting Behaviour, 1841–1852* (1967); Otis A. Singletary, *The Mexican War* (1960).

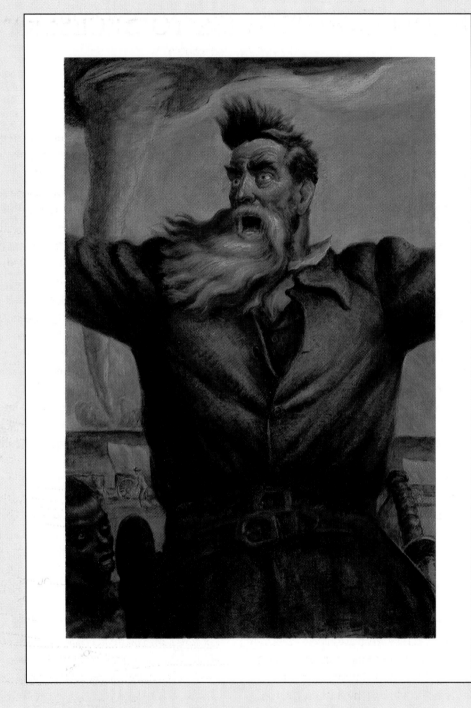

John Brown
by John Steuart Curry, 1939

14

FROM COMPROMISE TO SECESSION
1850–1861

Between December 1859 and February 1860, collisions between northerners and southerners in Congress produced a prolonged deadlock over the election of the Speaker of the House of Representatives. Tempers flared as never before. A South Carolinian observed that "the only persons who do not have a revolver and a knife are those who have two revolvers." Although the election of an obscure and inoffensive New Jersey congressman finally broke the deadlock, the tension and discord in Congress mirrored the division between the North and the South that would soon lead to the secession of the slave states from the Union.

Secession, a southern newspaper editor conceded in 1861, was a desperate measure. But, he quickly added, "We must recollect that we live in desperate times." A series of confrontations with the North over the status of slavery in the territories fed this growing sense of desperation in the South. Viewing the West as a boundless field of economic opportunity for themselves, northerners abhorred the idea of competing with slaves there for jobs and thus zealously resisted the westward advance of slavery. During the 1850s a growing number of northerners embraced the doctrine known as free soil, the belief that Congress had to prohibit slavery in all the territories. Free-soilers like New York's Republican senator William H. Seward and Illinois's senatorial candidate Abraham Lincoln did not call for the abolition of slavery in the southern states, but they did de-

fine the conflict between slavery and freedom as national in scope. In 1858 Seward spoke of an "irrepressible conflict" between slavery and freedom and predicted that either the wheat fields of the North would become slave or the cotton fields of the South free. Invoking the biblical warning that "a house divided against itself cannot stand," Lincoln made the same point in 1858: "I believe that this nation cannot exist permanently half slave and half free." In the eyes of these men, the only solution lay in a congressional prohibition of slavery in the territories.

The doctrine of free soil ultimately rested on an image of a good society as one in which free individuals worked to achieve economic self-sufficiency as landowning farmers, self-employed artisans, and small shopkeepers. Like free-soil northerners, white southerners valued economic independence, but they insisted that without slaves to do society's menial jobs, common white people could never attain economic self-sufficiency. By 1850 most southern whites had persuaded themselves that slavery was an institution that treated blacks humanely while enabling whites to enjoy comfortable lives.

These differing images of the good society made conflict over slavery in the territories virtually unavoidable. White southerners interpreted free-soil attacks on territorial slavery as slaps in their faces. Nothing infuriated them more than the idea that they could not take their property, slaves, anywhere that they chose. Increasingly, too, southerners viewed free-soilers' hostility as a thinly disguised attempt to corrode the foundations of slavery in both the territories and the South itself. When the abolitionist John Brown recklessly attempted to spark a southern slave insurrection in 1859, innumerable southerners concluded that only the extreme step of secession could safeguard the South against northern onslaughts. "Not only our property," a southern newspaper editor proclaimed in 1861, "but our honor, our lives and our all are involved."

THE COMPROMISE OF 1850

Ralph Waldo Emerson had predicted that an American victory in the Mexican War would be akin to swallowing arsenic, and his forecast proved disturbingly accurate. When the Treaty of Guadalupe Hidalgo was signed in 1848 to end the war, the United States contained an equal number (fifteen) of free and slave states. The vast territory ceded by Mexico (the Mexican cession) threatened to upset this balance in ways that few could have foreseen. Furthermore, all of the proposed solutions to the problem of slavery in the Mexican cession—a free-soil policy, extension of the Missouri Compromise line, and popular sovereignty—ensured controversy. The prospect of "Free Soilism, Wilmot Provisoism, and all such tomfoolery" horrified southerners. The idea of extending the Missouri Compromise line, 36°30', to the Pacific, which would allow slavery in New Mexico and southern California, antagonized northerners committed to free soil. (This second proposal simultaneously angered southern extremists, notably John C. Calhoun and his followers, by conceding to Congress the right to bar slavery in any of the territories.) The third solution, popular (or "squatter") sovereignty, which promised to ease the issue of slavery extension out of national politics by allowing each territory to decide the question for itself, offered the greatest hope for compromise. Yet popular sovereignty would appease neither those opposed in principle to the expansion of slavery nor those opposed to prohibitions on its expansion.

As statesmen fashioned their positions on slavery extension, the flow of events plunged the nation into a crisis. In the spring of 1849, the nonslaveholding Mor-

mons in Deseret drew up a constitution and sought admission to the Union. (The state of Deseret had been established by Brigham Young's followers on soil that had become part of the United States with the Treaty of Guadalupe Hidalgo.) Then in the fall of 1849, Californians, their numbers swollen by thousands of gold-rushers, framed a constitution that banned slavery, and in 1850 they petitioned for statehood. (From the standpoint of popular sovereignty, California had jumped the gun, for Congress had not yet recognized it as a territory.) To complicate matters, Texas, admitted as a slave state in 1845, laid claim to the eastern half of New Mexico, a region where the future of slaves remained in doubt.

By 1850 these territorial issues had become intertwined with two other concerns. Northern orators had long denounced slavery and the sale of slaves in the District of Columbia, within the shadow of the federal government. For their part, southerners had often complained that northerners were flouting the Fugitive Slave Act, which Congress had passed in 1793, and were actively frustrating slaveholders' efforts to catch runaways on northern soil and return them to the South. Any broad compromise between the sections would have to take into account northern demands for a restriction on slavery in the District of Columbia and southern insistence on a more effective fugitive-slave law.

Zachary Taylor at the Helm

Although elected president in 1848 without a platform, Zachary Taylor came to office with a clear position on the issue of slavery in the Mexican cession. A slaveholder himself, he took for granted the South's need to defend slavery. Taylor insisted that southerners would best protect slavery if they refrained from rekindling the issue of slavery in the territories. He rejected Calhoun's idea that the protection of slavery in the southern states ultimately depended on the expansion of slavery into the western territories. In Taylor's eyes, neither California nor New Mexico was suited to slavery; in 1849 he told a Pennsylvania audience that "the people of the North need have no apprehension of the further extension of slavery."

Although Taylor looked to the exclusion of slavery from California and New Mexico, his position differed from that embodied in the Wilmot Proviso, the free-soil measure proposed in 1846 by a northern Democrat. The proviso had insisted that *Congress* bar slavery in the territories ceded by Mexico. Taylor's plan, in contrast, left the decision to the states. Recognizing that most Californians opposed slavery in their state, Taylor had prompted California to bypass the territorial stage that normally preceded statehood, to draw up their constitution in 1849, and to apply directly for admission as a free state. The president strongly hinted that he expected New Mexico, where slavery had been abolished under Mexican rule, to do the same.

Taylor's strategy appeared to promise a quick, practical solution to the problem of slavery extension. It would give the North two new free states. At the same time, it would acknowledge a position upon which all southerners agreed: a *state* could bar or permit slavery as it chose. This conviction in fact served as the very foundation of the South's defense of slavery, its armor against all the onslaughts of the abolitionists. Nothing in the Constitution forbade a state to act one way or the other on slavery.

Despite its practical features, Taylor's plan dismayed southerners of both parties. Having gored the Democrats in 1848 as the party of the Wilmot Proviso, southern Whigs expected more from the president than a proposal that in effect yielded the proviso's goal—the banning of slavery in the Mexican cession. Many southerners, in addition, questioned Taylor's assumption that slavery could never take root in California or New Mexico. To one observer, who declared that the whole controversy over slavery in the Mexican cession "related to an imaginary negro in an impossible place," southerners pointed out that both areas already contained slaves and that slaves could be employed profitably in the mining of gold and silver. "California is by nature," a southerner proclaimed, "peculiarly a slaveholding State." Calhoun trembled at the thought of adding more free states. "If this scheme excluding slavery from California and New Mexico should be carried out—if we are to be reduced to a mere handful . . . wo, wo, I say to this Union." Disillusioned with Taylor, nine southern states agreed to send delegations to a southern convention that was scheduled to meet in Nashville in June 1850.

Henry Clay Proposes a Compromise

Taylor might have been able to contain mounting southern opposition if he had held a secure position in the Whig party. But the leading Whigs, among them Daniel Webster of Massachusetts and Kentucky's Henry Clay, each of whom had presidential aspirations, never reconciled themselves to Taylor, a political novice. Early in 1850 Clay boldly challenged Taylor's leadership by forging a set of compromise proposals to

Henry Clay

Eloquent but at the same time earthy, Clay was first elected to the Senate during Jefferson's administration. Subsequently, Clay himself made five unsuccessful bids for the presidency. A European visitor was struck by his penchant for chewing tobacco, drinking whiskey, putting his legs on the table, and spitting "like a regular Kentucky hog-driver."

resolve the range of contentious issues. Clay proposed (1) the admission of California as a free state; (2) the division of the remainder of the Mexican cession into two territories, New Mexico and Utah (formerly Deseret), without federal restrictions on slavery; (3) the settlement of the Texas–New Mexico boundary dispute on terms favorable to New Mexico; (4) as a pot-sweetener for Texas, an agreement that the federal government would assume the considerable public debt of Texas; (5) in the District of Columbia, the continuance of slavery but the abolition of the slave trade; and (6) a more effective fugitive-slave law.

Clay rolled all of these proposals into a single "omnibus" bill, which he hoped to steer through Congress. The debates over the omnibus during the late winter and early spring of 1850 witnessed the last major appearances on the public stage of Clay, Webster, and Calhoun, the trio of distinguished senators whose lives had mirrored every public event of note since the War of 1812. Clay played the role of the conciliator, as he had during the controversy over Missouri in 1820 and again during the nullification crisis in the early 1830s. He warned the South against the evils of secession and assured the North that nature would check the spread of slavery more effectively than a thousand Wilmot Provisos. Gaunt and gloomy, a dying Calhoun listened as another senator read his address, in which Calhoun summarized what he had been saying for years: the North's growing power, enhanced by protective tariffs and by the Missouri Compromise's exclusion of slaveholders from the northern part of the Louisiana Purchase, had created an imbalance between the sections. Only a decision by the North to treat the South as an equal could now save the Union. Three days later, Daniel Webster, who believed that slavery, "like the cotton-plant, is confined to certain parallels of climate," delivered his memorable "Seventh of March" speech. Speaking not "as a Massachusetts man, nor as a Northern man, but as an American," Webster chided the North for trying to "reenact the will of God" by legally excluding slavery from the Mexican cession and declared himself a forthright proponent of compromise.

However eloquent, the conciliatory voices of Clay and Webster made few converts. With every call for compromise, some northern or southern speaker would rise and inflame passions. The antislavery New York Whig William Seward, for example, enraged southerners by talking of a "higher law than the Constitution"—namely, the will of God against the extension of slavery. Clay's compromise became tied up in a congressional committee. To worsen matters, Clay, who at first had pretended that his proposals were in the spirit of Taylor's plan, broke openly with the president in May, and Taylor attacked Clay as a glory-hunter.

As the Union faced its worst crisis since 1789, a series of events in the summer of 1850 eased the way toward a resolution. When the Nashville convention assembled in June, extreme advocates of "southern rights," called the fire-eaters because of their recklessness, boldly made their presence felt. But talk of southern rights smelled suspiciously like a plot to disrupt the Union. "I would rather sit in council with the six thousand dead who have died of cholera in St. Louis," Senator Thomas Hart Benton of Missouri declared, "than go into convention with such a gang of scamps." Only nine of the fifteen slave states, most in the Lower South, sent delegates to the convention, and moderates took control and isolated the extremists. Then Zachary Taylor, after eating and drinking

too much at an Independence Day celebration, fell ill with gastroenteritis and died on July 9. His successor, Vice President Millard Fillmore of New York, quickly proved himself more favorable than Taylor to the Senate's compromise measure by appointing Daniel Webster as his secretary of state. Next, after the compromise suffered a devastating series of amendments in late July, Stephen A. Douglas of Illinois took over the floor leadership from the exhausted Clay. Recognizing that the compromise lacked majority support in Congress, Douglas jettisoned Clay's strategy by chopping the omnibus into a series of separate measures and seeking to secure passage of each bill individually. This ingenious tactic worked beautifully. By summer's end, in the Compromise of 1850, Congress had passed each component of Clay's plan: statehood for California; territorial status for Utah and New Mexico, allowing popular sovereignty; resolution of the Texas–New Mexico boundary disagreement; federal assumption of the Texas debt; abolition of the slave trade in the District of Columbia; and a new fugitive-slave law.

Assessing the Compromise

President Fillmore hailed the compromise as a "final settlement" of sectional divisions, and Clay's reputation for conciliation reached new heights. Yet the compromise did not bridge the underlying differences between the two sections. Far from leaping forward to save the Union, Congress had backed into the Compromise of 1850; the majority of congressmen in one or another section opposed virtually all of the specific bills that made up the compromise. Most southerners, for example, voted against the admission of California and the abolition of the slave trade in the District of Columbia; the majority of northerners opposed the Fugitive Slave Act and the organization of New Mexico and Utah without a forthright congressional prohibition of slavery. These measures passed only because the minority of congressmen who genuinely desired compromise combined with the majority in either the North or the South who favored each specific bill.

Each section both gained and lost from the Compromise of 1850. The North won California as a free state, New Mexico and Utah as likely future free states, a favorable settlement of the Texas–New Mexico boundary (most of the disputed area was awarded to New Mexico, a probable free state), and the abolition of the slave trade in the District of Columbia. The

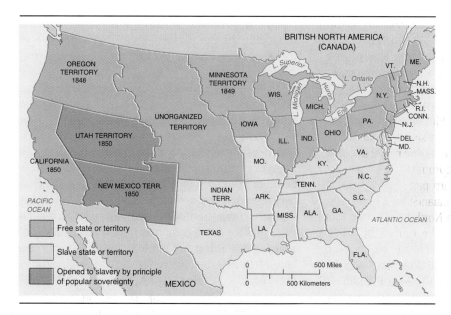

The Compromise of 1850
The Compromise of 1850 admitted California as a free state. Utah and New Mexico were left open to slavery or freedom on the principle of popular sovereignty.

South's benefits were cloudier. By stipulating popular sovereignty for New Mexico and Utah, the compromise, to most southerners' relief, had buried the Wilmot Proviso's insistence that Congress formally prohibit slavery in these territories. But to southerners' dismay, the position of the free-soilers remained viable, for the compromise left open the question of whether Congress could prohibit slavery in territories outside of the Mexican cession.

Not surprisingly, southerners reacted ambivalently to the Compromise of 1850. In southern state elections during the fall of 1850 and in 1851, procompromise, or Unionist, candidates thrashed anticompromise candidates who talked of southern rights and secession. But even southern Unionists did not dismiss the possibility of secession. Unionists in Georgia, for example, forged the celebrated Georgia platform, which threatened secession if Congress either prohibited slavery in New Mexico or Utah or repealed the fugitive-slave law.

The one clear advantage gained by the South, a more stringent fugitive-slave law, quickly proved a mixed blessing. Because few slaves had been taken into the Mexican cession, the question of slavery there had a hypothetical quality. However, the issues raised by the new fugitive-slave law were far from hypothetical; the law authorized real southerners to pursue real fugitives on northern soil. Here was a concrete issue to which the average northerner, who may never have

seen a slave and who cared little about slavery a thousand miles away, would respond with fury.

Enforcement of the Fugitive Slave Act

Northern moderates accepted the Fugitive Slave Act as the price the North had to pay to save the Union. But the law contained a string of features distasteful to moderates and outrageous to staunchly antislavery northerners. It denied alleged fugitives the right of trial by jury, did not allow them to testify in their own behalf, permitted their return to slavery merely on the testimony of the claimant, and enabled court-appointed commissioners to collect ten dollars if they ruled for the slaveholder but only five dollars if they ruled for the fugitive. In authorizing federal marshals to raise posses to pursue fugitives on northern soil, the law threatened to turn the North into "one vast hunting ground." In addition, the law targeted not only recent runaways but also those who had fled the South *decades* earlier. For example, it allowed slave-catchers in 1851 to wrench a former slave from his family in Indiana and return him to the master from whom he had fled in 1832. Above all, the law brought home to northerners the uncomfortable truth that the continuation of slavery depended on their complicity. By legalizing the activities of slave-catchers on northern soil, the law reminded northerners that slavery was a national problem, not merely a peculiar southern institution.

Antislavery northerners assailed the law as the "vilest monument of infamy of the nineteenth century." "Let the President . . . drench our land of freedom in blood," proclaimed Ohio's Whig congressman Joshua Giddings, "but he will never make us obey that law." His support for the law turned Senator Daniel Webster of Massachusetts into a villain in the eyes of the very people who for years had revered him as the "godlike Daniel." The abolitionist poet John Greenleaf Whittier wrote of his fallen idol:

> *All else is gone; from those giant eyes*
> *The soul has fled:*
> *When faith is lost, when honor dies,*
> *The man is dead.*

Efforts to catch and return fugitive slaves inflamed feelings in both the North and the South. In 1854 a Boston mob, aroused by antislavery speeches, broke into a courthouse and killed a guard in an abortive effort to rescue the fugitive slave Anthony Burns. Determined to prove that the law could be enforced "even in Boston," President Franklin Pierce sent a detachment of federal troops to escort Burns to the harbor, where a ship carried him back to slavery. No witness would ever forget the scene. As five platoons of troops marched with Burns to the ship, some fifty thousand people lined the streets. As the procession passed, one Bostonian hung from his window a black coffin bearing the words "THE FUNERAL OF LIBERTY." Another draped an American flag upside down as a symbol that "my country is eternally disgraced by this day's proceedings." The Burns incident shattered the complacency of conservative supporters of the Compromise of 1850. "We went to bed one night old fashioned conservative Compromise Union Whigs," the textile manufacturer Amos A. Lawrence wrote, "and waked up stark mad Abolitionists." A Boston committee later successfully purchased Burns's freedom, but the fate of many fugitives was far less happy. One such unfortunate was Margaret Garner, who, about to be captured and sent back to Kentucky as a slave, slit her daughter's throat and tried to kill her other children rather than witness their return to slavery.

In response to the Fugitive Slave Act, vigilance committees sprang up in many northern communities to spirit endangered blacks to safety in Canada. As another ploy, lawyers used obstructive tactics to drag out legal proceedings and thus raise the slave-catchers' expenses. Then during the 1850s, nine northern states passed "personal-liberty laws." By such techniques as forbidding the use of state jails to incarcerate alleged fugitives, these laws aimed to bar state officials from enforcing the law.

The frequent cold stares, obstructive legal tactics, and occasional violence encountered by slaveholders who ventured north to capture runaway slaves helped demonstrate to southerners that opposition to slavery boiled just beneath the surface of northern opinion. In the eyes of most southerners, the South had gained little more from the Compromise of 1850 than the Fugitive Slave Act, and now doubts surrounded even that northern concession. After witnessing riots against the Fugitive Slave Act in Boston in 1854, a young Georgian studying law at Harvard wrote to his mother, "Do not be surprised if when I return home you find me *a confirmed disunionist.*"

Uncle Tom's Cabin

The publication in 1852 of Harriet Beecher Stowe's novel *Uncle Tom's Cabin* aroused wide northern sympathy for fugitive slaves. Stowe, the daughter of the famed evangelical Lyman Beecher and the younger sister of Catharine Beecher, the stalwart advocate of domesticity for women, greeted the Fugitive Slave Act with horror and outrage. In a memorable scene from the novel, she depicted the slave Eliza escaping to freedom, clutching her infant son while bounding across ice floes on the Ohio River. Yet Stowe targeted slavery itself more than merely the slave-catchers who served the institution. Much of her novel's power derives from its intimation that even good intentions cannot prevail against so evil an institution. Torn from his wife and children by sale and shipped on a steamer for the Lower South, the black slave Uncle Tom rescues little Eva, the daughter of kindly Augustine St. Clare, from drowning. In gratitude, St. Clare purchases Tom from a slave-trader and takes him into his home in New Orleans. But after St. Clare's death, his cruel widow sells Tom to the vicious (and northern-born) Simon Legree, who whips Tom to death. Stowe played effectively on the emotions of her audience by demonstrating to an age that revered family life how slavery tore the family apart.

Three hundred thousand copies of *Uncle Tom's Cabin* were sold in 1852, and 1.2 million by the summer of 1853. Dramatized versions, which added dogs to chase Eliza across the ice, eventually reached perhaps fifty times the number of people as the novel itself. As a play, *Uncle Tom's Cabin* enthralled working-

Harriet Beecher Stowe, *1853*
Although her direct knowledge of slavery had been gleaned during a single visit to a Kentucky plantation, Stowe did extensive research before writing Uncle Tom's Cabin. *By making the demonic Simon Legree a northerner and by portraying southerners as well meaning, she effectively indicted slavery as an institution.*

class audiences normally indifferent, if not hostile, to abolitionism. During one stage performance, a reviewer for a New York newspaper observed that the gallery was filled with men "in red woollen shirts, with countenances as hardy and rugged as the implements of industry employed by them in the pursuit of their vocations." Astonished by the silence that fell over these men at the point when Eliza escapes across the river, the reviewer turned to discover that many of them were in tears.

The impact of *Uncle Tom's Cabin* cannot be precisely measured. Although the novel stirred deep feelings, it reflected the prevailing stereotypes of blacks far more than it overturned commonly held views. Stowe

portrayed only light-skinned blacks as aggressive and intelligent; she depicted dark-skinned blacks such as Uncle Tom as docile and submissive. In addition, some of the stage dramatizations softened the novel's antislavery message. In one version, which P. T. Barnum produced, Tom was rescued from Legree and returned happily as a slave to his original plantation.

Surgery on the plot, however, could not fully excise the antislavery message of *Uncle Tom's Cabin*. Though the novel hardly lived up to the prediction of a proslavery lawyer that it would convert 2 million people to abolitionism, it did push many waverers toward a more aggressively antisouthern and antislavery stance. Indeed, fear of its impact inspired a host of southerners to pen anti–Uncle Tom novels. As historian David Potter has concluded, the northern attitude toward slavery "was never quite the same after *Uncle Tom's Cabin*."

The Election of 1852

The issue of the enforcement of the Fugitive Slave Act fragmented the Whig party. The majority of northern Whigs, strongly supportive of free soil, had opposed the passage of the Fugitive Slave Act and now were leading defiance of the law. This vocal and potent northern free-soil wing put southern Whigs on the spot, for these southerners had long come before the southern electorate as the party best able to defend slavery within the Union.

The Whigs' nomination in 1852 of General Winfield Scott, the Mexican War hero, in place of the pro-compromise Millard Fillmore, widened the sectional split in their party. Although a Virginian, Scott had fallen under the influence of Senator William H. Seward of New York, a leader of the party's free-soil wing, and owed his nomination to northern votes. During the campaign Scott issued only a single, feeble endorsement of the Compromise of 1850, far less than southern Whigs needed if they were to brand the Democrats as the party of disunion and portray themselves as the party of both slavery and the Union.

The Democrats suffered from divisions of their own. In 1848 defectors from the Democratic party, led by Martin Van Buren, had formed the core of the Free-Soil party, which had gained over 10 percent of the popular vote. By 1852, however, most of the Free-Soilers of 1848, hungry for the spoils of office, returned to the Democratic party. As an idea rather than as a third party, free soil continued to win adherents between 1848 and 1852, but most converts to the idea of free

The Election of 1852

Candidates	Parties	Electoral Vote	Popular Vote	Percentage of Popular Vote
FRANKLIN PIERCE	Democratic	254	1,601,117	50.9
Winfield Scott	Whig	42	1,385,453	44.1
John P. Hale	Free-Soil		155,825	5.0

soil gravitated to the Whig rather than the Democratic party.

The Democratic convention began as a three-sided struggle among Lewis Cass of Michigan, James Buchanan of Pennsylvania, and Stephen A. Douglas of Illinois but ended with the nomination of a dark horse, Franklin Pierce of New Hampshire. Handsome, charming, and friendly, Pierce had served in Congress and in the Mexican War. But his appeal to the Democrats rested less on his political experience or his undistinguished war record (during a battle near Mexico City, he had passed out after having been thrown from his horse) than on his acceptability to all factions of the party. The "ultra men of the South," a friend of Pierce noted, "say they can cheerfully go for him and none, none say they cannot." In both the North and the South, the Democrats rallied not only behind the Compromise of 1850 but behind the idea of applying popular sovereignty to *all* the territories. In the most one-sided election since 1820, Pierce swept twenty-seven of the thirty-one states and won the electoral vote 254–42. The outcome was particularly galling for southern Whigs, who had soared to new heights four years previously. Compared to the 49.8 percent of the popular vote in the South won by Zachary Taylor in 1848, in 1852, Scott could claim only 35 percent of the southern vote. In state elections during 1852 and 1853, moreover, the Whigs were devastated in the South; one Whig stalwart lamented "the decisive breaking-up of our party."

THE COLLAPSE OF THE SECOND PARTY SYSTEM

Franklin Pierce had the dubious distinction of being the last presidential candidate for eighty years to win the popular and electoral vote in both the North and the South. Not until 1932 did another president, Franklin D. Roosevelt, repeat this accomplishment.

Pierce was also the last president to hold office under the second party system—Whigs against Democrats. For two decades the Whigs and the Democrats had battled, often on even terms. Then, within the four years of Pierce's administration, the Whig party disintegrated. In its place two new parties, first the American (Know-Nothing) party, and then the Republican party, arose.

Unlike the Whig party, the Republican party was a purely sectional, northern party. Its support came from former northern Whigs and from discontented northern Democrats. The Democrats survived as a national party, but with a base so shrunken in the North that in 1856, the Republican party, although scarcely a year old, swept two-thirds of the free states.

For decades the second party system had kept the conflict over slavery in check by giving Americans other issues—banking, internal improvements, tariffs, and temperance—to argue about. By the 1850s the debate over slavery extension was pushing such issues into the background and exposing raw divisions in each party. Of the two parties, Whig and Democratic, the Whigs had the larger, more aggressive free-soil wing, and hence they were more vulnerable than the Democrats to disruption. When Stephen A. Douglas in 1854 put forth a proposal to organize the vast Nebraska territory without restrictions on slavery, he ignited a firestorm that consumed the Whig party.

The Kansas-Nebraska Act

Signed by President Pierce at the end of May 1854, the Kansas-Nebraska Act dealt a shattering blow to the already weakened second party system. Moreover, the law triggered a renewal of the sectional strife that many Americans believed the Compromise of 1850 had buried. The origins of the act lay in the seemingly uncontroversial advance of midwestern settlement. Farm families in Iowa and Missouri had long dreamed of establishing homesteads in the vast prairies to their west, and their congressional repre-

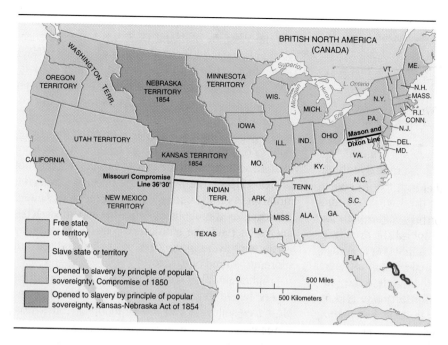

The Kansas-Nebraska Act, 1854

Kansas and Nebraska lay within the Louisiana Purchase, north of 36°30', and hence were closed to slavery until Stephen A. Douglas introduced his bills in 1854.

sentatives had repeatedly introduced bills to organize the territory west of these states, so that Native American land titles could be extinguished and a basis for government provided. Too, since the mid-1840s, advocates of national expansion had looked to the day when a railroad would link the Midwest to the Pacific; and St. Louis, Milwaukee, and Chicago had vied to become the eastern end of the projected Pacific railroad.

In January 1854 Senator Stephen A. Douglas of Illinois proposed a bill to organize Nebraska as a territory. An ardent expansionist, Douglas had formed his political ideology in the heady atmosphere of Manifest Destiny during the 1840s. As early as the mid-1840s, he had embraced the ideas of a Pacific railroad and the organization of Nebraska as ways to guarantee a continuous line of settlement between the Midwest and the Pacific. Although he preferred a railroad from his hometown of Chicago to San Francisco, Douglas dwelled on the national benefits that would attend construction of a railroad from *anywhere* in the Midwest to the Pacific. Such a railroad would enhance the importance of the Midwest, which could then hold the balance of power between the older sections of the North and South and guide the nation toward unity rather than disruption. In addition, westward expansion through Nebraska with the aid of a railroad struck Douglas as an issue, comparable to Manifest Destiny, around which the

contending factions of the Democratic party would unite.

Douglas recognized two sources of potential conflict over his Nebraska bill. First, some southerners advocated a rival route for the Pacific railroad that would start at either New Orleans or Memphis. Second, Nebraska lay within the Louisiana Purchase and north of the Missouri Compromise line of 36°30', a region closed to slavery. Unless Douglas made some concessions, southerners would have little incentive to vote for his bill, because the organization of Nebraska would simultaneously create a potential free state and increase the chances for a northern, rather than a southern, railroad to the Pacific. As the floor manager of the Compromise of 1850 in the Senate, Douglas thought that he had an ideal concession to offer to the South. The Compromise of 1850 had applied the principle of popular sovereignty to New Mexico and Utah, territories outside of the Louisiana Purchase and hence unaffected by the Missouri Compromise. Why not assume, Douglas reasoned, that the Compromise of 1850 had taken the place of the Missouri Compromise *everywhere*? Believing that expansion rather than slavery was uppermost in the public's mind, Douglas hoped to avoid controversy over slavery by ignoring the Missouri Compromise. But he quickly came under pressure from southern congressmen, who wanted an explicit repudiation of the Missouri Compromise. Soon southerners forced Douglas to state publicly that the Nebraska bill "superseded" the Missouri Compromise and rendered it "void." Still under pressure, Douglas next agreed to a division of Nebraska into two territories: Nebraska to the west of Iowa, and Kansas to the west of Missouri. Because Missouri was a slave state, most congressmen assumed that the division aimed to secure Kansas for slavery and Nebraska for free soil.

The modifications of Douglas's original bill set off a storm of protest. Congress quickly tabled the Pacific railroad (which, in the turn of events, would not be built until after the Civil War) and focused on the issue of slavery extension. A group of "Independent Democratic" northern congressmen, composed of antislavery Whigs and free-soil Democrats, assailed the bill as "part and parcel of an atrocious plot" to violate the "sacred pledge" of the Missouri Compromise and to turn Kansas into a "dreary region of despotism, inhabited by masters and slaves." Their rage electrified southerners, many of whom initially had reacted indifferently to the Nebraska bill. Some southerners had opposed an explicit repeal of the Missouri Compromise from fear of stimulating sectional discord; others doubted that Kansas would attract many slaveholders. But the furious assault of antislavery northerners united the South behind the Kansas-Nebraska bill by turning the issue into one of sectional pride as much as slavery extension.

Despite the uproar, Douglas successfully guided the Kansas-Nebraska bill through the Senate, where it passed by a vote of 37 to 14. In the House of Representatives, where the bill passed by little more than a whisker, 113 to 100, the true dimensions of the conflict became apparent. Not a single northern Whig representative in the House voted for the bill, whereas the northern Democrats divided evenly, 44 to 44.

The Surge of Free Soil

Douglas obviously had miscalculated the reaction to his Kansas-Nebraska bill. Amid the clamor over the bill, he conceded that he could now travel to Chicago by the light of his own burning effigies. Yet Douglas was neither a fool nor a political novice. Rather, he was the victim of a political force, the surge of feeling for free soil, that exploded under his feet.

Support for free soil united northerners who could agree on little else. Many northern free-soilers were racists who opposed letting any blacks, free or slave, into the West. In 1851 and 1853, racist free-soil advocates in Iowa and Illinois secured the passage of laws prohibiting settlement by black people; and in Iowa, Michigan, and Wisconsin, free-soilers refused by overwhelming majorities to allow blacks to vote. In Oregon, after rejecting slavery by a three-to-one majority in 1857, voters excluded all blacks from the state by an eight-to-one majority. But laws excluding blacks from western settlement were not always enforced, and not all free-soilers were racist. Some rejected slavery on moral grounds and opposed blatantly racist legislation. However, as the abolitionist George W. Julian accurately observed, the antislavery convictions of many westerners were grounded on a "perfect, if not supreme" hatred of blacks.

Although split over the morality of slavery, free-soilers agreed that slavery impeded whites' progress. Most free-soilers accepted Abraham Lincoln's portrayal of the North as a society of upwardly mobile farmers, artisans, and small businessmen and subscribed to the doctrine of "free labor"—the idea that in America, any enterprising individual could escape the class of wage labor and attain self-employment. "The man who labored for another last year," Lincoln insisted, "this year labors for himself, and next year he will hire others to labor for him." Because a slave worked for nothing, the free-soil argument ran, no free laborer could compete with a slave. A territory might contain only a handful of slaves or none at all, but as long as Congress refused to prohibit slavery in the territories, the institution could gain a foothold. Then slavery would grow, and free labor would wither; competition with slave labor would either drive out free labor or deter free labor from entering. Wherever slavery appeared, a free-soiler proclaimed, "labor loses its dignity; industry sickens; education finds no schools; religion finds no churches, and the whole land of slavery is impoverished."

Furthermore, free-soilers flatly rejected the idea that slavery had natural limits. As long as slaves could enter a territory, they believed, slaveholders would find tasks for them. In 1851 a free-soiler warned that "slavery is as certain to invade New Mexico and Utah, as the sun is to rise." By 1854 free-soilers were predicting that once secure in Kansas, slavery would invade the Minnesota Territory.

One free-soiler articulated the growing suspicions of many when he branded the Kansas-Nebraska Act "a part of a continuous movement of slaveholders to advance slavery over the entire North." At every turn, the free-soilers contended, the spread of slavery depended on the complicity of politicians. At the heart of the free-soil argument lay the belief that southern planters, southern politicians, and their northern dupes like Stephen A. Douglas were conspiring to spread slavery. And rather than any single event, there emerged a *pattern* of events—the Fugitive Slave Act, the repeal of the Missouri Compromise, and the Kansas-Nebraska division—that convinced free-soilers that a diabolical Slave Power was spreading its tentacles like an octopus. "I voted for the compromise measures of 1850, with the exception of the fugitive slave law," wrote a Whig congressman from Massachusetts, "and had little sympathy with abolitionists, but the repeal of the Missouri Compromise, that most wanton and wicked act, so obviously designed to promote the extension of slavery, was too much to bear. I now advocate the freedom of Kansas under all circumstances and at all hazards, and the prohibition of slavery in all territories now free."

The Ebbing of Manifest Destiny

The Kansas-Nebraska Act strained Democratic harmony and embarrassed the Pierce administration. The hubbub over the law doomed Manifest Destiny, the issue that had unified the Democrats in the 1840s.

Pierce had come to office as a champion of Manifest Destiny. In 1853 his emissary James Gadsden concluded a treaty with Mexico for the purchase of a strip of land south of the Gila River (now southern Arizona and part of southern New Mexico), an acquisition favored by advocates of a southern railroad route to the Pacific. The fiercely negative reaction to the so-called Gadsden Purchase, however, pointed up the mounting suspicions of expansionist aims. Encountering stiff northern opposition, Gadsden's treaty gained Senate approval in 1854 only after an amendment slashed nine thousand square miles from the purchase. Clearly, the same sectional rivalries that were brewing conflict over the existing territory of Nebraska were threatening to engulf proposals to gain *new* territory.

Pierce encountered even more severe buffeting when he tried to acquire the island of Cuba. Even as Congress was wrestling with the Kansas-Nebraska bill, Mississippi's former senator John A. Quitman was planning a massive filibustering (unofficial) military expedition—to seize Cuba from Spain. Pierce himself wanted to purchase Cuba and may have encouraged

Quitman as a way to scare Spain into selling the island. However, northerners, aroused by the Kansas-Nebraska bill, increasingly viewed filibustering as another manifestation of the Slave Power's conspiracy to grab more territory for the "peculiar institution." Pierce, alarmed by northern reaction to the Kansas-Nebraska bill and by signs that Spain planned to defend the island militarily, forced Quitman to scuttle the planned expedition.

Pierce still hoped to purchase Cuba, but events quickly slipped out of his control. In October 1854 the American ambassadors to Great Britain, France, and Spain, two of them from the South, met in Belgium and issued the unofficial Ostend Manifesto, which called upon the United States to acquire Cuba by any necessary means, including force, and then to welcome the island "into that great family of states of which the Union is the Providential Nursery." Already beset by the storm over the Kansas-Nebraska Act, and faced by northern outrage at the threat of aggression against Spain, Pierce quickly repudiated the manifesto.

Despite the Pierce administration's opposition to the Ostend Manifesto, the idea of expansion into the Caribbean continued to attract southerners, including the Tennessee-born adventurer William Walker. Slightly built and so shy and unassuming that he usually spoke with his hands in his pockets, Walker seemed an unlikely soldier of fortune. Yet between 1854 and 1860, the year he was executed by a firing squad in Honduras, Walker led a succession of filibustering expeditions into Central America. Taking advantage of civil chaos in Nicaragua, he made himself the chief political force in that nation, reinstituted slavery there, and talked openly of making Nicaragua a U.S. colony. Southern expansionists also kept the acquisition of both Cuba and parts of Mexico at the top of their agenda and received some support from northern Democrats. As late as 1859, President James Buchanan, Pierce's successor, tried to persuade Congress to appropriate funds for the purchase of Cuba.

For all of the proclamations and intrigues that surrounded the movement for southern expansion in the 1850s, the expansionists' actual strength and goals remained open to question. Many planned filibustering expeditions never got off the ground. With few exceptions the adventurers were shady characters whom southern politicians might admire but upon whom they could never depend. Moreover, a sizable body of southerners did not support the idea of southward expansion. The largely Whig sugar planters in Louisiana, for example, opposed acquiring Cuba, on grounds that once Cuba was annexed, its sugar would enter the United States duty-free and compete with American sugar.

Still, southern expansionists created enough commotion to worry antislavery northerners that the South aspired to establish a Caribbean slave empire. Like a card in a poker game, the threat of expansion southward was all the more menacing for not being played. As long as the debate over the extension of slavery focused on territories in the continental United States, slavery's prospects for expansion were limited and, Kansas aside, seemed fairly dim. If parts of the Caribbean were added to the United States, however, all these calculations would have to change.

The Whigs Disintegrate

While straining Democratic unity, the Kansas-Nebraska Act wrecked the Whig party. In the law's immediate aftermath, most northern Whigs hoped to blame the Democrats for the act and to entice free-soil Democrats to their side. In the state and congressional elections of 1854, the Democrats were decisively defeated. But the Whig party failed to benefit from the backlash against the Democrats. However furious they felt at Douglas for initiating the act, free-soil Democrats could not forget that the southern Whigs had supported Douglas. In addition, the northern Whigs themselves were deeply divided between antislavery "Conscience" Whigs, led by Senator William Seward of New York, and conservatives, led by former president Millard Fillmore, who were convinced that the Whig party had to adhere at all costs to the Compromise of 1850 to maintain itself as a national party.

Divisions within the Whig party not only repelled antislavery Democrats from affiliating with it but also prompted many antislavery Whigs to look for an alternative party. By 1856 the new Republican party would become the home for most of these northern refugees from the traditional parties; but in 1854 and 1855, when the Republican party was only starting to organize, the American, or Know-Nothing, party emerged as the principal alternative to the established parties.

The Rise and Fall of the Know-Nothings

The Know-Nothings evolved out of a secret nativist organization, the Order of the Star-Spangled Banner, founded in 1850. (The party's popular name, Know-

Nothing, derived from the standard response of its members to inquiries about its activities: "I know nothing.") One of many such societies that mushroomed in response to the unprecedented immigration of the 1840s, the Order of the Star-Spangled Banner had sought to rid the United States of immigrant and Catholic political influence by pressuring the existing parties to nominate and appoint only native-born Protestants to office, and by advocating an extension of the naturalization period before immigrants could vote.

Throughout the 1840s nativists usually voted Whig, but their allegiance to the Whigs started to buckle during Winfield Scott's campaign for the presidency in 1852. In an attempt to revitalize his party, which was badly split over slavery, Scott had courted the traditionally Democratic Catholic vote. But Scott's tactic backfired, for most Catholics voted for Franklin Pierce. Nativists, meanwhile, felt betrayed by their party, and, after Scott's defeat, many gravitated toward the Know-Nothings. The Kansas-Nebraska Act cemented their allegiance to the Know-Nothings, who in the North opposed both the extension of slavery and Catholicism. Indeed, an obsessive fear of conspiracies unified the Know-Nothings. Just as they denounced the pope for allegedly conspiring to subvert the American republic, they saw the evil influence of Slave Power everywhere.

The Know-Nothings' surge was truly stunning. In 1854 they captured the governorship, all the congressional seats, and almost all the seats in the state legislature in Massachusetts. Know-Nothings were sufficiently strong in the West to retard the emergence of the Republican party, and so strong in the East that they exploded any hopes that the Whigs had of capitalizing on hostility to the Kansas-Nebraska Act.

After rising spectacularly between 1853 and 1855, the star of Know-Nothingism nevertheless plummeted and gradually disappeared from the horizon after 1856. The Know-Nothings proved as vulnerable as the Whigs to sectional conflicts over slavery. Although primarily a force in the North, the Know-Nothings had a southern wing, composed mainly of former Whigs who loathed both the antislavery northerners who were abandoning the Whig party and the southern Democrats, whom they viewed as disunionist firebrands. In 1855 these southern Know-Nothings combined with northern conservatives to make acceptance of the Kansas-Nebraska Act part of the Know-Nothing platform, and thus they blurred the attraction of Know-Nothingism to those northern voters who were more antislavery than anti-Catholic. One such Whig refugee, Illinois congressman Abraham Lincoln, asked pointedly: "How can anyone who abhors the oppression of negroes be in favor of degrading classes of white people?" "We began by declaring," Lincoln continued, "that 'all men are created equal.' We now practically read it 'all men are created equal except negroes.' When the Know-Nothings get control, it will read 'all men are created equal, except Negroes and foreigners and Catholics.'" Finally, even most Know-Nothings eventually came to conclude that, as one observer put it, "neither the Pope nor the foreigners ever can govern the country or endanger its liberties, but the slavebreeders and slave-traders *do* govern it, and threaten to put an end to all government but theirs." Consequently, the Know-Nothings proved vulnerable to the challenge posed by the emerging Republican party, which did not officially embrace nativism and which had no southern wing to blunt its antislavery message.

The Origins of the Republican Party

Born in the chaotic aftermath of the Kansas-Nebraska Act, the Republican party sprang up in several northern states in 1854 and 1855. With the Know-Nothings' demise after 1856, the Republicans would become the main opposition to the Democratic party, and they would win each presidential election from 1860 through 1880; but in 1855 it was unclear whether the Republicans had any future. While united by opposition to the Kansas-Nebraska Act, the party held various shades of opinion in uneasy balance. At one extreme were conservatives who merely wanted to restore the Missouri Compromise; at the other was a small faction of former Liberty party abolitionists; and the middle held a sizable body of free-soilers.

In addition to bridging these divisions, the Republicans confronted the task of building organizations on the state level, where the Know-Nothings were already well established. Politicians of the day knew that the voters' allegiances were often shaped by state issues, including temperance. Maine's passage of the nation's first statewide prohibition law in 1851 spurred calls elsewhere for liquor regulation. Linking support for temperance with anti-Catholicism and antislavery, the Know-Nothings were well positioned to answer these calls.

Frequently, the same voters who were antislavery were also pro-temperance and anti-Catholic. The common thread here was the belief that addiction to alcohol and submission to the pope were forms of enslavement that had to be eradicated. Intensely moralistic, such voters viewed the traditional parties as controlled by unprincipled hacks, and they began to search for a new party. In competing with the Know-Nothings on the state level, the Republicans faced a dilemma, created by the fact that both parties were targeting many of the same voters. The Republican leadership had clearer antislavery credentials than did the Know-Nothing leadership, but this fact alone did not guarantee that voters would respond more to antislavery than to anti-Catholicism or temperance. Thus, if the Republicans attacked the Know-Nothings for stressing anti-Catholicism over antislavery, they ran the risk of alienating the very voters whom they had to attract. If they conciliated the Know-Nothings, they might lose their own identity as a party.

Sometimes attacking, sometimes conciliating, the Republicans won some successes in state elections in 1855; but as popular ire against the Kansas-Nebraska Act cooled, they also suffered setbacks. Even at the start of 1856, they were organized in only half the northern states and lacked any national organization. The Republicans desperately needed a development that would make voters worry more about the Slave Power than about rum or Catholicism. No single occurrence did more to unite the party around its free-soil center, to intensify voters' antislavery feelings, and, consequently, to boost the Republicans' fortunes than the outbreak of violence in Kansas, which quickly gained for the territory the name Bleeding Kansas.

Bleeding Kansas

In the wake of the Kansas-Nebraska Act, Boston-based abolitionists had organized the New England Emigrant Aid Company to send antislavery settlers into Kansas. The abolitionists' aim was to stifle escalating efforts to turn Kansas into a slave state. But antislavery New Englanders arrived slowly in Kansas; the bulk of the territory's early settlers came from Missouri or elsewhere in the Midwest. Very few of these early settlers opposed slavery on moral grounds. Some, in fact, favored slavery; others wanted to keep all blacks, whether slave or free, out of Kansas. "I kem to Kansas to live in a free state," exclaimed a clergyman, "and I don't want niggers a-trampin' over my grave."

Despite most settlers' racist leanings and utter hatred of abolitionists, Kansas became a battleground between proslavery and antislavery forces. In March 1855 thousands of proslavery Missourian "border

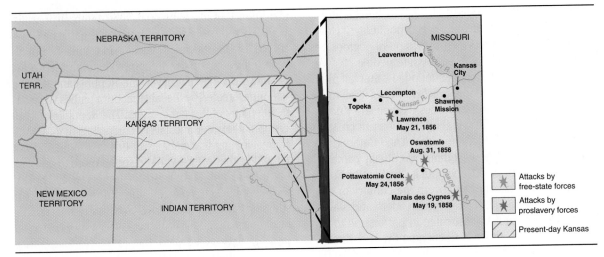

Bleeding Kansas
Kansas became a battleground between free-state and slave-state factions in the 1850s.

ruffians," led by Senator David R. Atchison, crossed into Kansas to vote illegally in the first election for a territorial legislature. Drawing and cocking their revolvers, they quickly silenced any judges who questioned their right to vote in Kansas. These proslavery advocates probably would have won an honest election, because they would have been supported by the votes both of slaveholders and of nonslaveholders horrified at rumors that abolitionists planned to use Kansas as a colony for fugitive slaves. But by stealing the election, the proslavery forces committed a grave tactical blunder. A cloud of fraudulence thereafter hung over the proslavery legislature subsequently established at Lecompton, Kansas. "There is not a proslavery man of my acquaintance in Kansas," wrote the wife of an antislavery farmer, "who does not acknowledge that the Bogus Legislature was the result of a gigantic and well planned fraud, that the elections were carried by an invading mob from Missouri." This legislature then further darkened its image by expelling several antislavery legislators and passing a succession of outrageous acts. These laws limited officeholding to individuals who would swear allegiance to slavery, punished the harboring of fugitive slaves by ten years' imprisonment, and made the circulation of abolitionist literature a capital offense.

The legislature's actions set off a chain reaction. Free-staters, including a small number of abolitionists and a much larger number of settlers enraged by the proceedings at Lecompton, organized a rival government at Topeka, Kansas, in the summer and fall of

1855. In response, the Lecompton government in May 1856 dispatched a posse to Lawrence, where free-staters, heeding the advice of antislavery minister Henry Ward Beecher that rifles would do more than Bibles to enforce morality in Kansas, had taken up arms and dubbed their guns "Beecher's Bibles." Riding under flags emblazoned "SOUTHERN RIGHTS" and "LET YANKEES TREMBLE AND ABOLITIONISTS FALL," the proslavery posse tore through the town like a hell-bent mob. Although the intruders did not kill anyone, they burned several buildings and destroyed two free-state printing presses—enough to earn their actions in the Republican press as "THE SACK OF LAWRENCE."

The next move belonged to John Brown. The son of a Connecticut abolitionist, Brown had drifted through business failures, bankruptcy, and even a charge of embezzlement, sustained only by his belief that God had ordained his misfortunes to test him. The sack of Lawrence convinced Brown that God now beckoned him, in the words of a neighbor, "to break the jaws of the wicked." In late May, Brown led seven men, including his four sons and his son-in-law, toward the Pottawatomie Creek near Lawrence. Setting upon five men associated with the Lecompton government, they shot one to death and hacked the others to pieces with broadswords. Brown's "Pottawatomie massacre" struck terror into the hearts of southerners and completed the transformation of "bleeding Kansas" into a battleground between the South and the North. A month after the massacre, a South Carolinian living in Kansas wrote to his sister:

I never lie down without taking the precaution to fasten my door and fix it in such a way that if it is forced open, it can be opened only wide enough for one person to come in at a time. I have my rifle, revolver, and old home-stocked pistol where I can lay my hand on them in an instant, besides a hatchet and an axe. I take this precaution to guard against the midnight attacks of the Abolitionists, who never make an attack in open daylight, and no Proslavery man knows when he is safe in this Ter[ritory.]

In Kansas popular sovereignty flunked its major test. Instead of quickly resolving the issue of slavery extension, popular sovereignty merely institutionalized the division over slavery by creating two rival governments, in Lecompton and Topeka. The Pierce administration then shot itself in the foot by denouncing the Topeka government and recognizing only its Lecompton rival. Pierce had forced northern Democrats into the awkward position of appearing to ally with the South in support of the fraudulently elected legislature at Lecompton. Nor did popular sovereignty keep the slavery issue out of national politics. On the day before the sack of Lawrence, Republican senator Charles Sumner of Massachusetts delivered a bombastic and wrathful speech, "The Crime Against Kansas," in which he verbally whipped most of the United States Senate for complicity in slavery and singled out Senator Andrew Butler of South Carolina for his choice of "the harlot, slavery" as his mistress and for the "loose expectoration" of his speech (a nasty reference to the aging Butler's tendency to drool). Sumner's oration stunned most senators. Douglas wondered aloud whether Sumner's real aim was "to provoke some of us to kick him as we would a dog in the street." Two days later a relative of Butler, Democratic representative Preston Brooks of South Carolina, strode into the Senate chamber, found Sumner at his desk, and struck him repeatedly with a cane. The hollow cane broke after five or six blows, but Sumner required stitches, experienced shock, and did not return to the Senate for three years. Brooks became an instant hero in the South, and the fragments of his cane were "begged as sacred relics." A new cane, presented to Brooks by the city of Charleston, bore the inscription "Hit him again."

Now "Bleeding Kansas" and "Bleeding Sumner" united the North. The sack of Lawrence, Pierce's recognition of the proslavery Lecompton government, and Brooks's actions seemed to clinch the Republican argument that an aggressive slaveocracy held white northerners in contempt. Abolitionists remained unpopular in northern opinion, but southerners were becoming even less popular than abolitionists. Northern migrants to Kansas coined a name reflecting their feelings toward southerners: "the pukes." Other northerners attacked the slaveholding migrants to Kansas as the "Missouri savages." By denouncing the Slave Power more than slavery itself, Republican propagandists sidestepped the issue of slavery's morality, which divided their followers, and focused on portraying southern planters as arrogant aristocrats and the natural enemies of the laboring people of the North.

The Election of 1856

The election of 1856 revealed the scope of the political realignments of the preceding few years. In this, its first presidential contest, the Republican party nominated John C. Frémont, the famed "pathfinder" who had played a key role in the conquest of California during the Mexican War. The Republicans then maneuvered the northern Know-Nothings into endorsing Frémont. The southern Know-Nothings picked the last Whig president, Millard Fillmore, as their candidate, and the Democrats dumped Pierce for the seasoned James Buchanan of Pennsylvania. A four-term congressman and long an aspirant to the presidency, Buchanan finally secured his party's nomination because he had the good luck to be out of the country (as minister to Great Britain) during the furor over the Kansas-Nebraska Act. As a signer of the Ostend Manifesto, he was popular in the South: virtually all of his close friends in Washington were southerners.

The campaign quickly turned into two separate races—Frémont versus Buchanan in the free states and Fillmore versus Buchanan in the slave states. In the North the candidates divided clearly over slavery extension; Frémont's platform called for a congressional prohibition of slavery in the territories, whereas Buchanan pledged congressional "non-interference." In the South Fillmore appealed to traditionally Whig voters and called for moderation in the face of secessionist threats. But by nominating a well-known moderate in Buchanan, the Democrats undercut some of Fillmore's appeal. Although Fillmore garnered more than 40 percent of the popular vote in ten of the slave states, he carried only Maryland. In the North Frémont outpolled Buchanan in the popular vote and won eleven of the sixteen free states; if Frémont had carried

The Election of 1856

Candidates	Parties	Electoral Vote	Popular Vote	Percentage of Popular Vote
JAMES BUCHANAN	Democratic	174	1,832,955	45.3
John C. Frémont	Republican	114	1,339,932	33.1
Millard Fillmore	American	8	871,731	21.6

Pennsylvania and either Illinois or Indiana, he would have won the election. As it turned out, Buchanan, the only truly national candidate in the race, secured the presidency.

The election yielded three clear conclusions. First, the American party was finished as a major national force. Having worked for the Republican Frémont, most northern Know-Nothings now joined that party, and in the wake of Fillmore's dismal showing in the South, southern Known-Nothings gave up on their party and sought new political affiliations. Second, although in existence scarcely more than a year, lacking any base in the South, and running a political novice, the Republican party did very well. A purely sectional party had come within reach of capturing the presidency. Finally, as long as the Democrats could unite behind a single national candidate, they would be hard to defeat. To achieve such unity, however, the Democrats would have to find more James Buchanans—"dough-face" moderates who would be acceptable to southerners and who would not drive even more northerners into Republican arms.

THE CRISIS OF THE UNION

No one ever accused James Buchanan of impulsiveness or fanaticism. Although he disapproved of slavery, he believed that his administration could neither restrict nor end the institution. In 1860 he would pronounce secession a grave wrong, but he would again affirm that his administration could not stop it. Understandably, contemporaries hailed his election as a victory for moderation. Yet his administration encountered a succession of controversies, first over the famed *Dred Scott* decision of the Supreme Court, then over the proslavery Lecompton constitution in Kansas, next following a raid by John Brown on Harpers Ferry,

Virginia, and finally concerning secession itself. Ironically, a man who sought to avoid controversy presided over one of the most controversy-ridden administrations in American history. Buchanan's problems arose less from his own actions than from the fact that the forces driving the nation apart were already spinning out of control by 1856. By the time of Buchanan's inauguration, southerners who looked north saw creeping abolitionism in the guise of free soil, whereas northerners who looked south saw an insatiable Slave Power. Once these images had taken hold in the minds of the American people, politicians like James Buchanan had little room to maneuver.

The Dred Scott Case

Pledged to congressional "non-interference" with slavery in the territories, Buchanan had long looked to the courts for a judicious and nonpartisan resolution of the vexatious issue of slavery extension. A case that appeared to promise such a solution had been winding its way through the courts for years; on March 6, 1857, two days after Buchanan's inauguration, the Supreme Court handed down its decision in *Dred Scott* v. *Sandford.*

Dred Scott, a slave, had been taken by his master during the 1830s from the slave state Missouri into Illinois and the Wisconsin Territory, areas respectively closed to slavery by the Northwest Ordinance of 1787 and by the Missouri Compromise. After his master's death, Scott sued for his freedom on the grounds of his residence in free territory. A jury sided with Scott and set him free. On appeal, however, the Missouri Supreme Court overturned the jury's decision in 1852 and returned Scott to slavery. Subsequently, Scott's new owner moved to New York while leaving Scott in Missouri, a turn of events that encouraged Scott to sue in the federal courts (which had jurisdiction over suits brought by citizens of one state against those of another). In 1856 the case finally reached the Supreme Court.

The Court faced two key issues. Did Scott's residence in free territory during the 1830s make him free? Next, regardless of the answer to this question, did Scott, again enslaved in Missouri, have a right to sue in the federal courts? The Court could have resolved the case on narrow grounds by answering the second question in the negative, but Buchanan wanted a far-reaching decision that would deal with the broad issue of slavery in the territories.

In the end, Buchanan got the broad ruling that he sought, but one so controversial that it settled little. In the most important of six separate majority opinions, Chief Justice Roger B. Taney, a seventy-nine-year-old Marylander whom Andrew Jackson had appointed to succeed John Marshall in 1835, began with the narrow conclusion that Scott, a slave, could not sue for his freedom. Then the thunder started. No black, whether a slave or a free person descended from a slave, could become a citizen of the United States, Taney continued. Next Taney whipped the thunderheads into a tornado. Even if Scott had been a legal plaintiff, Taney ruled, his residence in free territory years earlier did not make him free, because the Missouri Compromise, whose provisions prohibited slavery in the Wisconsin Territory, was *itself* unconstitutional. The compromise, declared Taney, violated the Fifth Amendment's protection of property (including slaves) from deprivation without due process of law.

Contrary to Buchanan's hopes, the decision touched off a new blast of controversy over slavery in the territories. The antislavery press flayed it as a "willful perversion" filled with "gross historical falsehoods." Taney's ruling gave Republicans more evidence that a fiendish Slave Power conspiracy gripped the nation. Although the Kansas-Nebraska Act had effectively repealed the Missouri Compromise, the Court's majority now rejected even the *principle* behind the compromise, the idea that Congress could prohibit slavery in the territories. Five of the six justices who rejected this principle were from slave states. The Slave Power, a northern paper bellowed, "has marched over and annihilated the boundaries of the states. We are now one great homogenous slaveholding community."

Like Stephen Douglas after the Kansas-Nebraska Act, President Buchanan now appeared as another northern dupe of the slaveocracy. Republicans restrained themselves from open defiance of the decision only by insisting that it did not bind the nation; Taney's comments on the constitutionality of the Missouri Compromise, they contended, amounted merely

to *obiter dicta*, opinions unnecessary to settling the case.

Reactions to the decision underscored the fact that by 1857 no "judicious" or nonpartisan solution to slavery extension was possible. Anyone who still doubted this needed only to read the fast-breaking news from Kansas.

The Lecompton Constitution

While the Supreme Court wrestled with the abstract issues raised by the expansion of slavery, Buchanan sought a concrete solution to the gnawing problem of Kansas, where the free-state government at Topeka and the officially recognized proslavery government at Lecompton viewed each other with profound distrust. Buchanan's plan for Kansas looked simple: an elected territorial convention would draw up a constitution that would either permit or prohibit slavery; Buchanan would submit the constitution to Congress; Congress would then admit Kansas as a state.

Unfortunately, no sooner had Buchanan devised his plan than it began to explode in his face. Popular sovereignty, the essence of Buchanan's plan, demanded fair play, a scarce quality in Kansas. The territory's history of fraudulent elections left both sides reluctant to commit their fortunes to the polls. An election for a constitutional convention took place in June 1857, but free-staters, by now a majority in Kansas, boycotted the election on grounds that the proslavery side would rig it. Dominated by proslavery delegates, a constitutional convention then met and drew up a frame of government, the Lecompton constitution, that protected the rights of those slaveholders already living in Kansas to their slave property and provided for a referendum in which voters could decide whether to allow in more slaves.

The Lecompton constitution created a dilemma for Buchanan. A supporter of popular sovereignty, he had gone on record in favor of letting the voters in Kansas decide the slavery issue. Now he was confronted by a constitution drawn up by a convention that had been elected by less than 10 percent of the eligible voters, by plans for a referendum that would not allow voters to remove slaves already in Kansas, and by the prospect that the proslavery side would conduct the referendum no more honestly than it had others. Yet Buchanan had compelling reasons to accept the Lecompton constitution as the basis for Kansas's admission as a state. The South, which had provided him

The Little Giant in the Character of Gladiator,
1858
Douglas and his supporters are shown as gladiators menacing President Buchanan and his administration's newspaper, the Washington Union, *for approving the Lecompton constitution.*

with 112 of his 174 electoral votes in 1856, supported the constitution. Buchanan knew, moreover, that only about two hundred slaves resided in Kansas, and he believed that the prospects for slavery in the remaining territories were slight. The contention over slavery in Kansas struck him as another example of how extremists could turn minor issues into major ones. To accept the constitution and speed the admission of Kansas as either a free state or a slave state seemed the best way to pull the rug from beneath the extremists and quiet the commotion in Kansas. Accordingly, in December 1857 Buchanan formally endorsed the Lecompton constitution.

Buchanan's decision provoked a bitter attack from Senator Stephen A. Douglas. What rankled Douglas and many others was that the Lecompton convention, having drawn up a constitution, then allowed voters to decide only whether more slaves could be brought into the territory. "I care not whether [slavery] is voted down or voted up," Douglas declared. But to refuse to allow a vote on the constitution itself, with its protection of existing slave property, smacked of a "system of trickery and jugglery to defeat the fair expression of the will of the people."

Even as Douglas broke with Buchanan, events in Kansas took a new turn. A few months after electing delegates to the convention that drew up the Lecompton constitution, Kansans had gone to the polls to elect a territorial legislature. So flagrant was the fraud in this election—one village with thirty eligible voters returned more than sixteen hundred proslavery votes—that the governor disallowed enough proslavery returns to give free-staters a majority in the legislature. After the drafting of the Lecompton constitution, this territorial legislature called for a referendum on the entire document. Whereas the Kansas constitutional convention's goal had been to restrict the choice of voters to the narrow issue of the future introduction of slaves, the territorial legislature sought a referendum that would allow Kansans to vote against the protection of existing slave property as well as the introduction of more slaves.

In December 1857 the referendum called earlier by the constitutional convention was held. Boycotted by free-staters, the constitution with slavery passed overwhelmingly. Two weeks later, in the election called by the territorial legislature, the proslavery side abstained, and the constitution went down to crushing defeat. Having already cast his lot with the Lecompton convention's election, Buchanan simply ignored this second election. But he could not ignore the obstacles that the division in Kansas created for his plan to bring Kansas into the Union under the Lecompton constitution. When he submitted the plan to Congress, a deadlock in the House forced him to accept a proposal for still another referendum. This time, Kansans were given the choice between accepting or rejecting the entire constitution, with the proviso that rejection would delay statehood. Despite the proviso, Kansans overwhelmingly voted down the constitution.

Not only had Buchanan failed to tranquilize Kansas, but he had alienated northerners in his own party. His support for the Lecompton constitution confirmed the suspicion of northern Democrats that the southern Slave Power pulled all the important strings in their party. Douglas became the hero of the hour for northern Democrats and even for some Republicans. "The bone and sinew of the Northern Democracy are with you," a New Yorker wrote to Douglas. Yet Douglas himself could take little comfort from the Lecompton fiasco, as his cherished formula of popular sovereignty increasingly looked like a prescription for civil strife rather than harmony.

The Lincoln-Douglas Debates

Despite the acclaim he gained in the North for his stand against the Lecompton constitution, Douglas faced a stiff challenge in Illinois for reelection to the United States Senate. Of his Republican opponent, Abraham Lincoln, Douglas said: "I shall have my hands full. He is the strong man of his party—full of wit, facts, dates—and the best stump speaker with his droll ways and dry jokes, in the West."

Physically as well as ideologically, the two men formed a striking contrast. Tall (6′4″) and gangling, Lincoln once described himself as "a piece of floating driftwood." Energy, ambition, and a passion for self-education had carried him from the Kentucky log cabin where he was born in 1809 through a youth filled with odd occupations (farm laborer, surveyor, rail-splitter, flatboatman, and storekeeper) into law and politics in his adopted Illinois. There he had capitalized on westerners' support for internal improvements to gain election to Congress in 1846 as a Whig. Having opposed the Mexican War and the Kansas-Nebraska Act, he joined the Republican party in 1856.

Douglas was fully a foot shorter than the towering Lincoln. But his compact frame contained astonishing energy. Born in New England, Douglas appealed primarily to the small farmers of southern origin who populated the Illinois flatlands. To these and others, he was the "little giant," the personification of the Democratic party in the West. The campaign quickly became more than just another Senate race, for it pitted the Republican party's rising star against the Senate's leading Democrat and, thanks to the railroad and the telegraph, received unprecedented national attention.

Although some Republicans extolled Douglas's stand against the Lecompton constitution, to Lincoln nothing had changed. Douglas was still Douglas, the author of the infamous Kansas-Nebraska Act and a man who cared not whether slavery was voted up or down as long as the vote was honest. Opening his campaign with the "House Divided" speech ("this nation cannot exist permanently half slave and half free"), Lincoln reminded his Republican followers of the gulf that still separated his doctrine of free soil from Douglas's popular sovereignty. Douglas dismissed the house-divided doctrine as an invitation to secession. What mattered to him was not slavery, which he viewed as merely an extreme way to subordinate an allegedly inferior race, but

the continued expansion of white settlement. Like Lincoln, he wanted to keep slavery out of the path of white settlement. But unlike his longtime rival, Douglas believed that popular sovereignty was the surest way to attain this goal without disrupting the Union.

The high point of the campaign came in a series of seven debates held from August 21 to October 15, 1858. The idea for the debates was proposed by Lincoln, who hoped to gain by them public recognition, and accepted by Douglas, who viewed the encounters as a way of putting an end to Lincoln's practice of speaking in each Illinois town as soon as Douglas had left. The Lincoln-Douglas debates mixed political drama with the atmosphere of a festival. For the debate at Galesburg, for example, dozens of horse-drawn floats descended on the town from nearby farming communities. One bore thirty-two girls dressed in white, one for each state, and a thirty-third, who dressed in black with the label "Kansas" and carried a banner proclaiming "THEY WON'T LET ME IN."

Douglas used the debates to portray Lincoln as a virtual abolitionist and advocate of racial equality. Both charges were calculated to doom Lincoln in the eyes of the intensely racist Illinois voters. In response, Lincoln affirmed that Congress had no constitutional authority to abolish slavery in the South, and in one debate he asserted bluntly that "I am not, nor ever have been in favor of bringing about the social and political equality of the white, and black man." However, fending off charges of extremism was getting Lincoln nowhere; so in order to seize the initiative, he tried to maneuver Douglas into a corner.

In view of the *Dred Scott* decision, Lincoln asked in the debate at Freeport, could the people of a territory lawfully exclude slavery? In essence, Lincoln was asking Douglas to reconcile popular sovereignty with the *Dred Scott* decision. Lincoln had long contended that the Court's decision rendered popular sovereignty as thin as soup boiled from the shadow of a pigeon that had starved to death. If, as the Supreme Court's ruling affirmed, Congress had no authority to exclude slavery from a territory, then it seemingly followed that a territorial legislature created by Congress also lacked power to do so. To no one's surprise, Douglas replied that notwithstanding the *Dred Scott* decision, the voters of a territory *could* effectively exclude slavery simply by refusing to enact laws that gave legal protection to slave property.

Douglas's "Freeport doctrine" salvaged popular sovereignty but did nothing for his reputation among southerners, who preferred the guarantees of the *Dred*

Stephen A. Douglas
Douglas's politics were founded on his unflinching conviction that most Americans favored national expansion and would support popular sovereignty as the fastest and least controversial way to achieve it. Douglas's self-assurance blinded him to rising northern sentiment for free soil.

Abraham Lincoln
Clean-shaven at the time of his famous debates with Douglas, Lincoln would soon grow a beard to give himelf a more distinguished appearance.

Scott decision to the uncertainties of popular sovereignty. Whereas Douglas's stand against the Lecompton constitution had already tattered his reputation in the South ("he is already dead there," Lincoln affirmed), his Freeport doctrine stiffened southern opposition to his presidential ambitions.

Lincoln faced the problem throughout the debates that free soil and popular sovereignty, although distinguishable in theory, had much the same practical impact. Neither Lincoln nor Douglas doubted that popular sovereignty, if fairly applied, would keep slavery out of the territories. In order to keep the initiative and sharpen their differences, Lincoln shifted in the closing debates toward attacks on slavery as "a moral, social, and political evil." He argued that Douglas's view of slavery as merely an eccentric and rather unsavory southern custom would dull the nation's conscience and facilitate the legalization of slavery everywhere. But Lincoln compromised his own position by rejecting both abolition and equality for blacks.

Neither man scored a clear victory in argument, and the senatorial election itself settled no major issues. Douglas's supporters captured a majority of the seats in the state legislature, which at the time was responsible for electing U.S. senators. But despite the racist leanings of most Illinois voters, Republican candidates for the state legislature won a slightly larger share of the popular vote than did their Democratic rivals. Moreover, in its larger significance, the contest solidified the sectional split in the national Democratic party and made Lincoln famous in the North and infamous in the South.

John Brown's Raid

Although Lincoln explicitly rejected abolitionism, he often spoke of free soil as a step toward the "ultimate extinction" of slavery in the South. Predictably, many southerners ignored the distinction between free soil and abolition and concluded that Republicans and abolitionists were inseparable components of an unholy alliance against slavery. Indeed, to many southerners, the entire North seemed locked in the grip of demented leaders bent on civil war. One of the South's more articulate defenders of slavery, for example, equated the doctrine of the abolitionists with those of "Socialists, of Free Love and Free Lands, Free Churches, Free Women and Free Negroes—of No-Marriage, No-Religion, No-Private Property, No-Law and No-Government."

No single event did more to rivet this image of the North in southerners' minds than the raid in 1859 on the federal arsenal at Harpers Ferry, Virginia, by John Brown, the brooding religious zealot responsible for the Pottawatomie massacre in Kansas three years earlier. At the head of twenty-one men, Brown seized the arsenal on October 16, 1859, in the hope of igniting a massive slave uprising, first in Virginia and then throughout the South. But Brown neglected to inform the slaves of his plans and even failed to provision his men with enough food to last a day. A detachment of federal troops, commanded by Lieutenant Colonel Robert E. Lee, quickly overpowered the raiders. Convicted of treason, Brown was hanged on December 2, 1859.

If this had been the whole story, southerners might have dismissed the raid as the act of an isolated lunatic. Captured correspondence, however, revealed that Brown, far from acting alone, had extensive ties to prominent northern abolitionists. These northerners had provided both moral and financial support for Brown's plan to invade Virginia, free the slaves, and "purge this land with blood." Any lingering southern doubts about the scope of the conspiracy vanished when parts of the North responded to Brown's execution with memorial services and tolling bells. Ralph Waldo Emerson exulted that Brown would "make the gallows as glorious as the cross," and William Lloyd Garrison proclaimed his support for "every slave insurrection at the South and in any slave country." Republicans, including Lincoln and Senator William Seward of New York, denounced Brown's raid, but southerners suspected that Brown's failure, rather than the deed itself, provoked the repudiation.

Although Brown had failed to start a slave insurrection, his abortive raid rekindled southern fears of slave uprisings. In the wake of Brown's raid and throughout 1860, rumors flew around the South of assorted slave plots to devastate the region. Vigilantes turned out to battle conspiracies that existed only in their own minds. For example, a horde of southern defenders mobilized to rout the thousands of abolitionists who were rumored to be conspiring to pillage northeastern Texas. In various other incidents, vigilantes rounded up thousands of slaves, whipped some into confessing to nonexistent plots, and then lynched them. The hysteria played into the hands of the southern-rights extremists known as the fire-eaters. Indeed, this faction actively encouraged the witch hunt by spreading tales of slave conspiracies in the press so that southern voters would turn to them as alone able to "stem the current of Abolition."

Although southern fears of slave insurrections proved unfounded, nothing calmed those apprehensions. Nor did it make any difference to southerners that Seward and Lincoln denounced Brown's raid. Most southerners interpreted the evidence linking Brown to abolitionists as just the tip of an iceberg and concluded that the abolitionists themselves were mere agents of the Republican party. Had not the Republicans repeatedly assailed slavery and sought unconstitutionally to bar its expansion? Had not Seward spoken of an "irrepressible conflict" between freedom and slavery? The incident at Harpers Ferry, declared resolutions passed by the Tennessee legislature, was "the natural fruit of this treasonable 'irrepressible conflict' doctrine put forth by the great head of the Black Republican party and echoed by his subordinates." In the

John Brown, *c. 1850*
*Brown ran to extremes of
kindness and brutality, sympathy and egotistic self-righteousness, all threaded together by his
Calvinist religious beliefs. Convinced
of humans' utter dependency on God,
he was sure that God had destined him
to start a slave insurrection. Brown contracted for the production of one thousand
pikes like the one shown here, with which he
planned to arm the slaves.*

final analysis, southerners contended, John Brown, abolitionists, and Republicans all rested their case on the same premise: that slaves were somehow an illegitimate form of property and that the South deserved only scorn for its "peculiar institution."

The South Contemplates Secession

Convinced that they were menaced not only by the eccentric William Lloyd Garrisons of the North but also by the Republican party that had swept two-thirds of the northern states in the election of 1856, southerners increasingly spoke of secession from the United States as their only recourse. "The South must dissever itself," a South Carolinian insisted, "from the rotten Northern element."

Southerners reached this conclusion gradually, and often reluctantly. In 1850 few southerners could have conceived of transferring their political and emotional allegiances from the United States to some new nation. Relatively insulated from the main tide of immigration, southerners thought of themselves as the most American of Americans. The fire-eaters, many of whom ardently desired secession, by no means represented southern thought. But the events of the 1850s

brought a growing number of southerners to the conclusion that the North had deserted the true principles of the Union. Southerners interpreted northern resistance to the Fugitive Slave Act and to slavery in Kansas as either illegal or unconstitutional, and they viewed headline-grabbing phrases like "irrepressible conflict" and "a higher law" as virtual declarations of war on the South. In southerners' eyes, it was the North, not the South, that had grown peculiar.

This sense of the North's deviance tinged reports sent home by southern visitors to the North during the 1850s. A Mississippi planter could scarcely believe his eyes, for example, when he witnessed a group of northern free blacks refusing to surrender their seats to a party of white women. Abolitionist hecklers rankled southern lecturers in the North. When assured by their northern friends that such hostility to the South's institutions did not reflect the whole of northern opinion, southerners could only wonder why northerners kept electing Republicans to office. Southern visitors increasingly described their northern trips as ventures into "enemy territory" and "a totally different country."

In this context of fraying sectional ties, John Brown's raid had an electrifying effect on southern opinion. Thousands of southerners, a Richmond newspaper editor observed after the raid, "who, a month ago, scoffed at the idea of a dissolution of the Union as a madman's dream . . . now hold the opinion that its days are numbered, its glory perished." A pamphlet published in 1860 embodied in its title the growing conviction of southerners that *The South Alone Should Govern the South*.

Viewed as a practical tactic to secure concrete goals, secession did not make a great deal of sense. Some southerners contended that secession would make it easier for the South to acquire more territory for slavery in the Caribbean; yet the South was scarcely united in desiring additional slave territory in Mexico, Cuba, or Central America. States like Alabama, Mississippi, and Texas contained vast tracts of unsettled land that could be converted to cotton cultivation far more easily than the Caribbean. Other southerners continued to complain that the North blocked the access of slaveholders to territories in the continental United States. But it is unclear how secession would solve this problem. If the South were to secede, the remaining continental territories would belong exclusively to the North, which could then legislate for them as it chose. Nor would secession stop future John Browns from infiltrating the South to provoke slave insurrections.

Yet to dwell on the impracticality of secession as a choice for the South is to miss the point. Talk of secession was less a tactic with clear goals than an expression of the South's outrage at the irresponsible and unconstitutional course that southerners viewed the Republicans as taking in the North. It was not merely that Republican attacks on slavery sowed the seeds of slave uprisings. More fundamentally, southerners believed that the North was treating the South as its inferior—indeed, as no more than a slave. "Talk of Negro slavery," exclaimed southern proslavery philosopher George Fitzhugh, "is not half so humiliating and disgraceful as the slavery of the South to the North." Having persuaded themselves that slavery made it possible for them to enjoy unprecedented freedom and equality, white southerners took great pride in their homeland. They bitterly dismissed Republican portrayals of the South as a region of arrogant planters and degraded white common folk. Submission to the Republicans, declared the Democratic senator Jefferson Davis of Mississippi, "would be intolerable to a proud people."

Nevertheless, as long as the pliant James Buchanan occupied the White House, southerners did no more than *talk* about secession. Once aware that Buchanan had declined to seek reelection, however, they anxiously awaited the election of 1860.

The Election of 1860

As a single-issue, free-soil party, the Republicans had done well in the election of 1856. To win in 1860, however, they would have to broaden their appeal in the North, particularly in states like Pennsylvania and Illinois, which they had lost in 1856. To do so, Republican leaders had concluded, they needed to forge an economic program to complement their advocacy of free soil.

A severe economic slump following the so-called Panic of 1857 furnished the Republicans a fitting opening. The depression shattered more than a decade of American prosperity and thrust economic concerns to the fore. In response, in the late 1850s, the Republicans developed an economic program based on support for a protective tariff (popular in Pennsylvania) and on two issues favored in the Midwest, federal aid for internal improvements and the granting of free 160-acre homesteads to settlers out of publicly owned land. By proposing to make these homesteads available to immigrants who were not yet citizens, the Republicans went far to shed their nativist image that lingered from their early association with the Know-Nothings. Carl Schurz, an 1848 German political refugee who had campaigned for Lincoln against Douglas in 1858, now labored mightily to bring his antislavery countrymen over to the Republican party.

The Republicans' desire to broaden their appeal also influenced their choice of a candidate. At their convention in Chicago, they nominated Abraham Lincoln over the early front-runner, William H. Seward of New York. Although better known than Lincoln, Seward failed to convince his party that he could carry the key states of Pennsylvania, Illinois, Indiana, and New Jersey. (Rueful Republicans remembered that their presidential candidate John C. Frémont would have won in 1856 if he had carried Pennsylvania and one of the remaining three states.) Lincoln held the advantage not only of hailing from Illinois but also of projecting a more moderate image than Seward on the slavery issue. Seward's penchant for controversial phrases like "irrepressible conflict" and "higher law" had given him a radical image. Lincoln, in contrast, had repeatedly affirmed that Congress had no constitutional right to interfere with slavery in the South and had explicitly rejected the "higher law" doctrine. The Republicans now needed only to widen their northern appeal.

The Democrats, however, who still claimed to be a national party, had to bridge their sectional divisions. The *Dred Scott* decision and the conflict over the Lecompton constitution had weakened the northern Democrats and emboldened the southern Democrats. Whereas Douglas desperately defended popular sovereignty against the free-soil doctrine, southern Democrats increasingly abandoned popular sovereignty for the crisp assurances of the *Dred Scott* decision. Heartened by Chief Justice Taney's ruling that Congress lacked the power to exclude slavery from the territories, many southerners now concluded that Congress had an obligation to safeguard slavery in any territory. In February 1860 Senator Jefferson Davis of Mississippi introduced a set of resolutions calling for the federal government to enforce the *Dred Scott* decision by actively protecting territorial slavery.

The Davis resolutions never stood a chance of adoption by Congress. Nevertheless, they embarrassed the Douglas Democrats. No northern Democrat could win an election on a platform calling for the congressional protection of slavery in the territories. As a Georgia Democrat opposed to the Davis resolutions commented, "Hostility to Douglas is the sole motive of the movers of this mischief. I wish Douglas defeated . . . , but I do not want him and his friends crippled or driven off. Where are we to get as many or as good men in the North to supply their places?"

The Democratic party's internal turmoil boiled over at its Charleston convention in the spring of 1860. Failing to force acceptance of a platform guaranteeing federal protection of slavery in the territories, the delegates from the Lower South stalked out. The convention adjourned to Baltimore, where a new fight broke out over the question of seating hastily elected, pro-Douglas slates of delegates from the Lower South states that had seceded from the Charleston convention. The decision to seat these pro-Douglas slates led to a walkout by delegates from Virginia and other states in the Upper South. The remaining delegates nominated Douglas; the seceders marched off to another hall in Baltimore and nominated Buchanan's vice president, John C. Breckinridge of Kentucky, on a platform calling for the congressional protection of slavery in the territories. Unable to rally behind a single nominee, the divided Democrats thus ran two candidates, Douglas and Breckinridge. The disruption of the Democratic party was now complete.

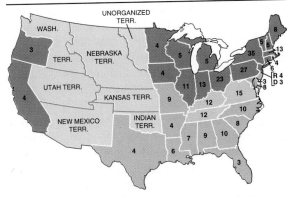

	Electoral Vote	Popular Vote	Percentage of Popular Vote
Republican Abraham Lincoln	180	1,865,593	39.8
Democratic, Southern John C. Breckinridge	72	848,356	18.1
Democratic, Northern Stephen A. Douglas	12	1,382,713	29.5
Constitutional Union John Bell	39	592,906	12.6
Divided	3 4		

The Election of 1860

The South still contained an appreciable number of moderates, often former Whigs who had joined with the Know-Nothings behind Fillmore in 1856. In 1860 these moderates, aided by former northern Whigs who opposed both Lincoln and Douglas, forged the new Constitutional Union party and nominated John Bell, a Tennessee slaveholder who had opposed both the Kansas-Nebraska Act and the Lecompton constitution. Calling for the preservation of the Union, the new party took no stand on the divisive issue of slavery extension.

With four candidates in the field, voters faced a relatively clear choice. Lincoln conceded that the South had a constitutional right to preserve slavery but demanded that Congress prohibit its extension. At the other extreme, Breckinridge insisted that Congress had to protect slavery in any territory that contained slaves. This left the middle ground to Bell and Douglas, the latter still committed to popular sovereignty but in search of a verbal formula that might reconcile it with the *Dred Scott* decision. Despite this four-way race, Lincoln won a clear majority of the electoral vote, 180 to 123 for his three opponents combined. Although Lincoln gained only 39 percent of the popular vote, his popular votes were concentrated in the North, the majority section, and were sufficient to carry every free state. Douglas ran a respectable second to Lincoln in the popular vote but a dismal last in the electoral vote. As the only candidate to campaign in both sections, Douglas suffered from the scattered quality of his votes and carried only Missouri. Bell won Virginia, Kentucky, and Tennessee, and Breckinridge captured Maryland and the Lower South.

The Movement for Secession

As the dust from the election settled, southerners faced a disconcerting fact: a man so unpopular among southerners that his name had not even appeared on the ballot in much of their section was now president. Lincoln's election struck most of the white South as a calculated northern insult. The North, a South Carolina planter told a visitor from England, "has got so far toward being abolitionized as to elect a man avowedly hostile to our institutions." Few southerners believed that Lincoln would fulfill his promise to protect slavery in the South, and most feared that he would act as a mere front man for more John Browns. "Now that the black radical Republicans have the power I suppose they will Brown us all," a South Carolinian lamented. An uneducated Mississippian residing in Illinois expressed his reaction to the election more bluntly:

> It seems the north wants the south to raise cotton and sugar rice tobacco for the northern states, also to pay taxes and fight her battles and get territory for the purpose of the north to send her greasy Dutch and free niggers into the territory to get rid of them. At any rate that was what elected old Abe President. Some professed conservative Republicans Think and say that Lincoln will be conservative also but sir my opinion is that Lincoln will deceive them. [He] will undoubtedly please the abolitionists for at his election they nearly all went into fits with Joy.

Some southerners had threatened secession at the prospect of Lincoln's election; now the moment of choice had arrived. On December 20, 1860, a South Carolina convention voted unanimously for secession; and by February 1, 1861, Alabama, Mississippi, Florida, Georgia, Louisiana, and Texas had followed South Carolina's lead (see "A Place in Time"). On February 4 delegates from these seven states met in Montgomery, Al-

Jefferson Davis
Davis brought an abundance of public experience to the Confederate presidency. Wounded in the Mexican War, he had served in the U.S. Senate, become secretary of war under President Franklin Pierce, and negotiated the Gadsden Purchase.

abama, and established the Confederate States of America.

Despite the abruptness of southern withdrawal from the Union, the movement for secession had been, and continued to be, laced with uncertainty. Many southerners had resisted calls for immediate secession. Even after Lincoln's election, fire-eating secessionists had met fierce opposition in the Lower South from so-called cooperationists, who called upon the South to act in unison or not at all. Many cooperationists had hoped to delay secession in order to wring concessions from the North that might remove the need for secession. Jefferson Davis, who was inaugurated in February 1861 as the first president of the Confederacy, was a most reluctant secessionist, and he remained in the United States Senate for two weeks after his own state of Mississippi had seceded. Even zealous advocates of secession had a hard time reconciling themselves to secession and believing that they were

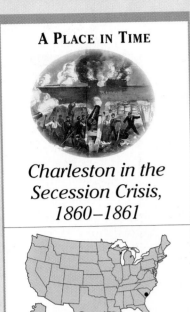

Charleston in the Secession Crisis, 1860–1861

After securing the nomination of Pennsylvania's James Buchanan for the presidency in 1856, northern Democrats made a conciliatory gesture to the South. They agreed to hold their party's 1860 convention in Charleston, South Carolina. Time would give northerners many opportunities to regret that gesture. Long in decline, with only a few overpriced hotels, Charleston offered little as a convention city. The supporters of Stephen A. Douglas had to convert the second floor of a meeting hall into a giant dormitory, where they slept in rows of beds and baked in one-hundred-degree heat. Far more troubling to the delegates who descended on the city in April 1860 was the hysteria that consumed Charleston in reaction to John Brown's raid on Harpers Ferry in Virginia six months earlier. Mounted police, armed with swords and muskets, patrolled the streets, and vigilantes combed the byways in search of abolitionists. Panicked Charlestonians viewed every northerner in the city—whether a politician, a traveling salesman, or a schoolteacher—as "necessarily imbued with doctrines hostile to our institutions."

Suspicion and harassment greeted northern sojourners, but Charleston's blacks endured a virtual reign of terror after "the late outrage at Harpers Ferry." A little under half the city's population in 1860 was black, and 81 percent of the blacks were slaves. White southerners distrusted urban slaves, most of whom lived apart from their rural masters and were hired out to city employers. Indeed, some slaves took advantage of their distance from their masters to hire themselves out for wages, a practice that whites feared would infect slaves with the notion that they were free. In addition, white workingmen resented competition from urban slaves in the skilled trades, and they used the furor over John Brown's raid to pressure the city's mayor into enforcing an old and long-neglected ordinance that slaves working away from their masters wear badges. Those without badges were rounded up and jailed, and their masters fined.

Charleston's enslaved blacks were not the sole targets of the city's increasingly repressive mood. Few southern cities had more visible or well-organized communities of free blacks than Charleston. Composed mainly of mulattos who took pride in their light skin and assembled in the Brown Fellowship Society, Charleston's free people of color formed a brown aristocracy of skilled tailors, carpenters, and small tradesmen. Free blacks like John Marsh Johnson worshiped in the same Episcopal church as such elite whites as Christopher G. Memminger, a prominent lawyer and politician who would soon become the Confederacy's secretary of the treasury. The financial prosperity of these free blacks depended on the white aristocrats who frequented their stores, admired their thrift and sobriety, and took comfort in their apparent loyalty. When a bill calling for the enslavement or expulsion of South Carolina's free blacks came before the state legislature in 1859, Memminger reminded the legislators that a free black had helped to expose Denmark Vesey's planned uprising of slaves back in 1822. Heartened by the support of Memminger and others, John Marsh Johnson congratu-

Slave Badges
The badges that they were forced to wear constantly reminded Charleston's slaves of their bondage.

Saluda Sentinels, Always Ready
Secessionist sentiment also flared in interior areas of South Carolina such as Saluda. This militia flag of the Saluda Sentinels, featuring an officer in Revolutionary War garb, shows how secessionists invoked memories of the American struggle for independence.

First Shots of the Civil War
Stunned Charleston residents crowded the city's rooftops to view the firing on Fort Sumter—a siege that lasted thirty-four hours.

lated himself for predicting "from the onset that nothing would be done affecting our position."

Johnson little realized the extent to which the world of Charleston's free blacks was in danger of falling apart. The city had been a center of southern-rights radicalism since the days of the nullification crisis. Charleston was the home of the fire-eater, Robert Barnwell Rhett; and it always rolled out the welcome carpet for Edmund Ruffin, a Virginia drumbeater for slavery. Furthermore, after John Brown's raid, even moderate citizens, including former Unionists, were embracing secession. The cause of secession demanded, in turn, that elite whites unite with working-class whites in a common front against the North. During the 1850s Charleston's working-class whites had grown increasingly powerful and aggressive; the increase in their numbers gave the city a white majority in 1860, for the first time in its history. Working-class whites feared competition from any blacks but had a special loathing for free blacks, who on Sundays dared "to draw up in fine clothes" and "wear a silk hat and gloves" and who celebrated weddings by drinking champagne and riding to the church in elegant carriages.

Soon free blacks became the victims of the growing cooperation between elite and working-class whites. Indeed, by August 1860 Charleston was in the grip of an "enslavement crisis." The same police dragnets that had snared urban slaves without badges now trapped innumerable free blacks as well. Unenslaved blacks suddenly had to prove that they were free, a tall order inasmuch as South Carolina had long prohibited the freeing of slaves. For decades white masters who wanted to free favored slaves had resorted to complicated legal ruses, with the result that many blacks who had lived for years as free people could not prove that they were free and were forced back into slavery. Abandoning his initial optimism, John Marsh Johnson wrote nervously to his brother-in-law to report "cases of persons who for 30 yrs. have been paying capitation Tax [as free persons of color] & one of 35 yrs. that have to go back to bondage & take out their Badges." Many other free African-Americans fled to the North.

A religious man, Johnson believed that God helped those who helped themselves. Rather than "supinely wait for the working of a miracle by having a Chariot let down to convey us away," he resolved in late August 1860 to stay and endure the "present calamity." By then, however, the Democratic party had snapped apart under the pressure of southern demands for the congressional recognition of slavery in all the territories. "The last party pretending to be a national party, is broken up," the secessionist Charleston *Mercury* exulted, "and the antagonism of the sections of the Union has nothing to arrest its fierce collision." In December 1860 another convention meeting in Charleston would proclaim South Carolina's secession from the United States. In April 1861, only a year after the Democratic delegates had assembled in Charleston for their party's convention, shore batteries along Charleston's harbor would open fire on Fort Sumter. This action set in motion a train of events leading to the extinction of slavery itself. Ironically, after the Civil War, the free blacks who had weathered the enslavement crisis of 1860 would emerge as the leaders of the city's black people, all of them now free.

no longer citizens of the United States. "How do you feel now, dear Mother," a Georgian wrote, "that *we* are in a foreign land?"

In the month after the establishment of the Confederate States of America, moreover, secessionists suffered stinging disappointments in the Upper South. Virginia, North Carolina, Tennessee, Arkansas, and the border slave states of Maryland, Kentucky, Delaware, and Missouri all rejected calls for secession. Various factors account for the Upper South's reluctance to embrace the movement. In contrast to the Lower South, which had a guaranteed export market for its cotton, the Upper South depended heavily on economic ties to the North, bonds that would be severed by secession. Furthermore, with proportionately far fewer slaves than the Lower South, the states of the Upper South and the border states doubted the loyalty of their sizable nonslaveholding populations to the idea of secession. Virginia, for example, had every reason to question the allegiance to secession of its nonslaveholding western counties, which would soon break away to form Unionist West Virginia. Few in the Upper South could forget the raw nerve touched by the publication in 1857 of Hinton R. Helper's *The Impending Crisis of the South*. A nonslaveholding North Carolinian, Helper had described slavery as a curse upon poor white southerners and thereby questioned one of the most sacred southern doctrines, the idea that slavery rendered all whites equal. If secession were to spark a war between the states, moreover, the Upper South appeared to be the likeliest battleground. Whatever the exact weight assignable to each of these factors, one point is clear: the secession movement that South Carolina so boldly started in December 1860 seemed to be falling apart by March 1861.

The Search for Compromise

The lack of southern unity confirmed the long-standing belief of Lincoln and most Republicans that the secessionists' talk, and even their actions, contained more bluster than substance. Seward described secession as the work of "a relatively few hotheads," and Lincoln expected that the loyal majority of southerners would soon wrest the initiative from the fire-eating minority.

This perception among the Republicans stiffened their resolve to resist the compromises that some moderates were trying to forge. In the immediate

wake of South Carolina's secession, Senator John J. Crittenden of Kentucky brought forth the most important of the compromises. Crittenden's plan included calls for the compensation of owners of runaway slaves, the repeal of the North's personal-liberty laws, a constitutional amendment to prohibit the federal government from ever interfering with slavery in the southern states, and another constitutional amendment that would restore the Missouri Compromise line for the remaining territories and guarantee federal protection of slavery below the line. This last amendment proved to be the sticking point. Lincoln stood firm against any abandonment of free soil. "On the territorial issue," he wrote to a southerner, "I am inflexible." In the face of steadfast Republican opposition, the Crittenden plan collapsed.

Lincoln's opposition to compromise rested partly on his belief that a loyal majority of southerners would soon overturn secession. The president-elect, however, almost certainly exaggerated the strength and dedication of southern Unionists. In reality, many of the southern opponents of the fire-eating secessionists were sitting on the fence and hoping for major concessions from the North; their allegiance to the Union was conditional, not unconditional. Lincoln can be faulted for his misreading of southern opinion. But even if his assessment had been accurate, it is unlikely that he would have accepted the Crittenden plan. Republicans viewed the plan as a surrender rather than a compromise, because it hinged on the abandonment of free soil, the principle on which the Republican party had been founded. In addition, as Lincoln well knew, some southerners still talked of seizing more territory for slavery in the Caribbean. In proposing to extend the 36°30′ line, the Crittenden plan specifically referred to territories "hereafter acquired," a veiled reference to future Caribbean expansion. If he were to accept the Crittenden compromise, Lincoln feared that it would be only a matter of time "till we shall have to take Cuba as a condition upon which they [the seceding states] will stay in the Union."

Beyond these considerations, the precipitous secession of the Lower South subtly changed the question that Lincoln faced. The issue was no longer slavery extension but secession. The Lower South had left the Union in the face of losing a fair election. For Lincoln to have caved in to such pressure would have violated majority rule, the principle upon which the nation, not just his party, had been founded.

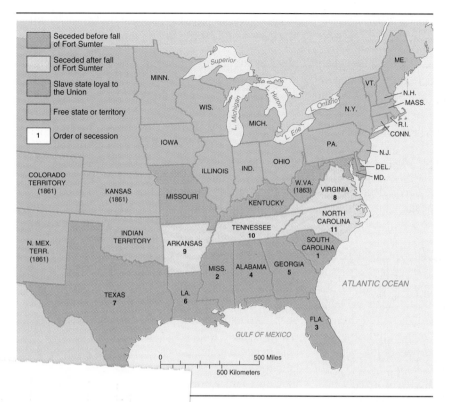

Secession

Four key states—Virginia, Arkansas, Tennessee, and North Carolina—did not secede until after the fall of Fort Sumter. The border slave states of Maryland, Delaware, Kentucky, and Missouri stayed in the Union.

in March 1861, little to ignite a war. Lin- ddress to "hold, oc- operty in the seven rtion that committed ns in Florida and Fort ston, South Carolina. had appointed secre- essed with the idea of order to hold the Up- dition to advising the m Fort Sumter, Seward the nation by provok- n. But Lincoln brushed ead, the president in- n Carolina of his inten- th much-needed provi- mmunition. To gain the dubious military advantage of attacking Fort Sumter before the arrival of relief ships, Confederate batteries began to bombard the fort shortly before dawn on April 12. The next day, the fort's garrison surrendered.

Proclaiming an insurrection in the Lower South, Lincoln now appealed for seventy-five thousand militiamen from the loyal states to suppress the rebellion. His proclamation pushed citizens of the Upper South off the fence upon which they had perched for three months. "I am a Union man," one southerner wrote, "but when they [the Lincoln administration] send men south it will change my notions. I can do nothing against my own people." In quick succession, Virginia, North Carolina, Arkansas, and Tennessee leagued with the Confederacy. After acknowledging that "I am one of those dull creatures that cannot see the good of secession," Robert E. Lee resigned from the United States Army rather than lead federal troops against his native Virginia.

The North, too, was ready for a fight, less to abolish slavery than to punish secession. Worn out from his efforts to find a peaceable solution to the issue of slavery extension, and with only a short time to live, Stephen Douglas assaulted "the new system of resistance by the sword and bayonet to the results of the ballot-box" and affirmed: "I deprecate war, but if it must come I am with my country, under all circumstances, and in every contingency."

CONCLUSION

During the 1850s the gap widened between northerners and southerners on the vexing issue of slavery extension. Popular sovereignty, which in 1850 struck many Americans as a practical solution to slavery in the territories, foundered in Kansas amid civil strife and turmoil over the Lecompton constitution. As support for popular sovereignty withered, sentiment for free soil gained ground in the North. In the South the *Dred Scott* decision provided judicial support for the position that Congress had to protect slavery in whatever territories it appeared.

Although the differences between northern and southern opinion on the slavery-extension issue sharpened and widened during the tempestuous decade, the two sections stood far apart by 1850. The Compromise of 1850 merely papered over an already considerable gulf. Decades of industrial expansion had convinced northerners of the value of free labor, a view that excluded competition with slaves. Yet decades of agricultural prosperity had persuaded southerners of the economic and moral value of slavery. The success of their system made southerners antagonistic to any suggestion that slave property was inferior to other property.

Despite this clear division by 1850, secession festered for ten years before erupting. More than a broad disagreement over slavery in the territories was needed to push the South into secession. Before the South took that drastic step, it had to convince itself that the North aimed not merely to bar the spread of slavery but also to corrode the moral and political foundations of southern society. Several events persuaded the South that such was indeed the North's intention: northern fury over the Kansas-Nebraska bill, the emergence of the purely sectional Republican party, northern opposition to the *Dred Scott* decision, and John Brown's raid on Harpers Ferry. Once southerners came to believe that northern attacks on slavery's expansion were tactics in a wider campaign to reduce the South to subjection and "slavery," secession became a natural recourse.

As an expression of principled outrage, secession fittingly capped a decade in which each side had clothed itself in principles. The conflicts over principle that marked the 1850s were deeply embedded in the nation's political heritage. Both sides, North and South, laid claim to the ideals of the Constitution, but each understood those ideals differently. For northerners wedded to free soil, liberty meant an individual's freedom to pursue self-interest without competition from slaves. For white southerners, liberty meant their freedom to dispose of their legally acquired property as they saw fit. Similarly, both sides subscribed to the rule of law, which each accused the other of deserting. Northerners found evidence of southern treachery in the voting fraud that culminated in the Lecompton constitution. Southerners pointed to northern defiance of the Fugitive Slave Act and, later, of the *Dred Scott* decision, and to northern complicity in John Brown's raid. In the end, war broke out between siblings who, although they claimed the same inheritance, had become virtual strangers to each other.

CHRONOLOGY

1846　Wilmot Proviso.

1848　Treaty of Guadalupe Hidalgo ends MexicanWar.
　　　　Free-Soil party formed.
　　　　Zachary Taylor elected president.

1849　California seeks admission to the Union as a free state.

1850　Nashville convention assembles to discuss the South's grievances.
　　　　Compromise of 1850.

1852　Harriet Beecher Stowe, *Uncle Tom's Cabin*.
　　　　Franklin Pierce elected president.

1853　Gadsden Purchase.

1854　Ostend Manifesto.
　　　　Kansas-Nebraska Act.
　　　　William Walker leads a filibustering expedition into Nicaragua.

1854–1855　Know-Nothing and Republican parties emerge.

1855　Proslavery forces steal the election for a territorial legislature in Kansas.
　　　　Proslavery Kansans establish a government in Lecompton.
　　　　Free-soil government established in Topeka, Kansas.

1856　The "Sack of Lawrence."

1856   John Brown's Pottawatomie massacre.
James Buchanan elected president.

1857   *Dred Scott* decision.
President Buchanan endorses the Lecompton constitution in Kansas.
Panic of 1857.

Dred Scott

1858   Congress refuses to admit Kansas to the Union under the Lecompton constitution.
Lincoln-Douglas debates.

1859   John Brown's raid on Harpers Ferry.

1860   Abraham Lincoln elected president.
South Carolina secedes from the Union.

1861   The remaining Lower South states secede.
Confederate States of America established.
Crittenden compromise plan collapses.
Lincoln takes office.
Firing on Fort Sumter; Civil War begins.
Upper South secedes.

FOR FURTHER READING

William W. Freehling, *The Road to Disunion: Secessionists at Bay, 1776–1854* (1990). A major study that traces the roots of secession.

Eric Foner, *Free Soil, Free Labor, Free Men: The Ideology of the Republican Party Before the Civil War* (1970). An outstanding analysis of the thought, values, and components of the Republican party.

William E. Gienapp, *The Origins of the Republican Party, 1852–1856* (1987). A comprehensive account of the birth of a major party.

Michael F. Holt, *The Political Crisis of the 1850s* (1978). A lively reinterpretation of the politics of the 1850s.

Allan Nevins, *The Ordeal of the Union* (vols. 1–2, 1947). A detailed, highly regarded account of the coming of the Civil War.

David Potter, *The Impending Crisis, 1848–1861* (1976). The best one-volume overview of the events leading to the Civil War.

ADDITIONAL BIBLIOGRAPHY

The Compromise of 1850 and Its Aftermath

Stephen W. Campbell, *The Slave Catchers* (1968); Thomas F. Gossett, *Uncle Tom's Cabin and American Culture* (1985); Holman Hamilton, *Prologue to Conflict: The Crisis and Compromise of 1850* (1964); Thelma Jennings, *The Nashville Convention* (1980); Thomas D. Morris, *Free Men All: The Personal Liberty Laws of the North, 1780–1861* (1974); Chaplain W. Morrison, *Democratic Politics and Sectionalism: The Wilmot Proviso Controversy* (1967).

Political Realignment, 1852–1856

Tyler Anbinder, *Nativism and Slavery: The Northern Know Nothings and the Politics of the 1850s* (1992); Eugene Berwanger, *The Frontier Against Slavery: Western Anti-Negro Prejudice in the Slavery Extension Controversy* (1967); Michael F. Holt, *Political Parties and American Political Development from the Age of Jackson to the Age of Lincoln* (1992); James A. Rawley, *Race and Politics: "Bleeding Kansas" and the Coming of the Civil War* (1969); Geoffrey W. Wolff, *The Kansas-Nebraska Bill* (1977).

The South and the Sectional Crisis

Charles H. Brown, *Agents of Manifest Destiny: The Lives and Times of the Filibusters* (1978); John Hope Franklin, *The Militant South, 1800–1861* (1970) and *A Southern Odyssey: Travelers in the Antebellum North* (1976); Michael P. Johnson and James L. Roark, eds., *No Chariot Let Down: Charleston's Free People of Color on the Eve of the Civil War* (1984); John McCardell, *The Idea of a Southern Nation: Southern Nationalists and Southern Nationalism, 1830–1861* (1979); Robert E. May, *The Southern Dream of a Caribbean Empire, 1854–1861* (1973); Rollin G. Os-

terweiss, *Romanticism and Nationalism in the Old South* (1949); Ronald L. Takaki, *A Proslavery Crusade: The Agitation to Reopen the African Slave Trade* (1971); J. Mills Thornton, *Politics and Power in a Slave Society* (1978).

The Disruption of the Union

William L. Barney, *The Road to Secession* (1972); Steven A. Channing, *Crisis of Fear: Secession in South Carolina* (1970); David Donald, *Charles Sumner and the Coming of the Civil War* (1960); Don E. Fehrenbacher, *The Dred Scott Case* (1978) and *Prelude to Greatness: Lincoln in the 1850s* (1962); George B. Forgie, *Patricide in the House Divided: A Psychological Interpretation of Lincoln and His Age* (1979); Henry V. Jaffa, *Crisis of the House Divided: An Interpretation of the Lincoln-Douglas Debates* (1959); Robert W. Johannsen, *Stephen A. Douglas* (1973); Michael Johnson, *Secession and Conservatism in the Lower South: The Social and Ideological Bases of Secession in Georgia, 1860–1861* (1983); Albert J. Kirwan, *John J. Crittenden: The Struggle for the Union* (1962); Milton Klein, *President James Buchanan: A Biography* (1962); Paul C. Nagel, *One Nation Indivisible: The Union in American Thought* (1964); Allan Nevins, *The Emergence of Lincoln* (2 vols., 1950); Roy F. Nichols, *The Disruption of American Democracy* (1948); Stephen B. Oates, *To Purge This Land with Blood: A Biography of John Brown* (1970); David Potter, *Lincoln and His Party in the Secession Crisis* (1942); Elbert B. Smith, *The Presidency of James Buchanan* (1975); Kenneth Stampp, *And the War Came: The North and the Secession Crisis, 1860–1861* (1970); R. A. Wooster, *The Secession Conventions of the South* (1962).

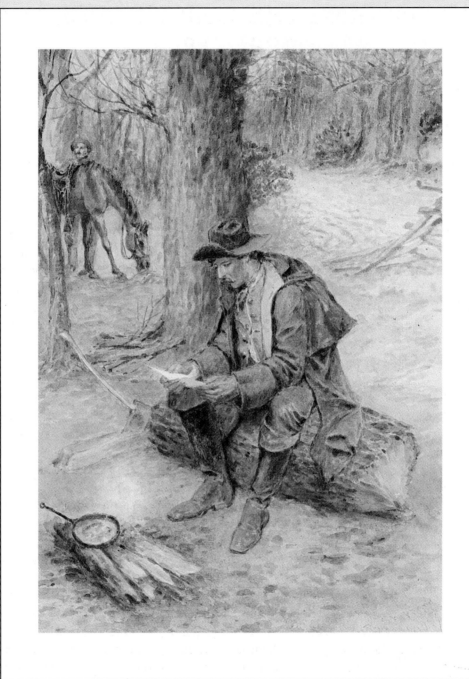

News from Home
by William Ludwell Sheppard

15

REFORGING THE UNION: CIVIL WAR 1861–1865

With the fall of Fort Sumter in April 1861, northerners and southerners rushed to arms. "They sing and whoop, they laugh: they holler to de people on de ground and sing out 'Good-bye,'" remarked a slave watching rebel troops depart. "All going down to die." Longing for the excitement of battle, the first volunteers enlisted with hopes of adventure and glory. Garish uniforms reflected their expectation of martial romance. Gaudiest of all were the northern Zouave regiments, whose members patterned their dress on that of French troops in North Africa, who, in turn, modeled their uniforms on a notion of what the Turks wore into battle: baggy red pantaloons, spotless white gaiters, and fezzes. Marching to war in dashing attire provided more than an outlet for romantic yearnings: it also gave boys a chance to act like men. A contemplative New Yorker, who sent two teenaged sons to enlist, marveled how the war provided "so much manhood suddenly achieved." In their early letters home, victorious soldiers exulted over their transformation in battle. "With your first shot you become a new man," an Alabama volunteer wrote to his father. Neither volunteers nor politicians expected a long or bloody war. Most northern estimates ranged from one month to a year. Southerners also looked forward to a speedy war. One rebel could lick ten Yankees, southerners liked to think, because "the Yankee army is filled with the scum of creation."

These expectations of military glory and quick fame proved the first of many miscalculations. Actual

battlefield experiences scarcely conformed to the early volunteers' rosy visions. For most soldiers, achieving manhood meant surviving in fetid army camps and inuring themselves to the stench of death. "We don't mind the sight of dead men no more than if they were dead hogs," a Union soldier claimed after one engagement. Soldiers rapidly learned the value of caution in battle. When "solid shot is cracking skulls like eggshells," a northern volunteer wrote, "the consuming passion is to get out of the way." You learn, a southerner wrote, to become "cool and deliberate."

These were the reactions of the lucky ones. One out of every five soldiers who fought in the Civil War died in it. The 620,000 American soldiers who lost their lives between 1861 and 1865 nearly equaled the number of American soldiers killed in all the nation's earlier and later wars combined. The war's gruesome destructiveness shattered politicians' expectations as well as soldiers' romantic visions. Once it became clear that the war could not be ended by a few battles, leaders on both sides contemplated strategies once unpalatable and even unthinkable. The South, where the hand of government had always fallen lightly on the citizenry, found that it had to draft men into its army and virtually extort supplies from its civilian population. By the end of the war, the Confederacy was even prepared to arm its slaves in an ironically desperate effort to save a society founded on slavery. The North, which began the war with the restricted objective of overcoming secession, and which explicitly disclaimed any intention of interfering with slavery, found that in order to win, it had to shred the fabric of southern society by destroying slavery. For politicians as well as soldiers, the war turned into a series of surprises.

MOBILIZING FOR WAR

North and South alike were unprepared for war. In April 1861 the Union had only a small army of sixteen thousand men, scattered all over the country, mostly in the West. One-third of the officers of the Union army had resigned to join the Confederacy. The Union seemed to hang by a thread politically. The nation had not had a strong president since James K. Polk in the 1840s. Its new president, Abraham Lincoln, struck many observers as a yokel. That such a government could marshal its people for war seemed a doubtful proposition. The federal government had levied no direct taxes on its citizens for decades, and it had never drafted anyone into its army. The Confederacy was even less prepared, for it had no tax structure, no navy, only two tiny gunpowder factories, and poorly equipped, unconnected railroad lines.

During the first two years of the war, both sides would have to overcome these deficiencies, raise and supply large armies, and finance the heavy costs of war. In each region mobilization for war expanded the powers of the central government to an extent that few had anticipated.

Recruitment and Conscription

The Civil War armies were the largest organizations ever created in America; by the end of the war, over 2 million men would have served in the Union army and 800,000 in the Confederate army. In the first flush of enthusiasm for war, volunteers rushed to the colors. "I go for wiping them out," a Virginian wrote to his governor. A similar zest for enlistment engulfed the North. "War! and volunteers are the only topics of conversation or thought," an Oberlin College student wrote to his brother in April 1861. "I cannot study. I cannot sleep. I cannot work, and I don't know as I can write."

At first, the raising of armies depended on local efforts rather than on national or even state direction. Cit-

izens opened recruiting offices in their hometowns, held rallies, and signed up volunteers. As a consequence, regiments were usually composed of soldiers from the same locale. Localism and voluntarism did not stop with the recruitment of troops. In the South cavalrymen were expected to provide their own horses, and uniforms everywhere were left mainly to local option. In both armies officers up to the rank of colonel were elected by other officers and enlisted men.

This informal and democratic way of raising and organizing soldiers conformed to the nation's political traditions. Americans had argued for generations that the freely given consent of the people, not the dictates of the government, could alone create an army in a republic. Because of its length and gruesome destructiveness, the Civil War would place insupportable stress on this tradition, however. As early as July 1861, the Union instituted examinations for officers, and its practice of electing officers gradually died out. In addition, as casualties mounted, military demand soon exceeded the supply of volunteers. Because nearly half of its 1861 volunteers had enlisted for only a year, the Confederacy felt the pinch first and in April 1862 enacted the first conscription law in American history. All able-bodied white males aged eighteen to thirty-five would be required to serve in the military for three years. Subsequent amendments raised the age limit to forty-five and then to fifty, and lowered it to seventeen.

The Confederacy's Conscription Act aroused little enthusiasm among southerners. Opponents charged that the draft was an assault on state sovereignty by a despotic regime and that the law would "do away with all the patriotism we have." Exemptions applied to many occupations, from religious ministry to shoe-making, and these angered the nonexempt. So did a loophole, closed in 1863, that allowed the well-off to purchase substitutes. Hostility also mounted over an amendment, the so-called 20-Negro law, that exempted an owner or overseer of twenty or more slaves from service. Although southerners widely feared that the slave population could not be controlled if all able-bodied white males were away in the army, the 20-Negro law evoked complaints about "a rich man's war but a poor man's fight."

Despite opposition, the Confederate draft became increasingly hard to evade, and this fact stimulated volunteering. Only one soldier in five was a draftee, but four out of every five eligible white southerners served in the Confederate army. In addition, a new conscription law, passed in 1864, required all soldiers then in the army to stay in for the duration of the war. This requirement ensured that a high proportion of Confederate soldiers would be battle-hardened veterans.

Once the army was raised, the Confederacy faced the challenge of supplying it. At first, the South lacked facilities to produce arms and ammunition and relied on imports from Europe, weapons confiscated from federal arsenals situated in the South, and guns captured on the battlefield. These stopgap measures bought time until an industrial base was established. By 1862 the Confederacy had a competent head of ordnance (weaponry), Josiah Gorgas. Working through Gorgas and other officials, the Confederacy assigned ordnance contracts to privately owned factories like the Tredegar Iron Works in Richmond, provided loans to establish new factories, and created government-owned industries like the giant Augusta Powder Works in Georgia. The South lost few, if any, battles for want of munitions.

The Confederacy was less successful in supplying its troops with clothing and food. Southern soldiers frequently went without shoes; during the South's invasion of Maryland in 1862, thousands of Confederate soldiers had to be left behind because they could not march barefoot on Maryland's gravel-surfaced roads. Late in the war, Robert E. Lee's Army of Northern Virginia ran out of food but never out of ammunition. The South's supply problems had several sources: railroads that fell into disrepair or were captured, an economy that relied more heavily on producing tobacco and cotton than growing food, and Union invasions early in the war that overran the livestock and grain-raising districts of central Tennessee and Virginia. Close to desperation, the Confederate Congress passed the Impressment Act in 1863, which authorized army officers to take food from reluctant farmers at prescribed rates. This law was even more unpopular than the Conscription Act. It also empowered agents to impress slaves into labor for the army, a provision that provoked yet more resentment. Slaveowners were willing to give up their relatives to military service, a Georgia congressman noted, "but let one of their negroes be taken and what a howl you will hear."

The industrial North could more easily supply its troops with arms, clothes, and food than could the South. However, keeping a full army was another matter. When the initial tide of enthusiasm for enlistment passed and the terms of the early recruits ended, Congress followed the Confederacy's example and turned to conscription. The Enrollment Act of March 1863 made every able-bodied white male citizen aged twenty to forty-five eligible for draft into the Union army.

Like the Confederate conscription law of 1862, the Enrollment Act granted exemptions, although only to high government officials, ministers, and men who were the sole support of widows, orphans, or indigent parents. It also offered two means of escaping the draft: substitution, or paying another man who would serve instead; and commutation, paying a $300 fee to the government. To provide draft machinery, the law divided each state into enrollment districts and gave them quotas to meet, first through volunteers and then through the draft. The new system was difficult to administer and chaotic in practice. Enrollment districts often competed for volunteers by offering cash payments (bounties); dishonest "bounty jumpers" repeatedly registered and deserted after collecting their payment. And as in the South, conscription aroused opposition. Democrats denounced it as a violation of individual liberties and states' rights. Ordinary citizens of little means resented the commutation and substitution provision and leveled their own "poor man's fight" charges. Still, as the Confederates had learned, the law stimulated volunteering. Only 8 percent of Union soldiers were draftees or substitutes.

Financing the War

The recruitment and supply of huge armies lay far beyond the capacity of American public finance at the start of the war. During the 1840s and 1850s, annual federal spending had averaged only 2 percent of the gross national product.* With such meager expenditures, the federal government could meet its revenue needs from tariff duties and from income brought in by the sale of public lands. In fact, the government had not imposed any direct taxes on its citizens for thirty years. During the war, however, annual federal expenditures gradually rose to 15 percent of the gross national product, and the need for new sources of revenue became urgent. Yet neither the Union nor the Confederacy initially showed much enthusiasm for imposing taxes. Americans were unaccustomed to paying taxes to their national government, both sides expected the war to be short, and neither wanted the

---

*Gross national product (GNP): the sum, measured in dollars, of all goods and services produced in a given year. By contrast, in the 1980s the federal budgets averaged about 25 percent of the GNP.

Union Forces

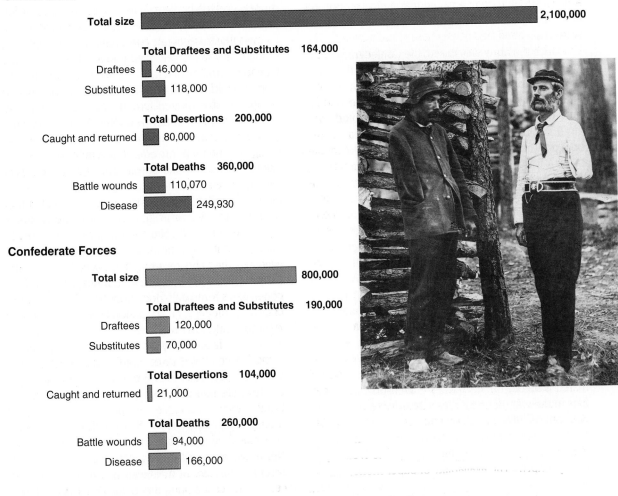

Total size — 2,100,000

Total Draftees and Substitutes   164,000
Draftees — 46,000
Substitutes — 118,000

Total Desertions   200,000
Caught and returned — 80,000

Total Deaths   360,000
Battle wounds — 110,070
Disease — 249,930

Confederate Forces

Total size — 800,000

Total Draftees and Substitutes   190,000
Draftees — 120,000
Substitutes — 70,000

Total Desertions   104,000
Caught and returned — 21,000

Total Deaths   260,000
Battle wounds — 94,000
Disease — 166,000

Total Civil War Deaths Compared to U.S. Deaths in Other Wars

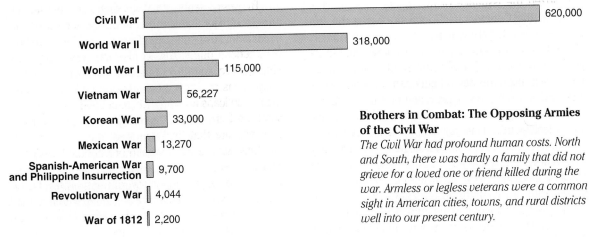

Civil War — 620,000
World War II — 318,000
World War I — 115,000
Vietnam War — 56,227
Korean War — 33,000
Mexican War — 13,270
Spanish-American War and Philippine Insurrection — 9,700
Revolutionary War — 4,044
War of 1812 — 2,200

Brothers in Combat: The Opposing Armies of the Civil War

The Civil War had profound human costs. North and South, there was hardly a family that did not grieve for a loved one or friend killed during the war. Armless or legless veterans were a common sight in American cities, towns, and rural districts well into our present century.

knock of the tax collector to dampen patriotic spirit. In August 1861 the Confederacy enacted a small property tax and the Union an income tax, but both measures were halfhearted, and neither raised much revenue. The Union's first income-tax law actually postponed collection until 1863.

Still needing revenue, both sides turned to war bonds; that is, to loans from citizens, to be repaid by future generations. The patriotic fervor of the early war years helped to sell these bonds. Southerners quickly bought up the Confederacy's first bond issue ($15 million) in 1861. That same year, a financial wizard, Philadelphia banker Jay Cooke, led a successful campaign to induce the northern public to subscribe to a much larger bond issue ($150 million). But in themselves bonds did not answer the requirements of wartime finance, because they had to be paid for in gold or silver coin (specie), which was in short supply. Soaking up most of its available specie, the South's first bond issue threatened to be its last. In the North many hoarded their gold rather than spend it on bonds.

Recognizing the limitations of taxation and of bond issues, the Union and the Confederacy began to print paper money. Early in 1862 Lincoln signed into law the Legal Tender Act, which authorized the issue of $150 million of the so-called greenbacks. Christopher Memminger, the Confederacy's treasury secretary, and Salmon P. Chase, his Union counterpart, shared a distrust of paper money, but each came around to the idea because, as Chase bluntly put it, *"The Treasury is nearly empty."* The availability of paper money would make it easier to pay soldiers, to levy and raise taxes, and to sell war bonds. The Legal Tender Act not only authorized the issuance of the greenbacks but also provided for the emission of $500 million of war bonds purchasable with greenbacks.

Yet doubts about paper money lingered. Unlike gold and silver, which had established market values, the value of paper money depended mainly on the public's confidence in the government that issued it. To bolster that confidence, Union officials made the greenbacks legal tender (that is, acceptable in payment of most public and private debts) and overcame their early reservations about taxes by imposing increasingly stiff taxes on everything from income to liquor and billiard tables. The steady flow of tax revenue into the federal treasury strengthened public confidence in the government's ability to meet its obligations and helped check the inflationary tendency inherent in paper money.

In contrast, the Confederacy never made its paper money legal tender. This omission raised the suspicion that the southern government had little confidence in its own paper issues. To compound the problem, the Confederacy raised less than 5 percent of its wartime revenue from taxes. (The comparable figure for the North was 21 percent.) The Confederacy did enact a comprehensive tax measure in 1863, but Union invasions disrupted its ability to collect taxes. In addition, the South's relatively undeveloped system of internal transportation made tax collection a hit-or-miss proposition. For example, the Confederacy's tax measures of 1863 included a tax-in-kind, a sort of tithe. After feeding their families, farmers had to pledge one-tenth of their crops to the government. Because thousands of agents were sent to collect it, the tax-in-kind brought results, but it fell disproportionately on farmers who lived near the railroads traveled by tax collectors. Some of the food collected, moreover, rotted in government warehouses for want of transportation. To many farmers, the Confederacy's tax policies seemed unfair and incompetently administered.

In the face of the Confederacy's sorry performance in collecting taxes, confidence in the South's paper money quickly evaporated, and the value of Confederate paper in relation to gold plunged. The Confederacy responded by printing more paper money, a billion dollars by 1865, but this action merely accelerated southern inflation. Whereas prices in the North rose about 80 percent during the war, the Confederacy suffered an inflation rate of over 9,000 percent. What cost a southerner one dollar in 1861 cost forty-six dollars by 1864.

By raising taxes, floating bonds, and printing paper money, both the Union and the Confederacy broke with the hard-money, minimal-government traditions of American public finance. For the most part, these changes occurred as unanticipated and often reluctant adaptations to wartime conditions. But in the North the Republicans took advantage of the departure of the southern Democrats from Congress to push through one measure that they and their Whig predecessors had long advocated, a system of national banking. In February 1863 Congress passed the National Bank Act over the concerted opposition of the northern Democrats. This law established criteria by which a bank could obtain a federal charter and issue national bank notes (notes backed by the federal government). It also gave private bankers an incentive to purchase war bonds, because once a private bank had obtained a federal charter, it could issue national bank notes up to 90 percent of the value of the war bonds that it held.

The North's ability to revolutionize its system of public finance reflected not only its longer experience with the complex financial transactions required by its industrial and commercial economy but its greater political cohesion during the war.

Political Leadership in Wartime

The Civil War pitted rival political systems as well as armies and economies against each other. The South entered the war with several apparent political advantages. Lincoln's call for militiamen to suppress the rebellion had transformed hesitators in the South into tenacious secessionists. "Never was a people more united or more determined," a New Orleans resident wrote in the spring of 1861. "There is but one mind, one heart, one action." Moreover, since the founding of the United States, the South had produced a disproportionate share of the nation's strong presidents: Washington, Jefferson, Madison, Monroe, Jackson, and Polk. Now President Jefferson Davis of the Confederacy, as a former war secretary and U.S. senator, possessed experience, honesty, courage, and what one officer described as "a jaw sawed in *steel*."

In contrast, the Union's list of political liabilities appeared lengthy. Loyal but contentious, northern Democrats wanted to prosecute the war without conscription, without the financial centralization represented by the National Bank Act, and without the abolition of slavery. Within the rival Republican party, Lincoln had trouble commanding respect. Unlike Davis, he had served in neither the cabinet nor the Senate, and his informal western manners inspired little confidence among eastern Republicans. Northern setbacks early in the war convinced most Republicans in Congress that Lincoln was an ineffectual leader. Vocal criticism of Lincoln sprang from a group of Republicans who became known as the Radicals and who included Secretary of the Treasury Salmon P. Chase, Senator Charles Sumner of Massachusetts, and Representative Thaddeus Stevens of Pennsylvania. The Radicals never formed a tightly knit cadre; on some issues they cooperated with Lincoln. But they did criticize him early in the war for failing to make the emancipation of the slaves a war goal and later for being too eager to readmit the conquered rebel states into the Union.

Abraham Lincoln
When Lincoln became president in March 1861, he faced more severe problems than any predecessor. Washington photographer Mathew Brady captured this image of the solemn President-elect on February 23, 1861, a few weeks after the formation of the Confederacy and shortly before Lincoln's inauguration.

Lincoln's distinctive style of leadership encouraged and simultaneously disarmed opposition within the Republican party. Keeping his counsel to himself until ready to act, he met criticism with homespun anecdotes that caught his opponents off guard. The Radicals frequently concluded that Lincoln was a prisoner of the conservative wing of the party, whereas conservatives complained that Lincoln was too close to the Radicals. But Lincoln's cautious reserve had the dual benefit of leaving open his lines of communication with both wings of the party and fragmenting his opposition. Lincoln shrewdly brought several of his critics into his cabinet, including Chase. Chase not only moderated his criticism of Lincoln but proved a fine administrator.

In contrast, Jefferson Davis had a knack for making enemies. A West Pointer, he would rather have led the army than the government, and he used his sharp tongue to win arguments rather than to win over his foes. Davis's cabinet suffered from frequent resignations; the Confederacy had five secretaries of war in four years, for example. In particular, Davis's relations with his vice president, Alexander Stephens of Georgia, bordered on disastrous. A wisp of a man, Stephens weighed less than a hundred pounds and looked like a boy with a withered face. But he compensated for his slight physique with a tongue as acidic as Davis's. Leaving Richmond, the Confederate capital, in 1862, Stephens spent most of the war in Georgia, where he sniped at Davis as "weak and vacillating, timid, petulant, peevish, obstinate."

The conflict between Davis and Stephens involved not only a clash of personalities but also an ideological division, a rift, in fact, like that at the heart of the Confederacy. Although the Confederate Constitution, drafted in February 1861, resembled the U.S. Constitution in several ways, the southern charter explicitly guaranteed the sovereignty of the Confederate states and prohibited the Confederate Congress from enacting protective tariffs and from supporting internal improvements (measures long opposed by southern voters). For Stephens and other influential Confederate leaders—among them, governors Joseph Brown of Georgia and Zebulon Vance of North Carolina—the Confederacy existed not only to protect slavery but, equally important, to enshrine the doctrine of states' rights. (Brown condemned the Confederate Conscription Act as the most severe blow to constitutional liberty in American history.) In contrast, Davis's main objective was to secure the independence of the entire South from the North, a goal that frequently led him to override the wishes of state governors for the good of the Confederacy as a whole.

This difference between Davis and Stephens bore some resemblance to the discord between Lincoln and the northern Democrats. Like Davis, Lincoln believed that winning the war demanded an enhancement of the central government's power; like Stephens, northern Democrats resisted governmental centralization. But Lincoln could control his opponents more effectively than Davis, not only because, by temperament, he was more suited than Davis to conciliation but also because of the different nature of party politics in the two sections.

In the South the Democrats and the remaining Whigs agreed to suspend party rivalries for the duration of the war. However, this decision, made to promote southern unity, actually encouraged disunity. Without the institutionalization of conflict that party rivalry provided, southern politics tended to disintegrate along personal and factional lines. Lacking a party organization to back him, Davis could not mobilize votes to pass measures that he favored through the Confederate Congress, nor could he depend on the support of party loyalists throughout the slave states. In contrast, in the Union, northern Democrats' organized opposition to Lincoln tended to unify the Republicans. In the 1862 elections, which occurred at a low ebb of Union military fortunes, the Democrats won control of five large states, including Lincoln's own Illinois. Republican leaders learned a lesson: no matter how much they disdained Lincoln, they had to rally behind him or risk being driven from office. Ultimately, the Union would develop more political cohesion than the Confederacy, not because it had fewer divisions but because it managed its divisions more effectively.

Securing the Union's Borders

Even before large-scale fighting began, Lincoln moved to safeguard Washington, which was bordered by two slave states (Virginia and Maryland) and filled with Confederate sympathizers. A week after Fort Sumter, a Baltimore mob attacked a Massachusetts regiment bound for Washington, but enough troops slipped through to protect the capital. Lincoln then dispatched federal troops to Maryland, where he suspended the writ of habeas corpus*; federal troops could now arrest prosecession Marylanders without formally charging them with specific offenses. Mindful that strong Unionist sentiment flourished in the western part of the state, and cowed by Lincoln's bold moves, the Maryland legislature rejected secession. Delaware, another border slave state, followed suit.

Next Lincoln authorized the arming of Union sympathizers in Kentucky, a slave state with a Unionist legislature, a secessionist governor, and a thin chance of staying neutral. Lincoln also stationed troops under General Ulysses S. Grant just across the Ohio River from Kentucky, in Illinois. When a Confederate army invaded Kentucky early in 1862, the state's legislature turned to Grant to drive it out. Officially, at least, Kentucky

---

*Habeas corpus: a court order requiring that the detainer of a prisoner bring the person in custody to court and show cause for his or her detention.

became the third slave state to declare for the Union. The fourth, Missouri, was ravaged by four years of fighting between Union and Confederate troops and between sundry bands of guerrillas and bushwackers, including William Quantrill, a Confederate desperado, and his murderous apprentices, Frank and Jesse James. Despite savage fighting and the divided loyalties of its people, Missouri never left the Union.[*]

By holding these four border slave states—Maryland, Delaware, Kentucky, and Missouri—in the Union, Lincoln kept open his lines to the free states and gained access to the river systems in Kentucky and Missouri that led into the heart of the Confederacy. (In 1862 invasions of the South by river would provide the North with most of its early military successes.) Lincoln's firmness, particularly in the case of Maryland, scotched charges that he was weak-willed, and it demonstrated how the crisis forced the president to exercise long-dormant powers. Although in the case *Ex parte* Merryman (1861), Chief Justice Roger B. Taney ruled that Lincoln had exceeded his authority in suspending the writ of habeas corpus in Maryland, the president, citing the Constitution's authorization of the writ's suspension in "Cases of Rebellion" (Article I, Section 9), insisted that he, rather than Congress, would determine whether a rebellion existed; and he ignored Taney's ruling.

IN BATTLE, 1861–1862

The Civil War was the first war to rely extensively on railroads, the telegraph, mass-produced weapons, joint army-navy tactics, iron-plated warships, rifled guns and artillery, and trench warfare. All of this lends some justification to its description as the first modern war. But to the participants, slogging through muddy swamps and weighed down with equipment, the war hardly seemed modern. In many ways, the soldiers had the more accurate perspective, for the new weapons did not always work, and both sides employed tactics that were more traditional than modern.

---

[*]Admitted to the Union in 1863, West Virginia became the fifth border state. This state originated in the refusal of thirty-five counties in the predominantly nonslaveholding region of Virginia west of the Shenandoah Valley to follow the state's leaders into secession in 1861.

Armies, Weapons, and Strategies

Compared to the Confederacy's 9 million people, of whom over one-third were slaves, the Union had 22 million people in 1861. The North also had 3.5 times as many white men of military age, 90 percent of all U.S. industrial capacity, and two-thirds of its railroad track. Yet the Union faced a daunting challenge. Its goal was to force the South back into the Union, whereas the South was fighting merely for its independence. To subdue the Confederacy, the North would have to sustain offensive operations over an area comparable in size to the part of Russia that the French emperor Napoleon had invaded in 1812 with disastrous results.

Measured against this challenge, the Union's advantages in population and technology shrank. The North had more men, but needing to defend long supply lines and occupy captured areas, it could commit a smaller proportion of them to frontline duty. The South, on the other hand, with black slaves as the basis of its labor force, could assign a higher proportion of its white male population to combat. As for technology, the North required, and possessed, superior railroads. Fighting defensively on so-called interior lines, the South could shift its troops relatively short distances within its defensive arc without relying on railroads, whereas the North had to move its troops and supplies huge distances around the exterior of the arc. Not only could guerrillas easily sabotage northern railroads, but once Union troops moved away from their railroad bases, their supply wagons often bogged down on wretched southern roads, which frequently became watery ditches in bad weather. Even on good roads, horses and mules, which themselves consumed supplies, were needed to pull wagons; an invading army of 100,000 men required 35,000 horses or mules. Finally, southerners had an edge in soldiers' morale, for Confederate troops battled on home ground. "No people ever warred for independence," a southern general acknowledged, "with more relative advantages than the Confederates."

The Civil War witnessed experiments with a variety of newly developed weapons, including the submarine, the repeating rifle, and the multibarreled Gatling gun, the forerunner of the machine gun. Yet these futuristic innovations had less impact on the war than did the perfection in the 1850s of a bullet whose powder would not clog a rifle's spiraled internal grooves after a few shots. Like the smoothbore muskets that both armies had employed at the start of the

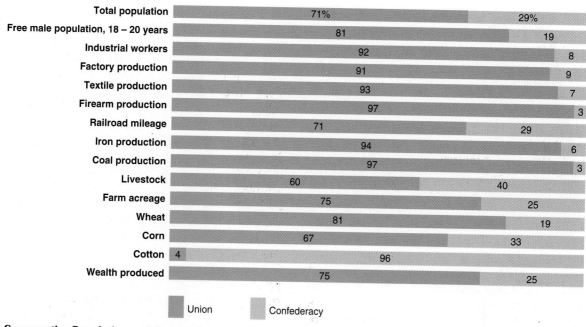

Total population	71%	29%
Free male population, 18 – 20 years	81	19
Industrial workers	92	8
Factory production	91	9
Textile production	93	7
Firearm production	97	3
Railroad mileage	71	29
Iron production	94	6
Coal production	97	3
Livestock	60	40
Farm acreage	75	25
Wheat	81	19
Corn	67	33
Cotton	4	96
Wealth produced	75	25

Union   Confederacy

Comparative Population and Economic Resources of the Union and the Confederacy, 1861
At the start of the war, the Union enjoyed huge advantages in population, industry, railroad mileage, and wealth produced.
SOURCE: *The Times Atlas of World History* (New Jersey: Hammond, Inc., 1978).

war, most improved rifles had to be reloaded after each shot. But where the smoothbore musket had an effective range of only eighty yards, the Springfield or Enfield rifles widely employed by 1863 could hit targets accurately at four hundred yards.

The development of the rifle posed a challenge to long-accepted military tactics. The tactical manuals used at West Point in the 1840s and 1850s had identified the mass infantry charge against an opponent's weakest point as the key to victory. These manuals assumed that defenders armed with muskets would be able to fire only a round or two before being overwhelmed. The same assumption led tacticians to disdain trenches; against assaulting infantry, trenches would become mere traps for defenders. Armed with rifles, however, a defending force could fire several rounds before closing with the enemy. Attackers would now have far greater difficulty getting close enough to thrust bayonets; less than 1 percent of the casualties in the Civil War resulted from bayonet wounds.

Thus the rifle produced some changes in tactics during the war. Both sides gradually came to under-

stand the value of trenches, which provided defenders with some protection against the withering fire of attacking forces. By 1865 trenches pockmarked the landscape in Virginia and Georgia. In addition, growing use of the rifle forced generals to rely less on cavalry. Traditionally, the cavalry had ranked among the most prestigious components of an army, in part because cavalry charges were often devastatingly effective and in part because the cavalry helped maintain class distinctions within the army. Indeed, at the start of the war, one of the clearest Confederate advantages lay in the quality of its cavalry. But rifles reduced the effectiveness of cavalry by increasing the firepower of foot soldiers. Bullets that might miss the rider would at least hit the horse. Thus as cavalry charges against infantry became more difficult, both sides relegated cavalry to reconnaissance missions and to raids on supply trains.

Although the rifle exposed traditional tactics to new hazards, it by no means invalidated those tactics. The attacking army still stood an excellent chance of success if it achieved surprise. The South's lush forests provided abundant opportunities for an army to sneak up on its opponent. For example, at the Battle of Shiloh

Life in the Field
*The implements in this Union
army-owned field surgical kit could remove bullets but not stop infection.
The British-made five-shot revolver reached the South despite the Union blockade.
A Confederate officer owned the brass-and-leather-adorned field glass. The bullet-rent trousers
belonged to a Union officer wounded at Peachtree Creek. Although he survived the war, he endured
repeated operations in the remaining forty-five years of his life to remove tissue infected by the bullet.*

in 1862, Confederate attackers surprised and almost defeated a larger Union army despite the rumpus created by green rebel troops en route to the battle, many of whom fired their rifles into the air to see if they would work.

Achieving such complete surprise normally lay beyond the skill or luck of generals. In the absence of any element of surprise, disaster became a likely result for the attacking army. At the Battle of Fredericksburg in December 1862, Confederate troops inflicted appalling casualties on Union forces attacking uphill over open terrain, and at Gettysburg in July 1863, Union riflemen and artillery shredded charging southerners. But generals might still achieve partial surprise by hitting an enemy before it had concentrated its troops; in fact,

this is what the North tried to do at Fredericksburg. Because surprise often proved effective, most generals continued to believe that their best chance of success lay in striking an unwary or weakened enemy with all the troops they could muster rather than in relying on guerrilla or trench warfare.

Much like previous wars, the Civil War was fought basically in a succession of battles during which exposed infantry traded volleys, charged, and countercharged. Whichever side withdrew from the field usually was thought to have lost the battle, but the losing side frequently sustained lighter casualties than the supposed victors. Both sides had trouble exploiting their victories, for neither had airplanes to hammer or tanks to envelop retreating columns. As a rule, the beaten army moved back a few miles from the field to lick its wounds; the winners stayed in place to lick theirs. Politicians on both sides denounced their generals as timorous fools for not pursuing a beaten foe, but these politicians rarely understood how difficult it was for a mangled victor to gather horses, mules, supply trains, and exhausted soldiers for a new attack. Until the end of the war, the only cases of entire armies actually surrendering arose from captured garrisons. Not surprisingly, for much of the war, generals on both sides concluded that the best defense was a good offense.

To the extent that the North had a long-range strategy in 1861, it lay in the so-called Anaconda plan. Devised by the Mexican War hero General Winfield Scott, the plan called for the Union to blockade the southern coastline and to thrust, like a huge snake, down the Mississippi River. Scott expected that this sealing off and severing of the Confederacy would make the South recognize the futility of secession and restore southern Unionists to power. The Anaconda plan promised a relatively bloodless end to the war, but Scott, a southern Unionist, exaggerated the strength of Unionist spirit in the South. Furthermore, although Lincoln ordered a blockade of the southern coast a week after the fall of Fort Sumter, the North hardly had the troops and naval flotillas to seize the Mississippi in 1861. So while the Mississippi was an obvious objective, northern strategy did not unfold according to any blueprint like the Anaconda plan.

Early in the war, the pressing need to secure the border slave states, particularly Kentucky and Missouri, dictated Union strategy west of the Appalachian Mountains. Once in control of Kentucky, northern troops plunged southward into Tennessee. The Appalachians tended to seal this western theater off from the eastern theater, where the Confederacy's decision to move its capital from Montgomery, Alabama, to Richmond, Virginia, shaped the Union strategy. "Forward to Richmond" became the Union's first war cry in 1861.

Stalemate in the East

Before they could reach Richmond, one hundred miles southwest of Washington, Union troops would have to dislodge a Confederate army brazenly encamped at Manassas Junction, only twenty-five miles from the Union capital. Lincoln ordered General Irvin McDowell to attack his former West Point classmate, Confederate general P. G. T. Beauregard. "You are green, it is true,"

Lincoln told McDowell, "but they are green also; you are all green alike." In the resulting First Battle of Bull Run (or First Manassas),* amateur armies clashed in bloody chaos under a blistering July sun. The engagement was a spectacle that contrasted vividly with the picnicking of the well-dressed Washington dignitaries who had gathered to view the action. Aided by last-minute reinforcements and by the disorganization of the attacking federals, Beauregard routed the larger Union army.

After Bull Run, Lincoln replaced McDowell with General George B. McClellan as commander of the Union's Army of the Potomac. Another West Pointer, McClellan had served with distinction in the Mexican War and mastered the art of administration by managing various midwestern railroads in the 1850s. Few generals could match his ability to turn a ragtag mob into a disciplined fighting force. His soldiers adored him, but Lincoln quickly became disenchanted with his new commander. Lincoln believed that the key to a Union victory lay in simultaneous, coordinated attacks on several fronts. In this way, the North could exploit its advantage in manpower and resources and negate the South's advantage of interior lines. McClellan, a proslavery Democrat, hoped to maneuver the South into a relatively bloodless defeat and then negotiate a peace that would readmit the Confederate states with slavery intact.

McClellan soon got an opportunity to demonstrate the value of his strategy. After Bull Run, the Confederates had pulled back behind the Rappahannock River and awaited the Union onslaught against Richmond. Rather than directly attack the Confederate army, McClellan formulated a plan in the spring of 1862 to move the Army of the Potomac by water to the tip of the peninsula formed by the York and James rivers and then move northwestward up the peninsula to Richmond. McClellan's plan had several advantages. Depending on water transport rather than on railroads (which Confederate cavalry could cut), the McClellan strategy reduced the vulnerability of northern supply lines. By dictating an approach to Richmond from the southeast, it threatened the South's supply lines. By aiming for the capital of the Confederacy rather than for the Confederate army stationed northeast of Richmond, finally, McClellan hoped to maneuver the

---

*Because the North sometimes named battles after local landmarks, often bodies of water, and the South after the nearest town, several Civil War battles are known by two names.

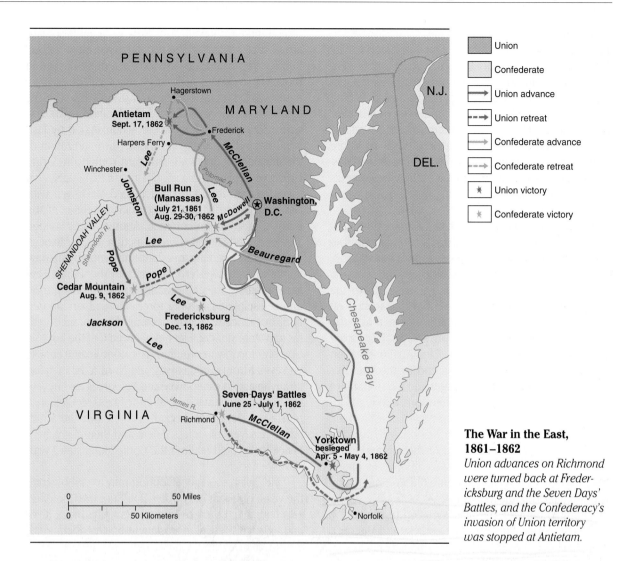

	Union
	Confederate
	Union advance
	Union retreat
	Confederate advance
	Confederate retreat
	Union victory
	Confederate victory

The War in the East, 1861–1862

Union advances on Richmond were turned back at Fredericksburg and the Seven Days' Battles, and the Confederacy's invasion of Union territory was stopped at Antietam.

southern troops into a futile attack on his army in order to avert a destructive siege of Richmond.

By far the most massive military campaign in American history to that date, the Peninsula Campaign at first unfolded smoothly. Three hundred ships transported seventy thousand men and huge stores of supplies to the tip of the peninsula. Reinforcements swelled McClellan's army to one hundred thousand. Although Confederate troops also poured into the peninsula, by late May McClellan was within five miles of Richmond.

If the war had been a chess game, McClellan would have become a grand master. But after luring the Confederacy to the brink of defeat, McClellan hesitated. Overestimating the Confederates' strength, he refused to launch a final attack on Richmond without

the reinforcements that he expected, which were turned back by Confederate general Thomas "Stonewall" Jackson in the Shenandoah Valley. While McClellan delayed, General Robert E. Lee took command of the Confederacy's Army of Northern Virginia. A foe of secession and so courteous that at times he seemed too gentle, Lee nevertheless possessed the qualities that McClellan most lacked, boldness and a willingness to accept casualties. Seizing the initiative, Lee attacked McClellan in late June 1862. The ensuing Seven Days' Battles, fought in the forests east of Richmond, cost the South nearly twice as many men as the North and ended in a virtual slaughter of Confederates at Malvern Hill. But it was his own northern casualties that unnerved McClellan, and he began to send increasingly panicky reports to Washington. Lincoln, who cared little for McClellan's peninsula strategy, ordered McClellan to call off the campaign and return to Washington.

With McClellan out of the picture, Lee and his lieutenant, Stonewall Jackson, now boldly struck north and, at the Second Battle of Bull Run (Second Manassas), routed a Union army under General John Pope that had been held back from the peninsula to guard Washington. Lee's next stroke was even bolder. Crossing the Potomac River in early September 1862, he invaded western Maryland, where the forthcoming fall harvest could provide him with desperately needed supplies. By seizing western Maryland, moreover, Lee could threaten Washington, indirectly relieve pressure on Richmond, improve the prospects of peace candidates in the North's upcoming fall elections, and possibly induce Britain and France to recognize the Confederacy as an independent nation. But McClellan met Lee at the Battle of Antietam (or Sharpsburg) on September 17. Although a tactical draw, Antietam proved a strategic victory for the North, for Lee subsequently called off his invasion and retreated south of the Potomac. Heartened by the apparent success of northern

arms, Lincoln then issued the Emancipation Proclamation, a war measure that freed all slaves under rebel control (see below). The carnage of the twenty-four thousand casualties at Antietam, however, made it the bloodiest day of the entire war. A Union veteran recollected that one part of the battlefield contained so many bodies that a man could have walked through it without stepping on the ground.

Complaining that McClellan had "the slows," Lincoln faulted his commander for not pursuing Lee after the battle and replaced him with General Ambrose Burnside, who thought himself, and soon proved himself, unfit for high command. In December 1862 Burnside led 122,000 federal troops against 78,500 Confederates at the Battle of Fredericksburg. Burnside captured the town of Fredericksburg, northeast of Richmond, but then sacrificed his army in futile charges up the heights west of the town. Even Lee was shaken by the northern casualties. "It is well that war is so terrible—we should grow fond of it," he told an aide during the battle. Richmond remained, in the words of a southern song, "a hard road to travel." The war in the East had become a stalemate.

Dead Soldiers at Antietam
These dead rebel gunners lie next to the wreckage of their battery at Antietam. The building, a Dunker church, was the site of furious fighting.

The War in the West

The Union fared better in the West. Unlike the geographically limited eastern theater, the war in the West shifted over a vast and crucial terrain that provided access to rivers leading directly into the South. The West also spawned new leadership. During the first year of war, an obscure Union general, Ulysses S. Grant, proved his competence. A West Point graduate, Grant had fought in the Mexican War and retired from the army in 1854 with a reputation for heavy drinking. He then had embarked on ventures in farming and in business, all of them dismal failures. When the Civil War began, he had gained an army commission through political pressure.

In 1861–1862 Grant retained control of two border states, Missouri and Kentucky. Moving into Tennessee, he captured two strategic forts, Fort Henry on the Tennessee River and Fort Donelson on the Cumberland. Grant then headed south to attack Corinth, Mississippi.

Corinth was a major railroad junction through which troops and supplies could be transported from the east to Memphis on the Mississippi River. In early April 1862, Confederate forces under generals Albert Sidney Johnston and P. G. T. Beauregard tried to relieve the Union pressure on Corinth by a surprise attack on Grant's army, encamped twenty miles north of the town, in southern Tennessee near a church named Shiloh. Hoping to whip Grant before the imminent arrival of twenty-five thousand Union reinforcements under General Don Carlos Buell, the Confederates exploded from the woods near Shiloh before breakfast and almost drove the federals into the Tennessee River. Beauregard cabled Richmond with news of a splendid Confederate victory. But Grant and his lieutenant, William T. Sherman, steadied the Union line. Buell's reinforcements arrived in the night, and a Union counterattack drove the Confederates from the field the next day. Although Antietam would soon erase the distinction, the Battle of Shiloh was the bloodiest in Ameri-can history to that date. Of the seventy-seven thousand men engaged, twenty-three thousand were killed or wounded, including Confederate general Albert Sidney Johnston, who bled to death from a leg wound. Defeated at Shiloh, the Confederates soon evacuated Corinth.

To attack Grant at Shiloh, the Confederacy had stripped the defenses of New Orleans, leaving only three thousand militia to guard its largest city. A combined Union land-sea force under General

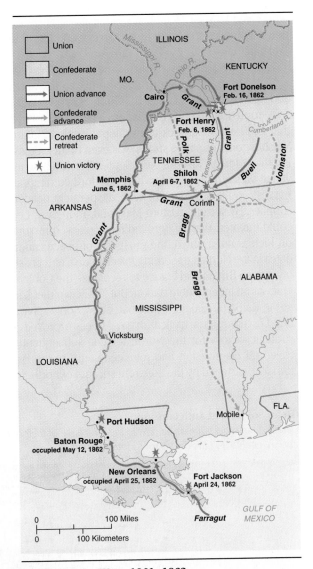

The War in the West, 1861–1862
By the end of 1862, the North held New Orleans and the entire Mississippi River except for the stretch between Vicksburg and Port Hudson.

Benjamin Butler, a Massachusetts politician, and Admiral David G. Farragut, a Tennessean loyal to the Union, quickly capitalized on the opportunity. Blasting his way past two river forts south of New Orleans, Farragut took the city in late April and soon added Baton Rouge and Natchez to his list of conquests. Meanwhile, another Union flotilla moved down the Mississippi and captured Memphis in June. Now the North controlled the entire river, except for a two-hundred-mile stretch between Port Hudson, Louisiana, and Vicksburg, Mississippi.

Union and Confederate forces also clashed in 1862 in the Trans-Mississippi West, the vast region of states and territories stretching from the Midwest to the Pacific coast. On the banks of the Rio Grande, Union volunteers, joined by Mexican-American companies, drove a Confederate army from Texas out of New Mexico. "Fight for your rights and repel the invaders!" the territorial governor had urged the Mexican-American recruits. A thousand miles to the east, in northern Arkansas and western Missouri, opposing armies vied to secure the Missouri River, a crucial waterway that flowed into the Mississippi. In Pea Ridge, Arkansas, in March 1862, forewarned northern troops scattered a Confederate force of sixteen thousand that included three Cherokee regiments. (Indian units fought on *both* sides in Missouri, where guerrilla combat raged until the war's end.)

These Union victories changed the nature of the Trans-Mississippi war. As the rebel threat faded, regiments of western volunteers that had mobilized to crush Confederates turned to fighting Indians. Conflict between the Dakota Sioux and Minnesota volunteers in the fall of 1862 spread to the north and west. Indian wars erupted in Arizona, Nevada, Colorado, and New Mexico, where California volunteers and the New Mexico cavalry, led by Colonel Kit Carson, overwhelmed the Apaches and Navajos. After 1865 federal troops moved west to complete the rout of the Indians that had begun in the Civil War (see Chapter 17).

Ironclads and Cruisers: The Naval War

By plunging its navy into the Confederacy like a dagger, the Union was exploiting one of its clearest advantages. The North began the war with over forty active warships against none for the South, and with the technology and industrial capacity to produce many more. Indeed, by 1865 the United States had the largest navy in the world. Steam-driven ships could penetrate the South's excellent river system from any direction and thereby turn a peacetime advantage into a wartime liability. For example, the Confederacy had stripped New Orleans's defenses in the belief that the real threat to the city would come from the north, only to find Farragut slipping in from the south.

Despite its size, the Union navy faced an extraordinary challenge in its efforts to blockade the South's thirty-five hundred miles of coast. Early in the war, small, sleek Confederate blockade-runners darted in and out of southern harbors and inlets with little

Deck of the *Monitor*
Although much smaller than its famous rival the Merrimac (*C.S.S.* Virginia), *the Union ironclad* Monitor *benefited from its shallow draft, speed, and maneuverability. Its flat, raftlike shape made it hard to hit.*

chance of capture. The North gradually tightened the blockade by outfitting tugs, whalers, excursion steamers, and ferries as well as frigates to patrol southern coasts. The proportion of Confederate blockade-runners that made it through dropped from 90 percent early in the war to 50 percent by 1865. Even more than tightening the blockade, however, northern seizure of rebel ports and coastal areas shrank the South's foreign trade. In daring amphibious assaults during 1861 and 1862, the Union captured the excellent harbor of Port Royal, South Carolina, the coastal islands off South Carolina, and most of North Carolina's river outlets. Naval patrols and amphibious operations contributed to a decline in the South's ocean trade to one-third its prewar level.

Although its resources were meager, the South made impressive efforts to offset the North's naval advantage. Early in the war, the Confederacy raised the scuttled Union frigate *Merrimac*, sheathed its sides with an armor of iron plate, rechristened it *Virginia*, and dispatched it to attack wooden Union ships in Hampton Roads, Virginia. The *Merrimac* quickly destroyed two northern warships but met its match in the hastily built Union ironclad the *Monitor*. In the first engagement of ironclads in history, the two ships fought an indecisive battle on March 9, 1862. The South constructed other ironclads and even the first submarine, which dragged a mine through the water to sink a Union ship off Charleston in 1864. Unfortunately, the "fish" failed to resurface and went down with its victim. But short of mechanics and iron-fabricating shops, the South could never build enough ironclads to overcome the North's supremacy in home waters. The Confederacy had more success on the high seas, where wooden, steam-driven commerce raiders like the *Alabama* and the *Florida* (both built in England) wreaked havoc on the Union's merchant marine. Commerce raiding, however, would not tip the balance of the war in the South's favor, because the North, unlike its opponent, did not depend on imports for war materials. The South would lose the naval war.

The Diplomatic War

While armies and navies clashed in 1861–1862, conflict developed on a third front, diplomacy. At the outbreak of the war, the Confederacy began a campaign to gain European recognition of its status as an independent nation. Southern confidence in a swift diplomatic victory ran high. Planning to establish a colonial empire in Mexico, Napoleon III of France had grounds to welcome the permanent division of the United States. Moreover, the upper classes in France, and also in Britain, were widely viewed as sympathetic to the aristocratic South and eager for the downfall of the brash Yankee republic. Furthermore, for years such influential southerners as South Carolina's senator and governor James Henry Hammond had contended that an embargo of cotton exports would bring Britain to its knees. These southerners reasoned that Britain, dependent on the South for four-fifths of its cotton, would break the Union blockade and provoke a war with the North rather than watch its textile workers sink into revolutionary discontent under the weight of an embargo.

Leaving nothing to chance, the Confederacy in 1861 dispatched emissaries James Mason to Britain and John Slidell to France to lobby for recognition of the South as an independent nation. When a Union ship captain, acting without orders, boarded the British vessel the *Trent*, which was carrying Mason and Slidell, and brought the two men to Boston as prisoners, British tempers exploded. "You may stand for this," Britain's prime minister, Lord Palmerston, roared to his cabinet, "but damned if I will." But cooler heads prevailed. Considering one war at a time enough, President Lincoln released Mason and Slidell.

Settlement of the *Trent* affair did not eliminate friction between the United States and Britain. The construction in British shipyards of two Confederate commerce raiders, the *Florida* and the *Alabama*, evoked protests from Union diplomats. In 1863 the U.S. minister to London, Charles Francis Adams (the son of former president John Quincy Adams), threatened war if two British-built ironclads commissioned by the Confederacy, the so-called Laird rams, were turned over to the South. Armed with long spikes below the water, the powerful rams posed a genuine threat to the Union blockade of the South. Britain, however, capitulated to Adams's protests and purchased the rams for its own navy.

On balance, the South fell far short of its diplomatic objectives. Although recognizing the Confederacy as a belligerent, neither Britain nor France ever recognized it as a nation. Basically, the Confederacy overestimated its hand. For several reasons, the South's vaunted "cotton diplomacy" failed dismally. The Confederate government talked of embargoing cotton exports in order to bring the British to their knees, but in reality, the government never controlled

CAVING IN, OR A REBEL "DEEPLY HUMILIATED".

more than 15 percent of the South's cotton. Planters conducted business as usual by raising cotton and trying to slip it through the blockade. The South ultimately lost its share of the British market anyway; with 77 percent of that market in 1860, it held only 10 percent by 1865. But this loss resulted from forces beyond southern control. Bumper cotton crops in the late 1850s had glutted the British market by the start of the war and weakened British demand for cotton. In addition, Britain had responded to the threat of a cotton embargo by developing new suppliers in Egypt and India, thereby buffering itself from southern pressure. Gradually, too, the North's tightened blockade restricted southern exports.

The South also exaggerated Britain's stake in helping the Confederacy. As a naval power that had frequently blockaded its own enemies, Britain's diplomatic interest lay in supporting the Union blockade in principle; from Britain's standpoint, to help the South break the blockade would set a precedent that could easily boomerang. Finally, although France and Britain often talked of recognizing the Confederacy, the timing never seemed quite right. The Union's success at Antietam in 1862 and Lincoln's subsequent issuance of the Emancipation Proclamation dampened

Europe's enthusiasm for recognition at a crucial juncture. By transforming the war into a struggle to end slavery, the Emancipation Proclamation produced an upsurge of pro-Union feeling in antislavery Britain, particularly among liberals and the working class. Workingmen in Manchester, England, wrote Lincoln to praise his resolve to free the slaves. The proclamation, wrote Henry Adams (diplomat Charles Francis Adams's son) from London, "has done more for us here than all of our former victories and all our diplomacy."

EMANCIPATION TRANSFORMS THE WAR

"I hear old John Brown knocking on the lid of his coffin and shouting 'Let me out! Let me out!'" abolitionist Henry Stanton wrote to his wife after the fall of Fort Sumter. "The Doom of Slavery is at hand." In 1861 this prediction seemed wildly premature. In his inaugural that year, Lincoln had stated bluntly, "I have no purpose, directly or indirectly, to interfere with the institution of slavery in the states where it exists." Yet in two years, the North's priorities underwent a decisive transformation. A mix of practical necessity and ideological conviction thrust the emancipation of the slaves to the forefront of northern war goals.

The rise of emancipation as a Union war goal reflected the changing character of the war itself. As late as July 1862, General George McClellan had written to Lincoln to restate his conviction that "neither confiscation of property . . . or forcible abolition of slavery should be contemplated for a moment." As the struggle dragged on, however, demands for the prosecution of "total war" intensified in the North. Even northerners who saw no moral value in abolishing slavery were starting to recognize the military value of emancipation as a technique to cripple the South's resources.

From Confiscation to Emancipation

Union policy on emancipation developed in stages. As soon as northern troops began to invade the South, questions arose about the disposition of captured rebel property, including slaves. Slaves who fled behind the Union lines were sometimes considered "contra-band"—enemy property liable to seizure—and were put to work for the Union army. Whereas some northern commanders viewed this practice a useful tool of war, others did not, and the Lincoln administration was evasive. To establish an official policy, Congress in August 1861 passed the first Confiscation Act, which authorized the seizure of all property used in military aid of the rebellion, including slaves. By the terms of this act, slaves who had been employed directly by the Confederate armed services and who later fled to freedom became "captives of war." But nothing in the act actually freed these contrabands, nor did the law apply to contrabands who had not worked for the Confederate military.

Several factors underlay the Union's cautious approach to the confiscation of rebel property. Officially maintaining that the South's rebellion lacked any legal basis, Lincoln argued that southerners were thus still entitled to the Constitution's protection of property. The president also had practical reasons to walk softly. The Union not only contained four slave states but also held a sizable body of proslavery Democrats who flatly opposed turning the war into a crusade against slavery. If the North in any way tampered with slavery, these Democrats feared, "two or three million semi-savages" might come north and compete with white workers. Aware of strong northern opposition to turning a limited policy of confiscation into a general program of emancipation, Lincoln assured Congress in December

1861 that the war would not become a "remorseless revolutionary struggle."

From the start of the war, however, Lincoln faced pressure from the loosely knit but determined Radical Republicans to adopt a policy of emancipation. Radicals hailed the war as a second American Revolution, one that would abolish slavery. Pennsylvanian Thaddeus Stevens urged that the Union "free every slave—slay every traitor—burn every Rebel mansion, if these things be necessary to preserve this temple of freedom." Radicals agreed with black abolitionist Frederick Douglass that "to fight against slaveholders without fighting against slavery, is but a half-hearted business."

With every new northern setback, support for the Radicals' point of view grew. Each Union military defeat reminded northerners that the confederacy, with a slave labor force in place to harvest southern crops and run southern factories, could commit a higher proportion of its white men to battle. As a military measure, the idea of emancipation thus gained increasing favor in the North, and in July 1862 Congress passed the second Confiscation Act. This law authorized the seizure of the property of all persons in rebellion and stipulated that slaves who came within Union lines "shall be forever free." Finally, the law opened the door to blacks' military service by authorizing the president to employ blacks as soldiers.

Nevertheless, Lincoln continued to stall, even in the face of rising pressure for emancipation. "My paramount object in this struggle *is* to save the Union, and is *not* either to save or destroy slavery," Lincoln told antislavery journalist Horace Greeley. "If I could save the Union without freeing *any* slave, I would do it, and if I could save it by freeing *all* the slaves, I would do it; and if I could save it by freeing some and leaving others alone, I would also do that." Yet Lincoln had always loathed slavery, and by the spring of 1862, he had come around to the Radical position that the war must lead to its abolition. He hesitated principally because he did not want to be stampeded by Congress into a measure that might disrupt northern unity and because he feared that a public commitment to emancipation in the summer of 1862, on the heels of the northern defeat at Second Manassas and the collapse of the Peninsula Campaign, might be interpreted as an act of frantic desperation. After failing to persuade the Union slave states to emancipate slaves in return for federal compensation, he drafted a proclamation of emancipation, circulated it within his cabinet, and waited for a right moment to issue it. Finally, after the

Union victory in September 1862 at Antietam, Lincoln issued the Preliminary Emancipation Proclamation, which declared all slaves under rebel control free as of January 1, 1863. Announcing the plan in advance softened the surprise, tested public opinion, and gave the states still in rebellion an opportunity to preserve slavery by returning to the Union—an opportunity that none, however, took. The final Emancipation Proclamation, issued on January 1, 1863, declared "forever free" all slaves in areas in rebellion.

The proclamation had limited practical impact. Applying only to rebellious areas, where the Union had no authority, it exempted the Union slave states and those parts of the Confederacy then in Union hands (Tennessee, West Virginia, southern Louisiana, and sections of Virginia). Moreover, it mainly restated what the second Confiscation Act had already stipulated: if rebels' slaves fell into Union hands, those slaves would be free. Yet the proclamation was a brilliant political stroke. By issuing it as a military measure, in his role as commander in chief, Lincoln pacified northern conservatives. Its aim, he stressed, was to injure the Confederacy, threaten its property, heighten its dread, sap its morale, and thus hasten its demise. By issuing the proclamation himself, Lincoln stole the initiative from the Radicals in Congress and mobilized support for the Union among European liberals far more dramatically than could any act of Congress. Furthermore, the declaration pushed the border states toward emancipation: by the end of the war, Maryland and Missouri would abolish slavery. Finally, it increased slaves' incentives to escape as northern troops approached. Fulfilling the worst of Confederate fears, it enabled blacks to join the Union army.

The Emancipation Proclamation did not end slavery everywhere or free "*all*" the slaves." But it changed the war. From 1863 on, the war for the Union would also be a war against slavery.

Crossing Union Lines

The attacks and counterattacks of the opposing armies turned many slaves into pawns of war. Some slaves became free when Union troops overran their areas. Others fled their plantations at the approach of federal troops to take refuge behind Union lines. A few were freed by northern assaults, only to be reenslaved by Confederate counterthrusts. One North Carolina slave celebrated liberation on twelve occasions, as many times as Union soldiers marched

through his area. By 1865 about half a million slaves were in Union hands.

In the first year of the war, when the Union had not yet established a policy toward contrabands (fugitive slaves), masters were able to retrieve them from the Union army. After 1862, however, the thousands of slaves who crossed Union lines were considered free. The continual influx of freed slaves created a huge refugee problem for army commanders. "What shall I do about the negroes?" wrote a Union general in Louisiana to army headquarters in 1862:

> *You can form no idea of . . . the appearance of my brigade as it marched down the Bayou. . . . Every soldier had a negro marching in the flanks, carrying his knapsack. Plantation carts, filled with negro women and children, with their effects; and of course compelled to pillage for their subsistence, as I have no rations to issue them. I have a great many more negroes in my camp now than I have whites.*

As 1862 drew to a close, Union commanders in the South were appointing superintendents of freedmen to supervise large contraband camps. Many freedmen served in army camps as cooks, teamsters, and laborers. Some worked for pay on abandoned plantations or were leased out to planters who swore allegiance to the Union and who paid them wages stipulated by the army. Whether in camps or working outside of them, freedmen had reason to question the value of their liberation. Deductions for clothing, rations, and medicine ate up most, if not all, of their earnings. Labor contracts frequently tied them to their employers for prolonged periods. Moreover, freedmen encountered fierce prejudice among Yankee soldiers, many of whom feared that emancipation would propel blacks north after the war. The best solution to the "question of what to do with the darkies," wrote one northern soldier, "would be to shoot them."

But this was not the whole story. Contrabands who aided the Union army as spies and scouts helped to break down ingrained bigotry. "The sooner we get rid of our foolish prejudice the better for us," a Massachusetts soldier wrote home. Before the end of the war, northern missionary groups and freedmen's aid societies sent agents into the South to work among the freed slaves, distribute relief, and organize schools. In March 1865, just before the hostilities ceased, Congress created the Freedmen's Bureau, which had responsibility for the relief, education, and employment

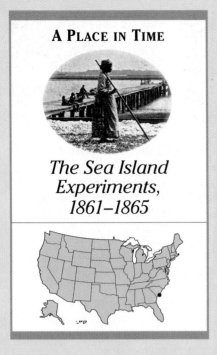

The Sea Island Experiments, 1861–1865

The Sea Islands

The island chain, famous for the production of what had come to be called sea-island cotton, was the site of unique wartime experiments in new social policies.

In November 1861 a Union fleet sailed into Port Royal Sound, an inlet among the South Carolina Sea Islands, and bombarded the port's defenses. Before Union troops could occupy the islands, the white residents, many of them slaveowning planters, fled to the mainland. Left behind were elegant mansions, sprawling cotton plantations, and ten thousand slaves, who would remember the invasion as the "gun shoot at Bay Point."

Lying just off the southern coast between Charleston and Savannah, the conquered islands—including Port Royal, Hilton Head, and St. Helena—provided an operating base for the Union blockade fleet. They were of potential value to the Treasury Department, too. The Sea Islands were known for their high-grade cotton, which could be used to supply northern textile mills and to bolster the Union economy. But the takeover of the islands presented the Union with a challenge as well as a triumph.

Before the invasion, slaves had composed 83 percent of the Sea Island population. Long isolated from the mainland, they retained a distinctive culture and perpetuated many African customs. Their syntax and vocabulary were West Indian, and their Gullah dialect was almost incomprehensible to outsiders. Since the late eighteenth century, they had endured a harsh slave system similar to that of the West Indies. To the northerners who now arrived on the Sea Islands—army personnel, treasury agents, plantation managers, teachers, and missionaries—the very numbers of the black inhabitants seemed overwhelming. "Negroes, negroes, negroes," wrote Elizabeth Botume, a Boston teacher. "They hovered around like bees in a swarm. . . . Every doorstep, box, or barrel was covered with them." With the war barely under way and victory still a vision on the distant horizon, the Union suddenly had to forge a policy toward these thousands of "contrabands." While warfare occupied the rest of the nation, Sea Island administrators embarked on a series of experiments in emancipation.

These experiments revealed deep divisions in northerners' thinking about the future of blacks. Some northerners on the scene focused on blacks' potential as soldiers. In May 1862 General David Hunter, who commanded the Union forces occupying the Sea Islands, formed a black army regiment; by August Sea Island men were being impressed into the First South Carolina "Volunteers," commanded by Massachusetts minister Thomas Wentworth Higginson. The drafting of blacks infuriated idealistic teachers and missionaries, who saw education as the blacks' primary need. "The negroes . . . will do anything for us, if we will only teach them," another teacher from Boston claimed. "The majority learn with wonderful rapidity," reported the free black Charlotte Forten of Philadelphia, "and they are said to be among the most degraded negroes of the South."

Equally sharp disagreements swirled around the question of economic opportunity for blacks. Edward Philbrick of Boston, an engineer who worked as a plantation superintendent on the islands, embodied one approach to the issue. Philbrick hoped to make the islands a showcase for free labor by turning the freed slaves into wage earners on the large cotton plantations there. For blacks to produce more cotton as wage earners than they had as slaves, Philbrick reasoned, would squelch northern "gabble about the danger of immediate emancipation" and buttress the position of those northerners who wanted emancipation to become the Union's main war goal. But the freedmen themselves had little enthusiasm for working in gangs on plantations, even if for wages. The practice smacked too much of their conditions under slavery. Instead, most Sea Island blacks would have preferred to plant food for themselves rather than cotton for northern factories, and many dreamed of owning their own land. "I should like to buy the very spot on which I live," an elderly freedman wrote to President Abraham Lincoln in a dictated letter. "I had rather work for myself . . . than work for a gentleman for wages."

Union administrators made some concessions to blacks' wishes. When, in the fall of 1863, Sea Island officials sold sixty thousand acres of confiscated rebel

Sea Island Teachers
The teachers and missionaries who arrived in the Sea Islands to work among the freed slaves were known as Gideon's Band. Above, a Gideonite group gathers in front of a stately home in Port Royal.

Sea Island Wage Labor
Free blacks sort cotton on an Edisto Island plantation. Northern managers who ran plantations on the Sea Islands during the war hoped to prove the virtues of free labor by turning freedmen into wage earners.

estates, only sixteen thousand acres were reserved for freedmen. The rest of the land was open to purchase by northern investors and speculators. Protesting the injustice of reserving a mere quarter of the acreage for those who composed the vast majority of the Sea Island residents, General Rufus Saxton, the islands' military governor and a "thoroughgoing Abolitionist, of the radical sort," secured approval in Washington for a plan to allow blacks to claim unsold land merely by squatting on it (a practice called preemption). Pressured by Saxton's rivals, however, the fed-

eral government reversed itself early in 1864 and forbade squatter claims.

The policy shifts continued. In December 1864 General William T. Sherman, fresh from his sweep across Georgia, arrived on the Sea Islands in the company of thousands of black camp followers who had gathered around his army during its march to the sea. To provide for these people, Sherman took steps to establish a class of black freeholders. General Sherman's Order No. 15 granted blacks the right to preempt unsold land not only on the Sea Islands but for thirty miles inland, on the mainland. By 1865 the islands had become a haven for black refugees from all over the South.

The new land policy would yet again be reversed: in August 1865 President Andrew Johnson would order all Sea Island lands returned to their original owners, thus dispossessing most of the blacks anew and leaving them no better or worse off than emancipated slaves elsewhere in the South. But during the Civil War, the islands had fulfilled a unique function. They had provided an arena wherein the Union first supervised emancipation and abolitionists first confronted large numbers of slaves. The scene of pioneer ventures in freedmen's education, black wage labor, and land redistribution, the Sea Islands had served as a testing ground for new social policies.

of former slaves. The Freedmen's Bureau law also provided that forty acres of abandoned or confiscated land could be leased to each freedman or southern Unionist, with an option to buy after three years. This was the first and only time that Congress provided for the redistribution of confiscated Confederate property.

Black Soldiers in the Union Army

During the first year of war, the Union had rejected black soldiers. Black applicants at northern recruiting offices were sent home, and black companies that had been formed in the occupied South were disbanded. After the second Confiscation Act, Union generals formed black regiments in occupied New Orleans and on the Sea Islands off the coasts of South Carolina and Georgia. Only after the Emancipation Proclamation did large-scale enlistment begin. Leading blacks such as Frederick Douglass and Harvard-educated physician Martin Delany worked as recruiting agents in northern cities. Douglass voiced the connection between black military service and black claims as citizens. "Once let the black man get upon his person the brass letters, U.S.; let him get an eagle on his button, and a musket on his shoulder and bullets in his pocket, and there is no power on earth which can deny that he has earned the right to citizenship." Union drafts now included blacks, recruiting offices arose in the loyal border

states, and freedmen in refugee camps throughout the occupied South were enlisted. By the end of the war, 186,000 blacks had served in the Union army, one-tenth of all Union soldiers. Fully half came from the Confederate states.

White Union soldiers commonly objected to the new recruits on racial grounds. But some, including Colonel Thomas Wentworth Higginson, a liberal minister and former John Brown supporter who led a black regiment, welcomed the black soldiers. "Nobody knows anything about these men who has not seen them in battle," Higginson exulted after a successful raid in Florida in 1863. "There is a fierce energy about them beyond anything of which I have ever read, except it be the French Zouaves [French troops in North Africa]." Even Union soldiers who held blacks in contempt pragmatically came to approve of "anything that will kill a rebel." Furthermore, black recruitment offered new opportunities for whites to secure commissions, for blacks served in separate regiments under white officers. Colonel Robert Gould Shaw of the Fifty-fourth Massachusetts Infantry, an elite black regiment, died in combat—as did half his troops—in an attack on Fort Wagner in Charleston harbor in July 1863.

Black soldiers suffered a far higher mortality rate than white troops. Typically assigned to labor detachments or garrison duty, blacks were less likely than whites to be killed in action but more likely to die of

Flag of the Second Regiment of U.S. Colored Troops; Black Artillerymen
Black troops, organized after the Emancipation Proclamation, fought under flags such as the Second Regiment colors. The soldiers in the photograph belonged to the Second U.S. Colored Light Artillery, which took part in the Battle of Nashville in 1864.

disease in the bacteria-ridden garrisons. In addition, the Confederacy refused to treat captured black soldiers as prisoners of war, a policy that denied captured blacks the opportunity to be exchanged for Confederate prisoners. Instead, Jefferson Davis ordered all blacks taken in battle to be sent back to the states from which they came, where they were reenslaved or executed. In an especially gruesome incident, when Confederate troops captured Fort Pillow, Tennessee, in 1864, they massacred 262 blacks—an action that provoked outcries but no retaliation from the North.

Well into the war, black soldiers faced inequities in their pay. In contrast to white soldiers, who earned $13.00 a month plus a $3.50 clothing allowance, black privates received only $10.00 a month, with clothing deducted. "We have come out Like men and we Expected to be Treated as men but we have bin Treated more Like Dogs then men," a black soldier complained to Secretary of War Edwin Stanton. In June 1864 Congress belatedly equalized the pay of black and white soldiers.

Although fraught with hardships and inequities, military service was a symbol of citizenship for blacks. It proved that "black men can give blows as well as take them," Frederick Douglass declared. "Liberty won by white men would lose half its lustre." A black private explained: "If we hadn't become sojers, all might have gone back as it was before. But now things can never go back because we have showed our energy and our courage . . . and our natural manhood." Above all, the use of black soldiers, especially former slaves, was seen by northern generals as a major strike at the Confederacy. "They will make good soldiers," General Grant wrote to Lincoln in 1863, "and taking them from the enemy weakens him in the same proportion they strengthen us."

Slavery in Wartime

Anxious white southerners on the home front felt as if they were perched on a volcano. "We should be practically helpless should the negroes rise," declared a Louisiana planter's daughter, "since there are so few men left at home." When Mary Boykin Chesnut of South Carolina learned that her cousin had been murdered in bed by two trusted house slaves, she became almost frantic. "The murder," Chesnut wrote, "has clearly driven us all wild." To maintain control over their 3 million black slaves, white southerners resorted to a variety of measures. They tightened slave patrols,

at times moved entire plantations to relative safety in Texas or in the upland regions of the coastal South, and spread scare stories among the slaves. "The whites would tell the colored people not to go to the Yankees, for they would harness them to carts . . . in place of horses," reported Susie King Taylor, a black fugitive from Savannah.

Wartime developments had a mixed effect on the slaves. Some remained faithful to their owners and helped hide treasured family belongings from marauding Union soldiers. Others were torn between loyalty and lust for freedom: one body servant, for example, accompanied his master to war, rescued him when he was wounded, and then escaped on his master's horse. Given a clear choice between freedom and bondage, slaves usually chose freedom. Few slaves helped the North as dramatically as Robert Smalls, a hired-out slave boatman who turned over a Confederate steamer to the Union navy, but most slaves who had a chance to flee to Union lines did so. The idea of freedom held irresistible appeal. Upon learning from a Union soldier that he was free, a Virginia coachman dressed in his master's clothes, "put on his best watch and chain, took his stick, and . . . told him that he might for the future drive his own coach."

The majority of slaves, however, had no escape and remained on their plantations under the nominal control of their masters. Despite the fears of southern whites, no general uprising of slaves occurred; and the Confederate war effort continued to utilize slave labor. The Confederacy impressed thousands of slaves to work in war plants, to toil as teamsters and cooks in army camps, and to serve as nurses in field hospitals. But wartime conditions reduced the slaves' productivity. With most of the white men off at war, the master-slave relationship weakened. The women and boys who remained on plantations complained of their difficulty in controlling slaves, who commonly refused to work, performed their labors inefficiently, or even destroyed property. A Texas wife contended that her slaves were "trying all they can, it seems to me, to aggravate me" by neglecting the stock, breaking plows, and tearing down fences. "You may give your Negroes away," she finally wrote despairingly to her husband in 1864.

Whether southern slaves fled to freedom or merely stopped working, they effectively undermined the plantation system. Thus southern slavery disintegrated even as the Confederacy fought to preserve it. Hard pressed by Union armies, short of manpower, and unsettled by the erosion of plantation slavery, the

Confederate Congress in 1864 considered the drastic step of impressing slaves into its army as soldiers in exchange for their freedom at the war's end. Robert E. Lee favored the use of slaves as soldiers on the grounds that if the Confederacy did not arm its slaves, the Union would. Others, however, were adamantly opposed. "If slaves will make good soldiers," a Georgia general argued, "our whole theory of slavery is wrong." Originally against arming slaves, Jefferson Davis changed his mind in 1865. In March 1865 the Confederate Congress narrowly passed a bill to arm three hundred thousand slave soldiers, although it omitted any mention of emancipation. As the war ended a few weeks later, however, the plan was never put into effect.

Although the Confederacy's decision to arm the slaves came too late to affect the war, the debate over arming them damaged southern morale by revealing deep internal disagreements concerning war goals. Even before these conflicts had become obvious, the South's military position had started to deteriorate.

The Turning Point of 1863

In the summer and fall of 1863, Union fortunes dramatically improved in every theater of the war. Yet the year began badly for the North. The slide, which had started with Burnside's defeat at Fredericksburg, Virginia, in December 1862, continued into the spring of 1863. Burnside's successor, General Joseph "Fighting Joe" Hooker, a windbag fond of issuing pompous proclamations to his troops, devised a plan to dislodge the Confederates from Fredericksburg by crossing the Rappahannock River north of the town and descending on the rebel rear. But Lee and Stonewall Jackson beat Hooker to the punch by routing him at Chancellorsville, Virginia, early in May 1863. The battle proved costly for the South, because Jackson was accidentally shot by Confederate pickets and died a few days later. Because Hooker had twice as many men as Lee, however, the Union defeat at Chancellorsville was especially humiliating for the North. "What will the country say?" Lincoln moaned. News from the West was no more heartening for the Union. Although repulsed at Shiloh in western Tennessee, the Confederates still had a powerful army in central Tennessee under General Braxton Bragg. Furthermore, despite repeated efforts, Grant was unable to take Vicksburg; the two-hundred-mile stretch of the Mississippi between Vicksburg and Port Hudson remained in rebel hands.

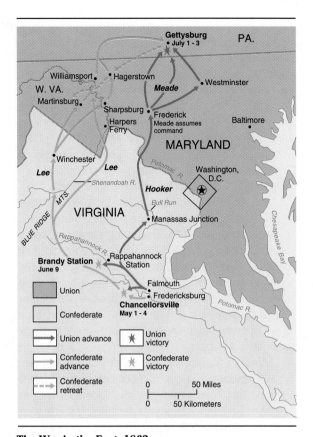

The War in the East, 1863
Victorious at Chancellorsville in May 1863, Lee again invaded Union territory but was decisively stopped at Gettysburg.

The upswing in Union fortunes began with Lee's decision after Chancellorsville to invade the North. The decision provoked dissent within the Confederate government, and Lincoln suspected that Lee was making a big mistake, but Lee had his reasons. He needed supplies that war-wracked Virginia could no longer provide, he hoped to panic Lincoln into moving troops from besieged Vicksburg to the eastern theater, and he thought that a major Confederate victory on northern soil would tip the balance in northern politics to the pro-peace Democrats and gain European recognition of the Confederacy. Moving his seventy-five thousand men down the Shenandoah Valley, Lee crossed the Potomac into Maryland and pressed forward into southern Pennsylvania. At this point, with Lee's army far to the west of Richmond, Hooker recommended a Union stab at the Confederate capital. But Lincoln brushed aside the advice. "Lee's *army*, and not *Richmond*, is

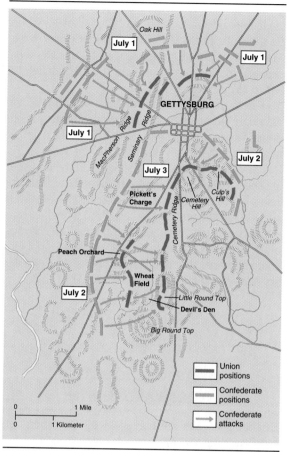

Gettysburg, 1863

The failure of Pickett's charge against the Union center on July 3 was the decisive action in the war's greatest battle.

and instead attacked the Union flanks, with some success. But because the Confederate assaults were uncoordinated, and some southern generals disregarded orders and struck where they chose, the Union was able to move in reinforcements and regain its earlier losses.

By the afternoon of July 3, believing that the Union flanks had been weakened, Lee attacked Cemetery Ridge in the center of the North's defensive line. After southern cannon shelled the line, a massive infantry force of fifteen thousand Confederates, Pickett's charge, moved in. But as the Confederate cannon sank into the ground and fired a shade too high, and as Union fire wiped out the rebel charge, rifled weapons proved their deadly effectiveness. At the end of the day, Confederate bodies littered the field. "The dead and the dying were lying by the thousands between the two lines," a dazed Louisiana soldier wrote. "The enemy seemed to be launching his cavalry to sweep the remaining handful of men from the face of the earth." A little more than half of Pickett's troops were dead, wounded, or captured in the horrible encounter. When Lee withdrew to Virginia on July 4, he had lost seventeen generals and over one-third of his army. Total Union and Confederate casualties numbered almost fifty thousand. Despite the Confederate defeat, Gettysburg was not a model Union victory, since Meade failed to pursue and destroy the retreating rebels. Still, because he had halted Lee's foray into the North, the Union rejoiced.

Almost simultaneously, the North won a less bloody but more strategic victory in the West, where Grant finally solved the puzzle posed by Vicksburg's defenses. Situated on a bluff on the east bank of the Mississippi, Vicksburg was protected on the west by the river and on the north by hills, forests, and swamps. Vicksburg could be attacked only over a thin strip of dry land to its east and south. Positioned to the north of Vicksburg, Grant had to find a way to get his army south of the city and onto the Mississippi's east bank. His solution lay in moving his troops far to the west of the city and down to a point on the river south of Vicksburg. Meanwhile, Union gunboats and supply ships ran past the Confederate batteries overlooking the river at Vicksburg (not without sustaining considerable damage) to rendezvous with Grant's army and transport it across to the east bank. Grant then swung in a large semicircle, first northeastward to capture Jackson, the capital of Mississippi, and then westward back to Vicksburg. After a six-week siege, during which famished soldiers and civilians in Vicksburg

your true objective," Lincoln shot back, and then he replaced Hooker with the more reliable George G. Meade.

Early in July 1863, Lee's offensive ground to a halt at a Pennsylvania road junction, Gettysburg. Confederates foraging for shoes in the town encountered some Union cavalry. Soon both sides called for reinforcements, and the war's greatest battle commenced. On July 1 Meade's troops installed themselves in hills south of town along a line that resembled a fishhook: the shank ran along Cemetery Ridge and a northern hook encircled Culp's Hill. By the end of the first day of fighting, most of the troops on both sides had arrived: Meade's army outnumbered the Confederates ninety thousand to seventy-five thousand. On July 2 Lee rejected advice to plant the Confederate army in a defensive position between Meade's forces and Washington

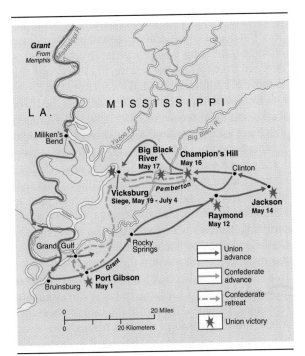

The War in the West, 1863: Vicksburg
Grant first moved his army west of Vicksburg to a point on the Mississippi south of the town. Then he marched northeast, taking Jackson, and finally west to Vicksburg.

were reduced to eating mules and even rats, General John C. Pemberton surrendered his thirty-thousand-man garrison to Grant on July 4, the day after Pickett's charge at Gettysburg. Port Hudson, the last Confederate holdout on the Mississippi, soon surrendered to another Union army. "The Father of Waters flows unvexed to the sea," Lincoln declared.

Before the year was out, the Union won another crucial victory in the West. General William S. Rosecrans fought and maneuvered Braxton Bragg's Confederate army out of central Tennessee and into Chattanooga, in the southeastern tip of the state, and then forced Bragg to evacuate Chattanooga. Bragg defeated the pursuing Rosecrans at the Battle of Chickamauga (September 19–20, 1863), one of the bloodiest of the war, and drove him back into Chattanooga. But the arrival of Grant and of reinforcements from the Army of the Potomac enabled the North to break Bragg's siege of Chattanooga in November. With Chattanooga secure, the way lay open for a Union strike into Georgia.

Coming on the heels of reverses that had driven northern morale to its lowest point of the war, Union successes in the second half of 1863 stiffened the North's will to keep fighting and plunged some rebel leaders into despair. Hearing of the fall of Vicksburg, Confederate ordnance chief Josiah Gorgas wrote, "Yesterday we rode the pinnacle of success—today absolute ruin seems our portion. The Confederacy totters to its destruction."

Totter it might, but the South was far from beaten. Although the outcome at Gettysburg quashed southerners' hopes for victory on northern soil, it did not significantly impair Lee's ability to defend Virginia. The loss of Vicksburg and the Mississippi cut the Confederate states west of the river—Arkansas, Louisiana, and Texas—off from those to the east; but these western states could still provide soldiers. Even with the loss of Chattanooga, the Confederacy continued to hold most of the Carolinas, Georgia, Florida, and Mississippi. Few contemporaries thought that the fate of the Confederacy had been sealed.

WAR AND SOCIETY, NORTH AND SOUTH

Extending beyond the battlefields of Gettysburg and Vicksburg, the Civil War engulfed two economies and societies. By 1863 the progress of the war provided stark contrasts: with its superior resources, the Union could meet wartime demands as the imperiled Confederacy could not. But both regions experienced labor shortages and inflation. As the conflict dragged on, both societies confronted problems of disunity and dissent, for war issues opened fissures between social classes. In both regions war encroached on everyday life. Families were disrupted and dislocated, especially in the South. Women on both sides took on new roles at home, in the workplace, and in relief efforts.

The War's Economic Impact: The North

The war had an uneven effect on the Union's economy. Some industries fared poorly. For instance, the loss of southern markets damaged the shoe industry in Massachusetts, where output declined from 45 million pairs in 1855 to 32 million pairs in 1865. A shortage of raw cotton sent the cotton-textile industry into a tailspin that was only partly offset by a rise in the production of woolens. On the other hand, industries directly related to the war effort, such as the manufacture of arms and clothing, benefited from huge government contracts. By 1865, for example, the ready-made clothing industry was receiving orders for more than a million uniforms a year. Military demand also provided abundant business for the railroads. Some privately owned lines, which had overbuilt before the war, doubled the volume of their traffic during the war. In 1862 the federal government itself went into the railroad business by establishing the United States Military Railroads (USMRR) to carry troops and supplies to the front. "The quicker you build the railroad," Union general William T. Sherman told his troops, "the quicker you'll get something to eat." By 1865 the USMRR was the largest railroad in the world.

The Republicans in Congress actively promoted business development during the war. Holding 102 of 146 House seats and 29 of 36 Senate seats in 1861, they overrode Democratic foes and hiked the tariff in 1862 and again in 1864 to protect domestic industries. The Republican-sponsored Pacific Railroad Act of 1862 provided for the development of a transcontinental railroad, an idea that had foundered before the war on disagreements over which route such a railroad should follow. With the South out of the picture and no longer able to demand a southern route from New Orleans across the Southwest, Congress chose a northern route from Omaha to San Francisco. Chartering the Union Pacific and Central Railroad corporations, Congress then gave to each large land grants and generous loans. These two corporations combined received more than 60 million acres in land grants and $20 million in loans from the government. The issuance of greenbacks and the creation of a national banking system, meanwhile, brought a measure of uniformity to the nation's financial system.

By raising the federal government's profile in the North's economy, the Republicans hoped to benefit a variety of social classes. To a degree, they succeeded. Republican measures like the Homestead Act, passed in 1862, embodied the party's ideal of "free soil, free labor, free men" by granting 160 acres of public land to settlers after five years of residence on the land. By 1865 twenty thousand homesteaders occupied new land in the West under the Homestead Act. To bring higher education within the reach of the common people, the Republicans secured passage in 1862 of the Morrill Land Grant Act. This law gave to the states proceeds of public lands—to fund the establishment of universities emphasizing "such branches of learning as

are related to agriculture and mechanic arts." The Morrill Act spurred the growth of large state universities, mainly in the Midwest and West. Michigan State, Iowa State, and Purdue universities, among many others, profited from the law.

Despite the idealistic goals behind some Republican laws, the war benefited the wealthy more than the average citizen. Corrupt contractors grew fat by selling the government substandard merchandise such as the notorious "shoddy," clothing made from compressed rags, which quickly fell apart. Speculators who locked their patriotism in the closet made millions in the gold market. Because the price of gold in relation to greenbacks rose whenever public confidence in the government fell, those who bought gold in the hope that its price would rise actually gained from Union defeats, and even more from Union disasters. Businessmen with access to scarce commodities also reaped astounding profits. For example, manpower shortages stimulated wartime demand for the mechanical reaper that Cyrus McCormick had patented in 1834. McCormick also profited from his distrust of the greenbacks. When paid for reapers in greenbacks, he immediately reinvested them in pig iron and then watched in glee as wartime demand drove the price of pig iron from twenty-three dollars to forty dollars a ton.

The war had a far less happy impact on ordinary workers. Protected from foreign competition by higher tariffs, northern manufacturers hoisted the prices of finished goods. Wartime excise taxes and inflation combined to push prices still higher. At the same time, wages lagged 20 percent or more behind cost increases for most of the war. This lag in wages, common in most periods of rapid inflation, became especially severe during the war because boys and women poured into government offices and factories as replacements for adult male workers who had joined the army. Not only did the new workers draw lower pay than the men whom they had replaced, but employers' mere threats of hiring more youths and females undercut the bargaining power of the men who remained in the work force.

Some workers organized to decry their low wages. "We are unable to sustain life for the price offered by contractors who fatten on their contracts," Cincinnati seamstresses declared in a petition to President Lincoln. Cigar makers and locomotive engineers formed national unions, a process that would accelerate after the war. But organized protests had little impact on wages; employers often denounced worker protests as unpatriotic hindrances to the war effort. In 1864 army troops were diverted from combat to put down protests in war industries from New York to the Midwest.

The War's Economic Impact: The South

Although stimulating some sectors of the North's economy, the war shattered the South's. Indeed, if both regions are considered together, the overall impact of the war was to retard *American* economic growth. For example, the commodity output of the American economy, which had registered huge increases of 51 percent and 62 percent in the 1840s and 1850s, respectively, rose only 22 percent during the 1860s. Even this modest gain depended wholly on the North, for in the 1860s commodity output in the South actually *declined* 39 percent.

Substantial wartime industrial growth by the South was more than offset by other factors. For example, the war wrecked the South's railroads; in 1864 Union troops, marching through Georgia under General William T. Sherman, tore up railroad tracks, heated them in giant fires, and twisted them into "Sherman neckties." Cotton production, once the foundation of the South's prosperity, sank from more than 4 million bales in 1861 to 300,000 bales in 1865 as Union invasions took their toll on production, particularly in Tennessee and Louisiana.

Invading Union troops also occupied the South's food-growing as well as cotton-producing regions. Moreover, in agricultural areas under Confederate control, the drain of manpower into the army decreased the yields per acre of crops like wheat and corn. Even the loss of a few carpenters and blacksmiths could disrupt the economy of rural districts. For example, the drafting of certain of their craftsmen, complained some Alabama petitioners to the federal government in 1863, had left their county "entirely Destitute of any man that is able to keep in order any kind of Farming Tules." Food shortages abounded late in the war. "The people are subsisting on the ungathered crops and nine families out of ten are left without meat," a Mississippi citizen lamented in 1864.

Agricultural shortages worsened the South's already severe inflation. By 1863 salt selling for $1.25 a sack in New York City cost $60.00 in the Confederacy. Food riots erupted in 1863 in Mobile, Atlanta, and Richmond; in Richmond the wives of ironworkers paraded to demand lower food prices.

Part of the blame for the South's food shortages rested with the planter class itself. Although some planters heeded government pleas to shift from cotton to food production, and cotton crops declined sharply

Destroying Railroad Track

As the Union general William T. Sherman invaded Georgia, his troops demolished Confederate property of military value, such as arsenals and railroads. These Union soldiers in Atlanta break up a railroad track before setting forth on their march to the sea. The damaged rails that they left behind, often bent out of shape to form "Sherman neckties," may still be found in parts of the South.

overall, many planters still raised more cotton than they could market abroad. The consequences were far-reaching. Slave labor, which could have been diverted to army camps, where slaves might have relieved soldiers of menial tasks, remained essential on the cotton plantations. This increased the Confederacy's reliance on its unpopular conscription laws. Moreover, cotton continued to sprout from land that could have been used for food production. To feed its hungry armies, the Confederacy had to resort to impressing food from civilians. This policy not only elicited resentment of planters but contributed to the South's mounting military desertions. Food-impressment agents usually concentrated on the easiest targets—farms run by the wives of active soldiers. Soldiers found it hard to resist desperate pleas to return home. The wife of an Alabama soldier wrote to him: "We haven't got nothing in the house to eat but a little bit o meal. I don't want you to stop fighting them Yankees . . . but try and get off and come home and fix us all up some and then you can go back." By the end of 1864, half of the Confederacy's soldiers were absent from their units.

In one respect, the persistence of cotton growing did aid the South, because cotton became the basis for the Confederacy's flourishing trade with the enemy. The U.S. Congress virtually legalized this trade in July 1861 by allowing northern commerce with southerners loyal to the Union. In practice, of course, it proved impossible to tell loyalists from disloyalists, and for most traders it hardly mattered. As long as Union textile mills stood idle for lack of cotton, northern traders happily swapped bacon, salt, blankets, and other necessaries for southern cotton. The Union's penetration of the Confederate heartland eased business dealings between the two sides. By 1864 traffic through the lines was providing the South with enough food daily to feed the entire Army of Northern Virginia. To a northern congressman, it seemed that the Union's policy was "to feed an army and fight it at the same time."

Trading with the enemy alleviated the South's food shortages but intensified its morale problems. The prospect of traffic with the Yankees gave planters an incentive to keep growing cotton, and it fattened merchants and middlemen. "Oh! the extortioners," complained a Confederate war-office clerk in Richmond. "Our patriotism is mainly in the army and among the ladies of the South. The avarice and cupidity of men at home could only be exceeded by ravenous wolves."

Dealing with Dissent

Both wartime governments faced mounting dissent and disloyalty. Within the Confederacy, dissent took two basic forms. First, a vocal group of states' rights activists, notably Vice President Alexander Stephens and governors Zebulon Vance of North Carolina and Joseph Brown of Georgia, spent much of the war attacking Jefferson Davis's government as a despotism. Second, loyalty to the Union flourished among a segment of the Confederacy's common people, particularly those living in the Appalachian Mountain region that ran from western North Carolina through eastern Tennessee and into northern Georgia and Alabama. The nonslaveholding small farmers who predominated here saw the Confederate rebellion as a slaveowners' conspiracy. Resentful of such measures as the 20-Negro exemption from conscription, they were reluctant to fight for what a North Carolinian defined as "an adored trinity, cotton, niggers, and chivalry." "All they want," an Alabama farmer complained of the planters, "is to get you pupt up and to fight for their infurnal negroes and after you do there fighting you may kiss there hine parts for o they care." On the whole, the Confederate government responded mildly to popular disaffection. In 1862 the Confederate Congress gave Jefferson Davis the power to suspend the writ of habeas corpus, but Davis used his power only sparingly, by occasionally and briefly putting areas under martial law, mainly to aid tax collectors.

Lincoln faced similar challenges in the North, where the Democratic minority opposed both emancipation and the wartime growth of centralized power. Although "War Democrats" conceded that war was necessary to preserve the Union, "Peace Democrats" (called Copperheads by their opponents, to suggest a resemblance to a species of easily concealed poisonous snakes) disagreed. Demanding a truce and a peace conference, they charged that administration war policy was intended to "exterminate the South," make reconciliation impossible, and spark "terrible social change and revolution" nationwide.

Strongest in the border states, the Midwest, and the northeastern cities, the Democrats mobilized the support of farmers of southern background in the Ohio Valley and of members of the urban working class, especially recent immigrants, who feared losing their jobs to an influx of free blacks. In 1863 this volatile brew of political, ethnic, racial, and class antagonisms in northern society exploded into antidraft protests in several cities. By far the most violent eruption occurred in July in New York City. Catalyzed by the first drawing of names under the Enrollment Act, and by a long-shoremen's strike in which blacks had been used as strikebreakers, mobs of Irish working-class men and women roamed the streets for four days until suppressed by federal troops. The city's laboring Irish loathed the idea of being drafted to fight a war on behalf of the slaves, who, once emancipated, might migrate north to compete with them for low-paying jobs. Too, they bitterly resented the provision of the draft law that allowed the rich to purchase substitutes. The Irish mobs' targets revealed the scope of their grievances. The rioters lynched at least a dozen blacks, injured hundreds more, and burned draft offices, the homes of wealthy Republicans, and the Colored Orphan Asylum.

President Lincoln's speedy dispatch of federal troops to quash these riots typified his forceful response to dissent. Throughout the war, Lincoln imposed martial law with far less hesitancy than Davis. After suspending the writ of habeas corpus in Maryland in 1861, he barred it nationwide in 1863 and authorized the arrest of rebels, draft resisters, and those engaged in "any disloyal practice." The differing responses of Davis and Lincoln to dissent underscored the differences between the two regions' wartime political systems. As we have seen, Davis lacked the institutionalization of dissent provided by party conflict and thus had to tread warily, lest his opponents brand him a despot. In contrast, Lincoln and other Republicans used dissent to rally patriotic fervor against the Democrats. After the New York City draft riots, for example, the Republicans blamed the violence on New York's antidraft Democratic governor, Horatio Seymour. When Seymour, rushing to the city to quell the disturbances, addressed a crowd of rioters as "my friends," the Republican press had a field day branding the Democrats as disloyal.

Forceful as he was, Lincoln did not unleash a reign of terror against dissent. In general, the North preserved freedom of the press, speech, and assembly. In 1864 the Union became the first warring nation in history to hold a contested national election. Moreover, although some fifteen thousand civilians were arrested during the war, most were quickly released. A few cases, however, aroused widespread concern. In 1864 a military commission sentenced an Indiana man to be hanged for an alleged plot to free Confederate prisoners. The Supreme Court reversed his conviction two years later when it ruled that civilians could not be tried by military courts when the civil courts were open (*Ex parte* Milligan, 1866). Of more concern were the arrests of politicians, notably Clement L. Vallandigham, an Ohio Peace Democrat. Courting arrest, Vallandigham challenged the administration, denounced the suspension of habeas corpus, proposed an armistice, and in 1863 was sentenced to jail for the rest of the war by a military commission. When Ohio Democrats then nominated him for governor, Lincoln changed the sentence to banishment. Escorted to enemy lines in Tennessee, Vallandigham was left in the hands of bewildered Confederates and eventually escaped to Canada. The Supreme Court refused to review his case.

The Medical War

Despite the discontent and disloyalty of some citizens, both the Union and the Confederacy witnessed a remarkable wartime patriotism that propelled civilians, especially women, to work tirelessly toward alleviating the suffering of soldiers. The United States Sanitary Commission, organized early in the war by civilians to assist the Union's medical bureau, consisted mainly of women volunteers. Described as a "great artery that bears the people's love to the army," the commission raised funds at "sanitary fairs," bought and distributed supplies, ran special kitchens to supplement army rations, tracked down the missing, and inspected army camps. The volunteers' exploits became legendary. One poor widow, Mary Ann "Mother" Bickerdyke, served sick and wounded Union soldiers as both nurse and surrogate mother. When asked by a doctor by what authority she demanded supplies for the wounded, she shot back, "From the Lord God Almighty. Do you have anything that ranks higher than that?"

Women also reached out to aid the battlefront through the nursing corps. Before the war ended, some thirty-two hundred women served the Union and the Confederacy as nurses. Already famed for her tireless campaigns on behalf of the insane, Dorothea Dix became the head of the Union's nursing corps. Clara Barton began the war as a clerk in the U.S. Patent Office, but she, too, greatly aided the medical effort, finding ingenious ways of channeling medicine to the sick and wounded. Catching wind of Union movements before Antietam, Barton showed up at the battlefield on the eve of the clash with a wagonload of supplies. When army surgeons ran out of

Andersonville Prison
*Started in early 1864, the overcrowded Andersonville prison in southwest Georgia provided no shel-
ter for its inmates, who built tent-like structures out of blankets, sticks, or whatever they could find.
Exposure, disease, and poor sanitation contributed to a mortality rate almost double that in other
Confederate prison camps, and made Andersonville a scandal that outlived the war.*

bandages and started to dress wounds with corn husks, she raced forward with lint and bandages. "With what joy," she wrote, "I laid my precious burden down among them." After the war, in 1881, she would found the American Red Cross. The Confederacy, too, had extraordinary nurses. One, Sally Tompkins, was commissioned a captain for her hospital work; another, Belle Boyd, served the Confederacy as both a nurse and a spy and once dashed through a field, waving her bonnet, to give Stonewall Jackson information. Danger stalked nurses even in hospitals far from the front. Author Louisa May Alcott, a nurse at the Union Hotel Hospital in Washington, D.C., contracted typhoid. Wherever they worked, nurses witnessed haunting, unforgettable sights. "About the amputating table," one reported, "lay large piles of human flesh—legs, arms, feet, and hands . . . the stiffened membrances seemed to be clutching oftentimes at our clothing."

Pioneered by British reformer Florence Nightingale in the 1850s, nursing was a new vocation for women and, in the eyes of many, a brazen departure from women's proper sphere. Male doctors were unsure about how to react to female nurses and sanitary workers. Some saw the potential for mischief in attractive women's roaming around male hospital wards. But other doctors viewed nursing and sanitary work as potentially useful. The miasm theory of disease (see Chapter 11) won wide respect among physicians and stimulated some valuable sanitary measures, particularly in hospitals behind the lines. In partial consequence, the ratio of disease to battle deaths was much lower in the Civil War than in the Mexican War.

Still, for every soldier killed during the Civil War, two died of disease. "These Big Battles is not as Bad as the fever," a North Carolina soldier wrote. The scientific investigations that would lead to the germ theory of disease were only commencing during the 1860s. Arm and leg wounds frequently led to gangrene or tetanus, and typhoid, malaria, diarrhea, and dysentery raged through army camps.

Prison camps posed a special problem. Prisoner exchanges between the North and the South, common early in the war, collapsed by midwar, partly because the South refused to exchange the black prisoners it held and partly because the North gradually concluded that exchanges benefited the manpower-short Confederacy more than the Union. As a result, the two sides had far more prisoners than either could handle. Prisoners on both sides suffered gravely from camp conditions. "This cold weather is not just suited to Southern Constitutions," a Mississippian imprisoned in a Union camp in Illinois wrote home. The worst conditions, however, plagued southern camps. Squalor and insufficient rations turned the Confederate prison camp at Andersonville, Georgia, into a virtual death camp; three thousand prisoners a month (out of a total of thirty-two thousand) were dying there by August 1864. After the war an outraged northern public secured the execution of Andersonville's commandant. Although the commandant was partly to blame, the deterioration of the southern economy had contributed massively to the wretched state of southern prison camps. The Union camps were not much better, but the fatality rate among northerners held by the South exceeded that of southerners imprisoned by the North.

The War and Women's Rights

Female nurses and Sanitary Commission workers were not the only women to serve society in wartime. In both northern and southern government offices and mills, thousands of women took over jobs vacated by men. Moreover, home industry revived at all levels of society. In rural areas, where manpower shortages were most acute, women often did the plowing, planting, and harvesting.

Few women worked more effectively for their region's cause than Philadelphia-born Anna E. Dickinson. After losing her job in the federal mint (for denouncing General George McClellan as a traitor), Dickinson threw herself into hospital volunteer work and public lecturing. Her lecture "Hospital Life," recounting the soldiers' sufferings, won the attention of Republican politicians. In 1863, hard pressed by the Democrats, these politicians invited Dickinson, then

scarcely twenty-one, to campaign on behalf of the Republican tickets in New Hampshire and Connecticut. This decision paid handsome dividends for the party. Articulate and poised, Dickinson captured the hearts and votes of her listeners. Soon Republican candidates who had dismissed the offer of aid from a woman begged her to campaign for them.

Mindful of the contributions of Dickinson and others, northern women's rights advocates hoped that the war would yield equality for women as well as for slaves. Not only should a grateful North reward women for their wartime services, these women reasoned, but it should recognize the link between black rights and women's rights. In 1863 feminists Elizabeth Cady Stanton and Susan B. Anthony organized the National Woman's Loyal League. Although the league's main activity was to gather four hundred thousand signatures on a petition calling for a constitutional amendment to abolish slavery, Stanton and Anthony used the organization to promote woman suffrage as well.

Despite high expectations, the war did not bring women significantly closer to economic or political equality. Women in government offices and factories continued to be paid less than men. Sanitary Commission workers and most wartime nurses, as volunteers, earned nothing. Nor did the war produce a major change in the prevailing definition of woman's sphere. In 1860 that sphere already included charitable and benevolent activities; during the war the scope of benevolence grew to embrace organized care for the wounded. Yet men continued to dominate the medical profession, and for the rest of the nineteenth century, nurses would be classified in the census as domestic help.

The keenest disappointment of women's rights advocates lay in their failure to capitalize on rising sentiment for the abolition of slavery to secure the vote for women. Although the North had compelling reasons to abolish slavery in the rebellious areas of the South, northern politicians could see little practical value in woman suffrage. The *New York Herald*, which supported the Loyal League's attack on slavery, dismissed its call for woman suffrage as "nonsense and tomfoolery." Stanton wrote bitterly, "So long as woman labors to second man's endeavors and exalt his sex above her own, her virtues pass unquestioned; but when she dares to demand rights and privileges for herself, her motives, manners, dress, personal appearance, and character are subjects for ridicule and detraction."

THE UNION VICTORIOUS, 1864–1865

Despite successes at Gettysburg and Vicksburg in 1863, the Union stood no closer to taking Richmond at the start of 1864 than in 1861, and most of the Lower South still remained under Confederate control. The constant press of Union invasion had taken its toll on the South's home front, but the North's persistent inability to destroy the main Confederate armies had eroded the Union's will to keep attacking. Northern war weariness strengthened the Democrats and jeopardized Lincoln's prospects for reelection in 1864.

The year 1864 proved crucial for the North. While Grant occupied Lee in the East, a Union army under William T. Sherman attacked from Tennessee into northwestern Georgia and took Atlanta in early September. The fall of Atlanta not only boosted northern morale but contributed to Lincoln's reelection. Now the curtain rose on the last act of the war. After taking Atlanta, Sherman marched across Georgia to Savannah, devastated the state's resources, and cracked its morale. Pivoting north from Savannah, Sherman then moved into South Carolina. Meanwhile, having backed Lee into trenches around Petersburg and Richmond, Grant forced the evacuation of both cities and brought on the Confederacy's collapse.

The Eastern Theater in 1864

Early in 1864 Lincoln made Grant commander of all Union armies and promoted him to lieutenant general. At first glance, the stony-faced Grant seemed an unlikely candidate for so exalted a rank, held previously only by George Washington. Grant, a contemporary noted, "padlocks his mouth, while his countenance in battle or repose . . . indicates nothing." Grant's only distinguishing characteristics were his ever-present cigars and a penchant for whittling sticks into chips. "There is no glitter, no parade about him." But Grant's success in the West had made him the Union's most popular general, perhaps even the Union's most popular person. With his promotion, Grant moved his headquarters to the Army of the Potomac in the East and mapped a strategy for final victory.

Like Lincoln, Grant believed that the Union had to coordinate its attacks on all fronts in order to exploit its numerical advantage and prevent the South from shifting troops back and forth between the eastern and western theaters. (The South's victory at Chickamauga in September 1863, for example, had rested in part on reinforcements sent by Lee to Braxton Bragg in the West.) Accordingly, Grant planned a sustained offensive against Lee in the East while ordering William T. Sherman to attack the rebel army in Georgia commanded by Bragg's replacement, General Joseph Johnston. Sherman's mission was "to break it [the Confederate army] up, and to get into the interior of the enemy's country . . . inflicting all the damage you can."

In early May 1864, Grant led 118,000 men against Lee's 64,000 in a forested area near Fredericksburg, Virginia, called the Wilderness. After being checked by Lee in a series of bloody engagements (the Battle of the Wilderness, May 5–7), Grant tried to swing around Lee's right flank, only to suffer new reverses at Spotsylvania on May 12 and Cold Harbor on June 3. These engagements were among the war's fiercest; at Cold Harbor, Grant lost 7,000 men in one hour. Oliver Wendell Holmes, Jr., a Union lieutenant and later a Supreme Court justice, wrote home how "immense the butcher's bill has been." But Grant refused to interpret repulses as defeats. Rather, he viewed the engagements at the Wilderness, Spotsylvania, and Cold Harbor merely as less than complete victories. Pressing on, he forced Lee to pull back to the trenches guarding Petersburg and Richmond.

Grant had accomplished a major objective, because once entrenched, Lee could no longer swing around to the Union rear, cut Yankee supply lines, or as at Chancellorsville, surprise the Union's main force. Lee did dispatch General Jubal A. Early on raids down the Shenandoah Valley, which the Confederacy had long used both as a granary and as an indirect way to menace Washington. But Grant countered by ordering General Philip Sheridan to march up the valley from the north and so devastate it that a crow flying over would have to carry its own provisions. The time had come, a Union chaplain wrote, "to peel this land." After defeating Early at Winchester, Virginia, in September 1864, Sheridan controlled the valley.

Sherman in Georgia

While Grant and Lee grappled in the Wilderness, Sherman advanced into Georgia at the head of 98,000 men. Opposing him with 53,000 Confederate troops (soon reinforced to 65,000), General Joseph Johnston

The Election of 1864

Candidates	Parties	Electoral Vote	Popular Vote	Percentage of Popular Vote
ABRAHAM LINCOLN	Republican	212	2,206,938	55.0
George B. McClellan	Democratic	21	1,803,787	45.0

retreated toward Atlanta. Johnston's plan was to conserve strength for a final defense of Atlanta while forcing Sherman to extend his supply lines. But Jefferson Davis, dismayed by Johnston's defensive strategy, replaced him with the adventurous John B. Hood. Hood, who lost the use of an arm at Gettysburg and a leg at Chickamauga, had to be strapped to his saddle; but for all his disabilities, he liked to take risks. In a prewar poker game, he had bet $2,500 with "nary a pair in his hand." Hood gave Davis what he wanted, a series of attacks on Sherman's army. The forays, however, failed to dislodge Sherman and severely depleted Hood's army. No longer able to defend Atlanta's supply lines, Hood evacuated the city, which Sherman took on September 2, 1864.

The Election of 1864

Atlanta's fall came at a timely moment for Lincoln, who was in the thick of a tough reelection campaign. Indeed, Lincoln had secured the Republican renomination with great difficulty. The Radicals, who had earlier flayed Lincoln for delay in adopting emancipation as a war goal, now dismissed his plans to restore the occupied parts of Tennessee, Louisiana, and Arkansas to the Union. The Radicals insisted that Congress, not the president, could alone set the requirements for readmission of conquered states and criticized Lincoln's reconstruction standards as too lenient. Whereas the Radicals rallied around Secretary of the Treasury Salmon P. Chase for the nomination, the Democrats attacked from a different direction. They had never forgiven Lincoln for making emancipation a war goal, and now the Copperheads, or Peace Democrats, demanded an immediate armistice, followed by negotiations between the North and the South to settle outstanding issues.

Although facing formidable challenges, Lincoln benefited from both his own resourcefulness and that of his political enemies. Playing his hand too quickly and openly, Chase turned the early boom for his nom-

ination into a bust. By the time of the Republican convention in July, Lincoln's managers were firmly in control. Moreover, to isolate the Peace Democrats and attract prowar Democrats, the Republicans formed a temporary organization, the National Union party, and replaced Lincoln's vice president, Hannibal Hamlin, with a prowar southern Unionist, Democratic senator Andrew Johnson of Tennessee. This tactic helped exploit the widening division among the Democrats, who nominated George B. McClellan, the former commander of the Army of the Potomac and an advocate of continuing the war until the Confederacy's collapse, and then ran him on a platform written by the Peace Democrats. McClellan spent much of his campaign distancing himself from his party's peace-without-victory platform.

Despite the Democrats' disarray, as late as August 1864, Lincoln seriously doubted that he would be reelected. Leaving little to chance, he arranged for furloughs so that Union soldiers, most of whom supported Lincoln, could vote in states lacking absentee ballots. But in the end it was chance, the timely fall of Atlanta, that aided him. Although Hood's army had escaped from the city, a Richmond newspaper conceded that the "disaster at Atlanta" had punctured the northern antiwar movement and saved Lincoln's presidency. With 55 percent of the popular vote and 212 out of 233 electoral votes, Lincoln swept to victory.

Sherman's March Through Georgia

Meanwhile, Sherman gave the South a new lesson in total war. After evacuating Atlanta, Hood led his Confederate army north toward Tennessee in the hope of luring Sherman out of Georgia. But Sherman did not rise to the bait. The war would never be won, he concluded, by chasing Hood around Tennessee and stretching his own supply lines to the breaking point. Rather, Sherman proposed to abandon his supply lines altogether, march his army across Georgia to Savannah, and live off the countryside as he moved along. He

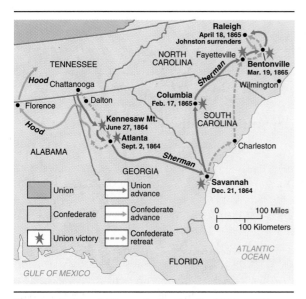

Sherman's March Through the South, 1864–1865

would break the South's will to fight, terrify its people, and "make war so terrible . . . that generations would pass before they could appeal again to it."

Sherman began by burning much of Atlanta and forcing the evacuation of most of its civilian population. This harsh measure relieved him of the need to feed and garrison the city. Then, sending enough troops north to ensure the futility of Hood's campaign in Tennessee, he led the bulk of his army, sixty-two thousand men, out of Atlanta to start the 285-mile trek to Savannah. Soon thousands of slaves were following the army. "Dar's de man dat rules the world," a slave cried on seeing Sherman. Sherman's four columns of infantry, augmented by cavalry screens, moved on a front sixty miles wide and at a pace of ten miles a day. They destroyed everything that could aid southern resistance—arsenals, railroads, munitions plants, cotton gins, cotton stores, crops, and livestock. The ruin far exceeded Sherman's orders. Moreover, although Sherman's troops were told not to destroy civilian property, foragers carried out their own version of total war, ransacking and sometimes demolishing homes. Indeed, the havoc seemed a vital part of Sherman's own strategy. By the time he occupied Savannah and made contact with the Union navy, he estimated that his army had destroyed about a hundred million dollars worth of property. After taking Savannah in December 1864, Sherman's army wheeled north toward South Carolina, the first state

to secede and, in the general's view, one "that deserves all that seems in store for her." Sherman's columns advanced unimpeded to Columbia, South Carolina's capital. After fires set by looters, slaves, soldiers of both sides, and liberated Union prisoners gutted much of the city, Sherman headed for North Carolina. By the spring of 1865, his army had left over four hundred miles of ruin. Other Union armies moved into Alabama and Georgia and took thousands of prisoners. Northern forces had penetrated the entire Confederacy, except for Texas and Florida, and crushed its wealth. "War is cruelty and you cannot refine it," Sherman wrote. "Those who brought war into our country deserve all the curses and maledictions a people can pour out."

Toward Appomattox

While Sherman headed north, Grant renewed his assault on the entrenched Army of Northern Virginia. Grant's main objective was Petersburg, a city south of Richmond through which most of the rail lines to the Confederate capital passed. Although Grant had failed on several occasions to overwhelm the Confederate defenses in front of Petersburg, the fall of Atlanta and Sherman's subsequent march through Georgia and into the Carolinas had taken their toll on Confederate morale. Rebel soldiers were accustomed to shortages of food and clothing, but now they were burdened as well by growing hopelessness. Rebel desertions, proportionately about the same as Union desertions until 1864, reached epidemic proportions in the winter of 1864–1865. Lee reported hundreds of his men deserting every night. Reinforced by Sheridan's army, triumphant from its campaign in the Shenandoah Valley, Grant late in March 1865 swung his forces around the western flank of Petersburg's defenders. Lee could not stop him. On April 2 Sheridan smashed the rebel flank at the Battle of Five Forks. A courier bore the grim news to Jefferson Davis, attending church in Richmond: "General Lee telegraphs that he can hold his position no longer."

Davis left his pew, gathered his government, and fled the city. In the morning of April 3, Union troops entered Richmond, pulled down the Confederate flag, and ran up the Stars and Stripes over the capitol. As white and black regiments entered in triumph, explosions set by retreating Confederates left the city "a sea of flames." "Over all," wrote a Union officer, "hung a canopy of dense smoke lighted up now and then by

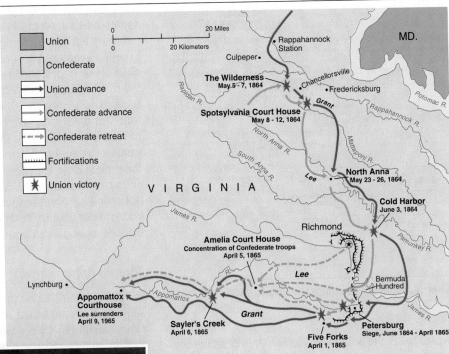

The Final Virginia Campaign, 1864–1865
Refusing to abandon his campaign in the face of enormous casualties, Grant finally pushed Lee (below) into defensive fortifications around Petersburg, whose fall doomed Richmond. When Lee tried to escape to the west, Grant cut him off and forced his surrender.

the bursting shells from the numerous arsenals throughout the city." Fires damaged the Tredegar Iron Works. Union troops liberated the town jail, which housed slaves awaiting sale, and its rejoicing inmates poured into the streets. On April 4 Lincoln toured the city and, for a few minutes, sat at Jefferson Davis's desk with a dreamy expression on his face.

Meanwhile, Lee was making a last-ditch effort to escape from Grant and from Sheridan's enveloping movements. Lee's destination was Lynchburg, sixty miles west of Petersburg. He planned to use the rail connections at Lynchburg to join General Joseph Johnston's army, which Sherman had pushed into North Carolina. But Grant and Sheridan swiftly choked off Lee's escape route, and on April 9 Lee bowed to the inevitable. He asked for terms of surrender and met Grant in a private home in the village of Appomattox Courthouse, Virginia, east of Lynchburg. While stunned troops gathered outside, Lee appeared in full dress uniform, with a sword. Grant entered in his customary disarray, smoking a cigar. When Union troops began to fire celebratory salutes, Grant put a stop to it. The final surrender of Lee's army occurred four days later. Lee's troops laid down their arms between federal ranks. "On our part," wrote a Union officer, "not a sound of trumpet . . . nor roll of drum; not a cheer ... but an awed stillness rather." Grant paroled Lee's twenty-six thousand men and sent them home with their horses and mules "to work their little farms." The remnants of Confederate resistance collapsed within a month of Appomattox. Johnston surrendered to Sherman on April 18. While jubilation swept the North, Jefferson Davis was captured in Georgia on May 10.

Grant returned to Washington. On April 14 he turned down a theater date with the Lincolns, because Julia Grant found first lady Mary Lincoln overbearing. That night at Ford's Theater, an unemployed pro-Confederate actor, John Wilkes Booth, entered Lincoln's box and shot him in the head. Waving a knife, Booth leaped onstage shouting the Virginia state motto, *"Sic semper tyrannis"* ("Such is always the fate of tyrants") and then escaped, despite having broken his leg. That same night, a Booth accomplice stabbed Secretary of State Seward, who later recovered, while a third conspirator, assigned to Vice President Johnson, failed to attack. Union troops hunted down Booth and shot him within two weeks, or else he shot himself. Of eight accused accomplices, including a woman boardinghouse keeper, four were hanged and the rest imprisoned. On April 15, when Lincoln died, Andrew Johnson became president. Six days later Lincoln's funeral train departed on a mournful journey from Washington to Springfield, Illinois, with crowds of thousands gathering at stations to weep as it passed.

CONCLUSION

The Civil War took a larger human toll than any other war in American history. The death count stood at 360,000 Union soldiers and 260,000 Confederates. Most families in the nation suffered losses. Vivid reminders of the human toll remained beyond the end of the century. For many years armless and legless veterans gathered at regimental reunions. Citizens erected monuments to the dead in front of town halls and on village greens. Soldiers' widows collected pensions well into the twentieth century.

The economic costs were staggering, but the war did not ruin the national economy, only the southern part of it. The vast Confederate losses, about 60 percent of southern wealth, were offset by northern advances. At the war's end, the North had almost all of the nation's wealth and capacity for production. Spurring economic modernization, the war provided a hospitable climate for industrial development and capital investment. "The truth is," wrote Ohio senator John Sherman to his brother, General William T. Sherman, "the close of the war with our resources unimpaired gives an elevation, a scope to the ideas of leading capitalists, far higher than anything undertaken in this country before." No longer the largest slaveowning power in the world, the United States would now become a major industrial nation.

The war had political as well as economic ramifications. It created a "more perfect Union" in place of the prewar federation of states. The doctrine of states' rights did not disappear, but it was shorn of its extreme features. There would be no further talk of secession, nor would states ever again exercise their antebellum range of powers. The national banking system, created in 1863, gradually supplanted state banks. The greenbacks provided a national currency. The federal government had exercised powers that many in 1860 doubted it possessed. By abolishing slavery and imposing an income tax, it asserted power over kinds of private property once thought untouchable. The war also promoted large-scale organization in both the business world and public life. The giant railroad corporation, with its thousands of employees, and the huge Sanitary Commission, with its thousands of auxiliaries and volunteers, pointed out the road that the nation increasingly would take.

Finally, the Civil War fulfilled abolitionist prophecies as well as Unionist goals. The war produced the very sort of radical upheaval within southern society that Lincoln originally said that it would not induce. Beaten Confederates had no idea of what to expect. Some wondered whether blacks and Yankees would permanently take over the South. The same thought occurred to the freedmen. "Hello, massa," a black Union soldier called out when he spotted his former owner among a group of Confederate prisoners whom he was guarding. "Bottom rail top dis time." The nation now turned its attention to the reconstruction of the conquered South and to the fate of 3.5 million newly freed slaves.

CHRONOLOGY

1861 President Abraham Lincoln calls for volunteers to suppress the rebellion (April).

Virginia, Arkansas, Tennessee, and North Carolina join the Confederacy (April–May).

Lincoln imposes a naval blockade on the South (April).

First Battle of Bull Run (July).

First Confiscation Act (August).

Sheet Music

1862 Legal Tender Act (February).

George B. McClellan's Peninsula Campaign (March–July).

Battle of Shiloh (April).

Confederate Congress passes the Conscription Act (April).

David G. Farragut captures New Orleans (April).

Homestead Act (May).

Seven Days' Battles (June–July).

Pacific Railroad Act (July).

Morrill Land Grant Act (July).

Second Confiscation Act (July).

Second Battle of Bull Run (August).

Battle of Antietam (September).

1862 Preliminary Emancipation Proclamation (September). Battle of Fredericksburg (December).

1863 Emancipation Proclamation issued (January).

Lincoln suspends writ of habeas corpus nationwide (January).

National Bank Act (February).

Congress passes the Enrollment Act (March).

Battle of Chancellorsville (May).

Battle of Gettysburg (July).

Surrender of Vicksburg (July).

New York City draft riots (July).

Battle of Chickamauga (September).

1864 Ulysses S. Grant given command of all Union armies (March).

Battle of the Wilderness (May).

Battle of Spotsylvania (May).

Battle of Cold Harbor (June).

Surrender of Atlanta (September).

Lincoln reelected (November).

William T. Sherman's march to the sea (November–December).

1865 Sherman moves through South Carolina (January–March).

Grant takes Richmond (April).

Robert E. Lee surrenders at Appomattox (April).

Lincoln dies (April).

Joseph Johnston surrenders to Sherman (April).

FOR FURTHER READING

Iver Bernstein, *The New York Draft Riots: The Significance for American Society and Politics in the Age of the Civil War* (1990). An exploration of the social, economic, and political facets of the riots, and their ramifications.

Catherine Clinton and Nina Silber, eds., *Divided Houses: Gender and the Civil War* (1992). Essays focusing on changes in women's roles and activities.

Leon Litwack, *Been in the Storm So Long: The Aftermath of Slavery* (1979). A prizewinning examination of slaves' responses to the process of emancipation, continuing into the Reconstruction era.

James M. McPherson, *Battle Cry of Freedom: The Civil War Era* (1988). An award-winning study of the war years, skillfully integrating political, military, and social history.

Phillip Shaw Paludan, *The Presidency of Abraham Lincoln* (1994). An assessment of Lincoln as statesman, party leader, commander-in-chief, and emancipator.

Charles Royster, *The Destructive War: William Tecumseh Sherman, Stonewall Jackson, and the Americans* (1991). An exploration of the meaning of violence and nationality in the Civil War era.

Emory M. Thomas, *The Confederate Nation, 1861–1865* (1979). An engaging narrative history, emphasizing the rise and fall of southern nationalism.

ADDITIONAL BIBLIOGRAPHY

General

Daniel Aaron, *The Unwritten War* (1973); William L. Barney, *Flawed Victory* (1975); David P. Crook, *Diplomacy During the Civil War* (1975); David Donald, ed., *Why the North Won the Civil War* (1960); Eric Foner, *Politics and Ideology in the Age of the Civil War* (1980); Paul G. Gates, *Agriculture and the Civil War* (1965); Harold Hyman, *A More Perfect Union* (1975); James M.

McPherson, *Ordeal by Fire* (1982); Mary Elizabeth Massey, *Bonnet Brigades: American Women and the Civil War* (1966); Allan Nevins, *The War for the Union*, 4 vols. (1959–1971); Lewis P. Simpson, *Mind and the American Civil War* (1989); Maris A. Vinovskis, *Toward a Social History of the American Civil War: Exploratory Essays* (1990); Edmund Wilson, *Patriotic Gore* (1961).

Lincoln

LaWanda Cox, *Lincoln and Black Freedom* (1981); David Donald, *Lincoln Reconsidered: Essays on the Civil War Era*, 2d ed. (1956); James M. McPherson, *Abraham Lincoln and the Second American Revolution* (1990); Mark E. Neely, Jr., *The Last Best Hope on Earth: Abraham Lincoln and the Promise of America* (1993); Stephen B. Oates, *With Malice Toward None: The Life of Abraham Lincoln* (1979); James R. Randall, *Lincoln the President*, 4 vols. (1944–1955); Benjamin Thomas, *Abraham Lincoln* (1952); T. Harry Williams, *Lincoln and the Radicals* (1941) and *Lincoln and His Generals* (1952); Garry Wills, *Lincoln at Gettysburg: The Words That Remade America* (1992).

The Military Experience

Michael Barton, *Good Men: The Character of Civil War Soldiers* (1981); Richard G. Beringer et al., *Why the South Lost the Civil War* (1986); Bruce Catton, *Mr. Lincoln's Army* (1951), *Glory Road* (1952), *A Stillness at Appomattox* (1953); Shelby Foote, *The Civil War: A Narrative*, 3 vols. (1958–1974); Joseph T. Glatthaar, *The March to the Sea and Beyond* (1985) and *Partners in Command: The Relationships Between Leaders in the Civil War* (1994); Edward Hagerman, *The American Civil War and the Origins of Modern Warfare* (1988); Herman Hattaway and Archer Jones, *How the North Won: A Military History of the Civil War* (1984); Alvin M. Josephy, Jr., *The Civil War in the American West* (1991); Gerald F. Linderman, *Embattled Courage: The Experience of Combat in the American Civil War* (1987); James M. McPherson, *What They Fought for, 1861–1865* (1994).

The Black Experience

Dudley Cornish, *The Sable Arm: Negro Troops in the Union Army* (1956); John Hope Franklin, *The Emancipation Proclamation* (1963); Louis S. Gerteis, *From Contraband to Freedman: Federal Policy Toward Southern Blacks, 1861–1865* (1973); Joseph T. Glatthaar, *Forged in Battle: The Civil War Alliance of Black Soldiers and White Officers* (1990); James M. McPherson, ed., *The Negro's Civil War* (1965); Benjamin Quarles, *The Negro in the Civil War* (1953); Willie Lee Rose, *Rehearsal for Reconstruction: The Port Royal Experiment* (1964).

The Southern Experience

Thomas B. Alexander and Richard E. Beringer, *The Anatomy of the Confederate Congress* (1972); Paul D. Escott, *After Secession: Jefferson Davis and the Failure of Southern Nationalism* (1978); Eli N. Evans, *Judah P. Benjamin* (1987); Drew Gilpin Faust, *The Creation of Confederate Nationalism* (1988) and *Southern Stories: Slaveholders in Peace and War* (1992); Douglas Southall Freeman, *R. E. Lee: A Biography*, 4 vols. (1934–1935); Clarence Mohr, *On the Threshold of Freedom: Masters and Slaves in Civil War Georgia* (1986); Robert M. Myers, ed., *The Children of Pride: A True Story of Georgia and the Civil War* (1972); Alan T. Nolan, *Lee Considered: General Robert E. Lee and Civil War History* (1991); George C. Rable, *Women and the Crisis of Southern Nationalism* (1989); James L. Roark, *Masters Without Slaves: Southern Planters in the Civil War and Reconstruction* (1978); Emory M. Thomas, *The Confederacy as a Revolutionary Experience* (1971); Bell I. Wiley, *The Plain People of the Confederacy* (1943) and *Road to Appomattox* (1956).

The Northern Experience

Adrian Cook, *Armies of the Streets: The New York City Draft Riots of 1863* (1974); George M. Fredrickson, *The Inner Civil War: Northern Intellectuals and the Crisis of the Union* (1965); David Gilchrist and W. David Lewis, eds., *Economic Change in the Civil War Era* (1965); Frank L. Klement, *The Copperheads of the Middle West* (1960) and *Dark Lanterns: Secret Political Societies, Conspiracies, and Treason Trials in the Civil War* (1984); William S. McFeely, *Grant: A Biography* (1981); James H. Moorhead, *American Apocalypse: Yankee Protestants and the Civil War* (1978); Philip Shaw Paludan, *"A People's Contest": The Union and the Civil War, 1861–1865* (1988); Joel Silbey, *A Respectable Minority: The Democratic Party in the Civil War Era, 1860–1868* (1977); George W. Smith and Charles Judah, eds., *Life in the North During the Civil War* (1968); Hans L. Trefousse, *The Radical Republicans* (1968).

Personal Narratives

Eliza Frances Andrews, *Wartime Journal of a Georgia Girl* (1908); David Donald, ed., *Inside Lincoln's Cabinet: The Civil War Diaries of Salmon P. Chase* (1959); Ulysses S. Grant, *Memoirs and Selected Letters* (1990); Rupert S. Hallard, ed., *The Letters and Diaries of Laura M. Towne* (1970); T. W. Higginson, *Army Life in a Black Regiment* (1867); Mary Ashton Livermore, *My Story of the War* (1881); W. T. Sherman, *Memoirs* (1990); C. Vann Woodward, ed., *Mary Chesnut's Civil War* (1982).

Freedmen in Jacksonville, Florida
mid–1870s

16

THE CRISES OF RECONSTRUCTION 1865–1877

When the Civil War ended, parts of the South resembled a wasteland. The landscape "looked for many miles like a broad black streak of ruin and desolation," wrote a Union general. Homes, crops, and railroads had been destroyed; farming and business had come to a standstill; and uprooted southerners wandered about. As the Confederate armies dispersed, remnants of regiments made their way home. White refugees who had fled Union armies and burned-out plantations traveled the roads. So did black refugees. Some former slaves returned to areas where they had once lived, in search of relatives from whom they had been separated. Others moved off plantations to test their freedom, to look for work, or to seek relief. "Right off colored folks started on the move," a Texas freedman recalled. "They seemed to want to get closer to freedom—so they'd know what it was—like a place or a city."

The mood of the ex-Confederates was often as grim as the landscape. "The South lies prostrate—their foot is on us—there is no help," a Virginia woman lamented in her diary. Unable to face "southern Yankeedom," some planters considered emigrating to the American West or to Europe, Mexico, or Brazil, and a few thousand did. A large northern presence increased the rebels' dismay: two hundred thousand federal troops occupied the former Confederacy. Northern journalists and officials also

ventured south to investigate conditions and assess rebel attitudes. Their conclusions varied. Chief Justice Salmon P. Chase, on a self-appointed fact-finding mission, insisted that southerners were conciliatory and flexible. "The people are now in a mood to accept almost anything which promises of a definite settlement," he wrote from North Carolina in May 1865. A few days later, a *New York Tribune* reporter, also in North Carolina, offered a harsher view of the ex-Confederates. "They are haughty, exacting, unsubdued, and if possible, *more* devilish than they ever were," he contended. "One would think that we were the subjugated and conquered people and not the rebels."

In previous wars, the mood of the vanquished had rarely, if ever, concerned victors. But the Civil War was a special case, for the Union had sought not merely victory but the return of national unity. The questions the federal government faced in 1865 were therefore unprecedented. First, how could the Union be restored and the defeated South reintegrated into the nation? Would the Confederate states be treated as conquered territories, or would they quickly be readmitted to the Union with the same rights as other states? Who would set requirements for readmission—Congress or the president? Would Confederate leaders be punished for treason? Would their property be confiscated and their political rights curtailed? Most important, what would happen to the more than 3.5 million former slaves? The future of the freedmen constituted *the* crucial issue of the postwar era, for emancipation had set in motion the most profound upheaval in the nation's history. Before the war slavery had been the distinguishing feature of southern society. A labor system and a means of racial control, it had determined the South's social, economic, and political structure. What would replace slavery in the postwar South? The end of the Civil War, in short, posed two problems that had to be solved simultaneously: how to readmit the South to the Union and what status the free blacks would have in American society.

Between 1865 and 1877, the drama of Reconstruction unfolded in several theaters. In Washington a conflict between President Andrew Johnson and Congress led to the enactment of a stringent Republican plan for restoring the South to the Union. In the defeated Confederate states, first readmitted to the Union under presidential directives, state governments were reorganized according to the new congressional plan, and Republicans took power. Throughout the South, the Reconstruction years spawned far-reaching social and economic changes.

Emancipation reshaped black communities, where former slaves sought new identities as free people, and it transformed the southern economy as a new labor system replaced slavery. The North, meanwhile, hurtled headlong into an era of industrial expansion, labor unrest, and financial crises. By the mid-1870s northern politicians were ready to discard the Reconstruction policies that Congress had imposed in the 1860s. Simultaneously, the southern states returned to "home rule," or Democratic control, as Republican regimes toppled one by one. In 1877 Reconstruction collapsed. But the nature and causes of its failure have engaged historians ever since.

RECONSTRUCTION POLITICS

At the end of the Civil War, President Johnson might have exiled, imprisoned, or executed Confederate leaders and imposed martial law indefinitely. Demobilized Confederate soldiers might have continued armed resistance to federal occupation forces. Freed

The Devastated South in 1865
As the Civil War ended, demoralized ex-Confederates confronted bleak prospects—"a joyless future of probable ignominy, poverty, and want," wrote one planter's daughter, "a life robbed of every blessing and already becoming intolerable." Here, a family in Fredericksburg, Virginia, returns to its war-shattered dwelling in a mood of resignation or despair. Significantly, no men of military age remain.

slaves might have taken revenge on former owners and the rest of the white community. But none of these drastic possibilities occurred. Instead, intense *political* conflict dominated the three years immediately after the war. In national politics unparalleled disputes produced new constitutional amendments, a presidential impeachment crisis, and some of the most ambitious domestic legislation ever enacted by Congress, the Reconstruction Acts of 1867–1868. The major outcome of Reconstruction politics was the enfranchisement of black men, a development that few had expected when Lee surrendered.

In 1865 only a small group of politicians supported black suffrage. These advocates were all Radical Republicans, a minority faction that had emerged during the war. Led by Senator Charles Sumner of Massachusetts and Congressman Thaddeus Stevens of Pennsylvania, the Radicals had clamored for the abolition of slavery, just as they supported a demanding reconstruction policy, both in wartime and after. Any valid plan to restore the Union, Stevens contended, must "revolutionize Southern institutions, habits, and manners . . . or all our blood and treasure have been spent in vain." But the Radicals, outnumbered in Congress by moderate and conservative Republicans and opposed by the Democratic minority, seemingly had little chance of success. Nonetheless, in the complex political battles of 1865–1868, the Radicals managed to win broad Republican support for parts of their Reconstruction program, including black male enfranchisement. Just as civil war had led to emancipation, a goal once supported by only a minority of Americans, so Reconstruction policy became bound to black suffrage, a momentous change that originally had only narrow political backing.

Lincoln's Plan

Conflict over Reconstruction began even before the war ended. In December 1863 President Lincoln issued the Proclamation of Amnesty and Reconstruction, which outlined a path by which each southern state could rejoin the Union. Under Lincoln's plan a minority of voters (equal to at least 10 percent of those who had cast ballots in the election of 1860) would have to take an oath of allegiance to the Union and accept emancipation. This minority could then create a loyal state government. But Lincoln's plan excluded some southerners from taking the oath: Confederate government officials, army and naval officers, as well

as those military or civil officers who had resigned from Congress or from U.S. commissions in 1861. All such persons would have to apply for presidential pardons. Also excluded, of course, were blacks, who had not been voters in 1860. Lincoln hoped through his "10 percent plan" to undermine the Confederacy by establishing pro-Union governments within it. Characteristically, Lincoln had partisan goals, too. He wanted to win the allegiance of southern Unionists (those who had opposed secession), especially former Whigs, and to build a southern Republican party.

Radical Republicans in Congress, however, envisioned a slower readmission process that would exclude even more ex-Confederates from political life. Their plan won the backing of almost all Republicans, who agreed that Lincoln's program was too weak. Thus in July 1864 Congress enacted the Wade-Davis bill, which provided that each former Confederate state would be ruled by a military governor. Under the Wade-Davis plan, after at least half the eligible voters took an oath of allegiance to the Union, delegates could be elected to a state convention that would repeal secession and abolish slavery. But to qualify as a voter or delegate, a southerner would have to take a second, "ironclad" oath, swearing that he had never voluntarily supported the Confederacy. Like the 10 percent plan, the congressional plan did not provide for black suffrage, a measure then supported by only some Radicals. Unlike Lincoln's plan, however, the Wade-Davis scheme would have delayed the readmission process almost indefinitely.

Claiming that he did not want to bind himself to any single restoration policy, Lincoln pocket-vetoed* the Wade-Davis bill. The bill's sponsors, Senator Benjamin Wade of Ohio and Congressman Henry Winter Davis of Maryland, blasted Lincoln's act as an outrage. By the end of the war, the president and Congress had reached an impasse. Arkansas, Louisiana, Tennessee, and parts of Virginia under Union army control moved toward readmission under variants of Lincoln's plan. But Congress refused to seat their delegates, as it had a right to do. Lincoln, meanwhile, gave hints that a more rigorous Reconstruction policy might be in store. In his last speech (April 1865), he revealed that he favored some form of black suffrage, perhaps for blacks who had served in the Union army. He also entertained Secretary of War Stanton's proposal for temporary

---

*Pocket veto: failure to sign a bill within ten days of the adjournment of Congress.

military occupation of the South. What Lincoln's ultimate policy would have been remains unknown. But at the time of his death, Radical Republicans turned with hope toward his successor, Andrew Johnson of Tennessee, in whom they felt they had an ally.

Presidential Reconstruction Under Johnson

The only southern senator to remain in Congress when his state seceded, Andrew Johnson had worked amicably with Radical Republicans in wartime and had served as military governor of Tennessee from 1862 to 1864. He had taken a strong anti-Confederate stand, declaring, for example, that "treason is a crime and must be made odious." Above all, Johnson had long sought the destruction of the planter aristocracy, a goal that dominated his political career. A self-educated man of humble North Carolina origins, Johnson had moved to Greenville, Tennessee, in 1826 and become a tailor. His wife, Eliza McCardle, had taught him how to write. An ardent Jacksonian, he had entered politics in the 1830s as a spokesman for nonslaveowning whites and risen rapidly from local official to congressman to governor to senator. Once the owner of eight slaves, Johnson reversed his position on slavery during the war. When emancipation became Union policy, he supported it, and as military governor, he assured Tennessee blacks that he would be their "Moses." But Johnson neither adopted abolitionist ideals nor challenged racist sentiments. He hoped mainly that the fall of slavery would injure southern aristocrats. Andrew Johnson, in short, had his own political agenda, which, as Republicans would soon learn, did not coincide with theirs. Moreover, he was a lifelong Democrat who had been added to the Republican, or National Union, ticket in 1864 to broaden its appeal and who had become president by accident.

Many Republicans voiced shock when Johnson announced a new plan for the restoration of the South in May 1865—with Congress out of session and not due to convene until December. The president presented his program as a continuation of Lincoln's plan, but in fact, it was very much his own. He explained in two proclamations how the seven southern states still without reconstruction governments—Alabama, Florida, Georgia, Mississippi, North Carolina, South Carolina, and Texas—could return to the Union. Almost all southerners who took an oath of allegiance would receive a pardon and amnesty, and all their property except slaves would be restored. Oath takers could elect

Andrew Johnson
When Vice President Johnson became president at Lincoln's death in April 1865, many Republicans expected him to impose "harsh terms" upon the defeated South.

delegates to state conventions, which would provide for regular elections. Each state convention, Johnson later added, would have to proclaim the illegality of secession, repudiate state debts incurred when the state belonged to the Confederacy, and ratify the Thirteenth Amendment, which abolished slavery. (Proposed by an enthusiastic wartime Congress early in 1865, the amendment would be ratified in December of that year.) As under Lincoln's plan, Confederate civil and military officers would be excluded from the oath needed for voting. But Johnson added a new disqualification. All well-off ex-Confederates, those with taxable property worth $20,000 or more, would also be barred from political life. This exclusion, said Johnson, would benefit "humble men, the peasantry and yeomen of the South, who have been decoyed . . . into rebellion." Johnson seemed to be planning a purge of aristocratic leaders. Poorer whites would now be in control.

Presidential Reconstruction took effect in the summer of 1865, supervised by provisional governors. But it had unforeseen consequences. Those southerners disqualified on the basis of wealth or high Confederate position applied for pardons in droves. Either gratified by their supplications or seeking support for reelection in 1868, Johnson handed out pardons liberally—some thirteen thousand of them. He also dropped plans for the punishment of treason. By the end of 1865, all seven states had created new civil governments to replace the imposed military rule, but in other ways the states had almost returned to the status quo ante bellum. Confederate army officers and large planters assumed state offices. Former Confederate congressmen, state officials, and generals were elected to Congress. (Most of these new representatives were former Whigs who had not supported secession; southerners thought that they were electing "Union" men.) Georgia sent Alexander Stephens, the former Confederate vice president and a one-time Unionist, back to Congress as a senator. Some states refused to ratify the Thirteenth Amendment or to repudiate their Confederate debts.

Most important, all states took steps to ensure a landless, dependent black labor force—in one Alabamian's words, to "secure the services of the negroes, teach them their place." This goal was achieved through the "black codes," which replaced the slave codes, the state laws that had regulated slavery. Because the ratification of the Thirteenth Amendment was assured by the terms of Johnson's Reconstruction plan, all states guaranteed the freedmen some basic rights. They could marry, own property, make contracts, and testify in court against other blacks. But the important parts of the black codes were their restrictions, which varied from state to state. Some codes established racial segregation in public places; most prohibited racial intermarriage, jury service by blacks, and court testimony by blacks against whites. All codes included economic restrictions that would prevent former slaves from leaving the plantations. South Carolina required special licenses for blacks who wished to enter nonagricultural employment. Mississippi prohibited blacks from buying and selling farmland. Most states required annual contracts between landowners and black agricultural workers and provided that blacks without lawful employment would be arrested as vagrants and auctioned off to employers who would pay their fines.

The black codes established a halfway status for the southern freedmen, who, though no longer slaves, were not really liberated either. Although "free" to sign labor contracts, for instance, those who failed to sign them would be considered in violation of the law and swept back into involuntary servitude. In practice,

many clauses in the codes never took effect: the Union army and the Freedmen's Bureau swiftly suspended the enforcement of racially discriminatory provisions of the new laws. But the black codes were important indicators of white southern intentions. They showed what "home rule" would have been like without federal interference.

When former abolitionists and Radical Republicans decried the black codes, Johnson defended the codes and his restoration program. Ex-Confederates, he contended, should not be forced back into the Union as "a degraded and debased people." Many northerners, however, perceived signs of southern defiance: voters had elected ex-rebels to public office; southern conventions had been reluctant to repudiate secession or slow to pronounce slavery dead; and new laws had robbed freedmen of basic rights. "What can be hatched from such an egg but another rebellion?" asked a Boston newspaper. Republicans in Congress agreed. When the Thirty-ninth Congress convened in December 1865, it refused to seat the delegates of the ex-Confederate states. Establishing the Joint (House-Senate) Committee on Reconstruction, Republicans prepared to dismantle the black codes and lock ex-Confederates out of power.

Congress Versus Johnson

The status of the southern blacks now became the major issue in Congress. "This is not a 'white man's government,'" exclaimed Republican congressman Thaddeus Stevens. "To say so is political blasphemy." But Radical Republicans like Stevens—who hoped to impose black suffrage on the former Confederacy and delay the readmission of the southern states into the Union—still constituted a congressional minority. Conservative Republicans, who tended to favor the Johnson plan, formed a minority too, as did the Democrats, who also supported the president. Moderate Republicans, the largest congressional bloc, agreed with the Radicals that Johnson's plan was too feeble. But they did not believe that northern voters would support black suffrage, and they wanted to avoid a dispute with the president. Since none of the four congressional blocs even approached the two-thirds majority required to overturn a presidential veto, Johnson's program would stay in place unless the moderates and the Radicals joined forces. The impetus for this alliance came from an unexpected source—Andrew Johnson himself, who soon alienated a majority of moderates and pushed them into the Radicals' arms.

The moderate Republicans supported two proposals drafted by one of their own, Senator Lyman Trumbull of Illinois, to invalidate the black codes. These measures won wide Republican support. In the first, Congress voted to continue the Freedmen's Bureau, established in 1865, whose term was coming to an end. This agency, headed by former Union general O. O. Howard and staffed mainly by army officers, was a major federal arm in the South. It provided relief, rations, and medical care; built schools for the freed blacks; put them to work on abandoned or confiscated lands; and tried to protect their rights as laborers. Congress voted to extend the bureau's life for three years and to give it new power: it could run special military courts to settle labor disputes and could invalidate labor contracts forced on freedmen by the black codes. In February 1866 Johnson vetoed the Freedmen's Bureau bill. The Constitution, he declared, did not sanction military trials of civilians in peacetime, nor did it support a system to care for "indigent persons."

In March 1866 Congress passed a second measure proposed by Trumbull, a bill that made blacks U.S. citizens with the same civil rights as other citizens and gave the federal government the right to intervene in the states to ensure black rights in court. Johnson vetoed the civil rights bill also. He argued that it would "operate in favor of the colored and against the white race." But in April Congress overrode his veto; the Civil Rights Act of 1866 was the first major law ever passed over a presidential veto. Then in July Congress enacted the Supplementary Freedmen's Bureau Act over Johnson's veto as well.

Johnson's vetoes bewildered many Republicans because the new laws did not undercut the basic structure of presidential Reconstruction. The president insisted, however, that both bills were illegitimate because southerners had been shut out of the Congress that passed them. His stance won support not only from the South but from northern Democrats, who were fast becoming Johnson's constituency. But the president had alienated the moderate Republicans, who began to work with the Radicals against him. Johnson had lost "every friend he has," one moderate legislator declared.

Some historians view Andrew Johnson as a political incompetent who, at this crucial turning point, bungled both his readmission scheme and his political future. Others contend that he was merely trying to forge a coalition of the center, made up of Democrats

King Andrew
This Thomas Nast cartoon, published in Harper's Weekly *just before the 1866 congressional elections, conveyed Republican antipathy to Andrew Johnson. The president is depicted as an autocratic tyrant. Radical Republican Thaddeus Stevens, upper right, has his head on the block and is about to lose it. The Republic sits in chains.*

and non-Radical Republicans. In either case, Johnson underestimated the possibility of Republican unity. Once united, the Republicans moved on to a third step: the passage of a constitutional amendment that would prevent the Supreme Court from invalidating the new Civil Rights Act and would block Democrats in Congress from repealing it.

The Fourteenth Amendment

In April 1866 Congress adopted the Fourteenth Amendment, which had been proposed by the Joint Committee on Reconstruction. To protect blacks' rights, the amendment declared in its first clause that all persons born or naturalized in the United States were citizens of the nation and citizens of their states and that no state could abridge their rights without due process of law or deny them equal protection of the law. This section nullified the *Dred Scott* decision of 1857 (see Chapter 14), which had declared that blacks were not citizens. Second, the amendment guaranteed that if a state denied suffrage to any of its male citizens, its representation in Congress would be proportionally reduced. This clause did not guarantee black suffrage, but it threatened to deprive southern states of some legislators if black men were denied the vote. Third, the amendment disqualified from state and national office *all* prewar officeholders—civil and military, state and federal—who had supported the Confederacy, unless Congress removed their disqualifications by a two-thirds vote. In so providing, Congress intended to invalidate Johnson's wholesale distribution of amnesties and pardons. Finally, the amendment repudiated the Confederate debt and maintained the validity of the federal debt.

The Fourteenth Amendment was the most ambitious step that Congress had yet taken. It revealed the growing receptivity among Republican legislators to the Radicals' demands, including black male enfranchisement. It reflected the Republican consensus that southern states would not deal fairly with blacks unless forced to do so. Most important, it was the first national effort to limit state control of civil and political rights. With its passage a huge controversy erupted. Abolitionists decried the second clause as a "swindle" because it did not explicitly ensure black suffrage. Southerners and northern Democrats condemned the third clause as vengeful. Southern legislatures, except for Tennessee's, refused to ratify the amendment, and President Johnson denounced it. His intransigence solidified the new alliance between moderate and Radical Republicans. It also turned the congressional elections of 1866 into a referendum on the Fourteenth Amendment.

Over the summer Johnson set off on a whistle-stop train tour from Washington to St. Louis and Chicago and back, speaking to the public at railroad stations along the way. But this innovative campaign tactic—the "swing around the circle," as Johnson called it—was a debacle. Humorless and defensive, the president argued with his audiences and made fresh enemies. His hope of creating a new National Union party, composed of Democrats and conservative Republicans who opposed the Fourteenth Amendment, thus cap-

sized. Moderate and Radical Republicans, meanwhile, defended the amendment, condemned the president, and branded the Democratic party "a common sewer . . . into which is emptied every element of treason, North and South."

When the votes in the congressional elections were tallied, Republican candidates won in a landslide, often with even greater margins of victory than in 1864. In the Fortieth Congress, which would convene in March 1867, Republicans would outnumber Democrats almost two to one in the House and almost four to one in the Senate. In the interim the Republicans had secured a mandate to overcome southern resistance to the Fourteenth Amendment and to enact their own Reconstruction program, even if the president vetoed every part of it.

Congressional Reconstruction

The congressional debate over how to reconstruct the South began in December 1866 and lasted three months. To stifle a resurgence of Confederate power, Radical Republican leaders called for black suffrage, federal support for public schools, confiscation of Confederate estates, and an extended period of military occupation in the South. Moderate Republicans, who once would have rejected such a plan as too extreme, were now willing to accept parts of it. Legislators debated every ramification, including the constitutional question of whether the southern states had in fact seceded from the Union during the war. In February 1867 after complex legislative maneuvers and many late-night sessions, Congress passed the Reconstruction Act of 1867 and, after Johnson vetoed it, repassed the law on March 2. Later that year and in 1868, Congress passed three further Reconstruction acts, all enacted over presidential vetoes, to refine and enforce the first.

The Reconstruction Act of 1867 invalidated the state governments formed under the Lincoln and Johnson plans and all the legal decisions made by those governments. Only Tennessee, which had ratified the Fourteenth Amendment and had been readmitted to the Union, escaped further reconstruction. The new law divided the other ten former Confederate states into five temporary military districts, each run by a Union general. Voters—all black men, plus those white men who had not been disqualified by the Fourteenth Amendment—could elect delegates to a state convention that would write a new state constitution granting black suffrage. When eligible voters ratified

Major Reconstruction Legislation

Law and Date of Congressional Passage	Provisions	Purpose
Civil Rights Act pf 1866 (April 1866)*	Declared blacks citizens and guaranteed them equal protection of the laws. →	→ To invalidate the black codes.
Supplementary Freedmen's Bureau Act (July 1866)*	Extended the life of the Freedmen's Aid Bureau and expanded its powers.	To invalidate the black codes.
Reconstruction Act of 1867 (March 1867)*	Invalidated state governments formed under Lincoln and Johnson.	To replace presidential Reconstruction with a more stringent plan.
	Divided the former Confederacy into five military districts.	
	Set forth requirements for readmission of ex-Confederate states to the Union.	
Supplementary Reconstruction Acts		To enforce the First Reconstruction Act.
Second Reconstruction Act (March 1867)*	Required military commanders to initiate voter enrollment.	
Third Reconstruction Act (July 1867)*	Expanded military commanders' powers.	
Fourth Reconstruction Act (March 1868)*	Provided that a majority of voters, however few, could put a new state constitution into force.	
Army Appropriations Act (March 1867)*	Declared in a rider that only the general of the army could issue military orders.	To prevent President Johnson from obstructing Reconstruction.
Tenure of Office Act (March 1867)*	Prohibited the president from removing any federal official without the Senate's consent.	To prevent President Johnson from obstructing Reconstruction.
Omnibus Act (June 1868)†	Readmitted seven ex-Confederate states to the Union.	To restore the Union, under the terms of the First Reconstruction Act.
Enforcement Act of 1870 (May 1870)‡	Provided for the protection of black voters.	To enforce the Fifteenth Amendment.
Second Enforcement Act (February 1871)	Provided for federal supervision of southern elections.	To enforce the Fifteenth Amendment.
Third Enforcement Act (Ku Klux Klan Act) (April 1871)	Strengthened sanctions against those who impeded black suffrage.	To combat the Ku Klux Klan and enforce the Fourteenth Amendment.
Amnesty Act (May 1872)	Restored the franchise to almost all ex-Confederates.	Effort by Grant Republicans to deprive Liberal Republicans of a campaign issue.
Civil Rights Act of 1875 (March 1875)§	Outlawed racial segregation in transportation and public accommodations and prevented exclusion of blacks from jury service.	To honor the late senator Charles Sumner.

*Passed over Johnson's veto.

†Georgia was soon returned to military rule. The last four states were readmitted in 1870.

‡Sections of the law declared unconstitutional in 1876.

§Invalidated by the Supreme Court in 1883.

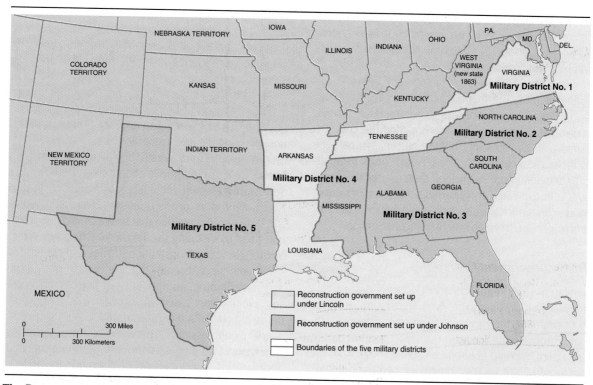

The Reconstruction of the South

The Reconstruction Act of 1867 divided the former Confederate states, except Tennessee, into five military districts and set forth the steps by which new state governments could be created.

the new constitution, elections could be held for state officers. Once Congress approved the state constitution, once the state legislature ratified the Fourteenth Amendment, and once the amendment became part of the federal Constitution, Congress would readmit the state into the Union—and Reconstruction, in a constitutional sense, would be complete.

The Reconstruction Act of 1867 was far more radical than the Johnson program because it enfranchised blacks and disfranchised many ex-Confederates. It fulfilled a central goal of the Radical Republicans: to delay the readmission of former Confederate states until Republican governments could be established and thereby prevent an immediate rebel resurgence. But the new law was not as harsh toward ex-Confederates as it might have been. It provided for only temporary military rule. It did not prosecute Confederate leaders for treason or permanently exclude them from politics. Finally, it made no provision for the confiscation or redistribution of property.

During the congressional debates, Radical Republican congressman Thaddeus Stevens had argued for the confiscation of large Confederate estates to "humble the proud traitors" and to provide for the former slaves. In March 1867 he had proposed subdividing such confiscated property into forty-acre tracts to be distributed among the freedmen. The remainder of the confiscated land, some 90 percent of it, would be sold to pay off war debts. Stevens wanted to crush the planter aristocracy and create a new class of self-sufficient black yeoman farmers. Political independence rested on economic independence, he contended; land grants would be more valuable to the freedmen than the vote, although both were deserved. Stevens's land-reform bill won the support of other Radicals, but it never made progress, for most Republicans held property rights sacred. Tampering with such rights in the South, they feared, would jeopardize those rights in the North. Moreover, Stevens's proposal would alienate southern ex-Whigs from the Republican cause, antagonize other white southerners, and thereby endanger the rest of Reconstruction. Thus land reform never came about. The "radical" Reconstruction acts were a compromise.

Congressional Reconstruction took effect in the spring of 1867. But it could not be enforced without military power, and Johnson, as commander in chief, controlled the army. When he impeded the congressional plan by replacing military officers sympathetic to the Radical cause with conservative ones, Republicans seethed. More suspicious than ever of the president and frustrated by his roadblocks, congressional moderates and Radicals once again joined forces to block Johnson from obstructing Reconstruction.

The Impeachment Crisis

In March 1867 Republicans in Congress passed two laws to limit presidential power. The Tenure of Office Act prohibited the president from removing civil officers without Senate consent. Cabinet members, the law stated, were to hold office "during the term of the president by whom they may have been appointed" and could be fired only with the Senate's approval. The goal was to bar Johnson from dismissing Secretary of War Stanton, the Radicals' ally, whose support Congress needed to enforce the Reconstruction acts. The other law, a rider to an army appropriations bill, barred the president from issuing military orders except through the commanding general, Ulysses S. Grant, who could not be removed without the Senate's consent.

The Radicals' enmity to Johnson, however, would not die until he was out of office. They began to look for grounds on which to impeach him and convict him and thereby remove all potential obstacles to congressional Reconstruction. The House Judiciary Committee, aided by private detectives, could at first uncover no valid charges against Johnson. On a second try, they produced some charges, but the House found them inadequate. Just as impeachment efforts seemed a lost cause, Johnson again came to his opponents' rescue by providing the charges they needed.

In August 1867, with Congress out of session, Johnson suspended Secretary of War Stanton and replaced him with General Grant. In early 1868 the reconvened Senate refused to approve Stanton's suspension, and Grant, sensing the Republican mood, vacated the office. Johnson then removed Stanton and replaced him with an aged general, Lorenzo Thomas. Johnson's

defiance forced Republican moderates, who had at first resisted impeachment, into yet another alliance with the Radicals: the president had "thrown down the gauntlet," a moderate charged. The House approved eleven charges of impeachment, nine of them based on violation of the Tenure of Office Act. The other charges accused Johnson of being "unmindful of the high duties of office," of seeking to disgrace Congress, and of not enforcing the Reconstruction acts.

Johnson's trial, which began in the Senate in March 1868, riveted public attention for eleven weeks. Seven congressmen, including leading Radical Republicans, served as prosecutors or "managers." Johnson's lawyers maintained that he was merely seeking a court test by violating the Tenure of Office Act, which he thought was unconstitutional. They also contended, somewhat inconsistently, that the law did not protect Secretary Stanton, an appointee of Lincoln, not Johnson. Finally, they asserted, Johnson was guilty of no crime indictable in a regular court.

The congressional "managers" countered that impeachment was a political process, not a criminal trial, and that Johnson's "abuse of discretionary power" constituted an impeachable offense. Although Senate opinion split along party lines and Republicans outnumbered Democrats, some Republicans wavered, fearing that the removal of a president would destroy the balance of power among the three branches of the federal government. They also distrusted Radical Republican Benjamin Wade, the president pro tempore of the Senate, who, because there was no vice president, would accede to the presidency if Johnson were thrown out.

Intense pressure from colleagues and constituents bombarded the wavering Republican senators, whose votes would prove crucial. Late in May 1868, the Senate voted against Johnson 35 to 19, one vote short of the two-thirds majority needed for conviction. Seven Republicans had risked political suicide and sided with the twelve Senate Democrats in voting against removal. In so doing, they set a precedent. Future presidents would not be impeached solely on political grounds or because two-thirds of Congress disagreed with them. But the anti-Johnson forces had also achieved their goal: Andrew Johnson had no future as president. After serving out the rest of his term, he returned to Tennessee, where he was reelected to the Senate five years later. Republicans in Congress, meanwhile, pursued their last major Reconstruction objective: to guarantee black male suffrage.

The Reconstruction Amendments

Amendment and Date of Congressional Passage	Provisions	Ratification
Thirteenth (January 1865)	Prohibited slavery in the United States.	December 1865
Fourteenth (June 1866)	Defined citizenship to include all persons born or naturalized in the United States.	July 1868, after Congress made ratification a prerequisite for readmission of ex-Confederate states to the Union.
	Provided proportional loss of congressional representation for any state that denied suffrage to any of its male citizens.	
	Disqualified prewar officeholders who supported the Confederacy from state or national office.	
	Repudiated the Confederate debt.	
Fifteenth (February 1869)	Prohibited the denial of suffrage because of race, color, or previous condition of servitude.	March 1870; ratification required of Virginia, Texas, Mississippi, and Georgia for readmission to the Union.

The Fifteenth Amendment

Black suffrage was the linchpin of congressional Reconstruction. Only with the support of black voters could Republicans secure control of the ex-Confederate states. The Fourteenth Amendment had promoted black suffrage indirectly, by threatening a penalty where it was denied. The Reconstruction Act of 1867, however, forced every southern state legislature to enfranchise black men as a prerequisite for readmission to the Union. But though black voting had begun in the South, much of the North had rejected it. At the end of the Civil War, only five New England states enfranchised black men; so did New York, on the condition that they owned property. Between 1867 and 1869, nine referenda in northern states defeated proposals for black suffrage. Iowa voters alone extended the franchise to blacks. Congressional Republicans therefore had two aims. They sought to protect black suffrage in the South against future repeal by Congress or the states and to enfranchise northern and border-state blacks, who would presumably vote Republican. To achieve these goals, Congress in 1869 proposed the Fifteenth Amendment, which prohibited the denial of suffrage by the states to any citizen on account of race, color, or previous condition of servitude.

Democrats argued that the proposed amendment violated states' rights by denying each state the power to determine who would vote. But Democrats did not control enough states to defeat the amendment, and it was ratified in 1870. Four votes came from those ex-Confederate states—Mississippi, Virginia, Georgia, and Texas—that had delayed the Reconstruction process and were therefore forced to approve the Fifteenth Amendment, as well as the Fourteenth, in order to rejoin the Union. Some southerners contended that the new amendment's omissions made it acceptable, for it had, as a Richmond newspaper pointed out, "loopholes through which a coach and four horses can be driven." What were these loopholes? The Fifteenth Amendment did not guarantee black officeholding, nor did it prohibit voting restrictions such as property requirements and literacy tests. Such restrictions might be used to deny blacks the vote, and indeed, ultimately they were so used.

The debate over black suffrage not only pervaded national politics but drew new participants into the fray. Since the end of the war, a small group of abolitionists, men and women, had sought to revive the cause of women's rights. In 1866, when Congress adopted the Fourteenth Amendment, women's rights advocates tried to join forces with their old abolitionist allies to promote both black suffrage and woman suffrage. Most Radical Republicans, however, did not want to be saddled with the woman-suffrage plank; they feared it would impede their primary goal, black enfranchisement.

This defection provoked disputes among women's rights advocates. Some, who continued to support black suffrage, contended that it would pave the way for the women's vote and that black men deserved priority. "If the elective franchise is not extended to the Negro, he is dead," explained Frederick Douglass, a longtime women's rights supporter. "Woman has a thousand ways by which she can attach herself to the ruling power of the land that we have not." But the women's rights leaders Elizabeth Cady Stanton and Susan B. Anthony, who repudiated black suffrage without attendant woman suffrage, decried the Fifteenth Amendment and denounced the Republicans for supporting it. The amendment, insisted Stanton, would establish an "aristocracy of sex." Moreover, she argued, if suffrage were extended without including women, their disabilities would merely increase. The battle over black suffrage and the Fifteenth Amendment divided women's rights advocates into two rival suffrage associations, both formed in 1869. It also severed reformers such as Stanton and Anthony from the abolitionist tradition in which they had matured politically and inspired the development of an independent women's rights movement.

By the time the Fifteenth Amendment was ratified in 1870, Congress could look back on five years of momentous achievement. Since the start of 1865, federal legislators had broadened the scope of American democracy by passing three constitutional amendments. The Thirteenth Amendment abolished slavery, the Fourteenth affirmed the rights of federal citizens, and the Fifteenth prohibited the denial of suffrage on the basis of race. Congress had also readmitted the former Confederate states into the Union. But after 1868 congressional momentum slowed. And in 1869, when Ulysses S. Grant became president, the fierce battle between Congress and the chief executive ceased. The theater of action now shifted to the South, where an era of tumultuous change was under way.

RECONSTRUCTION GOVERNMENTS

During the unstable years of presidential Reconstruction, 1865–1867, the southern states had to create new governments, revive the war-torn economy, and face the impact of emancipation. Social and economic problems abounded. War costs had cut into southern wealth, cities and factories lay in rubble, plantation-

labor systems disintegrated, and racial tensions flared. Beginning in 1865, freedmen organized black conventions, political meetings at which they protested ill treatment and demanded equal rights. These meetings took place in a climate of violence. Race riots erupted in major southern cities. In Memphis in May 1866, white crowds attacked black veterans, charged through black neighborhoods, and killed forty-six people; in New Orleans two months later, a white mob and police assaulted black delegates on their way to a political convention and left forty people dead. Even when Congress reimposed military rule in 1867, ex-Confederates did not feel defeated. "Having reached bottom, there is hope now that we may rise again to the surface in the course of time," a South Carolina planter wrote in his diary.

Congressional Reconstruction, supervised by federal troops, took effect in the spring of 1867. Despite efforts to stall it—many southern whites preferred military rule to the prospect of new civil governments based on black suffrage—the process moved forward. The Johnson regimes were dismantled, state constitutional conventions met, and voters elected new state governments, which Republicans dominated. In 1868 a majority of the former Confederate states rejoined the Union, and two years later, the last four states—Virginia, Mississippi, Georgia, and Texas—followed.

Readmission to the Union did not end the *process* of Reconstruction, for Republicans still held power in the South. Republican rule was very brief, lasting less than a decade in all southern states, far less in most of them, and on average under five years. Opposition from southern Democrats, the landowning elite, thousands of vigilantes, and indeed, most white voters proved insurmountable. Still, the governments formed under congressional Reconstruction were unique, because black men, including ex-slaves, participated in them. In no other society where slaves had been liberated—neither Haiti, where slaves had revolted in the 1790s, nor the British Caribbean islands, where Parliament had ended slavery in 1833—had freedmen gained democratic political rights.

A New Electorate

The Reconstruction laws of 1867–1868 transformed the southern electorate by temporarily disfranchising 10 percent to 15 percent of potential white voters and by enfranchising more than seven hundred thousand freedmen. Outnumbering registered white voters by

The Carpetbaggers

Southern Democrats disparaged carpetbaggers as interlopers who hoped to "fatten on our misfortunes." In reality, most were Union army officers, businessmen, and professionals with capital and energy to invest in the South. This 1869 sheet-music cover caricatures the carpetbaggers by depicting a predatory northern migrant casting a greedy eye upon the defeated Confederacy.

one hundred thousand, blacks gained voting majorities in five states.

The new electorate provided a base for the Republican party, which had never existed in the South. To their Democratic opponents, southern Republicans comprised three types of scoundrels: northern "carpetbaggers," who had allegedly come south seeking wealth and power (with so few possessions that they could be stuffed into traveling bags made of carpet material); southern "scalawags," predominantly poor and ignorant, who sought to profit from Republican rule; and hordes of uneducated freedmen, who were ready prey for Republican manipulators. Although the "carpetbag" and "scalawag" labels were derogatory and the stereotypes that they conveyed inaccurate, they remain in use as a form of shorthand. Crossing class and racial lines, the hastily established Republican party

was in fact a loose coalition of factions with varied and often contradictory goals.

To northerners who moved south after the Civil War, the former Confederacy was an undeveloped region, ripe with possibility. The carpetbaggers' ranks included many former Union soldiers who hoped to buy land, open factories, build railroads, or simply enjoy the warmer southern climate. Albion Tourgee, a young lawyer who had served with the New York and Ohio volunteers, for example, relocated in North Carolina after the war to improve his health. There he worked as a journalist, politician, and Republican judge, until Republican rule collapsed. Perhaps no more than twenty thousand northern migrants like Tourgee—including veterans, missionaries, teachers, and Freedmen's Bureau agents—headed south immediately after the war, and many returned north by 1867. But those who remained played a disproportionate part in Reconstruction politics, for they held almost one out of three state offices. Carpetbaggers recruited black support through a patriotic society called the Union League, which held meetings and rallies, urged blacks to vote, and escorted them to the polls.

Scalawags, white southerners who supported the Republicans, included some entrepreneurs who applauded party policies such as the national banking system and high protective tariffs as well as some prosperous planters, former Whigs who had opposed the South's secession. They also comprised a few prominent politicians, among them James Orr of South Carolina and Mississippi's governor James Alcorn, who became Republicans for practical reasons: they wanted to retain influence and limit Republican radicalism. Republicans appreciated such important recruits and hoped to attract more of them. Most scalawags, however, were small farmers from the mountain regions of North Carolina, Georgia, Alabama, and Arkansas. Former Unionists who had owned no slaves and had no allegiance to the landowning elite, they sought to improve their economic position. Unlike carpetbaggers, they lacked commitment to black rights and black suffrage; most came from regions with small black populations and cared little whether blacks voted or not. Scalawags held the most political offices during Reconstruction, but they proved the least stable element of the southern Republican coalition: eventually, many drifted back to the Democratic fold.

Freedmen, the backbone of southern Republicanism, provided eight out of ten Republican votes. Republican rule lasted longest in states with the largest

RADICAL·MEMBERS
OF THE S°. CA. LEGISLATURE.

Republicans in the South Carolina Legislature, *c. 1868*
Only in South Carolina did blacks comprise a majority in the legislature and dominate the legislative process during Reconstruction. This photographic collage of "Radical" legislators, black and white, suggests the extent of black representation. In 1874, blacks won the majority of seats in South Carolina's state senate as well.

black populations, such as South Carolina, Mississippi, Alabama, and Louisiana. Introduced to politics in the black conventions of 1865–1867, the freedmen sought land, education, civil rights, and political equality. Even when land was not forthcoming, they continued to vote Republican. As an elderly freedman announced at a Georgia political convention in 1867, "We know our friends."

Although Reconstruction governments would have collapsed without black votes, freedmen held at most one in five political offices. Blacks served in all southern legislatures and filled many high posts in Louisiana, Mississippi, and South Carolina. They constituted a majority, however, only in the legislature of South Carolina, a state in which more than 60 percent of the population was black. No blacks won the office of governor, and only two served in the U.S. Senate, Hiram Revels and Blanche K. Bruce, both of Mississippi.

In the House of Representatives, a mere 6 percent of southern members were black, and almost half of these came from South Carolina.

Black officeholders on the state level formed a political elite. They often differed from their black constituents in background, education, wealth, and complexion. A disproportionate number were literate blacks who had been free before the Civil War. (Many more former slaves held office on the local level than on the state level.) South Carolina's roster of elected officials illustrates some distinctions between high-level black officeholders and the freedmen who voted for them. Among those blacks sent to Congress, almost all claimed some secondary education, and some held advanced degrees. In South Carolina's state legislature, most black members, unlike the majority of their constituents, came from large towns and cities; many had spent time in the North; and some were well-off property owners or even former slave-owners. Color differences were evident, too: 43 percent of South Carolina's black state legislators were mulattos, as were only 7 percent of the state's black population.

The status gap between high-level black officials and black voters was significant. Most freedmen cared mainly about their economic future, especially about acquiring land, whereas black officeholders cared most about attaining equal rights. Still, both groups shared high expectations, and both prized enfranchisement. "We are not prepared for this suffrage," averred William Beverly Nash, an uneducated former slave, at the South Carolina constitutional convention. "But we can learn. Give a man tools and let him commence to use them and in time he will learn a trade. So it is with voting. We may not understand it at the start, but in time we shall learn to do our duty."

Republican Rule

Large numbers of blacks participated in American government for the first time in the state constitutional conventions of 1867–1868. The South Carolina convention had a black majority, and in Louisiana half the delegates were freedmen. The conventions forged democratic changes in their state constitutions. Delegates abolished property qualifications for officeholding, made many appointive offices elective, and redistricted state legislatures more equitably. All states established universal manhood suffrage, and some conventions offered further innovations: the new constitutions of Louisiana and South Carolina opened public schools to both races. These provisions integrated the New Orleans public schools as well as the University of South Carolina, from which whites withdrew. But most states did not provide for integrated schools, and no state instituted land reform. When proposals for land confiscation and redistribution arose at the state conventions, they fell to defeat, as they had in Congress. Hoping to attract northern investment to the reconstructed South, southern Republicans hesitated to threaten property rights or to adopt land-reform measures that northern Republicans had rejected. South Carolina did set up a commission to buy land and make it available to freedmen, and several states changed their tax structures to force uncultivated land onto the market, but in no case was ex-Confederate land confiscated.

Once civil power shifted from the federal army to the newly formed state governments, the Republican administrations began ambitious programs of public works. They built roads, bridges, and public buildings; promoted railroad development by endorsing railroad bonds; and funded institutions to care for orphans, the insane, and the disabled. The Republican regimes also expanded state bureaucracies, raised salaries for government employees, and formed state militia, in which blacks were often heavily represented. Finally, they created public-school systems, almost nonexistent in the South until then.

Because rebuilding the devastated South and expanding the state governments cost millions, state debts and taxes skyrocketed. During the 1860s the southern tax burden rose 400 percent. State legislatures increased poll taxes or "head" taxes (levies on individuals); enacted luxury, sales, and occupation taxes; and imposed new property taxes. Before the war southern states had taxed property in slaves but had barely taxed landed property at all. Now for the first time, state governments assessed even small farmers' holdings, and big planters paid what they considered an excessive burden. Although northern tax rates still exceeded southern rates, southern landowners resented the new levies. In their view, Reconstruction strained the pocketbooks of the propertied, who were already beset by labor problems and falling land values, in order to finance the vast expenditures of Republican legislators, or what one Alabamian called the "no property herd."

To Reconstruction's opponents, moreover, Republican rule was wasteful and corrupt, if not the "most stupendous system of organized robbery in history." A state like Mississippi, which had an honest government, provided little basis for such charges. But critics could justifiably point to Louisiana, where the governor pocketed thousands of dollars of state funds and corruption permeated all government transactions (as indeed it had before the war). Or they could cite South Carolina, where bribery ran rampant. The main postwar profiteers, besides the government officials who took bribes, were the railroad promoters who doled them out, and these were not necessarily Republicans. Nor did the Republican regimes in the South hold a monopoly on big spending or corruption. After the war bribery pervaded government transactions North and South, and far more money changed hands in the North. But Reconstruction's critics assailed Republican rule for additional reasons.

Counterattacks

Vexed as they were by northern interference, scalawag "treachery," and high taxes, ex-Confederates especially chafed at black enfranchisement and spoke with dread about the "horror of Negro domination." As soon as congressional Reconstruction took effect, a clamorous campaign began to undermine it. When the state constitutional conventions met, the Democratic press stood ready. Newspapers assailed North Carolina's delegates as an "Ethiopian minstrelsy . . . baboons, monkeys, mules . . . and other jackasses." They demeaned Louisiana's constitution as "the work of ignorant Negroes cooperating with a gang of white adventurers." A Little Rock newspaper denigrated the Arkansas convention as "a foul gathering whose putridity stinks in the nostrils of all decency."

The Democrats delayed political mobilization until the southern states were readmitted to the Union. After readmission, however, the Democrats swung into action, calling themselves Conservatives so as not to repel those former Whigs who might join them. At first they sought to win the votes of blacks; but when that effort failed, they tried other tactics. In 1868–1869 Georgia Democrats challenged the eligibility of black legislators and expelled them from office. In response, the federal government reestablished military rule in Georgia, but determined Democrats still undercut Republican power. In every southern state, they contested elections, backed dissident Republican factions, and were able to elect some

The Ku Klux Klan

*The menacing symbol and hooded disguise charac-
terized the Ku Klux Klan's campaign of intimidation
during Reconstruction. A Klan flag of 1866 (below)
features a fierce emblem and a threatening Latin
motto ("Because it always is, because it is everywhere, because it is abominable"). Hooded Klansmen, like this Tennessee nightrider (right), wore
colored robes with astrological symbols, such as the
moon and stars. The Klan strove to end Republican
rule, restore white supremacy, and obliterate, in a
southern editor's words, "the preposterous and
wicked dogma of negro equality."*

Democratic legislators. They also made steady inroads among the scalawags, siphoning some of their
votes from the Republicans.

Vigilante efforts to reduce black votes bolstered
the Democrats' campaigns to win white ones. Antagonism toward free blacks, long a prominent motif in
southern life, resurged after the war. During presidential Reconstruction, when the white South sought to
control freedmen's mobility, antiblack violence often
erupted. Freedmen's Bureau agents in 1865 itemized a
variety of outrages against blacks, including shooting,
murder, rape, arson, roasting, and "severe and inhuman beating." Vigilante groups sprang up sponta-
neously in all parts of the former Confederacy under
names like moderators, regulators, and in Louisiana,
Knights of the White Camelia. A new group soon rose
to dominance. In the spring of 1866, when the Johnson governments were still in power, six young Confederate war veterans in Tennessee formed a social
club, the Ku Klux Klan, distinguished by elaborate rituals, hooded costumes, and secret passwords. New
Klan dens spread through the state, and within a year

Democratic politicians and former Confederate officers took control of them. By the election of 1868,
when black suffrage had become a reality, Klan dens
existed in all the southern states, and Klansmen embarked on night raids to intimidate black voters. One of
its founders now denounced the Klan as "perverted"
and "pernicious," and indeed, it was no longer a social
club but a widespread terrorist movement. Reminiscent of the antebellum slave patrols, the Ku Klux Klan
became a violent arm of the Democratic party.

The Klan's goals were to suppress black voting,
reestablish white supremacy, and topple the Reconstruction governments. Its members attacked Union
League officers, Freedmen's Bureau officials, white
Republicans, black militia units, economically successful blacks, and black voters. Concentrated in areas
where the black and white populations were most
evenly balanced and racial tensions greatest, Klan
dens adapted their strategies and timing to local conditions. In Mississippi the Klan targeted black schools;
in Alabama it concentrated on Republican officeholders. In Arkansas terror reigned in 1868; in Georgia and

Florida Klan strength surged in 1870. Some Democrats denounced Klan members as "cut-throats and riff-raff." But prominent ex-Confederates were also known to be active Klansmen, among them General Nathan Bedford Forrest, the leader of the 1864 Fort Pillow massacre (see Chapter 15). Vigilantism united southern whites of different social classes and drew on the energy of many Confederate veterans. In areas where the Klan was inactive, other vigilante groups took its place.

Republican legislatures outlawed vigilantism through laws providing for fines and imprisonment of offenders. But the state militia could not enforce the laws, and state officials turned to the federal government for help. In May 1870 Congress passed the Enforcement Act to protect black voters. Even this law was unenforceable, because witnesses to violations were afraid to testify against vigilantes, and local juries refused to convict them. The Second Enforcement Act, which provided for federal supervision of southern elections, followed in February 1871. Two months later Congress passed the Third Enforcement Act, or Ku Klux Klan Act, which strengthened the sanctions against those who prevented blacks from voting. It also empowered the president to use federal troops to enforce the law and to suspend the writ of habeas corpus in areas that he declared in insurrection. President Grant suspended the writ in nine South Carolina counties that had been devastated by Klan attacks.

After Congress enacted the three laws, a joint congressional committee launched a full-scale investigation of Klan activities. Victimized blacks and southern politicians of both parties testified. "I have heard of any quantity of horrible deeds," Henry M. Turner, a black minister, politician, and former Union army chaplain told government investigators. "Every man in Georgia who has got any brains must be satisfied, that there are organized bands of night assassins, murderous villains, who have banded themselves together and roam about and kill Republicans, kill any man who has got the name of radical attached to him." While Turner and others testified, the Ku Klux Klan Act generated thousands of arrests; most terrorists, however, escaped conviction.

By 1872 the federal government had effectively suppressed the Klan, but vigilantism had served its purpose. Only a large military presence in the South could have protected black rights, and the government in Washington never provided it. Instead, federal power in the former Confederacy diminished. President Grant steadily reduced troop levels in the South; Congress allowed the Freedmen's Bureau to die in 1869; and the Enforcement acts became dead letters. White southerners, a Georgia politician explained to congressional investigators in 1871, could not discard "a feeling of bitterness, a feeling that the Negro is a sort of instinctual enemy of ours." The battle over Reconstruction was in essence a battle over the implications of emancipation, and it had begun as soon as the war ended.

THE IMPACT OF EMANCIPATION

"The master he says we are all free," a South Carolina slave declared in 1865. "But it don't mean we is white. And it don't mean we is equal." Emancipated slaves faced extreme handicaps. They had no property, tools, or capital and usually possessed meager skills. Only a minority had been trained as artisans, and more than 95 percent were illiterate. Still, the exhilaration of freedom was overwhelming, as slaves realized, "Now I am for myself" and "All that I make is my own." At emancipation they gained the right to their own labor and a new sense of autonomy. Under Reconstruction the freed blacks asserted their independence by seeking to cast off white control and shed the vestiges of slavery.

Confronting Freedom

For the former slaves, mobility was often the first perquisite of liberty. Some moved out of the slave quarters and set up dwellings elsewhere on their plantations; others left their plantations entirely. Landowners found that one freed slave after another vanished, with house servants and artisans leading the way. "I have never in my life met with such ingratitude," one South Carolina mistress exclaimed when a former slave ran off. Field-workers, who had less contact with whites, were more likely to stay behind or more reluctant to leave. Still, flight remained tempting. "The moment they see an opportunity to improve themselves, they will move on," diarist Mary Chesnut observed.

Emancipation stirred waves of migration within the former Confederacy. Some freed slaves left the Upper South for the Deep South and the Southwest— Florida, Mississippi, Arkansas, and Texas—where planters desperately needed labor and paid higher wages. Even more left the countryside for towns and cities, traditional havens of independence for blacks. Urban black populations sometimes doubled or tripled after emancipation. Overall during the 1860s, the urban black population increased by 75 percent, and the number of blacks in small rural towns grew as well. Many migrants eventually returned to their old locales, in search of their families or out of an attachment to the land. But they tended to settle on neighboring plantations rather than with their former owners. Freedom was the major goal. "I's wants to be a free man, cum when I please, and nobody say nuffin to me, nor order me roun'," an Alabama freedman declared to a northern journalist.

Freed blacks' yearnings to find lost family members prompted considerable movement. "They had a passion, not so much for wandering as for getting together," a Freedmen's Bureau official commented. Parents sought children who had been sold; husbands and wives who had been separated by sale, or who lived on different plantations, reunited; and families reclaimed youngsters who were being raised in masters' homes. The Freedmen's Bureau helped former slaves get information about missing relatives and travel to find them. Bureau agents also tried to resolve entanglements over the multiple alliances of spouses who had been separated under slavery.

Reunification efforts often failed. Some fugitive slaves had died during the war or were untraceable. Other ex-slaves had formed new partnerships and could not revive old ones. "I am married," one husband wrote to a former wife (probably in a dictated letter), "and my wife [and I] have two children, and if you and I meet it would make a very dissatisfied family." But there were success stories, too. "I's hunted an' hunted till I track you up here," one freedman told his wife, whom he found in a refugee camp twenty years after their separation by sale.

Once reunited, freed blacks quickly legalized unions formed under slavery, sometimes in mass ceremonies of up to seventy couples. Legal marriage had a tangible impact on family life. Men asserted themselves as household heads; wives and children of able-bodied men often withdrew from the labor force. "When I married my wife, I married her to wait on me and she has got all she can do right here for me and the children," a Tennessee freedman explained. Black women's desire to "play the lady," as southern whites described it, caused planters severe labor shortages.

Before the war at least half of field-workers had been women; in 1866, a southern journal claimed, men performed almost all the field labor. Nevertheless, by the end of Reconstruction, many black women had returned to agricultural work as part of sharecropper families. Others took paid work in cities, as laundresses, cooks, and domestic servants. (Many white women sought employment as well, for the war had incapacitated white breadwinners, reduced the supply of future husbands, and left families destitute or in diminished circumstances.) Still, former slaves continued to view stable, independent domestic life, especially the right to bring up their own children, as a major blessing of freedom. In 1870 eight out of ten black families in the cotton-producing South were two-parent families, about the same proportion as among whites.

Black Institutions

The freed blacks' desire for independence also led to the postwar growth of black churches. During the late 1860s, some freedmen congregated at churches operated by northern missionaries in the South; others withdrew from white-run churches and formed their own. The African Methodist Episcopal church, founded by Philadelphia blacks in the 1790s, gained thousands of new southern members. Negro Baptist churches sprouted everywhere, often growing out of plantation "praise meetings," religious gatherings organized by slaves.

The black churches offered a fervent, participatory experience. They also provided relief, raised funds for schools, and supported Republican policies. From the outset black ministers assumed leading political roles, first in the black conventions of 1865–1866 and later in the Reconstruction governments. After southern Democrats excluded most freedmen from political life at Reconstruction's end, ministers remained the main pillars of authority within black communities.

Black schools played a crucial role for freedmen as well. The ex-slaves eagerly sought literacy for themselves and above all for their children. At emancipation blacks organized their own schools, which the Freedmen's Bureau soon supervised. Northern philanthropic societies paid the wages of instructors, about half of whom were women. These teachers sometimes felt like pioneers in a foreign land. "Our work is just as much missionary work as if we were in

The Freedmen's School
Supported by the Freedmen's Bureau, northern freedmen's aid societies, and black denomina-
tions, freedmen's schools reached about 12 percent of school-age black children in the South by
1870. Here, a northern teacher poses with her students at a school in rural North Carolina.

India or China," a Sea Islands teacher commented. In 1869, just before it expired, the bureau reported more than four thousand black schools in the former Confederacy. Within three years each southern state had a public-school system, at least in principle, generally with separate schools for blacks and whites. Advanced schools for blacks opened as well, to train tradespeople, teachers, and ministers. The Freedmen's Bureau and northern organizations like the American Missionary Association helped to found Howard, Atlanta, and Fisk universities (all started in 1866–1867) and Hampton Institute (1868).

Despite these advances, black education remained limited. Located in towns, most freedmen's schools could not reach the large black rural population. Black public schools, similarly inaccessible to most rural black children, held classes only for very short seasons. Underfunded and inferior, they were sometimes the targets of vigilante attacks. At the end of Reconstruction, more than 80 percent of the black population were illiterate. Still, the proportion of youngsters who could not read and write had declined

and would continue to fall (see table, p. 518). "Perhaps some *will* get an education in a little while. I *knows* de *next generation will*," a freedman told a missionary in 1865. "But . . . we has been kep down *a hundred years* and *I* think it will take *a hundred years to get us back again.*"

School segregation and other forms of racial separation were taken for granted. Some black codes of 1865–1866 had segregated public-transit conveyances and public accommodations. Even after the invalidation of the codes, the custom of segregation had continued on streetcars, steamboats, and trains as well as in churches, theaters, inns, and restaurants. On railroads, for example, whites could ride in the "ladies' car" or first-class car, whereas blacks had to stay in smoking cars or boxcars with benches. In 1870 Senator Charles Sumner began campaigning in Congress for a bill that would desegregate schools, transportation facilities, juries, and public accommodations. After Sumner's death in 1874, Congress honored him by enacting a new law, the Civil Rights Act of 1875, which encompassed many ideas from his program, except

Percentage of Persons Unable to Write, by Age Group, 1870–1890, in South Carolina, Georgia, Alabama, Mississippi, and Louisiana

Age Group	1870	1880	1890
10–14			
Black	78.9	74.1	49.2
White	33.2	34.5	18.7
15–20			
Black	85.3	73.0	54.1
White	24.2	21.0	14.3
Over 20			
Black	90.4	82.3	75.5
White	19.8	17.9	17.1

Source: Roger Ransom and Richard Sutch, *One Kind of Freedom* (Cambridge: Cambridge University Press, 1978), 30.

for the controversial school-integration provision. But the law was rarely enforced, and in 1883, in the *Civil Rights Cases*, the Supreme Court invalidated it. The Fourteenth Amendment did not prohibit discrimination by individuals, the Court ruled, only that perpetrated by the state.

White southerners adamantly rejected the prospect of racial integration, which they insisted would lead to racial amalgamation. "If we have social equality, we shall have intermarriage," one white southerner contended, "and if we have intermarriage, we shall degenerate." Urban blacks, the most likely to be affected by segregation practices, sometimes challenged them, and black legislators promoted bills to desegregate public transit. Some black officeholders decried all forms of racial separatism. "The sooner we as a people forget our sable complexion," said a Mobile official, "the better it will be for us as a race." But most freed blacks were less interested in "social equality," in the sense of interracial mingling, than in black liberty and community. The newly formed postwar elite—teachers, ministers, and politicians—served black constituencies and therefore had a vested interest in separate black institutions. Rural blacks, too, widely preferred all-black institutions. They had little desire to mix with whites. On the contrary, they sought freedom from white control. Above all else, they wanted to secure personal independence by acquiring land.

Land, Labor, and Sharecropping

"The sole ambition of the freedman," a New Englander wrote from South Carolina in 1865, "appears to be to become the owner of a little piece of land, there to erect a humble home, and to dwell in peace and security, at his own free will and pleasure." Indeed, to freed blacks everywhere, "forty acres and a mule" promised emancipation from plantation labor, from white domination, and from cotton, the "slave crop." Just as garden plots provided a measure of autonomy under slavery, so did landownership signify economic independence afterward. "We want to be placed on land until we are able to buy it and make it our own," a black minister had told General Sherman in Georgia during the war. Some freedmen defended their right to the land on which they lived, by pointing out that they and their forebears had worked on it for decades without pay.

But freedmen's visions of landownership failed to materialize, for, as we have seen, large-scale land reform never occurred. Proposals to confiscate or redistribute Confederate property failed in Congress as well as in the southern state legislatures. Some freedmen did obtain land with the help of the Union army or the Freedmen's Bureau, and black soldiers sometimes pooled resources to buy land, as on the Sea Islands (see Chapter 15). The federal government also attempted to provide ex-slaves with land. In 1866 Congress passed the Southern Homestead Act, which set aside 44 million acres of land in five southern states for freedmen and loyal whites. Not only did this acreage contain poor soil, but few former slaves had the resources to survive even until their first harvest. Thus although about four thousand blacks were resettled on homesteads under the law, most were unable to establish farms. (White southern homesteaders fared little better.) By the end of Reconstruction, only a small minority of former slaves in each state owned working farms. In Georgia in 1876, for instance, blacks controlled a mere 1.3 percent of total acreage. Without large-scale land reform, the obstacles to black landownership remained overwhelming.

What were these obstacles? First, most freedmen lacked the capital to buy land and the equipment needed to work it. Furthermore, white southerners on the whole opposed selling land to blacks. Most important, planters sought to preserve a black labor force. They insisted that freedmen would work only under coercion, and not at all if the possibility of landownership arose. As soon as the war ended, the white South took steps to make sure that black labor would remain available where it was needed, on the plantations.

During presidential Reconstruction, southern state legislatures tried to limit black mobility and to preserve a captive labor force through the black codes. Under labor contracts in effect in 1865–1866, freedmen received wages, housing, food, and clothing in exchange for fieldwork. With cash so scarce, wages usually took the form of a very small share of the crop, often one-eighth or less, divided among the entire plantation work force. Serving as mediators between former slaves and landowners, Freedmen's Bureau agents actively promoted the new labor system; they encouraged freedmen to sign labor contracts and tried to ensure adequate wages. Imbued with the northern free-labor ideology, which held that wage workers could rise to the status of self-supporting tradesmen and property owners, bureau officials and agents endorsed black wage labor as an interim arrangement that would lead to economic independence. "You must begin at the bottom of the ladder and climb up," Freedmen's Bureau head O. O. Howard exhorted a group of Louisiana freedmen in 1865.

But the freedmen disliked the new wage system, especially the use of gang labor, which resembled the work pattern under slavery. Planters had complaints, too. In some regions the black labor force had shrunk to half its prewar size or less, due to the migration of freedmen and to black women's withdrawal from fieldwork. Once united in defense of slavery, planters now competed for black workers. Moreover, their labor problems mounted, for the freedmen, whom planters often scorned as lazy and incorrigible, did not intend to work as long or as hard as they had labored under slavery. One planter estimated that workers accomplished only "two-fifths of what they did under the old system"; and as productivity fell, so did land values. Some planters considered importing white immigrant labor, but they doubted that whites would perform black fieldwork for long. To top off the planters' problems, cotton prices plummeted, for during the war northern and foreign buyers had found new sources of cotton in Egypt and India, and the world supply had vastly increased. Finally, the harvests of 1866 and 1867 were extremely poor. By then an agricultural impasse had been reached: landowners lacked labor and freedmen lacked land. But free blacks, unlike slaves, had the right to enter into contracts—or to refuse to do so—and thereby gained some leverage.

Planters and freedmen began experimenting with new labor schemes, including the division of plantations into small tenancies (see "A Place in Time"). Sharecropping, the most widespread arrangement, evolved as a compromise. Under the sharecropping system, landowners subdivided large plantations into farms of thirty to fifty acres, which they rented to freedmen under annual leases for a share of the crop, usually half. Freedmen preferred this system to wage labor because it represented a step toward independence. The decentralized plan enabled heads of households to use the labor of family members. Moreover, a half-share of the crop far exceeded the fraction that freedmen had received as wages under the black codes. Planters often spoke of sharecropping as a capitulation, but they gained as well. Landowners retained power over tenants, because annual leases did not have to be renewed; they could expel undesirable tenants at the end of the year. Planters also shared the risk of planting with tenants: if a crop failed, both suffered the loss. Most important, planters retained control of their land and in some cases extended their holdings. The most productive land, therefore, remained in the hands of a small group of owners, as before the war. Sharecropping forced planters to relinquish day-to-day control over the labor of freedmen, but it helped to preserve the planter elite.

Sharecropping arrangements varied widely and were not universal. On sugar and rice plantations, the wage system continued. Some freedmen remained independent renters. Some landowners leased areas to white tenants who then subcontracted with black labor. But by the end of the 1860s, the plantation tradition had given way to sharecropping in the cotton South, and the new system continued to expand. A severe depression in 1873 drove many black renters into sharecropping. By then thousands of independent white farmers had become sharecroppers as well. Stung by wartime losses and by the dismal postwar economy, they sank into debt and lost their land to creditors. Many backcountry residents, no longer able to get by on subsistence farming, shifted to cash crops like cotton and suffered the same fate. At the end of Reconstruction, one-third of the white farmers in Mississippi, for instance, worked as sharecroppers.

By 1880, 80 percent of the land in the cotton-producing states had been subdivided into tenancies, most of it farmed by sharecroppers, white and black. Indeed, white sharecroppers now outnumbered black ones, although a higher proportion of southern blacks,

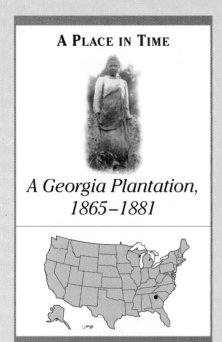

A Georgia Plantation, 1865–1881

The transformation of the Barrow plantation in Oglethorpe County, Georgia, is a microcosmic illustration of the striking changes that occurred in southern agriculture during Reconstruction. Before the Civil War, David Crenshaw Barrow had been the absentee owner of a two-thousand-acre plantation long known as the Pope Place. He had inherited the land through his first wife, Sarah Elizabeth Pope. The owner of several other plantations as well, Barrow had possessed some 400 slaves, about 135 of whom had lived on the "Pope Place." Assisted by slave foremen, an overseer had run the plantation. The overseer had lived in the main plantation house, from where he had kept a watchful eye on the slave quarters.

After the war the plantation changed in so many ways that by 1881, according to Barrow's son, David Crenshaw Barrow, Jr., "the place would now hardly be recognized." But the changes had occurred in stages.

The critical period immediately followed the war. At emancipation some of Barrow's former slaves had left the plantation, probably for nearby towns or other plantations. Those remaining had signed annual labor contracts with Barrow. Divided into two competing squads and supervised by a hired foreman, the freedmen grew cotton under the gang system. They received wages in the form of a share of the crop, with a reward going to the squad that worked more efficiently. Barrow liked the new system, but the freedmen did not. Within a few years, they rebelled against the hired foreman, "each man feeling the very natural desire to be his own 'boss' and farm to himself," Barrow's son wrote. The squads split into smaller groups and spread over the plantation. Still working for a small share of the crop, they continued to use the owner's mules and equipment. Now Barrow found the system unsatisfactory. He claimed that the freedmen mistreated the mules and failed to deliver his full share of the crop.

In the late 1860s, life on the Barrow plantation entered a third phase. One of the first planters in his area to subdivide his land, Barrow transformed the plantation into tenant farms of twenty-five to thirty acres. With this change, the freedmen moved their households from the old slave quarters to their own farms. They typically set up their log cabins at springs around

Tenants on the Barrow Plantation
Children pick cotton on the Barrow plantation in the late nineteenth century.

David Crenshaw Barrow, Jr.
The young Barrow posed for this photograph around the time that his article in Scribner's Monthly *appeared.*

The Barrow Plantation, 1860 and 1881
These maps show the changes that transformed the Barrow plantation after the Civil War.

the plantation and then added outhouses, stables, corncribs, and fodderhouses. Each head of family signed an annual contract, agreeing to pay a rent of 500 to 750 pounds of cotton plus varied amounts of other crops. As tenant farmers, the freedmen raised cotton (about half their crop), corn, and vegetables; the men did the plowing, and women and children the hoeing. Using uncultivated land for pasture, the tenants also raised hogs, chickens, and a few cattle. Barrow sold each farmer a mule on credit, and he set aside an acre on the edge of the plantation for a church and a school, which was open three months a year.

In 1881 David Crenshaw Barrow lived in the main house with two family members, probably his second wife (a former New Englander) and an unmarried daughter, Clara. The plantation's tenants numbered 162, at least half of them children. One out of four families was named Barrow. When David Crenshaw Barrow, Jr., summed up plantation life in 1881 for the readers of *Scribner's Monthly,* he emphasized "how completely the relations between the races at the South have changed." For instance, his father's tenants needed little supervision. "Very many negro farmers are capable of directing the working of their own crops," he explained,

"and not a few object to directions." The younger Barrow expressed pride that no tenant on his father's land had joined the "exodus" movement that had drawn blacks out of the South in the late 1870s. He also took pleasure in the fact that the most troublesome slave, Lem Bryant, once beyond the overseer's control, had become the most industrious tenant—a transformation Barrow, Jr., attributed to the impact of freedom.

Claiming satisfaction with the changes that he and his father had seen, planter Barrow's son assured his readers that southern freedmen were content with their lives as tenant farmers. "In Georgia, the negro has adapted himself to his new circumstances, and freedom fits him as if it had been cut out and made for him," he reported. "As a people, they are happy; they have become suited to their new estate and it to them." The younger Barrow's positive view of postwar farming arrangements might well have been challenged by the growing number of southerners, black and white, who had become mired in debt as sharecroppers. His article in *Scribner's,* however, written for a northern audience, was intended to convey a political message. Not only had the one-time slaves adjusted to emancipation, Barrow, Jr., sug-

gested, but so had their former owners. This concession was part of the national celebration of reunion that followed the collapse of Reconstruction.

Few if any of David Crenshaw Barrow's nine offspring, all born on the "Pope Place," found a vocation in southern agriculture. Two sons had died as young men, and another in a Civil War battle. By 1881 the surviving Barrow children, save Clara, had moved away from their father's home and chosen a variety of occupations. Pope Barrow, the oldest, became a lawyer and a judge and would later serve as U.S. senator from Georgia. Thomas Barrow, who had fought with the Confederate army, first turned to business and then became a Baptist minister. Lucy Barrow married the son of a prominent Georgian, Howell Cobb, who had once been considered for the post of president of the Confederacy. Nellie Barrow also married and moved to Sapelo Island off the coast of Georgia. David Crenshaw Barrow, Jr., began his career as a lawyer but in 1879 became a mathematics teacher at the University of Georgia in Athens, not far from the Oglethorpe County plantation. Barrow, Jr., retained an avid interest in farming, which he later practiced in partnership with the son of his father's former overseer.

Southern Share-cropping, 1880

The depressed economy of the late 1870s caused poverty and debt, increased tenancy among white farmers, and forced many renters, black and white, into sharecropping. By 1880 the sharecropping system pervaded most southern counties, with the highest concentrations in the cotton belt from South Carolina to eastern Texas.

SOURCE: U.S. Census Office, Tenth Census, 1880, *Report of the Production of Agriculture* (Washington, D.C.: Government Printing Office, 1883), Table 5.

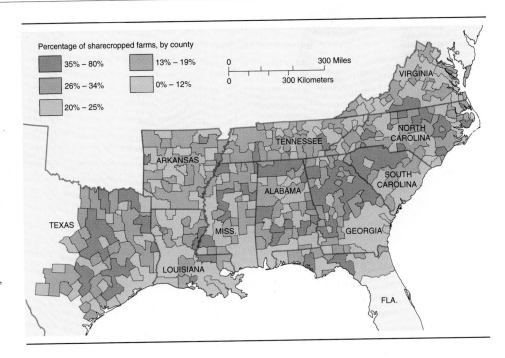

Percentage of sharecropped farms, by county

- 35% – 80%
- 26% – 34%
- 20% – 25%
- 13% – 19%
- 0% – 12%

about 75 percent, were involved in the system. Changes in marketing and finance, meanwhile, made the sharecroppers' lot increasingly precarious.

Toward a Crop-Lien Economy

Before the Civil War, planters had depended on factors, or middlemen, who sold them supplies, extended credit, and marketed their crops through urban merchants. These long-distance credit arrangements were backed by the high value and liquidity of slave property. When slavery ended, the factorage system collapsed. The postwar South, with hundreds of thousands of tenants and sharecroppers, needed a far more localized network of credit.

Into the gap stepped the rural merchants (often themselves planters), who advanced supplies to tenants and sharecroppers on credit and sold their crops to wholesalers or textile manufacturers. Because renters had no property to use as collateral, the merchants secured their loans with a lien, or claim, on each farmer's next crop. They charged exorbitant interest of 50 percent or more and quickly drew many tenants and sharecroppers into a cycle of indebtedness. Owing part of the crop to a landowner for rent, a sharecropper also owed a rural merchant a large sum (perhaps amounting to the rest of his crop, or more)

for supplies. Often, an illiterate tenant could not keep track of his financial arrangements, and a merchant could easily take advantage of him. "A man that didn't know how to count would always lose," an Arkansas freedman later explained. Once a tenant's debts or alleged debts exceeded the value of his crop, he was tied to the land, to cotton, and to sharecropping.

By the end of Reconstruction, sharecropping and crop liens had transformed southern agriculture. They bound the entire region to staple production and prevented crop diversification, for despite plunging cotton prices, creditors—landowners and merchants—insisted that tenants raise only easily marketable cash crops. Short of capital, planters could no longer invest in new equipment or improve their land by such techniques as crop rotation and contour plowing. Soil depletion, land erosion, and agricultural backwardness soon locked much of the South into a cycle of poverty. Overall, postwar changes in southern agriculture left the region with extremely bleak economic prospects.

But the major victims of the new agricultural arrangements were the indebted tenant farmers, who had been trapped in a system of what has been called debt peonage. Raising cotton for distant markets, for prices over which they had no control, remained the only survival route open to poor farmers, regardless of race. But the low income thus derived often forced them into sharecropping and crop liens, from which escape was difficult. Black tenants, for whom neither landownership nor economic independence ever materialized, suffered further handicaps. Not only were their rights as workers limited, but when Reconstruction ended, their political rights dwindled too. As one southern regime after another returned to Democratic control, freedmen could no longer look to the state governments for protection. Nor could they turn to the federal government, for northern politicians were preoccupied with their own problems.

New Concerns in the North

The nomination of Ulysses S. Grant for president in 1868 launched a chaotic era in national politics. Grant's two terms in office featured political scandals, a party revolt, a massive depression, and a steady retreat from Reconstruction policies. By the mid-1870s, northern voters cared more about the economic climate, unemployment, labor unrest, and currency problems than about the "southern question." Responsive to the shift in popular mood, Republicans became eager to end sectional conflict and consequently turned their backs on the freedmen of the South.

Grantism

Republicans had good reason to pass over longtime party leaders and nominate the popular Grant. A war hero, Grant was endorsed by Union veterans and admired throughout the North. Although identified with Radical Republican views by 1867, he had nonetheless escaped the bitter feuds of Reconstruction politics. At first a Johnson adviser, Grant had broken with Johnson during the tenure-of-office crisis and become his com-

petitor. Even before Grant's nomination, important visitors to Washington called on him as well as Johnson.

To oppose Grant in the 1868 election, the Democrats nominated New York governor Horatio Seymour, arch-critic of the Lincoln administration during the war. Seymour opposed Reconstruction and advocated "sound money," or the withdrawal of greenbacks from circulation, a policy begun by Hugh McCulloch, Johnson's treasury secretary. Grant, who defended Reconstruction, ran on his personal popularity more than on issues. Although he carried all but eight states in the election, the popular vote was very close; in the South, the votes of newly enfranchised freedmen provided the margin of victory. When he was inaugurated, Grant vowed to execute all the laws whether he agreed with them or not, to support sound money, and to follow a humane policy toward the Indians.

A strong leader in war, Grant proved a passive president. Although he lacked Johnson's instinct for disaster, he had little skill at politics. Many of his cabinet appointees—business executives, army men, and family friends—were mediocre if not unscrupulous, and a string of scandals plagued his administration. In 1869 financier Jay Gould and his partner Jim Fisk attempted to corner the gold market with the help of Grant's brother-in-law, a New York speculator. When gold prices tumbled, Gould salvaged his own fortune, but investors were ruined and Grant's reputation was tarnished. Then before the president's first term ended, his vice president, Schuyler Colfax, was found to be linked to the Crédit Mobilier, a fraudulent construction company created to skim off the profits of the Union Pacific Railroad. Using government funds granted to the railroad, the Union Pacific directors awarded padded construction contracts to the Crédit Mobilier, of which they were also the directors. Discredited, Colfax was dropped from the Grant ticket in 1872. More trouble lay ahead. Grant's private secretary, Orville Babcock, was unmasked in 1875 after taking money from the "whiskey ring," a group of distillers who bribed federal agents to avoid paying millions in

The Election of 1868

Candidates	Parties	Electoral Vote	Popular Vote	Percentage of Popular Vote
ULYSSES S. GRANT	Republican	214	3,013,421	52.7
Horatio Seymour	Democratic	80	2,706,829	47.3

Boss Tweed
Thomas Nast's cartoons in Harper's Weekly *helped topple New York Democratic boss William M. Tweed (photo at far left), who, with his associates, embodied corruption on a large scale. The Tweed Ring had granted lucrative franchises to companies they controlled, padded construction bills, practiced graft and extortion, and exploited every opportunity to plunder the city's funds.*

whiskey taxes. And in 1876 voters learned that Grant's secretary of war, William E. Belknap, had taken bribes to sell lucrative Indian trading posts in Oklahoma. Impeached and disgraced, Belknap resigned.

Although Grant was not personally involved in the scandals, he loyally defended his subordinates. To his critics, "Grantism" came to stand for fraud, bribery, and corruption in office. Such evils spread far beyond Washington. In Pennsylvania, for example, the Standard Oil Company and the Pennsylvania Railroad controlled the legislature. Urban politics also provided rich opportunities for graft and swindles. The New York City press revealed in 1872 that Democratic boss William M. Tweed, the "Grand Sachem" of Tammany Hall, led a ring that looted the city treasury and collected an estimated $200 million in kickbacks and payoffs. When Mark Twain and coauthor Charles Dudley Warner published their satiric novel *The Gilded Age** (1873), readers recognized the book's speculators, self-promoters, and maniacal opportunists as familiar types in public life.

Grant had some success in foreign policy. In 1872 his competent secretary of state, Hamilton Fish, engineered the settlement of the *Alabama* claims with

---

*The term "Gilded Age" was subsequently used to refer to the decades from the 1870s to the 1890s.

England. To compensate for damage done by British-built raiders sold to the Confederacy during the war, an international tribunal awarded the United States $15.5 million. But the Grant administration undercut this success with a fiasco when it tried to add nonadjacent territory to the United States, as the Johnson administration had done. In 1867 Johnson's secretary of state, William H. Seward, had negotiated a treaty in which the United States bought Alaska from Russia at the bargain price of $7.2 million. Although the press mocked "Seward's Ice Box," the purchase kindled expansionists' hopes. In 1870 Grant decided to annex the Caribbean island nation of Santo Domingo. Formerly known as Hispaniola and today called the Dominican Republic, Santo Domingo had been passed back and forth since the late eighteenth century among France, Spain, and Haiti. Annexation, Grant believed, would promote Caribbean trade and provide a haven for persecuted southern blacks, who might settle among the Dominicans. American speculators anticipated windfalls from land sales, commerce, and mining in Santo Domingo. But Congress disliked Grant's plan. Senator Charles Sumner denounced the scheme as an imperialist "dance of blood." The Senate rejected the annexation treaty and further diminished Grant's reputation.

The Election of 1872

Candidates	Parties	Electoral Vote	Popular Vote	Percentage of Popular Vote
ULYSSES S. GRANT	Republican	286	3,596,745	55.6
Horace Greeley*	Democratic		2,843,446	43.9

*Upon Greeley's death shortly after the election, the electors supporting him divided their votes among minor candidates.

As the election of 1872 approached, dissident Republicans expressed fears that "Grantism" at home and abroad would ruin the party. Even Grant's new running mate, Henry Wilson, referred to the president privately as a millstone, or burden, on his fellow Republicans. The dissidents took action. Led by a combination of former Radicals—including Sumner (now Grant's enemy), Senator Carl Schurz of Missouri, and Congressman George Julian of Indiana—and Republicans left out of Grant's "Great Barbecue," the president's critics formed their own party, the Liberal Republicans.

The Liberals' Revolt

The Liberal Republican revolt marked a turning point in Reconstruction history. By splitting the Republican party, it undermined support for Republican southern policy. The Liberals attacked the "regular" Republicans on several key issues. Denouncing "Grantism" and "spoilsmen" (political hacks who gained party office), they demanded civil-service reform to bring the "best men" into government. Rejecting the usual Republican high-tariff policy, they espoused free trade. Most important, the Liberals condemned "bayonet rule" in the South. Even some Republicans once known for radicalism did a turnabout, claiming that Reconstruction had achieved its goal: blacks had been enfranchised and could henceforth manage for themselves. Corruption in government, North and South, they asserted, now posed a greater danger than Confederate resurgence. In the South, indeed, corrupt Republican regimes were *kept* in power, the Liberals said, because the "best men"—the most capable politicians—were ex-Confederates who had been barred from officeholding.

For president the new party bypassed Charles Sumner and nominated *New York Tribune* editor Horace Greeley, who had inconsistently supported both a stringent reconstruction policy and leniency toward former rebels. The Democrats endorsed Greeley as well, despite his longtime condemnation of them. Their campaign slogan explained their support: "Anything to Beat Grant." Republican reformers were suddenly allied with the Democratic party that they had recently castigated as a "sewer" of treasonous sentiments.

Horace Greeley proved so diligent a campaigner that he worked himself to death making speeches from the back of a campaign train. He died a few weeks after the election. Grant, who won 56 percent of the popular vote, carried all the northern states as well as a majority of the sixteen southern and border states. But the division among Republicans affected Reconstruction. To deprive the Liberals of a campaign issue, Grant Republicans in Congress, the "regulars," passed an amnesty act that effectively allowed all but a few hundred ex-Confederate officials to hold office. The flood of private amnesty acts that followed convinced white southerners that any ex-Confederate save Jefferson Davis could rise to power. During Grant's second term, Republican desires to discard the "southern question" mounted as a depression of unprecedented scope gripped the whole nation.

The Panic of 1873

With the postwar years came accelerated industrialization, rapid economic expansion, and frantic speculation. Investors rushed to take advantage of rising prices, new markets, high tariffs, and seemingly boundless opportunities. Railroads provided the biggest lure. In May 1869 railroad executives drove a golden spike into the ground at Promontory Point, Utah, joining the Union Pacific and Central Pacific lines (see Chapter 17). The first transcontinental railroad heralded a new era. By 1873 almost four hundred railroad corporations crisscrossed the Northeast, consuming tons of coal and miles of steel rail from the mines and mills of Pennsylvania and neighboring states. Transforming the northern economy, the railroad boom led entrepreneurs to overspeculate, with drastic results.

Philadelphia banker Jay Cooke, who had helped finance the Union effort with his bond campaign during the Civil War, had taken over a new transcontinental line, the Northern Pacific, in 1869. Northern Pacific securities sold briskly for several years, but in 1873 the line's construction costs outran new investments. In September of that year, his vaults full of bonds he could no longer sell, Cooke failed to meet his obligations, and his bank, the largest in the nation, shut down. Smaller firms collapsed, as did the stock market. This Panic of 1873 triggered a five-year depression that wrought widespread devastation. Banks closed, farm prices plummeted, steel furnaces stood idle, and one out of four railroads failed. Within two years, eighteen thousand businesses went bankrupt, and by 1878 3 million employees were out of jobs. Those still at work suffered repeated wage cuts, labor protests mounted, and industrial violence spread (see Chapter 18). The depression of the 1870s revealed the conflicts of a new, industrial America.

The depression also fed a dispute over currency that had begun in 1865. The Civil War had created fiscal chaos. During the war, Americans had used both national bank notes, yellow in color, which would eventually be converted into gold, and greenbacks, a paper currency not "backed" by a particular weight in gold. To stabilize the postwar currency, greenbacks would have to be withdrawn from circulation. This "sound-money" policy, favored by investors, was implemented by Treasury Secretary Hugh McCulloch with the backing of Congress. But those who depended on easy credit, both indebted farmers and manufacturers, wanted an expanding currency; that is, more greenbacks. Once the depression began, demands for such "easy money" rose. The issue divided both major parties and was compounded by another one: how to repay the federal debt.

During the war the Union government had borrowed what were then astronomical sums, on whatever terms it could get, mainly through the sale of war bonds—in effect, short-term federal IOUs—to private citizens. By 1869 the issue of war-debt repayment was straining the Republican party, whose support came from voters with diverse financial interests. To pacify bondholders, Senator John Sherman of Ohio and other Republican leaders obtained passage of the Public Credit Act of 1869, which promised to pay the war debt in "coin." Holders of war bonds expected no less; in fact, they expected payment in coin, although many had bought their bonds with greenbacks!

With investors reassured by the Public Credit Act, Sherman guided legislation through Congress that swapped the old short-term bonds for new ones payable over the next generation. In 1872 another bill in effect defined "coin" as "gold coin" by dropping the traditional silver dollar from the official coinage. Through a feat of ingenious compromise, which placated investors and debtors, Sherman preserved the public credit, the currency, and Republican unity. In 1875 he engineered the Specie Resumption Act, which promised to put the nation effectively on the gold standard in 1879, while tossing a few more immediate but less important bones to Republican voters who wanted "easy money." Grant, no financial theorist, signed this act.

The Republican leadership acted not a moment too soon, because when the Democrats gained control of the House in 1875, with the depression in full force, a verbal storm broke out. Many Democrats and some Republicans passionately demanded that the silver dollar be restored in order to expand the currency and relieve the depression. These "free-silver" advocates secured passage of the Bland-Allison Act of 1878, which partially restored silver coinage. The law required the treasury to buy $2 million to $4 million worth of silver each month and turn it into coin but did not revive the silver standard. In 1876 other expansionists formed the Greenback party, which adopted the debtors' cause and fought to keep greenbacks in circulation. But despite the election of fourteen Greenback congressmen, they did not get even as far as the free-silver people had. As the nation emerged from depression in 1879, the clamor for "easy money" subsided, only to resurge in the 1890s (see Chapter 21). The controversial "money question" of the 1870s, never permanently solved, gave politicians and voters another reason to focus on new northern issues and forget about the South.

Reconstruction and the Constitution

The Supreme Court of the 1870s also played a role in weakening northern support for Reconstruction. In the wartime crisis, few cases of note had come before the Court. After the war, however, constitutional questions surged into prominence.

First, would the Court support congressional laws to protect freedmen's rights? The decision in *Ex parte* Milligan (1866) suggested not. In this case, the Court declared that a military commission established by the president or Congress could not try civilians in areas remote from war where the civil courts were functioning. Thus special military courts to enforce the Supplementary Freedmen's Bureau Act were doomed. Second, would the Court sabotage the congressional Reconstruction plan, as Republicans feared? Their qualms were valid, for if the Union was indissoluble, as the North had claimed during the war, then the concept of *restoring* states to the Union would be meaningless. In *Texas* v. *White* (1869), the Court ruled that although the Union was indissoluble and secession was legally impossible, the process of Reconstruction was still constitutional. It was grounded in Congress's power to ensure each state a republican form of government and to recognize the legitimate government in any state.

The 1869 decision protected the Republicans' Reconstruction plan. But during the 1870s, when cases arose involving the Fourteenth and Fifteenth amendments, the Court backed away from Reconstruction policy. Significantly, most of the justices at this time were Republicans who had been appointed to the Court by Lincoln and Grant.

In the *Slaughterhouse* cases of 1873, the Supreme Court began to chip away at the Fourteenth Amendment. The cases involved a business monopoly rather than freedmen's rights, but they provided an opportunity to interpret the amendment narrowly. In 1869 the Louisiana legislature had granted a monopoly over the New Orleans slaughterhouse business to one firm and had closed down all other slaughterhouses in the interest of public health. The excluded butchers brought suit. The state had deprived them of their lawful occupation without due process of law, they claimed, and such action violated the Fourteenth Amendment, which guaranteed that no state could "abridge the privileges or immunities" of U.S. citizens. The Supreme Court upheld the Louisiana legislature by issuing a doctrine of "dual citizenship." The Fourteenth Amendment, declared the Court, protected only the rights of *national* citizenship, such as the right of interstate travel or the right to federal protection when on the high seas. It did not protect those basic civil rights that fell to citizens by virtue of their *state* citizenship. Therefore, the federal government was not obliged to protect such rights against violation by the states. The

Slaughterhouse decision came close to nullifying the intent of the Fourteenth Amendment—to secure freedmen's rights against state encroachment.

The Supreme Court again backed away from Reconstruction in two cases involving the Enforcement Act of 1870. The case of *U.S. v. Reese* (1876) centered on Kentucky officials who, after barring blacks from voting, had been indicted in 1873 by a Kentucky federal court under the First Enforcement Act. In its decision in favor of the officials, the Supreme Court stated that the Fifteenth Amendment did not "confer the right of suffrage upon anyone." It merely prohibited the hindrance of voting on the basis of race, color, or previous condition of servitude. Since the Enforcement Act prohibited the hindrance of *anyone* from voting for *any* reason (that is, since it did not repeat the exact wording of the amendment), the Court declared its crucial sections, and the Kentucky indictment, invalid. Another 1876 case, *U.S.* v. *Cruikshank*, concerned the indictment under the 1870 Enforcement Act of white Louisianians after the Colfax massacre, a battle between armed whites and black state militiamen in which seventy blacks had surrendered, half of whom were then murdered. The Fourteenth Amendment, contended the Court, prohibited only the encroachment on individual rights by a *state*, not by other individuals; "ordinary crime" was not the target of federal law. The decision threw out the indictments and, with them, the effectiveness of the Enforcement Act.

Continuing its retreat from Reconstruction, the Supreme Court in 1883 invalidated both the Civil Rights Act of 1875 and the Ku Klux Klan Act of 1871 and later upheld segregation laws (see Chapter 21). These decisions cumulatively dismantled the Reconstruction policies that Republicans had sponsored after the war. The 1870s rulings that initiated the judicial retreat had a more immediate impact as well. They confirmed rising northern sentiment that Reconstruction's egalitarian goals could not be enforced.

Republicans in Retreat

The Republicans did not reject Reconstruction suddenly but rather disengaged from it gradually. The withdrawal process began with Grant's election to the presidency in 1868. Although not one of the architects of Reconstruction policy, Grant defended that policy and tried to enforce the laws. But he shared with most Americans a belief in decentralized government and a reluctance to assert federal authority in local and state affairs.

During the 1870s, as the northern military presence shrank in the South, Republican idealism waned in the North. The Liberal Republican revolt of 1872 eroded what remained of radicalism. Although the "regular" Republicans, who backed Grant, continued to defend Reconstruction in the 1872 election, many held ambivalent views. Commercial and industrial interests now dominated both wings of the party, and Grant supporters had greater zeal for doing business in and with the South than for rekindling sectional strife. After the Democrats showed renewed strength by winning control of the House in the 1874 elections, in a nationwide sweep, Reconstruction became a political liability.

By 1875 the Radical Republicans, so prominent in the 1860s, had vanished from the political scene. Chase, Stevens, and Sumner were dead. Other Radicals had lost office or had abandoned their former convictions. "Waving the Bloody Shirt," or defaming Democratic opponents by reviving wartime animosity, now struck many Republicans, including former Radicals, as counterproductive. Party leaders reported that voters were "sick of carpet-bag government" and tiring of both the "southern question" and the "Negro question." It now seemed pointless to continue the unpopular and expensive policy of military intervention in the South to prop up Republican regimes that even President Grant found corrupt. Finally, few Republicans shared the egalitarian spirit that had animated Stevens and Sumner. Politics aside, Republican leaders and voters generally agreed with southern Democrats that blacks, although worthy of freedom, were inferior to whites. To insist on black equality would be a thankless, divisive, and politically suicidal undertaking. Moreover, it would quash any hope of reunion between the regions. The Republicans' retreat from Reconstruction set the stage for its demise in 1877.

RECONSTRUCTION ABANDONED

"We are in a very hot political contest just now," a Mississippi planter wrote to his daughter in 1875, "with a good prospect of turning out the carpetbag thieves by whom we have been robbed for the past six to ten years." Similar contests raged through the South in the

The White League

Alabama's White League, formed in 1874, strove to oust Republicans from office by intimidating black voters. To political cartoonist Thomas Nast, such vigilante tactics suggested an alliance between the White League and the outlawed Ku Klux Klan.

1870s, as the resentment of white majorities grew and Democratic influence surged. By the end of 1872, the Democrats had regained power in Tennessee, Virginia, Georgia, and North Carolina. Within three years they won control in Texas, Alabama, Arkansas, and Mississippi. As the 1876 elections approached, Republican rule survived in only three states—South Carolina, Florida, and Louisiana. Democratic victories in the state elections of 1876 and political bargaining in Washington in 1877 abruptly ended what little remained of Reconstruction.

Redeeming the South

After 1872 the Republicans' collapse in the South accelerated. Congressional amnesty enabled almost all ex-Confederate officials to regain office, divisions among the Republicans loosened their party's weak grip on the southern electorate, and attrition diminished Republican ranks. Some carpetbaggers gave up and returned North, whereas others, including supporters of Liberal Republicans in the divisive 1872 election, shifted to the Democratic party. Scalawags de-

The Duration of Republican Rule in the Ex-Confederate States

Former Confederate States	Readmission to the Union Under Congressional Reconstruction	Democrats (Conservatives) Gain Control	Duration of Republican Rule
Alabama	June 25, 1868	November 14, 1874	6½ years
Arkansas	June 22, 1868	November 10, 1874	6½ years
Florida	June 25, 1868	January 2, 1877	8½ years
Georgia	July 15, 1870	November 1, 1871	1 year
Louisiana	June 25, 1868	January 2, 1877	8½ years
Mississippi	February 23, 1870	November 3, 1875	5½ years
North Carolina	June 25, 1868	November 3, 1870	2 years
South Carolina	June 25, 1868	November 12, 1876	8 years
Tennessee	July 24, 1866*	October 4, 1869	3 years
Texas	March 30, 1870	January 14, 1873	3 years
Virginia	January 26, 1870	October 5, 1869[†]	0 years

*Admitted before start of Congressional Reconstruction.
[†]Democrats gained control before readmission.
Source: John Hope Franklin, *Reconstruction After the Civil War* (Chicago: University of Chicago Press, 1962), 231.

serted in even larger numbers. Southerners who had joined the Republicans to moderate rampant radicalism tired of northern interference; once "home rule" by Democrats became a possibility, staying Republican meant going down with a sinking ship. Scalawag defections ruined Republican prospects. In some states, as white southerners fled the Republican party, blacks became more powerful within it, thus polarizing voters into white and black camps. Unable to win new white votes or retain the old ones, the always precarious Republican coalition fell apart.

Meanwhile, the Democrats mobilized grass roots support and overcame the white voter apathy that had plagued the early days of Reconstruction. The resurrected southern Democratic party was not a pillar of unity. Within it, businessmen who envisioned an industrialized "New South" opposed an agrarian faction called the Bourbons, who represented the old planter elite. But all Democrats shared a major goal: to oust the Republicans from office. Their tactics varied from state to state. Alabama Democrats won by promising to cut taxes and by getting out the white vote. In Louisiana the "White League," a vigilante organization formed in 1874, undermined the Republicans' hold. Intimidation also proved effective in Mississippi, where violent incidents—like the 1874 slaughter in Vicksburg of about three hundred blacks by rampaging whites—terrorized black voters. In 1875 the "Mississippi plan" took ef-

fect: local Democratic clubs armed their members, dispersed Republican meetings, patrolled voter-registration places, and marched through black areas. "The Republicans are paralyzed through fear and will not act," the anguished carpetbag governor of Mississippi wrote to his wife. "Why should I fight a hopeless battle . . . when no possible good to the Negro or anybody else would result?" In 1876, South Carolina's "Rifle Clubs" and "Red Shirts," armed groups that threatened Republicans, continued the scare tactics that had worked so well in Mississippi.

New outbursts of intimidation did not completely squelch black voting. Many southern blacks continued to vote until the end of Reconstruction and after. But the Democrats deprived the Republicans of enough black votes to win state elections. In some counties they encouraged freedmen to vote Democratic at supervised polls where voters cast their ballots in public by placing a card with a party label in a box. In other instances employers and landowners impeded black suffrage. Labor contracts included clauses barring attendance at political meetings; planters used the threat of eviction to keep sharecroppers in line. Since the Enforcement acts could not be enforced, intimidation and economic pressure succeeded.

Redemption, the word Democrats used to describe their return to power, meant more than a mere rotation in personnel. When the Democrats took office,

The Exodus to Kansas
Benjamin "Pap" Singleton, once a fugitive slave from Kentucky, returned there to promote the "exodus" movement of the late 1870s. Forming a real-estate company, Singleton traveled the South recruiting parties of freedmen who were disillusioned with the outcome of Reconstruction. These emigrants, boarding a riverboat at Vicksburg, Mississippi, looked forward to political equality, freedom from violence, and homesteads in Kansas.

they made changes as sweeping as those imposed by the Republicans in 1867–1868. Some states called constitutional conventions to reverse Republican policies. All cut back expenses, wiped out social programs, lowered taxes, and revised their tax systems to relieve landowners of large burdens. State courts limited the rights of tenants and sharecroppers. Most important, the Democrats used the law to ensure a stable black labor force. Legislatures restored vagrancy laws and revised crop-lien statutes to make landowners' claims superior to those of merchants. The redeemers extended their inventiveness to criminal law. Local ordinances in heavily black counties might restrict hunting, fishing, gun carrying, and ownership of dogs and thereby curtail the everyday activities of freedmen who lived off the land. States passed severe laws against trespassing and theft; stealing livestock or wrongly taking part of a crop became grand larceny with a penalty of up to five years

at hard labor. By the end of Reconstruction, a large black convict work force had been leased out to private contractors, who profited from their labor.

For the freedmen, whose aspirations had been raised by Republican rule, the impact of redemption was demoralizing. The new laws, Tennessee blacks contended at an 1875 convention, would impose "a condition of servitude scarcely less degrading than that endured before the late civil war." In the late 1870s, as the political climate grew more oppressive, an "exodus" movement spread through Mississippi, Tennessee, Texas, and Louisiana. "We . . . seed that there was no way on earth that we could better our condition," a Louisiana "colonization council" declared in 1877. Seeking a way out of the South, some freed blacks decided to become homesteaders in Kansas. After a major outbreak of "Kansas fever" in 1879, four thousand "exodusters" from Mississippi and Louisiana

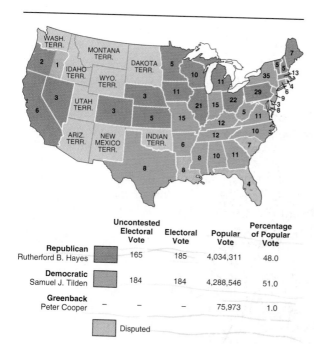

	Uncontested Electoral Vote	Electoral Vote	Popular Vote	Percentage of Popular Vote
Republican Rutherford B. Hayes	165	185	4,034,311	48.0
Democratic Samuel J. Tilden	184	184	4,288,546	51.0
Greenback Peter Cooper	–	–	75,973	1.0
Disputed				

The Disputed Election of 1876

joined about ten thousand who had reached Kansas in smaller groups earlier in the decade. But the vast majority of freedmen, devoid of resources, had no migration options or escape route. Mass movement of southern blacks to the North and Midwest would not gain momentum until the twentieth century.

The Election of 1876

By the autumn of 1876, with redemption almost complete, both parties moved to discard the heritage of animosity left by the war and Reconstruction. The Republicans nominated Rutherford B. Hayes, three times Ohio's governor, for president. Untainted by the scandals of the Grant years and popular with all factions in his party, Hayes presented himself as a "moderate" on southern policy. He favored "home rule" in the South and a guarantee of civil and political rights for all—two planks that were clearly contradictory. The Democrats nominated Governor Samuel J. Tilden of New York, a millionaire corporate lawyer and political reformer. Known for his assaults on the rapacious Tweed Ring that had plundered New York City's treasury, Tilden campaigned against fraud and waste. The candidates had much in common. Fiscal conservatives, both fa-

vored sound money. Both endorsed civil-service reform and decried corruption, an irony since the 1876 election would be extremely corrupt.

Tilden won the popular vote by a small margin and seemed destined to capture the 185 electoral votes needed for victory. But the Republicans challenged the pro-Tilden returns from South Carolina, Florida, and Louisiana. If they could deprive the Democrats of these nineteen electoral votes, Hayes would triumph. The Democrats, who needed only one of the disputed electoral votes for victory, challenged the validity of Oregon's single electoral vote, which the Republicans had won, on a technicality. Twenty electoral votes, therefore, were in contention. Republicans, however, still controlled the electoral machinery in the three unredeemed southern states, where they threw out enough Democratic ballots to declare candidate Hayes the winner.

The nation now faced an unprecedented dilemma: each party claimed victory in the contested states, and each accused the other of fraud. In fact, both sets of southern results had been obtained by fraud: the Republicans had discarded legitimate Democratic ballots, and the Democrats had illegally prevented freedmen from voting. To resolve the conflict, Congress in January 1877 created a special electoral commission to determine which party would get the contested electoral votes. Made up of senators, representatives, and Supreme Court justices, the commission included seven Democrats, seven Republicans, and one independent, Justice David Davis of Illinois. When Davis resigned to run for the Senate, Congress replaced him with a Republican, and the commission gave Hayes the election by an 8 to 7 vote.

Congress now had to certify the new electoral vote. But since the Democrats controlled the House, a new problem loomed. Some Democrats threatened to obstruct debate and delay approval of the electoral vote. Had they carried out their scheme, the nation would have been without a president on inauguration day. But there remained room for compromise, for many southern Democrats accepted Hayes's election. Among them were former scalawags with commercial interests to protect, who still favored Republican financial policies, and railroad investors, who hoped that a Republican administration would help them build a southern transcontinental line. Other southerners cared mainly about Democratic state victories and did not mind conceding the presidency as long as the new Republican administration would leave the South alone.

Republican leaders, although sure of eventual triumph, were willing to bargain as well, for candidate Hayes desired not merely victory but southern approval.

A series of informal negotiations ensued, at which politicians of both parties exchanged promises. Ohio Republicans and southern Democrats who met at the Wormley House, a Washington hotel, reached an agreement that if Hayes won the election, he would remove federal troops from South Carolina and Louisiana, and Democrats could gain control of those states. In other bargaining sessions, southern politicians asked for federal patronage, federal aid to railroads, and federal support for internal improvements. In return, they promised to drop the filibuster, to accept Hayes as president, and to treat freedmen fairly.

With the threatened filibuster broken, Congress ratified Hayes's election. Once in office, Hayes fulfilled some of the promises his Republican colleagues had made. He appointed a former Confederate as postmaster general and ordered federal troops who guarded the South Carolina and Louisiana statehouses back to their barracks. Although federal soldiers remained in the South after 1877, they no longer served a political function. The Democrats, meanwhile, took control of state governments in Louisiana, South Carolina, and Florida. When Republican rule toppled in these states, the era of Reconstruction finally ended, though more with a whimper than with a resounding crash.

But some of the bargains struck in the Compromise of 1877, such as Democratic promises to treat southern blacks fairly, were forgotten, as were Hayes's pledges to ensure freedmen's rights. "When you turned us loose, you turned us loose to the sky, to the storm, to the whirlwind, and worst of all . . . to the wrath of our infuriated masters," Frederick Douglass had charged at the Republican convention in 1876. "The question now is, do you mean to make good to us the promises in your Constitution?" The answer provided by the 1876 election and the 1877 compromises was "No."

CONCLUSION

The end of Reconstruction brought benefits to both political parties. Although unable to retain a southern constituency, the Republican party was no longer burdened by the unpopular "southern question." And it had firm support in New England, the Middle Atlantic states, and the Great Lakes states. The Democrats, who had regained power in the ex-Confederate states, would remain entrenched there for almost a century. To be sure, the South was now tied to sharecropping and economic backwardness as securely as it had once been tied to slavery. But "home rule," or Democratic control, was firmly in place.

Reconstruction's end also signaled a triumph for nationalism and the spirit of reunion. In the fall of 1877, President Hayes made a rousing goodwill tour of the South to champion reconciliation, and similar celebrations continued through the 1880s and 1890s. When former president Grant died in 1885, veterans of both Civil War armies served as pallbearers. Jefferson Davis, imprisoned for two years after the war but never brought to trial, urged young men to "lay aside all rancor, all bitter sectional feeling." The federal government turned battlefields into national parks where veterans of both armies could gather for reunions. As the nation applauded reconciliation, the reputation of Reconstruction sank. Looking back on the 1860s and 1870s, most late-nineteenth-century Americans dismissed the congressional effort to reconstruct the South as a fiasco—a tragic interlude of "radical rule" or "black reconstruction," fashioned by carpetbaggers, scalawags, and Radical Republicans.

With the hindsight of over a century, historians continue to regard Reconstruction as a failure, though of a different kind. No longer viewed as a misguided scheme that collapsed because of radical excess, Reconstruction is now widely seen as a democratic experiment that did not go far enough. Historians cite two main causes. First, Congress did not promote freedmen's independence through land reform; without property of their own, southern blacks lacked the economic power to defend their interests as free citizens. Property ownership, however, does not necessarily ensure political rights, nor does it invariably provide economic security. Considering the depressed state of southern agriculture in the postwar decades, the freedmen's fate as independent farmers would likely have been perilous. Thus the land-reform question, like much else about Reconstruction, remains a subject of debate. A second cause of Reconstruction's collapse is less open to dispute: the federal government neglected to back congressional Reconstruction with military force. Given the choice between protecting blacks' rights at whatever cost and promoting reunion, the government opted for reunion. Reconstruction's failure, therefore, was the federal government's failure to fulfill its own goals and create a biracial democracy in the South. As a result, the nation's adjustment to the consequences of emancipation would continue into the twentieth century.

The Reconstruction era left some significant legacies, including the Fourteenth and Fifteenth amendments, both products of an extraordinary chain of postwar political crises. Although neither amendment would be used to protect minority rights for almost a century, they remain monuments to the democratic zeal that swept Congress in the 1860s. The Reconstruction years also hold a significant place in black history. During this brief respite between slavery and repression, southern blacks reconstituted their families, created new institutions, took part in the transformation of southern agriculture, and participated in government, for the first time in American history. The aspirations

and achievements of the Reconstruction era left an indelible mark on black citizens, as is vividly conveyed in an excerpt from a federal document. In the 1880s a congressional committee investigating southern labor conditions solicited the testimony of James K. Green of Montgomery, Alabama, a black politician during Reconstruction and subsequently a carpenter and contractor. At the end of the war, Green reported,

> *I knew nothing more than to obey my master, and there were thousands of us in the same attitude, that didn't know the Lord's prayer, but the tocsin of freedom sounded and knocked at the door and we walked out like free men and we met the exigencies as they grew up, and shouldered the responsibilities.*

Green's proud memory of blacks' achievements reflected one kind of postwar experience. Consigning the Reconstruction era to history, other Americans of the 1880s turned their energies to their economic futures—to their railroads, factories, and mills, and to the exploitation of the country's bountiful natural resources.

CHRONOLOGY

1863 President Abraham Lincoln issues Proclamation of Amnesty and Reconstruction.

1864 Wade-Davis bill passed by Congress and pocket-vetoed by Lincoln.

1865 Freedmen's Bureau established.
Civil War ends.
Lincoln assassinated.

Lincoln Mourning Shield

Andrew Johnson becomes president.
Johnson issues Proclamation of Amnesty and Reconstruction.

1865 Ex-Confederate states hold constitutional conventions (May–December).
Black conventions begin in the ex-Confederate states.
Thirteenth Amendment added to the Constitution.
Presidential Reconstruction completed.

1866 Congress enacts the Civil Rights Act of 1866 and the Supplementary Freedmen's Bureau Act over Johnson's vetoes.
Ku Klux Klan founded in Tennessee.
Congress proposes the Fourteenth Amendment.
Tennessee readmitted to the Union.
Race riots in southern cities.
Republicans win congressional elections.
Thirty-ninth Congress begins debates over Reconstruction policy.

1867 Reconstruction Act of 1867.
William Seward negotiates the purchase of Alaska.
Constitutional conventions meet in the ex-Confederate states.
Howard University founded.

1868 President Johnson is impeached, tried, and acquitted.
Omnibus Act.
Fourteenth Amendment added to the Constitution.
Ulysses S. Grant elected president.

1869 Transcontinental railroad completed.

1870 Congress readmits the four remaining southern states to the Union.
Fifteenth Amendment added to the Constitution.
Enforcement Act of 1870.

1871 Second Enforcement Act.
Ku Klux Klan Act.

1872 Liberal Republican party formed.
Amnesty Act.
Alabama claims settled.
Grant reelected president.

1873 Panic of 1873 begins (September–October), setting off a five-year depression.

1874 Democrats gain control of the House of Representatives.

1875 Civil Rights Act of 1875.
Specie Resumption Act.

1876 Disputed presidential election: Rutherford B. Hayes versus Samuel J. Tilden.

1877 Electoral commission decides election in favor of Hayes.
The last Republican-controlled governments overthrown in Florida, Louisiana, and South Carolina.

1879 "Exodus" movement spreads through several southern states.

FOR FURTHER READING

Eric Foner, *Reconstruction: America's Unfinished Revolution, 1863–1877* (1988). A thorough exploration of Reconstruction that draws on recent scholarship and stresses the centrality of the black experience.

John Hope Franklin, *Reconstruction After the Civil War* (1961). An overview that dismantles the traditional view of Reconstruction as a disastrous experiment in radical rule.

William Gillette, *Retreat from Reconstruction, 1869–1879* (1979). A survey of the era's national politics, indicting Republican policy makers for vacillation and lack of commitment to racial equality.

Leon Litwack, *Been in the Storm So Long: The Aftermath of Slavery* (1979). A comprehensive study of the black response to emancipation in 1865–1866.

Michael Perman, *Emancipation and Reconstruction, 1862–1879* (1987). A brief, readable interpretive survey of the period.

Roger L. Ransom and Richard Sutch, *One Kind of Freedom: The Economic Consequences of Emancipation* (1977). Two economists' assessment of the impact of free black labor on the South and explanation of the development of sharecropping and the crop-lien system.

Kenneth M. Stampp, *The Era of Reconstruction, 1865–1877* (1965). A classic revisionist interpretation of Reconstruction, focusing on the establishment and fall of Republican governments.

Joel Williamson, *The Negro in South Carolina During Reconstruction, 1861–1877* (1965). A pioneer study of black life and institutions after emancipation.

ADDITIONAL BIBLIOGRAPHY

Reconstruction Politics

Richard H. Abbott, *The Republican Party and the South, 1855–1877* (1986); Herman Belz, *Emancipation and Equal Rights: Politics and Constitutionalism in the Civil War Era* (1978); Michael Les Benedict, *A Compromise of Principle: Congressional Republicans and Reconstruction, 1863–1869* (1974) and *The Impeachment and Trial of Andrew Johnson* (1973); W. R. Brock, *An American Crisis: Congress and Reconstruction, 1865–1867* (1963); Fawn Brodie, *Thaddeus Stevens: Scourge of the South* (1959); Richard O. Curry, ed., *Radicalism, Racism, and Party Realignment: The Border States During Reconstruction* (1969); David Donald, *Charles Sumner and the Rights of Man* (1970) and *The Politics of Reconstruction, 1863–1867* (1965); Ellen Carol DuBois, *Feminism and Suffrage: The Emergence of an Independent Women's Movement in America, 1848–1869* (1978); William Gillette, *The Right to Vote: Politics and Passage of the Fifteenth Amendment* (1969); Harold Hyman, *A More Perfect Union: The Impact of the Civil War and Reconstruction on the Constitution* (1973); Stanley I. Kutler, *Judicial Power and Reconstruction* (1968); Eric McKitrick, *Andrew Johnson and Reconstruction* (1960); James C. Mohr, *Radical Republicans in the North: State Politics During Reconstruction* (1976); William E. Nelson, *The Fourteenth Amendment* (1988); Hans Trefousse, *Andrew Johnson: A Biography* (1989).

The South

Dan C. Carter, *When the War Was Over: Self-Reconstruction in the South, 1865–1867* (1985); Richard Nelson Current, *Those Terrible Carpetbaggers* (1988); Stephen Hahn, *The Roots of Southern Populism* (1983); William C. Harris, *The Day of the Carpetbagger: Republican Reconstruction in Mississippi* (1979); Otto Olsen, ed., *Reconstruction and Redemption in the South* (1980); Michael Perman, *Reunion Without Compromise: The South and Reconstruction, 1865–1868* (1973) and *The Road to*

Redemption: Southern Politics, 1869–1879 (1984); Howard N. Rabinowitz, *Race Relations in the Urban South, 1865–1890* (1978); George C. Rable, *But There Was No Peace: The Role of Violence in the Politics of Reconstruction* (1984); Mark W. Summers, *Railroads, Reconstruction, and the Gospel of Prosperity* (1984); Allen W. Trelease, *White Terror: The Ku Klux Klan Conspiracy and Southern Reconstruction* (1971); Ted Tunnell, *Crucible of Reconstruction: War, Radicalism, and Race in Louisiana, 1862–1877* (1984); Jonathan M. Wiener, *Social Origins of the New South: Alabama, 1860–1885* (1978); Gavin Wright, *Old South, New South: Revolutions in the Southern Economy Since the Civil War* (1986).

Emancipation and the Freedmen

Ira Berlin et al., eds., *Freedom, A Documentary History of Emancipation, 1861–1867* (1982–1993); Carol Rothrock Bleser, *The Promised Land: The History of the South Carolina Land Commission, 1869–1890* (1969); W. E. B. Du Bois, *Black Reconstruction in America, 1860–1880* (1935); Barbara Jeanne Fields, *Slavery and Freedom on the Middle Ground: Maryland During the Nineteenth Century* (1985); Eric Foner, *Nothing but Freedom: Emancipation and Its Legacies* (1983) and *Politics and Ideology in the Age of the Civil War* (1980), Chapters 6–7; Herbert G. Gutman, *The Black Family in Slavery and Freedom, 1750–1925* (1976); Robert Higgs, *Competition and Coercion: Blacks in the American Economy, 1865–1914* (1977); Thomas Holt, *Black over White: Negro Political Leadership in South Carolina During Reconstruction* (1977); Gerald Jaynes, *Branches Without Roots: Genesis of the Black Working Class in the American South, 1862–1882* (1986); Jacqueline Jones, *Soldiers of Light and Love: Northern Teachers and Georgia Blacks, 1865–1873* (1980) and *Labor of Love, Labor of Sorrow: Black Women, Work, and the Family from Slavery to the Present* (1985), Chapter 2; Peter Kolchin, *First Freedom: The Responses of Alabama's Blacks to Emancipation and Reconstruction* (1972); Lawrence W. Levine, *Black Culture and Black Consciousness: Afro-American Folk Thought from Slavery to Freedom* (1977); William S. McFeely, *Yankee Stepfather: General O. O. Howard and the Freedmen* (1966); Nell Irvin Painter, *Exodusters* (1977); James Roark, *Masters Without Slaves: Southern Planters in the Civil War and Reconstruction* (1978); William Preston Vaughan, *Schools for All: The Blacks and Public Education in the South, 1865–1877* (1974); Joel Williamson, *The Crucible of Race: Black-White Relations in the American South Since Emancipation* (1984).

National Trends

Paul H. Buck, *The Road to Reunion, 1865–1900* (1937); Adrian Cook, *The Alabama Claims* (1975); Ari M. Hoogenboom, *Outlawing the Spoils: A History of the Civil Service Reform Movement* (1961); William S. McFeely, *Grant: A Biography* (1981); David Montgomery, *Beyond Equality: Labor and the Radical Republicans, 1862–1872* (1967); Walter T. K. Nugent, *The Money Question During Reconstruction* (1967) and *Money and American Society, 1865–1880* (1968); Keith I. Polakoff, *The Politics of Inertia: The Election of 1876 and the End of Reconstruction* (1973); John C. Sproat, *"The Best Men": Liberal Reformers in the Gilded Age* (1968); Irwin Unger, *The Greenback Era: A Social and Political History of American Finance* (1964); Allen Weinstein, *Prelude to Populism: Origins of the Silver Issue, 1867–1878* (1970); C. Vann Woodward, *Reunion and Reaction: The Compromise of 1877 and the End of Reconstruction* (rev. ed., 1956).

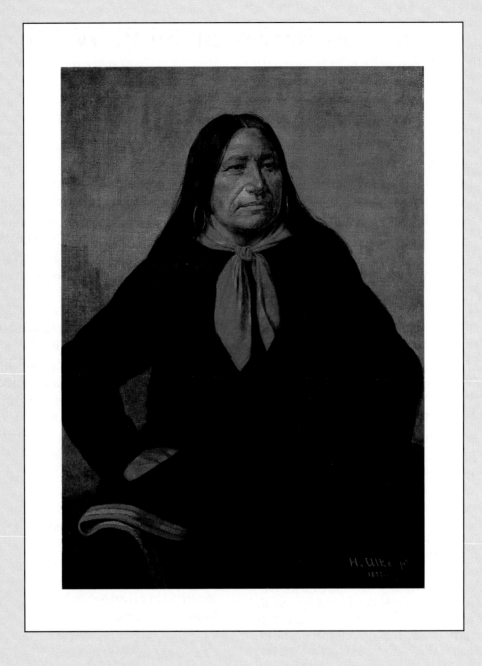

Spotted Tail, or Sinte-Galeshka,
of the Brulé Sioux
by Henry Ulke, 1877

17

THE TRANS-MISSISSIPPI WEST

In January 1855, braving freezing winds and deep snows, forty-year-old John W. North (inset), a New England abolitionist, lawyer, and land speculator, searched for a town site along the Cannon River in the southern Minnesota Territory. He found the perfect spot fourteen miles downstream from Faribault. Six months later, the new community, bearing the name "Northfield" in honor of its founder, consisted of a small store, two mills, several houses, and a ramshackle hotel with a cloth roof.

The following year, town resident E. J. Doolittle, writing to a friend back east, glowingly described the community:

Northfield commenced new a year ago last April.   we have one flowering mill that cost thirteen thousand dollars   1 water saw mill . . . three hotels, one of them cost Eleven thousand dollars 4 stores well filled with goods & our other Building a school house that cost nine hundred   a meeting house building   about 40 good nice dwelling houses . . . it is a very healthy place, & is going to be a great Farming country . . . I wish you could take a trip out here. . . . I know you would like the country   we do not have to dig stone nor cast manure to raise crops . . . I have just been up West of here about 75 miles I found it to be a fine country   I set out to drive my team through a prairie to get to a piece of timbered land   was obliged to stop   the grass was so thick & high that I could not get through, it was on an average 9 feet high for some way, you may think it a great story   If you don't believe it come out here & I will show to you wild geese, Ducks, Pigeons & fish in abundance.

Doolittle's enthusiastic letter expressed the wonderment and optimism that led many Americans in the second half of the nineteenth century to take part in one of the great migrations in modern history, exploring and developing nearly half the North American continent. Thirsting for a fresh start, they were lured west by the prospect of land and fortune.

Westward migration before the Civil War had helped create the image of the West as a land of adventure, opportunity, and inexhaustible natural resources. Trailblazing adventurers had raced pellmell across the huge expanses of the nation's midsection to reach the Pacific and join the gold rush of 1849, which brought quick settlement to the West Coast. When California was admitted as a state in 1850, it boasted a population of more than three hundred thousand newcomers. Other midcentury migrants—including farmers, land speculators, railroad developers, and various entrepreneurs— flooded into the fertile prairies of Iowa, Minnesota, eastern Kansas, and Nebraska, carving the land into farms and communities.

By the end of the Civil War, this image of the trans-Mississippi West as a land of unparalleled economic opportunities and bountiful natural resources beckoned to a new generation. Eager to exploit the million square miles of territory within this region, settlers victimized and elbowed aside the Native Americans, and swarmed onto the rolling prairies of the Great Plains. They quickly bought up the rich farmlands in present-day Wisconsin, Illinois, Minnesota, Iowa, and the eastern sections of the Dakotas, Nebraska, and Kansas where soils were fertile and rainfall plentiful. Some pushed past the hundreth meridian onto the semiarid high Plains of the western Dakotas and into eastern Montana, Wyoming, Colorado, and New Mexico in the hopes of making their fortune in mining or ranching. And some trudged on to the Rocky Mountains and farther still to the Great Basin of Nevada, where rainfall was scant (less than fifteen inches a year) and farming possible only in a few river valleys.

The same impulse that inspired settlers such as E. J. Doolittle to view the West as a symbol of economic opportunity drove some individuals to exploit the land's natural resources ruthlessly. The pell-mell quest for property and profit proved destructive to the Native Americans, to the environment, and often to the settlers themselves. Convinced of their own cultural superiority, farmers, ranchers, and miners saw nothing unjust in appropriating Native Americans' hunting and agricultural lands through flimsy, easily broken treaties. They stereotyped as alien and backward both the Mexicans who had lived in the Southwest for centuries and the Chinese immigrants who helped work the West's mines and build its railroads. Under the banner of civilization and progress, industrious western entrepreneurs stripped the landscape of trees, slaughtered millions of buffalo for their hides, skinned the mountainsides in search of minerals, and tore up the prairie sod to build farms.

But the drive to exploit western lands did not always succeed. The Indians strongly resisted, stalling settlement for several decades. Moreover, the rugged landscape of the high Plains proved more than a match for many. Seared by hot winds in summer and lashed by blinding blizzards in winter, this stark, weather-beaten country took the measure of all who ventured there, and drove thousands away.

In this same post–Civil War era, it was obvious that the West's economic development required considerable support by the federal government in the form of military intervention, land subsidies, and aid to railroad builders. Investments by eastern banks and foreign capitalists were also crucial, as was access to international markets. Yet westerners clung to their ideal of the self-reliant, independent individual who could successfully contend with any obstacle, whether natural, human, or economic. That ideal, though often sorely tested, survived to form the bedrock of western Americans' outlook even today.

NATIVE AMERICANS AND THE TRANS-MISSISSIPPI WEST

The trans-Mississippi West was far from empty when the newcomers arrived. An estimated 360,000 Indians lived in this region in the mid-nineteenth century. Contact with non-Indians had powerfully shaped these native cultures. Many southwestern pueblo peoples such as the Hopis and Zuñis, who initially had been subjugated by Hispanic conquerors, had gradually achieved accommodation with the relatively small Spanish-speaking population. Maintaining their traditional way of life based on agriculture and sheepherding, the Hopis and Zuñis traded mutton and produce with the Mexican *rancheros* (ranchers) for metal hoes, glass beads, knives, and guns. Pueblo Indians and *rancheros* alike endured terrifying raids by the Jicarilla Apaches and the Navajos, although by the nineteenth century, even these fierce fighters were trading extensively with non-Indians for manufactured goods, and the Navajos were gradually giving up nomadism in favor of settled agriculture.

Among the Indians dwelling on the Great Plains, the introduction of horses by the Spanish at the end of the sixteenth century, and of firearms by British traders in the eighteenth century, had created the armed and mounted warrior tribes encountered by nineteenth-century westward migrants. Commercial and other contacts with the non-Indian world continued to be important to the Plains Indians as new settlers moved in.

But beyond these generally positive exchanges, contact with advancing non-Indians massively disrupted Indian life everywhere. Disease, which had devastated Native Americans since the earliest European contact, continued its ravages among nineteenth-century western Indians. All tribes suffered severely from measles, diphtheria, and other diseases contracted from traders and settlers. By 1840 two major smallpox epidemics had reduced the Pawnees in Nebraska by nearly a third, to about six thousand people. The scattered tribes in California were similarly scourged by smallpox epidemics after the gold rush of 1849. Farther north, in present-day Oregon and Washington, the peaceful Klamath, Chinook, Yurok, and Shasta tribes, who lived in permanent villages and fished extensively, were periodically decimated by disease. So were the native inhabitants of Nevada's starkly beautiful Great Basin.

However, by the mid-nineteenth century, it was the physical disruption of Indian life on the Great Plains, where nearly half the Native Americans of the trans-Mississippi West dwelled, that caught the public eye and weighed on the public conscience. The non-Indians who descended on the Plains after 1850 had no understanding of traditional Indian culture and little inclination to respect or preserve the "savages'" ways. Military defeat and occasional massacres, forced removal to reservations, and devastation by disease, alcohol, and impoverishment demoralized the Plains Indian peoples. Neither the occasional Indian victories over federal troops nor the well-meaning but misguided efforts of reformers to "uplift" the surviving Indians reversed the downward spiral. By the 1890s relocation to distant, often inferior, and generally inadequate lands had become the fate of almost every Indian nation of the Great Plains. But there were also signs that the Native Americans were evolving a strong cultural response to conquest and forced modernization.

The Plains Indians

The Indians of the Great Plains inhabited two major subregions. The northern Plains, from the Dakotas and Montana southward to Nebraska, were dominated by several large tribes who spoke Siouan languages, as well as by the Flatheads, Blackfeet, Assiniboins, northern Cheyennes, Arapahos, and Crows. Some of these were allies, but others were bitter enemies who fought one another endlessly.

The other major concentration of Plains Indians lived in the central and southern Plains. The so-called Five Civilized Tribes driven there from the Southeast in the 1830s (see Chapter 9) pursued an agricultural life in their new home in the Indian Territory (present-day Oklahoma). In western Kansas the Pawnees maintained the older, more settled tradition characteristic of Plains river-valley culture before the introduction of horses, spending at least half the year in villages of earthen lodges along watercourses. Surrounding these were the truly nomadic tribes of western Kansas, Colorado, eastern New Mexico, and Texas—the Comanches, Kiowas, southern Arapahos, and Kiowa Apaches.

Considerable diversity flourished among the Plains tribes, and customs varied even within subdivisions of the same tribe. For example, the easternmost branch of the great Sioux Nation, the Dakota Sioux of Minnesota, who inhabited the wooded edge of the prairie, led a semisedentary life based on small-scale agriculture, deer and bison hunting, wild-rice harvesting, and maple-sugar production. In contrast, the Lakota Sioux,

American Buffaloe,
by M. E. D. Brown
The Sioux and other Plains Indians looked upon hunting as a test of bravery. As Sioux Chief Standing Bear insisted, "To endure pain, to bear the scars of life and battle, to defy the elements and laugh and sing in the face of death, a man had to possess the prime requisite of a Lakota brave—courage" [Land of the Spotted Eagle]

Buffalo Head Trophies
To encourage buffalo hunting as a sport, railroads crossing the Great Plains had the animal heads mounted by their own taxidermists for display at ticket stations.

who roamed the high Plains to the west, followed the buffalo migrations.

Despite the diversity, however, life for all the Plains Indians revolved around extended family ties and tribal cooperation. Within the various Sioux-speaking tribes, for example, children were raised without physical punishment and were taught to treat each adult clan member with the respect accorded to relatives. Families and clans joined forces to hunt and farm and reached decisions by consensus. Extended families, whose members followed the leadership of an older adult male in the tribe, gathered to form small winter villages or large summer encampments. Although non-Indians, steeped in their own notions of hierarchical social organization, called these men chiefs, the Indian leaders' power rested largely on persuasion. They reinforced their authority by example, giving their food and supplies to the needy and initiating projects in the hope that others would follow.

For the various Sioux bands, religious and harvest celebrations provided the cement for village and camp life. Sioux religion was complex and entirely different from the Judeo-Christian tradition. The Lakota Sioux thought of life as a series of circles. Living within the daily cycles of the sun and moon, Lakotas were born into a circle of relatives, which broadened to the band, the tribe, and the Sioux Nation. The Lakotas also believed in a hierarchy of plant and animal spirits that were often more powerful than human beings and whose help could be invoked in the Sun Dance. To

gain access to spiritual power and to benefit the weaker members of the community, young men would "sacrifice" themselves by suffering self-torture—for example, by fastening skewers to their chest from which they dragged buffalo skulls; by hanging suspended from poles; or by cutting pieces of their own flesh and placing them at the foot of the Sun Dance pole. Painter George Catlin, who recorded Great Plains Indian life before the Civil War, described such a ceremony: "Several of them, seeing me making sketches, beckoned me to look at their faces, which I watched through all this horrid operation, without being able to detect anything but the pleasantest smiles as they looked me in the eye, while I could hear the knife rip through the flesh, and feel enough of it myself, to start involuntary and uncontrollable tears over my cheeks."

Many Plains tribes—not only the Lakota Sioux but also the Blackfeet, Crows, and Cheyennes—followed the buffalo migration. The huge herds, which at their peak contained an estimated 32 million bison, filled an amazing array of tribal needs. The Indians utilized every part of the animal. They ate its meat, either fresh or dried. They used its hide for tepee covers, shields, boats, shirts, and robes. Sinews became bowstrings; bones were fashioned into hoes, knives, awls, fishhooks, chisels, hide fleshers, spatulas, flint knapping tools, and wedges. They rendered buffalo fat into grease, ground up hooves to make glue, carved horn tips into toy tops for the children, and used buffalo dung ("chips") for fuel. They even used the skull for religious purposes, as in the Sun Dance.

By the 1870s the eastern vogue for wearing buffalo robes on carriages and sleighs, coupled with the use of the animals' hides for industrial belting, encouraged white hunters to slaughter the herds upon which the Plains peoples depended. Ruthless entrepreneurs used the expanding railroad networks to kill the animals and transport their prized pelts swiftly to market. William F. "Buffalo Bill" Cody, a famous scout, Indian fighter, and organizer of Wild West shows, in 1867–1868 killed nearly 4,300 bison in eight months to feed construction crews building the Union Pacific railroad. The herds dwindled further as eastern sport hunters and even sightseers chartered trains and headed west to shoot the animals for profit or adventure. Army commanders, seeing in the destruction of the buffalo a means of undermining the resistance of buffalo-dependent Indians, encouraged the slaughter. The carnage that resulted was almost inconceivable in its scale. Between 1872 and 1875, hunters killed 9 million buffalo, taking only the skin and leaving the carcass to rot. A railroad conductor then recalled that "one could have journeyed more than 100 miles along the railroad right-of-way, without stepping off the carcass of a slaughtered bison." By the 1880s the once thundering herds had been reduced to a few thousand animals, a Native American way of life dependent on the buffalo had been ruined, and the path was cleared for American farmers to settle on former Indian hunting grounds.

The Transformation of Indian Life

Non-Indians not only wiped out most of the buffalo but also seized control of much of the land. Between 1837 and 1867, for example, the Ojibwa and Dakota Sioux in the Minnesota Territory ceded 24 million acres to the federal government in a series of treaties. These agreements established two large reservations (under the control of the Department of the Interior's Bureau of Indian Affairs) and promised the tribes annual government support. When the federal authorities failed to give the Dakota Sioux their yearly payments on time, however, they returned to their former hunting grounds. Driven by hunger and angered by unfulfilled promises, they rose up in August 1862, killing more than 500 white settlers. With reinforcements from the U.S. Army, the settlers crushed the uprising in two weeks, hanged 38 Indians, imprisoned more than 200, and exiled the rest to poor-quality

reservation land in the Dakotas and northeastern Nebraska. By 1866 the number of Sioux in Minnesota had been cut from 7,000 to 374.

By the 1860s the federal government had abandoned its previous policy of treating much of the West as a vast Indian reserve and had introduced a system of smaller, separate tribal reservations where the Indians were to be concentrated, by force if necessary, and where they were expected to exchange nomadism for a settled agricultural life. Some Native Americans, like the Pueblos of the Southwest, the Crows of Montana, and the Hidatsas of North Dakota (see "A Place in Time") peacefully accepted their fate. Others, among them the Navajos of Arizona and New Mexico, as well as the Dakota Sioux, initially opposed the new policy, but to no avail.

The remaining tribes, however, with a population of more than one hundred thousand, resisted. From the 1860s through the 1880s, these tribes—the western Sioux, Cheyennes, Arapahos, Kiowas, and Comanches on the Great Plains; the Nez Percés and Bannocks in the northern Rockies; and the Apaches in the Southwest—faced the U.S. Army in a series of final battles for the West.

In this protracted and bitter conflict, precipitated by the expansion of western settlement and by Washington's new reservation policy, both sides committed atrocities. Two examples illustrate the tragic pattern. In 1864 the Cheyennes and Arapahos of southern Colorado, weary of fighting the gold miners who had intruded upon their traditional lands in the Pikes Peak region, sued for peace and encamped by Sand Creek. There they were viciously attacked by the Colorado militia. Even after the Native Americans had raised a white surrender flag, the militia clubbed and scalped the terrified Indian women and children. "Kill and scalp all, big and little," shouted Colonel John M. Chivington, the militia leader; "Nits make lice." Two years later the Teton Sioux, defending hunting lands along Wyoming's Powder River that in their view had been fraudulently ceded to the United States by their Crow enemies, fought a ferocious war with the U.S. cavalry. Trying to stop construction of the Bozeman Trail (a new road angling northwestward from Fort Laramie, Wyoming, to the gold fields of Virginia City, Montana), the Teton Sioux killed Captain William J. Fetterman and his seventy-nine soldiers and mutilated their bodies.

These massacres—one, of Indians; the other, of whites—rekindled public debate over federal Indian policy. Western settlers had long pressed Congress to set up a tighter reservation policy controlled by the army rather than by the civilian "Indian agents" employed by the Bureau of Indian Affairs. Other critics, led by Wisconsin senator James R. Doolittle and supported by an Episcopal bishop from Minnesota, Henry Benjamin Whipple, opposed army control and simply urged a cessation of violence on both sides.

Responding to this debate in 1867, Congress halted construction of the Bozeman Trail, sent a peace commission to end the fighting, and set aside two large districts, one north of Nebraska, the other south of Kansas. There, it was hoped, the nomadic tribes would settle down and convert to Christianity. Behind the federal government's persuasion lay the threat of force. Any Native Americans who refused to "locate in [the] permanent abodes provided for them," warned Commissioner of Indian Affairs Ely S. Parker (himself a Seneca Indian), "would be subject wholly to the control and supervision of military authorities, [and] . . . treated as friendly or hostile as circumstances might justify."

At first the plan appeared to work. Representatives of sixty-eight thousand southern Kiowas, Comanches, Cheyennes, and Arapahos signed a treaty at Medicine Lodge Creek, Kansas, and pledged to live on land in present-day Oklahoma recently taken from Choctaw and Chickasaw reservations. The following year, scattered bands of Sioux, representing nearly fifty-four thousand northern Plains Indians, agreed to move to reservations on the so-called Great Sioux Reserve in the western part of what is now South Dakota in return for money and provisions.

But Indian dissatisfaction with the treaties ran deep. As a Sioux chief, Spotted Tail, told the commissioners: "We do not want to live like the white man. . . . The Great Spirit gave us hunting grounds, gave us the buffalo, the elk, the deer, and the antelope. Our fathers have taught us to hunt and live on the Plains, and we are contented." Rejecting the new system, many Indians refused to move to the reservations or to remain on them once there.

In August 1868 war parties of defiant Cheyennes, Arapahos, and Sioux raided settlements in Kansas and Colorado, burning homes and killing whites. In retaliation, army troops attacked Indians, even peaceful ones, who refused confinement. That autumn Lieutenant Colonel George Armstrong Custer's raiding party struck a sleeping Cheyenne village, killing more than a hundred warriors, shooting their more than eight hundred horses, and taking fifty-three women and children prisoner. Other hostile Cheyennes and Arapahos were pursued, captured, and returned to the reservations.

Spurred on by Christian reformers, Congress in 1869 established the Board of Indian Commissioners to mold reservation life along lines that the reformers thought desirable. The new board delegated to the major Protestant denominations the responsibility for appointing the agents who would run the reservations. The board's goal was to break, once and for all, the Indians' nomadic tradition and force them to remain on their reservations, where, under the supervision of benevolent agents, they would be Christianized, taught to farm on individual plots of land, and given government assistance. A comment by one federal official summed up the sense of cultural superiority that underlay U.S. Indian policy in these years: "A fundamental difference between Barbarians and a civilized people is the difference between a herd and an individual."

The new and inexperienced church-appointed Indian agents quickly encountered obstacles in trying to implement the board's policies. The pacifist Quaker agent Lawrie Tatum, a big-boned Iowa farmer, failed to persuade the Comanches and Kiowas to stay on their reservations in Oklahoma rather than raid Texas settlements; two Kiowa chiefs, Satanta and Big Tree, insisted that they could be at peace with the federal government while remaining at war with Texans. Other agents were unable to restrain scheming whites who fraudulently purchased reservation lands from the Indians. Moreover, the various Protestant denominations squabbled among themselves, all hoping to control the reservations that had the greatest number of potential converts. By the 1880s the federal government, frustrated with the churches, ignored their nominations for Indian agents and made its own appointments.

Caught in the sticky web of an ambiguous and faltering federal policy, and enraged by continuing non-Indian settlement of the Plains, defiant Native Americans struck back in the 1870s. On the southern Plains, the Kiowas, Comanches, and Cheyennes raided a trading post called Adobe Walls in the Texas panhandle in 1874, thereby setting off the so-called Red River War. In this conflict regular army troops, in a fierce winter campaign, destroyed Indian supplies and slaughtered a hundred Cheyenne fugitives near the Sappa River in Kansas. With the exile of seventy-four "ringleaders" in this uprising to reservations in Florida, Native American independence on the southern Plains came to an end. In the Southwest, in present-day Arizona and New Mexico, the Apaches fought an intermittent guerrilla war until their leader, Geronimo, surrendered in 1886.

Custer's Last Stand

Of all the acts of Indian resistance against the new reservation policy, none aroused more passion or caused more bloodshed than the conflict between the western Sioux tribes and the U.S. Army in the Dakotas, Montana, and Wyoming. The problems went back to the 1868 Treaty of Fort Laramie, which had ended the Powder River War and had set aside the Great Sioux Reserve "in perpetuity." But not all the Sioux bands had fought in the war or signed the treaty. For example, the highly respected chief Sitting Bull had carefully kept his band of Hunkpapa Sioux away from the fighting. Furthermore, certain western Sioux bands that did sign the treaty, among them the Oglala Sioux and the Brulé Sioux, had no intention of actually moving to the reservation.

Skillfully playing local officials against the federal government, Chief Red Cloud's Oglala band and Chief Spotted Tail's Brulé band in 1873 won the concession of staying near the Indian agencies along the upper reaches of the White River in Nebraska, near their traditional hunting grounds. Shuttling back and forth between the agencies and the camps of Sitting Bull and

the other nontreaty chiefs, they enjoyed the best of both worlds: they obtained government provisions but still hunted on their customary range. To protect these precious hunting grounds, they raided encroaching non-Indian settlements in Nebraska and Wyoming, intimidated federal agents, and harassed miners, railroad surveyors, and others who ventured onto their lands.

The Indian agents' inability to prevent the Sioux from entering and leaving the reservations at will, coupled with increasing pressures from would-be settlers and developers, prompted the army to take action. In 1874 General William Tecumseh Sherman sent a force under Colonel George Armstrong Custer into the Black Hills of South Dakota, near the western edge of the Great Sioux Reserve. Lean and mustachioed, with shoulder-length reddish-blond hair, the thirty-four-year-old Custer had been a celebrity since his days as an impetuous young Civil War officer, known for the black velvet uniform, embellished with gold braid, that he wore on the battlefield. Now he had switched to a fringed buckskin uniform set off by a crimson scarf. Flamboyant and ambitious, he had just published an autobiography, *My Life on the Plains,* casting himself in the heroic mold of Davy Crockett and Kit Carson.

Custer's ostensible purpose was to find a location for a new fort and to keep an eye on renegade Indians. But his real objective was to confirm rumors about the existence of gold there. In this he was spurred on by

Indian Chiefs
Early photographs of the Indian leaders Sitting Bull (left) and Joseph (right) captured both their pride and the frustration they felt after years of alternately negotiating and battling with the U.S. Army. "I don't want a white man over me," Sitting Bull insisted. "I want to have the white man with me, but not to be my chief. I ask this because I want to do right by my people. . . ."

the Northern Pacific Railroad, which wanted to attract settlers to the area. While Custer's troops mapped the lush meadows and chose a site for the fort, two "practical miners" panned the streams for gold. In a report that he telegraphed to the *New York World,* Custer described the region as excellent farm country and casually mentioned finding "gold among the roots of the grass." The gold stampede that predictably followed gave the army a new justification for interceding against the Indians.

Custer had in fact become part of a deliberate army plan to force concessions from the Sioux. In November 1875, when negotiations to buy the Black Hills broke down because the Indians' asking price was deemed too high, President Grant and his generals decided to remove all roadblocks to the entry of miners. Indians still outside the reservations after January 31, 1876, the government announced, would be hunted down by the army and taken in by force.

When the Indians refused to return to the reservations, the army mobilized for an assault. In June 1876, leading 600 troops of the Seventh Cavalry, Custer proceeded to the Little Bighorn River area of present-day Montana, a hub of Indian resistance. On the morning of June 25, seriously underestimating the Indian enemy and unwisely dividing his force, Custer, with 209 men, recklessly advanced against a large company of Indians, later estimated at from 1,500 to 5,000 warriors, encamped along the Little Bighorn. Soon the outnumbered troops found themselves surrounded and under heavy fire. Desperately some of the men shot their own horses and tried to use the bodies as protection; but with bullets pelting them from all sides, their situation was hopeless. Custer and his entire force were wiped out. Two days later, another company of cavalry troops came upon the scene of carnage and buried the bodies where they lay. A single creature was found alive: a horse that had belonged to one of Custer's captains.

Americans reeled from this unexpected Indian victory. Metropolitan newspaper columnists groped to assess the meaning of "Custer's last stand." Some went beyond criticism of Custer's leadership to question the wisdom of current federal policy toward the Indians. Others worried that an outraged public would demand retaliation and the outright extermination of the Sioux. Most, however, endorsed the federal government's determination to quash the Native American rebellion. "It is inconsistent with our civilization and with common sense," trumpeted a writer in the *New York Herald,* "to allow the Indian to roam over a country as fine as that around the Black Hills, preventing its development in

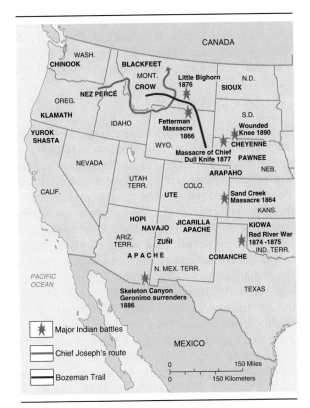

Major Indian-White Clashes in the West
Although they were never recognized as such in the popular press, the battles between Native Americans and the U.S. Army on the Great Plains amounted to a major undeclared war.

order that he may shoot game and scalp his neighbors. That can never be. This region must be taken from the Indian."

The Indians' surprising coup at Little Bighorn made the army more cautious. In Montana troops harassed various Sioux bands for more than five years. The army attacked Indian camps in the dead of winter and destroyed all supplies. Even Sitting Bull, a leader at Little Bighorn, who had led his tribe to Canada to escape the army, surrendered in 1881 for lack of provisions: the slaughter of the buffalo had wiped out his tribe's major food supply. For a time after his surrender, Sitting Bull suffered the ignominy of appearing as an attraction in Buffalo Bill's Wild West show.

Similar measures were used elsewhere in the West against Chief Joseph and his Nez Percés of Oregon and against the Northern Cheyennes, who had been forcibly transported to Oklahoma after the Battle of Little Bighorn. Some 150 survivors, including men, women, and children, led by Chief Dull Knife, escaped north in September 1878 to join the Sioux. But the army chased them down and imprisoned them in Fort Robinson, Nebraska. When the army denied their request to stay nearer to their traditional northern lands, tribal leaders refused to leave the fort. The post commander then withheld all food, water, and fuel. On a frigid night in January 1879, a desperate Dull Knife and his followers shot the guards and broke for freedom. Members of the startled garrison chased the Indians and gunned down half of them in the snow, including women and children as well as Dull Knife himself. The *Atlanta Constitution* condemned the incident as "a dastardly outrage upon humanity and a lasting disgrace to our boasted civilization." But although sporadic Indian resistance continued until the end of the century, these brutal tactics had sapped the Indians' will to resist.

"Saving" the Indians

Bloody massacres were not America's only answer to the "Indian problem." In 1879, the same year that Dull Knife led his followers on their doomed dash for freedom, army officer Richard H. Pratt founded the Carlisle Indian School in Pennsylvania. The school's objective seemed laudable: to equip individual Indians with the skills and cultural attitudes necessary to succeed in modern American society. As Pratt put it, he wanted to "kill the Indian and save the man." But the young Indians who came to Pratt's boarding school were uprooted from their families and tribes, and teachers there made no pretense of respecting traditional Indian culture. Carlisle became the prototype for a number of other Indian schools that would be established, well into the twentieth century, with the avowed purpose of reeducating Indian youth in whites' skills and outlooks. Culturally, reeducation represented as determined an assault on the Native American world as the slaughter of the buffalo, the seizure of hunting land, and military repression. Moreover, because it appealed to humanitarians' sincere concern for the Indians' well-being, it was more insidious.

These humanitarians, most of them well-educated easterners, were outraged not only by bloody atrocities like the Fort Robinson massacre but also by the federal government's flagrant abuse of its Indian treaties. A lecture tour by Chief Standing Bear, whose peaceful Ponca tribe had been driven from land north of the Missouri River guaranteed them by an 1865 treaty, further aroused the reformers' indignation. The Women's National Indian Rights Association, founded in 1883,

and other groups took up the cause. Standing Bear's eloquence particularly affected Helen Hunt Jackson, a Massachusetts widow who had recently married a rich Quaker businessman and moved to Colorado. In *A Century of Dishonor* (1881), Jackson sought to rally public opinion against the government's record of broken treaty obligations. In the reform tradition of Harriet Beecher Stowe's antislavery novel *Uncle Tom's Cabin*, Jackson proclaimed in her book, "It makes little difference . . . where one opens the record of the history of the Indians; every page and every year has its dark stain."

Genuinely concerned about the Indians' plight, well-intentioned humanitarians concluded that the Indians' interests would best be served by breaking up the reservations, ending all recognition of the tribes, and propelling individual Native Americans into mainstream society. In short, they proposed to eliminate the "Indian problem" by eliminating the Indians as a culturally distinct entity. Inspired by this vision, they threw their support behind a plan that resulted in the passage in 1887 of the Dawes Severalty Act.

The Dawes Act was designed to reform what well-meaning whites perceived to be the weaknesses of Indian life—the absence of private property, and the native peoples' nomadic tradition—by turning Indians into farmers and landowners. The law emphasized severalty, or the treatment of Indians as individuals rather than as members of tribes, and called for the breakup of the reservations. It provided for the distribution of 160 acres of reservation land for farming, or 320 acres for grazing, to each head of an Indian family who accepted the law's provisions. The remaining reservation lands (often the richest) were to be sold to speculators and settlers, and the income thus obtained would go toward purchase of farm tools. To prevent unscrupulous people from gaining control of the lands granted to individual Indians, the government would hold the property of each tribal member in trust for twenty-five years. Under the Dawes Act, those Indians who accepted allotments would in twenty-five years also be declared citizens of the United States with all the rights and responsibilities that attended such status, including the protection of federal laws and the requirement to pay taxes.

Western speculators who coveted reservation lands, as well as military authorities who wanted to break up the reservations for security reasons, had lobbied heavily for the Dawes Act. Nevertheless, the bill's strongest support had come from the "friends of the Indian" like Helen Hunt Jackson. Although they

Carrie Anderson (12 years), Anne Dawson (10 years), and Sarah Walker (13 years) *The Hampton Institute in Virginia took these "before" and "after" photographs of three young Crow Indian girls who had been sent East from their reservation in the 1880s. The doll, the checkers, the book, and the new dresses signified, for benefactors and the public, that they had been "civilized."*

genuinely hoped that the law would alleviate the Indians' suffering, these reformers also believed in the innate superiority of American culture. Like those nineteenth-century social reformers who set up relief organizations to impose middle-class values on the urban poor (see Chapter 19), and like the would-be uplifters of the southern freedmen, the "friends of the Indian" believed that teaching Indians English and farming would open the doors of opportunity to them. Convinced that citizenship would best protect the Indians, and that full assimilation into society would enable them to get ahead, the reformers systematically tried to "civilize" the Indian peoples and wean them from their traditional culture. To publicize the success of his Carlisle Indian School, Richard H. Pratt published a series of "before" and "after" photographs in which Indian girls with long, braided hair and traditional tribal dress were transformed into proper young ladies.

The Dawes Act did not specify a timetable for the breakup of the reservations. Because land surveys took time, few allotments were made to the Indians until the 1890s. The act eventually proved to be a boon not to the Indians but to speculators, who commonly evaded the law and obtained the Indians' most arable land. By 1934 the act had slashed the total Indian acreage by 65 percent. Much of what remained in Indian hands was too dry and gravelly for farming.

Although some Native Americans who received land under the Dawes Act prospered enough to expand their holdings and go into large-scale farming or ranching, countless others languished. Hunting restrictions on the former reservation lands prevented many Indians from supplementing their limited farm yields. At the same time, various forms of government support steadily increased Indians' dependence on federal

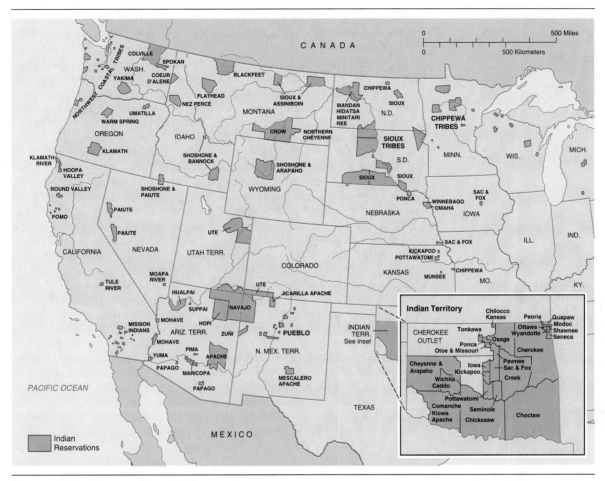

Western Indian Reservations, 1890

Native-American reservations were almost invariably located on poor-quality lands. Consequently, when the Dawes Severalty Act broke up the reservations into 160-acre farming tracts, many of the semiarid divisions would not support cultivation.

aid. Alcoholism, a continuing problem, and one exacerbated by the prevalence of whiskey as a trade item (and by the boredom that resulted from the disruption of hunting and other traditional pursuits), became more prevalent as Native Americans strove to adapt to the constraints of reservation life.

The Ghost Dance and the End of Indian Resistance on the Great Plains

The plight of the Sioux became desperate in the late 1880s as the federal government reduced their meat rations and saddled them with more and more restrictions, and as disease killed a third of their cattle. The Sioux, who still numbered almost twenty-five thousand, turned to Wovoka, a new prophet popular among the

Great Basin Indians in Nevada. Wovoka promised to restore the Sioux to their original dominance on the Plains if they performed the Ghost Dance.

Wearing sacred Ghost Shirts—cotton or leather vestments decorated to ward off evil—the dancers moved in a circle, accelerating until they reached a trancelike state and experienced visions of the future. In some cases, the dancers claimed special powers to kill non-Indian settlers. Many also believed that the Ghost Shirts would protect them from harm. Rituals such as the Ghost Dance enabled Indians to reaffirm their own culture.

In the fall of 1890, as the Ghost Dance movement spread among the Sioux in the Dakota Territory, Indian officials and military authorities grew alarmed. The local reservation agent, Major James McLaughlin,

Like-a-Fishhook, 1845–1900

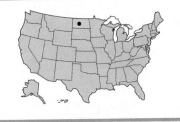

When Lewis and Clark visited the Hidatsa and Mandan Indians at the mouth of the Knife River in present-day North Dakota in 1804, they found a series of substantial villages, each protected by a palisade and consisting of forty to sixty large, round, earth-walled houses (earthlodges). The Mandans and the Hidatsas were closely knit, clan-oriented tribes that practiced subsistence agriculture supplemented with buffalo hunting. A century later, Goodbird, a Hidatsa, told a visiting anthropologist that "my family and I own four thousand acres of land, and we have money coming to us from the government. I own cattle and horses. I can read English, and my children are in school. . . . I am not afraid." In less than two generations, the Mandans and Hidatsas had abandoned ancient tribal ways closely adapted to the northern Plains and had become independent ranchers in a modern industrial society.

For Lewis and Clark, the communal nature of the traditional Mandan and Hidatsa cultures had been evident in every aspect of the native peoples' lives. Because members of the same clan, or extended kinship group, could not wed, marriage joined a man and a woman from different clans. Children were thus tied to a large clan network, encompassing the members of both parent's village. Clans were responsible for disciplining their members, providing for the sick and orphaned, and cooperating in sacred ceremonies.

Children treated all elders with the respect accorded their own parents.

Tradition carefully defined social roles. Young Hidatsa girls learned to separate ordinary knowledge about growing crops, dressing skins, cutting wood, and cooking from ancient and sacred knowledge of basket weaving and pottery making, teepee and house construction, beading, and quill weaving. These sacred skills had to be purchased from tribal leaders, and those who mastered them became valued members of the community. For example, in return for paying an elder with a suit of finely tanned skins, a young woman might learn how to raise the four sacred foundation posts and the four great beams of an earthlodge. When another tribal member requested the young woman's help in constructing a new earthlodge, he would pay her with tanned buffalo skins and food.

Young boys, too, learned the importance of reciprocal obligations. If a youth received his first bow and arrow from a maternal grandfather, he presented his elder with the first rabbits or prairie chickens killed with the weapons. At fifteen or sixteen, boys proved their toughness and willingness to go to war by fasting, enduring the torture of hanging from a tree by thongs laced through the skin, or cutting off a finger.

Religion pervaded the Hidatsa world. The people believed that they could acquire supernatural powers by practicing certain religious rites. Paralleling the seasons, their religious ceremonies celebrated the planting of corn in the spring and buffalo-hunting expeditions in the summer and winter. The buffalo-calling ceremony, staged in winter, required the village to be silent so that the buffalo would be attracted into the rivers along which the tribe dwelled. If the tribe failed to observe this ritual, a mild winter might set in. Unseasonably warm weather might in turn cause the buffalo to remain on the Plains, with the result that the Hidatsas might starve.

In 1837 a smallpox epidemic introduced by white settlers wiped out half the Hidatsas and most of the neighboring Mandans. Then in 1845, the remaining members of both tribes formed the village of Like-a-Fishhook. French fur traders moved in and exchanged cast-iron pots,

Bird's Eye View of the Mandan Village, 1800 Miles Above St. Louis, *by George Catlin, 1839*

Buffalo Dance Headdress
Headdresses such as this one worn by a member of the Buffalo Bulls, a warrior society, symbolized the achievements of the wearer and were featured at ritual dances and other social occasions. Indian societies prepared men and women for leadership roles and provided social experiences outside family and clan groups.

knives, beads, and guns for buffalo skins. In the 1850s, faced with the encroachment of white settlers on their hunting grounds and with the depletion of their wood supplies by the steamboats that plied the river and carried away timber for fuel, the Hidatsas signed a treaty with the U.S. government and were granted fifty thousand dollars a year for fifty years.

Contact with non-Indians slowly reshaped Hidatsa culture. With each new influx of settlers, more wild game disappeared. The Indians became dependent on the federal agents who distributed coffee, flour, sugar, and soap. To keep the Indians and non-Indians separated and to maintain the peace, the U.S. government set up Fort Berthold in 1864, established a permanent Indian agency there in 1868, sent in Congregational missionaries, and built schools. In 1887, under the Dawes Severalty Act, the government dispersed the communal villages and forced the Indians onto separate farms.

Those Indians who, like Goodbird, prospered, did so by adapting traditional culture to fit the government's regulations. Before establishing a farm, Goodbird held a spiritual vigil to choose the site. Breaking with his heritage, he lived in a wooden house but was careful to place the stove in the center and to leave the door open in good weather, following Hidatsa customs. Goodbird also learned how to work within the new federal system. He served in turn as a reservation policeman, an assistant farmer, a distributor for government rations, a store owner, a cattle rancher, and a Congregational minister.

Some members of his family did not adapt as easily. His mother, Buffalo Bird Woman, a skilled house builder and gardener born before the move to Like-a-Fishhook, lost her valued status when the tribe became assimilated. Her brother, Wolf Chief, wrote yearly letters to the Bureau of Indian Affairs, chronicling the folly of a government policy that asked Indians to farm 160 acres of semiarid land. He also resisted regulations prohibiting Indians from leaving the reservation and buying cattle.

By 1900 many Hidatsa had become thriving ranchers, using modern equipment like horse-drawn wagons and threshers. But the tribe preserved elements of the communal society that its members had once so treasured—by accommodating traditions to the modern world. Hidatsa culture was not dead in 1900, but in less than fifty years, it had been transformed.

(Left to right) **Son of a Star, Goodbird, and Buffalo Bird Woman, 1906**
Dressed in his best Sunday suit, Goodbird graphically demonstrates his movement away from the world of his parents. His father, Son of a Star, retains traditional garb, with the two feathers symbolizing his conquest of enemies in battle. Goodbird's mother, Buffalo Bird Woman, is wrapped in a traditional blanket.

decided that Chief Sitting Bull, whose cabin on the reservation had become a rallying point for the Ghost Dance movement, must be arrested. On a freezing, drizzly December morning, McLaughlin dispatched a company of forty-two Indian policemen from the agency to take Sitting Bull into custody. As two policemen pulled the chief from his cabin, his bodyguard Catch-the-Bear shot one of them. As the policeman fell, he in turn shot Sitting Bull at point-blank range. Bloody hand-to-hand fighting immediately broke out. As bullets whizzed by, Sitting Bull's horse sat down and began to perform the tricks remembered from its days in the Wild West show. Some observers were terrified, convinced that the spirit of the dead chief had entered his horse.

Sitting Bull's violent death preceded by only two weeks one of the bloodiest episodes of Indian-white strife on the Plains. On December 29, 1890, the Seventh Cavalry was rounding up 340 starving and freezing Sioux at Wounded Knee, South Dakota, when an excited Indian fired a gun hidden under a blanket. The

General Colby and Child
In keeping with his missionary vision, Brigadier General L. W. Colby, commander of the troops at Wounded Knee, proudly holds his adopted Indian daughter whose parents had been killed in the bloody massacre.

Wounded Knee
Piled up like cordwood, the frozen bodies of the Sioux slaughtered at Wounded Knee were a grim reminder that the U.S. Army would brook no opposition to its control of Indian reservation life.

soldiers retaliated with Hotchkiss cannons. Within minutes 300 Indians, including 7 infants, were slaughtered. Three days later, a baby who had miraculously survived was found wrapped in a blanket under the snow. She wore a buckskin cap on which a beadwork American flag had been embroidered. Brigadier General L. W. Colby, who adopted the baby, named her Marguerite, but the Indians called her Lost Bird.

As the frozen corpses at Wounded Knee were dumped into mass graves, a generation of Indian-white conflict on the Great Plains shuddered to a close. Lost Bird, with her poignantly patriotic beadwork cap, highlights the irony of the Plains Indians' response to the tragic dilemma confronting them. Many did try, with varying success, to adapt to alien non-Indian ways. But few succeeded fully, and many others were understandably devastated at being forced to abandon age-old religious beliefs and a way of life rooted in hunting, cooperative living, and nomadism. Driven onto reservations, the Plains Indians were reduced to a status of almost complete dependency, as once strong cultural traditions, modes of survival, and forms of social organization were crushed. By 1900 the Plains Indian population had shrunk from nearly a quarter of a million to just over a hundred thousand. Nevertheless, after 1900 the population began slowly to rise. Against overwhelming odds, the pride, group memory, and cultural identity of the Plains Indians survived all efforts to trample them.

Unlike the nomadic western Sioux, for whom the encounter with onrushing white civilization was most traumatic, the more settled Navajos of the Southwest adjusted more successfully to the reservation system, preserving traditional ways while incorporating elements of the new order in a complex process of cultural adaptation. By 1900 the Navajos had tripled their reservation land, dramatically increased their numbers and their herds, and carved out for themselves a distinct place in Arizona and New Mexico.

These extraordinary changes were forced on the Indian population by the advance of non-Indian settlement. In the name of civilization and progress, non-Indians in the generation after the Civil War pursued a course that involved a strong mixture of sincere (if misguided) benevolence, coercion wrapped in an aura of legality, and outbursts of naked violence. Many white Americans felt toward the Indians only contempt, hatred, and greed for their land. Others, however, like General Colby in his gesture of adopting the infant survivor of a massacre in which he himself had

participated, viewed themselves as divinely chosen instruments for uplifting and Christianizing the Indians. Both groups, however, were equally blind to any inherent value in Native American life and traditions. The humanitarians, no less than the most brutal advocates of extermination, played their part in shattering a proud people and an ancient culture. The Indians' fate would weigh on the American conscience for generations.

Settling the West

The successive defeats of the Native Americans opened up for settlement a vast territory that reached from the prairie Plains to the Sierra Nevada and the Cascade Mountains. In the 1840s, when nearly a quarter-million Americans had trudged overland to Oregon and California, they had typically endured a six- to eight-month trip in ox-drawn wagons. Provisions were meager and the journey perilous. After 1870, as railroad expansion made the trip to the Great Plains and the Far West not only faster but considerably easier, migration accelerated. In the next three decades, new settlers started up 2.5 million farms in the Dakotas, Nebraska, and Kansas alone. More land was parceled out into farms than in the previous 250 years of American history combined, and agricultural production doubled.

The First Transcontinental Railroad

On May 10, 1869, church bells clanged and cannons boomed across the nation as Americans celebrated the completion of the first railroad spanning North America. As the two sets of tracks—the Union Pacific's, stretching westward from Omaha, Nebraska, and the Central Pacific's, reaching eastward from Sacramento, California—met at Promontory Point, Utah, beaming officials drove in a final ceremonial golden spike with a silver hammer. With the coming of the transcontinental, Americans could make in a week's time the same coast-to-coast journey that earlier took travelers to California several *months*.

Building the railroad took backbreaking labor. Finding American muscle in inadequate supply, the railroads turned to immigrants. The Central Pacific employed numerous Chinese to chip and blast railbed out

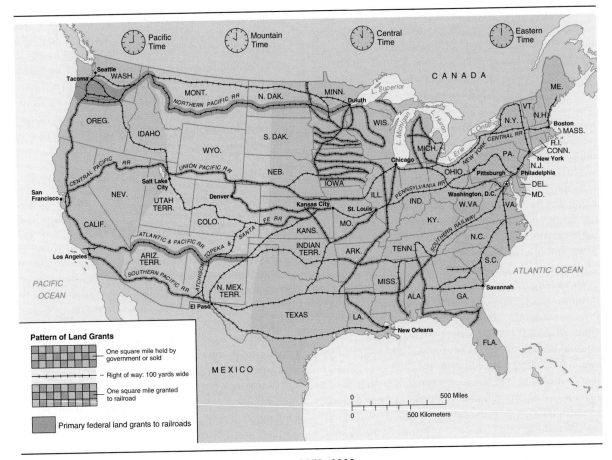

Transcontinental Railroads and Federal Land Grants, 1850–1900

Despite the laissez-faire ideology that argued against government interference in business, Congress heavily subsidized American railroads and gave them millions of acres of land. As illustrated in the box, belts of land were reserved on either side of a railroad's right of way. Until the railroad claimed the exact one-mile-square sections it chose to possess, all such sections within the belt remained closed to settlement.

of solid rock in the Sierra Nevada. The Union Pacific's construction gangs included countless Irish immigrants who dug their way across Nebraska and Wyoming. Americans of many other national and racial backgrounds, including blacks and Mexican-Americans, also joined in.

The Pacific Railroad Act of July 1, 1862, had authorized the construction of the transcontinental (see Chapter 15). The grants of land and other subsidies given to the railroads for each mile of track laid made them the single largest landholders in the West. Ultimately nine major routes ran from the South or Midwest to the West.

Settlers and the Railroad

By 1872, under the Pacific Railroad Act, Congress had awarded the railroads 170 million acres, worth at the time over half a billion dollars. By 1893 the states of Minnesota and Washington had also deeded to railroad companies a quarter of their state lands; Wisconsin, Iowa, Kansas, North Dakota, and Montana had turned over to them a fifth of their acreage. As mighty landowners, the railroads had a unique opportunity to shape settlement in the region—and to reap enormous profits.

The railroads used several different ploys to attract inhabitants. They created land bureaus and sent agents to the East Coast and Europe to recruit settlers. While the agents glorified the West as a new Garden of Eden, the land bureaus, which offered long-term loans and free transportation to prospective buyers, egged on the hesitant. "How can any young man of spirit settle himself down to earning a bare existence," exhorted one enthusiastic writer, "when all this vast region, . . . with its boundless, undeveloped resources before him, is inviting him on? They will be nobodies where they are—they can be somebodies in building up a new society." Acknowledging that life on the Great Plains could be lonely, the promoters advised young men to bring their own wives (because "maidens are scarce") and to emigrate as entire families and with friends.

In addition to the millions of Americans who migrated from nearby states, the railroads between 1870 and 1900 helped bring nearly 2.2 million foreign-born settlers to the trans-Mississippi West. Some agents recruited whole villages of Germans and eastern Europeans to relocate to the North Dakota plains, where they found soils similar to those of their homelands. By 1905 the Santa Fe Railroad alone had transported sixty thousand Mennonites from the Ukraine (to which they had migrated long before from their original homeland in Germany) to the fertile Kansas plains.

The railroads influenced agriculture as well. To ensure quick repayment of the money owed to them, the railroads urged new immigrants to specialize in cash crops—wheat on the northern Plains, corn in Iowa and Kansas, cotton and tobacco in Texas. Although these crops initially brought in high revenues, many farmers grew dependent on income from a single crop and ultimately became vulnerable to fluctuating market forces.

Homesteaders on the Great Plains

Liberalized land laws were another powerful magnet pulling settlers westward. The Homestead Act, which Congress passed in 1862 to benefit small farmers and urban workers, had offered 160 acres of land to any individual who would pay a $10 registration fee, live on the land for five years, and cultivate and improve it. Because getting to the Great Plains was costly, most settlers migrated from nearby states. In 1860 Kansas contained thirty-one thousand people from Illinois but only about forty-two hundred from New England. The majority had come from towns and small cities. On the Dakota frontier, only a third of the native-stock settlers had been farmers before emigrating.

The Homestead Act also proved quite attractive to immigrants from the British Isles as well as from

Homesteading in Nebraska, 1886
Not all Plains households were headed by males. The Chrisman sisters in Nebraska each staked a claim to 160 acres and took turns living with one another to fulfill the U.S. land office's residence requirements. Quilting was a relaxing diversion from the drudgery of farm work.

Scandinavia and other regions of Europe where good-quality land was prohibitively expensive. Urged on by land promoters, waves of English, Irish, Germans, Swedes, Danes, Norwegians, and Czechs immigrated to the United States in the 1870s and 1880s and formed their own communities. Soon the countryside in Minnesota and other states was dotted with towns bearing such names as New Ulm, New Prague, and New Sweden. Within a generation the Red River Valley in Minnesota could boast the largest Norwegian population outside Norway.

Although nearly four hundred thousand families claimed land under the provisions of the Homestead Act between 1860 and 1900, the law did not function as Congress had envisioned. Advance agents representing unscrupulous speculators filed false claims for the choicest locations, and railroads and state governments acquired huge landholdings. Despite the good intentions of the Homestead Act's authors, only one acre in every nine went to the pioneers for whom it was intended.

A second problem resulted from the 160-acre limit specified by the Homestead Act. On the rich soils of Iowa or Minnesota a 160-acre farm was ample, but in the drier areas west of the hundredth meridian, a farmer needed more land. To rectify this problem, Congress in 1873 passed the Timber Culture Act, which gave homesteaders an additional 160 acres if they planted trees on 40 acres. For states with little rainfall, Congress enacted the Desert Land Act in 1877, which made available 640 acres at $1.25 an acre on condition that the owner irrigate part of it within three years. However, this act, along with the Timber and Stone Act of 1878, which permitted the purchase of up to 160 acres of forest land for $2.50 an acre, was abused by grasping speculators, lumber-company representatives, and cattle ranchers seeking to expand their holdings. But even though families did not receive as much land as Congress had intended, federal laws kept alive the dream of the West as a place for new beginnings.

New Farms, New Markets

Railroad expansion and the liberalization of the land laws coincided with advances in farm mechanization and the development of improved strains of wheat and corn. Progress on these fronts enabled farmers to boost production dramatically. Efficient steel plows; spring-tooth harrows that broke up the dense prairie soil more effectively than earlier models; specially designed wheat planters; and improved grain binders, threshers, and windmills all allowed the typical Great Plains farmer of the late nineteenth century to grow and harvest ten times more wheat than would have been possible a few decades earlier. Another crucial invention was barbed wire, patented in 1874, which permitted farmers to keep roving livestock off their land—and which touched off violent conflicts between farmers and the cattle ranchers, who demanded the right to let their herds roam freely until the roundup. Generally the farmers won.

Fueling the leap in wheat production was a spiraling demand for the commodity, attributable to a 400 percent increase in the eastern urban population between 1870 and 1910. This demand was further stimulated by the development of milling techniques that improved the taste and texture of wheat flour. Before the 1870s, wheat was ground with large millstones that crushed the kernel to produce a coarse, strong-tasting, dark whole-wheat flour. In 1876 Minnesota millers used steel rollers to crack the kernel, allowing the husk to be blown off and the bran to be separated. This technique produced a silky, all-white flour that won first prize at the Philadelphia World's Fair that year. The Washburn Mills in Minneapolis (later renamed General Mills) used this new technology to produce tons of the better-tasting, though less nutritious, white flour. Harnessing the water power of St. Anthony Falls on the Mississippi and taking advantage of the Northern Pacific Railroad's extensive lines, the Washburn Mills soon gained both a national and an international market for its flour.

Farming seemed to be entering a period of unparalleled prosperity, and enthusiastic promoters nourished the idea that anyone could make an easy living in the West. But few fully understood the costs and perils of pursuing agriculture as a livelihood. Land was expensive, even at the reduced prices offered by the federal government and the railroads. The cost of the horses, machinery, and seed needed to start up a farm could exceed twelve hundred dollars, far more than the annual earnings of the average industrial worker. Faced with substantial mortgage payments, many farmers had to specialize in a crop such as wheat or corn that would fetch high prices. This specialization, in turn, made them dependent on the railroads for shipping and put them at the mercy of the international grain market's shifting currents.

Far from being an independent producer, the western grain grower was a player in a complex world market economy. Railroad and steamship transport allowed the American farmer to compete in the international market. High demand could bring prosperity, but when world overproduction forced grain prices down, the heavily indebted grower faced ruin. The emergence of a global grain trade also created economic pressures for peasant farmers in Europe— many of whom immigrated to the Plains, where their presence heightened the competition for land and for a slice of this tempting market. Faced with these realities, many Plains farmers quickly abandoned the illusion of frontier independence and easy wealth.

Exacerbating homesteaders' difficulties on the western Great Plains, normal rainfall was less than twenty inches a year. Farmers compensated through "dry farming"—plowing deeply to stimulate the capillary action of the soils and harrowing lightly to raise a covering of dirt that would retain precious moisture after a rainfall. They also built windmills and diverted creeks for irrigation. But the onset of unusually dry years in the 1870s, together with grasshopper infestations and the major economic depression that struck the United States between 1873 and 1878 (see Chapter 16), made the plight of some midwesterners desperate.

Building a Society and Achieving Statehood

Whether they hailed from the East, the nearby Midwest, or foreign lands, homesteaders faced difficult psychological adjustments to frontier life. Working from dawn to dusk in an unfamiliar place and facing fierce storms and natural disasters, many settlers became discouraged and returned East. But those who persisted eventually established ties to the land and built successful communities.

The first years of settlement were the most difficult. Toiling to build a house, plow the fields, plant the first crop, and drill a well, the pioneers put in an average of sixty-eight hours of tedious, backbreaking work a week, in isolated surroundings. Howard Ruede, a Pennsylvania printer who migrated to Kansas to farm, wrote home in 1877 complaining about the mosquitoes and bedbugs infesting his sod house. He and countless others coping with the severe Plains conditions saw their shining vision of Edenic farm life quickly dim. For blacks who emigrated from the South to Kansas and other parts of the Plains after the Civil War, prejudice and racism compounded the psychological burdens of adjusting to a different life.

Many middle-class women settlers, swept up in the romantic conventions of the day, found adaptation to Plains frontier life especially difficult. At least initially, some were enchanted by the haunting landscape, and in letters they described the undulating open plains as arrestingly beautiful. But far more were struck by the "horrible tribes of Mosquitoes"; the violent weather— drenching summer thunderstorms with hailstones as "big as hen's eggs" and blinding winter blizzards; and the crude sod huts that served as their early homes because of the scarcity of timber. One woman burst into tears upon first seeing her new sod house. The young bride angrily informed her husband that her father had built a better house for his hogs.

The high transiency rate on the frontier in these years reflected the frequent failures in adapting to the new environment. Nearly 66 percent of those who settled in Wapello County, Iowa, in 1850 had left within ten years. Seventy-nine percent of the families in a typical Wisconsin county in 1880 had moved on by 1895. Many were forced out by the rigors of frontier life, but others succumbed to speculative fever and sold out in the hope of finding better land farther west. However, in places that were populated largely by Germans and other immigrants with a tradition of family prosperity tied to continuous landownership, the persistence rate (or percentage of people staying for a decade or more) could be considerably higher.

Many who weathered the lean early years eventually came to identify closely with the land. Within a decade the typical Plains family that had "stuck it out" had moved into a new wood-frame house and had fixed up the front parlor. The women of these surviving households worked hard and learned to accept their lot. "Just done the chores," wrote one such woman to a friend. "I went fence mending and getting out cattle . . . and came in after sundown. I fed my White Leghorns, and then sat on the step to read over your letter. I forgot my wet feet and shoes full of gravel and giggled joyously." Despite their arduous existence, such settlers often spoke positively about life on the Great Plains. But they missed their old friends.

Some remote farm settlements blossomed into thriving communities. Churches and Sunday schools, among the first institutions to appear, became humming centers of social activity as well as of worship. Farmers gathered for barn raisings and group threshings, and families pooled their energies in quilting and husking bees. Neighbors readily lent a hand to the farmer whose barn had burned or whose wife or child

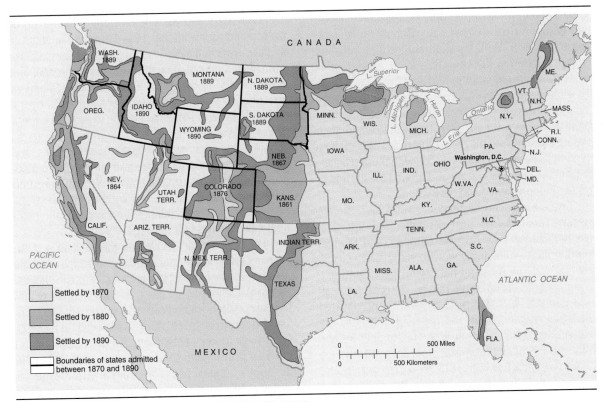

The Settlement of the Trans-Mississippi West, 1860–1890

The West was not settled by a movement of peoples gradually creeping westward from the East. Rather, settlers first occupied California and the Midwest and then filled up the nation's vast interior.

was sick. Cooperation was a practical necessity and a form of insurance in a rugged environment where everyone was vulnerable to instant misfortune or even disaster.

As settlements grew into small towns, their inhabitants labored to reverse easterners' images of the Midwest as unrefined and backward. They eagerly set up lyceums and libraries to uplift and enlighten local residents. Masonic lodges and social clubs soon followed. Larger communities established fashionable hotels, the symbol of urban sophistication and culture, and brought in entertainers to perform at their new "opera houses."

Like the farmers in the surrounding countryside, townspeople closed ranks when misfortune struck. At the first outbreak of fire or violence, the whole town mobilized. When the notorious ex-Confederate raider and outlaw Jesse James rode into Northfield, Minnesota, and held up the town bank in 1876, local mer-

chants grabbed their shotguns and drove him off, killing two of his gang.

The new settlers on the frontier tended to be conservative. They patterned their churches, schools, courts, and government structures after familiar institutions in the communities from which they had come. Achieving statehood required that the residents of a territory petition Congress to pass an enabling act establishing the territory's boundaries and authorizing an election to select delegates for a state constitutional convention. Once the state constitution had been drawn up and ratified by popular vote, the territory applied to Congress for admission as a state.

Under these procedures Kansas entered the Union in 1861, followed by Nevada in 1864 and Nebraska in 1867. Colorado joined in 1876. Not until 1889 did North Dakota, South Dakota, Montana, and Washington gain statehood. Wyoming and Idaho came into the Union the following year. Utah, long prevented from joining because of the Mormon practice of polygamy, finally declared plural marriages illegal and entered in 1896. With Oklahoma's admission in 1907 and Arizona's and New Mexico's in 1912, the process of creating permanent political institutions in the trans-Mississippi West was complete.

Although generally conservative, the new state governments did support woman suffrage. As territories became states, pioneer women, encouraged by women's rights activists like Susan B. Anthony and Elizabeth Cady Stanton, battled for the vote. Seven western states held referenda on this issue between 1870 and 1910. Success came first in the Wyoming Territory, where the tiny legislature enfranchised women in 1869 in hopes of improving the territory's reputation as a haven of rowdy mining camps by attracting females, then outnumbered six to one. The Utah Territory followed in 1870 and reaffirmed its support for woman suffrage when it became a state. Nebraska in 1867, and Colorado in 1876, permitted women to vote in school elections. Although these successes were significant, by 1910 only four states—Idaho, Wyoming, Utah, and Colorado—had granted women full voting rights. The very newness of their place in the Union may have sensitized legislators in these states to women's important contributions to settlement and made them open to experimentation; but by and large, familiar traditions persisted.

The Grange

As we have seen, Plains farming proved far riskier than many had anticipated. Terrible grasshopper infestations between 1873 and 1877 consumed nearly half the midwestern wheat crop. Although overall production surged after 1870, the abundant harvests undercut prices. Wheat tumbled from a high of $2.95 a bushel in 1866 to $1.06 in 1880. Countless farmers who had borrowed heavily to finance their homesteads and expensive new machinery went bankrupt or barely survived. One struggling elderly Minnesota farmer wrote the governor in 1874: "[W]e can see nothing but starvation in the future if relief does not come."

When relief did not come, the farmers responded by setting up cooperative ventures. Under the leadership of Oliver H. Kelley, a Department of Agriculture clerk, midwestern farmers in 1867 formed the Grange, or "Patrons of Husbandry," as the organization was officially called. Membership climbed to more than 1.5

million in the trying years of the early 1870s. Patterned after the Masonic Order, the Grange offered a program of education, emotional support, and fellowship. For the inexperienced homesteader, it made available a library of the latest information on planting and livestock raising. For the lonely farm family, the Grange organized biweekly social gatherings, including cooperative meals and lively songfests.

But the heart of the Grange was concern over farmers' economic plight. An 1874 circular announced the organization's central purpose: to help farmers "buy less and produce more, in order to make our farms more self-sustaining." Grangers embraced the older Jacksonian belief that the products of the soil were the basis of all honorable wealth and that the producer classes—people who worked with their hands—formed the true backbone of society. Members sought to restore self-sufficiency to the family farm. Ignoring the contradiction implicit in farmers' banding together to help individuals become independent tillers of the soil, they negotiated special discounts with farm-machinery dealers and set up "cash-only" cooperative stores and grain-storage elevators to cut out the "middlemen"—the bankers, grain brokers, and merchants who made money at their expense.

Grangers vehemently attacked the railroads, which routinely gave discounts to large shippers, bribed state legislators for special land favors, and charged higher rates for short runs than for long hauls. These practices stung hard-pressed farmers. Although professing to be nonpolitical, Grangers in Illinois, Wisconsin, Minnesota, and Iowa lobbied state legislatures in 1874 to pass laws fixing maximum rates for freight shipments.

The railroads responded by appealing to the Supreme Court to declare these "Granger laws" unconstitutional. But in *Munn* v. *Illinois* (1877), the Court not only ruled against the railroads' objections but also upheld an Illinois law fixing a maximum rate for the storage of grain. The regulation of grain elevators, declared the Court's majority, was legitimate under the federal Constitution's clause granting police powers to states. When the Court in *Wabash* v. *Illinois* (1886) modified this position by prohibiting states from regulating *interstate* railroad rates, Congress passed the Interstate Commerce Act (1887), reaffirming the federal government's power to investigate and oversee railroad activities and establishing a new agency, the Interstate Commerce Commission (ICC), to do just that. Although the commission failed to curb the railroads' monopolistic practices, it did establish the principle of federal regulation of interstate transportation.

Despite promising beginnings, however, the Grange movement soon faltered. The railroads, having lost their battle on the national level, lobbied state legislatures and won repeal of most of the rate-regulation laws by 1878. Moreover, the Grange system of cash-only cooperative stores failed because few farmers had ample cash. Ultimately the Grange ideal of complete financial independence proved unrealistic. Under the conditions that prevailed on the Plains after the Civil War, it was impossible to farm without borrowing money.

How valid was the Grangers' analysis of the farmers' problems? The Grangers blamed greedy railroads and middlemen for their economic difficulties, but the situation was not that simple. The years 1873–1878 saw the entire economy caught in a grinding depression, in which railroad operators and merchant middlemen, no less than farmers, had to scramble to survive. And although farm commodity prices did fall between 1865 and 1900, the wholesale prices of manufactured goods, including items needed on the farm, fell in the same period as well—often faster than farm prices. Even the railroads' stiff freight charges could be justified in part by the thin pattern of western settlement and the seasonality of grain shipments.

Notwithstanding, the farmers and the Grange leaders who articulated their grievances had plenty of reasons to complain. Farmers who had no control over the price level of their crops were at the mercy of local merchants and farm-equipment dealers who exercised monopolistic control over the prices that *they* could charge. Similarly, railroads sometimes insisted on transporting wheat to only one mill. Occasionally they even refused to stop at small towns to pick up local wheat shipments. Policies like these struck the farmers as completely arbitrary and made them feel powerless. Hamlin Garland captured the hardship and despair of frustrated farmers in his *Main-Travelled Roads* (1891) and *Son of the Middle Border* (1917), describing barely surviving families who "rose early and toiled without intermission, till the darkness fell on the plain, then tumbled into bed, every bone and muscle aching with fatigue."

When the prices of corn, wheat, and cotton briefly revived after 1878, many farmers deserted the Grange. Although the Grange lived on as a social and educational institution, it lost its economic clout because it was ultimately unable to improve the financial position of the farmers it served. For all its weaknesses, the Grange movement did lay the groundwork for an even more powerful wave of agrarian protest in the 1880s and 1890s, to be discussed in Chapter 21.

The Southwestern Frontier

Until 1848, when the Treaty of Guadalupe Hidalgo ended the Mexican War and ceded to the United States an immense territory—part of which became California, Arizona, and New Mexico—Mexicans had controlled wide-open expanses of the Southwest. They had built their own churches, maintained large ranching operations, and as we have seen, traded with the Indians. Although the peace treaty pledged the United States to protect the liberty and property of Mexicans who remained on American soil, in the next three decades, aggressive American ranchers and settlers took over the territorial governments and forced the Spanish-speaking population off much of the land. Mexicans who stayed behind adapted to the new Anglo society with varying degrees of success.

In Texas, where the struggle for independence from Mexico and the Mexican War had left a legacy of bitterness and misunderstanding, Anglos in the 1840s and 1850s frequently harassed local Mexican-Americans and confiscated their lands. Small numbers of Mexican bandits retaliated by raiding American communities, stealing from the rich and giving to the poor. Tensions peaked in 1859, when Juan Cortina, a local Mexican rancher, attacked the Anglo border community of Brownsville, Texas, and freed all the prisoners in jail. Pursued by the U.S. Army, Cortina battled the Americans for years, slipping back and forth across the border until the Mexican government, fearing a U.S. invasion, imprisoned him in 1875.

Similar violence erupted in California in the 1850s and 1860s after a cycle of flood and drought, together with a slumping cattle industry, ruined many of the large southern California ranches owned by the *californios*, the Spanish-speaking descendants of the original Spanish settlers. The collapse of the ranch economy forced many of these Mexican-Americans to retreat into socially segregated urban neighborhoods, called barrios. In Santa Barbara, California, Spanish-surnamed citizens made up nearly half the town's 2,640 residents in 1870. Ten years later, however, overwhelmed by an influx of Anglos, they composed barely a quarter of the population. Maintaining a tenacious hold on their traditions, Spanish-speaking people in

Adobe House, Santa Barbara, c. 1890

Although Spanish-speaking families in Santa Barbara were excluded from certain sections of town, they posed as proudly in front of their homes as did local Anglos.

Santa Barbara and other towns survived by working as low-paid day laborers.

The cultural adaptation of Spanish-speaking Americans to Anglo society unfolded more smoothly in Arizona and New Mexico, where the initial Spanish settlement was sparse and a small class of wealthy Mexican landowners had long dominated a poor illiterate peasantry. Moreover, beginning in the 1820s, well-to-do Mexicans in Tucson, Arizona, had educated their children in the United States and had formed trading partnerships and business alliances with Americans. Perhaps the most successful was Estevan Ochoa, who began a long-distance freighting business in 1859 with a U.S. partner and then expanded it into a lucrative merchandising, mining, and sheep-raising operation.

The success of hard-working businessmen such as Ochoa, who became mayor of Tucson, helped moderate American settlers' antagonistic attitudes toward the indigenous Mexican-American population. So, too, did the work of popular writers like Bret Harte and Helen Hunt Jackson. By sentimentalizing the old Spanish-Mexican ways in their writings, these authors in-creased public sympathy for Spanish-speaking Americans. Jackson's 1884 romance *Ramona,* a tale of doomed love set on a California Spanish-Mexican ranch overwhelmed by the onrushing tide of Anglo civilization, was enormously popular.

Not all was harmony, however. In Arizona and New Mexico, Mexican-American and Anglo ranchers became embroiled in fiery land disputes in the 1880s. Organizing themselves as *Las Gorras Blancas* (The White Caps) in 1888, Mexican-American ranchers tore up railroad tracks and intimidated and attacked both Anglo newcomers and those Hispanics who had fenced acreage in northern New Mexico previously considered public grazing land. But this vigilante action gained them little, as Anglo-dominated corporate ranching steadily impinged on their operations. Relations changed in the urban centers as well, as Mexican-American businessmen increasingly restricted their business dealings to their own people, and the Spanish-speaking population as a whole became more impoverished. Even in Tucson, where the Mexican-American elite enjoyed considerable economic and political success, 80 percent of the Mexican-Americans in the work force were laborers in 1880, taking jobs as butchers, barbers, cowboys, and railroad workers.

As increasing numbers of Mexican-American males lost title to their land and were forced to search for seasonal migrant work, Mexican-American women bore the responsibility of holding families and communities together. Households were headed by women when their husbands were away, and women fostered group identification through their emphasis on traditional customs, kinship, and allegiance to the Catholic Church. They served as *madrinas*, or godmothers, for others' children; tended garden plots; and traded food, soap, and produce with other women. This economy, invisible to those outside the village, stabilized the community in times of drought or persecution by Anglos.

Violence and discrimination against Spanish-speaking citizens of the Southwest escalated in the 1890s, a time of rising racism in the United States. Riots against Mexican-Americans broke out in the Texas communities of Beeville and Laredo in 1894 and 1899. Expressions of anti-Catholicism, as well as verbal attacks on the Mexican-Americans as violent and lazy, increased among hostile Anglos. For Spanish-speaking citizens, the battle for fair treatment and cultural respect would continue into the twentieth century.

EXPLOITING THE WEST

For a generation of Americans who watched enviously as astounding fortunes were being made in railroading, steel, and other businesses (see Chapter 18), the spectacular gold-mining, cattle-raising, and farming enterprises that lit up the western landscape from the 1850s to the 1880s appeared to offer great opportunities for the individual to strike it rich. Publicized in banner headlines across the land, these "bonanzas" promised unheard of wealth and seemed to confirm the myth of the frontier as a place of boundless opportunity. In reality, however, the bonanzas set in motion a boom-and-bust economy in which a few people became fabulously wealthy but most barely survived or lost their shirts. Of all the groups that surged onto the Great Plains and beyond in the late nineteenth century, none had to revise their expectations more radically than the speculators and adventurers thirsting for quick fortunes.

The Mining Frontier

Beginning with the California gold rush in 1849, a series of mining booms over the next three decades swept from the Southwest northward into Canada. The sensational discoveries in California's Sierra Nevada that produced more than $81 million worth of gold bullion in 1852 were followed by gold strikes on the Fraser River in British Columbia in 1857. The following year, Henry Comstock (who for obscure reasons bore the nickname "Old Pancake") stumbled upon the rich Comstock Lode along Nevada's Carson River. Months later, feverishly pursuing rumors of new strikes, prospectors swarmed into the Rocky Mountains near present-day Denver and uncovered deep veins of gold and silver along a little stream called Clear Creek. Over the next two decades, gold was discovered in Idaho, Montana, Wyoming, South Dakota, and, in 1896, in the Alaskan Klondike. Although the popular press clearly exaggerated reports of miners scooping up gold by the panful, by 1900 more than a billion dollars worth of gold had been mined just in California. The Comstock Lode alone produced more than $300 million worth of gold and silver.

The early discoveries of "placer" gold, panned from riverbeds and streams, reinforced the myth of the mining country as "a poor man's paradise." By 1860, when census takers asked Californians to report their occupations, more than 82,000 out of a population of 380,000 described themselves as miners. Of these, 35,000 were Chinese, many of whom were forced by prejudice to work claims that others had abandoned.

Although a few prospectors became fabulously wealthy, the experience of Henry Comstock, who sold out one claim for eleven thousand dollars and another for two mules, was more typical. The illusions of the frontier myth notwithstanding, most of the West's mining wealth fell into the hands of investment bankers and mining-company owners. Because the larger gold and silver deposits lay buried in veins of quartz deep within the earth, extracting them required huge investments in expensive equipment as well as substantial legal help for protection against competing claims. No sooner had the major discoveries been made, therefore, than large mining companies, backed by eastern or British capital, took them over.

But if the Comstock Lode, the Clear Creek strike, and the other ore discoveries failed to bring great riches to the average miner, they did stimulate flurries of secondary economic activity, and then wildly transformed normal patterns of social behavior. During the heyday of the Comstock Lode in the 1860s and 1870s, Virginia City, Nevada, erupted in an orgy of speculation and building. Like many boom towns near mining claims, it had sprung into being almost overnight. Started as a shantytown in 1859, it swelled by 1873 into a thriving metropolis of twenty thousand people, complete with elaborate mansions, a six-story hotel, an opera house, 131 saloons, 4 banks, and uncounted brothels. Males outnumbered females by three to one. Money quickly earned was even more rapidly lost.

In the chaotic rush to stake new claims, inhibitions about stealing and cheating fell by the wayside. Because Virginia City's police force was too small and too corrupt to maintain order, vigilantes took over the town during the economic downturn of 1871, hanged two notorious outlaws, and forced others off the lode. Justice on the mining frontier was occasionally a rough affair, but most communities, unlike Virginia City, established stable police forces and a regular system of courts.

The boom-and-bust cycle evident in Virginia City was repeated in towns across the west between 1870 and 1900. Mark Twain captured the thrill of the mining "stampedes" in his book *Roughing It* (1872). "Every few days," wrote Twain, "news would come of the discovery of a brand-new mining region: immediately the papers would teem with accounts of its richness, and away the surplus population would scamper to take possession. By the time I was fairly inoculated with the disease, 'Esmeralda' had just had a run and 'Humboldt' was beginning to shriek for attention. 'Humboldt! Humboldt!' was the new cry, and straightway Humboldt, the newest of the new, the richest of the rich, the most marvelous of the marvelous discoveries in silver-land, was occupying two columns of the public prints to 'Esmeralda's' one."

Word of new ore deposits lured to the mining towns transient populations salivating to get rich. Miners typically earned about $2,000 a year at a time when teachers made $450 to $650 and domestic help $250 to $350. But meals and a tiny room cost between $480 and $720 annually. Furthermore, mining was difficult and dangerous work. Serious accidents occurred daily. In less than two decades, more than three hundred workers died in the Virginia City mines. And when miners exhausted the major ore veins, they quickly packed up for new territories. By 1900 Virginia City's population had shrunk below four thousand. Although a few got rich, most miners at best earned only enough to go elsewhere, perhaps buy some land, and try again. But if the myth of the frontier exaggerated the opportunities of the mining West, it contained just enough reality to sustain people's hopes.

Cowboys and the Cattle Frontier

As Mark Twain had so colorfully related, the popular press's rousing accounts of big gold strikes had helped fuel the feverish expansion of the mining frontier during the 1860s and 1870s. Similar stories, romanticizing the life of the hardy cowboy, driving large herds of

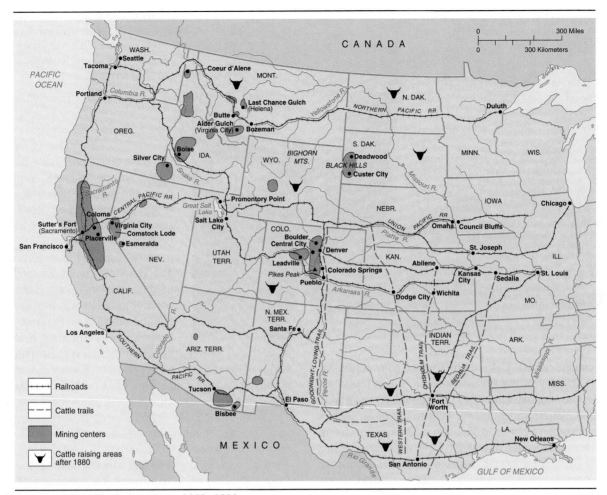

The Mining and Cattle Frontiers, 1860–1890

The western mining and ranching bonanzas lured thousands of Americans hoping to get rich quick.

longhorns northward from Texas through Oklahoma to markets in Dodge City and Abilene, Kansas, sparked the transformation of the cattle industry in these same decades. In this case, astute businessmen and railroad entrepreneurs, eager to fund their new investments in miles of track, promoted cattle herding as the new route to fame and fortune, and the eastern press took up the theme. The cowboy, once scorned as a ne'er-do-well and drifter, was now glorified as a man of rough-hewn integrity and self-reliant strength who lived a life of adventurous simplicity on the Shawnee, Chisholm, and other fabled cattle trails of the Southwest.

In 1868 Joseph G. McCoy, a young cattle dealer from Springfield, Illinois, shrewdly combined organizational and promotional skills to make the cattle indus-

try a new bonanza. Having grown up in a moderately wealthy family, McCoy had avoided military service and reaped an enviable profit trading livestock during the Civil War. He was well aware that attempts in the 1850s to drive longhorn cattle from south Texas grasslands northward to markets in Arkansas, Illinois, and Missouri had been unprofitable and dangerous, owing to frequent Indian attacks and outbreaks of "Texas fever" that had killed thousands of cattle. But with the relocation of the Plains Indians onto reservations and the extension of the railroads into Kansas in the post–Civil War period, McCoy realized that cattle shipping now had a renewed potential.

Forming a partnership in 1867 with his brothers' Illinois company that shipped cattle to New Orleans and New York, McCoy traveled to Kansas and oversaw the construction of a new stockyard in Abilene. By guaranteeing to transport his steers in railcars to hungry eastern markets, he obtained a five-dollar kickback from the railroads on each cattle car shipped. To make the overland cattle drives from Texas to Abilene easier, McCoy also helped survey and shorten the Chisholm Trail in Kansas. Finally, in a clever feat of showmanship, he organized the first Wild West show, sending four Texas cowboys to St. Louis and Chicago, where they staged roping and riding exhibitions that attracted exuberant crowds. At the end of his first year in business, thirty-five thousand steers were sold in Abilene; the following year the number more than doubled, to seventy-five thousand.

The great cattle drives of the 1860s and 1870s turned into a bonanza for herd owners. Steers purchased in Texas at $9 a head could be sold in Abilene, after deducting $4 in trail expenses, for $28. A herd of two thousand head could thus bring a tidy $30,000 profit. But the cattlemen, like the grain growers farther north on the Great Plains, lived at the mercy of high interest rates and an unstable market. During the financial panic of 1873, cattle drovers, unable to get extensions on their loans, fell into bankruptcy by the hundreds. Glossing over the market's instability, railroad promoters suggested that a 25 percent yearly profit was normal, and a 50 percent profit not unusual.

Persuaded by these claims and ever questing for the quick dollar, former miners, farmers, and countless other ambitious types turned to ranching. Foreign investors sank huge sums into the cattle business. The English alone put $45 million into ranch companies in the 1870s and 1880s—and by 1883 owned or controlled nearly 20 million acres of western grazing land. American businesses followed suit. For example, in the 1880s twenty domestically owned cattle companies, each worth between $20,000 and $3 million, operated in Wyoming.

As in mining, little of the money made by large-scale ranchers found its way into the pockets of the cowboys themselves. The typical cowpunchers who drove two-thousand-head herds eight hundred miles through the dirt and dust from southern Texas to Abilene during the 1870s earned a mere thirty dollars a month, about the same as common laborers. They also braved the gangs of cattle thieves that operated along the trails. The most notorious of the cattle rustlers, William H. Bonney, better known as Billy the Kid, may have murdered as many as eleven men before he was killed by a sheriff in 1881 at the age of twenty-one. The long hours, low pay, and hazardous work discouraged older ranch hands from applying. Most cowboys were young men in their teens and twenties who worked for a year or two and then pursued different livelihoods.

Of the estimated thirty-five thousand to fifty-five thousand men who rode the trails in these years, nearly one-fifth were black or Mexican. Barred by discrimination from many other trades, black cowboys enjoyed the freedom of life on the trail. Although they were excluded from the position of trail boss, they distinguished themselves as resourceful and shrewd cowpunchers. Nat Love, the son of Tennessee slaves, left for Kansas after the Civil War to work for Texas cattle companies. As chief brander, he moved through Texas and Arizona "dancing, drinking, and shooting up the town." By his own account, he was "wild, reckless, free," and "afraid of nothing." On July 4, 1876, when the Black Hills gold rush was in full swing, Love delivered three thousand head of cattle to a point near the hills and rode into Deadwood to celebrate. Local miners and gamblers had raised prize money for roping and shooting contests, and Nat Love won both, as well as a new title, Deadwood Dick. Close relationships sometimes developed between black and white cowboys. Shortly before Charles Goodnight, a white pioneer trailblazer, died in 1929, he recalled of the black cowboy Bose Ikard, a former slave, that "he was my detective, banker, and everything else in Colorado, New Mexico, and the other wild country I was in. The nearest and only bank was at Denver, and when we carried money I gave it to Bose." Goodnight revealed much about the economic situation of blacks on the Plains, however, when he added that "a thief would never think of robbing him [Ikard]—never think of looking in a Negro's bed for money."

Although the typical real-life cowboy led a lonely, dirty, and often boring existence, a mythic version of the frontier cowboy who might with equal ease become a gunslinging marshal or a dastardly villain was glamorized in the eastern press as early as the 1870s. The image of the West as a wild and lawless land where vigilantes battled with brutish bandits fired easterners' imaginations. Edward L. Wheeler, a writer for the publishing house of Beadle and Adams, in 1877 penned his first dime novel, *Deadwood Dick, The Prince of the Road: or, the Black Rider of the Black Hills.* Over the next eight years, Wheeler turned out thirty-three Deadwood Dick novels relating the adventures of the muscular young hero who wore black clothes and rode a black horse. Cast alternately as outlaw, miner, gang leader, and cowboy, Deadwood Dick turned his blazing six-shooters on ruthless ruffians and dishonest desperadoes. He had much in common with the real-life Deadwood Dick except that Wheeler, to please his white readership, made him a white man. The vigilante justice and lynch law celebrated in these novels portrayed the western frontier as a throwback to a semi-legendary earlier age in which honor had triumphed when the righteous took matters into their own hands.

The reality was a good deal less picturesque. Although Abilene, for example, went through an early period of violence and turmoil that saw cowboys pulling down the walls of the jail as it was being built, the town had quickly established a local police force to maintain law and order. City ordinances forbade the carrying of firearms and regulated saloons, gambling, and prostitution. James B. ("Wild Bill") Hickok served as town marshal in 1871, but his tenure was less eventful than legend had it. Dime novelists described him as "a veritable terror to bad men on the border," but during his term as Abilene's lawman, Hickok killed just two men, one of them by mistake.* Transient, unruly types certainly gave a distinctive flavor to cattle towns like Abilene, Wichita, and Dodge City, but the overall homicide rates there were not unusually high.

More typical of western conflicts were the "range wars" that pitted "cattle kings" (who thought that the open range existed for them alone to exploit) against farmers. Gaining the upper hand in state legislatures, farming interests sought to cripple the freewheeling cattlemen with quarantine laws and inspection regulations. Ranchers retaliated against the spread of barbed-wire farm fencing on the Plains, first by cutting the settlers' fences and then by buying up and enclosing thousands of acres of their own. Meanwhile, dozens of small-scale shooting incidents broke out between inhabitants of isolated farms and livestock drovers, as well as between rival cattlemen and sheep ranchers.

Peaking during 1880–1885, the bonanza produced more than 4.5 million head of cattle for eastern markets. Prices began to sag as early as 1882, however, and many ranchers, having expanded too rapidly, plunged heavily into debt. When President Grover Cleveland, trying to improve federal observance of Indian treaties, ordered cattlemen to remove their stock from the Cheyenne-Arapaho reservation in 1885, two hundred thousand more cattle were crowded onto al-

Ned Huddleston, alias Isom Dart
Outlaws and gunfighters, although small in number, created an image of the trans-Mississippi West as lawless and dangerous. Isom Dart, a member of Brown's Park outlaw faction in Colorado and Wyoming, here poses with his six-shooters.

ready overgrazed ranges. That same year and the following, two of the coldest and snowiest winters on record combined with summer droughts and Texas fever to destroy nearly 90 percent of the cattle in some regions, pushing thousands of ranchers into bankruptcy. Those who survived were forced to irrigate, fence their lands, and raise cattle on smaller ranches. The cattle industry lived on, but railroad expansion and the increasing numbers of steers raised outside the Great Plains brought the days of the open range and the great cattle drives to an end. As had the mining frontier, the early years of the cattle frontier left behind memories of individual daring, towering fortunes for some, and hard times for many.

---

*Hickok eventually moved on to Deadwood, where he was murdered in 1876 by Jack McCall as he played poker, ensuring his place in the pantheon of western heroes.

Bonanza Farms on the Plains

The heady enthusiasm that permeated mining and ranching in the 1870s and 1880s also percolated into agriculture. Like the gold rushes and cattle bonanzas, the wheat boom in the Dakota Territory started small but rapidly attracted large capital investments that produced the nation's first "agribusinesses."

The boom began during the Panic of 1873, when the failure of numerous banks caused the price of Northern Pacific Railroad bonds to plummet. The railroad responded by exchanging land for its depreciated bonds. Speculators, including the railroad's own president, George W. Cass, jumped at this wonderful opportunity and purchased more than three hundred thousand acres in the fertile Red River valley of North Dakota for between fifty cents and a dollar an acre.

Operating singly or in groups, the speculators established enormous, factorylike ten-thousand-acre farms, each run by a hired manager, and invested heavily in labor and equipment. On the Cass-Cheney-Dalrymple farm near Fargo, North Dakota, which covered an area six miles long by four miles wide, fifty men did the initial plowing. An additional one hundred were hired for harvesting. Together they used 66 plows, 21 seeders, 60 harrows, 30 self-binding harvesters, and 5 steam-powered threshers. On a typical spring day, 50 or 60 plows rumbled across the flat landscape in unison. The *New York Tribune* reported that Cass, who had invested fifty thousand dollars for land and equipment, paid all his expenses plus the cost of the ten thousand acres with his first harvest alone.

The publicity generated by the tremendous success of a few large investors like Cass and Oliver Dalrymple, the "king" of the wheat growers, led to an unprecedented wheat boom in the Red River valley in 1880. Eastern banking syndicates and small farmers alike rushed to buy land. North Dakota's population tripled in the 1880s. Wheat production skyrocketed to almost 29 million bushels by the end of the decade. But the profits so loudly celebrated in the eastern press soon evaporated. By 1890 some Red River valley farmers were destitute.

The wheat boom collapsed for a variety of reasons. Overproduction, high investment costs, too little or too much rain, excessive reliance on one crop, and depressed grain prices on the international market all undercut farmers' earnings. Large-scale farmers who had invested in hopes of getting rich felt lucky just to survive. Oliver Dalrymple lamented in 1889 that "it seems as if the time has come when there is no money in wheat raising."

The Oklahoma Land Rush

Even as farmers in the Dakotas and Minnesota were enduring poor harvests and falling prices, hard-pressed would-be homesteaders greedily eyed the enormous Indian Territory, as present-day Oklahoma was then known. The federal government, considering much of the land in this area virtually worthless, had reserved it for the Five Civilized Tribes, who had dwelled there since the 1830s. Because these tribes had sided with the Confederacy during the Civil War (except for some Cherokees), Washington had punished them by settling thousands of Indians from *other* tribes on lands in the western part of the territory. By the 1880s, recognizing the actual value of the Oklahoma lands, land-hungry non-Indians argued

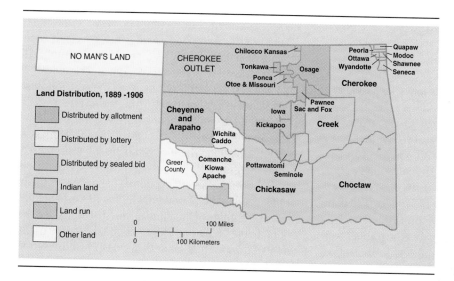

The Oklahoma Land Rush, 1889–1906

Lands in Oklahoma not settled by "sooners" were sold by lotteries, allotments, and sealed-bid auctions. By 1907 the major reservations had been broken up, and each Native American had been given a small farm.

that the Civilized Tribes' betrayal of the Union justified further federal confiscation of their land.

Over the Native Americans' protests, Congress in 1889 transferred to the federally owned public domain nearly 2 million acres in the central part of the Oklahoma Territory that had not been specifically assigned to any Indian tribe. At noon on April 22, 1889, thousands of men, women, and children in buggies and wagons stampeded into the new lands to stake out homesteads. (Other settlers, the so-called Sooners, had earlier infiltrated the lands illegally and were already plowing the fields.) Before nightfall tent communities had risen at Oklahoma City and Guthrie near stations on the Santa Fe Railroad. Nine weeks later, six thousand homestead claims had been filed. During the next ten years, as the Dawes Severalty Act freed up additional acres by breaking up the Indian reservations into individual allotments and opening the surplus to non-Indian settlement, homesteaders continued to pour into the territory.

The Oklahoma land rush demonstrated the continuing power of the frontier myth, which tied "free" land to the ideals of individual opportunity and self-determination. Despite early obstacles—the 1889 rush occurred too late in the season for most settlers to plant a full crop, and a drought parched the land the following year—Oklahoma farmers remained optimistic about their chances of "making it" on the last frontier. Most did survive, because they were fortunate enough to have obtained fertile land in an area where the normal rainfall was thirty inches, ten inches more than in the semiarid regions farther west. Still, a combination of exploitative farming, poor land management, and sporadic drought would within two generations place Oklahoma at the desolate center of what in the 1930s would be called the dust bowl.

The West of Life and Legend

In 1893, four years after the last major tract of Western Indian land, the Oklahoma Territory, was opened to non-Indian settlement, a young Wisconsin historian, Frederick Jackson Turner, delivered a lecture entitled "The Significance of the Frontier in American History." "[T]he frontier has gone," declared Turner, "and with its going has closed the first period of American history." Although Turner's assertion that the frontier was closed was inaccurate (more land would be settled there in the twentieth century than in the nineteenth), his linking of economic opportunity with the development of the trans-Mississippi West caught the popular imagination and launched a new school of historical inquiry into the effects of the frontier on U.S. history.

Scholars now recognize that Turner's inaccurate "frontier thesis," with its ethnocentric omission of Native Americans' claims to the land, was part of an idealized view of the West that became popular in the 1890s. As farmers, miners, ranchers, Indian agents, and prostitutes had pursued their varied activities in the *real* West, a parallel *legendary* West had taken deep root in the American imagination. In the nineteenth century, this mythic West was a product of novels, songs, and paintings. In the twentieth century, it would be perpetuated by movies, radio programs, and television shows. The legend merits attention, for its evolution is fascinating, and its influence far-reaching.

The American Adam and the Dime-Novel Hero

In the early biographies of frontiersmen like Daniel Boone, and in the wilderness novels of James Fenimore Cooper, the western hero's personal development sometimes parallels, but more often runs counter to, the interests of society. Mid-nineteenth-century writers, extending the theme of the western wilderness as an alternative to society, presented the frontiersman as a kind of mythic American Adam—simple, virtuous, and innocent, untainted by a corrupt social order. For example, an early biographer of Kit Carson, the Kentucky-born guide who in 1830 made one of the first recorded crossings of California's Mojave Desert, depicted him as a perfect antidote to the evils of refined society, an individual of "genuine simplicity, . . . truthfulness . . . [and] bravery." At the end of Mark Twain's *Huckleberry Finn,* Huck rejects the constraints of settled society as represented by Aunt Sally and heads west with the declaration, "I reckon I got to light out for the territory ahead of the rest, because Aunt Sally she's going to adopt me and sivilize me, and I can't stand it. I been there before." In this version of the legend, the West is a place of adventure, romance, or contemplation where one can escape from society and its pressures.

But even as this conception of the myth was being popularized, another powerful theme had emerged as well. The authors of the dime novels that blanketed the nation in the 1860s and 1870s offered the image of the western frontiersman as a figure deeply immersed in society and its concerns. In *Buffalo Bill: King of the*

Border Men (1869), a dime novel loosely based on real-life William F. ("Buffalo Bill") Cody, Edward Judson (who published under the name Ned Buntline) created an idealized hero who is a powerful force for morality and social order as he drives off treacherous Indians and rounds up horse thieves and no-good cattle rustlers.

So enthusiastically did the public welcome this new fictional frontiersman that Cody was inspired in 1883 to start his Wild West show. A former army scout and pony express rider, Cody was a natural showman, and his exhibitions proved immensely popular. Cody presented mock "battles" of army scouts and Indians—in effect, morality dramas of good versus evil. Along with entertainment, in short, the Wild West show reinforced the dime-novel image of the West as an arena of moral encounter where virtue always triumphed.

Revitalizing the Frontier Legend

Both versions of the myth—the West as a place of escape from society and the West as a stage on which the moral conflicts confronting society could be played out—figured prominently in the histories and essays of young Theodore Roosevelt, the paintings and sculptures of artist Frederic Remington, and the short stories and novels of writer Owen Wister. These three young members of the eastern establishment spent much time in the West in the 1880s, and each was intensely affected by the adventure. All three had felt thwarted by the constraints and enervating influence of the genteel urban world in which they had grown up, and each went West to experience the physical challenges and moral simplicities extolled in the dime novels. When Roosevelt arrived in 1884 at the ranch he had purchased in the Dakota Badlands, he at once bought a leather scout's uniform, complete with fringed sleeves and leggings.

Each man also found in the West precisely what he was looking for. The frontier that Roosevelt glorified in such books as *The Winning of the West* (four volumes, 1889–1896), and that the prolific Remington portrayed in his work, was a stark physical and moral environment that stripped away all social artifice and tested an individual's true ability and character. Drawing on a popular version of English scientist Charles Darwin's evolutionary theory, which characterized life as a struggle in which only the fittest and the best survived, Roosevelt and Remington exalted the disappearing frontier as the last outpost of an honest and true social order.

This version of the frontier myth reached its apogee in Owen Wister's enormously popular novel *The Virginian* (1902), later reincarnated as a 1929 Gary Cooper movie and a 1960s television series. In Wister's tale the elemental physical and social environment of the Great Plains produces individuals like his unnamed cowboy hero, "the Virginian," an honest, strong, and compassionate man, quick to help the weak and fight the wicked. The Virginian is one of nature's aristocrats—ill-educated and unsophisticated but upright, steady, and deeply moral. The Virginian sums up his own moral code in describing his view of God's justice: "He plays a square game with us." For Wister, as for Roosevelt and Remington, the cowboy was the Christian knight on the Plains, indifferent to material gain as he upheld virtue, pursued justice, and attacked evil.

Needless to say, the western myth in all its forms was far removed from the actual reality of the West. Critics delighted in pointing out that not one scene in *The Virginian* actually showed the hard physical labor of the cattle range. The idealized version of the West also glossed over the darker underside of frontier expansion—the brutalities of Indian warfare, the forced removal of the Indians to reservations, the racist discrimination against Mexican-Americans and blacks, the risks and perils of commercial agriculture and cattle growing, and the boom-and-bust mentality rooted in the selfish exploitation of natural resources.

Further, the myth obscured the complex links between the settlement of the frontier and the emergence of the United States as a major industrialized nation increasingly enmeshed in a global economy. Eastern and foreign capitalists controlled large-scale mining, cattle, and agricultural operations in the West. The technical know-how of industrial America underlay the marvels of western agricultural productivity. And without the railroad, that quintessential symbol of the new industrial order, western expansion would have been quite unthinkable.

Beginning a Conservation Movement

Despite its one-sided and idealistic vision, Owen Wister's celebration of the western experience reinforced a growing popular recognition, encouraged also by the enthusiastic writings of Theodore Roosevelt, Frederick Jackson Turner, and others, that many unique features of the western landscape were susceptible to misuse and might be ruined by overeager entrepreneurs. One important by-product of the western legend, therefore,

The Castle Geyser, Upper Basin, Yellowstone National Park, *by Thomas Moran, 1876 Dazzled by the bubbling sulfurous hot springs and roaring geysers, painters strove to portray the western landscape as one of God's wonders. In the process, they stimulated a new popular interest in preserving the spectacular features of the land.*

was a surge of public support for creating national parks and the beginning of an organized conservation movement.

Those who went west in the 1860s and 1870s to map the rugged terrain of the high Plains and the Rocky Mountains were often awed by the natural beauty of the landscape. Major John Wesley Powell, the one-armed veteran of the Civil War who charted the Colorado River in 1869, waxed euphoric about its towering rock formations and powerful cataracts. In *The Exploration of the Colorado River of the West and Its Tributaries* (1875), he wrote that, in coursing through one stretch of rapids: "A beautiful view is presented. The river turns sharply to the east, and seems enclosed by a wall, set with a million brilliant gems. What can it mean? Every eye is engaged, every one wonders. On coming nearer, we find fountains bursting from the rock, high overhead, and the spray in the sunshine forms the gems which bedeck the way. The rocks below the fountain are covered with mosses, and ferns, and many beautiful flowering plants. We name it Vasey's Paradise. . . ." In his important study, *Report on the Lands of the Arid Regions of the United States* (1878), Powell not only recognized the unique beauty of the Colorado River basin, but he also argued that settlers needed to readjust their expectations about the use of water in the dry western terrain.

As Powell educated the public about the significant differences between the natural landscape of the East Coast and that of the far West, and focused attention on the beauty of the Colorado River and the Grand Canyon in the Southwest, a group of adventurers, led by General Henry D. Washburn, visited the hot springs and geysers near the Yellowstone River in northwestern Wyoming and eastern Montana in 1870. They were stunned by what they saw. "You can stand in the valley of the Yosemite," wrote one of the party, "and look up its mile of vertical granite, and distinctly recall its minutest feature; but amid the canyon and falls, the boiling springs and sulphur mountain, and, above all, the mud volcano and the geysers of the Yellowstone, your memory becomes filled and clogged with objects new in experience, wonderful in extent, and possessing unlimited grandeur and beauty." Overwhelmed by the view, the Washburn explorers changed their plan to claim this area for the Northern Pacific Railroad and instead petitioned Congress to protect it from settlement, occupancy, and sale. Congress responded in 1872 by creating Yellowstone National Park to "provide for the preservation . . . of all time, mineral deposits, natural curiosities, or wonders within said park . . . in their natural condition."

These first steps to conserve the West's finest natural resources and safeguard them against exploitation by unscrupulous entrepreneurs represented the beginning of a changed awareness of the environment. In this same period George Perkins Marsh, an architect and politician from Vermont, in his influential study *Man and Nature* (1864), attacked the older view that nature existed to be tamed and conquered. Cautioning Americans to curb their destructive use of the landscape, he warned the public to change its ways. "Man," he wrote, "is everywhere a disturbing agent. Wherever he plants his foot, the harmonies of nature are turned to discords."

Marsh's impassioned plea for conservation of natural resources found its most eloquent support in the work of John Muir, a Scottish immigrant who had grown up in Wisconsin. Temporarily blinded by an accident, Muir left for San Francisco in 1869 and quickly fell in love with the redwood forests of the nearby Yosemite Valley. For the next forty years he tramped the rugged mountains of the West and campaigned for their preservation. A romantic at heart, he struggled to experience the wilderness at its most elemental level. Once trekking high in the Rockies during a summer storm, he climbed the tallest pine he could find and swayed back and forth in the raging wind.

Muir became the late nineteenth century's most articulate publicist for wilderness protection. "Climb the mountains and get their good tidings," he advised city dwellers. "Nature's peace will flow into you as the sunshine into the trees. The winds will blow their freshness into you, and the storms their energy, while cares will drop off like autumn leaves." Muir's spirited campaign to protect the wilderness contributed strongly to the establishment in 1890 of Yosemite National Park and the creation two years later of the Sierra Club, an organization committed to encouraging the enjoyment and protection of the wilderness in the mountain region of the Pacific Coast.

Despite the crusades of Muir, Powell, and Marsh to educate the public about the rapacious destruction of the environment, the campaign for wilderness preservation ironically reaffirmed the image of the West as a unique region whose magnificent landscape produced tough individuals of superior ability. Overlooking the senseless violence and ruthless exploitation of the land, contemporary writers, historians, and publicists proclaimed that the settlement of the final frontier marked a new stage in the history of civilization, and they kept alive the legend of the western frontier as a seedbed of American virtues.

CONCLUSION

It is precisely the divergence between the mythic West and the real West that offers a clue to the power and importance of the myth. In an era when industrialization, urbanization, and immigration were altering the nation in ways unsettling to many, Americans embraced the legend of the West as an uncomplicated, untainted Eden of social simplicity and moral clarity. The mythic West represented what the entire society had once been like (or so Americans chose to believe), before the advent of cities, factories, and masses of immigrants.

The myth was the cumulative work of many hands, from dime-novel writers, newspaper correspondents, and railroad publicists to novelists, politicians, and artists. It sank deeply into the American consciousness and influenced the public response to social change. The more tenaciously Americans clung to the myth, the harder it became for them to understand and adjust to the transformations around them.

Of all the people who tried to come to terms with the meaning of the West, Frederick Jackson Turner remains one of the most fascinating. In his 1893 lecture, Turner went on to insist that the frontier experience was the key to understanding American history. "The expansion westward with its new opportunities, its continuous touch with the simplicity of primitive society," he argued, "furnish the forces dominating [the] American character." The frontier experience, he continued, had produced a practical, inventive, self-reliant people who valued individualism and freedom because they had experienced them firsthand in the wide-open spaces and face-to-face communities of the West.

As an actual description of social reality, Turner's analysis left much to be desired. Contemporary historians have moved away from his monolithic interpretation of the "American character" and his optimistic, broad-brush characterization of the frontier social order. They have also critiqued his cavalier disregard of Native Americans and his view of the natural environment as resources to be exploited. But in his articulation and distillation of prevailing ideas about the West, Turner unconsciously demonstrated the powerful hold of the frontier on the national imagination. Caught up himself in a myth that expressed the vast opportunities for personal gain, Turner unwittingly became one of its most persuasive advocates.

The settlement of the West thus can be considered from two perspectives: on the one hand, as a formidable episode in the social, economic, and political history of the United States, and on the other, as a great mythic process that would live on in the American imagination long after the actual frontier had vanished, influencing our thinking about society, government, and ourselves.

CHRONOLOGY

1849   California gold rush.

1858   Henry Comstock strikes gold on the Carson River in Nevada.
Gold discovered at Clear Creek, Colorado.

1862   Homestead Act.
Sioux War breaks out in Minnesota.

1864   Nevada admitted to the Union.
Massacre of Cheyennes at Sand Creek, Colorado.
George Perkins Marsh, *Man and Nature.*

1866   Teton Sioux wipe out Captain William J. Fetterman's troops.
Railroad Enabling Act.

1867   Joseph McCoy organizes cattle drives to Abilene, Kansas.
The Grange (Patrons of Husbandry) founded.
New Indian policy of smaller reservations adopted.
Medicine Lodge Treaty.

1868   Fort Laramie Treaty.

1869   Board of Indian Commissioners established to reform Indian reservation life.

1872   Mark Twain, *Roughing It.*
Yellowstone National Park established.

1873   Panic allows speculators to purchase thousands of acres in the Red River valley of North Dakota cheaply.
Timber Culture Act.
Biggest strike on Nevada's Comstock Lode.

1874   Invention of barbed wire.
Gold discovered in the Black Hills of South Dakota.
Red River War pits the Kiowas, Comanches, and Cheyennes against the United States Army.
Grasshopper infestations ruin crops in Iowa and Kansas.

1875   John Wesley Powell, *The Exploration of the Colorado River.*

1876   Colorado admitted to the Union, gives women the right to vote in school elections.
Massacre of Colonel George Armstrong Custer and his troops at Little Bighorn.

1877   *Munn* v. *Illinois.*
Desert Land Act.

1878   Timber and Stone Act.
John Wesley Powell, *Report on the Lands of the Arid Regions of the United States.*

1879   Massacre of northern Cheyennes at Fort Robinson, Nebraska.

1881   Helen Hunt Jackson, *A Century of Dishonor.*

1883   William ("Buffalo Bill") Cody organizes Wild West show.

1886   Severe drought on the Plains destroys cattle and grain.
Wabash v. *Illinois.*

1887   Dawes Severalty Act.

1888   *Las Gorras Blancas* (The White Caps) raid ranchers in northern New Mexico.

Poster, c.1890

1889   Oklahoma Territory opened for settlement.

1889–1896   Theodore Roosevelt, *The Winning of the West.*

1890   Ghost Dance movement spreads to the Black Hills.
Massacre of Teton Sioux at Wounded Knee, South Dakota.
Yosemite National Park established.

1891   Hamlin Garland, *Main-Travelled Roads.*

1892   John Muir organizes the Sierra Club.

1893   Frederick Jackson Turner, "The Significance of the Frontier in American History."

1902   Owen Wister, *The Virginian.*

FOR FURTHER READING

William Cronon, George Miles, and Jay Gitlin, eds., *Under the Open Sky: Rethinking America's Western Past* (1992). Perceptive essays on western race relations, Native Americans, and regional identity.

Peter Iverson, *The Navajos* (1990). A brief, insightful history of the Navajos' culture and everyday life.

Patricia Nelson Limerick, *The Legacy of Conquest: The Unbroken Past of the American West* (1987). A critique of writing on the history of the West that argues for replacing Turner's frontier thesis with a theory of cultural conquest and domination.

Clyde A. Milner II, Carol A. O'Connor, and Martha A. Sandweiss, eds., *The Oxford History of the American West* (1994). A comprehensive reference work with chapters on many facets of the western experience.

Ruth B. Moynihan, Susan Armitage, and Christiane Fischer Dichamp, eds., *So Much to Be Done: Women Settlers on the Mining and Ranching Frontier* (1990). Firsthand accounts by women who struggled to adapt to living in the West.

Richard White, *"It's Your Misfortune and None of My Own": A New History of the American West* (1991). An excellent overview of the ways in which different racial and ethnic groups interacted in the trans-Mississippi West and exploited the area's natural resources.

ADDITIONAL BIBLIOGRAPHY

The Western Mystique

Gunther Barth, *Fleeting Moments: Nature and Culture in American History* (1990); William H. Goetzmann, *Exploration and Empire* (1966) and *The West of the Imagination* (1986); Anne F. Hyde, *The American Vision: Far Western Landscape and National Culture, 1820–1920* (1990); Howard R. Lamar, *The Far Southwest, 1846–1912* (1966); Roderick Nash, *Wilderness and the American Mind* (1973); Kevin Starr, *Americans and the California Dream, 1850–1915* (1973); William H. Truettner, ed., *The West as America: Reinterpreting Images of the Frontier, 1820–1920* (1991).

Native Americans

Gary Anderson and Alan Woolworth, eds., *Through Dakota Eyes: Narrative Accounts of the Minnesota Indian War of 1862* (1988); Robert F. Berkhofer, Jr., *The White Man's Indian* (1978); Mario T. Garcia, *Desert Immigrants* (1981); John S. Gray, *Custer's Last Campaign* (1991); Michael Green, *The Creeks* (1990); Jerome A. Greene, *Yellowstone Command: Colonel Nelson A. Miles and the Great Sioux War, 1876–1877* (1991); Frederick E. Hoxie, *A Final Promise: The Campaign to Assimilate the Indians, 1880–1920* (1984) and *The Crow* (1989); Janet A. McDonnell, *The Dispossession of the American Indian, 1887–1934* (1991); William G. McLoughlin, *After the Trail of Tears: The Cherokees' Struggle for Sovereignty, 1839–1880* (1993); John G. Neihardt, *Black Elk Speaks* (1932); Theda Perdue, *The Cherokee* (1989); Francis Paul Prucha, *The Great Father: The United States Government and Indians* (2 vols., 1984); Glenda Riley, *Women and Indians on the Frontier, 1825–1915* (1984); Willard H. Rollings, *The Comanche* (1989); Robert M. Utley, *The Last Days of the Sioux Nation* (1963), *Frontier Regulars: The United States Army and the Indian, 1866–1891* (1973), *The Indian Frontier of the American West, 1846–1890* (1984), and *The Lance and the Shield: The Life and Times of Sitting Bull* (1993); Richard White, *The Roots of Dependency: Subsistence, Environment, and Social Change Among the Choctaws, Pawnees, and Navajos* (1983).

The Process of Settlement

Peter G. Boag, *Environment and Experience: Settlement Culture in Nineteenth-Century Oregon* (1992); Albert Camarillo, *Chicanos in a Changing Society* (1979); Ricard Griswold del Castillo, *La Familia: Chicano Families in the Urban Southeast, 1848 to the Present* (1984); Arnoldo De Leon, *They Called Them Greasers: Anglo Attitudes Toward Mexicans in Texas, 1821–1900* (1983); Sarah Deutsch, *No Separate Refuge: Culture, Class, and Gender on the Anglo-Hispanic Frontier in the Overland Trail* (1979); Katherine Harris, *Long Vistas: Women and Families on Colorado Homesteads* (1993); Robert V. Hine, *Community on the American Frontier* (1980); Richard Hogan, *Class and Community in Frontier Colorado* (1990); Julie R. Jeffrey, *Frontier Women* (1979); D. Aidan McQuillan, *Prevailing over Time: Ethnic Adjustment on the Kansas Prairies, 1875–1925* (1990); Timothy R. Mahoney, *River Towns in the Great West* (1990); David Montejano, *Anglos and Mexicans in the Making of Texas, 1836–1986* (1987); Peggy Pascoe, *Relations of Rescue: The Search for Female Moral Authority in the American West, 1874–1939* (1990); Jane M. Pederson, *Between Memory and Reality: Family and Community in Rural Wisconsin, 1870–1970* (1992); Robert J. Rosenbaum, *Mexicano Resistance in the Southwest* (1981); Thomas Sheridan, *Los Tucsonenses: The Mexican Community in Tucson, 1854–1941* (1986); Kenneth L. Stewart and Arnoldo De Leon, *Not Room Enough: Mexicans, Anglos, and Socioeconomic Change in Texas, 1850–1900* (1993); John F. Stover, *American Railroads* (1961); Thomas A. Woods, *Knights of the Plow: Oliver H. Kelley and the Origins of the Grange in Republican Ideology* (1991).

The Bonanza West

Susan Armitage and Elizabeth Jameson, eds., *The Woman's West* (1987); Anne M. Butler, *Daughters of Joy, Sisters of Misery* (1985); William Cronon, *Nature's Metropolis: Chicago and the Great West* (1991); Hiram M. Drache, *The Day of the Bonanza* (1964); Monroe L. Billington, *New Mexico's Buffalo Soldiers, 1866–1900* (1991); Marion S. Goldman, *Gold Diggers & Silver Miners: Prostitution and Social Life on the Comstock Lode* (1968); Wilson P. Rodman, *Mining Frontiers of the Far West* (1963); William R. Savage, *The Cowboy Hero* (1986) and Savage, ed., *Cowboy Life: Reconstructing an American Myth* (1980); Richard W. Slatta, *Cowboys of the Americas* (1990); Duane A. Smith, *Mining America: The Industry and the Environment* (1987); Donald E. Worcester, *The Chisholm Trail* (1980).

The Frontier Legend

Stephen Fox, *John Muir and His Legacy* (1981); Roderick Nash, *The Rights of Nature: A History of Environmental Ethics* (1989) and Nash, ed., *American Environmentalism: Readings in Conservation History* (3d ed., 1990); Albert Runte, *Yosemite: The Embattled Wilderness* (1990); Henry Nash Smith, *Virgin Land: The American West as Symbol and Myth* (1950); Frederick Jackson Turner, *Frontier in American History* (1920); Frederick Turner, *Rediscovering America: John Muir in His Time and Ours* (1985); G. Edward White, *The Eastern Establishment and the Western Experience* (1968); Rupert Wilkinson, *American Tough: The Tough-Guy Tradition and American Character* (1984); Donald Worster, *Nature's Economy: A History of Ecological Ideas* (1977) and *Rivers of Empire* (1985).

Coal Miners
Detail of photograph by Lewis Hine

18

THE RISE OF
INDUSTRIAL AMERICA

On October 21, 1892, before a crowd of more than two hundred thousand onlookers, presidential candidate Grover Cleveland stepped proudly into the Grand Court of Honor to open the World's Columbian Exposition in Chicago. Grasping a small electric key connected to a two-thousand-horsepower engine, he proclaimed, "As by a touch the machinery that gives life to this vast Exposition is now set in motion, so in the same instant let our hopes and aspirations awaken forces which in all time to come shall influence the welfare, the dignity, and the freedom of mankind." A moment later, amid enthusiastic cheers, electric fountains shot streams of water high into the air, officially marking the exposition's opening.

The Chicago world's fair represented the triumph of thirty years of industrial development. The country's largest corporations displayed their newest products. Machinery Hall housed two gigantic steam engines, each capable of pumping 12 million gallons of water daily. In the Electricity Building, the Westinghouse Company's dynamos mysteriously lit a model Egyptian temple and a tower of incandescent light bulbs (inset); American Bell Telephone offered the first long-distance telephone calls to the East Coast; and inventor Thomas A. Edison exhibited his latest phonograph.

The largest structure at the fair, the Manufactures and Liberal Arts Building, was a monument to American industrial development. Its immense size, the fair's guidebooks boasted, was emblematic of a generation of technological achievement. Containing more than forty-four acres of floor space, 3 million feet of lumber, and five railroad carloads of nails, and housing the exhibits of numerous corporations, the structure easily accommodated the thousands of people milling about expectantly at the opening ceremonies.

The fair's splendor dazzled the more than 25 million visitors who entered the gates between October 1892 and October 1893. General Lew Wallace, author of the popular novel *Ben-Hur*, described the exposition as "the fairest city that ever the sun shown [*sic*] on." Historian Henry Adams, impressed by the electrical dynamos, spinning silently at unbelievable speeds, later described them as symbols for the infinite force and energy of the modern world. But Isabelle Garland, mother of writer Hamlin Garland, who visited the fair from a small midwestern farm community, was simply stunned. "[M]y mother sat in her chair, visioning it all yet comprehending little of its meaning," Garland later observed. "Her life had been spent among homely small things, and these gorgeous scenes dazzled her, ... letting in upon her in one mighty flood a thousand stupefying suggestions of art and history and poetry of the world.... At last utterly overcome, she leaned her head against my arm, closed her eyes and said, 'Take me home, I can't stand any more of it.' "

Isabelle Garland's emotional reaction captured the ambivalence of many late-nineteenth-century Americans, who found themselves both unsettled and exhilarated as the nation was transformed by industrialization. In less than thirty years, through innovations in management, technology, production, and distribution, business leaders had built the United States into the world's greatest industrial power. America's real gross national product grew between 1860 and 1900 by an average of nearly 4 percent annually, a rate one-third better than that of Germany and nearly double that of Great Britain. In these same years, U.S. textile and iron production doubled, the number of people engaged in manufacturing quadrupled, rail production quintupled, and new companies, operating nationwide, brought a host of new products into urban, small-town, and rural homes across the country. Overall, manufacturing output soared from $1.8 billion in 1860 to $13 billion in 1900. All the more remarkably, this growth came amid the disruptions of a boom-and-bust business cycle that produced crippling depressions in 1873–1879 and 1893–1897.

For the next several chapters—indeed, in a very real sense, for the rest of this book—we shall examine the consequences of this remarkable period of industrial growth. But first, we will look more closely at how this transformation occurred and at how it affected the men and women whose labor made it possible.

THE CHARACTER OF INDUSTRIAL CHANGE

Five features dominated the birth of modern industrial America after the Civil War: first, the exploitation of immense coal deposits as a source of cheap energy: second, the rapid spread of technological innovation and the factory system; third, the constant pressure on firms to compete tooth-and-nail by cutting costs and prices—as well as the impulse to elim-

inate rivals and create monopolies; fourth, the relentless drop in price levels (a stark contrast to the inflation of other eras); and finally, the failure of the money supply to keep pace with productivity, a development that drove up interest rates and restricted the availability of credit.

All five factors were closely related. The great bituminous coal deposits in Pennsylvania, West Virginia, and Kentucky provided the cheap energy that fueled the railroads, the factories, and explosive urban growth. Exploiting these inexpensive energy sources, new technologies stimulated productivity and catalyzed breathtaking industrial expansion. Technology also enabled manufacturers to cut costs and hire cheap unskilled or semiskilled labor. This cost cutting in turn drove firms to undersell each other, destroying weaker competitors and prompting stronger, more efficient (and more ruthless) ones to consolidate. At least until the mid-1890s, cost reduction, new technology, and fierce competition forced down overall price levels. Farmers and industrial workers suffered from chronically low agricultural commodity prices and wages, but in their capacity as consumers, they (and all Americans) benefited as store-bought goods cheapened. Meanwhile, high interest rates and the difficulty of obtaining credit added to the burdens of farmers and small entrepreneurs. And almost everyone suffered terribly during the depression years, when the government did nothing to relieve distress. "The sufferings of the working classes are daily increasing," wrote a Philadelphia worker in 1874. "Famine has broken into the home of many of us, and is at the door of all." Above all, business leaders' unflagging drive to maximize efficiency both created colossal fortunes at the top of the economic ladder and forced millions of wage earners to live near the subsistence level.

Out of the new industrial system poured dismal clouds of haze and soot—as well as the first tantalizing trickle of what would become an avalanche of consumer goods. In turn, mounting demands for consumer goods stimulated heavy industry's production of "capital goods"—machines to boost farm and factory output. Together with the railroads, the corporations that manufactured capital goods, refined petroleum, and made steel became the driving force in the nation's economic growth.

A stunning expansion in the *scale* of industry offered tangible evidence of the magnitude of eco-

Singer Sewing Machines

The Singer Company's success was built not only on its innovative use of interchangeable parts but also on advertising campaigns that stressed how easy its machines were to use.

nomic change. By the turn of the century, mammoth corporations dominated industrial production. The Singer Sewing Machine Company, for example, with capitalization (operating capital) of $20 million in 1905, boasted eight factories and more than 90,000 employees who made and sold 1.25 million sewing machines annually. Huge companies similarly achieved marvels of production in the railroad, meatpacking, steel, sugar, and oil industries.

Competition among the aggressive and innovative capitalists who headed American heavy industry was intense—and as the post–Civil War era opened, nowhere was it more intense than among the nation's railroads, which to many Americans most symbolized industrial progress.

Railroad Innovations

By 1900, 193,000 miles of railroad track crisscrossed the United States—more than in all of Europe, including Russia. These rail lines connected every state in the Union and opened up an immense new internal market. The omnipresent steam engine, rushing forward with what poet Walt Whitman called its "pant and roar," epitomized the new technological order. Most important, railroad companies pioneered crucial aspects of large-scale corporate enterprise, including the issuance of stock to meet their huge capital needs, the separation of ownership from management, the diver-sification of production facilities, the creation of national distribution and marketing systems, and the formation of new organizational and management structures.

Early railroad entrepreneurs such as Thomas A. Scott, who in the 1850s integrated seventy-three smaller companies and more than five thousand rail miles into the Pennsylvania Railroad, faced financial and organizational problems that would have ruined most smaller firms. The cost of buying land, laying track, building engines and cars, and setting up stations was horrendous. To meet these start-up costs and to carry on their extensive operations, railroads needed staggering sums. For large lines like the Pennsylvania, the necessary level of capitalization could approach $35 million.

How were sums like this raised? The railroads, of course, received enormous land and loan subsidies from federal, state, and local governments. But even so, the larger lines had to borrow heavily by selling bonds to the public. By 1900 the combined debt of all U.S. railroads stood at an astounding $5.1 billion, nearly five times that of the federal government. Another way the railroads raised capital was by selling stock. Unlike bond holders, who earned a fixed rate of interest, stockholders received dividends only when the company earned a profit.

Although the stockholders owned the railroad, day-to-day operations remained in the hands of company officials. Because of the railroads' heavy indebtedness and the disastrous consequences of scheduling mistakes (at a time when a single track carried trains traveling in both directions), railroad managers had a high stake in systematizing their operations for maximum safety and efficiency. To coordinate the complex flow of cars across the country, railroads relied heavily on the magnetic telegraph. Invented in 1837, telegraph service had expanded quickly. By the end of the Civil War, Western Union's forty-four thousand miles of wire and more than a thousand offices formed the backbone of a communications network that linked the entire nation. To improve efficiency, the railroads set up clearly defined, hierarchical organizational structures and divided their lines into separate geographic units, each with its own superintendent. Elaborate accounting systems documented the cost of every operation for each division, from coal consumption to the repair of engines and cars. Using these reports, railroad officials could set rates and accurately predict profits as early as the 1860s, a time when most businesses had no idea of their total profit until they closed their books at year's end. Railroad management innovations thus became a model for many other businesses seeking a national market.

Creativity, Cooperation, and Competition

Collis P. Huntington, Jay Gould, James J. Hill, and the other larger-than-life figures who reorganized and expanded the railroad industry in the 1870s and 1880s were often depicted by their contemporaries as villains and robber barons who manipulated stock markets and company policies to line their own pockets. For example, one competitor scorned Jay Gould, the short, secretive president of the Union Pacific, as a "perfect eel," and newspaper publisher Joseph Pulitzer called him "one of the most sinister figures that have ever flitted batlike across the vision of the American people." Recent historians, however, have pointed out that the great industrialists were a diverse group, and far from all bad. Although some were ironfisted pirates who engaged in deceptive and fraudulent practices, others were upstanding businessmen who managed their companies with sophistication and innovation. Indeed, some of their ideas were breathtaking in their originality and inventiveness.

The expansion and consolidation of railroading reflected both the ingenuity and the dishonesty flourishing on the corporate-management scene. Although by the 1870s railroads had replaced the patchwork of canal and stagecoach operations that dominated domestic transportation before the Civil War, the industry itself was in a state of chaos. Hundreds of small companies used widely different standards for car couplers, rails, track width, and engine size. Financed by large eastern and British banks, Huntington, Gould, and others devoured these smaller lines to create large, integrated track networks. In the Northeast four major trunk lines emerged. In the South four hundred small companies averaging less than forty miles of track apiece were consolidated into five major systems. West of the Mississippi five great lines—the Union Pacific (1869); the Northern Pacific (1883); the Atchison, Topeka, and Santa Fe (1883); the Southern Pacific (1883); and the Great Northern (1893)—controlled most of the track by 1893.

As they consolidated a hodgepodge of small railroads into a few interlocking systems, the masterminds of the giant trunk lines standardized all basic equipment and facilities, from engines and cars to outhouses (now provided in standard one-, two-, and three-hole sizes), automatic couplers, air brakes, and signal systems. In 1883, independently of the federal government, the railroads unilaterally divided the country into four time zones. This sweeping action

Jay Gould

In a commentary on Gould's vicious manipulation of the railway industry, a disapproving cartoonist depicted him as having amassed his fortune by destroying others' lives with as little concern as a bowler knocking down ninepins.

outraged those, like Isabelle Garland, who believed in "God's time," based on the rising and setting of the sun. Then in May 1886 all railroads shifted simultaneously to the new standard 4′ 8½″–gauge track. Finally, cooperative billing arrangements and accounting procedures enabled the railroads to ship cars from other roads, including dining and sleeping cars owned by the Pullman Palace Car Company, at uniform rates nationwide. Even steamship lines and urban commuter rail lines were incorporated into the railroads' tightly organized system.

This newly integrated transportation and communications network brought advantages to factory owners and consumers alike. Companies gained access to a national market in which to buy their raw materials and sell their goods. Farmers and storekeepers across the country could buy food, hardware, and clothing once available only in the major East Coast cities.

But the expansion and consolidation of the railroads had its costs. Competition between lines saddled the great trunk lines with massive debts. In 1879 Jay Gould, the guiding force behind the expansion of the Union Pacific, gained control of the Kansas Pacific Railroad. To squeeze out his southwestern competition, he ran tracks parallel to those of his rivals, engineered fluctuations in the price of their stock, and undercut their business by setting his rates below his own cost. One by one his competitors toppled into bankruptcy while he consolidated his holdings. Meanwhile, to increase his own income, he "watered" the company's stock by issuing stock certificates far in excess of the actual value of the assets. By 1885 other unprincipled operators had watered a third of the nation's railroad stock, badly pinching small investors.

Entangled in heavy indebtedness, overextended systems, and crooked business practices, the railroads fought each other recklessly for traffic. They cut rates for large shippers, offered special arrangements for handling bulk goods, showered free passes on politicians who supported their operations, and granted substantial rebates and kickbacks to favored clients. Major customers soon fought back by negotiating their own lower prices. The competition became so ferocious that railroads tried to end it by establishing pools—negotiated agreements to divide the traffic proportionally and charge uniform rates.

None of these tactics, however, shored up the railroads' precarious financial position. A pooling agreement between two railroads would soon be undermined by pressure from a third. Rebates given by one system prompted retaliation from another. And the continuous push to expand drove some overbuilt lines into bankruptcy.

Caught in the middle of the railroads' tug-of-war and stung by exorbitant rates and secret kickbacks, farmers and small business owners turned to state governments for help. In the 1870s many midwestern state legislatures, responding to Granger-led protests, outlawed rate discrimination. Initially upheld by the Supreme Court, these and other decisions were negated in the 1880s as the Court broke down local autonomy and supported the capitalist integration of the economy. Then in 1887, persuaded by Illinois senator Shelby M. Cullom's detailed study of devious railroad practices, Congress, as we have seen, passed the Interstate Commerce Act, which established the five-member Interstate Commerce Commission (ICC) to oversee the practices of railroads passing through more than one state. The law also banned monopolistic activity like pooling, rebates, and discriminatory short-distance rates. The railroads challenged the commission's rulings in the federal courts, however, and of sixteen cases brought to the Supreme Court before 1905, the justices found in favor of the railroads in all but one, essentially nullifying the ICC's regulatory clout. The Hepburn Act (see Chapter 22), passed in 1906, strengthened the ICC by finally empowering it to set rates.

The railroads' vicious competition did not abate until a national depression that began in 1893 forced a number of roads into the hands of the investment bankers on whom they had become increasingly dependent. Supported by the major investment houses in Boston, New York, and Philadelphia, J. Pierpont Morgan, a massively built man with piercing eyes and a commanding presence, took over the weakened systems, reorganized their administration, refinanced their debts, and built intersystem alliances by purchasing substantial blocks of stock in the competing roads. By 1906, thanks to the bankers' centralized management, seven giant networks controlled two-thirds of the nation's rail mileage.

In short, by the late nineteenth century, competition, corruption, mismanagement, and overextension had created a paradox in the railroad industry. The massive trunk systems had become the largest business enterprises in the world, towering over state and federal governments in the size and scale of their operations. They had pioneered the most advanced methods of accounting and large-scale organization. Their voracious appetite for rails and engines had stimulated the demand for iron, steel, and a host of secondary products. The integrated transportation network that they composed opened up exciting possibilities for the national distribution of new consumer products. Yet despite their enormous power and many innovations, the nation's railroads remained unstable. Cutthroat expansion had inflated operating costs, reduced revenues, and made them particularly vulnerable to economic downswings. During the depression of 1893, only intervention by investment bankers saved the industry from collapse.

Applying the Lessons of the Railroads to Steel

The close connections between railroad expansion and the growth of heavy industry are well illustrated in the career of steelmaker Andrew Carnegie. A diminutive dynamo of a man, only 5'3" tall, Carnegie combined the business expertise of a Jay Gould with the showmanship of a P. T. Barnum. His achievements rested heavily on his salesmanship and his managerial skill, both of which played a major role in his success at transferring to steel making the organizational and financial methods first developed in the railroad industry.

Carnegie's life was the embodiment of the rags-to-riches dream. Born in Dunfermline, Scotland, he had immigrated to America in 1848, at the age of twelve, and had taken a job at $1.20 a week as a bobbin boy in a Pittsburgh textile mill. Although he worked a sixty-hour week, the ambitious youngster also enrolled in a night course to learn double-entry bookkeeping.

The following year, Carnegie became a Western Union messenger boy. Taking over when the telegraph operators wanted a break, he soon became the city's fastest telegraph operator. Because he had to decode the messages for every major business in Pittsburgh, Carnegie gained an insider's view of their operations.

Carnegie's big break came in 1852, when Tom Scott, superintendent of the Pennsylvania Railroad's western division, hired him as his secretary and personal telegrapher. Only seventeen years old, Carnegie quickly mastered the complex details of what was the most innovative business at the time. When Scott became vice president of the Pennsylvania Railroad seven years later, Carnegie took over as head of the line's western division.

A daring innovator, Carnegie, in his six years as division chief, used the complex cost-analysis techniques developed by Scott to more than double the road's mileage and quadruple its traffic. He instituted the first night-train dispatchers and ran trains around the clock. When wrecks blocked the tracks, he burned the cars or laid new track around them. He slashed commuter fares to keep ridership at capacity and developed various cost-cutting techniques. Investing his earnings in telegraph, sleeping-car, and bridge companies, Carnegie by 1868 was earning more than fifty-six thousand dollars a year from his investments alone, a substantial fortune in that era.

In the early 1870s, Carnegie decided to build his own steel mill. His connections within the railroad industry, the country's largest purchaser of steel, made this a logical choice. Starting with the J. Edgar Thomson Mills, named for the president of the Pennsylvania Railroad, he introduced the new Bessemer production technology, which shot a blast of air through an enormous crucible of molten iron to burn off carbon and impurities. Carnegie combined the new technology with the cost-analysis approach learned from his railroad experience. Developing special scales to weigh the different materials used in the mill, he became the first steelmaker to establish the actual production cost per ton of steel. With this data, he not only cut expenses but also developed a solid basis for deciding when to invest in new furnaces and machine tools.

Carnegie's philosophy was deceptively simple: "Watch the costs, and the profits will take care of

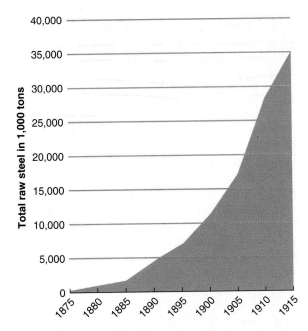

Iron and Steel Production, 1875–1915
New technologies, improved plant organization, economies of scale, and the vertical integration of production brought a dramatic spurt in iron and steel production.
NOTE: short ton = 2,000 pounds.
SOURCE: *Historical Statistics of the United States.*

themselves." From the start he priced his rails at sixty-five dollars per ton, five dollars below the competition. Then, through rigorous cost accounting, he lowered his production costs to fifty dollars per ton. Furthermore, he was not above asking for favors from his railroad-president friends or giving "commissions" to railroad purchasing agents. When other producers tried to get him to join a pool to fix prices, he initially agreed but then broke away; his efficient production methods enabled him to undersell all rivals.

As output climbed, Carnegie discovered the benefits of vertical integration—that is, controlling all aspects of manufacturing, from extracting raw materials to selling the finished product. In Carnegie's case this control embraced every stage from the mining and smelting of ore to the selling of steel rails. His movement toward vertical integration prompted him in 1881 to establish a partnership with Henry Clay Frick, the owner of a large coke* company, who in 1889 would

---

*Coke: the solid residue obtained from coal after the removal of volatile material.

Andrew Carnegie
Despite his well-polished image as a hard-working industrial leader, Carnegie left the details of management to others and spent a considerable amount of time playing golf near his castle in Scotland.

Andrew Carnegie Sums Up the Steel Business

The eighth wonder of the world is this:

two pounds of iron-stone purchased on
the shores of lake Superior and
    transported to Pittsburgh;

two pounds of coal mined in Connellsville
and manufactured into coke and
    brought to Pittsburgh;

one half pound of limestone mined
east of the Alleghenies and
    brought to Pittsburgh;

a little manganese ore,
mined in Virginia and
    brought to Pittsburgh.

And these four and one half pounds of
material manufactured into one pound of
solid steel and sold for one cent.

That's all that need be said
    about the steel business.

SOURCE: Harold C. Livesay, *Andrew Carnegie and the Rise of Big Business* (Boston: Little, Brown, 1975), 189.

become the chairman of Carnegie Steel while continuing as head of Frick Coke Company. In 1892 Carnegie also bought into an ore company in the newly opened Mesabi Range in Minnesota. Under Frick's aggressive leadership, Carnegie Steel's annual profits rose each year in the 1890s despite severe labor troubles and a crippling national depression, reaching $40 million in 1900. Carnegie Steel thus became the classic example of how sophisticated new technology might be combined with innovative management (and brutally low wages) to create a mass-production system that could slash consumer prices. By 1900 Carnegie was producing steel rails at a cost of $11.50 per ton.

Frick's management of daily operations left Carnegie free to pursue philanthropic activities. While still in his early thirties, Carnegie concluded that all great fortunes corrupted their possessors, and he resolved to donate his money to charitable projects. (He also knew full well that such actions would buttress his popularity.) Carnegie set up foundations and eventually donated more than $300 million for libraries, universities, and international-peace causes.

By 1900 Carnegie Steel, employing twenty thousand people, had become the world's largest industrial corporation. Yet the company was torn by internal divisions and beset by newly aggressive rivals. Many of Carnegie's able lieutenants chafed under his domineering management style. In January 1900, when Frick, who had verbally agreed to sell coke to Carnegie Steel at a price considerably below the market rate, tried to raise his price, Carnegie forced him out in an angry confrontation. Said Carnegie of his former partner (who was fourteen years his junior): "He's too old, too infirm in health *and mind.* . . . I have nothing but pity for Frick." (Later, when Carnegie suggested that they renew their old friendship, Frick responded, "Tell Mr. Carnegie I'll meet him in Hell.") The competitive challenge came from Federal Steel, a large complex put together in 1898 by J. Pierpont Morgan, and from Illinois Steel. The success of these imposing rivals threatened to choke off Carnegie's sales to the wire, nail, and pipe industries.

Carnegie responded with typical cunning, by cornering the patents (exclusive rights to manufacturing and sales) on a new process for producing seamless pipes and by announcing plans to build a new pipe plant. His competitors immediately sought a compromise. At Morgan's request Charles Schwab, Carnegie Steel's president, met Carnegie on the golf course early in 1901 to ask what he wanted for his share of Carnegie Steel. The next day Carnegie gave Schwab a penciled note asking for nearly half a billion dollars. Morgan's response was simple: "Tell Carnegie I accept his price." Combining Carnegie's companies with Federal Steel, Morgan set up the United States Steel Corporation, the first business capitalized at more than $1 billion. The corporation, with its two-hundred-member companies employing 168,000 people, marked a new scale in industrial enterprise.

Throughout his chain of corporate-world triumphs, Carnegie consistently portrayed himself as an entrepreneur who had risen through self-discipline and hard work. In a series of essays, he stressed that thrift, patience, and quick action in the face of opportunity were the keys to his success. The full story was more complex. He did not mention his uncanny ability to see the larger picture, his cleverness in hiring talented associates who would drive themselves (and the company's factory workers) mercilessly, his ingenuity in transferring organizational systems and cost-accounting methods from railroads to steel, and his callousness in keeping wages as low as possible. To a public little interested in corporate-management techniques, however, Carnegie's success simply reaffirmed the openness of the American economic system. For the new immigrants flooding the nation's shores, Carnegie's career gave credence to the idea that anyone might rise from rags to riches.

Consolidating the Industrial Order

Between 1870 and 1900, the same grasping competition that had stimulated railroad consolidation and reduced the number of iron and steel firms from 808 to 669 (see table) also swept the oil, salt, sugar, tobacco, and meatpacking industries. Like steel, these businesses required large capital investments and sold their products in highly competitive markets. Entrepreneurs in each industry therefore raced to reduce costs and dominate rivals. Chicago meatpackers Philip Armour and Gustavus Swift, for example, raised the process of making bacon, pork chops, and steak from hogs and cattle to a high level of efficiency. Using refrigerated railcars, they reaped a fortune supplying eastern cities with meat.

Industrial Consolidation: Iron and Steel Firms, 1870 and 1900

	1870	1900
No. of firms	808	669
No. of employees	78,000	272,000
Output (tons)	3,200,000	29,500,000
Capital invested	$121,000,000	$590,000,000

Source: Robert L. Heilbroner and Aaron Singer, *The Economic Transformation of America: 1600 to Present,* 2d ed. (San Diego: Harcourt Brace Jovanovich, 1984), 92.

The evolution of the oil industry typifies the consolidation process. After Edwin L. Drake drilled the first successful petroleum (or "crude-oil") well in 1859 near Titusville in northwestern Pennsylvania, entry into the oil business came relatively easily. Entrepreneurs sank wells, erected small refineries nearby, and distilled the petroleum into oil, which soon replaced animal tallow as the major lubricant, and into kerosene, which became the leading fuel for household and public lighting. By the 1870s the landscape near Pittsburgh and Cleveland, the sites of the first discoveries, was littered with rickety drilling rigs, assorted collection tanks, and ramshackle refineries. The almost festive atmosphere that pervaded this early oil boom—speculators flew homemade flags and banners over their rigs—diverted attention from the environmental pollution created at the drilling sites. "So much oil is produced," reported one Pennsylvania newspaper in 1861, "that it is impossible to care for it, and thousands of barrels are running into the creek; the surface of the river is covered with oil for miles. . . ."

In this rush for riches, John D. Rockefeller, a young Cleveland merchant, gradually achieved dominance. Although he did not share Andrew Carnegie's outgoing personality, the solemn Rockefeller resembled the opportunistic steelmaker in other respects. Like Carnegie, Rockefeller had a passion for cost cutting and efficiency. Having founded the Standard Oil Company in 1870, he daily scrutinized every aspect of the firm's operation. In one case he insisted that a manager find 750 missing barrel stoppers; in another he reduced from 40 to 39 the number of drops of solder used to seal a kerosene can. He realized that in a mass-production enterprise, small changes could save thousands of dollars.

Rockefeller constantly stressed the importance of providing a reliable product in winning consumer loy-

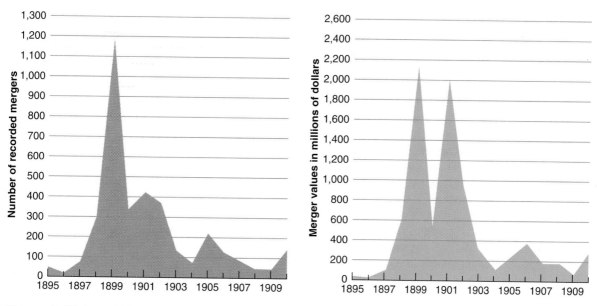

Mergers in Mining and Manufacturing, 1895–1910

A wave of business mergers occurred after the Supreme Court's 1897 and 1898 rulings that any firms concluding price-fixing or market-allocating agreements violated the Sherman Anti-Trust Act. But the merger mania died down when business leaders quickly discovered that companies could remain profitable only through vertical integration.

alty. He built a system of bulk depots and tank wagons for local kerosene distribution and insisted that all equipment be kept neat and clean. Like Carnegie, he adopted the latest refining technologies to improve the quality of his fuels and lubricants. To boost sales volume, he advertised heavily. Packaged in a familiar red five-gallon can, Standard Oil kerosene was instantly recognizable by consumers.

Rockefeller resembled Carnegie, too, in his extraordinary ability to understand the inner workings of an entire industry. He particularly focused on transportation. The firm that controlled the shipment of oil between the well and the refinery, and between the refinery and the retailers, he realized, could dominate the industry. Accordingly in 1872 he purchased his own tanker cars and wangled not only a 10 percent rebate from the railroads for hauling his oil shipments but also a kickback on his competitors' shipments. When new pipeline technology became available, Rockefeller set up his own massive interregional pipeline network.

Like Carnegie, Rockefeller used aggressiveness and deception to force out his competitors. When local refineries rejected his offers to buy them out, he priced his product line below cost and strangled their

business. If a storekeeper refused to sell Standard Oil's kerosene, the company supported the store's competitors. When rival firms teamed up against him, Rockefeller set up a pool—an agreement among several companies—that established production quotas and fixed prices. "The Standard Oil Company brooks no competition," a congressional investigating committee observed; ". . . its settled policy and firm determination is to crush out all who may be rash enough to enter the field against it; . . . it hesitates at nothing in the accomplishment of this purpose." Using such tactics, Rockefeller had seized control of 90 percent of the country's oil-refining capacity by 1879.

Convinced that competition wasted resources, Rockefeller tried to eliminate it in 1882 by establishing the Standard Oil Trust. Where the pool lacked legal status, the trust was a legal device that centralized control over a number of different companies by setting up a board of trustees to run all of them. To implement his trust, Rockefeller and his associates persuaded the stockholders of forty companies to exchange their stock for trust certificates. Within three years the Standard Oil Trust had consolidated crude-oil buying throughout its member firms and slashed the number of refineries by half. In this way Rockefeller integrated the petroleum industry both *vertically,* by controlling every function from production to local retailing, and *horizontally,* by merging the competing oil companies into one giant system.

Having neutralized the competition, Rockefeller reaped the profits. Standard Oil enlarged its refinery and pipeline capacity and expanded its distribution network not only in North America but also in Asia, Africa, and South America. Over the next decade, as he reinvested his profits in iron-ore deposits, steamship lines, and other enterprises, Rockefeller's personal fortune mushroomed to more than $800 million.

Taking a leaf from Rockefeller's book, companies in other industries such as copper, sugar, whiskey, and lead established their own trust arrangements. But their rapacious tactics, monopolistic control, and sky-high earnings soon provoked a public outcry. Beginning in New York State in 1879 and progressing to the federal level in 1888, legislative committees exposed the unscrupulous practices of these national trusts, and in the presidential election of 1888, both parties denounced them. When Rockefeller testified that the Standard Oil Trust had greatly reduced prices, his opponents pointed out that monopolies in the copper and sugar industries had pushed prices higher.

Fearful that the trusts would stamp out all competition, Congress, in 1890, under the leadership of Senator John Sherman of Ohio, passed the Sherman Anti-Trust Act, which outlawed trusts and any other contracts or combinations in restraint of trade and slapped violators with fines of up to five thousand dollars and a year in jail. But the loosely worded act failed to define clearly either *trust* or *restraint of trade.* As a result, between 1890 and 1904, the government prosecuted only eighteen antitrust suits. When Standard Oil's structure was challenged in 1892, its lawyers, invoking a New Jersey law that permitted corporations to own property in other states, simply reorganized the trust as an enormous holding company.* The same nine trustees became the new board of directors for Standard Oil (New Jersey), and the business made more money than ever.

The Supreme Court further hamstrung congressional antitrust efforts by interpreting the Sherman Act in ways sympathetic to big business. In 1895, for example, the federal government brought suit against the

---

*Holding company: a corporation that owns a controlling share of the stock of one or more other firms.

sugar trust in *United States* v. *E. C. Knight Company,* arguing that the Knight firm, together with four other corporations, controlled more than 90 percent of all U.S. sugar refining and therefore operated in illegal restraint of trade. The Court threw out the suit, however, drawing a distinction between commerce and manufacturing and defining the latter as a local concern, not a part of interstate commerce. The Court's decision ignored the fact that most trusts dominated the market through their extensive interstate distribution webs. Thus vindicated, corporate mergers and consolidations surged ahead at the turn of the century. By 1900 these mammoth firms accounted for nearly two-fifths of the capital invested in the nation's manufacturing sector.

The Triumph of Technology

Along with business mergers and consolidations, the invention and patenting of new machines offered another means of driving up profits, lowering costs, and improving efficiency. Furthermore, mechanical inventions had the added advantage of piquing demand for new products. The development of a safe, practical system of generating electricity, for example, made possible an ever-growing range of electrical motors and household appliances. After 1870 business corporations stepped up their research efforts and introduced a remarkable variety of consumer goods.

The major inventions that stimulated industrial output and underlay mass production in these years were largely hidden from public view. Few Americans had heard of the Bessemer process for manufacturing steel or of the improved technologies that facilitated bottle and glassmaking, canning, flour milling, match production, and petroleum refining. Fewer still knew much about the refrigerated railcars that enabled Gustavus Swift's company to slaughter beef in Chicago and ship it east or about the Bonsack cigarette-making machine that could roll 120,000 cigarettes a day, replacing sixty skilled handworkers.

The innovations that people did see were the fruits of this technology—products like the sewing machine, mass-produced by the Singer Sewing Machine Company beginning in the 1860s; the telephone, developed by Alexander Graham Bell in 1876; and the light bulb, perfected by Thomas A. Edison in 1879. These inventions eased the drudgery of everyday life and in some cases reshaped social interactions. With the advent of

Thomas A. Edison and His Inventions

At a time when Americans increasingly identified a corporation with a single individual, Edison made sure that he was directly associated with his inventions, either by being photographed with them or by using his name on product labels.

the sewing machine, for example, clothing could be factory-stitched at high speed, and women were relieved of the tedium of sewing the family apparel by hand; inexpensive mass-produced clothing thus led to a considerable expansion in personal wardrobes. The spread of telephones—by 1900 the Bell Telephone Company had installed almost eight hundred thousand in the United States—not only transformed communication but undermined social conventions for polite behavior that had been premised on face-to-face or written exchanges. The light bulb, by further freeing people from dependence on daylight, made possible longer and more regular working hours. These wonders in turn inspired optimism that future technologies might lead to the betterment of society itself. The commissioner of patents proudly declared in 1892, "America has become known the world around as the home of invention."

In the eyes of many, Thomas A. Edison epitomized the inventive impulse. Born in 1847 in Milan, Ohio, Edison, like Andrew Carnegie, was largely self-educated and got his start in the telegraphic industry. Also like the shrewd Scot, Edison was a born salesman and self-promoter. When he modestly averred that "genius is one percent inspiration and ninety-nine per-

cent perspiration," he tacitly accepted the popular identification of himself as an inventing "wizard." Edison moreover shared Carnegie's vision of a large, interconnected industrial system resting on a foundation of technological innovation.

In his early work, Edison concentrated on the telegraph. His experimentation in the 1860s with machines that would send multiple messages on the same wire and automatically print the results led in 1868 to his first major invention, a stock-quotation printer. The money earned from the patents on this machine enabled Edison to set up his first "invention factory," in Newark, New Jersey, a research facility that he moved to nearby Menlo Park in 1876. Assembling a staff that included university-trained scientists, Edison boastfully predicted "a minor invention every ten days, and a big one every six months."

When the telegraph market was undercut by Bell's invention of the telephone, Edison turned his attention to the electric light. He realized that practical electrical lighting had to be part of a complete system containing generators, voltage regulators, electric meters, and insulated wiring—a system that could be easily installed and repaired. It also had to be cheaper than lighting with natural gas, its main competitor.

Buoyed by the success and popularity of his invention in 1877 of a phonograph, or "sound writer" (*phono:* "sound"; *graph:* "writer"), Edison set out to develop a new filament for incandescent light bulbs. Characteristically, he announced his plans for an electricity-generation process before he perfected his inventions and then scrambled feverishly, testing hundreds of materials before he found a carbon filament that would glow dependably in a vacuum. Backed financially by banker J. Pierpont Morgan, the Edison Illuminating Company in 1882 opened a power plant in the heart of New York City's financial district, furnishing lighting for eighty-five buildings.

On the heels of Edison's achievement, other inventors rushed into the electrical field. In 1887 engineer Frank J. Sprague used Edison's ideas to develop the first electric streetcar system, in Richmond, Virginia. But Edison competitors such as George Westinghouse, the inventor of the railroad air brake, were dissatisfied with the high cost of electrical transmission in Edison's system. Applying the ideas of the young electrical engineer and inventor William Stanley, Westinghouse designed a more efficient, high-voltage, alternating-current system, in the process stealing many of Edison's ideas. Edison angrily sued his competitors for patent violation. Although he successfully defended his electric light from patent infringement, the lawsuits cost him more than $2 million. Embittered by the legal battles, Edison relinquished control of his enterprises in the late 1880s. In 1892, with financier Morgan's help, Edison's company merged with a major competitor to form the General Electric Company (GE). Four years later, GE and Westinghouse agreed to exchange patents under a joint Board of Patent Control. Such corporate patent-pooling agreements became yet another mechanism of market domination.

Although no longer a corporate leader, Edison continued to pump out invention after invention, including the mimeograph machine, the microphone, the motion-picture camera and film, and the storage battery. By the time of his death in 1931, he had patented 1,093 inventions and had amassed an estate worth more than $6 million. Yet Edison's greatest achievement remained his laboratory at Menlo Park. A model for the industrial research labs established at the turn of the century by Kodak, General Electric, and Du Pont, Edison's laboratory demonstrated that the systematic use of science in support of industrial technology paid large dividends. Invention itself, in short, had become big business.

Mass Production, Mass Marketing

The technological and managerial innovations of such figures as Edison, Carnegie, and Rockefeller proved readily adaptable throughout American industry, spurring marvels of productivity. Indeed, late-nineteenth-century industrialists often discovered that their factories spewed out more goods than the market could absorb. This was particularly true in two kinds of businesses: those that manufactured devices for individual use such as sewing machines and farm implements, and those that mass-produced consumer goods such as matches, flour, soap, canned foods, and processed meats. Not surprisingly, these industries were pathbreakers in developing advertising and marketing techniques. Strategies for whetting consumer demand and for differentiating one product from another represented an important component of the post–Civil War industrial transformation.

The growth of the flour industry illustrates both the spread of mass production and the emergence of new marketing concepts. In the 1870s the nation's

Product Merchandising
Eye-catching Quaker Oats and Ivory Soap advertisements helped turn the products they touted into household words.

flour mills adopted the most advanced European manufacturing technologies and installed continuous-
process machines that graded, cleaned, hulled, cut,
and packaged their product in one rapid operation.
These companies, however, soon produced more flour
than they could sell. To unload this excess and recoup
production costs, the mills thought up new product
lines such as cake flours and breakfast cereals and sold
them through hard-hitting advertising. Flour miller
Henry P. Crowell, for example, heavily advertised his
new milled oat product under an easy-to-remember
brand name, Quaker Oats.

Through brand names, trademarks, guarantees,
slogans, endorsements, and other gimmicks, manufacturers built demand for their products and won remarkable consumer loyalty. Americans bought Ivory
Soap, first made in 1879 by Procter and Gamble of
Cincinnati, because of the absurdly overprecise but impressive pledge that it was "99 and $^{44}/_{100}$ths percent
pure." James B. ("Buck") Duke's American Tobacco
Company used trading cards, circulars, boxtop premi-
ums, prizes, testimonials, and scientific endorsements
to convert Americans to cigarette smoking.

In the photographic field, George Eastman in the
1880s developed a paper-based photographic film as
an alternative to the bulky, fragile glass plates then in
use. But professional photographers resisted the innovation, and Eastman realized that "in order to make a
large business we would have to reach the general
public and create a new class of patrons." Manufacturing a cheap camera for the masses, the Kodak, and devising a catchy slogan ("You press the button, we do
the rest"), Eastman introduced a system whereby customers returned the one-hundred-exposure film *and
the camera* to his Rochester factory, where the film
was developed, the camera reloaded, and everything
shipped back to them—for a charge of ten dollars. In
marketing a new technology, Eastman had revolutionized an industry and democratized a visual medium
previously confined to a few.

Many other companies with names well known
today contributed to the production and marketing
revolution—H. J. Heinz of Pittsburgh, Campbell Soup
Company of Camden, Pabst Beer of Milwaukee, Borden Milk and Swift Meat Company of Chicago, to name
a few. Benefiting from the savings made possible by
new machinery, organizational efficiencies, high volume, and national distribution, such firms won a large
share of the market with advertising that stressed their
products' high quality and low cost.

Industrialization: Costs and Benefits

By 1900 the chaos of early industrial competition,
when thousands of small companies had struggled to
enter a national market, had given way to an economy
dominated by a few enormous firms. An industrial
transformation that had originated in railroading and
expanded to steel and petroleum had spread to every
nook and cranny of American business. For those who
fell by the wayside in the era's unforgiving economic
environment, the cost could be measured in ruined
fortunes, bankrupted companies, and shattered
dreams. John D. Rockefeller put things with characteristic bluntness. In the Standard Oil Trust, he said he
wanted "only the big ones, only those who have already proved they can do a big business. As for the others, unfortunately they will have to die."

Pittsburgh in the 1890s
*For many Americans, the price of progress was often pollu-
tion. Lacking the technology to filter carbon and gases from
smoke, factory owners had no choice but to fill the skies
with soot.*

The cost was high, too, for millions of American workers, immigrant and native-born alike. The new industrial order was built on the backs of a vast army of laborers who were paid subsistence wages and who could be fired on a moment's notice when hard times or new technologies made them expendable. Moreover, industrialization often devastated the environment. Polluted rivers fouled by oil or chemical waste, smoky skies filled with clouds of soot, and a landscape littered with reeking garbage and toxic materials bore mute witness to the relentless drive for efficiency and profit.

To be sure, what some called the second industrial revolution brought social benefits as well, in the form of labor-saving products, lower prices, and advances in transportation and communications. The benefits and liabilities sometimes seemed inextricably interconnected. The sewing machine, for example, created thousands of new factory jobs, made available a wider variety of clothing, and eased the lives of millions of housewives. At the same time, it encouraged avaricious entrepreneurs to operate sweatshops in crowded tenements and unsafe lofts, where they heavily employed the immigrant poor—often vulnerable young women—to toil long hours for pitifully low wages.

Whatever the final balance sheet of social gains and costs, one thing was clear: the United States had muscled its way onto the world stage as an industrial titan. Between 1870 and 1900, the percentage of the world's manufactured goods produced by Americans jumped from under a quarter to nearly a third. The ambition and drive of countless inventors, financiers, managerial innovators, and marketing wizards had combined to lay the groundwork for a new social and economic order in the twentieth century.

THE NEW SOUTH

The South entered the industrial era far more slowly than the North. As late as 1900, total southern cotton-mill output, for example, remained little more than half that of the mills within a thirty-mile radius of Providence, Rhode Island. Moreover, the South's $509 average per capita income was less than half the $1,165 income of northerners.

The reasons for the South's late economic blossoming are not hard to discern. The Civil War's physical devastation of the region, the scarcity of southern towns and cities, lack of capital, illiteracy, northern control of financial markets and patents, and a low rate of technological innovation crippled efforts by southern business leaders to promote industrialization and urban expansion.

Economic progress was also impeded by the myth of the Lost Cause, which, through its nostalgic portrayal of pre–Civil War society, perpetuated an image of the South as traditional and unchanging. So although sharing many features of northern industrial growth, including the use of new technology, southern industrialization inched forward haltingly and was shaped in distinctive ways.

Obstacles to Southern Economic Development

Much of the South's difficulty in industrializing arose from its lack of capital. Although the South had relatively few banks before the Civil War, the average loanable assets of southern banks had been quite high. Furthermore, a long-standing self-sufficient barter economy had functioned well for whites living in hilly upcountry areas where, as small farmers, they had raised their own food and paid their bills through trade of farm produce. One blacksmith's ledger entries from the period before the Civil War recorded payment with a hundred pounds of seed cotton, fifteen pounds of flour, a hundred split rails, buttons, four bushels of corn, and small amounts of cash.

But the Civil War shattered the South's credit system. Four years of fierce fighting saw cities burned, fields trampled, livestock slaughtered, and farms and plantations ruined. Moreover, the war caused banks to fail in large numbers. By 1865 the South, with more than a quarter of the nation's population, possessed just 2 percent of its banks.

Additionally, federal government policies adopted during the war restricted the expansion of the southern banking system. The Republican-dominated wartime Congress, which had created a national currency and banking structure, required anyone wishing to start a bank to have fifty thousand dollars in capital in order to obtain a charter. Few southerners could meet this test after the war. Even those with the necessary capital faced obstacles, since federal laws passed by northerners prohibited the extension of mortgages on real estate. With limited assets and restricted loan options, southern banks in effect were confined to urban cen-

14) B

ters and could lend only considerably smaller amounts than their northern counterparts.

With banks in short supply, country merchants and storekeepers became bankers by default, lending supplies rather than cash to local farmers in return for a lien, or mortgage, on their crops (see Chapter 16). Short of cash to pay their own debts, many southern storekeepers insisted that farmers increase their cotton and tobacco acreage because those crops initially brought the highest returns. Yet even though they marked up the goods sold on credit to farmers by 40 to 70 percent, storekeepers rarely became rich. Few merchants in Georgia during the last quarter of the century had a net worth over five thousand dollars.

The shift from planting corn to raising cotton and tobacco made small southern farmers particularly vulnerable to the fluctuations of commercial agriculture. By the 1880s many southerners who had been largely self-sufficient now depended on outside producers for food, shoes, and agricultural implements. Selling cotton in a national and international market, postbellum farmers became prey to forces beyond their control. When the price of cotton fell from eleven cents per pound in 1875 to less than five cents in 1894, well under the cost of production, many southern farmers grew desperate.

The South not only suffered from an overspecialization in cash crops, particularly cotton, and a shortage of cash and banking facilities but it also remained the victim of federal policies designed to aid northern industry. High protective tariffs raised the price of machine technology imported from abroad; the demonetization of silver (see Chapter 16) further limited capital availability; and discriminatory railroad freight rates hiked the expense of shipping finished goods and raw materials to outside markets.

The South's chronic shortage of funds affected the economy in indirect ways as well, by limiting the resources available for education. During Reconstruction northern philanthropists such as Georgia-born George Peabody, together with the Freedmen's Bureau, the American Missionary Association, and other relief agencies, had begun a modest expansion of public schooling for both blacks and whites. But Georgia and many other southern states operated segregated schools and refused to tax property for school support until 1889. As a result, school attendance remained low, severely limiting the number of educated people able to staff technical positions in business and industry.

Southern states, like those in the North, often contributed what modest funds they had to war veterans' pensions. In this way, southern state governments built a white patronage system for Confederate veterans and helped reinforce southerners' lingering idealization of the old Confederacy—the South's Lost Cause. As late as 1911, veterans' pensions in Georgia ate up $1.2 million, or 22 percent of the state's entire budget, leaving little for economic or educational development.

The New South Creed and Southern Industrialization

Despite the limited availability of state and federal funds for industrialization, energetic southern newspaper editors such as Henry W. Grady of the *Atlanta Constitution* and Henry Watterson of the *Louisville Courier Journal* beat the drums to encourage southern economic growth in the 1870s and proclaimed the boundless industrial potential of "this glorious sunny South." Fearful that the South would become an economic backwater, these writers and a cadre of planters, merchants, and industrialists championed what became known as the New South creed. The South's unprecedented natural resources and cheap labor, they argued, made it a natural site for industrial development. As one editor declared, "The El Dorado* of the next half century is the South. The wise recognize it; the dull and the timid will ere long regret their sloth or their hesitancy."

The movement to industrialize the South gained momentum in the 1880s. To attract northern capital, southern states offered tax exemptions for new businesses, set up industrial and agricultural expositions, and leased convicts from the state prisons to serve as cheap labor. Florida, Texas, and other states gave huge tracts of lands to railroads, which expanded dramatically throughout the South and in turn stimulated the birth of new towns and villages. Other states sold forest and mineral rights on nearly 6 million acres of federal lands to speculators, mostly from the North, who significantly expanded output. The production of iron, sulfur, and coal catapulted. Denuding the forests of Alabama and Louisiana, northern lumber syndicates between 1869 and 1899 increased lumber production by 500 percent.

---

*El Dorado: a legendary place in Spanish America sought out for its precious metals and jewels.

Pig Iron Scene, Birmingham, Alabama,
by Charles Graham, 1886
Although Birmingham Alabama's extensive foundries turned out inexpensive iron ingots, the northern owners forced factory operators to price their products at the same rate as ingots produced in Pittsburgh.

Following the lead of their northern counterparts, the southern iron and steel industries expanded as well. Birmingham, Alabama, founded in 1871 in the heart of a region blessed with rich deposits of coal, limestone, and iron ore, grew in less than three decades to a bustling iron-producing city with noisy railroad yards and roaring blast furnaces. By 1900 it was the nation's largest pig-iron shipper. In these same years, Chattanooga, Tennessee, housed nine furnaces, seventeen foundries, and numerous machine shops.

As large-scale recruiters of black workers, the southern iron and steel mills contributed to the migration of blacks cityward. By 1900, 20 percent of the southern black population was urban. Many of these urban blacks toiled as domestics or in similar menial capacities, but others entered the industrial work force in places like Birmingham and Chattanooga. Southern industry reflected the patterns of racism permeating other aspects of southern life. Tobacco companies used black workers, particularly women, to clean the tobacco leaves while white women, at a different location, ran the machines that made cigarettes. The bur-

geoning textile mills of the piedmont were lily-white, whereas in the iron and steel industry, blacks, who composed 60 percent of the work force by 1900, had practically no chance of advancement. Nevertheless, in a rare reversal of the usual pattern, southern blacks in the iron and steel industry on average earned more than did southern white textile workers.

The Southern Mill Economy

Unlike the urban-based southern iron and steel industry, the textile mills that mushroomed in the South in the 1880s took southern industrialization down a path different from that of the North and Midwest. Above the Mason-Dixon line, factories and mills were concentrated in cities. But the southern textile industry sprang up in the countryside and often became a catalyst for the formation of new towns and villages. (This same pattern had occurred in rural New England in the 1820s.) In those southern districts that underwent the gradual transition from an agricultural to a mill economy, country ways and values suffused the new industrial workplace.

The cotton-mill economy grew largely in the piedmont, a beautiful country of rolling hills and rushing rivers stretching from central Virginia to northern Georgia and Alabama. Until the 1850s the piedmont had been the South's backcountry, a land of subsistence farming and limited roads, far from the thriving coastal plantations. The Civil War had disrupted even the modest gains in railroad expansion and factory construction that had come in the 1850s. Then, struggling to rebuild their lives in the late 1860s, most of the piedmont's white yeoman farmers and freed blacks became ensnared in the crop-lien and sharecropping systems. In the two decades following the war, falling cotton and tobacco prices, laws that required the fencing of livestock, and higher taxes to support railway and road construction trapped farmers in the new commercial economy and undercut their semi-independent existence.

But postwar railroad construction also opened the region to outside markets and sparked a period of intense town building and textile-mill expansion. Between 1880 and 1900, track mileage in North Carolina grew more than 2½ times; the number of towns and villages jumped, quickening the pulse of commerce; and the construction of textile mills accelerated. During this same period, some 120 new mills were built in North Carolina alone; Augusta, Georgia, with twenty-eight hundred mill workers, became known as the Lowell of the South. The expansion of the southern textile industry nurtured promoters' visions of a new, more prosperous, industrialized South.

Merchants and newspaper editors hailed the prospect that proliferating cotton mills would lift the South out of its Civil War legacy of poverty and defeat. And sharecroppers and tenant farmers at first turned hopeful eyes toward mill work, realizing that a deepening agricultural depression was driving them into destitution and despair. Sharecropper Eula Durham, recalling a day spent picking cotton, vividly evoked the plight of the South's rural populace: "I got through picking that evening, . . . and [the owner of the cotton field] said 'Well, I don't know, I reckon you're worth a dime.' And he give me a dime for picking cotton all day. I went home and I cried, I was so mad. Papa said, 'If you don't sit down and hush I'm going to tear you all to pieces. That's all that old man had.' I said, 'Well, he ought to have told me that before I picked that cotton.' " For Eula Durham and countless others like her, the mills seemed to offer a way out of rural poverty.

But appearances were deceptive. The chief cotton-mill promoters were drawn from the same ranks of merchants, lawyers, doctors, and bankers who had profited from the commercialization of southern agriculture (and from the misfortunes of poor black and white tenant farmers and sharecroppers enmeshed in the new system). R. R. Haynes, a planter and merchant from North Carolina's Rutherford County, was typical of the new entrepreneurs. Starting out as a storekeeper, he expanded his operation to include a sawmill, cotton gins, and a wheat thresher. In 1884 he purchased land and water rights on Second Broad Creek and formed a company to finance construction of the Henrietta Mills. By 1913 Haynes owned not only one of the South's largest gingham-producing operations but also banks, railroads, lumber businesses, and a line of general stores.

Haynes and other prosperous southern textile industrialists had first constructed the mills and had purchased the most advanced cotton-spinning and cloth-weaving machinery from northern suppliers. They then recruited northern technicians and managers to set up the business and hired low-skilled laborers to be the backbone of their operation.

Mill superintendents drew their workers from impoverished nearby farms and commonly hired whole families (almost exclusively poor whites). In their public pronouncements, they promised that textile work would free these families from poverty and instill in them the virtues of punctuality and industrial discipline. While chanting these benefits, however, the cotton-mill entrepreneurs shamelessly exploited the South's deep pool of cheap labor. By the 1880s, when the mills were earning their investors from 30 percent to 75 percent profit, the superintendents were paying mill workers twelve to eighteen years of age from seven cents to eleven cents an hour, a rate 30 percent to 50 percent less than comparable mill wages in New England.

The mill dominated most piedmont textile communities. The mill operator not only built and owned the workers' housing and the company store but also supported the village church, financed the local elementary school, and pried into the morals and behavior of the mill hands. To curb the workers' tendency to move from one mill to another seeking better opportunities, the mill owner usually paid them just once a month, often in scrip—a certificate redeemable only in goods from the company store. Since few families had enough money and supplies to get through a month without buying on credit, they usually overspent and fell behind in their payments. In these cases, the charges were deducted from the workers' wages the following month. In this way, the mill drew workers and their families into a cycle of indebtedness very much like that faced by sharecroppers and tenant farmers.

Southern mill superintendents accommodated themselves to local customs. Unlike northern mill workers, predominantly female and single, southern mill employees comprised men, married and single women, and children. Mothers commonly brought babies into the mills and kept them in baskets nearby while tending their machines. Little children visiting older siblings in the mills sometimes learned to operate the machines themselves. Laboring a twelve-hour day, the mill hands relieved their tedium by deliberately stationing themselves near friends so that they might converse as they worked. Ties among the workers were strong. One employee put it simply: "The mill community was a close bunch of people . . . like one big family. We just loved one another." The mill managers adjusted to other local practices as well. Since many southerners traditionally ate their major meal at midday, mills often let most of their hands go home between twelve and one. In addition, mill hands worked cooperatively, as they had during planting and harvesting on the farm, and watched over the looms of coworkers who were taking a break.

Textile Workers
Textile mills hired both adults and children. Here a man and two boys stand before the machines that they operated for sixty hours a week. Child laborers in the mills often went home so tired that they fell asleep before supper and could not be wakened until morning.

To help make ends meet, mill workers kept their own garden patches and raised chickens and an occasional cow and pig. Southern mill hands thus brought communal farm values, nurtured through cooperative planting and harvesting, into the mills and mill villages. Although they had to adapt to machine-paced work and received barely enough pay to live on, the working poor in the mill districts, like their prewar counterparts in the North, eased the shift from rural to village-industrial life by clinging to a cooperative country ethic.

Like northern cotton mills before the Civil War, southern textile companies exploited the cheap rural labor around them, settling transplanted farm people in paternalistic company-run villages. Using these tactics, the industry underwent a period of steady growth. Between 1860 and 1900, cotton-mill capacity shot up 1,400 percent, and by 1920 the South was the nation's leading textile-mill center.

The Southern Industrial Lag

Still, industrialization in the South occurred on a smaller scale and at a slower rate than industrialization in the North and also depended far more on outside financing, technology, and expertise. Despite leaps in southern lumber, iron, and cotton production, the late-nineteenth-century southern economy remained essentially in a colonial status, subject to control by northern industries and financial syndicates. Except for the American Tobacco Company, southern industry was dominated by northern companies and northern bankers. U.S. Steel, for example, controlled the foundries in Birmingham, and in 1900 its executives began to price Birmingham steel according to the "Pittsburgh plus" formula based on the price of Pittsburgh steel, plus the freight costs of shipping from Pittsburgh. As a result, southerners paid higher prices for steel than did northerners, despite the fact that southern steel production was less costly than northern production.

An array of factors thus combined to retard industrialization in the South. Restrictive banking regulations, scarce capital, absentee ownership, unfavorable railroad rates, cautious state governments, wartime debts, lack of industrial experience, and control by profit-hungry northern enterprises all hampered the region's economic development. Dragged down by a poorly educated white population unskilled in modern technology and by an equally poorly trained, indigent black population excluded from skilled jobs, southern industry languished. Not until after the turn of the century did southern industry as a whole undergo the restructuring and consolidation that had occurred in northern business enterprise two decades earlier. As in the North, industrialization brought significant environmental damage, including polluted rivers and streams, decimated forests, grimy coal-mining towns, and soot-infested steel-making cities. Although Henry Grady's vision of a New South may have inspired many southerners to work toward industrialization, economic growth in the South, limited as it was by outside forces, progressed in its own distinctly regional way.

INDUSTRIAL WORK AND THE WORK FORCE

As we have seen in the contrasting experiences of the North and South, industrialization proceeded unevenly nationwide. In fact, during the late nineteenth century, *most* Americans still worked in small factories and locally run businesses. In cities like Philadelphia and Cincinnati, a variety of small-scale work settings coexisted. Tiny sweatshops where women and children hand-stitched clothing operated in the same neighborhoods as small factories employing a mix of skilled and unskilled laborers. But in more and more locales as the century unfolded, large factories sprang onto the industrial scene with armies of workers who turned out leather soles for shoes, veneer-covered plywood for furniture, and castings for plows. Thus for all the variety, the pattern of change was evident. Between 1860 and 1900, the number of industrial workers jumped from 885,000 to 3.2 million, and the trend toward large-scale production became unmistakable.

From Workshop to Factory

The transition to a factory economy came not as an earthquake but rather as a series of jolts varying in strength and duration. But whether they occurred quickly or slowly, the changes in factory production had a profound impact on skilled artisans and unskilled laborers alike, for they involved a fundamental restructuring of work habits and a new emphasis on workplace discipline.

The impact of these changes can be seen by examining the boot and shoe industry. As late as the 1840s, almost every shoe was custom-made by a single skilled artisan, who worked in a small, independent shop where he and four or five other shoemakers set their own hours and agreed on the stint, or the number of pairs, to be produced each day. These shoemakers were aristocrats in the world of labor. Taught in an apprentice system, they took pride in their work and controlled the quality of their product. In some cases they hired and paid their own helpers.

Around these shoemakers there evolved a distinctive working-class culture, subdivided along ethnic lines. Foreign-born English, German, and Irish shoe workers each set up ethnic trade organizations and joined affiliated benevolent associations (see Chapter 9). They took time off for religious observances, funerals, and holidays; drank sociably on the job; and helped each other weather accidents or sicknesses. Bound together by their potent religious and ethnic ties, they also attended common churches, observed weddings and funerals according to old-country traditions, and relaxed together at the local saloon after work. Living in tenements and boardinghouses within the same tight-knit ethnic neighborhood, they developed a strong ethnic and community pride.

As early as the 1850s, even before the widespread use of machinery, changes in the ready-made shoe trade began to erode the role and status of skilled labor. When Cincinnati's Filey and Chapin Company in 1851 moved its growing production staff into a large warehouse, the owners broke down the manufacturing process into a sequence of repetitive, easily mastered tasks. Skilled shoe artisans now worked in a "team" of four men, each responsible for one function: putting the shoe on the last (a form shaped like a

The Shoemakers
by E. B. and E. C. Kellogg, 1855
In antebellum America skilled shoemak-ers custom-made their products and sold them directly to the purchaser, cut-ting out the retailer. After the Civil War, the mass production of shoes spelled the end of many small shops, such as the one depicted in this lithograph.

person's foot), attaching the heel, trimming the sole, "finishing" the leather with stain and polish, and so forth. Thus instead of crafting a pair of shoes from start to finish, each team member specialized in only one part of the process. The Ohio commissioner of labor statistics in 1878 voiced a common artisan lament about this narrowing of skills: "[F]ew machinists can build an engine, few shoemakers . . . can make a shoe. . . . The machinist may be a first class vise hand, the shoemaker may be a splendid trimmer . . . [but] their future is dependent upon their ability to secure employment at such a specialty."

Not only did the nature of the work change under the new factory system of shoe manufacture, but workers lost the freedom to drink on the job and to take time off for special occasions. A working-class culture that had reinforced group solidarity was now dismissed by owners and shop foremen as wasteful and inefficient.

In the 1880s, as shoe factories became larger and more mechanized, traditional skills largely vanished. Sophisticated sewing and buffing machines allowed shoe companies to replace skilled operatives with lower-paid, less skilled women and children. By 1890 women made up more than 35 percent of the work-force in an industry once dominated by men.

In many other industries, skilled artisans found their responsibilities and relation to the production process changing. With the exception of some skilled construction crafts such as carpentry and bricklaying, artisans no longer participated in the production process *as a whole*. Like the laborer whose machine nailed heels on forty-eight hundred shoes a day, even "skilled" workers in the new factories specializing in consumer goods found themselves performing numb-ingly repetitive and monotonous tasks. Factory work, which writers and ministers had praised in the 1830s and 1840s as the foundation of happiness and the mark of social progress, had become specialized, machine-paced, and deadeningly routine.

The Hardships of Industrial Labor

The expansion of the factory system not only altered the nature of skilled work but also spawned an unprecedented demand for unskilled labor. By the 1880s nearly one-third of the 750,000 workers employed in the railroad and steel industries, for example, were common laborers.

In the construction trades, the machine and tool industries, and garment making, the services of unskilled laborers were procured under the so-called contract system. To avoid the problems of hiring, managing, and firing their own workers, large companies negotiated an agreement with a subcontractor to take responsibility for employee relations. A foreman or boss employed by the subcontractor supervised gangs of unskilled day laborers. These common workers were seasonal help, hired in times of need and laid off in slack periods. The steel industry employed them to shovel ore, coal, and lime around the yards and to move ingots inside the mills. The foremen drove the gangs hard; in the Pittsburgh area, the workers called the foremen "pushers."

Notoriously transient, unskilled laborers drifted from city to city and from industry to industry. As the first hired during good times and the first let go in bad, they sometimes worked for one-third the wages of a typical skilled artisan. In the late 1870s, unskilled laborers earned $1.30 a day, whereas bricklayers and blacksmiths earned more than $3.00. Only unskilled southern mill workers, whose wages averaged a meager 84¢ a day in these years, earned less.

Unskilled and skilled workers alike not only put in up to twelve-hour shifts but also faced grave hazards to their health and safety. The alarming incidence of industrial accidents stemmed from a variety of circumstances, including dangerous factory conditions, workers' inexperience, the rapid pace of the production process, and the employers' unconcern for plant safety. Hamlin Garland graphically described the perilous environment of a steel-rail mill at Carnegie's Homestead Steel Works in Pittsburgh (see "A Place in Time"). One steelworker recalled that on his first day at the mill, "I looked up and a big train carrying a big vessel with fire was making towards me. I stood numb, afraid to move, until a man came to me and led me out of the mill." Under such conditions the accident rate in the steel mills was extremely high.

In the coal mines and cotton mills, child laborers typically entered the workforce at age eight or nine. These youngsters not only faced the same environmental hazards as adults but were especially prone to injury because of the pranks and play that they engaged in on the job. (When supervision was lax in the cotton mills, for example, child workers would grab the belts that powered the machines and see who could ride them farthest up toward the drive shaft in the ceiling before letting go and falling to the floor.) In the coal industry, children were commonly employed as slate pickers. Sitting at a chute beneath the breakers that crushed the coal, they removed pieces of slate and other impurities. The cloud of coal dust that swirled around them made them vulnerable to black lung disease—a disorder that could progress into emphysema and tuberculosis. Children and others who toiled in the cotton mills, constantly breathing in cotton dust, fell ill with brown lung, another crippling disease.

For adult workers, the railroad industry was one of the most perilous. In 1889, the first year that the Interstate Commerce Commission compiled reliable statistics, almost two thousand railwaymen were killed on the job and more than twenty thousand were injured.

Disabled workers and widows received only minimal financial aid from employers. Until the 1890s the courts considered employer negligence to be one of the normal risks borne by the employee. Railroad and factory owners regularly fought against the adoption of state safety and health standards, on the grounds that the economic costs would be excessive. For sickness

and accident benefits, workers joined fraternal organizations and ethnic clubs, part of whose monthly dues benefited those in need. But in most cases, the amounts set aside were too low to be of much help. When a worker was killed or maimed in an accident, the family became dependent on relatives or kindly neighbors for assistance and support.

Immigrant Labor

Outside the South factory owners turned to unskilled immigrant laborers for the muscle needed in the booming factories, mills, railroads, and heavy-construction industries. In Philadelphia, where native-born Americans and recent German immigrants dominated the highly skilled metalworking trades, Irish newcomers remained mired in unskilled horse-carting and construction occupations until the 1890s, when the "new immigrants" from southern and eastern Europe replaced them (see Chapter 19). In the Northeast poverty-stricken French-Canadians filled the most menial positions in the textile mills. On the West Coast Chinese immigrants performed the dirtiest and most physically demanding jobs in mining, canning, and railroad construction.

Writing home in the 1890s, eastern European immigrants described the hazardous and draining work in the steel mills. "Wherever the heat is most insupportable, the flames most scorching, the smoke and soot most choking, there we are certain to find compatriots bent and wasted in toil," reported one Hungarian. Yet those immigrants disposed to live frugally in a boardinghouse and to work an eighty-four-hour week could save fifteen dollars a month, far more than they could have earned in the old country.

Intent on improving their families' economic standing, many immigrants readily accepted the steel mills' and factories' exhausting work schedules. One worker tersely summed up the typical routine: "A good job, save money, work all time, go home, sleep, no spend." Willing to make short-term sacrifices for long-term gains, immigrants commonly volunteered for overtime work on Sundays. If the immigrant workers stayed healthy, they often accumulated small savings and lived better than ever before.

Although most immigrants worked hard, few adjusted easily to the rat race of the factory world. The rural peasants from southern and eastern Europe who immigrated after 1890 found it especially difficult to abandon their irregular work habits for the unrelenting factory schedules. Unlike farm routines, which followed seasonal changes in daylight hours, factory operations were dictated by the invariable speed of the machines. A brochure that the International Harvester Corporation used to teach English to its Polish workers attempted to instill the "proper" values. Lesson 1 read:

> *I hear the whistle. I must hurry.*
> *I hear the five minute whistle.*
> *It is time to go into the shop.*
> *I take my check from the gate board and hang*
>   *it on the department board.*
> *I change my clothes and get ready to work.*
> *The starting whistle blows.*
> *I eat my lunch.*
> *It is forbidden to eat until then.*
> *The whistle blows at five minutes of starting*
>   *time.*
> *I get ready to go to work.*
> *I work until the whistle blows to quit.*
> *I leave my place nice and clean.*
> *I put all my clothes in the locker.*
> *I must go home.*

As this "lesson" reveals, factory work tied the immigrants to a rigid timetable very different from the pace of farm life.

When immigrant workers resisted the tempo of factory work, drank on the job, or took unexcused absences, employers used a variety of tactics to enforce discipline. Some sponsored temperance societies and Sunday schools to teach habits of punctuality and sobriety. Others published rule books dictating specific codes of behavior. When efforts at persuasion proved ineffective, employers cut wages and put workers on the piecework system, paying them only for the items produced. Employers sometimes also provided low-cost housing to build employee allegiance to the company and gain leverage against work stoppages: if the workers went on strike, the boss could simply evict them. To keep skilled artisans from leaving, a few companies paid bonuses, set up pension plans, and promised steady employment.

In some cases workers fought attempts to tighten factory discipline by demanding a say in production quotas or asserting traditional rights, such as the custom in the cigar-making industry of allowing one employee to read to others as they worked. Seeking to recreate a village atmosphere within the workplace,

immigrant factory help often persuaded employers to hire friends, and family members.

In the face of immigrant labor's desires for a more sociable, humane working environment, the proliferation of machines in the factories frequently sparked employer-employee tensions. When the factory owner's interest in increasing output corresponded with the immigrant's desire to maximize income, the offer of long hours at the machines was accepted and even welcomed. But when the employer cut wages or unreasonably accelerated the work schedule, unrest boiled to the surface.

Women and Work in Industrializing America

Women's work experiences in the nineteenth century were shaped both by marital status and by social class. Married women in all classes widely accepted an ideology of domesticity based on the idea of separate spheres for men and women (see Chapter 20). Believing that women possessed a unique talent for caring for children, married women tended to remain at home and raise children and look after the household as men labored in offices and factories. Although all married women supported their families by cooking, cleaning, and taking care of youngsters, the well-to-do could hire maids and cooks to ease their burdens. Working-class married women, in contrast, not only lacked such assistance but also often had the added responsibility of earning money at home to make ends meet.

For working-class married women, home work—working for wages at home by sewing, button-making, taking in borders, or doing laundry—had predated industrialization. The growth of cities and the expansion of the economy enabled unscrupulous entrepreneurs to exploit this captive workforce. Cigar manufacturers would buy or lease a tenement and require their twenty families to live and work there. In the clothing industry, similarly, manufacturers hired out finishing needlework tasks to lower-class married women and their children, who labored long hours in their crowded apartments.

In contrast to lower-class married women who had no choice but to accept home work, young, working-class single women often viewed outside work as an opportunity. In 1870 only 13 percent of all women worked outside the home. Sixty percent of these found jobs in domestic employment as cooks, maids, cleaning ladies, and laundresses. But most working women

Women in the Workplace
Crowded together at their sewing machines, these women endured the tedium of factory work by chatting with nearby friends. Despite long hours and congested conditions, unmarried laborers could earn enough to supplement their parent's income and occasionally have some extra funds to spend on themselves.

intensely disliked the long hours, dismally low pay, and social stigma attached to being a "servant." Therefore, when jobs in industry expanded in the last quarter of the century, growing numbers of single women abandoned domestic employment for the better-paying, less-demeaning work in the textile, food-processing, and garment industries. Between 1870 and 1900, the number of women working outside the home nearly tripled, and by the turn of the century, women made up 17 percent of the country's labor force.

A variety of factors propelled this rise in the employment of single females. Changes in agriculture prompted many young farm women to seek employment in the industrial sector (see Chapter 19), and immigrant parents often sent their daughters to the factories to supplement their meager family incomes. Plant managers, in turn, welcomed young immigrant women as a ready source of inexpensive, unskilled labor. But factory owners assumed that many of these women would marry within a short time, and thus treated them as temporary help and kept their wages low. Late in the century, young women in the clothing industry earned as little as five dollars for seventy hours of work.

Despite their paltry wages, long hours, and often unpleasant working conditions, many young women relished the independence they gained through factory employment. Even though most of their income went to their parents, they looked forward to having a little spending money for themselves. Mary Antin, a young Jewish immigrant, later captured in writing the excitement that she and her friends felt while shopping after a day of work in turn-of-the-century Boston, "noses and fingers on plate glass windows ablaze with electric lights and alluring with display."

When the typewriter and the telephone came into general use in the 1890s, office work became more specialized, and women with a high-school education moved into clerical and secretarial jobs earlier filled primarily by men. They were attracted by the clean, safe working conditions and relatively good pay. First-rate typists could earn six dollars to eight dollars a week, which compared favorably with factory wages. Even though women were excluded from managerial positions, office work carried higher prestige and was generally steadier than work in the factory or shop.

Despite the growing number of women workers, when the late-nineteenth-century popular press touted the possibilities of moving up the ladder of success in industrial America, it left out women completely. Women's work outside the home was seen as temporary. Their real achievement was defined in terms of marriage and the family. For women, success might be measured, for example, in the vicarious satisfaction they experienced when a husband received a promotion or a son earned a raise. Few people even considered the possibility that a woman could attain national or even local prominence in the emerging corporate order.

Hard Work and the Gospel of Success

Although women were generally excluded from the equation, influential opinion molders in these years preached that any man could achieve success in the new industrial era. In *Ragged Dick* (1867) and scores of later tales, Horatio Alger, a Unitarian minister turned dime novelist, recounted the adventures of poor but honest lads who rise through ambition, initiative, and self-discipline. Life is a struggle in Alger's fictional America, but the key to success lies in seizing the unexpected opportunities that fortune thrusts in one's path. In his stories shoe-shine boys stop runaway horses and are rewarded by rich benefactors who give them a start in business. The career of Andrew Carnegie was often offered as proof that the United States remained the land of opportunity and "rags to riches."

Not everyone embraced this belief. In an 1871 essay, Mark Twain chided the public for its naïveté and cynically suggested that business success was more likely to come to those who lied and cheated. In testimony given in 1883 before a Senate committee investigating labor conditions, a New Yorker named Thomas B. McGuire dolefully recounted how he had been forced out of the horse-cart business by larger, better-financed concerns. Declared McGuire: "A man in the express business today owning one or two horses and a wagon cannot even eke out an existence. . . . The competition . . . from these monopolies . . . is too great. . . . I live in a tenement house, three stories up, where the water comes in through the roof, and I cannot better myself. My children will have to go to work before they are able to work. Why? Simply because this present system . . . is all for the privileged classes, nothing for the man who produces the wealth." Only with starting capital of ten thousand dollars—then a large sum—said McGuire, could the independent entrepreneur hope to compete with the large companies.

What are the facts? Certainly Carnegie's rise from abject poverty to colossal wealth was the rare exception, as recent studies of nearly two hundred of the largest corporations reveal. Ninety-five percent of the industrial leaders came from middle- and upper-class backgrounds. However, even if skilled immigrants and native-born working-class Americans had little chance to move into management in the largest corporations, they did have considerable opportunity to rise to the top in *small* companies. In Paterson, New Jersey, the most successful owners of small- to medium-size iron,

machinery, and locomotive companies between 1850 and 1880 invariably had started their careers as workers, broadened their skills through apprenticeship, and then opened their own factories. Although few of them reaped immense fortunes, many attained substantial incomes.

For unskilled immigrant laborers, the opportunities for advancement were considerably more limited. Many did, however, move to semiskilled or skilled positions. And with new jobs came higher earnings and sometimes the means to purchase a house. In nineteenth-century Boston, except for blacks, significant numbers of unskilled workers advanced into the next higher occupational stratum. Yet most immigrants, particularly the Irish and Italians, moved far more slowly than the sons of middle- and upper-class Americans who began with greater educational advantages and family financial backing. The upward mobility possible for such unskilled workers was generally mobility *within* the working class. Immigrants who got ahead in the late nineteenth century went from rags to respectability, not rags to riches.

One positive economic trend in these years was the rise in real wages, representing gains in actual buying power. Average real wages climbed 31 percent for unskilled workers and 74 percent for skilled workers between 1860 and 1900. Overall gains in purchasing power, however, were often offset by personal injuries and unemployment during slack times or economic slumps. The position of unskilled immigrant laborers was particularly shaky. Even during a prosperous year like 1890, one out of every five nonagricultural workers was unemployed at least one month. During the depressions of the 1870s and 1890s, wage cuts, extended layoffs, and irregular employment pushed those at the very base of the industrial workforce to the brink of starvation.

Thus the overall picture of late-nineteenth-century economic mobility is complex. At the top of the scale, the rich grew even wealthier and amassed enormous fortunes. In 1890 a mere 10 percent of American families owned 73 percent of the nation's wealth. At the bottom of the scale, the most recent immigrants, particularly the unskilled, struggled to make ends meet. During the 1890s only about 45 percent of American industrial laborers earned more than the five-hundred-dollar poverty line annually. Nevertheless, in between the very rich and the very poor, skilled immigrants and small shopkeepers were swelling the ranks of the middle class. So although the standard of living for millions of Americans rose, the gap between the poor and the well-off remained a yawning abyss.

LABOR UNIONS AND INDUSTRIAL CONFLICT

Toiling long hours for low wages, often under dangerous and degrading conditions, some late-nineteenth-century workers turned to labor unions for help. But the unions faced formidable obstacles to increasing their membership. With desperately poor immigrants pouring into the country, employers could always hire newcomers willing to work for lower wages and even to serve as strikebreakers.

Ethnic and racial divisions within the workforce further hampered unionizing efforts. In mill towns like Troy, New York, for example, French-Canadian and Irish Catholic workers worshiped, socialized, and married largely within their own ethnic group. The same was true of Pennsylvania coal miners and steelworkers who had immigrated from various southern and eastern European countries.

Furthermore, relatively prosperous skilled crafts-workers felt little kinship with low-paid common laborers. And even the skilled artisans were divided among themselves, depending on their particular craft. Iron molders, cigar makers, carpenters, and printers all worked in radically different environments and saw little reason for cooperative effort. Thus when craft-based unions did challenge management and go on strike, they represented only a tiny percentage of the workforce.

Labor-organizing efforts reflected these realities. Two groups, the National Labor Union and the Knights of Labor, attempted to build a mass labor movement that would unite skilled and unskilled workers regardless of their specialty. After impressive initial growth, however, both efforts collapsed. The most successful labor movement of the period, the American Federation of Labor (AFL), represented an amalgamation of powerful independent craft unions. The AFL survived and grew, but it still represented only a small portion of the total labor force.

With unions so weak, labor unrest generally took the form of unplanned, wildcat walkouts when conditions became intolerable, and these actions born of desperation sometimes exploded into violence. This, in turn, whipped up middle-class fears of labor unrest, further impeding the development of a strong labor movement.

Organizing the Workers

The Civil War marked a watershed in the development of labor organizations. Labor unions were nothing new. From the eighteenth century on, carpenters, bricklayers, and other skilled workers had organized local trade unions to fight wage reductions and provide rudimentary benefits for their members in times of illness or accident. By the 1850s tradesmen in the printing, cigar-making, and iron-working businesses had even organized national associations along craft lines. But the effectiveness of these organizations was limited. The main challenge that labor leaders faced in the postwar period was how to boost the unions' clout. Some believed that this goal could be achieved by forming one big association that would transcend craft lines and pull in a mass membership.

One person inspired by this vision was Philadelphian William H. Sylvis, who in 1863 was elected president of the Iron Moulders' International Union, an organization of iron-foundry workers. Strongly built and bearded, with a "face and eyes beaming with intelligence," Sylvis traveled the country exhorting iron molders to organize. When he had no money for train fare, he rode in the cab with the engineer. A compelling speaker, he lambasted "the monied aristocracy—proud, imperious and dishonest, . . . blasting and withering everything it [comes] in contact with." Within a few years, Sylvis had built his union from "a mere pygmy" to a membership of eighty-five hundred.

In 1866, acting on his dream of a nationwide association to represent all workers, Sylvis called a convention in Baltimore that formed the National Labor Union (NLU). The new organization not only endorsed the eight-hour-day movement but also, reflecting the lingering aura of pre–Civil War utopianism, embraced a wide range of goals, including currency and banking reform, an end to convict labor, a federal department of labor, and restriction on immigration—especially Chinese immigration—since many regarded immigrants as responsible for driving wages down. The NLU under Sylvis's leadership also endorsed the cause of working women and elected the head of a Troy, New York, union of female laundry workers as one of its

25) C

**The Eight-Hour
Movement**

*Striking artisans from more than
three hundred companies filled
New York streets for weeks in
1872 in a campaign to reduce the
workday from ten hours to eight
hours. As is evident in this illustration, the eight-hour movement
gained additional support from
local saloons catering to German
immigrants.*

national officers. It urged black workers to organize as
well, though in racially separate unions.

In the winter of 1866–1867, Sylvis's own iron
founders' union became locked in a harrowing strike
when the nation's foundry owners cut wages and laid
off workers. After the strike failed miserably, Sylvis believed more deeply than ever before that the answer
lay not in strikes but in national political reform. He
invited a number of reformers to the 1868 NLU
convention, including woman-suffrage advocates Susan B. Anthony and Elizabeth Cady Stanton, who, according to a reporter, made "no mean impression on
the bearded delegates." But the NLU suffered a shattering blow when Sylvis died suddenly in 1869. Despite a claim of three hundred thousand members, it
faded quickly. After a brief incarnation in 1872 as the
National Labor Reform party, it vanished from the
scene.

But the dream of a national labor movement lived
on in a new organization, the Noble and Holy Order of
the Knights of Labor, founded in 1869 by nine Philadelphia tailors led by Uriah H. Stephens, head of the Garment Cutters of Philadelphia. A secret society modeled
on the Masonic order (see Chapter 10), the Knights
welcomed all wage earners or former wage earners;
they excluded only bankers, doctors, lawyers, stockbrokers, professional gamblers, and liquor dealers.
Calling for a great association of all workers, the
Knights demanded equal pay for women, an end to
child labor and convict labor, a graduated income tax,
and the cooperative employer-employee ownership of
factories, mines, and other businesses.

The Knights grew slowly at first, in part because
the Catholic church forbade Catholics to join. But
membership rocketed in the 1880s after the church
lifted its prohibition and Terence V. Powderly replaced
Stephens as the organization's head, or Grand Master
Workman, in 1879. A young Scranton machinist of
Irish-Catholic immigrant origins, Powderly was an unlikely labor leader. He was short and slight, with a
blond drooping mustache, elegant attire, and a fastidi-
ous, somewhat aloof manner. One journalist expressed surprise at finding such a fashionable and sophisticated man as the leader of "the horny-fisted sons
of toil." But Powderly's oratorical eloquence, coupled
with a series of successes in labor clashes, brought in
thousands of new members.

During its growth years in the early 1880s, the
Knights of Labor reflected both its idealistic origins and
Powderly's collaborative vision. Powderly opposed
strikes, which he considered "a relic of barbarism,"
and organized producer and consumer cooperatives.
A teetotaler, he also urged temperance upon the membership. Powderly advocated the admission of blacks
into local Knights of Labor assemblies, although he
recognized the strength of racism and allowed local assemblies to be segregated in the South. Under his leadership the Knights welcomed women members; by
1886 women organizers such as the feisty Irish-born
Mary Harris Jones, known as Mother Jones, had recruited thousands of workers, and women made up an
estimated 10 percent of the union's membership.

Powderly also supported restrictions on immigration—and a total ban on Chinese immigration. This

Ethnic and Racial Hatred

Conservative business owners used racist advertising such as this trade card stigmatizing Chinese laundry workers to promote their own products and to associate their company with patriotism.

policy reflected the widespread fear among union members of immigrants working so cheaply that they would steal jobs from others. In the West such fears were directed particularly against the Chinese, and they were heightened when California railroad magnate Leland Stanford declared, "[O]pen the door and let everybody come who wants to come . . . until you get enough [immigrants] here to reduce the price of labor to such a point that its cheapness will stop their coming." In 1877 San Francisco workers demonstrating for an eight-hour workday destroyed twenty-five Chinese-run laundries and terrorized the local Chinese population. In 1880 both major party platforms included anti-Chinese immigration plans. Two years later, Congress passed the Chinese Exclusion Act, placing a ten-year moratorium on Chinese immigration. Nevertheless, sporadic labor violence against the Chinese continued.

Although inspired by Powderly's vision of a harmonious and cooperative future, most rank-and-file Knights of Labor were more interested in immediate issues such as wage cuts, production speedups, and deteriorating working conditions. Specifically, they strongly disagreed with Powderly's antistrike position. In 1883–1884 local branches of the Knights led a series of spontaneous strikes that elicited only reluctant support from the national leadership. In 1885, however, when Jay Gould tried to eradicate the Knights of Labor from his Wabash railroad by firing active union members, Powderly and his executive board recognized that the survival of their organization was at stake. They instructed all Knights employed by the Wabash line to walk off the job and those working for other lines to refuse to handle Wabash cars. This highly effective action crippled the Wabash's operations. To the nation's amazement, the arrogant Jay Gould met with Powderly and agreed to halt his campaign against the Knights of Labor. "The Wabash victory is with the Knights," declared a St. Louis newspaper; "no such victory has ever before been secured in this or any other country."

With this apparent triumph, membership in the Knights of Labor soared. By 1886 more than seven hundred thousand workers were organized in nearly six thousand locals. Turning to political action that fall, the Knights mounted campaigns in nearly two hundred towns and cities nationwide, electing several mayors and judges (Powderly himself had served as mayor of Scranton since 1878) and claimed a role in electing a dozen congressmen. In state legislatures they secured passage of laws banning convict labor, and at the national level they lobbied successfully for a law against the importation of foreign contract labor. Conservatives warned darkly that the Knights could cripple the economy and take over the country if they chose.

But in fact, the organization's strength soon waned. The leadership lost control of the membership during the period of explosive growth, and with the failure of a series of unauthorized strikes in 1886—including one targeted at Jay Gould, who had resumed his vendetta against the Knights—disillusionment spread. The national reaction to the Haymarket riot (see below) contributed to the decline. By the late 1880s, the Knights of Labor was but a shadow of its former self. Nevertheless, the organization had given a major impetus to the labor movement and had awakened in thousands of workers a sense of group solidarity and potential strength. Powderly, who survived to 1924, always remained proud of his role "in forcing to the forefront the cause of misunderstood and downtrodden humanity."

As the Knights of Labor weakened, another national labor organization, pursuing more immediate and practical goals, was gaining strength. The skilled craft unions had long been uncomfortable with labor organizations like the Knights that welcomed skilled and unskilled alike. They were also concerned that the Knights' emphasis on broad reform goals would undercut their own commitment to better wages and to protecting the interests of their particular crafts. The break came in May 1886 when the craft unions left the Knights of Labor to form the American Federation of Labor (AFL).

From the first the AFL replaced the Knights' grand visions with practical tactics aimed at bread-and-butter issues. The AFL approach was aptly expressed in 1885 by Adolph Strasser, president of the International Cigar Makers' Union. Asked by a Senate labor committee about his union's "ultimate ends," Strasser responded, "We have no ultimate ends. We are going on from day to day. We fight only for immediate objectives. . . ."

This philosophy was vigorously pursued by Samuel Gompers, the English immigrant cigar maker who became head of the AFL in 1886 and led it for nearly forty years, until his death in 1924. Gompers believed in "trade unionism, pure and simple." The stocky, mustachioed labor leader had lost faith in utopian social reforms and catchall labor organizations in the 1870s, quickly recognizing that "the poor, the hungry, have not the strength to engage in a conflict even when life is at stake." To stand up to the corporations, Gompers asserted, labor would have to harness the bargaining power of the *skilled* workers, whom employers could not easily replace, and concentrate on the practical goals of raising wages and reducing hours.

A master tactician, Gompers believed that the trend toward large-scale industrial organization necessitated a comparable degree of organization by labor. He also recognized, however, that the skilled craft unions that had come together to form the AFL retained a strong commitment to controlling their own affairs. The challenge was to persuade the craftsworkers from the various trades to join forces without violating their sense of craft autonomy. Gompers's solution was to organize the AFL as a *federation* of trade unions, each retaining control of its own members but all linked by an executive council to coordinate strategy during boycotts and strike actions. "We want to make the trade union movement under the AFL as distinct as the billows, yet one as the sea," he told a national convention.

Focusing the federation's efforts on short-term improvements in wages and hours, Gompers carefully sidestepped divisive political issues. The new organization's platform did, however, demand an eight-hour workday, employers' liability, and mine-safety laws. By 1904, under Gompers's conservative tutelage, the AFL had grown to more than 1.6 million strong.

Although the unions held up an ideal toward which many might strive, labor organizations as a whole in the late nineteenth century remained rather weak. Less than 5 percent of the workforce joined union ranks. Split between skilled artisans and common laborers, separated along ethnic and religious lines, and divided over tactics, the unions battled with only occasional effectiveness against the growing power of corporate enterprise. Lacking financial resources, they typically watched from the sidelines during economic hard times as unorganized workers launched wildcat strikes that sometimes turned violent.

Strikes and Labor Violence

Americans had lived with a high level of violence from the nation's beginnings, and the nineteenth century, with its international and civil wars, urban riots, and Indian-white conflict, was no exception. Terrible labor clashes toward the end of the century were part of this continuing pattern, but they nevertheless shocked and dismayed contemporaries. From 1881 to 1905, there erupted close to thirty-seven thousand strikes, in which nearly 7 million workers participated. Some of these strikes involved property damage and looting. To a shaken middle class, unaware of the hardships suffered by workers, the United States seemed on the verge of a class war.

In a period of chronic labor unrest, certain years stood out. One such year was 1877. The trouble actually began in 1873, when a Wall Street crash triggered a major depression. Six thousand businesses closed the following year, and many more cut wages and laid off workers in a desperate effort to survive. Striking Pennsylvania coal miners were fired and evicted from their homes. Tramps roamed the streets in New York and Chicago. The tension took a deadly turn in 1877 during a wildcat railroad strike. Ignited by a wage reduction on the Baltimore and Ohio Railroad in July, the strike exploded up and down the railroad lines, spreading quickly to New York, Pittsburgh, St. Louis, Kansas City, Chicago, and San Francisco. Rioters in Pittsburgh torched Union Depot and the Pennsylvania Railroad

Attention Workingmen!

GREAT

MASS-MEETING

TO-NIGHT, at 7.30 o'clock,

AT THE

HAYMARKET, Randolph St., Bet. Desplaines and Halsted.

Good Speakers will be present to denounce the latest
atrocious act of the police, the shooting of our
fellow-workmen yesterday afternoon.

THE EXECUTIVE COMMITTEE.

Achtung, Arbeiter!

Große

Massen-Versammlung

Heute Abend, ½8 Uhr, auf dem

Heumarkt, Randolph-Straße, zwischen
Desplaines- u. Halsted-Str.

Labor Rally Poster, 1886
*Business interests tried to
smear labor unions as violence-prone and dominated
by foreign radicals. Pub-
lished in both German and
English, this labor poster
lent credence to such
attacks.*

The same middle-class Americans who worried about corporate abuse of power also grew terrified of mob violence from the bottom ranks of society.

Employers capitalized on the public hysteria to crack down on labor. Many required their workers to sign "yellow dog" contracts in which they promised not to strike or join a union. Some hired Pinkerton agents to serve as their own private police force and, when necessary, turned to the federal government and the U.S. Army to suppress labor unrest.

More strikes and violence followed in the 1880s. On May Day 1886, 340,000 workers walked off their jobs in support of the campaign for an eight-hour workday. Strikers in Cincinnati virtually shut down the city for nearly a month. Also in 1886, Chicago police shot and killed four strikers at the McCormick Harvester plant on May 3. At a protest rally the next evening in the city's Haymarket Square, someone threw a bomb from a nearby building, killing or fatally wounding seven policemen. The police in turn fired wildly into the crowd and killed four demonstrators.

Public reaction was immediate. Business leaders and middle-class citizens lashed out at labor activists and particularly at the sponsors of the Haymarket meet-

roundhouse. By the time the newly installed president Rutherford B. Hayes had called out the troops and quelled the strike two weeks later, nearly one hundred people had died, and two-thirds of the nation's railroads stood idle.

The railroad strike stunned middle-class America. The religious press responded hysterically. "If the club of the policeman, knocking out the brains of the rioter, will answer, then well and good," declared one Congregational journal, "[but if not] then bullets and bayonets . . . constitute the one remedy. . . . Napoleon was right when he said that the way to deal with a mob was to exterminate it."

ing, most of whom were associated with a German-language anarchist newspaper, the *Arbeiter Zeitung.* Eight were arrested and tried. Declared the Illinois attorney general: "Convict these men, make examples of them. Hang them, and you save our institutions." Although no evidence connected them directly to the bomb throwing, all were convicted, and four were executed. One committed suicide in prison. In Haymarket's aftermath still more Americans became convinced that the nation was in the grip of a deadly foreign conspiracy, and animosity toward labor unions intensified.

Stormy confrontations between business and labor continued into the 1890s. Federal troops were called out to crush a strike of silver miners in the Coeur d'Alene district of northern Idaho in 1892. Federal forces intervened again that same year when violence flared after managers cut wages, locked out the workers, and crushed the labor union at the Carnegie Steel Company plant in Homestead, Pennsylvania (see "A Place in Time").

The most systematic use of troops to smash union power came in 1894, during a strike against the Pullman Palace Car Company. George Pullman, a self-taught entrepreneur who had pioneered in the manufacture of elegant dining, parlor, and sleeping cars for the nation's railroads, in 1880 had constructed a factory and town, called Pullman, ten miles south of Chicago. The carefully planned community provided solid brick houses for the workers; beautiful parks and playgrounds; a large central building housing a bank, a theater, and a public library; and even its own sewage-treatment plant. But despite the benefits he gave the workers, Pullman closely policed their activities, outlawed saloons, and insisted that his properties turn a profit.

When the depression of 1893 hit, Pullman responded to a decline in orders by slashing workers' wages without reducing their rents. In reaction thousands of workers joined the newly formed American Railway Union and went on strike. They were led by a fiery young organizer, Eugene V. Debs, who vowed "to strip the mask of hypocrisy from the pretended philanthropist and show him to the world as an oppressor of labor." Union members working for the nation's largest railroads refused to switch Pullman cars, thus paralyzing rail traffic in and out of Chicago.

In response to the crisis, the General Managers' Association, an organization of top railroad executives, set out to break the union. The General Managers' first step was to import strikebreakers from among jobless easterners. Next they asked U.S. attorney general

Homestead:
The Town and the Mill,
1870–1907

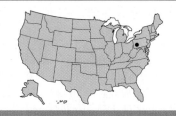

Homestead Workers

Shirts rolled up to expose their brawny arms, Homestead workers prided themselves on possessing the strength and toughness to work in the dangerous mills.

On a rainy fall day in 1893, the writer Hamlin Garland crossed the Monongahela River on a ferry and debarked at a grimy industrial town near Pittsburgh. On assignment for *McClure's* magazine, Garland was investigating the "perilous trade" of steel making at Homestead, Pennsylvania, where the Carnegie Steel Company ran a major mill. One year before, state troops had suppressed a violent strike there. Garland had been sympathetic to the strikers, and he harbored grim expectations as he approached the plant.

From the banks of the polluted Monongahela, he could see the town and the mill sprawled over a hillside. Near the water's edge stood clusters of large sheds topped by tall smokestacks. Farther up the hill, Garland noted rows of dingy workers' houses, covered with soot and dust. All in all, the place seemed "as squalid and unlovely as could be imagined," he reported. "The streets of the town were horrible; the buildings were poor; the sidewalks were sunken and full of holes." Everywhere "groups of pale, lean men slouched in faded garments, grimy with the soot and grease of the mills."

Barely two decades earlier, the site of Homestead had been pastureland. In 1870 two large farms, the McClure and West homesteads, dominated the area, surrounded by smaller farms. The next year, a commercial venture, the Homestead Bank and Life Insurance Company, bought up the land and subdivided it into building lots. The company planned to create a residential suburb from which commuters could easily reach Pittsburgh—only seven miles away—on a new railroad line. But Homestead's suburban days were short-lived. In 1878, when the town's population reached six hundred, a glass factory was built. Three years later a steel mill was constructed on the riverbank, and in 1886 Carnegie's company purchased the mill. The Homestead facilities proved ideal for steel making. The Monongahela ensured an ample water supply. Running through a region of bituminous coal mines, the river provided a conduit for fuel as well. New railroads brought in iron ore from Michigan mines and later from Minnesota. Within five years Carnegie had doubled the mill's capital and expanded its work force. By 1892 the sheds of the Carnegie works ranged over sixty acres. The town had eleven thousand residents, of whom thirty-eight hundred were mill employees.

Producing steel was inherently dangerous. Deaths from burns and other accidents were commonplace. Men worked twelve-hour shifts, and daily faced white-hot ingots, fast-moving overhead cranes, and exploding furnaces. To Garland, the mill was hell itself: "A roar of a hundred lions, a thunder as of cannons, flames that made the electric light look like a twinkling blue star, jarring clang of falling iron, burst of spluttering flakes of fire, scream of terrible saws, shifting of mighty trucks with hiss of Steam!"

From within this industrial inferno, the Amalgamated Association of Iron and Steel Workers had won recognition in 1889. Andrew Carnegie had at first accepted the union, but he later had decided, despite public statements to the contrary, that it had to be destroyed. Following Carnegie's instructions, company president Henry Clay Frick informed the union of its dismissal in June 1892. One by one, the mills were shut down and the workers locked out. Mobilizing in self-defense, the workers on the night of July 6 identified two barges making their way up the river toward the mills. The boats carried more than 300 armed men from the Pinkerton

Homestead Life

An oppressive atmosphere hung over Homestead. The heat, particularly unbearable in summer, provided work for numerous water boys in the mills. As for the quality of the air, one observer noted that "the idiosyncrasy of this town is smoke. It rolls sullenly in slow folds from the great chimneys of the iron-foundries, and settles down in black, slimy pools on the muddy streets."

National Detective Agency. When the Pinkertons tried to disembark, a day-long battle ensued in which seven union members and three Pinkertons died. A week later, the governor of Pennsylvania sent 8,000 National Guardsmen to restore order.

By December the mills had resumed full operation, the union had been broken, and the town of Homestead had been transformed by the influx of nearly 3,000 strikebreakers lured by the promise of jobs during a downturn in the national economy. Although the steel mills that Hamlin Garland visited seemed unchanged, Homestead as a community was devastated. Many former workmen were ruined. "The atmosphere was at times heavy with disappointment and hopelessness," commented another visitor. Not until after World War I would steel workers again try to reform the oppressive work conditions in the steel industry.

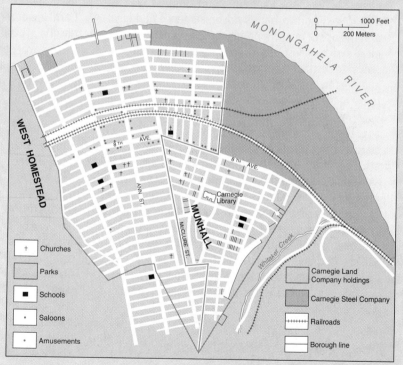

Homestead

The Carnegie Steel mills not only physically dominated the town but also occupied the most desirable land near the river. This location provided easy access to the barges that brought in supplies.

SOURCE: Pittsburgh Survey. Maps under direction of Shelby Harrison, 1908.

597b

Richard Olney, who sat on the board of directors of three major railroad networks, for a federal injunction (court order) against the strikers for allegedly refusing to move railroad cars carrying U.S. mail.

In fact, union members had volunteered to switch mail cars onto any trains that did not carry Pullman cars, and it was the railroads' managers who were delaying the mail by refusing to send their trains without the full complement of cars. Nevertheless, Olney, supported by President Grover Cleveland and citing the Sherman Anti-Trust Act, secured an injunction against the leaders of the American Railway Union for restraint of commerce. When the union refused to obey the injunction and order its members back to work, Debs was arrested and federal troops poured in. During the ensuing riot, seven hundred freight cars were burned, thirteen people died, and fifty-three were wounded. By July 18 the strike had been crushed.

By playing upon a popular identification of strikers with anarchism and violence, crafty corporate leaders like Frick and Pullman persuaded state and federal officials to cripple organized labor's ability to bargain with business. When the Supreme Court (in the 1895 case *In re Debs*) upheld Debs's prison sentence and legalized the use of injunctions against labor unions, the judicial system gave business a potent new weapon with which to restrain labor organizers. Despite successive attempts by the National Labor Union, Knights of Labor, American Federation of Labor, and American Railway Union to build a strong working-class movement, aggressive employer associations and conservative state and local officials hamstrung their efforts. In sharp contrast to Great Britain and Germany, where state officials often mediated disputes between labor and capital, federal and state officials in the United States increasingly sided with manufacturers. American unions—ineffective in the political arena, blocked by state officials, and frustrated by court decisions—failed to expand their base of support. Post–Civil War labor turmoil had sapped the vitality of organized labor and given it a negative public image that it would not shed until the 1930s.

Social Thinkers Probe for Alternatives

The widespread industrial disorder was particularly unsettling when juxtaposed with the growing evidence of working-class destitution. In 1879, after observing three men rummaging through garbage to find food, Walt Whitman wrote, "If the United States, like the

countries of the Old World, are also to grow vast crops of poor, desperate, dissatisfied, nomadic, miserably-waged populations, such as we see looming upon us of late years . . . , then our republican experiment, notwithstanding all its surface-successes, is at heart an unhealthy failure."

Whitman's bleak speculations were part of a general public debate over the social meaning of the new industrial order. At stake was a larger issue: should government become the mechanism for helping the poor and regulating big business?

Defenders of capitalism preached the laissez-faire ("hands-off") argument, insisting that government should never attempt to control business. They buttressed their case by citing Scottish economist Adam Smith, who had argued in *The Wealth of Nations* (1776) that self-interest acted as an "invisible hand" in the marketplace, automatically regulating the supply of and demand for goods and services. In "The Gospel of Wealth," an influential essay published in 1889, Andrew Carnegie justified laissez-faire by applying to human society the evolutionary theories of British scientist Charles Darwin. "The law of competition," Carnegie argued, "may be sometimes hard for the individual, [but] it is best for the race, because it insures the survival of the fittest in every department." Ignoring the scramble among businesses in the late nineteenth century to *eliminate* competition, Carnegie praised an unregulated competitive environment as a source of positive long-term social benefits.

Tough-minded Yale professor William Graham Sumner shared Carnegie's disapproval of government interference. In his combative book *What Social Classes Owe to Each Other* (1883), Sumner asserted that inexorable natural laws controlled the social order: "A drunkard in the gutter is just where he ought to be. . . . The law of survival of the fittest was not made by man, and it cannot be abrogated by man. We can only, by interfering with it, produce the survival of the unfittest." The social theorists, sentimental humanitarians, and "labor fakers" intent on uplifting the poor and needy, he insisted, were actually harming the "forgotten man"—the hard-working individual whose taxes were expected to fund their do-good schemes. The state, declared Sumner, owed its citizens nothing but law, order, and basic political rights.

This conservative, laissez-faire brand of Social Darwinism (as such ideas came to be called) did not go unchallenged. In *Dynamic Sociology* (1883), Lester Frank Ward, a geologist with the U.S. Geological Survey, argued that contrary to Sumner's claim, the supposed "laws" of nature *could* be circumvented by human will. Just as scientists had applied their knowledge to breeding superior livestock, government experts could use the power of the state to regulate big business, protect society's weaker members, and prevent the heedless exploitation of natural resources.

Henry George, a self-taught San Francisco newspaper editor and economic theorist, proposed to solve the nation's uneven distribution of wealth through what he called the single tax. In *Progress and Poverty* (1879), he noted that speculators reaped huge profits from the rising price of land that they neither developed nor improved. By taxing this "unearned increment," the government could obtain the funds necessary to ameliorate the misery caused by industrialization. The result would bring the benefits of socialism—a state-controlled economic system that distributed resources according to need—without socialism's great disadvantage, the stifling of individual initiative. George's program was so popular that he lectured around the country and only narrowly missed being elected mayor of New York in 1886.

The vision of a harmonious industrialized society evoked by labor leaders like William H. Sylvis and Terence V. Powderly was even more vividly expressed in the utopian novel *Looking Backward* (1888) by Massachusetts newspaper editor Edward Bellamy. Cast as a fantastic glimpse into the future, Bellamy's novel tells of Julian West, who falls asleep in the year 1888 and awakens in the year 2000 to find a nation without poverty or strife. In this future world, West learns, a completely centralized, state-run economy and a new religion of solidarity have combined to create a society in which everyone works for the common welfare. "Let but the famine-stricken nation . . . regulate for the common good the course of the life-giving stream," declares West, "and the earth would bloom like one garden, and none of its children lack any good thing." Bellamy's vision of a conflict-free society where all shared equally in industrialization's benefits so inspired middle-class Americans fearful of corporate power and working-class violence that nearly five hundred local Bellamyite organizations, called Nationalist clubs, sprang up to try to turn his dream into reality.

Ward, George, and Bellamy did not deny the benefits of the existing industrial order; they simply sought to humanize it. These utopian reformers envisioned a harmonious society whose members all worked together. Marxist socialists advanced a different view. Elaborated by German philosopher and radical agitator Karl Marx (1818–1883) in *Das Kapital* (1867) and other works, Marxism rested on the proposition (which Adam Smith had also accepted) that the labor required to produce a commodity was the only true measure of that commodity's value. Thus any profit made by the capitalist employer was "surplus value" appropriated from the exploited workers. As competition among capitalists increased, Marx predicted, wages would decline to starvation levels, and more and more capitalists would be driven out of business. At last society would be divided between a shrinking bourgeoisie (capitalists, merchants, and middle-class professionals) and an impoverished proletariat (the workers). At this point the proletariat would revolt and seize control of the state and of the means of production and distribution. Although Marx's thought was dominated by an insistence on class struggle as the essence of modern history, his eyes were also fixed on the shining vision of the communist millennium that the revolution would eventually usher in—a classless utopia in which the state would "wither away" and all exploitation would cease. To lead the working class in its coming showdown with capitalism, Marx and his collaborator Friedrich Engels helped found a series of socialist parties in Europe, whose strength grew steadily beginning in the 1870s.

Despite Marx's keen interest in the United States, Marxism proved to have little appeal in late-nineteenth-century America outside a tiny group of primarily German-born immigrants. The Marxist-oriented Socialist Labor party (1877) had attracted only about fifteen hundred members by 1890. More alarming to the public at large was the handful of anarchists, again mostly immigrants, who rejected Marxist discipline and preached the destruction of capitalism, the violent overthrow of the state, and the immediate introduction of a stateless utopia. In 1892 Alexander Berkman, a Russian immigrant anarchist, attempted to assassinate Henry Clay Frick, the manager of Andrew Carnegie's Homestead Steel Works. Entering Frick's office with a pistol, Berkman shot him in the neck and then tried to stab him. But a carpenter by chance working in Frick's office overpowered him. Rather than igniting a workers' insurrection that would usher in a new social order, as he had hoped, Berkman's act simply earned him a long prison sentence and confirmed the middle-class stereotype of "labor agitators" as lawless and violent.

CONCLUSION

By 1900 industrialization had propelled the United States into the forefront of the world's major powers, lowered the cost of goods through mass production, generated thousands of jobs, and made available a wide range of new consumer products. Few Americans would readily have given up their new material benefits.

Despite these advantages, all thinking people recognized that industrialization's cost was high. The rise of the giant corporations had been achieved through savage competition, exploited workers, shady business practices, polluted factory sites, and the collapse of an economic order built on craft skills and an apprenticeship system that had forged bonds between skilled and unskilled labor. Outbursts of labor violence, and the ominous phenomenon of urban slums and grinding poverty, showed starkly that all was not well in industrial America.

To improve their reputations, the great capitalists channeled at least a part of their fortunes into ostentatious public benefactions, including art museums, university endowments, and symphony orchestras. In contrast to Europe, where fortune remained within the family, some U.S. millionaires developed a lively tradition of private philanthropy.

Nevertheless, Americans remained profoundly ambivalent about the new industrial order. Caught between their desire for the higher standard of living that industrialization made possible and their fears of capitalist power and social chaos, Americans of the 1880s and 1890s sought strategies that would preserve those benefits while alleviating the undesirable social by-products. Efforts to regulate railroads at the state level, and such national measures as the Interstate Commerce Act and the Sherman Anti-Trust Act, as well as the fervor with which the ideas of a utopian theorist like Edward Bellamy were embraced, represented early manifestations of this impulse. In the Progressive Era of the early twentieth century, Americans would redouble their efforts to formulate political and social responses to the nation's economic transformation after the Civil War.

CHRONOLOGY

1837 Magnetic telegraph invented.

1859 First oil well drilled in Titusville, Pennsylvania.

1866 National Labor Union founded.

1869 First transcontinental railroad completed.
Knights of Labor organized.

1870 Standard Oil Company established.

1873 Panic of 1873 triggers a depression lasting until 1879.

1876 Alexander Graham Bell invents and patents the telephone.
Thomas A. Edison opens research laboratory at Menlo Park, New Jersey.

1877 Edison invents the phonograph.
Railway workers stage the first nationwide strike.

1879 Henry George, *Progress and Poverty.*
Edison perfects the incandescent lamp.

1881 Standard Oil Trust established.

1882 Edison opens the first electric power station on Pearl Street in New York City.
Chinese Exclusion Act.

1883 Railroads divide the country into time zones.

1883 William Graham Sumner, *What Social Classes Owe to Each Other.*
Lester Frank Ward, *Dynamic Sociology.*

1886 American Federation of Labor (AFL) formed.
Police and demonstrators clash at Haymarket Square in Chicago.

1887 Interstate Commerce Act establishes the Interstate Commerce Commission.

1888 Edward Bellamy, *Looking Backward.*

1889 Andrew Carnegie, "The Gospel of Wealth."

1890 Sherman Anti-Trust Act.

1892 Standard Oil of New Jersey and General Electric formed.
Steelworkers strike at Homestead, Pennsylvania.
World's Columbian Exposition opens in Chicago.
Miners strike at Coeur d'Alene, Idaho.

1893 Panic of 1893 triggers a depression lasting until 1897.

1894 Pullman Palace Car workers strike, supported by the National Railway Union.

1901 J. Pierpont Morgan organizes United States Steel.

FOR FURTHER READING

Edward L. Ayers, *The Promise of the New South: Life After Reconstruction* (1992). A comprehensive overview of economic and social change within the post–Civil War South.

Albro Martin, *Railroads Triumphant: The Growth, Rejection, and Rebirth of a Vital American Force* (1992). An excellent analysis of the railroads' impact on industrial and urban development in the late nineteenth century.

J. Carroll Moody and Alice Kessler-Harris, eds., *Perspectives on American Labor History: The Problems of Synthesis* (1989).

Essays on the role of gender and class within the American labor movement.

William Serrin, *Homestead: The Glory and Tragedy of an American Steel Town* (1992). A balanced account of a steel-making community.

Kim Voss, *The Making of American Exceptionalism: The Knights of Labor and Class Formation in the Nineteenth Century* (1993). A comparative analysis of American labor's attempts to mobilize workers in the face of business opposition.

ADDITIONAL BIBLIOGRAPHY

The Character of Industrial Change

Stephen Brier, ed., *Who Built America? Working People and the Nation's Economy, Politics, Culture, and Society* (1992); Alfred D. Chandler, Jr., *The Visible Hand: The Managerial Revolution in American Business* (1977); Victoria C. Hattam, *Labor Visions and State Power: The Origins of Business Unionism in the United States* (1993); Ari and Olive Hoogenboom, *A History of the ICC: From Panacea to Palliative* (1976); Thomas P. Hughes, *Networks of Power: Electrification in Western Society, 1880–1930* (1983); Maury Klein, *The Flowering of the Third America: The Making of An Organizational Society, 1850–1920* (1993); Naomi R. Lamoreaux, *The Great Merger Movement in American Business, 1895–1904* (1985); Harold Livesay, *Andrew Carnegie and the Rise of Big Business* (1975); Martin V. Melosi, *Coping with Abundance: Energy and Environment in Industrial America* (1985); Andre Millard, *Edison and the Business of Innovation* (1990); Alan Trachtenberg, *The Incorporation of America: Culture and Society in the Gilded Age* (1982); Olivier Zunz, *Making America Corporate, 1870–1920* (1990).

The New South

James C. Cobb, *Industrialization and Southern Society, 1877–1984* (1984), and *The Most Southern Place on Earth: The Mississippi Delta and the Roots of Regional Identity* (1992); Paul M. Gaston, *The New South Creed: A Study in Southern Mythmaking* (1970); Janette T. Greenwood, *Bittersweet Legacy: The Black and White "Better Classes" in Charlotte, 1850–1910* (1994); Steven Hahn and Jonathan Prude, eds., *The Countryside in the Age of Capitalist Transformation: Essays in the Social History of Rural America* (1985); Jacquelyn D. Hall et al., *Like a Family: The Making of a Southern Cotton Mill World* (1987); Robert Higgs, *Competition and Coercion: Blacks in the American Economy, 1865–1904* (1977); Roger L. Ransom and Richard Sutch, *One Kind of Freedom: The Economic Consequences of Emancipation* (1977); Peter Wallenstein, *From Slave South to New South: Public Policy in Nineteenth-Century Georgia* (1987); Jonathan M. Wiener, *Social Origins of the New South: Alabama, 1860–1885* (1978); C. Vann Woodward, *Origins of the New South, 1877–1913* (1951); Gavin Wright, *Old South, New South: Revolutions in the Southern Economy Since the Civil War* (1986).

Industrial Work and the Work Force

Ava Baron, *Work Engendered: Toward a New History of American Labor* (1991); John Bodnar, *Immigration and Industrialization: Ethnicity in an American Mill Town* (1977); David Brody, *In Labor's Cause: Main Themes on the History of the American Worker* (1993); John T. Cumbler, *Working-Class Community in Industrial America* (1979); Ileen A. DeVault, *Sons and Daughters of Labor: Class and Clerical Work in Turn-of-the-Century Pittsburgh* (1990); Melvin Dubovsky, *The State and Labor in Modern America* (1994); William F. Hartford, *Working People of Holyoke: Class and Ethnicity in a Massachusetts Mill Town, 1850–1960* (1990); Alice Kessler-Harris, *Out to Work: A History of Wage-Earning Women in the United States* (1982); S. J. Kleinberg, *The Shadow of the Mills: Working-Class Families in Pittsburgh, 1870–1907* (1989); Bruce Levine, ed., *Who Built America?* (1991); David Montgomery, *The Fall of the House of Labor: The Workplace, the State, and American Labor Activism, 1865–1925* (1987); Daniel Nelson, *Managers and Workers: Origins of the New Factory System in the United States, 1850–1920* (1975); Peter Rachleff, *Black Labor in Richmond, 1865–1890* (1984); Stephen J. Ross, *Workers on the Edge: Work, Leisure, and Politics in Industrializing Cincinnati, 1788–1890* (1985); Peter R. Shergold, *Working Class Life* (1982); Stephan Thernstrom, *The Other Bostonians: Poverty and Progress in the American Metropolis, 1880–1970* (1973).

Industrial Conflict

Paul Avrich, *The Haymarket Tragedy* (1984); Robert C. Bannister, *Social Darwinism: Science and Myth in Anglo-American Social Thought* (1979); Stanley Bruder, *Pullman* (1967); Mari Jo Buhle, *Women and American Socialism, 1870–1920* (1983); David P. Demarest, Jr., ed., *"The River Ran Red": Homestead 1892* (1992); Margaret M. Marsh, *Anarchist Women, 1870–1920* (1981); David Montgomery, *Workers' Control in America: Studies in the History of Work, Technology, and Labor Struggles* (1979); Alun Munslow, *Discourse and Culture: The Creation of America, 1870–1920* (1992); Richard J. Oestreicher, *Solidarity and Fragmentation: Working People and Class Consciousness in Detroit* (1986); Shelton Stromquist, *A Generation of Boomers: The Pattern of Railroad Labor Conflict in Nineteenth-Century America* (1993); John L. Thomas, *Alternative America: Henry George, Edward Bellamy, Henry Demarest Lloyd, and the Adversary Tradition* (1983); Daniel J. Walkowitz, *Worker City, Company Town: Iron and Cotton Workers Protest in Troy and Cohoes, New York, 1855–1884* (1978).

Washington Street, Indianapolis at Dusk
by Theodore Groll, c. 1892–1895 (detail)

THE TRANSFORMATION OF URBAN AMERICA

Incensed by the appalling crowding in New York City tenement housing in 1890, newspaper reporter Jacob Riis exploded in anger. He had toured congested inner-city apartments, poking into attics and cellars where families were jammed together so tightly that their members had to sleep in shifts. Riis published his findings in a dramatic exposé entitled *How the Other Half Lives* (1890).

With a sure eye for the distressing detail, he guided the reader into a typical Cherry Street tenement. "Be a little careful, please!" he warned. "The hall is dark and you might stumble over the children pitching pennies back there. . . . Here is a door. Listen! That short hacking cough, that tiny, helpless wail—what do they mean? They mean that the soiled bow of white you saw on the door downstairs will have another story to tell—Oh! a sadly familiar story—before the day is at an end. The child is dying of measles. With half a chance it might have lived; but it had none. That dark bedroom killed it."

To Riis, such tenements were significant not only as the homes of the immigrant poor and destitute but also as the incubators of disease and vice. With three of its wards averaging more than 285,000 people per square mile, New York City in 1890 epitomized for Riis the depths to which conditions in urban America had sunk. "In the tenements all the influences make for evil," he warned, "because they are the hotbeds of the epidemics that carry death to rich and poor alike [and] the nurseries of pauperism and crime that fill our jails and police courts."

Riis's grim view of tenement life, which reflected his secure middle-class position, contrasted sharply with many immigrants' remembrances of the tenement districts' vibrant street life, resonating with the melodies of organ grinders and the cries of peddlers, baked-potato and hot-corn vendors, and soda dispensers. Although their new homes in the tenements were crowded, immigrants often congregated elbow-to-elbow in the hallways; left apartment doors open to invite visitors; and joked, sang, and played music to recreate the village intimacy remembered from their homelands. "How the people did enjoy that music," reminisced one East Sider from New York. "Everyone would be at their windows listening. . . . Then the people would clap their hands; it was inspiring in a neighborhood like that."

Their perspectives differed markedly, but Riis and the East Sider each recalled an era of bounding population growth that had transformed New York and other American cities in the late nineteenth century. Not only on the East Coast but south to New Orleans and west to San Francisco, cities had swelled at an astonishing pace. Between 1870 and 1900, New Orleans's population nearly doubled, Buffalo's tripled, and Chicago's increased more than fivefold. By the turn of the century, Philadelphia, New York, and Chicago had each passed the 1-million-person mark, and 40 percent of all Americans lived in cities. In 1900 New York's 3.4 million inhabitants alone almost exactly equaled the nation's entire urban population in 1850.

The spectacular urban growth, fueled by migration from the New England countryside and an influx of nearly 11 million foreign immigrants between 1870 and 1900, created a dynamic new environment for economic development. Lured by the expectation of bountiful jobs, these new arrivals on the urban scene provided an inexpensive work force for countless small businesses and industries. Mushrooming cities thus made possible an unparalleled concentration of resources and markets that in turn dramatically stimulated national economic expansion. Like the frontier, the city symbolized opportunity for all comers.

Yet the city's unprecedented scale and diversity threatened traditional expectations about community life and social stability. Rural America had been a place of face-to-face personal relations, a clearly recognized social hierarchy, and a homogeneous population sharing the same likes and dislikes. In contrast, the city was a seething cauldron where a medley of immigrant groups contended with each other and with native-born Americans for jobs, power, and influence. Moreover, the same rapid growth that energized manufacturing and production strained city services and generated terrible housing and sanitation problems.

Native-born American city dwellers found the noise, stench, and congestion of this transformed landscape disturbing. Like Jacob Riis, they worried about the newcomers' squalid tenements, fondness for drink, and strange social customs. Thus when native-born reformers set about cleaning up the city and "Americanizing" the foreigners, they sought not only to improve the physical environment but also to destroy the distinctive customs that made immigrant culture different from their own. Resenting the attack on their way of life, the recent arrivals fought back and resisted change.

The late nineteenth century thus witnessed an intense struggle among these diverse urban constituencies to control the city politically and benefit from its

economic and cultural potential. The stakes were high, for America was increasingly becoming an urban nation.

URBAN EXPANSION

Between 1840 and 1900, the physical appearance of American cities was transformed. Responding to a critical need for factory sites, housing, and offices, land speculators, developers, and builders broke up urban space into residential neighborhoods, parks, downtown business districts, and commercial and manufacturing areas. Opportunistic business leaders pioneered transportation systems that moved thousands of urban commuters from home to work and back again by means of streetcars, trains, and eventually electric trolleys and subway cars. Working feverishly to keep pace with the demand for new housing, local carpenters and construction companies expanded the cities' boundaries by developing new suburban communities along railroad lines in the countryside, where land was cheaper and residents could enjoy a less crowded environment than the bustling downtown afforded.

The New Urban World

The rapid growth of cities large and small after the Civil War created a national urban network—an interconnected web of regional metropolises, specialized manufacturing cities, and smaller subordinate communities of varying size and function. Linked by rail lines and waterways, major cities like Boston, New York, Philadelphia, Chicago, Cincinnati, and San Francisco became regional centers that provided manufacturing plants and financial services for the surrounding countryside. Chicago, for example, emerged in the 1850s in the upper Midwest as the region's center for the shipping and marketing of lumber, meat, and grain. A scant thirty years later, its factories employed the largest industrial work force—over seventy-five thousand people—west of the Appalachians. Manufacturing nearly a quarter of a billion dollars worth of goods, the city's diverse industries also polluted the region's waterways and littered the landscape. Smaller cities, while equally destructive of the environment, often specialized in particular products or processes: for example, Holyoke, Massachusetts, in paper; Birmingham, Alabama, in steel; Minneapolis, Minnesota, in milling

Law Sakes Alive! What Are You Doing Baby? *(Detail) by Charles Markham, c. 1870 This spirited painting of a New York market in the 1870s captures the bustle of urban life in post–Civil War America.*

and lumber; Butte, Montana, in mining; Corning, New York, in glass; and Kansas City, Missouri, in processing and shipping beef.

Whatever the source of their growth, hundreds of cities expanded so briskly in the post–Civil War years that the nature of urban life was forever changed. In contrast to rural and small-town America, where the seasonality of agriculture dictated the rhythms of daily existence, cities pulsed with people rushing to beat deadlines. Moreover, whereas small-town residents knew their neighbors and shared their outlook, city dwellers lived in a world of strangers and confronted ethnic and class differences at every turn. Even the concept of time took on a new meaning in the city. Rural dwellers went to bed early, but urbanites walked about, played, and shopped late into the night. One social worker wrote, "Every night the brightly lighted main thoroughfares, with the gleaming store-windows, . . . , provide a promenade for thousands who find in walk and talk along the pavement a cheap form of social entertainment."

A Revolution in Transportation

Until the first quarter of the nineteenth century, most cities functioned as compact communities covering perhaps a three-square-mile area. Within these "walking" cities, so called because a person could easily walk from one end to the other, rich and poor lived in close proximity, with the wealthy near the commercial center and the poor scattered in basements around town. The development of new transportation systems, beginning in the 1830s with the stagecoach and continuing with the steam ferry and the horse-drawn streetcar, created a technological revolution that turned these older cities literally inside out. The rich and wellborn moved to the city's edge, while the poor migrated inward, settling in abandoned mansions that were subdivided and then subdivided again to accommodate their increasing numbers.

The first urban transportation networks, operating regularly scheduled city stagecoaches (omnibuses) over fixed routes, appeared in New York in the 1820s. Over the next two decades, smoother-riding horse-drawn streetcars, pulled by a single powerful horse along railway tracks in the streets, replaced them. By the 1880s, 415 horsecar companies carried 188 million passengers a year over more than six thousand miles of track. The horsecars provided easy transportation between city dwellers' places of work and their residences, which increasingly were separated.

The horsecars did have drawbacks. Extra animals were sometimes needed to pull the cars up hills, and hitching and unhitching them could take ten minutes. Observers recoiled as they watched panting horses, whipped by drivers, strain to pull the crowded cars. Many looked away in disgust as creatures that had stumbled and fallen were destroyed where they lay. In New York alone, an estimated fifteen thousand overworked beasts died each year in the 1880s.

Horse droppings were another problem. Health officials in Rochester, New York, estimated in 1900 that

Los Angeles Electric Railway Company, 1887
Electric trolley cars were quieter, cleaner, and less smelly than horse-pulled cars. Like most trolley lines in Los Angeles, this one was built to provide access to a new real estate development. Within three days, all building lots had been sold.

the excrement produced yearly by the city's fifteen thousand horses would fill a hole one acre in area and 175 feet deep and would breed 16 billion flies. Added to the mud and garbage that befouled city streets, the stinking heaps of dung moved officials to explore alternate transportation options.

Steam railroads were an obvious first choice. As early as 1849, fifty-nine commuter trains chugged into Boston daily from as far as fifteen miles away. But although steam engines could do the work of a hundred horses, they were designed for long hauls rather than short runs, and they functioned most efficiently when they pulled a large number of cars. To improve travel within the city, local officials explored more flexible alternatives that included cable cars and electric streetcars.

Chicago pioneered the most extensive cable-car system. Run by a circulating underground cable to which a conductor attached each vehicle, Chicago's cable cars by 1887 operated over more than eighty-six miles of track. More sanitary, better on hills, and quieter than horsecars and steam railways, cable cars marked a significant improvement in urban transportation. But high construction costs restricted cable operation to the most heavily traveled routes, and eventually cable cars proved profitable only in hilly cities such as San Francisco.

By the 1890s electric streetcars, called trolleys because of the four-wheeled spring mechanism that trolled along the overhead wires, had replaced horsecars and cable cars in most cities. First installed in Richmond, Virginia, and Montgomery, Alabama, electric streetcar systems shaped the urban environment in important ways. Unlike European transportation companies, which charged according to the distance traveled, American streetcar firms adopted a flat-fee policy, usually five cents per ride with free transfers. By subsidizing commuting with a uniform-fare system, streetcar companies enabled families to move farther and farther from the city's center without increasing their transportation expenses, thereby encouraging urban sprawl. Recognizing that streetcar lines required a certain density of population to be profitable, and that the expansion of the lines would substantially raise land values, most streetcar companies ran their transportation operations at a loss, purchased land at the city's periphery, and earned towering profits from the sale of real estate. When the suburban lands became fully settled, however, many streetcar companies went broke.

Streetcar lines, which radiated outward from the heart of the city like spokes on a wheel, also helped revitalize the city center. With crosstown routes so limited, commuters who wished to visit a different part of the city had to pass through the downtown. The practical effect of this arrangement was to improve commercial opportunities in the central business district. In 1874 Philadelphia merchant John Wanamaker, recognizing the potential created by the growing streetcar network, turned an old downtown railroad freight depot into an elaborate department store. Wanamaker's success in Philadelphia was duplicated by Morris Rich in Atlanta, Adam Gimbel and Rowland H. Macy in New York, Marshall Field in Chicago, and Joseph L. Hudson in Detroit. The inexpensive convenience of traveling by trolley made shopping downtown a new form of recreation for millions of Americans.

A Mobile Population

The expansion of streetcar systems, coupled with the completion of regional railroad networks, dramatically affected urban residential stability. Historians have long recognized that the immigrants and transplanted farm people who flooded into American cities in the late nineteenth century tended to move frequently. Only recently has it been discovered that the old elites in most of these cities were highly transient as well. Indeed, a fever to move seized much of the population in these years.

The reasons for this frenzied mobility were many. As city neighborhoods became crowded with people and congested with traffic, those who could headed for outlying residential areas, now conveniently accessible by streetcar. Others pulled up stakes in quest of the fashionable homes available on the city's periphery. Still others relocated because one could own a larger house for a lower cost in the new areas.

Omaha, Nebraska, typified many cities around the nation in the dizzying pace of its population's mobility. In the two decades before 1900, fewer than one-third of all Omaha residents lived in the same place for more than five years. In 1888 only 12.2 percent resided at the same address as they had in 1880. As the city's business district spread, rich and poor alike shifted residences rapidly.

A parallel movement *between* cities matched the frenetic residential shifts *within* cities. Both upper- and working-class urban families drifted from city to city in hopes of increasing their income or bettering their living conditions. Most cities, although growing in overall numbers because of the inpouring of newcomers, lost more than half their current inhabitants every decade. The actual population turnover was even greater, because many residents remained in town only a few

months or a year or two and therefore never even showed up in decade-by-decade reports. Historical demographers calculate that most U.S. cities in this period experienced an astonishing turnover of about three or four times their total population every ten years.

Contemporaries like Jacob Riis deplored the unprecedented rapidity and scale of residential change. Riis viewed the migration of the middle and upper classes to the suburban fringe, away from downtown congestion, as a selfish attempt to escape responsibility for improving inner-city neighborhoods. An immigrant himself, Riis complained that the privileged classes were deserting the poor. In a sense, he was correct. Although many well-to-do city dwellers were concerned about the destitute, they placed the happiness, health, and safety of their own families first.

Thus mobility and change were the norm in nineteenth-century urban society. New transportation systems facilitated considerable residential movement. Searching for new ways to better their lives, both rich and poor changed residences and jobs frequently. Just as the frontier West lured seekers of fresh beginnings and extravagant wealth, the city beckoned to the restless and ambitious with myriad exciting opportunities for advancement.

Migrants and Immigrants

The growing concentration of industries in urban settings produced demands for thousands of new workers in these years. The promise of good wages and a broad range of jobs drew many rural and small-town dwellers to the cities. So great was the migration from rural areas, especially New England, that some farm communities vanished from the map.

Young farm women led the exodus cityward. With the growing commercialization and specialization of farming in the late nineteenth century, farm work was increasingly male work. At the same time, rising sales of factory-produced goods through mail-order catalogs serving country areas reduced rural needs for women's labor on subsistence tasks. So young farm women flocked to the cities, where they competed for jobs with immigrant, black, and city-born white women.

From 1860 to 1890, the prospect of a better life also attracted nearly 10 million northern European immigrants to East Coast and midwestern cities, where they joined the more than 4 million who had settled

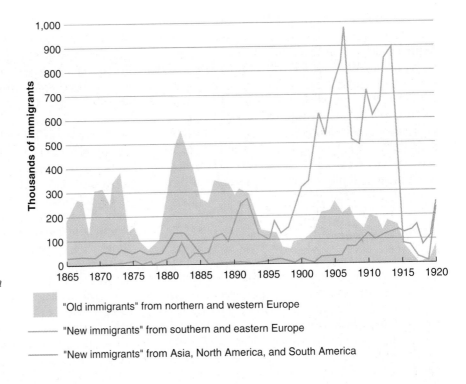

The Changing Face of U.S. Immigration, 1865–1920

Between 1865 and 1895, the majority of newcomers to America hailed from northern and western Europe. But the early twentieth century witnessed a surge of immigration from southern and eastern Europe.

"Old immigrants" from northern and western Europe

"New immigrants" from southern and eastern Europe

"New immigrants" from Asia, North America, and South America

there in the 1840s and 1850s. Germans made up the largest group, numbering close to 3 million. Behind them nearly 2 million English, Scottish, and Welsh immigrants and almost 1.5 million Irish came in search of new jobs and new opportunities. Moreover, by 1900 more than 800,000 French-Canadians had migrated south to work in the New England mills, and close to a million Scandinavian newcomers had put down roots in the rich farmlands of Wisconsin and Minnesota.

In the 1890s these "old immigrants" from northern and western Europe were joined by swelling numbers of "new immigrants"—Italians, Slavs, Greeks, and Jews from southern and eastern Europe, and Armenians from the Middle East. In the next three decades, these new immigrants, often from peasant backgrounds, would boost America's foreign-born population by more than 18 million.

Whether old immigrants or new, the surge of foreigners owed much to improvements in steam-powered vessels. After the Civil War, the introduction of large, swift, oceangoing steamships had not only reduced the time required for the Atlantic voyage from three months to two or three weeks but it also spawned a competition for passengers that drove down the cost of ocean passage.

The overwhelming majority of immigrants settled in cities in the northeastern and north-central states, with the Irish predominating in New England and the Germans in the Midwest. Fired up by the extravagant claims of the steamship lines, state immigrant bureaus, and railroad agencies, the new arrivals came in search of work and fresh beginnings. The impact of their numbers was staggering. In 1890 New York City (including Brooklyn, still a legally separate municipality) contained twice as many Irish as Dublin, as many Germans as Hamburg, half as many Italians as Naples, and 2½ times the Jewish population of Warsaw. That same year four out of five people living in greater New York had been born abroad or were children of foreign parents.

Many of these recent immigrants had come voluntarily, in pursuit of economic betterment. Others were forced out of their home countries by overpopulation, crop failure, famine, violence, or industrial depression. Emigration from England, for example, spurted during downswings in the British economy in 1873 and 1883. On the Continent, German peasants and artisans, squeezed by overpopulation and threatened by church reorganizations that they opposed, left in large numbers in the 1880s. In Norway severe job shortages coupled with a depression in agriculture and shipping

Jakob Mithelstadt and Family, 1905
*The Mithelstadts were Russian Germans who arrived in New York City on the
S.S.* Pretoria. *The poorest immigrants traveled in steerage, below-deck cargo areas
that lacked portholes and originally housed the cables to the ship's rudder.*

drove out more than 260,000 people between 1879 and 1893.

Some ambitious individuals, including many single young men, immigrated in the belief that their opportunities would be better in the United States than in their homeland. Birger Osland, an eighteen-year-old Norwegian, explained his reasons for leaving to a friend: "My father is a schoolteacher and has, besides me, two younger sons, so that it often strains his resources to keep us in school here. . . . Besides . . . as I now probably have a foundation upon which I can build my own further education, I have come to feel that the most sensible thing I can do is to emigrate to America." Although single women were less likely than men to come on their own, Irish women often did so and sent their earnings back home. Most commonly, however, wives and children waited in the old country until the family breadwinner had secured a job

and saved enough money to pay for their passage to America.

Would-be immigrants first had to travel to a European port city—Hamburg was a major port of embarkation—where they booked passage on a steamship. The cramped, often stormy Atlantic journey featured poor food, little privacy, and rudimentary sanitary facilities. Immigrants arrived tired, fearful, and in some cases very sick.

Further complications awaited the travelers upon reaching their destination, usually New York City. Before customs officials allowed them to enter the country, they inspected the newcomers for physical handicaps and contagious diseases. After 1892, those with "loathsome" infections such as leprosy, trachoma (a contagious viral disease of the eye), or venereal disease were refused admittance and deported. Immigrants who passed the physical examination then had their names recorded. If a customs inspector had difficulty pronouncing a foreign name, he often Anglicized it. One German Jew became flustered when asked for his name and mumbled "Schoyn vergessen [I forget]." The inspector, who did not understand Yiddish, wrote "Sean Ferguson" on the man's roster. In this manner, numerous immigrants ended up with "Americanized" names.

New York state established a special facility for admitting immigrants in 1855 at Castle Garden. Later, when the numbers swelled, the federal government took control and built a new station on Ellis Island in 1892. Here America's newest residents exchanged foreign currency for U.S. dollars, purchased railroad tickets, and arranged lodgings. In other cities immigrants were hounded by tavernkeepers, peddlers, and porters who tried to exploit their ignorance of the English language and American ways. "When you land in America," wrote one Swedish resident to friends back home, "you will find many who will offer their services, but beware of them because there are so many rascals who make it their business to cheat the immigrants."

Those who arrived with sufficient cash, including many German artisans and Scandinavian farmers, commonly traveled west to Chicago, Milwaukee, and the rolling prairies beyond. But most of the Irish, and later the Italians, who hailed largely from poor peasant backgrounds, remained in eastern cities like Boston, New York, and Philadelphia. Those Irish and Italians who did go west typically made the trip in stages, moving from job to job on the railroad and canal systems.

Adjusting to an Urban Society

For many immigrants the stress of adjusting to urban life in a new society was eased by the fact that they could settle among compatriots who had preceded them. If a map of New York City's streets and neighborhoods were colored in by nationality, Jacob Riis observed in 1890, it "would show more stripes than on the skin of a zebra, and more colors than any rainbow." The streets of Manhattan between the West Side Irish neighborhoods and the East Side German neighborhoods teemed with tenements housing Poles, Hungarians, Russians, and Italians.

Late-nineteenth-century social commentators often assumed that each nationality group clumped together for reasons of national clannishness. But in fact, the process was far more subtle and complex. Most immigrants preferred to live near others not merely of

their own nationality but from their own village or region in the old country. On New York's Lower East Side, for example, Italians did not form a single "Little Italy" but rather divided into many different subgroups: Neapolitans and Calabrians at Mulberry Bend, Genoese on Baxter Street, northern Italians west of Broadway, and Tyrolese Italians on Sixty-ninth Street near the Hudson River.

Within these ethnic neighborhoods, immigrants suffered incredibly crowded conditions. The congestion was worst in New York City, where, with real estate at a premium, landlords built four- and five-story buildings with few windows on lots only twenty-five feet wide. As early as 1853, the five-story Gotham Court tenement housed five hundred people. A decade later, when the owner added limited plumbing, the number of occupants jumped to eight hundred.

In 1879 New York reformers, concerned about the lack of light and fresh air in the tenements, passed a law that forced landlords to construct buildings with central ten-foot by four-foot air shafts. Dubbed "dumbbell tenements" because of their shape, the new buildings represented only a slight improvement over their predecessors. By the 1890s a single New York City block typically contained ten dumbbell tenements with between two thousand and four thousand immigrant residents. Although overcrowding was worst in Manhattan, cramped, low-grade housing also characterized immigrant districts in Boston, Philadelphia, San Francisco, and other cities. In 1902 investigators in Buffalo, New York, found sixty Polish immigrants—men, women, and children—living in a single small row house. Mattresses were piled up in the daytime and at night spread out over every available inch.

For all the adversity, many immigrant families enjoyed richly satisfying lives. Within the tight ethnic neighborhoods of major U.S. cities, immigrants could speak their native language, purchase traditional foods, attend old-world church services, and celebrate their festivals. Ironically, the attempts of well-intentioned reformers to change the immigrants' behaviors often served to heighten the newcomers' sense of ethnic identity and to encourage them to preserve their native customs.

Some recent arrivals, however, eagerly shed their old ways in hopes of achieving success quickly. For these immigrants and especially their children and grandchildren, the dream of upward mobility frequently became a reality. Husbands, sons, and daughters, whose work and social activities drew them into the currents of city life, generally embraced U.S. cul-

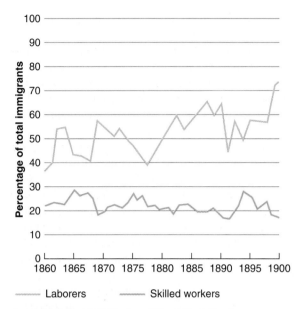

— Laborers   — Skilled workers

Immigration of Skilled and Unskilled Workers, 1860–1900

Far more laborers than skilled workers immigrated to American shores in the years from the Civil War to 1900.

NOTE: Laborers include unskilled workers, domestics, and farm hands.

SOURCE: Figure created by Thomas J. Archdeacon from data in U.S. Bureau of the Census, *Historical Statistics of the United States: Colonial Times to 1970* (Washington, D.C.: Government Printing Office, 1975), series C120–137.

ture faster than older immigrant women, whose world revolved around their tenement flats and immediate neighborhoods. As immigrant children learned English and "American" ways in the public schools, many rejected their elders' old-world accents, dress, and customs. For the second and third generation of immigrant families, the ethnic neighborhoods gradually lost their appeal. But much later, in the closing years of the twentieth century, many Americans would try to rediscover the lost world of their immigrant ancestors, finding in it long-neglected meaning and value.

Some immigrant groups adjusted far more easily than others. Those with a background in the skilled trades and a familiarity with Anglo-American customs had relatively few problems. English-speaking immigrants from the British Isles, particularly those from mill, mining, and manufacturing districts, found comparable work and established a comfortable life. Ethnic groups that formed a substantial percentage of a city's population also had a major advantage. The Irish, for example, who by the 1880s made up nearly 16 percent of New York's population, 8 percent of Chicago's, and 17 percent of Boston's, facilitated Irish immigrants' entry into the American mainstream by dominating Democratic politics and controlling the hierarchy of the Catholic church in all three cities. Similarly the Germans in Milwaukee, composing about a third of the city's population in 1880, owned several major breweries, tanneries, and iron foundries and held leadership positions in local government and civic organizations.

The larger the immigrant group, the more effectively organized were its churches, newspapers, schools, banks, and benevolent associations. Germans, Poles, Russian Jews, and other immigrants who arrived in large numbers in the 1880s and 1890s formed numerous self-help organizations. The New York Hebrew Free Loan Society, founded in 1892, gave interest-free loans of ten dollars to two hundred dollars to Jewish immigrants who wanted to set up their own businesses. By 1904 the society's treasury overflowed with more than a hundred thousand dollars donated by former loan recipients eager to support a benefactor that had helped them prosper.

Ironically, however, the larger immigrant groups' domination of urban institutions often made the adjustment to American society *more* difficult for members of smaller immigrant groups. Germans and other well-organized and skilled foreigners tended to exclude less-skilled newcomers from lucrative jobs. English and German dominance of the building trades, for example, enabled those nationalities to limit the numbers of Italians hired. Not surprisingly, Italians accounted for only 18 percent of New York City's skilled brick masons in 1900 but made up 55 percent of the male barbers and 97 percent of the poorly paid bootblacks.

Another reason smaller immigrant groups had difficulty adjusting to American society was that many of their members had no intention of staying permanently. Young Chinese and Italian males often journeyed to American shores simply to earn enough money to return home and buy land or set themselves up in business. Expecting only a brief stay, they made little effort to learn English or understand American customs. Of the Italians who immigrated to New York before 1914, nearly 50 percent went back to Italy. Although the rate of re-migration was greatest among Chinese and Italians, significant numbers of immigrants of other nationalities eventually returned to their homelands as well.

Various factors thus influenced the ability of immigrants of different national origins to adapt to urban

Garbage Box, First Ward, Chicago, ca. 1900
Lacking space for recreation, immigrant children played atop garbage boxes in crowded alleys. Concerned for their health, Jane Addams wrote that "this slaughter of the innocents, this infliction of suffering on the newborn, is so gratuitous and so unfair, that it is only a question of time until an outraged sense of justice shall be aroused on behalf of these children."

society in America. Nevertheless, as the number of foreigners in U.S. cities ballooned toward the turn of the century, all immigrant groups, irrespective of size, faced increasing hostility from native-born Americans, who not only disliked the newcomers' social customs but also feared their growing influence.

Slums and Ghettos

Every major city had its share of run-down, overcrowded slum neighborhoods. Generally clustered within walking distance of manufacturing districts, slums developed when landlords subdivided old buildings and packed in too many residents. The poorer the renters, the worse the slum. Slums became ghettos when laws, prejudice, and community pressure prevented the tenement inhabitants from renting elsewhere. During the 1890s Italians in New York, blacks in Philadelphia and Chicago, Mexican-Americans in Los Angeles, and Chinese in San Francisco increasingly became locked in segregated ghettos.

For a number of reasons, foreigners of Italian origin in particular were pushed into substandard housing. As we have seen, most unskilled young Italian

male immigrants in these years had little alternative to accepting the lowest-paying jobs. To maximize their meager savings, they took the cheapest housing available—generally badly deteriorated tenements. Because many viewed their stay in America as temporary, they endured terrible filth and congestion.

To urban reformers like Danish-born Jacob Riis, who brought their own cultural biases to the effort to improve urban sanitation and housing, the Italians themselves appeared to be at the heart of the slum problem. Riis despised the Italians' custom of congregating in the streets to purchase food, chat with friends, or simply pass the time. In *How the Other Half Lives,* he singled out a district called the Bend, at the intersection of Mulberry and Baxter streets, as the worst of New York's slums, and he emphasized its Italian character. "Half of the people in 'the Bend' are christened Pasquale . . . ," he wrote patronizingly. "When the police do not know the name of an escaped murderer, they guess at Pasquale and send the name out on an alarm; in nine cases out of ten it fits." While acknowledging the destructive effects of substandard housing, inadequate health care, unsanitary conditions, and the social disruption associated with immigration, Riis nonetheless blamed the Italian residents themselves for the district's crime, filth, disease, and appallingly high infant death rate. Other middle-class observers of urban poverty used the terms *slum* and *foreign colony* interchangeably. This tendency to fault the slum dwellers for their own plight, and to hold particular immigrant groups responsible for their living conditions, was characteristic of even well-intentioned reformers and helped shape—as well as distort—middle-class perceptions of the immigrant city.

Meanwhile, sobering evidence of the decay of urban America under the pressure of unremitting population growth mounted. Social workers in Chicago in the 1890s found conditions that matched those in New York City. Surveying a thirty-block section between Halsted Street and the Chicago River that was home to twenty-six different ethnic groups, they found that only about a quarter of the people had access to a bathroom with running water. The rest relied on repulsive outhouses, called privy vaults, located in yards or under porches. In an especially graphic report, the social workers deplored the district's "filthy and rotten tenements, the dingy courts and tumble-down sheds, the foul stables and dilapidated outhouses, the broken sewer-pipes, the piles of garbage fairly alive with diseased odors, and the numbers of children filling every nook, working and playing in every room, eating and sleeping in every window-sill, pouring in and out of every door, and seeming literally to pave every scrap of 'yard.'"

Health conditions in such districts almost defied description. Epidemics of typhoid fever, smallpox, and diphtheria periodically ravaged the slums, while slower killers like tuberculosis claimed many more victims (see "A Place in Time"). The immigrant city was particularly unsparing of its children. Juvenile diseases such as whooping cough, measles, and scarlet fever took a fearful toll, and infant mortality was very high. In one immigrant ward in Chicago in 1900, 20 percent of all infants died in their first year of life.

Furthermore, because tenements often bordered the industrial districts, residents had to put up with the noise, pollution, and foul odors of tanneries, foundries, factories, and packing houses. Because most factories used coal-fired steam engines as their energy source, and because coal was also the preferred heating fuel for most apartment houses and businesses, vast quantities of soot and coal dust drifted skyward daily. In tenements near factories and warehouses, the atmosphere was hazy-gray with smoke, and the buildings themselves took on a dingy, grimy patina.

Although the immigrants' situation was grim, the position of blacks was worse. In contrast to most immigrants, who stayed in the shabbiest tenements only until they could afford better housing, blacks were trapped in segregated districts. Driven out of the skilled trades and excluded from most factory work, blacks took menial jobs whose low pay left them little income for housing. Racist city dwellers used high rents, real-estate covenants, and neighborhood pressure to exclude them from areas inhabited by whites. Because the numbers of northern urban blacks in 1890 remained relatively small—for example, they composed only 1.2 percent of Cleveland's population and 1.3 percent of Chicago's—they could not overcome whites' concerted campaigns to shut them out.

By the turn of the century, growing competition between immigrants and black migrants moving up from the South led to further efforts to segregate blacks in the poorest sections of northern cities—in Chicago, a long, narrow "Black Belt" on the South Side; in Cleveland, the Central Avenue District. Blacks in such cities faced intimidation as well as segregation. A Washington, D.C., black newspaper, the *Bee*, asserted in the 1880s that white police officers, particularly the Irishmen on the force, "delight in arresting every little colored boy they see on the street, who may be doing something not at all offensive, and allow the white boys to do what they please."

Rivalry over housing and jobs sometimes sparked racial violence. Most frequently the victim of an attack was a single individual, but sometimes interracial clashes escalated into a full-scale riot, as in New York City during the summer of 1900. The melee was touched off when Arthur J. Harris, a young black man, knifed and killed a plainclothes policeman in lower Manhattan who he believed was mishandling his wife. News of the murder spread quickly among whites, and the district seethed with anger. "Men and women poured by the hundreds from the neighboring tenements," reported a local newspaperman. "Negroes were set upon wherever they could be found and brutally beaten."

Fashionable Avenues and Suburbs

As remains true today, the same cities that harbored slums, suffering, and violence also boasted neighborhoods of dazzling opulence. The wealthy built monumental residences on exclusive thoroughfares just outside the downtown: Fifth Avenue in New York, Commonwealth Avenue in Boston, Euclid Avenue in Cleveland, and Summit Avenue in St. Paul. In Chicago, after a devastating fire in 1871, the city's elite, including meatpacking magnate Philip Armour and department-store developer Marshall Field, moved south to Prairie Avenue around Eighteenth Street. Then in the 1880s, with the extension of Chicago's street-railway system, wholesale merchant and real-estate promoter Potter Palmer and other rich businessmen moved to Lake Shore Drive, the so-called Gold Coast on the near North Side. The city's upper crust soon followed. The gradual northward migration of Chicago's well-to-do was paralleled by the expansion of the immigrant districts on the South Side, where once fashionable mansions were converted into cramped apartments and quickly filled with newcomers from Europe.

In the 1870s and 1880s, wealthy city dwellers began moving to the suburbs to distance themselves further from the crowded tenement districts. Promoters of the suburban ideal, playing on the romantic rural nostalgia popular at the time, skillfully contrasted the rolling lawns and sheltered houses on the city's periphery with the teeming streets, noisy saloons, and mounds of garbage and excrement downtown. Soon

Immigrant Milwaukee in the 1890s

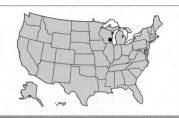

On August 5, 1894, a mob of more than three thousand furious Polish citizens on Milwaukee's South Side fought a pitched battle with police and health-department officials. A smallpox epidemic had broken out in the city, and the health department had ordered infected persons to be taken by ambulance to a city isolation hospital. A distraught mother who had recently lost another child to smallpox refused to let the city "kill" her sick two-year-old daughter by hospitalizing her. "I can give better care and nourishment here than they can give in the hospital," she yelled at the authorities. Confronted by a violent crowd armed with clubs, knives, and stones, the health-department crew beat a hasty retreat. The local newspaper later reported that for more than a month after this incident, "mobs of Pomeranian and Polish women armed with baseball bats, potato mashers, clubs, bed slats, salt and pepper, and butcher knives, lay in wait all day for . . . the Isolation Hospital van."

The smallpox riots of 1894 reflected deep antagonisms between city officials and ethnic groups in Milwaukee. The confrontations pitted reform-minded political appointees and sanitary engineers seeking to establish citywide health ordinances against immigrants seeking to preserve their traditions. The conflicts exposed the reformers' mixed motives, for beneath their drive to improve city sanitation lay a

East Water St. Looking South, Color Lithograph (Detail), c. 1898
By 1890 the thriving downtown center of Milwaukee, with its efficient trolley-car system and tall office buildings, was surrounded by immigrant neighborhoods on the near north and near south sides.

desire to destroy the foreign customs of Milwaukee's immigrants.

Tensions first surfaced in Milwaukee during a period of rapid growth. Settled in 1836 at a natural harbor formed on Lake Michigan, the city witnessed a tenfold population gain from 1850 to 1890, swelling from twenty thousand to more than two hundred thousand residents. Germans, who made up Milwaukee's largest immigrant group, predominated in the early years of settlement and concentrated heavily on the city's West Side. Then in the 1870s, large numbers of Poles and other eastern Europeans poured in, drawn by the unskilled jobs available in the rolling mills and blast furnaces of heavy industries such as the Milwaukee Iron Company and the E. P. Allis Company. Bartholomew Koperski, a Polish laborer, was typical of the many Poles who clustered in small, ill-ventilated houses in wards on the city's South Side. A railroad-car inspector, Koperski lived with his wife and six children in the upstairs of a twenty-two- by forty-foot cottage. He rented the basement to George Krzyzaniak, a twenty-nine-year-old Polish carpenter, his wife, and their two children. Although the city's health-department inspectors reported that most immigrants' homes were in "good sanitary condition," less than half had indoor plumbing.

The Koperskis and their compatriots belonged to a close ethnic community whose ties were cemented by their common language and their powerful religious bonds. Milwaukee's Poles founded their own Catholic churches; published their own Polish-language newspaper, *Krytyka* (The Critic); and figured prominently in ward politics. During smallpox epidemics the Milwaukee health department tried to establish citywide health policies that quarantined infected houses, banned public funerals, and forced diseased persons into isolation hospitals, but the cohesive Polish wards fought back. Accustomed to nursing the sick at home, the Poles protested city efforts to cart invalids off to hospitals and then ban family members from visiting them. Furthermore, with a strong tradition of elaborate church funerals for their deceased loved ones, they refused to accept the idea of burials without formal church rites.

At the height of the epidemic, a local alderman spoke out for his constituents.

Milwaukee's Polish Community
Polish residents of Milwaukee stand proudly before St. Josephat's Church, still under construction in this photograph from the early twentieth century.

He raged that the Poles were being treated as "the scum of Milwaukee." "I don't blame the people down here for being worked up," he told a newspaper reporter. "The patients at the hospitals are not treated like human beings, and the way the dead are buried is brutal." He was particularly incensed by the position taken by Milwaukee's health commissioner, Walter Kempster, a native-born American who asserted, "I am here to enforce the laws, and I shall enforce them if I have to break heads to do it."

The debate over city quarantine policies between Kempster and Milwaukee's South Siders rekindled a conflict dating from nearly six months earlier, when Kempster was first appointed health commissioner. Hired because of his medical credentials, Kempster, a Republican, had ignored his party's suggested list of candidates to fill the twenty-six openings in his department. Incensed by Kempster's failure to reward any of their constituents with a job, Polish city-council members had agitated for his removal. Now the smallpox epidemic provided an additional avenue for those longing to unseat Kempster. In

the crisis his adversaries denounced him as a symbol of arbitrary government authority and a subverter of immigrant culture and personal liberty.

As the deadly epidemic continued into the autumn months, the city council passed a new ordinance barring the health commissioner from hospitalizing victims without their consent. Still upset by his handling of the Polish South Siders, the council dismissed Kempster in February 1895. Milwaukee's battle over city health policies thus revealed a larger struggle between immigrant groups and public administrators: a tug-of-war for political control of the city.

Not until after 1900 did Milwaukee and other cities establish enforceable health regulations and vaccination policies that in time lowered the nationwide mortality rate from smallpox and other diseases. And only with massive educational campaigns in the Progressive Era were ethnic groups persuaded that local government had a legitimate need to interfere with their social customs in matters that concerned the welfare of all citizens.

Planning for the Garden City: Cleveland's Shaker Heights Suburb

As this promotional view of Shaker Heights indicates, the developers used the stately boulevards characteristic of the City Beautiful movement to give their design an element of formality and monumentality.

many major cities could boast of their own stylish suburbs: Haverford, Ardmore, and Bryn Mawr outside Philadelphia; Brookline near Boston; and Shaker Heights near Cleveland.

Middle-class city dwellers followed the precedents set by the wealthy. Skilled artisans, shopkeepers, clerks, accountants, and sales personnel moved either to new developments at the city's edge or to outlying suburban communities (although those at the lower fringe of the middle class typically rented apartments in neighborhoods closer to the city center). In the 1890s Chicago developer Samuel Eberly Gross created entire low-cost subdivisions north and west of the city and advertised homes for as little as ten dollars a month. Lawyers, doctors, small businessmen, and other professionals moved farther out along the main thoroughfares served by the street railway, where they purchased homes with large lots.

In time, a pattern of informal residential segregation by income took shape in the cities and suburbs. Built up for families of a particular income level, cer-tain neighborhoods and suburbs developed remarkably similar standards for lot size and house design. Commuters who rode the new street railways out from the city center could identify the changing neighborhoods along the way as readily as a geologist might distinguish different strata on a washed-out riverbank.

So by 1900 whirring trolley cars and hissing steam-powered trains had burst the boundaries of the compact midcentury city. Within this expanded city, sharp dissimilarities in building height and neighborhood quality set off business sectors from fashionable residential avenues and strikingly differentiated squalid manufacturing districts from parklike suburban subdivisions. Musing about urban America in 1902, James F. Muirhead, a popular Scottish guidebook author, wrote that New York and other U.S. cities reminded him of "a lady in a ball costume, with diamonds in her ears, and her toes out at her boots." To Muirhead, urban America had become a "land of contrasts" in which the spatial separations of various social groups and the radically unequal living conditions for rich and poor had heightened the sense of ethnic and class consciousness. Along with the physical change in American cities, in short, had come a new awareness of class and cultural disparities.

THE URBAN CHALLENGE

Although middle- and upper-class Americans were abandoning their downtown residences in the 1880s and 1890s, the business and professional activities of countless merchants, journalists, manufacturers, lawyers, and others remained centered in the vibrant heart of the city. These old-stock citizens were deeply troubled by the strikes and riots that periodically swept through the cities. Urban critics blamed the disorder on the immigrant masses, who did not, they concluded, share their own cultural views on self-discipline and moral improvement.

Convinced that urgent steps must be taken to stem what seemed a rising tide of riot, robbery, and rotten government, concerned citizens waged a continuous battle in the late nineteenth century to eradicate urban crime, reform "boss" politics, and assimilate the immigrants into mainstream American society. Their efforts were catalyzed by a powerful blend of altruism and self-interest.

Policing the City

Would-be reformers worried not only about the organized mass protests of disgruntled workers but about the crime that inevitably increased as city populations grew denser. In his novel *Ragged Dick* (1868), Unitarian minister Horatio Alger detailed the variety of scams and tricks that victimized rural visitors to the city. Shopkeepers swindled the unsuspecting by giving them incorrect change. Pickpockets and thieves stole handbags and purses. Con artists lured the unwary into giving them change for wallets stuffed with phony bills. Worst of all, Irish street gangs, led by toughs like Alger's fictional Mickey Maguire, sometimes beat up and robbed the innocent.

Horatio Alger and other writers who associated crime with the growth of cities did not exaggerate. In Philadelphia, for example, which expanded in population from 409,000 to 1,294,000 between 1850 and 1900, the number of homicides nearly tripled in the second half of the century. As city dailies splashed reports of violence across their front pages, reformers worried publicly about urbanites' easy access to cheap handguns.

In their desire to maintain public order, city officials in the 1830s and 1840s had established police forces to supplement the traditional night watch that had patrolled the streets after dark to keep an eye out for fires. Unlike their European counterparts, these police forces were civilian enterprises, separate from the military and controlled by local officials. Following the example set by New York in 1853, other American cities had outfitted their municipal police forces with badges and uniforms and authorized officers to carry revolvers.

Initially, however, these new urban police forces had an odd, ill-defined assortment of responsibilities. Although officially hired to maintain order, prevent crime, and regulate morality by controlling drunks and other public nuisances, the police often performed additional functions. In New York City they cleaned streets and inspected boilers. In Baltimore, Philadelphia, and New York, they ran lodging houses for the homeless and distributed supplies to the poor. In St. Louis they supervised the sanitation of vegetable markets.

The police sometimes battled immigrant gangs like Baltimore's Blood Tubs and New York City's Bowery Boys, but they made little headway in suppressing the rowdy street life, drinking, gambling, and prostitution that flourished within the immigrant working class. Middle-class civic leaders grumbled about the "disorderly" laborers noisily clustering on tenement stoops to talk politics or listen to street musicians. But they feared even more the immigrants' neighborhood saloons, which offered a free lunch with a five-cent beer, provided meeting rooms, spread news of job openings, and sometimes, in back rooms, furnished gambling tables and offered prostitutes' services.

State legislatures, dominated in these years by rural, native-born citizens who deplored the immigrants' drinking and gambling, regularly passed laws banning these practices, curtailing Sunday business operations, and regulating saloons. Caught between moralistic state legislators and immigrant communities resentful of outside meddling, the police tried to steer a middle course, tacitly allowing the saloons to remain open on Sunday, for example, as long as their patrons behaved properly in public.

An investigation conducted in 1894 by New York State senator Clarence Lexow uncovered considerable evidence that the New York City police not only failed to suppress illegal activities but in effect often licensed them. In return for regular payoffs, Lexow reported, the police permitted gamblers, prostitutes, and saloonkeepers to operate more or less at will in poor neighborhoods where little organized opposition existed, provided that they remained discreet. A portion of these payoffs, Lexow further revealed, ended up in the hands of local political bosses who hired and fired the police. Instead of fighting vice, a shocked Lexow concluded, the police were conniving in it.

The complex symbiosis between the police and those whom they were supposed to be policing manifested itself in other ways as well. By the 1870s, in New York and most other major cities, police departments had squads of detectives who were often not easily distinguishable from the crooks and con men with whom they rubbed shoulders. These detectives sometimes even functioned as go-betweens for thieves and robbery victims, returning the stolen property in exchange for a reward. In some cities professional criminals reached an understanding with the detectives and gave back property stolen from individuals of high prestige and standing.

In city after city in the late nineteenth century, reformers strove to professionalize law enforcement by transferring the hiring and firing of police officers from political bosses to independent, nonpartisan boards of commissioners. Not until the 1890s, however, did most urban police forces adopt a professional attitude toward their work. Pressured by reformers such as young Theodore Roosevelt, who headed New York City's Board of Police Commissioners from 1895 to 1897, civic leaders gradually removed the police department from the political patronage system and set up regular hiring procedures. Unable to enforce the strict morality desired by rural, native-born state legislators, many urban police departments by the turn of the century had shifted their attention from trying to control the "dangerous classes" to deterring criminal behavior.

Governing the City

The competition for authority over the police revealed a deeper power struggle within urban politics. Amid the furiously haphazard growth of cities, political power had become fragmented and decentralized. The urgent demands placed on public utilities, rapid-transit systems, and fire and police departments forced cities to raise taxes, issue bonds, and create a host of new municipal departments and positions. Since large sums of money could be made by dominating any segment of this process, state and local politicians fought desperately for control of the city and the right to run these lucrative urban services.

Complicating the contest for control of city politics was the fact that both city governments and state legislatures claimed to have jurisdiction over the urban environment. Ostensibly to curb abuse in urban government, state legislatures altered city charters, bestowed special contracts and monopolies on certain railroad and utility magnates, and tried to minimize taxes by reducing the expenses of city government and limiting city services.

This kind of outside interference in local affairs had by midcentury encouraged the rise of a new kind of professional politician, the "boss." The boss presided over the city's "machine"—an unofficial political organization designed to keep a particular party or faction in office. Whether or not officially serving as mayor, the boss, assisted by local ward or precinct "captains," wielded enormous influence in city government. Often a former saloonkeeper or labor leader, the boss knew his constituents well. Cincinnati's George B. Cox was a typical boss, though more honest than many. The son of British immigrants, Cox worked his way up from being a newsboy and lookout for

gamblers to tending bar and eventually acquired his own saloon. Elected to the Cincinnati city council in 1879, Cox in time became head of the city's Republican machine, which swung elections to the GOP, controlled key public offices, and acted as a broker among competing corporate and political interests.

For better or worse, the political machine was America's unique contribution to the challenge of municipal government in an era of pell-mell urban growth. Typified by Tammany Hall, the Democratic organization that dominated New York City politics from the 1830s to the 1930s, machines emerged in Baltimore, Philadelphia, Atlanta, San Francisco, and a host of other cities in the Gilded Age. Organized in a pyramid, the machine consisted of precinct or election-district captains who worked on the block or neighborhood level and who in turn reported to ward bosses. The ward bosses, frequently saloonkeepers, turned out the vote at election time in return for patronage jobs, contracts, and political appointments from city hall. At the apex of this pyramid sat the city boss, who controlled party activities throughout the city.

By the turn of the century, many urban machines ruled supreme. The politicians who ran them controlled the jobs of thousands of policemen, firemen, sanitation workers, street crews, and other city employees; they exerted enormous influence over courts, schools, city hospitals, and other municipal agencies. Democratic in some cities and Republican in others, the machine hammered out compromises and resolved conflicts among competing urban interest groups.

Working through the local ward captains, the machine rode herd on the tangle of municipal bureaucracies, rewarding its friends and punishing its enemies through its control of taxes, licenses, and inspections. The machine gave tax breaks to favored contractors in return for large payoffs and slipped them insider information about upcoming street and sewer projects. At the neighborhood level, the ward boss sometimes acted as a welfare agent, helping the needy and protecting the troubled. It was important to the boss that he be viewed as being generous to his constituents. To pay ten dollars to cover a tenement dweller's rent or to spend three dollars to cover a fine for a juvenile offense meant a lot to the poor, but it was small change to a boss who raked in millions from public-utility contracts and land deals. If the machine helped alleviate some of the poor's suffering in the Gilded Age, however, it hopelessly entangled urban social services with

"Let Us Prey," 1871
Cartoonist Thomas Nast hated William Marcy Tweed's ostentatious style. Pictured here as the chief vulture standing over the body of New York City, Boss Tweed wears an enormous diamond, a symbol of his insatiable greed.

corrupt politics and often prevented the political process from responding to the real problems of the city's neediest inhabitants.

A particularly effective precinct captain could work his way up from running the ward to running the city machine and eventually influence state and national politics as well. In Kansas City, Missouri, "Big Jim" Pendergast, an Irish hotelkeeper and saloonkeeper in one of the city's industrial wards, clawed his way to power in the 1890s by providing welfare services for his black, Italian, and Irish constituents. By controlling his ward's delegates to the city's Democratic convention, he rose to city alderman. When opposition interests threatened to use their pull in the state legislature to clamp down on the Kansas City police, Pendergast used his influence with the governor to engineer the appointment of a new city police chief

sympathetic to his allies. By the turn of the century, Pendergast held near-absolute sway in Kansas City politics and wielded considerable clout at the state level as well.

Bosses like Cox and Pendergast—and even those in smaller cities such as Rochester, Omaha, and Memphis—transformed urban politics into a new form of entrepreneurship. They could be as ambitious and ruthless as any Gilded Age captain of industry. Like the Carnegies and the Rockefellers, the city bosses pioneered new forms of social organization and extemporized managerial innovations even as they consolidated their personal power, and in some cases they amassed vast fortunes. At times greedy and utterly unscrupulous, they nevertheless paid lip service to immigrant and working-class concerns in a society increasingly dominated by the middle and upper classes.

Under New York City's boss William Marcy Tweed, the Tammany Hall machine epitomized the slimy depths to which extortion and contract padding could sink. Although between 1869 and 1871, Tweed gave $50,000 to the poor and $2,250,000 to schools, orphanages, and hospitals, his machine also dispensed sixty thousand patronage positions and pumped up the city's debt by $70 million through graft and inflated contracts. The details of the Tweed ring's massive fraud and corruption were widely reported in newspapers and brilliantly satirized in *Harper's Weekly* by German immigrant cartoonist Thomas Nast, who in one cartoon portrayed Tweed and his cronies as vultures picking at the city's bones. Tweed bellowed in fury. "I don't care a straw for your newspaper articles—my constituents don't know how to read," he told *Harper's*, "but they can't help seeing them damned pictures." Convicted of fraud and extortion, Tweed was sentenced to jail in 1873, served two years, escaped to Spain, was reapprehended and reincarcerated, and died in jail in 1878.

Not all bosses were as crooked and covetous as Tweed. Boss Cox of Cincinnati, who steadfastly maintained he had never received an illegal payoff, gained the backing of local good-government reformers—"goo-goos" to their opponents—by supporting voter-registration laws and by placing the police and fire departments under independent bipartisan boards. Cox helped remove police appointments from the patronage system and agreed to rules that required new recruits to undergo extensive training before joining the force. He also supported the construction of a new city waterworks as well as the improvement of parks and recreational facilities. Although Cox's opponents never believed that his administration was as free from corruption as he claimed, they did not overthrow his political machine until 1897.

Despite the stereotype of city bosses as coarse and crude—British observer James Bryce described them as "vulgar figures with good coats"—not all bosses fit that mold. San Francisco boss Abraham Ruef had graduated from the University of California at eighteen years of age with highest honors and spoke seven languages. Ed Flynn, the boss of the Bronx, New York, was a brilliant lawyer. Whatever their backgrounds, however, bosses represented a new political organization that stressed grassroots ties to the neighborhood and ward. Standing amid the real-estate promoters, local businessmen, wealthy entrepreneurs, civic reformers, and other groups vying for power and pursuing their various agendas in the cockpit of urban politics, the boss made sure that the concerns of his constituents were heard. In this ceaseless struggle among competing groups with vastly different interests, the boss displayed a flexible, pragmatic, and opportunistic approach to meeting the day-to-day challenges of urban life.

Nevertheless, by the turn of the century, the bosses faced well-organized assaults on their power, led by an urban elite whose members sought to restore "good government." In this atmosphere the bosses increasingly forged alliances with civic organizations and reform leagues. The results, although never entirely satisfactory to any of the parties involved, paved the way for new sewer and transportation systems, expanded parklands, and improved public services—a record of considerable accomplishment, given the magnitude of the problems created by urban growth.

Battling Poverty

In contrast to the political bosses' piecemeal attempts to help the urban poor, middle-class city leaders sought comprehensive solutions for relieving poverty. Jacob Riis and other reformers believed that the basic cause of urban distress was the immigrants' lack of self-discipline and self-control. Consequently, Riis and the other charity reformers focused on moral improvement and ignored the crippling impact of low wages and dangerous working conditions. Although many reformers genuinely sympathized with the suffering of the lower classes, the humanitarians ultimately turned their campaigns to help the destitute into missions to Americanize the immigrants and eliminate customs that they perceived as offensive and self-destructive.

Poverty-relief workers first targeted their efforts at the young, who were thought to be most malleable. Energized by the religious revivals of the 1830s and 1840s (see Chapter 10), early Protestant social reformers started charitable societies to help transient youths and street waifs. In 1843 Robert M. Hartley, a former employee of the New York Temperance Society, mobilized New York City's business and professional classes to support his newly founded New York Association for Improving the Condition of the Poor. Convinced that slum children learned bad habits from their parents, Hartley organized a system of "home visitation" that sent volunteers into inner-city tenements to urge poor families to change their ways. Expanding to Baltimore, Philadelphia, and Boston, Hartley's association also demanded pure-milk laws, public baths, and better housing.

Hartley's voluntaristic approach was supplemented at midcentury by the more coercive tactics of Charles Loring Brace, who in 1853 founded the New York Children's Aid Society. Brace admired "these little traders of the city . . . battling for a hard living in the snow and mud of the street" but worried that they might join the city's "dangerous classes." Brace not only established dormitories, reading rooms, and workshops where the boys could learn practical skills but he also sometimes swept children off the streets without the consent of their parents, shipped them to the country, and auctioned them off as farmhands to the highest bidder. Using a combination of persuasion and coercion, the Children's Aid Society by the mid-1890s had transferred ninety thousand boys from the city to foster homes in such states as Illinois, Michigan, and Wisconsin, where local residents put them to work.

Where Brace's Children's Aid Society gave vulnerable adolescents an alternative to living in the slums, the Young Men's Christian Association (YMCA), founded in England in 1841 and exported to America ten years later, provided decent housing and wholesome recreational facilities for country boys new to the city. More than any other institutions, the YMCA and later the YWCA (Young Women's Christian Association) worked to overcome the dislocation experienced by the thousands of rural Americans who migrated to the city in the post–Civil War years. In the Protestant tradition of moral improvement, both organizations

YMCA, c. 1890
Designed to function as a wholesome alternative to the vices of city life, the Young Men's Christian Association (YMCA) helped newcomers adjust to an urban environment by providing reading room libraries and evening classes as well as gyms, swimming pools, handball courts, and other recreational facilities.

subjected their members to considerable supervision and expelled them for drinking and other forbidden behavior.

The departure of young people—especially farmers' daughters—from older rural areas was truly startling. Between 1840 and 1900, almost half the townships in Vermont lost more than a quarter of their population, and young adults led the exodus. In one Vermont town, 73 percent of those aged five to fourteen in the 1880 census had left by 1900. Like Carrie Meeber, the heroine in Theodore Dreiser's *Sister Carrie* (1900), youthful rural migrants drawn to the city's greater economic opportunities were awed by the glamour and glitter of urban life. Far from home, with few friends and no place to stay, they easily fell victim to the city's flashy con artists and fast talkers. The YMCA and the YWCA supplied such country innocents safe temporary lodgings and reassuring reminders of home.

By 1900 more than fifteen hundred YMCAs acted as a haven for nearly a quarter-million men. But YMCA (and YWCA) leaders reached only a small portion of the young adult population. Some whom they sought to help were put off by the organizations' close supervision and highly moralistic stance. Others, eager to assert their independence in the new urban environment, preferred not to ask for help. And although charity workers made some progress in their efforts to aid youth, the strategy was too narrowly focused to stem the rising tide of urban problems.

New Approaches to Social Work

The inability of the Children's Aid Society, the YMCA, the YWCA, and other relief organizations to cope with the urban poor's explosive growth in the 1870s and 1880s convinced many middle-class Americans that urban poverty had reached epidemic proportions. The Reverend Josiah Strong, secretary of the American Home Missionary Society and minister of Cincinnati's Central Congregational Church, expressed this fear in his book *Our Country; Its Possible Future and Its Present Crisis* (1885). Asserting that the cities were "multiplying and focalizing the elements of anarchy and destruction," Strong attributed the urban menace to immigration and Catholicism. Critical of the immigrants' attachment to their saloons and beer halls, he pleaded for a cooperative effort among the Protestant churches to battle the dual plagues of intemperance and destitution.

Even before Strong mounted the battlements, social reformers had begun developing more coercive strategies for fighting poverty. One of the earliest and most effective agencies to use tough-minded tactics was the Salvation Army. A church established along pseudomilitary lines in England in 1865 by Methodist minister "General" William Booth, the Salvation Army sent its uniformed volunteers to America in 1880 to provide food, shelter, and temporary employment for families. Known for its rousing music and attention-getting street meetings, the group ran soup kitchens and day nurseries and dispatched its "slum brigades" to carry the message of morality to the immigrant poor.

Funded by donations, the Salvation Army functioned both to aid and to control an urban lower-class population whose fondness for saloons, dance halls, and streetside entertainment threatened the middle-class conception of a stable society. The organization's strategy was simple. Attract the poor with marching bands and lively preaching; follow up with offers of food, assistance, and employment; and then teach them the solid middle-class virtues of temperance, hard work, and self-discipline.

A similar approach to poor relief was implemented by the New York Charity Organization Society (COS), founded in 1882 by Josephine Shaw Lowell. Of a prominent Boston family, the strong-willed Lowell had been widowed when her husband of a few months was killed during the Civil War, and she wore black for the rest of her life.

Adopting what they considered a scientific approach to make aid to the poor more efficient, the COS leaders divided New York City into districts, compiled files on all aid recipients, and sent "friendly visitors" into the tenements to counsel families on how to improve their lives. Convinced that moral deficiencies lay at the root of poverty, and that the "promiscuous charity" of overlapping welfare agencies undermined poor people's desire to work, the COS tried to foster self-sufficiency in its charges.

Although the COS and similar groups in Boston, Philadelphia, and other cities did serve as useful coordinators for relief efforts, critics justly accused them of being more interested in controlling the poor than in alleviating their suffering. More often than not, the friendly visitors wore cultural blinders and expected to effect change by imposing middle-class standards. In the 1890s Chicago journalist George Ade cruelly ridiculed the typical friendly visitor as "235 pounds of Sunshine." The earnest Salvation Army workers and COS volunteers no doubt accomplished some good, but unable to see slum problems from the vantage point of the poor, they failed, for the most part, in their underlying objective: to convert the poor to their own standards of morality and decorum.

The Moral-Purity Campaign

The failure of Josephine Shaw Lowell and other like-minded social disciplinarians to eradicate urban poverty and crime prompted other reformers to push for even tougher measures against sin and immorality. In 1872 Anthony Comstock, a pious young dry-goods clerk, founded the New York Society for the Suppression of Vice. The organization demanded that municipal authorities close down gambling and lottery operations and censor obscene publications. Toward the end of his career in the early twentieth century, Comstock became a target of ridicule for his naive judgments about literature and art. (He dismissed George Bernard Shaw as "a foreign writer of filth" and raided the New York Art Students' League for displaying nude sculptures.) But in his heyday, Comstock's purity crusade gained widespread public support from middle- and upper-class civic leaders deeply frustrated by the lack of progress in flushing away urban vice.

Nothing symbolized the contested terrain between middle- and lower-class culture better than prostitution. Considered socially degenerate by some and a source of recreation by others, prostitution both exploited women and offered them large salaries and unbounded personal freedom. After the Civil War, the number of brothels—specialized houses where prostitutes plied their trade—expanded rapidly. Then in the 1880s, saloons, tenements, and cabarets, often controlled by political machines, displaced them. Even though immigrant women do not appear to have made up the majority of big-city prostitutes, reformers often labeled them as the major source of the problem.

In 1892 houses of prostitution, along with gambling dens and saloons, became targets for the reform efforts of New York Presbyterian minister Charles Parkhurst. Blaming the "slimy, oozy soil of Tammany Hall" and the New York City police—"the dirtiest, crookedest, and ugliest lot of men ever combined in semi-military array outside of Japan and Turkey"—for the city's rampant criminal evil, he organized the City Vigilance League in 1892 to clean up the city. When Senator Lexow's committee spearheaded the investigation of urban vice two years later, Parkhurst's league swamped the panel with evidence of officially tolerated corruption. In September 1894 a nonpartisan Committee of Seventy, among its members J. Pierpont Morgan, William Bayard Cutting, and the younger Cornelius Vanderbilt, elected a new mayor who pressured city officials to enforce the laws against prostitution, gambling, and Sunday liquor sales.

The purity campaign, however, lasted scarcely three years. Irish and German neighborhoods boisterously rallied in defense of their cherished saloons. Individuals who once championed Parkhurst's efforts scoffed at his self-righteous and bombastic rhetoric and deserted his movement; the city's reform coalition fell apart. Regaining power in 1897, Tammany Hall installed a new police chief who was once again content to regulate rather than root out vice. Even though Parkhurst politically controlled the mayor's office and had the backing of a reform coalition, his attempt to legislate morality had failed. New York City's population was too large, and its ethnic constituencies were too diverse, for middle- and upper-class reformers to curb all the illegal activities flourishing within the sprawling metropolis.

The Social Gospel

Meanwhile, a handful of Protestant ministers in the 1870s and 1880s began to explore several radical alternatives for aiding impoverished city dwellers. Instead of focusing on their alleged moral flaws and character defects, these ministers argued that the rich and the wellborn deserved part of the blame for urban poverty and thus had a responsibility to do something about it.

William S. Rainsford, the Irish-born minister at New York City's Saint George's Episcopal Church, pioneered the development of the so-called institutional church movement, whereby large downtown churches in once elite districts that had been overrun by immigrants would provide their new neighbors with social services as well as a place to worship. With the financial help of his wealthy church warden J. Pierpont Morgan, Rainsford organized a boys' club, built church recreational facilities for the destitute on the Lower East Side, and established an industrial training program.

Some conservatives tongue-lashed the churchman and his unorthodox approach. Charles A. Dana of the *New York Sun* branded Rainsford a "conspicuous representative of a school of unwise and mischievous social agitators." Unfazed, Rainsford redoubled his criticism of middle-class churchgoers for their lack of concern for the immigrant poor. Dismissing the moralists' assumption that alcohol abuse resulted entirely from a lack of will power, Rainsford argued that excessive drinking in immigrant wards was simply a by-product of life in the slums, where millions were trapped in often desperate circumstances. For Rainsford and those who shared his view, moral-purity campaigns to close saloons on Sunday were far less important than the prosecution of slum landlords and sweatshop owners who victimized the poor.

Although Rainsford and the members of his Institutional Church League could claim some successes in their own neighborhoods, their efforts in the end fell short, owing to the magnitude of slum conditions. But their sympathetic approach to urban destitution marked an important dimension of a crusade by a group of late-nineteenth-century ministers to awaken American Protestants to the realities of the immigrant city.

Supporting that drive were the leaders of the so-called Social Gospel movement, another effort within Protestantism to right contemporary social wrongs. The Social Gospel movement was launched in the 1870s by Washington Gladden, who for most of his career served as the minister of a large Congregational church in Columbus, Ohio. Dismayed by the way many middle-class churchgoers ignored the plight of urban slum dwellers, Gladden insisted that true Christianity commits men and women to fight social injustice head on, wherever it exists. Thus, in response to the wave of violent strikes in 1877, he urged church leaders to become mediators in the conflict between business and labor.

If Gladden set the tone for the Social Gospel, Walter Rauschenbusch, a minister at a German Baptist church in New York's notorious "Hell's Kitchen" neighborhood, articulated the movement's central philosophy. Educated in Germany, Rauschenbusch returned to the United States in the 1880s and was strongly influenced by Henry George's and Edward Bellamy's criticism of laissez-faire ideology. Enlarging the traditional Protestant focus on individual conversion, Rauschenbusch sought in such books as *Christianity and the Social Crisis* (1907) to apply Jesus's teachings to society itself. A truly Christian society, he said, would unite all churches, reorganize the industrial system, and work for international peace.

Although the Social Gospel's appeal for Christian unity led in 1908 to the formation of the Federal Council of Churches, the movement's biting attack on what its leaders blasted as the complacent Christian support of the status quo attracted only a handful of Protestants. But their earnest voices blended with a growing chorus of critics bemoaning the nation's urban woes.

The Settlement-House Movement

By the 1880s many concerned citizens had become convinced that reform pressures applied from the top down by the Charity Organization Society and the purity crusaders, however well intentioned, were not

Greeting Neighbors at Hull House
Settlement house workers were eager to work with immigrant families in order to insure that the children received proper health care and nutrition. In addition to establishing its own nursery, Hull House in Chicago provided classes for parents and helped find them jobs.

The youngest daughter of a successful Illinois businessman, Addams had graduated from Rockford College in 1882 and toured Europe a year later with her friend Ellen Gates Starr. Impressed by Toynbee Hall, a charity workers' residence situated deep in a London slum, the two women returned to Chicago in 1889, purchased and repaired the dilapidated Charles J. Hull mansion on South Halsted Street, and opened Hull House as an experiment in the settlement-house approach. Living in the house and working in daily contact with poor immigrants, they hoped to provide an exemplar of a creative outlet for college-trained women like themselves.

Jane Addams's hostility toward the methods and philosophy of the Charity Organization Society and other coercive agencies came from disillusioning personal experience. During her first years at Hull House, Addams had accepted Josephine Shaw Lowell's model for managing the poor. But in her autobiography, *Twenty Years at Hull House* (1910), Addams explained why she later rejected Lowell's self-assured methods. Once, attempting to get a jobless shipping clerk to help himself, she encouraged him to take a job as a canal digger. Following her advice, the clerk had contracted pneumonia and died a week later. "I learned," Addams wrote sadly, "that life cannot be administered by definite rules and regulations; that wisdom to deal with man's difficulties comes only through some knowledge of his life and habits as a whole; and that to treat an isolated episode is almost sure to invite blundering."

Drawing on the popular middle-class ideal of true womanhood as supportive and self-sacrificing, the indefatigable Addams turned Hull House into a social center for recent immigrants and denied herself the luxuries that she might have purchased with her family wealth. Getting to know the Italian newcomers around her was a top priority. She invited them to plays; sponsored art projects; held classes in English, civics, cooking, and dressmaking; and encouraged them to preserve their traditional crafts. Disturbed by the depth of the neighborhood poverty that she witnessed, Addams set up a kindergarten, a laundry, an employment bureau, and a day nursery for working mothers. Hull House also sponsored recreational and athletic programs and dispensed legal aid and health care. In the hope of upgrading the shockingly filthy and overcrowded housing in the environs, Addams and her coworkers published systematic studies of city housing conditions and tirelessly pressured politicians to enforce sanitation regulations. For a time, demonstrating

only ineffective but wrongheaded. Simple passage of laws did not ensure obedience. Rejecting Parkhurst's contemptuous attitude toward the poor, and the Charity Organization movement's tendency to blame poverty on individual moral failure, a younger generation of charity workers led by Jane Addams developed a new weapon against destitution: the settlement house. Like the Social Gospelers, they began by recognizing that the physical hardships of slum life were often beyond the control of individuals. Stressing the environmental causes of poverty, settlement-house advocates insisted that relief workers take up residence in poor neighborhoods where, in Addams's words, they could see firsthand "the struggle for existence, which is so much harsher among people near the edge of pauperism."

her principle of direct engagement with the lives of the poor, Addams even served as garbage inspector for her immigrant ward.

By 1895 at least fifty settlement houses had opened in cities around the nation. Settlement-house leaders trained a generation of young college students, many of whom would later serve as state and local government officials. Florence Kelley, for example, who had worked at Hull House, in 1893 became the chief factory inspector in Illinois. For Kelley as for other young female settlement workers, settlement houses functioned as a supportive sisterhood of reform through which they developed skills in working with municipal governments. Many settlement-house veterans would later draw on their experience in these years and play an influential role in the regulatory movements of the Progressive Era (see Chapter 22). Through their sympathetic attitudes toward the immigrants and their systematic publication of data about slum conditions, settlement-house workers gave turn-of-the-century Americans new hope that the city's problems could be overcome.

But in their attempt to bridge the gap between rich and poor and to promote class cooperation and social harmony, settlement houses had mixed success. Although many immigrants deeply appreciated the settlement houses' resources and activities, they widely felt that the reformers were uninterested in increasing their political power. Limited by their own commitment to social order and class harmony, settlement-house advisers tended to overlook immigrant organizations and their leaders. Although Hull House, one of the most successful of these efforts, attracted two thousand visitors per week in 1894, this was only a fraction of the more than seventy thousand people who dwelled in a six-block radius of the building. "They're like the rest," complained one immigrant, "a bunch of people planning for us and deciding what is good for us without consulting us or taking us into their confidence."

RESHAPING THE URBAN ENVIRONMENT

While reformers battled slum conditions and municipal corruption in the decades after the Civil War, landscape architects and city planners who shared the social workers' goal of a stable, orderly urban society took a different approach. In contrast to those who stressed people-oriented remedies, these architects and planners sought to reshape the urban masses by transforming their physical surroundings. In city after city, they redesigned the street system, installed new sewer and water mains, leveled hills, filled in swamps, and created broad boulevards and tree-lined parkways. Entire sections of America's metropolises were rebuilt in an attempt to restore beauty, dignity, and order to the urban environment.

Convinced that the arts themselves could function as a civilizing force in society, these self-proclaimed saviors of America's cities also established monumental public libraries with extensive book collections and endowed large art museums with treasured paintings and sculpture. To enhance appreciation of drama and music, they constructed theaters and symphony halls and founded professional orchestras. To encourage healthy outdoor exercise, they expanded park and recreational facilities. All the while, real-estate and business interests were remodeling the city in their own way, punctuating the urban skyline with great towers of commerce and finance that rose as high as thirty stories.

Although the motivation behind the commercial construction was simple—profit and business growth—sponsors of the new urban landscape had more complex social objectives. They hoped that the cultural institutions and recreational facilities would make the city more appealing and attractive. But they also wanted, through urban redesign, to instill a sense of monumental order that would tame and restrain the masses. Although they never entirely achieved either goal, they did significantly restructure America's cities in the second half of the nineteenth century.

Parks and Public Spaces

Influenced by the work of English designers, and noting the popularity of parklike cemeteries such as Mount Auburn (1831) in Cambridge, Massachusetts, and Laurel Hill (1836) in Philadelphia, architects Andrew Jackson Downing and Frederick Law Olmsted envisioned a new urban landscape. With the backing of civic leaders, they proposed plans for the American city that contrasted sharply with the designs of the crowded, centralized cities of Europe. The ideal metropolis, they argued, should differentiate land use by clearly separating shopping and housing areas from the industrial district. The city should have a compact commercial nucleus, but even there spacious parks and roadways should open up the landscape. Most important, public buildings and boulevards should be built on a grand scale to inspire and awe ordinary citizens.

Olmsted was one of the earliest and most successful promoters of this vision. A self-taught scientific farmer, surveyor, and journalist, he had teamed up with English architect Calvert Vaux in 1858 to develop "Greensward," the original plan for Central Park in New York City. Olmsted and Vaux consciously designed the park as a spacious, tranquil country refuge within the city, a picturesque alternative to the monotonous straight-line grid of the urban streets. Buoyed by their success with Central Park, they went on to design major parks for Brooklyn, Chicago, Philadelphia, and Boston.

Boston's Back Bay

When Olmsted and other architects called for revitalizing the urban environment through the application of planning and design principles, they took as a model the development of Boston's fashionable Back Bay district.

Until 1857 this area was a 450-acre tidal flat covered with water. Beginning that year, the state undertook a massive engineering project to reclaim the land. Between 1857 and 1900, special gravel trains ran around the clock between the Back Bay and Needham, nine miles away, filling in the low areas and eventually raising the ground level by an average of twenty feet. The state deeded some of the lots thus created to the contractors as payment for the filling work, reserved others for educational and philanthropic organizations, and sold the rest as building lots. Each deed specified the height of the building that could be constructed on the lot, the distance that the building should be set back from the street, and the construction materials that could be used.

State engineers laid out Commonwealth Avenue, the Back Bay's main thoroughfare, along the lines of a

Boston Public Gardens, *by Edward Emerson Simmons, 1893*
Urban parks such as the Boston Public Garden brought the country into the city, creating a peaceful refuge from the din of downtown life.

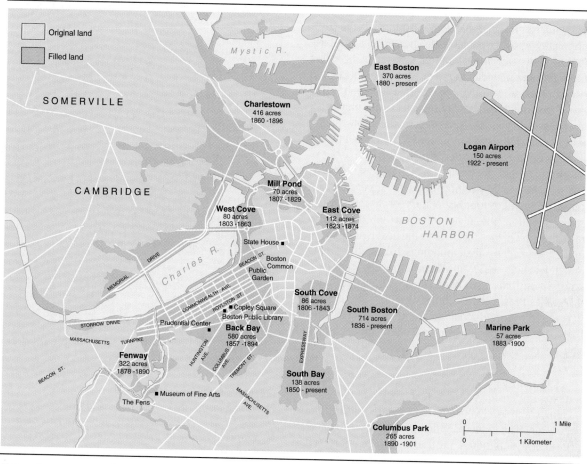

Original land

Filled land

Mystic R.

East Boston
370 acres
1880 - present

Charlestown
416 acres
1860 -1896

SOMERVILLE

Logan Airport
150 acres
1922 - present

CAMBRIDGE

Mill Pond
70 acres
1807 -1829

West Cove
80 acres
1803 -1863

East Cove
112 acres
1823 -1874

*BOSTON
HARBOR*

Charles R.

MEMORIAL   DRIVE

State House ■

BEACON ST.
Boston
Common
Public
Garden

COMMONWEALTH AVE.

BOYLSTON ST.

■ Copley Square
Boston Public Library

South Cove
86 acres
1806 -1843

South Boston
714 acres
1836 - present

Prudential Center ■

STORROW DRIVE

MASSACHUSETTS   TURNPIKE

Back Bay
580 acres
1857 -1894

HUNTINGTON   AVE.

COLUMBUS   AVE.

TREMONT ST.

EXPRESSWAY

Marine Park
57 acres
1883 - 1900

Fenway
322 acres
1878 -1890

BEACON ST.

■ Museum of Fine Arts

The Fens

MASSACHUSETTS   AVE.

South Bay
138 acres
1850 - present

Columbus Park
265 acres
1890 -1901

0   1 Mile

0   1 Kilometer

Urban Improvement: Expanding the City of Boston
*Contractors used round-the-clock gravel trains to fill in Boston's smelly tidal flats. The city
not only gained valuable new land but also cleverly transformed a storage basin for river
flood waters into the Back Bay Fens, the first in a string of connected urban parks.*

French boulevard, with a formal, central section graced by trees, stone benches, and statues. Elegant side streets branched off from the avenue, with back alleys for horse-cart deliveries. The uniform height of the district's five-story brownstone houses established a line of vision that imparted both formality and consistency.

A variety of cultural institutions, founded through donations from upper-class business owners, reinforced the Back Bay's image as a center of civilization and refinement. Architect Henry Hobson Richardson designed the imposing Trinity Church on Copley Square in 1875. Twelve years later, on the opposite side of the square, the New York firm of McKim, Mead, and White erected the monumental Boston Public Library. Space was also allocated for a fine-arts museum, a museum of science, and an orchestra hall. In 1881 Frederick Law Olmsted laid out the Fenway Park system near the Back

Bay, building up the roadways to form dikes along the banks of the meandering, low-lying Muddy River.

Under the careful regulations of the Back Bay commissioners, the district, with its array of cultural attractions, became a mecca for upper-class Bostonians. In addition to the public library, the Back Bay eventually contained two colleges, two museums, five schools, and twelve churches. In the eyes of many social reformers, Back Bay Boston thus represented the ideal urban environment that could be created through city planning.

Rebuilding Chicago

In contrast to Boston's achievements, the expansion of Chicago in the post–Civil War era was a planner's nightmare. Chicago was America's shock city, the extreme example of the many problems spawned by unregulated growth. Between 1850 and 1870, the city's population rose like a tidal wave, increasing from thirty thousand to nearly three hundred thousand. The influx not only strained city services but also inundated neighborhoods. So brisk was the rate of increase that architects, builders, and city officials could only react to crises as they arose. Nevertheless, the sheer magnitude of change forced Chicagoans to innovate in ways that were sometimes copied elsewhere.

For example, the expansion of the city in the 1840s left residents with swampy, unpaved streets that remained quagmires for most of the year. To remedy this soggy situation, the city council in 1855 decided to raise the level of the streets. Over the next twenty years, owners jacked up their buildings to meet the new grade level. In 1857 one British traveler noted in amazement that "the Briggs House, a gigantic hotel, five stories high, solid masonry, weighing 22,000 tons, was raised four and a half feet, and new foundations built below. The people were in it all the time, coming and going, eating and sleeping—the whole business of the hotel proceeding without interruption."

Chicago faced a new crisis in October 1871 when a raging fire destroyed more than sixty-one thousand buildings and leveled nearly four square miles in the central city. The entire commercial district was gutted, and nearly a hundred thousand people were left homeless. The urgent need for downtown reconstruction provided an unprecedented opportunity for Chicago architects, engineers, and civic leaders. In the next two decades, these groups cooperatively pioneered exciting new methods for tall-office-building construction. Their experimentation made possible a new American building type, the skyscraper.

The skyscraper depended on three technological innovations: fireproofing, the internal metal frame, and the elevator. Although all three were available before the fire, not until the 1880s did Chicago architects, hectically rebuilding the city's business district, combine them in a distinctive commercial style. Given the city's recent experience, officials insisted that all new structures be built out of noncombustible materials. Stone was the obvious choice, but its great weight sharply limited the size of stone buildings that could be erected on Chicago's marshy soil. Louis Sullivan and other architects developed a far lighter alternative—a central metal skeleton, fireproofed with a fired-clay (or terracotta) tile, to support the exterior walls. By placing the metal frame on an expanded foundation and installing

Chicago's First Skyscraper
The Home Insurance Company building, designed in 1885 by William Le Baron Jenney, pioneered the new skyscraper structure by using an internal skeleton of steel to support its thin masonry walls.

motorized steam and electric elevators, Chicago architects increased the city's building heights from four to twenty-two stories. Once the commanding size and elevation of the Reliance Building (1890), Masonic Temple (1891), and other Chicago skyscrapers had demonstrated the technical feasibility and commercial advantages of constructing tall, metal-supported buildings on small, expensive urban lots, other American cities began to raise their skylines as well.

The dramatic rebuilding of the urban environment in Boston and Chicago, together with the inspiring example of Chicago's World's Columbian Exposition in 1892–1893 (see Chapter 18), encouraged business leaders and reformers in many smaller cities to swing into action. By the turn of the century, municipal-art societies, park and outdoor-art associations, and civic-improvement leagues had sprung up around the country. City after city launched planning programs to replace muddy streets and unsightly billboards in the downtown business districts with broad boulevards, sparkling fountains, and gleaming marble public buildings.

Known collectively as the city-beautiful movement, this crusade favored the interests of the well-born and the wealthy. Although advocates of the movement asserted that improving the urban landscape would benefit both rich and poor alike, they were less interested in upgrading the quality of immigrant housing and sanitary conditions in the slums than in making the city's public buildings impressive and monumental. Like the followers of the architect Richard Morris Hunt, they believed that attractive, more imposing civic architecture and landscape design would inevitably produce better citizens and reduce the dangers of urban immorality and social disorder. In the early twentieth century, the city-beautiful impulse would evolve into a comprehensive city-planning movement (see Chapter 22) inspired by even more soaring visions of a transformed urban environment.

Toward a Metropolitan America

While the city-beautiful advocates drafted their plans for the urban future, harried city-hall bureaucrats, municipal administrators, and civic engineers wrestled with such practical matters as inadequate water supplies, antiquated sewer systems, and basic municipal services that seemed continually to lag behind the pace of urban growth. As they worked to upgrade city services, these administrators developed more efficient and more centralized mechanisms of municipal organization and supervision. Little by little, new citywide agencies took over matters once handled at the neighborhood and ward level.

But while city administration became centralized, urban power remained widely dispersed. Urban elites, particularly business and real-estate interests, had difficulty cooperating. Immigrants often opposed the centralizing tendency, particularly when it disrupted familiar ties with the ward captain or involved plans to force them out of dilapidated though relatively inexpensive housing. Such conflicts among different segments of the urban population ultimately encouraged compromise arrangements necessary for the smooth functioning of the entire city.

Around midcentury, city dwellers began to recognize that the most dangerous aspect of urban life was the deplorable quality of the water and sewer systems. Most urbanites in the 1870s still relied on private wells, outhouses, and cesspools. Sewer systems, where they existed, were primitive and ineffective. One sanitary engineer described city sewer systems as "reservoirs of liquid filth, ever oozing through the defective joints, and polluting the very earth upon which the city stands."

Chicago poured its sewage directly into Lake Michigan, continually contaminating the source of its water supply and contributing directly to the frequent cholera, typhoid, and diphtheria epidemics that ravaged the city; Chicago's typhoid death rate alone reached 174 per 100,000 people in 1891. In New Jersey, Paterson and Passaic dumped their sewage directly into the Passaic River right above Newark's freshwater intakes.

Early attempts by city officials to construct interconnected sewer systems fell victim to local politics. In Washington, D.C., for example, the first contractors hired to build the system, who were chosen for their political contacts, proved grossly incompetent. They produced lateral sewers that could not run uphill into the main trunk lines. In New Orleans, a city subject to outbreaks of yellow fever and malaria, efforts to construct a citywide system in 1892 failed because of political ineptitude and contractor inexperience. Similarly, in St. Louis and Cincinnati, where politicians awarded contracts based on patronage, early, inadequate systems had to be replaced within a decade, at enormous expense.

Gradually and painfully, however, cities began to develop the centralized administrative structures that their size required, including the managerial tools to build and run effective sewer and water systems. To halt the further pollution of Lake Michigan, Chicago city officials in 1889 persuaded the state legislature to create a 185-square-mile sanitary district encompassing the city and its environs, supervised by elected officials with independent taxing authority. Between 1894 and 1899, the city built the enormous Ship and Sanitary Canal, which reversed the flow of the Chicago River to carry the city's processed sewage downstate. In Boston, too, engineers and civic officials in 1889 set up the centralized Metropolitan Sewage Commission, a permanent bureaucracy empowered to acquire land, oversee sewer construction, and formulate long-term expansion plans. By 1900 sewer and water systems established elsewhere had cut mortality rates from typhoid fever nationwide by 65 percent.

The movement to centralize control over water and sewer facilities was emblematic of a broader process of physical and political consolidation in urban America in the late nineteenth century. As cities exploded in size, they added unincorporated surrounding land (a process called annexation) and absorbed adjacent municipalities (consolidation). Through annexation and consolidation, city governments found that they could better coordinate transportation, water, and sewer networks and also increase tax revenues. In 1859 Philadelphia annexed five surrounding suburbs, quadrupling its population with the stroke of a pen. Chicago followed suit in 1889, adding 133 square miles in an area that is now the far South Side. The largest such consolidation occurred in 1898, when Brooklyn, Queens, Staten Island, and the Bronx joined Manhattan to form the New York City that we know today. In the process, New York added nearly 2 million people to its population and ballooned in size from forty-four to nearly three hundred square miles.

Practically every large American city broadened its boundaries in these years. The trend toward annexation was supported by merchants and business elites who saw it as another way to undercut the political power of the immigrant wards that in their view stood in the way of progress. The good-government reformers, waving the banner of civic efficiency, hailed annexation as a step toward making the police and fire departments and other municipal agencies more professional. Land speculators and real-estate promoters welcomed annexation as a way of securing the municipal water and sewer systems that would sharply increase the worth of their holdings. Most middle-class suburbanites, eager for access to efficient city services, went along with the process. Not until the mid-twentieth century would outlying suburban communities, valuing local autonomy and wary of big-city tax rates and social problems, successfully fight off annexation.

CONCLUSION

The movement toward a metropolitan America represented the culmination of a long struggle to control the changing urban world in the decades after the Civil War. The mind-boggling urban expansion of these years, drawing in millions of rural Americans and foreign immigrants alike, brought a concentration of economic power, an expansion of consumer markets, and a cornucopia of lucrative investment possibilities. For a nation in which seven out of ten people still lived on farms or in towns of fewer than twenty-five hundred inhabitants, as was true of America in 1880, the big cities' sheer size and diversity sometimes seemed overwhelming, while the battles for power and wealth that raged in urban America proved both exciting and deeply disturbing. It is hardly surprising that observers of the time like Jacob Riis threw up their hands at conditions in the nation's metropolises.

While the social critics had their say, the urban population itself wrestled with the stresses and tensions of a social environment unfamiliar to many and undergoing tremendous flux. Middle- and upper-class urban residents were troubled not only by the new industrial city's massive physical problems—housing, schooling, transportation, sanitation, police and fire protection, and all the rest—but even more

by the city's corrosive effect on traditional values and expectations. Migrants from America's farms and homogeneous small towns suddenly found themselves in an impersonal, ever-changing, fast-paced commercial world where antagonistic economic interests and ethnic and racial groups grappled for influence and power.

Predictably many of the native-born urban newcomers responded by attempting to re-create in the city the familiar features of rural life. They agitated for parks and playgrounds to bring nature into the metropolis, crusaded for temperance to dam the river of alcohol that washed over the immigrant wards, and campaigned for political reforms that would end boss rule and restore to them familiar forms of local government.

Immigrants, too, had to adjust to city life. Recently uprooted, in many cases, from centuries-old rhythms of peasant life or from the ghettos of eastern Europe, these newly arrived aliens had to adapt to the unremitting demands of industrial labor, to a babble of unfamiliar languages, to the mortal hazards and casual indignities of tenement-house life, and to the head-spinning diversity of the American urban scene. Faced with discrimination and hostility, older immigrants clung as long as they could to their traditional ways, their ethnic foods, their street and saloon culture, and their cherished religious institutions. Remarkably impervious to the assaults of middle-class political opponents, the pieties of would-be uplifters, or the efforts of moral reformers to legislate behavior, the immigrants rallied round a familiar figure, the boss. Of all the urban actors in these years the bosses demonstrated the most versatility in learning how to wield the levers of power in the strange new world of the Gilded Age city.

The city, then, was a place of constant contention among wildly different groups—poverty-stricken foreign immigrants, recent arrivals from the American hinterland, old urban elites, newly minted capitalist tycoons, an uneasy middle class, growing numbers of blacks—that eyed each other warily through layers of suspicion and mistrust. In view of these social realities, it is hardly surprising that the beautifiers and planners who sought through monumental architecture, classic statuary, and broad avenues to force the city into a single cultural mold only partially achieved their aims.

What finally emerged from the boisterous and bruising conflict was a gradual recognition that all city dwellers shared a basic interest in such mundane matters as clean water, adequate sewers, regular garbage collection, and reliable fire protection. Out of this realization blossomed a conception of what some called the service city—a city that could efficiently meet the collective needs of its diverse inhabitants while they pursued their personal or group interests. By 1900 cities across America had established administrative structures and developed trained bureaucracies with broad responsibility for sanitation, transportation, street lights, public health, parks, police, and so on. A metropolitan America had taken shape.

Despite dark warnings of chaos and social upheaval, a remarkable degree of order and stability prevailed in urban America as the nineteenth century closed. After a generation of unchecked growth, political struggle, and social unrest, the nation's cities had evolved governmental forms sufficient to assure at least an adequate quality of life for all and to intervene when necessary to protect the welfare of the urban populace. This enlarged conception of government only slowly penetrated the arena of national politics, but the lessons so painfully learned in the late-nineteenth-century cities would profoundly shape the progressive movement that lay ahead.

CHRONOLOGY

1843 Robert M. Hartley founds the New York Association for Improving the Condition of the Poor.

1851 The American branch of the Young Men's Christian Association (YMCA) opens.

1853 Charles Loring Brace founds the New York Children's Aid Society.

1855 New York opens its Castle Garden immigrant center.

1857 Filling in of Boston's Back Bay begins.

1858 Frederick Law Olmsted and Calvert Vaux design Central Park.

1859 Philadelphia annexes five surrounding suburbs.

1869 Boss William Marcy Tweed gains control of New York's Tammany Hall political machine.

1871 The Great Chicago Fire.

1872 Anthony Comstock founds the New York Society for the Suppression of Vice and leads a "purity" campaign.

1874 John Wanamaker opens his Philadelphia department store.

1875 Henry Hobson Richardson designs Trinity Church in Boston.

1879 The New York "dumbbell" tenement law is passed.

1880 William Booth's followers establish an American branch of the Salvation Army.

1882 Josephine Shaw Lowell founds the New York Charity Organization Society (COS).

1888 First electric-trolley line, in Richmond, Virginia.

1889 Jane Addams and Ellen Gates Starr open Hull House.

1890 Jacob Riis,
How the Other Half Lives.

Jacob Riis

1892 Immigrant-admitting station is opened on Ellis Island in the New York City harbor.

Reverend Charles Parkhurst organizes the City Vigilance League.

"Big Jim" Pendergast gains control of the Kansas City political machine.

1894 The Chicago Ship and Sanitary Canal is built.

Clarence Lexow's investigation of New York City reveals widespread police corruption.

1898 New York City consolidates five boroughs into Greater New York.

1900 Theodore Dreiser, *Sister Carrie.*

1907 Walter Rauschenbusch, *Christianity and the Social Crisis.*

1910 Jane Addams, *Twenty Years at Hull House.*

For Further Reading

Paul Boyer, *Urban Masses and Moral Order in America, 1820–1920* (1978). A richly detailed analysis of reformers' attempts to control city life.

Ruth H. Crocker, *Social Work and Social Order: The Settlement Movement in Two Industrial Cities, 1889–1930* (1992). An important, balanced assessment of the settlement-house movement.

William Cronon, *Nature's Metropolis: Chicago and the Great West* (1991). An innovative study of the link between urban growth and regional economic prosperity in the Midwest.

Kenneth T. Jackson, *Crabgrass Frontier: The Suburbanization of the United States* (1985). A stimulating comparative study of city expansion and suburban development in Europe and America.

Peter McCaffery, *When Bosses Ruled Philadelphia: The Emergence of the Republican Machine, 1867–1933* (1993). A revi-

sionist look at political bosses that downplays their welfare role.

Martin V. Melosi, ed., *Pollution and Reform in American Cities, 1870–1930* (1980). A pioneering examination of the environmental impact of U.S. industrial and urban growth.

Walter Nugent, *Crossings: The Great Transatlantic Migrations, 1870–1914* (1992). A thoughtful overview of the reasons for the major migrations to the Americas.

Kathy Peiss, *Cheap Amusements: Working Women and Leisure in Turn-of-the-Century New York* (1986). A forceful, provocative analysis of immigrant women's lives.

David Ward, *Poverty, Ethnicity, and the American City, 1840–1925* (1989). A penetrating analysis of the relationship among immigration, ethnicity, and the changing structure of industrial capitalism.

Additional Bibliography

Urban Growth and Expansion

Thomas J. Archdeacon, *Becoming American: An Ethnic History* (1983); Gunther Barth, *Instant Cities: Urbanization and the Rise of San Francisco and Denver* (1975) and *City People: The Rise of Modern City Culture in Nineteenth-Century America* (1978); John E. Bodnar, *The Transplanted: A History of Immigrants in Urban America* (1985); Howard P. Chudacoff, *Mobile Americans: Residential and Social Mobility in Omaha, 1880–1920* (1972); Brian J. Cudahy, *Cash, Tokens, and Transfers: A History of Urban Mass Transit in North America* (1990); Roger Daniels, *A History of Immigration and Ethnicity in American Life* (1990); Lawrence H. Fuchs, *The American Kaleidoscope: Race, Ethnicity, and the Civic Culture* (1990); Donna R. Gabaccia, *From Sicily to Elizabeth Street: Housing and Social Change Among Italian Immigrants, 1880–1930* (1982); Susan A. Glenn, *Daughters of the Shtetl: Life and Labor in the Immigrant Generation* (1990); John Higham, *Send These to Me: Jews and Other Immigrants in Urban America* (1975) and ed., *Ethnic Leadership in America* (1978); Alan M. Kraut, *The Huddled Masses: The Immigrant in American Society, 1880–1921* (1982); Judith W. Leavitt, *The*

Healthiest City: Milwaukee and the Politics of Health Reform (1982); Stephen J. Leonard and Thomas J. Noel, *Denver: Mining Camp to Metropolis* (1990); Virginia Yans-McLaughlin, ed., *Immigration Reconsidered: History, Sociology, Politics* (1990); Stanley Nadel, *Ethnicity, Religion, and Class in New York City, 1845–1880* (1990); Roy Rosenzweig, *Eight Hours for What We Will: Workers and Leisure in an Industrial City, 1870–1920* (1983); Rudolph J. Vecoli and Suzanne M. Sinke, eds., *A Century of European Migrations, 1830–1930* (1991); Sam B. Warner, Jr., *The Urban Wilderness: A History of the American City* (1972).

The Problems of the City

Jane Addams, *Twenty Years at Hull House* (1910); Alexander B. Callow, Jr., *The Tweed Ring* (1966) and *The City Boss in America* (1976); Allen F. Davis, *Spearheads for Reform: The Social Settlements and the Progressive Movement 1890–1914* (1967); Robert M. Fogelson, *Big-City Police* (1977); Lawrence M. Friedman, *Crime and Punishment in American History* (1993); Timothy J.

Gilfoyle, *City of Eros: New York City, Prostitution, and the Commercialization of Sex, 1790–1920* (1992); Lori Ginzberg, *Women and the Work of Benevolence: Morality, Politics, and Class in the Nineteenth-Century United States* (1990); Sidney L. Harring, *Policing a Class Society: The Experience of American Cities, 1865–1915* (1983); Alan M. Kraut, *Silent Travelers: Germs, Genes, and the "Immigrant Menace"* (1994); Kenneth L. Kusmer, *A Ghetto Takes Shape: Black Cleveland, 1870–1930* (1976); Roger Lane, *Policing the City: Boston, 1822–1885* (1967) and *William Dorsey's Philadelphia and Ours: On the Past and Future of the Black City in America* (1991); Elisabeth Lasch-Quinn, *Black Neighbors: Race and the Limits of Reform in the American Settlement House Movement, 1890–1945* (1993); Terrence J. McDonald, *The Parameters of Urban Fiscal Policy: Socioeconomic Change and Political Culture in San Francisco, 1860–1906* (1986) and ed., William Riordon, *Plunkitt of Tammany Hall* (1994); Henry F. May, *Protestant Churches and Industrial America* (1963); Zane L. Miller, *Boss Cox's Cincinnati: Urban Politics in the Progressive Era* (1968); Gwendolyn Mink, *Old Labor and New Immigrants in American Political Development: Union, Party, and State, 1875–1920* (1986); Eric H. Monkkonen, *Police in Urban America, 1860–1920* (1981) and *America Becomes Urban: The Development of U.S. Cities and Towns, 1780–1980* (1988); Christine M. Rosen, *The Limits of Power: Great Fires and the Process of City Growth in America* (1986); Sheila M. Rothman, *Living in the Shadow of Death: Tuberculosis and the Social Experience of Illness in American History* (1994); Henry L. Taylor, Jr., ed., *Race and the City: Work, Community, and Protest in Cincinnati, 1820–1970* (1993).

Transforming the City's Physical Environment

Elizabeth C. Cromley, *Alone Together: A History of New York's Early Apartments* (1990); John Duffy, *The Sanitarians: A History of American Public Health* (1990); Albert Fein, *Frederick Law Olmsted and the American Environmental Tradition* (1972); James Gilbert, *Perfect Cities: Chicago's Utopias of 1893* (1991); David C. Hammack, *Power and Society: Greater New York at the Turn of the Century* (1982); William H. Jordy, *American Buildings and Their Architects* (Vol. 3 of *Progressive and Academic Ideals at the Turn of the Century*) (1972); Lawrence W. Kennedy, *Planning a City upon a Hill: Boston Since 1630* (1992); John Ottensmann, *The Changing Spatial Structure of American Cities* (1975); Harold L. Platt, *The Electric City: Energy and the Growth of the Chicago Area, 1880–1930* (1991); David Schuyler, *The New Urban Landscape: The Redefinition of City Form in Nineteenth-Century America* (1986); Jon C. Teaford, *City and Suburb: The Political Fragmentation of Metropolitan America, 1850–1970* (1979) and *The Unheralded Triumph: City Government in America, 1870–1900* (1984); Robert C. Twombly, *Louis Sullivan: His Life and Work* (1986).

Practice Makes Perfect
c. 1900

DAILY LIFE, POPULAR CULTURE, AND THE ARTS
1860–1900

In 1894 Walter Teller Post (inset), a recently married junior clerk for the Northern Pacific Railway in St. Paul, Minnesota, wrote in high spirits to his father on the family farm in Michigan. "I am hunting for a house," he noted. "Lillie and I have decided that it will be much nicer to go to housekeeping than to board. . . . We have to pay $35.00 per month for board. . . . We want to get a house [to rent] for about $15 or $20.00 per mo."

Several weeks later, Post proudly sent his father a sketch of their new rented house, showing the placement of all furniture and including stick figures of himself and his wife tucked cozily in their bed. The young couple had tried to furnish their home inexpensively, turning down, for example, a "wonderful opportunity" to purchase a $300 piano for only $10 down and $10 a month. Nevertheless, they had run up a $150 bill at a St. Paul department store. Post had put $100 down and promised to pay the balance in two months.

Post's father did not approve. Buying on credit was dangerous, he wrote back. And what about Walter's promise to send home ten dollars a month to help out his parents? Knowing only the long hours and hard work of farm life, the elder Post counseled restraint and warned his son not to spend beyond his means.

Post's father's concerns were well founded. Dazzled by the growing availability of consumer

goods, Walter had gotten in over his head. In less than two months, staggered by an unanticipated heating bill on his rented house, Post defaulted on his debt to the department store. Frustrated with his long hours and low pay, Post began to complain to his superiors. In September 1896 the railroad dismissed him. Soon he was searching for work among relatives in Indiana.

Walter Post's experience was hardly unique. Countless other people faced similar difficulties in adjusting to the emerging consumer culture. American society was slowly shifting from a producer economy that valued hard work and thrift to a new consumer economy wherein material possessions and leisure-time activities became the hallmarks of personal identity. For the throngs of native-born Americans who, like Walter Post, moved from farm to city to work for national corporations, and for the millions of foreign immigrants to the United States in these years, the process of adjusting expectations and learning to live in a rapidly changing industrial society was not easy.

Although the heyday of consumer goods lay in the future, a torrent of new products poured out of American factories, promising a transformation of everyday life and unimagined levels of comfort and convenience. Hot-air furnaces, electric lights, indoor plumbing, sewing machines, and cast-iron kitchen ranges eased the drudgery of running a home. Kellogg's Corn Flakes, Hires Root Beer, Jell-O, Borden's Evaporated Milk, and other prepared foods reduced meal-preparation time as well.

But these products were not equally accessible to everyone; their greater variety, in fact, widened the gulf between the haves and the have-nots and intensified the sense of class consciousness among rich and poor. The middle and upper classes, which included lawyers, doctors, accountants, store managers, engineers, and other white-collar workers, increasingly defined their status in terms of comfortable houses, material possessions, education, genteel cultural standards, and leisure activities. In contrast, farmers and the urban working classes— the overwhelming majority of the population—although attracted (like Walter Post) to the new consumer products dangled before them, gained access to them slowly. Restricted by low income and frequent unemployment, they plucked whatever small benefits they could.

Despite a roller-coaster economy and major depressions in 1873 and 1893, many men and women did improve their families' economic position and social standing. For all the upward mobility, however, the gulf between the classes widened. While the very rich lived in a world apart, and the middle class embraced its own particular behavior code and cultural pursuits, a vigorous working-class culture took form in the streets, churches, dance halls, saloons, vaudeville theaters, social clubs, and amusement parks of the bustling immigrant cities. Middle-class reformers strove to remake this working-class culture into their own image of propriety. In the long run, however, it was the culture of the masses that would prove the more influential in shaping modern America.

EVERYDAY LIFE IN FLUX

In the closing decades of the nineteenth century, industrialization not only introduced an unprecedented range of innovative products but also opened up new jobs and destroyed older ones, in the process rearranging the occupational structure and altering the

distribution of income within society. These changes, together with the expansion of white-collar occupations, created new expectations for family life and fostered a growing sense of class awareness. "The stratification of our society, and its crystallization into social groups," wrote New York lawyer John Jay Chapman in 1898, "is little short of miraculous."

Rising Standards of Living

In the second half of the nineteenth century, in virtually every industry, mechanization increased output, decreased prices, and encouraged the development of new products that revolutionized life for many Americans. In the clothing trades, for instance, the widespread use of sewing machines profoundly changed the apparel industry. Before the Civil War, handmade shirts required nearly thirty thousand stitches and took fourteen hours to complete. Most people wore hand-me-downs, and styles were simple. By the 1880s, however, complete shirts of standardized size could be machine-sewn in less than two hours.

Because of these changes, personal wardrobes for the middle and elite classes expanded dramatically. Clothes closets became commonplace household features, supplementing the small bureaus or armoires that had previously sufficed to hold the family apparel. Dress became an ever-more-important badge of social class. Immigrants and rural migrants rushed to purchase cheap factory-made clothes and lose the "greenhorn" or "hayseed" look.

Innovations in food technology, among them breakfast cereals, changed eating habits. In 1878, following on the heels of pre–Civil War dietary reformer Sylvester Graham (see Chapter 11), physician John Harvey Kellogg of Battle Creek, Michigan, marketed Granola—a wheat, corn, and oat mixture that he advertised as healthier than the then standard breakfast of sausage, eggs, and potatoes. In the next three decades, Kellogg produced a variety of new cereals, including wheat flakes, shredded wheat, and Kellogg's Corn Flakes.

Soon competitors rushed into the field. Charles W. Post, for example, developed Grape Nuts Flakes and Postum, a breakfast drink made from bran, wheat, and molasses that he touted as an alternative to overstimulating, unhealthful coffee. By the turn of the century, health-conscious middle- and upper-class Americans had shifted to the new cereals and hot drinks as simpler, more easily prepared substitutes for the traditional heavy breakfast.

The Veribest

By the turn of the century, Armour and other meat packing companies promoted their trimmed and packaged meats not only as time-savers for busy homemakers but also as a guarantee of high quality. As the product name and the medals on the young cook suggest, Armour hoped that customers would think that this canned meat had won prestigious awards at the recent world's fairs in Chicago or St. Louis.

Not all inventions lived up to their promoters' claims. Lydia Pinkham's famous vegetable extract "for all those painful Complaints and Weaknesses so common to our best female population" contained nearly 23 percent alcohol. Other so-called health compounds featured significant amounts of opium. Countless patent medicines, including one that promised to "POSITIVELY CURE" backache in two hours and deafness in two days, were totally ineffective. But they were eagerly snatched up by a society that had come to believe that material and physical improvements were now within everyone's reach.

Although some products failed to work as claimed, the overall impact of late-nineteenth-century industrialization was to significantly improve the level of comfort and convenience for many American families. In 1870 most urban women had shopped daily, baked their own bread, and canned their own fruits and vegetables. Hours and hours were spent preparing food, doing laundry by hand, firing up smoky stoves and furnaces, and carrying "slop jars" containing human excrement to malodorous waste-collection tanks. By 1900, in contrast, the spread of indoor plumbing, better stoves and furnaces, commercially prepared foods, and mechanical washing machines had greatly eased this domestic burden. Urban middle- and upper-class families began to take for granted central heating, electric lights, telephone service, and a range of other household innovations unknown earlier. Refrigerated railroad cars now brought fresh meat to local butchers, and housewives used iceboxes to store it for up to a week. In place of canning, homemakers purchased inexpensive commercially canned vegetables, Heinz pickles, and Campbell's soups. Campbell's jingle—"It only takes a ten-cent can to make enough for six"—targeted an economy-minded mass market.

Bringing New Commodities to Rural and Small-Town America

While the new products made possible by swift industrialization gradually changed the lives of city dwellers, mail-order houses and chain stores reoriented the standards of rural and small-town consumers. The changes began with Aaron Montgomery Ward, a traveling salesman from Chicago. In the 1860s Ward realized how dependent rural Americans were on local merchants selling a limited range of goods at high prices. Scraping together his savings and joining forces with the Grangers, who had pledged to reduce farmers' costs by cutting out the middleman (see Chapter 17), Ward in 1872 circulated a list of products for sale at a 40 percent discount. For farmers hesitant to deal with a distant, unknown merchant, he promised the unconditional right to return merchandise. By 1884 Ward's catalog offered nearly ten thousand items to rural customers.

Ward soon ran into competition from Richard Warren Sears, a flamboyant young Minnesota railroad agent whose taste for marketing was first whetted when he sold a case of watches left at his station. Moving to Chicago in 1887, he established a mail-order company (now Sears, Roebuck) that could ship farmers a wide range of products, including agricultural implements, clothing, medicine, furniture, stoves, guns, tools, and baby carriages. Sears built customer loyalty by guaranteeing low prices and publishing testimonials from satisfied patrons. The firm carried many products at different prices to suit all pocketbooks. Pump organs, for example, ranged from "Our AA Grade Home Favorite" at $64.95 to "Our Happy Home Organ, Grade B," at $22.00.

Distributed to millions of rural families, the encyclopedic Sears and Ward's catalogs, available in German and Swedish as well as English, opened the door to a new world of consumer goods and, coincidentally, educated their readers in the canons of middle-class taste. "The prevailing style in furniture," advised the 1897 Sears catalog, "is to have the various odd pieces upholstered in harmonizing colors of different shades." Similarly, consumers had only to browse through the mail-order catalog to learn to distinguish a fish fork from a pickle fork or to appreciate the differences between cheap and expensive sewing machines, sleighs, and carriages.

Marketing like this inspired such trust in rural and small-town readers that they sometimes sought advice on personal problems. One lonely farmer wrote to Montgomery Ward's proposing marriage to the "girl wearing hat number —— on p. 153 of your catalog."

The chain store offered another mechanism for bringing low-priced mass-produced goods to consumers outside large cities. F. W. Woolworth, a farm boy from upstate New York, in 1879 opened a "Five and Ten Cent Store" in Utica that sold goods like crochet needles, safety pins, soap, harmonicas, and thimbles from a "five-cent counter." Increasing his volume and multiplying his stores, Woolworth appealed to those Americans who either lacked the money to buy more expensive goods or simply wished to economize. Woolworth's, together with the Great Atlantic and Pacific Tea Company (A&P), which consolidated several separate food stores into one operation in 1859, pioneered the creation of nationwide "chains" that stressed low prices and consumer savings.

Under a barrage of advertising, consumers by the 1890s faced new choices daily about what they should buy. More conscious than ever before of the sparkling array of material options open to them, the American people were slowly drawn into a milieu in which the goods and services purchased increasingly dictated one's position and status in society. At the same time

that material possessions made possible new realms of comfort and convenience, they also reinforced a pervasive sense of widening class differences.

A Shifting Class Structure

Patterns of consumption, culture, and everyday life reflect a society's class structure, and in late-nineteenth-century America, this structure underwent important modifications. From the colonial period on, social class had been loosely defined by occupation and income. Contemporaries readily identified the rich, the "middling ranks," and the poor in every community. But in the post–Civil War era, fundamental changes in the nature of work, together with shifts in residential location, massive immigration, and new patterns of consumption, redefined and sharpened the conception of social class. In addition to income and occupation, lifestyle and self-identification now became important determinants of social rank.

The working class felt the impact of these changes first and most keenly. At midcentury skilled artisans, who exercised considerable authority over their work and viewed themselves as independent entrepreneurs, had dominated the working class. Common laborers, who exchanged simple muscle power for a daily wage, identified with the artisans above them and hoped eventually to acquire skilled positions themselves. Although skilled artisans earned between five hundred and nine hundred dollars yearly, or from two to ten times the wages of common laborers, both segments of the working class shared a common outlook and sense of class identity. In Pittsburgh and other cities, craftsworkers and laborers lived on the same streets, attended the same churches, and patronized the same saloons. They believed in the value of hard physical labor, prided themselves on their physical strength, and helped each other in times of need.

Beginning in the 1870s, however, the bond between craftsworkers and unskilled laborers began to dissolve as new production methods restructured the work process. By the 1880s the widespread use of machinery had destroyed the jobs of many skilled artisans. The Bessemer steel-making process, for example, eliminated the need for the skilled puddlers who controlled production in the iron industry. With fewer skilled positions available, the only people willing to undertake the dangerous, low-paying steel-mill jobs were unskilled foreign immigrants who desperately needed work. Thus by the turn of the century, a rift had

Telephone Operators, 1885
The anonymity of the new technology of the telephone sometimes led to flirtations between male callers and the young women who manually transferred calls. Mark Twain's narrator in A Connecticut Yankee in King Arthur's Court *(1889) is so infatuated with telephone operators that he names his first child Hello Central.*

developed within the working class. Craftsworkers now commonly looked down on the newcomers. Cut off from the common laborers who formed a substratum below them, skilled artisans identified more and more with the middle class.

As the working class fragmented, the expansion of the middle class, which would vastly accelerate in the early twentieth century, was already under way. After the Civil War, the demand for trained personnel increased in all economic sectors. Growing municipal bureaucracies, school systems, police forces, and fire departments required specially trained employees. Large businesses and national corporations hired armies of clerks, accountants, and salespeople to manage their operations. Bustling department stores, insurance agencies, and food companies established accounting and sales divisions. These middle-class personnel worked in clean company headquarters and city offices physically separated from the sooty factories and dirty mills that employed manual laborers.

In contrast to members of the working class, who were paid by the hour or according to the level of production, middle-class clerical and professional workers received fixed weekly or monthly salaries. The salaries of the middle class, moreover, were considerably higher than even those of skilled craftsworkers. In Detroit, where very few skilled artisans took home more than $500 yearly, city clerks, bookkeepers, and inspec-

tors earned between $500 and $1,000, and other middle-class jobs often paid more than $1,000 a year.

Middle-class employees' higher earnings and steady work significantly changed their outlook and expectations. Freed from worries about making ends meet, many adopted long-term strategies for maximizing their purchasing power. They devoted more resources to educating their children, buying expensive items such as sewing machines and pianos on credit, and otherwise improving household comforts and conveniences. A shorter workweek, moreover, gave middle-class employees more time to spend with their families and greater opportunities for socializing and recreation.

The very wealthy, meanwhile, did not hesitate to flaunt their riches, thus honing public awareness of growing class divisions in industrial America. The Carnegies, Morgans, Rockefellers, Goulds, Huntingtons, and Fricks used their immense fortunes to build elaborate houses and country estates. Railroad financier Jay Gould, the owner of Lyndhurst—a Gothic castlelike home in Tarrytown, New York, with a 380-foot-long greenhouse filled with exotic plants—was typical of a generation for whom a palatial house offered the ultimate proof of success on the capitalist battlefield. In Newport (Rhode Island), Bar Harbor (Maine), and other fashionable resort areas, the wealthy built great mansions (euphemistically called cottages), kept stables of racehorses, joined exclusive country clubs, and cruised on their magnificent personal yachts. Many also amassed lavish art collections, endowed museums, and traveled abroad.

As a result of workplace restructuring, the expansion of the middle class, and the rise in enormous fortunes, income distribution in America by the turn of the century had become severely skewed. Statistics are imprecise, but a knowledgeable observer estimated in 1896 that of the nation's 12.5 million families, approximately 5.5 million were working class and earned less than $500 annually; 5.5 million were middle class and had incomes from $500 to $5,000; and the remaining 1.5 million, or the 12 percent whose incomes were over $5,000, were rich. This privileged 12 percent, however, owned *86 percent* of the nation's wealth. In contrast, the middle class, whose families made up 44 percent of the population, possessed only 12.5 percent of the aggregate wealth, and the working class, who composed the bottom 44 percent of the nation's people, struggled to survive with a mere 1.5 percent of the wealth.

The Changing Family

This skewed distribution of resources had an important impact on family life. The level of family income not only determined access to household technology and consumer goods but also affected family size, life expectancy, infant mortality, and relationships between parents and children. Historians are cautious in their use of aggregate federal census statistics from the era, which blur differences among social classes as well as between rural and urban Americans and between ethnic groups and the native-born. Nevertheless, such data *can* give us a broad overview of the changes in family structure in the post–Civil War years.

Between 1860 and 1900, these statistics reveal, most Americans lived in nuclear families; that is, families made up of only parents and children. Often boarders and servants resided with the nuclear family, but grandparents and other relatives typically did not. And families were becoming smaller, largely because mothers bore fewer children, continuing a trend begun in the early nineteenth century. For white women, the number of live births* fell from an average of 5.42 children in 1850 to 3.56 in 1900. But those children

---

*As measured by the fertility rate: the average number of children born to each female between the ages of fourteen and forty-five.

who were born had a better chance of surviving to adulthood, as indicated statistically by a rise in life expectancy from 38.4 years to 46.3 years for males and from 40.5 years to 48.3 years for females. Overall, the size of the average nuclear family stabilized at five or six members.

Like all averages, however, these figures obscure the significant differences created by social class, race, and ethnicity. For example, because of a very high rate of infant mortality among black males, their average life expectancy at birth in 1900, the first year for which we have statistics, was only 22.5 years, less than half that for whites. Similarly, the decline in family size was not uniformly distributed. Farmers and the urban working class, relying on the labor of their children to make ends meet, continued to have large families. Immigrant and farm families with six to eight children remained common. The urban middle and upper classes, by contrast, who did not need their children's earnings, chose to limit their family size. In Buffalo, New York, an industrial city with many immigrants, the difference in the average number of children in families of various occupational groups in 1900 was striking: 5.7 for laborers, 5.2 for skilled workers, and only 3.5 for business owners and company managers.

These statistics reveal how significantly middle- and upper-class families differed from their working-class counterparts. The correlation of high income with smaller family size indicates that the middle and upper classes were practicing birth control, either by periodically abstaining from sexual intercourse, by other forms of contraception, or by abortion. Whatever the method, smaller families meant more free time for women, more attention to the education and training of children, and greater opportunity for leisure and recreation.

Working-Class Family Life

The dramatic impact of income level on the nature of family life becomes most evident when we look at black and immigrant working-class households. Because many such households hovered at or fell below the poverty level, they had to rely on the labor of the children and on a network of relatives who could pitch in during times of need. The poorer the family, the more dependent it became on the cooperative work of all its members simply to survive.

Black families in the post–Civil War South, freed from slavery with few possessions and little money,

**The Walters,
Lubert County, Georgia,
1896**

Southern black families such as the Walters clan depended on extended kin networks for assistance and emotional support.

Thanks to these strong family bonds, Sutton overcame the loss of his own parents and eventually was able to buy a farm and form a stable family of his own.

Although often better off than their black counterparts, poor white farm families in the South and Midwest also depended heavily on the effort of all family members to survive. While the men and older boys worked in the fields, the farm wife with her younger children ran the house and kept the kitchen garden. In addition to preparing meals, drawing water, tending the stove fire, cleaning the house, feeding chickens, taking care of the milk shed, and doing wash, farm women sewed and mended clothes, knitted hats and gloves, wove tablecloths, churned butter, made soap, and trimmed the oil lamps that illuminated the home in this age before electricity.

When necessary, rural white women and their daughters took over the duties normally performed by the men. "There were nine children in our family," reminisced Margaret Mitchell Womer about her childhood on the Great Plains, "six girls and three boys, and as the girls were older and my father not strong, the hard toil of the pioneer life fell to the lot of the girls. . . . Our house was made of logs and the girls helped in the construction of it." Some mothers and daughters even plowed the fields and helped with the harvest. Farm families thus owed their survival to the hard work and resourcefulness of everyone involved.

The same was true for urban working-class families, for whom the contributions of women, young adults, and children often spelled the difference

relied heavily on their extended families for help and support. Although most blacks lived in nuclear, two-parent families, they counted on the close proximity of cousins, aunts, uncles, and other relatives to assist them with child care, housing, and expenses. For blacks, the extended kinship network replaced the nuclear family as the dominant institution in their daily lives. (In rural North Carolina and Mississippi, kinship networks containing between fifty and two hundred people practiced a remarkable degree of mutual cooperation, making decisions jointly, sharing economic resources, providing emotional support at funerals, and strengthening ties within the group through reciprocal visiting, family reunions, and membership in the same church.)

The case of Joseph Sutton, who lived at Miles River Neck in Talbot County, Maryland, typified postwar blacks' reliance on relatives. In 1889, when Sutton was four, his father died. His mother, unable to run the farm by herself, moved to Baltimore to find work, leaving Sutton with his grandmother, who became, in effect, his surrogate parent. Three years later, at age seven, he moved in with his uncle, a nearby tenant farmer. There, for several years, Sutton took care of a baby cousin who was named after his great-grandmother, a common practice that symbolically reinforced the cohesiveness of the extended family.

between survival and modest prosperity. The average urban family of five or six members in the 1890s needed an annual income of between six hundred and eight hundred dollars to live comfortably. Although prices for food, rent, and other necessities dropped between 1865 and 1890, and real wages increased by almost 50 percent, most working-class families still did not have a high enough income to live on the father's earnings alone. As in rural America, survival thus became a cooperative family effort.

To supplement their income, urban working-class families often rented rooms to boarders, and the women commonly took in laundry. Under the latter circumstance, washing became a heavy, all-day chore. Beyond washing and cooking, urban working-class women who could not afford store-bought apparel continued to sew the family's clothes.

If a husband became sick or lost his job, a wife might even take a job in a garment factory alongside her elder daughters, who usually worked in manufacturing plants until they married. Immigrant children commonly went to work at the age of ten or twelve and were expected to turn over their earnings to their parents. Children grew up quickly under the weight of such responsibilities, but they also developed a strong family loyalty.

For many working-class families, the cooperative family ethic was the key to improving their financial position. In Detroit, for example, a fifty-year-old German carpenter and his three working children in the 1890s generated a combined income of $1,428, well within middle-class earning levels. By pooling the wages of all family members, working-class families were often able to set aside enough money to purchase a house, which functioned as both a residence and a kind of insurance. If the principal breadwinner fell sick or became unemployed, families could take in boarders or use the house as collateral on a loan.

The other common strategy used by working- and middle-class families alike to support elderly parents was the creation of what historians call a stem family arrangement. In the stem phase, as children grow up, get married, and move away from home to form their own nuclear families, one child remains in the parental household even after marrying. That child provides old-age care for the parents, often continuing in the same line of work or in some cases taking over the family farm or business, in return for assuming ownership of the house when the parents die. Particularly for

working-class Americans, the stem family brought security to infirm and aged parents.

Successful working-class families took pleasure not only in their material gains but also in their accomplishments in the face of difficult odds. "We had to live pretty close," proudly commented a Massachusetts carpenter in 1890 who was raising six children, "but we did it, and now we have the house all paid for, so there is no longer any rent." The cooperative family ethic, which stressed mutual support and reliance on a network of relatives, thus enabled working-class Americans to survive and in some cases even get ahead in the rapidly changing economic environment of the late nineteenth century. But the cooperative pattern also accentuated the differences between poor families and their middle- and upper-class counterparts who managed comfortably on the salary of the main breadwinner alone.

MIDDLE-CLASS SOCIETY AND CULTURE

Spared the struggle for survival that confronted most Americans after the Civil War, society's middle and upper ranks faced a different challenge: how to explain and rationalize their access to the material benefits of the emerging consumer society. To justify the position of society's wealthier members, ministers, advice-book writers, and other commentators appealed to Victorian morality, a set of social ideas widely extolled by the privileged classes of England and America during the long reign (1837–1901) of Britain's Queen Victoria.

Proponents of Victorian morality argued that the financial success of the middle and upper classes was linked to their superior talent, intelligence, morality, and self-control. They also believed that women were the driving force for moral improvement: while men engaged in the world's work, women would provide the gentle, elevating influence that would lead society in its upward march.

While authoritative voices preached the certitudes of Victorian morality, thereby defending the status of America's upper classes, a network of institutions, from elegant department stores and hotels to elite colleges and universities, reinforced the privileged position of these groups in society.

Manners and Morals

The Victorian world view, which first took shape in the 1830s and 1840s, rested on several fundamental assumptions. Cautiously optimistic about human nature, Victorian Americans believed that progress would only come through strenuous effort. This view energized a variety of reform movements against suffering and injustice, including slavery.

But this intense moralism also often led to an obsessive preoccupation with the details of personal behavior. Because most members of the elite and middle classes had achieved their status (or so they believed) through sobriety, industriousness, and self-restraint, they stressed these virtues. Thus "Victorian morality" became synonymous with an intense emphasis on self-discipline and self-control. Although this moral outlook was often violated in practice, especially among the very rich, it was widely preached as the standard for all society.

In addition to emphasizing sobriety and self-control, preachers of Victorian morality stressed the importance of "culture" (by which they meant a knowledge of the social graces, literature, the fine arts, and classical music) as an agency of social uplift. In the post–Civil War years, prominent clergymen like Henry Ward Beecher of Brooklyn and Phillips Brooks of Boston urged cultural refinement on both the middle class and those aspiring to middle-class status. Beecher proclaimed in 1876, "The laborer ought to be ashamed of himself" who after twenty years "has not his China plates, who has not his chromos [cheap copies of famous paintings], who has not some books nestling on the shelf." To further the cause, the elite founded, and the middle class supported, a network of cultural institutions in these years, including the Metropolitan Museum of Art in New York (1870), the Museum of Fine Arts in Boston (1870), and similar institutions in Philadelphia, Chicago, and other cities.

At its most petty, the middle-class focus on conduct and behavior often degenerated into a preoccupation with manners and social rituals. Middle- and upper-class families increasingly defined their own social standing in terms not only of income but also of behavior. Good manners, including a knowledge of proper etiquette in all social occasions, especially dining and entertaining, became an important badge of status.

In her popular advice book *The American Woman's Home* (1869), Catharine Beecher (the sister of Henry Ward Beecher) reflected a typical Victorian self-consciousness about proper manners. The following list of dinner-table behaviors, she said, should be avoided by those of "good breeding":

> *Reaching over another person's plate; standing up to reach distant articles, instead of asking to have them passed; . . . using the table-cloth instead of napkins; eating fast, and in a noisy manner; putting large pieces in the mouth; . . . [and] picking the teeth at the table. . . .*

For Beecher and other molders of manners, meals became important rituals that differentiated the social classes. Not only were they occasions for displaying the elaborate china and silver that wealthy families exclusively possessed, but they also provided telltale clues to a family's level of refinement and sophistication.

The Victorian code—with its emphasis on morals, manners, and proper behavior—thus served to heighten the sense of class differences for the post–Civil War generation and to create visible distinctions among social groups. Prominent middle- and upper-class Victorians made bold claims about their sincere interest in helping others improve themselves. More often than not, however, their self-righteous, intensely moralistic outlook simply widened the gap that income disparities had already opened.

The Cult of Domesticity

Victorian views on morality and culture, coupled with rising pressures on consumers to make decisions about a mountain of domestic products, had a subtle but important impact on middle-class expectations about women's role within the home. From the 1840s on, many architects, clergymen, and other promoters of the so-called cult of domesticity (see Chapter 9) had idealized the home as "the woman's sphere," a protected retreat where she could express her special maternal gifts, including a sensitivity toward children and an aptitude for religion. "The home is the wife's province," asserted one writer; "it is her natural field of labor . . . to govern and direct its interior management."

During the 1880s and 1890s, advocates of this cult of domesticity added a new obligation to the traditional woman's role as director of the household: to foster an artistic environment that would nurture her family's cultural improvement. For many Victorian Americans of the comfortable classes, houses became statements of cultural aspiration. Elaborately

"The Wife and Children of Robert Gordon at Home" on West 33d Street, New York, *by Seymour J. Guy, 1866 Middle- and upper-class Victorian Americans identified the home as a protected environment, enhanced by art and music, where mothers could raise their imaginative and playful children.*

ornamented architectural styles were popular. Like intricate sculptures, these structures featured detailed, mass-produced spindle ornamentation on the front porches; windows of varying dimensions; and ornate projecting chimneys. Women took charge of arranging the furniture and the overflowing decoration of the front parlor, turning it into a treasure house whose furnishings and curios would reflect the family's social standing and refinement. Souvenir spoons and other knickknacks collected during family travels were displayed to demonstrate the household's cosmopolitanism. Excluded from the world of business and commerce, many middle- and upper-class women devoted considerable time and energy to decorating their home, seeking to make it, as one advice book suggested, "a place of repose, a refuge from the excitement and distractions of outside . . . , provided with every attainable means of rest and recreation."

Not all middle-class women pursued the domestic ideal. For some, housework and family responsibilities overwhelmed the concern for artistic accomplishment. For others, the artistic ideal itself was not to their taste. Sixteen-year-old Mary Putnam complained privately to a friend that she played the piano because of "an abstract general idea . . . of a father coming home

regularly tired at night (from the plow, I believe the usual legend runs), and being solaced by the brilliant yet touching performance of a sweet only daughter upon the piano." She then confessed that she detested the piano. Increasingly, women in the 1880s and 1890s sought other outlets for their creative energies. Some, such as temperance crusader Frances Willard, would even use the cult of domesticity as a rationale for political causes.

Department Stores and Hotels

Although Victorian social thought justified the privileged status of the well-to-do, many thrifty people who had grown up in the early nineteenth century found it difficult to accept the new preoccupation with accumulation and display. To dull their pangs of guilt, merchandisers in the 1880s stressed the high quality and low cost of the artistic objects they sold, encouraging Americans to loosen their purse strings and enjoy prosperity without inner reservations.

A key agent in modifying attitudes toward consumption was the department store. In the final quarter of the nineteenth century, innovative entrepreneurs led by Rowland H. Macy in New York, John

Rike's Department Store, Dayton, Ohio, 1893
Department stores set new standards for customer comfort and service in this era.

Wanamaker in Philadelphia, and Marshall Field in Chicago built the giant department store into an urban institution and transformed the shopping experience for the millions of middle- and upper-class consumers who were their greatest patrons.

The merchandising innovations of the large urban department store represented a radical departure from earlier techniques. Unlike the rural general store, which offered a limited choice of food and clothing, department stores borrowed the economy-of-scale principle from the new mass-production industries, purchased their goods in large volume at low cost, and sold every conceivable household and clothing item. Where the small-shop owner haggled over prices and offered adjustments for unsatisfactory merchandise grudgingly if at all, the department store sold goods at a fixed price, allowed unconditional exchanges, and provided free delivery.

Merchants like Wanamaker and Macy helped overcome the middle and upper classes' reluctance to spend by advertising their products at "rock-bottom" prices and fighting price wars to convince customers of the validity of their claims. To avoid keeping their stock too long, they held giant end-of-the-season clearance sales at drastically marked-down prices.

The major downtown establishments sought to make shopping an adventure. Not only did the rapid turnover of merchandise create a sense of constant novelty, but the mammoth stores themselves became imitation palaces, complete with stained-glass skylights, marble staircases, brilliant chandeliers, and plush carpets. When it opened in 1876, John Wanamaker's Grand Depot in Philadelphia, which boasted a gaslit "tent" where women could examine silk evening gowns under ballroom conditions, welcomed more than seventy thousand people. Marshall Field's Chicago emporium contained a stained-glass dome, blue English carpets, and rare walnut paneling.

Department stores lavished care and attention on shoppers, especially women. Richly decorated lounges supplied with newspapers and stationery, elegant restaurants serving modestly priced lunches, salespeople who greeted shoppers at the door, and glittering holiday decorations enticed visitors to linger and buy on impulse. Brigades of female salesclerks answered questions and made the women feel at home. Such personal attention suggested to middle- and upper-class customers that they were of the ranks that deserved to be served. The large urban department store thus functioned as a kind of social club and home away from home for comfortably fixed women.

The great department stores' merchandise, interior decor, and deferential staff reinforced middle-class standards of behavior and consumption. The lower-class heroine in O. Henry's short story "The Trimmed Lamp," Nan, who hopes to rise into the middle class by marrying the right suitor, explains to her friend Lou that her job as a department-store salesgirl has taught her proper manners and ideals. Although poor, she sews her jacket to match exactly that of a frequent customer, the well-to-do Mrs. Van Alstyne Fisher. Appealing to the status consciousness of their middle- and upper-class customers, department stores implicitly promised higher social standing for the upwardly mobile. For the financially secure, shopping became an adventure, a form of entertainment, and a means of affirming one's place in society.

The stately metropolitan hotels that proliferated in the late nineteenth century provided further examples of high fashion and elite taste. After Boston's Tremont Hotel established a prototype for refined elegance and technological innovation in the 1830s by offering its guests indoor plumbing and speaking tubes (the predecessor of telephones), cities across America aspired to build top-notch hotels. By the 1880s innovative hotels were setting new standards for design excellence.

The Waldorf Astoria in New York, the Palmer House in Chicago, and San Francisco's Palace became public shrines, epitomizing efficient organization and upper-class taste. Built in 1892 in the German Renaissance style, the Waldorf Astoria was a self-contained community with offices, restaurants, ballrooms, courtyards, and five hundred guest rooms. Household reformers writing in the 1890s held up the highly organized restaurants and laundry systems of the big hotels as models for efficient cooperative-apartment complexes.

Whether one marveled at their efficiency or gazed in wonder at their splendid gilt mirrors and plush carpets, the grand hotels, like the giant department stores, set the pattern for luxury, convenience, and service. In his 1904 travel book *The American Scene,* writer Henry

James described the first-class hotel as "a synonym for civilization." In a society that shunned aristocratic pretensions, hotels and department stores made luxury acceptable by clothing it in the guise of efficiency and simple good taste. They provided a setting where newly affluent members of society could indulge and pamper themselves, if only for a few minutes or a day.

The Transformation of Higher Education

At a time when relatively few Americans possessed even a high-school education, U.S. colleges and universities represented another institutional stronghold of the business and professional elite and of the moderately well-to-do middle class. In 1900, despite enrollment increases in the preceding decades, only 4 percent of the nation's eighteen- to twenty-one-year-olds were enrolled in institutions of higher learning.

Wealthy capitalists gained status and a measure of immortality by endowing colleges and universities. Leland Stanford and his wife Jane Lathrop Stanford launched Stanford University in 1885 with a bequest of $24 million in memory of a dead son; John D. Rockefeller donated $34 million to the University of Chicago in 1891. Industrialists and businessmen dominated the boards of trustees of many educational institutions and forced their conservative views on the faculty and administrators. Sardonic economist Thorstein Veblen called these business-oriented academic managers "Captains of Erudition."

Not only the classroom experience but also social contacts and athletic activities—especially football—prepared affluent young men for later responsibilities in business and the professions. Adapted by American college students in 1869 from English rugby, football was largely an elite sport. But the game, initially played without pads or helmets, was marred by violence in its early years. In 1905, eighteen students died of playing-field injuries. Many college presidents therefore dismissed football as a dangerous waste of time and money. When the University of Michigan in 1873 challenged Cornell to a game in Ann Arbor, Cornell's president Andrew D. White huffily telegraphed back, "I will not permit thirty men to travel four hundred miles merely to agitate a bag of wind."

But eager alumni and coaches strongly defended the new sport. Some—among them Henry Lee Higginson, the Civil War veteran and Boston banker who gave Harvard "Soldier's Field" stadium as a memorial to

Army and Navy Football Players
The first Army-Navy football game was played in 1891. Walter Camp, the popular Yale coach, thought that the new sport provided excellent training for war. "The knowledge of when, where, and how to make an attack," he wrote, "is the critical thing which distinguishes great generalship, whether in war or football."

those who had died in battle—praised football as a character-building sport. A Social Darwinist who fervently believed that life was a struggle, Higginson insisted that football could improve the strength, courage, and self-discipline of American college youth. Other defenders of the sport, including famed Yale coach Walter Camp, insisted that football could function as a surrogate frontier experience in an increasingly urbanized society. By 1900 football had become a popular fall ritual, and team captains were campus heroes. The sport served to stimulate alumni giving and built goodwill for these elite institutions that otherwise remained far outside the experience of the average American.

Although postsecondary education remained confined to a small minority, more than 150 new colleges and universities were founded between 1880 and 1900, and enrollments more than doubled. While wealthy capitalists endowed some institutions, others, such as the state universities of the Midwest, were financed largely through public funds. Many colleges, including some that would evolve into first-rate institutions, were founded and largely funded by various religious denominations.

These years also witnessed a fundamental debate in higher education over what should be taught and how it should be presented. Impetus for reform came

from new discoveries in science and medicine. Most physicians in the 1850s had attended medical school for only two sixteen-week terms. They typically received their degree without ever having visited a hospital ward or examined a patient. Then came the Civil War, which graphically exposed the abysmal state of American medical education. Twice as many soldiers died from infections as from wounds. Doctors were so poorly trained and ignorant about sanitation that they often infected soldiers' injuries when they probed wounds with hands wiped on pus-stained aprons. "The ignorance and general incompetency of the average graduate of American medical schools, at the time when he receives the degree which turns him loose upon the community," wrote Harvard president Charles W. Eliot in 1870, "is something horrible to contemplate."

In the 1880s and the 1890s, the public's well-justified skepticism about doctors encouraged leading medical professors, many of whom had studied in France and Germany, to begin restructuring American medical education. Using the experimental method developed by German scientists, they insisted that medical students in graduate-school programs be trained in biology, chemistry, and physics, including laboratory experience. By 1900 graduate medical education had been placed on a firm professional foundation. Similar reforms took place in graduate programs in architecture, engineering, and law.

These changes were part of a larger transformation in higher education after the Civil War that gave rise to a new institution, the research university. Unlike even the best of the mid-nineteenth-century colleges, whose narrow, unvarying curriculum focused on classical languages, theology, logic, and mathematics, the new research universities offered courses in a wide variety of subject areas, established various professional schools, and encouraged faculty members to pursue basic research. For Andrew D. White, the first president of Cornell University (1869), the objective was to create an environment "where any person can find instruction in any study." At Cornell, the University of Wisconsin at Madison, Johns Hopkins, Harvard, and other institutions, this new conception of higher education laid the groundwork for the central role that America's universities would play in the intellectual, cultural, and scientific life of the twentieth century. Despite these significant changes, with all their portents for the future, however, higher education still remained largely the privilege of a few as the nineteenth century ended. The era when college attendance would become the norm rather than the rare exception lay many years ahead.

WORKING-CLASS LEISURE IN THE IMMIGRANT CITY

In colonial America the subject of leisure time had been linked by ministers to "idleness," the dangerous first step leading to sin and wickedness. Disapproval of leisure also characterized the overwhelmingly rural culture of the early nineteenth century, in which the unremitting routines of farm labor left little time for relaxation. Family picnics, horse races, county fairs, revival meetings, and holiday observances such as the Fourth of July and Christmas had provided occasional permissible diversion, but most Americans continued to view leisure activities skeptically, and the line between relaxation and laziness was never clearly drawn. Henry Clay Work's popular song "My Grandfather's Clock" (1876), which praised the ancient timepiece for "wasting no time" and working "ninety

years, without slumbering," bore witness to the tenacity of this deep-seated reverence for work and suspicion of leisure.

After the Civil War, as immigration soared, urban populations shot up, and factories multiplied, striking new patterns of leisure and amusement emerged, most notably among the urban working class. Middle-class educators and moralists continued to ponder the distinction between "wholesome" and "unwholesome" recreation, but they were little heeded in the throbbing immigrant cities. After spending long hours in factories, mills, and behind department-store counters, or working as domestic servants in the homes of the wealthy, working-class Americans eagerly sought relaxation and diversion. They thronged the streets, patronized saloons and dance halls, cheered at boxing matches and baseball games, and organized boisterous group picnics and holiday celebrations. As amusement parks, vaudeville theaters, sporting clubs, and racetracks provided further outlets for workers' need for entertainment, leisure became a big business catering to a mass public.

For millions of working-class Americans, leisure time took on increasing importance as factory work became ever more routinized and impersonal. Immigrants in particular cherished their few opportunities for interaction and recreation. Ironically, the same ethnic divisions that fragmented the immigrant work force and retarded the emergence of a strong labor movement provided the foundation for a vigorous working-class culture beyond the factory gates, since ethnic bonds often underlay neighborhood-based pastimes.

Although many recreational activities involved both men and women, others particularly attracted one gender or the other. Whereas saloons offered an intensely male environment where patrons could share good stories, discuss and bet on sporting events, and momentarily put aside pressures of job and family, young working women shared confidences with friends in informal social clubs, tried out new fashions in street promenading, and found excitement in neighborhood dance halls and amusement park excursions.

Streets, Saloons, and Boxing Matches

No segment of the population had a greater need for amusement and recreation than the urban working class. Hours of tedious, highly disciplined, and physically exhausting labor left workers tired but thirsting for excitement and escape at the end of the day. A

German Singing Society, Wausau, Wisconsin, 1884
Singing, camaraderie, and beer drinking were all part of membership in a German singing club. Participation in such clubs provided immigrants with a network of friends and ties to their ethnic heritage.

banner carried by the Worcester, Massachusetts, carpenters' union in an 1889 demonstration for the eight-hour workday summed up the importance of workers' leisure hours: "EIGHT HOURS FOR WORK, EIGHT HOURS FOR REST, AND EIGHT HOURS FOR WHAT WE WILL."

City streets provided recreation that anyone could afford. Relaxing after a day's work, shop girls and laborers clustered on busy corners, watching shouting pushcart peddlers and listening to organ grinders and buskers play familiar melodies. For a penny or a nickel, they could buy bagels, baked potatoes, soda, and a variety of other foods and drinks. Especially in the summer, when the heat and humidity within the tenements reached unbearable levels, the streets became a buzzing hive of neighborhood social life. One immigrant later fondly recalled his boyhood on the streets of New York's Lower East Side: "Something was always happening, and our attention was continually being shifted from one excitement to another."

The streets were open to all, but other leisure institutions drew mainly a male clientele. For example, in cities like Baltimore, Milwaukee, and Cincinnati with a strong German immigrant flavor, gymnastic clubs (called *Turnverein*) and singing societies (*Gesangverein*) provided both companionship and the opportunity to perpetuate old-world cultural traditions.

For workmen of all ethnic backgrounds, saloons offered companionship, conviviality, and five-cent beer, often with a free lunch thrown in. New York City

had an estimated ten thousand saloons by 1900 and Denver nearly five hundred. As neighborhood gathering places, saloons reinforced group identity and became centers for immigrant politics. Saloonkeepers, who often doubled as local ward bosses, performed small services for their patrons, including finding jobs and writing letters for illiterate immigrants. Sports memorabilia and pictures of prominent prizefighters adorned saloon walls. With their rich mahogany bars, etched glass, shiny brass rails, and elegant mirrors, saloons provided a taste of high-tone luxury to their factory patrons. Although working-class women rarely joined their husbands at the saloon, they frequently sent a son or daughter to the corner pub for a "growler"—a large tin pail of beer.

The conventions of saloon culture thus stood in marked contrast to both the socially isolating routines of factory labor and the increasingly private and family-centered social life of the middle class. Nevertheless, it would be a mistake to view the old-time saloon through a haze of sentimental nostalgia. In the rougher saloons, prostitution and criminal activity flourished. Moreover, the problem of family violence related to drunkenness was a real one, and the widespread custom of "treating," or buying drinks for one's friends, although revealing an appealing spirit of comradeship, often meant that even less money from a workman's limited weekly pay was available to meet urgent family needs.

McSorley's Bar,
by John Sloan, 1912
Neighborhood saloons were
places where friends could
get together. In his novel Sister
Carrie, *Theodore Dreiser*
admiringly described "the
long bar . . . [with its] blaze
of lights, polished woodwork,
colored and cut glassware
and many fancy bottles."

For working-class males, bare-knuckles prizefighting became one of the most popular amusements. Drawing its heroes from the poorer ranks of society, the ring became an arena where lower-class men could assert their individuality and physical prowess. In East Coast cities, blacks, Irish, and Germans formed their own "sporting clubs" and used athletics to bolster their self-confidence and reaffirm their racial or ethnic identity.

Despite its origins and continued popularity within the working class, amateur boxing gained unexpected elite support in the 1880s and 1890s as an antidote to what some considered a dangerous tendency toward male effeteness among the privileged classes. Theodore Roosevelt, a New York patrician and rising figure in Republican politics, did much to make the sport more respectable. The introduction of the Marquis of Queensbury code—a set of rules devised in England, requiring the use of gloves, outlawing wrestling holds, standardizing the three-minute round with a one-minute rest period, and changing the time required for a knockout from thirty seconds to ten—increased boxing's acceptability to the upper crust. Meanwhile, the sport, like other popular leisure-time diversions, was becoming professionalized.

The Rise of Professional Sports

Contrary to the prevailing myth, schoolboy Abner Doubleday did not invent baseball in Cooperstown, New York, in 1839. As an English game called rounders, the pastime had existed in one form or another since the seventeenth century. But if Americans did not create baseball, they unquestionably took this informal children's game and turned it into a major professional sport. The first organized baseball team, the New York Knickerbockers, was formed in 1845. Then in the 1860s the rules were codified, and the sport assumed its modern form. Overhand pitches replaced those formerly thrown underhand. Fielders, who now wore gloves, had to catch the ball on the fly to make an out instead of fielding it on one bounce. Games were standardized at nine innings, and bases were spaced ninety feet apart, as they are today.

In that same decade, promoters organized professional clubs and began to charge admission and compete for players. The Cincinnati Red Stockings, the first team to put its players under contract for the whole season, gained fame in 1869 by touring the country and ending the season with fifty-seven wins and no losses. Team owners organized the National League in

World's Heavyweight Boxing Championship, 1892

In dethroning ring champion John L. Sullivan, "Gentleman Jim" Corbett demonstrated that speed and finesse were more than a match for brute strength.

1876, took control from the players by requiring them to sign a reserve contract that forbade them to play for a rival organization, and limited each city to one professional team. Soon the owners were filling baseball parks with crowds of from ten thousand to twelve thousand fans and earning enormous profits. By the 1890s baseball had become big business. As today, clubs scheduled doubleheaders, ran promotions such as children's day and ladies' day, and made money by selling beer, peanuts, and hot dogs.

Although baseball attracted a national following at all social levels, the working class particularly took the sport to heart. The most profitable teams were those from major industrial cities with a large working-class population. Workers attended the games when they could and avidly followed their team's progress when they could not. Some saloons reported scores on blackboards. In Cleveland just after the turn of the century, Mayor Tom Johnson erected a bulletin board downtown that recorded game results.

Newspapers thrived on baseball. Joseph Pulitzer introduced the first separate sports page when he bought the *New York World* in 1883, and much of the sporting news in the *World* and other papers was devoted to baseball. For the benefit of German immigrants, the New York *Staats Zeitung* published a glossary of German equivalents of baseball terms: for example, "umpire" was *Umparteiischer*. Baseball, declared novelist Mark Twain in a burst of hyperbole, had become "the very symbol . . . and visible expression of the drive and push and rush and struggle of the raging, tearing, booming nineteenth century."

Although no other organized sport attracted as large a following as baseball, horse racing and boxing contests were also widely covered in the popular press and drew big crowds of spectators and bettors. But whereas races like Louisville's Kentucky Derby became important social events for the rich, professional boxing aroused more passionate devotion among the working class. By far the most popular sports hero of the nineteenth century was heavyweight fighter John L. Sullivan, "the Boston Strong Boy." Of Irish immigrant stock, Sullivan began boxing in 1877 at the age of nineteen. His first professional fight came in 1880 when he knocked out John Donaldson, "the Champion of the West," in a Cincinnati beer hall. With his massive physique, handlebar mustache, and arrogant swagger, Sullivan was enormously popular among immigrants. Barnstorming across the country, he vanquished a succession of local strong men, invariably wearing his trademark green tights with an American flag wrapped around his middle. Cleverly, Sullivan also refused to fight blacks, in deference, he said, to the wishes of his fans. This policy conveniently allowed him to avoid facing the finest boxer of the 1880s, the Australian black Peter Jackson.

Sullivan loved drink and high living, and by the end of the eighties, he was sadly out of shape. But when the editor of the *Police Gazette*, a sensational tabloid, designed a new heavyweight championship belt—allegedly containing two hundred ounces of silver and encrusted with diamonds and pure gold—and awarded it to Sullivan's rival Jake Kilrain, the champion had to defend himself. The two met on a sweltering, hundred-degree day in New Orleans in July 1889, in the last bare-knuckles championship match. After seventy-five short but grueling rounds, Kilrain's managers threw in the towel. Newspapers around the nation banner-headlined the story. Contemptuously returning the championship belt to the *Police Gazette* after having had it appraised at $175, Sullivan went on the road in a melodrama written specifically for him. Playing the role of a blacksmith, he (in the words of a recent historian of bare-knuckles boxing) "pounded an anvil, beat a bully, and mutilated his lines." But his fans did not care: he was one of them, and they adored him. As one admirer wrote:

His colors are the Stars and Stripes,
He also wears the green,
And he's the grandest slugger that
The ring has ever seen.

Vaudeville, Amusement Parks, and Dance Halls

In contrast to the male preserve of saloons and prizefights, the world of vaudeville shows, amusement parks, and neighborhood dance pavilions not only welcomed all comers regardless of gender but in some cases proved particularly congenial to working-class women.

Vaudeville evolved out of the pre–Civil War minstrel shows, in which white comedians made up as blacks had performed songs and comic sketches (see Chapter 11). Vaudeville performances offered a succession of acts, all designed for mass appeal. The shows typically opened with a trained animal routine or a dance number, followed by a musical interlude featuring sentimental favorites such as "On the Banks of the Wabash Far Away" mixed in with new hits such as "Meet Me in St. Louis, Louis," a jaunty spoof of a young wife's frustration with her stick-in-the-mud husband.

Comic skits followed, ridiculing the trials of urban life, satirizing the ineptitude of the police and municipal officials, poking fun at the babel of accents in the immigrant city, and mining a rich vein of broad ethnic humor and stereotypes. After further musical numbers and acts by ventriloquists, pantomimes, and magicians, the program ended with a "flash" finale such as flying-trapeze artists swinging against a black background. By the 1880s vaudeville was drawing larger crowds than any other form of theater, and understandably so: not only did it provide an inexpensive evening of lighthearted entertainment, but in the comic sketches, immigrant audiences could laugh at their own experience as they saw it translated into slapstick and caricature.

Where vaudeville offered psychological escape from the stresses of working-class life by exploiting its comic potential, amusement parks provided physical escape, at least for a day. The prototype of the sprawling urban amusement parks was New York's Coney Island, a section of Brooklyn's oceanfront that in the 1870s evolved into a resort for the masses. At the turn of the century, the opening of several large amusement centers bearing names like Luna Park and Dreamland and featuring performers, fun houses, thrill rides, and games of skill boosted Coney Island's popularity. Taking the train from Manhattan, thousands of young people poured into Coney Island each summer seeking fun and amusement. Young couples who rode through the dark Tunnel of Love, sped down the dizzying roller coaster in Steeplechase Park, or watched belly dancers in the carnival atmosphere of the sideshows were encouraged to surrender to the spirit of exuberant play, forget the restrictions and demands of the industrial world, and lose themselves in fantasy.

By the end of the nineteenth century, New York City had well over three hundred thousand female wage earners, most of them young, unmarried women working as seamstresses, laundresses, typists, domestic servants, or department-store clerks. For this army of low-paid young working women and their counterparts in other cities, the amusement parks with their exhilarating rides and glittering dance pavilions, together with the dance halls that dotted the immigrant districts of most cities, exerted a powerful lure. Here they could meet friends, spend time with young men beyond the watchful eyes of parents, show off their new dresses, and try out the latest dance steps. As a twenty-year-old German immigrant woman who worked as a servant in a wealthy household observed: "I have heard some of the high people with whom I have been living say that Coney Island is not tony. The trouble is that these high people don't know how to dance. I have to laugh when I see them at their balls

Coney Island
Denounced by conservative reformers as "Sodom by the Sea," the Coney Island amusement park, as its guidebook implied, offered thrilling rides and a carnival atmosphere which stood in marked contrast to the decorous manners of starched, straight-laced, polite society.

and parties. If only I could get out on the floor and show them how—they would be astonished." For such women, the brightly decorated dance pavilion, the exciting music, and the spell of a warm summer night could seem a magical release from the drudgery of daily life.

Ragtime

Since slavery days, black Americans had sustained a strong, creative musical culture, and thus it is not surprising that blacks made a major contribution to the popular music of the late nineteenth century, in the form of ragtime. Nothing could illustrate more sharply the differences between the culture of the middle class and that of the working class than the contrasting styles of popular music each favored. The middle class

preferred hymns or songs that taught a lesson or conveyed a moral. Ragtime, by contrast, which originated in the 1880s with black musicians in the saloons and brothels of the South and Midwest, was played strictly for entertainment (see "A Place in Time").

Ragtime developed out of the rich tradition of sacred and secular songs through which African-Americans had long eased the burdens of their lives. Like spirituals, ragtime used syncopated rhythms and complex harmonies, but it blended these with marching-band musical structures to create a distinctive style. A favorite of "honky-tonk" piano players, ragtime was introduced to the broader public in the 1890s by the music publishers of New York's Tin Pan Alley and became a national sensation.

The reasons for the sudden ragtime craze were complex. Inventive, playful, with catchy syncopations and an infectious rhythm in the bass clef, the music displayed a fresh originality that had an appeal all its own. But part of ragtime's popularity also came from its origin in brothels and its association with blacks, who were widely stereotyped in the 1890s as sexual, sensual, and uninhibited by the rigid Victorian social conventions that restricted whites' behavior. The "wild" and complex rhythms of ragtime, therefore, were widely interpreted to be a freer and more "natural" expression of elemental feelings about love and affection. John Philip Sousa, the composer of "Stars and Stripes Forever," reflected this common middle-class stereotype in his assertion that ragtime's "primitive rhythms . . . excite the basic human instincts." The rejection of ragtime by genteel critics like Sousa, however, made the new dance music all the more attractive to an urban working class that largely rejected the middle-class Victorian moral code.

Ragtime's best-known composer, Scott Joplin, a talented black piano player from St. Louis, introduced his music at Chicago's Columbian Exposition in 1893. "Maple Leaf Rag," published in 1899, earned him a national reputation. Hoping to win recognition as a serious composer, Joplin moved to New York in 1907 and wrote an opera, *Tremonisha*, which was never staged during his lifetime. He died a decade later, penniless and largely forgotten.

Ragtime's great popularity thus proved a mixed blessing for blacks. It testified to the achievements of brilliant composers like Joplin, helped break down the barriers faced by blacks in the music industry, and contributed to a spreading rebellion against the repressiveness of Victorian standards. But for some whites, ragtime simply confirmed their stereotype of blacks as

New Orleans in the 1890s

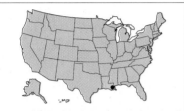

From its French and Spanish beginnings in the eighteenth century, New Orleans remained a unique city in the 1890s. Its popular culture fused elements from the culinary and musical traditions of the varied groups in its population, especially its free blacks and Creoles of color. The latter were the offspring of Africans and "Cajuns"—descendants of the Acadians, the eighteenth-century exiles from French Canada who had settled along the swampy bayous of the Mississippi Delta south of the city.

During the early nineteenth century, New Orleans's large free black and "colored" Creole population had enjoyed a degree of independence found nowhere else in the South among people of color. Free blacks had established their own churches and fraternal societies, formed their own militia, and borne arms. Both wealthy and poor free blacks had created a distinctive culture melding African and French customs. In the Vieux Carré, the old French part of the city, slaves and free blacks joined together on Sunday afternoons to play drums, banjos, and violins. Young people danced and sang, mingling African voodoo rhythms with Catholic church liturgical melodies.

During the Civil War and Reconstruction, however, the humiliating occupation of New Orleans by Federal troops had left a legacy of southern white bitterness against the black population. Then in the 1880s and 1890s, as Italian immigrants swelled the city's population, racial tensions were rekindled. Despite the discord, festivals like Mardi Gras, with its riotous parades and boisterous balls, continued. The city won notoriety for its racetrack betting, gambling, and prostitution. Sightseers flocked to New Orleans to savor its spicy Creole food, drink in its smoky bars, and visit its seedy bordellos and raunchy dance halls. Its sidewalks thronged with commercial travelers, longshoremen, country folk in the city for a day, and racetrack bettors. "One is apt to see here at some hour of the day anybody from a St. Louis capitalist to the man who came the night before with no change of linen, and seven dollars sewn in his waistcoat," wrote a visiting journalist. Appropriately, promoters chose New Orleans as the site of the September 1892 championship boxing match in which "Gentleman Jim" Corbett defeated John L. Sullivan.

Among the city's liveliest traditions was the marching band. A product of the eighteenth-century military, whose drummers and fifers helped identify regiments' locations amidst battlefield chaos, the marching band by the mid-nineteenth century had become a fixture in cities and towns across America, and prominently so

The Buddy Bolden Band
Charles "Buddy" Bolden, a local barber and cornet player (second from left), started a jazz band near New Orleans's Congo Square in the 1890s. So popular was the group that fans nicknamed its creator King Bolden.

Valve Trombone

Members of New Orleans's Reliance Brass Band played this pre–World War I vintage trombone. The band's founder, "Papa" Jack Laine, was known as the father of white jazz.

in New Orleans. Saturday nights, young and old alike ambled to the city-park bandstand to hear local groups belt out the stirring marches of John Philip Sousa and other composers.

New Orleans's black brass bands in particular pioneered new playing styles that captured national attention. Having snapped up the affordable used musical instruments piled high in pawn shops after the Civil War, blacks in New Orleans—unfettered by written scores and formal music lessons—developed innovative styles for bugles, trombones, and the newly invented piston-valve trumpets. Every black social organization, club, fire station, and lodge boasted its own twelve-member brass marching band. The bands played at picnics, parades, dances, church socials, circuses, minstrel shows, athletic contests, and holiday gatherings. By the 1880s many brass bands gained fame for playing in the new "ratty," "raggy," unscored, syncopated style, with its echoes of the older call-and-response African-American singing style that featured one person shouting a phrase and in turn being answered by the group. Brass bands were also known for their custom of playing religious hymns "straight" on the way to the cemetery and then "jazzing them up" on the way home. Within the bands—which often also played in bars and brothels—individual soloists such as

coronetist Charles "Buddy" Bolden became famous for improvisational blues solos. These soulful performances were the forerunners of a new musical style,

Ragtime Sheet Music

The nearly universal popularity of ragtime music was confirmed when sheet-music publishers on New York's 28th Street, an area nicknamed Tin Pan Alley, brought out Irving Berlin's "Alexander's Ragtime Band." Although Berlin was a Russian Jewish immigrant and the song had hardly a trace of ragtime in it, the connection with the New Orleans ragtime tradition made the tune an instant hit.

"jazz," that emerged in the 1890s and became a national rage after the turn of the century.

Although the popularity of these musicians—later immortalized in Irving Berlin's song "Alexander's Ragtime Band"—increasingly attracted middle-class white audiences and seemed to imply a growing general acceptance of black musicians, racial prejudice in New Orleans continued to shape local practices. If a black band marched into a white neighborhood, the residents commonly pelted the musicians with rocks.

In 1897, seeking to isolate and regulate prostitution, city administrators created a special district, named Storyville after Sydney Story, the councilman who proposed the new quarter. Storyville's glittering saloons and ubiquitous houses of prostitution hired some of the best black ragtime piano players. Other black musicians, excluded from some white establishments, could find jobs only in the racially segregated bars and cabarets of the two-block "Tango Belt" surrounding Storyville. Musically talented Creoles of color—the proud descendants of free-black mulattos whose musical training had assured them positions in local orchestras and opera houses—could secure employment only in these districts, where they worked alongside criminals and prostitutes.

For all its uniqueness, New Orleans typified larger strands in turn-of-the-century American life. (The city's cultural diversity also anticipated trends that in the twentieth century would make all the United States a truly multicultural society.) And the complex history of early jazz in New Orleans paralleled the ironic relationship of popular culture and racism in the larger society. White middle-class America, like the one of New Orleans, would soon embrace this African-American musical contribution. Captivated by New Orleans "Dixieland" jazz, they would idolize its best practitioners, including the great trumpeter Louis Amstrong, a veteran of the New Orleans brass marching bands. Yet these middle-class Americans, like their counterparts in New Orleans, would see no contradiction in celebrating jazz while harboring deep prejudices against the very people from whose culture this vital new music had emerged.

primitive and sensual, a bias that underlay the racism of the period and helped justify segregation and discrimination.

In sum, from many perspectives the factories and immigrant slums of late-nineteenth-century America present a grim picture. The realities of overwork, poverty, disease, and inhumane living conditions hover darkly over the history of the period. Yet in the face of such realities, the laboring masses avidly pursued a colorful variety of leisure-time activities that affirmed their social solidarity and sustained their spirits. The vitality, gaiety, and sheer energy of this working-class culture remind us that however bleak their lives, the members of the urban working class remained strong and resilient in these years, conscious of their human worth and determined to assert it.

CULTURES IN CONFLICT

In the late nineteenth century the United States was embroiled in class conflict and cultural unrest. Part of this turmoil raged within the middle class itself. Victorian morality and genteel cultural standards were never totally accepted even within the elite and middle classes, and as the century ended, ethical questionings and new cultural stirrings intensified. Women stood at the center of the era's cultural turbulence. Thwarted by a restrictive code of feminine propriety, middle-class women made their dissatisfactions heard. Developments as diverse as the rise of women's clubs, the growth of women's colleges, and an 1890s bicycle fad contributed to the emergence of what some began to call the new woman.

But although Victorian culture was challenged from within the middle class itself, a widening chasm divided the well-to-do from the immigrant cities' teaming hordes of laborers. Perhaps in no period of American history have class conflicts—cultural as well as economic—been more open and raw. As native-born middle-class leaders nervously eyed the rambunctious and sometimes disorderly culture of city streets, saloons, boxing clubs, dance halls, and amusement parks, they correctly perceived a massive if unconscious challenge to their own cultural and social standing. While some middle-class reformers promoted the public school as an institution for imposing middle-

class values on the urban masses, others battled the hydra-headed manifestations of urban "vice" and "immorality." But ultimately it was the genteel mores of the middle class, not urban working-class culture, that proved the more vulnerable. By 1900 the Victorian social and moral ethos was crumbling on every front.

The Genteel Tradition and Its Critics

What was this genteel culture that aroused such opposition? In the 1870s and 1880s, a group of upper-class writers and magazine editors, led by Harvard art-history professor Charles Eliot Norton and New York editors Richard Watson Gilder of *The Century* magazine and E. L. Godkin of *The Nation*, codified Victorian standards for literature and the fine arts. With the support of artistic allies in Boston and New York, they joined forces in a campaign designed to improve American taste in interior furnishings, textiles, ceramics, wallpaper, and books. By fashioning rigorous criteria for excellence in writing and design, they hoped to create a coherent national artistic culture.

The drive to improve the arts was prompted in part by the flood of cheap reproductions and sensationalistic novels that poured off the nation's presses after the Civil War. Despondent about what Godkin called a "chromo civilization" enamored of trashy books and garish chromolithographic prints, Norton, Godkin, and Gilder, joined by the editors of other highbrow periodicals such as the *Atlantic Monthly* and *North American Review*, set up new guidelines for serious literature. They lectured the middle class about the value of high culture and the insights to be gained from the fine arts. They also censored their own publications to remove all sexual allusions, vulgar slang, disrespectful treatments of Christianity, and unhappy endings. In a characteristic gesture, Norton tried unsuccessfully to persuade dime-novel publisher Erastus Beadle to print Shakespeare's plays instead of western adventures and crime stories.

Expanding their combined circulation to nearly two hundred thousand copies and opening their magazines to a variety of new authors, Godkin and the other editors of these "quality" periodicals created an important forum for serious writing. Novelists Henry James, who published virtually all of his work in the *Atlantic*, and William Dean Howells, who served as editor of the same magazine, helped to lead this elite literary establishment. James believed that "it is art that *makes* life, . . . [There is] no substitute whatever for [its] force and beauty. . . ." This so-called art for art's sake movement also made its influence felt through the work of architects, jewelers, and interior decorators.

Although the genteel magazines initially provided an important forum for new writers, their editors' strident elitism and imperialistic desire to control the nation's literary standards soon aroused opposition. Samuel Langhorne Clemens, better known as Mark Twain, spoke for many young writers when he declared as early as 1869 that he was through with "literature and all that bosh." Attacking aristocratic literary conventions, Twain and other authors who shared his concerns explored new forms of fiction and worked to broaden literature's appeal to the general public.

These efforts by a younger generation of writers to chart new directions for American literature rested on fundamental changes taking place in the publishing industry. To compete with elite periodicals costing twenty-five to thirty-five cents, new magazines like *Ladies' Home Journal, Cosmopolitan,* and *McClure's* lowered their prices to a dime or fifteen cents and tripled or quadrupled their circulation. Supporting themselves through advertising rather than subscriptions, these magazines encouraged new trends in fiction while they mass-marketed new products and services. They provided an audience for young authors seeking to move beyond idealized romances and literary conventions to write about real people in everyday life.

Some of these authors have been labeled regionalists because they captured the distinctive dialect and details of local life in their environs. In *The Country of the Pointed Firs* (1896), for example, Sarah Orne Jewett wrote of the New England village life that she knew from her own neighbors in South Berwick, Maine. Others, most notably William Dean Howells, have been called realists because of their focus on a truthful depiction of the commonplace and the everyday, especially in urban areas. Still others have been categorized as naturalists because their stories take on a fatalistic cast and stress the economic and psychological determinants of life. Stephen Crane's *Maggie: A Girl of the Streets* (1892), a bleak story of an innocent girl's exploitation and ultimate suicide in the harsh environment of an urban slum, is generally considered the first American naturalistic novel. Yet in practice, these categories are imprecise and often overlap. What many of these writers shared, irrespective of labels, was a skepticism toward literary conventions and an intense desire to understand the society around them.

The careers of Mark Twain and Theodore Dreiser highlight the changes in the publishing industry and the evolution of new forms of writing. Both authors grew up in the Midwest, outside the East Coast literary establishment; Twain was born near Hannibal, Missouri, in 1835, and Dreiser in Terre Haute, Indiana, in 1871. As young men both worked as newspaper reporters and traveled widely in search of new financial opportunities. Both learned from direct and sometimes bitter personal experience about the greed, speculation, and fraud that figured centrally in Gilded Age life.

Of the two, Twain more incessantly sought a mass-market audience. With his drooping mustache, white hair, and white suits, Twain deliberately turned himself into a media personality, lecturing from coast to coast, founding his own publishing house, and selling his books through door-to-door salesmen. The name Mark Twain became his trademark, identifying him to readers as a literary celebrity much as the labels Coca-Cola and Ivory Soap won instant consumer recognition.* Although Dreiser possessed neither Twain's flamboyant personality nor his instinct for salesmanship, he, too, learned to crank out feature articles for mass magazines heavily dependent on advertising.

Drawing on their own experiences, Twain and Dreiser wrote about the human impact of the wrenching social changes taking place around them: the flow of people to the expanding cities and the relentless scramble for power, wealth, and fame. In the *Adventures of Huckleberry Finn* (1884), Twain presents a classic narrative of two runaways, the rebellious Huck and the slave Jim, drifting down the Mississippi in search of freedom. Their journey southward, which contrasts the idyllic life on the raft with the tawdry, fraudulent world of the small riverfront towns, is at the same time a journey of identity that brings with it a deeper understanding of contemporary American society.

Dreiser's *Sister Carrie* (1900) also tells of a journey. But in this case, the main character, Carrie Meeber, an innocent and attractive girl on her way from her Wisconsin farm home to Chicago, is first seduced by a traveling salesman and then moves in with Hurstwood, the married proprietor of a fancy saloon. Driven by her desire for expensive department-store clothes

---

Mark Twain was originally a boatman's term indicating the two-fathom depth at which steamboats could safely navigate on the Mississippi River, which flows past Clemens's native Hannibal.

Sarah Orne Jewett and Mark Twain

Jewett and Twain not only broke from genteel literary standards but also created unique personal styles through their studied poses and distinctive attire.

and lavish entertainment, Carrie is an opportunist incapable of feeling guilt. She follows Hurstwood to New York, knowing that he has stolen the receipts from his saloon, abandons him when his money runs out, and pursues her own career in the theater.

Twain and Dreiser broke decisively with the genteel tradition's emphasis on manners and decorum. *Century* magazine readers complained that *Huckleberry Finn* was coarse and "destitute of a single redeeming quality." The publisher of *Sister Carrie* was so repelled by Dreiser's novel that he printed only a thousand copies (to fulfill the legal terms of his contract) and then stored them in a warehouse, refusing to promote them.

Growing numbers of scholars and critics similarly challenged the self-serving certitudes of Victorian mores, including assumptions that moral worth and economic standing were closely linked and that the status quo of the 1870s and 1880s represented a social order decreed by God and nature alike. Whereas Henry George, Lester Ward, and Edward Bellamy elaborated their visions of a cooperative and harmonious society (see Chapter 18), economist Thorstein Veblen in *The Theory of the Leisure Class* (1899) offered a caustic critique of the life-styles of the new capitalist elite. Raised in a Norwegian farm community in Min-

nesota, Veblen looked at the captains of industry and their families with a jaundiced eye, mercilessly documenting their "conspicuous consumption" and lamenting the widening economic gap between "those who worked without profit" and "those who profited without working."

Within the new discipline of sociology, Annie MacLean exposed the exploitation of department-store clerks, Walter Wyckoff uncovered the hand-to-mouth existence of unskilled laborers, and W. E. B. Du Bois documented the suffering and hardships faced by blacks in Philadelphia. The publication of these social scientists' writings, coupled with the economic depression and seething labor agitation of the 1890s, made it increasingly difficult for turn-of-the-century middle-class Americans to accept the smug, self-satisfied belief in progress and genteel culture that had been a hallmark of the Victorian outlook.

Modernism in Architecture and Painting

The challenge to the genteel tradition also found strong support among architects and painters. By the 1890s Chicago architects William Holabird, John Wellborn Root, and others had tired of copying European designs. Breaking with established architects such as Richard Morris Hunt, the designer of French chateaux for New York's Fifth Avenue, these Chicago architects followed the lead of Louis Sullivan, who argued that a building's form should follow its function. In their view, banks should look like the financial institutions they were, not like Greek temples. Rejecting the pretentiousness of prevailing elite mores and striving to evolve functional American design standards, the Chicago architects looked for inspiration to the future—to modernism—not to the past.

Frank Lloyd Wright's "prairie-school" houses, first built in the Chicago suburb of Oak Park in the 1890s, represented a typical modernist break with past styles. Wright scorned the bulky Victorian house with its large attic and basement. His designs, which featured broad, sheltering roofs and low silhouettes, used interconnecting rooms to create a sense of spaciousness.

The call of modernism, with its rejection of Victorian gentility, influenced late-nineteenth-century American painting as well. The watercolors of Winslow Homer, a magazine illustrator during the Civil War, revealed nature as brutally tough and unsentimental. In Homer's grim, elemental seascapes, lone men struggle against massive waves that constantly threaten to overwhelm them. Thomas Eakins's canvases of swimmers, boxers, and rowers (such as his well-known *Champion Single Sculls,* painted in 1871) similarly captured moments of vigorous physical exertion in everyday life. To make his paintings realistic, Eakins studied anatomy and dissected cadavers at a medical school. He also insisted on using nude models in his drawing classes at the Pennsylvania Academy of Fine Arts. When he removed the loincloth of a male model, proper Philadelphians demanded his dismissal, even though his students overwhelmingly supported him. In contrast to the realist Eakins, Albert Pinkham Ryder, a reclusive New York painter, turned to the inner world of dreams. The self-taught Ryder painted in a simple, almost primitive style. His landscapes blurred color and form, evoking a mood of reverie and mystery. Stubbornly independent, he escaped the pressures of the refined artistic establishment by retreating into a natural environment re-created from memory.

The revolt by architects and painters against Victorian standards was symptomatic of a larger shift in middle-class thought. This shift resulted from fundamental economic changes that had spawned a far more complex social environment than that of the past. As Protestant minister Josiah Strong perceptively observed in 1898, the transition from muscle to me-chanical power had "separated, as by an impassable gulf, the simple, homespun, individualistic world of the . . . past, from the complex, closely associated life of the present." The increasingly evident gap between rural or small-town life—a world of quiet parlors and flickering kerosene lamps—and life in the big, glittering cities of iron and glass made nineteenth-century Americans acutely aware of differences in upbringing and wealth. Given the disparities between rich and poor, between rural and urban, and between native-born Americans and recent immigrants, it is no wonder that pious Victorian platitudes about proper manners and the genteel arts seemed out of touch with the new social realities.

Distrusting the idealistic Victorian assumptions about social progress, middle-class journalists, novelists, artists, and politicians nevertheless remained divided over how to replace them. Not until the progressive period would social reformers draw on a new expertise in social research and an enlarged conception of the federal government's regulatory power to break sharply with their Victorian predecessors' social outlook.

From Victorian Lady to New Woman

Although middle-class women figured importantly in the revolt against Victorian refinement, their role was complex and ambiguous. Dissatisfaction with the cult of domesticity did not necessarily lead to open rebellion. Many women, although chafing against the constraints of the genteel code and the assumption that they should limit their activities to the home, remained committed to playing a nurturing and supportive role within the family. In fact, early advocates of a "widened sphere" for women often fused the traditional Victorian ideal of womanhood with a firm commitment to political action.

The career of temperance leader Frances Willard illustrates how the cult of domesticity, with its celebration of special female virtues, could evolve into a broader view of women's social and political responsibilities. Like many of her contemporaries, Willard believed that women by nature were compassionate and nurturing. She was also convinced that drinking encouraged thriftlessness and profoundly threatened family life. Resigning as dean of women and professor of English at Northwestern University in 1874, Willard devoted her energies full-time to the temperance cause. Five years later she was elected president of the newly formed Woman's Christian Temperance Union (WCTU).

Willard took the traditional cult of domesticity's belief that women had unique moral virtues and transformed it into a rationale for political action. The domestication of politics, she asserted, would protect the family and improve public morality. Choosing as the union's badge a bow of white ribbon, symbolizing the purity of the home, she launched a crusade in 1880 to win the franchise for women so that they could vote to outlaw liquor. Willard soon expanded the WCTU's activities to include welfare work, prison reform, labor arbitration, and public health. Under her leadership the WCTU, with a membership of nearly 150,000 by 1890, became the nation's first mass organization of women. Through it, women gained experience as lobbyists, organizers, and lecturers, in the process undercutting the assumption of "separate spheres."

An expanding network of women's clubs offered another means by which middle- and upper-class women could hone their skills in civic affairs, public speaking, and intellectual analysis. In the 1870s many well-to-do women met weekly to study topics of mutual interest. These club women soon became involved in social-welfare projects, public-library expansion, and tenement reform. By 1892 the General Federation of Women's Clubs, an umbrella organization established that year, boasted 495 affiliates and a hundred thousand members.

Another major impetus to an expanded role for women came from a younger generation of college women. Following the precedent set by Oberlin College in 1836, coeducational private colleges and public universities in the Midwest enrolled increasing numbers of women in these years, whereas Columbia, Brown, and Harvard universities in the East admitted women to the affiliated but separate institutions of Barnard (1889), Pembroke (1891), and Radcliffe (1894), respectively. Nationally, the percentage of colleges admitting women jumped from 30 percent to 71 percent between 1880 and 1900. By the turn of the century, women made up more than one-third of the total college-student population.

Initially, female collegiate education reinforced the prevailing concepts of femininity. The earliest women's colleges—Mount Holyoke (1837), Vassar (1865), Wellesley and Smith (1875), and Bryn Mawr (1884)—were founded to prepare women for marriage, motherhood, and Christian service. But participation in college organizations, athletics, and dramatics enabled female students to learn traditionally

Cigar-Box Label, c. 1910
Vassar College promoted the new image of womanhood by stressing the interconnections among education, athletics, and ethics.

"masculine" strategies for gaining power. The generation of women educated at female institutions in the late nineteenth century developed the self-confidence to break with the Victorian ideal of passive womanhood and to compete on an equal basis with men by displaying strength, aggressiveness, and intelligence—popularly considered male attributes. By 1897 the U.S. commissioner of education noted, "[I]t has become an historical fact that women have made rapid strides, and captured a greater number of honors in proportion to their numbers than men."

Victorian constraints on women were further loosened at the end of the century when a bicycling vogue swept urban America. Fearful of waning vitality, middle- and upper-class Americans explored various ways to improve their vigor. Some used health products such as cod liver oil and sarsaparilla for "weak blood." Others played basketball, invented in 1891 by a physical-education instructor at Springfield College in Massachusetts to keep students in shape during the winter months. But bicycling, which could be done individually or in groups, quickly became the most popular sport for those who wished to combine exercise with recreation.

Bicycles of various designs had been manufactured since the 1870s, but bicycling did not become a national craze until the invention in the 1880s of the so-called safety bicycle, with its smaller wheels, ball-bearing axles, and air-filled tires. By the 1890s over a million Americans owned bicycles. In Boston alone more than twenty-five thousand cyclists jammed the streets on a

Bicycling Lithograph, 1887
The first high-wheeler bicycles were difficult and dangerous to ride. One bump might pitch the rider forward over the handlebars. Therefore, the sport at first was restricted to males. Females who wished to accompany their male friends, as shown in this lithograph, could ride the more cumbersome, "fairy tricycle."

typical Sunday afternoon, and thousands attended bike races in Franklin Park.

Bicycling especially appealed to young women who had chafed under the restrictive Victorian attitudes toward female exercise, which held that proper young ladies must never sweat and that the female body must be fully covered at all times. The young women who rode bikes were immediately on display. Pedaling along without restrictive corsets or padded clothing, sporting instead a shirtwaist or "split" skirt, a woman bicyclist made an implicit feminist statement suggesting that she had broken with genteel conventions and wanted to explore new activities beyond the traditional sphere.

Changing attitudes toward femininity and women's proper role also found expression in gradually shifting ideas about marriage. Charlotte Perkins

Gilman, a suffrage advocate and speaker for women's rights, asserted that women would make an effective contribution to society only when they won economic independence from men through work outside the home (see Chapter 22). One very tangible indicator of women's changing relationship to men was the substantial rise in the divorce rate between 1880 and 1900. In 1880 one in every twenty-one marriages ended in divorce. By 1900 the rate had climbed to one in twelve. Women who brought suit for divorce increasingly cited their husbands' failure to act responsibly and to respect their autonomy. Accepting such arguments, courts frequently awarded the wife alimony, a monetary settlement payable by the ex-husband to support her and their children.

Contemporary assessments of all these changes differed widely, often along gender lines. "Molly Donahue have up an' become a new woman!" complained Mr. Dooley, humorist Finley Peter Dunne's satirical newspaper character, in 1898. By riding a bicycle, demanding the vote, and "wearin' clothes that no lady shud wear," Molly had announced her independence. A more sympathetic male observer, magazine illustrator Charles Dana Gibson, captured the popular image of this new woman with his folio of "Gibson girls." In contrast to the stiff, corseted Victorian lady of formal engravings, the Gibson girl exuded a spirit of independence and freedom. Pictured playing tennis or riding her bicycle, Gibson's tanned, vigorous young woman enjoyed the healthy outdoor life and active participation in the community.

Women writers generally welcomed the new female commitment to independence and self-sufficiency. In the short stories of Mary Wilkins Freeman, for example, women's expanding role is implicitly compared to the frontier ideal of freedom. Freeman's characters fight for their beliefs without concern for society's reaction. Feminist Kate Chopin pushed the debate to the extreme by having Edna Pontellier, the married heroine of her 1899 novel *The Awakening*, violate social conventions by first falling in love with another man and then taking her own life when his ideas about women prove as narrow and traditional as those of her husband.

Despite the efforts of these and other champions of the new woman, attitudes changed slowly. The enlarged conception of women's role in society exerted its greatest influence on middle-class women who had enjoyed the privilege of higher education, possessed some leisure time, and could reasonably hope for success in journalism, education, social work, and nursing. For female immigrant factory workers and for shop girls who worked sixty hours a week to try to make ends meet, however, the ideal remained a more distant goal. So although many women were seeking more independence and control over their lives, most still viewed the home as their primary responsibility.

Public Education as an Arena of Class Conflict

The agitation over women's role remained largely confined to the middle class, but a very different controversy, over the scope and function of public education, engaged Americans of all socioeconomic levels. This debate starkly highlighted the class and cultural divisions in late-nineteenth-century society. Viewing the public schools as an instrument for indoctrinating and controlling the lower ranks of society, middle-class educators and civic leaders from the 1870s on campaigned to expand public schooling and bring it under centralized control. Not surprisingly, the reformers' efforts aroused considerable opposition from ethnic and religious groups whose outlook and interests differed sharply from theirs.

Thanks to the crusade for universal public education started by Horace Mann and other antebellum educational reformers, most states by the Civil War had public-school systems, and more than half the nation's children were receiving some formal education. But most attended school for only three or four years, and few went on to high school. Concerned that many Americans lacked sufficient knowledge to participate wisely in public affairs or function effectively in the labor force, middle-class educational activists in the 1870s worked to raise the overall educational level and to increase the number of years that children spent in school.

One such reformer was William Torrey Harris, a Victorian moralist who viewed the public schools as a "great instrumentality to lift all classes of people into . . . civilized life." First as superintendent of the St. Louis public schools in the 1870s, and later as the federal commissioner of education, Harris urged teachers to instill in their students a sense of order, decorum, self-discipline, and civic loyalty. Believing that modern industrial society depended on citizens' conforming to the timetables of the factory and the train, he envisioned the schools as models of punctuality and precise scheduling: "The pupil must have his lessons ready at the appointed time, must rise at the tap of the

San Diego, California, Schoolhouse, c. 1890
The stained-glass windows, elaborate bell tower, and ornate entranceway of this San Diego school testified to the community's pride in and commitment to public education.

bell, move to the line, return; in short, go through all the evolutions with equal precision."

To achieve these goals and to wrest control of the schools from neighborhood leaders and ward politicians, reform-minded educators like Harris elaborated a philosophy of public education stressing punctuality, centralized administration, compulsory-attendance laws, and a tenure system to insulate teachers from political favoritism and parental pressure. By 1900 thirty-one states required school attendance of all children from eight to fourteen years of age.

But the steamroller methods used by Harris and like-minded administrators to systematize public education quickly prompted protests. New York pediatrician Joseph Mayer Rice, who in 1892 toured thirty-six cities and interviewed twelve hundred teachers, scornfully criticized an educational establishment that stressed singsong memorization and prisonlike discipline. Writing in *Forum* magazine, Rice told of a Chicago teacher who drilled her students mercilessly and yelled at them, "Don't stop to think, tell me what you know!" In city after city, he discovered teachers more concerned about students' posture than their learning.

Rice's biting attack on public education overlooked the real advances in reading and computation made in the previous two decades. Nationally, despite the influx of immigrants, the illiteracy rate for individuals ten years and older dropped from 17 percent in 1880 to 13 percent in 1890, largely because of the expansion of urban educational facilities. But Rice was on target in assailing many teachers' rigid emphasis on silence, docility, and unquestioning obedience to the rules. When a Chicago school inspector found a thirteen-year-old boy huddled in the basement of a stockyard building and ordered him back to school, the weeping boy blurted out, "[T]hey hits ye if yer don't learn, and they hits ye if ye whisper, and they hits ye if ye have string in yer pocket, and they hits ye if yer seat squeaks, and they hits ye if ye don't stan' up in time, and they hits ye if yer late, and they hits ye if ye ferget the page."

By the 1880s several different groups found themselves in opposition to centralized urban public-school bureaucracies. Although many working-class families valued education, those who depended on their children's meager wages for survival resisted the attempt to force their sons and daughters to attend school past the elementary grades. Although some immigrant families made great sacrifices to enable their children to get an education, many withdrew their offspring from school as soon as they had learned the rudiments of reading and writing, and sent them to work.

Furthermore, Catholic immigrants objected to the overwhelmingly Protestant orientation of the public schools. Distressed by the use of the King James Bible and by the schools' failure to observe saints' days, Catholics set up separate parochial-school systems. In response, Republican politicians, resentful of the Catholic immigrants' overwhelming preference for the Democratic party, tried unsuccessfully in 1875 to pass a constitutional amendment cutting off all public aid to church-related schools. Catholics in turn denounced federal aid to public schools as intended "to suppress Catholic education, gradually extinguish Catholicity in this country, and to form one homogeneous American people after the New England Evangelical type."

At the other end of the social scale, upper-class parents who did not wish to send their children to immigrant-thronged public schools enrolled their daughters in female seminaries such as Emma Willard's in Troy, New York, and their sons in private academies and boarding schools like St. Paul's in Concord, New Hampshire. Shielding their privileged students from the temptations of urban life and preparing them to go on to college, these institutions reinforced the elite belief that higher education should be the preserve of the well-to-do.

The proliferation of private and parochial schools, together with the controversies over compulsory education, school funding, and classroom decorum, reveal the extent to which public education had become entangled in ethnic and class differences. Unlike Germany and Japan, which standardized and centralized their national education systems in the late nineteenth century, the United States, reflecting its social heterogeneity, instead created a diverse system of locally run public and private institutions that allowed each segment of society to retain some influence over the schools attended by its own children. Amid the disputes, school enrollments dramatically expanded. In 1870 fewer than seventy-two thousand students attended the nation's 1,026 high schools. By 1900 the number of high schools had jumped to more than 5,000, and the number of students to more than half a million.

CONCLUSION

By the 1890s class conflict was evident not just in the struggles to control public education but in practically every area of daily life, from mealtime manners to popular entertainment and recreation. Caught up in the material benefits of a prospering industrial society, middle- and upper-class Americans battled against what they deemed "indecent" lower-class behavior in all its forms, from dancing, gambling, and prizefighting to playing baseball on Sunday and visiting bawdy boardwalk sideshows. Even public parks became arenas of class conflict. Whereas the elite favored the large, impeccably groomed urban parks that would serve as models of gentility and propriety, working people fought for neighborhood parks where they could picnic, play ball, drink beer, and escape the stifling heat of tenement apartments.

Although the well-to-do classes often appeared to have the upper hand in these clashes, significant dissension surfaced early within their own ranks. The aged poet Walt Whitman was not alone in his sentiments when he lamented, in his essay *Democratic Vistas* (1881), how "certain portions of the people" were trying to force their cultural standards and moral values on the great mass of the population, who were thereby made to feel "degraded, humiliated, [and] of no account." Other critics, among them Charlotte Perkins Gilman, faulted middle-class society broadly for its obsession with polite manners and empty social rituals.

By the end of the century, this contest for power between the elite classes on the one hand and the immigrants and workers on the other seemed headed toward a partial resolution in a series of compromises that neither side had anticipated or expected. As Victorian morality eroded, undercut by dissension from within and opposition from without, new standards emerged that blended elements of earlier positions. In the sports of boxing and baseball, for example, new rules regulated behavior in the ring and on the field. Despite the professionalization of sports, however, it was immigrant heroes who captured the popular imagination as the older elite vision of sport as a vehicle for instilling self-discipline and self-control was transformed into a new commitment to sports as spectacle and entertainment. Like it or not, sports had become big business and an important part of the new consumerism.

Similar patterns of compromise and change took place in other areas. Vaudeville houses, lambasted by the well-to-do for their risqué performances, evolved into the nation's first movie theaters. Ragtime music, with its syncopated rhythms, gave rise to jazz. Primitive pleasure parks like Coney Island paved the way for such multimillion-dollar theme parks and amusement complexes as Disneyland and the Mall of America. In short, the raffish, disreputable, raucous, and frequently denounced working-class culture of the late-nineteenth-century immigrant city can be seen, in retrospect, as nothing less than the fertile seedbed of twentieth-century mass culture. And everywhere, popular culture became increasingly dominated by commercial interests that capitalized on the disposable income created by the nation's explosive industrial growth and encouraged the popular fondness for material goods, leisure, sports, and other entertainments.

CHRONOLOGY

1865   Vassar College founded.

1869   Cornell University founded.
First intercollegiate football game.
The Great Atlantic & Pacific Tea Company (A&P) organizes a chain of food stores.

1871   Thomas Eakins, *The Champion Single Sculls.*

1875   Smith College founded.
Frances Willard joins the Woman's Christian Temperance Union.
Henry Clay Work, "My Grandfather's Clock."

1876   National League of baseball players organized.

1879   F. W. Woolworth opens his "Five and Ten Cent Store" in Utica, New York.

1884   Mark Twain, *Adventures of Huckleberry Finn.*
Bryn Mawr College founded.

1886   Richard Warren Sears starts Sears, Roebuck.

1891   Stanford University founded.
University of Chicago founded.
Columbia University adds Barnard College as a coordinate institution for women.
Basketball invented at Springfield College in Massachusetts.

1892   Joseph Mayer Rice writes his exposé of public education in *Forum* magazine.
General Federation of Women's Clubs organized.

1893   Stephen Crane, *Maggie: A Girl of the Streets.*

1895   Coney Island amusement parks open in Brooklyn.

1899   Scott Joplin, "Maple Leaf Rag."
Kate Chopin, *The Awakening.*
Thorstein Veblen, *The Theory of the Leisure Class.*

1900   Theodore Dreiser, *Sister Carrie.*

FOR FURTHER READING

Elliot Gorn and Warren Goldstein, *A Brief History of American Sports* (1993). A skillful analysis of the impact of urbanization, industrialization, and commercialization on American sports.

William Leach, *Land of Desire: Merchants, Power, and the Rise of a New American Culture* (1993). A balanced examination of the innovative advertising and merchandising strategies that underlay the shift to a consumer culture in the 1890s.

Jessica Foy and Thomas J. Schlereth, eds., *American Home Life, 1880–1930* (1992). A probing look at the impact of technology and changing social practices on family life at the turn of the century.

Sheila M. Rothman, *Woman's Proper Place: A History of Changing Ideals and Practices, 1870 to the Present* (1978). A perceptive study of shifting attitudes toward women's proper role in society.

Olivier Zunz, *Making America Corporate, 1879–1920* (1990). A pioneering exploration of corporate capitalism's impact on the creation of a consumer culture.

ADDITIONAL BIBLIOGRAPHY

Daily Life

Stuart Blumin, *The Emergence of the Middle Class: Social Experience in the American City, 1760–1900* (1989); Clifford E. Clark, Jr., *The American Family Home, 1800–1960* (1986); Francis G. Couvares, *The Remaking of Pittsburgh: Class and Culture in an Industrializing City, 1877–1919* (1984); William F. Hartford, *Working People of Holyoke: Class and Ethnicity in a Massachusetts Mill Town, 1850–1960* (1990); Jacqueline Jones, *Labor of Love, Labor of Sorrow: Black Women, Work, and the Family from Slavery to the Present* (1985) and *The Dispossessed: America's Underclasses from the Civil War to the Present* (1992); S. J. Kleinberg, *The Shadow of the Mills: Working-Class Families in Pittsburgh, 1870–1907* (1989); Thomas J. Schlereth, *Victorian America: Transformations in Everyday Life, 1876–1915* (1991); Olivier Zunz, *The Changing Face of Inequality: Urbanization, Industrial Development, and Immigrants in Detroit, 1880–1920* (1982).

The Culture of the Middle Class

Martha Banta, *Imaging American Women: Idea and Ideals in Cultural History* (1987); Lawrence A. Cremin, *American Education: The Metropolitan Experience, 1876–1980* (1988); Helen L. Horowitz, *Alma Mater: Design and Experience in Women's Colleges from Their Nineteenth-Century Beginnings to the 1930s* (1984); John F. Kasson, *Rudeness and Civility: Manners in Nineteenth-Century Urban America* (1990); Steven Mintz and Susan Kellogg, *Domestic Revolutions: A Social History of American Family Life* (1988); Michael Oriard, *Reading Football* (1993); Lewis O. Saum, *The Popular Mood of America, 1860–1890* (1990); Thomas Schlereth, ed., *Victorian America: Transformations in Everyday Life* (1991); Barbara M. Solomon, *In the Company of Educated Women: A History of Women and Higher Education in America* (1985); Louise L. Stevenson, *The Victorian Homefront: American Thought and Culture, 1860–1880* (1991); Susan Strasser, *Satisfaction Guaranteed: The Making of the American Mass Market* (1989); David Tyack and Elisabeth Hansot, *Learning Together: A History of Coeducation in American Schools* (1990); Laurence R. Veysey, *The Emergence of the American University* (1965).

Working-Class Leisure and Recreation

Robert C. Allen, *Horrible Prettiness: Burlesque and American Culture* (1991); John C. Burnham, *Bad Habits: Drinking, Smoking, Taking Drugs, Gambling, Sexual Misbehavior, and Swearing in American History* (1993); John T. Cumbler, *Working-Class Community in Industrial America: Work, Leisure, and Struggle in Two Industrial Cities, 1880–1930* (1979); Perry Duis, *The Saloon: Public Drinking in Chicago and Boston, 1880–1920* (1983); Elliot J. Gorn, *The Manly Art: Bare-Knuckle Prize Fighting in America* (1986); Karen Halttunen, *Confidence Men and Painted Women: A Study of Middle-Class Culture in America, 1830–1870* (1982); Neil Harris, *Cultural Excursions: Marketing Appetites and Cultural Tastes in Modern America* (1990); John F. Kasson, *Amusing the Million: Coney Island at the Turn of the Century* (1978); Peter Levine, *A. G. Spalding and the Rise of Baseball: The Promise of American Sport* (1985); Benjamin G. Rader, *Baseball: A History of America's Game* (1992); Steven A. Riess, *City Games: The Evolution of American Urban Society and the Rise of Sports* (1989); Roy Rosenzweig, *Eight Hours for What We Will: Workers and Leisure in an Industrial City, 1870–1920* (1983); Robert W. Snyder, *The Voice of the City: Vaudeville and Popular Culture in New York* (1989); James C. Whorton, *Crusaders for Fitness: The History of Health Reformers* (1984).

The Clash of Cultures

Edward A. Berlin, *King of Ragtime: Scott Joplin and His Era* (1993); Burton J. Bledstein, *The Culture of Professionalism: The Middle Class and the Development of Higher Education in America* (1976); Ruth Borodin, *Francis Willard: A Biography* (1986); Robert Crunden, *American Salons: Encounters with European Modernism, 1885–1917* (1993); Emory Elliott, ed., *Columbia Literary History of the United States* (1988); Lori Ginsberg, *Women and the Work of Benevolence: Morality, Politics, and Class in the Nineteenth-Century United States* (1990); T. J. Jackson Lears, *No Place of Grace: Antimodernism and the Transformation of American Culture, 1880–1920* (1981); Lawrence W. Levine, *Highbrow/Lowbrow: The Emergence of Cultural Hierarchy in America* (1988); R. Laurence Moore, *Selling God: American Religion in the Marketplace of Culture* (1994); David Nasaw, *Schooled to Order: A Social History of Public Schooling in the United States* (1979); Burton W. Peretti, *The Creation of Jazz: Music, Race, and Culture in Urban America* (1992); Daniel J. Singal, *The War Within: From Victorian to Modernist Thought in the South, 1919–1945* (1982); David B. Tyack, *The One Best System: A History of American Urban Education* (1974); Morton White, *Social Thought in America: The Revolt Against Formalism* (1947).

Early Train
by George Edward Anderson, c. 1880

POLITICS AND EXPANSION IN AN INDUSTRIALIZING AGE

Rain fell steadily in Chicago on June 6, 1884, as Republican delegates crowded into the city's cavernous convention hall. But the weather did not dampen excitement, for the party's presidential candidate was to be chosen. Visitors crowded the galleries; gaslights illuminated the flags and the orators droning on stage. As the popular front-runner, Senator James G. Blaine, was nominated, the hall exploded in a wild demonstration. The *New York Herald Tribune* reported:

J. G. BLAINE, THE SONOROUS SENATOR OF THE SANGUINARY SHIRT.

> *Whole delegations mounted their chairs and led the cheering which instantly spread to the stage and deepened into a roar fully as deep and deafening as the voice of Niagara. The scene was indescribable. The air quivered, the gaslights trembled and the walls fairly shook. The flags were stripped from the gallery and stage and frantically raised, while hats, umbrellas, handkerchiefs and other personal belongings were tossed to and fro like bubbles over the great dancing sea of human heads.*

Late-nineteenth-century politics was an exuberant affair. Elections aroused enormous interest, and voters participated in record numbers. Songs, parades, banners, and buttons transformed presidential campaigns into national festivals.

The Republicans gathered in Chicago could well cheer. Their party had held the White House since 1861. Despite the Republicans' stranglehold on the presidency, however, the two parties were very evenly matched. In national elections, the outcome was rarely certain.

But beneath the hoopla, serious issues were at stake. Matters such as tariff rates, veterans' pensions, railroad development, and monetary policy vitally affected important interest groups as well as millions of ordinary Americans. Political feelings ran high over local issues as well. Religious, ethnic, and cultural differences between immigrant and native-born voters, and even between immigrant groups, shaped the politics of the big cities and of states like Wisconsin and Minnesota.

Yet while industrialization and urbanization were transforming the nation, politicians in Washington often seemed unable or unwilling to grapple with the social consequences. In part, this passivity reflected a deeply entrenched tradition of localism in American public life. To nineteenth-century Americans, "government" meant primarily the local authorities, not distant Washington.

But the federal government's lack of engagement with the social consequences of industrialization also arose from the fact that the nation's new corporate elite played an important role in both major parties in this era, and these leaders firmly opposed government intervention in the economy. Wages, hours, working conditions, and even the appalling urban-slum conditions, they insisted, were determined by rigid "economic laws" that must not be tampered with. These same capitalists welcomed government economic policies that aided business, such as protective tariffs or railroad subsidies, but otherwise they preached "hands off."

While government sidestepped social problems that in retrospect seem of central importance, politicians from the president down spent an amazing amount of time passing out government jobs. By the 1880s, the excesses of the spoils system, culminating in a shocking presidential assassination, had become so notorious that a demand for civil-service reform swept the nation.

As corporations restructured the economy and manipulated the political system to their advantage, major social groups became either political outcasts or political victims. In the cotton South and on the wheat-growing western plains, natural catastrophes and economic grievances exploded in the 1880s in a grass-roots agrarian protest movement. Southern blacks, meanwhile, endured not only disfranchisement but segregation, exploitation, and terrorism in an avowedly racist society.

Agrarian discontent turned even more political in the early 1890s when the People's, or Populist, party emerged, demanding far-reaching government programs to remedy economic and social problems. When a terrible depression struck in 1893, unrest deepened. In 1896 voters for the first time in decades chose between two candidates, William McKinley and William Jennings Bryan, with radically different political and economic philosophies.

As the century ended, a potent combination of sensational journalism, humanitarianism, nationalistic fervor, and capitalistic pressures fueled a drive for expansion. In a short war in 1898, the United States defeated Spain and acquired Caribbean and Pacific island territories. Further expansion in Latin America and Asia soon followed.

PARTY POLITICS IN AN ERA OF SOCIAL AND ECONOMIC UPHEAVAL

Geography, ethnic loyalties, economic interests, and myriad state and local alignments shaped American politics in the 1870s and 1880s. Two major issues preoccupied lawmakers nationally. The first involved the

nature and size of the money supply. The second issue was how to staff the government bureaucracy. In the 1870s critics began to attack the time-honored practice of awarding government jobs to the party faithful. In the Pendleton Act (1883), civil-service reformers took a step toward their goal of awarding government jobs on the basis of merit rather than political connections.

Patterns of Party Strength

Although voters elected only one Democratic president, Grover Cleveland, between 1857 and 1912, presidential elections often proved extremely close. In 1876 and again in 1888, the defeated Democrat actually received more popular votes than the Republican victor. Control of the two houses of Congress was frequently divided between Republicans and Democrats.

Each party had its centers of regional strength. The Democrats ruled the South; southern sections of border states like Ohio, Indiana, and Illinois; and major northern cities with large immigrant populations. In the South the white elite that controlled the Democratic party dominated political life. White southerners, Democratic since President Andrew Jackson's day and embittered by the Civil War, viewed Republicans as villains who had devastated the South, set up carpetbag governments in the defeated Confederacy, and elected General Grant as president. In election after election, the "solid South" rolled up overwhelming Democratic majorities. Similarly, in Boston, New York, and other northern cities, powerful Democratic bosses ensured the national party ticket strong support at election time. Not all big-city political machines were Democratic, but enough were to boost the Democratic cause mightily.

The Republican base was rural and small-town New England, Pennsylvania, and the upper Midwest. The Republicans could also count on votes in the northern cities from the native-born middle class and business and professional men, including the growing ranks of white-collar workers.

Northern Civil War veterans who after the war formed a social and political lobbying organization known as the Grand Army of the Republic (GAR) represented another potent Republican bloc. The letters GAR, one wit suggested, stood for "Generally All Republican." To solidify this vote, the Republicans ran a series of former Union Army generals for president and voted generous veterans' benefits.

Nor did economic standing always determine party affiliation. Most businessmen were Republican, but not all. In 1888 a top Republican cautioned party workers not to assume that "the influence and money of the great corporation interest" would automatically flow to the Republicans.

State and local party leaders managed electoral campaigns. They chose the candidates, raised money, organized rallies, and—if their candidate won—distributed public jobs to party workers. In Indiana ten thousand local Republican workers canvassed the state in 1884, gathering data about party affiliation from every voter.

Chieftains like the former saloonkeepers "Big Jim" Pendergast, the Democratic boss of Kansas City, and George B. Cox, the Republican boss of Cincinnati, controlled urban politics (see Chapter 19). These bosses turned out the vote by taking care of constituents, repaying ward leaders and party loyalists with municipal jobs, and on occasion financing campaigns with "contributions" extracted from city employees or from companies doing business with the city.

With the two parties so evenly matched, "swing states" where elections could go either way—Connecticut, New York, New Jersey, Indiana, and Illinois—held the balance of power. By no coincidence, most presidential and vice-presidential candidates came from these critical states.

Compared to today, voter participation was remarkably high. Of course, most women did not yet have the vote, and blacks were losing it in the post-Reconstruction South. But among eligible northern voters, participation rates of more than 80 percent were not unusual, and in particularly hard-fought state and local elections, the rate could rise to 95 percent. Voter participation a century later would equal scarcely half that level.

Because only men could vote in most states, political parties functioned in part as male social organizations. This is one reason woman suffrage aroused such resistance: it threatened the male political subculture that offered men so many material and emotional rewards.

The Stakes of Politics

Late-nineteenth-century electoral campaigns centered on issues important to large numbers of voters—among them the tariff, the currency supply, and the benefits paid to war veterans. The import duties

Immigrant Entrepreneurship
This 1888 photograph picturing the entire staff and stock of William C. Raue's house- and sign-painting business in Watertown, Wisconsin (a center of German immigrant culture), captures the expansive spirit of the 1880s—an exuberance reflected in the era's politics.

These regional political divisions also reflected different economic interests. Politically powerful groups frequently clashed over the tariff, currency, public-land policy, and government support for railroads and internal improvements.

These geographic patterns of party strength were not always clear cut. The Republicans made frequent, if unsuccessful, efforts to dent the "solid South" and worked tirelessly to attract urban-immigrant voters. Democratic candidates often fared well in the Republican strongholds of New England and the Midwest. Family tradition, ethnic ties, religious affiliation, and local issues often determined how an individual voted.

charged on hundreds of commodities, from steel to sugar, had a direct impact on powerful economic interests and even entire regions. Government policies affecting the money supply or veterans' pensions similarly concerned millions of Americans very directly.

To be sure, elections frequently involved emotional side issues. Orators resorted to windy patriotic rhetoric or shamelessly flattered various immigrant groups. Southern office seekers made crude racist appeals to white voters, whereas Republican candidates in the North often "waved the bloody shirt," reminding voters that the Republicans had led the nation during the Civil War and that the Confederacy's leaders had all been Democrats. As Rutherford B. Hayes advised a Republican campaigner in 1876: "Our strong ground is the dread of a solid south, rebel rule, etc., etc. . . . [M]ake these topics prominent in your speeches. It leads people away from 'hard times,' which is our deadliest foe."

And although national party candidates of the 1870s and 1880s addressed some issues of contemporary concern, they rarely confronted the most glaring problems. Except for the Interstate Commerce Act of 1887 and the largely symbolic Sherman Anti-Trust Act of 1890, Washington generally ignored the social consequences of industrialization. Indeed, the nation's capital sometimes seemed caught in a time warp as the rest of society plunged headlong into the modern era.

Why this neglect? The most important reason is that the capitalist elite, with massive political clout, firmly resisted public regulation or oversight. But the federal government's weakness had other causes as well. After Johnson's impeachment, Grant's passivity, and Hayes's disputed election, the presidency was a much diminished office.

In the legislative branch, party discipline hardly existed as senators jealously guarded their political turf and displayed little concern for large national issues. The parties were well organized to win elections, not to govern. One former senator, looking back on these years, recalled that each senator "kept his own orbit and shone in his sphere, within which he tolerated no intrusion from the President or from anybody else." As for the House of Representatives, political scientist (and future president) Woodrow Wilson described it in 1885 as a "mass of jarring elements."

Furthermore, most Americans did not *expect* the federal government to intervene in economic or social affairs. The doctrine of laissez-faire—the belief that un-

regulated competition represented the best path to progress—was widely preached. By this view, the federal government should promote economic development but not regulate the industries that it subsidized.

When people did want help from government, they tended to turn to local or state authorities. Some of the fiercest political contests erupted far from Washington. On the Great Plains, angry farmers demanded that their state legislatures regulate railroad rates. In the cities, immigrant groups contended for political power while native-born reformers periodically attempted to oust the political machines.

Moreover, city and state governments vied furiously with each other for control. In many states, cities could not change their system of government, alter their tax structure, or regulate municipal utilities without state approval. When Chicago wanted to issue permits to street popcorn vendors, a special act of the Illinois legislature was required.

In most state legislatures the rural districts held disproportionate influence. In Connecticut, for example, where the legislature had last been reapportioned in 1818, villages of a few hundred people had the same voting strength in the legislature as Hartford and Bridgeport. This issue, too, sparked countless political battles.

These grass-roots political rivalries frequently pitted ethnic and social groups against one another. In New York City immigrant Catholics and native-born Protestants locked horns over tax support to parochial schools. In 1889 the native-born Republican legislators of Wisconsin passed a law requiring all children to attend English-language schools. This was a direct slap at the Catholic and Lutheran parochial schools where immigrant children studied mainly in German, Swedish, or Norwegian.

Electoral skirmishes between ethnic groups often centered on cultural differences, as native-born Protestants tried to force on the immigrants their own views on gambling, prostitution, temperance, and Sabbath observance. No issue aroused more conflict than prohibition. Irish whiskey drinkers, German beer drinkers, and Italian wine drinkers were equally outraged by anti-liquor legislation. In state after state, as well as in many cities and counties, prohibition proposals on the ballot always roused passionate voter interest.

Thus Gilded Age politics formed an intricate mosaic of individuals, groups, and political parties pursuing varied interests in city halls, statehouses, and Washington, D.C. But despite all the activity, the political system still lagged behind in addressing the social problems of an increasingly urbanized and industrialized nation.

The Hayes White House: Virtue Restored

In this era of locally based politics and a diminished presidency, the state leaders who ran party politics tended to favor appealing but pliable presidential candidates.

Rutherford B. Hayes perfectly embodied this narrow view of the office. A lawyer and Civil War general wounded in action, Hayes had won admiration as an honest postwar governor of Ohio. His major presidential achievement was to restore respect for the office after the Grant scandals. With his flowing beard, the benevolent Hayes brought dignity and decorum to the White House. In part, this reflected the influence of his wife, Lucy, an intelligent, college-educated woman of great moral earnestness. The Hayeses and their five children often gathered after dinner for hymns and family prayers.

In contrast to Grant, who was given to periodic drinking bouts, Hayes drank only moderately. He also recognized the political strength of the temperance movement. "Lemonade Lucy" Hayes actively supported the Woman's Christian Temperance Union (WCTU). After one alcohol-free White House dinner, Hayes's secretary of state grumbled, "It was a brilliant affair. The water flowed like champagne."

Regulating the Money Supply

In the 1870s a political issue surfaced that would agitate American politics for decades: how to create a money supply adequate for a growing and diverse economy without producing inflation. Before the Civil War, with currency from some sixteen hundred state banks in circulation, the monetary situation was chaotic. A uniform national currency was needed, but what should the medium of exchange be? The only truly trustworthy money, many believed, was gold or silver, or certificates exchangeable for these scarce and precious metals. Reflecting this notion, all the *federally* issued currency in circulation in 1860, about $228 million, consisted of gold or silver coins or U.S. Treasury notes redeemable for gold or silver. Americans' almost superstitious reverence for gold and silver added to the difficulty of establishing a coherent monetary policy.

To complicate matters, opposing groups clashed over the money question. Bankers and creditors, most business leaders, economists, and politicians believed that economic stability required a strictly limited currency supply. But too tight a money supply would drive interest rates up and prices down. Debtors—especially southern and western farmers—and some manufacturers favored expanding the money supply. Expansion would make it easier for them to pay off their obligations and also, by increasing consumer buying power, help prop up falling farm prices.

After the Civil War, the monetary debate focused on a specific question: should the wartime greenbacks still in circulation be retained and even expanded, or gradually phased out, leaving only a currency backed by gold (see Chapter 16)? The hard times associated with the Panic of 1873 rendered this dispute even more bitter.

The money issue entered electoral politics in the mid-1870s with the formation of the Greenback party, advocating an expanded money supply and other measures to benefit workers and debtor farmers of the West and South. In the 1878 midterm elections, with the support of labor organizations embittered by the government's hostility in the labor unrest of 1877, Greenback candidates garnered more than a million votes and won fourteen seats in Congress.

As prosperity returned after 1878, the Greenback party faded, but the money issue, vital to so many people, did not. The debate now focused on the coinage of silver. Up to 1873 the U.S. Treasury purchased and minted into coins all the gold and silver offered to it for sale. However, by the early 1870s little silver was being sold to the treasury, and in the Coinage Act of 1873, Congress instructed the U.S. mint to stop making silver coins. Silver had been "demonetized." But just then, new discoveries in Nevada increased the silver supply, and the same debtor groups agitating for more greenbacks now also demanded that the government resume the purchase and coinage of silver. Enthusiastically backed by the silver-mine owners, they denounced the demonetization of silver as "the Crime of '73."

Silver forces won a partial victory in 1878, when Congress passed the Bland-Allison Act over Hayes's veto. This law required the treasury to buy from $2 million to $4 million worth of silver each month and mint it into silver dollars. But the treasury, dominated by monetary conservatives, sabotaged the law's intent by purchasing the minimum quantity of silver specified by the law and then refusing to circulate the silver dollars that it minted.

Frustrated silver advocates tried a new approach in the Sherman Silver Purchase Act of 1890. This measure instructed the treasury to buy, at current market prices, 4.5 million ounces of silver monthly—by no coincidence, almost precisely the amount then being produced by the nation's silver mines. It further required the government to issue treasury notes, redeemable in gold or silver, equivalent to the cost of these purchases. The Sherman Silver Purchase Act did slightly increase the money supply; but as world silver prices plummeted in 1893 and after, the government paid far less each month for its purchases and therefore issued fewer treasury notes. The tangled controversy over silver went on.

The Spoils System

Since the Jacksonian era, successful candidates in national elections had rewarded supporters and contributors with government positions ranging from cabinet posts and ambassadorships to post-office and customs-service jobs. The pattern of filling public jobs with political appointees also prevailed at the city and state level. This system, originally called rotation in office, had its defenders: it seemed the most democratic means of filling government positions, and it provided upward mobility for lucky appointees.

But the system had its less desirable side. Unqualified and incompetent applicants sometimes got jobs simply because of their party loyalty. Once in office, these appointees often had to contribute to the reelection campaigns of their political patrons. Because of such abuses, this mode of filling public jobs came to be called the spoils system after the old expression "To the victor belongs the spoils."

The battle over patronage among party chieftains led in the 1870s to a split in the Republican party between rival factions nicknamed the Stalwarts and the Half-Breeds. The two differed over little except who would control the party machinery and thus have the right to distribute patronage jobs. The Stalwarts' leader, the vain and strutting senator Roscoe Conkling of New York, had gained control of his state's patronage in President Grant's day. Senator James G. Blaine of Maine led the Half-Breeds.

For years, a small but influential group of reformers of the native-born elite class had campaigned for a professional civil service based on merit. Well bred, well educated, and well heeled, these reformers little understood the immigrants for whom the public payroll could be a ticket out of poverty. They favored a civil service staffed by "gentlemen . . . who need nothing and want nothing from government except the satisfaction of using their talents." Whatever their class biases, these conservative reformers had a point. As government grew more complex, a professional civil service became essential.

Advocates of professionalization included Missouri senator Carl Schurz, editor E. L. Godkin, and social-welfare leader Josephine Shaw Lowell. Civil-service reformers displayed an almost religious fervor. "I have spent my life in fighting the spoils system," gasped one on his deathbed. They gave speeches, wrote editorials, and in 1881 founded the National Civil Service Reform League.

Cautiously embracing the civil-service cause, President Hayes in 1877 launched an investigation of the corruption-riddled New York City customs office and demanded the resignation of two high officials. Both men had close ties to Conkling: one, Chester A. Arthur, was Conkling's top lieutenant in distributing patronage jobs. When the two ignored Hayes's resignation order, the president suspended them. Hayes's action won praise from civil-service reformers and Conkling's lasting hatred. The New York senator sneered about "snivel service" and Rutherfraud B. Hayes.

Civil-Service Reform

At the Republican convention of 1880, when neither the Stalwarts nor the Half-Breeds could win the nomination for their favored candidates, the delegates at last turned to a dark horse, Congressman James A. Garfield of Ohio. Because Garfield had well-known links to the Half-Breeds, and to soften the blow to Conkling, the convention chose as Garfield's running mate Chester A. Arthur, the Conkling loyalist recently fired by Hayes! Since Garfield enjoyed excellent health, the choice of the totally unqualified Arthur seemed safe.

The Democrats nominated a career army officer from Pennsylvania, Winfield Scott Hancock, and the Greenbackers gave the nod to Congressman James B. Weaver of Iowa. All three candidates had served as Civil War generals, Hancock with particular distinction. Garfield's managers stressed his war record and his humble log-cabin birth. By a razor-thin margin of under 40,000 votes (of 9.2 million cast), Garfield edged out Hancock; Weaver trailed far behind with 308,578.

The Election of 1880

Candidates	Parties	Electoral Vote	Popular Vote	Percentage of Popular Vote
JAMES A. GARFIELD	Republican	214	4,453,295	48.5
Winfield S. Hancock	Democratic	155	4,414,082	48.1
James B. Weaver	Greenback-Labor		308,578	3.4

When Garfield chose the Half-Breed leader James G. Blaine as secretary of state and named a Conkling opponent as the New York City customs collector, the Stalwart leader Roscoe Conkling tried a political maneuver that backfired. Together with New York's other senator, Thomas Platt, a Conkling loyalist nicknamed "Me Too," he resigned from the Senate. He hoped that the New York legislature would at once reelect him and thereby strengthen his political power. But Conkling miscalculated. The legislature chose another senator and ended Conkling's career.

The Sacred Elephant

Having yielded to reformers' pressure and enacted a civil-service law, the Republican party prepared for the 1884 electoral campaign. This cartoon by Thomas Nast represents an early use of the elephant as symbol of the Republican party.

But the civil-service reformers sought more than the defeat of individual spoilsmen; they wanted a civil-service law. A tragic event helped them realize their wish. On July 2, 1881, as President Garfield walked through the Washington railway station, a man burst from the shadows, pulled out a pistol, and shot him twice. It seemed at first that Garfield might survive, but the war veteran knew better. "I am a dead man," he told his doctors. He was right. Garfield's death on September 19, 1881, brought to the White House Vice President Chester A. Arthur, the very symbol of patronage corruption. The assassin, a drifter named Charles J. Guiteau, was tried and hanged despite his obvious insanity, which took the form of a delusion that the Stalwarts would hail him as a hero and give him a prestigious job.

Civil-service reformers shrewdly capitalized on public shock at Garfield's assassination to build support for their cause, portraying the fallen president as a spoils-system martyr. In 1883 Congress enacted a civil-service law introduced by Senator George Pendleton of Ohio (Garfield's home state) and drafted by the Civil Service Reform League. The Pendleton Civil Service Act set up a civil-service commission to prepare competitive examinations and establish standards of merit for a variety of federal jobs; it also forbade political candidates from soliciting contributions from government workers.

The Pendleton Act initially covered only about 12 percent of federal employees but was gradually expanded. The creation of a professional civil service independent of party politics helped to bring the federal government in step with the modernizing trends transforming society.

As for Chester A. Arthur, the fact that he proved to be a mediocre president pleasantly surprised those who had expected him to be an utter disaster. Ex-president Hayes feared that Roscoe Conkling would be "the power behind the throne," but in fact, Arthur supported civil-service reform and proved remarkably independent. Still, the easygoing and rather indolent Arthur was at best a caretaker president. Fed up with the feuding Republicans, the voters in 1882 gave the Democrats an overwhelming majority in the House of Representatives. In 1884, for the first time since the 1850s, they would put a Democrat in the White House, in the person of Grover Cleveland.

POLITICS OF PRIVILEGE, POLITICS OF EXCLUSION

Although hardly radical, Grover Cleveland challenged powerful interests by calling for cuts in the tariff and in veterans' pensions. Aroused interest groups rallied to defeat him in the 1888 election, one of the most corrupt in American history. During the Republican administration of 1889–1893, corporate interests and the veterans' lobby seemed firmly in the driver's seat. Meanwhile, debt-ridden, drought-stricken farmers from Georgia to the Dakotas mounted a spirited protest movement. And in the South so recently wracked by war, new forms of social and moral devastation emerged as the white majority denied the region's black citizens their most basic rights.

1884: Cleveland Victorious

At that tumultuous Chicago convention in 1884, the Republicans nominated their best-known party leader, James G. Blaine. A gifted and witty orator with a keen memory for names and faces, Blaine represented the younger, more dynamic wing of the Republican party eager to shed the taint of "Grantism" and build a truly national party that would promote economic development and take a greater interest in foreign policy.

But like many others, Blaine's name had been smirched in the tawdry politics of the Gilded Age. Historian Henry Adams surely had Blaine in mind when he wrote that the political history of this era offered "little but damaged reputations." In Blaine's 1876 senatorial campaign, his opponents had published incriminating letters in which Blaine, as speaker of the house, appeared to offer political favors to a railroad company in exchange for stock. One of these communications ended with the directive "Burn this letter," which Democrats gleefully chanted whenever Blaine ran for office thereafter. For civil-service reformers, Blaine epitomized the hated patronage system. To E. L. Godkin, he "wallowed in spoils like a rhinoceros in an African pool."

Sensing Blaine's vulnerability, the Democrats chose a sharply contrasting nominee, Grover Cleveland of New York. In a meteoric political rise from reform mayor of Buffalo to governor, Cleveland had fought the bosses and spoilsmen. Short, rotund, and resembling a bulldog, Cleveland was his own man in an era of back-room political bargainers.

The shrewdness of the Democrats' choice became apparent when Godkin, Carl Schurz, and other Republican reformers bolted to Cleveland. These independent-minded Republicans were promptly nicknamed Mugwumps, an Algonquian Indian term for a renegade chief.

But Cleveland had liabilities, including rumors that as a young man he had fathered an illegitimate child. With characteristic honesty, Cleveland admitted the accusation, but the Republicans still jeered at rallies: "Ma, Ma, where's my pa?" ("He's gone to the White House, ha, ha, ha!" responded defiant Democrats.)

A more serious problem for Cleveland was opposition by Tammany Hall, the New York City Democratic machine that he had fought as governor. If Tammany's

The Election of 1884

Candidates	Parties	Electoral Vote	Popular Vote	Percentage of Popular Vote
GROVER CLEVELAND	Democratic	219	4,879,507	48.5
James G. Blaine	Republican	182	4,850,293	48.2
Benjamin F. Butler	Greenback-Labor		175,370	1.8
John P. St. John	Prohibition		150,369	1.5

Steelworkers in Pittsburgh; Shoeworker in Lynn, Massachusetts
The complex battles over tariff rates in the late nineteenth century reflected the diverse interests of a wide array of industries and economic groups.

immigrant voters stayed home on election day, Cleveland could lose his own state. But in late October a prominent New York City clergyman denounced the Democrats as the party of "Rum, Romanism, and Rebellion." Blaine failed to repudiate the remark immediately. The Cleveland campaign managers widely publicized this triple insult—to Roman Catholics, to patriotic Democrats tired of the "bloody shirt," and to drinkers. This blunder and the Mugwumps' defection allowed Cleveland to carry New York State by twelve hundred votes, and with it the election.

Tariffs and Pensions

In some respects, Cleveland adapted comfortably to the dim role expected of Gilded Age presidents. He had early embraced the belief that progress and prosperity depended on the government's not meddling in the economy. In Andrew Jackson's day, laissez-faire had been a radical idea, eagerly endorsed by ambitious small entrepreneurs who wanted business conditions favorable to competition; by the 1880s it had become the rallying cry of a corporate elite staunchly opposed to any public regulation or oversight.

Holding fast to the political views of his youth, Cleveland displayed limited grasp of the impact of industrialization. Vetoing a bill that would have provided seeds to drought-stricken farmers in Texas, he warned that people should not expect the government to bail them out of their troubles. It is little wonder, then, that ordinary working Americans often found national politics irrelevant. A trade-union leader, testifying in 1885 before a congressional committee investigating labor conditions, challenged both parties to "take up some live issue instead of raking over the dead ashes of the past."

One public matter, however, did arouse Cleveland's energies: the tariff. This issue, dating from the 1790s, involved a tangle of conflicting economic and political interests. Tariff duties were a major source of public revenue in this era before a federal income tax, so the tariff was really a form of taxation. But which imported goods should be subject to duties, and how high should rates be? Opinions diverged radically.

The producers of such commodities as coal, hides, timber, and wool demanded tariff protection against foreign competition, and industries that had prospered behind tariff walls—iron and steel, textiles, machine tools—wanted protection to continue. Many

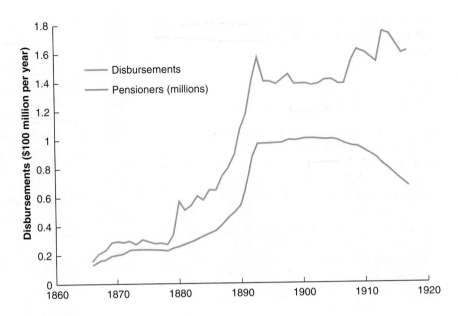

Civil War Pensions and Pensioners, 1866–1917

The pension system for Union army veterans represented a major federal welfare program in the late nineteenth and early twentieth centuries.

SOURCE: William H. Glasson, *Federal Military Pensions in the United States* (New York: Oxford University Press, 1918), p. 273

workers in these industries agreed, convinced that high tariffs meant higher wages. Other manufacturers, however, while seeking protection for their finished products, wanted low tariffs on the raw materials they required. Massachusetts shoe manufacturers, for example, urged high duties on imported shoes but low duties on imported hides. Farmers of the West and South, by contrast, hated the protective tariff, charging that it inflated farm-equipment prices and, by impeding international trade, made it hard to sell American farm products abroad.

Above all, the tariff was a political football. In general, the business-oriented Republicans advocated high tariffs and the Democrats, with their agrarian base, favored lower rates. But in reality a legislator's vote on a tariff bill depended almost entirely on the economic interests of his state or district. As a Democratic senator from Indiana put it in 1883, he supported his party's low-tariff position—except when it threatened Indiana's economic interests.

Cleveland's call for lower tariffs arose initially from the fact that in the 1880s the high tariff, generating millions of dollars in annual federal revenue, was feeding a growing budget surplus. This surplus continually tempted legislators to distribute it in the form of veterans' pensions or expensive public-works programs, commonly called pork-barrel projects, in their home districts. With his horror of paternalistic government, Cleveland viewed the budget surplus as a corrupting influence.

In his annual message to Congress in 1887, Cleveland argued that lower tariffs would not only cut the federal surplus but also reduce prices and slow the development of trusts. Although the Democratic campaign of 1888 gave little attention to the issue, Cleveland's tariff message dismayed many corporate boardrooms, where talk of lowering the tariff seemed a dangerous assault on business prosperity.

Cleveland stirred up another hornet's nest when he took on the Grand Army of the Republic. Veterans' disability pensions cost the government millions of dollars annually. No one opposed pensions for the deserving, but by the 1880s fraudulent claims had become a public scandal. The GAR urged veterans to file claims; and no matter how outrageous, these were routinely approved by Congress and the president. One veteran got a disability pension for poor eyesight that he blamed on wartime diarrhea. Not all Civil War veterans abused the system, of course. When Samuel Whisler, an Ohio farmer and minister, received a pension check from Washington, he promptly returned it with a note: "I cannot prove that my disabilities were directly the result of the exposure and hardship of war; therefore, I cannot honestly accept this money." But abuses were widespread enough to become a matter of partisan political controversy.

Unlike his predecessors, Cleveland investigated these claims—and rejected many of them. In 1887 he vetoed a bill that would have pensioned all disabled veterans (even if their disability had nothing to do with military service) and their dependents. The pension list should be an honor roll, he declared, not a refuge for frauds.

1888: Big Business and the GAR Strike Back

By 1888 some influential interest groups had concluded that Cleveland must go. He won renomination but faced a grimly determined Republican opposition. When Blaine decided not to run, the Republican kingmakers turned to Benjamin Harrison of Indiana.

A corporation lawyer and former senator, Benjamin Harrison exhibited such personal coldness that some ridiculed him as the human iceberg. His campaign managers learned to whisk him away after speeches before anyone could talk with him or experience his flabby handshake. Capitalizing on the fact that he was the grandson of William Henry Harrison, they incongruously called their aloof candidate Young Tippecanoe.

Harrison's managers also developed a new style of electioneering. Instead of sending the candidate around the country, they brought delegations to Indianapolis, where Harrison read them flowery speeches targeted to their interests. Solemnly Harrison told an audience of awed little girls, "Some of the best friends I have are under ten years of age."

The Republicans zeroed in on the tariff issue. Falsely portraying Cleveland as an advocate of "free trade"—the elimination of all tariffs—they warned of the dire consequences of such a step. The high protective tariff, they argued, ensured business prosperity, decent wages for industrial workers, and a healthy home market for farmers.

The Republicans amassed a $4 million campaign fund from worried business leaders. (Because the Pendleton Civil Service Act had outlawed the solicitation of campaign contributions from government workers, political parties depended more than ever on corporate contributors.) This war chest purchased not only posters and buttons but also votes.

In one of the campaign's "dirty tricks," a California Republican leader, pretending to be a British-born naturalized citizen named Charles Murchison, wrote to the British ambassador to ask how he should vote. The ambassador fell into the trap and advised "Murchison" to vote for Cleveland. Capitalizing on the anti-British feeling then prevalent in the United States, especially among Irish immigrants, the Republicans cynically publicized the "Murchison letter" as a shocking attempt by a foreign power to meddle in an American election.

Despite such Republican chicanery, Cleveland received almost one hundred thousand more votes than Harrison. But Harrison carried the key states of Indiana and New York and thus won in the electoral college. The Republicans held the Senate and regained the House. When Harrison piously observed that Providence had aided the Republican cause, his campaign chairman, Matthew Quay, snorted: "Providence hadn't a damn thing to do with it. . . . [A] number of men . . . approach[ed] the gates of the penitentiary to make him president."

Harrison swiftly rewarded his supporters. He appointed as commissioner of pensions a past GAR commander who on taking office declared "God help the surplus!" Within five years the pension rolls ballooned from 676,000 to nearly a million. Sociologist Theda Skocpol has described this massive pension system (which was coupled with medical care in a network of veterans' hospitals) as America's first large-scale public-welfare program.

So freely did money flow for pensions and pork-barrel legislation that the Republican Congress of 1890 became known as the Billion-Dollar Congress. In 1890

The Election of 1888

Candidates	Parties	Electoral Vote	Popular Vote	Percentage of Popular Vote
BENJAMIN HARRISON	Republican	233	5,477,129	47.9
Grover Cleveland	Democratic	168	5,537,857	48.6
Clinton B. Fisk	Prohibition		249,506	2.2
Anson J. Streeter	Union Labor		146,935	1.3

the triumphant Republicans also enacted the McKinley Tariff, which pushed rates to an all-time high.*

Rarely has the federal government been so subservient to entrenched economic interests, so saturated in the native-born Protestant cultural outlook, and so out of touch with the plight of the disadvantaged as during the 1880s.

But discontent was rising. Voters rebuffed the Republicans in the midterm election of 1890, when the Democrats gained sixty-six congressional seats to win control of the House of Representatives. This voter response reflected not only a stinging rebuke of the Billion-Dollar Congress and the business-ruled Harrison administration but also immigrant resentment at the efforts of the WCTU and other organizations dominated by Protestant, native-born Americans to "uplift" newcomers by force of law. Above all, however, the 1890 election awakened the nation to a tide of political activism engulfing the agrarian South and West.

Southern and Western Farmers Organize

Millions of farmers felt abandoned by the political process in the late nineteenth century. Agricultural acreage and production grew impressively in these years (see Chapter 17), but many farmers confronted a demoralizing cycle of falling prices, scarce money, and debt. These problems hit the chronically impoverished South and the boom-and-bust Great Plains with stinging severity.

In the cotton South, small planters found themselves trapped by the crop-lien system, endlessly mortgaging future harvests to finance current expenses. Mired in debt, many had to give up their land and become tenants or sharecroppers. About a quarter of southern farmers were tenants in 1880; by 1900, the figure had risen to one-third. One historian has aptly called the South in these years "a giant pawnshop."

Wheat farmers on the Great Plains also faced bewildering problems. Plunging into debt to buy land at high interest rates, many found themselves owing not only the bank but also the farm-implement dealer, the grain-elevator operator, and the railroad. In the 1870s farmers had looked to the Greenback and Grange movements for help, but by 1880 these efforts had faded.

From these trying circumstances emerged the alliance movement, the most significant outburst of grass-roots protest and reform in the late nineteenth century. It began in Texas in the late 1870s as poor farmers gathered to discuss their hardships. Soon an organization took shape, promoted by activists like farmer William Lamb, who organized more than a hundred local alliances.

The alliance idea advanced eastward across the lower South, especially after a farsighted Texan, Charles W. Macune, self-trained as both a lawyer and a physician, assumed leadership in 1887. By 1889 Macune had merged several regional farmers' organizations into a single body, the National Farmers' Alliance and Industrial Union, or Southern Alliance. A parallel organization of black farmers, the National Colored Farmers' Alliance, had meanwhile emerged in Arkansas and spread to other southern states.

Like the Grange, the alliance initially advocated farmers' cooperatives to purchase equipment and supplies for members and to market their cotton. These cooperatives mostly failed, however, because farmers lacked the capital to finance them.

Still, by 1890 the Southern Alliance boasted 3 million members, with an additional 1.2 million claimed by the National Colored Farmers' Alliance. Alliance members generally comprised not only the poorest farmers but also those most dependent on a single crop and most geographically isolated. As they attended alliance rallies and picnics, read the alliance newspaper, and listened to alliance speakers, hard-hit farm families felt less cut off—and increasingly recognized the political potential of their collective undertaking. As a member farmer in Hardy, Arkansas, wrote in 1889, "Reform never begins with the leaders, it comes from the people."

Meanwhile, alliance fever was burning across the Great Plains as well. In the drought-plagued years 1880 and 1881, alliances sprang up in Kansas, Nebraska, Iowa, and Minnesota. But the protest spirit faded as six years of abundant rainfall revived confidence and lured many thousands of settlers to the northern plains. In parts of Kansas, the boom triggered frenzied land speculation; farms that had sold for $6.25 an acre in the 1860s went for $270.00 an acre in 1887. Railroads, eager to promote settlement along their routes, fed the boom mentality.

In 1886–1887, however, came a painful awakening as killing winter blizzards and ice storms gave way to drought. From 1887 to 1897, only two Great Plains

---

*To pass the tariff, the Republican leadership did agree to a measure of interest to farmers and debtors: the Sherman Silver Purchase Act (see p. 668).

Consumer Prices and Farm-Product Prices, 1865–1913

As cycles of drought and debt battered Great Plains wheat growers, a Kansas farmer wrote: "At the age of 52, after a long life of toil, economy, and self-denial, I find myself and family virtually paupers."

wheat crops were worth harvesting. Searing winds shriveled the half-ripe grain as locusts and chinch bugs gnawed away the rest. To make matters worse, wheat prices fell as world production increased.

Many families packed up and returned East. "In God we trusted, in Kansas we busted," some scrawled on their wagons. Western Kansas lost 50 percent of its population between 1888 and 1892. But others hung on, and the Northwestern Alliance, although never as large as its southern counterpart, grew rapidly. By 1890 the Kansas Alliance claimed 130,000 members, followed closely by alliances in Nebraska, the Dakotas, and Minnesota. Like the Southern Alliance, the Northwestern Alliance initially experimented with cooperatives and gradually turned to politics.

Southern Alliance leaders Tom Watson of Georgia and Leonidas L. Polk of North Carolina urged southern farmers, black and white, to recognize their common plight and act together. For a time, this message of racial cooperation in the interest of reform offered promise. In Kansas, meanwhile, Jerry Simpson, a witty, intelligent rancher who lost his stock in the hard winter of 1886–1887, became a major alliance leader.

Mary E. Lease, a fiery Wichita lawyer, burst on the scene in 1890 as a spellbinding alliance orator.

Lease was only one of many women active in the alliance. Often veterans of the Granger and prohibition causes, they now rallied to the new movement, founding the National Women's Alliance (NWA) in 1891. Declared the NWA: "Put 1,000 women lecturers in the field and revolution is here." By no coincidence, a strong feminist strain pervades Ignatius Donnelly's *The Golden Bottle* (1892), a novel portraying the agrarian reformer's social vision.

As the movement swelled, the opposition turned nasty. When Jerry Simpson mentioned the expensive silk stockings of a conservative politician in his district and noted that *he* had no such finery, a hostile newspaper editor labeled him "Sockless Jerry" Simpson, the nickname he carried to his grave. When Mary Lease advised Kansas to "raise less corn and more hell," another conservative editor sneered: "[Kansas] has started to raise hell, as Mrs. Lease advised, and [the state] seems to have an overproduction. But that doesn't matter. Kansas never did believe in diversified crops."

Watermelon Time in Texas
Two Norwegian immigrant farm children of the 1890s pose winsomely in their family's fields. Farm life was far from idyllic, however, as drought, insects, and economic problems stalked rural America.

From all this feverish activity, a political agenda took form. In 1889 the Southern and Northwestern alliances loosely merged and adopted a political litmus test for candidates in the 1890 midterm elections. Their objectives included tariff reduction, a graduated income tax, public ownership of the railroads, federal funding for irrigation research, a ban on landownership by aliens, and "the free and unlimited coinage of silver."

The 1890 elections revealed the depth of agrarian disaffection in the South and West. Southern Democrats who endorsed alliance goals won four governorships and gained control of eight state legislatures. On the Great Plains, alliance-endorsed candidates secured control of the Nebraska legislature and gained the balance of power in Minnesota and South Dakota. In Kansas the candidates of the alliance-sponsored People's party demolished all opposition. Three alliance-backed senators, together with some fifty congressmen (including Watson and Simpson), went to Washington in 1890 as angry winds from the hinterlands buffeted the political system.

But differences soon surfaced. Whereas Northwestern Alliance leaders favored a third party, the Southern Alliance, despite Watson and Polk's advice, rejected such a move, fearing it would weaken the southern Democratic party, the bastion of white supremacy.

By 1892, however, some Southern Alliance leaders had reluctantly adopted the third-party idea, since many Democrats whom they had backed in 1890 had ignored the alliance agenda once in office. In February 1892 alliance leaders organized the People's Party of the United States—a title quickly shortened to the Populist party. At the party convention that August, thirteen hundred cheering delegates nominated for president the former Civil War general and Greenback nominee James B. Weaver of Iowa, now white-maned. Courting the South, they chose as Weaver's running mate the Virginian James Field, who had lost a leg fighting for the Confederacy.

The Populist platform restated the goals drawn up by the alliance leaders in 1889 while adding a call for the direct popular election of senators and other electoral reforms. It also endorsed a plan devised by alliance leader Charles Macune by which farmers could store their nonperishable commodities in government warehouses, receive low-interest loans using the crops as collateral, and then sell the stored commodities when market prices rose. Ignatius Donnelly's ringing preamble pronounced the nation on "the verge of moral, political, and material ruin" and declared, "[W]e seek to restore the government of the Republic to the hands of 'the plain people' with which class it originated."

As the Populists geared up for the 1892 campaign, another group of citizens with far more profound grievances found themselves pushed even further to the margins of American public life.

African-Americans After Reconstruction

The end of Reconstruction in 1877 and the restoration of power to the southern white elites, the so-called redeemers (see Chapter 16), spelled bad news for the nation's blacks, most of whom still lived in the South. The redeemer coalition of large landowners, merchants, and "New South" industrialists had little interest in the ex-slaves except as a docile labor force or as political pawns. However, southern white opinion demanded an end to the hated "Negro rule," and local Democratic party officials pursued this objective. Suppressing the black vote was a major goal. At first, black disfranchisement was achieved by intimidation, terror, and blatant vote fraud, as blacks were either kept from the polls or forced to vote Democratic. Then in 1890 Mississippi amended its state constitution in ways that effectively excluded most black voters, and other southern states soon followed suit.

Because the Fifteenth Amendment (1870) guaranteed all male citizens' right to vote, disfranchisement had to be accomplished indirectly by such means as literacy tests, poll taxes, and property requirements. The racist intent of these devices became obvious when procedures were introduced to ensure that they affected only *black* voters. One stratagem, the so-called grandfather clause, exempted from these electoral requirements anyone whose ancestor had voted in 1860.

Black disfranchisement proceeded erratically over the South—North Carolina elected a black congressman as late as 1898. But by the early twentieth century, it was essentially complete.

Disfranchisement was only the keystone of the solid arch of white supremacy laboriously erected in the South. In a parallel development that culminated in the early twentieth century, state after state passed laws imposing strict racial segregation in many realms of life (see Chapter 22). Black caterers, barbers, contractors, bricklayers, carpenters, and other artisans lost their white clientele.

Blacks who went to prison—sometimes for minor offenses—faced the convict-lease system, by which cotton planters, coal-mine operators, and other employers "leased" prison gangs and forced them to work under slave-labor conditions. One survivor of the system recalled: "A Georgia [convict-lease] camp is hell itself!" The ultimate enforcer of southern white supremacy was the lynch rope. Through the 1880s and 1890s, an average of about a hundred blacks were lynched annually in the United States, mainly in the South. The stated reasons, often the rape of a white woman, frequently arose from rumor and unsubstantiated accusations. (The charge of "attempted rape" could refer to a wide range of loosely defined behavior unacceptable to whites.) The lynch mob enforced social control, terrorizing blacks and demonstrating whites' absolute power. By no coincidence, lynching peaked in 1892 as many poor blacks embraced the farmers' alliance movement and rallied to the Populist party banner. Fifteen black Populists were killed in

Georgia alone, one historian has estimated, during that year's acrimonious campaign.

The relationship between southern agrarian protest and white racism was complex. Some Populists, like Georgia's Tom Watson, sought to build a genuinely interracial movement. Watson denounced lynching and the convict-lease system. When a black Populist leader pursued by a lynch mob took refuge in his house during the 1892 campaign, Watson summoned two thousand armed white Populists to defend him. But most white Populists, abetted by rabble-rousers like "Pitchfork Ben" Tillman of South Carolina, clung to racism; Watson complained that most poor whites "would joyously hug the chains of . . . wretchedness rather than do any experimenting on [the race] question."

The white elite, eager to drive a wedge in the protest movement, inflamed lower-class white racism. Addressing an alliance audience in 1889, conservative Atlanta editor Henry W. Grady warned against division among white southerners; the region's only hope, he said, was "the clear and unmistakable domination of the white race." But even as they raised the bugaboo of "Negro rule," the white elite manipulated the urban black vote as a weapon against agrarian radicalism, driving Tom Watson to despair. On balance, the rise of southern agrarian protest deepened racial hatred and ultimately worsened blacks' situation.

While southern blacks suffered racist oppression, the federal government stood aside. In 1877 President Hayes noted that black rights were being trampled, but he kept these observations to himself. In this he typified a generation of northern politicians who paid lip service to egalitarian principles but failed to apply them to blacks.

The Supreme Court similarly abandoned blacks to their fate. The Fourteenth Amendment (1868) had granted blacks citizenship and the equal protection of the laws, and the Civil Rights Act of 1875 outlawed racial discrimination on juries and in public places such as hotels and theaters, as well as on railroads, streetcars, and other such conveyances; but the Supreme Court soon ripped gaping holes in these protective laws.

In the *Civil Rights Cases* (1883), the Court declared the Civil Rights Act of 1875 unconstitutional. The Fourteenth Amendment protected citizens only from *governmental* infringement of their civil rights, the justices ruled, not from acts by private citizens such as railroad conductors. In *Plessy* v. *Ferguson* (1896), the justices upheld a Louisiana law requiring segregated railroad cars. Racial segregation was constitutional, the Court held, provided that equal facilities were made available to each race. (In a prophetic dissent, Associate Justice John Marshall Harlan observed, "Our Constitution is color blind." Segregation, he added, violated the constitutional principle of equality before the law.)

With the Supreme Court's blessing, the South segregated its public-school system, ignoring the caveat that such separate facilities must be equal. (In reality, white children studied in nicer buildings, used newer equipment, and were taught by higher-paid teachers than black children.) Not until 1954 did the Court abandon this "separate but equal" doctrine. Rounding out their dismal record, the justices in 1898 upheld the poll tax and literacy tests by which southern states had disfranchised blacks.

Few northerners protested the South's white-supremacist society. Until the North condemned lynching outright, declared the aged abolitionist Frederick Douglass in 1892, "it will remain equally involved with the South in this common crime." The restoration of sectional harmony, in short, came at a high price: acquiescence by the North in the utter debasement of a people whose freedom had cost the lives of many thousands of northern young men.

Blacks responded in various ways to their plight. The best-known black southerner of the period, Booker T. Washington, counseled patience, accommodation, and the acquisition of skills (see Chapter 22). Many blacks did adapt to a racist society and even managed a precarious happiness. Black churches provided emotional support, as did black fraternal lodges like the Knights of Pythias.

Some blacks established businesses to serve their community. Two black-owned banks, in Richmond and Washington, D.C., were chartered in 1888. The North Carolina Mutual Insurance Company, organized in 1898 by John Merrick, a prosperous Durham barber, eventually evolved into a major enterprise. Bishop Henry M. Turner of the African Methodist Episcopal church urged blacks to return to Africa and build a great Christian nation. Turner made several trips to Africa in pursuit of his proposal.

African-American protest never wholly died out. Frederick Douglass urged that blacks press for full equality; "Who would be free, themselves must strike the first blow," he proclaimed in 1883. Blacks should meet violence with violence, insisted militant New York black leader T. Thomas Fortune.

The Knights of Labor
Black delegate Frank J. Farrell introduces Terence V. Powderly, head of the Knights of Labor, at the organization's 1886 convention. The Knights were unusual in accepting both black and female workers.

Other blacks answered southern racism by leaving the region. In 1879 several thousand moved to Kansas (see Chapter 16). Some ten thousand migrated to Chicago between 1870 and 1890. Blacks who moved north soon found, however, that although white supremacy was not official policy, public opinion sanctioned many forms of de facto discrimination. Northern black laborers, for example, like their southern counterparts, encountered widespread prejudice. Although the Knights of Labor welcomed blacks and by the mid-1880s had an estimated sixty thousand black members, its successor, the American Federation of Labor, despite a policy that officially forbade racial discrimination, in practice looked the other way as many of its member unions informally excluded blacks.

The rise of the so-called solid South, firmly established on racist foundations, had important implications for American politics. For one thing, it made a mockery of the two-party system in a vast region of the nation. For years, the only meaningful election south of the Potomac was the Democratic primary. Only in the

1960s, in the wake of sweeping social and economic changes, would a genuine two-party system emerge in the South. Furthermore, the large bloc of southern Democratic senators and congressmen who trooped off to Washington each year, accumulating seniority and power, exerted a great and often reactionary influence on public policy. Above all, they mobilized instantly to quash any threat to southern white supremacy. Finally, the solid South wielded enormous clout in the national Democratic party. No Democratic contender for national office unacceptable to the white South stood a chance.

But above all, the rigid caste system that evolved in the post-Reconstruction South profoundly shaped the consciousness of those immediately caught up in it, white and black alike. As white novelist Lillian Smith has written, describing her girlhood in turn-of-the-century Florida and Georgia, "From the day I was born, I began to learn my lessons. . . . I learned it is possible to be a Christian and a white southerner simultaneously; to be a gentlewoman and an arrogant callous creature at the same moment; to pray at night and ride a Jim Crow car the next morning; . . . to glow when the word *democracy* was used, and to practice slavery from morning to night."

THE 1890s: POLITICS IN A DEPRESSION DECADE

The 1890s was one of the most difficult and unsettled decades in American history. Grover Cleveland, elected to a second term in 1892, faced a business panic, an erosion of the government's fiscal stability, and a depression that took a terrible human toll. The early 1890s also brought bloody labor strikes as well as the

emergence [...]
1890s laid [...]
ment—dom [...]
the principle of laissez-fa [...]
social consequences of ind [...]
tion. Yet from these same c [...]
found changes in American po [...]

1892: Populists Challenge the Statu[...]

The year 1892 brought evidence of gath[...] tent. The Populist party platform, adopt[...] fered an angry catalog of agrarian deman[...] month, thirteen people died in a gun b[...] between strikers and strikebreakers at the Homestead steel plant near Pittsburgh, and President Harrison sent federal troops to Coeur d'Alene, Idaho, where a silver-mine strike had turned violent. Events seemed to justify the Populists' warnings of a nation verging on ruin.

Faced with domestic turmoil and fearful that the powerful European socialist movement would spread to the United States, both major parties acted cautiously. The Republicans renominated Harrison and adopted a platform that ignored escalating unrest. The Democrats turned again to Grover Cleveland, who in four years out of office had made clear his growing conservatism and his opposition to the Populists.

In contrast to 1888, the tide this time flowed in the Democrats' direction. Cleveland won by more than 360,000 votes—a decisive margin in this era of close elections.

Populist strength proved spotty. James B. Weaver got just over a million votes—8.5 percent of the total—and the Populists elected five senators, ten congressmen, and three governors. The new party carried Kansas and showed some appeal in the West and in Georgia, Alabama, and Texas, where the alliance movement had taken deep root. But it made no dent in New England or the urban East, did poorly in the

The Election of 1892

Candidates	Parties	Electoral Vote	Popular Vote	Percentage of Popular Vote
GROVER CLEVELAND	Democratic	277	5,555,426	46.1
Benjamin Harrison	Republican	145	5,182,690	43.0
James B. Weaver	People's	22	1,029,846	8.5
John Bidwell	Prohibition		264,133	2.2

n regions of the Midwest, broad strength in the upper l! Whipped! Smashed!" moaned pulist Ignatius Donnelly in his diary. ut most of the South, racism, ingrained loyalty, distaste for a ticket headed by a for- ion general, and widespread intimidation and fraud kept the Populist vote under 25 percent. This ailure killed the prospects for interracial agrarian re- form in the region. After 1892 southern politicians seeking to appeal to poor whites—including a disillu- sioned Tom Watson—stayed within the Democratic fold and laced their populism with virulent racism.

The Panic of 1893: Capitalism in Crisis

Cleveland soon confronted the worst crisis to face any president since the Civil War: an economic collapse in the railroad industry, which quickly spread. In the rapid industrial growth of the 1880s, railroads had led the way, unleashing a wave of speculation among investors. Some railroads had fed the speculative mania by issuing more stock (and enticing investors with higher dividends) than their business prospects warranted.

Weakened by agricultural stagnation, railroad growth slowed in the early 1890s. This, in turn, affected many related industries, including iron and steel. In 1893 the bubble burst. The first hint of trouble ahead came in February with the failure of the Philadelphia and Reading Railroad.

This bankruptcy would not alone have triggered a general business collapse had it not come at a time of weakened confidence in the gold standard—the gov- ernment's pledge to redeem paper money for gold on demand. This diminished confidence had several sources. First, when a leading London investment bank collapsed in 1890, hard-pressed British investors unloaded millions of dollars worth of stock in Ameri- can railroads and other corporations and converted their dollars to gold. As a result, $68 million in U.S. gold reserves flowed across the Atlantic. Second, Con- gress's generous veterans' benefits and pork-barrel ap- propriations during the Harrison administration re- duced the government's financial resources just as tariff revenues were dropping because of the prohibi- tively high McKinley Tariff. Third, the 1890 Sherman Sil- ver Purchase Act further strained the gold reserve. This measure required the government to pay for its monthly silver purchases with treasury certificates re-

deemable for either silver or gold. When new silver dis- coveries in the early 1890s pushed silver's market value down, many holders of these treasury certificates con- verted them to gold. Finally, the election of Grover Cleveland in 1892 eroded confidence in the dollar even more. Although Cleveland personally endorsed the gold standard, his party was known to harbor many advocates of inflationary policies.

In January 1892 the gold reserve stood at $192 million. By the time Cleveland took office in March 1893, it had dwindled to $100 million, the bare mini- mum considered necessary to support the dollar. This decline alarmed those who believed—as most people did—that the gold standard offered the only sure evi- dence of the government's financial stability.

The collapse of a railroad early in 1893 thus trig- gered an economic crisis whose preconditions already existed. Fear now fed on itself as panicky investors converted their stock holdings to gold. Stock prices plunged in May and June; the gold reserve plummeted to $59 million; by the end of the year, seventy-four rail- roads and more than fifteen thousand commercial in- stitutions, including six hundred banks, had failed. So unfolded the Panic of 1893, the forerunner of four years of hard times.

The Depression of 1893–1897

The economic crisis worsened in 1894: by June nearly two hundred railroads had failed. By 1897 about a third of the nation's railroad mileage was in bankruptcy. Just as the railroad boom had been the key to the industrial prosperity of the 1880s, so the railroad crisis of the early 1890s sent shudders through the entire economy as hundreds more banks and other businesses failed. A full-scale depression clamped down on the nation.

In human terms, the depression of 1893–1897 took a heavy toll. Estimates of industrial unemploy- ment ranged from 20 percent to 25 percent. Upward of one-fifth of factory workers had no money with which to feed their families and heat their homes. Re- cent immigrants faced disaster. Jobless men tramped the streets and rode freight trains from city to city seek- ing work. Immigrant wives and mothers faced with caring for their families found the depression equally devastating.

The unusually harsh winters of 1893 and 1894 ag- gravated the misery. In New York City, where the crisis quickly swamped local relief agencies, a minister re- ported numerous instances of starvation. Amid the suf-

Coxey's Army
Jacob Coxey's "army" of the unemployed reaches the outskirts of Washington, D.C., in 1894. Note the new electrical or telephone poles.

March 1894 to lobby for his scheme. Thousands joined him en route, and several hundred actually reached Washington in late April.

Police arrested Coxey and other leaders when they attempted to enter the Capitol grounds, however; and his "army" broke up. Jacob Coxey may have been eccentric (he named a son Legal Tender Coxey), but his proposal closely resembled programs that the government would adopt during the depression of the 1930s.

As unrest intensified, fear and anger clutched middle-class Americans. A church magazine demanded that troops put "a pitiless stop" to all outbreaks of unrest. To some observers, a bloody upheaval seemed imminent.

Conservatives Hunker Down

In the face of mass suffering and turmoil, Cleveland retreated into a laissez-faire fortress. Boom-and-bust economic cycles were inevitable, he insisted, echoing the conventional wisdom of the day; the government could only huddle and ride out the storm.

Failing to grasp the complex causes of the depression, Cleveland focused on a single peripheral issue: defending the gold standard. As the gold reserve dwindled, he blamed the Sherman Silver Purchase Act, and in August 1893 he called a special session of Congress to repeal it. Silver advocates resisted fiercely, but Congress followed Cleveland's wishes.

Nevertheless, the gold drain continued and the depression deepened. In early 1895, with the gold reserve down to $41 million, Cleveland turned to Wall Street.

fering, a rich New Yorker named Bradley Martin threw a lavish costume ball costing several hundred thousand dollars. The partygoers spent as much as ten thousand dollars on their costumes. Popular outrage over this flaunting of wealth in a prostrate city forced Martin and his family to move abroad.

In rural America, already hard-hit by declining agricultural prices, the depression turned trouble into ruin. Farm prices dropped by more than 20 percent between 1890 and 1896. Corn plummeted from 50¢ to 21¢ a bushel; wheat, from 84¢ to 51¢. Cotton sold for 5¢ a pound in 1894.

Some desperate Americans turned to protest. The populist movement, already strong, gained more adherents. In Chicago workers at the Pullman factory reacted to successive wage cuts by walking off the job in June 1894 (see Chapter 18). The strikers' statement summed up their plight: "We struck at Pullman because we were without hope." In Massillon, Ohio, self-taught monetary expert Jacob Coxey concluded that the answer to unemployment was a $500 million public-works program funded with paper money not backed by gold but simply designated "legal tender" (just as it is today). A man of action as well as ideas, Coxey organized a march on Washington in

Bankers J. P. Morgan and August Belmont agreed to lend the government $62 million in exchange for U.S. bonds at a special discount. With this loan, the government purchased 3.5 million ounces of gold, half from foreign sources. Meanwhile, Morgan and Belmont resold the bonds to the public for a substantial profit. Despite public indignation about Cleveland's hat-in-hand appeal to private bankers, this complicated deal did help restore confidence in the government's economic stability. The gold drain was stemmed, and when the treasury offered $100 million in bonds in January 1896, they sold quickly.

Cleveland saved the gold standard, but at a high price. His dealings with Morgan and Belmont, and the bankers' handsome profits on the gold-purchase deal, confirmed agrarian radicals' suspicions of an unholy alliance between Washington and Wall Street. Cleveland's readiness to use force against the Pullman strikers and Jacob Coxey's peaceful marchers suggested insensitivity to the downtrodden.

Politics in the early 1890s, as always, reflected the maneuverings of competing interest groups. In this case corporate interests held the whip hand, as a battle over the tariff made clear. Although Cleveland favored tariff reform, the Congress of 1893–1895—despite its Democratic majorities—proved more responsive to high-tariff lobbyists. The Wilson-Gorman Tariff of 1894 lowered duties somewhat but made so many concessions to protectionist interests that Cleveland disgustedly allowed it to become law without his signature.

One feature of the Wilson-Gorman Tariff hinted at changes ahead: the act imposed a modest income tax of 2 percent on all income over $4,000 (about $40,000 in purchasing power today). But in 1895 the Supreme Court declared this measure unconstitutional. On a 5 to 4 vote, the Court held that the Constitution forbade direct federal taxation of individuals. Whether one looked at the executive, the legislature, or the judiciary, Washington's subordination to a single interest group, the corporate elite, seemed nearly complete.

Cleveland's policies split the Democratic party. Agrarian leaders and silver Democrats condemned his opposition to the Sherman Silver Purchase Act. South Carolina's Ben Tillman, running for the Senate in 1894, proclaimed, "[T]his scoundrel Cleveland . . . is an old bag of beef and I am going to Washington with a pitchfork and prod him in his fat old ribs." This split in the Democratic ranks decisively affected the elections of 1894 and 1896 and reshaped political alignments as the century ended.

The depression also contributed to a fundamental reorientation of social thought. Middle-class charitable workers who had been taught that individual defects of character caused poverty now realized—as socialists had long insisted and as the poor knew only too well—that even sober and hardworking people could succumb to economic forces beyond their control. As the social-work profession took form in the early twentieth century, its members spent less time preaching to the poor and more time investigating the social sources of poverty.

Laissez-faire ideology suffered a grievous setback in the 1890s as depression-worn Americans widely adopted a broadened conception of the government's role in dealing with the social consequences of industrialization. In the Progressive movement of the early twentieth century, this new perspective would activate powerful political energies. The depression was memorable, in short, not only for the suffering that it brought but also for the lessons that it taught.

THE WATERSHED ELECTION OF 1896

Galloping Republican gains in the 1894 midterm election revealed the depths of popular revulsion against Cleveland and the Democrats, who were blamed for the hard times. As politicians geared up for the 1896 presidential election, the monetary question became the overriding symbolic issue. Whereas conservatives clung to the gold standard, agrarian radicals rallied to the banner of "free silver." The silverites' moment of triumph came at the 1896 Democratic convention, when the nomination went to a young champion of the silver cause, William Jennings Bryan. Despite Bryan's eloquence, Republican William McKinley emerged victorious. His triumph laid the groundwork for a political realignment that would influence American politics for a generation.

1894: Protest Grows Louder

With the depression at its worst and President Grover Cleveland increasingly unpopular, the midterm election of 1894 spelled Democratic disaster. The blizzard of protest votes, commented one observer, buried the Democrats "a thousand feet deep." Gaining 5 seats in the Senate and 117 in the House, the Republicans won both houses of Congress. They also secured control of several key states—including New York, Illinois, and Wisconsin—as immigrant workers, battered by the depression, abandoned their traditional Democratic allegiance.

Populist candidates garnered nearly 1.5 million votes in 1894—an increase of more than 40 percent over their 1892 total. Populism's most impressive gains occurred in southern states such as North Carolina, Alabama, and Georgia. Although several western states that had voted Populist in 1892 returned to their traditional Republican allegiance in 1894, the overall results that year heartened Populist leaders.

The Silver Issue

As serious economic divisions split Americans in the mid-1890s, Supreme Court justice Stephen J. Field described the situation as "a war of the poor against the rich: a war constantly growing in intensity and bitterness." But this "war" involved mostly words and raged over a symbolic issue: free silver.

By clutching the gold standard so bulldoggishly, Cleveland forced his opponents into an equally exaggerated obsession with silver. Thus the genuine issues that divided rich and poor, creditor and debtor, and farmer and city dweller were obscured by murky debates over two semimythic precious metals. Whereas conservatives warned of the nightmarish dangers of abandoning the gold standard, agrarian radicals in the South and West extolled silver as a universal panacea. They were urged on and in some instances financed by western silver-mine owners who stood to profit handsomely if silver again became a monetary metal.

Beneath the rhetoric, each side had a point. Gold advocates recognized that a nation's paper money must be based on more than a government's ability to run printing presses and that uncontrolled inflation could be catastrophic. The silver advocates knew from personal experience how tight-money policies depressed prices and devastated farmers. Unfortunately, these underlying realities were rarely expressed clearly.

The silverites' most influential propaganda, William H. Harvey's *Coin's Financial School* (1894), explained the monetary issue in simplified partisan terms, denounced "the conspiracy of Goldbugs," and insisted that the free coinage of silver would banish debt and "revivify all the industries of the country." More than four hundred thousand copies of Harvey's

booklet were sold or given away by silver-mine owners.

Silver Advocates Capture the Democratic Party

At the 1896 Democratic convention in Chicago, conservatives protested in vain as western and southern delegates adopted a platform—including a demand for the free and unlimited coinage of silver at the ratio of sixteen to one—that in effect repudiated the Cleveland administration.

Who would be the nominee? The front-runner was Congressman Richard Bland of Missouri, a pillar of the silver cause. But behind the scenes, the groundwork was being laid for the nomination of a dark horse: William Jennings Bryan of Nebraska. A thirty-six-year-old Illinois native, Bryan had entered politics as a young lawyer in Lincoln, Nebraska. During two terms in Congress (1891–1895), he had fought for silver and against repeal of the Sherman Silver Purchase Act.

Bryan had honed his oratorical talents in college debating contests and in his early political campaigns. After his first political speech, he told his wife, "Mary, . . . last night I found that I had power over the audience. I could move them as I chose." His moment at Chicago came when he delivered a major speech in the debate over the platform. In an era before electronic amplification, his booming voice and broad

"Dubious"
A Republican poster pointed to poor nations that had a silver coinage, implying that the same fate awaited the United States if it adopted Bryan's panacea.

William McKinley's "Front-Porch" Campaign, 1896
McKinley (front row, sixth from left) poses with an Italian-American brass band from Buffalo, New York, in front of his home in Canton, Ohio.

gestures easily reached the upper gallery of the cavernous hall. In this famous speech, Bryan praised western farmers as the bedrock of the republic and scorned advocates of the gold standard. By the time he reached his rousing conclusion—"You shall not press down upon the brow of labor this crown of thorns, you shall not crucify mankind upon a cross of gold"— the wildly cheering delegates had identified their candidate (see "A Place in Time").

The silverites' capture of the Democratic party presented a dilemma to the Populists. They, too, advocated free silver, but only as one reform among many. To jump aboard the Bryan bandwagon would be to abandon the broad-ranging Populist program. Furthermore, fusion with the Democrats could destroy their influence as a third party. Yet the Populist leaders recognized that the most likely effect of a separate Populist ticket would be to siphon votes from Bryan and ensure the election of a conservative Republican. Reluctantly, the Populists endorsed Bryan, while preserving a shred of independence (and confusing voters) by naming their own vice-presidential candidate, Tom Watson, now a Georgia congressman. The Populists were learning the difficulty of organizing an independent political movement in a nation where the two-party system had taken deep root.

The Republicans, meanwhile, had nominated former governor William McKinley, who as an Ohio congressman had given his name to the McKinley Tariff of 1890. The Republican platform extolled the high protective tariff and endorsed the gold standard.

1896: Conservatism Triumphant

Bryan did his best to sustain the momentum of the Chicago convention. Crisscrossing the nation by train, he delivered his free-silver campaign speech to more than six hundred audiences in twenty-nine states. Not everyone found Bryan irresistible. One skeptical editor compared him to Nebraska's notoriously shallow Platte River: six inches deep and a mile wide at the mouth.

McKinley's campaign was shrewdly managed by his political mentor Mark Hanna, a Cleveland industrialist. A dignified, somewhat aloof figure, McKinley could not match Bryan's popular touch; to one critic, he always seemed to be "determinedly looking for his pedestal." Accordingly, Hanna built the campaign not around the candidate but around posters, pamphlets, and newspaper editorials that warned of the dangers of free silver, caricatured Bryan as a rabid radical, and portrayed McKinley and the gold standard as twin

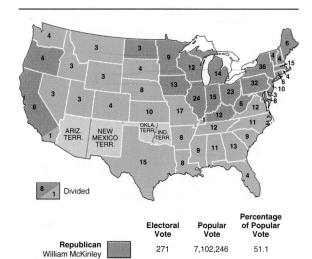

The Election of 1896

	Electoral Vote	Popular Vote	Percentage of Popular Vote
Republican William McKinley	271	7,102,246	51.1
Democratic William J. Bryan	176	6,492,559	47.7
Minor parties	–	–	315,398	1.2

The Election of 1896

pillars of prosperity. One poster pictured businessmen and factory workers carrying a giant gold coin on which stood a regal McKinley holding the American flag as the sun of "PROGRESS" rose behind him.

Drawing on a war chest possibly as large as $7 million, Hanna spent lavishly. J. P. Morgan and John D. Rockefeller together contributed half a million dollars, far more than Bryan's total campaign contributions. Taking a leaf from the 1888 Harrison campaign, McKinley stayed home in Canton, Ohio, emerging from time to time to read prepared speeches to visiting delegations. Carefully orchestrated by Hanna, McKinley's deceptively bucolic "front-porch" campaign was actually a marvel of organization. All told, some 750,000 people trekked to Canton that summer.

On election day, McKinley swamped Bryan by over six hundred thousand votes. He swept the Northeast and the Midwest and even carried three farm states beyond the Mississippi—Iowa, Minnesota, and North Dakota—as well as California and Oregon. Bryan's strength was limited to the solid South and the sparsely settled Great Plains and Rocky Mountain states. The Republicans retained control of Congress.

Why did Bryan lose despite the depression's heavy toll and the protest spirit abroad in the land? Certainly the scare tactics of the free-spending Republicans played a role. But Bryan's candidacy carried its own heavy liabilities. His core constituency, while passionately engaged politically, was limited. Seduced by free silver and Bryan's lung power, the Democrats had committed themselves to a platform and a candidate with little appeal for factory workers, the urban middle class, or the settled family farmers of the midwestern corn belt. The cities went heavily for McKinley. Urban voters realized that higher farm prices, a major free-silver goal, also meant higher food prices—hardly an attractive prospect. Bryan's weakness in urban America reflected cultural differences as well. To urban Catholics and Jews, this moralistic, teetotaling Nebraskan thundering like a Protestant revival preacher seemed utterly alien.

Finally, despite their telling critique of laissez-faire capitalism, the Populists' effort to define a humane and democratic alternative relied heavily on visions of a premodern economic order of independent farmers and entrepreneurs. Although appealing, this vision seemed increasingly anachronistic as the new corporate order steadily extended its reach.

While the forces of reform assessed their defeat, the McKinley administration translated its conservative platform into law. The Dingley Tariff (1897) pushed rates to all-time high levels, and the Currency Act of 1900 officially committed the United States to the gold standard. With returning prosperity, rising farm prices

The Election of 1900

Candidates	Parties	Electoral Vote	Popular Vote	Percentage of Popular Vote
WILLIAM McKINLEY	Republican	292	7,218,491	51.7
William Jennings Bryan	Democratic; Populist	155	6,356,734	45.5
John C. Wooley	Prohibition		208,914	1.5

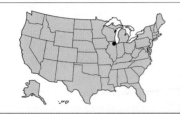
Barely sixty years old in the 1890s, Chicago was already a booming, bustling city of more than 1.5 million people, second only in population to New York. The Midwest's commercial, industrial, railroad, and agricultural hub, the city's stockyards teemed with livestock destined for slaughter and the packing houses. Along fashionable North Side streets like Lake Shore Drive stood the proud mansions of the city's great tycoons—men like Leander McCormick, who made farm equipment; Potter Palmer, who built hotels; Marshall Field, who owned a big department store; and Philip Armour, who slaughtered hogs. In the sprawling South Side working-class wards, immigrants from scores of countries crowded in tenements but somehow preserved their distinctive ethnic identity. Along the notorious Levee, saloons and brothels flourished, including the elegant Everleigh Club, run by two sisters from Kentucky, Ada and Minna Everleigh. A maze of elevated trains brought Chicagoans to the crowded downtown area, the Loop, where in the 1880s the world's first skyscrapers, thrusting eight and ten stories in the air, had transformed the skyline. Presiding over it all were colorful, easygoing politicians with nicknames like Bathhouse John and Hinky Dink.

Visiting Chicago in the 1890s was a must for European tourists, who were invariably overwhelmed by its throbbing vitality and stark contradictions. A British journalist in 1897 called Chicago the "queen and guttersnipe of cities, cynosure and cesspool of the world," where public spiritedness and flagrant civic corruption existed side by side.

Native-born writers, too, found the metropolis on Lake Michigan both alluring and repellent. The novelist Theodore Dreiser, who worked in Chicago as a journalist in the early 1890s, later tried to recapture his mixed impressions: "By its shimmering lake it lay, a king of shreds and patches, a . . .yokel with an epic in its mouth, a tramp, a hobo among cities, with the grip of Caesar in its mind, the dramatic force of Euripides in its soul. A very bard of a city this, singing of high deeds and high hopes, its heavy brogans buried deep in the mire of circumstance." A fictional Chicago reformer in Henry B. Fuller's *With the Procession* (1895) complains, "This town of ours labors under one peculiar disadvantage: it is the only great city in the world to which all its citizens have come for the

A Busy Chicago Slaughterhouse

From across the Midwest and Great Plains, the railroads funneled cattle, hogs, and other livestock into Chicago. Workers in blood-drenched slaughterhouses like this converted the animals into steaks, chops, and sausage for the dining tables of urban America.

685a

The 1893 Chicago World's Fair
The fair's harmonious architecture and sylvan tranquillity, captured in this painting by Theodore Robinson, contrasted sharply with the grimy, throbbing city beyond.

one common, avowed object of making money."

In 1893 Chicago organized the magnificent Columbian Exposition, ostensibly to honor Christopher Columbus but mostly to celebrate itself. In a swampy area along Lake Michigan rose glistening exhibition halls, statuary, and a shimmering reflecting lagoon. A dizzying array of mechanical, artistic, and agricultural exhibits was on display from many states and nations. The Woman's Building, organized by Bertha Palmer, Potter Palmer's wife, housed exhibits from nearly fifty countries. Numerous conferences were held, including a "world's parliament of religions." On the Midway Plaisance—the fair's popular amusement section—farm folk gaped at belly dancers from the Middle East and rode the world's first Ferris wheel. At night the exhibition buildings were outlined by strands of electric lights—the first that many Americans had seen. For hundreds of thousands of visitors, the Chicago world's fair provided memories for a lifetime. For urban planners, the "White City" that sprang up as if by magic that summer was a tantalizing foretaste of beautiful cities of the future. The man chiefly re-

sponsible for the fair's design, Chicago architect Daniel H. Burnham, more than lived up to his motto: "Make no little plans, they have no magic to stir men's blood." The fair ended literally with a bang. On the last day, as Mayor Carter H. Harrison was attending the closing ceremonies, he was shot and killed by a disappointed office seeker.

The world's fair delayed the arrival of the depression of 1893–1897 to Chicago, but when the crisis hit, it hit hard. More than two hundred thousand Chicagoans were out of work during the winter of 1893–1894. Many crowded into city hall each night to sleep on the floor; there, at least, they could be warm. In the city's dumps, men, women, and even small children picked over the garbage, searching for food. Tension gripped the city. When Governor John Peter Altgeld, charging a miscarriage of justice, in 1893 pardoned three men sentenced to hang after the Haymarket bombing of 1886, he was denounced by the city's elite, and his political career was over. In 1894, when workers at George Pullman's factory went out on strike, federal troops put down the disturbances.

Then in the hot July of 1896, the Democrats poured into town for their convention. The Nebraska delegation arrived in a special fourteen-car train festooned with banners for William Jennings Bryan. Reflecting the desperate economic plight of the Great Plains, they took rooms at the Clifton House, a cheap, run-down hotel. The delegation of wealthy New York "Gold Democrats," led by millionaire financier and horse-racing enthusiast William C. Whitney, arrived in a special New York Central train and stayed at the city's finest hotel.

On the convention's second night, Bryan dined with his wife Mary and a friend at the Saratoga Restaurant. They watched as delegates surged along Dearborn Street, demonstrating for the Democratic front-runner, Missouri congressman Richard Bland. Said Bryan quietly, "These people don't know it, but they will be cheering for me just this way by this time tomorrow night. I will make the greatest speech of my life tomorrow." He was right. The next day, he gave his rousing "Cross of Gold" speech, and the nomination was his.

Even for Chicago, the overgrown boomtown of the West, it had been quite a week—and quite a decade.

William Jennings Bryan

after 1897, and the discovery of gold in Alaska and elsewhere, these measures aroused little protest. Bryan won renomination in 1900, but the fervor of 1896 was missing. The Republican campaign theme of prosperity, summed up in the slogan "A Full Dinner Pail," easily won McKinley a second term.

The elections of 1894 and 1896 produced a Republican majority that, except for Woodrow Wilson's two presidential terms (1913–1921), would dominate national politics until the election of Franklin D. Roosevelt in 1932. Bryan's crushing defeat and the Republicans' emergence as the party of prosperity and the sound dollar killed the Populist party and drove the Democrats back to their regional base in the South. But although populism collapsed after 1896, a new reform movement called progressivism was picking up momentum. Many of the Populists' reform proposals would be enacted into law in the progressive years.

All this lay in the future, however. The most stirring events of the McKinley years occurred abroad. As prosperity returned at home, the United States flexed its muscles beyond the seas.

◆

EXPANSIONIST STIRRINGS AND WAR WITH SPAIN

The same corporate elite that dominated late-nineteenth-century domestic politics influenced U.S. foreign policy as well, contributing to surging expansionist pressures as the century ended. Not only business leaders but also politicians, statesmen, editorial writers, and Fourth-of-July orators insisted that national greatness required America to match Europe's imperial powers in making its weight felt in the world. Fanned by sensationalistic newspaper coverage of a Cuban struggle for independence and elite calls for greater American international assertiveness, war between the United States and Spain broke out in 1898.

Roots of Expansionist Sentiment

Since the early 1600s, when European settlers first established colonies along North America's Atlantic coast, the newcomers had been an expansionist people. By the 1840s the drive for more territory had acquired a name: "Manifest Destiny." The expansionist impulse had faded somewhat after the Civil War as industrialization absorbed American energies, but it revived strongly after 1880 as innumerable politicians and other opinion molders hammered into the public mind the conviction that America had a global destiny.

The example set by European nations and Japan contributed to this welling-up of expansionist sentiment. In 1897, the sixtieth anniversary of Queen Victoria's reign, Great Britain staged a great celebration to remind the world of its far-flung colonial empire. Meanwhile, France, Belgium, Italy, Germany, and Japan were busily collecting colonies from North Africa to distant Pacific islands. True national greatness, many opinion molders advised, demanded an empire.

In corporate circles, meanwhile, the opinion spread that continued prosperity required overseas markets. Secretary of State James Blaine voiced this view when he warned in 1890 that national productivity was outrunning "the demands of the home market" and insisted that American business must look abroad.

The proponents of a stronger navy contributed to the expansionist movement as well. In *The Influence of Sea Power upon History* (1890), Alfred T. Mahan, former head of the Navy War College at Newport, Rhode Island, equated sea power with national greatness and urged a U.S. naval buildup. Since a strong navy required bases abroad where vessels could dock for repairs, supplies, and fuel, Mahan and other naval advocates supported the movement to acquire foreign territories, especially Pacific islands with good harbors.

Some religious leaders proclaimed America's divine mission to spread Christianity. With American Protestant missionaries already fanning out over the globe, this call exerted a powerful appeal. The expansionist argument sometimes took on a racist tinge. As the Reverend Josiah Strong put it in his influential 1885 work *Our Country,* "God is training the Anglo-Saxon race for its mission"—a mission of bringing Christianity and civilization to the world's "weaker races."

All these themes were woven together by a group of Republican expansionists. Senator Henry Cabot Lodge of Massachusetts; diplomat John Hay; and Theodore Roosevelt, a rising New York Republican, tirelessly preached the gospel of imperial greatness and military might. "I should welcome almost any war," declared Roosevelt in 1897, "for I think this country needs one." A series of diplomatic skirmishes between 1885 and 1895 starkly revealed the newly assertive American mood and paved the way for the war that Roosevelt desired.

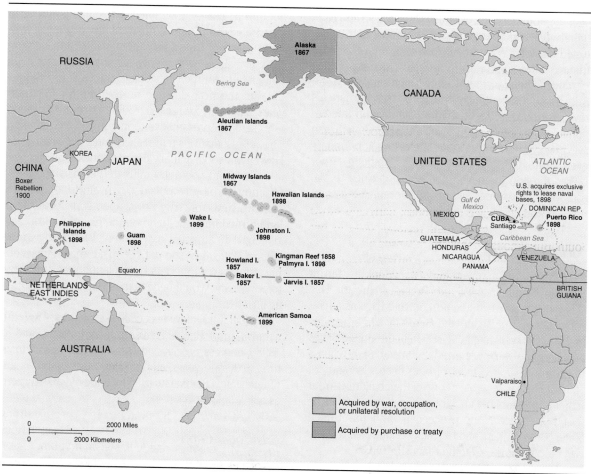

U.S. Territorial Expansion in the Late Nineteenth Century
The major period of U.S. territorial expansion abroad came in a short burst of activity in the late 1890s, when newspapers and some politicians beat the drums for empire.

In the mid-1880s, quarrels flared between the United States and Great Britain over fishing rights in the North Atlantic and in the Bering Sea off Alaska. These disputes reawakened Americans' latent anti-British feelings as well as the old dream of acquiring Canada. A poem published in the *Detroit News* (adapted from an English music-hall song) supplied the nickname that critics would apply to the promoters of expansion—jingoists:

> *We do not want to fight,*
> *But, by jingo, if we do,*
> *We'll scoop in all the fishing grounds*
> *And the whole dominion too!*

The fishing-rights dispute was settled by compromise in 1898, but by then attention had shifted to Latin America. In 1891 the United States seized a Chilean vessel that was attempting to buy guns in San Diego for one faction in a civil war then raging in Chile. A short time later, a mob in Valparaiso, Chile, killed two unarmed American sailors and injured seventeen others on shore leave. A furious President Harrison practically called for a declaration of war against Chile. Only when the Chilean government apologized and paid an indemnity was the incident closed.

Another Latin American conflict, in 1895, arose from a dispute between Venezuela and Great Britain over the boundary line of British Guiana. The disagreement worsened after gold was discovered in the contested territory. When the British rejected a U.S. arbitration offer, Secretary of State Richard Olney reminded them of the Monroe Doctrine. When the British condescendingly retorted that America's revered Monroe Doctrine had no standing in international law, a livid Grover Cleveland asked Congress to set up a commission to settle the disputed boundary even without Britain's approval. As patriotic fervor pulsed through the nation, the British decided to placate the United States and in 1897 accepted the commission's findings.

Pacific Expansion

Meanwhile, U.S. strategists focused on the far-off Samoan Islands in the South Pacific, where the U.S. Navy sought access to the port of Pago Pago as a refueling station. But Britain and Germany had ambitions in Samoa as well, and in March 1889 the United States and Germany narrowly avoided a naval clash when a hurricane destroyed most of both fleets. Secretary of State Blaine's wife wrote to one of their children, "Your father is now looking up Samoa on the map." Once he found it, negotiations proceeded, and the United States, Great Britain, and Germany established a three-way "protectorate" over the islands.

Attention had by that time shifted to the Hawaiian Islands, twenty-five hundred miles west of California. The islands had both strategic and economic significance for the United States. New England trading vessels had visited Hawaii as early as the 1790s, and in the 1820s had come Yankee missionaries. In 1835 a young Boston merchant had established a thousand-acre sugar plantation. Within a generation, American-owned plantations worked by Chinese and Japanese laborers dotted the islands. Under an 1887 treaty, the United States built a naval base at Pearl Harbor, near Honolulu. American economic dominance and the influx of foreigners angered Hawaiians. In 1891 they welcomed to the Hawaiian throne Liliuokalani, a strong-willed, independent woman hostile to Americans.

Meanwhile, a crisis had come in 1890, when the framers of the McKinley Tariff, pressured by domestic sugar growers, eliminated the duty-free status enjoyed by Hawaiian sugar. Hawaii's wholesale sugar prices plunged 40 percent as a result. Facing ruin, the planters in January 1893 deposed Queen Liliuokalani, proclaimed the independent Republic of Hawaii, and requested U.S. annexation. A leader in this coup was Sanford B. Dole, a prominent pineapple planter. The U.S. State Department's representative in Hawaii, who had supported Dole's revolution, cabled Washington: "The Hawaiian pear is now fully ripe, and this is the golden hour for the United States to pluck it."

But the pear dangled on the tree for five more years. The grab for Hawaii troubled Grover Cleveland, who sent a representative to investigate the situation. This representative's report shed doubt on whether the Hawaiian people actually desired annexation.

Cleveland's scruples infuriated expansionists. "In ordering Old Glory pulled down at Honolulu," declared a New York City newspaper, "President Cleveland turned back the hand on the dial of civilization." "Queen Lil" attracted a sentimental following in the United States, but she did not make matters easy for her American supporters by declaring that if restored to power, she would behead those who had conspired against her.

When McKinley succeeded Cleveland in 1897, the acquisition of Hawaii moved rapidly forward, and in 1898 Congress proclaimed Hawaii an American territory. Sixty-one years later, it joined the Union as the fiftieth state. Liliuokalani lived to a ripe old age, revered as a link to Hawaii's past.

Crisis over Cuba

By 1898 American attention had shifted to an island much closer to home: the Spanish colony of Cuba, ninety miles off Florida, where in 1895 an anti-Spanish rebellion had broken out. This revolt, organized by the brilliant Cuban writer José Martí and other Cuban exiles in New York City, won little support from U.S. business. Americans had $50 million invested in Cuba and annually imported $100 million worth of sugar and other products from the island, and turmoil could jeopardize these interests. Nor did the rebels initially secure the backing of either the Cleveland or the McKinley administration, both of which urged Spain to grant Cuba a degree of autonomy.

But the rebels' cause aroused much popular sympathy in the United States. This support increased with revelations that the Spanish commander in Cuba, Valeriano Weyler, was herding Cuba's civilian population into concentration camps to isolate the rebels. Brutality, malnutrition, and disease turned these camps into hellholes in which perhaps two hundred thousand Cubans died.

Fueling American anger was the sensationalized reporting of two New York City newspapers, William

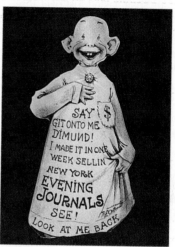

Yellow Journalism

Joseph Pulitzer's World *(left) and William Randolph Hearst's* Journal—*whose comic-strip character "the Yellow Kid" (below) gave rise to the term* yellow journalism—*had a field day when an explosion ripped the U.S.S.* Maine *in Havana harbor.*

Randolph Hearst's *Journal* and Joseph Pulitzer's *World,* which were embroiled in a fierce circulation war. One of Hearst's gimmicks was a color comic strip, "The Yellow Kid," which provided a name for his debased editorial approach: yellow journalism. The Hungarian immigrant Pulitzer normally had higher standards, but in the cutthroat competition for readers, Pulitzer's *World* matched the *Journal*'s lurid sensationalism. Both editors exploited the Cuban crisis. Headlines screamed the latest developments, and feature stories detailed "Butcher" Weyler's atrocities. When a young Cuban woman was jailed for resisting a rape attempt by a Spanish officer, a Hearst reporter helped the woman escape and brought her triumphantly to New York.

In 1897 a new, more liberal Spanish government softened its Cuban policy, and a peaceful resolution of the crisis seemed possible. But Hearst and Pulitzer continued to inflame the public. On February 8, 1898, Hearst's *Journal* published a private letter written by Spain's minister to the United States that described McKinley as "weak" and "a bidder for the admiration of the crowd." Many Americans agreed (Theodore Roosevelt once said that McKinley had "no more backbone than a chocolate eclair"), but they resented hearing it from a Spanish diplomat.

Irritation over this incident turned to outrage when on February 15, 1898, an explosion rocked the U.S. battleship *Maine* in Havana harbor and killed 266 American crewmen. A painstaking review of all the evidence in 1976 concluded that a shipboard ammunition explosion, set off by a fire in a coal-storage bunker, had caused the blast. But in 1898 neither Washington nor the yellow press was in any mood to view the tragedy as accidental. A navy inquiry blamed the blast on an underwater mine; newspaper headlines blazed with accusations of a "Spanish mine"; and war spirit flared high.

President McKinley, however, still hung back from war. He paced the White House at night and at least once broke down in tears. But McKinley was not prepared to risk his popularity by resisting an aroused America. (Of his sensitivity to public opinion, one Washington politician commented, "McKinley keeps his ear to the ground so close that he gets it full of grasshoppers much of the time.") Despite further Spanish concessions, McKinley sent a war message to Congress on April 11, and legislators enacted a joint resolution recognizing Cuba's independence and authorizing force to expel the Spanish. An amendment introduced by Senator Henry M. Teller of Colorado renounced any U.S. interest in "sovereignty, jurisdiction, or control" in Cuba and pledged that America would leave the island alone once independence was assured.

The Spanish-American War

The conflict with Spain lasted just over three months, with only a few days of actual combat. The first action came on May 1, 1898, when a U.S. fleet under the command of Admiral George Dewey, chief of the U.S. Asiatic Squadron based at Hong Kong, steamed into Manila Bay in the Philippines and destroyed or captured all ten Spanish ships anchored there, at the cost of 1 American and 381 Spanish lives. In mid-August U.S. troops occupied the capital, Manila.

In Cuba the fighting centered on the Spanish military stronghold of Santiago de Cuba on the southeastern coast. On May 19 a Spanish battle fleet of seven aging vessels under Admiral Pascual Cervera sailed into the Santiago de Cuba harbor, where five U.S. battleships and two cruisers at once blockaded them. On July 1, in the war's only significant land action, American troops seized two strongly defended Spanish garrisons on El Caney Hill and San Juan Hill overlooking Santiago de Cuba. Leading the volunteer "Rough Riders" unit in the capture of San Juan Hill was none other than Theodore Roosevelt, who at last got his taste of war. "I am entitled to the medal of honor, and I want it," he wrote his friend Senator Lodge.

On July 3 Cervera attempted to pierce through the American blockade to the open sea. U.S. naval fire raked the archaic Spanish vessels and sank them. Spain lost 474 men in this gallant but doomed show of the flag. Americans might have found a cautionary lesson in this sorry end to four hundred years of Spanish rule in the New World, but few had time for somber musings on the Fourth of July, 1898. The *Washington Post* observed,

> *A new consciousness seems to have come upon us—the consciousness of strength—and with it a new appetite, the yearning to show our strength. . . . [t]he taste of empire . . .*

John Hay was more succinct. It had been, he wrote Roosevelt, "a splendid little war."

Many who served in Cuba found the war far from splendid. Ill trained and poorly equipped, the troops went into summer combat in the tropics wearing heavy woolen uniforms. Medical care was abysmal.

Food poisoning, yellow fever, malaria, and other diseases killed more than 5,000 American soldiers during and after the war; in contrast, 379 had died in battle.

Despite the racism they faced at base camps and on transport ships, blacks served with distinction. The black Tenth Cavalry, a part of the Rough Riders, played a crucial role in taking San Juan Hill. One enthusiastic New York newspaper exclaimed: "All honor to the black troopers of the gallant Tenth. . . . Firing as they marched, their aim was splendid, their coolness superb, and their courage aroused the admiration of their comrades."

The Spanish sought an armistice on July 17, and in the peace treaty signed that December in Paris, Spain recognized Cuba's independence and, after much pressure and a payment of $20 million, ceded the Philippines, Puerto Rico, and the Pacific island of Guam to the United States. As 1899 dawned Americans possessed an island empire stretching from the Caribbean to the Pacific.

DEEPENING IMPERIALIST VENTURES: THE PHILIPPINES, CHINA, PANAMA

The end of the Spanish-American War proved only an interlude in this period of expansionism. A few anti-imperialists protested, but they were no match for the jingoists. In the Philippines, America fought a brutal four-year war against Filipinos struggling for independence. In China, Washington took diplomatic and military steps to ensure an "open door" for U.S. commercial interests. Closer to home some highly dubious maneuvering by President Theodore Roosevelt cleared the way for the construction of an American canal across the Isthmus of Panama.

The Platt Amendment

For four years after the war (1898–1902), the U.S. Army governed Cuba under the command of General Leonard Wood. Wood's administration improved public health, education, and sanitation but nevertheless violated the spirit of the 1898 Teller Amendment, by which the United States had pledged to leave after Spain's expulsion.

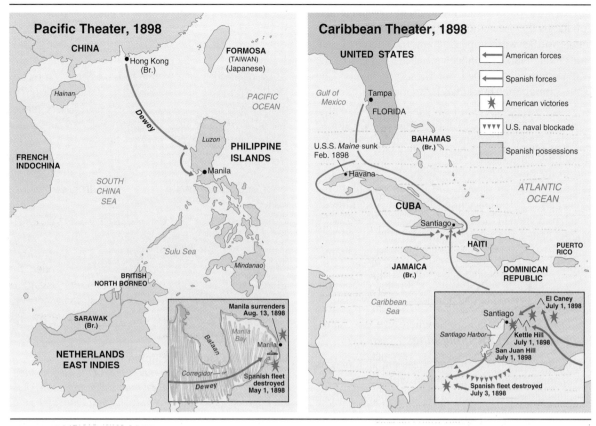

Pacific Theater, 1898

CHINA
FORMOSA (TAIWAN) (Japanese)
Hong Kong (Br.)
Hainan
PACIFIC OCEAN
Dewey
FRENCH INDOCHINA
Luzon
PHILIPPINE ISLANDS
SOUTH CHINA SEA
Manila
Sulu Sea
Mindanao
BRITISH NORTH BORNEO
SARAWAK (Br.)
NETHERLANDS EAST INDIES

Manila surrenders Aug. 13, 1898
Bataan
Manila Bay
Manila
Corregidor
Spanish fleet destroyed May 1, 1898
Dewey

Caribbean Theater, 1898

UNITED STATES

→ American forces
← Spanish forces
✴ American victories
▼▼▼▼ U.S. naval blockade
☐ Spanish possessions

Gulf of Mexico
Tampa
FLORIDA
U.S.S. *Maine* sunk Feb. 1898
BAHAMAS (Br.)
Havana
ATLANTIC OCEAN
CUBA
Santiago
HAITI
PUERTO RICO
JAMAICA (Br.)
DOMINICAN REPUBLIC
Caribbean Sea

Santiago
Santiago Harbor
El Caney July 1, 1898
Kettle Hill July 1, 1898
San Juan Hill July 1, 1898
Spanish fleet destroyed July 3, 1898

Major Battles in the Spanish-American War

The Spanish-American War was a short, sharp, one-sided encounter between the oldest European empire in the New World and the youngest power on the global stage. The conflict itself involved only a few limited U.S. engagements with out-matched Spanish forces in Cuba and the Philippines. The subsequent U.S. campaign to suppress an independence movement in the Philippines, however, proved long and costly.

The Gatling Guns,

by Charles Johnson Post, Cuba, 1898
Patented by Richard Jordan Gatling in 1862 this rapid-firing machine gun saw ser-vice in the Spanish-American War a generation later.

The troops eventually withdrew, though under conditions that limited Cuban sovereignty. An amendment to a 1901 army appropriations bill offered by Senator Orville Platt of Connecticut at the request of the War Department spelled out these conditions. The Platt Amendment authorized American withdrawal only after Cuba agreed not to make any treaty with a foreign power limiting its independence and not to borrow beyond its means. The United States also reserved the right to intervene in Cuba when it saw fit and to maintain a naval base there. With U.S. troops still occupying the island, the Cuban constitutional convention of 1901 accepted the Platt Amendment, which remained in force until 1934. Under its terms the United States reoccupied Cuba in 1906–1909 and again in 1912 and established a naval base at Guantánamo Bay, near Santiago de Cuba, which it still maintains. U.S. investments in Cuba, estimated at $50 million in 1898, soared to half a billion dollars by 1920.

Guerrilla War in the Philippines

An urgent problem confronted President McKinley as the Spanish-American War ended: what to do about the Philippines. This group of seven thousand remote Pacific islands, four hundred of them inhabited, had a population of more than 5 million in 1898. At the war's outset, few Americans knew that the Philippines belonged to Spain or even where they were. Without a map, McKinley later confessed, "I could not have told where those darn islands were within two thousand miles."

But the victory over Spain whetted the appetite for expansion. To the American business community, the Philippines offered a stepping-stone to the inviting China market. Reflecting the prevailing mood as always, McKinley reasoned that it would be dishonorable to return the Philippines to Spain and dangerous to leave them on their own. The Filipinos were unready for self-government, he believed, and would be gobbled up if set adrift in the shark-infested waters of imperial rivalries. McKinley further persuaded himself that American rule would enormously benefit the Filipinos, whom he called "our little brown brothers." A devout Methodist who easily fell into the language of the pulpit, he explained that America's mission was "to educate the Filipinos, and to uplift and civilize and Christianize them, and by God's grace do the very best we could by them. . . ." (In fact, most Filipinos were already Christian—a legacy of centuries of Spanish rule.) Having prayerfully reached his decision, McKinley in-

U.S. Soldiers Question Filipino Women
The United States' military repression of the Filipino independence movement brought much suffering to the civilian population. As many as two hundred thousand people died of disease, malnutrition, and other wartime hazards.

structed the American peace negotiators in Paris to insist on U.S. acquisition of the Philippines.

But uplifting the Filipinos required a struggle. As early as 1896, twenty-seven-year-old Emilio Aguinaldo had organized a Filipino independence movement to drive out Spain. In the summer of 1898, with arms supplied by Commodore Dewey, Aguinaldo's forces had captured most of Luzon, the Philippines' main island. When the Spanish surrendered, Aguinaldo proclaimed Filipino independence and drafted a democratic constitution. Feeling betrayed when the Paris peace treaty ceded his country to the United States, Aguinaldo in February 1899 ordered his rebel force to attack Manila, the American base of operations. Seventy thousand more U.S. troops were ordered to the Philippines, and by the end of the year, this initial Filipino resistance had been crushed.

But these hostilities represented only the opening phase of a long guerrilla conflict. Before it ended, over 125,000 American men had served in the Philippines, and 4,000 had been killed—more than ten times the

American battle deaths in the Spanish-American War. As many as 20,000 Filipino independence fighters died. As in the later Vietnam War, casualties and suffering ravaged the civilian population as a result of U.S. military action. The American forces captured Aguinaldo in March 1901, but large-scale guerrilla fighting went on through the summer of 1902.

In 1902 a special Senate committee heard sobering testimony from soldiers back from the Philippines about the execution of prisoners, the torture of suspects, and the burning of Filipino villages. The humanitarian mood of 1898, when Americans had rushed to save Cuba from the Spaniards, seemed remote indeed.

By the Philippine Government Act (1902), Congress vested authority in a governor general to be appointed by the president. But the act also provided for an elected Filipino assembly and promised eventual self-government. Progress toward independence inched forward, with intervals of semimilitary rule. (The U.S. farm lobby strongly supported Philippine self-government, because only with independence could tariff barriers be erected against Filipino agricultural products.) On July 4, 1946, nearly half a century after Admiral Dewey's guns had boomed in Manila Bay, independence finally came to the Filipinos.

Critics of Empire

Not all Americans applauded imperialism. Although few in number, the critics, like the Mugwumps who had challenged the spoils system, were influential. Indeed, some of them, like Carl Schurz and E. L. Godkin, *were* former Mugwumps. Other anti-imperialists included William Jennings Bryan, settlement-house founder Jane Addams, novelist Mark Twain, and Harvard philosopher William James. A somewhat unexpected recruit, steel king Andrew Carnegie, gave thousands of dollars to the cause. In November 1898, with the United States poised to take over not only Hawaii but perhaps the Philippines as well, these critics of empire formed the Anti-Imperialist League.

For the United States to subjugate other peoples, the anti-imperialists believed, was to violate the principles embodied in the Declaration of Independence and the Constitution. As one of them wrote, "Dewey took Manila with the loss of one man—and all our institutions." The military fever that accompanied expansionism also dismayed the anti-imperialists. Jane Addams reported that Chicago street children were playing violent games and carrying out mock murders of "Spaniards" during the Spanish-American War.

In February 1899 the anti-imperialists failed by one vote to prevent Senate ratification of the expansionist peace treaty with Spain. McKinley's overwhelming re-election victory in 1900 and the defeat of the expansionist critic William Jennings Bryan eroded the anti-imperialists' causes. Nevertheless, at a time of jingoistic rhetoric and militaristic posturing, they had upheld an older and finer vision of America.

The "Open Door": Competing for the China Market

As the Philippines war dragged on, American policy makers turned their attention still farther west—to China. Their objective was not territorial expansion but protection of U.S. commercial opportunities. Business interest in foreign markets had increased sharply with the depression of 1893–1897. Proclaimed Indiana senator Albert J. Beveridge in 1898, "American factories are making more than the American people can use; American soil is producing more than they can consume. Fate has written our policy for us; the trade of the world must and shall be ours."

The China market beckoned invitingly. Textile producers dreamed of massive sales to China's millions; investors saw opportunities for large-scale railroad construction. China was especially vulnerable to foreign intervention as the enfeebled Manchu Dynasty was tottering after a 250-year reign. In 1896 a consortium of New York capitalists formed the American China Development Company to promote trade and railroad investment in China.

But other nations, too, were eyeing the China market. Some went so far as to pressure the weak Chinese government to designate certain ports and even entire regions as spheres of influence where they would have exclusive trading and development rights. In 1896 Russia won both the right to build a railway across Manchuria and a twenty-five-year lease on a large section of the region. In 1897 Germany forcibly secured a ninety-nine-year lease on the port of Chaozhou (Kiaochou) as well as mining and railroad rights in the adjacent Shandong (Shantung) province. The British won various concessions, too.

When it appeared that U.S. businesses might be squeezed out of China, Washington intervened. In September 1899 Secretary of State John Hay addressed notes to the major European powers with economic interests in China, asking them not to interfere with American trading rights in China. Specifically,

U.S. Troops in China, 1900
On a dirt road flanked by stone elephants, mounted American troops sent by President McKinley prepare to march on Beijing as part of an international force assembled to suppress the Boxer Rebellion. This intervention signaled a deepening U.S. involvement in Asia.

Hay requested that they open the ports within their spheres of influence to all nations and not grant special privileges to the traders of their own country. The six nations gave noncommittal answers, but Hay blithely announced that the principle of an "Open Door" to American business had been accepted.

These Open Door notes illuminate the way commercial considerations influenced American foreign policy. They reflected what has been called a quest for "informal empire," in contrast to the acquisition of overseas colonies favored by the more openly imperialistic powers. In this kind of economic expansionism, Washington played a subordinate and supporting role to private enterprise—a kind of "imperialism" that fit neatly with the ideology of laissez-faire. Although U.S. trade with China remained minuscule in these years, visions of an enormous potential market there helped introduce a global perspective into American economic thinking.

As Hay pursued his Open Door efforts, a more immediate threat to American interests—indeed, to all foreign interests—emerged in China. For years, antiforeign feeling had been building in China, fanned by an aged Manchu Dynasty empress disgusted by the growth of Western influence. In 1899 a fanatical antiforeign secret society known as the Harmonious Righteous Fists (called "Boxers" by Western journalists) went on a rampage throughout China and killed thousands of foreigners as well as Chinese converts to Christianity. In June 1900 the Boxers occupied Beijing (Peking), the Chinese capital, and laid siege to the district housing the foreign legations. The United States contributed twenty-five hundred soldiers to an international army that in August 1900 marched on Beijing, drove back the Boxers, and rescued the occupants of the besieged legations.

The defeat of the Boxer uprising further weakened China's government. Fearing total collapse of the regime, which would allow the imperial powers to carve up China, John Hay in 1900 issued a second, more important series of Open Door notes. He reaffirmed the principle of free and open trade in China for all nations and announced America's determination to preserve China's territorial and administrative integrity. In the 1930s, when Japanese expansionism menaced China's survival, John Hay's policy helped shape the American response.

The Panama Canal: Hardball U.S. Diplomacy

The next episode in this cycle of foreign involvements left the most tangible legacy: the Panama Canal. Traders had long dreamed of a navigable canal across the ribbon of land joining North and South America that would eliminate the long and hazardous voyage around South America. In 1879 a French company headed by Ferdinand de Lesseps, builder of the Suez Canal, had secured a twenty-five-year concession from Colombia to build a canal across the Isthmus of Panama, then part of Colombia. But mismanagement and yellow fever plagued the project, and ten years and $400 million later, it went bankrupt, with the canal only half completed. Seeking to recoup some of its losses, the French company offered its assets, including the still-unexpired concession from Colombia, to the United States for $109 million.

In the expansionist climate of the 1890s, this offer aroused interest. An alternative route across Nicaragua also had its proponents, but when the French lowered their price to $40 million in 1901, this did the trick. In 1902 Congress authorized President Theodore Roosevelt* to accept the French offer. The following year, Secretary of State Hay signed an agreement with the Colombian representative, Tomás Herrán, granting the United States a ninety-nine-year lease on a strip of land for the construction of a canal, in return for a down payment of $10 million and an annual fee of $250,000.

But the Colombian senate rejected the Hay-Herrán agreement, deciding instead to wait for the French concession to expire and then negotiate a new concession with the United States. This shrewd action outraged Roosevelt, who privately denounced the Colombians as "greedy little anthropoids."

Determined to have his canal, Roosevelt found a willing collaborator in Philippe Bunau-Varilla, an official of the bankrupt French company. Dismayed that his company might lose its $40 million, Bunau-Varilla, from his room in New York's Waldorf Astoria Hotel, organized a "revolution" in Panama. While his wife stitched a flag, he wrote a declaration of independence and a constitution for the new nation. When the "revolution" occurred as scheduled on November 3, 1903, a U.S. warship hovered offshore as a warning to Colombia not to interfere. Proclaiming Panama's independence, Bunau-Varilla appointed himself its first ambassador to the United States. Three days later, Washington recognized the newly hatched nation. Bunau-Varilla next quickly signed a treaty with John Hay granting the United States a ten-mile-wide strip of land across Panama "in perpetuity" (that is, forever) on the same financial terms earlier rejected by Colombia. A few years later, Theodore Roosevelt summed up the episode: "I took the Canal Zone, and let Congress debate, and while the debate goes on, the canal does also."

The first challenge confronting the U.S. canal builders was the yellow fever that had haunted the French. A drainage project directed by army colonel William Gorgas eradicated the fever-bearing mosquito—a remarkable public-health achievement. Construction began in 1906, and in August 1914 the first ship passed through the canal.

In 1921, implicitly acknowledging the dubious methods used to acquire the Canal Zone, the Senate voted a payment of $25 million to Colombia. But the price paid by the United States for the Panama Canal cannot be measured in dollars alone. For decades after, the ill feeling generated by Theodore Roosevelt's high-handed actions, combined with other instances of U.S. interventionism, shadowed U.S.–Latin American relations.

---

*Elected vice president in 1900, Roosevelt had become president upon McKinley's assassination in September 1901.

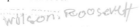

CONCLUSION

The opening of the Panama Canal concluded thirty years of expansionism that proclaimed the debut of the United States on the world stage and underscored the global reach of U.S. capitalism. But foreign involvements never fully diverted attention from the fundamental question of late-nineteenth-century domestic American politics: could a government designed for the needs of a small agrarian society serve a nation of factories and immigrant-crowded cities? Down to 1900, the answer was by no means clear. Although issues such as patronage, the tariff, veterans' benefits, and monetary policy generated much oratory and some action, the dominant ideology of laissez-faire severely limited government activism.

Rising agrarian discontent in the 1890s, sharpened by the depression of 1893–1897, underscored the urgency of certain social problems in these years. The Populist party, spawned by rural hardship, boldly challenged the assumptions of the laissez-faire ideologists and corporate leaders who largely determined public issues. Although populism as an organized political force disintegrated after Bryan's ill-fated free-silver campaign of 1896, and despite its nostalgic aspects, the movement's insistence that government play an assertive role in solving social and economic problems helped form the political environment of the progressive movement, to which we now turn.

CHRONOLOGY

1873　Panic of 1873.
　　　　Coinage Act demonetizes silver.

1877　Rutherford B. Hayes becomes president after disputed election.

1878　Bland-Allison Act requires U.S. Treasury to purchase silver.

1880　James Garfield elected president.

1881　Assassination of Garfield; Chester A. Arthur becomes president.

1883　Pendleton Civil Service Act.

1884　Grover Cleveland elected president.

1887　Cleveland urges tariff reform and vetoes veterans' pension bill.

1888　Benjamin Harrison elected president.

1889　United States, Great Britain, and Germany establish protectorate over Samoan Islands.

1890　Sherman Silver Purchase Act.
　　　　Sherman Anti-Trust Act.
　　　　McKinley Tariff pushes tariffs to all-time high.

1891　Crisis between United States and Chile over attack on U.S. sailors.

1892　Cleveland elected to second term as president.

1893　Panic of 1893; depression of 1893–1897 begins.
　　　　Drain of treasury's gold reserve.
　　　　Repeal of Sherman Silver Purchase Act.
　　　　Overthrow of Queen Liliuokalani of Hawaii.

1894　"Coxey's Army" marches on Washington.
　　　　Pullman strike.
　　　　Wilson-Gorman Tariff.

Queen Liliuokalani

1895　Supreme Court declares federal income tax unconstitutional.
　　　　Banker's loans end drain on gold reserve.
　　　　United States intervenes in Venezuela–Great Britain boundary dispute.

1896　Free-silver forces capture Democratic party and nominate William Jennings Bryan.
　　　　William McKinley elected president.

1897　Dingley Tariff.

1898　Spanish-American War.

**1898–
1902**　United States suppresses guerrilla uprising in Philippines.

1899　First United States Open Door notes on China.
　　　　United States helps put down Boxer uprising.

1900　Currency Act officially places United States on gold standard.
　　　　Second Open Door notes on China.
　　　　McKinley reelected; Theodore Roosevelt elected vice president.

1901　Platt Amendment retains U.S. role in Cuba.
　　　　Assassination of McKinley; Theodore Roosevelt becomes president.

1902　Philippines Government Act.

1903　Hay–Herrán Treaty rejected by Colombia.
　　　　"Revolution" in Panama organized by Philippe Bunau-Varilla.
　　　　Hay–Bunau-Varilla Treaty.

1914　Completion of Panama Canal.

William McKinley

FOR FURTHER READING

Edward L. Ayers, *The Promise of the New South: Life After Reconstruction* (1992). A richly textured work that explores the complexity of the topic and pays close attention to nonelite men and women.

Robert L. Beisner, *From the Old Diplomacy to the New, 1865–1900,* 2d ed. (1986). A valuable study tracing the roots of expansionism.

W. Fitzhugh Brundage, *Lynching in the New South: Georgia and Virginia, 1880–1930* (1993). A careful analysis of lynching in two southern states over a fifty-year period.

William F. Holmes, ed., *American Populism* (1994). A well-se-
lected set of nineteen scholarly essays interpreting the agrarian reform movement and surveying its varied aspects.

Morton Keller, *Affairs of State: Public Life in Late-Nineteenth-Century America* (1977). An excellent account of politics and government.

Robert C. McMath, *American Populism: A Social History, 1877–1898* (1993). A well-written study summing up recent scholarship on populism, especially its social and cultural dimensions.

John Offner, *An Unwanted War* (1992). A good recent history of the diplomacy leading up to the Spanish-American War.

ADDITIONAL BIBLIOGRAPHY

Gilded Age Politics and Voting Patterns: General

Peter H. Argersinger, "The Value of the Vote: Political Representation in the Gilded Age," *Journal of American History* 76 (June 1989): 59–90; Paula Baker, "The Domestication of Politics: Women and American Political Society, 1780–1920," *American Historical Review* 89 (June 1984): 620–647, and *The Moral Framework of Public Life: Gender, Politics and the State in Rural New York, 1870–1930* (1991); Richard J. Jensen, *The Winning of the Midwest: Social and Political Conflict, 1888–1896* (1971); Paul Kleppner, *The Cross of Culture: A Social Analysis of Midwestern Politics, 1850–1900* (1970); J. Morgan Kousser, *The Shaping of Southern Politics: Suffrage Restriction and the Establishment of the One-Party South, 1880–1910* (1974); David J. Rothman, *Politics and Power: The United States Senate, 1869–1901* (1966).

Monetary Issues and Civil-Service Reform

Milton Friedman and A. J. Schwartz, *A Monetary History of the United States* (1963); Ari A. Hoogenboom, *Outlawing the Spoils: The Civil Service Movement* (1961); Gerald W. McFarland, *Mugwumps, Morals, and Politics, 1884–1920* (1975); Thomas C. Reeves, *Gentleman Boss: The Life of Chester Alan Arthur* (1975); John Sproat, *"The Best Men": Liberal Reformers in the Gilded Age* (1968); Allen Weinstein, *Prelude to Populism: Origins of the Silver Issue* (1970).

Pensions, the Tariff, Agrarian Protest, Populism

Peter H. Argersinger, *Populism and Politics: William Alfred Peffer and the People's Party* (1974); Gene Clanton, *Populism: The Humane Preference in America, 1890–1900* (1991); Lawrence Goodwyn, *The Populist Moment: A Short History of the Agrarian Revolt in America* (1978); Steven Hahn, *The Roots of Southern Populism: Yeoman Farmers and the Transformation of the Georgia Upcountry, 1850–1890* (1983); Donald B. Marti, *Women of the Grange: Mutuality and Sisterhood in Rural America, 1866–1920* (1991); Martin Ridge, *Ignatius Donnelly: Portrait of a Politician* (1962); Theda Skocpol, *Protecting Soldiers and Mothers: The Political Origins of Social Policy in the United States* (1992); Tom E. Terrill, *The Tariff, Politics, and American Foreign Policy, 1874–1901* (1973).

Black History in the Late Nineteenth Century

Kenneth M. Hamilton, *Black Towns and Profit: Promotion and Development in the Trans-Appalachian West, 1877–1915* (1991); Louis R. Harlan, *Booker T. Washington: The Making of a Black Leader, 1865–1901* (1972); J. Morgan Kousser, *The Shaping of Southern Politics: Suffrage Restriction and the Establishment of the One-Party South* (1974); Neil R. McMillan, *Dark Journey: Black Mississippians in the Age of Jim Crow* (1989); August Meier and Elliott Rudwick, *From Plantation to Ghetto*, 3d ed. (1976); Howard N. Rabinowitz, *Race Relations in the Urban South* (1978); C. Vann Woodward, *The Origins of the New South, 1877–1913* (1971).

The Election of 1896, McKinley, and Bryan

Peter H. Argersinger, "'A Place on the Ballot': Fusion Politics and Antifusion Laws," *American Historical Review* 85 (April 1980): 287–306; Paolo E. Coletta, *William Jennings Bryan* (3 vols., 1964–1969); Robert F. Durden, *The Climax of Populism: The Election of 1896* (1965); Paul W. Glad, *McKinley, Bryan, and the People* (1964); Lewis L. Gould, *The Presidency of William McKinley* (1980).

Roots of American Expansion; Anti-Imperialism

Robert L. Beisner, *Twelve Against Empire: The Anti-Imperialists, 1898–1900* (1968); Walter LaFeber, *New Empire: American Expansionism, 1860–1898* (1963); Ernest R. May, *American Imperialism* (1968); Thomas J. Osborne, *"Empire Can Wait": American Opposition to Hawaiian Annexation, 1893–1898* (1981); Emily S. Rosenberg, *Spreading the American Dream: American Economic and Cultural Expansion, 1890–1945* (1982); Robert Seager II, *Alfred Thayer Mahan* (1977); Merze Tate, *The United States and the Hawaiian Kingdom* (1965); E. Berkeley Tompkins, *Anti-Imperialism in the United States: The Great Debate, 1890–1920* (1970).

The Spanish-American War and the Philippines

H. W. Brands, *Bound to Empire: The United States and the Philippines* (1992); Walter LaFeber, *Inevitable Revolutions: The United States in Central America* (1983); Gerald F. Linderman, *The Mirror of War: American Society and the Spanish-American War* (1974); Glenn A. May, *Social Engineering in the Philippines: The Aims, Execution, and Impact of American Colonial Policy, 1900–1913* (1980); Stuart Creighton Miller, *"Benevolent Assimilation": The American Conquest of the Philippines, 1899–1903* (1982); Hyman Rickover, *How the Battleship Maine Was Destroyed* (1976); John Edward Weems, *The Fate of the Maine* (1992); Richard E. Welch, *Response to Imperialism: The United States and the Philippine-American War* (1979).

U.S.-Chinese Relations; The Panama Canal

Kenton Clymer, *John Hay: The Gentleman as Diplomat* (1975); Michael L. Coniff, *Panama and the United States: The Forced Alliance* (1992); Michael Hunt, *The Making of a Special Relationship: The United States and China to 1914* (1983); Akira Iriye, *Across the Pacific: An Inner History of American East-Asian Relations* (1967); Walter LaFeber, *The Panama Canal* (1979); Sheldon B. Liss, *The Canal: Aspects of United States–Panamanian Relations* (1967): Thomas J. McCormick, *China Market: America's Quest for Informal Empire, 1893–1901* (1967); David McCullough, *The Path Between the Seas: The Creation of the Panama Canal, 1870–1914* (1977); Marilyn B. Young, *The Rhetoric of Empire: American China Policy, 1895–1901* (1968).

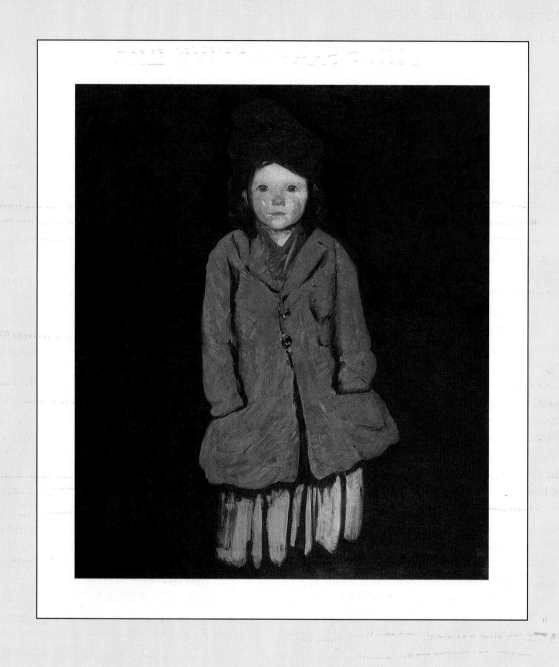

Lily Williams
by George Luks, 1909

THE PROGRESSIVE ERA

It was late Saturday afternoon on March 25, 1911, but at the Triangle Shirtwaist factory on Washington Place in New York City, hundreds of young women and a few men were still at work. The clatter of fifteen hundred sewing machines jammed into the eighth- and ninth-floor workrooms filled the air. Suddenly fire broke out. Feeding on the bolts of cloth hanging over the sewing machines, the fire soon transformed the upper floors into an inferno. Panicked workers rushed for the doors, only to find some of them locked. Other doors opened inward (a violation of the fire laws) and were jammed shut by the crush of bodies.

There were a few miraculous escapes. Breaking through the outer doors of the elevator shaft, twenty-two-year-old Cecilia Walker and others slid down the elevator cable eight floors to ground level. Young Pauline Grossman crawled to safety across a narrow alleyway when three male employees formed a human bridge. As others tried to cross, however, the weight became too great, and the three men fell to their death. In desperation, dozens of workers leaped from the windows to certain death on the sidewalk below. One falling woman became entangled in a utility wire and hung there until the fire burned through her dress, when she plunged to the ground.

Distraught immigrant parents wandered amid the scenes of death all night, in search of their daughters; newspaper reporters could hear "a dozen pet names in Italian and Yiddish rising in shrill agony above the deeper moan of the throng." Sunday's *New York Times* summed up the horror in a banner headline:

141 MEN AND GIRLS DIE
IN WAIST FACTORY FIRE;
TRAPPED HIGH IN
WASHINGTON PLACE BUILDING;
STREET STREWN WITH BODIES;
PILES OF DEAD INSIDE.

The Triangle fire offered terrible evidence that all was not well in urban-industrial America. Industrialization had brought many benefits, but it had also taken a heavy human toll and changed American life forever. The fabled "land of opportunity" seemed a myth as large corporations grew still larger. For the immigrant millions in unsafe factories and unhealthy slums, life was often a desperate cycle of poverty, exhausting labor, and early death. As a new middle class of white-collar workers and urban professionals consolidated its position, a revived women's movement demanded full participation in the political process.

From this volatile social stew surged a current of reform energy that came to be called the progressive movement. For decades, historians have argued about how to interpret this movement. Originally they portrayed it in a kind of political-cartoon fashion as an inspiring triumph of "the people" over sinister corporations and crooked bosses. More recently, historians have added complexity to this picture, noting the role of special-interest groups (sometimes including big business) in promoting specific reforms as well as the movement's darker side and its blind spots. Above all, historians now try to distinguish the diverse and sometimes contradictory impulses once lumped under the catchall label "progressivism."

But despite the interpretive shifts, historians have always recognized progressivism as a highly significant reform movement spawned by the vast changes that since the Civil War had obliterated many of the familiar contours of an older, simpler America. Whatever their specific agenda, all progressives grappled with the new social world of corporations, factories, cities, and immigrants.

Of course, reform was nothing new in the early 1900s; indeed, the impulse to correct dangerous trends and to steer society back to its proper course is a constant in American history.

But progressivism was quite different from earlier reform movements. For example, the reformers of the 1830s and 1840s had typically viewed government as irrelevant or even hostile to their purposes. Individuals and small, self-selected groups, they had insisted, must take the lead in achieving a better social order. The progressives, by contrast, viewed *government* as a major ally in the reform cause. And far from glorifying the individual or withdrawing from society, they saw organizations and social engagement as essential to reform.

Emerging around 1900, first at the city and state levels, myriad organizations, many composed exclusively of women, pursued varied reform objectives. Under the influence of journalists, novelists, religious leaders, social thinkers, and politicians, this diffuse progressive impulse coalesced and took on national dimensions. At the federal level, a spirit of government activism turned Washington into a hotbed of activity. By 1917, when reform gave way to war, American government and society had been altered in fundamental ways. This chapter looks first at the social changes that spawned progressivism and then at the movement itself.

THE CHANGING AMERICAN SOCIETY AND ECONOMY

Explosive urban growth and corporate consolidation transformed the United States in the early twentieth century. As native-born Americans poured cityward, they met a tide of immigrant newcomers, producing, in the words of one historian, the "swirling confusion that occurs in the mouth of a harbor when a river discharges its waters against the force of a rising ocean tide." The American city, with its business elite, its growing middle class, and its new immigrants, gave these early-twentieth-century decades their unique social character. Simultaneously, in these years of booming prosperity, new forms of business organization transformed American capitalism. As we saw in Chapter 18, however, not everyone benefited equally from economic growth. Millions of industrial workers endured long hours, low wages, dangerous working conditions, and pressures to increase productivity. Through labor unions and the ballot box, workers organized to improve their lot.

Immigrant Masses and a New Urban Middle Class

Through all the political turbulence of the early twentieth century, humanity continued to flow inexorably toward the cities. By 1920, when the nation's urban population for the first time passed the 50 percent mark, sixty-eight American cities boasted more than 100,000 inhabitants. New York City grew by 2.2 million from 1900 to 1920, Chicago by 1 million, and Detroit by 425,000.

Like the heroine of Theodore Dreiser's novel *Sister Carrie* (1900), who left her rural home to work in Chicago, many of the new urbanites came from farms and small towns. But the big source of urban growth continued to be immigration. New York City's immigration center, Ellis Island, hummed busily at the start of the twentieth century, as immigration soared to all-time highs. More than 17 million newcomers arrived from 1900 to 1917, and most of them became city dwellers.

As in the 1890s, the influx was mainly from southern and eastern Europe, but more than 200,000 Japan-

1890–1920

change in urban areas

immigrants (work force)

middle class

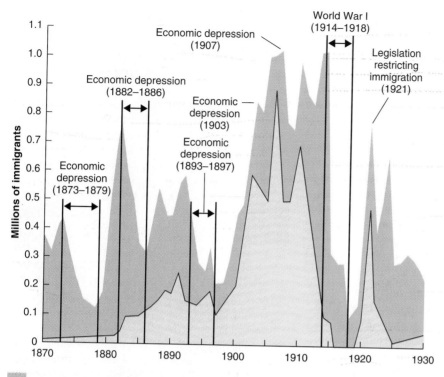

Immigration to the United States, 1870–1930

With the end of the depression of the 1890s, immigrants from southern and eastern Europe poured into America's cities, spurring an immigration-restriction movement, urban moral-control campaigns, and efforts to improve the physical and social conditions of immigrant life.

SOURCES: *Statistical History of the United States from Colonial Times to the Present* (Stamford, Conn.: Fairfield Publishers, 1965); and report presented by Senator William P. Dillingham, Senate document 742, 61st Congress, 3rd session, December 5, 1910: Abstracts of Reports to the Immigration Commission.

Total number of immigrants

Southern and eastern European immigrants

ese and 40,000 Chinese also arrived between 1900 and 1920, as well as thousands of Mexicans who migrated northward to work on the railroad. As before, most immigrants came out of economic necessity. But other factors influenced their decision as well. Whereas many Mexicans fled revolutionary upheavals in their country, religious persecution figured importantly in the emigration of eastern European Jews. The Jews of the Russian Empire were confined to a region of Poland and western Russia known as the Pale, where even in the best of times they suffered discrimination. Periodically, anti-Semitic campaigns called pogroms swept over Russia, leading to the massacre of many Jews and forcing others to flee for their lives. Thousands of these eastern European Jewish immigrants settled on New York's Lower East Side, which by 1915 had a Jewish population of 1.4 million.

The immigrants of the early twentieth century, like their predecessors, found city life harsh and unforgiving as they crowded into slum tenements, row

Japanese Immigrant Railroad Workers
America's phenomenal post–Civil War industrial growth would have been impossible without the millions of immigrants who labored long hours for low wages.

houses, and rickety three-story structures called triple deckers. The ability of authorities to provide such basic necessities as safe water, sewage facilities, garbage collection, and fire protection—not to mention decent schools and parks—chronically lagged behind the pace of urban growth. In many cities municipal corruption compounded the problem. Health conditions remained shockingly bad, with death rates in the most crowded immigrant wards twice the national average.

For years, Social Gospel ministers, settlement-house leaders, and reform-minded journalists like Jacob Riis had been reminding middle-class America of the conditions festering in the immigrant slums. In the early twentieth century, the message began to sink in and to affect the political process. A growing awareness of the urban problem helped lay the groundwork for the progressive reform movement.

While the immigrants attracted much attention, a subtler change was transforming the cities as well: the vast expansion of a native-born middle class. From 1900 to 1920, the white-collar work force jumped from 5.1 million to 10.5 million—more than double the growth rate for the work force as a whole. As industry grew, the number of people in advertising doubled; the ranks of civil engineers more than tripled; and the number of secretaries increased by nearly 600 percent, from 134,000 to 786,000.

Included in this new white-collar class were such diverse groups as the engineers, technicians, and bureaucrats of big corporations; the owners and managers of medium-size local businesses; and professionals such as lawyers, physicians, and teachers. As these groups grew, so, too, did their sense of professional identity. Long-established professional societies such as the American Bar Association and the National Education Association grew rapidly. Scores of new professional groups arose, from the American Association of Advertising Agencies (1917) and the National Association of Accountants (1919) to the U.S. Chamber of Commerce (1912), the American Association of University Professors (1915), and the Farm Bureau Federation (1919). This truly was an age of organization.

The rise of this newly self-conscious middle class had wide-ranging effects. Ambitious, well educated, and valuing self-discipline and social stability, the members of this class were aware of their numbers and eager to make their influence felt. They had a keen and often uneasy sense of their rank in the urban social order: beneath the aristocratic old families and new corporate elite, above the immigrant masses in the

Women Enter the Labor Force
A fare collector on an electric streetcar in Milwaukee, 1917.

sprawling slums. For many middle-class Americans, membership in a national professional organization provided a sense of identity that might earlier have come from neighborhood, political-party affiliation, or local community standing.

For the women of this new urban middle class, the city offered both opportunities and frustrations. Whereas immigrant girls took jobs as servants or factory operatives, middle-class women became schoolteachers, secretaries, typists, librarians, clerks, and telephone operators. The number of women in such white-collar jobs surged from 949,000 in 1900 to 3.4 million in 1920. Higher education offered another outlet for women. The number of women earning college degrees, although still a small proportion of the total female population, more than tripled in this twenty-year period. Of the 5 percent of college-age Americans attending college in 1910, 40 percent were women.

But for married women of the middle class, hedged in not only by the demands of home and children but by an ideology of domesticity, city life could mean isolation and frustration. The divorce rate crept up, from one in twelve marriages in 1900 to one in nine by 1916. As we shall see, many middle-class women joined the new female white-collar workers and college graduates in leading a resurgent women's movement.

African-Americans in a Racist Age

Of the nation's 10 million blacks in 1900, more than two-thirds lived in the rural South as sharecroppers and tenant farmers. For them, infestations of the cotton boll weevil, which spread to the United States from Mexico in the 1890s, and devastating floods that periodically poured over eroded farmlands worsened an already difficult situation. Seeking economic betterment, many southern blacks left the land. By 1910 over 20 percent of the southern black population was urban-dwelling. Whereas black men in the cities took jobs in factories, mines, docks, and railroads or became carpenters, plasterers, or bricklayers, many black women became domestic servants, seamstresses, or workers in laundries and tobacco factories. By 1910, 54 percent of America's black women held jobs.

Across the South, legally enforced racism peaked in the early twentieth century. Local "Jim Crow" laws strictly segregated streetcars, trains, schools, parks, public buildings, and even cemeteries. The facilities provided for blacks, including the schools, were invari-ably far inferior. Legally imposed residential segregation also existed in a number of southern cities until the Supreme Court outlawed it in 1917. Most labor unions excluded black industrial workers, and skilled black artisans earned about one-third less than whites. In some courts, black and white witnesses took the oath on separate Bibles! Trapped in a cycle of poverty, poor education, and discrimination, and prevented from voting through a variety of stratagems, southern blacks faced formidable obstacles.

Meanwhile, the trek northward continued. Fleeing poverty and racism, and drawn by job opportunities, two hundred thousand blacks migrated to the North between 1890 and 1910. Wartime conditions drew still more in 1917–1918 (see Chapter 23), and by 1920, 1.4 million African-Americans lived in the North. For the growing ranks of northern blacks, conditions were only slightly better. In northern cities, as in the South, open racism intensified after 1890, as depression and massive immigration heightened social tensions. (Ironically, the immigrants themselves, competing with blacks for jobs and housing, sometimes exhibited the most intense racial prejudice.) Segregation, though not imposed by law, was a fact of life, supported by informal social pressure and sometimes violence. Blacks lived in run-down "colored districts," attended dilapidated schools, and worked at the lowest-paying jobs. Although northern blacks could vote, their ballots—usually cast for the Republican party, the party of Lincoln—brought little political influence. Republican leaders tolerated only those black politicians who confined themselves to distributing low-level patronage jobs and kept silent on more fundamental issues. Even the newest of the mass media, the movies, reinforced racism. D. W. Griffith's 1915 classic *The Birth of a Nation* disparaged blacks and glorified the Ku Klux Klan.

Founding of the Ku Klux Klan as Portrayed in D. W. Griffith's *The Birth of a Nation* (1915) *Brilliant and innovative technically, the movie also reinforced racist attitudes.*

Smoldering racism occasionally exploded in violence. Antiblack rioters in Atlanta in 1906 murdered four blacks and burned many black homes. A white police officer severely beat the president of a black theological seminary. Lynching had peaked in the 1880s and 1890s, but from 1900 to 1920, an average of about seventy-five still occurred yearly. The victims were usually black men accused of murder, rape, or some other crime. In certain cases, trumped-up charges justified the murder of blacks whose assertive behavior or economic aspirations whites found intolerable. Some lynchings involved incredible sadism, with large crowds in attendance, and the victim's body mutilated. Authorities did little to stop the practice. At a 1916 lynching in Texas, the mayor warned the mob not to damage the hanging tree, since it was on city property. Nor were all lynchings in the South. In Springfield, Ohio, in 1904, the body of a lynch victim was left hanging all day.

For all their adversity, or in part because of it, blacks developed self-reliance, group cohesion, and a vigorous culture. Black religious life, centered in the African Methodist Episcopal church, was a bulwark of support for many. African-American women in northern cities, drawing on strategies dating back to the slavery era, relied on networks of relatives and neighbors to provide child care when both parents worked. A handful of black colleges and universities such as Fisk in Nashville and Howard in Washington, D.C., carried on against heavy odds.

The urban black community included several black-owned insurance companies and banks and boasted a small elite of entrepreneurs, teachers, ministers, and lawyers. A black achiever in a different field, Jack Johnson of Galveston, Texas, won the world's heavyweight boxing championship in 1908. Although major-league baseball excluded blacks, a thriving "Negro League" attracted a big following in black America.

Meanwhile, new African-American musical idioms emerged. Scott Joplin turned the music of black bars and "honky-tonks" into ragtime, a catchy rhythmic style that became highly popular. The blues, rooted in the chants of southern sharecroppers, gained recognition with the songs of W. C. Handy, including the classic "St. Louis Blues" (1914). Among urban blacks, jazz was gaining popularity (see "A Place in Time," Chapter 20). Originating in New Orleans with the band of Buddy Bolden in the 1890s, jazz moved northward to Chicago and other cities around the First World War, eventually to win recognition as America's greatest musical achievement.

Corporate Boardrooms, Factory Floors

The late-nineteenth-century corporate consolidation that produced such behemoths as Carnegie Steel and the Standard Oil Trust accelerated in the early twentieth century. Indeed, this process proceeded so rapidly that for a time around 1900, more than 260 companies annually were swallowed up in mergers. This era also gave rise to holding companies—giant conglomerates that owned a number of corporations engaged in the same kind of business. The most famous holding company arose in 1901 when, as we saw in Chapter 18, financiers led by J. P. Morgan bought Andrew Carnegie's steel business and combined it with others to form the United States Steel Company. This corporate titan, capitalized at $1.4 billion, controlled 80 percent of all U.S. steel production. Repeating the same pattern, Morgan in 1902 consolidated six competing companies into the International Harvester Company to gain control of 85 percent of the farm-implement business. In the automotive field, William C. Durant in 1908 founded the General Motors Company, which, with financial backing from the Du Pont Corporation, bought up various independent automobile manufacturers, from the inexpensive Chevrolet to the luxury Cadillac.

Many workers benefited from the prevailing good times. Industrial workers' average annual real wages (defined, that is, in terms of actual purchasing power, after allowing for inflation) rose from $532 in the late nineteenth century to $687 by 1915. In railroading and other unionized industries, wages climbed still higher. But even with the dollar's buying power many times greater than today (a loaf of bread cost seven cents in 1915), such wages could barely support a family and left little cushion for emergencies.

To survive, entire immigrant families went to work. Two-thirds of immigrant girls entered the labor force in the early 1900s, working as factory help or domestics or in small establishments like laundries and bakeries. Child-labor statistics, although unreliable, suggest that in 1910 the nonfarm labor force included at least 1.6 million children aged ten to fifteen—15 percent of that age group—working in factories, mills, tenement sweatshops, and street trades such as shoe shining, flower selling, and newspaper vending. The

A Young Girl Sells Newspapers Near an Elevated Train Station in New York City, 1896.

total may have been higher, since many of the "women workers" listed in the census were in fact young girls. One investigator found a girl of five working at night in a South Carolina textile mill.

For all laborers, the hours were long and the hazards great. Despite the 8-hour movement of the 1880s, the average worker in 1900 still toiled 9½ hours a day, and much longer in certain industries. Some southern textile mills required workdays of 12 and even 13 hours. The Triangle fire was a particularly gruesome reminder of the unsafe conditions in many industries. Few employers accepted responsibility for work-related accidents and illnesses. Vacations and retirement benefits were practically unheard of. With rare exceptions, capitalists extracted the maximum of labor from their work force and gave a bare minimum in return.

For immigrants and other new industrial workers accustomed to a casual, task-oriented pattern of rural labor, the demands of the time clock and the machine forced major and often bitterly resented adjustments. A new specialist, the efficiency expert, used time-and-motion studies to speed up the production process. The efficiency expert dreamed of making human workers as predictable as machines. In *Principles of Scientific Management* (1911), Frederick W. Taylor explained his ideas for increasing efficiency by standardizing job routines and rewarding the fastest workers. In business circles and the larger culture, *efficiency* and *Taylorism* became popular catchwords.

Children in the Labor Force, 1880–1930

	Children Gainfully Employed, Nonagricultural Work		
Year	Total number of children aged 10–15 (in milions)	Total number of children employed (in millions)	Percentage of children employed
1880	6.6	1.1	16.8
1890	8.3	1.5	18.1
1900	9.6	1.7	18.2
1910	10.8	1.6	15.0
1920	12.5	1.4	11.3
1930	14.3	0.7	4.7

SOURCE: *The Statistical History of the United States from Colonial Times to the Present* (Stamford, Conn.: Fairfield Publishers, 1965).

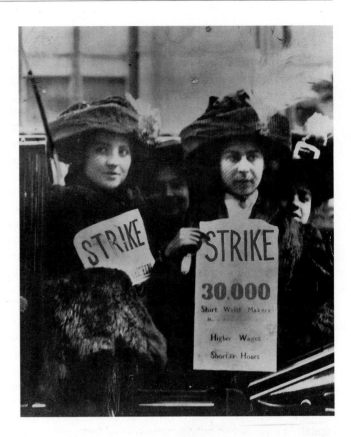

Rumblings of Labor Militance
*(Above) Emblem of the radical IWW;
(right) striking garment workers, New York City,
1909. Declared Clara Lemlich at a strike rally, "I
am a working girl . . . on strike against intolerable
conditions. I am tired of listening to speakers who
talk in general terms."*

Workers Organize; Socialism Advances

Confronting such conditions, workers continued to organize. The American Federation of Labor (AFL) grew from fewer than half a million members in 1897 to some 4 million by 1920. But this number still represented only about 20 percent of the nonfarm labor force. With thousands of immigrants hungry for jobs, union activities could be risky. The boss could always fire an "agitator" and hire a docile newcomer instead. Judicial hostility also plagued the labor movement. In one of many anti-union court decisions, a unanimous Supreme Court in the 1908 *Danbury Hatters* case curtailed unions' right to set up boycotts in support of strikes. A union boycott was a "conspiracy in restraint of trade," said the Court, and thus a violation of the Sherman Anti-Trust Act.

As in the past, the AFL's strength lay in the skilled trades and not in the factories and mills where most immigrants and women worked. A few unions did try to reach the laborers at the lower end of the scale. The International Ladies' Garment Workers' Union (ILGWU), organized in 1900 by immigrants working in New York City's needle trades, conducted a suc-

cessful strike in 1909 and another after the 1911 Triangle fire.

For the women who walked the picket lines, these strikes were at once exhilarating and frightening. Some were beaten by police; others lost their jobs. The 1909 strike began when young Clara Lemlich, herself a victim of police brutality, jumped to her feet as the speechmaking droned on at a protest rally and passionately called for a strike. Twenty thousand women garment workers stayed off the job the next day.

Another union that targeted the most exploited workers was the Industrial Workers of the World (IWW), nicknamed the Wobblies, founded in Chicago in 1905. The IWW's colorful leader was William D. "Big Bill" Haywood, a giant of a man and a compelling orator who sometimes wore a black eyepatch to cover an old injury. After leading a knockabout life in Utah and Nevada, Haywood in 1893 joined the newly founded Western Federation of Miners. In 1895 he and two other union leaders were acquitted on charges of complicity in the murder of the governor of Idaho.

Never large, and torn by dissent, the Wobblies' membership probably peaked at around thirty thousand, comprising mostly western miners, lumbermen, fruit pickers, and itinerant laborers. But it captured the imagination of the cultural rebels of New York City's Greenwich Village, where Haywood often visited. Its greatest success came in 1912, when it won a bitter textile strike in Lawrence, Massachusetts. This victory owed much to two women. Elizabeth Gurley Flynn, a fiery Irish-American orator who had joined the IWW in 1906, and Margaret Sanger, a leader of the birth-control movement, who publicized the cause by sending strikers' children to sympathizers in New York City for temporary foster care.

In contrast to the conservative AFL, the IWW preached revolution. In 1908 it proclaimed, "[The] struggle must go on until the workers of the world . . . take possession of . . . the machinery of production, and abolish the wage system." Despite such fire-breathing rhetoric, however, the IWW's reputation for violence was much exaggerated. Nevertheless, it faced unremitting harassment through arrests and prosecution by government officials, and by 1920 its strength was broken.

Other workers, as well as some middle-class Americans dismayed by capitalism's human toll, turned to socialism. All socialists advocated an end to capitalism and backed public ownership of factories, utilities, railroads, and communications systems, but they differed sharply on how to achieve these goals. Whereas the revolutionary ideology of German social theorist Karl Marx won a few converts, the vision of democratic socialism achieved at the ballot box attracted more adherents. In 1900 democratic socialists formed the Socialist Party of America (SPA). They included Morris Hillquit, a Russian-Jewish immigrant and New York City labor organizer; Victor Berger, the leader of the German socialists of Milwaukee; and Eugene V. Debs, the Indiana labor leader who had converted to socialism during his imprisonment following the 1894 Pullman strike. The SPA's most popular spokesperson, Debs was its presidential candidate five times between 1900 and 1920.

The high tide of socialist strength came around 1912, when SPA membership stood at 118,000. Debs won over 900,000 votes for president that year (about 6 percent of the total), and the Socialists elected a congressman (Berger) and hundreds of municipal officials. The Intercollegiate Socialist Society, headed by eloquent lecturer Rose Pastor Stokes, a Russian-Jewish immigrant who had married a wealthy New Yorker with radical sympathies, carried the message to college and university campuses. The party also boasted

thirteen daily newspapers and some three hundred weeklies, many published in foreign languages for immigrant members.

The upsurge in Socialist votes represented only one sign of rising discontent with politics as usual. As the ill effects of rampant industrial growth became ever more palpable, the demand for government action first voiced by the Populists in the 1890s grew more insistent.

THE PROGRESSIVE MOVEMENT TAKES SHAPE

At the start of the century, intellectuals increasingly challenged the ideological foundations of a business-dominated social order, and writers and journalists publicized the human toll of industrialization. Soon reform thundered over the nation as activists sought to make government more democratic, eradicate unhealthful and dangerous conditions in cities and factories, and curb corporate power. Awed by the diversity of these efforts and the political energies they unleashed, Americans grouped them under a single label: the progressive movement.

Progressivism: An Overview

What was progressivism? On a few points, all students of the movement agree. First, it was a political response to industrialization and its social by-products: immigration, urban growth, the concentration of corporate power, and the widening of class divisions. Second, it was in most cases distinct from populism, the reform movement that preceded it. Whereas populism attracted aggrieved farmers, progressivism's strength lay in the cities. Progressivism enlisted far more journalists, academics, and social theorists than did populism. Finally, the progressives were *reformers*, not radicals or revolutionaries. They wanted to remedy the social evils spawned by capitalism, not destroy the system itself.

But which aspects of the new urban-industrial capitalist order most needed attention, and what remedies were required? These basic questions stirred deep disagreements. Indeed, progressivism never constituted a cohesive movement with a unified program but rather a diverse array of reform activities that

A Poor Neighborhood in Philadelphia, ca. 1915
Scenes like this in the immigrant wards of America's great cities stirred middle-class reformers to action at the turn of the century.

sometimes overlapped and sometimes diverged. Many reformers insisted that restoring democracy required stricter regulation of business, from local transit companies to the almighty trusts. Other reformers, emphasizing the humanitarian theme, called for laws to protect workers and the urban poor. Other progressives concentrated on schemes for reforming the structure of government, especially at the municipal level. Finally, some reformers, viewing immigration, urban immorality, and incipient social disorder as the central problems, fought for immigration restriction, the abolition of prostitution and saloons, and other social control strategies. All this contributed to the mosaic of progressive reform.

And who were the progressives? Like the movement itself, they comprised a diverse lot, aligned in shifting coalitions that might unite on one issue, then divide on another. The native-born Protestant middle class, including the new white-collar professionals, was certainly central, but on issues affecting the welfare of factory workers and slum dwellers, the urban-immigrant political machines—and workers themselves—provided critical support. Even corporate leaders at times helped to shape business-regulation measures, especially when the pressure for such regulation became irresistible.

The impetus for reform came at first not from the political parties but from private groups with names like the Playground Association of America and the American League for Civic Improvement. In this era of organizations, all the major progressive reforms, from woman suffrage and the abolition of child labor to antiprostitution and prohibition, drew strength from organized interest groups.

Closely related to this organizational impulse was the progressives' emphasis on a "scientific" approach to social problems. Scientific and technological expertise underlay the new industrial order, and progressives tended to believe that such expertise would also solve the social problems spawned by industrialism. Progressives marshaled social research, expert opinion, and statistical data to support their various causes.

Some historians, stressing progressivism's technological and managerial aspects, portray it as an example of an organizational stage that all modernizing societies pass through. This is a useful way to think of the movement, provided one realizes that "progressivism" was not some automatic process unfolding independently of human will. Eloquent leaders, gifted journalists, earnest ministers, and energetic organizers all played a role. Human emotion—whether indignation over child labor, visions of a happier future, or political

Progressive Era Social Thinkers
(Left to right) Oliver Wendell Holmes, Jr., Jane Addams, John Dewey, Thorstein Veblen. Wrote one reform-minded intellectual, "We shall demand perfection and never expect to get it."

ambition—propelled the movement forward. Progressivism, in short, is not an impersonal historical abstraction. It is a useful general term for the activities and concerns of many thousands of individual Americans in the early twentieth century.

Intellectuals Lay the Groundwork

Building on the writings of such figures as Lester Ward, Edward Bellamy, and the Social Gospel leaders, a group of turn-of-the-century thinkers helped reorient American social thought. In the process, they laid the ideological foundation for progressivism.

William Graham Sumner and other Gilded Age intellectuals had argued that Charles Darwin's theory of evolutionary progress through natural selection supported an ideology of unrestrained economic competition. The intellectual assault on this version of Social Darwinism launched by Lester Ward intensified in the opening years of the new century. Scholars in many disciplines produced work skeptical of the established order and the old intellectual consensus and implicitly supporting far-reaching changes.

One such reshaper of economic thought was the eccentric but brilliant Thorstein Veblen. A Norwegian-American from rural Minnesota, Veblen earned a Ph.D. from Yale in 1884 but had trouble holding a job, partly because of sexual affairs that offended conventional mores. Nevertheless, in *The Theory of the Leisure Class* (1899), Veblen brilliantly satirized the values and

life-styles of the Gilded Age business elite. Later he would argue that engineers, shaped by the discipline of the machine, were better fitted to lead society than the business class. Veblen epitomized the admiration for efficiency, science, and technical expertise that lay at the heart of the progressive impulse.

Historians, too, contributed to the new currents of thought. In "The Significance of the Frontier in American History" (see Chapter 17), Frederick Jackson Turner argued that the central dynamic of American history was not the actions of Washington policy-makers but the social and political experience of generations of western pioneers. Other historians generalized Turner's point. In *The New History* (1912), James Harvey Robinson argued that historians should probe beneath political and military events to explore the evolution of societies as a whole.

In *An Economic Interpretation of the Constitution* (1913), Charles A. Beard gave ammunition to progressive reformers seeking to curb big business by arguing that the Constitution makers of 1787 had served the interests of the moneyed class of their day. Mary Ritter Beard (Charles Beard's wife and collaborator), in such books as *Woman's Work in Municipalities* (1915) and *A Short History of the American Labor Movement* (1920), spotlighted groups that traditional histories ignored.

Harvard philosopher William James, meanwhile, in his influential 1907 essay *Pragmatism*, argued that truth emerges not from universal laws or abstract theorizing but from experience, as we test our ideas in practice. Truth is what *works*. James's emphasis on the fluidity of knowledge and the importance of practical action contributed to the progressive mood of reformism and skepticism toward established orthodoxies.

James enormously admired Jane Addams, whose settlement house serving Chicago's immigrants exemplified his pragmatic philosophy. While others theorize about reality, he wrote her, "you *inhabit* reality." In *Democracy and Social Ethics* (1902), Addams criticized individualism and called for a new social ideology rooted in awareness of modern society's complex interdependence.

No thinker better captured progressives' faith in the power of ideas to transform society than Herbert Croly. The son of Manhattan journalist David Croly and the woman's club founder Jane Cunningham, Croly grew up in a cosmopolitan world where social issues were hotly debated. In his masterpiece, *The Promise of American Life* (1909), Croly called for an activist federal government of the kind Alexander Hamilton had advocated in the 1790s, but one that would serve *all* citizens, not merely the capitalist class. To build public support for such a transformed conception of government, Croly argued, socially engaged intellectuals must play a key role. In 1914 he founded the *New Republic* magazine as a forum for progressive ideas.

New Ideas About Education and the Law

With public-school enrollment leaping from about 7 million children in 1870 to more than 23 million in 1920, progressive intellectuals realized that here was a potent engine of social change. John Dewey, a mild-mannered philosopher who taught at the University of Chicago and after 1904 at Columbia University, led the campaign to transform educational ideas. Dewey's boyhood in a small Vermont town shaped his social values. A just and harmonious society, he insisted, could be built through the intelligent application of the scientific method to social problems. Viewing intelligence as above all an instrument of social action, he called his philosophy Instrumentalism.

The public schools, Dewey maintained, could be incubators of reform if they embraced the new ethic of social interdependence. Banishing bolted-down chairs and desks from the model school that he started at the University of Chicago in 1896, he encouraged children to interact with each other as well as with the teacher.

In *Democracy and Education* (1916), Dewey argued that schools must not only *teach* democracy and cooperation but *embody* those values through their methods and curriculum. The ideal school, he said, would be an "embryonic community" where children worked together in a harmonious process of intellectual inquiry and social growth. A democratic socialist deeply skeptical of capitalism, Dewey saw educational reform as one step in a broad social and economic transformation.

The nation's colleges and universities also caught the new spirit of civic idealism. No longer a haven of "useless and harmless recluses," proclaimed the University of Michigan's president in 1899, the university must dedicate itself to the public good. Princeton's president Woodrow Wilson summed up the new mood in the title of his 1902 inaugural address: "Princeton for the Nation's Service."

Even the natural sciences felt the lure of social activism. At the Massachusetts Institute of Technology, for example, Ellen Richards pioneered in applying chemistry to the issues of nutrition, food adulteration, and public hygiene. Statisticians used their skills to study labor conditions, epidemic diseases, and urban housing density.

Fresh ideas suffused the legal profession as well. For decades, conservative judges, citing ancient precedents, had routinely upheld corporate interests and struck down reform legislation. A few jurists, however, had argued for a more flexible view. The most influential champion of the new legal philosophy was the patrician Boston law professor Oliver Wendell Holmes, Jr. In *The Common Law* (1881), Holmes had insisted that law must evolve as society changes. In an aphorism much quoted by progressives, he had declared, "The life of the law has not been logic; it has been experience." Appointed to the Supreme Court in 1902, as the progressive movement began, Holmes issued a series of eloquent dissents from the opinions of the conservative Court majority.

In many ways, then, intellectuals and academics chipped away at laissez-faire ideology and laid the foundation for a new social ethic.

Novelists and Journalists Spread the Word

Novelists and journalists helped transform progressivism into a national movement by conveying to middle-class readers the seamy details of corporate wrongdoing, municipal corruption, and the harsh reality of slum and factory life. Advances in high-speed printing and photographic reproduction assured their message a mass audience and sharpened its emotional impact.

A pathbreaking early work came in the depression year 1894, when Chicago journalist and reformer Henry Demarest Lloyd produced *Wealth Against Commonwealth,* a biting exposé of the Standard Oil Company. In the wake of Lloyd's book, early-twentieth-century novelists offered compelling indictments of corporate greed and heedless urban growth. In *The Octopus* (1901), Frank Norris portrayed the struggle between railroad owners and the wheat growers of California's San Joaquin Valley. In *Susan Lenox: Her Fall and Rise* (1917), David Graham Phillips explored the links between slum life, political corruption, and prostitution. Theodore Dreiser's *The Financier* (1912) offered a memorable portrait of a hard-driving business tycoon utterly devoid of a social conscience.

Most influential of all in forging the progressive spirit were dozens of articles exposing urban political corruption and corporate wrongdoing published in mass-circulation magazines such as *McClure's* and *Collier's.* President Theodore Roosevelt, who considered some of these articles too one-sided, disparagingly nicknamed the authors "muckrakers," but the name stuck as a badge of honor. New York journalist Lincoln Steffens began the muckraking vogue in October 1902 with a *McClure's* article on municipal dishonesty in St. Louis, and soon such exposés were appearing everywhere.

The muckrakers' stark journalistic prose, emphasizing facts rather than abstractions, could be very powerful. In a 1903 series on working women, for example, Maria Van Vorst grippingly described a Massachusetts shoe factory where women's fingernails literally rotted off as they continually immersed their hands in caustic dyes.

The muckrakers touched a nerve. *McClure's* circulation soared to 750,000 and *Collier's* to more than 1 million during their heyday in 1901–1903. Many magazine exposés later appeared in book form, including Lincoln Steffens's *The Shame of the Cities* (1904); the damning *History of the Standard Oil Company* (1904) by another *McClure's* reporter, Ida Tarbell; and David Graham Phillips's *Treason of the Senate* (1906).

Artists and photographers supplied a visual counterpoint to the prose of journalists and novelists. Painters George Luks, John Sloan, and others, a group later dubbed the "Ashcan School," painted realistic canvases of New York's teeming immigrant life. Lewis

Hine continued the tradition of Jacob Riis by photographing factory laborers, especially children with their stunted bodies, pale skin, and sad expressions.

Reforming the Political Process

If one had to pinpoint progressivism's beginning, it would be in the 1890s, in the well-to-do neighborhoods of America's cities. To the native-born urban elites and middle classes, the immigrant-based "boss system" of city government represented the essence of evil, and in the 1890s a series of middle-class political reform crusades burst on the urban scene. New York City went through a succession of anti-Tammany reform spasms in which Protestant clergy helped to mobilize the forces of righteousness against the bosses. In Detroit the reform administration of Mayor Hazen Pingree (1890–1897) brought honesty to city hall, lowered transit fares, and made the tax structure more equitable. Pingree also provided public baths and in other ways improved the quality of life. A shrewd politician as well as a reformer, he once slapped a health quarantine on a brothel where a local business leader was paying a visit, and refused to let the man leave until he promised to back Pingree's reforms.

Stimulated by the writings of Lincoln Steffens and others, the municipal-reform impulse grew stronger after 1900. In 1907, for example, newspaper editor Fremont Older led a crusade against San Francisco's notoriously corrupt boss Abe Reuf. Attorney Hiram Johnson, who took over the prosecution of the Reuf machine when the original prosecutor was gunned down in court, obtained a conviction of the mayor and his cronies. Sternly self-righteous, Johnson perfectly embodied the reform fervor of the day—one observer called him "a volcano in perpetual eruption"—and he rode the fame of the Reuf case to the California governorship in 1910 and the U.S. Senate in 1916.

In Toledo, Ohio, a colorful eccentric named Samuel M. "Golden Rule" Jones led the reform crusade. A self-made businessman converted to the Social Gospel, Jones introduced profit sharing in his factory, and as mayor he established playgrounds, free kindergartens, lodging houses for tramps, and an open-air church for all faiths.

But as the urban political-reform movement matured, it moved beyond good works or simply "throwing the rascals out." It now also involved a systematic attack on the roots of urban misgovernment, including the uncontrolled private monopolies that provided such basic city services as water, gas, electricity, and public transportation. Municipal reformers passed laws regulating the rates these utilities could charge, taxing them more equitably, and curbing their political influence. In some cases, reformers advocated public ownership of these companies. Public ownership of utilities, for example, was part of the reform program of Mayor Tom Johnson of Cleveland, praised by Lincoln Steffens as "the best mayor of the best governed city in the United States."

Reflecting the Progressive Era enthusiasm for expertise and efficiency, some municipal reformers advocated *structural* changes in city government. Specifically, they wanted to substitute professional managers and administrators, chosen in citywide elections, for mayors and aldermen elected on a ward-by-ward basis. Natural disasters sometimes gave a boost to this particular reform. A ruinous hurricane and flood led Galveston, Texas, to adopt a city commission form of government in 1900. Dayton, Ohio, went to a city-manager system in the chaotic aftermath of a ruinous flood in 1913. Supposedly above politics, these experts were expected to run the city like an efficient business.

Who were these municipal reformers? Depending on the issue, virtually all elements of the urban population took part in reform efforts at one time or another. The native-born middle class, led by clergymen, newspaper editors, and other opinion molders, provided the initial impetus and core support for urban political reform. Business interests often pushed for citywide elections and the city-manager system—structural changes that diminished the immigrant wards' political clout and increased that of the corporate elite. On matters of immediate practical concern to ordinary city dwellers, such as improved municipal services, the urban-reform movement won support from the immigrants and even from political bosses who realized that massive urban growth was swamping the old, informal system of providing for their constituents.

The municipal-reform movement soon expanded to encompass electoral reform at the state level. By 1910, for example, all states had replaced the old system of voting, by which the voter brought to the polls a preprinted ballot bearing the name of a specific candidate, with the new system of secret balloting, which made it hard to rig elections. Another Progressive Era electoral reform, the direct primary, originated in Wisconsin in 1903. In a direct primary party members (rather than the leadership) selected the party's nominees for public office.

Some western states inaugurated electoral reforms known as initiative, referendum, and recall. By an initiative, voters can instruct the legislature to consider a specific bill. In a referendum, they can actually enact a law or (in a nonbinding referendum) express their views on a proposed measure. By a recall petition, voters can remove a public official from office if they muster enough signatures. This flurry of electoral reform crested in 1913 with the ratification of the Seventeenth Amendment to the Constitution, providing for the direct election of U.S. senators by the voters at large.

These electoral changes were intended to democratize voting, but party leaders and organized interest groups soon learned to manipulate the new electoral machinery very effectively. Ironically, the new procedures appear to have served mainly to weaken the ties of party loyalty and reduce voter interest. Overall voter-participation rates declined steeply in the early twentieth century, whereas political activity by organized interest groups increased.

Protecting Workers, Beautifying the City

If municipal governance, utility regulation, and electoral reform represented the brain of progressivism, the impulse to improve conditions in factories, mills, and slums represented its heart. By 1907, despite some employers' claims that abolishing child labor would produce "a nation of sissies," some thirty states had done just that. A 1903 Oregon law limited women in industry to a ten-hour workday. Other reformers concentrated on industrial safety, welfare programs, and disability benefits for workers injured on the job. (At the federal level, this impulse would soon produce a series of important laws.)

Such measures won support from political bosses in cities with large immigrant populations, such as New York, Cleveland, and Chicago. State senator Robert F. Wagner, a leader of Tammany Hall, New York City's Democratic machine, headed the New York State Factory Investigating Committee, set up after the 1911 Triangle fire. Thanks to this committee's efforts, New York enacted fifty-six worker-protection laws, including ones tightening factory-safety standards, permitting pregnancy leaves, and requiring chairs with backs for garment workers. By 1914 twenty-five states had passed laws making employers liable for job-related injuries or deaths.

Other urban reformers pursued such practical goals as better garbage collection and street cleaning, milk inspection, public-health programs, and stricter housing codes. In a reform measure that served as a model for many cities and states, the New York legislature in 1901 tightened the regulations governing tenement houses. Building on the earlier efforts of Frederick Law Olmsted and others (see Chapter 19), urban-beautification advocates campaigned for more parks, boulevards, and street lights and called for laws against billboards, smoky factories, and unsightly overhead electrical wires.

An influential voice for urban beautification was Daniel Burnham, chief architect of the 1893 Chicago world's fair. In 1902 Burnham and others organized a successful drive to revive Charles L'Enfant's beautiful original plan for Washington, D.C. Burnham also developed innovative city plans for Cleveland and San Francisco, though the latter effort fell victim to the 1906 San Francisco earthquake and fire. But his most impressive achievement was his master plan of 1909 for Chicago.

Burnham recognized that only bold and comprehensive plans would capture the public imagination. Consequently, he proposed for Chicago a visionary blueprint that would make the city both efficient and aesthetically harmonious. Burnham recommended transforming the lakefront by building a new park, museum, and recreational complex; speeding traffic flow by constructing diagonal avenues across the city's rigid street-grid system; eliminating slums by constructing wide streets and enforcing sanitation regulations; and revitalizing the city's congested major thoroughfare, Michigan Avenue, by raising the grade level to allow cross traffic to pass under it.

In Burnham's dream city, Chicago's focal point would be a great new civic center containing a majestic neoclassical city hall and a vast plaza. Although the grandeur of Burnham's plan made its implementation difficult, many of its features eventually became a reality. Between 1910 and 1920, Chicago spent more than $300 million on urban-development projects. Many urban beautifiers in the Progressive Era shared Burnham's conviction that parks, grand boulevards, imposing squares, and monumental public buildings would surely create an orderly, civic-minded urban populace.

Corporate Regulation

The conviction that big business must be brought to heel, inherited from the populists and reinforced by the muckrakers, suffused the progressive outlook. Few

Americans wanted to destroy the giant corporations, but many became convinced that these enterprises that had benefited so enormously from the government's economic policies should also be subject to government supervision. One state after another enacted legislation regulating railroads, mines and mills, telephone companies, and other businesses. Public-health officials, factory inspectors, and other regulators monitored corporate America as never before.

No state pursued regulation more avidly than Wisconsin under Governor Robert La Follette (1901–1906). La Follette served in Congress in the 1880s as a loyal Republican, but he feuded with the state party leadership and in 1900 won the governorship as an independent. Soon "Fighting Bob" began transforming state government just as Cleveland's Tom Johnson and other reform mayors were transforming municipal government. Challenging the business interests long dominant in Wisconsin politics, the La Follette administration adopted the direct primary system, set up a railroad regulatory commission, increased corporate taxes, and passed a law limiting campaign spending.

In drafting these measures, La Follette consulted regularly with reform-minded professors at the nearby University of Wisconsin. He also set up a legislative reference library so that lawmakers could inform themselves about complicated issues rather than relying on political lobbyists. This novel approach to state government gained national attention as the "Wisconsin Idea."

Regulating national corporations at the municipal and even state level posed obvious problems. Once progressivism reached into national politics, however, the regulatory impulse, rooted in grass-roots activism, moved to the center of the reform agenda.

Progressivism and Social Control: The Movement's Coercive Dimension

Although troubled by the social consequences of urban-industrial growth, progressives believed that they could restore order through research, legislation, and enlightened social tinkering. This outlook underlay progressivism's confident spirit but also gave it a repressive, moralistic edge. While some progressives focused on such problems as child labor, industrial

Instructing Movie Audiences in Proper Behavior
Managers struggled to impose decorum as early movie audiences, drawn mainly from the ranks of urban immigrants, freely commented on the film or otherwise made their opinions known.

safety, and corporate regulation, others addressed issues of personal behavior and morality. The social problems these reformers addressed were real and serious. But their moralistic rhetoric and the remedies they proposed often betray an impulse to force the urban poor to conform to their own middle-class code.

Moral Control in the Cities

Fearful of urban social disorder, some reformers sought to impose morality by law. They campaigned against gambling, amusement parks, dance halls, and the newest moral menace, the movies. The first commercial films were brief comic sequences like *The Kiss* or *The Sneeze*, but with *The Great Train Robbery* (1903), which lasted for eight minutes, the movies began to tell stories. In 1914 came Theda Bara in *A Fool There Was*, with its famous line "Kiss me, my fool!" (Bara, one of the first silent-movie stars, was actually Theodosia Goodman of Cincinnati.)

Quaint as they seem today, these early movies struck many middle-class Americans as dangerously immoral. The fact that they were screened in immigrant neighborhoods in five-cent halls called nickelodeons intensified such feelings. Here immigrant youth could briefly escape parental supervision. As a New York City garment worker who lived with her Ital-

ian-immigrant parents later recalled, "The one place I was allowed to go by myself was the movies. My parents wouldn't let me go anywhere else, even when I was twenty-four."

This freedom from moral oversight was precisely what worried progressives. Warning of "nickel madness," they demanded film censorship. Several states and cities did, in fact, set up censorship boards. Chicago's police chief was empowered to ban movies that he considered immoral.

The moral reformers also targeted prostitution, a major social problem in urbanizing America. Male procurers lured newly arrived young women into the business and then took a share of their income. Women's paltry wages for factory work or domestic service attracted many to this illicit but more lucrative occupation. One prostitute wrote that she was unwilling "to get up at 6:30 to be at work at 8 and work in a close stuffy room . . . until dark for $6 or $7 a week" when an afternoon with a man could bring in far more. Her math, if not her moral judgment, was accurate. Early-twentieth-century prostitutes could earn five times more than the typical woman worker.

Addressing this issue in true progressive fashion, the reformers investigated and quantified what they called "the social evil." The American Social Hygiene Association (1914), financed by John D. Rockefeller, Jr., sponsored medical research on venereal disease, underwrote "vice investigations" in various cities, and drafted model municipal statutes against prostitution.

Soon this legitimate social issue took on heavy symbolic overtones for middle-class reformers as a lurid symptom of urban America's rampant immorality. A "white slave" hysteria gripped the country. Sensationalized books, articles, and films warned that innocent farm girls were being kidnapped and forced into a life of sin in the city. The Mann Act (1910) made it a federal crime to transport a woman across a state line "for immoral purposes." Amid much fanfare, the red-light districts of New Orleans, Chicago, and other cities were shut down or forced to operate more discreetly.

Battling Alcohol and Drugs

With the prohibition crusade, the progressive moral-control effort reached its zenith. Temperance had long been part of the American reform agenda, but in the Progressive Era the reformers' tactics and objectives shifted significantly. Earlier campaigns had focused on persuading individuals to give up drink. But with the founding of the Anti-Saloon League (ASL) in 1895, the emphasis shifted to the *legal* abolition of alcoholic beverages.

The ASL was a typical progressive organization. Full-time professionals staffed the national office, and Protestant ministers served on a network of state committees. The ASL presses in Westerville, Ohio, produced propaganda documenting the role of alcohol and the saloon in health problems, family disorder, political corruption, and workplace inefficiency. The ASL promoted nationwide prohibition as the answer to these problems.

Like prostitution, alcohol abuse was serious. Annual per capita consumption in 1906–1910 was a staggering 2.6 gallons. As the ASL charged, alcoholism contributed to various public health problems as well as to poverty, domestic abuse, and other social pathologies. But like the antiprostitution crusade, the prohibition campaign also represented a battleground in the culture wars between native-born citizens and the new immigrants. The ASL, while it raised legitimate issues, also embodied Protestant America's impulse to control and tame the immigrant city.

Supported by the Woman's Christian Temperance Union and influential church agencies, the ASL's crusade picked up steam. Congress in 1919 ratified the Eighteenth Amendment, outlawing the manufacture, sale, or transport of alcoholic beverages. The most controversial of the Progressive Era social reforms had achieved its goal.

The Progressive Era also marks the moment when Americans first addressed the issue of drug abuse—and for good reason. Opium, derived from the juice of poppies, not only was smoked by Chinese immigrants in "opium dens" dedicated to the purpose but also was widely used in medicines. Physicians and patent-medicine manufacturers freely used the opium derivatives morphine and heroin. (The Bayer drug company first marketed heroin commercially in 1898). Cocaine, extracted from coca leaves, was widely used as well. Coca-Cola contained cocaine until about 1900.

The Progressive Era regulatory impulse quickly zeroed in on these dangerous drugs. Numerous local and state laws addressed the problem. Federal efforts included not only the Pure Food and Drug Act but also the Hague Opium Treaty of 1912, a twelve-nation agreement undertaken at U.S. initiative. The Harrison Narcotics Act of 1914, a follow-up to the Hague Treaty, strictly regulated heroin, morphine, cocaine, and other addictive substancees. In their battle against drugs, as in their environmental concerns, the progressives at the dawn of the twentieth century uncannily antici-

pated some of the central issues that still confront the nation as the century closes.

Immigration Restriction

If the immigrant city posed threats, some reformers concluded, the answer lay in excluding immigrants. As one reformer declared, "All the great problems . . . are tied up with the one great problem of foreign immigration." As early as 1894 prominent Bostonians formed the Immigration Restriction League to promote a literacy test as a means of cutting the influx of immigrants. The American Federation of Labor, fearing immigrant job competition, also endorsed restriction.

This reform also won support from many, though not all, progressives. Characteristically, they documented their case with a flourish of scientific expertise. In 1911 a congressional commission produced a massive study bristling with statistics allegedly proving the new immigrants' innate degeneracy. Sociologist Edward A. Ross, a prominent progressive, in 1914 described the typical recent immigrants as "low-browed, big-faced persons of obviously low mentality."

Led by Senator Henry Cabot Lodge of Massachusetts, Congress enacted literacy-test bills in 1896, 1913, and 1915, only to see them vetoed by a succession of presidents. In 1917, however, such a bill became law over President Woodrow Wilson's veto. This, too, was part of progressivism's ambiguous legacy.

Eugenics: Scientific Bigotry

The starkest example of the perversion of "science" in the Progressive Era was the eugenics movement. Eugenics is the control of reproduction to alter the characteristics of a plant or animal species. Some American eugenicists believed that society itself could be improved through genetic control. In 1904 the Carnegie Foundation funded a genetics research center on Long Island. The director, Charles B. Davenport, was not only a well-known zoologist but also a racist, anti-Semite, and advocate of immigration restriction. Inspired by Davenport and other eugenicists, certain states legalized the forced sterilization of criminals, sex offenders, and persons adjudged mentally deficient. In the 1927 case *Buck* v. *Bell*, the Supreme Court upheld the constitutionality of such laws.

This ugly underside of early-twentieth-century social thought pervaded Madison Grant's *The Passing of the Great Race* (1916). In many respects, Grant embodied the best in progressivism. Of an old New York family, he supported numerous civic causes. Yet in *The Passing* he concocted a rancid brew of pseudoscientific data and spewed out a vicious diatribe against Jews, blacks, and southern and eastern Europeans. Jesus Christ, he insisted, was not really a Jew but an unrecognized "Nordic." Grant called for racial segregation, immigration restriction, and the forced sterilization of "unfit" groups, including "worthless race types." Writing at the height of the Progressive Era, he chillingly previewed ideas that within a few years Adolf Hitler would bring to fruition.

Racism and Progressivism

As Grant's work suggests, racism rose to a high pitch during the Progressive Era. Although individual progressives like settlement-house leader Lillian Wald and muckraker Ray Stannard Baker spoke out against racial injustice, the progressive movement as a whole did little as blacks were lynched, disfranchised, and discriminated against. Like the immigrants, blacks represented for many progressives not potential reform allies but a source of social menace and danger to be studied, controlled, and kept out of public life.

In the South, progressive reformers often led the movement for black disfranchisement and segregation. Southern woman-suffrage leaders pointed out that with most blacks disfranchised in the region, granting women the vote would strengthen white supremacy. Numerous southern politicians—including Governor James K. Vardaman of Mississippi and Senator Ben Tillman of South Carolina—supported a variety of progressive reforms while simultaneously pursuing viciously antiblack policies.

Progressive Era racism pervaded Washington during the presidency of Woodrow Wilson (1913–1921). Born in Virginia and reared in Georgia, Wilson displayed a patronizing attitude toward blacks all his life. He praised the racist movie *The Birth of a Nation* and acquiesced as southerners in his cabinet and in the Congress (some of them powerful committee chairmen) imposed rigid segregation on all levels of the government.

Some progressives, however, spoke up for immigrants and blacks. Settlement-house worker Mary White Ovington, for example, helped found the National Association for the Advancement of Colored People (see below) and wrote *Half a Man* (1911), a study of the effects of racial prejudice on New York City's blacks. Yet progressive social thought included a number of disturbing ingredients—an assurance of moral and intellectual superiority, an exaggerated confidence in the social applications of science, a readiness to use state power to coerce individual behavior—that all too readily could turn repressive and destructive.

BLACKS AND WOMEN ORGANIZE

For blacks and women, especially those of the urban middle class, the early twentieth century was a time of intense activity and intellectual ferment. Both groups had ample reason for dissatisfaction, and both organized to address those grievances.

Controversy Among African-Americans

The nation's foremost black leader from the 1890s until his death in 1915 was Booker T. Washington. Born in slavery in Virginia in 1856, the son of a slave woman and her white master, Washington at the age of sixteen enrolled at a freedmen's school in Hampton, Virginia, founded by a Civil War general, Samuel Chapman Armstrong. In 1881 Washington organized in Tuskegee, Alabama, a state vocational school for blacks that eventually became Tuskegee University.

Washington set forth his racial views in a famous address in Atlanta in 1895. The first task of America's blacks, he insisted, must be to acquire useful vocational skills. Once blacks proved their economic value to society, he predicted, racism would fade away; meanwhile, they must patiently accept their lot. Although Washington secretly contributed to organizations fighting racial discrimination, the public message of his "Atlanta Compromise" speech was one of accommodation to a racist society.

Washington traveled widely, lectured often, and once dined at the White House with Theodore Roosevelt. His autobiography, *Up From Slavery* (1901), recounted his rise from poverty through honesty, hard work, and the help of kindly patrons—themes familiar to a generation reared on Horatio Alger.

Many blacks revered Washington, especially in the South, but northern blacks increasingly challenged his ideas. With racism rising and blacks' status worsening, Washington's accommodationist message and his optimistic predictions seemed unrealistic. One critic, William Monroe Trotter, the editor of a black

A New Black Leadership
Ida Wells-Barnett, crusader against lynching, and W. E. B. Du Bois, outspoken critic of Booker T. Washington and author of the classic The Souls of Black Folk. *The challenge, wrote Du Bois, was to find a way "to be both a Negro and an American."*

newspaper, the *Boston Guardian,* in 1902 called Washington's acceptance of black disfranchisement "a fatal blow . . . to the Negro's political rights and liberty." Another black who rejected Washington's views was antilynching crusader and editor Ida Wells-Barnett. Driven from Memphis in 1892 when a mob destroyed her offices, she settled in Chicago and mounted a national anti-lynching campaign. A formidable woman with powerful flashing eyes, Wells-Barnett sharply criticized Booker T. Washington's virtual silence on the subject.

Washington's most potent challenge came from W. E. B. Du Bois (1868–1963). America's first black Ph.D. (from Harvard in 1895), Du Bois taught from 1896 to 1910 at Atlanta University, a black institution that competed with Tuskegee for contributions from northern philanthropists. A cultivated scholar of refined manners and a distinguished appearance, Du Bois set forth his differences with Washington in *The Souls of Black Folk* (1903). Rejecting Washington's call for patience and the exclusive cultivation of manual skills, Du Bois demanded for blacks the same intellectual opportunities open to whites. Furthermore, he declared, blacks must actively resist all forms of racial dis-

crimination. In his assertiveness and militance, Du Bois set the direction of African-American activism in the new century.

The Founding of the NAACP

For a time in the 1890s, an organization called the Afro-American Council served as a forum for blacks who favored vigorous resistance to racism. But when Booker T. Washington gained control of this organization around 1900, his opponents turned elsewhere. In 1905, under Du Bois's leadership, they held a conference at Niagara Falls, and for the next few years, participants in the "Niagara Movement" met annually.

Meanwhile, a small group of white reformers had also grown dissatisfied with Washington's cautiousness. Prominent among them was newspaper publisher Oswald Garrison Villard, grandson of abolitionist William Lloyd Garrison. In 1909 Villard and his allies, with Du Bois and other blacks from the Niagara Movement, formed the National Association for the Advancement of Colored People (NAACP). Rejecting Washington's approach, the NAACP called for political equality for blacks and an end to racial discrimination.

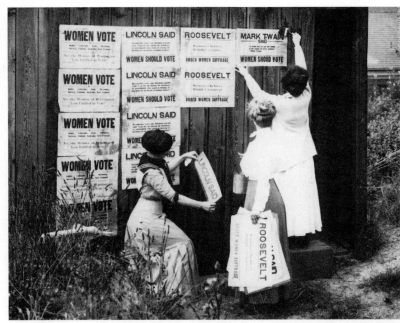

A Revived Women's Movement

A poster prepared by the Massachusetts Woman Suffrage Association;as the drive for woman suffrage gained momentum, these activists in Washington State put up posters for the cause.

Attracting the urban black middle class, the NAACP by 1914 had six thousand members in fifty branches. The cause of racial equality had gained a robust new voice.

Revival of the Woman-Suffrage Movement

As late as 1910, women could vote in only four sparsely populated western states: Wyoming, Utah, Colorado, and Idaho. In six state referenda after 1896, woman suffrage failed. But rushing social and ideological currents infused the movement with new vitality after 1900. The growing ranks of middle-class women found disfranchisement galling, particularly when recently arrived immigrant men, often less well educated than themselves, could vote. A vigorous suffrage movement in Great Britain reverberated in America as well. Finally, the larger climate of the progressive movement, in which women played a leading role, powerfully boosted the cause.

Like progressivism itself, the renewal of the women's movement started at the grass-roots level. In New York, Chicago, Los Angeles, and other cities, local suffragists developed innovative forms of publicity, in-

cluding street meetings and parades. Suffrage campaigns in California (1911) and New York (1915), though unsuccessful, gave evidence of a fresh drive and militancy.

New leaders, drawing on the rhetoric of progressive reform, translated this energy into a revitalized national movement. When the revered Susan B. Anthony retired in 1900 from the presidency of the National American Woman Suffrage Association (NAWSA), she passed the mantle to Carrie Chapman Catt of Iowa. Although family illness forced her to resign in 1904, Catt remained active in NAWSA and in 1915 again became its president. Under her shrewd direction, NAWSA adopted the so-called Winning Plan: grass-roots organization with tight central coordination.

Following NAWSA's plan, women lobbied legislators, distributed literature, conducted referenda, and organized parades and rallies. State after state, most in the Far West and Midwest, fell into the suffrage column. A key victory came in 1917 when New York State voters approved a woman-suffrage referendum.

With some exceptions, NAWSA's membership remained largely white, native-born, and middle class. Few black, immigrant, or working-class women

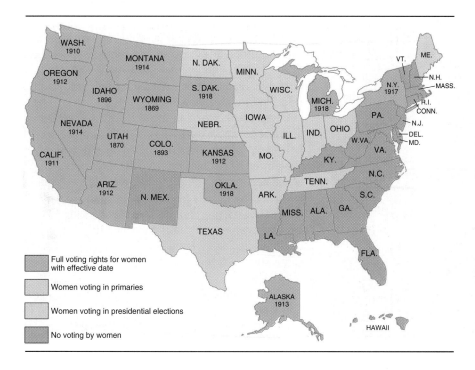

Woman Suffrage Before the Nineteenth Amendment
Beginning with Wyoming in 1869, woman suffrage made steady gains in western states before 1920. Further east, key victories came in New York (1917) and Michigan (1918). But much of the East remained an anti-woman-suffrage bastion throughout the period.

joined, and some upper-class women *opposed* suffrage reform. The leader of the "Antis" was Josephine Dodge, a very wealthy New York City widow who in 1911 formed the National Association Opposed to Woman Suffrage, based in her Fifth Avenue apartment. Women already had behind-the-scenes influence, Dodge argued; to invade the male realm of politics could only tarnish their moral and spiritual role.

Nor did all suffragists accept Catt's strategy. One who did not was Alice Paul, who as a student in Great Britain had observed the militant tactics of the British suffragists. Impatient with NAWSA's state-by-state approach, Paul in 1913 founded the Congressional Union, later renamed the Woman's party, to bring direct pressure on the federal government to enact a woman-suffrage amendment. Insisting that "the party in power"—in this case, the Democrats—must be held accountable for the continued denial of votes to women, Paul and her followers in the war year 1917 picketed the White House round the clock. They posted large signs that read:

> PRESIDENT WILSON IS DECEIVING THE WORLD . . .
> AS THE PROPHET OF DEMOCRACY. . . . HE IS
> RESPONSIBLE FOR THE DISFRANCHISEMENT OF
> MILLIONS OF AMERICANS. WE IN AMERICA KNOW
> THIS. THE WORLD WILL FIND HIM OUT.

Several of the demonstrators were arrested, jailed, and when they went on a hunger strike, force-fed.

Thanks in part to women's active participation in the war effort (see Chapter 23), the tide turned at last. The Nineteenth Amendment, granting women the vote, narrowly passed Congress in 1919, and by August 1920 it was ratified. That November, seventy-two years after the first American women's rights convention, in 1848, women across America went to the polls.

Breaking Out of the "Woman's Sphere"

The suffrage movement did not exhaust the organizational energies of American women. The 1890s had seen the founding of such groups as the General Federation of Women's Clubs, the National Council of Jewish Women, and the National Association of Colored Women; and these organizations grew vigorously in the early twentieth century. Women's club members, settlement-house leaders, and individual female activists joined in a wide range of reform efforts. These included the campaigns to bring playgrounds and day nurseries to the slums, to abolish child labor, to improve conditions for women workers, and to ban unsafe foods and quack remedies. Concern over such issues knew no gender boundaries. As Jane Addams

Birth-Control Pioneer Margaret Sanger
One of eleven children, Sanger saw her exhausted mother die at age forty-nine. Sanger's National Birth Control League was the forerunner of the Planned Parenthood Federation of America.

observed, the same nurturing impulse that led women to care for their own children also drew them into broader political activism in an industrial era when hazards often came from outside the home as well as inside.

Entrenched cultural assumptions about woman's "sphere" crumbled as women became active on many fronts. Penologist Katherine Bement Davis, with a Ph.D. from the University of Chicago, served in these years as the innovative superintendent of a woman's reformatory in Bedford Hills, New York, and then as New York City's commissioner of corrections. Anarchist Emma Goldman crisscrossed the country delivering riveting lectures on politics, feminism, and modern drama while coediting a radical monthly, *Mother Earth*. And in 1914 Margaret Sanger began her crusade · birth control, a term that she coined. A nurse as

well as a radical feminist, Sanger witnessed the tragedy of unwanted pregnancies among slum women. She fled to Europe to escape arrest on obscenity charges directed against her journal *The Woman Rebel* but returned in 1916 to open the nation's first birth-control clinic, in Brooklyn, New York.

Representative of a vanguard group of women in higher education were Marion Talbot, professor of household administration and first dean of women at the University of Chicago; Ellen Richards, who taught home economics and promoted women's education at the Massachusetts Institute of Technology; and M. Carey Thomas, president of Bryn Mawr College. Many of these women educators belonged to the Association of Collegiate Alumnae (1881), which in 1921 became known as the American Association of University Women.

The leading feminist intellectual of these years, Charlotte Perkins Gilman, was divorced and living in California when she wrote *Women and Economics* (1898). This influential work traced the history of sexual discrimination; explored the cultural process of gender stereotyping; and linked the legal, political, and social subordination of women to their economic dependence upon men. Drawing on the ideas of Lester Ward and Edward Bellamy, Gilman argued that confining women to the domestic sphere, though necessary at an earlier evolutionary stage, had become outdated and inefficient. She advocated economic independence for women through equality in the workplace; the consolidation of cooking, cleaning, and other domestic tasks; and state-run day-care centers.

Both Alice Hamilton and Florence Kelley typify women's central role in progressive reform. Hamilton, a professor of bacteriology at Northwestern University, worked closely with Jane Addams at Hull House. In 1910, combining her scientific expertise with her social-welfare impulses, she conducted a pathbreaking study of lead poisoning in industry. Appointed an investigator for the U.S. Bureau of Labor in 1911, she became an expert on—and campaigner against—work-related health hazards.

Florence Kelley, the daughter of a Republican congressman from Pennsylvania, became a resident of Hull House in 1891. Investigating conditions in factories and tenement sweatshops, Kelley in 1893 helped secure passage of an Illinois law prohibiting child labor and limiting working hours for women. In 1899 she became general secretary of the National Consumers' League, which mobilized consumer pressure to lobby for improved factory conditions. Campaigning for a federal child-labor law, Kelley angrily asked, "Why are seals, bears, reindeer, fish, wild game in the national parks, buffalo, [and] migratory birds all found suitable for federal protection, but not children?" Kelley's efforts helped to awaken Americans to the evils of child labor.

◆

NATIONAL PROGRESSIVISM— PHASE I: ROOSEVELT AND TAFT

By around 1905 these varied reform activities were coalescing into a national movement. Symbolically, in 1906 Robert La Follette left the Wisconsin statehouse to go to Washington as a U.S. senator. He arrived just as progressivism found its first national leader, Theodore Roosevelt.

Bombastic, self-righteous, and jingoistic—but also brilliant, politically savvy, and endlessly interesting—Roosevelt, "TR," became president in 1901 and, for the next 7½ years, made the White House a volcano of activism far different from the rather somnolent days of Rutherford B. Hayes or Benjamin Harrison. Skillfully orchestrating public opinion as an instrument of political power, the popular young president pursued his goals: labor mediation, consumer protection, conservation, business virtue, and activism abroad. TR's hand-picked successor, William Howard Taft, lacked the master's political genius, however, and his administration floundered amid sniping among former allies.

Roosevelt's Path to the White House

On September 6, 1901, in Buffalo, an anarchist named Leon Czolgosz shot William McKinley. It seemed at first that the president would survive, and Vice President Theodore Roosevelt proceeded with a planned hiking trip in New York's Adirondack Mountains. But several days later, a guide arrived with an urgent message: McKinley's condition was worsening. All night long Roosevelt traveled by horse and wagon the forty miles over mountain roads to the nearest railroad station. Here, learning of McKinley's death, he boarded a train for Buffalo. On September 14 the forty-two-year-old Roosevelt took the presidential oath of office.

Many politicians shuddered at the thought of the impetuous Roosevelt as president. Republican king-maker Mark Hanna exclaimed, "My God, that damned cowboy in the White House!" Although not a cowboy, Roosevelt did display many traits associated with the West. The son of an aristocratic New York family of Dutch origins, the sickly and nearsighted Theodore had seemed almost a caricature of the pampered rich kid. But at the age of eleven, he began a bodybuilding program that, combined with summers in Wyoming, transformed him into a model of physical fitness.

Teddy Roosevelt Cream Pitcher, ca. 1910 *TR captivated the national imagination like no president since Lincoln. With a gun in one hand and a book in the other, this bit of Americana suggested two of Roosevelt's many interests: hunting and scholarship.*

When his young wife died in 1884, he stoically carried on. "I have never believed it did any good to flinch . . . from any blow," he wrote; "nor does it lighten the blow to cease from working." Two years on a Dakota ranch (1884–1886) further toughened him, eased his grief, and deepened his enthusiasm for what he termed "the strenuous life."

Plunging into politics at a time when most members of his social class considered it unfit for gentlemen, he served as a state assemblyman, New York City's police commissioner in a reform administration, and a U.S. civil-service commissioner. In 1898, fresh from his Cuban exploits (see Chapter 21), he was elected New York's governor. Two years later, the state's Republican boss, eager to be rid of a governor he could not control, arranged for Roosevelt's nomination as vice president. (Angered by this maneuver, Roosevelt wrote, "I would a great deal rather be anything, say a history professor, than Vice-President.")

In contrast to some of his predecessors, who seemed worn down by the presidency, Roosevelt found it energizing. "While President I have been President emphatically . . . ," he once boasted; "I believe in a strong executive." He enjoyed public life and loved the limelight. "When Theodore attends a wedding he wants to be the bride," a relative observed, "and when he attends a funeral he wants to be the corpse." Americans took to their rambunctious young president with his toothy grin, machine-gun speech, and passion for the outdoors. When he refused to shoot a bear cub on a hunting trip, a shrewd toy maker marketed a cuddly new product, the Teddy Bear.

After Teddy Roosevelt, the American presidency was never quite the same. He enlarged the office in ways that permanently affected the balance of power within American government.

Labor Disputes and Corporate Regulation

The new president's political skills were quickly tested. In May 1902 the United Mine Workers Union (UMW) called a strike to gain not only higher wages and shorter hours but also recognition as a union. The mine owners refused even to talk to the UMW leaders. After five months, with winter looming and coal reserves dwindling, TR acted. Summoning the deadlocked parties to the White House and threatening to take over the mines, he won their reluctant acceptance of an arbitration commission to settle the dispute. The commission's findings, issued in 1903, granted the miners a 10 percent wage increase and reduced their working day from ten to nine hours.

TR's approach to labor disputes, illustrated in the coal strike, differed sharply from that of his predecessors, who typically called out the troops to break strikes. Though not consistently prolabor, he defended workers' right to organize. When a prominent mine owner unctuously urged that the miners' welfare be left to "the Christian men to whom God in his infinite wisdom has given control of the property interests of the country," Roosevelt derided such "arrogant stupidity."

With his privileged background, TR neither feared nor much respected the capitalists who had clawed their way to the top in Gilded Age America. The prospect of spending time with "big-money men," he once wrote a friend, "fills me with frank horror." Conservative at heart, he had no desire to abolish big corporations, which he believed essential to national greatness. Nevertheless, he embraced the progressive conviction that corporate behavior must be regulated. A strict moralist, he believed that corporations, like individuals, must be held to a high standard of virtue.

At the same time, Roosevelt the political realist understood that many powerful Washington figures did not share such views—among them Senator Nelson W. Aldrich of Rhode Island, a wily defender of business interests. Roosevelt's presidency thus involved continuing tension among his moralism, his aristocratic conservatism, his cautious embrace of progressive ideas, and his recognition of the realities of power in capitalist America. The first test soon came.

When J. P. Morgan in 1901 formed the United States Steel Company, the nation's first billion-dollar corporation, public uneasiness over business consolidation deepened. As always, TR dashed to the head of the parade. In his 1902 State of the Union message, he gave high priority to breaking up business monopolies, or "trust-busting." Roosevelt's attorney general soon filed suit against the Northern Securities Company, a holding company recently formed by railroad and banking interests to control railroading in the Northwest, for violation of the Sherman Anti-Trust Act. Railroad tycoon E. H. Harriman struck back, ridiculing "political adventurers" who did nothing but "pose and draw a salary." But Roosevelt easily handled Harriman. On a speaking tour that summer, he called for a "square deal" for all Americans and denounced special treatment for powerful capitalists. "We don't wish to destroy corporations," he insisted, "but we do wish to make them subserve the public good." In 1904, on a 5 to 4 vote, the Supreme Court ordered the Northern Securities Company dissolved.

The Roosevelt administration sued forty-three other companies for antitrust violations. In two key cases not finally decided until 1911, the Supreme Court ordered the breakup of the Standard Oil Company, the granddaddy of all the trusts, and the reorganization of the American Tobacco Company to make it less monopolistic.

As the 1904 election neared, Roosevelt made peace with the Republicans' big-business wing, writing cordial letters to J. P. Morgan, E. H. Harriman, and other tycoons. When the convention that unanimously nominated Roosevelt in Chicago adopted a conservative, probusiness platform, $2 million in corporate campaign contributions poured in. Conservative Democrats, meanwhile, eager to purge their party of the free-silver heresies of William Jennings Bryan, nominated a conservative New York judge and party loyalist, Alton B. Parker, and crafted a platform that firmly embraced the gold standard.

Easily defeating the lackluster Parker, Roosevelt turned to one of his major goals: railroad regulation. He now regarded corporate regulation, rather than dramatic bursts of trust-busting, as a more promising long-term role for government, and this shift of outlook

The Election of 1904

Candidates	Parties	Electoral Vote	Popular Vote	Percentage of Popular Vote
THEODORE ROOSEVELT	Republican	336	7,628,461	57.4
Alton B. Parker	Democratic	140	5,084,223	37.6
Eugene V. Debs	Socialist		402,283	3.0
Silas C. Swallow	Prohibition		258,536	1.9

was reflected in the central role that he played in the passage of the Hepburn Act (1906). The Elkins Act (1903) had stiffened the penalties against railroad rebates to favored shippers, and the Hepburn Act further tightened existing railroad regulation. This measure empowered the Interstate Commerce Commission to set maximum railroad rates and to examine railroads' financial records. It also required standardized bookkeeping to make such inspection easier and curtailed the railroads' distribution of free passes.

The Hepburn Act displayed TR's knack for political bargaining, as he skillfully fenced with Senator Aldrich and other conservatives opposed to the measure. In one basic compromise, he agreed to delay tariff reform in return for enactment of the Hepburn bill. Although the measure did not entirely satisfy reformers like La Follette, it did significantly increase the government's ability to regulate the railroads.

Consumer Protection and Racial Issues

No progressive reform aroused a more gut-level popular response than the campaign against unsafe and falsely labeled food, drugs, and medicine. Upton Sinclair's *The Jungle* (1906) graphically described the foul conditions in some meatpacking plants. Wrote Sinclair in one vivid passage: "It was too dark in these [packing-house] storage places to see well, but a man could run his hand over these piles of meat and sweep off handfuls of dried dung of rats. These rats were nuisances, and the packers would put poisoned bread out for them, they would die, and then rats, bread, and meat would go into the hoppers together." (The socialist Sinclair also detailed the exploitation of immigrant workers but this message proved less potent. "I aimed at the nation's heart, but hit it in the stomach," he later lamented.)

Other muckrakers exposed useless and even dangerous patent medicines. As we have seen, many popular nostrums, including children's medicines, contained cocaine, opium, or a large percentage of alcohol. "Colden's Liquid Beef Tonic," for example, "recommended for treatment of the alcohol habit," itself contained 26.5 percent alcohol! In the absence of regulation, the peddlers of these potions freely claimed that they could cure cancer, grow hair, and restore sexual potency.

Ever sensitive to the public mood, Roosevelt supported the Pure Food and Drug Act and the Meat Inspection Act, both passed in 1906. The former outlawed the sale of adulterated foods or drugs and required accurate ingredient labels; the latter imposed strict sanitary requirements for meatpackers and created a program of federal meat inspection still in effect today. A Department of Agriculture chemist, Dr. Harvey W. Wiley, had for years waged war on adulterated foods, and by 1906 the more reputable food-processing, meatpacking, and medicinal companies, eager to regain public confidence, supported regulatory measures as well. Thanks to the muckrakers' revelations, TR's leadership, and pressure from the affected industries themselves, Wiley's lonely crusade at last succeeded.

On racial matters, Roosevelt compiled a marginally better record than that of many other politicians in this dismally racist age. On the positive side, he appointed a black as head of the Charleston customhouse despite white opposition, and he closed a Mississippi post office rather than yield to demands that he dismiss the black postmistress. In a gesture of symbolic import, he met with Booker T. Washington at the White House. The worst blot on his record came in 1906, when he summarily discharged an entire regiment of black army troops charged with rioting in Brownsville, Texas. The "Brownsville Incident" incensed black Americans. (In 1972, when most of the men involved were long dead, Congress removed the dishonorable discharges from their records.)

The Conservation Movement

Of Roosevelt's many domestic concerns, none speaks more directly to the present than his commitment to conservation. By 1900, decades of urban-industrial growth and western expansion had taken a heavy toll on the land. In the West disputes over land use burst into the political arena as mining and timber interests, farmers, ranchers, sheep growers, and preservationists advanced competing claims.

Whereas western business interests and boosters preached exploitation of the region's resources, groups such as the Sierra Club sought to preserve wilderness areas for their beauty and aesthetic appeal. Socially prominent easterners also embraced the wilderness cause. Thanks to their efforts, Congress in 1891 authorized the president to designate public lands as forest reserves. Under this act, presidents Benjamin Harrison and Grover Cleveland set aside some 35 million acres.

In the early twentieth century, a wilderness vogue swept America. Amid congested cities and clanging factories, the wilderness with its unspoiled lakes, virgin forests, and inspiring vistas offered harried Americans the promise of tranquility and spiritual solace. As Sierra Club president John Muir observed, "I never saw a discontented tree." Popular writers like Owen Wister, Gene Stratton Porter, and Edgar Rice Burroughs evoked the tang of the campfire and the lure of the primitive. Summer camps, which began in the 1890s, as well as the Boy Scouts (1910) and Girl Scouts (1912), gave city children a taste of wilderness living.

The wilderness vogue seeped into politics. Resource-management issues frequently pitted state and local authorities against the federal government. Local politicians, echoing their region's business groups, charged that the preservationists' wilderness campaign jeopardized western economic development.

Between the wilderness enthusiasts and the fans of unrestrained development stood a cadre of government professionals who saw the public domain as a resource to be managed scientifically. This characteristically progressive position found its ablest advocate in Gifford Pinchot, the nation's first professional forester. In 1905 President Roosevelt named Pinchot, then chief forester of the U.S. Department of Agriculture, to head the new U.S. Forest Service. In this position he campaigned not for preservation but for conservation—the planned, regulated use of the nation's forest lands for public and commercial purposes.

Wilderness advocates viewed Pinchot's Forest Service warily. They saw it as a safeguard against mindless exploitation but worried that Pinchot's multiuse approach would lead to commercial development in unspoiled wilderness areas. As one Sierra Club member wrote, "It is true that trees are for human use. But there are aesthetic uses as well as commercial uses—uses for the spiritual wealth of us all, as well as for the

Women and Conservation
Women embraced the early wilderness-preservation movement. In this turn-of-the-century photograph, Sierra Club members enjoy a picnic lunch in the great outdoors.

Teddy Roosevelt at Yosemite

TR loved the West, where he had found revitalization as a youth. As president he promoted wilderness preservation and better management of natural resources.

material wealth of some." Professional conservationists, in turn, dismissed the wilderness advocates as sentimental amateurs.

Theodore Roosevelt was by temperament a preservationist. He had passed the happiest hours of his youth on the western plains, and though a big-game hunter, he championed wilderness and wildlife preservation. In 1903 he spent a blissful few days camping in California's Yosemite National Park with John Muir. "When I hear of the destruction of a species," he wrote, "I feel just as if all the works of some great writer had perished."

But Roosevelt the politician understood the conservationists' call for planned development of the nation's natural resources. In this spirit he supported the National Reclamation Act of 1902 that earmarked the proceeds of public-land sales for water management

in the Southwest and set up the Reclamation Service, a federal bureau to plan irrigation projects.

In arid regions, the Reclamation Service faced intense political pressures. In one notorious instance, the mayor of Los Angeles derailed a vast Reclamation Service irrigation project intended for the farmers of California's Owens Valley and diverted the precious water to his city instead.

Despite his love of the wilderness, Roosevelt backed Pinchot's multiuse land-management program. Following Pinchot's advice, Roosevelt set aside 200 million acres of public land (85 million of them in Alaska) as national forests, mineral reserves, and potential water-power sites.

But this approach, too, provoked opposition in the West, and in 1907 Congress rescinded the president's authority to create national forests in six timber-rich western states. Roosevelt signed the bill, but only after designating twenty-one new national forests totaling 16 million acres in the six states!

To reassert the conservationist gospel, Pinchot, with Roosevelt's blessing, organized a White House conservation conference for the nation's governors in 1908. Here experts discussed the utilitarian benefits of resource management. John Muir and others who stressed the spiritual and aesthetic value of the wilderness were not invited. But the struggle between wilderness purists and multiuse advocates went on, surfacing again in the 1912–1913 fight over proposals to dam the Tuolumne River in Yosemite National Park (see "A Place in Time").

Skillfully using magazine articles to rally public support, preservationists won key victories in these years. For example, campaigns by private citizens saved a large grove of California's giant redwoods and a lovely stretch of the Maine coastline from commercial depredation. Women reformers played a key role in many of these efforts.

The national-park system also grew stronger in these years. Beginning with Yellowstone in 1872, thirteen national parks had been created by 1916, but with no overall management. The number of park visitors surged from 69,000 in 1908 to 335,000 in 1915. Addressing the problem, Congress in 1916 created the National Park Service to oversee these preserves, which the writer Wallace Stegner once called the nation's "crown jewels." To protect archaeological sites, especially in the Southwest, Congress in 1906 passed the Antiquities Act. A number of sites preserved by presidential action under this law eventually became national parks.

Hetch Hetchy Valley in 1913

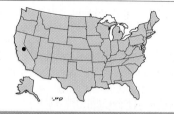

At the turn of the century, one of the loveliest spots in California's Sierras was Hetch Hetchy Valley. The Indian name referred to the Valley's grassy meadows. Here glaciers and the Tuolumne River had carved deep, sharp-edged gorges of spectacular beauty.

But when officials of San Francisco, 150 miles away, visited Hetch Hetchy, they saw not only beauty but a solution to their city's serious water problems. A dam at the valley's mouth would create a vast reservoir that could supply water for San Francisco and pay for itself as a hydroelectric power source.

Because Hetch Hetchy lay within Yosemite National Park, created by Congress in 1890, the secretary of the interior at first rejected San Francisco's application to dam the Tuolumne. But the city applied again in 1908, two years after an earthquake and fire devastated San Francisco, and this time the secretary approved. The application needed congressional approval as well, however. Opponents of the plan geared up confidently for a campaign to defeat it.

The Sierra Club and its president, John Muir, a revered nature writer and wilderness advocate, led the opposition. Muir loved Yosemite, and the plan for a

water-power project in the park dismayed him. Going public, Muir and his associates alerted wilderness groups across the nation and published magazine articles describing the beauty of the valley that would be forever hidden under the waters of the reservoir.

Muir compared the flooding of Hetch Hetchy to the willful destruction of a great cathedral. Amid rampant urban growth, he argued, Americans needed wilderness for their spiritual well-being. He wrote bitterly, "These temple destroyers, devotees of ravaging commercialism, seem to have a perfect contempt for Nature, and instead of lifting their eyes to the God of the Mountains, lift them to the Almighty Dollar."

But the project had attracted powerful backers, including Gifford Pinchot, head of the U.S. Forest Service. Pinchot advocated a multiuse approach to national forests and wilderness areas, and the Hetch Hetchy project fit his vision.

San Francisco authorities pushed hard for the plan. The reservoir, they argued, could support a variety of recreational activities. The San Francisco *Chronicle* called the dam's critics "hoggish and mushy esthetes." San Francisco's chief engineer ridiculed them as "short-haired women and long-haired men."

President Theodore Roosevelt at first endorsed the plan. However, he then vacillated as opposition grew. In the national parks, he said in 1908, "all wild things should be protected and the scenery kept wholly unmarred."

The battle culminated in 1913 with hearings before the Public Lands Committee of the U.S. House of Representatives. Both sides mounted a final effort. Opponents rallied public opinion through more magazine articles; backers lobbied members of Congress. Pinchot, testifying in support of the application, offered his own utilitarian definition of conservation: "The fundamental principle . . . is that of use, to take every part of the land and its resources and put it to that use . . . which . . . will serve the most people." A California congressman pointed out that the "old barren rocks" of Hetch Hetchy Valley had a market value of only about $300,000, whereas the proposed dam would be worth many

John Muir in Hetch Hetchy Valley, 1895, *by Gilbert Dellinger, 1963 This painting, based on a photograph, portrays the influential nature writer and Sierra Club president in the valley he loved and fought unsuccessfully to save.*

Hetch Hetchy: From the Sublime to the Utilitarian

California's lovely Hetch Hetchy Valley was a favorite subject of nineteenth-century artists, as this romantic painting by Albert Bierstadt, dating from the 1870s, reveals. When the Tuolumne River was dammed to create a reservoir for San Francisco, only the mountainous peaks above the waterline stood, silent reminders of the wild grandeur that had been sacrificed.

times that amount. Another legislator posed the issue in dramatic terms: "We all love the sound of whispering winds amid the trees," he said, but "the wail of a hungry baby will make us forget it."

Late in 1913, despite a blizzard of opposition mail, both houses of Congress passed the Hetch Hetchy dam bill by large margins. Within a year John Muir was dead of pneumonia—but really, some said, he had died of a broken heart.

The dam project proceeded slowly, at twice the estimated cost. The first water reached San Francisco in 1934. The vision of Hetch Hetchy reservoir as a vacation paradise remained unfulfilled. Writes environmental historian Stephen Fox: "As the water level rose and fell with the changing seasons the shoreline was marred by slimy mud and decaying vegetation. Nothing could grow at the edge of the artificial lake. Under moonlight, with tree trunks scattered around like so many bodies, it resembled a battlefield one day after the fight: a wasteland bearing stark testimony to man's befuddled ingenuity."

But though the dam's opponents lost this battle, historian Roderick Nash points out that the struggle had a larger meaning: for the first time, over a five-year period, the American public debated the aesthetic implications of a major public-works project. In the nineteenth century, such a debate would have been unthinkable. Hetch Hetchy helped put wilderness preservation on the public agenda.

Hetch Hetchy retains its power to stir emotions. In 1987 Secretary of the Interior Donald Hodel made headlines by proposing that the reservoir be drained and the valley be restored to its natural state. This, Hodel said, would relieve overcrowding in Yosemite Valley, forty miles to the south. Environmentalists expressed interest; San Francisco officials reacted with the same outrage their predecessors had shown seventy-five years before toward opponents of their cherished project. Whether Hodel's ideas will ever be implemented remains to be seen. Meanwhile, Hetch Hetchy Valley lies submerged under 300 feet of water, buried but not forgotten.

The Election of 1908

Candidates	Parties	Electoral Vote	Popular Vote	Percentage of Popular Vote
WILLIAM H. TAFT	Republican	321	7,675,320	51.6
William Jennings Bryan	Democratic	162	6,412,294	43.1
Eugene V. Debs	Socialist		420,793	2.8
Eugene W. Chafin	Prohibition		253,840	1.7

Environmental health hazards, although lower on most progressives' agenda than conservation, roused concern as well. With factories polluting the air and discharging poisons into rivers, some urban reformers campaigned with varied success for restrictive legislation. Roosevelt was sympathetic, especially when personally affected. A power plant spewing black smoke near the White House roused him to threaten legal action.

Despite the differences of approach, environmental issues stood high on the national agenda in the Progressive Era. Roosevelt played a crucial part in this process. Along with millions of acres of national forest, he created fifty-three wildlife reserves, sixteen national monuments, and five new national parks. Just as important, Roosevelt kept environmental concerns in the public mind. Declaring conservation "the most vital internal question" facing America in his first State of the Union message, he gave priority to an issue that reverberates still. "We are not building this country of ours for a day," Roosevelt said; "It is to last through the ages."

Roosevelt's chosen successor, Secretary of War William Howard Taft, for president but chose a conservative vice-presidential nominee and, influenced by the National Association of Manufacturers, drafted an extremely conservative platform. (It called for "revision" of the tariff but neglected to say in which direction.)

On the Democratic side, the defeat of conservative Alton B. Parker in 1904 opened the door for a last hurrah by William Jennings Bryan. Nominating the Nebraskan for a third White House run, the Democrats adopted a platform that called for a lower tariff, denounced the trusts, and embraced the cause of labor.

The Bryan of 1908 aroused neither the unreasoning horror nor the passionate support of 1896. With Roosevelt's endorsement, Taft coasted to victory. But the Democrats made significant gains—Bryan bested Parker's 1904 vote total by 1.3 million—and progressive Republican state candidates outran the conservative national ticket. Overall, the 1908 election outcome suggested a lull in the reform movement, not its end.

Taft in the White House

Roosevelt had pledged not to run in 1908, and to the disappointment of millions, he kept his promise. The Republican party's most conservative elements easily regained party control. They nominated

**"Goodness Gracious!
I Must Have Been Dozing"**
This 1910 cartoon in the humor magazine Puck *lampoons President Taft's mounting political difficulties and suggests ex-president Theodore Roosevelt's unhappiness with his designated successor.*

After the inaugural Roosevelt departed to hunt big game in Africa, to the delight of conservatives. Quipped Senator Aldrich, "Let every lion do its duty." Even with TR an ocean away, his presence remained vivid. "When I am addressed as 'Mr. President,'" Taft wrote Roosevelt, "I turn to see whether you are not at my elbow."

Taft, from an old political family in Cincinnati, differed markedly from Roosevelt. Whereas TR kept in fighting trim, the sedentary Taft was grossly overweight. Roosevelt sparred in a boxing ring that he set up in the White House; Taft preferred golf. TR loved speech-making and dramatic battles with the forces of evil; Taft had little taste for political conflict and avoided the limelight. His happiest days would come after he left the presidency, as chief justice of the Supreme Court.

Pledged to carry on TR's program, Taft supported the Mann-Elkins Act (1910), which strengthened the Interstate Commerce Commission's rate-setting powers and extended its regulatory authority to the nation's telephone and telegraph companies. On the antitrust front, the Taft administration actually outdid Roosevelt, prosecuting no fewer than ninety cases. But Taft characteristically pursued these cases without much publicity; and in the public mind, TR remained the quintessential "trustbuster."

A Divided Republican Party

During the Roosevelt administration, a small but vocal group of reform-minded Republican legislators, nicknamed the Insurgents, challenged their party's congressional leadership. Influential Insurgents included senators La Follette and Albert Beveridge of Indiana and congressman George Norris of Nebraska. In 1909 the Insurgents turned against President Taft after a bruising battle over the tariff.

Taft at first shared the Insurgents' belief that the tariff should be lowered. But in 1909, when high-tariff advocates in the Senate, led by Nelson W. Aldrich, pushed through the Payne-Aldrich Act, raising the rates on hundreds of items, Taft abandoned the fight. Signing the measure into law, Taft, to the Insurgents' disgust, praised it as "the best tariff bill that the Republican party ever passed." The battle lines between conservative and progressive Republicans were drawn.

A major Insurgent target was the Speaker of the House, Joseph G. Cannon of Illinois, a poker-playing, to-bacco-chewing Republican whose benevolent nickname, Uncle Joe, belied his reactionary and ruthless politics. Wielding near-absolute power, Cannon kept most reform bills from even reaching a vote. The Insurgents' resentment against "Cannonism" burst out in March 1910, when they joined with the Democrats to remove Cannon from the pivotal Rules Committee and revoke his power to appoint its members. This Insurgent victory was a direct slap at Taft, who supported Cannon.

Relations between Taft and Roosevelt eroded in 1909–1910, as TR's allies sent him stormy letters detailing Taft's ineptitude and lack of reform zeal. The so-called Ballinger-Pinchot affair brought matters to a head. Taft's secretary of the interior, Richard A. Ballinger, was a conservative Seattle lawyer who disliked federal controls and believed in private development of natural resources. In one of a series of decisions galling to conservationists, Ballinger approved the sale, to a group of Seattle businessmen, of several million acres of public lands in Alaska containing rich coal deposits. This group in turn sold its holdings to a consortium of New York bankers that included J. P. Morgan, the very symbol of the money power. When Department of the Interior official Louis R. Glavis protested these actions, he was fired. In true muckraking style, Glavis published an article in *Collier's* blasting Ballinger's actions. When Gifford Pinchot of the Forestry Service likewise criticized Ballinger in congressional testimony in January 1910, he, too, got the ax. TR's supporters seethed.

Upon Roosevelt's return to the United States in June 1910, Pinchot met the boat. In the 1910 midterm election, Roosevelt campaigned for Insurgent candidates. In a speech that alarmed conservatives, the former president appealed for more federal regulation of business, censured judges who struck down progressive laws, and endorsed the radical idea of reversing judicial rulings by popular vote. Giving a name to his reviving political crusade, TR borrowed from Herbert Croly's *The Promise of American Life* and proposed a "New Nationalism" that would make the federal government a powerful reform instrument.

The Democrats captured the House of Representatives in 1910, and a coalition of Democrats and Insurgent Republicans controlled the Senate. As the reform tide rose, Theodore Roosevelt sounded more and more like a presidential candidate. Meanwhile, however, a new challenger for the national leadership of the progressive movement was coming forth, this time from the ranks of the Democrats.

NATIONAL PROGRESSIVISM— PHASE II: WOODROW WILSON

In the 1912 election, Theodore Roosevelt and Woodrow Wilson, together with Socialist Eugene Debs, offered competing visions of reform. Wilson won, and in his first term he played a pivotal leadership role as Congress enacted an imposing array of reform measures.

The Four-Way Election of 1912

In February 1912, now openly opposed to Taft, Roosevelt announced that he would seek the 1912 Republican nomination. But Taft had no intention of withdrawing, and a Republican battle royal loomed. Two other factors complicated the picture: the growing strength of the Socialist party and the presidential ambitions of Senator Robert La Follette. For a time, La Follette's candidacy attracted reform-minded Republicans, but when Roosevelt entered the race, it quickly collapsed.

Challenging Taft in six state primaries and four Republican state conventions, Roosevelt was almost uniformly victorious. But Taft controlled the party machinery, and the Republican convention that met in Chicago in June disqualified many of Roosevelt's hard-won delegates. Outraged, TR's backers stalked out of the convention. In August they reassembled in Chicago to form a third party, the Progressive party. What had been the label of an amorphous reform movement became the official name of a political organization.

Roosevelt exploited his macho image to the hilt, declaring himself "stripped to the buff and ready for the fight." "I feel fit as a bull moose," he trumpeted, thereby giving his organization its nickname: the Bull Moose party. Riding an emotional high, the cheering delegates nominated their hero by acclamation, designated Hiram Johnson as his running mate, and adopted a platform that endorsed practically every reform cause of the day, including tariff reduction, woman suffrage, business regulation, the abolition of child labor, the eight-hour workday, workers' compensation, the direct primary, and the popular election of senators. The revivalistic mood crested as the

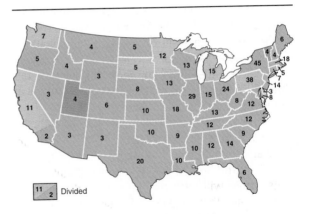

	Electoral Vote	Popular Vote	Percentage of Popular Vote
Democratic Woodrow Wilson	435	6,296,547	41.9
Progressive (Bull Moose) Theodore Roosevelt	88	4,118,571	27.4
Republican William H. Taft	8	3,486,720	23.2
Socialist Eugene V. Debs	—	900,672	6.1

The Election of 1912

delegates joined in such songs as "Onward Christian Soldiers" and "The Battle Hymn of the Republic." The new party attracted a diverse array of followers, from a former partner of J. P. Morgan to settlement-house leader Jane Addams, united by their admiration for the charismatic Roosevelt.

Meanwhile, the new political spirit had also infused the Democratic party, spawning reform administrations at the local and state level. One of these was in New Jersey, where in 1910 voters elected a political novice, Woodrow Wilson, as governor. A "Wilson for president" boom soon arose, and when the Democrats assembled in Baltimore in late June, Wilson won the nomination.

In the electoral campaign, Taft more or less gave up, taking comfort that he had kept his party safe for conservatism. Whereas Debs championed an end to capitalism and a socialized economic order, Roosevelt and Wilson offered differing and less radical prescriptions. TR continued to preach his New Nationalism: government regulation of big business in the public interest. Wilson, by contrast, speaking of the "New Freedom," evoked an earlier era of small entrepreneurs and free competition. "The history of liberty is the history of the limitation of governmental power, not the increase of it," he declared.

Roosevelt did well for a third-party candidate, winning more than 4 million votes to Taft's 3.5 million, and eighty-eight electoral votes to Taft's eight. But the divided Republicans proved no match for the united Democrats. Wilson glided to victory with 6.3 million votes; the Democrats also took both houses of Congress. More than 900,000 voters cast their ballots for Debs and socialism.

The 1912 election linked the triumphant Democrats firmly with reform (except on the issue of race)—a link that Franklin D. Roosevelt would build upon in the 1930s. And the breakaway Progressive party of 1912 demonstrated the strength of the reform impulse among grass-roots Republicans while leaving the Republican party itself in the grip of its most conservative elements.

Woodrow Wilson: The Scholar as President

The son, grandson, and nephew of Presbyterian ministers, Wilson grew up in various southern towns in a churchly atmosphere that shaped his oratorical style and his moral outlook. Although slow in school (probably because of the learning disorder dyslexia), Wilson graduated from Princeton and earned a Ph.D. in political science from Johns Hopkins University. He taught at Princeton and in 1902 became its president. Admired at first for his educational ideas, Wilson gradually lost support because of a rigid unwillingness to compromise. In 1910, having lost several battles at Princeton, he left the academic world. Two years later he was president of the United States.

As national leader, Wilson exhibited the same strengths and weaknesses he had earlier displayed at Princeton. With an impressive bearing and piercing gray eyes, he was an eloquent orator with a masterly command of language. But the same idealism that so inspired people could also alienate them. When he chose, Wilson could be a master of political statesmanship and compromise. "He can walk on dead leaves and make no more noise than a tiger," declared one awed politician. But he could also retreat into a fortress of absolute certitude that tolerated no opposition. During his eight years as president, all these facets of his complex personality would come into play.

Tariff and Banking Reform

Tariff reform—a hot political issue and long a goal of southern and agrarian Democrats—headed Wilson's agenda. Breaking a precedent dating from Thomas Jefferson's day, Wilson on April 8, 1913, read his tariff message to Congress in person. A low-tariff bill quickly passed the House, but the Senate bill bogged down in partisan conflict. Demonstrating his flair for dramatic leadership, Wilson publicly denounced the tariff lobbyists flooding into Washington. His censure led to a Senate investigation of lobbyists and of senators who personally profited from high tariffs. In the aftermath of the publicity, the Senate passed a bill slashing tariff rates even more than the House version. The Underwood-Simmons Tariff reduced rates by an average of 15 percent and placed a number of items, including iron and steel, on the free list. It also imposed an income tax, as authorized by the newly ratified Sixteenth Amendment.

In June 1913 Wilson again went before Congress, this time to call for banking and currency reform. Everyone agreed that the nation's antiquated banking system was inadequate for a modern industrial economy. Totally decentralized and independent, American banks needed a strong central institution—a "lender of last resort" to help them to weather fiscal crises such as the Panic of 1907, in which many banks had failed. But beyond a general agreement on the need for reform, the consensus evaporated. The nation's bankers, whose Senate spokesman was Nelson Aldrich, favored a privately controlled central bank similar to the old Bank of the United States that Andrew Jackson had attacked in the 1830s. Progressive reformers wanted a publicly controlled central banking system. Others, including influential Virginia congressman Carter Glass, were leery of any central banking authority, public or private.

No monetary expert, Wilson listened to all sides. He did, however, insist that the banking system must ultimately be under public control. Through the summer and fall of 1913, the complex bargaining went on, with Wilson playing a critical behind-the-scenes role. The result was the Federal Reserve Act of December 1913, Wilson's greatest legislative achievement.

A compromise among the various viewpoints before Congress, the Federal Reserve Act created a network of twelve regional Federal Reserve banks under mixed public and private control. Each regional bank was authorized to issue currency, called Federal Reserve notes, to the private banks in its district. These banks, in turn, could use this money to make loans to corporations and individual borrowers. (Look at a dollar bill: in the circle to the left of Washington's portrait, you will find the name of the specific Federal Reserve Bank that issued your bill.) Overall control of the system was placed in the hands of the heads of the twelve regional banks and a Washington-based Federal Reserve Board consisting of the secretary of the treasury, the comptroller of the currency, and seven other members appointed by the president for fourteen-year terms. All national banks were required to join the new system and deposit a portion of their assets in their regional Federal Reserve Bank.

As established in 1913, the Federal Reserve's decision-making authority was badly diffused. But eventually—and particularly after the 1930s—"the Fed" would grow into a strong central monetary institution. In addition to providing a safeguard against financial panics, the Federal Reserve Board shapes monetary policy to promote economic growth and dampen inflationary pressures. The Board accomplishes these objectives in three ways: by setting the percentage of their assets that member banks must keep on deposit in the Federal Reserve system; by buying and selling government securities; and, most important, by raising or lowering the interest rate on funds advanced to member banks. By this means the Fed can ease or tighten credit and thus affect the rate of business expansion.

Corporate Regulation

Wilson and his congressional allies turned next to that quintessential progressive cause, business regulation. Although candidate Wilson had shown little sympathy for the regulatory approach (with its implicit acknowledgment that giant corporations were here to stay), as president he shepherded through Congress two important regulatory measures. These embodied somewhat different strategies. The first, the Federal Trade Commission Act (1914), reflected an administrative approach. This law created a five-member federal "watchdog" agency, the Federal Trade Commission (FTC), with power to investigate suspected violations of federal regulatory statutes, to require regular reports from corporations, and to issue "cease and desist" orders (subject to court review) when it found unfair methods of business competition.*

The second of these measures, the Clayton Antitrust Act (1914), took the more traditional approach of listing specific illegal activities. The Sherman Anti-Trust Act of 1890, although outlawing business practices "in restraint of trade," had remained vague about details. The Clayton Act spelled out a series of illegal practices, such as selling at a loss to monopolize a market.

Because some of the "watchdogs" Wilson appointed to the FTC were conservatives with big-business links, this agency did not play the active role reformers had hoped. But with the added clout of the Clayton Act, the Wilson administration filed antitrust suits against nearly a hundred corporations.

Labor Legislation and Farm Aid

Sympathetic to labor, and leading a party historically identified with working people, Wilson supported the American Federation of Labor, defended workers' right to organize, and endorsed a Clayton Act clause that exempted strikes, boycotts, and peaceful picketing from the antitrust laws' prohibition of actions "in restraint of trade." During the 1916 presidential campaign, Wilson and the Democratic congressional leadership pushed through three important worker-protection laws: the Keating-Owen Act, barring from interstate commerce products manufactured by child labor†; the Adamson Act, establishing an eight-hour workday for interstate railway workers; and the Workmen's Compensation Act, providing accident and injury protection to federal workers.

Wilson also strongly supported the Federal Farm Loan Act and the Federal Warehouse Act (1916), which enabled farmers, using land or crops as security, to secure low-interest federal loans. The Federal High-

---

*The Federal Trade Commission replaced an earlier agency, the Bureau of Corporations, set up in 1903.

†This measure was declared unconstitutional in 1918. Later a 1919 law that placed a special tax on all goods manufactured by child labor was also ruled unconstitutional. But these laws paved the way for the final abolition of child labor by the Fair Labor Standards Act of 1938.

way Act (1916), which provided federal matching funds for state highway-construction programs, benefited not only the new automobile industry but also farmers plagued by bad roads.

Progressivism and the Constitution

The probusiness tilt typical of the courts in the late nineteenth century faced increasing criticism in the Progressive Era. Dramatic evidence of the changing judicial climate came in *Muller* v. *Oregon* (1908), in which the Supreme Court upheld an Oregon ten-hour law for women laundry workers. Defending the constitutionality of the Oregon law was Boston attorney Louis Brandeis, who offered economic, medical, and sociological evidence of the harmful effects of long hours on women workers. This evidence came mainly from the research of Brandeis's sister-in-law Josephine Goldmark, a staff member of Florence Kelley's National Consumers' League. The Court's acceptance of this "Brandeis brief" marked a breakthrough in making the legal system more responsive to new social realities.

In 1916 Woodrow Wilson nominated Brandeis, who had helped fashion Wilson's New Freedom campaign theme in 1912, to the Supreme Court. Disapproving of Brandeis's innovative approach to the law, the conservative American Bar Association protested, as did the *New York Times,* the president of Harvard, and Republican leaders in Congress. Bigots opposed Brandeis because he was a Jew. But Wilson stood by his nominee, and after a fierce battle, the Senate approved.

The Progressive Era also produced four amendments to the Constitution, the first since 1870. The Sixteenth (ratified in 1913) granted Congress the authority to tax income, thus ending a long legal battle. A Civil

War income tax had been phased out by 1872. The Wilson-Gorman Tariff Act of 1894 had included a provision for an income tax (see Chapter 21), but a conservative U.S. Supreme Court, in *Pollack* v. *Farmers' Loan and Trust* (1895), had not only ruled this measure unconstitutional but blasted it as "communistic." The *Pollack* decision spurred the campaign for a constitutional amendment that succeeded in 1913. Quickly exercising its new authority, Congress in 1913 imposed a graduated federal income tax with a maximum rate of 7 percent on incomes in excess of $500,000.

The Seventeenth Amendment (1913) mandated the direct election of U.S. senators by the people, rather than senators' selection by state legislatures as was provided in Article I of the Constitution. This amendment brought to fruition a reform first advocated by the Populists as a way of trimming the power of corporations and political bosses and of making the Senate more responsive to the popular will.

The next two amendments culminated great reform campaigns that we have already examined. Nationwide prohibition was established by the Eighteenth (1919), and the Nineteenth (1920) granted women the vote. This remarkable wave of amendments vividly demonstrated how profoundly the progressive impulse had transformed the political landscape.

1916: Wilson Edges Out Hughes

Wilson easily won renomination in 1916. The Republicans turned to the bearded Charles Evans Hughes, a Supreme Court justice and former New York governor. The Progressive party leaders tried to nominate Theodore Roosevelt again, but TR's reformist interests had given way to an obsession with drawing the United States into the European war. At his urging, the

The Election of 1916

Candidates	Parties	Electoral Vote	Popular Vote	Percentage of Popular Vote
WOODROW WILSON	Democratic	277	9,127,695	49.4
Charles E. Hughes	Republican	254	8,533,507	46.2
A. L. Benson	Socialist		585,113	3.2
J. Frank Hanly	Prohibition		220,506	1.2

Progressives endorsed Hughes and effectively ended their role as a third party. Because of the war, the issue of military preparedness figured importantly in the campaign (see Chapter 23).

With the Republicans now more or less reunited, the election was extremely close. Wilson won in the popular vote (9.1 million votes to Hughes's 8.5 mil-lion), but the electoral-college outcome remained in doubt for several weeks as the California tally see-sawed back and forth. Ultimately, Wilson carried the state by fewer than four thousand votes, and with it, the election.

But war and its aftermath, not reform, would oc-cupy Wilson's second term.

CONCLUSION

With the flurry of worker-protection legislation in the fall of 1916, the progressive movement lost momentum as the nation's attention turned from reform to war. A few reform measures enacted in the 1920s and a 1924 presidential campaign by Senator Robert La Follette under a revived Progres-sive party banner, would offer reminders that pro-gressivism remained a force. But the movement's zest and drive clearly waned with the coming of World War I.

Yet progressivism left a remarkable legacy, not only in specific laws but also in a changed view of government. To be sure, this altered perspective had ideological roots in the American past, including Jef-fersonian optimism about human perfectibility, Jack-sonian opposition to special privilege, conservative fears of "the masses," and the rising status of science and social research that had come with advances in higher education and the growing confidence of such academic disciplines as economics, sociology, and statistics.

But the progressives combined these diverse in-gredients in creative new ways. By 1916 a consensus had taken hold that it was proper and necessary for government to play a central social and economic role. Thus a major progressive achievement was to expand the meaning of democracy and to challenge the cynical view that government was nothing but a tool of the economic elite. Theodore Roosevelt and Woodrow Wilson, together with governors like Robert La Follette and mayors like Tom Johnson, vastly enlarged the role of the executive in American government. But progressives did not seek "big gov-ernment" for its own sake. Rather, they recognized that in an era of gargantuan industries, sprawling cities, and concentrated corporate power, govern-ment's role had to grow correspondingly if the public interest were to be served, a decent common life achieved, and the more vulnerable members of soci-ety protected.

Unquestionably, this high progressive ideal often faltered in practice. Moral indignation and a vision of social justice were sufficient to create reform laws and regulatory agencies, but those laws and agencies were often unable to fulfill their purpose, as emo-tional fervor gave way to bureaucratic routine. In-deed, reforms that the progressives originally envi-sioned as serving the larger society sometimes in practice mainly benefited special interests. Corpora-tions that initially fought regulation proved remark-ably adept at manipulating the new regulatory state to their own advantage. Unquestionably, too, pro-gressivism had its repressive, illiberal, and coercive dimensions; and on the issue of racial justice, its record was generally dismal.

After all this has been acknowledged, however, the Progressive Era shines forth as a time when American politics seriously began to confront the so-cial upheavals wrought by industrialization. It was also a time when Americans learned to think of their government neither as remote and irrelevant nor as a plaything of the powerful but rather as an arena of possibility where public issues and social problems could be meaningfully addressed. Twenty years later, another great reform movement, the New Deal, would draw heavily on progressivism's legacy.

CHRONOLOGY

1895 Anti-Saloon League founded.

1898 Charlotte Perkins Gilman, *Women and Economics.*

1899 Thorstein Veblen, *The Theory of the Leisure Class.*

Charlotte Perkins Gilman

1900 International Ladies' Garment Workers' Union (ILGWU) founded.

Socialist Party of America organized.

Theodore Dreiser, *Sister Carrie.*

Carrie Chapman Catt becomes president of the National American Woman Suffrage Association (NAWSA).

1901 Assassination of McKinley; Theodore Roosevelt becomes president.

1902 Roosevelt mediates coal strike.

National Reclamation Act.

Jane Addams, *Democracy and Social Ethics.*

1903 W. E. B. Du Bois, *The Souls of Black Folk.*

1904 Roosevelt elected president.

Northern Securities case.

Lincoln Steffens, *The Shame of the Cities.*

Ida Tarbell, *History of the Standard Oil Company.*

1905 Industrial Workers of the World (IWW) organized.

Niagara Movement established by W. E. B. Du Bois and others.

Gifford Pinchot appointed head of U.S. Forest Service.

1906 Hepburn Act.

Upton Sinclair, *The Jungle.*

Pure Food and Drug Act.

Meat Inspection Act.

Lochner v. *New York.*

Antiquities Act.

1907 Walter Rauschenbusch, *Christianity and the Social Crisis.*

William James, *Pragmatism.*

1908 *Muller* v. *Oregon.*

William Howard Taft elected president.

1909 Payne-Aldrich Tariff.

Ballinger-Pinchot controversy.

National Association for the Advancement of Colored People (NAACP) founded.

Herbert Croly, *The Promise of American Life.*

1910 Mann Act.

Mann-Elkins Act.

1911 Triangle Shirtwaist Company fire.

Supreme Court orders dissolution of Standard Oil Company.

1912 Republican party split; Progressive (Bull Moose) party founded.

Woodrow Wilson elected president.

1913 Underwood-Simmons Tariff.

Federal Reserve Act.

Sixteenth Amendment added to the Constitution.

Seventeenth Amendment added to the Constitution.

Thirty thousand march for woman suffrage in New York.

1914 Federal Trade Commission Act.

Clayton Antitrust Act.

1915 D. W. Griffith, *The Birth of a Nation.*

1916 Federal Farm Loan Act.

Keating-Owen Act.

Adamson Act.

Workmen's Compensation Act.

Wilson reelected.

John Dewey, *Democracy and Education.*

Margaret Sanger opens nation's first birth-control clinic in Brooklyn, New York.

National Park Service created.

1919 Eighteenth Amendment added to the Constitution.

1920 Nineteenth Amendment added to the Constitution.

FOR FURTHER READING

Alan Dawley, *Struggle for Justice: Social Responsibility and the Liberal State* (1991). A thoughtful study placing the progressive movement in a larger historical and ideological context.

Noralee Frankel and Nancy S. Dye, eds., *Gender, Class, Race, and Reform in the Progressive Era* (1991). Selected essays exploring progressivism from various social perspectives.

Arthur S. Link and Richard L. McCormick, *Progressivism* (1983). Lucid, sensible unraveling of progressivism's diverse strands and comprehensive discussion of current interpretations.

William A. Link, *The Paradox of Southern Progressivism, 1880–1930* (1992). A regional study tracing the emergence of a reform-minded new administrative order in the urban South.

Robert B. Westbrook, *John Dewey and American Democracy* (1991). The definitive intellectual biography of an influential philosopher and social thinker.

ADDITIONAL BIBLIOGRAPHY

Society and the Economy

David Brody, "The American Worker in the Progressive Age: A Comprehensive Analysis" in David Brody, *Workers in Industrial America: Essays on the Twentieth-Century Struggle*, 2d ed. (1985); Ardis Cameron, *Radicals of the Worst Sort: Laboring Women in Lawrence, Massachusetts, 1860–1912* (1993); Susan A. Glenn, *Daughters of the Shtetl: Life and Labor in the Immigrant Generation* (1990); Alice Kessler-Harris, *Out to Work: A History of Wage-Earning Women in the United States* (1982); Elaine Tyler May, *Great Expectations: Marriage and Divorce in Post-Victorian America* (1980); Bruno Ramirez, *When Workers Organize: The Politics of Industrial Relations in the Progressive Era, 1898–1916* (1978).

The Progressive Impulse

John D. Buenker, *Urban Liberalism and Progressive Reform* (1973); David M. Chalmers, *The Social and Political Ideas of the Muckrakers* (1964); Nancy F. Cott, *A Woman Making History: Mary Ritter Beard Through Her Letters* (1991); Ruth H. Crocker, *Social Work and Social Order: The Settlement Movement in Two Industrial Cities, 1889–1930* (1992); Lawrence A. Cremin, *The Transformation of the Schools: Progressivism in American Education, 1876–1957* (1971); Robert Crunden, *Ministers of Reform: The Progressives' Achievement in American Civilization* (1982); Allen F. Davis, *Spearheads for Reform: The Social Settlements and the Progressive Movement, 1890–1914*, 2d ed. (1984); Robert W. Gordon, *The Legacy of Oliver Wendell Holmes, Jr.* (1992); Dewey W. Grantham, *Southern Progressivism: The Reconciliation of Progress and Tradition* (1983); Richard L. McCormick, *From Realignment to Reform: Political Change in New York State, 1893–1910* (1981), and "The Discovery That Business Corrupts Politics: A Reappraisal of the Origins of Progressivism," *American Historical Review* 86 (1981): 247–274; Jean B. Quandt, *From the Small Town to the Great Community: The Social Thought of Progressive Intellectuals* (1970); Judith Ann Trolander, *Professionalism and Social Change: From the Settlement House Movement to Neighborhood Centers* (1987); Walter I. Trattner, *Crusade for Children* (1970); Robert Wiebe, *Businessmen and Reform: A Study of the Progressive Movement* (1962) and *The Search for Order, 1877–1920* (1967); Clarence E. Wunderlin, Jr., *Visions of a New Industrial Order: Social Science and Labor Theory in America's Progressive Era* (1992).

Reforming Municipal Government

Samuel P. Hays, "The Politics of Reform in Municipal Government in the Progressive Era," *Pacific Northwest Quarterly* 55 (1964): 157–169; Melvin G. Holli, *Reform in Detroit: Hazen S. Pingree and Urban Politics* (1969); Bradley R. Rice, *Progressive Cities: The Commission Government Movement in America, 1901–1920* (1977); Martin J. Schiesl, *The Politics of Efficiency: Municipal Administration and Reform in America, 1880–1920* (1977).

Moral Reform and Social Control

Paul Boyer, *Urban Masses and Moral Order in America, 1820–1920* (1978); Mark T. Connelly, *The Response to Prostitution in the Progressive Era* (1980); Mark H. Haller, *Eugenics: Hereditarian Attitudes in American Thought* (1963); Barbara Meil Hobson, *Uneasy Virtue: The Politics of Prostitution and the American Reform Tradition* (1987); Jack Temple Kirby, *Darkness at Dawning: Race and Reform in the Progressive South* (1972); Alan M. Kraut, *Silent Travelers: Germs, Genes, and the "Immigrant Menace"* (1994); John F. McClymer, *War and Welfare: Social Engineering in America, 1890–1925* (1980); Mark Moore and Dean Gerstein, eds., *Alcohol and Public Policy: Beyond the Shadow of Prohibition* (1981); W. J. Rorabaugh, *The Alcoholic Republic* (1979); Ruth Rosen, *The Lost Sisterhood: Prostitution in America: 1900–1918* (1982); Peter Temin, *Taking Your Medicine: Drug Regulation in the United States* (1980); James H. Timberlake, *Prohibition and the Progressive Movement, 1900–1920* (1963); William O. Walker III, *Opium and Foreign Policy: The Anglo-American Search for Order in Asia, 1912–1954* (1991).

Women in the Progressive Movement

Ellen Chesler, *Woman of Valor: Margaret Sanger and the Birth Control Movement in America* (1992); Ellen Fitzpatrick, *Endless Crusade: Women Social Scientists and Progressive Reform* (1990); Lynn D. Gordon, *Gender and Higher Education in the Progressive Era* (1990); Ann J. Lane, *To Herland and Beyond: The Life and Work of Charlotte Perkins Gilman* (1990); Marian J. Morton, *Emma Goldman and the American Left* (1992); Robyn Muncy, *Creating a Female Dominion in American Reform, 1890–1935* (1991); Rosalind Rosenberg, *Beyond Separate Spheres: The Intellectual Roots of Modern Feminism* (1982).

African-American Life and Thought

Louis R. Harlan, *Booker T. Washington: Wizard of Tuskegee, 1901–1915* (1983); Charles F. Kellogg, *NAACP: The History of the National Association for the Advancement of Colored People, 1909–1920* (1967); Elliott M. Rudwick, *W. E. B. Du Bois* (1969); Joe W. Trotter, Jr., ed., *The Great Migration in Historical Perspective: New Dimensions of Race, Class, and Gender* (1991).

Progressivism in National Politics

Kendrick A. Clements, *The Presidency of Woodrow Wilson* (1992); Paolo E. Coletta, *The Presidency of William Howard Taft* (1973); Lewis L. Gould, *The Presidency of Theodore Roosevelt* (1991); Arthur S. Link, *Woodrow Wilson and the Progressive Era* (1963); Nick Salvatore, *Eugene V. Debs* (1982); David Thelen, *Robert La Follette and the Insurgent Spirit* (1976); Melvin I. Urofsky, *Louis D. Brandeis and the Progressive Tradition* (1981).

Progressives and the Environment

Stephen R. Fox, *The American Conservation Movement: John Muir and His Legacy* (1981); Samuel P. Hays, *Conservation and the Gospel of Efficiency: The Progressive Conservation Movement, 1890–1920* (1959); Clayton R. Koppes, "Shifting Themes in American Conservation," in Donald Worster, ed., *The Ends of the Earth* (1988); Carolyn Merchant, "Women of the Progressive Conservation Movement, 1900–1916," *Environmental Review* 8 (Spring 1984): 57–85; Roderick Nash, *Wilderness and the American Mind* (1967); James Penick, Jr., *Progressive Politics and Conservation: The Ballinger-Pinchot Affair* (1968); Elmo R. Richardson, "The Struggle for the Valley: California's Hetch Hetchy Controversy, 1905–1913," *California Historical Society Quarterly* 38 (1959): 249–258.

Infantryman
by Harry Everett Townsend

23

WORLD WAR I

On the evening of April 2, 1917, a somber Woodrow Wilson was driven from the White House to the Capitol. His mission: to ask Congress for a declaration of war against Germany. War had engulfed Europe in 1914, and by 1917 it had already taken a ghastly toll. The president spent the moments before his speech in a small room adjacent to the House of Representatives. Now flushed and trembling, he stared into a mirror until he had mastered his emotions. At 8:32 P.M. he strode into the House chamber and began his address.

Halfway through, Wilson uttered a memorable phrase: the world, he proclaimed, must be made "safe for democracy." Applause and shouts reverberated through the hall. Many senators and congressmen waved little silk American flags that someone had distributed beforehand. As the speech ended, cheers echoed through the House chamber. Senator Henry Cabot Lodge of Massachusetts, one of Wilson's staunchest political opponents, rushed forward to shake his hand. "Mr. President," said Lodge, "you have expressed in the loftiest manner the sentiments of the American people."

But Wilson's own mood remained muted. "Think what it was they were applauding," he mused to an aide; "my message today was a message of death for our young men. How strange it seems to applaud that."

This message of death, which did indeed send thousands of American men to their graves, came reluctantly from Wilson, after months of trying to keep the United States out of war. Elected on a tide of reformist enthusiasm, Wilson found himself enmeshed in foreign affairs as his presidential term proceeded. Preoccupied at first with problems in Asia and Latin America, Wilson was soon caught up in—and ultimately consumed by—the struggle engulfing Europe. Wilson brought to these foreign crises the same self-assured moralism that he had long applied to issues closer to home.

Whereas Woodrow Wilson's international involvements focused on Europe, his Republican predecessors in the White House, Theodore Roosevelt and William Howard Taft, had asserted a more active world role for the United States in Asia and Latin America. In contrast to William McKinley, a reluctant and clumsy imperialist, Theodore Roosevelt had no doubts about America's mission in Asia: to provide a balance of power, preventing any other nation from controlling the region. With his customary energy and highly personal approach, Roosevelt pursued this objective. President Taft, on the other hand, relied less on a grand geopolitical design than on a practical desire to open the markets of the developing part of the world to American business. Taken together, the foreign policies pursued by each of these early-twentieth-century presidents—Roosevelt's balance-of-power chess game, Taft's focus on business opportunities, and Wilson's moralism—illustrate the diverse and sometimes contradictory motives that would continue to shape the United States' world role as the twentieth century unfolded.

DEFINING AMERICA'S WORLD ROLE

Wilson's call for war in 1917 came against a backdrop of intensified U.S. involvement abroad, especially in Asia and Latin America, following the Spanish-American War and the occupation of the Philippines. These foreign engagements clearly reflected the United States' growing determination to assert its might, to protect and extend American business investments abroad, and to impose its own standards of good government throughout the world.

The Roosevelt Corollary in Latin America and the Balance of Power in Asia

Although building the Panama Canal remains Theodore Roosevelt's most famous foreign-policy coup, his response to other foreign crises further illuminated his belief that the United States must strengthen its world role, protect U.S. interests in Latin America, and preserve the balance of power in Asia.

In 1904, when several European nations threatened to invade the Dominican Republic, a small Caribbean island nation that had defaulted on its debts, Roosevelt concluded that such an assault would threaten American interests. If any big power were to intervene in Latin America, he believed, it should be the United States. Accordingly, in his annual message to Congress in December 1904, Roosevelt declared that although the United States had no territorial ambitions in Latin America, "chronic wrongdoing" by any Latin American nation would justify intervention by the United States, acting as international policeman.

This pronouncement soon came to be known as the Roosevelt Corollary to the Monroe Doctrine. The original "doctrine," promulgated by President James Monroe in 1823, had warned European powers against meddling in Latin America; the Roosevelt Corollary announced that under certain circumstances, the United States had the right to precisely such meddling. Suiting actions to words, the United States operated the Dominican Republic's customs service for two years and took over the management of its foreign debt.

Meanwhile, on the other side of the world, the imperial rivalries that swirled over China in the 1890s continued unabated in the new century, briefly casting President Theodore Roosevelt in the unfamiliar role of peacemaker. In 1900, taking advantage of the turmoil caused by the Boxer uprising (see Chapter 21), one hundred thousand Russian troops occupied the Chinese province of Manchuria, where Russia sought to promote its commercial interests by building railroads. This action alarmed the Japanese, who had their own plans for southern Manchuria and the nearby Korean peninsula. In February 1904 the Japanese launched a surprise attack that destroyed the Russian naval force at Port Arthur, Manchuria. In the Russo-Japanese War that followed, the Japanese completely dominated the Russians.

Roosevelt was quite happy to see Russian expansionism checked, but a total Japanese defeat of the Russians would not only disrupt the balance of power that TR considered essential to peace in the Far East but also threaten America's role in the Philippines. Accordingly, in June 1905 TR invited Japan and Russia to send delegates to a peace conference at Portsmouth, New Hampshire. In September the two rivals signed a peace treaty. By its terms, Russia recognized Japan's rule in Korea and made other territorial concessions. After this outcome, curbing Japanese expansionism—peacefully, if possible—became America's major objective in Asia. For his role in ending the Russo-Japanese War, Roosevelt received the Nobel Peace Prize in 1906.

Meanwhile, American relations with Japan soured when the San Francisco school board, in 1906, reflecting growing West Coast hostility to Asian immigrants, herded all Asian children into segregated schools. Summoning the school-board members to Washington, Roosevelt persuaded them to reverse this discriminatory policy. In return, the Roosevelt administration in 1908 negotiated a "gentlemen's agreement" with Japan by which Tokyo pledged to stop the emigration of Japanese laborers to the United States. Racist attitudes on the West Coast continued to poison U.S.–Japanese relations, however. In 1913 the California legislature prohibited Japanese aliens from owning land.

While Californians warned of the "yellow peril," Japanese journalists, eyeing America's increasing military strength and involvements in Asia, began to speak of a "white peril." In 1907 Roosevelt ordered a flotilla of sixteen gleaming white U.S. battleships on a "training operation" to Japan and on around the world. Although officially treated as a courtesy call, the visit of this "Great White Fleet" to Japan pointedly underscored America's growing naval might.

Wilson J Rac...

Dollar Diplomacy in China and Nicaragua

The foreign policy of President William Howard Taft, who took office in 1909, focused mainly on advancing American commercial interests abroad—a policy that critics called dollar diplomacy. Since 1899, when Secretary of State John Hay wrote the first of his "Open Door" notes (see Chapter 21), Washington had tried with scant success to secure from the European powers and Japan a share in China's economic development. Pursuing this goal, the Taft administration persuaded a group of U.S. bankers to explore investments in China. But when their agent in China proposed an American-financed railroad in northern Manchuria, he got nowhere. Not only did the U.S. bankers reject the idea, but the Russians and Japanese at once signed a treaty carving up Manchuria for commercial purposes, freezing out the Americans. When Woodrow Wilson took office in 1913, the Taft policy of promoting U.S. commercial expansion in China was, for the time being, shelved.

Closer to home, in Nicaragua, dollar diplomacy enjoyed more success. In 1911 a U.S.–supported revolution in Nicaragua brought to power Adolfo Díaz, an officer of an American-owned Nicaraguan mining property. "Under proper administration," suggested Díaz in a message to the United States, Nicaragua could be "a field for American commerce, instead of a pest under your nose." Prodded by the U.S. Depart-

ment of State, American bankers lent the Díaz government $15 million in exchange for control of the Nicaraguan national bank, the customs service, and the national railroad.

When a revolt against Díaz broke out in 1912, Taft put the Roosevelt Corollary into action: he ordered in twenty-five hundred marines to protect the American bankers' investment. Except for one brief interval, marines occupied the Nicaraguan capital, Managua, until 1933 as a reminder of U.S. military might.

Wilson and Latin America

Criticizing the expansionist policies of his Republican predecessors, Wilson pledged in 1913 that the United States would "never again seek one additional foot of territory by conquest." Nevertheless, Wilson, too, became entangled in Latin American politics. In 1915, after bloody upheavals in Haiti and the Dominican Republic (two tiny nations sharing the same Caribbean island, Santo Domingo), Wilson ordered in the marines. A Haitian constitution favorable to U.S. commercial interests was ratified in 1918 by a margin of 69,377 in favor, 355 against—in a vote supervised by the marines. Under the command of Major General Smedley ("Old Gimlet Eye") Butler, marines brutally suppressed Haitian resistance to U.S. rule. The marines remained in the Dominican Republic until 1924, and in Haiti until 1934.

P.R. – 1924
H – 1934

U.S. Marines in Nicaragua, 1912
These troops were part of the twenty-five hundred marines sent by President Taft to support Nicaragua's pro–U.S. ruler, Adolfo Díaz. The marines remained for most of the next twenty-one years.

Woodrow Wilson, Schoolteacher
This 1914 political cartoon captures the patronizing self-righteousness of Wilson's approach to Latin America that planted the seeds of long-term resentments.

In 1913–1914, Wilson's major foreign preoccupation was with Mexico, a nation divided between a tiny elite of wealthy landowners and a mass of poor peasants. In a turbulent era for Mexico, Wilson tried to promote good government in Mexico City, to protect the large U.S. capital investments in the country, and to safeguard the U.S. citizens traveling in Mexico or living along its border.

In 1911 rebels led by the democratic reformer and mystic Francisco Madero had ended the thirty-year rule of the autocratic president Porfirio Díaz. Forty thousand Americans had settled in Mexico under Díaz's regime, and U.S. investors had poured some $2 billion into Mexican oil wells and other ventures. Madero briefly succeded Díaz, but early in 1913, just as Wilson took office, Mexican troops loyal to general Victoriano Huerta, a full-blooded Indian, overthrew and murdered Madero.

Reversing the long-standing American policy of recognizing all governments regardless of how they came to office, Wilson refused to recognize Huerta's regime: "I will not recognize a government of butchers," he declared. Authorizing arms sales to Huerta's rival, General Venustiano Carranza, Wilson also ordered the port of Vera Cruz blockaded to prevent a shipment of German arms from reaching Huerta. Announced Wilson, "I am going to teach the South American republics to elect good men."

In April 1914, seven thousand U.S. troops occupied Vera Cruz and began fighting Huerta's forces. Sixty-five Americans and some five hundred Mexicans were killed or wounded. Bowing to U.S. might, Huerta abdicated, Carranza took power, and the U.S. troops withdrew.

But the turmoil in Mexico continued, as local rebels and bandits challenged Carranza's authority. In January 1916 a bandit chieftain operating in northern Mexico, Pancho Villa, murdered sixteen young American mining engineers whom he had pulled from a train. Soon after, Pancho Villa's gang burned the town of Columbus, New Mexico, and killed nineteen of its inhabitants. Enraged, the American people demanded action. Wilson dispatched a punitive expedition that eventually totaled twelve thousand U.S. troops into Mexico under the command of General John J. Pershing. Many of these troops were black. When Pancho Villa not only eluded Pershing but brazenly staged another raid across the border into Texas, Wilson ordered 150,000 National Guardsmen to the Mexican border. This massive military response to a comparatively minor problem would long prove a sore point in U.S.–Mexican relations.

Early in 1917, with the United States edging toward war in Europe, Wilson withdrew the U.S. forces from Mexico. When Carranza was formally elected president later that year, Wilson extended U.S. recognition. That same year, curbing the freewheeling operations of U.S. capitalists, Mexico adopted a new constitution that gave the central government rather than regional administrators control of the nation's oil and mineral resources and imposed strict regulations on foreign investors and developers.

Although soon overwhelmed by the larger drama of World War I, these involvements in Asia and Latin America illuminate American foreign-policy goals in these years. These goals reflected a search for world order on U.S. terms—an international system founded on the uniquely American ideological blend of liberalism, democracy, and capitalistic enterprise. Sometimes explicitly, often implicitly, Washington planners envisioned a harmonious, stable global order of democratic societies that would welcome both American political values and American corporate expansion.

President Wilson summed up this view in a speech to a business conference: "Let your thoughts and your imagination run . . . throughout the whole world, and with the inspiration . . . that you are Americans and are meant to carry liberty and justice and the principles of humanity wherever you go, go out and sell goods that will make the world more comfortable and more happy, and convert them to the principles of America."

These involvements in Asia and Latin America also foreshadowed future trends. The diplomatic maneuvering between the United States and Japan signaled a developing clash of interests, compounded by racism, that in 1924 would lead the United States to ban Japanese immigration and in 1941 culminate in war. The revolutionary and nationalistic energies stirring in Latin America would explosively transform the politics of this region half a century later. And of more immediate concern, the vision of an American-based world order that underlay these episodes would soon find its fullest expression in Woodrow Wilson's response to the crisis now unfolding in Europe.

WAR IN EUROPE

When war burst upon Europe in August 1914, most Americans wished only to remain aloof. For nearly three years, as the conflict raged in the trenches and on the high seas, the United States stayed officially neutral. But the tide of opinion gradually shifted. Emotional ties to the British and French, powerful economic considerations, the vision of a world remade in America's image, and German violations of Woodrow Wilson's definition of neutral rights all combined by April 1917 to suck the United States into the maelstrom.

The Coming of War

With a few exceptions, Europe remained at peace through much of the nineteenth century and the early years of the twentieth. Some prophesied that war was a thing of the past. Beneath the surface, however, ominous developments, including a complex network of military alliances, belied such hopeful predictions. As early as 1882, Germany, Austria, and Italy signed a mu-

tual-defense treaty. In turn, France signed military treaties with Russia (1894) and Great Britain (1904).

Beyond the formal alliances stirred imperial ambitions and nationalistic passions. The ancient Ottoman Empire, centered in Turkey, which had once controlled much of southeastern Europe, lost its grip in the 1870s, leaving in its wake such newly independent nations as Romania, Bulgaria, and Serbia. While parts of the Ottoman Empire had converted to Islam, the Serbs adhered to Eastern Orthodox Christianity.

Nationalistic and religious passions ran high in these new states, and particularly in Serbia. Serbian patriots dreamed of achieving the cultural and political unification of the large ethnic group known as Slavs, including those living in Bosnia-Herzegovina, which bordered Serbia to the west. This dream, called Pan-Slavism, powerfully molded turn-of-the-century politics in southeastern Europe. Russia, the homeland of millions of Slavs, supported the Pan-Slavic cause.

Meanwhile, however, the Austro-Hungarian Empire, with its capital in Vienna, also saw opportunities for expansion as the Ottoman Empire receded. In 1908 Austria-Hungary annexed Bosnia-Herzegovina. This move aroused alarm in Russia and fury in Serbia.

Germany, under the rule of Kaiser Wilhelm II, also displayed expansionist impulses. Many Germans believed that their nation, recently forged from a collection of independent principalities, had lagged in the race for national greatness and empire. Expansion, modernization, and military power became the order of the day in Berlin, the German capital.

At a level deeper than diplomacy and politics, many Europeans felt a vague restlessness in the opening years of the twentieth century. Life seemed soft, boring, and stale. Like Theodore Roosevelt on the eve of the Spanish-American War, some openly speculated that a war might strengthen the national character and add excitement to a languid age.

These elements of European political culture combined to kindle an explosion that had horrendous consequences. In June 1914 Archduke Franz Ferdinand of Austria made a state visit with his wife to Bosnia. As they rode in an open touring car through Sarajevo, the Bosnian capital, a young Pan-Slavic nationalist gunned them down. In response, Austria delivered a harsh ultimatum to Serbia on July 23 and five days later declared war on Serbia. Now Europe's intricate system of alliances came into play. Russia, which had a secret treaty with Serbia, mobilized for war. Germany declared war on Russia and on Russia's ally France. Great Britain, linked by treaty to France, declared war on Germany. A lone assassin's bullet had plunged Europe into a war that would change history.

The American People's Initial Responses

President Wilson immediately proclaimed American neutrality and called on the nation to be neutral "in thought as well as in action." Most Americans, grateful that three thousand miles of salt water lay between them and the war, supported Wilson's position. A popular song of the day summed up the national mood: "I Didn't Raise My Boy to Be a Soldier."

For Woodrow Wilson, the unfolding European crisis strangely paralleled a crisis in his own life. His wife, Ellen, long a source of wise advice and nurturing support, died on August 6, 1914. Thus while the president dealt with the international crisis, he also had to cope with his own grief and loss.

Although most Americans shared Wilson's desire to stay out of the war, his call to remain neutral in thought proved more difficult. Extensive economic ties linked the United States and Britain. Many Americans of British ancestry, including Wilson himself, felt an emotional bond with England. As early as August 1914, Wilson mused to a relative that victory for militaristic Germany would spell disaster for the world. Countless well-to-do Americans had traveled in England. School textbooks stressed the English origins of American institutions. The English language itself—the language of Shakespeare, Dickens, and the King James version of the Bible—deepened the tie between Britons and Americans. The British government subtly reinforced this pro-British mood by propaganda stressing the British-American link.

But not all Americans felt spontaneous ties with the British. Millions were of German origin, and many sympathized with Germany's cause. Irish-Americans found little reason for dismay in the prospect of a German victory that might free Ireland from the British colonial yoke. Some Scandinavian immigrants initially identified more with Germany than with England on a cultural level.

Even though a variety of cultural and ethnic crosscurrents influenced American attitudes toward the war, they did not at first override the fundamental commitment to neutrality. For most Americans, as for the Wilson administration itself, keeping the United States out of the conflict became the chief goal.

The Perils of Neutrality

Despite its embrace of neutrality in 1914, the U.S. government went to war in 1917, with strong popular support. What caused this turnabout?

First of all, Wilson's vision of a world order built on American political and economic values conflicted with his neutrality. The international system that he favored, based on liberalism, democracy, and freedom for American capitalistic enterprise, would have been impossible, he believed, in a world dominated by imperial Germany and its autocratic ruler Kaiser Wilhelm II. Furthermore, Wilson gradually became convinced that even an Allied* victory would not ensure a liberal peace without a U.S. role in the postwar settlement. And to help shape the peace, America would have to help fight the war.

This global vision influenced Wilson's handling of the immediate issue that dragged the United States into the conflict: the question of neutral nations' rights on the high seas. Within days of the war's outbreak, the British had intercepted American merchant ships bound for Germany, declaring their cargo contraband that could aid Germany's war effort. Wilson had protested vehemently. These seizures evoked distant memories of earlier conflicts with England over neutral rights. "Madison and I are the only two Princeton men that have become president," Wilson mused to an adviser; "the circumstances of the War of 1812 and now run parallel. I sincerely hope they will not go further."

Wilson's protests intensified in November 1914, when Britain declared the North Sea a war zone and planted it with deadly explosive mines. By choking off Germany's maritime imports, including food, Britain hoped to bring Germany to its knees. In March 1915 the British blockaded all German ports. Once more, the United States protested in vain. Britain was determined to exploit its naval advantage to the fullest, even if it meant alienating American public opinion.

But Germany, not England, ultimately violated Wilson's conception of neutral rights so grossly that the United States went to war. If Britannia ruled the waves, Germany controlled the ocean depths with a new weapon: the torpedo-equipped submarine, or

---

*During World War I, Great Britain, Russia, France, and later Italy were called the Allies. Germany and Austria-Hungary were called the Central Powers. The United States entered the war in 1917 as an "Associate Power" of the Allies, thereby distinguishing its war conduct and aims from those of the other nations with whom it sided.

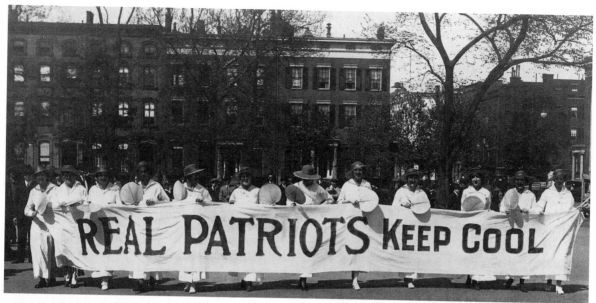

Woman's Peace Party Parade
With fans to symbolize their point, these marchers urged President Wilson to "Keep Cool"
and continue the search for peace despite German provocations.

U-boat. In February 1915 Berlin proclaimed the waters around the British Isles a war zone and warned off all ships. Again Wilson protested; Germany would be held to "strict accountability," he declared, for any loss of American ships or lives. Nevertheless, several Americans died in the succeeding months as U-boats torpedoed British ships and a U.S. tanker.

Then on May 1, 1915, in a small announcement published in U.S. newspapers, the German embassy cautioned Americans against travel on British or French vessels. Six days later, a U-boat without warning sank the British liner *Lusitania* off the Irish coast, with the loss of 1,198 lives, including 128 Americans. As newspapers screamed the news in bold headlines, U.S. public opinion turned sharply anti-German. (The *Lusitania*'s cargo holds, historians later discovered, had carried munitions destined for England.)

In increasingly strong messages to Berlin, collectively called the *Lusitania* notes, Wilson demanded specific pledges that Germany would cease unrestricted submarine warfare. A few days after the *Lusitania* sinking, Wilson insisted that America, without going to war, could persuade the belligerents to recognize the principle of neutral rights. The president said, "There is such a thing as a man being too proud to fight."

The *Lusitania* disaster exposed deep divisions in U.S. public opinion. Many Americans, concluding that war with Germany had become inevitable, ridiculed Wilson's "too proud to fight" speech. Theodore Roosevelt, the Nobel Peace Prize winner, beat the drums for war and heaped scorn on the president's "abject cowardice and weakness." A lobby of bankers and industrialists called the National Security League promoted armament and universal military training and organized "preparedness" parades in New York, Washington, and other cities. By the fall of 1915, Wilson himself was calling for a military buildup.

Many others, however, including not only German-Americans and pacifists but millions who had taken Wilson's neutrality speeches seriously, deplored the drift toward war. Some leading feminists and social-justice reformers warned that the militant war spirit eroded the humanitarian values central to progressive reform. Jane Addams, for example, pointed out that the international movements to reduce infant mortality and provide better care to the aged had been "scattered to the winds by the war."

As early as August 1914, fifteen hundred black-clad women had marched down New York's Fifth Avenue, protesting the war. Early in 1915 Jane Addams,

Carrie Chapman Catt, and other feminists formed the Woman's Peace party to strengthen the cause. Late in 1915 automaker Henry Ford chartered a vessel dubbed the Ford peace ship to take a group of pacifists and other war opponents, including Addams, to Scandinavia in an effort to persuade the belligerents to accept neutral mediation and fulfill his dream of ending the war by Christmas.

Serious divisions surfaced even within the Wilson administration. Believing Wilson's *Lusitania* notes too hostile, and dismayed by what he saw as the abandonment of true neutrality, Secretary of State William Jennings Bryan resigned in June 1915. His successor, the ineffectual Robert Lansing, usually let Wilson act as his own secretary of state.

Some neutrality advocates concluded that incidents like the *Lusitania* crisis were inevitable if Americans continued to sail belligerent ships. Early in 1916 a congressman and a senator introduced legislation to forbid such travel (the Gore-McLemore Resolutions), but it failed under opposition from President Wilson, who insisted that the principle of neutral rights must be upheld.

For a time, Wilson's firm but restrained approach seemed to work. Although Germany did not specifically answer the *Lusitania* notes, it secretly ordered U-boat captains to spare passenger ships and eventually agreed to pay compensation for the loss of American lives in the *Lusitania* sinking. In August 1915, when a U-boat violated orders and sank a British passenger vessel, the *Arabic*, killing two Americans, Germany pledged that such incidents would not recur. In March 1916, however, when a German sub sank a French passenger ship, the *Sussex*, in the English Channel, injuring several Americans and violating the *Arabic* pledge, Wilson threatened to break diplomatic relations—a step toward war. In response, Berlin pledged not to attack merchant vessels without warning provided that Great Britain, too, observed "the rules of international law." Ignoring this qualification, Wilson announced Germany's acceptance of American demands; for the rest of 1916, the crisis over neutral rights eased.

The debate over the meaning of neutrality also involved questions of U.S. financial support to the warring nations. Soon after the war had begun, when banker J. P. Morgan sought permission to extend a loan to France, Secretary of State Bryan had rejected the request as "inconsistent with the true spirit of neutrality."

But towering economic considerations, combined with outrage over the *Lusitania* sinking, undermined this policy. In August 1915 Treasury Secretary William G. McAdoo warned Wilson of dire economic consequences if a lack of funds forced cuts in Allied purchases of munitions and agricultural commodities in the United States. "To maintain our prosperity, we must finance it," McAdoo insisted. Only substantial loans to Great Britain, agreed Secretary of State Lansing, could prevent "a serious financial situation" in the United States, including "unrest and suffering among the laboring classes." Asked Lansing rhetorically, "Can we afford to let a declaration as to our conception of the 'true spirit of neutrality' made in the early days of the war, stand in the way of our national interests?"

Swayed by such arguments, and personally sympathetic to the Allied cause, Wilson permitted the Morgan bank to lend $500 million to the British and French governments. By April 1917, U.S. banks had lent $2.3 billion to the Allies, in contrast to only $27 million to Germany. And although U.S. trade with the Central Powers dropped sharply from 1914 to 1917, trade with the Allies increased nearly fourfold in these years. Despite American neutrality, the Allies depended upon the United States economically, strengthening corporate America's position in the world economy.

Stalemate in the Trenches

While Americans focused on neutral rights and the war at sea, the land war in Europe degenerated into a bloody and costly stalemate. The German high command initially planned to defeat the French and British in six weeks, but an autumn 1914 German drive across Belgium and into France bogged down along the Marne River in the face of dogged British and French resistance. The two sides then dug in, forming a line of trenches that snaked across France from the English Channel to the Swiss border. For more than three years, this line remained essentially unchanged. Occasional offensives gained little ground while taking a terrible human toll. A German offensive in February 1916 began with the capture of two forts near the town of Verdun and ended that June with the French recapture of the same two forts, now nothing but rubble, at a cost of hundreds of thousands of casualties. This war in the trenches was nightmarish for those caught up in it: a ghastly inferno of mud, lice, rats, artillery bursts, poison gas, and sudden, random death.

In the struggle to capture the minds of Americans, the British stepped up their propaganda campaign. Posters and articles portrayed the atrocities allegedly committed by "the Huns" (a derogatory wartime term for the Germans), such as impaling babies on the tips of bayonets. After the war, much of this propaganda was exposed as false. In this climate, Americans who supported Germany increasingly faced suspicion as potential traitors. Documents seized in July 1915 revealing that German embassy officials were financing espionage in U.S. war plants further discredited the German cause.

The Election of 1916

The war loomed large in the 1916 presidential election, in which, as we have seen, Woodrow Wilson edged out Charles Evans Hughes to win a second term. The Democrats' campaign theme emerged when their convention's keynote speaker, in describing Wilson's handling of a series of foreign crises, aroused wild applause as he ended each account with the refrain "We didn't go to war."

The Republican Hughes flip-flopped, both criticizing Wilson for not being aggressive enough and rebuking him for pursuing policies that might lead to war. An ever more bloodthirsty Theodore Roosevelt, prodding Hughes toward greater militance (and thereby hurting Hughes's chances with antiwar voters), campaigned more for war than for the Republican ticket. The only difference between Wilson and the bearded Hughes, Roosevelt jeered, was a shave. Hughes did well among Irish-Americans and German-Americans, who considered Wilson excessively pro-British; Wilson's policies, on the other hand, won him solid support from women voters in those western states that had adopted woman suffrage. Above all, Wilson's victory, close as it was, revealed the strength of the American people's desire for peace as late as November 1916, five months before Wilson led the nation into war.

The United States Enters the War

Early in 1917 Germany's leaders took a fateful step: they resumed unrestricted submarine warfare. From 1914 on, a sharp debate had raged in Berlin between Chancellor Theobald von Bethmann-Hollweg, who favored limiting U-boat warfare to keep the United States neutral, and military leaders who wanted to utilize Ger-

many's U-boats to the maximum. As the war dragged on and a German victory seemed no nearer, Bethmann-Hollweg's position weakened. Even if the United States declared war, the generals argued, unrestricted U-boat use could bring victory before an American army reached the front. With billions in American loans already financing the Allied war effort, they further argued, a formal U.S. declaration of war meant little. The military significance of an American war declaration, said one German naval official, would be "zero, zero, zero."

The generals ultimately prevailed, and on January 31, 1917, Germany proceeded once again with unlimited U-boat attacks—a decision almost certain to pull the United States into the war.

Events now rushed forward with the rapidity of a torpedo speeding toward its target. Wilson broke diplomatic relations on February 3. During February and March, U-boats sank five American ships. On February 24, British intelligence informed Washington of a telegram from the German foreign secretary, Alfred Zimmermann, to the German ambassador in Mexico. If Mexico would join in a war against the United States, the cable said, Germany would pledge to restore Mexico's "lost territories" of Texas, Arizona, and New Mexico.

On April 2 Wilson delivered his war message to Congress. A short but bitter debate followed. Senator Robert La Follette of Wisconsin spoke passionately in opposition. The Senate voted 82 to 6 for war, and the House 373 to 50. Three key factors—German attacks on American shipping, U.S. economic investment in the Allied cause, and American cultural links to the Allies, especially England—had converged to draw the United States into the war.

MOBILIZING AT HOME, FIGHTING IN FRANCE

Compared to European nations, the United States was touched relatively lightly by World War I. The European states fought for more than four years; the United States, for nineteen months. Their armies suffered casualties of 70 percent or more; the American army's casualty rate was 8 percent. The fighting left parts of France and Belgium brutally scarred; the American homeland was untouched. Nevertheless, the war marked a profound turning point in American history. Not only did it change the lives of the hundreds of thousands of men who fought in it, but it deeply affected the American home front and transformed the nation's government and economy.

Raising an Army

The U.S. declaration of war in April 1917 found America's military woefully unprepared. The regular army consisted of 120,000 enlisted men, few with combat experience, plus some 80,000 recently federalized National Guardsmen. An aging officer corps dozed away the years until retirement.* Enough ammunition was on hand for only two days of fighting. The War Department was a snake pit of jealous bureaucrats, one of whom hoarded twelve thousand typewriters as the war approached.

To raise an army and organize the military constituted the most immediate challenges. The brilliant army chief of staff Peyton C. Marsh handled the latter task, and Wilson's secretary of war, Newton D. Baker, took on the former. The fast-talking reform mayor of Cleveland, Baker was a poor administrator but a public-relations genius. The Selective Service Act of May 18, 1917, required all young men between twenty-one and thirty (later expanded to eighteen and forty-five) to register for military service. Mindful of the Civil War draft riots, Baker carefully planned the first official draft-registration day, June 5, 1917, as a "festival and patriotic occasion."

Each registrant received a number, and draftees were chosen by lottery, with a blindfolded Newton D. Baker presiding. In contrast to the policy during the Civil War, local civilian draft boards rather than the military managed the draft. By November 1918 more than 24 million men had registered, of whom nearly 3 million were drafted. Volunteers and National Guardsmen swelled the total to 4.3 million.

Thanks to a precedent-breaking decision by Secretary of the Navy Josephus Daniels, eleven thousand women served in the navy in World War I, and several hundred in the marines. Shielded from combat duty, these women worked as nurses, secretaries, and telephone operators.

The War Department originally planned for several months of training, but some draftees embarked

Building an Army
Uniformed young women dubbed "Marinettes" post marine recruitment posters in New York City.

for France after only a few weeks. Thousands of draftees sweated through the American Psychological Association's new "IQ" (intelligence quotient) tests. The results revealed not only the low educational level of many recruits but also the class and cultural biases of the test writers. One question, for example, asked whether *mauve* was a drink, a color, a fabric, or a food. When the psychologists announced that 50 percent of the whites and 90 percent of the blacks taking the tests had scored at the "moron" level, editorial writers anxiously discussed the rising tide of imbecility supposedly sweeping the nation.

In the training camps, young men got their first taste of military discipline and, for many, their first experience of the world beyond their hometown or native farm. When not taking tests, doing calisthenics, peeling potatoes, or mastering the bayonet, the soldiers watched movies, attended vaudeville shows, or read books supplied by the American Library Association.

---

*The last Civil War veteran in the army, Colonel John Clem (a drummer boy at the Battle of Shiloh), had retired only two years before.

Entertainment and recreational facilities were provided by volunteer organizations whose activities were coordinated by the Commission on Training Camp Activities, a War Department agency responsible for the recruits' moral welfare.

Organizing the Economy for War

The coming of war in 1917 brought not only military mobilization but also unprecedented government oversight of the economy. Populists and progressives had long urged more public control of corporations and had taken steps in this direction. Now, wartime saw the construction of an elaborate framework of oversight and supervision.

In 1916 Congress had created an advisory body, the Council of National Defense, to oversee the government's preparedness program. In 1917 this council set up the War Industries Board (WIB) to coordinate military purchasing, assure production efficiency, and meet the military's needs for weapons, equipment, and supplies. The WIB limped along until March 1918, when Wilson reorganized it and put Bernard Baruch in charge.

A courtly South Carolinian of German-Jewish background, Baruch had made a fortune as a Wall Street stock speculator. Wilson, awed by Baruch's practical knowledge, called him Dr. Facts. Under Dr. Facts, the WIB exercised enormous control over the industrial sector. In addition to allocating raw materials, the board established production priorities and introduced all kinds of efficiencies. As a war measure, the WIB induced companies that had been bitter competitors to standardize and coordinate their production processes to save steel, rubber, and other scarce commodities. The standardization of bicycle manufacturing, for example, saved two thousand tons of steel. Acting under the authority of the Lever Food and Fuel Control Act of August 1917, one of the most far-reaching laws ever enacted in America, Wilson set up two more powerful new agencies, the Fuel Administration and the Food Administration. The Fuel Administration, under Williams College president Harry Garfield, controlled coal output, regulated fuel prices and consumption, and in March 1918 introduced daylight-saving time. Benjamin Franklin, in the 1770s, had first proposed adjusting the clocks to take advantage of the longer summer daylight hours, but it took the war emergency to bring it about.

Herbert Hoover headed the Food Administration. Born in poverty in Iowa, Hoover had prospered as a mining engineer in Asia. He was organizing food relief in Belgium when Wilson brought him back to Washington. The Food Administration oversaw the production

Home-Front Mobilization
The U.S. Food Administration flooded the nation with posters urging wartime food conservation.

Herbert Hoover, Humanitarian
During and after the war, the future president coordinated relief efforts to send food and clothing to war-torn Europe. In 1917–1918 he also headed the U.S. Food Administration.

and allocation of foodstuffs—especially wheat, meat, and sugar—to assure adequate supplies for the army as well as for the desperately food-short Allies. By Hoover's calculations, in 1918 the Allies needed America to supply nearly 2 million tons of meat, 9 million tons of grain, and 1.5 million tons of sugar.

Insofar as possible, these wartime regulatory agencies relied on voluntary cooperation—reinforced by heavy official pressure—to achieve the government's objectives. For example, a barrage of Food Administration posters, magazine advertisements, and other propaganda urged Americans to conserve food. Housewives signed pledges to observe "meatless days" and "wheatless days." President Wilson pitched in by allowing a flock of sheep to be pastured on the White House lawn. Slogans such as "Serve Beans by All Means" promoted substitutes for scarce commodities. In one Food Administration film, a young man wondering how he can help the war effort as he heaps sugar into his coffee is approached by a stern Uncle Sam, who challenges him: "Why don't you help save sugar?"

Harriot Stanton Blatch, a woman-suffrage leader and daughter of women's rights pioneer Elizabeth Cady Stanton, headed the Speakers' Bureau of the Food Administration, which helped spread the conservation message. Blatch also organized the Woman's Land Army, which recruited female volunteers as replacements for male farm workers who had been drafted.

The War Industries Board, the Fuel Administration, and the Food Administration represented only the tip of the regulatory iceberg. Nearly five thousand government agencies supervised home-front activities during the war. The Overman Act of May 1918 gave President Wilson ultimate control of this tangle of federal agencies, including the Railroad Administration, the Shipping Board, and the National War Labor Board, which resolved labor-management disputes that jeopardized production. When a massive railroad tie-up during the snowy winter of 1917–1918 threatened the flow of supplies to Europe, the government simply took over the system. Within a few months, the Railroad Administration, headed by Secretary of the Treasury William G. McAdoo, transformed the four hundred thousand miles of track owned by nearly three thousand competing companies into an efficient national transportation system.

American business, much criticized by progressive reformers, utilized the war emergency to improve its image. Corporate executives poured into Washington as consultants, advisers, and administrators of the wartime regulatory agencies. Factory owners distributed prowar propaganda to their workers. Trade associations mobilized the nation's productive strength behind the war.

The war sped up a process of corporate consolidation and economic integration that had been under way for years. Prodded by Washington, businesses undertook coordinated efforts to make the production and distribution process more rational and efficient. In place of trust-busting, the government now waived the antitrust laws and encouraged industrial cooperation. The number of major corporate mergers in 1917 approached two hundred, more than twice the annual average for the immediate prewar years. Commenting in 1918 on the epidemic of "mergeritis," one magazine observed, "Never before has the civilized world been so committed as now to a policy of giant mergers in industry, to concentration, combination, and consolidation. . . . The war has accelerated . . . a tendency that was already irresistible. . . . Instead of punishing companies for acting in concert, the government is now in some cases forcing them to unite."

While promoting corporate consolidation, the war also proved highly profitable for U.S. business. Although Congress imposed an excess-profits tax to discourage profiteering, the system had many loopholes, and wartime profits mushroomed. Among the nation's leading copper companies, for example, after-tax profits jumped from 12 percent in 1913 to 24 percent in 1917.

This colossal regulatory apparatus fell apart quickly when the war ended, but its influence lingered. The corporate mergers and coordination of the war years, coupled with the climate of business-government cooperation, profoundly affected the evolution of American business. And the old laissez-faire suspicion of government, already weakened, eroded still further in 1917–1918. In the 1930s, when the nation faced a different kind of crisis, the government activism of World War I would be remembered. Many of the government agencies set up in response to the Great Depression (see Chapter 25) were closely modeled on the wartime agencies of 1917–1918.

With the AEF in France

About 2 million soldiers went to France in 1917–1918 as members of the American Expeditionary Force (AEF) under General John J. Pershing. Ironically, Pershing was of German origin; his family name had originally been Pfoersching. A West Point graduate and commander of the 1916 Mexican expedition against

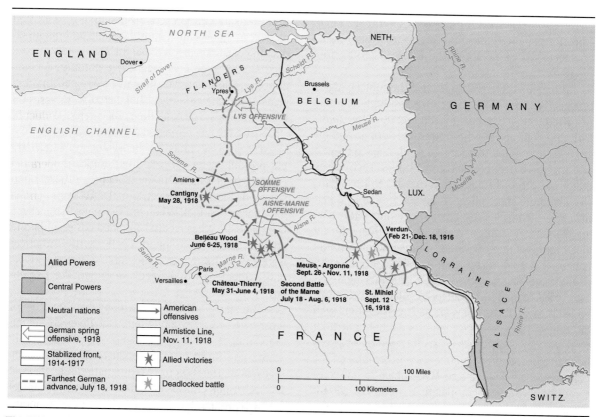

The United States on the Western Front, 1918

American troops first saw action in the campaign to throw back Germany's spring 1918 offensive in the Somme and Aisne-Marne sectors. The next heavy American engagement came that autumn as part of the Allies' Meuse-Argonne offensive that ended the war.

Pancho Villa, Pershing was an iron-willed officer with a ramrod bearing, steely eyes, and trim mustache. The death of his wife and three of their four children in a San Francisco fire in 1915 had further hardened him.

For most men of the AEF, the war at first seemed what Theodore Roosevelt called it: a great adventure. Most had never journeyed far from home, and now they were en route to Europe! They made the voyage on crowded freighters or, for a lucky few, captured German passenger liners. Once in France, freight cars marked "HOMMES 40, CHEVAUX 8" (40 men, 8 horses) transported them to the front. Then began the routine of marching, training—and waiting. The Young Men's Christian Association (YMCA), Red Cross, and Salvation Army provided recreation and a touch of home. Many young American women volunteered in these centers for servicemen. AEF members who spent the war behind the lines would recall French hospitality and culture fondly.

France offered other diversions as well, and the U.S. military conducted a massive campaign, including lectures, posters, and films, warning of the danger of venereal disease. One poster declared, "A German bullet is cleaner than a whore." When the French premier, Georges Clemenceau, offered to provide prostitutes for the American troops (as was the custom for French soldiers), Secretary of War Baker exclaimed, "For God's sake, don't show this to the President, or he'll stop the war."

On the Western Front, aerial dogfights between German and Allied reconnaissance planes offered spectacular sideshows. The most famous of the World War I air aces, Germany's legendary "Red Baron," Manfred von Richthofen, shot down eighty British and French planes before his luck finally ran out in April 1918. In 1916 a group of American volunteers joined the French air corps as the *Lafayette Escadrille*. Secretary of War Baker, convinced of the airplane's military possibilities, persuaded Congress to appropriate large sums for plane construction. Few were actually built, however—a rare failure of the U.S. war-production program.

When the United States entered the conflict, Allied prospects looked bleak. Germany's resumption of unrestricted U-boat warfare took a horrendous toll on Allied shipping: six hundred thousand tons in March 1917, nine hundred thousand in April. A failed French offensive on the Marne that spring caused such losses that French troops mutinied. A massive British offensive along the French-Belgian border ground to a halt near Passchendaele, Belgium, in November 1917, having gained four miles at a cost of more than 100,000 killed and wounded per mile. That same month, the Italian army suffered a disastrous defeat at Caporetto near the Austrian border, losing 275,000 prisoners.*

To make matters worse for the Allies in 1917, Russia left the war. Russia for years had been seething with discontent. Landless peasants, exploited industrial workers, university intellectuals inspired by Western liberal values, and revolutionaries who embraced the communist ideology of Karl Marx joined in hatred of the repressive and incompetent government of Tsar Nicholas II. In March 1917 a revolutionary uprising including all these elements overthrew the tsar. A provisional government under the liberal Alexander Kerensky took power.

But Kerensky's government faltered as the Marxist revolutionaries maneuvered to seize power. One faction of the divided revolutionary party, called bolsheviks (the Russian word for *majority*), gained the initiative in April when its top leaders, including Vladimir Lenin, returned from exile in Switzerland. (The Germans, hoping that a victorious Lenin would take Russia out of the war, had permitted him and his party to pass through Germany in a sealed train.)

On November 6, 1917 (October 24 by the Russian calendar), a bolshevik armed coup led by Lenin and Leon Trotsky, another exile who had recently arrived from New York City, overthrew Kerensky and seized power. Capitalizing on the war weariness of the Russian people, the new leaders signed an armistice with Germany, which freed many thousands of German troops on the Russian front for fighting in France.

In these desperate circumstances, the French and British generals urgently wished to incorporate the Americans into already established units. But for both military and political reasons, Pershing and his superiors in Washington insisted that the AEF be "distinct and separate." A believer in aggressive combat, Pershing abhorred the defensive mentality ingrained by three years of trench warfare. Further, he correctly surmised that America's voice at the peace table would be stronger if the AEF remained a distinct fighting force.

The first AEF units reached France in June 1917, but not until early 1918 did the Americans see much combat. In March, Germany launched a major offensive along the Somme River, aimed at France's ports on the English Channel. When the Germans made alarming gains, the Allies created a unified command under French general Ferdinand Foch. Some American troops were thrown into the fighting around Amiens and Armentières that finally stemmed the German advance.

The second phase of Germany's spring 1918 offensive came in May along the Aisne River. By the end of the month, the Germans had broken through to the Marne and faced a nearly open route to Paris, fifty miles away. The French government prepared for evacuation. At this critical moment, on June 4, American forces arrived in strength. Parts of three U.S. divisions* and a marine brigade helped stop the Germans at the town of Château-Thierry and nearby Belleau Wood, a huge German machine-gun nest.

These two German offensives had punched deep holes (or *salients*, in military language) in the Allied line. A final German drive aimed at the cathedral city of Rheims in the middle of the line between these two salients was stopped with the help of some eighty-five thousand American troops. This Allied rebuff represented the war's crucial turning point. At enormous cost, the Germans' desperate effort to break the Allied line had been defeated.

Turning the Tide

The Allied offensive that would end the war began on July 18, 1918. Of the 1 million American soldiers now on French soil, 270,000 fought in a successful drive to push the Germans back from their positions along the Marne. Rain pelted down as the Americans moved into position on the night of July 17. One wrote in his diary,

---

*Initially neutral, Italy entered the war in 1915 on the side of the Allies.

*In World War I an AEF division at full strength consisted of 27,000 men and 1,000 officers, plus 12,000 support troops. Each division was split into four infantry regiments.

Oppy Wood,
by John Nash, 1917
This stark painting of a front-line strongpoint near Arras in northern France conveys the unearthly desolation of trench warfare after three years of often stalemated combat.

"Trucks, artillery, infantry columns, cavalry, wagons, caissons, mud, MUD, utter confusion." Meanwhile, more than 100,000 AEF members joined in a British offensive north of the Somme that at last expelled the Germans.

Pershing's first independent command came in September, when Foch authorized an American campaign to close a German salient around the town of St. Mihiel on the Meuse River, about 150 miles east of Paris. Seizing the chance to test his strategy of hard-hitting offense, Pershing assembled nearly 500,000 American and 100,000 French soldiers. Shelling of German positions began at 1:00 A.M. on September 11. Recorded an American in his diary, "It was zero hour and in one instant the entire front . . . was a sheet of flame, while the heavy artillery made the earth quake." Within four days the salient was closed, in part because some German units were already withdrawing when the attack began. Even so, St. Mihiel cost the United States seven thousand casualties.

The war's last major battle began on September 26, as some 1.2 million Americans joined in the struggle to drive the Germans from the Meuse River and the dense, ravine-filled Argonne Forest north of Verdun, a region scarred by four years of trench warfare. The stench of poison gas hung in the air, and bloated rats scurried in the mud, gorging on human remains. Whole areas reeked of decaying flesh. Americans now endured the filth, vermin, and dysentery from polluted water familiar to veterans of the trenches. Frontline troops would never forget the terror of combat. As shells whizzed overhead one particularly dark night, recalled a veteran, "We simply lay and trembled from sheer nervous tension." Some welcomed injuries as a ticket out of the battle zone. Others collapsed emotionally and were hospitalized for "shell shock."

The Allied high command assigned the AEF to advance to the city of Sedan and cut the four-track Sedan-Mezières Railroad, a major German supply route. In the way lay three long, heavily fortified German trenches, called *Stellung*. Teddy Roosevelt's joyous adventure seemed far away in the Meuse-Argonne campaign. "We are not men anymore, just savage beasts," wrote a young American after the battle. Wholesale death came in many forms, and without ceremony. Bodies, packs, rifles, photos of loved ones, and letters from home sank indiscriminately into the all-consuming mud.

Adding to the horror was an influenza epidemic that took many lives on the battle front as well as in training camps and cities back home. The strain reached even the iron-willed Pershing. One day as he rode in his staff car, he buried his head in his hands and moaned his dead wife's name: "Frankie, Frankie, my God, sometimes I don't know how I can go on."

Religious principles and ethical scruples seemed irrelevant as young men struggled to survive in a setting where the only rule was kill or be killed. "Love of thy neighbor is forgotten," recalled one, together with "all the falsities of a sheltered civilization." The war's obscene brutality would shape the literature of the 1920s as writers such as Ernest Hemingway stripped away the illusions obscuring the reality of mass slaughter.

But the AEF at last overran the dreadful *Stellung*, and the survivors slogged northward. In early November the Sedan-Mezières railroad was cut. The AEF had fulfilled its assignment, at a cost of 26,277 dead.

African-Americans in the AEF

More than 260,000 blacks volunteered or were drafted in World War I, and 50,000 of them went to France. Racism pervaded the military, as it did American society itself. The navy assigned blacks only to menial positions, and the marines excluded them altogether. When the war began, the army hastily retired its senior black officer, Colonel Charles Young, on dubious medical grounds. Young rode on horseback from Ohio to Washington, D.C., to prove his fitness, but to no avail.

One racist senator from Mississippi, warning that the sight of "arrogant, strutting," black soldiers would trigger race riots, urged that blacks not be drafted at all. Indeed, blacks in many training camps experienced crude racial abuse. Tension reached the breaking point in Houston in August 1917, when some black members of the Twenty-fourth Infantry, endlessly goaded by local whites, seized weapons from the armory and killed seventeen whites. After a hasty trial with no opportunity for appeal, thirteen black soldiers were hanged and forty-one imprisoned for life. Not since the Brownsville Incident of 1906 (see Chapter 22) had black confidence in military justice been so shaken.

Once in France, blacks worked mainly as messboys (mealtime aides), laborers, or stevedores (ship-cargo handlers). Although reflecting a pattern of discrimination, these assignments in fact significantly aided the war effort. Working sometimes in twenty-four-hour shifts, black stevedores unloaded mountains of supplies from America with impressive efficiency.

One all-black division, the 92d, saw combat in the Meuse-Argonne. In addition, four black infantry regiments served with distinction under French command. One entire regiment (the 369th) received the French Croix de Guerre, and several hundred individual black soldiers were awarded French decorations for bravery.

The Germans showered the blacks of the 92d division with leaflets describing racism in America and urging them to cross over to the German lines, but none did. Some whites of the AEF, seeking to infect the French with their own racism, urged them to treat the blacks as inferiors. Most French people ignored this advice, however, and at least superficially treated blacks as equals. For black members of the AEF, this eye-opening experience would remain with them after the war.

PROMOTING THE WAR AND SUPPRESSING DISSENT

As neutralist sentiment faded, patriotic fervor pervaded American society in 1917–1918. It reflected in part an elaborate government propaganda campaign to whip up enthusiasm for the war. As patriotism spread, it brought in its wake stifling intellectual conformity as well as intolerance for radical ideas and dissent of all kinds. Fueling this repressive spirit, government authorities and private vigilante groups hounded and arrested socialists, pacifists, and other dissidents and in the process trampled the constitutional rights of thousands.

Advertising the War

President Wilson viewed the war at home as no less important than the war in France. "It is not an army we must shape and train for war, it is a nation," he declared. Wilson's rhetoric revealed his awareness that millions of Americans opposed the war. Indeed, immediately after the president's call for war, a thousand anti-war demonstrators besieged Senator Lodge and his prowar congressional colleagues on the Capitol steps. The opponents of the war represented many diverse viewpoints, but collectively they posed a formidable barrier to Wilson's dream of rallying the nation behind his crusade for a new and finer world order.

Liberty Bond Rally, New York City, 1917
The Wilson administration was especially eager to persuade immigrant and ethnic groups to support the war effort. In this war-bond rally, Chinese-Americans portray (left to right) China, Miss Liberty, and Uncle Sam.

Seeking initially to overcome domestic opposition by persuasion rather than coercion, the administration drew upon the new professions of advertising and public relations to sell the war to Americans. Treasury Secretary McAdoo (who had married Woodrow Wilson's daughter Eleanor in 1914) orchestrated a series of government bond drives, called Liberty Loans, that financed a good share of the $35.5 billion (including loans to the Allies) that World War I cost the United States. The five Liberty Loan campaigns conducted between 1917 and 1919 raised more than $21 billion, or about two-thirds of the nation's war costs. As a consequence of this heavy wartime borrowing, the national debt rose from $1 billion in 1914 to nearly $27 billion in 1919.

McAdoo promoted the Liberty Loan drives with enormous ballyhoo. Posters exhorted citizens, "FIGHT OR BUY BONDS." Liberty Loan parades featured flags, banners, and marching bands. Movie stars like Douglas Fairbanks, Mary Pickford, and Charlie Chaplin worked for the cause. Schoolchildren contributed nickels and dimes for "thrift stamps" convertible into government bonds. Beneath the hucksterism ran an undercurrent of coercion. Only "a friend of Germany," McAdoo warned, would refuse to buy bonds.

The remaining one-third of the government's war costs came from taxes. Taking advantage of its new power to tax individual incomes granted by the Sixteenth Amendment (ratified in 1913), Congress imposed stiff wartime income taxes that rose as high as 70 percent at the top income levels. War-profits taxes, excise taxes on liquor and luxuries, and increased estate taxes also helped finance the war.

George Creel, a progressive reformer and journalist, headed Washington's most effective wartime propaganda agency, the Committee on Public Information (CPI). Established in April 1917, ostensibly to combat wartime rumors with facts, the Creel committee in reality functioned as a propaganda agency, proclaiming the government's version of reality and discrediting all who questioned that version.

Brimming with energy and ideas, Creel set up twenty-one separate divisions to handle different aspects of the CPI's campaign. One division, for example, distributed thousands of posters drawn by leading illustrators. Still another wrote propaganda releases that appeared in the press as "news" with no indication of their source. The *Saturday Evening Post* and other popular magazines published CPI ads that warned against spies, saboteurs, and anyone who "spreads pessimistic stories" or "cries for peace." Theaters screened CPI propaganda films bearing such titles as *The Kaiser: The Beast of Berlin*.

The CPI particularly targeted recent immigrants, who were presumed to be of dubious loyalty. It poured foreign-language pamphlets into immigrant neighborhoods and supplied prowar editorials to the foreign-language press. At a CPI media event held at Mount Vernon on July 4, 1918, an Irish-born tenor sang "The Battle Hymn of the Republic" while immigrants from thirty-three nations filed reverently past George Washington's tomb.

The CPI also targeted the working class. Factory posters refuted the socialists' charge that the war was a capitalists' war. Creel's committee quietly financed an "American Alliance for Labor and Democracy" headed by labor leader Samuel Gompers.

Creel hatched the idea of the "four minute men": a network of seventy-five thousand speakers across the nation who gave short, patriotic talks to audiences of all kinds on topics assigned by the CPI. Creel later calculated that this small army of propagandists delivered 7.5 million speeches.

Intellectuals, Cultural Leaders, and Reformers Present Arms

The nation's teachers, writers, religious leaders, and magazine editors overwhelmingly supported the war. These custodians of culture saw the conflict as a struggle to defend threatened values. Historians wrote essays contrasting Germany's glorification of brute force with the Allies' loftier ideals. Novelist Robert Herrick predicted a "resurrection of nobility" due to the war. In *The Marne* (1918), expatriate American writer Edith Wharton expressed her love for her adopted nation, France. The war poems of Alan Seeger enjoyed great popularity in wartime America. A Harvard graduate who volunteered to fight for France in 1914 and died in action in 1916, Seeger held a romantic vision of war that many Americans longed to share. An artillery barrage was for him "the magnificent orchestra of war." The "sense of being the instrument of Destiny," wrote Seeger, represented the "supreme experience" of combat.

Many progressive reformers who had applauded Wilson's domestic program now cheered his war. The wartime climate of government activism and sacrifice for the common good, they believed, would encourage further reform activity. Some of George Creel's coworkers in the Committee on Public Information were former muckraking writers. Herbert Croly, Walter Lippmann, and other progressive intellectuals associated with the *New Republic* magazine zealously supported the war. In gratitude, Wilson administration officials met regularly with the *New Republic*'s editors to brief them on the government's policies.

The liberal philosopher and educational reformer John Dewey joined the prowar chorus. In a series of *New Republic* pieces in 1917–1918, Dewey condemned the war's opponents. Socially engaged intellectuals, he said, must accept reality as they found it and shape it toward positive social goals, not stand aside in self-righteous isolation. The war, he went on, presented exciting "social possibilities" as an instrument for betterment at home and abroad. Domestically, the wartime growth of government power could be channeled to reform purposes once peace returned. Internationally, America's entry into the war could transform a crude imperialistic clash into a global democratic crusade. Dewey's seductive argu-

ments persuaded many progressive reformers to support the war.

Other intellectuals exploited the war for their own purposes. Harvard psychologist Robert M. Yerkes, for example, trumpeted the IQ tests administered to draftees as evidence of psychology's importance and social usefulness. A 1918 article in *Science* magazine proclaimed that the war offered all American scientists "an immediate opportunity of proving their worth to their country."

Wartime Intolerance

Responding to this drumfire of propaganda, some Americans became almost hysterical in their hatred of all things German, their hostility to aliens and dissenters, and their strident patriotism. Isolated acts by German saboteurs, including the blowing up of a New Jersey munitions dump, fanned the flames. German-Americans, as well as citizens suspected of harboring pro-German sentiments, were forced to kiss the flag or recite the Pledge of Allegiance. A woman in Canton, Ohio, was wrapped in a flag, marched to a bank, and ordered to buy a war bond. In Collinsville, Illinois, a mob of five hundred lynched the German-born Robert Prager in April 1918. When a jury exonerated the mob leaders, a jury member shouted, "Nobody can say we aren't loyal now." The *Washington Post*, although deploring the lynching, viewed it as evidence of "a healthful and wholesome awakening in the interior of the country."

An Iowa politician announced that "90 percent of all the men and women who teach the German language are traitors." German books vanished from libraries, towns with German names changed them, and on some restaurant menus, "liberty sandwich" and "liberty cabbage" replaced "hamburger" and "sauerkraut." A popular evangelist, Billy Sunday, proclaimed, "If you turn hell upside down you will find 'Made in Germany' stamped on the bottom."

Even the music world suffered. The Boston Symphony Orchestra dismissed its conductor, Karl Muck, for accepting a decoration from the kaiser. Leopold Stokowski of the Philadelphia Orchestra dropped German opera, songs, and contemporary orchestral music from the repertoire but asked President Wilson whether Bach, Beethoven, Mozart, and Brahms might not be retained.

The zealots fell with special ferocity on war critics and radicals. A mob hauled a Cincinnati pacifist minister off to a woods and partially stripped and whipped him. Theodore Roosevelt branded antiwar senator Robert La Follette "an unhung traitor." Columbia University's president fired two antiwar professors. In Bisbee, Arizona, a vigilante mob forced twelve hundred miners who belonged to the Industrial Workers of the World onto a freight train and shipped them into the New Mexico desert without food, water, or shelter.

Opponents of the War

Despite the overheated conformist climate, a few Americans refused to support the war. Some were German-Americans with ties of memory and ancestry to the land of their forebears. Others were religious pacifists, including Quakers, Mennonites, and members of other historic peace churches. Of the more than sixty-five thousand men who registered as conscientious objectors (COs), twenty-one thousand were drafted. The army assigned most of these to "noncombatant" duty on military bases, such as cleaning latrines. In some camps these COs experienced great abuse. When two Hutterite brothers who had refused to wear military uniforms died in prison, their bodies were dressed in uniforms before they were shipped home.

Jane Addams, a founder of the Woman's Peace party in 1915, remained a pacifist throughout the war, alienating many of her friends and reform colleagues. (She did, however, lecture for the Food Administration's Speakers' Bureau, because she viewed increased food production as a way to help the war's innocent victims.) In *Peace and Bread in Time of War* (1922), Addams described the loneliness and ostracism that she experienced during the war as a result of her unpopular pacifist stance.

Woodrow Wilson heaped scorn on the pacifists. "What I am opposed to is not [their] feeling . . . , but their stupidity," he told a labor audience in November 1917; "my heart is with them, but my mind has contempt for them. I want peace, but I know how to get it, and they do not."

Socialist leaders, including Eugene V. Debs and Victor Berger, opposed the war on political grounds. They regarded it simply as a capitalist contest for world markets, with the soldiers on both sides as cannon fodder. The U.S. declaration of war, they insisted, reflected mainly Wall Street's desire to protect its loans to England and France.

The war split the American women's movement. Whereas some leaders like Jane Addams opposed the war, others endorsed it. Most offered qualified support while keeping their own goals firmly in view. Anna Howard Shaw, for example, a former president of the National American Woman Suffrage Association (NAWSA), agreed to chair the Woman's Committee of the wartime Council of National Defense. Despite her seventy years, Shaw did her stubborn best in this largely symbolic post to bring a feminist perspective to bear on wartime policy.

Carrie Chapman Catt
The head of the National American Woman Suffrage Association supported the U.S. war effort in 1917–1918 while insisting that the suffrage campaign go forward as well.

Although Carrie Chapman Catt, Shaw's successor as president of NAWSA, joined Jane Addams in founding the Woman's Peace party in 1915, she supported U.S. entry into the war in 1917, sharing to some extent Wilson's vision of a more liberal postwar world order. But Catt continued to direct her primary energies to the suffrage cause, insisting that this remained NAWSA's "number one war job." For this, some superpatriots accused her of disloyalty.

One of the votes against Wilson's call for a declaration of war in the House of Representatives was cast by the pacifist Jeannette Rankin of Montana, the first woman elected to Congress. "I want to stand by my country," she declared emotionally on the House floor, "but I cannot vote for war." The war's most incisive critic was Randolph Bourne, a young journalist. Although Bourne admired John Dewey, he rejected Dewey's prowar position and dissected his arguments in penetrating essays published in 1917–1918. Like moths near a flame, Bourne said, intellectuals found action and power mesmerizing. He dismissed as a self-serving delusion the belief that liberal reformers could direct the war to their own purposes. War took on its own terrible momentum, he wrote, and could no more be controlled by intellectuals than a rogue elephant crashing through the bush. "If the war is too strong for you to prevent," he asked, "how is it going to be weak enough for you to control and mould to your liberal purposes?"

Ultimately, Dewey, Lippmann, and other prowar intellectuals came to agree with Bourne. By 1919 Dewey conceded that the war, far from promoting liberalism, had unleashed the forces of reaction and intolerance. Randolph Bourne did not live to see his vindication, however. He died, at thirty-two, in the influenza epidemic of 1918–1919.

Suppressing Dissent by Law

Wartime intolerance also found expression in federal laws and in the actions of government officials. The Espionage Act of June 1917 prescribed fines of up to ten thousand dollars and prison sentences of up to twenty years for a variety of loosely defined antiwar activities. The even more severe Sedition Amendment to the Espionage Act (May 1918) imposed heavy penalties on anyone convicted of using "disloyal, profane, scurrilous, or abusive language" about the government, the Constitution, the flag, or the military.

Wilson's reactionary attorney general, Thomas W. Gregory of Texas, employed these measures to stamp out dissent. Opponents of the war, proclaimed Gregory, should expect no mercy "from an outraged people and an avenging government." Under this sweeping legislation and similar state laws, the authorities arrested some fifteen hundred pacifists, socialists, and others who dared to speak or write against the war. One socialist, Rose Pastor Stokes, found herself facing ten years behind bars (the sentence was later commuted) for telling an audience of women, "I am for the people, and the government is for the profiteers." Kate Richards O'Hare, a midwestern socialist organizer, served more than a year in prison for allegedly telling a small audience in Bowman, North Dakota, "The women of the United States are nothing more than brood sows, to raise children to get into the army and be made into fertilizer." (O'Hare denied having used these words, though she readily admitted to delivering antiwar lectures.) Eugene V. Debs was sentenced to ten years in a federal penitentiary for a noninflammatory speech discussing the economic causes of war.

The Espionage Act also authorized the postmaster general to bar from the mail a wide variety of suspect material—a provision enforced by Postmaster General Albert S. Burleson, a pompous, radical-hating superpatriot. Burleson suppressed a number of socialist periodicals. In January 1919 Congressman-elect Victor Berger received a twenty-year prison sentence (later set aside by the Supreme Court) and was denied his seat in the House of Representatives for publishing antiwar articles in his socialist newspaper, the *Milwaukee Leader*. According to socialist Norman Thomas, Burleson "didn't know socialism from rheumatism," but he blundered ahead with his repressive crusade. A patriotic outfit designating itself the American Protective League, and local volunteer groups called "Councils of Defense," operating with vague governmental authorization, further enforced ideological conformity and sniffed out anyone who expressed reservations about the war.

A few citizens protested. Muckraking journalist Upton Sinclair wrote to President Wilson to deplore that a man of Albert Burleson's "pitiful and childish ignorance" should wield such power; but Wilson did little to restrain either his postmaster general or his attorney general. Nor did the U.S. Supreme Court. In three 1919 decisions, the Court upheld the Espionage Act convictions of antiwar activists. In one, *Schenck* v. *United States*, Justice Oliver Wendell Holmes, Jr., justified such repression when the exercise of the constitutional right of free speech posed a "clear and present danger" to the nation. In another decision, the Supreme Court upheld the conviction of Eugene V. Debs under the Espionage Act. Although the war was over, a vindictive Woodrow Wilson refused to commute Debs's sentence.*

The wartime mood, originally one of idealism and high resolve, had degenerated into fearful suspicion, narrow ideological conformity, and persecution of those who failed to meet the zealots' notions of "100 percent Americanism." The effects of this ugly wartime climate would linger long after the armistice was signed.

ECONOMIC AND SOCIAL TRENDS IN WARTIME AMERICA

Like all wars, World War I brought unanticipated economic and social changes. The war affected the lives of millions of industrial workers, farmers, women, and blacks in important ways. The wartime mood also furthered some progressive reforms and gave a significant boost to the moral-reform movement in American life.

---

*President Warren Harding released the aging Debs in December 1921, but his rights as a U.S. citizen were not restored.

Boom Times in Industry and Agriculture

For all its horrendous toll, World War I brought glowing prosperity to the American economy. From 1914 to 1918, factory output grew by more than one-third. Despite the mobilization of several million men into military service, the civilian work force grew by 1.3 million from 1916 to 1918, including many women and blacks, and unemployment dwindled. The "Help Wanted" signs appeared most often in war-related industries such as shipbuilding, munitions, steel, and textiles. Wages rose as well, but so did prices, which soared by 60 percent during the war. With manual labor in demand in factories and mills, however, the real wages of *unskilled* workers increased by nearly 20 percent from 1914 to 1918.

A no-strike rule prevailed in American industry during the war. Samuel Gompers, the prowar head of the American Federation of Labor, ordered AFL workers to stay on the job for the duration. (Some maverick AFL locals, as well as members of the more radical Industrial Workers of the World, ignored Gompers and went on strike anyway.) Despite the strike ban, union membership rose from 2.7 million in 1916 to more than 5 million by 1920. In part, this growth reflected the pro-union policies of the National War Labor Board, which guaranteed workers' right to organize and to bargain collectively with management.

The economic boom brought social disruption as well as prosperity. The stream of job seekers pouring into industrial centers strained housing, schools, and municipal services to the limit (see "A Place in Time"). The changes in social behavior took many forms. For example, the consumption of cigarettes, which soldiers and workers could conveniently carry in their uniform pockets, increased nearly 350 percent, from 14 billion in 1914 to 48 billion in 1918. Automobile production quadrupled, from 460,000 in 1914 to 1.8 million in 1917. (The output of cars dipped briefly in 1918, when the government appropriated extra steel for military production.)

Agriculture profited, too. With European farm production disrupted, U.S. agricultural prices more than doubled in 1913–1918, and farmers' real income rose significantly. Planters who sold cotton for 12¢ a pound in 1913 received 29¢ a pound by 1918. Corn prices soared from 70¢ a bushel to $1.52 a bushel in the same five-year period.

This agricultural boom proved a mixed blessing. Many farmers borrowed heavily to expand production, and when the artificially high prices of agricultural commodities collapsed after the war, they faced a credit squeeze. During tough times in the 1920s and 1930s, many farmers would look back to the war years as the last period of real prosperity.

Blacks Migrate Northward

The war speeded up the exodus of southern blacks. An estimated half-million African-Americans moved northward during the war, and most of them settled in cities. Each day, fresh arrivals from the South trudged through the railroad stations of Chicago, Cleveland, Philadelphia, New York, Detroit, and Pittsburgh. Chicago's black population grew from 44,000 in 1910 to 110,000 in 1920; Cleveland's, from 8,000 to 34,000.

What lured these thousands? Above all, it was economic opportunity. The war dried up the flow of immigrant workers from Europe, and American industry turned to the black population, still heavily southern and rural, to help take up the slack. Black newspapers like the *Chicago Defender,* widely circulated in the South, spread the word of job opportunities. Some companies sent labor agents south to recruit black workers. Letters and word-of-mouth reports swelled the ranks of blacks heading north. One southern black, newly settled near Chicago, wrote home, "Nothing here but money, and it is not hard to get." A Pittsburgh newcomer presented a more balanced picture: "They give you big money for what you do, but they charge you big things for what you get."

To the black sharecropper mired in poverty and confronting blatant racism, the prospect of a salary of three dollars a day or more, in a region where racism seemed less intense, appeared a heaven-sent opportunity. The migration grew steadily; by 1920, 1.5 million American blacks were working in northern factories or other urban-based jobs.

These newcomers brought with them their social institutions—above all, the church. In the black neighborhoods of the North, storefront "holiness" churches sprang up to meet the spiritual needs of deeply religious migrants from the South. The concentration of blacks in New York City laid the groundwork for the Harlem Renaissance, a cultural flowering of the 1920s. This migration also provided recruits for black activist organizations. Membership in the recently founded National Association for the Advancement of Colored People (NAACP) doubled in 1918–1919. Jamaican black nationalist Marcus Garvey saw the opportunities of this

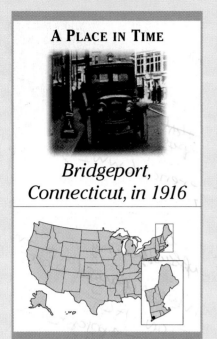
Even before the United States went to war in April 1917, the European conflict had transformed scores of American cities. Financed in part by loans from the Morgan bank and other U.S. financial houses, war orders rolled in from London and Paris—and, more rarely, Berlin—to factories in Pittsburgh, Schenectady, Dayton, Providence, Toledo, Birmingham, and the Du Pont Corporation's munitions plants in Delaware and New Jersey.

The city of Bridgeport, Connecticut, exemplifies both the prosperity and the disruption that the outbreak of hostilities brought to many U.S. industrial centers. Founded as a Puritan settlement on Long Island Sound in 1639, the community had grown slowly and sedately. In the nineteenth century, one of Bridgeport's major claims to fame was as the home of P. T. Barnum. When the irrepressible showman died in 1891, the city turned his lavish mansion, "Iranistan," into a museum.

Bridgeport had a good harbor at the mouth of the Poquonock River, and in the nineteenth century had come mills and factories that produced everything from corsets to Singer sewing machines. In 1914 Bridgeport was a stable, quiet city of about 100,000 inhabitants, its factory district balanced by solid middle-class neighborhoods and tree-lined suburbs.

But within a few months of the onset of war in Europe, Bridgeport found itself in a maelstrom of explosive growth as old factories expanded and new ones sprouted. The Locomobile Company doubled its work force to manufacture thousands of open-bed military trucks (contemporaries called them motor wagons). After being tested on the city's streets with heavy loads of scrap iron, the vehicles were driven to the piers of New York City for the hazardous voyage to Europe. Most of the city's war production went to the Allies—but not all. One large firm, the Bridgeport Projectile Company, secured a major contract to make shells for the Central Powers. With the initiation of the U.S. preparedness program, military contracts from Washington supplemented those from abroad. Bridgeport's Torpedo Boat Company, for example, quadrupled its capacity in 1915 to manufacture submarines for the U.S. Navy.

Among Bridgeport's largest employers before the war was the Union Metallic Cartridge Company, owned by industrialist Marcellus Hartley Dodge. With close ties to the Rockefeller family as well as to the Morgan interests, Dodge secured millions of dollars in European war contracts, and employment at his cartridge company zoomed from 2,200 to 7,000. Early in 1915

Main Street in Bridgeport

Dodge decided to expand his Remington Arms Company in Bridgeport. By early autumn contractors had erected eighteen large interconnected buildings for the manufacture of bayonets and rifles. Hordes of would-be workers lined up at Remington's gates, and for several months the company hired a new person on the average of every ten minutes. By 1916 fifteen thousand men and women were working at Remington.

This sudden prosperity, coming after a business slowdown in 1914, created a boom mentality in the nation's manufacturing belt. After the war the financiers and industrialists who prospered from these military contracts would be criticized as "merchants of death." But in 1915–1916 only a few socialists and pacifists pointed out that the munitions flowing from U.S. factories were contributing to an appalling slaughter on the Western Front. The talk was only of fat payrolls and humming factories. As the news magazine *World's Work* observed in January 1916, "Bridgeport bears witness . . . that war orders pay. . . . Each man, asking his neighbor, 'How's business?' gets the hearty response, 'Never better!' "

The war boom also ushered in unexpected social changes. As fifty thousand workers, most of them single young men and women, flooded Bridgeport, the population explosion strained the city's municipal services to the limit. Half the newcomers were recent immigrants from southern and eastern Europe who introduced strange languages and unfamiliar ways into this staid Yankee town. An obsession with loyalty and security gripped the city. Workers with German-sounding names were denied employment or fired unless they could prove their patriotism to the satisfaction of company management. The two hundred armed guards patrolling the Remington plant admitted workers by special pass only.

Housing posed an urgent problem. Rents and house prices shot sky-high, and soon no accommodations were available at any price. With the factories running twenty-four hours a day, landlords would rent a room to three different tenants, who would then occupy it in eight-hour shifts. When builders put up little new housing, fearing that the war boom would not last, Remington itself erected more than eighty brick residences, as well as temporary dormitories for four thousand young female employees.

Civic and religious leaders worried about the morals of the thousands of young people who thronged the city's streets after work. The few movie theaters and other recreational centers practically burst at the seams. Remington built a gymnasium and organized amateur baseball leagues for its workers. Moralists pointed out the necessity of banning alcohol and prostitutes from wartime Bridgeport.

The sudden boom spawned a series of labor disputes. Employees in the city's other factories demanded the same high wages as the war workers, and during the summer of 1916, fifty-five strikes broke out in Bridgeport. Eager to keep their workers happy in an intensely competitive labor market, employers quickly granted their demands. Wages went up and working hours fell. By the end of 1916, the city's major employers had all adopted the eight-hour workday.

Long before Woodrow Wilson's fateful war message to Congress, the conflict in distant France had transformed an American city. As a magazine writer observed in September 1916, "In the course of a few months, a typical New England town became one of the busiest hives of war industry in America." The ghost of P. T. Barnum, roaming the halls of "Iranistan," must have marveled at what was happening to Bridgeport.

A Laborer at Bridgeport's Remington Arms Company Stamping Out a Bayonet

Women War Workers in the Remington Arms Plant

wartime migration as well. In 1916 Garvey moved his recently founded Universal Negro Improvement Association (UNIA) from Jamaica to New York City. By 1919, with branches in most northern cities, the UNIA stood poised for explosive growth in the 1920s.

Once the initial elation faded, African-Americans newly arrived in northern cities often found that they had exchanged one set of problems for another. White workers resented the labor competition, and white homeowners lashed out as jammed black neighborhoods spilled over into surrounding areas.

A bloody outbreak of violence occurred on July 2, 1917, in East St. Louis, Illinois—home to ten thousand blacks who had recently come from the South. In a well-coordinated action, a white mob torched many black homes and then shot the residents as they fled for their lives. At least thirty-nine blacks perished, including a two-year-old infant who was shot and then thrown into the doorway of a burning house.

A few weeks later, a silent march down New York's Fifth Avenue organized by the NAACP protested racist violence. One banner bore the slogan "Mr. President, Why Not Make AMERICA Safe for Democracy?" Despite the protests, racial enmity in northern cities, like other wartime social trends, did not end with the return of peace.

Women and the War

From one perspective, World War I seems a uniquely male experience. Male politicians and statesmen made the decisions that led to war. Male generals issued the orders that sent other men into battle. Yet any event as vast as war touches all of society, not just half of it. The war affected women differently than men, but it affected them profoundly.

Women's movement leaders like Carrie Chapman Catt and Anna Howard Shaw hoped that the war would lead to equality and greater opportunity for women. In *Mobilizing Woman-Power* (1918), Harriot Stanton Blatch offered a feminist variant of Woodrow Wilson's theme: women should actively support the war, she said, in order to have a role in shaping the peace.

For a brief moment, the war did indeed seem to promise dramatic gains for women. Not only did thousands of women serve directly in the military and in volunteer agencies at home and in France, but in 1917–1918, about 1 million women worked in industry. More thousands held other jobs, from streetcar conductors to bricklayers. "Out of . . . repression into opportunity is the meaning of the war to thousands of women," wrote Florence Thorne of the American Federation of Labor in 1917; "[w]e ought to plan boldly for a splendid world after the war."

Such hopes glowed brightly as the woman suffrage movement sped toward victory in 1917–1918 on a tide of wartime idealism. "The services of women during the supreme crisis have been of the most signal usefulness and distinction," President Wilson wrote Catt; "it is high time that part of our debt should be acknowledged." New York in 1917 passed a state woman-suffrage referendum that had been rejected two years before. Twenty-six states in 1917–1919 petitioned Congress to pass a woman-suffrage amendment to the Constitution, and in 1919, by overwhelming margins, the House and Senate did just that. The Nineteenth Amendment was ratified in 1920.

Beyond this achievement, however, hopes that the war would permanently better women's status proved unfounded. Relatively few women actually entered the work force for the first time in 1917–1918; most simply moved from poor-paying jobs to somewhat better-paying ones. And despite women's protests and War Labor Board rulings, even in these better-paying jobs most earned less than the men they replaced.

As the war ended, women lost their jobs to returning veterans. The New York labor federation advised, "The same patriotism which induced women to enter industry during the war should induce them to vacate their positions after the war." Male streetcar workers in Cleveland went on strike to force women conductors off the job. Twenty women judges in New York were compelled to resign; they had simply been hired as temporary wartime help, officials informed them.

Despite the short-lived rise in employment during the war, the percentage of working women actually declined slightly from 1910 to 1920. As industrial researcher Mary Van Kleeck wrote in 1921, when the emergency ended, traditional male attitudes toward women "came to life once more." Randolph Bourne's bleak vision again proved prophetic. The dark underside of the war spirit—the prejudice, the intolerance, the conformism—survived and flourished after the return of peace; the war's more positive side effects, such as the beginnings of gender equality in the workplace, proved more ephemeral.

The War and Progressivism

The United States entered World War I during a period of intense reform activity at home (see Chapter 22), and many historians have explored the war's effect on the progressive movement. They paint a mixed picture. In the long run, the war unquestionably stifled reform energies and ushered in a decade of reaction. During the war itself, socialists and others who favored a radical overhaul of the capitalist system endured hostility and persecution. And while the war brought increased corporate regulation—a major progressive goal—the wartime regulatory agencies were often dominated by the very business interests supposedly being supervised.

Yet some reform causes clearly did benefit from the war's coming. Not only did the woman-suffrage campaign surge forward, but the years 1917–1918 saw real gains in the movement to better the condition of industrial workers. The War Labor Board not only encouraged workers to join unions but also pushed war plants to introduce the eight-hour workday, which by the war's end became the norm in U.S. industry. The War Department and the War Labor Board also pressed factory owners to observe the federal ban on child labor, to provide worker-compensation benefits, to open their plants to safety and sanitation inspectors, and to observe all state labor legislation. William McAdoo's Railroad Administration, moreover, recognized railway workers' right to unionize. Another wartime agency, the United States Housing Corporation, built housing projects for workers, including some that encompassed schools, playgrounds, and recreational centers.

Social-justice progressives, who had long campaigned for worker-protection laws, now pointed out that such measures would help to win the war by promoting social stability and industrial efficiency. Responding to this appeal, several states during the war banned child labor, set wage-and-hour rules, and enacted various protections and benefits for factory laborers.

Like the wartime movement toward greater employment opportunities for women, this flurry of social-justice reform activity quieted with the return of peace. But the laws remained on the books, creating precedents for future reform efforts.

The war also strengthened the coercive, moral-reform component of the progressive movement, including the drive for prohibition. Nineteen states had already gone dry by 1917, but the war gave a decisive boost to the cause. Exploiting the anti-German hysteria, prohibitionists pointed out that the nation's biggest breweries bore such German names as Pabst, Schlitz, and Anheuser-Busch. Beer, they hinted, was part of a German plot to undermine America's moral fiber and

Counting the Cost
By 1915 the prohibition campaign, reinforced by speakers, tracts, and cartoons like this, was entering its final phase. America's entry into war in 1917 provided the final impetus to ratification of the Eighteenth Amendment.

fighting qualities. And with Herbert Hoover preaching food conservation, they portrayed as unpatriotic and wasteful the use of grain to make whiskey and gin. Secretary of War Baker prohibited liquor sales near military camps and even forbade soldiers in uniform to buy a drink. Thus when the Eighteenth Amendment—banning the manufacture, shipment, or sale of alcoholic beverages—passed Congress in December 1917, it was widely seen as a war measure. Ratified in 1919, the prohibition amendment went into effect on January 1, 1920.

The war also strengthened the Progressive Era antiprostitution campaign, not only in France but on the home front. The War Department closed all brothels near military bases; Congress appropriated $4 million to combat prostitution and venereal disease, especially among war workers; and sixty Young Women's Christian Association (YWCA) lecturers toured the nation for the Commission on Training Camp Activities, warning women to uphold strict standards of sexual morality.

"Do Your Bit to Keep Him Fit," urged one wartime pamphlet addressed to women.

In San Antonio, Texas, a major military hub, the leader of a 1918 antiprostitution meeting reflected the war mood when he declared, "We propose to fight vice and its allies with the cold steel of the law, and to drive in the steel from the point to the hilt until the law's supremacy is acknowledged." Among the 110 red-light districts closed on military orders was New Orleans's famed Storyville. Jazz musicians who had been performing in Storyville's brothels and clubs moved up the Mississippi, carrying their music to Memphis, St. Louis, Kansas City, and Chicago. Thus the moral reformism of World War I helped to bring jazz northward.

The wartime ground swell of moral-reform activity convinced some that traditional codes of behavior, under heavy challenge before the war, had now been restored to dominance. One antiprostitution crusader wrote, "Young men of today . . . are nearer perfection in conduct, morals, and ideals than any similar generation of young men in the history of the world. Their minds have been raised to ideals that would never have been attained save by the heroism of . . . the World War."

JOYOUS ARMISTICE, BITTER AFTERMATH

In November 1918 the war that had battered Europe for more than four years ended at last. Woodrow Wilson dominated the peace conference but failed in his most cherished objective: American membership in the League of Nations. At home, as racism and intolerance worsened, the electorate repudiated Wilsonianism and in 1920 sent Republican Warren G. Harding to the White House.

Wilson's Fourteen Points

From the moment the United States went to war, President Wilson planned to put a "Made in America" stamp on the peace that would follow. U.S. involvement, he and his liberal supporters believed, could transform a sordid power conflict into nothing less than a struggle for a more democratic world order. Many Americans counted on the president to translate that vision into reality.

As the nation mobilized in 1917, Wilson strove to translate his vision into specific war aims. When the Allies failed to agree on a common statement of purpose, Wilson recruited a group of scholarly advisers called the Inquiry and proceeded on his own. The need for a clear statement of America's war objectives grew urgent after the bolsheviks seized power in Russia late in 1917 and published many of the self-serving secret treaties signed by the European powers prior to 1914.

In a speech to Congress in January 1918, Wilson summed up U.S. war aims. These came to be called the "Fourteen Points." Eight of these goals dealt with territorial settlements in postwar Europe, pledging self-determination and autonomy for peoples formerly dominated by the Austro-Hungarian or the Ottoman empires. A ninth point vaguely insisted that colonial disputes must be resolved in the interests of the colonized peoples as well as of the European colonial powers. The remaining five points offered Wilson's larger postwar vision: a world of unrestricted navigation, freer trade, reduced armaments, openly negotiated treaties rather than secret pacts of the kind that had helped bring on war in 1914, and "a general association of nations" to assure permanent peace and resolve conflicts peacefully. The Fourteen Points helped solidify American support for the war, especially among liberals. The high-minded objectives seemed proof that the nation had gone to war not for selfish reasons but out of noble motives. Could Wilson achieve his goals? That remained to be seen.

Armistice

With the failure of Germany's spring 1918 offensive and Allied advances in the Meuse-Argonne and elsewhere, the German high command in early October proposed to Wilson an armistice based on the Fourteen Points. The British and French hesitated, but when Wilson threatened a separate peace, they agreed to make peace on the basis of the Fourteen Points. Meanwhile, in Berlin, Kaiser Wilhelm II had abdicated and a German republic had been proclaimed.

As dawn broke over the Forest of Compiègne on November 11, 1918, Marshal Foch and his German counterparts, seated in Foch's private railway car, signed an armistice. Word spread quickly across the lines: hostilities would cease at 11:00 A.M. An American air ace, Captain Edward Rickenbacker, flew over the lines at precisely 11:00 A.M. and watched as the

The End of the War: Starting Home, *by Horace Pippin, 1931 Americans celebrated the armistice of November 1918 with joy and relief. But for Pippin, a black ex-soldier and folk artist, the war's end was an occasion to reflect on the violence and carnage of the struggle.*

First Lieutenant Harry S Truman
Prevented by weak eyesight from enrolling at West Point, Truman served in the Missouri National Guard and commanded an artillery battalion in France during the First World War. The experience of leadership bolstered his confidence and helped lay the groundwork for his later political career.

booming guns fell silent and as troops cautiously emerged and approached each other. Rockets burst over the front that night, not in anger now but in relief and celebration. Back home, cheering throngs filled the streets, many carrying hand-lettered signs. "LONG LIVE PEACE," blazed one in Chicago. "Everything for which America has fought has been accomplished," Wilson's armistice message hopefully proclaimed.

Soon crowded troop transports were ferrying proud and relieved soldiers home. One returnee, artillery captain Harry S Truman of Missouri, in a letter to his fiancée, Bess Wallace, described his feelings upon entering New York Harbor:

Dear Bess,

I've never seen anything that looks so good as the Liberty Lady in New York Harbor and the mayor's welcoming boat, which came down the river to meet us. You know the men have seen so much and have been in so many hard places that it takes something real to give them a thrill, but when the band on that boat played "Home Sweet Home" there were not many dry eyes. The hardest of hard-boiled cookies even had to blow his nose a time or two.

The Versailles Peace Conference

The fighting was over, but the task of forging a peace treaty remained. Determined to play a central role, Wilson made a crucial decision: he would lead the American delegation to the peace conference. This was probably a mistake. The strain of protracted bargaining quickly took its toll on his frail nerves and slim reserve of energy.

Wilson compounded his mistake in choosing his fellow peace commissioners: the sole Republican was an elderly diplomat who lacked influence in his party's circles. The appointment of one or two prominent Republicans might have spared Wilson much future grief. A further ill omen came in the November 1918 congressional elections. Despite Wilson's plea to the electorate to strengthen his hand at the peace conference by voting Democratic, the Republicans gained control of both houses of Congress.

Nevertheless, spirits soared on December 4, 1918, as the *George Washington,* a converted German liner, steamed out of New York bearing Woodrow Wilson to Europe—the first president to cross the Atlantic while in office. Ships' whistles blared; small planes buzzed overhead; and a jaunty Wilson waved his hat to the crowd on the docks. The giddy mood continued when the *George Washington* arrived at the French port of Brest. In Paris shouts of "Voodrow Veelson" rang out as Wilson and the French president rode in a parade up the Champs-Élysées, the city's ceremonial boulevard. When Wilson visited England, children at the dock in Dover spread flowers in his path. In Italy an exuberant local official compared his visit to the Second Coming of Jesus Christ.

The exhilaration evaporated quickly, however, when the peace conference began on January 18, 1919, at the palace of Versailles near Paris. A so-called Council of Four, comprising the Allied heads of state, dominated the proceedings: Wilson; Italy's Vittorio Orlando; the aged and cynical Georges Clemenceau of France, determined to avenge Germany's humiliating defeat of France in 1871; and David Lloyd George of Great Britain, of whom Wilson said, "He is slippery as an eel, and I never know when to count on him."

These European statesmen represented bitter, vindictive nations that had suffered horrendously in the war. Their objectives bore little relationship to Wilson's vision of a liberal peace. As Clemenceau remarked, "God gave us the Ten Commandments and we broke them. Mr. Wilson has given us the Fourteen Points. We shall see."

Woodrow Wilson in Paris, December 1918
Citizens of the victorious Allied nations greeted Wilson deliriously, but back home the Republicans had gained control of both houses of Congress, and the political climate would soon turn sharply hostile.

Debates raged as the former Allies wrangled. Orlando demanded a port for Italy on the eastern Adriatic. Japan insisted on keeping the trading rights that it had seized from the Germans in the Chinese province of Shandong (Shantung). Clemenceau was obsessed with revenge. At one point, an appalled Wilson threatened to leave the conference.

Reflecting this poisonous political climate, the peace treaty signed by a sullen German delegation in Versailles's Hall of Mirrors on June 28, 1919, was harshly punitive. Germany was disarmed, stripped of its colonies, forced to admit sole blame for the war, and saddled with whopping reparation payments to the Allies.* France regained the provinces of Alsace and Lorraine lost to Germany in 1871 and took control for fifteen years of Germany's coal-rich Saar Basin. The

---

*These reparations were set at $56 billion, including the pensions that the Allied governments would ultimately pay their veterans, but quickly negotiated downward. When Germany stopped reparations in 1932, only $9 billion had been paid.

treaty demilitarized a zone thirty miles east of the Rhine to the French border and transferred a slice of eastern Germany to Poland. All told, Germany lost one-tenth of its population and one-eighth of its territory under the Versailles treaty. The treaty granted Japan's Shandong claims and gave Italy a slice of Austrian territory around the Brenner Pass in which lived two hundred thousand German-speaking inhabitants.

Wilson's idealistic emphasis on self-determination and democracy influenced some of the treaty's provisions. Germany's former colonies (as well as those of Turkey in the Middle East) went to the various Allies under a "mandate" or trusteeship system that in theory would eventually lead to independence. The treaty also recognized the independence of Poland; the Baltic states of Estonia, Latvia, and Lithuania (territories that Germany had seized in a harsh peace treaty with bolshevik Russia in March 1918); and two new nations carved from the old Austro-Hungarian and Ottoman empires: Czechoslovakia and Yugoslavia.

On balance, however, the Versailles treaty proved a disaster. Not only did it arouse festering resentment in Germany, but its framers made little effort to come to terms with revolutionary Russia. Indeed, in August 1918 a fourteen-nation Allied army had landed at various Russian ports on the Baltic and at Vladivostok in Siberia, ostensibly to protect Allied war matériel and secure the ports from German attack. But these troops were soon assisting a counterrevolutionary Russian force (including both tsarists and liberal democrats) seeking to overthrow Lenin and Russia's new bolshevik government.

Some seven thousand U.S. troops participated in this intervention, remaining until April 1920. Like nearly every political leader of his day, Woodrow Wilson strongly opposed bolshevism. Having welcomed the liberal Russian revolution of March 1917, he viewed Lenin's October coup and Russia's withdrawal from the war as a betrayal of the Allied cause and of his hopes for a liberal Russian future.

The Versailles treaty reflected this hostility. Its territorial settlements in eastern Europe were designed to keep Russia as weak as possible. Before leaving Versailles, Wilson and the other Allied leaders agreed to support a Russian military leader, Admiral Aleksandr Kolchak, who was continuing to fight the bolsheviks. Wilson, who had earlier refused to recognize Huerta and his government of "butchers" in Mexico, now refused to recognize Lenin's communist government. (Indeed, not until 1933 did the United States recognize the Soviet Union.)

The Fight over the League of Nations

Exhausted by months of bargaining and dismayed by the treaty's vindictive features, Wilson focused his attention in the summer of 1919 on his one shining achievement at Versailles: the creation of a new international organization, the League of Nations. The agreement or "covenant" to establish the League, written into the peace treaty itself, engaged Wilson's deepest emotions. The League embodied his vision of a liberal, harmonious, and rational world order. As he wrote an adviser, "At least . . . we are saving the Covenant, and that instrument will work wonders [and] bring the blessing of peace. . . . [W]hen the war psychosis has abated, it will not be difficult to settle all the disputes that baffle us now."

But within a few months, Wilson's dream would lie in ruins. A warning sign had come in February 1919, when thirty-nine Republican senators and senators-elect, including Henry Cabot Lodge, signed a letter rejecting the League in its present form. Wilson

A 1918 cartoon portrays Senate opposition to U.S. membership in the League of Nations. At President Wilson's insistence, the covenant to establish the League had been incorporated in the Versailles treaty.

had retorted defiantly, "You cannot dissect the Covenant from the treaty without destroying the whole vital structure."

When Wilson returned to the United States in July 1919 and submitted the Versailles treaty to the Senate for ratification, Lodge bottled it up in the Foreign Relations Committee. Furious at Lodge's tactics, and convinced that he could rally popular opinion to his cause, Wilson abruptly left Washington on September 3 for a western speaking tour. Covering more than nine thousand miles by train, Wilson defended his beloved League in thirty-seven speeches in twenty-two days. Crowds were large and friendly. People wept as Wilson described his visits to American war cemeteries in France, and cheered his vision of a world free of war.

But the grueling trip left Wilson totally exhausted. On September 25, as his train chugged eastward from Pueblo, Colorado, he collapsed. "I just feel as if I am going to pieces," the president, bursting into tears, told his physician, Cary Grayson. The train rushed back to Washington, where Wilson suffered a devastating stroke on October 2. For a time, he lay paralyzed and near death. Despite a partial recovery, Wilson spent the rest of his term mostly in bed or in a wheelchair, a reclusive invalid, his mind clouded, his fragile emotions betraying him into vindictive actions and petulant outbursts. He broke with his closest advisers; refused to see the British ambassador, Sir Edward Grey; and dismissed Secretary of State Lansing, whom he accused of disloyalty. In January 1920 Dr. Grayson advised resignation on medical grounds, but Wilson refused.

Wilson's strong-willed second wife, Edith Galt, whom the president had married in December 1915, played a highly manipulative role during these difficult months. The second Mrs. Wilson fiercely guarded her incapacitated husband. She and Dr. Grayson hid his condition from the public, controlled his access to information, and decided who could see him. Cabinet members, congressional leaders, and even the vice president, Thomas R. Marshall, were barred from the White House. When the leader of one political delegation told Mrs. Wilson that "the welfare of the country" could be affected by the delegation's meeting with the president, she snapped, "I am not thinking of the country now, I am thinking of my husband."[*]

Under these trying circumstances, the final act of the League drama unfolded. On September 10, 1919,

the Foreign Relations Committee at last reported the Versailles treaty to the Senate, but with a series of amendments. The Senate split into three groups over the League issue: Democrats who supported the League covenant without changes; Republican "Irreconcilables," led by Hiram Johnson, Robert La Follette, and Idaho's William Borah, who opposed the League completely; and Republican "Reservationists" led by Lodge, who demanded changes in the League covenant before they would support U.S. membership. The Reservationists' key objection focused on Article 10 of the covenant, which pledged each member nation to preserve the political independence and territorial integrity of all other members. This blank-check provision, the Reservationists believed, limited America's freedom of action in foreign affairs and Congress's constitutional right to declare war. That right must be spelled out explicitly in the League covenant, they insisted.

Had Wilson been willing to compromise, the Senate would certainly have ratified the Versailles treaty, and the United States would surely have joined the League. But the invalid president dug in his heels as his illness aggravated his tendency toward rigidity. From his isolation in the White House, Wilson instructed the Democratic senators to vote against the treaty with Lodge's reservations. Although international-law specialists believed that these reservations would not significantly weaken American participation in the League of Nations, Wilson rejected them as "a knife thrust at the heart of the treaty."

Despite the positive response of audiences on Wilson's western tour, the American people did not rise up in support of the League. The reactionary political mood that Wilson's own administration had helped create during the war did not encourage a grand gesture of political idealism once the war was over. As the editor of *The Nation* magazine observed, "If [Wilson] loses his great fight for humanity, it will be because he was deliberately silent when freedom of speech and the right of conscience were struck down in America."

In a Senate vote on November 19, 1919, pro-League Democrats loyally following Wilson's instructions and anti-League Irreconcilables joined forces to defeat the Versailles treaty with Lodge's reservations. A second vote the following March produced the same result. The United States would not join the League. A president elected amid soaring popular enthusiasm in 1912, applauded when he called for war in 1917, and adulated when he arrived in Europe in 1918, lay isolated and sick, his political leadership repudiated.

---

*The Twenty-fifth Amendment to the Constitution, ratified in 1967, set up procedures for the transfer of power to the vice president from a president unable to perform the duties of the office.

What should have been Woodrow Wilson's moment of supreme triumph had turned to ashes in his grasp.

Racism and Red Scare

The wartime spirit of "100 percent Americanism" left a bitter aftertaste in the United States. The years 1919–1920 saw new racial violence and fresh antiradical hysteria.

Lynch mobs murdered seventy-six blacks in 1919, the worst toll in fifteen years. The victims included ten veterans, several of them still in uniform. Some lynchings involved incredible brutality. In Omaha a mob shot a black prisoner more than a thousand times, mutilated him, and hanged his body in a busy intersection.

The bloodiest violence occurred in 1919 in Chicago, where the influx of southern blacks had pushed racial tension to a high level. On a hot July afternoon, whites at a Lake Michigan beach threw stones at a black youth swimming offshore. When he sank and drowned, word quickly flashed through the black neighborhoods. A thirteen-day reign of terror followed as white and black marauders roamed the streets and randomly attacked innocent victims. Black gangs stabbed an Italian peddler; white gangs pulled blacks from streetcars and shot or whipped them. The violence and arson left fifteen whites and twenty-three blacks dead, over five hundred injured, and more than a thousand families, mostly black, homeless.

The wartime antiradical panic crested in the Red Scare of 1919–1920. The fear of "bolshevism" deepened when a rash of 3,630 strikes, representing an accumulation of grievances, broke out in 1919. When Seattle's labor unions organized an orderly general strike early in 1919, the mayor, accusing the strikers of seeking to "duplicate the anarchy of Russia," called for federal troops. Anxiety crackled again in April, when packages mailed to various public officials proved to contain bombs. One such bomb blew off the hands of a senator's maid; another damaged the home of the U.S. attorney general.

In September 350,000 steelworkers went on strike protesting low pay and a workweek of nearly seventy hours. Mill owners broke the strike by using brutally repressive tactics and by taking out newspaper ads describing the walkout as a bolshevik plot engineered by "Red agitators."

The antiradical paranoia soon took political form. In November 1919 the House of Representatives refused to seat prominent Milwaukee socialist Victor Berger. Berger's district promptly reelected him, but

J. Edgar Hoover, Newly Appointed Director of the Federal Bureau of Investigation, 1924
Earlier, during the postwar "Red Scare" of 1919–1920, Hoover headed the Justice Department's General Intelligence Division that investigated radicals and alleged subversives.

the House stood firm. The New York legislature expelled several socialist members. The Justice Department, hastily setting up a countersubversion division under young J. Edgar Hoover, future head of the Federal Bureau of Investigation, arrested hundreds of suspected communists and radicals. In December 1919, 249 Russian-born aliens were deported aboard the USS *Buford*, nicknamed the Red Ark. One deportee was the radical Emma Goldman, whose departure deprived the birth-control movement of an important leader. The government's antiradical crusade won enthusiastic support from the American Legion, a newly founded veterans' association, as well as the National Association of Manufacturers.

On January 2, 1920, in a national dragnet coordinated by the Justice Department, federal marshals and local police in thirty-two cities raided the homes of suspected radicals and the headquarters of radical organizations. Without bothering with search warrants or arrest warrants, these authorities arrested more than 4,000 persons (of whom some 550 were eventually deported), and ransacked homes and offices, seizing papers and records.

These raids involved gross violations of civil rights and simple decency. Marshals barged into one woman's bedroom to arrest her. In Lynn, Massachusetts, police arrested thirty-nine men and women meeting to plan a cooperative bakery. In Boston, police paraded scores of arrested persons through the streets in handcuffs and chains. In a prison in Boston Harbor, the arrestees were confined in crowded, unheated, and unsanitary cells.

The rabidly antiradical and politically ambitious attorney general, A. Mitchell Palmer, coordinated these "Red raids." A Quaker who had compiled a strong reform record as a member of Congress, Palmer totally succumbed to the anticommunist hysteria of the early postwar period. Defending his actions, Palmer later described the menace he believed the nation faced in 1919:

> *The blaze of revolution was sweeping over every American institution of law and order . . . eating its way into the homes of the American workman, its sharp tongues of revolutionary heat . . . licking at the altars of the churches, leaping into the belfry of the school bell, crawling into the sacred corners of American homes, seeking to replace marriage vows with libertine laws, burning up the foundations of society.*

The more outrageous manifestations of the Red Scare subsided as Palmer's lurid predictions failed to materialize and attention turned to other matters. When a bomb exploded in New York City's financial district in September 1920, killing thirty-eight people, most Americans saw the event as the work of an isolated fanatic, not evidence of approaching revolution.

The Election of 1920

In this unsettled climate, the election of 1920 approached. Wilson, now wholly out of touch with political reality, toyed with seeking a third term but was dissuaded. At least two cabinet members, Treasury Secretary McAdoo and Attorney General Palmer, harbored presidential aspirations. But when the Democrats convened in San Francisco, the delegates sang "How Dry I Am" (prohibition had just taken effect), halfheartedly endorsed Wilson's League position, and nominated James M. Cox, the mildly progressive governor of Ohio. They chose as Cox's running mate the young assistant secretary of the navy, Franklin D. Roosevelt, who possessed a potent political name.

The confident Republicans, meeting in Chicago, had trouble finding a candidate who could secure a majority of convention votes. Party leaders at last turned to Senator Warren G. Harding of Ohio, an amiable politician whose principal qualification was his availability. As one Republican leader observed: "There ain't any first raters this year. . . . We got a lot of second raters, and Harding is the best of the second raters." For vice president, they chose Governor Calvin Coolidge of Massachusetts, who won attention in 1919 with an outspoken denunciation of a Boston policemen's strike.

Wilson proclaimed the election a "solemn referendum" on the League, but his prediction of a landslide victory for Cox proved wildly inaccurate. The nation was spiritually drained, both by the war and by the emotional roller-coaster ride—from idealism to disillusionment—on which Wilson had taken it. "The bitterness toward Wilson is everywhere . . .," wrote a Democratic campaign worker; "he hasn't a friend."

Sensing the popular mood, Harding promised a return to "normalcy"—no more crusades, no more cavalcades of reform. His campaign addresses were empty of content but vaguely reassuring. William McAdoo would later describe Harding's speeches as "an army of pompous phrases moving over the landscape in search of an idea." Harding himself called them "bloviations."

Harding and Coolidge piled up a memorable landslide victory: 16 million popular votes against 9 million for Cox and Roosevelt. Nearly a million voters, at least in part to protest the wartime repression of radicals, defiantly cast their ballots for the socialist Eugene V. Debs, then serving time in an Atlanta penitentiary.

The election dashed all hope for American entry into the League of Nations. During the campaign Harding had spoken vaguely of some form of "international organization," but with victory assured, he bluntly announced that the question of American membership in the League was "dead." "Let it rest in the deep grave to which it has been consigned," he added for good measure in 1923. Senator Lodge exulted that the voters had ripped "Wilsonism" up by the roots. The misty sense of national destiny and high purpose that Woodrow Wilson had evoked so eloquently in April 1917 survived only as an ironic memory as Americans impatiently turned to a new president, a new decade, and a new era.

The Election of 1920

Candidates	Parties	Electoral Vote	Popular Vote	Percentage of Popular Vote
WARREN G. HARDING	Republican	404	16,143,407	60.4
James M. Cox	Democratic	127	9,130,328	34.2
Eugene V. Debs	Socialist		919,799	3.4
P. P. Christensen	Farmer-Labor		265,411	1.0

CONCLUSION

By conservative estimate, the First World War cost 10 million dead and 20 million wounded. Included in this toll were 112,000 American dead—49,000 in battle and the rest from influenza and other diseases. For those not in uniform, the war often produced a flush of prosperity but also hardships, ranging from sugar shortages to the loss of loved ones.

The war's social, political, economic, and technological impact extended far beyond the battlefield. The conflict brought marked advances in the technology of slaughter, for example, from U-boat torpedoes and primitive aerial bombs to toxic gases and more efficient machine guns.

The war furthered the goals of some reformers, bringing to fruition the woman-suffrage and prohibition causes, for example. To promote economic mobilization, the federal government expanded its regulatory power over corporations (even though business leaders themselves often ran the wartime Washington agencies), and measures were enacted to assure war workers' well-being and efficiency. But in a larger sense, the war and its aftermath severely undermined the best side of progressivism: its openness to new ideas, its commitment to social justice, and its humanitarian concern for the underdog. As conformism and fear of radicalism set in, the prewar reform impulse withered. This climate of reaction intensified in 1919–1920, as an emotionally spent American people sharply repudiated Woodrow Wilson and his idealism.

The war also introduced major changes in the lives of millions of ordinary workers, farmers, blacks, and women, and enhanced the standing of social workers, psychologists, engineers, public-relations specialists, advertisers, and other professionals who contributed expertise to the cause. Internationally, despite the wrangles that kept the United States out of the League of Nations, the conflict propelled the United States to the center of world politics and left the nation's businesses and financial institutions poised for global expansion.

Some of these changes endured; others proved fleeting. Cumulatively, however, their effect was profound. The United States that celebrated the armistice in November 1918 was a very different society from the one that Woodrow Wilson had so solemnly summoned to war only nineteen months earlier.

CHRONOLOGY

1905 President Theodore Roosevelt mediates the end of the Russo-Japanese War.

1906 At the request of Roosevelt, San Francisco ends segregation of Asian schoolchildren.

1907 Roosevelt sends the "Great White Fleet" around the world.

1912 U.S. Marines occupy Nicaragua.

Theodore Roosevelt

1914 U.S. troops occupy Vera Cruz, Mexico.

Archduke Franz Ferdinand of Austria assassinated.

World War I begins; President Woodrow Wilson proclaims American neutrality.

Wilson protests British interception of U.S. merchant ships.

1915 U.S. Marines occupy Haiti and the Dominican Republic.

Woman's Peace party organized.

Wilson's "strict accountability" note protests German U-boat attacks.

1915 British liner *Lusitania* sunk by German U-boat.

U.S. "preparedness" movement begins.

Germany restricts U-boat campaign.

Wilson permits U.S. bank loans to Allies.

1916 U.S. punitive expedition invades Mexico, seeking Pancho Villa.

After *Sussex* sinking, Germany pledges not to attack merchant ships without warning.

Wilson reelected president.

1917 U.S. troops withdraw from Mexico.

Germany resumes unrestricted U-boat warfare; United States breaks diplomatic relations.

United States enters the war.

Selective Service Act sets up national draft.

War Industries Board, Committee on Public Information, and Food Administration created.

Espionage Act passed.

NAACP march in New York City protests antiblack riot in East St. Louis and upsurge in lynchings.

Bolsheviks seize power in Russia; Russia leaves the war.

1917 New York State passes woman-suffrage referendum.

U.S. government seizes the nation's railroads.

1918 Wilson outlines Fourteen Points for peace.

Sedition Amendment to Espionage Act passed.

American Expeditionary Force (AEF) helps stop Germans at Château-Thierry and Belleau Wood, closes St. Mihiel salient, and plays key role in the Meuse-Argonne campaign.

Armistice signed (November 11).

1919 Eighteenth Amendment added to the Constitution.

Peace treaty, including League of Nations covenant, signed at Versailles.

Racial violence in Chicago.

Wilson suffers paralyzing stroke.

Versailles treaty, with League covenant, rejected by Senate.

1920 "Red raids" organized by Justice Department.

Nineteenth Amendment added to the Constitution.

Warren G. Harding elected president.

FOR FURTHER READING

Robert H. Ferrell, *Woodrow Wilson and World War I, 1917–1921* (1985). A vigorously written critical synthesis; especially good on the peace negotiations.

Frank Freidel, *Over There: The Story of America's First Great Overseas Crusade* (1964). Excellent, readable overview of the AEF experience based on soldiers' diaries and reminiscences.

Martin Gilbert, *The First World War: A Complete History* (1994). Weak on strategy, but vividly conveys the grim experience of ordinary soldiers.

David M. Kennedy, *Over Here: The First World War and American Society* (1980). Deeply researched interpretive study of the home front during the war.

Thomas J. Knock, *To End All Wars: World War I and the Quest for a New World Order* (1992). A compelling study of the origins of Wilson's internationalism and of the links between domestic reform and foreign policy.

Ronald Schaffer, *America in the Great War: The Rise of the War Welfare State* (1991). Explores the war's effect on corporate organization and business-government links, as well as wartime initiatives to benefit industrial workers.

ADDITIONAL BIBLIOGRAPHY

The United States in Asia and Latin America

Lester E. Langley, *The Banana Wars: An Inner History of American Empire, 1900–1934* (1983); D. G. Munro, *Intervention and Dollar Diplomacy in the Caribbean, 1900–1921* (1964); James Reed, *The Missionary Mind and America's East Asian Policy, 1911–1915* (1983); Thomas Schoonover, *The United States in Central America, 1860–1911* (1991); Robert Freeman Smith, *The United States and Revolutionary Nationalism in Mexico* (1972).

The Road to War and Wartime Diplomacy

Lloyd E. Ambrosius, *Woodrow Wilson and the American Diplomatic Tradition* (1987); John M. Blum, *Woodrow Wilson and the Politics of Morality* (1956); John L. Gaddis, *Russia, the Soviet Union, and the United States* (1978); Lloyd C. Gardner, *Safe for Democracy: The Anglo-American Response to Revolution,* *1913–1923* (1984); N. Gordon Levin, Jr., *Woodrow Wilson and World Politics: America's Response to War and Revolution* (1968); Arno J. Mayer, *Political Origins of the New Diplomacy, 1917–1918* (1963).

The Battlefield Experience

John Whiteclay Chambers II, *To Raise an Army: The Draft in Modern America* (1987); Edward M. Coffman, *The War to End All Wars: The American Military Experience in World War I* (1968); Robert Jackson, *At War with the Bolsheviks: The Allied Intervention into Russia, 1917–1920* (1972); Lee Kennett, *The First Air War, 1914–1918* (1991); Bernard Nalty, *Strength for the Fight: A History of Black Americans in the Military* (1986); Frank E. Vandiver, *Black Jack: The Life and Times of John J. Pershing* (1977).

The Government Mobilizes for War

Daniel R. Beaver, *Newton D. Baker and the American War Effort, 1917–1919* (1966); Kathleen Burk, *Britain, America and the Sinews of War* (1985); Robert D. Cuff, *The War Industries Board* (1973); Charles Gilbert, *American Financing of World War I* (1970); Franz Samelson, "Putting Psychology on the Map: Ideology and Intelligence Testing," in Allan R. Buss, ed., *Psychology in Social Context* (1979): 103–168; Jordan A. Schwarz, *The Speculator: Bernard M. Baruch in Washington, 1917–1965* (1981).

American Society and Culture in World War I

Allen F. Davis, "Welfare, Reform and World War I," *American Quarterly* 19 (1967): 516–533; Melvyn Dubofsky, "Abortive Reform: The Wilson Administration and Organized Labor, 1913–1920," in James E. Cronin and Carmen Sirianni, eds., *Work, Community, and Power: The Experience of Labor in Europe and America, 1900–1925* (1983); Maurine W. Greenwald, *Women, War and Work* (1980); Ellis W. Hawley, *The Great War and the Search for a Modern Order: A History of the American People and Their Institutions, 1917–1933*, 2d ed. (1992); Florette Henri, *Black Migration: Movement Northward, 1900–1920* (1975); Frederick C. Luebke, *Bonds of Loyalty: German-Americans and World War I* (1974); John F. McClymer, *War and Welfare: Social Engineering in America, 1890–1925* (1980); Barbara J. Steinson, *American Women's Activism in World War I* (1982); Jacqueline van Voris, *Carrie Chapman Catt: A Public Life* (1987).

Patriotism, Dissent, and Repression

Ray H. Abrams, *Preachers Present Arms: The Role of the American Churches and Clergy in World Wars I and II* (1969); George T. Blakey, *Historians on the Homefront: American Propagandists for the Great War* (1970); Charles Chatfield, *For Peace and Justice: Pacifism in America, 1914–1941* (1971); Carl H. Chrislock, *Watchdog of Loyalty: The Minnesota Commission of Public Safety During World War I* (1991); Bruce Clayton, *Forgotten Prophet: The Life of Randolph Bourne* (1984); Alfred E. Cornebise, *War as Advertised: The Four Minute Men and America's Crusade, 1917–1918* (1984); Christopher Gibbs, *The Great Silent Majority: Missouri's Resistance to World War I* (1988); Carol S. Gruber, *Mars and Minerva: World War I and the Uses of Higher Learning in America* (1975); Michael T. Isenberg, *War on Film* (1981); Michael Pearlman, *To Make Democracy Safe for America: Patricians and Preparedness in the Progressive Era* (1984); Harold C. Peterson and Gilbert Fite, *Opponents of War, 1917–1918* (1968); William Preston, Jr., *Aliens and Dissenters: Federal Suppression of Radicals, 1903–1933* (1966); Maurice Rickards, *Posters of the First World War* (1968); Stephen Vaughn, *Holding Fast the Inner Lines: Democracy, Nationalism, and the Committee on Public Information* (1980); Larry Wayne Ward, *The Motion Picture Goes to War: The U.S. Government Film Effort During World War I* (1985).

Aftermath: Red Scare, Failed Peace, and Disillusionment

Wesley M. Bagley, *The Road to Normalcy: The Presidential Campaign and Election of 1920* (1962); David Brody, *Labor in Crisis: The Steel Strike of 1919* (1965); Stanley A. Coben, *A. Mitchell Palmer: Politician* (1963); Stanley Cooperman, *World War I and the American Novel* (1970); Arno Mayer, *Politics and Diplomacy of Peacemaking* (1967); Robert K. Murray, *Red Scare: A Study in National Hysteria, 1919–1920* (1955); Stewart I. Rochester, *American Liberal Disillusionment in the Wake of World War I* (1977); Klaus Schwabe, *Woodrow Wilson, Revolutionary Germany, and Peacemaking, 1918–1919* (1985); Ralph Stone, *The Irreconcilables: The Fight Against the League of Nations* (1970); William M. Tuttle, Jr., *Race Riot: Chicago in the Red Summer of 1919* (1970); Arthur J. Walworth, *Wilson and His Peacemakers* (1986); William C. Widenor, *Henry Cabot Lodge and the Search for an American Foreign Policy* (1980).

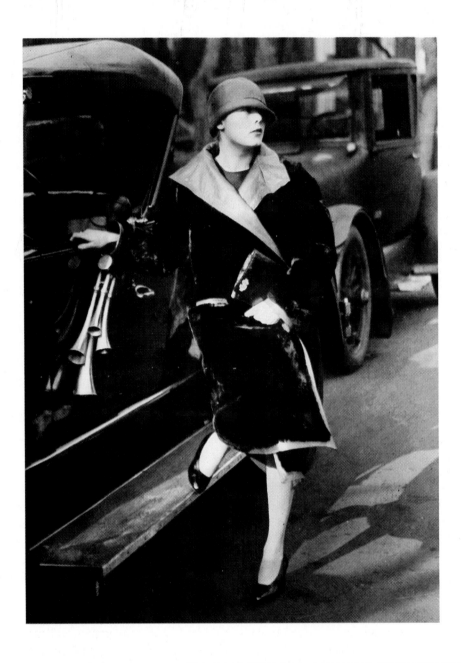

A 1920s Flapper
Suzette Dewey, the daughter of a Treasury Department
official poses beside her roadster, December 1927

24

Alisha Adato

THE 1920s

Sam Groipen of Medford, Massachusetts, was washing the windows of his little grocery store, the Cooperative Cash Market, one day in June 1928 when he saw a meat truck pull up in front of the A&P supermarket next door. Sam knew the meaning of this seemingly ordinary event: his days as an independent grocer were numbered. A Jewish immigrant who had come from Russia with his family as a sixteen-year-old in 1914, Sam had opened his market in 1923, the year that he married. At first Sam and his wife did well. Sam served the customers; his wife did the bookkeeping. They knew their patrons by name, advertised in the local newspaper, and extended credit to those short on cash.

In 1925, however, the chain-store invasion began. A&P moved in next door, then First National and Stop & Shop across the street. At first the chains did not hurt Sam's business. Small by today's standards, they carried only brand-name groceries, not meat or fish. But the Medford A&P added meat and fish in 1928. To save his declining business, Sam at one point put a large "MAIN ENTRANCE" sign over the door of his small shop amid a forest of supermarkets. But nothing helped. He watched his former customers—some of whom still owed him money—walk past his door on their way to a supermarket. "I felt like I was being strangled," he later recalled; "those bastard chains were destroying me."

In 1935 Sam Groipen sold out. Abandoning his dream of prospering as an independent business-man, he took a sales job with the giant Prudential Life Insurance Company. Looking back years later, Sam's bitterness toward the chains had softened. "When I bought the store I was young and ambitious," he recalled, "but I have been mellowed by the system."

Groipen's experience paralleled that of many independent entrepreneurs in the 1920s who found themselves competing with, and in many cases swallowed up by, great consolidated corporations. This economic transformation was only one of many developments in a decade that ushered in profound changes in American society.

In the 1920s the nation's vast productive capacity, resting on the industrial base laid down in the late nineteenth century, burst forth with a tidal wave of automobiles, radios, electrical appliances, and other consumer goods. This torrent of new products brought prosperity to the economy and major changes to the lives of ordinary Americans. The prosperity proved fragile; the changes did not. Ingrained patterns of diet, dress, housekeeping, travel, entertainment, and even thought shifted markedly as the economic order evolved.

These technological changes, following several decades of immigration and urban growth, also spawned severe social tensions. While Republican presidents espoused conservative political and cultural values, deep conflicts ripped at the fabric of society. But this same ferment also stimulated creativity in literature and the arts.

When the decade ended, Americans tried to sum up in a phrase their kaleidoscopic memories of these turbulent and change-filled years: they called them the Roaring Twenties.

A NEW ECONOMIC ORDER

Fueled by new consumer products, sophisticated advertising, and innovative forms of corporate organization, the economy surged in the 1920s. But not everyone benefited. Key industries declined, workers lost jobs as factories were automated, and farmers suffered chronic economic troubles. Still, the overall picture seemed rosy, and most Americans celebrated a thriving business culture.

A Decade of Prosperity

The war-induced boom lasted until late 1920, when the rush of demobilization disrupted the economy. As the government abruptly canceled contracts, and returning veterans swamped labor markets, a sharp recession struck. Consumers welcomed falling prices, but the recession's other effects hurt badly. Business slowed, bankruptcies increased, and unemployment jumped. Among nonfarm workers, the jobless rate surged from 2.4 percent in 1918 and 1919 to 19.5 percent in 1921. Recovery came in 1922, however, and for the next few years the economy grew spectacularly. Unemployment fell to as low as 3 percent, prices held steady, and the gross national product climbed from about $70 billion in 1922 to nearly $100 billion in 1929.

An array of new consumer goods, including home electrical products, contributed to the prosperity. Factories had started to electrify in the late nineteenth century; and with the construction of hydroelectric generating plants at Niagara Falls and elsewhere, the age of electricity dawned for urban American households as well. By the mid-1920s, with more than 60 percent of the nation's homes wired for electric power, a mind-boggling parade of electrical appliances, from refrigerators, ranges, washing machines, and vacuum cleaners to fans, razors, and mixers, stood gleaming in the stores. The manufacture of such appliances, as well as of heavy-duty equipment for the electrical industry itself, provided a massive economic stimulus.

Economic Expansion, 1920–1929
After a brief postwar downturn, the American economy surged in the 1920s.
SOURCE: U.S. Department of Commerce, *Long-Term Economic Growth* (Washington, D.C.: U.S. Government Printing Office, October 1966), 169.

The 1920s business boom rested, too, on the automobile. At first a plaything of the rich, the automobile had started to reach a larger market even before the war. As early as 1904, Ransom E. Olds had sold five thousand of his sporty Oldsmobiles for $650 each. Henry Ford of Detroit, who had built his first prototype automobile in 1896, introduced the low-priced Model T in 1908; by 1916 seven hundred thousand had been sold.

But in the 1920s the automobile came into its own. Passenger-car registrations jumped from about 8 million in 1920 to more than 23 million in 1930. Ford led the market until mid-decade, when General Motors Corporation (GM) spurted ahead by touting a range of colors (the Model T came only in black) and improved passenger comfort. GM's lowest-priced car, named for French automotive designer Louis Chevrolet, proved especially popular. Responding to the challenge, Ford in 1927 introduced the stylish Model A in a variety of colors. By the end of the decade, the automobile industry accounted for about 9 percent of all wages in manufacturing and had stimulated such related industries as rubber, gasoline and petroleum, advertising, and highway construction.

The rosy business climate stimulated capitalist expansion. To supply their overseas markets, Ford, GM, General Electric, and other big corporations invested heavily in production facilities abroad. Other American firms acquired foreign processing facilities or sources of raw materials. Swift, Armour, and other U.S. meatpackers built packing plants in Argentina; Anaconda Copper acquired Chile's biggest copper mine; and the mammoth United Fruit Company established processing factories throughout Latin America. By 1930 U.S. private investment abroad totaled over $15 billion.

New Modes of Producing, Managing, and Selling

Building on the industrial feats of the war years, the 1920s saw striking increases in productivity. New assembly-line techniques of mass production boosted the per capita output of industrial workers by some 40 percent during this decade. At the sprawling Ford plants near Detroit, workers stood in one place and performed simple, repetitive tasks as an endless chain conveyed the partly assembled vehicles past them. Engines entered the final line from their own separate assembly lines.

Assembly-line production quickly spread. *Fordism* became a synonym worldwide for American industrial prowess. In the Soviet Union, which purchased twenty-five thousand Ford tractors in the 1920s, the people "ascribed a magical quality to the name of Ford," a 1927 visitor reported.

Corporate consolidation, spurred by the war, continued. By the end of the 1920s, over a thousand companies a year vanished through merger. A few corporate giants dominated the major industries: Ford, GM, and Chrysler in automobiles; General Electric and Westinghouse in electricity; U.S. Steel in the steel industry. In the public-utilities field, consolidation became epidemic. Samuel Insull of the Chicago Edison Company, for example, built an empire of local power companies that by 1929 had assets of $3.5 billion. By the end of the decade, one hundred corporations controlled nearly half the nation's business activity.

Merger mania was only one expression of the process of corporate consolidation. Even when corporations did not actually merge, companies that made the same product often cooperated through trade associations on such matters as pricing, product specifications, and division of markets.

This effort by American capitalism to streamline its operations also led to more bureaucratic management structures. A few business leaders, to be sure, perpetuated the individualistic management style characteristic of the nineteenth century. Henry Ford ruled his company autocratically, bullying his subordinates, including his own son Edsel, and making decisions largely by impulse. But this was atypical. Like the federal government and many professional societies, corporations rationalized their management in the twenties. They set up specialized divisions responsible for such varied spheres as product development, market research, economic forecasting, and employee relations. The day-to-day oversight of this new corporate structure increasingly fell to professionals trained in the techniques of management.

The modernization of business affected wage policies as well as production and organization. Rejecting the conventional economic wisdom that advised employers to pay the lowest wages possible, "enlightened" business leaders began to argue that higher wages would generate higher productivity. Henry Ford led the way in 1914 by paying his workers an unprecedented five dollars a day, at a time when the *yearly* wages of factory workers averaged under seven hundred dollars. Other companies followed his lead in the 1920s.

New systems for distributing goods emerged as well. Automobiles reached consumers through vast dealer networks. By 1926 the number of Ford dealerships approached ten thousand. Manufacturers pressured dealers to sell a specified quota of cars. As one ex–Ford dealer confessed in 1927, "You can sell [some people] anything if you hammer them hard enough." An expanding network of chain stores accounted for about a quarter of all retail sales by 1930. The spread of the automobile encouraged some family businesses such as roadside diners and tourist cabins, but in general, small, locally owned businesses like Sam Groipen's grocery store were squeezed out of business by the chains. The A&P grocery chain expanded from 5,000 stores in 1922 to 17,500 in 1928. Installment buying was another mass-marketing innovation. By 1929, credit purchases accounted for 75 percent of automobile sales, and the total amount consumers owed in their charge accounts, installment plans, and so on stood at $7.1 billion—$4.5 billion more than in 1919.

Above all, the 1920s business boom bobbed along on a frothy sea of advertising. In 1929 corporations spent an estimated $1.8 billion promoting their wares,

**A Standard Oil Station
in New Jersey, 1927**
*While the driver chats with
her friends on a rainy day, the
attendant manually pumps
the gasoline into the tank.*

and the advertising business employed some six hundred thousand people. Radio, the newest of the mass media, relied entirely on advertising for its income. The barons of the advertising business stood high among the corporate elite of the 1920s. Chicago ad man Albert Lasker owned the Chicago Cubs baseball team as well as his own eighteen-hole golf course.

Like their counterparts today, the advertisers of the twenties used celebrity endorsements ("Nine out of ten screen stars care for their skin with Lux toilet soap"), promises of social success, and threats of social embarrassment. Beneath a picture of a sad young woman, for example, a 1923 Listerine mouthwash ad proclaimed,

> *She was a beautiful girl and talented too. She
> had the advantages of education and better
> clothes than most girls of her set. She possessed
> that culture and poise that travel brings. Yet in
> the one pursuit that stands foremost in the mind
> of every girl and woman—marriage—she was a
> failure.*

The young woman's problem was *halitosis,* a hitherto little-known term for bad breath. The remedy, of course, was Listerine, and lots of it.

Helen Resor of New York's big J. Walter Thompson Agency worked her way up in a male-dominated business. Resor specialized in advertising copy directed to women. Her most famous slogan promoted Woodbury soap: "For the Skin You Love to Touch."

Beyond touting specific products, advertisers redefined popular aspiration by offering a seductive vision of a new era of consumption. Ads created a fantasy world of elegance, grace, and boundless pleasure. Enticing Americans to partake of the technological abundance, advertisers aroused desires that the new consumer-oriented capitalist system happily fulfilled. As one critic wrote in 1925,

> *[W]hen all is said and done, advertising . . . cre-
> ates a dream world: smiling faces, shining teeth,
> school girl complexions, cornless feet, perfect fit-
> ting [underwear], distinguished collars, wrinkle-
> less pants, odorless breath, regularized bowels,
> . . . charging motors, punctureless tires, perfect
> busts, shimmering shanks, self-washing dishes—
> backs behind which the moon was meant to rise.*

Business influence in the 1920s extended far beyond the factory and the advertising pages; it saturated all areas of life. A 1921 article in *Independent* magazine summed up the prevailing mood: "America stands for one idea: Business. . . . Thru business, properly conceived, managed, and conducted, the human race is finally to be redeemed."

Postwar America venerated the magnates of business and the new world of material comfort they had created. Presidents Harding and Coolidge lauded business values and hobnobbed with businessmen. Magazines profiled corporate leaders. A 1923 public-opinion poll placed Henry Ford far ahead of Warren Harding as

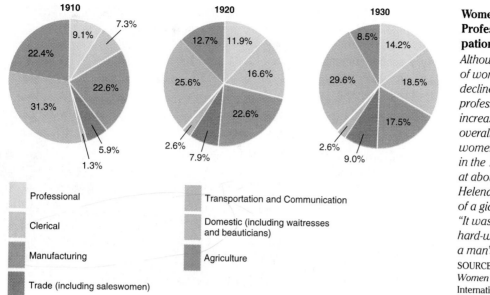

1910

7.3%
9.1%
22.4%
22.6%
31.3%
5.9%
1.3%

1920

12.7% 11.9%
16.6%
25.6%
22.6%
2.6%
7.9%

1930

8.5%
14.2%
18.5%
29.6%
17.5%
2.6%
9.0%

Professional

Clerical

Manufacturing

Trade (including saleswomen)

Transportation and Communication

Domestic (including waitresses and beauticians)

Agriculture

Women Employed in Professions and Occupations, 1910–1930
Although the percentage of women farm workers declined and that of professional women increased slightly, the overall proportion of women in the work force in the 1920s held steady at about 25 percent. Said Helena Rubenstein, head of a giant cosmetics firm, "It was not easy being a hard-working woman in a man's world."
SOURCE: Grace Hutchins, *Women Who Work* (New York: International, 1934), 24.

a 1924 presidential prospect. In *The Man Nobody Knows* (1925), ad man Bruce Barton, son of a Protestant minister, described Jesus Christ as a managerial genius who "picked up twelve men from the bottom ranks of business and forged them into an organization that conquered the world." Rarely have business values so pervaded American life. In *Middletown,* a study of Muncie, Indiana, published in 1929, sociologists Robert and Helen Lynd observed, "More and more of the activities of life are coming to be strained through the bars of the dollar sign."

Women in the New Economic Era

As we shall see, the new electrical appliances, the automobile, and the other technological wonders of the 1920s profoundly affected the lives of American women. In the decade's advertising, glamorous women smiled behind the steering wheel, happily operated electric appliances, smoked cigarettes in romantic settings, and vacationed in exotic resorts. One resourceful ad man promoted cigarettes for women as "torches of freedom." In the advertisers' dream world, housework became an exciting technological challenge. As one ad put it: "Men are judged successful according to their power to delegate work. Similarly the wise woman delegates to electricity all that electricity can do."

But what of women in the workplace? The rise of the assembly line, offering physically less demanding work, theoretically should have increased job opportunities for women; but in fact, males dominated the work force in automobile plants and other assembly-line factories. Although the number of women holding jobs outside the home increased by more than 2 million in the 1920s, the *proportion* of such women continued essentially unchanged, hovering at about 24 percent. The gains of 1917–1918 receded quickly in the 1920s.

Women who did find work in industry often faced wage discrimination. In 1929, for example, a male trimmer in the meatpacking industry received fifty-two cents an hour, a female trimmer, thirty-seven cents an hour. Assuming that women entered the labor market only temporarily prior to marriage, employers relegated them to low-paying piece-rate jobs. The weakening of the union movement in the 1920s (see below) particularly hit women workers. As the decade wore on, the proportion of women workers who belonged to unions fell to a miniscule 3 percent.

The bureaucratization of business increased female job opportunities somewhat. By 1930 some 2 million women—one-fifth of the total female labor force—had become secretaries, typists, or filing clerks. Very few women gained admission to capitalism's managerial ranks, however. Women like Helena Rubenstein, founder of a cosmetics empire, were exceptional. With medical schools imposing a 5 percent quota on female admissions, the number of women physicians actually declined from 1910 to 1930.

The proportion of female high-school graduates going to college slowly increased, however, from 8 percent in 1920 to 12 percent in 1930. Whereas fewer than 17,000 women received college degrees in 1920, in 1930 the total neared 50,000. And despite the hurdles, more and more college-educated women combined marriage and career. Indeed, the proportion of working women who were married rose by about 25 percent in the 1920s. Most took clerical jobs, worked in the lower ranks of business, or entered traditional "women's professions" such as nursing, librarianship, social work and teaching. A handful followed the lead of Progressive Era feminist trailblazers to become researchers and scholars in colleges and universities. As today, the balancing of marriage and a career was not easy. Phyllis Blanchard, a psychologist, wrote in the 1920s of the strain of juggling her "two greatest needs—the need for love and the need for independence."

Workers in a Business Age

The labor movement faced tough sledding in the twenties. Union membership declined from 5 million in 1920 to 3.4 million in 1929. Several factors underlay this decline. For one thing, overall wage rates moved steadily upward in the 1920s. In the steel industry, for example, real hourly wages rose about 17 percent from 1923 to 1929. Aggregate statistics on wage increases conceal many inequities and regional variations, but the prevailing pattern of fatter pay envelopes helped undermine the union movement.

Changes in the industrial process figured importantly as well. The trade unions' traditional strength lay in old, established industries like printing, railroading, coal mining, and the building trades. This older craft-based pattern of union organization was ill suited to the new mass-production industries.

Management hostility further weakened organized labor. Henry Ford hired thugs and spies to intimidate would-be union organizers. In Marion, North Carolina, deputy sheriffs shot and killed six striking textile workers. The deputies were acquitted, but a union organizer went to jail.

More typically, however, the anti-union campaign took subtler forms. Manufacturers' associations renamed the non-union shop the "open shop" and

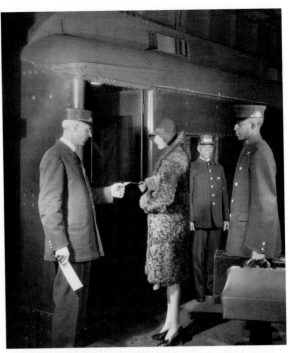

Railroad Employees of the 1920s
The Brotherhood of Sleeping Car Porters was one of the few unions with black members in a decade when the American workplace was strictly segregated.

praised it as the "American Plan" of labor relations. Some firms set up company-sponsored employee associations and, in consultation with these groups, provided cafeterias, recreational facilities, and so on. A few big corporations such as U.S. Steel and Standard Oil sold their workers company stock at special prices. Some corporate leaders treated "welfare capitalism" (the phrase used to describe this new approach to labor relations) as evidence of a heightened ethical awareness in American business. In reality, corporate paternalism arose mainly from the desire to prevent the formation of independent unions with real clout.

Black membership in labor unions by 1929 stood at only about eighty-two thousand—mostly longshoremen, mine workers, and railroad porters. The American Federation of Labor officially prohibited racial discrimination, but the unions that made up the AFL discriminated in many ways. Some had clauses in their constitutions limiting membership to whites; others simply followed a de facto exclusionary policy. Corporations often hired blacks as strikebreakers, and this increased organized labor's hostility toward them. Black strikebreakers, denounced as "scabs," took such work out of dire need. As a jobless black character says in Claude McKay's 1929 novel *Home to Harlem*, "I got to live, and I'll scab through hell to live."

Had the climate been different, a vast pool of workers might have been prime candidates for unionization. Belying the general prosperity, wage rates of unskilled workers barely budged. Concluded one labor economist, "The failure of the unskilled to share in the general advance . . . is indeed startling."

Of the regional variations that skewed the wage picture, that between North and South loomed largest. In 1928 the average unskilled laborer in New England earned forty-seven cents an hour, whereas the same labor in the South paid twenty-eight cents an hour. Textile corporations moved south in search of lower wage rates, devastating many historic New England mill towns.

Not only women but also blacks, Mexican-Americans, and recent immigrants from southern and eastern Europe clustered at the bottom of the wage scale. Black workers, many of them recent migrants from the South new to the industrial labor force, faced special difficulties. "Last hired and first fired," they performed the most menial jobs and rarely held supervisory positions.

Ailing Agriculture

Agriculture's wartime prosperity gave way to hard times in the 1920s. The prices of wheat, corn, and hay plummeted by 50 percent and more as the government's heavy wartime purchases for the army dwindled, as European agriculture revived, and as the nation's high protective tariff depressed agricultural exports. Between 1919 and 1921, farm income fell from $10 billion to just over $4 billion. When farmers compensated for low prices by increasing productivity, large surpluses and weak prices resulted. The real annual earnings of full-time agricultural workers, which had risen to $528 by 1920, fell to $344 in 1921 and only inched up for the rest of the decade. Farmers who had borrowed heavily to buy land and equipment during the war now felt the squeeze as loans and mortgage payments came due. Banking suffered, too, as farmers defaulted.

The major farm organizations, including the American Farm Bureau Federation (1920), turned to Washington for help. In 1924 the so-called farm bloc backed a complicated price-support plan, the McNary-

Haugen bill. Under this plan, the government would annually purchase the surplus of six basic farm commodities—cotton, corn, rice, hogs, tobacco, and wheat—at the average price that these commodities had brought in 1909–1914 (when farm prices were high) and then sell these surpluses on the world market at prevailing prices. The government would make up the resulting losses through a tax on domestic sales of these commodities—a tax that consumers ultimately would have paid in the form of higher food prices. Defeated in Congress in 1924 and 1926, the bill passed in 1927 and 1928, but President Calvin Coolidge vetoed it both times. This abortive effort to help financially strapped farmers offered one of many evidences of the conservative political climate of the 1920s.

REPUBLICANS IN POWER

Politics in the 1920s reflected the decade's business orientation. The Republicans controlled Congress and supplied two presidents who mirrored the prevailing cultural mood. In this climate former progressives and feminists faced difficult times.

The Harding and Coolidge Years

The dominant Republican party continued in the 1920s to draw support from northern farmers, corporate leaders, small businesspeople, and some skilled workers. The Democrats drew their votes mainly from the white South and the political machines of the immigrant cities.

With Republican progressives in the doghouse for having bolted to Theodore Roosevelt in 1912, party conservatives controlled the 1920 Republican convention. As we have seen, they settled upon Senator Warren G. Harding of Ohio as their presidential candidate. In 1891, a struggling newspaper editor, Harding had married the local banker's daughter and with her prodding launched the political career that brought him to the Senate in 1915. A genial backslapper, the floridly handsome Harding enjoyed good liquor, good stories, poker with his cronies, and occasional furtive encounters with his mistress, Nan Britton.

Yet this amiable nonentity overwhelmed his Democratic opponent and fellow Ohioan James M. Cox (see Chapter 23). Harding's very ordinariness appealed to voters longing for stability after the ordeal of war. Compared to Wilson's lofty sermons, even Harding's vacuous oratory had a soothing appeal.

In partial compensation for his lack of qualifications, Harding made some notable cabinet appointments: Henry A. Wallace, the respected editor of an Iowa farm periodical, became secretary of agriculture; Charles Evans Hughes, former New York governor and 1916 presidential candidate, secretary of state; and Andrew W. Mellon, a Pittsburgh banker and financier, treasury secretary. Herbert Hoover, the wartime food administrator, dominated the cabinet as secretary of commerce.

Unfortunately, Harding also made some disastrous appointments: his political manager, Harry M. Daugherty, as attorney general; a Senate pal, Albert B. Fall of New Mexico, as secretary of the interior; and a wartime draft dodger whom Harding had met in Hawaii, Charles Forbes, as director of the Veterans' Bureau. These men, not the high-minded Hughes or Hoover, set the tone of the Harding years: an aura of back-room sleaze reminiscent of the Grant administration.

By 1922, as Washington rumor hinted at criminal activity in high places, Harding confessed to a friend, "I have no trouble with my enemies. . . . But . . . my goddamn friends . . . , they're the ones that keep me walking the floor nights." Seeking escape, Harding in 1923 vacationed in Alaska. In late July he suffered a heart attack, and on August 2, in a San Francisco hotel room, he died.

In 1924 a Senate investigation exposed the full scope of the scandals. Charles Forbes, convicted of stealing Veterans' Bureau funds, evaded prison by fleeing abroad. The bureau's general counsel committed suicide, as did an associate of Attorney General Daugherty accused of influence peddling. Daugherty himself, forced from office in 1924, escaped conviction in two criminal trials.

The seamiest scandal involved Interior Secretary Fall, who went to jail for secretly leasing government oil reserves in Elk Hills, California, and Teapot Dome, Wyoming, to two oilmen while accepting "loans" from them totaling four hundred thousand dollars. Like "Watergate" in the 1970s, "Teapot Dome" became a shorthand label for an entire legacy of presidential scandals.

Vice President Calvin Coolidge, on a family visit in the village of Plymouth, Vermont, took the presidential oath by lantern light from his father, a local magistrate.

Calvin Coolidge Throwing Out the First Ball
Coolidge, one wit said, must have been weaned on a pickle. Government's "greatest duty," he once observed, "is not to embark on any new ventures."

Coolidge brought a distinctly different style to the White House. Whereas Harding was convivial and talkative, Coolidge's naps and taciturnity became legendary. As he was leaving after a presidential visit to California, a radio reporter asked for a parting message to the people of the state. "Good-bye," Coolidge responded. When he died in 1933, humorist Dorothy Parker asked, "How could they tell?"

Apart from matters of style, the advent of Coolidge brought little change. Government policies in the 1920s reflected the prevailing probusiness climate. The Fordney-McCumber Tariff (1922) and the Smoot-Hawley Tariff (1930) pushed rates to all-time highs, benefiting domestic manufacturers. Thanks to the efforts of Treasury Secretary Andrew Mellon, Congress lowered the income-tax rates for the well-to-do. (To his credit, Mellon also balanced the federal budget every year from 1921 to 1928.) The Supreme Court under Chief Justice William Howard Taft, appointed by Harding in 1921,

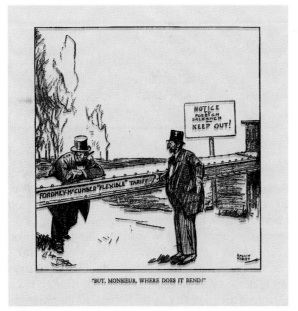

NOTICE
FOREIGN
SALESMEN
KEEP OUT!

FORDNEY-M^CUMBER "FLEXIBLE" TARIFF

"BUT, MONSIEUR, WHERE DOES IT BEND?"

The high U.S. tariffs of the 1920s reflected the postwar decade's isolationist mood. Despite certain "flexible" rate features, the Fordney-McCumber Tariff of 1922 reversed the downward trend of several earlier tariffs and erected prohibitive barriers against imported goods.

overturned several progressive reform measures opposed by influential business interests, including a 1919 federal law imposing punitive taxes on the products of child labor and a minimum-wage act for women workers in Washington, D.C. Coolidge rejected an aid request from Mississippi River flood victims with the prim reminder that the government had no duty to protect citizens "against the hazards of the elements."

Coolidge's veto of the McNary-Haugen farm bill further illuminated his philosophy of government. Warning of "the tyranny of bureaucratic regulation and control" that the plan would entail, he denounced the measure as an unconstitutional price-fixing scheme that would benefit farmers at the expense of "the general public welfare." Although his party had long championed high tariffs and other measures of benefit to business, Coolidge chafed when farmers pursued the same kind of special-interest politics.

Foreign Policy in an Isolationist Age

The arena of international relations produced Harding's most notable achievement: the Washington Naval Arms Conference. After the war ended in 1918,

the United States, Great Britain, and J ward a naval-arms race that none of ther. In July 1921 President Harding called for to deal with the problem. When the gat vened in Washington, Secretary of State Hu tled the delegates by proposing the destructic ur specific vessels to achieve an agreed-upon ratio of ships among the world's naval powers. When the admiral heading the British delegation heard Hughes's proposal, one observer recalled, he "came forward in his chair with the manner of a bulldog, sleeping on a sunny doorstep, who has been poked in the stomach."

In February 1922 the three nations, together with Italy and France, signed a treaty pledging to reduce their battleship tonnage by specified amounts and to observe a ten-year moratorium on battleship construction. The United States and Japan also agreed to respect each other's territorial holdings in the Pacific. Although this treaty ultimately failed to prevent war, it did represent an early arms-control effort.

Apart from the naval-arms conference, America followed an isolationist foreign policy in the 1920s. As U.S. corporate and financial interests spread worldwide, politically the nation turned inward, joining neither the League of Nations nor the Court of International Justice (the World Court), a League-sponsored agency to resolve international disputes. The United States did participate informally in some League agencies and conferences; but in general, symbolic gestures replaced meaningful international engagement. In 1928 the United States and France, eventually joined by sixty other nations, signed the Kellogg-Briand Pact renouncing aggression and calling for the outlawry of war. Lacking any enforcement mechanism, this high-sounding document did nothing to prevent the militarism that within a decade would again plunge the world into war.

U.S. insistence that its wartime allies repay their war debts in full produced much ill will. As President Coolidge laconically put it, "They hired [borrowed] the money, didn't they?" According to calculations by the Senate in 1922, the total Allied war debt and German reparations payments came to $22 billion, including interest. With the Allies' economies foundering and Germany wracked by inflation, the Allies in 1924 created a commission to address the reparations crisis. Charles G. Dawes, President Harding's budget director and Coolidge's 1924 running mate, chaired this commission. The resulting arrangement, called the Dawes Plan, scaled back U.S. war-debt and reparations

The Election of 1924

Candidates	Parties	Electoral Vote	Popular Vote	Percentage of Popular Vote
CALVIN COOLIDGE	Republican	382	15,718,211	54.0
John W. Davis	Democratic	136	8,385,283	28.8
Robert M. La Follette	Progressive	13	4,831,289	16.6

demands. But high U.S. tariff barriers and Germany's deepening financial crisis made it difficult for foreign powers to earn the dollars necessary to pay even the reduced levies.

Progressive Stirrings, Democratic Divisions

The progressive spirit survived in the legislative branch. Congress staved off Andrew Mellon's proposals for even deeper tax cuts for the rich. Senator George Norris of Nebraska successfully prevented the Coolidge administration from selling a federal hydroelectric facility at Muscle Shoals, Alabama, to automaker Henry Ford for a fraction of its value. And with the creation of the Federal Radio Commission (1927), Congress extended to this new industry the progressive principle of government regulation of business activity.

In 1922, a midterm election year, labor and farm groups formed the Conference for Progressive Political Action (CPPA), which helped defeat conservative Republican candidates. Meeting in Cleveland in July 1924, CPPA delegates revived the Progressive party; adopted a prolabor, profarmer platform that called for government ownership of railroads and nominated Wisconsin senator Robert La Follette for president. The Socialist party and the American Federation of Labor endorsed the nomination as well.

The Democratic party, split between its urban and rural wings, met in New York city for its 1924 convention. The depth of this split became evident when a resolution condemning the Ku Klux Klan failed by one vote, 542 to 541. In the contest for the presidential nomination, Woodrow Wilson's treasury secretary, William G. McAdoo, championed the party's rural, Protestant, southern wing, whereas the big-city delegates rallied behind Governor Alfred E. Smith of New York, a Roman Catholic of Irish immigrant origins.

As the delegates cast ballot after ballot in the stifling convention hall, neither McAdoo nor Smith could gain the necessary two-thirds majority. Joked humorist Will Rogers: "New York invited you folks here as guests, not to live." After 102 ballots the exhausted delegates nominated an obscure compromise candidate, John W. Davis, a conservative New York corporation lawyer. Despite the Democrats' support for some progressive reforms in the Wilson era, the party's close identification with the interests of the poor and minorities still lay ahead. In a gesture to the party's agrarian wing, however, Davis did choose as his running mate Governor Charles Bryan of Nebraska, the younger brother of William Jennings Bryan.

Calvin Coolidge easily won the Republican nomination. The Republican platform praised the high Fordney-McCumber Tariff, urged tax and spending cuts, and applauded the Washington Naval Arms Conference. With the economy humming, Coolidge cruised to victory with nearly 16 million votes, about twice Davis's total. La Follette garnered 4.8 million votes—a significant achievement for a third-party candidate but far short of victory. Indeed, La Follette's Progressive party candidacy, which divided the Democratic vote, helps to explain the magnitude of Coolidge's margin over Davis.

Women and Politics in the 1920s: A Dream Deferred

Suffragists' hope that votes for women would transform politics survived briefly after the war. The major parties added women to their national committees and in 1920 endorsed several platform planks drafted by the newly organized League of Women Voters. Polling places shifted from saloons to schools and churches; states that had not done so earlier passed laws permitting women to serve on juries and hold public office. The Women's Joint Congressional Committee, formed by a coalition of women's groups in 1919, lobbied for child-labor laws, protection of women workers, and federal support for education. The Sheppard-Towner Act (1921), passed in response to such lobbying, appropriated $1.2 million for rural prenatal and baby-care centers staffed by public-health nurses.

Alice Paul (1885–1977)
A student in England during the British suffrage campaign, Paul brought its militant tactics back to America. In the 1920s and after, she advocated an equal rights amendment to the Constitution.

Overall, however, the Nineteenth Amendment had little political impact. Women who had marched for suffrage and cooperated on other progressive reforms now scattered to all points on the political spectrum. Some voted Republican, others Socialist. Some joined the La Follette campaign in 1924, others worked to rebuild the Democratic party. Many withdrew from politics altogether. A midwestern women's club leader lamented that the hall where reformers once delivered passionate speeches "now rings with such terms as 'no trump' and 'grand slam.' "

As the women's movement splintered, it lost focus. Drawing mainly middle-class and professional women, the League of Women Voters abandoned activism for the "nonpartisan" study of civic issues. Some feminists worked for peace. Carrie Chapman Catt founded the National Conference on the Cause and Cure of War, and Jane Addams turned her energies to the Women's International League for Peace and Freedom.

Meanwhile, Alice Paul and her National Woman's party campaigned for an equal-rights amendment to the Constitution. Paul even opposed legislation protecting women workers because such laws supposedly implied women's inferiority. Most feminists, as well as radicals and labor activists, condemned her position. The amendment might benefit professional women, these critics charged, but it could hurt female factory workers if it meant the abolition of protective legislation. In any event, the proposed amendment got nowhere.

The conservative political atmosphere and materialistic mass culture of the 1920s underlay this disarray. Jane Addams and other women's rights leaders faced accusations of communist sympathies by right-wing groups. Countless young women, bombarded by advertising that defined liberation in terms of the purchase of consumer goods, found the prewar feminists' earnest civic idealism embarrassingly passé. One young woman in 1927 ridiculed "the old school of fighting feminists" for their lack of "feminine charm" and scorned the hard-core activists "who antagonize men with their constant clamor about maiden names, equal rights, [and] women's place in the world."

In such a climate, the few reforms achieved by organized women's groups often proved short-lived. The women's movement suffered serious setbacks when the Supreme Court struck down child-labor laws (1922) and women's protective laws (1923). A 1924 child-labor constitutional amendment opposed by business interests passed the Congress after heavy lobbying by women's organizations, but only a few states ratified it. And the Sheppard-Towner program of rural prenatal aid and baby care, denounced by the American Medical Association as an assault on physicians' monopoly of the health business, expired in 1929.

MASS SOCIETY, MASS CULTURE

The automobiles, electrical appliances, and myriad other products that flowed from the assembly lines in the 1920s reflected more than a change in the technological order. They heralded a new social and cultural era. Not only did these products themselves change Americans' everyday lives, but the standardized mass production that spawned them proved as adaptable to the realm of ideas as to the realm of roadsters and refrigerators.

A Nation of Cities, Consumer Goods, and Automobiles

The 1920 census confirmed that the United States had become a nation of cities. For the first time, the urban population outnumbered the rural. The census recorded a dozen cities of more than 600,000.

Blacks led the way in the migration cityward. By 1930 more than 40 percent of the nation's 12 million blacks lived in cities, 2 million of them in Chicago, Detroit, New York, and other metropolitan centers of the North and West. Signaling political changes to come, the first black congressman since Reconstruction, Oscar De Priest, was elected in 1928 from Chicago's South Side.

This urban growth had wide cultural ramifications. Although small-town values remained strong, the nation in the 1920s became increasingly urbanized, not only numerically but also, as one historian has written, "in the cast of its mind, in its ideals, and in its folkways." The powerful shaping agencies of the culture—radio, the movies, the corporations, the advertising agencies, the mass magazines—all operated from the urban centers. Even when these cultural voices nostalgically evoked rural values, they did so from big-city editorial offices and studios. It was in the cities, too, that the new consumer goods, particularly electrical appliances such as refrigerators, ranges, and vacuum cleaners, had the greatest impact.

For women, these innovations significantly reduced the hours and physical effort expended on housework. When Robert and Helen Lynd interviewed working-class women in Muncie in 1925, nearly 75 percent said that they spent less time on housework than had their mothers. Vacuum cleaners supplanted brooms, dustpans, and carpet beaters. The time-consuming task of firing up a wood stove became a memory. Store-bought clothes replaced homemade apparel. Even the refrigerator saved labor. One young woman of the 1920s, Florence Hunt of Madison, Wisconsin, later recalled: "I remember when we got our first electric refrigerator. Before that, we had the old oak icebox with the big cake of ice in the metal-lined chest below. The ice would melt into a pan underneath, and the pan would run over and make a big mess."

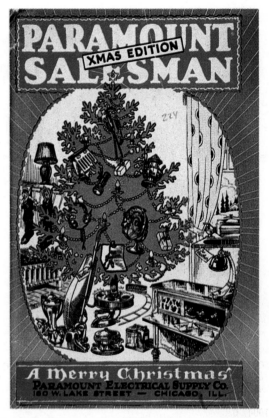

Christmas in Consumerland
Giving a modern twist to an ancient symbol, this advertising catalog of the 1920s offered an enticing array of new electric products for the home.

In the early twentieth century, many urban wives had patronized commercial laundries to spare themselves the onerous chore of home laundering. But with the arrival of the electric washing machine and iron, this task moved back into the home. In this respect, the new technology reversed the trend toward the socialization of housework that reformers like Charlotte Perkins Gilman had welcomed.

Food preparation and even diet also shifted in response to economic and technological change. The rise of the supermarket, for example, made sharp inroads on the annual ritual of canning. As one housewife commented in the mid-1920s, "You just spent your summer canning in 1890, but the canned goods you buy today are so good that it isn't worth your while." Similarly, before World War I, most housewives still baked their own bread, but by 1925 nearly 75 percent of the Muncie housewives told the Lynds

The Automobile Age: Passenger Cars Registered in the United States, 1900–1990

From a plaything for the rich, the automobile emerged after 1920 as the basic mode of transportation for the masses, in the process transforming American life in countless ways.

SOURCES: *Historical Statistics of the United States, Colonial Times to 1970* (Washington, D.C.: U.S. Government Printing Office, 1975), 716; *Statistical Abstract of the United States, 1994* (Washington, D.C.: U.S. Government Printing Office, 1994), 630.

that they used commercially baked bread. In earlier times fresh fruits, vegetables, and salads had vanished from American tables in winter. With the advent of refrigeration, supermarkets, and motor transport, fruits and vegetables became available year-round.

For social and cultural impact, nothing matched the automobile. Urban planners worriedly discussed traffic jams, parking problems, and the soaring accident rate. More than twenty-six thousand Americans died in traffic accidents in 1924. A Muncie resident challenged the Lynds: "Why on earth do you need to study what's changing this country? I can tell you what's happening in just four letters: A-U-T-O."

Like electrical appliances, the A-U-T-O reached into the lives of ordinary Americans. Family vacations, rare a generation earlier, now enjoyed a great vogue. City dwellers rediscovered the natural beauty of the land—though they often found that thousands of their fellow Ford owners had the same goal in mind! The automobile diminished the isolation of rural life and gave farm dwellers easier access to the city for shopping and entertainment.

Although the automobile could bring the family together, it could also erode family cohesion. Young people welcomed the freedom from parental oversight that it offered. As the Lynds observed, young people could now on a whim drive to a dance or party in a distant city. Complained one father, "It's getting so a fellow has to make a date with his family to see them."

The automobile's effects on individuality were similarly mixed. In contrast to train passengers, compelled to follow a fixed route and schedule, car owners could travel where they wished, when they wished. But in other ways, the automobile furthered standardized American life. Millions chugged around in identical black vehicles. One-room schoolhouses stood empty as buses carried children to consolidated schools. Neighborhood shops and markets declined as people drove to more distant chain stores. By no coincidence, the advent of the automobile age also brought the first suburban department stores, the first shopping center (in Kansas City), and the first fast-food chain (A & W Root Beer).

Even at $300 or $400, the automobile remained too expensive for the poor. A used-car market developed, but even so, car ownership only gradually penetrated the lowest economic ranks. Thus the "automobile suburbs" that sprang up beyond the streetcar lines attracted mainly the prosperous; the urban poor, including the growing black population, remained behind. This pattern laid the groundwork for urban-suburban social divisions that would widen in the decades ahead.

At the same time, the automobile's farm cousin, the tractor, transformed agriculture. The number of tractors soared from 246,000 in 1920 to 920,000 in 1930. In this period of low farm prices, many farmers went into debt to buy mechanized equipment, thus contributing to the worsening agricultural crisis.

Soaring Energy Consumption and a Threatened Environment

The proliferation of electrical products and of passenger cars had long-term implications for the environment and natural resources. With electrical use more than tripling in the 1920s, U.S. generating plants in 1929 consumed 42 million tons of coal, 10 million barrels of oil, and 112 million cubic feet of natural gas. And the 20 million automobiles clogging the nation's highways by 1929 not only embodied tons of steel but endlessly guzzled fuel. In 1916 U.S. refineries had

East River from the 30th Story of the Sheraton Hotel, *by Georgia O'Keeffe, 1928 Better known for her later paintings inspired by the New Mexico desert, O'Keeffe in this painting of a New York City scene incidentally recorded the atmospheric pollution issuing from factory smokestacks—one of many warnings of environmental problems ahead.*

produced under 50 million barrels of gasoline. In 1929 they refined 435 million barrels, using more than a billion barrels of crude oil in the process.

The need for gasoline set off fevered activity in the oilfields of Texas, Oklahoma, southern California, and elsewhere. The Teapot Dome scandal arose directly from the decade's rising oil demand. As wildcatters made and lost fortunes, oil company giants like Standard, Texaco, Gulf, and Atlantic solidified their dominance of the industry. Domestic oil production rose by some 250 percent in these years, and annual oil imports crept up from 61 million barrels to 76 million barrels.

The natural gas found with petroleum deposits seemed so abundant that much of it was simply burned off. Throughout most of the 1920s, the U.S. Bureau of Mines calculated, more than a billion cubic feet of natural gas went up in smoke *every day* in America's oil fields.

In short, the heavy consumption of nonrenewable fossil fuels, though still small by later standards, already characterized American society by the 1920s.

The wilderness that had inspired early nineteenth-century Americans with its sublimity came under heavy siege a hundred years later. Power plants, steel mills, and automobile engines pumped tons of pollutants into the atmosphere. The automobile opened more regions to easy human access—and human pollution. As ribbons of asphalt and cement snaked across the land, gas stations, billboards, restaurants, and tourist cabins followed.

Isolated voices protested. The Sierra Club and the Audubon Society worked to preserve wilderness and wildlife. *Outdoor America*, the magazine of the Izaak Walton League, published articles by well-known writers and public figures extolling the wilderness. In 1923 the Walton League persuaded Congress to halt a private-development scheme to drain the wetlands along a three-hundred-mile stretch of the Mississippi from Lake Pepin in Minnesota to Rock Island, Illinois. Instead this beautiful span of the river was declared a wildlife preserve.

Aldo Leopold of the U.S. Forest Service warned of the dangers of unchecked technology. For too long in the United States, wrote Leopold in 1925, "a stump was our symbol of progress." Americans accustomed to a seemingly boundless wilderness, he added, "are *unconscious* of what the disappearance of wild places would mean." Wilderness preservation demanded not just sentimental pronouncements, Leopold stressed, but careful planning and political savvy.

Few listened. To most Americans of the 1920s, pollution and a contracting wilderness seemed small prices to pay for the manifold benefits of the electric motor and the internal-combustion engine. The resources that were being depleted seemed almost limitless, and the industries that used them represented jobs, economic growth, and industrial development. The expansive, confident generation of the 1920s had little time for the environmental issues that would raise alarms two generations later.

Radio Mania

A 1920s furniture store capitalizes on the radio vogue with a display of the latest Atwater Kent models.

hours the fulfillment that jobs often failed to provide.

Just as Henry Ford offered standardized transportation, so entrepreneurs in other fields offered standardized amusement. The mass production of culture had started at least as early as the 1830s, of course, with the rise of the penny press, the dime novel, and the sentimental romance. But the process vastly accelerated in the twenties.

Mass-circulation magazines flourished. By 1922 ten American magazines boasted a circulation of more than 2.5 million each. Some of these trumpeted sex, crime, and "true confessions"; others presented a blend of fiction, cartoons, and stories. The venerable *Saturday Evening Post,* with its bucolic Norman Rockwell covers and its fiction featuring small-town life, specialized in prepackaged nostalgia. Onetime muckraking magazines like *Collier's* now offered far more soothing fare.

In 1921 the husband-and-wife team of DeWitt and Lila Wallace started *Reader's Digest,* a magazine that condensed articles originally published elsewhere. Perfectly attuned to the times, the *Digest* offered traditionalist, probusiness views in a standardized format and simple prose. Pitched to the mass market, it represented the journalistic counterpart of the Model T or the A&P.

Even bookselling saw major changes. The old-style bookstores, with their musty, individualistic flavor, declined as publishers marketed their products through department stores or mail-order houses such as the Book-of-the-Month Club and the Literary Guild, both established in 1926.

Routinized Work, Mass-Produced Pleasure

The new assembly-line techniques affected the way industrial employees viewed their work and themselves. The essence of the assembly line was repetitive labor, with a minimum of individual initiative or variation.

Managers in mass-production factories actively discouraged expressions of individuality and even communication among employees. Because talking or laughter could divert workers from their task, Ford employees learned to whisper without moving their lips and adopted a fixed, impassive mask that some called "Fordization of the face."

As work became more routine, its psychic rewards diminished. Life on the assembly line did not foster pride in one's skills or the specialized knowledge that came from years of farming or mastering a craft. Nor did the assembly line offer much prospect of advancement. In Muncie, factories employing over four thousand workers announced only ten openings for foremen in 1924 and 1925—less than one chance in four hundred for upward job mobility. These changes in the nature of work may have contributed—along with higher wages and a shorter workweek—to the rising interest in leisure-time activities in these years, as workers sought in their free

Radio and the movies contributed even more dramatically to the standardization of culture. As a mass-culture phenomenon, the radio era began on November 2, 1920, when station KDKA in Pittsburgh broadcast the news of Warren Harding's election. In 1921 New York's WEAF began a regular news program featuring H. V. Kaltenborn, and that autumn a Newark station broadcast the World Series (the Giants beat the Yankees). In 1922 five hundred new stations began operations. "There is radio music in the air, every night, everywhere," proclaimed a San Francisco newspaper; "anybody can hear it at home on a receiving set." By 1927 radio sales approached 7 million.

In 1926 three big corporations—General Electric, Westinghouse, and the Radio Corporation of America—formed the first radio network, the National Broadcasting Company (NBC). The Columbia Broadcasting System (CBS) followed in 1927. Consolidating the new medium, the networks soon ruled radio broadcasting. Programming reflected audience preferences as revealed through market research. From Maine to California, Americans laughed at the same jokes, hummed the same tunes, and absorbed the same commercials.

New York's WEAF broadcast the first commercially sponsored program in 1922, and soon the commercialization of the new medium was complete. The first network comedy show, the enormously popular (and mildly racist) "Amos 'n' Andy" (1928), brought millions in sales to its sponsor, Pepsodent toothpaste.

The movies, too, attracted a huge audience at all social levels as they expanded from the immigrant slums into elegant uptown theaters with names like "Majestic," "Ritz," and "Palace." First came the silent-film era, with such stars as the comedian Charlie Chaplin, the swashbuckling Douglas Fairbanks, the romantic Rudolph Valentino, and "America's sweetheart" Mary Pickford. Director Cecil B. De Mille won fame and fortune for lavish biblical spectacles such as *The Ten Commandments* (1923).

After Al Jolson's *The Jazz Singer* (1927) introduced sound to the movies, they became even more popular and spawned a new generation of screen idols, including the western hero Gary Cooper and the aloof Scandinavian beauty Greta Garbo. Another enduring Hollywood favorite, Mickey Mouse, made his debut in a 1928 animated cartoon, *Steamboat Willy*, produced by the young Walt Disney. By 1930 weekly movie attendance was nearly 80 million.

Like radio programming, movie production became more and more standardized. By 1930 such Hollywood giants as Metro-Goldwyn-Mayer, Warner Brothers, and Columbia turned out the vast majority of American films. Predictable plots and typecast stars prevailed.

Moviegoers entered a celluloid world far removed from reality. One movie ad in the *Saturday Evening*

Moviemaking at Warner Brothers Hollywood Studio
Pioneering in sound films in a movie-mad decade, Warner Brothers Pictures earned profits of more than $17 million in 1929.

Post promised "all the adventure, all the romance, all the excitement you lack in your daily life." These mass-produced fantasies shaped popular behavior and values, especially those of the impressionable young. In the words of writer John Dos Passos, Hollywood offered a "great bargain sale of five-and-ten-cent lusts and dreams."

The film industry also stimulated consumption by presenting alluring images of the good life. As a black high-school student told a social researcher in the 1920s, "The movies have often made me dissatisfied with my neighborhood, because when I see a movie [with] the beautiful castle, palace, . . . and beautiful house, I wish my home was something like these."

Fads, Celebrities, and Heroes

In this era of mass communication, when news could reach every corner of the nation in a few seconds, a succession of fads and media-promoted events—or pseudoevents—preoccupied millions of Americans. In 1921 Atlantic City promoted itself with a bathing-beauty competition grandly called the Miss America Pageant. In 1922 came the vogue for a Chinese game called mah-jongg. In 1924 a crossword-puzzle craze swept the country.

In professional sports massive publicity focused on a few larger-than-life celebrities: Babe Ruth of the New York Yankees, who hit sixty home runs in 1927; Ty Cobb, the Detroit Tigers' manager, whose earlier record of 4,191 major-league hits stood for many years; Gertrude Ederle, the first woman to swim the English Channel; prizefighters Jack Dempsey and Gene Tunney, whose heavyweight title fights in 1926 and 1927 attracted crowds totaling more than two hundred thousand and radio audiences many times larger.

The lives of some of these sports celebrities had a seamy side. Ruth was a coarse, heavy-drinking womanizer; Cobb, an ill-tempered racist. Yet the alchemy of publicity transformed them into exciting gladiators with lovable nicknames like the Sultan of Swat (Ruth) or the Georgia Peach (Cobb).

The ballyhoo extended to college sports as well. When Notre Dame played Army in 1924, sportswriter Grantland Rice memorably described Notre Dame's backfield:

> *Outlined against a blue-gray October sky, the Four Horsemen rode again. In dramatic lore, they are known as Famine, Pestilence, Destruction,*

> *and Death. These are only aliases. Their real names are Stuhldreher, Miller, Crowley, and Layden.*

Another 1920s legend was born. The four young players, looking acutely uncomfortable, even posed on horseback in their football uniforms as a publicity stunt.

This media-induced idolization of celebrities illuminates the anxieties and aspirations of ordinary Americans in these years. The young woman trying to define a role for herself in a period of confusing social change could find in the beauty pageants one kind of ideal to which she could aspire. For the man whose sense of mastery had been shaken by numerous developments from feminism to Fordism, cheering a sports hero like Dempsey or Ruth could momentarily restore a sense of pride and self-confidence.

The psychological meaning of this hero worship emerged with particular clarity in the response to Charles A. Lindbergh, the unknown young pilot who flew solo across the Atlantic on May 20–21, 1927. A Minnesotan of Swedish ancestry, Lindbergh spent the

Ty Cobb Displays His Batting Technique
In reality a mean-tempered racist, baseball's Ty Cobb enjoyed celebrity status in the 1920s as the "Georgia Peach." Here he met a group of boys with polio who were guests at a major-league game.

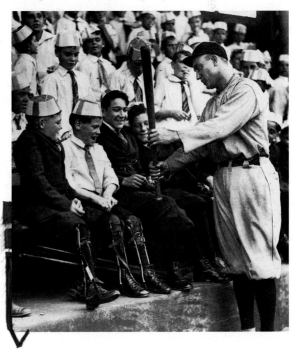

early twenties as a stunt flyer and airmail pilot and then decided to compete for a $25,000 prize offered by a New York hotel for the first nonstop New York–Paris flight. Lindbergh's daring flight in his silver-winged monoplane, *The Spirit of St. Louis,* captured the popular imagination. From the moment he touched down in Paris, the glare of media attention enveloped him. In blasé New York, thousands turned out for a ticker-tape parade. President Coolidge held a White House reception; radio, newspapers, magazines, and movie newsreels provided saturation coverage. With his shy smile and self-effacing modesty, the "Lone Eagle" handled his celebrity with dignity. In an age of scandals and scams, he proved an authentic hero.

Coolidge praised Lindbergh's flight as a triumph of corporate technology, but many editorialists saw his achievement as evidence that the individual still counted in an era of standardization and mechanization. To conservatives Lindbergh's solid virtues proved that the old verities survived in a time of moral disarray. Native-born midwesterners embraced the Minnesotan as one of their own and insisted that he, not urban immigrants, most truly represented America.

Clearly the social effects of the new mass media were neither all good nor all bad. The technologies of mass communication promoted cultural standardization and uniformity of thought and to a degree stifled local and regional diversity. But radio, the movies, and the mass magazines also helped forge a national culture and introduced millions of Americans to fresh viewpoints and new ways of behaving. While they entertained, the mass media also hammered home a powerful message: an individual's horizons need no longer be limited by his or her immediate environment. The spread of mass culture in the 1920s opened a larger world for ordinary Americans. If that world was often vacuous and tawdry, it was also sometimes exciting, stimulating, and provocative.

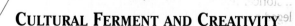

CULTURAL FERMENT AND CREATIVITY

The American experience in the 1920s involved more than political scandals, triumphs of productivity, and short-lived fads. This was also a decade of bubbling creativity. While some highly visible young people—and their parents—flouted the manners and morals of the prewar generation, writers, artists, musicians, and scien-

tists compiled a record of remarkable achievement. African-Americans, meanwhile, asserted their pride and collective energy through a remarkable cultural flowering known as the Harlem Renaissance. Pulsing through the decade were the rhythms of jazz, a black musical idiom that appealed to whites as well as blacks.

The Jazz Age and the Postwar Crisis of Values

The war and its sour aftermath brought to boil the simmering cultural restlessness of the prewar years. As Randolph Bourne, one of the first to grasp the war's profound cultural implications, wrote in 1918, "One has a sense of having come to a sudden, short stop at the end of an intellectual era." The postwar period confirmed Bourne's premonition. In *The Wasteland* (1922), poet T. S. Eliot evoked images of a shattered culture. Another poet, Ezra Pound, made the same point more brutally in *Hugh Selwyn Mauberley* (1920). America had gone to war, he wrote, to save "a botched civilization; . . . an old bitch gone in the teeth."

The postwar crisis of values took many forms. Some members of the younger generation—especially affluent college students—boisterously assailed older conventions of decorous behavior. Taking advantage of the decade's prosperity and the freedom offered by the automobile, they threw noisy parties, consumed bootleg liquor, flocked to jazz clubs, and danced the Charleston. When asked about her favorite activity, a California college student replied, "Of course, I adore dancing; who doesn't?"

The young also discussed sex more freely than their elders and in some cases indulged more openly in premarital sexual experimentation. Wrote novelist F. Scott Fitzgerald, "None of the Victorian mothers had any idea how casually their daughters were accustomed to be kissed." The ideas of Sigmund Freud, the Viennese physician whose studies of human sexuality first appeared in the 1890s, enjoyed a popular vogue in the 1920s—often in grossly oversimplified form.

Our knowledge of the 1920s "sexual revolution" derives largely from journalistic accounts and anecdotal reminiscences. Premarital sexual intercourse may have increased, but it was still exceptional, and widely disapproved of by the young as well as the older. What can be documented is a change in courtship patterns. In earlier periods "courting" implied a serious intention of marriage. In the 1920s the more informal ritual of dating evolved. Casual dating allowed young people

Doing the Charleston: A St. Louis Dance Contest in 1925
Media events like this helped shape the image of the 1920s as frivolous and pleasure mad. Originating among African-Americans of Charleston, South Carolina, the Charleston was popularized by the all-black Broadway musical review of 1923, Runnin' Wild.

to test compatibility and gain confidence in relating to the opposite sex without necessarily contemplating marriage. The twenties also brought greater erotic freedom, but within clear bounds. Despite moralists' charges of a total collapse of standards, most 1920s youth drew a distinct line between permissible and impermissible behavior.

The double standard, which held women to a stricter code of sexual conduct than men, remained in force. Whereas young men could boast of their sexual adventures, young women reputed to be "fast" could face ostracism. The male's traditional role in initiating sexual activity also survived intact in the 1920s, as revealed by the decade's elaborate etiquette of kissing. One male student summed up this etiquette: "Although a girl will not always let you kiss her when you ask her, she usually appreciates your asking her, often so much that she has to tell her friends."

Despite the double standard, the postwar changes in behavior did have a liberating effect on women. Female sexuality was acknowledged more openly. Skirt lengths crept up, makeup (once the badge of a prostitute) appeared on many female faces, and the elaborate armor of petticoats and corsets was drastically reduced. The awesome matronly bosom of the late nineteenth century mysteriously deflated in the twenties as a trimmer, more boyish figure became the fashion ideal.

With the medical risks of smoking as yet undiscovered, many thousands of American young women took up this habit. In a survey at Ohio State University, one-third of the women students said that they had tried cigarettes. Many of these new female smokers viewed the matter as a women's rights issue. As a woman student at the University of Illinois put it, "In this day one has a perfectly good right to ask why men should be permitted to smoke while girls are expelled for doing it."

Moral guardians protested these changes. A Methodist bishop denounced the new dances that brought "the bodies of men and women in unusual relation to each other." When the president of the women's college Bryn Mawr permitted students to smoke on campus in 1925, denunciations erupted. "Nothing has occurred in higher education that has so shocked our sense of social decency as the action of Bryn Mawr," fulminated the president of a Kansas teachers' college.

According to F. Scott Fitzgerald, around 1922 adults began to imitate the rebelliousness of the young. "[T]ired of watching the carnival with ill-concealed envy," he wrote, middle-aged Americans "discovered that young liquor will take the place of young blood, and with a whoop the orgy began." But cultural generalizations by novelists do not necessarily reflect historical reality. During the years of Fitzgerald's alleged national orgy, for example, the U.S. divorce rate remained constant.

The most enduring twenties stereotype is that of the flapper—the sophisticated, fashionable, pleasure-mad young woman. The term *flapper* apparently originated with a drawing by magazine illustrator John Held jr. depicting a young woman dressed in the latest fashion but with her rubber boots open and flapping.

(Held himself typified the 1920s. The product of a Mormon upbringing in Utah, he both lived and chronicled the fast life of this so-called Jazz Age. When that era ended in 1929, his career collapsed.)

Although many young women vaguely fit the flapper stereotype, it was largely a creation of journalists, fashion designers, and advertisers. But like all stereotypes, it played a cultural role. In the nineteenth century, the idealized woman on her lofty moral pedestal had symbolized an elaborate complex of cultural ideals. The semimythic flapper stereotype, with her bobbed hair, defiant cigarette, dangling beads, heavy makeup, and shockingly short skirt, similarly epitomized the rebelliousness pervading the youth culture of the twenties and signaled more changes ahead.

Indeed the entire Jazz Age was partially a mass-media and novelistic creation. F. Scott Fitzgerald's romanticized treatment of the affluent postwar young, *This Side of Paradise* (1920), spawned many imitators. A Catholic boy from St. Paul who left Princeton when he failed chemistry, Fitzgerald was only twenty-four when his best-selling novel appeared. With his sculpted good looks, wavy blond hair, and striking green eyes, he, like John Held jr., not only wrote about the Jazz Age but lived it. Flush with royalties, he and his wife Zelda partied away the early twenties in New York, Paris, and the French Mediterranean.

A moralist at heart, Fitzgerald both admired and deplored Jazz Age behavior. His finest novel, *The Great Gatsby* (1925), brilliantly captures not only the gilded existence of the superrich and the social climbers of the 1920s but also the coldhearted selfishness and romantic illusions that ruled their lives.

As a description of the 1920s, the "Jazz Age" label must be applied with care. The upheaval in manners and morals was genuine but limited to a narrow social stratum. Old values did not vanish in a hazy blur of alcoholic parties, suggestive dances, and backseat sex. Millions of Americans adhered to traditional ways and traditional standards. Most farmers, blacks, industrial workers, and recent immigrants found economic survival more pressing than the latest dance craze or the newest flapper fads and fashions.

But like the "flapper," the "Jazz Age" stereotype did capture a part of the postwar scene, especially the brassy, urban-based mass culture and the hedonism that contrasted so sharply with the idealism and social commitment of the Progressive Era and the war years. After the stock market crash of 1929 (see Chapter 25), nostalgia-tinged memories of the "Jazz Age" would underscore the differences between the supposedly carefree 1920s and the grim 1930s.

Alienated Writers

Like Fitzgerald, many young writers found the cultural turbulence of the 1920s a creative stimulus. The decade's most talented writers forged a remarkable body of work that was equally hostile to the moralistic pieties of the old order and the business pieties of the new.

The definitive literary skewering of postwar American society came in the novels of Sinclair Lewis, who had left his native Sauk Centre, Minnesota, in 1902 and rarely returned except in imagination. In *Main Street* (1920), Lewis caustically depicted the cultural barrenness and smug self-satisfaction of a fictional midwestern farm town, Gopher Prairie. In *Babbitt* (1922) he wielded his satirical scalpel upon a larger city, Zenith. In the character of George F. Babbitt, a middle-aged real-estate agent trapped in stifling middle-class conformity, Lewis created one of the memorable figures of American fiction.

The scorn for middle-class America that dripped from Lewis's novels found its journalistic counterpart in the work of H. L. Mencken, a Baltimore newspaperman of German stock who in 1924 founded and became coeditor of *The American Mercury* magazine, the bible of the decade's alienated intellectuals. An influential cultural arbiter, Mencken championed writers like Sinclair Lewis and Theodore Dreiser while ridiculing small-town Americans, Protestant fundamentalists, the middle class (Mencken called it the Booboisie), and mainstream American culture generally. His devastating essays on Wilson, Harding, Coolidge, and Bryan are classics of political satire. Asked why he remained in a nation so contemptible, Mencken replied, "Why do people visit zoos?"

A visual equivalent of Mencken's raucous iconoclasm was offered by photographer Alfred Stieglitz. In a 1923 show in New York, Stieglitz displayed a close-up photo of a gelded horse's underside with the caption "Spiritual America."

Some young writers spent the 1920s abroad, often in France. Even before the war, Eliot, Pound, and Gertrude Stein had become expatriates, and after the armistice other aspiring writers joined them. The most famous expatriate, Ernest Hemingway, had grown up in Oak Park, Illinois, become a reporter, and suffered serious wounds while serving as a Red Cross volunteer on the Italian front during the war. In 1921, at the age of twenty-two, Hemingway settled in Paris and began to write. In *The Sun Also Rises* (1926), he portrayed a group of American and English young people, variously shattered by the war, as they drift around Spain. Even writers who stayed home often underwent a kind of inner expatriation, distancing themselves from the dominant business culture. Willa Cather, for example, produced a series of novels that implicitly repudiated modern mass society by evoking alternatives ranging from early New Mexico (*Death Comes for the Archbishop*, 1927) to seventeenth-century Quebec (*Shadows on the Rock*, 1931).

For this generation of writers, World War I represented a seminal experience. The best of the war novels, Hemingway's *A Farewell to Arms* (1929), loosely based on the author's own experiences in Italy, powerfully depicted the war's futility and the leaders' inflated rhetoric. Avoiding the elaborate style and lofty abstractions of much prewar literature, Hemingway invented a terse, pared-down style. In a famous passage of *A Farewell to Arms*, the narrator says

> *I was always embarrassed by the words sacred, glorious, and sacrifice and the expression in vain. We had heard them . . . and had read them, on proclamations that were slapped up by billposters over other proclamations, now for a long time, and I had seen nothing sacred, and the things that were glorious had no glory and the sacrifices were like the stockyards at Chicago if nothing was done with the meat except to bury it. There were many words that you could not stand to hear and finally only the names of places had dignity.*

But though writers gagged at Wilsonian rhetoric, village narrowness, and chamber-of-commerce cant, they remained at heart deeply American. A hopeful, often buoyantly confident desire to create a vital and authentic national culture inspired their literary efforts, just as it had earlier inspired Hawthorne, Melville, and Whitman.

The social changes of these years energized African-American cultural life as well. Blacks' growing concentration in the urban North, especially in New York City, contributed to a black cultural flowering of the 1920s known as the Harlem Renaissance. This surge of artistic creativity took many forms, from all-black Broadway musical reviews to poems and novels exploring the African-American experience (see "A

Place in Time"). Harlem Renaissance figures flocked to memorable parties at Dark Towers, the elegant penthouse apartment of A'Lelia Walker, whose mother, known as Madame C. J. Walker, had amassed a fortune in the hair-preparation business.

Achievements in Architecture, Painting, and Music

The creative energies of the 1920s found other outlets as well. A burst of architectural activity, for example, transformed the urban skyline, especially in the larger cities. Chaotically eclectic in style, this architecture nevertheless displayed tremendous vitality. By the end of the decade, the United States boasted 377 buildings over 70 stories tall. The skyscraper, proclaimed one architectural writer, "epitomizes American life and American civilization."

Not everyone was enamored of the skyscraper and urbanization. Cultural critic Lewis Mumford, for example, lashed out at cities, with their "labyrinths of subways, . . . audacious towers, [and] . . . endless miles of asphalted pavements." As an alternative to ever more gargantuan and impersonal cities, Mumford advocated decentralization and a revitalization of the nation's regional roots.

Artists of the twenties turned to America itself for inspiration—either the real nation around them or the one that they held in memory. Whereas muralist Thomas Hart Benton evoked a vanished, half-mythic America of cowboys, pioneers, and riverboat gamblers, Edward Hopper starkly portrayed a nation of faded small towns and lonely cities. In such paintings as *Sunday* (1926), in which an elderly man slumps on the curb of an empty sidewalk in front of a row of abandoned stores, Hopper conveyed both the dreariness and the potential beauty of urban America.

Other 1920s painters offered more upbeat images. John Sloan's vibrant and colorful *Main Street Gloucester* (1921), conveys a very different mood from that of Sinclair Lewis's novel *Main Street*, published the year before. Charles DeMuth painted boldly geometric grain elevators, factories, and urban scenes, and painter and photographer Charles Sheeler recorded on film a dramatic series of images of Ford's River Rouge plant near Detroit. Wisconsin native Georgia O'Keeffe came to New York City in 1918 when Alfred Stieglitz (whom she married in 1924) mounted a show of her work. O'Keeffe's 1920s paintings evoked both the congestion and the excitement of Manhattan.

Harlem in the Twenties

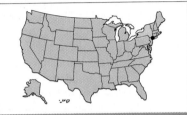

Braving chilly breezes, New Yorkers cheered warmly on February 17, 1919, as the all-black Fifteenth Infantry Regiment, back from France, paraded up Fifth Avenue. Led by Lieutenant James Europe's band, thousands of black troops marched in formation. Banners blazed: "OUR HEROES — WELCOME HOME." When the parade reached Harlem, north of Central Park, discipline collapsed amid joyous reunions. A new day seemed at hand for black America, and Harlem stood at its center.

The part of Manhattan Island that the early Dutch settlers had called Nieuw Haarlem was in transition by 1920. An elite suburb in the late nineteenth century, Harlem evolved rapidly during the First World War as its black population swelled. Some 400,000 southern blacks in search of wartime work migrated northward from 1914 to 1918, and the influx continued in the 1920s. That decade, New York City's black community surged from 152,000 to 327,000. Most of the newcomers settled in Harlem, where handsome old brownstone apartments were subdivided to house them. But racism and lack of education took their toll. Black Harlem had a small middle class of entrepreneurs, ministers, and funeral directors, but most Harlemites held low-paying, unskilled jobs. Many found no work at all. Overcrowding and the population spurt gave rise to social problems and high rates of tuberculosis, infant mortality, and venereal disease.

Poet and Novelist Langston Hughes,
by Winold Reiss

But Harlem also became a vibrant center of black cultural activity in the twenties. On the musical-comedy stage, the 1921 hit *Shuffle Along* launched a series of popular all-black reviews. The 1923 show *Runnin' Wild* sparked the Charleston dance craze. The Cotton Club and other Harlem cabarets featured such jazz geniuses as Duke Ellington, Fletcher Henderson, and Jelly Roll Morton. Muralist Aaron Douglas, concert tenor Roland Hayes, and singer-actor Paul Robeson contributed to the cultural ferment.

Above all, the Harlem Renaissance was a literary movement. The poet Langston Hughes drew upon the oral traditions of transplanted southern blacks in *The Weary Blues* (1926). The Jamaican writer Claude McKay evoked Harlem's throbbing, sometimes sinister nightlife in *Home to Harlem* (1928). In his avant-garde work *Cane* (1923), Jean Toomer used poems, drama, and short stories to convey the thwarted efforts of a young northern mulatto to penetrate the mysterious, sensual world of the black South. In her novel *Quicksand* (1928), Nella Larsen, a native of the Danish West Indies, told of a mulatto woman's struggle with her own sexuality and with the divergent cultural worlds of Denmark, the West Indies, the American South, and Harlem.

In essays and conversations at late-night parties, talented young blacks explored the challenge of finding a distinct cultural voice in white America. The gentle philosopher Alain Locke, a former Rhodes scholar who taught at Howard University in Washington, D.C., assembled essays, poems, and short stories in *The New Negro* (1925), a landmark work that hailed the Harlem Renaissance as black America's "spiritual coming of age." Wrote Locke: "Harlem, I grant you, isn't typical, but it is significant. It is prophetic."

White America quickly took notice. Book publishers courted black authors. Charlotte Mason, a wealthy Park Avenue matron, funded the aspiring writers Langston Hughes and Zora Neale Hurston. The novelist and photographer Carl Van Vechten introduced black artists and writers to editors, publishers, and producers. White writers discovered and sometimes distorted black life. Eugene O'Neill's play *The Emperor Jones*, produced in 1921, starred Charles Gilpin as a fear-crazed

Jazz Pianist, Composer, and Band Leader Ferdinand (Jelly Roll) Morton
Rooted in the rich musical traditions of African-Americans, jazz shaped the rhythm and beat of the Harlem Renaissance.

tunately I did not feel the rhythms of the primitive surging through me ... I was only an American Negro. I was not Africa. I was Chicago and Kansas City and Broadway and Harlem."

The Harlem Renaissance lacked a political framework or organic ties to the larger African-American experience. Indeed, Alain Locke in *The New York Negro* urged talented blacks to shift from "the arid fields of controversy and debate to the productive fields of creative expression." The writers and artists of the Renaissance ignored the racism, discrimination, and economic troubles faced by most African-Americans in the 1920s. They reacted with hostility to Marcus Garvey and his efforts to mobilize the urban black masses.

With the stock market crash in 1929 and the onset of the Great Depression, the Harlem Renaissance ended. In the 1930s, a new generation of writers led by Richard Wright would launch a more politically engaged black cultural movement. Looking back in 1935, Alain Locke would write sadly: "The rosy enthusiasm and hopes of 1925 were cruelly deceptive mirages. [The Depression] revealed a Harlem that the social worker knew all along, but had not been able to dramatize. There is no cure or saving magic in poetry and art for precarious marginal employment, high mortality rates, and civic neglect." Langston Hughes tersely assessed the movement in his 1940 autobiography: "The ordinary Negroes hadn't heard of the Negro Renaissance. And if they had, it hadn't raised their wages any."

But for all its naïveté, the Harlem Renaissance left an important legacy. The post–World War II literary flowering that began with Ralph Ellison's *Invisible Man* (1952) and continued with the works of James Baldwin, Toni Morrison, Alice Walker, and others owed a substantial debt to the Harlem Renaissance. Walker, in particular, would pay generous tribute to Zora Neale Hurston. For black writers in the West Indies and in French West Africa, "Harlem" would become a core motif, a symbol of both racial oppression and racial achievement. A fragile flower battered by the cold winds of the depression, the Harlem Renaissance nevertheless stands as a monument to African-American cultural creativity even under difficult circumstances.

West Indian tyrant. King Vidor's 1929 movie *Hallelujah,* featuring an all-black cast, romanticized plantation life and warned of the city's dangers. The 1925 novel *Porgy,* by Dubose and Dorothy Heyward, offered a sympathetic but sentimentalized picture of Charleston's black community. Reworked as a drama, *Porgy* won the Pulitzer Prize in 1927; George Gershwin's musical adaptation, *Porgy and Bess,* appeared in 1935.

In a decade of prohibition and shifting sexual mores, Harlem seemed to offer sensuality, eroticism, and escape from taboos. Prostitutes, speakeasies, and cocaine were indeed readily available. The whites who packed the late-night jazz clubs and the pulsating dance reviews and who patronized black writers and artists widely praised black culture for its "spontaneous," "primitive," or "spiritual" quali-

ties. Harlem, writes historian Nathan Huggins, offered the hope of recovering "that essential self one somehow lost on the way to civility." Few whites bothered to examine the more prosaic realities of Harlem life. The Cotton Club, controlled by gangsters, featured black performers but barred most blacks from the audience. Observed black writer Rudolph Fisher in 1927: "White people [once] went to Negro cabarets to see how Negroes acted; now Negroes go to these same cabarets to see how white people act."

And with patronage came subtle attempts at control. When Langston Hughes in the 1930s began to write about urban poverty rather than Africa or black spirituality, Charlotte Mason angrily withdrew her support. Wrote Hughes later: "Concerning Negroes, she felt that they were America's great link with the primitive. . . . But unfor-

The Great White Way,
by Howard Thain, 1925
This painting radiates the
vibrancy, bright lights, and
raucous commercialism of
New York City, the nation's
premier metropolis in the
booming 1920s.

Musical performers and composers, too, exploited the cultural resources that they knew best. As composer Aaron Copland later recalled, describing his days as a music student in Paris in the early twenties, "The conviction grew inside me that the two things that seemed always to have been so separate in America—music and the life about me—must be made to touch."

Whereas Copland and other composers drew upon folk-music traditions, still others evoked the new urban-industrial America. Composer Frederick Converse's 1927 tone poem about the automobile, "Flivver Ten Million," for example, featured such episodes as "Dawn in Detroit," "May Night by the Roadside," and "The Collision." Employing the new medium of radio, conductor Walter Damrosch brought classical music to millions with his "Music Appreciation Hour" on NBC.

Above all, American music in the 1920s meant jazz. The Original Dixieland Jazz Band—five white musicians imitating the black jazz bands of New Orleans—debuted at Reisenweber's Cabaret in New York City in January 1917, and a jazz vogue soon began. "A college existence without jazz," insisted one student newspaper, "would be like a child's Christmas without Santa Claus."

The white bands that introduced jazz to a larger audience in the twenties also drained it of much of its energy. The most popular white band leader of the decade, Paul Whiteman, offered watered-down "jazz" versions of standard tunes and light classical works. Of the white composers who wrote in a jazz idiom, George Gershwin, with his *Rhapsody in Blue* (1924) and *An American in Paris* (1928), was the most original.

Meanwhile, black musicians were replenishing the springs of authentic jazz. Guitar picker Hudie Ledbetter (nicknamed Leadbelly) performed his field shouts and raw songs before appreciative black audiences in the South. Singers like Bessie Smith and Gertrude ("Ma") Rainey drew packed audiences on Chicago's South Side and recorded on black-oriented labels produced by the major record companies. Trumpeter Louis ("Satchmo") Armstrong and band leader Fletcher Henderson did some of their most creative work in the 1920s, while the enormously talented black pianist, composer, and band leader Duke Ellington performed to packed audiences at Harlem's Cotton Club.

Advances in Science and Medicine

In a quite different field of endeavor, the creativity of the 1920s bubbled up as well in a diversity of scientific developments that would reverberate for decades to come. The first long-range television transmission, from New York City to Washington, occurred in 1927. In nuclear physics Arthur H. Compton of the University of Chicago won the Nobel Prize in 1927 for his studies on the nature of X rays, and Ernest O. Lawrence of the University of California laid the theoretical groundwork that led to the construction of the first cyclotron in the early thirties.

The 1920s also witnessed important gains in medical research. Harvey Cushing of Harvard Medical School made dramatic advances in neurosurgery, and at the University of Wisconsin, chemist Harry Steenbock discovered how to create vitamin D in milk by bombarding it with ultraviolet rays. Advances in the treatment of such killers as diphtheria, whooping cough, measles, and influenza helped produce a significant lengthening of life-expectancy rates.

Meanwhile, in 1919 a physicist at Clark University in Massachusetts, Robert Goddard, published a little-noticed scientific article entitled "A Method of Reaching Extreme Altitudes." Throughout the 1920s Goddard studied the problem of rocketry and even performed rudimentary experiments including, in 1926, the first successful launch of a liquid-fuel rocket. Ridiculed at the time, Goddard's predictions of lunar landings and deep-space exploration proved prophetic.

A few observers sensed the stirrings of a new era of scientific advance. In *Science and the Modern World* (1925), Harvard philosopher Alfred North Whitehead underscored science's growing role. Although "individually powerless," Whitehead concluded, scientists were "ultimately the rulers of the world." Although some found this prospect exhilarating, for many others it was simply one more in an array of disorienting social changes that made the 1920s an unusually stressful and conflict-ridden decade.

A SOCIETY IN CONFLICT

Despite prosperity and superficial gaiety, American society faced severe strains in the 1920s. The cultural homogeneity of an earlier day had collapsed under the combined assault of immigration, technology, urban growth, and Darwinian evolutionary theory. As a consequence, rural Americans uneasily surveyed the mushrooming cities; native-born Protestants apprehensively eyed the swelling ranks of Catholics and Jews;

and upholders of traditional standards viewed the revolution in manners and morals with dismay. These complex crosscurrents manifested themselves in a series of highly charged episodes and movements that cast in harsh relief the social tensions of these years.

Immigration Restriction

Fed by wartime superpatriotism, the venerable impulse to turn America into a nation of like-minded, culturally identical people crested in the 1920s. In 1921 Congress limited annual immigration to about 350,000. The National Origins Act of 1924 slashed the total to 164,000 and restricted immigration from any one nation to 2 percent of the total number of persons of that "national origin" already in the United States in 1890. Since the great influx of southern and eastern Europeans had come after 1890, the intent of this provision was clear: to reduce the immigration of these people. As Calvin Coolidge observed upon signing the law, "America must be kept American." Furthermore, by excluding Asians entirely, the 1924 law gratuitously insulted the Chinese and Japanese.

In 1929 Congress advanced the base year for determining "national origins" forward to 1920, but even under this formula, the annual quota for Poland stood at a mere 6,500; for Italy, 5,800; and for Russia, 2,700. This quota system, which survived into the 1960s, represented the most enduring counterattack of rural, native-born America against the immigrant cities.

Because most restrictionists viewed Asia and southern and eastern Europe as the sources of "undesirables," the laws placed no restraints on immigration from the Western Hemisphere. In fact, immigration from French Canada and Latin America soared in the 1920s. Poverty and domestic political turmoil propelled many thousands of Mexicans northward. By 1930 at least 2 million Mexican-born people lived in the United States, half of them in Texas, California, and Arizona. California's Mexican-American population soared from 90,000 to nearly 360,000 in the 1920s. Many of these newcomers to the Southwest became migratory farm workers who lived in shacks and earned miserably low wages in the region's large-scale agribusinesses.

The Sacco-Vanzetti Case

The same nativist, antiradical sentiments that produced the postwar Red Scare and underlay the immigration-restriction movement emerged starkly in a controversy over a Massachusetts murder case that quickly became a *cause célèbre*. On April 15, 1920, robbers shot and killed the paymaster and guard of a shoe factory in South Braintree, Massachusetts, and stole two cash boxes containing $17,776.51. Three weeks later the police arrested two Italian immigrants, Nicola Sacco and Bartolomeo Vanzetti, and charged them with the murders. A jury found them guilty in 1921, and after repeated delays and appeals, they died in the electric chair on August 23, 1927.

These bare facts do not begin to convey the texture of the case or the emotions it aroused. Sacco and Vanzetti were not only immigrants but avowed anarchists, and from the start the prosecution harped on their radicalism. The judge, a conservative Yankee Republican, made plain his hostility to the defendants, whom he privately called "those anarchist bastards."

The Sacco-Vanzetti case encapsulated divisions in the larger society. Nativists dwelled on the defendants' immigrant origins. Conservatives, brushing aside issues raised by the defense, insisted that these alien anarchists must die. By contrast, prominent liberals such as Felix Frankfurter of the Harvard Law School (a future Supreme Court justice); socialist Eugene Debs; and writers and artists like John Dos Passos, Edna St. Vincent Millay, and Ben Shahn rallied around the convicted men.

In 1927, a prestigious commission appointed by the governor of Massachusetts to review the case upheld the verdict. As Sacco and Vanzetti went to the chair twenty-seven days later, John Dos Passos summed up his feelings in a bitter poem that concluded:

> *All right you have won you will kill the brave*
> *   men our friends tonight*
> *. . . all right we are two nations.*

Whether Sacco and Vanzetti actually committed the murders remains uncertain. The case against them was circumstantial and far from airtight. However, recent findings, including research on Boston's anarchist community and ballistics tests on Sacco's gun, suggest that they may have been guilty. But the poisonous political climate that tainted the trial remains indisputable, as does the case's symbolic importance in exposing the splits in American society in the 1920s.

The Ku Klux Klan

The nativism of the immigration-restriction movement erupted even more viciously in the revived Ku Klux Klan. The original Klan had faded by the 1870s, but in

A Ku Klux Klan Ceremony on Long Island in the Early 1920s
The baby has been outfitted with its own white hood and robe. During its brief heyday after World War I, the revived Klan won many adherents all over the country to its message of white supremacy, moral purity, and 100 percent Americanism.

November 1915, a group of hooded men gathered at Stone Mountain, Georgia, and revived it. D. W. Griffith's glorification of the Klan in *The Birth of a Nation* provided further inspiration.

The movement attracted little notice until 1920, when two Atlanta public-relations specialists organized a national membership drive. Sensing the appeal of the Klan's nativist, white-supremacist ideology and its secret ritualism, they devised a recruitment campaign involving a ten-dollar membership fee divided among the salesman (called the Kleagle) signing up new members, the local sales manager (King Kleagle), the district sales manager (Grand Goblin), and "Imperial Wizard" William J. Simmons—with a rake-off to themselves. The enterprising pair also negotiated exclusive rights to sell Klan robes and masks ($6.50), the horse robe that every member had to buy whether or not he owned a horse ($8.00), and the genuine Chattahoochee River water used in initiation rites ($10.00 a bottle). This elaborate scam succeeded beyond anyone's wildest dreams.

Estimates of the new recruits to the Klan or its auxiliary, Women of the Klan, in the early twenties range as high as 5 million. From its southern base, the Klan spread through the Midwest and Far West, especially in cities and towns where the native-born Protestant population remained dominant. The Klan drew from both blue-collar and lower-white-collar ranks, including salespeople, clerks, and small businesspeople.

For a time, the Klan exerted real political power in Texas, Oklahoma, Oregon, Indiana, and other states. In Oklahoma the Klan-controlled legislature impeached and removed an anti-Klan governor. The Klan elected a governor in Oregon and pushed through legislation requiring public-school attendance of all children. Although the U.S. Supreme Court eventually judged this law unconstitutional, the state's Catholic school system suffered.

In 1922 a dentist from Texas, Hiram Wesley Evans, who described himself as "the most average man in America," became Imperial Wizard. Disarmingly admitting the Klan's image as a haven of "hicks" and "rubes," Evans urged the college-bred to support the great cause.

Under the umbrella term "100 percent Americanism," the thrust of Klan bigotry varied from region to region. In the South the antiblack theme loomed large. Klaverns in the North and West more often targeted Catholics and Jews. In the Southwest the Klan singled out violators of prohibition for vigilante action.

The Klan of the 1920s filled important needs for its members. Although riddled with corruption at the top, it was not a movement of criminals or fanatics; observers commented on the ordinariness of the members. The Klan's promise to restore the nation to an imagined purity—ethnic, moral, and religious—appealed powerfully to ill-educated, deeply religious, and economically marginal Americans threatened by a rapidly changing society.

For small businessmen caught between organized labor and the new corporate order, the Klan's ideology of white supremacy offered a racist vocabulary for articulating economic anxieties. For men made uneasy by woman suffrage and by changing sexual mores among the young, the Klan's pledge to fight for the "purity of white womanhood" had a powerful pull.

Klan membership also gave a sense of importance and group cohesion to native-born citizens who felt disoriented and marginalized by the new social order of immigrants, big cities, radio, and the movies. The ritual, the ceremonials, and the burning crosses lit up drab lives with drama and excitement. As one member wrote, "Who can look upon a multitude of white-robed Klansmen without thinking . . . of that throng of white-robed saints in the Glory Land?"

But if the individual Klan member seems more weak and alienated than sinister, the movement as a whole was far from benign. Klan members resorted to intimidation, threats, beatings, and even murder in their racist quest for a purified America.

The Klan collapsed with shocking suddenness. In March 1925 Indiana's politically influential Grand Dragon, David Stephenson, pressed bootleg liquor on a young secretary, forced her on a Pullman train bound for Chicago, and raped her. When she swallowed poison the next day, Stephenson and his henchmen refused to call a physician. The woman died several weeks later, and the Grand Dragon went to jail for first-degree manslaughter. From prison he revealed details of pervasive political corruption in Indiana. Its high moral pretensions in shreds, the Klan faded rapidly. The social tensions that had incubated its growth eased in the altered climate of the 1930s. The Klan did not die, however, and after World War II again surfaced as a malignant influence in American life.

The Garvey Movement

Among African-Americans the decade's social strains produced a different kind of mass movement. For most blacks, escape from southern rural poverty made worse by racism led only to northern ghetto poverty made worse by racism. Many poor urban blacks turned to the spellbinding orator Marcus Garvey and his Universal Negro Improvement Association (UNIA). In a society where white represented the ideal, Garvey inverted the formula and glorified all things black. He urged black economic cooperation and founded a chain of UNIA grocery stores and other businesses. Finally, Garvey called on the world's blacks to return to "Motherland Africa" and establish a nation "strong enough to lend protection to the members of our race scattered all over the world."

An estimated eighty thousand blacks joined the UNIA, and many thousands more felt the lure of Garvey's hypnotic oratory; the uplift of the colorful UNIA parades, uniforms, and flags; and the seduction of Garvey's dream of a mass return to Africa. Garvey's mobilization of the black masses unsettled not only white America but also the middle-class leaders of the NAACP and the black church. W. E. B. Du Bois of the NAACP was one of Garvey's sharpest critics.

In 1923 a federal court convicted Garvey of fraud in connection with the Black Star Steamship Company, one of his business ventures. In 1927, after two years' imprisonment, Garvey was deported to Jamaica. Without its charismatic leader, the UNIA collapsed. But as the first mass movement in black America, it revealed the discontent seething in the urban ghettos and the potential for large-scale activism. "In a world where black is despised," commented a black newspaper upon Garvey's deportation, "he taught them that black is beautiful."

Fundamentalism and the Scopes Trial

American Protestantism had undergone severe trials in the half-century before 1920. The prestige of science had increased steadily, challenging religion's high cultural standing. Scholars had dissected the Bible's historical origins, and psychologists had explained the religious impulse in terms of human emotional needs. And all the while, Catholic and Jewish immigrants had poured in.

Liberal Protestantism had responded by accepting the findings of science and emphasizing social service to the immigrants. By around 1910 the Social Gospel seemingly had taken firm root. But a reaction was building. This reaction came to be known as fundamentalism, after *The Fundamentals*, a series of pamphlets published in 1909–1914. Protestant fundamentalists insisted on the divine inspiration of every word in the Bible, on the Genesis version of Creation, and on the virgin birth and resurrection of Jesus. Social Gospelers and "modernists," they insisted, had abandoned these truths.

In the early 1920s, fundamentalists focused especially on a single issue: the theory of evolution. The evolutionary theory that Charles Darwin had advanced in *On the Origin of Species* (1859) seemed to fundamentalists to be a blatant rejection of biblical truth. Fundamentalist legislators in twenty states in 1921–1922 introduced bills to prohibit the teaching of evolution in the public schools, and several southern states enacted such legislation. In Texas, Governor Miriam ("Ma") Ferguson personally censored textbooks that discussed evolution. "I am a Christian mother," Ferguson declared, "and I am not going to let that kind of rot go into Texas textbooks." Fundamentalism's best-known champion in these years, aging politician William Jennings Bryan, vigorously endorsed the anti-evolution cause.

When the Tennessee legislature in 1925 outlawed the teaching of evolution in the public schools, the American Civil Liberties Union (ACLU) volunteered to defend any teacher willing to challenge this law. A young high-school biology teacher in the town of Dayton, Tennessee, John T. Scopes, accepted the offer. Scopes read to his class a textbook description of Darwin's theory, and his arrest duly followed.

Chicago criminal lawyer Clarence Darrow headed the ACLU's team of lawyers, and William Jennings Bryan assisted the prosecution. Journalists and photographers poured into Dayton, Chicago radio station WGN broadcast the proceedings live, and the Scopes "monkey trial" became an overnight sensation.

The trial's symbolic climax came when Darrow cross-examined Bryan on his religious beliefs and his scientific knowledge. As Bryan doggedly insisted on the literal accuracy of every story in the Bible, his ignorance of vast realms of human knowledge became painfully clear. Darrow amply succeeded in humiliating Bryan and ridiculing his "fool ideas." The local jury found Scopes guilty, but the larger verdict, the one that really counted, differed sharply. The Dayton trial marked an embarrassing setback for fundamentalism. When Bryan died of a heart attack a few days after the trial's end, H. L. Mencken wrote a harshly satirical column that mercilessly derided Bryan and the "gaping primates" who idolized him.

Fundamentalism diminished as a force in mainstream Protestantism after the Scopes trial, but many local congregations and scores of radio preachers still embraced the traditional faith. So, too, did the popular evangelist Billy Sunday, a former professional baseball player. In tabernacles seating up to 10,000 people, Sunday used publicity techniques, skilled musicians, and a flamboyant pulpit style to spread his fundamentalist message and denounce the loose living and modernism of the 1920s.

Zealous new denominations and independent "full gospel" churches carried on the cause. Charismatic evangelist Aimee Semple McPherson, for example, regularly filled her cavernous Angelus Temple in Los Angeles and reached thousands more by radio. Radiating drama and beauty, the white-gowned McPherson won an enormous following through her cheerful sermons and theatrical talent. On one occasion she employed a gigantic electric scoreboard to illustrate the triumph of good over evil. Her followers, predominantly transplanted midwestern farmers, embraced her fundamentalist theology while reveling in her mastery of the techniques of mass entertainment. In many ways, McPherson anticipated the television evangelists of a later day. When she died in 1944, her International Church of the Foursquare

Aimee Semple McPherson
Offering a beguiling blend of religious fundamentalism, faith healing, and show-biz glitz, the Los Angeles–based McPherson won countless devoted followers.

Gospel had over six hundred branches in the United States and abroad. Fundamentalism suffered a setback at Dayton, but it was far from dead as the 1920s ended.

Prohibition

The societal fissure so evident in the Klan movement and in the Scopes trial extended as well to the decade-long struggle to rid the United States of alcoholic beverages. Temperance reform stretched far back into the nineteenth century, and, as we saw in Chapter 23, prohibition won wide support among progressives in the years before World War I as a legitimate response to the serious social problems associated with alcohol abuse. But the prohibition cause also had a symbolic dimension, as a sign of the struggle of native-born Americans to maintain cultural and political dominance over the immigrant cities. Both components of the anti-alcohol crusade loomed large in the 1920s.

When the Eighteenth Amendment took effect in January 1920, prohibitionists rejoiced. Billy Sunday proclaimed,

The reign of tears is over. The slums will soon be only a memory. We will turn our prisons into factories and our jails into storehouses and corn-cribs. Men will walk upright now. Women will smile and children will laugh.

At first, Sunday's dream seemed attainable. Saloons closed; liquor advertising stopped; arrests for drunkenness dwindled. In 1921 alcohol consumption stood at about one-third the prewar level—an impressive decline. Yet prohibition was discredited by the end of the decade, and in 1933 it came to an end. What went wrong? Essentially, the prohibition debacle illustrates the virtual impossibility, in a democracy, of enforcing rules of behavior with which substantial numbers of citizens disagree.

From the beginning, enforcement of the Volstead Act, the 1919 law that established a Prohibition Bureau within the Treasury Department, was underbudgeted and sporadic, especially in strongly antiprohibition states. New York, for example, repealed its prohibition-enforcement law as early as 1923. Further, the Volstead Act contained significant loopholes. Alcohol could be purchased for medicinal or religious purposes, or manufactured in private homes for consumption by family or friends. And, unlike later antidrug laws, the act did not outlaw the possession of alcoholic beverages, only their commercial manufacture, sale, and distribution.

Would-be drinkers grew bolder as enforcement faltered. For rebellious young people, the illegality of alcohol simply added to its appeal. "Without doubt," declared a University of Wisconsin student, "prohibition has been an incentive for young folks to learn to drink. . . . It is the natural reaction of youth to rules and regulations." Every city boasted its speakeasies where customers could buy drinks, and rumrunners routinely smuggled in liquor from Canada and the West Indies. Shady entrepreneurs sold flavored but highly toxic industrial-grade alcohol to an unsuspecting public. Many people concocted their own home brew, and the demand for sacramental wine increased amazingly. By 1929, thanks to such diverse stratagems, alcohol consumption had risen to about 70 percent of the prewar level.

Organized crime helped drinkers circumvent the law. In Chicago the police looked the other way as rival gangs engaged in bloody wars to control the city's liquor business. Chicago witnessed 550 gangland killings in the 1920s, with few arrests or convictions. By 1929 Chicago mob king Al Capone controlled a vast network of speakeasies producing annual profits of $60 million. Although far from typical, Chicago's heavily publicized crime wave appeared to offer dramatic

Prohibition Alley Scene, *by Ben Shahn, ca. 1934 In this fanciful painting, incorporating a portrait of gangster Al Capone, Shahn linked the crime and violence of bootlegging with the respectable citizenry who patronized speakeasies that sold illicit liquor.*

proof of prohibition's failure. A reform designed to produce a more orderly, law-abiding America seemed to be having precisely the opposite effect.

Thus prohibition, too, became a battleground in the decade's cultural wars. The "drys"—usually native-born Protestants—praised prohibition as a necessary and legitimate social reform. The "wets"—liberals, alienated intellectuals, Jazz Age rebels, big-city immigrants—condemned it as moralistic meddling. Many college and university students regarded prohibition as a joke. At Trinity College in Connecticut, the student newspaper suggested that as their class gift, the seniors erect a distillery on the campus "with the proceeds going to the college."

Prohibition figured prominently in the 1928 presidential campaign. Although the Democratic platform halfheartedly endorsed it, Democratic candidate Al Smith made no secret of his support for repeal of the Eighteenth Amendment. By contrast, Republican Herbert Hoover praised prohibition as "a great social and economic experiment, noble in motive and far-reaching in purpose." Once elected, Hoover appointed a commission to study the matter. In a confusing 1931 report, the commission acknowledged the breakdown of prohibition but nevertheless urged its retention. A New York journalist parodied the findings in a doggerel verse:

> *Prohibition is an awful flop.*
> *We like it.*
> *It can't stop what it's meant to stop.*
> *We like it.*

> *It's left a trail of graft and slime,*
> *It's filled our land with vice and crime,*
> *It don't prohibit worth a dime,*
> *Nevertheless we're for it.*

By 1933, the year that brought repeal of the Eighteenth Amendment, the nation had other matters on its mind, and prohibition seemed little more than a relic from another age.

◆ HOOVER AT THE HELM

Herbert Hoover, elected president in 1928, seemed an excellent bet to sustain the nation's prosperity. Unlike his two predecessors, Hoover was no standpat conservative. He brought to the White House a distinctive social and political philosophy that reflected his background in engineering.

The Election of 1928

A Hollywood casting agent could not have chosen two individuals who better personified the social and cultural schisms of the 1920s than the presidential candidates of 1928: Al Smith and Herbert Hoover. Both self-made men, they were in other ways "as far apart as Pilsner and Coca Cola," as H. L. Mencken put it.

Smith, the four-term governor of New York, easily won the 1928 Democratic nomination. The urban-

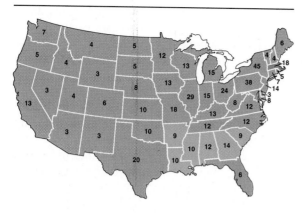

	Electoral Vote	Popular Vote	Percentage of Popular Vote
Republican Herbert C. Hoover	444	21,391,993	58.2
Democratic Alfred E. Smith	87	15,016,169	40.9
Minor parties	–	–	330,725	0.9

The Election of 1928

immigrant wing of the party that Smith represented had gained strength in the four years since the deadlocked convention of 1924. A Catholic and a "wet," Smith, with his brown derby hat perpetually askew, exuded the flavor of immigrant New York City. Originally a machine politician, and fundamentally conservative in his social ideas, he represented progressivism's urban-immigrant component through his championing of social welfare and civil rights. His political intimates included several reform-minded women, notably Frances Perkins, the head of the state industrial board, and Belle Moskowitz, a key adviser.

Herbert Hoover won the Republican nomination with equal ease. In August 1927, when Calvin Coolidge cryptically declared, "I do not choose to run for president in 1928," Secretary of Commerce Hoover announced his own candidacy. Hoover faced no real competition, although some conservative party leaders remained suspicious of the highly intelligent but aloof progressive figure who had never run for public office and indeed had spent much of his pre-1920 adult life abroad.

Born in West Branch, Iowa, and orphaned at an early age, Hoover had put himself through Stanford University and made a fortune as a mining engineer in China and Australia. His notable service as wartime food administrator won him a place in the Harding and Coolidge cabinets.

Hoover, disdaining handshaking and baby kissing, instead issued "tons of reports on dull subjects" (in Mencken's jaundiced view) and delivered laboriously composed radio speeches in a boring monotone. So dull was Hoover's campaign that the originality of some of his ideas went unnoticed. Smith, by contrast, campaigned spiritedly throughout the country. This may actually have hurt his cause, however, because many Americans west of the Hudson did not warm to his big-city wisecracking and accent.

Smith's Catholicism figured importantly in the campaign. Whether, on balance, the religious issue helped or hurt his candidacy remains debatable, but he unquestionably faced a strong backlash of prejudice. Hoover urged religious tolerance, and Smith denied any conflict between his faith and the duties of the presidency, but to some Protestants, especially rural southerners and urban fundamentalists, the issue seemed vital. Rumors circulated of the relocation of the Vatican to the United States if Smith won. (A postelection joke had the defeated Smith sending the pope a one-word telegram: "Unpack.") Long discredited anti-Catholic propaganda such as Maria Monk's *Awful Disclosures* of 1836 (see Chapter 13) were revived.

The decisive campaign issue, however, was probably not religion but prosperity. Republican orators freely took credit for the nation's booming economy and warned that a Smith victory would mean "soup kitchens instead of busy factories." In his nomination acceptance speech, Hoover foresaw "the final triumph over poverty." Seeking to defuse the prosperity issue, Smith chose as his campaign manager a General Motors vice president who moved the Democratic party headquarters to the GM building in New York and released lists of well-known capitalists who backed Smith.

Nevertheless, Hoover won in a landslide, grabbing 58 percent of the vote and even making deep inroads in the Democratic "solid South." Smith won a meager 87 electoral votes, compared to 444 for Hoover. In a stark comment on the prevailing political climate, the Socialist party candidate, Norman Thomas, received only 267,000 votes—less than a third of Debs's 1920 total.

Beneath the Hoover landslide, however, lay evidence of an emerging political realignment. Smith did well in the midwestern farm belt, where financially strapped farmers abandoned their normal Republican allegiance. In northern cities, Catholic and Jewish immigrants (and their children, now coming of voting age) voted Democratic in record numbers. In 1924 the

Presidential Voting by Selected Ethnic Groups in Chicago, 1924, 1928 and 1932

| | *Percent Democratic* | | |
	1924	1928	1932
Blacks	10	23	21
Czechoslovaks	40	73	83
Germans	14	58	69
Italians	31	63	64
Jews	19	60	77
Lithuanians	48	77	84
Poles	35	71	80
Swedes	15	34	51
Yugoslavs	20	54	67

SOURCE: John M. Allswang, *A House for All Peoples: Ethnic Politics in Chicago, 1890–1936* (Lexington: University Press of Kentucky, 1971).

nation's twelve largest cities had all gone Republican; in 1928 Smith carried all twelve. Should prosperity end, these portents suggested, the Republican party would be in trouble.

Herbert Hoover's Social Thought

As 1929 dawned, Americans looked hopefully to their new president, whom admirers dubbed the Great Engineer. Not only had Hoover compiled a notable record of achievement, but he entered the White House with a well-developed social creed expounded most fully in his 1922 book *American Individualism*. Although his own life had followed the classic self-made-man pattern, Hoover did not mindlessly champion laissez-faire competition. Nor, in contrast to Harding and Coolidge, did he uncritically cheer for big business. His Quakerism, humanitarian activities, and engineering experience combined with his Republican party loyalties to produce a unique social outlook.

Like Theodore Roosevelt, whom he had supported in 1912, Hoover believed that cutthroat capitalist competition had become anachronistic. Rational economic development, he insisted, demanded corporate cooperation in marketing, wage policy, raw-material allocation, and product standardization. The economy, in short, should operate like an efficient machine.

Capitalism, he argued, had broad social obligations. He welcomed the growth of welfare capitalism and urged further movement in this direction. But above all, Hoover believed in voluntarism. The cooperative, socially responsible economic order that he envisioned must come about through the voluntary action of capitalist leaders, not through government coercion—down that path lay totalitarianism—or through power struggles pitting labor against management.

Hoover had put his philosophy into practice as secretary of commerce. Reorganizing the Commerce Department along more rational lines, he had made it a model for private industry. Seeking to accelerate the decade's trend toward corporate consolidation and cooperation, he had convened more than 250 conferences at which business leaders discussed such issues as unemployment, pricing policies, labor-management relations, and the virtues of trade associations. He urged higher wages to increase consumer purchasing power and in 1923, arguing on grounds of efficiency, he persuaded the steel industry to shift to an eight-hour workday. At the same time, he opposed the McNary-Haugen farm bill and other proposals for direct government intervention in the economy.

Hoover's ideology had its limitations. He showed more interest in cooperation among capitalists than among consumers or workers. His belief that American capitalism was embracing cooperation, social service, and enlightened labor policies overestimated the role of altruism in business decision making. And his unqualified opposition to government economic intervention brought him grief later in his administration, when such intervention became urgently necessary.

Applying his ideology to specific issues, Hoover in his early months as president compiled an impressive record. He set up the President's Council on Recent Social Trends to gather data for policy makers' guidance. He created commissions to study public-policy issues. Responding to the farm problem, he secured passage of legislation that established a Federal Farm Board (1929) to promote cooperative commodity marketing. This, he hoped, would raise farm prices while preserving the voluntarist principle.

As the summer of 1929 turned to autumn, the Hoover administration seemed off to a promising start. But while Hoover methodically applied his engineering skills to the business of government, ominous long-term economic trends were converging toward a crisis that would overwhelm and ultimately destroy his presidency.

CONCLUSION

The 1920s stay vividly etched in America's historical consciousness partly because memorable events so decisively bracket the decade: World War I at the beginning, a catastrophic stock-market crash at the end. But another reason the era remains restlessly alive is the picture it presents of an entire people grappling with massive technological and social change. Like world travelers made half-groggy by jet lag, Americans of the twenties sought to adapt to the rise of a mass-production, mass-culture metropolitan world that had emerged, seemingly almost overnight. Radio, the automobile, the movies, a parade of electrical appliances—so familiar today as hardly to merit a second thought—were still exciting novelties in post–World War I America.

The most interesting responses to these changes unfolded outside the political arena. Whereas the conservative political leadership of the twenties typically fell back on ideologies inherited from an earlier, less complex era, the rest of society seethed in ferment. Ironically, the same stresses and disorientation that produced bitter social conflicts also made the decade one of the most creative in American cultural history. The champions of prohibition and fundamentalism, the troubled folk who donned the robes of the Klan, the urban blacks who cheered Marcus Garvey, the artists and writers of the Harlem Renaissance, the early jazz musicians, and the novelists and poets who revitalized American literature were all, in their different ways, trying to make sense of an unfamiliar and often threatening new social order. Historians rightly deplore the political failures and reactionary social movements of the twenties, but that ought not obscure the positive and lasting aspects of this remarkable decade's achievements.

CHRONOLOGY

1915   Modern Ku Klux Klan founded.

1919   Volstead Act.

1920–1921 Sharp postwar recession; agricultural prices plummet.

1920   Warren G. Harding elected president.

Radio station KDKA, Pittsburgh, broadcasts election returns.

Eighteenth Amendment to the Constitution takes effect.

F. Scott Fitzgerald, *This Side of Paradise*.

Sinclair Lewis, *Main Street*.

1921   Recovery from recession; economic boom begins; agriculture remains depressed.

Sheppard-Towner Act.

National Woman's party founded by Alice Paul.

Shuffle Along, all-black musical review.

1921–1922 Washington Naval Arms Conference.

1922   Supreme Court declares child-labor law unconstitutional.

Fordney-McCumber Tariff restores high rates.

Herbert Hoover, *American Individualism*.

1922   Sinclair Lewis, *Babbitt*.

T. S. Eliot, *The Wasteland*.

1923   Harding dies; Calvin Coolidge becomes president.

Supreme Court strikes down minimum-wage law for women.

Jean Toomer, *Cane*.

1924   Teapot Dome scandals investigated.

National Origins Act.

Calvin Coolidge elected president.

McNary-Haugen farm bill introduced.

1925   Scopes trial.

Ku Klux Klan scandal in Indiana.

Alain Locke, *The New Negro*.

Dorothy and DuBose Heyward, *Porgy*.

F. Scott Fitzgerald, *The Great Gatsby*.

1926   Ernest Hemingway, *The Sun Also Rises*.

Langston Hughes, *The Weary Blues*.

1927   *The Jazz Singer*, first sound movie.

Coolidge vetoes the McNary-Haugen bill.

Henry Ford introduces the Model A.

1927   Willa Cather, *Death Comes for the Archbishop*.
Execution of Sacco and Vanzetti.
Charles A. Lindbergh's transatlantic flight.

1928   Kellogg-Briand Pact.
Herbert Hoover elected president.

1929   Federal Farm Board created.
Sheppard-Towner program terminated.
Hallelujah, first all-black movie.
Ernest Hemingway, *A Farewell to Arms*.
Robert and Helen Lynd, *Middletown*.

1933   Repeal of the Eighteenth Amendment.
Smoot-Hawley Tariff.

The passion of
Sacco and Vanzetti,
by Ben Shahn

FOR FURTHER READING

Charles C. Alexander, *Here the Country Lies: Nationalism and the Arts in Twentieth Century America* (1980). A useful revisionist study whose chapters on the 1920s stress the decade's positive achievements.

Loren Bartiz, ed., *The Culture of the Twenties* (1970). A rich collection of primary documents with a helpful introductory essay.

Paul Carter, *The Twenties in America* (1968) and *Another Part of the Twenties* (1977). Two essays offering refreshingly personal interpretive judgments.

Lynn Dumenil, *The Modern Temper: America in the 1920s* (1995). Offers a wealth of fresh insights, especially on often neglected groups and movements.

Ellis W. Hawley, *The Great War and the Search for a Modern Or-*

der (1979). An economic study that traces the emergence (and collapse in 1929) of the first mass-consumption society.

William E. Leuchtenberg, *The Perils of Prosperity, 1914–1932* (1970). A cogent examination of the serious thinkers and mass culture of the twenties.

Nancy MacLean, *Behind the Mask of Chivalry: The Making of the Second Ku Klux Klan* (1994). Explores Klan members' anxieties about corporate growth, feminism, sexuality, and other issues of the 1920s.

Joan Shelley Rubin, *The Making of Middle-Brow Culture* (1992). An interpretive study of the Book-of-the-Month Club and other 1920s institutions by which high culture reached a larger public.

ADDITIONAL BIBLIOGRAPHY

Economic Trends

Guy Alchon, *The Invisible Hand of Planning: Capitalism, Social Science, and the State in the 1920s* (1985); David Brody, "The Rise and Decline of Welfare Capitalism," in John Braeman et al., *Change and Continuity in Twentieth-Century America: The 1920s* (1968); Gilbert C. Fite, *American Farmers: The New Minority* (1981); Roland Marchand, *Advertising the American Dream: Making Way for Modernity, 1920–1940* (1985); Mira Wilkins, *The Maturing of Multinational Enterprise: American Business Abroad from 1914 to 1970* (1974).

Politics and International Relations

Thomas Buckley, *The United States and the Washington Conference, 1921–1922* (1970); Douglas B. Craig, *After Wilson: The Struggle for the Democratic Party, 1920–1934* (1992); L. Ethan El-

lis, *Republican Foreign Policy, 1921–1933* (1968); John D. Hicks, *Republican Ascendancy, 1921–1933* (1960); Charles L. Mee, *The Ohio Gang: The World of Warren G. Harding* (1981); Robert K. Murray, *The Politics of Normalcy: Governmental Theory and Practice in the Harding-Coolidge Era* (1973); Joan Hoff-Wilson, *American Business and Foreign Policy* (1971).

Mass Culture

James J. Flink, *The Car Culture* (1975); Fred J. MacDonald, *Don't Touch That Dial* (1979); Lary May, *Screening Out the Past: The Birth of Mass Culture and the Motion Picture Industry* (1980); Susan Smulyan, *Selling Radio: The Commercialization of American Broadcasting, 1920–1934* (1994).

Jazz Age Youth, Dissident Writers and Intellectuals, Black Culture

Beth A. Bailey, *From Front Porch to Back Seat: Courtship in Twentieth-Century America* (1988); Stanley Coben, *Rebellion Against Victorianism: The Impetus for Cultural Change in 1920s America* (1991); Paula Fass, *The Damned and the Beautiful: American Youth in the 1920s* (1977); Fred Hobson, *Mencken: A Life* (1994); Frederick J. Hoffman, *The Twenties: American Writing in the Postwar Decade,* rev. ed. (1962); Arthur Mizener, *The Far Side of Paradise: A Biography of F. Scott Fitzgerald* (1951).

Women in the 1920s

Lois W. Banner, *American Beauty* (1983); Kathleen M. Blee, *Women and the Klan: Racism and Gender in the 1920s* (1991); Dorothy M. Brown, *Setting a Course: American Women in the 1920s* (1987); Stanley Lemons, *The Woman Citizen: Social Feminism in the 1920s* (1973); Estelle B. Freedman, "The New Woman: Changing Views of Women in the 1920s," *Journal of American History* 61 (1974): 372–392; Frank Stricker, ". . . Career Women in Twentieth-Century America," *Journal of Social History* 10 (Fall 1976): 1–19; Leslie Woodcock Tentler, *Wage-Earning Women: Industrial Work and Family in the United States, 1900–1930* (1979); Daniel J. Walkowitz, "The Making of a Feminine Professional Identity: Social Workers in the 1920s," *American Historical Review* 95 (October 1990): 1051–1075; Nancy Woloch, *Women and the American Experience,* 2d ed. (1994), Chapter 16.

African-Americans, Jazz, the Harlem Renaissance

Robert E. Hemenway, *Zora Neale Hurston: A Literary Biography* (1977); Nathan Huggins, *Harlem Renaissance* (1971); David L. Lewis, *When Harlem Was in Vogue* (1981); Kathy H. Ogren, *The Jazz Revolution: Twenties America and the Meaning of Jazz* (1989); Gilbert Osofsky, *Harlem: The Making of a Ghetto* (1968);
Arnold Rampersand, *The Life of Langston Hughes* (2 vols., 1986–1988); Judith Stein, *The World of Marcus Garvey: Race and Class in Modern Society* (1985); Tyrone Tillery, *Claude McKay* (1992).

Religious Trends

Edith L. Blumhofer, *Aimee Semple McPherson* (1993); Lyle W. Dorsett, *Billy Sunday and the Redemption of Urban America* (1991); George M. Marsden, *Fundamentalism and American Culture* (1980); William Vance Trollinger, *God's Empire: William Bell Riley and Midwestern Fundamentalism* (1990).

Cultural Tensions and Symbolic Events

Paul Avrich, *Sacco and Vanzetti: The Anarchist Background* (1991); Norman H. Clark, *Deliver Us from Evil: An Interpretation of American Prohibition* (1976); Kenneth T. Jackson, *The Ku Klux Klan in the City, 1915–1930* (1967); Shawn Lay, ed., *The Invisible Empire in the West: Toward a New Historical Appraisal of the Ku Klux Klan in the 1920s* (1992); Lawrence W. Levine, *Defender of the Faith; William Jennings Bryan: The Last Decade, 1915–1925* (1965); Leonard J. Moore, *Citizen Klansmen: The Ku Klux Klan in Indiana, 1921–1928* (1991); Francis Russell, *Tragedy in Dedham: The Story of the Sacco-Vanzetti Case* (1971); John W. Ward, "The Meaning of Lindbergh's Flight," *American Quarterly* 10 (1958): 3–16.

Herbert Hoover and the 1928 Election

David Bruner, *Herbert Hoover: The Public Life* (1979); E. Paula Elder, *Governor Alfred E. Smith: The Politician as Reformer* (1983); Ellis W. Hawley, ed., *Herbert Hoover as Secretary of Commerce* (1981); Joan Hoff-Wilson, *Herbert Hoover: Forgotten Progressive* (1975); Allan J. Lichtman, *Prejudice and the Old Politics: The Presidential Election of 1928* (1979).

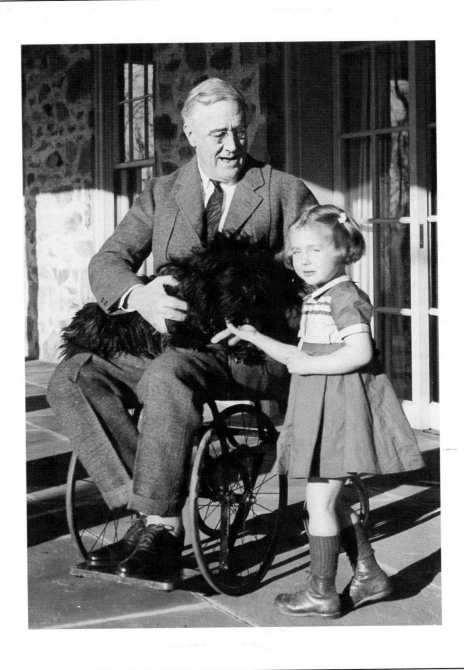

**President Franklin D. Roosevelt
with His Dog Fala and a Future Voter**

25

CRASH, DEPRESSION, AND NEW DEAL

Rugged Campobello Island, lying off Eastport, Maine, was green and sunlit that August afternoon in 1921. In the waters off the island, a small sailboat bobbed and darted. At the helm, with several of his children, was thirty-nine-year-old Franklin D. Roosevelt. A rising Democrat, Roosevelt had served as assistant secretary of the navy during World War I and as his party's vice-presidential candidate in 1920. But all this was far from his mind now. He loved sailing, and he loved Campobello Island. His parents had vacationed there, and he had introduced his future wife Eleanor to the island in 1904.

Suddenly the idyllic afternoon took an ominous turn. First, Roosevelt, though an experienced sailor, unaccountably lost his footing and fell into the bay. Then he spotted the smoke of a fire on the heavily wooded island. Beaching the boat, he and the children frantically cut evergreen branches and beat back the spreading flames. With typical energy, Roosevelt insisted that he and the children jog the two miles to the family's rambling summer cottage on the beach.

That night, Roosevelt felt unusually fatigued. Next morning his left leg dragged as he tried to walk. Soon all sensation in both legs disappeared. He had suffered an attack of poliomyelitis (infantile paralysis), a crippling viral infection that most often struck children but sometimes adults as well. Except for a cumbersome shuffle with crutches and heavy metal braces, he would never walk again.

This illness changed the lives of both Franklin and Eleanor Roosevelt. For Franklin, it seemed the end of his career. But he endured long hours of therapy and gradually resumed political activity. In June 1928, laboriously mounting the podium at the Democratic National Convention, he nominated his friend Al Smith for president. Soon after, the New York Democratic party nominated Roosevelt for governor, and he went on to victory.

Somewhat superficial and even arrogant before 1921, this privileged only child became, through his ordeal, more thoughtful, more understanding of the disadvantaged, and far more determined. "If you had spent two years in bed trying to wiggle your big toe," he once said, "after that everything else would seem easy!"

Eleanor Roosevelt at first devoted herself entirely to her husband's care—he could not even urinate without help with a catheter—and to the child-rearing responsibilities that now fell upon her. But she also encouraged him to return to politics. After years of subservience to her domineering mother-in-law, Sara Roosevelt, she firmly resisted Sara's efforts to take her son back to the family home at Hyde Park, New York, and turn him into a permanent invalid.

Eleanor became her husband's eyes and ears. Already actively involved with social issues, she now joined the executive board of the New York State Democratic party and edited the women's division newsletter. Though painfully shy, she forced herself to make public speeches, overcoming an embarrassing tendency to giggle nervously at inappropriate moments.

The Roosevelts would soon need the qualities of character they had acquired during Franklin's fight back from incapacitating illness. Eight years after that afternoon at Campobello, a devastating stock-market collapse signaled the onset of the worst depression in American history. Herbert Hoover grappled with the economic crisis through most of his term and then in 1933 made way for his successor: Franklin Roosevelt. Franklin and Eleanor, in their different ways, left their imprint on American history.

President Roosevelt dominated U.S. politics from 1933 until his death in 1945, first as leader of the effort to overcome the depression and then as wartime commander in chief. The depression-fighting phase of Roosevelt's presidency, commonly called the New Deal, was characterized by a dizzying array of laws, agencies, and programs that historians ever since have tried to whip into coherent form. And, indeed, certain patterns do emerge. In the years 1933–1935, sometimes called the First New Deal, the dual themes were relief and recovery. While Roosevelt urged national unity, his administration and a heavily Democratic Congress grappled with massive unemployment, business stagnation, and agricultural distress. Around 1935, responding to political challenge on the Left and buoyed by a ringing endorsement in the 1934 midterm election, the New Deal shifted toward a more reformist course. In the so-called Second New Deal of 1935–1938, the administration placed less emphasis on unity and more on business regulation and on social programs and tax policies benefiting working people, small farmers, sharecroppers, migrant laborers, and others at the lower end of the scale. Historians still argue over specific New Deal programs, and Americans of differing political persuasions even debate its overall merits. But few would disagree that the New Deal stands as a watershed in twentieth-century American history.

The laws and agencies that made up the New Deal were a complex amalgam of approaches shaped by many political crosscurrents and countless individuals. But in the public mind, the New Deal

meant Roosevelt. Loved by some in his own day almost as a member of the family and reviled by others as a demagogue and an opportunist, Roosevelt is recognized today as a consummate politician whose administration set the national political agenda for a generation.

CRASH AND DEPRESSION

Like a joyride that ends in a blur of screeching tires and crunching metal, the prosperity of the 1920s came to a jolting climax in October 1929 with the collapse of the stock market. The Wall Street crash proved only the overture to a depression that reached every household in the land. President Hoover struggled resolutely with the crisis, but his ideological commitment to private initiative and his horror of governmental coercion limited his effectiveness. In November 1932 a nation sorely disillusioned with Hoover gave an overwhelming electoral mandate to the Democratic party and its new leader, Franklin Roosevelt.

Black Thursday

Stock prices had risen steadily through much of the 1920s as investors responded optimistically to growing prosperity and advances in productivity. But in 1928–1929, this upward movement turned into a frenzied spiral as more and more speculators plunged into the market. Prices of automotive, radio, aviation, and other glamour stocks floated into what one contemporary called "the blue and cloudless empyrean." Stock speculation in early 1929 seemed the perfect form of gambling for an egalitarian society: everybody won.[*]

In 1925 the market value of all stocks had stood at about $27 billion; in early October 1929 it hit $87 billion. An estimated 9 million Americans played the market in these heady months, often on borrowed money. With stockbrokers willing to lend speculators

---

[*]The speculative mania also fed a Florida real-estate boom that ended abruptly in September 1926 when a killer hurricane devastated Miami—an eerie local preview of the stock market crash that would batter the entire nation three years later.

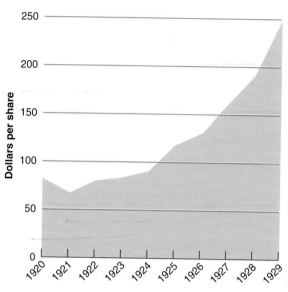

Stock Market Prices in the 1920s

After rising moderately in the early 1920s, stock market prices shot up later in the decade. Looking at such statistics, Herbert Hoover declared in 1929: "I have no fears for the future of our country. It is bright with hope."

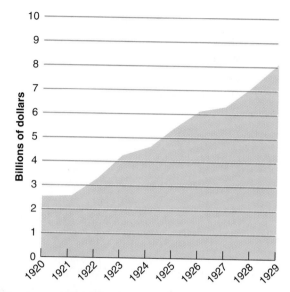

Consumer Borrowing in the 1920s

Americans plunged heavily into debt in the 1920s to play the stock market and to buy their new Fords, Chevrolets, and other consumer products. By 1929 their total debt stood at about $8 billion.

up to 75 percent of a stock's purchase price, credit or "margin" buying became the rule. By the summer of 1929, such brokers' loans totaled $6 billion. The Federal Reserve Board's easy-credit policies and Treasury Secretary Andrew Mellon's continual pressure for income-tax cuts had increased the volume of money available for speculation.

A torrent of optimistic pronouncements drew more and more people into the market. "Everybody Ought to Be Rich," proclaimed General Motors executive John Raskob in the title of a *Ladies' Home Journal* article. President Calvin Coolidge, as he left office in March 1929, declared stocks "cheap at current prices."

With the nation's corporations eager for their share of the speculators' money, new securities, in the words of one historian, "were manufactured almost like cakes of soap" simply because money could be made from their sale. A few years before, Kleagles and Goblins had prospered by selling Ku Klux Klan memberships; now brokerage agents grew rich peddling American Can, Studebaker, Houston Oil, and Westinghouse. "Investment trusts," akin to the mutual funds of a later day, though totally unregulated, offered novices

the benefit of the supposedly superior wisdom of more seasoned investors.

This speculative frenzy ignored some hard economic realities. The prosperity on which it rested was in fact precarious. Agriculture remained depressed, as did mining, textiles, and other industries. Automobile production slowed as the 1920s wore on. The construction industry declined sharply in 1928–1929—an omen few heeded.

In July 1928 the Federal Reserve Board tried to dampen speculation by increasing the interest rate on federal reserve notes, and early in 1929 "the Fed" warned member banks not to lend money for stock-market speculation. But with speculators willing to pay up to 20 percent interest for money to buy more stock, major banks and large corporations poured additional millions into the money market—an act akin to dumping gasoline on an already raging fire. The Fed tightened credit again in September. This time the action was effective, but with catastrophic consequences.

On October 24, 1929, "Black Thursday"—the collapse finally came. As prices suddenly dropped, trading grew panicky. Some stocks found no buyers at all: they had literally become worthless pieces of paper.

Life

January 24, 1930   PRICE 10 CENTS

The Long and the Short of it

Coping with the Crash

In January 1930, three months after the stock market crash, the humor magazine Life *offered a wry comment on the few investors who rode out the crash as well as the vast majority who were devastated by it.*

Mounted police broke up the crowds milling outside the New York Stock Exchange. Their faces frozen with anxiety, speculators huddled around the ticker-tape machines in brokers' offices—"like friends around the bedside of a stricken friend," according to the *New York Times.* At midday a group of powerful New York bankers temporarily allayed the panic by issuing a reassuring statement and ostentatiously buying some $30 million worth of major stocks. But after a weak rally on Friday, prices plunged still lower early the next week. The climax came on Tuesday, October 29, when a record 16 million stocks changed hands in frantic trading, most at inconceivably low prices. The big bankers who had earlier tried to restore confidence remained grimly silent. In the ensuing weeks, feeble up-swings in stock prices alternated with further plunges.

On Black Thursday Herbert Hoover, issuing the first of what would become a long series of optimistic statements, pronounced the economy fundamentally "sound and prosperous." But Hoover was wrong. By mid-November the loss in the market value of stocks stood at $30 billion. Stock prices stabilized and even recovered somewhat in early 1930. For a fleeting moment, the worst appeared to be over. But the economy had deeper problems.

Onset of the Depression

Many economists shared Hoover's hope of quick recovery. After a stock-market shakeout, analysts predicted, business activity would quickly revive. Instead, the economy went into a long tailspin. The nation soon found itself locked in a full-scale depression that did not bottom out until 1933 and whose effects lingered through the decade.

What were the underlying causes of this depression? Some economists focus on the structural factors that made the prosperity of the 1920s fragile and unstable. For example, increased productivity did not generate corresponding wage increases for workers but rather took the form of higher corporate profits. Between 1920 and 1929, the share of total personal income going to the top 5 percent of America's income earners rose from 22 percent to 26 percent. By contrast, the 40 percent of Americans at the lower end of the economic scale received only about 12 percent of the total national income in 1929. The well-to-do spent a larger share of their income on nonessentials and luxuries, and this discretionary spending diminished sharply when the 1929 crash came. The decade's gains in productivity also encouraged overproduction. By the summer of 1929, the automobile, housing, textile, tire, and other durable-goods industries were overextended and cutting back.

Economists who trace the depression's causes to structural weaknesses in the economy also point to the decline in farm prices in the 1920s as a major weak spot. Others argue that important sectors of industry—including railroads, steel, textiles, and mining—were lagging technologically as early as the 1930s and could not attract the kind of investment needed to stimulate recovery.

A second interpretation, the "monetarist" school launched by Milton Friedman and Anna Jacobson Schwartz in *Monetary History of the United States* (1963), focuses on the collapse of the banking system in the early 1930s (see below), which they in turn blame on Federal Reserve System policies. The Fed, they charge, failed to assure an adequate money supply that would have enabled the economy to bounce back from the shock of the crash. The money supply did indeed shrink by 38 percent in the early 1930s, though the reasons remain under debate.

All analysts emphasize that the U.S. depression occurred within the context of a global economic crisis. European economies—already enfeebled as a result of the First World War, massive debt payments, and a heavy trade imbalance with the United States—collapsed in 1931. Austria's biggest bank failed in May; Germany imposed currency controls in July; Great Britain abandoned the gold standard in September. This larger crisis had a variety of unpleasant effects upon the American economy, including plummeting exports. By heightening the cautiousness of U.S. business leaders, the world economic collapse also intensified the fearful psychological climate that nurtured the crisis.

While economists debate the depression's causes, its chilling impact on the U.S. economy is all too clear. Statistics tell the bleak story. The gross national product dropped from $104 billion in 1929 to $59 billion in 1932. Farm prices, already low, fell by nearly 60 percent from 1929 to 1932. Wheat, which had sold for $1.04 a bushel in 1929, yielded only 51¢ a bushel in 1933. Railroad corporations controlling a third of the nation's track mileage fell into bankruptcy in the early thirties.

The banking system tottered toward collapse. Between 1930 and early 1933, more than fifty-five hundred banks closed their doors. Industrial production rose slightly in the summer of 1932, but by the beginning of 1933, conditions had grown worse than ever. The unemployment rate rose from 3 percent in 1929 to 25 percent in 1933. This meant that the number of jobless Americans soared from 1.6 million to nearly 13 million in this four-year period. Many Americans who still had jobs faced cuts in pay and hours.

The Depression's Human Toll

The grim message embedded in these figures found confirmation as Americans looked around them—at idle factories, bankrupt farms, and closed banks; at the hopelessness etched in the expressions of the jobless waiting in breadlines, sleeping on park benches, or trudging the streets looking for work. Men hopped freight trains and rode from city to city, hoping to find work. Others sold pencils or apples on the streets to earn a few dollars. Americans reared on the ethic of hard work, self-support, and the promise of upward mobility through persistent effort found chronic unemployment a shattering psychic blow.

Because most of those thrown out of work had families to support, the unemployment figures must be multiplied several times over to reflect the magnitude of the distress. Similarly, the epidemic of bank closings not only worsened the liquidity crisis but deprived millions of small depositors and their families of savings they could ill afford to lose. Blacks, Mexican-Americans, southern sharecroppers, and other groups endured particular hardships in the depression (see Chapter 26).

Their Only Roof, by Harry Gottlieb Many 1930s artists, writers, and photographers evoked the hardships of the Great Depression.

Heartrending scenes were played out across rural America as thousands of farm families lost their homes. In 1933 alone over 5 percent of the nation's farms underwent mortgage foreclosures or forced sales because of tax delinquency, with Iowa and the Dakotas especially hard hit. At some of these forced sales, angry friends and neighbors dominated the auction, bought the foreclosed farm for a trivial sum such as a penny or a dollar, and then returned it to the evicted family.

For the children of the depression, poor diet and inadequate medical and dental care laid the groundwork for long-term health problems. City health departments and rural clinics reported alarming increases in malnutrition, rickets, pellagra, and other diet-related ills among children. By early 1933, as local school boards stung by dwindling tax revenues shortened the school year and even closed schools, more than three hundred thousand children were out of school.

Newspapers of the early thirties conveyed the human meaning of the crisis by focusing on dramatic vignettes. The *New York Times* described "Hoover Valley"—a section of Central Park where jobless men had built makeshift shelters of boxes and packing crates. In winter, the homeless sometimes wrapped themselves in thick layers of newspapers they sardonically called Hoover blankets. Washington State suffered an epidemic of forest fires deliberately set by men hoping to earn a few dollars as fire fighters. In a woods near Danbury, Connecticut, police discovered a woman and her daughter near starvation. For five days they had eaten nothing but wild berries and apples.

Some gave up altogether. The suicide rate climbed nearly 30 percent between 1928 and 1932. In Youngstown, Ohio, a fifty-seven-year-old jobless father of ten jumped to his death from a bridge as the authorities prepared to evict his family from their home. Although extreme, such stories represented part of the terrible social cost of the nation's worst depression.

Hoover's Response

Historically, Americans had viewed depressions as acts of nature; little could be done but to ride out the storm. Some members of Hoover's administration, including Treasury Secretary Mellon, continued to espouse such views. Hoover himself disagreed. Drawing upon the legacy of progressive reform and his experiences as U.S. food administrator during World War I, he initially responded to the economic crisis with energy and de-

termination. But the steps he took also reflected his ideological commitment to localism and to private initiative. "Every time we find solutions outside of government," he told one audience, "we have not only strengthened character, but we have preserved our sense of real self-government."

Acting on these beliefs, Hoover summoned business leaders to the White House soon after the crash and pledged them to maintain wages and employment. Viewing the unemployment crisis as a local issue, he called on municipal and state governments to create public-works projects. In October 1930 he set up an Emergency Committee for Employment to coordinate the efforts of voluntary relief agencies. Seeking a private rather than a government response to the liquidity crisis, Hoover in 1931 persuaded the nation's largest banks to set up a private lending agency, the National Credit Corporation, from which hard-pressed smaller banks could borrow funds to make business loans.

But rather than improving, the crisis worsened. As early as November 1930, the voters rendered a harsh verdict on Hoover's policies. In the midterm election that year, the Republicans lost control of the House of Representatives and gave up eight Senate seats to the Democrats.

In fact, Hoover's well-intentioned antidepression strategy failed dismally. Unemployment mounted, and in 1931, pledges to the president notwithstanding, U.S. Steel, General Motors, and other big corporations announced major wage cuts. The unemployment crisis quickly swamped private charities and local welfare agencies. In Philadelphia, where joblessness soared to more than three hundred thousand by early 1932, the city first cut weekly relief payments to $4.23 per family and then in June suspended them entirely. One charitable leader later described conditions in the city: "[People] kept alive from day to day, catch-as-catch-can, reduced for actual subsistence to something of the status of a stray cat prowling for food, for which a kind soul occasionally sets out a plate of table scraps or a saucer of milk."

By 1932, with an election looming and his voluntarist approach discredited, Hoover took a series of steps that together constituted an unprecedented federal response to economic crisis. In January, at the president's recommendation, Congress set up and provided $2 billion in funding for a new agency, the Reconstruction Finance Corporation (RFC), to make loans to major economic institutions such as banks, insurance companies, and railroads. By July the RFC had

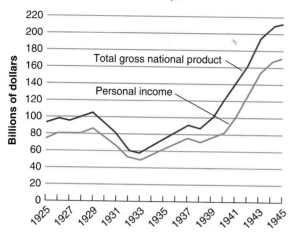

The Decline and Recovery of the U.S. Economy, 1925–1945

Billions of dollars

Total gross national product

Personal income

Business Failures, 1929–1945

Thousands of failures

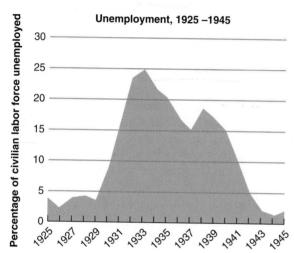

Unemployment, 1925–1945

Percentage of civilian labor force unemployed

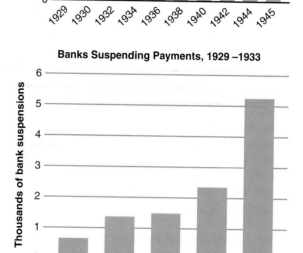

Banks Suspending Payments, 1929–1933

Thousands of bank suspensions

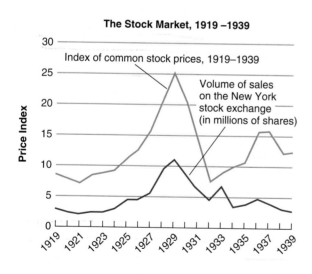

The Stock Market, 1919–1939

Index of common stock prices, 1919–1939

Volume of sales on the New York stock exchange (in millions of shares)

Price Index

The Sagging of the Building Boom, 1919–1939

Value of new building permits (1930 = 100)

Index of value

The Statistics of Hard Times

SOURCES: C. D. Bremmer, *American Bank Failures* (New York: Columbia University Press, 1935), 42; Thomas C. Cochran, *The Great Depression and World War II: 1929–1945* (Glenview, Illinois: Scott, Foresman, 1968); *Historical Statistics of the United States, Colonial Times to 1970* (Washington, D.C.: U.S. Government Printing Office, 1975).

pumped $1.2 billion into the economy. In February Hoover signed the Glass-Steagall Act, allocating $750 million of the government's gold reserves for loans to private businesses. And in July, although he had earlier vetoed similar measures backed by the Democrats, Hoover signed legislation authorizing the RFC to give $2 billion to state and local governments for job-creating public-works programs.

Ironically, however, Hoover reaped little political benefit from these measures. He supported the RFC idea only reluctantly, after the private National Credit Corporation's failure became obvious. He signed the $2 billion public-works bill very grudgingly, issuing a dire warning that it could open the door to "socialism and collectivism."

Hoover increasingly blamed the depression on great global forces and argued that only international measures would help. Some of the actions he advocated, such as a one-year moratorium on war-debt and reparations payments by European nations, made sense but seemed irrelevant to the urgent plight of ordinary Americans. Dreading an unbalanced budget, Hoover in 1931 called for a tax increase and thereby further alienated voters trying desperately to make ends meet.

Sensing the public's rising hostility, Hoover grew sullen and withdrawn. He communicated with the American people through impersonal White House press releases that urged self-help and local initiative, denounced proposals for an expanded federal role, and endlessly saw prosperity "just around the corner." His relations with the news media soured. When his press secretary resigned and Hoover replaced him with a man disliked by the Washington press corps, one reporter joked that the appointment was the first known instance of a rat boarding a sinking ship.

The man once portrayed as a great humanitarian and a managerial genius now emerged in the press as bumbling and hard-hearted. Digging in his heels, Hoover told an aide, "No president must ever admit that he has been wrong." He even stubbornly continued to endorse prohibition long after its unpopularity had become obvious. A presidency launched so auspiciously in 1929 was ending in bitterness and failure.

Mounting Discontent and Protest

An ominous mood spread over the nation. In 1931 hard-hit midwestern farmers organized the Farmers' Holiday Association to force prices up by withholding grain and livestock from the market. Dairy farmers who had watched wholesale milk prices sink to two cents a quart dumped thousands of gallons of milk in Iowa and Wisconsin. Farmers who did not participate in the boycott faced angry reprisals. Violence threatened some city streets when people were evicted from homes and apartments for nonpayment of rent, their meager possessions piled up on the sidewalk.

The most alarming protest came from World War I veterans. In 1924 Congress had voted a veterans' bonus in the form of twenty-year endowment policies against which the veterans might receive government loans. In 1931 a Texas Democratic congressman introduced a bill to change these endowments into immediate cash payments, and in June 1932 some ten thousand veterans, many jobless, descended on Washington to lobby for its passage. When Congress rejected the bill on June 17, most of the "bonus marchers" went home, but about two thousand stayed on, organizing protest parades and building a makeshift settlement in an outlying section of the city called Anacostia Flats. At one march, when a black veteran carrying an American flag was shoved and racially taunted, he shot back, "Don't try to push me, I fought for this flag in France and I'm going to fight for it here on Pennsylvania Avenue."

A nervous Herbert Hoover ordered the army to confine the veterans to Anacostia Flats. The officer given this duty, General Douglas MacArthur, decided to break up the settlement entirely. On July 28 a force of one thousand soldiers armed with tear gas, tanks, and machine guns drove the veterans from their encampment and burned it to the ground. Assisting this operation were two young army officers who, like MacArthur himself, would win fame in World War II: Dwight D. Eisenhower and George S. Patton, Jr. For many Americans, the image of armed troops using force on peaceful demonstrators—and veterans at that—symbolized the Hoover administration's insensitivity to the depression's human dimension.

The Election of 1932

In the absence of other volunteers, Herbert Hoover easily won renomination at the 1932 Republican convention. Smelling defeat, the delegates gloomily adopted a platform offering perfunctory praise for Hoover's antidepression measures.

The Democrats, by contrast, scented victory as they gathered in Chicago. Their platform, crafted to

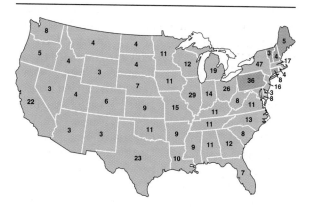

	Electoral Vote	Popular Vote	Percentage of Popular Vote
Democratic Franklin D. Roosevelt	472	22,809,638	57.4
Republican Herbert C. Hoover	59	15,758,901	39.7
Minor parties	–	–	1,153,306	2.9

The Election of 1932

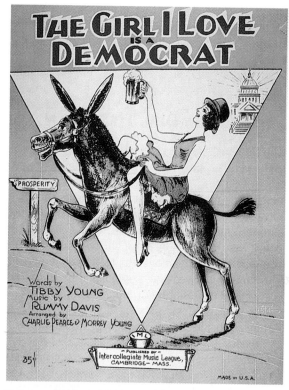

Democratic Sheet Music, c. 1932
Though linking prosperity to prohibition repeal, this long-forgotten tune never attained the popularity of the song the Democrats made their own in 1932, "Happy Days Are Here Again."

erase the divisions that had weakened the party in the 1920s, appealed to the party's urban wing with a call for an end to prohibition, to farmers with support for agricultural aid programs, and to fiscal conservatives with a demand for a balanced budget and a 25 percent cut in federal spending.

Who would win the nomination remained unclear, however, as Democratic hopefuls vied to challenge Hoover. These included Al Smith of New York, the party's 1928 standard-bearer; Texas's favorite son, John Nance ("Cactus Jack") Garner, Speaker of the House of Representatives; and Franklin D. Roosevelt, Smith's political protégé and the current governor of New York.

When Roosevelt failed to secure the necessary two-thirds majority in the early ballots, the possibility of a dark-horse candidate arose. But then the veteran Democratic leader William McAdoo, a delegate from California, announced his state's switch from Garner to Roosevelt. The Californians had not come to Chicago to see a deadlocked convention, he proclaimed, but to elect a president. The nomination was Roosevelt's. Breaking precedent, FDR flew to Chicago to accept the nomination in person. Not realizing that he was naming an era, Roosevelt in his rousing acceptance speech pledged "a new deal for the American people."

Despite this ringing phrase, Roosevelt's campaign oratory gave no clear sense of his presidential agenda. He called for "bold persistent experimentation" and for more attention to "the forgotten man at the bottom of the economic pyramid," yet he also attacked Hoover's "reckless" spending and insisted that "only as a last resort" should the federal government play a larger economic role.

If his campaign lacked specifics, Roosevelt exuded confidence and high spirits. Above all, he was not Hoover! On November 8, FDR and his running mate John Nance Garner received nearly 23 million votes, as compared to fewer than 16 million for Hoover. (Roosevelt's margin in electoral votes was even more lopsided: 472 to 59.) Both houses of Congress went Democratic by heavy margins. After twelve years of Republican rule, the Democrats were back in the saddle. But what did this mean in terms of a program to fight the depression? During the lengthy interval between the election and Roosevelt's inauguration on March 4, 1933,* no one, probably including Roosevelt himself, could confidently answer that question.

THE NEW DEAL TAKES SHAPE

The Roosevelt years began on a note of excitement and feverish activity. Enjoying overwhelming majorities in Congress, FDR proposed a staggering array of emergency measures in his early months in office, most of which passed by large margins. These measures reflected differing and sometimes contradictory policy perspectives. But through the confusion the contours of a depression-fighting strategy emerged. This strategy involved three components: *industrial recovery* through business-government cooperation and pump-priming federal spending; *agricultural recovery* through subsidized crop reduction; and *short-term emergency relief for the jobless*—funneled through state and local agencies when possible, but provided directly by the federal government if necessary. Hovering over this bustle loomed the larger-than-life figure of a smiling Franklin Roosevelt, cigarette holder jauntily tilted upward, for millions a symbol of confidence and renewed hope.

New Beginnings

FDR's inaugural address set the tone of his administration. Although characteristically short on specifics, the new president dedicated his administration to helping the people in their time of crisis. "The only thing we have to fear," he intoned, "is fear itself." Americans responded with an outpouring of support. Within days half a million approving letters deluged the White House.

Fulfilling one Democratic campaign pledge, Congress a few days before the inaugural had passed an amendment to repeal the Eighteenth Amendment, which the states soon ratified. The thirteen-year experiment with prohibition was over. Repeal would stimulate recovery, supporters argued, by producing a bonanza of local, state, and federal taxes on the sale of alcoholic beverages.

---

*The Twentieth Amendment, which shifted the date of the presidential inauguration from March to January 20, took effect after the 1933 inauguration.

Attention now turned to the main event: fighting the depression. In some ways, Franklin Roosevelt seemed an unlikely figure to rally Americans in their moment of crisis. Like his distant cousin Theodore Roosevelt, FDR was of the social elite. His Dutch-immigrant ancestors had been merchants and landed aristocrats in New York for nearly three centuries, and he himself was the product of Groton Academy, Harvard College, and Columbia Law School. But during a term in the state senate (1911–1913) and as governor of New York, he had established close links with the urban-immigrant wing of the state Democratic party. When the depression struck, he had proposed to the New York legislature an innovative series of measures, including unemployment insurance, emergency relief, and a public-works program.

Roosevelt thus entered the Oval Office a seasoned, affable politician with a fine-tuned sensitivity to the public mood and a generalized desire to restore the nation to economic health within a framework of capitalism and democracy. But he had no detailed agenda for achieving these goals. Little interested in theory, Roosevelt encouraged competing proposals, compromised (or papered over) differences, and then threw his weight behind the measures that he sensed could be sold to Congress and the American people.

From his gubernatorial days, he had built up a circle of advisers nicknamed the brain trust. This group included Columbia University professors Raymond Moley and Rexford G. Tugwell and lawyer Adolph A. Berle. Of these, Moley was the most conservative; indeed, he eventually repudiated the New Deal. But Tugwell and Berle, heirs of the progressive reform tradition, rejected laissez-faire ideology and advocated broad programs of federal economic planning and corporate regulation.

Roosevelt heeded his advisers, but they did not (as some critics charged) manipulate him like sinister puppet masters. In fact, the New Deal reflected many ideological and political crosscurrents. FDR by temperament sought a range of opinions rather than relying on a single core of advisers.

Eleanor Roosevelt played a key White House role. A niece of Theodore Roosevelt, the president's wife had a keen social conscience and a background in Progressive Era settlement-house work. At age eighteen she had joined Florence Kelley's National Consumers' League. She helped shape FDR's ideas by exposing him to the reformers, social workers, and advocates of minority rights whose causes she shared. Through Eleanor Roosevelt the ideas of a generation of reform-

Eleanor Roosevelt Visits a West Virginia Coal Mine, 1933

A New Yorker *cartoon of 1933 portrayed one coal miner exclaiming to another: "Oh migosh, here comes Mrs. Roosevelt." But reality soon caught up with humor, as the First Lady immersed herself in the plight of the poor and the exploited.*

ers found a voice in the White House. Wrote Rexford Tugwell: "No one who ever saw Eleanor Roosevelt sit down facing her husband, and holding his eyes firmly, say to him 'Franklin, I think you should . . . ,' or 'Franklin, surely you will not . . .' will ever forget the experience."

She traveled ceaselessly—40,000 miles in 1933 alone—and served as an astute observer for her wheelchair-bound husband. (With sly wit a Washington newspaper headlined midway through FDR's first term, "MRS. ROOSEVELT SPENDS NIGHT AT WHITE HOUSE.") In 1935 she began a regular syndicated newspaper column, "My Day." The poorest and most obscure Americans wrote her letters pouring out their troubles as they would to a personal friend.[*]

---

[*]Ironically, this couple who had such emotional rapport with the American people had long been emotionally distant from each other. Each found intimacy outside marriage: Franklin through a long-term relationship with his wife's social secretary, Lucy Mercer, and Eleanor with Lorena Hickok, a former journalist and aide to the New Deal relief administrator Harry Hopkins. Only years later did these personal details become generally known.

Roosevelt's top political adviser, James A. Farley, had managed FDR's two gubernatorial campaigns (1928 and 1930) and done the spadework that won his patron the presidential nomination in 1932. As postmaster general, he spent more time on politics than on the mails. He distributed patronage jobs, managed FDR's 1932 and 1936 campaigns, and smoothed White House relations with state and local Democratic machines. Bored by policy issues, Jim Farley had a master's sense of the treacherous currents of presidential politics.

Roosevelt's cabinet reflected the New Deal's diversity. Secretary of Labor Frances Perkins, the first woman cabinet member, had served as industrial commissioner of New York during FDR's years as governor. Interior Secretary Harold L. Ickes, a prickly but able Republican progressive from Chicago, had helped organize liberal Republicans for Roosevelt in 1932. Secretary of Agriculture Henry A. Wallace of Iowa held the same post his father had occupied in the Harding and Coolidge administrations. Editor of an influential agricultural weekly, Wallace excelled as an agricultural economist, crop experimenter, and farm-policy theorist. Treasury Secretary Henry Morgenthau, Jr., FDR's neighbor and political ally from New York days, though a fiscal conservative, tolerated the unbalanced budgets necessary to finance New Deal antidepression programs.

Below the cabinet rank, a host of newcomers poured into Washington in 1933—former progressive reformers, settlement-house workers, political scientists, economics professors, bright young lawyers recommended by Felix Frankfurter of Harvard Law School. These newcomers energized the capital. They drafted bills, vied for the president's ear, and debated conflicting strategies of reform and recovery. From this hectic, pressure-cooker environment emerged a torrent of laws, programs, and agencies that historians try to encompass within a single catchall label: the New Deal.

The Hundred Days

Between March 9 and June 16, 1933, Congress enacted more than a dozen important measures, making the turbulent "Hundred Days" a period of remarkable legislative productivity. Rooted in the political experience of the Progressive Era and World War I, and even in the Hoover presidency, these measures sharply increased the level of federal involvement in the nation's economic life.

The banking crisis represented FDR's most urgent challenge. To gain time, the president on March 5 ordered all banks to close for four days. At the end of this so-called bank holiday, he proposed an Emergency Banking Act, which sailed through Congress. This law permitted healthy banks to reopen with a Treasury Department license, provided for the orderly management of failed banks, and enlarged the government's regulatory power over money and banking. In the first of a series of informal radio talks dubbed "fireside chats," the president assured Americans that they could again entrust their money to banks. A second banking act, passed in June, further restored the nation's confidence in the banks by creating the Federal Deposit Insurance Corporation (FDIC) to insure all bank deposits up to five thousand dollars and to separate deposit banking from investment banking.

In keeping with the budget-balancing pledges of the Democratic platform, FDR on March 10 proposed, and Congress soon passed, an economy measure cutting federal workers' salaries, slashing veterans' pensions and benefits, and otherwise seeking to trim spending.

Other measures revealed the early New Deal's more innovative side. On March 31, for example, on FDR's recommendation Congress created the Civilian Conservation Corps (CCC) to employ jobless youths in such projects as reforestation, park maintenance, and erosion control. By 1935 half a million young men were earning $35 a month plus room and board in CCC camps from Maine to California. Even this small sum made a difference for families with no income at all.

Two federal agencies established during the Hundred Days addressed the heartbreak of mortgage foreclosure. The Home Owners Loan Corporation (HOLC) helped needy citizens refinance their home mortgages. Eventually HOLC refinanced about one-fifth of all U.S. mortgages. The Farm Credit Administration did the same for rural Americans facing the loss of their farms.

The most comprehensive relief measure of the early New Deal, the Federal Emergency Relief Act (May 1933), revealed the continued strength of Herbert Hoover's conviction that relief must remain a local matter. This measure appropriated $500 million to replenish the empty relief coffers of states and cities. To administer this program, FDR appointed Harry Hopkins, a former social worker who would emerge as one of the New Deal's most powerful figures. A gaunt chain smoker who enjoyed parties and the racetrack, Hopkins enlivened the Washington scene. In his first two hours on the job, from a makeshift desk in a hallway, he distributed $5 million to state and local relief agencies.

Another early New Deal measure incorporating ideas from the past was the Tennessee Valley Authority (TVA). During World War I, the government had built a hydroelectric plant on the Tennessee River at Muscle Shoals, Alabama, to power a nearby nitrate plant. In the 1920s Senator George W. Norris of Nebraska had unsuccessfully urged the reactivation of this facility to supply electric power to nearby farmers who still lived in a world of wood stoves and kerosene lamps.

With the TVA the Roosevelt administration vastly expanded Norris's idea through a commitment to the economic and social development of the entire Tennessee River valley—one of the nation's poorest areas. The TVA built a hydroelectric network that supplied cheap power to the region while also developing a flood-control system, recreational facilities, and a soil-conservation program. Under director David E. Lilienthal, the TVA proved one of the New Deal's most popular achievements.

TVA ultimately failed to fulfill its advocates' high hopes, and it eventually met controversy on several fronts. The agency's policy of displacing private landowners to build dams, reservoirs, and parks roused criticism. Private power interests distrusted TVA, and President Dwight Eisenhower in the 1950s called it an example of "creeping socialism." Environmentalists, advocates of energy conservation, and critics of nuclear power (which TVA later championed) all found reason in subsequent years to attack TVA. During the early New Deal, however, TVA, and the planning vision it embodied, met with little but admiration and praise.

The two most important measures of the Hundred Days, the Agricultural Adjustment Act and the National Recovery Act, addressed the urgent task of economic recovery. Both measures evolved from debates among advocates of differing ideas that had been around for some time.

On the agricultural front, some favored the approach embodied in the McNary-Haugen bill of the 1920s by which the government would purchase agricultural surpluses and sell them abroad. Others, however, insisted that reduced production offered the key to agricultural recovery. They noted that farmers, seeking to maintain incomes, had responded to declining prices by *increasing* output, a process that drove prices still lower.

The advocates of production cuts won out. As a first step to this goal, the government in the summer of

Building the Norris Dam on the Clinch River in Tennessee, 1935
This dam, part of the New Deal's Tennessee Valley Authority, honored Senator George W. Norris, long an advocate of public-power projects in this region of the South.

Major Measures Enacted During the "Hundred Days" (March 9–June 16, 1933)

March 9	Emergency Banking Relief Act
20	Economy Act
31	Unemployment Relief Act (Civilian Conservation Corps)
May 12	Agricultural Adjustment Act
12	Federal Emergency Relief Act
18	Tennessee Valley Authority
27	Federal Securities Act
June 13	Home Owners' Refinancing Act
16	Farm Credit Act
16	Banking Act of 1933 (Federal Deposit Insurance Corporation)
16	National Industrial Recovery Act (National Recovery Administration; Public Works Administration)

1933 paid southern cotton planters to plow under much of their crop and midwestern farmers to slaughter some 6 million piglets and pregnant sows. The slaughter of pigs when many people lacked food proved a public-relations gaffe that the New Deal never fully lived down.

Pursuing the same goal in a more systematic fashion, the Agricultural Adjustment Act of May 1933 set up a program by which producers of the major agricultural commodities—including hogs, wheat, corn, cotton, and dairy products—received payments, called subsidies, in return for cutting production. A tax on food processors, such as the mills that converted grain into flour or cereals, financed these subsidies. (The nation's consumers, who eventually paid this tax in the form of higher food prices, ultimately financed the New Deal's farm program.) A new federal agency, the Agricultural Adjustment Administration (AAA), supervised the complex program. The goal was *parity*: a restoration of farmers' purchasing power to what it had been in 1909–1914—a time of prosperity in rural America.

The National Industrial Recovery Act (NIRA), passed in June 1933, drew upon the trade associations that President Hoover had promoted. It also recalled the 1917–1918 era, when American business, prodded by Washington, had cooperated in the war-mobilization campaign. Now in 1933 the enemy was the depression rather than the German kaiser, but something of the same spirit of cooperation and shared purpose again united the nation—at least for a brief interval.

Under this law representatives of the major industries, granted immunity from antitrust prosecution, drafted codes of "fair competition" for their industries. These codes set production limits, prescribed wages and working conditions, and forbade price cutting and unfair competitive practices. The National Recovery Administration (NRA) oversaw the codes.

The NRA aimed to promote recovery by breaking the cycle of wage cuts, falling prices, and layoffs. But reformers like Frances Perkins and union advocates like Senator Robert F. Wagner of New York saw further potential. Under pressure from Perkins, the NRA's textile-industry code banned child labor—long a goal of reformers. And through Wagner's efforts Section 7a of the law gave a boost to organized labor by prohibiting employers from discriminating against union members and affirming workers' legal right to organize and bargain collectively.

The head of the NRA, Hugh Johnson, who had served with the War Industries Board in 1917–1918, brought to the job energy, mercurial emotions, and a knack for publicity. Johnson quickly organized a national campaign, complete with parades in major cities, to persuade consumers to buy only from companies that subscribed to an NRA code. The campaign's symbol, the blue eagle, and its slogan, "We Do Our Part," adorned roadside billboards and magazine advertisements.

The National Industrial Recovery Act also appropriated some $3.3 billion for a public-works program to employ the jobless and pump money into the economy. To oversee this vast program, the law created another new agency, the Public Works Administration (PWA). Under Secretary of the Interior Harold Ickes, the PWA eventually spent more than $4 billion on some thirty-four thousand public-works projects, including dams, bridges, and public buildings.

The NRA echoed Herbert Hoover's theme of business-government cooperation. In his speeches of 1933–1935, FDR always included the corporations as key players in the "all-American team" fighting the depression. Although the NRA codes, once signed by the president, had the force of law, their implementation depended on voluntary business support. Caught up in the spirit of national unity prevailing in 1933, most business leaders cooperated—at least initially.

Moreover, the probusiness Reconstruction Finance Corporation, a carryover from the Hoover era, remained active. FDR appointed as RFC chairman the Houston banker Jesse H. Jones. Under Jones, the RFC lent billions of dollars at favorable rates to banks, insurance companies, railroads, and even a large department-store chain. Jones not only helped endangered financial institutions but also extended government loans for new business ventures, making the RFC a potent financial instrument serving corporate America.

A few early New Deal measures, however, anticipated a more adversarial approach to business. In fact, the 1929 crash had produced a bitter reaction against business executives. This reaction found expression in a Senate investigation of Wall Street conducted in 1932–1934 under the direction of a tough New York lawyer, Ferdinand Pecora. Pecora's probe revealed that not one of the twenty partners of the Morgan Bank had paid a penny of income tax in 1931 or 1932. People

jeered when the president of the New York Stock Exchange told a Senate committee considering regulatory legislation: "You gentlemen are making a big mistake. The Exchange is a perfect institution."

Reflecting this public mood, Congress in May 1933 passed the Federal Securities Act, regulating the sale of stocks. This law required corporate executives to inform the Federal Trade Commission fully on all stock offerings and made them personally liable for any misrepresentation of securities issued by their companies. The following year Congress curbed the purchase of stock on credit (a practice that had contributed to the 1929 debacle) and created a new agency, the Securities and Exchange Commission (SEC), to oversee the stock market.

Congress adjourned for the summer on June 16, 1933, and the Hundred Days ended. For many Americans this initial burst of legislative activity came to symbolize the dynamism, as well as the confusion, of the Roosevelt years. The Hundred Days spawned an array of "alphabet-soup" agencies whose initials few could keep straight. How all these new programs and agencies would work in practice remained to be seen.

The NRA Bogs Down

The economy improved briefly in the summer of 1933, but recovery proved illusory. Economic indicators remained bleak through 1934, and problems and controversy plagued the New Deal.

The National Recovery Administration encountered particular problems, related in part to the erratic personality of its head, the hard-driving, hard-drinking Hugh Johnson. But the NRA's difficulties went deeper. As the crisis-induced national unity of early 1933 faded, corporate America grew increasingly unhappy with NRA regulation. Charges of code violations increased. Small businesses objected that the codes served the interests of large businesses. Republicans and some jurists attacked the NRA as unconstitutional. The agency itself, meanwhile, became bogged down in drafting trivial codes. The shoulder-pad industry had its own code; the nation's burlesque houses adopted an NRA code specifying the degree of nudity strippers could display. Fundamentally, the trade associations that wrote and supervised the codes used them to restrict competition and maintain prices, not to stimulate economic expansion.

Beset by myriad problems, the NRA gradually sank of its own weight. Johnson departed in 1934, and in

May 1935 the Supreme Court unanimously declared the NRA unconstitutional. The Court based its ruling on two grounds: first, the act delegated to the president regulatory powers that constitutionally belonged to the legislative branch; second, the NRA was regulating commerce within individual states, violating the constitutional provision limiting federal regulation to *interstate* commerce. Few New Dealers mourned. As an economic-recovery measure, the NRA had failed.

Troubled Agriculture

The New Deal's early agricultural program proved more successful, but it, too, generated controversy. Aided by drought as well as by New Deal policies, agricultural production declined and commodity prices rose, as planners had hoped. From 1933 to 1937, total farm income increased by 50 percent.

But the AAA did little to help landless farm laborers, migrant workers, or the tenants and sharecroppers of the cotton South. Indeed, the AAA crop-reduction subsidies hurt tenants and sharecroppers, because the landowners often banked the subsidy checks, removed the acreage from production, and left the sharecroppers to shift for themselves. One Georgia

sharecropper wrote Harry Hopkins: "I have Bin farming all my life But the man I live with Has Turned me loose taking my mule [and] all my feed. . . . I can't get a Job so Some one said Rite you."

Some victims of this process resisted. In 1934 the interracial Southern Tenant Farmers' Union, led by the Socialist party, emerged in Arkansas. Declared one elderly black sharecropper at the organizing meeting: "The same chain that holds my people holds your people too. . . . The landlord is always betwixt us, beatin' us and starvin' us and makin' us fight each other. There ain't but one way . . . and that's for us to get together and stay together." The landowners struck back with a campaign of terror, chasing down union organizers as their ancestors had once hunted runaway slaves.

Nature itself seemed to conspire against the farmers at the bottom of the economic ladder, as parching drought in the mid-1930s turned the Great Plains into a dust bowl (see "A Place in Time"). Battered by depression and drought alike, many poor farmers of the South and Great Plains abandoned the land. Some migrated to the cities, expanding already huge relief rolls. Others packed their humble belongings into old cars and headed west to become migrant agricultural workers in California and Arizona. The hardships they

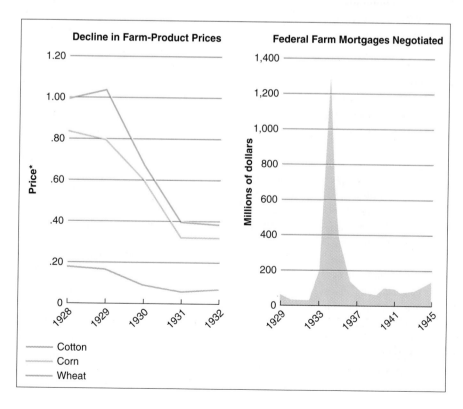

Agriculture During the Great Depression

The depression hit rural America with brutal fierceness, as the statistics on commodity prices and farm mortgages show.

*The graph shows the price per pound for cotton and the price per bushel for corn and wheat.

SOURCE: *Historical Statistics of the United States, Colonial Times to 1970* (Washington, D.C., Government Printing Office, 1975), 511, 517.

Cimarron County, Oklahoma: Heart of the Dust Bowl

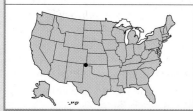

As though the Depression were not enough, searing drought and howling dust storms compounded the misery of the 1930s across the Great Plains. Journalists dubbed the region the Dust Bowl, and the name stuck.

The rains failed in 1930, devastating wheat and livestock on the southern Plains. The dust came in 1934. A storm that began in early May whipped 350 tons of dust across the nation. Twelve million tons filtered down on Chicago alone. Before finally blowing out to sea, the storm darkened East Coast cities from Boston to Savannah.

Through 1939 each spring and summer brought a new scourge of dust. The worst year was 1937, with seventy-two major storms. The locus shifted from year to year, but hardest hit were western Kansas and Oklahoma, northwestern Texas, and eastern Colorado and New Mexico. Some storms—"black blizzards"—arose suddenly. One in Kansas roared in so quickly that the date, April 14, 1935, became known as Black Sunday. "Sand blows" started more insidiously but proved equally nerve-racking. By 1938 some 10 million acres had lost five inches or more of topsoil; another 13.5 million acres had suffered less severe but still serious erosion.

Survivors never forgot the experience. The skies blackened; trains derailed; blinded automobile drivers proceeded on foot, only to become hopelessly lost. A child died when he wandered away and suffocated in a dust drift. The dust sifted into houses and coated everything with a thick film. Night brought little relief: "A trip for water to rinse the grit from our lips," wrote a Kansas woman, "and then back to bed with washcloths over our noses. We try to lie still, because every turn stirs the dust on the blankets."

Some reacted with resignation; others, with gallows humor. Proclaimed one sign: "Great Bargains in Real Estate. Bring Your Own Container." Religious fundamentalists saw the dust storms as a portent of the Second Coming. Dorothea Lange and other New Deal photographers compiled a memorable visual record of

Fleeing a Dust Storm, Cimarron County, 1934
This famous photograph by Arthur Rothstein captured the desolation of the dust-choked Oklahoma land.

Credit for "A Place in Time" vignette above:
Hogue, Alexandre. **Dust Bowl, 1933**. National Museum of Art, Washington, D.C., U.S.A.

Oklahoma Farm Family, 1939

Battered by drought, dust, debt, and depression, rural Oklahomans endured especially hard times in the 1930s. Many gave up and moved on, sometimes in the dark of night to evade bank creditors.

the storms' aftermath; amateur photographers caught scenes of the dust clouds rolling in. Painter Alexandre Hogue created haunting images of dead cattle and abandoned tractors in mounds of dust. Woody Guthrie, the balladeer of the Dust Bowl, grew up in Okemah, Oklahoma, and Pampa, Texas, before migrating to California in 1937. Guthrie's song "The Great Dust Storm" began:

It fell across our city like a
* curtain*
* of black rolled down,*
We thought it was our judgment,
* we thought*
* it was our doom.*

In the heart of the Dust Bowl lay Cimarron County, Oklahoma, at the tip of the state's panhandle. After the displacement of the local Plains Indians to reservations, the region had been settled by Mexican shepherds, Anglo cattle ranchers, and, in the 1890s, wheat growers. In the 1920s the Santa Fe Railroad chugged in, and some people prospered. Farm-implement dealers in the principal town, Boise City, did a thriving business. The 1931 wheat harvest approached 6 million bushels. But then spreading drought and swirling dust spelled catastrophe. As early as 1933, a Texas news-

paper reported: "Not a blade of wheat in Cimarron County, Oklahoma; cattle dying.... Humans suffering from dust fever—milk cows going dry, turned into pasture to starve, hogs in such pitiable shape that buyers will not have them." Newspapers reported forced sales of farms.

With their livelihood destroyed, families packed their scant possessions into old jalopies, abandoned foreclosed farms and bank debts, and rumbled off in the night. The county's population fell by 40 percent in the 1930s, from over 4,000 to about 2,500.

The farmers who fled Cimarron County were part of a vast tide of migrants. From 1935 to 1937, a government study found, 34 percent of the farm families in forty Dust Bowl counties pulled up stakes, leaving ten thousand empty houses and 9 million abandoned acres. During the decade as a whole, nearly 3.5 million people left the Great Plains; Oklahoma's population sank more than 18 percent. Most moved only a short distance, into a city or a nearby state, but many pushed on to California or the Pacific Northwest. Though coming from various states, they all bore a derisive nickname: Okies.

The federal government tried to help. Congress voted $525 million in emergency drought relief in 1934. The Roosevelt

administration sent fact-finding teams, launched public-works projects, and provided emergency farm loans. Dust Bowl wheat farmers gladly accepted federal payments under the Agricultural Adjustment Act for not cultivating their bone-dry land. The Taylor Grazing Act of 1934 addressed another environmental problem on the Plains: overgrazing by cattle herds. This law created the Grazing Service (later the Bureau of Land Management) to protect the remaining public lands in the West.

Although journalists sometimes portrayed the drought as unnatural and wholly unforeseen, agricultural specialists had long recognized that periodic drought and low rainfall make grain farming precarious beyond the 100th meridian, which bisects central Kansas. Drought had laid waste the region in the 1890s, and climatologists traced extended dry spells as far back as the thirteenth century. Nor were dust storms simply an inevitable corollary of drought. Environmental historian Donald Worster, in *Dust Bowl: The Southern Plains in the 1930s* (1979), documents the practices that caused the erosion that in turn produced the dust storms. Through the early twentieth century, settlers had used ever more powerful tractors and combines (which harvest and thresh wheat in one operation across a sixteen-foot swath) to cultivate more and more acres. Going into debt to buy farm equipment, wheat-planting "sodbusters" had plowed up the grama-buffalo grass and other native short grasses, leaving 33 million acres exposed to parching winds.

Even without the drought, the transition to large-scale mechanized farming would have driven many small farmers off the land, prey to debt and tumbling wheat prices. Indeed, from 1910 to 1930, *before* the drought, notes James Gregory in *American Exodus* (1989), the number of agricultural workers on the southern Plains fell by some 340,000. And even in the 1930s, most who left the region did not come from the areas hardest hit by drought and dust. In short, the depression-era crisis on the southern Plains was a complex phenomenon with complex causes. But because of journalists, photographers, novelists, and folk singers, it was the "Dust Bowl" image that captured the popular imagination and shaped perceptions of the depression years on the Great Plains.

experienced became symbolic of the suffering and disruption of the 1930s.

In 1933–1935 debate raged between those New Dealers whose goal was to restore prosperity to the agricultural sector as a whole and those, like Rexford Tugwell and Jerome Frank of the Department of Agriculture, who urged special attention to the nation's poorest farmers. At first FDR sided with those who took a less reformist view, and early in 1935 Frank and several of his allies in the Department of Agriculture were dismissed. The policy debate continued, however, and in the later New Deal, the advocates of a farm policy reflecting broader social objectives would score significant legislative victories (see below).

Controversy over Relief Strategy

Intense discussion focused, too, on the issue of aid for the unemployed. Relief administrator Harry Hopkins grew increasingly impatient with the slowness and inefficiency of many state and local relief agencies. By November 1933 Hopkins had convinced Roosevelt that only direct federal relief could prevent mass suffering and perhaps violent upheaval that winter. FDR put Hopkins in charge of a new but temporary public works agency, the Civil Works Administration (CWA). Through the cold winter, the CWA expended nearly a billion dollars on short-term work projects for the jobless. When the CWA check arrived, one Iowa woman recalled, "The first thing I did was to go out and buy a dozen oranges. I hadn't tasted any for so long that I had forgotten what they were like."

With the coming of spring, however, FDR abolished the CWA. No one would starve in warm weather, he believed. Although his conservative critics did not realize it, FDR shared with them a horror of creating a permanent underclass subsisting on welfare payments. But the persistence of mass unemployment, coupled with the inability of local agencies to cope with the challenge, rendered further federal relief programs nearly inevitable.

Hopkins's growing influence sharpened an intense behind-the-scenes struggle between him and Harold Ickes to control federal relief policy. Ickes, a supercautious man, went over every PWA proposal with a fine-tooth comb. The PWA built many projects of enduring value, but in the short run the deliberate approach of "Honest Harold" left billions in relief funds stalled in the pipeline while he and his staff painstak-ingly reviewed every detail of their large-scale undertakings.

In contrast, the more impatient Hopkins sought above all to put people to work and get money circulating. Even make-work projects like raking leaves, filling potholes, and collecting litter had merit, in his view, if they achieved these goals. Given the urgency of the unemployment crisis, Hopkins won the power struggle with Ickes for dominant influence in shaping federal relief policy.

The New Deal in Midstream: Popularity and Problems

Despite the New Deal's brave beginnings, the depression continued as 1934 drew to a close. Major problems afflicted the NRA, conflict flared over farm policy, and the need for federal relief spending seemed to be expanding rather than tapering off.

But the New Deal remained highly popular. This popularity reflected both the administration's achievements and FDR's political skills. Assisted by speechwriters and publicists, Roosevelt commanded the political stage, marshalling support for his programs with buoyancy, good humor, and self-assurance. Although many staunchly Republican newspaper publishers remained hostile, FDR enjoyed excellent relations with the working press. He loved bantering with reporters, and they reciprocated by presenting an overwhelmingly favorable picture of his administration.

In contrast to his tense and edgy predecessor, Roosevelt savored public appearances and took naturally to radio. He treated radio listeners not as an anonymous mass but as three or four family members in a living room, and in his "fireside chats," he described his goals to the American people. To many, he seemed almost a family member himself. Frances Perkins later described his manner during these radio talks: "His head would nod and his hands would move in simple, natural, comfortable gestures. His face would smile and light up as though he were actually sitting on the front porch or in the parlor with them." Roosevelt, in short, displayed an easy mastery of radio that his successors in the era of television would emulate.

The midterm election of November 1934 ratified the popular verdict on the New Deal. Reversing the usual midterm pattern, the incumbent Democrats *increased* their majorities in both the House and the Senate. As for FDR, Kansas journalist William Allen White observed, "He's been all but crowned by the people." Where would Roosevelt go now? Some observers viewed the New Deal as essentially complete and anticipated a period of consolidation. But a different mood prevailed in the White House and in Congress. As the 1934 election returns rolled in, Harry Hopkins turned to a group of New Deal friends and declared, "Boys, this is our hour!" A new surge of activism, rivaling that of the Hundred Days, lay ahead.

THE NEW DEAL CHANGES COURSE

As the mood of national unity initially roused by Roosevelt faded, the New Deal faced criticism from conservatives for going too far and from radicals for not going far enough. Shelving the unity theme, Roosevelt veered sharply leftward and took up the cause of the underdog. Buoyed by the results of the 1934 midterm election and with an eye on the forthcoming presidential contest, FDR in 1935 pushed through a bundle of reform measures so impressive that historians call this phase the Second New Deal. The landslide reelection victory that followed in 1936 cemented a new Democratic coalition that would long remain a potent political force.

Challenges from Right and Left

Although the early New Deal was hardly radical, some conservative business leaders soon concluded that it posed a mortal threat to the capitalist system. In 1934 several top corporate figures, joined by an increasingly conservative Al Smith and other disgruntled Democrats, formed an anti–New Deal organization called the American Liberty League, dedicated to the proposition that the Roosevelt program restricted individual freedom and pointed the way to socialism. Early in 1935 the U.S. Chamber of Commerce blasted the New Deal. Anti-Roosevelt jokes circulated among the rich, many of whom denounced FDR as a traitor to his class and sputtered in rage at "that man in the White House."

More potent opposition came from demagogues who targeted those in the lower ranks of American life by offering a variety of social and economic panaceas. Detroit Catholic priest and radio spellbinder Charles E. Coughlin won an audience of some 40 million for his volatile brew of economics, politics, and piety. At first Coughlin supported the New Deal, but by 1935 he was condemning FDR as a "great betrayer and liar," making anti-Semitic allusions, and peddling his own panaceas, including nationalization of the banks. As a priest and a native of Canada, Coughlin himself could not run for office, but his radio followers, organized as the National Union of Social Justice and drawn mainly from the ranks of the urban lower-middle class with a sprinkling of small businessmen, threatened FDR's 1936 electoral hopes.

Millions of older Americans, meanwhile, rallied to the banner of an elderly California physician, Francis E. Townsend, who proposed that the government pay two hundred dollars each month to all retired citizens over sixty, requiring only that the money be spent within thirty days. Such a plan would not only help elder Americans and stimulate the economy, Townsend insisted, but also open up jobs by encouraging early retirement. The scheme would have quickly bankrupted the nation, but many older citizens, especially in southern California, embraced it.

FDR's wiliest rival was Huey Long of Louisiana, a flamboyant political hell raiser. A country lawyer who won the Louisiana governorship in 1928, Long ruled the state as his personal fiefdom while building highways, schools, and public housing. He roared into Washington as a senator in 1932, preaching his "Share Our Wealth" program: a 100 percent tax on all annual incomes over $1 million and appropriation of all fortunes in excess of $5 million. With this money Long proposed to give every American family a comfortable income, a house, a car, old-age benefits, and free educational opportunities. Although he sometimes played the buffoon, Long was highly intelligent. One senator, describing his debating style, compared him to a horsefly: "He would light on one part of you, sting you, and then, when you slapped at him, fly away to land elsewhere and sting again."

"Every man a king," proclaimed Long, and millions responded. His baiting of the rich and powerful appealed to many Americans resentful of the nation's gaping disparities of wealth. Like Father Coughlin, Long fleetingly endorsed the New Deal, but as his book *My First Days in the White House* (published posthumously in 1935) made clear, the presidential bug had bitten him badly. By 1935 "the Kingfish" (a nickname drawn from the radio comedy show "Amos 'n' Andy") boasted 7.5 million supporters. An assassin's bullet cut

Long down that September, but his close associate, the even more demagogic Gerald L. K. Smith, quickly took over his Share Our Wealth organization.

Adding to Roosevelt's worries, economic recovery eluded his grasp. National income in 1934 rose about 25 percent above the disastrous year 1933 but still hovered far below the 1929 level. Millions had been jobless for three or four years and were deeply demoralized. The rising frustration found expression in nearly two thousand strikes, some of them communist-led, that disrupted labor in 1934, from New York taxi drivers to San Francisco dockworkers.

Rather than withdrawing in the face of adversity, as Hoover had done, Roosevelt outflanked his opponents and regained the political high ground in 1935 with an impressive series of legislative initiatives—the so-called Second New Deal.

The Second New Deal: Expanding Federal Relief

Roosevelt set the stage for the Second New Deal in his January 1935 State of the Union address in calling for broad social reform. He soon fleshed out the rhetoric with a program involving six central elements: an enlarged and reorganized federal program of relief for the jobless, assistance to the rural poor, support for organized labor, social-welfare benefits for older Americans and other disadvantaged groups, stricter business regulation, and heavier taxes on the well-to-do.

With unemployment still alarmingly high, Congress in April 1935 passed the Emergency Relief Appropriation Act, granting Roosevelt $5 billion to spend more or less as he wished. He swiftly set up a new agency, the Works Progress Administration (WPA), headed by Harry Hopkins. Like the temporary Civil Works Administration that had helped the nation through the winter of 1933–1934, the WPA funneled relief assistance directly from the federal government to individuals.

But Roosevelt's horror of "the dole" led him to insist that the WPA provide *work* rather than handouts for the jobless. Over its eight-year life, the WPA employed more than 8 million jobless Americans, pumped $11 billion into the economy, and completed a mind-boggling number of projects: 650,000 miles of roads constructed or improved; 124,000 bridges built or repaired; 125,000 schools, hospitals, post offices, and other public buildings erected.

Although most WPA workers performed manual labor, the agency also assisted writers, performers, and artists. The Federal Writers' Project employed out-of-work authors to produce a series of state guides as well as the histories of ethnic and immigrant groups. Black novelist Richard Wright's first book, a short-story collection called *Uncle Tom's Children* (1938), was written with support from the Federal Writers' Project. In Massachusetts, WPA workers transcribed hundreds of pages of handwritten legal documents from the witchcraft episode of 1692. In the South they collected the reminiscences of aged ex-slaves.

The Federal Theatre Project (FTP) put unemployed actors to work in theaters across the nation. One FTP undertaking, the Living Newspaper, which dramatized contemporary social issues, was dismissed by some critics as New Deal propaganda. But the FTP drama companies touring small-town America gave millions their first taste of live theater. Artists working for the Federal Arts Project designed posters, taught painting in schools, and decorated post offices and courthouses with murals. These WPA arts agencies helped thousands of creative people survive the depression; they also enlivened a dismal decade and created an unprecedented federally supported popular-culture program.

Other New Deal agencies distributed relief funds as well. The National Youth Administration provided part-time work for more than 2 million high school and college youths. And Harold Ickes's Public Works Administration, after its slow start, now picked up a full head of steam. Expending more than $4 billion over its entire life span, PWA employed many thousands of workers on some thirty-four thousand construction projects, including such diverse undertakings as the Triborough Bridge and the Lincoln Tunnel in New York City, the awesome Grand Coulee Dam on the Columbia River in Washington State, and a strikingly beautiful library for the University of New Mexico.

With monumental relief spending came budget deficits. The federal budget dipped into the red by $461 million in 1932, and deficits persisted through the decade. They fluctuated from highs of $3.6 billion in 1934 and $4.4 billion in 1936 to a low of $1.2 billion in 1938. These deficits were covered by government borrowing. According to the British economist John Maynard Keynes, deficit spending in a depression was good policy. When faced with an economic downturn and chronic unemployment, said Keynes, governments should adopt a policy of deficit spending to fund

Construction of a Dam, *by William Gropper (1897–1977)*
The New Deal's Federal Arts Project commissioned murals for post offices and other
public buildings. Gropper, whose work exposed social injustice and class inequalities,
painted this mural for the Department of the Interior building in Washington, D.C.

public-works programs, thereby increasing purchasing power and stimulating recovery. The New Deal, however, was not Keynesian in philosophy. Because all the dollars that flowed into public-works programs were withdrawn from the economy through taxation or government borrowing, the stimulus effect was nil. FDR always viewed deficit spending as a deplorable necessity, not as a positive instrument of government policy.

The Second New Deal: Turning Leftward

Roosevelt's legislative proposals of 1935 reflected a sharp turn to the left. In 1933, buoyed by a burst of national unity, Roosevelt had played down class differences, stressed the shared goal of recovery, and attempted an unprecedented degree of centralized economic planning and control. By 1935 the political struggles inevitable in a democracy made up of conflicting social classes and diverse interest groups were reviving. Reflecting the new political reality, the Second New Deal abandoned the effort to devise programs with universal appeal. Stung by conservative criticism and gathering discontent, Roosevelt now offered a program frankly geared to the poor, the disadvantaged, and the laboring masses.

Social-justice advocates like Secretary of Labor Frances Perkins and federal Children's Bureau director Grace Abbott, as well as Eleanor Roosevelt, helped shape this program. But so, too, did hard-headed political calculations. Looking ahead to 1936, Roosevelt's

political advisers feared that the followers of Coughlin, Townsend, and Long could siphon off enough votes to deny Roosevelt a second term. This worry figured prominently in shaping FDR's 1935 political agenda.

The New Deal's leftward turn was evident in its agricultural policy, as the plight of sharecroppers, tenants, migrants, and other poor farmers aroused fresh attention. This plight, as we have seen, had been worsened by the New Deal's own AAA and its payments to large landowners to take acreage out of production. The Resettlement Administration, created by Congress in May 1935 and directed by Rexford Tugwell, made loans to help small farmers buy their own farms and to enable sharecroppers and tenants tilling exhausted soil to resettle in more productive areas. Although Tugwell's agency achieved less than he had hoped and lasted only two years, it did keep the difficulties of tenants and sharecroppers alive as an issue of government concern.

The Rural Electrification Administration (REA), another agency created in the spring of 1935, made low-interest loans to utility companies and farmers' cooperatives to extend electricity to the 90 percent of rural America that still lacked it. By 1941, 40 percent of American farms enjoyed electric power.

Meanwhile, the agricultural-recovery program suffered a setback in January 1936 when the Supreme Court declared the Agricultural Adjustment Act unconstitutional. The processing tax that funded the AAA's subsidies was an illegal use of the government's tax

Major Later New Deal Legislation (November 1933–1938)

1933 (Nov.)	Civil Works Administration	**1935**	Emergency Relief Appropriations Act (Works Progress Administration) National Labor Relations Act (Wagner Act) Revenue Act of 1935 Social Security Act Public Utilities Holding Company Act Banking Act of 1935 Resettlement Administration Rural Electrification Act
1934	Civil Works Emergency Relief Act Home Owners' Loan Act Securities Exchange Act (Securities and Exchange Commission) Communications Act (Federal Communications Commission) Federal Farm Bankruptcy Act National Housing Act (Federal Housing Administration)	**1937**	National Housing Act of 1937 Bankhead-Jones Farm Tenancy Act
		1938	Fair Labor Standards Act Agricultural Adjustment Act of 1938

power, the Court ruled. To replace the AAA, Congress passed the Soil Conservation and Domestic Allotment Act, which paid farmers to cut production of soil-depleting crops such as wheat and cotton (which also happened to be the major surplus commodities) and to plant soil-conserving grasses and legumes instead. When agricultural prices remained depressed, Congress passed another major farm law in 1938 (see below).

Organized labor won a key victory during the Second New Deal, again thanks to the efforts of New York senator Robert Wagner. At first FDR had opposed Wagner's campaign for a prolabor law, viewing such "special-interest" legislation as discordant with the early New Deal's national-unity theme. Wagner patiently built congressional support for his bill, however. In May 1935, when the Supreme Court ruled the NIRA unconstitutional, including Section 7a protecting union members' rights, FDR announced his support for a labor law that would survive constitutional scrutiny.

The National Labor Relations Act of July 1935 guaranteed collective-bargaining rights, permitted closed shops,* and outlawed such management practices as spying on unions and blacklisting labor "agitators." The law also created a new agency, the National Labor Relations Board (NLRB), to supervise shop elections and deal with labor-law violations. The Wagner Act, as it was called, stimulated a wave of unionization (see Chapter 26).

Of all the measures of the Second New Deal, one stands out for its long-range significance: the Social Security Act of 1935. Drafted by a committee chaired by Secretary of Labor Frances Perkins, this measure had a complex parentage, including the ideas of Progressive Era reformers and the example of social-welfare programs in England and Germany. It established a mixed federal-state system of old-age pensions for workers; survivors' benefits for the victims of industrial accidents; unemployment insurance; and aid for dependent mothers and children, the blind, and the crippled.

Taxes paid in part by employers and in part by wages withheld from workers' paychecks funded the pension and survivors' benefit features of the program. In the short run, this payroll-withholding provision withdrew money from circulation and contributed to a sharp recession in 1937. But it made sense politically, because workers would fight any effort to repeal a social-security plan to which they themselves had contributed. As President Roosevelt put it, "With those taxes in there, no damned politician can ever scrap my social security program."

The Social Security Act set benefit payments at an extremely low level; contained no provision for health insurance; and excluded millions of farmers, domestic workers, and self-employed workers. However, it established the principle of federal responsibility for social welfare and created the basic framework for a welfare system that would evolve and expand in the decades ahead.

The Second New Deal's more radical thrust found expression, also, in two business regulatory measures of 1935. The Banking Act strengthened the Federal Reserve Board's control over the nation's banking system

---

*In a closed shop, all employees must join the union as a condition of employment, so that the union bargaining agent can negotiate with management as the representative of the entire work force.

and money supply. The Public Utilities Holding Company Act regulated the interstate transmission of electricity and—targeting the sprawling public-utility empires that had proliferated in the 1920s—restricted gas and electric companies to one geographic region.

And finally, the Revenue Act of 1935 raised personal taxes at the higher income levels, increased corporate taxes, and boosted the levies on gifts and estates. Though this tax law had numerous loopholes and was not quite the "soak the rich" measure some believed, it did express the somewhat more class-conscious spirit of the Second New Deal.

By September 1935, when Congress finally adjourned, the Second New Deal was complete. A set of laws had been enacted promoting the interests of the jobless, the elderly, the rural poor, and the blue-collar workers; regulating major business enterprises more strictly; and somewhat increasing the taxes paid by the wealthy. Without fully embracing any of the radical panaceas espoused by Coughlin, Townsend, or Long, FDR had directed his program to the fears and inequities on which they had thrived. But despite the "antibusiness" label that his enemies pinned on him, FDR remained a firm supporter of the capitalist system. In his view the New Deal had saved capitalism by reforming its excesses and addressing some of its less desirable social consequences.

The Election of 1936: The New Deal at High Tide

With the Second New Deal in place and unemployment declining, FDR faced the 1936 electoral campaign with confidence. "There's one issue in this campaign," he told an aide; "it's myself, and people must be either for me or against me."

The Republicans' presidential candidate, Governor Alfred Landon of Kansas, belonged to his party's long dormant progressive wing. A fiscal conservative

who nevertheless believed that government must be responsive to social issues, Landon proved an earnest though inept campaigner. "Wherever I have gone in this country, I have found Americans," he revealed in one speech. Desperate Republican campaigners lambasted Roosevelt's alleged dictatorial ambitions and charged that soon all workers would be forced to wear metal dog tags engraved with their social-security numbers.

Campaigning more against the fading memory of Herbert Hoover than against the inoffensive Alf Landon, FDR struck back with his usual zest. Only the forces of "selfishness and greed" opposed him, he declared at an election-eve rally in New York City, adding: "Never before in history have these forces been so united against one candidate as they stand today. They are united in their hatred for me—and I welcome their hatred."

In the most crushing electoral victory since 1820, FDR carried every state but Maine and Vermont. Landon failed to carry even his home state of Kansas. Pennsylvania went Democratic for the first time since 1856. While Roosevelt was swamping Landon by a margin of 11 million popular votes, the Democrats increased their already top-heavy majorities in the Senate and the House of Representatives. The 1936 election underscored the message of 1932: decades of Republican dominance in national politics lay in ruin.

The Roosevelt landslide buried his minor-party opponents as well. Socialist Norman Thomas received under two hundred thousand votes. The Communist party's presidential candidate, Earl Browder, garnered only about eighty thousand votes despite the party's strenuous recruitment and organizing efforts. And Congressman William Lemke of North Dakota—the candidate of the coalition of Coughlinites, Townsendites, and Share Our Wealth enthusiasts that had appeared so formidable early in 1935—polled fewer than nine hundred thousand votes.

The Election of 1936

Candidates	Parties	Electoral Vote	Popular Vote	Percentage of Popular Vote
FRANKLIN D. ROOSEVELT	Democratic	523	27,752,869	60.8
Alfred M. Landon	Republican	8	16,674,665	36.5
William Lemke	Union		882,479	1.9

The New Democratic Coalition

As a minority party much of the time from 1860 to 1930, the Democrats had counted on three bases of support: the white South, parts of the West, and big-city Democratic organizations like Tammany Hall in New York City and the Kansas City machine of boss Tom Pendergast. FDR retained these centers of strength. The "solid South" went solidly for Roosevelt in 1936, and the urban Democratic machines delivered equally lopsided victory margins.

FDR rarely challenged state or local Democratic leaders who produced electoral pluralities, whether they supported the New Deal or not. In Virginia he withdrew support from a pro–New Deal governor who clashed with the state's conservative but powerful Democratic senators, Harry Byrd and Carter Glass. When the Democratic boss of Jersey City, New Jersey, Frank Hague, faced mail tampering charges, FDR told Jim Farley: "Forget prosecution. . . . Tell Frank to knock it off . . . , but keep this thing quiet because we need Hague's support if we want New Jersey."

FDR pushed far beyond this traditional base in forging a new Democratic majority, however. Five partially overlapping voter groups made up the cornerstone of this new majority: farmers, urban immigrants, unionized industrial workers, northern blacks, and women.

The midwestern farm belt, long a Republican bastion, found the New Deal's agricultural program congenial and switched to Roosevelt. In Iowa, for example, where Democratic candidates had been lucky to garner 20 percent of the vote in the 1920s, FDR won decisively in 1936.

Urban voters, many of them immigrants or the offspring of immigrants, followed the same pattern. Building on Al Smith's urban breakthrough in 1928, FDR carried the nation's twelve largest cities in 1936. Not only did the New Deal relief programs aid the urban masses, but Roosevelt wooed them persuasively at election time. When the presidential campaign entourage swept through cities like New York and Boston, cheering crowds lined the route for miles. Further solidifying his urban support, FDR appointed many representatives of the newer urban-immigrant groups, including unprecedented numbers of Catholics and Jews, to high New Deal positions.

Organized labor, led by prominent figures like Sidney Hillman of the Amalgamated Clothing Workers and John L. Lewis of the United Mine Workers, also joined the New Deal coalition. The unions pumped money into Roosevelt's reelection campaigns (although not nearly as much as big business gave to the Republicans), and the rank-and-file union members voted overwhelmingly for Roosevelt. Despite his early foot dragging on the Wagner bill, FDR's reputation as a "friend of labor" proved unassailable.

The administration's ties to organized labor had by 1936 helped give rise to a strong anti–New Deal mood in business circles. But FDR won some business support, particularly from officials of corporations that benefited from his programs, such as the electrical companies that provided equipment for the TVA and PWA hydroelectric projects, and exporters who profited from the later New Deal's aggressive free-trade policies.

Although most southern blacks remained disfranchised, the swelling black population of the northern cities played a growing role in electoral politics. As late as 1932, two-thirds of this northern black vote had gone to Hoover. One black editor, annoyed by black voters' Republican allegiance, advised his readers to "turn Lincoln's picture to the wall. That debt has been paid in full."

The advent of the New Deal produced a historic shift. Chicago's black voters signaled the new order in 1934 when they elected a Democrat in place of their popular Republican congressman, Oscar DePriest. In 1936 northern blacks voted in record numbers, and 76 percent of them cast their ballots for FDR. In Harlem, Roosevelt won a crushing 81 percent of the vote.

Solid reasons underlay this turnaround. Last hired and first fired, blacks experienced unemployment rates in the depression even higher than those for the work force as a whole. Thus jobless blacks in the urban North benefited heavily from New Deal relief programs. (The AAA's crop-reduction program uprooted many southern black sharecroppers, but as a disfranchised group, they could not express their frustration at the polls.)

Many blacks also perceived the New Deal as a force for racial justice. The record does not fully bear out this perception. The racially discriminatory clauses written into some NRA codes led black activists to dismiss the agency as "Negroes Ruined Again." Some New Deal agencies tolerated racial bias. The TVA, for example, barred blacks from Norris, its "model town" in Tennessee.

Harlem Voters, 1936
A rushing tide of northern black votes contributed mightily to Roosevelt's victory margin in his second presidential campaign.

Roosevelt kept aloof from an NAACP campaign to make lynching a federal crime. After declining in the 1920s, lynchings increased in the 1930s, as some Americans translated their economic woes into racial aggression. Although an anti-lynching bill passed the House of Representatives in 1935, southern racist senators—all Democrats—organized a filibuster against it. Concerned about his legislative program, and fearful of alienating southern white voters, FDR stood aside from the struggle. Concluded the NAACP bitterly, "[Blacks] ought to realize by now that the powers-that-be in the Roosevelt administration have nothing for them." Roosevelt remained similarly passive in 1938 when an anti-lynching bill again was narrowly defeated.

In other ways, however, FDR and the New Deal did work modestly to advance the black cause. Assuring an audience at Howard University, a black institution in Washington, D.C., that there would be "no . . . forgotten races" in his administration, Roosevelt supported those seeking to eradicate racism from New Deal agencies and appointed more than a hundred blacks to policy-level positions. The highest-ranking of these, Mary McLeod Bethune, served as director of minority affairs in the National Youth Administration.

The daughter of ex-slaves, Bethune was a Florida educator who headed the National Council of Negro Women from 1935 to 1949. An influential figure in New Deal Washington and a close friend of Eleanor Roosevelt's, Bethune led the so-called black cabinet that acted as a link between the Roosevelt administration and black organizations.

Roosevelt appointed William Hastie, a black NAACP lawyer, to a federal judgeship. In addition, the "Roosevelt Supreme Court" that took shape after 1936 made a series of important antidiscrimination rulings in cases involving voting rights, wage inequity, jury selection, and real-estate bias.

Thanks in large part to Eleanor Roosevelt, the New Deal also supported racial justice in symbolic ways. In 1938, for example, when a meeting in Birmingham, Alabama, of the interracial Southern Conference for Human Welfare was segregated in compliance with the city's Jim Crow statutes, Mrs. Roosevelt pointedly placed her chair in the area separating the white and black delegates. In 1939, when the Daughters of the American Revolution barred a performance by black contralto Marian Anderson in Washington's Constitution Hall, Mrs. Roosevelt resigned from the organization and New Deal officials arranged for an Easter Sunday concert by Anderson on the steps of the Lincoln Memorial. Seventy-five thousand turned out.

White racists, including many powerful Democrats, seethed at the New Deal's overtures to blacks. When a black minister rose to deliver the invocation at the 1936 Democratic convention in Philadelphia, Senator "Cotton Ed" Smith of South Carolina noisily stalked out. "This mongrel meeting ain't no place for a white man," he fumed. Boasting of his walkout to a white audience back home, Smith declared, "It seemed to me that old John Calhoun leaned down from his mansion in the sky and whispered, 'You did right, Ed.' "

In short, black support for Roosevelt reflected more than purely economic calculations. Although civil rights did not appear on the New Deal's legislative agenda, racial justice and black advancement did win support in Roosevelt's White House.

The Roosevelt administration worked strenuously to attract women voters. The head of the Democratic party's women's division, Molly Dewson, a former National Consumers' League official and a close friend of the Roosevelts, led this effort. In the 1936 campaign, Dewson mobilized fifteen thousand women who went door to door distributing more than 80 million colorful flyers describing New Deal programs. "[W]e did not make the old-fashioned plea that our nominee was charming," she later recalled; "instead we appealed to [women's] intelligence."

Dewson believed that women had a particular interest in issues relating to the home, an3d her campaign materials stressed how social security, the National Youth Administration, federal school-lunch programs, and other New Deal initiatives strengthened the family. Unlike earlier feminists, Dewson did not push a specifically feminist agenda or women's rights legislation. The New Deal programs of economic recovery and social welfare, she argued, offered the best promise of advancement for both men and women.

Dewson did, however, advocate the appointment of more women to federal policy-level positions, and she knew which strings to pull to place women in key New Deal posts. FDR appointed not only the first woman cabinet member (Frances Perkins) but also the first woman ambassador and more female federal judges than any of his predecessors. Through Dewson's efforts, the proportion of women postmasters increased significantly, and the 1936 Democratic platform committee reflected a fifty-fifty gender balance.

But despite the visibility of a few blacks and women in New Deal circles, and symbolic gestures of support, advancing the cause of these groups was not high on the New Deal agenda. Racism and sexism pervaded American society when FDR took office, and his administration, preoccupied with the economic crisis,

did relatively little to change that state of affairs. Those conditions would await a later reform generation.

The New Deal and the Environment

Environmental issues loomed large in the 1930s. Indeed, had Franklin Roosevelt not been preoccupied with the depression, he might outrank Theodore Roosevelt as the president who did most to spur national awareness of conservation.

Roosevelt's commitment to conservation went deep. His Hyde Park estate nestled in an unspoiled wooded region along the Hudson. As early as 1910, as chair of the Fish and Game Committee of the New York Senate, he had sought to regulate tree cutting that threatened wildlife. As president, Roosevelt approached conservation passionately. Under his prodding, the Civilian Conservation Corps thinned forests, built hiking trails and fire lookout towers, and planted hundreds of thousands of trees.

Soil conservation emerged as a New Deal priority. The terrible Great Plains dust storms of 1933–1935 resulted not only from drought but from decades of overgrazing and unwise farming practices. Less dramatic than the dust bowl but no less damaging was soil erosion in the South and elsewhere. By the 1930s, 9 million acres of farmland had been lost to erosion, with another 80 million acres in jeopardy.

Under director Hugh Bennett, the Soil Conservation Service of the Department of Agriculture set up demonstration projects and research stations across the nation. Farmers learned the value of contour plowing, terracing, crop rotation, and planting soil-strengthening grasses. The Taylor Grazing Act of 1934—enacted as dust clouds from the West darkened the skies over Washington, D.C.—restricted the grazing on public lands that had contributed to the problem.

We have already noted the TVA's important environmental component, in controlling the devastating floods that worsened soil erosion in the nation's heartland. In a larger sense, TVA's planners dreamed of harnessing the region's natural resources to serve its people—the goal of such earlier conservationists as Gifford Pinchot. Though the TVA fell short of this lofty vision, it achieved much and became a model for similar multipurpose watershed projects in the United States and abroad.

Despite the depression, New Deal planners found time to further the national-park movement. Olympic

The Arts and Conservation Under the New Deal
This striking poster illustrates the work of two New Deal agencies. Designed by Albert Bender, an artist employed by the WPA's Federal Arts Project, it promoted the Civilian Conservation Corps (CCC), which put city youth to work in the great outdoors. Above, a CCC volunteer plants Ponderosa pines in 1938 in a Montana national forest.

National Park in Washington, Shenandoah National Park in Virginia, and Kings Canyon National Park in California all date from the 1930s.

Wildlife preservation also gained ground. Jay Darling, an Iowa political cartoonist and avid duck hunter named by FDR to head the Biological Survey of the Department of Agriculture, vigorously promoted wildlife preservation, especially midwestern duck-breeding grounds. By 1940 the government had established some 160 new wildlife refuges, comprising more than 7.5 million acres. Roosevelt even closed a Utah artillery range that threatened a nesting site of the endangered trumpeter swan. (In 1939 the Biological Survey became part of a new agency, the U.S. Fish and Wildlife Service, in the Department of the Interior.)

The wilderness movement, earlier championed by John Muir and Aldo Leopold, won powerful new adherents, including Robert Marshall of the U.S. Forest Service. In 1935 Marshall, Leopold, and others formed the Wilderness Society to lobby for the cause. Wilderness, said the society, was not "a luxury or plaything" but "a human need." Under pressure from wilderness advocates, Congress set aside a large portion of Kings Canyon National Park as wilderness area.

The wilderness and wildlife movements brought together an unusual coalition of New Deal planners; men and women who cherished the wilderness on aesthetic grounds; and corporations, particularly firearms companies, financially interested in preserving wildlife for hunters. The National Wildlife Federation (1936), for example, which joined with the Roosevelt administration to sponsor a major wildlife conference in Washington in 1936, was largely funded by the gun industry.

From a contemporary perspective, the New Deal's environmental record presents gaps and blind spots.

Matters of grave concern today, such as atmospheric pollution, dwindling fossil fuels, pesticide hazards, and the pressures of an ever-growing population on limited global resources, received little attention. Most New Dealers viewed ever-rising levels of mass consumption as desirable. The vast hydroelectric projects of the Tennessee Valley Authority and the Public Works Administration, while they made sense at a time when much of rural America still lacked electric power, fed an ideology of boundless energy consumption that would come to seem heedless and wasteful in a later era when energy conservation and restraint became high priorities.

Nevertheless, viewed in the context of the 1930s, the New Deal's environmental record remains impressive. The Roosevelt administration focused attention on conserving nature to a degree that had not been true for twenty years and would not again be true for a generation.

THE NEW DEAL DRAWS TO A CLOSE

No sooner had Roosevelt won reelection by a mountainous majority in 1936 than he launched an ill-conceived attack on the Supreme Court that weakened him politically. In the wake of this divisive fight, an embattled FDR confronted a newly energized conservative opposition that helped bring the New Deal to an end. But the New Deal's legacy remained; in the span of a few years, the nation's political agenda had been rewritten.

FDR and the Supreme Court

Fresh from electoral triumph, Roosevelt early in 1937 went after the one branch of government that seemed immune to his New Deal vision: the Supreme Court. The Court in 1937 comprised nine elderly men; one had served as a justice since 1910, another since 1914. Four justices were archconservatives who abhorred the New Deal. Joined by others of more moderate views, these conservatives had invalidated the NRA, the AAA, and progressive state laws. They seemed determined, in the words of Harlan Fiske Stone, a liberal Court member, to "tie Uncle Sam up in a hard knot."

Roosevelt feared that key measures of the Second New Deal, including the Social Security Act and the Wagner Act, would meet a similar fate. Indeed, some lawyers were so sure that the Social Security Act would

be found unconstitutional that they advised their business clients to ignore it.

In February 1937 FDR unexpectedly proposed a sweeping court-reform bill that would have allowed the president to appoint an additional Supreme Court member for each justice over the age of seventy, up to a total of six. Roosevelt blandly insisted that this proposal reflected his concern for the heavy workload of aging justices. However, his political motivation escaped no one.

FDR evidently believed that his enormous personal popularity would translate into a ground swell of support for his Court plan, but this did not happen. Congress and the public greeted it with skepticism that soon turned to sharp disapproval. The size of the Supreme Court (unspecified in the Constitution) had been modified several times in the early years of the Republic, but the membership of nine, set by Congress in 1869, had taken on an almost sacrosanct quality. Conservatives blasted the "court-packing" scheme. Some feared a Rooseveltian grab for power in the wake of the president's electoral triumph; others resented the disingenuous way that FDR had presented the plan. Even some New Dealers abandoned the president on this issue.

For several months FDR pushed his reform bill, but when the Senate voted down the scheme in July, he quietly gave up the fight. For one of the rare times in his long presidency, Roosevelt had suffered an embarrassing defeat.

But in fact, the Supreme Court had yielded to Roosevelt's pressure. One of the most conservative justices retired in May 1937; others announced retirement plans. In April and May, the Court upheld several key New Deal measures, including the Wagner Act (*National Labor Relations Board* v. *Jones and Laughlin Steel Corporation*) as well as a state minimum-wage law. This outcome may have been Roosevelt's objective all along. From 1937 to 1939, to replace justices who retired or died, FDR appointed four new members to the Supreme Court—Hugo Black, Stanley F. Reed, Felix Frankfurter, and William O. Douglas—laying the groundwork for a liberal majority that would long outlive Roosevelt and his New Deal.

The Roosevelt Recession

Just as the Supreme Court fight ended, FDR confronted a far more serious crisis: after improving in 1936 and early 1937, the economy again plunged ominously in

August 1937. Industrial production slumped to 1934 levels. Steel output sank from 80 percent to 19 percent of capacity. Menacing unemployment statistics again dominated the headlines: after dropping to around 7 million in early 1937, the jobless toll soared to 11 million in early 1938—more than 20 percent of the work force.

What caused this short but severe "Roosevelt recession"? Federal policies that steeply reduced consumer income played a role. The new social-security program's payroll taxes withdrew some $2 billion from circulation. Furthermore, FDR, concerned about mounting deficits, had seized upon the signs of recovery to terminate the PWA and to cut the WPA and other New Deal relief programs sharply. Although these economies did reduce the federal deficit, they also contributed directly to the economic downturn of 1937–1938. So, too, did a drastic contraction of the money supply instigated by the Federal Reserve Board to forestall inflation.

Echoing Hoover, FDR assured his cabinet, "Everything will work out all right if we just sit tight and keep quiet." Meanwhile, however, some key New Dealers had been persuaded by the Keynesian call for deficit spending as the key to recovery. Aware that FDR would have to be persuaded by political rather than economic arguments, they recruited Harry Hopkins to warn the president of a political backlash if breadlines and soup kitchens returned. Only a renewal of massive relief spending, Hopkins insisted, offered hope. Convinced, FDR in April 1938 authorized heavy new spending. Once more the WPA money machine clanked into action, and work-relief checks rained down on the parched economy. The PWA received a new lease on life. By the end of 1938, conditions were improving. Unemployment declined, and industrial output increased.

The End of the New Deal

Preoccupied by the Supreme Court fight, the 1937–1938 recession, and a menacing world situation (see Chapter 26), FDR offered few reform initiatives in his second term. Congress, however, enacted several significant measures. The Bankhead-Jones Farm Tenancy Act of 1937, for example, created a new agency, the Farm Security Administration (FSA), replacing Rexford Tugwell's short-lived Resettlement Administration. FSA made low-interest loans enabling tenant farmers and sharecroppers to buy family-size farms of their own. Although the FSA did little to help the poorest tenants and sharecroppers (who were considered bad credit risks), it lent more than $1 billion by the end

Life in a Small Southern Town

In a fleeting moment captured on film by Dorothea Lange, this 1936 shot of a Clarksdale, Mississippi, plantation owner speaks volumes about racial and class realities in the rural South.

of 1941, assisting many thousands of tenant families to become farm owners.

The FSA also established a network of well-run camps offering clean, sanitary shelter and medical services to migrant farm workers, many of whom lived in wretched, unhealthful conditions as they pursued their low-paying seasonal occupation. In its most innovative program, the FSA commissioned talented photographers, among them Dorothea Lange of San Francisco, to preserve on film the lives of tenants, migrants, and uprooted dust bowl families. In carrying out this assignment, Lange and other FSA photographers created a haunting album of stark depression-era images.

Other measures of the later New Deal set important precedents for the future. The National Housing Act of 1937, sponsored by Senator Wagner, appropriated $500 million for urban slum clearance and public-housing projects. The Fair Labor Standards Act of 1938 banned child labor and established a national minimum wage of forty cents an hour and a maximum workweek of forty hours. Passed after intense political logrolling, this measure reflected not only humanitarianism but also some northern legislators' desire to undermine the competitive edge of the South, with its low wage scales. Although riddled with exceptions, this law did establish important regulatory precedents and improve conditions for some of the nation's hardest-working and lowest-paid workers.

The Agricultural Adjustment Act of 1938, adopted as surpluses and low prices continued to beset farmers, set up procedures for limiting production of basic agricultural commodities such as cotton, wheat, corn, and tobacco. It also created a mechanism by which the government, in years of big harvests and low prices, would make loans to farmers and store their surplus crops in government warehouses.[*] In years of poor harvests and higher prices, farmers could repay their loans and market their commodities at a profit. This measure helped stabilize farm prices and established the basic framework of federal agricultural policy for decades to come.

The later 1930s also brought a dramatic leap in union membership (see Chapter 26). This labor activism, stimulated in part by Section 7a of the NIRA and by the Wagner Act, demonstrated the New Deal's con-

tinuing role in transforming the social contours of American life.

Despite such achievements, the New Deal after 1935 clearly lost momentum. The slackened pace partly reflected the growing strength of an anti–New Deal congressional coalition of Republicans and conservative southern Democrats. Sensing FDR's vulnerability after the Supreme Court fight, this opposition became more outspoken. Virginia Democrat Carter Glass, for example, in a denunciation of the New Dealers, proclaimed, "Thomas Jefferson would not speak to these people."

In 1937, at a moment when nerves were already rubbed raw by the Court fight, an aroused Congress rejected FDR's proposal to reorganize the executive branch by regrouping existing agencies, bureaus, and commissions into twelve superdepartments under the president's direct authority. The plan made administrative sense, but FDR's congressional critics claimed that it would create a virtual White House dictatorship.

The conservative coalition also slashed relief appropriations, launched an investigation of the NLRB, cut corporate taxes in 1938, and in July 1939 spitefully killed the WPA's Federal Theatre Project. Suspecting FDR of using WPA staff members for campaign purposes, the conservatives in 1939 passed the Hatch Act, forbidding federal workers from participating in electoral campaigns.

The Fair Labor Standards Act of 1938 became law only after intense White House lobbying and watering down by conservatives. As recovery proceeded, noted Harry Hopkins, Congress and the public seemed to become "bored with the poor, the unemployed, the insecure."

Although FDR campaigned actively in the midterm election of 1938, the Republicans gained heavily in the House and Senate and won a net of thirteen governorships. Roosevelt also campaigned against several prominent anti–New Deal Democratic senators in 1938, but the major targets of his attempted purge, including senators Walter George of Georgia, "Cotton Ed" Smith of South Carolina, and Millard Tydings of Maryland, all won renomination and went on to victory in the general election.

Focusing mainly on ominous foreign developments in his January 1939 State of the Union message, FDR proposed no new domestic measures and spoke merely of the need to "preserve our reforms." The New Deal was over.

---

[*]These payments came directly from the federal treasury rather than from a processors' tax, a feature that had caused the Agricultural Adjustment Act of 1933 to be declared unconstitutional (see above).

CONCLUSION

The New Deal in its six-year life compiled a stunning record. To be sure, not all New Deal programs succeeded. Nor did the New Deal achieve full economic recovery. As late as 1939, unemployment still hovered at around 9.5 million, or more than 17 percent of the labor force. Only in 1943, in the midst of a war-induced economic boom, did the vast pool of the jobless finally evaporate.

Yet when all this is acknowledged, the New Deal still constitutes a watershed in American history. The Roosevelt administration began by assuming a government responsibility to promote economic prosperity and the well-being of all citizens. Such measures as social security, the Wagner Act, and the Fair Labor Standards Act defined the basic contours of the modern activist welfare state.

In the 1920s, as through much of post–Civil War U.S. history, the business class had dominated Washington while other groups were largely frozen out. Certainly the favored treatment of business did not suddenly end in 1933, as the Reconstruction Finance Corporation's massive loans to large corporations make clear. However, as the New Deal evolved, it increasingly acted as a broker for *all* organized interest groups—not just business, but also agriculture, labor, and other sectors. Although this still left the unorganized—southern sharecroppers and tenants, for example—with little influence, government gradually became more responsive to varied interests.

The New Deal stood for reforms of a new kind. The progressives, convinced of the righteousness of their cause, had set out to eradicate evil from American life, whether exploitative corporate power or gambling, drink, and prostitution. The New Dealers' aim by contrast, was not to purify the nation but to bring their expertise to bear on the practical problems of business stagnation, unemployment, and the maldistribution of economic resources. The New Deal *style* differed markedly from that of earlier reform eras. As historian William E. Leuchtenberg has written, "If the archetypical progressive was Jane Addams singing 'Onward Christian Soldiers,' the representative New Dealer was Harry Hopkins betting on the horses at Laurel Race Track."

The New Deal vastly increased the power and prestige of the presidency. Roosevelt so dominated the politics of this era, and peppered Congress with so many messages and proposals, that Americans began to expect their president to formulate "programs" and to shape the terms of public debate. This development decisively altered the balance of power between the White House and Congress.

Any evaluation of the New Deal must come to grips with Franklin D. Roosevelt. Neither a saint nor a superman, he could be maddeningly devious, as in the Supreme Court fight, and his administrative skills left much to be desired. But Roosevelt's strengths outweighed his liabilities. Unlike some of his challengers on the Left and ideologues of the Right like Hoover, he adopted an open, experimental approach in grappling with the nation's problems. He once compared himself to a football quarterback, deciding which play to call next after seeing how the last one worked out. In the desperate conditions of the early depression years, the nation urgently needed such tolerance for innovation.

Above all, Roosevelt's infectious optimism brought renewed confidence to a demoralized people. "We Americans of today . . . ," observed the president to an audience of young people in 1939, "are characters in the living book of democracy. But we are also its author. It falls upon us now to say whether the chapters that are to come will tell a story of retreat or a story of continued advance."

CHRONOLOGY

1929	Stock market crash; onset of depression.
1930	President Hoover's Emergency Committee for Employment.
1931	Farmers' Holiday Association.
1932	Reconstruction Finance Corporation. Glass–Steagall Act.
1932	Veterans' bonus march. Franklin D. Roosevelt elected president.
1933	Repeal of Eighteenth Amendment (end of Prohibition). Federal Deposit Insurance Corporation created. Emergency Banking Act.

1933	Civilian Conservation Corps (CCC).	**1935**	Public Utilities Holding Company Act.
	Federal Emergency Relief Act (FERA).		NAACP campaign for federal antilynching law.
	Tennessee Valley Authority (TVA).		Huey Long assassinated.
	Agricultural Adjustment Administration (AAA).		Revenue Act.
	National Recovery Administration (NRA).	**1936**	Supreme Court declares AAA unconstitutional.
	Public Works Administration (PWA).		Soil Conservation and Domestic Allotment Act.
	Civil Works Administration (CWA).		Roosevelt wins landslide reelection victory.
1934	Securities and Exchange Commission (SEC).	**1937**	Roosevelt's "court-packing" plan defeated.
	Civil Works Emergency Relief Act.		Hugo Black appointed to the Supreme Court.
	Democrats gain in midterm elections.		Farm Security Administration (FSA).
	Taylor Grazing Act.		National Housing Act.
1935	Supreme Court declares NRA unconstitutional.	**1937–1938**	The "Roosevelt recession."
	Emergency Relief Appropriation Act.	**1938**	Fair Labor Standards Act.
	Works Progress Administration (WPA).		Agricultural Adjustment Act of 1938.
	National Youth Administration.		Republicans gain heavily in midterm elections.
	Resettlement Administration.		Stanley Reed appointed to the Supreme Court.
	Rural Electrification Administration (REA).	**1939**	Hatch Act.
	National Labor Relations Act (Wagner Act).		Marian Anderson concert at Lincoln Memorial.
	Social Security Act.		Felix Frankfurter and William O. Douglas appointed to the Supreme Court.
	Banking Act.		

FOR FURTHER READING

Anthony J. Badger, *The New Deal: The Depression Years, 1933–1940* (1989). Good recent overview of the period and its politics.

Paul Conkin, *The New Deal,* 2d ed. (1975). A concise, balanced assessment.

Steve Fraser and Gary Gerstle, eds., *The Rise and Fall of the New Deal Order, 1930–1980* (1989). Incisive critical essays on the New Deal's long-term legacy.

John A. Garraty, *The Great Depression* (1986). Especially valuable on the global aspects of the crisis.

William E. Leuchtenberg, *Franklin D. Roosevelt and the New Deal* (1983). A comprehensive, readable overview, rich in illuminating detail.

Albert U. Romasco, *The Politics of Recovery: Roosevelt's New Deal* (1983). A study particularly useful for the New Deal's policies toward business.

Harvard Sitkoff, *A New Deal for Blacks* (1978). An exploration of the Roosevelt administration's policies toward black Americans.

Studs Terkel, *Hard Times* (1970). An oral history that poignantly conveys the depression's human toll.

Susan Ware, *Beyond Suffrage: Women and the New Deal* (1981). A study of the network of women who held high office in the New Deal.

ADDITIONAL BIBLIOGRAPHY

Onset of the Great Depression

Roger Daniels, *The Bonus March* (1971); Milton Friedman and Anna J. Schwartz, *Monetary History of the United States, 1867–1960* (1963), Chapter 7, "The Great Contraction"; John Kenneth Galbraith, *The Great Crash, 1929* (1961); Susan Estabrook Kennedy, *The Banking Crisis of 1933* (1973); Albert U. Romasco, *The Poverty of Abundance: Hoover, the Nation, the Depression* (1965); John Shover, *Cornbelt Rebellion: The Farmers' Holiday Association* (1965); Peter Temin, *Did Monetary Forces Cause the Great Depression?* (1976) and *Lessons from the Great Depression* (1989).

The Early New Deal

Richard P. Adelstein, "'The Nation as an Economic Unit': Keynes, Roosevelt, and the Managerial Idea," *Journal of American History* 78 (June 1991): 160–187; Bernard Bellush, *The Failure of NRA* (1975); Blanche Wiesen Cook, *Eleanor Roosevelt,* Vol. I (1992); Searle F. Charles, *Minister of Relief: Harry Hopkins and the Depression* (1963); Walter L. Creese, *TVA's Public Planning: The Vision, the Reality* (1990); Frank Friedel, *Franklin D. Roosevelt* (1990); Gerald H. Gamm, *The Making of New Deal Democrats: Voting Behavior and Realignment in Boston, 1920–1940* (1989); Otis L. Graham, Jr., *Toward a Planned Society: From Roosevelt to*

Nixon (1976); Nancy L. Grant, *TVA and Black Americans: Planning for the Status Quo* (1990); James N. Gregory, *American Exodus: The Dust Bowl Migration and Okie Culture in California* (1989); William Ivy Hair, *The Kingfish and His Realm: The Life and Times of Huey P. Long* (1991); Peter H. Irons, *The New Deal Lawyers* (1982); Mark Leff, *The Limits of Symbolic Reform: The New Deal and Taxation, 1933–1939* (1984); Richard H. Maidment, *The Judicial Response to the New Deal* (1991); Van L. Perkins, *Crisis in Agriculture: The AAA and the New Deal* (1969); Sean J. Savage, *Roosevelt: The Party Leader, 1932–1945* (1991); Geoffrey C. Ward, *A First-Class Temperament: The Emergence of Franklin Roosevelt* (1989); Donald Worster, *Dust Bowl* (1979).

The Later New Deal

Alan Brinkley, *Voices of Protest: Huey Long, Father Coughlin, and the Great Depression* (1982); David E. Conrad, *The Forgotten Farmers: The Story of the Sharecroppers and the New Deal* (1965); Jane DeHart-Mathews, *The Federal Theatre* (1967); Lyle Dorsett, *Franklin D. Roosevelt and the City Bosses* (1977); J.

Joseph Huthmacher, *Robert F. Wagner and the Rise of Urban Liberalism* (1968); Richard Lowitt, *The New Deal and the West* (1984); Roy Lubove, *The Struggle for Social Security* (1968); William F. MacDonald, *Federal Relief Administration and the Arts* (1969); Charles McKinley and Robert W. Frase, *Launching Social Security* (1970); Frank E. Smith, *The Politics of Conservation* (1966); Charles H. Trout, *Boston, the Great Depression, and the New Deal* (1977); Nancy J. Weiss, *Farewell to the Party of Lincoln: Black Politics in the Age of FDR* (1983).

The End of the New Deal

Dewey W. Grantham, *The Democratic South* (1963); James T. Patterson, *Congressional Conservatives and the New Deal* (1967); Milton Plesur, "The Republican Congressional Comeback of 1938," *Review of Politics* 24 (1962): 525–562; Richard Polenberg, *Reorganizing Roosevelt's Government* (1966); Charles M. Price and Joseph Boskin, "The Roosevelt Purge . . . ," *Journal of Politics* 28 (1966): 660–670.

From Arkansas
by Georges Schreiber, 1939

26

AMERICAN LIFE IN A DECADE OF CRISIS AT HOME AND ABROAD

It was January 11, 1937, and in Flint, Michigan, the temperature was sixteen above zero. For ten days some one hundred strikers had occupied Fisher Body plant No. 2, which made bodies for General Motors cars. A few miles away, other strikers were occupying the larger Fisher Body plant No. 1. Determined to force a showdown, GM executives cut off the heat to plant No. 2 and locked the main gate, preventing supporters from carrying food to the strikers inside. As evening fell, some 150 picketers and a crowd of onlookers milled about uneasily.

Around 8:00 P.M., after strikers had broken the lock on the main gate, thirty Flint policemen in riot gear rolled up in squad cars; some time later, they were joined by fifty more. When the police fired tear-gas canisters into the plant, the occupiers doused them with fire hoses.

Masterminding the strategy was Victor Reuther, a brother of Walter Reuther, president of the local United Auto Workers (UAW) union. Victor issued directions to the strikers through a loudspeaker powered by his car battery. One participant later recalled his voice as "an inexhaustible, furious flood pouring courage into the men."

As the police moved closer, the workers beat them back with a shower of empty bottles, nuts and bolts, and two-pound car-door hinges. When the picketers overturned a sheriff's car—with the overweight sheriff inside—the outraged police fired into their ranks, injuring fourteen.

As Victor Reuther's battery grew weaker, Genora Johnson, the young wife of a striker, took the loudspeaker and urged women in the crowd to join the picketers. Many did so, running a gauntlet of police who tore at their coats. As the ranks of the picketers grew, the police gunfire stopped. After a five-hour standoff, the police withdrew. Thanks in part to Victor Reuther's bullhorn and the quick thinking of Genora Johnson, the UAW's strike against GM went on to eventual victory.

To grasp the full meaning of the Great Depression, which touched so many millions of Americans, we must move from Wall Street, the halls of Congress, and New Deal agencies out into the world of auto plants, harvest fields, artists' studios, and ordinary people's homes. And we must turn our attention abroad as well, for in these economically cataclysmic years, powerful nations across the seas came under the control of brutal militaristic dictatorships that raised again the specter of war and added to the pervasive sense of crisis.

THE AMERICAN PEOPLE IN THE DEPRESSION DECADE

Like a raging natural catastrophe, the depression crashed over 1930s America, leaving economic, social, and emotional havoc in its wake. A bird's-eye view of its awesome human toll conveys some of the reality, but a full understanding of the depression's impact also demands attention to particular groups of Americans—defined by occupation, gender, race, or ethnic origin—to whom the crisis brought special hardships and, in some cases, unique opportunities.

For millions of industrial workers, the New Deal created a more favorable climate for unionization. But union growth still did not come easily. Workers often had to fight a hostile management for the right to organize. Some female and minority members of the labor force shared in the benefits that came with union membership, but for others, the depression worsened an already difficult situation. The 1930s witnessed a backlash against working women and feminist goals in general, and the circumstances of hard-pressed blacks and Hispanic-Americans grew even more desperate.

Native Americans, meanwhile, became the objects of well-meaning but in some ways misguided attention from New Dealers. And the depression profoundly affected the most basic social group of all, the family. Some families experienced conflict and disruption in these difficult years; others grew closer in the face of adversity.

The Plight of a People

In terms of human suffering, the depression took an enormous toll. For all the New Deal's efforts, unemployment in the 1930s never fell below about 14 percent, and during much of the decade, it was considerably higher. (A generation later, in the 1960s, the government would define 5 percent unemployment as the maximum tolerable level.) The percentages represent masses of jobless men and women; as late as 1939, the total stood at nearly 9 million. In rural America bankruptcies, foreclosures, and abandoned farms multiplied. A quarter of all farm families had to accept public or private assistance during the 1930s.

In some cities the jobless rate soared far beyond the national average. In Toledo in 1932, for example, it stood at an incredible 80 percent. And many workers were forced to take jobs below their level of training: college alumni pumped gas; business-school graduates sold furniture. A retired navy captain employed in a movie theater wore his usher's outfit with as much dignity as he had once worn his naval uniform.

Others eked out a few dollars by peddling products to neighbors as poor as themselves. "I'll never forget watching my mother trying to sell Two-in-One Shoe Polish door to door," one child of the depression later remarked.

Poor diet and people's inability to pay for medical and dental visits laid the groundwork for long-term problems. "You have to have money to be sick—or [you] did then," novelist John Dos Passos recalled; "any dentistry also was out of the question, with the result that my teeth went badly to pieces. Without dough you couldn't have a tooth filled." The savings of older Americans quickly evaporated when hard times hit. By the mid-thirties, 1 million Americans over sixty-five were on relief.

Psychologists counseled victims of "unemployment shock": jobless persons who walked the streets by day seeking work and then lay awake at night worrying. Small humiliations provided a constant reminder of failure. When shoe soles wore out, cardboard or folded newspapers had to serve. Shoe tacks pierced worn rubber heels, cutting the skin. "You pass a thousand shoe-shops where a tack might be bent down," one young man recalled; "but you can't pull off a shoe and ask to have *that* done—for nothing."

As for the young people of the 1930s, one observer compared it to a team of runners waiting impatiently for a starting gun that never sounded. High-school enrollment increased sharply, as many youths, who would otherwise have entered the job market simply stayed on in school.

For the chronically disadvantaged, the depression represented simply one more in a series of hardships. But the jobless rolls also included millions who had been earning good wages and had even achieved a measure of affluence before 1929. These newly impoverished individuals experienced intense psychological stress over their sudden decline in income and status. Some went to great lengths to maintain appearances, even when they had barely enough to eat. One carpet-cleaning firm made extra money by clandestinely renting out Oriental rugs, brought in for cleaning, to families that had been forced to sell their own carpets. Advertisements of the 1930s, promoting products ranging from mouthwashes and deodorants to encyclopedias and correspondence courses, exploited feelings of shame. Building on techniques already established, the ads played on people's fears of being found out, of having their failings and pretenses exposed. Ads in *Good Housekeeping* and similar women's magazines extolled low-cost meals and other budget-trimming strategies.

Decades later, survivors of the depression would recognize how deeply they had been marked by it. Habits of scrimping and saving acquired in the 1930s, for example, often survived into more affluent times. As Caroline Bird has written in *The Invisible Scar*, her aptly titled social history of the 1930s, the depression for many boiled down to "a dull misery in the bones."

Industrial Workers Unionize

The economic crisis energized and transformed organized labor. Between 1900 and 1930, the number of unskilled or semiskilled factory workers had more than doubled, soaring from 3.7 million to 7.7 million. Yet at the outset of the depression, these workers remained almost completely unorganized. For years managers of such major industries as steel, automobiles, and textiles had blocked all attempts to unionize their workers, seeing such efforts as a threat to their right to run their businesses as they saw fit. The prosperity and probusiness mood of the 1920s had further sapped the energies of the labor movement.

But in the 1930s hard times and a favorable government climate gave rise to a new labor militancy and a surge of unionization. When the National Labor Relations Act of 1935 guaranteed labor's right to organize and to engage in collective bargaining, tremors of activism shook the rather stodgy American Federation of Labor. More militant AFL leaders like John L. Lewis of the United Mine Workers (UMW) and Sidney Hillman of the Amalgamated Clothing Workers, chafing at the AFL's slowness in organizing factory workers, decided to act. In November 1935 Lewis and Hillman started the Committee for Industrial Organization (CIO) within the AFL. Drawing upon a war chest supplied by the UMW, young CIO activists preached unionization to workers in Pittsburgh's steel mills, Detroit's auto plants, Akron's rubber factories, and southern textile mills. Unlike the restrictive, craft-based AFL unions, these CIO unions welcomed all workers in a particular industry, regardless of race, gender, or degree of skill.

In 1936 a CIO-sponsored Steel Workers Organizing Committee (SWOC) headed by Lewis's lieutenant Philip Murray geared up for a major strike to win union recognition. SWOC's target was giant U.S. Steel, described by John L. Lewis as "the crouching lion in the pathway of labor." In fact, Lewis had already secretly worked out a settlement with the head of U.S. Steel, Myron C. Taylor, who had decided to stop fighting unionization in the face of labor militance and the prolabor climate in Washington. In March 1937 U.S. Steel recognized the steelworkers' union, granted a wage increase, and accepted a forty-hour workweek. Other big steel companies followed suit, and by the end of the year, four hundred thousand steelworkers had signed their union cards.

Meanwhile, organizers led by the fiery, redheaded young autoworker and labor activist Walter Reuther had mapped a campaign to unionize General Motors, where hostility to organized labor ran deep. In December 1936 thousands of workers at GM's two body plants in Flint stopped work and occupied the factories. This "sit-down strike" in two key plants paralyzed GM's production.

Keeping their action peaceful, the sit-down strikers carefully protected the equipment and the cars on the assembly lines. Recalled one striker, "If anybody got careless with company property—such as sitting on an automobile cushion without putting burlap over it—he was talked to."

Women played a key role in the Flint strike. Although women workers did not participate in the actual occupation of the plants (to avoid gossip that might discredit the strike), they picketed on the outside. In addition, strikers' wives, sisters, and daughters organized the Women's Auxiliary to support the strike. This auxiliary opened a kitchen to feed the striking workers, set up a speakers' bureau to present the union's version of the issues, paraded with their children through downtown Flint, and even produced a drama called *The Strike Goes On*.

The showdown with the police at Fisher Body plant No. 2 on January 11, 1937, led to the formation of the Women's Emergency Brigade, whose members remained on twenty-four-hour alert for picket duty wherever needed. Complete with red berets and armbands, the four-hundred-member Emergency Brigade played a key role during the rest of the strike. Though male leaders overall led the direction of the strike, female participants discovered the exhilaration of working with others on a common cause. As one woman wrote

**Striking Auto Workers
Hold Impromptu
Dance, March 1937**
*The campaign to organize
auto workers, centered in
Michigan, spread to other areas as well, reaching these
workers at a Chevrolet body
plant in St. Louis.*

in the UAW newspaper, "I
only wish I'd gotten mad
long ago . . . , but I didn't
have time for anything outside of my own small circle.
I'm living for the first time
with a definite goal."

At first, GM fought
unionization. Company of-
ficials called in the police to
harass the sit-down strik-
ers, sent spies to union meetings, and warned workers' families that strikers would be fired. GM also tried
to persuade the Roosevelt administration and the governor of Michigan to summon troops and expel the
strikers by force. Although Roosevelt disapproved of
the sit-down tactic, he refused to mobilize federal
troops against the participants.

On February 11, General Motors backed down
and signed a contract recognizing the United Automobile Workers (UAW). Bearded workers who had
vowed not to shave until victory was won streamed jubilantly out of the plants. Chrysler soon fell into line,
and by the end of 1937, the UAW boasted more than
four hundred thousand members. Unionization of the
electrical and rubber industries also moved forward
rapidly.

In 1938 the Committee for Industrial Organization
formally broke with the AFL to become the Congress of
Industrial Organizations, a 2-million-member association of six major industrial unions including the autoworkers, steelworkers, and electrical workers. In response to the CIO challenge, the AFL itself showed new
flexibility in adapting to the changed nature of the labor force. Overall, union membership in the United
States shot from under 3 million in 1933 to well over 8

million in 1941, with much of the increase taking place
after 1936.

These victories often came hard, as some big corporations battled unionization. Henry Ford, for example, hated unions, and his loyal lieutenant, a tough
brawler named Harry Bennett, organized a squad of
union-busting thugs—the "Service Department"—to
fight the UAW. In 1937, in a bloody encounter later
memorialized as the "Battle of the Overpass," Bennett's men viciously beat Walter Reuther and other
UAW officials outside Ford's River Rouge plant near
Detroit. Not until 1941 did Ford yield to the union's
pressure.

The Republic Steel Company, headed by a union
hater named Tom Girdler, dug in its heels as well. Even
after U.S. Steel and the other major steelmakers signed
with the CIO in March 1937, Republic and a group of
smaller companies known collectively as "Little Steel"
adamantly refused.

In May 1937 workers in twenty-seven Little Steel
plants, including Republic's factory in South Chicago,
walked off the job. Anticipating the strike, Girdler had
assembled an arsenal of riot guns and tear gas. On May
30, Memorial Day, a mass of strikers approached a

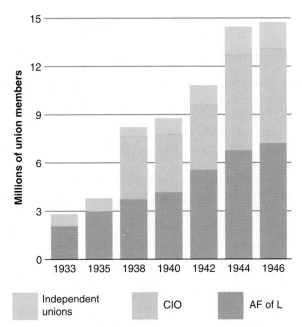

The Growth of Labor Union Membership, 1933–1946

Independent unions

CIO

AF of L

force of 264 police guarding the factory. When someone threw a large stick at the police, they responded with a hail of gunfire that left four strikers dead, six others dying, and more than eighty wounded. A coroner's jury ruled the killings "justifiable homicide," but an investigative committee headed by Senator Robert M. La Follette, Jr., found that what the newspapers were branding the Memorial Day Massacre had been "clearly avoidable by the police." In 1941 Tom Girdler and the rest of Little Steel threw in the towel and signed union agreements with the CIO.

Another holdout against unionization was the textile industry, with over six hundred thousand workers in 1930, mostly in the South and 40 percent female. The United Textile Workers (UTW), an AFL affiliate, had faltered badly in the 1920s owing to a series of failed strikes, a lack of strong AFL support, and a policy of admitting only skilled workers. In 1934 the CIO set up a Textile Workers Organizing Committee (TWOC) that in effect took over the feeble TWU. However, the mill owners viciously fought the TWOC's massive recruitment drive, and the 1930s ended with most textile workers still unorganized.

Virtually untouched by the unionizing wave of the 1930s was a large pool of workers at the lower end of the wage scale—domestics; agricultural laborers; department-store clerks; and restaurant and laundry workers, for example—who tended to be women,

blacks, or recent immigrants. Although union membership grew from 11 percent to 23 percent of the nonfarm labor force in the 1930s, more than three-quarters of nonfarm workers remained unorganized as the decade ended. Yet when the exceptions have been noted, the unionization of key sectors of America's industrial work force in the 1930s must rank as one of the decade's most memorable developments.

Why did powerful corporations finally cave in to unionization after years of resistance? Certainly workers' militance and the tactical skill of a new generation of labor leaders played a major role. So, too, did management's fear of violence and sabotage (even though nearly every instance of strike-related violence in the 1930s involved attacks on workers by management or by the police).

But above all, labor's successes after 1936 reflected a changed government climate. Where government officials had once helped break strikes by force and legal intimidation, Roosevelt and key state officials like the governor of Michigan refused to intervene on the side of management. (The willingness of the South Chicago police to act as a kind of private army for Tom Girdler represents a rare exception to this pattern.) The Fair Labor Standards Act of 1938 and the role of the National Labor Relations Board in assuring fair union votes (see Chapter 25) made clear that Washington would no longer line up with management in labor disputes. Once the heads of the nation's major industries realized this, most quickly came to terms with the union leaders.

Mixed Blessings for Women

Senator Robert Wagner called the working woman in the depression years "the first orphan in the storm." Indeed, for the 25 percent of American women gainfully employed in 1930, the depression brought difficult times. The female jobless rate eventually rose to more than 20 percent, and it hovered there through much of the decade. Women who were determined to continue working often did so only by taking lower-paying, lower-status jobs. A female factory worker who lost her job, for example, might take work as a sales clerk, waitress, or maid. Of the young women entering the job market for the first time, many had to settle for temporary or part-time work.

As a result of heavy competition from displaced male workers, the proportion of women even in such white-collar "women's professions" as librarianship, social work, and public-school teaching declined in the 1930s. Women who did manage to cling to their jobs confronted blatant wage discrimination. In 1939, for example, the average woman schoolteacher in the United States earned nearly 20 percent less than her male counterpart with comparable experience.

Married women workers encountered enormous resentment. They were accused of merely seeking to earn "pin money," whereas in fact most worked out of economic necessity. Nevertheless, people complained that married women had no right to hold jobs with so many men out of work. In a 1936 Gallup poll, 82 percent of Americans said that a wife should not work if her husband had a job. Many cities refused to employ married women as schoolteachers and even fired women teachers who got married.

Secretary of Labor Frances Perkins, though a woman and a long-time supporter of the Women's Trade Union League, lined up with the labor leaders and others critical of married women who worked. A number of the NRA codes gave the stamp of approval to lower pay for women workers. The minimum-wage clause of the Fair Labor Standards Act of 1938 helped thousands of women workers whose hourly wage fell below the new minimum but did not cover many categories of women workers, including the more than 2 million who worked for wages in private households.

The unionization drive of the later 1930s had a similarly mixed effect on women workers. Some women benefited from the campaign to organize the mass-production industries. For example, a big GM parts factory in Detroit employed more than six thousand women, and these female workers helped plan and carry out the "slowdown" strategy that led to a union contract in 1937.

But the most heavily female sectors of the labor force—the textile industry and the clerical, service, and sales occupations—were precisely the ones where the union movement made the least headway. The failed campaign to unionize the textile industry was paralleled by an equally unsuccessful drive to organize clerical workers. By the 1930s office work had been almost completely feminized, and most women office employees earned far less than male factory workers. When the CIO chartered an office workers' union in 1937, many secretaries responded with enthusiasm, and several strikes were carried out. (The secretaries who struck a brassiere company in 1940 showed wit as well as determination when they demanded, as their union newspaper reported, "an uplift in wages because their company keeps them flat-busted.") But

the CIO campaign to unionize clerical workers not only riled male bosses but also many male union leaders, and it made little progress.

Despite the celebrity of a few women like Eleanor Roosevelt, Frances Perkins, and Amelia Earhart (the first woman to fly solo across the Atlantic), the depression represented a low point for the women's movement. Battling the economic crisis, the nation had little patience for feminist issues or the struggle for gender equality.

Notwithstanding the many roadblocks, the proportion of women working for wages crept up slightly, from 25 percent in 1930 to 26 percent in 1940. Furthermore, the percentage of gainfully employed *married* women increased markedly, from 11.7 percent in 1930 to 15.6 percent a decade later. In short, neither depression nor widespread criticism could reverse the long-term movement of women into the workplace; indeed, the economic crisis may have accelerated that movement, as married women took jobs to supplement the family income. As one working wife explained: "One day in '32 [my husband] just went fishing . . . and he fished for the rest of the bad times. . . . So at twenty-eight, with two little girls, . . . I took a job as a salesclerk in the J. C. Penney, and worked through the Depression."

Blacks, Hispanic-Americans, and Native Americans Cope with Hard Times

The depression markedly slowed the urbanization of African-Americans. Some 400,000 southern blacks moved to northern cities in the 1930s—far fewer than in the 1920s or the 1940s. In 1940 about 77 percent of the nation's 12 million blacks still lived in the South.

Rural and urban blacks alike endured extreme hardships. Black tenant farmers and sharecroppers frequently faced eviction, in part because of the New Deal's agricultural policies. Among black industrial workers the jobless rate far exceeded the rate for whites, largely because of deep-seated racism and discriminatory union policies intensified by fierce job competition. A 1936 Chicago study reported "a prevailing sentiment that Negroes should not be hired as long as there are white men without work." Although black workers benefited from the CIO's nondiscriminatory policy, workplace racism remained an ugly fact of life.

Lynchings and miscarriages of justice continued for blacks as well, especially in the South. Twenty-four blacks died by lynching in 1933. In 1931 eight black youths were sentenced to death by an all-white jury in

Scottsboro, Alabama, on highly suspect charges of raping two white women in a freight car. After heavy publicity and an aggressive defense, the Supreme Court in 1935 ordered a new trial for the "Scottsboro Boys" because of the unconstitutional exclusion of blacks from the jury and the denial of legal counsel to the defendants. Five of the group were again convicted in 1936–1937, however, and served lengthy prison terms.

Blacks did not accept racism and discrimination passively. The National Association for the Advancement of Colored People battled in courts and legislatures against lynching, racial segregation, and the denial of voting rights. Urban blacks particularly resented white-owned businesses in black neighborhoods that employed only whites. A campaign against this situation organized by the St. Louis Urban League in the early 1930s spread to Chicago, Philadelphia, New York, and other cities. Under the banner "DON'T SHOP WHERE YOU CAN'T WORK," black protesters marched and boycotted businesses that hired only whites. In March 1935 hostility against white-owned businesses in Harlem, fueled by more generalized anger over racism and chronic unemployment, ignited a riot that caused an estimated $200 million in property damage and left three blacks dead.

The American Communist party called attention to racist conditions as part of a depression-era recruitment effort in the black community. The International Labor Defense Committee, a group linked to the Communist party, publicized the "Scottsboro Boys" case and supplied lawyers for the defense. But despite a few notable recruits (including, for a time, the young black writer Richard Wright), blacks did not join the Communist party at any higher rate than other Americans.

To some extent, the depression diverted attention from racial issues and the desperate economic straits of black Americans in the 1930s. But the rising tempo of activism gave warning that blatant racial discrimination and inequality could not be ignored forever.

The more than 2 million Hispanic-Americans, too, faced trying times in the 1930s. Some of these were citizens who had long lived in the Southwest, but most were recent arrivals from Mexico, Puerto Rico, Cuba, and elsewhere in Latin America and South America. All but a handful were manual laborers. Some worked in the steel or meatpacking industries, whereas others, especially those from Mexico, were migratory agricultural laborers. As the depression deepened, the Mexican-born farm workers of the Southwest, welcomed for years as a source of cheap labor, faced rising hostility. The influx into California and Arizona of thousands

Young Mexican Cotton Picker in the 1930s
Whether in agricultural labor or urban barrios, Mexican-Americans endured harsh conditions during the Great Depression.

Alabama Sharecropper
By paying landowners to take acreage out of production, New Deal agricultural policies often worsened the plight of sharecroppers.

of "Okies" fleeing the dust bowl worsened the job crisis for local farm workers. By 1937 more than half the cotton workers of Arizona were out-of-staters who had supplanted Mexican-American laborers.

With their traditional patterns of migratory work disrupted, Mexican-Americans poured into southwestern cities, swelling the population of the Hispanic urban neighborhoods, called barrios. In the cities, too, they met discrimination, sometimes in the form of such crude signs as "NO NIGGERS, MEXICANS, OR DOGS ALLOWED."

Finding themselves expendable, some half a million Mexicans returned to their native land in the 1930s. Many did so voluntarily; others, through court-ordered repatriation. In 1932, for example, more than two hundred thousand Mexican aliens were expelled by immigration officials and local authorities (see "A Place in Time").

Mexican-American agricultural workers who remained endured appalling labor conditions and near-starvation wages. A wave of protests and strikes (some led by Communist party organizers) swept California in these years. In 1933 strawberry pickers in El Monte, pea pickers in Hayward, grape pickers in Lodi and Fresno, and cotton workers in the San Joaquin Valley struck for higher wages. A labor organization called the Confederación de Uniones de Campesinos y Obreros Mexicanos (Confederation of Unions of Mexican Workers and Farm Laborers) emerged from the El Monte strike. Under the impetus of CUCOM, more strikes erupted in 1935–1936, from the celery fields and citrus groves of the Los Angeles region to the lettuce fields of the Salinas Valley.

Agribusiness organizations like the Associated Farmers of California and the California Fruit Growers Exchange (which marketed its citrus under the brand name Sunkist) fought the unions. With a war chest of $225,000, the Associated Farmers broke the Salinas Valley lettuce workers' strike. Sometimes the owners' anti-union resistance turned violent. In October 1933, bullets ripped into a cotton pickers' union hall in Pixley, California, killing two men and wounding several others.

Fighting heavy odds, the labor movement among Mexican-American farm workers achieved a few successes. Striking cotton pickers, for example, increased the rate for a hundred pounds of cotton to 75¢—less than the $1 they had demanded but 25 percent higher than the 60¢ that they had been receiving. These strikes awakened at least some Americans to the inhu-

A Navajo Family near Arizona's Grand Canyon
Under reformer John Collier the Bureau of Indian Affairs in the 1930s sought a renewal of tribal life and an end to the gradual transfer of tribal lands to whites.

mane working conditions and shamefully low wages of one of the nation's most exploited groups.

The 1930s also revived attention to the nation's 170,000 Native Americans, most of whom existed in a world of poverty, scant education, poor health care, and bleak prospects. The Dawes Act of 1887 (see Chapter 17) had dissolved the tribes as legal entities and sought to promote the assimilation of Indians into the American mainstream by allocating tribal lands to individual Indians and offering the rest for sale. By the early 1930s, whites held about two-thirds of the land that Native Americans had possessed in 1887, including much of the most valuable acreage.

Meanwhile, officials of the Bureau of Indian Affairs, among them several Quaker humanitarians appointed by Herbert Hoover, had become convinced that the Dawes Act approach should be reversed. John Collier, a reformer who had lived for a time among the Pueblo Indians of New Mexico, supported this view as well. To preserve what he saw as the spiritual beauty and harmony of traditional Indian life, Collier in 1923 had founded the American Indian Defense Association.

Appointed commissioner of Indian affairs in 1933, Collier cadged funds from the CCC, the PWA, and the WPA to construct schools, hospitals, and irrigation systems on reservations. Native American workers for whom these projects provided jobs would in later years look back to the 1930s as a time of prosperity.

But Collier also sought to implement his larger vision of a renewed tribal life. In 1934 he presented to Congress an omnibus bill halting the sale of tribal land, restoring the remaining unallocated lands to tribal control, creating new reservations, and expanding existing ones. Collier's bill also provided for tribal councils with broad powers of home rule and required Indian schools to focus on Native American history and to encourage traditional arts and handicrafts.

Collier's visionary bill sparked angry opposition in western states. Some Indian leaders criticized it as a plan to transform the reservations into a kind of living museum and to treat Native Americans as an exotic minority set apart from modern life. Collier's sweeping bill did, indeed, reflect the sentimental idealism of a benevolent outsider rather than the actual views of the nation's highly diverse Native American population.

The law that emerged, the Indian Reorganization Act of 1934, hailed by some as the Indians' New Deal, represented a compromise between Collier and his critics. The new law halted the sale of tribal lands and enabled tribes to regain title to their unallocated lands. But Congress scaled back Collier's vision of tribal self-government and dropped the original bill's rhetorical calls for the renewal of traditional tribal culture.

As the New Deal ran out of gas in the later 1930s, so, too, did Indian reform. Collier resigned in 1945, and by the late 1940s his dream of a revitalized tribal life had faded. The Indian tribes' special standing with the federal government had been largely terminated, and Native Americans were once more encouraged to abandon the reservation, give up traditional ways, and take their chances with everyone else in the treacherous currents of contemporary American life.

Family Life and Population Trends

For parents, life in the 1930s often meant an endless struggle to make ends meet and hold the family together. They patched clothes, stretched food resources to the limit, and when all else failed, turned to public assistance. A young college-educated wife described in a *Scribner's* magazine article the humiliation of welfare-office visits and the frustration of not being allowed to buy such "luxuries" as fresh fruit with her food coupons.

For the neediest, among them blacks, Hispanic-Americans, and the sharecropper families of the rural South, the depression imposed added misery on lives already blighted by poverty. In his novel *Native Son* (1940), Richard Wright drew upon personal experience to describe the desperate conditions of depression-era family life in the black slums of Chicago.

Ironically, however, life at the bottom had forced blacks, as well as others among the very poor, to develop survival skills lacked by more affluent families. Social workers marveled at the emotional resilience and the patterns of mutual aid that helped black families get through the depression despite appallingly high unemployment rates. In New York's Harlem, a charismatic black religious leader named Father Divine institutionalized this cooperative spirit by organizing soup kitchens that distributed three thousand free meals a day.

Hard times disrupted marital patterns. The marriage rate tumbled in the early thirties, as couples confronted harsh economic realities. When John Anderson graduated from the University of Wisconsin in 1931, for example, he anticipated finding a good job and marrying the classmate he had been dating. But months as a door-to-door salesman in Ohio shattered his hopes. "We corresponded for a couple of years," Anderson recalled, "but as time passed our letters were farther and farther apart. The . . . breaking up of young people who wanted to get married was the cause of much unhappiness and suffering during the Depression."

The birthrate also dropped sharply in the early depression years, as couples postponed a family or decided to have only one or two children. Such planning became easier with the spread of birth-control devices such as condoms and diaphragms. The Federal Council of Churches, an association of Protestant denominations, declared contraception by artificial means morally acceptable in 1931, and in 1936 a federal court lifted the ban against importing or mailing birth-control information. Soon even the Sears, Roebuck catalog advertised contraceptives.

A declining birthrate combined with restrictions on immigration to hold population growth in the 1930s to a scant 7 percent, in contrast to an average of 20 percent in the 1900–1930 decades. The economic crisis also temporarily slowed the growth of cities. The urban share of the population held steady in the 1930s at about 56 percent. In fact, many jobless young people returned to live with their parents on farms.

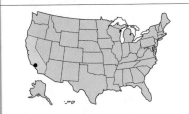

The Los Angeles Barrio in the 1930s

In the early 1930s, the depths of the depression, a party went on in the heart of Los Angeles's Mexican barrio. The members of the Nava family planned to return to their native Mexico the next day, and their friends bade them good-bye. Without work or money, the Navas had accepted an offer made to all barrio residents by the welfare authorities: free transportation back to Mexico . . . one-way only.

But as it happened, the Navas never boarded the train for Mexico. That night their eight-year-old son Julián suffered a ruptured appendix and was rushed to the hospital. He survived, but in the aftermath of the crisis, the family decided to remain in Los Angeles.

The Navas were only one of many thousands of Los Angeles families of Mexican origin whose lives were disrupted by the depression. Mexicans had first migrated to the city in large numbers in the early twentieth century, to take jobs laying track for the Pacific Electric Railroad. The 1910 census reported 8,917 Mexicans in Los Angeles, but knowledgeable local observers put the figure at closer to 20,000.

Mexicans continued to pour into the city even after the railroad-construction boom ended. They took the lowest-paying urban jobs and found seasonal employment as agricultural workers. By 1930 the Mexican population of Los Angeles County stood at 167,000—the largest concentration of Mexicans in the world outside Mexico City. Most lived in "Sonora Town," the sprawling barrio of East Los Angeles.

When the depression hit, unemployment soared in the barrio, and the newcomers, once welcomed as a source of cheap labor, were now denounced as a drain on scarce relief funds. In January 1931 the Los Angeles County welfare director telegraphed Washington, asking that a team of immigration officials be sent to the city to supervise the deportation of Mexicans. The presence of federal representatives, he said, would "have a tendency to scare many thousands of alien deportables out of this district, which is the result intended."

Arriving as requested, immigration officers conducted dragnet raids in the barrio and made highly publicized arrests of Mexican aliens lacking proper documentation. In one raid in February 1931, police surrounded a downtown park popular with the Mexicans and held some four hundred adults and children captive for over an hour.

Meanwhile, Los Angeles welfare officials announced their plan of free one-way transportation to Mexico. The cost of sending a full trainload of returnees (called *repatriados*) to Mexico, they calculated, would be more than offset by annual savings in relief payments. Though the plan was "voluntary," those who refused to become *repatriados* found their relief payments cut off and, later in the 1930s, their

Los Angeles Barrio, *c. 1930*
This photograph was taken in Chavez Ravine, now the site of Dodger Stadium.

applications for jobs in the WPA, PWA, or other New Deal work programs rejected. Under combined federal and local pressure, an estimated seventy thousand Mexicans left Los Angeles in 1931 alone.

Underlying this deportation drive was not only concern about welfare costs but prejudice. Some native-born Angelenos referred to the newcomers contemptuously as "greasers"; papers played up stories of barrio gang wars and crimes involving Mexicans. The Mexican community did not accept this injustice passively, however. The city's Spanish-language newspaper, *La Opinión,* and the barrio's business association denounced the intimidating tactics of immigration and welfare officials.

As the worst of the depression passed and the deportations and "voluntary" departures diminished, the rhythm of life in the barrio resumed, presenting a fascinating picture of a community suspended between two cultures. Radios covered with colorful *serapes* broadcast both the latest popular songs and the native folk melodies of Mexico, called *rancheros.* Supermarket food supplemented such traditional fare as enchiladas, tamales, and burritos. Though influenced by the cosmopolitan life around them, the Mexicans of Los Angeles spoke Spanish in the barrio, lit votive candles to the Virgin Mary in their churches, and perpetuated traditional remedies and folk beliefs dating back centuries.

The younger generation, gathering on the barrio's sidewalks in the warm southern California evenings, developed a distinctive street culture involving endless conversation, dramatic hairdos, a swaggering air of bravado, and flamboyant styles of dress: short skirts, black stockings, and perilously high heels for the girls; widely draped, deeply pleated "zoot suits" for the boys.

Whereas some of the barrio's young people turned to the vibrant street life, others concentrated on making their way in the larger society. Among the latter was Julián Nava. After high school and World War II naval service, Nava went on to Pomona College and Harvard University. In the 1960s, by then a history professor at San Fernando State College, he was elected to the Los Angeles School Board. In 1971 he became the board's president, with responsibility for a school system enrolling 650,000 students and operating on an annual budget of $750 million.

Julián Nava had come a long way since that depression-era night when an appendicitis attack had changed the course of his life. And Los Angeles had come a long way as well. The once-despised Mexican minority had become an integral part of the city's fabric, affecting in countless ways its culture, its music, its religion, its cuisine, and the very texture of its life.

Designer's Sketch for a "Zoot Suit"

Mexican Men Outside Los Angeles Relief Office

By contrast, another long-term demographic trend, the westward movement, continued unabated, with profound implications for the future. Not only dust-bowl farmers but many thousands of American families responded to hard times by seeking brighter opportunities in the West, especially in California. The proportion of the population living in the Pacific region rose dramatically in this decade, and Los Angeles advanced from tenth to fifth among U.S. cities, leapfrogging such older urban centers as Boston, Baltimore, Cleveland, and St. Louis.

The depression's searing psychological effects struck families as well as individuals. In households with a strong tradition of male authority, the husband's loss of a job and consequent erosion of self-esteem often had a devastating impact. One man expressed the depression's threat to his masculinity in extreme form when he told a social investigator, "I would rather turn on the gas and put an end to the whole family than let my wife support me." Desertions increased, and the divorce rate, after a dip in the early and mid-thirties, edged upward, reaching a then all-time high by 1940.

Children found vacation plans canceled, hoped-for birthday presents not materializing, and mealtimes tense with anxious discussions of family finances. Maria Tighe of Long Island, who was seven years old when the stock market crash threw her father out of a job, could recall years later sneaking to 6:00 A.M. mass so that her friends would not see her ugly dresses and shoes provided by the welfare bureau. Elena Columbo, who grew up in Maynard, Massachusetts, in the thirties, remembered her dread at being sent to collect the food distributed by municipal authorities: "I used to cry. I didn't want to go, but I had to; I was the oldest. Everyone would see you there. I was ashamed."

But the crisis also led people to rediscover traditional skills. They painted their own houses and repaired their own cars. Home baking and the canning of fruits and vegetables revived. Many would later look back on the depression as a time when adversity had strengthened social feelings and the spirit of mutual help. A man who grew up in small-town Wisconsin said of those years: "The feeling among people was beautiful. Supposing some guy was a hunter. He'd go out and get a hold of some ducks or some game, [and] they'd have their friends over and share it."

Sharing and making do could soften the depression's harsh impact on family life but not eliminate it entirely. The experience of a Cleveland railroad worker's family, recalled years afterward by one of the daughters, conveys that impact with particular vividness:

My father lost his job and we moved into a double-garage. The landlord didn't charge us rent for seven years. We had a coal stove, and we had to each take turns, the three of us kids, to warm our legs. It was awfully cold when you opened those garage doors. We would sleep with rugs and blankets over the top of us [and] dress under the sheets. . . . In the morning we'd get out and get some snow and put it on the stove and melt it and wash around our faces. . . . [We] put on two pairs of socks on each hand and two pairs of socks on our feet, and long underwear and . . . Goodwill shoes. Off we'd walk, three, four miles to school.

Recollections such as this make clear why the depression remained etched in the memory of those who lived through it.

THE AMERICAN CULTURAL SCENE IN THE THIRTIES

The depression's cultural impact matched its social effects. Whereas radio and the movies presented mostly escapist fare, writers, artists, and social thinkers offered a more personal and probing view of American life and ideology. In the demoralized days of the early thirties, this view tended to be highly critical. But the tone shifted as the decade proceeded, and by the end of the thirties, the nation's cultural creators were discovering new value in America's history and traditions, and unexpected strength in its people. This more positive tone reflected the renewal of hope stimulated by the New Deal as well as the rallying of American intellectuals against the rise of militaristic dictatorships abroad—dictatorships that made American democracy seem both more fragile and more meritorious than some intellectuals had once appeared to think.

The Golden Age of Radio

Radio provided an antidote to hard times. Each evening, millions of Americans gathered around their Silvertone or Atwater Kent radio consoles to listen to their favorite network news commentators, musical programs, and—above all—comedy shows. Radio humor reached its zenith in the 1930s, when the real

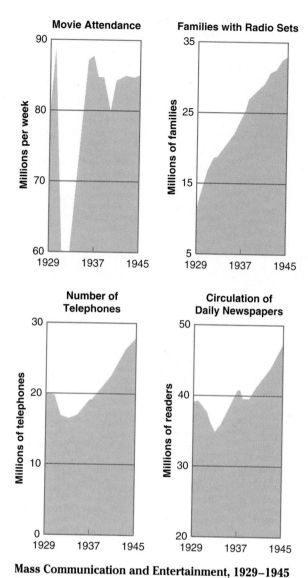

Mass Communication and Entertainment, 1929–1945
The media provided both information and diversion amid hard times. Boasted one movie-industry leader in 1934: "No medium has contributed more greatly than film to . . . the national morale during a period featured by revolution . . . in other countries."

SOURCES: American Telephone and Telegraph Company, Federal Communications Commission, *The Film Daily,* and the National Broadcasting Company.

soap companies usually sponsored them). So deeply did many listeners become involved with these daily dollops of idealized romance and melodramatic crises that the line between fantasy and reality often blurred. Listeners wrote earnest letters to the soap-opera characters advising them how to handle their problems. When a New York City woman who was sentenced to be executed for murder lamented to a newspaper reporter that now she would miss the forthcoming episodes of her favorite soap opera, *Abie's Irish Rose,* the program's producers considerately gave her a synopsis of the next six months' fictional developments.

Housewives made up the overwhelming majority of soap-opera listeners. Identifying with the ordeals and traumas of the radio heroines, these women gained at least temporary escape from the difficulties of their own housebound lives. As one female listener put it, "I can get through the day better when I hear they have sorrows, too."

The standardization of mass culture, under way in the 1920s, proceeded apace in the 1930s. As with television today, a successful radio show spawned a spate of imitations, producing a dead level of sameness across the radio band. Soap operas in particular took on a monotonous, assembly-line quality. Yet this formulaic and commercialized programming satisfied most listeners, perhaps because they had experienced little else.

The Silver Screen

The major movie studios tottered toward bankruptcy in 1931 and 1932, but in true Hollywood fashion, they staged a dramatic recovery in 1933 and for the rest of the decade enjoyed remarkable prosperity. Like radio, the movies proved extremely popular in depression America, when most people could still afford the quarter that it cost to see a show. The introduction of double features in 1931 and of drive-in theaters in 1933 also helped boost attendance. During some weeks in the 1930s, as many as 75 million Americans went to the movies. In 1939, 65 percent of the population attended at least once a week. The motion picture, declared one Hollywood executive, had become "as necessary as any other daily commodity."

What did these millions see? A few movies of the decade dealt realistically with such contemporary social issues as labor unrest in the coal industry (*Black Fury*) and the sharecroppers' plight (*Cabin in the Cotton*). Two brilliant documentaries made by Pare Lorentz for the Farm Security Administration, *The*

world was hardly laughable. Comedians like Jack Benny, Fred Allen, and the husband-and-wife team George Burns and Gracie Allen won fiercely loyal audiences.

So, too, did the fifteen-minute afternoon domestic dramas known as soap operas (thus called because

**Movies in a
Depression Decade**
*Hollywood prospered in
the 1930s as Americans
sought escape from eco-
nomic worries.* Animal
Crackers *(1930) starred
the Marx Brothers.*

River and *The Plow That
Broke the Plains*, evoked
the human and emotional
toll of a century of westward expansion.

Warner Brothers stu-
dio (which had close ties
with the Roosevelt admin-
istration) made a series of
movies in 1934–1936 that
portrayed the New Deal in
glowing terms. And in *Mr. Deeds Goes to Town* (1936)
and *Mr. Smith Goes to Washington* (1939), director
Frank Capra, the son of Italian immigrants, offered an
unabashedly patriotic and idealistic message: that
"the people" would always triumph over entrenched
interests.

The gangster movies of the early thirties, drawing
inspiration from real-life criminals like "Public Enemy
Number One" John Dillinger and the legendary Bonnie
Parker and Clyde Barrow, served up a different style of
film realism. Photographed in stark black and white
and taking advantage of the advent of sound, motion
pictures like *Little Caesar* (1930) and *The Public Enemy* (1931) offered gritty, memorable images of urban
America: looming skyscrapers; squealing tires in menacing, rain-swept streets; lonely bus depots and all-
night diners; the rat-tat-tat of machine guns as rival
gangs battled it out. When civic groups protested the
glorification of crime in the gangster movies, Hollywood simply reversed the formula to make the police
and "G-men" (FBI agents) the heroes, while retaining
the same level of violence.

The lead characters in the gangster movies, especially those played by Edward G. Robinson and James
Cagney, represented 1930s-style variants of the individ-

ualistic Horatio Alger heroes of an earlier day, fighting
their way upward against incredible odds. Their portrayals struck a responsive chord with depression-era
moviegoers, for whom the odds often seemed equally
discouraging and the social environment equally menacing in daily life.

But above all, the movies offered escape—the
chance to forget the depression for a couple of hours.
The Hollywood publicist who claimed that the movies
"literally laughed the big bad wolf of the depression
out of the public mind" obviously exaggerated, but cin-
ema's narcotic function in the thirties is clear. Lush
musicals such as *Gold Diggers of 1933* (with its theme
song "We're in the Money") offered dancing, catchy
tunes, and cheerful plots involving the triumph of
pluck over adversity. Walt Disney's *Snow White and
the Seven Dwarfs* (1937) brought new sophistication
to animation, and *The Wizard of Oz* (1939) became
an American classic, beloved by generations of children and adults alike.

The Marx Brothers, Groucho, Chico, and Harpo,
provided some of the depression decade's zanier
movie moments. In comedies like *Animal Crackers*,
Duck Soup, and *A Night at the Opera*, these vaudeville
troupers of Jewish-immigrant origins created an anar-

Patrons line the block to see the latest Marx Brothers' comedy, Horse Feathers, *plus a full program of cartoons and newsreels.*

chic world that satirized authority, fractured the English language, and demolished all known rules of logic. In *Animal Crackers,* for example, Groucho and Chico planned a search for a stolen painting:

GROUCHO: *Suppose nobody in the house took the painting?*

CHICO: *Go to the house next door.*

GROUCHO: *Suppose there isn't any house next door?*

CHICO: *Then we gotta build one.*

At a time when the established order and the traditional wisdom often seemed unreliable at best, the Marx Brothers' madcap mockery precisely matched the American mood.

Hollywood in the thirties dealt with blacks and women largely in stereotypes. Paul Robeson pursued a brief movie career in the thirties, re-creating his stage role in *The Emperor Jones,* for example, but for the most part, talented black performers found themselves confined to such roles as the weepy, scatterbrained maid played by Butterfly McQueen in *Gone with the Wind* or the indulgent house servant patronized by child star Shirley Temple and played by tap dancer Bill

Robinson in *The Little Colonel* (1935). Under the denigrating screen name Stepin Fetchit, black actor Lincoln Perry played a slapstick role as the slow-moving, slow-talking butt of humor in many movies of the 1930s and later.

Hollywood continued to preach that women could find fulfillment only in marriage and domesticity. A few films, however, at least chipped away at the traditional stereotype. In the 1936 comedy *Wedding Present,* for example, Joan Bennett played a strong-willed professional. A top female star of the thirties, Mae West, invented a new, far more assertive stereotype. Tough, brassy, openly sexual, and fiercely independent, West in *I'm No Angel, She Done Him Wrong,* and other hits mocked conventional morality, cut her suitors down to size with a razor-sharp wit, and made it clear that she would take orders from no one.

The Literature of the Early Thirties

Matching the nation's discouraged mood, the American fiction of the early depression era exuded disillusionment, cynicism, and despair. Sinclair Lewis and H. L. Mencken had satirized the middle class in the 1920s, but their successors in the early thirties challenged the fundamental premises of American ideology far more radically.

In his bleak *Studs Lonigan* trilogy (1932–1935), Chicago-born James T. Farrell offered a depressing picture of the hero's empty existence. The product of a chaotic working-class Irish-immigrant neighborhood much like the one that Farrell himself had known as a boy, young Lonigan lacks any framework of meaning for making sense of his fragmented urban world. He stumbles through life, trying to piece together a coherent world view from the bits of mass culture that drift his way. At the end of the third volume, nearing thirty, jobless, and alone, Lonigan dies of tuberculosis in an impersonal hospital.

In *U.S.A.*, (1930–1936), a highly innovative three-volume work, John Dos Passos drew a dark and intricate panorama of twentieth-century American history. Dos Passos's United States is a bloated, money-mad, exploitive society devoid of social or spiritual coherence. As one character says, "Everything you've wanted crumbles in your fingers as you grasp it."

Of all these downbeat writers of the early thirties, the bleakest was surely Nathanael West. Drawing on his experiences as a night clerk in a seedy Manhattan hotel, West in *Miss Lonelyhearts* (1933) created a surreal story of a newspaper advice columnist so oppressed by the stream of human misery endlessly flowing across his desk that he retreats into apathy and ultimately insanity. In West's *A Cool Million* (1934), a bitter parody of the Alger success novels, brave and virtuous young Lemuel Pitkin comes to New York to seek his fortune only to be cheated, betrayed, beaten, imprisoned, and eventually murdered.

Some radical novelists of the early thirties wrote even more explicitly of the decadence of capitalism, the exploitation of workers, and an approaching revolution. The American Communist party encouraged such writing through its John Reed* Clubs for writers and through contests to discover literary talent among the proletariat. Amid much dross, some interesting work emerged. Jack Conroy's *The Disinherited* (1933), a novel dealing with exploitation and labor violence in the Missouri coal fields, gained force from the fact that Conroy's father and brother had died in a mine disaster. In a trilogy of novels beginning with *Pity Is Not Enough* (1933), Iowa-born proletarian writer Josephine Herbst offered a cold-eyed view of the shifting fortunes and muddled ideological gropings of a family from the Gilded Age through the 1930s.

Radical playwrights brought the class struggle to the stage. Clifford Odets's *Waiting for Lefty* (1935) of-fered cartoonlike stereotypes of noble workers and evil bosses and ended with the audience chanting "Strike! Strike! Strike!" Marc Blitzstein's radical musical *The Cradle Will Rock* (1937) was originally funded by the WPA's Federal Theatre Project. When nervous WPA officials ordered the performance postponed shortly before the opening-night curtain, the cast and audience defiantly walked down the street to another theater, and the show went on.

The Later Thirties: The Popular Front and Cultural Nationalism

In 1933 and 1934, the U.S. Communist party vehemently attacked Franklin Roosevelt and the New Deal. But in 1935 Soviet dictator Joseph Stalin promulgated a new policy. Increasingly fearful of attack by Nazi Germany under its fascist* dictator Adolf Hitler, Stalin now called for a worldwide alliance, or "Popular Front," of all those who opposed Hitler and his Italian fascist counterpart, Benito Mussolini. Responding to the new Soviet line, American communist leaders began to praise Franklin Roosevelt, to describe communism as "twentieth century Americanism," and to recruit noncommunist writers and intellectuals to the antifascist cause.

For those who rallied to the Popular Front, and for many who did not, few events aroused more passionate emotions in these years than the Spanish Civil War of 1936–1939. In July 1936 Spanish army units led by fascist general Francisco Franco launched a revolt to overthrow Spain's legally elected left-wing government, a coalition of liberals, socialists, communists, and anarchists. Franco's cause won support from Spanish conservatives and monarchists, as well as from landowners, industrialists, and the Roman Catholic hierarchy. His fellow fascists Hitler and Mussolini provided extensive military aid.

The cause of the anti-Franco Spanish Loyalists (who continued to back the elected government in Madrid) won support from writers, artists, and intellectuals who sympathized with the Popular Front. Archibald MacLeish, speaking at a writers' congress in New York City in 1937, pleaded eloquently for the Loyalist cause. No longer could writers stand aloof from

---

*John Reed (1887–1920) was a pre–World War I American radical who wrote *Ten Days That Shook the World* (1919), an account of the Bolshevik Revolution.

---

*Fascism (derived from the *Fascisti*, a political organization founded in Italy in 1919): a form of government involving one-party dictatorship, state control of production, extreme nationalism, hostility to minority groups, and the forcible suppression of all opposition, including labor unions.

their society, he insisted. The time for political commitment had come:

> These battles [in Spain] are not symbols of other battles to be fought elsewhere at some other time. They are the actual war itself. And in that war, that Spanish war on Spanish earth, we writers who contend for freedom are—whether we wish or not—engaged.

Writer Ernest Hemingway, who visited Spain as a war correspondent in 1936–1937, firmly supported the Loyalists. His novel *For Whom the Bell Tolls* (1940) told of a young American, Robert Jordan, who joins a Loyalist guerrilla band in the Spanish mountains and eventually dies for the cause. *For Whom the Bell Tolls* contrasted sharply with Hemingway's novels of the 1920s, with their disillusionment and skepticism about abstract ideals. Reflecting on his new-found capacity for political engagement, Hemingway later wrote, "The Spanish Civil War offered something which you could believe in wholly and completely, and in which you felt an absolute brotherhood with the others who were engaged in it."

The Popular Front collapsed on August 24, 1939, when the Soviet Union and Nazi Germany signed a pact agreeing not to make war on each other and dividing Poland between them. Stalin's cynical exercise in power politics shocked idealistic Americans who had allied themselves with the Popular Front. Almost overnight, enthusiasm for cooperating with the communists under the banner of "antifascism" evaporated. Membership in the American Communist party dwindled as well. But although it was short-lived, the Popular Front influenced U.S. politics and culture in the later 1930s and alerted Americans to the rise of fascism in Europe.

The emergence of fascism and the renewal of political engagement inspired by the Popular Front, coupled with the achievements of the Roosevelt administration, stimulated a broad shift in the American cultural climate in the mid-1930s. The New Deal's programs for writers, artists, and musicians contributed to this cultural resurgence as well. The cynicism of the early depression years now gave way to a more hopeful view of America—its people, its history, and its political system. Abandoning the satirical tone characteristic of the 1920s, writers now voiced admiration for the solid virtues of ordinary Americans. Even Sinclair Lewis, in a work far removed from the tone of *Main Street* and *Babbitt*, soberly warned of the dangers facing American democracy in his 1935 novel *It Can't Happen Here.*

Walker Evans Photograph
Together with contemporaries such as Dorothea Lange and Ben Shahn, Evans created a memorable portfolio of depression-era images for the Farm Security Administration. (At the time there was only one kind of Coca-Cola; it came in glass bottles and cost five cents.)

This more affirmative cultural mood expressed itself in many ways. In John Steinbeck's *The Grapes of Wrath* (1939), for example, an uprooted dust-bowl family, the Joads, experience many setbacks as they make their way from Oklahoma to California along Route 66 in their battered old Hudson. But they never give up, and they always help others. As Ma Joad puts it, "They ain't gonna wipe us out. Why, we're the people—we go on."

Another eloquent expression of the new cultural spirit had its beginnings in 1936 when Tennessee-born journalist James Agee and photographer Walker Evans spent several weeks living with Alabama sharecropper families while researching an article on rural poverty for the business magazine *Fortune*. But

Fortune rejected the intensely personal work that Agee produced, and not until 1941 did it appear under the title *Let Us Now Praise Famous Men*. Enhanced by Walker Evans's haunting photographs, Agee's beautifully written masterpiece evoked not only the precariousness of life at the bottom but also the strength and decency of Americans living at that level.

The more positive assessment of American life found expression on the stage as well. Thornton Wilder's play *Our Town* (1938) warmly portrayed a turn-of-the-century New England town where the deceptively ordinary routines of everyday life become, in memory, infinitely precious. In the same vein, William Saroyan's *The Time of Your Life* (1939) affectionately celebrated the foibles and virtues of a colorful collection of American "types" whom the playwright assembled in a San Francisco waterfront bar.

American music, too, reflected this swell of cultural nationalism. In such compositions as *Billy the Kid* (1938), Aaron Copland drew upon a rich store of American legends and folk melodies. George Gershwin turned to a popular 1920s play about black life in Charleston for the inspiration of his 1935 opera *Porgy and Bess*.

And jazz, that quintessentially American music, surged in popularity in the later thirties, thanks to the big bands of Benny Goodman, Count Basie, Glenn Miller, and others who developed a smoother, more flowing style of jazz known as swing. Goodman, the product of a Chicago immigrant upbringing, got his start on the clarinet at Jane Addams's Hull House. The beginning of the swing era dates from August 1935, when the Goodman band played to an enthusiastic sellout audience at the Palomar Ballroom in Los Angeles, featuring arrangements by the great Fletcher Henderson. Another unforgettable moment in jazz history came in 1938, when the Goodman band performed at New York's Carnegie Hall, citadel of classical music. Jazz had arrived. One of Goodman's important contributions to jazz was to include black musicians like pianist Teddy Wilson and vibraphonist Lionel Hampton in live performances as well as in recording sessions of his predominantly white orchestra.

The Count Basie band got its start at Kansas City's Reno Club, where, as Basie later recalled, "We played from nine o'clock in the evening to five or six the next morning, including the floor shows, and the boys in the band got eighteen dollars a week and I got twenty one." In 1936 Basie moved to a club on New York's Fifty-second Street called the Famous Door, and word

soon spread. For the next decade, swing dominated popular music.

The cultural nationalism of the later 1930s also heightened interest in regional literature and art. Wallace Stegner wrote about Iowa in *Remembering Laughter* (1937), and Zora Neale Hurston's *Their Eyes Were Watching God* (1937) explored a black woman's search for fulfillment in her rural Florida community. In such works as *Absalom, Absalom!* (1936) and *The Hamlet* (1940), the best of the regional novelists, William Faulkner of Mississippi, continued the complex and often tragic saga of his mythic Yoknapatawpha County and its fictional population of McCaslins, Compsons, Sartorises, and the upstart Snopses.

Artists Thomas Hart Benton of Missouri (a descendant of the nineteenth-century Missouri senator of the same name), John Steuart Curry of Kansas, and Grant Wood of Iowa contributed a strongly regional note to painting. Wood's best ideas, he insisted, "came while milking a cow." But Curry, who taught art at the University of Wisconsin, reminded his students that regionalism could not substitute for talent. He noted, "Some of us . . . look forward to a great and alive art in the Middle West, but . . . [y]our greatness will not be found in Europe or in New York, or in the Middle West, or in Wisconsin, but within yourself."

Americans in these years also began to recognize the richness of their folk-art heritage. Galleries mounted shows of Amish quilts, New Hampshire weather vanes, itinerant portraiture from the colonial era, and lovingly crafted children's toys. A 1938 show at New York's Museum of Modern Art entitled "Masters of Popular Painting" introduced Horace Pippin, a black Philadelphia laborer whose right arm had been shattered by a sniper's bullet in World War I. In such painting as *John Brown Going to His Hanging*, Pippin revealed a genuine, if untutored, talent. A small private show at the Museum of Modern Art in 1939, "Contemporary Unknown American Painters," featured seventy-nine-year-old Anna "Grandma" Moses of Hoosick Falls, New York. One of many folk artists "discovered" in this era of cultural nationalism, Grandma Moses and her simple but charming paintings of scenes from her girlhood would become highly popular in the 1940s and 1950s.

The patriotic absorption in all things American as the thirties ended generated a fascination as well with the nation's past. Americans flocked to historical recreations such as Henry Ford's Greenfield Village near Detroit and Colonial Williamsburg in Virginia, the latter

Bringing in the Maple Sugar, *by Anna "Grandma" Moses, c. 1939*
A mood of patriotism and nostalgia for simpler times contributed to the popularity of folk artists in the later 1930s.

elaborately restored by the Rockefeller Foundation. Texans restored the Alamo in San Antonio, the "Cradle of Texas Liberty," between 1936 and 1939. Americans also made best sellers of historical novels like Margaret Mitchell's romantic epic of the Old South, *Gone with the Wind* (1936). Poet Carl Sandburg won a Pulitzer Prize in 1939 for a four-volume biography that elevated Abraham Lincoln to near-mythic status. And critic Van Wyck Brooks, who in the 1920s had dismissed the American literary tradition as pallid and second-rate, struck a new note with *The Flowering of New England* (1936), a warm appreciation of the writers who had flourished in New England a century earlier.

As the 1930s drew to a close, Americans viewed their society, their history, and their political system with a newly appreciative eye. The nation had survived the worst economic crisis in its history. The social fabric remained whole; revolution had not come. As other societies collapsed into totalitarian dictatorships, American democracy thrived. The intellectuals, writers, and creative artists of a decade earlier now led the way in celebrating America and its people.

The Age of Streamlining

This mood of restored confidence was neatly captured in a bold style of industrial design called streamlining, which transformed the appearance of thousands of products. Streamlining originated in the 1920s with a visionary group of industrial designers including Norman Bel Geddes of Michigan, Walter Teague of Indiana, and Raymond Loewy, a native of Paris who emigrated to New York City in 1919. Inspired by the romance of flight, Geddes, Teague, Loewy, and others preached the gospel of streamlining: the substitution of graceful, smoothly flowing curves and parabolas for gewgaws and clunky, square shapes in industrial designs. The goal, said Geddes, was to reduce products to their "utmost simplification in terms of function and form."

Behind these aesthetic principles lay a social vision: that harmonious and functional consumer products would inspire a more harmonious and functional society. As cultural historian Jeffrey Meikle puts it, "The streamlined society would be as smooth and uncomplicated as an egg—a mechanical egg with no possibility of unruly life breaking out from within."

Streamlining appealed to American business in the 1930s. It made many products more attractive to consumers—a vital consideration at a time of economic stagnation. When Sears, Roebuck hired Raymond Loewy to streamline its line of Coldspot refrigerators in the 1930s, sales surged upward. Streamlining also helped business rebuild a reputation severely tarnished by the stock market crash of 1929. At first, business had tried to bolster its image with advertisements and pronouncements in defense of the free-enterprise system. But by mid-decade corporations began to

Streamlining
*Industrial designers of the 1930s whetted consumer de-
mand and shaped the decade's aesthetics with their radically redesigned products. This experimental locomotive of
1934 was a gleaming triumph of streamlining.*

stress the wonderful material benefits that business
brought to society. The slogan of the Du Pont Corporation, "Better Things for Better Living Through Chemistry," summed up the new theme. Streamlined product designs fit in perfectly with this effort of corporate
America to enhance its image as the benevolent
shaper of the future.

Soon products ranging from automobiles to toast-
ers, alarm clocks, and cigarette lighters emerged in
sleek new forms. The prosaic pencil sharpener meta-
morphosed into a gleaming, aerodynamically sound
work of art poised for takeoff. Museum exhibits featured streamlined product designs. The sleekly mod-
ernistic service stations Geddes designed for Texaco,
he boasted, would make lubrication "a stimulating experience" rather than merely "a casual necessity of
motoring."

Under the theme "The World of Tomorrow," the
New York World's Fair of 1939 represented the high
point of both the streamlining vogue and corporate
America's public-relations counteroffensive in the late
1930s. The heart of the fair, and its heavily publicized
logo, was the Trylon and Perisphere: the former a
seven-hundred-foot needle symbolizing the event's
"lofty purpose" and the latter a smooth globe two hundred feet in diameter that seemed to float on a large circular pool of water. Inside the Perisphere, visitors
found "Democracity," a large revolving diorama portraying an orderly, harmonious city of the future.

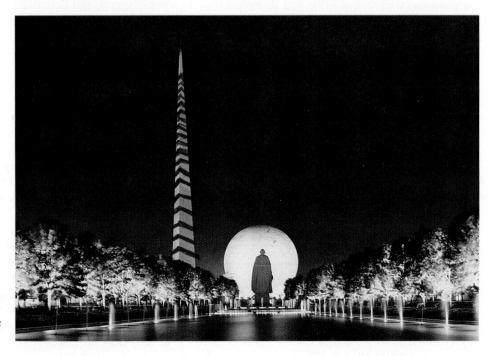

ork World's
39

e fair's
on of a
bright
world
im as

The hit of the fair was Futurama, the General Motors exhibit designed by Norman Bel Geddes. Visitors entered a darkened circular auditorium where, to the accompaniment of piped-in music and a resonant recorded narration, a vision of America in the distant year 1960 unfolded before their eyes—an America dominated by a complex highway network complete with multiple lanes, cloverleafs, and stacked interchanges. A brilliant public-relations investment, Futurama not only promoted GM vehicles but also built public support for the costly interstate highway system that the increasing number of cars and trucks would soon make essential—a system that would become a reality in the 1950s.

Along with such wonders as television and automatic dishwashers, the 1939 World's Fair did, indeed, offer its millions of visitors a first glimpse of "The World of Tomorrow."—a benign, smoothly functioning technological utopia made possible by the nation's corporations. As a business magazine editorialized, "If there are any doubters left, a visit to the New York World's Fair should convince them that American business has been the vehicle which carried the discoveries of science and the benefits of machine production to the doorstep of American consumers." In one seductive, streamlined package, this fair epitomized corporate capitalism's version of the cultural nationalism and the reviving optimism that characterized the American mood as the thirties ended.

Undercurrents of Apprehension

But a muted note of fear belied the surface confidence. For although the economic crisis had eased, dangers loomed on the international front. The anxiety triggered by the menacing world situation sometimes surfaced in unexpected ways. One such moment came on October 31, 1938, when the Columbia Broadcasting System aired a dramatic adaptation of H. G. Wells's science-fiction story *War of the Worlds* directed by twenty-three-year-old Orson Welles. In realistic detail, the broadcast reported the landing of a spaceship near Princeton, New Jersey, the emergence of aliens with lethal ray guns, and their deadly advance toward New York City. An actor mimicking the voice of President Roosevelt urged citizens to flee for their lives.

This vivid dramatization sparked a national panic. For a few hours, horrified listeners from coast to coast firmly believed that aliens had landed, that New York lay in ruins, and that the end of the world was at hand. Social scientists who later studied the event concluded that of a listening audience of some 6 million people, 20 percent had reacted in fear and even hysteria. Some jumped in their cars and sped off into the night. Others prayed. A few attempted suicide. Not for several hours did the nation's heartbeat return to normal.

Beneath the panic about "Martians" that autumn night lay a far more rational fear: of approaching war. For a decade, while Americans had been preoccupied by the depression, the international situation had steadily worsened. By October 1938 global conflict seemed a distinct possibility. For weeks radio news bulletins had warned of impending war between Germany and England. In fact, some listeners to *War of the Worlds*, blurring the broadcast's details, concluded that a foreign nation had launched a surprise attack against the United States. Recalled one young woman, "People saw how excited I was and tried to quiet me, but I kept saying over and over again to everybody I met: 'Don't you know New Jersey is destroyed by the Germans—it's on the radio.' "

The panic triggered by Orson Welles's Halloween prank quickly changed to sheepish embarrassment, but the fear aroused by more realistic dangers only escalated. By the time the New York World's Fair offered its shining vision of "The World of Tomorrow," the actual world of 1939 had become very scary indeed.

THE UNITED STATES IN A MENACING WORLD

Apart from efforts to improve relations with Latin America, the early Roosevelt administration remained largely aloof from the rest of the world. But while the United States grappled with the depression, Italy, Germany, and Japan pursued an increasingly aggressive and militaristic course. Americans reacted with ambivalence, torn between an impulse to resist fascism and an even stronger desire for peace. Vowing not to bumble into war once again as in 1917, millions in the United States supported neutrality and peace. Others, however, insisted that America should help embattled democracies abroad. All the while, the world edged steadily closer to the precipice.

FDR's Nationalism and the Good Neighbor Policy

Focusing on domestic recovery, President Roosevelt initially pursued a policy that put American economic interests above all other considerations. His secretary of state, Cordell Hull, believed passionately in free trade and international economic cooperation, but FDR showed little interest.

Indeed, in the summer of 1933, while Hull was representing the United States at a London economic conference called by the leading trading nations to stabilize the value of their currencies, Roosevelt dispatched his adviser Raymond Moley to England bearing a blunt message: the president had no interest in any currency-stabilization plans that might undercut his New Deal recovery program. Without the cooperation of the United States, the London conference broke up in angry frustration.

Roosevelt did, however, commit himself to an internationalist approach in Latin America, where bitterness over decades of "Yankee imperialism" ran high. In his 1932 inaugural address, FDR announced a "Good Neighbor" policy toward Latin America, rejecting the blustery "Big Stick" tactics of his cousin Theodore, who had moralistically insisted on Washington's right to use force to correct "wrongdoing" in Latin America. At a conference in Montevideo, Uruguay, in 1933, the United States endorsed a statement of principles that declared, "No state has the right to intervene in the internal or external affairs of another."

Under this policy Roosevelt withdrew the last U.S. troops from the Dominican Republic and Haiti and persuaded the National City Bank of New York to transfer its control of Haiti's central bank to the Haitian government. He also worked out a treaty with the president of Panama reducing the U.S. role in Panamanian affairs and increasing Panama's commercial rights in the Canal Zone. At the same time, however, the United States remained closely identified with the repressive regimes of Raphael Trujillo in the Dominican Republic and Anastasio Somoza in Nicaragua.

The major tests of the Good Neighbor policy came in Cuba and Mexico. In Cuba falling sugar exports related to U.S. quotas imposed by the protectionist Smoot-Hawley Tariff of 1930 triggered an economic crisis. This in turn led to a revolutionary uprising in 1933 that brought to power the leftist radical Grau San Martín. The United States opposed the San Martín government and refused to recognize it. But rather than sending in the marines as Theodore Roosevelt might have done, the administration pursued a less direct but no less effective course of action. Early in 1934, with the connivance of the U.S. ambassador to Cuba, Sumner Welles, and after a "visit" by U.S. warships, San Martín was overthrown by a conservative coalition dominated by strongman Fulgencio Batista. Moving quickly to help the Batista regime, Washington lowered the tariff on Cuban sugarcane. As Cuban exports to the United States rose, Batista consolidated his power. He would rule Cuba on and off until 1959, when he was in turn overthrown by Fidel Castro.

In Mexico a reform government headed by Lázaro Cárdenas came to power in 1936 and promptly nationalized several big oil companies owned by U.S. and British corporations. Washington once again refrained from military intervention. Conceding Mexico's right to nationalize the oil companies but insisting on fair compensation, the United States pressured Cárdenas economically by suspending U.S. purchases of Mexican silver. After lengthy negotiations, Mexico and the oil companies hammered out a compensation figure agreeable to both parties.

In summary, although the Roosevelt administration continued to intervene in Latin America in various indirect ways, the Good Neighbor policy eventually brought an end to the more heavy-handed forms of interference, including direct military occupation.

The Rise of Fascism in Europe and Asia

Meanwhile, powerful political forces raged across much of the world—forces that would ultimately pull the United States once more into war. As early as 1922, exploiting Italy's postwar economic problems and social unrest, Benito Mussolini and his Fascist party came to power in Rome and within a few years suppressed all dissident voices and imposed one-party rule.

A greater menace unfolded in Germany with the rise of the Austrian-born Adolf Hitler. An embittered war veteran with a gift for demagogic harangues, Hitler capitalized on the German people's resentment of the harsh Versailles treaty and the inability of Germany's democratic government to control runaway inflation in the 1920s. Briefly jailed in 1923 after an unsuccessful grab for power, Hitler took the opportunity to dictate his political manifesto, *Mein Kampf* (My Struggle), replete with fanatic nationalism and anti-Semitism.

Depression struck Germany in 1929 as it did the United States. As the economic situation deteriorated,

Hitler's National Socialist (Nazi) party won broad support. On January 30, 1933, five weeks before Franklin Roosevelt took the oath as president of the United States, Hitler became the chancellor of Germany. Roosevelt and Hitler thus rose to power almost simultaneously, and their lives would fatefully intertwine for the next twelve years until they died within two weeks of each other in April 1945—Roosevelt as the leader of a victorious nation; Hitler, a suicide in his Berlin bunker.

Crushing potential rivals within his own movement, Hitler quickly established a brutal dictatorship. Young Nazis in the major cities staged bonfires to burn the works of authors—many of them Jewish—espousing "un-German" ideas. A racist who believed that Germany must be purified of all "inferior" taint, Hitler instituted a program to drive out German Jews, whom he further blamed for Germany's defeat in World War I.

Pursuing a militaristic and expansionist foreign policy, Hitler in 1935 announced plans for a half-million-man army. A year later Nazi troops reoccupied the German-speaking Rhineland, a region that the Versailles treaty had ordered demilitarized. Early in 1938, to the cheers of Austria's Nazi sympathizers, Hitler proclaimed an *Anschluss* (union) between Austria and Germany, and German tanks rolled into Vienna, Austria's capital. Mussolini, intent on building for Italy an African empire to match those of other European powers, invaded helpless Ethiopia in 1935. These hostile moves caused much hand wringing but little firm action in London, Paris, Washington, and Geneva, the headquarters of the League of Nations.

After Austria, Hitler turned to the Sudetenland, a large region belonging to neighboring Czechoslovakia containing some 3 million ethnic Germans and 700,000 Czechs. Ethnically the Sudetenland was part of Germany, Hitler insisted, and he thundered his determination to take it, by force if necessary. At a conference in Munich on September 29–30, 1938—a conference that excluded the Czechs—British prime minister Neville Chamberlain and his French counterpart Edouard Daladier yielded to Hitler's demands and agreed to turn over the Sudetenland to Germany. A weakened Czechoslovakia, stripped of a third of its population and territory by this agreement, faced the massed tanks and troops of the German army. Interpreting this appeasement of the Germans as a diplomatic victory, Chamberlain proclaimed "peace in our time." Millions sighed in relief; war had been avoided.

Meanwhile, halfway around the world in Tokyo, fanatically nationalistic militarists had gained control of the Japanese government and inaugurated a fateful course of expansion. In 1931–1932 Japanese troops occupied the vast Chinese province of Manchuria, installed a puppet government, and gave the region a Japanese name: "Manchukuo." In July 1937 the Japanese launched a full-scale war against China itself.

The individual pieces of this frightening puzzle had begun to come together in 1936, when Germany, Italy, and Japan signed treaties of alliance and mutual defense. The alignment that would soon join forces in war had been forged.

The American Mood: No More War

The American people's response to these developments reflected a deep revulsion against war. Novelists of the 1920s like Ernest Hemingway had repudiated the exalted rhetoric of the World War I era, and by the mid-1930s, millions of Americans had concluded that the decision for war in April 1917 had been a ghastly mistake.

A series of books published in mid-decade reinforced this conclusion. The United States had been dragged into war, their authors argued, by banking and corporate interests desperate to protect their millions in loans and weapons sales to England and France. Walter Millis, a *New York Herald Tribune* reporter, documented this charge in *The Road to War: America, 1914–1917* (1935). More sensational exposés of the international arms traffic bore such titles as *Merchants of Death* and *One Hell of a Business*. Other works probed the propaganda techniques by which Americans had allegedly been brainwashed into supporting the war.

Public concern over the "merchants of death" issue led to the creation of a congressional investigating committee headed by Senator Gerald Nye, a North Dakota Republican, to look into the charges. In a series of hearings between 1934 and 1936, the Nye committee compiled evidence of the involvement of U.S. banks and corporations in financing World War I and supplying arms to the Allies. It also documented these groups' lobbying and public-relations activities in support of U.S. intervention. The Nye committee hearings gave new life to the old Progressive Era suspicions of "Wall Street" and "big business."

These books and investigations hit home. A Gallup poll in January 1937 revealed that an astonishing 70 percent of Americans believed that the United States should have stayed out of World War I. What

European Aggression Before World War II

Less than twenty years after the end of World War I, war again loomed in Europe as Hitler launched Germany on a course of military and territorial expansion.

had seemed at the time an act of high idealism now appeared to many a surrender to corporate interests.

All this produced a widespread determination to keep the United States out of future wars. Mistakenly equating Hitler with Kaiser Wilhelm, and the rise of fascism with the militaristic posturing of the pre-1914 European powers, many Americans concluded that the United States, protected by two oceans, could safely remain aloof from the upheavals convulsing other parts of the world. A *New York Times* book reviewer said that Walter Millis's *Road to War* should be made "required reading before anything more [is] said or written about American participation in another European war."

Reflecting this outlook, a peace movement spread across the nation's college and university campuses in 1935–1938. Led by the American Student Union and various peace groups, students organized antiwar rallies and marched with banners bearing such slogans

as "SCHOLARSHIPS, NOT BATTLESHIPS." In a "peace strike" in the spring of 1936, half a million students boycotted classes and attended antiwar events.

Novelists and playwrights expressed the national mood as well. As early as 1930, the German antiwar novel *All Quiet on the Western Front* became a best seller in the United States, and two popular antiwar dramas of 1936—Irwin Shaw's *Bury the Dead* and Robert E. Sherwood's *Idiot's Delight*—strengthened the mid-decade peace movement. In Shaw's play six American soldiers killed in battle refuse to be buried despite the generals' desperate try to get them underground and out of sight.

A series of Neutrality Acts passed in 1935–1937 gave legislative expression to the popular longing for peace. Trying to prevent a repetition of the circumstances that had dragged the United States into war in 1917, these measures outlawed arms sales or loans to

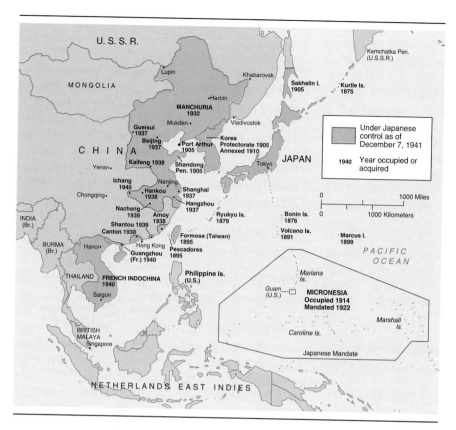

Japanese Expansion Before World War II
Dominated by militarists, Japan pursued an expansionist policy in Asia in the 1930s, extending its sphere of economic and political influence. In July 1937, having already occupied the Chinese province of Manchuria, Japan attacked China proper.

nations at war and forbade Americans from traveling on the ships of belligerent powers. In 1937, responding to the civil war in Spain, Congress extended the neutrality legislation to cover that conflict as well.

Critics of the Neutrality Acts (including President Roosevelt, who had signed them reluctantly) pointed out that these laws failed to distinguish between aggressors and victims, and might actually embolden a nation bent on conquest. When Japan invaded China in 1937, FDR refused to invoke the provisions of the Neutrality Act (on the technicality that neither side had formally declared war) in order to remain free to extend loans to the embattled Chinese.

The high point of the effort to promote peace legislatively came early in 1938, when Indiana congressman Louis Ludlow proposed a constitutional amendment requiring a national referendum on any U.S. declaration of war except in cases of actual attack. Only by a narrow margin, and after a direct appeal from President Roosevelt, did Congress reject the Ludlow Amendment.

Hesitant Response to the Fascist Challenge

The American people reacted only slowly to the fascist and militaristic regimes in Italy, Germany, and Japan. Indeed, many Americans initially admired Mussolini. He had imposed discipline, made the trains run on time, and in general energized Italy with a flurry of government activity.

Even Hitler found some American fans. As late as 1939, the German-American Bund, a pro-Nazi organization, filled New York's Madison Square Garden with twenty thousand sympathizers. A Hollywood writer and anti-Semite named William Dudley Pelley organized a U.S. fascist movement called the Silver Shirts. (The initials echoed Hitler's S.S., an elite corps of Nazi fanatics.) Pelley's recruits, he boasted, represented "the flower of our Christian manhood." Some Americans—including Joseph P. Kennedy, U.S. ambassador to Great Britain (and father of future president John F. Kennedy)—found Hitler praiseworthy, or at least tolerable, because of his rabid anticommunism.

Benito Mussolini in a Characteristic Pose

The Italian fascist initially won some American admirers for his dynamism and his stern insistence on order.

Even for Americans unsympathetic to fascism, Hitler and Mussolini seemed at first less figures of menace than of ridicule. Political cartoonists had a field day with Mussolini's jutting jaw. The goose-stepping marches of fascist troops appeared more like comic-opera routines than an omen of horrors. Through much of the thirties, the news magazine *Time* treated the posturing Italian and German dictators as more humorous than dangerous.

From the first, however, some Americans viewed fascism with grave apprehension. The Popular Front was one expression of this antifascist impulse. As early as 1933, Harvard literature professor Howard Mumford Jones, addressing the American Library Association, warned that the Nazi book burnings and suppression of free speech menaced freedom everywhere. And newspaper columnist Dorothy Thompson, expelled from Nazi Germany in 1934, emerged as one of America's most powerful voices denouncing Hitlerism.

Whatever their feelings about fascism, most Americans strongly opposed a U.S. military response. Since neither the League of Nations nor Europe itself seemed capable of effective resistance to Hitler and Mussolini, why should the United States become involved?

President Roosevelt, fascinated by global politics and recognizing the role of power in world affairs, advocated adequate defenses and as early as 1933 promoted naval expansion. At the same time, personalizing international affairs just as he did domestic issues, he communicated constantly with world leaders, including Hitler and Mussolini, seeking avenues of accommodation.

Bowing to antiwar sentiment at home, FDR never pushed ahead of U.S. public opinion. In 1935 he even assured a visiting Australian leader that America would never again enter a foreign war, regardless of the circumstances. In a 1937 speech, he suggested the possibility of a "quarantine" of aggressor nations to stop "the epidemic of world lawlessness," but when the public reacted coolly, he backed off.

Throughout much of the decade, FDR urged negotiations as the best way to deal with Hitler. Thus, he sent a telegram of praise to Prime Minister Chamberlain after the signing of the Munich Pact in September 1938 and assured a State Department official that he was "not a bit upset" over the agreement to hand the Sudetenland over to Germany. The American public shared the president's support for the Munich Pact. A *New York Times* editorial summed up the prevailing consensus: "Let no man say that too high a price has been paid for peace in Europe until he has searched his soul and found himself willing to risk in war the lives of those who are nearest and dearest to him."

Various factors figured in America's hesitant response to the disturbing events in Europe. Since the 1790s, the shapers of U.S. foreign policy had made it a priority to avoid entanglement in Old World quarrels and disputes. This deep-seated isolationist impulse was reinforced in the interwar years by the widespread conviction that American intervention in World War I had been a mistake, and by the fact that since 1929 the domestic economic crisis had driven events abroad far to the background of American public awareness.

The only real confrontation with Hitlerism had come in the arena of sports. At the 1936 Summer Olympics in Berlin, African-American track star Jesse Owens had confounded Nazi racial theories by winning four gold medals and breaking or tying three world records. And then in 1938, in a sports event heavy with symbolic overtones, black American boxer Joe Lewis knocked out German fighter Max Schmeling in the first round of their heavyweight championship fight in New York City. But while Americans might cheer these pinpricks at Hitler's pretensions, they shied away from any action that might threaten war.

Washington responded with more uneasiness to Japanese aggression against China than to the maneuverings of Hitler and Mussolini though with little more action. Thanks to a long involvement in China by U.S. business interests and Christian missionaries, Americans regarded that nation with special sympathy and interest. Whereas religious groups looked upon China as a vast mission field ripe for harvest, top government policy makers held firmly to the old dream of China's boundless economic potential as an outlet for American goods. As U.S. corporations increasingly felt "the need of foreign markets," Secretary of State Hull wrote

FDR in 1935, they would turn to Asia, "for in that region lie the great potential markets of the world." On such grounds the United States had long advocated its Open Door policy, guaranteeing all nations equal commercial access in China.

Japan's expansionist moves of the 1930s, first in Manchuria and then against all China, threatened this Open Door principle. On a practical and immediate level, as Commerce Department officials pointed out, the closing of China to U.S. trade meant the loss of $100 million in annual cotton sales. Concern that Japanese goods, particularly textiles, might someday flood the world market sharpened Washington's uneasiness over Tokyo's aggressive policies. As early as 1934, General William "Billy" Mitchell, an advocate of air power, declared, "Japan is our most dangerous enemy, and our planes should be designed to attack her." At the same time, in the privacy of the cabinet, Roosevelt was speculating about the possibility of eventual war with Japan.

Publicly, however, Washington (which was in no position militarily to carry out a threat of war) reacted to Japan's moves in China with largely symbolic gestures. Both the Hoover and Roosevelt administrations refused to recognize Japan's puppet regime in Manchuria, and after the Japanese invasion of 1937, Washington extended modest loans to China and urged Americans to boycott Japanese silk. (At a student convention in 1938, college women stripped off their silk hose and threw them in a bonfire, while the male students did the same with their silk neckties.) In October 1938 the U.S. ambassador to Japan, Joseph Grew, protested Japan's violation of the Open Door principle. The Japanese responded that the Open Door was "inapplicable" to the conditions of "today and tomorrow." Apart from these cautious steps, the United States did little as the Japanese tightened their grip on China.

1938–1939: The Gathering Storm

The interlude of reduced tension that followed the Munich Pact proved pathetically brief. Chamberlain's "peace in our time" lasted precisely 5½ months. At 6:00 A.M. on March 15, 1939, Nazi troops crashed across the border into Czechoslovakia. By evening they had lofted the Nazi swastika flag in Prague. Within another 5 months came the Nazi-Soviet Pact, giving Hitler a green light to invade Poland.

In the United States, the worsening European situation intensified the debate over America's role. Some continued almost desperately to urge the United States to keep free of the approaching conflict. Recalling how U.S. involvement in the 1914–1918 war had shattered the progressive reform movement and spawned a climate of repressiveness and reaction, the opponents of intervention warned that the same thing could happen again. The nation should concentrate on its own social problems, they urged. As historian Carl Becker put it, "The place to save democracy is at home."

But opinion was shifting rapidly. As pacifist and neutralist sentiment weakened, the voices urging greater activism grew insistent. Warning of the "malignant character and cancerous spread" of fascism, cultural critic Lewis Mumford in 1938 issued "A Call to Arms" in the *New Republic* magazine. Archibald MacLeish, having earlier championed the cause of Spain, now exhorted his fellow citizens to mobilize against Hitlerism itself. MacLeish (appointed to the prestigious position of Librarian of Congress in 1939) coupled his calls for intervention with attacks on the alienated writers and intellectuals of the 1920s who, he claimed, had undermined American patriotism and made it harder for the nation to rouse itself against fascism.

After the fall of Czechoslovakia and Albania early in 1939, a now thoroughly aroused President Roosevelt publicly called on Hitler and Mussolini to pledge not to invade thirty-one specific nations, which he listed. A jeering Hitler, reading FDR's message before the German Reichstag (legislative assembly) as his Nazi followers roared with laughter, proclaimed sarcastically: "Mr. President, I fully understand that the vastness of your nation and the immense wealth of your country allow you to feel responsible for . . . the whole world. . . . I, sir, am placed in a much more modest and smaller sphere. . . ." In Rome Mussolini mocked Roosevelt's physical disability, joking that the president's paralysis had apparently reached his brain.

Roosevelt did more than send messages. In October 1938 he asked Congress for a $300 million military appropriation; in November he instructed the Army Air Corps to plan for an annual production of twenty thousand planes; in January 1939, calling for actions against "aggressor nations . . . more effective than mere words," he submitted to Congress a $1.3 billion defense budget. Hitler and Mussolini, he said, were "madmen" who "respect force and force alone."

America and the Jewish Refugees

Once in power, Hitler and the Nazis had quickly translated their hatred of Jews into official policy. In 1935 a series of measures known as the Nuremberg Laws denied German Jews citizenship and many legal rights. In 1938 the anti-Semitic campaign grew more brutal, with the objective of forcing all Jews out of the country. The Nazis barred Jews from attending concerts or plays, expelled Jewish students from schools and universities, and required Jews to register all their property. Using as a pretext the assassination of a German official in Paris by a distraught Jewish youth, Hitler levied a "fine" of $400 million on the entire Jewish population of Germany.

This remorseless campaign reached a crescendo of violence on November 9–10, 1938: *Kristallnacht,* or "the Night of Broken Glass." In a systematic and well-coordinated rampage carried out all over Germany and Austria, Nazi thugs vandalized Jewish homes, burned synagogues (while firemen stood by to make sure that adjacent structures did not ignite), and wrecked and looted thousands of Jewish-owned businesses. Not even Jewish hospitals, old people's homes, or children's boarding schools escaped the terror.

No longer could anyone mistake Hitler's malignant intent. Indeed, this brutish repression foreshad-owed the policy of outright extermination that would emerge during World War II as Hitler's "final solution" to the "Jewish problem." Jews, who had been leaving Germany in great numbers since 1933, now streamed out by the tens of thousands, seeking whatever haven they could find. From 1933 through 1938, some sixty thousand came to the United States.

Among the victims of fascism who found refuge in America were several hundred distinguished scholars, musicians, writers, artists, and scientists. (Although mostly Jewish, this group also included some non-Jews who opposed Hitler, such as novelist Thomas Mann and theologian Paul Tillich.) The illustrious company of immigrants included pianist Rudolph Serkin, composer Béla Bartók, architect Walter Gropius, political theorist Hannah Arendt, future secretary of state Henry Kissinger, and scores more of equal distinction. It also comprised a brilliant cadre of physicists—Leo Szilard, James Franck, Edward Teller, Enrico Fermi—who would soon play a central role in building the atomic bomb.

Although driven to America involuntarily, these men and women quickly rebuilt their smashed careers. As the director of one university art center commented wryly: "Hitler is my best friend. He shakes the tree and I collect the apples." American cultural and intellectual life in the second half of the twentieth cen-

Refugees from Nazism: Pianist Rudolph Serkin, Political Theorist Hannah Arendt
Thousands of Jewish writers, musicians, scientists, and scholars sought refuge in America from the tide of anti-Semitism unleashed by Adolf Hitler in the 1930s. Non-Jewish opponents of fascism like the novelist Thomas Mann immigrated to the United States as well.

tury would have been immeasurably diminished had it not been for these talented refugees from the turmoil in Europe.

Although welcoming famous and distinguished Jewish refugees, however, the United States proved far more reluctant to grant sanctuary to the mass of Nazism's Jewish victims. The sixty thousand Jews admitted to the United States by the end of 1938 composed but a small ripple of the refugee tide, and Congress consistently rejected all efforts to open the doors more widely by liberalizing the immigration law with its discriminatory quotas (see Chapter 24).

President Roosevelt bears some responsibility for this failure. To be sure, Roosevelt deplored Hitler's persecution of the Jews. Shocked by *Kristallnacht,* he told a news conference that he "could scarcely believe such things could occur in a twentieth-century civilization." And through Roosevelt's efforts, a conference held at Evian, France, in 1938 set up an Inter-Governmental Committee on Refugees. But apart from this largely symbolic gesture, Roosevelt did little to translate his generalized sympathy for the Jews into political efforts to liberalize the immigration statute.

Roosevelt's attitude mirrored that of the American populace as a whole. Although practically all Americans, according to the public-opinion polls, professed to deplore the persecution of the Jews, only a minority favored admitting more refugees. When the pollsters asked early in 1938 if the immigration act should be amended to admit "a larger number of Jewish exiles from Germany," 75 percent responded no. The president of Sears, Roebuck wrote a senator, "I hope our natural sympathy with the plights of the Jews in Germany and Austria will not allow us to relax our immigration laws for one moment." When Senator Wagner and Congresswoman Edith Nourse Rogers of Massachusetts offered a joint bill in 1939 to admit twenty thousand German refugee children (most of whom would have been Jewish), 66 percent of Americans opposed even this humanitarian measure! Isolationist and anti-immigrant sentiments, perhaps intensified by latent anti-Semitism, severely limited America's response to the tragedy of European Jewry.

The consequences of such attitudes was graphically illustrated in June 1939 when the *St. Louis,* a vessel loaded with nine hundred Jewish refugees, after being denied a landing permit in Havana, asked permission to discharge its human cargo at Fort Lauderdale, Florida. Not only did immigration officials refuse this request, but according to the *New York Times,* a Coast Guard cutter stood by "to prevent possible attempts by refugees to jump off and swim ashore." With the lights of America within view, the *St. Louis* turned slowly eastward and sailed back across the Atlantic, carrying its stateless passengers to a fate that for many meant death at the hands of the Nazis.

CONCLUSION

The ordeal of the *St. Louis* provides an appropriately somber finale to a decade that began with Americans dazed by the stock market crash and ended with the nation teetering on the brink of war. Between those bleak events, to be sure, the thirties brought bright moments of political creativity, social advance, and cultural achievement. American society reeled under the impact of the depression but also displayed sturdy resilience. While hard times stimulated unionizing activity from the factories of the East to the agricultural fields of the West, corporate America demonstrated its capacity for renewal with bold design innovations in consumer goods and vigorous public-relations campaigns. The thirties was hardly a high point for black America, but the NAACP and other organizations continued the struggle against lynching and discrimination, laying the groundwork for later advances. And while radio and the movies provided standardized amusement for the masses, writers, photographers, and painters not only conveyed the decade's sad realities but also rediscovered the vitality and richness of America's regional cultures. All the while, menacing events clouded the horizon. By 1939 the world looked dark; it would soon look darker still.

CHRONOLOGY

1930   *Little Caesar,* gangster movie starring Edward G. Robinson.

Animal Crackers, classic Marx Brothers comedy.

1930–1936   John Dos Passos, *U.S.A.* trilogy.

1931–1932   Japan invades Manchuria and creates puppet government.

1932–1935   James T. Farrell, *Studs Lonigan* trilogy.

1933   Nathanael West, *Miss Lonelyhearts.*

Jack Conroy, *The Disinherited.*

She Done Him Wrong and *I'm No Angel,* Mae West movie hits.

Roosevelt's economic nationalism undermines London Economic Conference.

United States plays role in rise of Cuban strongman Fulgencio Batista.

Adolf Hitler becomes chancellor of Germany and assumes dictatorial powers.

1934   Indian Reorganization Act.

Nathanael West, *A Cool Million.*

1934–1936   Nye committee investigations.

Strikes by Mexican-American agricultural workers in the West.

1935   Supreme Court reverses conviction of the "Scottsboro Boys."

Harlem ghetto riot.

Clifford Odets, *Waiting for Lefty.*

Walter Millis, *The Road to War: America, 1914–1917.*

Sinclair Lewis, *It Can't Happen Here.*

1935–1937   Neutrality Acts.

1935–1938   Peace movement sweeps U.S. campuses.

1935–1939   Era of the Popular Front.

1936   William Faulkner, *Absalom, Absalom!*

Mr. Deeds Goes to Town, Frank Capra movie.

1936–1937   Autoworkers' sit-down strike against General Motors (December 1936–February 1937).

1936–1939   Spanish Civil War.

1937   U.S. Steel, General Motors, and Chrysler sign union contracts.

Ten strikers shot dead in "Memorial Day Massacre" at Republic Steel Company in South Chicago.

Japan invades China.

1938   Formation of Congress of Industrial Organizations (CIO).

Thornton Wilder, *Our Town.*

Carnegie Hall concert by Benny Goodman.

War of the Worlds broadcast on CBS radio.

Nazis occupy Austria.

Munich Pact gives Sudetenland to Hitler.

Kristallnacht, night of Nazi terror against German and Austrian Jews.

United States protests Japanese violation of Open Door principle in China.

1939   John Steinbeck, *The Grapes of Wrath.*

New York World's Fair.

Nazis invade Czechoslovakia.

Nazi-Soviet Pact.

FDR submits $1.3 billion military budget.

St. Louis, carrying Jewish refugees from Naziism, refused landing permission in Florida.

1940   Richard Wright, *Native Son.*

William Faulkner, *The Hamlet.*

Ernest Hemingway, *For Whom the Bell Tolls.*

The Grapes of Wrath, movie directed by John Ford.

1941   James Agee and Walker Evans, *Let Us Now Praise Famous Men.*

FOR FURTHER READING

Caroline Bird, *The Invisible Scar* (1966). Moving look at the depression's human and psychological toll.

Lizabeth Cohen, *Making a New Deal: Industrial Workers in Chicago, 1919–1939* (1990). A well-researched interpretive study of working-class culture and the union movement.

Robert Dallek, *Franklin D. Roosevelt and American Foreign Policy, 1932–1945* (1979). A fine study stressing FDR's responsiveness to domestic political currents.

Anthony Heilbut, *Exiled in Paradise: German Refugee Artists and Intellectuals in America from the 1930s to the Present* (1983). Good account of a refugee movement that profoundly influenced American culture.

Jacqueline Jones, *The Dispossessed: America's Underclass from the Civil War to the Present* (1992). A broad-ranging work placing the plight of the Depression-era poor in a larger historical context.

Jeffrey Meikle, *Twentieth Century Limited: Industrial Design in America, 1925–1939* (1979). Fascinating study of the streamlining movement, with a good chapter on the New York World's Fair.

Arnold A. Offner, *American Appeasement: United States Foreign Policy and Germany, 1933–1938* (1969). A comprehensive and well-written study.

Susan Ware, *Holding Their Own: American Women in the 1930s* (1982). A good overview incorporating recent scholarly research.

ADDITIONAL BIBLIOGRAPHY

American Society in the 1930s

Robert F. Berkhofer, Jr., *The White Man's Indian: Images of the American Indian from Columbus to the Present* (1978); John A. Clausen, *American Lives: Looking Back at the Children of the Great Depression* (1993); Sidney Fine, *Sitdown: The General Motors Strike of 1936–1937* (1969); Mario T. García, *Mexican Americans: Leadership, Ideology and Identity, 1930–1960* (1989); Cheryl Lynn Greenberg, *"Or Does It Explode?": Black Harlem in the Great Depression* (1991); Abraham Hoffman, *Unwanted Mexican-Americans in the Great Depression* (1974); Robert S. McElvaine, ed., *Down and Out in the Great Depression* (1983); Michael A. Malone and Richard W. Etulain, *The American West: A Twentieth Century History* (1989); Ruth M. Milkman, "Women's Work and the Economic Crisis: Some Lessons from the Great Depression," in Nancy Cott and Elizabeth Pleck, eds., *A Heritage of Her Own* (1979), pp. 507–541; Richard A. Reiman, *The New Deal and American Youth* (1992); Lois Scharf, *To Work and to Wed: Female Employment, Feminism, and the Great Depression* (1980); Lois Scharf and Joan M. Jensen, eds., *Decade of Discontent: The Woman's Movement, 1920–1940* (1983); Catherine McNichol Stock, *Main Street in Crisis: The Great Depression and the Old Middle Class on the Northern Plains* (1992); Winifred D. Wandersee, *Women's Work and Family Values, 1920–1940* (1981); Susan Ware, *Still Missing: Amelia Earhart and the Search for Modern Feminism* (1993); Jill Watts, *God, Harlem U.S.A.: The Father Divine Story* (1992); Nancy Woloch, *Women and the American Experience,* 2d ed. (1994), Chapters 17–18.

Cultural Trends in the Depression Decade

Matthew Baigell, *The American Scene: Painting in the 1930s* (1974); Andrew Bergman, *We're in the Money: Depression America and Its Films* (1971); Hadley Cantril, *Invasion from Mars: A Study in the Psychology of Panic* (1940); Malcolm Goldstein, *The Political State: American Drama and Theatre of the Great Depression* (1974); Nancy Helber and Julia Williams, *The Regionalists* (1967); Henry Jenkins, *Who Made Pistachio Nuts? Early Sound Comedies and the Vaudeville Aesthetic* (1992); Harvey Klehr, *The Heyday of American Communism: The Depression Decade* (1984); Marlene Park and Gerald Markowitz, *Democratic Vistas: Post Offices and Public Art in the New Deal* (1984); Richard H. Pells, *Radical Visions and American Dreams: Culture and Social Thought in the Depression Years* (1973); William Stott, *Documentary Expression and Thirties America* (1973); Martin Williams, *Jazz in Its Own Time* (1989).

U.S. Foreign Policy and the Fascist Challenge

Robert Cohen, *When the Old Left Was Young: America's First Mass Student Movement, 1929–1941* (1993); Wayne S. Cole, *Roosevelt and the Isolationists, 1932–1945* (1983); Charles DeBenedetti, *The Peace Reform in American History* (1980); Robert A. Divine, *The Illusion of Neutrality* (1962) and *The Reluctant Belligerent* (1979); Robert H. Ferrell, *American Diplomacy in the Great Depression* (1957); Lloyd C. Gardner, *Economic Aspects of New Deal Diplomacy* (1964); Thomas N. Guinsburg, *The Pursuit of Isolation in the United States Senate from Versailles to Pearl Harbor* (1982); Deborah E. Lipstadt, *Beyond Belief: The American Press and the Coming of the Holocaust* (1993); Arnold A. Offner, *The Origins of the Second World War: American Foreign Policy and World Politics, 1917–1941* (1975); John E. Wiltz, *In Search of Peace: The Senate Munitions Inquiry, 1934–1936* (1963); David S. Wyman, *Paper Walls: America and the Refugee Crisis, 1938–1941* (1985).

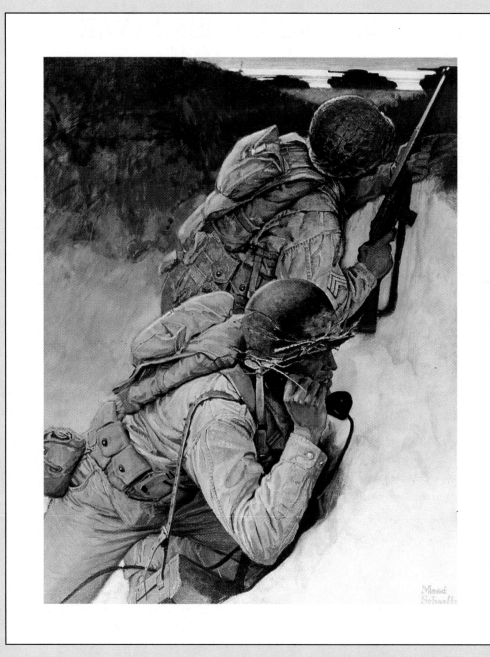

The Signal Corps
by Mead Schaffer

27

WAGING GLOBAL WAR
1939–1945

Americans who lived through World War II retained vivid images of the war's beginning and end long afterward. Even years later, most recalled their shock and indignation upon hearing the news on December 7, 1941, of the Japanese attack on the American naval base at Pearl Harbor, Hawaii, that brought the United States into the conflict. And they cherished their memories of the celebrations that greeted President Harry S Truman's announcement of the Japanese surrender on August 14, 1945.

Their forty-five months of global war finally over, Americans celebrated with exuberance. Virtually all Americans had considered the nation's participation in the war as just and necessary, and they now rejoiced in triumph. "Any girl . . . in downtown San Diego got kissed and thrown in Horton Plaza fountain," recalled Patricia Livermore. "I got thrown in ten times." Thousands of people snakedanced through a drenching thunderstorm in Salt Lake City, and nearly half a million cavorted in the streets in front of San Francisco's city hall. The society editor of the *Boston Herald,* Alison Arnold, remembered hearing the news on her car radio while driving home. "At almost every house the door opened and children poured out waving flags. The church bells were ringing. Everybody got in their cars and drove around town with the horns blowing." Some 2 million people frolicked in New York's Times Square. "The victory roar that greeted the announcement beat upon the eardrums until it numbed the senses," the *New York Times* reported the next day. "Restraint was thrown to the winds. Those in the crowds tossed hats, boxes and flags in the air. From those leaning perilously out of the windows of office buildings and hotels came a shower of paper, confetti, streamers. Men and women embraced—there were no strangers in New York yesterday."

Most Americans would remember it as "the good war." Although the United States was no stranger to the the tragic toll of the war—some 300,000 Americans lost their lives, and twice as many were wounded—U.S. losses paled beside the tens of millions of casualties suffered by European and Asian peoples. The American home front, moreover, suffered none of the devastation that swept Europe and Asia: it was neither bombed nor invaded; it endured few serious material deprivations. To the contrary, the war made the United States once again a land of opportunity and hope. It provided a shock cure for a sick economy, lifting the nation out of depression, redistributing income, and transforming the United States into a largely middle-class society. It gave millions of Americans languishing in the depression a second chance; and for millions more, a first chance. Women and African-Americans especially savored the novel joys of independence. Simultaneously, "total war" profoundly transformed behavior and institutions. It reshaped the economy and fostered an increasingly powerful and active federal government. It disrupted family relationships and laid bare social problems. And it ended American isolationism, pushing the United States to the forefront of a strange, new era in world affairs. As the poet Archibald MacLeish noted in 1943, "This war is not a war only, but an end and a beginning—an end to things known and a beginning of things unknown. We have smelled the wind in the streets that changes weather. We know that whatever the world will be when the war ends, the world will be different."

INTO THE STORM, 1939–1941

Twenty years after the conclusion of World War I, Germany, Italy, and Japan unleashed a campaign of expansion and invasion that ultimately drew the United States into a second global conflict. The Roosevelt administration initially hoped that neutrality would keep America at peace and secure. When German victories in western Europe in the spring of 1940 smashed that prospect, the president tried economic intervention as an alternative to military involvement, lending aid to those nations resisting aggression by the Rome-Berlin-Tokyo Axis. As the fascist menace loomed larger, Roosevelt spurred an American rearmament program and provided more and more materials to the Allies, stretching his executive authority to the legal limit and beyond. Although reluctant to ask a divided Congress to declare war against the Axis, the president understood that his uncompromising conduct toward Germany and Japan could cause the United States to be "pushed," as he said, into a worldwide war. The push came with Japan's attack on the U.S. fleet at Pearl Harbor. As the New World girded to redress the balance of power in two older worlds in 1942, Americans suffered their grimmest year of the war. Military officials gloomily contemplated a prolonged war of seven to fifteen years.

Storm in Europe

Adolf Hitler precipitated war by demanding that Poland restore to Germany the city of Danzig (Gdansk), lost after World War I. When Poland refused, the Führer's troops poured into Poland at dawn

on September 1, 1939. Two days later, Britain and France, honoring their commitments to Poland, declared war on Germany. Roosevelt dutifully invoked the Neutrality Acts, a series of laws passed in the mid-1930s to prohibit the specific actions, such as supplying arms to belligerents, that had drawn the United States into World War I. But the president did not repeat Woodrow Wilson's appeal to Americans to be "impartial in thought as well as in action." Even a neutral, Roosevelt declared, "cannot be asked to close his mind or his conscience."

Determined to avoid an Allied defeat, which would force the United States to confront Nazi Germany alone, the president in mid-September 1939 asked a special session of Congress to revise the Neutrality Act's prohibition against the sale of weapons to belligerents. Adopted in November, the amended neutrality law still prohibited U.S. ships from entering war zones but now allowed nations engaged in the war to purchase arms in the United States—if the belligerents paid cash and carried the arms away in their own ships. Roosevelt had tailored the "cash-and-carry" provision to fit a public mood that favored *both* aiding the Allies *and* staying out of the war.

After a long, quiet lull in the European war (a "phony war," some said), Hitler's armies attacked suddenly and massively. German troops seized Denmark and conquered Norway in April 1940, overran the Dutch and Belgians in May, and then dashed toward the English Channel. Using almost every craft in England that could float, the British staged a spectacular rescue operation, evacuating most of its army and some French troops across the English Channel from Dunkirk in northern France. Prime Minister Winston Churchill rallied the British people: "We shall fight on the beaches, we shall fight on the landing grounds, we shall fight in the fields; we shall never surrender." Still, the Germans sliced southward and westward through France, bypassing the Maginot Line,* and Italian troops attacked northward. On June 22 France surrendered. A jubilant Hitler dictated the armistice to the French in the same railway car at the same spot where German representatives had been forced to sign the armistice of November 11, 1918.

Hitler now took aim at his last surviving opponent, Great Britain. During the summer and fall of 1940, in the Battle of Britain, Hitler first sought to use his air

---

*Maginot Line: an extensive system of fortifications built by France in the 1930s to guard against a German invasion.

Historic Guildhall in London, January 1941
The massive German bombing of England prompted President Roosevelt to propose legislation which would permit him to lend or lease supplies to nations whose defense was vital to American security.

force to destroy the British air force so that the Germans could then invade England. Failing that, Hitler turned to terror-bombing British cities, hoping to demoralize the people and force their government to sue for peace. With Coventry destroyed and parts of London reduced to rubble, Churchill pleaded for all possible American aid short of troops. Most Americans favored additional support for Britain. But a large and articulate minority opposed such assistance, criticizing it either as a waste of materials needed by the United States for its own defense or as a subterfuge to involve Americans in a war not vital to their interests.

The Election of 1940

As the war escalated, Americans speculated about Roosevelt's political intentions. Would he run for an unprecedented third term? Not until the eve of the Democratic convention in July did the president reveal that, given the world crisis, he would consent to a "draft" from his party. The Nazi menace forced conservative Democrats to accept FDR for another possible term and even to accept as his running mate Secretary of Agriculture Henry Wallace, an ultraliberal disliked by many leaders.

The German victories in Europe had an even greater impact on the Republicans' nominating process. Whereas the anti-interventionist front-runners, Senator Robert A. Taft of Ohio and District Attorney Thomas E. Dewey of New York, criticized Roo-

sevelt's handling of foreign affairs, a dark-horse candidate, Wendell L. Willkie of Indiana, championed greater aid to the British. Backed by internationalists in the Republican party, especially those in corporate business and publishing, Willkie, a former Democrat and utility magnate, stampeded the GOP convention and won the nomination.

To counter Willkie's vigorous campaigning, Roosevelt played the role of a national leader too busy with defense and diplomacy to engage in partisan politics. He undercut GOP criticisms by appointing Hoover's secretary of state, Henry L. Stimson, as his new secretary of war and Landon's running mate, Frank Knox, as his secretary of the navy. Encouraged by large bipartisan majorities in Congress, Roosevelt approved the nation's first peacetime draft and another dramatic increase in defense spending. Then in September, with Willkie's public support, the president concluded an executive agreement with Churchill to transfer fifty American destroyers used in World War I to Britain in exchange for leases on British air and naval bases in the Western Hemisphere. Although he had taken the nation closer to war, Roosevelt evaded a congressional vote on the matter and described the agreement as a way of preventing U.S. entry into the war.

The president's anti-interventionist critics condemned Roosevelt's "dictatorial" methods and accused him of scheming to entangle the United States in the European conflict. To mobilize public opinion against the drift toward war, isolationists organized the

The Election of 1940

Candidates	Parties	Electoral Vote	Popular Vote	Percentage of Popular Vote
FRANKLIN D. ROOSEVELT	Democratic	449	27,307,819	54.8
Wendall L. Willkie	Republican	82	22,321,018	44.8

Committee to Defend America First. Largely financed by Henry Ford and his associates, the America First Committee featured aviator Charles Lindbergh as its most popular speaker. Under the slogan "Fortress America," these isolationists claimed that the United States had the strength to stand alone regardless of Hitler's victories in Europe. Although America First attracted backers from virtually every region, ideology, and ethnic group, most Americans supported Roosevelt's effort to assist Great Britain while avoiding fighting in the war. Heartened by Roosevelt's pledge— "I will never send an American boy to fight in a European war"—most voters chose to stay with FDR. Carrying thirty-eight states, Roosevelt won reelection with 55 percent of the ballots cast.

From Isolation to Intervention

Assured of four more years in power, Roosevelt moved resolutely in support of Britain. He called upon the United States to be the "great arsenal of democracy" and proposed a new system for supplying Britain without requiring cash payment: "lend-lease." The plan would allow the president to lend or lease war supplies to any nation deemed "vital to the defense of the United States." Although bitterly attacked by isolationists as the end of American nonintervention and as a declaration of economic war against Germany, Congress approved the bill in March 1941. Shipments to England began at once, and after Hitler invaded the U.S.S.R. in June, U.S. war supplies flowed to the Soviet Union. Despite American hostility toward communism, Roosevelt insisted that Nazi Germany was the chief danger to the United States. To defeat Hitler, FDR confided, "I would hold hands with the Devil."

Roosevelt next turned his sights on the German submarines that were destroying British ships more rapidly than England could replace them, and were hindering Britain's ability to transport war materials across the Atlantic from the United States. First Ameri-

can ships began to assist the British in tracking German U-boats. Then the U.S. Navy started convoying British ships carrying lend-lease supplies, with orders to destroy enemy ships if necessary to protect the shipments. U.S. forces also occupied Greenland and Iceland to keep these strategic Danish islands out of the hands of the Nazis, who had overrun Denmark itself.

In mid-August Roosevelt met with Churchill aboard a warship off Newfoundland to discuss joint military strategy. The two leaders' concluding public statement, soon known as the Atlantic Charter, expressed their mutual ideal of a postwar world. Recalling Woodrow Wilson's Fourteen Points (see Chapter 23), the charter condemned aggression, affirmed national self-determination, and endorsed the principles of collective security and disarmament. The following month, a German submarine opened fire on an Amer-

The Lend-Lease Act, 1941
As part of the program adopted by Congress to lend and lease goods and weapons to countries fighting against aggression, an M-3 tank is loaded aboard a ship destined for Africa.

ican destroyer. Roosevelt denounced the Nazis as "the rattlesnakes of the Atlantic" and authorized naval patrols to shoot on sight at all Axis vessels operating between the United States and Iceland. In mid-October an American destroyer was torpedoed, and on the final night of the month, a submarine sank the destroyer *Reuben James,* killing 115 of its 160 officers and enlisted men.

On a collision course with Germany, Roosevelt persuaded Congress in November to permit the arming of merchant ships and their sailing all the way into belligerent ports. Virtually nothing now remained of the neutrality legislation adopted by Congress in the 1930s to keep the United States out of war. Although not prepared for a major war, America was already fighting a limited one, and full-scale war seemed imminent.

Toward Pearl Harbor

Hitler's triumphs in western Europe encouraged the Japanese to expand further into Asia. They also left the United States virtually alone to oppose Japan's expansion. Viewing Germany as the primary threat to American security, the Roosevelt administration sought to apply just enough pressure to deter the Japanese without provoking Tokyo to war before the United States had built the "two-ocean navy" authorized by Congress in 1940. "It is terribly important for the control of the Atlantic for us to keep peace in the Pacific," Roosevelt told Harold Ickes, his secretary of the interior, in mid-1941. "I simply have not got enough navy to go around—and every episode in the Pacific means fewer ships in the Atlantic." American military leaders agreed. As late as November 17, 1941, a report of the Joint Board of the Army and Navy counseled the president to prolong negotiations with Japan, emphasizing that "the most essential thing now, from the United States standpoint, is to gain time."

Both Japan and the United States hoped to avoid war, but neither would compromise its goals in return for peace. Japan's desire to create a Greater East Asia Co-Prosperity Sphere (an empire embracing much of China, Southeast Asia, and the western Pacific) matched America's insistence on the Open Door in China and the maintenance of the status quo in the rest of Asia. The Japanese considered the U.S. demand that they give up their Asian conquests just a ploy to deny Japan's rise to world power. And the United States viewed Japan's talk of legitimate national aspirations a

smoke screen to hide its brutalizing of Chinese peasants and its bullying of Europeans to rob them of their Asian colonies. Decades of "yellow-peril" propaganda, as well as Tokyo's aggression in China, hardened Washington's firm attitude toward Japan; and unlike the isolationists so strongly opposed to U.S. involvement in European affairs, no American pressure groups organized to prevent a clash with Japan.

Initially, Roosevelt hoped that economic pressure would stop Japanese expansion in Asia. In mid-1939 the United States ended its 1911 Treaty of Trade and Navigation with Japan, and a year later banned the sale of aviation fuel and scrap metal to Japan. Then, following the signing of the Tripartite Pact by Germany, Italy, and Japan in September 1940, whereby each of the Axis nations agreed to help the others in case of an attack by a new enemy, namely the United States, Roosevelt extended the embargo to steel and other metals. That same month, Japan occupied northern Indochina, a French colonial possession, and Washington responded by adding other vital products to the embargo list.

In July 1941 the Japanese overran the rest of Indochina. Roosevelt retaliated by freezing all Japanese assets in the United States and clamping a total embargo on trade with Japan. Tokyo now had to choose between submitting to the United States to gain a resumption of trade or conquering new lands to obtain the supplies vital to its war machine. In October the expansionist war minister Hideki Tojo replaced the more conciliatory Fumimaro Konoye as prime minister of the imperial government. Tojo, who opposed compromise with the United States, set the first week in December as the deadline for Japanese forces to take the offensive if the United States did not capitulate and resume trade relations with Japan. The embargoed Japanese, watching their fuel meters drop toward empty, believed they had no other option.

U.S. intelligence's deciphering of the top code used in messages sent to Japanese ambassadors alerted the Roosevelt administration by late November that war was imminent. It made no concessions, however, during the eleventh-hour negotiations still under way in Washington. Hull insisted that the resumption of American trade depended on the complete withdrawal of Japanese troops from China and Indochina. "I have washed my hands of it," Hull informed Stimson on November 27, "and it is now in the hands of you and Knox—the Army and the Navy." The Japanese, he added, "mean to fight and you will have to watch out."

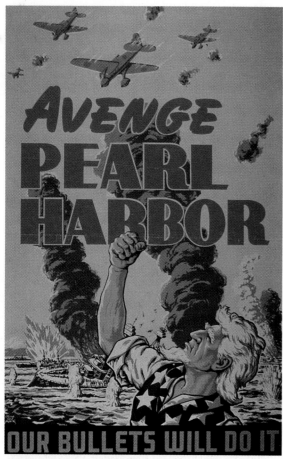

The Attack on Pearl Harbor
In this poster designed to whip up American workers'
support for the war, a defiant Uncle Sam shakes his fist
at Japanese bombers over Pearl Harbor.

War warnings went out to all commanders in the Pacific that same day, advising that negotiations were deadlocked and that a Japanese attack was imminent. U.S. officials expected that the Japanese would move first against British or Dutch possessions to the south, or perhaps strike the Philippines. But the Japanese were gambling on a knockout punch. They hoped that a surprise aerial raid on the U.S. naval base at Pearl Harbor would destroy the U.S. Pacific Fleet and compel a Roosevelt preoccupied with Germany to seek accommodation with Japan.

Unopposed waves of Japanese dive-bombers and torpedo planes soared across the Hawaiian island of Oahu on the morning of December 7, 1941, to bomb the ships anchored in Pearl Harbor and to strafe the

planes parked wingtip to wingtip—as protection against sabotage—at the nearby air bases. American forces suffered their most devastating defeat in history. In less than three hours, 188 aircraft had been destroyed and nearly as many damaged, and eight battleships, three light cruisers, and three destroyers had been sunk or crippled. The attack killed almost 2,400 Americans. Japan's spectacular victory would open the way for an advance to the threshold of Australia by April 1942. It would also ensure Roosevelt an aroused and united America to avenge what he termed this "date which will live in infamy."

When Roosevelt asked Congress to declare war on Japan on December 8, it took the Senate only fifteen minutes to proclaim unanimous approval. After forty minutes of discussion in the House, just one dissenting vote was cast—by Montana's Jeannette Rankin, who had also cast a nay vote against U.S. entry into World War I. The president still hesitated to request a declaration of war against Germany. Hitler quickly resolved his dilemma. Although the Tripartite Pact required Germany to assist Japan only if it were attacked first, and Hitler's advisers begged him not to add the United States to the long list of anti-Nazi belligerents, he went before a cheering Reichstag on December 11 to declare war on the "half Judaized and the other half Negrified" American people. Mussolini chimed in with his declaration of war against the United States, and Congress reciprocated that same afternoon. America faced a global war that it was not yet ready to fight.

On the Defensive

In the days after Pearl Harbor, German U-boats wreaked havoc in the North Atlantic and freely prowled the Caribbean and the East Coast of the United States. Every twenty-four hours, five more Allied vessels went to the bottom. Scores of tankers and freighters flying the Stars and Stripes sank within sight of U.S. shores. U-boats even bottled up the Chesapeake Bay for nearly six weeks. By the end of 1942, Admiral Karl Dönitz's U-boat "wolf packs" had sunk more than a thousand Allied ships, offsetting the tremendous pace of American ship production. The United States was losing the Battle of the Atlantic.

Similarly, the war news from Europe and Africa was, as Roosevelt admitted, "all bad." Hitler had planted the swastika across an enormous swath of territory, from the outskirts of Moscow and Leningrad—a thousand miles deep into Russia—to the Pyrenees on the Spanish-French border, and from the northern tip of Norway to the Libyan desert. In the spring of 1942, the onrushing Germans inflicted more than 250,000 casualties on the Soviet army in the Crimea, and Hitler launched a powerful offensive to seize the Caucasian oil fields. Just as relentlessly, German forces lunged eastward in North Africa, threatening to seize the Suez Canal, the British oil lifeline. It seemed only a matter of months before the Mediterranean would be an Axis sea and Hitler would be in India to greet Tojo marching across Asia from the east.

Apparently as invincible as the Nazis, the Japanese inflicted defeat after defeat on the Allied forces in the Pacific. Tojo followed up his victory at Pearl Harbor by taking Guam, a U.S. possession, three days later. Wake Island and Hong Kong followed. The British fortress of Singapore, the key to Southeast Asia, surrendered in February; that same month, Tojo's naval squadrons shattered Allied warships in the Battle of the Java Sea. March brought the fall of the oil-rich Dutch East Indies, and April of Burma, the last mainland link to China. Having pushed the U.S. garrison on the Philippines first onto the Bataan peninsula and then onto the island of Corregidor, Japan took more than 11,000 American soldiers prisoner early in May. At that point, Japan's rising-sun flag waved over hundreds of islands in the central and western Pacific and over the entire eastern perimeter of the Asian mainland from the border of Siberia to the border of India.

AMERICA MOBILIZES FOR WAR

The United States had begun to prepare for war after the fall of France in mid-1940. But many businesses, fearful that the demand for combat equipment might be short-lived, hesitated to convert to war production. Constant bickering among the military, industry, and labor also hindered preparedness, as each selfishly jockeyed for influence and power. And Roosevelt's own reluctance to speed mobilization, arising from his concern that his political opponents would depict him as a warmonger, further slowed the nation's preparations for global warfare. In December 1941 the American armed forces had a combined total of only 1.6 million. With war production composing just 15 percent

of industrial output, the military f... ages. Moreover, Washington had s... efficient bureaucratic structure to...

Pearl Harbor changed everyth... Congress passed the War Powers Act, ... president unprecedented authority. Hundreds ... cial wartime agencies soon regulated almost every facet of American life. Increased draft calls and voluntary enlistments vastly enlarged the army and the navy. By the end of the war, more than 15 million men had been trained and equipped for the armed forces; and nearly 350,000 women had served in the women's branches of the military, especially the WAC (Women's Army Corps) and the WAVES (Women Accepted for Voluntary Emergency Service in the Navy). To direct this military complex, Roosevelt formed the Joint Chiefs of Staff, which, with Admiral William D. Leahy as chief, was made up of representatives of the army, the navy, and the army air force. Only a minor "corps" within the army as late as June 1941, the air force grew more dramatically than any other branch of the service and achieved virtual autonomy as it assumed a vital role in American combat strategy. The changing nature of modern warfare also led the Joint Chiefs of Staff to create the Office of Strategic Services (OSS) to conduct espionage, analyze the enemy's strengths and weaknesses, and gather the intelligence information required for strategic planning. In 1942 the managers of America's increasingly diversified and huge war machine moved into the world's largest building, the newly constructed Pentagon, in which some 35,000 military personnel worked. And like the Pentagon, the far-reaching domestic changes under way outlasted the war and greatly altered American attitudes, behavior, and institutions.

Organizing for Victory

Shortly after Pearl Harbor, Roosevelt called upon Americans to produce in 1942 an unprecedented 60,000 planes, 45,000 tanks, 20,000 anti-aircraft guns, 8 million tons of shipping, and immense quantities of other supplies for the American and the Allied fighting forces. To organize this effort, Roosevelt established the War Production Board (WPB). Its tasks included allocating scarce materials, limiting or stopping the production of civilian goods, and distributing contracts among competing manufacturers. In addition, the War Manpower Commission (WMC) supervised the mobilization of men and women for the military, war industry, and

ιculture; the National War Labor Board (NWLB) me-
ιated disputes between management and labor, seeking to prevent strikes and runaway wage increases; and
the Office of Price Administration (OPA) imposed strict
price controls to check inflation as more and more personal income pursued fewer consumer goods.

In October 1942 Roosevelt persuaded James F.
Byrnes to leave the Supreme Court to become the "assistant president" in charge of America's domestic war
effort. His assignment was to increase the coordination
of and cooperation between the many government
agencies and representatives of industry and the military involved in carrying out the war effort. In May 1943
the president formally appointed Byrnes to head the
new Office of War Mobilization (OWM), which exercised control over all aspects of the economy, as
Bernard Baruch had done during World War I.

"The Americans can't build planes," a Nazi commander had jeered, "only electric iceboxes and razor
blades." But soon after February 1942, when the last
new civilian car came off a wartime assembly line, the
United States achieved a miracle of war production. "It
was not so much industrial conversion," noted a business leader, "as industrial revolution, with months and
years condensed into days." Automobile manufacturers retooled to produce planes and tanks; a merry-go-
round factory switched to fashioning gun mounts; a
pinball-machine maker converted to armor-piercing
shells. By late 1942 the proportion of the economy
committed to war production had more than doubled,
to 33 percent, and more new industrial plants would
be built during the first three years of war than in the
previous fifteen years of peace. Whole new industries
were created. The government invested $700 million in
some fifty new synthetic-rubber-making plants, to
compensate for the loss of 97 percent of the nation's
crude-rubber supply stemming from Japanese conquests in rubber-producing regions. By 1944 more
than 80 percent of the rubber consumed in the United
States came from the close to 1 million tons of synthetic rubber manufactured that year. At the war's
close, Americans, once the world's largest importers of
crude rubber, were the world's largest exporters of
synthetic rubber.

The United States also became the world's greatest manufacturer of armaments. The nation produced
more war matériel than its Axis enemies combined. By
the end of the war, Americans had assembled some
300,000 military aircraft, as well as more than 86,000
tanks, 372,000 artillery pieces, 2.6 million machine

guns, and 6 million tons of aircraft bombs. In addition,
the United States turned out more than 5,000 cargo
ships and 86,000 warships. When the government
started its emergency crash shipbuilding program in
1941, it took about six months to produce a Liberty-
class merchant ship. In 1943 Henry J. Kaiser, who had
supervised the construction of Boulder Dam, used the
revolutionary technique of prefabrication to reduce the
time to less than two weeks; and in 1945 Kaiser,
dubbed "Sir Launchalot," and his fellow shipbuilders
were completing a cargo ship a day.

Such breakneck production came at a significant
cost. The size and powers of the government expanded
far more than they had even during the New Deal, as
the sum of defense spending zoomed from 9 percent of
the GNP in 1940 to 46 percent in 1945, and the federal
budget leaped from $9 billion to $98 billion. The number of civilian employees of the federal government
mushroomed from 1.1 million to 3.8 million. The executive branch, which managed the war effort, grew the
most, and an alliance formed between the defense industry and the military. (A generation later, Americans
would call these concentrations of power the imperial
presidency and the military-industrial complex.) And
because the government sought the greatest volume of
war production in the shortest possible time, it encouraged corporate profits. "If you are going to try to go to
war in a capitalist country," Secretary of War Stimson
pointed out, "you have to let business make money out
of the process or business won't work."

"Dr. New Deal," Roosevelt aptly put it in 1943, had
given way to "Dr. Win the War." To encourage business to convert to war production and to expand its industrial capacity, the government guaranteed profits
through a system of cost-plus-fixed-fee contracts, generous tax write-offs, and suspension of antitrust prosecutions. Such measures chiefly benefited the giant corporations. Two-thirds of all federal war-production
dollars went to the one hundred largest firms. The ten
biggest businesses received 30 percent of the dollar total of all defense contracts, a development greatly accelerating trends toward economic concentration.

A War Economy

The United States spent about $250 million a day to de-
feat the Axis. Federal expenditures totaled more than
$320 billion between 1941 and 1945, ten times more
than the cost of World War I and nearly twice the
amount that had been spent by the government since

Home Front, *by Golan Gross-Bettelheim*
Responding to the government's plea to join the defense effort, more than six million women entered the labor force during the war. Despite continued discrimination in pay and the inadequacy of child-care facilities, by 1945 women were over a third of all workers on the home front.

its founding in 1788. Wartime spending and the military draft vanquished the unemployment of the Great Depression and stimulated an industrial boom that produced unprecedented prosperity for most Americans. War spending doubled U.S. industrial output, created 17 million new jobs, and increased the GNP per capita from $573 in 1940 to $1,074 in 1945. By the end of the war, net farm income was more than twice the 1940 level; corporate profits after taxes had leaped 70 percent; and the real wages, or purchasing power, of industrial workers had risen 50 percent.

Full employment, longer workweeks, payment of time and a half for overtime, and the increased hiring of minorities, women, youth, and the elderly brought a middle-class standard of living to millions of families. The war years produced the only significant shift in the distribution of U.S. income in the twentieth century. Even without considering the effect on the most affluent of the graduated income tax, which went up sharply during the war, the fraction of total income going to the richest 5 percent sank from 26 percent to 20

percent, whereas the share of the least affluent 40 percent climbed from 13 percent to 16 percent of all income. The earnings of the bottom fifth of workers rose by 68 percent; and the middle class doubled.

The war reversed the hard times of the 1920s and 1930s for U.S. farmers. The parity rate paid by the government jumped from 72 percent in 1939 to 110 percent in 1943, and covered more commodities than ever before. At the same time, agricultural productivity soared. With over a million more new tractors in use in 1945 than in 1940, and with the utilization of improved fertilizers and cultivation techniques, by the end of the war, farmers produced 477 million more bushels of corn than they had at the start of the conflict, as well as 324 million more bushels of wheat and 500 million more pounds of rice. The combination of higher prices, increased productivity, and a 17 percent decline in the agricultural population enabled those who remained on the land to add $20 billion to the value of their farm property and to accumulate $11 billion in savings. Radio comedians changed the words of a nursery rhyme to sing "The farmer's in the dough." As mechanization and the consolidation of small farms into fewer large ones proceeded, farming became "agribusiness," and organized agriculture took its seat in the council of power alongside organized labor, big government, and big business.

Meanwhile, organized labor expanded and grew wealthier. Union membership rose from 9 million workers in 1940 to 14.8 million in 1945 (to embrace 35 percent of nonagricultural employment). The jump resulted from the increase in the work force, combined with the National War Labor Board's "maintenance-of-membership" rule, which required all workers already enrolled in a union to continue their membership for the term of the existing contract. At the same time, the NWLB limited wage increases to restrain inflation. Many unions flexed their new muscles, however, to negotiate unprecedented fringe benefits for their members, including paid vacation time and health and pension plans. Although most labor leaders obeyed the "no-strike" pledge they had given the president immediately after Pearl Harbor, "wildcat" strikes not authorized by union officials periodically stopped work. Most were resolved with no marked effect on war production. The days lost during the war because of strikes amounted to less than one-tenth of 1 percent of total working time. The single major exception to the NWLB's success came in mid-1943 when the iron-willed head of the United Mine Workers, John L. Lewis, led more than half a million coal-field workers out of the pits three times in two months. These coal strikes cost the union movement dearly. Over Roosevelt's veto Congress passed the Smith-Connally War Labor Disputes Act in June 1943, which limited workers' right to strike in any facility deemed essential to the war effort and empowered the president to seize and operate any such strike-bound plant. This legislation paved the way for the antilabor laws enacted in the postwar years.

Far more than strikes, inflation threatened the wartime economy. The Office of Price Administration fought a constant battle against the upward trend of wartime prices that was fueled by the combination of greater American spending power and fewer available goods and services. In the aftermath of Pearl Harbor, however, the OPA could do little but decry the steady 2-percent-a-month rise in prices. Gallup polls indicated that about 90 percent of Americans favored price controls, yet Congress hesitated to act. Each interest group resisted a maximum limit on its own wages or prices and demanded a ceiling on everyone else's. Not until the end of 1942 did Congress give the president the authority to freeze wages, prices, and rents. This freeze enabled the OPA to stop the upward spiral. Consumer prices rose only 8 percent in the last two years of the war; and the total 28 percent increase in the cost of living between 1940 and 1945 stood in marked contrast to the 62 percent rate of inflation between 1914 and 1918.

The OPA also instituted a rationing program to combat inflation and to conserve scarce materials. Under the slogan "Use it up, wear it out, make it do or do without," the OPA rationed gasoline, coffee, sugar, butter, cheese, and meat. Accepting rationing as a contribution to the security of loved ones fighting the war, most Americans endured "meatless Tuesdays" and cuffless trousers. They formed car pools, ate sherbet instead of ice cream, and put up with imitation chocolate that tasted like soap and imitation soap that did not lather. Only a minority patronized the black market to purchase scarce items. Americans also planted 20 million victory gardens, served as air-raid wardens, and organized collection drives to recycle cooking grease, used paper and rubber, and scrap metal.

The sale of war bonds, by draining consumer purchasing power, helped decrease inflation; and the purchase of the bonds gave civilians a sense of involvement in the war effort. The Treasury Department sold about $40 billion in "E" bonds to small investors through payroll-deduction plans and organized bond drives, and nearly twice that amount in higher-denom-ination bonds to wealthy individuals and corporations. The bonds raised half the money needed to pay for the war. Roosevelt sought to pay for the war as much as possible by increasing taxes. Congress, however, gave the president less tax revenue than he wanted. Expenditures outstripped taxes by $22 billion in 1942 and by $57 billion in 1943. Congress also refused to legislate as progressive a tax system as Roosevelt desired. Still, the Revenue Act of 1942 raised the top income-tax rate from 60 percent to 90 percent and added middle- and lower-income groups to the tax rolls for the first time, quadrupling the number of Americans who had to file returns and pay taxes. Begun in 1943 as a *temporary* wartime expedient, the payroll-deduction system automatically withheld income taxes from wages and salaries. By 1945 the federal government was receiving nearly twenty times the tax revenue that it had in 1940.

Science and the War

To emphasize the decisiveness of scientific and technological developments in the Second World War, Winston Churchill dubbed it "a wizard war." The talents of scientists were extensively exploited, and even before the United States entered the war, Roosevelt had formed a National Defense Research Committee to organize scientists for a weapons race against the Axis. Later in 1941 he created the Office of Scientific Research and Development (OSRD) as the contracting agency for the development of new ordnance and medicines. The OSRD spent more than $1 billion to produce improved radar and sonar devices, rocket weapons, and proximity fuses for mines and artillery shells. Its funds advanced the development of jet aircraft, pressurized cabins for pilots, and high-altitude bombsights, and its employment of scientists to devise the best methods for utilizing new weapons resulted in a brand-new field called operational analysis. OSRD also hastened the widespread use of DDT and other insecticides, contributed to improvements in blood-transfusion techniques, and helped produce copious supplies of "miracle drugs," notably penicillin, to combat infections, and synthetic drugs like Atabrine to substitute for scarce quinine. These advances saved thousands of lives during the war and prolonged life expectancy in peacetime. But in these endeavors, neither government nor industry evidenced much concern for the environment. The toxicity of DDT and other insecticides was largely ignored. The production of synthetic rubber fouled the air with sulfur dioxide and carbon monoxide. Vapors from the Kaiser steel plant in Fontana, California, destroyed the grapefruit crop. And the production of plutonium for an atomic bomb led to the dumping of radioactive waste at Hanford, Washington.

The project to develop an atomic bomb began in August 1939 when physicist Albert Einstein, a Jewish refugee from Hitler's Germany, warned Roosevelt that Nazi scientists were seeking to use atomic physics to construct a weapon of extraordinary destructiveness. The president promptly established an advisory committee on uranium and in late 1941 launched a massive Anglo-American secret program—the Soviets were excluded—to produce an atomic bomb before the Germans did. With the aid of European colleagues, American physicists in 1942 successfully achieved a controlled atomic chain reaction and acquired the basic knowledge necessary to develop an atomic bomb. In 1943 and 1944 the Manhattan Engineering District—the code name given to the atomic research project—worked to stockpile U-235, a rare uranium isotope, and plutonium, a synthetic element, and in 1945 to assemble a bomb that could utilize the fissionable material for an atomic explosion. By July 1945 the Manhattan Project had secretly employed more than 120,000 people and spent nearly $2 billion.

Just before dawn on July 16, 1945, a blinding fireball, flashing with "the brightness of several suns at midday," arose over the desert at Alamogordo, New Mexico. A huge, billowing mushroom cloud followed. With a force of twenty thousand tons of TNT, the blast from the atomic test explosion could be felt more than a hundred miles from the detonation point. The awesome spectacle reminded J. Robert Oppenheimer, the Manhattan Project's scientific director, of a line from Hindu scripture: "Now I am become death, the destroyer of worlds." The atomic age had begun.

Propaganda and Politics

People as well as science and machinery had to be mobilized for the global conflict. To sustain a spirit of unity, the Roosevelt administration managed public opinion. Both to restrict the flow of secret military information and to intensify the American people's determination to destroy the Axis, the government regulated the media. In December 1941 Roosevelt established the Office of Censorship. This bureau examined all letters going overseas and worked with publishers and broadcasters to suppress information

★ SILENCE MEANS SECURITY ★

Silence Means Security
Widespread wartime worries about domestic spies led propagandists to order up security posters like this one featuring a WAC.

that might damage the war effort, such as details of troop movements. At its peak the Office of Censorship employed more than fourteen thousand people. Although Americans saw and heard more news coverage than in any previous war, much was concealed. A year passed before the casualty figures and the extent of damage to the naval fleet from the attack on Pearl Harbor were disclosed. Photographs of American dead on battlefields did not appear in newspapers until 1943, and only a few such pictures were approved for publication during war years.

To shape public opinion, Roosevelt created the Office of War Information (OWI) in June 1942. Headed by respected pioneer radio news commentator Elmer Davis, the OWI employed more than four thousand artists, writers, and advertising specialists to explain the war and to counter enemy propaganda. But rather than stressing the U.S. commitment to the preservation of democratic values, the OWI played up the barbarism of the Axis nations and the need to crush them.

Hollywood producers answered the OWI directive—"Will this help win the war?"—by portraying American soldiers as freedom-loving heroes and

Axis troops as sadistic murderers. Comics and strips illustrated similarly sinister and dehu-ed enemies. Jukeboxes blared songs like "Let's Put the Axe to the Axis." Because the American home front was spared the terrible sufferings commonplace in Europe and East Asia, government propaganda emphasized the enemy's "bestiality" in order to motivate Americans to contribute to the war effort. Anti-Japanese propaganda contained a strong dose of racism.

While the Roosevelt administration concentrated on fighting the war, Republican critics seized the initiative on domestic political matters. They were aided by the American people's tendency to blame wartime shortages and losses on the party in power and by the decreasing vitality of economic issues. Full employment and high wages undercut the Democrats' class appeal. The low voter turnout in the 1942 election, moreover, disproportionately hurt liberal Democrats. The Roosevelt coalition in urban areas relied heavily on draft-age and working-class men and women; but many of them in 1942 had recently migrated or gone into the armed services and failed to meet residency requirements or to obtain absentee ballots.

The Republicans gained nine seats in the Senate and forty-six in the House in the 1942 elections, and congressional politics shifted to the right. The power to make or break legislation was held by the conservative bloc of Republicans and southern Democrats. This coalition resented the wartime expansion of executive authority and aimed to protect states' rights and to curb labor unions and welfare spending. The conservatives abolished the CCC and the WPA and rebuffed liberal proposals to extend the New Deal.

Despite the strength of the conservative coalition in Congress, the war expanded government and executive power to an unprecedented degree. To an extent unimaginable in the 1930s, the federal government's budget, size, and powers ballooned during the war. As never before, Washington managed the economy, molded public opinion, funded scientific research, and intruded in the day-to-day lives of the American people.

But with more than $300 billion expended on the war effort, economic despondency gave way to buoyant prosperity. Unemployment ended. Millions moved above the poverty line, and millions more entered the middle class as organized labor and agriculture thrived. Big business also prospered and grew bigger, more highly concentrated, and increasingly intertwined with the military. The "miracle of production," as Americans termed their industrial success, strength-ened confidence in business leaders and in the government's fiscal role in maintaining a robust economy. The achievements of mobilization made the United States second to none in economic and military power and transformed Americans' expectations of what their federal government could and should be.

WAR AND AMERICAN SOCIETY

Some 15 million American men and 350,000 U.S. women went to war. They called themselves GIs, for like their equipment, they were "government issue" machines, mobilized by a society that hated Hitler and ached to avenge Pearl Harbor. Like cartoonist Bill Mauldin's scruffy GI characters Willy and Joe, they were more interested in dry socks than in ideology. They fought because fighting was necessary. Reluctant warriors, they had few aims beyond destroying the enemy and returning to a familiar, secure United States.

But as the war dragged on for almost four years, servicemen and servicewomen were transformed by the military experience. Millions of GIs who had never been far from home traveled to unfamiliar cities, remote parts of the country, and foreign nations. Sharing tents, bunks, and foxholes with Americans of different religions, nationalities, and social backgrounds helped instill in them perspectives that erased some pre-1941 prejudices. The thousands of gay men and lesbians who served in the armed forces (despite the military's efforts to exclude them) also found wartime liberating, as they were freed from traditional expectations and from the scrutiny of family and neighbors. Some of those suspected of being gay, however, were discharged as undesirables, sent to psychiatric hospitals, or imprisoned in so-called queer stockades. Wartime service sowed the seeds of a more homogenized, national culture and broadened personal horizons. It modified how GIs saw themselves as well as how they viewed others.

The wartime experience also changed the GIs' sense of future possibilities. Many enlistees acquired skills in jobs and professions that they had barely known existed. Under the Servicemen's Readjustment Act, or "GI Bill of Rights," enacted by Congress in June 1944, which provided living allowances, tuition fees, and supplies to veterans pursuing their ambitions, several million ex-GIs who had been unable to afford education before the war would be studying for a high-school diploma or enrolled in college in 1946.

Returning GIs also found that America had changed as much as they had. "Home, the one really profound goal that obsesses every one of the Americans marching on foreign shores," wrote combat journalist Ernie Pyle, would never be the same again. Sweeping alterations in society challenged established values, redefined traditional relationships, and created unaccustomed problems. Readjusting to this new world could be difficult, often painful, and for some GIs impossible.

The New Mobility

Nothing did more to transform the social topography than the vast internal migration of an already mobile people. Along with the 15 million men who moved because of military service, as least as many Americans relocated to be near their husbands and fathers in the armed forces or to secure new economic opportunities. Throughout the country, women and men, young and old, black and white, pulled up stakes and swarmed to the centers of war production, especially to the Pacific Coast states, which did half the wartime shipbuilding and airplane manufacturing. California added nearly 2 million people to its growing population, many of them from the Southwest or Mexico. Some 6 million people left farms to work in the cities, particularly those near the manufacturing complexes of the Midwest and the West Coast. Several million whites and blacks from the South migrated northward and westward, as well as to naval shipyards from Norfolk, Virginia, to Houston, and aircraft plants from Marietta, Georgia, to Fort Worth. This mass uprooting of people from familiar settings made Americans both more cosmopolitan and tolerant of differences, and more lonely, alienated, and frustrated. Furthermore, life-styles became increasingly freewheeling as Americans moved far from their hometowns and their traditional values. Almost everywhere near war plants, housing shortages caused severe social problems. Millions of Americans lived in converted garages, tent cities, dilapidated shacks, overpriced hotels and rooming houses, trailer camps, or even their automobiles. Overcrowding as well as wartime separations placed strains on family and community life. High rates of divorce, mental illness, family violence, and juvenile delinquency reflected the disruptions caused in part by

the lack of privacy, the sense of impermanence, the absence of familiar settings, and the competition for scarce facilities. Few boom communities had the resources to supply their suddenly swollen populations with needed transportation, recreation, and social services. Urban blight, as well as conflicts between newcomers and oldtimers, accelerated.

Education and Entertainment

The war-production boom that created both over-crowded communities and ghost towns played havoc with the nation's school systems. More than 350,000 experienced teachers quit their jobs to join the armed services or to take on better-paying war work. Many rural schools were left without any teachers, and countless schools in congested boom towns were understaffed. Students, too, abandoned the schools in record numbers. High-school enrollments sank as the full-time employment of teenagers rose from 900,000 in 1940 to 3 million in 1944.

The loss of students to war production and the armed services forced colleges to admit an unprecedented number of women and to contract themselves out to the military. The navy's V-12 program and the army's specialized-training program sent nearly a million servicemen to college campuses during the war to acquire skills in engineering, foreign languages, economics, and the sciences. The military presence was all-pervasive. Harvard University awarded four military-training certificates for every academic degree it conferred, and the chancellor of one branch of the University of California announced that his school was "no longer an academic tent with military sideshows. It is a military tent with academic sideshows." Higher education became ever more dependent on the federal government, and most universities sought increased federal contracts and subsidies, despite their having to submit to greater government interference and regulation.

The war also had a profound impact on American culture. All the media placed a stronger emphasis than ever before on mass production and mass audiences; and all emerged from the war more highly organized and with greater concentrations of power. Expenditures on books and theater entertainment doubled between 1941 and 1945. Between 60 million and 100 million Americans a week (in a population of 135 million) went to the movies, and the film industry reached its zenith in 1945–1946. Hollywood turned out a spate of war-oriented films in the aftermath of Pearl Harbor that reinforced the image of Nazis and Japanese as fiends and intensified Americans' appetite for unconditional victory. Such films as *Mission to Moscow* and *Song of Russia,* moreover, glorified Soviet heroism. As the war dragged on, however, and people tired of propaganda, Hollywood emphasized romance and adventure with such popular stars as Katharine Hepburn, Spencer Tracy, and Ingrid Bergman. Numerous films, like *Meet Me in St. Louis* with Judy Garland, nostalgically portrayed a mythically serene America.

Similarly, popular music early in the war featured patriotic themes. Published ten days after the attack on Pearl Harbor, "Goodbye, Mama, I'm Off to Yokohama" became the first hit of 1942. As the war continued, themes of lost love and loneliness dominated lyrics. Numbers like "They're Either Too Young or Too Old" expressed the laments and yearnings of women separated from the men they loved. So, too, did the dozens of "dream songs," in which love denied by the real world could be achieved only in a dream. By 1945 bitterness rather than melancholy pervaded the lyrics of the best-selling records. Songs like "Saturday Night Is the Loneliest Night of the Week" revealed a frustrated impatience for the war's end.

In bookstores, nonfiction rapidly overshadowed novels, although mysteries and historical romances remained popular. Few war novels were published, but Marion Hargrove's *See Here, Private Hargrove,* a semiautobiographical account of boot-camp experiences, and John Hersey's *A Bell for Adano,* the story of an Italian-American in the occupation of Sicily, became instant classics. Magazines, however, were the biggest sellers: every popular periodical increased its circulation. *Life, Look, The Saturday Evening Post,* and *Time* were the major fare to satisfy America's hunger for reports of battle actions and of the prospects for peace. Wendell Willkie's *One World* (1943) became the fastest-selling title in publishing history to that time, with 1 million copies snapped up in two months and 2 million in two years. A euphoric vision of a world without military alliances and spheres of influence, this brief volume by the 1940 Republican presidential candidate expressed hope that an international organization would extend the blessings of peace and democracy through the postwar world. The military's need for huge quantities of inexpensive reading materials led the Government Printing Office to publish the Armed Services Editions,

reprints of classic novels and new works on every conceivable topic, in a double-column paperback format. The nearly 350 million copies distributed free to soldiers markedly speeded up the American acceptance of quality paperbacks, first introduced in 1939 by the Pocket Book Company.

An avid interest in wartime news also spurred a significant jump in radio listening during the war. The quest for up-to-the-minute information kept radio audiences at record levels. The voices of Edward R. Murrow and Eric Sevareid reporting from the battlefields became as familiar as those of Jack Benny and Eddie Cantor on their comedy shows. An RCA advertisement expressed the excitement: "Radio annihilates distance, sweeps away the barriers of time, penetrates through mountain and sea, stone and steel." Programs analyzing current issues, like *Town Meeting of the Air,* reached the height of their popularity.

Women and the Family

While the soap operas and comedies continued to broadcast traditional images of family life, millions of American women donned pants, put their hair in bandannas, and went to work in defense plants. Reversing a decade of efforts to exclude women from the labor force, the federal government in 1942 urged women into war production and pressured employers to hire them. Songs like "We're the Janes Who Make the Planes" appealed to women to take up war work, and every avenue of mass propaganda called upon them to "help save lives" and to "release able-bodied men for fighting." Women who never before had worked outside the home found employment in shops and factories, and others quit their menial positions as maids and clerks for the higher pay and union benefits of industry. More than 6 million women entered the labor force during the war, increasing the number of employed women to 19 million. The proportion of unionized female workers rose from 9 percent to 22 percent. Less than a quarter of the labor force in 1940, women constituted well over a third of all workers in 1945.

Even more startling to many, the characteristics of female wage earners changed. Predominantly young and single before the war, 75 percent of the new women workers were married, 60 percent were over thirty-five, and more than 33 percent had children under the age of fourteen. Women performed almost every kind of job, even those previously typed "man's work." They tended blast furnaces, ran lathes, operated cranes, greased locomotives, drove taxis, welded hulls, loaded shells, and worked in coke plants, rolling mills, and shipyards, once the exclusive preserves of men. "Rosie the Riveter," holding a large pneumatic gun in arms bulging with muscle, became the familiar symbol of the woman war worker: she was, in the words of a popular song, "making history working for victory."

By doing the work of men, women implicitly challenged a fundamental justification for sexual inequality. Yet wartime also strengthened traditional convictions. Men fought. Women were neither drafted nor expected to volunteer. This mind set would have powerful consequences after the war, and it allowed gender discrimination to flourish throughout the war. Women earned only about 65 percent of what men did for the same work. Few women during the war challenged the traditional view of gender roles; and gender equality was never a goal for the federal government. Government propaganda portrayed women's war work as only a temporary response to an emergency. "A woman is a substitute," claimed a War Department brochure, "like plastic instead of metal." Training films stressed the similarity between operating industrial machinery and women's familiar work running sewing machines and vacuum cleaners. The work to be done, moreover, was pictured as an extension of women's traditional roles as wives and mothers. One American newspaperwoman wrote of the "deep satisfaction which a woman of today knows who has made a rubber boat which may save the life of her aviator husband, or helped fashion a bullet which may avenge her son!" Given the concern about the availability of jobs for veterans after the war, moreover, the public attitude toward women's employment changed little in World War II. In 1945 only 18 percent of the respondents in a poll approved of married women working.

Traditional notions of a woman's place, and the stigma attached to working mothers, were also reflected in the government's resistance to establishing child-care centers for women employed in defense. "A mother's primary duty is to her home and children," the Labor Department's Children's Bureau stated. "This duty is one she cannot lay aside, no matter what the emergency." New York Mayor Fiorello LaGuardia proclaimed that the worst mother was better than the best nursery, and few officials publicly disagreed. Accordingly, funds for federal child-care centers covered few defense workers' children, the Extended Schools Services program never received adequate funding, and the young suffered. Terms like *eight-hour orphans* and *latch-key children* entered the language to describe unsupervised children forced to fend for themselves. Social workers' reports cited instances of infants locked in cars in war-plant parking lots while their mothers completed their shifts. Fueling the fears of those who believed that the employment of women outside the home would cause the family to disintegrate, juvenile delinquency increased fivefold during the war, and the divorce rate zoomed from 16 per 100 marriages in 1940 to 27 per 100 in 1944.

Yet the impact of war on women and the family proved multifaceted and even contradictory. As the number of divorces sailed to record heights, the marriage rate and birthrate increased to their highest levels in two decades. Although some women remained content to roll bandages for the Red Cross, more than three hundred thousand women joined the armed forces and for the first time in American history served in positions other than that of nurse. Despite the prevalence of traditional beliefs about gender roles and a woman's place, female workers gained unprecedented employment opportunities and public recognition. Although many eagerly gave up their jobs in defense plants in search of domestic stability at the end of the war, just as many did not relish losing the income and self-esteem they had gained in contributing to the war effort. As Inez Sauer, who went to work for Boeing in Seattle, recalled:

> My mother warned me when I took the job that I would never be the same. She said, "You will never want to go back to being a housewife." She was right, it definitely did. At Boeing I found a freedom and an independence I had never known. After the war I could never go back to playing bridge again, being a clubwoman and listening to a lot of inanities when I knew there were things you could use your mind for. The war changed my life completely.

Overall, women gained a new sense of their potential. They proved their capability and experienced the autonomy of participating in society outside the home. Although most aspired to be a wife and mother, not a WAC or riveter, the war had nevertheless widened the public sphere for women and challenged sexist notions as nothing ever had before.

African-Americans and the War

Even more dramatically, the war opened doors of opportunity for many blacks. The wartime experience heightened blacks' aspirations and produced major cracks in the wall of white racist attitudes and policy.

Recognizing that the government needed the loyalty and labor of a united people, black leaders entered World War II determined to secure equal rights. Far from repeating W. E. B. Du Bois's call during World War I for blacks to put aside grievances and "close ranks" behind the president, in 1942 civil-rights spokesmen insisted that African-American support of the war hinged on America's commitment to racial justice. Black politicians demanded that the battle against the Axis be a "Civil War II" to destroy racism at home as well as Nazi racism abroad, and that the fight be a "Double V" campaign waged for victory over racial discrimination as well as triumph on the battlefield. Many blacks responded to the slogan "democracy in our time" with a militancy rarely before seen in African-American communities.

Membership in the NAACP multiplied nearly ten times, reaching half a million in 1945. The association pressed for enactment of anti–poll tax and antilynching legislation, decried discrimination in defense industries and in the armed services, and sought to end black disfranchisement. The campaign for voting rights gained momentum when the Supreme Court, in *Smith* v. *Allwright* (1944), ruled Texas's all-white primary unconstitutional. The decision eliminated a bar that had existed in eight southern states, although these states promptly resorted to other devices to minimize voting by blacks.

A new civil-rights organization, the Congress of Racial Equality (CORE), founded in 1942, advanced the strategy of nonviolent resistance to challenge Jim Crow. Employing the same forms of direct action that Mohandas Gandhi used in his campaign for India's independence, CORE staged a sit-in in 1942 in a Chicago restaurant that refused to serve blacks. CORE's success inspired interracial groups in other cities to begin experimenting with nonviolent direct action to end racial discrimination. Also during 1942, A. Philip Randolph, president of the Brotherhood of Sleeping Car Porters, labored to build his March-on-Washington Committee into an all-black mass protest movement that would engage in civil disobedience to protest racial discrimination.

In 1941 Randolph had called for a "thundering march" of one hundred thousand blacks on Washington "to wake up and shock white America as it has never been shocked before." He warned Roosevelt that if the president did not abolish discrimination in the armed services and the defense industry, African-Americans would besiege Washington. The president agreed to compromise.

In June 1941 Roosevelt issued Executive Order 8802, the first presidential directive on race since Reconstruction. It prohibited discriminatory employment practices by federal agencies and all unions and companies engaged in war-related work, and it established the Fair Employment Practices Commission (FEPC) to enforce this new policy. Although the FEPC lacked effective enforcement powers, booming war production and a labor supply depleted by the draft resulted in the employment of some 2 million African-Americans in industry and another 200,000 in the federal civil service. Between 1942 and 1945, the proportion of blacks in war-production work rose from 3 percent to 9 percent. By the end of the war, black membership in labor unions had doubled to 1,250,000, and the number of skilled and semiskilled black workers had almost tripled. The average wage for African-Americans increased from $457 to $1,976 a year, compared with a gain of $1,064 to $2,600 for white workers.

Preparing for Battle

Recognizing that its racial discrimination and segregation practices resulted in an inefficient and wasteful use of manpower and depressed the morale of African-Americans, the armed services gradually provided blacks with a greater role in combat, including the establishment of the 99th Pursuit Squadron, the first African-American aerial fighting unit.

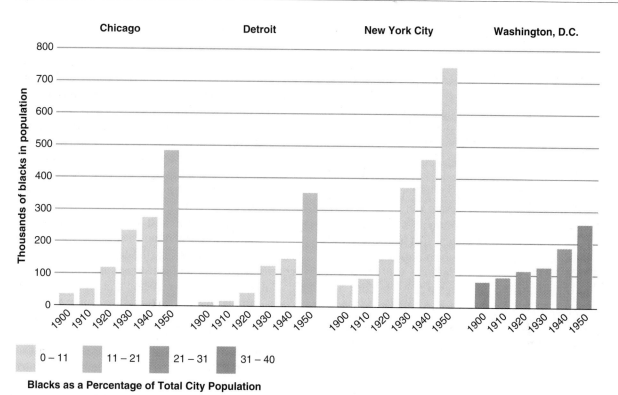

Growth of the Black Population in Select Northern Cities, 1900–1950

The migration of blacks from the rural South to northern cities dramatically increased when the labor shortages of the Second World War created new opportunities in industry and civil service for blacks.

About 1 million African-Americans served in the armed forces. Wartime needs slowly forced the military to end policies of excluding blacks from the marines and coast guard, restricting them to jobs as mess boys in the navy, and confining them to non-combatant units in the army. The all-black 761st Tank Battalion gained distinction fighting in Germany, and the 99th Pursuit Squadron won eighty Distinguished Flying Crosses for its combat against the *Luftwaffe* in Europe. In 1944 both the army and navy began experiments in integration in their training facilities, on ships, and on the battlefield. The great mass of blacks, however, served throughout the war in segregated service units commanded by white officers. Post exchanges, the USO, and the base chapels barred or discriminated against them. Ironically, the Red Cross maintained separate black and white blood banks, even though a black physician, Dr. Charles Drew, had invented the process of storing blood plasma. The failure of military authorities to protect black servicemen off the post, and the use of white military police to keep blacks "in their place," sparked conflict and rioting on many army bases in the South and overseas. At least fifty black soldiers died in racial encounters during the war. "I used to sing gospel songs until I joined the Army," recalled blues-guitar great B. B. King, "then I sang the blues."

The violence within the military mirrored the growing racial tensions on the home front. As blacks militantly protested against discrimination and rejected all pleas to "go slow" in their campaign for first-class citizenship, many whites stiffened their resistance to any changes in blacks' inferior economic and social positions. Numerous clashes occurred, and in mid-1943 scores of cities reported pitched battles between whites and African-Americans. The bloodiest race riot exploded in Detroit that June. After thirty hours of racial beatings, shootings, burning, and looting, twenty-five African-Americans and nine whites lay dead, more than seven hundred had been injured, and over $2 million of property had been destroyed. The fear of continued violence led both to a greater emphasis on racial tolerance by liberal whites and to a reduction in the militancy of African-American leaders.

Realizing that few Americans would tolerate a war against racism at home that impeded the war effort abroad, most African-American organizations began emphasizing programs to lessen aggressive behavior by blacks.

Yet the war brought significant changes that would eventually result in a successful drive for black civil rights. Over seven hundred thousand blacks migrated from the South. This exodus turned a southern problem into a national concern. It created a new attitude of independence in blacks suddenly freed from the stifling constraints of caste. And greater educational and employment opportunities for the blacks who left the rural South engendered a spirit of hopefulness. As the growing numbers of blacks in the industrial cities of the North began to vote, moreover, they held the balance of power in close elections. This prompted politicians in both major parties to extend greater recognition to blacks and to pay more attention to civil rights.

Blacks' optimism also flowed from the new prominence of the United States as a major power in a predominantly nonwhite world. Japanese propaganda appeals to the peoples of Asia and Latin America emphasized lynchings and race riots in the United States. For the first time, Americans had to confront the peril that white racism posed to their national security. In addition, the horrors of Nazi racism made Americans more sensitive to the harm caused by their own white-supremacist attitudes and practices. As a former governor of Alabama complained, Nazism has "wrecked the theories of the master race with which we were so contented so long."

Summing up these developments, Swedish economist Gunnar Myrdal, in his massive study of race problems, *An American Dilemma* (1944), concluded that "not since Reconstruction had there been more reason to anticipate fundamental changes in American race relations." Black veterans especially, with a new sense of self-esteem that came from participating in the victorious war effort, returned to civilian life with high expectations. Like the athlete Jackie Robinson, who as a young lieutenant had refused to take a seat at the rear of a segregated bus and had fought and won his subsequent court martial, and like the black enlistee who, after spending four years in the army, declared, "I'm damned if I'm going to let the Alabama version of the Germans kick me around," blacks faced the postwar era with a firm resolve to gain all the rights possessed by the white majority.

Native Americans, Mexican-Americans, and Jews in Wartime

The wartime winds of change also brought new opportunities as well as problems to other American minorities. Some twenty-five thousand Native Americans served in the armed forces during the war. Navajo "code talkers," for example, performed a valuable service for the U.S. military, confounding the Japanese by using the Navajo language to relay secret messages between U.S. command centers. Another seventy-five thousand Indians left the reservations to work in defense plants and shipyards. It was the first time most of them had lived in a non-Indian world. After the war many preferred to remain in the cities and hoped to become assimilated into mainstream life. The continuation of anti-Indian discrimination and of efforts to keep Native Americans in a subordinate status, however, forced a majority of those who had left the reservations to return. They found that their reservations had suffered severely from congressional cuts in Indian budgets. Prodded by those who coveted Indian lands, lawmakers demanded that Indians be taken off the backs of the taxpayers and "freed from the reservations" so that they could make their own way like other Americans. To mobilize against the campaign to end all reservations and trust protections, Native Americans from various parts of the country organized the National Congress of American Indians. At the same time, Native American veterans who chose to return to the reservations after the war found themselves ineligible for veterans' loans, hospitalization, and other GI benefits. Living on federal lands, they learned, canceled all the advantages that other veterans received after the war.

To relieve labor shortages in agriculture, caused by conscription and the movement of rural workers to city factories, the government negotiated an agreement with Mexico in July 1942 to import *braceros,* or temporary workers. Classified as foreign laborers and not as immigrants, an estimated 200,000 *braceros,* half of them in California, received short-term contracts guaranteeing adequate wages, medical care, and decent living conditions. But farm owners not only frequently violated the terms of these contracts but also encouraged an influx of illegal migrants from Mexico desperate for employment. Unable to complain about their working conditions without risking their own arrest and deportation, hundreds of thousands of Mexicans became illegal aliens, persistently exploited by

Anglo planters and ranchers. At the same time, an equally large number of Mexicans and Mexican-Americans moved to Los Angeles, Chicago, Detroit, and other large cities, where for the first time significant numbers found jobs in defense plants, garment factories, shipbuilding yards, and steel mills. As their occupational status and material conditions improved, signs of acculturation grew. However, most Mexican-Americans remained in separate communities, called *colonias,* sealed off from the larger society.

Much of the hostility toward Mexican-Americans focused on young gang members who wore "zoot suits"—a fashion that originated in Harlem and emphasized long, broad-shouldered jackets and pleated trousers tightly pegged at the ankles. Known as *pachucos,* zoot-suited Mexican-Americans particularly aroused the ire of servicemen stationed in Los Angeles. After a series of minor clashes, bands of sailors from nearby bases and soldiers on leave in Los Angeles rampaged through the city in early June 1943, stripping *pachucos,* cutting their long hair, and beating them. Military authorities looked the other way. City police intervened only to arrest Mexican-Americans. *Time* magazine described the violence as "the ugliest brand of

mob action since the coolie race riots of the 1870s," yet Los Angeles officials praised the servicemen for having rioted, and the city council made the wearing of a zoot suit a misdemeanor. Spanish-speaking Americans also suffered many of the same kinds of discrimination in the military as blacks did. Nevertheless, nearly 350,000 Mexican-Americans served in the armed forces, volunteering in much higher numbers than that warranted by their percentage of the population and earning a disproportionate number of citations for distinguished service and Medals of Honor. And much like black and Native-American veterans, returning Mexican-American veterans organized new groups, among them the American GI Forum, to press for equal rights after the war.

Despite the lip service paid to tolerance, American Jews also discovered that even a war against Nazism did not end traditional prejudices. Anti-Semitism persisted in restrictive covenants to prevent the sale of homes to Jews, in employment ads that stated that only Protestants or Catholics need apply, in rigid quota systems to limit the number of Jews in universities, and in "gentlemen's agreements" to exclude Jews from certain professions. Public-opinion polls throughout the war revealed that a significant minority of Americans blamed either Wall Street Jews or Jewish communists for the war and thought that Hitler was justified in his treatment of Jews in Germany.

The Holocaust
Entering Germany in 1945, American and Russian soldiers discovered the horrors that the Nazis had perpetrated on European Jews and others. One anonymous American GI wrote of the ghastly concentration-camp scenes, "I've seen what wasn't ever meant for human eyes to see."

When the Holocaust—the name later given to the Nazis' systematic effort to exterminate all European Jewry—became known in the United States early in 1942, most Americans viewed it as just a Jewish problem, of small concern to them. Even well-intentioned people, remembering that accounts of German atrocities during World War I had often turned out to be propagandists' lies, tended to discount what they were hearing of Nazi massacres. Not until late November, by which time some 2.5 million Jews had perished, did the State Department admit knowledge of Hitler's genocide. And fourteen more months passed before Roosevelt established a special agency, the War Refugee Board (WRB), to assist in the rescue and relocation of those condemned to the extermination camps and slave-labor concentration camps. Even then, most American officials doubted the possibility, in wartime, of freeing and transporting large numbers of Jews to safety. Despite having aerial photographs of the death camp at Auschwitz in Poland, moreover, the Allies bombed factories in the vicinity but left intact the gas chambers and crematoria, as well as the railway lines leading to them, claiming that attacking them would divert air power from more vital raids elsewhere, and thus prolong the war. "How could it be," historian David Wyman has asked, "that Government officials knew that a place existed where 2,000 helpless human beings could be killed in less than an hour, knew that this occurred over and over again, and yet did not feel driven to search for some way to wipe such a scourge from the earth?"

Although probably little could have been done to save most of Hitler's victims, the feeble U.S. response to Germany's "final solution" reflected American leaders' single-minded concentration on winning the war as quickly and with as little suffering to the United States as possible. U.S. inaction was also colored by Britain's wish to placate its Arab allies by keeping Jewish settlers out of Palestine, the congressional and public fears of an influx of destitute Jews into the United States, and the hesitancy of many American Jewish leaders to press the matter and risk increasing anti-Semitism at home. Because of the State Department's obstruction of rescue efforts, the WRB saved the lives of only 200,000 Jews and 20,000 non-Jews. Six million other Jews, about 75 percent of the European Jewish population, were gassed, shot, and incinerated, as were several million gypsies, Poles, communists, and gay men.

The Internment of Japanese-Americans

Only a tiny minority of Americans refused to support the war effort. While about 37,000 conscientious objectors to war, mostly Quakers and Mennonites, accepted noncombat service as medical corpsmen and as orderlies in public-health hospitals, some 5,500, primarily Jehovah's Witnesses, refused to serve in any way and were imprisoned. The worst abuse of civil liberties, however, was the internment of 112,000 Japanese-Americans, two-thirds of them native-born U.S. citizens, in relocation centers guarded by military police. The policy reflected more than forty years of anti-Japanese sentiment on the West Coast, rooted in racial prejudice and economic rivalry, as well as fear of Japanese sabotage in the immediate aftermath of Pearl Harbor. Self-seeking politicians and farmers who sought to take over the landholdings of Japanese-Americans had long decried the "yellow peril," and following the attack on Pearl Harbor, they whipped up the rage and fears of many white Californians. Numerous patriotic associations and newspapers clamored for action. The army general in charge of the Western Defense Command proclaimed, "A Jap is a Jap. It makes no difference whether he is an American citizen or not." In February 1942 Roosevelt gave in to the pressure and authorized the evacuation of all Japanese-Americans from the West Coast, despite the fact that not a single Japanese-American had been apprehended for espionage or sedition and neither the FBI nor military intelligence had uncovered any evidence of disloyal behavior by Japanese-Americans. Hawaii was the exception to this policy. Despite the large number of Hawaiians of Japanese ancestry, no internment policy was implemented there (see A Place in Time).

Forced to sell their lands and homes at whatever prices they could obtain, Japanese-Americans were herded into barbed-wire-encircled detention camps in the most desolate areas of the West. Few Americans protested their incarceration. Stating that it would not question government claims of military necessity during time of war, the Supreme Court upheld the constitutionality of the evacuation in the *Korematsu* case (1944). By then the hysteria had subsided and the government had begun a program of gradual release. Indeed, the 442d Regimental Combat Team, made up entirely of Japanese-Americans, became the most decorated unit in all the military service. In 1982 a special government commission formally blamed the Roo-

Mother in Jerome Camp, *by Henry Sugimoto, 1943 This painting expresses the loyalty and patriotism of the Japanese-Americans detained in concentration camps, who, despite losing their liberty and most of their worldly goods, volunteered for combat duty and fought gallantly in the European theater.*

sevelt administration's action on "race prejudice, war hysteria, and a failure of political leadership" and apologized to Japanese-Americans for "a grave injustice." In 1988 Congress voted to pay $20,000 compensation to each of the nearly 62,000 Japanese-American internees still alive.

THE BATTLEFRONT, 1942–1944

"No matter how long it may take us to overcome this premeditated invasion," President Roosevelt had promised in his war message to Congress on December 8, 1941, "the American people in their righteous might will win through to absolute victory." In the same spirit, as the new year began, Britain, the Soviet Union, the United States, and twenty-three other coun-

tries signed the Declaration of the United Nations. The "Grand Alliance" of 26 nations opposing the Axis promised to devote its full resources to battle to a triumphal conclusion. But in early 1942 the Allied outlook remained bleak. Nazi forces had conquered much of Europe and threatened the Suez Canal, and Japan controlled the western half of the Pacific and a significant part of Asia.

The mobilization of America's military might turned the tides of war. Fighting on two oceans as well as in the desert sands of Africa, the snows of continental Europe, and the jungles of Pacific islands, Americans played a key role in stopping the Axis advance and liberating conquered areas. Diplomacy followed the fortunes of war. The Allies' unity, strongest at the height of the Axis menace, gradually dimmed as Germany and Japan weakened and as the United States, Britain, and the Soviet Union each sought wartime strategies and postwar arrangements best suited to its own national interest.

The Allied Drive in Europe

Immediately after the raid on Pearl Harbor, British and American officials agreed first to concentrate on defeating Germany and then to smash Japan. But they differed on where to mount an attack. To relieve the beleaguered Russians, who in 1942 were facing the full fury of the German armies, General George C. Marshall, army chief of staff, proposed an invasion of France that would force Hitler to transfer troops to the west and thus lessen the pressure on the Red armies. But England's prime minister Churchill insisted on clearing the Mediterranean before invading France. Recalling the frightful loss of a generation of young Britons in the bloody trench warfare of World War I, Churchill feared that a premature landing in France would lead to another slaughter. In addition, Churchill wanted the Americans to assist the British army fighting against the Germans in North Africa and to protect England's control of the Suez Canal. Over Soviet protests the prime minister persuaded Roosevelt to attack the Germans in North Africa and to delay a "second front" in western Europe. In November 1942, in Operation Torch, an Allied army of more than a hundred thousand American and British troops, commanded by General Dwight D. Eisenhower, landed in Morocco and Algeria. They pressed eastward to entrap the German army being pushed across Libya by British

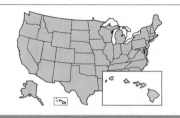
Much as the war came to the United States initially and most dramatically at Pearl Harbor, the outlines of an increasingly multicultural United States emerging from the Second World War could be seen first and most clearly in Hawaii. The nearly one million soldiers, sailors, and marines stopping in Hawaii on their way to the battlefront, as well as the more than one hundred thousand men and women who left the mainland to find war work on the islands, expected the Hollywood image of a simple Pacific paradise: blue sky, green sea, and white sand; palm trees and tropical sunsets; exotic women with flowers in their hair. They found instead a complex multiracial and multiethnic society. The experience would change them, as they in turn would change the islands.

Before December 7, 1941, few Americans knew where Pearl Harbor was or even that Hawaii was a part of their country, a colonial possession, a territory annexed by the U.S. government in 1898.

Few realized that Honolulu, a tiny fishing village when Captain James Cook sailed by the difficult entrance to its harbor in 1778, had subsequently become the major maritime center of a kingdom, the seat of a territorial government, and a gritty port city that would serve as the major staging ground for the war to be waged in the Pacific. And few knew that this American outpost, as a result of successive waves of immigration beginning in the 1870s by Chinese, Portuguese, Japanese, and Filipinos, had a population in 1940 in which native Hawaiians and white Americans (called *haoles,* which in Hawaiian means "strangers") each constituted only 15 percent of the islands' inhabitants.

The approximately 160,000 Hawaiians of Japanese ancestry—including some 100,000 second-generation Japanese, or *Nisei,* who had been born in Hawaii and were therefore U.S. citizens—composed Hawaii's largest ethnic group, more than a third of the population.

Japanese-Americans Go to War
The 442d Regimental Combat Team fought some of the bloodiest battles of the war.

Japan's attack on Pearl Harbor immediately raised fears of sabotage or espionage by Hawaiians of Japanese descent. Rumors flew of arrow-shaped signs cut in the sugarcane fields to direct Japanese planes to military targets and of *Nisei* women waving kimonos to signal Japanese pilots. But in stark contrast to the wholesale incarceration of the Japanese in the Pacific coast states, where the dangers of subversive activities were slight in comparison to Hawaii, official military and administrative policy in the islands was to maintain traditional interracial harmony throughout the war, and to treat all law-abiding inhabitants of Japanese ancestry justly and humanely. "This is America and we must do things the American way," announced Hawaii's military governor. "We must distinguish between loyalty and disloyalty among our people." There was no mass internment of the *Nisei* and *Issei* (those who emigrated from Japan) as there was on the mainland; and they committed no acts of sabotage.

For the *Issei,* loyalty to the United States had become an obligation, a matter of honor. To eliminate potential associations with the enemy, they destroyed old books, photographs of relatives, and brocaded *obi* (kimono sashes) and replaced portraits of the Japanese emperor with pictures of President Roosevelt. A burning desire to prove that they were true Americans prompted many of their Hawaiian-born children, often referred to as AJAs (Americans of Japanese ancestry), to become "superpatriots." AJAs contributed heavily to war-bond drives and sponsored their own "Bombs on Tokyo" campaign; they cleared areas for new military camps; and they converted the halls of Buddhist temples, Shinto shrines, and Japanese-language schools (all closed for the duration, and reopened after the war) into manufactories of bandages, knit socks, sweaters, and hospital gowns (the latter sewed for the Red Cross and Office of Civil Defense). Their newly expanded contact with other Hawaiians, including *haoles,* hastened their assimilation into the larger Hawaiian society. In addition, AJAs served in the military campaigns in the Pacific as interpreters—translating, interrogating, intercepting transmissions, and cracking enemy

Coming Home
Returning to Hawaii, a member of the "Fighting 442d" Regimental Combat Team is embraced by his grateful father.

codes; and they fought in Europe with the all-*Nisei* 442d Regimental Combat Team, the most highly decorated organization in the U.S. Army. These contributions gave the Japanese in Hawaii, as it did other ethnic groups, a new sense of their worth and dignity. The war experience aroused expectations of equal opportunity and treatment, of full participation in island politics, of no longer accepting a subordinate status to *haoles.*

Additionally, the attitudes of many Hawaiians toward *haoles* changed as native islanders witnessed a large number of whites doing manual labor for the first time. Their view that whites would always hold superior positions in society—as bosses, plantation owners, business leaders, and politicians—was turned topsy-turvy by the flood of Caucasian mainland war workers, mostly from the fringes of respectability, and easily stereotyped as drunks and troublemakers. The hordes of white servicemen crowding into Hon-

olulu's Hotel Street vice district for liquor, for tattoos, for posed pictures with hula girls in grass skirts, for three-dollar sex at the many brothels, and then for treatment at prophylaxis stations to ward off venereal diseases also tarnished traditional notions of white superiority. And the hundreds of white prostitutes (mostly from California) who brazenly operated in Honolulu further mocked the belief that those with white skin had a "natural" right to rule those of a darker hue.

Much as the influx of mainland whites changed the attitudes of the people of Hawaii, the Hawaiian experience, in turn, changed the outlooks of many of the servicemen and war workers stationed there. In Honolulu, they grew accustomed to women's holding full-time jobs as a far higher percentage of women worked outside the home than was the case on the mainland. Given the scarcity of "available" white women, moreover, the men gradually became less uneasy about interracial dating, joking that "the longer you were on the island, the lighter [skinned] the girls became." And not a few GIs ultimately married women of Chinese, Filipino, or Hawaiian ancestry. Most of the whites who had come to Hawaii had never lived where whites did not constitute a majority and where *they* were the ones who were different. Most had never before encountered or conversed with those of African or Asian ancestry. Suddenly, they were in the midst of a mixture of ethnic and racial groups unmatched anywhere in the United States, in the midst of a society of people of diverse cultures working together for a common cause. So also were the nearly thirty thousand African-American servicemen and workers who arrived in the islands before the war's end. Having experienced nothing like the fluid and relaxed racial relations of Hawaii's multiethnic society, blacks discovered an alternative to the racist America they knew. Some chose never to go back to the mainland. Others returned home to the states to press for the rights and freedoms they had first tasted in Hawaii. In so many ways, wartime Hawaii, termed "the first strange place" by historians Beth Bailey and David Farber, would anticipate the "strangeness" of U.S. society today.

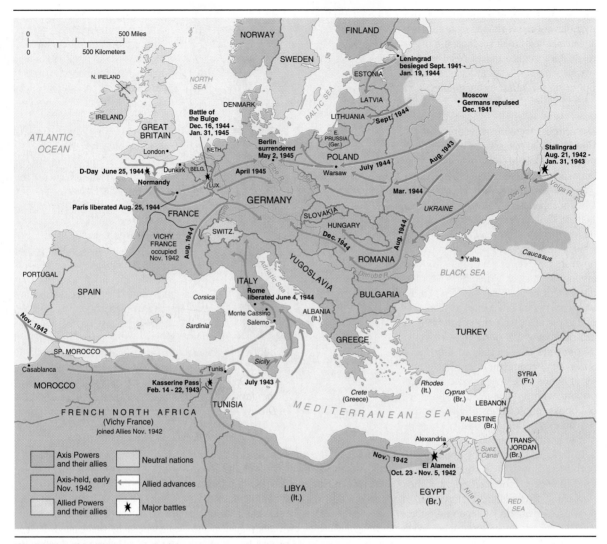

World War II in Europe and Africa

The momentous German defeats at Stalingrad and in Tunisia early in 1943 marked the turning point in the war against the Axis. By 1945 the Allied conquest of Hitler's "thousand-year" Reich was imminent.

forces from Egypt. Eventually surrounded by Allied troops, over a quarter of a million Germans surrendered in Tunisia in May 1943, despite Hitler's orders to fight to the death.

Germany lost even more men on its eastern front. Thousands died every day as huge Soviet and German armies fought the Battle of Stalingrad. By the end of 1942, the Russian snow had turned red with blood. In the fighting at Stalingrad, the Soviet Union suffered more battle deaths in four months than the United States did in the entire war. The Red Army, however, emerged victorious; it saved Stalingrad, hung on at besieged Leningrad, and went on the offensive across a front a thousand miles wide.

Stalin renewed his plea for a "second front" against Germany as the Soviet Union continued to bear the brunt of the dying. But when Churchill again objected, Roosevelt agreed to the British plan for an invasion of Sicily in the summer of 1943. In little more than a month, the Allies seized control of Sicily. Italian military leaders deposed Mussolini and surrendered to the Allies on September 8. But as British and American troops began the crawl up the boot-shaped Italian peninsula, German soldiers poured into Italy and rescued Mussolini. Having to face elite German divisions in defensive positions, the Allies spent eight months inching their way 150 miles to Rome. They would still be battling through the mud and snow of northern Italy when the war in Europe ended.

In 1943 and 1944, the Allies turned the tide in the Atlantic, began to send thousands of bombers over Germany, and pushed the Nazis out of the Soviet Union. The Battle of the Atlantic was won by American science and industry as much as by the American navy. The utilization of advanced radar systems and the development of high-frequency direction finders; the invention of special torpedoes and depth charges; breakthroughs in signals intelligence; and the increasing number of planes and destroyer escorts produced in the United States turned the tide. By December 1943 the Allies had essentially won the Battle of the Atlantic. At the start of that year, moreover, Britain's Royal Air Force and the United States Army Air Force began round-the-clock bombardment of Germany. The British by night and the Americans by day rained thousands of tons of bombs on German cities. In raids on Hamburg in July 1943, Allied planes killed some sixty thousand people and leveled vast areas of the city, much as they had done earlier to Cologne.

Meanwhile, the Soviet offensive in 1943 reclaimed Russian cities and towns held by the Nazis. In July German and Soviet divisions fought the largest tank battle in history near the city of Kursk: the victorious Red Army gained the strategic offensive and the defeated Germans faced perpetual retreat. By mid-1944 the Red Army had largely cleared the Germans out of the Soviet Union. The Soviet troops advanced swiftly. They reached the outskirts of Warsaw, Poland, in July and established a puppet government in Lublin, took control of Romania in late August and of Bulgaria two weeks later, and assisted communist guerrillas led by Josip Broz Tito in liberating Yugoslavia in October.

As eastern Europe fell under Soviet domination, Allied forces prepared for a sweep across France. The long-delayed "second front" would be launched by General Dwight D. Eisenhower, who had been chosen supreme allied commander in Europe. Neither as inspirational a leader as Douglas MacArthur nor as heroic a warrior as George Patton, Eisenhower nevertheless had the diplomatic and administrative talents to

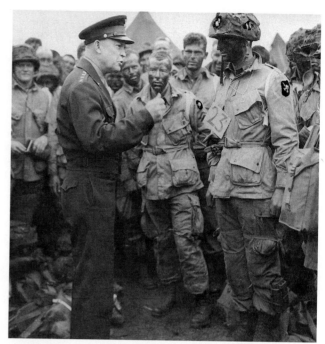

"Full Victory—nothing else!"
Commander-in-Chief of the Allied Expeditionary Force General Dwight D. ("Ike") Eisenhower gives the order of the day to U.S. paratroopers in England on the eve of D-Day.

supervise Operation Overlord, as the combined land-sea-air assault on France was called. Early on the morning of June 6, 1944—"D-Day"—the largest amphibious invasion in history began. Ferried across the English Channel in thousands of vessels, and supported by more than 10,000 airplanes, nearly 200,000 American, British, and Canadian troops stormed the beaches of Normandy. Despite ferocious German resistance, they succeeded in establishing beachheads and gradually pushed inland as almost a million more Allied soldiers waded ashore in the following six weeks. A major breakthrough at Saint Lo late in July enabled Allied troops to delve deep into the countryside and to liberate Paris a month later. By summer's end the British had secured Belgium and the Americans had recovered Luxembourg and most of France.

As the Allies prepared for their attack on Germany, Hitler on December 16 threw the last of his reserves, a quarter of a million men, against the American position in the Forest of Ardennes in Belgium and Luxembourg. In ten days Hitler's troops drove a bulge eighty miles long and fifty miles deep into the Allied line. On

Entry into Coutances, *by Aaron Bohrad*
Breaking the lodgment in which the Germans had them contained in Normandy,
General Omar Bradley's First Army and the U.S. Eighth Air Force turned the German
Seventh Army's retreat into a rout by late July 1944.

Christmas Day the Allies stopped the German counterattack and within a month had driven the Nazis back to the Rhine. Hitler had lost his final gamble in the Battle of the Bulge and had exhausted Germany's reserves. The way to Germany was now open. But the fierce fighting in the Ardennes took a toll of American casualties that eclipsed the Battle of Gettysburg as the bloodiest fight in American history: fifty-five thousand combatants killed or wounded and eighteen thousand taken prisoner.

The War in the Pacific

The day after the Philippines fell to Japan in mid-May 1942, an American naval force confronted a Japanese fleet in the Coral Sea off northeastern Australia. For the first time in history, a naval battle was fought entirely from aircraft carriers. Although both sides lost one carrier and many planes, the Battle of the Coral Sea thwarted the Japanese advance on Australia. Less than a month later, the Japanese navy turned eastward to-

ward Midway Island, the most important American outpost between Hawaii and Japan. A superior imperial armada aimed to knock out the decimated American fleet in the Pacific. But because the U.S. Signal Corps had deciphered the Japanese naval code, Admiral Chester Nimitz knew the plans and locations of the Japanese ships. In a decisive victory, American dive-bombers sank four major aircraft carriers and destroyed several hundred planes. The Japanese reverted to the defensive, seeking to hold what they had previously won.

On August 7, 1942, marines waded ashore at Guadalcanal in the Solomon Islands to protect Australia from attack. Facing suicidal resistance—as well as rampant malaria, dysentery, fungus, and all the ravages of the disease-infested tropics—U.S. troops were stalemated for almost three months, until Admiral William Halsey's fleet destroyed the Japanese ships in the area, isolating those Japanese remaining on Guadalcanal. Yet it would take another three months before the Japanese were driven off the island, leaving behind more than twenty-five thousand

World War II in the Pacific

American ships and planes stemmed the Japanese offensive at the Battles of the Coral Sea and Midway Island. Thereafter, the Japanese were on the defensive against American amphibious assaults and air strikes.

[handwritten annotations on map: "stepping stone to Hawaii → we broke their code + met then", "after → Japanese couldn't project power over Pacific Islands b/c didn't have that many aircraft carriers"]

[handwritten below caption: "of Pacific 2 turning points ① Midway ② Guadalcanal"]

[handwritten: "after: Japanese never launched lost ~1/6 aircraft carriers"]

of their dead—a gruesome preview of the island battles to come.

In fall 1943 the United States began a two-pronged advance toward Japan. Under General MacArthur, who had commanded the heroic but futile defense of the Philippines and had vowed that "I shall return" to the islands, the army advanced north from Australia, "leapfrogging" from one strategic island to the next. A second force, led by Admiral Nimitz, "island-hopped" across the central Pacific, capturing key islands from which U.S. aircraft could bomb Japan. Taking one of the first islands, Tarawa, cost over a thousand marine lives in four days. His men, said the commanding general, "looked older than their fathers, dirty, unshaven, with gaunt, almost sightless eyes; they had survived

the ordeal but it had chilled their souls." The price of vanquishing Japan would not be cheap.

Although Pacific operations remained secondary to the defeat of Germany, the American forces under MacArthur and Nimitz steadily increased. By late 1944 the United States had deployed nearly 1.5 million marines and soldiers, as well as the navy's fastest and largest aircraft carriers, in the Pacific theater. Though suffering heavy casualties in capturing New Guinea before liberating Manila in early 1945, MacArthur lost fewer than 28,000 men overall, less than the number killed in some individual battles in Europe. Nimitz, meanwhile, seized strategic bases on the Gilbert Islands in November 1943 and the Marshall Islands in February 1944, and went on to capture the Marianas in the summer, putting Tokyo within range of the mighty B-29s, which could each carry seven tons of bombs. By late 1944 they were incinerating cities in Japan. Simultaneously, the American navy destroyed the remaining combat effectiveness of the imperial fleet at the battles of the Philippine Sea and Leyte Gulf. Japan's sea and air power was totally shattered. Despite their disastrous losses, however, Japanese military leaders stymied every attempt by civilians in the government to negotiate a peace.

The Grand Alliance

Roosevelt's goals throughout the war had remained the total defeat of the Axis in Europe and Asia at the least possible cost in American lives, and the establishment of a world order strong enough to preserve peace, open trade, and ensure national self-determination in the postwar era. Aware that only a common enemy fused the Grand Alliance together, Roosevelt tried to promote harmony by concentrating on military victory and postponing divisive postwar matters.

But Churchill and Stalin had other goals. Britain sought to retain its imperial possessions and a balance of power against the U.S.S.R. on the Continent. The Soviet Union aspired to weaken Germany permanently and to create a sphere of influence in Eastern Europe to protect itself against possible future military attacks from the West. To hold this uneasy alliance together, Roosevelt put his faith in personal diplomacy and met frequently with foreign leaders to plan strategy and to mediate conflicts.

Speeding across the war-ravaged Atlantic in a Pan American Clipper in January 1943, Roosevelt was the first president to fly in office and the first to leave the United States in wartime. His destination was Casablanca, Morocco's main port. There, in the midst of the North African campaign, FDR and Churchill resolved to attack Italy before invading France and to proclaim that the war would be pursued until the Axis

accepted "unconditional surrender." In this proclamation they had sought to reduce Soviet mistrust of the West, which had been worsened by the postponement of the promised "second front," and to deter Stalin from offering Hitler a separate peace. In Cairo, in November 1943, Roosevelt had met with Churchill and Jiang Jieshi (Chiang Kai-shek), the anticommunist head of the Chinese government. To induce Jiang to fight until Japan surrendered unconditionally, FDR had promised that Manchuria and Taiwan would be returned to China and that there would be a "free and independent Korea."

The president and prime minister had then continued on to Tehran, the capital of Iran, to confer with Stalin. The Allied triumvirate (known as the Big Three) set the invasion of France for May or June 1944 and agreed to divide Germany into zones of occupation and to impose reparations on the Reich. Most important to Roosevelt, Stalin had also promised to enter the war against Japan after Hitler's defeat. On his return to the United States, the president predicted, "We are going to get along with him [Stalin] and the Russian people—very well indeed."

The Election of 1944

Roosevelt then turned his attention to domestic politics. The Republicans had made important gains in the 1942 congressional elections, and conservatives in both parties looked forward to consolidating their position in 1944. Although conservative Democrats could not deny Roosevelt renomination in 1944, they did force him to dump the liberal Henry Wallace from the ticket and to accept Harry S Truman. A moderate senator from Missouri, Truman had gained national attention by chairing a subcommittee investigating waste in the defense effort. Not strongly opposed by any major faction in the party, Truman, "the new Missouri Compromise," restored a semblance of unity to the Democrats for the 1944 campaign.

The Election of 1944

Candidates	Parties	Electoral Vote	Popular Vote	Percentage of Popular Vote
FRANKLIN D. ROOSEVELT	Democratic	432	25,606,585	53.5
Thomas E. Dewey	Republican	99	22,014,745	46.0

Similarly hoping that unity would carry them to victory, the GOP shunned the liberal and internationalist Wendell Willkie and nominated the moderate New York governor Thomas E. Dewey. To conciliate right-wing Republicans, Dewey selected John W. Bricker of Ohio as his running mate. More a contest of personalities than of issues, the campaign featured the Republicans harping on FDR's failing health and Roosevelt exploiting the American military victories in Europe and the Pacific.

In November the electorate sent FDR back to the White House for an unprecedented fourth term. The president amassed 432 electoral votes to Dewey's 99. But with just 53 percent of the popular vote, Roosevelt won by his narrowest margin ever. As never before, he owed his triumph to the urban vote and to the involvement of organized labor in Democratic politics. Most voters, eager to enjoy their new prosperity, showed little inclination for further New Deal programs. They also left the power of the conservative coalition in Congress intact. A weary Roosevelt now directed his waning energies toward vanquishing the Axis and constructing a new international order that would prevent future wars.

Yalta Conference, 1945
The palaces where Roosevelt, Churchill, Stalin, and their advisers gathered were still standing, but the rest of Yalta had been reduced to ruin during the German occupation.

Triumph and Tragedy, 1945

By the time of Roosevelt's last meeting with Churchill and Stalin, in February 1945 in the Soviet city of Yalta, the realities of the military situation favored the Soviet Union. The victorious Soviet offensives were nearly complete, but U.S. forces were still recovering from the Battle of the Bulge and were facing fanatical resistance on the route to Japan. The Red Army had overrun much of Eastern Europe, begun to organize Poland, Romania, and Bulgaria as communist states, and massed its troops just fifty miles from Berlin. The Joint Chiefs of Staff insisted to Roosevelt that it was worth almost any price to obtain Stalin's military assistance in the Far East. They expected the invasion of Japan to cost a million American casualties. Stalin was in a position to make demands. He already dominated eastern Europe, and there was little that Churchill and Roosevelt could do to alter that; the United States still faced a long, bloody battle with the Japanese, and Stalin had the luxury of deciding whether or not to remain a nonparticipant in the Pacific war.

The Yalta agreements mirrored the new balance of power. Stalin again promised to declare war on Japan "two or three months" after the surrender of Germany, and in return Churchill and Roosevelt reneged on their arrangement with Jiang Jieshi, made at Cairo, and promised the Soviet Union concessions in Manchuria and the territories that it had lost in the Russo-Japanese War forty years earlier. Stalin then recognized Jiang as the ruler of China and promised to persuade Mao Zedong's (Mao Tse-tung's) Chinese communists to end the nation's long civil war and cooperate with Jiang. The Soviet dictator also dropped his demands for $20 billion in reparations from Germany and the permanent dissolution of the Reich, accepting a temporary partitioning of Germany and future discussions by a reparations commission. On the matter dearest to Roosevelt's heart, Stalin approved plans for a United Nations Conference to be held in San Francisco in April 1945 to establish a permanent international organization for collective security.

Stalin, however, proved adamant on the issue of Soviet dominance in Eastern Europe, particularly

Poland. Twice in the twentieth century, Poland had been the pathway for German troops invading Russia. Stalin would not expose his land again, and after the Soviets had captured Warsaw in January 1945, he encouraged the Polish communists to brutally subdue a noncommunist majority. Roosevelt and Churchill refused to recognize the communist Lublin regime. But in consideration of the Soviet power in the area, they reluctantly accepted Stalin's vague pledge to reorganize the government to include noncommunist Poles and to allow free elections as soon as possible to determine the future government of Poland. Short of going to war against the Soviet Union while simultaneously battling Hitler and the Japanese, Roosevelt could only hope that Stalin would keep his promises.

The Defeat of Germany

As the diplomats at Yalta delayed resolving their differences, the Allied armies closed the vise on Germany. Early in March American troops captured Cologne and then encircled the Ruhr Valley, Germany's industrial heartland. To counter the threat of Soviet power in a postwar Europe, Churchill now proposed a rapid, concentrated Anglo-American thrust to Berlin. General Eisenhower, with Roosevelt's backing, overruled the British. The Americans, wishing to minimize their casualties and to reassure Stalin, who continued to fear that his allies might sign a separate peace with Germany, methodically advanced on a broad front extending from the North Sea to the border of Switzerland. In the last week of April, American and Russian troops joined hands at the Elbe River. By then, however, the Soviets had taken Vienna and reached the suburbs of Berlin. On April 30 Hitler committed suicide in a bunker under the streets of Berlin, and the city fell to the Soviets on May 2. A hastily assembled new German government surrendered unconditionally on May 8.

Jubilant Americans celebrated Victory in Europe (V-E) Day with ticker-tape parades and dancing in the streets. But the rejoicing quickly subsided. The United States now had to turn its attention to the war in the Pacific. Moreover, in the last weeks of the German campaign, as Allied troops liberated those remaining in the concentration camps, Americans saw newsreels of the gas chambers in Auschwitz, the human ovens of Dachau, and the corpses stacked high like cordwood in Belsen. They learned with horror that 6 million Jews and several million others had been systematically murdered in these Nazi death and forced-labor camps. And they mourned a tragedy closer to home, the death of Franklin Roosevelt. Throughout the early months of 1945, the once robust FDR had appeared frail and weary. On April 12 the exhausted president, sitting for a portrait at his second home in Warm Springs, Georgia, abruptly clutched his head and moaned "I have a terrific headache." A cerebral hemorrhage ended his life. His unprepared successor would inherit leadership of the most powerful nation in history as well as troubles with the Soviet Union that seemed more intractable every day.

A New President

"I don't know whether you fellows ever had a load of hay or a bull fall on you," Harry S Truman told reporters on his first full day in office, "but last night the moon, the stars, and all the planets fell on me." An unpretentious politician, awed by his new responsibilities, Truman struggled to continue FDR's policies. But Roosevelt had made no effort to familiarize his vice president with the course of world affairs. Truman distrusted the Soviets and counted on American military power to maintain the postwar peace. In office less than two weeks, he lashed out at Soviet ambassador V. M. Molotov that the United States was tired of waiting for the Russians to carry out the Yalta agreement on free elections in Poland, and he threatened to cut off lend-lease aid if the Soviet Union did not cooperate. The Truman administration then reduced U.S. economic assistance to the Russians and stalled on the decision to grant them a $1 billion reconstruction loan. But Stalin strengthened his domination of Eastern Europe, breaking the promises he had made at Yalta. The bluster of both Stalin and Truman did nothing to arrest the dissolution of the Grand Alliance.

The United States would neither concede the Soviet sphere of influence in Eastern Europe nor take decisive steps to terminate it. Although Truman insisted on a free Poland, he still eagerly sought Stalin's cooperation in establishing the United Nations and in defeating Japan. Soviet-American relations deteriorated. By June 1945, when the Allied countries succeeded in framing the United Nations Charter, hopes for a new international order had dimmed, and the United Nations emerged as a diplomatic battleground for the Americans and Soviets. Truman, Churchill, and Stalin met at Potsdam, Germany, from July 16 to August 2, to

Garden at Hiroshima, *by Standish Backus*
A few years after the triumphant celebrations that came with the war's end, an American painter produced this powerful antiwar statement.

complete the postwar arrangements begun at Yalta. Each seeking to preserve and enlarge his nation's sphere of influence in the world, the Allied leaders could barely agree even to demilitarize Germany and to punish Nazi war criminals. All the major divisive issues were postponed and left to the Council of Foreign Ministers to resolve later. Given the diplomatic impasse, only military power remained to determine the contours of the postwar world.

The Atomic Bombs

Meanwhile, the war with Japan ground on. Early in 1945 an assault force of marines invaded Iwo Jima, a speck of an island 700 miles from Japan. There the marines battled thousands of Japanese soldiers hidden in tunnels and behind concrete bunkers and pillboxes. Securing the five-square-mile island would cost the marines twenty-five thousand casualties. A month later, American troops waded ashore on Okinawa, only 350 miles from Japan and a key staging area for the planned U.S. invasion of the Japanese home islands. Death and destruction engulfed Okinawa: after eighty-three days of fighting, some 80,000 civilians had suffered casualties and nearly the entire Japanese garrison of 110,000 men lay dead. Subduing the armed resistance on the island had required some forty thousand American casualties.

If the capture of these small islands had brought such bloodshed, officials wondered, what would the assault on the Japanese home islands be like? Although a naval blockade and daily bombing were exhausting Japan (on March 9–10 a fleet of B-29s dropped napalm- and magnesium-bombs on Tokyo, entirely burning to the ground sixteen square miles of the city and killing some eighty-four thousand), the imperial government showed little disposition to surrender. Consequently, Truman scheduled an invasion of the Japanese island of Kyushu for late 1945 and one of Honshu, the main island, for early 1946.

The successful detonation of an atomic blast at Alamogordo in mid-July, however, gave Truman an alternative to the costly planned invasion. While meeting with Stalin and Churchill at Potsdam, Truman issued an order on July 25 that an atomic bomb be dropped if Japan did not surrender before August 3. The next day he warned Japan to surrender unconditionally or face "prompt and utter destruction." Japan rejected the Potsdam Declaration on July 28, and Truman gave the military the go-ahead. On August 6 a B-29 named the *Enola Gay* took off from the Marianas island of Tinian and dropped a uranium bomb on Hiroshima, plunging the city into what Japanese novelist Masuji Ibuse termed "a hell of unspeakable torments." The three hundred thousand degrees centigrade fireball incinerated houses and pulverized people. More than seventy thousand died in the searing flash of heat, and many of the additional seventy thousand injured later died of radiation poisoning. On August 8, as promised, Stalin declared war on Japan. The next day, at high noon, a B-29 dropped a plutonium bomb on Nagasaki, killing forty thousand, injuring more than sixty thousand, and obliterating much of the city. On August 14 Japan accepted the American terms of surrender, which implicitly permitted the emperor to retain his throne but subordinated him to the U.S. commander of the occupation forces. On the battleship *Missouri*, General MacArthur formally received the Japanese surrender on September 2, 1945. The war was over.

Subsequently, many have questioned whether the fighting had to end with the United States resorting to the dreaded new atomic weapons. Some believe that racist American attitudes toward the Japanese motivated the decision to drop the bombs. As war correspondent Ernie Pyle wrote, "The Japanese are looked upon as something inhuman and squirmy—like some people feel about cockroaches or mice." Yet from the very beginnings of the Manhattan Project, those involved regarded Germany as the target; and considering the indiscriminate ferocity of the Allied bombings of Hamburg and Dresden that killed many tens of thousands of civilians, there is little reason to assume that the Allies would not have dropped atomic bombs on German cities if they had been available before the German surrender. Others contend that demonstrating the bomb's terrible destruc-

tiveness on an uninhabited island would have moved Japan to surrender. We will never know for sure. American policy makers had ruled against a demonstration bombing as impractical and too risky because the United States had an atomic arsenal of only two bombs, and they did not know whether the mechanism for detonating them in the air would work. Still others argue that Japan was ready to surrender and that an invasion of the home islands was unnecessary. Again, we cannot know for sure. All that is certain is that as late as July 28, 1945, Japan flatly rejected a demand for surrender, and not until after the bombing of Hiroshima did the Japanese government discuss acceptance of the Potsdam Declaration.

The rapid worsening of relations between the United States and the Soviet Union, moreover, strengthened the conviction of some that Truman ordered the use of the atomic bombs primarily to intimidate Stalin. The failure of the Americans and Soviets to resolve their differences had led Truman and his key advisers to seek an end to the war in the Pacific before Stalin's entry into the conflict. They had also recognized the need to brandish an awesome weapon that might give the United States the leverage to oust the communists from Eastern Europe. Referring to the Soviets, President Truman noted just before the atomic test at Alamogordo, "If it explodes, as I think it will, I'll certainly have a hammer on those boys." Secretary of War Henry Stimson contended that the bomb was "a badly needed equalizer" in the struggle with the Soviet Union and that it emboldened the president to "get tough with the Russians." And Truman's new secretary of state, James Byrnes, thought that the bomb would "make Russia more manageable" and would "put us in a position to dictate our own terms at the end of the war."

The president and his advisers believed that the atomic bombs would strengthen their hand against the Soviets; but that was not the foremost reason why the bombs were dropped. As throughout the war, American leaders in August 1945 relied on production and technology to win the war with the minimum loss of American life. Every new weapon was put to use; the concept of "total war" easily accommodated the terror bombing of masses of civilians; and the atomic bomb was simply one more item in an awesome arsenal that had already wreaked enormous destruction on the Axis. No responsible official counseled that the United States should accept the deaths of thousands of Americans while not using a weapon developed with 2 billion taxpayer dollars. Indeed, to the vast majority of

Americans, the atomic bomb was, in Churchill's words, "a miracle of deliverance" that shortened the war and saved lives. "I was a 21-year-old second lieutenant leading a rifle platoon," wrote one veteran later:

When the bombs dropped and news began to circulate that the invasion of Japan would not take place, that we would not be obliged to run up the beaches near Tokyo, assault-firing while being mortared and shelled, for all the fake manliness of our façades, we cried with relief and joy. We were going to live. We were going to grow up to adulthood after all.

CONCLUSION

The atomic bombs ended the deadliest war in history. More than 14 million men under arms, including more than 300,000 Americans, had died. Another 25 million civilians had perished. Much of Asia and Europe was reduced to rubble. Although the United States emerged physically unscathed, the war had had a profound impact on American life that would become starkly apparent in the postwar decades. Mobilization altered the structure of the economy; accelerated trends toward bigness in business, agriculture, and labor; and drastically enlarged the role of the military in many aspects of American life. World War II transformed the scope and authority of the federal government, especially the presidency. It catalyzed vital changes in racial and social relations. Fighting and winning the greatest war in history, moreover, was a vital coming-of-age experience for an entire generation that did much to give postwar American society a "can do" spirit.

Isolationism all but disappeared. The United States had grown too big and the world too small. By far the strongest nation in the world, the United States now played a role in global affairs that would have seemed inconceivable to most Americans just five years before. Taunting the few remaining isolationist diehards in Congress, the *New Yorker* asked them: "If you do not know that your country is now entangled beyond recall with the rest of the world, what *do* you know?" Having stopped the Nazi onslaught in Europe and the Japanese conquest of Asia, many hoped that the newly established United Nations would ensure peace. But the mass destruction of the war and the total defeat of the Axis left in their wake a new international conflict—the Cold War—whose influence would be at least as significant as that of World War II itself.

CHRONOLOGY

1939 Germany invades Poland; World War II begins.
Soviet Union invades Poland.

1940 Germany conquers the Netherlands, Belgium, France, Denmark, Norway, and Luxembourg.
Germany, Italy, and Japan sign the Tripartite Pact.
Selective Service Act.
Franklin Roosevelt elected to an unprecedented third term.

1941 Lend-Lease Act.
Roosevelt establishes the Fair Employment Practices Commission (FEPC).
Germany invades the Soviet Union.
Japan attacks Pearl Harbor; the United States enters World War II.
War Powers Act.

1942 Battle of Midway halts Japanese offensive.
Internment of Japanese-Americans.
Revenue Act expands graduated income-tax system.
Allies invade North Africa (Operation Torch).
First successful atomic chain reaction.
CORE founded.

1943 Soviet victory in Battle of Stalingrad.
Coal miners strike; Smith-Connally War Labor Disputes Act.

UNITED WE WIN

1943 Detroit race riot.
          Allied invasion of Italy.
          Big Three meet in Tehran.

1944 Allied invasion of France (Operation Overlord).
          GI Bill of Rights.
          Roosevelt wins fourth term.
          Battle of the Bulge.

1945 Big Three meet in Yalta.
          Battles of Iwo Jima and Okinawa.
          Roosevelt dies; Harry S Truman becomes president.
          Germany surrenders.
          Truman, Churchill, and Stalin meet in Potsdam.
          United States drops atomic bombs on Hiroshima and
          Nagasaki; Japan surrenders.

FOR FURTHER READING

Beth Bailey and David Farber, *The First Strange Place: The Alchemy of Race and Sex in World War II Hawaii* (1992). A wide-ranging survey of the war's impact on Hawaiian society.

John Dower, *War Without Mercy* (1986). An insightful look at racism among the Americans and the Japanese.

Patrick Heardon, *Roosevelt Confronts Hitler: American Entry into World War II* (1987). An economic interpretation of U.S. foreign policy.

Warren Kimball, *The Juggler: Franklin Roosevelt as Wartime Statesman* (1991). A study of the president's war aims and postwar vision.

Gordon W. Prange, *At Dawn We Slept: The Untold Story of Pearl Harbor* (1981). A thoroughly researched, balanced examination of the controversies surrounding the Japanese attack.

Holly Cowan Shulman, *The Voice of America* (1991). An in-depth account of America's wartime propaganda policies and programs.

David Wyman, *The Abandonment of the Jews* (1985). A critical assessment of the United States' role in the Holocaust.

ADDITIONAL BIBLIOGRAPHY

Military Operations

Stephen E. Ambrose, *The Supreme Commander: The War Years of General Dwight D. Eisenhower* (1970); Akira Iriye, *Power and Culture: The Japanese-American War, 1941–1945* (1981); John Keegan, *Six Armies in Normandy: From D-Day to the Liberation of Paris, June 6–August 25, 1944* (1982); Lee Kennett, *G.I.: The American Soldier in World War II* (1987); Gordon W. Prange, *Miracle at Midway* (1982); Michael Sherry, *The Rise of American Air Power* (1987); Ronald H. Spector, *Eagle Against the Sun: The American War with Japan* (1984); Mark A. Stoler, *The Politics of the Second Front: American Military Planning and Diplomacy in Coalition Warfare, 1941–1945* (1977).

Mobilization

Alan Clive, *State of War: Michigan in World War II* (1979); George Q. Flynn, *The Mess in Washington: Manpower Mobilization in World War II* (1979); Paul A. C. Koistinen, *The Military-Industrial Complex: A Historical Perspective* (1980); Nelson Lichtenstein, *Labor's War at Home: The CIO in World War II* (1983); Geoffrey Perrett, *Days of Sadness, Years of Triumph: The American People, 1939–1945* (1974); Bradley F. Smith, *The Shadow Warriors: The OSS and the Origins of the CIA* (1983); Peter Soderbergh, *Women Marines: The World War II Era* (1992); Allan M. Winkler, *The Politics of Propaganda: The Office of War Information, 1942–1945* (1978).

American Society

Karen Anderson, *Wartime Women: Sex Roles, Family Relations, and the Status of Women During World War II* (1981); Allan Berube, *Coming Out Under Fire: The History of Gay Men and Women in World War II* (1990); Dominic Capeci and Martha Wilkerson, *Layered Violence: The Detroit Rioters of 1943* (1991); Roger Daniels, *Prisoners Without Trial* (1993); John D'Emilio, *Sexual Politics, Sexual Communities: The Making of a Homosexual Minority in the United States* (1983); Lillian Faderman, *Odd Girls and Twilight Lovers, A History of Lesbian Life in Twentieth-Century America* (1994); Mario T. García, *Mexican-Americans: Leadership, Ideology, and Identity, 1930–1960* (1989); Bill Gilbert, *They Also Served: Baseball and the Homefront* (1992); Susan M. Hartmann, *The Home Front and Beyond: American Women in the 1940s* (1982); Maureen Honey, *Creating Rosie the Riveter: Class, Gender, and Propaganda During World War II* (1984); Peter Irons, *Justice at War: The Inside Story of the Japanese-American Internment* (1983); Walter Jackson, *Gunnar Myrdal and America's Conscience* (1990); Amy Kesselman, *Fleeting Opportunities: Women Shipyard Workers in Portland and Vancouver During World War II and Reconversion* (1990); Nicholas Lemann, *The Promised Land: The Great Black Migration and How It Changed America* (1991); Ruth Milkman, *Gender at Work: The Dynamics of Job Discrimination by Sex During World War II* (1987); Merl Reed, *Seedtime for the Modern Civil Rights Movement* (1991); Viki Ruiz, *Cannery Women, Cannery Lives: Mexican Women, Unionization, and the California Food Processing Industry* (1987); William Tuttle, Jr., *"Daddy's Gone to War": The Second World War in the Lives of America's Children* (1993); Michi Weglyn, *Years of Infamy: The Untold Story of America's Concentration Camps* (1976).

Diplomacy

John H. Backer, *The Decision to Divide Germany: American Foreign Policy in Transition* (1978); Russell D. Buhite, *Decision at Yalta* (1986); Wayne S. Cole, *Roosevelt and the Isolationists, 1932–1945* (1983); Waldo Heinrichs, Jr., *Threshold of War* (1988); James H. Madison, ed., *Wendell Wilkie: Hoosier Internationalist* (1992); Keith Sainsbury, *Churchill and Roosevelt at War* (1994); Michael Schaller, *The United States Crusade in China, 1938–1945* (1979); Michael Sherry, *Preparing for the Next War: American Plans for Postwar Defense, 1941–1945* (1977); Christopher Thorne, *Allies of a Kind: The United States, Britain and the War Against Japan, 1941–1945* (1978); Jonathan Utley, *Going to War with Japan* (1985); Donald Watt, *How War Came* (1989).

The Atomic Bomb

Gar Alperovitz, *Atomic Diplomacy: Hiroshima and Potsdam*, rev. ed. (1985); Herbert Feis, *The Atomic Bomb and the End of World War II* (1966); Gregg Herken, *The Winning Weapon: The Atomic Bomb in the Cold War, 1945–1950* (1980); J. Hershberg, *James B. Conant: Harvard to Hiroshima and the Making of the Nuclear Age* (1993); Martin Sherwin, *A World Destroyed* (1975); Leon Sigal, *Fighting to a Finish* (1988); John Ray Skates, *The Invasion of Japan, Alternative to the Bomb* (1994).

Her World
by Philip Evergood, 1948

28

COLD WAR AMERICA
1945–1952

On the day that Franklin Roosevelt died, the new president, Harry S Truman (inset), hurried to console his predecessor's widow. "Is there anything *I* can do for you?" he inquired. "Is there anything *we* can do for you?" Eleanor Roosevelt responded, "for *you* are the one in trouble now." The Truman administration, the first in a turbulent era that began with the atomic clouds over Hiroshima and Nagasaki, faced a succession of crises at home and abroad. Truman would often quip, "If you can't stand the heat, get out of the kitchen." And Truman's kitchen remained hot, as domestic discord deepened, his conflicts with Congress and the Republicans grew rancorous, and U.S.–Soviet relations crackled with nuclear tensions.

Americans hoped that the postwar era would bring, in the words of the title of MGM's academy-award-winning 1946 film about servicemen's homecoming, "the best years of our lives." Optimistic that there would not soon be another war, confident that the nation could solve any problems that arose, Americans rushed to grab a share of the good life. They married, had babies, made Dr. Benjamin Spock's child-care manual the hottest-selling title since the sales lists began in 1895, took instant pictures of their families on the first Polaroid cameras, bought cars with automatic transmissions, and moved to split-level houses in suburbs. But the peace of mind that they yearned for eluded most, for the Second World War had wrought decisive and disturbing changes in American society and in the global balance of power.

As never before, foreign developments affected American lives. The failure to secure a solution to the problem of Eastern Europe's fate sparked a confrontation in which the Soviet Union and the United States each sought to reshape the postwar world to serve its own national interests. An uncompromising Truman squared off against an obsessive Stalin. Each action by one intensified the insecurities of the other. A new form of international conflict—a Cold War—emerged, in which the two superpowers avoided a direct military clash yet used all their available resources around the globe to thwart the other's objectives.

The Cold War fundamentally changed America. Abandoning its historic aloofness from events outside the Western Hemisphere, the United States plunged into a global struggle to contain the Soviet Union and stop communism. The nation that only a few years before had had no military alliances, a small defense budget, and limited troops now built a massive military establishment, signed mutual-defense pacts with some forty countries, directly intervened in the affairs of allies and enemies alike, erected military bases on every continent, and embarked on a seemingly limitless nuclear-arms race with the Soviets. In the drive to halt the expansion of communism, the United States dispatched many thousands of Americans to fight in Korea, as their sons and younger brothers would later fight in Vietnam.

The Cold War's political and social effects proved equally decisive. The national preoccupation with the Soviet threat discredited the Left and sapped the vitality of liberalism. Focusing on the communist menace, the Truman administration did little to extend the New Deal reform agenda.

The Cold War affected the American Right as well. From the late nineteenth century through the 1930s, politically conservative Americans had deplored the growth of federal power and called for sharp limits on government. Conservatives of the Cold War era continued to hold these views on domestic social and economic issues, but when it came to military expansion, sniffing out domestic subversion and disloyalty, and leading the world fight against communism, they applauded a far-reaching expansion of government power. This ambivalence about the federal government's proper role would shape conservative ideology for decades to come.

The Cold War also stifled the free expression of ideas in America, as the anxieties of the early postwar period spawned a second "Red Scare" reminiscent of 1919. Provoked by popular fears of communist aggression abroad and of subversion from within the United States, a spate of public and private witch hunts undermined the liberties of the American people. The reckless hurling of unfounded charges of disloyalty added a new word to the American vocabulary—*McCarthyism.* Sounding an alarm of communism, McCarthyism destroyed careers, silenced criticisms of the status quo, and fueled political intolerance. It also discredited President Truman, who ironically had taken the lead in arousing American fears of communism. Renouncing Truman's leadership, the American people in 1952 turned to Dwight Eisenhower, a hero of the Second World War, to deliver the stability for which they so longed.

THE POSTWAR POLITICAL SETTING

Truman's sudden elevation to the presidency in 1945 caught both the new chief executive and the American people unprepared. Few outside his home state of Missouri or official Washington knew much about him, other than that in background and bearing he could

not have been more unlike FDR. Born in 1884, the son of a Lamar, Missouri, mule trader, Truman grew up in Independence, where he was remembered as a shy and bookish youth. After high school he worked on his grandfather's farm until America's entry into the First World War gave him the opportunity to serve overseas in the field artillery. Returning to Kansas City after the war, Truman operated a men's clothing store and dabbled in local politics. When his haberdashery business failed in 1922, he became a full-time member of the party machine run by Tom Pendergast, the Democratic "boss" of Kansas City. First as county judge, and after 1934 as a U.S. senator, Truman gained a reputation as a diligent but colorless partisan, a supporter of Franklin Roosevelt yet not a committed New Dealer. Neither experienced in world affairs nor supported by any major interest group within the Democratic party, Truman won the vice-presidential nomination on the 1944 ticket because he was a safe alternative to the liberal Henry Wallace and the southern conservative James F. Byrnes.

The very idea of this "usurper" in the White House initially dismayed liberals. "How I wish you were at the helm," the mayor of Minneapolis, Hubert H. Humphrey, wrote to Henry Wallace. Liberal displeasure mounted as the feisty Truman let it be known that he intended to rule in his own way. He replaced New Dealers in the cabinet with moderates, and he gave key executive posts to old political cronies, whom the press, recalling Warren Harding's corrupt "Ohio Gang," dubbed the "Missouri Gang." At the same time, Truman unsettled conservatives by urging Congress to adopt a twenty-one-point economic-reform program and by emphasizing his role as the champion of the common people against the special interests.

Deeply concerned for the public welfare, Truman displayed on his desk a motto of Mark Twain: "Always do right. This will gratify some people, and astonish the rest." He wanted government to do more than in the past to help the average American—but without significantly altering the existing economic and social system. "I want to keep my feet on the ground," Truman confided to an aide. "I don't want any experiments; the American people have been through a lot of experiments and they want a rest." Neither rest nor an end to experiments would mark the Truman presidency, however. Instead, aggressive Republican partisanship, a deeply divided Democratic party, and intense legislative suspicion of executive leadership would mark the political era.

Demobilization and Reconversion

As tangible proof of the war's end, most Americans wanted the 12 million men and women serving in the military "home alive in '45." Demonstrating for more transport ships to return them to the United States, American troops in Guam and Manila barraged members of Congress with threats of "no boats, no votes." In Paris and Frankfurt, thousands of GIs surged through the streets chanting "Service yes, serfdom no!" On a single day in December, more than sixty thousand postcards arrived at the White House bearing the message "Bring the Boys Home by Christmas." Truman bowed to the pressure. By mid-1946 the navy had been reduced from 4 million to 1 million, and the army from 8 to fewer than 2 million. By 1948 the American military totaled just 1.5 million.

The rapid demobilization pleased and frightened Americans. Some in Congress worried that veterans would bring back a blood lust for killing and proposed "demilitarization centers" to rehabilitate them before their release from the military. Hundreds of magazine articles focused on the readjustment problems that ex-GIs faced. The more than half a million divorces recorded in 1945 gave the United States the highest divorce rate in the world. The veterans came home, moreover, to a drastic housing shortage. In Chicago former servicemen were forced to live in coal sheds; in San Francisco they slept in automobiles.

As the GIs became civilians and war plants closed, Americans most feared the return of mass unemployment and economic depression. Following Japan's surrender, the government immediately canceled $35 billion in war contracts. Within ten days a million defense workers had lost their jobs. Defense spending plummeted from $76 billion in 1945 to less than $20 billion in 1946. Instead of the feared depression, however, an economic boom began in late 1946. U.S. economic output, which had risen from $91 billion in 1939 to $200 billion in 1946, soared to $318 billion in 1950.

The Servicemen's Readjustment Act of 1944, popularly called the GI Bill of Rights, helped to stimulate this economic growth. Under the GI Bill, 2.3 million veterans, receiving $500 a year for tuition and $50 a month for living costs, constituted half of the total college enrollment between 1945 and 1950. The more than $15 billion they received in educational benefits, medical treatment, and loans to purchase homes or farms or to start businesses aided the economic recovery. The reconversion of industry further catalyzed economic activity. Benefiting from a 1945 tax cut of almost $6 billion and the accumulation of huge wartime profits, businesses invested massively in new factories and equipment.

The United States' emergence as economic leader of the noncommunist world had been signaled in 1944 when the Allied governments met at a New Hampshire resort to hammer out the Bretton Woods Agreement. Under this treaty, foreign currencies were to be valued ("pegged") in relation to the dollar, and several important institutions were created to oversee international trade and finance: the International Monetary Fund (IMF), the General Agreement on Tariffs and Trade (GATT), and the World Bank.

The United States' favorable position in international trade and finance bolstered the idea that the postwar years marked the dawn of "the American century." Fears of a depression faded into vistas of limitless economic growth. With many nations in ruin after the war, American firms could cheaply import raw materials; and with little competition from other industrial nations, they could increase their sales of export goods to record levels. In addition, wartime advances in science and

The Postwar Housing Shortage
Would-be homeowners and contractors waited in line for as long as three days for the building permits the FHA began issuing after V-J Day.

technology, especially in electronics and synthetic materials, led to the development of new industries and radically boosted productivity in others.

Wartime savings and the pent-up demand for consumer goods further kindled postwar industrial growth and economic prosperity. The men and women who had endured the Great Depression and the Second World War yearned for the good life, and by the end of 1945, they possessed some $140 billion in bank accounts and government bonds. The rage to consume, and the widespread ability to do so, more than compensated for the decline in defense spending. Advertisements promising "a Ford in your future" and an "all-electric kitchen-of-the-future" became reality as sales of homes, furniture, cars, appliances, and clothing skyrocketed. Scores of new products—televisions, filter cigarettes, electric clothes dryers, freezers, automatic transmissions, tubeless tires, air conditioners, hi-fis—emerged as hallmarks of the middle-class lifestyle.

Truman's Troubles

Americans' hunger to enjoy the fruits of affluence left them with little appetite for an extension of New Deal reforms. The Employment Act of 1946 proved to be Truman's only major legislative accomplishment in the Seventy-ninth Congress. It committed the federal government to assuring economic growth and established the president's Council of Economic Advisers. Congress, however, gutted from the proposed bill both the goal of providing *full* employment and the broad executive authority necessary to attain that objective. Congress also blocked Truman's requests for public housing, a higher minimum wage, social-security expansion, a permanent Fair Employment Practices Commission, an anti–poll tax bill, federal aid to education, and government medical insurance.

Congressional eagerness to dismantle wartime controls, coupled with inconsistent leadership by the president, hobbled the administration's ability to deal with the major postwar economic problem: inflation. As consumer demand outran the supply of goods, the pressure on prices in the immediate postwar period grew intense. The wartime Office of Price Administration (OPA) continued to enforce price controls for a time after the end of the war, but food producers, manufacturers, and retailers opposed controls. Although many consumers favored a continuation of OPA, others disliked it as a symbol of wartime regulation. Reflecting these conflicting demands, Congress in June 1946 passed a bill that would have extended OPA's life while

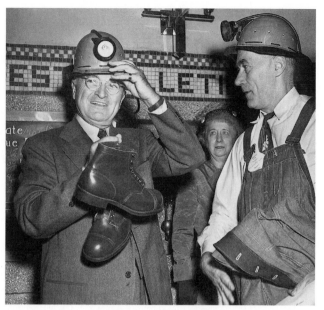

President Truman with Union Supporters
Following his veto of the Taft-Hartley bill and 1948 election victory, won, in large part, by the strong backing of organized labor, a smiling Truman dons a hard hat with copper miners in Butte, Montana.

curtailing its powers. Truman vetoed the bill, effectively ending all price controls. Within a week food costs rose more than 16 percent. The price of beef doubled. "PRICES SOAR, BUYERS SORE, STEERS JUMP OVER THE MOON" headlined the *New York Daily News*.

Now Congress passed a second bill extending price controls in weakened form, and Truman signed it. But farmers and meat producers, opposing price controls, threatened to withhold food from the market. Observing that "meatless voters are opposition voters," Truman lifted controls on food prices just before the November 1946 midterm elections. Democratic candidates fared badly anyway, and Truman soon announced the end of all price controls. By then the consumer price index had jumped nearly 25 percent since the end of the war, and food prices had risen at a far faster rate than that.

Driven by the sharp rise in prices and the shrinking paychecks that came with the end of wartime bonuses and overtime, organized labor demanded higher wages. When employers resisted, strikes tore across the postwar labor landscape: more hours were lost in work stoppages in the twelve months after V-J Day than in any previous year in all American history. In January 1946, 3 percent of the entire labor force was on strike, and more than 4.5 million men and women went on strike that year, including the powerful United Mine Workers, headed by John L. Lewis. Following forty days of closed coalfields, the president ordered government seizure of the mines, in this way forcing the miners back to work. Truman then pressured the mine owners to grant the union most of the demands that he had earlier denounced as inflationary. Six months later, Lewis called for and got another strike, and again the government took over the mines.

In the spring of 1946, railway engineers and trainmen also struck and, for the first time in the nation's history, totally shut down the railroad system. Truman exploded. "If you think I'm going to sit here and let you tie up this whole country," the president shouted at the heads of the two unions, "you're crazy as hell." Emboldened by public hostility to unions ignited by work stoppages, Truman went before Congress on May 25, 1946, to demand authority to draft workers who struck in vital industries. Only when the rail employees gave in did the Senate reject Truman's proposal. His threat alienated labor leaders, and his encouragement of inflationary wage-price agreements between powerful unions and industries forced consumers to pay the bill in the form of higher prices.

By the fall of 1946, Truman had angered most major interest groups and seemed unable to govern effectively. Less than a third of those polled approved of his performance. "To err is Truman," some gibed. One commentator suggested that the Democrats nominate Hollywood humorist W. C. Fields for president: "If we're going to have a comedian in the White House, let's have a good one." Summing up the public discontent with inflation, strikes, and shortages, the Republicans asked, "Had enough?" In the 1946 elections they captured twenty-five governorships and, for the first time since 1928, won control of Congress.

ANTICOMMUNISM AND CONTAINMENT

Compounding Truman's problems, simmering antagonisms between Moscow and Washington had come to a boil by the end of 1946. With their common enemy, Hitler, dead, the "shotgun marriage" of the Soviet Union and the United States ended in a fight for advantage in the power vacuum left by the defeat of Ger-

many and Japan, the exhaustion and bankruptcy of Western Europe, and the crumbling of colonial empires in Asia and Africa. In a postwar setting ripe for misperception and misunderstanding, the two nations each sought security and their own national interests in a manner that fed the fears of the other. Fundamental ideological differences widened the chasm between the two powers. The stage was set for a dangerous conflict.

Confrontation and Polarization

As in the closing months of the war, the destiny of Eastern Europe, especially Poland, continued to be at the heart of U.S.–Soviet contention. Ravaged twice in a quarter-century by German troops sweeping eastward across the plains of Poland, the Soviet Union wanted to ensure that it would never again be vulnerable to such invasions. Stalin insisted not only on a demilitarized and deindustrialized Germany but on a buffer of nations friendly to the Soviet Union along its western flank. The communist dictator considered such a Soviet sphere of influence in Eastern Europe essential to his country's security, a just reward for the U.S.S.R.'s bearing the brunt of the war against Germany, and no different from the American spheres of influence in Western Europe, Japan, and Latin America. Moreover, Stalin believed that a pro-Soviet zone in Eastern Europe had been implicitly accepted by Roosevelt and Churchill at Yalta.

With the 10-million-strong Red Army occupying roughly half of Europe at the end of the war, Stalin installed governments subservient to Moscow in Bulgaria, Hungary, and Romania. (Pro-Soviet revolutionary governments gained power independently of Moscow in Albania and Yugoslavia.) Disregarding the Yalta Declaration of Liberated Europe, the Soviets in 1945 barred free elections in Poland and brutally suppressed the Polish democratic parties. The Soviet Union would tolerate no government in Poland that it could not control. In Stalin's view, Poland was "not only a question of honor for Russia, but one of life and death."

Stalin's refusal to abandon dominance in Eastern Europe was matched by Truman's unwillingness to concede Soviet supremacy beyond Russia's own borders. What Stalin saw as critical to Russia's national security the Truman administration viewed as a violation of the right of nations to self-determination, a betrayal of democratic principles, and a cover for the spread of communism. Stalin's demands also violated a basic diplomatic tenet embraced by Truman and his foreign-policy advisers: that a policy of appeasement toward aggressive dictators leads not to peace but to greater violence and bloodshed. The Munich conference of 1938, at which British prime minister Neville Chamberlain had capitulated to Hitler's territorial demands and thereby helped bring on World War II, was very much in their minds as they dealt with Stalin. America needed a tough policy on Poland, advised W. Averell Harriman, the American ambassador in Moscow, since any "generous and considerate attitude" by the United States would be regarded as weakness by Soviet leaders and would result in a "barbarian invasion of Europe." Moreover, many of Truman's advisers believed that traditional balance-of-power diplomacy and the division of the world into spheres of influence had caused the two world wars. Peace, they argued, could be ensured only through a new world order based on the self-determination of all nations working in good faith within the structure of the United Nations.

Truman believed that accepting the "enforced sovietization" of Poland and Eastern Europe would betray the U.S. war aims. Both the Atlantic Charter and the Yalta declaration had pledged self-government through free and open elections to the people of war-torn Europe. The president did not want the nations rescued from Hitler's tyranny to fall under the sway of another totalitarian dictatorship. Too, Truman worried that a Soviet stranglehold in Eastern Europe would imperil the American economy, whose health, he believed, depended on export outlets and on access to raw materials in the countries that Stalin appeared determined to control solely for Soviet economic betterment.

Domestic political considerations further shaped the Truman administration's response to Stalin. As had Roosevelt, Truman fully understood the political importance of the overwhelmingly Democratic 6 million Polish-Americans as well as of the millions of other Americans of Eastern European origin. Because these peoples retained a keen interest in the fates of their homelands, the Democratic party would face disaster, Truman realized, if the administration reneged on the Yalta accords. The president also recognized the political strength of anticommunism in American politics and knew that any appearance of administration support for the Soviet control of Eastern Europe would give his conservative opponents an enormous advantage. Many Republicans had already grumbled about Roosevelt's concessions to the Soviets at Yalta, and the new president was determined not to appear "soft" on communism.

A combative posture fit the temperament of the feisty Truman. Eager to show his foes that he was in command, the president matched Stalin's intransigence on Polish elections with his own demands for self-determination and the reorganization of Poland's government along democratic lines. Emboldened by America's monopoly of atomic bombs and its undisputed position as the world's economic superpower, the president hoped that the United States could control the terms of postwar settlements.

The Cold War Begins

Truman's assertiveness inflamed Stalin's compulsive mistrust of the West and deepened the Soviets' obsession with their own security. Stalin both stepped up his confiscation of materials and factories from occupied territories and forced his Eastern European satellites to close their doors to Anglo-American trade and influence. In early February 1946, warning that there could be no lasting peace with capitalism, Stalin proclaimed new plans to overcome the American edge in weapons technology.

Two weeks later, a sixteen-page telegram from George F. Kennan, the American chargé d'affaires in Moscow, arrived in Washington. A leading student of Soviet politics, Kennan, who had been stationed in the U.S.S.R. since the 1930s, warned that the Soviet Union was "a political force committed fanatically to the belief" that there could be no permanent peace with the United States, and that the only answer was "a long-term, patient but firm and vigilant containment of Russian expansive tendencies." The idea that only strong, sustained U.S. resistance could "contain" Soviet expansionism suited the mood of Truman, who a month earlier had insisted that the time had come "to stop babying the Soviets" and "to get tough with Russia." It also suited the mood of the many in the government who wanted "no compromise" with the communists, and "containment" soon became Washington gospel. On February 27 Senator Arthur Vandenberg of Michigan, the top-ranking Republican on the Senate Foreign Relations Committee, condemned Soviet actions in Europe and Asia and demanded that the United States "draw the line" with Moscow. The next day Secretary of State James F. Byrnes, who had been trying to negotiate an accommodation with the Soviet Union, so echoed the senator's call for a hard line that the press dubbed his speech "the Second Vandenberg Concerto."

A Cold War Confection
Celebrating the first public American atom-bomb tests, conducted on the Bikini Atoll in 1946, navy admirals Blandy and Lowery, assisted by Mrs. Blandy, slice an "atomic cake" in the Pentagon.

A week later, Truman accompanied Winston Churchill to Westminster College in Missouri, where the former British prime minister delivered a speech warning of a new threat to the democracies, this time from Moscow. Stalin, Churchill intoned, had drawn an iron curtain across the eastern half of Europe. "This is certainly not the liberated Europe we fought for," he exclaimed, calling for an alliance of the English-speaking peoples against the Soviet Union. "[T]here is nothing they admire so much as strength," he argued, "and nothing for which they have less respect than for military weakness."

Truman in the spring of 1946 shifted his foreign policy in the direction prescribed by Kennan and Churchill. To force Stalin to keep an earlier promise to withdraw Soviet soldiers from the north of oil-rich Iran, Truman dispatched part of the Sixth Fleet to the Black Sea and threatened to send in American combat troops. Then in June, the president submitted an atomic-energy control plan to the United Nations, requiring the Soviet Union to cease all work on atomic weaponry and to submit to a comprehensive system of control and inspection by a U.N. agency. Only then, the

administration's plan specified, would the United States destroy its own atomic arsenal. As expected, the Soviets rejected the American proposal and offered an alternative plan equally unacceptable to the United States. With mutual hostility escalating, the Soviets and Americans rushed to develop their own doomsday weapons. In 1946 Congress passed the Atomic Energy Act, which established the Atomic Energy Commission (AEC) to control nuclear development and declared that the utilization of fissionable materials should be for civilian purposes "so far as practicable." From the outset, however, at least 90 percent of the AEC's effort focused on military weapons.

Thus, less than a year after American and Soviet soldiers had jubilantly joined hands at the Elbe River to celebrate Nazism's defeat, the U.S.–Soviet peace had been lost. The Cold War had begun. This conflict between the two superpowers and their allies would be waged largely by economic pressure, nuclear intimidation, propaganda, and subversion rather than by direct U.S.–Soviet military confrontation. It would nevertheless affect American life as decisively as any military engagement that the nation had ever fought.

European Crisis, American Commitment

A formal proclamation of America's commitment to contain the Soviet sphere of influence came in early 1947. On February 21 the British informed the United States that they could no longer afford to keep up their assistance to the governments of Greece and Turkey in their respective struggles against a communist-supplied insurgent guerrilla movement and against Soviet pressure for access to the Mediterranean. With more than half its industrial plants idled by a lack of fuel, a stricken Britain asked the United States to bear the costs of thwarting communism in the eastern Mediterranean. The harsh European winter, the most severe in memory, intensified the sense of urgency in Washington. The economies of Western Europe had come to a standstill. Famine and tuberculosis plagued the Continent. European nations' colonies in Africa and Asia were in revolt. Cigarettes and candy bars circulated as currency in Germany, and the communist parties in France and Italy appeared on the verge of toppling the precarious democratic coalition governments. Truman resolved to meet the challenge.

The president's first task was to mobilize support for a major departure from America's powerful tradition of no entangling alliances. In a tense meeting at

**American Food for
a Hungry Europe**
*Grateful English mothers
line up for orange juice sent
by the United States to assist
Europeans devastated by the
Second World War.*

the White House on February 27, Truman's new secretary of state, former army chief of staff George C. Marshall, presented the case for providing massive aid to Greece and Turkey. More concerned about inflation at home than about a civil war in Greece, however, most of the assembled members of Congress balked. Then Dean Acheson seized the moment. The newly installed undersecretary of state defined the issue not as one of assisting the Greek oligarchy and the Turkish military regime but rather as a universal struggle of freedom against tyranny. "Like apples in a barrel infected by the corruption of one rotten one," he warned, the fall of Greece or Turkey would open Asia, Western Europe, and the oil fields of the Middle East to the Red menace. "The Soviet Union [is] playing one of the greatest gambles in history," Acheson concluded. "We and we alone are in a position to break up that play." Shaken, the congressional leaders agreed to support the administration's request if the president could "scare hell out of the country."

Truman could and did. On March 12, 1947, in an address to a joint session of Congress, the president requested military assistance to Greece and Turkey. He starkly portrayed the struggles there as a conflict between liberty and oppression, and declared that the United States must support free peoples everywhere

"resisting attempted subjugation by armed minorities or by outside pressures." If we fail to act now, the president concluded, "we may endanger the peace of the world—and we shall surely endanger the welfare of our own nation." Called the Truman Doctrine—and meant to be as comprehensive as the Monroe Doctrine's "Keep Out" sign posted on the Western Hemisphere—the president's declaration committed the United States in theory to the role of global policeman. Endorsed by the Republican-controlled Congress in its mid-May vote in favor of aid to Greece and Turkey, the Truman Doctrine laid the foundation for American Cold War policy for much of the next four decades.

A month later, the administration proposed massive American assistance for European recovery. The resulting program was called the Marshall Plan after the secretary of state, who had earlier advocated such aid in a Harvard commencement address. Truman envisioned the Marshall Plan as another weapon in the American arsenal against the spread of communism. With food in Western Europe scarce, the president wanted to end the economic devastation that could readily be exploited by communists. Although the Marshall Plan was ostensibly an effort to help the hungry and homeless of *all* the European countries, Truman correctly calculated that Russia and its communist

The Postwar Division of Europe

The wartime dispute between the Soviet Union and the Western Allies over Poland's future hardened after World War II into a Cold War that split Europe into competing American and Russian spheres of influence. Across an "iron curtain," NATO countries faced the Warsaw Pact nations

allies would reject American economic assistance because of the conditions and controls linked to the aid. The administration also accurately predicted that economic recovery in Western Europe would expand sales of American goods abroad and thus promote prosperity in the United States. Although denounced by the Left as a "Martial Plan" and by isolationist voices on the Right as a "Share-the-American-Wealth Plan," the Marshall Plan fulfilled its sponsors' hopes. Congress appropriated $17 billion for economic recovery in sixteen nations over a five-year period. By 1952 the economic and social chaos thought to provide a seedbed for communism had been overcome in those nations. Western Europe revived, prospered, and achieved an unprecedented unity, and U.S. business, not incidentally, boomed.

Confrontation

While the United States implemented the Truman Doctrine and the Marshall Plan, the Soviet Union tightened its grip on Moscow-backed Eastern European governments in Poland, Bulgaria, Albania, and Romania. In 1947–1948 communist takeovers added Hungary and Czechoslovakia to the Soviet sphere. Stalin then sought to abort the prospect of a reborn Germany. The 1945 Potsdam Agreement had divided Germany into four separate zones (administered by France, Great Britain, the Soviet Union, and the United States) and had created a joint four-power administration for Germany's capital, Berlin, lying 110 miles within the Soviet-occupied eastern zone. As the Cold War unfolded, however, the West began to view a revived Germany as a buffer against the Soviet-controlled East. The Western powers gradually united their zones, and Stalin responded in April 1948 by impeding the flow of supplies and people from the west of Germany into Berlin. To thwart the creation of a new anticommunist German nation (which would also include West Berlin), the Russians in June blocked all rail and highway routes through the Soviet zone into Berlin. Stalin calculated that the Western powers, obstructed from provisioning the 2 million pro-Western Berliners under their control in the non-Russian sector of the city, would either have to abandon any plans to create an independent West Germany or withdraw and accept a communist Berlin.

Truman resolved neither to abandon Berlin to the Soviets nor to shoot his way into the city and possibly set off World War III. Instead he ordered a massive airlift to provide Berliners with the thousands of tons of food and fuel necessary for their survival. "We are going to stay, period," the president declared to end a cabinet discussion on the matter. American cargo planes were soon landing at West Berlin's Templehof Airport almost every three minutes around the clock, bringing a mountain of supplies each day. To prevent the Soviets from shooting down the defenseless planes, Truman ordered a fleet of B-29s, the only planes capable of delivering atomic bombs, to bases in England in July 1948. Truman hinted that he would use "the bomb" if necessary. Tensions rose. The president confided in his diary that "we are very close to war." Meanwhile, for nearly a year, "Operation Vittles," as the Berlin airlift was called, provided the blockaded city with a precarious lifeline.

In May 1949 the Soviets suddenly ended the blockade. Stalin's gambit had failed. The airlift highlighted America's determination and technological prowess, revealed Stalin's stubborn willingness to use innocent citizens as pawns in pursuit of his goals, and drastically intensified anti-Soviet feelings in the West. Public-opinion polls in the United States in late 1948 revealed an almost unanimous belief that "Russia is an aggressive, expansion-minded nation" and an overwhelming demand for "firmness and increased 'toughness' in relations with Russia."

The continuing fear of a Soviet assault on Western Europe fostered support for a revitalized West German state and for an Atlantic collective security alliance. In May 1949 the United States, Britain, and France ended their occupation of Germany and approved the creation of the Federal Republic of Germany (West Germany). A month earlier, ten nations of Western Europe had adopted the North Atlantic Treaty establishing a military alliance with the United States and Canada and declaring that an attack on any member of the alliance would be considered an attack against all. For the first time in its history, the United States had entered into a peacetime military alliance. Support for the treaty was not unanimous, however. Senator Robert Taft of Ohio, speaking for a small band of Republican senators, warned that such an agreement would provoke the Soviets to respond in kind, stimulate a massive arms race, and open the floodgates of American military aid to Europe. But the Senate overwhelmingly approved the treaty, and in July the United States officially joined the North Atlantic Treaty Organization (NATO), marking the formal end of U.S. isolationism.

Two days after the Senate ratification, Truman asked Congress to authorize $1.3 billion for military assistance to NATO nations. To underscore his determination to contain communism, especially after the outbreak of the Korean War in June 1950 (see below), the president persuaded General Dwight D. Eisenhower to become the supreme commander of the new mutual defense force and authorized the stationing of four American army divisions in Europe as the nucleus of the NATO armed force. The Soviet Union responded by creating the German Democratic Republic (East Germany) in 1949, by exploding its own atomic bomb that same year, and by setting up a rival Eastern bloc military alliance, the Warsaw Pact, in 1955. A mere decade after the Second World War, the United States and the Soviet Union had divided Europe into two armed camps.

The Cold War in Asia

Moscow-Washington hostility similarly led to the division of Asia into contending military and economic camps. The Soviets carved out a sphere of influence in Manchuria, the United States denied the U.S.S.R. any role in the postwar military occupation of Japan, and the two superpowers partitioned a helpless Korea.

As the head of the U.S. occupation forces ruling Japan after the war, General Douglas MacArthur oversaw the country's transformation into a prosperous democracy. With the end of the occupation in 1952, the Mutual Security Treaty between the two countries allowed the United States to retain its military bases and troops in Japan, near the Soviet Union's Asian rim. Effectively a U.S. military protectorate, Japan welcomed the security provided by the American nuclear umbrella, which allowed the Japanese to devote almost all their resources to economic development;

and the United States had gained a staunch anticommunist ally in the Pacific. Other efforts by the Truman administration to contain communism in Asia as well as in Europe included aiding the newly independent Philippine government in crushing a leftist Huk guerrilla movement, and assisting the French to reestablish their colonial rule in Indochina (the region of Southeast Asia comprising Cambodia, Laos, and Vietnam), despite American declarations in favor of national self-determination and in opposition to imperialism.

In China, however, U.S. efforts to stop the triumph of communism failed. The Truman administration initially tried to mediate the civil war raging in China between the Guomindang (Koumintang), or Nationalist, regime of Jiang Jieshi (Chiang Kai-shek) and the communist armies led by Mao Zedong (Mao Tse-tung). But U.S. opposition to a communist victory in China led the administration to escalate its assistance to Jiang's eroding forces. The United States sent nearly $3 billion in aid to the Nationalists between 1945 and 1949. American dollars, however, could not force the inefficient Guomindang government to reform itself and to win the support of the Chinese people. Jiang had alienated both peasants, by suppressing agrarian reform, and city dwellers, at whose expense he had profiteered. His armies, moreover, suffered from poor morale. As Mao's well-disciplined and motivated forces marched south, Jiang's soldiers mutinied and surrendered without a fight. Jiang's armies "did not have to be defeated," said Dean Acheson; "they disintegrated." Unable to stem the growth of revolutionary sentiment or to hold the countryside—where the communists, in Mao's words, "swam like fishes in the peasant sea"—Jiang's regime collapsed. By the end of 1949, he had fled to an exile government on the island of Taiwan (Formosa).

Americans reacted with shock to Mao's establishment of the communist People's Republic of China. The most populous nation in the world, looked to as a counterforce to communism in Asia and a major market for American trade, had become "Red China." John Foster Dulles, a major Republican authority on foreign policy, called the communization of China "the worst defeat the United States has suffered in its history." Denying that it could have done more to alter the outcome of the civil war, the Truman administration faulted Jiang's failure to achieve the reforms necessary to hold the Chinese people's loyalty. But the government's explanation failed to persuade most Americans. The fall of China to communism particularly embittered conservatives who had long believed that America's future lay in Asia rather than Europe. In particular, many on the Right blamed "pro-Communists in the State Department" for Jiang's failure.

As the China debate raged, the president announced in September 1949 that the Soviet Union had successfully exploded an atomic bomb. In an instant the world had changed (see "A Place in Time"). The loss of the U.S. nuclear monopoly shattered illusions of American invincibility. Taken together with the news of Mao's victory, the reports of Moscow's atomic capability spawned anticommunist hysteria in the United States and led to irrational searches for scapegoats and subversives to explain American setbacks in world affairs.

A reeling Truman administration began a major reassessment of its Cold War strategy. Stung by Republican charges that he was soft on communism, the president decisively ended the dispute among his scientific advisers in January 1950 by ordering the Atomic Energy Commission to mount an all-out effort to develop a fusion-based hydrogen bomb (H-bomb)—one with power measured in millions of tons of TNT rather than in thousands of tons like the existing A-bombs. Edward Teller, a Hungarian-born physicist who had worked on the Manhattan Project, had long argued for a fusion bomb, in which explosive power is created by forcing hydrogen atoms together. But leading scientists in America's nuclear establishment, led by J. Robert Oppenheimer and Harvard University president James B. Conant, had rejected Teller's proposed weapon as too complex to construct and too immorally destructive to use. Given the fearful mood in Washington early in 1950, however, Truman quickly accepted the report of his secretaries of defense and state recommending a crash thermonuclear program. In November 1952 the United States exploded its first H-bomb in the Marshall Islands, projecting a radioactive cloud twenty-five miles into the stratosphere and blasting a canyon a mile long and 175 feet deep in the ocean floor. Nine months later the Russians also detonated a hydrogen bomb. The balance of thermonuclear terror escalated.

Early in 1950 Truman had also established a blue-ribbon committee of State and Defense Department officials to conduct a top-secret review of national defense policy. They devised NSC-68, a report emphasizing the Soviet Union's aggressive intentions and military strength. To counter what the report termed the U.S.S.R.'s "design for world domination"—the mortal challenge posed by the Soviet Union "not only to this Republic but to civilization itself"—NSC-68 called for a massive U.S. military buildup. The report advocated a

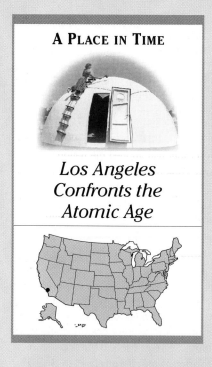

Los Angeles Confronts the Atomic Age

Early in January 1951, a Los Angeles construction company staged a major ground-breaking ceremony for the television cameras to promote its backyard family atomic-bomb shelters. As Hollywood stars applauded, Mrs. Ruth Calhoun, mother of three, smilingly dug the first spadeful of dirt. For $1,995 she had bought an underground cubicle at the edge of her patio that would include green plastic carpeting, beige-painted concrete walls, and even a lightweight Geiger counter to test for radioactivity. "I do a lot of canning and bottling in the summer," Mrs. Calhoun explained to reporters, "and it will make a good storehouse." She added, "It will make a wonderful place for the children to play in, too."

California Bomb Shelter Under Construction, 1951
The manufacturer stocked this model with water, oxygen, and shovels.

Despite the reassuring tone of the ceremony, atmospheric nuclear testing and the possibility of nuclear war troubled Americans. Tales of the dire effects of radioactivity and images of mushroom-shaped clouds became part of American popular culture. Country-music lyrics warned of "peace in the world, or the world in pieces." Radio programs offered chilling descriptions of the atomic destruction of American cities. An NBC broadcast on the hypothetical bombing of Chicago exclaimed,

Most of those in the center of the city were violently killed by the blast or by the following vacuum which explosively burst their stomachs and intestines, and violently ruptured their tissue. Those few who escaped the blast, but not the gamma rays, died slowly but inevitably after they had left the ruined city.

Similarly graphic portrayals of people vaporized in a nuclear flash and the earth incinerated in a giant atomic fireball appeared in Ray Bradbury's 1950 science-fiction best seller *The Martian Chronicles*. Book titles by eminent scientists trumpeted *There Is No Defense*, and the 1949 best-seller *No Place to Hide* (offered by the Book-of-the-Month Club and condensed by the *Reader's Digest*) warned grimly of the horrifying effects of radioactivity.

In September 1949 the White House had stunned the American people with a terse announcement that the Soviet Union had successfully detonated an atomic explosion: the United States had lost its nuclear monopoly. When Soviet-supplied North Korean troops invaded South Korea in June 1950, apprehensive Americans sought security in renewed nuclear superiority, and safety in civil defense.

In 1950 the president created the Federal Civil Defense Administration (FCDA). The agency flooded the country with booklets, movies, and exhibits stressing that surviving an atomic war was possible through preparedness. It urged women to "never go out bare-legged" and cautioned men to wear wide-brimmed hats for protection against the "heat flash" of a nuclear attack. Public schools held atomic-air-raid drills and frequently showed the civil-defense film in which Bert the Turtle taught children to "duck and cover." To identify bodies in the event of a nuclear attack, New York City and San Francisco issued free metal identification tags, modeled after military dog tags, to all schoolchildren. Philadelphia sold them in local stores. Four million Americans volunteered to be Sky Watchers, scanning the shorelines and rooftops for Soviet planes; and millions more marked the numbers 640 and 1240 on their radio dials, where they could find communications in an atomic attack. Major corporations invested in underground facilities to safeguard their company records. Real-estate advertisements offered "good bomb immunity" in secluded parts of the country. Clever entrepreneurs found a market for aluminum pajamas and lead-foil brassieres, and California governor Earl Warren urged citizens to build family shelters.

Like Ruth Calhoun, many other Los Angeles residents in 1951 purchased or constructed bomb shelters, ranging from wood-covered dirt holes to septic tanks that could be converted into six-person shelters to multithousand-dollar refuges outfitted with radio and telephone. For three thousand dollars, Sam Markell bought a "Kidde Kokoon." It came equipped with all that his family of five desired for a three-to-five-day underground stay, including a chemical toilet, nonelectric clock, canned food and water, protective apparel, and pick-and-shovel tool ("for digging out after the blast"). To reduce his family's anxieties, Ronald Bates enlarged his backyard barbecue pit into a bomb shelter and stocked it with board games

The Kidde Kokoon

The Kidde Kokoon's exterior hatch and interior living quarters are shown.

and puzzles as well as first-aid kits and other emergency supplies. Those who could not afford shelters learned the FCDA's "survival secrets" ("jump in any handy ditch or gutter . . . drop flat on the ground . . . bury your face in your arms . . . never lose your head").

The cease-fire in Korea in 1953 diminished the dread of imminent nuclear disaster that had gripped the nation. Resigned to living with the threat of nuclear destruction, Americans now laughed as Doris Day sang "Tic, Tic, Tic," poking fun at the dangers of radioactivity, and satirist Tom Lehrer in "The Wild West Is Where I Want to Be" sang of wearing lead BVDs at the Nevada test site contaminated by radioactive fallout. Yet the fears remained. In 1954, two-thirds of those polled expected that hydrogen bombs would be used against the United States in a world war; later that year, *Time* reported that "talk and worry over the H-bomb's radioactive 'fall-out' is spreading." Soon more than a million families had their own bomb shelters.

large standing army and the quadrupling of defense expenditures to wage a global struggle against communism. The National Security Council, organized in 1947 to advise the president on all matters concerning America's preparedness, approved NSC-68 in principle in April. But Truman hesitated to swallow his advisers' expensive prescription. An aide to Secretary of State Acheson recalled, "We were sweating over it, and then, with regard to NSC-68, thank God Korea came along." By the end of 1950, Truman had ordered the implementation of NSC-68 and more than tripled the defense budget.

The Korean War

On June 24, 1950, as Truman pondered the implications of NSC-68, North Korean troops swept across the thirty-eighth parallel and invaded the Republic of Korea (South Korea). Following Japan's defeat in 1945, the Korean peninsula, previously part of the Japanese Empire, had been temporarily divided at the thirty-eighth parallel for the purpose of military occupation by Soviet and U.S. troops. This dividing line had solidified into a political frontier between the Soviet-backed People's Democratic Republic in North Korea and the American-supported Republic of Korea. Each sector of the Korean peninsula, nevertheless, had continued to hope that Korea would soon be a unified nation governed by its own regime.

North Korea's move seemed to Truman more a case of Soviet-directed aggression than an internal Korean matter. Despite conflicting evidence of Stalin's role, Truman never doubted that Stalin saw Korea as a test of the containment policy and U.S. will.

"Korea is the Greece of the Far East," the president explained shortly after receiving the news of the invasion. "If we are tough enough now, if we stand up to them like we did in Greece three years ago, they won't take any next steps. But if we just stand by, they'll move into Iran and they'll take over the whole Middle East." Ever mindful of the failure of appeasement at Munich, Truman announced that "if aggression is successful in Korea, we can expect it to spread through Asia and Europe to this hemisphere." Failure to act would embolden the communists and lead to an even bloodier "third world war, just as similar incidents had brought on the second world war." Politically, moreover, Truman had to prove to Republican critics that the Democrats would stand up to "the Reds" and not allow another country to "fall" to the communists.

The president decided to intervene. Without consulting Congress or asking for a formal declaration of war, Truman quickly secured the United Nations'

U.S. Marines Battling for Seoul, September 1950
From the start Truman believed that the Soviet Union had orchestrated the North Korean invasion of South Korea. He steadfastly maintained that "if the Russian totalitarian state was intending to follow in the path of the dictatorship of Hitler and Mussolini, they [had to] be met head on in Korea."

sanction for a common "police action" against the aggressor. (Because the Soviet Union was then boycotting the Security Council, to protest the U.N.'s failure to seat Mao Zedong's Chinese government in place of the exiled Jiang Jieshi regime in Taiwan, it could not utilize its veto.) On June 27 Truman ordered American air and sea forces to the aid of the South Koreans and appointed seventy-year-old General Douglas MacArthur to command the U.N. effort in Korea. Although the intervention was officially a U.N. "police action," most of the naval and air support and nearly half the troops fighting under the U.N. flag came from the United States; South Korea supplied some 43 percent of the forces, and fourteen other nations contributed fewer than 10 percent of the U.N. troops.

The North Koreans rapidly pushed the U.N. forces back to the southeastern tip of the peninsula. Then in a brilliant amphibious maneuver on September 15, MacArthur's troops landed at Inchon, a port city near Seoul, and forced the North Koreans to retreat across the thirty-eighth parallel. Heartened by this success, the Truman administration on September 27 permitted MacArthur to order the U.N. armies across the thirty-eighth parallel and toward the Yalu River, the boundary between North Korea and China. The police action to restore the original border between the two Koreas now became a war of liberation to create "a unified, independent, and democratic" single nation of Korea.

As MacArthur's troops neared the Yalu River, Mao Zedong warned that China would not "stand idly by" if its border were threatened. Ignoring Mao's admonition, an overconfident MacArthur deployed the U.N. forces in a thin line below the river. On November 25 thirty-three Chinese divisions (about 300,000 men) counterattacked. Within two weeks they had driven MacArthur's stunned troops below the thirty-eighth parallel. By March 1951 the fighting had stabilized at roughly the original border between North Korea and South Korea.

Truman again reversed course and in the spring of 1951 sought a negotiated peace based on the original objective of reestablishing the integrity of South Korea. But MacArthur rocked the boat. He urged that he be allowed to bomb and blockade China, to "unleash" Jiang Jieshi's troops against the communist regime, and to seek total victory even at the risk of an all-out war with China. Truman rejected such proposals: "We are trying to prevent a world war—not to start one." He further worried that the Soviet Union would take

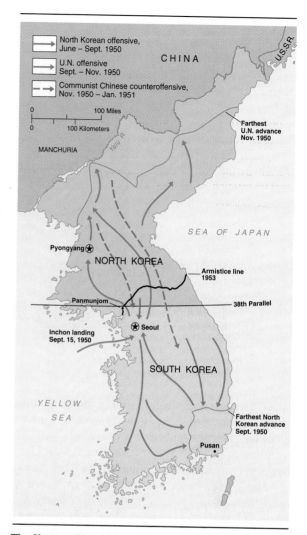

The Korean War, 1950–1953
The experience of fighting an undeclared and limited war for the limited objective of containing communism confused the generation of Americans who had just fought an all-out war for the total defeat of the Axis. General MacArthur spoke for the many who were frustrated by the Korean conflict's mounting costs in blood and dollars: "There is no substitute for victory."

advantage of American involvement in a major war on the Asian mainland to pursue an aggressive course in Europe. Therefore, the conflict remained a limited war for a limited objective—to hold the line in Korea. But MacArthur had no stomach for stalemate, "In war," he declared, "there is no substitute for victory," and he persisted in publicly criticizing administration policy.

General MacArthur in Korea
Opposing President Truman's 1951 efforts to negotiate a settlement, MacArthur publicly called for the bombing and blockade of China.

When his open opposition to the president's conduct of the war hindered White House progress toward negotiation, the president relieved MacArthur of command on April 10, 1951, provoking a dramatic clash between civil and military authority.

MacArthur's public insubordination amounted to a direct attack upon civilian control of the military. But public opinion backed the general; only 29 percent of those polled in May 1951 favored the president's strategy of limited war. Most Americans were baffled by Truman's objective of containing rather than defeating the enemy and were angered by the steady toll of U.S. casualties. An increasing number began to listen sympathetically to Republican criticisms of the president, such as Indiana senator William Jenner's charge that "this country today is in the hands of a secret coterie which is directed by agents of the Soviet Union."

In July 1951 truce talks began in Korea, but they dragged on for two years as both sides fought a restricted yet deadly war. By the time the wrangling over prisoner repatriation and the location of the cease-fire line finally ended on July 26, 1953, this "limited" war had cost the United States 54,246 American lives, another 103,284 wounded and missing, and some $54 billion. The conflict in Korea also speeded up the implementation of NSC-68 and the transformation of containment into a general global policy. Between

1950 and 1953, defense expenditures zoomed from 5 percent to 13 percent of the gross national product, from one-third to two-thirds of the entire federal budget. In these years the United States also acquired new bases around the world, committed itself to rearm West Germany, and joined a mutual-defense pact with Australia and New Zealand. Increased military aid flowed to Jiang Jieshi's forces on Taiwan, and American military assistance was extended to the French army fighting the communist Ho Chi Minh in Indochina. With the United States now supporting any and all perceived enemies of communism, the State Department declared the French struggle against the guerrillas of the Vietminh (the league for Vietnamese independence) "an integral part of the worldwide resistance by the Free Nations to communist attempts at conquest." By 1954 the United States would be paying three-quarters of the French war costs in Vietnam.

Truman's intervention in Korea preserved a precarious balance of power in one arena of Cold War conflict, by preventing the South Korean regime from falling to its rival in the north. The president's action underscored the administration's commitment to the anticommunist struggle as well as the shift of that struggle's focus from Europe to Asia. George Kennan's containment doctrine, originally advanced to justify U.S. aid to Greece and Turkey, served in the early 1950s as the ideological foundation for a major war in Korea and, more ominously, for a deepening U.S. involvement with France's colonial war in Vietnam. Furthermore, by committing U.S. troops to battle with neither a declaration of war nor congressional approval, Truman set precedents for future undeclared wars, further expanded presidential powers, and helped to institutionalize the "warfare" state. The inconclusive outcome in Korea, moreover, combined with the shock over China's fall to stir deep frustrations and renew hatred of communism among Americans. The chain of unsettling developments would have broad political and cultural consequences in the 1950s and beyond.

THE TRUMAN ADMINISTRATION AT HOME

When Japan surrendered in 1945, Americans most wanted to bring the boys home and enjoy the peace. Since the crash of 1929, the nation had known little but the privations of depression and the sufferings and shortages of war. Now it was time to forget the past and again enjoy life! Widespread postwar affluence gave substance to these dreams. By 1953 the average U.S. family enjoyed twice as much real income as in the go-go 1920s. Americans flocked to suburbia, launched a baby boom of howling proportions, and borrowed or saved to purchase the stoves, refrigerators, and new cars that had long been out of reach or unavailable. Sales of TV sets soared from fewer than 7,000 in 1946 to over 7 million by 1949; by 1953 half of all U.S. homes had at least one television.

Not all Americans shared equally in the good times. Poverty remained a stark fact of life for millions in the cities and on farms. Black Americans, who had loyally supported the war and in many cases fought on foreign battlefields, felt special bitterness as they experienced once again the grim reality of racism at home. Many refused to acquiesce, and this early postwar period saw the emergence of a civil-rights movement that in a few years would sweep the nation.

But with the coming of peace, most Americans turned away from public issues and preoccupied themselves with career and family. The New Deal's achievement remained a proud memory, but the reform energies responsible for those achievements subsided into complacency.

The spirit of the times was not ref[...] conservative trend in Congress suppo[...] of the power of both the federal g[...] groups such as organized labor tha[...] prominence in the 1930s. In additio[...] obsessions among the American people sharpened a tendency to associate radicalism with disloyalty, and undercut liberal efforts to alter the status quo. The popular mood meshed with the administration's own priorities, especially after 1949, to use federal expenditures primarily for rearmament, not for social welfare. Anticommunism came first, not reform.

The Eightieth Congress

The Republicans of the Eightieth Congress, which convened in January 1947, interpreted the 1946 elections as a mandate to reverse the New Deal. As "Mr. Republican," Senator Robert A. Taft of Ohio declared, "We have got to break with the corrupting idea that we can legislate prosperity, legislate equality, legislate opportunity." The Republican-controlled Congress passed tax measures favorable to the rich and defeated proposals to raise the minimum wage and to provide federal funds for education and housing. The chief battleground between the president and conservatives, however, was the New Deal's pro-union Wagner Act of 1935 (see Chapter 25).

The rash of postwar strikes had created a national consensus—fostered by frequent media depictions of union leaders as labor barons, goons, and Reds—for curbing the unions' power. In 1947 more than twenty states passed laws to restrict union activities, and Congress followed suit with the Labor-Management Relations Act, better known as the Taft-Hartley Act. The new law modified the Wagner Act by outlawing such union practices as the closed shop and by permitting the president to call an eighty-day cooling-off period to delay any strike that might endanger national safety or health. Although the act increased the difficulty of organizing non-unionized workers, it hardly became the "slave labor bill" that the union leadership had predicted. Still, the rank and file protested the act, and labor leaders demanded that Truman veto it.

With an eye on the upcoming 1948 election, Truman vetoed the measure. Congress easily overrode the veto, but Truman had taken his first major step toward gaining organized labor's endorsement for the election. He needed that support, and a lot more. Neither widely admired nor especially liked, Truman realized that his only hope in 1948 rested on his success in forging FDR's New Deal coalition. He counted on the solid South to stay Democratic; courted the midwestern farm belt; and devoted most of his effort to winning the metropolitan areas, appealing particularly to laborers, liberals, ethnic Catholics, Jews, and African-Americans. Like Franklin D. Roosevelt in the 1930s, Truman proposed one liberal reform bill after another to the Eightieth Congress. He urged legislators to extend the New Deal concept to education, housing, and health insurance, to repeal the Taft-Hartley Act, and to raise price supports for farmers. At the same time, Truman courted voters of Eastern European ancestry by emphasizing his opposition to Soviet communism. And, overriding the objections of the State Department, which feared losing support in the Arab world—home to the world's richest petroleum resources—the president extended diplomatic recognition to the new state of Israel immediately after it proclaimed independence on May 14, 1948. Deeply sympathetic toward the Jewish survivors of the Holocaust who had immigrated to Israel, Truman also understood the strategic importance of Jewish-American voters.

Fun, Forties-Style

After the war Americans grabbed for the good life, whether that meant enjoying a thrill-inducing ride at Coney Island, planning a family vacation, or jiving to a jukebox.

The Politics of Civil Rights

Much like FDR, President Truman wanted the support of southern white Democrats and initially hesitated to get involved in racial issues. But the growing civil-rights movement, and the violence if provoked, demanded a White House response.

Many African-Americans, but especially those who had served in the armed forces, demanded the right to vote after the war. In 1945 and 1946, various African-American civil-rights groups conducted voter-registration drives, raising the number of blacks registered to vote in the South to 12 percent in 1947, up from a mere 2 percent in 1940. The majority of southern blacks, however, still risked intimidation, repression, and even murder in pursuing their constitutional right to vote. Leading white-supremacist politicians, among them Georgia governor Eugene Talmadge and Mississippi senator Theodore G. Bilbo, urged their followers to resort to any means to keep blacks from voting.

Fearful of blacks' assertiveness in seeking the vote, of their increasing refusal to move aside or doff their caps when white men approached, and of other signs of a bold new spirit among African-Americans, some southern whites brutally asserted their dominance. In 1946 whites killed several black war veterans in rural Georgia who had voted that year, flogged to death an "uppity" black tenant farmer in Mississippi, blow-torched a young black in Louisiana for daring to enter a white woman's house, and blinded a black soldier for failing to sit in the rear of a bus in South Carolina. In Columbia, Tennessee, in 1946, whites rioted against blacks who insisted on their rights. In this incident police arrested seventy blacks and looked away as a white mob broke into the jail to murder two black prisoners. An aroused civil-rights movement called for federal action to end the violence. Many liberals and leftists joined former first lady Eleanor Roosevelt in establishing the National Committee for Justice in Columbia, Tennessee, and nearly fifty religious and civil-liberties groups united with the NAACP in the National Emergency Committee Against Violence.

In September 1946 Truman met with a delegation from these organizations to discuss racial terrorism in the South. Horrified by their accounts, the president vowed to act. Not only did Truman personally believe that every American should enjoy the full rights of citizenship, but he also understood the importance of the growing black vote and took note of the continuing heavy migration of southern blacks to northern cities

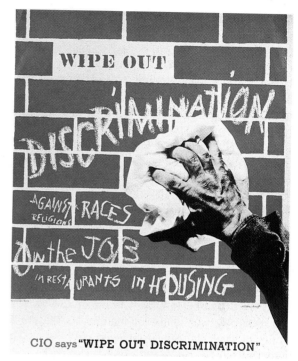

Wipe Out Discrimination, *by Milton Ackoff, 1949 The publication of* To Secure These Rights *catapulted civil-rights issues to the forefront during the Truman years.*

in states with large electoral votes. He realized, moreover, that white racism damaged American relations with much of the rest of the world. The Soviet Union repeatedly highlighted the ill treatment of blacks in the United States, both to undercut American appeals to the racially diverse peoples of Africa, Asia, and Latin America and to counter U.S. condemnations of repression behind the iron curtain. Shortly after the 1946 elections, therefore, Truman established the first President's Committee on Civil Rights to investigate race relations. Its report, *To Secure These Rights,* proposed antilynching and anti–poll tax legislation and called for an end to racial discrimination and segregation in American life. Boldly, Truman in February 1948 sent a special message to Congress urging the enactment of most of the committee's proposals.

Southern segregationists immediately denounced the president, accusing him of "kissing the feet of minorities" and "stabbing the South in the back." Key southern leaders warned of a boycott of the national Democratic ticket. Truman backtracked. Cowed by the prospect of a major southern defection from Democratic ranks, he dropped his plans to submit specific civil-rights bills to Congress and endorsed a weak civil-rights plank for the Democratic platform that made no mention of his own proposals.

But at the Democratic convention in July 1948, liberals and urban politicians who needed the backing of black voters rejected the president's feeble civil-rights plank. They amended the platform to commit the Democratic party to press for action on Truman's initial proposals. Thirty-five dissenting delegates from Mississippi and Alabama stalked out of the convention. They soon joined with other southern segregationists to form the States' Rights Democratic party and to nominate Governor Strom Thurmond of South Carolina for the presidency.

Running on a platform that emphasized opposition to civil rights, Thurmond's Dixiecrats, as they were nicknamed, hoped to win a hundred electoral votes in the South. If successful, they planned to use their political power as leverage to restore their dominance in the Democratic party and to protect "the southern way of life" against what they deemed an oppressive central government. Determined to preserve white supremacy, the Dixiecrats placed their electors on the ballot as the regular Democratic ticket in the several states in which they controlled the party machinery and thus erected a major roadblock to Truman's chances of victory.

The Election of 1948

Truman's hopes for election became even more remote when a band of Democratic left-wingers joined with the communists to launch a new Progressive party that nominated Henry A. Wallace for president. Truman had fired Wallace, his secretary of commerce and FDR's vice president (1941–1945), in September 1946 for publicly questioning the administration's "get tough" stance toward the Soviet Union. The Wallace candidacy especially threatened Truman's chances in the key populous northern states, where many urban Democrats viewed Wallace as the true heir of New Deal liberalism.

Facing a divided Democratic party, the Republicans sought to win by avoiding controversy and playing it safe. They adopted a platform that vaguely approved much of the New Deal policy and the administration's bipartisan foreign policy; they nominated the moderate governor of New York, Thomas E. Dewey, as their standard-bearer, and the popular governor Earl Warren of California as his vice presidential

running mate. Confident of victory, they ran a complacent campaign aimed at offending the fewest people. Dewey devoted most of his public appearances to bland appeals for national unity. Although sound in principle, the strategy backfired by making Dewey seem aloof and smug.

In contrast, Harry Truman and his folksy running mate, Senator Alben Barkley of Kentucky, tirelessly kept up the offensive against the "no-good, do-nothing" Republican-controlled Eightieth Congress. To shouts of "Give 'em hell, Harry," the president hammered away at the GOP as the party of "privilege, pride, and plunder." Although Truman earned applause for his spunk, pollsters predicted a sure Dewey victory.

A surprised nation awoke the day after the election to learn that the president had squeaked to the biggest upset in U.S. history. Truman received 24.1 million votes (49.5 percent) to Dewey's 22 million (45.1 percent). Ironically, the Progressives and the Dixiecrats had helped Truman. The prominence of the communists in the Wallace campaign forced most disgruntled liberals back into the Democratic column and made the president look moderate by comparison. Wallace received only about a million popular votes and won no electoral votes. Thurmond col-

The Election of 1948

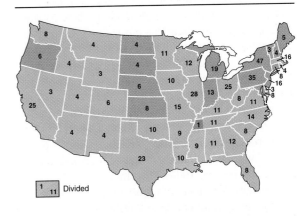

	Electoral Vote	Popular Vote	Percentage of Popular Vote
Democratic Harry S Truman	303	24,105,812	49.5
Republican Thomas E. Dewey	189	21,970,065	45.1
States' Rights Strom Thurmond	39	1,169,063	2.4
Minor parties	–	1,442,667	3.0

Harlem Residents Greet President Truman
Although stymied by Congress, Truman put forth unprecedented, sweeping civil-rights proposals that brought thousands of African-Americans out to see the president campaign in Harlem on October 29, 1948.

lected fewer than 1.2 million votes and carried only the four southern states where the Dixiecrats ran under the regular Democratic party emblem. Although many white southerners despised Truman's advocacy of civil rights, they were not yet ready to revolt. As the attorney general of Virginia explained, "The only sane and constructive course to follow is to remain in the house of our fathers—even though the roof leaks, and there be bats in the belfry, rats in the pantry, a cockroach in the kitchen and skunks in the parlor." Moreover, Thurmond's failure to spark a major defection of southerners from the Democratic fold had freed Truman in the months before the election to campaign as a proponent of civil rights.

In July 1948 Truman had issued executive orders barring discrimination in federal employment and creating a committee to ensure "equality of treatment and opportunity for all persons in the armed services without regard to race, color, religion or national origin." This presidential edict proved good politics, though the navy, marine corps, and army moved haltingly to lower their racial barriers. Truman also benefited politically as a result of Supreme Court decisions in favor of civil rights. In 1946 the Court had declared segregation in

interstate bus transportation unconstitutional (*Morgan* v. *Virginia*); and in the election year of 1948, it outlawed restrictive housing covenants that forbade the sale or rental of property to minorities (*Shelley* v. *Kraemer*). Blacks similarly took heart in 1948 from the number of cities and states that had passed fair-employment-practices and public-accommodations laws and from the change in social attitudes symbolized by the Brooklyn Dodgers' 1947 decision to break major-league baseball's color barrier with Jackie Robinson, the grandson of a slave. They voted accordingly. Truman won a higher percentage of the black vote than had even FDR in his four victories.

Most of all, Truman won in 1948 because he recreated the New Deal coalition forged by Roosevelt. With the crisis in Berlin helping to rally the American people behind the president, Truman took every opportunity to remind farmers and laborers that the Republican "gluttons of privilege" planned to "turn the clock back" and deny them the benefits they had gained under the New Deal. "In a sense," observed one political commentator in a post-mortem of Truman's success, "Roosevelt won his greatest victory after his death."

The Fair Deal

Although he had chalked up less than half the popular vote, winning by the narrowest margin since 1916, Truman viewed his election a mandate for liberalism. In his 1949 State of the Union message, he proposed an ambitious social and economic program that he called the Fair Deal. He asked Congress to enlarge the New Deal programs in the areas of economic security, conservation, and housing and to go far beyond FDR's initiatives in civil rights, national health insurance, federal aid to education, and agricultural subsidies.

The Eighty-first Congress complied with most of Truman's appeals to extend existing programs. Lawmakers boosted the minimum wage to seventy-five cents an hour; increased social-security coverage and benefit payments; expanded appropriations for public power, reclamation, soil conservation, flood control, and slum clearance; and authorized the construction of 810,000 subsidized low-income housing units, as well as the National Science Foundation. Following up on the popular War Brides Act of 1945, which enabled 117,000 wives and children of servicemen who had married while overseas to migrate to the United States, Congress also enacted the Displaced Persons Act, which allowed entry to 205,000 homeless survivors of the Nazi forced-labor and death camps. But legislators rejected Truman's calls for repeal of the Taft-Hartley Act, federal aid to education, a comprehensive national health-insurance plan, and a cropsubsidy system that would both maintain farm income and hold down food prices. Southern Democratic lawmakers, with conservative Republican help, stymied all of Truman's efforts to enact civilrights legislation.

Truman's failure to persuade Congress to adopt the new measures of his Fair Deal resulted, in part, from his own lessening commitment to domestic reform as the Cold War and then the Korean War increasingly absorbed his time and energy. Furthermore, the Cold War strengthened the conservative coalition's power by making the president ever more reliant on conservatives for their support of his military and foreign policies. In part, too, the postwar prosperity enjoyed by most Americans sapped the public enthusiasm that had sustained FDR's New Deal. In 1949, according to the Hickock Manufacturing Company, the belt size of the average American man had expanded to thirty-four inches, up from a depression-years average of thirty-one inches. The postwar Congresses mirrored the sense of well-being that most voting Americans felt. They also reflected the popular apprehensions over communism that doomed liberal hopes for a resurgence of reform.

THE POLITICS OF ANTICOMMUNISM

As the Cold War worsened, a growing number of Americans came to believe that the country's foreign difficulties were rooted in treason and subversion at home. How else could the Chinese communists have gained power over all of China and the Soviets have exploded their own atomic bomb? Unhinged by fear, millions of Americans enlisted in a postwar crusade that blamed scapegoats for the nation's problems and equated dissent with disloyalty.

Similar intolerance had prevailed in the Know-Nothing campaign of the 1850s and the Red Scare of 1919–1920. The tendency to link radicalism with foreign conspiracies, moreover, was deeply rooted among American conservatives. Since its establishment in 1938, the House Committee on Un-American Activities (later called the House Un-American Activities Committee, or HUAC) had served as a platform for reactionaries' denunciation of the New Deal as a communist plot to sovietize America. Only the extreme Right had taken such fulminations seriously at first. But after the Second World War, mounting numbers of Democrats as well as Republicans climbed on the anti-Red bandwagon.

The second Red Scare deeply influenced both government actions and the behavior of ordinary Americans. Millions of men and women—in labor unions, schools and universities, and government jobs at every level—were subjected to oaths and security investigations. Anticommunist hysteria destroyed the Left, discredited liberalism, and undermined labor militancy. The trampling of civil liberties spawned a "silent generation" of college students and widespread political apathy, and the purge of controversial government officials ensured foreign-policy rigidity and the postponement of liberal domestic reforms.

Loyalty and Security

As the Cold War began, reasons abounded for legitimate concern about American security. The Communist party had claimed some eighty thousand members at its height during the Second World War, and many more Americans, openly or secretly, had sympathized with its goals. No one knew how many of these individuals occupied sensitive government positions or directed their primary loyalty to the Soviet Union. In mid-1945 a government raid on the offices of a pro-communist magazine, *Amerasia*, uncovered a cache of classified documents that had been passed to the periodical by two State Department employees and a naval intelligence officer. Ten months later the Canadian government exposed a major spy network that had given American military information and atomic secrets to the Soviets during the war. In response to the communist threat and to growing Republican criticism that the administration was lax in its internal security, Truman late in 1946 appointed a commission to study the loyalty problem.

Nine days after his "Truman Doctrine" speech of March 1947, he issued Executive Order 9835 establishing the Federal Employee Loyalty Program to root out subversives in government service. The order provided for a loyalty check on all government employees. Although the program initially had certain safeguards, the drive for absolute security overrode concerns about the rights of civil servants. Soon those suspected of disloyalty could neither face their accusers nor require the investigators to reveal the source of their information. Rather than focusing on potential subversives in high-risk areas, the probe extended to the associations and beliefs of *every* government worker.

Local review boards sometimes accused employees of disloyalty solely because they criticized American foreign policy or espoused the unionization of federal workers. "Of course the fact that a person believes in racial equality doesn't *prove* that he's a communist," mused an Interior Department loyalty board chairman, "but it certainly makes you look twice, doesn't it?" Government employees were asked whether they provided religious training for their children and what they thought of female chastity. Some were discredited because they owned books on socialism or liked foreign films. Others lost their jobs because of guilt by association with radical friends and relatives, or because of previous membership in, or contributions to, organizations now listed by the attorney general as disloyal to the United States. By 1956 the probe had led to 2,700 dismissals and 12,000 resignations but had uncovered no evidence of subversion or espionage. But it did spread fear and a mood of caution among government employees. "Why lead with your chin?" became a dominant reflex. "If communists like apple pie and I do," claimed one federal worker, "I see no reason why I should stop eating it. But I would."

The Anticommunist Crusade

The very existence of a federal loyalty inquest fed the fears of communist hysteria. It promoted widespread fears of communist infiltrators and legitimized other efforts to expose subversives. Universities banned controversial speakers. Popular magazines featured such articles as "Reds Are After Your Child." Even Marvel comics joined the fray: "Beware, commies, spies, traitors, and foreign agents! Captain America, with all loyal, free men behind him, is looking for you, ready to fight until the last one of you is exposed for the yellow scum you are."

By the end of Truman's term, thirty-nine states had enacted antisubversion laws and loyalty programs with even fewer procedural safeguards than the federal government's. In legislation reminiscent of the Sedition Act of 1918, Connecticut made it a crime to print any "scurrilous or abusive matter" about the government, the armed forces, military uniforms, and the flag. Michigan invalidated all bequests to organizations judged subversive. Imprisonment awaited anyone in Massachusetts who knowingly allowed a meeting place to be used by communists. Schoolteachers, college professors, and state and city employees throughout the nation had to sign loyalty oaths or lose their jobs.

In 1947 a series of House Un-American Activities Committee hearings to expose communist influence in American life dominated the news. HUAC's probes blurred the distinctions between dissent and disloyalty, between radicalism and subversion. The committee perfected the tactic of threatening recalcitrant witnesses with the loss of their livelihoods. In Washington, D.C., a man lost his license to sell secondhand furniture because he had invoked the Fifth Amendment when questioned about his past; a woman who did the same was so effectively boycotted that she had to sell her thriving drugstore and leave town. HUAC also frightened labor unions into expelling communist members and steering clear of progressive causes. Fearing that to champion leftist causes would make them appear procommunist, unions now concentrated solely on better pay and benefits for their members. Rather than the social-democratic movement that many unions aspired to become in the 1930s, postwar organized labor became a highly bureaucratic special-interest pressure group.

HUAC also left its mark on the entertainment industry. When a group of prominent film directors and screenwriters refused to cooperate with the committee in 1947, HUAC had them cited for contempt and sent to federal prison. The threat of further investigations prompted the movie colony, financially dependent on favorable press and public opinion, to exile its dissenters. Hollywood established an unofficial blacklist barring the employment of anyone with even a slightly questionable past. Familiar faces disappeared from the movie screen; a similar blacklist in broadcasting silenced some of radio's most talented voices. Between 1948 and 1954, Hollywood churned out more than forty anticommunist films, bearing such titles as *The Red Menace* and *I Married a Communist.* One studio even canceled a film on Longfellow, explaining that Hiawatha had tried to stop wars between Indian tribes and that some might see the Indian's effort as communist propaganda for peace. Another withdrew plans to film the story of Robin Hood because he took from the rich and gave to the poor.

The presidential campaign of 1948 poured yet more fuel on the fires of national anxiety. Truman depicted rival candidate Henry Wallace as a Stalinist dupe, and Wallace's Progressive party as a tool of Moscow. Truman even accused the Republicans of being "unwittingly the ally of the communists in this country." The GOP responded in kind, dubbing the Democrats as "the party of treason." Republican Richard M. Nixon, running for reelection as a congressman from California, charged the Democrats with responsibility for "the unimpeded growth of the communist conspiracy in the United States."

To blunt the force of such accusations, Truman's Justice Department in 1948 prosecuted eleven top leaders of the American Communist party under the Smith Act of 1940, which outlawed any conspiracy to advocate the overthrow of the government. The result was the conviction and jailing of American citizens for their rhetoric, not for any actual acts of violence or espionage. In 1951 in *Dennis* v. *U.S.,* the Supreme Court upheld the constitutionality of the Smith Act, declaring that Congress had the power to curtail freedom of speech when national security required such restriction. This decision cleared the way for the prosecution of nearly one hundred other communist functionaries.

Ironically, the Communist party was fading into obscurity at the very time when politicians magnified the threat that it posed. By 1950 its membership had shrunk to fewer than thirty thousand. Yet Truman's attorney general that year warned that American Reds "are everywhere—in factories, offices, butcher stores, on street corners, in private businesses—and each carries in himself the germ of death for society."

Hiss and the Rosenbergs

No single episode did more to set off alarms of a diabolic Red conspiracy within the national government than the case of Alger Hiss. In the midst of the 1948 presidential campaign, HUAC conducted a hearing in which Whittaker Chambers, a senior editor at *Time* magazine and former Soviet agent who had broken with the communists in 1938, identified Hiss as an underground party member in the 1930s. The contrasts between the two men could not have been more dramatic. Chambers, the rumpled, repentant ex-communist, appeared a tortured soul crusading to save the West from the Red peril. The elegant Hiss seemed the very symbol of the liberal establishment. A graduate of Johns Hopkins University and Harvard Law School, Hiss had clerked for Supreme Court Justice Oliver Wendell Holmes before joining the Department of Agriculture in the New Deal. During World War II, he had worked for the State Department (even serving as a presidential adviser at Yalta and helping to organize the founding conference of the United Nations), and after the war he directed the Carnegie Endowment for International Peace, a private foundation promoting ways to avert war. Hiss initially denied any communist affiliation and claimed not even to know Chambers.

Most liberals believed Hiss. They thought he was being persecuted by a conservative congressional committee bent on tarnishing New Deal liberalism. The administration rushed to his defense. Truman denounced Chambers's allegation as a "red herring" to deflect attention from the failures of the Republican Eightieth Congress in an election year.

But to many of those who harbored suspicions about the Rooseveltian liberal tradition, Chambers's persistence and Hiss's fumbling retreat intensified fears that the Democratic administration might be teeming with communists. Under rigorous questioning by Congressman Richard Nixon, a HUAC member, the former New Dealer relented and admitted that he had known Chambers and had even let Chambers have his car and live in his apartment. Still, Hiss denied ever having been a communist. Chambers then broadened his accusation, claiming that Hiss had committed espionage in the 1930s by giving him secret State Department documents to be transmitted to the Soviet Union. To prove his charge, Chambers produced microfilm copies of confidential government papers that had been reproduced on a typewriter once owned by Hiss.

Hiss protested his innocence, but a grand jury indicted him for perjury, or lying under oath. (The statute of limitations for espionage prevented a charge of treason.) A first trial ended in a hung jury, but a second resulted in a conviction in January 1950. Hiss was sentenced to five years in federal prison. Congressional conservatives were emboldened. Who knew how many other bright young New Dealers had betrayed the country?

Just as the Hiss affair ended, another shocking case of espionage alarmed Americans about their government's internal security. In early February 1950, the

Ethel and Julius Rosenberg
The couple are shown in 1951 leaving the New York City federal court after their arraignment on spy charges. They would later be electrocuted for what the trial judge called their "loathsome offense."

British arrested Klaus Fuchs, a German-born scientist involved in the Manhattan Project, for having passed atomic secrets to the Soviets during the Second World War. Fuchs's confession led to the arrest of his American accomplice, Harry Gold, who then implicated David Greenglass, a machinist who had worked at Los Alamos. Greenglass named his sister and brother-in-law, Ethel and Julius Rosenberg, as co-conspirators in the wartime atomic spy network. The children of Jewish immigrants, the Rosenbergs insisted that they were victims of anti-Semitism and were being persecuted for their leftist beliefs. Primarily on the testimony of Gold and Greenglass, a jury in March 1951 found the Rosenbergs guilty of conspiring to commit espionage. The trial judge sentenced them to die by electrocution in New York's Sing Sing prison.

The severity of the punishment reflected the anticommunist fever during the Korean War years. Although offered clemency if they named other spies, neither Rosenberg would confess. On June 19, 1953, the Rosenbergs were executed.

Few Americans could separate fact from fantasy. For many only a conspiracy theory could explain U.S. weakness and Russian might. Frustrated by their unexpected failure to unseat Truman in 1948, Republicans seized on such a theory. Doomed to four more years of the longest exile from the White House that either party had endured since the Civil War, the GOP seemed to be abandoning all restraint when it hurled such accusations as one senator's charge that the Democratic administration was a "crazy assortment of collectivist cutthroat crackpots and Communist fellow-traveling appeasers."

McCarthyism

No individual would scourge Democrats as audaciously and inflict as many mortal wounds as Republican senator Joseph R. McCarthy of Wisconsin. Desperate for a winning issue on which to run for reelection in 1952, McCarthy noted the attention accorded his fellow Republicans for their attacks on the Democrats as "soft on communism." Following suit, on February 9, 1950, McCarthy boldly trumpeted to a GOP women's meeting in Wheeling, West Virginia, that communists in the State Department were undermining American power in world affairs. "I have here in my hand a list of 205," McCarthy announced to the audience as he waved a laundry list, "a list of names known to the Secretary of State as being members of the Communist party and who nevertheless are still working and shaping policy." Although he could not produce evidence to back up his statement, the combination of his senatorial stature and brazen style gave him a national forum. McCarthy repeated his accusation in other speeches in the next few days, reducing his numbers to 81 and then 57 and toning down the rhetoric of his indictment from "card-carrying communists" to "subversives" to "bad risks." A Senate committee investigating the matter branded McCarthy's charges "a fraud and a hoax," but the junior senator from Wisconsin persisted.

Buoyed by the partisan usefulness of Senator McCarthy's onslaught, Republicans encouraged even more accusations. "Joe, you're a dirty s.o.b.," declared Ohio senator John Bricker, "but there are times when you've got to have an s.o.b. around, and this is one of them." Even the normally fair-minded Robert Taft urged McCarthy "to keep talking, and if one case doesn't work, try another." He did just that, and *McCarthyism* became a synonym for public charges of disloyalty without sufficient regard for evidence.

As the Korean War dragged on and Americans became increasingly vulnerable to demogoguery, McCarthy's efforts to (in his words) "root out the skunks" escalated. He ridiculed Secretary of State Dean Acheson as the "Red Dean" and lashed out at Truman's dismissal of General Douglas MacArthur as "the greatest victory the communists have ever won." In mid-1951 the senator charged that Secretary of Defense George C. Marshall, "a man steeped in falsehood," had "aided and abetted a communist conspiracy so immense as to dwarf any previous such venture in the history of man."

McCarthy's attacks appealed most to midwestern Republicans indignant about the welfare state, restrictions on business, and the Europe-first emphasis of Truman's foreign policy. For them anticommunism was a weapon of revenge against the liberals and internationalists, and a means to regain the controlling position that conservative forces had once held in American life. McCarthy also won a devoted following among blue-collar workers who identified with the senator's charge that a person was either a true American or one of those "egg-sucking phony liberals." Laborers widely praised his insistence that the war against communism had to be fought with brass knuckles, not kid gloves. His flag-waving patriotic appeals held a special attraction for traditionally Democratic Catholic ethnics, who sought to gain acceptance as "100 percent Americans" through displays of anti-

communist zeal. Countless Americans also shared McCarthy's hatred of privilege and gentility, of the "bright young men who are born with silver spoons in their mouths," of the "striped-pants boys in the State Department." And his conspiratorial explanation offered a simple answer to the perplexing questions of the Cold War.

McCarthy's political power rested on the Republican establishment's support and on Democrats' fears of antagonizing him. The widespread backing of McCarthy by his GOP colleagues made Democratic condemnations of the senator's tactics seem like mere partisan criticism. And when he helped Republican candidates in the 1950 congressional elections to unseat Democrats who had denounced him, McCarthy appeared invincible. "Look out for McCarthy" became the Senate watchword. "Joe will go that extra mile to destroy you," warned the new majority leader, Lyndon B. Johnson of Texas. However much Democratic members of Congress detested him, few now dared incur his wrath.

Over Truman's veto federal lawmakers in 1950 adopted the McCarran Internal Security Act, requiring organizations deemed to be communist by the attorney general to register with the Department of Justice and to furnish membership lists and financial statements. The measure also barred communists from employment in defense plants, empowered the government to deny passports to communists and to deport any alien suspected of subversion, and authorized the arrest and detention during a national emergency of "any person as to whom there is reason to believe might engage in acts of espionage or sabotage." The McCarran-Walter Immigration and Nationality Act, passed in 1952, again over Truman's veto, maintained the discriminatory quota system, based on national origins, in which immigrants from northern and western Europe received 85 percent of annual admissions. Although it formally ended the long-standing principle of Oriental exclusion, allowing token quotas to Asian nations, the measure also strengthened the attorney general's authority to exclude and deport aliens suspected of supporting communism.

The Election of 1952

By 1952 public apprehension about the loyalty of government employees combined with frustration over the Korean stalemate to sink Democratic presidential

The Election of 1952

Candidates	Parties	Electoral Vote	Popular Vote	Percentage of Popular Vote
DWIGHT D. EISENHOWER	Republican	442	33,936,234	55.1
Adlai E. Stevenson	Democratic	89	27,314,992	44.4

hopes to their lowest level since the 1920s. Moreover, both business and labor resented Truman's decision to freeze wages and prices during the Korean conflict. And evidence of corruption in government further plagued the Democratic party. Revelations of bribery and influence peddling by some of Truman's old political associates gave the Republicans ammunition for charging the party in power with "plunder at home, and blunder abroad." In a late-1951 Gallup poll, Truman's standing dropped to an all-time low of 23 percent. Early in 1952 he announced that he would not seek reelection.

In his place the dispirited Democrats drafted the governor of Illinois, Adlai Stevenson. Although a reluctant candidate, Stevenson promised to "talk sense to the American people," and his eloquence and wit made liberal intellectuals campaign "madly for Adlai." But Stevenson could not disassociate himself from the unpopular Truman, and his lofty speeches failed to stir the average voter. Most of all, he could not overcome the popular sentiment that twenty years of Democratic rule was enough and that, as the Republicans proclaimed, "It's time for a change."

Compounding Democratic woes, the GOP nominated popular war hero Dwight D. Eisenhower. In 1948 the nonpartisan Eisenhower had rejected Democratic pleas that he head their ticket, insisting that "lifelong professional soldiers should abstain from seeking higher political office." But in 1952 he answered the call of the moderate wing of the Republican party, which needed a strong candidate to challenge the isolationist and conservative forces arrayed with Ohio senator Robert A. Taft. Eisenhower's supporters outmaneuvered Taft's in a battle over contested delegates and succeeded in getting "Ike" nominated on the first ballot. As a concession to the hard-line anticommunists in the party, Eisenhower accepted as his running mate Senator Richard M. Nixon of California, the former HUAC Red hunter who had exposed Alger Hiss and

had won a seat in the Senate in 1950 by redbaiting his opponent, Helen Gahagan Douglas, as "pink right down to her underwear."

Eisenhower and Nixon proved unbeatable. With his captivating grin and unimpeachable record of public service, Eisenhower projected both personal warmth and the vigorous authority associated with military command. His smile, wrote one commentator, "was also a philosophical statement. It was a smile of infinite reassurance," promising benevolence and caring. Ike symbolized the stability for which Americans yearned. At the same time, Nixon kept public apprehensions at the boiling point. He accused the Democrats of treason, derided the Democratic candidate as "Adlai the appeaser . . . who got a Ph.D. from Dean Acheson's College of Cowardly Communist Containment," and charged that a Stevenson victory would bring "more Alger Hisses, more atomic spies."

The GOP ticket momentarily stumbled when newspapers revealed the existence of a "slush fund" collected by California business leaders to keep Richard Nixon in "financial comfort." However, Nixon saved his candidacy with a heart-tugging television defense of his actions in which he explained the gifts as intended to benefit his family. Eisenhower then ensured a GOP landslide by his last-minute pledge to "go to Korea" to end the stalemated war. He won 55 percent of the popular vote and cracked the solid South to carry thirty-nine states. Ike also managed to pull enough Republicans into office on his coattails to give the GOP control of both houses of Congress, though by small margins.

Dan Collins was typical of the many Americans who voted for Eisenhower in 1952. Collins had suffered through the Great Depression and fought in World War II. In 1946 he returned to Boston and civilian status, "hoping to relax, get rich, and enjoy a bit of the good life." He earned more money in construction than he had previously dreamed possible and gained reassurance from his family values, religion, and patriotism. But Soviet expansionism abroad, coupled with fears of communist infiltration at home, intruded on his peace of mind. By 1951 Collins had concluded that "McCarthy must be on target in attacking those liberals in Washington." The following year, believing the Truman administration "riddled with Reds and corruption," Collins, a staunch Democrat, decided that "it was time to give the other guys a chance."

CONCLUSION

Voters like Dan Collins thus terminated two decades of uninterrupted Democratic rule in the White House. The 1952 election also marked the close of the early postwar era. That period had seen notable economic successes. Confounding the pessimists who had predicted that the depression would come roaring back once wartime production ended, the nation not only made the transition to a peacetime economy but achieved high levels of prosperity and employment.

But the postwar years were also a time of irony. The costly military triumph that Americans celebrated in 1945 opened up a different but equally dreadful conflict with the Soviet Union. Whether the Cold War would ignite a global nuclear war remained very much in doubt as the Truman administration ended. Domestically, the era that was to have ushered in tranquillity instead brought bitter partisanship and an ugly mood of suspicion and repression.

The early postwar period laid the groundwork for trends that would mold American history for half a century. The Cold War rhetoric of the Truman years influenced an entire generation's perceptions of the world. The imperatives of the anticommunist offensive provided the rationale for a vast strengthening of presidential power that would fundamentally reorient the nature of the federal government. And the first stirrings of civil-rights activism and of America's involvement in Vietnam forecast issues that would dominate American life in the 1960s.

But most Americans had little inkling of these long-term historical currents in 1952. They vaguely sensed that the bright promise of August 1945 had somehow slipped away, but they looked with hope to a new president. Ike's infectious grin seemed an omen of better times ahead.

CHRONOLOGY

1945 Truman proposes twenty-one-point program of economic reforms.

1946 Employment Act.
Winston Churchill delivers his "iron curtain speech.
Coal miners' strike.
More than a million GIs enroll in college.
Inflation soars to more than 18 percent.
Republicans win control of Congress.

1947 Truman Doctrine.
Truman orders Federal Employee Loyalty Program.
Taft-Hartley Act.
Marshall Plan proposed to aid Europe.
President's Committee on Civil Rights issues *To Secure These Rights.*

1948 Communist coup in Czechoslovakia.
State of Israel founded.
Soviet Union begins blockade of Berlin; United States begins airlift.
Congress approves Marshall Plan.
Truman orders an end to segregation in the armed forces.
Communist leaders put on trial under the Smith Act.
Truman elected president.

1949 North Atlantic Treaty Organization (NATO) established.

East and West Germany founded as separate nations.

Communist victory in China.

Soviet Union detonates an atomic bomb.

1950 Truman authorizes building a hydrogen bomb.

Soviet spy ring at Los Alamos uncovered.

Alger Hiss convicted of perjury.

Joseph McCarthy launches anticommunist crusade.

Korean War begins.

Julius and Ethel Rosenberg arrested as atomic spies.

1950 McCarran Internal Security Act.

Truman accepts NSC-68.

China enters the Korean War.

1951 Douglas MacArthur dismissed from his Korean command.

Supreme Court upholds Smith Act.

Rosenbergs convicted of espionage.

1952 First hydrogen bomb exploded.

Dwight D. Eisenhower elected president; Republicans win control of Congress.

FOR FURTHER READING

John Diggins, *The Proud Decades, 1941–1960* (1989). A wide-ranging survey of U.S. culture and politics.

Richard M. Fried, *Nightmare in Red: The McCarthy Era in Perspective* (1990). A cogent account of McCarthyism's rise and fall.

John L. Gaddis, *The United States and the Cold War* (1992). A probing reexamination of the major issues.

Robert Griffith and Athan Theoharis, eds., *The Specter: Original Essays on the Cold War and the Origins of McCarthyism* (1974). A collection of revisionist interpretations.

Alonzo L. Hamby, *Beyond the New Deal: Harry S. Truman and American Liberalism* (1973). A positive assessment of Truman's efforts to preserve and extend the New Deal.

Athan Theoharis and John Stuart Cox, *The Boss: J. Edgar Hoover and the Great American Inquisition* (1988). A biographical analysis highlighting the FBI's role in the 1950s Red Scare.

Melvyn Leffler, *A Preponderance of Power: National Security, the Truman Administration, and the Cold War* (1992). The most comprehensive and incisive history of the Cold War's early stages.

ADDITIONAL BIBLIOGRAPHY

General Works

William Graebner, *The Age of Doubt: American Thought and Culture in the 1940s* (1991); David Halberstam, *The Fifties* (1993); William Pemberton, *Harry S. Truman: Fair Dealer and Cold Warrior* (1989); Gary W. Reichard, *Politics as Usual: The Age of Truman and Eisenhower* (1988).

The Cold War

H. W. Brands, *The Devil We Knew: Americans and the Cold War* (1993); Gregory Fossedal, *Our Finest Hour: Will Clayton, The Marshall Plan, and the Triumph of Democracy* (1993); John L. Gaddis, *Strategies of Containment: A Critical Appraisal of Postwar American National Security Policy* (1982); Gregg Herken, *The Winning Weapon: The Atomic Bomb in the Cold War, 1945–1950* (1980); Michael Hogan, *The Marshall Plan* (1987); Timothy P. Ireland, *Creating the Entangling Alliance: The Origins of NATO* (1981); Bruce R. Kuniholm, *The Origins of the Cold War in the Near East* (1980); T. J. McCormick, *America's Half Century: United States Foreign Policy in the Cold War* (1992); Robert L. Messer, *The End of an Alliance* (1982); Wilson Miscamble, *George F. Kennan and the Making of American Foreign Policy* (1992); David Painter, *Oil and the American Century* (1986); H. Schaffer, *Chester Bowles: New Dealer in the Cold War* (1993).

The Cold War in Asia

Roy Appleman, *Disaster in Korea* (1992); Clay Blair, *The Forgotten War* (1988); June Grasso, *Harry Truman's Two-China Policy* (1987); John Halliday and Bruce Cumings, *Korea: The Unknown War* (1989); Gary Hess, *The U.S. Emergence as a Southeast Asian Power* (1986); Robert J. McMahon, *Colonialism and the Cold War* (1981); Robert Newman, *Owen Lattimore and the "Loss" of China* (1992); Andrew Rotter, *The Path to Vietnam* (1987); Howard Schonberger, *Aftermath of War: Americans and the Remaking of Japan* (1989); Shu Guang Zhang, *Deterrence and Strategic Culture: Chinese-American Confrontations* (1993).

The Cold War at Home

Paul Boyer, *By the Bomb's Early Light* (1985); Steven Gillon, *Politics and Vision: The ADA and American Liberalism* (1987); Robert Griffith, *The Politics of Fear: Joseph R. McCarthy and the Senate* (1970); Joel Kovel, *Red Hunting in the Promised Land* (1994); Stanley Kutler, *The American Inquisition* (1982); Gary May, *Un-American Activities: The Trials of William Remington* (1994); David M. Oshinski, *A Conspiracy So Immense: The World of Joe McCarthy* (1983); Ronald Radosh and Joyce Milton, *The Rosenberg File* (1983); Thomas C. Reeves, *The Life and Times of Joe McCarthy* (1982); Ellen Schrecker, *No Ivory Tower: McCarthyism and the Universities* (1986); Allen Weinstein, *Perjury: The Hiss-Chambers Case* (1978); Stephen Whitfield, *The Culture of the Cold War* (1991).

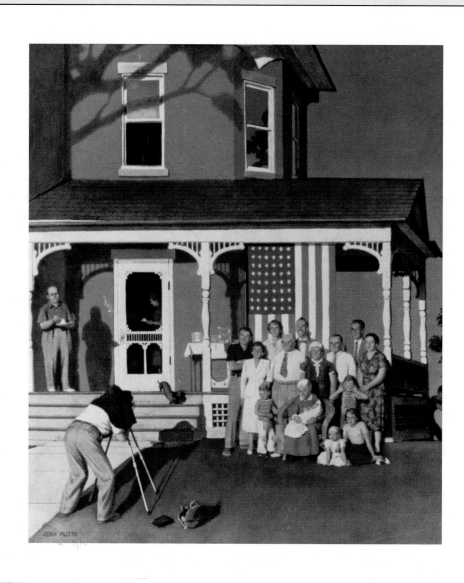

Family Photograph
by John Falter, 1952

29

AMERICA AT MIDCENTURY

It starts with these giant ants that crawl out of the ground from that place in New Mexico where they tested the atomic bomb—Alamogordo. They're desperate for sugar, and they rip apart anybody who gets in their way. It ends in the sewers of Los Angeles—and it's *really* scary!"

The year was 1954, and moviegoers all across America were shivering in terror at *Them!*, the giant-ant film that was part of a wave of mutant movies pouring out of Hollywood in the fifties. The atomic bomb and nuclear radiation played a big role in these productions. In *The Incredible Shrinking Man* (inset), the unlucky hero is accidentally exposed to "atomic dust" and begins to shrink. In *The Attack of the Fifty-Foot Women*, the process is reversed. Nuclear testing also spawned a giant octopus in *It Came from Beneath the Sea,* unleashed *The Attack of the Crab Monsters,* and was even responsible for the *Invasion of the Body Snatchers* by pods from outer space.

The vogue for science-fiction and monster movies revealed anxieties underlying the apparent complacency of the 1950s, particularly the fear of radioactive fallout from the atmospheric nuclear tests that pumped into the world's environment radioactive clouds containing strontium 90, a cancer-causing chemical that accumulates in the teeth and bone marrow, especially of children.

Public apprehension about nuclear tests was one component of this complex and fascinating period. Fears of communism, of juvenile delinquency, and of homosexuality were others. Critics condemned the "alien" life-styles of lesbians and gay men and warned of their susceptibility to blackmail by Soviet agents; the Eisenhower administration prohibited homosexuals from holding government jobs. But many such painful realities of the 1950s either were hidden from Americans or dimmed in the public consciousness in subsequent years. Indeed, the late sixties brought an outpouring of nostalgia for the "nifty fifties." In the distorting mirror of memory, the decade came to seem a peaceful time of prosperity and easy living, of cheap gasoline and big cars, of comfortable suburban homes and family togetherness. The mass media portrayed the fifties as a sunny time when almost everybody liked Ike and loved Lucy. Hollywood films and TV programs re-created the lives of the "typical" fifties teenagers, who wore pedal pushers and circle skirts, did the bunny hop and hand jive, danced to "Sh-Boom" and "The Purple People-Eater," and idolized Elvis Presley.

Like most historical generalizations, this image of the fifties contains elements of truth. Many Americans did in fact enjoy the fruits of the decade's consumer culture. Having endured the hard times of the depression and war years, they reveled in a prosperity presided over by a popular and trustworthy president. They had confidence in Dwight Eisenhower and welcomed the thaw in the Cold War that came after the Korean War. And no doubt some high schoolers did lead the carefree, fun-filled existence captured in later media images.

Yet for a full picture of the fifties, we must look beyond the stereotypes. The decade also saw the birth of the space age, of a private nuclear-power industry, and of hydrogen bombs and intercontinental ballistic missiles (ICBMs). Scientists unraveled the structure of DNA, the nucleic-acid molecule in cells that determines inherited characteristics. The decade also brought Women Strike for Peace, an organization of mostly middle-class housewives concerned about radioactivity in the atmosphere and the possibility of nuclear war. It was an era, too, of intense political passions, kindled by such influential voices as Senator Joseph McCarthy, the Warren Court, and civil-rights leader Martin Luther King, Jr. The advent of an automated and computerized postindustrial society, television's growing power, and the baby boom transformed society, as did mass suburbanization and a remarkable internal migration. Midcentury America encompassed peace and a widening Cold War, prosperity and persistent poverty, civil-rights triumphs and rampant racism. Although the fifties were good years for many Americans, they were also a time when the seeds of future crises were sown.

THE EISENHOWER PRESIDENCY

Rarely in our history has a president better fit the national mood than did Dwight David Eisenhower. By 1953 Americans had endured a quarter-century of upheaval—first a stock market crash and crippling depression, and then a world war and a menacing Cold War. Americans craved peace and stability. This is what Eisenhower delivered. Ending "Truman's folly" in Korea, he kept the nation prosperous and out of war. Although Eisenhower's moderate policies frustrated both conservatives and liberals, they proved to be just what most Americans desired. Seemingly an amateur outside the political fray, Eisenhower gave a people weary of partisanship a sense of unity. In place of continued insecurity, he inspired confidence.

Two Eisenhower Grins
On one of his many vacations from office, President Eisenhower (right) and his brother, Dr. Milton Eisenhower, admire each other's catch of trout near Pennsylvania State College.

Immensely popular throughout his two terms, Eisenhower epitomized the virtues as well as the hopes of many Americans. The most distinguished general of the Second World War, he projected the image of a plain but good man. He expressed complicated issues in simple terms yet governed a complex urban, technological society. At once the hero who had vanquished Hitler and a grandfatherly figure with twinkling blue eyes, Ike comforted an anxious people.

The General as Chief Executive

Born on October 14, 1890, in Denison, Texas, Dwight Eisenhower grew up in Abilene, Kansas, in a poor yet loving, strongly religious family. More athletic than studious, he graduated from the U.S. Military Academy at West Point in 1915. Appointed primary aide to army chief of staff General George Marshall just five days after the bombing of Pearl Harbor, he quickly demonstrated his flair for war planning and organization. In 1942 he directed the American invasion of North Africa, and in 1944 he assumed the post of supreme commander of the Allied forces on the Western Front. Well liked for his genial manner, and respected for his managerial ability and talent for conciliation, Ike became as an inspirational figure of heroic stature.

Eisenhower's approach to the presidency, reflecting his wartime leadership style, differed from that of his Democratic predecessors. He devoted his energy to major matters only, and he worked to bring contending factions together. His restrained view of presidential authority stemmed in part from his respect for the constitutional balance of power. It also reflected Eisenhower's sense of the dignity of the Oval Office. The new president rarely intervened publicly in the legislative process, shunned using his office as a "bully pulpit," and assured his cabinet members that he would "stay out of [their] hair." He established an orderly chain of command in which everything moved through channels. Although derided by the Democrats as a bumbler who preferred golf to government, who "reigned but did not rule," Eisenhower skillfully operated to great effect behind a cultivated façade of passivity.

"Dynamic Conservatism"

Determined to govern the nation on business principles, Eisenhower staffed his administration predominately with corporate executives. "Eight millionaires and a plumber," jested one journalist describing the new cabinet. The president hoped to make good on one cabinet member's boast that "we're here in the saddle as an administration representing business and industry." Eisenhower in his first year worked with Congress to reduce farm-price subsidies, to cut the number of government employees, and to slash the federal budget. He also promoted private rather than public development of hydroelectric and nuclear power and won congressional approval of a bill that turned over to the coastal states oil-rich "tidelands" that the Supreme Court had previously awarded to the federal government.

Mainly, the Eisenhower administration stayed on a centrist, middle-of-the-road course. The corporate outlook espoused by Eisenhower rejected an extreme shift to the right or a return to pre–New Deal Republican policies. More pragmatic than ideological, he wished to reduce government spending and taxes, contain inflation, and govern efficiently. Facing powerful pressure groups and, after 1954, Democratic majorities in both houses of Congress, he accommodated himself to large-scale labor organizations and social welfarism. Summing up the president's views, his brother and adviser Milton Eisenhower declared, "We should keep what we have, catch our breath for a while, and improve administration; it does not mean moving backward."

Eager to avoid a depression, President Eisenhower vetoed conservative Republican senator Robert Taft's demand to abolish the Council of Economic Advisers. Indeed, under the leadership of Arthur Burns, who advocated a strong government effort to "fine-tune" the economy, the council emerged as Ike's key domestic agency. (Burns was the only government official other than the secretary of state who had a fixed weekly appointment with the president.) The president advocated using "any and all weapons in the federal arsenal, including changes in monetary and credit policy, modifications of the tax structure, and a speed-up in the construction of public works" to stimulate the economy and check business downturns. When recessions struck in 1953 and 1957, Eisenhower abandoned his goal of a balanced budget in favor of increased spending to restore prosperity.

The president labeled his credo "dynamic conservatism" and "modern Republicanism." Whatever the slogan, Eisenhower went along with Congress when it extended social-security benefits to more than 10 million Americans; raised the minimum wage from seventy-five cents to a dollar an hour; added 4 million workers to those eligible for unemployment benefits; and increased federally financed public housing for low-income families. He also approved the construction of the St. Lawrence Seaway, linking the Great Lakes and the Atlantic Ocean, and the creation of the Department of Health, Education and Welfare. In 1956 Eisenhower backed the largest and most expensive public-works program in American history: the Interstate Highway Act, authorizing the building of a forty-one-thousand-mile system of expressways. The freeways snaking across America accelerated suburban growth, heightened dependency on cars and trucks, hastened the decline of the nation's rail lines, contributed to the decay of its central cities and the pollution of its air, and drastically increased gasoline consumption.

The Republicans renominated Eisenhower by acclamation in 1956, and the electorate handed him a landslide victory. Running on a record of "peace, progress, and prosperity," Ike trounced Democrat Adlai Stevenson for a second time. With the GOP crowing "Everything's booming but the guns," the president won two-thirds of the nonunion labor vote and 45 percent of union members' ballots. Eisenhower garnered nearly 36 million popular votes to Stevenson's 26 million and carried all but seven states.

The Election of 1956

Candidates	Parties	Electoral Vote	Popular Vote	Percentage of Popular Vote
DWIGHT D. EISENHOWER	Republican	457	35,590,472	57.6
Adlai E. Stevenson	Democratic	73	26,022,752	42.1

The Downfall of Joseph McCarthy

Although the president despised Joseph McCarthy—whom he once derided as a "pimple on the path to progress"—Eisenhower feared confronting the senator. Instead, he tried to steal McCarthy's thunder by tightening security requirements for government employees; when that failed, he allowed McCarthy to grab plenty of rope in hopes that the demagogue would hang himself. McCarthy did so in 1954, when he accused the army of harboring communist spies. The army counterattacked by accusing McCarthy of using his influence to gain preferential treatment for a member of his staff who had been drafted.

Congress voted to investigate the charges hurled by McCarthy and by the army, and on April 22, 1954, televised hearings commenced. A national audience witnessed McCarthy's boorish behavior firsthand. His dark scowl, raspy voice, endless interruptions ("point of order, Mr. Chairman, point of order"), and disregard for the rights of others repelled many viewers. He behaved like the bad guy in a TV western, observed novelist John Steinbeck: "He had a stubble of a beard, he leered, he sneered, he had a nasty laugh. He bullied and shouted. He looked evil." In June, McCarthy slurred the reputation of a young lawyer assisting Joseph Welch, the army counsel. Suddenly the mild-mannered Welch turned his wrath on McCarthy—"Until this moment, Senator, I think I really never gauged your cruelty or your recklessness. . . . Have you no sense of decency?" The gallery burst into applause.

The spell of the inquisitor broken, President Eisenhower moved to destroy McCarthy. With the GOP no longer needing him to drive the "Commiecrats" from power, and the Democrats eager to be rid of their scourge, the Senate voted 67 to 22 in December 1954 to censure the Wisconsin senator for contemptuous behavior. This powerful rebuke—only the third in the Senate's history—demolished McCarthy as a political force. McCarthyism, Ike gloated, had become "McCarthywasism."

McCarthy died in 1957, but the fears that he had exploited lingered. Throughout the 1950s, Congress annually funded the House Un-American Activities Committee's search for suspected radicals, and state and local governments still required teachers to take loyalty oaths. McCarthyism also remained a rallying call of conservatives disenchanted with the postwar consensus on both foreign and domestic matters. The

Caught in His Web

After four years of cowing opponents with accusations and intimidation, Joesph McCarthy's attacks on officers of the U.S. Army led in 1954 to a congressional investigation of the senator; six weeks of televised hearings in which McCarthy revealed his crude, bullying behavior to the American people; and, in December, to a Senate vote to censure him.

"I Can't Do This To Me!"

radio news commentaries of Fulton Lewis, Jr., and Clarence Manion; articles in the *National Review* (founded in 1955 by William F. Buckley, Jr., a recent Yale graduate); and the mailings of organizations like the Christian Anti-Communist Crusade and the John Birch Society all warned of a major subversive threat posed by domestic communism. Stressing victory over communism rather than its containment, the "new conservatives" (or radical right, as their opponents called them) also bemoaned the "creeping socialism" of Truman and Eisenhower and advocated a return to older moral standards. A particular target of their criticism was the Supreme Court.

The Warren Court

Considerably liberalized by the presence of a new chief justice, Earl Warren (1953), and three other Eisenhower appointees, the Supreme Court incurred conservatives' wrath for defending the constitutional rights of persons accused of subversive beliefs. In *Jencks* v. *United States* (1957), the Court held that the accused had the right to inspect government files used by the prosecution. In *Yates* v. *United States* (also 1957), the justices overturned the convictions of Communist party officials under the Smith Act (see Chapter 28), emphasizing the distinction between the specific advocacy of unlawful acts and the teaching of general revolutionary ideology. Right-wing opponents demanded limitations on the Court's powers and plastered "Impeach Earl Warren" posters on highway billboards.

These condemnations, however, paled beside those of segregationists following the Supreme Court's decision in *Brown* v. *Board of Education of Topeka* (May 17, 1954). In a unanimous ruling reversing *Plessy* v. *Ferguson* (see Chapter 21), the Court held that separating schoolchildren "solely because of their race generates a feeling of inferiority as to their status in the community that may affect their hearts and minds in a way unlikely ever to be undone" and thus violated the equal-protection clause of the Fourteenth Amendment. "In the field of public education," the nine justices concluded, "the doctrine of 'separate but equal' has no place. Separate educational facilities are inherently unequal." A year later, the Court ordered the states to desegregate their schools "with all deliberate speed."

As the border states complied, Eisenhower directed the school officials of Washington, D.C., to end segregation in the public classrooms of the nation's

capital. But he refused to force white southerners to accept the Court's ruling. "I don't believe you can change the hearts of men with laws or decisions," he observed. Although not a racist, he never publicly endorsed the *Brown* decision, and he privately regretted his appointment of Earl Warren as "the biggest damn fool mistake I ever made."

Encouraged by the lack of presidential support for *Brown,* southern white opposition stiffened. White Citizens Councils sprang up, and the Ku Klux Klan revived. Declaring *Brown* "null, void, and of no effect," southern legislatures claimed the right to "interpose" themselves against the federal government and adopted a strategy of "massive resistance" to thwart compliance with the law. They denied state aid to local school systems that chose to desegregate and even closed down desegregated public schools.

In 1956 more than a hundred members of Congress signed the Southern Manifesto, denouncing *Brown* as "a clear abuse of judicial power." White southern politicians competed to "outnigger" each other in opposition to desegregation. When a gubernatorial candidate in Alabama promised to go to jail to defend segregation, his opponent swore that he would die for it. Segregationists also resorted to violence and economic reprisals against blacks to maintain all-white schools. At the end of 1956, not a single black attended school with whites in the Deep South, and few did so in the Upper South.

The Laws of the Land

Southern resistance reached a climax in September 1957 when Arkansas governor Orval E. Faubus mobilized the state's National Guard to bar nine African-American students from entering Little Rock's Central High School under a federal court order. After a new court order forced Faubus to withdraw the guardsmen their place was taken by a mob of nearly a thousand jeering whites who blocked the black students' entry.

Responding to Faubus's challenge of federal authority, Eisenhower went on television that night to condemn this "disgraceful occurrence." He ordered the obstructors of federal law "to disperse forthwith." The next day, when the mob defied him, the president defended national supremacy and the prestige of his office by placing the Arkansas National Guard under federal command and, for the first time since Reconstruction, by dispatching federal troops to protect the rights of African-Americans. The troops patrolled the high school for the rest of the year, to ensure blacks' safety. But rather than accept desegregation, Faubus shut down all of Little Rock's public high schools in 1958 and 1959. As the fifties ended, fewer than 1 percent of the African-American students in the Deep South were enrolled in desegregated schools.

Even so, the *Brown* decision and Little Rock were key episodes in the emergence of the struggle for civil rights. They galvanized the federal government's powers to use the law to mandate changes in the South. And Little Rock in particular foreshadowed television's vital role in the demise of Jim Crow. The contrast between the images of howling white racists and those of the clean-cut and resolute black students, projected so vividly on the TV screen, immensely aided the civil-rights cause. According to a 1957 public-opinion poll, fully 90 percent of whites outside the South approved the use of federal troops in Little Rock.

Most nonsouthern whites also favored legislation to enfranchise southern African-Americans. Despite his personal reservations, Eisenhower proposed a voting-rights bill in the midst of the 1956 presidential campaign. Passed the following year, the Civil Rights Act of 1957, the first civil-rights law enacted since Reconstruction, established a permanent commission on civil rights with broad investigatory powers. Unfortunately, the law did little to guarantee the ballot to blacks. The Civil Rights Act of 1960 only slightly strengthened the first measure's enforcement provisions. Neither act empowered federal officials to register African-Americans to vote. Like the *Brown* decision, however, they implied a new attitude toward racial matters on the part of the federal government and further encouraged blacks to fight for their due.

THE COLD WAR CONTINUES

The Eisenhower administration maintained the containment policy inherited from the Truman years. Joseph Stalin's death in 1953 and Dwight Eisenhower's resolve to reduce the risk of nuclear war gradually brought a thaw in the Cold War. But an ideological deadlock still gripped the United States and the Soviet Union. The Cold War did not end. Changing times modified the East-West conflict, but containment remained the crux of American foreign policy throughout the 1950s.

Truce in Korea

As his first priority, Eisenhower honored his campaign pledge to go to Korea. Visiting in December 1952, he could not, however, bring home a settlement. The sticking point in negotiations remained the fate of thousands of North Korean and Chinese prisoners of war, held by U.N. forces, who did not want to return to communist rule. In the summer of 1953, the Asian leaders agreed to a compromise, influenced by the uncertainty reigning in the communist world following Stalin's death in March and by Eisenhower's veiled threat to use nuclear weapons to break the stalemate. The armistice signed on July 23, 1953, set the boundary between North and South Korea close to the thirty-eighth parallel, the prewar demarcation line, and established a panel of neutral nations to administer the POWs' return. The end of the fighting brought relief to many Americans but left Korea divided and its political problems unresolved.

Ike and Dulles

Eager to ease Cold War hostilities through diplomacy, Eisenhower first had to mollify the Republican Old Guard. Right-wingers in Congress rejected containment and clamored for forceful efforts to roll back the Red tide. To placate them while he sought to relax tensions with the Soviet Union, the president chose as his secretary of state John Foster Dulles.

A rigid Presbyterian whose humorlessness led some to dub him "Dull, Duller, Dulles," the secretary of state talked of a holy war against "atheistic communism." He called for an offensive aimed at "liberating" the captive peoples of Eastern Europe and unleashing Nationalist leader Jiang Jieshi (Chiang Kai-shek) against Communist China. Condemning neutralism on the part of other nations as "immoral," he threatened "an agonizing reappraisal" of American commitments if its allies did not follow the U.S. lead in each twist and turn of the Cold War. Believing that the Soviet Union understood only force, Dulles insisted on the necessity of "brinkmanship," the art of never backing down in a crisis, even if it meant risking war.

Such saber rattling pleased the Right, but Eisenhower preferred conciliation to bring the Cold War under control. Partly because he feared a nuclear war with the Soviet Union, which had tested its own H-bomb in 1953, Eisenhower refused to translate Dulles's rhetoric into action. The president insisted on making his administration's key foreign-policy decisions, and he understood the limits of American power. When East German workers rioted in 1953 and the Hungarians and Poles revolted in 1956, the United States did nothing to prevent the Soviets from crushing these insurrections. And despite talk of "unleashing" Jiang, the 1954 mutual-defense treaty concluded with Taiwan specifically prohibited the Nationalists from any aggressive ventures without prior consultation with the United States.

Waging Peace

As Hiroshima-size atomic bombs gave way to multi-megaton thermonuclear weapons in the American and Soviet arsenals, Eisenhower labored to reduce the probability of mutual annihilation. Speaking at the United Nations, he proposed an "atoms for peace" plan, whereby both superpowers would contribute fissionable materials to a new U.N. agency for use in industrial projects. Meanwhile, mounting fears over radioactive fallout from atmospheric atomic tests, especially the 1954 U.S. test series in the Pacific that spread strontium 90 over a wide area, heightened world concern about the nuclear-arms race.

In 1955 Eisenhower and the Soviet leaders met in Geneva for the first East-West summit conference since the Second World War. The discussions produced no concrete results, but mutual talk of "peaceful coexistence" led reporters to hail the "spirit of Geneva." Although the two nations could not agree on a specific plan for nuclear-arms control, Moscow suspended further atmospheric tests of nuclear weapons in March 1958 and did not resume them for the remainder of Eisenhower's term. The United States followed suit.

Still, the Cold War continued. Dulles negotiated mutual-defense pacts with any nation that would join the United States in opposing communism. Dulles's "pacto-mania," as some called it, committed the United States to the defense of forty-three nations. Primarily, however, the administration relied on the U.S. nuclear arsenal to deter the Soviets. Tailored to suit a fiscally conservative administration, Washington's "New Look" defense program emphasized nuclear bombs and the planes to deliver them while it cut back on the army and navy. The "New Look" stressed threatening Moscow with "massive retaliation" rather than utilizing U.S. troops in costly "brushfire" wars in remote places. "More bang for the buck," Republicans bragged. But the "New Look"

The Space-Age Toy Shop, 1950s
Through the eyes of two innocent children ogling a fantastic assortment of toy doomsday weapons, the cartoonist captured modern society's fascination with the space-age tools of global destruction.

spurred the Soviets to seek "more rubble for the ruble" by enlarging their own nuclear stockpile.

Meanwhile, the focus of the Cold War shifted from Europe to the Third World, the largely nonwhite, developing nations. There the two superpowers waged war by proxy, using local guerrillas and military juntas to battle in isolated deserts and steamy jungles. There too, the Central Intelligence Agency (CIA) fought a covert war against those thought to be imperiling American interests.

The Clandestine CIA

To command the CIA, Eisenhower chose Allen Dulles, a veteran of wartime OSS cloak-and-dagger operations and the brother of the secretary of state. Established by the National Security Act of 1947 mainly to conduct espionage and to analyze information on foreign nations, the CIA soon became involved in various undercover operations to topple regimes believed hostile to the United States. In 1953 the agency plotted with Iranian army officers to overthrow the popularly elected government that had taken possession of the rich oil resources long exploited by Britain. Fearing a precedent that might jeopardize Western oil interests in the Middle East, the CIA secretly returned the deposed shah of Iran to power and restored the oil wells to British firms. As a result, the United States gained a loyal ally on the Soviet border, and American oil companies prospered from Iranian oil concessions. But the seeds of Iranian hatred of America had been sown—an enmity that would haunt the United States a quarter-century later.

In 1953, to ensure a pro-American government, the CIA intervened in elections in the Philippines. In 1954 it equipped and trained a force of Guatemalans to stage a military coup against the incumbent regime, which had seized 225,000 acres from the American-owned United Fruit Company. After destroying the leftist government, the CIA's Guatemalan agents instituted a military dictatorship subservient to the United States, restored United Fruit's properties, and trampled all political opposition. The few Washington officials who knew of these clandestine operations approved them.

During his second term, Eisenhower allowed the CIA even greater leeway, and by 1957 more than half of the agency's personnel and 80 percent of its budget were devoted to "covert action." It subverted governments, bribed foreign politicians, and subsidized foreign newspapers and labor unions that hewed to a pro-American line. Unwilling to be pulled into long, costly military conflicts as Truman had been drawn into the Korean War, Eisenhower relied on clandestine CIA activities to bolster the United States' allies and weaken its opponents.

Conflict in Vietnam

Of all the secret CIA operations in the 1950s, the most extensive were in Vietnam. Following Mao Zedong's victory in China in 1949, and especially after the outbreak of the Korean conflict, the United States had begun to view Indochina as an area of strategic importance. The Truman administration had furnished the French (who were seeking to reconquer their former colony of Vietnam) with large-scale military assistance to wage war against the Vietminh, a broad-based Vietnamese nationalist coalition of guerrilla fighters led by the communist Ho Chi Minh (see Chapter 28). By 1954 American aid accounted for three-quarters of the French expenditures in the struggle. Still, the French

tottered near defeat. In early 1954 the Vietminh trapped some twelve thousand French troops in the valley of Dienbienphu.

France appealed for U.S. intervention. High-ranking Eisenhower administration officials urged the use of American armed power, including atomic weapons, to assist the French. But the president demurred, unwilling to commit U.S. troops to a jungle war against a popular liberation movement. "No one could be more bitterly opposed to ever getting the United States involved in a hot war in that region than I am," he stressed in 1954; "I cannot conceive of a greater tragedy for America." On May 7, 1954, the French surrendered at Dienbienphu, and in July an international conference in Geneva arranged a cease-fire and divided Vietnam at the seventeenth parallel pending elections in 1956 to choose the government of a unified nation.

Though opposed to committing the United States to another Asian land war, Eisenhower feared the consequences of a communist takeover in Vietnam and refused to sign the Geneva Peace Accords. He made his concern graphic in his "domino theory": "You have a row of dominoes set up, and you knock over the first one, and what will happen to the last one is the certainty that it will go over very quickly. So you have a beginning of a disintegration that would have the most profound influences." If Vietnam fell, Eisenhower warned, nearby Thailand, Burma, and Indonesia, and ultimately all of America's Asian allies, would follow.

Eisenhower ignored the Geneva settlement. The CIA Mission in Vietnam helped install Ngo Dinh Diem, a fiercely anticommunist Catholic, first as premier of France's puppet state and then in 1955 as president of an independent South Vietnam. CIA agents worked with Diem to train his armed forces and secret police, to eliminate political opposition, and to block the election to reunify Vietnam that the Geneva agreements had specified. As Eisenhower later candidly admitted, the United States did not want the election held because "possibly 80 percent of the population would have voted for the communist Ho Chi Minh as their leader." Washington pinned its hopes on Diem to maintain a noncommunist South Vietnam.

But the autocratic Diem could not rally public support. His Catholicism alienated the predominantly Buddhist population; and his refusal to institute land reform for the peasants and to end government corruption created widespread opposition. In 1975 Vietminh guerrillas began sporadic attacks against the Saigon regime, and in December 1960 they organized as the National Liberation Front of South Vietnam (NLF). Backed by North Vietnam, the insurgents attracted wide support. Diem's position, meanwhile, grew weaker. In conflict with the peasantry, and even with major units of his own army, he relied on the billions of dollars and the growing corps of U.S. advisers that the Eisenhower administration supplied. Although Diem spurned U.S. requests to make the reforms that might undercut the NLF's appeal, the United States resolved to "sink or swim with Ngo Dinh Diem."

Antiwesternism in the Middle East

Vietnam would become America's gravest world problem in the 1960s, but Eisenhower faced his greatest crisis in the Middle East. The Arab nationalist Gamal Abdel Nasser came to power in Egypt in 1954, determined to modernize his country. To woo him, the United States offered financing for a dam at Aswan to harness the Nile River. But when Nasser declared neutrality in the Cold War and purchased arms from Czechoslovakia, Dulles canceled the loan. In retaliation, Nasser nationalized the foreign-owned Suez Canal. Nasser's action outraged Britain, which depended on the canal for most of its oil shipments; and his growing appeal to the restive Arabs of Algeria alarmed France, which was trying to retain control of that North African country. For its part, Israel saw Nasser as a menacing force. Egyptian-Israeli tensions and cross-border raids increased, culminating in Nasser's 1955 blockade of the Gulf of Aqaba, Israel's only Red Sea outlet. To protect their interests, Israel, France, and Britain attacked Egypt in October 1956.

The invasion of Egypt enraged Eisenhower. America's closest allies had not consulted the United States, and Moscow was threatening intervention, raising the specter of a great-power nuclear confrontation. The president condemned the invasion and supported a U.N. resolution to that effect while simultaneously ordering the Strategic Air Command on alert against the U.S.S.R. "If those fellows start something, we may have to hit 'em—and if necessary, with everything in the bucket," he warned. On November 6 Britain, France, and Israel promised to leave Egypt, and by March 1957 the last troops (the Israelis) were gone.

The Suez crisis had two vital consequences. It swelled antiwestern sentiment in the Third World, and in its aftermath the United States replaced Britain and France as the protector of Western interests in the Middle East. Eisenhower announced in January 1957 that

"the existing vacuum in the Middle East must be filled by the United States before it is filled by Russia." Anxious to secure the oil needed by western industry and consumers, the president proclaimed—and Congress approved—what became known as the Eisenhower Doctrine, an announcement that the United States would send military aid and, if necessary, troops to any Middle Eastern nation that asked for help against "international communism."

Eisenhower acted on the doctrine in July 1958. A nationalist coup in Iraq overthrew the monarchy and brought to power the first of many antiwestern regimes. Worried that more such coups would occur, Eisenhower sent fourteen thousand American marines to Lebanon at the request of its beleaguered prowestern government. The marines soon left Lebanon, but U.S. policymakers continued to interpret Third World nationalism as communist inspired.

Frustrations Abroad

Such interventions augmented the anti-Americanism of neutralists and nationalists in many small nations. When Vice President Nixon visited Peru and Venezuela in 1958, after the overthrow of dictators who had been personally decorated by Eisenhower, crowds spat at him and stoned his car. The following year, Fidel Castro overturned a dictatorial regime in Cuba and denounced "yanqui imperialism." When anti-American rioting rocked Japan in 1960, Eisenhower canceled his announced trip to the United States' strongest Asian ally.

The beleaguered president suffered a tougher blow on May 1, 1960, when, two weeks before a scheduled summit conference with Khrushchev in Paris, the Soviets shot down a high-altitude U.S. spy plane twelve hundred miles inside Soviet borders. Prior to this incident, Eisenhower had worked diligently to improve Soviet-American relations. His diplomacy in 1958 had defused a crisis over the fate of Berlin. In 1959 Nixon had visited the Soviet Union, and Khrushchev had toured the United States. At the presidential retreat at Camp David, Maryland, the two heads of state had held a cordial meeting and agreed to confer in Paris during the coming year.

But they would never meet again. The plane's downing exposed the U-2 reconnaissance missions that the United States had been flying over the Soviet Union since 1956 to spy on military installations. When Khrushchev announced the downing, the Eisenhower administration, denying the charge of espionage, initially maintained that a flight to collect weather data

The Great Debate, July 24, 1959

At the opening of the American National Exhibit in Moscow, Vice President Richard Nixon and Soviet Premier Nikita Khrushchev engaged in a "kitchen debate," arguing not about the strength of their rockets or bombs but about the relative merits of American and Soviet washing machines and television sets.

had strayed off course. An angry Khrushchev then displayed to the world the captured CIA pilot, the U-2's spy cameras, and photos taken of Soviet missile sites. Belatedly, Washington admitted the spying; but Eisenhower refused the Soviet premier's demands that he apologize for the flights. The summit collapsed.

The Eisenhower Legacy

Three days before leaving office, Eisenhower delivered a prophetic message to the American people. Like George Washington, he used the occasion of his farewell address to issue a somber warning. The demands of national security, observed the former soldier who had spent nearly two-thirds of his life in uniform, had produced the "conjunction of an immense military establishment and a large arms industry that is new in the American experience." Swollen Cold War defense budgets, he said, had made the health of the nation's economy dependent on military expenditures. Defense contracts had become the staff of life for scholars at research universities, for politicians from districts housing air and naval bases, and for executives at the United States' largest corporations. This intertwined combination of interests, Eisenhower believed, exerted enormous leverage in the councils of government and threatened the traditional subordination of the military in American life. He warned, "We must guard against the acquisition of unwarranted influence, whether sought or unsought, by the military-industrial complex. The potential for the disastrous rise of misplaced power exists and will persist."

The president concluded with an assessment of his foreign policy: he had avoided war but could not affirm that lasting peace was in sight. Most scholars agreed. He had ended the war in Korea, kept the peace for the next seven and a half years, avoided direct military intervention in Vietnam, begun the process of relaxing tensions with the Soviet Union, and even cooperated in achieving a lull in the atmospheric testing of doomsday weapons. Yet he had also presided over an accelerating nuclear-arms race and a widening Cold War, and he had given the CIA the green light to intervene in local conflicts around the globe.

In domestic affairs, the moderate Eisenhower pleased neither Left nor Right. His acceptance of the social-welfare legislation of the New Deal so annoyed the Republican Right that conservatives grumbled that Ike's memoir of his first term should have been titled *More of the Same* rather than *Mandate for Change*. Liberals, on the other hand, faulted Eisenhower for not doing enough to quash McCarthyism and racism. Ike gave the majority of voters what they wanted, not what ideologues thought they should want. Americans yearned for reassurance, and Eisenhower supplied it. He restored dignity to the presidency and a sense of harmony to the nation. As lucky as he was skillful, Eisenhower led the nation during a great economic boom; and in an age of upheaval, he furnished what Americans most desired: a breathing spell in which to relish the comforts of life. "Eisenhower did his best to make time stand still," summed up historian William O'Neill, "and for a little while it did."

THE AFFLUENT SOCIETY

When economist John Kenneth Galbraith published a book about postwar America in 1958, he called it *The Affluent Society.* A broad-based prosperity had indeed made the 1950s a period of economic abundance. The material aspects of the American dream had seemingly come true. By the end of the 1950s, about 60 percent of all American families owned homes; 75 percent, cars; and 87 percent, at least one TV. The gross national product in the 1950s increased 50 percent as a consequence of heavy government spending, a huge upsurge in productivity, and a steadily increasing demand for consumer goods and services.

Not all was rosy on the economic front. Three brief recessions marred the prosperity of the Eisenhower Era. In the 1957–1958 downturn, the unemployment rate inched up to 7.6 percent, the highest since the Great Depression. A rising national debt, which reached almost $290 billion by the end of 1960, evoked further worry.

But overall, the economic growth of the fifties brought the United States the highest standard of living the world had ever known. When corrected for inflation, the average American worker's real income in 1960 was 35 percent higher than it had been in 1945, and twice the level of the prosperous 1920s. With just 6 percent of the world's population, the United States produced and consumed nearly half of everything made and sold on earth.

The New Industrial Society

Federal expenditures, a major source of the nation's economic growth, nearly doubled in the 1950s, and the outlays of state and local governments more than kept pace. Although federal expenditures composed just 1 percent of the GNP in 1929, by the mid-1950s they had soared to 17 percent. They constructed roads and airports, financed home mortgages, supported farm prices, paid pensions and unemployment benefits, and provided stipends for education. But more than *half* the federal budget each year—about 10 percent of the

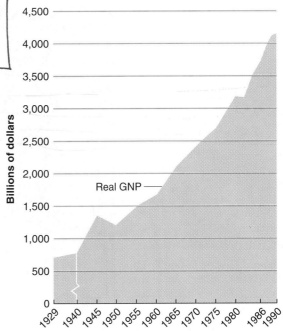

Gross National Product, 1929–1990

Following World War II, the United States achieved the highest living standard in world history. Between 1950 and 1970, the real GNP, which factors out inflation and reveals the actual amount of goods and services produced, steadily increased. However, in 1972, 1974–1975, 1980, and 1982 the real GNP declined.

NOTE: Data shown in 1982 dollars.

SOURCE: *Economic Report of the President,* 1991.

GNP—went to defense expenditures. And with continued U.S.–Soviet rivalry in the production of atomic munitions, the development of missile-delivery systems, and the space race, the federal government was the nation's chief sponsor of scientific and technological research and development (R&D) in the 1950s.

Startling breakthroughs in science revolutionized U.S. industry, with both positive and negative consequences. Funded by the Atomic Energy Commission and utilizing U.S. Navy and Westinghouse scientists, the Duquesne Light Company in 1954 began construction in Shippingport, Pennsylvania, of the nation's first nuclear-power plant. It came on line in 1957, and a second one, near Morris, Illinois, followed. No one warned the public of the problem of accidental releases of radiation or of the dilemma over where to store spent fuel rods. As a result of ongoing R&D, chemicals surged from the fiftieth-largest industry before the war to the nation's fourth-largest in the 1960s.

General Electric Assembly Line
As Americans in the postwar years satisfied their pent-up demand for household conveniences like these washing machines, their consumption of dwindling natural resources increased dramatically, as did the amount of pollution they produced.

As chemical fertilizers and pesticides contaminated groundwater supplies, and as the expansion of plastics for consumer products reduced landfill space, Americans—unaware of the hidden perils—marveled at the plentiful fruits and vegetables they could buy and delighted in their Dacron suits, Orlon shirts, Acrilan socks, and Teflon-coated pots and pans.

Electronics spurted to become the fifth-biggest industry in the United States. The industry sold electrical equipment to other businesses and electrical appliances to consumers. Electric consumption tripled in the 1950s as industry turned to automation and as Americans, urged by advertisers to "live better electrically," purchased electric washers and dryers, freezers, blenders, television sets, and stereos, as well as electric blankets, electric garage-door openers, and electric pencil sharpeners. Essential to the expansion in both the chemical and the electronics industry was the availability of inexpensive petroleum. With domestic crude-oil production increasing close to 50 percent and petroleum imports rising from 74 million to 371 million barrels between 1945 and 1960, petroleum replaced coal as the nation's main energy source. Hardly anyone paid attention when a physicist, in remarks before the American Geophysical Society in 1953 on escalating energy consumption, warned that "adding 6 billion tons of carbon dioxide to the atmosphere each year is warming up the Earth."

Bountiful cheap gasoline also underlay the expansion of the aircraft and automobile industries. The continued growth of aircraft manufacture, the nation's third-largest industry throughout the fifties, rested on massive government defense spending, on the switch to jet propulsion by commercial aviation, and on the enormous sums poured into space research in the latter 1950s. The titan of the American economy, the automobile industry, spending nearly one-fifth of its budget on R&D, utilized technology to increase productivity. Where the auto industry had once partially replaced human labor with machinery, it now used automation to control the machines. Between 1945 and 1960, the industry halved the number of hours and workers required to produce a car. Other manufacturers followed suit, investing an average of $10 billion a year throughout the fifties on new labor-saving machinery.

The Age of Computers

One key to the postwar technological revolution was the electronic computer. A new era dawned in 1944 when the International Business Machines Corporation (IBM), cooperating with scientists at Harvard University on devices to decipher the secret codes of the Axis powers, produced the Mark I calculator. Although slow and enormously cumbersome—a maze of five hundred miles of wiring and more than three thousand electromechanical relays—it proved a vital first step. Two years later, to improve artillery trajectory, the U.S. Army began operating ENIAC, the first electronic computer. Still vast and complex, with tens of thousands of vacuum tubes and resistors, ENIAC reduced the time required to multiply two tenth-place numbers from Mark I's three seconds to less than three-thousandths of a second. Then came the development of operating instructions, or programs, that could be stored inside the computer memory; the substitution of printed circuits for wired ones; and in 1948, at Bell Labs, the invention of tiny, solid-state components, called transistors, that ended reliance on radio tubes.

The computer fundamentally changed the American economy and society. Sales of electronic computers to industry rose from twenty in 1954 to more than a thousand in 1957, and to more than two thousand in 1960. By then, with the government as its major client, the electronic-computer industry had become a billion-dollar business. The government, which used three machines in computing the 1950 census returns, employed several hundred on the 1960 census. They became as indispensable to Pentagon strategists playing war games as to the Internal Revenue Service, as integral to the work of the Weather Bureau as to aerospace scientists "flying" rockets still on the drawing board. By the mid-1960s more than thirty thousand computers were being utilized by banks, insurance companies, airline- and hotel-reservation departments, stock-brokerage firms, hospitals, and universities. By making industrial automation possible, computers also transformed the nature of work. Greater quantities of products could be manufactured in less time and with fewer workers than ever before.

Concentration and Consolidation in Industry and Agriculture

Rapid technological advances accelerated a long-term economic trend: the growth and power of big business. In 1950, twenty-two U.S. firms had assets of more than $1 billion; ten years later more than fifty did. By 1960 one-half of 1 percent of all companies earned more than half the total corporate income in the United States. The wealthiest, which could afford huge R&D outlays, became oligopolies as they swallowed up weak competitors. Just as three television networks monopolized the nation's airwaves, so three automobile and three aluminum companies produced more

The American Farmer, 1940–1993

The postwar years saw a fundamental transformation of American agriculture.
While the small family farmer joined the rural exodus to the cities, large farms prospered.

SOURCE: U.S. Bureau of the Census, *Statistical Abstract of the United States, 1993* (Washington, D.C.)

Scientific Agriculture, 1955
*A Pennsylvania farmer survey-
ing the array of synthetic fertilizers, insecticides, and chemicals
he annually uses on his
78-acre farm.*

than 90 percent of the cars and aluminum in the United States; and a handful of firms in steel, petroleum, aircraft, chemicals, and electrical machinery controlled the lion's share of their industries' assets and sales. Major corporations also increased their power by forming conglomerates (mergers of companies in unrelated industries) and by acquiring facilities overseas, thus becoming "multinational" enterprises. Despite talk of "people's capitalism," the oil-rich Rockefeller family alone owned more corporate stock than all the nation's wage earners combined.

Along with growth and consolidation came further bureaucratization. In a process under way since the early twentieth century, "executives" continued to replace "capitalists," so that by the mid-1950s American industry employed more than a quarter-million vice presidents. The new professional managerial class, largely divorced from ownership of the corporations they controlled, administered the many diverse departments involved in R&D, production, advertising, sales, accounting, investment, and labor relations. As standard-setters for the hosts of salaried, white-collar workers whom they supervised, managers placed a

premium on conformist behavior—on giving in to social pressure rather than adhering to personal values. Sociologist David Riesman contrasted their "other-directed" behavior—an obsession to fit in and gain acceptance by bowing to the dictates of a group or organization—with the "inner-directed" orientation of small businesspeople and professionals of earlier years, who were guided by the values they had learned in their youth. Deploring this development, radical sociologist C. Wright Mills depicted members of the white-collar class as selling "not only their time and energy but their personalities as well."

Changes in American agriculture paralleled those in industry. Farming grew increasingly scientific and mechanized. Between 1945 and 1960, technology cut the work-hours necessary to grow and harvest crops by more than half. Many farm families migrated to urban America. In 1956 alone one-eleventh of the farm population left the land. But the big, heavily capitalized farm businesses prospered by employing new machinery and by saturating their acreage with chemicals.

Few Americans understood the extent to which chemical fertilizers, herbicides, and pesticides poisoned the environment until the publication of Rachel Carson's *Silent Spring* in 1962. A former researcher for the Fish and Wildlife Service, Carson argued for selective methods of pest control. Attacking the rain of toxic DDT released "indiscriminately from the skies," she painstakingly demonstrated that the poison could not be contained. DDT did not degrade in water, was absorbed by plants and then stored in the tissues of birds and fish, and was eventually recycled throughout the food chain. Gradually, the states banned the use of DDT, and the federal government followed suit in 1972.

Meanwhile, agribusiness benefited from the increased profitability of farming with chemicals. They also grew rich from the $5 billion spent by the government on farm subsidies in the 1950s—payments proportional to farm size and output. Moreover, a new soil-conservation program adopted in 1956, which paid farmers to take cropland out of production, primarily enriched the businesses that owned extensive property and could allow tens of thousands of their acres to lie fallow.

Blue-Collar Blues

Consolidation also transformed the labor movement. After twenty discordant years, the AFL and CIO merged in 1955. The new AFL-CIO brought 85 percent of all union members into a single administrative unit, with the AFL's George Meany as president and the CIO's Walter Reuther as senior vice president. The leadership promised aggressive unionism, but the movement could not recapture its old militancy.

Organized labor was a victim of its own past successes. Victories at the bargaining table had secured so many benefits for workers that their solidarity gave way to complacency. By the mid-fifties most unionized Americans earned decent wages and pensions, worked fewer than forty hours a week, and received paid vacations as well as sickness and hospitalization benefits. In the late 1940s, the United Automobile Workers and General Motors had signed a trend-setting contract providing for automatic wage hikes whenever productivity increased or the cost of living rose. Then in 1953, in negotiations with the Ford Motor Company, the UAW led the way again, winning a guaranteed annual wage and the provision that laid-off workers would be paid two-thirds of their normal earnings in addition to government unemployment benefits. Complacent management preferred higher costs to strikes. As Chrysler executive Lee Iacocca recalled: "Because

we had a lock on the market, we could continually spend more money on labor and simply pass the additional costs along to the consumer in the form of price increases." The labor turbulence of the early postwar years subsided.

The decrease in the number of blue-collar workers further sapped organized labor. As automation reduced the number of laborers in coal mines, auto plants, and steel mills, membership in those once mighty industrial unions dropped by more than half. Most of the new jobs in the 1950s were in the traditionally union-resistant white-collar service sector and in public employment, which banned collective bargaining by labor unions. Unwilling or unable to woo the unskilled and semiskilled minority workers in the low-paying service nonagricultural jobs, organized labor saw its portion of the labor force drop from a high of 36 percent in 1953 to 31 percent in 1960.

Prosperity, Suburbanization, and Mobility

As real income rose, Americans satisfied their desires for the goods and services they had longed for. Spending less of their income on basic necessities, they purchased electric lawn mowers, air conditioners, and striped toothpaste. They heaped their shopping carts with food that had been frozen, sprayed, dehydrated, and fortified. When they lacked cash, they borrowed. In 1950, Diner's Club issued the first credit card, and American Express followed in 1958. Installment buying, home mortgages, and auto loans raised Americans' total private indebtedness in the 1950s from $73 billion to $196 billion. A consumer culture dominated American life. To further stimulate consumerism, advertising expenditures leaped nearly 250 percent in the fifties. Throughout the decade business annually allocated more for advertising than the nation spent on public education.

The car-selling slogan of the 1950s, "You auto buy now," encouraged Americans to purchase a record 58 million new cars that decade. The number of registered automobiles increased by 21 million, the total of motor-vehicle miles traveled rose by 75 percent, and critics complained of "autosclerosis"—the clogging of urban arteries. In an era when nobody spoke of quality as "Job One," the auto industry kept the public buying by promising glamour and status in bigger and flashier models with gleaming chrome, two-tone colors, and tail fins. Although seat belts remained an unadvertised

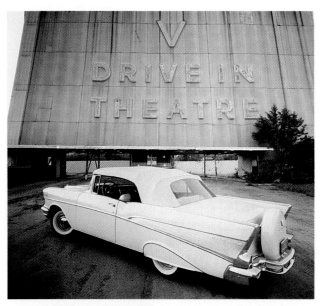

1957 Chevrolet Bel Air
In addition to hyping its shiny chrome and elongated tail fins, advertisements alliteratively described this car's automatic transmission as the Triple-Turbine Turbo-Glide.

extra-cost option, the 1955 Ford featured "Trigger-Torque 'Go' Power," and that year's Pontiac boasted the "Sensational Strato-Streak V–8!" Other gas-guzzling road chariots—sporting such names as "Marauder" and "Barracuda"—came in colors ranging from "passion pink" to "lilac mist" and were powered by engines capable of propelling them more than twice as fast as any existing speed limit. Hand in hand came rises in highway deaths, air pollution, and oil consumption, as well as a creeping sprawl of motels, gas stations, and fast-food outlets.

"Auto-mania" spurred white flight to Beechwood, Ohio; Glenview, Illinois; and suburbs throughout the country. So did government policies. As federal spending on highways skyrocketed from $79 million in 1946 to $2.9 billion in 1960, and as state and local expenditures for roads kept pace, areas once considered too remote by urban workers became desirable places to live. The tax code further induced home buying by permitting deductions for home-mortgage interest payments and for property taxes. And the Federal Housing Administration (FHA) and the Veterans Administration (VA) stimulated home sales by offering low-interest loans.

Eighty-five percent of the phenomenal 13 million new homes built in the 1950s were in the suburbs. A variety of attractions lured Americans to suburbia. Some moved in search of affordable single-family dwellings. Others became suburbanites to escape the crime and grime of the central cities and to distance themselves from the millions of newly urbanized minorities. And many newly married Americans headed for suburbia in quest of communities oriented toward children and education (see "A Place in Time").

Although social critics complained about endless acres of cookie-cutter houses inhabited by bored housewives and harried husbands desperate to keep up with their neighbors, most suburbanites enjoyed their new life-style, tranquil surroundings, and like-minded neighbors. They gained a sense of belonging and of influence in the community. To a nation of immigrants, most from countries where property ownership was denied to all but an elite few, taking title to a home of one's own formed the very core of the American dream.

Whereas the population of central cities rose 10 percent during the 1950s, the number of suburban dwellers nearly *doubled.* About a million New Yorkers migrated to communities ringing the city. Bordering Los Angeles, Orange County doubled in population in the 1940s and then tripled that in the 1950s. Nationwide some 18 million moved to the suburbs. For the first time in the twentieth century, a majority of Americans lived in their own homes rather than in rented quarters. The suburban population of 60 million in 1960 equaled that of the central cities. And by 1970 the suburbs would contain two-thirds of the metropolitan-area population and the cities only one-third—exactly the reverse of 1950.

Americans migrated not only from city to suburb but from North to South and from East to West. Lured by employment opportunities, droves of Americans descended on the Houston–Beaumont–Port Arthur complex, as well as on Phoenix and Mobile. Attracted by the jobs in the aircraft industry, others headed for the Northwest. Most, however, like the Brooklyn Dodgers and the New York Giants, migrated to California, which added some 5 million to its numbers and accounted for fully one-fifth of the nation's population growth in the 1950s. The fifth-largest state in 1940, California would supplant New York in 1963 as the most populous. The shift of millions from the frosty North and East to the balmy South and West altered the nation both economically and politically. Drawn to the Sun Belt by right-to-work laws, which outlawed the union shop, and by low taxes and energy costs, countless industrialists moved their plants and corporate headquarters

Central-city dwellers	

Suburban dwellers

Rural and small-town dwellers

Urban, Suburban, and Rural Americans, 1940–1960

In the fifteen years following World War II, more than 40 million Americans migrated to the suburbs, where, as one father put it, "a kid could grow up with grass stains on his pants." Over the same period, fourteen of the fifteen largest U.S. cities lost population.

SOURCE: Adapted from U.S. Bureau of the Census, *Current Censuses, 1930–1970* (Washington, D.C.: U.S. Government Printing Office).

there, also transplanting their conservative outlooks. By 1980 the population of the Sun Belt—an area stretching from the Old Confederacy across Texas and the Southwest to southern California—would exceed that of the North and East; and the political power of the Republican party would rise accordingly.

An American magically transported from the depression-wracked 1930s to the prosperous nation of twenty years later would have had trouble believing her eyes. Financial worry had given way to affluence. An industrial system rooted in an era of cheap immigrant labor and belching smokestack factories was being transformed by automation, the computer, new management techniques, and the flow of businesses to the Sun Belt. A union movement that had long struggled for recognition now found itself in decline, and people that for a century had crowded in ever-greater numbers into city apartments now turned their gaze to the mass-produced houses of the suburbs. Inexorably, all these changes molded future social contours and political issues.

◆

CONSENSUS AND CONSERVATISM

Of course, not everyone embraced the fifties' materialism or sank unquestioningly into a deep cushion of contentedness. Disaffected intellectuals criticized conformity and consumerism, especially in middle-class suburbia. They condemned American religion for tepidness; denounced the young as a "silent generation"; bemoaned identical "ticky-tacky" houses and monotony in "disturbia"; and lampooned the shallow quality of life in "an America of mass housing, mass markets, massive corporations, massive government, mass media, and massive boredom." These critics targeted "organization men" bent on getting ahead by going along, "status seekers" pursuing external rewards to compensate for inner insecurities, and "other-directed" personalities highly vulnerable to peer-group pressure. The United States, the dissenters charged, had become a "packaged society" and its people "all items in a national supermarket—categorized, processed, labeled, priced, and readied for merchandising."

But the attack on homogeneity and materialism oversimplified reality. It ignored the increasing ethnic, racial, and religious diversity of U.S. society; it overlooked the acquisitiveness and conformity of earlier generations—the peer-group pressures in small-town America; and it failed to gauge the currents of dissent swirling beneath the placid surface. Too eager to sneer at the middle class that shunned them, the fault finders of the 1950s caricatured rather than characterized American society.

Still, their criticism did spotlight the elevation of comfort over challenge, safety over risk, and private pleasures over public affairs. Americans hungered for security, and they sought refuge in the good life.

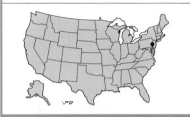

Alfred and William Levitt revolution-ized home construction much as Henry Ford did automobile production and Henry Kaiser shipbuilding. Their pio-neering use of mass-production tech-niques to construct a large, inexpensive housing development opened the gates for an exodus from the cities to the sub-urbs. Their success stimulated a host of imitators and a record 1.65 million hous-ing starts in 1955.

Following the Second World War, Levitt & Sons purchased fifteen hundred acres of potato fields on Long Island's Hempstead Plain, some thirty miles from midtown Manhattan. In response to the housing shortage, the Levitts quickly built 2,000 homes and rented them for just sixty-five dollars a month to married veter-ans eager to escape from their in-laws' residences or cramped apartments where landlords frowned on children. Using the standardized construction techniques that they had first employed in erecting low-cost housing units for wartime navy work-ers in Norfolk, Virginia, the Levitts then rapidly built and rented 2,000 more homes. In 1948 they began to offer the houses for sale. The company recognized that working Americans' ever-greater de-mand for suburban housing—a demand fueled by the easy availability of low-cost mortgages from the FHA and the VA, ex-tensive car ownership, and the expanding U.S. highway system—promised a bo-nanza of profits. By 1951 the Levitts had built and sold another 13,500 homes.

To erect their 720-square-foot Cape Cod or ranch-style houses as quickly and cheaply as possible, the Levitts estab-lished their own lumber mill, nail factory, and electrical-supply company. They em-ployed mainly unskilled, nonunion labor-ers, each of whom was trained to perform just one task. Everything moved on a fixed timetable as Levitt & Sons made "a factory of the whole building site." First came the bulldozers and trenching machines to strip and ditch each 60- by 100-foot lot in twenty-seven minutes. Another crew poured the concrete foundation. Trucks then brought the precut and preassem-bled materials to each site, where a suc-cession of teams hammered the prefabri-

Levittown, Long Island, in 1949
The popularity of this typical Levittown house, providing comfortable living space for this family of five on a lot sixty feet by one hundred feet, made the Levitts the nation's largest home builder.

cated siding, connected the plumbing, strung the electrical wires, fitted the windows, laid the flooring, shingled the roof, and spray-painted the walls. One man did nothing but move from house to house bolting Bendix washing machines to the floor.

Levittown initially radiated uniformity. Each house had two bedrooms; a bath; a kitchen equipped with an electric refrigerator, a range, and a washing machine; an expansion attic; and a living room with a fireplace, picture window, and built-in television set. Deeds to the property required door chimes, not buzzers, prohibited picket fences, mandated regular lawn mowing, and even specified when the wash could be hung to dry in the backyard. All the town streets curved at the same angle, and a tree was planted every twenty-eight feet.

Critics decried the tasteless, monotonous conformity of Levittown; but young marrieds, as they were called, avidly purchased the Levitts' houses. Levittown's comforts and conveniences sharply contrasted with living conditions in the Quonset huts, trailer parks, and stuffy apartments to which many postwar Americans had become accustomed. One veteran, Wilbur Schaetzl, considered the crowded, violence-ridden Brooklyn neighborhood from which he had moved "so awful I'd rather not talk about it. Getting into this house was like being emancipated." Laura Forman, who had one child and was expecting a second, found Levittown to be a "paradise for children—and mothers. Soon after we moved in, neighbors I hadn't even met yet came in to help. Because my husband was working, they packed my bags, drove me to the hospital, and took care of my other baby. And they wouldn't let me buy anything for the new baby either. That carriage isn't mine and neither is the crib." Such small-town friendliness also appealed to Izzy Stark, who had previously lived in an apartment house without ever knowing his neighbors. Stark's Levittown friends "were closer than kin. When the girls go to a garden club meeting, we boys get together and baby-sit and play poker. Or one night we'll all go bowling or to the movies. And now we're all taking some of these adult education courses down at the school one night a week. I'm taking 'How to Finish

Suburban Leisure Time
Working and/or relaxing in one's backyard became the primary weekend activity in the nation's burgeoning suburbs in the 1950s.

Your Attic' and Bob and Harry are learning photography." Despite the long commute to his office in Manhattan (he would travel half a million miles, or twenty times around the world, before he retired), Stark had achieved "his dream house."

To meet the galloping demand for its low-cost homes, in the early 1950s Levitt & Sons bought eight square miles of spinach farmland on the Delaware River in Bucks County, Pennsylvania, and constructed a second Levittown of sixteen thousand homes. Still another followed in Willingboro, New Jersey. Each endeavor mirrored the Levitts' concern for planned orderliness. In the Bucks County development, they situated schools, churches, baseball fields, shopping centers, parking lots, and offices for doctors and dentists at symmetrical points outside the residential clusters. In Willingboro they integrated the houses and the recreational and shopping facilities within the various neighborhoods. But that was all that the Levitts wished to inte-

grate. Fearful that the admission of blacks would provoke "white flight" from the communities that they designed, Levitt & Sons excluded African-Americans. Not until the mid-1960s, when blacks brought suit to be allowed to purchase a home in Levittown, New Jersey, did the Levitts sell their first home to a nonwhite. As late as 1990, Long Island's Levittown had an African-American population of just 0.03 percent.

The enormous success of the Levittown ventures reflected the shift in population in the 1950s. The United States in these years increasingly became a nation of white suburbs and nonwhite cities. As the suburbs attracted not only more and more private homeowners but also more and more commerce and industry, the cities fell victim to shrinking tax bases just as their need for social services zoomed. Levittown and such similar suburban communities as Oak Meadows outside Chicago and Parkmerced near San Francisco had changed the face of America.

Postwar Population Growth
As the baby boom took off, 1950s popular magazines placed a renewed emphasis on family life and commonly featured stories and portraits of five- and six-member families.

Togetherness and the Baby Boom

In 1954 *McCall's* magazine coined the term *togetherness* to celebrate the "ideal" couple: the man and woman who married young, had a large family, and centered their lives on home and children. The combination of economic prosperity and Cold War saber rattling led Americans in the 1950s to wed at an earlier age than their parents, to have babies sooner, and to have more of them. The fertility rate (the number of births per thousand women) rose from 80 in 1940 to 106 in 1950 and peaked at 123 in 1957, when an American baby was born every seven seconds.

At the same time, medical science made tremendous advances against childhood disease. Infection-fighting drugs—particularly streptomycin in 1945 and aureomycin in 1948—virtually eliminated diphtheria, influenza, and typhoid fever. In the mid-1950s the Salk and Sabin vaccines ended the dreaded poliomyelitis (polio), the major scourge of children. The dramatic drop in the mortality of the young helped raise life expectancy in the United States from 65.9 years in 1945 to 70.9 years in 1970. In tandem with the baby boom, this decline contributed to a 19 percent population increase. At a time of negligible immigration, the U.S. population jumped from 151 million to 180 million in

the 1950s, a larger spurt than in any previous decade. Most significantly, the percentage of children under fourteen in the total population leaped from less than a quarter in 1945 to nearly a third in 1960.

The sheer size of the baby-boom generation ensured its continuing historical importance. In the 1950s it helped fuel the economic boom and expand the nation's educational system. It also made child rearing a preeminent concern and reinforced the idea that women's place was in the home. With Americans convinced that early-childhood experiences influenced individuals psychologically for their entire lives, motherhood became a vital, demanding calling.

No one did more to emphasize the presumed close connection between full-time mothers and healthy children than Dr. Benjamin Spock: only the Bible outsold his *Baby and Child Care* (1946) in the fifties. Popularizing the theories of Sigmund Freud and John Dewey as an alternative to authoritarian child rearing, Spock urged mothers to create an atmosphere of warmth and intimacy for their children so that they could mature into well-adjusted adults. Crying babies were to be comforted so that they would not feel rejected. Breast feeding came back into vogue. Spock's advice led to less scolding and spanking and more "democratic" family discussions. In some homes it produced a "filiarchy," where children's wants dominated. "Do it for the kids" ruled the roost. Spock's teachings placed a premium on mothers' full-time devotion to child rearing; anything less, he argued, might result in maladjustment. Spock even wanted the government to pay mothers so that they would not have to work outside the home. Seldom had motherhood been so exalted.

Domesticity

Popular culture throughout the fifties glorified marriage and parenthood and depicted a woman's devotion to life in the home with her children as the most cherished goal. Television almost always pictured mother at home—usually in the kitchen. Hollywood films perpetuated the stereotype of career women as neurotics and of loving mothers as happy. As the "girl next door" star Debbie Reynolds explained in the film *The Tender Trap* (1955), "A woman isn't a woman until she's been married and had children."

The educational system promoted the same notion. Whereas girls learned typing, etiquette, and cooking, boys were channeled into carpentry, auto mechanics, and courses leading to careers. Extracurricular activities reinforced the belief in males as leaders and females as assistants. Guidance counselors cautioned young women not to "miss the boat" of marriage by pursuing a higher education. "Men are not interested in college degrees, but in the warmth and humanness of the girls they marry," stressed one textbook on family living. Overall, women constituted a smaller percentage of college students in the 1950s than in the 1920s or 1930s and received fewer advanced degrees than in those decades. Almost two-thirds of the college women in the fifties failed to complete a degree, and except in the most prestigious colleges, most of those who did graduate concentrated in such fields as home economics and primary education.

Even as the culture celebrated domesticity, profound changes were under way. Despite the layoffs of women immediately after World War II, women returned to the labor force. By 1952, 2 million more women worked outside the home than had been employed during the war; and by 1960 nearly 40 percent of American women would hold full- or part-time jobs. The proportion of working wives, moreover, rose from 15 percent in 1940 to 30 percent in 1960. Reversing earlier patterns, some 40 percent of all working women in 1960 had school-age children.

Most worked to add to family income, not to challenge stereotypes. To help pay for the knotty-pine rumpus room, they took low-paying, low-prestige jobs where women remained "girls" whatever their age. Although the rise in female employment fostered conditions that would lead to a feminist resurgence in the late 1960s, organized feminism ebbed to its lowest point of the century during the fifties. The great majority of women responded to prosperity and atomic jitters by concentrating on private satisfactions and trying to make the home a haven in an uncertain world.

Religion and Education

"Today in the U.S.," *Time* claimed in 1954, "the Christian faith is back in the center of things." Signs of the revival abounded. Leading religious popularizers—fiery evangelist Billy Graham, riveting Roman Catholic bishop Fulton J. Sheen, and "positive-thinking" Protestant minister Norman Vincent Peale—had syndicated newspaper columns, best-selling books, and radio and television programs. Hollywood's biggest box-office attractions included *The Robe, The Ten Commandments, Ben Hur,* and other religious extravaganzas. While popular singers crooned such hits as "I Believe" and "The Man Upstairs," TV commercials pronounced that "the family that prays together stays together."

The American Legion organized a "Back to God" campaign. Dial-a-Prayer offered formulaic telephone solutions for various spiritual problems. Congress added the phrase "under God" to the Pledge of Allegiance and made "IN GOD WE TRUST" mandatory on all U.S. currency. Church attendance swelled from 64.5 million (48 percent of the population) in 1940 to 110 million (63 percent) in 1958.

Augmenting a trend that would escalate in the future, millions of Americans embraced evangelical fundamentalism and became "born-again" Christians. Most Americans turned to religion for reassurance in an anxious age—for peace of mind and a sense of belonging. President Eisenhower himself opined, "Everybody should have a religious faith, and I don't care what it is." Thus, despite an aura of religiosity in the fifties, the *intensity* of religious belief diminished for many men and women as mainstream churches downplayed sin and evil and preached Americanism and fellowship.

Similarly, education flourished in the 1950s yet seemed more intellectually shallow than in previous decades. As a result of the baby boom, primary-school enrollment, which had risen by less than a million in the 1940s, jumped by nearly 10 million in the 1950s. California opened a new school an average of every seven days throughout the decade and still faced a classroom shortage. Likewise, the proportion of college-age Americans enrolled in institutions of higher learning soared from 15 percent in 1940 to 32 percent in 1957 and topped 40 percent in the early 1960s. At every level a watered-down version of the doctrine of "Education for Life Adjustment," attributed to John Dewey, held sway. Legions of Dewey disciples promoted sociability and self-expression over science, math, and history. Community needs took precedence over intellectual rigor, and the "well-rounded" student became more prized than the highly skilled and knowledgeable one.

Numerous surveys of college students in the 1950s described them as conservative, conformist, and careerist, as a "silent generation" more interested in security and comfort than in distinguishing themselves. Campus passivity was the norm, except when it came to panty raids or competitions to determine how many undergraduates could be stuffed into a phone booth. When Oklahoma A&M surveyed its students about their greatest concern, number one was finding a parking space. Overall, students' attitudes closely mirrored those of their elders.

Affirmation and Anxiety: The Culture of the Fifties

American culture at midcentury reflected both the upbeat spirit of a prosperous era and an undercurrent of discontent with the quality of life. Enjoying more leisure time and bigger paychecks, Americans spent one-seventh of the gross national product in 1950 on entertainment. Spectator sports boomed, new symphony halls opened, and book sales doubled.

New York replaced Paris as the capital of the art world, and abstract expressionism was the rage. Like the immense canvases of painters Jackson Pollock and Mark Rothko, and the cool jazz of trumpeter Miles Davis, the major novels of the 1950s were characterized by psychological introspection and an improvisational style of expression. This set them apart from the literature of the 1930s, with its social realism and political engagement. In such novels as Sloan Wilson's *The Man in the Gray Flannel Suit* (1955) and John Updike's *Rabbit Run* (1960), the heroes feel dissatisfaction with their jobs and their domestic situation and long for a more vital and authentic existence. Yet the characters

are incapable of decisive action. J. D. Salinger's popular *The Catcher in the Rye* (1951) offered an adolescent version of the alienated, ineffectual 1950s literary hero. Young Holden Caulfield, expelled from prep school, is repelled by the "phoniness" of the adult world and vaguely considers a break for freedom. But he returns home, suffers a nervous collapse, and retreats to an inner realm of imagined heroic exploits.

The most vital fiction of the fifties came from southern, African-American, and Jewish-American writers. William Faulkner continued his dense saga of the Snopses of Yoknapatawpha County, Mississippi, in *The Town* (1957) and *The Mansion* (1960), and Eudora Welty offered her evocation of small-town Mississippi life in *The Ponder Heart* (1954). Aspects of the black experience were memorably presented in James Baldwin's *Go Tell It on the Mountain* (1953) and Ralph Ellison's *Invisible Man* (1951). Bernard Malamud's *The Assistant* (1957) explored the Jewish immigrant world of New York's Lower East Side, and Philip Roth's *Goodby Columbus* (1959) dissected the very different world of upwardly mobile Jews.

Hollywood, too, reflected the diminished concern with social issues. Movie moguls concentrated on westerns, musicals, and lavish costume spectacles. When film producers did turn from chariot races to life in the 1950s, they generally portrayed Americans as one big, happy, white, middle-class family. The movies glorified material success and romantic love. And Hollywood now reserved the scarlet letter *A* for women intent on ambition rather than adultery. In place of the independent career-woman-in-tailored-suit types featured in films of the 1940s were the subordinated child-women roles played by Sandra Dee and June Allyson; the cute, cozy helpmates portrayed by Doris Day and Debbie Reynolds; and the "dumb blondes," especially Marilyn Monroe.

But even as motion pictures entertained the American people, the industry declined. Between 1948 and 1960, as television viewing soared, weekly movie attendance dropped from nearly 90 million to about 45 million, the number of feature films produced fell from more than 400 to only 154, and a fifth of the nation's theaters became bowling alleys and supermarkets. Hollywood tried to recoup by developing such new visual techniques as Cinerama and the highly touted 3-D films, for which viewers donned special glasses that gave the illusion of depth. Nothing, however—including Smell-O-Vision and its rival Aroma-Rama, which emitted smells corresponding to what was depicted on

American business capitalized on the phenomenon. Introduced in 1952, *TV Guide* soon outsold all other periodicals and by 1960 was published in fifty-three separate regional editions for its 7 million subscribers. The TV dinner, first marketed in 1954, altered the nation's eating habits. By the mid-fifties the three networks that controlled the television airwaves were each grossing larger advertising revenues than any other communications medium in the world.

In television's youth, producers showcased talent and creativity. A spectrum of high-quality shows appeared during prime time, including opera performances, notable documentaries like the "See It Now" series hosted by Edward R. Murrow, sophisticated comedies like "Your Show of Shows," and critically acclaimed original dramas on "Playhouse 90" and "Studio One."

But all too soon, the networks' race for profits combined with McCarthy-era anxieties to transform the innovative young medium into a cautious celebrator of conformity and consumerism. "The message of the media is the commercial," one critic noted, as corporations spent fortunes hawking their products. Expenditures for television advertising rose to $170 million in 1950, then doubled in 1951, passed $1 billion in 1955, and nearly doubled again in the next six years. To reap the greatest possible share of the revenue bonanza, the networks competed for the largest audiences by appealing to the lowest common denominator of taste. (As radio comedian Fred Allen observed, "They call television a medium because it's rare when it is well done.")

Critics reviled television as an "idiot box" rotting viewers' minds with a bland menu of situation comedies punctuated by outbursts of canned laughter. TV frequently portrayed women as either zany madcaps ("My Friend Irma," "I Love Lucy") or saccharine-sweet housewives ("The Donna Reed Show," "Ozzie and Harriet"). Such popular programs as "Father Knows Best" and "Make Room for Daddy" celebrated the family's paternal protector. Few of the complexities of modern family life were depicted, beyond Theodore "Beaver" Cleaver's disdain for baths and homework on "Leave It to Beaver." An ongoing series of police dramas and westerns, however, affirmed the value of violence in overcoming evil. "Gunsmoke" and "Have Gun, Will Travel" led the list of the most widely watched shows. And although millions of youngsters tuned in to "The Howdy Doody Show" and donned mouseketeer ears as they watched "The Mickey Mouse Club," children's programs also featured mayhem and gunplay.

Marilyn Monroe
Shown here in a poster promoting her 1956 film Bus Stop, *Monroe was the all-time movie sex symbol. Exuding carnality, she teased: "I love to do the things the censors won't pass."*

the screen—could stem television's exploding popularity. By 1960 TV showed more than five times as much film footage as Hollywood produced, and dozens of abandoned movie lots and theaters had been converted into TV locations and studios.

The Message of the Medium

No cultural medium ever grew so huge so quickly, and none so boldly reinforced the mood of the times as American television in the 1950s. The number of households with TV sets shot up from several thousand in 1946 to 5 million in 1950. Thereafter set ownership rose at a rate of some 5 million a year. By the mid-fifties more than two-thirds of all homes in the United States sported a rooftop television antenna; and early in the 1960s, 90 percent of all households had at least one TV, and 13 percent owned more than one. The number of transmitting stations jumped from six in 1946 to nearly five hundred in 1960.

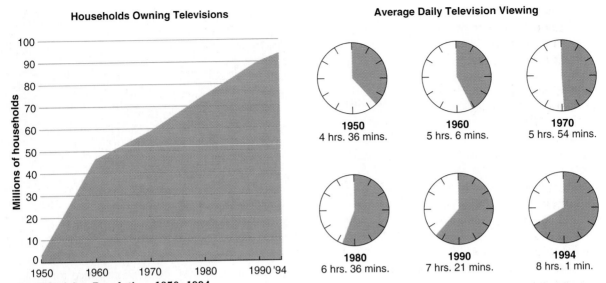

Households Owning Televisions

Millions of households

Average Daily Television Viewing

1950
4 hrs. 36 mins.

1960
5 hrs. 6 mins.

1970
5 hrs. 54 mins.

1980
6 hrs. 36 mins.

1990
7 hrs. 21 mins.

1994
8 hrs. 1 min.

The Television Revolution, 1950–1994

As televisions became commonplace in the 1950s, TV viewing altered the nature of American culture and politics.

SOURCE: *Statistical Abstracts of the United States.*

Television reinforced consumerism and conformity, spawning such nationwide mass fads as Davy Crockett coonskin fur caps and Barbie dolls, as well as hula hoops, whiffle balls and silly putty. It strengthened gender and racial stereotypes and encouraged passivity. And it had a pronounced effect on American politics, where video images dominated reality. Richard Nixon's televised appeal for support in 1952 saved his beleaguered vice presidential candidacy. In 1960 the "telegenic" image projected by candidate John F. Kennedy would help tip the presidential election his way. At another political level, TV's portrayal of the United States as a nation of contented citizens both reinforced complacency and obscured the existence of "the other America."

TV Favorites from the Fifties

Lucy and Ricky in "I Love Lucy" were popular visitors to America's living rooms in the 1950s.

THE OTHER AMERICA

"I am an invisible man," declared the African-American narrator of Ralph Ellison's *Invisible Man*; "I am invisible, understand, simply because people refuse to see me." Indeed, few white, middle-class Americans perceived the extent of social injustice in the United States. "White flight" from cities to suburbs produced physical separation of the races and classes. Newly constructed expressways walled off decaying ghettos and pockets of rural poverty from middle-class motorists speeding by. The popular culture focused overwhelmingly on affluent Americans enjoying the "good life" and depicted minorities almost exclusively as servants, criminals, or buffoons. In such an America, there was no need for fundamental social change. Material abundance would suffice. A bit of economic fine-tuning would perfect the system. After all, both Adlai Stevenson and *Time* magazine assured the nation in 1956 that the total elimination of poverty was in sight.

Poverty and Urban Blight

Economic realities belied such optimism. True, the number of families living in poverty (defined by the federal government in the fifties as a family of four earning less than three thousand dollars a year) declined from 34 percent in 1947 to 22 percent in 1960, but some 35 million Americans, more than one-fifth of the nation, still lived below the poverty level, victims of malnutrition, disease, and squalor. Millions more existed just above the poverty line. Many were senior citizens, without medical or hospital insurance, and approximately 8 million of the aged had incomes below a thousand dollars a year.

At least a third of the poor lived in depressed rural areas, where the 2 million migrant farm workers experienced the most abject poverty. The secretary of labor in 1959 estimated their average hourly wage at fifty cents, but in fact, many worked for considerably less. Observing a Texas migratory-labor camp in 1955, a journalist reported that 96 percent of the children had consumed no milk in the previous six months; eight out of ten adults had eaten no meat; and most slept "on the ground, in a cave, under a tree, or in a chicken house." In California's Imperial Valley, the infant death

The Other America
The quality of life for citizens like these poor white children and the black North Carolina grandmother substantiated Michael Harrington's claim that too much had been made of American affluence in the 1950s.

rate among migrant workers was more than seven times the statewide average.

The bulk of the poor, however, huddled in decaying inner-city slums. Masses of Deep South blacks,

Appalachian whites, Native Americans forced off reservations, Puerto Ricans, and Mexican migrants strained the cities' already inadequate schools and housing. Nearly two hundred thousand Mexican-Americans herded into San Antonio's Westside barrio; a local newspaper described them as living like cattle in a stockyard, "with roofed-over corrals for homes and chutes for streets." A visitor to New York City's slums in 1950 found "25 human beings living in a dark and airless coal cellar ten feet below the street level. . . . No animal could live there long, yet here were 17 children, the youngest having been born here two weeks before." Trapped in a vicious cycle of want and a culture of poverty, the children of the poor started school at a disadvantage, quickly fell behind in their learning, and lacking encouragement or expectation of success, dropped out. Living with neither hope nor the necessary skills to enter the mainstream of American life, they bequeathed a similar legacy to their own children.

The migration to the city by those most in need of services paralleled the exodus of affluent residents and businesses to suburbia. "We turned our cities into doughnuts," an urban planner commented, "with all the dough around the center and nothing in the middle." With their tax base shrinking, city governments watched helplessly as antiquated schools and mass-transit facilities deteriorated.

The pressing need for low-cost housing went unanswered. Slum-clearance and urban-renewal projects frequently shunted the poor from one ghetto to another to open up space for new parking garages and cultural centers. The Los Angeles barrio of Chavez Ravine was bulldozed to allow for construction of Dodger Stadium; the Mexican-American community of South Phoenix was uprooted to make way for a highway. At the same time, landlords, realtors, and bankers deliberately excluded nonwhites from decent housing. Half of the housing in New York's heavily black Harlem predated 1900. There it was not uncommon for more than a dozen people to share a tiny apartment with broken windows, faulty plumbing, and gaping holes in the walls. Harlem's rates of illegitimate births, infant deaths, narcotics use, and crime towered above the averages for the city and the nation. "Where flies and maggots breed, where the plumbing is stopped up and not repaired, where rats bite helpless infants," black social psychologist Kenneth Clark observed, "the conditions of life are brutal and inhuman."

Blacks' Struggle for Justice

In the black South the collision between the high hopes raised by the 1954 *Brown* decision and the indignities of persistent racial discrimination and segregation had sparked a new phase in the civil-rights movement. To sweep away the separate but rarely equal facilities that demeaned them in the "Jim Crow" South, African-Americans developed new tactics, organizations, and leaders in the 1950s to engage large numbers of blacks in their own freedom fight and to arouse the conscience of white Americans, on whom the enforcement of constitutional rights ultimately depended.

Symbolic of the racism that touched even the smallest details of everyday living, black passengers on the Montgomery, Alabama, public bus system had to surrender their seats so that no white rider would have to stand. Although they composed more than three-quarters of all passengers, blacks had to pay their fares at the front of the bus, leave and reenter through the back door, sit only in the rear, and then give up their seats to any standing white passengers. In December 1955 a strong-willed black woman named Rosa Parks refused to get up so that a white man could sit. She was arrested. In protest, Montgomery's black leaders organized a massive boycott of the buses. "There comes a time when people get tired," intoned Martin Luther King, Jr., an eloquent twenty-seven-year-old African-American minister who articulated the anger of Montgomery blacks, "tired of being segregated and humiliated; tired of being kicked about by the brutal feet of oppression." The time had come, King continued, to cease being patient "with anything less than freedom and justice." With this speech what would become a year-long bus boycott by fifty thousand black Montgomerians began.

Whites tried to crush the boycott by intimidating and harassing blacks and by firebombing the homes of King and other black leaders, but the blacks stayed off the buses and gained greater self-respect. "My soul has been tired for a long time," an old woman told a minister who had stopped his car to offer her a ride; "now my feet are tired, and my soul is resting."

But the city leaders would not budge. This resistance forced the blacks to take their case to court and to file suit to challenge the constitutionality of bus segregation. In November 1956 the U.S. Supreme Court affirmed a lower-court decision outlawing segregation on the buses.

The Montgomery bus boycott demonstrated African-American strength and determination. It cracked the southern white myth that blacks liked segregation and that outside agitators alone sought to topple Jim Crow. It affirmed for blacks everywhere the possibility of social change. It gave the nation in Dr. King a persuasive African-American leader whose oratory could both inspire black activism and touch the white conscience.

King's philosophy of civil disobedience fused the spirit of evangelical Christianity's sacrifice and redemption with the strategy of nonviolent resistance to authority. King's emphasis on direct action gave every African-American an opportunity to become actively involved; and his insistence on nonviolence diminished the likelihood of bloodshed. Preaching that they must lay their bodies on the line to provoke crises that would force whites to confront their racism, he nevertheless urged his people to continue to love their enemies. By so doing, King prophesied, blacks would convert their oppressors and build a community of true brotherhood. To direct this new campaign against Jim Crow, King and a network of black ministers formed the Southern Christian Leadership Conference (SCLC) in 1957.

The Hispanic-American and Native American Predicament

Although aware of the black struggle, Mexican-Americans and Native Americans made little headway in their own efforts to end discrimination. The same was true for Puerto Ricans, who, coming from a U.S. territory as American citizens, could enter the mainland without restriction. Many Puerto Ricans wanted to leave their island because of a decline in commercial agriculture and the absence of industries that could absorb rural migrants. Lured by the demand for labor on the mainland and by fifty-dollar flights to New York City, their numbers in the United States swelled from seventy thousand in 1940 to a quarter of a million in 1950, and to nearly a million by 1960. Crowded mainly into the low-rent barrio of New York's East Harlem, Puerto Ricans suffered from inadequate schools, sanitation services, and police protection and were denied access to middle-class jobs and political influence. Still, like countless immigrants before them, they gained greater personal freedom in the United States while losing the security of a strong cultural tradition.

Family frictions flared in the transition from Puerto Rican to American ways. Parents felt upstaged by children who learned English and obtained jobs that were closed to them. The relationship between husbands and wives changed as women found readier access to jobs than did men. One recent migrant explained, "Whether I have a husband or not I work . . . and if my husband dare to complain, I throw him out. That is the difference; in Puerto Rico I should have to stand for anything a man asks me to do because he pays the rent. Here I belong to myself." However, although old values weakened and Puerto Ricans tried to embrace American ways, they encountered prejudice because of their skin color and Spanish language.

Mexican-Americans suffered the same indignities as did Puerto Ricans. Most of them were also underpaid and overcharged, cheated and discriminated against, forced to attend segregated schools, and excluded from the mainstream of American life. The presence among them of countless "undocumented aliens" added to their woes.

In the decade after the Second World War, new irrigation systems added 7.5 million acres to the agricultural lands of the Southwest and stimulated a demand for cheap Mexican labor. To stem the tide of illegal Mexican immigrants, Congress in 1951 enacted a "temporary worker" program that brought in tens of thousands of seasonal laborers, called *braceros.* Many stayed on without authorization, joining a growing but unknown number of other illegal Latino migrants. Between 1953 and 1955 the Eisenhower administration located and deported more than 3 million allegedly undocumented entrants, in many cases without recourse to due process. Periodic roundups, however, did not substitute for a sound labor policy or an effective enforcement strategy, and millions of Mexicans continued to cross the poorly guarded two-thousand-mile border. Neither the Asociación Nacional México-Americana (founded in 1950) nor the League of United Latin American Citizens could stop the exploitation of resident aliens by U.S. employers or the violations of the rights of Mexican-American citizens. Often arrested and detained while walking the streets, Mexican-Americans frequently had to prove to authorities their legal right to be in the United States. Such civil-rights violations reinforced Mexican-Americans' mistrust of the government and intensified their alienation from Anglo society.

Although the GI Bill of Rights had helped some Mexican-Americans to make it into the middle class, and several cities in the Southwest had passed antidiscrimination laws as a result of Mexican-American

A Periodic Roundup

Los Angeles police remove a group of undocumented Mexican immigrants from a freight train and prepare to send them back across the border.

political activism, the lot of the one-third who lived below the poverty line worsened. Both the existence of millions of undocumented aliens and the continuation of the *bracero* program depressed wages for Mexican-American workers. Whereas the new arrivals worked in the fields, most Mexican-Americans moved to urban *colonias* during the 1950s. By 1960 more than half a million Mexican-Americans resided in the Los Angeles metropolitan area, and the *colonias* of Denver, El Paso, Phoenix, and San Antonio were proportionately as large. First-generation Mexican-Americans generally worked in construction, light manufacturing, and the garment trades; those of the second generation typically obtained higher status than their parents.

Native Americans remained the poorest, most ignored minority. Between 1900 and 1930 Indian tribes had lost more than half the land they possessed. In 1953, pressured by the agricultural, lumber, and mining interests that coveted the remaining Indian lands, Congress adopted House Concurrent Resolution 108. This ended the Indians' status as wards of the United States and called for the liquidation of the reservation system and the termination of special federal services to tribes.* First applied to the Menominees of Wisconsin and the Klamaths of Oregon, who owned valuable timberlands, the policy proved disastrous. Further impoverishing the Indians whom it affected, the law

---

*All Native Americans were granted citizenship by an act of Congress in 1924.

transferred more than five hundred thousand acres of Native American lands to non-Indians. To speed the sale of Indian lands to developers, the government established the Voluntary Relocation Program. Designed to lure Indians off the reservations and into urban areas, relocation offices provided Native Americans with moving costs, assistance in finding housing and jobs, and living expenses until they obtained work. "We're like wheat," said one Hopi woman who went to the city. "The wind blows, we bend over. . . . You can't stand up when there's wind."

By the end of the decade, more than sixty thousand Indians had left the reservations for urban America. Some became middle class; some ended up in the run-down shantytowns at the cities' edge; and nearly a third returned to their tribes. The National Congress of American Indians and many tribal councils officially protested termination and relocation. A Seminole petition to President Eisenhower voiced the Native Americans' common concern: "We do not say that we are superior or inferior to the White Man and we do not say that the White Man is superior or inferior to us. We do say that we are not White Men but Indians, do not wish to become White Men but wish to remain Indians, and have an outlook on all things different from the outlook of the White Man." But the Native Americans' pleas went unanswered. They remained the most invisible of America's "invisible" men and women. Another decade would pass before the nation began to acknowledge their plight.

Seeds of Disquiet

Late in the fifties a new mood of self-scrutiny and apprehension ruffled the placid surface of American life. Academics spotlighted shortcomings in the system and questioned the nation's goals and values. Periodic business recessions, rising unemployment, and the growing national debt made Khrushchev's 1959 threat to bury the United States economically, and his boast that "your grandchildren will live under communism," ring in American ears. At the same time, anticolonial movements in the Third World, especially Fidel Castro's takeover of Cuba, diminished Americans' sense of national power and pride. Adding to the disquiet were an alienated American youth and a sophisticated display of technolgy by the United States' Cold War arch-rival.

Sputnik

On October 4, 1957, the Soviet Union launched into orbit the first artificial earth satellite, called *Sputnik* ("Little Traveler"). Weighing 184 pounds and measuring a mere twenty-two inches in diameter, it circled the earth at eighteen thousand miles per hour. *Sputnik* dashed the American myth of unquestioned technological superiority; and when *Sputnik II,* carrying a dog, went into a more distant orbit on November 3, the event loosed a torrent of indignation that Eisenhower had allowed a "technological Pearl Harbor." Democrats warned that a "missile gap" between the United States and the Soviet Union imperiled the American republic.

The Eisenhower administration initially disparaged the Soviet achievement. But Eisenhower pushed behind the scenes to have the American Vanguard missile hastily readied to launch a satellite into orbit. On December 6, with many millions watching on TV, the Vanguard rose just a few feet in the air before exploding. Newspapers around the globe mockingly rechristened the missile "Flopnik" or "Sputternik." When asked what Americans would find if they ever

reached the moon, physicist Edward Teller joked, "Russians."

Eisenhower did not find it a laughing matter; he doubled the funds for missile development to $4.3 billion in 1958 and raised the level to $5.3 billion in 1959. To quiet national self-doubt, he also established the Science Advisory Committee, whose recommendations led to the creation of the National Aeronautics and Space Administration (NASA) in July 1958. By the end of the decade, the United States had launched several space probes and successfully tested the Atlas intercontinental ballistic missile (ICBM) system.

Part of the fallout from *Sputnik* was a feverish effort to reshape American education. Critics blamed the schools' emphasis on "life adjustment" for the fact that the Soviet Union was producing twice as many scientists and engineers as the United States and complained that the United States reserved for its football stars the laurels that the U.S.S.R. awarded to outstanding students. Progressive education fell into disfavor.

"Wonder Why We're Not Keeping Pace?"
A Response to *Sputnik*
To account for the U.S.S.R.'s lead in the space race, cartoonist Herblock focuses on American weaknesses rather than Soviet strengths.

Sputnik provided the impetus for a crash program aimed at raising educational standards and swept aside the educational establishment's resistance to curriculum reform. Political barriers to federal aid to education tumbled as funds from Washington went to construct new classrooms and laboratories, improve teacher salaries, and install instructional television systems in American schools. In 1958 Congress passed the National Defense Education Act, which provided loans to undergraduate and graduate students, as well as funds for teacher training and for the development of new instructional materials in the sciences, mathematics, and foreign languages.

Americans now banked on higher education to ensure national security. The number of college students, 1.5 million in 1940 and 2.5 million in 1955, skyrocketed to 3.6 million in 1960. That year the U.S. government funneled $1.5 billion to universities, a hundredfold increase over 1940.

The hike in education spending was directly linked to the Cold War. By 1960 nearly a third of the scientists and engineers on university faculties were engaged in full-time research for the federal government, mostly on defense projects. Although it channeled millions of dollars to the nation's campuses, this new liaison between the Pentagon and America's colleges and universities raised unsettling questions about what some were dubbing a military-industrial-*educational* complex.

A Rebellion of Youth

Even as the education of America's children underwent scrutiny, adolescents experienced a cultural restiveness and search for self-definition. Few adults considered the social implications of their affluence on the young, or the consequences of having a generation of teenagers who could stay in school rather than have to go to work. Few gave much thought to the impact on children of growing up in an age when traditional values like thrift and self-denial had declining relevance, and of maturing at a time when young people had the leisure and money to shape their own subculture. Moreover, despite talk of family togetherness, fathers were often too busy to give much attention to their children, and mothers sometimes spent more time chauffeuring their young than communicating with them. Much of what adults knew about teenage mores they learned from the mass media, which tended to focus on the sensational and the superficial.

The media thrived on accounts of juvenile delinquency, for example. News stories depicted high schools as war zones, city streets as jungles ruled by youth gangs, and teenagers as zipgun-armed hoodlums. Although in the mid-fifties some four hundred thousand youths were annually convicted of delinquency, this figure did not represent a dramatic spurt over the wartime delinquency rate. And although less than 10 percent of teenagers had anything to do with gangs and switchblades, the many who sported black-leather motorcycle jackets, bandied street slang, and slicked back their hair in the "ducktail" look aroused adult disapproval and alarm.

Also dismaying to parents, young Americans passionately embraced rock-and-roll. In 1951 Alan Freed, the host of a classical-music program on Cleveland radio, had observed white teenagers dancing to and buying rhythm-and-blues records. Rhythm-and-blues had traditionally been recorded by and for blacks. Freed surmised that teens were drawn to the music, with its heavy beat and sexually suggestive lyrics, because of its contrast with the syrupy pop songs then flowing across the airwaves. In 1952 he started a new radio program called "Moondog's Rock and Roll Party." Its popularity soared, and in 1954 Freed took his program to New York City, where he propelled rock-and-roll into a national craze.

Just as white musicians in the 1920s and 1930s had adapted black jazz for white audiences, so white performers in the 1950s transformed rhythm-and-blues into "Top Ten" rock-and-roll records for white youth. Bill Haley and the Comets in 1954 dropped some of the sexual allusions from Joe Turner's version of "Shake, Rattle, and Roll," added country-and-western guitar riffs, and produced the first major rock-and-roll hit. When Haley performed his "Rock Around the Clock" in *The Blackboard Jungle*, a 1955 film about juvenile delinquency, many parents linked rock-and-roll with sex and rebellion.

Nothing confirmed this connection more than the phenomenal success of Elvis Presley. Born in Tupelo, Mississippi, Elvis Aron Presley was a nineteen-year-old truck driver in 1954 when, on impulse, he recorded two songs at a Memphis studio. Melding the pentecostal music of his boyhood Assembly of God church with the hillbilly boogie that he heard on the "Grand Ole Opry" radio shows, and peppering in the frank sexuality of rhythm-and-blues, Presley added his voice to the cacophony transforming a bland popular music that the restless youth of the fifties found wanting.

"Tutti Frutti, Aw rutti"
During a 1956 concert, the hip-bucking, tight-panted, Elvis "the Pelvis" Presley elicits the usual passionate reactions from his female fans.

From January 1956, with the release of "Heartbreak Hotel," to March 1958, when he was drafted, Elvis produced fourteen consecutive million-selling records. Girls screamed at his voice and swooned at his pouty-surly expression; boys wore their hair long and greasy in imitation of the superstar.

Ironically, Presley himself craved respectability. Even as his lyrics invited rebelliousness, he was collecting mainstream society's material symbols of success and status, including a fleet of pink Cadillacs and a Memphis mansion that would become a shrine for his fans after his death.

But his raw energy and swaggering sensuality shocked middle-class white adults, who saw in Presley's smirking lips and bucking hips a threat to all they held dear. The more adults condemned rock-and-roll,

however, the more teenagers loved it. Record sales tripled between 1954 and 1960, and Dick Clark's "American Bandstand," first broadcast nationwide in 1957, became the decade's biggest TV hit.

Much as teens cherished rock-and-roll for its frankness and exuberance, they elevated the characters played by Marlon Brando in *The Wild One* (1954) and by James Dean in *Rebel Without a Cause* (1955) to cult status for their overturning of respectable society's mores, and they delighted in *Mad* magazine's ridiculing of the phony and pretentious in middle-class America. Rejecting Detroit's standards, teenagers customized their cars to make personal statements—which parents rarely understood.

Portents of Change

A group of nonconformist writers known as the Beats expressed a more fundamental revolt against middle-class society. In such works as Allen Ginsberg's *Howl* (1956) and Jack Kerouac's *On the Road* (1957), the Beats scorned the competition and materialism of the fifties corporate world and scoffed at the "square" America described by Kerouac as "rows of well-to-do houses with lawns and television sets in each living room with everybody looking at the same thing and thinking the same thing at the same time." Romanticizing society's outcasts, they also glorified uninhibited sexuality, spontaneity, and spirituality.

The educated college-age youth who were among the Beats' greatest admirers gradually rejected the complacency and cautiousness of the era. Protesting capital punishment and the continuing investigations of the House Un-American Activities Committee, they also decried the nuclear-arms race. In 1958 and 1959, thousands participated in Youth Marches for Integrated Schools in Washington. Together with the Beats and rock music, this vocal minority of the "silent generation" heralded a youth movement that would explode in the 1960s.

CONCLUSION

The disquiet of the late fifties underlined the paradox of American society at midcentury. On the one hand, the United States was mightier than any nation in history and basked in a prosperity that enabled many citizens to enjoy "the good life." On the other hand, Americans felt unease as the U.S.–Soviet arms race heated up and as booming times brought unsettling social changes.

Still, most Americans concentrated on the sunny facets of the 1950s. Applauding Eisenhower's moderation and genial leadership, they ignored his warnings about the military-industrial complex and closed their eyes to the persistent poverty within segments of society and to the concentration of power in the economy. America's white middle class looked ahead to continued affluence and peace. Tuning in to coverage of the 1960 campaign on their TV sets, they viewed two presidential candidates who themselves were glowing representatives of the consumer culture. The Democrat John Kennedy and the Republican Richard Nixon affirmed the premises on which America's consensus of anticommunism and economic abundance was based. Each promised to outdo his rival in expanding prosperity and containing communism. Few citizens who followed the campaign imagined that the United States would soon be waging both a domestic war against poverty and a land war in Asia, or that the new rock-and-oll generation would help topple the South's institutions of white supremacy, challenge the older generation's most cherished values, and usher in an era of confrontation.

CHRONOLOGY

1944 Mark I calculator begins operation.

1946 Dr. Benjamin Spock, *Baby and Child Care*.
ENIAC, the first electronic computer, begins operation.

1947 Levittown, New York, development started.

1948 Bell Labs develops the transistor.

1950 Asociación Nacional México-Americana established.

1952 Dwight D. Eisenhower elected president.

1953 Korean War truce signed.
CIA-supported coup in Iran.
Earl Warren appointed U.S. chief justice.
House Concurrent Resolution 108.

1954 Army-McCarthy hearings.
Brown v. *Board of Education of Topeka*.
Fall of Dienbienphu; Geneva Conference.
CIA intervention in Guatemala.

1955 Salk polio vaccine developed.
AFL-CIO merger.
First postwar U.S.– Soviet summit meeting.
James Dean stars in *Rebel Without a Cause*.
Montgomery bus boycott begins.

1956 Interstate Highway Act.
Suez crisis.
Soviet intervention in Poland and Hungary.
Allen Ginsberg, *Howl*.
Eisenhower reelected.

1957 Eisenhower Doctrine announced.
Civil Rights Act (first since Reconstruction).
Jack Kerouac, *On the Road*.
Little Rock school-desegregation crisis.
Soviet Union launches *Sputnik*.
Peak of "baby boom" (4.3 million births).

1958 U.S. troops sent to Lebanon.
National Defense Education Act.
United States and Soviet Union halt atomic tests.
National Aeronautics and Space Administration (NASA) founded.

1959 Fidel Castro comes to power in Cuba.
Khrushchev and Eisenhower meet at Camp David.

1960 National Liberation Front of South Vietnam (NLF) established.
U-2 incident.
Second Civil Rights Act.

1961 Eisenhower notes military-industrial complex.

1962 Rachel Carson, *Silent Spring*.

Rachel Carson

FOR FURTHER READING

William H. Chafe, *The American Woman: Her Changing Social, Economic, and Political Roles, 1920–1970,* rev. ed. (1988). An incisive examination of discrimination against women and their efforts to overcome it.

Kenneth Jackson, *Crabgrass Frontier: The Suburbanization of the United States* (1985). An indispensable social history of suburban growth.

Jacqueline Jones, *The Dispossessed: America's Underclasses from the Civil War to the Present* (1992). A thorough analysis of the roots of modern poverty.

Walter A. McDougall, . . . *The Heavens and the Earth: A Political History of the Space Age* (1985) A probing investigation of the diplomatic and political factors affecting the space program.

Elaine Tyler May, *Homeward Bound: American Families in the Cold War Era (*1988). A social history of how the Cold War influenced gender roles, marriage, parenting, and family life.

Larry May, ed., *Recasting America: Culture and Politics in the Age of the Cold War* (1989). A stimulating collection of essays.

John Modell, *Into One's Own: From Youth to Adulthood in the United States, 1920–1975* (1989). An important, insightful survey of the coming of age of American youth.

Chester Pach, Jr., and Elmo Richardson, *The Presidency of Dwight D. Eisenhower* (1991). A fair, balanced, and thoughtful overview.

ADDITIONAL BIBLIOGRAPHY

The Eisenhower Administration

Fred Greenstein, *The Hidden-Hand Presidency* (1982); Elizabeth Huckaby, *Crisis at Central High: Little Rock, 1957–1958* (1980); Richard Melanson and David Mayers, eds., *Reevaluating Eisenhower* (1986); Nicol Rae, *The Decline and Fall of the Liberal Republicans* (1989); David W. Reinhard, *The Republican Right Since 1945* (1983); Bernard Schwartz, *Super Chief: Earl Warren and His Supreme Court* (1983).

Foreign Affairs and Policies

David Anderson, *Trapped by Success: The Eisenhower Administration and Vietnam* (1991); Howard Ball, *Justice Downwind: America's Nuclear Testing Program in the 1950s* (1986); Henry Brands, Jr., *Cold Warriors* (1988); Richard Immerman, *The CIA in Guatemala* (1982); Burton Kaufman, *Trade and Aid: Eisenhower's Foreign Economic Policy* (1982); Gabriel Kolko, *Confronting the Third World* (1988); Andrew Rotter, *The Path to Vietnam* (1987).

The Economy and the Affluent Society

David P. Calleo, *The Imperious Economy* (1982); Gilbert C. Fite, *American Farmers* (1981); Mark I. Gelfand, *A Nation of Cities* (1975); James R. Green, *The World of the Worker* (1980); Dolores Hayden, *Redesigning the American Dream* (1984); Donald Katz, *Home Fires: An Intimate Portrait of One Middle-Class Family in Postwar America* (1992); Zane L. Miller, *Suburb: Neighborhood and Community in Forest Park, Ohio, 1935–1976* (1981); J. R. Oakley, *God's Country: America in the Fifties* (1986); Gwendolyn Wright, *Building the Dream: A Social History of Housing in America* (1981).

Culture and Conservatism

James Baughman, *The Republic of Mass Culture: Journalism, Filmmaking, and Broadcasting Since 1941* (1992); Barbara B. Clowse, *Brainpower for the Cold War: The Sputnik Crisis and the National Defense Education Act of 1958* (1981); Jeffrey Hart, *When the Going Was Good: American Life in the Fifties* (1982); Landon Y. Jones, *Great Expectations: America and the Baby Boom Generation* (1980); George Lipsitz, *Class and Culture in Cold War America* (1981); William O'Neill, *American High* (1986); Richard Pells, *The Liberal Mind in a Conservative Age: American Intellectuals in the 1940s and 1950s* (1984); Lynn Spigel, *Make Room for TV* (1992); Ella Taylor, *Prime-Time Families: Television Culture in Postwar America* (1989); Alan M. Wald, *The New York Intellectuals* (1987).

Feminism and Women's History

Wini Breines, *Young, White, and Miserable: Growing Up Female in the Fifties* (1992); Stephanie Coontz, *The Way We Never Were* (1992); Ruth Schwartz Cowan, *More Work for Mother* (1983); Myra Dinnerstein, *Women Between Two Worlds* (1992); Eugenia Kaledin, *Mothers and More: American Women in the 1950s* (1984); Leila Rupp and Verta Taylor, *Survival in the Doldrums* (1987); Rickie Solinger, *Wake Up Little Susie: Single Pregnancy and Race Before Roe v. Wade* (1992).

The Other America

Rodolfo Acuna, *Occupied America: A History of Chicanos* (1981); Taylor Branch, *Parting the Waters* (1988); Larry W. Burt, *Tribalism in Crisis: Federal Indian Policy, 1953–1961* (1982); Thomas Cripps, *Making Movies Black: The Hollywood Message Movie from World War II to the Civil Rights Era* (1993); Donald Fixico, *Termination and Relocation: Federal Indian Policy, 1945–1970* (1986); J. Wayne Flynt, *Dixie's Forgotten People: The South's Poor Whites* (1979); Steven Lawson, *Running for Freedom* (1991); Elena Padilla, *Up from Puerto Rico* (1958); James T. Patterson, *America's Struggle Against Poverty, 1900–1980* (1981); Linda Reed, *Simple Decency & Common Sense* (1992); Harvard Sitkoff, *The Struggle for Black Equality, 1954–1992* (1993).

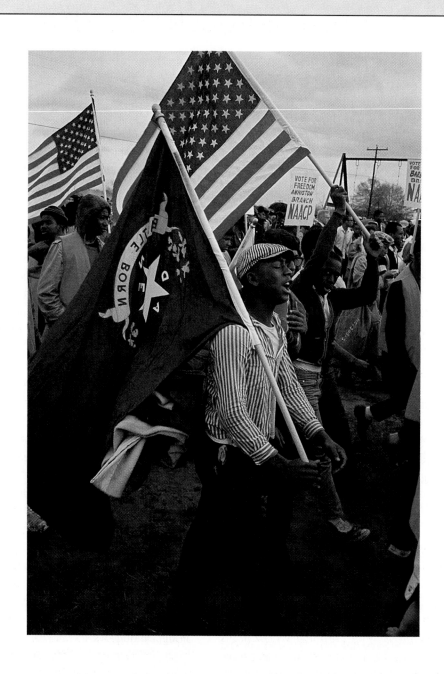

The Selma to Montgomery March
1965

30

THE TURBULENT SIXTIES

In January 1960, four African-American freshmen at North Carolina Agricultural and Technical (A & T) College in Greensboro discussed their humiliation over not being allowed to eat alongside white diners at lunch counters in the South. Middle class in aspirations, the children of urban civil servants and industrial workers, they believed that the Supreme Court's *Brown* decision of 1954 should have ended the indignities of racial discrimination and segregation. But the promise of change had outrun reality. Massive resistance to racial equality still proved the rule throughout Dixie. In 1960 most southern blacks could neither vote nor attend integrated schools. They could not enjoy a cup of coffee alongside whites in a public restaurant. Impatient yet hopeful, the A & T students could not accept the inequality that their parents had endured. They had been inspired by the Montgomery bus boycott led by Martin Luther King, Jr., as well as by successful African independence movements in the late fifties in Ghana, the Belgian Congo, and other former European colonial possessions.

On the afternoon of February 1, the four young African-Americans entered the local Woolworth's and sat down at the lunch counter. "We don't serve colored here," the waitress replied when the freshmen asked for coffee and doughnuts. The students remained seated. They would not be moved. They vowed to sit in until the store closed and to repeat their request the next day and beyond, until they were served. On February 2 more than twenty A & T students joined them in their protest. The following day, over sixty sat in. By the end of the week, the students overflowed Woolworth's and sat in at the lunch counter in the nearby S. H. Kress store. Six months later, after prolonged peaceful sit-ins, boycotts, and demonstrations, Greensboro's white civic leaders grudgingly allowed blacks to sit down at a restaurant and be served.

Meanwhile, the example of the Greensboro "coffee party" had inspired similar sit-ins throughout North Carolina and in neighboring states. By April 1960 sit-ins had disrupted seventy-eight southern communities, and by September 1961 some seventy thousand students had sat in to desegregate eating facilities as well as to "kneel in" in churches, "sleep in" in motel lobbies, "wade in" on restricted beaches, "read in" at public libraries, "play in" at city parks, and even "watch in" at segregated movie theaters.

The courage of the students transformed the struggle for racial equality. Their activism emboldened black adults to voice their dissatisfaction, and it brought young African-Americans a new sense of self-respect and strength. "I myself desegregated a lunch counter, not somebody else, not some big man, some powerful man, but little me," claimed a student. "I walked the picket line and I sat in and the walls of segregation toppled." Each new victory convinced thousands more that "nothing can stop us now."

The winds of change stirred by the sit-ins swept away the complacency that characterized much of the 1950s. Watching the film footage of demonstrations and arrests each evening on his television set in Harlem in 1960, a young African-American teacher named Robert Moses felt their impact. "The students in that picture had a certain look on their faces, sort of sullen, angry, determined," recalled Moses, who would soon lead the drive to register black voters in Mississippi. "Before, the Negro in the South had always looked on the defensive, cringing. This time they were taking the initiative. They were kids my age, and I knew this had something to do with my life." That same year, socialist Michael Harrington began to investigate the plight of the poor in an America that barely acknowledged their existence; Ralph Nader, a recent graduate of Harvard Law School, sounded the alarm that many automobiles were "unsafe at any speed"; and mother and writer Betty Friedan started writing what would become a pathbreaking 1963 book on sexism, *The Feminine Mystique.*

These endeavors symbolized the sense of new beginnings in the early sixties. Impatience and idealism, especially on the part of young Americans, led many to embrace John Kennedy's New Frontier and to rally behind Lyndon Johnson's Great Society. Both administrations' rhetorical emphasis on social justice generated fervent hopes and soaring expectations among the dispossessed. But the assassinations of cherished national leaders, widespread racial strife, and U.S. involvement in Vietnam dampened optimism, and a reaction by the majority who opposed radical change curtailed social reform. The promise of a new decade would end in discord and disillusionment.

THE NEW FRONTIER, 1960–1963

In 1960 John Fitzgerald Kennedy personified the energy and self-confidence of American youth. On television Kennedy projected an image of commitment and vigor (or "vigah," as he pronounced it). Capitalizing on his wealth and good looks, he became the symbol of new approaches to old problems.

His father, Joseph P. Kennedy, had earned a fortune from shipping, investment, liquor, and real-estate interests. A generous contributor to the Democratic party, he had secured appointive posts from Franklin Roosevelt. But his prewar isolationism had prevented him from gaining elective office and admittance to the party's inner circles. Seething with unfulfilled ambitions, Joe Kennedy raised his sons to attain the political power that had eluded him. He drove them unrelentingly, instilling in each a passion to excel and to rule. Despite a severe back injury, John Kennedy played sports at Harvard and served in the navy during World War II. Behind the scenes the elder Kennedy persuaded a journalist to rework John's senior thesis into the book *Why England Slept* (for which John got full credit); and he prevailed upon a popular novelist to publish articles lauding John's heroism in rescuing sailors after their PT boat had been sunk in the South Pacific.

Esteemed as a war hero and scholar, John Kennedy employed his charm and his father's political connections to win election in 1946 to the House of Representatives from a Boston district where he had never lived. Kennedy did little to distinguish himself in the Congress, but the voters of Massachusetts, captivated by his personality and pleased with his moderately liberal voting record, sent him to the Senate in 1952 and overwhelmingly reelected him six years later. By then Kennedy had a beautiful wife, Jacqueline, and a Pulitzer Prize for *Profiles in Courage,* a book written primarily by a staff member.

Only Kennedy's religion, Roman Catholicism, threatened his political future. No Catholic had ever been elected president; and the 1928 defeat of Alfred E. Smith had convinced many politicians that none ever could be. Nevertheless, Kennedy's popularity and formidable political organization gained him a first-ballot victory at the 1960 Democratic convention. Just forty-two years old when he accepted the nomination, Kennedy sounded the theme of a "New Frontier"—for reform at home and victory abroad, for "more sacrifice instead of more security."

The Election of 1960

"All at once you had something exciting," recalled Don Ferguson, a University of Nebraska student. "You had a guy who had little kids and who liked to play football on his front lawn. Kennedy was talking about pumping new life into the nation and steering it in new directions." But middle-aged, middle-class Americans, the bulk of the electorate, seemed to be looking for something else: stability and the continuation of Eisenhower's "middle way" promised by the Republican candidate, Vice President Richard M. Nixon. Although scorned by liberals for his McCarthyism, Nixon had the advantage of being better known and more experienced than his Democratic rival. Furthermore, he was a Protestant and was closely identified with the still popular Ike.

Nixon fumbled his opportunity. He conceded that he and Kennedy shared the same policies, and he devoted most of his time to defending Eisenhower's record. His greatest mistake, however, was agreeing to meet Kennedy in four debates.

An audience of more than 70 million tuned in to the nation's first televised encounter between presidential candidates, an event that established the dominance of television in American politics. The contrast between a haggard, pale Nixon, still recuperating from a knee infection that had hospitalized him for two weeks, and a dynamic, tanned Kennedy was striking. The telegenic Democrat radiated confidence; his opponent appeared insecure as he sweated visibly. Although radio listeners considered the contest a draw, the far larger number that watched on TV believed that the Democratic challenger had bested the front-running vice president. Kennedy shot up in the polls, and Nixon never regained the lead.

Kennedy benefited from the embarrassing U-2 incident and an economic recession that had marred Eisenhower's final year in office. He also boosted his chances by choosing Senate majority leader Lyndon B. Johnson, a Protestant and moderate from Texas, as his running mate.

Still, the 1960 presidential election was the closest since 1888. Kennedy's hairbreadth margin of victory (see map) reflected a widespread desire to keep things as they were, as well as a hostility to the idea of a Catholic president. Kennedy failed to secure the votes of more than 4 million usually Democratic Protestants, mainly in the South and trans-Mississippi West. This significantly lowered his popular tally, although most of the South remained in the Democratic column. However, Kennedy's capture of 80 percent of the Catholic vote in the closely contested midwestern and northeastern states played a crucial role in his electoral college victory. Although Nixon carried more states than Kennedy, the Democrat's popularity with urban minorities gave Kennedy a slender triumph.

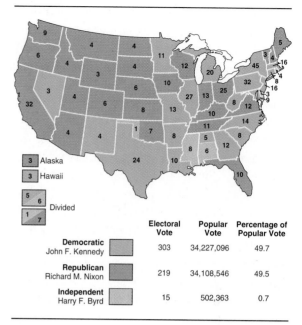

	Electoral Vote	Popular Vote	Percentage of Popular Vote
Democratic John F. Kennedy	303	34,227,096	49.7
Republican Richard M. Nixon	219	34,108,546	49.5
Independent Harry F. Byrd	15	502,363	0.7

The Election of 1960

"To Get America Moving Again"

Kennedy set the tone of a new era at his inauguration, proclaiming that "the torch has been passed to a new generation of Americans." He recruited for his administration a host of young technocrats and academics—the "best and brightest" in author David Halberstam's wry phrase—who contrasted sharply with the staid businessmen of the Eisenhower administration. His closest advisers included McGeorge Bundy, a youthful dean of Harvard University, as special assistant for national-security affairs; Robert McNamara, a statistical wizard and president of the Ford Motor Company, as secretary of defense; and Walter Heller, a University of Minnesota professor, as chairman of the Council of Economic Advisers. For attorney general the president selected his thirty-five-year-old brother Robert Kennedy. "I see nothing wrong with giving Robert some legal experience before he goes out to practice law," JFK joked.

"America's leading man," novelist Norman Mailer termed John Kennedy. The president adopted a dynamic style calculated to broaden his popular support. In his many TV appearances, he exuded promise and purpose. Aided by his wife Jacqueline, who became the epitome of elegance and poise for millions of women, the president filled his administration with the trappings of culture and excellence. Distinguished

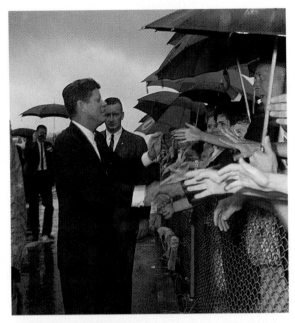

John Fitzgerald Kennedy
Of the Kennedy years, historian Arthur Schlesinger observed: "Washington seemed engaged in a collective effort to make itself brighter, gayer, more intellectual, more resolute. It was a golden interlude."

artists performed at the White House, and the president embellished his speeches with quotations from Emerson and references to Aristotle. Kennedy's taste and grace, as well as wit and wealth, awed the media, and news reporters routinely extolled the president as a heroic, vibrant family man. Knowing nothing of his fragile health, frequent use of mood-altering drugs, or extramarital affairs, many Americans idolized the television image crafted by JFK.

Kennedy's Domestic Record

The media focus on Kennedy's charismatic leadership, on his moral exhortations and demands for sacrifice, obscured the reality of Kennedy's unexceptional domestic record. There was hardly a New Frontier in legislation. Kennedy simply lacked the votes in Congress to overcome the barriers to reform erected by Republicans and southern Democrats, the same conservative coalition that had stifled Truman's Fair Deal. Kennedy rarely pressed the legislators to enact his reform measures, maintaining that "there is no sense in raising hell and then not being successful."

Instead, JFK made economic growth his domestic priority. To stimulate the economy, Kennedy combined increased defense and space expenditures with inducements to private enterprise to invest in capital growth. The president persuaded Congress in 1961 to boost the defense budget by nearly 20 percent, procuring not only five times more intercontinental ballistic missiles than Eisenhower had thought necessary but also a vastly augmented stockpile of medium-range missiles and nuclear submarines armed with Polaris missiles. To checkmate insurgencies in the Third World—what the communists called wars of national liberation—the president strengthened the military's conventional forces and established Special Forces units ("Green Berets") trained in guerrilla warfare. Both to stimulate the economy and to enhance American prestige, Kennedy persuaded Congress to finance a multibillion-dollar crash effort to place a man on the moon by 1970. (It would eventually cost the United States more than $25 billion to land astronaut Neil Armstrong on the lunar surface in 1969.)

Accepting unbalanced budgets as a price of stimulating economic growth, Kennedy proposed lower business taxes through investment credits and generous depreciation allowances. Most business groups, however, remained suspicious of Kennedy. In April 1962 their uneasiness turned to wrath when Kennedy marshaled all the presidency's power to enforce informal wage-and-price restraints to curb inflation. Reacting angrily when U.S. Steel jacked up steel prices by six dollars a ton just after he had pressured the steelworkers' union to accept a noninflationary contract with minimal wage increases, the president denounced the steel company, threatened it with antitrust lawsuits and cancellation of government contracts, and mobilized the Federal Trade Commission and the FBI to investigate price agreements among steel producers. U.S. Steel rescinded its price hike. But the business community's resentment also forced Kennedy to relent. When the steel companies subsequently raised prices twice within a year, Kennedy said and did nothing. Trying to woo the business community and to promote private investment and consumption, the president in 1963 proposed that the government hold the line on social expenditures and reduce both corporate and personal taxes.

When the Kennedy presidency tragically ended in November 1963, his tax cut remained bottled up in Congress. His management of the economy, however, had already more than doubled the rate of economic growth, decreased unemployment, and held inflation to just 1.3 percent a year. He had introduced the longest uninterrupted era of economic expansion in American history. Still, liberal critics grumbled about "the third Eisenhower administration." They deplored Kennedy's failure to effect any redistribution of income or to plug the large tax loopholes that benefited the rich. They regretted that corporate profits had risen five times more than personal income and that Kennedy had promoted military spending at the expense of social welfare. They especially condemned Kennedy for neglecting the needs of the public sector and the environment.

By the early 1960s environmental pollution had become a matter of deepening public concern. Awareness of the fragility of the earth's ecosystem, initially awakened during the fallout scare of the 1950s, intensified with the publication of Rachel Carson's *Silent Spring* in 1962. Carson's somber documentation of the hazards of DDT and other pesticides set off a national furor comparable to the impact of Upton Sinclair's 1906 exposé of the meat-packing industry, *The Jungle.* Kennedy appointed an advisory committee on pesticides, and federal regulation followed. In 1963 Congress also passed the Clean Air Act, regulating automotive and industrial emissions. After decades of heedless pollution, hardly helped by the introduction of aluminum pop-top cans in 1963, Washington hesitatingly began to deal with the major environmental problems resulting from a modern industrial order and consumer society.

Kennedy and Civil Rights

When Kennedy enumerated the nation's "unfinished and neglected tasks" in his first State of the Union address, he did not even mention racial injustice. The president did not anticipate the intensity of the crusade for civil rights that would soon engulf the South, nor did he welcome it. He straddled the issue for two years of his presidency, worrying that the fight for racial equality would split the Democratic party and entangle Congress in lengthy filibusters. That would jeopardize the rest of his legislative program and his reelection hopes.

Thus Kennedy treated racial problems as a thorny thicket to be tiptoed around rather than a preeminent issue requiring decisive leadership. He balanced his selection of an unprecedented number of African-Americans for high office with the appointment of white racists to federal judgeships. He sought to speed deseg-

regation by litigation yet remained aloof from attempts by congressional liberals to enact civil-rights legislation. After stalling for two years on his campaign pledge to ban discrimination in federally financed housing with "a stroke of the pen," the president issued a weak executive order that did little to lessen the residential segregation that both symbolically and in fact set African-Americans apart from white Americans.

But agitators for civil rights kept pressure on the president. In the spring of 1961, the Congress of Racial Equality (CORE), an interracial protest group founded in 1942, organized a "freedom ride" through the Deep South to dramatize the widespread violation of a 1960 Supreme Court decision outlawing segregation in interstate transportation. In Anniston, Alabama, Ku Klux Klansmen savagely beat the freedom riders and burned their bus; a white mob in Birmingham mauled a CORE contingent. Not until whites in Montgomery even more viciously assaulted the freedom riders did Kennedy finally dispatch federal marshals to end the violence. And not until after scores more freedom rides and the arrest of hundreds of young protesters did the president press the Interstate Commerce Commission to enforce the Supreme Court's ruling.

Kennedy again used federal force to quell white racist violence in the fall of 1962. When a federal court ordered the University of Mississippi to enroll James Meredith, a black air-force veteran, angry whites, egged on by Mississippi's defiant governor Ross Barnett, rioted. Rallying behind Confederate flags, students and troublemakers attacked the federal marshals who had escorted Meredith to "Ole Miss." The Battle of Oxford left two dead, hundreds injured, and the campus shrouded in tear gas. Only the presence of federal troops finally restored order—and upheld the right of a black American to attend the university of his home state.

The African-American Revolution

With mounting numbers of African-Americans demonstrating to secure racial equality, Kennedy could no longer temporize. The climax came in Birmingham, Alabama. Determined to provoke a confrontation that would expose the violent extremism of southern white racism and force Kennedy's hand, Martin Luther King, Jr., initiated a series of marches, sit-ins, and pray-ins on Good Friday, 1963. With each protest bringing more arrests, Birmingham police commissioner Eugene "Bull" Connor scoffed that King would soon "run out of niggers." But as thousands of schoolchildren joined King's

Birmingham, 1963

President Kennedy said this photograph of an African-American being attacked by a police dog during the protest demonstrations in Birmingham made him "sick." It helped galvanize the the nation's conscience, leading Kennedy to submit a comprehensive civil-rights bill to Congress.

the desegregating of stores and the upgrading of black workers. By mid-1963 the rallying cry "Freedom Now!" reverberated through the land as the number and magnitude of the protests soared. Concerned about America's image abroad and about the "fires of frustration and discord" raging at home, Kennedy believed that if the federal government did not lead the way toward "peaceful and constructive" changes in race relations, blacks would turn to far more militant leaders and methods. When Governor George Wallace refused to allow two black students to enter the University of Alabama in June 1963, Kennedy acted forthrightly. He forced Wallace—who had pledged "Segregation now! Segregation tomorrow! Segregation forever!"—to capitulate to a court desegregation order.

On June 11 the president went on television to define civil rights as "a moral issue" and to declare that "race has no place in American life or law." Describing the plight of blacks in the Jim Crow America of 1963, he asked, "Who among us would be content to have the color of his skin changed and stand in his place? Who among us would then be content with the counsels of patience and delay?" A week later Kennedy proposed a comprehensive civil-rights measure. Although House liberals moved to toughen Kennedy's proposal, most members of Congress seemed immune to the president's plea.

To compel Congress to act, nearly 250,000 Americans converged on the Capitol on August 28 (see "A Place in Time"). But neither Kennedy's nor King's eloquence could quell the rage of the bitterest opponents of civil rights. The night of the president's address, Medgar Evers, the head of the Mississippi branch of the NAACP, was murdered by a sniper in Jackson, Mississippi. In September the bombing of a black church in Birmingham killed four girls attending Sunday school. And still, southern obstructionism kept the civil-rights bill stymied in Congress, with little hope of passage.

crusade, Connor grew impatient and tried to crush the black movement with overwhelming force. He unleashed his men, armed with electric cattle prods, high-pressure water hoses, and snarling attack dogs, on the nonviolent demonstrators. The ferocity of Connor's attacks, chronicled on the television news programs of many nations, filled the world with revulsion.

"The civil-rights movement should thank God for Bull Connor," JFK remarked. "He's helped it as much as Abraham Lincoln." Indeed, Connor's vicious tactics seared the nation's conscience. And the combination of growing white support for equal rights, and African-American activism, pushed Kennedy to work to end segregation. Behind the scenes the president persuaded Birmingham's leaders to accept a compromise settlement that ended the demonstrations in return for

New Frontiers Abroad, 1960–1963

Having proclaimed in his inaugural address that "we shall pay any price, bear any burden, oppose any foe to assure the survival and success of liberty," Kennedy launched a major buildup of the nation's military

JFK at the Berlin Wall
June 26, 1963, President John F. Kennedy and East German policemen stare at each other across the wall dividing East and West Berlin.

arsenal. He adopted a strategy of "flexible response" to give him "a wider choice than humiliation or all-out nuclear action." He tripled the United States' overall nuclear capabilities, increased conventional military forces, and established the counterinsurgency Green Berets to fight Third World guerrilla revolutionaries.

To reduce communism's appeal in Africa, Asia, and Latin America, Kennedy gained congressional backing for his program of economic assistance in the Third World. A new Agency for International Development coordinated foreign aid. The Food for Peace program distributed surplus agricultural products. The Alliance for Progress envisioned a $100 billion joint public and private effort aimed at social reform and economic development in Latin America. Everyone in the Western Hemisphere had "a right to social justice," Kennedy affirmed, and this meant "land for the landless, and education for those who are denied education." In addition, the president in 1961 created the Peace Corps. By 1963 some five thousand volunteers were serving two-year stints as teachers, sanitation engineers, crop specialists, and health workers in more than forty Third World nations.

Cold War Activism

Kennedy's first foreign-policy crisis came in the spring of 1961. To eliminate a communist outpost on America's doorstep, Kennedy approved plans drawn up by the Eisenhower administration for fifteen hundred anti-Castro exiles, "La Brigada," to storm Cuba's Bay of Pigs. The scheme, conceived by the CIA and endorsed by the Joint Chiefs of Staff, assumed that the invasion would trigger a general uprising of the Cuban people to dethrone Fidel Castro. It was a fiasco.

An opportunity to prove his fighting ardor came in June 1961, when he met with Soviet leader Nikita Khrushchev to try to resolve the matters of a peace treaty with Germany and the presence of Western forces in Berlin (see Chapter 28). Comparing the American troops in that divided city to "a bone stuck in the throat," Khrushchev threatened war unless the West retreated. Perceiving the young president as inexperienced and easily intimidated, Khrushchev announced that he would sign a separate German peace agreement with East Germany that would imperil Western occupation rights in Berlin. A shaken Kennedy returned to the United States and declared the defense of West Berlin "the great testing place of Western courage and will." He doubled draft calls, ordered more than 150,000 reservists to active duty, and asked Congress for an additional $3 billion defense appropriation. The threat of thermonuclear war increased until mid-August, when the Soviets settled for a stalemate. Leaving unchanged the American role in West Germany and Berlin, Moscow signed a peace treaty with East Germany and constructed a wall of concrete and barbed wire to seal off their zone of Berlin. Designed to stop the flow of Germans from the communist sector (about a thousand refugees a day in July 1961), the Berlin Wall ended the exodus of talent

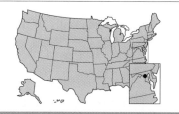
In 1963 the racially separate and unequal nation's capital more closely resembled a divided southern city than a showplace of democracy. Beyond the gleaming marble façades of Washington's public buildings sprawled slums as appalling as any in the nation. The flight of the white middle class to suburban Maryland and Virginia had abandoned large residential sections of Washington to African-Americans. Within the shadow of the Capitol, more than 40 percent of the city's families lived below the poverty level in a ghetto of wretched, rat-infested rooming houses. No other American city exceeded the District of Columbia in rates of infant mortality, venereal disease, and arrests for prostitution and drugs. And although, as the seat of the federal government, Washington could boast the highest per capita income of any American city, a large proportion of

its citizens subsisted on welfare. Most African-Americans fortunate enough to have jobs held low-paying government posts or served as the waiters, maids, and cooks for the whites in power. Many had no work at all.

It was to the Washington of stately white monuments that civil-rights groups planned to march in 1963 to dramatize grass-roots support for federal action against racial discrimination and segregation. To improve the chances of the civil-rights bill proposed by President Kennedy, they bypassed the drab streets of the black ghetto and rallied on the Mall, the very symbol of American nationhood and democracy.

As the sun rose over Washington on August 28, radio news bulletins predicted that the crowd would fall short of the 100,000 people expected. But throughout

A National Disgrace   *Abject poverty flourished just minutes from the Capitol Building as the civil-rights crusaders gathered on the Mall.*

the morning a seemingly endless caravan of cars, buses, trains, and planes brought in an estimated quarter-million pilgrims from every part of the country and from abroad—powerful evidence of the new consensus in favor of a strong civil-rights act. More than 150,000 blacks mingled with some 75,000 whites on the grassy slopes surrounding the Washington Monument. In the spirit of a church outing, they shared picnic lunches, sang songs of the movement, and then surged toward the Lincoln Memorial, holding aloft banners proclaiming such messages as "WE SEEK THE FREEDOM IN 1963 PROMISED IN 1863" and "A CENTURY-OLD DEBT TO PAY." Massed along the banks of the reflecting pool, the crowd gloried in its immense size and patiently endured several hours of speechmaking by African-Americans deploring discrimination and by whites confessing guilt over their belated commitment to racial justice.

Finally, in the late afternoon, after the wilting Washington heat and humidity had turned their clothes soggy, after many on the fringes of the crowd had withdrawn to the shade of old elms and oaks, the huge assemblage stilled as Martin Luther King, Jr., stood at the lectern in the shadow of the Great Emancipator. In a husky voice, King described the oppression of blacks, promised to continue the struggle until they gained all their civil rights, and in rising tones claimed that African-Americans would never be satisfied as long as they remained victimized by ghettoization and powerlessness. "[W]e will not be satisfied," King thundered, "until justice rolls down like the waters and righteousness like a mighty stream." As his followers shouted their approval, King put aside his text and, in the familiar cadences of the southern preacher that he was, spoke of a broader vision.

"I have a dream," King chanted again and again as the crowd roared amens in response, that someday, in the red hills of Georgia, the sons of former slaves and slave owners could sit together at the table of brotherhood ... that even Mississippi could become an oasis of freedom and justice ... that boys and girls of both races in Alabama could join hands "and walk together as sisters and brothers" ... that his

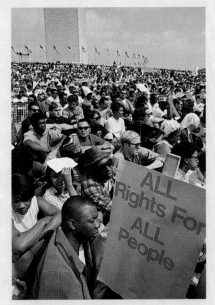

March on Washington for Jobs and Freedom, 1963
Originally proposed by African-American trade unionist A. Philip Randolph, the March on Washington generated an outpouring of support far too powerful for President Kennedy to ignore.

four children could live in a nation where they would be judged on the basis of their character and not the color of their skin ... that freedom could ring throughout America ... that "all of God's children, black men and white men, Jews and Gentiles, Protestants and Catholics, will be able to join hands and sing in the words of that old Negro spiritual 'Free at last! Free at last! Thank God almighty, we are free at last!'"

King's oratory on that muggy August afternoon in 1963 did not speed the slow progress of the civil-rights bill through Congress. It did not end racism or erase poverty and despair. It did not prevent the ghetto riots that lay ahead, or the white backlash that would ultimately smother the civil-rights movement and destroy King himself. But King had turned a political rally into a historic event. In one of the great speeches of history, he recalled America to the ideals of justice and equality, proclaiming that the color of one's skin ought never be a burden or a liability in American life. In five years King would be dead, murdered by a white racist. But his dream lives. It is the promise of America, a vital reminder of what the United States could be.

Martin Luther King, Jr.
King warned of the "whirlwind of revolt" that would consume the nation if blacks' civil rights continued to be denied.

that had menaced the economic survival of the East German state. Yet at the same time, it became an enduring symbol of communist failure and denial of personal freedom. Although neither the Soviets nor the Americans could claim total victory, Kennedy believed that his toughness had paid off. In early 1962 he proposed a $3.5 billion five-year plan to construct fallout shelters for all Americans. *Life*, as it had a decade earlier, featured a variety of shelter models complete with detailed building plans.

To the Brink of Nuclear War

In mid-October 1962 American aerial photographs revealed that the Soviet Union had begun to construct missile bases and to place both medium-range (one-thousand-mile) and intermediate-range (two-thousand-mile) missiles in Cuba. Smarting from the Bay of Pigs affair, fearing unchecked Soviet interference in the Western Hemisphere, and believing that his own credibility was at stake, Kennedy responded assertively. Rejecting the military's advice to order an immediate invasion of the island or air strikes against the Soviet missiles in Cuba, the president went on television on October 22 to denounce "this clandestine, reckless, and provocative threat to world peace" and to issue an ultimatum that the missiles be removed. The United States would "quarantine" Cuba—that is, impose a naval blockade—to prevent the delivery of more missiles and would dismantle by force the missiles already in Cuba if the Soviets did not do so.

Kennedy's announcement rocked the world. Never before had the two superpowers appeared to be on such a collision course toward a nuclear war. For four days apprehension mounted as the Soviets' technicians worked feverishly to complete missile launch pads and as Soviet missile-carrying ships steamed toward the U.S. blockade. Americans stayed glued to their radios and television sets. As they waited, 180 U.S. naval ships in the Caribbean prepared to confront the Soviet freighters; B-52s armed with nuclear bombs took to the air; and nearly a quarter-million troops assembled in Florida to invade Cuba. A solemn secretary of state Dean Rusk reported, "We're eyeball to eyeball."

"I think the other fellow just blinked," a relieved Rusk announced on October 25. The Cuba-bound Soviet ships stopped dead in the water, and Kennedy received a conciliatory message from Khrushchev guaranteeing that Moscow would remove the missiles in exchange for an American promise never to invade Cuba. But just as Kennedy prepared to respond positively to the Soviet offer, he received a second letter from Khrushchev. The Kremlin now insisted that the United States dismantle its missile sites in Turkey as part of the deal. Hours later an American U-2 reconnaissance plane was shot down over Cuba. It was "the blackest hour of the crisis," wrote a Kennedy aide. As the military urged an invasion of Cuba, Robert Kennedy persuaded his brother to accept the proposal in Khrushchev's first letter and to ignore the second one. In the early morning hours of October 27, Khrushchev pledged to remove the missiles in return for Kennedy's noninvasion promise.

The full dimensions of the crisis became known only after the end of the Cold War. In January 1992 the Russian military disclosed that Soviet forces in Cuba had possessed thirty-six nuclear warheads for their twenty-four intermediate-range missiles (capable of hitting most of the United States), as well as nine tactical nuclear weapons intended to be used against invading U.S. troops. Soviet field commanders had independent authority to use these weapons. Worst of all, Kennedy, McNamara, and other decision makers in Washington had not known that the Soviets already had the capability to launch a nuclear strike from Cuba.

"We do not need to speculate," said a shaken McNamara in 1992, "about what would have happened had the U.S. attack been launched, as many in the U.S. government—military and civilian alike—were recommending to the President on October 27th and 28th. We can predict the results with certainty. . . . No one should believe that U.S. troops could have been attacked by tactical nuclear warheads without the U.S.'s responding with nuclear warheads. . . . And where would it have ended? In utter disaster."

Staring over the brink of nuclear war chastened both Kennedy and Khrushchev. They agreed to install a Kremlin–White House "hot line" so that the two sides could communicate instantly in future crises. In June 1963 Kennedy advocated a step-by-step relaxation of superpower tensions. Two months later, they agreed to the Limited Test Ban Treaty, which prohibited atmospheric and undersea nuclear testing.

These efforts tentatively moved the two superpowers toward a new phase of the Cold War that would later be called détente. The United States and the U.S.S.R. began to accept each other as adversaries who could settle their differences by negotiation. But détente did not end the Soviet-American nuclear-arms race. Rather, the Cuban missile crisis had the unintended consequences of unleashing a massive U.S. arms buildup and of prompting a Kremlin decision to amass a much larger arsenal of intercontinental ballistic missiles and nuclear-missile submarines. The arms race escalated to a far greater degree than ever before, and so did the widening contest for power in the Third World.

Kennedy and Indochina

On retiring from the presidency, Eisenhower had apologized to his successor for the "mess" in Laos, a tiny, landlocked section of former French Indochina that had been created by the Geneva agreement in 1954 (see Chapter 29). A civil war between an American-backed regime and the procommunist Pathet Lao rebels appeared headed in early 1961 for a communist triumph. Although convinced of the need to fight communists in "brushfire wars" in the Third World, Kennedy considered Laos strategically insignificant compared to Berlin and Cuba and signed an accord in July 1962 that restored a neutralist premier to Laos but did little to weaken communist power in the countryside. Ironically, while stiffening Kennedy's resolve to allow no further communist gains in neighboring South Vietnam, the Laotian settlement confirmed North Vietnam's impression of American weakness.

Determined not to give further ground in Southeast Asia, Kennedy expanded Eisenhower's commitment by ordering massive shipments of weaponry to the South Vietnamese government and by increasing the number of American forces stationed in South Vietnam from less than 700 in early 1961 to more than 16,000 by the end of 1963. Like his predecessor, JFK thought that letting "aggression" go unchecked could lead to a wider war and believed that if communists forcibly took over one nation in a region, others would soon follow (the domino theory). Like Eisenhower, Kennedy assumed international communism to be a monolithic force, a single global enemy under the direct control of Moscow and Beijing. He viewed the conflicts fomented by the communist leadership as tests of America's, and his own, will. He would show the world that the United States was not the "paper tiger" that Mao Zedong (Mao Tse-tung) mocked.

As the unpopular South Vietnamese regime of Premier Ngo Dinh Diem, who had assumed power in 1954, came under attack from the National Liberation Front, or Vietcong, the Americans initiated a "strategic

hamlet" program to isolate the Vietcong by moving South Vietnamese peasants into fortified villages. Kennedy also pressed Diem to make the reforms that might gain him the support of his people. Diem refused, choosing to crush the demonstrations against him by students and Buddhists. By mid-1963 Buddhist monks were immolating themselves in public to protest Diem's repression, and Diem's own military leaders were plotting a coup to depose the premier.

In the fall of 1963, American policy makers concluded that their effort to stave off a Vietcong victory required a new government in Saigon. They gave assurances of support to South Vietnamese army officers planning Diem's overthrow. On November 1 the military leaders staged their coup, captured Diem and his brother, and shot them. The United States promptly recognized the new government (the first of nine South Vietnamese regimes in the next five years) but found it no better able than Diem's to defeat the Vietcong. Kennedy would either have to use many more American combat forces to reverse the tide of war or withdraw and seek a face-saving negotiated settlement.

What he would have done next is unknown, for less than a month after Diem's murder, John F. Kennedy fell victim to assassination. His admirers contend that Kennedy's disillusionment with South Vietnam's efforts to defend itself had led the president by late 1963 to advocate privately the withdrawal of American forces after the 1964 election. And the president in the fall of 1963 seemingly rejected publicly the sending of combat troops to Vietnam: "It is their war. We can help them, we can send them equipment, we can send our men out there as advisers, but in the final analysis it is their people and their government who have to win or lose the struggle."

Yet skeptics note that the president followed this utterance with a ringing restatement of his belief in the domino theory and a promise that America would not withdraw from the conflict. Virtually all his closest advisers, moreover, held that an American victory in Vietnam was essential to check the advance of communism in Asia. They would also counsel Kennedy's successor accordingly.

The Thousand-Day Presidency

In the fall of 1963, to improve his chances for victory in the 1964 presidential election, Kennedy traveled to Texas with Lyndon Johnson. On November 22 a smiling Jack and Jackie Kennedy rode in an open car past cheering crowds lining the streets of Dallas. As the motorcade slowed to turn, shots rang out. The president slumped. Bullets had shattered his skull and throat. While the driver sped the mortally wounded president to a nearby hospital—where the doctors soon pronounced Kennedy dead—Secret Service agents rushed a benumbed Vice President Johnson to Air Force One to be sworn in as president.

In the aftermath of the assassination, sorrow and disbelief reverberated throughout the nation. Most Americans ceased their regular activities for the next four days. They sat stunned in front of their televisions and stared at the countless replays of the murder of Kennedy's accused assassin, Lee Harvey Oswald, in the Dallas city jail by a minor underworld figure; of the somber state funeral, with the president's small son saluting his father's casket; of the grieving family lighting an eternal flame at Arlington National Cemetery. Few of the hundred million who watched would ever forget. Television, which had made the "Camelot" president a celebrity, raised the fallen leader to heroic, lovable stature. "Mr. Kennedy always seemed like the kind of father I would have wanted, the perfect father," an American teenager wrote to Jacqueline Kennedy after the assassination. "He seemed so warm, sincere, intelligent and just plain wonderful when I saw him on television." Millions worldwide would say the same today; the Kennedy magic has never died.

A balanced judgment on Kennedy remains elusive, partly because historians are still too close in time to the Camelot years to assess them dispassionately and partly because the Kennedy family has denied researchers access to many important documents relating to the man and his presidency. Kennedy loyalists have always stressed the "might have beens" and insisted on JFK's intelligence and grace, his potential for greatness, and his ability to change and grow. His detractors—whose ranks have swollen in recent years—point to the discrepancy between his glowing but essentially artificial public image and his recklessly amoral private sexual behavior. Liberal historians often deplore his eagerness to pursue an aggressive Cold War strategy. Conservatives blame him for stirring unrealistic expectations and for setting in motion the enormous expansion of federal power that would continue to surge through his successor Lyndon Johnson's Great Society years.

Some conclusions about the Kennedy presidency seem reasonably clear. Domestically, JFK felt badly

President Kennedy's Grave, May 29, 1964
"The death of a democratic prince, but a prince who . . . had become part of everyone's psychic and emotional life" was how one commentator described the assassinated president. Here, Jacqueline Kennedy and her children, John Jr. and Caroline, are shown at Arlington National Cemetery marking JFK's forty-seventh birthday.

constrained by the lack of a liberal majority in Congress, which forced him to compromise frequently with conservative, often segregationist, congressional leaders. Only about one-third of his legislative proposals became law. Partly because his personal behavior made him vulnerable to blackmail by J. Edgar Hoover, Kennedy allowed the FBI unprecedented authority to infringe on civil liberties—even as the CIA was apparently conniving with the Mafia to assassinate Fidel Castro. (The tangled web of plots and policies that enmeshed John and Robert Kennedy, Hoover, organized crime, and the national security agencies remains to be sorted out by scholars.) Although the Kennedy administration helped to launch the longest sustained economic recovery in the nation's history, this upturn resulted from spending far more on missiles than on humans, more on the space race than on social welfare. And there was no "New Frontier" for environmental protection or for slowing corporate consolidation. Internationally, Kennedy left an equally mixed record. On the one hand, he secured the world's first nuclear-test-ban treaty; on the other, he initiated a massive (and strategically unnecessary) nuclear-arms buildup. While recognizing the need for social reform in Latin America, he failed to fund the Alliance for Progress adequately. He compromised on Laos but deepened U.S. involvement in Vietnam. Despite talk of policy change, Kennedy in the main shared his predecessors' assumptions about the threat of international communism, insisted on maintaining U.S. global superiority, and dangerously heated up the rhetoric of Cold War confrontation.

A balanced judgment must recognize both Kennedy's significant impact on his contemporaries and his political and personal shortcomings. By conveying a sense of concern for the underprivileged and by shaking the nation out of complacency, he gave reformers new hope, aroused the poor and powerless (especially African-Americans), and challenged the young to struggle for what ought to be. He stimulated a flowering of social criticism and political activism in the 1960s rare in American history. But Lyndon Johnson—sworn in as president on the same plane that carried the murdered JFK's body back to Washington—inherited a dangerous combination of soaring expectations at home and a deteriorating, unwinnable entanglement in Vietnam. Like so many heroes in history, Kennedy left the stage before his glory tarnished. During the five years after Kennedy's assassination that Johnson would occupy the White House, one illusion after another was destined to be shattered; the American people would suffer a loss of confidence in their nation and its leaders—the consequences of which still endure.

THE GREAT SOCIETY

Lyndon Baines Johnson, who enjoyed being referred to by his initials in the manner of his idol FDR, immediately faced crises abroad and a stalled Kennedy program in Congress. Distrusted by liberals as "a Machiavelli in a Stetson," regarded as a usurper by the Kennedy loyalists who surrounded him in the Oval Office, LBJ had achieved his highest ambition—yet he had achieved it through the assassination of a popular president in Johnson's home state. Only nine years older than Kennedy, he seemed nevertheless a relic of a past era, a back-room wheeler-dealer. Indeed, many Americans compared the crude and domineering Johnson unfavorably to Kennedy, who

in death appeared even more elegant and gifted than he had in life.

The new president, however, possessed advantages that enabled him to provide healing balm and effective leadership for the mourning nation. Johnson had served in Washington almost continuously since 1932, as congressional aide, New Deal administrator, congressman, senator, majority leader, and vice president. No modern president came to office with more national political experience. He displayed persuasive skill in wooing allies, neutralizing enemies, forging compromise among conflicting interests, and achieving legislative results. The fact that Johnson was a Protestant, a southerner, a reputed moderate, and a close associate of Capitol Hill power brokers, moreover, significantly improved the chances of the blocked Kennedy agenda.

His first two years as president were extraordinarily successful. He deftly handled the awkward transition of power, won a landslide victory in 1964, and in 1965 guided through Congress the greatest array of social-reform legislation in American history.

But Johnson would not rest on his laurels. LBJ's swollen yet fragile ego could not abide the sniping of the Kennedy crowd, and he frequently complained that the media did not give him "a fair shake as president." Wondering aloud, "Why don't people like me?" Johnson pressed on—to do more, to do it bigger and better—to surpass his predecessors and vanquish all foes at home and abroad. Ironically, in seeking consensus and the love of the American people, Johnson would hopelessly divide the nation and leave office repudiated.

Toward the Great Society

The new president called for early passage of the tax-cut and civil-rights bills as a memorial to John Kennedy, and he overcame the congressional obstacles that had stymied his predecessor. In February 1964 Congress passed a bill reducing income taxes by $10 billion. The measure spurred economic growth by driving up consumer spending and driving down unemployment, and the budget deficit shrank from nearly $6 billion in 1964 to under $4 billion in 1966.

Johnson also engaged in cloakroom bargaining that, for the first time in history, produced a cloture vote to end a southern filibuster against a civil-rights bill. The resulting law was the most far-reaching legislation since Reconstruction. The 1964 Civil Rights Act

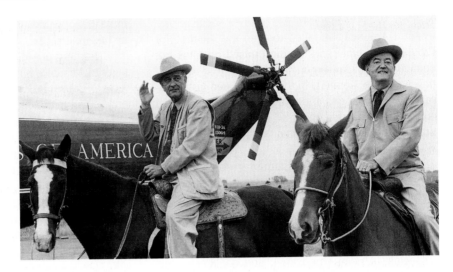

LBJ with Hubert Humphrey
Visiting LBJ's Texas ranch in 1964, Johnson's Minnesotan future vice president posed on horseback with the boss. The democratic ticket would win an overwhelming majority of the popular and electoral votes that year.

outlawed segregation in public accommodations, granted the federal government new powers to fight black disfranchisement and school segregation, and created the Equal Employment Opportunity Commission (EEOC) to prevent job discrimination because of race, religion, national origin, and gender.

In his boldest domestic initiative, Johnson then declared "unconditional war on poverty in America." The public approval that greeted this sweeping effort owed much to Michael Harrington's *The Other America* (1962), which documented that one-fifth to one-fourth of the nation lived in poverty. Largely invisible in an affluent America, some 40 million people—including destitute senior citizens, isolated farmers, blacks in urban ghettos, Hispanics in barrios and migrant-labor camps, Indians on reservations, miners in Appalachia, and families headed by a single mother—dwelled in substandard housing and subsisted on inadequate diets. Unaided or minimally assisted by a social-welfare bureaucracy, they lived with little hope in a culture of poverty, deprived of the education, medical care, and employment opportunities that most Americans took for granted.

To bring these "internal exiles" into the mainstream, President Johnson proposed a wide variety of training programs and support services. Enacted by Congress in August 1964, his Economic Opportunity Act far exceeded any previous government effort to aid the poor. The legislation established the Office of Economic Opportunity to fund and coordinate a Job Corps that would train young people in marketable skills; VISTA (Volunteers in Service to America), a domestic

peace corps of young volunteers who would work in poverty areas; Project Head Start, which would provide compensatory education for preschoolers from disadvantaged families; the Community Action Program, to encourage the "maximum feasible participation" of the poor themselves in the decisions that affected them; and an assortment of public-works and training programs.

Summing up his goals in 1964, Johnson offered a cheering crowd in Ann Arbor, Michigan, a vision of what he called the Great Society. First must come "an end to poverty and racial injustice," proclaimed LBJ, but that would be just the beginning:

> *The Great Society is a place where every child can find knowledge to enrich his mind and to enlarge his talents. It is a place where leisure is a welcome chance to build and reflect, not a feared cause of boredom and restlessness. It is a place where the city of man serves not only the needs of the body and the demands of commerce but the desire for beauty and the hunger for community. It is a place where man can renew contact with nature. It is a place which honors creation for its own sake and for what it adds to the understanding of the race. It is a place where men are more concerned with the quality of their goals than the quantity of their goods.*

A cornucopia of liberal programs targeting health, education, conservation, the environment, and racial equality appeared ready to flow from Washington if Johnson won election in November.

The Election of 1964

Lyndon Johnson's Great Society vision unsettled conservatives. Though lacking a leader of national stature since the death of Robert A. Taft in 1953, conservatism remained a potent force. Frederick Hayek's classic laissez-faire manifesto *The Road to Serfdom* (1944), Whittaker Chambers's *Witness* (1952), and Russell Kirk's *The Conservative Mind* (1953) kept the conservative flame aglow. The movement's foremost journalist, William F. Buckley, impressed even opponents with his wit and intellectual rigor. The student organization Young Americans for Freedom was active on college campuses, and the *Reader's Digest* spread the message to millions of households. And from the Right's extremist fringe, the John Birch Society stridently denounced communist influence everywhere.

Leaders of the Right scorned the paternalism and welfarism of Kennedy-Johnson politics, as well as the moderate "me-too" Republicans (many put Eisenhower in this category) who often went along with the liberal Democrats. Although conservatives supported strong government and bountiful federal spending when the goal was to defeat communism, they reacted in dismay at similar levels of government activism when the goal was to fight poverty, injustice, and lack of opportunity at home. To such conservatives, Johnson's Great Society was anathema—high-sounding rhetoric masking still more government infringement of basic American freedoms.

At the same time, the Great Society's racial liberalism frightened southern segregationists as well as a growing number of white laborers in northern cities who feared that the integration of their lily-white neighborhoods, schools, and workplaces would be the price paid for racial justice. Their support of Alabama's segregationist governor George Wallace in democratic primaries in Maryland, Wisconsin, and Indiana in the spring of 1964 revealed a "white backlash" against the civil-rights movement. At the Republican convention in July, these dissatisfied groups coalesced to gain control of the GOP. They nominated the right-wing senator Barry Goldwater of Arizona as their presidential candidate and the equally staunch conservative congressman William Miller from upstate New York as his running mate and wrote a platform that repudiated liberal republicanism.

Determined to offer the nation "a choice, not an echo," Goldwater extolled his Senate votes against the civil-rights act and against the censure of Joseph McCarthy; suggested abolishing the graduated income tax and the Tennessee Valley Authority; advocated the elimination of the union shop and of "compulsory" social security; and intimated that he might use nuclear weapons against Cuba and North Vietnam if those nations did not accede to American demands. Goldwater combined classical laissez-faire ideology with a characteristically southwestern suspicion of Washington. He appealed to Americans disturbed by the Cold War stalemate and by centralized decision making by the federal government. With TV imagemaking increasingly shaping politics, Goldwater projected integrity and forthrightness. His campaign slogan "In Your Heart You Know He's Right" summed up his supporters' feelings.

Goldwater's conservative crusade enabled Johnson to run as a liberal reformer yet still pose as the more moderate candidate. Together with his running mate, Senator Hubert Humphrey of Minnesota, Johnson depicted Goldwater as a trigger-happy extremist who would press the nuclear button in a crisis. When Goldwater charged that the Democrats had dillydallied in Vietnam rather than pursuing a total victory, Johnson appeared the apostle of restraint. "We are not going to send American boys nine or ten thousand miles from home," the president assured the American people in October, "to do what Asian boys ought to be doing for themselves."

To no one's surprise, LBJ surged to victory with 43 million votes to Goldwater's 27 million. The GOP

The Election of 1964

Candidates	Parties	Electoral Vote	Popular Vote	Percentage of Popular Vote
LYNDON B. JOHNSON	Democratic	486	43,126,506	61.1
Barry M. Goldwater	Republican	52	27,176,799	38.5

carried only Arizona and five Deep South states. Many commentators proclaimed the death of both conservatism and the GOP. In fact, Goldwater's nomination and the support that he garnered from white southerners and blue-collar workers presaged the future triumph of conservatism in American politics. Despite the Democrats' success in branding Goldwater an irresponsible reactionary, nearly 40 percent of the electorate cast their ballots for an uncompromising conservative who demanded total victory over communism and an end to the welfare state. In the short run, the Democrats secured huge majorities of 68 to 32 in the Senate and 295 to 140 in the House, which nullified the conservative coalition's power to block the president's proposals. For the first time in a quarter-century, the liberals had a working majority.

Triumphant Liberalism

"Hurry, boys, hurry," an exhilarated LBJ urged his aides. "Get that legislation up to the hill and out. Eighteen months from now ol' Landslide Lyndon will be Lame-Duck Lyndon." Wanting it all, and all at once, Johnson flooded Congress with Great Society proposals—sixty-three of them in 1965 alone. And he got most of what he requested (see box, p. 975).

The Eighty-ninth Congress—"the Congress of Fulfillment" to the president, and Johnson's "hip-pocket Congress" to his opponents—enormously enlarged the War on Poverty and passed another milestone civil-rights act. The Congress enacted a Medicare program that provided health insurance for the aged under social security, and a Medicaid program that allocated federal funds to the states to provide medical care for the indigent. The legislators also enacted the first-ever general aid to education, granting federal funds to every level from kindergarten to graduate school. Appalachia, one of the nation's poorest regions, received redevelopment aid. New laws provided federal funds to revitalize inner-city neighborhoods, to construct low-income housing, and to supplement the rents paid by impoverished tenants. These acts marked a substantial expansion of the "guarantor state" initiated by the New Deal. Other measures passed by Congress reflected the Great Society's quality-of-life concerns. These included laws to promote automobile safety and consumer rights and to establish the National Endowments for the Arts and Humanities as well as new departments of transportation and of housing and urban development (the latter to be headed by Robert Weaver, the nation's first African-American cabinet member). In addition, Congress in 1965 passed a revolutionary immigration law abolishing the discriminatory national-origins quotas. "Those who come will come because of what they are," said the president, "not because of the land from which they sprung." Reversing the previous pattern, the great bulk of newcomers to the United States would now emigrate from Asia and the Western Hemisphere, not Europe.

The Great Society also sought to reduce pollution and to protect and preserve nature, and significantly expanded federal responsibility for the environment. The President's Commission on Natural Beauty pressed to lessen the number of billboards on highways and to eliminate junkyards. Secretary of the Interior Stewart Udall—a strong advocate for the environment—played a major role in gaining the establishment of Redwood National Park and in defeating efforts to build dams on the Colorado River that would have flooded the lower Grand Canyon. Under Udall's prodding, moreover, Congress strengthened the 1960 Clean Water and 1963 Clean Air acts and passed legislation to protect endangered species and the wildlands and to preserve scenic rivers and millions of acres of wilderness.

Summing up the array of Great Society legislation, a presidential aide asserted, "There was no child we could not feed, no adult we could not put to work, no disease we could not cure, no toy, food or appliance we could not make safer, no air or water we could not clean." But the Great Society did not materialize. Although some programs endured and improved the quality of life, as many failed or faded away—in part because they were flawed, ill conceived and based on phony assumptions; in part because the liberal consensus that supported Johnson's proposals rapidly unraveled, allowing promising beginnings to die prematurely; in part because they were underfunded. Although the number of poor decreased, the war against poverty was, in the words of Martin Luther King, Jr., "shot down on the battlefields of Vietnam."

While annual expenditures for the Office of Economic Opportunity averaged $1.7 billion in 1965–1968, less than 1.5 percent of the federal budget, appropriations for the military in these years annually averaged $64 billion. LBJ's shift of emphasis from welfare to warfare shattered his consensus and enraged

Major Great Society Programs

1964

Tax Reduction Act cuts by some $10 billion the taxes paid primarily by corporations and wealthy individuals.

Civil Rights Act bans discrimination in public accommodations, prohibits discrimination in any federally assisted program, outlaws discrimination in most employment, and enlarges federal powers to protect voting rights and to speed school desegregation.

Economic Opportunity Act authorizes $1 billion for a "war on poverty" and establishes the Office of Economic Opportunity to coordinate Head Start, Upward Bound, VISTA, the Job Corps, and similar programs.

1965

Elementary and Secondary Education Act, the first general federal-aid-to-education law in American history, provides more than $1 billion to public and parochial schools for textbooks, library materials, and special-education programs.

Voting Rights Act suspends literacy tests and empowers "federal examiners" to register qualified voters in the South.

Medical Care Act creates a federally funded program of hospital and medical insurance for the elderly (Medicare) and authorizes federal funds to the states to provide free health care for welfare recipients (Medicaid).

Omnibus Housing Act appropriates nearly $8 billion for low- and middle income housing and for rent supplements for low-income families.

Immigration Act ends the discriminatory system of national-origins quotas established in 1924.

Appalachian Regional Development Act targets $1 billion for highway construction, health centers, and resource development in the depressed areas of Appalachia.

Higher Education Act appropriates $650 million for scholarships and low-interest loans to needy college students and for funds for college libraries and research facilities.

National Endowments for the Arts and the Humanities are created to promote artistic and cultural development.

1966

Demonstration Cities and Metropolitan Development Act provides extensive subsidies for housing, recreational facilities, welfare, and mass transit to selected "model cities" and covers up to 80 percent of the costs of slum clearance and rehabilitation.

Motor Vehicle Safety Act sets federal safety standards for the auto industry and a uniform grading system for tire manufacturers.

Truth in Packaging Act broadens federal controls over the labeling and packaging of foods, drugs, cosmetics, and household supplies.

---

the millions still mired in poverty. A tide of black militancy and urban riots alienated "middle America." At the same time, growing bitterness engendered by the war in Vietnam focused the wrath of liberals, particularly the young, on LBJ. The Democrats' loss of forty-seven seats in the House of Representatives in 1966 sealed the Great Society's fate.

The Warren Court in the Sixties

Although the Supreme Court remained a bulwark of liberalism, by 1966 it, too, was under siege. Beginning with its 1954 school-desegregation decision, and continuing with 1956–1957 rulings that affirmed the rights of alleged communists (see Chapter 29), the Court, headed by Chief Justice Earl Warren, had incensed the far right. Then, with Kennedy's substitution of two liberals for moderates on the High Court in 1962, and with Johnson's appointment of the even more liberal Abe Fortas and Thurgood Marshall—the latter, the Court's first black justice—the Warren Court handed down decisions in the 1960s that both changed the tenor of American life and further offended conservatives.

Major Decisions of the Warren Court

1954

Brown v. *Board of Education of Topeka* rejects the separate-but-equal concept and outlaws segregation in public education.

1957

Watkins v. *U.S.* restricts Congress's investigatory power to matters directly pertinent to pending legislation.

Yates v. *U.S.* limits prosecutions under the Smith Act to the advocacy of concrete revolutionary action and disallows prosecutions for the preaching of revolutionary doctrine.

1962

Baker v. *Carr* holds that the federal courts possess jurisdiction over state apportionment systems to ensure that the votes of all citizens carry equal weight.

Engel v. *Vitale* prohibits prayer in the public schools.

1963

Abington v. *Schempp* bans Bible reading in the public schools.

Gideon v. *Wainwright* requires states to provide attorneys at public expense for indigent defendants in felony cases.

Jacobellis v. *Ohio* extends constitutional protection to all sexually explicit material that has any "literary or scientific or artistic value."

1964

New York Times Co. v. *Sullivan* expands the constitutional protection of the press against libel suits by public figures.

Wesberry v. *Sanders* and *Reynolds* v. *Sims* hold that the only standard of apportionment for state legislatures and congressional districts is "one man, one vote."

1966

Miranda v. *Arizona* requires police to advise a suspect of his or her constitutional right to remain silent and to have a counsel present during interrogation.

1967

Loving v. *Virginia* strikes down state antimiscegenation laws, which prohibit marriage between persons of different races.

1968

Katzenbach v. *Morgan* upholds federal legislation outlawing state requirements that a prospective voter must demonstrate literacy in English.

Green v. *County School Board of New Kent County* extends the *Brown* ruling to require the assignment of pupils on the basis of race, to end segregation.

In a series of landmark constitutional rulings (see box), the Warren court prohibited Bible reading and prayer in public schools, limited the power of communities to censor books and films, and declared unconstitutional various state bans on the use of contraceptives. In *Baker* v. *Carr* (1962) and related decisions, the Warren court ruled that the principle of "one man, one vote" must prevail in both state and national elections and that representation in all legislative bodies be allocated on the basis of "people, not land or trees, or pastures." Especially unsettling to many Americans was the Court's commitment to a rigorous standard of due process for everyone caught up in the criminal-justice system. Rulings decreeing that a poor defendant charged with a felony must be provided with an attorney, and that the accused had the right to counsel during interrogation, appeared to some to be handcuffing the law-enforcement process at a time of rising crime in the streets.

Criticism of the Warren court reached a climax in 1966 when it ruled in *Miranda* v. *Arizona* that police must warn all arrested suspects that anything they said could be used against them in court and that they could choose to remain silent. Two years later both Richard Nixon and George Wallace would win votes by promising to appoint new justices who would emphasize "law and order" over individual rights and liberties.

THE CHANGING STRUGGLE FOR EQUALITY, 1964–1968

The drive for black equality crested and then receded in the two years following the 1963 March on Washington. The movement ended legal discrimination and black disfranchisement and gained improved opportunities for education and employment. But those victories did not vanquish the major problems that beset blacks because of caste and poverty: crime and drug addiction, family disorganization, and feelings of inadequacy rooted in three centuries of oppression. The persistence of white racism, moreover, discouraged blacks; they questioned whether they would ever be seen as equals in America. Many who struggled for racial justice grew disenchanted with American society and increasingly hostile to whites. For some, the movement had generated aspirations that it could not fulfill and had kindled a racial pride that rejected integration as a desirable goal. "The paths of Negro-white unity that had been converging," wrote Martin Luther King, Jr., "crossed at Selma and like a giant X began to diverge."

The Voting Rights Act of 1965

Initially, Lyndon Johnson had proved a loyal ally for the civil-rights movement. He had demonstrated his commitment by championing the Civil Rights Act of 1964. In outlawing discrimination in public accommodations and facilities, the act destroyed the legal basis of the South's caste system. But by 1964 activists in SNCC and CORE, believing that the ballot box held the key to power for southern blacks, had mounted a major campaign to register blacks to vote.

Focusing on the state most hostile to equal rights, field-workers for the two groups organized the Mississippi Freedom Summer Project of 1964 to dramatize the need for black enfranchisement. A thousand college-student volunteers assisted blacks in registering to vote and in organizing "Freedom Schools," which taught black history and emphasized African-American self-worth. Harassed by Mississippi law-enforcement officials and Ku Klux Klansmen, the young volunteers endured the firebombing of black churches and civil-rights headquarters, as well as arrests, beatings, kidnappings, and murders. Although they added

a mere twelve hundred blacks to the registration rolls, the volunteers enrolled nearly sixty thousand disfranchised blacks in the Mississippi Freedom Democratic party (MFDP) to take their case to the national Democratic convention that August. The MFDP challenged the right of the all-white Mississippi delegation to represent the state's Democrats and insisted that the Democratic nominating convention seat the MFDP delegates instead. President Johnson, concentrating on heading off a white southern walkout from the convention, proposed to grant two at-large seats to the MFDP and to bar delegations from states that disfranchised blacks at all future conventions. His compromise carried, but at the price of alienating militants in the movement.

In 1965 Martin Luther King, Jr., and his Southern Christian Leadership Conference (SCLC) planned a confrontation that would force the federal government to assure blacks of the franchise. Determined to gain a strong voting-rights law, they organized mass protests in Selma, Alabama. Blacks constituted approximately half the voting-age population of Dallas County, where Selma was located, but only 1 percent of them were registered to vote, in contrast to 65 percent of whites. Selma also had county sheriff Jim Clark, every bit as ill tempered and violence-prone as Birmingham's "Bull" Connor. As expected, Clark's men attacked black protesters and bystanders indiscriminately and brutally. Sheyann Webb, aged eight, recalled the troopers' charging of those who attempted to march peacefully across a bridge: "I was terrified. I saw those horsemen coming toward me and they had those awful masks on; they rode right through the cloud of tear gas. Some of them had clubs, others had ropes, or whips, which they swung about them like they were driving cattle." Showcased on the television news, the vicious attack provoked yet another burst of national outrage and support for a voting-rights bill.

Signed by the president in August 1965, the Voting Rights Act spectacularly expanded black suffrage in the South and transformed southern politics. The law authorized federal examiners to register qualified voters and to suspend the literacy test in all areas where fewer than half the minority residents of voting age were registered. Together with the Twenty-fourth Amendment, ratified in 1964, which outlawed the poll tax in federal elections, and a 1966 Supreme Court decision striking down the poll tax in *all* elections, the Voting Rights Act boosted the number of registered Alabama blacks from 24 percent of those eligible in 1964 to 57 percent in 1968. In Mississippi in these four years,

Voter Registration of African-Americans in the South, 1964–1971

As blacks overwhelmingly registered to vote as Democrats, some former segregationist politicians, among them George Wallace, started to court the black vote, and many southern whites began to cast their ballots for Republicans, inaugurating an era of real two-party competition in the South.

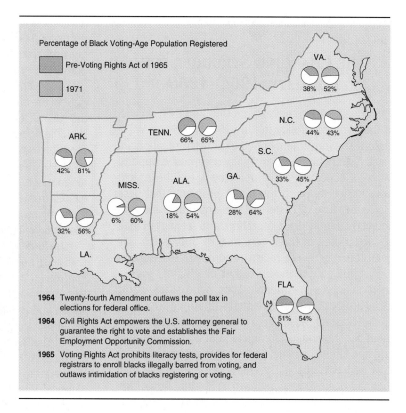

Percentage of Black Voting-Age Population Registered

▨ Pre-Voting Rights Act of 1965

▢ 1971

VA.   38%   52%

TENN.   66%   65%

N.C.   44%   43%

ARK.   42%   81%

S.C.   33%   45%

MISS.   6%   60%

ALA.   18%   54%

GA.   28%   64%

LA.   32%   56%

FLA.   51%   54%

1964 Twenty-fourth Amendment outlaws the poll tax in elections for federal office.

1964 Civil Rights Act empowers the U.S. attorney general to guarantee the right to vote and establishes the Fair Employment Opportunity Commission.

1965 Voting Rights Act prohibits literacy tests, provides for federal registrars to enroll blacks illegally barred from voting, and outlaws intimidation of blacks registering or voting.

the proportion of black registrants leaped from 7 percent to 59 percent; and the number of black voters throughout the South rose from 1 million to 3.1 million. For the first time since Reconstruction, African-Americans constituted a force to be reckoned with in southern politics.

The civil-rights movement had altered, not revolutionized, race relations in America. Blacks' new voting power led to the defeat of Sheriff Jim Clark and numerous other white supremacists. Other once ardent segregationists found it politically prudent to change their stance and seek black support. Equal access to public accommodations gave African-Americans a new sense of dignity. "Now if we do want to go to McDonald's we can go to McDonald's," mused a black woman in Atlanta. "It's just knowing! It's a good feeling." But with discrimination lingering in many spheres and black unemployment still disproportionately high, the anger bubbling below the surface of the urban ghetto finally boiled over.

The Long, Hot Summers

On August 11, 1965, five days after the voting-rights-bill signing, a confrontation between white police and young blacks in Watts, Los Angeles's largest black district, ignited the most destructive race riot in more than two decades. For six days nearly fifty thousand blacks, venting long-repressed anger, looted shops, firebombed white-owned businesses, and sniped at police officers, fire fighters, and National Guard troops. When the melee ended, thirty-four people had been

killed, some nine hundred injured, nearly four thousand arrested, and $30 million worth of property devastated. In rapid succession blacks in Chicago and in Springfield, Massachusetts, took to the streets, looting, burning, and battling police.

Then in the summer of 1966, more than a score of ghetto outbreaks erupted in northern cities. Black youths rioted to force whites to pay heed to the squalor of the slums, to the savage behavior of police in the ghetto, and to urban poverty—issues that the civil-rights movement had ignored. Frustrated by the allure of America's wealth portrayed on TV and by what seemed the empty promise of civil-rights laws, African-American mobs stoned passing motorists, ransacked stores, torched white-owned buildings, and hurled bricks at the troops sent to quell the disorder. The following summer brought nearly 150 racial outbreaks and 40 riots. It was the most intense and destructive outpouring of racial violence that the United States had ever witnessed. In Newark, New Jersey—the city with the nation's highest rates of African-American unemployment and maternal mortality—the arrest of a black taxi driver triggered five days of arson and looting that culminated in the killing of twenty-five blacks by the police. A week later Detroit, plagued by constant conflict between black citizens and white police, exploded in the bloodiest race riot in half a century: forty-three dead, more than a thousand wounded, nearly $50 million worth of property destroyed, and a large part of the country's fifth-largest city ravaged by some four thousand fires.

Within hours of the announcement of the assassination of Martin Luther King, Jr., in 1968 (see Chapter 31), black uprisings flared in the ghettos of over a hundred cities. The week's upheavals left another forty-six dead. Overall, the riot toll from 1964 to 1968 included nearly $200 million in destroyed property, forty thousand arrests, seven thousand injured, and some two hundred deaths.

A frightened, bewildered nation wondered why such widespread rioting was occurring just when blacks were beginning to achieve their goals. Militant blacks explained the riots as revolutionary violence to overthrow a racist, reactionary society. The extreme Right saw them as evidence of a communist plot. Conservatives described the riots as senseless outbursts— "engaged in by a few but bringing great distress to all." An investigation conducted by the government's National Advisory Commission on Civil Disorders (the Kerner Commission) indicted "white racism" for fostering an "explosive mixture" of poverty, slum housing, poor education, and police brutality in America's cities. Warning that "our nation is moving toward two societies, one black, one white—separate and unequal," the commission recommended the creation of 2 million new jobs, the construction of 6 million units of public housing, an attack on de facto school segregation in the North, and massive funding for a "national system of income supplementation." President Johnson, aware of a swelling white backlash, ignored the advice of the commission that he had established, and most whites approved of Johnson's inaction. Alarmed by the demands for "Black Power" that had resounded during the recent riots, they preferred that their taxes be spent on strengthening local police forces rather than on government programs to improve ghetto conditions.

"Black Power"

Paralleling the desperation expressed by African-Americans in the urban riots, a demand for Black Power in 1966 flowed from bitter disappointment at the limited pace of racial change, as well as from black outrage to-

Malcolm X
Rejecting the nonviolent, integrationist civil-rights movement, militant black nationalist Malcolm X urged African-Americans to get their freedom "by any means necessary."

ward a white society that continued to block the most minimal advances by African-Americans. Less on ideology than an exclamation of fury and frustration, the rhetoric of Black Power evolved mainly from the teachings of Malcolm X. A former pimp, drug addict, and street hustler, Malcolm X had converted to the Nation of Islam, or Black Muslim, faith while in prison. Founded in Detroit in 1931 by Elijah Poole (who took the Islamic name Elijah Muhammad), the Nation of Islam insisted that blacks practice self-discipline and self-respect, and rejected integration as a goal. Exhorting African-Americans to separate themselves from the "white devil," Malcolm X urged them to be proud of their blackness and their African roots, to view themselves with their "own eyes not the white man's." Blacks, he proclaimed, must control their own destinies, rely on armed self-defense rather than nonviolence, and seize their freedom "by any means necessary." Malcolm X was assassinated by members of the Nation of Islam in February 1965, after he had broken with and criticized Elijah Muhammad. But his death hardly silenced his voice. Malcolm's account of his life,

The Autobiography of Malcolm X (1965), became the preeminent text for the burgeoning Black Power movement.

In the summer of 1966, Stokely Carmichael led SNCC away from its original commitment to nonviolence and integration: "The only way we gonna stop them white men from whippin' us is to take over. We been saying freedom for six years and we ain't got nothin'. What we gonna start saying now is Black Power!" Carmichael's successor as head of the SNCC, H. Rap Brown, encouraged African-Americans "to get you some guns. . . . I mean, don't be trying to love that honky [white man] to death. Shoot him to death." Taking SNCC at its word, two college students in Oakland, California, Huey Newton and Bobby Seale, organized the Black Panthers in 1966. Brandishing firearms and wearing bandoliers, the Black Panthers gained national publicity from a series of violent confrontations with the police and from Newton's repeated claim that "quoting from Chairman Mao . . . political power comes through the barrel of a gun."

The "Black Power" slogan was adopted by African-American leaders of virtually every persuasion. Revolutionaries used it to preach guerrilla warfare; liberals, to demand reform; and conservatives, to emphasize self-help. For many who adopted it, the phrase simply meant self-pride. "Say it loud—I'm black and I'm proud," chanted soul singer James Brown, and a generation of African-Americans affirmed that "black is beautiful." Rejecting skin bleaches and hair straighteners, young blacks donned dashikis, wore Afro hairstyles, enjoyed soul music and soul food, and established black-studies programs at colleges. Black Power reflected an insistence that African-Americans shape their own culture and define their own destiny. "I may have lost hope," Jesse Jackson, a young SCLC leader in Chicago, frequently asked students to repeat after him, "but I am . . . somebody. . . . I am . . . black . . . beautiful . . . proud. . . . I must be respected." This theme would soon reverberate through other social movements.

Native-American and Chicano Power

Activist Native Americans, whose peoples numbered nearly eight hundred thousand, half of them on reservations, organized demonstrations during the sixties to publicize their plight and to awaken self-respect and cultural pride. The Eisenhower termination policy, which had sought to assimilate Indians into the urban

Native Americans on Alcatraz Island, 1969
After taking over the island, the American Indian Movement demanded government funds to develop it into an Indian cultural center and university. In 1971 federal officials removed the demonstrators.

César Chávez
To dramatize the plight of migrant workers, Chávez drew on the tactics of the civil-rights movement. In 1965 he led striking grape pickers with the slogan "God is Beside You on the Picket Line."

mainstream of American life, had enormously disrupted Indian ways. In 1961 representatives of sixty-seven tribes gathered in Chicago to draw up a Declaration of Purposes; three years later hundreds of Indians assembled in Washington to lobby for recognition in the War on Poverty. Native Americans, they pointed out, suffered the worst poverty, the highest disease and death rates, and the poorest education and housing of any group in the United States. President Johnson responded by establishing the National Council on Indian Opportunity in 1965, to channel antipoverty funds into Indian communities, and in 1968 Johnson became the first president to send Congress a special message seeking greater federal aid for the Indians.

By then, young activists on the National Indian Youth Council were demanding "Red Power" and insisting on the name "Native American." They agitated for preferential hiring, Native-American studies in colleges, and government reimbursement for the lands that whites had illegally taken from them in violation of federal laws and treaties. Adopting the civil-rights movement's tactics of direct action and confrontation, Indians in Washington State in 1968 held "fish-ins" to assert old treaty rights to fish in the Columbia River and Puget Sound. Native Americans also seized an abandoned federal penitentiary on Alcatraz Island in San Francisco Bay, mockingly claiming it "by right of discovery" and offering to buy it from the government for twenty-four dollars in beads and cloth (the sum allegedly paid by the Dutch to Indians for Manhattan Island in 1626). In Massachusetts, Wampanoag Indians transformed Thanksgiving Day, 1970, into a National Day of Mourning. The most highly publicized Indian group, the American Indian Movement (AIM), founded by Chippewas in Minneapolis in 1966, emphasized the right of Native Americans to control their own affairs. Like the Blank Panthers, AIM established armed patrols to protect Indians from harassment by the police.

Mexican-Americans also challenged the dominance of whites. Their ethnic pride and solidarity were kindled by the efforts of César Estrada Chávez, a World War II veteran who founded the National Farm Workers Association to gain union recognition and improved working conditions for farm laborers. A devout Roman Catholic, Chávez followed Martin Luther King, Jr., in utilizing religion and nonviolent resistance as weapons in the battle for social justice. Portraying the farm workers' struggle—*La Causa*—as part of the larger national movement for civil rights and social justice, Chávez organized a strike of grape pickers in Cali-

fornia in 1965 and a nationwide consumer boycott of grapes (and later, lettuce) picked by nonunion workers. His efforts led to better wages for field hands and strengthened ethnic consciousness among Mexican-Americans.

Most Mexican-Americans living in the United States in the sixties did not work on farms. Although in 1940 they had been the most rural of the major ethnic groups in the United States, by 1970, 85 percent of all Mexican-Americans lived in urban areas. Neighborhoods such as Pacoima and North Hollywood in Los Angeles became centers of Mexican-American businesses. While some Mexican newcomers embraced U.S. culture, others, particularly young activists, rejected assimilation and shunned mainstream values. They demanded that other Americans refer to them by their self-designation, *Chicanos* and *Chicanas,* as a mark of respect for their ethnic identity. They called for bilingual and bicultural education, for Chicano Studies in universities, and for Chicana-only organizations. In New Mexico, they founded the Alianza to recapture territory usurped by whites. In Colorado the Crusade for Justice, and in Texas La Raza Unida, exemplified the new militancy, as did the United Mexican-American Students on campuses in the Southwest. Young Chicanos in California organized the Brown Berets, modeled on the Black Panthers, and began to speak of "Chicano Power." They demanded control over the institutions most affecting them, particularly the Immigration and Naturalization Service. Owing to the ending of the *bracero* program and to the annual ceilings imposed by the 1965 immigration law, many Mexicans seeking seasonal work or permanent residence entered the United States surreptitiously—and hundreds of thousands each year were arrested and deported.

The "Black Power," "Red Power," and "Brown Power" movements did not sustain the intense activism and media attention that they attracted in the late sixties. But in elevating the consciousness and nurturing the confidence of the younger generation, each contributed to the cultural pride within its respective group.

A Second Feminist Wave

Following the victory of the woman-suffrage campaign in 1920, the feminist movement in the United States had fallen on hard times. Individual feminists had carried on the tradition of Susan B. Anthony and Elizabeth Cady Stanton, but the movement as a whole had lost momentum. In the 1950s feminist consciousness had hit a low point.

But with the rising tempo of activism sparked by the civil-rights movement, a new spirit of self-awareness and dissatisfaction stirred middle-class women. It resulted in a revived feminist movement that profoundly altered women's view of themselves and their role in American life.

Several events coalesced the stirrings of discontent into a movement. John F. Kennedy, who personally exploited women in a series of fleeting sexual encounters both before and after his marriage, established the Presidential Commission on the Status of Women. Its 1963 report on sexual discrimination in employment documented occupational inequities suffered by women that were similar to those endured by minority groups. Women received less pay than men for comparable or even identical work and had far less chance of moving into professional or managerial careers. Although women composed 51 percent of the population, only 7 percent of the nation's doctors and less than 4 percent of its lawyers were female. The women who served on the presidential commission and on the state commissions that it inspired successfully urged that the Civil Rights Act of 1964 prohibit sexual as well as racial discrimination in employment.

These women then monitored the Equal Employment Opportunity Commission's handling of discrimination complaints by women. Dismayed by the EEOC's reluctance to enforce the ban on discrimination by gender, Bella Abzug, Aileen Hernandez, and others formed the National Organization for Women (NOW) in 1966. Defining itself as a civil-rights group for women, NOW lobbied for equal opportunity, filed lawsuits against gender discrimination, and mobilized public opinion "to bring American women into full participation in the mainstream of American society NOW."

The popularity of NOW and its rapid gains in membership owed much to the publication in 1963 of Betty Friedan's *The Feminine Mystique.* Calling it "the problem that has no name," Friedan condemned the narrow postwar view that women should seek fulfillment solely as wives and mothers. The trap of suburban domesticity, Friedan argued, left many women with feelings of emptiness, with no sense of accomplishment, and afraid even to ask "the silent question—'Is this all?'" To escape the mystique, Friedan asserted, women must pursue independent careers and establish "goals that will permit them to find their own

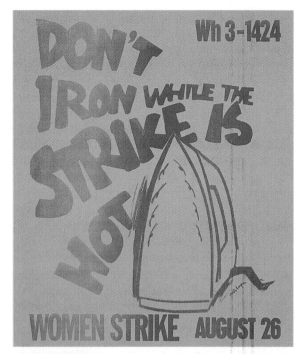

Women's Strike
Initially ridiculed or considered ultraradical, the women's movement grew throughout the 1970s, demanding wage parity with men, pressuring the media to cease gender stereotyping, urging the creation of child-care centers, and advocating the legalization of abortion.

identity." *The Feminine Mystique* revealed to disillusioned women that they were not alone in their unhappiness. Friedan's demand for "something more than my husband, my children, and my home" rang true to many educated middle-class women who found the creativity of homemaking and the joys of motherhood exaggerated.

Still another catalyst for feminism came from the involvement of younger women in the civil-rights and anti–Vietnam War movements. Women who joined these causes gained confidence in their own potential, an ideology to describe oppression and justify revolt, and experience in the strategy and tactics of organized protest. At the same time, their involvement made them conscious of their own second-class status, as men in these movements had monopolized the positions of power, relegated women to menial jobs like typing and making coffee, and sexually exploited them. In 1967 female veterans of the antiwar and civil-rights movements launched a new drive for women's liberation that borrowed the concept of class oppression from Marxist theory, the tactics and rhetoric of African-American liberation, and the loose organization of the student antiwar movement.

In 1968 militant feminists adopted the technique of "consciousness raising" as a recruitment device and a means of transforming women's perceptions of themselves and society. Tens of thousands of women assembled in small discussion groups to share experiences and air grievances. As they talked, they gradually realized that others felt dissatisfaction similar to their own. "When I saw that what I always felt were my own personal hangups was as true for every other woman in that room as it was for me! Well, that's when *my* consciousness was raised," a New York City participant related. In this way, women learned to regard personal problems as shared problems with social causes and political solutions, rather than as just psychological issues to be resolved individually. Recalling how "eye-opening" these women-only rap sessions had been for her, one housewife explained: "It wasn't just whining, it was trying to figure out *why,* why we felt things and what we could do to make our marriages more equal and our lives better." With this new consciousness came a sense of "sisterhood" and a commitment to end women's subordination to men.

Across the nation, women's liberation groups sprang up, employing a variety of tactics and techniques. In 1968 radical feminists crowned a live sheep Miss America to dramatize that such contests degraded women, and set up "freedom trash cans" in which women could discard high-heeled shoes, bras, curlers, and other items that they considered demeaning. They invaded all-male bars and social clubs and sat in at lawyers' associations and medical societies to dramatize discrimination against women in professional careers. Highlighting the relationship between personal life and politics, and questioning all traditional notions of "women's sphere," they established health collectives and day-care centers, founded abortion-counseling services, demanded equality in education and the workplace, and protested the negative portrayals of women in the media, in advertising, and in language. Terms such as *sexism* and *male chauvinist pig* entered the American vocabulary.

Despite a gulf between radicals and reformers, quarreling factions set aside their differences in August 1970 to join in the largest women's rights demonstration ever. Commemorating the fiftieth anniversary of woman suffrage, the Women's Strike for Equality brought out tens of thousands of women nationwide to parade for the right to equal employment and safe, legal abortions. By then the women's movement had already pressured many financial institutions to issue credit to single women and to married women in their own name; filed suit against hundreds of colleges and universities to secure salary raises for women faculty members victimized by discrimination; ended newspapers' practice of listing employment opportunities under separate "Male" and "Female" headings; and gained government guidelines that required corporations receiving federal funds to adopt nondiscriminatory hiring practices and equal pay scales. By 1970, moreover, more than 40 percent of all women held full-time jobs outside the home.

In sharp contrast to the 1950s, when the ideologists of domesticity and "togetherness" had sought to force all women into a single mold, the changed consciousness born of the feminist movement of the sixties opened up for millions of young women—and many older women as well—a larger world of choices and opportunities. Of course, domesticity remained an option, but it was no longer the *only* option. Women were taking control of their own lives and defining their own goals, in their own language. Accepting a Grammy award for "I Am Woman," singer Helen Reddy thanked God for all "She" had done.

THE LOST CRUSADE IN VIETNAM, 1964–1968

The militancy of women, blacks, Native Americans, and Chicanos chipped away at the consensus that LBJ so desired, but more than any other issue, America's deepening involvement in Vietnam unraveled his hopes for a united society. Although he had intended to concentrate on domestic affairs, Johnson was sidetracked by the situation in South Vietnam. Diem's successors proved unable to wage the war effectively, and the Vietcong in 1964 stepped up attacks on noncommunist South Vietnam with equipment supplied by North Vietnam.

Johnson had to choose either to intervene in a more decisive manner than his predecessors or to extricate the United States from Southeast Asia. The president was ambivalent. He privately described Vietnam as "a raggedy-ass fourth-rate country" undeserving of American blood and dollars. He feared that an all-out American military effort would provoke Chinese or Soviet entry and lead to World War III. And he foresaw that a full-scale American engagement in "that bitch of a war" would destroy "the woman I really loved—the Great Society." On the other hand, Johnson could not abide the thought that America might appear weak to its communist enemies. "We learned from Hitler at Munich that success only feeds the appetite of aggression," he told a press conference. If America abandoned Vietnam, he added, invoking the domino theory, "The battle would be renewed in one country and then in another country." Only American resolve and strength, Johnson believed, would deter a wider war. Having witnessed the McCarthyite assault on Truman and the Democrats after the "loss" of China in 1949, moreover, the president refused to consider any move that would leave him vulnerable to conservative attack. "I am not going to lose Vietnam," he insisted. "I am not going to be the president who saw Southeast Asia go the way China went."

Trapped between unacceptable alternatives, Johnson widened America's limited war, hoping that American firepower would force Ho Chi Minh to the bargaining table. But the North Vietnamese and NLF were determined to win at any cost. They calculated that they would gain more by outlasting the United States than by negotiating. So the war ground on, devastating Southeast Asia and dividing the United States as no event in American history had since the Civil War.

The Vietnam War, to 1968
Wishing to guarantee an independent, noncommunist government in South Vietnam, Lyndon Johnson remarked in 1965: "We fight because we must fight if we are to live in a world where every country can shape its own destiny. To withdraw from one battlefield means only to prepare for the next."

The Gulf of Tonkin Resolution

In 1964 Johnson took steps to impress North Vietnam with America's commitment to defend South Vietnam and to block his vigorously anticommunist opponent, Barry Goldwater, from capitalizing on Vietnam in the presidential campaign. In February he ordered the Pentagon to prepare plans for air strikes against North Vietnam. In May his advisers drafted a congressional resolution authorizing an escalation of American military action, and in June the president appointed General Maxwell Taylor, a proponent of greater American involvement in the war, as ambassador to Saigon. Then, in early August, North Vietnamese patrol boats allegedly clashed with two American destroyers in the Gulf of Tonkin (see map). Evidence of the attack was unclear, yet Johnson announced that Americans had

Infantry Patrol in a Clearing, *by Roger Blum*
An unconventional war without fronts or territorial objectives, the Vietnam War generally involved small units of American troops engaging NLF and NVA forces in rice paddies, jungles, and swamps.

been victims of "open aggression on the high seas." Withholding the fact that the U.S. ships had been assisting South Vietnamese raids against North Vietnamese islands in a clandestine operation planned by American advisers, the president condemned the attacks as unprovoked.

Ordering limited, retaliatory air strikes against North Vietnam for the first time, Johnson called on Congress to pass the previously drafted resolution giving him the authority to "take all necessary measures to repel any armed attack against the forces of the United States and to prevent further aggression." Assured by the president that this meant no "extension of the present conflict," the Senate passed the so-called Gulf of Tonkin Resolution 88 to 2; the House vote was 416 to 0. Johnson had not only signaled America's determination to stand by its allies but also stymied Gold-

water's effort to make Vietnam a campaign issue. He also now had a resolution that he likened to "grandma's nightshirt—it covered everything." His attorney general would soon describe the resolution as "the functional equivalent of a declaration of war," and the president would consider it a mandate to commit American forces to Vietnam as he saw fit. But the Gulf of Tonkin Resolution also created a credibility problem for Johnson, as opponents of the war charged that he had misled Congress and misinformed the American public.

Americanization of the War

Interpreting the Gulf of Tonkin Resolution as a blank check to widen the war, Johnson in early 1965 ordered the sustained bombing of North Vietnam, "Operation

Rolling Thunder." Designed to inflict just enough damage to persuade Hanoi to negotiate, while simultaneously boosting the morale of the Saigon government and arresting the flow of soldiers and supplies southward from North Vietnam, the bombing accomplished none of its purposes. Furthermore, for all of LBJ's concern about restraint, the United States dropped eight hundred tons of bombs daily on North Vietnam between 1965 and 1968, three times the tonnage that had rained on all of Europe, Africa, and Asia during World War II.

Unable to turn the tide by bombing, Johnson made a fateful decision to escalate the U.S. commitment by sending combat troops to Vietnam. Adopting a "meat-grinder" strategy of victory through attrition, Johnson aimed to push the communists to the peace table by inflicting losses on their forces at a rate that exceeded the enemy's ability to recruit additional troops. Hanoi, however, was prepared to battle on until the United States lost the will to fight, and steadily became more directly involved in the conflict. Determined to prevent North Vietnam from winning, Johnson had stationed some 485,000 American troops in Vietnam by the end of 1967, a greater military force than the United States had deployed in Korea at the peak of that war. Each escalation had been matched by North Vietnam; yet the end was still not in sight, and the Joint Chiefs of Staff kept asking for more fighting men.

Opposition to the War

First on college campuses and then in cities and small towns across the country, a growing number of Americans doubted the wisdom of the nation's involvement in Vietnam and vocally opposed it. A week after the marines splashed ashore at Danang, South Vietnam, in March 1965, students and faculty at the University of Michigan conducted the first teach-in to raise questions about U.S. intervention. All-night and two- or three-day discussions of the war followed at other universities; and some twenty-five thousand people, mainly students, attended a rally in Washington that spring to applaud the denunciation of an unjust and unnecessary war by senators Wayne Morse of Oregon and Ernest Gruening of Alaska, the only members of Congress to vote against the Gulf of Tonkin Resolution.

The following year, paralleling new draft calls, large-scale campus protest against the war erupted. Students staged disruptive demonstrations against military recruitment and university research for the Pentagon and began a draft-resistance movement.

Likewise in 1966, a galaxy of liberal intellectuals and members of the clergy spoke out against the war. Some described it as a civil conflict in which the United States had no business meddling. Others doubted that the United States could win at any reasonable cost and feared the prospect of spiraling escalation. Still others worried about the negative impact of the war on U.S. relations with the rest of the world. And many decried the drastic cutbacks in Great Society programs made necessary by the costs of the war. Opposition to the war by J. William Fulbright and Robert Kennedy in the Senate, by such foreign-policy experts as George Kennan and Walter Lippmann, and by Dr. Benjamin Spock and Martin Luther King, Jr., spurred hundreds of thousands of Americans to participate in antiwar marches and demonstrations in 1967.

Critics also noted that the war's toll fell most heavily on the nation's poor. Thanks to college deferments, the subtle use of influence, and a military-assignment system that shunted the better educated to desk jobs, lower-class youths were twice as likely to be drafted and, if drafted, twice as likely to be assigned to combat duty as those from the middle class. About 80 percent of the enlisted men who fought in Vietnam came from poor and working-class families.

TV coverage of the war further eroded support for American involvement. Scenes of shocking cruelty, of fleeing refugees, of children maimed by U.S. bombs, and of dying Americans, replayed in the nation's living rooms night after night, laid bare the horror of the war and undercut the official optimism of government press agents. Relentlessly pursuing action stories, TV crews uncovered the nastiest aspects of a dirty war. Americans shuddered as they watched napalm (a burning glue that adheres to skin and clothing) and defoliants lay waste Vietnam's countryside and leave thousands of civilians dead or mutilated. They viewed American troops, supposedly winning the hearts and minds of the Vietnamese, forcibly uprooting peasants, burning their villages, and desecrating their ancestral burial grounds.

It would be a mistake, however, to conclude that most Americans opposed the war. In 1965 opinion polls revealed that 65 percent of Americans, including a majority of college students, backed Johnson's war policy. Even at the height of the antiwar movement—when campus and street demonstrations dominated the headlines and the TV screens—the majority of Americans initially either supported the war or remained undecided. But key sectors of the religious, academic, and media communities were in opposition;

LBJ's Vietnam Nightmare
The Vietnam War spelled Johnson's undoing. Young peace demonstrators made known their feelings about the president's role in the war during a massive antiwar protest at the Pentagon in October 1967 (top); a cartoonist caricatured Johnson as being haunted by the ghosts of Vietnam (inset).

and as casualty figures surpassed those of the Korean War, and total costs approached $100 billion, the war's unpopularity, even among the ambivalent majority, deepened. "I want to get out, but I don't want to give up" was a common response expressed to public-opinion pollsters. In mid-1967 Secretary of Defense Robert McNamara admitted that "the picture of the world's greatest superpower killing or seriously injuring a thousand noncombatants a week, while trying to pound a tiny backward country into submission on an issue whose merits are hotly disputed, is not a pretty one."

Equally disturbing was the manner in which the war had polarized the nation. Compromise, and even civil discourse, had become impossible. "Hawks" demanded a quick and total victory. "Doves" insisted on negotiating rather than fighting. All the while, the vast middle group of ordinary Americans, though not opposed to the war on principle, was being driven to the conclusion that it was unwinnable. As Johnson lashed out at his critics as "nervous Nellies" and refused to de-escalate the conflict, the young paraded outside the White House taunting "Hey, hey, LBJ, how many kids did you kill today?" By 1968 Johnson had become a virtual prisoner in the White House—unable to speak in public without drawing hecklers—and his dream of a Great Society lay in ruins.

CONCLUSION

Despite President Lyndon Johnson's mountain of woes in 1968, much had been accomplished during his administration. Under his predecessor, John Kennedy, high hopes prevailed that society could be reformed and communism contained. Idealistic Americans, especially the young, widely believed that the time had come to rid the nation of racism and poverty. The civil-rights movement that took form in the Kennedy years ultimately vanquished legally enforced segregation, disfranchisement, and racial discrimination, and it nurtured the self-respect of black Americans. Its triumphs also inspired other disadvantaged and minority Americans and women to fight for equality, develop self-pride, and determine their own destinies.

The reform impulse peaked during Lyndon Johnson's first two years in the White House. Millions benefited from Great Society legislation directed toward education, the arts, economic growth, environmental and consumer protection, and medical care and financial relief for the needy. The Great Society made the United States a more caring and just nation.

Yet the Great Society promised much more—far too much more—than it could deliver. As Kennedy and Johnson had overestimated U.S. power abroad, both relied primarily on economic growth to resolve domestic problems. And in the end, the Great Society spent too little money for too short a period to be effective. Despite LBJ's boast that the United States could afford both guns and butter (that is, fund a major war abroad while continuing a high level of spending on social programs at home), the skyrocketing costs of the war in Vietnam reduced the "War" on Poverty to a skirmish. As the American commitment in Vietnam skyrocketed to $30 billion a year by 1968, and as the casualties mounted, increasing numbers of college-age youth and militant African-Americans questioned both the war in Vietnam and the kind of society that could support such a war. Some turned to violence to end what they perceived as evil, and, in turn, a conservative reaction eroded support for further reform. Floundering in a futile, faraway war, Johnson and the Democratic party—like the American people as a whole—faced the election year of 1968 in confusion and disarray.

CHRONOLOGY

1960 Sit-ins to protest segregation begin.
John F. Kennedy elected president.

1961 Peace Corps and Alliance for Progress created.
Bay of Pigs invasion.
Freedom rides.
Berlin Wall erected.

1962 Michael Harrington, *The Other America*.
Cuban missile crisis.

1963 Civil-rights demonstrations in Birmingham.
March on Washington.
Test-Ban Treaty between the Soviet Union and the United States.
Kennedy assassinated; Lyndon B. Johnson becomes president.
Betty Freidan, *The Feminine Mystique*.

1964 "Freedom Summer" in Mississippi.

1964 Civil Rights Act.
Gulf of Tonkin incident and resolution.
Economic Opportunity Act initiates War on Poverty.
Johnson elected president.

1965 Bombing of North Vietnam and Americanization of the war begin.
Assassination of Malcolm X.
Civil-rights march from Selma to Montgomery.

Marchers on the road to Montgomery

1965 Teach-ins to question U.S. involvement in War in Vietnam begin.
Voting Rights Act.
Watts riot in Los Angeles.

1966 Stokely Carmichael calls for Black Power.
Black Panthers formed.
National Organization for Women (NOW) founded.

1967 Massive antiwar demonstrations.
Race riots in Newark, Detroit, and other cities.

FOR FURTHER READING

Irving Bernstein, *Promises Kept: John F. Kennedy's New Frontier* (1991), and Thomas Reeves, *A Question of Character: A Life of John F. Kennedy* (1991). Two conflicting interpretations of the man and his presidency.

William Chafe, *The Unfinished Journey: America Since World War II*, rev. ed. (1995). An interpretive history of social change emphasizing issues of class, gender, and race.

John Dittmer, *Local People: The Struggle for Civil Rights in Mississippi* (1994). An important study of the African-American freedom movement.

Sara Evans, *Personal Politics* (1979). An analysis of the roots of modern feminism in the civil-rights movement and in the New Left.

Samuel Hays, *Beauty, Health, and Permanence: Environmental Politics in the United States, 1955–1985* (1987). A pathbreaking account of modern environmentalism.

George Herring, *America's Longest War*, rev. ed. (1985). A comprehensive account of the reasons for America's involvement and ultimate failure in Vietnam.

Harvard Sitkoff, *The Struggle for Black Equality, 1954–1992* (1993). A dramatic account of the terror-laced struggle against white racism.

ADDITIONAL BIBLIOGRAPHY

John F. Kennedy and the New Frontier

Thomas Brown, *JFK: History of an Image* (1988); James Giglio, *The Presidency of John F. Kennedy* (1991); Jim F. Heath, *Decade of Disillusionment: The Kennedy-Johnson Years* (1975); Bruce Miroff, *Pragmatic Illusions: The Presidential Politics of JFK* (1976); Herbert Parmet, *Jack* (1980) and *JFK* (1983); Garry Wills, *The Kennedy Imprisonment* (1983).

Foreign Affairs in the Sixties

James Arnold, *The First Domino* (1991); Michael Beschloss, *The Crisis Years* (1991); Bernard Firestone, *The Quest for Nuclear Stability* (1982); John Girling, *America and the Third World* (1980); Walter LaFeber, *Inevitable Revolutions: The United States in Central America* (1985); Richard Mahoney, *JFK: Ordeal in Africa* (1983); Peter Wyden, *Bay of Pigs* (1980).

Lyndon B. Johnson and the Great Society

E. Berkowitz and Kim McQuaid, *Creating the Welfare State* (1992); Richard Cloward and Frances Fox Piven, *Poor People's Movements* (1978); Mark Gelfand, *A Nation of Cities* (1975); Michael Katz, *The Undeserving Poor: From the War on Poverty to the War on Welfare* (1989); Doris Kearns, *Lyndon Johnson and the American Dream* (1977); Charles Morris, *A Time of Passion* (1984); Charles Murray, *Losing Ground: American Social Policy, 1950–1980* (1984); D. Zarefsky, *President Johnson's War on Poverty: Rhetoric and History* (1986).

The Pursuit of Equality

Taylor Branch, *Parting the Waters: America in the King Years* (1988); James Button, *Black Violence: Political Impact of the 1960s Riots* (1978); Clayborne Carson, *In Struggle: SNCC and the Black Awakening of the 1960s* (1981); William Chafe, *Civilities and Civil Rights: Greensboro, North Carolina, and the Black Struggle for Freedom* (1980) and *The Paradox of Change: American Women in the 20th Century* (1991); David Chappell, *Inside Agitators: White Southerners in the Civil Rights Movement* (1994); E. C. Clark, *The Schoolhouse Door: Segregation's Last Stand at the University of Alabama* (1993); W. M. Dulaney and Kathleen Underwood, eds., *Essays on the American Civil Rights Movement* (1993); Mario García, *Mexican-Americans: Leadership, Ideology, and Identity* (1989); David J. Garrow, *Protest at Selma: Martin Luther King, Jr., and the Voting Rights Act of 1965* (1978); Hugh Davis Graham, *The Civil Rights Era* (1989); Cynthia Harrison, *On Account of Sex: The Politics of Women's Issues, 1945–1968* (1988); Steven F. Lawson, *Black Ballots* (1976); K. Mills, *This Little Light of Mine: The Life of Fannie Lou Hamer* (1993); Carlos Munoz, Jr., *Youth, Identity, Power: Chicano Movement* (1989); Mark Stern, *Calculating Visions: Kennedy, Johnson and Civil Rights* (1992).

The Vietnam War at Home and at the Front

David Anderson, *Trapped by Success* (1991); C. Appey, *Working Class War* (1992); Eric Bergerud, *The Dynamics of Defeat* (1991); Larry Berman, *Lyndon Johnson's War* (1989); Phillip Davidson, *Vietnam at War* (1991); Gloria Emerson, *Winners and Losers* (1976); Frances FitzGerald, *Fire in the Lake* (1972); Gary Hess, *Vietnam and the United States* (1990); David Levy, *The Debate over Vietnam* (1990); Thomas Powers, *The War at Home* (1973); Neil Sheehan, *A Bright Shining Lie* (1988); Kathleen J. Turner, *Lyndon Johnson's Dual War: Vietnam and the Press* (1981); Marilyn Young, *The Vietnam Wars* (1991).

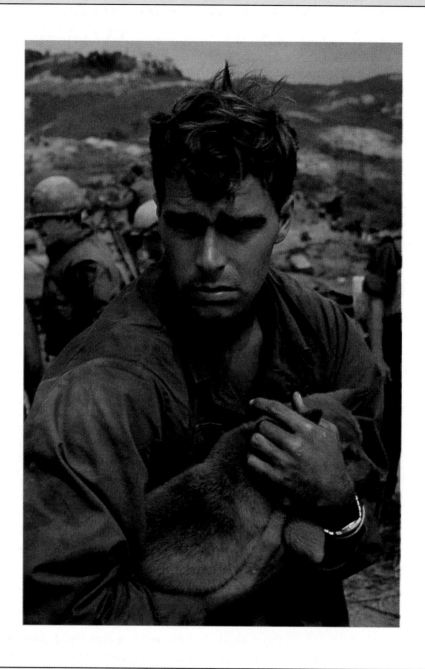

American Soldier in Vietnam
by Larry Burrows, 1972

The Port Huron Statement—SDS's inaugural political manifesto—signaled the passing of the campus apathy of the Eisenhower years. Written primarily by Tom Hayden, a twenty-two-year-old former editor of the University of Michigan student newspaper, and adopted in June 1962 by the sixty or so founding members of SDS, the statement offered a broad critique of American society and expressed a yearning for more genuine human relationships: "We would replace power rooted in possession, privilege or circumstances, with power rooted in love, reflectiveness, reason and creativity." Citing the success of the southern sit-ins and freedom rides, SDS envisioned a nonviolent youth movement transforming the United States into a "participatory democracy": a society in which individuals directly controlled the decisions that affected their lives. That, in turn, would cure such ills as materialism, militarism, careerism, and racism.

The red-diaper babies provided most of SDS's earliest recruits. These were altruistic youth, often raised in strongly Jewish or Christian homes that encouraged high ethics and political engagement. Many other idealistic students never joined SDS, preferring to be associated with what they vaguely called the Movement. But whatever the label, a generation of activists found their agenda for change in the Port Huron Statement and other SDS manifestos. Suiting action to rhetoric, SDS volunteers moved into working-class neighborhoods to lay the groundwork, they hoped, for a grassroots political awakening.

Like the Berkeley free-speech activists, thousands of students were similarly radicalized by what they perceived as the impersonality and rigidity of campus administrators, the insensitivity of the nation's bureaucratic processes, and mainstream liberalism's inability to bring far-reaching change. Only by a radical rejection of the politics of compromise and consensus, many concluded, could the system be restructured along truly humane and democratic lines. By 1965 Mario Savio's call for students to throw their bodies upon "the machine" until it ground to a halt was reverberating on campuses nationwide.

From Protest to Resistance

The movement took many forms. Students held sit-ins to halt compulsory ROTC (Reserve Officer's Training Corps) programs. They protested dress codes and parietal rules. They marched to demand changes in the grading system and in the number of required courses. They threatened to close down universities that would

neither cease research for the military nor admit more minority students. But more than any other issue, the escalation of the war in Vietnam in 1965 gave the so-called New Left an opportunity to kindle a mass student movement. When the Johnson administration abolished automatic student deferments from the draft in January 1966, more than two hundred new campus chapters of SDS appeared.

Popularizing the slogan "Make Love—Not War," SDS in 1966 disrupted ROTC classes, organized draft-card burnings, and harassed campus recruiters for the military and for the Dow Chemical Company—the chief producer of napalm and Agent Orange, the chemicals used in Vietnam to burn villages and defoliate forests. The next year, as the organization adopted the rallying cries "From Protest to Resistance" and "The Streets Belong to the People," SDS leaders encouraged more provocative acts of defiance. They orchestrated civil disobedience at selective-service centers and openly counseled students to flee to Canada or Sweden rather than submit to the draft. At the Spring Mobilization to End the War in Vietnam, which attracted nearly a half-million antiwar protesters to New York's Central Park, SDS members led chants of "Burn cards, not people" and "Hell, no, we won't go!" as hundreds of supporters tossed their draft cards into a bonfire. By year's end SDS claimed about 100,000 members in some three hundred campus chapters.

In the spring of 1968, at least forty thousand students on some one hundred campuses took part in demonstrations against war and racism. Occasionally the confrontations turned violent, as in April at Columbia University. To denounce the university's proposed expansion into neighboring Harlem to construct a gymnasium, militant students, shouting "Gym Crow must go," occupied the administration building and held a dean against his will. The protest quickly expanded into a demonstration against the war and university military research. Almost a thousand students occupied campus buildings, barricaded them, and converted them into "revolutionary communes." "We are fighting to recapture a school from business and war," wrote student James Kunen, "and rededicate it to learning and life." Outraged by the brutality of the police who retook the buildings by storm, the moderate majority of Columbia students then joined in a boycott of classes that shut down the university. A pitched battle between police and some five thousand antiwar demonstrators at the Democratic National Convention in Chicago that summer (see below) offered further evidence that the antiwar movement in which student

Homeless in Vietnam, 1968
As antiwar protest escalated in the United States, these two little South Vietnamese girls walked in the rubble of their homes in Hué. The area was demolished after brutal fighting.

activists figured prominently was hurtling the nation toward social convulsion.

Despite its passion, the student movement was, in the main, peaceful. It adhered to nonviolence and sought an end to the war and to racism by awakening the nation's conscience, not by provoking disorder and bloodshed. Opponents who warned darkly of revolutionary plots or trivialized the demonstrations as juvenile antics staged for television misrepresented the earnestness of the students' effort and the careful planning that went into their protests.

A high point of the movement came in the autumn of 1969 with the New Mobilization, a series of mass antiwar demonstrations on campuses across the nation culminating in mid-November with the March Against Death in Washington, D.C. As three hundred thousand protesters descended on the wintry city, they joined the nonstop march that began at Arlington National Cemetery, snaked past the White House, and ended at the Capitol, where twelve old-fashioned wooden coffins had been set up. For forty hours, from

Thursday afternoon to Saturday morning, they marched in single file, each person carrying a candle and a cardboard plaque bearing the name of a soldier killed or a village destroyed in Vietnam. Writer Garry Wills, watching the slow line of young people move through Washington's darkened streets in the middle of the night, reflected: "They were ragged kids, comically self-important, a Halloween crew of trick-or-treaters; but the men they walked for could not be treated now, and they had no tricks to play—unless this were their last one, this haunting by proxy." Richard Nixon, Lyndon Johnson's Republican successor in the White House, pointedly let it be known that he had spent the weekend watching football on TV.

The Waning of Student Radicalism

A crescendo of violence in the spring of 1970 marked the effective end of the student movement as a political force. On April 30, 1970, President Nixon jolted a war-weary nation with the announcement that he had ordered U.S. troops to invade Cambodia. This neutral Southeast Asian nation, the president said, had become a staging area for North Vietnamese troops. Nixon's action was part of his plan for extricating the United States from Vietnam by "Vietnamizing" the ground conflict while stepping up the bombing to force the North Vietnamese to the negotiating table. His expansion of the war stunned students who had been lulled by his periodic announcements of U.S. troop withdrawals from Vietnam. Infuriated, frightened, and feeling betrayed, they exploded in hatred for Nixon and the war.

At Kent State University in Ohio, as on scores of other campuses, these frustrations loosed a new wave of student turmoil. A few hard-core radicals smashed windows, pelted police cars with rocks, and even attempted to firebomb the ROTC building. Reacting to the tumult, Nixon lashed out at the college protesters as "bums," and his vice president Spiro Agnew compared them to Nazi storm troopers. In the same spirit, Ohio governor James Rhodes, who was waging an uphill campaign for the Republican senatorial nomination, slapped martial law on Kent State University and on May 3 ordered some three thousand National Guardsmen to the tense town of Kent. Donning full battle gear, the troops rolled onto the Kent State campus in armored personnel carriers, appropriated the gym for their headquarters, and pitched tents. Rhodes, presenting himself as the "law-and-order" candidate, hurried to Kent, where he denounced the protesters as

National Guardsmen at Kent State University, 1970

President Nixon's Commission on Campus Unrest concluded that "the [National Guard's] timing and manner of dispersal was disastrous. . . . The rally was peaceful and there was no impending violence."

"worse than the [Nazi] Brown Shirts and the communists" and vowed "to eradicate the problem."

The next day, May 4, about six hundred Kent State students held a peaceful demonstration against the escalation of the war. Catching the students by surprise, the voice of a campus police officer boomed through a bullhorn: "This assembly is unlawful! This is an order—disperse immediately!" Students shouted back: "Pigs off campus!" Some threw stones. "Prepare to move out," the guard commander ordered his men, "and disperse this mob." With bayonets outthrust, the guardsmen moved toward the rally and laid down a blanket of tear gas. Hundreds of demonstrators and onlookers, choking and weeping, ran from the advancing guard. The members of Troop G, apparently panicking, suddenly raised their rifles and fired a volley.

"My God," a girl screamed, "they're killing us!" Thirteen seconds later, when the guardsmen stopped shooting at the students hundreds of yards away, thirteen bodies lay sprawled on the ground. Nine students had been wounded, including one who was paralyzed by a bullet entering his spine. Four were dead. None of those killed was a campus radical. Two had simply been passing by on their way to lunch.

The guardsmen later claimed that they had fired to protect themselves from a "charging mob." But an FBI investigation branded this defense a fabrication, and the commission appointed by Nixon to examine the incident denounced the action as "indiscriminate firing" and "unnecessary, unwarranted and inexcusable."

Nationwide, students and others reacted with stunned disbelief and then a torrent of angry protest demonstrations. On May 15 Mississippi highway patrolmen looking into a campus demonstration fired into a women's dormitory at Jackson State College, killing two students and wounding eleven. This senseless act heightened student resentment of the war and of the president who continued to wage it. Roughly three-quarters of a million students, out of 7 million, identified themselves as "radical or far Left." About 80 percent of all U.S. campuses thereafter experienced protests, although most were peaceful. More than four hundred colleges and universities suspended normal operations as students boycotted classes.

Popular reactions to the campus convulsions revealed the further polarization of an already divided nation. A majority of college students blamed Nixon for widening the war, and many applauded the demonstrators' goals. But far more Americans charged the *victims* with responsibility for the deaths at Kent State and criticized campus protesters for undercutting Nixon's foreign policy. Although a majority of Americans now conceded that the Vietnam War had been a "mistake," 69 percent also believed that the antiwar protesters were "harmful to American life." Underlying the censure were a deep resentment of college students and an impatience for an end to the social chaos of recent years. In reactions that were symptomatic of the nation's division, while Kent State students expressed profound alienation after the shootings, many Kent townspeople shared the sympathies of a local merchant who observed that the National Guard "made only one mistake—they should have fired sooner and longer." A local ditty promised, "The score is four, and next time more."

In fact, the campus protests after Kent State were the final spasm of an expiring, fragmenting movement. When a bomb planted by three antiwar radicals destroyed a science building at the University of Wisconsin in the summer of 1970, killing a graduate student (who himself opposed the war), the overwhelming majority of students, including those who were against the war, reacted with strong disapproval. When classes resumed that fall, the mood on the nation's campuses was dramatically different. A short-lived fad of "streaking"—racing across campus in the nude—more reminiscent of the twenties than the sixties, signaled the end of the student uprising. Frustrated by their failure to end the war, much less to revolutionize American society, former antiwar activists turned to other causes—especially the women's and ecology movements—to mystic cults and rural communes, or to careers and parenthood. The once influential SDS, having shunned doctrinaire ideology and authoritarian leadership, fell prey to disciplined, hard-line followers of Chinese communist leader Mao Zedong (Mao Tse-tung) or Cuban revolutionary Che Guevara. A handful of frustrated radicals went underground, planning and in a few cases carrying out acts of terrorism that provided a justification for government repression of the remnants of the antiwar movement. In 1970 FBI director J. Edgar Hoover added twelve hundred agents to the nearly two thousand FBI agents and many more paid informants already engaged in a crackdown on the New Left. The FBI, moreover, was just one of several government agencies then working, in Hoover's words, "to expose, disrupt, misdirect, discredit, or otherwise neutralize the activities" of radicals. The New Left succumbed, a victim of government harassment, of its own internal contradictions, and of President Nixon's success in winding down the war in Vietnam. The movement's failure to win or hold the support of workers and students left it without adherents.

But the aftereffects of the campus activism outlived the New Left's demise. Student radicalism had catalyzed the resentments of millions of ordinary people into a rejection of liberalism. Youths' militancy had helped to unite fundamentalist Protestants upset by changing moral standards, white southerners angered by school desegregation, and blue-collar workers fed up with welfare expenditures, in a new conservatism whose leaders would restore stability, patriotism, and traditional values.

Propelled to prominence was the conservative Ronald Reagan of California, who won his state's governorship in 1966 in part because of his firm opposition to the Berkeley demonstrators. The actor-turned-politician then gained a resounding reelection victory by taking an even harder line than before against student militancy. Railing against the radicals who continued to disrupt the University of California, Reagan declared, "If it takes a bloodbath, let's get it over with. No more appeasement!" Sounding the same theme, conservatives gained elective office nationwide. Memories of the student revolt would weaken liberalism's appeal throughout much of the 1970s and 1980s.

Yet at the same time, the New Left spurred the growth of wider public opposition to the Vietnam War. The movement not only mobilized the campuses into a force that the government could not ignore but made continued U.S. involvement in the Asian conflict more difficult. Too, the New Left's efforts aided in liberalizing many facets of student life and in rendering university governance less authoritarian. Following the campus protests, dress codes and curfews virtually disappeared; ROTC became an elective rather than a requirement; colleges recruited minorities; and students sat on the committees that shaped their education, often pushing for "relevant" or contemporary courses as supplements to the traditional curriculum.

Some New Left veterans maintained their activism in post-1970 causes: environmentalism, consumer advocacy, and the antinuclear movement. For example, Tom Hayden became a reforming California state legislator in the 1980s. Female students who learned organizing skills and also endured blatant male chauvinism in the sixties' antiwar movement formed the backbone of a resurgent women's movement in the seventies.

All this fell far short of the original New Left vision, however. The New Left never came near its goal of reconstructing the American social and political order. Students could be mobilized in the short run against the war in Vietnam, but only a few made a long-term commitment to radical politics. For the most part, the generation that the New Left had hoped to organize as the vanguard of radical change preferred pot to politics, and rock to revolution.

The Youth Culture

The sense of alienation and desire for change that led some youth to want to remake society led others to pursue altered states of consciousness and life-styles contrary to dominant cultural ways. Rejecting order, reason, monogamy, and social responsibility as "hang-ups," some joined communes or tribes—group living arrangements in which the members renounced individualism and private property and sought to coexist in noncompetition and harmony. In Chicago's Old Town and Atlanta's Fourteenth Street, among others, places where "you could take a trip without a ticket," the quest for a new consciousness usually led to drugs. Giving a name to this new pattern of behavior, historian Theodore Roszak wrote in the late 1960s, "It would hardly seem an exaggeration to call what we see arising among the young a 'counter culture': meaning, a culture so radically disaffiliated from the mainstream assumptions of our society that it scarcely looks to many as a culture at all, but takes on the alarming appearance of a barbarian intrusion." Experimenting with drugs would have a greater personal effect on more young Americans than the political activities of the New Left.

The mores of these culturally radical youths owed a debt to the Beats of the fifties (see Chapter 29). Substituting the pleasure ethic for the work ethic, these "hippies" scandalized the middle class with their sexual promiscuity and indulgence in drugs. Surveys estimated that at least half the college students in the late sixties tried marijuana and that a minority used hallucinogenic or mind-altering drugs, particularly LSD and mescaline. Drug use came easy to a generation that had been conditioned to find happiness through consumption—one whose parents used nicotine and alcoholic beverages to make it through the day and depended on amphetamines and tranquilizers, society's acceptable "uppers" and "downers." The high priest of LSD was Timothy Leary, a former Harvard psychologist fired in 1963 for encouraging students to experiment with drugs—to "tune in, turn on, drop out." On the West Coast, writer Ken Kesey and his followers, the Merry Pranksters, promoted hallucinogens by conducting "acid tests" (distributing free tablets of LSD in orange juice) and created the "psychedelic" craze of Day-Glo-painted bodies gyrating to electrified rock music under flashing strobe lights. Influenced by LSD's reality-bending effects, the counterculture sought a world without rules, one in which magic and mysticism replaced science and reason. Jim Morrison's rock group the Doors took inspiration and its name from Aldous Huxley's paean to hallucinogens, *The Doors of Perception,* and bands like the Grateful Dead, closely associated with Kesey, launched the San Francisco sound of "acid rock"—the perfect marriage of "sex, drugs, and rock-and-roll."

To further distance themselves from middle-class respectability, many youths flaunted outrageous personal styles. Young men and women showed their disdain for America's high-consumption society by dressing in surplus military garments, torn jeans, and tie-dyed T-shirts. Some embellished their outfits with love beads and Indian ornaments. Especially galling to adults, young men sported long hair and beards. Indeed, long hair became the badge of the countercultural life-style. To the young, it meant freedom to do as they pleased, but to parents it symbolized disrespect and contempt for social conventions.

Trends in popular music both echoed and shaped the changing youth culture. Early in the sixties, folk music had been the vogue on college campuses. Songs protesting racism and injustice mirrored the idealistic, nonviolent commitment of the civil-rights movement. Bob Dylan sang hopefully of changes "blowin' in the wind" that would transform society. African-American musicians like Stevie Wonder and Mexican-American rockers like Richie Valens were also "hip happenings." Then Beatlemania swept the country in 1964. It was time to heed one's hormones and have fun. Moving quickly beyond their early romantic songs like "I Want to Hold Your Hand," the English group soon gloried in the youth culture's drugs ("I'd love to turn you on"), sex ("why don't we do it in the road?"), and radicalism ("you say you want a revolution?"). They would be joined by Rolling Stones mayhem, the Motown beat, and scores of acid rockers.

The counterculture celebrated its vision of a life of freedom and harmony for all in August 1969, when nearly four hundred thousand young people gathered on farmland in New York's Catskill Mountains for the Woodstock festival. They reveled for three days and nights in the music of dozens of rock stars, swam nude in the lake, and openly shared drugs, sexual partners, and their contempt for the Establishment. The counterculture heralded the festival as the dawning of an era of love and peace, the Age of Aquarius.

In fact, however, the counterculture's luster had already dimmed. The pilgrimage of the "flower children" to the Haight-Ashbury district of San Francisco (see "A Place in Time") and to New York's East Village in 1967 had brought in its wake a train of muggers, rapists, and dope peddlers pushing hard drugs. With the end of the decade came the shattering of the counterculture dream. In December 1969 the deranged Charles Manson and his "family" of runaways

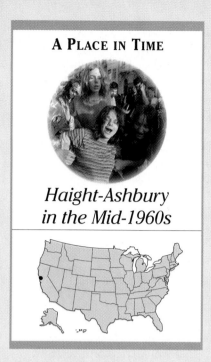

Haight-Ashbury in the Mid-1960s

Bordering Golden Gate Park by the bay, the Haight-Ashbury district of San Francisco in 1965 became a haven for dropouts seeking an alternative to the competitive, materialistic values of the "straight" world. They were attracted to the two-square-mile area of run-down Victorian homes by the seemingly carefree life-style of the artists and "beatniks" who had moved there after being forced out of nearby North Beach. Fittingly, in a city once notorious for its opium dens, and whose original name, Yerba Buena, meant "good herb," Haight-Ashbury emerged as the capital of hippiedom, mainly because of the availability there of hallucinogenic drugs, which California did not outlaw until late 1966.

A distinctive counterculture developed in "Hashbury," as some called the district. The Psychedelic Shop on Haight Street supplied drug paraphernalia. Restaurants served organic or macrobiotic

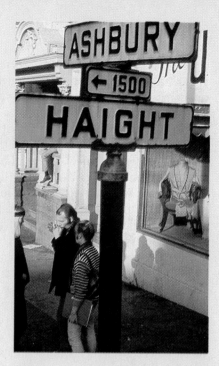

Janis Joplin with Big Brother and the Holding Company
Joplin once summed up her approach to her career and life for a reporter: "If I miss, I'll never have a second chance. . . . I gotta risk it. I never hold back, man. I'm always on the outer limits of probability." Along with Jim Morrison and Jimi Hendrix, other musical stars of the counterculture, Joplin died from a drug overdose.

The Haight-Ashbury Scene
By 1967, as the popular song "Are You Going to San Francisco?" drifted over American airwaves, Haight-Ashbury was the scene of a mass immigration of youth. (Left) Two street people; (center) orange-gowned Hare Krishnas; (right) a Merry Prankster outside a bus adorned with psychedelic imagery.

meals. The Free Medical Clinic dispensed aid for bad drug trips and venereal diseases. Disciples of the Radha Krishna Temple roamed the streets in flowing orange robes, preaching universal peace and chanting the Hare Krishna. Underground newspapers like *The Oracle* provided commentaries on drugs, radical politics, mysticism, and rock music.

Such local groups as the Grateful Dead and Country Joe and the Fish gave free concerts in the park and popularized psychedelic ballrooms like the Fillmore West. The Diggers—who took their name from the seventeenth-century English radicals who defined property owning as theft—distributed free food and clothing. And many residents lived communally, sharing work, meals, and sex.

Early in 1967, the first Human Be-In at Golden Gate Park made Haight-Ashbury a focus of media attention. Seeking to titillate their audiences, reporters and television crews dwelled on the twenty thousand "flower children" who rang bells, danced ecstatically, shared drugs, and handed sticks of smoking incense to the police.

Accounts of the festival played up Timothy Leary's preaching of the virtues of LSD, Beat poet Allen Ginsberg's chanting of Buddhist mantras, and the Jefferson Airplane's "acid rock" music. Soon everyone was talking about hippies. *Time* put them on its cover. About seventy-five thousand runaways, drug addicts, and bewildered children crowded into the Haight for the 1967 "summer of love."

Close behind them came gawking tourists, "weekend hippies" looking for easy sex and exotic drugs, heroin addicts, and a legion of robbers and rapists. The Haight-Ashbury denizens' complete trust in strangers and faith in love and peace faded quickly as crime soared, drug users died, and narcotics agents cracked down on the abusers. "Love is the password in the Haight-Ashbury," observed one reporter, "but paranoia is the style. Nobody wants to go to jail."

"Hashbury" deteriorated into a slum overrun by dope dealers and criminals. Those who could, pursued their dream of living a life of love and sharing on communal farms in northern California, in Colorado, in southern Illinois. But whether in the hills of Vermont or the "big island" of Hawaii or the deserts of New Mexico, they often found, as did one disillusioned hippie, that "we were together at the level of peace and freedom and love. We fell apart over who would cook and wash the dishes and pay the bills."

Avenue of the Americas, 1969, *by Raphael Soyer*
To distance themselves from the traditional norms of middle-class respectability, the disaffected young adopted new life-styles and new forms of dress and recreation. Their sense of alienation and rebelliousness are captured in this painting of a late sixties urban street scene.

recruited in Haight-Ashbury ritually murdered a pregnant movie actress and four of her friends. The Manson tragedy revealed that something had gone profoundly wrong. Then a Rolling Stones concert at the Altamont Raceway near San Francisco deteriorated into a violent melee in which several concertgoers died. In 1970 the Beatles disbanded. On his own, Beatle John Lennon sang: "The dream is over. What can I say?"

The Sexual Revolution

The counterculture's "do your own thing" and "if it feels good, do it" idea of sex blended with a relaxation of sexual taboos in the broader U.S. culture. There was greater permissiveness in actual sexual behavior, although the media exaggerated such change. (To some extent Americans were simply becoming more open in pursuing previously hushed-up sexual activity.) The result of these shifts in attitude and behavior was the widely trumpeted sexual revolution that flourished un-

til the mid-1980s, when the AIDS epidemic—as well as the "graying" of the 1960s generation—chilled the ardor of open sexuality.

Most commentators linked the increase in sexual permissiveness to waning fears of unwanted pregnancy. In 1960 oral contraceptives came on the market. By 1970 "the Pill" was being taken by some 12 million women. Even more women used the intrauterine device (or IUD, subsequently banned as unsafe) or the diaphragm. Some states legalized abortion. In 1970 in New York state, one fetus was legally aborted for every two babies born. Then in 1973 the Supreme Court in *Roe* v. *Wade* struck down all remaining state laws that infringed on a woman's right to an abortion during the first trimester (three months) of pregnancy.

The Supreme Court also declared unconstitutional most laws restricting "sexually explicit" materials, and the mass culture quickly exploited the new permissiveness. *Playboy* featured ever-more-explicit erotica, and women's periodicals encouraged their readers to enjoy worry-free recreational sex. Hollywood's filmmakers filled the movie screens with explicit sex, provoking outrage from parental groups and religious organizations. These protests forced the Motion Picture Association to introduce a rating system in 1968 that indicated a film's suitability for viewers of different ages and sensibilities. The enormous commercial success of films given "R" or "X" ratings led Broadway producers to present plays featuring frontal nudity, mimed sex acts, and mock orgies. Even television taboos tumbled as network censors allowed off-color jokes and frank discussions of previously forbidden subjects. By 1970, when the Federal Commission on Obscenity and Pornography recommended the end of all restrictions on pornographic materials available to adults, most barriers to public expressions of sexuality had already fallen.

The casual acceptance of sexuality undoubtedly influenced behavior. The divorce rate nearly doubled in the 1970s; many couples chose to live together without benefit of a marriage license; and by the mid-1970s, according to surveys, three-quarters of all college students, male and female, had engaged in sexual intercourse before their senior year. The use of contraceptives (and to some extent, even of abortion) spread to women of all religious backgrounds—including Roman Catholics, despite the Catholic church's impassioned stand against "artificial" birth control.

Stimulated by the other protest movements in the sixties, gay liberation emerged publicly in late June 1969 after New York City police raided the Stonewall Inn, a gay bar in Greenwich Village, and the homosexual patrons defiantly fought back. The new Gay Power movement had built on the quiet and mostly secretive reform-minded homosexual discussion groups that had formed after World War II, as well as on the "homophile" movement of the early sixties that had lobbied government officials to end discrimination and legal oppression. Its adherents came primarily from the semi-underground gay communities that had sprouted in the big cities in the 1960s. By 1973 some eight hundred openly gay groups were fighting for equal rights for homosexuals, for incorporating lesbianism into the women's movement, and for removing the stigma of immorality and depravity attached to being gay. That year, they succeeded in getting the American Psychiatric Association to rescind its official view of homosexuality as a mental disorder.

What some hailed as sexual liberation, many bemoaned as moral decay. Offended by the sudden visibility of openly gay men and lesbians and by the proliferation of "topless" bars, X-rated pornographic theaters, and "adult" bookstores, millions of Americans who cherished monogamy and family values applauded politicians who promised a war on smut. Questions of morality and social behavior became volatile issues at the polls as images of pubescent promiscuity, sex education in the schools, rising abortion rates, and homosexuals "coming out of the closet" merged in many ordinary Americans' minds with pictures of student demonstrators and ghetto riots. In defense of embattled traditional morality, a host of normally Democratic voters swelled the tide of conservatism as the decade ended.

1968: THE POLITICS OF STRIFE

The social and cultural turmoil of the sixties had unfolded against a backdrop of frustration with the course of events in Vietnam and an intensifying political crisis at home. The stormy year 1968 brought all of these developments together in a particularly explosive fashion. The year began with a thunderclap. In early January the North Koreans seized the American naval spy vessel USS *Pueblo* in international waters. They would hold the crew prisoners for almost a year. Even more jarring events followed: political assassinations, escalating protests against the war, a presidential nominating convention marred by violence, and rioting in the nation's ghettos. Converging in the presidential campaign of that year, the swirling currents of strife precipitated the first major realignment in American politics since the New Deal.

The Tet Offensive in Vietnam

Early in January 1968, liberal senator Eugene McCarthy of Minnesota, a critic of the Vietnam War, surprised the nation by announcing that he would enter the New Hampshire primary to challenge Lyndon Johnson for the presidential nomination. Experts thought that McCarthy, a witty intellectual, had no chance of unseating Johnson, who had won the presidency in 1964 by the largest margin of votes in American history. The last time such an insurgency had been attempted, in 1912, even the charismatic Teddy Roosevelt had failed. Yet McCarthy persisted, determined that at least one Democrat enter the primaries on an antiwar platform.

The Tet Offensive, January–February 1968
Although the Tet offensive proved a major tactical defeat for the communists, it effectively undermined American public support for the war.

Suddenly America's hopes for victory in Vietnam sank, and with them LBJ's political fortunes. On January 31—the first day of Tet, the Vietnamese New Year—the National Liberation Front (NLF) and the North Vietnamese mounted a massive offensive. They attacked more than a hundred South Vietnamese towns and cities and even the U.S. embassy in Saigon. After a month of ferocious fighting, American troops repelled the offensive, killing thirty-seven thousand enemy forces and inflicting a major military defeat on the communists.

The media, however, emphasized the staggering number of American casualties and the audacious scope of the Tet offensive. The realization that no area of South Vietnam was secure from the enemy, and that a foe whom the president had repeatedly claimed was

beaten could initiate such daring attacks, jolted Americans. Many no longer believed reports of battlefield successes streaming from the White House and doubted that the United States could win the war at an acceptable cost.

After Tet increasing numbers of voters listened with newly sympathetic ears to McCarthy's criticism of the war. *Time, Newsweek,* and the *Wall Street Journal* published editorials urging a negotiated settlement. NBC anchorman Frank McGee concluded that "the grand objective—the building of a free nation—is not nearer, but further, from realization." The nation's most respected newscaster, Walter Cronkite of CBS, opined that "it seems now more certain than ever that the bloody experience of Vietnam is to end in a stalemate." "If I've lost Walter," President Johnson sighed, "then it's over. I've lost Mr. Average Citizen." Johnson's approval rating dropped to 35 percent after Tet, the lowest of any president since Truman's troubled times. The number of Americans who described themselves as prowar "hawks" slipped from 62 percent in January to just 41 percent in March, whereas the proportion of antiwar "doves" climbed from 22 percent to 42 percent.

A Shaken President

A beleaguered Lyndon Johnson pondered a change in American policy. When the Joint Chiefs of Staff requested an additional 206,000 men for Vietnam, the president turned to old friends and advisers. Former secretary of state Dean Acheson told the president that "the Joint Chiefs of Staff don't know what they're talking about." Clark Clifford, the new secretary of defense, also doubted the wisdom of further escalation. Questioning the top military commanders, Clifford became "convinced that the military course we were pursuing was not only endless but hopeless."

Meanwhile, nearly five thousand college students had dropped their studies to stuff envelopes and ring doorbells for Eugene McCarthy in the New Hampshire primary contest. To be "clean for Gene," they cut their long hair and dressed conservatively so as not to alienate potential supporters. McCarthy astonished the experts by winning nearly half the popular vote as well as twenty of the twenty-four nominating-convention delegates in a state regarded as conservative.

After this upset, twice as many students converged on Wisconsin to canvass its more liberal Democratic voters. They expected a resounding McCarthy triumph in the nation's second primary. Hurriedly, on

Robert Kennedy

Running an energy-charged campaign in 1968, the dynamic "Bobby" seemed to inspire either wild devotion or deep dislike. He became the Democrats' chief advocate for the disadvantaged and leading critic of the Vietnam War.

March 16, Senator Robert Kennedy also entered the Democratic contest, and like McCarthy, he campaigned on a promise to end the war. Projecting the familiar Kennedy glamour and magnetism, Kennedy, who had resigned as attorney general and won election to the Senate from New York in 1964, was the one candidate who Johnson feared could deny him renomination. Indeed, millions of Americans viewed Kennedy as the rightful heir to the White House. Having secured the passionate support of minorities, the poor, and working-class ethnic whites, Kennedy was described by one columnist as "our first politician for the pariahs, our great national outsider."

On March 31, exactly three years after the marines had first splashed ashore at Danang, Johnson informed a surprised television audience, "I'm taking the first step to de-escalate the conflict": a halt to the bombing in North Vietnam. Catching even his closest aides off guard, LBJ added that he wanted time to devote all his efforts to the search for peace. "Accordingly," he concluded, "I shall not seek, and I will not accept, the nomination of my party for another term as your president." Believing that he had done what was best for the nation, Johnson was embittered by the abuse he had suffered: "I tried to make it possible for every child of every color to grow up in a nice house, eat a solid breakfast, to attend a decent school and to get a good and lasting job," he grumbled. "But look at what I got instead. Riots in 175 cities. Looting. Burning. Shooting. . . . Young people by the thousands leaving the university, marching in the streets. . . ." Not wanting to risk further polarizing the Democrats and the nation, he called it quits. "The only difference between the [John F.] Kennedy assassination and mine," he lamented, "is that I am alive and it has been more tortuous." Two days later, pounding the final nail into Johnson's political coffin, McCarthy trounced the president in the Wisconsin primary.

Assassinations and Turmoil

On April 4, three days after the vote in Wisconsin, chilling news issued from Memphis, Tennessee. Martin Luther King, Jr., who had gone to the city to support sanitation workers striking for union recognition and better working conditions, had been shot and killed on the balcony outside his motel room. The assassin was James Earl Ray, a white convict who had escaped from the Missouri state penitentiary. Ghetto blacks in nearly 125 cities surged through the streets in anger. As twenty blocks of Chicago's West Side went up in flames, Mayor Richard Daley ordered police to shoot to kill arsonists. In Washington, D.C., more than 700 fires illuminated the night sky. Rioting blacks there forced army units in combat gear to set up machine-gun emplacements outside the Capitol and White House. The nationwide rioting left forty-six dead, more than three thousand injured, and nearly twenty-seven thousand in jail.

Meanwhile, a three-cornered scramble had developed for the Democratic presidential nomination. Johnson's vice president, Hubert Humphrey, entered the race as the standard-bearer of the Democratic coalition forged in the New Deal and of the party regulars who supported Johnson's Vietnam policies. McCarthy remained the candidate of the "new politics"—a moral crusade against war and injustice directed to affluent and educated liberals. And Robert Kennedy campaigned as the tribune of the less privileged, the sole candidate who appealed to white ethnics and the minority poor. But on June 5, 1968, as he celebrated victory in the California presidential primary

George Wallace Supporters, 1968
As he chalked up primary victories in a string of southern states as well as in northern states such as Maryland and Michigan, Wallace proudly took credit for rattling "the eye-teeth of the Democratic party."

at a Los Angeles hotel, the brother of the murdered president was himself assassinated, by a Palestinian refugee, Sirhan Sirhan, who loathed Kennedy's pro-Israeli views.

The assassination smashed the dream of the proponents of peace and racial justice to capture the Democratic party. Many despaired of politics as an avenue of change. "I won't vote," one youth said. "Every good man we get they kill." A young black woman in Oregon grieved: "I knew it was all over, that there was no more reason for hope." Several weeks later, she joined the Black Panthers.

Other Democrats, rejecting a party that seemed helpless in the face of mass disorder, turned to the third-party candidate George Wallace or to the Republican nominee Richard Nixon. Projecting a new image of maturity and inner tranquillity, Nixon played the role of harmonizer and allowed his vice presidential running mate, Spiro Agnew, to act the shrill partisan. Appealing to those who yearned for a cessation of discord, Nixon promised to end the war in Vietnam honorably, to restore "law and order," and to heed "the voice of the great majority of Americans, the forgotten Americans, the non-shouters, the non-demonstrators, those who do not break the law, people who pay their taxes and go to work, who send their children to school, who go to their churches, . . . who love this country."

Third-party candidate George Wallace capitalized on the same wellspring of reaction as Nixon. Complaining that there was not "a dime's worth of difference" between the Democrats and Republicans, Wallace, the American Independence party candidate, pitched a fiery yet folksy message to blue-collar workers and southern whites fed up with antiwar protesters, black militants, hippies, and the liberal intellectuals who praised them.

Violence outside the Democratic National Convention in Chicago in August 1968 swelled the appeal of both Wallace and Nixon. Thousands had descended on the city to demonstrate their opposition to the Vietnam War. Most of the protesters hoped to pressure the delegates to repudiate the administration's Vietnam policy. Others, associated with the radicals within SDS, wanted to provoke a confrontation that would discredit the Democrats. A small number of alienated young Americans, seeking to ridicule the system, created the Yippies (Youth International party). Its guerrilla-theater stunts fascinated the media, which did much to publicize Yippie threats to dump LSD in Chicago's water system and to release greased pigs in the city's crowded Loop area.

Remembering the rioting that Chicago had suffered in the wake of King's assassination, Mayor Richard Daley took a hard line against the demonstrators, giving his police a green light to attack "the hippies, the Yippies, and the flippies." The savagery of the Chicago police, however, fulfilled the radicals' wish for mass disorder. On August 28, as a huge national television audience looked on and as protesters chanted, "The whole world is watching," Daley's bluecoats clubbed demonstrators and bystanders alike, shoving them through plate-glass windows, and beating them bloody. The brutality on the streets overshadowed the convention's nomination of Hubert Humphrey and ripped the Democrats further apart. The tumult fixed Americans' image of the Democrats as the party of dissent and disarray.

Conservative Resurgence

Nixon capitalized on the turmoil. His television commercials flashed images of campus and ghetto uprisings. He castigated the Supreme Court and Justice Department for safeguarding the rights of criminals and revolutionaries rather than those of law-abiding citizens. He made a special appeal to white southerners, asserting that "our schools are for education—not in-

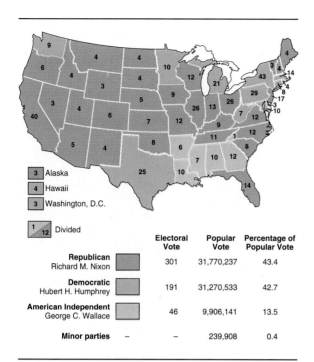

	Electoral Vote	Popular Vote	Percentage of Popular Vote
Republican Richard M. Nixon	301	31,770,237	43.4
Democratic Hubert H. Humphrey	191	31,270,533	42.7
American Independent George C. Wallace	46	9,906,141	13.5
Minor parties	–	239,908	0.4

Legend:
- 3 Alaska
- 4 Hawaii
- 3 Washington, D.C.
- 1/12 Divided

The Election of 1968

tegration." He portrayed himself as the representative of the great Silent Majority.

George Wallace, likewise appealing to Americans' revulsion against radicalism, raged across the political landscape in 1968. He fired up the fury of the working class against school integrationists, welfare mothers, and radical college professors alike. Promising to keep peace in the streets if it took "thirty thousand troops armed with three-foot bayonets," he vowed that "if any demonstrator ever lays [sic] down in front of my car, it'll be the last car he'll ever lie down in front of."

Wallace climbed steadily in voter-preference polls, inching up from 11 percent in February 1968 to 16 percent in July and to 21 percent in September. Although many liked Wallace's views, few believed that he had any serious chance of winning, and they either did not vote or grudgingly switched to his opponents. Even so, 14 percent of the electorate—primarily young, lower-middle-class, small-town workers—cast their vote for Wallace.

Despite a last-minute Humphrey surge that enabled the Democratic candidate to come almost even with Nixon, the Republicans squeaked to victory with 43.4 percent of the popular vote. Nixon garnered only 301 electoral votes, the narrowest victory since

Woodrow Wilson's slender triumph in 1916. Nevertheless, a new conservative majority had supplanted the long-dominant New Deal coalition, as Humphrey received just 38 percent of the white vote (12 million votes less than Johnson in 1964).

The 57 percent of the electorate who voted for Nixon or Wallace would dominate American presidential politics into the 1990s. While the national Democratic party fractured into a welter of contending interest groups, the Republicans attracted a new majority of Americans who lived in the suburbs and the Sun Belt, regarded the federal government as wasteful, disdained student radicalism and the forced busing of schoolchildren, and objected to special efforts to assist minorities and persons on welfare. Yearning for restraint abroad and stability at home, a new majority of citizens looked hopefully to their new president to end the Vietnam War and to restore social harmony.

NIXON AND WORLD POLITICS

When Richard Milhous Nixon took the oath of office, he was already a familiar figure on the political scene. A Californian of Quaker origins, Nixon had worked briefly in wartime Washington with the Office of Price Administration before joining the navy and serving in the Pacific. Elected to Congress in 1946 on a strong anticommunist platform, he won national prominence as a member of the House Un-American Activities Committee for his role in investigating accused spy Alger Hiss. Nixon advanced to the Senate four years later in a campaign involving innuendos of disloyalty against his liberal Democratic opponent, Helen Gahagan Douglas, whom he labeled "the Pink Lady." After two terms as Dwight Eisenhower's vice president, his loss to John Kennedy in 1960 and his unsuccessful bid for the California governorship seemingly had ended his political career. In 1968, however, the perception that liberalism meant discord at home and defeat abroad propelled him to the presidency.

Nixon sought to make his mark in foreign affairs. He considered himself a master of realpolitik—a pragmatic politics focusing on the advancement of the national interest. He promoted a grand design that would both check Soviet expansionism and bring stability to the world, as well as limit the nuclear-arms race and

The Vietnam War: A Chronology

1945 Ho Chi Minh announces Declaration of Independence from France.

1950 French-controlled Vietnam receives U.S. financial aid and military advisers.

1954 Dienbienphu falls to Ho's Vietminh.
Geneva Accords end Indochina War and temporarily divide Vietnam at the seventeenth parallel.
Ngo Dinh Diem becomes South Vietnam's premier.

1955 Diem establishes the Republic of Vietnam.
U.S. advisers take over training of South Vietnamese army (ARVN).

1960 National Liberation Front (Vietcong) formed.

1961 President John Kennedy markedly increases military aid to South Vietnam.

1962 Strategic-hamlet program put in operation.

1963 Buddhist protests commence.
ARVN coup overthrows and assassinates Diem.
16,000 U.S. military personnel in Vietnam.

1964 General William Westmoreland takes charge of U.S.Military Assistance Command in South Vietnam.
Gulf of Tonkin incident and subsequent U.S. congressional resolution.
United States bombs North Vietnam.
23,300 U.S. military personnel in Vietnam.

1965 First American combat troops arrive in South Vietnam, at Danang.
184,000 U.S. military personnel in Vietnam.

1966 B-52s attack North Vietnam for first time.
Senate Foreign Relations Committee opens hearings on U.S. in Vietnam.
385,000 U.S. military personnel in Vietnam.

1967 Major antiwar demonstrations in New York and San Francisco; protest march on the Pentagon.
485,600 U.S. military personnel in Vietnam.

1968 North Vietnamese forces surround Khesanh.
Tet offensive.
My Lai massacre.
President Lyndon Johnson announces partial bombing halt and decision not to run for reelection.
Peace talks begin in Paris.
General Creighton Abrams replaces Westmoreland as commander of American troops in Vietnam.
536,000 U.S. military personnel in Vietnam.

enhance America's economic well-being. Nixon recognized that the war in Vietnam had eroded American support for similar armed interventions and that the widening Sino-Soviet split had outdated his predecessors' monolithic anticommunist policies. He planned to get the United States out of Vietnam and begin a new era of détente—an easing of tensions—with the communist world.

To manage American diplomacy, Nixon chose Henry Kissinger. A refugee from Nazi Germany and a professor of international relations at Harvard University, Kissinger served as national security adviser until 1973, when he became secretary of state. He shared Nixon's desire to concentrate the power to make foreign policy in the White House, bypassing the bureaucracies at the State and Defense departments. Both men believed that effective diplomacy required se-crecy. Indulging their penchant for intrigue, they refashioned foreign policies in a way that kept their actions hidden from the American people and key government officials.

Vietnamization

The Nixon-Kissinger grand design, as a White House aide noted, required disgorging "the bone in the nation's throat" that Vietnam had become. Continued involvement in the war not only sapped America's military strength but also worsened inflation. In addition, it thwarted détente with the Soviet Union and the People's Republic of China and threatened to tarnish Nixon's reputation. "I'm not going to end up like LBJ," the new president vowed, "holed up in the White House afraid to show my face on the street. I'm going

1969 United States begins bombing North Vietnamese bases in Cambodia.

Provisional Revolutionary Government (PRG) formed by Vietcong.

First U.S. troop withdrawal announced after American military personnel in Vietnam reach peak strength of 543,400 in April.

Ho Chi Minh dies.

Nationwide antiwar protests in October.

475,200 U.S. military personnel in Vietnam.

1970 United States and South Vietnamese forces join in Cambodian incursion.

Student protests force some four hundred colleges and universities to close following Kent State killings.

Cooper-Church amendment limits U.S. role in Cambodia.

Senate repeals Gulf of Tonkin Resolution.

334,600 U.S. military personnel in Vietnam.

1971 United States provides air support for South Vietnamese invasion of Laos.

Antiwar rally of 400,000 in Washington.

Daniel Ellsberg releases Pentagon Papers to the *New York Times.*

1972 North Vietnam launches first ground offensive since 1968.

U.S. bombing and mining of North Vietnamese ports.

Last U.S. ground troops leave South Vietnam.

Preliminary peace agreement reached; National Security Adviser Henry Kissinger announces that "peace is at hand."

South Vietnam rejects peace treaty.

United States bombs Hanoi and Haiphong.

24,200 U.S. military personnel in Vietnam.

1973 Peace agreement signed in Paris by North and South Vietnam, the Vietcong, and the United States.

End of U.S. draft.

Congress passes War Powers Act.

First American POWs released in Hanoi.

U.S. bombing in Southeast Asia ends.

Fewer than 250 U.S. military personnel in Vietnam.

1974 South Vietnam announces new outbreak of war.

1975 North Vietnamese offensive captures Danang.

Senate rejects President Gerald Ford's request for emergency aid for South Vietnam.

South Vietnam surrenders following North Vietnam's capture of Saigon.

Khmer Rouge takes control in Cambodia.

Pro-Hanoi People's Democratic Republic established in Laos.

to stop that war." Speaking in Guam during an Asian tour in August 1969, the president unveiled what became known as the Nixon Doctrine, which redefined America's role in the Third World as that of a helpful partner rather than that of a military protector. Asian nations facing communist subversion could count on America's financial and moral support, Nixon explained, but the United States would expect them to defend themselves.

The Nixon Doctrine reflected the president's understanding of the war weariness of both the electorate and the U.S. troops in Vietnam. Johnson's decision to stop escalating and start negotiating had left American fighting men with a sense that nothing counted any longer but survival. Morale had plummeted; discipline had collapsed. Army desertions had risen from twenty-seven thousand in 1967 to more than seventy-six thou-

sand in 1970, and the desertion rate in the marines had increased even more precipitously. Racial conflict among American soldiers had become commonplace, and more than half the soldiers in Vietnam in 1970 used drugs. The army reported over eight hundred cases of "fragging"—the killing of officers by enlisted men—and suspected that there might have been another fourteen hundred instances.

The fears and frustrations of the U.S. fighting forces led to atrocities against the Vietnamese. A T-shirt popular among American soldiers read "KILL THEM ALL! LET GOD SORT THEM OUT!" Especially after 1967, instances of Americans' dismembering enemy bodies, torturing captives, torching villages, and murdering civilians came to light. In March 1968, in the hamlet of My Lai, an army unit under the command of inexperienced lieutenant William Calley massacred several hundred defenseless civilians. The soldiers gang-raped girls, blew apart children with hand grenades, lined up women and old men in ditches and shot them, and then burned the village. Revelations of such incidents, and the increasing number of returning soldiers who joined the Vietnam Veterans Against the War and who renounced their medals and citations, undercut the already diminished support for the war.

Nixon was still determined to salvage the United States' prestige. To achieve what he called "peace with honor," he pursued three courses of action simultaneously. First, he replaced American fighting forces with South Vietnamese troops, a process that became known as Vietnamization. By transferring responsibilities for the ground war to South Vietnam, Nixon reduced the number of American troops in Vietnam from more than half a million to fewer than thirty thousand by 1972. Second, taking the reins from the Saigon government, whose leaders feared that any accord with the communists would doom them, Nixon sent Henry Kissinger to negotiate secretly with North Vietnam's foreign minister, Le Duc Tho. Finally, to force the communists to compromise even as American forces withdrew, the president in March 1969 authorized an escalation of American bombing. To maximize the harm done to the enemy—Kissinger called the tactic "jugular diplomacy"—Nixon secretly ordered the bombing of North Vietnamese supply routes in neighboring Cambodia and Laos, as well as the intensification of bombing raids on North Vietnam. By playing "the mad bomber," he hoped to force concessions from the enemy. As the president told an aide,

> *I want the North Vietnamese to believe I've reached the point where I might do anything to stop the war. We'll just slip the word to them that "for God's sake, you know Nixon is obsessed about communism. We can't restrain him when he's angry—and he has his hand on the nuclear button"—and Ho Chi Minh himself will be in Paris in two days begging for peace.*

LBJ's War Becomes Nixon's War

The president's authorization of secret B-52 bombing raids against Cambodia (they would not become public knowledge until reported by the *New York Times* in 1972) neither convinced Hanoi to beg for peace nor disrupted communist supply bases in Cambodia. They did help to undermine the precarious stability of that tiny republic and to precipitate a civil war there between pro-American and communist forces. To aid the Cambodian communists (the Khmer Rouge) and to facilitate North Vietnam's use of Cambodia as a staging area for attacks on South Vietnam, the North Vietnamese stepped up their infiltration of troops into

"The Blind Leading the Blind," 1971
Cartoonist David Levine depicted four presidents as being blind with regard to American involvement in Vietnam: Eisenhower, who first made an equivocal U.S. commitment in the faraway Asian nation; Kennedy, who deepened that commitment; Johnson, under whose administration the war escalated into a major conflict; and finally Nixon, who expanded American bombing targets to neutral Cambodia.

Reprinted with permission from The New York Review of Books, Copyright © 1971 NYREV, Inc.

Cambodia in early 1970. In turn, Nixon ordered a joint U.S.–South Vietnamese incursion into Cambodia at the end of April. The invading soldiers captured significant caches of enemy weapons, and their success bought time for Vietnamization. But the costs were high. The invasion ended Cambodia's neutrality, widened the war throughout Indochina, and provoked massive American protests against the war, culminating in the student deaths at Kent State and Jackson State universities.

The following year Nixon again combined the continued withdrawal of American troops with renewed blows against the enemy. In February 1971, at the administration's initiative, the South Vietnamese army invaded Laos to destroy communist bases there and to restrict the flow of supplies southward from North Vietnam. The South Vietnamese, however, were routed. American television vividly conveyed their disorderly retreat and their desperate attempts to escape the enemy by clinging to the skids of departing U.S. helicopters.

Emboldened by this success, the North Vietnamese in 1972 mounted the so-called Easter Offensive, their largest campaign since 1968. With less than one hundred thousand U.S. troops still in Vietnam, Nixon retaliated by mining North Vietnam's harbors and unleashing B-52s on its major cities. "The bastards have never been bombed like they are going to be bombed this time," he vowed.

America's Longest War Ends

On October 26, 1972, just days before the U.S. presidential election, Kissinger announced that "peace is at hand." The cease-fire agreement that he had secretly negotiated with Le Duc Tho required the withdrawal of all remaining U.S. troops; provided for the return of American prisoners of war; and, giving in to the communists' primary objective, allowed North Vietnamese troops to remain in South Vietnam.

Kissinger's negotiations had sealed Nixon's reelection but had failed to gauge Thieu's obstinacy. The South Vietnamese president refused to sign a cease-fire agreement that permitted North Vietnamese troops to remain in the South. Meanwhile, Le Duc Tho, angered by Thieu's rebuff, pressed for even greater concessions at the negotiating table. Once again Nixon resorted to massive B-52 raids. The 1972 Christmas bombing of Hanoi and Haiphong, the heaviest and most destructive of the entire war, roused fierce opposition in Congress and denunciations in the United Nations. But it helped to force the North Vietnamese to relent at the same time that Nixon's secret assurances to Thieu that the United States would "respond with full force should the settlement be violated by North Vietnam" ended Saigon's recalcitrance.

On January 23, 1973, the day on which Lyndon Johnson died of a heart attack, President Nixon announced a settlement agreement. The Paris Accords, signed four days later, essentially restated the terms of the October truce. The agreement ended hostilities between the United States and North Vietnam yet left unresolved the differences between North Vietnam and the Thieu regime, guaranteeing that Vietnam's future would yet be settled on the battlefield.

Thus, for all practical purposes, ended the United States' longest war—a war that did not involve vital U.S. interests, whose costs far outweighed potential benefits, and which worsened domestic problems and social divisions. It had cost at least $150 billion and resulted in some 58,000 American deaths and more than 300,000 wounded, including at least 10,000 paraplegics. Nearly half a million of the 2.7 million Americans who served in the war, moreover, received less-than-honorable discharges—a measure of the high desertion rate, the rampant drug use, the spread of antiwar sentiment even in the military, and the immaturity of the troops (the average U.S. soldier in Vietnam was just nineteen years old, seven years younger than the average American GI in World War II).

Virtually all who survived, wrote marine rifleman William Jayne, came back "as immigrants to a new world. For the culture we had known dissolved while we were in Vietnam, and the culture of combat we lived in so intensely . . . made us aliens when we returned." Reminders of a war that Americans wished to forget, most veterans were ignored when they returned home. Beyond media attention to the psychological difficulties that they faced in readjusting to civilian life, which principally fostered an image of veterans as disturbed and dangerous, the nation paid little heed to those who had served and sacrificed.

Relieved that the long nightmare was past, most Americans tried to forget the war. Even the bitterness of many veterans faded. Few Americans gave much thought to how the war had devastated Vietnam, causing two million casualties. Laos, too, had suffered; Cambodia paid perhaps the most terrible price of all. After the war had widened to engulf previously peaceful Cambodia, a fanatical communist insurgency called the Khmer Rouge emerged victorious in 1975. Three million Cambodians—40 percent of the country's population—died in the mass killings and "relocations" that ensued, until the Khmer Rouge itself was driven from power by the Vietnamese in 1979.

"We've adjusted too well," complained Tim O'Brien, a veteran and novelist of the war, in 1980. "Too many of us have lost touch with the horror of war. . . . It would seem that the memories of soldiers should serve, at least in a modest way, as a restraint on national bellicosity. But time and distance erode memory. We adjust, we lose the intensity. I fear that we are back where we started. I wish we were more troubled."

Détente

The disengagement of American troops from Vietnam helped Nixon achieve a turnabout in Chinese-American relations and détente with the communist superpowers. These dramatic developments marked the most significant shift in U.S. foreign policy since the start of the Cold War and created a new relationship among the United States, the Soviet Union, and China.

Since the Korean War, the United States had refused to recognize the People's Republic. Treating the mainland Chinese regime as an outlaw, the United States had vetoed the admission of "Red China" to the United Nations and pressured American allies to restrict trade with the communist giant. But by 1969 a widening Sino-Soviet split made the prospect of improved relations attractive both to Chinese leader Mao Zedong and to Nixon and Kissinger. China wanted to end its isolation, the United States wanted to play one communist power off against the other, and both wanted to thwart U.S.S.R. expansionism in Asia.

As Nixon's first move in what Kissinger called "the three-dimensional game," the president in the fall of 1970 began to refer to China as the People's Republic rather than Red China. He also publicly intimated that he wished to visit "that vast, unknown land." Then in April 1971, the Chinese hosted an American table-tennis team that had been touring Japan. Behind this "ping-pong diplomacy" lay serious maneuverings. Talks between the two nations' ambassadors in Poland led to a secret trip to Beijing by Kissinger in June and a startling mid-1971 announcement by Nixon that he would travel to the People's Republic "to seek the normalization of relations."

On February 22, 1972, the president's plane landed in China. Not since 1879, when Ulysses Grant

Nixon in China, 1972
American TV networks covered Nixon's dramatic visits to legendary landmarks such as the Great Wall, as well as his impromptu conversations with the Chinese people. One reporter remarked that "the White House was playing [the visit] as a pageant, not as a news story."

had visited after leaving office, had a U.S. president journeyed to China, the most populous country in the world. Accompanied by an entourage of reporters and television camera crews, a beaming Nixon toured the Great Wall and exchanged rice-liquor toasts with Mao Zedong and Chinese premier Zhou Enlai (Chou Enlai). Although differences between the two powers delayed official diplomatic relations until 1979, the Nixon visit signaled the end of more than twenty years of Sino-American hostility—a historic milestone.

In an equally significant step, Nixon visited Moscow in May 1972. "There must be room in this world for two great nations with different systems to live together and work together," the president proclaimed. He concluded agreements with the Soviets on trade* and technological cooperation, and signed the first Strategic Arms Limitation Treaty (SALT I). Overwhelmingly ratified by the Senate in October 1972, the treaty limited the two superpowers to two hundred an-

---

*Specifically, the Soviets agreed to buy at least $750 million in American grain over a three-year period—a boon to U.S. farmers.

tiballistic missiles (ABMs) and two ABM systems apiece, and also froze for five years the number of offensive intercontinental missiles and submarine-launched missiles both nations could have. The major effect of the agreement, Kissinger later explained in his memoirs, was to intensify "the concept of deterrence through mutual terror: By giving up missile defense, each side was leaving its popuation hostage to a strategic missile attack. Each side therefore had an ultimate interest in preventing a war that could only be mutually destructive." Although largely a symbolic step toward control of the nuclear arms race, SALT I both reduced Cold War tensions and enhanced Richard Nixon's stature as a proponent of peace.

A Multipolar World

Rapprochement with China and détente with the Soviet Union could not alone ensure international stability. Conditions in the Middle East had grown more volatile. In the 1967 Six-Day War, Israel, fearing that a massive Arab attack was imminent, had launched a preemptive offensive that in six days routed Nasser's Egyptian army and air force, decimated Jordan's forces, and defeated the Syrian army. In the war's aftermath, Israel had occupied the Egyptian-controlled Sinai and Gaza Strip, the Jordanian-ruled West Bank and East Jerusalem, and Syria's Golan Heights.

Israel promised to give up most of these lands in return for direct negotiations and peace, but the Arab states refused to negotiate with Israel or to recognize its right to exist. The Palestinian population, which to this point had relied mainly on support by the Arab governments, now looked to the Palestinian Liberation Organization, or PLO (founded by the Arab states in 1964), to defend its interests. The PLO sought international recognition for Palestinian rights while also calling for Israel's destruction. Competing PLO factions hijacked Western airliners, raided Israel, and murdered Israeli athletes at the 1972 Olympic Games. To retaliate, Israel assassinated PLO agents abroad and bombed the PLO's bases and its installations in refugee camps, especially in Lebanon.

War exploded again in October 1973. Egypt and Syria launched surprise attacks against Israel on the Jewish high holy day of Yom Kippur. Israel struggled to survive and then, with the aid of military equipment airlifted by the United States, stopped the assault and counterattacked. At that point, the United States pressured Israel to accept a cease-fire rather than press its

DICK WALLMEYER
Long Beach Press-Telegram
© Register and Tribune Syndica

Oil, the Ultimate Weapon
American support for Israel in the Yom Kippur War prompted OPEC in October 1973 to impose an embargo on crude-oil shipments to the United States and its allies. The embargo stung the economies of Western Europe and Japan and brought not only fuel shortages but also steep rises in inflation and petroleum prices in the United States.

advantage. Nevertheless, the oil-producing Arab states, in retaliation, embargoed shipments of crude oil to the United States and its allies. U.S. oil imports had leaped from 8 to 36 percent in the previous two decades, and Europe depended on Arab oil for 60 percent of its energy. The oil embargo, in effect from October 1973 to March 1974, spawned acute fuel shortages and, as the cost of a barrel of crude oil soared from $3 to more than $12, a steep rise in the cost of petroleum products and the rate of inflation. (Among other consequences, the oil embargo spurred the use of nuclear power; by the end of 1975, there were 157 nuclear plants in operation around the world, and even more were under construction.)

The Nixon administration, which generally had sided with Israel, now sought better relations with moderate Arab regimes so as to isolate Arab hardliners. The dual shock of an energy crisis at home and

Imports of Crude Oil

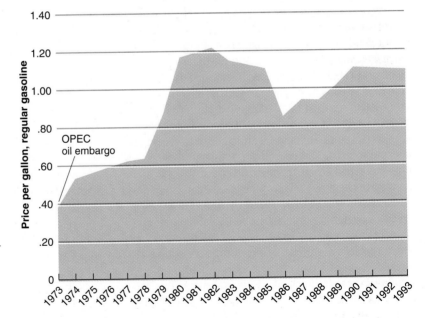

Gasoline Prices

The Energy Crisis: Crude-Oil Imports and Gasoline Prices

Not until the 1980s, through the combination of a deep recession and fuel conservation, did U.S. petroleum imports finally begin dropping off (top). OPEC's ability to act as a supercartel in setting oil prices sent the cost of filling a car's gas tank skyrocketing in the 1970s (bottom).

SOURCE: Energy Information Administration, *Annual Energy Review,* 1993.

renewed Soviet influence among Arab hard-liners spurred Nixon and Kissinger to win Egypt for the prowestern camp, to conciliate the oil-rich Arab rulers of the Persian Gulf, and to force Arab-Israeli peace talks. Beginning in October 1973, Kissinger spent two years pursuing "shuttle diplomacy." Flying from one capital to another, he engineered two Israeli-Egyptian disengagement accords (in which Israel gave up slices of Sinai) and one between Israel and Syria (separating their forces and ending Israeli occupation of a small part of the Golan Heights). He also persuaded the Arabs to drop their oil embargo. Kissinger's diplomacy, designed to establish the United States as the sole Middle Eastern peacemaker and to exclude the Soviets, had a limited but notable success. Splits among the Arabs widened. Egypt moved closer to Washington, receiving American aid at the price of Arab condemnation. Syria broke with Sadat and gradually became even more intransigent against Israel. The PLO itself began to divide into moderate and hard-line factions. Increasingly isolated, some Palestinian insurgents struck all the harder against Israel and against U.S. citizens abroad.

To counter Soviet influence and to protect American interests, the Nixon administration also supplied arms to the shah of Iran, Reza Pahlavi; to President Ferdinand Marcos in the Philippines; and to the white-supremacist regime of South Africa. The realpolitik of the Nixon-Kissinger diplomacy based American aid on a nation's willingness to oppose the Soviet Union rather than on the nature of its government. Thus the administration provided assistance to antidemocratic regimes in Argentina, Brazil, Nigeria, and South Korea, as well as to the Portuguese colonial authorities in Angola.

After the election of the Marxist Salvador Allende to the presidency of Chile in 1970, Nixon secretly funneled $10 million to the CIA to fund opponents of the leftist Chilean government. The United States also cut off economic aid to Chile, blocked private banks from granting the nation loans, and successfully pressed the World Bank to drop Chile's credit rating. Believing that it had the tacit approval of Washington, a military junta in September 1973 overthrew the Chilean government and killed Allende. Nixon quickly recognized the new dictatorship, and substantial economic aid and private investment once again flowed to Chile.

The administration's active opposition to Allende reflected the extent to which American policy remained committed to containing communist influence. At the same time, Nixon understood the limits of American might and the changed realities of world affairs. Discarding the model of a globe torn by a bipolar conflict between capitalism and communism—a perspective that had dominated State Department thought since 1945—Nixon took advantage of the rift between China and the Soviet Union to improve U.S. relations with both communist nations. The Nixon administration also ended American involvement in the Vietnam War and improved the United States' position in the Middle East. Perhaps most significantly, the politician who had built his reputation as a hard-line Cold Warrior initiated a new era of détente with the communist powers.

DOMESTIC PROBLEMS AND DIVISIONS

Richard Nixon hoped to be remembered as an international statesman; yet domestic affairs kept intruding. In some respects, Nixon displayed resourcefulness and creativity in the domestic realm. He made a significant initiative in welfare reform and, rejecting the hands-off approach of traditional Republican conservatism, grappled with inflation and other complex economic problems that the nation confronted in the early seventies.

But there was another side to the Nixon administration that appealed to the darker recesses of the national character and exacerbated the fears and hatreds that divided Americans. This underside of the Nixon years was rooted in the complex character of Richard Nixon himself.

Richard Nixon: Man and Politician

Reporters who observed Nixon invariably commented on the multiple levels of his personality: the calculated public persona of the politician, beneath which lurked a different and shadowy Nixon that rarely revealed itself. Nixon the politician exhibited many impressive traits. He was highly intelligent, with phenomenal endurance and a capacity for total concentration.

Yet Nixon also displayed the rigid self-control of a man monitoring his every move and shunning self-revelation. A basic rule of the Nixon White House, wrote one reporter, was to avoid any situation that would "expose to general view the man within the shell." Hidden was the insecure Nixon, suspicious and angry. He was almost paranoid in his conviction that enemies lurked on all sides, waiting to destroy him. He seethed with resentments, often acted as though he were locked in mortal combat, and viewed his life as a never-ending series of battles and crises.

Driven as he was, Nixon sought to annihilate, not merely defeat, his partisan enemies, particularly those of the "eastern liberal establishment" who had long opposed him and whom he despised in return. "Nixonland," Adlai Stevenson had observed in the fifties, was a place of "slander and scare, of sly innuendo, of a poison pen, the anonymous phone call, and hustling, pushing, shoving—the land of smash and grab and anything to win." Nixonland lived on after Nixon's accession to the presidency.

President Nixon in Vietnam

In May 1969, Nixon announced a "phased withdrawal" of American troops and a program of "Vietnamization," whereby South Vietnamese forces would "take over some of the fighting fronts now being manned by Americans."

Probing for the source of his furies, some observers viewed him as the classic outsider: reared in pinched surroundings, physically awkward, unable to relate easily to others. Although he propelled himself to the heights of national power, Nixon remained the outsider, sensing that he would never be fully accepted. Nagging suspicions that others more cultivated and privileged than he were always laughing at him, holding him in contempt, led him, in return, to sneer at "the so-called best circles in America."

Whatever forces shaped Nixon's personality, many Americans identified with his biases. That identification, indeed, helped him to attain the presidency. As historian Garry Wills has observed, Nixon's strengths and deficiencies uncannily matched what was "best and weakest in America." At the beginning of his administration, it was the new president's strengths that were most apparent. He spoke of national reconciliation, appointed a well-qualified team, took bold initiatives in the international arena, and dealt with domestic problems responsibly. But the darker side soon came to the fore. This side of Nixon ultimately prevailed and would drive him from office in disgrace.

The Nixon Presidency

Having urged Americans to stop shouting at one another, Nixon began his presidency with a moderation reminiscent of Eisenhower. His calm rhetoric and appointment of a cabinet of flexibly conservative men promised the respite from unrest that most Americans desired. Symbolic of this beginning, a united country joined the new president in celebrating the first successful manned space mission to the moon. Seven years after President John Kennedy had launched a massive effort to meet the Russian challenge in space (see Chapter 30), Apollo 11 landed its lunar module *Eagle* on the moon's Sea of Tranquillity. On July 21, 1969, astronaut Neil Armstrong walked on the moon's surface and announced to television audiences back on earth, "That's one small step for man, one giant leap for mankind." Americans took pride in the fact that the United States had come from behind to win the space race. Millions thrilled as astronauts Armstrong and Buzz Aldrin planted an American flag and a plaque reading, "Here men from planet earth first set foot on the moon, July 1969 A.D. We came in peace for all mankind."

The first newly elected president since 1849 to face both houses of Congress controlled by the opposition party, Nixon initially had approved a moderate extension of Great Society programs. He signed bills to increase social-security benefits, to produce subsidized housing for low- and middle-income families, to expand the Job Corps, and to grant the vote to eighteen-year-olds.

Although Nixon sided with corporate leaders who claimed that the cost of meeting stringent environmental standards would make U.S. industry uncompetitive with foreign enterprises, the Democrat-controlled Congress enacted legislation targeting the adverse effects of material growth. Laws passed during the Nixon presidency limited pesticide use, further protected endangered species and marine mammals, controlled strip-mining practices, safeguarded coastal lands, regulated consumer-product safety and the transportation of hazardous materials, and established maximum levels for the emissions of pollutants into the air. Increasing concerns about the environment, deepened by a major oil spill off the coast of Santa Barbara in 1969 that befouled beaches and killed many seabirds and aquatic creatures, also resulted in the National Environmental Policy Act (1969), requiring federal agencies to prepare an environmental-impact analysis of all pro-

Moonwalk, July 1969
In this photograph taken by fellow astronaut Neil Armstrong, Edwin Aldrin, Jr., descends the steps of the lunar-module ladder just before his historic walk on the moon.

posed projects and establishing the Environmental Protection Agency in 1970 to enforce environmental regulations. That year, as well, Congress created the Occupational Safety and Health Administration (OSHA) to ensure workers' well-being.

The increased attention to the environment culminated in the celebration of the first Earth Day in April 1970. Largely the effort of former antiwar and civil-rights activists, Earth Day spotlighted such problems as thermal pollution, the profusion of solid waste, and dwindling resources. Emphasizing that the obsession with industrial growth and consumerism was straining the environment to the breaking point, Earth Day introduced many Americans to the idea of "living lightly on the earth." Soon in vogue were various alternative ways of living: organic gardening, vegetarianism, solar power, recycling, composting, and preventive health care. Also in 1970, Nixon's Commission on Population Growth and the American Future promoted zero population growth: the idea that birthrate should not exceed the death rate.

The growth of a bigger, more intrusive government—under Nixon, the number of pages in the *Federal Register* detailing federal regulations tripled—provoked conservatives to grumble. They became more displeased when race-conscious employment policies (including quota systems to increase blacks' access to skilled jobs) were mandated to cover all federal contractors. And they grew even angrier when Nixon unveiled his Family Assistance Plan (FAP) in mid-1969. A bold effort to overhaul the inefficient and unwieldy welfare system, the FAP proposed a guaranteed annual income for all Americans—$1,600 plus food stamps for a family of four, which could be supplemented by outside earnings. The House approved FAP, but it expired in the Senate,* caught in an ideological crossfire between liberals who considered the benefits inadequate and conservatives who opposed on principle the notion of a guaranteed income for all.

Congress proved more receptive to another Nixon innovation: revenue sharing. To reverse the flow of power and resources from the states to Washington, Nixon proposed that the federal government distribute funds to the states to use as they saw fit. Revenue sharing particularly appealed to suburbanites opposed to federal "giveaway programs for the poor." Nixon hailed the measure, enacted in 1972, as a "New Federalism" that would invigorate local government. But in the wake of accompanying slashes in federal spending for social services, the nation's financially pressed cities complained that the new system left them worse off than before.

A Troubled Economy

Inheriting the fiscal consequences of Lyndon Johnson's effort to wage the Vietnam War and to finance the Great Society—"guns and butter"—by massive deficit financing rather than raising taxes, Nixon assumed the presidency facing what in those days was considered a whopping budget deficit ($25 billion) and an inflation rate of 5 percent. Nixon's $2.5 billion tax cut in 1969 only worsened the problem, so he then encouraged the Federal Reserve Board to raise interest rates and contract the money supply. The rate of inflation continued to go up, but economic growth declined and unemployment soared. Economists coined

*In 1988 Moynihan, now a Democratic senator from New York, would finally see key elements of his Family Assistance Plan enacted into law.

Inflation, 1946–1993

Inflation, which had been moderate during the two decades following the Second World War, began to soar with the escalation of the war in Vietnam in the mid-1960s. In 1979 and 1980 the nation experienced double-digit inflation in two consecutive years for the first time since World War I.

a new word, *stagflation,* to describe this combination of rising prices and economic recession, or stagnation.

In 1971 Nixon lurched from one policy to another in a futile effort to curb inflation and to cure the recession. Declaring "I am now a Keynesian," he first tried deficit spending to stimulate economic growth in the private sector. It produced the largest budget deficit since World War II, as well as a spurt in the GNP, but did little to halt the long-term economic decline. To correct the balance-of-payments deficit and the drop in the nation's international trade, he then devalued the dollar. Rather than being arbitrarily fixed in relation to other currencies, the dollar would now be left to find its own fluctuating level—to "float"—in the international monetary exchanges. But this measure did not halt the growth of foreign competition or stem the increasing cost of imported raw materials, especially oil. Finally, in a reversal of his earlier refusal to consider wage-and-price controls, the president froze wages, prices, and rents for ninety days and imposed limits on future increases. These policies worked somewhat until the 1972 election. As soon as he was reelected, however, Nixon again reversed course, replacing the controls with voluntary, and ineffective, guidelines. Inflation

and sluggish economic growth would remain major problems throughout the decade.

Law and Order

Despite his public appeals for unity, Nixon took divisive actions in an effort to outflank George Wallace and attract the support of southern whites, northern ethnics, blue-collar workers, and suburbanites—the voters that political theorist Kevin Phillips described as "in motion between a Democratic past and a Republican future." One part of Nixon's political strategy involved a tough stand against crime and drug use, and a war on domestic radicalism.

To combat the militants he despised, Nixon drew upon the full resources of the federal government. The Internal Revenue Service audited the tax returns of antiwar and civil-rights activists, and the Small Business Administration denied them loans. The Federal Bureau of Investigation illegally wiretapped leftist individuals and organizations, and the National Security Agency intercepted their telecommunications. The FBI also infiltrated the ranks of the SDS and black radical groups with informers and agents who provoked violence within these movements to discredit them. The Justice Department and the FBI worked closely with local police forces in 1969–1970 to arrest Black Panthers on dubious charges and to disrupt their operations by disinformation programs. Gunfights between police and the Panthers killed some forty members of this radical black organization. Contrary to the specific prohibitions written into the National Security Act of 1947, moreover, the CIA investigated, and compiled dossiers on, thousands of American dissidents. To focus the nation's fears on the radical threat, Nixon authorized the Department of Justice to prosecute antiwar activists and militant blacks in highly publicized trials.

Nixon also moved secretly to crush his opponents. Drawing from unspent 1968 campaign funds, he created a covert task force in 1969 to spy on liberal columnists and congressional critics of his administration. Viewing his political adversaries as personal assailants, the president compiled an "enemies list" of prominent Americans who would be harassed by the government. "Anyone who opposes us, we'll destroy," warned a top White House official. "As a matter of fact, anyone who doesn't support us, we'll destroy." To coordinate the government vendetta against his opponents, Nixon chose his aide Charles Colson, a self-described "anti-press, anti-liberal Nixon fanatic."

Widening the offensive against the antiwar movement, Nixon in 1970 approved a scheme, known as the Huston Plan, which would employ the CIA and FBI in a variety of illegal missions. The plan involved the recruitment of students to infiltrate radical organizations, extensive wiretapping and electronic surveillance, break-ins and burglaries to ferret out or plant evidence of illegal activity, and a new agency to centralize domestic covert operations under White House supervision. FBI chief J. Edgar Hoover, however, perceiving the Huston Plan as a threat to the FBI's power, emphatically opposed it. Blocked, Nixon secretly created his own White House unit to discredit his opponents and ensure executive secrecy. Nicknamed "the plumbers" by White House insiders because of their assignment to stop government leaks, the team was headed by an ex-FBI agent, G. Gordon Liddy, and a former CIA operative, E. Howard Hunt.

The plumbers' first target was Daniel Ellsberg. Previously an analyst for the Department of Defense, Ellsberg in mid-1971 had turned over to the press the secret Pentagon Papers, a documentary history of American involvement in Vietnam prepared by the department during the Johnson administration. On June 13 the *New York Times* began to publish the papers. Although the documents contained nothing damaging about the Nixon administration, they revealed a long history of government lies—to foreign leaders, to Congress, and to the American people. Fearing that the Pentagon Papers would further undermine public trust in the government and establish a precedent for publishing classified material, Nixon obtained a court injunction barring further publication of the papers. The *Times*, protesting the unprecedented use of prior restraint against the press, appealed to the Supreme Court. The Court lifted the injunction, ruling that the First Amendment forbade such censorship. A livid Nixon directed the Department of Justice to indict Ellsberg for theft and espionage and ordered the plumbers to discredit him. In August 1971 Hunt and Liddy broke into the office of Ellsberg's psychiatrist to search for information that might denigrate the man who had become an instant hero to the antiwar movement.

The Southern Strategy

Along with his attacks on crime and radicalism, Nixon's strategy included courting whites upset by the African-American drive for equality, especially southerners fearing school desegregation. Turning its back on the black vote, the administration testified before Congress against extending the Voting Rights Act of 1965 and in favor of modifications in the Fair Housing Act of 1968 that would have crippled its enforcement provisions. Moreover, it pleaded for a postponement in the desegregation of Mississippi's schools and filed suits to prohibit transporting children to desegregate public schools. When the Supreme Court in 1971 unanimously upheld busing as a constitutional and necessary tactic to achieve racial balance in the schools (*Swann* v. *Charlotte-Mecklenburg Board of Education*), Nixon went on television to condemn the ruling and to ask Congress to enact a moratorium on busing.

The strategy of wooing the white South similarly dictated Nixon's approach to nominations for the Supreme Court. To reverse the liberalism of the Warren court, he tried to fill the Court with strict constructionists, judges who would not "meddle" in social issues or "be soft on criminals." In 1969 Nixon appointed Warren Burger, a conservative federal judge, to replace the retiring Earl Warren as chief justice. Nixon then tried to appoint a Deep South conservative to halt the pace of desegregation. But the Senate twice rejected his nominees. The president used these defeats to portray the Democrats as contemptuous of the South. By 1972 Nixon had succeeded in appointing three justices with reputations as strict constructionists to the Supreme Court: Harry Blackmun of Minnesota, Lewis Powell of Virginia, and William Rehnquist of Arizona. Joining forces with Chief Justice Burger, the Nixon appointees steered the Court in a moderate direction. Although ruling liberally in cases involving abortion, desegregation, and the death penalty, the Burger court shifted to the right in rulings on civil liberties, community censorship, and the power of the police.

The Silent Majority Speaks

In his drive to build a Republican majority, Nixon denounced the Democrats as the party of New Left "hooligans, hippies, and radical liberals" and blamed them for fostering drug use, supporting abortion, and cultivating social disorder. To gain control of Congress in the off-year elections of 1970, Nixon encouraged his vice president, Spiro Agnew, to attack the liberal opposition. Crisscrossing the nation, the vice president assailed students as "parasites of passions," Democrats as "sniveling hand-wringers," and intellectuals as "an effete corps of impudent snobs." He relentlessly attacked the news media, which Nixon viewed as bent on discrediting him. Implying that the television networks were run by a "tiny and closed fraternity of privileged men," Agnew described newscasters as "curled-lip boys in eastern ivory towers" and, in a memorable epithet, "nattering nabobs of negativism."

Although liberals deplored Agnew's alarming alliterative allegations, many Democratic candidates joined their Republican opponents in appealing for law and order, patriotism, and a rejuvenation of traditional family values. The 1970 electoral result proved a draw. The Democrats increased their majority in the House by nine, and the GOP picked up two Senate seats. Since the party of the president in power had suffered losses in every off-year congressional election except that of 1934, the White House took comfort in the standoff.

The Election of 1972

Nixon's reelection appeared assured. He counted on his diplomatic successes with China and the Soviet Union and his winding down of the war in Vietnam to attract moderate voters. He expected his southern strategy and law-and-order posture to appeal to the conservative Democrats who had voted for Wallace in 1968. Continued Democratic divisions boosted Nixon's optimism.

Nixon's only major worry, another third-party candidacy by George Wallace, dissolved on May 15, 1972. During a campaign stop at a Maryland shopping center, Wallace was shot by a deranged young man named Arthur Bremer. Paralyzed from the waist down, the Alabamian withdrew from the race, leaving Nixon a monopoly of the white-backlash, law-and-order vote.

The Senate's most outspoken dove, the "prairie populist" George McGovern of South Dakota, capitalized on the support of antiwar activists to blitz the Democratic primaries. New party rules (adopted after the 1968 convention) that required every state delegation at the nominating convention to include minority, female, and youthful delegates in approximate proportion to their numbers among the populace also aided the liberal McGovern. One supporter, actress Shirley MacLaine, gleefully described California's delegation as "looking like a couple of high schools, a grape boycott, a Black Panther rally, and four or five politicians who walked in the wrong door." A disapproving labor leader grumbled about "too much hair and not

enough cigars at this convention." McGovern won the nomination on the first ballot.

Perceptions of McGovern as inept and radical, however, drove away all but those most committed to him. After pledging to stand behind his vice presidential running mate Thomas Eagleton "1,000 percent" when it became known that the Missouri senator had received electric-shock therapy for nervous depression, McGovern dumped him from the ticket and suffered the embarrassment of having several prominent Democrats publicly decline to run with him. McGovern's endorsement of income redistribution, the decriminalization of marijuana, an immediate withdrawal from Vietnam, and a whopping $30 billion defense-budget cut exposed him to GOP ridicule as the candidate of the radical fringe. Tagging McGovern the apostle of "abortion, acid, and amnesty" (he also advocated a pardon for the nearly 120,000 young Americans who had fled the United States to avoid the draft), the Republicans ensured that the Democrats never gained the offensive.

Nixon left no stone unturned, remembering his narrow loss to John F. Kennedy in 1960 and his too-slender victory over Hubert Humphrey in 1968. He created the Committee to Re-Elect the President (CREEP) to do everything necessary to ensure his reelection, and appointed his attorney general, John Mitchell, as its head. The many millions in contributions collected by CREEP financed a series of "dirty tricks" that spread dissension within Democratic ranks and paid for a special internal espionage unit to spy on the opposition. Led by Liddy and Hunt of the White House plumbers, the Republican undercover team gained Mitchell's approval for a plan to wiretap telephones at the Democratic National Committee headquarters in the Watergate apartment/office complex in Washington. Early in the morning of June 17, 1972, a security guard foiled the break-in to install the bugs. Arrested were James McCord, the security coordinator of CREEP, and several other burglars associated with Liddy and Hunt.

A White House cover-up began immediately. Nixon proclaimed "categorically" that "no one in the White House staff, no one in this administration, presently employed, was involved in this bizarre incident." Consequently (as the American people would learn after the election), Nixon ordered key staff members to expunge Hunt's name from the White House telephone directory, to buy the silence of those arrested with some four hundred thousand dollars in hush money and hints of a presidential pardon, and to

The Election of 1972

Candidates	Parties	Electoral Vote	Popular Vote	Percentage of Popular Vote
RICHARD M. NIXON	Republican	520	47,169,911	60.7
George S. McGovern	Democratic	17	29,170,383	37.5

direct the CIA to halt the FBI's investigation of the Watergate break-in on the pretext that the inquiry would damage national security.

With the McGovern campaign a shambles and Watergate seemingly safely contained, Nixon won the election overwhelmingly. He polled nearly 61 percent of the popular vote and took the electoral college 520 to 17. He carried all of the once solidly Democratic South and won over a large majority of such traditionally Democratic voters as union members and Catholics. McGovern edged Nixon out in just one state, Massachusetts, and the District of Columbia. Only blacks, Mexican-Americans, Jews, and low-income voters strongly supported the Democratic contender. The 1968 realignment in presidential balloting had been solidified.

The GOP, however, gained only twelve seats in the House, and the Democrats added two more seats to bolster their majority in the Senate. This outcome demonstrated the growing difficulty of unseating incumbent legislators as well as the decline of party loyalty and the prevalence of ticket splitting among voters. In addition, in 1972, only 55.7 percent of the eligible electorate went to the polls (in 1960, 63.8 percent of those eligible had voted, and that figure had dropped in each intervening election). Whether indifferent to politics or disenchanted with the choices offered, a growing number of citizens no longer bothered to participate in the electoral process.

THE CRISIS OF THE PRESIDENCY

In his second inaugural address, Nixon pledged "to make these four years the best four years in America's history." Ironically, they would rank among its sorriest, and the worst in Nixon's career. He would see his vice president resign in disgrace and his closest confidants go to jail. He himself would serve barely a year and a half of his second term before resigning office to escape impeachment and possibly a criminal trial.

The Watergate Cover-Up

The scheme to conceal the connection between the White House and the accused Watergate burglars had succeeded during the 1972 campaign. But after the election federal judge "Maximum John" Sirica, known for his tough treatment of criminals, refused to accept the claim of those on trial for the break-in that they had acted on their own. Threatening severe prison sentences, Sirica coerced James McCord of CREEP into confessing that highly placed White House aides had known in advance of the break-in and that the defendants had committed perjury during the trial. McCord also stated that the White House had pressured him and his codefendants "to plead guilty and remain silent." Meanwhile, two *Washington Post* reporters, Carl Bernstein and Bob Woodward, following clues furnished by "Deep Throat,"* an unnamed informant in the Nixon administration, wrote a succession of front-page stories linking the break-in to illegal contributions and to "dirty tricks" against the Democrats paid for by CREEP.

In February 1973 the Senate established the Special Committee on Presidential Campaign Activities to investigate the alleged election misdeeds. As the trail of revelations led closer to the Oval Office, Nixon fired his special counsel, John Dean, after Dean refused to be a scapegoat. Then on April 30 the president announced the resignations of his two major assistants, H. R. Haldeman and John Ehrlichman, and pledged to get to the bottom of the scandal: "There can be no whitewash at the White House." He appointed Secretary of

---

*Deep Throat was also the title of a notorious pornographic film of the time.

Defense Elliot Richardson, a Boston patrician of unassailable integrity, as his new attorney general, and, bowing to Senate demands, instructed Richardson to appoint a special Watergate prosecutor with broad powers of investigation and subpoena. Richardson selected Archibald Cox, a Harvard law professor and a Democrat.

In May the special Senate committee began a televised investigation. Chaired by the wily Sam ("I'm just a plain country lawyer") Ervin of North Carolina, an expert on constitutional law, the hearings revealed the existence of a White House "enemies list," the president's use of government agencies to harass his opponents, and administration favoritism in return for illegal campaign donations. Most damaging to the president, the hearings exposed the White House's active involvement in the Watergate cover-up. But the Senate still lacked concrete evidence of the president's criminality, the so-called smoking gun that would prove Nixon's guilt. Because it was simply his word against that of his former counsel, John Dean, who had testified that Nixon personally directed the cover-up, the president expected to survive the crisis.

Then another presidential aide surprised the committee and the nation by revealing that Nixon had installed a secret taping system in the White House that recorded all conversations in the Oval Office. Both the Ervin committee and special prosecutor Cox insisted on access to the tapes, but Nixon refused, claiming executive privilege and national-security considerations. In October, when Cox sought a court order to obtain the tapes, Nixon ordered Attorney General Richardson to fire him. Instead, Richardson resigned in protest, as did the deputy attorney general. It was then left to the third-ranking official in the Department of Justice, Solicitor General Robert Bork, to dump Cox. The furor stirred by this "Saturday Night Massacre" sent Nixon's public-approval rating rapidly downward. Even as Nixon named a new special prosecutor, Leon Jaworski, the House Judiciary Committee began impeachment proceedings.

A President Disgraced

Adding to Nixon's woes that October, Vice President Agnew, having been charged with income-tax evasion and accepting bribes, pleaded no contest—"the full equivalent to a plea of guilty," according to the trial judge. Dishonored, Agnew left government service with a three-year suspended sentence, a ten-thousand-dollar fine, and a letter from Nixon expressing "a great

"I Am the Law!"
The Supreme Court case of United States v. Richard M. Nixon (1974) tested the constitutionality of President Nixon's claim to absolute executive privilege as a basis for not turning over subpoenaed White House tapes. But in a unanimous decision, the Court ruled that neither "the doctrine of the separation of powers nor the need for confidentiality of high-level communications, . . . can sustain an absolute, unqualified presidential privilege of immunity from judicial process under all circumstances."

sense of personal loss." The president nominated the popular House minority leader, Gerald R. Ford of Michigan, to replace Agnew. Nevertheless, the unrelenting legal and political processes unfolding against Nixon made his continued residence at 1600 Pennsylvania Avenue highly uncertain.

In March 1974 special prosecutor Jaworski and the House Judiciary Committee subpoenaed the president for the tape recordings of Oval Office meetings following the Watergate break-in. Still trying to cover up the conspiracy, Nixon in April released edited transcripts of the tapes, filled with gaps and numerous repetitions of the phrase "expletive deleted." Despite the excisions, the president emerged as petty and vindictive. Even in the absence of a smoking gun implicating the president directly, what remained of Nixon's standing was destroyed. "We have seen the private man and we are appalled," declared the staunchly Republican *Chicago Tribune.*

Nixon's sanitized version of the tapes satisfied neither Jaworski nor the House Judiciary Committee. Both pressed for unedited recordings of key Oval Office conversations. In late July the Supreme Court rebuffed the president's claim to executive privilege. Citing the president's obligation to provide evidence necessary for the due process of law, Chief Justice Burger ordered Nixon to release the unexpurgated tapes.

On July 27 the House Judiciary Committee adopted the first article of impeachment. Six of the seventeen Republicans voted with the twenty-one Democrats to charge Nixon with obstruction of justice for impeding the Watergate investigation. An additional Republican voted with the majority on July 29 to condemn the president's abuse of power, particularly his partisan use of such agencies as the FBI and IRS. By a smaller margin, the committee on July 30 added as a third article of impeachment the president's contempt of Congress in refusing to obey a congressional subpoena to release the tapes.

Nixon was now checkmated. On August 5, 1974, he conceded in a televised address that he had withheld relevant evidence from the special prosecutor and the Judiciary Committee. He then surrendered the subpoenaed tapes. They contained the smoking gun proving that the president had ordered the cover-up, obstructed justice, subverted one government agency to prevent another from investigating a crime, and then lied about his role in the matter for more than two years. Shocked by the disclosures, even the die-hard Nixon loyalists on the Judiciary Committee publicly switched their votes in favor of impeaching the president. Still, Nixon wavered, refusing to surrender. On August 7 Republican congressional leaders informed him of the certainty of his impeachment and conviction. Two days later, Richard Nixon became the first American president to resign, and Gerald Ford took office as the nation's first chief executive to have been elected neither president nor vice president.

CONCLUSION

The shocking dénouement of Watergate marked the end of a period of extraordinary rancor in the nation's history. It capped a turbulent time in which a president elected by a majority that broke all records had feared to run for reelection, and his successor, who had garnered the next greatest percentage of the popular vote, resigned in disgrace. Coming on the heels of the U.S. withdrawal from Vietnam, the cultural and political rebellion of the young, severe energy shortages, and a deteriorating economy, Watergate intensified the American people's loss of confidence in their government and its future.

The optimism of Americans is closely correlated with their belief that Washington can govern effectively. In the 1940s and 1950s, the people had faith in their government, which decisively won the Second World War, ushered in unprecedented prosperity, provided social security, and built an impressive highway system. But in the 1960s, presidents Kennedy and Johnson raised expectations they did not fulfill. They failed to deliver on their promise of better schooling, good health care at a reasonable cost, reduced crime, and harmonious race relations. As a result, the percentage of Americans who trusted Washington to do the right thing most of the time dropped precipitously in the mid-sixties. A rising number of Americans came to see Democratic liberals as upper-middle-class intellectuals unable to address the main concerns of ordinary people and unwilling to uphold the most cherished American institutions and values— the family, patriotism, and traditional sexual morality.

Capitalizing on anti-Washington, antiliberal sentiment, President Richard Nixon fashioned a new majority coalition to succeed the bloc forged by Franklin Roosevelt during the New Deal. Although Nixon masterfully reduced international tensions, he too became victimized by the gulf between popular expectations and such domestic woes as worsening stagflation, an energy crisis, and continuing disorder and crime in the streets. Promising to unite a divided people, he polarized them further. Stressing law and order, he employed illegal means to secure his goals and then tried to conceal the facts from investigative bodies. Nearly fifty Nixon administration officials were indicted for fraud, extortion, perjury, obstruction of justice, and other crimes, and more than a score of the president's associates, including White House aides and Attorney General John Mitchell, went to prison.

The man left to pick up the pieces—Nixon's successor, Gerald Ford—proclaimed, "Our long national nightmare is over." But as Americans contemplated the bicentennial of their Declaration of Independence in 1976, the malaise spread. Coping with the realities of relative economic and international decline, a pessimistic nation—disillusioned with its leaders' mendacity, panicked by the end of the postwar economic boom, and helpless before foreign terrorists, oil sheiks, and street criminals—distrusted its political system and thus further limited its ability to govern effectively.

CHRONOLOGY

1960 Birth-control pill marketed.

1964 Berkeley Free Speech Movement (FSM).

1965 Ken Kesey and Merry Pranksters stage first "acid test."

1966 Abolition of automatic student deferments from the draft.

1967 March on the Pentagon.
Israeli-Arab Six-Day war.

1968 Tet offensive.
President Lyndon Johnson announces that he will not seek reelection.
Martin Luther King, Jr., assassinated; race riots sweep nation.
Students take over buildings and strike at Columbia University.
Robert F. Kennedy assassinated.
Violence mars Democratic convention in Chicago.
Vietnam peace talks open in Paris.
Richard Nixon elected president.

1969 Apollo 11 lands first Americans on the moon.
Nixon begins withdrawal of U.S. troops.
Woodstock festival.
March Against Death in Washington, D.C.
Lieutenant William Calley charged with murder of civilians at My Lai.

Woodstock Poster

1970 United States invades Cambodia.
Students killed at Kent State and Jackson State universities.
Nixon proposes Huston Plan.
Environmental Protection Agency established.

1970 OSHA created.
Earth Day first celebrated.

1971 United States invades Laos.
Swann v. *Charlotte-Mecklenburg Board of Education.*
New York Times publishes Pentagon Papers.
Nixon institutes wage-and-price freeze.
South Vietnam invades Laos with the help of U.S. air support.

1972 Nixon visits China and the Soviet Union.
SALT I agreement approved.
Break-in at the Democratic National Committee headquarters in Watergate complex.
Nixon reelected in landslide victory.
Christmas bombing of North Vietnam.

1973 Vietnam cease-fire agreement signed.
Trial of Watergate burglars.
Senate establishes Special Committee on Presidential Campaign Activities to investigate Watergate.
President Salvador Allende ousted and murdered in Chile.
Vice President Spiro Agnew resigns; Gerald Ford appointed vice president.
Roe v. *Wade.*
Yom Kippur War; OPEC begins embargo of oil to the West.
Saturday Night Massacre.

1974 Supreme Court orders Nixon to release Watergate tapes.
House Judiciary Committee votes to impeach Nixon.
Nixon resigns; Ford becomes president.

Nixon's Farewell

FOR FURTHER READING

William Berman, *America's Right Turn: From Nixon to Bush* (1994). A valuable overview of the politics of conservatism.

William Chafe, *Never Stop Running: Allard Lowenstein and the Struggle to Save American Liberalism* (1993). The strife of the 1960s through the prism of a key liberal activist.

Kim McQuaid, *The Anxious Years* (1989). A chronicle of national passions and struggles from 1968 to Nixon's resignation.

Herbert Parmet, *Richard Nixon and His America* (1990). A solid survey of the presidency and the era.

W. J. Rorabaugh, *Berkeley at War* (1989). A lively analysis of the events that rocked Berkeley in the 1960s.

Robert Schulzinger, *Henry Kissinger: Doctor of Diplomacy* (1989). A balanced examination of Kissinger-Nixon foreign policies.

ADDITIONAL BIBLIOGRAPHY

The New Left and Student Movements

Edward Bacciocco, Jr., *The New Left in America* (1974); Ronald Berman, *America in the Sixties* (1968); Wini Breines, *Community and Organization in the New Left* (1989); Peter Clecak, *Radical Paradoxes* (1973); Peter Collier and David Horowitz, *Destructive Generation: Second Thoughts About the Sixties* (1989); C. DeBenedetti and C. Chatfield, *An American Ordeal: The Antiwar Movement of the Vietnam Era* (1990); David Farber, *Chicago '68* (1988); Todd Gitlin, *The Sixties: Years of Hope, Days of Rage* (1987); Kenneth Heineman, *Campus Wars* (1992); Maurice Isserman, *If I Had a Hammer: The Death of the Old Left—and the Birth of the New Left* (1989); Charles Kaiser, *1968 in America* (1988); Joseph Kelner and James Munves, *The Kent State Coverup* (1980); Kenneth Keniston, *Youth and Dissent* (1971); Richard King, *The Party of Eros* (1972); James Kunen, *The Strawberry Statement* (1968); C. Manes, *Green Rage: Radical Environmentalism* (1990); James Miller, *Democracy Is in the Streets* (1987); Charles Reich, *The Greening of America* (1970); Theodore Roszak, *The Making of a Counterculture* (1969); M. Small and W. Hoover, eds., *Give Peace a Chance: Exploring the Vietnam Antiwar Movement* (1992); Jon Wiener, *Come Together* (1983).

The Politics of 1968

Marshall Frady, *Wallace* (1970); Louis Gould, *1968: The Election That Changed America* (1993); Richard Lemons, *The Troubled Americans* (1970); Joe McGinniss, *The Selling of the President, 1968* (1969); Kevin Phillips, *The Emerging Republican Majority* (1969); Richard Scammon and Ben Wattenberg, *The Real Majority* (1970); Herbert Schandler, *The Unmaking of a President* (1977); Irwin Unger and Debi Unger, *Turning Point: 1968* (1988).

Nixon-Kissinger Foreign Policies

Lloyd Gardner, *A Covenant with Power* (1984) and *The Great Nixon Turnaround* (1973); Arnold Isaacs, *Without Honor: Defeat in Vietnam and Cambodia* (1983); Henry Kissinger, *White House Years* (1979) and *Years of Upheaval* (1982); Robert Litwack, *Détente and the Nixon Doctrine* (1984); Timothy Lomperis, *The War Nobody Lost—and Won* (1984); Gareth Porter, *Vietnam* (1979); Stephen Rabe, *The Road to OPEC* (1982); Franz Schurmann, *The Foreign Policies of Richard Nixon* (1987); William Shawcross, *Side-Show: Kissinger, Nixon, and the Destruction of Cambodia* (1979); Melvin Small, *Johnson, Nixon, and the Doves* (1988).

The Nixon Administration

Jonathan Aitken, *Nixon: A Life* (1994); Stephen Ambrose, *The Triumph of a Politician* (1989); Fawn Brodie, *Richard Nixon: The Shaping of His Character* (1981); Vincent Burke, *Nixon's Good Deed: Welfare Reform* (1974); David Calleo, *The Imperious Economy* (1982); Jody Carleson, *George Wallace and the Politics of Powerlessness* (1981); Ronald Formisano, *Boston Against Busing: Race, Class, and Ethnicity in the 1960s and 1970s* (1991); J. Greene, *The Limits of Power: The Nixon and Ford Administrations* (1992); James Reichley, *Conservatives in an Age of Change: The Nixon and Ford Administrations* (1981); Kirkpatrick Sale, *Power Shift* (1976); Michael Tanzer, *The Energy Crisis* (1974).

Watergate

John Dean, *Blind Ambition* (1976); James Doyle, *Not Above the Law* (1977); John Ehrlichman, *Witness to Power* (1982); Jim Houghan, *Secret Agenda: Watergate, Deep Throat and the CIA* (1984); J. Anthony Lukas, *Nightmare: The Underside of the Nixon Years* (1976); Richard Nixon, *RN: The Memoirs of Richard Nixon* (1978); John Sirica, *To Set the Record Straight* (1979); Maurice Stans, *The Terrors of Justice* (1984); Athan Theoharis, *Spying on Americans* (1978).

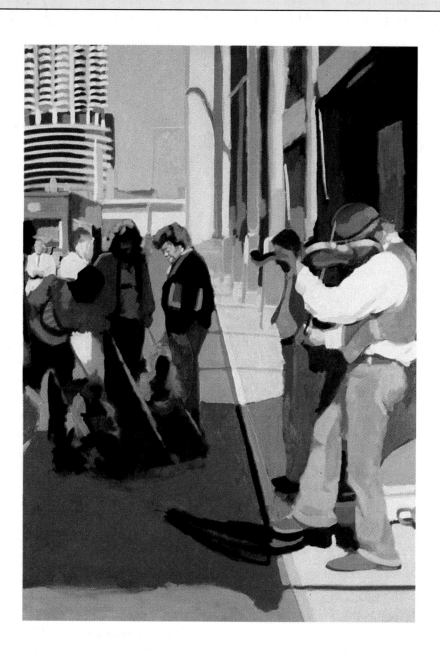

Fiddler Player (detail)
by Nick Paciorek

TURNING INWARD: SOCIETY AND POLITICS FROM FORD TO REAGAN

In October 1985 *Forbes* business magazine hailed "the richest man in America": Sam Walton of Bentonville, Arkansas. The name meant nothing to many readers, but those familiar with the world of discount merchandising knew it well. Walton was founder and chair of the Wal-Mart Corporation, one of the discount chains that transformed mass marketing in the United States after 1960. Walton's story was the stuff of legend. Estimating his net worth at "$20 or $25 billion," he lived modestly in Bentonville, generally wore a "Wal-Mart" baseball cap, and still went to the local barbershop for his haircuts.

Born in Kingfisher, Oklahoma, in 1918, Walton grew up in various small towns in Missouri. While his father, a mortgage agent, repossessed farms during the Great Depression, young Sam sold milk, rabbits, and magazine subscriptions door-to-door. The youngest Eagle Scout in Missouri's history, he was also voted "Most Versatile" by his high school classmates. After graduation from the University of Missouri, World War II army service, and marriage to Helen Robson, he began a retailing career in September 1945 as manager of a Ben Franklin variety store in Newport, Arkansas.

Sam and Helen (with a loan from Helen's father, a wealthy rancher and businessman) opened their own Walton's Five and Dime in Bentonville, Arkansas, in 1950, and a second one in nearby Fayetteville two years later. From the first, he demonstrated the single-minded initiative that characterized his career: he scoured the region for bargain-priced merchandise that he then sold on a high-volume basis at a small markup. As the Fayetteville store manager recalled: "Sam used to come down . . . driving an old fifty-three Plymouth. He had that car so loaded up he barely had room to drive. And would you like to guess what he had in it? Ladies' panties. Three for $1.00 and four for $1.00 and nylon hose." Remarked another early associate: "What motivates the man is the desire to absolutely be on top of the heap."

The first Wal-Mart store opened in Rogers, Arkansas, in 1962, and soon Wal-Marts were spreading across rural and small-town Arkansas, Oklahoma, Missouri, and beyond. "We just started repeating what worked, stamping out stores cookie-cutter style," Walton recalled. The time was right, as the boom years created rich opportunities for merchandisers. Walton innovated discount retail selling, together with Zayre's in New England, the Target chain of Minneapolis's Dayton-Hudson Company, Woolco (spun off from the Woolworth five-and-dime empire), and K-Mart, started by the S. S. Kresge Company, another dime-store pioneer. Three-quarters of the early discounters failed, but others prospered. Wal-Mart went public in 1970, and its period of phenomenal growth began. With jobs tight and inflation eroding consumer buying-power in the 1970s, the chain's rock-bottom prices helped low-income families to make ends meet. Thanks to successive stock splits, 100 shares of Wal-Mart stock purchased for $1,650 in 1970 were worth about $3 million by 1990.

Sam Walton also created a unique corporate culture that included promotional gimmicks such as "shopping cart bingo," rousing employee gatherings punctuated by cheers and company songs, and stunts including Walton's 1984 grass-skirted hula dance on Wall Street because he lost a bet with Wal-Mart's chief executive officer about annual sales volume.

Wal-Mart had its critics. Sam Walton fought off unions by introducing a profit-sharing plan to supplement the low wages he paid his workers. Many of Wal-Mart's senior officers resigned in 1974 amid a bitter management battle. Above all, criticism came from the hundreds of small-town merchants driven out of business by Wal-Mart's high-volume, price-slashing approach to marketing. Walton felt no sympathy for these failed competitors. "[Their] customers were the ones who shut [them] down. They voted with their feet. . . . Wal-Mart has actually kept quite a number of small towns from becoming practially extinct by offering low prices and saving literally billions of dollars for the people who live there, as well as by creating hundreds of thousands of jobs in our stores."

On March 17, 1992, President George Bush flew to Bentonville to give its most famous resident the Medal of Freedom, the nation's highest civilian award. Said Bush: "An American original, Sam Walton embodies the entrepreneurial spirit and epitomizes the American dream." Two weeks later, Walton died of bone cancer. When his autobiography, *Made in America,* appeared soon after, another admirer, H. Ross Perot, proclaimed: "Every person who dreams of building a great business *must* read this book."

The business lived on. In 1994 some 2,600 Wal-Mart Discount Department Stores, Warehouse Outlets, supercenters, and "Sam's Wholesale Clubs" could be found across forty-five states, Canada, and Puerto Rico. Wal-Mart Corporation, employing 525,000, that year reported sales of $67.3 billion.

The Wal-Mart phenomenon was part of a transformation in the U.S. economy. The service sector grew rapidly as fast-food outlets like McDonald's and Wendy's and discount stores such as Wal-Mart spread. High-tech industries prospered as well. But other sectors of the economy, notably the steel mills, auto plants, tool-and-die factories, and appliance and electronics manufacturers of the old industrial heartland, grew weaker, battered by imports. Sam Walton's career may have proved, as George Bush claimed, that "the American dream" remained alive, but for millions of people the dream was proving more and more elusive.

AFTER THE SIXTIES: CHANGING SOCIAL AND CULTURAL CONTOURS

American social and cultural trends of the 1970s and 1980s reflected both the afterglow of 1960s activism and a reaction against the upheavals of that turbulent decade. Some causes of the sixties, notably environmentalism and feminism, gained ground in the seventies. Women in record numbers poured into the work force, enrolled in professional schools, and launched careers. But the violence and divisiveness of 1968–1970 left a painful legacy, and in their aftermath many young adults turned to personal goals, material acquisition, and sometimes narcissistic self-indulgence. Others found meaning and social identification in celebrating their ethnicity.

Even as the quest for material advancement pervaded the post-sixties climate, millions of Americans remained mired in poverty. The African-American experience epitomizes the decade's divergent trends. While many blacks moved into the middle class, others became even more deeply alienated and cut off from the traditional avenues of upward mobility.

Radicals of the 1960s had celebrated sexual freedom and feminists had demanded reproductive choice, but the post-1970 years brought fierce debates over abortion, as well as greater caution in sexual behavior as AIDS wreaked its deadly havoc. Simultaneously, the unsettling pace of change led to a search for moral certitude and spiritual solace, producing a resurgence of religion in U.S. life. Despite their apparent diversity, these crosscurrents of post-1960s society were interconnected. Indeed, many of the era's cultural and social trends become fully comprehensible only in the context of political and economic developments.

America Turns Inward

Social activism did not disappear in the aftermath of the 1960s, but while some issues attracted even more attention, others faded. Although the reform impetus in the sixties had initially come from the Left, after 1968 it was just as likely to surface on the Right.

The revived women's movement, a major development of the sixties, gained ground in the seventies. And the heightened environmental consciousness stimulated by the publication of Rachel Carson's *Silent Spring* (1962) and by President Lyndon B. Johnson's Great Society programs remained central as Americans expressed rising concern about air and water pollution and the peril to endangered species. A campaign to save the whales from extinction at the hands of the whaling fleets of various nations won many recruits. The hazards of nuclear power aroused particular attention in the later 1970s, culminating in 1979 when a near-catastrophic accident crippled the Three Mile Island nuclear-power plant near Harrisburg, Pennsylvania. For several days, the nation watched anxiously as the accident threatened to turn into a major catastrophe. A Hollywood movie released at the same time, *China Syndrome,* raised further alarms about the dangers of nuclear power. *China Syndrome* starred Jane Fonda, a leading antiwar activist of the sixties, illustrating some political activists' shift of focus to new issues.

But millions of young people turned from public to private concerns. The sour political atmosphere and constricted economy of the seventies did not inspire the kind of civic idealism that John F. Kennedy and Martin Luther King, Jr., had once aroused. While the burial of the Kennedy-Johnson liberal consensus in the wreckage of Vietnam and the fragmentation of the New Left in 1968–1970 left a vacuum of political leadership on the Left, the Watergate debacle of 1973–1974 temporarily derailed the forward momentum of the political Right. With politics in disarray, more personal preoccupations beckoned. And after 1980, Ronald Reagan's message of individualism easily translated into a self-centered materialism. Apart from calls for more military spending, Reagan offered little in the way of a national agenda. In these circumstances, the "campus radical" of the 1960s gave way to

Save the Whales
Protests against the commercial whaling industries of Japan and other nations arose in the 1970s and gained momentum in later decades. These 1988 demonstrators gathered across from the White House during a visit by Japanese prime minister Noboru Takeshita.

a new social stereotype, the "yuppie" (young urban professional), preoccupied with physical fitness, psychic harmony, and a consumption-obsessed life-style. Reversing the middle-class flight from the city, many yuppies purchased run-down inner-city apartments or town houses and expensively restored them. This process, known as gentrification, often had the effect of pushing out poorer residents, including countless elderly citizens.

Physical well-being became a middle-class obsession—sometimes to good effect. Yuppies jogged and exercised with sweaty determination. A vogue for "natural" foods free of pesticide residues and chemical additives spread, and the rate of cigarette smoking declined as medical evidence linked the habit to lung cancer, heart disease, and other maladies. Transcendental meditation and other "consciousness-raising" techniques won devoted followers in the seventies. But self-improvement could easily turn selfish. Historian Christopher Lasch summed up his view of the era in the title of his 1978 book *The Culture of Narcissism;* writer Tom Wolfe called it simply the Me Generation.

No single age group had a monopoly on this post-sixties pursuit of private goals and pleasures. Encouraged by the mass media and an ever expanding entertainment industry, that pursuit helped to define the era. Average daily TV viewing time crept up from about six hours in 1970 to nearly seven by 1990. Prime-time soap operas like "Dallas," chronicling the steamy affairs of a mythical Texas oil family, captivated millions each week. At the same time, the rise of cable television gave birth to a variety of new channels offering everything from business reports to rock music. For an added fee, viewers had a still broader choice, including first-run films on HBO (Home Box Office). Faced with such competition, the networks' share of the market declined to under 75 percent by the early 1990s.

The Disney Corporation, already enjoying great success with its Southern California theme park, Disneyland (opened in 1955), launched the even bigger Disneyworld in Florida in 1982. Blockbuster movies like *Jaws* (1975), *Star Wars* (1977), *Close Encounters of the Third Kind* (1977), and *E.T.* (1982) offered escapist fare for millions. Professional sports grew more popular than ever. Baseball's World Series, football's Super Bowl, and the National Basketball Association playoffs attracted vast television audiences. Superstar sports celebrities earned multimillion-dollar salaries and even more from product endorsements.

A revolution in consumer electronics shaped the era as well. The introduction of the videocassette recorder (VCR) enabled Americans to tape TV shows for later viewing and to rent movies on cassette. By the early 1990s, 70 percent of U.S. households had VCRs; entertainment had become highly privatized. Instead of going out to the movies, many families now spent Saturday night at home with the VCR. In the music field, the compact disc, in which tiny laser beams "read" millions of dots molded into three miles of concentric circles on each disc, offered remarkably high-quality sound. Americans bought millions of CD players in the late 1980s and early 1990s.

And this was the era of the personal computer. A product of World War II, the computer moved into the home in the late 1970s when two young Californians, Steven Jobs and Stephen Wozniak, developed a small-scale model. In 1977 the Apple II computer hit the market. Sales reached $118 million by 1980, and computer businesses mushroomed in a region south of San Francisco nicknamed "Silicon Valley" (after the silicon computer chip). IBM, which launched its PC (personal computer) in 1981, quickly grabbed 40 percent of the market. By 1994, 37 percent of all U.S. households owned personal computers. Computer dealers that year purchased $8 billion worth of new equipment to keep pace with the surging demand.

The Women's Movement: Gains and Uncertainties

Of all the legacies of the 1960s, perhaps the most far-reaching was a revitalized women's movement and basic changes in the status of women in American life. Betty Friedan's *The Feminine Mystique* (1963) had heralded a new cycle of feminist activism, and as the civil-rights and antiwar movements politicized thousands of middle-class young women, many began to examine their own subordinate status in society. The National Organization for Women (NOW), founded by Friedan and others in 1966, boasted nearly fifty thousand members by the mid-1970s. Feminist support groups and Gloria Steinem's *Ms.* magazine (founded in 1972) spread the message.

With the movement's growth came political clout. The National Women's Political Caucus (1971) promoted a feminist agenda in Washington and state capitals. By 1972 many states had liberalized their abortion laws and outlawed gender discrimination in hiring. That same year, Congress passed an Equal Rights Amendment (ERA) to the Constitution ("Equality of rights under the law shall not be denied or abridged by the United States or any State on the basis of sex"). When twenty-eight states quickly ratified it, ultimate adoption seemed assured.

In 1973 came *Roe* v. *Wade,* a profoundly important Supreme Court decision. In a case involving a Texas woman (called Jane Roe in the case record to preserve her anonymity) seeking to end her pregnancy, the Supreme Court, by a 7–2 vote, proclaimed women's constitutional right to abortion. The majority decision, written by Justice Harry Blackmun, relied heavily on the right to privacy, which Blackmun grounded in the due-process clause of the Fourteenth Amendment.

The women's movement remained strong in the later 1970s and the 1980s, but the early unity waned as radical and moderate camps emerged. Although both camps espoused gender equality, moderates deplored the radicals' sometimes strident rhetoric. Movement activists also remained overwhelmingly middle-class and white. Many homemakers were put off by some feminists' tendency to downgrade family values while praising female autonomy and careerist goals. In *The Second Stage* (1981), Betty Friedan urged feminists to add family issues to their agenda and not leave this potent theme to their opponents.

As the movement gained visibility, its opposition hardened. In 1972 President Nixon vetoed a bill that would have set up a national network of day-care cen-

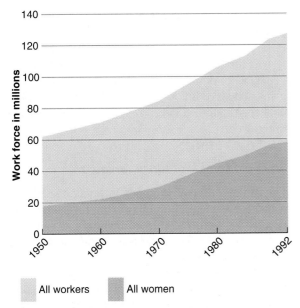

Women in the Work Force, 1950–1992

Since 1960 the proportion of American women who are gainfully employed has surged upward. As a result, young women coming of age in the 1990s have far different expectations about their lives than did their grandmothers or even their mothers.

SOURCES: *Statistical Abstract of the United States,* 1988 (Washington, D.C.: U.S. Government Printing Office, 1987), 373; *World Almanac and Book of Facts, 1989* (New York: Pharos Books, 1988), 152; *Statistical Abstract of the United States, 1993* (Washington, D.C., U.S. Government Printing Office, 1993), 400, 401.

ters; its "communal approach to child-rearing," he charged, was "family weakening." After the initial spurt of support for the ERA, the ratification process bogged down. In 1979 Congress gave advocates an additional three years to achieve ratification, but the amendment died in 1982, three states short of the required three-fourths.

No issue relating to women aroused more anguished controversy than abortion. In the wake of *Roe v. Wade*, a well-organized "Right to Life" movement pressed for a constitutional amendment outlawing abortions. This effort, led by Roman Catholic and conservative Protestant groups, generated intense controversy. Abortion, opponents charged, undermined respect for human life; it was "the murder of the unborn." "Pro-life" advocates held mass rallies and picketed pregnancy-counseling centers. Phyllis Schlafly, a prominent conservative and longtime Cold War polemicist, emerged as a leading crusader against

abortion rights, the Equal Rights Amendment, and other feminist causes. In 1976 Congress cut off Medicaid funding for most abortions, in effect putting this procedure out of reach of the poor.

Most feminists adopted a "pro-choice" stance, arguing that the abortion decision should rest with the individual woman and her physician and not be subject to legal prohibition. Public-opinion polls reflected the nation's polarization, but a majority favored the "pro-choice" position. The number of women seeking abortions rose from about 750,000 in 1973 to more than 1.5 million in 1980 and then leveled off.

The proportion of women working outside the home leaped from 35 percent in 1960 to about 58 percent in 1992. Along with the women's movement, another reason for this trend was the soaring cost of living in these years. Many families found they could not get ahead, or even maintain their standard of living, on a single income. Although many women workers remained at the low end of the pay scale, this pattern, too, was changing. From 1977 to 1992, the proportion of corporate-management positions held by women rose from 24 percent to 42 percent (though *top* management still remained an overwhelmingly male preserve). The ratio of female lawyers and physicians edged upward after 1960, reaching about 18 percent by 1992. Among the under-thirty age group, the proportion of women approached one-third, while steeply rising female enrollments in medical schools, law schools, and Ph.D. programs guaranteed a continuation of this trend.

These changes affected fertility patterns. After the postwar baby boom's peak in 1960, the birthrate dropped steadily for sixteen years, reaching a low in 1976. Couples not only were marrying later but postponed starting a family and had fewer children. By 1980 the statistically average American family had 1.6 children. The number of unmarried couples living together—most of them childless—jumped from 523,000 in 1970 to 3.5 million by 1993. And 1993 saw 508 divorces for every 1,000 marriages, up from 258 per 1,000 in 1960.

Some conservatives worried that women's changing roles would lead to a weakening of the family. Working women themselves acknowledged the stresses of their situation. Torn between career and family pressures, some yielded to the "super-woman" syndrome, pushing themselves to be successful professionals, attentive mothers, superb cooks, efficient housekeepers, and seductive wives all at the same time.

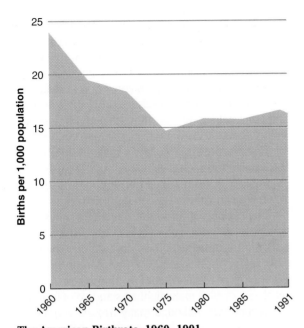

The American Birthrate, 1960–1991

Families of four or five children or even more were once common in the United States. But from 1960 to the mid-1970s, the U.S. birthrate fell by nearly half.

SOURCE: *Statistical Abstract of the United States, 1994* (Washington, D.C.: U.S. Government Printing Office, 1994), 76.

Older feminists worried that younger women, taking for granted opportunities won in earlier struggles, were losing sight of the movement's original goals. Could women function as equals in the male world, they asked, without absorbing the competitiveness, the status preoccupations, and the careerism characteristic of that world? Feminists recognized, too, that a long road lay ahead in overcoming ingrained patterns of gender discrimination. Working women's average earnings still lagged well behind those of men. And although the pattern was shifting, the workplace remained largely gender segregated. Such fields as nursing and secretarial work overwhelmingly employed women, whereas men dominated the higher-prestige professions like law and medicine, particularly at the upper ranks.

The eighties was not a favorable decade for confronting these inequities. The Reagan administration, suspicious of government activism on social issues, opposed many feminist goals. The Reagan budget cuts fell especially harshly on social-welfare programs serving women and children. As women heading single-parent families increasingly swelled the welfare rolls, observers spoke of the "feminization of poverty."

As the 1980s ended, feminist leaders and women generally could take legitimate satisfaction in many gains achieved. But they also recognized that major challenges loomed and complex issues remained unresolved.

The Two Worlds of Black America

The same conservative trends in public life that affected the women's movement in the 1970s and 1980s had ramifications for African-Americans as well. The Reagan administration, distrusting government generally, was cool toward calls for positive government action to remedy past racial injustices. Reagan's appointees to the United States Civil Rights Commission, the agency charged with enforcing civil-rights laws, shared the president's doubts about government's role in such matters. This governmental foot dragging came at a time of worsening crisis for the African-American community.

The story of black America in the 1970s and 1980s was really two very different stories. On one hand, millions of blacks experienced significant upward mobility. Thanks to the civil-rights movement, blacks could pass through doors long closed. In 1965 black students accounted for under 5 percent of college enrollments; by 1990 the figure had risen to 12 percent, as the proportion of black high-school graduates going on to college nearly matched that of their white classmates. By 1990 some 46 percent of black workers held white-collar jobs. TV's *Cosby Show,* a popular family comedy of the later 1980s in which Bill Cosby played an obstetrician married to a lawyer, portrayed this successful, upwardly mobile black world. Many African-Americans worked steadily in blue-collar jobs as well.

But outside this world of employed, often upwardly mobile blacks lay the grim world of inner-city slums where blacks who had missed the "Up" escalator found themselves trapped. In this world, comprising about a third of the black population, up to half the young people never finished high school and the jobless rate in the late 1980s hovered as high as 60 percent.

Although racism contributed to this situation, economic trends played a role as well. Structural changes in the economy since World War II had eliminated

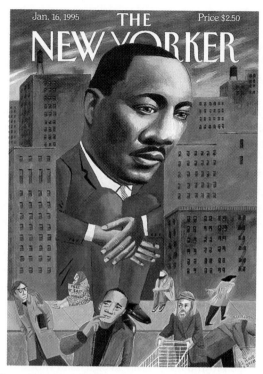

Cover Drawing "I Had a Dream," *by Mark Ulriksen In this 1995* New Yorker *cover, the spirit of Martin Luther King, Jr., broods over a scene of Americans displaced and marginalized in a rapidly changing economy.*

(© 1995 The New Yorker Magazine, Inc. All Rights Reserved.)

many unskilled jobs once held by the urban poor. The recessions of the 1970s and early 1980s battered the already struggling black underclass, and job cuts in steel, automaking, and other basic industries hit black skilled workers. Inflation and rising demands for an educated work force further battered the poor and those with little schooling, while welfare payments failed to keep up with the rising cost of living.

Cocaine, including the particularly potent "crack," pervaded the urban ghettos in the 1970s and 1980s. Black children as young as eight or nine earned up to a hundred dollars a day working as lookouts for drug dealers. By their early teens, some became dealers themselves, earning in two days what they would make in a year working at McDonald's.

This is not to suggest that only the poor or minorities abused drugs. All social levels in the 1970s, including the world of yuppies, sports celebrities, show-business figures, and young corporate executives indulged in cocaine and other drugs. Despite the enactment of a supposedly tougher antidrug law (the Comprehensive Drug Abuse Act of 1970), the consumption of such substances was widely tolerated and was even glorified in some movies, popular songs, and rock concerts. But among the inner-city poor, drug use was particularly pervasive—and devastating.

This was also a violent world. In the 1980s a young black male was six times as likely to be murdered as a young white male. Sixty black children under the age of seventeen were murdered in Detroit in 1987, most in gang-related violence. In Los Angeles two major gangs, the Bloods and the Crips, accounted for more than four hundred killings that year. Jewelle Taylor Gibbs of the School of Social Welfare at Berkeley summed up the situation in 1988: "Young black males in America's inner cities are an endangered species. . . . They are [the] rejects of our affluent society."

Among unmarried young black women of the slums, the pregnancy rate soared. Single women—most of them young, poor, and uneducated—accounted for 66 percent of all black births in 1994. Millions of these single mothers, many scarcely beyond childhood themselves, depended on welfare payments for survival. Caught in a vicious cycle of dependence, these millions threatened to become a permanent undercaste in American society.

Although unemployment, drug use, illegitimacy, and welfare dependency affect Americans of all races and ethnic groups, these problems emerged most starkly among inner-city black and Hispanic populations. Buffeted by complex social and economic forces, the United States' predominantly nonwhite inner cities came to pose a major social challenge.

New Patterns of Immigration

America's recent population growth—from 204 million in 1970 to more than 260 million in 1995—reflects a steady influx of immigrants, both legal and illegal. In contrast to former eras, when most immigrants came from Europe, some 45 percent of the new arrivals since 1960 have come from the Western Hemisphere and 30 percent from Asia.

Thanks to both immigration and a high birthrate, Hispanics compose the nation's fastest-growing ethnic group. The 1995 Hispanic population stood at more

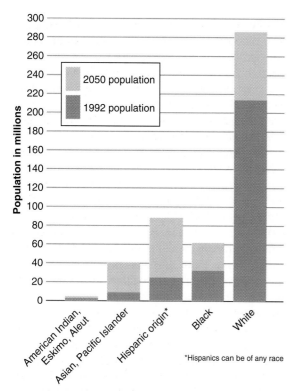

Changing Demographics

The U.S. population by race and hispanic origin in 1992 and 2050 (Census Bureau projections).

SOURCE: *Statistical Abstract of the United States, 1994* (Washington, D.C.: U.S. Government Printing Office, 1994), 17, 18.

than 26 million (up from 9 million in 1970), consisting mainly of Mexican-Americans concentrated in the Southwest; and Cubans, Puerto Ricans, Haitians, and other West Indians living mainly in New York, Florida, Illinois, and New Jersey.

As with immigrants of the past, economic necessity propelled these newcomers to America. In oil-rich Mexico, for example, with its appalling unemployment and per capita annual income of just over two thousand dollars, the collapse in world oil prices in the 1980s worsened the nation's chronic poverty, spurring many to seek new opportunities in the north (and graphically illustrating the interconnectedness of economic and social history). But these recent immigrants, like their predecessors, often faced hardship and poverty in their adopted land as well. In 1990 nearly 20 percent of Mexican-Americans and 30 percent of Puerto Ricans lived below the poverty line.

Proudly upholding their language and traditions, these Hispanic newcomers strongly influenced American culture. In Los Angeles, with nearly a million Mexican-Americans, one could drive for miles in the 1980s and see only Spanish business signs and movie marquees; large parts of Miami, such as the open-air market of the Calle Oche district, seemed wholly Hispanic (see Chapter 33, "A Place in Time").

Estimates of the number of illegal aliens in the United States ranged as high as 12 million by the early

New Americans, 1994

Beneath the political icons and popular-culture imagery of their adopted nation, children of Hmong (Laotian) immigrants study at Lincoln Elementary School, Wausau, Wisconsin.

1990s. Working long hours under harsh conditions with few legal protections, these impoverished migrants, mostly Mexicans and Haitians (as well as Puerto Ricans, who are U.S. citizens), performed hard manual labor, sweated in the garment trades, cleaned houses and cared for children, and bent their backs in agricultural fields. Addressing this growing problem, the Immigration Reform and Control Act of 1986 outlawed the hiring of illegal aliens and strengthened immigration controls at the border. At the same time, the new law offered legal status to aliens who could prove that they had lived in the United States since January 1, 1982.

Immigration from Asia also climbed as newcomers from Korea, Vietnam, and the Philippines joined already well-established Japanese and Chinese communities in California and spread eastward. These newest Americans worked hard, sought higher education, and moved up rapidly. The younger generation, torn between the new and the old, faced stresses and tensions but generally retained a strong group identity while taking advantage of the larger society's opportunities. All these ethnic trends made contemporary America a far more diverse and vibrant place than it had been a generation earlier.

Brightening Prospects for Native Americans

The status of American Indians sank to a low point in the 1950s, when the federal government sought to terminate all Indian-aid programs and promote Indians' relocation in cities—where, it was tacitly hoped, they would gradually disappear as a distinct ethnic group. Aroused by this destructive and ill-conceived policy, and influenced by the social-protest climate of the sixties, members of the militant American Indian Movement (AIM) dramatized their cause by occupying Alcatraz Island in San Francisco Bay in 1969, the Bureau of Indian Affairs in Washington in 1972, and a trading post at Wounded Knee, South Dakota (site of the 1890 Indian massacre by the U.S. Army), in 1973.

This militance helped bring about an important shift in federal policy. Rejecting both the "termination" approach and Washington's traditional paternalism toward Indians, President Nixon in 1970 called for greater autonomy for the Native Americans in managing their own affairs. The Indian Self-Determination Act of 1974 granted tribes the right to control federal-aid programs on the reservations and to oversee their own schools.

The seventies also brought a heightened sense of Indian pride. By 1990 more than 1.7 million persons identified themselves as American Indians, in contrast to fewer than 800,000 in 1970. Since natural increase could not account for this rate of growth, census analysts concluded that more Americans were choosing to identify themselves as Indians. This upsurge doubtless reflected not only growing ethnic pride but also certain advantages associated with tribal membership, including the sharing of tribal revenues from casinos and other enterprises, and employment opportunities available to officially designated minorities under federal affirmative-action guidelines.

Wounded Knee, South Dakota, 1973
In a gesture of symbolic protest, activists of the American Indian Movement (AIM) occupied Wounded Knee, scene of the 1890 massacre of 300 Sioux by the U.S. army.

This flowering of ethnic pride inspired efforts to promote economic development on the reservations. Federal legislation in 1961 had given tribes the right to buy or develop land for commercial or industrial projects, and a number of tribes undertook commercial ventures ranging from resorts to mining and logging operations. Other tribes permitted food-processing companies, electronics firms, and other businesses to build factories on tribal lands, providing much-needed jobs to help alleviate the severe unemployment problem. Certain tribes took advantage of their exemption from state gambling laws to open casinos, although this source of revenue aroused opposition both from antigambling groups and from Native Americans who saw in casinos a threat to Indian culture.

Indian tribes have also reasserted long-ignored treaty rights. The Indian Claims Commission, a federal agency set up in 1946, has worked overtime since 1970 to resolve Indian land claims. In 1971 the Eskimos, Aleuts, and other native peoples of Alaska won 40 million acres of land and nearly $1 billion in settlement of their long-standing claims. In 1980 the Sioux were awarded $107 million for lands in South Dakota illegally taken from them more than a century earlier, and the Penobscot Indians in Maine won claims based on a federal law of 1790. In 1988 the tiny Puyallup tribe of Washington State received $162 million in settlement of their claim that the city of Tacoma occupied land granted them by treaty in the 1850s. The Puyallups announced plans to restore the salmon runs on the Puyallup River and to construct a deep-water port on Puget Sound.

High rates of unemployment, alcoholism, and disease persisted both on the reservations and in the cities. But the renewal of tribal life, the new direction of federal policy, and the willingness of the white majority to honor ancient treaties clearly represented an advance. The changed attitude was reflected in popular culture as well. Movies such as *Little Big Man* (1970) and *Dances with Wolves* (1990), and the popular TV series of the 1990s "Northern Exposure," while prone to sentimentalizing Indian culture, were an improvement over the hostile stereotypes purveyed in cowboy-and-Indian movies in earlier decades.

Sexuality in the Era of AIDS

The greater openness about sex that was one of the sixties' legacies had a particular impact on the homosexual community. In June 1969—in an event that

The AIDS Quilt, Washington, D.C., 1987
Each panel commemorates a person who died of AIDS. Wrote one woman who quilted a panel in honor of her grandson: "We were so close. I was there when he was born, and I was there when he passed away."

would later assume great symbolic import—a routine police raid on a Greenwich Village gay bar, the Stonewall Inn, took an unexpected turn when the patrons fought back with a barrage of bottles and beer cans (see Chapter 31). Beginning in the 1970s, many gay men and lesbians "came out of the closet" and openly acknowledged their sexual preference. They rallied, paraded, and organized to fight job discrimination and other forms of harassment. As one leader told a throng of fifty thousand demonstrators in Washington, D.C., in 1979: "We are twenty million strong in this nation. We are moving from gay pride to gay politics."

Religious conservatives, meanwhile, deplored this trend as evidence of society's moral disintegration. Declared evangelist Jerry Falwell: "Homosexuality is . . . so abominable in the sight of God that he destroyed the cities of Sodom and Gomorrah because of this terrible sin."

The loosening of traditional sexual mores received a jolting setback in the 1980s, however, with the proliferation of various sexually transmitted diseases, including AIDS (acquired immune deficiency syndrome), first diagnosed in the United States in 1981. By 1995 more than 270,000 Americans had died of AIDS, and an estimated 1 million more carried HIV, the causative virus. Public-health officials warned that a vaccine against the deadly virus lay far in the future. Despite widespread fears of a "breakout" into the general population, AIDS remained confined mainly to sexually active homosexuals and bisexuals, intravenous drug users sharing needles, and those having sexual intercourse with members of these high-risk groups. Nevertheless, medical authorities soberly warned of the need for caution and urged the wider use of condoms. This somber message was driven home in 1991 when basketball superstar Earvin ("Magic") Johnson of the Los Angeles Lakers announced that he had tested positive for the HIV virus. In 1995 the Olympic gold-medal-winning diver Greg Louganis made a similar revelation.

The AIDS scare provided some Americans with an excuse to express their hatred of homosexuals. But others responded admirably. The disease's mysterious nature stimulated a massive medical-research effort, although AIDS- and HIV-advocacy groups called for much larger allocations of funds to this research. Hospices in many communities provided care and support to sufferers; a large AIDS quilt bearing the names of victims toured the nation; candlelight marches memorialized those who had died.

Fearful of AIDS and other sexually transmitted diseases, both the homosexual and heterosexual populations grew more cautious in their sexual behavior. The exuberant slogan of the 1960s, "Make Love, Not War," had given way to a more somber exhortation, "Safer Sex."

The Evangelical Renaissance

A striking aspect of post-1970 American society was the high visibility of religion. Amid sometimes tumultuous social change, many Americans sought the assurance of beliefs that would give meaning to life and provide ethical guidance. Religious faith has always loomed large in American history, but after 1970 it played a more decisive cultural and political role than it had for years.

This intensification of religious interest assumed many forms. Some joined cults such as the Reverend Sun Myung Moon's Unification church (whose adherents some called "moonies") and the International Society for Krishna Consciousness, whose chanting, saffron-robed followers added an exotic note on city streets and college campuses. The more significant expression of this religious resurgence was the rapid growth of evangelical Protestant denominations such

as the 2-million-member Assemblies of God church and the 14-million-strong Southern Baptist Convention. Though these groups differed among themselves, all believed in the Bible's verbatim truth, in a "born-again" religious conversion, and in an earthly life governed by personal piety and strict morality.

Evangelical Christians had pursued social reform before the Civil War, and many twentieth-century evangelicals also turned to political activity, but of a conservative variety. As a California evangelical minister observed in 1985: "I always thought that churches should stay out of politics. Now it seems almost a sin *not* to get involved." Jerry Falwell's pro-Reagan Moral Majority registered an estimated 2 million new voters in 1980 and 1984. While targeting specific issues such as abortion, pornography, and public-school prayer, evangelicals also embraced a strongly conservative, anticommunist world view.

Falwell disbanded his organization after 1984, but the Reverend Pat Robertson's well-organized Christian Coalition took its place. Mobilizing grass-roots efforts by conservative Christians to elect candidates to school boards and the like, the coalition had the long-range aim of expanding political influence at the state and national level.

Evangelicalism's rejuvenation was fueled by a network of religious bookstores, by radio stations featuring religious programming, and, above all, by television evangelists. Along with Falwell's "Old Time Gospel Hour," popular broadcasts included Pat Robertson's "700 Club," Jim and Tammy Bakker's "PTL" (Praise the Lord) program, Oral Roberts's telecasts from Oklahoma, and Jimmy Swaggart's from Louisiana. Many of these shows aired on Robertson's CBN (Christian Broadcasting Network), the nation's fourth-largest cable network. With their constant pleas for money, the televangelists repelled many Americans, but millions of others found their spiritual message reassuring.

The "electronic church" suffered severe jolts after 1987. Jim Bakker, who resigned after acknowledging a sexual encounter with a church secretary and subsequent payoffs to buy her silence, went to prison on fraud charges. The fiercely moralistic Jimmy Swaggart fell from grace when his repeated trysts with prostitutes became known. But the TV preachers' tribulations could not obscure the growing influence of evangelical religion. In *The Culture of Disbelief* (1993), Stephen J. Carter, an evangelical believer and a professor at Yale Law School, called on politicians, the media, and the legal profession to cease "trivializing" religion and to recognize its vital importance for millions of Americans. Confronting change on all sides, evangelicals found certitude in their faith. In the process, they profoundly influenced American life in the late twentieth century.

Years of Malaise: Post-Watergate Politics and Diplomacy

The social changes and public discontents of the 1970s helped to shape the era's political culture. With Richard Nixon's graceless exit from the White House, the nation seemed to lose spirit and direction. First Gerald Ford and then Jimmy Carter grappled with a tangle of domestic and foreign problems. As the Organization of Petroleum Exporting Countries (OPEC) forced up oil prices, the U.S. economy fell prey to inflation, unemployment, and recession. A foreboding sense of limits—both on economic growth and on the ability of government to solve problems—gripped many Americans. Globally, the period 1974–1980 brought mostly humiliations and setbacks, from the final withdrawal of U.S. personnel from Vietnam to the seizure of American citizens as hostages in Iran. What had once been the stark simplicities of a bipolar world blurred as complex problems arose in Asia, the Mideast, Latin America, and Africa—a region coming to be called the Third World.

The nation's spirit, sapped by Vietnam and Watergate and by widening social and cultural divisions, flagged further. Remote were the confident days of the 1950s and early 1960s, when Americans, enjoying a dynamic, expansive economy, had felt the masters of their fate, assured of their role as leaders of the "Free World" and equal to whatever challenges arose. Despite some notable achievements, post-Watergate America wallowed in a collective funk. A nation long convinced that it was exceptional, and immune to the historical forces that hedged in other societies, seemed diminished, enervated, and adrift, buffeted by forces beyond its control. By 1980 the accumulation of frustration and anger had generated powerful currents of political revolt.

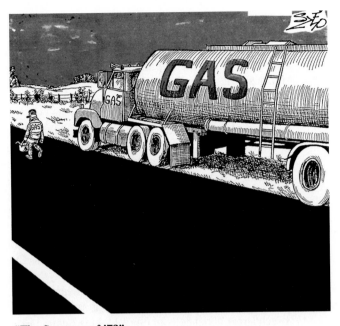

"The Summer of '73"
Most Americans found the economic crisis spawned by the Arab oil embargo no laughing matter.

The Caretaker Presidency of Gerald Ford

Gerald R. Ford took the presidential oath on August 9, 1974. A Michigan congressman who had served as minority leader before becoming vice president, Ford conveyed decency, if little evidence of brilliance. TV comedians parodied his verbal gaffes ("If Lincoln were alive today, he'd roll over in his grave"), but the visceral revulsion that many Americans felt toward Nixon never extended to his likable successor.

Ford's honeymoon period ended a month into his term, however, when he pardoned Richard Nixon for "any and all crimes" committed while in office—thus shielding the ex-president from prosecution for his Watergate role. Ford insisted that this action would help to heal the body politic, but many Americans reacted with outrage.

On domestic issues Ford proved more conservative than Nixon, vetoing a variety of environmental, social-welfare, and public-interest measures, among them a 1974 "freedom of information" bill granting citizens greater access to government records. The heavily Democratic Congress, however, overrode most of these vetoes.

Economic problems occupied much of Ford's attention. Beginning in 1973, oil prices shot up as a result of the Arab oil embargo (see Chapter 31) and stiff OPEC price hikes. The impact of these increases on the United States, which imported more than one-third of its oil, was devastating. The soaring cost of gasoline, home heating oil, and other petroleum-based products drastically worsened already serious inflation. Consumer prices rose by 12 percent in 1974 and 11 percent in 1975.

In October 1974 Ford unveiled a program of voluntary restraint dubbed "Whip Inflation Now" (WIN). Although he gamely wore a big "WIN" button in his lapel, prices continued to zoom. Ford also cut federal spending and endorsed the Federal Reserve Board's effort to cool the overheated economy by raising the discount rate.

A severe recession resulted. The economy stalled badly in 1974–1975. Unemployment approached 9 percent in 1974 and 11 percent in 1975. Tax receipts dropped as business stagnated, and the federal deficit, already a problem in the Vietnam War years, spurted to then record levels. Ford proposed a tax cut and other measures to stimulate consumer spending, but economic headaches plagued his administration to the end.

The oil crisis devastated the U.S. auto industry. As gas prices skyrocketed, Americans stopped buying Detroit's inefficient gas-guzzlers. GM, Ford, and Chrysler laid off more than 225,000 workers in 1974. Smaller, fuel-efficient imports increased their market share from 17 percent in 1970 to 33 percent in 1980.

On the diplomatic front, Ford retained Henry Kissinger as secretary of state and supported the Nixon-Kissinger initiatives aimed at improving relations with China and the Soviet Union (see Chapter 31). Meeting at Vladivostok, Siberia, in 1974, Ford and Soviet leader Leonid Brezhnev made progress toward a new arms-control treaty, SALT II, limiting each side to twenty-four hundred nuclear missiles. The following year in Helsinki, Finland, Ford and Brezhnev joined thirty-one European nations in adopting a set of accords formalizing Europe's post-1945 political boundaries and avowing respect for human rights and freedom of travel. The Helsinki Accords boosted the forces of change in the Soviet bloc and in retrospect may represent Ford's most important accomplishment.

The battered national morale suffered another blow in April 1975 when the South Vietnamese government fell, writing a bleak finis to two decades of U.S. effort to prevent just such an outcome. The nation's TV networks chronicled desperate helicopter evacuations from the roof of the U.S. embassy in Saigon (soon renamed Ho Chi Minh City) as North Vietnamese troops closed in. A few weeks later, when the new communist government of Cambodia seized a U.S. merchant ship, the *Mayagüez,* a frustrated Ford ordered a military rescue. This hasty show of force freed the thirty-nine *Mayagüez* crew members but cost the lives of forty-one U.S. servicemen.

As the nation entered the election year 1976—also the bicentennial of the Declaration of Independence—Americans found little cause for cheer and reasons aplenty to repudiate the party in power.

The Outsider as Insider: President Jimmy Carter

Gerald Ford won the Republican nomination in 1976 despite a strong challenge from the former governor of California, Ronald Reagan. In a large field of Democratic hopefuls, the candidacy of Jimmy Carter, a wealthy Georgia peanut grower who had served as governor of his home state but remained unknown nationally, initially aroused scant attention. But Carter swept the primaries in early 1976 by stressing themes that appealed to post-Watergate America. He made a virtue of his status as an outsider to Washington, pledged never to lie to the American people, and freely avowed his religious faith as a "born-again" Christian.

Winning the nomination handily, Carter chose as his running mate Senator Walter Mondale, a liberal Democrat from Minnesota. Democratic campaigners attacked the Ford administration's high inflation and unemployment rates. But Carter's early lead in the polls eroded as voters sensed a lack of clarity in his program and reacted against some of his mannerisms, including a toothy grin that seemed to flash on and off like a neon sign.

But Carter hung on to win by a narrow margin: 49.9 percent of the popular vote to Ford's 47.9. His electoral-college plurality was 297 to 240. (Less than 54 percent of those eligible had bothered to vote at all—a gauge of post-Watergate apathy.) The vote broke sharply along class lines: the well-to-do went for Ford; the disadvantaged, overwhelmingly for Carter. The Georgian swept the South and received 90 percent of the black vote.

The Election of 1976

Candidates	Parties	Electoral Vote	Popular Vote	Percentage of Popular Vote
JIMMY CARTER	Democratic	297	40,827,394	49.9
Gerald R. Ford	Republican	240	39,145,977	47.9

As chief executive, Carter rejected the trappings of what some in Nixon's day had labeled the imperial presidency. On inauguration day, with his wife and daughter, he walked from the Capitol to the White House. In an echo of Franklin D. Roosevelt's radio chats, he delivered some of his television speeches wearing a casual sweater and seated in an easy chair by a fireplace.

But populist symbolism could not ensure a successful presidency. Carter entered the White House without a clear political philosophy, and he never overcame this liability. Liberals and conservatives both claimed him; no one knew where he stood. Intensely private, Carter relied on a tight circle of young staff members from Georgia and avoided socializing with politicians. "Carter couldn't get the Pledge of Allegiance through Congress," groused one legislator. An intelligent, disciplined man who had worked as an engineer in the nuclear-submarine program after graduating from the U.S. Naval Academy, Carter focused well on specific problems. But he lacked a larger political vision, or at least the capacity to convey such a vision.

Carter fought the recession during his first year with a tax cut and public-works programs. Thanks in part to these efforts, the unemployment rate dropped to around 5 percent by late 1978. But this activist strategy did not extend to social-welfare measures involving federal spending, for which he showed little sympathy.

Putting his logical skills to good use, Carter introduced notable administrative reforms in the civil service and the executive branch of government. But his poor relations with Congress often frustrated even these efforts. His attempts to promote a national health-insurance program, overhaul the welfare system, and reform the loophole-ridden income-tax laws had little success. Responding to major social movements, however, he did appoint a number of women and members of minority groups to federal judgeships.

Carter's foreign-affairs achievements outshone his domestic record, but here, too, the negatives ultimately outweighed the positives. As a candidate he had urged increased attention to human-rights violations around the globe, and his secretary of state, Cyrus Vance, worked to combat abuses in Chile, Argentina, Ethiopia, South Africa, and other nations. Human-rights problems in countries considered critical to U.S. security, such as South Korea and the Philippines, were treated more gingerly.

Carter also tried to adapt U.S. foreign policy to a world no longer dominated by the superpowers. He sought better relations, for example, with the new black nations of Africa. As one State Department official summed up the administration's view: "It is not a sign of weakness to recognize that we alone cannot dictate events elsewhere. It is rather a sign of maturity in a complex world."

Carter, like Ford, also pursued initiatives launched by his predecessors. Since 1964, when anti-American riots had rocked Panama, successive administrations in Washington had been negotiating a more equitable treaty relationship between the two nations. The Carter administration completed negotiations on two treaties transferring the Panama Canal and the Canal Zone to the Panamanians by 1999. Although these agreements amply protected U.S. security interests, conservatives attacked them as proof of America's post-Vietnam loss of nerve. Why should the United States give up the Panama Canal, harrumphed a California senator; "we stole it fair and square." But in a rare congressional success, Carter won Senate ratification of the treaties in 1977 by a vote of 68–32, 1 more than the two-thirds required.

The strengthening of ties with China accelerated after China's long-time leader Mao Zedong (Mao Tsetung) died in 1976 and his successor, Deng Xiaoping, expressed interest in closer links with the United States. Carter restored full diplomatic relations with the People's Republic of China on January 1, 1979, thus

A Step Toward Peace in the Middle East
In 1979 President Anwar el-Sadat of Egypt (left), President Carter, and Prime Minister Menachem Begin of Israel signed the Camp David Accords.

opening the door to scientific, cultural, academic, and commercial exchanges.

Toward the Soviet Union Carter showed both conciliation and toughness, with toughness eventually winning out. In a June 1979 meeting in Vienna, Carter and Leonid Brezhnev signed the SALT II agreement, which Carter submitted to the Senate for ratification. It ran into trouble from advocates of a strong military, however, who charged that it favored the Soviets.

The fatal blow to SALT II came in January 1980 when the Soviet Union invaded Afghanistan, its neighbor to the south. The reasons for the invasion were complex, but in the United States many viewed it as proof of Moscow's expansionist designs on the Middle East. In this unfavorable political environment, Carter not only withdrew the SALT II agreement from the Senate but adopted a series of anti-Soviet measures, including a boycott of the 1980 Summer Olympics in Moscow. Carter's hard-line Soviet policy reflected the influence of his national security adviser, Zbigniew Brzezinski, a Polish-born political scientist who viewed détente with suspicion and advocated a tough stance toward Moscow. Owing in part to Brzezinski's influence, the administration's human-rights pronouncements focused increasingly on the Soviet Union.

The Middle East: Peace Accords and Hostages

Jimmy Carter reaped both his proudest achievement and his bitterest setback in the Middle East. Despite Kissinger's efforts, a state of war still prevailed between Israel and Egypt. When Egyptian leader Anwar el-Sadat surprised the world by flying to Israel in November 1977 to negotiate with Israeli prime minister Menachem Begin, Carter saw an opening. In September 1978, at Carter's invitation, Sadat and Begin met at Camp David, the presidential retreat in Maryland, where they hammered out the "framework" of a peace treaty. Further bargaining followed, but on March 26, 1979, the two leaders signed a formal peace treaty at the White House.

At the heart of the Camp David Accords lay a timetable for a gradual transition to autonomy for the West Bank and Gaza Strip Palestinians. Only after such autonomy was established would negotiations on the territories' final status begin. But events soon dashed Carter's hopes for a comprehensive Middle Eastern settlement. Prime Minister Begin announced that the Camp David Accords would not bar Israel from continuing to build Jewish settlements in the occupied

Hanging Jimmy Carter in Effigy in Tehran
Under Ayatollah Khomeini, anti-American demonstrations became a feature of Iranian public life.

territories. The other Arab states rejected the accords and shunned Egypt, and in 1981 Islamic fundamentalists assassinated Sadat, in part because he had dared to negotiate with Israel. (His successor, Hosni Mubarak, continued Sadat's policies, and in 1982 Israel completed its withdrawal from Sinai.) Tension among Israel, the Palestinians, and hard-line Arab "rejectionists" led by Syria remained electric. Limited though it was, Camp David nevertheless constituted the high point of Carter's presidency.

A fresh Middle Eastern crisis erupted in 1979. For years, Iran had been ruled by a U.S. ally, the shah Mohammed Reza Pahlavi, who had been restored to power with CIA help in 1953 and erected a repressive regime that tortured and intimidated its opponents. Resistance was led by the spiritual head of Iran's Shiite Islamic population, Ayatollah Ruhollah Khomeini, who rallied opposition forces from his exile in Paris. In January 1979, as the Shiite revolution peaked, the shah fled Iran. Khomeini, returning in triumph, imposed strict Islamic rule and preached hatred of the United States.

In early November Carter admitted the shah to the United States for cancer treatment. Shortly after, militant Iranian students stormed the U.S. embassy in Tehran and seized more than fifty American hostages. Thus began the Iranian hostage crisis, a 444-day ordeal that traumatized Americans and nearly paralyzed the Carter administration. TV images from Tehran of blindfolded hostages, anti-American mobs, and embassy occupiers using U.S. flags as garbage bags rubbed American nerves raw. A rescue attempt in April 1980 failed as an American helicopter and transport plane collided in the Iranian desert, killing eight U.S. servicemen. Secretary of State Vance, who had opposed the high-risk rescue effort, resigned.

To Carter's chagrin, the hostage crisis persisted through the 1980 presidential campaign. Not until inauguration day, January 20, 1981, did the Iranian authorities at last release the hostages, allowing Carter's successor, Ronald Reagan, to greet them as they returned.

A Sea of Troubles as Carter's Term Ends

Inflation, already a problem, assumed horrendous proportions as Carter's term wore on. Prices increased by more than 13 percent in both 1979 and 1980. As before, the primary blame lay with staggering energy costs. The decade's second oil crisis hit in 1979. As OPEC boosted oil prices to more than $30 a barrel, Americans accustomed to paying 30¢ for a gallon of gasoline saw prices edging toward $1 a gallon. As long lines formed at gas stations, tempers flared. An array of energy-related costs fed the runaway inflation. In 1979 alone, U.S. consumers paid $16.4 billion in added costs related to the oil-price increases. Like Ford, Carter relied on voluntarism to curb the inflationary spiral. His Council on Wage and Price Stability exhorted workers and manufacturers to hold the line. But repeated oil-price hikes stymied his efforts.

As the Federal Reserve Board pushed the discount rate higher, bank interest rates reached an unheard-of 20 percent by 1980. With mortgages and business loans prohibitively expensive, economic activity remained in the doldrums, producing "stagflation"—a dismal combination of business stagnation and price inflation. As the government borrowed money to make up for slumping tax revenues, the upward pressure on interest rates increased.

Pondering the oil crisis, Carter drew a larger lesson: the nation's wasteful approach to dwindling fossil-fuel resources must give way to a new ethic of conservation. Carter recognized that two key factors underlying a generation of U.S. economic growth—cheap, unlimited energy and the lack of foreign competition—could no longer be counted on. Americans, he concluded, must learn to survive in a "zero-sum society" that could no longer anticipate endless future expansion. Appointing himself the bearer of this bad news, he tried to formulate policies reflecting a philosophy of restraint.

Congress in 1975 had set fuel-efficiency standards for automobiles and established a national speed limit of fifty-five miles per hour, but Carter sought to do more. As early as 1977, he created the Department of Energy and proposed various taxes on oil and gasoline consumption, tax credits for conservation measures, and research on alternative-energy resources. A considerably watered-down energy bill emerged from Congress in 1978.

As with Herbert Hoover earlier, Americans turned against the remote figure in the White House. When Carter's approval rating dropped to 26 percent in the summer of 1979 (lower than Nixon's at the depths of Watergate), the president retreated to Camp David for a period of reflection and consultation and then delivered a television address that seemed to shift the blame to the American people, in whom he discerned a collective "crisis of confidence." A major cabinet reshuffle followed, but the whole exercise deepened suspicions that Carter himself was a large part of the problem. Rising frustration over the Iranian hostage crisis deepened Carter's unpopularity. By mid-1980 his approval rating had sunk to an appalling 23 percent.

The Democrats glumly renominated Jimmy Carter in 1980. But with double-digit inflation, 20 percent interest rates, an 8 percent unemployment rate, and the hostage crisis, Carter had scant hope of reelection.

Despite his single star-crossed term in office, Carter remains a fascinating political figure. His sudden emergence in 1976 vividly illustrated how, in the TV era, a relative unknown could bypass party power brokers and organized interest groups and gain a national following almost overnight. Emerging at a moment when Americans longed to see integrity and competence restored to the presidency, he seemed at first to fill the bill precisely. Keenly analytical, he identified many issues that would dominate the national agenda in future years: energy policy; tax, welfare, and health-care reform; the need to redefine America's world role. But he lacked the political skills that might have inspired the nation to confront those problems productively. By the end of his term, a victim both of his own flaws and of forces largely beyond his control, Carter was lonely and discredited. A notable postpresidential career devoted to humanitarian service and the resolution of international conflicts helped to restore Carter's reputation, but when he left office in January 1981, few were sorry to see him go.

THE REAGAN REVOLUTION

In 1980 voters turned to a presidential candidate who promised to break with the recent past: Ronald Reagan. Reagan's unabashed patriotism appealed to a nation still traumatized by Vietnam. He promised to reverse the "tax and spend" policies that many saw as one cause of the nation's economic woes. His attacks on the liberal ideology of the New Deal, the Fair Deal, and the Great Society resonated with millions of middle-class and blue-collar Americans.

As president, Reagan revived national pride and confidence. His economic policies at first caused a sharp recession but eventually brought down inflation and triggered a consumer buying spree and a surge of speculative investment. But these same policies laid the groundwork for serious economic difficulties after his departure.

Détente, already ebbing by the end of Carter's term, faltered in the early 1980s as Reagan revived the belligerent rhetoric of the early Cold War, raised the stakes in the arms competition with the Soviets, and supplied weapons and money to anticommunist forces in Latin America. But even Reagan, the quintessential Cold Warrior, found himself enmeshed in foreign problems that did not readily fit into his bipolar, highly ideological world view.

Background of the Revolution

Several economic, ideological, and social trends contributed to Reagan's appeal. First, voters were angry and frightened by the prospect of chronic stagflation, and Carter's orthodox economic policies offered little hope for change. Reagan promoted a seemingly painless panacea: he would propose a dramatic tax cut, and the resulting stimulus to the economy would boost federal tax revenues so that the budget could be balanced, reducing inflationary pressures. His Republican rival George Bush ridiculed this plan as "voodoo economics," but it impressed many voters as an idea worth trying. Moreover, Reagan's tributes to self-help and private enterprise exerted great appeal despite the New Deal–Great Society ideology of government activism. Simultaneously, decades of Cold War rhetoric had imprinted deeply on the American consciousness a determination to remain ahead of the Soviets militarily and in general to play a forceful world role. Carter struck many voters as vacillating in his dealings with Moscow and unwilling to stand up firmly for U.S. interests. Reagan's uncomplicated patriotism, his calls for strengthening the military, and his eloquent assertions of the United States' continued greatness acted as a balm to a wounded national psyche.

Reagan also embraced the ideology of the so-called New Right as it had evolved in the 1970s: a cultural conservatism stressing social and moral issues. The social turmoil and sexual revolution of the 1960s; the women's movement; the rising rates of abortion and divorce; the more open expression of homosexuality; the pervasiveness of pornography, sex and violence in the mass media; and "secular humanism" in school textbooks—all gravely upset millions of Americans, who responded with a call for a restoration of morality and "traditional values." Jerry Falwell's Moral Majority was only one of many groups eager to translate such concerns into political action.

Population shifts in the seventies also played a role in Reagan's success. Whereas New York City, Chicago,

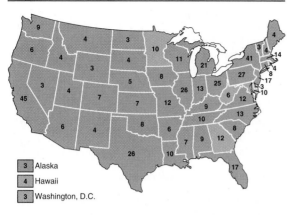

	3	Alaska
	4	Hawaii
	3	Washington, D.C.

		Electoral Vote	Popular Vote	Percentage of Popular Vote
Republican Ronald Reagan		489	43,899,248	50.8
Democratic Jimmy Carter		49	35,481,435	41.0
Independent John B. Anderson	–	–	5,719,437	6.6
Minor parties	–	–	1,395,558	1.6

The Election of 1980

Detroit, and other cities of the Northeast and upper Midwest lost population during the decade, Texas, California, Florida, Arizona, and other Sun Belt states rapidly gained. These states represented regions that historically had been both conservative politically and suspicious of Washington. In 1978 Californians passed Proposition 13, a referendum calling for sharp cuts in state taxes. Elsewhere in the West, ranchers and developers organized the so-called Sagebrush Rebellion to demand a return of federal lands to state control.

Ronald Reagan, a skillful actor and seasoned public speaker with a likable manner and ready smile, combined these themes and concerns into a potent and appealing message. Belying his sixty-nine years, he conveyed a youthful zest and jauntiness. At a time of deepening national malaise, he confidently offered the kind of assured leadership for which the nation longed. Time would reveal quite a gap between substance and image in Reagan's program, but in 1980 a majority of voters found his appeal irresistible.

The Man Behind the Movement

Reagan grew up in Dixon, Illinois, the son of an alcoholic father and a pious mother active in the Disciples of Christ church. After graduating from Eureka College near Peoria, he worked as a sports announcer in Des Moines before setting out for Hollywood in 1937. His fifty-four films enjoyed only moderate success, but after 1954 he made a name for himself as a corporate spokesman for the General Electric Company. A New Dealer in the 1930s, Reagan had moved to the right in the 1950s. He won national visibility in 1964 with a TV speech for presidential candidate Barry Goldwater in which he eloquently praised American individualism and the free-enterprise system.

Recognizing Reagan's flair for politics, a group of California millionaires engineered his election as governor in 1966. In Sacramento he continued to popularize conservative ideas while proving himself capable of compromise. Reagan nearly won the Republican presidential nomination in 1976, and in 1980 he had little trouble disposing of his principal opponent, former CIA director George Bush, whom he then chose as his running mate.

Like his one-time political hero Franklin Roosevelt, Reagan promised the American people a new deal.

Ronald Reagan, Outdoorsman
Despite photo opportunities like this, President Reagan gave little support to the environmental cause.

But unlike the New Deal of the 1930s, Reagan's version offered diminished government intervention, reduced taxes and spending, and an unleashing of the free-enterprise system. Internationally, Reagan called for a restoration of U.S. leadership and pride.

Hammering at the question "Are you better off now than you were four years ago?" Reagan garnered almost 51 percent of the popular vote to Carter's 41 percent. An independent candidate, liberal Republican congressman John Anderson, collected most of the balance. In the Senate races Republicans gained eleven seats, and with them, for the first time since 1955, a majority. These Senate victories revealed the power of conservative political-action groups (PACs), which used computerized mass mailings focusing on emotional issues like abortion and gun control to defeat specifically targeted liberal Democrats. (PACs were not the exclusive tool of conservatives; organizations of all ideological stripes used them with great effectiveness.)

Reaping the benefits of a Republican southern strategy dating to Richard Nixon's day, Reagan carried every southern state except Carter's own Georgia as well as every state west of the Mississippi except Minnesota and Hawaii. Over half the nation's blue-collar workers voted Republican. Of the political alliance forged by Roosevelt in the 1930s, only black voters remained firmly Democratic.

Reagan's term began auspiciously as the Iranian hostages boarded planes for home. With this trauma past, the nation sized up its new leader. Few had a clear notion of his program beyond a rhetorical commitment to patriotism, military strength, the free market, and traditional values, but Reagan soon gave concrete substance to these generalities.

Reaganomics

The new president's economic program, called Reaganomics by the media, boiled down to the belief that American capitalism, if freed from the burden of heavy taxes and government regulation, would surge to new heights of productivity. Reagan's first budget message proposed a five-year, $750 billion tax cut built around a 30 percent reduction in federal income taxes over three years. Trimming down this proposal slightly, Congress in May 1981 voted a 25 percent income-tax cut: 5 percent in 1981 and 10 percent in 1982 and 1983. Middle-class and working-class Americans, who had already organized grass roots "tax revolts" from Massachusetts to California, generally applauded.

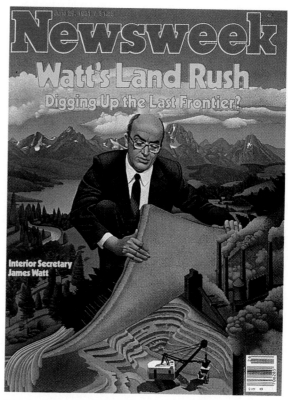

The Sagebrush Rebellion
As secretary of the interior (1981–1983), James Watt of Wyoming championed the movement to open public lands in the West to commercial development—the so-called Sagebrush Rebellion.

To make up for the lost revenues, Reagan proposed massive spending reductions in such programs as school lunches, student loans, job training, and urban mass transit. Congress went along to some extent, slashing more than $40 billion from domestic spending in 1981 (less than Reagan had requested). Conservative Democrats, called boll weevils because many of them hailed from the South, joined Republicans in voting these cuts. Journalists harked back to FDR's "Hundred Days" of 1933 to find a comparable time when government had shifted gears so dramatically. Many economists warned that the tax cut, even with reduced spending, would produce huge federal deficits, but Reagan continued to insist that his program of lower tax rates would stimulate business growth and thereby push up total tax revenues.

Reagan's appointees to key agencies implemented another component of Reaganomics: drastic cutbacks in federal regulation of business. As Reagan

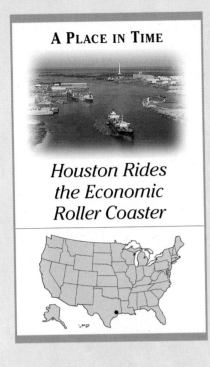

Houston Rides the Economic Roller Coaster

The ups and downs of oil prices in the 1970s and 1980s took Houston, Texas, on a wild economic roller-coaster ride—a ride that reversed the experience of the rest of the country. While most of America reeled under skyrocketing energy costs, Houston's economy boomed. But when oil prices fell, stimulating recovery elsewhere, Houston suffered terribly.

Houston was no stranger to boom-and-bust cycles. Founded in 1837 on Buffalo Bayou and named for Texas hero Sam Houston, the town flourished in the nineteenth century as a railroad center. But its history changed forever on January 10, 1901, when prospector Anthony Lucas brought in the world's mightiest oil well, Spindletop, in nearby Beaumont. For nine days the gusher roared on before it could even be capped. As more oil was discovered, new corporations emerged, including Gulf and Texaco, and Houston became the nerve center of the new industry. A channel to Galveston Bay in the Gulf of Mexico, completed in 1914, made the city a deep-water port. Hard times came in the early 1930s, but World War II brought renewed growth.

The city's most spectacular boom came in the 1970s, when OPEC pushed world oil prices to unheard-of levels. Though Middle Eastern nations dominated OPEC, its pricing policies benefited U.S. petroleum companies as well, by increasing the value of *all* oil. The profits of the five biggest U.S. oil firms quadrupled in the seventies, reaching $14.5 billion by the end of the decade. Exxon's first-quarter profits in 1980 approached $2 billion, the largest ever recorded by any company in history.

Basking in the glow of prosperity, Houston outdistanced its long-time rival Dallas. The city boasted more than 1.5 million inhabitants by 1980, a 26 percent increase in a decade, making it the fifth largest in the United States. Home to 440,000 blacks and 280,000 Hispanics, the city reflected the Southwest's ethnic diversity. With Nuevo Laredo, Mexico, only 275 miles away, a steady stream of Mexican immigrants arrived to work in the city's thriving industries. In Houston's vibrant Mexican-American district, Magnolia, a low-lying area near the docks once noted for its lush magnolia trees, family and community networks assured a stable cul-

Houston's Dramatic Skyline at Dusk

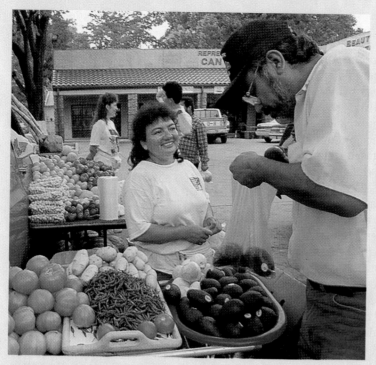

Estella Ortiz's Fruit Stand, Magnolia Park

Quinceañera Celebration
A Mexican-American Magnolia Park resident prepares for this traditional rite-of-passage celebration for fifteen-year-old girls of Spanish background. The event often is considered more important than a wedding.

ture and provided avenues of economic opportunity.

Unfettered by zoning laws, sprawling Houston led the nation in new construction in the 1970s. Skyscrapers formed a stunning downtown skyline. "If business takes you [to Houston]," advised *Forbes* magazine, "be prepared to work over lunch, dinner, and even breakfast."

Not all was work, however. In the exclusive suburb of River Oaks, where the oil barons' mansions stood in opulent array, the country club charged $35,000 for a membership—and had a long waiting list. Seeking to shed its rowdy boom-town image, Houston poured money into the symphony, the ballet, the opera, and a new cultural center. The nearby Johnson Space Center contributed to the city's prosperity as well, but, above all, that prosperity rested on the sticky black substance that Houstonians persisted in calling "awl."

Plummeting oil prices in the 1980s, however, battered the domestic oil industry. Three hundred thousand oil workers lost their jobs from 1982 to 1987. In Houston tens of thousands of jobs vanished. High-salaried young geologists took work as hotel bellhops, while unemployed drill

hands had to poach game to feed their children. Houston's half-finished skyscrapers stood dark and silent; a multimillion-dollar suburban development, Heritage Plaza, looked like a ghost town. The exclusive Brae Burn Country Club slashed its membership fee from fifteen thousand dollars to eight thousand dollars.

By 1986 the Texas unemployment rate stood at 9 percent, two full percentage points above the national rate, and in Houston it was even higher. A national financial crisis in the savings and loan industry hit Houston hard, as several of the city's giant S&Ls, having extended millions of dollars in high-risk loans in the boom years, collapsed.

But even in hard times, Houstonians took a kind of perverse Texas pride in the magnitude of the disaster that had befallen them. Declared chamber of commerce president Gerald Griffin, "There is no other place on this planet hit as hard as Houston."

As the 1980s ended and oil prices turned up once again, evidence of recovery began to appear. Houston's unemployment rate dropped, and fewer "For Sale" signs stood on front lawns. But hard times

persisted for Houston's Mexican-Americans. The recession of the early 1990s hit the Magnolia district hard. Houston's Hispanic population grew by 72 percent in the 1980s, owing to continued immigration and a high birthrate, but opportunities shrank. Jobs in industry declined; the new jobs that did open up were either high-tech or service-sector positions requiring advanced training or menial, low-paying, unskilled work. "It's been hard to keep our dignity sometimes, but we still have our hopes," said Maria Jimenez, the wife of a Houston janitor, in 1992. At Magnolia's Austin High School, nearly 75 percent of students dropped out before graduating. Drug use and teenage pregnancy rose, and the conflict between traditional ways and "Anglo" culture caused severe family stress. On Magnolia's streets, Taco Bells and Pizza Huts stood side by side with dark *cantinas* where old men gathered to drink and remember and with *yerberías* offering traditional herbal remedies and potions. The problems of Magnolia, Houston's fastest-growing district, were typical of those faced by the nation's 14 million Mexican-Americans in the harsh economic climate of the early 1990s.

put it, "Government is not the solution to our problems: government *is* the problem." Deregulation had begun under Carter, but in the Reagan years it was vastly expanded and extended into new areas such as banking, the savings-and-loan industry, transportation, and communications. The head of the Federal Communications Commission hacked away at federal rules governing the broadcast industry. The secretary of transportation cut back many of the regulations Congress had passed in the 1970s to reduce air pollution and improve efficiency and safety in cars and trucks. Secretary of the Interior James Watt, a leader in the Sagebrush Rebellion, opened federal wilderness areas, forest lands, and coastal waters to developers. But although the Reagan administration's attack on "big government" profoundly affected certain federal functions, particularly in the regulatory realm, it had little overall effect. The steady growth of the federal budget and of the federal bureaucracy, under way throughout the twentieth century, continued in the 1980s.

While implementing Reaganomics, the administration also had to cope with the immediate problem of inflation. The Federal Reserve Board led the charge, pushing the discount rate ever higher. This harsh medicine, coupled with a sharp drop in world oil prices, did its job. Inflation fell to around 4 percent in 1983 and held steady thereafter. (Although overall inflation dropped, health-care costs skyrocketed, setting the stage for a major political issue of the 1990s.)

But the high interest rates necessary to curb inflation again spawned a severe recession. This downturn, which began late in 1981, exceeded even those of the Ford and Carter years. By late 1982 one of ten American workers was jobless. As funding for social programs dried up, the plight of the poor worsened. Blacks and Hispanics of the inner cities suffered severely.

The Reagan recession had another component as well: falling exports. As foreign investors bought dollars in order to earn high American interest rates, the dollar rose in value vis-à-vis foreign currencies. This in turn made U.S. goods more expensive abroad. The decline in exports—coupled with big increases in imports of TVs, stereos, and automobiles from Japan and other countries—propelled the U.S. trade deficit (the gap between exports and imports) from $31 billion in 1981 to $111 billion in 1984. The trade gap with Japan alone widened to a staggering $33 billion in 1984.

The nation's industrial heartland reeled under the triple blow of slumping exports, foreign competition,

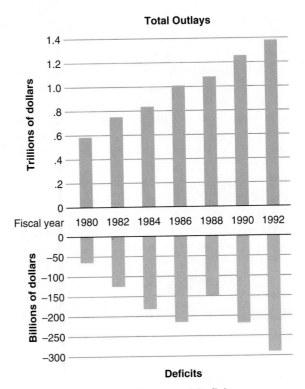

Federal Budget Expenditures and Deficits, Fiscal Years 1980–1992

After soaring to more than $200 billion in 1986, the runaway federal deficit declined somewhat, then surged again in 1990. Driven by mushrooming health-care costs, it could surpass $400 billion by 2002.

SOURCES: U.S. Department of the Treasury; Office of Management and Budget; *New York Times*, 1 March 1992, p. 1; *Statistical Abstract of the United States, 1993* (Washington, D.C., 1993), p. 328.

and technological obsolescence. The aging steel mills, machinery and automobile companies, and other smokestack industries of the Midwest and Great Lakes region laid off hordes of workers; some plants closed. From 1979 through 1983, 11.5 million American workers lost jobs as a result of plant closings or slack work.

The drop in exports hurt farmers as well. Wheat exports fell 38 percent from 1980 to 1985, and corn exports by 49 percent. In heartbreaking foreclosure sales evocative of the 1930s, Americans lost farms that their families had run for generations.

Soaring federal deficits added to the economic muddle. Reagan's tax cuts reduced federal revenues without immediately bringing about the predicted business boom, while increases in military appropriations more than offset domestic spending cuts. With the economy in crisis, the government awash in red ink, and critics denouncing him as callous toward the poor, Reagan offered assurances that his program would soon take effect. Still, in 1982–1983, he accepted a reduced rate of military spending, a slowing of funding cuts in social programs, emergency job programs to relieve unemployment, and various tax increases euphemistically called "revenue-enhancement measures."

Despite a stock-market upturn, the public remained deeply worried about the economy throughout 1982, and in the congressional elections that fall, the Democrats gained twenty-six House seats. Like other recent administrations, the Reagan presidency appeared headed for failure. But early in 1983 an economic rebound became obvious. Encouraged by tax cuts, by a long-awaited decline in interest rates, and, above all, by evidence that inflation had been tamed at last, consumers went on a buying binge. The stock market surged, unemployment dropped, and the gross national product shot up by nearly 10 percent.

The Great Bull Market

The revival of consumer spending unleashed a wave of stock-market speculation reminiscent of the 1920s. The great bull market began on August 12, 1982, when the Dow Jones average stood at 777, and it lasted for five years. Entrepreneurs like Donald Trump, a Manhattan real-estate tycoon, and Ivan Boesky, who seemed to have a magic touch when it came to stock transactions, became celebrities. E. F. Hutton and other brokerage firms advertised heavily to lure people into the market. The 1984 autobiography of Lee Iacocca, who had rescued Chrysler Corporation from near bankruptcy (thanks to a federal loan guarantee program in 1980), became a best-seller. Reports of corporate mergers filled newspaper business columns. Chevron bought Gulf for $13 billion in 1984; GE acquired RCA (and its NBC subsidiary) for $6.3 billion in 1986. Through it all, the stock market roared on. Banks and savings-and-loan companies, newly deregulated and flush with the deposits of investors seeking high interest rates, lent billions to developers planning shopping malls, luxury apartments, retirement villages, research parks, and high-rise office buildings.

Meanwhile, however, the downside of the Wall Street feeding frenzy had surfaced. In 1985 E. F. Hutton officials pled guilty to manipulating funds in ways that defrauded hundreds of banks. Ivan Boesky went to prison after his 1986 conviction for insider trading (profiting through advance knowledge of planned corporate actions). Then on October 19, 1987, "Black Monday," came a stock market crash. In the largest single-day drop in stock market history, the Dow plunged 508 points as one-fifth of the paper value of the nation's stocks evaporated. Newspapers recalled the 1929 crash that had ushered in the Great Depression. The 1987 collapse had no such long-term effects, thanks to prompt government action to ease credit, but it did remind a new generation of investors that stocks can go down as well as up.

Even during the great bull market, serious economic problems remained. The trade gap widened; the deficit surpassed $200 billion in 1986; and millions of farmers, inner-city poor, and displaced industrial workers did not share in the renewed prosperity. But—just in time to brighten Reagan's reelection prospects—the overall economic picture looked more hopeful than it had in years.

Reagan Confronts the "Evil Empire"

Unsettledness at the State Department, anti-Soviet pronouncements from the White House, and setbacks in the Middle East characterized U.S. foreign policy in the early eighties. Reagan's first secretary of state, Alexander Haig, alienated many administration leaders, including outspoken U.N. ambassador Jeane Kirkpatrick, with his flamboyant, self-promoting style. In 1982 Reagan replaced Haig with George Shultz, who had served as secretary of labor and the treasury under Richard Nixon.

Détente had already started to fade in the late 1970s, but the level of anti-Soviet rhetoric intensified during Reagan's first term. Addressing a convention of Protestant evangelicals, the president blasted the Soviet Union as an "evil empire" and "the focus of evil in the modern world." Anti-Soviet fury exploded in September 1983, when the Soviets shot down a Korean passenger plane that had strayed into Soviet airspace, killing all 269 aboard. Moscow claimed that the plane had been spying, but Reagan, as well as most Americans, rejected this explanation.

The administration's initial obsession with the Soviets influenced its policy toward El Salvador and Nicaragua, two poor Central American nations caught up in revolutionary turmoil. The Reagan White House steadfastly supported the ruling Salvadoran military junta in its ruthless suppression of a leftist insurgency

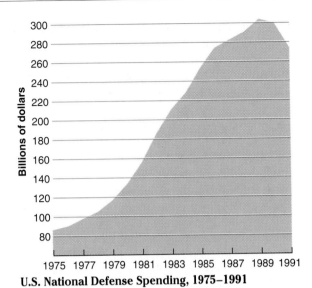

U.S. National Defense Spending, 1975–1991

SOURCE: *Statistical Abstract of the United States, 1993* (Washington D.C., 1993), p. 328.

backed by Cuba and Nicaragua. A moderate, José Napoleón Duarte, won the 1984 presidential election with U.S. support, but the killing of suspected leftists went on.

In Nicaragua the Carter administration had at first extended financial assistance to the Sandinista revolutionaries who overthrew dictator Anastasio Somoza in 1979. But Reagan quickly reversed this policy, claiming that the leftist Sandinistas were turning Nicaragua into a procommunist state like Castro's Cuba and a staging area for Soviet expansion. Under director William Casey, the CIA in 1982 organized and financed a ten-thousand-man anti-Sandinista guerrilla army, called the contras, based in neighboring Honduras and Costa Rica. The contras, many with links to the deposed Somoza regime, conducted raids, planted mines, and carried out sabotage inside Nicaragua.

Fearing another Vietnam, Americans grew alarmed as details of this U.S.–run "covert" war leaked out. Congress voted a yearlong halt in U.S. military aid to the contras in December 1982 and imposed a two-year ban in October 1984. But Reagan's enthusiasm for the contras, whom he lauded as "the moral equivalent of our Founding Fathers," held steady. Secret contra aid, funded from private right-wing sources and foreign governments, and organized within the White House itself by Lieutenant Colonel Oliver North of the National Security Council staff and others, continued despite congressional prohibitions. A 1988 truce between the Sandinistas and the contras, arranged by President

Oscar Arias Sánchez of Costa Rica and other Central American leaders, won only grudging backing by Reagan, who still hoped for a contra victory.

Reagan's militarization of American foreign policy fell heavily on the tiny West Indian island of Grenada, where a 1983 coup had replaced the leftist government with an even more radical, and unpopular, regime. On October 25, 1983, two thousand U.S. Marines invaded Grenada, overthrew the offending government, and installed one friendly to the United States. Democrats voiced sharp criticism, but the administration claimed that U.S. strategic interests in the region justified the action. Most Grenadians, as well as other West Indian governments, expressed their approval.

Tragedy and Frustration in the Middle East

Its concerns focused elsewhere, the Reagan administration at first paid relatively less attention to the Middle East. Hoping to stem the spread of radical Islamic fundamentalism, the United States generally tilted toward Saddam Hussein's Iraq in its long, bloody war with Iran, although Washington also tried covertly to court perceived "moderates" in Iran.* Meanwhile, the administration viewed the smoldering conflicts among Israel, the faction-ridden PLO, and Syria through the prism of Soviet-Western rivalries.

In August 1981 Israel and the PLO concluded a cease-fire, but the PLO continued building up its forces and carved out a sanctuary in southern Lebanon from which it could threaten Israel and defend itself against Syrian- and Lebanese-government hostility. In June 1982, when the Abu Nidal group—extremists within the PLO who opposed its leader, Yasir Arafat, and who advocated an all-out struggle against Israel—critically wounded the Israeli ambassador to Great Britain, Prime Minister Begin took action against all Palestinian guerrillas. Israeli troops invaded Lebanon to destroy the PLO and, by so doing, to break the West Bank Palestinians' loyalty to it. The invasion defeated the PLO militarily and forced its leaders to evacuate Lebanon. It also intensified the civil war among various Lebanese Christian and Muslim factions. A Christian militia took the opportunity to massacre Palestinians in a refugee camp near Beirut.

Initially sympathetic to the Israeli intervention, the Reagan administration found itself drawn into the tur-

---

*These efforts drew the Reagan administration into a morass of secret arms-for-hostages deals with Iran, which were exposed in 1985 as the Iran-contra scandal unfolded. See p. 1053.

moil. After the Beirut massacre, two thousand American marines entered Lebanon as part of a multinational peacekeeping force. But the Muslim militias saw the Americans as favoring Israel and the Christian side and began firing on the marines, in turn provoking U.S. naval shelling of the Lebanese coast. The tragic climax came in October 1983, when a Shiite Muslim crashed an explosive-laden truck into a poorly guarded barracks, killing 239 marines. Reagan had not made clear how the deployment served U.S. interests, and the disaster underscored the failure of his Lebanese policy. By early 1984 he withdrew the marines, leaving Lebanon to its warring factions and to the Syrians.

Disappointment also dogged Reagan's attempt to promote a wider Middle Eastern settlement. By announcing the "Reagan Plan" in September 1982, the president tried to use the Lebanese crisis to jump-start Arab-Israeli peace talks along the lines envisioned by the Camp David Accords, and he stressed the need to address the Palestinian question. Over the next four years the administration tried to bring Arafat and Jor-

dan's King Hussein together for a "Jordanian solution" to the West Bank question. But this effort was scuttled by Syrian opposition to being excluded from the process, by the PLO's reluctance to come under a Jordanian "umbrella," and by Israel's security fears.

Military Buildup and Antinuclear Protest

Convinced that the United States had grown dangerously weak militarily since Vietnam, Reagan launched the most massive military expansion in American peacetime history. The Pentagon's budget swelled from $171 billion in 1981 to more than $300 billion by 1985.

With the decline and eventual collapse of the Soviet Union in the later 1980s and early 1990s (see Chapter 33), Reagan's supporters would claim that Moscow's efforts to match Reagan's costly military buildup had dealt the final blow to an already weak Soviet economy. Others, however, saw these developments as arising primarily from the internal dynamic of events

The Nuclear-Freeze Campaign, 1982
A movement to halt the nuclear arms race arose in the early Reagan years. These New York City marchers on June 12, 1982, were part of a rally that drew eight hundred thousand demonstrators to Central Park.

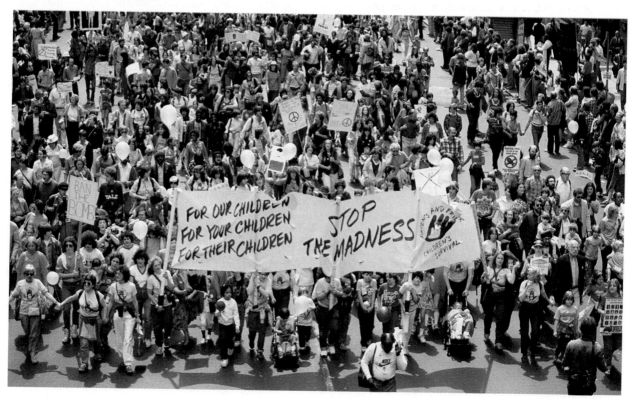

in the U.S.S.R. itself, and relatively unaffected by Reagan's policies.

The Reagan military buildup included a strong nuclear-weapons thrust. To head the Arms Control and Disarmament Agency, the president appointed a critic of arms control. Secretary of State Haig spoke of the possible utility of "nuclear warning shots" in a conventional war, and other administration officials mused about the "winnability" of nuclear war. With the support of its NATO allies (despite protests in England, West Germany, and elsewhere), the administration in 1983 deployed 572 cruise and Pershing II missiles in Western Europe in fulfillment of a 1979 NATO decision, counterbalancing Soviet missiles in Eastern Europe.

The Federal Emergency Management Agency promulgated a civil-defense plan whereby city residents would flee to remote "host communities" when nuclear war threatened. A Defense Department official argued that backyard shelters would save millions of people in a nuclear conflagration. "If there are enough shovels to go around," he asserted, "everybody's going to make it."

Such talk, coupled with the military buildup of the early 1980s, the faltering arms-control process, and Reagan's anti-Soviet rhetoric sparked a grass-roots reaction as millions of Americans perceived a growing threat of nuclear war. This response—the first sustained popular challenge to Reaganism—took the form of a campaign for a verifiable superpower freeze on the manufacture and deployment of nuclear weapons. Early in 1982 several New England town meetings adopted freeze resolutions; that summer, eight hundred thousand antinuclear protesters—the largest political demonstration in American history—rallied in New York's Central Park; in the fall elections, freeze resolutions passed in nine states, including California and Wisconsin.

Responding to the antinuclear clamor, the administration in June 1982 proposed the total removal of medium-range nuclear missiles from Europe and began talks with the Soviets in Geneva on strategic-arms reductions. Seeking to neutralize the freeze movement, Reagan in March 1983 proposed the Strategic Defense Initiative (SDI), a vast system of space-based lasers and other high-tech defenses against nuclear missiles. Quickly nicknamed Star Wars after the 1977 movie, SDI drew upon Americans' deep faith in technology. The Pentagon launched an SDI research program, but critics pointed out not only the project's prohibitive cost and technical implausibility but also the

likelihood that it would provoke another escalation in the nuclear-arms race.

Reagan Reelected

As the 1984 election neared, liberal Democrats and many independents found much to criticize in the Reagan presidency, including runaway military spending, worsening Cold War tensions, massive budget deficits, a cavernous foreign-trade gap, cuts in social programs, and the assault on the government's well-established regulatory function. To critics, jingoism abroad and selfishness at home summed up the meaning of Reaganism.

But many Americans applauded Reagan's attacks on big government and his get-tough policy toward the Soviets. Rhetoric aside, the administration had some solid achievements to its credit, notably an end to rampant inflation and a booming economy. Reagan's personal popularity, moreover, remained high. Some dubbed him the Teflon president—nothing seemed to stick to him. Even his liberal opponents found occasional reason to cheer, as in 1981, when he nominated Sandra Day O'Connor as the first woman justice on the U.S. Supreme Court. And Americans admired Reagan's courageous, even jaunty response when a ricocheting bullet fired by a mentally disturbed young man struck him in the chest as he left a Washington hotel on March 30, 1981. Rushed to the hospital, Reagan walked in under his own steam, quipping to the physicians, "Please tell me you're all Republicans."*

By 1984 many citizens believed that Reagan had delivered on his promise to revitalize the free-enterprise system, rebuild U.S. military might, and make the nation again "stand tall" in the world.

The 1984 Republican convention, carefully staged for television, accented themes of patriotism, prosperity, and the personality of Ronald Reagan. The Democratic hopefuls included Gary Hart, a former Colorado senator, whom some accused of mimicking John F. Kennedy's mannerisms, and Jesse Jackson, a black Chicago minister and one-time civil-rights associate of Martin Luther King, Jr., who proposed a "rainbow coalition" of African-Americans, Hispanics, displaced workers, and other outsiders in Reagan's America.

But former vice president Walter Mondale won the nomination the old-fashioned way, securing en-

---

*The attack permanently disabled Reagan's press secretary, James Brady. With his wife, Sarah, Brady later became a leader in the campaign for toughened gun-control laws.

The Election of 1984

Candidates	Parties	Electoral Vote	Popular Vote	Percentage of Popular Vote
RONALD REAGAN	Republican	525	54,451,521	58.8
Walter Mondale	Democratic	13	37,565,334	40.5

dorsements from labor unions, party bigwigs, and various interest groups. His campaign's high point came when he announced his vice-presidential choice, New York congresswoman Geraldine Ferraro, the first woman to run on a major-party presidential ticket.

Riding the tide of prosperity, Reagan and Bush won 59 percent of the popular vote and carried every state but Mondale's Minnesota and the District of Columbia. Once again, many traditionally Democratic voters, especially blue-collar workers, defected to Reagan. The "gender gap" that had emerged in earlier polls measuring Reagan's support largely dissolved in 1984. Despite Ferraro's presence on the Democratic ticket, a higher percentage of women voted Republican in 1984 than in 1980.

The appeal of Reagan's ideology and his mastery of television, combined with a booming economy, had won him a solid second-term victory. Though the Democrats retained control of Congress and remained strong at the state and local level, the Republicans' post-1968 dominance of presidential politics—interrupted only by Jimmy Carter's single term—continued.

CONCLUSION

More than at any time since the 1950s, the United States of the later 1970s and 1980s seemed almost two societies with little in common and barely aware of each other's existence. Millions of upwardly mobile young Americans abandoned the social activism of the 1960s to concentrate on personal goals, whether economic or psychological. Whereas the billions of dollars amassed by the likes of Donald Trump and Ivan Boesky remained a distant fantasy for the nation's yuppies, the materialistic obsessions so flaunted by these entrepreneurial overachievers merely intensified values far more widely shared.

The other America, as always, was the world of the poor, the minorities, and the recent immigrants, gathered predominantly in the inner cities. In decaying housing projects and urban streets that resembled battle zones, crime, drugs, and public-health hazards posed constant threats, and a failing educational system and inadequate public services had equally dire long-term implications. In sharp contrast to earlier political eras, from FDR's New Deal to Lyndon Johnson's Great Society, when the plight of the poor and the inequities of American life had gripped the nation's attention, the 1970s and 1980s saw little apparent concern among the middle and elite classes for the social problems festering outside their own charmed circles.

The collapse of the Nixon presidency shaped national politics through the rest of the 1970s as presidents Gerald Ford and Jimmy Carter tackled complex problems at home and abroad with little success. The year 1980 marked a defining moment in American politics: voters put in the White House a candidate pledged to radical and fundamental changes in the role of the government in American life. In retrospect, the "Reagan revolution" delivered far less than it promised, though in his first term Reagan's policies did put his personal stamp on American public life to a degree that invited comparison with Franklin Roosevelt's New Deal.

On the international front, Reagan's first-term militarism and rhetorical bellicosity helped ratchet Cold War animosities sharply upward and convinced many Americans that full-scale nuclear war was far from unthinkable. But in Reagan's second term, to the amazement of nearly everyone, profound seismic shifts rumbled across the Soviet Union, transforming the Cold War and altering the world power balance in ways that few would have imagined in 1984.

CHRONOLOGY

1963   Betty Friedan, *The Feminine Mystique.*

1966   Founding of National Organization for Women (NOW).

1969   Police raid on Stonewall Inn, Greenwich Village gay bar, sparks resistance.

1972   Equal Rights Amendment passed by Congress.

1973   Major rise in OPEC prices; Arab oil boycott.
Roe v. *Wade.*

1974   Richard Nixon resigns presidency; Gerald Ford sworn in.
Whip Inflation Now (WIN) program.
Indian Self-Determination Act.
Ford-Brezhnev meeting.

Ford takes oath of office.

1975   South Vietnamese government falls.
Mayagüez incident.

1976   Jimmy Carter elected president.

1977   Panama Canal treaties ratified.
Introduction of Apple II computer.

1978–1980 Double-digit inflation and soaring interest rates.

1979   Menachem Begin and Anwar el-Sadat sign peace treaty at White House.
Second round of OPEC price increases.
Accident at Three Mile Island nuclear plant.
Carter and Leonid Brezhnev sign SALT II agreement in Vienna.
Carter restores full diplomatic relations with the People's Republic of China.

1980   Carter withdraws SALT II agreement from Senate after Soviet invasion of Afghanistan.
Iran hostage crisis preoccupies nation.
Ronald Reagan elected president.

1981   Major cuts in taxes and domestic spending, coupled with large increases in military budget.

1981–1983 Severe recession (late 1981–early 1983).

1982   Equal Rights Amendment dies.
CIA organizes contra war against Nicaragua's Sandinista government.
800,000 rally in Central Park for nuclear-weapons freeze.
Stock-market boom begins.

1983   239 U.S. Marines die in Beirut terrorist attack.
U.S. invasion of Grenada.
U.S. deploys Pershing II and cruise missiles in Europe.
Reagan proposes Strategic Defense Initiative (Star Wars).
Soviets down Korean airliner, killing 269.

1984   Geraldine Ferraro chosen as vice presidential running mate on Democratic ticket.
Reagan defeats Walter Mondale in landslide.

Geraldine Ferraro

1986   Immigration Reform and Control Act.
Federal deficit rises to $221 billion.

FOR FURTHER READING

James L. Baughman, *The Republic of Mass Culture: Journalism, Filmmaking, and Broadcasting in America Since 1941* (1992). Thorough, readable survey of the mass media's expanding role in contemporary America.

Paul Boyer, ed., *Reagan as President* (1990). Contemporary speeches, articles, and editorials commenting on Reagan and his program, with an introduction by the editor.

Peter Carroll, *It Seemed Like Nothing Happened* (1983). A perceptive overview history of the 1970s.

Thomas Byrne Edsall with Mary D. Edsall, *Chain Reaction: The Impact of Race, Rights, and Taxes on American Politics* (1992). Insightful analysis of the social and economic sources of the rise of a conservative voting majority.

Haynes Johnson, *Sleepwalking Through History: America in the Reagan Years* (1991). A thoughtful account of American poli-

tics and culture in the 1980s by a seasoned *Washington Post* reporter.

Carl H. Nightingale, *On the Edge: A History of Poor Black Children and Their American Dreams* (1993). Moving presentation of the effect of inner-city poverty on its most vulnerable victims.

Gaddis Smith, *Morality, Reason, and Power* (1986). Evaluation of Jimmy Carter's foreign policy by an able diplomatic historian.

Garry Wills, *Reagan's America: Innocents at Home* (1987). A stimulating, wide-ranging work by a distinguished political writer.

Daniel Yankelovich, *New Rules: Search for Self-Fulfillment in a World Turned Upside Down* (1981). An assessment of the American mood on the basis of public-opinion interviews and surveys.

ADDITIONAL BIBLIOGRAPHY

The Ford and Carter Years

William C. Berman, *America's Right Turn: From Nixon to Bush* (1994); James Bill, *The Eagle and the Lion: . . . American-Iranian Relations* (1987); James Cannon, *Time and Chance: Gerald Ford's Appointment with History* (1993); Raymond L. Garthoff, *Détente and Confrontation: American-Soviet Relations from Nixon to Reagan* (1987); Steven B. Hunt, *The Energy Crisis* (1978); Burton I. Kaufman, *The Presidency of James Earl Carter, Jr.* (1993); David P. McCaffrey, *The Politics of Nuclear Power* (1991); Michael P. Malone and F. Ross Peterson, "Politics and Protests," in Clyde A. Milner II, et al., *Oxford History of the American West* (1994); George D. Moffett III, *The Limits of Victory: . . . The Panama Canal Treaties* (1983); Peter R. Odell, *Oil and World Power*, 5th ed. (1979); William B. Quandt, *Camp David* (1987); A. James Riechley, *Conservatives in an Age of Change* (1980); Barry Rubin, *Paved with Good Intentions* (1983) [relations with Iran]; David Schoenbaum, *The United States and the State of Israel* (1993); Lars Shoultz, *Human Rights and U.S. Policy Toward Latin America* (1981); Strobe Talbott, *Endgame* (1979) [SALT II].

The Reagan Presidency

Raymond Bonner, *Weakness and Deceit: U.S. Policy and El Salvador* (1984); William J. Broad, *Teller's War: The Top-Secret Story Behind the Star Wars Deception* (1992); Thomas Carothers, *In the Name of Democracy: U.S. Policy Toward Latin America in the Reagan Years* (1991); Robert Dallek, *Ronald Reagan: The Politics of Symbolism* (1984); Jack W. Germond and Jules Witcover, *Blue Smoke and Mirrors: How Reagan Won and Why Carter Lost the Election of 1980* (1981); David E. Kyvig, ed., *Reagan and the World* (1990); Jonathan Lash, *A Season of Spoils: The Story of the Reagan Administration's Attack on the Environment* (1984); Frances Fox Piven and Richard A. Cloward, *The New Class War: Reagan's Attack on the Welfare State and Its Consequences* (1982); Kirkpatrick Sale, *Power Shift: The Rise of the Southern Rim and Its Challenge to the Eastern Establishment* (1975); Michael Schaller, *Reckoning with Reagan: America and Its President in the 1980s* (1992); C. Brant Short, *Ronald Reagan and the Public Lands: America's Conservation Debate, 1979–1984* (1989); Charles D. Smith, *Palestine and the Arab-Israeli Conflict*, 2d ed. (1992); David A. Stockman, *The Triumph of Politics: How the Reagan Revolution Failed* (1986); Stephen Vaughn, *Ronald Reagan in Hollywood: Movies and Politics* (1994); Sidney Weintraub and Marvin Goodstein, eds., *Reaganomics in the Stagflation Economy* (1983).

Social and Cultural Trends Since 1970

Carl Abbott, *The New Urban America: Growth and Politics in the Sunbelt Cities* (1981); Ken Auletta, *The Underclass* (1981); Frank D. Bean et al., *Mexican and Central American Population and U.S. Immigration Policy* (1989); Michael A. Bernstein and David A. Adler, eds., *Understanding American Economic Decline* (1994); Albert Camarillo, "Latin Americans: Mexican Americans and Central Americans," in Mary Kupiec Cayton, Elliott J. Gorn, and Peter W. Williams, eds., *Encyclopedia of American Social History*, II (1993), 855–872; Bongyoun Choy, *Koreans in America* (1979); John Crewden, *The Tarnished Door: The New Immigrants and the Transformation of America* (1983); Roger Daniels, "Asian Americans," in Cayton, Gorn, and Williams, *Encyclopedia of American Social History*, II, 873–890; Douglas Glasgow, *The Black Underclass* (1980); Andrew Hacker, *Two Nations: Black and White, Separate, Hostile, Unequal* (1992); James D. Hunter, *Culture Wars: The Struggle to Define America* (1991); Christopher Lasch, *The Culture of Narcissism* (1978); Michael Moritz, *The Little Kingdom: The Private Story of Apple Computer* (1984); Edwin Shur, *The Awareness Trap: Self-Absorption Instead of Social Change* (1976); Carol B. Stack, *All Our Kin: Strategies for Survival in a Black Community* (1975); James B. Stewart, *Den of Thieves* (1991) [Wall Street trading scandals of the 1980s]; Vance Trimble, *Sam Walton: The Inside Story of America's Richest Man* (1990); Reed Ueda, *Postwar Immigrant America* (1994); Sam Walton, *Made in America* (1992); William Julius Wilson, *The Truly Disadvantaged: The Inner City, the Underclass, and Public Policy* (1987).

Women's Issues; Gay and Lesbian History; Sexuality

Barbara Hinkson Craig and David M. O'Brien, *Abortion and American Politics* (1993); Martin Duberman, *Stonewall* (1993); Sara Evans, *Personal Politics: The Roots of Women's Liberation in the Civil Rights Movement and the New Left* (1979); Elizabeth Fee and Daniel M. Fox, eds., *AIDS* (2 vols., 1988, 1992); Jo Freeman, *The Politics of Women's Liberation* (1979); David J. Garrow, *Liberty and Sexuality: The Right to Privacy and the Making of Roe v. Wade* (1994); Leigh W. Rutledge, *The Gay Decades: From Stonewall to the Present* (1992); Barry D. Schoub, *AIDS and HIV in Perspective* (1994); Suzanne Staggenborg, *The Pro-Choice Movement* (1991); Mark Thompson, ed., *Long Road to Freedom: . . . The Gay and Lesbian Movement* (1994); Winifred D. Wandersee, *On the Move: American Women in the 1970s* (1988).

Religion in Modern America

Paul Boyer, *When Time Shall Be No More: Prophecy Belief in Modern American Culture* (1992); Donald W. Dayton and Robert K. Johnston, eds., *The Variety of American Evangelicalism* (1991); Ethics and Public Policy Center, *No Longer Exiles: The Religious New Right in American Politics* (1993); George M. Marsden, *Understanding Fundamentalism and Evangelicalism* (1991); Mark Noll, *One Nation Under God? Christian Faith and Political Action in America* (1988); Garry Wills, *Under God: Religion and American Politics* (1990); John Woodridge, *The Evangelicals* (1975); Robert Wuthnow, *The Restructuring of American Religion: Society and Faith Since World War II* (1988).

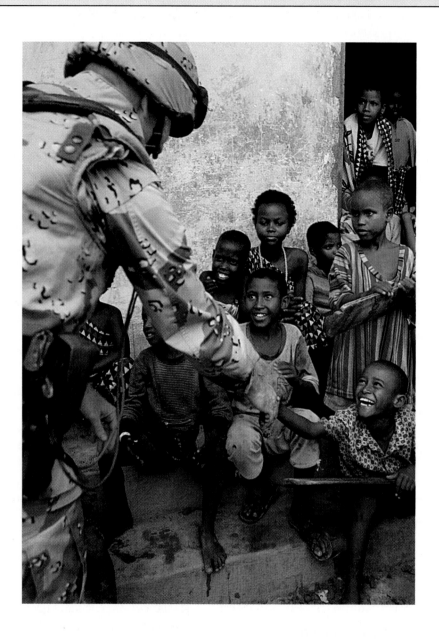

U.S. Marine with Somali Children
1992

BEYOND THE COLD WAR

It was a sunny morning in March 1991. At Langley Air Force Base in Virginia, thousands of people waited anxiously as six F-15 fighters flew overhead in close formation. Many hands gripped small U.S. flags. At last a giant C-141 transport plane touched down. As the first soldiers emerged, the crowd cheered. The mass scene soon broke up into intimate private dramas of clutching embraces and tearful reunions. The first GIs had come home from the war in the Persian Gulf. As more men and women returned daily all that spring, such scenes were repeated again and again across America.

For two months Operation Desert Storm, undertaken to drive the invading Iraqis from neighboring Kuwait, had mesmerized the nation. Initial fears had given way to euphoria as the war had proceeded better for the nations allied against Iraq than anyone had anticipated. Yellow ribbons decorated trees and front doors across the land. Desert Storm T-shirts and even golf balls bearing the likeness of Iraqi dictator Saddam Hussein sold briskly.

Now the Gulf War was over, and the nation welcomed home its heroes. Bull-necked General H. Norman Schwarzkopf, commander of the Persian Gulf force, was feted in an old-fashioned ticker-tape parade in New York City.

Like Woodrow Wilson in 1917, President George Bush defined the war as a moral crusade: "We went halfway around the world to do what is moral and just and right. . . . We're coming home now proud, confident, heads held high. . . . We are Americans."

The president also found a deeper psychological meaning of the war: "By God, we've kicked the Vietnam syndrome once and for all." Indeed, Vietnam was on many minds. Bush proclaimed that Desert Storm would help erase bitter memories of the failed effort in Southeast Asia. "It's Vietnam . . . as it should have been," commented one observer, *"Vietnam, The Movie: Part II*—and this time it comes out right."

A nation that had endured not only defeat in Vietnam but frustrations abroad, economic setbacks, and chronic domestic problems briefly indulged a burst of patriotism. Said one returning soldier, "I can't see how anybody, right now, could not feel proud to be an American." A Vietnam veteran made the point even more explicitly: "VCRs may be made in Japan and Mercedes [in Germany], but what's going on in the Middle East is undeniably made in the U.S.A. I think that's a source of pride we have not had since World War II."

A few Americans expressed sorrow that a war should unleash such an orgy of self-congratulation. The fighting, after all, had brought death to thousands of young men conscripted into Saddam's army, and suffering to Iraqi civilians, many of whom were victims of Saddam no less than the Kuwaitis. But reflections of this kind rarely intruded as the victory party rolled on. The Persian Gulf success seemed an appropriate coda to a still more seismic event—the end of the Cold War itself.

Of course, the euphoria did not last. Other concerns, other realities, soon soured the sweet tang of victory, especially as Saddam stubbornly clung to power. But for a fleeting moment, the United States again had seemed to occupy what Americans had understood to be its rightful place: front and center on the world stage, defender of righteousness and justice.

This vision would become increasingly difficult to sustain as the United States grappled with a new and unfamiliar post–Cold War world order. President Bush, who seemed to dither as recession battered the economy, lost his reelection bid in 1992. His successor, Democrat Bill Clinton, took office amid a wave of hope but soon struggled with image problems, policy disputes, and global complexities that cumulatively took a heavy toll. The "revolt against government" that had underlain Ronald Reagan's victory in 1980 continued into the 1990s.

Despite economic recovery and the end of the Cold War, the national mood remained sour and edgy. Battered by political setbacks and misjudgments, Clinton saw his popularity steadily erode. The 1994 midterm election brought a stunning repudiation of the Democrats. As the twentieth century drew to a close, America's course both domestically and internationally remained highly uncertain.

PROBLEMS AND OPPORTUNITIES IN REAGAN'S SECOND TERM

In his first term, Ronald Reagan had set the political agenda with his program of tax cuts, deregulation, and expanded military spending. In his second term, however, events began to overtake the Reagan White House. A growing budget deficit and trade gap raised alarm signals, and the long-running Iran-contra scandal erupted in 1986. But these developments were eclipsed as events in the Soviet Union promised a dramatic easing of Cold War tensions. With a historic trip to Moscow in 1988, Reagan gave his blessing to the new era of Soviet-American relations. Despite prob-

lems and scandals, Reagan left office in 1989 with high approval ratings, the first president since Dwight Eisenhower to complete two full terms.

Tax Reform, Budget Deficits, and Trade Gaps

On the domestic front, Reagan's second term brought some significant legislative achievements, including a new immigration law (see Chapter 32) and an administration-sponsored tax-reform law that made the system fairer by eliminating many deductions and establishing uniform rates for people at comparable income levels. The law also removed some 6 million low-income Americans from the income-tax rolls. Reagan also, as we shall see, played an important role in reshaping the Supreme Court in his own conservative image.

But sky-high federal deficits—the legacy of Reaganomics—remained a serious problem. The deficit gushed to over $200 billion in 1985 and 1986 and hovered at about $150 billion in 1987 and 1988. Gargantuan federal deficits, coupled with an enormous trade gap, which surged to more than $152 billion in 1986 and 1987, represented long-term economic problems bequeathed by Reagan to his successor.

Middle East Encore: Talks and Terrorism

In Reagan's second term, as in his first, the Middle East spelled trouble. In December 1987 the Intifada, a Palestinian uprising against Israeli occupation, began in Gaza and spread to the West Bank. In response, Secretary of State Shultz made yet one more effort at a settlement in 1988, in which he attempted to bring Jordan and the Palestinians into negotiations with Israel over an accelerated Palestinian autonomy plan. But the Israeli government, led by Prime Minister Yitzhak Shamir, rejected the "land for peace" formula and refused to negotiate with the Palestinians until the Intifada ended; and the Palestinians rejected Shultz's proposals as not going far enough toward creating a Palestinian state. Despite U.S. opposition, Israel continued to build Jewish settlements on the West Bank.

A deadly by-product of the conflict in the Middle East came in the later 1980s in the form of a rash of kidnappings, airplane hijackings, airport attacks, a cruise-ship seizure, and other terrorist acts linked to Palestinians and their backers, including Colonel Muammar el-Qaddafi, Libya's ruler. In April 1986, after a Libyan-directed bombing of a Berlin nightclub popular with

American GIs, Reagan ordered a U.S. bombing raid on five Libyan military sites. In the worst of the terrorist incidents, a Pan Am jet flying from London to New York in December 1988 crashed in Scotland, killing all 259 aboard, including a great many Americans. Authorities quickly established that a concealed bomb had sparked a midflight explosion. In 1991, the U.S. and British governments formally charged Libya with complicity in the Pan Am bombing, presumably in retaliation for the earlier U.S. raid on Libya. But Qaddafi denied the charges and refused to extradite the accused officials. Despite tightened airport security, terrorist groups remained difficult to combat.

The Mideast was also the spawning ground for a crisis that would rock the Reagan presidency to its core.

The Iran-Contra Scandal

On November 3, 1986, a Beirut newspaper reported that in 1985 the United States had shipped, via Israel, 508 antitank missiles to the vehemently anti-American government of Iran. Thus began the worst scandal of the Reagan administration. Admitting the sale, Reagan said that the aim had been to encourage "moderate elements" in Tehran and to secure the release of American hostages held in Lebanon by pro-Iranian radical groups. In February 1987 a presidentially appointed investigative panel placed heavy blame on the administration—particularly on Donald Regan, then chief of staff, who promptly resigned.

But more details soon spilled out, including the bizarre sidelight that national-security adviser Robert McFarlane had accompanied a second arms shipment to Tehran in May 1986, bringing with him, as a gift to the Ayatollah Khomeini, a Bible autographed by President Reagan. The most explosive revelation, however, was that Lieutenant Colonel Oliver North, a National Security Council aide, had diverted millions in profits from the Iran arms sales to pay for military assistance to the Nicaraguan contras (opponents of Nicaragua's Sandinista government) at a time when Congress had forbidden such aid. In November 1986, just before FBI investigators arrived, North and his secretary, as they later acknowledged, altered and deleted computer files of official memoranda and held a "shredding party" to destroy incriminating documents. North also implicated CIA director William Casey in illegalities, but Casey's death of a brain tumor in May 1987 thwarted this line of investigation.

Trying to Stanch a Flood
Despite White House efforts to defuse the crisis, the Iran-contra scandal preoccupied the nation by early 1987, when this cartoon appeared.

In the summer of 1987, a joint House-Senate committee chaired by Senator Daniel Inouye of Hawaii investigated the charges. The nation watched in fascination as "Ollie" North, resplendent in his bemedaled marine uniform, portrayed himself as a true patriot, and as former national security adviser John Poindexter testified that he had deliberately concealed the fund-diversion scheme from Reagan.

The Inouye committee found no evidence that Reagan had personal knowledge of illegalities, but roundly criticized the lax management style and disregard for the law that had fed the scandal. Meanwhile, early in 1988, a court-appointed special prosecutor, Lawrence Walsh, issued criminal indictments against Poindexter, North, and others. In 1989 a federal jury convicted North of obstructing a congressional inquiry, destroying and falsifying Security Council documents, and accepting an illegal gratuity. Federal judge Gerhard Gesell reversed this conviction in 1991 on the technical grounds that certain incriminating testimony against North had been given under a promise of immunity.* Although less damaging than Watergate, the Iran-contra scandal dogged the Reagan administration's final years as a shocking abuse of executive power.

---

*Proclaiming himself vindicated, North continued his lucrative public-speaking career, published a book claiming that Reagan had been fully aware of his activities, and in 1994 narrowly lost a U.S. Senate race in Virginia.

More Scandals and Embarrassments

Other revelations plagued Reagan's second term, including allegations of bribery and conspiracy in military-procurement contracts involving some of the Pentagon's largest suppliers. But ironically, Reagan's closest associates caused some of his worst problems. His old friend Attorney General Edwin Meese became a target of investigation for allegedly using his influence to promote ventures in which he had a financial interest, including a billion-dollar oil-pipeline project in Iraq. Meese resigned in July 1988, declaring himself "vindicated" when a special prosecutor decided not to press criminal charges. In *For the Record* (1988), former chief of staff Donald Regan, still smarting over his forced resignation and his feuds with the president's wife, Nancy, portrayed Reagan as little more than an automaton: "Every moment of every public appearance was scheduled, every word was scripted, every place where Reagan was expected to stand was chalked with toe marks." In 1989 came revelations that former interior secretary James Watt and other prominent Republicans had been paid hundreds of thousands of dollars for interceding with the Department of Housing and Urban Development on behalf of developers seeking federal subsidies.

Reagan's popularity seemed unaffected by all this dirty linen. His admirers did not really look to him for administrative brilliance or conventional political skills; the sources of his popularity lay far deeper. Drawing on his own conservative convictions as well as on his years of training as an actor, Reagan possessed an uncanny ability to articulate the beliefs, aspirations, and fears of millions of Americans. Moreover, Reagan benefited from an unanticipated turn of events abroad that would end his presidency on a note of triumph.

Reagan's Mission to Moscow

A dramatic warming of Soviet-American relations began early in Reagan's second term. Meeting at Geneva in 1985 and Reykjavík, Iceland, in 1986, Reagan and Soviet leader Mikhail Gorbachev explored the arms-control issues that the two nations had been negotiating since 1983. Beset by a mounting economic crisis at home, Gorbachev eagerly pursued an easing of superpower tensions to provide a breathing space for domestic reform.

In 1987 negotiators reached agreement on a treaty providing for the removal of twenty-five hundred

President Reagan Visits Red Square
As the Cold War crumbled, President Reagan flew to Moscow in 1988 to sign a nuclear-arms reduction treaty with Soviet premier Mikhail Gorbachev.

American and Soviet missiles from Europe. This Intermediate Nuclear Forces (INF) Treaty, signed by Gorbachev and Reagan in Washington that December, for the first time eliminated an entire class of *existing* nuclear weapons rather than merely limiting the deployment of *future* weapons as SALT I had done. In another first, the INF Treaty provided for on-site inspection to verify compliance.

This agreement, in turn, led to Reagan's historic visit to Moscow in May 1988. Not only did the two leaders sign the INF Treaty (which meanwhile had won Senate ratification), but they established a cordial personal relationship. Asked about his 1983 "evil empire" remark, Reagan responded amiably that he had been talking about an earlier era, not Gorbachev's U.S.S.R.

Milestones in Nuclear-Arms Control

Year	Event	Provisions
1963	Limited Test Ban Treaty	Prohibits atmospheric, underwater, and outer-space nuclear testing.
1967	Outer Space Treaty	Prohibits weapons of mass destruction and arms testing in space.
1968	Non-Proliferation Treaty	Promotes peaceful international uses of nuclear energy; aims to stop the global proliferation of nuclear weaponry.
1972	Strategic Arms Limitation Treaty (SALT I)	Limits for five years U.S. and Soviet deployment of strategic weapons systems.
	Anti-Ballistic Missile (ABM) Treaty	Restricts U.S. and Soviet testing and deployment of defensive systems.
1974	Threshold Test Ban Treaty	Establishes limits on size of underground tests.
1979	Strategic Arms Limitation Treaty (SALT II) (Unratified)	Limits strategic launch vehicles and delivery craft and restricts the development of new missiles. (The treaty was never ratified, but the United States and the Soviet Union observed its terms.)
1982	Strategic Arms Reduction (START) Talks	Seeks 50 percent reduction in U.S. and Soviet strategic nuclear weapons.
1988	Intermediate-Range Nuclear Forces (INF) Treaty	Commits the United States and the Soviet Union to withdraw their intermediate-range nuclear missiles from Eastern and Western Europe and to destroy them.
1991	START Treaty	Provides for a 25 percent cut in U.S. and Soviet strategic nuclear weapons.

Resolving one sticky point in U.S.–Soviet relations, Gorbachev announced Soviet withdrawal from Afghanistan after eight years of warfare.

Détente, derailed in the late 1970s, was not only back on track but barreling ahead. Reagan's role in this process stirred applause that must have warmed the old actor's heart. Many who remained sharply critical of Reagan's domestic policies praised the INF Treaty and the Moscow summit. The vigorous Cold Warrior, denouncer of earlier arms-control treaties, and champion of massive military spending seemed destined to be remembered for his part in bettering relations with the Soviets and reducing the risk of global war. Such are the paradoxes of politics and the endless fascination of history.

The Election of 1988

As 1988 approached, Reagan's would-be successors emerged. On the GOP side, Vice President George Bush pulled away from his strongest rival, Kansas senator Robert Dole, and soon had the nomination sewn up.

A large group of contenders battled for the Democratic nomination. The field eventually narrowed to two: Jesse Jackson and Massachusetts governor Michael Dukakis. Jackson, preaching concern for the poor and urging a full-scale war on drugs, ran well in

the primaries, winning a larger margin of white votes than in 1984. But Dukakis victories in major primary states like New York and California proved decisive. As his running mate, Dukakis chose Texas senator Lloyd Bentsen.

On the Republican side, Bush surprised everyone by selecting a little-known young senator from Indiana, J. Danforth Quayle III, the son of a wealthy newspaper publisher, as his vice-presidential choice. The press soon revealed that in 1969, when his family's newspapers had strongly supported the Vietnam War, Quayle had pulled strings to evade service in Vietnam. But the issue faded; indeed, it may have helped Quayle by casting him as a victim of media persecution.

Accepting the nomination, Bush called for a "kinder, gentler America" and pledged: "Read my lips: no new taxes." In the campaign he stressed Reagan's achievements while distancing himself from the Iran-contra scandal and other embarrassments. Emphasizing peace and prosperity, he pointed to better Soviet relations, low inflation, and the 14 million new jobs created during the eighties—an achievement unmatched by any other industrial nation.

A TV commercial aired by Bush supporters, playing on racist stereotypes, featured a black man who committed rape and murder after his release by Dukakis under a Massachusetts prisoner-furlough

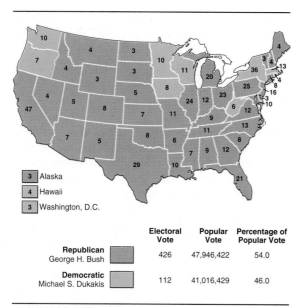

	Electoral Vote	Popular Vote	Percentage of Popular Vote
Republican George H. Bush	426	47,946,422	54.0
Democratic Michael S. Dukakis	112	41,016,429	46.0

The Election of 1988

ten states plus the District of Columbia. Bush's electoral college plurality was a lopsided 426–112. The Democrats, however, retained control of both houses of Congress and most state legislatures.

After Richard Nixon's political disgrace, the caretaker presidency of Gerald Ford, and the problem-ridden tenure of Jimmy Carter, Ronald Reagan had served two full terms and helped restore national pride. Internationally, he had the good fortune to hold office as the Cold War thawed and the Soviet menace faded.

Domestically, Reagan chalked up a mixed record. Inflation was tamed, and after 1983 the economy showed a bloom of health. But the administration largely ignored serious social issues and structural weaknesses in the economy. Despite Reagan's popularity, his image faded quickly. From the perspective of the mid-1990s, the Reagan years seemed more an interlude of nostalgia and drift than of positive achievement—a time when individual gain took precedence over the public sphere.

program. Bush assailed Dukakis's veto of a bill requiring Massachusetts schoolchildren to recite the Pledge of Allegiance, even though the Supreme Court had long ago declared such laws unconstitutional. In response, Dukakis emphasized his accomplishments as governor. "This election is not about ideology, it's about competence," he insisted. He hammered at the failures of the "Swiss-cheese" Reagan economy and wooed the "Reagan Democrats" who had deserted the party in 1980 and 1984.

But Dukakis seemed edgy and defensive, and his dismissal of ideology made it difficult for him to define his vision of America. He denounced Bush's "soft-on-crime" charges as "garbage," but the garbage stuck. Even Dukakis's own backers wearied of his stock phrases and his repeated boasts of his managerial skills.

Both candidates avoided serious issues in favor of TV-oriented "photo opportunities" and "sound bites." Bush visited flag factories and military plants. Dukakis tried to prove his toughness on defense by posing in a tank. Editorial writers grumbled about the "junk-food" campaign, but fleeting visual images, catchy phrases, and twenty-second spots on the evening news had seemingly become the essence of presidential politics.

On November 8, Bush carried forty states and garnered 54 percent of the vote. Dukakis prevailed in only

THE BUSH YEARS: RESOLVE ABROAD, DRIFT AT HOME

George Bush was a patrician in politics. The son of a powerful Connecticut senator, he had attended Yale and fought in World War II before entering the Texas oil business. He had served in Congress, lost a Senate race, directed the CIA, and sought the Republican presidential nomination in 1980 before being tapped as Ronald Reagan's running mate that year.

As president, Bush compiled a curiously uneven record. Internationally, his administration responded positively to upheavals in the Soviet Union, reacted decisively when Iraq invaded Kuwait, took positive steps in Latin America, and worked to ease Israeli-Palestinian tensions. But on domestic issues, Bush often appeared asleep at the switch, substituting platitudes for policy. In retrospect, the Bush interlude seems primarily a postscript to the Reagan era.

The Cold War Ends

Amid the changing of the guard in Washington, the collapse of Soviet power proceeded with breathtaking rapidity. When Gorbachev refused to send troops to prop

End of the Berlin Wall, November 1989
As East German border guards watch passively, a West Berliner pounds away at the hated symbol of a divided city.

up unpopular Marxist governments in Eastern Europe, they quickly fell. New, democratic, noncommunist governments sprang up behind what Winston Churchill had long ago called the Iron Curtain. In November 1989, the Berlin Wall, a grim symbol of Cold War hostilities, was opened. The Soviets announced the withdrawal of all troops from East Germany by 1994. With Germany reunited for the first time since 1945, the Bonn government took on the massive task of incorporating the poverty-stricken East Germans into the West German economy. The Baltic republics—Estonia, Latvia, and Lithuania—forcibly annexed by the Soviet Union on the eve of World War II, declared independence. As Moscow's power faltered, calls for autonomy resounded within the other Soviet republics as well.

The Cold War was over. In August 1991 President Bush and Mikhail Gorbachev signed a treaty in Moscow reducing their strategic nuclear arsenals by 25 percent. The nuclear-arms race, the Cold War's evil twin, seemed over as well. Secretary of Defense Dick Cheney proposed a 25 percent reduction in U.S. military forces over five years. With the Soviet-sponsored Warsaw Pact ended, NATO announced plans for a 50 percent troop reduction.

As the Soviet Communist party's centralized control collapsed, the nation's economy sank ever deeper into crisis. Soviet reformers called for a market economy on the Western capitalist model, but the difficulties of such a transition were formidable, and the opposition still a threat. On August 21, 1991, hard-line Communist party leaders in Moscow tried to overthrow Gorbachev. But, the Russian people, rallied by Boris Yeltsin, president of the Russian Republic, defied the plotters and their tanks. Hundreds of thousands of Muscovites protectively surrounded the Russian parliament. Within days the coup leaders were under arrest. Gorbachev briefly returned to power, but Yeltsin increasingly assumed the dominant role.

The coup failure accelerated the demise of the Soviet Communist party and of the Soviet Union itself. Exuberant crowds toppled statues of Lenin and other communist leaders across the Sovet Union. Leningrad reverted to its tsarist name, St. Petersburg. As the various Soviet republics rushed to independence, Mikhail Gorbachev was overwhelmed by forces he himself had unleashed. Gorbachev had risen to power hoping to reform the political and economic system, but he also wished to preserve the Soviet Union and manage the reform process through a democratized Communist party. In these latter goals he failed. The coup attempt stripped the last shred of legitimacy from the Soviet Communist party. And later that year most of the Soviet republics, led by Russia's forceful Yeltsin, proclaimed the end of the U.S.S.R. and formed a new, vaguely defined Commonwealth of Independent States. Bowing to the inevitable, Gorbachev resigned.

Dealing with these complexities was Secretary of State James Baker, a longtime Bush ally who had served as chief of staff and treasury secretary under Reagan. Bush and Baker proceeded cautiously as the Soviet empire disintegrated. America's influence was limited, in any event, as long-suppressed forces of nationalism and ethnicity burst forth in Eastern Europe and in the former Soviet Union itself.

As the apparatus of central planning collapsed and prices mounted, economic chaos and social upheaval threatened, especially in the Russian Republic.

Chronic civil war, 1992 – .

Soviet war in Afghanistan, 1979 – 1989.

Armenian-Azerbaijan conflict, 1990 – .

Persian Gulf crisis, 1990.

Iran-Iraq War, 1980 – 1988.

Gulf War, 1991

Russia intervenes in Chechnya, 1994 – .

Gorbachev assumes power, 1985; Moscow coup fails, and U.S.S.R. dissolved, 1991.

Palestinian Intifada begins, 1987.

Rise of Solidarity, 1980.

Fall of Berlin Wall, 1989; Germany unified, 1990.

Yugoslavia dissolves in civil war, 1991 – 1992.

Communist regimes overthrown since 1989

Soviet Union, dissolved in 1991 and replaced by Commonwealth of Independent States (Estonia, Latvia, and Lithuania did not join the Commonwealth)

Yugoslavia, dissolved in civil war, 1991-1992

500 Miles
500 Kilometers

The Breakup of Yugoslavia

Some Western economists and political leaders argued for massive Western aid, but others opposed it, contending that a flood of outside relief could swamp Russia's transition to a free-market economy and slow the nation's shift of resources from the military to the civilian sector. Early in 1992 the Bush administration proposed a program of some $35 billion in aid to Russia by the United States, other nations, and various international monetary agencies.

One issue of vital concern was the future of the Soviet arsenal of 27,000 nuclear weapons, based not only in Russia but in newly independent Ukraine, Belarus, and Kazakhstan. Baker worked strenuously to assure the security and orderly dismantling of these weapons and to prevent the flow of nuclear-weapons technology and know-how to Third World nations eager to develop their own nuclear capability. As strategic talks with Yeltsin and other leaders went forward, Bush announced further major reductions in the U.S. nuclear arsenal.

In some respects, the Cold War's end created a climate more favorable to the resolution of regional conflicts. For decades the superpowers had given military, economic, and diplomatic aid to their allies, client states, and rebel forces throughout the Third World. In a globe no longer dominated by the Cold War face-off, the prospect for resolving local disputes brightened.

Evidence for this change appeared in Latin America, the scene of bloody civil wars in the Cold War era. In Nicaragua, Bush abandoned Reagan's policy of financing the contra's war against the leftist Sandinista government. Observed Secretary of State Baker, "I think we all have to admit that the policy basically failed." Instead, Bush and Congress worked out a program aimed at reintegrating the contras into Nicaraguan life and politics. In a 1989 accord, the Sandinistas and the contras agreed on national elections in 1990, greater press freedom, the release of political prisoners, and an end to the war. In the elections the victory went to newspaper publisher Violetta Chamorro, leader of a multiparty anti-Sandinista coalition.

(left) **Eastern Europe and the Mideast: Regions in Turmoil**

The collapse of the Soviet Union brought both hope and upheaval in its wake. In Yugoslavia and parts of the former Soviet sphere, the end of the old order unleashed bitter fighting. The Mideast, too, has seen deadly conflict in recent years, from guerrilla skirmishes to full-scale war.

In tiny El Salvador, where the United States had spent more than $1 billion to keep leftist guerrillas from power, the right-wing government and the opposition leaders signed a peace treaty early in 1992. The treaty provided for expansive reforms and ended a twelve-year civil war that had left 75,000 dead.

With the waning of the Cold War, the underlying sources of Latin America's social turbulence came more sharply into focus. Monumental problems linked to poverty, ignorance, and economic exploitation still plagued the region, and open guerrilla war continued in Peru. The flow of cocaine and heroin to U.S. cities from South America and Central America posed a serious problem. Indeed, in December 1989 concern over the drug traffic led to a U.S. invasion of Panama to capture the nation's strongman ruler, General Manuel Noriega. Formerly on the CIA payroll, Noriega had become wholly corrupt, accepting bribes to permit drugs to pass uninterruptedly through Panama on their way north. Jailed in Miami in 1991, Noriega was convicted of drug trafficking and given a life prison term.

America's relations with the Philippines, a former colony and longtime U.S. ally, shifted as well. Resistance to the corrupt government of President Ferdinand Marcos intensified after the 1983 assassination of the popular opposition leader Benigno Aquino. After a fraud-ridden election in 1986, Aquino's widow, Corazon, rejected Marcos's victory assertions and proclaimed herself president. While Marcos went into exile in Hawaii, the United States recognized Aquino's government. In 1991, over Aquino's opposition, the Philippines legislature ended the long-term agreement by which the United States had maintained two naval bases in the islands. In the post–Cold War climate of eased world tensions, the Bush administration accepted this decision and withdrew from the bases.

South Africa had emerged as a focus of debate in Reagan's second term; Anglican bishop Desmond Tutu, a leader of South Africa's blacks, had rallied American support for his people's cause against the government's policy of racial segregation, called apartheid. In 1986, overriding a Reagan veto, Congress had imposed stiff economic sanctions against South Africa, including a ban on South African products and a prohibition on U.S. business investments in South Africa. These sanctions, with the coercive measures of other nations, brought change to South Africa. In 1990 President F. W. de Klerk released black leader Nelson Mandela after a twenty-seven-year imprisonment and opened negotiations with Mandela's African National

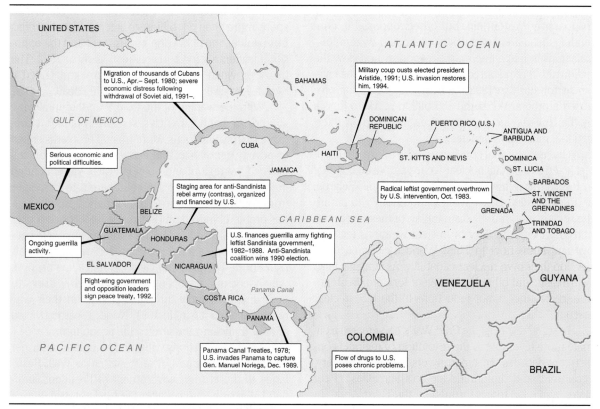

UNITED STATES

ATLANTIC OCEAN

Migration of thousands of Cubans to U.S., Apr.– Sept. 1980; severe economic distress following withdrawal of Soviet aid, 1991–.

BAHAMAS

Military coup ousts elected president Aristide, 1991; U.S. invasion restores him, 1994.

GULF OF MEXICO

DOMINICAN REPUBLIC

PUERTO RICO (U.S.)

ANTIGUA AND BARBUDA

CUBA

Serious economic and political difficulties.

HAITI

ST. KITTS AND NEVIS

DOMINICA

ST. LUCIA

JAMAICA

MEXICO

Staging area for anti-Sandinista rebel army (contras), organized and financed by U.S.

BELIZE

Radical leftist government overthrown by U.S. intervention, Oct. 1983.

BARBADOS

ST. VINCENT AND THE GRENADINES

GRENADA

GUATEMALA

CARIBBEAN SEA

HONDURAS

TRINIDAD AND TOBAGO

Ongoing guerrilla activity.

U.S. finances guerrilla army fighting leftist Sandinista government, 1982–1988. Anti-Sandinista coalition wins 1990 election.

EL SALVADOR

NICARAGUA

VENEZUELA

GUYANA

Right-wing government and opposition leaders sign peace treaty, 1992.

Panama Canal

COSTA RICA

PANAMA

COLOMBIA

PACIFIC OCEAN

Panama Canal Treaties, 1978; U.S. invades Panama to capture Gen. Manuel Noriega, Dec. 1989.

Flow of drugs to U.S. poses chronic problems.

BRAZIL

The United States in Latin America and the Caribbean
Plagued by poverty, population pressures, repressive regimes, and drug trafficking, Latin America saw turmoil and conflict—but also some hopeful developments—in the 1980s and 1990s.

Congress. When the South African parliament scrapped much of the nation's apartheid laws in 1991, President Bush lifted the economic sanctions. In 1992, a strong majority of the nation's whites voted to endorse de Klerk's program of dismantling apartheid and extending political rights to the black majority.

China proved a notable exception to the world trend from repressiveness to freedom. The United States' improved relations with China suffered a grievous setback in 1989, when the Chinese army brutally crushed a prodemocracy demonstration by masses of unarmed students in Beijing's Tiananmen Square, killing an estimated four hundred to eight hundred young men and women. A wave of repression, arrests, and public executions followed. The Bush administration protested sharply, curtailed diplomatic contacts, and urged international financial institutions to postpone loans to China. But Bush refrained from breaking

diplomatic relations or canceling trade agreements with China, leaving these and a host of other foreign-policy headaches to his successor.

As Cold War worries diminished, international-trade issues loomed large. The towering U.S. trade deficit with Japan stirred special concern. Although this gap dropped somewhat from its 1987 high of more than $55 billion, it hovered at $43 billion in 1991. Early in 1992, facing a stubborn recession and rising unemployment in an election year, President Bush turned a planned Asian trip into a trade mission. He took along a team of U.S. business leaders, including the heads of the "big three" American auto companies, who tried, with little success, to persuade the Japanese to buy more U.S. products. The trip was widely viewed as a failure. When Bush collapsed and vomited from a sudden attack of flu at a state dinner in Tokyo, some found the mishap unhappily symbolic. As the Bush administration grappled with a tangle of global issues in a world no longer dominated by superpower rivalry, one regional provocation elicited a dramatic, clear-cut response.

Operation Desert Storm

On August 2, 1990, Iraq invaded its neighbor, the oil-rich sheikdom of Kuwait, with which it had a long-running dispute over the vast Rumaila oilfield. Iraq's dictator, Saddam Hussein, had dismissed Kuwait's independent-nation status as a creation of Western imperialists and asserted Iraq's historic claims to the region.

Under Saddam, Iraq for years had threatened not only Israel but the Arab nations as well. The Iraqi military buildup, including both chemical- and nuclear-weapons programs, had worried many governments in the 1980s.

During the Iran-Iraq war that had raged from 1980 to 1988, however, the United States had tilted in Iraq's favor because Iran was rabidly anti-American. But Iranian hostility to the United States moderated after the death of Ayatollah Khomeini in 1989, so this incentive to placate Iraq was removed. When Iraq invaded Kuwait, Washington immediately denounced the act.

Avoiding the mistakes of Lyndon Johnson in the Vietnam era, Bush built a consensus for action against Iraq in the Congress, in the United Nations, and among the American people. He also articulated a clear military objective—Iraq's withdrawal from Kuwait—and deployed more than 400,000 troops in Saudi Arabia to achieve that goal. Secretary of Defense Dick Cheney, formerly a Wyoming congressman, played a key role in this effort.

A series of U.N. resolutions imposed economic sanctions against Iraq and insisted that Saddam withdraw from Kuwait by January 15, 1991. On January 12, after somber debate, the Senate and the House endorsed military action against Iraq. The vote was 52 to 47 in the Senate; 250 to 183 in the House. Most Democrats voted against war, favoring continued economic sanctions instead.

The war began on January 16 with a massive air assault. For nearly six weeks, U.S. B-52 and F-16 bombers, flying up to 3,000 sorties daily, pounded Iraqi troops in the field, Iraqi supply depots, and command and communications targets in Iraq's capital, Baghdad. The air forces of other nations participated as well.

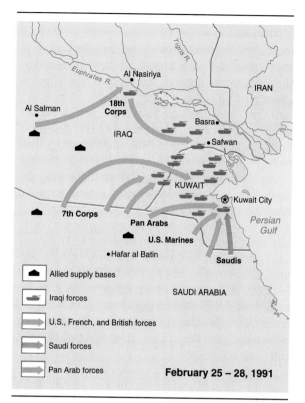

Operation Desert Storm: The Ground War
Preceding the ground operations that ended the war was a massive air assault. Iraq's Scud missile attacks on Israel and Saudi Arabia provided TV drama but had little effect on the war's outcome.

Although Iraq offered little direct resistance to this air attack, Saddam ordered Soviet-made Scud missiles fired against Tel Aviv and other Israeli cities, as well as against the Saudi capital, Riyadh. These did little damage, but Americans watched transfixed as the Cable News Network carried live coverage of U.S. Patriot missiles streaking off to intercept incoming Scuds.

Indeed, for Americans viewing a carefully edited version of the war on TV, it often seemed a glorified video game. The reality of an estimated 100,000 Iraqi deaths, both military and civilian, hardly impinged on the national consciousness.

On February 23, after diversionary maneuvers to mislead Iraqi commanders, 200,000 U.S. troops under General H. Norman Schwarzkopf moved across the desert toward Kuwait. Although heavy rains turned the roadless sands to soup, the army ground on. Within three days of the ground war Iraqi soldiers were in full flight or surrendering en masse. U.S. forces destroyed 3,700 Iraqi tanks while losing only three. One hundred hours after the ground war had begun, with Iraqi resistance crushed, President Bush declared a cease-fire. After U.S. forces liberated Kuwait City, members of Kuwait's ruling al-Sabah family gradually filtered back from Cairo and other safe havens where they had sat out the war. Total American casualties numbered 148 dead—including 35 killed inadvertently by U.S. firepower—and 467 wounded.

As the victory celebrations receded, the war's political aftermath came into focus. Kuwait expelled many thousands of Palestinian laborers for their support of Iraq, creating a major refugee problem. Within Iraq, amid widespread civilian hardship and malnutrition, Saddam still held power. His army brutally suppressed uprisings against his rule by Shiite Muslims in the south and a large Kurdish ethnic minority in the north. United Nations inspectors found convincing evidence of Iraq's advanced nuclear-weapons project, and the halting of this sinister undertaking was viewed with general relief.

Capitalizing on the favorable diplomatic climate created by its military effort in the Persian Gulf, Bush called for a renewed Middle Eastern peace effort. Syria, with its Soviet patron in collapse, supported this move. Talks involving Israel, the Palestinians, and various Arab states began in November 1991 in Madrid and soon shifted to Washington. The two sides progressed slowly as they confronted decades of mistrust, as the Shamir government continued to promote Jewish settlement on the disputed West Bank, and as Palestinians resorted to violence and the killing of Jewish settlers. But polls showed 80 percent of Israelis in favor of the peace process, and a majority in support of some form of Palestinian self-rule. Frustrating though it was, the peace process continued as Bush's term ended, and under his successor it would bear fruit.

Domestic Discontents

The tax cuts, Pentagon spending, and deregulatory fervor of the "Reagan revolution" had roused entrepreneurial energies, fueled a stock-market surge, and set off an economic boom that gave the 1980s a glow of prosperity. In the 1990s, however, the longer-term effects of Reaganism began to be felt. As the economy soured, the go-go eighties seemed remote. During Bush's term, America seethed with economic discontent, especially among the middle class.

A Soured Economy
The savings-and-loan crisis, part of the aftermath of the expansive economic climate of the 1980s, was projected to cost U.S. taxpayers billions of dollars.

First came the collapse of the savings-and-loan (S&L) industry, which for decades had provided home loans to borrowers and a secure return to depositors. In the late seventies, double-digit inflation had forced the S&Ls to pay high interest to attract deposits, even though most of their assets were tied up in long-term, fixed-rate mortgages. In the early eighties, capital freed up by the Reagan tax cuts flowed into S&Ls, with their high rates of return. In the fever to deregulate, the rules governing S&Ls were eased excessively. Caught up in the high-flying economic mood of the eighties, S&Ls nationwide made risky loans on speculative real-estate ventures. As the economy cooled, many of these investments went bad. In 1988–1990, nearly six hundred S&Ls failed, especially in the Southwest, wiping out the savings of many depositors.

Because the federal government insures savings-and-loan deposits, the Bush administration in 1989 set up a program to repay depositors and sell millions of dollars worth of foreclosed office towers and apartment buildings in an already depressed real-estate market. Estimates of the cost of the bailout topped $400 billion. By 1990, wrote a journalist, " 'Savings and loan' had become synonymous with 'bottomless pit.' "

The federal deficit, another problem worsened by the Reagan tax cuts and runaway military spending, continued to mount. In the fall of 1990, after acrimonious negotiations, Congress and Bush agreed on a five-year deficit-reduction package involving drastic spending cuts and tax increases. Under the lash of upward-spiraling deficits, Bush had retreated from his 1988 campaign pledge, "Read my lips: no new taxes." He would pay a high political price for this "betrayal."

Despite the budget-balancing agreement, the red ink flowed on. The deficit reached $269 billion in 1991 and $290 billion in 1992. The total federal debt surpassed $3 trillion. The Gulf War, the S&L bailout, and soaring welfare and Medicare/Medicaid payments combined to wreak havoc with the budget-balancing effort.

To make matters worse, recession struck in the summer of 1990. Retail sales slumped; housing starts declined; unemployment rose. A weak recovery in 1991 faltered, and hard times hung on into 1992, with a jobless rate of more than 7 percent. As the economic slowdown chipped away at tax revenues, states slashed social-welfare funding. Michigan reduced AFDC payments by 17 percent. New Jersey and California, the latter facing a budget deficit of more than $12 billion, planned similar cuts. The number of Americans below the poverty line rose by 2.1 million in 1990, to about 34 million. As the economy stumbled, the plight of the poor roused resentment rather than sympathy. Declared Ohio's governor, "Most Ohioans have had enough welfare, enough poverty, enough drugs, enough crime." Political strategists diagnosed a middle-class phenomenon they called "compassion fatigue." In November 1991 David Duke, a former Grand Wizard of the Ku Klux Klan, running as a Republican, captured a majority of the white votes in an unsuccessful campaign for governor of Louisiana.

The U.S. auto industry, battered by Japanese imports, fared disastrously in 1991. A week before Christmas, GM unveiled plans to close twenty-one plants and cut its work force by more than seventy thousand.

Personal and national economic woes made many Americans look back on Reagan's policies with skepticism. If 1984 was "morning in America," wrote a columnist, quoting a Reagan campaign slogan, 1989–1990 was the "morning after." For most middle-class Americans, the situation was more frustrating and anxiety-producing than desperate. Still, a gloomy economic picture clouded much of Bush's term.

Hard times worsened already bleak conditions in the inner cities, unaffected by Reagan-era prosperity. In April 1992 an outbreak of civil disorder, arson, looting, and violence erupted in a poor black district of Los Angeles and quickly spread to other parts of the city. The

immediate cause was black rage and incredulity (shared by many others) over a jury's acquital of four white Los Angeles police officers whose brutal beating of a black motorist had been filmed on videotape. For several days the explosion of anger and pent-up frustration raged, leaving some forty persons dead and millions in property damage, and reminding a complacent nation yet again of the desperate conditions in its inner cities. Across the continent in Miami, a large portion of the African-American community similarly found itself mired in poverty (see "A Place in Time").

Reflecting the priorities of the middle-class white majority, the Bush administration did little to address these issues. In 1990, when Congress passed a bill broadening federal protection against job discrimination, Bush vetoed it. With an eye to disgruntled white voters, the president claimed that the bill encouraged racial quotas in hiring.* When Bush showed up in Atlanta in 1992 to sing "We Shall Overcome" on the birthday of Martin Luther King, Jr., King's daughter, the Reverend Bernice King, asked bitterly, "How dare we celebrate in the midst of a recession, when nobody is sure whether their jobs are secure?"

The recession also stung public-school budgets. Despite much handwringing over the shortcomings of the United States' educational system, especially in poor neighborhoods, remedies proved elusive. Bush ballyhooed himself as the "education president" and held a conference on the subject but addressed the issue only fitfully. Bush called for standardized national testing of schoolchildren, supported a voucher system by which parents could withdraw their children from public schools and enroll them in private schools, and urged corporate America to support a fund for experimental schools. But such proposals hardly matched the magnitude of the problem.

The environmental issue was spotlighted in March 1989 when a 987-foot oil tanker, the *Exxon Valdez,* ran aground in Alaska's beautiful Prince William Sound and spilled more than 10 million gallons of crude oil. The accident fouled six hundred acres of coastal and marine habitats, killed thousands of sea otters and shore birds, and jeopardized Alaska's vital herring and salmon industries.

In the hot summer of 1989, the Environmental Protection Agency (EPA) reported that air pollution in more than one hundred cities exceeded federal

---

*In 1991, announcing that his concerns had been met, Bush signed a similar bill.

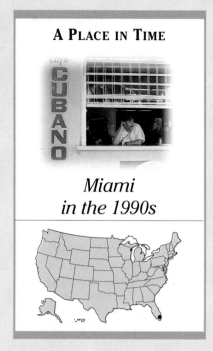

Miami in the 1990s

So tangled and complex has the U.S. social web become by the 1990s that some observers fear its unraveling. No American city poses the issue of multiculturalism more starkly than Miami, where ethnic diversity is not simply a *part* of the story; in many respects, it *is* the story.

Thrusting up along Biscayne Bay near Florida's southern tip, Miami's fifteen miles of sun-drenched beaches, breathtaking skyline of flamboyant skyscrapers, and pastel-tinted Art Deco buildings all proclaim the nation's southernmost major city. When Ponce de Leon reached the bay in 1513, Calusas Indians inhabited the area. Spain claimed the region until 1819, when the Adams-Onís Treaty ceded title to the United States. Florida entered the union in 1845, about the time the settlement on Biscayne Bay began to be called Miami. Sporadic Indian resistance—the so-called Seminole Wars—persisted into the 1850s. (A small tribe of Native Americans, the Miccosukee, lives on a nearby reservation.)

A frenzied land boom in the 1920s collapsed in the wake of a killer hurricane, but Miami prospered after 1945 as GIs who had trained in the area returned to live and as northern "snowbirds" fled south each winter, many eventually to become permanent residents. Miami Beach proved es-

The Café Cubano in Miami's "Little Havana"

pecially popular with Jewish retirees from New York. One of these, the novelist I. B. Singer, recalled his first visit in 1948: "Miami Beach resembled a small Israel. . . . Yiddish resounded around us in accents as thick as those you would hear in Tel Aviv." By 1975 Miami's Jewish population had reached 300,000, most of them over age sixty.

But today's Miami exudes primarily a Hispanic flavor. Cubans fled their island country en masse after Fidel Castro seized power in 1959, and by 1973, 300,000 had settled in Miami. Thousands more, the so-called Mariel boat people who left with Castro's approval, arrived in 1980. By 1990, 49 percent of the 2 million inhabitants of Dade County (comprising Miami and its environs) were of Cuban birth or descent.

Cuban-Americans influence not only Miami's cultural ambience but its political and economic agenda. Cuban-born Xavier Saurez became mayor in 1985. Far from being a struggling minority, Cuban-Americans compose a confident, fully developed ethnic community. "Little Havana," the sprawling downtown district centered on *Calle Ocho* (Eighth Street), boasts not only churches, restaurants, and shops but also banks, medical centers, law offices, insurance companies, and construction firms, employing professionals of all kinds.

Other Hispanic groups also call Miami home. Jamaicans have long been present, and the 1980s brought emigrants from troubled Nicaragua, El Salvador, and especially Haiti. Although U.S. immigration officials intercept and repatriate Haitian refugees arriving by sea, this community continues to grow. "Little Haiti," a district of some 60,000 people anchored by Notre Dame d'Haiti Church, enhances Miami's ethnic ambience.

The African-American community, making up some 18 percent of the population, is centered in Liberty City, Richmond Heights, and other enclaves. While Richmond Heights is middle class and well-to-do, the black population overall ranks among the city's poorest. In contrast to the situation in other multiethnic cities, Miami's African-Americans and Hispanics have not collaborated in pursuit of common goals. While many native-born blacks feel alienated and exploited, Hispanic newcomers of whatever skin color tend to view the United States more posi-

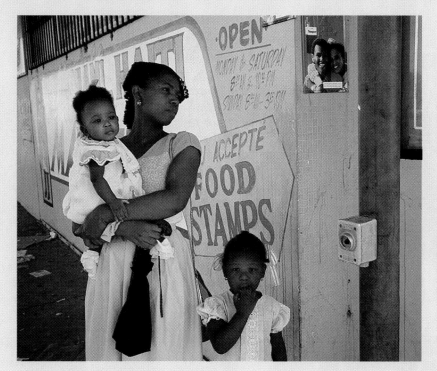

A Mother and Two Daughters in Miami's Little Haiti District

In 1994 a reporter observed a Vietnamese, a Spanish-speaking Colombian, and a French-speaking Haitian vainly trying to communicate at an auto-repair shop. (They eventually diagnosed the problem: a faulty distributor.) In 1980 the Dade County commissioners proclaimed English the official language for government business. Florida voters imposed the same rule statewide in 1988. But many thousands of Miamians continue to conduct their daily lives without resort to English.

Miami's links with organized crime go far back. Rum-running and gambling proliferated in the 1920s, and underworld figures wielded great political and economic clout. Mobster Al Capone retired here in the 1930s. Today, a $12 billion annual wholesale drug traffic drives up the crime statistics. Fast boats smuggle in cocaine from "mother ships" hovering offshore; commercial aircraft arriving from South America unwittingly transmit drugs. Dade County's 1981 homicide toll of 621 earned it the dubious title "Murder Capital USA." A popular TV show of 1984–1989, "Miami Vice," glamorized the city's sleazy underside along with its tropical setting, laid-back fashions, and stage-set architecture. While drug wars and domestic disputes account for most of the bloodshed, the killing of several tourists during robbery attempts tarnished the city's appeal in the early 1990s. "Miami wears its crime like cheap perfume," observes a guidebook half boastfully; "it's hard to ignore."

On another front, decades of development have taken a heavy toll on fragile wetlands and unspoiled wilderness areas. The nearby Everglades, once spread over four million acres, has dwindled to one-tenth its former size. Of the exotic wildlife that formerly inhabited this fragile ecosystem, only a fraction survives.

tively as a place of freedom and opportunity. Politically, the two communities diverge radically. While African-Americans generally vote Democratic, the staunchly anticommunist Cubans are mostly conservative Republicans.

Ethnic diversity generates a distinctive Miami style. Jewish delis coexist with Hispanic restaurants. Snapper, *paella*, conch fritters, stone crabs, Haitian curried goat, potent Cuban coffee, black beans and rice, and an array of salsas tempt local palates. In prosperous times, ethnic lines blur in a shared pursuit of the good life. A recession in the 1970s drove the jobless rate to 13 percent, but the economy bounced back in the 1980s. For the affluent, a prevailing love of sports finds many outlets: sailing, windsurfing, sports-car rallies, horseracing at Hialeah, the annual Orange Bowl extravaganza, and avid support for the Miami Dolphins professional football team, the Miami Heat basketball team, and the University of Miami Hurricanes.

With its ceaseless round of parades, fairs, and festivals, the city seems dedicated to the pleasure principle. Casual dress and gold jewelry for both sexes set the tone. One annual event draws thousands of chocolate lovers. The beaches encourage a narcissism that some call Miami's "body culture." Cosmetic surgery thrives. Fashion photography, capitalizing on the ever-present sunlight, is big business. Journalist Patrick May sums up the city this way: "Non-stop entertainment. Over a stage backdropped by fruit salad sunsets and palm tree props, the curtain for 100 years has risen faithfully each dawn. And there it stands, tongue firmly in cheek, hogging the spotlight. The show-off of American cities admiring itself in a full-length mirror."

But behind the façade lie problems. Indeed, Miami is a microcosm of troubling contemporary issues. Racial tensions simmer near the surface. Black neighborhoods erupted in violence in 1968 and again in 1980 when a Tampa jury acquitted a white police officer in a black man's death. As the Hispanic population has grown, non-Hispanic whites have moved out. Civic leaders bemoan "Anglo flight," and a commonly seen bumper sticker gibes: "Will the last American leaving Miami please bring the flag?"

With Spanish the native tongue of half the residents, language is contested terrain. In many neighborhoods, English is rarely spoken, heard on radio or TV, or seen on billboards, magazine stands, or store signs. Other languages thrive as well.

Crime, ethnic tensions, environmental degradation, cultural diversity, hedonistic pleasure seeking—for better or worse, Miami has it all. In this vibrant, garish, future-oriented city, many of the most urgent social issues facing contemporary America emerge in particularly stark fashion.

Cleaning Up After the *Exxon Valdez* Disaster
Volunteers collect and bag sea otters killed in the Exxon
Valdez *oil spill of March 1989, a catastrophe that focused
attention on industrialization's mounting ecological toll.*

ment began the multibillion-dollar task of disposing of
radioactive wastes and cleaning up nuclear-weapons
facilities and nuclear-power plants that in some cases
had been contaminating the surrounding soil and
ground water for years.

But the Bush administration, like the Reagan
regime before it, more often dismissed environmental
concerns. Vice President Quayle ridiculed environmentalists; the administration scuttled international
treaties on global warming and mining in Antarctica,
recommended oil exploration in Alaskan wilderness
preserves, and proposed to open vast tracts of protected wetlands to development. In 1992 Bush addressed Earth Summit, a United Nations–sponsored international environmental conference in Rio de
Janeiro, but his defensive, self-serving speech further
alienated environmental activists.

The Supreme Court Moves Right

Like all presidents, Reagan and Bush sought to perpetuate their political ideology through their Supreme
Court appointments. In addition to the Sandra Day
O'Connor nomination, Reagan in 1986 elevated
William Rehnquist to chief justice to replace the retiring Warren Burger and chose another judicial conservative, Antonin Scalia, to fill the Burger vacancy. When
a third vacancy opened in 1987, Reagan nominated
Robert Bork, a judge and legal scholar whose intellectual rigidity and doctrinaire opposition to judicial activism led the Senate to reject him. Reagan's next
nominee withdrew after admitting that he had
smoked marijuana. Reagan's third choice, Anthony
Kennedy, a conservative jurist from San Francisco,
won quick confirmation.

President Bush made two Court nominations:
David Souter in 1990 and Clarence Thomas in 1991.
Souter, a New Hampshire judge, won easy confirmation. The Thomas nomination, however, proved very
controversial. Bush nominated him to fill the seat vacated by the retiring Thurgood Marshall, a black who
had fought segregation as an NAACP lawyer in the
1950s and 1960s. Thomas, though also an African-
American, was notable mainly for espousing conservative causes (he praised Oliver North as a maligned
hero, for example) and opposing affirmative-action
programs. Having grown up in poverty and gone on to
attend Yale Law School and to head the Equal Employment Opportunity Commission (EEOC) in the Reagan
years, Thomas viewed individual effort, not govern-

standards. In Louisiana, the EPA said, industry was
pumping nearly 2 million pounds of pollutants into the
air daily. In 1991 the EPA reported that the ozone shield
over the United States—the layer that protects human
life from cancer-causing solar radiation—was being
depleted by pollutants at twice the rate scientists had
predicted.

Squeezed between rising public concern and corporate calls for a go-slow policy, the Bush administration compiled a mixed record on the environment.
Bush called the *Exxon Valdez* spill a "major tragedy"
but insisted that oil exploration and drilling must go
on. In a rare bipartisan effort, the White House and the
Democratic Congress passed a toughened Federal
Clean Air Act in 1990. (California and other states enacted even stricter laws, tightening automobile-emis-
sion standards, for example.) In addition, the govern-

ment programs, as the avenue of black progress. Noting Thomas's right-wing ideology and his thin record as a federal appeals judge, critics charged Bush with cynically playing the politics of race.

The nomination became even more controversial when a former Thomas associate at EEOC, law professor Anita Hill, charged him with sexual harassment. For several days, as the Senate Judiciary Committee explored Hill's accusations, the face-off dominated the nation's TV screens and heightened national awareness of the harassment issue. In the end Thomas narrowly won confirmation, 52–48.

With these Reagan-Bush appointments, the liberal, social-activist thrust of the Court that had been inaugurated in Franklin Roosevelt's day and sustained in the 1950s and 1960s under Earl Warren and other justices was at least temporarily blunted. In a series of 5–4 rulings in 1989, the Court upheld a Missouri law limiting women's right to an abortion and imposed restrictive new definitions on civil-rights laws aimed at protecting the employment rights of women and minorities and remedying past inequities. In the 1990–1991 term, the Court narrowed the rights of arrested persons and upheld federal regulations barring physicians in federally funded family-planning clinics from discussing abortion with their clients. (A poll found that 71 percent of Americans opposed this intrusion in the doctor-patient relationship.) In a 5–4 decision in 1992, the Supreme Court upheld a Pennsylvania law placing various restrictions on abortion. The majority, however, led by a centrist group comprising Souter, O'Connor, and Kennedy, affirmed *Roe* v. *Wade,* the 1973 decision upholding women's constitutional right to an abortion. To overturn this right after nineteen years, said the majority, would cause "profound and unnecessary damage to the Court's legitimacy, and to the nation's commitment to the rule of law."

The Politics of Frustration

George Bush's shifting political fortunes served as a barometer of the public mood. In the afterglow of Operation Desert Storm, his approval ratings shot up to a startling 88 percent—only to plummet below 50 percent as the war-induced euphoria evaporated and the recession eroded the nation's confidence. In a 1991 election to fill a Senate vacancy in Pennsylvania, Bush's attorney general (and the former governor of the state) lost to a liberal Democrat who articulated middle-class concerns about high taxes and health-care costs.

Milking His Popularity
Despite President Bush's efforts to milk the Gulf War for political advantage, his bumbling approach to domestic issues cost him support.

Heeding such warnings, Bush proclaimed economic recovery his "No. 1 priority." But in a damning editorial late in 1991, the *New York Times* commented: "Nearly three years into his term, George Bush remains mystifyingly incomplete: shrewd and energetic in foreign policy and . . . , clumsy and irresolute—at home. . . . The domestic Bush flops like a fish, leaving the impression that he doesn't know what he thinks or doesn't much care, apart from the political gains to be extracted from an issue." Capitalizing on voter frustration, the Democrats attacked Bush's preoccupation with foreign affairs. When Bush flew to Rome in November 1991, the Democrats released a list of U.S. towns named Rome, with their unemployment rates.

In his State of the Union message in January 1992, Bush unveiled a package of recession-fighting proposals, including tax breaks for first-time home buyers, lower taxes on capital gains, and tax incentives for business investment. Democrats dismissed this belated focus on domestic issues as politically motivated and inadequate to the problem.

With Bush seemingly invulnerable after Operation Desert Storm, top Democrats stayed out of the 1992 presidential race. But Governor Bill Clinton of Arkansas took the plunge and, despite surfacing doubts about his character and stories of marital infidelity, defeated other hopefuls in a grueling round of primaries. As his running mate, Clinton chose Senator Al Gore of

Tennessee, an advocate for the environment. At the party's convention in July, Clinton pledged change and an activist government addressing jobs, the environment, health care, and the economic squeeze on the middle class. On abortion, he was strongly pro-choice. As Clinton oriented the party toward the middle class and muted its concern with the poor, traditional liberals as well as some black leaders, including Jesse Jackson, expressed uneasiness.

President Bush quashed a primary challenge by conservative columnist Pat Buchanan, and the Bush-Quayle ticket coasted to renomination. But the Republican right dominated the party convention. Buchanan and evangelist Pat Robertson gave divisive speeches summoning the GOP to a crusade against abortion, sexual permissiveness, radical feminism, gay rights, and perceived threats to "family values." Delegates who belonged to Robertson's Christian Coalition cheered, but moderate Republicans deplored this rightward turn.

One gauge of voter disaffection was the presidential race of H. Ross Perot, a political outsider who scorned politics-as-usual. At the peak of "Perotmania," nearly 40 percent of the voters supported the Texan, who had amassed billions as founder and head of a data-processing firm. The nation's economic problems were simple, Perot insisted; only party politics stood in the way of solving them. As president he would conduct electronic "town meetings" by which voters would pass judgment on his proposals. Where this left Congress in the governing process remained unclear. Perot's autocratic ways and thin-skinned response to criticism turned off many supporters, and in July 1992 he left the race. But he reentered in October, spent millions on TV advertising, and participated in the televised presidential debates.

Bush ran a negative campaign, attacking Clinton's character and charging that the Arkansas governor not only had evaded the draft during the Vietnam War but later tried to obscure the truth. Sensing voter anger over his failure to confront economic distress, Bush promised to put James A. Baker in charge of domestic affairs in a second term. Toward the campaign's end, as the polls remained bleak, Bush became abusive, ridiculing Clinton and Gore as "crazies" and "bozos." Clinton, meanwhile, focused on the stagnant economy and the eroding position of the middle class. He pledged to work for a national health-care system, welfare reform, and a federal industrial policy that

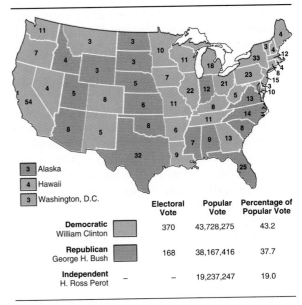

	Electoral Vote	Popular Vote	Percentage of Popular Vote
Democratic William Clinton	370	43,728,275	43.2
Republican George H. Bush	168	38,167,416	37.7
Independent H. Ross Perot	–	19,237,247	19.0

The Election of 1992

would promote economic recovery and innovative new technologies.

The voters spoke on November 3, when 43 percent chose Clinton. Bush trailed with 38 percent, and Perot amassed 19 percent—the largest share for a third party since Teddy Roosevelt's Bull Moose party got 27 percent in 1912. In the electoral tally, Clinton won 370 votes to Bush's 168.

Clinton swept the Northeast and the Pacific Northwest, did well in the Midwest, and carried such key swing states as California, Ohio, and New Jersey. He lured back many blue-collar and suburban "Reagan Democrats" and made long strides toward reclaiming the South for the Democrats. Voters aged eighteen to twenty-nine, who had tilted Republican in 1984 and 1988, went solidly for Clinton in 1992. Reflecting the high voter interest in the campaign, 55 percent of eligible voters cast ballots, up from barely 50 percent in 1988.

Most incumbents in Congress won reelection. In Pennsylvania, Republican senator Arlen Specter, a Judiciary Committee member who had roused women's anger by his harsh questioning of Anita Hill, narrowly beat back a challenge by a feminist political novice. But Congress was becoming less of a white male club and more representative of U.S. society as a whole.

Thirty-eight African-Americans and seventeen Hispanics won election to the 1993–1994 Congress, up from twenty-five and ten respectively. Colorado elected Native American Ben Nighthorse Campbell to the Senate, and a California congressional district sent the first Korean-American to Washington.

Women candidates fared well. California became the first state to elect two women senators, Barbara Boxer and Diane Feinstein. Illinois elected the first African-American woman to the Senate, Carol Moseley Braun. Overall, the new Congress included fifty-three women: six in the Senate and forty-seven in the House. This outcome, together with the advent of Hillary Clinton, the first presidential spouse to have a career in her own right, gave credence to those who had proclaimed 1992 the "Year of the Woman."

The 1992 election marked a shift of voter attention to domestic issues as the Cold War faded. New, urgent world problems would arise—indeed, they already existed—but for the moment, Americans clearly wished their government to address neglected matters at home. With Democrats in control of both the legislative and executive branches of government, the end of the much-deplored Washington "gridlock" seemed possible. Formidable challenges confronted the new Congress and the new White House team. In the hopeful beginnings of his term, President Bill Clinton eagerly engaged those challenges.

THE CLINTON YEARS: DEMOCRATIC DISARRAY, REPUBLICAN RESURGENCE

William Jefferson Clinton—or Bill Clinton, as he preferred—represented a new political generation. George Bush was a World War II veteran, shaped by memories of Pearl Harbor, FDR, and Bing Crosby. Bill Clinton was a baby boomer, formed by Vietnam, JFK, and the Beatles.

Born in Hope, Arkansas, in 1946, he admired Elvis Presley, played the saxophone, and thought of becoming a pop musician. But graduation from Georgetown University in Washington, D.C., a stint at Oxford University as a Rhodes scholar, and attendance at Yale Law School deepened his growing interest in politics. After marrying his law-school classmate Hillary Rod-

ham, he returned to Arkansas and won the governorship in 1979, at age thirty-two.

Clinton began his presidency in January 1993 with confidence and high energy. But grueling difficulties on both the domestic and foreign-policy fronts quickly propelled his administration into rough waters. In the 1994 midterm election, a disgruntled electorate generated a Republican landslide of major proportions.

Struggling to Shape a Domestic Agenda

Both Clinton and Vice President Albert Gore belonged to the New Democratic Coalition, a group of moderates who sought to shed the party's reputation for ultra-liberalism and wasteful spending on social programs. Courting the middle-class and blue-collar voters who had once composed the party's backbone, Clinton ran a campaign that stressed Middle America's concerns: the recession, health care, runaway welfare costs, and a sputtering economy. Clinton also embraced the causes that had inspired many activists in the sixties and seventies, including feminism, abortion rights, and environmental concerns.

Signaling one goal of his presidency, Clinton named women to head the Justice Department, the Department of Energy, the Department of Health and Human Services, the Council of Economic Advisors, the Environmental Protection Agency, the United Nations delegation, and (beginning in 1994) the Bureau of the Budget. To fill his first Supreme Court vacancy in 1993, he nominated Judge Ruth Bader Ginsberg of New York, a champion of women's rights. (When the retirement of Harry A. Blackmun created a second vacancy on the High Court in 1994, Clinton nominated moderate liberal Stephen G. Breyer, a federal appeals-court judge in Boston.) Clinton appointed his wife, Hillary Rodham Clinton, to head the Task Force on National Health-Care Reform.

Clinton's early weeks in office taught some hard lessons as he made a rocky transition from Little Rock to Washington. His effort to fulfill a campaign pledge to end the exclusion of homosexuals from military service roused a hornet's nest of protest. A study commission eventually drafted a compromise summed up in the phrase "Don't ask, don't tell."

Elected amid a recession, Clinton promised to focus "like a laser beam" on the economy. His economic program, offered in February 1993, represented an amalgam of viewpoints among his advisers, including budget hawks eager to cut the deficit, advocates of more spending on social programs, and economists convinced that federally funded research and training programs would stimulate long-term economic growth.

The bill proposed spending cuts (especially in military appropriations) and tax increases aimed at a net deficit reduction of $325 billion over four years. Clinton also proposed $169 billion in new spending to stimulate job creation and economic growth. In August Congress narrowly passed a five-year economic plan that incorporated Clinton's spending cuts and tax increases while gutting his economic-stimulus package. Enactment of even a modified budget plan spared Clinton a major early embarrassment.

Clinton's economic program included the North American Free Trade Agreement (NAFTA). Negotiated by the Bush administration, this pact admitted Mexico to the free-trade zone earlier created by the United States and Canada. While critics including Ralph Nader and H. Ross Perot warned that low-wage jobs would flee to Mexico, NAFTA backers, including most economists, predicted a net gain in jobs as Mexican markets opened to U.S. products. After frenzied White House deal making, the House in November 1993 passed NAFTA by a comfortable 234–200 margin, thus handing Clinton another welcome victory. As predicted, trade with Mexico shot up in 1994.

An improving economy eased pressures on the administration to devise an economic-stimulus program. A rebound that began in 1992 picked up steam in 1993 and 1994. Retail sales rose, notably in durable goods and building materials—key indicators of consumer confidence. The Big Three automakers recovered strongly, earning some $14 billion in 1994. The steel industry bounced back as well and posted 1994 profits of around $1 billion. Thanks to the addition of 3.5 million jobs in 1994, the unemployment rate fell to 5.4 percent by year's end, the lowest in more than four years.

Inflation remained under control as well, owing in part to a succession of interest-rate increases imposed by the Federal Reserve Board to cool the surging economy. A weakening of the OPEC oil cartel also helped hold inflation in check. In constant dollars, crude oil cost about the same in 1993 as in 1973, before the cycle of price spurts. And the federal deficit, while still massive, declined from the scary levels of the late 1980s. The 1994 deficit dropped to $220 billion, with $167 billion forecast for 1995. Structural economic

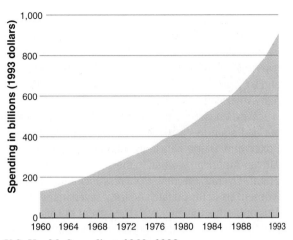

U.S. Health Spending, 1960–1993

SOURCE: Department of Health and Human Services, in *The Economist*, March 19, 1994.

problems remained, but the short-term picture brightened in the mid-1990s.

Meanwhile, Hillary Rodham Clinton's health-care task force, supported by a staff that eventually grew to more than 500 and working mainly behind closed doors, devised a sweeping reform plan incorporated in a massive bill of 1,342 pages. President Clinton launched the debate with a speech to a joint session of Congress in September 1993. Extending coverage to all Americans, including the estimated 39 million lacking medical insurance, the plan mandated that employers pay 80 percent of workers' health-insurance costs and, to cover the $100 billion in start-up costs, proposed stiff new taxes on tobacco. The proposal also addressed the problem of spiraling costs. From 1980 to 1992, Medicare and Medicaid payments ballooned from $48 billion to $296 billion, growing from 8 percent to 14 percent of the federal budget. Health-insurance premiums soared as well. Without controls, analysts calculated, U.S. health spending would consume 19 percent of the Gross Domestic Product by the year 2000, twice the rate in most other industrialized nations. The plan's cost-containment provisions, summed up in the phrase "managed competition," included regional health-care purchasing cooperatives, caps on health-insurance premiums and on Medicare and Medicaid payments, and a national health board to monitor costs.

As Congress debated, lobbyists for the insurance industry, tobacco companies, the medical profession,

Last Heartbeat for Health-Care Reform

Launched with great fanfare, the Clinton administration's health-care reform program soon bogged down amid public confusion, congressional politics, and intense lobbying by interest groups.

retired persons, business organizations, and hospital associations, as well as advocates of a Canadian-style national health system, all mobilized. Business groups denounced the employer-mandate provision. President Clinton offered to compromise on various points but insisted that universal coverage was not negotiable.

About half of Americans initially supported the Clinton plan, but by mid-1994, after months of lobbying and partisan wrangling, support had fallen sharply. By the fall of 1994, health-care reform was stalled, at a heavy cost to the Clinton presidency. "We're just sick of talking about this," groused one senator. The American people seemed to agree. Public sentiment for piecemeal, incremental change had been misinterpreted by the new administration as support for a total overhaul of the health-care system—a system accounting for one-seventh of the nation's economy. Appearing secretive and patronizing, Hillary Clinton's task force had ignored political realities. But although the effort failed, the problems that had given rise to it remained. One way or another, health care seemed certain to return to the political agenda.

As Congress debated health care, crime and welfare reform topped voter concerns. In response, the administration in 1994 pushed an anti-crime bill providing $30 billion to fund drug treatment, more prisons and police officers, boot camps for first-time offenders, a ban on assault weapons, and various prevention programs. After much debate and partisan maneuvering, Congress enacted a crime bill similar to Clinton's initial proposal.

In addition, Clinton in June 1994 introduced a welfare-reform bill, fulfilling his campaign pledge to "end welfare as we know it." This measure reflected concerns that the biggest welfare system, Aid to Families with Dependent Children (AFDC), was creating a permanent dependent class and spiraling out of control. With 14.3 million women and children on AFDC's rolls—a 31 percent jump since 1989—at an annual cost of $63 billion in direct payments, food stamps, and Medicaid benefits,

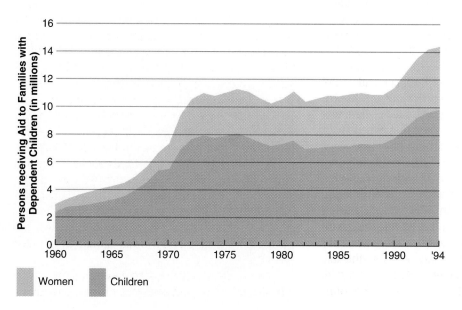

The Welfare Rolls, 1960–1994

SOURCE: House Ways and Means Committee, in *New York Times,* "News of Week in Review," June 19, 1994, p. 4.

such concerns were hardly surprising. The Clinton bill proposed to end AFDC payments after two years, at which time the recipient would have to go to work, in a public-service job if necessary. The bill included job training and child-care provisions, as well as measures to force absent fathers ("deadbeat dads") to support their offspring. It also permitted states to deny extra payments to mothers who bore more children while on welfare.

Critics pointed out that AFDC recipients were often ill educated and among the least employable in the job market. By one estimate, the plan would require 1.5 million public-sector jobs. Some found the proposed reform harsh, but supporters quoted the 1935 warning of President Franklin D. Roosevelt that "continued dependence on relief induces a spiritual and moral disintegration." With the midterm elections approaching, Congress took no action on welfare reform.

President Clinton's slumping approval ratings, which by mid-1994 had dropped to 42 percent, complicated his task. Many found him too ready to compromise, too eager to please, and too inclined to flit from issue to issue. Exploiting the "character issue," critics publicized Clinton's financial dealings while governor, including a real-estate speculation in the Whitewater Development Company. Hillary Rodham Clinton's profit of $100,000 in commodities trading on an investment of $1,000 raised more questions, as did the 1993 suicide of the Clintons' close friend, assistant White House counsel Vincent W. Foster, Jr. Charges of sexual impropriety on Clinton's part, first aired during the campaign, resurfaced in 1994 when an Arkansas state employee alleged in a lawsuit that as governor, Clinton had solicited sexual favors.

As Clinton proved vulnerable, the political climate turned nasty. Radio commentator Rush Limbaugh won celebrity with his jeering attacks on liberals and his cynical ridicule of the very idea of government. Televangelist Jerry Falwell offered a videotape that hinted (with no evidence) that Clinton had arranged the murder of political enemies. The Christian Coalition, founded by TV preacher Pat Robertson, conducted training sessions and church-based voter-registration drives to win political power at the local level. By 1994, with 1.2 million evangelical supporters and some nine hundred chapters nationwide, the Christian Coalition had gained control of the Republican parties of Virginia, Minnesota, Iowa, Texas, South Carolina, and Oregon.

Clinton angrily denounced his foes on the Right, but the symbolic politics of personal vituperation and hot-button cultural issues increasingly preempted public discourse, thus obscuring social and economic problems of urgent importance. Although composing a minority of the electorate, the religious Right, with its passion and organizational energy, represented a powerful and unpredictable force in American politics of the 1990s.

The Quest for a Coherent Foreign Policy

In contrast to George Bush, Bill Clinton preferred domestic issues to foreign policy. In the Clinton White House, complained a British journalist, world affairs seemed "a rude interruption to the president's busy domestic schedule." Yet the United States remained the world's only superpower after the Soviet collapse, and its world role inevitably invited scrutiny.

In Eastern Europe, the Soviet collapse unleashed bitter ethnic conflicts. As Yugoslavia broke up in 1991, Serbian forces in Bosnia launched a murderous campaign of "ethnic cleansing" to drive out Muslims and Croats. Advised by Secretary of State Warren Christopher, Clinton supported a U.N.-peacekeeping effort and contributed U.S. airpower to NATO bomb-

Sarajevo, May 1995
Grieving relatives bury a five-year-old boy killed in the shelling of Sarajevo by Bosnian Serbs. As the Serbs pursued their campaign of "ethnic cleansing" against Bosnia's Muslim population, scenes like this became tragically frequent.

ing raids on Serb positions. But when the Serbs took hundreds of U.N. peacekeepers hostage following NATO air strikes in May 1995, NATO quickly backed down and suspended the attacks. Encouraged, the Serbs overran the Muslim enclave of Srebrenica in August 1995 and menaced other U.N.-designated "safe areas" including Bosnia's capital, Sarajevo. As Washington tried to mobilize further air attacks without committing U.S. ground troops, the crisis underscored the difficulty of coordinating international peacekeeping efforts in the absence of a Soviet threat that could unify Western governments and rally public opinion.

In the former Soviet Union, Russia endured inflation, shortages, and economic chaos as centralized control yielded to a market-oriented system. Extortionist gangs flourished, and an antiwestern nationalist party showed alarming strength in the December 1993 elections. Again, the Clinton administration played a peripheral role, supporting President Boris Yeltsin (who came to Washington for a summit meeting in September 1994) and pledging economic aid to Russia and the Ukraine but otherwise watching from the sidelines. Despite worsening conditions in Russia and strained diplomatic relations following Moscow's brutal attack on the breakaway republic of Chechnya early in 1995, the administration continued to insist that Yeltsin represented Russia's best hope for stability and democratization.

The domestic political constraints on U.S. power in the post–Cold War era became clear in Africa and the Caribbean. In the East African nation of Somalia, a U.S. military intervention undertaken by President Bush in 1992 as a humanitarian response to famine and starvation ended bleakly in 1994 as U.S. forces became embroiled in conflict between warring Somali factions. In the tiny central African nation of Rwanda, ancient hatreds between two rival groups, the Hutu majority and the Tutsi minority, flared into genocidal violence in 1994. Roving bands of Hutu militia massacred as many as a half-million Tutsi. When Tutsi rebels struck back, up to a million terrified Hutus fled into neighboring Zaire, creating a massive refugee crisis. Traumatized by the Somali fiasco, the Clinton administration pledged equipment to a planned U.N. intervention but otherwise did little.

A similar pattern unfolded in Haiti, where in September 1991 a military junta overthrew President Jean-Bertrand Aristide and terrorized his supporters. As thousands of Haitians fleeing poverty and repression set out for Florida in small, unseaworthy craft, Washington vacillated, adopting various policies toward the refugees. African-American political leaders kept attention focused on the crisis, as did the 300,000 U.S.-born Haitians. Unable to dislodge the junta, Clinton in July 1994 assembled a potential invasion flotilla off Haiti's coast. The picture changed in September, however, when ex-president Jimmy Carter persuaded the

Haitian Youths Greet U.S. Army Helicopter, Port-au-Prince, Haiti, September 1994

Another Step on the Rocky Path to Mideast Peace
President Clinton presides as Israeli Prime Minister Yitzhak Rabin and PLO Chairman Yasir Arafat shake hands after signing a peace accord at the White House, September 13, 1993.

junta leaders to accept voluntary exile. Backed by a peaceful occupation force of twenty thousand U.S. troops, Aristide resumed the presidency. Periodic attacks on Aristide supporters by the Haitian police continued, however, and the chasm between the island's wealthy elite and its impoverished masses remained as wide as ever. For Clinton, even this qualified diplomatic success had a bittersweet edge because of the crucial role played by Carter, from whom he had sought to distance himself.

Elsewhere, patient U.S. diplomatic effort bore fruit. South Africa's move to multiracial democracy, hastened by the economic sanctions imposed by the United States and other nations, advanced dramatically in 1994 as Nelson Mandela, long imprisoned by the nation's apartheid government, won the presidency in the nation's first free elections.

In the Middle East, negotiations between the Israelis and the Palestine Liberation Organization produced in 1994 an agreement on limited Palestinian self-rule in the Gaza Strip and the West Bank city of Jericho. Acknowledging the United States' role in the accord, PLO leader Yasir Arafat and Israeli prime minister Yitzhak Rabin signed the agreement in Washington with a smiling President Clinton looking on. As Israel and Jordan began talks, a broader Mideast peace accord seemed possible. Incidents of terrorism continued, however, including the February 1993 bombing of

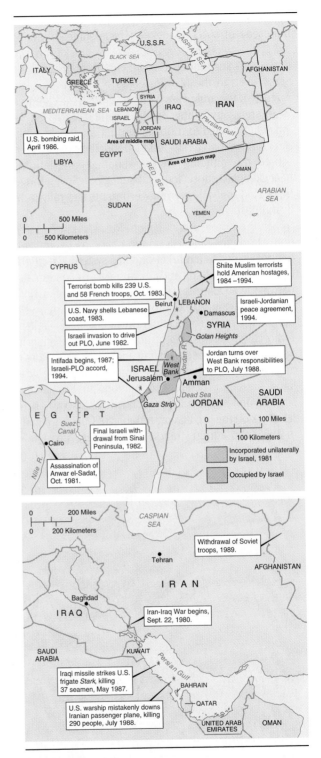

The Mideast Crises, 1980–Present
Despite the long history of Mideast violence and animosity, the end of the Cold War and negotiations among the hostile parties gave promise by the mid-1990s of at least a partial easing of tensions in the region.

the World Trade Center in New York City by Shiite fundamentalists linked to a radical Egyptian sheik.

Another apparent diplomatic success for Clinton came in his dealings with North Korea, ruled since 1948 by communist strongman Kim Il Sung. In brazen violation of the 1970 Nuclear Nonproliferation Treaty, the North Koreans began reprocessing spent fuel rods from nuclear-power plants into plutonium, a key component of nuclear bombs. In June 1994, under pressure from Washington and facing U.N. economic sanctions (and following a visit by Jimmy Carter), Kim pledged to stop making plutonium, to open North Korea's nuclear program to U.N. inspection, and to join in talks in Geneva on adherence to the nonproliferation pact. Kim died soon after, but prospects remained good for a peaceful resolution of the crisis. Clinton faced questions about Jimmy Carter's increasingly visible diplomatic role, however, and criticism from Republicans that he had conceded too much to the wily North Koreans. Indeed, after their electoral triumph in 1994 (see next section), Senator Dole and other GOP leaders in Congress subjected all aspects of Clintonian diplomacy to sharp critical scrutiny.

As the NAFTA agreement made plain, the expansion of foreign trade figured prominently on Clinton's foreign-policy agenda. The U.S. trade deficit, after several years of decline, shot up to $133 billion in 1993 as consumer spending improved. Of this, $59 billion represented the trade gap with Japan. Emulating George Bush, Clinton utilized a 1993 Asian economic summit in Seattle and a trade mission to Japan to pressure the Japanese to buy more U.S. goods.

Again like President Bush, Clinton chose to preserve trading ties with China despite Beijing's human-rights abuses. In 1994, while deploring the repression of dissidents, Clinton extended China's "most favored nation" trading status with the United States. This decision reflected economic realities: China had become the fourth most important U.S. trading partner.

In July 1994 Clinton traveled to Naples for the annual meeting of the Group of Seven (G-7), the world's leading economic powers: the United States, Japan, Great Britain, France, Germany, Italy, and Canada. (One journalist dubbed the G-7 the "Board of Directors of Planet Earth.") Addressing the assembly, the president stressed the G-7 leaders' role in promoting trade, investment, economic development, and job creation—familiar Clintonian themes. "Trade as much as troops," he declared, "will increasingly define the ties that bind nations in the twenty-first century."

Certainly trade increasingly defined U.S. relations with Europe. In 1993, by ratifying a treaty negotiated at Maastricht, Holland, the nations of the European Community (EC) created a new and stronger organization, the European Union (EU). With fifteen member states pledged to closer economic and political integration, including a common currency and coordinated economic policies, the EU loomed as a trading bloc of intimidating proportions. President Clinton downplayed the risks of economic competition between the EU and the NAFTA bloc. Instead, in a 1994 speech in Berlin, once the outpost of a divided Europe, he emphasized broad cooperation on economic and other global issues.

A practical step in this direction came in 1994 when the Clinton administration signed, and the Senate ratified, a new trading agreement negotiated by the member nations of GATT (the General Agreement on Tariffs and Trade, established in 1947 and now renamed the World Trade Organization). The agreement provided for a gradual lowering of trade barriers worldwide and set up mechanisms for resolving trade disputes. Economists foresaw significant economic benefits to the United States.

The link between trade and diplomacy was illustrated early in 1995 on two different fronts. When the Mexican peso collapsed, jeopardizing not only foreign investors but the flow of foreign trade, President Clinton, concluding that the crisis affected America's vital interests, quickly proposed $40 billion in loan guarantees to stabilize the situation.

At about the same time, Clinton threatened heavy punitive tariffs on many imports from China as a way of pressuring Beijing to halt the black-market pirating of U.S. movies, CDs, and computer software. This tough approach reversed the more lenient U.S. policy of 1993, but in the administration's view the economic issues clearly outweighed the resulting strained relations. Commented Lloyd Bentsen, the recently retired secretary of the treasury: "Everyone's been saying for a long time that foreign policy is becoming economic, but . . . it's taken a while for the message to sink in."

While offering no grand strategic vision, the Clinton administration in its first two years grappled with an array of regional issues and crises. Some criticized Clinton's diplomacy as indecisive; "[A] series of deals does not constitute a foreign policy," complained the *New York Times*. But the challenge of applying U.S. power appropriately in highly diverse situations was no simple matter in a post–Cold War world.

THE 1994 ELECTIONS AND AFTER: A SHARP RIGHT TURN

As the midterm elections approached, frustration with the administration, and with Washington politics generally, intensified. Commented Governor Lawton Chiles of Florida: "There's a feeling loose in the land of utter frustration." A bumper sticker captured this mood succinctly: "I'M FED UP." Bill Clinton had won in 1992 as a "new Democrat" offering fresh ideas, but by 1994 many voters viewed him as simply an old Democrat of the big-government, "tax-and-spend" variety. His early call for an end to the ban on homosexuals in the military, while applauded by some, convinced others that narrow special-interest groups controlled the White House agenda. To his critics, Clinton's failed health-care plan represented the dead end of a discredited New Deal/Great Society style of top-down reform. The "character issues" swirling around Clinton made his political setbacks even more damaging. Opponents saw him as hopelessly indecisive. Commented the Rev. Jesse Jackson: "When the president comes to a fork in the road, he chooses the fork."

At the same time, a movement to downsize government, reform the welfare system, slash taxes and spending, and shift power to the states gained momentum among the middle class. As the private sector downsized, the reasoning went, so should Washington. A bubbling brew of cultural and social issues added to the disaffection. These included such diverse but emotional topics as abortion, pornography, crime, school prayer, "radical feminism," rising rates of out-of-wedlock births, the cultural dominance of "secular humanism," and an alleged collapse of "family values." Illegal immigration (estimated at 1.9 million in 1994, mostly from Mexico and Central America) stirred resentment as well. Adding to the brew, a sour mood spread among white males angered by affirmative-action programs designed to aid minorities and women.

A network of conservative organizations orchestrated the rightward swing. As Pat Robertson's Christian Coalition mobilized evangelicals, the National Rifle Association (NRA) contributed generously to candidates who opposed restrictions on firearms. Conservative think tanks such as the Heritage Foundation funded studies critiquing liberal policies. Right-wing

Speaker of the House Newt Gingrich
A key architect of the Republican electoral victory in 1994, Gingrich led a right-wing assault on sixty years of welfare-state liberalism.

radio commentators and talk-show hosts continued to fill the airwaves with denunciations of the "liberal elite."

All this occurred during a period of economic recovery, minimal inflation, and a declining federal deficit. Normally, good economic news helps the party in power, but the Democrats reaped few political benefits from the boom. In part, this was because the recovery did little for ordinary Americans. The actual buying power of the average worker's paycheck rose for a few years in the early 1980s, but then fell from 1986 to 1990, and remained flat thereafter. Automation, foreign competition, and the weakness of organized labor all combined to keep wages down. In an October 1994 poll, an ominous 58 percent of Americans said they did not feel personally better off despite the economic upturn.

In the campaign summer of 1994, Republican Congressman Newt Gingrich of Georgia shrewdly translated the disgruntled mood into Republican votes. Displaying his media savvy, Gingrich drafted a "Contract with America," including tax cuts, congressional term limits, tougher crime laws, a balanced-budget amendment, and other popular reforms. In a photogenic ceremony on the Capitol steps, some 300 Republican candidates signed the Contract. Gingrich's strategy effectively nationalized the midterm election, normally dominated by local issues.

The resulting Republican landslide transformed the political landscape. By solid majorities, voters gave the Republicans control of both houses of Congress for the first time since 1954; increased the number of Republican governors to thirty-one; and cut down such Democratic giants as New York governor Mario Cuomo, Chicago congressman Dan Rostenkowski (plagued by an ethics investigation), and Speaker of the House Tom Foley—the first Speaker since 1860 to fail in a reelection bid. In Texas' gubernatorial race, George W. Bush, son of the former president, defeated the Democratic incumbent, Ann Richards. California voters passed Proposition 187, denying social services—including schooling and most medical care—to illegal immigrants and their children.

Sixty-three percent of white males voted Republican; evangelical Christians flocked to the polls, mostly to cast ballots for GOP candidates. Republican strategists hailed the election as the death knell of an activist, big-government tradition dating to the New Deal, and a giant further step in a conservative resurgence launched by Barry Goldwater and Richard Nixon in the 1960s. Liberals, feminists, environmentalists, and leaders of the Hispanic and African-American communities, by contrast, reacted with dismay. "Race was at the heart of this election," charged African-American historian Roger Wilkins angrily; "There was a fierce anti-black and anti-immigrant undertone to this switch to the Republican party. The message was, 'Let us take this country back and make it a white country—a white male country—again.' "

The new order quickly solidified its gains. Republican governors like Wisconsin's Tommy Thompson and Christine Todd Whitman of New Jersey insisted that the states, not Washington, D.C., were now the best source of policy ideas. In the nation's capital, Republicans took over congressional committees long chaired by Democrats. Robert Dole of Kansas became the new Senate majority leader; the reactionary Jesse Helms of North Carolina ascended to the chairmanship of the Foreign Relations Committee; and ninety-two-year-old Strom Thurmond of South Carolina, presidential candidate of the States Rights (Dixiecrat) party in 1948, headed the Arms Services Committee. New York's Alphonse D'Amato, eager to investigate the Clintons' tangled financial dealings, became chair of the Banking Committee.

In the House of Representatives, a jubilant horde of 230 Republicans, 73 of them newly elected, proclaimed Newt Gingrich Speaker by acclamation, made Rush Limbaugh an "honorary member," and set about translating the "Contract with America" into law. On its first day—a record session that lasted until 2:23 A.M.—the House adopted various procedural reforms and extended to the 40,000 employees of Congress and its agencies the protection of civil-rights laws and labor laws from which Congress had hitherto exempted itself. Another early bill forbade unfunded mandates, by which Washington had imposed regulations and programs on the states without providing money to cover the costs.

The House also soon passed a constitutional amendment requiring a balanced federal budget by the year 2002. (The amendment included several escape clauses: it could be waived in wartime, or overridden by a three-fifths vote of Congress.) The Senate, however, rejected the admendment by a one-vote margin. On the cultural front, House Republicans targeted such "liberal elite" institutions as the Public Broadcasting Corporation, the National Endowment for the Arts, and the National Endowment for the Humanities.

Other issues including budget cuts, a shift of power to the states, repeal of the 1993 ban on assault weapons (the NRA's top priority), and a constitutional amendment permitting prayer in the schools, awaited their turn. The Republicans also pledged increased defense appropriations. Despite the Cold War's end and the absence of significant threats to the nation's security, some conservative strategists, proposing frightening hypothetical scenarios, urged continued high levels of military spending, and key Republican leaders agreed.

The new Republican majority especially spotlighted tax cuts and welfare reform. On the tax front, GOP leaders promised an array of tax credits and benefits for the middle class and the wealthy that, if enacted, would reduce federal revenues by nearly $200 billion over a five-year period. It would also gut the Tax Reform Act of 1986, designed to eliminate tax breaks and loopholes.

As in the early Reagan years, the promise of tax cuts coupled with increased defense spending seemed fatal to any hope of balancing the budget, but Republican leaders insisted that large savings could be achieved in other parts of the budget. Where these savings would come from was unclear, since the biggest budget items apart from defense were interest payments on the national debt and two programs sacred to the middle class, Social Security and Medicare, which the Republicans pledged not to touch.

On welfare reform, early GOP proposals included measures to encourage or force welfare recipients off the dole and into the labor market; terminate benefit increases for children born out of wedlock; and stop benefits to immigrant aliens, even legal immigrants. Some plans also called for annual welfare appropriations in place of entitlement programs that grew automatically as more individuals met the mandated criteria. Republican governors pressed for block grants to the states, which states could allocate as they chose, as an alternative to the crazy-quilt of federal welfare programs that had grown up over the years.

The impetus for welfare reform had two sources. The first was cost. The two major welfare programs, Medicaid and Aid to Families with Dependent Children (AFDC), together with food stamps, cost about $125 billion in 1994. Though dwarfed by the benefits that flowed to the middle class through Social Security, Medicare, farm subsidies, and a variety of tax deductions, this sum still contributed substantially to the annual budget deficits.

The second argument for welfare reform, proclaimed by Newt Gingrich and many others, was ideological: the belief that the system undermines the work ethic and traps the poor in a permanent cycle of dependence. Despite the absence of data proving this hypothesis, it appealed strongly to hard-working Americans only too ready to view the poor as lazy and shiftless.

The proliferating welfare-reform proposals raised serious policy issues and ethical questions. Would the proposed changes penalize children for their parents' actions? In urban areas lacking job opportunities, would the government provide public employment to individuals dropped from the welfare rolls, or leave their survival to the vagaries of private charity? And could one assume that fifty state welfare programs

would be any more successful than federally mandated ones?

Overall, the torrent of bills, hearings, and press releases pouring out of Washington early in 1995 recalled the heady days of Lyndon Johnson's Great Society and even the first Hundred Days of FDR's New Deal. Now, however, the new ideas and activist energy came from conservatives, not from liberals.

President Clinton appeared stunned by his plummeting fortunes. In a maladroit bit of symbolism, he went hunting the day the new Congress convened, and was photographed carrying a dead duck. A rambling State of the Union address offered little more than a feeble echo of the Republican agenda, including tax cuts, welfare reforms, and a slimmed-down federal government. While Senator Dole and others maneuvered for the 1996 GOP nomination, Democratic leaders speculated about a possible challenge to Clinton from within his own party.

House Speaker Newt Gingrich, meanwhile, exercised a degree of personal power that evoked memories of "Uncle Joe" Cannon, who ruled the House in the early twentieth century (see Chapter 22). A one-time history teacher, Gingrich displayed an intellectual cockiness and a shoot-from-the-hip style that won the admiration of some and struck others as know-it-all arrogance. Gingrich stumbled in January 1995 when he accepted a $4.5 million book-royalty advance from a publishing house owned by Rupert Murdoch, a publishing tycoon with vital interests in federal legislation. Gingrich backed away from the advance under a hail of adverse criticism, but his reputation for impetuousness grew. Journalists also focused on Gingrich's network of political action groups, dubbed "Newt, Inc.," through which corporate contributors and others placed at Gingrich's personal disposal a $16 million war chest.

No one questioned Gingrich's political genius. Lampooning liberals as "left-wing elitists" and "counterculture McGoverniks," the Georgia firebrand challenged the entire structure of social programs and federal-state relations that had evolved since the New Deal, and articulated the political values of an earlier era of laissez-faire, sink-or-swim individualism.

Gingrich dismissed liberals as trapped in the past and unable to think creatively about the future. A technological enthusiast, he predicted that all Americans will soon possess laptop computers, fax machines, cellular phones, and instant access to the global electronic internet. Space enthralled him as well. In *Window of Opportunity* (1984), he anticipated "a mirror system in space [that] could provide the light equivalent of many full moons so that there would be no need for nighttime lighting of highways." The weightlessness of space stations, he suggested, could transform life for persons confined to wheelchairs on earth. He envisioned a "virtual Congress" dispersed around the nation and linked electronically.

Gingrich admired the futurologists Alvin and Heidi Toffler, whose *Future Shock* (1970) and *The Third Wave* (1980) foretold electronic wonders ahead. Linking the Tofflers' utopian vision to his own conservative politics, Gingrich envisioned a future of free-flowing information and decentralized power in which technology would free individuals from the constraints of centralized government.

On the foreign-relations front, the Republican landslide signaled a further turn inward. The Contract with America largely ignored foreign policy, and key Republican legislators openly espoused isolationist views. Jesse Helms, the new chair of the Senate Foreign Relations Committee, denounced the United Nations as an enemy of U.S. interests, criticized international environmental treaties, saw little good in U.N. peacekeeping efforts, and compared foreign aid to throwing money down a rat hole. Like the domestic welfare program, suggested another GOP senator, America's $14 billion foreign-aid program trapped the recipient nations in a "devastating cycle of dependence." This upsurge of isolationism and hyper-nationalism dismayed many citizens who saw an intimate link between America's long-term prospects and the fate of the world as a whole, including those societies mired in grinding poverty.

For all the rhetoric, the larger meaning of the 1994 election remained unclear. The party in power often loses ground in midterm—though rarely so dramatically. For some observers, the election's most troubling aspect was not the choices made by those who voted, but the apparent apathy of those who did not. Only 38 percent of eligible voters went to the polls in 1994, so the great shift rightward was actually achieved by about one-fifth of the total electorate.

Still, a significant ideological change did appear to be under way, challenging a legacy of federal social-welfare activism stretching back through the Great Society and the New Deal to the progressive era. In their railings against "Washington," the conservative ideologists of the 1990s echoed the language of the anti-Federalists of the 1780s, terrified of the tyrannical centralized power the new Constitution would create.

Anti-Washington rhetoric holds a continuing appeal for Americans, evoking as it does a vanished era when one could pull up stakes and head for a supposedly empty wilderness, beyond the reach of government and irksome social constraints.

Embattled liberals did not entirely retreat from the ideological fray. To be sure, they conceded, the Tenth Amendment does reserve "to the States . . . or to the people" all powers not delegated to the central government. Yet America is one nation, they insisted, not simply a collection of states—a single society with an integrated economy, transportation grid, national media, and mass culture. The most urgent problems we face are national in scope, transcending state boundaries.

All political wisdom does not lie in Washington, D.C., liberals granted, and the reach of federal power has definite limits. But neither is "Washington" a Great Satan deserving only contempt and ridicule. Time and again in our history, the federal government, in its three branches, has taken the lead in making America a more equitable and humane society. If rampant individualism and hostility to government wins the day, liberals asked, who will speak for the general welfare, the social bond that unites us as a society, and the plight of the poorest and most vulnerable among us?

The disputes of the 1990s were, in fact, part of a very old debate. American political discourse has always oscillated between the claims of states' rights and individual freedom, on the one hand, and the claims of the nation and of society as a whole, on the other. The process of negotiating these rival claims is often painful, controversial, and messy. But such is the nature of decision-making in a free society. As Winston Churchill once observed, democracy is the worst possible form of government—except for all the others.

A BROADER PERSPECTIVE

For teaching purposes, the history of the United States is often divided into presidential administrations. There are good reasons for this approach. Our quadrennial presidential elections stimulate debate on vital public issues, and presidents shape the national agenda as they present their legislative programs.

But the "presidential synthesis" has its drawbacks. It can narrow one's perspective to short-term issues and partisan conflict, obscuring a broader view of the nation's direction. These drawbacks have become particularly evident in the late twentieth century, as the nation has undergone profound changes that clearly will outlast any one president's term.

A look beyond specific presidential administrations reveals that the United States has confronted social divisions, economic transformations, a shifting demographic profile, and cultural tensions as the century has closed. Globally, the Cold War's end has posed problems and challenges that seem in some ways even more maddeningly complex than those the nation faced before the collapse of the Soviet Union.

Economic and Social Trends: Coping with Change

Changes in the economic and social arena are especially evident. Women's entry into the workplace, for example, described in Chapter 32, has continued unabated. By 1993, over 57 percent of American women were in the labor force; by 2005, the Bureau of Labor Statistics estimates, the figure will approach 64 percent. In opinion polls, most high-school girls assume a career in their future. Even Dagwood Bumstead's spouse Blondie, the ultimate comic-strip housewife, started a catering business in 1991. (By contrast, the 1994 Disney movie *The Lion King* has been criticized for reinforcing stereotypes of female subordination.) The entry of women into the workplace has had far-reaching implications. Employers commonly offer pregnancy leave and flexible work schedules, for example, to accommodate parental duties.

More broadly, despite the economic recovery of the early 1990s, a nagging sense of narrowing possibilities continues to trouble many Americans. The United States remains an economic powerhouse but is not the colossus it was in the early post–World War II decades. The nation's share of the world's total output of goods and services, for example, tumbled from one-third in 1950 to one-fifth in 1990.

And Americans have continued each year to buy far more in foreign products than they have sold. The U.S. trade deficit in 1994 soared to $108 billion, up 42 percent from 1993. Some of the dollars spent on foreign products have returned in the form of capital investment. By 1990 foreign holdings in U.S. banks, businesses, and real estate stood at a staggering $1.5 trillion. In the face of such statistics, Cold War fears of

East Meets West: Beijing, 1993
An awestruck Chinese tyke poses with a mannequin of Ronald McDonald, corporate symbol of the McDonald fast-food chain. The global spread of U.S. mass culture, a key long-term trend, accelerated in the 1990s.

military vulnerability have given way to fears of *economic* vulnerability.

As recessions have come and gone, the decline of jobs in the industrial sector and the growth of the service sector have continued. Manufacturing employed only 17 percent of all nonagricultural workers in the mid-1990s, with further declines predicted. The steel industry illustrates the pattern. Domestic steel production revived dramatically in the 1980s and early 1990s, and by 1994, plants were operating at 98 percent of capacity. Yet as a consequence of automation and cost-cutting efficiencies, the number of steelworkers fell from some 240,000 in 1983 to 140,000 in 1992.

As industrial employment has declined, so has union membership. In 1945 some 35 percent of U.S. workers belonged to unions; in 1993 the figure was about 15 percent. Ronald Reagan and George Bush won the presidency despite vigorous labor opposition, and Reagan broke a 1981 strike by the air-traffic controllers' union at little political cost. Clinton promoted the NAFTA treaty despite anguished protests from organized labor. Since most service workers today are not unionized, further decline in organized labor's influence seems inevitable.

In the service sector's upper ranks, one finds high-income managers, physicians, lawyers, teachers, engineers, computer programmers, and so forth. But many service-sector workers hold low-paying, low-skilled jobs in sales, fast-food vending, custodial work, and similar jobs. Much of the job growth of the mid-1990s, like that of the 1980s, has been at this low end of the service sector, often in temporary positions. (Some call them "McJobs.") Indeed, more than one-fifth of the U.S. labor force in 1994 was either temporary or part-time, enjoying few benefits or advancement prospects. Such jobs rarely provide sufficient income or benefits to live comfortably or raise a family.

And even the service sector, the primary source of new jobs, has faced slow growth, periodic shakeouts, and uncertainty as employers have coped with over-expansion and rising competition by trimming labor costs. In 1992 the *New York Times* reported, "Most economists expect the great American job machine . . . to run at just half speed through much of the 1990s." The same newspaper two years later found "uncertainty, insecurity, and anxiety" in all sectors of the labor force. The low voter turnout in 1994, and the absence of serious attention to economic issues in that election, suggested a widespread view that politics could do little to alleviate such concerns.

White-collar and blue-collar workers alike often feel themselves on an economic treadmill. With little cushion, a medical crisis or protracted retirement expenses can quickly erase a family's life savings.

Success in the job market increasingly has required not just a willingness to work but advanced training and special skills. For young people seeking work, and for displaced industrial workers, this has been bleak news. Indeed, even as joblessness declined in 1993–1994, it remained disturbingly high for younger workers. About 14 percent of workers aged 16–25 were unemployed in 1993, twice the national average. Nor has a college degree guaranteed employment in the volatile job market of the nineties. Small wonder that 75 percent of young people have told pollsters that they expect to be worse off than their parents.

While politicians debated welfare reform, social conditions continued to deteriorate in the inner cities, where the structural problems besetting the economy have been vastly magnified. Detroit's jobless rate in 1994 was 18 percent; among young people, it approached 50 percent. Some observers have spoken of an alienated "outer class" lacking work, uneducated, politically apathetic, socially adrift, warehoused in decaying housing projects, the children easy prey to crime, street gangs, and drugs. These densely populated urban slums accounted for most of the 15 percent of the American population living below the poverty line in 1993—up from 12 percent in 1977.

For the nation's 30 million African-Americans, the chasm between the suburban middle class and the inner-city poor, explored in Chapter 32, has widened. Among middle-class blacks, statistics continue to be encouraging. The number of black college graduates grew from 1 million in 1980 to over 2.2 million in 1994. More than 8,000 blacks held elective public office in America in 1993, a fivefold increase over 1970. The 1990s saw the election of New York City's first black mayor (David Dinkins) and the first black governor (Douglas Wilder of Virginia). President Bush appointed African-Americans Colin Powell as chairman of the Joint Chiefs of Staff, Louis Sullivan as secretary of health and human services, and Clarence Thomas to the Supreme Court. President Clinton's high-level black appointees have included Ronald Brown as secretary of commerce and Joycelyn Elders as surgeon general. (Elders resigned in 1994 amid controversy over her pronouncements on such sensitive issues as federal drug policy and sex education.)

But middle-class black achievement cannot efface the reality of life for the one-third of blacks who live below the poverty line. In 1994 the number of incarcerated juveniles, most of them black or Hispanic, surpassed 100,000. Periodic explosions of urban violence, and movies like Spike Lee's *Do the Right Thing* (1989) and John Singleton's *Boyz 'N the Hood* (1991), a harrowing depiction of gang warfare in Los Angeles, have dramatized the situation.

With more than 220 million guns in America in the mid-1990s and a shooting every fourteen minutes, firearms violence obviously has not been confined to the inner cities, yet it has taken a fearful toll there. On April 29, 1994, James Darby, a black third-grader in New Orleans, as part of a class assignment, wrote to President Clinton expressing his fear of urban violence. On May 8, walking home from a Mother's Day picnic, James was shot and killed.

Much of the violence has been spawned by the drug traffic, which has remained at epidemic levels despite much-publicized preventive efforts. While cocaine use has declined somewhat in the 1990s, the use of heroin, LSD, and other drugs has risen. In some inner-city neighborhoods, drug dealers are the biggest employers of teenage youths. Heroin-related emergency-room admissions rose 44 percent in the first six months of 1994 over the corresponding period in 1993.

The epidemic of out-of-wedlock pregnancies among young black women has continued as well, drastically reducing the young mothers' opportunities for education and employment and narrowing the children's life prospects. A 1994 Census Bureau report found 57 percent of all African-American children living with a single parent, usually the mother. Declared Marian Wright Edelman of the Children's Defense Fund in 1994: "We have a major black child crisis, the worst since slavery." The *Economist* of London has called the plight of the United States' inner-city welfare children "a disaster as pressing as any in the world."

A similar social dichotomy has characterized the Hispanic population. Growing numbers of Hispanics have advanced economically and academically in the 1980s and 1990s, and Hispanics have begun to exercise the political clout their numbers warranted. In California alone, more than 4,000 Hispanics held public office in 1991. President Clinton's Hispanic appointees include Henry G. Cisneros as secretary of housing and urban development and Federico F. Peña as secretary of transportation.

But more than a quarter of all Hispanics have remained trapped in poverty, either in urban barrios or on the migrant-labor circuit. Among the Hispanic poor, the all-too-familiar social patterns associated with economic deprivation have manifested themselves, including street gangs, drug addiction, and teen pregnancy. The same 1994 Census Bureau study found one-third of all Hispanic children living with a single parent who had never married. The high-school dropout rate among Hispanic youths neared 30 percent in 1991, three times the national rate.

On the cultural front, meanwhile, the right-wing savaging of President Clinton, and the Christian Coalition's efforts to take over the Republican party, have formed only part of a larger backlash, under way since the 1960s, against what conservatives saw as the moral decay of society. This reaction had abated somewhat in the 1980s, when the conservative Ronald Reagan occupied the White House, but with Clinton's victory it again rocketed into prominence, polarizing public discourse to a disturbing degree. In earlier times, the cul-

tural wars had been waged along sectarian lines, with native-born Protestants battling Catholic and Jewish immigrants. Now the lines were redrawn as former antagonists drew together and found common ground on a shifting array of emotion-laden cultural issues touching deeply held values.

During the Cold War, the full diversity of conservative ideology was muted, as anticommunism provided a common theme around which all could rally. In the nineties, with this unifying theme gone, religious and cultural conservatives are articulating their distinctive fears more openly and vigorously.

The cultural war has unfolded on many fronts, from radio talk shows and magazine columns to protests at school-board meetings and boycotts of TV shows and magazines considered morally offensive. History textbooks have become contested terrain as conservatives have attacked them for promoting "multiculturalism" and for allegedly pandering to the forces of "political correctness." The intensity and bitterness of the conflict have borne witness to the level of anxiety of once-dominant groups dismayed by the changes overwhelming the nation and convinced that society's moral destiny hangs in the balance.

The abortion controversy shows no sign of abating. As the rhetoric of the "pro-life" campaign has escalated, some individuals have, with tragic irony, crossed the line from peaceful protest to life-threatening violence. In July 1994, an anti-abortion activist shot and killed a physician and his bodyguard outside a Pensacola, Florida, abortion clinic. That December, an unstable young man murdered two people and wounded five others at clinics in Brookline, Massachusetts.

A far deadlier outburst of violence came on April 19, 1995, when a car bomb demolished an Oklahoma City federal building, killing more than 150 people, including many children in a day-care center. The attack occurred precisely two years after a federal raid on the Waco, Texas, compound of the Branch Davidians, a religious sect charged with firearms violations. The Waco raid ended tragically when a fire of uncertain origin killed some eighty Branch Davidians. After the Oklahoma City blast, authorities arrested a suspect , Timothy McVeigh, who had expressed outrage over the Waco incident. McVeigh and other suspects in the case had links to the Michigan Militia, one of many secretive paramilitary organizations that sprang up in the 1990s. President Clinton (and many other observers) blamed such shadowy antigovernment hate groups, and the outer fringe of right-wing radio talk-show hosts, for

**Oklahoma City,
April 19, 1995**
*Street workers and media
gather around the Alfred P.
Murrah Federal Building
after a massive bomb shattered its facade. The blast
took a heavy toll in human
life.*

contributing to a climate that had apparently driven a
few extremists to criminal violence. At the same time,
however, Clinton's call for beefed-up federal powers to
investigate the hate groups merely intensified their
fears of a vast conspiracy to destroy freedom in America — fears often linked to racist and anti-Semitic ideas
as well. The poisonous climate created by the peddlers
of paranoia, punctuated by acts of violence, worsened
the prospects for the kind of calm discussion of public
issues, marked by reasoned argument and mutual respect, that was essential if the nation was to solve the
urgent problems it faced.

An Imperiled Environment

Environmental protection is another long-term issue
that transcends any one presidential administration.
Three Mile Island and the *Exxon Valdez* disaster were
but two of a series of events dramatizing the threat to
our increasingly vulnerable planet. In 1982 authorities
permanently evacuated the community of Times
Beach, Missouri, when they realized that for years the
town had oiled its roads in summer with industrial
sludge containing the poison dioxin. In 1984 poison-

ous gases escaping from a U.S.-owned chemical plant
in Bhopal, India, killed seventeen hundred nearby
villagers.

With the Cold War over, Americans confronted the
cost of cleaning up the nation's nuclear-weapons facilities: $150 billion, according to one estimate. In 1994 the
Energy Department revealed that the United States possessed nearly one thousand metric tons of weapons-
grade uranium and twenty-six metric tons of plutonium
stockpiled in ten states from California to New York.

The most polluted site, the Hanford Nuclear
Reservation near Richland, Washington, was a vast
dump of radioactive waste where clean-up estimates
ran as high as $57 billion. The permanent disposal of
the waste from Hanford and other nuclear-weapons
sites, as well as of spent fuel from the nation's aging
nuclear-power plants, roused intense political passions. With every new site proposed, local resistance
was immediate and fierce.

The environmental threat has taken many forms.
Acid rain, bearing sulfur dioxide and other pollutants
from U.S. factories and auto exhaust, has destroyed
marine life in Canadian lakes and killed Appalachian
forests. As carbon dioxide from factories burning fossil

fuels has generated a layer of heat-retaining gases in the lower atmosphere, and as fluorocarbons from spray cans, refrigeration equipment, and other sources have depleted the upper-atmosphere ozone layer shielding the earth from solar radiation, scientists warn of a global warming trend—the "greenhouse effect"—with catastrophic potential.

The Oil Pollution Act of 1990, passed in the angry aftermath of the *Exxon Valdez* disaster, vividly illustrates the problem of translating environmental concerns into public policy. This law, which vastly enlarged the definition of persons legally entitled to compensation because of oil spills, has proved an administrative nightmare, and after four years enforcement procedures are not yet in place.

A New World Order?

Globally, the twentieth century's closing decades have witnessed what diplomat George Kennan called "a turning point of the most momentous historical significance": the end of the Cold War and the demise of the Soviet Union. As the bipolar world that had emerged after World War II collapsed, so too did the epic struggle that for forty years had shaped the United States' foreign policy, economy, and culture. Victory in the Cold War has brought a sense of long effort rewarded and an occasion to reaffirm such basic principles as democracy, individual rights, and freedom of expression that had proved more enduring than the dogmas of totalitarianism.

But with the Cold War's end has come a disorienting realization that the world is suddenly a more complicated place than before. As a character in John Updike's 1990 novel *Rabbit at Rest* puts it: "It's like nobody's in charge of the other side any more. I miss it, the cold war. It gave you a reason to get up in the morning." Victory in the Cold War produced "a good deal of talk about a new world order," observed political scientist Richard Barnet in the same vein in 1992, "but, for all the talk, the nightly news is a kaleidoscope of disorder."

Totalitarian regimes had collapsed, and the threat of a thermonuclear holocaust had blessedly subsided, but in their place trouble spots around the world clamored for attention. Like firefighters battling countless small blazes rather than one raging conflagration, policymakers accustomed to Cold War strategizing coped with a mare's nest of seemingly unrelated issues.

The global order coming into focus in the 1990s differs radically from that faced by Harry Truman in 1945 or even by John F. Kennedy in 1961. The task has been to define a constructive role for the United States in a world of powerful regional, economic, and political alignments. In 1993 Clinton concentrated on trade relations with Asia; in 1994, with the Soviet threat no longer assuring transatlantic unity, he sought to redefine U.S. relations with Europe.

In the post–Cold War era, however, the globe's central polarity increasingly has seemed not East-West but North-South: between the industrialized societies of the Northern Hemisphere, with their generally high living standards and stable birthrates, and a Southern Hemisphere scourged by poverty, hunger, disease, illiteracy, crushing population growth, and a dangerous gap between the masses and the ruling elites. As Americans have focused on their domestic problems, the need to keep larger global realities constantly in view has become especially urgent.

Many hope that in the post–Cold War era, the United Nations, long a pawn of the superpowers' conflict, will at last function in the way envisioned by its more idealistic supporters in 1945. And indeed, in 1994 more than seventy thousand blue-helmeted U.N. representatives from seventy nations performed peacekeeping duties in fourteen world trouble spots from El Salvador to Somalia. U.N. agencies also addressed environmental and public-health issues that transcended national boundaries. How the world organization will evolve in the future, particularly as the U.S. electorate turns to the right, remains to be seen.

Clearly, it will take Americans time to adjust to a new historical age in which international issues have to be addressed on their own terms rather than reduced to simplistic Cold War slogans. A stable, humane, and open international order will not arise automatically from the ruins of the old. It will require clear thinking, committed effort, and active engagement by citizens as well as policymakers. In confronting that challenge, the United States will continue to play a central role.

CONCLUSION

U.S. society has evolved with dizzying rapidity in the closing years of the twentieth century. Many Americans are thriving in the new service-based economy dominated by computers and an array of interactive communications technologies dubbed "the electronic highway" by President Clinton, and once envisioned only by science-fiction writers. But as millions lag behind, fears deepen of a nation permanently divided between an educated, professional elite and prosperous middle class, on the one hand, and an outer class stuck in poverty and despair. The pace of social and demographic change has brought uneasiness, cultural tensions, and sometimes explosions of reactionary venom. Internationally, as familiar power alignments have dissolved before their eyes, Americans have watched anxiously to discern the shape of the new order and their place in it.

In the mid-1990s politicians, the media, and citizens in general are only beginning to come to terms with the scope of these changes. Is the political system equal to the challenge, they ponder, or will fear, demagoguery, and reaction triumph? Will a multicultural society comprising diverse ethnic groups, cultural values, and religious beliefs find the resources to sustain a sense of common national identity, or will fragmentation and mistrust prevail? As the United States moves further into its third century as a nation, no one can be certain of the answers to these questions.

CHRONOLOGY

1984–1986 Congress bars military aid to contras.

1985 Rash of airline hijackings and other terrorist acts.

1986 Congress passes South African sanctions.
U.S. air raid on Libya.
William Rehnquist becomes chief justice of the United States.
Antonin Scalia joins Supreme Court.

1987 Congressional hearings on Iran-contra scandal.
Stock market crash.
Trade deficit reaches $170 billion.

1988 Oliver North, John Poindexter, and other Iran-contra figures indicted.
Reagan signs INF Treaty in Moscow.
George Bush elected president.
Anthony Kennedy joins Supreme Court.

Oliver North

1989 Oliver North convicted of Iran-contra role.
Massive Alaskan oil spill by *Exxon Valdez.*
Supreme Court, in several 5–4 decisions, restricts civil-rights laws.
U.S. invasion of Panama; Manuel Noriega overthrown.

1989 China's rulers crush prodemocracy movement.
Berlin Wall is opened.

1990 Federal Clean Air Act passed.
President Bush and Congress agree on five-year budget-deficit reduction package.
Iraq invades Kuwait.
Recession begins.
Germany reunified; Soviet troops start withdrawal from Eastern Europe.
David H. Souter joins Supreme Court.

1991 Gulf War (Operation Desert Storm).
United States and U.S.S.R. sign treaty reducing strategic nuclear arms by 25 percent.
Upheavals in Soviet Union as economy nears collapse, Communist party is disbanded, and Soviet republics declare independence.
Clarence Thomas seated on Supreme Court.

1992 Recession recovery is slow, joblessness high.
Supreme Court approves Pennsylvania restriction on abortion but upholds *Roe* v. *Wade.*
U.S. intervention in Somalia to provide humanitarian aid.

Clarence Thomas

Arkansas governor Bill Clinton elected president.

1993   Congress enacts modified version of Clinton
economic plan.

Congress approves NAFTA treaty.

Recession ends.

Congress debates health-care reform
(1993–1994).

Ruth Bader Ginsberg joins Supreme Court.

World Trade Center bombed.

1994   Christian Coalition gains control of Republican
party in several states.

1994   Somalia intervention ends.

United States seeks ouster of military junta in
Haiti.

Nelson Mandela elected president of South
Africa.

Israeli-PLO accord on limited Palestinian self-
rule in Gaza and Jericho.

G-7 nations meet in Naples.

Stephen G. Breyer joins Supreme Court.

Republican victory in 1994 elections.

FOR FURTHER READING

Many titles listed in Chapter 32's bibliography are relevant for
Chapter 33 as well. Discussions of trends in contemporary Amer-
ica may also be found in such journals as *The Atlantic Monthly,
Business Week, Christianity Today, Commentary, The Economist*
(London), *Fortune, Harper's Magazine, Monthly Labor Review*
(U.S. Department of Labor), *New Republic, National Review,
The Nation, Nation's Business, The New Leader, New York
Times Magazine, The Progressive, Scientific American,* and *U.S.
News and World Report.*

Mary Jo Bane and David T. Ellwood, *Welfare Realities: From
Rhetoric to Reform* (1994). Ellwood, assistant secretary of
health and human services in the Clinton administration, and
his co-author explore the complexities of welfare reform.

Robert Bellah et al., *The Good Society* (1991). Thoughtful reflections on the sources of community in the American historical
experience.

Al Gore, *Earth in the Balance: Ecology and the Human Spirit*
(1992). A soon-to-be vice president assesses the environmental challenges facing humankind.

Philip K. Howard, *The Death of Common Sense: How the Law is
Suffocating America* (1995). A lawyer looks at how well-intentioned but overly detailed government regulations can get out
of hand.

James Davison Hunter, *Culture Wars: The Struggle to Define
America* (1991). A sociologist's analysis of the sources of
moral and cultural conflict in contemporary U.S. society.

Haynes Johnson, *Divided We Fall: Gambling with History in the
Nineties* (1994). A journalist's disturbing report, based on
grass-roots interviews, on a divided and apprehensive populace.

David Maraniss, *First in His Class: A Biography of Bill Clinton*
(1995). Explores the sources of Clinton's political drive and his
almost desperate need to be liked.

Mark Robert Rank, *Living on the Edge: The Realities of Welfare
in America* (1994). A compelling look at the human face of
some of society's most marginal members.

*Statistical Abstract of the United States, 1995: The National Data
Book* (1995). A treasure trove of information on economic and
social trends, from the budget deficit to college enrollments.

U.S. News and World Report, *Triumph Without Victory: The Un-
reported History of the Persian Gulf War* (1992). The most
complete early history of Operation Desert Storm, by the editors of a leading news magazine.

Lawrence E. Walsh, *Iran-Contra: The Final Report* (1994). Independent counsel Walsh's full record of the crimes and cover-
ups associated with the Iran-Contra affair.

ADDITIONAL BIBLIOGRAPHY

Politics and Political Trends

Charles F. Allen, *The Comeback Kid* [Bill Clinton] (1992); Sidney
Blumenthal, "Christian Soldiers," *New Yorker,* July 18, 1994, pp.
31–37; Michael Duffy, *Marching in Place: The Status Quo Presi-
dency of George Bush* (1992); Ken Gross, *Ross Perot: The Man
Behind the Myth* (1992); Roderick P. Hart, *Seducing America:
How Television Charms the Modern Voter* (1994); Kevin P.
Phillips, *The Politics of Rich and Poor: Wealth and the American
Electorate in the Reagan Aftermath* (1990); Richard Rose, *The
Post-Modern President: George Bush Meets the World* (1991);

Paul Starr, *The Logic of Health Care Reform* (1992); Bob Woodward, *The Agenda: Inside the Clinton White House* (1994).

Economic Prospects

Michael A. Bernstein and David A. Adler, eds., *Understanding
American Economic Decline* (1994); Larry N. Gerston et al., *The
Deregulated Society* (1988); Otis L. Graham, Jr., *Losing Time:
The Industrial Policy Debate* (1992); Martin Lowy, *High Rollers:*

Inside the Savings and Loan Debacle (1991); Wallace C. Peterson, *Silent Depression: The Fate of the American Dream* (1994); Clyde V. Prestowitz, Jr., *Trading Places: How We Allowed Japan to Take the Lead* (1988); Robert Reich, *The Work of Nations: Preparing Ourselves for 21st Century Capitalism* (1991).

Social Issues

Children's Defense Fund, *The State of America's Children, 1991* (1991); Ellis Cose, *The Rage of a Privileged Class: Why Are Middle-Class Blacks Angry?* (1993); Sylvia Ann Hewlett, *When the Bough Breaks: The Cost of Neglecting Our Children* (1991); Denis Heyck, ed., *Barrios and Borderlands: Cultures of Latinos and Latinas in the United States* (1993); Arlie Hochschild, *Second Shift: Working Parents and the Revolution at Home* (1989); Christopher Jencks, *The Homeless* (1994); Lloyd D. Johnston et al., *Trends in Drug Use and Associated Factors Among American High School Students, College Students, and Young Adults, 1975–1989* (National Institute on Drug Abuse, 1991); Alex Kotlowitz, *There Are No Children Here: The Story of Two Boys Growing Up in the Other America* (1991); Patricia Nelson Limerick, Clyde Milner, and Charles Rankin, eds., *Trails: Toward a New History of the American West* (1991); Paul Light, *Baby Boomers* (1988); J. Anthony Lukas, *Common Ground: A Turbulent Decade in the Lives of Three American Families* (1986); Ronald B. Mincy, *Nurturing Young Black Males: Challenges to Agencies, Programs, and Social Policies* (1994); Christopher Pierson, *Beyond the Welfare State? The New Political Economy of Welfare* (1991); Roger Rosenblatt, *Life Itself* (1992) [the abortion debate]; Philip Shabecoff, *A Fierce Green Fire: The American Environmental Movement* (1994); Judith B. Schor, *The Overworked American: The Unexpected Decline of Leisure* (1991); Lisbeth B. Schorr with Daniel Schorr, *Within Our Reach: Breaking the Cycle of Disadvantage* (1988); Harvard Sitkoff, *The Struggle for Black Equality, 1954–1992,* rev. ed. (1993); Arlene S. Skolnick, *Embattled Paradise: The American Family in an Age of Uncertainty* (1991);

Richard White, *Rude Awakenings: What the Homeless Crisis Tells Us* (1992).

Popular Culture and Cultural Conflicts

"America's Hottest Export: Pop Culture," *Fortune,* December 31, 1990, pp. 50–60; Stephen L. Carter, *The Culture of Disbelief: How American Law and Politics Trivialize Religious Devotion* (1993); "Fancy Free: A Survey of the [American] Entertainment Industry," *The Economist* (London), December 23, 1989, pp. 3–18; Gerald Graff, *Beyond the Culture Wars: How Teaching the Conflicts Can Revitalize American Education* (1992); Robert Hughes, *The Culture of Complaint: The Fraying of America* (1993); Edward Palmer, *Televison and America's Children: A Crisis of Neglect* (1988); Neil Postman, *Amusing Ourselves to Death: Public Discourse in the Age of Show Business* (1985); Arthur M. Schlesinger, Jr., *The Disuniting of America* (1991); Michael Winship, *Television* (1988).

America and the World

Steve Albert, *The Case Against the General: Manuel Noriega and the Politics of American Justice* (1993); Michael R. Beschloss and Strobe Talbott, *At the Highest Levels: The Inside Story of the End of the Cold War* (1994); Michael L. Coniff, *Panama and the United States: The Forced Alliance* (1992); John Lewis Gaddis, *The United States and the End of the Cold War* (1992); Roger Hilsman, *George Bush vs. Saddam Hussein* (1992); Dilip Hiro, *Desert Shield to Desert Storm: The Second Gulf War* (1992); Michael J. Hogan, ed., *The End of the Cold War: Its Meaning and Implications* (1992); John R. MacArthur, *Second Front: Censorship and Propaganda in the Gulf War* (1992); Joseph S. Nye, *Bound to Lead: The Changing Nature of American Power* (1990); Gale Stokes, *The Walls Came Tumbling Down: The Collapse of Communism in Eastern Europe* (1993); Robert W. Tucker and David C. Hendrickson, *The Imperial Temptation: The New World Order and America's Purposes* (1992).

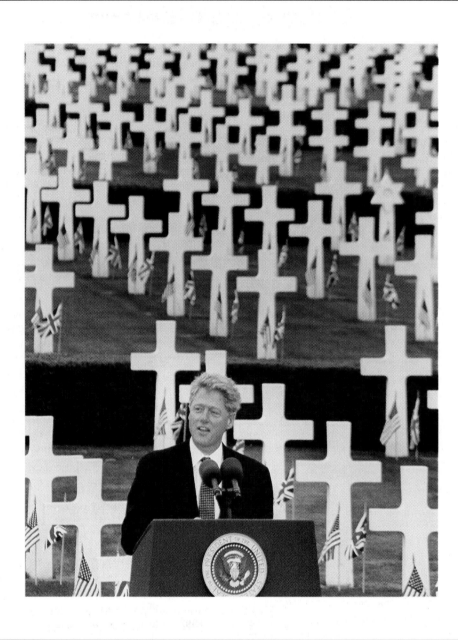

President Clinton at D-Day Ceremonies in Cambridge, England
June 4, 1994

LOOKING AHEAD—
LOOKING BACK

Anniversaries pregnant with historical meaning for Americans crowded in heavily in the early 1990s. In 1992 came the quincentennial of Christopher Columbus's epic voyage that opened the lands and civilizations of the New World to European discovery and exploitation. Nineteen ninety-four brought the twenty-fifth anniversary of two very different events that had helped to define the sixties: the Woodstock festival and Neil Armstrong's moonwalk. In 1995, a planned exhibit by the Smithsonian Institution marking the fiftieth anniversary of the atomic bombing of Hiroshima and Nagasaki stirred passionate disagreements over how the event should be remembered.

Of all these landmarks, the most poignant for many older Americans was June 6, 1994, the fiftieth anniversary of D-Day, the cross-Channel invasion into Nazi-occupied Normandy that marked a turning point in the war against Nazi tyranny. As the leaders of France, Great Britain, the United States, and other nations assembled to mark the occasion, aging veterans returned for a final sentimental journey to the scene of their youthful adventure. Many visited military cemeteries in France to pay tribute to thousands of GIs who did not survive the invasion.

The D-Day ceremonies starkly reminded Americans of the vast differences between 1944 and 1994. Then, the nation had been united; few doubted the monstrousness of the enemy or the righteousness of the American cause. In 1994 the United States seemed more fragmented than united, and the nation's role in a confusing post–Cold War world was far from clear.

President Bill Clinton, addressing the Polish parliament after the D-Day commemoration, noted the contrast. Yet he insisted that the historical role of today's generation, if less dramatic than that of those who had fought in World War II or even those who had stood on the ramparts in the Cold War, was no less meaningful. Said the president:

The challenges our generation faces are different than those our parents faced. They are problems that in many cases lack pressing drama. They require quiet and careful solutions. And if we meet them well, our reward will not be stunning moments of glory, but gradual and real improvements in the lives of our people.

We must find the will to unite around these opportunities of peace, as previous generations have united against war's life-or-death threats and oppression's fatal grip. To the courage that enables men and women to drop behind enemy lines, face down rumbling tanks or advance freedom's cause underground, we must add a new civil courage—the energy and optimism and patience to move forward through peaceful but hard and rapidly changing times.

As Clinton acknowledged, the United States' situation as the twentieth century winds down poses uncertainty and frustration. Yet there is cause for confidence as well. The anniversaries of the early 1990s have invited Americans to look back on their history; to reflect on the diverse, contentious, and creative society of today; and to contemplate their future as a people. Many have found reason for reassurance as well as uneasiness.

Changes and Challenges Ahead

Experts forecast steady U.S. population growth in the twenty-first century. Immigration, increased life expectancy, and a continued high birthrate among some groups are predicted to produce a population of 310 million by 2080—sixty million more than in 1990. Clearly, the task of providing education, health care, housing, and jobs to nearly a third of a billion citizens will stretch political skills and society's resources to the limit.

This growing population is also aging. In 1950, 8 percent of Americans were sixty-five or older; by 1990 the figure stood at 13 percent, with a rise to 17 percent projected by 2020. The social-security, nursing-care, and medical systems will clearly face heavy strains

i

in maintaining the health and dignity of the swelling ranks of the elderly.

And future U.S. society will be increasingly diverse, both ethnically and culturally. As a percentage of the total population, the native-born white population is diminishing each year and will continue to do so. By 2020, demographers predict, Hispanics will form the nation's largest minority, with some 16 percent of the population. African-Americans will follow closely behind, at 14 percent, while Asian-Americans will make up 7 percent. In a little more than two decades, in short, these three groups, plus Native Americans, will compose nearly 40 percent of the population. By 2050 "minorities" once considered outsiders will make up almost half the population.

On the economic front, as we have seen, the United States, after a century of undisputed industrial leadership and an exceptional post–World War II interlude of global economic supremacy, no longer can take its dominance for granted. The U.S. economy will probably remain the world's largest for some time, but it will undergo wrenching structural adjustments and face heavy competition from the thriving and integrated European powerhouse and from Pacific-rim producers with automated factories, highly efficient work forces, lower labor costs, and far greater research-and-development budgets than most U.S. businesses can boast.

Along with these broad social and economic trends, other social problems and challenges already evident will persist. Domestically, the grim phenomena of inner-city alienation and social fragmentation, marked by crime, drug abuse, lethal gang warfare, and out-of-wedlock pregnancy, seem deeply entrenched, though the partisans of welfare reform believe they have a formula for change. On the world scene, the United States in the mid-1990s was clearly only in the earliest stage of defining its international role in a post–Cold War global economy.

Facing Up to Change

Simply to list the problems confronting the nation can quickly produce a mood of discouragement. And the gloom deepens as one listens to the raucous cacophony of voices intent on widening the divisions in U.S. society and on deepening mistrust of the government, the media, and the schools. The contemptuous hostility toward the United States' institutions, democratic processes, and civic traditions expressed in some groups, and among some influential shapers of popular opinion, represents a disturbing trend.

At the same time, many Americans are turning inward, fearful of the diversity that has been the nation's strength and hallmark. The nineteenth-century British thinker John Stuart Mill once wrote: "It is hardly possible to overrate the value . . . of placing human beings in contact with persons dissimilar to themselves, and with modes of thought and action unlike those with which they are familiar. . . . Such communication has always been . . . one of the primary sources of progress." Yet in the concluding decades of the twentieth century, some groups have turned away from the common arena of American public life, identifying only with those who share their background or outlook, and viewing the larger society with suspicion and hostility.

Yet there are also signs of positive trends. If the U.S. economy faces strains, it also possesses an enormous capacity for growth and adaptation. The nation's educational system, for all its problems, remains one of the strongest, most open in the world. And while some voices in the culture promote embittered and divisive outlooks, concentrating on what drives Americans apart, others seek solutions and address the nation's problems in a serious and thoughtful way. Indeed, the early 1990s saw an outpouring of books and essays (many of them listed in the bibliographies of Chapters 32 and 33) exploring society's problems and probing for creative solutions. These works, sharply contrasting with the stridency of extremist groups and the pronouncements of demagogues all too ready to rip at the United States' sadly frayed social fabric, offer heartening evidence that despite the great challenges confronting their society, many Americans feel far from demoralized.

This hopeful note emerged, too, in Judge Stephen Breyer's 1994 testimony before the Senate Judiciary Committee weighing his Supreme Court nomination. Reflecting on his service as counsel to the Judiciary Committee in the 1970s, Breyer expressed his belief in the fundamental merit of the American system of government, for all its shortcomings:

> There were disagreements to resolve, but everyone shared the same basic ground rules, basic assumptions about democracy, freedom, fairness, and the need to help others. . . .
>
> [The] vast array of Constitution, statutes, rules, regulations, practices, procedures—that

*huge vast web—has a single basic purpose.
That purpose is to help the many different
individuals who make up America from so
many different backgrounds and circumstances,
with so many different needs and hopes . . . [to]
live together productively, harmoniously, and
in freedom.*

Drawing Strength from the Past

Yet in contemplating the present tangle of problems, Americans understandably feel apprehensive. Will we be equal to the task? Is our era of social creativity behind us, with only a long twilight ahead? A best-seller of 1988, Paul Kennedy's *The Rise and Fall of the Great Powers*, suggested that the United States might soon go the way of Spain, Great Britain, and other world leaders of yesteryear.

Journalist Haynes Johnson, after touring fifteen states and talking to hundreds of Americans, assessed the national mood in his 1994 book with the sobering title *Divided We Fall*. Johnson found citizens oppressed by economic worries, fearful that the nation's greatness lay in the past, and gloomily aware of the forces of ethnicity, race, and class that seemed to be tearing society apart. "Everywhere, people express a gnawing uneasiness about what kind of country America is becoming," Johnson wrote.

Despite this dark analysis, Johnson also found a sober determination to revive the American spirit and redefine the national vision—not necessarily in Washington, but at the local level. "After listening to these people," he summed up, ". . . I do not feel that I have been writing the obituary of the American Dream. I believe I have been writing about an interlude in the reclaiming of that Dream."

In this process of reclamation and renewal, American history offers grounds for hope as well as for pessimism. The philosopher William James once spoke of the "blooming, buzzing confusion" of the universe; and U.S. history, too, when viewed from too close up, can seem merely a mass of facts and dates, signifying nothing. When considered broadly, however, our national experience furnishes reason for encouragement. Despite wrong turns and missed opportunities, our history is one of challenges confronted and problems solved.

Underlying this record of achievement is the strength and adaptive capacity of the U.S. government. The Constitution drafted in Philadelphia in 1787 for a struggling new nation of 4 million people, most of them farmers of British origin, today provides a strong and responsive government for a modern industrial society of 255 million people drawn from all around the world. The intricate political machinery invented by the founders—with checks and balances among the three branches of the federal government and a further parceling-out of power among federal, state, and local authorities—still works remarkably well. It provides a continuity and stability almost unheard of in the world's troubled political history.

American democracy has also become more inclusive. In 1787 the franchise was confined to white male property owners. By 1920—after workingmen's movements in the Jacksonian era, the bloody Civil War, and a long battle for woman suffrage—all adult Americans had the constitutional right to vote regardless of race, gender, or economic standing. For blacks, that right was often denied in practice, and not until the civil-rights struggles of the 1950s and 1960s did it become a full reality. Of course, many social and cultural problems defy the simple remedy of the ballot box, but the right to vote is the essential prerequisite to righting social wrongs. The process of translating the franchise into meaningful political power is a matter of organization, and this process, too, has been a continuing one. Many different groups have played a part, from the Civil War veterans and farmers of the late nineteenth century to the industrial workers of the 1930s to the Hispanics, feminists, evangelicals, elderly Americans, and gay-rights organizations of the 1990s.

Although the "lessons of history" are rarely simple or obvious, Americans of earlier generations confronted circumstances that in interesting ways parallel those that bedevil us today. Their success in coping with the challenges of their day offers reason for confidence as we nervously anticipate future problems.

Large-scale economic change, for example, is nothing new to Americans. The transformations of the nineteenth century, when industrialization altered the very nature of society, were as sweeping as any that we face. The vast technological processes that turned an agrarian society into an urban-industrial one seemed as unsettling to those who experienced them as the problems we wrestle with today. Yet our forebears emerged from this era of radical change with their government and their basic social institutions robustly intact.

Similarly, present-day environmental and public-health menaces had their counterparts in earlier times, when vile factory smoke blackened urban skies, open sewers emptied into rivers, freewheeling entrepreneurs pillaged the wilderness, dangerous machines killed and maimed thousands of workers, and unscrupulous firms foisted tainted food and dangerous medicines on an unsuspecting public. But the nation took action. Stimulated by journalistic exposés, laws were enacted and agencies created to protect society against the treacherous side effects of the new industrial order. The hazards today differ, of course, but the tradition of rising to the challenge survives.

Another asset from our past is the tradition of respect for human rights and freedom of speech—a hard-won legacy rooted in Judeo-Christian religious teachings, the English common law tradition, the Bill of Rights, and a host of landmark judicial decisions. To be sure, this legacy has often been betrayed, but it lives on, and it sets us apart from millions who still live under repressive regimes.

Ironically, the dissidents who have struggled against authoritarian governments elsewhere in recent years have displayed an appreciation for political freedom that we Americans too often take for granted. In 1989 the Chinese student demonstrators in Beijing erected a makeshift statue modeled on the Statue of Liberty, and they displayed banners proclaiming "We Shall Overcome" before hundreds of them were slaughtered by China's rulers. And in a moving speech to Congress in 1990, the dissident Czech playwright

Václav Havel, who within weeks went from prison to the presidency of his nation, invoked Thomas Jefferson and Abraham Lincoln as his inspiration.

Perhaps the greatest domestic challenge facing America is to summon up a sense of common purpose in an increasingly fragmented society. In a 1991 book disturbingly titled *The Rise of Selfishness in America*, James Lincoln Collier wrote:

> *What we must do, if we are to make any improvement in our visibly decaying society is, by means of our intelligence and imagination, understand . . . that this America is our community, and that, as members of it, we are going to be damaged one way or another if we do not from time to time put the interests of the whole above our own concerns. A people who will not sacrifice for the common good cannot expect to have any common good.*

Such warnings remind us that awareness of the United States' role in inspiring democratic strivings throughout the world is no cause for complacency or smugness. Rather, this realization can nurture in us a quiet determination to live up more fully to our national ideals, to strengthen the bonds that unite us rather than dwelling on what divides us, and to pass on to future generations the enduring vision of freedom and common purpose that others have transmitted to us from the past.

DECLARATION OF INDEPENDENCE

IN CONGRESS, JULY 4, 1776

THE UNANIMOUS DECLARATION OF THE THIRTEEN UNITED STATES OF AMERICA

When, in the course of human events, it becomes necessary for one people to dissolve the political bands which have connected them with another, and to assume, among the powers of the earth, the separate and equal station to which the laws of nature and of nature's God entitle them, a decent respect to the opinions of mankind requires that they should declare the causes which impel them to the separation.

We hold these truths to be self-evident: That all men are created equal; that they are endowed by their Creator with certain unalienable rights; that among these are life, liberty, and the pursuit of happiness; that, to secure these rights, governments are instituted among men, deriving their just powers from the consent of the governed; that whenever any form of government becomes destructive of these ends, it is the right of the people to alter or to abolish it, and to institute new government, laying its foundation on such principles, and organizing its powers in such form, as to them shall seem most likely to effect their safety and happiness. Prudence, indeed, will dictate that governments long established should not be changed for light and transient causes; and accordingly all experience hath shown that mankind are more disposed to suffer, while evils are sufferable, than to right themselves by abolishing the forms to which they are accustomed. But when a long train of abuses and usurpations, pursuing invariably the same object, evinces a design to reduce them under absolute despotism, it is their right, it is their duty, to throw off such government, and to provide new guards for their future security. Such has been the patient sufferance of these colonies; and such is now the necessity which constrains them to alter their former systems of government. The history of the present King of Great Britain is a history of repeated injuries and usurpations, all having in direct object the establishment of an absolute tyranny over these states. To prove this, let facts be submitted to a candid world.

He has refused his assent to laws, the most wholesome and necessary for the public good.

He has forbidden his governors to pass laws of immediate and pressing importance, unless suspended in their operation till his assent should be obtained; and, when so suspended, he has utterly neglected to attend to them.

He has refused to pass other laws for the accommodation of large districts of people, unless those people would relinquish the right of representation in the legislature, a right inestimable to them, and formidable to tyrants only.

He has called together legislative bodies at places unusual, uncomfortable, and distant from the depository of their public records, for the sole purpose of fatiguing them into compliance with his measures.

He has dissolved representative houses repeatedly, for opposing, with manly firmness, his invasions on the rights of the people.

He has refused for a long time, after such dissolutions, to cause others to be elected; whereby the legislative powers, incapable of annihilation, have returned to the people at large for their exercise; the state remaining, in the mean time, exposed to all the dangers of invasions from without and convulsions within.

He has endeavored to prevent the population of these states; for that purpose obstructing the laws of naturalization of foreigners; refusing to pass others to encourage their migration hither, and raising the conditions of new appropriation of lands.

He has obstructed the administration of justice, by refusing his assent to laws for establishing judiciary powers.

He has made judges dependent on his will alone, for the tenure of their offices, and the amount and payment of their salaries.

He has erected a multitude of new offices, and sent hither swarms of officers to harass our people and eat out their substance.

He has kept among us, in times of peace, standing armies, without the consent of our legislatures.

He has affected to render the military independent of, and superior to, the civil power.

He has combined with others to subject us to a jurisdiction foreign to our constitution, and unacknowledged by our laws, giving his assent to their acts of pretended legislation:

For quartering large bodies of armed troops among us;

For protecting them, by a mock trial, from punishment for any murders which they should commit on the inhabitants of these states;

For cutting off our trade with all parts of the world;

For imposing taxes on us without our consent;

For depriving us, in many cases, of the benefits of trial by jury;

For transporting us beyond seas, to be tried for pretended offenses;

For abolishing the free system of English laws in a neighboring province, establishing therein an arbitrary government, and enlarging its boundaries, so as to render it at once an example and fit instrument for introducing the same absolute rule into these colonies;

For taking away our charters, abolishing our most valuable laws, and altering fundamentally the forms of our governments;

For suspending our own legislatures, and declaring themselves invested with power to legislate for us in all cases whatsoever.

He has abdicated government here, by declaring us out of his protection and waging war against us.

He has plundered our seas, ravaged our coasts, burned our towns, and destroyed the lives of our people.

He is at this time transporting large armies of foreign mercenaries to complete the works of death, desolation, and tyranny already begun with circumstances of cruelty and perfidy scarcely paralleled in the most barbarous ages, and totally unworthy of the head of a civilized nation.

He has constrained our fellow-citizens, taken captive on the high seas, to bear arms against their country, to become the executioners of their friends and brethren, or to fall themselves by their hands.

He has excited domestic insurrection among us, and has endeavored to bring on the inhabitants of our frontiers the merciless Indian savages, whose known rule of warfare is an undistinguished destruction of all ages, sexes, and conditions.

In every stage of these oppressions we have petitioned for redress in the most humble terms; our repeated petitions have been answered only by repeated injury. A prince, whose character is thus marked by every act which may define a tyrant, is unfit to be the ruler of a free people.

Nor have we been wanting in our attentions to our British brethren. We have warned them, from time to time, of attempts by their legislature to extend an unwarrantable jurisdiction over us. We have reminded them of the circumstances of our emigration and settlement here. We have appealed to their native justice and magnanimity; and we have conjured them by the ties of our common kindred, to disavow these usurpations, which would inevitably interrupt our connections and correspondence. They, too, have been deaf to the voice of justice and of consanguinity. We must, therefore, acquiesce in the necessity which denounces our separation, and hold them, as we hold the rest of mankind, enemies in war, in peace friends.

We, therefore, the representatives of the United States of America, in General Congress assembled, appealing to the Supreme Judge of the world for the rectitude of our intentions, do, in the name and by the authority of the good people of these colonies, solemnly publish and declare, that these United Colonies are, and of right ought to be, FREE AND INDEPENDENT STATES; that they are absolved from all allegiance to the British crown, and that all political connection between them and the state of Great Britain is, and ought to be, totally dissolved; and that, as free and independent states, they have full power to levy war, conclude peace, contract alliances, establish commerce, and do all other acts and things which independent states may of right do. And for the support of this declaration, with a firm reliance on the protection of Divine Providence, we mutually pledge to each other our lives, our fortunes, and our sacred honor.

JOHN HANCOCK [*President*]
[*and fifty-five others*]

THE ARTICLES OF CONFEDERATION AND PERPETUAL UNION

BETWEEN THE STATES OF NEW HAMPSHIRE, MASSACHUSETTS BAY, RHODE ISLAND AND PROVIDENCE PLANTATIONS, CONNECTICUT, NEW YORK, NEW JERSEY, PENNSYLVANIA, DELAWARE, MARYLAND, VIRGINIA, NORTH CAROLINA, SOUTH CAROLINA, GEORGIA.*

Article 1.

The stile of this confederacy shall be "The United States of America."

Article 2.

Each State retains its sovereignty, freedom and independence, and every power, jurisdiction, and right, which is not by this confederation expressly delegated to the United States, in Congress assembled.

Article 3.

The said states hereby severally enter into a firm league of friendship with each other for their common defence, the security of their liberties and their mutual and general welfare; binding themselves to assist each other against all force offered to, or attacks made upon them, or any of them, on account of religion, sovereignty, trade, or any other pretence whatever.

Article 4.

The better to secure and perpetuate mutual friendship and intercourse among the people of the different states in this union, the free inhabitants of each of these states, paupers, vagabonds, and fugitives from justice excepted, shall be entitled to all privileges and immunities of free citizens in the several states; and the people of each State shall have free ingress and regress to and from any other State, and shall enjoy therein all the privileges of trade and commerce, subject to the same duties, impositions, and restrictions, as the inhabitants thereof respectively; provided, that such restrictions

*This copy of the final draft of the Articles of Confederation is taken from the *Journals,* 9:907–925, November 15, 1777.

shall not extend so far as to prevent the removal of property, imported into any State, to any other State of which the owner is an inhabitant; provided also, that no imposition, duties, or restriction, shall be laid by any State on the property of the United States, or either of them.

If any person guilty of, or charged with treason, felony, or other high misdemeanor in any State, shall flee from justice and be found in any of the United States, he shall, upon demand of the governor or executive power of the State from which he fled, be delivered up and removed to the State having jurisdiction of his offence.

Full faith and credit shall be given in each of these states to the records, acts, and judicial proceedings of the courts and magistrates of every other State.

Article 5.

For the more convenient management of the general interests of the United States, delegates shall be annually appointed, in such manner as the legislature of each State shall direct, to meet in Congress, on the 1st Monday in November in every year, with a power reserved to each State to recall its delegates, or any of them, at any time within the year, and to send others in their stead for the remainder of the year.

No State shall be represented in Congress by less than two, nor by more than seven members; and no person shall be capable of being a delegate for more than three years in any term of six years; nor shall any person, being a delegate, be capable of holding any office under the United States, for which he, or any other for his benefit, receives any salary, fees, or emolument of any kind.

Each State shall maintain its own delegates in a meeting of the states, and while they act as members of the committee of the states.

In determining questions in the United States, in Congress assembled, each State shall have one vote.

Freedom of speech and debate in Congress shall not be impeached or questioned in any court or place out of Congress: and the members of Congress shall be protected in their persons from arrests and imprisonments, during the time of their going to and from, and attendance on Congress, *except for treason,* felony, or breach of the peace.

Article 6.

No State, without the consent of the United States, in Congress assembled, shall send any embassy to, or receive any embassy from, or enter into any conference, agreement, alliance, or treaty with any king, prince, or state; nor shall any person, holding any office of profit or trust under the United States, or any of them, accept of any present, emolument, office or title, of any kind whatever, from any king, prince, or foreign state; nor shall the United States, in Congress assembled, or any of them, grant any title of nobility.

No two or more states shall enter into any treaty, confederation, or alliance, whatever, between them, without the consent of the United States, in Congress assembled, specifying accurately the purposes for which the same is to be entered into, and how long it shall continue.

No State shall lay any imposts or duties which may interfere with any stipulations in treaties entered into by the United States, in Congress assembled, with any king, prince, or state, in pursuance of any treaties already proposed by Congress to the courts of France and Spain.

No vessels of war shall be kept up in time of peace by any State, except such number only as shall be deemed necessary by the United States, in Congress assembled, for the defence of such State or its trade; nor shall any body of forces be kept up by any State, in time of peace, except such number only as, in the judgment of the United States, in Congress assembled, shall be deemed requisite to garrison the forts necessary for the defence of such State; but every State shall always keep up a well regulated and disciplined militia, sufficiently armed and accoutred, and shall provide, and constantly have ready for use, in public stores, a due number of field pieces and tents, and a proper quantity of arms, ammunition and camp equipage.

No State shall engage in any war without the consent of the United States, in Congress assembled, un-less such State be actually invaded by enemies, or shall have received certain advice of a resolution being formed by some nation of Indians to invade such State, and the danger is so imminent as not to admit of a delay till the United States, in Congress assembled, can be consulted; nor shall any State grant commissions to any ships or vessels of war, nor letters of marque or reprisal, except it be after a declaration of war by the United States, in Congress assembled, and then only against the kingdom or state, and the subjects thereof, against which war has been so declared, and under such regulations as shall be established by the United States, in Congress assembled, unless such States be infested by pirates, in which case vessels of war may be fitted out for that occasion, and kept so long as the danger shall continue, or until the United States, in Congress assembled, shall determine otherwise.

Article 7.

When land forces are raised by any State for the common defence, all officers of or under the rank of colonel, shall be appointed by the legislature of each State respectively, by whom such forces shall be raised, or in such manner as such State shall direct; and all vacancies shall be filled up by the State which first made the appointment.

Article 8.

All charges of war and all other expences, that shall be incurred for the common defence or general welfare, and allowed by the United States, in Congress assembled, shall be defrayed out of a common treasury, which shall be supplied by the several states, in proportion to the value of all land within each State, granted to or surveyed for any person, as such land and the buildings and improvements thereon shall be estimated according to such mode as the United States, in Congress assembled, shall, from time to time, direct and appoint.

The taxes for paying that proportion shall be laid and levied by the authority and direction of the legislatures of the several states, within the time agreed upon by the United States, in Congress assembled.

Article 9.

The United States, in Congress assembled, shall have the sole and exclusive right and power of determining on peace and war, except in the cases mentioned in the

6th article; of sending and receiving ambassadors; entering into treaties and alliances, provided that no treaty of commerce shall be made, whereby the legislative power of the respective states shall be restrained from imposing such imposts and duties on foreigners as their own people are subjected to, or from prohibiting the exportation or importation of any species of goods or commodities whatsoever; of establishing rules for deciding, in all cases, what captures on land or water shall be legal, and in what manner prizes, taken by land or naval forces in the service of the United States, shall be divided or appropriated; of granting letters of marque and reprisal in times of peace; appointing courts for the trial of piracies and felonies committed on the high seas, and establishing courts for receiving and determining, finally, appeals in all cases of captures; provided, that no member of Congress shall be appointed a judge of any of the said courts.

The United States, in Congress assembled, shall also be the last resort on appeal in all disputes and differences now subsisting, or that hereafter may arise between two or more states concerning boundary, jurisdiction or any other cause whatever; which authority shall always be exercised in the manner following: whenever the legislative or executive authority, or lawful agent of any State, in controversy with another, shall present a petition to Congress, stating the matter in question, and praying for a hearing, notice thereof shall be given, by order of Congress, to the legislative or executive authority of the other State in controversy, and a day assigned for the appearance of the parties by their lawful agents, who shall then be directed to appoint, by joint consent, commissioners or judges to constitute a court for hearing and determining the matter in question; but, if they cannot agree, Congress shall name three persons out of each of the United States, and from the list of such persons each party shall alternately strike out one, in the petitioners beginning, until the number shall be reduced to thirteen; and from that number not less than seven, nor more than nine names, as Congress shall direct, shall, in the presence of Congress, be drawn out by lot; and the persons whose names shall be drawn, or any five of them, shall be commissioners or judges to hear and finally determine the controversy, so always as a major part of the judges who shall hear the cause shall agree in the determination; and if either party shall neglect to attend at the day appointed, without shewing reasons which Congress shall judge sufficient, or, being present, shall refuse to strike, the Congress shall proceed to nominate three persons out of each State, and the secretary of Congress shall strike in behalf of such party absent or refusing; and the judgment and sentence of the court to be appointed, in the manner before prescribed, shall be final and conclusive; and if any of the parties shall refuse to submit to the authority of such court, or to appear or defend their claim or cause, the court shall nevertheless proceed to pronounce sentence or judgment, which shall, in like manner, be final and decisive, the judgment or sentence and other proceedings being, in either case, transmitted to Congress, and lodged among the acts of Congress for the security of the parties concerned: provided, that every commissioner, before he sits in judgment, shall take an oath, to be administered by one of the judges of the supreme or superior court of the State where the cause shall be tried, "well and truly to hear and determine the matter in question, according to the best of his judgment, without favour, affection, or hope of reward": provided, also, that no State shall be deprived of territory for the benefit of the United States.

All controversies concerning the private right of soil, claimed under different grants of two or more states, whose jurisdictions, as they may respect such lands and the states which passed such grants, are adjusted, the said grants, or either of them, being at the same time claimed to have originated antecedent to such settlement of jurisdiction, shall, on the petition of either party to the Congress of the United States, be finally determined, as near as may be, in the same manner as is before prescribed for deciding disputes respecting territorial jurisdiction between different states.

The United States, in Congress assembled, shall also have the sole and exclusive right and power of regulating the alloy and value of coin struck by their own authority, or by that of the respective states; fixing the standard of weights and measures throughout the United States; regulating the trade and managing all affairs with the Indians not members of any of the states; provided that the legislative right of any State within its own limits be not infringed or violated; establishing and regulating post offices from one State to another throughout all the United States, and exacting such postage on the papers passing through the same as may be requisite to defray the expences of the said office; appointing all officers of the land forces in the service of the United States, excepting regimental officers; appointing all the officers of the naval forces, and commissioning all officers whatever in the service of the United States; making rules for the government and regulation of the said land and naval forces, and directing their operations.

The United States, in Congress assembled, shall have authority to appoint a committee to sit in the recess of Congress, to be denominated "a Committee of the States," and to consist of one delegate from each State, and to appoint such other committees and civil officers as may be necessary for managing the general affairs of the United States, under their direction; to appoint one of their number to preside; provided that no person be allowed to serve in the office of president more than one year in any term of three years; to ascertain the necessary sums of money to be raised for the service of the United States, and to appropriate and apply the same for defraying the public expences; to borrow money or emit bills on the credit of the United States, transmitting, every half year, to the respective states, an account of the sums of money so borrowed or emitted; to build and equip a navy; to agree upon the number of land forces, and to make requisitions from each State for its quota, in proportion to the number of white inhabitants in such State; which requisitions shall be binding; and, thereupon, the legislature of each State shall appoint the regimental officers, raise the men, and cloathe, arm, and equip them in a soldier-like manner, at the expence of the United States; and the officers and men so cloathed, armed, and equipped, shall march to the place appointed and within the time agreed on by the United States, in Congress assembled; but if the United States, in Congress assembled, shall, on consideration of circumstances, judge proper that any State should not raise men, or should raise a smaller number than its quota, and that any other State should raise a greater number of men than the quota thereof, such extra number shall be raised, officered, cloathed, armed, and equipped in the same manner as the quota of such State, unless the legislature of such State shall judge that such extra number cannot be safely spared out of the same, in which case they shall raise, officer, cloathe, arm, and equip as many of such extra number as they judge can be safely spared. And the officers and men so cloathed, armed, and equipped, shall march to the place appointed and within the time agreed on by the United States, in Congress assembled.

The United States, in Congress assembled, shall never engage in a war, nor grant letters of marque and reprisal in time of peace, nor enter into any treaties or alliances, nor coin money, nor regulate the value thereof, nor ascertain the sums and expences necessary for the defence and welfare of the United States, or any of them: nor emit bills, nor borrow money on the credit of the United States, nor appropriate money, nor agree upon the number of vessels of war to be built or purchased, or the number of land or sea forces to be raised, nor appoint a commander in chief of the army or navy, unless nine states assent to the same; nor shall a question on any other point, except for adjourning from day to day, be determined, unless by the votes of a majority of the United States, in Congress assembled.

The Congress of the United States shall have power to adjourn to any time within the year, and to any place within the United States, so that no period of adjournment be for a longer duration than the space of six months, and shall publish the journal of their proceedings monthly, except such parts thereof, relating to treaties, alliances or military operations, as, in their judgment, require secrecy; and the yeas and nays of the delegates of each State on any question shall be entered on the journal, when it is desired by any delegate; and the delegates of a State, or any of them, at his, or their request, shall be furnished with a transcript of the said journal, except such parts as are above excepted, to lay before the legislatures of the several states.

Article 10.

The committee of the states, or any nine of them, shall be authorized to execute, in the recess of Congress, such of the powers of Congress as the United States, in Congress assembled, by the consent of nine states, shall, from time to time, think expedient to vest them with; provided, that no power be delegated to the said committee for the exercise of which, by the articles of confederation, the voice of nine states, in the Congress of the United States assembled, is requisite.

Article 11.

Canada acceding to this confederation, and joining in the measures of the United States, shall be admitted into and entitled to all the advantages of this union; but no other colony shall be admitted into the same, unless such admission be agreed to by nine states.

Article 12.

All bills of credit emitted, monies borrowed and debts contracted by, or under the authority of Congress before the assembling of the United States, in pursuance of the present confederation, shall be deemed and considered as a charge against the United States, for payment and satisfaction whereof the said United States and the public faith are hereby solemnly pledged.

Article 13.

Every State shall abide by the determinations of the United States, in Congress assembled, on all questions which, by this confederation, are submitted to them. And the articles of this confederation shall be inviolably observed by every State, and the union shall be perpetual; nor shall any alteration at any time hereafter be made in any of them, unless such alteration be agreed to in a Congress of the United States, and be afterwards confirmed by the legislatures of every State.

These articles shall be proposed to the legislatures of all the United States, to be considered, and if approved of by them, they are advised to authorize their delegates to ratify the same in the Congress of the United States; which being done, the same shall become conclusive.

CONSTITUTION OF THE
UNITED STATES OF AMERICA

PREAMBLE

We the people of the United States, in order to form a more perfect union, establish justice, insure domestic tranquillity, provide for the common defense, promote the general welfare, and secure the blessings of liberty to ourselves and our posterity, do ordain and establish this CONSTITUTION for the United States of America.

Article I

Section 1. All legislative powers herein granted shall be vested in a Congress of the United States, which shall consist of a Senate and a House of Representatives.

Section 2. The House of Representatives shall be composed of members chosen every second year by the people of the several States, and the electors in each State shall have the qualifications requisite for electors of the most numerous branch of the State Legislature.

No person shall be a Representative who shall not have attained to the age of twenty-five years, and been seven years a citizen of the United States, and who shall not, when elected, be an inhabitant of that State in which he shall be chosen.

Representatives and direct taxes shall be apportioned among the several States which may be included within this Union, according to their respective numbers, *which shall be determined by adding to the whole number of free persons, including those bound to service for a term of years and excluding Indians not taxed, three-fifths of all other persons.* The actual enumeration shall be made within three years after the first meeting of the Congress of the United States, and within every subsequent term of ten years, in such manner as they shall by law direct. The number of Representatives shall not exceed one for every thirty thousand, but each State shall have at least one Representa-

tive; *and until such enumeration shall be made, the State of New Hampshire shall be entitled to choose three, Massachusetts eight, Rhode Island and Providence Plantations one, Connecticut five, New York six, New Jersey four, Pennsylvania eight, Delaware one, Maryland six, Virginia ten, North Carolina five, South Carolina five, and Georgia three.*

When vacancies happen in the representation from any State, the Executive authority thereof shall issue writs of election to fill such vacancies.

The House of Representatives shall choose their Speaker and other officers; and shall have the sole power of impeachment.

Section 3. The Senate of the United States shall be composed of two Senators from each State, *chosen by the legislature thereof,* for six years; and each Senator shall have one vote.

Immediately after they shall be assembled in consequence of the first election, they shall be divided as equally as may be into three classes. The seats of the Senators of the first class shall be vacated at the expiration of the second year, of the second class at the expiration of the fourth year, and of the third class at the expiration of the sixth year, so that one-third may be chosen every second year; *and if vacancies happen by resignation or otherwise, during the recess of the legislature of any State, the Executive thereof may make temporary appointments until the next meeting of the legislature, which shall then fill such vacancies.*

No person shall be a Senator who shall not have attained to the age of thirty years, and been nine years

---

Note: Passages that are no longer in effect are printed in italic type.

a citizen of the United States, and who shall not, when elected, be an inhabitant of that State for which he shall be chosen.

The Vice President of the United States shall be President of the Senate, but shall have no vote, unless they be equally divided.

The Senate shall choose their other officers, and also a President *pro tempore,* in the absence of the Vice President, or when he shall exercise the office of the President of the United States.

The Senate shall have the sole power to try all impeachments. When sitting for that purpose, they shall be on oath or affirmation. When the President of the United States is tried, the Chief Justice shall preside: and no person shall be convicted without the concurrence of two-thirds of the members present.

Judgment in cases of impeachment shall not extend further than to removal from the office, and disqualification to hold and enjoy any office of honor, trust or profit under the United States; but the party convicted shall nevertheless be liable and subject to indictment, trial, judgment and punishment, according to law.

Section 4. The times, places and manner of holding elections for Senators and Representatives shall be prescribed in each State by the legislature thereof; but the Congress may at any time by law make or alter such regulations, except as to the places of choosing Senators.

The Congress shall assemble at least once in every year, and such meeting *shall be on the first Monday in December, unless they shall by law appoint a different day.*

Section 5. Each house shall be the judge of the elections, returns and qualifications of its own members, and a majority of each shall constitute a quorum to do business; but a smaller number may adjourn from day to day, and may be authorized to compel the attendance of absent members, in such manner, and under such penalties, as each house may provide.

Each house may determine the rules of its proceedings, punish its members for disorderly behavior, and with the concurrence of two-thirds, expel a member.

Each house shall keep a journal of its proceedings, and from time to time publish the same, excepting such parts as may in their judgment require secrecy; and the yeas and nays of the members of either house on any question shall, at the desire of one-fifth of those present, be entered on the journal.

Neither house, during the session of Congress, shall, without the consent of the other, adjourn for more than three days, nor to any other place than that in which the two houses shall be sitting.

Section 6. The Senators and Representatives shall receive a compensation for their services, to be ascertained by law and paid out of the treasury of the United States. They shall in all cases except treason, felony and breach of the peace, be privileged from arrest during their attendance at the session of their respective houses, and in going to and returning from the same; and for any speech or debate in either house, they shall not be questioned in any other place.

No Senator or Representative shall, during the time for which he was elected, be appointed to any civil office under the authority of the United States, which shall have been created, or the emoluments whereof shall have been increased, during such time; and no person holding any office under the United States shall be a member of either house during his continuance in office.

Section 7. All bills for raising revenue shall originate in the House of Representatives; but the Senate may propose or concur with amendments as on other bills.

Every bill which shall have passed the House of Representatives and the Senate, shall, before it become a law, be presented to the President of the United States; if he approve he shall sign it, but if not he shall return it with objections to that house in which it originated, who shall enter the objections at large on their journal, and proceed to reconsider it. If after such reconsideration two-thirds of that house shall agree to pass the bill, it shall be sent, together with the objections, to the other house, by which it shall likewise be reconsidered, and, if approved by two-thirds of that house, it shall become a law. But in all such cases the votes of both houses shall be determined by yeas and nays, and the names of the persons voting for and against the bill shall be entered on the journal of each house respectively. If any bill shall not be returned by the President within ten days (Sundays excepted) after it shall have been presented to him, the same shall be a law, in like manner as if he had signed it, unless the Congress by their adjournment prevent its return, in which case it shall not be a law.

Every order, resolution, or vote to which the concurrence of the Senate and House of Representatives may be necessary (except on a question of adjournment) shall be presented to the President of the United

States; and before the same shall take effect, shall be approved by him, or being disapproved by him, shall be repassed by two-thirds of the Senate and House of Representatives, according to the rules and limitations prescribed in the case of a bill.

Section 8.   The Congress shall have power

To lay and collect taxes, duties, imposts, and excises, to pay the debts and provide for the common defense and general welfare of the United States; but all duties, imposts and excises shall be uniform throughout the United States;

To borrow money on the credit of the United States;

To regulate commerce with foreign nations, and among the several States, and with the Indian tribes;

To establish an uniform rule of naturalization, and uniform laws on the subject of bankruptcies throughout the United States;

To coin money, regulate the value thereof, and of foreign coin, and fix the standard of weights and measures;

To provide for the punishment of counterfeiting the securities and current coin of the United States;

To establish post offices and post roads;

To promote the progress of science and useful arts by securing for limited times to authors and inventors the exclusive right to their respective writings and discoveries;

To constitute tribunals inferior to the Supreme Court;

To define and punish piracies and felonies committed on the high seas and offenses against the law of nations;

To declare war, grant letters of marque and reprisal, and make rules concerning captures on land and water;

To raise and support armies, but no appropriation of money to that use shall be for a longer term than two years;

To provide and maintain a navy;

To make rules for the government and regulation of the land and naval forces;

To provide for calling forth the militia to execute the laws of the Union, suppress insurrections, and repel invasions;

To provide for organizing, arming, and disciplining the militia, and for governing such part of them as may be employed in the service of the United States, reserv-

ing to the States respectively the appointment of the officers, and the authority of training the militia according to the discipline prescribed by Congress;

To exercise exclusive legislation in all cases whatsoever, over such district (not exceeding ten miles square) as may, by cession of particular States, and the acceptance of Congress, become the seat of government of the United States, and to exercise like authority over all places purchased by the consent of the legislature of the State, in which the same shall be, for erection of forts, magazines, arsenals, dock-yards, and other needful buildings;—and

To make all laws which shall be necessary and proper for carrying into execution the foregoing powers, and all other powers vested by this Constitution in the government of the United States, or in any department or officer thereof.

Section 9.   *The migration or importation of such persons as any of the States now existing shall think proper to admit shall not be prohibited by the Congress prior to the year 1808; but a tax or duty may be imposed on such importation, not exceeding $10 for each person.*

The privilege of the writ of habeas corpus shall not be suspended, unless when in cases of rebellion or invasion the public safety may require it.

No bill of attainder or ex post facto law shall be passed.

No capitation, or other direct, tax shall be laid, unless in proportion to the census or enumeration herein before directed to be taken.

No tax or duty shall be laid on articles exported from any State.

No preference shall be given by any regulation of commerce or revenue to the ports of one State over those of another; nor shall vessels bound to, or from, one State, be obliged to enter, clear, or pay duties in another.

No money shall be drawn from the treasury, but in consequence of appropriations made by law; and a regular statement and account of the receipts and expenditures of all public money shall be published from time to time.

No title of nobility shall be granted by the United States: and no person holding any office of profit or trust under them, shall, without the consent of the Congress, accept of any present, emolument, office, or title, of any kind whatever, from any king, prince, or foreign state.

Section 10. No State shall enter into any treaty, alliance, or confederation; grant letters of marque and reprisal; coin money; emit bills of credit; make anything but gold and silver coin a tender in payment of debts; pass any bill of attainder, ex post facto law, or law impairing the obligation of contracts, or grant any title of nobility.

No State shall, without the consent of Congress, lay any imposts or duties on imports or exports, except what may be absolutely necessary for executing its inspection laws: and the net produce of all duties and imposts, laid by any State on imports or exports, shall be for the use of the treasury of the United States; and all such laws shall be subject to the revision and control of the Congress.

No State shall, without the consent of Congress, lay any duty of tonnage, keep troops or ships of war in time of peace, enter into any agreement or compact with another State, or with a foreign power, or engage in war, unless actually invaded, or in such imminent danger as will not admit of delay.

Article II

Section 1. The executive power shall be vested in a President of the United States of America. He shall hold his office during the term of four years, and, together with the Vice President, chosen for the same term, be elected as follows:

Each state shall appoint, in such manner as the legislature thereof may direct, a number of electors, equal to the whole number of Senators and Representatives to which the State may be entitled in the Congress; but no Senator or Representative, or person holding an office of trust or profit under the United States, shall be appointed an elector.

The electors shall meet in their respective States, and vote by ballot for two persons, of whom one at least shall not be an inhabitant of the same State with themselves. And they shall make a list of all the persons voted for, and of the number of votes for each; which list they shall sign and certify, and transmit sealed to the seat of government of the United States, directed to the President of the Senate. The President of the Senate shall, in the presence of the Senate and the House of Representatives, open all the certificates, and the votes shall then be counted. The person having the greatest number of votes shall be the President,

if such number be a majority of the whole number of electors appointed; and if there be more than one who have such majority, and have an equal number of votes, then the House of Representatives shall immediately choose by ballot one of them for President; and if no person have a majority, then from the five highest on the list said house shall in like manner choose the President. But in choosing the President the votes shall be taken by States, the representation from each State having one vote; a quorum for this purpose shall consist of a member or members from two-thirds of the States, and a majority of all the States shall be necessary to a choice. In every case, after the choice of the President, the person having the greatest number of votes of the electors shall be the Vice President. But if there should remain two or more who have equal votes, the Senate shall choose from them by ballot the Vice President.

The Congress may determine the time of choosing the electors and the day on which they shall give their votes; which day shall be the same throughout the United States.

No person except a natural-born citizen, *or a citizen of the United States at the time of the adoption of this Constitution,* shall be eligible to the office of President; neither shall any person be eligible to that office who shall not have attained to the age of thirty-five years, and been fourteen years a resident within the United States.

In case of the removal of the President from office or of his death, resignation, or inability to discharge the powers and duties of the said office, the same shall devolve on the Vice President, and the Congress may by law provide for the case of removal, death, resignation, or inability, both of the President and Vice President, declaring what officer shall then act as President, and such officer shall act accordingly, until the disability be removed, or a President shall be elected.

The President shall, at stated times, receive for his services a compensation, which shall neither be increased nor diminished during the period for which he shall have been elected, and he shall not receive within that period any other emolument from the United States, or any of them.

Before he enter on the execution of his office, he shall take the following oath or affirmation:—"I do solemnly swear (or affirm) that I will faithfully execute the office of the President of the United States, and will to the best of my ability preserve, protect and defend the Constitution of the United States."

Section 2. The President shall be commander in chief of the army and navy of the United States, and of the militia of the several States, when called into the actual service of the United States; he may require the opinion, in writing, of the principal officer in each of the executive departments, upon any subject relating to the duties of their respective offices, and he shall have power to grant reprieves and pardons for offenses against the United States, except in cases of impeachment.

He shall have power, by and with the advice and consent of the Senate, to make treaties, provided two-thirds of the Senators present concur; and he shall nominate, and by and with the advice and consent of the Senate, shall appoint ambassadors, other public ministers and consuls, judges of the Supreme Court, and all other officers of the United States, whose appointments are not herein otherwise provided for, and which shall be established by law: but Congress may by law vest the appointment of such inferior officers, as they think proper, in the President alone, in the courts of law, or in the heads of departments.

The President shall have power to fill up all vacancies that may happen during the recess of the Senate, by granting commissions which shall expire at the end of their next session.

Section 3. He shall from time to time give to the Congress information of the state of the Union, and recommend to their consideration such measures as he shall judge necessary and expedient; he may, on extraordinary occasions, convene both houses, or either of them, and in case of disagreement between them, with respect to the time of adjournment, he may adjourn them to such time as he shall think proper; he shall receive ambassadors and other public ministers; he shall take care that the laws be faithfully executed, and shall commission all the officers of the United States.

Section 4. The President, Vice President and all civil officers of the United States shall be removed from office on impeachment for, and on conviction of, treason, bribery, or other high crimes and misdemeanors.

Article III

Section 1. The judicial power of the United States shall be vested in one Supreme Court, and in such inferior courts as the Congress may from time to time ordain and establish. The judges, both of the Supreme and inferior courts, shall hold their offices during good behavior, and shall, at stated times, receive for their services a compensation which shall not be diminished during their continuance in office.

Section 2. The judicial power shall extend to all cases, in law and equity, arising under this Constitution, the laws of the United States, and treaties made, or which shall be made, under their authority;—to all cases affecting ambassadors, other public ministers and consuls;—to all cases of admiralty and maritime jurisdiction;—to controversies to which the United States shall be a party;—to controversies between two or more States;—*between a State and citizens of another State;*—between citizens of different States;—between citizens of the same State claiming lands under grants of different States, and between a State, or the citizens thereof, and foreign states, citizens or subjects.

In all cases affecting ambassadors, other public ministers and consuls, and those in which a State shall be party, the Supreme Court shall have original jurisdiction. In all the other cases before mentioned, the Supreme Court shall have appellate jurisdiction, both as to law and fact, with such exceptions, and under such regulations, as the Congress shall make.

The trial of all crimes, except in cases of impeachment, shall be by jury; and such trial shall be held in the State where said crimes shall have been committed; but when not committed within any State, the trial shall be at such place or places as the Congress may by law have directed.

Section 3. Treason against the United States shall consist only in levying war against them, or in adhering to their enemies, giving them aid and comfort. No person shall be convicted of treason unless on the testimony of two witnesses to the same overt act, or on confession in open court.

The Congress shall have power to declare the punishment of treason, but no attainder of treason shall work corruption of blood, or forfeiture except during the life of the person attainted.

Article IV

Section 1. Full faith and credit shall be given in each State to the public acts, records, and judicial proceedings of every other State. And the Congress may by general laws prescribe the manner in which such acts, records, and proceedings shall be proved, and the effect thereof.

Section 2.   The citizens of each State shall be entitled to all privileges and immunities of citizens in the several States.

A person charged in any State with treason, felony, or other crime, who shall flee from justice, and be found in another State, shall on demand of the executive authority of the State from which he fled, be delivered up, to be removed to the State having jurisdiction of the crime.

No person held to service or labor in one State, under the laws thereof, escaping into another, shall, in consequence of any law or regulation therein, be discharged from such service or labor, but shall be delivered up on claim of the party to whom such service or labor may be due.

Section 3.   New States may be admitted by the Congress into this Union; but no new State shall be formed or erected within the jurisdiction of any other State; nor any State be formed by the junction of two or more States, or parts of States, without the consent of the legislatures of the States concerned as well as of the Congress.

The Congress shall have power to dispose of and make all needful rules and regulations respecting the territory or other property belonging to the United States; and nothing in this Constitution shall be so construed as to prejudice any claims of the United States, or of any particular State.

Section 4.   The United States shall guarantee to every State in this Union a republican form of government, and shall protect each of them against invasion; and on application of the legislature, or of the executive (when the legislature cannot be convened), against domestic violence.

Article V

The Congress, whenever two-thirds of both houses shall deem it necessary, shall propose amendments to this Constitution, or, on the application of the legislatures of two-thirds of the several States, shall call a convention for proposing amendments, which, in either case, shall be valid to all intents and purposes, as part of this Constitution, when ratified by the legislatures of three-fourths of the several States, or by conventions in three-fourths thereof, as the one or the other mode of ratification may be proposed by the Congress; provided *that no amendments which may be made prior to the year one thousand eight hundred and eight shall in any manner affect the first and fourth clauses in the ninth section of the first article;* and that no State, without its consent, shall be deprived of its equal suffrage in the Senate.

Article VI

All debts contracted and engagements entered into, before the adoption of this Constitution, shall be as valid against the United States under this Constitution, as under the Confederation.

This Constitution, and the laws of the United States which shall be made in pursuance thereof; and all treaties made, or which shall be made, under the authority of the United States, shall be the supreme law of the land; and the judges in every State shall be bound thereby, anything in the Constitution or laws of any State to the contrary notwithstanding.

The Senators and Representatives before mentioned, and the members of the several State legislatures, and all executive and judicial officers, both of the United States and of the several States, shall be bound by oath or affirmation to support this Constitution; but no religious test shall ever be required as a qualification to any office or public trust under the United States.

Article VII

The ratification of the conventions of nine States shall be sufficient for the establishment of this Constitution between the States so ratifying the same.

Done in Convention by the unanimous consent of the States present, the seventeenth day of September in the year of our Lord one thousand seven hundred and eighty-seven and of the Independence of the United States of America the twelfth. In witness whereof we have hereunto subscribed our names.

[Signed by]
G° WASHINGTON
Presidt and Deputy from Virginia
[*and thirty-eight others*]

AMENDMENTS TO THE CONSTITUTION

Article I*

Congress shall make no law respecting an establishment of religion, or prohibiting the free exercise thereof; or abridging the freedom of speech, or of the press; or the right of the people peaceably to assemble, and to petition the government for a redress of grievances.

Article II

A well-regulated militia being necessary to the security of a free State, the right of the people to keep and bear arms shall not be infringed.

Article III

No soldier shall, in time of peace, be quartered in any house without the consent of the owner, nor in time of war, but in a manner to be prescribed by law.

Article IV

The right of the people to be secure in their persons, houses, papers, and effects, against unreasonable searches and seizures, shall not be violated, and no warrants shall issue but upon probable cause, supported by oath or affirmation, and particularly describing the place to be searched, and the persons or things to be seized.

Article V

No person shall be held to answer for a capital, or otherwise infamous crime, unless on a presentment or indictment of a grand jury, except in cases arising in the land or naval forces, or in the militia, when in actual service in time of war or public danger; nor shall any person be subject for the same offense to be twice put in jeopardy of life or limb; nor shall be compelled in any criminal case to be a witness against himself, nor be deprived of life, liberty, or property, without due process of law; nor shall private property be taken for public use without just compensation.

Article VI

In all criminal prosecutions, the accused shall enjoy the right to a speedy and public trial, by an impartial jury of

---

*The first ten Amendments (Bill of Rights) were adopted in 1791.

the State and district wherein the crime shall have been committed, which district shall have been previously ascertained by law, and to be informed of the nature and cause of the accusation; to be confronted with the witnesses against him; to have compulsory process for obtaining witnesses in his favor, and to have the assistance of counsel for his defense.

Article VII

In suits at common law, where the value in controversy shall exceed twenty dollars, the right of trial by jury shall be preserved, and no fact tried by a jury shall be otherwise reexamined in any court of the United States, than according to the rules of the common law.

Article VIII

Excessive bail shall not be required, nor excessive fines imposed, nor cruel and unusual punishments inflicted.

Article IX

The enumeration in the Constitution, of certain rights, shall not be construed to deny or disparage others retained by the people.

Article X

The powers not delegated to the United States by the Constitution, nor prohibited by it to the States, are reserved to the States respectively, or to the people.

Article XI
[*Adopted 1798*]

The judicial power of the United States shall not be construed to extend to any suit in law or equity, commenced or prosecuted against one of the United States by citizens of another State, or by citizens or subjects of any foreign state.

Article XII
[*Adopted 1804*]

The electors shall meet in their respective States, and vote by ballot for President and Vice President, one of whom, at least, shall not be an inhabitant of the same State with themselves; they shall name in their ballots the person voted for as President, and in distinct ballots the person voted for as Vice President, and they shall make distinct lists of all persons voted for as President, and of all persons voted for as Vice President, and of the number of votes for each, which lists they shall sign and certify, and transmit sealed to the seat of government of the United States, directed to the President of the Senate;—the President of the Senate shall, in the presence of the Senate and House of Representatives, open all the certificates and the votes shall then be counted;—the person having the greatest number of votes for President shall be the President, if such number be a majority of the whole number of electors appointed; and if no person have such majority, then from the persons having the highest numbers not exceeding three on the list of those voted for as President, the House of Representatives shall choose immediately, by ballot, the President. But in choosing the President, the votes shall be taken by States, the representation from each State having one vote; a quorum for this purpose shall consist of a member or members from two-thirds of the States, and a majority of all the States shall be necessary to a choice. And if the House of Representatives shall not choose a President whenever the right of choice shall devolve upon them, before *the fourth day of March* next following, then the Vice President shall act as President, as in the case of the death or other constitutional disability of the President.

The person having the greatest number of votes as Vice President shall be the Vice President, if such a number be a majority of the whole number of electors appointed; and if no person have a majority, then from the two highest numbers on the list the Senate shall choose the Vice President; a quorum for the purpose shall consist of two-thirds of the whole number of Senators, and a majority of the whole number shall be necessary to a choice. But no person constitutionally ineligible to the office of President shall be eligible to that of Vice President of the United States.

Article XIII
[*Adopted 1865*]

Section 1. Neither slavery nor involuntary servitude, except as a punishment for crime whereof the party shall have been duly convicted, shall exist within the United States, or any place subject to their jurisdiction.

Section 2. Congress shall have power to enforce this article by appropriate legislation.

Article XIV
[*Adopted 1868*]

Section 1. All persons born or naturalized in the United States, and subject to the jurisdiction thereof, are citizens of the United States and of the State wherein they reside. No State shall make or enforce any law which shall abridge the privileges or immunities of citizens of the United States; nor shall any State deprive any person of life, liberty, or property, without due process of law; nor deny to any person within its jurisdiction the equal protection of the laws.

Section 2. Representatives shall be apportioned among the several States according to their respective numbers, counting the whole number of persons in each State, excluding Indians not taxed. But when the right to vote at any election for the choice of Electors for President and Vice President of the United States, Representatives in Congress, the executive and judicial officers of a State, or the members of the legislature thereof, is denied to any of the male inhabitants of such State, being twenty-one years of age and citizens of the United States, or in any way abridged, except for participation in rebellion, or other crime, the basis of representation therein shall be reduced in the proportion which the number of such male citizens shall bear to the whole number of male citizens twenty-one years of age in such State.

Section 3. No person shall be a Senator or Representative in Congress or Elector of President and Vice President, or hold any office, civil or military, under the United States, or under any State, who, having previously taken an oath, as a member of Congress, or as an officer of the United States, or as a member of any State legislature, or as an executive or judicial officer of any State, to support the Constitution of the United States, shall have engaged in insurrection or rebellion against the same, or given aid and comfort to the enemies thereof. Congress may, by a vote of two-thirds of each house, remove such disability.

Section 4. The validity of the public debt of the United States, authorized by law, including debts incurred for payment of pensions and bounties for services in suppressing insurrection or rebellion, shall not be questioned. But neither the United States nor any State shall assume or pay any debt or obligation incurred in aid of insurrection or rebellion against the United States, or any claim for the loss or emancipation of any slave; but all such debts, obligations, and claims shall be held illegal and void.

Section 5. The Congress shall have the power to enforce, by appropriate legislation, the provisions of this article.

Article XV
[*Adopted 1870*]

Section 1. The right of citizens of the United States to vote shall not be denied or abridged by the United States or by any State on account of race, color, or previous condition of servitude.

Section 2. The Congress shall have power to enforce this article by appropriate legislation.

Article XVI
[*Adopted 1913*]

The Congress shall have power to lay and collect taxes on incomes, from whatever source derived, without apportionment among the several States, and without regard to any census or enumeration.

Article XVII
[*Adopted 1913*]

Section 1. The Senate of the United States shall be composed of two Senators from each State, elected by the people thereof, for six years; and each Senator shall have one vote. The electors in each State shall have the qualifications requisite for electors of [voters for] the most numerous branch of the State legislatures.

Section 2. When vacancies happen in the representation of any State in the Senate, the executive authority of such State shall issue writs of election to fill such vacancies: Provided, that the Legislature of any State may empower the executive thereof to make temporary appointments until the people fill the vacancies by election as the Legislature may direct.

Section 3. This amendment shall not be so construed as to affect the election or term of any Senator chosen before it becomes valid as part of the Constitution.

Article XVIII
[*Adopted 1919; repealed 1933*]

Section 1. *After one year from the ratification of this article the manufacture, sale, or transportation of intoxicating liquors within, the importation thereof into, or the exportation thereof from the United States and all territory subject to the jurisdiction thereof, for beverage purposes, is hereby prohibited.*

Section 2. *The Congress and the several States shall have concurrent power to enforce this article by appropriate legislation.*

Section 3. *This article shall be inoperative unless it shall have been ratified as an amendment to the Constitution by the legislatures of the several States, as provided by the Constitution, within seven years from the date of the submission thereof to the States by the Congress.*

Article XIX
[*Adopted 1920*]

Section 1. The right of citizens of the United States to vote shall not be denied or abridged by the United States or by any State on account of sex.

Section 2. The Congress shall have the power to enforce this article by appropriate legislation.

Article XX
[*Adopted 1933*]

Section 1. The terms of the President and Vice President shall end at noon on the 20th day of January, and the terms of Senators and Representatives at noon on the 3d day of January, of the years in which such terms would have ended if this article had not been ratified; and the terms of their successors shall then begin.

Section 2. The Congress shall assemble at least once in every year, and such meeting shall begin at noon on the 3d of January, unless they shall by law appoint a different day.

Section 3. If, at the time fixed for the beginning of the term of the President, the President-elect shall have died, the Vice President-elect shall become President. If a President shall not have been chosen before the time fixed for the beginning of his term, or if the President-elect shall have failed to qualify, then the Vice President-elect shall act as President until a President shall have qualified; and the Congress may by law provide for the case wherein neither a President-elect nor a Vice President-elect shall have qualified, declaring who shall then act as President, or the manner in which one who is to act shall be selected, and such persons shall act accordingly until a President or Vice President shall have qualified.

Section 4. The Congress may by law provide for the case of the death of any of the persons from whom the House of Representatives may choose a President whenever the right of choice shall have devolved upon them, and for the case of the death of any of the persons from whom the Senate may choose a Vice President whenever the right of choice shall have devolved upon them.

Section 5. Sections 1 and 2 shall take effect on the 15th day of October following the ratification of this article.

Section 6. This article shall be inoperative unless it shall have been ratified as an amendment to the Constitution by the Legislatures of three-fourths of the several States within seven years from the date of its submission.

Article XXI
[*Adopted 1933*]

Section 1. The eighteenth article of amendment to the Constitution of the United States is hereby repealed.

Section 2. The transportation or importation into any State, Territory, or Possession of the United States for delivery or use therein of intoxicating liquors, in violation of the laws thereof, is hereby prohibited.

Section 3. This article shall be inoperative unless it shall have been ratified as an amendment to the Constitution by conventions in the several States, as provided in the Constitution, within seven years from the date of submission thereof to the States by the Congress.

Article XXII
[*Adopted 1951*]

Section 1. No person shall be elected to the office of President more than twice, and no person who has held the office of President, or acted as President, for more than two years of a term to which some other person was elected President shall be elected to the office of President more than once. But this article shall not apply to any person holding the office of President when this article was proposed by the Congress, and shall not prevent any person who may be holding the office of President, or acting as President, during the term within which this article becomes operative from holding the office of President or acting as President during the remainder of such term.

Section 2. This article shall be inoperative unless it shall have been ratified as an amendment to the Constitution by the legislatures of three-fourths of the several States within seven years from the date of its submission to the States by the Congress.

Article XXIII
[*Adopted 1961*]

Section 1. The District constituting the seat of Government of the United States shall appoint in such manner as the Congress may direct:

A number of electors of President and Vice President equal to the whole number of Senators and Representatives in Congress to which the District would be entitled if it were a State, but in no event more than the least populous State; they shall be in addition to those appointed by the States, but they shall be considered for the purposes of the election of President and Vice President, to be electors appointed by a State; and they shall meet in the District and perform such duties as provided by the twelfth article of amendment.

Section 2. The Congress shall have the power to enforce this article by appropriate legislation.

Article XXIV
[*Adopted 1964*]

Section 1. The right of citizens of the United States to vote in any primary or other election for President or Vice President, for electors for President or Vice President, or for Senator or Representative in Congress, shall not be denied or abridged by the United States or any State by reason of failure to pay any poll tax or other tax.

Section 2. The Congress shall have the power to enforce this article by appropriate legislation.

Article XXV
[*Adopted 1967*]

Section 1. In case of the removal of the President from office or of his death or resignation, the Vice President shall become President.

Section 2.   Whenever there is a vacancy in the office of the Vice President, the President shall nominate a Vice President who shall take office upon confirmation by a majority vote of both Houses of Congress.

Section 3.   Whenever the President transmits to the President pro tempore of the Senate and the Speaker of the House of Representatives his written declaration that he is unable to discharge the powers and duties of his office, and until he transmits to them a written declaration to the contrary, such powers and duties shall be discharged by the Vice President as Acting President.

Section 4.   Whenever the Vice President and a majority of either the principal officers of the executive departments or of such other body as Congress may by law provide, transmit to the President pro tempore of the Senate and the Speaker of the House of Representatives their written declaration that the President is unable to discharge the powers and duties of his office, the Vice President shall immediately assume the powers and duties of the office as Acting President.

Thereafter, when the President transmits to the President pro tempore of the Senate and the Speaker of the House of Representatives his written declaration that no inability exists, he shall resume the powers and duties of his office unless the Vice President and a majority of either the principal officers of the executive department[s] or of such other body as Congress may by law provide, transmit within four days to the President pro tempore of the Senate and the Speaker of the House of Representatives their written declaration that the President is unable to discharge the powers and duties of his office. Thereupon Congress shall decide the issue, assembling within forty-eight hours for that purpose if not in session. If the Congress, within twenty-one days after receipt of the latter written declaration, or, if Congress is not in session, within twenty-one days after Congress is required to assemble, determines by two-thirds vote of both Houses that the President is unable to discharge the powers and duties of his office, the Vice President shall continue to discharge the same as Acting President; otherwise, the President shall resume the powers and duties of his office.

Article XXVI
[Adopted 1971]

Section 1.   The right of citizens of the United States, who are eighteen years of age or older, to vote shall not be denied or abridged by the United States or by any State on account of age.

Section 2.   The Congress shall have power to enforce this article by appropriate legislation.

Article XXVII*
[Adopted 1992]

No law, varying the compensation for services of the Senators and Representatives, shall take effect, until an election of Representatives shall have intervened.

---

*Originally proposed in 1789 by James Madison, this amendment failed to win ratification along with the other parts of what became the Bill of Rights. However, the proposed amendment contained no deadline for ratification, and over the years other state legislatures voted to add it to the Constitution; many such ratifications occurred during the 1980s and early 1990s as public frustration with Congress's performance mounted. In May 1992 the Archivist of the United States certified that, with the Michigan legislature's ratification, the article had been approved by three-fourths of the states and thus automatically became part of the Constitution. But congressional leaders and constitutional specialists questioned whether an amendment that took 202 years to win ratification was valid, and the issue had not been resolved by the time this book went to press.

Growth of U.S. Population and Area

Census	Population	Percentage of Increase over Preceding Census	Land Area Square Miles	Population per Square Mile
1790	3,929,214		867,980	4.5
1800	5,308,483	35.1	867,980	6.1
1810	7,239,881	36.4	1,685,865	4.3
1820	9,638,453	33.1	1,753,588	5.5
1830	12,866,020	33.5	1,753,588	7.3
1840	17,069,453	32.7	1,753,588	9.7
1850	23,191,876	35.9	2,944,337	7.9
1860	31,443,321	35.6	2,973,965	10.6
1870	39,818,449	26.6	2,973,965	13.4
1880	50,155,783	26.0	2,973,965	16.9
1890	62,947,714	25.5	2,973,965	21.2
1900	75,994,575	20.7	2,974,159	25.6
1910	91,972,266	21.0	2,973,890	30.9
1920	105,710,620	14.9	2,973,776	35.5
1930	122,775,046	16.1	2,977,128	41.2
1940	131,669,275	7.2	2,977,128	44.2
1950	150,697,361	14.5	2,974,726*	50.7
1960†	178,464,236	18.4	2,974,726	59.9
1970	204,765,770	14.7	2,974,726	68.8
1980	226,504,825	10.6	2,974,726	76.1
1990	248,709,873	9.8	2,974,726	83.6

*As remeasured in 1940.
†Not including Alaska (pop. 226,167) and Hawaii (632,772).

Admission of States into the Union

State	Date of Admission	State	Date of Admission
1. Delaware	December 7, 1787	26. Michigan	January 26, 1837
2. Pennsylvania	December 12, 1787	27. Florida	March 3, 1845
3. New Jersey	December 18, 1787	28. Texas	December 29, 1845
4. Georgia	January 2, 1788	29. Iowa	December 28, 1846
5. Connecticut	January 9, 1788	30. Wisconsin	May 29, 1848
6. Massachusetts	February 6, 1788	31. California	September 9, 1850
7. Maryland	April 28, 1788	32. Minnesota	May 11, 1858
8. South Carolina	May 23, 1788	33. Oregon	February 14, 1859
9. New Hampshire	June 21, 1788	34. Kansas	January 29, 1861
10. Virginia	June 25, 1788	35. West Virginia	June 20, 1863
11. New York	July 26, 1788	36. Nevada	October 31, 1864
12. North Carolina	November 21, 1789	37. Nebraska	March 1, 1867
13. Rhode Island	May 29, 1790	38. Colorado	August 1, 1876
14. Vermont	March 4, 1791	39. North Dakota	November 2, 1889
15. Kentucky	June 1, 1792	40. South Dakota	November 2, 1889
16. Tennessee	June 1, 1796	41. Montana	November 8, 1889
17. Ohio	March 1, 1803	42. Washington	November 11, 1889
18. Louisiana	April 30, 1812	43. Idaho	July 3, 1890
19. Indiana	December 11, 1816	44. Wyoming	July 10, 1890
20. Mississippi	December 10, 1817	45. Utah	January 4, 1896
21. Illinois	December 3, 1818	46. Oklahoma	November 16, 1907
22. Alabama	December 14, 1819	47. New Mexico	January 6, 1912
23. Maine	March 15, 1820	48. Arizona	February 14, 1912
24. Missouri	August 10, 1821	49. Alaska	January 3, 1959
25. Arkansas	June 15, 1836	50. Hawaii	August 21, 1959

Presidential Elections, 1789–1992

Year	States in the Union	Candidates	Parties	Electoral Vote	Popular Vote	Percentage of Popular Vote
1789	11	GEORGE WASHINGTON	No party designations	69		
		John Adams		34		
		Minor candidates		35		
1792	15	GEORGE WASHINGTON	No party designations	132		
		John Adams		77		
		George Clinton		50		
		Minor candidates		5		
1796	16	JOHN ADAMS	Federalist	71		
		Thomas Jefferson	Democratic-Republican	68		
		Thomas Pinckney	Federalist	59		
		Aaron Burr	Democratic-Republican	30		
		Minor candidates		48		
1800	16	THOMAS JEFFERSON	Democratic-Republican	73		
		Aaron Burr	Democratic-Republican	73		
		John Adams	Federalist	65		
		Charles C. Pinckney	Federalist	64		
		John Jay	Federalist	1		
1804	17	THOMAS JEFFERSON	Democratic-Republican	162		
		Charles C. Pinckney	Federalist	14		
1808	17	JAMES MADISON	Democratic-Republican	122		
		Charles C. Pinckney	Federalist	47		
		George Clinton	Democratic-Republican	6		
1812	18	JAMES MADISON	Democratic-Republican	128		
		DeWitt Clinton	Federalist	89		
1816	19	JAMES MONROE	Democratic-Republican	183		
		Rufus King	Federalist	34		
1820	24	JAMES MONROE	Democratic-Republican	231		
		John Quincy Adams	Independent Republican	1		
1824	24	JOHN QUINCY ADAMS	Democratic-Republican	84	108,740	30.5
		Andrew Jackson	Democratic-Republican	99	153,544	43.1
		William H. Crawford	Democratic-Republican	41	46,618	13.1
		Henry Clay	Democratic-Republican	37	47,136	13.2
1828	24	ANDREW JACKSON	Democratic	178	642,553	56.0
		John Quincy Adams	National Republican	83	500,897	44.0
1832	24	ANDREW JACKSON	Democratic	219	687,502	55.0
		Henry Clay	National Republican	49	530,189	42.4
		William Wirt	Anti-Masonic	7 }	33,108	2.6
		John Floyd	National Republican	11 }		
1836	26	MARTIN VAN BUREN	Democratic	170	765,483	50.9
		William H. Harrison	Whig	73 }		
		Hugh L. White	Whig	26 }	739,795	49.1
		Daniel Webster	Whig	14 }		
		W. P. Mangum	Whig	11 }		
1840	26	WILLIAM H. HARRISON	Whig	234	1,274,624	53.1
		Martin Van Buren	Democratic	60	1,127,781	46.9
1844	26	JAMES K. POLK	Democratic	170	1,338,464	49.6
		Henry Clay	Whig	105	1,300,097	48.1
		James G. Birney	Liberty		62,300	2.3

cont.

Because candidates receiving less than 1 percent of the popular vote are omitted, the percentage of popular vote may not total 100 percent.

Before the Twelfth Amendment was passed in 1804, the electoral college voted for two presidential candidates; the runner-up became vice president.

Presidential Elections, 1789–1992 *(cont.)*

Year	States in the Union	Candidates	Parties	Electoral Vote	Popular Vote	Percentage of Popular Vote
1848	30	ZACHARY TAYLOR	Whig	163	1,360,967	47.4
		Lewis Cass	Democratic	127	1,222,342	42.5
		Martin Van Buren	Free Soil		291,263	10.1
1852	31	FRANKLIN PIERCE	Democratic	254	1,601,117	50.9
		Winfield Scott	Whig	42	1,385,453	44.1
		John P. Hale	Free Soil		155,825	5.0
1856	31	JAMES BUCHANAN	Democratic	174	1,832,955	45.3
		John C. Frémont	Republican	114	1,339,932	33.1
		Millard Fillmore	American	8	871,731	21.6
1860	33	ABRAHAM LINCOLN	Republican	180	1,865,593	39.8
		Stephen A. Douglas	Democratic	12	1,382,713	29.5
		John C. Breckinridge	Democratic	72	848,356	18.1
		John Bell	Constitutional Union	39	592,906	12.6
1864	36	ABRAHAM LINCOLN	Republican	212	2,206,938	55.0
		George B. McClellan	Democratic	21	1,803,787	45.0
1868	37	ULYSSES S. GRANT	Republican	214	3,013,421	52.7
		Horatio Seymour	Democratic	80	2,706,829	47.3
1872	37	ULYSSES S. GRANT	Republican	286	3,596,745	55.6
		Horace Greeley	Democratic	*	2,843,446	43.9
1876	38	RUTHERFORD B. HAYES	Republican	185	4,034,311	48.0
		Samuel J. Tilden	Democratic	184	4,288,546	51.0
		Peter Cooper	Greenback		75,973	1.0
1880	38	JAMES A. GARFIELD	Republican	214	4,453,295	48.5
		Winfield S. Hancock	Democratic	155	4,414,082	48.1
		James B. Weaver	Greenback-Labor		308,578	3.4
1884	38	GROVER CLEVELAND	Democratic	219	4,879,507	48.5
		James G. Blaine	Republican	182	4,850,293	48.2
		Benjamin F. Butler	Greenback-Labor		175,370	1.8
		John P. St. John	Prohibition		150,369	1.5
1888	38	BENJAMIN HARRISON	Republican	233	5,477,129	47.9
		Grover Cleveland	Democratic	168	5,537,857	48.6
		Clinton B. Fisk	Prohibition		249,506	2.2
		Anson J. Streeter	Union Labor		146,935	1.3
1892	44	GROVER CLEVELAND	Democratic	277	5,555,426	46.1
		Benjamin Harrison	Republican	145	5,182,690	43.0
		James B. Weaver	People's	22	1,029,846	8.5
		John Bidwell	Prohibition		264,133	2.2
1896	45	WILLIAM McKINLEY	Republican	271	7,102,246	51.1
		William J. Bryan	Democratic	176	6,492,559	47.7
1900	45	WILLIAM McKINLEY	Republican	292	7,218,491	51.7
		William J. Bryan	Democratic; Populist	155	6,356,734	45.5
		John C. Wooley	Prohibition		208,914	1.5
1904	45	THEODORE ROOSEVELT	Republican	336	7,628,461	57.4
		Alton B. Parker	Democratic	140	5,084,223	37.6
		Eugene V. Debs	Socialist		402,283	3.0
		Silas C. Swallow	Prohibition		258,536	1.9

*When Greeley died shortly after the election, his supporters divided their votes among the minor candidates.

Because candidates receiving less than 1 percent of the popular vote are omitted, the percentage of popular vote may not total 100 percent.

Presidential Elections, 1789–1992 *(cont.)*

Year	States in the Union	Candidates	Parties	Electoral Vote	Popular Vote	Percentage of Popular Vote
1908	46	WILLIAM H. TAFT	Republican	321	7,675,320	51.6
		William J. Bryan	Democratic	162	6,412,294	43.1
		Eugene V. Debs	Socialist		420,793	2.8
		Eugene W. Chafin	Prohibition		253,840	1.7
1912	48	WOODROW WILSON	Democratic	435	6,296,547	41.9
		Theodore Roosevelt	Progressive	88	4,118,571	27.4
		William H. Taft	Republican	8	3,486,720	23.2
		Eugene V. Debs	Socialist		900,672	6.0
		Eugene W. Chafin	Prohibition		206,275	1.4
1916	48	WOODROW WILSON	Democratic	277	9,127,695	49.4
		Charles E. Hughes	Republican	254	8,533,507	46.2
		A. L. Benson	Socialist		585,113	3.2
		J. Frank Hanly	Prohibition		220,506	1.2
1920	48	WARREN G. HARDING	Republican	404	16,143,407	60.4
		James N. Cox	Democratic	127	9,130,328	34.2
		Eugene V. Debs	Socialist		919,799	3.4
		P. P. Christensen	Farmer-Labor		265,411	1.0
1924	48	CALVIN COOLIDGE	Republican	382	15,718,211	54.0
		John W. Davis	Democratic	136	8,385,283	28.8
		Robert M. La Follette	Progressive	13	4,831,289	16.6
1928	48	HERBERT C. HOOVER	Republican	444	21,391,993	58.2
		Alfred E. Smith	Democratic	87	15,016,169	40.9
1932	48	FRANKLIN D. ROOSEVELT	Democratic	472	22,809,638	57.4
		Herbert C. Hoover	Republican	59	15,758,901	39.7
		Norman Thomas	Socialist		881,951	2.2
1936	48	FRANKLIN D. ROOSEVELT	Democratic	523	27,752,869	60.8
		Alfred M. Landon	Republican	8	16,674,665	36.5
		William Lemke	Union		882,479	1.9
1940	48	FRANKLIN D. ROOSEVELT	Democratic	449	27,307,819	54.8
		Wendell L. Willkie	Republican	82	22,321,018	44.8
1944	48	FRANKLIN D. ROOSEVELT	Democratic	432	25,606,585	53.5
		Thomas E. Dewey	Republican	99	22,014,745	46.0
1948	48	HARRY S TRUMAN	Democratic	303	24,105,812	49.5
		Thomas E. Dewey	Republican	189	21,970,065	45.1
		Strom Thurmond	States' Rights	39	1,169,063	2.4
		Henry A. Wallace	Progressive		1,157,172	2.4
1952	48	DWIGHT D. EISENHOWER	Republican	442	33,936,234	55.1
		Adlai E. Stevenson	Democratic	89	27,314,992	44.4
1956	48	DWIGHT D. EISENHOWER	Republican	457	35,590,472	57.6
		Adlai E. Stevenson	Democratic	73	26,022,752	42.1
1960	50	JOHN F. KENNEDY	Democratic	303	34,227,096	49.7
		Richard M. Nixon	Republican	219	34,108,546	49.5
		Harry F. Byrd	Independent	15	502,363	.7
1964	50	LYNDON B. JOHNSON	Democratic	486	43,126,506	61.1
		Barry M. Goldwater	Republican	52	27,176,799	38.5
1968	50	RICHARD M. NIXON	Republican	301	31,770,237	43.4
		Hubert H. Humphrey	Democratic	191	31,270,533	42.7
		George C. Wallace	American Independent	46	9,906,141	13.5

cont.

Because candidates receiving less than 1 percent of the popular vote are omitted, the percentage of popular vote may not total 100 percent.

Presidential Elections, 1789–1992 *(cont.)*

Year	States in the Union	Candidates	Parties	Electoral Vote	Popular Vote	Percentage of Popular Vote
1972	50	RICHARD M. NIXON	Republican	520	47,169,911	60.7
		George S. McGovern	Democratic	17	29,170,383	37.5
1976	50	JIMMY CARTER	Democratic	297	40,827,394	49.9
		Gerald R. Ford	Republican	240	39,145,977	47.9
1980	50	RONALD W. REAGAN	Republican	489	43,899,248	50.8
		Jimmy Carter	Democratic	49	35,481,435	41.0
		John B. Anderson	Independent		5,719,437	6.6
		Ed Clark	Libertarian		920,859	1.0
1984	50	RONALD W. REAGAN	Republican	525	54,451,521	58.8
		Walter F. Mondale	Democratic	13	37,565,334	40.5
1988	50	GEORGE H. W. BUSH	Republican	426	47,946,422	54.0
		Michael S. Dukakis	Democratic	112	41,016,429	46.0
1992	50	WILLIAM J. CLINTON	Democratic	370	43,728,275	43.2
		George H. W. Bush	Republican	168	38,167,416	37.7
		H. Ross Perot	Independent		19,237,247	19.0

Because candidates receiving less than 1 percent of the popular vote are omitted, the percentage of popular vote may not total 100 percent.

Vice President and Cabinet Members, 1789–1995

The Washington Administration (1789–1797)

Vice President	John Adams	1789–1797
Secretary of State	Thomas Jefferson	1789–1793
	Edmund Randolph	1794–1795
	Timothy Pickering	1795–1797
Secretary of Treasury	Alexander Hamilton	1789–1795
	Oliver Wolcott	1795–1797
Secretary of War	Henry Knox	1789–1794
	Timothy Pickering	1795–1796
	James McHenry	1796–1797
Attorney General	Edmund Randolph	1789–1793
	William Bradford	1794–1795
	Charles Lee	1795–1797
Postmaster General	Samuel Osgood	1789–1791
	Timothy Pickering	1791–1794
	Joseph Habersham	1795–1797

The John Adams Administration (1797–1801)

Vice President	Thomas Jefferson	1797–1801
Secretary of State	Timothy Pickering	1797–1800
	John Marshall	1800–1801
Secretary of Treasury	Oliver Wolcott	1797–1800
	Samuel Dexter	1800–1801
Secretary of War	James McHenry	1797–1800
	Samuel Dexter	1800–1801
Attorney General	Charles Lee	1797–1801
Postmaster General	Joseph Habersham	1797–1801
Secretary of Navy	Benjamin Stoddert	1798–1801

The Jefferson Administration (1801–1809)

Vice President	Aaron Burr	1801–1805
	George Clinton	1805–1809
Secretary of State	James Madison	1801–1809
Secretary of Treasury	Samuel Dexter	1801
	Albert Gallatin	1801–1809
Secretary of War	Henry Dearborn	1801–1809
Attorney General	Levi Lincoln	1801–1805
	Robert Smith	1805
	John Breckinridge	1805–1806
	Caesar Rodney	1807–1809
Postmaster General	Joseph Habersham	1801
	Gideon Granger	1801–1809
Secretary of Navy	Robert Smith	1801–1809

The Madison Administration (1809–1817)

Vice President	George Clinton	1809–1812
	Elbridge Gerry	1813–1814

cont.

The Madison Administration (1809–1817)   (cont.)

Secretary of State	Robert Smith	1809–1811
	James Monroe	1811–1817
Secretary of Treasury	Albert Gallatin	1809–1813
	George Campbell	1814
	Alexander Dallas	1814–1816
	William Crawford	1816–1817
Secretary of War	William Eustis	1809–1812
	John Armstrong	1813–1814
	James Monroe	1814–1815
	William Crawford	1815–1817
Attorney General	Caesar Rodney	1809–1811
	William Pinkney	1811–1814
	Richard Rush	1814–1817
Postmaster General	Gideon Granger	1809–1814
	Return Meigs	1814–1817
Secretary of Navy	Paul Hamilton	1809–1813
	William Jones	1813–1814
	Benjamin Crowninshield	1814–1817

The Monroe Administration (1817–1825)

Vice President	Daniel Tompkins	1817–1825
Secretary of State	John Quincy Adams	1817–1825
Secretary of Treasury	William Crawford	1817–1825
Secretary of War	George Graham	1817
	John C. Calhoun	1817–1825
Attorney General	Richard Rush	1817
	William Wirt	1817–1825
Postmaster General	Return Meigs	1817–1823
	John McLean	1823–1825
Secretary of Navy	Benjamin Crowninshield	1817–1818
	Smith Thompson	1818–1823
	Samuel Southard	1823–1825

The John Quincy Adams Administration (1825–1829)

Vice President	John C. Calhoun	1825–1829
Secretary of State	Henry Clay	1825–1829
Secretary of Treasury	Richard Rush	1825–1829
Secretary of War	James Barbour	1825–1828
	Peter Porter	1828–1829
Attorney General	William Wirt	1825–1829
Postmaster General	John McLean	1825–1829
Secretary of Navy	Samuel Southard	1825–1829

The Jackson Administration (1829–1837)

Vice President	John C. Calhoun	1829–1833
	Martin Van Buren	1833–1837
Secretary of State	Martin Van Buren	1829–1831
	Edward Livingston	1831–1833

The Jackson Administration (1829–1837) (cont.)

	Louis McLane	1833–1834
	John Forsyth	1834–1837
Secretary of Treasury	Samuel Ingham	1829–1831
	Louis McLane	1831–1833
	William Duane	1833
	Roger B. Taney	1833–1834
	Levi Woodbury	1834–1837
Secretary of War	John H. Eaton	1829–1831
	Lewis Cass	1831–1837
	Benjamin Butler	1837
Attorney General	John M. Berrien	1829–1831
	Roger B. Taney	1831–1833
	Benjamin Butler	1833–1837
Postmaster General	William Barry	1829–1835
	Amos Kendall	1835–1837
Secretary of Navy	John Branch	1829–1831
	Levi Woodbury	1831–1834
	Mahlon Dickerson	1834–1837

The Van Buren Administration (1837–1841)

Vice President	Richard M. Johnson	1837–1841
Secretary of State	John Forsyth	1837–1841
Secretary of Treasury	Levi Woodbury	1837–1841
Secretary of War	Joel Poinsett	1837–1841
Attorney General	Benjamin Butler	1837–1838
	Felix Grundy	1838–1840
	Henry D. Gilpin	1840–1841
Postmaster General	Amos Kendall	1837–1840
	John M. Niles	1840–1841
Secretary of Navy	Mahlon Dickerson	1837–1838
	James Paulding	1838–1841

The William Harrison Administration (1841)

Vice President	John Tyler	1841
Secretary of State	Daniel Webster	1841
Secretary of Treasury	Thomas Ewing	1841
Secretary of War	John Bell	1841
Attorney General	John J. Crittenden	1841
Postmaster General	Francis Granger	1841
Secretary of Navy	George Badger	1841

The Tyler Administration (1841–1845)

Vice President	None	
Secretary of State	Daniel Webster	1841–1843
	Hugh S. Legaré	1843
	Abel P. Upshur	1843–184
	John C. Calhoun	184

The Tyler Administration (1841–1845) (cont.)

Secretary of Treasury	Thomas Ewing	1841
	Walter Forward	1841–1843
	John C. Spencer	1843–1844
	George Bibb	1844–1845
Secretary of War	John Bell	1841
	John C. Spencer	1841–1843
	James M. Porter	1843–1844
	William Wilkins	1844–1845
Attorney General	John J. Crittenden	1841
	Hugh S. Legaré	1841–1843
	John Nelson	1843–1845
Postmaster General	Francis Granger	1841
	Charles Wickliffe	1841
Secretary of Navy	George Badger	1841
	Abel P. Upshur	1841
	David Henshaw	1843–1844
	Thomas Gilmer	1844
	John Y. Mason	1844–1845

The Polk Administration (1845–1849)

Vice President	George M. Dallas	1845–1849
Secretary of State	James Buchanan	1845–1849
Secretary of Treasury	Robert J. Walker	1845–1849
Secretary of War	William L. Marcy	1845–1849
Attorney General	John Y. Mason	1845–1846
	Nathan Clifford	1846–1848
	Isaac Toucey	1848–1849
Postmaster General	Cave Johnson	1845–1849
Secretary of Navy	George Bancroft	1845–1846
	John Y. Mason	1846–1849

The Taylor Administration (1849–1850)

Vice President	Millard Fillmore	1849–1850
Secretary of State	John M. Clayton	1849–1850
Secretary of Treasury	William Meredith	1849–1850
Secretary of War	George Crawford	1849–1850
Attorney General	Reverdy Johnson	1849–1850
Postmaster General	Jacob Collamer	1849–1850
Secretary of Navy	William Preston	1849–1850
Secretary of Interior	Thomas Ewing	1849–1850

The Fillmore Administration (1850–1853)

___ ___	None	
	Daniel Webster	1850–1852
	Edward Everett	1852–1853
	Thomas Corwin	1850–1853
	Charles Conrad	1850–1853

The Fillmore Administration (1850–1853) (cont.)

Attorney General	John J. Crittenden	1850–1853
Postmaster General	Nathan Hall	1850–1852
	Sam D. Hubbard	1852–1853
Secretary of Navy	William A. Graham	1850–1852
	John P. Kennedy	1852–1853
Secretary of Interior	Thomas McKennan	1850
	Alexander Stuart	1850–1853

The Pierce Administration (1853–1857)

Vice President	William R. King	1853
Secretary of State	William L. Marcy	1853–1857
Secretary of Treasury	James Guthrie	1853–1857
Secretary of War	Jefferson Davis	1853–1857
Attorney General	Caleb Cushing	1853–1857
Postmaster General	James Campbell	1853–1857
Secretary of Navy	James C. Dobbin	1853–1857
Secretary of Interior	Robert McClelland	1853–1857

The Buchanan Administration (1857–1861)

Vice President	John C. Breckinridge	1857–1861
Secretary of State	Lewis Cass	1857–1860
	Jeremiah S. Black	1860–1861
Secretary of Treasury	Howell Cobb	1857–1860
	Philip Thomas	1860–1861
	John A. Dix	1861
Secretary of War	John B. Floyd	1857–1861
	Joseph Holt	1861
Attorney General	Jeremiah S. Black	1857–1860
	Edwin M. Stanton	1860–1861
Postmaster General	Aaron V. Brown	1857–1859
	Joseph Holt	1859–1861
	Horatio King	1861
Secretary of Navy	Isaac Toucey	1857–1861
Secretary of Interior	Jacob Thompson	1857–1861

The Lincoln Administration (1861–1865)

Vice President	Hannibal Hamlin	1861–1865
	Andrew Johnson	1865
Secretary of State	William H. Seward	1861–1865
Secretary of Treasury	Samuel P. Chase	1861–1864
	William P. Fessenden	1864–1865
	Hugh McCulloch	1865
Secretary of War	Simon Cameron	1861–1862
	Edwin M. Stanton	1862–1865
Attorney General	Edward Bates	1861–1864
	James Speed	1864–1865
Postmaster General	Horatio King	1861

cont.

The Lincoln Administration (1861–1865)   (cont.)

	Montgomery Blair	1861–1864
	William Dennison	1864–1865
Secretary of Navy	Gideon Welles	1861–1865
Secretary of Interior	Caleb B. Smith	1861–1863
	John P. Usher	1863–1865

The Andrew Johnson Administration (1865–1869)

Vice President	None	
Secretary of State	William H. Seward	1865–1869
Secretary of Treasury	Hugh McCulloch	1865–1869
Secretary of War	Edwin M. Stanton	1865–1867
	Ulysses S. Grant	1867–1868
	Lorenzo Thomas	1868
	John M. Schofield	1868–1869
Attorney General	James Speed	1865–1866
	Henry Stanbery	1866–1868
	William M. Evarts	1868–1869
Postmaster General	William Dennison	1865–1866
	Alexander Randall	1866–1869
Secretary of Navy	Gideon Welles	1865–1869
Secretary of Interior	John P. Usher	1865
	James Harlan	1865–1866
	Orville H. Browning	1866–1869

The Grant Administration (1869–1877)

Vice President	Schuyler Colfax	1869–1873
	Henry Wilson	1873–1875
Secretary of State	Elihu B. Washburne	1869
	Hamilton Fish	1869–1877
Secretary of Treasury	George S. Boutwell	1869–1873
	William Richardson	1873–1874
	Benjamin Bristow	1874–1876
	Lot M. Morrill	1876–1877
Secretary of War	John A. Rawlins	1869
	William T. Sherman	1869
	William W. Belknap	1869–1876
	Alphonso Taft	1876
	James D. Cameron	1876–1877
Attorney General	Ebenezer Hoar	1869–1870
	Amos T. Ackerman	1870–1871
	G. H. Williams	1871–1875
	Edwards Pierrepont	1875–1876
	Alphonso Taft	1876–1877
Postmaster General	John A. J. Creswell	1869–1874
	James W. Marshall	1874
	Marshall Jewell	1874–1876
	James N. Tyner	1876–1877

The Grant Administration (1869–1877)   (cont.)

Secretary of Navy	Adolph E. Borie	1869
	George M. Robeson	1869–1877
Secretary of Interior	Jacob D. Cox	1869–1870
	Columbus Delano	1870–1875
	Zachariah Chandler	1875–1877

The Hayes Administration (1877–1881)

Vice President	William A. Wheeler	1877–1881
Secretary of State	William M. Evarts	1877–1881
Secretary of Treasury	John Sherman	1877–1881
Secretary of War	George W. McCrary	1877–1879
	Alex Ramsey	1879–1881
Attorney General	Charles Devens	1877–1881
Postmaster General	David M. Key	1877–1880
	Horace Maynard	1880–1881
Secretary of Navy	Richard W. Thompson	1877–1880
	Nathan Goff, Jr.	1881
Secretary of Interior	Carl Schurz	1877–1881

The Garfield Administration (1881)

Vice President	Chester A. Arthur	1881
Secretary of State	James G. Blaine	1881
Secretary of Treasury	William Windom	1881
Secretary of War	Robert T. Lincoln	1881
Attorney General	Wayne MacVeagh	1881
Postmaster General	Thomas L. James	1881
Secretary of Navy	William H. Hunt	1881
Secretary of Interior	Samuel J. Kirkwood	1881

The Arthur Administration (1881–1885)

Vice President	None	
Secretary of State	F. T. Frelinghuysen	1881–1885
Secretary of Treasury	Charles J. Folger	1881–1884
	Walter Q. Gresham	1884
	Hugh McCulloch	1884–1885
Secretary of War	Robert T. Lincoln	1881–1885
Attorney General	Benjamin H. Brewster	1881–1885
Postmaster General	Timothy O. Howe	1881–1883
	Walter Q. Gresham	1883–1884
	Frank Hatton	1884–1885
Secretary of Navy	William H. Hunt	1881–1882
	William E. Chandler	1882–1885
Secretary of Interior	Samuel J. Kirkwood	1881–1882
	Henry M. Teller	1882–1885

cont.

The Cleveland Administration (1885–1889)

Vice President	Thomas A. Hendricks	1885–1885
Secretary of State	Thomas F. Bayard	1885–1889
Secretary of Treasury	Daniel Manning	1885–1887
	Charles S. Fairchild	1887–1889
Secretary of War	William C. Endicott	1885–1889
Attorney General	Augustus H. Garland	1885–1889
Postmaster General	William F. Vilas	1885–1888
	Don M. Dickinson	1888–1889
Secretary of Navy	William C. Whitney	1885–1889
Secretary of Interior	Lucius Q. C. Lamar	1885–1888
	William F. Vilas	1888–1889
Secretary of Agriculture	Norman J. Colman	1889

The Benjamin Harrison Administration (1889–1893)

Vice President	Levi P. Morton	1889–1893
Secretary of State	James G. Blaine	1889–1892
	John W. Foster	1892–1893
Secretary of Treasury	William Windom	1889–1891
	Charles Foster	1891–1893
Secretary of War	Redfield Proctor	1889–1891
	Stephen B. Elkins	1891–1893
Attorney General	William H. H. Miller	1889–1891
Postmaster General	John Wanamaker	1889–1893
Secretary of Navy	Benjamin F. Tracy	1889–1893
Secretary of Interior	John W. Noble	1889–1893
Secretary of Agriculture	Jeremiah M. Rusk	1889–1893

The Cleveland Administration (1893–1897)

Vice President	Adlai E. Stevenson	1893–1897
Secretary of State	Walter Q. Gresham	1893–1895
	Richard Olney	1895–1897
Secretary of Treasury	John G. Carlisle	1893–1897
Secretary of War	Daniel S. Lamont	1893–1897
Attorney General	Richard Olney	1893–1895
	James Harmon	1895–1897
Postmaster General	Wilson S. Bissell	1893–1895
	William L. Wilson	1895–1897
Secretary of Navy	Hilary A. Herbert	1893–1897
Secretary of Interior	Hoke Smith	1893–1896
	David R. Francis	1896–1897
Secretary of Agriculture	Julius S. Morton	1893–1897

The McKinley Administration (1897–1901)

Vice President	Garret A. Hobart	1897–1899
	Theodore Roosevelt	1901

The McKinley Administration (1897–1901)   (cont.)

Secretary of State	John Sherman	1897–1898
	William R. Day	1898
	John Hay	1898–1901
Secretary of Treasury	Lyman J. Gage	1897–1901
Secretary of War	Russell A. Alger	1897–1899
	Elihu Root	1899–1901
Attorney General	Joseph McKenna	1897–1898
	John W. Griggs	1898–1901
	Philander C. Knox	1901
Postmaster General	James A. Gary	1897–1898
	Charles E. Smith	1898–1901
Secretary of Navy	John D. Long	1897–1901
Secretary of Interior	Cornelius N. Bliss	1897–1899
	Ethan A. Hitchcock	1899–1901
Secretary of Agriculture	James Wilson	1897–1901

The Theodore Roosevelt Administration (1901–1909)

Vice President	Charles Fairbanks	1905–1909
Secretary of State	John Hay	1901–1905
	Elihu Root	1905–1909
	Robert Bacon	1909
Secretary of Treasury	Lyman J. Gage	1901–1902
	Leslie M. Shaw	1902–1907
	George B. Cortelyou	1907–1909
Secretary of War	Elihu Root	1901–1904
	William H. Taft	1904–1908
	Luke E. Wright	1908–1909
Attorney General	Philander C. Knox	1901–1904
	William H. Moody	1904–1906
	Charles J. Bonaparte	1906–1909
Postmaster General	Charles E. Smith	1901–1902
	Henry C. Payne	1902–1904
	Robert J. Wynne	1904–1905
	George B. Cortelyou	1905–1907
	George von L. Meyer	1907–1909
Secretary of Navy	John D. Long	1901–1902
	William H. Moody	1902–1904
	Paul Morton	1904–1905
	Charles J. Bonaparte	1905–1906
	Victor H. Metcalf	1906–1908
	Truman H. Newberry	1908–1909
Secretary of Interior	Ethan A. Hitchcock	1901–1907
	James R. Garfield	1907–1909
Secretary of Agriculture	James Wilson	1901–1909
Secretary of Labor and Commerce	George B. Cortelyou	1903–1904
	Victor H. Metcalf	1904–1906
	Oscar S. Straus	1906–1909
	Charles Nagel	1909

cont.

The Taft Administration (1909–1913)

Vice President	James S. Sherman	1909–1912
Secretary of State	Philander C. Knox	1909–1913
Secretary of Treasury	Franklin MacVeagh	1909–1913
Secretary of War	Jacob M. Dickinson	1909–1911
	Henry L. Stimson	1911–1913
Attorney General	George W. Wickersham	1909–1913
Postmaster General	Frank H. Hitchcock	1909–1913
Secretary of Navy	George von L. Meyer	1909–1913
Secretary of Interior	Richard A. Ballinger	1909–1911
	Walter L. Fisher	1911–1913
Secretary of Agriculture	James Wilson	1909–1913
Secretary of Labor and Commerce	Charles Nagel	1909–1913

The Wilson Administration (1913–1921)

Vice President	Thomas R. Marshall	1913–1921
Secretary of State	William J. Bryan	1913–1915
	Robert Lansing	1915–1920
	Bainbridge Colby	1920–1921
Secretary of Treasury	William G. McAdoo	1913–1918
	Carter Glass	1918–1920
	David F. Houston	1920–1921
Secretary of War	Lindley M. Garrison	1913–1916
	Newton D. Baker	1916–1921
Attorney General	James C. McReynolds	1913–1914
	Thomas W. Gregory	1914–1919
	A. Mitchell Palmer	1919–1921
Postmaster General	Albert S. Burleson	1913–1921
Secretary of Navy	Josephus Daniels	1913–1921
Secretary of Interior	Franklin K. Lane	1913–1920
	John B. Payne	1920–1921
Secretary of Agriculture	David F. Houston	1913–1920
	Edwin T. Meredith	1920–1921
Secretary of Commerce	William C. Redfield	1913–1919
	Joshua W. Alexander	1919–1921
Secretary of Labor	William B. Wilson	1913–1921

The Harding Administration (1921–1923)

Vice President	Calvin Coolidge	1921–1923
Secretary of State	Charles E. Hughes	1921–1923
Secretary of Treasury	Andrew Mellon	1921–1923
Secretary of War	John W. Weeks	1921–1923
Attorney General	Harry M. Daugherty	1921–1923
Postmaster General	Will H. Hays	1921–1922
	Hubert Work	1922–1923
	Harry S. New	1923
Secretary of Navy	Edwin Denby	1921–1923
Secretary of Interior	Albert B. Fall	1921–1923
	Hubert Work	1923

The Harding Administration (1921–1923)   (cont.)

Secretary of Agriculture	Henry C. Wallace	1921–1923
Secretary of Commerce	Herbert C. Hoover	1921–1923
Secretary of Labor	James J. Davis	1921–1923

The Coolidge Administration (1923–1929)

Vice President	Charles G. Dawes	1925–1929
Secretary of State	Charles E. Hughes	1923–1925
	Frank B. Kellogg	1925–1929
Secretary of Treasury	Andrew Mellon	1923–1929
Secretary of War	John W. Weeks	1923–1925
	Dwight F. Davis	1925–1929
Attorney General	Henry M. Daugherty	1923–1924
	Harlan F. Stone	1924–1925
	John G. Sargent	1925–1929
Postmaster General	Harry S. New	1923–1929
Secretary of Navy	Edwin Denby	1923–1924
	Curtis D. Wilbur	1924–1929
Secretary of Interior	Hubert Work	1923–1928
	Roy O. West	1928–1929
Secretary of Agriculture	Henry C. Wallace	1923–1924
	Howard M. Gore	1924–1925
	William M. Jardine	1925–1929
Secretary of Commerce	Herbert C. Hoover	1923–1928
	William F. Whiting	1928–1929
Secretary of Labor	James J. Davis	1923–1929

The Hoover Administration (1929–1933)

Vice President	Charles Curtis	1929–1933
Secretary of State	Henry L. Stimson	1929–1933
Secretary of Treasury	Andrew Mellon	1929–1932
	Ogden L. Mills	1932–1933
Secretary of War	James W. Good	1929
	Patrick J. Hurley	1929–1933
Attorney General	William D. Mitchell	1929–1933
Postmaster General	Walter F. Brown	1929–1933
Secretary of Navy	Charles F. Adams	1929–1933
Secretary of Interior	Ray L. Wilbur	1929–1933
Secretary of Agriculture	Arthur M. Hyde	1929–1933
Secretary of Commerce	Robert P. Lamont	1929–1932
	Roy D. Chapin	1932–1933
Secretary of Labor	James J. Davis	1929–1930
	William N. Doak	1930–1933

The Franklin D. Roosevelt Administration (1933–1945)

Vice President	John Nance Garner	1933–1941
	Henry A. Wallace	1941–1945
	Harry S Truman	1945

cont.

The Franklin D. Roosevelt Administration (1933–1945) *(cont.)*

Secretary of State	Cordell Hull	1933–1944
	Edward R. Stettinius, Jr.	1944–1945
Secretary of Treasury	William H. Woodin	1933–1934
	Henry Morgenthau, Jr.	1934–1945
Secretary of War	George H. Dern	1933–1936
	Henry A. Woodring	1936–1940
	Henry L. Stimson	1940–1945
Attorney General	Homer S. Cummings	1933–1939
	Frank Murphy	1939–1940
	Robert H. Jackson	1940–1941
	Francis Biddle	1941–1945
Postmaster General	James A. Farley	1933–1940
	Frank C. Walker	1940–1945
Secretary of Navy	Claude A. Swanson	1933–1940
	Charles Edison	1940
	Frank Knox	1940–1944
	James V. Forrestal	1944–1945
Secretary of Interior	Harold L. Ickes	1933–1945
Secretary of Agriculture	Henry A. Wallace	1933–1940
	Claude R. Wickard	1940–1945
Secretary of Commerce	Daniel C. Roper	1933–1939
	Harry L. Hopkins	1939–1940
	Jesse Jones	1940–1945
	Henry A. Wallace	1945
Secretary of Labor	Frances Perkins	1933–1945

The Truman Administration (1945–1953)

Vice President	Alben W. Barkley	1949–1953
Secretary of State	Edward R. Stettinius, Jr.	1945
	James F. Byrnes	1945–1947
	George C. Marshall	1947–1949
	Dean G. Acheson	1949–1953
Secretary of Treasury	Fred M. Vinson	1945–1946
	John W. Snyder	1946–1953
Secretary of War	Robert P. Patterson	1945–1947
	Kenneth C. Royall	1947
Attorney General	Tom C. Clark	1945–1949
	J. Howard McGrath	1949–1952
	James P. McGranery	1952–1953
Postmaster General	Frank C. Walker	1945
	Robert E. Hannegan	1945–1947
	Jesse M. Donaldson	1947–1953
Secretary of Navy	James V. Forrestal	1945–1947
Secretary of Interior	Harold L. Ickes	1945–1946
	Julius A. Krug	1946–1949
	Oscar L. Chapman	1949–1953
Secretary of Agriculture	Clinton P. Anderson	1945–1948
	Charles F. Brannan	1948–1953

The Truman Administration (1945–1953)   (cont.)

Secretary of Commerce	Henry A. Wallace	1945–1946
	W. Averell Harriman	1946–1948
	Charles W. Sawyer	1948–1953
Secretary of Labor	Lewis B. Schwellenbach	1945–1948
	Maurice J. Tobin	1948–1953
Secretary of Defense	James V. Forrestal	1947–1949
	Louis A. Johnson	1949–1950
	George C. Marshall	1950–1951
	Robert A. Lovett	1951–1953

The Eisenhower Administration (1953–1961)

Vice President	Richard M. Nixon	1953–1961
Secretary of State	John Foster Dulles	1953–1959
	Christian A. Herter	1959–1961
Secretary of Treasury	George M. Humphrey	1953–1957
	Robert B. Anderson	1957–1961
Attorney General	Herbert Brownell, Jr.	1953–1958
	William P. Rogers	1958–1961
Postmaster General	Arthur E. Summerfield	1953–1961
Secretary of Interior	Douglas McKay	1953–1956
	Fred A. Seaton	1956–1961
Secretary of Agriculture	Ezra T. Benson	1953–1961
Secretary of Commerce	Sinclair Weeks	1953–1958
	Lewis L. Strauss	1958–1959
	Frederick H. Mueller	1959–1961
Secretary of Labor	Martin P. Durkin	1953
	James P. Mitchell	1953–1961
Secretary of Defense	Charles E. Wilson	1953–1957
	Neil H. McElroy	1957–1959
	Thomas S. Gates, Jr.	1959–1961
Secretary of Health, Education, and Welfare	Oveta Culp Hobby	1953–1955
	Marion B. Folsom	1955–1958
	Arthur S. Flemming	1958–1961

The Kennedy Administration (1961–1963)

Vice President	Lyndon B. Johnson	1961–1963
Secretary of State	Dean Rusk	1961–1963
Secretary of Treasury	C. Douglas Dillon	1961–1963
Attorney General	Robert F. Kennedy	1961–1963
Postmaster General	J. Edward Day	1961–1963
	John A. Gronouski	1963
Secretary of Interior	Stewart L. Udall	1961–1963
Secretary of Agriculture	Orville L. Freeman	1961–1963
Secretary of Commerce	Luther H. Hodges	1961–1963
Secretary of Labor	Arthur J. Goldberg	1961–1962
	W. Willard Wirtz	1962–1963
Secretary of Defense	Robert S. McNamara	1961–1963

cont.

The Kennedy Administration (1961–1963)   (cont.)

Secretary of Health, Education, and Welfare	Abraham A. Ribicoff	1961–1962
	Anthony J. Celebrezze	1962–1963

The Lyndon Johnson Administration (1963–1969)

Vice President	Hubert H. Humphrey	1965–1969
Secretary of State	Dean Rusk	1963–1969
Secretary of Treasury	C. Douglas Dillon	1963–1965
	Henry H. Fowler	1965–1969
Attorney General	Robert F. Kennedy	1963–1964
	Nicholas Katzenbach	1965–1966
	Ramsey Clark	1967–1969
Postmaster General	John A. Gronouski	1963–1965
	Lawrence F. O'Brien	1965–1968
	Marvin Watson	1968–1969
Secretary of Interior	Stewart L. Udall	1963–1969
Secretary of Agriculture	Orville L. Freeman	1963–1969
Secretary of Commerce	Luther H. Hodges	1963–1964
	John T. Connor	1964–1967
	Alexander B. Trowbridge	1967–1968
	Cyrus R. Smith	1968–1969
Secretary of Labor	W. Willard Wirtz	1963–1969
Secretary of Defense	Robert F. McNamara	1963–1968
	Clark Clifford	1968–1969
Secretary of Health, Education, and Welfare	Anthony J. Celebrezze	1963–1965
	John W. Gardner	1965–1968
	Wilbur J. Cohen	1968–1969
Secretary of Housing and Urban Development	Robert C. Weaver	1966–1969
	Robert C. Wood	1969
Secretary of Transportation	Alan S. Boyd	1967–1969

The Nixon Administration (1969–1974)

Vice President	Spiro T. Agnew	1969–1973
	Gerald R. Ford	1973–1974
Secretary of State	William P. Rogers	1969–1973
	Henry A. Kissinger	1973–1974
Secretary of Treasury	David M. Kennedy	1969–1970
	John B. Connally	1971–1972
	George P. Shultz	1972–1974
	William E. Simon	1974
Attorney General	John N. Mitchell	1969–1972
	Richard G. Kleindienst	1972–1973
	Elliot L. Richardson	1973
	William B. Saxbe	1973–1974
Postmaster General	Winton M. Blount	1969–1971
Secretary of Interior	Walter J. Hickel	1969–1970
	Rogers Morton	1971–1974
Secretary of Agriculture	Clifford M. Hardin	1969–1971
	Earl L. Butz	1971–1974

The Nixon Administration (1969–1974) (cont.)

Secretary of Commerce	Maurice H. Stans	1969–1972
	Peter G. Peterson	1972–1973
	Frederick B. Dent	1973–1974
Secretary of Labor	George P. Shultz	1969–1970
	James D. Hodgson	1970–1973
	Peter J. Brennan	1973–1974
Secretary of Defense	Melvin R. Laird	1969–1973
	Elliot L. Richardson	1973
	James R. Schlesinger	1973–1974
Secretary of Health, Education, and Welfare	Robert H. Finch	1969–1970
	Elliot L. Richardson	1970–1973
	Caspar W. Weinberger	1973–1974
Secretary of Housing and Urban Development	George Romney	1969–1973
	James T. Lynn	1973–1974
Secretary of Transportation	John A. Volpe	1969–1973
	Claude S. Brinegar	1973–1974

The Ford Administration (1974–1977)

Vice President	Nelson A. Rockefeller	1974–1977
Secretary of State	Henry A. Kissinger	1974–1977
Secretary of Treasury	William E. Simon	1974–1977
Attorney General	William Saxbe	1974–1975
	Edward Levi	1975–1977
Secretary of Interior	Rogers Morton	1974–1975
	Stanley K. Hathaway	1975
	Thomas Kleppe	1975–1977
Secretary of Agriculture	Earl L. Butz	1974–1976
	John A. Knebel	1976–1977
Secretary of Commerce	Frederick B. Dent	1974–1975
	Rogers Morton	1975–1976
	Elliott L. Richardson	1976–1977
Secretary of Labor	Peter J. Brennan	1974–1975
	John T. Dunlop	1975–1976
	W. J. Usery	1976–1977
Secretary of Defense	James R. Schlesinger	1974–1975
	Donald Rumsfeld	1975–1977
Secretary of Health, Education, and Welfare	Caspar Weinberger	1974–1975
	Forrest D. Mathews	1975–1977
Secretary of Housing and Urban Development	James T. Lynn	1974–1975
	Carla A. Hills	1975–1977
Secretary of Transportation	Claude Brinegar	1974–1975
	William T. Coleman	1975–1977

The Carter Administration (1977–1981)

Vice President	Walter F. Mondale	1977–1981
Secretary of State	Cyrus R. Vance	1977–1980
	Edmund Muskie	1980–1981

cont.

The Carter Administration (1977–1981) (cont.)

Secretary of Treasury	W. Michael Blumenthal	1977–1979
	G. William Miller	1979–1981
Attorney General	Griffin Bell	1977–1979
	Benjamin R. Civiletti	1979–1981
Secretary of Interior	Cecil D. Andrus	1977–1981
Secretary of Agriculture	Robert Bergland	1977–1981
Secretary of Commerce	Juanita M. Kreps	1977–1979
	Philip M. Klutznick	1979–1981
Secretary of Labor	Ray F. Marshall	1977–1981
Secretary of Defense	Harold Brown	1977–1981
Secretary of Health, Education, and Welfare	Joseph A. Califano	1977–1979
	Patricia R. Harris	1979
Secretary of Health and Human Services	Patricia R. Harris	1979–1981
Secretary of Education	Shirley M. Hufstedler	1979–1981
Secretary of Housing and Urban Development	Patricia R. Harris	1977–1979
	Moon Landrieu	1979–1981
Secretary of Transportation	Brock Adams	1977–1979
	Neil E. Goldschmidt	1979–1981
Secretary of Energy	James R. Schlesinger	1977–1979
	Charles W. Duncan	1979–1981

The Reagan Administration (1981–1989)

Vice President	George Bush	1981–1989
Secretary of State	Alexander M. Haig	1981–1982
	George P. Shultz	1982–1989
Secretary of Treasury	Donald Regan	1981–1985
	James A. Baker III	1985–1988
	Nicholas Brady	1988–1989
Attorney General	William F. Smith	1981–1985
	Edwin A. Meese III	1985–1988
	Richard Thornburgh	1988–1989
Secretary of Interior	James Watt	1981–1983
	William P. Clark, Jr.	1983–1985
	Donald P. Hodel	1985–1989
Secretary of Agriculture	John Block	1981–1986
	Richard E. Lyng	1986–1989
Secretary of Commerce	Malcolm Baldridge	1981–1987
	C. William Verity, Jr.	1987–1989
Secretary of Labor	Raymond Donovan	1981–1985
	William E. Brock	1985–1988
	Ann Dore McLaughlin	1988–1989
Secretary of Defense	Caspar Weinberger	1981–1988
	Frank Carlucci	1988–1989
Secretary of Health and Human Services	Richard Schweiker	1981–1983
	Margaret Heckler	1983–1985
	Otis R. Bowen	1985–1989
Secretary of Education	Terrel H. Bell	1981–1985
	William J. Bennett	1985–1988
	Lauro F. Cavazos	1988–1989

The Reagan Administration (1981–1989)   (cont.)

Secretary of Housing and Urban Development	Samuel Pierce	1981–1989
Secretary of Transportation	Drew Lewis	1981–1983
	Elizabeth Dole	1983–1987
	James L. Burnley IV	1987–1989
Secretary of Energy	James Edwards	1981–1982
	Donald P. Hodel	1982–1985
	John S. Herrington	1985–1989

The Bush Administration (1989–1993)

Vice President	J. Danforth Quayle III	1989–1993
Secretary of State	James Baker III	1989–1993
Secretary of Treasury	Nicholas Brady	1989–1993
Attorney General	Richard Thornburgh	1989–1991
	William Barr	1991–1993
Secretary of Interior	Manuel Lujan	1989–1993
Secretary of Agriculture	Clayton Yeutter	1989–1991
	Edward Madigan	1991–1993
Secretary of Commerce	Robert Mosbacher	1989–1992
	Barbara Franklin	1992–1993
Secretary of Labor	Elizabeth Dole	1989–1990
	Lynn Martin	1991–1993
Secretary of Defense	Richard Cheney	1989–1993
Secretary of Health and Human Services	Louis Sullivan	1989–1993
Secretary of Education	Lauro Cavazos	1989–1990
	Lamar Alexander	1990–1993
Secretary of Housing and Urban Development	Jack Kemp	1989–1993
Secretary of Transportation	Samuel Skinner	1989–1991
	Andrew Card	1992–1993
Secretary of Energy	James Watkins	1989–1993
Secretary of Veterans' Affairs	Edward Derwinski	1989–1993

The Clinton Administration (1993–   )

Vice President	Albert W. Gore, Jr.	1993–
Secretary of State	Warren Christopher	1993–
Secretary of Treasury	Lloyd Bentsen	1993–1994
	Robert Rubin	1995–
Attorney General	Janet Reno	1993–
Secretary of Interior	Bruce Babbitt	1993–
Secretary of Agriculture	Michael Espy	1993–1994
	Dan Glickman	1994–
Secretary of Commerce	Ronald Brown	1993–
Secretary of Labor	Robert Reich	1993–
Secretary of Defense	Les Aspin	1993–1994
	William Perry	1994–
Secretary of Health and Human Services	Donna Shalala	1993–
Secretary of Education	Richard Reilly	1993–
Secretary of Housing and Urban Development	Henry Cisneros	1993–
Secretary of Transportation	Federico Peña	1993–
Secretary of Energy	Hazel O'Leary	1993–
Secretary of Veterans' Affairs	Jesse Brown	1993–

Supreme Court Justices

Name	Terms of Service	Appointed By
JOHN JAY	1789–1795	Washington
James Wilson	1789–1798	Washington
John Rutledge	1790–1791	Washington
William Cushing	1790–1810	Washington
John Blair	1790–1796	Washington
James Iredell	1790–1799	Washington
Thomas Johnson	1792–1793	Washington
William Paterson	1793–1806	Washington
JOHN RUTLEDGE*	1795	Washington
Samuel Chase	1796–1811	Washington
OLIVER ELLSWORTH	1796–1800	Washington
Bushrod Washington	1799–1829	J. Adams
Alfred Moore	1800–1804	J. Adams
JOHN MARSHALL	1801–1835	J. Adams
William Johnson	1804–1834	Jefferson
Brockholst Livingston	1807–1823	Jefferson
Thomas Todd	1807–1826	Jefferson
Gabriel Duvall	1811–1835	Madison
Joseph Story	1812–1845	Madison
Smith Thompson	1823–1843	Monroe
Robert Trimble	1826–1828	J. Q. Adams
John McLean	1830–1861	Jackson
Henry Baldwin	1830–1844	Jackson
James M. Wayne	1835–1867	Jackson
ROGER B. TANEY	1836–1864	Jackson
Philip P. Barbour	1836–1841	Jackson
John Cartron	1837–1865	Van Buren
John McKinley	1838–1852	Van Buren
Peter V. Daniel	1842–1860	Van Buren
Samuel Nelson	1845–1872	Tyler
Levi Woodbury	1845–1851	Polk
Robert C. Grier	1846–1870	Polk
Benjamin R. Curtis	1851–1857	Fillmore
John A. Campbell	1853–1861	Pierce
Nathan Clifford	1858–1881	Buchanan
Noah H. Swayne	1862–1881	Lincoln
Samuel F. Miller	1862–1890	Lincoln
David Davis	1862–1877	Lincoln
Stephen J. Field	1863–1897	Lincoln
SALMON P. CHASE	1864–1873	Lincoln
William Strong	1870–1880	Grant
Joseph P. Bradley	1870–1892	Grant

NOTE: The names of Chief Justices are printed in capital letters.

*Although Rutledge acted as Chief Justice, the Senate refused to confirm his appointment.

Supreme Court Justices *(cont.)*

Name	Terms of Service	Appointed By
Ward Hunt	1873–1882	Grant
MORRISON R. WAITE	1874–1888	Grant
John M. Harlan	1877–1911	Hayes
William B. Woods	1881–1887	Hayes
Stanley Matthews	1881–1889	Garfield
Horace Gray	1882–1902	Arthur
Samuel Blatchford	1882–1893	Arthur
Lucious Q. C. Lamar	1888–1893	Cleveland
MELVILLE W. FULLER	1888–1910	Cleveland
David J. Brewer	1890–1910	B. Harrison
Henry B. Brown	1891–1906	B. Harrison
George Shiras, Jr.	1892–1903	B. Harrison
Howell E. Jackson	1893–1895	B. Harrison
Edward D. White	1894–1910	Cleveland
Rufus W. Peckham	1896–1909	Cleveland
Joseph McKenna	1898–1925	McKinley
Oliver W. Holmes	1902–1932	T. Roosevelt
William R. Day	1903–1922	T. Roosevelt
William H. Moody	1906–1910	T. Roosevelt
Horace H. Lurton	1910–1914	Taft
Charles E. Hughes	1910–1916	Taft
EDWARD D. WHITE	1910–1921	Taft
Willis Van Devanter	1911–1937	Taft
Joseph R. Lamar	1911–1916	Taft
Mahlon Pitney	1912–1922	Taft
James C. McReynolds	1914–1941	Wilson
Louis D. Brandeis	1916–1939	Wilson
John H. Clarke	1916–1922	Wilson
WILLIAM H. TAFT	1921–1930	Harding
George Sutherland	1922–1938	Harding
Pierce Butler	1923–1939	Harding
Edward T. Sanford	1923–1930	Harding
Harlan F. Stone	1925–1941	Coolidge
CHARLES E. HUGHES	1930–1941	Hoover
Owen J. Roberts	1930–1945	Hoover
Benjamin N. Cardozo	1932–1938	Hoover
Hugo L. Black	1937–1971	F. Roosevelt
Stanley F. Reed	1938–1957	F. Roosevelt
Felix Frankfurter	1939–1962	F. Roosevelt
William O. Douglas	1939–1975	F. Roosevelt
Frank Murphy	1940–1949	F. Roosevelt
HARLAN F. STONE	1941–1946	F. Roosevelt
James F. Byrnes	1941–1942	F. Roosevelt
Robert H. Jackson	1941–1954	F. Roosevelt
Wiley B. Rutledge	1943–1949	F. Roosevelt
Harold H. Burton	1945–1958	Truman

cont.

Supreme Court Justices *(cont.)*

Name	Terms of Service	Appointed By
FREDERICK M. VINSON	1946–1953	Truman
Tom C. Clark	1949–1967	Truman
Sherman Minton	1949–1956	Truman
EARL WARREN	1953–1969	Eisenhower
John Marshall Harlan	1955–1971	Eisenhower
William J. Brennan, Jr.	1956–1990	Eisenhower
Charles E. Whittaker	1957–1962	Eisenhower
Potter Stewart	1958–1981	Eisenhower
Byron R. White	1962–1993	Kennedy
Arthur J. Goldberg	1962–1965	Kennedy
Abe Fortas	1965–1970	L. Johnson
Thurgood Marshall	1967–1991	L. Johnson
WARREN E. BURGER	1969–1986	Nixon
Harry A. Blackmun	1970–1994	Nixon
Lewis F. Powell, Jr.	1971–1987	Nixon
William H. Rehnquist	1971–1986	Nixon
John Paul Stevens	1975–	Ford
Sandra Day O'Connor	1981–	Reagan
WILLIAM H. REHNQUIST	1986–	Reagan
Antonin Scalia	1986–	Reagan
Anthony Kennedy	1988–	Reagan
David Souter	1990–	Bush
Clarence Thomas	1991–	Bush
Ruth Bader Ginsburg	1993–	Clinton
Stephen Breyer	1994–	Clinton

PHOTOGRAPH CREDITS

Prologue

p. xxxii, (Detail) The Fine Arts Museums of San Francisco, Gift of Mrs. Harold R. McKinnon and Mrs. Harry L. Brown, 1962.21; p. xxxv, Eric Meola/The Image Bank; p. xxxvii, Cara Moore/The Image Bank; p. xxxviii(top), Steve Proehl/The Image Bank; p. xxxviii(bottom), Alan Becker/The Image Bank; p. xxxix, Tom Bean/Tony Stone Images; p. xl, Nathan Benn/Stock Boston; p. xlii, Gary S. Chapman/The Image Bank; p. xliii(top), Jim Brandenburg/Minden Pictures; p. xliii(bottom), Eric Meola/The Image Bank; p. xliv(left), Don Landwehrle/The Image Bank; p. xliv(right), Edward Bower/The Image Bank; p. xlv(top), Peter Cole/New England Stock Photo; p. xlv(bottom), John Aldridge/The Picture Cube; p. xlvi(top), Bo Zaunders/The Stock Market; p. xlvi(bottom), Steve Dunwell/The Image Bank; p. xlvii, James L. Amos/Photo Researchers, Inc.

Chapter 1

p. xlviii, Ohio Historical Society; p. 1, Courtesy, Peabody Essex Museum, Salem, MA. Photo by Mark Sexton; p. 3(top), Photo Archives/Denver Museum of Natural History; p. 3(bottom), Courtesy of the National Museum of the American Indian, Smithsonian Institution; p. 6, Werner Forman Archive/Art Resource; p. 7, Tozzer Library, Harvard University; p. 9(top), Tim Haste/Profiles West; p. 9(bottom), William M. Ferguson; p. 11(top), Georg Gerster/Comstock; p. 11(bottom), James A. Ford and Clarence H. Webb. "Poverty Point, a late archaic site in Louisiana." New York, American Museum of Natural History, 1956 (Anthropological Papers, Vol. 46, Part 1); p. 12, Field Museum of Natural History/Werner Forman Archive/Art Resource; p. 13a(both), Cahokia Mounds State Historic Site, Painting of Cahokia by Lloyd K. Townsend; p. 13b(both), Cahokia Mounds State Historic Site; p. 15, Santa Barbara Museum of Natural History; p. 19, Ohio Historical Society.

Chapter 2

p. 20, Courtesy of the John Carter Brown Library at Brown University; p. 21, (Detail) The Metropolitan Museum of Art, Gift of J.P. Morgan, 1900 (00.18.2); p. 24, Courtesy Entwistle Gallery, London/Werner Forman Archive/Art Resource; pp. 28, 30, The Granger Collection; p. 33; American Museum of Natural History, photo: Else Sackler; Lee Boltin; p. 37, © cliche Bibliotheque Nationale de France, Paris; p. 38, "Manuscrito Pictorico Mexicano de Mediados del Siglo XVI," by Lienzo de Tlaxcala. Tozzer Library/Harvard University; p. 41, Arizona State Museum, University of Arizona. Helga Teiwes, Photographer; p. 43, By permission of Houghton Library/Harvard University. Photo by Barry Donahue; p. 44, Print Collection Miriam and Ira. D. Wallach Division of Art, Prints & Photographs, The New York Public Library. Astor,

Lenox and Tilden Foundations; p. 46(all), Courtesy, Flowerdew Hundred Foundation; p. 47a(vignette), Copyright British Museum; p. 47a(bottom), The Granger Collection; p. 47b(all), Copyright The British Museum; p. 49, Courtesy, Plimoth Plantation, Inc., Plymouth, Massachusetts; p. 50, (Detail) National Portrait Gallery, London.

Chapter 3

p. 52, Courtesy of the Massachusetts Historical Society; p. 53, Courtesy of the John Carter Brown Library at Brown University; p. 54, American Antiquarian Society; p. 56(both right), Courtesy of the Pilgrim Society, Plymouth, Massachusetts; p. 56(left), Eliot Elisofon, LIFE MAGAZINE © Time Warner Inc.; p. 61(left), Courtesy of the Massachusetts Historical Society; p. 61(top right), Courtesy of the Pilgrim Society, Plymouth, Massachusetts; p. 61(bottom right), Courtesy, Museum of Fine Arts, Boston. Gift of Senator Leverett Saltonstall; p. 67, (Detail) "From the records of the Court of Oyer & Terminer 1692, property of the Supreme Judicial Court, Division of Archives and Records Preservation." On deposit at Peabody Essex Museum, Salem, Massachusetts; p. 71, Granger Collection; p. 74, Copyright The British Museum; p. 75, The New York Public Library, Arent's Tobacco Collection. Print Collection, Miriam and Ira D. Wallach Division of Art, Prints & Photographs. Astor, Lenox and Tilden Foundations; p. 78, Library Company of Philadelphia; p. 81; Burgerbiblithek Bern; p. 85, Collection of Albany Institute of History and Art, Gift of Governor and Mrs. Averill Harriman and Three Anonymous Owners; p. 87(left), Library of Congress; p. 87(right), The Historical Society of Pennsylvania; p. 87a(vignette), Jill Enfield/The Image Bank; p. 87a(right); Courtesy, Museum of New Mexico Neg. #11409; p. 87b; Photo by John K. Hillers. Courtesy, Museum of New Mexico. Neg. #16096; p. 90, The Granger Collection.

Chapter 4

p. 92, Courtesy, Winterthur Museum; p. 93, The Granger Collection; p. 96, Courtesy, Winterthur Museum; p. 101, Peabody Essex Museum, Salem, Massachusetts; p. 105, Wethersfield Historical Society; p. 110, Newport Historical Society #NHS53.3; p. 112, Courtesy, Maryland State Archives, Special Collections MSA SC 1497-277; p. 113, Peabody Museum, Harvard University. Photo by Hillel Burger; p. 114, Mackinac State Historic Park; p. 116, Courtesy, Winterthur Museum; p. 117, The Royal Library, Copenhagen; p. 117a, 117b(all), From the exhibition "Fort Mose: Colonial America's Black Fortress of Freedom" produced by the Florida Museum of Natural History; p. 118, Bob Daemmrich/Stock Boston; p. 122(both), John Neubauer; p. 123, Print Department, Public Library of the City of Boston; p. 124, (Detail) Yale University Art Gallery, Bequest of Eugene Phelps Edwards.

Chapter 5

p. 126, (Detail) Courtesy, Winterthur Museum. Bequest of Henry Francis du Pont; p. 127, The Granger Collection; p. 129, Library of Congress; p. 131, Courtesy, Winterthur Museum; p. 132, Indianapolis Museum of Art, The James E. Roberts Fund; p. 137, Manuscripts & Archives Division, New York Public Library; p. 139, Library of Congress; p. 142, "British Officials Doing the Devil's Work" from *Boston Gazette.* American Antiquarian Society; p. 145, Courtesy, Museum of Fine Arts, Boston, Deposited by the City of Boston; p. 146, Colonial Williamsburg Foundation; p. 148, Historical Society of Pennsylvania; p. 150, Library of Congress; p. 154, American Antiquarian Society; p. 156, Courtesy of the Decorative & Industrial Arts Department of the Chicago Historical Society; p. 157a(vignette), Photograph courtesy of the Concord Museum, Concord, MA #Pi414; p. 157a(bottom), American Antiquarian Society; p. 157b(top), Photograph courtesy of the Concord Museum, Concord, MA #Pi414; p. 157b(bottom), John Carter Brown Library at Brown University; p. 159, Peabody Essex Museum, Salem, Massachusetts.

Chapter 6

p. 162, West Point Museum Collections, United States Military Academy; p. 163, (Detail) Courtesy, Museum of Fine Arts, Boston, Deposited by City of Boston; p. 164, Print Collection, Miriam & Ira D. Wallach Division of Art, Prints and Photographs, The New York Public Library, Astor, Lenox and Tilden Foundations; p. 167, (Detail) Collection of the New-York Historical Society; p. 168, Visual Materials Division, Department of Rare Books & Special Collections, Princeton University Libraries; p. 172, (Detail) Independence National Historical Park; p. 175, Anne S.K. Brown Military Collection, Brown University Library; p. 178, Collection of Alexander A. McBurney; p. 179, (Detail) Boston Athenaeum; p. 180, New York State Office of Parks, Recreation and Historic Preservation, John Jay Homestead State Historic Site; p. 183a(vignette), Rochester Museum & Science Center, Rochester, New York; p. 183a(bottom), The New-York Historical Society; p. 183b, Courtesy of the National Museum of the American Indian, Smithsonian Institution #S3499; p. 189, National Gallery of Canada, Ottawa; p. 191, Henry Groskinsky, LIFE MAGAZINE © Time Warner Inc.; p. 192, (Detail) Colonial Williamsburg Foundation; p. 197, (Detail) National Portrait Gallery/Art Resource, NY.

Chapter 7

p. 200, National Museum of American History, Smithsonian Institution; p. 201, Chicago Historical Society; p. 205, Museum of the City of New York; p. 205a(vignette), "High Street, from Ninth Street, Philadelphia," © 1799 by William Birch. Monticello/Thomas Jefferson Memorial Foundation, Inc.; p. 205a(bottom), Rare Book Department, The Free Library of Philadelphia; p. 205b, (Detail) Delaware Art Museum, Wilmington. Gift of Absalom Jones School, Wilmington; p. 209, Collection of the New-York Historical Society; p. 210, Courtesy, Donaldson Lufkin & Jenrette Collection of Americana; p. 215, Smithsonian Institution Photo #BAE 1169-L-3; p. 218, (Detail) Chicago Historical Society; p. 220, The Brooklyn Museum, #39.536.1. Gift of the Crescent Hamilton Athletic Club; p. 221, Colonial Williamsburg Foundation; p. 224(left), Adams National Historic Site, Photo by Jeffrey Dunn; p. 224(right), National Museum of American Art, Washington, DC/Art Resource, N.Y.; p. 228, Monticello/Thomas Jefferson Memorial Foundation,

Inc.; p. 231, Monticello/Thomas Jefferson Memorial Foundation, Inc.; p. 232(left), Museum of American Political Life/University of Hartford. Photograph by Sally Anderson-Bruce; p. 232(right), Courtesy of Atwater Kent Museum.

Chapter 8

p. 234, (Detail) The Minneapolis Institute of Arts, William Hood Dunwoody Fund; p. 235, The Huntington Museum, San Marino, California; p. 237(left), Courtesy, Robert M. Hinklin Jr., Inc. Spartanburg, South Carolina; p. 237(right), Monticello/Thomas Jefferson Memorial Foundation; p. 238, Franklin D. Roosevelt Library; p. 240, Boston Athenaeum; p. 244(both top), Courtesy, Independence National Historical Park; p. 244(bottom), Peabody Museum, Harvard University. Photo by Hillel Burger; p. 248, The Print and Picture Collection, The Free Library of Philadelphia; p. 251, The Granger Collection; p. 254, The New Haven Colony Historical Society, Gift of Mrs. Philip Galpin; p. 256, Copyrighted by White House Historical Association; p. 257, Visual Materials Division, Department of Rare Books and Special Collections, Princeton University Libraries; p. 257a(vignette), "View of Boston and the South Boston Bridge, 1828." Boston Athenaeum; p. 257a(bottom), Courtesy of The Harvard University Portrait Collection. Gift of Francis V. Bulfinch 1933; p. 257b(top), Print Collection, Miriam & Ira D. Wallach Division of Art, Prints and Photographs, New York Public Library. Astor, Lenox and Tilden Foundations; p. 257b(bottom), Courtesy of Museum of Fine Arts, Boston. Gift of Mrs. Horatio A. Lamb in memory of Mr. & Mrs. Winthrop Sargent; p. 258, Bettmann; p. 264(left), (Detail) Courtesy, Independence National Historical Park; p. 264(right), Anne S K Brown Military Collection, Brown University Library.

Chapter 9

p. 266, (Detail) The Saint Louis Art Museum. Purchase: Ezra H. Lilly Fund; p. 267, Hudson Bay Company Archives/Provincial Archives of Manitoba; p. 269(left), The Walters Art Gallery, Baltimore; p. 269(top right), Buffalo Bill Historical Center, Cody, Wyoming; As a Memorial to Jeanette J. Leonard, on behalf of her husband Dr. Kenneth O. Leonard; p. 269(bottom right), Missouri Historical Society, St. Louis; p. 270, Metropolitan Museum of Art, Rogers Fund 1942 (42.95.12); p. 272, William L. Clements Library, University of Michigan, Ann Arbor; p. 273a(vignette), National Museum of American Art, Washington, DC/Art Resource, NY; p. 273a(left), Collection of The New-York Historical Society; p. 273a(right), National Portrait Gallery, Washington, DC/Art Resource, NY; p. 273b(top), National Museum of American Art, Washington, DC/Art Resource, NY; p. 273b(bottom), State Historical Society of Wisconsin; p. 277, Museum d'Histoire Naturelle, No. 62003-2; p. 278, Collection of The New-York Historical Society; p. 284, University of Massachusetts Lowell; p. 287, The Saint Louis Art Museum. Loan from the collection of Arthur Ziern, Jr.; p. 289, Witt Library/Courtauld Institute of Art; p. 293, Giampietro Gallery, 50 East 78th, New York, NY 10021; p. 296, Yale University Art Gallery. Gift of George Hoadley, B.A. 1801.

Chapter 10

p. 298, (Detail) The Walters Art Gallery, Baltimore; p. 299, Special Collections, Skillman Library, Lafayette College, Easton, PA; p. 302, The Metropolitan Museum of Art, Gift of I.N. Phelps Stokes, Edward S. Hawes, Alice Mary Hawes, Marion Augusta Hawes,

Chapter 16

p. 498, William Gladstone Collection; p. 499, Library of Congress; p. 500, "The Return to Fredericksburg After the Battle," by David English Henderson. Gettysburg National Military Park; p. 502, National Portrait Gallery, Washington, DC/Art Resource, NY; p. 504, *Harpers Weekly,* 1866; p. 511, The Granger Collection; p. 512, The Museum of the Confederacy, Richmond, Virginia. Photograph by Katherine Wetzel; p. 514(below), Decorative and Industrial Arts/Chicago Historical Society; p. 514(right), Tennessee State Museum Collection. Photograph by June Dorman; p. 517, William Gladstone Collection; p. 519a(vignette), Courtesy, Georgia Department of Archives and History; p. 519a, Courtesy, Georgia Department of Archives and History; p. 519b, Hargrett Rare Book and Manuscript Library, The University of Georgia; p. 522(left), *Harpers Weekly,* 1871; p. 522(right), Brown Brothers; p. 526, *Harpers Weekly,* October 24, 1874; p. 528(all), Kansas State Historical Society; p. 531, Museum of American Political Life/University of Hartford. Photo by Steve Laschever.

Chapter 17

p. 534, National Museum of American Art, Washington, DC/Art Resource, NY; p. 535, Minnesota Historical Society; p. 537, Library of Congress; p. 538, Kansas Pacific Railway Album, DeGolyer Library, Southern Methodist University; p. 541(both), Bettmann Archive; p. 544(both), Peabody Museum, Harvard University; p. 545a(both), National Museum of American Art, Washington, DC/Art Resource, NY; p. 545b(top), Peabody Museum, Harvard University, Photo by Hillel Burger; p. 545b(bottom), Minnesota Historical Society, Gilbert Wilson photo; p. 546(top), National Museum of Natural History, Smithsonian Institution; p. 546(bottom), The Huntington Library, San Marino, California; p. 549(right), Nebraska State Historical Society; p. 549(left), Solomon D. Butcher Collection/Nebraska State Historical Society; p. 555, Santa Barbara Historical Society; p. 557, Special Collections Division/University of Washington Libraries. Photo by E.A. Hegg. Negative No. 1312; p. 560, Denver Public Library, Western History Department; p. 564, Chromolithograph by Louis Prang of Thomas Moran's "Castle Geyser, Upper Geyser Basin, Yellowstone National Park," from F.V. Hayden's *Yellowstone National Park* 1876) Smithsonian Institution Libraries; p. 566, Buffalo Bill Historical Center, Cody, Wyoming. Gift of the Coe Foundation.

Chapter 18

p. 568, Library of Congress; p. 569, Culver Pictures; p. 571, Bettmann; p. 572, Bettmann; p. 575, Library of Congress; p. 579(left), U.S. Department of the Interior/National Park Service/Edison National Historic Site; p. 579(right), The Granger Collection; p. 580(both), Library of Congress; p. 581, Bettmann; p. 584, *Harpers Weekly,* March 26, 1877; p. 586, Library of Congress; p. 588, The Connecticut Historical Society, Hartford, Connecticut; p. 591, Photograph courtesy of the Lynn Historical Society; p. 594, Museum of American Political Life/University of Hartford. Photograph by Steven Laschever; p. 595, Library of Congress; p. 597, Chicago Historical Society; p. 597a(vignette), Library of Congress; p. 597a, Carnegie Library of Homestead. Reproduction by Randolph Harris; p. 597b(top left and right), Library of Congress.

Chapter 19

p. 602, Indianapolis Museum of Art, Gift of a Couple of Old Hoosiers; p. 603, Bettmann, UPI Newsphotos; p. 605, Collection of The New York Historical Society; p. 606, Security Pacific Collec-tion/Los Angeles Public Library; p. 609, Ellis Island Museum; p. 612, Chicago Historical Society; p. 613a(vignette), "Leslie's Weekly," September 27, 1894; p. 613a(bottom), Photo Courtesy of Milwaukee County Historical Society; p. 613b, State Historical Society of Wisconsin; p. 614, The Western Reserve Historical Society, Cleveland, Ohio; p. 617, North Wind Picture Archives; p. 619, The Granger Collection; p. 622, University of Illinois at Chicago. The University Library. Jane Addams Memorial Collection; p. 624, Edward Emerson Simmons (1852–1931), *Boston Public Garden,* 1893, oil on canvas, 18 × 26 in. (45.7 × 66 cm), Daniel J. Terra Collection, 34.1984. Photograph © 1996. Courtesy, of Terra Museum of American Art, Chicago; p. 626, Chicago Historical Society; p. 629, National Portrait Gallery, Washington, DC/Art Resource, NY.

Chapter 20

p. 632, State Historical Society of Wisconsin. Photo by Charles Van Schaick; p. 633, Minnesota Historical Society, Harry Sheperd photo; p. 635, Bettmann; p. 637, By Permission of AT&T Archives; p. 639, Courtesy, University Archives, Bancroft Library; p. 642, "The Contest for the Bouquet: The Family of Robert Gordon in Their New York Dining Room," 1866, by Seymour Joseph Guy. The Metropolitan Museum of Art, Purchase, Gift of William E. Dodge, by exchange, and Lila Acheson Wallace Gift. (1992.128); p. 643, Bettmann Archive; p. 645(both), West Point Museum Collections, United States Military Academy. Photograph by Paul Warchol; p. 647, State Historical Society of Wisconsin; p. 648, Photograph © The Detroit Institute of Arts, Founders Society Purchase; p. 649, From the collections of Henry Ford Museum and Greenfield Village; p. 651, Brooklyn Historical Society; p. 651a(vignette), The Granger Collection; p. 651a, New Orleans Jazz Club Collection, LA State Museum, Photo by Jan W. Brantley; p. 651b(all), Courtesy Louisiana Jazz Club Collection, Louisiana State Museum, Photo © 1992 Jan White Brantley; p. 654(left), Granger Collection; p. 654(right), North Wind Picture Archives; p. 656, The Gifted Line, John Grossman, Inc.; p. 657, The Granger Collection; p. 658, San Diego Historical Society — Ticor Collection.

Chapter 21

p. 662, Brigham Young University; p. 663, Library of Congress; p. 665, D. C. Heath Archives; p. 669, Harvard College Library; p. 671(left), Miriam and Ira D. Wallach Division of Arts, Prints and Photographs, New York Public Library, Astor, Lenox and Tilden Foundations; p. 671(right), Library of Congress; p. 676, glass plate negative, © 1900–1910, P1979.41.74, Amon Carter Museum, Fort Worth, Texas. Clifton, Texas Collection; p. 678, The Granger Collection; p. 681, Library of Congress; p. 683, Division of Political History, Smithsonian Institution; p. 684, Political History Division, National Museum of American History, Smithsonian Institution; p. 685a(vignette), Courtesy, The Manoogian Collection; p. 685a, The Chicago Historical Society; p. 685b(top), Courtesy, The Manoogian Collection; p. 685b(bottom), Library of Congress; p. 689(left), Library of Congress; p. 689(right), Granger Collection; p. 691, U.S. Army Center of Military History, Art/Exhibits Branch; p. 692, California Museum of Photography, University of California, Riverside; p. 694, U.S. Signal Corps Photo/National Archives; p. 696(left), Granger Collection; p. 696(right), Bettmann Archive.

Chapter 22

p. 698, Courtesy of The Jordan-Volpe Gallery, Inc.; p. 699, Granger Collection; p. 701, Denver Public Library/Western History Depart-